WEBSTER'S
NEW WORLD™

DICTIONARY

—— of ——

MUSIC

Nicolas Slonimsky

Edited by Richard Kassel

MACMILLAN • USA

Macmillan General Reference
A Simon & Schuster Macmillan Company
1633 Broadway
New York, NY 10019-6785

A Webster's New World™ book

MACMILLAN is a registered trademark of Macmillan, Inc.

ISBN: 0-02-862747-4

Manufactured in the United States of America

02 01 00 99 98 — 5 4 3 2 1

Slonimsky, Nicolas, 1984-
        Webster's New World dictionary of music/ Nicolas Slonimsky:
                p. cm
            ISBN 0-02-862747-4
                1. Dictionaries--Music,   2. Music--Bio-bibligraphy.   I. Kassel, Richard
ML100.S639   1998
780'.3--dc21   98-31029
                                                                            CIP
                                                                            MN

Editor's Preface:

Nicolas Slonimsky (1894-1995) was perhaps the greatest writer and editor of music dictionaries of all time. In 1937, after emigrating from Russia to the United States and teaching himself English, Slonimsky began his career with the first edition of *Music Since 1900*, a select chronology of music events. He next edited *Thompson's International Cyclopedia of Music and Musicians* (4th to 8th editions). He is perhaps best known for his remaking of *Baker's® Biographical Dictionary of Musicians* (5th to 8th editions), completely rewriting its entries in his unparalleled style. In 1989 Slonimsky published his *Lectionary of Music*, which was a dictionary of music written in a narrative style intended to be read for pleasure and general information.

From the *Lectionary of Music*, augmented by material from Slonimsky's vast archive of works, Schirmer Books published the comprehensive and highly acclaimed *Bakers® Dictionary of Music*. From this fine lineage Webster's New World has derived this concise and extraordinarily readable paperback dictionary of music. Thanks to the deft and experienced hand of editor Richard Kassel, virtually every entry has retained Slonimsky's renowned tone, wit, and scholarship. Amateur and professional musicians and music lovers alike will enjoy reading and learning about the world of music from the unique perspective of one of its greatest lexicographers.

Special thanks goes to Schirmer Books and Electra Yourke, Nicolas' daughter, for making the great wealth of Slonimsky's work available.

Acknowledgements:

I have attempted to put Mr. Slonimsky's innumerable thoughts and words into perspective, balancing his knowledge, personal experience, lively and opinionated outlook, humor, and sheer love of language (especially the less familiar aspects of it) with the needs of a music dictionary written for individuals new to the richness of music—its variegated history, major participants, and seemingly overwhelming vocabulary. To the extent that I have been able to reach a meeting of the minds with the indomitable Mr. Slonimsky is a tribute to his acuity and remarkable productivity; I hope that you find his way of expressing the pleasures of music salutiferous.

I am grateful to all those at Webster's New World—Suzanne Snyder, and especially my editor, Faunette Johnston, who made a potentially treacherous task feel like a walk along the beach on a lovely windy day, and who put up with my tribulations and laughed tactfully at my Slonimsky-like attempts at humor. For my entry into the publishing arena I owe a great deal to Richard Carlin, executive editor at Schirmer Books, longtime friend, fine musician, and editor's editor. I have also enjoyed the privilege of working with Mr. Slonimsky's daughter Electra Yourke, who has maintained and expanded her father's legacy with distinction.

I offer thanks to teachers, colleagues, friends, and lovers past (and present?), and to my amazing family, still close and supportive despite life's painful distractions and travails, and finally those who, by negative example, have taught me how (and how not) to treat others, and how to withstand the natural shocks that flesh is heir to.

To Z and E, then.

Richard Kassel
New York, NY
Summer 1998

Table of Contents

Introduction to Musical Terminology

Elements of Notation

Notation is a system of signs used in writing music. The written signs for the time value (length, duration) of musical tones are called *notes;* the written signs for pauses (intervals of silence) between the tones are called *rests.*

Notes and Rests

Whole note ○   Half note ♩   Quarter note ♩

Whole rest ▬   Half rest ▬   Quarter rest ⸝

Eighth note ♪   16th note ♬   32nd note ♬   64th note ♬

Eighth rest ⸜   16th rest ⸜   32nd rest ⸜   64th rest ⸜

Whole note ○ = 2 ♩, or 4 ♩, or 8 ♪, or 16 ♬, or 32 ♬, or 64 ♬

Half note ♩ = 2 ♩, or 4 ♪, or 8 ♬, or 16 ♬, or 32 ♬

Quarter note ♩ = 2 ♪, or 4 ♬, or 8 ♬, or 16 ♬

Eighth note = 2 ♬, or 4 ♬, or 8 ♬

Sixteenth note ♪ = 2 ♬, or 4 ♬

Thirty-second note ♪ = 2 ♬

The Staff

The staff consists of five parallel horizontal lines. Notes are written on the lines, or in the spaces between. For higher or lower tones, additional short lines are provided, called *ledger lines.*

‒‒ Ledger lines

5th line ——————
4th line ——————   4th space
3rd line ——————   3rd space
2nd line ——————   2nd space
1st line ——————   1st space

‒‒ Ledger lines

The Clefs

A *clef* is a sign written at the head (beginning) of the staff to fix the position of one note. The most common clefs are

the *G* clef (Treble Clef) 𝄞 fixing the place of the note g¹

the *F* clef (Bass Clef) 𝄢 fixing the place of the note f;

and

the *C* clef, which designates a line on the staff as c¹ (middle C); it acquires a different name according to the line used:

Tenor Clef   Alto Clef   Soprano Clef

The Scales

The staff and clefs together fix the pitch of the notes, showing whether they are high or low. A series of eight successive notes on the staff forms what is called a *scale.* To name the notes of the scale, we use the first seven letters of the alphabet, *A B C D E F G.* Scales are named after the notes on which they begin, which is called the *keynote.* The scale of *C,* written in whole notes, in the bass and treble clefs, is as follows:

The *C* written on the ledger line just below the treble staff and just above the bass staff is called middle C.

The notes in the same vertical line are of the same pitch and have the same name. For ordinary purposes, any note marked *C (c)* is called simply *"C."* But, in order to fix the place which any given note occupies among all the others (that is, to fix its "absolute pitch"), the whole range of musical tones is divided into sections of seven notes each, called "octaves," and lettered and named as shown:

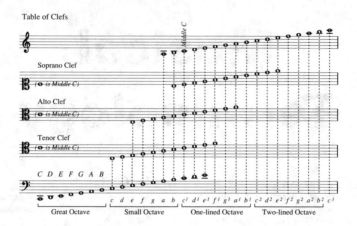

Table of Clefs

Pitch Registers

In order to indicate the exact location of a note in the total gamut, the following system is used in this dictionary:

C_1 C_2 c c^1 c^2 c^3 c^4 etc.

Chromatic Signs

The *chromatic signs* are set before notes to raise and lower their pitch.

The *sharp* ♯ raises its note a semitone;

The *flat* ♭ lowers its note a semitone;

The *natural* ♮ restores its note to the natural pitch on the staff (without chromatic signs);

The *double sharp* × raises its note two semitones;

The *double flat* ♭♭ lowers its note two semitones;

The sign ♮♯ restores a double sharped note to a sharped note;

The sign ♮♭ restores a double flatted note to a flatted note.

The Intervals

An *interval* is the difference in pitch between two notes. In measuring an interval, it is customary to take the lower note as the basis, and to measure up to the higher note. When the two notes are exchanged and the measurement is made downward, the interval is called "inverted."

Diatonic Intervals of the Major Scale

All Standard Intervals and Their Inversions

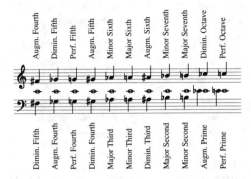

The Keys

A *key* is a scale employed harmonically, that is, employed to form chords and successions of chords. On the keynote C, or on any other note, two different species of scale or key may be built up:

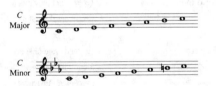

Such a key or scale is called *major* when its third and sixth are major intervals; it is minor when its third and sixth are *minor* intervals. The succession of intervals in every major key is the same as that in *C* major; in every minor key, as in *C* minor. To adjust the intervals properly, chromatic signs are employed.

Table of Major Keys

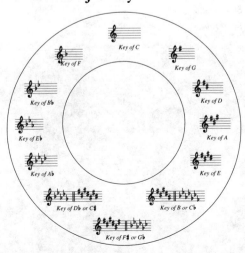

It will be seen, on passing around the circle in either direction, that the keynotes of the successive keys always follow each other at the interval of a perfect fifth; hence, this circle of keys, ending where it began, is called the circle of fifths.

Chords

A *chord* is formed by a succession of from three to five different tones, built up in intervals of diatonic thirds from a given tone, or *root*. A three-tone chord is a triad; a four-tone chord is a *seventh chord* (chord of the seventh); a five-tone chord is a *ninth chord* (chord of the *ninth*).

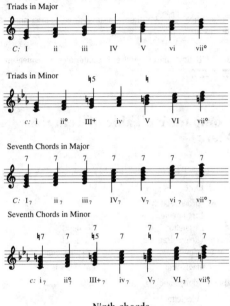

Ninth chords

When the root of the chord is the lowest tone, the chord is in the fundamental position; when some other tone is the lowest, the chord is inverted. Each triad has two inversions; each seventh chord has three.

Inversions of Triad   Inversions of Seventh Chord

The first inversion of a triad is called a 6 chord.

The second inversion of a triad is called a $^6_4$ chord.

The first inversion of a seventh chord is called a $^6_5$ chord.

The second inversion of a seventh chord is called a $^4_3$ chord.

The third inversion of a seventh chord is called a 2 chord.

Time Signatures

The *time signature* appears after the clef, at the beginning of the staff; the lower figure shows the *kind* of notes taken as the unit of measure, while the upper figure shows the number of these notes that can fit in a measure, and the groupings of beats.

For instance $\frac{3}{4}$ (3/4 time) means "three quarter-notes to the measure":

$\frac{12}{16}$ (12/16 time) means "twelve sixteenth-notes to the measure":

Comparative Table of Tempo Marks

CLASS I

INDICATING A STEADY RATE OF SPEED

Largo (broad, stately)		
Largamente		
Larghetto	Group I.	
Grave (heavy, dragging)	General	
Lento (slow)	signification	
Adagissimo	of terms is	
Adagio (slow, tranquil)	SLOW.	
Adagietto		
Andantino		

Andante (moving, going along)

Moderato

Allegretto	Group II.
Allegramente	General
Allegro (brisk, lively) [con moto,	signification
vivace] [agitato, appassionato]	of terms is
Presto (rapid) [con fuoco, veloce]	FAST.
Prestissimo	

CLASS II

INDICATING ACCELERATION

Accelerando   (with increasing rapidity)

Stringendo	(swiftly accelerating, usually
Affrettando	with a *crescendo*)
Incalzando	
Doppio movimento	(twice as fast)
Più mosso	(a steady rate of speed,
Più moto	*faster* than preceding
Veloce	movement)

CLASS III

INDICATING A SLACKENING IN SPEED

Rallentando	
Ritardando	
Allargando	(gradually growing slower)
Tardando	
Slentando	
Strascinando	
Molto meno mosso	($\flat = \flat$ del movimento precedente) (half as fast)
Ritenuto	(a steady rate of speed, Meno mosso *slower* than preceding movement)
Meno moto	
Calando	
Deficiendo	
Mancando	(growing slower
Morendo	and softer)
Sminuendo	
Smorzando	

A. The initial note of the alphabetical scale in German and English terminology; *A* corresponds to the note *La* of France, Italy, Spain, Portugal, Latin America, and Russia. Its alphabetical primacy was established by Glareanus, in his *Dodecachordon* (1547), fixed *A* as the tonic of the Aeolian mode; however, in 1571 Zarlino elevated the Ionian mode to primacy, relegating *A* to the 6th step of our C-major scale. In some methods of musical analysis, capital *A* stands for the A-major triad, small *a* for the A-minor triad. *A* is the note used for tuning an orch.; it is usually given out by the oboe because the oboe is the least affected by humidity or other weather conditions of all pitched instruments. The standard American frequency for A above middle C is 440 cycles (vibrations) per second.

a (It. preposition); **à** (Fr. preposition). By, at, in, with, for.

a cappella (It., as in chapel). Performed in the church style; choral singing without instrumental accompaniment. Generally, any unaccompanied vocal performance.

A major. A key often associated with springtime; Mendelssohn's Spring Song, from the Songs Without Words (op. 62), is cast in this key, although the title, not the composer's, was probably invented by a publisher. His "Italian" sym. (No. 4) is in A major, as is Tchaikovsky's Italian Capriccio, for Italy was poetically associated in the minds of northerners with sun and spirit. Beethoven's most joyful sym., No. 7, is in A major; Wagner grandiloquently described it as "the apotheosis of the dance." Many classical works catalogued as A minor end in A major, among them the Piano Concerto of Schumann and the Violin Concerto of Glazunov, with tonally assertive fanfares in the finale suggesting the triumph of the glow of optimism.

a mezza voce (It., half voice). With half the power of the voice (or instrument).

A minor. The key of resignation. Few syms. are set in it, although A minor is technically advantageous for string instruments: open violin strings provide for the tonic and dominant of A minor, and open strings of the viola and cello offering its tonic and subdominant. Mozart avoids A minor as a principal tonic, as does Beethoven, although the opening movement of the *Kreutzer Sonata* mixes A minor and major effectively. Mahler's Sym. No. 6, a work of mental depression in which he wrestles with Fate, is in A minor, as is Sibelius's Sym. No. 4, a work so unlike the robustly Finnish Sibelius that it must be regarded as exceptional. There are surprisingly few violin concertos in this eminently violinistic key: Glazunov, Bloch, and Dvořák wrote concertos in A minor.

Two great piano concertos are in A minor, by Schumann and Grieg. This introspective and essentially pessimistic key suits Tchaikovsky perfectly; his Piano Trio (dedicated to the memory of Nicholas Rubinstein) opens with a phrase on the cello in A minor that comes nearest to the sound of sobbing in music.

a poco a poco (It., little by little). Gradually. Correct adverbial form for *poco a poco*, but seldom used.

A string. The 2nd string (2nd highest) of a violin; the 1st of a viola or cello; the 3rd of a double bass; the 5th of a guitar.

A tempo (It., in time). Return to the preceding rate of speed.

Ab (Ger., off). In organ music, remove stop or coupler.

ABA. A symbolic representation of ternary form, in which the 1st section (A) is repeated after the 2nd (B). Many classical songs and arias follow this formula; ABA is therefore also known as song form.

Abbado, Claudio, b. Milan, June 26, 1933. Abbado received his early music training from his father, then enrolled in the Milan Cons., graduating in 1955 in piano; made his conducting debut in Trieste (1958); won the Koussevitzky conducting prize at Tanglewood; won the Mitropoulos Competition, N.Y. (1963). He made his American conducting debut with the N.Y. Phil. (1963); conducted at La Scala, Milan; the Vienna Phil; the London Sym. Orch.; Chamber Orch. of Europe; Chicago Sym. Orch.; Vienna State Opera. In 1989 he was named artistic director of the Berlin Phil., succeeding Karajan; also founded the European Community Youth Orch.; La Filarmonica della Scala in Milan; and Vienna's Mahler Orch. A fine technician, Abbado is capable of distinguished performances ranging from the Classic era to the cosmopolitan avant-garde.

abdampfen (Ger., evaporate). Deaden the sound, e.g., place hand on timpani; release piano damper pedal.

Abecedarianism (A-B-C-D-arianism). A reference to anything essentially alphabetarian. *Abecedarianism* is not necessarily pejorative; highly trained intellect and technical skill is required to create an Abecedarian masterpiece, e.g., the self-inverted redundant prose of Gertrude Stein. The same applies to musical Abecedarianism: Stravinsky's *Piano Pieces for 5 Fingers*, Bartók's *Mikrokosmos*, and Casella's *Valse diatonique* (from *Pezzi infantili*) illustrate sophisticated Abecedarianism. Abecedarian infantiloquy is naturally produced by small children banging at random on the white keys of the piano keyboard at the level of their heads, often resulting in the unintentional formation of interesting pandiatonic patterns vivified by asymmetrical rhythms. The walk across the keys by Domenico Scarlatti's cat inspired a fugue; critics who dismiss music as "cat music" misunderstand the constructivist potential of random tonal juxtaposition.

ablation. A decadent overuse of decorative and ornamental elaborations in early 20th-century music resulted in profound repugnance to such practices; an inevitable consequence was drastic ablation of all nonessential thematic excrescences and protuberances from a finished composition. A process of subjective ablation impelled some modern composers to revise early works and reduce their instrumental luxuriance to an economically functional organization. A very striking instance is Stravinsky's reorchestration of the score of his ballet The

Firebird, removing supernumerary instruments, excising florid cadenzas, and in effect plucking the fiery bird of its iridescent plumage; most audiences prefer the original luxuriant version to this later parsimonious arrangement. In his mature years Hindemith devised a harmonic theory so self-sufficient that he "corrected" several earlier works according to its principles, not unlike straining cheese through cloth.

Abravanel, Maurice, b. Saloniki, Jan. 6, 1903; d. Salt Lake City, Sept. 22, 1993. He was taken to Switzerland at the age of 6, then Berlin; took composition lessons with Weill. With the advent of the Nazis in 1933, he moved to Paris and conducted ballet; toured Australia (1934–35). In 1936 he joined the Metropolitan Opera in N.Y.; generally adverse reviews compelled his resignation (1938); turned to leading Broadway musicals; conducted the Chicago Opera Co. (1940–41). In 1947 he became conductor of the Utah Sym. Orch. at Salt Lake City; in the 32 years of his tenure, built it into one of the finest sym. orchs. in the U.S.; introduced many modern works into its repertoire. In 1976 he underwent open-heart surgery; retired in 1979.

Abschnitt (Ger.). Section.

absolute music. Music without extramusical connotation; music that is free from programmatic designs, psychological affiliations, or illustrative associations; its Latin etymology connotes independence. Functionally absolute music is nearly synonymous with abstract music, but the 2 terms differ in their temporal points of reference: the concept of absolute music is of ancient heritage, while abstract music is a relatively recent phenomenon, marked by structural athematism in an atonal context. See also ⇒ program music.

absolute pitch. Perfect pitch.

abstract music. A separation of sonic structures from representational images, whether pictorial or psychological; the antonym of all musical styles that are concrete or naturalistic. Abstract works are usually short, athematic, and rhythmically asymmetric; intellectual fantasy, rather than sensual excitation, is the generating impulse of abstract music; titles are often derived from constructivist and scientific concepts: *Structures, Projections, Extensions, Frequencies, Synchronisms*. Boris Blacher even developed the genre of abstract opera, lacking nearly all reference points to the genre. Abstract expressionism, a term applied to nonobjective painting, is sometimes used to describe abstract musical works with expressionistic connotations. A subsidiary genre of abstract music is aleatory music, in which the process of musical cerebration is replaced by random interplay of sounds and rhythms. See also ⇒absolute music.

absurd music (Eng., away from + irrational). Oxymoronic pairs, such as "passionate indifference" or "glacial fire," are intrinsically absurd and yet eloquent in their self-contradiction; absurd music cultivates analogous incompatibilities that are particularly effective in modern opera, where scenes of horror may be illustrated by a frivolous waltz, festive celebrations by a sombre funereal march; the scherzo in Mahler's 1st sym. is an instrumental example. The modern techniques of polytonality and atonality represent absurd music (and worse) to the withered sensitivity of an old-fashioned ear.

Abteilung (Ger.). Division or portion of a composition.

Accardo, Salvatore, b. Turin, Sept. 26, 1941. He won the Vercelli (1955), Geneva (1956), and Paganini (Genoa, 1958) violin competitions; pursued career as orch'l soloist and as recitalist; active in recent years as conductor; as violin virtuoso, excels in a vast repertoire; in addition to standard literature, performs many rarely heard works, including Paganini's concertos. His playing embodies fidelity to the classical school of violin playing, in which virtuosity is subordinated to stylistic propriety.

accelerando (It., accelerating). Gradually growing faster. Abbr. *accel.* or *acc.*, followed by dots or lines to indicate the continuity of the acceleration.

accelerato (It., accelerated). Livelier, faster.

accent. A stress, such as an increase in dynamic level.

acciaccatura (It.). 1. Short accented appoggiatura. 2. A note a 2nd above, and struck with, the principal note, and instantly released.

accidental. A chromatic sign not found in the key signature but placed in front of a note to alter its pitch in the course of a piece. Sharps, flats, naturals, double sharps, and double flats are the accidentals commonly used.

The flat sign (♭) lowers the note by a semitone. Derived from the small b, it was introduced as early as the 11th century to provide the perfect 4th in the major tetrachord on F (B♭), to avoid the forbidden tritone, called the *diabolus in musica* (devil in music). (This alteration was regarded as so obvious an necessity that the ♭ was dubbed *signum asininum* (mark of the ass), for the hopelessly stupid students who had to use this sign.) In medieval Latin, this B-flat was called *b rotundum* (round B) or *b mollis* (soft B; thus the French term *bémol* for flat). When a symbol for B natural was desired, a square was substituted for the gentle oval of *b*. This note received the name *b quadratum* (square b) or *b durum* (hard b). Because in Gothic script the square *b* looked like the letter h, the square *b* was eventually substituted for the sign of B natural; as a result, the German musical scale was extended to 8 letters of the alphabet, where *H* stands for B-natural. To this day, B-flat is designated in the German musical alphabet simply as *B*. A double flat is marked simply by 2 flats (♭♭).

The origin of the sharp (♯) is more complicated. Sharps originally appeared in medieval notation to cancel previously used flats; a sharp was therefore called *signum cancellatum* (sign of cancellation); in French this canceling sign was called *b carré* (squared *b*) so the term *bécarre* came to mean a natural sign. Further modifications of the signs for a sharp (raising a note by a semitone) and a natural (canceling a previous sharp or flat) helped differentiate between them: the sharp assumed the shape of a crisscrossed lattice (♯), and the natural was represented by a rhombus with an upward stem to the left and a downward stem to the right (♮). Double sharps are represented by a cross resembling the letter *x* (✕).

Accidentals usually retain their validity throughout 1 bar, but the rules are not absolute. Flats and sharps in Baroque scores were sometimes retroactive; the player had to know or guess where a leading tone led or how a passing note passed, based on subsequent accidentals; Baroque composers and copyists often omitted self-evident accidentals, to be supplied by the player relying on general usage. To add to the uncertainty, modern composers are not always strictly logical in their use of accidentals. In atonal music and 12-tone works, double sharps or double flats have no raison d'être, because only the absolute pitch counts, not its notation. Still, there are some preferences. Just as in tonal music B-flat and F-sharp are the harbingers of keyed tonality, so in atonal music B-flat is more common than its enharmonic equivalent A-sharp, and F-sharp preferred to G-flat.

accompaniment. Any part or parts (chords, bass lines, secondary parts) that attend or support the voices or instruments bearing the principal part or parts in a composition. It is *ad libitum* when the piece can be performed without it, *obbligato* when required. Accompaniment can be added by someone other than the original composer. In modern music, accompaniment transcends its traditional ancillary function and becomes an integral part of the entire composition. The simplest form of modern accompaniment is that of polytonality, in which the melody is set in one key and the harmony in another. Rhythmically, the modern accompaniment rarely follows the inflections of the melody; deliberate oxymoronic usages are enhanced by translocated accents.

accordion. A free-reed instrument patented by Cyrillus Demian of Vienna in 1829. The elongated body serves as bellows, to be drawn out and pushed together; the bellows is closed at either end by a keyboard. In older types the right hand plays a set of buttons having a diatonic or incomplete chromatic treble scale (button accordion); later models have piano-like chromatic keyboards. The left hand has up to 120 keys for harmonic bass tones. See also ⇒bandonéon; concertina.

acid rock. A heavier form of rock, developed in the California music scene in the later 1960s, with relatively light contrapuntal textures, emphasis on feedback guitar solos, and powerful amplification. Often, cryptic references to drugs such as LSD ("acid") are made in the lyrics. See ⇒rock.

acoustics. The physics of sound; the laws of the vibrations of strings and other solid materials, the transmission of air movement in the organ and wind instruments, and the effect of the superposition of the resulting sound waves on consonant or dissonant intervals and harmonies. Acoustics (Grk., audible) also establishes the causes of different tone colors and related problems, such as noise; the connecting link between physics and musical aesthetics.

Pitch depends on the length and tension of vibrating strings, length and diameter of the air column in a pipe of the organ, or size of a bell or a drum. The height of pitch is proportionate to the frequency of vibrations, the number of cycles (complete oscillations) of a string or air column per second (cps). If the thickness of a string remains the same, the frequency of vibrations decreases with its length. If a string is set in motion with greater force so that the amplitude of its vibrations is increased, then the resulting sound becomes louder without changing the actual pitch. The range of audible sounds for the human ear is between 16 and 25,000 cps; dogs hear sounds far above the human range; high-pitched whistles, inaudible to humans, are used to summon dogs.

Each string or air column naturally divides itself into component parts to produce overtones, or partials. Theoretically, each cycle produces also 2 vibrations of one-half that of the sounding body, 3 vibrations of one-third that of the sounding body, and so on; these partials are potentially audible. The simpler or smaller the whole-numbered fraction produced by the divided string, the more euphonious the interval created by such overtones; the perfect octave produced by the division of a string into 2 equal parts (1/2 or 2:1) is the most consonant interval; the interval between one-third of the string and one-half of the string produces the interval of the perfect 5th (2/3 or 3:2); between the division of the string into 3 parts and 4 parts, the perfect 4th (3/4); between the division of the string into 4 parts and 5 parts, the major 3rd (4/5). These intervals together constitute the major triad, acoustically the most natural consonant triad.

To the panoply of humanly audible sounds must be added whole series of combinational tones produced by either the difference or the summation of 2 tones, particularly those sounded in perfect tuning (just intonation). A violinist playing the double stop e^2 and g^2 on the 2 upper strings in the perfect acoustical ratio of a minor 3rd (5/6) will hear an unwelcome difference-tone, C below the G string. These intrusive sounds are also called Tartini tones, after the 18th-century violinist who 1st described them in detail. Furthermore, combinational tones form between the overtones of the individual sounds; fortunately, they cannot be heard in performances. Aware of this parasitic phenomenon, string players instinctively avoid using such acoustically perfect double stops; such intentional (and unintentional) playing and instrument manufacturing imperfections save music from nonharmonic pandemonium.

For more than 2,000 years theorists have wrestled with the problem of equalizing the perfect octave by having its ratio of vibrations 2:1 commensurate with that of a 5th that has a ratio of vibrations 3:2 (Pythagorean tuning). In the traditional cycle of 5ths, 12 perfect 5ths on the keyboard of the piano (or any instrument built on the tempered scale) is supposed to be identical to 7 octaves; but this is an impossible equation, because 2 to the 7th power (2^7) equals 3:2 to the 12th ($3/2^{12}$). Other tunings were tried (meantone, well temperament); but by the late 18th century, acousticians finally abandoned all hope of reconciling the pure harmonic series with practical instruments, and equal temperament became generally accepted. The acoustic perfection of the perfect 5ths was sacrificed (i.e., made slightly flat) in order to fit 12 3:2's into the compass of 7 octaves; similar adjustment was made in other intervals. As a result the tempered major chord is not an acoustically pure triad but an artificially adjusted harmony.

In the 20th century the prevalence of dissonance has forced reconsideration of the overtone series. The tritone, deprecated by medieval scholiasts, became a foundation of atonality, polytonality, and other modern techniques; acoustically it resembles the 45th partial, some 6 1/2 octaves from the fundamental note. Scriabin, theorizing ex post facto, regarded his Mystic Chord as consonant, as its constituents approximate higher partials. In Ravel's *Bolero* the melody is at 1 point accompanied by a group of flutes and piccolos constituting the 6th, 8th, 10th, and 12th overtones progressing in parallel formations; in the score, Ravel marks the gradually decreasing dynamics of these progressively higher notes, corresponding to the natural tapering of their strength; this calculated enhancement of overtones affects the timbre of the solo instrument, whose tone color changes of its own accord.

acoustics, architectural. Acoustical innovations and improvements in the purity of intonation are not without musical perils. The desire of modern architects to "attain" acoustical perfection can lead to orch'l pollution in the concert hall. Old-fashioned rococo architecture, with ornate brocades and heavy curtains, had the necessary dampening of sounds and echoes to secure harmonious euphony. Modern acousticians stripped away the decorations, tasseled seat covers, and cushioned surfaces, replacing them with plywood and plastic, while adding mobiles suspended from the ceiling to eliminate microsonic impurities. But these experiments often resulted in unwelcome side effects: While parasitical noises were neutralized, a slew of unanticipated musical microorganisms, overtones, and combination tones arose from the instruments themselves, flooding the hall in a harmonious plasma that destroyed the natural equilibrium of tonal imperfections and mutual reverberations that produced the rich resonance intuitively achieved in the past. The consequences of modernization were painfully evident in the scientifically designed Phil. (now Avery Fisher) Hall at Lincoln Center, N.Y.; when George Szell was invited to make suggestions, he allegedly recommended tearing the whole thing down and starting over. A version of Szell's suggestion was carried out years later; acoustical anarchy was corrected by ingenious rearrangements of the auditorium and the stage; natural heterogeneity of sonic euphony was restored.

act (It., *atto*). A primary division of an opera or scenic cantata. In opera each act may be subdivided into several scenes or tableaux.

action. In keyboard instruments, the mechanism set in motion by the fingers, or by the feet (organ pedals). In the harp the "action" (a set of pedals) does not directly produce the sound, but changes the key by shortening the strings by a semitone or whole tone.

action music. In the late 1950s and early 1960s, manifestations of mixed media, happenings with audience participation, or performance art in which spontaneous psychological and physiological excitations determine the course of events. Composers of action music may provide sets of instructions, leaving specific decisions to the performers; the actions of the performers are generally equal in importance to the sounds they make. Like impressionism, the term arose by analogy with painting; action painting implies a freely wielded brush in which the unpremeditated splash of color becomes a creative enzyme for the next projection. In action music there is no calculated design goal; the initial reflex generates successive series of secondary reflexes in a network of musico-neural synapses, resulting in the formation of dynamically propelled sounds.

action song. children's song in which bodily movements depict the action of the words, such as folding the hands and closing the eyes to represent sleep, fluttering of the fingers downward to represent rain, crossing the arms in circular movement

to represent the sun, flapping the hands to imitate birds in flight, etc. An example of this genre is *The Itsy Bitsy Spider.*

Acuff, Roy (Claxton), b. Maynardville, Tenn., Sept. 15, 1903; d. Nashville, Tenn., Dec. 23, 1992. He learned to play the fiddle, and later appeared as singer and guitarist. In 1938 he and his Smoky Mountain Boys became featured artists on the Grand Ole Opry radio program in Nashville; became famous with his renditions of *The Great Speckled Bird, Wabash Cannonball,* and *Wreck on the Highway;* composed *Precious Jewel;* was active as publisher. In 1962 he became the 1st living musician to be elected to the Country Music Hall of Fame; in 1988, celebrated his 50th anniversary at the Grand Ole Opry.

ad libitum (Lat., at will; abbr. *ad lib.*). 1. Employ the tempo or expression freely; 2. Indicates that vocal or instrumental parts may be left out. *Cadenza ad libitum,* cadenza that may be performed or not, have another substituted for it, or improvised, at the performer's will.

adagietto (It.). 1. A tempo or movement slightly faster than adagio. 2. A short adagio movement.

adagio (It., at ease). Quite slowly, leisurely; slow movement; often used for introductions to sonata-form movements. *Adagio adagio,* very slowly; *adagio assai,* very slowly; *adagio (ma) non tanto,* not too slowly; *adagio molto,* very slowly; *adagio non molto,* not too slowly; *adagissimo,* extremely slowly.

Adam, Adolphe (Charles), b. Paris, July 24, 1803; d. there, May 3, 1856. As one of the creators of French opera, he ranks with Auber and Boieldieu in the expressive power of melodic material and sense of dramatic development. He studied piano, then went to the Paris Cons.; devoted his entire career exclusively to theatrical music; obtained his 1st success with a short comic opera, *Le Chalet* (1834), which held the stage for 1,400 performances through the years. An even greater success was *Le Postillon de Longjumeau* (1836), an opera that achieved permanence throughout the operatic world. There followed a series of stage works; at times he produced 2 or more operas in a single season. In the process of inevitable triage, most of them went by the board, but a number remained in the repertoire, including the comic opera *Si j'étais roi* (1852). Adam wrote 53 operas in all, but his most durable and beloved work is the ballet *Giselle* (1841); the song *Cantique de Noël* also became popular.

Adam (Adan) de la Halle (Hale), called "Le Bossu d'Arras" (Hunchback of Arras), b. Arras, *c.* 1237; d. Naples, *c.* 1287. Adam was a famous trouvère; many of his works (monophonic and polyphonic) have survived, the most interesting being a dramatic pastoral, *Le Jeu de Robin et de Marion* (1285), written for the Anjou court at Naples and resembling an opéra comique in its plan. He was gifted in the dual capacity of poet and composer.

Adams, John (Coolidge), b. Worcester, Mass., Feb. 15, 1947. Minimalist composer best known for his topical operas *Nixon in China* (1987) and *The Death of Klinghoffer* (1991) as well as impressive orch'l works; his music covers a wide spectrum of other media.

adaptation. Arrangement.

added seventh. Minor or major 7th added to the major triad; in jazz, the minor 7th (e.g., in the seventh chord C, E, G, Bb) is a blue note. Depending on the context, the major 7th can be more or less acrid when added to a tonic major triad at the end of a piece. *Added sixth,* Major 6th added to the major tonic triad, often at the end of a phrase, and treated as consonant; 1st used by Debussy and others early in the 20th century, the added 6th chord (e.g., C, E, G, A) became commonplace in jazz piano playing.

Adderley, "Cannonball" (Julian Edwin), b. Tampa, Fla., Sept. 15, 1928; d. Gary, Ind., Aug. 8, 1975. He owes his nickname to mispronunciation of "cannibal," refering to his voracious eating habits; after receiving his B.A., directed a band in Fort Lauderdale (1948–50); jazz career began in a combo at a Greenwich Village (N.Y.) club; in 1956 formed group with his brother Nat Adderley (b. Tampa, Nov. 25, 1931), a cornetist; also played with Miles Davis. He achieved fame through his recordings, beginning with *African Waltz* (1961); others include *Dis Here, Sermonette, Work Song, Jive Samba, Mercy Mercy Mercy, Walk Tall,* and *Suite Cannon.* He died from a stroke suffered during a concert.

Adler, Richard, b. N.Y., Aug. 3, 1921. He was educated at the Univ. of North Carolina; served in the U.S. Navy (1943–46); became producer; staged shows at the White House during the Kennedy and Johnson administrations. He wrote musicals in collaboration with Jerry Ross. The most popular were *The Pajama Game* (1954), with its striking hit song *Hernando's Hideaway,* and *Damn Yankees* (1955). He also wrote *The Lady Remembers (The Statue of Liberty Suite)* for soprano and orch. (1985).

Adorno, Theodor (born Wiesengrund), b. Frankfurt am Main, Sept. 11, 1903; d. Visp, Switzerland, Aug. 6, 1969. In his early writings he used the hyphenated name Wiesengrund-Adorno. He studied with Sekles in Frankfurt and Berg in Vienna; for several years was prof. at the Univ. of Frankfurt; devoting himself mainly to music criticism, ed. the progressive music journal *Anbruch* in Vienna (1928–31); went to Oxford (1934); later emigrated to the U.S.; became connected with radio research at Princeton Univ. (1938–41); subsequently lived in Calif. He returned to Germany in 1949 and became director of the Institut für Sozialforschung, Frankfurt; publ. numerous essays dealing with the sociology of music, among them *Philosophy of the New Music* (1949); *Dissonances: Music in the Bureaucratic World* (1956); *Arnold Schönberg* (1957); *Form in New Music* (1966); *Alban Berg, Master of the Smallest Passages* (1968); advised Thomas Mann on the musical parts of his novel *Doktor Faustus.* He exercised deep influence on the trends in musical philosophy and general aesthetics, applying the sociological tenets of Karl Marx and the psychoanalytic techniques of Freud; in his speculative writings, introduced the concept of cultural industry, embracing all types of musical techniques, from dodecaphony to jazz.

aeolian harp or lyre (from Grk. *Aeolus,* god of wind). Stringed instrument sounded by the wind. It is a narrow, oblong wooden box with low bridges at either end, across which are stretched gut strings. The harp is placed in an open window or some other aperture where a draft of air will sweep the strings.

Aeolian mode. A church mode, codified in Glareanus's *Dodecachordon,* corresponding to the modern natural minor scale. Using the piano's white keys, the mode ranges from A to A (A–B–C–D–E–F–G–A).

aerophones (Grk. *aeros* + *phonos,* air sound). An older classification of music instruments that produce their sounds by the vibration of air, including the accordion, pipe and reed organ families, flutes, and mouth-blown reed instruments.

affects, doctrine of. A protopsychomusical theory treating the relationship between music and emotions. The affects doctrine (Lat. *affectus,* state of the soul) dates back to Greek antiquity, when the correlation between music and soul was accepted as scientific fact. The Greek word for *affectus* is *pathos,* which conveys the meaning of deep emotion. (The adjective *pathétique* still retains that meaning, as it is used in the subtitle of Tchaikovsky's Sym. No. 6.)

St. Augustine wrote, "Musica movet affectus." In medieval Latin treatises, the term *musica pathetica* was attached to music that represents emotions. The medieval description of the tritone as *diabolus in musica* is an early precursor of the doctrine of affects. In his *Musica practica* (1482), Ramos de Pareia draws a correspondence between the 4 temperaments of human condition and the 4 authentic church modes. An even more "scientific" tract is *Istitutioni harmoniche* by Zarlino (1558), in which all consonant intervals are divided into 2 categories: those consisting of whole tones (major 2nds, major 3rds, and their inversions) reflect the feeling of joy, and those containing fractional tones (minor 2nds, minor 3rds, and their inversions) express sadness.

The theorists of the Renaissance expanded the affects doctrine to include tempo, rhythm, registers, and dynamics. If some of these scholastic applications have retained their validity, it is because they generally correspond to observable physiological or psychological conditions. Rapid passages do not readily portray illness or death, and slow progressions in static harmonies do not easily evoke anger.

The establishment of major and minor tonality brought about the most durable affectus, associating major keys with joy and minor keys with sorrow; this dichotomy persists even to day. One cannot imagine Schumann's *The Happy Farmer* in minor or Chopin's *Funeral March* (from the op. 35 sonata) in major.

The doctrine of affects greatly influenced the melodic structure of vocal works. The symbolism of states of mind is evident in the works of Bach. Thus the verbal injunction "Get up, Get up!" is expressed by ascending major arpeggios; the phrase "Follow me" is illustrated by long ascending-scale passages; suffering is depicted by narrow chromatic configurations; the fall into Hell is punctuated by a drop of the diminished 7th.

During the Baroque period some musical philosophers actually drew comparative tables between states of mind and corresponding intervals, chords, tempos, and the like. The famous 18th-century lexicographer Mattheson stated in his treatise *Die neueste Untersuchung der Singspiele* (1744) that "it is possible to give a perfect representation of the nobility of soul, love, and jealousy with simple chords and their progressions." This exaggerated notion of the precise correspondence between emotions and musical progressions was tenaciously upheld in the annotations, mostly by German writers, of programmatic works. The diminished-7th chord, often used to enhance the dramatic tension in opera, received the nickname of *accorde di stupefazione*, a designation related to the doctrine of affects. The selection of registers by Romantic composers also frequently follows these psychological associations. The preference of Sibelius for the somber sonorities of the lower registers may reflect the severity of the Finnish landscape. Indeed it can be hypothesized that the music of the North tends toward greater exploitation of low registers, slower tempos, and minor modes, whereas the music of the South cultivates high registers and fast tempos.

The elaborate enumerations of leading motives and the analysis of their intervallic content by annotators of Wagner's music dramas and the symphonic poems of Richard Strauss are remnants of the affects doctrine. Even Schoenberg, who rejected programmatic interpretations of musical tones, yielded to the temptation of writing descriptive music in his score *Accompaniment to a Cinema Scene*, in which the subsections (Imminent Danger, Anxiety, and Catastrophe) follow in their dynamic content the precepts of the affects doctrine. In the 20th century the doctrine of affects has practically disappeared and been replaced by structural analysis unconnected with emotional content.

affettuoso (It., with affect). Passionately, emotionally, with great feeling, very expressively.

A-flat major. A key of joyous celebration and human devotion; an eminently pianistic tonality having 4 black keys and 3 white keys, conveniently disposed for melodies and harmonies. It lies uneasily for string instruments, however, and is therefore rarely if ever selected as the principal key for a large orch'l work; among individual symphonic movements in A-flat major, the 3rd movement of the Sym. No. 1 of Brahms is notable. A-flat major describes a festival mood in Schumann's *Carnaval*, and it is a romantic invocation in Liszt's *Liebestraum*.

African music. To the white people of Europe and America during the centuries of colonialism, Africa was the Dark Continent; Stanley, who "found" Livingstone and extended his famous superfluously genteel salutation, entitled his book *In Darkest Africa*. Joseph Conrad, who actually traveled in central Africa, summarized his experience in his novel *Heart of Darkness* with the words of its central character, "The Horror! The Horror!" In colonial times, European opera composers eagerly exploited reports from the mysterious continent as material for exotic libretti. Verdi's *Aida* is a prime example of melodrama depicting the collision of 2 civilizations. In Meyerbeer's opera *L'Africaine*, the woman of the title is a Malagasy beauty. While composers of such operas did not even attempt to find out what real African music was, the peoples of the African coastal regions absorbed the cultures, including music, of the various European and Asian powers. On its Mediterranean coast, Arabian modalities in song and dance held sway. The British influence was paramount on the coast of the Indian Ocean; the Portuguese were the colonial powers in Mozambique and Angola. Both the Dutch and the English established their artistic influence in South Africa. France and Belgium spread their cultures in western Africa and the Congo. The islands in the Indian Ocean, Madagascar and St. Mauritius, developed a unique mixture of European and Arabian musical cultures.

On the other hand, through modern technology and the development of ethnological research, it became possible to examine the reality of Africa beyond the archetypal figures of witch doctors and local chiefs holding court under an umbrella. One could now notate and record the indigenous music of Africa. Such knowledge could be exploited; the motion picture *The African Queen* includes a large section in which the indigenous people play drums and chant authentic music. But Europeans and Americans could not easily understand the powerful role of singing and drumming in African life.

The diversity of African chants and rhythms is extraordinary. The tonal progressions allow great variety of pitch, quasi-diatonic and ultrachromatic scales alternating with wide intervals but rarely exceeding a 5th. Remarkably, the tritone is freely used in African song cadences. The rhythmic figures are regular in meter, with some asymmetry and syncopation; in ensemble, however, they combine to form complex polyrhythmic designs with feelings of absolute spontaneity and improvisatory freedom. The strong beat may be emphasized by loud claps. Texts include invocations to the gods of the village, laments when disaster strikes, and celebrations for important local events, marriages, or the inauguration of new chiefs. There are hundreds of dialects among African tribes, and each language serves as a dynamic means of communication; thus the unique click of the Bushmen and others may serve to mark the end of a musical phrase. Intonation is of prime significance; slight rises or drops in pitch may change the meaning of a phrase.

The most common African ensemble contains drums of various sizes, gourds with rattling beads attached as shakers, metal bells, slit-log drums, and various manufactured products. Especially interesting is the talking drum, in the form of an hourglass with long strips of leather stretching down the sides from the head so that when the drum is squeezed under the arm it changes pitch; it is played with bent sticks. Another native instrument is the thumb piano, or mbira, a small wooden box with flexible nails or prongs of various lengths that are thumbed to produce sounds. For a larger gamut, harp-lutes are widely used, the largest being the kora with 21 strings. Animal horns are the most prominent aerophones.

There is much dispute as to the influence of the African diaspora on black and black-influenced musics of the Western hemisphere. The rhythmic element seems the most incontrovertible, with the drum kit of popular music and jazz adapted from African polyrhythmic drumming. Dance music is especially receptive to African rhythmic patterns. In addition to percussion, the banjo's ancestors came from West Africa. Less convincing are arguments supporting the presence of blues and pentatonic scale elements in African sources; given the lack of examples of pre-20th–century traditional African music and the intense confluence of white and black stylistic elements, such claims will probably remain speculative.

Earlier in the century, Cuban avant-garde composers such as Caturla (*Bembé*) and Roldán (*La Rebambaramba*) borrowed extensively from African music, as did Brazilians such as Villa-Lobos and Nobre. Western musicians now go to Africa to learn their music, e.g., the American composer Steve Reich took a course in African percussion techniques in Ghana and subsequently wrote a piece for voices and drums entitled *Drumming*. Conversely, African popular music has flourished with distinctive national and group-associated styles, incorporating large doses of Western popular music and contributing significantly to World Music.

aggregate. 1. Collection of notes in serial composition representing 1 instance of a pitch class. 2. A collection of notes heard at the same time.

agitato (It.). Agitated. *Mosso agitato,* very agitated; *agitato con passione* (It.), passionately agitated; *agitazione, con* (It.), with agitation, agitatedly.

Agnus Dei. The 5th and usually last section of the Catholic High Mass Ordinary, divided into 2 parts: *Agnus Dei* (Lamb of God) and *Dona nobis pacem* (Give Us Peace).

agogic (Grk., to lead). A slight deviation from the main rhythm for the purposes of accentuation. This legitimate performing practice may allow melodically important notes to linger without disruption of the musical phrase. Rubato is an agogical practice. The term was introduced by Riemann in 1884. In musical rhetoric, it is opposed to the concept of dynamics, which provides accentuation by varying the degree of intensity.

aguinaldo. Spiritual Spanish song glorifying Jesus and the saints, almost invariably in ternary form. Also called *adoración*.

Aida trumpet. A long trumpet specially constructed for use in Verdi's opera *Aida*. The original, manufactured in France, was called *trompette thébaine*, trumpet of Thebes. It produced only 4 notes: A-flat, B-flat, B-natural, and C.

air. Tune, melody; song. *Air varié* (Fr.), tema con variazioni.

al fine (It., to the end). Used in phrases like *Dal segno al fine*, instruction for the performer to play "from the sign to the place marked *fine*," or *Da capo al fine,* "from the beginning (*capo*, head) of the piece to the place marked *fine*." The latter instruction is associated with pieces in ternary form (ABA). *Al fresco* (It., in the open air), description of outdoor concerts, operatic performances, and other events, usually free of charge; *al segno* (It., to the sign), direction to play until the appearance of a sign 𝄋, usually indicating the end of a repeated section; *al tallone* (It., at the heel), to play near the nut of the bow.

alba (Prov., light of dawn). Provençal morning song, very popular with the troubadours, that corresponds to the serenade, or evening song. See ⇒alborada, aubade.

Albéniz, Isaac (Manuel Francisco), b. Camprodon, May 29, 1860; d. Cambo-les-Bains (Pyrenees), May 18, 1909. Exceptionally precocious, he was exhibited as a child pianist; began studying with N. Oliveros. At age 7 he was taken to Paris; studied with Marmontel, teacher of Bizet and Debussy. Returning to Spain, he studied at the Madrid Cons.; stowed away on a ship bound for Puerto Rico; made his way to the southern U.S.; earned a living by playing at places of entertainment. He returned to Spain and traveled in Europe; met Liszt in Budapest (1880);

settled in Barcelona (1883). He met Pedrell, who influenced him in the direction of national Spanish music; went to Paris for composition studies; abandoned concert career for composition.

Almost all of Albéniz's works are for piano and inspired by Spanish folklore; established the modern school of Spanish piano literature based on authentic rhythms and melodic patterns rather than imitations of national Spanish music by French and Russian composers. His piano suite *Iberia* (1906–1909) is a brilliant display of piano virtuosity.

Alberti bass. Type of arpeggiated tonal accompaniment in even tempo, traditionally for the left hand on the keyboard. Popularized (if not invented) by Domenico Alberti (Italian singer, harpsichordist, and composer; b. Venice, 1710; d. Rome, c. 1740) early in the 18th century, it was used extensively by Haydn, Mozart, and Beethoven, among others.

Albinoni, Tomaso (Giovanni), b. Venice, June 8, 1671; d. there, Jan. 17, 1751. Between 1694 and 1740 he produced 53 operas, mostly in Venice. However, his historical significance lies with his concertos, sonatas, and trio sonatas. Bach admired his music and made arrangements of 2 fugues taken from trio sonatas. However, the famous *Adagio* for strings and organ is almost totally the work of R. Giazotto, an Italian musicologist.

alborada (Sp.). Spanish morning song, orig. performed on a primitive oboe with drum accompaniment as a morning serenade. See ⇒alba, aubade.

Albumblatt (Ger.). Short and (usually) simple vocal or instrumental piece, often intended as a musical autograph or offering; album-leaf.

alcuno, -a (It.). Some; certain.

aleatory music (from Lat. *alea*, a die or dice game). Chance music, either in the compositional process or the performer's realization. Random composition can be generated by the throw of dice or some other way of producing numbers by chance. By drawing an arbitrary table of correspondences between numbers and musical parameters (pitch, duration, rests) it is possible to derive a number of desirable melorhythmic curves. In realizing aleatory scores, rhythmic values and pitches are subject to multiple choices by the performer; sometimes only duration is specified by the composer; in extreme cases even the length of the piece itself is aleatory.

Chance music is nothing new, having been practiced as early as the 18th century. Mozart amused himself by writing a piece with numbered bars that could be put together by throwing dice. Aleatory music in modern times, however, is a more serious business, especially as cultivated by Cage, who often used numbers derived from the Chinese *I Ching*. His classic aleatory works include *Music of Changes* for piano and the *Piano Concert*. Stockhausen wrote numerous aleatory pieces for piano and chamber ensembles, as did his many disciples and followers in Europe and Japan. The term *aleatoric* is sometimes used.

Human or animal phenomena may also serve as primary data. Configurations of fly specks on paper, curves and parabolas produced by geometry and trigonometry, flight patterns of birds over a specific location, etc. are possible materials for aleatory music.

Kagel has made use of partially exposed photographic film for aleatory composition. Xenakis organizes aleatory music in stochastic terms, providing the teleological quality absent in pure aleatory pursuits. Among related subjects of aleatory music are probability, information theory, stochastic composition, cybernetics, experimental music, computer music, empirical music, and indeterminacy.

Alkan, Charles-Valentin (born Morhange), b. Paris, Nov. 30, 1813; d. there, Mar. 29, 1888. His father, Alkan Morhange (1780–1855), operated a Parisian music school; he and his 4 brothers became well-known musicians who adopted their father's 1st name. Charles-Valentin entered the Paris Cons. (1819); made his public debut as pianist and composer in Paris (1826); developed friendships with Dumas *père,* Hugo, George Sand, Delacroix, and his neighbor Chopin. He appeared in a concert with Chopin (1838); despite the favorable reception, did not appear again until 1844. His piano work, *Le Chemin de fer,* op. 27 (1844), is the 1st to describe a railroad. In 1848 Zimmerman retired as piano prof. at the Paris Cons. and suggested Alkan as his successor; despite intercessions by Sand, the position went to Marmontel, propelling Alkan even further into seclusion. After Chopin's death he abandoned his circle of artistic friends and became a virtual recluse, not performing again until 1873. He publ. the remarkable *12 études dans les tons mineurs,* op. 39 (1857), in which études 4–7 constitute a sym., études 8–10 a concerto without orch.; became interested in the pedalier, a pedal board attached to a piano, on which he played organ works of Bach and for which he wrote compositions, including the unique *Bombardo-carillon for 4 Feet Alone.*

During his lifetime, Alkan was enigmatic; his pianistic skills were highly praised, compared to those of Chopin and Liszt, and yet his aberrant behavior and misanthropy caused his name to fade into the foreground. The claim that he was killed by falling volumes of the Talmud (of which he was a scholar) from his bookcase was absurd anti-Semitic calumny. Judging from the difficulty of his works, his skills must have been formidable. Since his death several pianists—notably Busoni, Petri, Raymond Lewenthal, and Ronald Smith—have kept his works alive.

all', alla (It.). To the, in the, at the; in the style of; like.

alla breve (It.). In modern music, a 2/2 meter, i.e., 2 beats per measure with the half note carrying the beat; also called *cut time* (from medieval terminology). Implies a faster tempo than 4/4.

all' ottava (It., at the octave). Play the notes an octave higher than written. The sign 8va ——————— or 8——————— is usually employed.

alla siciliana (It.). In Sicilian style; like a siciliana. *Alla stretta* (It., narrow, close together), 1. Growing ever faster. 2. In the style of a stretto (stretta). *Alla turca,* in Turkish style; *all'unisono,* in unison (or octaves).

allargando (It., widening). Growing slower; usually presages an ending.

allegretto (It., quite lively). Moderately fast; faster than andante, slower than allegro. Light; almost dancelike.

allegro (It., joyful). Fast, lively, brisk, rapid. Allegro is not as fast as presto. *Sonata allegro,* a formal structure found in many movements of Classic and Romantic music; the tempo is not necessarily allegro.

allein (Ger.). Alone; only.

alleluia. Latin form of the Hebrew *Hallelujah* (Praise the Lord!), acclamation found throughout the Roman Catholic liturgy. In the High Mass the alleluia chant follows the gradual. It is in ternary form, with a verse in the middle; the alleluia section ends with a lengthy melisma called a *jubilus.* When joy is not called for (e.g., the Requiem Mass), the alleluia is replaced by the tract.

allemanda (It.); **Allemande** (Fr.). 1. In the Renaissance, a German dance in 2/4. 2. In the Classic period, a German dance in 3/4 time, similar to the Ländler. 3. A movement in the Baroque suite (usually the 1st or following a prelude) in 4/4 time and moderate tempo (andantino). It is as much French in style as German.

Allison, Mose, b. Tippo, Miss., Nov. 11, 1927. After serving in the U.S. Army he formed his own trio; then played with Stan Getz and Gerry Mulligan. His earlier songs were heavily blues-influenced; his mature songs, often marked by satirical and cynical lyrics, have been performed by such notables as Van Morrison, the Who, John Mayall, Georgie Fame, and Bonnie Raitt. Some of his best-known songs include *7th Son* (a hit for Johnny Rivers), *One of These Days, Parchman Farm, Tell Me Something, I Don't Want Much,* and *Perfect Moment.*

Almeida, Laurindo, b. São Paulo, Sept. 2, 1917; d. Van Nuys, Calif., July 26, 1995. After mastering the guitar he settled in Rio de Janeiro and made appearances on the radio; led his own orch. at the Casino da Urca. In 1947 he moved to the U.S.; was a soloist with Stan Kenton's band; later led his own small groups. He gave numerous recitals and was a soloist with sym. orchs.; also appeared with his wife, the soprano Deltra Eamon. Almeida brought the Brazilian style of jazz, with its dance rhythms and modalities, into greater prominence, preparing the way for its burst of popularity in the 1960s.

alphorn (Ger.). Long wooden natural horn able to produce up to the 12th partial, used by shepherds in the Alps to call the sheep back home at sunset. Brahms notated an Alpine horn tune on a postcard he sent to Clara Schumann in 1868 with the words "Hoch auf 'm Berg, tief im Tal, grüss' ich dich viel tausendmal!" (High on the mountain, deep in the valley, I greet you many thousand times.) Eight years later he made use of it in the famous horn solo in the last movement of his Sym. No. 1, which contains an approximation (F♯, 3 1/2 octaves above the fundamental C) of the 11th partial note.

alt, in (alto; It.). Notes in the octave from f^2 to f^3.

Notes in the octave above this are said to be *in altissimo.*

alteration. 1. A generic term for raising or lowering a note's pitch by means of an accidental. 2. In mensural notation, the doubling of the value of the 2nd semibreve in duple time, thus converting it into triple ("perfect") time.

altered chords. Chords containing chromatic alterations of harmonies normally expected within the tonality of the music; also called chromatic chords.

alternativo (It.). Contrasting section in dance forms, such as a trio in a minuet; a substitute for such a section.

althorn (U.S. Eng., Ger.). The B♭ alto saxhorn, patented by Sax in 1845 and perfected by the Bohemian maker Václav Nervenv in 1859; the orig. Fr. name was *saxhorn ténor.*

alti naturali (It., naturally high ones). In the Middle Ages, male falsetto singers, as opposed to *voci artificiali,* the castratos.

altissimo, in (It., in the highest). Range of voices from g³ (an octave above the treble staff) to g⁴. Some medieval singers are reputed to have been able to sing in this range without falsetto. See ⇒alto.

alto (It., from Lat. *altus,* high; Ger., Alt). 1. The deeper of the 2 main divisions of women's or boys' voices, the soprano being the higher; the standard alto gamut ranges from g to c²; in voices of great range, down to d and up to f² or even higher. Alto singers possess resonant chest voices. In opera the parts of young swains who unsuccessfully court the heroine are often given to altos (trouser roles), e.g., Siebel in Gounod's *Faust.* Also called *contralto.* 2. Instrument of similar compass, such as the alto saxhorn, alto saxophone, alto recorder, alto flute, and alto clarinet (basset horn). 3. The counter-tenor voice. 4. (Fr.) The viola; tenor violin.

alto, -a (It.). High. *Alta viola,* tenor violin; *ottava alta,* octave higher.

alto clef. A C-clef placing middle C on the 3rd line.

amateur. An art lover who, while possessing understanding for and certain practical knowledge of it, does not pursue it as a profession. A noble word degraded during the past couple of centuries to connote persons who dabble in the arts without requisite skill or understanding, *amateur* (from Fr., one who loves) is often synonymous with *dilettante* (from It., one who delights), which itself has been unjustly degraded from its original meaning. In the 18th century the word *amateur* had a complimentary meaning. There was a flourishing society in Paris called Concerts des Amateurs. Composers dedicated their works to persons described as amateurs in the dedication. Such publications could also be directed at a specific market; C. P. E. Bach entitled a set of clavier sonatas "à l'usage des dames." In the 19th century the salon genres of instrumental and vocal chamber music were the true popular music of their day, along with the most successful operatic arias. By the next century the cultivated and vernacular traditions were more or less irreconcilable; classical composers wrote primarily pedagogical pieces, while most audiences turned to the succession of popular music styles that filled the air.

Many professions are notable for having very enthusiastic amateurs of music. A story is told about a famous pianist who played a concerto with a doctors' orch. Shortly afterward he suffered an attack of appendicitis; several surgeons from the orch. volunteered to operate on him, but he declined. "I prefer to have my appendix removed by a member of the New York Philharmonic," he declared in all solemnity. Albert Einstein was quite proficient on the violin, although an anecdote suggests that when he played a Mozart sonata with the famous pianist Schnabel, he could not keep time. "For pity's sake, Albert," his partner exclaimed, "can't you count?" The 18th-century composer Philidor earned a place in chess history by his opening known as Philidor's Defense. Prokofiev reached the rank of a top chess player in Russia. The famous French artist Ingres loved to play the violin, even though he could never quite master it. Hence the expression "violon d'Ingres" is applied to a passionate but inefficient amateur.

Conversely, many musicians show a respectable talent for painting; Schoenberg, Gershwin, and Robert Moran have had public exhibitions of their art. The Italian futurists, among them Russolo, painted canvases in an expressionistic manner that fetched high prices after their deaths. Ruggles devoted himself entirely to painting and stopped writing music during the last 40 years of his very long life. Rudhyar painted hundreds of pictures symbolic of his mystical beliefs.

Many royal personages were amateurs in the best sense of the word, among them Frederick the Great of Prussia (who performed regularly with C. P. E. Bach and Quantz) and Albert, Prince Consort of England. Francis Hopkinson, a signer of the Declaration of Independence, claimed the distinction of being the 1st American to produce a musical composition. Thomas Jefferson played the harpsichord, violin, and recorder; Benjamin Franklin perfected the glass harmonica. Presidents Harry Truman and Richard Nixon played the piano, but their repertory was limited; Bill Clinton is the finest presidential saxophonist the U.S. has ever had. On the other hand, the great Polish patriot Paderewski was a pianist 1st, a statesman 2nd. It is said that when he met the French prime minister Clemenceau at the Versailles Peace Conference following World War I, Clemenceau exclaimed, "So you are the famous pianist, and now you are Prime Minister! What a comedown!" Even Verdi was a member of the 1st Italian parliament.

Amati. Renowned Italian family of violin makers working at Cremona. (1) Andrea (b. between 1500 and 1505; d. before 1580) was the 1st violin maker of the family; established the prototype of Italian instruments, with characteristics found in modern violins. His sons were (2) Antonio (b. *c.* 1538; d. *c.* 1595), who built violins of varying sizes, and (3) Girolamo (b. *c.* 1561; d. Nov. 2, 1630), who continued the tradition established by his father, working together with his brother. (4) Nicola (Niccolò) (b. Dec. 3, 1596; d. Apr. 12, 1684) was the most illustrious of the family. Son of Girolamo, he built some of the "grand Amatis," large violins of powerful tone surpassing in clarity and purity those made by his father and grandfather. In Nicola's workshop both Andrea Guarneri and Antonio Stradivari received their training. (5) Girolamo (b. Feb. 26, 1649; d. Feb. 21, 1740), son of Nicola and the last of the family, produced violins inferior to those of his predecessors; he departed from the family tradition in many respects, seemingly influenced by Stradivari's method without equaling his superb workmanship.

ambitus. 1. In church mode theory, the range of scale degrees comprising a given mode. The determination of the ambitus can depend on the mode's being authentic, plagal, or mixed. 2. The range of a voice, instrument, or piece.

Ambrosian chant. System of plainchant associated with the 4th-century bishop of Milan, St. Ambrose (b. Trier [Treves], c. 333; d. Milan, Apr. 4, 397). It preceded by 2 centuries the codification of Gregorian chant. There are many musicological views of Ambrosian chant: inchoate predecessor of Gregorian chant; refreshing style free from the stricter Gregorian doctrine; extension of Eastern liturgical sources. The last interpretation is supported by its use of florid quasi-exotic melismas that adorn its melodies and move freely between modes; some such fioriituras comprise more than 100 notes. Perhaps the most rational theory about the historical place of the Ambrosian chant is its being a Milanese branch of the liturgical ritual; the other main branches are the Gregorian of Rome, the Gallican of France, and the Mozarabic of Moorish Spain. This division is analogous with the emergence of Romance languages from their common Latin source.

ambulation. The indicated movement of performers in the process of playing a piece. This is an example of spatial distribution, in which the player's position in physical space is treated as an independent parameter. Ambulation is related to vectorialism, in that the direction of the sound source depends on the placement, stationary or kinetic, of the performers. In an ambulatory composition the players may be instructed to make their entrances on, or exits off, the stage while playing their instruments; they may utilize the concert hall; they may be suspended from the flies or rise from beneath the stage; they may move during the piece, in random or specified directions; they may "interact" with each other, with varying degrees of improvisatory freedom; percussionists may have more than one setup on stage, and are required to move between them, sometimes quite rapidly.

Ameling, Elly (Elisabeth Sara), b. Rotterdam, Feb. 8, 1934. After studies in Rotterdam and the Hague, she completed her training with Bernac in Paris; won the Hertogenbosch (1956) and Geneva (1958) competitions; made her formal recital debut in Amsterdam (1961); appeared with the Concertgebouw Orch., Amsterdam, and the Rotterdam Phil.; made her London (1966) and N.Y. (1968) debuts. Her 1st operatic appearance was as Ilia in *Idomeneo* (Amsterdam, 1973); chose to concentrate on a concert career; gave numerous lieder recitals and appeared with many major European orchs; made a Knight of the Order of Oranje Nassau by the Dutch government (1971); established a prize to be awarded at 's Hertogenbosch.

Amen (Heb.). Concluding word in a Jewish or Christian prayer; expression of faith. Sometimes an Amen section in an oratorio is extended so as to become a concluding chorus of considerable length. *Amen cadence,* popular term for plagal cadence, to which *Amen* is often sung.

ametric. Without meter; lacking a regular, sustained pulse.

Amirkhanian, Charles (Benjamin), b. Fresno, Calif., Jan. 19, 1945. His early percussion compositions experimented with sound phenomena independent of traditional musical content, as in the 1965 Sym. I, scored for 12 players and 200-odd objects ranging from pitch pipes to pitchforks. With painter Ted Greer he developed a radical notational system based on visual images transduced by performers into sound events. He is perhaps best known for his developments in text-sound composition, featuring a voice percussively intoning and articulating decontextualized words and phrases; especially difficult but rewarding is *Dutiful Ducks* (1977). Since the early 1980s his works have used sampled ambient sounds manipulated by a Synclavier digital synthesizer.

amplifier. Electronic device used in all reproducing sound systems to control and heighten volume.

amplitude. Widest disturbance in a vibration; the scientific correlate to the sensation of loudness. *Amplitude modulation,* change made to the amplitude of a sound wave enabling information transfer to electromagnetic wave (AM).

Amram, David (Werner, III), b. Philadelphia, Nov. 17, 1930. Amram is best known for his cross-cultural experiments, combining jazz, world, and classical musical styles in his compositions and performances. He has also composed film scores, radio works, for the theater, and for orch. and smaller ensembles.

anacrusis (Gk., upbeat). Unaccented syllables beginning a verse of poetry. In music, the weak beat, or weak part of a measure, with which a piece or phrase may begin. See ⇒Auftakt.

anagram. Rearrangement of notes of a subject to generate plausible thematic variations; analogous to the literary anagram, where words and sentences are derived from a given meaningful matrix (e.g., "Flit on, cheering angel" from *Florence Nightingale*). The 12 notes of the chromatic scale yield 479,001,600 possible permutations suitable for dodecaphonic usages. Polyanagrams, formed by linear (melodic), vertical (harmonic), and oblique (fugal) parameters, are comprised in the generic term combinatoriality, introduced by Babbitt. The remarkably intricate *Anagrama* by Kagel, scored for speaking chorus, 4 vocalists, and instruments, to a text derived from Dante's *Divina Commedia*, executes a number of permutations forming plausible sentences in different languages.

analysis. The study of musical structure and form. Description of a musical composition in verbal terms offers 2 alternatives: to paint a word picture with poetic metaphors and psychological excursions, or to confine oneself to compiling an inventory of melodic phrases, rhythmic terms, harmonic progressions, contrapuntal combinations, and formal designs. The obvious defect of the 1st method is the impossibility of forming any idea of style or technique. The nickname "Moonlight" given to Beethoven's Piano Sonata "quasi una fantasia" (No. 2, op. 27) by a literary critic communicates little about the work's structure. Emotional similes such as *romantic, stormy, wistful,* and *fantastic* are no better. Stylistic designations can be a little more informative if their meaning is known (e.g., Baroque, rococo, traditional).

The alternative approach involves the bar-by-bar description of the music in its melodic, rhythmic, and harmonic content within a composer-selected form of composition. Finally there is the presumption of a working hypothesis, where the analyst proposes a widely ranging specific notion, e.g., that all of Beethoven's main themes are based on a falling 3rd, either major or minor. However, the elaboration of such a thesis, using the opening of his 5th Sym., requires either the avoidance of instances where the thesis does not apply or the derivation of "alternative" 3rds, such as a 6th (an inverted 3rd) or a 4th (an expanded 3rd).

Global hypotheses are made more impressive through the invention of their own nomenclatures and rationalizations. Several theories are based on the natural system of harmonics (overtones), which has the advantage of empirically studied structures and demonstrable import in melody and harmony. Schenker's system outlines a scientific looking terminology, of which Urlinie (primordial line) promises to trace any tonal melody of the Baroque, Classic, and Romantic eras (Common Practice Period) to its component elements; inversely, the fundamental presence of the triad makes it possible to reconstruct any tonal melody through arbitrary processes of interpolation and extrapolation of melodic notes. Any musical phrase, rhythm, and harmonic accompaniment can be reduced to a preselected form, in a process related to topological congruence.

Unfortunately, composers' own comments are often unenlightening or even misleading, e.g., Beethoven's "Pastoral" Sym., Mahler's early programmatic syms., Schoenberg's postdated titles for the 5 Orch'l Pieces (op. 16), and Tchaikovsky's 4th Sym. as described to Madame von Meck. Indeed, taking a composer's biography, personal observations, and psychological profile as the basis of musical analysis mistakes rhetoric and "inner meaning" for musical style and technique. The problem of analytical description of musical works remains unsolved.

anapest (Grk.). Metrical foot of 3 syllables, 2 short (unstressed) and 1 long (stressed); in music, corresponds to upbeat of 2 quick notes followed by a long note in 4/8 time.

ancor (from It. *ancora*). Again, also, yet, still, ever. *Ancora piano*, continue singing (or playing) softly; *ancora più piano*, still softer.

andante (It., going, moving, walking). Tempo mark indicating a moderately slow, easily flowing pace between adagio and allegretto. Often used ambiguously, its speed depends on other factors, such as the type of accompaniment. *Andante con moto*, flowing and rather more animated.; *andante mosso*, flowing and rather more animated; *andante un poco allegretto*, flowing and rather more animated.

andantino (It.). Diminutive of andante, used ambiguously; it literally means "a little slower than andante," but it is generally used to mean "a little faster than andante."

Anderson, Laurie, b. Chicago, June 5, 1947. Renouncing conventional modernism, her goal has been to unite all arts as they once coexisted in theatrical practice; makes use of all styles and technologies, from topical pop to electronics, incorporating images of herself projected on a screen; uses a variety of instrumentation, including a homemade violin activated by a luminous bow made of electronic tape. She has become particularly famous for her multimedia cyberpunk projections, applying cybernetic principles to deliberately commonplace movements,

behavior, and language; her performances combine speech, song, and bodily exertions; her programmed compositions are improvisations in which she alters her natural voice electronically, making free use of vocal techniques. Her 1st popular success was the minimalist *O Superman*, built on a repeating phrase (1981); produced the large-scale collage epic *United States* on themes of travel, politics, money, and love (1983).

Anderson, Marian, b. Philadelphia, Feb. 17, 1897, d. Portland, Oreg., Apr. 8, 1993. She sang in the choir of the Union Baptist Church, South Philadelphia. Funds were raised for her to study voice with G. Boghetti; won 1st prize at a Philadelphia singing contest (1923); received top honors at a contest held by the N.Y. Phil. at Lewisohn Stadium (1925), winning a solo appearance. She gave a recital at Carnegie Hall (1929); made her 1st European appearance in London (1930); subsequently toured Europe and the Soviet Union; her singing of Negro spirituals produced a sensation. She gained national attention when the Daughters of the American Revolution (DAR) refused to let her appear at their Constitution Hall in Washington, D.C. (1939), citing the organization's policy of racial segregation; this led to Eleanor Roosevelt's resigning from the DAR and Anderson's receiving an invitation to sing at the Lincoln Memorial on Easter Sunday; a huge audience attended the broadcast concert. She sang Ulrica in *Un ballo in maschera* at the Metropolitan Opera, N.Y. (1955), the 1st black singer to appear there. Her remaining years were filled with a seemingly unending list of honors.

Andrews, Julie (born Julia Elizabeth Wells), b. Walton-on-Thames, Oct. 1, 1935. Her mother was a pianist and her stepfather, whose surname she adopted, was a music-hall singer. She was praised for her performance in the Broadway musical *The Boy Friend* (1954), displaying considerable vocal range and technique; followed with her outstanding portrayal of Eliza Doolittle in *My Fair Lady* (1956–60), for which she received the Drama Critics Award; subsequently appeared in *Camelot* (1960–62). Turning her attention to films, she appeared in the whimsical *Mary Poppins* (1964), for which she won an Academy Award for best actress, and *The Sound of Music* (1966). In later years she appeared in several films directed by her husband, Blake Edwards, by which she hoped to alter her squeaky clean image. Their biggest success was *Victor, Victoria*, a farce on gender role-playing, made into a musical (1995) with Andrews in the lead.

Andrews Sisters, American popular singing group. (Members: LaVerne, b. Minneapolis, Minn., July 6, 1915; d. Brentwood, Calif., May 8, 1967; Maxene, b. Minneapolis, Jan. 3, 1918; and Patricia [Patti], b. Minneapolis, Feb. 16, 1920.) They formed the most successful "girl group" in history, selling over 60 million records. Among their most popular songs were *Bei Mir Bist Du Schoen* (1937), *Rum and Coca Cola* (1944), and *Winter Wonderland* (1947). They were excellent at boogie-woogie renditions, performed in close 3-part harmony, including *Beat Me Daddy 8 to the Bar* and *Boogie Woogie Bugle Boy*; the latter was reinterpreted by Bette Midler (1973, with Midler doing all vocal parts), setting off a resurgence of interest in their music.

Andriessen, Louis, b. Utrecht, June 6, 1939. He 1st studied with his father (the composer Hendrik Andriessen,

1892–1981) and van Baaren at the Royal Cons. in the Hague (1957–62); also studied with Berio in Milan (1962–63). He was a cofounder of a Charles Ives Soc. in Amsterdam. His works are idiomatically advanced, extending minimalist concepts into complex sonority (*De Tijd*) or emphatic, iconoclastic expression (*Hoketus, De Materie*). His brother Jurriaan (1925–) is also a leading Dutch composer.

Angeles, Victoria de los (born Victoria Gómez Cima), b. Barcelona, Nov. 1, 1923. Made her concert debut in Barcelona (1944) and her 1st operatic appearance there (1946); won the Geneva Competition (1947). She performed at the Paris Opera as Marguerite (1949); at Covent Garden, London as Mimi (1950). She 1st appeared at the Metropolitan Opera, N.Y. as Marguerite (1951); sang at the Metropolitan until 1961. She retired from the stage (1969); gave occasional recitals, excelling particularly in Spanish and French songs. Her extensive operatic repertoire included Manon, Donna Anna, Nedda, Mélisande, Cio-Cio-San, and Carmen.

Anglican chant. Liturgical singing generally adopted in English-speaking Protestant liturgy; usually harmonized with simple chords.

ängstlich (Ger.). Anxiously, fearfully.

Anhang (Ger.). 1. Coda, codetta. 2. Supplement, as in a Gesamtausgabe.

animals and animal music. Because birds are the primordial music-makers of the animal world, it is not surprising that composers have for centuries imitated birdcalls in their works. The cuckoo has the most immediately identifiable leitmotif: a falling major 3rd. Beethoven immortalized it, along with the trilling nightingale and the repetitive quail, in his *Pastoral Sym.* (A toy cuckoo is used in Leopold Mozart's *Toy Sym.*) The 18th-century French composer Daquin wrote a harpsichord piece entitled *The Cuckoo,* which became a universal favorite. The contemporary French composer Messiaen expanded the musical aviary by filling his compositions with painstakingly notated exotic birdcalls. The rooster is glorified in Rimsky-Korsakov's opera *Le Coq d'or,* sounding his call on the muted trumpet. Villa-Lobos reproduces the piercing cry of the araponga on high B-flat in one of his *Bachianas Brasileiras.*

Non-avian creatures are represented as well. Buzzing insects provide obvious sources of animal onomatopoeia. Rimsky-Korsakov's *Flight of the Bumble Bee* is a famous example; a more esoteric illustration is Bartók's *Diary of a Fly* from his *Mikrokosmos.* In the score of his opera *L'Enfant et les sortilèges,* Ravel includes a couple of meowing amorous cats. The bleating of sheep is imitated by a cacophonous ensemble of wind instruments in R. Strauss's *Don Quixote.* In the *Duet for 2 Cats* traditionally attributed to Rossini, 2 sopranos sing their parts to the most familiar phrase associated with felines. Saint-Saëns has a whole menagerie in his *Carnival of the Animals* (including pianists).

Actual reproductions of animal noises are used in modern scores: Respighi introduced a recording of a nightingale in his symphonic poem *The Pines of Rome.* The American composer Hovhaness had used recordings of the sounds of humpback whales. When a dog incidentally barked during a recording of

Piston's ballet suite *The Incredible Flutist,* the conductor decided to keep it in the final recording. In Kirk Nurock's *Sonata for Dog and Piano* the canine performer's role is obbligato and totally improvised.

animando (It.). With increasing animation; growing livelier. *Animando un poco* somewhat more animatedly.

animato (It.). With spirit, spiritedly, vivaciously.

Anon. Abbr. for *Anonymous,* used in the attribution of religious music of the Middle Ages, traditional music, and many other pieces. Most ecclesiastical chants are anonymous.

Ansatz (Ger.). 1. Proper adjustment of the lips in wind playing; embouchure. 2. Precise attack at the beginning of a phrase in string playing.

Anstimmen (Ger.). Tune; begin singing. *Anstimmung,* tuning, intonation.

answer. In a fugue, 2nd voice or part (comes), which takes up (in transposition) the subject (dux, fugal theme) given in the 1st voice or part. A *real answer* transposes the subject note-for-note to the dominant; a *tonal answer* requires modification, replacing a tonic note with its supertonic, to fulfill harmonic requirements.

antecedent. Theme or subject of a canon or fugue, proposed by the 1st part; the dux; any theme or motive proposed for imitation, or imitated further on.

Antheil, George (Georg Johann Carl), b. Trenton, N.J., July 8, 1900; d. N.Y., Feb. 12, 1959. He was famous in his day for composing music that glorified the age of the machine. He went to Europe in 1922; gave several concerts featuring his compositions as well as impressionist music; spent a year in Berlin; went to Paris, his domicile for several years; was one of the 1st American students of the legendary Nadia Boulanger. In Paris he made contact with Joyce and Pound; became the self-styled *enfant terrible* of modern music; naively infatuated with modern machinery, composed the *Ballet mécanique* with the avowed intention to "épater les bourgeoisie"; collaborated with Fernand Léger on a film to be synchronized with the music, but this proved impractical; the 1926 premiere was noncinematic. He returned to America, staging a spectacular *Ballet mécanique* in N.Y., employing airplane propellers, 8 pianos, and a large percussion battery, creating an uproar in the audience and much publicity in the newspapers (1927).

Subsequent works were less successful, and Antheil moved to Hollywood (1936); wrote film music and ran a syndicated lonely hearts column; wrote more syms., operas, and other works, but reduced his musical idiom to accessible masses of sound; these works were rarely performed; nevertheless, remains a herald of the avant-garde of yesterday.

anthem (Mid. Eng. *antem*). Hymnal song performed by a chorus, with or without accompaniment and of moderate length. Many anthem texts are based on Scripture, but others are newly composed. Liturgically the form corresponds to the Roman Catholic motet. Anthem singing arose in the Reformation; consequently, it had its most fruitful development in the Lutheran and Anglican churches. The term came to signify any solemn song performed by a community. *National anthems* are the patriotic extensions of prayerful religious songs.

anticipation. Resolution of a dissonant melodic note on the upbeat, without resolving other parts of the harmony; most commonly applied to the leading tone, moving to the tonic, thereby preempting its resolution. Such anticipation forms a highly dissonant chord combining elements of the dominant and tonic harmonies; thus the anticipatory element is enhanced.

antiphon(e) (from Grk. *anti* + *pho-næ*, countersound). 1. Orig., responsive system of singing by 2 choirs (or divided choir) in early Catholic service of song, where the same phrase would be repeated an octave higher by a 2nd chorus composed of women and boys. 2. Responsive or alternate singing, chanting, or intonation as practiced in the Greek, Roman, Anglican, and Lutheran churches. 3. A choral response after the singing of a psalm, usually sung syllabically. In large polyphonic compositions an antiphon may be set elaborately, vying in importance with the main section. 4. A short sentence, generally from Holy Scripture, sung before and after the psalms for the day.

antiphonal. 1. Liturgical book containing most of the Divine Office; antiphonary; antiphoner. 2. In antiphon style; responsive; alternating.

antique cymbals. Small hollow-sphere brass cymbals of definite pitch, played with a small mallet; orig. used to accompany dances in ancient Greece; used in modern scores for special effects. Also called crotales (Fr., from Lat. *crotalum*).

anvil. Metal bar struck by a hammer, 1st used in Auber's *Le Maçon* (1825); made famous in the so-called Anvil Chorus in Verdi's *Il Trovatore* (1853). In *Das Rheingold* Wagner introduces 18 anvils to illustrate the forging of the ring of the Nibelung. The anvil is also used by Varèse (*Ionisation*, 1931) and Orff (*Antigonae*, 1949).

aperiodicity. Nonrecurrence of musical time, with formants distributed unpredictably.

applause. (from Lat. *plaudere*, to clap hands) A culturally determined, seemingly instinctive reaction to an excellent artistic performance. Shouts of "Bravo!" often join the applause; outside Italy, "Bravo!" is shouted equally at men and women performers, although the proper grammatical form for female artists is "Brava!" (Kudos addressed to more than 1 performer take the form "Bravi!") In Islamic countries audiences cry out "Allah, Allah!" to commend singers; in Spain it is "Olé, olé!"

At the opera, applause often greets the entrance of a favorite singer. When there is an orch'l coda after a particularly successful aria, it is often drowned out by intemperate applause, as in the case of the soft instrumental conclusion to the famous tenor's aria in Leoncavallo's *Pagliacci*. A tug-of-war can ensue when the conductor tries seriously to proceed while the singer longs to prolong the applause. In the heyday of opera, a singer expiring at the end of an aria had to rise from the dead and bow to the public. Cries of "Bis!" (twice, encore) call for a repetition of an aria. It was once common among opera singers, especially in the 19th

century, to hire people to applaud them furiously; such a group was called a claque.

A peculiar type of responsorial applause emerged in Russia toward the middle of the 20th century, when the artists themselves applauded the audience, usually in a rhythmic measure of 1 long and 2 short claps. The origin of this custom can be traced to the practice of political leaders returning the applause of an enthusiastic audience. It is interesting that whistling, an expression of passionate pleasure at performances in England and America, is equivalent to hissing or booing in France and Russia. Shortly after the conclusion of World War II, American soldiers greeted the Russian dancers in Berlin with whistling; the performers were in tears, believing that they had been roundly dismissed. The so-called Bronx cheer, produced by sticking out the tongue between closed lips and exhaling vigorously, is the most emphatic American way of expressing displeasure at the quality of performance, short of physical violence.

appoggiatura (It., leaning note). 1. Dissonant note to be performed on the beat and immediately resolved; usually indicated by a note printed in small type before the principal note. In binary time it borrows half the value of the principal note; in ternary time, may borrow two-thirds of the principal dotted note; unclear usage can be frustrating for scholars, editors, and performers.

An *accented appoggiatura* is a grace note which takes the accent and part of the time value of the following principal note.

The *long appoggiatura*

performed ... is seldom written now.

The *short appoggiatura*

is performed .

The *unaccented appoggiatura*

is performed ,

and takes its time value from the preceding principal note, to which it is smoothly bound.

2. In analysis, any note that functions like an ornamental appoggiatura but is written out fully.

Arab music. The traditional music of Arab nations of the Mediterranean and Persian Gulf basins differs so greatly from the nature of Western music that transcription with any degree of fidelity into Western notation is fraught with difficulties. Arab musical meters and rhythms lack the four-square quality of Western songs; its melodic structure is somewhat microtonal, thus incommensurable with the tempered scale, at least in theory. Form is not divisible into even periods. The melodic range is narrow; the only development of the principal theme consists in florid melodic variations and embellishments (see ⇒arabesque).

The tuning of Arab music rarely coincides with the Western system of tetrachords; major and minor tonalities are nonexistent in the Western sense of those terms. There are 12 basic modes (each called maqa-m) in Arab music, which tend to emphasize the minor 3rd. Harmonization and polyphony in the Western sense of the word are nonexistent; the only combination of tones in Arab music results from simultaneous accompaniments on Arab instruments to singers, sometimes producing quasi-heterophonic textures.

Numerous medieval theoretical treatises by Arab mathematicians and philosophers have survived. Notation of Arab chants and rhythmic modes usually gives the hand positions on indigenous instruments, which have retained virtually the same construction and tuning throughout the centuries; besides the Arab lute (ūnd), a vertical flute (nāy), 1-string fiddle (rabāb), vase-shaped drum (darabukka), and tambourine (tār) are used.

Several Russian and French composers wrote pieces purporting to be of Arabian inspiration; their melodies invariably emphasize the melodic augmented 2nd and other progressions. Tchaikovsky included a *Danse Arabe* in his *Nutcracker*; the only suggestion of an exotic atmosphere is the avoidance of a perfect cadence, use of minor mode, and a continuous pedal point on the tonic and dominant. The most famous Arabian tale in Western music is Rimsky-Korsakov's symphonic suite *Scheherazade*, inspired by the Arabian Nights; but there is no ersatz Arab modality. Recent composers (e.g., Schuller, *7 Studies on Themes of Paul Klee*) have attempted more authentic-sounding borrowings.

arabesque. Type of character piece for piano, featuring ornamental passages accompanying or varying melodies, usually in a pronounced 2/4 time. The etymological reference to Arab design reflects the Romantic infatuation with exotica, in this case non-representational Islamic art. Schumann, Tchaikovsky, Debussy, and others wrote arabesques.

Arbeau, Thoinot (anagram of birth name Jehan Tabourot), b. Dijon, Mar. 17, 1520; d. Langres, July 23, 1595. He owes his fame to his *Orchésographie* (Langres, 1588; 2nd ed., 1589), a "manual in dialogue form so that everyone might learn and practice the virtuous activity of dancing"; in addition to instructions (based on a system of initial letters), contains invaluable observations on contemporaneous dance music.

arciorgano. Organ described by Vicentino (1561) with manuals or divided keys, designed to incorporate the diatonic, chromatic, and enharmonic genera of ancient Greek theory, so that modulation could occur in all keys without the necessity for temperament.

arco (It., bow). Return to the normal use of the bow; follows pizzicato or col legno passages.

Argento, Dominick, b. York, Pa., Oct. 27, 1927. In the pantheon of American composers, Argento occupies a distinct individual category, outside any certifiable modernistic trend or technical idiom. He writes melodious music in harmonious

treatment so deliberate in intent that even his apologists profess embarrassment at the unimpeded flow and bel canto style of his Italianate opera scores; most important, audiences and an increasing number of sophisticated critics profess their admiration for his unusual songfulness. Yet an analysis of Argento's productions reveals the presence of acerbic harmonies and artfully acidulated melismas. Long associated with the Minnesota Opera (which he co-founded); most of his works have premiered there. Among his operas: *Christopher Sly,* after Shakespeare (1963), *Postcard from Morocco* (1971), *The Voyage of Edgar Allan Poe* (1976), *Miss Havisham's Fire,* after Dickens (1979), *Casanova's Homecoming,* opera buffa (1985), and *The Aspern Papers* (1988). He has written many nonoperatic vocal works.

ärgerlich (Ger.). Angrily.

arhythmic. Without rhythm; lacking regular, sustained beat or pulse.

aria (It.; from Lat. *aer;* plural *arie;* Ger., *Arie*). Air, tune, or melody; common to all European languages, "aria" signifies a manner or model of performance or composition. In 17th-century England the spelling *ayre* designated a variety of songs, serious or popular. Baroque instrumental pieces of songful character were often called arias. The most common association of *aria* is with solo operatic song. Types of aria used in Italian opera include: *aria buffa,* comic or burlesque aria; *aria cantabile,* "songful" aria expressing sorrow or yearning; *aria da capo* or *da capo aria* (to the head), aria in symmetrical ternary form, where the 3rd part is the exact or slightly varied repetition of the 1st part (ABA, ABA'); popularized by the Neapolitan school in the 2nd half of the 17th century; became the most common form of operatic aria, especially among Italian and Italianate composers of the 18th and 19th centuries. In Romantic opera, the da capo evolved into the *grand aria* or *aria grande,* divided into (1) main theme, fully developed; (2) more tranquil and richly harmonized 2nd section; and (3) repetition *da capo* of the 1st, with more florid ornamentation; *aria da chiesa,* church aria, as opposed to secular operatic aria; *aria da concerto,* aria for concert singing; *aria d'entrata,* aria sung by an operatic character upon her or his 1st entrance; *aria di bravura,* rapid virtuosic song expressing violent passion through florid ornamentation; *aria parlante,* "talking aria," in declamatory manner.

arietta (It.). Short aria, lacking da capo repeat; similar to the cavatina found in Baroque Italian opera. *Ariette* (Fr.), short aria or song; usually inserted into French divertissement rather than opera.

arioso (It., like an aria). 1. In vocal music, style between full aria and lyric recitative; short melodious strain interrupted by or ending in recitative. Invented by the Florentine opera inventors, who called it *recitativo arioso.* 2. Impressive, dramatic style suitable for the *aria grande;* any vocal piece in that style. 3. In instrumental music, cantabile.

Arlen, Harold (born Hyman Arluck), b. Buffalo, Feb. 15, 1905; d. N.Y., Apr. 23, 1986. His collaborators included Ira Gershwin (*The Man That Got Away*), Johnny Mercer (the musicals *St. Louis Woman,* 1946, and *Saratoga,* 1959; *Ac-cent-tchu-ate the Positive*), Truman Capote (the 1954 musical

House of Flowers), Ted Koehler (*Get Happy, Between the Devil and the Deep Blue Sea, I Love a Parade, I Gotta Right to Sing the Blues,* and *Stormy Weather*), and his most frequent partner, E. Y. Harburg, with whom he wrote 3 musicals, several films (especially *The Wizard of Oz,* 1939, including *Over the Rainbow*), and songs such as *Satan's Li'l Lamb, It's Only a Paper Moon,* and *Happiness Is a Thing Called Joe.*

Armstrong, Louis, b. New Orleans, August 4, 1901; d. N.Y., July 6, 1971. Known as Satchmo, Satchelmouth, Dippermouth, and Pops. Thanks to a rediscovered birth record, it is now known that he was not born on July 4, 1900; grew up in Storyville, New Orleans's brothel district; a juvenile delinquent, was placed in the Home for Colored Waifs; played cornet in its brass band, with its repertoire of marches, rags, and songs; after his release, learned jazz style in blues bands in local honky-tonks; played in "Kid" Ory's band (1918–19). In 1922 he went to Chicago to play in "King" Oliver's Creole Jazz Band; made his 1st recordings (1923); joined Fletcher Henderson's band in N.Y. (1924–25); returned to Chicago; organized his own jazz combo, the Hot 5 (1925); made series of influential recordings with it, the Hot 7, and other groups he led (to 1928); from about 1926, concentrated on the trumpet. In 1929 he returned to N.Y.; became famous through appearances on Broadway, in films, and on radio; led own big band (1935–47); organized his All Stars ensemble (1947); in succeeding years, made innumerable tours of the U.S. and abroad; became enormously successful as entertainer; made television appearances and hit recordings, including a celebrated version of *Hello, Dolly* (1964). Although he suffered a severe heart attack in 1959, he made appearances until his death.

Armstrong was one of the greatest figures in the history of jazz, and one of the most popular entertainers of his time; revolutionary "hot" style of improvisation moved jazz irrevocably away from New Orleans style in the 1920s; unique gravelly voiced scatsinging and song renditions became as celebrated as his trumpet virtuosity. His 2nd wife was jazz pianist and composer Lil(lian) Hardin (b. Memphis, Tenn., Feb. 3, 1898; d. Chicago, Aug. 27, 1971), who played for both Oliver and Armstrong in the 1920s.

Arne, Thomas Augustine, b. London, Mar. 12, 1710; d. there, Mar. 5, 1778. He schooled at Eton; spent 3 years in a solicitor's office; at the same time, studied music and acquired considerable skill on violin; began composing settings "after the Italian manner" to various plays. His most important work was *Comus* (1738); in 1740, produced the masque *Alfred,* the finale of which contains the celebrated song *Rule Britannia,* which became a patriotic song of Britons everywhere. In addition to nearly 100 dramatic works, he contributed separate numbers to 28 theatrical productions and composed 2 oratorios, secular vocal pieces, and instrumental music. His sister was the celebrated actress Mrs. Cibber.

Arnold, Malcolm, b. Northampton, Oct. 21, 1921. He studied trumpet, conducting, and composition at the Royal College of Music, London (1938–40); played 1st trumpet with the London Phil. (1941–42; 1946–48); then devoted himself to composition, developing a melodious and harmonious style of writing which appealed immediately to the general public while avoiding obvious banality; many works reveal modalities common to English folk songs, often invested in acridly pleasing harmonies;

experience as trumpeter and conductor in popular concerts provided a secure feeling for propulsive rhythms and brilliant sonorities; composed effective film music. In 1970 Arnold was made Commander of the Order of the British Empire.

arpa (It.). 1. Harp. 2. Play arpeggio.

arpeggiando, arpeggiato, (It., playing like a harp; noun, *arpeggio;* plural, *arpeggi*). Sounding a chord's notes in steady succession; playing broken chords, usually from lowest to highest note; a chord thus played; broken or spread chord (or chordal passage).

arpeggione. String instrument about the size of a cello, having 6 strings and a guitarlike shape; invented by Johann Georg Staufer of Vienna (1824), its vogue was of a short duration; Schubert wrote a sonata for it, now usually played on cello.

arrangement. Adaptation, transcription, or reduction of a composition for performance on an instrument, or by any vocal or instrumental combination, for which it was not originally written; any composition so adapted or arranged.

19th-century reductions of classical syms. for piano 4-hands made it possible for amateurs to become acquainted with sym. literature when mechanical recordings did not exist. Piano albums published under such ingratiating titles as *Brother and Sister* made it possible to acquaint pianistic youth with popular operatic arias as well. Professional composers made such arrangements, with no sense of indignity about the task. With the advent of the phonograph this practice declined; composers wrote 4-hand music primarily for their own purposes. Stravinsky arranged *Le Sacre du Printemps* for his own convenience; Grieg arranged Mozart piano sonatas for 2 pianos, remaining faithful to the originals. Debussy and Ravel wrote 4-hand works for children. Rimsky-Korsakov arranged music by Mussorgsky, Borodin, and other composers, popularizing works while introducing bowdlerized elements. Ravel was probably the most active composer/arranger of his own piano music, including *Rapsodie Espagnole, Ma Mère L'Oye, Le Tombeau de Couperin,* and *Valses Nobles et Sentimentales.* When Rachmaninoff played his Piano Concerto No. 2 in Los Angeles, a lady rushed to him after the show, exclaiming, "Beautiful! Who is your arranger?" "Madam," Rachmaninoff replied, "in Russia, we composers were so poor we had to write our own music." Busoni's famous version for piano solo of Bach's *Chaconne* has become a popular virtuoso piece; Brahms arranged the Bach for piano left-hand.

A special form of reduction was the so-called theater arrangement, adaptations of symphonic works for small amateur productions. Theater arrangements usually contained indications for optional substitutions of one instrument by another, with the piano part filling in the harmonic vacuum. This practice is comparable to the Baroque's interchangeable scoring. The terminology surrounding arrangements is imprecise; works labeled transcriptions tend to be grander and freer, approaching a fantasy. Paraphrases may be said to be even freer, more inspired by than translating their models, such as Liszt's many lied and operatic paraphrases.

Arrau, Claudio, b. Chillan, Feb. 6, 1903; d. Murzzuschlag, Austria, June 9, 1991. He received his early training from his mother; as a child, played publicly in Santiago; in 1910, was sent to Berlin; gave piano recitals in Germany and Scandinavia (1914–15), attracting attention by his precocious talent. In 1921 he returned to Chile; in 1924, made his 1st American tour as concerto soloist; appointed to the faculty of the Stern Cons.; Berlin. Between 1928 and 1940, toured Russia several times; performed in Europe, Latin America, and the U.S. In 1941 he settled permanently in N.Y.; continued performing, teaching, and touring; recorded the complete Beethoven sonatas (1962–69); supervised an urtext ed. of those works. In 1978 he gave up Chilean citizenship to protest Pinochet regime; became naturalized U.S. citizen (1979), nevertheless remained revered figure in Chile; awarded the Chilean National Arts Prize (1983); toured Chile in 1984, after an absence of 17 years. In his playing, Arrau combined classical purity and precision of style with rhapsodic éclat.

ars antiqua (Lat., old art). Style associated with polyphonic musical developments of the 12th and early 13th centuries. *Ars antiqua* had its inception in France; its great early representatives were the masters of the Notre Dame or Paris school; Leoninus was the "best composer of the organum," polyphonic music with a slow moving cantus firmus in the lower voice and a florid melismatic upper voice with chantlike rhythm; the younger Perotin was the "best composer of discant," with durationally similar lower and upper voices, producing a somewhat note-against-note effect in modal rhythms; an intermediate type between organum and discant was copula, although this may refer to text rather than musical structure. Organum eventually engendered the clausula, short pieces à 2 providing flexible interludes within organum.

By adding a Latin liturgical text to the clausula's upper voice, the motet resulted; when applied to secular music, a seemingly chaotic practice evolved where different texts, in French as well as Latin, were performed simultaneously in the upper voices; the cantus firmus voice became an instrumental part; although a striking departure from earlier polyphonic forms, the polytextual motet proved the most fertile development in medieval music. The cantus firmus retained its dominant role during the ars antiqua, excepting the freely composed conductus.

The metrical system of ars antiqua is confined almost exclusively to ternary groupings in the tempus perfectum; binary meters were used in the tempus imperfectum (more incomplete than imperfect). The theoretical doctrine of ars antiqua was best expressed by Franco of Cologne, active in the 13th century, in *Ars cantus mensurabilis*, in which he codified the period's rhythmic modes, indicating the relative note values of mensural notation.

ars musica. (Lat. art of music) In medieval universities, music was regarded as one of 7 liberal arts (*septem artes*), taught in Latin like most subjects, as part of the *quadrivium*—arithmetica, geometria, musica, and astronomia. (The remaining *trivium* included *grammatica, rhetorica,* and *dicilectica*.) In medieval Latin, *ars* fell in between the more elevated concept of *scientia* (science), and above the more common category of *usus* (use); when Guido d'Arezzo taught singers with the aid of the Guidonian hand in the 11th century, he followed the precepts of practical *usus*; when he introduced *neumes,* 1st without lines and later with, ars musica was elevated to the state of the science of singing (*scientia canendi*). This marked the beginning of musical notation, which culminated in the treatise *Ars nova,* compiled c. 1320 by Philippe de Vitry and subtitled *Ars nova notandi* (The New Art of Notating Music). As this "scientific" musical aspect developed further in medieval universities, subdivisions were delimited, such as *ars cantus plani* (art of plainchant) and *ars componendi* (art of composing); Bach subtitled his *Musikalisches Opfer "ars canonica"* (art of writing canons).

ars nova (Lat., new art). Period of 14th-century music that contrasted with the ars antiqua by its more complex and controlled counterpoint and a return to lighter textures, even monophony, in secular music. The name stems from the eponymous treatise of Philippe de Vitry, compiled c. 1320, and from a work by Johannes de Muris, *Ars novae musicae* (1321). By themselves the 2 theorists' innovations were historically important: the extension of mensural notation to include small note values, down to the semiminima; and the formal acceptance of binary division of the measure, as contrasted with the previous designation of ternary division as the sole *tempus perfectum*. But the composers of ars nova went even further, dismissing ternary division as ars antiqua, old-fashioned and, by implication, inferior art.

Ars nova composers accepted 3rds and 6ths as consonances and the resulting phenomena of faburden and fauxbourdon, successions of ⁶⁄₃ chords in parallel motion; this interest in "sweet" consonance represents the beginning of vertically determined counterpoint. These "novelties" aroused opposition by adherents of *ars antiqua;* Jacques de Liège, in his treatise *Speculum musicae* (Mirror of Music, early 14th century) declares ruefully, "Regnat nova ars, exulat antiqua" (New art reigns, old art is exiled), and then excoriates the "unnatural" novelties of the modernists. Ironically, to modern ears the ars antiqua, with its quartal harmonies, sounds more progressive than the ars nova, with its 3rds and 6ths. In rhythmic patterns, too, ars antiqua cultivates more "modern" syncopated iambic prosody (short-long), whereas ars nova uses the more "natural" trochaic rhythmic figure (long-short).

There were three outstanding representatives of the ars nova. The Frenchman Machaut skillfully used the rhythms and melos of popular dances and song forms, including ballades, rondeaux, and virelais. The Italian Landini wrote fluid, direct works; he used but did not actually invent the Landini cadence. The Flemish Ciconia, active in Italy at the end of the 14th century, helped reverse the trend of ars nova toward further simplification and engaged in the exploration of a new polyphony. In this sense he was a forerunner of the great Netherlandish contrapuntal school that reached its height in the Renaissance.

articulation. By analogy to speech, manner in which notes are joined one to another by the performer; specifically, the art of clear enunciation in singing and precise rhythmic accentuation in instrumental playing; principal component of phrasing.

artificial harmonics. Harmonics produced on stopped strings rather than on open strings (e.g., of the violin). Two fingers of the left hand combine to perform these notes: the finger nearer the neck presses the string to establish the fundamental; the finger nearer the bridge lightly touches the string to produce the harmonic relative to the fundamental; e.g., a perfect 4th above the stopped fundamental produces a note 2 octaves higher than this fundamental.

Ashkenazy, Vladimir (Davidovich), b. Gorki, July 6, 1937. His parents were professional pianists who taught him at an early age; took lessons at the Central Music School and the Moscow Cons.; won 2nd prize at the International Chopin Competition, Warsaw (1955). A turning point in his career occurred when he won 1st prize in the Queen Elisabeth of Belgium International Competition, Brussels (1956); made his 1st U.S. tour (1958); with John Ogdon, shared 1st prizes in the Tchaikovsky International Competition, Moscow (1962). He has conducted various orchs. As a piano virtuoso, he holds an international reputation for penetrating insight and superlative technique; mastery extends from Haydn to early 20th-century composers; known for superb performances of the Rachmaninoff concertos; stated general antipathy toward avant-garde music. As conductor he has demonstrated an affinity for the 19th- and 20th-century repertoire; prepared and conducted his own effective orchestration of Mussorgsky's *Pictures at an Exhibition.*

Ashley, Robert (Reynolds), b. Ann Arbor, Mich., Mar. 28, 1930. He was active with Milton Cohen's Space Theater (1957–64), the ONCE Festival and ONCE Group (1958–69), and the Sonic Arts Union (1966–76); toured with them in the U.S. and Europe; directed the Center for Contemporary Music at Mills College in Oakland, Calif. (1969–81). In his independent compositions he pursues the ideal of "total musical events," absorbing gesticulation, natural human noises, and the entire planetary environment; known particularly for his highly original video operas, including *Music with Roots in the Aether* (1976), *Perfect Lives (Private Parts)* (1977–83), *Atalanta (Acts of God)* (1982), and *Improvement.*

aspramente (It.). Sternly, even cruelly.

assai (It.). Very.

assez doux (mais d'une sonorité large) (Fr.). Rather soft, but with ample sonority (Ravel, *Pavane pour une infante défunte*).

Astaire, Fred (born Frederick Austerlitz), b. Omaha, May 10, 1899; d. Los Angeles, June 22, 1987. With his sister Adele (b. Omaha, Sept. 10, 1897; d. Phoenix, Jan. 25, 1981) he appeared in dance and comedy routines from the age of 7; they worked on the vaudeville circuit, then starred in revues and musicals. Following his sister's retirement; went to Hollywood; teamed up with the dancer Ginger Rogers and gained renown through such films as *The Gay Divorcée* (1934), *Roberta* (1935), *Top Hat* (1935), *Swing Time* (1936), and *Shall We Dance* (1937). His mastery of the dance, ably abetted by an insouciant singing style, contributed greatly to the development of the musical film, earning him a special Academy Award in 1949.

asymmetry. Departure from the customary binary or ternary rhythm. Asymmetry is common outside of Western European and related music. Compound meters are intrinsically asymmetric, as are those typical of Serbian, Croatian, Bulgarian, Macedonian, and Rumanian folk music: subdivisions of binary and ternary meters into unequal groups. The ethnomusicologist Bartók used such meters, derived from the multiethnic folkways of his native Transylvania, in his own music. In modern primitivist music, asymmetry is artificially imposed, e.g. Stravinsky's *L'Histoire du soldat,* in which an asymmetrical melodic line is projected upon a steady bass, creating constant arhythmia and suggesting a missed heartbeat. In the opposite situation, an easily apprehended melody is deliberately thrown out of symmetry by the addition or elision of a rhythmic unit while the accompanying figure continues its preordained course.

Atempause (Ger., pause in breath). Slight break to catch breath before a strong beat.

athematic composition. Deliberate effort to separate the melodic line into segregated groups of phrases and motives bearing no relation to one another. Athematic music does not adhere to any formal organization; such music can therefore start and end at any point. Stockhausen (*Klavierstück XI*), Haubenstock-Ramati, and others organize some works in segments (mobile form) playable in any order whatsoever, with the stipulation that when a performer, accidentally or intentionally, arrives at an already-performed segment, the piece ends. Athematic composition tends toward atonality, where the nonrepetitive principle of melodic material is paramount. An athematic work need not be incoherent or inchoate; successive melodic statements may be related by preferential use of a certain interval or rhythmic configuration. In this sense it may be said that an athematic composition has either zero or an indefinitely large number of themes.

at(h)emlos (Ger.). Breathlessly.

Atkins, Chet (Chester Burton), b. Luttrell, Tenn., June 20, 1924. He began playing the guitar as a child, mastering it without formal instruction; from 1941, appeared on radio, including the *Grand Ole Opry,* Nashville; became an executive for RCA Victor (1957), managing its recording studio in Nashville; led the movement toward popular country-western music (Nashville sound), using electric instruments and modern techniques. A versatile guitarist, he felt at ease in many popular genres; played jazz and toured Europe, the Far East, and Africa; elected to the Country Music Hall of Fame in 1973.

atonality. The absence of tonality, avoiding the historic relationships between members of major and minor scales; traditional tonal structures are abandoned and the key signature is absent. The technique of atonal writing derives from the chromatic scale but resolutely shuns the use of semitonal passages; Rimsky-Korsakov's *Flight of the Bumblebee* is not an example of atonality. The term *atonality* became current among progressive musicians in Vienna at the turn of the 20th century. Schoenberg is generally credited (or blamed) for the invention of atonal composition; he expressly denied this honor (or dishonor). But his posttonal music avoided triadic constructions and harmonic relationships, letting the melody flow freely, unconstrained by the rigid laws of modulation, cadence, sequence, and other time-honored tonal devices. In 1924 he reached the theoretical apogee of his compositional approach, the 12-tone technique (dodecaphony, or serialism), in which all semitones (and melodies) are related to each other without reference to tonal center or epicenter.

Atonal composers (i.e., those not using serial technique) avoid a particular tone's repetition to avoid any tonal implication.

Atonal melodies cultivate wide intervallic leaps, avoiding the monotony of consecutive small intervals. Although individual phrases in atonal music are usually short, the cumulative melodic curve may appear long and sustained; moreover, there is a singular sense of equilibrium inherent in good atonal melodies, where the incidence of high notes is balanced by countervailing groups of low notes; the solid central range represents a majority of essential notes. Such melodies invite dissonant harmonization; the overwhelming desire to obviate the tonic-dominant relationship in atonality requires the replacement of the perfect 5th by the "neutral" tritone and of the octave by a major 7th; tertian melodies and harmonies—affiliated with triadic structures—give way to quartal and quintal progressions; melodic 4ths became hallmarks of atonal writing, potentially evolving into a chord comprising 12 perfect 4ths.

Schoenberg and Berg deprecated the use of the term *atonality*. Berg concluded a 1930 radio talk on the subject with these words: "Antichrist himself could not have thought up a more diabolical appellation than atonal!" A negative concept etymologically, the term was 1st applied by hostile critics as derisive description of this new style, but, as often happens, a perjorative term became the accepted one.

attacca (It., attack). 1. Begin what follows without pause or with a very short pause. 2. In singing, stroke of the glottis.

attack. Act or style of beginning a phrase, passage, or piece.

au mouvement (Fr.). A tempo.

aubade (from Fr. *aube*, dawn). Morning music, as contrasted with serenade, evening music. Aubades were popular in the 17th and 18th centuries, played by military and municipal ensembles on special occasions; the aubade corresponds to the Spanish *alborada*. Several 20th-century composers have written aubades as sophisticated or nostalgic evocations of the past. See also ⇒alba.

Auber, Daniel-François-Esprit, b. Caen, Normandy, Jan. 29, 1782; d. Paris, May 12, 1871. His father, a Parisian art dealer, sent him to London to acquire knowledge of the field; studied music and wrote songs for social entertainment there. Political tension between France and England forced return to Paris (1803); devoted himself exclusively to music. His 1st opera performed in Paris was *Le Séjour militaire* (1813); *La Bergère châtelaine* (1820) was his 1st success. From then on, almost every year saw the production of a new Auber opera; 45 operas were staged professionally in Paris between 1813 and 1869; fortunately collaborated with the best French librettist of the time, Scribe, who wrote (alone or with others) no fewer than 37 librettos for him. His greatest success was *Masaniello, ou La Muette de Portici* (1828); it laid the foundation of French grand opera along with Meyerbeer's *Robert le diable* and Rossini's *Guillaume Tell*; its vivid portrayal of nationalist fury stirred French and Belgian audiences; anti-Dutch riots followed its performance in Brussels (1830); another popular success was *Fra Diavolo* (1830), soon a repertory standard. Despite his successes with grand opera, he is best seen as a founder of later French *opéra comique*, worthy successor to Boïeldieu and at least an equal of Adam and Hérold; Rossini and Wagner valued

his music. Among his other operas are *Le Cheval de bronze* (1835); *Le Domino noir* (1837); and *Manon Lescaut* (1856).

audiences. As classical music's tendency toward formalization has limited audience participation to communal church singing, folk festivals, or Gebrauchsmusik, the primary role for the audience is its reception of works and performances. The response of an audience to new music or to an artist's debut is of crucial significance to public success. Yet there are numerous cases in which the premiere of a famous work was a fiasco: *The Barber of Seville, Tosca, Pelléas et Mélisande*, and *Tannhäuser*. On the other hand, rapturous applause has greeted many an artistic failure.

The reaction of music critics has been less indicative of final judgment than that of the audience. Because Italian operagoers often know the music as well as or better than the singers themselves, they often shout encouragement or condemnation. When a tenor sang flat in a Naples performance, a listener pointed his index finger upward and shouted: "Su! Su!" (higher, higher). When a weighty leader of brigands warned his followers not to attack the demure lady of the castle whom he recognized as his half-sister by saying, "Desist! On the same milk were we nurtured!" an audience member yelled, "You bastard! You must have lapped up all the cream!" When instead the male singer was slight and the prima donna ample, and the plot required him to carry her off the stage, someone in the audience suggested, "Make it in 2 trips!" At a futurist concert in Paris in 1913, several people actually mounted the stage and attacked the performers physically; the futurists, however, fought back; a dozen members of the audience had to be hospitalized.

Enthusiasm for popular pianists, violinists, and (especially) singers often carried the audience away to extremes. During the golden age of opera, admirers would unharness the carriage of a prima donna and pull her and it to her home or hotel. In the 1890s young girls with scissors invaded the stage after Paderewski concerts, intent on cutting off locks of his flowing hair. The adulation for serious artists in Russia was extraordinary both before and after the Revolution; music lovers stood in line all night to get tickets for a Chaliapin recital; one crooked entrepreneur in Leningrad collected many rubles in the 1920s by selling tickets for a phantom piano recital by Josef Hofmann. Russian audiences, insatiable in demands for encores, sometimes refuse to leave the hall until the lights are turned off.

None of these revelations of enthusiasm can approach the frenzy of rock concert fans, who have been known to abandon themselves to orgies of animal delight. Other groups of fans have been known to follow their favorite band literally, such as the Deadheads who traveled with their beloved Grateful Dead until its demise. While symphonic, operatic, and recital audiences are limited by the size of the hall, rock festivals have been taking place in the open air since the 1960s, most notably the 1969 Woodstock festival in N.Y. State, attended by about half a million people.

audition. Performance test given to an aspiring actor, singer, instrumentalist, or sym. conductor, preliminary to the offer of place in cons. or contract. In the professional world, the fate of trembling (or arrogant) hopefuls usually lies in the hands of an all-powerful manager, casting director, or talent scout. At its worst, theatrical or film audition depends on the applicant's willingness to share the "casting couch" with their interrogator. In more typically "humane" classical auditions, juries of professional musicians, usually retired concert players or obsolete opera singers, are engaged to sit in judgment. The greatest nightmare for an auditioning performer is to be suddenly interrupted while performing by a jury member who exercises his or her temporary power with a curt "thank you," 1st flashing a glance at jury colleagues for anticipated approbation of the verdict. Happily, the annals of the opera and concert hall are full of stories about budding celebrities ignominiously cast aside, only to rise to the heights as critically acclaimed artists and commercially successful stars.

auf (Ger.). On. *Sordinen auf,* put mutes on.

Aufführung (Ger.). Performance.

aufgeregt (Ger.). Agitated, excited.

aufhalten (Ger.). Stop, retard.

Auftakt (Ger.). Upbeat, anacrusis; fractional measure beginning movement, piece, or theme.

Auftritt (Ger.). Scene of an opera.

Aufzug (Ger.). Act of an opera.

Augenmusik. Eye music.

augmentation. Doubling (or otherwise multiplying) the duration of the notes of theme or motive; the subject is thereby presented at half speed. This simple arithmetical device looms large in contrapuntal and fugal writing; in Bach's fugues, augmentation is employed didactically to illustrate resources of tonal counterpoint; in his C-minor fugue in book II of *The Well-Tempered Clavier,* he combines the original theme with itself at half the speed. Augmentation lends itself naturally to the expression of Gothic grandiloquence, particularly in the conclusion of works; Reger and Bruckner produced fine effects of this type. In organ works, augmentation can be used impressively in the bass register of the pedals. An unusual augmentation occurs in the coda of the 1st movement of Debussy's *La Mer,* where the pervading whole-tone harmonies secure needed euphony. See also ⇒diminution.

augmented fourth. Interval an enharmonic semitone larger than the perfect 4th, as from C to F-sharp (not G-flat). *Augmented second,* interval an enharmonic semitone larger than major 2nd, found between the 6th and 7th degrees of the harmonic minor scale, such as F and G-sharp in the A-minor scale; characteristic of Eastern melodies; *augmented sixth,* interval an enharmonic semitone larger than major 6th, as from C to A-sharp (not B-flat); the framing interval of the so-called French 6th, German 6th, and Italian 6th chords; *augmented triad,* triad consisting of 2 ascending major 3rds, as in C, E, G-sharp.

aulos (Grk., reed, pipe). Ancient Greek wind instrument presaging the oboe; it usually had 2 connected pipes branching out in the shape of the letter *V,* blown simultaneously through bulbous mouthpiece holding single, sometimes double reed; made of reed, wood, ivory, or bone; both pipes had an equal number of symmetrically placed holes. While fingers of both hands could play either pipe, it seems possible that one of the pipes functioned as a drone. The aulos is associated with the corybantic dances of Dionysian worship, as opposed to the Apollonian music on the kithara.

Auric, Georges, b. Lodève, Hérault, Feb. 15, 1899; d. Paris, July 23, 1983. He studied music at the Montpellier Cons.; went to Paris; studied at the Cons. and at the Schola Cantorum; by age 20, had composed around 300 songs and piano pieces, ballet, and comic opera; following World War I, joined the anti-Romantic movement in France, led by Satie and Cocteau; Satie urged young composers to produce "auditory pleasure without demanding disproportionate attention from the listener," while Cocteau elevated artistic ugliness to an aesthetic ideal. Under Satie's aegis, Auric joined 5 composers of his generation in group 1st called Les Nouveaux Jeunes, later Les 6 (with Milhaud, Honegger, Poulenc, Durey, and Tailleferre); established connection with Diaghilev, who commissioned him to write ballets for the Ballets Russes; his facile yet felicitous manner of composing, with mock-Romantic connotations, fit perfectly into Diaghilev's scheme; particularly successful were *Les Facheux* (1924) and *Les Matelots* (1925); wrote music for numerous films, among them *Le Sang d'un poète* (1930), *A nous la liberté* (1932), *La Belle et la Bête* (1946), *Orphée* (1949), and *Lola Montes* (1955). His theatrical experience earned him important administrative posts; general administrator of both the Paris Opéra and the Opéra-Comique (1962–68); served as president of the French Union of Composers and Authors (1954–77); elected to the Academie (1962).

Ausdruck, mit (Ger.). With expression. *Mit innigem Ausdruck,* with heartfelt expression; *ausdrucklos* (Ger.), without expression (Berg, *Wozzeck*).

Ausgabe (Ger.). Edition. *Neue Ausgabe,* new edition; *revidierte Ausgabe,* revised edition.

Auszierungen (Ger.). Ornaments, ornamentations.

Auszug (Ger.). Arrangement or reduction, as in *Klavierauszug,* piano reduction from full score.

authentic cadence. Cadence in which the penultimate chord is the dominant, followed by the final tonic.

authentic mode. Mode in which the lower tonic or final is the lowest note of the mode. In Gregorian chant the 4 most frequently used modes are the Dorian, Phrygian, Lydian, and Mixolydian, with finals D, E, F, and G, respectively. The 1-octave gamut of authentic modes ranges from the lower tonic (final) to upper tonic (D to D, E to E, etc.). These modes are equivalent to the piano's white keys, although contrapuntal rules demand flexibility between B and B♭. In early church singing and theory, authentic modes were named by Latinized quasi-Greek ordinal numbers: Protus, Deuterus, Tritus, and Tetrardus. Later, a system of *tonoi* (modes) emerged, numbering authentic modes with odd numbers (1, 3, 5, 7) and plagal modes with even numbers. In the

16th century Glarean (Dodecachordon) added 4 more modes to reflect late Renaissance practice; the authentic modes were Aeolian (A to A) and Ionian (C to C). See also ⇒plagal mode.

autoharp. 19th-century zither invented by Charles Zimmerman. It has special harmony buttons that dampen all strings except the ones needed for the desired chord, so that the player can strum arpeggios freely with the fingers or plectrum; used to demonstrate harmonic progressions and accompany simple songs. The autoharp was also used in U.S. Appalachian traditional music.

automatic writing. Means of communication from beyond the grave, as employed by spiritualists. A British housewife, Rosemary Brown, appeared on television in the summer of 1969 and claimed that her diluted imitations of works by Schubert and Liszt were dictated to her by them, and that she wrote them down automatically. Her claims were never subjected to controlled examination, but if substantiated they would prove that prolonged state of death fatally affects the ability to compose even among celebrated musicians.

auxiliary note. Nonharmonic melodic note approached by step in one direction and left by step in the opposite direction; neighbor note.

avant-garde (Fr. *vanguard,* in advance). Term, dating from 1910, referring to radical or incomprehensible art as viewed in its own time; generally, yesterday's avant-garde becomes today's commonplace. The term *avant-garde* is the heir to long series of terms descriptive of progressive art: *modern, ultra-modern, new, modernistic, experimental, empiric.* Its unfortunate derivation from military vocabulary does not seem to dismay progressive composers, who accept the term as an honorable profession of artistic faith. At present the term usually denotes the musical ideas and practices of Europeans such as Boulez, Stockhausen, Berio, and others, as distinct from those of the American experimental school or tradition, e.g., Cage, Feldman, Wolff, and others. See ⇒experimental music.

avec abandon (Fr.). Emotionally; passionately; carried away by feeling. *Avec âme,* con anima; *avec charme,* gracefully; *avec*

élan, dashingly; con islancio; *avec emphase,* with emphasis; *avec énergie,* with energy, energetically; accent vigorously and phrase distinctly.

avec le chant (Fr.). See ⇒col canto.

Avison, Charles (born Aznavurian), b. Newcastle-upon-Tyne, 1709 (old style; baptized Feb. 16); d. there, May 9, 1770. He wrote concertos employing strings with basso continuo; orch'l sonatas in which keyboard dominates; concertos for strings *à* 7 with harpsichord; keyboard concertos with string quartet; quartets for keyboard with 2 violins and cello; trio sonatas for keyboard with 2 violins. His *Essay on Musical Expression* (London, 1752) is important as an early exposition of relative musical values by an English musician.

Ax, Emanuel, b. Lwów, June 8, 1949. He began playing the violin at age 6; studied piano with his father; moved to Warsaw when he was 8, to Winnipeg when he was 10; settled in N.Y. (1961); enrolled at the Juilliard School of Music. He toured South America (1969); became U.S. citizen (1970); made N.Y. debut (1973). After many frustrations he won 1st place in the Rubinstein International Piano Master Competition, Tel Aviv, earning an American concert tour; also appeared throughout Europe; awarded the Avery Fisher Prize (1979); In addition to fine interpretations of the standard repertoire, has distinguished himself as champion of contemporary music.

ayre. English court song of the 16th and 17th centuries, usually accompanied on the lute; old English spelling of air.

Aznavour, Charles (born Aznavurian), b. Paris, May 22, 1924. A son of an Armenian baritone from Tiflis, he received his early musical training at home; acted in Paris variety shows at age 5; learned to play the guitar. His songs became popular in the 1940s; championed by Mistinguette, Chevalier, and Piaf; made several American tours as nightclub entertainer; acted in films; composed a great number of songs, of the *tristesse chansons* and frustration ballads type; best-known songs in translation include *Yesterday When I Was Young, All the Pretty Girls, The Old-Fashioned Way,* and *She.* His operetta *Monsieur Carnaval* was produced in Paris (1965).

B (Ger. *H;* Fr., It., Rus., Sp. *Si*). 1. The 7th tone and degree in the diatonic scale of C major. 2. In musical theory, uppercase *B* designates the B-major triad, while lowercase *b* indicates the B-minor triad. 3. In Ger., B flat. This unique usage makes it possible to render Bach's name in musical notes, since the Ger. *H* corresponds to B natural (see ⇒B–A–C–H). 4. (Abbr.) Bass, basso; *c.B.*, col Basso; *b.c.*, basso continuo).

B dur (Ger.). B-flat major.

B major. A key of velvety warmth, rich in texture and emotionally ingratiating. The scale of B major, numbering all 5 black keys (F♯, C♯, G♯, D♯, A♯) and 2 white keys (B, E), is eminently pianistic, but the tonality is not suited for orch'l works. Only the subdominant of B major is represented by an open string on the violin and double bass. As for brass instruments, they are easier to play in flat keys, which B major certainly is not. Its enharmonic equivalent, C-flat major, with 7 flats in the key signature, has a certain affinity with the standard tuning of transposing wind instruments; Stravinsky's ballet *The Firebird* has a section in C-flat major, a rarity in orch'l music.

B minor. As described by the 17th-century French composer Charpentier, a *solitaire et mélancolique* key. The description has held true, as composers have demonstrated. Tchaikovsky's *Pathétique Sym.*, certainly one of the most melancholy pieces ever written, is in B minor, as are Mendelssohn's overture *Fingal's Cave* (suggesting aloofness and remoteness) and the bassoon solo in the 2nd movement of Rimsky-Korsakov's *Scheherazade*. Perhaps the epitome of dolor is achieved in the 1st movement of Schubert's *Unfinished Sym.*

B moll (Ger.). B-flat minor.

Babbitt, Milton (Byron), b. Philadelphia, May 10, 1916. He received his 1st musical training in Jackson, Miss.; revealed an acute flair for mathematical reasoning as well; studied with Philip James, Marion Bauer, and Sessions. He taught mathematics at Princeton Univ. (1942–45), then music (1948–84); taught at Juilliard School, N.Y. (from 1973); elected a member of the National Inst. of Arts and Letters (1965). For Princeton and Columbia Univs. he inaugurated a Center for Electronic Music with a newly constructed mainframe synthesizer.

Babbitt has promulgated a system of melodic and rhythmic sets ultimately leading to (integral) total serialism; extended Schoenberg's serial principle to embrace 12 different note values, time intervals between instrumental entries, dynamic levels, and instrumental timbres. In order to describe the potential combinations of the 4 basic aspects of a tone-row, he introduced the term "combinatoriality," with symmetrical parts of a tone-row designated as "derivations." His original music, some of it aurally beguiling, is best understood after a preliminary study of its underlying compositional plan. In 1982 he won a special citation of the Pulitzer Committee for "his life's work as a distinguished and seminal American composer."

baby grand. The smallest size of the grand piano.

baccheta di legno (It.). Wooden drumstick used for a dry (nonresonant) beat. *Baccheta di tamburo* (It.), a larger drumstick. *Bacchetto* (It.), a smaller drumstick.

bacchetta (It.). Conductor's baton.

B–A–C–H. The letters of Bach's name, which in German pitch nomenclature generate the notes B flat, A, C, and B natural. Bach used this chromatic theme in the unfinished last fugue of *The Art of the Fugue,* and many composers have since paid tribute to him by writing pieces based on the same 4 notes; their disposition (4 adjacent chromatic notes in alternation) makes it possible to use them as a cell within a 12-tone row.

Bach, Carl Philipp Emanuel, b. Weimar, Mar. 8, 1714; d. Hamburg, Dec. 14, 1788. The 3rd son of Johann Sebastian Bach; called the "Berlin" or "Hamburg" Bach; studied with his father at the Thomasschule, Leipzig; studied jurisprudence at the Univs. of Leipzig and Frankfurt-an-der-Oder; went to Berlin (1738); became chamber musician to Frederick the Great of Prussia (1740); arranged his father's visit to Potsdam (1747). In 1768 he became cantor at the Johanneum, Hamburg; held this post until his death; abandoning the strict polyphonic style of his father, became a leader of the new school of clavier music and a master of *Empfindsamkeit* (inner expressivity); directed several keyboard collections at "connoisseurs and amateurs." His *Essay on the True Art of Playing the Clavier* (1753–62) has been very influential, yielding much authentic information about musical practices of the latter 18th century.

Bach, Johann (John) Christian, b. Leipzig, Sept. 5, 1735; d. London, Jan. 1, 1782. The 11th surviving son of Johann Sebastian Bach; called the "London" Bach. He studied with his father and his stepbrother C. P. E. Bach; went to Italy (1754); studied with Padre Martini; converted to Roman Catholicism for work purposes; at the Milan Cathedral (1760–62); traveled throughout Italy; composed several successful operas there. In 1762 he moved to London; his acclaimed opera *Orione, ossia Diana vendicata* was premiered there (1763); appointed music master to the Queen (1764); with C. F. Abel, gave a famous series of London concerts (1764–81).

When young Mozart came to London (1764), Bach took interest in him and improvised with him at the keyboard. Mozart retained a lifelong affection for him, using Bach's keyboard sonatas as models for his early piano concertos. Bach was highly prolific; wrote syms., keyboard concertos, chamber music, violin sonatas, and piano sonatas. His music exhibited the galant style of the 2nd half of the 18th century; totally departed from his father's ideals; an important influence on the Classic era. Best known as an instrumental composer, he wrote successful operas, including *Catone in Utica* (1761), *Temistocle* (1772), *Lucio Silla* (to same libretto as Mozart's, 1774), *La clemenza di Scipione* (1778), and *Amadis de Gaule* (1779).

Bach, Johann Christoph Friedrich, b. Leipzig, June 21, 1732; d. Bückeburg, Jan. 26, 1795. The 9th son of Johann Sebastian Bach, he was called the "Bückeburg" Bach. He studied music with his father; attended the Univ. of Leipzig in jurisprudence; became chamber musician to Count Wilhelm of Schaumburg-Lippe of Bückeburg (1750); became "Concert-Meister" (1759); remained until his death. He was a virtuoso, but is less known as a composer than his brothers and stepbrothers; wrote sym., concertos, oratorios, cantatas, and keyboard music in the style galant.

Bach, Johann Sebastian. b. Eisenach, Mar. 21 (baptized Mar. 23), 1685; d. Leipzig, July 28, 1750. He attended the Latin school in Eisenacht. Bach began attending the Lyceum, Ohrdruf (1695); lived with his brother Johann Christoph; admitted to the Mettenchor of the Michaeliskirche, Lüneburg (1700); won a position in Weimar but didn't take post; appointed organist at the Neukirche, Arnstadt (1703); travelled to Lübeck to hear Buxtehude (1705), presumably hoping to obtain the older man's position as organist upon retirement, but Buxtehude expected successor to marry the eldest of his 5 unmarried daughters. Bach declined and returned to Arnstadt.

In 1707 he became organist at the Blasiuskirche, Mühlhausen; that year, married his cousin Maria Barbara Bach presented his cantata *Gott ist mein König* (BWV 71, 1708); resigned that year to accept the better-paying post of court organist to Duke Wilhelm Ernst of Weimar; became Konzertmeister (1714); in 1717, accepted the position of Kapellmeister and music director to Prince Leopold of Anhalt in Cöthen; but his departure was blocked by Wilhelm Ernst, who even imprisoned Bach before releasing him from his obligations.

The Cöthen period, one of the most productive and least troubled in Bach's life, was a time of instrumental music: the *Brandenburg Concertos, Clavierbüchlein für Wilhelm Friedemann Bach,* book I of *Das Wohltemperierte Clavier,* and the solo violin and cello works. While traveling with Prince Leopold, his wife Maria Barbara died, leaving him with 7 children; the following year, he married his 2nd wife, Anna Magdalena Wilcken (1701–60); they had 13 children. When Prince Leopold married a woman with no interest in music, Bach began looking for a new job; when Kuhnau, the cantor of Leipzig, died (1722), he applied for the post; Leipzig authorities, who offered it 1st to Telemann and then Christoph Graupner, elected Bach Leipzig city cantor; officially installed in 1723.

As director of church music, he supervised church musicians; provided music for services; taught at the Thomasschule; here wrote his greatest sacred works: the *St. Matthew Passion, St. John Passion,* B-minor Mass, Magnificat, the holiday oratorios, and most of the church cantatas. In 1729, he organized the famous Collegium Musicum, made up of professionals and students who gave weekly concerts; led this group until 1737, again from 1739 to 1741. He suffered from a cataract that gradually darkened his vision; an operation on his eyes in 1749, performed with the crude tools of the time, left him almost totally blind. The etiology of his last illness is unclear; it is said that his vision suddenly returned (possibly when the cataract receded spontaneously), but a cerebral hemorrhage supervened; a few days later he was dead.

Despite the musical supremacy of Bach, he was not isolated, but a mentor to young students, a master organist, and instructor whose non-sacred compositions were didactic in intent; indeed, the text of the dedication of his epoch-making *Das wohltemperierte Clavier oder Praeludia und Fügen* (book I, 1722; book II, 1742) reads: "The Well-Tempered Clavier, or Preludes and Fugues in all tones and semitones . . . composed and notated for the benefit and exercise of musical young people eager to learn, as well as for a special practice for those who have already achieved proficiency and skill in this study." He was not the 1st to attempt such a cycle; J. C. F. Fischer anticipated him in a 1702 collection *Ariadne musica,* comprising 20 preludes and fugues in different keys; undoubtedly Bach was aware of this work, as the subjects of several of Bach's pieces are similar or nearly identical to those in Fischer's work. This does not detract from the significance of Bach's accomplishment, however; the beauty and totality of development make his work vastly superior to those of his putative predecessors.

In the art of variations, Bach was supreme; a superb example is the *Goldberg Variations,* so named because it was commissioned by a Russian diplomat through the mediation of Bach's pupil J. G. Goldberg, Kayserling's harpsichordist. Bach's 6 *Concerts à plusieurs instruments,* known as the *Brandenburg Concertos* because of their dedication to the margrave of Brandenburg (possibly as a petition for an appointment), represent the crowning achievement of the secular Baroque; nos. 2, 4, and 5 of the set are examples of concerto grosso, contrasting a group of solo instruments (concertino) with an accompanying string orch. (ripieno).

Die Kunst der Fuge (The Art of Fugue), Bach's unfinished last composition (begun 1749), provides an encyclopedia of fugues, canons, and various counterpoints based on the same theme: inversion, canon, augmentation, diminution, double fugue, triple fugue, at times appearing in fantastic optical symmetry so that the written music itself forms a balanced design; here, art is designed to instruct the mind as well as delight the ear. Also extraordinary is *Das Musikalische Opfer* (Musical Offering), composed for Frederick the Great of Prussia, who had invited Bach to Potsdam (1747). The King gave him a subject (allegedly of his own invention); asked him to improvise a fugue upon it (which Bach did). Upon his return to Leipzig, Bach composed a set of contrapuntal pieces based on the King's theme.

Contrary to received wisdom, Bach was not unappreciated by his contemporaries (although his compositions were considered old-fashioned); Mozart, Beethoven, and Chopin studied the preludes and fugues. While Mendelssohn's Berlin revival of the *St. Matthew Passion* (1829) was important, Bach's reputation had never really dimmed. Even modern composers who have abandoned conventional tonality are irresistibly drawn to Bach, e.g., Berg's use of the chorale *Es ist genug* (from the cantata *O Ewigkeit, du Donnerwort,* BWV 60) in the bittersweet finale of his violin concerto (1935). The slogan "Back to Bach" may hold true for every musical era; yet his art never entirely disappears to begin with. The standard Bach thematic catalogue is W. Schmieder's *Thematisch-systematisches Verzeichnis der musikalischen Werke von J. S. B. (Bach-Werke-Verzeichnis)* (Leipzig, 1950; 3rd ed., 1961).

Bach, P. D. Q. See ⇒Schickele, Peter.

Bach, Wilhelm Friedemann, b. Weimar, Nov. 22, 1710; d. Berlin, July 1, 1784. The eldest son of Johann Sebastian Bach; called the "Halle" Bach. He studied with his father at the Thomasschule (1723–29) and violin with J. G. Graun in Merseburg (1726); enrolled at the Univ. of Leipzig in mathematics, philosophy, and law (1729); organist at the Sophienkirche, Dresden (1733), then the Liebfrauenkirche, Halle (1746);

offered the Kapellmeister position in Darmstadt, but somehow lost it (1762); walked out on the Halle post (1764); moved to Brunswick (1770), then Berlin (1774), where he taught Mendelssohn's great-aunt and gained favor at Anna Amalia's court; his intrigues there backfired; died in poverty. A highly gifted composer, he alternated between his father's style and the new Empfindsamkeit; career was flawed by personal instability; custodianship of part of Johann Sebastian's MSS was incompetent, if not criminal; claimed some of his father's music for his own; forged the older Bach's signature on at least 1 of his own pieces.

Bacharach, Burt, b. Kansas City, May 12, 1928. He played jazz piano in nightclubs; studied at McGill Univ., Montreal; took courses with Darius Milhaud and Henry Cowell at the New School for Social Research, N.Y.; toured with Marlene Dietrich as accompanist (1958–61); In 1962, joined forces with lyricist Hal David, producing such songs as *Reach Out for Me, Trains and Boats and Planes, Make It Easy on Yourself, Blue on Blue, Walk on By, Always Something There to Remind Me, What the World Needs Now Is Love, Do You Know the Way to San Jose?, Raindrops Keep Fallin' on My Head, The Look of Love,* and *I'll Never Fall in Love Again;* produced the successful Broadway musical *Promises, Promises* (1968). He wrote songs for the films *What's New Pussycat?, Wives and Lovers, Alfie, Send Me No Flowers, Promise Her Anything,* and *Butch Cassidy and the Sundance Kid.* The singer Dionne Warwick (b. 1941) was his best interpreter.

Backhaus, Wilhelm, b. Leipzig, Mar. 26, 1884; d. Villach, Austria, July 5, 1969. He studied with Reckendorf (1891–99) and briefly with d'Albert; went on a major tour in 1900; acquired a fine European reputation as pianist and teacher; made U.S. debut as soloist in Beethoven's *Emperor Concerto* under Walter Damrosch in N.Y. (1912); settled in Lugano (1930); continuing to teach, became a Swiss citizen; following World War II, resumed concert tours; made last U.S. appearance at a N.Y. recital in 1962, displaying undiminished virtuosic vigor; particularly distinguished in his interpretations of the works of Beethoven and Brahms.

Baez, Joan (Chandos), b. Staten Island, N.Y., Jan. 9, 1941. She learned the guitar by ear; studied drama at Boston Univ.; made her 1st important appearance at the Newport Folk Festival (1959); in 1965, founded the Inst. for the Study of Non-Violence; joined the anti-Vietnam War movement; supported the organizing fight of the United Farm Workers' Union; appeared at concerts promoting topical humanitarian causes. She was associated with Bob Dylan in the 1960s and 1970s (depicted in her *Diamonds and Rust*), and followed his lead into folk-rock; most recognizable trademark is her beautifully rich voice and superb diction.

bagatelle (Fr., trifle). Short, lighter piece with no specific form, usually for keyboard; the term was 1st used by Couperin for a rondeau (*Les Bagatelles,* 10th *ordre,* 2nd Book of Harpsichord Pieces, 1717); Beethoven wrote 3 sets for piano (opp. 33, 119, 126), many of which are far from trifling; other bagatelle composers are Smetana, Saint-Saëns, Sibelius, Bartók, Dvořák, Poulenc, and Webern. Liszt's *Bagatelle ohne Tonart,* written *c.* 1880 and publ. posth., is explicitly "without key," lacking a key signature, and cultivating tritones, major 7ths, and other "atonal" intervals.

bagpipe(s). Ancient wind instrument of Eastern origin, still popular in Great Britain, Ireland, and many European cultures. The basic instrument comprises an air-holding bag and pipes. The Scottish highland bagpipe has 4 pipes: 3 drone-pipes, single- or double-reed pipes tuned to a tone, its 5th, and its octave; and 1 chanter (melody-pipe), a single- or double-reed pipe with 6 or 8 holes. The bag is a leather sack filled with air either from the mouth (through a blowpipe) or from small bellows worked by the player's arm; the sounding pipes are inserted in and receive air from the bag. Scotland has several varieties of bagpipe; the best known is the highland pipe, a mouth-blown military instrument held upright, covered in plaid, and played by men in skirts. The most familiar Irish pipe is the smaller union or uilleann pipe, bellows-blown, lap-held, and with regulator pipes with keys played with the heel of the hand, allowing for chords.

Although the bagpipe is the national instrument of Scotland and Ireland, many similar instruments are found in Europe: Northumbrian small-pipe (England); musette, cornemuse, and biniou (France); gaita and zampoña (Spain, Portugal); Dudelsack (Germany); zampogna and cornamusa (Italy); gadje (Yugoslavia, Macedonia, Bulgaria); duda (Hungary, Belarus); cimpoi (Rumania); dudy (Czech Republic); gajdy (Slovakia); dudy and koziol (Poland); and mashq (India).

baguette (Fr.). Conductor's baton; also, a drumstick. *Baguette de bois,* wooden drumstick; *baguette d'eponge,* drumstick with a sponge head.

Baker, David (Nathaniel), b. Indianapolis, In., Dec. 21, 1931. He studied with G. Schuller, B. Heiden, J. Orrego-Salas, W. Russo, and G. Russell; taught in small colleges and public schools; appointed chairman of jazz studies at Indiana Univ. (1966); played trombone with S. Kenton, L. Hampton, and Q. Jones. His compositions fuse jazz improvisation with ultra-modern devices, including serial procedures; has composed extensively in most genres; his books include *Jazz Improvisation: A Comprehensive Method of Study for All Players* (1969) and *Techniques of Improvisation* (1971); he co-edited *The Black Composer Speaks* (1978).

Baker, (Dame) Janet (Abbott), b. Hatfield, Yorkshire, Aug. 21, 1933. She began singing lessons in London with H. Isepp and M. St. Clair; attended classes at the Mozarteum, Salzburg (1956); attended Lotte Lehmann's London master class; a decisive career turn came with her joining Britten's English Opera Group; created the role of Kate Julian in Britten's television opera *Owen Wingrave* (1971); made her successful American debut with the San Francisco Sym. in Mahler's *Das Lied von der Erde* and presented a solo recital in N.Y. (1966); subsequent engagements took her all over Europe. Queen Elizabeth II made her a Dame Commander of the Order of the British Empire (1976); gave operatic farewell in 1982. She was an outstanding artist of intellectual brilliance; her extensive operatic repertoire ranged from Monteverdi and Handel to R. Strauss and Britten; one of the great lieder artists of her day, excelling in Schubert and Schumann.

Baker, Josephine, b. St. Louis, June 3, 1906; d. Paris, Apr. 12, 1979. She was a street musician by age 13; toured on the vaudeville circuit; gained recognition in the show *Chocolate Dandies* (1924); went to Paris; starred in *La Revue nègre,* then the Folies-Bergère (1925); introduced bracelets-and-bananas costume. Her exotic, highly erotic, quixotic stage persona gained her fame; starred in a revival of Offenbach's *La Créole* (1934); became naturalized French citizen (1937); entertained troops and assisted in the French Resistance during the Nazi occupation (1940–44). After the war she turned to humanitarian causes, adopting orphans from various countries; also active in the U.S. civil rights movement.

Baker, Theodore, b. N.Y., June 3, 1851; d. Dresden, Oct. 13, 1934. Although trained in business, he decided to devote himself to music; went to Leipzig (1874); wrote 1st serious study of Native American music (Ph.D., 1882). Returning to the U.S. (1890), he became literary ed. and trans. for G. Schirmer (1892); retired; returned to Germany (1926). He publ. *A Dictionary of Musical Terms* (1895); *A Pronouncing Pocket Manual of Musical Terms* (1905); *The Musician's Calendar and Birthday Book* (1915–17). In 1900 he publ. *Baker's Biographical Dictionary of Musicians,* his imperishable monument; rectified lack of American musicians in earlier reference works; publ. a 2nd ed. (1905); subsequent eds. rev. by Alfred Remy (3rd, 1919); Carl Engel (4th, 1940); and Nicolas Slonimsky, who rev. 5th (1958), 6th (1978), 7th (1984), and 8th eds. (1991), and undertook 3 supplementary vols. (1949, 1965, 1971).

Balakirev, Mily (Alexeievich), b. Nizhny-Novgorod, Jan. 2, 1837 (new style; Dec. 21, 1836, old style); d. St. Petersburg, May 29, 1910. He went to Moscow; studied piano with A. Dubuque and theory with K. Eisrich; met A. Oulibishev, author and owner of an estate in Nizhny-Novgorod; Balakirev played piano in private musical evenings there; attended the Univ. of Kazan in mathematics (1853–54); went to St. Petersburg; met Glinka, who encouraged his musical interests (1855); made his compositional debut there (1856), playing the solo part in the 1st movement of his never compl. Piano Concerto; his *Overture on the Theme of 3 Russian Songs* was performed in Moscow (1859), his *Overture to King Lear* in St. Petersburg later that year.

In 1860 Balakirev took a boat ride down the Volga River from Nizhny-Novgorod to the Caspian Sea delta; collected, notated, and harmonized Russian folk songs; his 1866 collection included the *Song of the Volga Boatmen,* or *Song of the Burlaks* (peasants who pulled large grain boats upstream on the Volga). He organized a St. Petersburg group known as the Balakirev Circle (1863), to promote nationalist Russian music and oppose passive imitation of then dominant classical German compositions; founded the Free Music School in St. Petersburg; gave concerts of Russian and German compositions.

In 1867 Balakirev went to Prague to conduct Glinka's operas there; organized a concert of Russian and Czech works at his Free Music School that year; the program included pieces by Borodin, Cui, Mussorgsky, Rimsky-Korsakov, and himself. The occasion moved the critic Vladimir Stasov to declare that Russia, too, had its "mighty little handful" (*moguchaya kuchka*) of fine musicians; in English, the group became known as the "Mighty 5." In addition to a spiritual unity of Slavic nations, the Mighty 5 looked to exotic Islamic lands through the Caucasus to Persia in the south and to Central Asia in the east. Balakirev became fascinated with Caucasian quasi-oriental melodies and rhythms during visits there; wrote a brilliant oriental fantasy for piano, *Islamey* (1869); its technical difficulties rival Liszt's études.

Balakirev slackened the tempo of his work; consistently had trouble completing his scores; discontinued the Free Music School concerts (1872); worked for the railroad transport, then as administrator in women's educational insts. in St. Petersburg; returned to musical activities (1881); conducted the premiere of the Sym. No. 1 by the 16-year-old Glazunov (1882); rev. and completed earlier scores, including the *2nd Overture on Russian Themes,* renamed *Russia* (1864–82), the symphonic poem *Tamara* (1867–82), and the Sym. No. 1 in C Major (1864–97); composed his 2nd Sym. in D Minor (1909); took up the 2nd Piano Concerto (begun 1861) but left it unfinished (compl. Liapunov); retired (1894); spent his remaining years composing.

Balakirev made a tremendous impact on the destinies of Russian music, particularly because of his patriotic conviction that Russia could rival Germany and other nations in the art of music. His relatively small output can be attributed to illnesses, including encephalitis and severe depression; nonetheless, left powerful and exotically colored works that deserve more performances.

balalaika (Rus.). Popular Russian instrument of the guitar type, with a triangular body, long neck, and 3 strings. It became popular in the 18th century. Toward the end of the 19th century serious Russian musicians became interested in constructing differently sized balalaikas and combining with the more ancient domra in ethnic Russian ensembles.

Balanchine, George (born Gyorgy Melitonovich Balanchivadze), b. St. Petersburg, Jan. 22, 1904; d. N.Y., Apr. 30, 1983. He attended the Imperial Ballet School, St. Petersburg; studied music at the Petrograd Cons.; founded the Young Ballet; joined Diaghilev's Ballets Russes, Paris and choreographed for it (1924–29); at the invitation of American dance specialist Lincoln Kirstein, came to N.Y. (1933); they formed the School of American Ballet (1934), later known as American Ballet (1935–38), Ballet Caravan (1941), Ballet Soc. (1946–48), and finally the N.Y.C. Ballet (from 1948); toured Russia with the company (1962).

Balanchine was distinguished by his modern innovations in ballet, with music by old and new composers, especially Stravinsky: from Le Chant du Rossignol (1925) to Agon (1957). He retained his connections with Europe (Hindemith's Kammermusik No. 2, Mozart's Divertimento No. 15) but adapted quickly to the American landscape, setting dances to works by K. Swift, Gould, H. Kay, Sousa, Gershwin, and R. Rodgers (4 musicals); received the Presidential Medal of Freedom (1983); died shortly thereafter of the consequences of "progressive cerebral disintegration." In his long career he created nearly 200 ballets; he once said, "Music must be seen, and dance must be heard."

ballad (from Lat. *ballare,* to dance). 1. Orig., song intended for dance accompaniment; hence the air of such a song. 2. In modern usage, simple narrative poem, often sentimental or dramatic, generally meant to be sung. The ballad has been an especially fruitful genre in English-speaking countries, acquiring Romantic connotations in the choice of mysterious legends or horror stories as subject matter. 3. Orig., short, simple vocal melody set to 1 or more symmetrical stanzas, with a light instrumental accompaniment; the term now includes instrumental melodies of a similar character. 4. Compositions for single instruments or orch., embodying the idea of a narrative. 5. In the U.S., any folk song, regardless of content.

ballad opera. Musical stage work primarily made up of extant ballads and folk songs or at least their tunes; spoken dialogue is a component. Popular in 18th-century England and its northern colonies, the genre is stylistically close to the French vaudeville. The work that precipitated the genre's heyday was *The Beggar's Opera*, 1728, by John Gay, with music arranged by John Christopher (Johann Christoph) Pepusch (1667–1752); subsequent ballad operas drew freely on arias and choruses of past composers. The genre exhausted itself toward the end of the 18th century; gave way to the fertile development of German Singspiel. More than a century later the ballad opera was revived in Germany by Weill and others who used the mixed English-German designation *Songspiel* (*song* having acquired a German meaning for musical entertainment of any kind); the 20th-century model was usually newly composed.

ballade (Fr., from Lat. *ballare*, dance; Ger.). Term of widely ranging connotations, 1st applied to vocal compositions of the masters of the ars nova and to troubadour songs; despite the word's derivation, the choreographic aspect of this genre had disappeared by this time. Among the most significant polyphonic vocal ballades are Machaut's; later developments were bergerettes (from *bergère*, a shepherdess) and pastoral songs of the 18th century.

The Romantic ballade was either a balladlike art song or an instrumental solo piece. Ballades (ballads) were strophic poems as popularized by Goethe and Schiller; Schubert and Schumann set a multitude of these poems by having each stanza sung to the same music; the most prolific composer of German ballades was Loewe, who published 17 vols. of mostly strophic songs. A more elaborate type of ballade was through-composed (Ger. *durchkomponiert*), where each stanza could be set to different music. Instrumental ballades were designed as wordless narratives; Chopin's ballades for piano are the greatest examples of this genre; others were written by Liszt, Brahms, and Grieg; Medtner introduced a sonata-ballade hybrid; orch'l ballades were also composed, e.g., Glazunov's *Concerto Ballata* for Cello and Orch. (op. 108, 1931).

ballata (from Lat. *ballare*, dance). The most popular song form of the early Italian Renaissance, close in function and spirit to the French virelai and the Spanish villancico; each of several stanzas is followed by a *ripresa* (refrain). Despite the apparent derivation, no dance-related ballatas have been found. In the Trecento (14th century), Landini and others produced masterpieces in this genre.

ballet (Fr.; Ger. *Ballett*). 1. Integral dance work; dance introduced in an opera or other stage work. 2. Pantomime, with music and dances setting forth the thread of the story.

balletto (It.). 1. Ballet. 2. Title of an allegretto by Bach, in common time. 3. In the 17th century, dramatic madrigal for voices and instruments written in a free manner, with some passages suited for dance. 4. Purely instrumental compositions with no dance associations.

ballo (It.). 1. Dance. 2. Short theatrical work with dance. 3. Dramatic musical work with dance, e.g., Monteverdi's *Il Ballo delle ingrate*.

ballet de cour (Fr.). Court dance genre of French royalty, from Henry III to Louis XIV, with courtiers, including the King, participating in the performance. Subject matter included mythology, non-Christian "primitives and savages," and the glory of the royal state. Stylistically, the genre borrowed from the Italian mascherata and intermedio and French courtly pantomimes and fetes; similar to the English masque. Louis XIV danced from 1651 (at age 13) until 1670; thereafter the genre began a decline that, excepting a brief revival under Louis XV, saw its extinction by the mid-18th century. Composers of music for *ballets de cour* included P. Guérdon, Lully, de Lalande, Destouches, Campra, and Mouret.

band. 1. Instrumental ensemble consisting of brass, woodwind, and percussion instruments, excluding string instruments; applied to military bands, jazz bands, dance bands, and brass bands; in jazz a stylistic distinction exists between big bands (orch.) and small bands (combos, groups). In the hierarchy of musical ensembles, the band occupies a lower position than an orch.; the terms wind orch. or symphonic band are found; however, English and other kings had their royal bands, implying no condescension towards this designation; Lully's group of 24 violons du roy was called La grande bande. 2. Company of musicians playing military or sports-oriented music. 3. Section of the orch. playing instruments of the same family (brass band, string band, wind band, wood band).

band, big. See ⇒Big band.

band, brass. 1. Large ensemble consisting of brass instruments, with tubas of various sizes; mostly used for military and sports displays or municipal entertainments; sometimes present concerts of arranged classical music or original and commisioned works. In Britain, also called silver band. 2. Brass section of the orch.

band, marching. Military band used in more pacific pursuits, such as holiday parades and sporting events.

band, military. Large, mobile ensemble designed to accompany military activities. Since time immemorial, military activities have been accompanied by brass instruments, drums, and cymbals; as the apostle Paul asks rhetorically (I Corinthians 14:8), "If the trumpet gives an uncertain sound, who shall prepare himself to the battle?" Military bands arose in Europe during the Middle Ages; Frederick the Great added other melody instruments such as oboes and clarinets to them. In the latter 18th century the instrumentation of military bands incorporated Janizary music sonorities, with drums, Turkish crescents, and bells; in the mid-19th century French military bands adopted the newly invented saxophone. As a rule, each branch of the military service has its own band; in the U.S. the Marines, the Army, the Navy, and the Air Force maintain bands of the highest professional standard. In Great Britain there are several excellent military bands, notably that of the Scots Guard Royal Artillery, with its signature bagpipes. The French Garde Républicaine still presents regular concerts.

band, string. 1. American traditional music ensemble of the Appalachian and southern regions, evolved in the 19th century from black minstrelsy, work songs, and Anglo-Irish balladry; instrumentation generally included banjo, fiddle, and guitar; also called old-time. 2. String section of the orch.

band, symphonic. British or American ensemble intended for music on a symphonic scale. An American univ., college, or high school band includes more wind instruments than a regular sym. orch.; a large symphonic band may have up to 2 dozen clarinets, numerous brass and saxophones, and an impressive contingent of percussion; double basses may also be included. A considerable literature for symphonic band exists, beginning with the Harmoniemusik written for 18th-century Prussian regimental bands. Among modern composers, Holst, Vaughan Williams, Hindemith, Stravinsky, Prokofiev, and Milhaud contributed to the repertoire; Schoenberg made a significant departure from his 12-tone method by composing a perfectly tonal piece for an American school band. The activity and music of the symphonic band (also called concert band or wind orch.) is one of music's best-kept secrets.

band, wind. Wind section of the orch.

band, wood. Woodwind section of the orch.

banda (It.). 1. Military band. 2. Brass instruments and percussion in the orch. 3. Onstage ensemble in an opera.

bandmaster. Conductor of a military band.

bandola (Sp.). 1. Latin American relative of the Spanish bandurria, with a teardrop shape and concave back. *Bandolón* (Sp.), larger bandurria, with 6 sets of 3 or 4 strings.

Bandonéon (Sp., from Ger. *Bandoneon, Bandonion*). Large square concertina with single or double action, invented by the German instrument manufacturer Heinrich Band in the 1840s; now a staple of South American tango music and associated with the proponent of *nueva tango,* Astor Piazzolla (1921–92).

bandora (Sp.). Pandora.

bandoura (Ukr.). 1. Ukrainian archlute. 2. Hybrid Ukrainian psaltery with an unfretted lute, tuned chromatically and played with a plectrum; in Russia, it is sometimes used in homogenous ensembles; also called bandura.

bandurria (Sp.). Flat-backed member of the lute family from Spain, with 6 pairs of steel or gut strings and fretted short neck, and played in tremolo style with a plectrum; similar to the mandolin. See also ⇒bandola.

banjo. African-American traditional string instrument, strummed or picked with a plectrum, with a long neck connected to a tambourinelike, open-backed wooden body; striking of strings against the head is common; the standard instrument has 5 strings; the 5th, added in the 1830s, is the thumb string (*drone chanterelle*), about half the others' length. The 5-string instrument was supplanted by a 4-string, droneless type in the late 19th century, but returned to prominence with bluegrass. The tenor banjo has a shorter neck and no thumb string.

The 1st written references to a banjo forerunner occur in the 17th century, with references to a *strum-strum* and *banza;* later names include *banjer* and *banjar;* a nearly identical similar instrument called the *ramkie* was in use in southern Africa by the early 18th century; undoubtedly similar instruments existed before these. In the U.S. the banjo was an ingredient of blackface minstrelsy, Appalachian and southern old-time string-band music (played in a strummed style called variously "frailing," "rapping," or "knocking"), bluegrass (in which the player picks the strings with 3 fingers), and early jazz (using the tenor banjo).

bar. 1. Vertical line dividing measures on the staff, indicating where the strong downbeat falls; barline. The 1st regular usage of the bar occurs in 15th-century tablatures; downbeat and upbeat were not consistently notated until the Baroque. 2. American name for measure; thus, the notes and rests contained between 2 bars.

Barber, Samuel, b. West Chester, Pa., Mar. 9, 1910; d. N.Y., Jan. 23, 1981. His aunt was the esteemed operatic contralto Louise Homer (1871–1947), married to composer Sidney Homer (1864–1953). Barber began composing at age 7; played piano at school functions and organ in church; enrolled at 14 in the newly founded Curtis Inst. of Music, Philadelphia; studied with I. Vengerova, R. Scalero, E. de Gogorza, and Fritz Reiner. A baritone, he sang successfully in public; however, composition became his main interest. He avoided facile, fashionable modernism; adopted a lyrical and Romantic idiom with a distinct melodic and harmonic originality; early successes included the *Overture to "The School for Scandal,"* after Sheridan (1933); *Dover Beach* for Baritone and String Quartet, after Arnold (1933; rec. by him, 1939), *Music for a Scene from Shelley* (1935); and the 1-movement Sym. No. 1 (1937). In 1938 the *1st Essay for Orchestra* and the passionately serene *Adagio for Strings* (arranged from his 1936 String Quartet) were performed by Toscanini; the latter remains one of the most popular American works.

Barber taught intermittently at the Curtis Inst. (1939–42); joined the Army Air Force (1942), which commissioned him to write his 2nd Sym.; premiered by Koussevitzky (1944); a demilitarized version was premiered by the Philadelphia Orch. (1948); still dissatisfied, discarded the work except for the 2nd movement, rev. as *Night Flight* (1964; the complete work was rediscovered after his death). After being discharged (1945), he settled in Mount Kisco, N.Y., in a house ("Capricorn") purchased jointly with Menotti.

Barber, always devoted to the theater, wrote a ballet, *Medea (The Serpent Heart),* for Martha Graham (1946), rev. as *Cave of the Heart* (1947); a 3rd manifestation was *Medea's Meditation and Dance of Vengeance* (1956). He wrote a light operatic sketch, *A Hand of Bridge,* to a Menotti libretto (1953); a modern oratorio with *Prayers of Kierkegaard* for Soprano, Chorus, and Orch. (1954); his 1st full-length opera, *Vanessa,* to a Menotti libretto (1957), produced by the Metropolitan Opera, N.Y. (1958; his 1st Pulitzer Prize). He composed *Antony and Cleopatra,* after Shakespeare, a commission for the opening of the new Metropolitan Opera House (1966); premiere was haunted by a non-rotating revolving stage and faulty acoustics; annoyed critics damned the music along with the staging; rev. version (1975, with Menotti's help) received better responses.

Barber composed fine instrumental works: the Piano Concerto (1962, his 2nd Pulitzer Prize); the Piano Sonata, introduced by Horowitz (1949, with applications of 12-tone writing); a witty piano suite, *Excursions* (1945). His vocal works thrived melodically: *Knoxville: Summer of 1915* (1948); *Hermit Songs* (1953); *Andromache's Farewell* (1963); numerous songs and song cycles. Although his music remained fundamentally tonal, he used chromatic techniques freely, verging at times on atonality and polytonality; a mastery of modern counterpoint produced effective neo-Baroque canons and fugues; his opulent orchestration avoided turgidity; his virtuosic treatment of solo instruments was unfailingly idiomatic.

barbershop harmony. Type of American a cappella close harmony singing, replete with chromatic passing notes, crooned by men waiting for haircuts in the late 19th century; evolved from Austro-German choral society singing. Professional and amateur groups were very popular in the 1st quarter of the 20th century; in modern performances this style is usually presented satirically, with appropriately costumed singers gesticulating in mock eloquence.

Barbirolli, (Sir) John (Giovanni Battista), b. London, Dec. 2, 1899, of Italian-French parentage; d. there, July 29, 1970. He made his 1st appearance as a cellist at the Queen's Hall (1911); joined the Queen's Hall Orch. (1916); after serving in the British Army (1918–19), resumed his musical career. In 1924 he organized a chamber orch. in Chelsea; was a staff conductor with Sadler's Wells, London (1926–29); substituted for Beecham at a London Sym. Orch. concert (1927); guest conducted at Covent Garden, London (1929–33); named conductor of both the Scottish Orch., Glasgow, and the Leeds Sym. Orch. (1933). He made his American debut as a guest with the N.Y. Phil. (1936–37); engaged as its permanent conductor (1937–42); returned to England; named conductor of the Hallé Orch., Manchester (1943), its conductor-in-chief (1958), and its conductor laureate for life (1968). He returned to conducting at Covent Garden; led the Houston Sym. (1961–67) while continuing at the Hallé; knighted (1949) and made a Companion of Honour (1969).

Barbirolli was distinguished primarily in the Romantic repertoire; interpretations were marked by nobility, expressive power, and brilliance; his fine pragmatic sense of shaping the music according to inward style avoided projecting his own personality upon it; however, this very objectivity tempered his success with American audiences, accustomed to charismatic flamboyance. He had a special affinity for English musicm performing works of Elgar, Delius, and Britten; conducted the premieres of the 7th and 8th Syms. of Vaughan Williams; developed a fondness for Mahler; had little use for most modern music; composed an Oboe Concerto on themes by Pergolesi for his 2nd wife, oboist Evelyn Rothwell.

Barbosa-Lima, Carlos, b. São Paulo, Dec. 17, 1944. He began guitar study at age 7; principal teachers were Isaias Savio and Segovia; made his 1st U.S. tour (1967); toured South America, Europe, and Israel; commissioned works for guitar from Ginastera, Balada, and Mignone; transcribed works by Bach, Handel, and other composers. He combined his concert career with teaching at the Manhattan School of Music, N.Y.

barcarolle (barcarole; Fr., from It. *barce + rollo,* barkrower; It., *barcarola, barcarole;* Ger. *Barcarole*). 1. Song of the Venetian gondoliers; inseparably associated with the taxi-boaters who entertained and delighted tourists in the 19th century; usually set in 6/8 or 12/8 time, suggesting a lulling motion of the waters in the Venetian canals; also called *gondoliera.* The most famous operatic barcarolle is in Offenbach's *Tales of Hoffmann;* Gilbert and Sullivan turned the boatmen into sentimental lovers in their operetta *The Gondoliers.* 2. Vocal, instrumental, or concerted piece imitating the vocal barcarolle. Chopin wrote a poetic barcarolle for piano (op. 60, 1845), in which the accompaniment maintains a constant movement from the tonic to the dominant while the melody engages in artful fiorituras; Mendelssohn has 3 such pieces in his *Songs Without Words* for piano.

bard. Celtic epic poet or musician. The bards were 1st described in ancient Greek and Roman sources; but tradition dates to the pre-Christian Celtic British Isles. By the later Middle Ages, bards were included in a caste system which included the higher ranking *filidh.* The use of an elaborate metric system and classical Gaelic persisted into the 17th century in Ireland and the 18th century in Scotland; bards were accompanied by (or accompanied themselves on) the Irish harp or the crwth; medieval Welsh bards established an annual festival, the Eisteddfod, which was revived in 1880 as a choral festival.

Barenboim, Daniel, b. Buenos Aires, Nov. 15, 1942. He studied and played piano publicly in Buenos Aires; moved to Israel (1952); during the summers of 1954–55, studied with Fischer, Markevitch, and Enrico Mainardi in Salzburg; studied with Nadia Boulanger in Paris (1954–56), then C. Zecchi in Siena; performed in Paris (1955) and London (1956); in N.Y., played Prokofiev's First Piano Concerto under Stokowski (1957); gave 1st U.S. solo recital (1958).

Barenboim played all 32 Beethoven sonatas in a concert series in Tel Aviv (1960), then again in N.Y.; made conducting debut in Haifa (1957); toured with the Israel Phil. in the U.S. (1967); led the London Sym. Orch. in N.Y., then toured throughout the U.S. In 1967 he married Jacqueline DuPré; they appeared in numerous sonata programs until she was stricken with multiple sclerosis (1972). He 1st conducted opera at the Edinburgh Festival (1973); named music director of the Orch. de Paris (1975); named artistic director of the new Bastille Opéra, Paris (1988); artistic and financial disagreements led to his abrupt dismissal (1989); appointed Solti's successor as music director of the Chicago Sym. Orch.

As a pianist Barenboim sometimes emphasized Romantic flexibility over Classic balance of form and thematic content; conducted congenial performances of Romantic masterpieces; became engrossed in the music of Tchaikovsky, Elgar, and Bruckner; his early performances of Mozart were accused of sentimentality and excessive attention to detail, but his interpretations have gained in perspective and maturity.

barform (Ger.). Medieval German strophic structure; each stanza is divided into 2 sections, the *Aufgesang* (on song), followed by an *Abgesang* (off song); in musical settings, the 1st section is repeated before moving to the 2nd (not repeated); thus AAB. The term would have been long relegated to limbo had it not been for Wagner, who provides a surprisingly logical definition of barform in *Die Meistersinger von Nürnberg;* in a once famous series of analyses, Alfred Lorenz found Wagner's operas to consist of a string of barforms.

baritone (Grk., deep sound). 1. Medium-range male voice, lower than the tenor and higher than the bass; compass is from A to about f^1. An ideal baritone voice possesses the character of lyric masculinity; baritones are rarely given leading operatic roles, usually left to tenors; yet Mozart entrusted the role of Don Giovanni to a baritone; character baritones range from villainy to piety, from nefarious Scarpia in *Tosca* to saintly Amfortas in *Parsifal;* the imperious Wotan in Wagner's *Der Ring des Nibelungen* is a bass-baritone; the most famous dramatic baritone part is the toreador Escamillo in *Carmen*. Baritones are often given comic parts, e.g., Mr. Lavender-Gas, a literature professor in Menotti's *Help! Help! The Globolinks!* 2. Valved brass instrument in B♭, with the range of the trombone and a narrower bore than the euphonium. The baritone serves to fill harmony rather than play solo; the distinction between baritone and euphonium is maintained in the U.K., France, and Germany (*Tenorborn* and *Bariton,* respectively); in the U.S., used for either instrument.

baritone clef. The obsolete F clef on the 3rd line:

barline. See ⇒bar.

Baroque music. Classical music prominent between around 1600 and 1750. Although the term *Baroque* (from Port. *barroco,* irregularly shaped jewel) originally implied a bizarre, even crude quality, it has acquired the opposite meaning of dignity and precise craftsmanship; concept originated with French critics and was used derogatorialy; in his *Dictionnaire de Musique* (1768) Rousseau wrote that "a Baroque music is one in which harmony is confused, charged with modulations and dissonances; the melody is harsh and hardly natural; the intonation difficult; and the movement constrained." For the 18th century and early 19th centuries *goût baroque* meant having a taste for fanciful design in architecture and painting; a change of attitude came about in 19th-century Germany with the rehabilitation of the Baroque style as technically advanced art; Curt Sachs applied the term to music (1919); has come to refer to the greatest flowering of contrapuntal, instrumental, and vocal art. The inception of the Baroque coincided with the birth of opera, which challenged the highly intricate polyphony of the late Renaissance. Opera grew out of the rudimentary form envisioned by the Florentine Camerata, where melodic content of operatic recitative, arioso, and aria was essentially monodic; voice and text were determining factors of rhythm; but by the mid-18th century the 1st wave of Italian bel canto vocal virtuosity had overwhelmed monodic intelligibility. In other vocal genres the madrigal evolved into the cantata; unstaged religious operas called oratorios sidestepped the theatrical bans during Lent; in all vocal music the da capo aria became the primary formal structure.

More dramatic developments occurred in instrumental music, which developed an independent identity separate from vocal music. In addition to solo keyboards, brass ensembles, and string consorts that existed before 1600, orch'l and mixed chamber ensembles became popular; important genres included sonata, concerto, suite, prelude and fugue, theme and variations, and sinfonia (predecessor of sym.). Another development was the basso continuo, by which figures (i.e., ciphers) indicated the intervals from the bass note up, thus determining harmonic progressions and (in the later Baroque) modulations. By then German composers had revitalized the polyphonic style with the fugue, within or without the basso continuo framework. Sonata and sym. were still undifferentiated as the Baroque era was coming to an end. Style galant and Empfindsamer Stil introduced a less monumental and polyphonic music, with an idiosyncratic attention to the smallest affect; from the music of these style's proponents (Bach's sons, the Mannheim school), Haydn and Mozart brought these forms to perfection in the mature Classic period.

Another accomplishment of Baroque music was a decisive move from ambiguous modality to definitive tonality, culminating in Bach's *Well-Tempered Clavier;* prevailing Baroque techniques were derived not from postmedieval polyphonic modalities but from new principles of symmetry and self-consistency, allowing unlimited diversity of thematic transformation within a firm tonal system. A symbolic link was drawn between tonalities and musical intervals with the text; major keys became the expressions of joy, fortitude, and determination, whereas minor keys expressed melancholy, dejection, and depression; melodic intervals conveyed meaning even when words themselves could not be clearly understood.

The popular notion that Baroque music is analogous to architecture—metrical units in a melody corresponding to the severe proportions of a Doric column, and melodic ornaments of a Baroque phrase measured as precisely as the fanciful incrustations of a Gothic cathedral—is belied by contemporaneous descriptions of the state of mind and bodily actions of performers. In *Principles of Musick* (London, 1636) Charles Butler commented: "The composer is transported as it were with some musical fury, so that he himself scarce knoweth what he doth nor can presently give a reason for his doing." In *Musick's Monument* (London, 1676) Thomas Mace described the mental state of the Baroque listener: "Sensibly, fervently, and zealously captivated, we are drawn into raptures and contemplations by those unexpressible rhetorical, uncontrollable persuasions and instructions of musick's divine language, to quietness, joy, and peace; absolute tranquility." The anon. English translator of a 1702 French treatise described his impression of Corelli: "I never met with any man that suffered his passions to hurry him away so much whilst he was playing on the violin . . . . His eyes will sometimes turn as red as fire; his countenance will be distorted; his eyeballs roll as in an agony; and he gives in so much to what he is doing that he doth not look like the same man." In light of these reports it seems ironic that some 20th-century standards of "authentic" Baroque performance should be commanded by rigorous observation of the written notation with no tolerance for deviation from mathematical precision of meters and rhythms unless specifically indicated in contemporaneous writings, and the exclusion of personal or collective emotions from immutable music of Baroque masters. Inevitably, conflicting factions arose among specialists; music editors disagreed on the proper execution of trills, mordents, and other ornaments in Bach's works; yet diversity ruled the performance of Baroque music in its own time; one suspects the "truth" to be less marmoreal, if there be one at all.

Baroque suite. See ⇒suite.

barré (Fr.). In lute or guitar playing, stopping some or all strings with the left-hand forefinger. *Grand barré,* stopping more than 3 strings simultaneously.

barrel organ. Mechanical organ of ancient origins in which a wooden cylinder (or barrel) is mounted on a metal spindle attached to a board; the cylinder is slid into position and rotated with a hand crank; the brass staples or pins on the cylinder's circumference trigger the desired pitches; the wind required to produce sound is generated by a bellows operated by the hand crank. The most salient use of the barrel organ was in parishes unable to afford or find organists; also found on the streets; erroneously known as the hurdy-gurdy. Its popularity died out in the mid-19th century; substantial number of instruments have survived in playable condition, attesting to their practical and durable designs; related to the orchestrion and Maelzel's panharmonicon.

barrelhouse. Style of piano playing related to boogie-woogie, using ragtime, stomping, or walking basses, 4/4 meter, and blues-based melodies; in vogue in the 1920s and 1930s, beginning in the South and then moving north.

Bartók, Béla. b. Nagyszentmiklós (now Sinnicolau Mare, Rumania), Mar. 25, 1881; d. N.Y., Sept. 26, 1945. His mother gave him his 1st piano lesson. After his father's death (1888) and several itinerant years (during which he began composing), family settled in Pozsony; studied with László Erkel (son of Ferenc) and Hyrtl; enrolled at the Budapest Academy of Music (1899); studied with István Thomán, a Liszt pupil, and J. Koessler. In his early career he was best known as a pianist; early compositions reveal the accumulating influences of Liszt, Brahms, R. Strauss, and anti-German Hungarian nationalism.

In 1904 Bartók began exploring the resources of genuine traditional music, including Hungarian, Rumanian, Slovak, and other ethnic strains found in his native Transylvania; formed a scholarly and personal friendship with Kodály; they traveled throughout Hungary collecting folk songs and publ. *Magyar Népdalok* (1906); from then on, Bartók journeyed all over Hungary, doing fieldwork and making recordings; he helped changed the long-held notion that Hungarian music was bastardized Gypsy music. In 1907 he succeeded Thomán at the Academy of Music; collected traditional music in North Africa (1913); member of the musical directorate (with Dohnányi and Kodály) of the short-lived Hungarian Democratic Republic (1919); a brilliant pianist; limited his recitals primarily to own compositions; regularly toured throughout Europe; gave 2-piano concerts with his 2nd wife, Ditta Pásztory (b. c. 1902; d. Budapest, Nov. 21, 1982; married 1923).

In his compositions Bartók was influenced by tonal colors and impressionistic harmonies as cultivated by Debussy and other French composers; his ballet *The Wooden Prince* (1917) and opera *Bluebeard's Castle* (1918) made him an international figure; harmonic sonorities remained true to tonality, but expanded to embrace chromatic polymodal structures and unremittingly dissonant chordal combinations; in piano works, exploited the extreme registers of the keyboard, often as tone clusters to simulate pitchless drumbeats (*Allegro Barbaro,* 1911). The melodic line of his works sometimes veered toward atonality in its chromatic involutions, but folk song element grew pronounced; sometimes employed melodic figures comprising all 12 notes of the chromatic scale; however, never adopted integral techniques of serialism.

Bartók toured as a pianist in the U.S. (1927–28) and the Soviet Union (1929). After resigning from the Academy of Music (1934), realized (with Kodály) the long-planned *Corpus Musicae Popularis Hungaricae,* cataloguing 13,000 Hungarian and 2,500 Rumanian items; explored relationships between these and Slovak, Ruthenian, and Serbo-Croatian music. But the shadow of Nazism gradually made life intolerable, even as he continued composing important works; with increasing press attacks and withdrawal from public musical life, awaited his

mother's death (1939) and the outbreak of war to make his final voyage to the U.S. (1940). He had many setbacks: unsuccessful duo-recitals, rejected MSS on Rumanian and Turkish music, declining health; but worked on 2,600 discs of Yugoslav traditional music in a Harvard Univ. collection (1941–42). ASCAP helped support him in last years; the Concerto for Orch. (1944), commissioned by Koussevitzky at Szigeti and Reiner's behest, proved his most popular work (and last completed score); succumbed to polycythemia; 1st buried in N.Y. State; the 3rd Piano Concerto and Viola Concerto were finished by his pupil Tibor Serly (1901–78). Performances and recordings increased enormously after his death; remains were taken to Budapest (as he had requested) for a state funeral (1988).

No cerebral purveyor of abstract musical designs, Bartók was an ardent student of folk culture (especially Slavic); sought roots of meters, rhythms, and modalities in spontaneous songs and dances of the people; regarded his analytical studies of popular melodies as most important contribution to music. He was also interested in the natural musical expression of children; believed them capable of absorbing modalities and asymmetrical rhythmic structures with greater ease than adults trained in established rigid disciplines; his remarkable piano collection, *Mikrokosmos* (6 vols., 1940), is a method to initiate beginners into the world of unfamiliar tonal and rhythmic combinations, providing means of instruction parallel to Kodály's method of musical training.

For grownups Bartók left a considerable legacy: stage works (including *The Miraculous Mandarin,* 1926); choral music, notably the *Cantata Profana* (1934); songs dominated by folklike melody; orch'l music, including suites, folk music transcriptions, violin concertos and rhapsodies (2 apiece), and *Music for Strings, Percussion and Celesta* (1937); piano music, including *14 Bagatelles* (1908), Sonata (1926), *Out of Doors* (1926), Sonata for 2 Pianos and Percussion (1937); chamber music, featuring violin and piano duos, Sonata for Solo Violin (1944), the quirky *Contrasts* written for Szigeti and B. Goodman (1938), and 6 string quartets (1908–39), the most important set of works in this genre since Beethoven (if only he had lived to write a planned 7th quartet).

baryton. String instrument developed from the viola bastarda; it is about the size of the viola da gamba, with 6 or 7 gut strings and up to 20 wire sympathetic strings that could with difficulty be plucked; Josef Haydn wrote around 175 chamber works with baryton for his patron Count Nikolaus Esterházy, an avid amateur player; somewhat popular in the 18th century, sank into oblivion thereafter.

Basie, "Count" (William), b. Red Bank, N.J., Aug. 21, 1904; d. Hollywood, Fla., Apr. 26, 1984. After studying with his mother he met and learned from important stride pianists (J. P. Johnson, "Fats" Waller); toured on the vaudeville circuit; played for various bands in N.Y. (1923–26); while touring the country, was stranded in Kansas City (1927); played for local bands; joined Bennie Moten's Kansas City Orch., a pioneering swing band; after Moten's death (1935) he formed a new band with old and new colleagues (including saxophonist Lester Young, its most important soloist); in a few years it had gained fame, recording contracts, and a new name: the Count Basie Orch.

Basie attracted attention by his peculiar piano technique, emphasizing passages played by a single finger while directing his band with a glance or a movement of the eyebrow; adopted Waller's discursive brilliance on the keys but altered it in the direction of rich economy of means; led big bands, with a break for financial reasons; formed an octet (1950–51); however, soon organized a new big band; toured Europe successfully several times; played a command performance for the Queen of England (1957). In 1976 he suffered a heart attack; recuperated and returned to an active career; received the Kennedy Center Award for achievement in the performing arts (1981) and the Medal of Freedom (posth., 1985); among hits were *I O'Clock Jump* (his theme song), *Jumpin' at the Woodside, Goin' to Chicago, Lester Leaps In, Broadway, April in Paris,* and *L'il Darlin'.*

bass (Eng., Ger.; It. *basso*). 1. Lowest male voice, with an ordinary compass from F to e^1 (extreme compass from C to f^1). In his drama *The Sea Gull*, Chekhov tells of an Italian bass singer who sang at the Imperial Opera in St. Petersburg, rousing the audience to admiring frenzy when he reached low C, whereupon a choir bass singer in the audience shouted "Bravo" an octave lower (C^1). (Some speculate that the vast expanse of the Russian landscape contributes to the formation of powerful chest cavities, whereas the cerulean waters of the Bay of Naples favor the development of the Italian lyric tenor voice.) Bass singers are usually cast as sinners or devils, e.g., Mephistopheles in *Faust*, Mussorgsky's villainous usurper Boris Godunov, and the treacherous victim Hunding in *Die Walküre*. 2. Singer having such a voice. 3. The lowest tone in a chord; lowest part in a composition. 4. Double bass or electric bass. 5. Antiquated bass viola da gamba. 6. Family of organ stops on the pedals, e.g., Gemshornbass. 7. Valved brass instrument used in brass and military bands with tuba-like range.

bass clarinet. B-flat instrument an octave below the standard (soprano) clarinet, with upwardly curved bell; like other members of the clarinet family, evolved from the obsolete chalumeau; 1st extant instruments date from late 18th century; modern form patented by Sax in 1838; like other orig. "adjunct" woodwinds, the bass clarinet has been very popular among 20th-century composers.

bass clef. F clef on the 4th line:

bass drum. Large cylindrical drum of indefinite pitch with heads on both sides; orch'l instrument is at least 32 inches in diameter; entered classical orch. with Gluck and Mozart (*The Abduction from the Seraglio*); Beethoven used it 1st the finale of his Sym. No. 9. Its dramatic and often ominous sound was favored by R. Strauss and Mahler, who punctuated his symphonies with single drum strokes; in Leoncavallo's *Pagliacci* the bass drum is a prop used by the clown tormented by jealousy; in Litolff's overture *Robespierre* it illustrates Robespierre's beheading; commonly found in military bands.

bass flute. Lowest member of the flute family, requiring a wide cylinder and wound tubing; its range starts at C, an octave below the standard (soprano) flute; requires considerable lung power to blow and superlative lip technique to articulate. Although reported in the 16th century, a truly usable version did not appear until the early 20th century (e.g., albisifono).

bass guitar. Electric instrument with range of the double bass, a guitar-shaped body, and 4 strings; a solid-bodied and held against the body, like the electric guitar; provided rhythmic and harmonic underpinnings in rock, funk, soul, and other popular bands.

bass line. Since the Renaissance, the lowest voice; in addition since the Baroque, determinant of the melody and essential factor in the harmony; often and incorrectly regarded as "subsidiary," as each bass note serves as lowest pitch in a harmonic progression, determining chord positions; melody and bass are the most exposed lines, thus counterpoint between them must be absolutely correct according to stylistic rules in force.

bass-baritone. High bass voice.

basse danse (Fr., flat or low dance; It. *bassadanza*). Principal court dance of the late Middle Ages and Renaissance; *basse* describes the nature of the dance, in which partners move with striding steps without leaving the floor. The basse danse was usually accompanied by wind instruments, with a 3/2 meter and a slow and stately tempo; 1st cited by a troubadour in 1340; earliest extant choreography dates from the late 15th century; cantus firmus technique was used, improvisation the means of realization.

basset horn (Fr. *cor de basset;* Ger. *Bassetthorn;* It. *corno di bassetto*). Relative of the clarinet and chalumeau, now pitched in F, to c^3 with a bent or curved tube and a mellow, sombre timbre; the later, larger-bored instrument is virtually identical with the 19th-century alto clarinet. The orig. basset horn in G, with a narrow bore, was developed in the late 18th century; used by Mozart for the Masonic music, Serenade K. 361, Requiem, 3 operas, divertimentos, vocal and wind ensemble pieces, and the orig. plan for the Concerto K. 622; Beethoven, Mendelssohn, and R. Strauss also composed for it.

basso buffo (It.). Comic bass, such as the music master Don Basilio in Rossini's *The Barber of Seville.*

basso cantante (It.). Bass-baritone.

basso continuo (It., continuous bass; Eng. figured bass, thoroughbass; Fr. *basse continue, chifrée, figurée;* Ger. *Generalbass, bezifferter Bass;* abbr. *continuo*). In Baroque ensemble music, part played by 2 instruments: a keyboard or fretted string (harpsichord, organ, lute) and a low-pitched sustaining instrument (cello, viola da gamba, bassoon). Basso continuo also refers to its notational system: only the bass line is given; numerical figures (ciphers) below it indicate intervals to be played above it (realized), thereby spelling out the harmony within a given tonality; the number of notes or voicing is not designated. Historically the basso continuo developed as to aid improvisation and indicate the main harmony in the keyboard part, which supplied the accompaniment, e.g, 6/4/2 over a bass D in A major or minor would indicate (from bottom) D, E, G-sharp, and B, in closed or open voicings, and with free doublings. Ornamentation and additional counterpoint could be improvised, depending on the ability and taste of the player. Basso continuo continued its didactic role up through the 19th century.

basso obbligato (It.). An indispensable bass part or accompaniment.

basso ostinato (It., obstinate bass). Bass line consisting of a repeated motive or phrase; serves as foundation for variations in the upper voices; can be greatly diversified in realization or approach the more static quality of the English ground bass; the passacaglia and chaconne are forms based on it.

basso profondo (It., profound bass). The lowest bass voice; often misspelled *basso profumo*.

bassoon (It. *bassone, fagotto;* Fr. *basson;* Ger. *Fagotte*). Low-pitched woodwind instrument of the oboe family; its double reed is attached via a curved metal mouthpiece to a conical double bore, comprising 4 joints wrapped vertically, ending in a slightly flared bell; *fagotto* and *Fagott* mean "bundle of sticks" to describe its shape; pearlwood traditionally used in its manufacture. Its normal range is from Bb₁ to f², sometimes higher; its tone is soft, mellow, and nasal. The bassoon developed from the curtal in the mid-1600s, gradually expanding range and keys until the 19th century, when 2 schools of manufacturing—French and German—became distinct. 1st used for basso continuo, it was given independent parts from the mid-18th century on, including concertos (Vivaldi, Mozart); the opening of Stravinsky's *The Rite of Spring* (1913) provides a bassoon solo in its upper register, producing an unusual but memorable effect. See also ⇒contrabassoon, oboe.

baton (from Fr. *Bâton*, stick, roll; *baguette*). 1. Conductor's stick, common by the mid-18th century, with several predecessors. 2. In the U.S., the twirling stick of a drum major or majorette in a marching band.

battaglia (It., battle; Eng. battle piece). Compositions featuring imitations of trumpet flourishes, fanfares, drum rolls, and similar explosions of sound; evolved in the 14th century. Battle pieces were invariably in march time, a typical rhythmic figure consisting of a half note followed by 2 quarter notes. Characteristic of Renaissance battle music is *La Guerre de Marignan*, a 4-part chanson by Jannequin (1528); instrumental battaglias were written by Byrd, Sweelinck, Frescobaldi, and Couperin; Monteverdi introduced stile concitato in the *canto guerriero, Combattimento di Tancredi et Clorinda* (1624). Possibly the most durable battaglia is J. Kuhnau's portrayal of David and Goliath in the *Biblische Historien* (1700); Baroque battaglias were favored in operas and oratorios; later such works include *The Battle of Prague* by the Czech composer F. Koczwara (c. 1750–91), Beethoven's notorious *Wellington's Victory* (orig. for a mechanical instrument and often cited as a paradigm of exceptionally bad music written by an exceptionally great composer); Tchaikovsky's celebrated *Overture: 1812,* commemorating the Russian victory over Napoleon; and the orch'l interlude in Rimsky-Korsakov's *The Legend of the Invisible City of Kitezh,* describing the battle between Russians and Mongols.

battery (Fr. *batterie*). 1. Group of percussion instruments. 2. Drum roll. 3. 18th-century term for arpeggiated figures; also, the rasgueado. 4. Sonnerie.

Battle, Kathleen, b. Portsmouth, Ohio, Aug. 13, 1948. She studied voice with F. Bens; made her debut at the Spoleto Festival in the Brahms Requiem (1972); subsequently sang with the N.Y. Phil., Cleveland Orch., Los Angeles Phil., and other leading American orchs. She made her Metropolitan Opera, N.Y., debut as the Shepherd in *Tannhäuser* (1978); appeared for the 1st time at Covent Garden, London, as Zerbinetta (1985). Karajan chose her as soloist for the globally televised New Year's Day concert of the Vienna Phil. (1987). A dispute with management led to her departure from the Metropolitan (1993); nonetheless, she continues to perform widely, excelling in the light, lyric soprano repertoire, particularly Sophie, Despina, Blonde, Zerlina, Nanetta, and Adina; has also established a concert and recital career.

battuta (It., beat). Downbeat; measure; also, a return to strict time after a deviation.

Bax, (Sir) Arnold (Edward Trevor), b. London, Nov. 8, 1883; d. Cork, Ireland, Oct. 3, 1953. He studied with Matthay and Corder at the Royal Academy; visited Dresden (1905); went to Ireland, becoming profoundly interested in ancient Irish folklore; wrote poetry and prose; his compositions were inspired by Celtic legends. He returned to England (1910); that year, visited Russia, composing piano pieces in a pseudo-Russian style; wrote music for J. M. Barrie's skit *The Truth about the Russian Dancers;* remaining years were spent in Britain, with visits to visiting Ireland; by the 1930s, received official acknowledgment (knighthood, 1937; Master of the King's Musick, 1941), but his greatest creativity were past, replaced by deep depression.

Bax was extremely prolific; rooted in neo-Romanticism, impressionistic elements are in evidence in his instrumental works; harmony is elaborate and richly chromatic; contrapuntal fabric is free, emphasizing complete independence of component melodies. In folk-song settings, he succeeded in combining simple melodies with effective modern harmonies. His orch'l reinterpretations of Celtic images evoked archaic the twilight mood, among them *In the Faery Hills* (1909), *Spring Fire* (1913), *The Garden of Fand* (1916), *November Woods* (1917), *Tintagel* (1919), *The Happy Forest* (1921), *Winter Legends* 1930), and *A Legend* (1944); composed 7 syms., concert overtures, chamber and piano works. An excellent pianist, he rarely played in public, nor did he conduct own works; wrote a candid autobiography, *Farewell, My Youth* (London, 1943).

Be (Ger.). The flat sign ♭.

Beach, Amy Marcy Cheney (Mrs. H. H. A.), b. Henniker, N.H., Sept. 5, 1867; d. N.Y., Dec. 27, 1944. She studied with E. Perabo, C. Baermann, and J. W. Hill; made her debut as a pianist in Boston (1883), playing a Moscheles concerto; married Dr. H. H. A. Beach, a Boston surgeon (1885); thereafter used Mrs. H. H. A. Beach professionally. She 1st composed for piano; completed a Mass in E-flat, premiered in Boston (1892); her Gaelic Symphony, based on Irish folk tunes, was successfully performed by the Boston Sym. (1896, probably the 1st U.S. performance of a female composer's sym.) She premiered her Violin Sonata with Franz Kneisel (1897); appeared as soloist with the Boston Sym. in the premiere of her Piano Concerto in C-sharp Minor (1900); wrote a great many Romantic songs. Widowed in 1910, she traveled to Europe, playing her works in Berlin, Leipzig, and Hamburg; considered the 1st woman and American to compose music at a European level of excellence. Her music, unpretentious in its idiom and epigonic in its historical aspect, remains important as the work of a 2nd New England school and female pioneer composer; her opera *Cabildo* (1932) has recently received attention.

Beach Boys, The. (Leader/bass/vocal: Brian Wilson, b. Hawthorne, Calif., June 20, 1942; guitar/vocal: Carl Wilson, b. Hawthorne, Dec. 21, 1946 drums/vocal: Dennis Wilson, b. Hawthorne, Dec. 4, 1944; d. Dec. 28, 1973, Marina del Rey, Calif.; guitar/vocal: Al Jardine, b. Los Angeles, Sept. 3, 1942; lead vocal: Mike Love, b. Los Angeles, Mar. 15, 1941.) Surf-and-sun harmony group of the 1960s; formed around the Wilson family and their cousin Love, the group was led by Brian, the talented though troubled teenager who composed and arranged most of their material. After scoring hits with surf-oriented material, they expanded into the general Calif. teen lifestyle (*Fun Fun Fun, Help Me Rhonda, California Girls*). Brian learned to create complex arrangements, both vocal and instrumental, influenced by producer Phil Spector; reached the zenith of his creativity with the album *Pet Sounds* and the hit *Good Vibrations* (1967); increasing drug use, mental problems, and tensions within the group led him to withdraw from performing and composing; the quality of the group's work dropped precipitously; survived primarily as a nostalgia band; Brian has written and recorded solo material, with mixed results.

beam. Horizontal lines connecting adjacent notes.

Beardslee, Bethany, b. Lansing, Mich., Dec. 25, 1927. She made her N.Y. debut in 1949; known as a specialist in modern music; has an extraordinary technique with a flutelike sonority and impeccable intonation; mastered the art of Sprechstimme; gave classic renditions of such works as Schoenberg's *Pierrot Lunaire;* also a brilliant performer of vocal music by Berg, Webern, Babbitt, and Stravinsky; gave fine recitals; taught at the Westminster Choir College and Univ. of Tex., Austin.

beat. 1. Division or unit of musical time in a measure. 2. Movement of the hand in marking ("beating") time. 3. Pulsation of 2 consecutive tones in a trill. 4. Appoggiatura. 5. Throbbing caused by the interfering tone waves of 2 tones of different pitch; beats are used to tune instruments.

Beatles, The. (Leader/guitar/vocal: John [Winston] Lennon, b. Liverpool, Oct. 9, 1940; d. N.Y., Dec. 8, 1980; vocal/bass/piano: [John] Paul McCartney, b. Liverpool, June 18, 1942; lead guitar/vocal: George Harrison, b. Feb. 25, 1943; drums/vocal: Ringo Starr [Richard Starkey], b. Liverpool, July 7, 1940.) Original, innovative, and highly influential rock band of the 1960s. Influenced by the skiffle movement in England, Lennon formed his 1st band, the Quarry Men (named for their school); played at church bazaars and local events (1957); McCartney joined the band as a guitarist; brought in a younger school friend, Harrison; Lennon added his friend Stu Sutcliffe, an art student who tried (not too successfully) to play the bass. The group, known 1st as the Silver Beatles, became simply the Beatles, a name inspired by Buddy Holly's Crickets; the name "Beatles" puns on the coleopterous insect and popular music's "beat." The group opened at the Casbah Club in Liverpool (1959); soon moved to the more prestigious Cavern Club (1961), where they took on drummer Pete Best. In 1960 they played in Hamburg's Star Club, scoring a gratifyingly vulgar success by their loud, electrically amplified sound; returned to England. In 1961 they hired perspicacious promoter Brian Epstein, who owned a local record shop, as manager; he launched an extensive publicity campaign to put them over. Having left the group, Sutcliffe died of a brain hemorrhage (1962); Best was forced out of the group after their 1st audition tapes for the British Decca label; soon replaced by local drummer Richard Starkey, aka Ringo Starr.

The Beatles opened at the London Palladium (1963), driving the youthful audience to a frenzy, a scene repeated elsewhere in Europe, the U.S., Japan, and Australia. Lennon, McCartney, and to a much lesser extent Harrison were the songwriters; although American in origin, the rhythm and blues-country music mix plied by the quartet had an indefinably British lilt: square meter, accented primary beats, minimal syncopation, modal harmony, lowered submediants in major keys, and a preference for plagal cadences and consecutive triadic progressions, creating at times a curiously hymnal mood. Their lyrics were distinguished by suggestive allusions, sensuous but not flagrantly erotic, anarchistic but not destructive, cynical but also humane. Early hits began with *Love Me Do, Please Please Me, I Want to Hold Your Hand, Can't Buy Me Love, All My Loving, 8 Days a Week, Ticket to Ride,* and *Day Tripper.* They acted in or produced the highly original films *A Hard Day's Night, Help!, Yellow Submarine,* and *Let It Be.* The group abandoned touring with much fanfare to devote themselves to their recording activities (1966); the 1st result was the innovative single *Penny Lane* and *Strawberry Fields Forever,* both portraits of their Liverpool childhoods. They produced one of the 1st, and best, concept albums with *Sergeant Pepper's Lonely Hearts Club Band* (1967), featuring *A Day in the Life* (orig. banned by British radio). After Epstein's death that year, band members turned to Transcendental Meditation, spending some months in India; recorded the individually rather than group-oriented *White Album;* old strains within the group began to show; acrimoniously split up after recording *Abbey Road* (1970). For their subsequent careers, see individual entries.

bebop. Type of jazz developed in America during the 1940s, associated with Charlie Parker, Dizzy Gillespie, Thelonious Monk, and Bud Powell; its name derives from onomatopoeic vocables (*bebop, rebop, bop*) descriptive of jazz techniques; invention of the term and the technique is generally attributed to Gillespie. The most striking characteristic of bebop is its maximal velocity, sometimes reaching 20 notes a second in clear articulation, with a strong off-beat stress. Bebop is marked by irregular syncopation, a widely ranging melody of quasi-atonal configurations, and an accompaniment in rapidly changing modernistic harmonies, making use of unresolved dissonances and polytonal combinations. The improvisational element far outweighs the precompositional; bebop structures are almost invariably repetitions of 32-bar sections, and there is a fair amount of blues-based or borrowed composition.

bebung (Ger., trembling). Vibrato effect on stringed instruments or on a clavichord, the latter produced by pressing the key repeatedly so that the tangent vibrates the string slightly without releasing it.

bécarre (Fr.). Natural sign (♮).

Bechet, Sidney (Joseph), b. New Orleans, May 14, 1897; d. Garches, France, May 14, 1959. He learned to play blues and rags on clarinet in honky-tonks in Storyville in New Orleans; played with leading jazz musicians in New Orleans, Chicago, and on tour; purchased a soprano saxophone in London (c. 1919); made frequent trips to Europe (1920s); worked with Armstrong (in Clarence Williams's Blue Five and the Red Onion Jazz Babies), Ellington, Noble Sissle, Johnny Hodges, Tommy Ladnier, and Zutty Singleton; the 1930s saw a decline in his fortunes, but the Dixieland revival returned him to the forefront; during the 1940s, led his own jazz groups in N.Y.; made recordings with Mezz Mezzrow; settled in Paris (1951). He was one of the most important jazz musicians of his era, unchallenged on the soprano saxophone, admired for passionate playing and unbridled freedom of expression; his autobiography, *Treat It Gentle*, was publ. posth. (N.Y., 1960).

Becken (Ger.). Cymbal (singular); cymbals (plural).

Becker, John J(oseph), b. Henderson, Ky., Jan. 22, 1886; d. Wilmette, Ill., Jan. 21, 1961. He taught at Notre Dame Univ. (1917–27), the College of St. Thomas, St. Paul (1929–35), Barat College of the Sacred Heart, Lake Forest (1943–57), and sporadically at the Chicago Musical College; served as Minn. State Director for the Federal Music Project (1935–41). His early works are characterized by somewhat Germanic romantic moods; drawn into the circle of modern American music (c. 1930); on the editorial board of *New Music Quarterly* (founded by Cowell); associated with Ives (Becker scored his *General William Booth's Entrance into Heaven* for Chamber Orch., 1934). He conducted modern American works with various groups in St. Paul; striving for a style that combined modernity and Americanism, wrote 8 works for various instrumental groups called "Soundpieces"; developed a type of theatrical action with music. Becker's mature music is marked by sparse sonorities of an incisive rhythmic character, contrasted with dissonant conglomerates of massive harmonies.

bedächtig (Ger.). Meditatively.

bedeutungsvoll (Ger.). Full of meaning; significantly.

bedrohlich (Ger.). Menacing.

Beecham, (Sir) Thomas, b. St. Helens, near Liverpool, Apr. 29, 1879; d. London, Mar. 8, 1961. His father was a man of great wealth, derived from the once-famous Beecham pills to help anemics; Thomas could engage in life's pleasures and the arts without troublesome regard for economic limitations. After early studies, he organized an amateur orch. soc.; conducted a performance with the prestigious Hallé Orch. in Manchester (both in 1899); got a conducting job with a traveling opera company (1902); settling in London, gave his 1st professional sym. concert (1905); assembled and led the New Sym. Orch. (1906–1908); formed the Beecham Sym. Orch. (1909). Beecham appeared in a new role of operatic impresario, at Covent Garden and at His Majesty's Theatre (1910–13); boldly invited R. Strauss to Covent Garden to conduct his own operas. Beecham conducted at the Theatre Royal at Drury Lane; conducted the Royal Phil. Soc. concerts (1916); gave operatic performances with the Beecham Opera Co. By that time his reputation as a forceful and charismatic conductor was secure in England; his audiences grew; many critics, impressed by his imperious ways and spectacular operatic productions, sang his praise; however, others criticized a somewhat cavalier treatment of the classics. In appreciation of his services to British music, he was knighted in 1916; at the death of his father, he succeeded to the title of baronet; his inheritance could not redeem exorbitant disbursements in his enterprises; declared bankrupt (1919), but rebounded a few years later and continued his extraordinary career.

In 1928 Beecham made his American debut conducting the N.Y. Phil.; organized and conducted the Delius Festival in London (1929), which Delius, racked by tertiary syphilitic affliction, paralyzed and blind, attended; organized the London Phil. Orch. (1932); contemptuous of general distaste for the Nazi regime, took the London Phil. to Berlin for a concert attended by the Führer (1936). Returning to England, he continued his activities; as the Allied war situation deteriorated, went to the U.S. (1940); toured Australia; music director and conductor of the Seattle Sym. Orch. (1941–43); filled guest engagements at the Metropolitan Opera, N.Y. (1942–44). In America he received sharp criticism, which he haughtily dismissed as philistine; on his part, was outspoken in snobbish disdain for the cultural inferiority of England's wartime allies. Returning to England, he founded yet one more orch., the Royal Phil. (1946); resumed conducting at Covent Garden (1951); made a Companion of Honour (1957). He publ. an autobiography, *A Mingled Chime* (London, 1944).

Beer, Jacob Liebmann. See ⇒Meyerbeer, Giacomo.

Beeson, Jack (Hamilton), b. Muncie, Ind., July 15, 1921. He studied with B. Phillips, B. Rogers, H. Hanson, and Bartók; joined the staff of Columbia Univ. (1945); made a prof. there (1965); chairman of the music dept. (1968–72); named MacDowell Prof. of Music (1967). His music is marked by enlightened utilitarianism; particularly forceful are his operas, which recall the lyrical aesthetic of Douglas Moore's operas and also rely on American subject manner.

Beethoven, Ludwig van. b. Bonn, Dec. 15 or 16 (baptized Dec. 17), 1770; d. Vienna, Mar. 26, 1827. The family was of Dutch extraction (the name means "beet garden"); Johann van Beethoven (c. 1740–92) worked for the Elector of Bonn (from 1752); married a young widow, Maria Magdalena Leym (1767); they were the composer's parents.

In addition to his father, the young Ludwig studied with F. A. Ries and N. Simrock; his 1st important composition teacher was Christian Gottlob Neefe (1748–98), who saw his pupil's great potential; guided Beethoven through the study of Bach and keyboard improvisation; helped Beethoven's publ. his 1st work (1783); the Bonn Elector Maximilian Franz appointed him deputy court organist (1784–92); he also served as a violist in theater orchs. In 1787 the Elector sent him to Vienna for a brief stay; the report that he met and played for Mozart, who then pronounced him a future great composer, may be a figment of an eager imagination. Beethoven returned to Bonn; watched his mother die of tuberculosis; obliged to provide sustenance for his 2 younger brothers, as his alcoholic father could no longer meet his obligations; Ludwig successfully petitioned for half his father's salary (1789); supplemented income by giving piano lessons; met several wealthy patrons; continued to compose.

In 1790 Haydn was honored in Bonn by the Elector on his way to London; it is likely that Beethoven was introduced to him, and that Haydn encouraged him to come to Vienna to study with him. Beethoven went to Vienna (Nov. 1792) and began his studies with Haydn, who was a kindly but somewhat careless teacher; when Haydn went to London again (early 1794), Beethoven began a formal study of counterpoint with Johann Georg Albrechtsberger (1736–1809); these studies continued for about a year. Beethoven also took lessons in vocal composition with Salieri, then the Austrian Imperial Kapellmeister.

Beethoven found a generous benefactor in Prince Karl Lichnowsky, who awarded him an annual stipend (*c.* 1800), for which he was amply repaid by Beethoven's dedications to him, especially the *Sonate Pathétique* (op. 13) and the op. 1 piano trios. Another aristocratic Viennese patron was Prince Franz Joseph Lobkowitz: the 6 string quartets, op. 18; the *Eroica* Sym., after he dropped the dedication to Napoleon; Triple Concerto, op. 56; and—in conjunction with Prince Andrei Razumovsky—the 5th and 6th Syms. Razumovsky, the Russian ambassador to Vienna, maintained a string quartet (1808–14) in which he played the 2nd violin (the leader was Beethoven's friend Ignaz Schuppanzigh); to Razumovsky, he dedicated his 3 string quartets (op. 59), which use an authentic Russian folk melody in 2 of the works. Another Russian patron was Prince Nikolai Golitzyn, for whom he wrote his great string quartets opp. 127, 130, and 132.

Beethoven made his 1st public appearance in Vienna (1795) as soloist in one of his piano concertos (probably the B-flat Major Concerto, op. 19); played in Prague, Dresden, Leipzig, and Berlin (1796); participated in fashionable "competitions" with other pianists, including J. Wolffl (1799) and D. Steibelt (1800). At the threshold of the 19th century, new compositions included the 1st and 2nd Syms.; 5 piano sonatas, including the "Moonlight" and "Pastoral" (opp. 22, 36, 27/1–2, 28); 4th and 5th violin sonatas (opp. 23–24); the cello variations on Mozart's *Bei Männern, welche Liebe fühle;* the op. 18 string quartets; Septet in E-flat Major (op. 20); String Quintet (op. 29); and songs. His early Viennese career was most successful; was popular not only as a virtuoso pianist and composer, but as a social figure welcome in Vienna's aristocratic circles; his students included society ladies and even royal personages, notably Archduke Rudolf of Austria, to whom Beethoven dedicated the so-called *Archduke Trio* (op. 97, 1811) and other works.

But Beethoven's progress was fatefully affected by an inexplicably growing deafness; when the situation reached a crisis, he wrote (in Oct. 1802) a poignant document known as the "Heiligenstadt Testament," after the village he was then living in. In the document (discovered after his death), he voiced his despair at the inexorable failing of his most important sense; implored his brothers, in case of his early death, to consult his physician, who knew the secret of his "lasting malady" contracted in 1796; the etiology of his illness suggests that the malady was syphilis; however, the impairment may have been due to an otosclerosis, resulting in the shriveling of the auditory nerves and concomitant dilation of the accompanying arteries; there were also indications of tinnitus, a constant buzzing in the ears that also affected Schumann and Smetana. To the end of his life Beethoven hoped to find a remedy for his deafness among the latest "scientific" medications, to no avail.

Remarkably, Beethoven continued his creative work with his usual energy; there were few periods of interruption in the chronology of his works; similarly there was no apparent influence of his health or depression on the content of his music; tragic and joyful musical passages had equal shares in an inexhaustible flow of varied works. In 1803 he presented a concert of his compositions in Vienna; was soloist in his 3rd Piano Concerto (op. 37); later that year, played the Violin Sonata, op. 47, accompanying the mulatto virtuoso George Polgreen Bridgetower (*c.* 1779–1860); eventually dedicated the work to Rodolphe Kreutzer; Tolstoy's novella *The Kreutzer Sonata* (1889) concerns the risks of the unrestrained and adulterous emotions "inspired" by this work.

During 1803–05 Beethoven composed his great Sym. No. 3 in E-flat Major, op. 55, the *Eroica.* According to his student Ferdinand Ries (1784–1838), the orig. dedication to Napoleon was torn off the MS after he learned of Napoleon's self-proclamation as Emperor of France (1804); he supposedly exclaimed, "So he is a tyrant like all the others after all!" Ries's waiting 34 years to report this story throws some doubt on its credibility; in fact, a post-proclamation letter to the publisher Breitkopf & Härtel has Beethoven's reference to the actual title as "really Bonaparte"; his own MS shows he crossed out the designation "Inttitulata Bonaparte" but let the words, "Geschrieben auf Bonaparte," stand. In 1806, the sym. was publ. as the *Sinfonia eroica composta per festeggiare il sovvenire d'un grand' uomo* (Heroic sym. composed to celebrate the memory of a great man). But which great man? The Emperor was alive and leading his Grande Armée to new conquests (his forces entered Vienna in 1805); yet the famous funeral march (2nd movement) expressed a sense of loss and mourning. Is the tribute now a generalized one? Or is Beethoven mourning the passing of Napoleon, First Consul? The mystery remains.

In 1803 Mozart's librettist for *Die Zauberflöte,* Schikaneder, asked Beethoven to compose an opera to another of his librettos; the composer lost interest and instead began a work based on J. N. Bouilly's *Leonore, ou L'Amour conjugal.* The completed opera was eventually named *Fidelio, oder Die eheliche Liebe;* Fidelio is the heroine Leonore's transvestite name in her efforts to save her imprisoned husband; elements of Singspiel persist throughout an otherwise serious work. *Fidelio* (or *Leonore*) was premiered a few days after the French army entered Vienna (1805); after 3 performances, the opera was rescheduled for 1806; eventually a final and greatly rev. version was produced (1814). Beethoven wrote 3 overtures for the earlier versions (now known as *Leonore* 1, 2, and 3); the final version has a 4th overture, known as *Fidelio.*

In the extraordinary profusion of creativity of 1802–08, Beethoven brought out the 3 string quartets, op. 59; 4th, 5th, and 6th Syms.; Violin Concerto; 4th Piano Concerto; Triple Concerto; the Coriolan Overture; and 6 piano sonatas, including the *Tempest* (D minor, op. 31/2); the *Waldstein* (C major, op. 53); and the *Appassionata* (F minor, op. 57). Financial difficulties beset him: various annuities from patrons were uncertain, and the devaluation of Austrian currency played havoc with his calculations. In Oct. 1808 King Jerome Bonaparte of Westphalia offered the composer the post of Kapellmeister of Kassel at a substantial salary, but he chose to remain in Vienna.

Between 1809 and 1812 Beethoven wrote his 5th Piano Concerto, the "Emperor" (dedicated to Archduke Rudolf); the String Quartet, op. 74 ("Harp"); incidental music to Goethe's drama *Egmont;* 7th and 8th Syms.; and 3 piano sonatas, including the E-flat Major, op. 81a, whimsically subtitled *Das Lebewohl, Abwesenheit, und Wiedersehn* (also known as *Les Adieux, l'absence, et le retour*); explicit characterization was rare with Beethoven; even in the 6th Sym. (*Pastoral*), whose movements bear specific subtitles, birdsong imitations, and the realistic portrayal of a storm, he appended a cautionary phrase: "More as an expression of one's feelings than a picture." Nationalism underlies his designation of 4 late piano sonatas (opp. 101, 106, 109, and 110) as works for a *Hammerklavier,* "hammer keyboard," rather than fortepiano, since all of his piano sonatas were for fortepiano; he was expressing his Austro-German consciousness. Most notably, he specifically denied that the famous introductory 4-note call in the 5th Sym. represented the knock of Fate at his door; the characteristic iambic tetrameter (3 short beats followed by 1 accented long beat) was anticipated and echoed in several of his works. The figure served as an Allied call in World War II, appropriate as it spelled *V* for *Victory* in Morse code; the Germans could not very well jail people for whistling Beethoven, so they interpreted it as the 1st letter of the archaic German word *Viktoria* and trumpeted it blithely over their radios.

Personal misfortunes, chronic ailments, and intermittent quarrels with friends and relatives preoccupied Beethoven's entire life; a man who ardently called for peace among men never achieved peace within; yet he could afford to disdain the attacks in the press; on the margin of a critical but justified review of *Wellington's Victory,* he wrote, "You wretched scoundrel! What I shit is better than anything you could ever think up!" He was overly suspicious; exaggerated his poverty; was untidy in personal habits, often using preliminary drafts to cover soup and the chamber pots, leaving telltale circles on the MSS; studiously examined the winning numbers of the Austrian government lottery, hoping to find a numerological clue to winning a fortune. Because of nearly indecipherable handwriting, the copying of his MSS presented difficulties; not only were notes smudged, but he often failed to mark a crucial accidental; a copyist compared copying 20 pages of Rossini favorably with a single page of Beethoven. On the other hand, the sketchbooks, containing many alternative drafts, are extremely valuable, allowing a peek into the inner sanctum of his creative process.

Beethoven spent most of his life in solitude; deprived of the pleasures and comforts of family life, sought to find a surrogate son in his nephew Karl, son of his brother Caspar Carl, who died in 1815. Beethoven regarded his sister-in-law Johanna as an unfit mother; sought and won sole guardianship over the boy in court by pouring torrents of vilification upon her, implying that she was engaged in prostitution (1820); proceeded to make his nephew's life very difficult, particularly by banning visits to his mother. In 1826 Karl attempted suicide in desperation over Beethoven's stifling avuncular affection; he survived, went into the army, was his uncle's sole heir, and enjoyed a normal life.

That Beethoven dreamed of an ideal life companion is clear from his candid utterances and letters, but he never kept company with any particular woman in Vienna. He lacked social graces: he could not dance, was unable to carry on a light conversation, and of course was overwhelmed by the dreadful reality of deafness. There were several objects of his secret passions, but he either didn't propose marriage or chose unsuitable women; it became inevitable that he would seek escape through illusions. The best-known of these was the famous letter addressed to an "unsterbliche Geliebte" (Immortal Beloved), couched in exuberant emotional tones characteristic of the sentimental romances of the time and strangely reminiscent of Goethe's novel *The Sorrows of Young Werther* (1774); the letter, never mailed, was discovered in a secret desk compartment after his death. Clues to the lady's identity are maddeningly few; the current candidate for most-likely-to-have-been-the "Immortal Beloved" is Antonie Brentano, wife of a merchant and mother of 1 daughter. Beethoven was a frequent visitor at their house (1810–12), and he dedicated works to all 3 Brentanos. His letters to Antonie and her replies express mutual devotion, but they cannot be easily reconciled with the torrid protestation of undying love in the unmailed letter. Speculation regarding his courting other society women, consorting with prostitutes, or alleged repressed homosexuality have also caused ink to be spilt.

The last period of Beethoven's composing included the monumental 9th Sym. (op. 125), completed and 1st performed in Vienna (1824), and the Missa Solemnis (op. 123); it is reported that Caroline Unger, alto soloist in the Missa Solemnis, had to pull Beethoven by the sleeve at the end of the 2nd movement of the sym. to acknowledge the applause he could not hear. With the 9th Sym., Beethoven completed the evolution of the symphonic form as he envisioned it; the choral finale, with reminiscences of the previous 3 movements, was his manifesto addressed to all humanity to unite in universal love, using the text from Schiller's ode *An die Freude* (To Joy). Other late works included the "late" string quartets (opp. 127, 130, 131, 132, and 135), counterparts to his 9th Sym. in their striking innovations, dramatic pauses, and novel instrumental tone colors; 10th violin sonata (op. 96); the monumental *33 Variations on a Waltz by Diabelli* (op. 120); 2 sets of bagatelles (opp. 119 and 126); and numerous folk-song arrangements.

In Dec. 1826 Beethoven was stricken with a fever that developed into a mortal pleurisy; dropsy and jaundice supervened to this condition; surgery to relieve the accumulated fluid in his organism was unsuccessful; he died on the afternoon of Mar. 26, 1827; an electric storm struck Vienna as he lay dying, a fact confirmed by the contemporaneous Viennese weather bureau; but the story that he raised his clenched fist aloft as a gesture of defiance to an overbearing Heaven is fantasy. The funeral of Beethoven was held in all solemnity; his life and work has been honored since on many occasions and in many ways.

When von Bülow was asked for his favorite key signature, he replied that it was E-flat major, the tonality of the *Eroica,* for it had 3 flats—1 apiece for Bach, Beethoven, and Brahms. Beethoven became forever the "2nd B" in popular music books. Beethoven's music marks a division between the Classic period of the 18th century, exemplified by Mozart and Haydn, and the new spirit of Romantic music that characterized the entire 19th century. The music of the 18th century possessed the magnitude of mass production; according to his own count, Haydn wrote 104 syms.; Mozart wrote about 45 syms. during his short lifetime. Haydn's syms. were constructed according to an easily defined formal structure; while Mozart's last syms. show greater depth of penetration, they do not depart from Classic conventions. In sartorial matters, music before Beethoven was *Zopfmusik* (pigtail music); Haydn and Mozart are familiar to us by portraits with their heads crowned by elaborate wigs; Beethoven's hair was by contrast luxuriant in its unkempt splendor.

Beethoven's syms. were few in number and mutually different. The 1st and 2nd Syms. may still be classified as *Zopfmusik,* but with the 3rd Sym. he entered a new world of music: it was on a grander scale than previous syms., had the intense contrast of a funeral march, and merged the scherzo with the finale. Although the 5th Sym. had no designated program, its thematic unity was unprecedented. Wagner attached a bombastic label, "Apotheosis of the Dance," to the 7th Sym., with the memorably economical slow march movement. Beethoven called the 8th Sym. his "little sym.," in comparison with the mighty 9th Sym. With the advent of Beethoven, the manufacture of syms. en masse ceased; Schumann, Brahms, Tchaikovsky, and their Romantic contemporaries wrote but a few syms. apiece or turned to the concert overture or symphonic poem for orch. music. (Exceptions were Dvořák, Bruckner, and Mahler, who equaled Beethoven's total.)

Yet Beethoven's melody and harmony did not diverge from the sacrosanct laws of euphony and tonality; even the dissonant chord introducing the last movement of the 9th Sym. resolves to the tonic, giving only a moment's pause to the ear. His beloved device of pairing the melody in the high treble with triadic chords in close harmony in the deep bass was a stylistic peculiarity but not necessarily an infringement of Classic rules; yet contemporaneous critics found such practices repugnant and described him as an eccentric determined to create unconventional sonorities; equally strange to the untutored ear were pregnant pauses and sudden modulations in his instrumental works. Beethoven was not a natural contrapuntist, but like Haydn in his middle years he began to use fugal finals; his monumental *Grosse Fuge,* originally composed as the finale of the String Quartet, op. 130, was separated and publ. as op. 133. His fugal movements were usually free canonic imitations, with the structure but not the essence of the Baroque masters.

Beethoven attached opus numbers to most of his works; other works are catalogued as WoO (works without op. number, in the 1955 Kinsky and Halm catalogue) and Hess (works that appeared for the 1st time in the 1957 Hess catalogue).

begeisterung, mit (Ger.). With enthusiasm, spirit, and inspiration.

begleitung (Ger.). Accompaniment.

beguine. Latin American dance in a lively syncopated rhythm. Cole Porter made a brilliant play on words in his *Begin the Beguine* (from *Jubilee,* 1935), a song imitative of Latin rhythms that he composed after hearing the dance during a cruise in the West Indies.

behaglich (Ger.). Easily, comfortably; comodo.

Beiderbecke, (Leon) Bix, b. Davenport, Iowa, Mar. 10, 1903; d. N.Y., Aug. 6, 1931. He began to play music as a small child; developed a flair for ragtime and jazz; played cornet in various jazz groups in Chicago and St. Louis; developed a distinctive style of rhythmic lyricism; joined the Paul Whiteman band (1927); his closest musical associate was saxophonist Frank Trumbauer; although lacking formal musical education, wrote a few beguilingly attractive piano pieces of an impressionistic coloring (*In a Mist*). He succumbed to severe alcoholism. His musical legacy was preserved in recordings; although the settings were conventional, his unique tone and improvisational sensitivity to pitch choice and rhythm transcended ordinary harmonic progressions; one of the 1st white jazz musicians to be admired by black performers; after his death a cult formed around him and his tantalizingly small legacy.

Beinum, Eduard van, b. Arnhem, Sept. 3, 1900; d. Amsterdam, Apr. 13, 1959. He studied with J. B. de Pauw and Sem Dresden; 1st appeared as a pianist with the Concertgebouw Orch., Amsterdam (1920); thereafter devoted himself to choral conducting; in 1931, appointed associate conductor of the Concertgebouw Orch.; in 1945, became principal conductor, succeeding Mengelberg (who had been disfranchised for collaboration with the Germans during the occupation). He was a guest conductor of various European orchs.; made his American debut with the Philadelphia Orch. (1954); later that year toured the U.S. with the Concertgebouw Orch.; from 1957 until shortly before his death was principal guest conductor with the Los Angeles Phil. Beinum was regarded by most critics as an intellectual conductor whose chief concern was the projection of the music itself rather than his own musical personality; was equally capable in Classic, Romantic, and modern works.

bel canto (It., beautiful song). 1. Art of lyrical and virtuosic performance as exemplified by the finest Italian singers of the 18th and 19th centuries, by contrast to recitative and the declamatory singing style favored by Wagner; the term represents the once glorious tradition of vocal perfection for beauty's sake. The secret of bel canto was the exclusive property of Italian singing teachers who spread the technique to Russia, to England, and to America; the art of bel canto is still being taught in conservatories and music schools as a necessary precondition for an operatic career. 2. Operatic repertoire composed to highlight bel canto singers, notably late Baroque and early Romantic Italian opera; fell into disuse until after World War II, when singers such as Callas, Sutherland, and Sills revived the works of Bellini, Donizetti, Handel, and others.

belebt (Ger.). Animated, brisk.

bell. 1. Hollow metallic percussion instrument sounded by a clapper hanging inside or by a hammer outside. See ⇒bells. 2. The flaring, open end of wind instruments such as the trumpet, trombone, or English horn; the instruction "bells up" directs the player to hold the instrument upward for a louder sound.

Bell, Joshua, b. Bloomington, Ind., Dec. 9, 1967. He studied with Mimi Zweig, Josef Gingold, Ivan Galamian, and Szeryng; after winning a competition, appeared with the Philadelphia Orch. under Muti, becoming the youngest soloist to appear with it on a subscription concert; in 1985, made his Carnegie Hall debut in N.Y. as soloist with the St. Louis Sym. Orch.

bellicoso (It., bellicose). In a martial, warlike manner.

Bellini, Vincenzo, b. Catania, Sicily, Nov. 3, 1801; d. Puteaux, near Paris, Sept. 23, 1835. Bellini's grandfather and father were maestri di cappella in Catania; after studying with them he entered the Real Collegio di Musica di San Sebastiano (Naples), where he was instructed by Nicola Zingarelli and others; wrote several sinfonias, 2 Masses, and the cantata *Ismene* (1824). His 1st opera, *Adelson e Salvini,* was given at the Collegio in 1825; a production at the Teatro San Carlo in Naples of his 2nd opera, *Bianca e Gernando* followed (1826); went to Milan; an opera seria, *Il Pirata* for the Teatro alla Scala was successfully produced (1827); this was his 1st setting of a libretto by the noted Felice Romani (1788–1865); another successful opera seria, *La Straniera,* followed (1829); also produced *Zaira* that year, less successfully (Parma). He was commissioned to write for the Teatro La Fenice, Venice; the result, the Shakespearean *I Capuleti ed i Montecchi* (1830), had a decisive success; even more successful was *La Sonnambula* (Milan, 1831), with the celebrated soprano Giuditta Pasta as Amina; she also introduced the title role of his most famous opera, *Norma* (La Scala, 1831), which established Bellini's mastery of Italian operatic bel canto. *Beatrice di Tenda,* produced in Venice (1833), failed; it was his last collaboration with Romani; traveled to London and Paris; produced his last opera, *I Puritani* (1835), whose positive reception was due in part to a superb cast (Grisi, Rubini,

Tamburini, and Lablache). Bellini was contemplating future productions and marriage when stricken with an attack of amebiasis; died 6 weeks before his 34th birthday; his remains were reverently removed to his native Catania in 1876.

Bellini's music represents Italian bel canto at its most glorious melodiousness; words, rhythm, melody, harmony, and instrumental accompaniment unite in mutual perfection. The lyric flow and dramatic expressiveness of his music provide a natural medium for singers in the Italian language, so that his greatest masterpieces, *La Sonnambula* and *Norma*, remain in the repertoire of opera houses throughout the world. Limiting himself to opera seria and semiseria genres, he selected melodramatic subjects with Romantic female figures in the center of the action to appeal to the public: women who go mad (*Il Pirata, I Puritani*), walk in their sleep (*La Sonnambula*), or walk into funeral pyres with their lovers (*Norma*).

bells. Generic name for church bells, carillons, tubular chimes, and other types; for church bells, the collective name is a *ring*, and the sound they make together is a *peal*, e.g., "the peal of a ring of 5 bells." The largest church bell was the Czar's Bell, cast in Moscow (1733) but which fell and cracked; it weighed nearly 500,000 pounds and was about 20 feet in diameter. The Liberty Bell in Philadelphia is far smaller and is etched as an American patriotic symbol of the early days of the U.S.; it too is cracked. Church bells are rarely used in musical scores, but their sounds are produced by imitation.

Other bells: tubular bells (also called tubular chimes or simply chimes), suspended from a horizontal bar and struck with a hammer; sleighbells, like those attached to the harness of a horse-drawn sleigh, included in scores of Leopold Mozart, Mahler, and Varèse; cowbells, heavier bells with a clapper, found in a few classical scores but very common in popular music; domestic handbells, used for special operatic effects; handbell ensembles., comprising a set of handbells with varying pitches, popular in churches in the U.K. and U.S., played using the change-ringing system; glockenspiel, a set of bells in the form of metal bars; carillon, a tower of stationary bells (inside or outside churches), played on a large keyboard. The science of making and playing bells is called campanology (It. *campana*, bell).

bémol (Fr.). The flat sign (♭).

ben (It.). Well, good, very. *Ben articolato*, clearly and neatly pronounced and phrased; *ben marcato*, well marked; *ben pronunziato*, clearly enunciated; *ben ritmato*, observe the rhythm carefully and precisely; *ben sostenuto*, very sustained; *ben tenuto*, very sustained.

Benedictus (Lat., blessed). Concluding portion of the Sanctus in the Roman Catholic Mass; often appears as a separate movement.

benefit. Special performance whose proceeds go to the singer or director of an opera performance; a common practice in the 18th and 19th centuries that declined toward the middle of the 20th century, when benefits were usually given for charitable or patriotic purposes.

Bennett, Richard Rodney, b. Broadstairs, Kent, Mar. 29, 1936. He studied with Lennox Berkeley, Howard Ferguson, and Boulez; taught at the Royal Academy of Music, London

(1963–65); visiting prof. at the Peabody Cons., Baltimore (1970–71); made a Commander of the Order of the British Empire (1977). He composes in a typically British neoclassicism using more dissonance; is an excellent pianist. Among his many works are operas (*The Mines of Sulphur*, 1965; *Victory*, after the Conrad novel, 1970), ballets, numerous solo concertos, pieces for chamber and full orchs. (*Aubade*, 1964; 2 syms., 1966, 1968; *Zodiac*, 1976; *Dream Dancing*, 1986); vocal music, including choruses; piano and chamber music; and film scores: *The Nanny* (1965), *Billion Dollar Brain* (1967), *Nicholas and Alexandra* (1971); *Murder on the Orient Express* (1974); and *Equus* (1977).

Berberian, Cathy, b. Attleboro, Mass., July 4, 1925; d. Rome, Mar. 6, 1983. She studied singing, dancing, and pantomime; traveled to Italy; attracted wide attention by performing the ultrasurrealist *Fontana Mix* by Cage, producing a fantastic variety of sound effects (1958); noting her 3-octave vocal range, one bewildered music critic remarked that she could sing both Tristan and Isolde. Thanks to her uncanny ability to produce ultrahuman (and subhuman) tones, and her willingness to incorporate into her professional vocalization a variety of animal noises, guttural sounds, grunts and growls, squeals, squeaks and squawks, clicks and clucks, shrieks and screeches, hisses, hoots, and hollers, she instantly became the darling of inventive composers of the avant-garde, who eagerly dedicated to her their nearly unperformable works.

She married Luciano Berio (1950; separated and divorced by 1968); he wrote *Circles, Epifanie, Visage, Sequenza, Recital I (for Cathy)*, and *Folk Songs* for her; she also intoned earlier music, making a favorable impression with her recordings of Monteverdi. A composer in her own right, she wrote works such as *Stripsody*, an arresting soliloquy of labial and laryngeal sounds, and a piano piece, *Morsicat(h)y*; resented being regarded as a freak, insisting her objective was merely to meet the challenge of the new art of her time; claimed that, Steely Dan to the contrary, there were no roulades she couldn't sing.

berceuse (Fr. *berceau*, cradle). Cradle song or lullaby, usually set in 6/8 time, suggesting the rocking of a cradle, with an ostinato accompaniment on the tonic and the dominant. Chopin's famous Berceuse (op. 57) for piano has an ingeniously varie-gated melody against a steady accompaniment on a pedal point; Balakirev, Debussy, Ravel, Busoni, and Stravinsky wrote berceuses.

Berg, Alban (Maria Johannes), b. Vienna, Feb. 9, 1885; d. there, Dec. 24, 1935. He played piano and composed songs without formal training; in 1904, met Schoenberg, who became his teacher, mentor, and close friend; studied with him for 6 years; Webern was a fellow classmate; the 3 initiated the radical movement known as the 2nd Viennese school of composition. Berg assisted Schoenberg in organizing Vienna's Soc. for Private Musical Performances (Verein für Musikalische Privataufführungen, 1918–22) whose goal was to perform works unacceptable to established musical society; in 1925 Berg joined the newly created ISCM, which would promote fresh musical ideas. His early works reflected the late Romantic style of Wagner, Hugo Wolf, and Mahler, in numerous songs and the *Piano Sonata* (1908); also composed works of an aphoristic quality: *5 Orchestral Songs on Postcard Texts* (1912, premiered 1952), *4 Pieces for Clarinet* (1913), and *3 Pieces for Orchestra* (1915, premiered 1930).

In 1917 Berg began work on the opera *Wozzeck* (based on Georg Büchner's fragmentary play); the score represents an ingenious synthesis of Classic forms and modern techniques; organized as a series of purely symphonic sections in traditional forms, the 3 acts (each 5 scenes long) comprise an exposition of character pieces, a sym. of increasing despair, and a dénouement of inventions on different ostinatos, respectively. Its premiere at the Berlin State Opera (1925) precipitated a storm of protests and press reviews of extreme violence, as did the Prague premiere (1926); undismayed, Berg and his friends publ. a brochure incorporating the most vehement reviews so as to shame and denounce the critics. Stokowski, ever eager to defy convention, gave the American premiere in Philadelphia (1931); arousing great interest, it was received with cultured equanimity; thereafter, performances multiplied in Europe (including Russia); eventually became recognized as the masterpiece it is.

Berg then wrote the *Lyric Suite* for string quartet in 6 movements; premiered in Vienna by the Kolisch Quartet (1927). A long-suppressed vocal part for its finale, bespeaking his affection for a married woman, Hanna Fuchs-Robettin, was rediscovered through an annotated score found in a Viennese library (premiered 1979); his widow Helene had knowingly or unknowingly had donated it; the text proved to be Stefan Georg's translation of Baudelaire's *De Profundis clamavi* from *Les Fleurs du mal*. Berg also inserted semiotical and numerological clues to his feelings in a sort of symbolical synthesis, here and in other works.

Berg's 2nd opera, *Lulu* (1928–35), to a libretto derived from 2 plays by Wedekind, was left unfinished at his death; the 2 completed acts and music from the *Symphonische Stücke aus der Oper "Lulu"* (1934) were performed posth. in Zurich (1937). Helene Berg forestalled any attempt to have the work completed; his publishers, asserting their legal rights, secretly commissioned Friedrich Cerha to re-create the 3rd act from the *Symphonische Stücke,* Erwin Stein's unpubl. vocal score (1936), and other sources. Cerha's task required 12 years (1962–74); after Berg's widow's death (1976), a premiere of the complete opera was given at the Paris Opéra, with Stratas as Lulu and Boulez conducting (1979); an American premiere followed in Santa Fe later that year. As in *Wozzeck,* Berg organized *Lulu* in a series of Classic forms; but while *Wozzeck* was written before Schoenberg's formulation of the 12-tone method of composition, *Lulu* was set in full-fledged dodecaphonic techniques; even so, frequent divagations from the dodecaphonic code resulted in triadic tonal harmonies.

Berg's last completed work was the Violin Concerto, given its 1st performance at the Festival of the ISCM in Barcelona (1936); the score is dedicated "Dem Andenken eines Engels" (To the memory of an angel), a reference to the recently deceased young daughter of Alma Mahler and Walter Gropius; a deeply felt work, it is couched in the 12-tone technique, with free and frequent interludes of passing tonality and quotations from a Carinthian folksong and the Bach chorale *Es ist genug* (from *O Ewigkeit, du Donnerwort,* BWV 60).

bergerette (Fr. *berger,* shepherd). 1. Pastoral or rustic song popular in 18th-century France, and the poetry associated with it. 2. Instrumental dance of the 16th century.

Bergonzi, Carlo, b. Polisene, near Parma, July 13, 1924. He studied with Grandini; made his operatic debut as a baritone in Lecce, singing Figaro in *The Barber of Seville* (1948); switched to tenor, singing Andrea Chénier in Bari (1951); appeared at La

Scala, Milan, with much success (1953); sang in London (from 1953); made his U.S. debut with the Chicago Lyric Opera as Luigi in *Il Tabarro* (1955); made his 1st appearance at the Metropolitan Opera, N.Y., as Radames (1956); remained on its roster until 1974. His voice had well-modulated and beautiful tone; he possessed an elegant and lively sense of line and taste; was distinguished in Italian lyric dramatic operatic roles, such as Canio, Turiddu, Des Greux, Manrico, Riccardo (*Un Ballo in Mascera*), Cavaradossi, and Boito's Faust.

Berio, Luciano, b. Oneglia, Oct. 24, 1925. He studied music with his father, then with Ghedini, Giulini, and (in the U.S.) Dallapiccola; married an extraordinary singer, Cathy Berberian, who willingly sang his most excruciating soprano parts; they were divorced in 1968, but she magnanimously continued to sing his music thereafter. He returned to Italy; joined the staff of the Italian Radio; founded the Studio di Fonologia Musicale (1955) for experimental work on acoustics; ed. the progressive magazine *Incontri Musicali* (1956–60); joined the faculty of the Juilliard School of Music, N.Y. (1965–71), providing an alternative to its traditionally conservative atmosphere; subsequently maintained an infrequent but important connection with America. In the mid-1970s he joined the Inst. de Recherche et de Coordination Acoustique/Musique (IRCAM) in Paris, working closely with its director, Boulez; became the director of the Accademia Filarmonica Romana (1976); awarded Germany's Siemens Prize for his contributions to contemporary music (1989).

Perhaps the most unusual characteristic of his creative philosophy is his impartial eclecticism, permitting the use of the widest variety of resources, from Croatian folk songs to objets trouvés; is equally liberal in his use of graphic notation; some of his scores look like expressionist drawings. He is a rare contemporary composer who can touch the nerve endings of sensitive listeners and music critics, one of whom described his *Sinfonia* (1968–69), his best-known work) with ultimate brevity: "It stinks." But if *Sinfonia* stank, then by implication so did the ample quotes from Mahler, Ravel, and Richard Strauss used as found musical objects in this work. Apart from "pure" music, many of Berio's works use all manner of artifacts and artifices of popular pageants, including mimodrama, choreodrama, concrete noises, acrobats, clowns, jugglers, and organ grinders (*Opera,* 1970).

Berlin, Irving (born Israel Balin), b. Mogilev, May 11, 1888; d. N.Y., Sept. 22, 1989. Fearing anti-Semitic pogroms, his family emigrated when he was 5 years old and landed in N.Y. His father was a synagogue cantor; he worked as a newsboy, a busboy, and a singing waiter; improvised on the bar piano and wrote the lyrics to a song, *Marie from Sunny Italy;* when the song was publ. (1907), his name had changed to Berlin; soon acquired the American vernacular; never tried to experiment with sophisticated language, thus distancing himself from younger contemporaries such as Ira Gershwin and Cole Porter. He never learned to read or write music; composed most of his songs in F-sharp major for convenience's sake; to use other keys, he had a special hand clutch built at the piano keyboard, so that his later songs acquired an air of tonal variety; this piano is kept at the Smithsonian Institution, Washington, D.C.

Berlin worked as a song-plugger and performer of his own songs; his 1st big hit was *Alexander's Ragtime Band* (not a rag; 1911); wrote his 1st ballad, *When I Lost You,* which sold a million copies (1912). His 1st complete score was written for *Watch Your Step*, a musical comedy featuring the dancers Vernon and Irene Castle (1914). Berlin was drafted into the U.S. Army (1917) but did not serve in military action; instead wrote a revue, *Yip, Yip, Yaphank*, which orig. included the 1st version of *God Bless America*; omitted from the show, he revised it for singer Kate Smith (1938); the song, patriotic to the core, became an unofficial American anthem. After the war ended he helped produce the *Music Box Revues* (1921–25); the best-known song was *Say It With Music*.

Beginning in 1935, Berlin turned his attention to films and musicals; his most successful films were *Top Hat*, with Astaire and Rogers (1935); *Follow the Fleet* (1936); *On the Avenue* (1937); *Holiday Inn*, with Bing Crosby singing *White Christmas* (1942); and *Easter Parade* (1948); his 1st musical was *Louisiana Purchase* (1940); the most successful were *Annie Get Your Gun* (1946) and *Call Me Madam* (1950); his last musical was *Mr. President* (1962).

Berlin's 1st biographer, Alexander Woollcott, referred to him as a "creative ignoramus," meaning it as a compliment. Victor Herbert specifically discouraged him from learning harmony for fear that he would lose his natural genius for melody; indeed, despite a lack of formal training, he composed songs with unusual tonal and harmonic progressions, unlikely formal structures, and uneven phrase lengths. Herbert also encouraged him to join the American Soc. of Composers, Authors, and Publishers (ASCAP) as a charter member, the source of his fantastically prosperous commercial success. He was extremely generous with his enormous earnings; all of *God Bless America*'s royalties were donated to the Boy and Girl Scouts of America; another great song, *White Christmas*, became a sentimental hit among American troops stationed in the Pacific during World War II; in 1954 he received the Congressional Medal of Honor for his patriotic songs. But he was reclusive in his last years; he even avoided making a personal appearance when members of ASCAP gathered before his house to serenade him on his 100th birthday.

Berlioz, (Louis) Hector. b. La Côte-Saint-André, Isère, Dec. 11, 1803; d. Paris, Mar. 8, 1869. He played the flute and guitar; went to Paris to study medicine, which he abandoned (1824); studied composition with J. F. Le Sueur (1822); 1st important work was a *Messe solennelle* (1825; MS recently rediscovered); resumed studies with Le Sueur and Reicha (1826); wrote an opera, *Les Francs-juges*, never fully performed (MS partially extant); in 1828 presented a concert of works at the Paris Cons.; one, *Huit scènes de Faust* after Goethe, was later revised and produced as *La Damnation de Faust* (1845–46). In 1827 he began annual attempts to win the Prix de Rome for the "best" cantata, all candidates setting the same text; after 3 failures, won with *La Mort de Sardanapale* (1830).

In the meantime Berlioz became hopelessly infatuated with Irish actress Harriet Smithson after attending her portrayal of Ophelia in Shakespeare's *Hamlet* given by a British troupe in Paris (1827). He knew no English and Miss Smithson spoke no French; made no effort to engage her personally; temporarily found a surrogate in Camille Moke, a young pianist. Romantically absorbed in the ideal of love through music, he wrote his most ambitious work to date, the *Sym. fantastique*, as an offering of adoration and devotion to Miss Smithson. In the 5-movement work the object of the hero's passion haunts him through the device of the idée fixe; she appears 1st as an entrancing but unattainable vision; as an enticing ball dancer; then as a deceptively

pastoral image; he penetrates her disguise and kills her, a crime for which he is led to the guillotine. (This *March to the Scaffold* borrows from *Les Francs-juges* with a few bars of the idée fixe used melodramatically.) At the end she reveals herself as a wicked witch at a Sabbath orgy. The fantastic program and wild musical fervor are astutely subordinated to the symphonic form; the idée fixe itself serves merely as a recurring motif; the work emerges as a magnificent tapestry of sound, its unflagging popularity testifying to its evocative power; the work was premiered at the Paris Cons. (1830) with considerable success; Miss Smithson herself failed to materialize. Undeterred, Berlioz provided a sequel entitled *Lélio, ou Le Retour à la vie*, supposedly signaling the hero's renunciation of his morbid obsessions; the work is a pastiche. Both works were performed at a single concert in Paris (1832); Smithson finally made an appearance. Music proved to be the food of love; Berlioz and Smithson became emotionally involved and married (1833); alas, their marriage proved happy for only a brief time; they had 1 son, Louis; throughout their marriage she was beset by debilitating illnesses. He found a more convenient woman companion, the singer Marie Recio, whom he married shortly after Smithson's death in 1854; he also survived his 2nd wife, who died in 1862.

Whatever the peripeteias of his personal life, Berlioz never lost a lust for music; after his Prix de Rome sojourn in Italy, his next important work was *Harold en Italie* for Solo Viola with Orch., based on Byron's *Childe Harold* (1834); commissioned by Paganini, it had too little solo viola writing to satisfy him (but he let Berlioz keep the fee). Berlioz followed it with an opera semiseria, *Benvenuto Cellini* (1834–37), which premiered at the Paris Opéra unsuccessfully (1838); he rev. the score, which premiered in Weimar, conducted by Liszt (1852). Berlioz became a highly active music critic and *feuilletoniste*; in 1835 he began conducting. Now entrenched in the Parisian cultural world, he composed a *Grande messe des morts* (Requiem; 1837), which demanded a huge chorus and antiphonal forces. In late 1838 he conducted a successful concert of his works; legend has it that Paganini came forth after the concert, knelt in homage to him, and (according to Berlioz) subsequently gave him 20,000 francs. In 1839 he conducted the premiere of his dramatic sym. *Romeo et Juliette*, one of the most moving lyrical invocations of Shakespeare's tragedy, rich in melodic invention and instrumental interplay. In 1840 he premiered the *Grande symphonie funèbre et triomphale*, commemorating soldiers fallen in the fight for Algeria; apparently conducted it with a drawn sword through the streets of Paris, accompanying the ashes of the military heroes to their interment in the Bastille column. At an 1844 concert after the Exhibition of Industrial Products, he conducted Beethoven's 5th Sym. with 36 double basses, Weber's overture to *Der Freischütz* with 24 French horns, and the Prayer of Moses from Rossini's *Mosè in Egitto* with 25 harps; boasted that his 1,022 performers achieved an ensemble worthy of the finest string quartet. For his *L'Imperiale*, performed after the 1855 version of the same exhibition, he had 1,200 performers, augmented by huge choruses and a military band; in anticipation of a century later, installed 5 semiconductors and kept them in time with a "metronome" (his left hand) while holding the baton in his right.

Such indulgences generated derision on the part of classical musicians and critics; caricatures represented Berlioz as a madman commanding a heterogeneous mass of instrumentalists and singers driven to distraction by the music; he deeply resented these attacks, complaining bitterly about Paris's uncongenial artistic environment. But whatever obloquy he suffered, he also found satisfaction in his pervasive influence on his contemporaries, including Wagner, Liszt, and the Russian school; publ. his *Grand traité d'instrumentation et d'orchestration modernes* (Paris, 1843), which became a standard text in orchestration; wrote the *Roman Carnival Overture* (1844), based on music from *Benvenuto Cellini*. In 1846 he completed the oratorio-like "dramatic legend," *La Damnation de Faust*, incorporating an arrangement of the nationalistic Rákóczy March, rationalized when he took the liberty of conveying Goethe's Faust to Hungary; the march became an extremely popular concert piece.

Berlioz undertook successful tours of Russia and England (1847–48); in 1849, composed his grand Te Deum; wrote the uncharacteristically gentle oratorio *L'Enfance du Christ* (1854); despite past operatic failures, returned to stage composition; chose the *Aeneid* of Virgil, selecting the episodes concerning the Trojan War and Aeneas's visit to Carthage; composed the grand opera *Les Troyens* (1856–60); part of the work was produced at the Théâtre-Lyrique, Paris (1863); its opera's financial returns made it possible for him to abandon his occupation as music critic. His last operatic project was *Béatrice et Bénédict*, after Shakespeare's *Much Ado About Nothing*; conducted its premiere in Baden-Baden (1862). Despite frail health and a state of depression generated by his "failure" as composer and conductor in France, he achieved a final series of successes abroad; conducted *La Damnation de Faust* in Vienna (1866); went to Russia during the 1867–68 season and received an enthusiastic reception there; but the death of his beloved son Louis while serving in the military (1867) was a final blow to his well-being.

Posth. recognition came slowly to Berlioz; long after his death conservative critics still referred to his bizarre and willfully dissonant music; no cult comparable to the ones around the names of Wagner and Liszt coalesced; only the overtures, the *Sym. fantastique*, and the songs (particularly *Les nuits d'été*, 1841) entered the repertory; operatic performances were extremely rare; since he did not write solo works, concert recitals did not feature his name; however, literature about and recordings of his legacy mushroomed after World War II, particularly in English and by British artists; these have now secured his rightful place in music history.

Berman, Lazar (Naumovich), brilliant Soviet pianist; b. Leningrad, Feb. 26, 1930. He studied with Goldenweiser; after a modest beginning, made a highly successful tour of Italy (1970); toured the U.S. with tremendous acclaim (1976). In his repertoire he showed a distinct predilection for the Romantic period; among moderns he favored Scriabin and Prokofiev; his titanic technique, astounding in the facility of bravura passages, did not preclude excellent poetic evocation of lyric moods.

Bernac, Pierre (born Bertin), b. Paris, Jan. 12, 1899; d. Villeneuve-les-Avignon, Oct. 17, 1979. He started his singing career late in life, studying with Walter Straram; gave a recital in Paris, offering songs by Poulenc and Auric (1926); sang works by Debussy, Ravel, Honegger, and Milhaud; eager to learn the art of German lieder, studied with Reinhold von Warlich; returning to Paris, devoted himself to concerts and teaching. He became a lifelong friend to Poulenc, who wrote songs and song cycles for him and acted as his accompanist in many of their tours through Europe and America; younger composers such as Daniel-Lesur, Jolivet, Sauguet, and Françaix also wrote for him. He conducted master classes in the U.S. and taught at the American Cons.,

Fontainebleau; publ. a valuable manual, *The Interpretation of French Song* (N.Y., 1970), and a monograph, *Francis Poulenc: The Man and His Songs* (N.Y., 1977).

Bernstein, Elmer, b. N.Y., Apr. 4, 1922. He studied with Sessions and Wolpe; served in the U.S. Air Force during World War II; then settled in Hollywood and became a highly successful and versatile composer of background scores, particularly in dramatic films; of these the most effective were *The Man with the Golden Arm* (1955), *The 10 Commandments* (1956), *Desire under the Elms* (1958), *The Magnificent 7* (1960), *Summer and Smoke* (1958), *Walk on the Wild Side* (1962), *To Kill a Mockingbird* (1963), *The Great Escape* (1963), *Hawaii* (1966), *True Grit* (1969), *The Shootist* (1976), *Airplane!* (1980), and *Ghostbusters* (1984); also composed chamber music, the musical *How Now Dow Jones* (1967), 3 orch'l suites, chamber music, and songs.

Bernstein, Leonard (born Louis), b. Lawrence, Mass., Aug. 25, 1918, d. N.Y., Oct. 14, 1990. He studied piano with Helen Coates and Heinrich Gebhard; entered Harvard Univ. (1935) and studied with Piston, A. Tillman Merritt, and E. B. Hill; moved to Philadelphia (1939); studied with Reiner, R. Thompson, and I. Vengerova; attended Tanglewood (1940–41); worked with Koussevitzky. In 1943 he became assistant conductor to Artur Rodzinski of the N.Y. Phil. Bernstein's break came on Nov. 14, 1943, when he replaced Bruno Walter on short notice in a N.Y. Phil. concert; acquitted himself magnificently and was roundly praised in the press. He became the N.Y. Phil.'s 1st American-born music director (1958); toured with the orch. in South America, Russia, 16 other European and Near Eastern countries, Japan, Alaska, and Canada.

Bernstein was the 1st American to lead a regular performance at La Scala, Milan (Cherubini's *Medea*, 1953); made his Metropolitan Opera, N.Y., debut (1964), conducting *Falstaff*, the work chosen for his debut with the Vienna State Opera (1966); in 1969 he resigned from the N.Y. Phil. in order to pursue composition and other projects; the orch. named him the unprecedented title of "laureate conductor; " took the orch. on a tour of 11 European cities, giving 13 concerts in 17 days (1976). Ebullient with communicative talents, he initiated a televised series of "Young People's Concerts" (1958), serving as an astute and self-confident commentator; these concerts became popular with audiences of all ages; arranged a series of educational music programs for television. He taught at Brandeis Univ. (1951–55) and, concurrently, in Tanglewood; was the Charles Eliot Norton Prof. in Poetry at Harvard Univ. (1973); lectured at M.I.T. He was the recipient of many honors throughout Europe; elected to the American Academy of Arts and Letters (1981); made president of the London Sym. Orch. (1987) and laureate conductor of the Israel Phil. (1988). As interpreter and program maker he showed a unique affinity with the music of Mahler, whose syms. he repeatedly performed in cycles; in late 1989, conducted celebratory performances of Beethoven's 9th Sym. on both sides of the Berlin Wall, with an orch. made up of players from the Bavarian Radio Sym. Orch., Munich and N.Y., London, Paris, Dresden, and Leningrad orchs.

An excellent pianist, Bernstein often appeared as a soloist in classical or modern concerts, occasionally conducting the orch. from the keyboard. An intellectual by nature and *litterateur* and modernistically inclined poet by aspiration, he publ. some excellent sonnets; was outspoken on behalf of liberal causes and once dubbed a member of the "radical chic." His tremendous overflow of spiritual and purely animal energy impelled certain histrionic mannerisms on the podium that elicited some critics' derisive comments about his "choreography."

Bernstein seemed unique in his protean proficiency as a symphonic and operatic conductor as well as a composer of complex musical works and original and enormously popular stage productions; in *West Side Story* (1957), created a significant social drama, abounding in memorable tunes; other successful shows were *On the Town* (1944) and *Candide* (1956). In his 2nd Sym., *The Age of Anxiety* (1949; rev. 1965), he reflected the turbulence of modern life; ever true to his Jewish heritage, he wrote a devout choral sym., *Kaddish* (1963; rev. 1977); as a testimony to his ecumenical religious feelings, produced the semidramatic *Mass* (1971), with numerous departures from the Roman Catholic liturgy.

Berry, Chuck (Charles Edward Anderson), b. San Jose, Calif., Jan. 15, 1926. He was a chorister at the Antioch Baptist Church, St. Louis; learned to play guitar and improvised tunes in a then-current jazz manner; went to Chicago; recorded his song *Maybellene* for the Chess record company (1955); it quickly climbed the charts in all 3 major categories: rhythm and blues, country-western, and popular. He scored many more hits through the late '50s, including *Brown-Eyed Handsome Man, Roll Over Beethoven, Rock and Roll Music, Johnny B. Goode, Sweet Little 16,* and *Memphis, Tennessee.*

Around this time Berry opened the Chuck Berry Club Bandstand in St. Louis, which prospered; but his career was interrupted for 2 years while he served time in a federal penitentiary for violating the Mann Act (1961–63); while jail made him bitter, he maintained his onstage spirit of happy-go-lucky insouciance; rebounded with *Nadine, No Particular Place to Go,* and *My Ding-a-Ling,* his last big hit; maintained active career as a lively oldie-but-goodie, still doing his patented "duckwalk" across the stage.

Berry's guitar style was based on rapid rhythm-and-blues riffs and country influences; exploited the electric guitar's potential for highly rhythmic chording (the most distinctive feature of his playing) and ringing overtones; his songs were primarily blues-based, with strong emphasis on "a backbeat [so that] you can't lose it/Any old time you use it"; was certainly one of the most influential artists of the 1950s on later musicians.

beruhigend (Ger.). Becoming calmer, gradually calming down.

Berwald, Franz (Adolf), b. Stockholm, July 23, 1796; d. there, Apr. 3, 1868. Franz studied with his father and others; played violin and viola in the orch. of the Royal Chapel, Stockholm (1812–28); toured Finland and Russia with his brother (1819); moved to Berlin (1829); opened a flourishing orthopedic establishment (1835); went to Vienna (1841); obtained some success as a composer of symphonic poems; was highly prolific. He then returned to Stockholm (1842); secured a foothold with operettas and cantatas; in late 1843 his cousin Johan Fredrik conducted the premiere of the *Sinfonie sérieuse* (only 1 of 4 syms. performed in his lifetime); a poor performance hurt his cause.

Berwald returned to Vienna, where Jenny Lind sang in his stage cantata *Ein ländliches Verlobungsfest in Schweden* at the Theater an der Wien (1846); elected an honorary member of the Salzburg Mozarteum (1847); returned to his homeland in hopes of securing a position (1849); hopes dashed, became manager of a glassworks in Sandö (1850–58), part owner of a sawmill (1853), and operator of a brick factory. He was shunned by the Swedish musical establishment (which he disdained); his extraordinary gifts as a composer went almost totally unrecognized in his lifetime; finally made a member of the Swedish Royal Academy of Music, Stockholm (1864); named to its composition chair, despite an attempt to unseat him (1867).

Berwald's masterpiece is his *Sinfonie singulière* (1845), a forward-looking work not performed until the 20th century; wrote 3 other fine syms., worthwhile chamber music, and at least 1 fine opera (*Estrella de Soria*); his output reveals the influence of the early German Romantic school in general, but with an unmistakably individual voice, notable for modulatory audacity.

beschwingt (Ger.). Winged. *Leicht beschwingt,* lightly and swiftly, volante.

Besetzung (Ger.). The scoring of a work, enumerating the voices and instruments employed.

Bethune "Blind Tom" (Thomas Greene), (born Wiggins), b. Columbus, Ga., May 25, 1849; d. Hoboken, N.J., June 13, 1908. Born blind and into slavery, he was purchased along with his parents by James N. Bethune (1850); taught by Bethune's daughter when he showed great aptitude and retentive ability; exploitation of his musical abilities began when Bethune "exhibited" him throughout Ga. (1857); "leased" him for 3 years to Perry Oliver, a Savannah planter, who arranged concert appearances for him throughout the southern states and Washington, D.C. With the outbreak of the Civil War, Bethune took full charge of Tom's career, touring the Confederacy to raise money for the rebel cause; obtained legal custody and a major part of Tom's earnings (1865). Tom Bethune spent the rest of his career playing in Europe and North America; was unable to escape the Bethune family; a court upheld their "guardianship" in 1887; by the end of his public performing days he was working the vaudeville circuit, improvising on themes suggested by the audience. Tom Bethune was an excellent pianist; programs included Bach, Beethoven, Liszt, Chopin, Thalberg, Gottschalk, and his own compositions, mostly improvised character pieces in salon manner, supplied with programmatic titles by his managers: *Rainstorm* (1865); *The Battle of Manassas* (1866); *Wellenlänge* (Wavelength, 1882); *Imitation of the Sewing Machine* (1889).

bestimmt (Ger.). Decisively , with energy.

betont (Ger.). Accented, marked. *Betonung, mit,* accented, with emphasis.

betrübt (Ger.). Grieved, afflicted.

bewegt (Ger.). Moved, agitated., animated. *Bewegter,* faster; *più mosso,* movement; *Bewegung,* agitation.

Beyer, Johanna Magdalena, b. Leipzig, July 11, 1888; d. N.Y., Jan. 9, 1944. After studies in Germany, she emigrated to the U.S. (1924); earned a teacher's certificate (1928); studied with Rudhyar, Crawford Seeger, and Cowell; wrote music and several plays for various N.Y. projects. During Cowell's term in San Quentin prison (1937–41), she acted as his secretary and cared for his scores. Her compositional style is dissonant counterpoint; composed much chamber music; among her works are 4 string quartets (1934, 1936, 1938, 1943), *Cyrnah* for Chamber Orch. (1937), *Reverence* for Wind Ensemble (1938), and *Music of the Spheres* for 3 Electrical Instruments or Strings (from the unfinished opera *Status Quo*, 1938).

bezifferter Bass (Ger., figured bass). Basso continuo.

B-flat major. If any key can claim to be the key of the universe, it is B-flat major. Most machines of modern industry—electric motors, fans, and washing machines—buzz, whir, and hum on the 60-cycle B-flat, corresponding to the lowest state of the bassoon; transposing instruments of the orch., e.g., trumpets and clarinets, are usually in B-flat, enabling them to play in B-flat major as easily as pianists play in C major. B-flat major is the key of fanfares and of festival and military marches, especially with natural trumpets in B-flat playing an overwhelming role; B-flat major is the key for the march of the soldiers in *Faust*, the return of Radames from the conquest of Ethiopia in *Aida*, the march of the children and the signal call summoning Don José back to the barracks in *Carmen*, and the dramatic trumpet call in *Fidelio* announcing the arrival of the governor. In the orch'l repertory, Schubert's romantic Sym. No. 5 is in B-flat major; in a more introspective mood, Bruckner's Sym. No 5; Beethoven chose this key for his unpretentious Sym. No. 4, but for Schumann the key must have signified the joy of life, as shown by his Sym. No. 1, called the *Spring*; Prokofiev described the blinding pagan sunrise at the end of his *Scythian Suite* in blazing B-flat major. The song *Over There*, imitating the bugle calls of the doughboys of World War I, is in B-flat major, as is the bugle call that announces the opening of horse races; and there is that gloriously uninhibited upward sweep of a B-flat clarinet that opens Gershwin's *Rhapsody in Blue*.

B-flat minor. The key of B-flat minor is pianistically desirable as the relative key of D-flat major; both have a full complement of black keys. Tchaikovsky's famous Piano Concerto No. 1, nominally in this key, quickly explodes into action with the famous optimistic D-flat major theme. Chopin favored B-flat minor, as he wrote a scherzo (op. 31) and a piano sonata (op. 35) in this key; the sonata's slow movement is the well-known *Marche funèbre*. Few symphonic works are unambiguously set in B-flat minor; an example is the *Alpine* Sym. by R. Strauss, in which the ascent and the descent to and from the summit are illustrated by corresponding up-and-down scales of B-flat minor. Miaskovsky assigned the key to his Sym. No. 11, but then he wrote syms. in virtually every key.

Biber, Heinrich (Ignaz Franz von), b. Wartenberg, Bohemia, Aug. 12, 1644; d. Salzburg, May 3, 1704. After employment in smaller cities, he became a member of the royal chapel at Salzburg (1670); appointed vice-Kapellmeister (1679) and Kapellmeister (1684); served the Emperor Leopold I, who ennobled him in 1690; Salzburg archbishops were his patrons. Biber was a founder of the German school of violin playing and among the 1st to employ scordatura, a system of artificial mistuning to facilitate performance; collections included the so-called Mystery Sonatas and Passacaglia for Violin (*c.* 1676) and trios publ. as *Harmonia artificiosa* (1712); composed 3 operas, only 1 of which survived; sacred music, including a Mass and a Requiem; chamber music.

bicinium (Lat., double song). 16th-century term for a composition for 2 voices or instruments, the 1st significant collection of which was *Bicinia Gallica, Latina, Germanica*, publ. by Rhau (1545). The popularity of bicinia was primarily a reaction to the polyphonic structures of the Flemish school; they also served as teaching devices; remained popular until the early Baroque; Lassus was its greatest practitioner. A revival took place in the early 20th century; Bartók and Hindemith composed such pieces, using dissonant harmony.

Biedermeier. Genre of domestic furniture standard in petit bourgeois German homes in the 1st half of the 19th century; subsequently expanded meaning to include sentimental literature, painting, and music; acquired derogatory implications. The name came from the fictional Gottlieb Biedermeier, pseudonym of the writer of ostensibly naive and implicitly satirical stories publ. in the German magazine *Fliegende Blätter*.

big band. Primary ensemble of the swing era of American jazz and popular music of the 1930s and 1940s. Big band music is scored for multiple trumpets, trombones, clarinets, and saxophones (melody group), while small groups (combos) usually employ at most 1 of each; in both big and small bands the rhythm section comprises piano and/or guitar, drum kit, and double bass; in arrangments, melody instruments are often reinforced in unison. Big band nomenclature includes *front line* (soloists), *sidemen* (hired musical hands), and the *signature tune* (musical motto of a particular band).

Bigard, "Barney" (Alban Leon), b. New Orleans, Mar. 3, 1906; d. Culver City, Calif., June 27, 1980. He played E-flat clarinet, then tenor saxophone in local New Orleans bands; went to Chicago; worked with King Oliver (1925–27); recorded with Armstrong, Morton, and Johnny Dodds; began playing clarinet again. In 1927 he joined Ellington's band, with which he played until 1942; collaborated on *Clarinet Lament, Mood Indigo, Ducky Wucky*, and *Saturday Night Function;* later formed small bands of his own, working mostly in Los Angeles and N.Y.; played intermittently with Armstrong's All Stars (1947–61); one of the best jazz clarinet players, known for warm tone and a capacity for smooth glissandos and chromatic runs.

Biggs, E(dward George) Power, b. Westcliff, Mar. 29, 1906; d. Boston, Mar. 10, 1977. After studies and performances in the U.K., he went to the U.S. (1930), becoming a naturalized citizen (1937); made his N.Y. debut at the Wanamaker Auditorium (1932). He was an organist in Newport, R.I. (1930–31); moved to Cambridge, Mass. and became organist at Christ Church; became music director of the Harvard Church, Brookline. He toured Europe; surveyed old European church organs to find the type of instrument that Bach and Handel played; played mostly the Baroque masters; commissioned works from Piston, Harris, Hanson, Porter, and Britten. Biggs became well known through weekly organ recitals broadcast over the CBS network (1942–58); concertized until arthritis forced him to reduce concert activities; continued recording; ed. organ works. He refused to perform on electronic instruments, which he felt vulgarized and distorted classical organ sound.

Billings, William, b. Boston, Oct. 7, 1746; d. there, Sept. 26, 1800. A tanner's apprentice, he learned musical rudiments from treatises by British psalmodists; compensated for lack of training by a wealth of original ideas and determination to put them into practice; his 1st collection of choral music, *The New England Psalm Singer* (Boston, 1770), contained what he later described as "fuging pieces . . . more than 20 times as powerful as the old slow tunes"; these freely canonic pieces have "each part striving for mastery and victory"; other publ. books were *The Singing Master's Assistant* (1778); *Music in Miniature* (1779); *The Psalm Singer's Amusement* (1781); *The Suffolk Harmony* (1786); and *The Continental Harmony* (1794). His sense of humor is evident in *Jargon*, harmonized entirely in dissonances and prefaced by a "manifesto" to the Goddess of Discord. Several religious works became popular, particularly *Chester* and *the Rose of Sharon*; the *Lamentation over Boston* was written in Watertown while the capital was occupied by the British. Despite his skill, he could not make a living in music; dependent on charity, he died in poverty. 2 centuries later, the fresh combination of reverence and solemnity with humor in his works inspired many American musicians; Cowell wrote a series of "fuging tunes"; Schuman's *New England Triptych* is based on 3 Billings hymns.

binary. Dual; 2-part; in music, twofold form or rhythm. *Binary form,* structure founded on 2 principal themes (see ⇒sonata form), or divided into 2 distinct or contrasted sections; binary forms are common in Baroque songs and dances that lack a contrasting middle section. The harmonic plan in binary composition is symmetrical: the 1st section proceeds from the tonic to the dominant, and the 2nd section begins on the dominant and ends on the tonic; the allemande is a typical binary form. Even in ternary forms, the nucleus is always binary, with the 3rd section being a literal or oblique repetition of the 1st. While always possible to convert a binary to a ternary form through repetition, it is difficult if not impossible to shorten a ternary to a binary form without performing major surgery. Stravinsky is quoted, perhaps apocryphally, as saying that Mozart's music would gain if the contrasting developmental (middle) sections were removed from all his works. *Binary measure,* common time, where the 1st of every 2 components takes the accent; regular and equal alternation between downbeat and upbeat. Binary rhythms may contain 2 subdivisions per beat; in medieval music, binary division in metrical time was called *tempus imperfectum,* "incomplete rhythm," the ternary division being *tempus perfectum,* "complete rhythm."

Binchois (Binch, Binche), Gilles (de), b. probably Mons, Hainaut, *c.* 1400; d. Soignies, near Mons, Sept. 20, 1460. After training as a chorister, he was an "honorably chivalrous soldier," probably in the service of the Earl of Suffolk, who was among the English occupying France (1424); joined the Burgundian court (by 1427); advanced from 5th chaplain (1436) to 2nd; retained the latter position until his death; also held several prebends and titles. He greatly distinguished himself as composer of both sacred and secular works, noted for organic melodic constructions, characteristic rhythms, and contrapuntal independence; style is considered traditional when compared to his acquaintance Dufay's.

Bing, Sir Rudolf (Franz Joseph), b. Vienna, Jan. 9, 1902. He studied at the Univ. of Vienna; took singing lessons; worked at opera houses in Darmstadt (1928–30) and Berlin (1930–33); went to England (1934); became general manager at Glyndebourne (1936–49); became British subject (1946); was active at the Edinburgh Festival; was its artistic director (1947–50). In 1950 he was appointed general manager of the Metropolitan Opera, N.Y., inaugurating one of the most eventful and at times turbulent periods in the history of the Metropolitan; his controversial dealings with prima donnas were legendary. In 1971 Queen Elizabeth II of England made him a Knight Commander of the Order of the British Empire; resigned from the Metropolitan in 1972.

Bingen, Hildegard von. See ⇒Hildegard von Bingen.

Binkley, Thomas (Eden), b. Cleveland, Dec. 26, 1931; d. Bloomington, Ind., Apr. 28, 1995. He studied at the Univ. of Ill. (B.M., 1956); attended the Univ. of Munich before returning to the U.S. From 1960 to 1980 he directed the Studio der frühen Musik, Munich; taught and performed in the medieval program at the Schola Cantorum Basiliensis, Basel (1973–77); in 1979 became prof. of music and director of the Early Music Inst. at the Indiana Univ. School of Music, Bloomington. The Studio der frühen Musik quartet included Andrea von Ramm (mezzo-soprano), Sterling Jones (bowed strings), and a succession of tenors (Nigel Rogers, Willard Cobb, Richard Levitt) along with Binkley (plucked strings); their performances and recordings redefined early music realization through an improvisatory and free approach, tinged with an Arab flavor, and an innovative approach to instrumentation. Many performers learned greatly from Binkley, notably Benjamin Bagby of Sequentia.

biomusic. Biological events are electrochemical in nature. Because energy in any form can be transmuted into sound waves, musically inclined biologists have experimented in converting the electrical energy in the brain, heart, lungs, eyeballs, and blood into signals perceivable by the auditory nerve; brain activity can already be electronically metamorphosed into sounds. The brain as composer fascinates musicians who want their art to be scientifically reducible without losing human quality. Biomusical experimentation can work in reverse, measuring the effect of sounds upon auditory organs and the electrical signals produced by the organs of the body, whether human or animal; the ultimate aim is to connect emotional states with the sound waves produced by electronic transformation of biological impulses. The acceleration of the pulse under the influence of powerful emotion has obvious counterparts as accelerando and crescendo, while reduction in pulse rate is analogous to ritenuto and diminuendo.

Birtwistle, (Sir) Harrison (Paul), b. Accrington, Lancashire, July 15, 1934. He studied clarinet; entered the Royal Manchester College of Music (1952); studied composition; formed the New Music Manchester Group with P. M. Davies, Goehr, and Ogdon; studied clarinet with R. Kell in London. He was visiting fellow at Princeton Univ. (1966) and visiting prof. at Swarthmore College (1973); became music director at the National Theatre, South Bank, London (1975); received the Grawemeyer Award (1987); knighted (1988).

In his compositions he departed completely from the folkloric trends once popular in British modern music; adopted an abstract, complex idiom, often with satirical overtones; compositions include stage works: *Punch and Judy* (1966–67), *Down by the Greenwood Side* (1968–69), *Yan Tan Tethera* (1983–84), *The Mask of Orpheus* (1973–84), *Gawain* (1990–91); orch'l works: *The Triumph of Time* (1971–72) and

Silbury Air (1977); chamber vocal works: *Ring a Dumb Carillon* (1964–65) and *Nenia: The Death of Orpheus* (1970); instrumental works: *Refrains and Choruses* (1957), *Verses for Ensembles* and *Tragoedia* (both 1965), and *Secret Theater* (1984).

bis (Lat., twice). 1. Accolade used by European audiences to request an encore. 2. In printed music, indication that a passage is to be repeated.

bitonality. The simultaneous presence of 2 different tonalities; a form of polytonality. Before the advent of 20th-century modern music, playing in 2 different keys simultaneously could only be regarded as a joke. Mozart wrote a piece entitled *Ein musikalischer Spass* (A Musical Joke, K. 522) with bitonal writing; the subtitle of the piece, *Dorfmusikanten* (Village Musicians), betrays his sly intent to ridicule the inability of rustic players (and perhaps kleinmeisters) to perform correctly.

Bitonality is no longer a joke but a well-established practice calculated to add spice and sparkle to singular tonality. The most effective bitonal device is combining 2 major triads whose tonics form a tritone; the complex of C major and F-sharp major triads forms the harmonic foundation of Stravinsky's *Petrouchka* as the "Petrouchka chord." Acoustically the most advantageous position of these 2 chords is the open spacing of 1 in root position in the low register, the other in close harmony in the 1st inversion of the triad, e.g., from the lowest note, C, G, E; A-sharp, C-sharp, F-sharp). Bitonality of minor triads is seldom encountered, due to poor acoustical balance.

In neoclassical music a modal type of bitonality has come into existence, exemplified by such complexes as: C major and D major falling within the Lydian mode; a combination of 2 major or minor triads with a common tone, e.g., C major combined with E major or E-flat major, favored by those exploring ethnic associations, including Vaughan Williams and Harris; a noneuphonious homonymous complex of major and minor triads in close harmony (e.g., C, E, G; C, E-flat, G), with a conflict between the major and the minor 3rd above the same tonic; cultivated assiduously by Stravinsky from his earliest period; in its linear devolution it offers a stimulating quasi-atonal melodic design. In his variations on *America,* reportedly written in 1891, Ives combines F major with A-flat major; to bring out the bitonal resonance, he marks one of the tonalities pianississimo and the other fortissimo.

biwa. Japanese plucked flat lute, derived from the Chinese pipa.

Bizet, Georges (Alexandre-Cesar-Leopold), b. Paris, Oct. 25, 1838; d. Bougival, June 3, 1875. His father was a singing teacher and composer; his mother, an excellent pianist. At age 9 he entered the Paris Cons., studying with Marmontel, Benoist, and Halévy, whose daughter, Geneviève, married Bizet in 1869; won the Grand Prix de Rome (1857); shared (with Lecocq) a prize offered by Offenbach for a 1-act opéra comique, Le Docteur Miracle (1857); while in Rome, composed a 2-act Italian opera buffa, Don Procopio (1858–59; post. premiere); another 1-act opera was composed there (La Guzla de l'Emir; withdrawn). Returning to Paris, Bizet produced a grand opera, Les Pêcheurs de perles (Théâtre-Lyrique, 1863), but, like La Jolie Fille de Perth (Théâtre-Lyrique, 1867), it failed to win popular approval; a 1-act opera, Djamileh (Opéra-Comique, 1872),

fared no better. His incidental music for Daudet's play L'Arlèsienne (1872) was ignored by audiences and critics; received more attention at its revival (1885), and an orch'l suite (1872) was acclaimed (a 2nd suite was made by Guiraud after Bizet's death).

Bizet's last major work was his masterpiece, *Carmen,* based on an 1845 novel by Mérimée and produced, after many difficulties with management and talent, at the Opéra-Comique (1875); reception by the public was not enthusiastic; critics attacked the opera for its lurid subject and supposed adoption of Wagner's methods. Although the attendance was not high, the opera was maintained in the repertoire, with 37 performances during the 1st season. Bizet was chagrined by the opera's controversial reception, but it is melodramatic fiction to claim, as some have, that *Carmen*'s alleged failure precipitated the composer's death (on the night of the 33rd perf., of a heart attack resulting from years of quinsy attacks). *Carmen* became a triumphant success throughout Europe; the Metropolitan Opera in N.Y.1st produced it in Italian (1884), then in French (1893). The famous act 1 habanera is not Bizet's own, but a melody by the Spanish composer Yradier; Bizet inserted it in *Carmen* (with alterations), mistaking it for a folk song. He wrote or planned other stage works, composed a few notable orch'l works (Sym. in C Major, *Roma, Patrie*), piano music (including *Jeux d'enfants* for piano duet), choral works (notably *Vasco da Gama,* an "odesym."), and songs.

Björling, Jussi (Johan Jonatan), b. Stora Tuna, Feb. 5, 1911; d. Siaro, near Stockholm, Sept. 9, 1960. He studied singing with his father; joined the vocal Björling Male Quartet (1916–21); toured the U.S.; studied in Stockholm (from 1928); made operatic debut at the Royal Swedish Opera as the Lamplighter in *Manon Lescaut* (1930); remained a company member until 1938; sang with the Vienna State Opera, Dresden State Opera, and Salzburg Festival. He made his professional U.S. debut in a concert broadcast from Carnegie Hall, N.Y. (1937); made his 1st appearance with the Metropolitan Opera as Rodolfo (1938); sang there until 1941; returned to Sweden. He returned to the Metropolitan Opera (1945–54, 1956–57, 1959); in early 1960, suffered a heart attack while preparing to sing Rodolfo at Covent Garden, London; in spite of great discomfort he went ahead with the performance; appeared for the last time in a Stockholm concert later that year. Björling was highly regarded for the purity of his fine vocal technique, consistency of register, and interpretative restraint and sense of style; excelled in Puccini, Verdi, Gounod, and Russian roles.

Blacher, Boris, b. Newchwang, China (of half-German, quarter-Russian, and quarter-Jewish ancestry), Jan. 19, 1903; d. Berlin, Jan. 30, 1975. His family moved to Irkutsk, Siberia (1914–20); in 1922 he went to Berlin; studied architecture and then composition; from 1948 until 1970 was prof. at the Hochschule für Musik, Berlin (director, 1953–70). An exceptionally prolific composer, he was equally adept in classical forms and in experimental procedures; initiated a system of "variable meters," with time signatures following the arithmetical progression, alternatively increasing and decreasing, with permutations contributing to metrical variety; developed a sui generis "abstract opera," incorporating an element of organized improvisation. In 1960 he was appointed director of the Seminar of Electronic Composition at the Technological Univ. in Berlin;

subsequently made ample use of electronic resources in his own music.

Blades, Rubén, b. Panama City, July 16, 1948. He was self-taught in music; despite receiving a law degree at the Univ. Nacional de Panama (1974), went to work for Fania Records in N.Y.; discovered by Ray Barretto, made his singing debut at Madison Square Garden; collaborated with Willie Colon; gained reputation as a fine performer and songwriter; his lyrics were highly charged with social and political significance and under-girded by salsa rhythms; organizing his own band, Seis del Solar; produced the successful album *Buscando America* (1984). He wrote the score for and starred in the film *Crossover Dreams* (1985), and acted in Spike Lee's *Mo' Better Blues* (1990) and Paul Simon's *The Capeman* (1997).

Blake, Eubie (James Herbert), b. Baltimore, Feb. 7, 1883; d. N.Y., Feb. 12, 1983. He grew up in an atmosphere of syncopated music and sentimental ballads played on music boxes; had piano lessons from a church organist; at age 15 got a regular job as a pianist in a "hookshop" (bordello), where he improvised rag music (his long fingers could stretch 12 keys); soon began to compose in earnest. In 1899 he wrote his 1st hit *Charleston Rag;* joined a singer named Noble Sissle (1915); appeared on the vaudeville circuit together, advertised as the Dixie Duo; broke the tradition of blackface comedians (white and black) by devising an all-black musical, *Shuffle Along* (N.Y., 1921), billed as "a musical melange"; the score included *I'm Just Wild About Harry,* a big hit used as a campaign song for Harry Truman (1948). Another hit, *Memories of You,* was written by Blake for the musical *Blackbirds of 1930.* He was moved by a purely scholarly interest in music; as late as 1949, took courses in the Schillinger system of composition at N.Y. Univ.; recorded the album *The 86 Years of Eubie Blake* (1969), reviving interest in his music and performing; in 1972 formed his own record company. As his centennial approached, a Broadway revue billed simply *Eubie!* was produced successfully; received the Medal of Freedom from President Reagan (1981); made last public appearance at age 99 at Lincoln Center in N.Y. (1982). He composed musicals, rags, études, boogies, novelties, waltzes, and a plethora of popular songs, including *Love Will Find a Way, That Charleston Dance, Memories of You, Roll Jordan, Harlem Moon,* and *Ain't We Got Love.*

Blake, Rockwell (Robert), b. Plattsburgh, N.Y., Jan. 10, 1951. He sang with various small opera companies, attracting notice when he appeared as Lindoro with the Washington (D.C.) Opera (1976); sang with the Hamburg State Opera (1977–79) and the Vienna State Opera (1978); made his N.Y. City Opera debut as Count Ory (1979) and Metropolitan Opera debut as Lindoro (1981). He sang at the Chicago Lyric Opera (1983), the Rossini Opera Festival, Pesaro (1983), San Francisco Opera (1984), Paris Opéra (1985) and Opéra-Comique (1987), Bavarian State Opera, Munich (1987), Montreal (1989), and the Salzburg Festival (1989). In 1990 he appeared in the leading tenor role in Pergolesi's *Annibal* in Turin; sang widely in concerts. Blessed with a remarkable coloratura, he won notable distinction as a true *tenore di grazia,* excelling in Mozart and Rossini.

Blakey, Art (called Abdullah Ibn Buhaina), b. Pittsburgh, Oct. 11, 1919; d. N.Y., Oct. 16, 1990. He 1st studied piano, then turned to drums; played with Mary Lou Williams (1942); joined Fletcher Henderson (1942–43), Billy Eckstine (1944–47), and Buddy de Franco's quartet (1952–53). In 1947 he formed a group, the Jazz Messengers, which had everchanging membership over the years. In the 1940s he worked with Davis, Gordon, Navarro, and Monk; in the early 1950s, Parker, C. Brown, and Horace Silver. Silver joined with Blakey in the Jazz Messengers of 1955; Silver left the following year, and Blakey took full control. Numerous important musicians have jumped from the Blakey springboard into the spotlight. He participated in the "Giants of Jazz" tour with Gillespie and Monk (1971–72), and a memorable drum battle with Roach, E. Jones, and B. Rich (Newport, 1974). In 1984 the Jazz Messengers won a Grammy Award for *New York Scene.* Blakey's driving, freewheeling style was quintessential hard bop.

Bläser (Ger.). Wind instruments; also *Blasinstrumente.*

Blasquartett (Ger.). Wind quartet. *Blasquintett,* wind quintet.

Blech (Ger.). Brass. *Blechinstrumente,* brass instruments; *Blechmusik,* brass music.

blindness. Musically gifted blind children develop more rapidly than normal children as performers on an instrument; blind organists in particular can achieve great distinction in their profession (e.g., Helmut Walcha). The pianist Alec Templeton made a lucrative career as an entertainer; jazz pianists Ray Charles and George Shearing are also blind. Frederick Delius lost his sight because of a syphilitic infection, but continued to compose by dictating music, note by note, to Eric Fenby. Joaquín Rodrigo became blind as a child but composed guitar works, as does José Feliciano. Rahsaan Roland Kirk extended bop saxophone playing by inventing instruments. Stevie Wonder has been a significant force in popular music for more than a quarter century. Blues musicians such as Blind Blake, Rev. Gary Davis, Willie McTell, and Jeff Healey overcame their sightlessness with aplomb. "Blind Tom" Bethune, a former slave with great pianistic talent, was exploited for most of his life by his former owner, who gained custody and toured him throughout the U.S. and Europe for half a century.

Bliss, (Sir) Arthur (Edward Drummond), b. London, Aug. 2, 1891; d. there, Mar. 27, 1975. He studied with Stanford, Vaughan Williams, and Holst; served in the British Army during World War I; wounded (1916) and gassed (1918); resumed his musical studies after the Armistice; 2 early works, *Madam Noy* for Soprano and 6 Instruments (1918) and *Rout* for Soprano and Orch. (setting nonsense syllables, 1922), were highly successful, establishing him as a leading modernist. He taught in California (1923–25); returned to London; scored the film *Things to Come,* after H. G. Wells (1935); a succession of important ballets followed: *Checkmate* (1937), *Miracle in the Gorbals* (1944), and *Adam Zero* (1946); his most ambitious work is the opera *The Olympians,* after J. B. Priestly (1949). During World War II he was BBC music director (1942–44); knighted (1950); named Master of the Queen's Musick, succeeding Arnold Bax (1953).

Blitzstein, Marc, b. Philadelphia, Mar. 2, 1905; d. Fort-de-France, Martinique, Jan. 22, 1964. He studied with R. Scalero,

Siloti, N. Boulanger, and Schoenberg; back in the U.S., devoted himself chiefly to the cultivation of stage works of "social consciousness," modeled after the type created by Brecht and Weill; accordingly wrote theater works for performance in cabaret-type theaters. *The Cradle Will Rock*, a 1-act opera of "social significance," became a succès du scandale when its sponsor, the Federal Theatre Project, withdrew because of its theme (steel-union organization); John Houseman and Orson Welles produced it under the auspices of the Mercury Theatre (N.Y., 1937, with the composer at the piano). In 1940 he received a Guggenheim fellowship; stationed with the U.S. Armed Forces in England; composed *The Airborne Sym.* for Narrator and Orch. (N.Y., 1946); in 1952, he had his biggest success—as translator of Brecht and Weill's *Der Dreigroschenoper* into *The Threepenny Opera*, featuring Lenya; most successful of his postwar works were the opera *Regina*, after Hellman's play *The Little Foxes* (1949), and 2 musicals: *Reuben Reuben* (1955) and *Juno*, after O'Casey's *Juno and the Paycock* (1959). An opera commissioned by the Ford Foundation on the subject of Sacco and Vanzetti was never finished.

Bloch, Ernest, b. Geneva, July 24, 1880; d. Portland, Oreg., July 15, 1959. He studied with Jaques-Dalcroze and L. Rey in Geneva (1894–97); then with Ysaÿe and Rasse in Brussels (1897–99); earliest works demonstrated a natural attraction to non-European cultures and coloristic melos; in 1900 went to Munich to study with Iwan Knorr and Ludwig Thuille; composed his 1st Sym. in C-sharp minor (1901–02); its 4 movements orig. bearing titles expressive of changing moods; spent a year in Paris; met Debussy; 1st publ. work, the song cycle *Historiettes au crépuscule* (1903), shows Debussy's influence. In 1904 Bloch returned to Geneva; began composing his only opera, *Macbeth*, after Shakespeare (1904–09); as a tribute to his homeland, continued writing the orch'l *Helvetia*, based on Swiss motifs, begun in 1900 but not completed until 1928; during the 1909–10 season, he conducted symphonic concerts in Lausanne and Neuchâtel; during World War I began to express his Jewish identity musically in works such as *3 Jewish Poems, Israel* for Soloists, Chorus, and Orch., and *Schelomo*, "Hebrew rhapsody" for Cello and Orch.; these works mark the height of Bloch as a Jewish composer; long after his death, *Schelomo* retains its popularity.

In 1916 Bloch toured the U.S. as conductor for dancer Maud Allan's troupe; it was unsuccessful; taught at the Mannes School of Music, N.Y. (1917–20); became an American citizen (1924). In America he found sincere admirers and greatly talented students, among them Sessions, Bacon, Antheil, Moore, B. Rogers, R. Thompson, Porter, Stevens, Elwell, I. Freed, F. Jacobi, and Kirchner; directed the Inst. of Music, Cleveland (1920–25) and the San Francisco Cons. (1925–30). In 1927 he won 1st prize in a *Musical America* competition for his epic rhapsody *America;* performed with great publicity in 5 cities; did not impress critics or audiences, and remains a mere by-product of his genius. He returned to his native country (1930), but with the advent of war resettled in the U.S.; taught at the Univ. of Calif., Berkeley (1940–52); finally retired to Agate Beach, Oreg.

In general, Bloch's aesthetic shifted from a somewhat expressionist quality to a neoclassical approach; favored sonorities formed by the bitonal relationship of 2 major triads with the tonics a tritone apart (the "Petrouchka" chord), but even his dissonances were euphonious; in his last chamber works, experimented for the 1st time with themes comprising 12 different notes; never adopted strict dodecaphonic technique. In his early Piano Quintet, Bloch made expressive use of quarter tones in the string parts; in his Jewish works, emphasized the interval of the augmented 2nd without literally imitating Hebrew chants.

block chords, block harmony. Modern type of harmony in which the component chords move in parallel formation, whether triads, 7th chords, 9th chords, or more dissonant combinations.

Blockflöte (Blochflöte; Ger.). 1. The recorder; an old kind of *flute à bec.* 2. An organ stop having pyramid-shaped flue pipes of 2', 4', 8', or 16' pitch, sometimes stopped.

Blomdahl, Karl-Birger, b. Växjö, Oct. 19, 1916; d. Kungsängen, near Stockholm, June 14, 1968. He studied with Rosenberg, Wöldike, and Tor Mann in Stockholm; traveled in France and Italy (1946); taught students, including Pettersson, Bucht, and Karkoff; attended Tanglewood seminar (1954–55). Returning to Stockholm, he taught at the Royal Academy of Music; taught Rabe and Mellnäs (1960–64); appointed music director at the Swedish Radio (1964).

In the 1940s Blomdahl was an organizer (with Bäck, Carlid, Johanson, and Lidholm) of the "Monday Group" in Stockholm, dedicated to propagating an objective and abstract idiom as distinct from the prevalent type of Scandinavian Romanticism. His early works are in a neoclassical idiom influenced by Hindemith; then turned to advanced techniques, including the application of electronic music. He composed several major orch'l works and ballets; his 3rd Sym., subtitled *Facetter* ("Facets"), utilizes dodecaphonic techniques. In 1959 his opera *Aniara* made him internationally famous; it imagines a pessimistic future in which post-apocalyptic survivors of Earth are forced to emigrate to saner worlds; the score employs electronic sounds; its thematic foundation is derived from a series of 12 different notes and 11 different intervals. At the time of his death he was working on an opera entitled *The Saga of the Great Computer*, incorporating electronics, concrete sounds, and synthetic speech.

Blow, John, b. Newark-on-Trent, Nottinghamshire (baptized), Feb. 23, 1649; d. Westminster (London), Oct. 1, 1708. In 1660–61 he was chorister at the Chapel Royal under H. Cooke; studied organ with Christopher Gibbons; appointed organist of Westminster Abbey (1668). In 1679 he left this post; Purcell, who had been Blow's student, succeeded him; after Purcell's untimely death, Blow was reappointed (1695) and remained until his death; buried in the north aisle. He married Elizabeth Braddock in 1674; she died in childbirth, leaving 5 children (1683). He held the rank of Gentleman of the Chapel Royal (from 1674); succeeded Humfrey as Master of the Children of the Chapel Royal (1674); Master of the Choristers at St. Paul's (1687–1703); Composer of the Chapel Royal (1699).

While still a Chapel Royal chorister, Blow began to compose church music, including Anglican services, secular part songs, catches, and organ and instrumental music; composed odes for many occasions, including New Year's Day, 1682, *Great Sir, the Joy of All Our Hearts*, and 5 odes for St. Cecilia; numerous anthems, including 2 for the coronation of James II; *Epicedium for Queen Mary* (1695); *Ode on the Death of Purcell* (1696). Blow's collection of 50 songs, *Amphion Anglicus*, was publ. in 1700; his best-known work is the masque *Venus and Adonis* (*c.* 1685), his only complete score for the stage; contributed separate songs for numerous dramatic plays. Purcell regarded Blow as "one of the greatest masters in the world."

blue note. Pitches approximating the lowered 3rd and 7th degrees in a major scale, as B flat and E flat in the C-major scale; the diminished fifth may also be included (G flat in C major); the blue note is characteristic of jazz and blues melodies. While fixed instruments must allow blue notes to fall "between the cracks," string and wind instruments (including the voice) can bend pitch and thus produce the highly emotive tonal effects associated with blue notes.

bluegrass. Country style pioneered by mandolinist Bill Monroe with his famous group the Blue Grass Boys (named for his home state of Ky.). Monroe's aggressive mandolin style, high vocal harmonies, and bluesy compositions all became standard ingredients for bluegrass. The instrumentation of his most successful band—guitar, mandolin, banjo, fiddle, and bass—became the model for the standard bluegrass lineup; 2 key musicians in Monroe's 1945–48 group, Lester Flatt and Earl Scruggs, separated from the master and formed their own successful band, providing the music for the 1967 film *Bonnie and Clyde,* which helped to popularize the style. More recent bluegrass (known as newgrass) exhibits harmonic, melodic, and formal experimentation as well as the influence of other styles, primarily jazz and progressive rock.

blues. Traditional African-American ballad style; it is in 4/4 time, is based on major tonality with melodies characterized by lowered 3rd and 7th ("blue") notes, and has developed a stereotyped, 12-measure harmonic pattern: I (x 4) – IV (x 2) – I (x 2) – V (x 1) – IV (x 1) – I (x 2). The colloquialism "blues" (sadness) dates back to at least the early 19th century, but the musical form evolved from Negro spirituals, work songs, field hollers, and ballads, both Anglo- and African-American. The country blues style seems to have existed by the 1890s, with a singer self-accompanied by a banjo, later a guitar; the genre was associated with the southern states, going as far west as Texas; the standard and relatively unusual strophe scheme was already in place: line A, repeat line A, then a rhyming line B (like the medieval German Barform); country blues was popularized 1st by songsters, itinerant performers on the medicine-show circuit; by the 1920s the pure blues performer was replacing the songster.

The black composer and trumpet player W. C. Handy claimed to have "discovered" the blues; he publ. *Memphis Blues* (1911) and *St. Louis Blues* (1914), aimed at an urban clientele. The marketing approach worked, and Handy became a wealthy man. In the 1920s the urban or city blues style emerged: the 12-measure and the 16- or 32-measure (A–A–B–A, 4 x 4 or 4 x 8 measures long) strophic-harmonic patterns became standard; supporting instrumentation drew from the piano, trombone, cornet, saxophone, and drum kit, i.e., a jazz combo; the harmonica became significant in the 1930s. Urban blues reached its 1st height in N.Y. and other northern cities, growing out of the "chitlin circuit" tours in the South; many female urban blues singers became stars: Ma Rainey, Mamie Smith, Alberta Hunter, Ida Cox, and the great Bessie Smith; at the same time, rural performers continued and expanded the traditional blues genre: Charley Patton, Blind Lemon Jefferson, Son House, Blind Boy Fuller, Bukka White, Texas Alexander, Bo Carter, Blind Willie

McTell, Memphis Minnie, and the last great traditional blues musician, Robert Johnson. After the 2nd World War John Lee Hooker, Lightnin' Hopkins, Fred McDowell, Sonny Terry and Brownie McGhee, and Mance Lipscomb contributed to the style; a blues revival in the 1960s (paralleling the folk revival) led to the rediscovery of long-silent musicians: House, White, Sleepy John Estes, and Mississippi John Hurt.

Urban blues became predominant, and the scene shifted to Chicago after a period of important barrelhouse and boogie-woogie piano playing throughout the country; blues bands began to produce important music (Tampa Red, Big Bill Broonzy, Washboard Sam, the 1st Sonny Boy Williamson). After World War II the electrification of the guitar led to the development of rhythm and blues, combining elements of blues, swing, and boogie-woogie; but the urban blues developed into the electric blues known as Chicago style in the hands of Muddy Waters, Howlin' Wolf, James Cotton, Otis Spann, Little Walter, and the 2nd Sonny Boy Williamson; with its strong emphasis on improvisation, this style offered white musicians an opportunity to explore the blues: Paul Butterfield, Mike Bloomfield, Eric Clapton, the Yardbirds, and Canned Heat.

BMI (Broadcast Music Incorporated). Music licensing organization founded in N.Y. in 1940 as an alternative to ASCAP; it grants licenses to entertainment businesses, including radio and television stations, hotels, restaurants, ballrooms, airlines, even circuses, i.e., wherever music is performed. BMI purchases the rights from publishers, who in turn pay royalties to composers and lyricists; in other words, it serves as intermediary between the composer and/or lyricist and the public users of such productions.

Since BMI started out as a rival organization to ASCAP, it naturally tried to attract composers with prestigious names but who did not command a decent royalty income for performances; in its early years it offered large sums of money to such composers—up to $10,000 a year; more adventurous than its rival in attracting rock and other postwar popular music composers; the 2 organizations have reached a professional truce.

boat song. Barcarolle.

bocca (It.). Mouth. *Bocca chiusa, con,* with closed mouth.

Boccherini, (Ridolfo) Luigi, b. Lucca, Feb. 19, 1743; d. Madrid, May 28, 1805. In 1757 he was engaged as a cellist in the orch. of the Court Theater, Vienna; returned to Lucca (1761–66); undertook a concert tour with the violinist Filippo Manfredi; arriving in Paris, he appeared at the Concert Spirituel (1768); exceedingly popular as a performer; 1st publications were 6 string quartets and 2 books of string trios (Paris, 1767). In 1769 he became chamber composer to the Infante Luis at Madrid; after the latter's death (1785), remained in Spain and received a pension; appointed court composer *in absentia* to Friedrich Wilhelm II of Prussia (1786); after the King's death (1797), concentrated fully on his Spanish opportunities. In 1800 he enjoyed the patronage of Napoleon's brother, Lucien Bonaparte, French ambassador to Madrid (1800–1801). Despite successes at European courts, he lost his appeal to his patrons and public. He supposedly died in poverty; in a belated tribute to a native son, Lucca authorities had his remains transferred and reinterred with great solemnity in 1927.

Boccherini had profound admiration for Haydn; indeed, so close was Boccherini's style to Haydn's that he was known as "the wife of Haydn." An exceptionally fecund composer, he specialized almost exclusively in chamber music, including 26 chamber syms., 2 octets, 16 sextets, 125 string quintets, 12 piano quintets, 24 quintets for strings and flute (or oboe), 91 string quartets, 48 string trios, 21 violin sonatas, 6 cello sonatas, and 11 cello concertos; wrote secular and sacred vocal music, including a Christmas cantata.

Bock, Jerry (Jerrold Lewis), b. New Haven, Conn., Nov. 23, 1928. He studied at the Univ. of Wis.; settled in N.Y.; composed for revues (*Catch a Star!*, 1955) and television (*Your Show of Shows*); gained wide recognition with his musicals *Mr. Wonderful* (1956), *The Body Beautiful* (1958), *Fiorello!* (based on the life of N.Y. mayor LaGuardia, 1959), and *She Loves Me* (1963). His greatest success was *Fiddler on the Roof* (1964), also made into a movie.

Bockstriller (Ger.). Goat trill.

bodhran (Gael.). Traditional Irish drum with a goat hide stretched over a circular shallow frame, played with a 2-headed beater; used in uptempo dance pieces, it sets a steady fast beat, with accents and timbral changes interwoven.

Boehm system. System of playing the flute with keys replacing the holes in the old instruments; named after the 19th-century German inventor Theobald Boehm (1794–1881), one of the greatest flute players of his time; sought to produce a more acoustically correct instrument; fixed the position and size of the holes so as to obtain purity and fullness of tone; the keys assured prompt and accurate "speaking"; the bore was modified, rendering the tone much fuller and mellower.

Boethius (Anicius Manlius Torquatus Severinus Boetius), b. Rome, A.D. *c.* 480; d. 524, executed on suspicion of treason by Emperor Theodoric, to whom he was counselor for many years. He wrote a treatise in 5 books, *De Institutione Musica,* the chief sourcebook for the theorizing monks of the Middle Ages; 1st publ. in Venice (1491). Whether the notation commonly called "Boethian" (using Latin indices to denote traditional Greek notation) is properly attributable to him has been questioned for about 3 centuries.

Bogen (Ger.). 1. A bow. 2. Slur or tie.

Böhm, Karl, b. Graz, Aug. 28, 1894; d. Salzburg, Aug. 14, 1981. He studied law (Dr. Jur., 1919), then music with Mandyczewski and G. Adler at the Vienna Cons.; appointed conductor at the Municipal Theater, Graz (1917–21); conducted at the Bavarian State Opera, Munich (1921–27); appointed Generalmusikdirektor in Darmstadt (1927–31); having already mastered a number of works by Mozart, Wagner, and R. Strauss, added operas by Krenek and Hindemith to his repertoire; conducted Berg's *Wozzeck* and was praised by the composer (1931).

From 1931 to 1933 Böhm served as General Musikdirektor of the Hamburg Opera (1931–33); from 1934 to 1943 was music director of the Dresden State Opera; gave the 1st performances of 2 R. Strauss operas: *Die Schweigsame Frau* (1935) and

Daphne (1938; dedicated to Böhm); during the last 2 years of the raging war, conducted at the Vienna State Opera (1943–45); after the war he was not allowed by the Allied authorities to perform pending an investigation of his political past; was cleared and resumed his career (1947). He went to Buenos Aires; organized and conducted German opera seasons at the Teatro Colón (1950–53); returned to the Vienna State Opera (1954–56); conducted *Fidelio* at the opening of the reconstructed Vienna State Opera House (1955). He made his 1st U.S. appearance with the Chicago Sym. Orch. (1956); made his debut at the Metropolitan Opera, N.Y., with *Don Giovanni* (1957); conducted occasional performances there until 1974. In 1961 he took the Berlin Phil. to the U.S.; toured Japan with it (1963–64); led a U.S. tour with the Deutsche Oper, Berlin; took the Vienna State Opera for its 1st U.S. tour (1979). He also conducted radio and television performances.

In the annals of conducting, Böhm may be regarded as a worthy successor of the glorious pantheon of Austro-German conductors such as Muck, Walter, and Furtwängler; admired for impeccable rendition of Classic opera scores, particularly those of Mozart, in which he scrupulously avoided any suggestion of improper romanticization; equally extolled for productions of Wagner and Strauss; earned additional respect for his audacious espousal of modern music.

Boieldieu, François-Adrien, b. Rouen, Dec. 16, 1775; d. Jarcy, near Grosbois, Oct. 8, 1834. Boieldieu received his musical instruction from Charles Broche; appointed assistant organist at St. André, Rouen; his 1st opéra-comique, *La Fille coupable,* was produced in Rouen (1793) as was *Rosalie et Myrza* (1795); befriended by Cherubini, Méhul, L. E. Jadin, and Erard; his romances (popular songs) were printed in Paris (16 vols., 1794–1811), as were 9 piano sonatas (1795–1800); a facile composer, produced one opera after another; had no difficulties getting them Parisian performances; most successful was the opéra-comique *Le Calife de Bagdad* (1800), with its appealing orientalisms.

After a one-year marriage with the dancer Clotilde Mafleurai fell apart (1803), Boieldieu was invited to write for the Imperial theaters in St. Petersburg for a handsome salary; attended to his duties conscientiously, producing at least 1 opera annually; admired by Czar Alexander I; despite a salary increase and a comfortable life, decided to leave Russia and return to Paris (1811); resumed composing operas; appointed prof. of composition at the Paris Cons. (1817–26); named a Chevalier of the Legion of Honor (1821). His greatest success was the opéra-comique *La Dame blanche,* to a Scribe libretto after Walter Scott; the suspenseful story and effective and atmospheric music corresponded precisely to public taste of the time; premiered at the Opéra-Comique, Paris (1825). His estranged wife died in 1826, so he married the singer Jenny Phillis-Bertin the following year; in 1833 received a grant of 6,000 francs from the French government; retired to his country house at Jarcy; during the last years of his life, became interested in painting; also successful as a teacher; among his pupils were Fétis, Adam, and P. J. G. Zimmerman.

Boieldieu wrote about 40 operas; several were composed in collaboration with Méhul, Berton, Hérold, Cherubini, Catel, Paer, Isouard, Kreutzer, and Auber; 9 works are lost. His significance in the history of French opera is great, although the nationalistic hopes of French critics that he would rival Rossini (whom he admired) did not materialize; lacked the necessary power of invention, both in dramatic and comic aspects, that made Rossini a magician of 19th-century opera. Boieldieu's natural son, Adrien-Louis-Victor Boieldieu (1815–83), was also a composer; his mother was Thérèse Louise Antoinette Regnault, an Opéra-Comique singer.

bois (Fr., wood). Woodwind.

Boismortier, Joseph Bodin de, b. Thionville, Moselle, Dec. 23, 1689; d. Roissy-en-Brie, Oct. 28, 1755. After living in Metz and Perpignan he settled in Paris (1724); very little is known about his career; publ. 102 works between 1724 and 1747. A prolific composer of instrumental music, he wrote works for recorders and transverse flutes; 2 clavecin suites; trio sonatas, including 1 set using the viola da gamba (1732); pieces designed for amateurs (in the positive sense) scored with a drone instrument, either a musette or a vielle, and publ. pieces such as *Gentillesses* (1731) or *Divertissemens de campagne* (1734); also wrote 3 ballet-operas and a number of cantatas.

boîte à musique (Fr.). Music box.

Boito, Arrigo (birth name, Enrico), b. Padua, Feb. 24, 1842; d. Milan, June 10, 1918. He studied with Alberto Mazzucato and Ronchetti-Monteviti; 2 cantatas, written with Franco Faccio, attracted favorable attention; the Italian government granted them a gold medal and a 2-year foreign travel stipend; Boito visited Paris, Poland, Germany, Belgium, and England. He was strongly influenced by new French and German music; upon his return to Milan, began composition of his 1st opera and most significant work, *Mefistofele,* a mixture of conventional Italian opera and dramatic ideas stemming from Beethoven and Wagner; premiered at La Scala (1868), it was a disaster, with factions—for and against the unusual treatment of the subject—interrupting an already-long work (prologue and 5 acts) and Boito's inept conducting. The opera was then withdrawn; he undertook a revision with only 4 acts; successfully premiered in Bologna (1875); appears in the repertory of leading opera houses, but—although truer to Goethe—its success has never matched that of Gounod's *Faust.* Boito never completed his 2nd opera, *Nerone,* on which he worked for more than half a century (1862–1916). The score was heavily revised by Tommasini and Toscanini (including elimination of the 5th act) and premiered by the latter at La Scala (1924).

Boito's gift as a lyric poet is equal to his as a composer. He publ. a book of verses under the anagrammatic pen name of Tobia Gorrio (Turin, 1877); wrote his own operas' librettos; made admirable trans. of foreign works (*Armide, Der Freischütz, Rienzi, Russlan and Ludmilla,* the Wesendonk Lieder); wrote the librettos of *Otello* and *Falstaff* and revised *Simon Boccanegra* for Verdi; also wrote *La Gioconda* for Ponchielli, *Amleto* for Faccio, etc.; also publ. novels. He held many honorary titles from the King of Italy; in 1912, followed in Verdi's footsteps and became a senator.

Bolcom, William (Elden), b. Seattle, May 26, 1938. He studied with John Verrall, Milhaud, and Leland Smith; taught at the Univ. of Washington, Seattle (1965–66), Queens College, CUNY (1966–68), and the N.Y. Univ. School of the Arts (1969–70); joined the faculty of the Univ. of Mich.'s school of music (1973); made a full prof. (1983). He was composer-in-residence of the Detroit Sym. Orch. (from 1987); won the Pulitzer Prize for his *12 New Études* for Piano (1988); after absorbing a variety of techniques, experimented widely and wildly in serial thematics, musical collage, sophisticated intentional plagiarism, and microtonal electronics; also active as a pianist, recording and giving recitals of ragtime piano; with his wife, the singer Joan Morris, gave concerts of popular American songs from olden times. Bolcom's compositions include 5 syms., actors' opera *Dynamite Tonight* (1963), *Commedia* for Chamber Orch. (1971), secular oratorio *Songs of Innocence and of Experience* (1981), theater piece *Casino Paradise* (1990), and opera *McTeague* (1992); publ., with Robert Kimbass, *Reminiscing with Sissle and Blake* (N.Y., 1973); ed. Rochberg's collected essays as *The Aesthetics of Survival: A Composer's View of 20th Century Music* (Ann Arbor, Mich., 1984).

Bolden, "Buddy" (Charles Joseph), b. New Orleans, Sept. 6, 1877; d. Jackson, La., Nov. 4, 1931. He was a pioneering figure in early jazz, active in New Orleans; by 1901 had a 6-piece unit and was playing in the honky-tonks and dives of Storyville; career was destroyed by a cerebral dysfunction and alcoholism; confined to a state hospital in Jackson in 1906, remaining there until his death. While Bolden's life and contributions are clouded in legend and spurious anecdote, his tone, rhythmic power, and emotional slow-blues playing separated him from more mellow early jazz bands; his playing was more ornamented than improvisatory; influenced the next generation of New Orleans cornetists (Keppard, Bunk Johnson); helped standardize the ensemble and repertory of early jazz.

bolero (Sp.). 1. Spanish national dance in syncopated 3/4 time and lively tempo (allegretto), the dancers accompanying their steps with castanets; evolved from either the fandango or seguidilla; resembles the Andalusian cachucha. 2. Cuban dance in 2/4 time, close to the habanera. 3. Composition in bolero style, such as Chopin's piano piece (op. 19) and Ravel's orch'l work; boleros or bolero rhythms in classical music are also found in Beethoven, Weber, Méhul, Auber, Berlioz, and Moszkowski.

Bolling, Claude, b. Cannes, Apr. 10, 1930. He received grounding in piano, classical repertoire, and the jazz idiom; studied with Duruflé in Paris; immersed himself in the jazz scene. He became a prominent crossover figure for the *Sonata for 2 Pianists* (1970) for Jean-Bernard Pommier; *Suite for Flute and Jazz Piano Trio,* written for Rampal (1975), became an internationally successful recording (1981); also wrote *California Suite* (film score, 1976), *Suite for Violin and Jazz Piano Trio* (for P. Zukerman; 1978), *Suite for Chamber Orch. and Jazz Piano Trio* (1983), and *Suite for Cello and Jazz Piano Trio* (for Yo-Yo Ma; 1984).

bombard (Eng., Ger.; It. *bombardo;* Fr. *bombarde*). 1. Low-pitched member of the shawm family, common during the 14th to 16th centuries, now obsolete. See also ⇒posaune. 2. 32', 16', or 8' organ reed stop, popular in France.

bombardon (Eng., Ger., Fr.; It. *bombardone*). 1. Bass bombard. 2. 3- or 4-valve bass tuba, invented in the 1840s. 3. 32' or 16' organ reed stop, popular in France.

bomba. Traditional dance of Puerto Rico; also its music, a significant predecessor of salsa.

bones. Primitive rhythm instrument of 2 bones or pieces of wood clicked together by the fingers of 1 hand; used in Irish traditional music, American blackface minstrelsy, and old-time Appalachian music.

bongos. Paired, knee-held Cuban drums, struck by the fingertips; despite weak sonority, they furnish a distinct sound that stands out in percussive ensembles; have also been adopted by many symphonic composers.

Bonynge, Richard (Alan), b. Sydney, Sept. 29, 1930. He began his career as a pianist; after marrying soprano Joan Sutherland (1954), devoted himself to helping her master the bel canto operatic repertoire; made his conducting debut in concert with her in Rome (1962); 1st conducted opera in Vancouver (*Faust*, 1963); led *I Puritani* at Covent Garden, London (1964); made his Metropolitan Opera, N.Y., debut conducting *Lucia di Lammermoor* with his wife in the title role (1966). In subsequent years he conducted concerts and operas throughout the world; was music director of the Australian Opera, Sydney (1976–86); made a Commander of the Order of the British Empire (1977).

boogie-woogie. Piano-based jazz style developed in the late 1920s, beginning in Chicago and quickly spreading to N.Y. and elsewhere. Like many jazz terms, *boogie-woogie* is an onomatopoeic alliterative word suggesting a certain type of rhythmic beat; characteristic features are concentrated in the ostinato accompaniment: rapid 8th notes in broken octaves, following a walking bass pattern, and the so-called doubled blues bass, following the standard harmonic pattern (see ⇒blues). In the late 1930s a boogie-woogie craze swept the U.S.; many important pianists received due attention: Albert Ammons, Meade "Lux" Pete Johnson, Jimmy Yancey, and "Cripple" Clarence Lofton. The style was adopted or transmogrified by swing bands and songs, most notably *Boogie Woogie Bugle Boy* by the Andrews Sisters (1941); after World War II, boogie-woogie was incorporated into the blues, particularly as practiced by Chicago pianists; even Piet Mondrian, living in N.Y., painted a colorful grid-based abstract with broken straight lines crossing other broken straight lines; he called it *Broadway Boogie-Woogie*.

bop. Bebop.

bore. Shape of the body of woodwind and brass instruments, beginning with the diameter of the cylinder.

Borge, Victor (born Borge Rosenbaum), b. Copenhagen, Jan. 3, 1909, of Russian Jewish extraction. He developed a remarkable facility and prestidigital velocity on the piano keys; studied theory at the Copenhagen Cons.; went to Berlin; became a pupil of a pupil of Liszt, then a pupil of a pupil of Busoni; plans for a Swedish tour were prevented by the Nazi invasion of Denmark; emigrated (1940); became a U.S. citizen (1948). In America he changed his name and inaugurated a show under the rubric *Comedy in Music* (1953), giving a total of 849 performances—then unprecedented for a Broadway 1-man show; mastered idiomatic English to such an extent that he could improvise jokes that invariably elicited chuckles; developed a sepulchral voice imitating bass singers and an ornithological

coloratura à la Jenny Lind; thus equipped, made a television career; continued solo appearances well into his 80s.

Borodin, Alexander (Porfirievich), b. St. Petersburg, Nov. 12, 1833; d. there, Feb. 27, 1887. The illegitimate son of a Georgian prince, he received an excellent education; learned several foreign languages and to play the flute; played 4-hand arrangements of Haydn and Beethoven syms. with a friend; at age 14 wrote a piece for flute and piano and a String Trio on themes from *Robert le Diable*. He became a student of the Academy of Medicine, St. Petersburg (1850); later joined its staff and publ. important papers. Although mainly preoccupied with scientific pursuits, he continued to compose; he married Ekterina Protopopova (1863), an accomplished pianist who shared her appreciation of Chopin, Liszt, and Schumann with him.

A decisive influence on his compositional progress was a meeting with Balakirev in 1862; later formed friendships with the critic Stasov (who included him in the "Mighty 5"), Mussorgsky, and other musicians of the Russian national school. He adopted a style conforming with their new ideas; excelled in a type of Russian orientalism which greatly attracted Russian musicians at the time; never became a consummate craftsman, like Rimsky-Korsakov; although quite proficient in counterpoint, avoided purely contrapuntal writing. His feeling for rhythm and orch'l color was extraordinary; evocation of exotic scenes in his orch'l works and his masterpiece, the opera *Prince Igor* (1869–87; premiered 1890), was superb. Composition was a very slow process for Borodin; several of his works (e.g., *Prince Igor*) remained incomplete and were ed. after his death by Rimsky-Korsakov and Glazunov; other major works include 2 syms.; *In Central Asia*, a symphonic poem; 2 string quartets; piano quintet; *Petite Suite* for Piano; songs.

bossa nova (Port., new beat). Popular Brazilian song and dance music in diversely syncopated 2/4 time, derived from samba and influenced by jazz; in its purest form the vocal part is mostly improvised to rhythmic accompaniment, including a musical bow called the *marimban*. Bossa nova became internationally popular in the late 1950s and 1960s, thanks largely to Antonio Carlos Jobim (*Desafinado*, 1959), Stan Getz, Baden Powell, Astrud Gilberto, and others; it gradually became submerged in other popular styles.

Boston (Valse Boston). Hesitation waltz.

Bottesini, Giovanni, b. Crema, Dec. 22, 1821; d. Parma, July 7, 1889. He studied double bass with Rossi at the Milan Cons. (1835–39); played in various orchs.; visited the U.S. (1847); went to England (1848); appeared as a cello soloist; made his independent concert debut in London (1849). In 1853 he was once more in America; active as a conductor in Paris, Russia, and the Scandinavian countries; invited by Verdi to conduct the world premiere of *Aida* in Cairo (1871); eventually retired to Parma as cons. director.

Bottesini was the 1st great virtuoso on the double bass (3-stringed), usually regarded as unwieldy, and thus he became a paragon for the relatively few artists who have essayed that instrument after him; thus Koussevitzky was often described as the "Russian Bottesini" during his early career as a double-bass player. Bottesini also composed a number of passable operas with several performances in his lifetime.

bouche (Fr.). Mouth. *Bouche fermée* (with mouth closed; It. *bocca chiusa*), humming; effective device used in choral singing and especially opera, e.g.; act 4 of Verdi's *Rigoletto,* where it is used with great dramatic effect; other examples include Puccini's *Madama Butterfly,* Debussy's *Sirènes* (*Nocturnes*), and Berg's *Wozzeck;* distinct from vocalise, also sung without words but with mouth open.

bouffe (Fr.). Comic, burlesque. *Opéra bouffe,* comic opera.

bouffon (Fr., jester, comedian). Mime-dancers who performed exotic dances at French courts in the 16th century. The famous polemical exchange between adherents of Italian and French opera in mid-18th-century Paris became known as the guerre des bouffons.

Boulanger, Lili (Juliette Marie Olga), b. Paris, Aug. 21, 1893; d. Mezy, Seine-et-Oise, Mar. 15, 1918. She was the sister of Nadia (Juliette) Boulanger; studied composition with Vidal at the Paris Cons. (1909–13); attracted considerable attention by winning the Grand Prix de Rome with her cantata *Faust et Hélène,* the 1st woman to receive this distinction; her death less than 5 years later was justifiably lamented by French musicians as a great loss. Her talent, delicate and poetic, continued the tradition of French Romanticism on the borderline of Impressionism. Besides her prizewinning cantata she wrote 2 symphonic poems; choral music; *Clairières dans le ciel,* a beautiful cycle of 13 songs; individual songs; piano pieces; violin pieces; her opera to Maeterlinck's *La Princesse Maleine* remained incomplete.

Boulanger, Nadia (Juliette), b. Paris, Sept. 16, 1887; d. there, Oct. 22, 1979. She was the sister of Lili (Juliette Marie Olga) Boulanger. Her grandmother, father, and mother were professional musicians; her mother was her 1st teacher. At the Paris Cons., studied with Guilmant, Vierne, Vidal, Widor, and Fauré; received the 2nd Prix de Rome for her cantata *La Sirène* (1908); collaborated with Raoul Pugno on compositions, completing his opera *La Ville Morte* after his death; composed other works but, realizing that she could not compare with her sister Lili's compositional talent, devoted herself to teaching, a profession in which she found both her vocation and greatest fame. She assisted in a harmony class at the Paris Cons. (1909–24); engaged as a teacher at the École Normale de Musique (1920–39); when the American Cons. was founded at Fontainebleau (1921), joined its faculty as a teacher of composition and orchestration; became its director in 1950. She also had a large class of private pupils from all parts of the world, among them Copland, Harris, Piston, Thomson, Carter, Diamond, Siegmeister, I. Fine, Blackwood, Berger, J. Vincent, Shapero, Glass, Markevitch, Françaix, L. Berkeley, and Lipatti; whatever their feelings about her methods, all admired her insistence on formal and technical perfection.

Boulanger's tastes were far from catholic; a great admirer of Stravinsky, Debussy, and Ravel, she had little appreciation of Schoenberg and the 2nd Viennese school; visited the U.S. several times; played the organ part in Copland's Organ Sym. (which she advised him to compose) with the N.Y. Sym. Orch., under W. Damrosch's direction (1925); was also a fine conductor; led the premiere of Stravinsky's *Dumbarton Oaks Concerto;* 1st woman to conduct subscription concerts of the Boston Sym. Orch. (1938) and any N.Y. Phil. concert (1939) or any London orch. (Royal Phil. Soc., 1937). During World War II she stayed in America; taught classes at Radcliffe College, Wellesley College, and the Juilliard School of Music, N.Y.; returned to Paris (1946); took over a piano accompaniment class at the Paris Cons.; continued private teaching as long as her frail health permitted.

Boulez, Pierre, b. Montbrison, Mar. 26, 1925. He studied composition with Messiaen and R. Leibowitz, who initiated him into the procedures of serial music; became a theater conductor in Paris (1948); toured the U.S. with a French ballet troupe (1952); in 1954 organized in Paris a series of concerts, called "Domaine Musical," devoted mainly to avant-garde music; gave courses at the International Festivals for New Music in Darmstadt (1958). He delivered a course of lectures on music at Harvard Univ. (1963); made his American conducting debut in N.Y. (1964); engaged as guest conductor with the Cleveland Orch.

In 1971 Boulez was appointed music director of the N.Y. Phil., a choice that surprised many. From the outset, he asserted complete independence from public and managerial tastes, featuring works by Schoenberg, Berg, Webern, Varèse, and other modernists while giving a relatively small place to Romantic composers. This policy provoked the expected opposition on the part of many subscribers; the musicians themselves voiced their appreciation of his remarkable qualities as a professional of high caliber; they described him as a "French correction," with reference to his extraordinary sense of rhythm, perfect pitch, and memory but also a signal lack of emotional participation in the music. In America he showed little interest in social amenities and made no effort to ingratiate himself with men and women of power; his departure in 1977 and the accession of the worldly Zubin Mehta as successor were greeted with a sigh of relief, an antidote to Boulez's stern regimen. Boulez accepted outside obligations; served as chief conductor of the BBC Sym. Orch., London (1971); as a perfect Wagnerite, gave exemplary performances of the operas in Germany and elsewhere; was one of the few Frenchmen to conduct *Parsifal* in Germany; led the Ring cycle in Bayreuth (1976). The precision of his leadership and his knowledge of the score produced a profound impression on both the audience and the critics.

He founded the Inst. de Recherche et Coordination Acoustique/Musique (IRCAM) in Paris, a futuristic establishment generously subsidized by the French government (1974); in this post he and others could freely carry out experiments with electronic compositional techniques aided by digital synthesizers and a complex set of computers capable of acoustical feedback. His music is an embodiment of such avant-garde techniques; it is fiendishly difficult to perform and even more difficult to describe in terms of dissonant counterpoint, free serialism, or indeterminism; he was one of the 1st composers to pursue total serialism and electroacoustic technology, but disassociated himself from any particular modern school of music; even publ. a pamphlet with the shocking title *Schoenberg est mort,* shortly after Schoenberg's actual death.

Boult, (Sir) Adrian (Cedric), b. Chester, Apr. 8, 1889; d. London, Feb. 22, 1983. His mother and a science teacher gave him his 1st music instruction; sang in the Oxford Bach Choir; studied with Hans Sitt at the Leipzig Cons. (1912–13); attended rehearsals and concerts of the Gewandhaus Orch. under Nikisch; sang in its choir. He joined the staff of Covent Garden, London (1914); guest conducted the Liverpool Phil. (1916) and London Sym. Orch. (1918); principal conductor of Ballets Russes's 1919 London season; conducted the British Sym. Orch., made up of former British army soldiers (1919–24); taught conducting at the Royal College of Music, London (1919–30); music director of the City of Birmingham Orch. (1924–30); music director of the Bach Choir (1928–31).

Boult served as director of music for the BBC, London (1930–42); organized the BBC Sym. Orch. and led its 1st concert (1930); served as its chief conductor until 1950: led it on several tours abroad, including a notably successful one to Paris, Vienna, Zurich, and Budapest (1936); guest conducted the Vienna Phil. (1933), Boston Sym. Orch. (1935), NBC Sym. Orch., N.Y. (1938), N.Y. Phil. (1939), Chicago Sym. Orch. (1939), and Concertgebouw Orch., Amsterdam (1945). He was associate conductor of the Henry Wood Promenade Concerts in London (1942–50); music director of the London Phil. (1950–57), which he brought to the Soviet Union (1956); was again music director of the City of Birmingham Sym. Orch. (1959–60); taught again at the Royal College (1962–66). In addition to his knighthood (1937) and many other honors, he conducted at the coronations of King George VI (1937) and Queen Elizabeth II (1953).

Boult's style of conducting was devoid of glamorous self-assertion; his ideal was to serve the music with a minimum of display, for which he was greatly respected by the musicians of the orchs. he conducted. Throughout his long and distinguished career he championed the cause of British music; was particularly esteemed for his performances of Vaughan Williams, whose Pastoral Sym. (1922), 4th Sym. (1935), and 6th Sym. (1948) received their premiere performances under his direction in London.

bourdon (Fr., bumblebee; Lat. *vox obtusa;* Ger. *Gedackt*). 1. Organ stop of 32' or 16' pitch, having stopped wooden pipes, sometimes with metallic tops; French organs also have open bourdons of 8' and 4' pitch. 2. Great bell, as the bourdon of Notre Dame. 3. Sustained pedal tone or drone, as played on the bagpipes, hurdy-gurdy, lute, or bowed strings.

bourrée (Fr.). 1. Dance of French or Spanish origin, in rapid tempo, having 2 sections of 8 measures each, and in 2/4 or 4/4 time. 2. Optional movement in the Baroque instrumental suite, in alla breve time.

bow (Fr. *archet;* Ger. *Bogen;* Sp., It. *arco*). 1. Long and slender piece of subtle and flexible wood strung with a length of horsehair, brought into proper tension by a sliding nut worked by a screw at the bow-hand end; used to play string instruments such as the violin or cello. Originally curved (as in archery), earlier bows were shorter and had a greater distance between the bow itself and the hair. The modern type of straight bow was standardized early in the 19th century; cello and double-bass bows are usually heavier and shorter than the violin and viola bows. 2. Execute with a bow; mark a piece with signs indicating the bowing.

bow-arm or -hand. The right arm or hand.

bowed instrument. Any instrument played with a bow.

Bowie, David (born David Jones), b. South London, Jan. 8, 1947. He changed his name to avoid confusion with the British singer Davy Jones of the Monkees. He scored his 1st hit with *Space Oddity* (1969), associated with extraterrestrial visions;

dissatisfied with his direction, opened the innovative Arts Lab, but was talked into returning to rock. With the guitarist Mick Ronson and the drummer Woody Woodmansey, he put out a record, *The Man Who Sold the World* (1970), with the cover showing him in drag; it gave the impetus to a subdivision of rock known as "glitter rock." Carrying on his space obsession, Bowie released several "conceptual" albums, including the very successful *Ziggy Stardust* (1972), which he paid tribute to drug society in *Rock 'n' Roll Suicide* and offered the powerful *Suffragette City;* subsequent avatars were found in the problematic *Diamond Dogs* (1974), with the anthemic *Rebel, Rebel,* and *Young Americans* (1975), with the title song and the soul-influenced hit *Fame.*

Bowie decided to try his luck in the movies, and starred in the space fantasy *The Man Who Fell to Earth* (1976), in which his somewhat introspective image and emaciated appearance fitted the alien hero's image; had other important roles in *Christian F., Merry Christmas Mr. Lawrence, Absolute Beginners,* and the role of Andy Warhol in Julian Schnabel's film *Basquiat.* In the theater, he took the title role in the play *Elephant Man* (1980), and performed in Brecht's *Baal* (1982). He has also produced many other artists' albums, and written film songs and soundtracks; his most significant musical contributions in the last 2 decades include 3 moody synthesizer albums made with Brian Eno (1977–79); *Let's Dance,* with 4 hit singles; and several anthologies.

Bowie, Lester, b. Frederick, Md., Oct. 11, 1941. He began playing in St. Louis in the rhythm-and-blues bands of Albert King and Little Milton; moved to Chicago (1965); co-founded the Assoc. for the Advancement of Creative Musicians (AACM), a group composed of young avant-garde black jazz players. In 1969 he became a founding member of the Art Ensemble of Chicago; his performances, aside from those with the Ensemble, range from solo concerts to ones with his own bands, From the Root to the Source and Lester Bowie's Brass Fantasy. His most popular recordings include *Fast Last* (1974), *The 5th Power* (1978), and *All the Magic* (1982); *23 Facts in 2 Acts* for musicians, dancers, chorus, and actors was premiered at the Brooklyn Academy of Music (1989).

bowing. The art of playing with the bow on string instruments; a player's method or style, depending on the manner of applying the bow to the strings. Because a bow is of a finite length, a melody must be played alternately with up-bows and down-bows. Up-bows move against gravity, therefore more effort must be applied to the movement than to a down-bow, which follows the direction of gravity. When a composer wishes to produce a succession of strong sounds, down-bows are indicated by a specific sign that looks like a square bracket turned 90 degrees to the right (⊓). A succession of up-bows, used to produce lighter sounds, is indicated by a capital letter *V* above the note.

When several notes are used in the same stroke of a bow, the 1st and last notes are connected by a curved line. Because of the need to change direction of the bow, rhythmic figures such as a quarter note followed by an 8th note, when not played by the same type of bowing, cannot be performed evenly with the same amount of pressure and tone. Apart from legato, which should not have any interruption of sound, the most common stroke is *staccato,* Italian for "detached." For special effects, the player is instructed to bow *col legno,* with the wooden part of the bow; *sul ponticello,* close to the bridge; *sul tasto,* on the fingerboard.

Bowles, Paul (Frederic), b. Jamaica, N.Y., Dec. 30, 1910. As a youth he became fascinated with pictorial arts, belles lettres, and vocal projection of poetry; after a sojourn in Paris, returned to N.Y.; worked as a bookshop clerk and composed; impressed Copland by his early vocal pieces; Bowles studied with him privately. He returned to Paris; befriended Thomson; studied with Boulanger; became a habitué of the dadaist circles on the left bank of the Seine; composed the cantata *Par le détroit* (1933), and the pseudo-Grecian *Scènes d'Anabase* for tenor, oboe, and piano (1932). In 1936 he returned to the U.S.; wrote his 1st stage work, the ballet *Yankee Clipper* (1937); wrote theatrical incidental music and a short opera, *The Wind Remains* after Lorca, produced in N.Y. with Bernstein conducting (1943).

A total change in artistic orientation occurred in 1949 when he publ. the novel *The Sheltering Sky,* the 1st of many bone-chilling novels, short stories, and translations of Moroccan literature; although he completed his 3rd opera, *Yerma,* based on the Lorca play (1955), the N.Y. scene no longer satisfied his needs; moved permanently to Tangier (1959). While his writings are dark, even grim, his musical works recall those of the French neoclassical school, with nostalgia, wit, and evocations of jazz, Mexican, and Moroccan traditional music thrown in; he composed 16 film scores; the Concerto for 2 Pianos and Ensemble (1947); chamber and piano music; and the genteel *A Picnic Cantata* for Women's Voices, 2 Pianos, and Percussion (N.Y., 1954).

boy (boys') choir. Group of prepubescent males singing soprano parts, with the alto parts sung by countertenors or older boys; common in Anglican churches.

boy soprano. Prepubescent male singing in the upper register; an essential participant in chapel choirs and other religious settings that banned female involvement; many Renaissance, Baroque, and early Classic composers started their careers in this capacity, losing those jobs when their voices broke.

Boyce, William, b. London (baptized), Sept. 11, 1711; d. Kensington, Feb. 7, 1779. As a youth he was a chorister in St. Paul's Cathedral under Charles King; studied with Maurice Greene, the cathedral organist; organist at the Earl of Oxford's chapel (1734–36), then St. Michael's, Cornhill (1736–68); named composer to the Chapel Royal (1736). His main task was to provide sacred music; also contributed incidental music to theatrical productions; conducted the Festivals of the 3 Choirs (Gloucester, Worcester, Hereford, 1737); served as Master of the Royal Band in 1755. In 1757 he became Master of the King's Musick, succeeding Greene; but increasing deafness forced him to abandon active musical duties (1769).

In his last years Boyce compiled the remarkable collection *Cathedral Music* (3 vols., 1760, 1768, and 1773); this anthology comprises morning and evening services, anthems, and other church music by virtually all the major Baroque British composers. His own compositions were nearly all vocal music: anthems, odes, cantatas, and more than 15 stage works; but his remarkable instrumental works maintains his reputation: 12 sonatas for 2 Violins and Bass (London, 1747); 8 syms. (London, 1760); 12 overtures (London, 1770); and 10 voluntaries for organ or harpsichord (London, 1779).

brace. 1. Character { that connects 2 or more staves indicating that the parts on these staves are to be played simultaneously, whether by one instrument (e.g., piano) or more. 2. Group of staves so connected, as the *upper brace*.

Brahms, Johannes. b. Hamburg, May 7, 1833; d. Vienna, Apr. 3, 1897. His father, a double bassist in the Hamburg Phil. Soc., taught Brahms the rudiments of music; he then studied with Cossel and Marxsen. On his own, he eked out a subsistence by playing piano in taverns, restaurants, and other establishments (but not in brothels); met the Hungarian violinist Eduard Reményi (born Hoffmann), who taught him the fine points of the alla zingarese style; they made a successful concert tour (1853). In Göttingen, Brahms formed a friendship with Joachim, who gave him an introduction to Liszt in Weimar; saw differences in his own aesthetic from the "new German school." Of greater significance was his meeting with the Schumanns in Düsseldorf; Robert called him a "young eagle"; in his "Neue Bahnen" (New Paths) from the Neue Zeitschrift für Musik (1853), he described young Brahms as having come into life as Minerva sprang in full armor from the brow of Jupiter. Schumann's death in 1856 after years of agonizing mental illness deeply affected Brahms. He remained a devoted friend of Schumann's family; his correspondence with Clara (14 years his senior) reveals a deep affection and spiritual intimacy, but if there were more romantic feelings in their relationship, it was apparently only on his part; speculation about their friendship entering a more physical phase exists solely in fevered imaginations of wishful biographers. Indeed, Brahms exhibited a lifetime pattern of relationships with eligible women and contemplations of marriage, but, like Beethoven, never surrendered his bachelorhood.

From 1857 to 1859 Brahms was employed in Detmold as court pianist, chamber musician, and choir director; premiered his 1st piano concerto in Hannover, with Joachim as conductor (1859); returning to Hamburg, formed a women's chorus (1859–62); hoped to be named conductor of the Hamburg Phil. Soc., but the directoriat did not engage him (1863). He instead became conductor of the Viennese Singakademie (1863–64); focused on a cappella works, giving him the opportunity to study Baroque music; left to avoid political intrigue.

As early as 1857 Brahms began work on his choral masterpiece, *Ein deutsches Requiem;* deeply saddened by his mother's death (1865), he completed the score, premiered in Leipzig (1869); its title ("German Requiem") indicates that a German text drawn from Luther's Bible rather than the traditional Latin is used. Among his other vocal scores are *Rinaldo,* a cantata (1868); the *Liebeslieder* and *Zigeunerlieder* for Vocal Quartet and Piano (2 or 4 hands); the *Alto Rhapsody* (1869); the *Schicksalslied* (1871); *Nänie* (1881); and lieder. His instrumental music from this time includes 2 extremely successful vols. of *Hungarian Dances* for Piano 4-hands (1869–80); and chamber music, including the Piano Quintet, op. 34 (1864); String Sextet No. 2, op. 36 (1865); Trio for French Horn, Violin, and Piano, op. 40 (1865); 2 String Quartets, op. 51 (1873); and 3rd String Quartet, op. 67 (1876).

Brahms was named artistic director of the concerts of Vienna's famed Gesellschaft der Musikfreunde (1872–75); during this time he composed the *Variations on a Theme by Joseph Haydn,* op. 56a (1873), based on a chorale from a military *Feld-partita* then attributed to Haydn (the actual composer is unknown). For years friends and admirers had urged him to write a sym.; as early as 1855 he began work on one; by 1862 had nearly completed the 1st movement of what became his 1st Sym. Although still insecure about his symphonic capacity, he finally completed the great C-minor Sym. (op. 68), premiered in Karlsruhe, conducted by Dessoff (1876). Von Bülow, master of the telling phrase, called it "The 10th," thus placing Brahms on a direct line from Beethoven (who wrote 9); Brahms was both aware of his debt to the older composer and haunted by it.

Brahms composed his 2nd Sym., op. 73, premiered by the Vienna Phil. (1877); Violin Concerto, op. 77, dedicated to Joachim, who premiered it with the Gewandhaus Orch. (1879); 2nd Piano Concerto, op. 83, with Brahms as soloist at the Budapest premiere (1881). Then followed the 3rd Sym., op. 90, premiered by the Vienna Phil., under Richter (1883); finally, the 4th Sym., op. 98, premiered in Meiningen (1885). Brahms's symphonic cycle has fewer departures from the formal scheme than in Beethoven, and no extraneous episodes disturbing the general flow. He wrote music pure in design and eloquent in sonorous projection; his authentic Classicism endeared him to critics who were repelled by Wagnerian streams of sound, while alienating those seeking something more than a surface geometry of thematic configurations from music.

The chamber music possesses similar symphonic qualities: string quartets, violin sonatas, and the 1st Piano Trio, op. 8 (1854, rev. 1889). His piano writing is severe in its contrapuntal texture, but pianists keep the rhapsodies, intermezzos, and other character pieces in their repertoire. He imparted sheer delight through Hungarian rhapsodies and waltzes, which represented the Viennese side of his character, in contrast with the Germanic profundity of his syms. His song cycles continued the evolution of the lieder as composed by Schubert and Schumann; Brahms's cycles culminated in the starkly beautiful *4 Serious Songs* (op. 121, 1896).

Objectively seen, the private life of Brahms was that of a middle-class bourgeois who worked systematically and diligently on his current tasks while maintaining a fairly active social life. He made friends easily, traveled to Italy, and spent many summers in the solitude of the Austrian Alps. But he was essentially reserved, unsentimental, at times even callous; he needed his privacy for artistic and personal reasons; even Clara considered him "as much a riddle—I might almost say as much a stranger—as he was 25 years ago" (1880). But he was also a selfless family member who tried to save his parents' marriage and helped support his stepmother and stepbrother after his father's death. He was always ready and willing to help young composers (his earnest efforts on behalf of Dvořák were notable). Even during his Viennese period Brahms remained a sturdy Prussian; he hoped to see Germany a dominant force in Europe philosophically and militarily. (In his workroom he kept a bronze relief of Bismarck, crowned with laurel.) Extremely meticulous in his working habits (his MSS were clean and legible), he avoided wearing formal dress; dined in simple restaurants and drank a great deal of beer. He lived a good life, but died a painful death, stricken with cancer of the liver.

Brahms was indifferent to hostile criticism and entirely free of professional jealousy. His differences with Wagner were stylistic: Wagner was an opera composer, whereas Brahms never wrote for the stage (although he sought librettos). Some ardent admirers of Wagner (such as Hugo Wolf) found little of value in the music of Brahms, while admirers of Brahms (such as Hanslick) were sharp critics of Wagner. It is amazing to read the outpouring of invective against Brahms by G. B. Shaw and American critics, usually along the lines of dullness and turgidity. Yet at the

hands of successive Austro-German conductors, he became a standard symphonist in the northeastern U.S. Brahms now appears to be the greatest master of counterpoint after Bach; one can learn polyphony from a studious analysis of the chamber music and piano works; also excelled in variation forms: the piano variations on a theme of Paganini are exemplars of contrapuntal learning, and are among the most difficult piano works of the 19th century. Posterity gave him a full measure of recognition; Hamburg, which had never treated him well, celebrated his sesquicentennial in 1983 with great pomp.

Brain, Dennis, b. London, May 17, 1921; d. in an automobile accident, Hatfield, Hertfordshire, Sept. 1, 1957. He studied with his father, Aubrey (Harold) Brain, who had been a hornist with the London Sym. and BBC Sym. Orch. (1893–1955); served as 1st horn player in the Royal Phil. and later with the Philharmonia Orch.; rapidly acquired the reputation of a foremost performer on his instrument. Britten's *Serenade for Tenor, Horn, and Strings* was written for him. He was killed when he drove at a high speed, at night, from Edinburgh to London, and hit a tree; his death caused a profound shock among English musicians. His uncle (Alfred, 1885–1966) was a hornist; his brother Leonard (1915–75) chose to be an oboist.

Branca, Glenn, b. Harrisburg, Pa., Oct. 6, 1948. After drama studies, he moved to N.Y. (1976); cofounded the experimental group Theoretical Girls; began composing works for massed, overamplified electric guitars, later adding brass, percussion, and other electric instruments. Most of his works are called syms., in the orig. sense (concordance of sound); they are generally extremely loud and work best in a live setting; stylistically the syms. evoke Varèse, the futurists, 1930s percussion pieces, instrumental art-rock, and the 2nd minimalist school; but Branca's music is totally distinctive. He received considerable publicity in 1982 when Cage responded to a Branca performance by calling the piece "fascist."

branle, bransle (Fr.; Eng. *brangle,* brawl). Popular 16th-century French dance in which several persons joined hands and took the lead in turn. Derived from the generic basse danse type, the branle came in many varieties, in both binary and ternary meters; the latter is the putative predecessor of the minuet.

Brant, Henry, b. Montreal (of American parents), Sept. 15, 1913. He learned musical rudiments from his father; moved to N.Y. (1929); studied with L. Mannes, Riegger, Antheil, and Fritz Mahler (Gustav's nephew); taught at Columbia Univ., the Juilliard School, and Bennington College; settled in Santa Barbara, Calif. (1982). An audacious explorer of sonic potentialities, he drew without prejudice upon resources ranging from kitchen utensils to tin cans in search of superior cacophony.

Brant was a pioneer in the field of spatial music; participating instruments were placed at specified points in space, on the stage, in the balcony, and in the aisles; almost all of his music since the early 1950s has used spatial technique. In conducting spatial, music, he developed an appropriate body language, turning at 90°, 135°, and 180° angles to address his instrumentalists; gave cues by actually imitating the appearance of the entering instruments, miming the violin bow, a trombone valve, a piccolo, or a drum by the movement of his body or by facial movements; proposed a concert hall with movable plywood partitions, changing configurations according to acoustical requirements;

unfortunately, the closest (but unrelated) realization of this plan, at the Calif. Institute of the Arts, Valencia, is not designed for musical acoustics.

Among his many works are *Angels and Devils,* concerto for flute accompanied by 10 members of the flute family (1st version, 1931); *Signs and Alarms* for Chamber Ensemble (1953); *Kingdom Come,* spatial work for orch., circus band, organ (1970); *Meteor Farm,* spatial work for Javanese, West African, southern Indian, Western orch., jazz, and 2 choral ensembles (1982); and *Western Springs* for 2 Orchs., 2 Choruses, and 2 Jazz Groups (1984).

brass band. Band, brass.

brass instruments. Wind instruments made of metal, forming one of the Western orch'l instrument families. The 4 orch'l brass instruments today are the French horn, trumpet, trombone (the only modern unvalved brass instrument), and tuba; other brass instruments are or were found in brass, military, and wind bands: cornet, bugle, tenor horn, flugelhorn, baritone, euphonium, bombardon, saxhorn, ophicleide, and serpent. A refined definition of a brass instrument involves the size of the mouthpiece and shape of the bore, so the saxophone is technically a woodwind made of metal, while the serpent, popular in bands until the early 19th century, was a brass instrument made of wood.

Bratsche (Ger.). The viola.

bravo, -a (It.). Shout of acclaim for the performer, commonly a male or female opera singer, respectively. *Bravi,* acclaim for more than one performer.

bravura (It.; Ger., Bravour; Fr., *bravoure*). Boldness, spirit, dash, brilliancy; a resounding display of technical virtuosity. *Bravourstück,* a vocal or instrumental piece of a brilliant and difficult character; *con bravura* (It.), with boldness; brilliantly; with swaggering confidence; *valse de bravoure* (Fr.), instrumental waltz in brilliant, showy style.

Braxton, Anthony, b. Chicago, June 4, 1945. After early studies in both jazz and classical music, he joined the Assoc. for the Advancement of Creative Musicians (AACM; 1966); formed the Creative Construction Co. with Leroy Jenkins and Wadada Leo Smith (1967); went to N.Y.; played in the improvisation ensemble Musica Elettronica Viva (1970) and Chick Corea's free-jazz quartet, Circle (1970–71). Although his activities and influence have been most visible in avant-garde jazz improvisation based on graphic and other nontraditional notation, his output in the 1970s included compositions for band and piano; his album *For Alto* (1968) was the 1st recording for unaccompanied saxophone.

break (1). Short and lively improvised instrumental solo in jazz that momentarily disrupts the continuity of the tune without upsetting the symmetric period of the whole, usually in pre-arranged harmonic changes. Breaks can be of various lengths, can be improvised by 1 or more solo instrumentalists, and can result in ingenious, even complex contrapuntal settings.

break (2). 1. The point where one register of a voice or instrument passes over into another: in the voice, the junction of the head and chest registers; in the clarinet, between each of 4 reg-

isters. 2. False or imperfect tone produced by incorrect lipping of a horn or trumpet, or by difficulty with the reed of the clarinet (called "the goose"); in singing, by some defect in the vocal organs. 3. In an organ stop, when playing up the scale, the sudden return to the lower octave (caused by an incomplete set of pipes); in compound stops, any point in their scale where the relative pitch of the pipes changes.

breakdown. Lively Anglo-American traditional dance in 4/4, associated with the old-time fiddle and banjo style, dating from the late 19th century. In bluegrass, the breakdown became the genre for friendly rapid-finger competition between players.

breaking of the voice. See ⇒mutation.

Bream, Julian (Alexander), b. London, July 15, 1933. He was educated at the Royal College of Music in London; made his debut at age 17; founded the Julian Bream Consort (1960); directed the Semley Festival of Music and Poetry (from 1971). Through his numerous concerts and recordings he has helped to revive interest in Elizabethan lute music; named an Officer of the Order of the British Empire (1964) and a Commander of the Order of the British Empire (1985); several works have been written for him.

breath/ing mark. A sign (', *, ^, v, or ") inserted in a vocal part, indicating that the singer may (or must) take breath at that point, rather than elsewhere.

breit (Ger.). In a broad tempo. *Breiten Strich* (Ger.). Use a broad stroke of the bow (when playing a string instrument).

Brel, Jacques, b. Brussels, Apr. 8, 1929; d. Paris, Oct. 9, 1978. He rose to fame in France in the 1950s as a singer and writer of popular songs, which emphasized such themes as unrequited love, loneliness, death, and war; in 1967, quit the concert stage and turned to the theater and film as a producer, director, and actor. In 1968 the composer Mort Shuman brought Brel's songs to Broadway in the musical *Jacques Brel Is Alive and Well and Living in Paris;* the title soon proved ironic; stricken with cancer, Brel abandoned his career in 1974 and moved to the Marquesas Islands; in 1977, returned to Paris to record his final album, *Brel.*

Brendel, Alfred, b. Wiesenberg, Moravia, Jan. 5, 1931. His teachers were E. Fischer, Paul Baumgartner, Steuermann, and Michl; made his concert debut in Graz (1948); began a successful career in Europe; played for the 1st time in U.S. (1963); toured in South America, Japan, and Australia. He is particularly distinguished as an interpreter of the Vienna classics, but also included Schoenberg's difficult Piano Concerto in readiness. In 1983 he presented in N.Y. a 7-concert cycle of the complete piano sonatas of Beethoven; received honorary knighthood from Queen Elizabeth II of England (1989).

Brendel, Wolfgang, b. Munich, Oct. 20, 1947. He joined the Bavarian State Opera, Munich (1971); became Kammersänger (1977); made his Metropolitan Opera, N.Y., debut as Count Almaviva in *Le nozze di Figaro* (1975), at the San Francisco Opera as Rodrigo in *Don Carlo* (1979), Milan's La Scala as Count Almaviva (1981), Chicago Lyric Opera as Miller in *Luisa Miller* (1982), and at the Bayreuth Festival as Wolfram (1985). He made his debut at London's Covent Garden as Conte

Di Luna in *Il Trovatore* in 1985; appeared in opera centers throughout Europe and the U.S.; most noted roles include Rossini's Figaro, Papageno, Eugene Onegin, Amfortas, Silvio, and Pelleas.

breve (Lat. *brevis; nota brevis,* short note). Short note value; in medieval mensural notation, indicated by a black or open square; its value was half of a longa. However, a whole generation of even shorter notes made their appearance; the breve became incongruously the longest note in modern notation. This unnatural terminology is retained in contemporary British usage: the breve, written as an open oblong, equals 2 whole notes and can be used only in the time signature of 8/4.

Brian, Havergal, b. Dresden, Staffordshire, Jan. 29, 1876; d. Shoreham-by-the-Sea, Sussex, Nov. 28, 1972. He studied instruments with local teachers; taught himself elementary music theory, French, and German; engaged in musical journalism (1904–49); attained reputation in England as a harmless eccentric possessed by inordinate ambitions to become a composer; attracted supporters who in turn were derided as gullible admirers of a patent amateur. Brian continued to write music in large symphonic forms; some works were performed, mostly by nonprofessional organizations and often long after their composition, e.g., Sym. No. 1, the *Gothic* for Solo Voices, Chorus, Children's Chorus, Brass Bands, and Orch. (1919–27) had 1st complete performance in 1961. Amazingly he increased his productivity with age; wrote 22 syms. after reaching the age of 80, more after the age of 90; the total number was 32 syms.

Brian was not an innovator; followed the Germanic traditions of R. Strauss and Mahler in the spirit of unbridled grandiosity, architectural formidability, and rhapsodically quaquaversal thematicism. His modernism tended to be programmatic, as in the whole-tone progressions in the opera *The Tigers* (1916–19), illustrating the zeppelin attacks on London during World War I. His readiness to lend his MSS to anyone interested resulted in the loss of several of his works; a few of them were retrieved after years of search.

Brice, Fanny (born Fannie Borach), b. N.Y., Oct. 29, 1891; d. Los Angeles, May 29, 1951. After singing in her parents' tavern, she toured the burlesque circuit; discovered by Florenz Ziegfeld, he featured her in his Follies of 1910; subsequently she appeared in other eds. of the Follies and in Broadway musicals; most notable film role was self-portrayal in *The Great Ziegfeld* (1936); in the Follies of 1934 she created the role of little Baby Snooks, a character she portrayed on radio from 1938 until her death. Her 3rd husband was Billy Rose, the producer and songwriter (married 1929; divorced 1938); her career was the subject of the 1964 Broadway musical *Funny Girl,* made into a film starring Barbra Streisand (1968).

Brico, Antonia, Dutch-born American pianist, teacher, and conductor; b. Rotterdam, June 26, 1902; d. Denver, Aug. 3, 1989. She moved to California in 1906 and took courses at the Univ. of Calif., Berkeley, graduating in music in 1923; went to Berlin, where she took conducting lessons with Muck at the State Academy of Music; also studied piano with Sigismund Stojowski. She played piano recitals in Europe, but her main interest was in conducting; overcoming the general skepticism about feminine conductorship, raised funds to conduct a special concert with the Berlin Phil. in 1930, which aroused some curiosity; then received a conducting engagement in Finland, which gained her a commendation from Sibelius; later associated with Albert Schweitzer, visiting his hospital in South Africa and receiving from him suggestions for performing Bach. In 1974 she was the subject of a film documentary entitled *Antonia,* in which she eloquently pleaded for the feminist cause in music and especially in conducting; on the strength of this film, obtained some engagements, among them an appearance at the Hollywood Bowl; returned to Denver; maintained a piano studio.

bridge. 1. In bowed instruments, a thin, arching piece of wood set upright on the belly to raise and stretch the strings above the resonance box, to which the bridge communicates the vibrations of the strings. 2. In the piano and other stringed instruments, a rail of wood or steel over which the strings are stretched.

Bridge, Frank, b. Brighton, Feb. 26, 1879; d. Eastbourne, Jan. 10, 1941. He took violin lessons from his father; entered the Royal College of Music in 1899; studied composition with Stanford; graduated (1904); specialized in viola playing; member of the Joachim String Quartet in 1906 and later of the English String Quartet; also appeared as a conductor; led the New Sym. Orch. during Marie Brema's season (1910–11) at the Savoy Theatre in London; conducted at Covent Garden during the seasons of Raymond Roze and Beecham; appeared at the Promenade Concerts. He toured the U.S. in 1923, conducting his own works in Rochester, Boston, Detroit, Cleveland, and N.Y.; revisited the U.S. in 1934 and 1938. As a composer he received a belated recognition toward the end of his life and posthumously; despite his considerable instrumental music, works rarely appeared in the programs of modern music festivals.

Much of Bridge's music is generated by passionate emotionalism, soaring with euphonious dissonances, while his chamber music maintains a neoclassical spirit of Baroque construction; although greatly impressed by the works of the 2nd Viennese school, never embraced serial composition. Most remarkable of his more advanced works was the 4th String Quartet (1937). Britten, an ardent student and admirer, wrote his *Variations on a Theme of Frank Bridge* (1937) based on the Idyll No. 2 for string quartet (1906).

brillante (It.). Brilliant, showy, sparkling.

Brindisi (It., from Ger. *bring' dir's,* I bring it to you). Salutatory drinking song or toast; not connected to the Italian city of Brindisi. The earliest known operatic Brindisi is in Donizetti's *Lucrezia Borgia,* the best known in *La Traviata* (*Labiamo!*).

brio, con (It., with noise). With gusto; spiritedly; vigorously, brilliantly; *brioso.*

brisé (Fr., broken). 1. In string playing, short, detached strokes of the bow. 2. Arpeggiate a chord. 3. In the 18th century, a fioritura.

Britten, (Edward) Benjamin. Lord Britten of Aldeburgh, b. Lowestoft, Suffolk, Nov. 22, 1913; d. Aldeburgh, Dec. 4, 1976. He grew up in moderately prosperous circumstances; his father was an orthodontist, his mother an amateur singer. He played the piano and improvised facile tunes; many years later, used these youthful inspirations in the *Simple Sym.;* took viola lessons with Audrey Alston. At age 13 he was accepted as a pupil in composition by Bridge, whose influence was decisive on his development as a composer; entered the Royal College of Music in London (1930); studied piano with A. Benjamin and H. Samuel and composition with J. Ireland.

He progressed rapidly; his earliest works showed a mature mastery of technique and a fine lyrical talent of expression. His *Fantasy Quartet* for Oboe and Strings was performed at the Festival of the ISCM in Florence (1934); became associated with the theater and the cinema and began composing background music for films. He was in the U.S. at the outbreak of World War II; returned to England (spring 1942); exempted from military service as a conscientious objector. After the war he organized the English Opera Group (1947); co-founded the Aldeburgh Festival, in collaboration with Eric Crozier and Peter Pears (1948); devoted mainly to production of short English operas, it became an important cultural institution; many of Britten's own works were premiered at the Festivals, often under his own direction; also had productions at the Glyndebourne Festival.

In many of his operas Britten reduced the orch'l contingent to 12 performers, with the piano part serving as a modern version of the Baroque ripieno; this economy of means made it possible for small opera groups and univ. workshops to perform his works; yet he succeeded in creating a rich spectrum of instrumental colors, in an idiom ranging from simple triadic progressions, often in parallel motions, to ultrachromatic dissonant harmonies; upon occasion he applied dodecaphonic procedures, but never employed the formal design of the 12-tone method. Characteristic of his operas is the inclusion of orch'l interludes, which became independent symphonic poems related to the dramatic action of the work; the cries of seagulls in his most popular and musically most striking opera, *Peter Grimes* (1945), create a fantastic quasi-surrealistic imagery. He was equally successful in treating tragic subjects, as in *Peter Grimes* and *Billy Budd* (1951); comic subjects, exemplified by *Albert Herring* (1947); and mystical evocation, as in *The Turn of the Screw* (1954). He composed the patriotic *Gloriana* (1953), based on the life of Queen Elizabeth I, for the coronation of Elizabeth II; possessed a flair for writing music for children, in which he managed to present a degree of sophistication and artistic simplicity without condescension.

Britten was a versatile composer; he realized a version of Gay's *Beggar's Opera;* wrote modern parables for church performance and a contemporary retelling of the medieval English miracle play *Noye's Fludde* (1958). Among his other works the most remarkable is the *War Requiem* (1962), a profound tribute to the war dead, mixing the Latin Requiem with Wilfrid Owen's poetry. In 1952 he was made a Companion of Honour; in 1965, received the Order of Merit; in June 1976, created a life peer of Great Britain by Queen Elizabeth II, the 1st composer to be so honored.

broken chords. Harmonic units (chords) whose tones are sounded in succession instead of together, whether as self-contained progression or accompaniment. See ⇒arpeggio.

broken consort. An old description of a Renaissance ensemble having both strings and wind instruments, as opposed to *whole consort,* where the instruments were of the same family. *Broken music,* music for a broken consort.

broken octaves. 1. Series of octaves in which the higher tones alternate with the lower. 2. Short octave, the lowest octave

in keyboard instruments before 1700, in which rarely used chromatic bass notes were left out, leaving only 8 notes in that octave.

Broonzy, "Big Bill" (born William Lee Conley), b. Scott, Miss., June 26, 1893; d. Chicago, Aug. 14, 1958. He 1st took up the fiddle; made his way to Chicago (by 1920); learned the guitar and began his career as a blues singer. He was as popular in Europe as in the U.S., making tours in 1951, 1955, and 1957; an important participant in the transition to the Chicago blues style.

Broschi, Carlo. See ⇒Farinelli.

Broschi, Riccardo. See ⇒Farinelli.

Brown, Clifford ("Brownie"), b. Wilmington, Del., Oct. 30, 1930; d. in an automobile accident on the turnpike near Bedford, Pa., June 26, 1956. He studied at Del. State College and Md. State College; gained experience playing in college jazz bands; later joined Tadd Dameron's group; toured Europe in 1953 with Lionel Hampton's orch.; returning to the U.S., worked with Art Blakey; subsequently formed the Brown-Roach Quintet with Max Roach. Brown was particularly successful as a master of improvisation.

Brown, Earle (Appleton, Jr.), b. Lunenburg, Mass., Dec. 26, 1926. He played trumpet in school bands; enrolled in Northeastern Univ., Boston, to study engineering; played trumpet in the U.S. Army Air Force Band; was substitute trumpet player with the San Antonio Sym. Returning to Boston, he began to study the Schillinger system of composition; took private theory lessons with Rosalyn Brogue Henning; adopted the most advanced types of compositional techniques, experimenting in serial methods as well as aleatory improvisation; was fascinated by the parallelism existing in abstract expressionism in painting, mobile sculptures, and free musical forms; to draw these contiguities together, initiated the idea of open forms, using graphic notation with visual signs in musical terms. The titles of his works give clues to their contents: *Folio* (1952–53), a group of 6 compositions in which the performer may vary the duration, pitch, and rhythm; *25 Pages* (1953), played by any number of pianists up to 25, reading the actual pages in any desired order, and playing the notes upside down or right side up; and *Available Forms I* for 18 Instruments, consisting of musical "events" happening in accordance with guiding marginal arrows. Brown made much use of magnetic tape, both in open and closed forms.

Apart from Brown's creative endeavors, he had numerous lecturing engagements in Europe and the U.S.; was composer-in-residence with the Rotterdam Phil. in the Netherlands (1947); guest prof. at the Basel Cons. in Switzerland (1975); visiting prof. at the Univ. of Southern Calif. in Los Angeles (1978) and Yale Univ. (1980–81, 1986–87). He was composer-in-residence at the American Academy in Rome (1987); president of the American Music Center (1986–89). He professes no *parti pris* in his approach to composition, whether dissonantly contrapuntal or serenely triadic; rather, his music represents a mobile assembly of plastic elements; as a result, his usages range from astute asceticism and constrained constructivism to soaring sonorism and lush lyricism.

Brown, James, b. Barnwell, Ga., May 3, 1928. He originally played keyboards, drums, and string bass; formed a group which he called the Famous Flames; produced a triply emphatic song, *Please, Please, Please,* (1956) which made the top of the charts; other big hits were *Try Me, Prisoner of Love, It's a Man's World, Out of Sight,* and *Papa's Got a Brand New Bag.* He then formed the James Brown Revue and produced stage shows; his songs acquired a political flavor, such as his proclamatory *Black Is Beautiful, Say It Loud, I'm Black and I'm Proud,* and *Living in America;* cultivated vocal sex motifs in *I Got Ants in My Pants, Hot Pants, Body Heat,* and *Sex Machine;* made an admonitory gesture to junkies in *King Heroin;* at the height of his fame, known as "Soul Brother Number 1," "Godfather of Soul," and "King of Soul."

Brown, Rosemary, b. London, July 27, 1917. She led a middle-class life as a housewife, and liked to improvise at the piano; possessed of a certain type of musical mimicry, began playing passages in the manner of her beloved Mozart, Beethoven, Schubert, Chopin, or Liszt; they usually consisted of short melodies invariably accompanied by broken triads and 7th-chords. Under the influence of popular literature dealing with communication with ghosts, she became convinced that this music was being dictated to her by departed composers; she willingly recited stories about their human kindness to her (e.g., Chopin warning her to turn off the leaking faucet in the bathtub to prevent flooding). On a grocery errand as a small child, she was approached by a tall, gray-haired gentleman who, observing that she carried a music book, introduced himself as Franz Liszt and volunteered to teach her piano without remuneration; she had similar happy encounters with other famous composers; soon arranged to take dictation of posthumous works from them. She appeared on British television writing down notes under the dictation of Beethoven, but Beethoven's image failed to materialize, owing no doubt to some last-moment scruples on the part of the producers; she put out a couple of maudlin, maundering, meandering pamphlets dealing with her transcendental experiences, and a professional journalist publ. the story of her contacts with dead composers.

Brubeck, Dave (David Warren), b. Concord, Calif., Dec. 6, 1920. He received classical piano training from his mother; played in local jazz groups from age 13; studied at the College of the Pacific in Stockton, Calif. (1941–42); received instruction in composition from Milhaud at Mills College in Oakland, Calif., and from Schoenberg in Los Angeles. During military service in World War II he led a band in Europe; founded his own octet and trio (1949); organized the Dave Brubeck Quartet (1951), which acquired a reputation as one of the leading jazz groups of the era, known for its metric experiments and stylistic borrowings from classical sources.

His sons Darius (b. San Francisco, June 14, 1947), a keyboard player; Chris (b. Los Angeles, Mar. 19, 1953), a bass guitar and bass trombone player; and Danny (b. Oakland, May 5, 1955), a drummer, often performed with him. His works include 2 ballets, A Maiden in the Tower (1956) and Points on Jazz (1961); a musical, The Real Ambassador (1962); 2 oratorios: The Light in the Wilderness (1968) and Beloved Son (1978); 3 cantatas: The Gates of Justice (1969), Truth Is Fallen (1971), and La fiesta de la posada (1975); Festival Mass to Hope (1980); and piano pieces. His brother, Howard R(engstorff) Brubeck (b. Concord, Calif., July 11, 1916; d. La Jolla, Calif., Feb. 16, 1993), a composer, served as chairman of the music dept. at Palomar Junior College, San Marcos, Calif. (1953–78).

Bruch, Max, b. Cologne, Jan. 6, 1838; d. Friedenau, near Berlin, Oct. 2, 1920. His mother, a professional singer, was his 1st teacher; studied theory with Breidenstein in Bonn; in 1852, won a scholarship of the Mozart Foundation in Frankfurt for 4 years; a pupil of Hiller, Reinecke, and Breuning; at age 14, brought out a sym. at Cologne; at 20, produced his 1st stage work, *Scherz, List und Rache,* after Goethe (Cologne, 1858). He taught in Cologne (1858–61); made prolonged visits to Berlin, Leipzig, Dresden, and Munich; went to Mannheim; produced his 1st full-fledged opera, *Die Loreley* (1863); also wrote an effective choral work, *Frithjof,* presented with great success in various German towns and in Vienna.

Bruch became music director of a concert organization in Koblenz (1865–67); wrote his 1st Violin Concerto, a great favorite among violinists; went to Sonderhausen as court Kapellmeister; went to Berlin; his last opera, *Hermione,* based on Shakespeare's *The Winter's Tale,* was produced at the Berlin Opera (1872); accepted the post of conductor of the Liverpool Phil. (1880–83); visited the U.S. and conducted his choral work *Arminius* in Boston. He was director of an orch. society in Breslau (1883–90); in 1891, became prof. of composition at the Hochschule für Musik in Berlin, retiring in 1910. Bruch was married to the singer Clara Tuczek (d. 1919).

Bruch's music, although imitative in its essence and even in its melodic and harmonic procedures, has a great eclectic charm; he was a master of harmony, counterpoint, and instrumentation, and equally adept at handling vocal masses; contributed a great deal to the development of the secular oratorio. Among his instrumental works, the *Scottish Fantasy* for Violin and Orch. (1880) was extremely successful when Sarasate (its dedicatee) performed it all over Europe; his most popular work is *Kol Nidrei* for Cello and Orch., based on a melody associated with the Day of Atonement and composed for the Jewish community of Liverpool (1880); its success led to the erroneous assumption that Bruch himself was Jewish (he was from a clerical Protestant family). His Concerto for 2 Pianos and Orch. was commissioned by an American duo-piano team who rev. the original drastically for its premiere (Philadelphia Orch., Stokowski conducting, 1916); in 1971 the authentic version was discovered in Berlin and given its 1st performance by Nathan Twining and Mer Berkofsky with the London Sym., Dorati conducting (1974).

Bruckner, (Josef) Anton. b. Ansfelden, Sept. 4, 1824; d. Vienna, Oct. 11, 1896. He studied music with his father, a village schoolmaster and church organist; took music lessons at Hörsching with his cousin Johann Baptist Weiss. After his father's death in 1837, he enrolled as a chorister at St. Florian, attending classes in organ, piano, violin, and music theory; in 1840–41, entered the special school for educational training in Linz, also studied music theory with Leopold Edler von Zenetti in Enns.

While in his early youth, Bruckner held teaching positions in elementary public schools in Windhaag (1841–43), Kronstorf (1843–45), and St. Florian (1845–55); served as provisional organist there (1848–51); despite professional advance, felt a lack of basic compositional techniques; at age 31 went to Vienna to study with the renowned pedagogue Simon Sechter (1788–1867), continuing with him intermittently until 1861. He became cathedral organist in Linz (1856), successfully competing against several applicants; but, still determined to acquire more technical knowledge, he began taking orchestration lessons with Otto Kitzler, cellist of the Linz municipal theater

(1861–63); undertook an assiduous study of the Italian polyphonic school and of masters of German polyphony, especially Bach; these tasks preoccupied him so completely that he did not begin composing freely until nearly 40 years old.

Around this time Bruckner fell under the powerful influence of Wagner's music; this infatuation diverted him from classical polyphony; attended the premiere of *Tristan und Isolde* in Munich and met its composer (1865); met Liszt in Pest and Berlioz during his visit in Vienna. His adulation of Wagner was extreme; the dedication of his 3rd Sym. reads: "To the eminent Excellency Richard Wagner the Unattainable, World-Famous, and Exalted Master of Poetry and Music, in Deepest Reverence Dedicated by Anton Bruckner." But the personal differences between Wagner and Bruckner could not be more striking: Wagner, a man of the world who devoted his whole life to the promotion of his artistic and human affairs; Bruckner, insecure and desperately seeking recognition. Strangely enough, in his own music Bruckner never embraced the tenets and practices of Wagner, but followed the sanctified tradition of Germanic polyphony. Whereas Wagner strove toward the ideal union of drama, text, and music in a new type of opera, Bruckner kept away from the musical theater, confining himself to symphonic and choral music. Bruckner seldom followed Wagner's chromatic style of writing, and never tried to emulate the passionate rise and fall of Wagnerian "endless" melodies to depict the characters in his operas.

Although an inadequate conductor, Bruckner was a master organist; in 1869 he appeared in organ recitals in France; visited England, giving performances in the Royal Albert Hall and the Crystal Palace in London (1871); was esteemed as a pedagogue. He succeeded Sechter as prof. of harmony, counterpoint, and organ at the Vienna Cons. (1868); that year was also named provisional court organist, an appointment formally confirmed in 1878; concurrently taught piano, organ, and music theory at St. Anna College, Vienna (1870–74). In 1875 he was appointed lecturer in harmony and counterpoint at the Univ. of Vienna. In failing health, he retired from the Vienna Cons. in 1891, as court organist (1892), and as lecturer at the Univ. of Vienna (1894); the remaining years of his life were devoted to the composition of his 9th Sym., which remained unfinished at his death.

For Bruckner, the faith and the sacraments of the Roman Catholic Church were not mere rituals but profound psychological experiences. Following the practice of Haydn, he signed most of his works with the words "Omnia ad majorem Dei gloriam." From reports of his friends and contemporaries, it appears that he regarded each happy event of his life as a gift of God, each disaster as an act of divine wrath. His yearning for secular honors was none the less acute for that; was tremendously gratified upon receiving an honorary doctorate from the Univ. of Vienna in 1891, the 1st musician to be so honored there. (He unsuccessfully solicited similar degrees from other univs.) It was not until the end of his unhappy life that, thanks to a group of devoted friends among conductors, he finally achieved a full recognition of his greatness.

A signal testimony to Bruckner's lack of self-confidence was a willingness to revise works repeatedly, not always for the better, taking advice from conductors and ostensible well-wishers. The textual problems concerning his works are numerous and complex; his many revisions resulted in conflicting versions of his syms. appearing in circulation with the founding of the International Bruckner Soc., a movement was begun to publ. the original versions of his MSS, the majority of which he bequeathed to the Hofbibliothek, Vienna. A complete ed. of Bruckner's works began to appear in 1930.

To Bruckner, music was an apotheosis of symmetry, his syms. cathedrals of Gothic grandeur; he never hesitated to repeat a musical phrase several times so as to establish a work's thematic foundation. The syms. constitute a monumental achievement, characterized by a striking display of originality and a profound spiritual quality; his sacred works are similarly expressive of latent genius. He is usually paired with Mahler, who was a generation younger but whose music embodied qualities of grandeur akin to those that permeated the symphonic and choral works of Bruckner.

Bruckner suffered from periodic attacks of depression; his entire life seems to have been a study of unhappiness, most particularly in numerous attempts to find a woman to be his wife. He desperately made halfhearted proposals in marriage to women of the people; the older he grew, the younger were the objects of his misguided affections; a notorious episode was his proposal of marriage to a chambermaid at a Berlin hotel. He died a virgin.

Bruggen, Frans, distinguished Dutch recorder player, flutist, and conductor; b. Amsterdam, Oct. 30, 1934. He studied the recorder with Kees Otten and flute at the Amsterdam Muzieklyceum; took courses in musicology at the Univ. of Amsterdam; launched a major career as a virtuoso performer of music for the recorder. As a flute soloist he was equally at home in performances of the Baroque masters and contemporary avant-garde composers; gave informative lectures and illustrative performances of recorder music in Europe; taught at the Royal Cons. in the Hague. In 1981 he founded the Orch. of the 18th Century, which he conducted with fine success on both sides of the Atlantic.

bruitism (Fr. *bruitisme; bruit* = noise). Term, originally derogatory, denoting the use of noise as a compositional element. The pioneer work of bruitism was *Arte dei Rumori* by the Italian futurist Luigi Russolo, which codified noises of friction, attrition, sibilation, percussion, and concussion, and for which he created his noise-producers (*intonarumori*). Varèse elevated the inchoate bruitistic scheme to a purely musical form in his epoch-making work *Ionisation*.

Brummstimmen (Ger., humming voices; It. *bocca chiusa*). Vocal production of the tone without words, through the nose, and with closed mouth.

brunette (Fr., dark-haired woman). French song genre of the 17th and 18th centuries, similar to the bergerette, containing both authentic traditional and street ballad motives. Lully and Rameau wrote brunettes into their operas.

bruscamente (It.). Brusquely or forcibly accented; *Brusco,* brusque.

Brustregister (Ger.). Chest voice production.

Brustwerk (Ger., chest work). Group of pipes in front of the organ, usually played on the 2nd manual and having a softer sound than the larger main organ.

Bryars, Gavin, b. Goole, Yorkshire, Jan. 16, 1943. He studied philosophy at Sheffield Univ. and composition with Cyril

Ramsey and George Linstead; began his career as a bassist, turning in 1966 to composition and quickly emerging as one of England's most influential experimental composers. His academic appointments have included Portsmouth College of Art, where he founded the Portsmouth Sinfonia (made up of amateurs), and Leicester Polytechnic (from 1970); ed. the *Experimental Music Catalogue* (1972–81); official biographer of the eccentric English composer, novelist, and painter Lord Berners. His compositions, indeterminate and replete with repetition, often utilize electronic means; warmth and humor are evidenced in *The Sinking of the Titanic* (1969), a multimedia, meditative collage work composed of excerpts from pieces the drowning orch. might have been playing; other compositions include *Jesus' Blood Never Failed Me Yet* (1971), *Out of Laeski's Gazebo* (1977), *My 1st Homage* (1978), *The Vespertine Park* (1980), and *Effarene* (1984). He has collaborated with a number of well-known musicians, including Eno, Reich, and Cardew; a number of pieces have been choreographed by Lucinda Childs. In 1984 his opera *Medea*, in collaboration with Robert Wilson, was premiered at the Opera de Lyon.

buccina. Ancient Roman semicircular metal horn used during festivals, usually adorned with a metal ornament in the shape of an animal horn; similar to a shepherd's horn.

Buchla, Donald (Frederick), b. Southgate, Calif., Apr. 17, 1937. After studying physics at the Univ. of Calif., Berkeley, he became active with the San Francisco Tape Music Center, where in 1966 he installed the 1st Buchla synthesizer; founded Buchla Associates in Berkeley for the manufacture of synthesizers. In addition to designing and manufacturing electronic instruments, he also installed electronic-music studios at the Royal Academy of Music, Stockholm, and at IRCAM, Paris; in 1975, cofounded the Electric Weasel Ensemble, a live electronic-music group; in 1978, became codirector of the Artists' Research Collective in Berkeley. He held a Guggenheim fellowship in 1978.

Buffalo Springfield. (Leader/guitar/vocal: Stephen Stills, b. Dallas, Tex., Jan. 3, 1945; lead guitar/vocal: Neil Young, b. Toronto, Canada, Nov. 12, 1945; rhythm guitar/vocal: Richie Furay, b. Yellow Springs, Ohio, May 9, 1944; bass: Bruce Palmer, b. Liverpool, Ontario, Canada, 1946; drums: Dewey Martin, b. Chesterville, Ontario, Canada, Sept. 30, 1942. Jim Messina, b. Maywood, Calif., Dec. 5, 1947, replaced Palmer in late 1967.) Popular rock band of the 1960s; took its name from a brand of steamroller; its various members have gone on to illustrious careers. The original band was shortlived (1966–68), with 1 hit, Stephen Stills's social-protest song *For What It's Worth;* the band combined various influences, from folk and country to progressive rock. Stills went on to form Manassas and Crosby, Stills and Nash (CSN); Young undertook a solo career and also performed with Stills and CSN; Furay and Messina formed Poco; Messina formed a duo with Kenny Loggins; Furay formed a duo with John David Souther; Martin formed Medicine Ball.

buffa (It.). Comic, burlesque. *Buffo* (buffo-singer; *buffone,* jester), comic actor or operatic singer.

buffa, aria. See ⇒Aria buffa.

buffa, opera. See ⇒Opera buffa

bugaku. Japanese masked dance derived from Chinese and Korean court traditions. The slow and stately musical accompaniment emphasizes woodwinds and drums.

bugle. 1. Wind instrument of brass or copper, with cupped mouthpiece, used for military calls and infantry signals; a trumpet without valves. 2. The key-bugle, with 6 keys and a compass of over 2 octaves. 3. The valve-bugle. See ⇒saxhorn.

Bühnenmusik (Ger., stage music). Incidental music for plays or music performed on the stage, such as the finale of *Don Giovanni.*

buisine (from Lat. *buccina,* semicircular metal horn). Long straight slender Roman military trumpet, spread throughout Europe by conquering Roman armies.

Bull, John, b. probably in Old Radnor, Radnorshire, *c.* 1562; d. Antwerp, Mar. 12, 1628. He was a pupil of William Blitheman in the Chapel Royal; received his Mus.B. from Oxford, then sworn in as a Gentleman of the Chapel Royal (1586); became its organist (1591); on Queen Elizabeth's recommendation, appointed prof. of music at Gresham College (1596); elected 1st public lecturer (1597). He got into difficulties with Gresham College after impregnating a maiden named Elizabeth Walter; forced to resign (1607); hastened to take a marriage license 2 days later. In 1610 he entered the service of Prince Henry; charged with adultery (1613); fled England. He became assistant organist at the Antwerp Cathedral (1615), then principal organist (1617); in the Netherlands, became acquainted with the great Dutch organist and composer Sweelinck; both he and Bull exerted considerable influence on the development of contrapuntal keyboard music of the time; Bull also composed many canons and anthems; many works previously attributed to him are now considered doubtful.

bull-roarer. Aerophone consisting of a rhomboid piece of wood attached to a string passed through a small hole, pierced at one end and whirled through the air; the string may be held by the player's hand or on a stick.

Bülow, Hans (Guido) von, b. Dresden, Jan. 8, 1830; d. Cairo, Feb. 12, 1894. At the age of 9 he began to study piano with Friedrich Wieck and theory with Max Eberwein; went to Leipzig; studied law at the univ. and music with Moritz Hauptmann; studied piano with Plaidy; from 1846 to 1848, lived in Stuttgart; made his piano debut there; attended the Univ. of Berlin (1849), joining radical social groups; shortly afterward went to Zurich and met Wagner, who was there in exile. After a year in Switzerland conducting theater music, Bülow proceeded to Weimar; began studies with Liszt; toured Germany and Austria as a pianist (1853); appointed piano dept. head at the Stern Cons. in Berlin (1855–64); married Liszt's natural daughter, Cosima (1857).

In 1864 Bülow was called by Ludwig II to Munich as court pianist and conductor; the King also summoned Wagner from exile. Bülow himself became Wagner's ardent champion; at the Munich Court Opera, he led the 1st performances of *Tristan und Isolde* (1865) and *Die Meistersinger von Nürnberg* (1868). It was about this time that Wagner became intimate with Cosima; after her divorce she married Wagner (1870); despite this betrayal, Bülow continued to conduct Wagner's music; his growing admiration for Brahms cannot be construed as pique. By 1872 Bülow lived in Florence; resumed his career as a pianist; triumphantly successful in England and Russia; during an American tour (1875–76), gave 139 concerts; revisited there in 1889 and 1890. He took over the conductorship in Meiningen (1880–85); married an actress there, Marie Schanzer (1882); conducted the Berlin Phil. (1887–93); a lung ailment forced him to seek a cure in Egypt, but he died shortly after arriving in Cairo.

As a conductor Bülow was an uncompromising disciplinarian, insisting on perfection of detail; was able to project considerable emotional power on the music; one of the 1st conductors to dispense with the use of the score; allegedly could memorize a piano concerto by just reading the score, even while riding in a train. His repertoire focused on Classic and Romantic music, was receptive toward composers of the new school; when Tchaikovsky, unable to secure a performance of his 1st Piano Concerto in Russia, offered the score to Bülow, he accepted it; gave world premiere as soloist in Boston (1875); he also encouraged the young Richard Strauss, giving him his 1st position as conductor. His own works fall into the "Kapellmeister Musik" category: competent, well structured, but devoid of originality. He made masterly transcriptions; annotated and ed. Beethoven's piano sonatas; these eds. were widely used by piano teachers, even though criticism was voiced against liberties taken with some passages and occasional alterations of the original to enhance resonance. Bülow was renowned for his wit and alliterative punning; dubbed Brahms "the 3rd B of music," the 1st being Bach, the 2nd Beethoven. His writings are of elevated literary quality.

Bumbry, Grace (Melzia Ann), b. St. Louis, Jan. 4, 1937. She sang in church choirs as a child; in 1955 began voice studies with Lotte Lehmann; made her professional debut in a London concert (1959); made a spectacular appearance as Amneris at the Paris Opera (1960). Wieland Wagner engaged her to sing Venus in *Tannhäuser* at the Bayreuth Festival; she was the 1st African-American to play the role of a Wagnerian goddess; as a result, there were immediate repercussions, and she was invited by Jacqueline Kennedy to sing at the White House (1961); then undertook a grand tour of U.S. concerts; in 1963 she performed Venus again, at the Chicago Lyric Opera and at Lyons. In 1965 she made her Metropolitan Opera debut in N.Y. as Princess Eboli in *Don Carlos;* sang *Carmen* at the Salzburg Festival under Karajan (1966) and repeated the role at the Metropolitan with extraordinary success. The sensational element of her race was no longer the attraction; the public and the press judged her impartially as a great artist. In 1970 she sang Salome at Covent Garden, London (1970) and again at the Metropolitan Opera (1973); proved ability to perform mezzo-soprano and soprano roles with equal brilliance by singing both Aida and Amneris, and both Venus and Elisabeth.

Burgundian cadence. See ⇒Landini cadence; double leading-tone cadence.

Burgundian school. The ill-defined name of the composition style that formed a natural transition from the ars nova—in which the motet was the crowning achievement—to the great Flemish school, which achieved its luxuriant polyphonic flowering during the late Renaissance. The justification for the term *Burgundian* is that most of the musicians of this school served at the various courts in the duchy that comprised much of the Netherlands and Belgium, as well as Burgundy proper (although no major composer of the school was Burgundian). Dissatisfied music historians offered mostly chauvinistic alternatives: designating the entire 15th century as the Burgundian epoch; 1st Flemish school; *École franco-flamande;* and Italo-Burgundian. Finally, a compromise was achieved by retaining the name Burgundian school, or Burgundian music, to denote the courtly chanson cultivated primarily at the duchy's courts, and by applying the term Netherlands or Flemish school to other forms there: the Mass with a definite cantus firmus and the secular forms of the ballade and virelai. (Would the problem be solved by calling this period the Quattrocento school, after the Italian term for the 1400s?)

The Burgundian school shared features in common with the developing "English style" of polyphonic music; 3ds and 6ths were accepted as consonant harmonic intervals, parallel to the appearance of the fauxbourdon and faburden; tonic and dominant triads became the mainstays of the harmonic texture, particularly in cadences. The major key, described a century before by the pejorative term modus lascivus, now became common, particularly in secular music, although it was still not theoretically sanctioned. The simplification of counterpoint cleared the way for the advent of a new polyphonic school of northern Europe during the Renaissance. The greatest masters of this period were Guillaume Dufay, whose life covered the 1st three-quarters of the century, and Gilles Binchois, whose lifetime embraced the 1st 60 years. Dufay was known as "Cantor illustrissimi ducis burgundie" (court musician of the illustrious Duke of Burgundy), although his tenure at the duchy was relatively brief.

burla (It.). Burlesca. *Burlando,* joking, jesting, romping; *burlesca* (It., jest), short piece, usually for keyboard, in a lighter mood. Bach was one of the 1st to write a burlesca; *burlescamente,* in burlesque style; *burletta* (It., little joke), burlesque; a musical farce; short comic opera; *burlevole,* like a burlesque.

burlesque. Dramatic extravaganza, or farcical travesty of some serious subject, with more or less music; popular type of theatrical entertainment that flourished in the 18th century parallel to the ballad opera; usually included comic recitatives and songs with original texts set to preexisting popular tunes. In the 19th century the genre of burlesque was lifted from its vulgar connotations and became a dignified instrumental or vocal form; R. Strauss wrote a *Burleske* for Piano and Orch., as did Bartók and others. Stravinsky's ballet *Petrouchka* is subtitled *Scènes burlesques.* In the late 19th and 20th century, burlesque devolved into the burlesque show.

burlesque show. Popular type of entertainment, the staple of American musical theater in the 2nd half of the 19th century. Imported from England, the 1st true burlesque show was an exhibition called *British Blondes.* Burlesque differed from the minstrel show in its emphasis on "sensuality," mostly in the form of (relatively) scantily clad young women (hence the synonym "girlie show"); it had much in common with the musicals of the period, which were more like revues and featured chorus lines; striptease was added to the burlesque in the 20th century, one famous club was the subject of a film (*The Night They Raided Minsky's*); the "sexual revolution" of the 1960s killed off the burlesque show.

Burney, Charles, b. Shrewsbury, Apr. 7, 1726; d. Chelsea, Apr. 12, 1814. He was a pupil of Edmund Baker (organist of Chester Cathedral), of his eldest half brother, James, and, from 1744 to 1747, of Arne in London. In 1749 he became organist of St. Dionis-Backchurch and harpsichord player at the subscription concerts in the King's Arms, Cornhill (1749); resigned these posts (1751); appointed organist at King's Lynn, Norfolk (1760), where he planned and began work on his *General History of Music.* He returned to London in 1760; having begun and then exhausted such material as was available for his *History of Music,* visited France, Switzerland, and Italy in 1770 and Germany, the Netherlands, and Austria in 1772; consulted libraries, attended concerts, and formed contacts with the leading musicians and scholars of the period (C. P. E. Bach, Gluck, Hasse, Metastasio, Voltaire et al.). The immediate results of these journeys was *The Present State of Music in France and Italy* (publ. 1771, in diary form) and *The Present State of Music in Germany, the Netherlands* (1773); his *General History of Music* appeared in 4 vols. (1776–89; the 1st volume was publ. concurrently with the complete work of his rival, Sir John Hawkins); from 1806, received a government pension; composed for the stage and small ensembles.

Burns, Robert, b. Alloway, Jan. 25, 1759; d. Dumfries, July 21, 1796. He collected traditional songs, completed fragmentary songs, and wrote lyrics in traditional style, matching them to folk melodies; his major contribution in this field was *The Scots Musical Museum* (6 vols, 1787–1803), co-edited and published by James Johnson (*c.* 1750–1811).

Busoni, Ferruccio (Dante Michelangiolo Benvenuto), b. Empoli, near Florence, Apr. 1, 1866; d. Berlin, July 27, 1924. His father played the clarinet; his mother, Anna Weiss, was an amateur pianist; learned to play the piano as a child; at age 8 played in public in Trieste; gave a piano recital in Vienna when he was 10; included his own compositions. In 1877 the family moved to Graz, where he took piano with W. Mayer; conducted his *Stabat Mater* in Graz at age 12; at 15, accepted to the Accademia Filarmonica in Bologna. In 1886 he went to Leipzig; undertook a profound study of Bach's music; appointed prof. of piano at the Helsingfors Cons. (1889), where among his students was Sibelius.

In 1890 Busoni participated in the Rubinstein Competition in St. Petersburg, winning with his *Konzertstück* for Piano and Orch.; taught piano at the Moscow Cons. (1890–91); accepted the post of prof. at the New England Cons. of Music in Boston (1891–94); made several tours while maintaining his principal residence in Berlin. During the season of 1912–13 he made a triumphant tour of Russia; appointed director of the Liceo Musicale in Bologna (1913). The outbreak of the war in 1914 forced a move to neutral Switzerland, where he stayed in Zurich until 1923; went to Paris, then Berlin, remaining until his death (leaving his opera *Doktor Faust* unfinished). In various cities, at various times, he taught piano in music schools; among his students were Brailowsky, Ganz, Petri, Mitropoulos, and Grainger. He also taught composition; Weill, Jarnach, and Vogel were pupils; exercised great influence on Varèse, who greatly prized his advanced theories of composition.

Busoni was a philosopher of music who tried to formulate a universe of related arts; issued grandiloquent manifestos urging a return to classical ideals in modern forms; sought to establish a unifying link between architecture and composition; his eds. of Bach's works included drawings illustrating the architectonic plan of Bach's fugues. He incorporated his innovations in his grandiose piano work *Fantasia contrappuntistica,* which opens with a prelude based on a Bach chorale and closes with a set of variations on B–A–C–H. In his theoretical writings he proposed 113 different heptatonic modes; suggested the possibility of writing music in exotic scales and subchromatic intervals; expounded ideas in the influential essay *Entwurf einer neuen Aesthetik der Tonkunst* (Trieste, 1907; Eng. trans., 1911); other publications of significance were *Von der Einheit der Musik* (1923; Eng. trans., 1957) and *Über die Möglichkeiten der Oper* (Leipzig, 1926).

Despite Busoni's great innovations in composition and theoretical writing, his legend is kept alive mainly through his sovereign virtuosity as a pianist; introduced a concept of piano sonority as an orch'l medium; indeed, some listeners reported having heard simulations of trumpets and French horns sounded by his hands. The few extant recordings of his playing transmit a measure of the grandeur of his style, but betray a tendency, endemic in his era, towards free treatment of the musical text, despite his preaching an absolute fidelity to the written notes. In performance, Busoni's name appears most often associated with magisterial and eloquent Bach piano transcriptions; his gothic transfiguration of Bach's *Chaconne for Unaccompanied Violin* is a perennial favorite of pianists.

Buxtehude, Dietrich (Didericus), b. probably in Helsingborg, *c.* 1637; d. Lübeck, May 9, 1707. His father, Johannes Buxtehude (1601–74), an organist of German extraction, was active in Holstein, then under Danish rule. After receiving a thorough education, Dietrich became organist at St. Mary's in Helsingborg (1657 or 1658), then at St. Mary's in Helsingør (1660); appointed organist and Werkmeister, succeeding the recently deceased Franz Tunder at St. Mary's in Lübeck (1668); he submitted to the locally customary condition that he marry his predecessor's oldest unmarried daughter, marrying Anna Margaretha that year. He continued a Lübeck tradition of *Abendmusiken*—concerts of organ music and concerted pieces for chorus and orch.—held annually in late afternoon on 5 of the 6 Sundays immediately preceding Christmas. Mattheson and Handel visited Buxtehude in 1703, ostensibly to be considered as his successor; but it may be surmised that the notorious marriage clause deterred them from further negotiations; in 1705 J. S. Bach made a similar pilgrimage, although there is no proof that he left for similar reasons. (Buxtehude's daughter, 1st of 7, eventually married her father's successor, J. C. Schieferdecker, in 1707.) Buxtehude exerted a major influence on younger organists by virtue of the significant role he played in the transitional period of music history from Froberger to the contrapuntal mastery of Bach; though little of his music exists in MS, many composers were known to have made copies for their own study; his major student was Nicolaus Bruhns (1665–97). Buxtehude appears prominently in the painting *Domestic Music Scene* (1674) by Johannes Voorhout.

Byrd, Henry Roeland ("Professor Longhair"), b. Bogalusa, La., Dec. 19, 1918; d. New Orleans, Jan. 30, 1980. He received rudimentary instruction in music from his mother; subsequently developed an individual style of playing influenced by blues, New Orleans, and Caribbean elements; Fats Domino, Huey

Smith, and Allen Toussaint made his style popular outside New Orleans; his erudite synthetic techniques earned him his nickname.

Byrd (Byrde, Bird), William, b. probably in Lincoln, 1543; d. Stondon Massey, Essex, July 4, 1623. He may have studied with Tallis. In 1563 he was appointed organist of Lincoln Cathedral; sworn in as a Gentleman of the Chapel Royal (1568) while remaining at Lincoln Cathedral (to 1572); then assumed his duties, together with Tallis, as organist of the Chapel Royal. In 1575 they were granted a patent by Queen Elizabeth I for the exclusive privilege of printing music and selling music paper for a term of 21 years; the license proved unprofitable; successfully petitioned the Queen to give them an annuity in the form of a lease (1577); after the death of Tallis, the license passed wholly into Byrd's hands (1585).

The earliest publication by Byrd and Tallis was the 1st set of *Cantiones sacrae* for 5 to 8 voices (1575), dedicated to the Queen; works issued by Byrd alone under exclusive license were *Psalmes, Sonets and Songs* (1588), *Songs of Sundrie Natures* (1589), and 2 further vols. of *Cantiones sacrae* (1589, 1591). Many of his keyboard pieces appeared in the MS collection *My Ladye Nevells Booke* (1591) and Francis Tregian's collection *Fitzwilliam Virginal Book* (c. 1612–19); during the winter of 1592–93, moved to Stondon Massey, Essex; subsequently involved in various litigations and disputes concerning the property's ownership; between 1592 and 1595, publ. 3 masses; between 1605 and 1607, brought out 2 vols. of *Gradualia*. His last collection, *Psalmes, Songs and Sonnets*, was publ. in 1611. Byrd was unsurpassed in his time in compositional versatility; his masterly technique is revealed in his ecclesiastical works, instrumental music, madrigals, and solo songs.

Byrds, The. (Leader/guitar/vocal: Jim [later Roger] McGuinn, b. Chicago, Il., July 13, 1942; guitar/vocal: David Crosby, b. Los Angeles, Ca., Aug. 14, 1941; guitar/vocal: Gene Clark, b. Tipton, Mo., Nov. 17 1941; d. Sherman Oaks, Calif., May 24, 1991; bass/vocal: Chris Hillman, b. Los Angeles, Dec. 4, 1942; drums: Mike Clarke, b. New York, June 3, 1944; d. Treasure Island, Fl., Dec. 19, 1993.) Harmonious and inventive American folk-rock group of the 1960s; 1st scored hits with their sunny harmonies on folk-protest songs like Bob Dylan's *Mr. Tambourine Man* (1965), introduced by McGuinn's jangly electric 12-string guitar, and Pete Seeger's *Turn Turn Turn*. They then went psychedelic with extended improvisations on *8 Miles High* (1966), thought to refer to a drug experience (although McGuinn claimed it had to do with an airplane flight). The group dropped to a quartet when Clark left, and then a trio when Crosby bailed out; the lineup metamorphosed further until 1969, when McGuinn led a new country-rock lineup featuring bluegrass guitarist Clarence White (1944–73) until its demise in early 1973.

Byrne, David, b. Dumbarton, Scotland, May 14, 1952. His family moved to the U.S.; he entered the Rhode Island School of Design; developed a determined conviction that dance, song, instrumental music, drama, and cinema were parts of a total art. As his own medium he selected modern dance music and vocal works, stretching in style from folk music to rock; frequented the popular cabarets and dance halls of N.Y., where he absorbed the essence of urban folklore and the rhythmic ways of natural musicians. He joined the group Talking Heads, which specialized in exotic rhythms, especially Caribbean dance tunes, merengue, salsa, bomba, cha-cha, cambia, and the classical samba; as counterweight, his deadpan ironic lyrics and eccentric attitudes offered an alternative to punk and new wave. Much of Byrne's music concocted of these elements is multilingual; one album is titled *Speaking in Tongues;* also favors African sounds, such as Nigerian juju. The titles of his own songs are fashionably nonsensical, e.g., *Stop Making Sense,* which seems to make plenty of sense to his public; an accomplished guitarist, he displays unbounded physical energy, allowing himself a free voice that ranges from a hiccup to a cry, while urging the accompanying chorus to intone such anarchistic declarations as "don't want to be part of your world." His devotion to modern dance is exemplified by the remarkable score he wrote for *The Catherine Wheel,* choreographed by Twyla Tharp; it possesses the widely differing ingredients of new-wave rock and spiritual soul music, masculine and rough while being elegiac and devotional at the same time; the resulting complex incorporates African percussion. Taken as a whole, it represents a synthesis of urban beat and a largely unrelated Eastern rhythm. His 1989 solo album *Rei Momo* consists of songs that, backed by a 16-piece band, combine Latin and pop styles. There is a hypnopompic quality in his inspiration as a composer, asymptotically lying in both reality and irreality, like a half-waking state.

Byzantine chant. The church system of modes and monophony established in the Byzantine Empire of Constantine the Great (created A.D. 330), continuing until the fall of Constantinople to the Turks (1453). Byzantine hymnody is similar to Gregorian chant in its monophonic melos, diatonic structures, and asymmetrical sequences unsubordinated to meter. The development of Byzantine chant can be seen by considering the successive emergence of various types of hymns: *kontakion* in the 6th century, *troparion* in the 7th century, and *kanon* in the 8th century; the essentially syllabic chant began to be adorned with flowery melodic elaborations, but even these embellishments were sung to syllabic verbal formations, having no meaning in themselves. Byzantine music masters outlined a system of modes, or *echoi,* that paralleled the system of modes in the Western church. The language of Byzantine chant from its inception to its decline remained Greek, but there is no formal, tonal, or structural link between the Byzantine *echoi* and the ancient Greek modes; it is, rather, an autochthonous Christian type of hymnody. Its dependence on Oriental rites, particularly Jewish, has been a matter of speculation among scholars.

C (Eng., Ger.; Fr. *ut;* It. *do*). 1. 1st tone and degree of the C-major or C-minor scale; C major has neither sharps nor flats in the key signature. C is *ut,* the syllable assigned to it in Guido d'Arezzo's Latin hymn; in other Romance languages and Russian it is *do.* In our musical C-bound universe, C major is a "white" scale on the piano keyboard (i.e., lacks black keys), beloved of composers as Chopin, Rachmaninoff, and Prokofiev; also the generating point of "white" pandiatonic harmonies. The primacy of C in medieval notation is suggested by the term *clavis signata* attached to middle C. Robert Browning referred to his permanent abode as "the C major of this life." 2. In some theory systems, capital *C* designates the C-major triad, small *c* the C-minor triad. 3. *Middle C* is the note c¹ on the piano keyboard.

Tenor C is the lowest note in the tenor voice, c:

The tenor-C time signature symbol (**c**) indicates 4/4 and is not, as is sometimes suggested, a phonetic sign for the Spanish *cuatro,* Italian *quattuor,* French *quatre,* or English *common time;* actually a relic of the medieval half circle, meaning "imperfect" time, "perfect" time being triple meter. The *cut-time* time signature (**¢**) designates the tempo alla breve (It., quickened), corresponding to 2/2 or 2/4 time.

C clef. Movable clef indicating the position of middle C on the staff; its visual form varies, but a shape suggestive of a Gothic letter *K* is common. The standard types have been soprano, mezzo-soprano, alto, tenor, and baritone (see ⇒"The Clefs"); the tenor clef is still used for bassoon and cello parts; the alto is the standard viola clef; tenor vocal parts are now written on the treble clef, sounding an octave below written pitch; this can be indicated by a double treble clef, an 8 attached to the bottom of a treble clef, or a hybrid superimposition of the C clef onto the treble clef.

C dur (Ger.). C major.

C major. Key of exultant joy, triumphant jubilation, and communal celebration. Beethoven selected C major for his 1st Sym.

and 1st Piano Concerto, as well as the finale of the 5th Sym. The most Olympian of Mozart's syms., No. 41 (the Jupiter Symphony), is also in C major; when Schumann completed his own C-major sym. he was aware of the splendors of Mozart's work, for he remarked to a friend, "Yes, I think it will be a regular *Jupiter.*" Wagner set the prelude to his only comic opera, *Die Meistersinger von Nürnberg,* in C major. The key may be solemn and proclamatory, as in the opening of *Also sprach Zarathustra* of R. Strauss; Scriabin ended his *Poem of Ecstasy* with 53 measures of C major. Prokofiev was fond of C major; his most popular piano concerto, No. 3, goes on for pages of white-key music before modulating; in the fairy tale *Peter and the Wolf* Peter's opening theme is set in undiluted C major; the coda of the march from his *Love for 3 Oranges* ends on a loud C-major triad.

It is natural that pianists should be addicted to C major; it is the 1st scale they practice when beginning their lessons, being freed from bothering with black keys; naturally, pianists who become composers are apt to make full use of their beloved white keys. Multitudes of piano studies of Czerny and Hanon are set in the key. On the other hand, composers of atonal music are apt to exclude C-major associations from their musical vocabulary; Schoenberg used occasional triadic formations, but instances of an unadulterated C-major chord during his atonal and dodecaphonic period are minimal. Yet his disciple Berg did not hesitate to use C major in his atonal masterpiece, *Wozzeck,* in the recitative "Da wieder ist Geld, Marie" (Here is money again, Marie) to underline the vulgar essence of money.

C minor. The key of concentration in solemnity, of philosophical introspection, quite different from its parallel C major; but the 2 are intimately related, not through the traditional cycle of scales but with the Picardy 3rd, in which the minor 3rd of a minor triad is replaced by a major 3rd at the cadence or last movement. No matter how sepulchral, how lugubrious, how morbid a C-minor opening can be, there is always a promise of C major. The most famous sym. in C minor is unquestionably Beethoven's 5th, with its "fateful" opening of 4 notes falling from the dominant to the mediant in C minor; but even if we banish all previous knowledge of the work from our memory, the glorious explosion of a C-major finale seems inevitable; the 1st Sym. of Brahms in C minor reaches a similar apotheosis in the parallel C major finale.

For Mozart the key of C minor had tragic connotations, as heard in the angular convolutions in the opening of the 1st movement of his C-minor Piano Concerto (K.466), followed by chromatic modulations into alien regions. Beethoven's *Pathétique Sonata* is in C minor; the tragic connotations of its slow opening are unmistakable. Schubert's 4th Sym. bore the designation *Tragic* in the MS and is also in this key. Bruckner was possessed by C minor; his 1st, 2nd, and 8th Syms. are all in it; Mahler's 2nd Sym., which rivals in length the interminably revolving syms. of Bruckner, is in C minor.

Scriabin selected the key of C minor for 2 syms., the 2nd and the 3rd, which he named *Divine Poem;* both end in redeeming C major. The most frequently performed Saint-Saëns sym., his 3rd, with organ, is in C minor; but this sym. teleologically directs itself toward a C-major finale, with the organ literally pulling out all the stops. C minor is eminently pianistic: Beethoven's great 3rd Piano Concerto is set in the key, as is the most popular piano concerto of modern times, the 2nd by Rachmaninoff, with its overwhelming C-major finale. *Tod und Verklärung* by R. Strauss starts in C minor, representing the corruption of death, but concluding in triumphant C major, depicting transfiguration.

C moll (Ger.). C minor.

cabaletta (It., rhythmic verse). In 18th-century Italian opera, a cavatinalike form; later, the concluding section of an aria or duet, forming a summary in rapid tempo and with heightened intensity.

Caballé, Montserrat, b. Barcelona, Apr. 12, 1933. She learned to sing at a convent which she attended as a child; at age 8 was accepted at the Cons. del Liceo in Barcelona; her teachers included Conchita Badia; graduated (1953); went to Italy; sang some minor roles. After a successful appearance as Mimi at the Basel Opera, she advanced rapidly, singing Tosca, Aida, Violetta, and other standard opera parts; proved her ability to master difficult modern parts as Salome, Elektra, and Marie; filled guest engagements at the Vienna State Opera; toured in Germany; sang Manon in Mexico City (1964).

She made a triumphant American debut (1965) when summoned to substitute for Marilyn Horne as Lucrezia Borgia at Carnegie Hall in N.Y.; usually restrained N.Y. critics praised her without reservation for the beauty of her voice and expressiveness of her dramatic interpretation. There followed several other American appearances, all highly successful; made her debut at the Metropolitan Opera in N.Y. as Marguerite (1965); continued appearances with the Metropolitan Opera; among her most significant roles were Violetta, Mimi, Aida, Norma, and Donna Anna; created the role of Queen Isabella in Balada's *Cristobal Colón* in Barcelona (1989). In 1964 she married Bernabé Marti, a Spanish tenor (1964); appeared together in joint recitals.

cabaret. Form of nightclub entertainment dating from *c.* 1880 to the 1930s; especially popular in Paris and Berlin. Many cabarets sprang to life, notably the Chat Noir and Le Boeuf sur le Toit (Paris) and Überbrettl (Berlin); French cabaret featured numerous witty and slyly ironic songs and artists such as Yvette Guilbert (1885–1944), who inspired a host of 20th-century *chanteurs* and *chanteuses;* the Berlin cabaret world continued until the Nazi succession in the 1930s, having inspired the political music of Weill, Eisler, and Dessau.

caccia (It., chase, hunt). Italian medieval vocal form originating in Florence in the 14th century. Initially the caccia used words concerned with hunting; often arranged in the form of a canon wherein one voice "chased" another; its popularity grew when renowned composers wrote in this form. It often combined with a madrigal, in a compound form known as the canonic madrigal; motets containing canonic imitation were called *caccia motets. Alla caccia,* in hunting style, so accompanied by horns.

Caccini, Francesca "La Cecchina," b. Florence, Sept. 18, 1587; d. ?, Florence, *c.* 1640. The daughter of Giulio Caccini, she was probably the 1st woman composer of operas; her opera-ballet *La liberazione di Ruggiero dall'isola d'Alcina* was produced at a palace near Florence (1625), and a book of songs from it was publ. that same year. She wrote a *Ballo delle zingare* (Florence, 1615) and performed as one of the gypsies. Her sacred drama *Il martirio di Sant'Agata* was produced in Florence (1622).

Caccini, Giulio "Romano," b. probably in Tivoli, Oct. 8, 1551; d. Florence (buried), Dec. 10, 1618. The father of Francesca Caccini, his nickname "Romano" refers to time spent in Rome. He was a pupil of Scipione delle Palla in singing and lute playing; his 1st compositions were madrigals in traditional polyphonic style, but new ideas generated in the meetings of the Florentine Camerata inspired him to write vocal solos in recitative form (termed *musica in stile rappresentativo*), which he sang with consummate skill to his own theorbo accompaniment; these 1st dramatic compositions were followed by settings of separate scenes written by Bardi, including *Il combattimento d'Apolline col serpente;* next came 2 collaborations, *Euridice* (with Peri, libretto by Rinuccini, 1600) and *Il rapimento di Cefalo* (libretto by Chiabrera, 1600); he later composed his own *Euridice* (1602). He is best known for 2 vols. of *Le nuove musiche,* sets of "madrigals" for solo voice with bass, or monodies (Florence, 1601, 1614); *Amarilli mia bella* (vol. 1) became very popular. From the mid-1560s, he lived in Florence as a singer at the Tuscan court; considered "the father of a new style of music"; Bardi said that he had "attained the goal of perfect music"; but his claim to priority in writing in *stile rappresentativo* is not clearly supported by known chronology.

cachua. Traditional dance of the Quechua people of Peru, usually performed on indigenous flutes with the accompaniment of a small drum, usually in binary meter.

Cacioppo, George (Emanuel), b. Monroe, Mich., Sept. 24, 1927; d. Ann Arbor, Mich., Apr. 4, 1984. He studied with Ross Lee Finney at the Univ. of Mich. (M.A., 1952) and Leon Kirchner in Tanglewood; subsequently cofounded the ONCE Festival concerts in Ann Arbor (1960). His dodecaphonic technique of composition was subject to cautious deviation; experimented with "open end" forms of composition according to aleatory principles, e.g. *Piano Pieces* (1962–70) for any number of pianos, with their realization on tape sounding synchronously or nonsynchronously and lasting any practical (or impractical) length of time.

cacophony (Grk., bad sound). Raucous conglomeration of sound; a pejorative often applied by baffled conservative music critics, whose untutored ears cannot comprehend innovative concords. Thus an English writer reviewing Chopin's 1842 recital described his music as "excruciating cacophony"; Nikita Khrushchev, expressing an opinion on 12-tone music, said, "To you it may be dodecaphony, but to me it's plain cacophony." (*Dodecaphony* and *cacophony* also rhyme in Russian.) Other favorite targets of this accusation were Wagner, Debussy, R. Strauss, Schoenberg, Stravinsky, Bartók, and Prokofiev.

cadence. Generic term denoting the close or ending of a melody, phrase, section, or harmonized movement; many of these categories overlap. The purpose of a cadence (Lat. *cadere,* fall) is to establish the terminal key of a musical composition. At the minimum, a cadence contains the dominant triad followed by the tonic triad (V–I), a type called an *authentic cadence;* a cadence consisting of a subdominant triad leading to a tonic triad (IV–I) is a *plagal cadence* (also amen or oblique); in order to circumscribe the tonality more fully, 3 chords are used: the subdominant, the dominant, and the concluding tonic triads, forming a *full authentic cadence* (complete, full, perfect), which includes all 7 scalar notes, thus outlining the key unambiguously.

To enhance the tonality in a cadence, the 2nd inversion of the tonic triad ($I^6/_4$) is inserted between the subdominant and the dominant triad ($I-IV-I^6/_4-V-I$). Other surrogates of the fundamental chords are commonly adopted; thus the subdominant harmony can be substituted by the use of the 1st inversion of the supertonic triad ($II^6/_3$), sharing the same bass with the subdominant root position triad), in the so-called *Neapolitan cadence*, the subdominant is replaced by a 1st-inversion triad with flattened supertonic and submediant ($\flat II^6/_3$), which then moves through the dominant to the tonic. The dominant triad can be extended by adding a minor 7th, forming the dominant (or major-minor) 7th chord (V^7), or else be replaced by the 1st inversion of the leading-tone triad ($VII^6/_3$), which shares 3 notes of the dominant 7th chord, a substitution to be avoided at the final cadence of a tonal piece.

Non-final cadences that do not end on the tonic are essential to tonal music. The most common is the *half cadence* (imperfect), where the harmonic progression ends without difficulty on the dominant chord, approached from any number of chords. An important type of irregular cadence is the *deceptive cadence* (evaded, interrupted), in which the dominant 7th chord resolves unexpectedly to the submediant triad instead of the tonic triad, thus "deceiving" harmonic expectations. In major keys the deceptive submediant is a minor triad (e.g., in C major, A minor); in minor keys the submediant triad is major (e.g., in C minor, A-flat major). During the ars nova Landini was a consistent user of a cadence now bearing his name (although not his invention); in it the melodic leading tone is diverted to the submediant, a degree below, before resolving into the tonic (7–6–8).

Cadences can be endlessly ornamented—and the final resolution into the tonic chord tantalizingly delayed—creating harmonic suspense. A common delaying device is the insertion of a florid cadenza over the $I^6/_4$ chord, in anticipation of the inevitable arrival of the dominant harmony prior to arriving on the tonic; the concluding tonic triad is then repeated several times, in varying rhythmic figures and harmonic positions; the melody traverses through the 3rd or the 5th note of the tonic before arriving at the final tonic in the melody. It is most instructive to compile a statistical table of the number of such tonic chords in Classic syms; in the resonant C-major coda of Beethoven's 5th Sym., the tonic chord is repeated 15 times, after alternating with the dominant triad; his 8th Sym., 24 times.

While in Classic and Romantic music the final tonic normally consists of no more than 3 distinct notes, 20th-century composers have introduced a pandiatonic cadential type in which the tonic triad is supplemented by the submediant, supertonic, or major 7th in a major key, e.g., the C-major triad blossoms out into a chord of C–E–G–A, C–E–G–B, C–G–E–A–D, or other combinations of those ingredients, excepting the subdominant. (This exclusion could be explained by the absence of a subdominant derived from the fundamental by an 4-octave expansion of the overtone series.) Jazz musicians popularized harmonies with "added notes," culminating in final chords with added 6ths, 7ths (natural or flatted), 9ths, 11ths (often sharped), and 13ths, all technically tonal dissonances, but all sounding to the modern ear as equally or more satisfyingly concordant than undiluted sterile triadic tonic harmony.

cadence (2). 1. Cadenza. 2. The rhythm and/or tempo of a piece.

cadenza (It., cadence; from *cadere*, fall; Ger. *Kadenz*; Rus. *Kadentsia*). 1. In an aria or other accompanied vocal piece, brilliant improvisatory passage for the soloist in free time, usually near the end. During the Golden Age of Opera (18th and early 19th centuries) coloratura singers rolled out formidable lines of trills and arpeggios; composers began to rebel against this sometimes indulgent artistic license; Berlioz, Wagner, and Verdi did everything possible to prohibit such improvisation. By the 20th century the vocal cadenza was extinct per se, introduced solely at a composer's specific direction. 2. Elaborate passage or fantasia at the end of the 1st or last movement of a concerto, played by the solo instrument. In its orig. conception *cadenza* signified an improvisatory interpolation in an instrumental work, intended to display the technical brilliance of the virtuoso performer. Solo cadenzas in classical concertos were rarely written by the composer, but were contributed by performers and other composers; their products were not always compatible with the orig. work's style; emphasis on technical display sometimes jarred with the style of the unornamented original. In general, a well-written cadenza should incorporate the main themes of the orig.; in Romantic concertos, continued sequences and modulations into relative keys are common. Cadenzas are usually announced by a sustained tonic 2nd-inversion chord ($I^6/_4$), with the dominant pedal point in the bass. Most 20th-century composers have abandoned the virtuoso cadenza.

cadenza (It.). 1. Cadence. *Cadenza ad libitum*, the performer chooses whether to perform the written cadenza, substitute another cadenza, or improvise a cadenza.

Cæsura. Cesura.

café chantant (Fr., singing cafe). Predecessor of the cabaret; flourished during the 2nd Empire in Paris between 1852 and 1870; more like a nonsmoking saloon than the cabaret world painted by Toulouse-Lautrec; evolved into larger places of entertainment of which the most celebrated was the Folies-Bergère where increasingly explicit sexuality reigned. The orig. repertoire was dominated by sentimental ballads. When the café chantant was transferred to England it assumed the name music hall; scorned by Victorian society as a shocking institution of sensuality.

Cage, John, (born John Milton Cage, Jr.), Los Angeles, Sept. 5, 1912; d. N.Y., Aug. 12, 1992. He was a "composer whose work and revolutionary ideas profoundly influenced mid-20th-century music." His father was an inventor, his mother active as a clubwoman in California. John Cage, Jr. studied piano with Fannie Dillon and Richard Buhlig in Los Angeles; also with Lazare Levy in Paris; returned to the U.S.; studied composition in Calif. with A. Weiss and Schoenberg, and with Cowell in N.Y. In 1935, he married Xenia Kashevaroff; divorced amicably in 1945. In 1938–39 he served as a dance accompanist in Seattle; also organized a percussion group; expanded upon Cowell's piano technique by initiating a procedure called prepared piano, which consists of placing on the piano strings a variety of objects, such as screws, copper coins, and rubber bands, which alter the tone color or pitch of individual keys; the term and procedure gained acceptance among avant-garde composers.

Cage taught for a season at Chicago's School of Design (1941–42); moved to N.Y.; began a fruitful association with the dancer Merce Cunningham, with whom he collaborated on radically innovatory dance/music works; musical adviser to the Merce Cunningham's dance co. until 1987. Another important association was Cage's his collaboration with the pianist David Tudor, who reified Cage's exotic inspirations where the performer shares creative responsibility. At Black Mountain College, Cage presented a theatrical event historically marked as the earliest Happening (1952).

Cage gradually departed from the pragmatism of precise notation and defined ways of performance, electing to mark creative intentions through graphic symbols and pictorial representations; established the principle of indeterminacy in composition, producing works any 2 performances of which could never be "identical." He became immersed in an earnest study of mushrooms, acquiring formidable expertise and winning a prize in Italy in competition with professionals; became interested in chess, and played demonstration games with Marcel Duchamp, painter turned chessmaster, on a chessboard designed by Lowell Cross to operate on aleatory principles with the aid of a computer and a system of laser rays.

Wishing to achieve ultimate freedom in musical expression, Cage produced a piece entitled *4'33"*, in 3 movements, during which no sounds are intentionally produced; premiered in Woodstock, N.Y. by Tudor, sitting at a piano playing nothing for the length of time eventually stipulated in the title (1952). Another "silent" piece, *0'00"*, "to be played in any way by anyone," was premiered in Tokyo (1962). Any sound produced by the listeners were automatically regarded as integral to the pieces themselves.

Cage was a consummate showman; his exhibitions invariably attracted music lovers and music haters alike, expecting to be exhilarated or outraged. In such public events he departed from musical, unmusical, or even antimusical programs in favor of the exercise of surrealist imagination; the audience might be asked to participate actively, e.g., go out into the street and bring in garbage pails needed for percussion effects, with or without garbage.

To eliminate the subjective element in composition, Cage selected the components of his pieces by dice throwing, using the classic *I Ching* (Book of Changes), an ancient Confucian oracle book, resulting in a non-dodecaphonic system of total serialism, in which all parameters—acoustical pulses, pitch, noise, duration, relative loudness, tempi, combinatory superpositions—were determined by charts based on the thrown dice results. His stage work *Europeras 1 & 2* (1987), designed, staged, and directed by him, is a sophisticated collage built from excerpts from repertory operas selected and manipulated by computer software; composed 3 more *Europeras*.

Cage was a brilliant writer, much influenced by the manner, grammar, syntax, and glorified illogic of Gertrude Stein; among these works are *Silence* (1961), *A Year from Monday* (1967), *M* (1973), *Empty Words* (1979), and *X* (1983). He developed (but did not invent) the poetic genre called mesostic, anchored by a string of letters down the center of the page that spell a name, a word, or even a line of text relating to the poem's content. Mesostic poems were eventually composed by computer, pulverizing the "source material," in turn enhanced by Cage into a semicoherent, highly evocative poetic text. In 1988–89 Cage was Charles Eliot Norton Prof. of Poetry at Harvard Univ., for which he prepared a series of lengthy mesostic poems incorporating the writings of R. B. Fuller, Thoreau, McLuhan, and others. Since Cage's works are multigenetic, the scores are exhibited in galleries and museums; a series of 52 paintings, the New River Watercolors, were completed in 1987 at the Virginia Polytechnic Inst. and State Univ.; shown at the Phillips Collection, Washington, D.C. (1990).

Cahn (Kahn), Sammy (born Samuel Cohen), b. N.Y., June 18, 1913. He played violin in variety shows and organized a dance band; went to Hollywood (1940) and wrote songs with Jule Styne for several films: *Youth on Parade* (1942), *Carolina Blues* (1944), *Anchors Aweigh* (1945), *It Happened in Brooklyn* (1947), *Romance on the High Seas* (1948); in 1955 started a music publ. company. Among his best-known songs are *Bei Mir Bist Du Schoen, I Should Care, 3 Coins in the Fountain, I'll Never Stop Loving You, The Tender Trap,* and *High Hopes* (later J. Kennedy's 1960 campaign song); publ. *The Songwriter's Rhyming Dictionary* (N.Y., 1983).

caisse (Fr.). Drum. *Caisse à timbre, caisse claire,* snare drum; *grosse caisse,* bass drum; *caisse roulante* (rolling drum), tenor drum; *caisse sourde* (muffled drum), tenor drum.

cakewalk. African-American dance in quick 2/4 time; popular in blackface minstrelsy in the latter 19th century, its vogue soon spread all over the world. The cakewalk was used in the walk-around finale in the minstrel show (later vaudeville and burlesque). Its syncopated rhythm is essentially that of ragtime; Debussy included a cakewalk in his piano suite *Children's Corner* with the politically incorrect title of *Golliwog's Cakewalk.*

calando (It.). Decreasing in loudness and (usually) tempo.

Caldwell, Sarah, b. Maryville, Mo., Mar. 6, 1924. She learned to play violin at home; appeared at local events as a child; enrolled in psychology studies at the Univ. of Arkansas; undertook violin study at the New England Cons. with Richard Burgin, concertmaster of the Boston Sym. Orch.; also studied viola with Georges Fourel. In 1947 she was engaged by Boris Goldovsky, head of the opera dept. at the New England Cons., as his assistant, a valuable apprenticeship for her; engaged as head of the Boston Univ. opera workshop (1952); formed the Opera Group in Boston (1958), beginning an extraordinary career in which she displayed peculiar acumen for developing this enterprise with scant musical and financial resources; changed its name to the Opera Co. of Boston (1965); took over a former vaudeville theater. In most of her productions she acted as producer, conductor, administrator, stage director, scenery designer, and publicity manager.

Among her productions were *La Traviata, Falstaff, Benvenuto Cellini* by Berlioz, *Don Quichotte, I Capuletti ed i Montecchi,* and several modern operas, among them *War and Peace, Moses und Aron, Lulu, Intolleranza,* and *Montezuma;* produced the American premieres of Tippett's *The Ice Break* and Zimmermann's *The Soldiers;* induced singers such as Sills,

Horne, Gobbi, Gedda, and Domingo to sing with her co. Critics heaped praise on Caldwell for musicianship, physical and mental energy, imagination, and a sort of genius for opera productions; 1st woman to conduct at the Metropolitan Opera, N.Y. (*La Traviata*, 1976).

call and response. Synonym for antiphony, used in English-speaking religious contexts.

Callas, Maria (born Maria Anna Sofia Cecilia Kalogeropoulos), b. N.Y., Dec. 3, 1923; d. Paris, Sept. 16, 1977. Her father was a Greek immigrant; the family went back to Greece when she was 13; she studied voice at the Royal Academy of Music in Athens with Elvira de Hidalgo; made her debut as Santuzza in a school production of *Cavalleria rusticana* (1938); 1st professional appearance was in a minor role in Suppe's *Boccaccio* at the Royal Opera, Athens at 16; sang her 1st major role (Tosca) there (1942); returned to N.Y. (1945); auditioned for the Metropolitan Opera Co.; offered a contract, decided to go to Italy instead; made local debut in the title role of *La Gioconda* (Verona, 1947).

Callas was encouraged by famous conductor Tullio Serafin, who engaged her to sing Isolde and Aida in various Italian productions; became a member of La Scala, Milan (1951). Handicapped by her excessive weight, she slimmed down (from 210 to 135 pounds); with her classical Greek profile and penetrating eyes, made a striking impression on the stage; as Cherubini's Medea, mesmerized the audience by her dramatic representation of pity and terror. Some critics opined that she lacked a true bel canto quality and had a defective coloratura technique; but her power of interpretation was such that she was soon acknowledged as one of the greatest dramatic singers of the century.

Her professional and personal life was as tempestuous as that of any prima donna's; in 1949, married the Italian industrialist G. B. Meneghini (d. 1981), who became her manager; they separated 10 years later. Her romance with Greek shipping magnate Aristotle Onassis was a recurrent topic of sensational gossip; given to outbursts of temper, regularly made newspaper headlines by walking off the stage following an altercation, or failing to appear altogether at scheduled performances; her inevitable return to the stage was eagerly welcomed by her legion of admirers.

She left La Scala (1958), then returned (1960 to 1962); from 1952 to 1959, sang at Covent Garden, London, the Chicago Lyric Opera, and the Dallas Opera. Perhaps the peak of her career was her brilliant debut at the Metropolitan Opera in N.Y. as Norma (1956); but following a well-publicized disagreement with management, quit the company; returned there as Violetta (1958); left again that year, returning only in 1965 to sing Tosca (with her voice in near ruin). In 1971 she gave a seminar on opera at the Juilliard School of Music; she was enthusiastically received by students (1971); in 1974, went on a concert tour with Giuseppe Di Stefano; by now, any hopes of a theatrical comeback were dashed.

She retired to Europe, but died in Paris suddenly of a heart attack; her body was cremated and her ashes scattered on the Aegean Sea. A radio commentator's characterization of her artistry: "If an orgasm could sing, it would sound like Maria Callas." Pleonastically speaking, she was an incarnation of carnality.

calliope. Circus pipe organ with very loud whistles activated by steam. Raucous and vulgar, it became a musical symbol of the swashbuckling and aggressive late 19th century; went into a limbo of nostalgia with the advent of the modern sophisticated age. Calliope is the Muse of Eloquence.

Calloway, Cab(ell), b. Rochester, N.Y., Dec. 25, 1907; d. Cokebury Village, Del., Nov. 8, 1994). After making his way to Chicago he began his career as a singer and dancer; led the Alabamians (1928–29); took over the Missourians, with which he established himself in N.Y. (1929–30); appeared in the revue *Hot Chocolates* (1929); subsequently led other groups; led house band at the Cotton Club; performed on Broadway and in film. He was a proponent of scat singing, characterized by nonsense syllabification and rapid glossolalia with the melodic line largely submerged under an asymmetric inundation of rhythmic heterophony; he was known as the Hi-de-ho Man; biggest, most enduring hit was *Minnie the Moocher* (1931); compiled the *Hepster's Dictionary,* listing jazz terms (1938).

calma, con (It.). With calm; calmly, tranquilly. *Calmando(si)* (It.), growing calm, becoming tranquil; *calmato,* calming down.

calypso. Popular music of the West Indies, originating in Trinidad in the 1920s. Much influenced by American jazz, its meter is 4/4 with sharp syncopations. The mostly English lyrics often reflect topical subjects. Accompaniment may include drums, maracas, kitchen utensils, and bottles. Calypso is the wellspring from which many Caribbean dance and song genres have arisen.

Calzabigi, Ranieri (Raniero Simone Francesco Maria) di, b. Livorno, Dec. 23, 1714; d. Naples, July 1795. In 1750 he went to Paris; lived in Brussels (1760), Vienna (1761–72), and Pisa (by 1775). He engaged in polemics regarding the relative merits of French and Italian operas; lent energetic support to Gluck's ideas of operatic reform; wrote the librettos of *Orfeo ed Euridice, Alceste,* and *Paride ed Elena* for him; broke with Gluck when the latter handed over one of his librettos to another composer. Salieri and Paisiello were other important composers of his librettos. He publ. *Dissertazione su le poesie drammatiche del Sig. Abate Pietro Metastasio* (1755), a controversial work concerning Metastasio and Hasse.

cambiata (It., changed; Eng., changing note). Formerly, an accented passing tone; now, an auxiliary note placed on the weak beat below or above the principal note and left by a skip of a 3rd in a diatonic melody:

In the 1st half of the example the c² is the cambiata, auxiliary to the overall upper-neighbor motion (d²–e²–d²); in the 2nd half of the example the b² is the cambiata, auxiliary to and interrupting the overall passing-note motion (e²–d²–c²). In either case, a pleasing dissonance against the main harmony is formed. Unlike the echappée, the harmony does not change during this ornament.

camera (It.). Chamber, room, small hall. *Alla camera,* in the style of chamber music; *musica da camera,* chamber music.

Camerata. Historically important Florentine intellectual and artistic group organized by Giovanni de' Bardi (*c.* 1573–87); included aristocratic poets, philosophers, and music lovers. Besides functioning as a musical salon, it hoped to reinstate a "pure" singing manner without accompaniment, as they believed was the practice in ancient Greek drama; it was thus philosophically allied to the Renaissance. Renouncing the florid art of polyphonic writing, the Camerata cultivated lyric melody and homophonic monody, the basis for the imminent genesis of opera.

campana (It.). Bell. *Campanella, -o,* a small bell; *campanology,* science of bell making and ringing.

campestre (It.). Pastoral, rural, idyllic.

canary (Fr. *canarie;* Sp. *canario*). European dance popular in the 16th and 17th centuries, derived from an old Canary Islands dance. Most composers expressed the rhythm in triple (3/8, 3/4) or compound meters (6/4, 6/8); there are rare examples of duple-meter canaries; the music resembles that of the sarabande or passamezzo moderno; Quantz distinguishes the canary from the gigue, which "have the same movement, [by the fact that] the Gigue is played with a short and light bow, but in the Canarie, which consists always of dotted notes, the bowing is short and sharp."

cancan. Lively and mildly salacious Algerian dance; came to Paris *c.* 1830; set in rapid 2/4 time; musically similar to a galop or quadrille. At the height of its popularity under the 2nd Empire, the cancan, as danced by young women on the vaudeville stage, shocked the sensitivities of conservative French audiences because the beskirted choristers kicked their legs above their waists in time and performed leg splits. Early eds. of the *Oxford Companion to Music* characterized the cancan as "a boisterous and latterly indecorous dance," and demurred at further elucidation by stating that "its exact nature is unknown to anyone connected with this *Companion.*" Variants are still performed in stage shows (e.g., the Rockettes at New York's Radio City Music Hall).

cancel. The natural sign (♮); a term current in American schools in the 2nd half of the 19th century.

canción (Sp.). Song, specifically the poetic type of 15th-century Spanish popular ballad but more dignified semantically than the rustic villancico. The verse is usually strophic, the musical setting strictly symmetrical. *Cancionero,* gathered or published collection of Spanish-language songs. Many cancioneros of Spanish Renaissance secular music are preserved in Spanish archives; numerous collections of sacred music survive in Mexico.

cancrizans (Lat., crabwise). Retrogressive, moving backward. See ⇒canon.

canon. 1. Contrapuntal composition of 2 or more voices in which a subject (theme) introduced by 1 voice is strictly imitated by another voice, while the 1st voice continues with a suitable contrapuntal part. The most common type of canon is imitation on the same pitch or an octave higher, called *canon at the (in) unison.* A more difficult imitation is the *canon at the 5th,* which gave rise to the fugue. In a classical fugue the imitating voice is in the dominant, entering either a 5th higher or a 4th lower than the initial subject. The most popular canons are *a*2, but the earliest known canon, the English *Sumer is icumen in,* is *a*4. Examples of canons in 8, 16, 32, and even more voices exist, but the subjects of such canons are inevitably reduced to a series of broken tonic triads, with few auxiliary notes, and so contribute little to the contrapuntal essence of the form.

The canonic subject can be imitated *by augmentation,* doubling the note values of the original theme, or *by diminution,* halving the note values. In *canon by inversion,* the imitating voice inverts the melodic intervals of the subject, therefore producing a mirror image (hence the alternative name "mirror canon"). The most ingenious and difficult type to compose out is the *canon cancrizans,* "crab-walking canon," in which the melody is imitated by its retrograde, i.e., the same melody backwards. (Actually, crabs walk sideways, but the old contrapuntists were apparently not conversant with the ways of crabs.) If the crab-walking voice is inverted, the result is *imitation by retrograde inversion* (or by *inverted retrograde*). Most canons are furnished with an ending by way of an *authentic cadence;* canons that return to the beginning, called *perpetual canons* or *canon ad infinitum,* are popularly known as *rounds.*

Baroque composers enjoyed instructing the performer or the dedicatee of the canon to decide at what particular beat the imitating voice should enter, with a suitable Latin quotation, such as "seek, and ye shall find"; this type is fittingly called a *riddle canon* (or *puzzle canon*). The masters developed fantastic ingenuity in writing canons in all conceivable forms, carefully attending to the proper resolution of dissonance without breaking established rules of harmony and counterpoint. The art of canon suffered an inevitable decline in 20th-century music when dissonances became emancipated and canons could be written at any interval and in any form of inversion, retrograde, or the inversion of the retrograde, without fear of violating harmonic conventions. Yet Schoenberg, Webern, and Bartók wrote well-constructed canons; the technique itself has been revived in larger dodecaphonic contexts. 2. Established repertoire for a particular genre.

canon à l'écrivisse (Fr., canon cancrizans). See ⇒canon.

canon ad infinitum (Lat., infinite canon). See ⇒canon.

canon al rovescio (It, canon cancrizans or by inversion). See ⇒canon.

canon by inversion. See ⇒canon.

canon cancrizans (Lat., crab canon). See ⇒canon.

canon enigmaticus (Lat., riddle canon). See ⇒canon.

canon per arsin et thesin (Lat., canon by upbeat and downbeat). 1. Canon al rovescio (see ⇒canon). 2. Canon where the imitating voice begins 1 beat after the subject begins.

canon per augmentationem (Lat., canon by augmentation). See ⇒canon.

canon per diminutionem (Lat., canon by diminution). See ⇒canon.

canon per recte et retro (Lat.). Canon cancrizans. See ⇒canon.

canon perpetuus (Lat., perpetual canon). See ⇒canon.

canonic imitation. Use of canonic procedure; imitation of the subject in another voice.

Canonical Hours. The Divine Office's schedule of daily prayer within the Roman Catholic Church. Beginning in the morning, the present cycle (adopted in 1971) comprises *Lauds, Terce, Sext, Nones, Vespers,* and *Compline;* the old night Office, *Matins/Vigils,* is now an *Office of Readings,* which may be said at any time.

canso (Prov.). Song.

cantabile (It.). In a songful manner, songfully; achieved currency in the 18th century, when it became an aesthetic criterion of musical beauty. In vocal compositions, cantabile appears redundant (a singer ought to sing "songingly"), but it became aesthetically important in instrumental writing. Often cantabile is part of the movement's rubric, as in Mozart's Andante cantabile *con espressionione* in his A-minor Piano Sonata (K. 310) and Beethoven's Adagio cantabile in his 2nd Violin Sonata (op. 12/2). Romantic composers made increasing use of the term, e.g., Tchaikovsky, in the Andante cantabile of his 1st String Quartet (op. 11). In the piano music of Chopin, Schumann, and others, cantabile is in effect synonymous with legato.

cantando (*cantante;* It.). Singingly; smooth and flowing.

cantata (It., work to be sung). Originally, a solo vocal work with basso continuo; gradually enlarged to include solo voices (singing recitatives, arias, duets, etc.), chorus, and instruments; its development paralleled the emergence of opera and oratorio in the early 17th century. The genre is distinguished from the sonata, "a work to be sounded, or played."

In contrast to the religious oratorio, the cantata 1st appeared as a secular composition, a series of vocal stanzas in strophic form; the cantata later became a religious genre, evolving from German Lutheran 17th-century sacred concertos. A cantata is usually shorter than an oratorio, with a flexible form, so that it can admit lyrical and dramatic elements at will, appearing as a series of extended arias or as an operatic scene with recitatives.

Bach's cantatas contributed decisively to this standardization of the form; at his hands the common type of monodic cantata grew in fervent religious devotion and dramatic grandeur within a polyphonic framework of incomparable mastery. He was not averse to writing cantatas of a topical nature, such as his *Coffee Cantata.* Mozart wrote a Masonic cantata; one aria from it became the Austrian national hymn after World War I. Beginning early in the 19th century the composition of secular cantatas to prechosen texts was prescribed in order to obtain the Prix de Rome at the Paris Cons; since practically all French composers

worth their bouillabaisse competed for the Prix de Rome, the number of prize-winning and prize-losing French cantatas reached tens of thousands of MSS.

In the 20th century the borderline between an oratorio and a cantata became more difficult to trace. Prokofiev's patriotic film suite *Alexander Nevsky* partakes of the features of both oratorio in the solemnity of its invocation and of a cantata in the brevity of its individual numbers. Generally, modern composers resorted to the writing of cantatas when a festive occasion demanded it. Britten wrote 2 particularly memorable cantatas: *Cantata Accademica* (1960) and *Cantata Misericordium* (1963). Bartók's *Cantata Profana* (*The Enchanted Stags,* 1934) is a choral work with orch., with text and musical themes borrowed from Rumanian folklore. Ginastera wrote the highly effective *Cantata para América Mágica,* for Soprano and Percussion Ensemble, to pseudo-Indian texts and based on traditional South American melodies (1961).

cantatore (It.). Singer (male); *cantatrice* (Fr.), singer (female).

cante chico (Sp., small song). Lesser flamenco genre, distinct from the more developed cante jondo.

cante jondo (Andal., deep song; Sp. *cante hondo*). Chief flamenco genre, as opposed to cante chico.

Canteloube (de Malaret), (Marie-) Joseph, b. Annonay, near Tournon, Oct. 21, 1879; d. Grigny, Seine-et-Oise, Nov. 4, 1957. He studied piano in Paris with Amelie Doetzer (a Chopin pupil) and composition with d'Indy at the Schola Cantorum; became an ardent collector of French folk songs and arranged and publ. many of them for voice with instrumental accompaniment; his *Chants d'Auvergne* for Voice and Piano/Orch. (4 vols., 1923–30) are frequently heard. *Anthologie des chants populaires français* (4 vols., 1939–44) is a comprehensive collection of regional folk songs. He also publ. a biography of d'Indy (Paris, 1949).

canti carnascialeschi (It., carnival songs). Polyphonic songs performed at Florentine festivals; flourished during the reign of the Medicis in the 15th century; historically important because of their inclusion of work songs, e.g., those of tailors, scribes, and perfume makers; their form approximates that of the frottola.

canticle (Lat. *canticum,* song). Christian hymns whose texts are psalm-like and taken from the Bible, but not from the Book of Psalms itself; the term is sometimes extended to include non-scriptural texts and certain psalms. Canticles are called major when their texts comes from the New Testament, minor when they come from the Old Testament; parts of the Song of Solomon are also set. Britten composed 5 canticles (1947–75).

canticum (Lat., song). Canticle.

cantiga. Medieval Sp. or Port. song in the vernacular. Secular cantigas were categorized according to content, such as *cantigas de amor* (sung by a woman), *cantigas de amigo, cantigas de escarnio* (satires), and *cantigas de gesta* (narrative and epic songs); religious cantigas were most often sung in praise of the

Virgin Mary. The hypothesis of Arabic origin and their being brought to Spain by the Moors is unfounded; they are probably varieties of villancicos, with some influence from French and Provençal singers. Only 2 sets of cantigas have survived, the 6 secular love songs by the Galician Martin Codax (*c.* 1230) and the voluminous *Cantigas de Santa Maria* (*c.* 1250–80), more than 400 religious songs collected and illuminated by employees of King Alfonso X ("el Sabio," the Wise) of Castile and León.

cantilena (It., little song; Ger. *cantilene;* Fr. *cantilène*). 1. Orig., plainchant. 2. Medieval secular monophony. 3. English polyphonic song genre of the late 13th and 14th centuries, with a strong tendency toward homorhythm, therefore ideal for *contenance angloise* (frequent use of parallel 1st-inversion chords) to flourish; however, more typically free medieval counterpoint is present. 4. Flowing, songlike passage on an instrument (from the 19th century).

cantillation (Lat. *cantillare,* to sing softly). Solo religious chanting in the Jewish service, usually a naturally accented recitative based on the liturgy; the manner of the cantillation is peculiarly rhapsodic and often set in lamentation style.

cantique (Fr.). Hymn.

canto (It.). 1. Melody, song, chant. 2. The soprano, i.e., highest vocal or instrumental part. *Canto a cappella,* sacred song performed without accompaniment; *canto fermo, cantus firmus; canto figurato,* florid polyphony rich in melodic figuration; *col canto* (It., with the melody), accompanists are to follow the solo part's tempo and expression.

cantor (Lat. *cantare,* sing). 1. In the Roman Catholic Church, soloist in the liturgical chants; the chorus is called *schola.* 2. In Lutheran liturgy, the music director (as Bach was in Leipzig). 3. In the Jewish service, the soloist who sings the cantillation.

cantus ambrosianus (Lat.). Ambrosian chant.

cantus choralis (Lat., choral chant). Gregorian chant, when performed as notes of equal length.

cantus firmus (Lat., set song). Fixed or given melody used contrapuntally and to which other parts must be set correctly; historically, the main structural subject, traditionally a plainchant melody, in medieval and Renaissance polyphonic music; originated in the organum of the Parisian Notre Dame school in the 12th century, continuing to appear in Renaissance religious music. In 15th-century masses the cantus firmus melody often came from secular popular songs, notably *L'homme armé.* A cantus firmus was at 1st given to the tenor part and consisted of long notes of more-or-less even duration; but later Renaissance composers used the cantus firmus as thematic material (e.g., Des Prez's *Missa Pange lingua,* a paraphrase mass). In the Baroque the cantus firmus was often placed in the bass, as in organ chorales, where it was played on the pedals.

cantus fractus. Chant with subdivisions of long notes resulting in notes of different metrical value; distinct from *cantus planus* with notes of even values.

cantus gemellus (Lat., twin song; Eng. *gymel*). Type of 2-part writing in parallel 3rds or 6ths,.common during the Middle Ages. The historical relationship to faburden is not clear; the term dates from the 5th century.

cantus gregorianus (Lat.). Gregorian chant.

cantus mensuratus (Lat., measured song). Chant consisting of precisely measured notes, usually of equal duration.

cantus planus (Lat., plain chant). Gregorian chant, when performed as notes of equal length.

cantus transpositus (Lat., transformed song). In the theory of mensural notation, an indication to alter a given meter.

canzona, canzone (It.; pl, *canzone, canzoni*). 1. (usually *canzone*) Song or folk song; a vocal genre. In Dante's time, a lyrical poem consisting of several stanzas; also, settings of such poems. During the Renaissance the canzone melody acquired folk-song traits, becoming the *canzone alla napoletana,* a form of lyric ballad; also applied to a madrigal-style part song (as in *villanella*). 2. (usually *canzona*) Instrumental piece; 1st used for lute or keyboard works; during the Renaissance, was differentiated into the *canzona francese (canzona alla francese)*— in which musical differentiation of sections became significant—and the ensemble genre called *canzona da sonar.* As canzonas became more complex in contrapuntal settings, they soon resembled the ricercar, giving rise to a hybrid form of variation canzona, with a single theme followed by a free fantasy in variation form.

By the Baroque, canzona began to be identified with sonata, i.e., any instrumental piece, without connoting Classic sonata form; some German editors even equated the canzona with the fugue. Such terminological proliferation led to such semantic oversaturation that "canzona" became *passe-partout* for any melodious vocal or instrumental work; thus Tchaikovsky designated the slow movement of his 4th Sym. as "in modo di canzona." With the advent of neoclassicism in the 2nd quarter of the 20th century, the canzona was artificially revived as an instrumental form of a neo-Baroque type.

canzonet (It. *canzonetta,* little canzona). Solo song or part song; a brief instrumental piece.

capo (It.). Chief, head, beginning. *Da capo,* from the beginning.

capo tasto (It. *capotasto, capo,* head fret). 1. Wood, ivory, or metal bar placed on the fingerboard of guitars or lutes to shorten the length of all strings and thus raise their pitch, enabling transposition to other keys without changing fingerings. 2. The nut of stringed instruments having a fingerboard.

cappella (Lat., It., chapel). Chorus; orch.; court or chapel ensemble. The word has been used in 2 senses: as the place of worship itself, and for persons performing in the church service. *A (or alla) cappella* (It., as in chapel), without instrumental accompaniment; mostly polyphonic choral works composed and played according to the restrictions placed on chapel performance, beginning with the Renaissance.

capriccio (It., from Lat. caper, goat; pl. *capricci*). Caprice; a musical caper; originated in the Renaissance as a lively instrumental composition in a free improvisatory style; but the term was interchangeably used with ricercar, canzone, or toccata; in the 19th century the capriccio reasserted its capricious character. Weber, Brahms, Reger, and R. Strauss wrote instrumental capriccios; Bach entitled one of his few programmatic pieces *Capriccio on the Departure of His Beloved Brother;* Beethoven notated his rondo op. 129 (the so-called *Rage Over a Lost Penny*) "quasi un capriccio." Paganini composed 24 capriccios for solo violin, popular in numerous arrangements. The free form of capriccio makes it especially suitable for works of national character: Tchaikovsky wrote a *Capriccio Italien,* Rimsky-Korsakov a *Capriccio Espagnol,* Saint-Saëns a *Capriccio Arabe,* and Strauss an opera he called *Capriccio.* Empowered by neoclassicalism in the 20th century, the term regained its original meaning as a contrapuntal instrumental piece in the manner of a ricercar, e.g., Stravinsky's 1929 *Capriccio* for piano and orch.

Cardew, Cornelius, b. Winchcombe, Gloucester, May 7, 1936; d. London, Dec. 13, 1981. He sang in the chorus at Canterbury Cathedral until puberty; studied composition with Howard Ferguson at the Royal Academy of Music, London (1953–57); in 1957, went to Cologne; worked at the electronic studio as an assistant to Stockhausen (1958–60); returnedto England and organized concerts of experimental music. From 1963 to 1965 he was in Italy; studied with Goffredo Petrassi in Rome; in 1967, appointed to the faculty of the Royal Academy of Music; in 1969, with Michael Parsons and Howard Skempton, organized the Scratch Orch., a heterogeneous group for performances of new music, militantly latitudinarian and disestablishmentarian.

Under the influence of the teachings of Mao Zedong, Cardew renounced his modernistic past as a bourgeois deviation detrimental to pure Marxism; subsequently wrote the ominously titled *Stockhausen Serves Imperialism* (1974); repudiated his own magnum opus, *The Great Learning* (premiered at the 1968 Cheltenham Festival), setting Pound's trans. of Confucius, for a chorus instructed to bang on tapped stones, to whistle and shriek, but never to stoop to actual singing; in the rev. version he appended the slogan, "Apply Marxism-Leninism-Mao Zedong Thought in a living way to the problems of the present" (premiered by the Scratch Orch. in a London Promenade Concert, 1972). Another major works is *3 Winter Potatoes* for piano, assorted concrete sounds, newspapers, balloons, noise, and people working (Focus Opera Group, London, 1968); publ. several pamphlets containing some confusing confutations of Confucius, and a seminal manual, *Scratch Music* (1970); died after being hit by a car.

carezzevole (It.; Fr. *caressant*). Caressingly, soothingly.

carillon (Fr.; Ger. *Glockenspiel*). 1. Set of church bells suspended from a beam in the belfry, operated either by swinging them or playing them from a keyboard, with the keys connected to the clappers of the bells. Modern carillons may have as many as 50 bells and are capable of rapid scales, complete harmonies, and trills. 2. Tune played on this instrument; instrumental piece imitating its effect. 3. Mixture organ stop.

carioca. Brazilian dance in a fast 4/4 time, derived from the rhythm of the samba, originating in the vicinity of Rio de Janeiro (*carioca* is a colloquial term for an inhabitant of that city).

Carissimi, Giacomo, b. Marino, near Rome (baptized), Apr. 18, 1605; d. Rome, Jan. 12, 1674. He was organist at the Cathedral of Tivoli (1625–27); maestro di cappella in the Church of S. Apollinare in Rome (1628 to his death); also served as maestro di cappella of the Collegio Germanico in Rome. A prolific and original composer, he broke with the Palestrina tradition; devoted to perfecting the monodic style, as is evidenced by his highly developed recitative and more varied instrumental accompaniments; his MSS were dispersed and many are lost, but some printed works are still extant: the oratorios (*Jephte*—his masterpiece; *Judicium Salomonis; Jonas; Balthazar*); 2 collections of motets *a*2, 3, and 4 (Rome, 1664, 1667); masses *a*5 and 9 (Cologne, 1663, 1667); cantatas; and individual pieces in several collections.

Carlos, Wendy (born Walter), b. Pawtucket, R.I., Nov. 14, 1939. He played piano as a child; studied music and physics at Brown Univ. and Columbia Univ., where he studied with Ussachevsky; began working with Robert Moog in perfecting the Moog Synthesizer. The result of their experiments with versified tone colors was the record album *Switched On Bach* (1968), which became unexpectedly successful, especially among wide-eyed, susceptible American youth; this was followed by *The Well-Tempered Synthesizer,* engineered entirely by Carlos (1969). At age 32, he accepted his sexual duality, a woman's psyche imprisoned in a man's body; underwent a transsexual operation; on St. Valentine's Day, 1979, officially changed his 1st name from Walter to Wendy. She produced the film scores for *A Clockwork Orange, The Shining,* and *TRON.*

carmen (Lat.). In the Middle Ages, a song, lyric poem, or melody in a vocal composition.

Carmichael, Hoagy (Hoagland Howard), b. Bloomington, Ind., Nov. 22, 1899; d. Rancho Mirage, Calif., Dec. 27, 1981. His ambition was to become a lawyer, graduating from the Ind. Univ. Law School, and played the piano only for relaxation; in 1929, went to Hollywood but failed to obtain work as a musician; working on his own, he organized a swing band and composed for it. He revealed a natural gift for melody; had success with such songs as *Riverboat Shuffle* and *Washboard Blues;* his song *Stardust,* became the foundation of his fame and fortune; other popular tunes included *Georgia On My Mind* (popularized by Ray Charles), *Ivy, I Get Along Without You Very Well, Heart and Soul,* and *In the Cool, Cool, Cool of the Evening,* an Academy Award winner for best movie song (1951); active as a film and television.

Carnegie Hall. Most famous concert hall in the U.S.; opened in N.Y. (1891) through an endowment from the wealthy magnate Andrew Carnegie (1835–1919), who built an immense fortune from successful steel and oil investments. He believed in philanthropic programs to support education and art by establishing financial foundations. Tchaikovsky was the guest conductor at the opening of Carnegie Hall, 1st called Music Hall. The space is beloved by concert performers for its remarkable acoustics, although recent adjustments have been controversial; even so the name Carnegie Hall has assumed a magical aura as a passport to greatness in music. A smaller room was subsequently built adjoining the main hall, known as Carnegie Chamber Hall, then Carnegie Recital Hall, and finally Weill Recital Hall (not referring to the German-American composer).

Carnival (from Lat. *carne*, meat; + *vale*, from Lat. *levare*, abandon). Mardi Gras; Shrove Tuesday; the day before the beginning of Lent. Many composers wrote pieces glorifying the carnival season: Berlioz's orch. *Roman Carnival Overture;* Liszt's 9th Hungarian Rhapsody (subtitled *Carnaval de Pest*); Saint-Saëns's ingenious suite, *The Carnival of the Animals;* and Schumann's piano suite *Carnaval,* subtitled *Scenes mignonnes sur quatre notes.*

carnival songs. Generic description of festive songs that mark Mardi Gras celebrations in Europe and South America. For the Florentine variety, see ⇒canti carnascialeschi.

carol (from med. Fr. *carole,* round dance with singing). Joyous Christmas song; the most common type, established in the 19th century, is in 4-part harmony, symmetrical in structure, and usually in a major key; more ancient forms preserve the style of polyphonic modality.

Carolan (O'Carolan), Turlough, b. near Nobber, County Meath, *c.* 1670; d. near Kilronan, Mar. 25, 1738. He was an itinerant harper who improvised Irish verses and tunes; wrote around 220 orig. tunes; these were publ. in various 18th-century collections of Irish music.

Carpenter, John Alden, b. Park Ridge, Chicago, Feb. 28, 1876; d. Chicago, Apr. 26, 1951. He received his B.A. degree from Harvard Univ. (1897); studied with J. K. Paine; entered his father's shipping supply business; vice president of the firm (1909–36). During his earlier years in business he continued his musical studies in Rome (1906) and in Chicago with Bernard Ziehn (1908–12). After his retirement from business he devoted himself entirely to composing; awarded the Gold Medal of the National Inst. of Arts and Letters (1947). His 1st major work was the orch. suite *Adventures in a Perambulator* (1915); from musical contacts abroad, he absorbed mildly modernistic and impressionistic techniques; applied them to music based on American urban subjects, adding the resources of jazz rhythms; his 1st "American" work was a "jazz pantomime," *Krazy Kat,* after a well-known cartoon character (1921); wrote a large-scale musical panorama, *Skyscrapers* (1926), performed here and abroad, attracting much critical comment as the 1st symphonic work descriptive of modern American civilization (its primary historical significance).

Carreño, (Maria) Teresa, b. Caracas, Dec. 22, 1853; d. N.Y., June 12, 1917. As a child she studied with her father, an excellent pianist; driven from home by a revolution, the family settled in N.Y. (1862); there she studied with Gottschalk; at age 8, gave a public recital in N.Y.; began her career in 1866, after studying with G. Mathias in Paris and Anton Rubinstein; lived mainly in Paris (1866–70), then in England; developed a singing voice, making an unexpected appearance in Edinburgh as the Queen in *Les Huguenots* (1872); returned to the U.S. (1876); studied singing in Boston. For the Bolivar centenary celebration

in Caracas (1885), she appeared as singer, pianist, and composer of the festival hymn (not the same as *Gloria al bravo pueblo,* the national hymn, often misattributed to Carreño). She demonstrated her versatility once more by conducting the opera company managed by her husband, baritone Giovanni Tagliapietra, for 3 weeks; resumed her career as a pianist; made her German debut in Berlin (1889); toured Australia (1907). Her last orch. appearance was with the N.Y. Phil. (1916), her last recital in Havana (1917).

She impressed her audiences by the impetuous élan of her playing, and was known as "the Valkyrie of the piano." She married 4 times: to violinist Emile Sauret (1873), Tagliapietra (1876), pianist Eugene d'Albert (1892–95), and to Arturo Tagliapietra, a younger brother of Giovanni (1902). Early in her career she wrote a number of compositions, some publ.; one of the 1st pianists to play MacDowell's music in public; he studied with her in N.Y. She was greatly venerated in Venezuela; her mortal remains were solemnly transferred from N.Y. and reburied in Caracas (1938).

Carreras, José (Maria), b. Barcelona, Dec. 5, 1946. He studied with Jaime Francesco Puig at the Barcelona Cons.; sang Gennaro opposite Caballé's Lucrezia Borgia in Barcelona (1970); made his Italian debut as Rodolfo in Parma (1971) and his 1st appearance in London, as Leicester in *Maria Stuarda.* He made his N.Y. City Opera debut as Pinkerton (1972); continued to sing there until 1975; made his Metropolitan Opera debut in N.Y. as Cavaradossi (1974), then his 1st appearance at Covent Garden, London, and at La Scala, Milan (1975).

In 1987 he was stricken with acute lymphocytic leukemia; after exhaustive medical treatment, he appeared at a special Barcelona outdoor concert in 1988 for an audience of 150,000; founded the José Carreras Leukemia Foundation. In 1989 he sang in recital in Seattle and N.Y.; returned to opera, singing Jason in Cherubini's *Medea* in Mérida, Spain. He created the title role of Balada's *Cristobal Colón* in Barcelona (1989); among his other fine roles are Alfredo, Edgardo, Nemorino, Don Jose, Andrea Chenier, the Duke of Mantua, and Don Carlos. He is one-third of the "3 Tenors" tour, with Domingo and Pavarotti.

Carte, Richard D'Oyly, b. London, May 3, 1844; d. there, Apr. 3, 1901. He studied at Univ. College in London; wrote an opera, *Dr. Ambrosias,* and songs; turned to music management, representing Gounod, Adelina Patti, and the tenor Mario. He then became interested in light opera and introduced Lecocq's *Giroflé-Girofla,* Offenbach's *La Périchole,* and other popular French operettas to England. His greatest achievement was the launching of comic operas by Gilbert and Sullivan; he commissioned and produced their *Trial by Jury* (Royalty Theatre, 1875); formed a syndicate to stage other works by Gilbert and Sullivan at the London Opéra-Comique Theatre. Dissension within the syndicate induced him to build the Savoy Theatre (1881), celebrated as the home of Gilbert and Sullivan productions, with Carte himself as the leading "Savoyard"; he introduced many improvements in theatrical management, including the replacement of gaslight by electric illumination. He successfully operated the Savoy until his death; the enterprise was continued by his wife (Helen Lenoir) until her death (1913); thereafter by his sons, and finally by his granddaughter; it was disbanded in 1982. In 1887 Carte attempted to establish serious English opera through the building of a special theater (now known as the Palace Theatre), and the production in 1891 of Sullivan's grand opera *Ivanhoe*, followed by commissions to other English composers to write operas; he was in the end unsuccessful.

Carter, Benny (Bennett Lester), b. N.Y., Aug. 8, 1907. He was an autodidact musician; after learning to play the piano as a child, he took up the trumpet and the alto saxophone; worked with various bands (1923–28); gained wide recognition as an arranger; led his own band (1932–34); went to London, where he was an arranger for the BBC dance orch. (1936–38); concurrently active as an instrumentalist, bandleader, and recording artist. Upon his return to the U.S. (1938) he led his own orch. in N.Y. (to 1940); organized a big band and settled in Los Angeles (1942). After 1946 he devoted himself mainly to composing and arranging scores for films and television; worked as an arranger for major jazz singers; made occasional appearances as an instrumentalist in later years, including tours abroad; made a number of recordings; assumed a new role as a teacher, giving lectures at various univs. and colleges. One of the outstanding jazz alto saxophonists of his day, Carter also shone as a trumpeter, trombonist, clarinetist, and pianist.

Carter, Elliott (Cook, Jr.), b. N.Y., Dec. 11, 1908. He came from a well-to-do family; entered Harvard Univ. (1926), majoring in literature and languages; studied piano at the Longy School of Music in Cambridge, Mass; from 1930, devoted himself exclusively to music; studied harmony and counterpoint with Piston and orchestration with E. B. Hill; attended a Harvard course given by Gustav Holst (1932); obtained his M.A. (1932); went to Paris; studied with Nadia Boulanger, receiving a "licence de contrepoint"; also learned mathematics, Latin, and Greek.

In 1935 Carter returned to America; music director of the Ballet Caravan (1937–39); taught music, mathematics, physics, and classical Greek at St. John's College, Annapolis, Md. (1939–41). He taught at the Peabody Cons., Baltimore (1946–48), Columbia Univ. (1948–50), and Yale Univ. (1958–62). He served as American delegate at the East-West Encounter in Tokyo (1962); composer-in-residence at the American Academy in Rome (1963); held a similar post in West Berlin (1964). In 1967–68 he was a professor-at-large at Cornell Univ.; held Guggenheim fellowships (1945, 1950), and the American Prix de Rome (1953). That year, he received 1st prize in the Concours International de Composition in Liège for his 1st String Quartet; received the Pulitzer Prize (among others) for his 2nd String (1960) Quartet; won a 2nd Pulitzer for his 3rd String Quartet (1973); in 1985, awarded the National Medal of Arts.

Carter's reputation as one of the most important American composers grew with every new work; Stravinsky was quoted as saying that his Double Concerto for Harpsichord and Piano was the 1st true American masterpiece. The evolution of his style of composition is marked by his constant preoccupation with taxonomic considerations; the early works are neoclassical; then absorbed the Schoenbergian method of composition with 12 tones; finally developed a system of serial organization in which all parameters, including intervals, metric divisions, rhythm, counterpoint, harmony, and instrumental timbres, become parts of the total conception of each individual work. In this connection he introduced the idea of metric modulation, in which meters and tempos are subtly changed by realigning their

relationships to the note value of the beat (or its subdivision). Furthermore, he assigns to each participating instrument in a polyphonic work a special interval, a distinctive rhythmic figure, and a selective register, so that each part's individuality is clearly outlined, a distribution which is often reinforced by placing the players at a specified distance from one another.

Carter Family, The. (Guitar/autoharp/vocal: "Mother" Maybelle [Addington]; b. Nickelsville, Va., May 10, 1909; d. Nashville, Tenn., Oct. 23, 1978; vocal: A[lvin]. P[leasant]. Delaney Carter, b. Maces Spring, Va., Apr. 15, 1891; d. there, Nov. 7, 1960; autoharp/vocal: Sara Dougherty Carter, b. Flat Woods, Va., July 21, 1898; d. Lodi, Calif., Jan. 8, 1979.) Well-known country singing group, formed in 1927 by A. P. Carter, his wife, and his wife's cousin. Through recordings and radio broadcasts (1927–43) they led the way to the widespread popularity of mountain folk and country music; among their greatest successes were their versions of *Wildwood Flower, It Takes a Worried Man to Sing a Worried Song, Will the Circle Be Unbroken, Wabash Cannonball,* and *Amazing Grace*. In later years Maybelle appeared with her 3 daughters at the Grand Ole Opry in Nashville, where she displayed her talents as a guitarist, autoharpist, and songwriter; made appearances with her son-in-law, Johnny Cash.

Carter, Ron(ald Levin), b. Ferndale, Mich., May 4, 1937. He took up the cello at 10 and the double bass at 17; studied at the Eastman School of Music in Rochester, N.Y. (B.Mus., 1959) and at the Manhattan School of Music in N.Y. (M.Mus., 1961). After playing in the Chico Hamilton quintet, he did stints with Monk, Dolphy, C. Adderley, Monk, and others; a member of Miles Davis's quintet (1963–68); subsequently a member of the N.Y. Jazz Quartet; and led his own quartet and other groups. He has explored bowing techniques in addition to the more typical jazz pizzicato; publ. a method book, *Building a Jazz Bass Line* (1966; 2nd ed., 1970); teaches at the City College, City Univ. of N.Y.; has made a specialty of solo bass performances of Bach.

Caruso, Enrico (Errico), b. Naples, Feb. 25, 1873; d. there, Aug. 2, 1921. He sang Neapolitan ballads by ear; as a youth, applied for a part in *Mignon* at the Teatro Fondo in Naples, but could not follow the orch. at the rehearsal and had to be replaced. His 1st serious study was with Guglielmo Vergine (1891–94); continued with Vincenzo Lombardi; his operatic debut took place at the Teatro Nuovo in Naples (1894); appeared at the Teatro Fondo in *La Traviata, La Favorita,* and *Rigoletto*, later adding *Aida, Faust, Carmen, La Bohème,* and *Tosca.* The decisive turn in his career came when he sang the leading tenor role in the premiere of Giordano's *Fedora* (Teatro Lirico, Milan, 1898) and made a great impression; several important engagements followed, including St. Petersburg and Moscow (1899–1900); Buenos Aires (1899–1903); and the culmination of these successes, the coveted opportunity to sing at La Scala, where he performed in *La Bohème* (1900) and in the premiere of Mascagni's *Le Maschere* (1901).

At the Teatro Lirico in Milan Caruso took part in the 1st performances of Franchetti's *Germania* (1902) and Cilèa's *Adriana Lecouvreur* (1902); in 1902, appeared (with Melba) in Monte Carlo and was re-engaged for 3 more seasons. He made his Covent Garden debut as the Duke in *Rigoletto* (1902) and was immediately successful; gave 25 performances in London, appearing with Melba, Nordica, and Calvé. In 1902–03 he sang in Rome and Lisbon; in 1903, sang in South America and, finally, made his American debut at the Metropolitan Opera, N.Y., in *Rigoletto*. After that memorable occasion, he was connected with the Metropolitan to the end of his life. He traveled with various American opera companies from coast to coast; was in San Francisco when the 1906 earthquake nearly destroyed the city. He achieved his most spectacular successes in America, attended by enormous publicity; in 1907, sang in Germany (Leipzig, Hamburg, Berlin) and in Vienna; was acclaimed there as enthusiastically as elsewhere.

Caruso's fees soared from $2 as a boy in Italy in 1891 to the then fabulous sum of $15,000 for a single performance in Mexico City (1920). He made recordings in the U.S. as early as 1902; his annual income from this source alone was $115,000 at his peak. He excelled in Italian verismo; his Cavaradossi and Canio became models for all singers; sang several French operas. Only the German repertory remained alien to him; his only appearances in Wagnerian roles were 3 performances of *Lohengrin* in Buenos Aires (1901). His voice possessed such natural warmth and great strength in the middle register that as a youth he was thought a baritone. The sustained quality of his bel canto was exceptional; gave superb interpretations of lyrical parts; for dramatic effect he often resorted to the "coup de glotte" (also known as the "Caruso sob"); here the singing gave way to intermittent vocalization without tonal precision; while criticized for such approaches, his characterizations on the stage were overwhelmingly impressive.

Caruso's private life was turbulent; a liaison with Ada Giachetti, by whom he had 2 sons, was painfully resolved by court proceedings in 1912; there were also suits brought against him by 2 American women. In 1906 the celebrated "monkey-house case" (in which he was accused of improper behavior toward a lady while viewing the animals in Central Park) threatened for a time his American success; in 1918 he married Dorothy Park Benjamin of N.Y., over the strong opposition of her father, a rich industrialist.

Although of robust health, Caruso abused it by unceasing activity; stricken with a throat hemorrhage during a performance at the Brooklyn Academy of Music (1920), was able to sing in N.Y. only one more time that year; surgical operations were performed in an effort to arrest a pleurisy; taken to Italy, succumbed to the illness after a period of remission; the operatic world mourned. He was known as a convivial person and a lover of fine food (a brand of macaroni was named after him); possessed a gift for caricature (a collection of his drawings was publ. in N.Y. in 1922).

Casals, Pablo (Pau Carlos Salvador Defilló),

b. Vendrell, Catalonia, Dec. 29, 1876; d. San Juan, Puerto Rico, Oct. 22, 1973. He was the 2nd child of 11, 7 of whom died at birth; legend has it that he barely escaped the same fate when the umbilical cord became entangled around his neck, nearly choking him to death. Another legend, given his support—that he was conceived as Brahms began composing his B-flat-major Quartet, op. 67 and born as Brahms was finishing it—is rendered moot by the quartet's having been completed and performed before Casals was born. But even the ascertainable facts of Casals's life

make it a glorious legend. His father, the parish organist and choirmaster in Vendrell, gave him instruction in piano, violin, and organ; at age 11 he 1st heard the cello performed by a group of traveling musicians, and decided to study the instrument. In 1888 his mother took him to Barcelona; he enrolled in the Escuela Municipal de Música; studied cello, theory, and piano. His prodigious progress as a cellist led him to give a solo recital in Barcelona at 14 (1891); graduated with honors (1893). Albéniz, who heard him play in a cafe, gave him a letter of introduction to Maria Cristina, the Queen Regent, in Madrid; played at informal concerts in the palace; granted a royal stipend for study in composition with Tomas Bretón.

In 1893 Casals entered the Cons. de Musica y Declamación in Madrid; attended chamber music classes of Jesus de Monasterio; played in the newly organized Quartet Soc. there (1894–95). He went to Paris (1895); deprived of his stipend from Spain, earned a living by playing 2nd cello in the orch. of the Folies Marigny; returned to Spain; appointed to the faculty of the Escuela Municipal de Música in Barcelona (1896); principal cellist in the orch. of the Gran Teatro del Liceo; in 1897, appeared as soloist with the Madrid Sym. Orch.; awarded the Order of Carlos III from the Queen; his career as a cello virtuoso was now assured. In 1899 he played at the Crystal Palace in London; played for Queen Victoria at her summer residence in the Isle of Wight; twice appeared as a soloist at a prestigious Lamoureux Concert in Paris, obtaining exceptional public and critical success; toured Spain and the Netherlands with pianist Harold Bauer (1900–1901), made his 1st tour of the U.S. (1901–1902). In 1903 he toured South America; played at the White House for President Theodore Roosevelt (1904); in 1906, met the talented young Portuguese cellist Guilhermina Suggia, who studied with him and began to appear in concerts as Mme. P. Casals-Suggia, although not legally married to him; their liaison dissolved (in 1912; in 1914 he married the American socialite and singer Susan Metcalfe; they separated in 1928 but were not divorced until 1957.

Continuing his brilliant career, Casals organized a concert trio with Cortot (piano) and Thibaud (violin) in Paris (1905); they played together until 1937. He also became interested in conducting; organized the Orquesta Pau Casals in Barcelona and led its 1st concert in 1920; with the outbreak of the Spanish Civil War in 1936, the Orquesta Pau Casals ceased activities. He was an ardent supporter of the Spanish Republican government; after its defeat, vowed never to return to Spain until democracy was restored there; settled in the French village of Prades near the Spanish border; between 1939 and 1942, made sporadic appearances as a cellist in Free France and Switzerland. So fierce was his opposition to the Franco regime that he declined to appear in countries that recognized the totalitarian Spanish government, making an exception to take part in a chamber music concert at the White House (1961) at the invitation of President Kennedy, whom he admired.

In 1950 Casals resumed his career as conductor and cellist at the Prades Festival, organized to commemorate the bicentennial of Bach's death; led the Prades Festivals until 1966; moved to San Juan, Puerto Rico, where his mother was born (1956); an annual Festival Casals was inaugurated (1957). Over the years he energetically pursued pedagogy; led master classes, some televised, in Switzerland, Italy, Berkeley, Calif., and Marlboro, Vt.

Of Casals's compositions, perhaps the most effective is *La sardana* for cello ensemble (1926). His oratorio *El pessebre* (The Manger) was premiered in Acapulco, Mexico (1960), with numerous subsequent performances under his direction; one of his last compositions was the *Himno a las Naciónes Unidas* (Hymn of the United Nations; 1971). In 1957, he married his young pupil Marta Montañez; following his death, she married the pianist Eugene Istomin (1975). Casals did not live to see the liberation of Spain from Franco, but was posth. honored by the democratic Spanish government that followed, with a commemorative postage stamp in honor of his 100th birthday (1976).

Casella, Alfredo, b. Turin, July 25, 1883; d. Rome, Mar. 5, 1947. He began to play the piano at age 4, studying with his mother; went to Paris; studied with Diemer and Fauré at the Paris Cons. (1896); won 1st prize in piano (1899); toured Europe, including Russia; appeared as guest conductor with European orchs., including the Concerts Populaires at the Trocadero (1912); taught piano at the Paris Cons. (1912–15); returned to Rome; appointed prof. of piano at the Accademia di Santa Cecilia, succeeding Sgambati; founded the Soc. Nazionale di Musica (1917), known after 1923 as the Corporazione delle Musiche Nuove (Italian section of the ISCM).

In 1921 Casella made his U.S. debut with the Philadelphia Orch. as composer, conductor, and piano soloist; also appeared in Chicago, Detroit, Cincinnati, Cleveland, and Los Angeles; directed the Boston Pops (1927–29); introduced many modern works; failed to please the public. He received the $3000 1st prize given by the Musical Fund Soc. in Philadelphia (1928) and the Coolidge Prize (1934). In 1938 he returned to Italy, his home until his death. He was a prolific writer on music, publishing articles in Italy, France, Russia, Germany, and America; an enlightened cosmopolitan mind enabled him to penetrate various musical cultures while steadfastly proclaiming his adherence to the ideals of Italian art. In his music, although 1st cultivating extreme modernism, his style evolved into neoclassicism.

Cash, Johnny, b. in a railroad shack near Kingsland, Ark., Feb. 26, 1932. He worked as a water boy in a farmer's family; sang Baptist hymns in church; at age 17 won $5 at a local amateur talent contest. In 1950 he enlisted in the U.S. Air Force, stationed in Germany; learned to play guitar while in the service; returned to the U.S. (1954). In 1955, he began a series of radio appearances and played music circuits specializing in country-western music; soon began composing his own songs, although he never learned to read music. The subjects of his songs include the miseries of common folk as well as prison life; His most popular recordings include *Folsom Prison Blues* (inspired by his brief imprisonment in El Paso on the charge of smuggling tranquilizer tablets from Mexico), *Ring of Fire, A Boy Named Sue, The Ballad of Ira Hayes, Understand Your Man,* and *I Walk the Line.* In 1968 he married well-known country-music singer June Carter Cash (b. Maces Spring, Va., June 23, 1929); his daughter by an earlier marriage, Rosanne Cash (b. Memphis, Tenn., May 24, 1955), is a new-country singer and composer.

cassa (It., drum). Snare drum unless otherwise specified. *Cassa chiara,* snare drum; *cassa grande* (*cassa, gran*), bass drum; *cassa rullante,* tenor drum.

cassation. Late 18th-century multimovement instrumental genre combining the contiguous traits of a serenade, suite, divertimento, and sinfonia. There are many etymological theories regarding the term: from the It. *cassare,* dismiss, release; Fr. *casser,* break; *cassa,* drum; Ger. *gassatim gehen,* perform in the streets (18th century).

castanets (Sp. *Castaña,* chestnut). Pair of small concave pieces of wood or ivory, attached by a cord to a dancer's thumb and forefinger and struck together in time with the music; the name refers to the wood traditionally used for the instrument. In the orch. version of the castanets, the small concave pieces are attached to a central piece of wood ending in a handle, by which they are held and shaken or struck against the palm.

Castelnuovo-Tedesco, Mario, b. Florence, Apr. 3, 1895; d. Los Angeles, Mar. 16, 1968. He studied at the Cherubini Inst. with del Valle (piano) and Pizzetti (composition); began composing at an early age; his 1st organized composition, *Cielo di settembre* for Piano, revealed impressionistic tendencies; wrote the patriotic song *Fuori i barbari* during World War I. He attained considerable eminence in Italy between the 2 wars, his music often heard at European festivals. Political events forced him to leave Italy; settled in the U.S. (1939); became a naturalized citizen (1946). He was active as a film composer in Hollywood but continued to write large amounts of orch. and chamber music. His style is remarkably fluent and adaptable, often reaching rhapsodic eloquence.

castrato (It.; plur. *castratos, castrati*). Castrated adult male singer with soprano or alto voice. Young males were castrated at puberty to inhibit the maturation of their sexual glands, thereby preserving their high voices; this barbarous practice originated in the 16th century, shortly before the development of opera, which demanded "angelic" voices in mythological roles such as Orpheus. By the 18th century castratos commanded large fees to sing opera; Handel wrote parts for the famous castratos Senesino and Nicolini; perhaps the most celebrated castrato singer was Carlo Broschi, called Farinelli. After 1750 the production of castrato singers became a covert affair, and was completely forbidden by the latter 19th century. The last castrato singer was Alessandro Moreschi (1858–1922), known as the "Angelo di Roma" because of his celestially pure voice; recordings of Moreschi's singing (1903) have survived.

Catalani, Alfredo, b. Lucca, June 19, 1854; d. Milan, Aug. 7, 1893. He studied music with his father, a church organist; in 1872 studied with Fortunato Magi and Bazzini at the Inst. Musicale Pacini in Lucca; went to Paris, where he attended classes of Bazin (composition) and Marmontel (piano). He returned to Italy (1873); succeeded Ponchielli as prof. of composition at the Milan Cons. (1886); became acquainted with Boito, who encouraged him, and young Toscanini, who championed his music. Catalani tried to create a Wagnerian counterpart in Italian opera, choosing librettos with fantastic subjects suitable for dramatic action. After many unsuccessful productions he finally achieved his ideal in *La Wally* (1893), but died of tuberculosis a year later.

catcalls. Derogatory hissing at a performance. The term is unfair to cats, who never meow derogatorily.

catch. Popular type of English social song for 3 or more male parts, in the form of a canon or round; thus the need for each singer to "catch" or take up his part at the right moment. The word *catch* is probably derived from the Italian *caccia*, or chase, because one voice "chases" another as in a canon. Catches were favored in the aristocratic clubs of London in the late 16th, 17th, and 18th centuries, along with the glee; such clubs commissioned celebrated composers to write catches for them, which were collected and publ. in anthologies (by Ravenscroft, Hilton, Benson & Playford, Walsh & Hare). Purcell, Blow, and Handel were among those who composed catches. Among the earliest catches was *Three Blind Mice;* another begins with the famous line, "Catch that catch can." Texts often contained humorous allusions to topical events, puns, and even mild obscenities, at times scatological in character.

catgut. Common but misleading name for gut strings, which are generally made from lamb intestines.

cats. 1. *Katzenmusik* (Ger., cat music), ultimate term of opprobrium used by ailurophobic critics, thus alienating cat lovers. In his singing ballet *L'enfant et les sortilèges,* Ravel introduces an amorous baritone tomcat and a nubile mezzo-soprano kitten singing a fine atonal duet. In a modern piece, *Anatomy of Melancholy,* an anonymous composer scores a part for a cat, in which the cat player is instructed to pull the animal's tail at climactic moments. 2. 20th-century Americanism for musicians in popular bands; by extension, applicable to any human, mostly of the masculine gender; a bantering but friendly, even affectionate term.

Caturla, Alejandro García, b. Remedios, Mar. 7, 1906; d. assassinated there, Nov. 12, 1940. He studied with Pedro Sanjuán in Havana, then with Nadia Boulanger in Paris (1928); founder (1932) and conductor of the Orquesta de Conciertos de Caibarién in Cuba; served as district judge in Remedios. His works were performed in Cuba, Europe, and the U.S. In Caturla's music, primitive Afro-Cuban rhythms and themes are treated with modern techniques and a free utilization of dissonance, as in *Bembé* for 14 Instruments (1929); *Dos poemas Afro-Cubanos* for Voice and Piano (1929; also orch.); *Yambo-O,* Afro-Cuban oratorio (1931); *Rumba for Orch.* (1931); *Primera suite cubana* for Piano and 8 Wind Instruments (1930); *Manita en el Suelo,* "mitologia bufa Afro-Cubana" for Narrator, Marionettes, and Chamber Orch., to a text by Alejo Carpentier (1934).

Cavalli (Caletti), Pier Francesco, b. Crema, Feb. 14, 1602; d. Venice, Jan. 14, 1676. His father was Giovanni Battista Caletti detto Bruni, maestro di cappella at the Cathedral in Crema, who gave him his 1st musical instruction; as a youth, sang under his father's direction in the Cathedral. The Venetian nobleman Federico Cavalli, mayor of Crema, took him to Venice for further musical training; as was customary, he adopted his sponsor's surname. In 1616 he entered the choir of S. Marco in Venice, beginning a lifelong association; sang there under Monteverdi; organist at Ss. Giovanni e Paolo (1620–30); turned his attention to opera, organizing a company at the Teatro San Cassiano; his 1st opera, *Le nozze di Teti e di Peleo,* was performed there (1639); 9 more followed within the next decade.

In 1639 Cavalli successfully competed against 3 others for the post of 2nd organist at S. Marco; in 1660 Cardinal Mazarin invited him to Paris; he presented a restructured version of his *Serse* for the marriage festivities of Louis XIV and Maria Theresa; composed *Ercole amante,* premiered at the Tuileries (1662). He returned to Venice (1662); officially appointed 1st organist at S. Marco (1665); became maestro di cappella (1668). After Monteverdi, Cavalli stands as one of the most important Venetian composers of opera in the mid-17th century, as well as sacred music; several works are available in modern eds.

cavata (It., extraction). 1. Operatic arioso epitomizing the sentiment of a scene, in regular meter and placed at the end of a recitative (*recitativo con cavata*); evolved into the *cavatina,* a short song or operatic aria without a 2nd section or da capo, often preceded by an instrumental introduction and concluding with a cabaletta.

CD. See ⇒Compact disc.

CD-ROM (Compact Disc with Read-Only Memory). System of data storage that preserves an impressive amount of aural, written, and/or visual information on a CD-sized disk. The CD-ROM may be used on a properly equipped personal computer or through a MIDI into a synthesizer or sampler in order to access a large number of prerecorded sounds.

Cecilianism (after St. Cecilia, patron saint of music). Reform movement in Roman Catholic church music, intended to restore choral polyphony in all its purity, as opposed to romantic treatment of religious themes. The Cecilian movement had its inception in Germany in the 19th century, where numerous choral organizations were founded; Cecilianism later spread to the U.S., cultivated mostly by German emigré societies and their publ.

cedendo (It.). Gradually growing slower, receding. *Céder* (Fr.), recede, slow down; *cédez* (Fr.), go slower.

celesta (Fr. *Céleste,* heavenly). Keyboard instrument built on the principle of a glockenspiel, with keys activating hammers to strike the steel bars in its mechanism; once limited to 4 octaves, has been expanded to 5; has a soft ingratiating sound, hence the name given it by its Parisian inventor, Auguste Mustel (1886). Tchaikovsky discovered the celesta during his Parisian sojourn; was so enchanted with it that he warned his publisher not to tell other composers about its existence, specifically Rimsky-Korsakov and Glazunov; Tchaikovsky himself included a celesta in the movement describing the sugar-plum fairy in *The Nutcracker.* Another type of celesta, dating from the 1860s, is the *dulcitone,* which uses tuning forks instead of steel bars; it was invented by Mustel's father.

cell. Small group of notes, indicative of pitch or rhythm, serving as an organizing device; usually applied to atonal or dodecaphonic music.

cello (It.; plur. *cellos, celli*). Standard abbrev. of violoncello.

cembalo (It.). Harpsichord; later, pianoforte, clavier; formerly, dulcimer; often used interchangeably with basso continuo.

cencerros (Sp., lead-mule bell). Cuban cowbells, popular in Latin American dance music and used by Messiaen.

cercar la nota (It., seek the note). Vocal practice, in which the principal note is reached through a soft anticipatory grace note, to achieve a better projection of the voice.

Cerha, Friedrich, b. Vienna, Feb. 17, 1926. He studied violin with Vasa Prihoda and composition with Alfred Uhl at the Vienna Academy of Music (1946–51); studied musicology and philosophy at the Univ. of Vienna (Ph.D., 1950); upon graduation, became active in the modernistic movement as a violinist, conductor, and composer; with Schwertsik, organized the Viennese new music ensemble Die Reihe (1958); in 1960, became director of the electronic-music studio and a lecturer at the Vienna Academy, becoming a prof. in 1969. He was commissioned by Berg's publisher to complete the 3rd act of *Lulu* (1962–74), 1st performed at the Paris Opéra (1979). His own music pursues the aim of "atomization of thematic materials" as a means toward total integration of infinitesimal compositional quantities, with minimal variations of successive temporal units; his best-known work is the opera *Baal,* after Brecht (1973–81).

Ces (Ger.). C flat.

Cesti, Antonio (born Pietro), b. Arezzo (baptized), Aug. 5, 1623; d. Florence, Oct. 14, 1669. Although reference works give his 1st name as Marc Antonio, this is incorrect. He was a choirboy in Arezzo before joining the Franciscan order in Volterra (1637), adopting the name Antonio; received the patronage of the Medicis; served novitiate at S. Croce in Florence; assigned to the Arezzo monastery; reportedly received his musical training from Abbatini in Rome and Citta di Castello (1637–40) and Carissimi in Rome (1640–45); while in Volterra, received the patronage of the Medici family.

Cesti's 1st opera, *Orontea* (Venice, 1649), was highly successful; active at the court of Archduke Ferdinand Karl in Innsbruck (1652–57); sang tenor in the Papal Choir in Rome (1659–60). After being released from his vows, he quit the Papal Choir, intending to return to court duties in Innsbruck; in spite of a threat of excommunication, went to Innsbruck until the death of the Archduke (1665) led to the removal of its musical entourage to Vienna. Cesti was made assistant Kapellmeister (1666); returned to Italy (1668); served as maestro di cappella at the Tuscan court in Florence during the last years of his life. He was one of the most important composers of secular vocal music of his time; composed mostly operas and cantatas; his most notorious work was the overblown last opera, *Il pomo d'oro* (1668).

cesura (caesura; from Lat. *caedere,* cut). Dividing line between 2 melodic and rhythmical phrases within a period; called masculine or feminine dependent upon its occurring after a strong or weak beat.

Chabrier, (Alexis-) Emmanuel, b. Ambert, Puy de Dome, Jan. 18, 1841; d. Paris, Sept. 13, 1894. He studied law in Paris (1858–61); studied composition, piano, and violin; served in the government from 1861; cultivated his musical tastes; with Duparc, d'Indy, and others, formed a private group of music lovers; admired Wagner enthusiastically. He began to compose in earnest, producing the light operas *L'Etoile* (1877) and *Une éducation manquée* (1879); went to Germany with Duparc to hear Wagner's operas (1879); returned to Paris; publ. piano pieces; traveled to Spain; the fruit of this journey was his most famous work, the rhapsody *España* (1883), which produced a sensation when premiered by Lamoureux (1884); another "Spanish" work was the *Habanera* for Piano (1885). Chabrier served as chorus master for Lamoureux; this helped develop his knowledge of vocal writing; wrote the operas *Gwendoline* (1886), *Le Roi malgré lui* (1887), and *Briséïs* (incomplete; premiered 1897; staged 1899). In his operas he aimed for a grand style, oscillating between passionate Wagnerianism and more conventional French theater music; although enjoying a succès d'estime, they never became popular; more attention has been paid to them recently.

cha-cha. Latin American dance in an insistent binary rhythm, a variant of the mambo; sometimes called more emphatically *cha-cha-cha;* it had a wave of popularity in Europe and the U.S. in the 1950s.

chaconne (Fr.; Sp. *chacona;* It. *ciaccona*). 1. Spanish dance in triple meter, imported from Latin America in the early 17th century. 2. Instrumental piece, derived from the dance of the same name, consisting of a series of variations above a ground bass not over 8 measures in length, in 3/4 time and slow tempo; a contrapuntal genre consisting of a series of variations on a theme in a definite harmonic progression. The chaconne is close in structure to and often difficult to distinguish from the passacaglia.

Chaliapin, Feodor (Ivanovich), b. Kazan, Feb. 13, 1873; d. Paris, Apr. 12, 1938. He was of humble origin; at age 10, apprenticed to a cobbler; at 14, got a job singing in a chorus in a traveling opera co.; his companion was Maxim Gorky, who also sang in a chorus; together they made their way through the Russian provinces, often forced to walk the railroad tracks when they could not afford the fare. Chaliapin's wanderings brought him to Tiflis, in the Caucasus, where he was introduced to singing teacher Dimitri Usatov (1847–1913), who immediately recognized his extraordinary gifts; taught him free of charge, helping him besides with board and lodgings. In 1894 Chaliapin was employed in a summer opera company in St. Petersburg; shortly afterward, was accepted at the Imperial Opera; sang in Moscow with a private opera company (1896); produced a great impression by his dramatic interpretation of the bass parts in Russian operas; gave numerous solo concerts, which sold out almost immediately; young music lovers would stand in line all night long to obtain tickets.

Chaliapin's 1st engagement outside Russia was in 1901, at La Scala in Milan, singing the title role in Boito's *Mefistofele;* returned to La Scala (1904, 1908). In 1907 he made his American debut at the Metropolitan Opera, N.Y., as Mefistofele; then sang Méphistophélès in *Faust* and Leporello (1908); returned to America (1921) and sang one of his greatest roles, Boris Godunov; continued to appear at the Metropolitan until 1929; sang Russian roles at Covent Garden, London (1913); returned to Russia in 1914, remaining there during World War I and the Revolution. He was named a People's Artist by the Soviet government, but this title was withdrawn after he emigrated to Paris (1922), where he remained until his death, except for appearances in England and America.

The negative Soviet attitude towards Chaliapin after 1922 gradually changed to recognition of his stature as a great Russian artist who elevated the art of Russian opera to the summit of expressive perfection. He was one of the greatest singing actors of all time, dominating every scene in which he appeared; to the last, he never failed to move audiences, even though his vocal powers had declined considerably during his last years. In addition to his famed interpretations of Boris Godunov, Méphistophélès, and the buffo roles of Don Basilio and Leporello, he played the title role in the film *Don Quixote;* his last American recital took place in N.Y. (1935).

chalumeau. 1. Single-reed, cylindrical-bore woodwind, related to the clarinet; developed in the 17th century; orig. had no keys, which were added in the 18th century. While many view the chalumeau as the progenitor of the clarinet, the 2 instruments coexisted in the 18th century; the chalumeau was stronger in the lowest register than the clarinet of the era. By the end of the century the chalumeau had been superseded, but not before influencing the construction of the bass clarinet. 2. The lowest register of the clarinet.

chamber music. Vocal or instrumental music suitable for performance in a room or small hall; especially, quartets and similar concerted pieces for solo instrument ensembles. *Chamber opera,* opera suitable for chamber performance, with limited numbers of singers accompanied by a chamber orch.; *chamber orchestra,* small orch. with reduced string section and fewer winds and percussion; *chamber symphony,* work for a smaller orch., usually of lesser musical scale.

chance music. See ⇒chance operations; aleatory.

chance operations. Practice of composing music via chance means (throwing dice, consulting the *I Ching,* making use of random-number generators, etc.), resulting in works literally devoid of compositional taste or intention; pursued primarily by Cage.

change. 1. Harmonic modulation. 2. Vocal mutation. 3. Any melodic phrase or figure played on a chime of bells.

change-ringing. The art and practice of ringing a peal of bells in varying and systematic order.

changing note. Cambiata.

chanson (Fr.). 1. Song; specifically, the polyphonic type cultivated during the 15th and 16th centuries in France and the Netherlands; usually strophic in structure, with the same melody or music repeated for each stanza. 2. French equivalent to the lied; also called mélodie. 3. French popular song genres from the 17th century on.

chanson de geste (Fr., heroic song). Medieval lyric genre, of which *Chanson de Roland* is the most famous example; fantastically long, they could number more than 20,000 lines in an unchanging meter; sung to monotonous melodic phrases by professional minstrels; improvisation was an integral feature of the chanson de gests. Some melodies are preserved through quotations in *Jeu de Robin et Marion* by Adam de la Halle and *Aucassin et Nicolette.*

chansonette (Fr., small song). French song of a light nature, often containing scabrous verses; flourished in France in the 19th century in cafés chantants.

chant. 1. Sacred song. 2. Anglican song, adapted to canticles and psalms, consisting of 7 harmonized measures, where the time-value of the single note constituting the 1st and 4th measures is lengthened or shortened to fit the words, while the others are sung in strict time. Each of the 2 divisions of the chant (3 and 4 measures, respectively) begins on a reciting-note and ends with a final. 3. Gregorian song, with a melody repeated with the several verses of biblical prose text; it has 5 divisions: (1) the intonation, (2) the 1st dominant, or reciting-note, (3) the mediation, (4) the 2nd dominant, or reciting-note, and (5) the final. 4. (Fr.). Song; singing; melody; tune. 5. Vocal part, as distinguished from the accompaniment.

chanter. The melody-pipe of the bagpipe.

chanteur (Fr.). Singer (male). *Chanteuse,* singer (female).

chantey (chanty). Shanty.

chapel (Fr. *chapelle*). 1. Church building or assembly room where congregants worship. 2. Company of musicians attached to the establishment of any distinguished personage, e.g., the Chapel Royal of England.

character piece (Ger. *Charakterstück*). Musical genre cultivated in the 19th century, usually applied to piano pieces and furnished with titles suggesting a mood, impression, scene, event, landscape, or pictorial subject; typical titles are bagatelles, impromptus, *moments musicaux, Lieder ohne Worte,* and *Albumblätter.* Schumann composed character pieces under the titles *Fantasiestücke, Nachtstücke, Kinderszenen, Waldszenen,* and *Carnaval.* The genre was anticipated by Couperin and Rameau, who used such descriptive titles as *Les langueurs-tendres, La triomphante,* etc. Character pieces are usually short, symmetrically constructed, and not difficult to perform. Modern composers abandoned the German model, but were not averse to using imaginative titles, as illustrated by Prokofiev's *Visions fugitives* and Scriabin's mystical titles to some of his short piano pieces: *Flammes sombres, Desir,* and *Poème satanique.*

charango (Sp.). Peruvian guitar, usually with 10 strings, many of which are tuned to the same note for greater sonority.

charivari. Raucous and cacophonous serenade calculated to ridicule or upset a pompous official or a honeymooning couple; a type of entertainment that arose in France in medieval times. The word itself is onomatopoeic; its etymology is uncertain; its pronunciation is "shivaree."

Charles, Ray (born Ray Charles Robinson), b. Albany, Ga., Sept. 23, 1930. He was born to impoverished parents, stricken with glaucoma, and totally blind at age 6; nevertheless, began playing the piano; was sent to the St. Augustine (Fla.) School for the Deaf and Blind; received instruction in composition and Braille musical notation; learned to play the trumpet, alto saxophone, clarinet, and organ. He quit school at 15 and formed his own combo; settled in Seattle; acquired a popular following there. Shortening his name to Ray Charles to avoid confusion with boxer Sugar Ray Robinson, he scored his 1st hit recording with *Baby Let Me Hold Your Hand* (1951), followed by *I've Got a Woman* (1955), *Hallelujah, I Love Her So* (1956), *The Right Time* (1959), *What'd I Say* (1959), *Hit the Road Jack* (1961), *I Mint Julep* (1961), and *I Can't Stop Loving You* (1962); among his notable albums were *The Genius of Charles* (1960) and *Modern Sounds in Country and Western Music* (1962). He tours widely and frequently performs on radio and television.

Charleston (after city in South Carolina). Syncopated binary dance tune, orig. from the African-American revue *Runnin' Wild* (1923); launched one of the most obsessive dance fads in American history. The dance involves twisting knees and heels while hands and arms follow in alternation.

Charpentier, Gustave, b. Dieuze, Lorraine, June 25, 1860; d. Paris, Feb. 18, 1956. He studied at the Paris Cons. (1881–87); pupil of Massart (violin), Pessard (harmony), and Massenet (composition); received the Grand Prix de Rome in 1887 with the cantata *Didon*. He evinced great interest in social problems of the working classes; formed the society L'Oeuvre de Mimi Pinson (1900), devoted to the welfare of the poor; reorganized during World War I as an auxiliary Red Cross society. He owes his fame to 1 amazingly successful opera, *Louise,* a *roman musical* to his own libretto, produced at the Opéra-Comique in Paris (1900). The score is written in the spirit of naturalism, including such realistic touches as the street cries of Paris vendors. Its success was immediate; entered the operatic repertory all over the world; its U.S. premiere at the Metropolitan Opera, N.Y., took place in 1921. Encouraged by this success, Charpentier wrote a sequel, *Julien* (1913), but it failed to arouse interest comparable to that of *Louise.*

Charpentier, Marc-Antoine, b. Paris, *c.* 1645–50; d. there, Feb. 24, 1704. He studied with Carissimi in Italy; returned to Paris; active as composer to Molière's acting troupe; also in the service of Marie de Lorraine, the Duchess of Guise, later serving as her *haute-contre* and *maître de musique* until her death (1688); also served the grand Dauphin. Louis XIV granted him a pension (1683); taught music to Philippe, Duke of Chartres; *maître de musique* to the Jesuit church of St. Louis; held that post at Sainte-Chapelle (1698–1704). He was one of the leading French composers of his era, distinguishing himself in both sacred and secular works. His extensive output of sacred music includes masses, Magnificats, Te Deums, antiphons, hymns, psalms, and over 200 motets, many of which are akin to oratorios; also composed sacred instrumental works. He wrote some 30 works for the stage, including the *tragédies lyriques David et Jonathas* (1688) and *Medée* (1693); cantatas, overtures, ballet airs, pastorals, incidental pieces, *airs serieux, airs a boire;* also secular instrumental pieces, including dances for strings.

Chausson, (Amedee-) Ernest, b. Paris, Jan. 20, 1855; d. Limay, near Mantes, June 10, 1899 (in a bicycle accident). Possessing private means, he was an amateur in the best sense; studied with Massenet at the Paris Cons.; took private lessons with Franck. The influence of Wagner as well as that of Franck determined the harmonic and melodic elements in his music; despite these derivations, he established an individual style, tense in its chromaticism and somewhat flamboyant in its melodic expansion; its French character is unmistakable in the elegance and clarity of its structural plan. He was active in Parisian musical society; was secretary of the Soc. Nationale de Musique; composed relatively little music, but is known for his *Poème* for Violin and Orch., *Poème de l'amour et de la mer* for Voice and Orch., and the Concerto for Piano, Violin, and String Quartet.

Chávez (y Ramírez), Carlos (Antonio de Padua), b. Calzada de Tacube, near Mexico City, June 13, 1899; d. Mexico City, Aug. 2, 1978. He studied piano as a child with Pedro Luis Ogazon; studied harmony with Juan B. Fuentes and Manuel Ponce; began to composing very early in life; wrote a sym. at age 16; made effective piano arrangements of popular Mexican songs and wrote many piano pieces of his own. His 1st important work was a ballet on an Aztec subject, *El fuego nuevo* (1921); historical and national Mexican subjects remained the primary source of inspiration in many of his works, but he rarely resorted to literal quotations from authentic folk melodies; sublimated and distilled Mexican melorhythms, resulting in a sui generis style of composition.

In 1922–23 Chávez traveled in France, Austria, and Germany, becoming acquainted with new developments in composition; influences from this period is reflected in his abstract titles, e.g., *Aspectos, Energia, Unidad;* returned to Mexico; organized and conducted concerts of new music, giving the 1st Mexican performances of works by Stravinsky, Schoenberg, Satie, Milhaud, and Varèse; lived in N.Y. (1926–28); organized the Orquesta Sinfónica de Mexico, which he conducted (1928–49); its repertoire included 82 1st performances of Mexican works, many commissioned and encouraged by him; Revueltas was among them. During his tenure as conductor Chávez engaged a number of famous foreign musicians as guest conductors, as well as numerous soloists. In 1948 the orch. was renamed Orquesta Sinfónica Nacional; it remains a permanent institution. He directed the Cons. Nacional de Música (1928–33, 1934); general director of the Inst. Nacional de Bellas Artes (1946–52).

Beginning in 1936 Chávez conducted numerous concerts with major American orchs.; also conducted in Europe and South America. Culturally he maintained a close connection with progressive artists and authors of Mexico, particularly Diego Rivera; his *Sinfonía proletaria* for chorus and orch. reflects his political commitment. In 1958–59 he was Charles Eliot Norton Lecturer at Harvard Univ.; these lectures were publ. under the title *Musical Thought* (Cambridge, Mass., 1960); publ. a book of essays, *Toward a New Music* (N.Y., 1937). Chávez is best known for his ballets—*El fuego nuevo, Los cuatro soles, Caballos de Vapor/HP, Antigona, La hija de Colquide,* and *Piramide*—and his syms., including *Sinfonía India, Sym. No. 2* (1935), and *Sinfonía romántica, Sym. No. 4* (1952).

Checker, Chubby (born Ernest Evans), b. Philadelphia, Oct. 3, 1941. Adopting the name Chubby Checker as a takeoff on Fats Domino, he first attracted a following with his recording of *The Class* (1959). Fame, however brief, came with his recording of Hank Ballard's *The Twist* (1960); toured the U.S. to exploit the new dance craze. With the invasion of the Beatles in 1964, his career was aborted; in later years, performances were relegated to the U.S. nostalgia circuit.

chef d'attaque (Fr., chief of the start). Term occasionally used by orch. players for the concertmaster; more common is *premier violon.*

chef d'orchestre (Fr., chief of the orch.). Conductor; occasionally abbrev. *chef.*

cheironomy (Grk., law of the hand). Ancient system of leading a choir with the aid of a hand-sign language, in which finger positions indicate the tempo, intervals, and rhythm; iconographical representations indicate its use in ancient Egypt, Coptic Christian, India, Israel, and Byzantine and Roman chant.

cheng. See ⇒Zheng.

Cherry, Don(ald), b. Oklahoma City, Nov. 18, 1936; d. Malaga, Spain, Oct. 19, 1995. He studied trumpet and harmony while attending high school in Los Angeles; began his career in 1951, appearing with Red Mitchell, Dexter Gordon, and other jazz musicians; then went to N.Y., where he worked and recorded with Ornette Coleman; after 1963 he toured extensively in Europe and Africa. A proponent of free jazz, he adopted instruments of other folk cultures in his performances. His stepdaughter, Neneh (b. Stockholm, Sweden, Mar. 10, 1964), enjoyed brief success with 1989's dance hit *Buffalo Stance.*

Cherubini, (Maria) Luigi (Carlo Zenobio Salvatore), b. Florence, Sept. 14, 1760; d. Paris, Mar. 15, 1842. He 1st studied music with his father, the *maestro al cembalo* at the Teatro della Pergola in Florence, and others. In 1778 he received a grant from the Grand Duke Leopold of Tuscany, which enabled him to study with Sarti in Milan; by then, had composed music for the church and stage intermezzos; wrote arias for Sarti's opera as well as exercises in the early contrapuntal style. His 1st operatic success came with *Armida abbandonata* (1782).

In 1784 Cherubini went to London to write an opera for the King's Theatre; *La finta principessa* (1785) was followed by *Il Giulio Sabino* (1786), which brought him public acceptance and the admiration of the Prince of Wales; made his 1st visit to Paris in the summer of 1785; introduced to Marie Antoinette by the court musician Giovanni Battista Viotti. In the spring of 1786 he made Paris his home; made 1 last visit to Italy to oversee the production of his *Ifigenia in Aulide* (1788); his 1st opera for Paris, *Démophon* (1788), failed because of Marmontel's inept libretto and the composer's less than total command of French prosody.

In 1789 Cherubini became music director and conductor of the newly licensed Italian Opera at the Tuileries; after the company moved to a new theater in the rue Feydeau, he produced *Lodoïska* (1791) with notable success; developed a new dramatic style which would have profound impact on French opera: the increased breadth and force of its ensemble numbers, its novel and rich orch'l combinations, and its heightened dramatic effect inspired others, particularly Mehul and Le Sueur.

With the French Revolution in full swing, the Italian Opera disbanded (1792); Cherubini went to Normandy; returned to Paris (1793); became an inspector at the new Inst. National de Musique (later the Cons.). His *Medée* (1797), noteworthy for its startling characterization of Medea and masterful orchestration,

proved a major step in his development; with *Les Deux Journées, ou Le Porteur d'eau* (1800), scored his greatest public triumph as a theatrical composer; the work was performed throughout Europe to much acclaim.

In 1805 Cherubini visited Vienna, where he was honored at the court; met the foremost musicians of the day, including Haydn and Beethoven; composed *Faniska,* successfully premiered at the Kärnthnertortheater (1806); after Napoleon captured Vienna, received royal favor by the French emperor, who expressed his desire that Cherubini return to Paris. When *Pimmalione* (1809) failed to please Paris, he retired to the château of the Prince of Chimay, occupying himself with botanizing and painting.

At the request of the church of Chimay, Cherubini produced the celebrated 3-part Mass in F major; subsequently devoted much time to sacred music; commissioned by the Phil. Soc of London to compose a sym., a cantata, and an overture (1815); visited London for their performances; appointed co-superintendent (with Le Sueur) of the Royal Chapel (1816); became director of the Paris Cons. (1822), continuing until a month before his death; during his last years, composed 6 fine string quartets. He became a member of the Inst. and Chevalier of the Legion d'honneur; in 1841, a Commander of the Legion d'honneur, the 1st musician so honored. He was accorded a state funeral, during which his Requiem in D minor (1836) was performed.

Cherubini was an important figure in the transition from the Classic to the Romantic in music; his influence on French operatic history was of great significance; although his operas have not found a permanent place in the repertory, several have been revived recently. His valuable *Cours de contrepoint et de fugue* (written with Halévy; Paris, 1835; Eng. trans., 1837) remained for many years a fundamental study of the art of composition. He played a predominant role in French music education during his tenure at the Paris Cons., establishing an authoritarian regimen; in most of his faculty instruction, pursued the Italian type of composition, rejecting any novel deviations from strict form, harmony, counterpoint, or orchestration; regarded Beethoven's 9th Sym. as an aberration of a great composer's mind; rejected descriptive music, demonstratively refusing to attend rehearsals or performances of the *Sym. fantastique* by Berlioz, then a Cons. student.

chest register. Lower register of the male or female voice, the tones of which produce sympathetic vibration in the chest.

chest tone (chest voice). 1. Vocal quality of the chest register. 2. Manner of voice production recommended by Italian teachers for tenors and basses, subjectively felt as though traveling into the chest from the larynx; the corresponding expansion of the lungs produces a richer tone.

Chevalier, Maurice, b. Paris, Sept. 12, 1888; d. there, Jan. 1, 1972. He began his career as a singer in Parisian cafés and music halls; then acted in films; went to Hollywood (1929); soon established himself as a musical comedy star, speaking and singing in English with an ingratiating French accent, affecting a debonair mien, carrying a cane, and wearing a straw hat; early films included *The Innocents of Paris* (1929), *Love Me Tonight* (1932), and *The Merry Widow* (1934). He remained in France during the German occupation, giving shows for French prisoners of war in Germany; after the war, this activity led to accusations of collaboration with the enemy, but he explained his conduct as a desire to maintain public spirit among Frenchmen, and he was exonerated. His later films included *Gigi* (1958), *Can-Can* (1960), and *Fanny* (1961). A special Academy Award was presented to him in 1958 in appreciation of his contributions to popular entertainment.

chevrotement (Fr., like a goat; Ger. *Bockstriller*). Rather uncomplimentary reference to the goat trill; chevrotement is occasionally used for special comic effects in opera.

chiarezza, con (It.). Clearly, distinctly, limpidly. *Chiaro,* clear.

chiave (It.). Clef. *Chiavette,* little clefs used in the 16th and 17th centuries to change the range of the staff in order to avoid the use of extra lines above or below it; the baritone F clef, with the F on the 3rd line instead of the more common 4th line, is an example; C clefs placed on different lines of the staff are standard and therefore not considered chiavette.

chiesa (It.). Church. *Sonata da chiesa,* an instrumental piece suitable for church performance.

child prodigies. The idea of a child possessed of great musical talent was popular in the Romantic era, when childhood itself was revered as a time of behavior unspoiled by the hand of civilization. About 10 percent of child prodigies make good and become adult virtuosos; Jascha Heifetz was a prodigy with flowing locks of hair; Mischa Elman and Yehudi Menuhin also made good. Among piano prodigies of our time, Josef Hofmann was undoubtedly the greatest; his American tour (1887–88) was sensational, but he ran into trouble with the Soc. for the Prevention of Cruelty to Children, who objected to the heavy concert schedule; Hofmann's concert tours were curtailed for several years; returned to America only as an adult of 22.

While child violinists and pianists are relatively common occurrences in the prodigy market, composers are relatively rare; after all, it takes more ability and mature concentration to compose an organized piece of music than to play through a piano sonata or a violin concerto. Mozart's music composed at 15 shows unmistakable genius; Schubert wrote some of his greatest songs at 17, the same age that Mendelssohn composed the overture to Shakespeare's *A Midsummer Night's Dream.* Child conductors enjoyed a vogue in the 1940s, but only 1 continued a significant career in music: Lorin Maazel, who appeared with the N.Y. Phil. Orch. when he was just 11 years old; the newspaper *PM,* in its issue of July 6, 1941, succinctly described the event in the headline: "11-Year-Old Wrings Zing Out of Toscanini's Band." He showed considerable musical understanding and rhythmical vivacity as he led the orch. He has had a distinguished career in conducting, but his story is unusual in the world of prodigies, most of whom never mature into concert artists.

Child, Francis, b. Boston, Feb. 1, 1825; d. there, Sep. 16, 1896. He is remembered for his *English and Scottish Popular Ballads* (1882), a collection of more than 300 song texts, codified folklore, and compared variants. Although he is criticized for some of his editorial choices, particularly his Victorian attitude toward bawdiness, his collection is remains the starting point for any serious student of this repertory.

children's chorus. Choir of boys and girls, all singing treble parts, often called for in opera (*Carmen*), less often in symphonic works.

Childs, Barney (Sanford), b. Spokane, Wash., Feb. 13, 1926. He studied intermittently with Leonard Ratner, Chávez, Copland, and Elliott Carter; obtained degrees from the Univ. of Nevada (1949), Oxford Univ. as a Rhodes Scholar (1955), and Stanford Univ. (1959), all in literature; taught English at the Univ. of Arizona (1956–65); served as dean of Deep Springs College in Calif. (1965–69). From 1969 to 1971 he taught music theory at Wisconsin College-Cons. in Milwaukee; joined the faculty at Johnston College of the Univ. of Redlands in Calif. (1971); became a prof. there (1973). Not overly concerned with public tastes and current fashions, he cultivates indeterminate structures. He ed., with Elliott Schwarz, *Contemporary Composers on Contemporary Music* (N.Y., 1967).

chimes. 1. Set of between 5 and 12 bells tuned to the scale, played by swinging either the bells themselves or clappers hung within them; also, a tune so played. 2. Set of bells and hammers played by a keyboard; a carillon 3. Tubular bells.

ch'in. See ⇒Qin.

chin rest. Oval plate of ebony attached to the edge of the violin or viola, to the left of the tailpiece.

Chinese blocks. Hollowed out polished boxes of resonant wood; when struck with a drumstick or mallet they produce a xylophonelike tone. Chinese blocks, actually Caribbean in origin, are popular in jazz and popular percussion; may also be arranged in a scale-like set. Also called Chinese temple blocks, temple blocks, or woodblocks.

Chinese crescent (Chinese hat, Chinese pavilion). Turkish crescent.

chitarra (It.). Guitar. *Chitarrina,* small Neapolitan guitar; *chitarrone,* large double-necked archlute.

chiuso, -a (It.). Closed. *A bocca chiusa* (It., with closed mouth), humming.

chocalho (*kocalho;* Port.). Brazilian tube rattle in the form of a long cylinder filled with seeds or buckshot, held horizontally between the fingers of both hands and shaken rhythmically; the sound resembles the maracas; used to accompany the samba and other Brazilian dances.

choeur (Fr.). See ⇒Chorus.

choir. 1. Company of singers, especially in a church. 2. Choral society. 3. In the Anglican church, singers of the daily choral service, who sit divided between the *decani* and *cantoris* sides of the chancel. 4. Subdivision of a chorus; e.g., the 1st and 2nd choirs in 8-part music. 5. Instrumental groups, e.g., a brass choir.

Chopin, Frédéric, b. Fryderyk Franciszek Chopin, Zelazowa Wola, near Warsaw, probably Mar. 1, 1810 (his certificate of baptism gives the date Feb. 22, 1810); d. Paris, Oct. 17, 1849. His father, Nicolas Chopin, was a native of Marainville, France, who went to Warsaw as a French teacher; his mother, Tekla-Justyna Krzyżanowska, was Polish. At age 8, Chopin played in public a piano concerto by Gyrowetz; had already begun to compose polonaises, mazurkas, and waltzes; received his primary musical instruction from the Bohemian pianist Adalbert Żiwny, who resided in Warsaw at the time; Józef Elsner, director of the Warsaw School of Music gave him a thorough instruction in music theory and form. He was 15 years old when his Rondo for Piano was publ. (op. 1). In 1829 he set out for Vienna; gave 2 highly successful concerts; arranged to publ. his variations on Mozart's *Là ci darem la mano* (from *Don Giovanni*) for piano and orch. (op. 2); this work attracted the attention of Schumann, who saluted Chopin in the *Allgemeine Musikalische Zeitung* (1831), in an article wherein Schumann's alter ego, Eusebius, exclaims, "Hats off, gentlemen! A genius!" (The common assumption that Schumann "launched" Chopin is deceptive, as Schumann did not yet have the power or reputation to do so.) Returning to Warsaw in 1830, Chopin gave the premieres of his Piano Concerto in F minor, op. 21, and his Piano Concerto in E minor, op. 11.

Chopin spent the winter of 1830–31 in Vienna; the failed Polish rebellion against Russian domination determined his future course of action; then went to Paris, visiting Linz, Salzburg, Dresden, and Stuttgart on the way; arrived in Paris (1831); introduced to Rossini, Cherubini, Paer; Bellini, Meyerbeer, Berlioz, Alkan, Hugo, and Heine; became particularly friendly with Liszt. He presented his 1st Paris concert (1832), and taught the piano. The Paris critics called him "the Ariel of the piano"; in 1834 he went with Hiller to Germany; met Mendelssohn, Clara Wieck, and Robert Schumann; in July 1837, went with Camille Pleyel to London.

In 1836 Chopin met the novelist Amandine Aurore Lucie Dupin Dudevant, whose literary pseudonym was George Sand. They became intimate, despite being quite incompatible in character and interests: Sand was involved in social affairs and held radical views; Chopin was a poet confined within his inner world; it could be said that she was the masculine and he the feminine partner in their companionship. In the winter of 1838–39 he accompanied Sand to the island of Majorca; she attended to him with total devotion, yet, in a personal letter dated 1838, wrote that she had difficulty in inducing him to submit to a sensual embrace, implying that she lived as an immaculate virgin most of the time they were together.

They parted in 1847; by that time Chopin was quite ill with tuberculosis; a daguerreotype taken of him represents a prematurely aged man with facial features showing sickness and exhaustion, with locks of black hair partly covering his forehead. Yet he continued his concert career; undertook a tour as pianist in England and Scotland (1848); gave his last concert in Paris. *La Revue et Gazette Musicale* reported, "The finest flower of feminine aristocracy in the most elegant attire filled the Salle Pleyel," the paper reported, "to catch this musical sylph on the wing." He played his last concert in London, a benefit for Polish émigrés, in late 1848; died the following year. Mozart's Requiem was performed at his funeral at the Madeleine, with Habeneck conducting the orch. and chorus of the Paris Cons. and Pauline Viardot and Lablache singing the solo parts. He was buried at Père-Lachaise between the graves of Cherubini and Bellini;

however, at his own request his heart was sent to Warsaw for entombment in his homeland.

Chopin represents the full liberation of the piano from traditional orch.l and choral influences and the authoritative assumption of its role as a solo instrument. Not seeking orch.l sonorities, he may have paled as a virtuoso beside the titanic Liszt, but the poesy of his pianism, its fervor of expression, the pervading melancholy in his nocturnes and ballades, and the bounding exultation of his scherzos and études were never equaled. From a purely technical standpoint, his figurations (influenced by bel canto colorature) and bold modulatory transitions seem to presage the elaborate transtonal developments of modern music.

choral. Relating or pertaining to a chorus or vocal concerted music. *Choral notes,* the square notes used for writing plainsong; *choral service,* a church service with music by the choir.

chorale (Lat. *choralis,* of the chorus). Religious choral compositions employed in German Protestant churches. The development of the chorale within the German Protestant service is intimately connected with the activities of Luther himself, who had the Latin hymns of the Roman Catholic Church translated into the vernacular, thus making it possible for the congregation to take part in the singing; thus *Te deum laudamus* became *Herr Gott, Dich loben wir,* and the Credo opening became *Wir glauben all' an einen Gott.* But the Lutheran Church also boldly borrowed melodies from secular songs; one of the most popular was *Durch Adams Fall ist ganz verderbt* (Through Adam's Fall We Sinned All). Collections of Lutheran chorales were published in Germany as early as 1524, when the Protestant movement was still fighting the stigma of heresy; soon these chorales became the sources for polyphonic compositions, thus effectuating a link between chorale and instrumental music. The chorale reached its peak in the works of Bach, who harmonized hundreds of known chorale melodies and arranged many more. Thus the purely practical movement of the Protestant chorale, begun in the early 16th century with the purpose of forming a sacred repertory of songs in the German tongue, grew into a great art, embracing all genres of sacred and secular music.

chorale cantata. A religious vocal work in which harmonized chorales are used in some or all sections of the cantata, along with free recitatives and homophonic arias. Most of Bach's cantatas are of this type.

chorale prelude. Organ composition based on a chorale or hymn tune; used to open Protestant church services; in Roman Catholic usage this genre corresponds to the organ hymn.

chorale variations. Keyboard genre, particularly of the 17th and 18th centuries; the rhythms of the variations could derive from the movements of the Baroque instrumental suite compositions

choralmässig (Ger.). In the style of a chorale.

chord. 1. All tonal combinations containing 3 or more pitch classes. The major triad (3-note chord) is colloquially described as a "common chord"; this does not make other chords "uncommon." Before the advent of modern music, triadic chords (chords derived from triads by inversion and distribution in various registers) constituted a statistical majority in all Classic and Romantic music. The final chords in a cadence in every composition written before 1900 are tonic triads or unisons, discounting duplications in octaves. Any chord that contains more than 3 different notes was regarded as a dissonance, requiring resolution into a consonance according to traditional academic rules. Discrimination against unrestricted use of dissonant chords has been abolished in the music of the 20th century. 2. Harmony of from 3 to 7 tones forming an ascending series of diatonic 3rds (see ⇒Chords). *Block, flat, or solid chord,* one whose notes are played simultaneously; *broken or rolled chord,* arpeggiated chord.

chord organ. Electronic keyboard instrument invented by Laurens Hammond (1950) which allows harmonies to be produced by pressing the appropriate button; the principle is analogous to the accordion family and autoharp.

chordophones (Grk., string sound). Older classification of instruments that produce their sound by means of vibrating strings stretched between fixed points.

chorea (Grk., row of dancers). Medieval term for a dancing melody, or dance in general.

choree (Grk.; Lat. *chorea*). In Greek prosody, a foot of 2 syllables in which the 1st is accented; also called trochee. Modern examples include the polka and galop.

choreography (Grk. *choreo* + Fr. *graphie*). 1. Composition and arrangement of dances, particularly ballet and modern types. 2. Notation of such a composition, indicating the position and movement of the dancer(s).

choro. Generic term used to describe Brazilian urban instrumental music beginning in the 1870s; the music performed is played by an ensemble with a soloist. All kinds of music are performed by choro groups: polka, waltz, modinha, samba, maxixe, and the Brazilian tango. *Chôros,* music written in a Brazilian style; closely associated with Villa-Lobos, who wrote 14 works for various instrumental groups under this name; the most engaging is No. 5 for Piano (1926), subtitled *Alma Brasileira* (Brazilian Soul).

chorus. 1. Ensemble of voices, consisting of sopranos, altos, tenors, and basses, abbreviated SATB. A female or boys' chorus consists of sopranos and altos (e.g., SSAA); a male chorus consists of tenors, basses and sometimes baritones (TTBarB). A double chorus often involves a spatially separated ensemble (SSAATTBB). In any choral music, there are usually 2 or more singers to a part. 2. Refrain in traditional music, popular songs, show tunes, jazz, and similar music.

Chou Wen-chung, b. Chefoo, June 29, 1923. He studied civil engineering at the National Univ. in Chungking (1941–45); went to the U.S. on a scholarship to study architecture; turning his attention to music, studied composition with Slonimsky in Boston (1946–49), Varèse in N.Y. (1949–54), and Luening at Columbia Univ. (M.A., 1954); held 2 Guggenheim fellowships (1957, 1959); became a naturalized U.S. citizen. He was composer-in-residence at the Univ. of Illinois in Urbana (1958) and

on the faculties of Brooklyn College (1961–62), Hunter College (1963–64), and Columbia Univ. (from 1964); elected to the Inst. of the American Academy and Inst. of Arts and Letters (1982); ed. several Varèse works. His music combines Chinese elements of structure and scale formation with free dissonant counterpoint related to Varèse's theory of "organized sound."

Christe eleison (Grk., Christ have mercy). Part of the Kyrie. See ⇒Mass.

Christian, Charlie, b. Bonham, Tex., July 29, 1916; d. N.Y., Mar. 2, 1942. His parents and his 4 brothers were musicians; as a child, played in the family band; at maturity, began playing an amplified guitar; played in Benny Goodman's Sextet (1939–41); later played with Gillespie and Monk. Christian was among the first electric jazz guitarists; his single-string leads were much admired and copied by others; one of the finest early bebop performers, he was stricken with tuberculosis and died at age 25.

Christie, William (Lincoln), b. Buffalo, N.Y., Dec. 19, 1944. He studied with Igor Kipnis, Ralph Kirkpatrick, Palisca, Krigbaum, and Temperley; moved to France (1971); performed with the Concerto Vocale, a Renaissance and Baroque ensemble; in 1978, formed Les Arts Florissants (named after an M.-A. Charpentier opera), an ensemble dedicated to Baroque French and Italian repertory. His performances and recordings of works by Charpentier, Lambert, Lully, Monteverdi, Purcell, Rameau, Rossi, Gesualdo, Montéclair, and Bouzignac have been enthusiastically received in Europe and the U.S.

Christoff, Boris (Kirilov), b. Plovdiv, May 18, 1914; d. Rome, June 28, 1993. He sang in the Gusla Choir in Sofia; he was heard by King Boris, who provided the means for him to go to Rome to study with Stracciari; later studied in Salzburg with Muratti; made his debut in a Rome concert (1946); made his opera debut there at the Teatro Argentina as Colline in *La Bohème;* made his 1st appearance at La Scala in Milan (1947), Covent Garden in London (1949), and his U.S. debut as Boris Godunov with the San Francisco Opera (1956). During his distinguished career he appeared at many leading opera houses, singing most of the principal bass roles in the operas of Verdi as well as Gurnemanz, Ivan Susanin, Hagen, Rocco, Konchak, and King Mark; renowned for his dramatic portrayal of Boris, which recalled Chaliapin; his brother-in-law was Tito Gobbi.

chromatic (Grk. *chroma*, color). 1. Progression of notes by semitone, or half step. 2. Tones foreign to a given diatonic scale or harmony.

chromatic signs. Accidentals; the sharp (♯), flat (♭), natural (♮), double sharp (𝄪), and double flat (♭♭).

chromaticism. Consistent use of chromatic (semitonal) progressions; the systematic insertion of intermediary notes between two diatonic degrees. In the key of C major every sharp and every flat constitutes a chromatic note a semitone apart from the preceding diatonic degree or the following one. A distinction is made between a chromatic and a diatonic semitone. The interval from E to F is a diatonic semitone (moving up the alphabetic scale), but the interval between F and F sharp is a chromatic semitone, because the same letter-note is used twice: 1st as a diatonic scale degree (F) and then as a chromatic note, F sharp. In the progression F-F sharp-G, the F sharp constitutes a chromatic passing note.

In musical analysis, it is necessary to consider the prevalence of diatonic melody and harmony relative to the frequency of chromatic passages. A convoluted melody weaving its way around principal triadic tones impresses the ear as highly chromatic, even when 2 consecutive semitones do not occur. On the other hand, a clearly tonal melody with a plethora of chromatic passage notes will register as diatonic if such a melody is harmonized in triads or 7th chords belonging to the principal key, e.g., the chromatic runs in Rimsky-Korsakov's *Flight of the Bumblebee* and Bach's *Chromatic Fantasy*. But there is no question as to the chromatic nature of the prelude to Wagner's *Tristan und Isolde,* for the harmonies proceed by half steps.

Post-Wagnerian music was swept by a tidal wave of chromaticism; many composers abandoned key signatures altogether because the triadic resting point occurred too infrequently to justify their use. Chromatic melody and chromatic harmony achieved their ultimate development in the method of composition with 12 different notes related only to one another, as formulated by Schoenberg. As a coup de grâce to triadic diatonicism, he avoided triads and their inversions, particularly major triads. However, chromaticism for its own sake was not Schoenberg's aim; rejecting tonality as a governing principle, he organized harmony and melody according to the new dodecaphonic principle. A reaction to chromaticism developed in the 2nd and 4th quarters of the 20th century when diatonicism returned as waves of neoclassicism and postmodernism.

Chung, Kyung-Wha, b. Seoul, Mar. 26, 1948. Sister of Myung-Wha Chung and Myung-Whun Chung, she began to study the violin as a small child; made solo orch. debut in Seoul at age 9, playing the Mendelssohn Concerto; went to the U.S.; (1961); studied with Ivan Galamian at the Juilliard School of Music, N.Y. In 1967 she shared 1st prize with Pinchas Zukerman in the Leventritt Competition; appeared as soloist with the N.Y. Phil. (1968); made her European debut with the London Sym. Orch. (1970); embarked upon a wide-flung tour in Europe and Asia. She gave numerous trio concerts with her sister and brother; appeared as a soloist with her brother acting as conductor.

Chung, Myung-Wha, b. Seoul, Mar. 19, 1944. Sister of Kyung-Wha Chung and Myung-Whun Chung, she studied cello in Seoul; made her orch. debut there (1957); went to the U.S. (1961); studied with L. Rose at the Juilliard School of Music, N.Y.; attended Piatigorsky's master class at the Univ. of Southern Calif. in Los Angeles. She made her U.S. debut in San Francisco (1967); her European debut in Spoleto (1969); won 1st prize in the Geneva Competition (1971) the same year she became a naturalized U.S. citizen. She appeared as soloist with orchs. in Europe and America; also played trio concerts with her sister and brother.

Chung, Myung-Whun, b. Seoul, Jan. 22, 1953. Brother of Myung-Wha Chung and Kyung-Wha Chung, he played piano as a child, making his debut as soloist with the Seoul Phil. at age 7; went to the U.S.; studied with Nadia Reisenberg (piano) and Carl Bamberger (conducting) at the Mannes College of Music in N.Y., and at the Juilliard School (diplomas in piano and conducting,

1974); received further study in conducting there from Sixten Ehrling (1975–78); made his conducting debut in Seoul (1971); won 2nd prize in piano at the Tchaikovsky Competition in Moscow (1974); became a naturalized U.S. citizen in 1973. He pursued a dual career as a pianist and conductor; gave trio concerts with his sisters; assistant conductor of the Los Angeles Phil. (1978–81); chief conductor of the Saarland Radio Sym. Orch., Saarbrucken (1984–90); made his Metropolitan Opera debut in N.Y. conducting *Simon Boccanegra* (1986); in 1990, began in the prestigious position of music director of the new Bastille Opéra, Paris. This appointment, considering his relative youth and his absence from the customary engagements at European musical centers, created a sensation among impresarios and the press.

church modes. Octave scales employed in medieval and Renaissance church music. See ⇒authentic modes; plagal modes.

church sonata. Sonata da chiesa.

ciaccona (It.). Chaconne.

Ciconia, Jean (Johannes), b. Liège, *c.* 1335; d. Padua, between Dec. 11 and Dec. 24, 1411. Little is known about his life; he was in Italy from 1358 to 1367; in Liège from 1372 until 1401; arrived in Padua (1402), where he was a canon. He wrote the treatise *De proportionibus musicae* (latter 14th century); his significance lies in the early use of musical devices that became current only much later; he applied the technique of French isorhythmic style as well as canonic imitation.

Cilèa, Francesco, b. Palmi, Calabria, July 23, 1866; d. Varazze, Nov. 20, 1950. He studied at the Naples Cons. (1881–89); taught piano there (1894–96) and harmony at the Istituto Musicale in Florence (1896–1904); head of the Palermo Cons. (1913–16); director of the Cons. di San Pietro a Majella in Naples (1916–35); member of the Reale Accademia Musicale in Florence (1898). He wrote relatively few works, most of them operas; his most famous is *Adriana Lecouvreur,* after Scribe (Milan, 1902).

Cimarosa, Domenico, b. Aversa, near Naples, Dec. 17, 1749; d. Venice, Jan. 11, 1801. He was the son of a stonemason. After his father's death, his mother placed him in the monastery school of the church of S. Severo dei Padri Conventuali in Naples; began his musical training with the monastery organist; enrolled at the Cons. di S. Maria di Loreto (1761); studied voice, violin, and keyboard playing; following his graduation (1771), studied voice with the castratro Giuseppe Aprile. His 1st opera, *Le stravaganze del conte,* was staged in Naples (1772); from 1776, composed operas prolifically, producing about 65 works for the major Italian theaters as well as those abroad; in 1779, named supernumerary organist of the Royal Chapel in Naples; in 1785, the 2nd organist; served as maestro of the Ospedaletto, a cons. for girls in Venice.

In 1787 Cimarosa was appointed maestro di cappella to the court of Catherine the Great in St. Petersburg, where he wrote 3 operas and various other works for the court and the nobility; when the court cut back on its funding of music, his contract was allowed to lapse in 1791. He proceeded to Vienna, where

Emperor Leopold II appointed him Kapellmeister; composed his masterpiece, *Il matrimonio segreto*, premiered with great acclaim at the Burgtheater (1792); the Emperor was so pleased that he ordered it to be repeated that evening; while its fame spread throughout Europe, Cimarosa returned to Italy in 1793 as one of the most celebrated musicians of the age; appointed 1st organist of the Royal Chapel in Naples (1796).

In 1799 Cimarosa welcomed the Neapolitan republican movement by composing a patriotic hymn for the burning of the royal flag; however, the monarchy was restored later that year and his efforts miscarried; arrested in late 1799 and sent to prison for 4 months; released only after the intervention of prominent individuals; went to Venice, where he died while working on his opera *Artemisia*. It was rumored that he had been poisoned by order of Queen Caroline of Naples; persistent cries of foul play led to the Pope's personal physician's being sent to Venice to make an autopsy; according to a sworn statement (Apr. 5, 1801), Cimarosa died of a gangrenous abdominal tumor. He was an outstanding composer of Italian opera buffa in his day; his melodic inventiveness, command of form, superb vocal writing, and masterly orchestration were unexcelled until Rossini arrived upon the scene.

cimbalom. Large dulcimer associated primarily with Hungarian and other Gypsy bands; the range is 4 octaves (from E to e^3). Trapezoidal in form, it is laid out on a table and is played with two mallets. A type with a chromatic scale and damper pedal was developed in the 1870s. Kodály uses the cimbalom in his orch'l work *Háry János;* Stravinsky employs it in his *Renard* and a provisional version of *Les Noces*. Liszt imitates the sound of the cimbalom in his Hungarian Rhapsody No. 11 for piano, specifically indicating the passage as *quasi-Zimbalo* (like a cimbalom).

cinelli (It.). Cymbals.

cipher. 1. Practice of basing a composition on pitches that are tonal equivalents to letters of the alphabet; see ⇒B–A–C–H. 2. On the organ, a note that, owing to some derangement of the action, persists in sounding.

circle of fifths (cycle of fifths). 1. Series of 5ths tuned (as on the piano) in equal temperament, so that the 12th note of the series has the same letter name as the 1st note. 2. Chart showing the 12 major and 12 minor keys, arranged by ascending 5ths and represented graphically by the face of a clock beginning at 12 o'clock with C major and A minor, each having no sharps or flats. The direction of sharp keys is clockwise, while the direction of flat keys moves counterclockwise. When the 6 o'clock position is reached, going in the sharp direction, the key of F-sharp major enharmonically meets G-flat major; similarly, its relative key—D-sharp minor—is changed to E-flat minor.

It is theoretically possible to continue the accumulation of sharps in key signatures, moving clockwise, reaching the key of B-sharp major at the 12 o'clock position, with 12 sharps in the key signature; similarly, the accumulation of flats in key signatures, moving counterclockwise, arrives at the 12 o'clock position in the key of D-double-flat major, with 12 flats in the signature. But equally tempered key signatures of more than 7 sharps or flats are totally impractical, superfluous, and avoided

in actual usage. Among the exceptions: the scale passages in B-sharp major (enharmonically C major) in the 4-hand piano arrangement of Stravinsky's *Le Sacre du printemps;* the D-double-flat major scale outlined in the piano part of Ravel's Piano Trio; and, in 1 amazing instance, in *The Legend of the Invisible City of Kitezh,* Rimsky-Korsakov modulates clockwise until he is forced to use an accidental triple-sharp. See ⇒Intro., The Keys.

circuitry. The stipulation of spatial, visual, or lighting requirements. Modern scores for mixed-media performances often have the appearance of blueprints for the electric circuits of scientific instruments and digital computers. An early example of musical circuitry is the color organ part in Scriabin's *Prométhée,* intended to fill halls with changing colors corresponding to fluctuations in instrumental timbre; the detailed lighting given by Schoenberg in his monodrama *Erwartung* are in the same category. The Russian composer Nikolai Obouhov (1892–1954), who called himself "Nicolas L'illumine," designed an electronic instrument in the form of a cross.

circular breathing. Modern (although ancient) technique, primarily among vocalists and wind players, where the performer inhales breath through the nose while simultaneously exhaling breath through the mouth, thus sustaining sound for an indefinite length of time.

circular canon. Canon closing in the key a semitone above that in which it begins; 12 repetitions would thus carry it through the circle of 12 keys.

circus music. Type of band music associated with circuses, fairs, etc.; early on, performed with fiddles and drums, later with bands of up to 36 players, mostly brass and timpani; the repertoire, like early extemporized accompaniment to silent film, is determined by the character of the acts being supported.

Cis (Ger.). C sharp.

Cis dur (Ger.). C-sharp major.

Cis moll (Ger.). C-sharp minor.

citole (Ger. *Citole, Zitole;* It. *cetula*). Medieval and early Renaissance fretted string instrument with a body in 1 piece and 4 strings; plucked with a quill.

cittern (*cithern, cithren;* Fr. *cistrel;* Ger. *Cister, Cither, Zitter*). Fretted string instrument with a pear-shaped body, strung with wire and played with a plectrum; used in the 16th and 17th centuries. There were many variants of construction, but the most common instruments had 4 to 6 double-strung courses and a neck cut half away from behind the fingerboard; there are diatonic and chromatic models.

Čiurlionis, Mikolajus Konstantinas, b. Varena, Oct. 4, 1875; d. Pustelnik, near Warsaw, Apr. 10, 1911. He studied composition with Noskowski and at the Leipzig Cons. with Carl Reinecke and Jadassohn; active in Warsaw as a choral conductor (1902–09). His music reflects Germanic Romantic tendencies, but he also developed interesting theories of so-called tonal ground formations, anticipating the serial methods of

Schoenberg and Hauer. Čiurlionis was also a painter of the abstract expressionist manner; many of his paintings carry musical titles, such as *Prelude and Fugue, Spring Sonata,* etc.; compositions include the symphonic poems *In the Forest* (1901) and *The Ocean* (1907); cantata, De profundis (1899); String Quartet; numerous piano pieces and songs.

clang (Ger. *Klang*). Fundamental with its harmonics. *Clang-color, clang-tint,* tone color or timbre in relation to the harmonic spectrum.

clappers. Pair of wooden or metal disks or sticks held between the fingers and struck together to mark the beat in a dance; rudimentary type of castanets, perhaps the most ancient percussion instrument.

Clapton, Eric (Patrick), also called "Slowhand," b. Ripley, Surrey, Mar. 30, 1945. He played guitar as a youth; at 18, joined the Metropolis Blues Quartet, which later changed its name to the Yardbirds. He played with this group for a short time until turned off by its increasing commercialism; in 1965, joined John Mayall's Bluesbreakers; a year later, formed a trio named Cream with bassist Jack Bruce and drummer Ginger Baker; the group turned the rock world upside down by introducing prolonged improvisational jams and breadth of influences. When Cream soured, Clapton organized the "supergroup" Blind Faith, with Baker, Stevie Winwood, and Ric Grech, but Blind Faith soon gave up the ghost, even with his spiritual hymn *In the Presence of the Lord* maintaining the flame briefly.

After a brief fling with Delaney and Bonnie, Clapton formed Derek and the Dominoes, winners of a certified Gold Award for its album *Layla* (1971); they disbanded after a year or so of feverish and drug-addled activity. Depressed by these recurrent dissolutions, he went into relative obscurity; but in 1979 he hit the jackpot with *Lay Down Sally.* After paying homage to the middle-class fascination with coke by covering the tunes *Tulsa Time* and *Cocaine,* he was finally able to kick his own drug habit. In 1980 he finally found his niche with the album *Just One Night;* subsequent successful albums include *Another Ticket* (1981), *Money and Cigarettes* (1983), *August* (1986), and *Unplugged* (1992). In 1995 he scored a hit with *Tears in Heaven,* inspired by the accidental death of his young son, who fell from an apartment window.

claque (Fr., clapping). Mercenary applause, hired by operatic stars, bosomy prima donnas, self-inflated tenors, and occasional seemingly normal pianists and desperate violinists. The practice of engaging a claque began in the early 19th century in Italy; it rapidly spread to France, Victorian England, and America. Occasionally an ambitious opera star would engage an anticlaque to drown out a rival's claque. Well-paid enthusiasm might spill out onto the street, with opera lovers unharnessing the horses of a prima donna's carriage and pulling her home by manpower. A list for services circulating Paris in the mid–19th century quoted the following prices:

Applause sufficient for a single curtain call	150 francs
Overwhelming applause.	225 francs
Hissing a rival singer.	250 francs
Ovation after the last act, serenading before the window of the artist's home	price by special arrangement

The claquers were officially banned at the Metropolitan Opera House in N.Y. in 1935 but were still prospering in the 1960s, at the cost of up to $100 for a group of vociferous young males on Saturday afternoons.

clarinet. Transposing woodwind instrument related to and probably derived from the 18th-century chalumeau; a standard member of the classical orch. since the latter part of the 18th century; 1st mentioned in 1710. The Bohemian composer Johann Stamitz (1717–57) was the 1st to include a clarinet part in an orch'l score (1755). The clarinet (It. *clarinetto, clarino;* from Lat. *claro, clear;* Ger. *Klarinette;* Fr. *clarinette*) is a single-reed instrument, by contrast with the double-reed oboe and bassoon. It has a cylindrical tube of African blackwood pierced by 18 holes, 13 being closed by keys; its compass comprises 3 octaves in 4 different registers: low (chalumeau), medium (throat, break), high (clarinetto), and extreme. The player blows into a beak at one end; the other end is a bell-shaped aperture; like all woodwinds, opening and closing the holes vary the length of the instrument, enabling it to change pitch. Unique among wind instruments, the acoustic spectrum of clarinet tone reveals only the odd-numbered harmonics, producing both its special timbre and the difficulties in constructing an instrument capable of overblowing the higher pitches in tune. The clarinet is the most expressive and the most versatile instrument of the woodwinds, capable of attaining a zephyrlike waft in the low and middle registers and an overwhelming fortissimo in the upper register.

The written range of the clarinet is from E below the treble clef to the high G or beyond above (i.e., e–g^3); it is a transposing instrument, so that the written note sounds higher or lower than written, e.g., the most commonly used clarinet, the soprano in B flat, sounds that pitch when playing a written C (for the A clarinet, the written C sounds A, etc.). A clarinet in C was formerly popular, but it was awkward to play in tonalities with several sharps or flats in the key signature; modern clarinets avoid these technical difficulties, for the B-flat clarinet automatically provides 2 flats in the key signature and the A clarinet 3 sharps; thus the player uses the B-flat clarinet for flat keys and the A clarinet for sharp keys. Orch'l transpositions result in key signatures in the clarinet parts differing from those in the strings. Some modern composers prefer to write orch'l clarinet parts in the conductor's score without transposition, while writing the individual clarinet parts in B flat and A, sparing the conductor's having to compute the proper transposition while providing the correct transpositions to the players themselves.

The clarinet family includes 2 small (sopranino) clarinets, tuned in D and E flat (transposing, respectively, a major 2nd and a minor 3rd up); the clarinet in F (transposing down a 5th), called the basset horn and favored by Mozart; the alto clarinet in E flat, which appears rarely in orch'l scores. The bass clarinet in B flat transposes an octave below the soprano clarinet (i.e., major ninth). There also exists a contrabass clarinet which transposes 2 octaves lower than either of the soprano instruments; playing on the contrabass requires exceptionally strong lungs, and, on the rare occasions that it is required, there is usually a special pedal that blows in additional air.

A large repertory of clarinet music exists. Stamitz was only one of the Mannheim composers to write for the new instrument. Mozart bemoaned the absence of clarinets at Salzburg in 1778; but he soon had 2 fine clarinetists (the Stadler brothers) and wrote the 1st significant corpus of clarinet music. Among the most popular clarinet concertos are those by Mozart, Weber, Spohr, Nielsen, Debussy (*Première rapsodie*), Hindemith, Copland, Musgrave, and Corigliano. Gershwin's *Rhapsody in Blue* is practically a double concerto for clarinet and piano; the opening clarinet solo reaches a high B flat, approached by a glissando, an effect that only modern virtuosos are capable of. The clarinet was an essential instrument in jazz ensembles through the Dixieland/New Orleans, Chicago/"hot," and swing/big band eras. Stravinsky wrote his *Ebony Concerto* for jazz clarinetist Woody Herman; the title plays on the slang term for clarinet, *ebony stick*.

clarinet stop. See ⇒crumhorn.

clarino. 1. High register of the trumpet, where it is possible to produce a complete diatonic scale in natural harmonics. 2. The long-tubed Baroque high trumpet, capable of fast tempo and clear articulation, made obsolete by the modern trumpet. 3. 4' reed organ stop of shrill, piercing tone; clarion stop.

Clarke, Rebecca (Thacher), b. Harrow, Aug. 27, 1886; d. N.Y., Oct. 13, 1979. She studied violin with Hans Wessely at the Royal Academy of Music (1902–04) and composition with Stanford at the Royal College of Music, London (1904–10); switched to the viola; took a few lessons from L. Tertis; 1st female member of Henry Wood's Queen Hall Orch. (1912); formed and played with the English Ensemble (1928–29). She made history by tying E. Bloch for 1st place in the 1919 Coolidge Competition (Viola Sonata); the award eventually went to Bloch, due in large part to Mrs. Coolidge's discomfort with a woman composer's being equal to any man. She married composer-pianist James Friskin (1944); moved to N.Y.

Her fine music, comprising entirely chamber works, was quite advanced, being on the fringe of atonality in outline but remaining firmly rooted in English Impressionism; for some of her compositions she used the name Anthony Trent. They include the Violin Sonata (1909), *Morpheus* for Viola (1917), Piano Trio (1921), *Rhapsody* for Cello (1923), String Quartet (1924), *Passacaglia on an Old English Tune* for Viola (1941), *Prelude, Allegro, and Pastorale* for Clarinet and Viola (1942); over 60 songs.

clarsach (Gael.). Irish harp.

Classic era (from Lat. *classis*, aristocratic pedigree; always capitalized). The classical music style dating *c.* 1750–1825,

preceded by the ornate Baroque style and leading to the expansiveness of the Romantic period of composition. Stylistically, Classic music is distinguished by formal symmetry, set in either binary or ternary structures, strict observance of the proper sequence of tonalities in modulation, incisive but relatively simple rhythms, articulate polyphony, and harmonic euphony. Instrumental technique in the Classic era was conservative; virtuosity, encouraged for its own sake during the Baroque, became subservient to the dignified formality of the general design; the Romantic shifted the emphasis from clarity of form to a humanistic concern for emotional expression. Since the formulas of Classic harmony, melody, and rhythm were standardized to a considerable degree, composers of the period were able to turn out hundreds of syms., concertos, sonatas, and dozens of operas, cantatas, and other works, all tailored to a fairly uniform model, no matter how different their stylistic contents.

Like all historical concepts, the Classic era does not yield to temporal delimitation. The roots of Beethoven's music were firmly lodged in the Classic spirit, while his last period anticipates Romanticism; a similar dichotomy applies to the music of Schubert. To account for this historic indeterminacy, the term Viennese Classicism was introduced to describe the productions of European composers active between 1800 and 1830. Inevitably, composers of the 20th century, weary of the endless self-projections of the Romantic composers, turned for relief to the clear, unambiguous, and in some respects impersonal ways of the 18th century; a modern "version" of the Classic style arose under the guise of neoclassicism (which, however, was equally neo-Baroque).

classical music (always lowercase). Colloquially, any highly evolved music where a significant written element has helped preserve it, as opposed to popular or folk music, whose survival has depended on some form of oral tradition. For better or worse, classical music is also called *serious music, highbrow music, cultivated music,* or *art music*; etymologically derived from the ancient Roman notion of *classis* (Lat., aristocratic pedigree), suggesting order, purposeful behavior, high morality, aesthetic perfection, productivity, efficiency, and the ability to create attractive artifacts. Renaissance scholars applied the term to the arts, emphasizing those selfsame qualities, as they found in the surviving literature, architecture, and statuary of ancient Greece and Rome. However, the term *classical music* does not apply only to the period of Haydn, Mozart, and Beethoven (*c.* 1750–1825), which in this dictionary is called the Classic period. (Similarly, "romantic" is a qualitative assessment; "Romantic" is a 19th-century style period.)

classical suite. See ⇒suite.

classicism. Historically recurring aesthetic emphasizing purity of design, perfection of form, and the meeting of the highest cultivated demands, applied to literature, art, and music. These qualities were connected historiographically with remote ages, particularly of Greece and Rome; negative aspects of ancient society were overlooked, so as not to detract from the artistic glory of Greece and the grandeur of Rome. The flowering of the arts during the Renaissance was marked by the renascence of interest in these classical cultures. The emergence of opera at the threshold of the 17th century was an outgrowth of the search for the artistic essence of Greek tragedy; since the dramatic performances in ancient Greece were accompanied by music, the theorists of opera urged a return to monodic simplicity in melody and rhythm and the abandonment of the intricate polyphony of the Franco-Flemish (Netherlandish) mode. See also ⇒neoclassicism.

clausula (Lat. *claudere*, conclude). Type of formalized ending in early sacred polyphony. Clausulae were usually sung to a single vowel or syllable derived from a melisma of a chant such as Alleluia; the singing of a clausula signaled the termination of a polyphonic work and thus served a cadential-like function in performance. Yet there is a distinction: the cadence signifies a homophonic rather than a polyphonic ending in a harmonic setting. During the Renaissance period the distinction between the clausula and the cadence tended to disappear.

clavecin (Fr.; It. *clavicembalo*). Harpsichord or virginal.

claves (Sp.). Percussion instrument with a sharp sound produced by a pair of sticks of resonant polished hardwood struck against each other; used in Latin American popular music.

clavichord (Lat. *clavis*, key + Grk. *chorda*, string). Keyboard instrument popular during the Renaissance and Baroque periods, particularly in Germany, where it was the favored domestic instrument. A precursor of the pianoforte, it differs in action from the latter in having upright brass wedges called tangents on the rear end of the keys (instead of hammers); upon pressing a key, the tangent strikes the wire and remains pressed against it until the finger is lifted, causing only 1 section of the string to vibrate. It thus differs in construction from its musical siblings, the harpsichord and the virginal, in that the strings are not plucked but struck, therefore closer to the sound production means of a modern piano. The clavichord has a delicate intimate sound far softer than that of the harpsichord; it possesses the unique capacity of producing a peculiar vibrato governed by varying the pressure on the keys even after they are depressed (Bebung); its range was between 3 and 5 octaves; it was C. P. E. Bach's favorite instrument. While the harpsichord has regained its significance in performance contexts, the clavichord has retreated to the sidelines.

clavier. 1. Keyboard or manual of any keyboard instrument; defined thus from the early 16th century. 2. Any strung keyboard instrument. This spelling was used in the late 17th and 18th centuries; in the 19th century *clavier* generally referred to the piano; in 20th-century Germany the spelling was changed to *Klavier*.

clavier de récit (Fr.). Swell manual.

clef (Fr., key). Character set in a staff at the beginning of a composition, fixing the pitch or position of 1 note, and by analogy the rest.

Two clefs are used in piano music, the G clef 𝄞, indicating the position of the note G above middle C on the 2nd line, and the F clef 𝄢, indicating the position of the note F below middle C on the 4th line. The G clef is also called treble or violin clef, because it is used for high vocal parts or violin music; the F clef is called bass clef because it covers the lower register. The present shape of the G clef evolved from the Gothic capital letter *G* (G); the F clef was 1st indicated as a red line; it later evolved from the capital letter *F*.

Another group of clefs indicate the position of middle C on the staff. The present shape of the C clef (𝄡) evolved from the letter *C*. The most current C clefs are the viola (alto) clef, placing middle C on the 3rd line, and the tenor clef, with middle C on the 4th line. The viola clef dominates viola parts and is found occasionally in upper-register trombone parts; the tenor clef is used for upper-register cello and bassoon parts. Several C clefs are obsolete, among them the soprano clef, with middle C on the 1st line, and the baritone clef, with middle C on the 5th line of the staff.

The lower the clef is posted the more room it affords to high notes; conversely, when a clef is placed high on the staff the available range lies in the low register. A hybrid tenor and treble clef is sometimes used in the tenor parts of operatic scores to replace the inaccurate G clef, which covers the register an octave above the common tenor range and is most suited to soprano parts. Bach made use of various C clefs even in his keyboard compositions; the Invention No. 15 in F major is notated in the soprano clef for the right hand and the tenor clef for the left; this notation is apt to startle a piano-minded clef reader who stumbles upon the facsimile edition. See also ⇒Intro., The Clefs.

Clementi, Muzio (baptized Mutius Philippus Vincentius Franciscus Xaverius), b. Rome, Jan. 23, 1752; d. Evesham, Worcestershire, England, Mar. 10, 1832. He began to study music as a child with Antonio Buroni; at age 7, commenced studies with the organist Cordicelli; studied voice with Giuseppe Santarelli; by 1766, was organist of the parish San Lorenzo in Damaso. About this time Peter Beckford, cousin of the English novelist William Beckford, visited Rome; struck by Clementi's youthful talent and with the permission of Clementi's father, he took the boy to England. For the next 7 years he lived, performed, and studied at Beckford's estate of Stepleton Iwerne, Dorset.

During the winter of 1774–75 Clementi settled in London; made his 1st appearance as a harpsichordist in a benefit (1775); was harpsichordist at the King's Theatre, where he led operatic performances. In 1779 his 6 sonatas, op. 2, were publ., bringing him his 1st public success, both in England and on the Continent; toured the Continent, giving piano concerts in Paris (1780); continued touring with appearances in Strasbourg, Munich, and Vienna (1781); during his Viennese stay, his famous piano contest with Mozart took place at court before Emperor Joseph II (1781). Several of his syms. were performed in London (1786), but were soon eclipsed by the syms. of Haydn; in 1790, retired from public performances as a pianist; continued to lead orch. concerts from the keyboard; after 1796, withdrew from all performances, devoting himself to teaching, and collected large fees. He lost part of his fortune through the bankruptcy of Longman and Broderip, music publishers and piano builders (1798); however, with John Longman, formed a partnership on the ruins of the old company; became highly successful; his business acumen led to great success with subsequent partners during the next 3 decades.

From 1802 to 1810 Clementi traveled extensively on the Continent, pursuing business interests, teaching, composing, and giving private concerts; while in Vienna in 1807, met Beethoven and arranged to become his major English publisher; returned to England in 1810; helped organize the Phil. Soc. of London; appeared as conductor (1813). In 1816–17 he conducted his syms. in Paris, followed by engagements in Frankfurt (1817–18); revisited Paris (1821); went to Munich (1821–22); in Jan. 1822, conducted his works with the Gewandhaus Orch. in Leipzig; returned to England; conducted more concerts with the Phil. Soc. (to 1824); as with Haydn before, however, his syms. soon fell from the repertory, as Beethoven's masterpieces eclipsed his own works. In 1830 he retired from his mercantile ventures; made his last home at Evesham, Worcestershire. As a teacher, Clementi had many distinguished pupils, including Johann Baptist Cramer, John Field, Karl Zeuner, Alexander Klengel, Friedrich Kalkbrenner, and Ludwig Berger.

Cleveland, James, b. Chicago, Dec. 5, 1931; d. Los Angeles, Feb. 9, 1991. He was reared in a gospel milieu; was encouraged to develop his natural musical talent by the pianist Roberta Martin; he was a pianist and singer with the Caravans; formed the Gospel Chimes (1959); became a licensed minister of the Church of God in Christ. His song *Grace Is Sufficient* (1948) became a gospel standard; his album *Peace Be Still* (1963) added further to his renown. In 1970 he founded the Cornerstone Institutional Baptist Church, for which he also served as pastor.

Cliburn, Van (Harvey Lavan, Jr.), b. Shreveport, La., July 12, 1934. His mother, Rildia Bee Cliburn, a pupil of Arthur Friedheim, was his only teacher until 1951, when he entered the Juilliard School of Music in N.Y. to study with Rosina Lhevinne, graduating in 1954. He was 4 when he made his 1st appearance in public in Shreveport; after winning the Texas State Prize (1947), appeared as a soloist with the Houston Sym. Orch; won the National Music Festival Award (1948), the Dealy Award and the Kosciuszko Foundation Chopin Prize (1952), and the Roeder Award and the Leventritt Competition in N.Y. (1954); also appeared as a soloist with the N.Y. Phil. that year. In 1958 he captured 1st prize at the Tchaikovsky Competition in Moscow, the 1st American to do so; upon his return to N.Y., received a hero's welcome and a ticker tape parade; in subsequent years toured extensively, appearing as a soloist and recitalist. In 1978 he withdrew from public performances, but reappeared in a concert for President Reagan and Soviet General Secretary Gorbachev at the White House in Washington, D.C. (1987); appeared in the Liszt and Tchaikovsky 1st piano concertos with the Philadelphia Orch. (1989); later accepted Gorbachev's invitation to perform in Moscow. Cliburn's playing combines a superlative technique with a genuine Romantic sentiment, particularly effective in the music of Tchaikovsky and Rachmaninoff. The Van Cliburn International Piano Competition was organized by him in 1962 and is held quadrennially in Fort Worth, Tex., the home of the Van Cliburn Foundation.

Cline, Patsy (born Virginia Patterson Hensley), b. Winchester, Va., Sept. 8, 1932; d. in an airplane crash, Camden, Tenn., Mar. 5, 1963. She was an accomplished singer of country music; in 1957, won national recognition on Arthur Godfrey's *Talent Scouts* television program with her rendition of *Walkin' After Midnight;* among her hits were *Heartaches, I Fall to Pieces,* and *Sweet Dreams of You;* she was at the peak of her

popularity when she met her untimely death. In 1973 she was elected to the Country Music Hall of Fame.

cloche (Fr.). Bell. *Cloches,* chimes; *clochette,* a small bell.

clog box. Chinese block.

Clooney, Rosemary, b. Maysville, Ky., May 23, 1928. She sang on a Cincinnati radio station at 13; toured as a soloist with Tony Pastor's Orch. (1945–49); acquired popular success with her recording of *Come On-a My House* (1951); pursued a lively career as a nightclub singer and on recordings, radio, and television. A long-standing dependence on drugs resulted in a mental collapse in 1968; she was able to resume her career in 1976.

close. Cadential ending of a section, movement, or piece.

close harmony. 4-voice arrangement in which the 3 upper voices are confined within an octave.

cluster. Tone cluster.

coda (It., tail). Closing passage after the formal structure of a movement has been fulfilled. The imminent arrival of a coda is often indicated by a dominant pedal point in the bass; other ways include a rapid acceleration followed by a prolonged retardation, a forceful crescendo, or an equally eloquent diminuendo. In fugal writing the coda often annexes additional voices, forming a harmonic section, with the pedal point on the tonic. Bach's fugue in C minor in the 1st book of the *Well-Tempered Clavier* is an example. *Codetta* (It., little tail), short coda.

Cohan, George M(ichael), b. Providence, R.I., July 3, 1878 (Cohan believed that he was born on July 4, but his birth certificate proves July 3 to be correct); d. N.Y., Nov. 5, 1942. He was a vaudeville performer with a natural talent for writing verses and simple melodies in the ballad style. His greatest song, *Over There* (1917), became sweepingly popular during World War I (to the extent that Caruso made a "phonetic" recording of it for the Allied cause); he received a Medal of Honor for it. The film *Yankee Doodle Dandy* (1942) and the Broadway musical *George M!* (1968) were both based on his life.

col legno (It., with the wood). In bowed string playing, strike the strings with the wooden part of the bow rather than with the horsehair.

col pugno (It., with the fist). Percussive effect on the piano keyboard. Prokofiev marked *col pugno* in an episode in his 6th Piano Sonata, and it is probably the sole example of fist pounding in piano concert literature before the 1950s; similar to the tone clusters introduced by Cowell, which are played with forearms or fists.

Cole, "Cozy" (William Randolph), b. East Orange, N.J., Oct. 17, 1906; d. Columbus, Ohio, Jan. 29, 1981. After taking up the drums, he began his career in 1928; played with Jelly Roll Morton, Stuff Smith, and others before joining Cab Calloway's band (1938); appeared on radio; played on Broadway in the musical *Carmen Jones* (1943), displaying his expertise in *Beat Out Dat Rhythm on a Drum;* appeared in *The 7 Lively Arts* with Benny Goodman's Quintet (1945). He later played with Louis Armstrong; formed his own band and toured Africa (1962); a member of the Jonah Jones Quintet (1969–76); artist-in-residence at Capital Univ. in Columbus, Ohio.

Cole, Nat "King" (born Nathaniel Adams Coles), b. Montgomery, Ala., Mar. 17, 1917; d. Santa Monica, Calif., Feb. 15, 1965. He worked as a jazz pianist in Los Angeles nightclubs; in 1939 formed the original King Cole Trio (piano, guitar, bass); gradually shifted to singing. He was the 1st black artist to acquire a sponsor on a radio program; had a brief television series. He created a distinct style of velvet vocalization and satin softness in the rendition of intimate, brooding, sentimental songs; his appeal was universal such that tours in South America, Europe, the Middle East, and the Far East attracted great multitudes of admirers who knew him by his recordings. The sole exception was his home state; at a concert in Birmingham, Ala., on Apr. 10, 1956, he was attacked by 6 white men and suffered a minor back injury.

Coleman, Cy (born Seymour Kaufman), b. N.Y., June 14, 1929. He studied at the N.Y. College of Music; began as a composer for radio and television; with lyricist Joseph A. McCarthy, composed *I'm Gonna Laugh You Out of My Life* and *Why Try to Change Me Now?* To the words of Carolyn Leigh he wrote the song *Witchcraft;* as propelled through the pharynx and larynx of Frank Sinatra it became a hit; wrote the musical *Wildcat* (1960), best remembered for the song *Hey, Look Me Over; Little Me* followed in 1962. He achieved further success with *Sweet Charity* (1966) and *Seesaw* (1973); among other works were *I Love My Wife* (1977), *On the 20th Century* (1978), *Barnum* (1980), *City of Angels* (1989), *The Will Rogers Follies* (1991), and *The Life* (1997).

Coleman, Ornette, b. Fort Worth, Tex., Mar. 9, 1930. He was largely an autodidact; served his apprenticeship playing in carnival and rhythm-and-blues bands; his studies of harmony and theory led him to develop a distinctive style in which the improvised melodic line is independent of the preassigned harmonic scheme. In addition to performing on saxophones, he has written concert music in a respectable modernistic idiom; among his works are *Forms and Sounds* for woodwind quintet (1965), *Skies of America* for orch. (1972), and *Sex Spy* (1977).

Coleridge-Taylor, Samuel, b. London, Aug. 15, 1875; d. Croydon, Sept. 1, 1912. He studied violin at the Royal College of Music (1890); won a composition scholarship (1893); studied under Stanford (to 1896). In 1903 he founded at Croydon a successful amateur string orch.; later added professional woodwind and brass. He was appointed a violin teacher at the Royal Academy of Music (1898); prof. of composition at Trinity College, London (1903) and the Guildhall School (1910); conducted the London Handel Soc. (1904–12); composed and taught in Croydon; made 3 concert tours of the U.S. (1904, 1906, 1910) conducting his works. From the beginning his compositions showed an individuality that rapidly won them recognition; his short career was watched with interest. His most successful work was the trilogy *The Song of Hiawatha,* including *Hiawatha's Wedding Feast* (London, 1898), *The Death of Minnehaha* (North Staffordshire, 1899), and *Hiawatha's*

Departure (London, 1900); the 1st complete performance was presented in Washington, D.C. (1904).

colla parte (It.). Yield to and follow discreetly the solo part or voice.

colla punta dell'arco, at the point (tip) of the bow; *colla sinistra,* with the left hand; *colla voce* (It., with the voice), col canto.

collage. As in the visual arts, heterogeneous compositions in which unexpected or inharmonious elements are juxtaposed, frequently with reference to other, earlier musics.

collective composition. The practice of parceling out the composition of an opera, musical, or other large work among several composers. Handel, Bononcini, and Amadei wrote 1 act each for the opera *Muzio Scevola* for a London performance (1721); it served also as a test of excellence which Handel apparently won. The brothers Paul and Lucien Hillemacher collaborated on a number of operas and even adopted a joint signature, P. L. Hillemacher. The Russian Mighty Five began but never completed a collaborative opera *Mlada*. The *F-A-E Sonata* for violin and piano (1853) was put together by Schumann, Brahms, and the otherwise forgotten Albert Dietrich.

During the early years of the Soviet regime the idea of musical collectivism fascinated student composers at the Moscow Conservatory; they formed the Productive Collective of Student Composers of the Moscow Cons. (PROCOLL), hoping to represent the collectivism of the masses. Chinese musicians have also contributed to musical collectivism, notably *The Yellow River Concerto* for piano and orch.; produced by the Peking Opera Troupe in Shanghai, it was purportedly written by committee, but only 4 musicians, presumably members thereof, acknowledged the applause after its production. See also ⇒pasticcio.

collective nouns. Singular nouns referring to groups of like animals or things. The following are suggestions for collective nouns to designate groups of musical instruments: a fluviality of flutes, an exhalation of piccolos, a conviviality of clarinets, a scabrosity of bassoons, a promiscuity of saxophones, an oriflamme of French horns, a plangency of oboes, an ambrosia of harps, a flourish of trumpets, a pomposity of trombones, a phlogiston of tubas, a circumspection of pianos, an enfilade of violins, a reticence of violas, an elegance of cellos, a teratology of double basses, a titillation of triangles, and the Brobdingnagian borborygmuses of bass drums.

Collegium musicum (Lat.). Group organized to make music for pleasure. The 1st Collegium musicum was formed in Prague (1616); a similar group was organized by Bach in Leipzig. A contemporary description of the Collegium musicum in Frankfurt (1718) stated that its purpose was "to quicken the spirit after a day of work by providing innocent pastime." At such gatherings amateur musicians were given an opportunity to play instrumental music and also discuss musical matters. The practice was revived in colleges and universities in Europe and America in the 20th century, primarily with the purpose of studying and reviving early music.

coll'ottava (It.). Play in octaves; double at the octave.

Colombina (It., Fr. *Columbine*). Stock female character in the commedia dell'arte, the sweetheart of Arlecchino (Harlequin).

colophane. Rosin applied to the hair of string instrument bows to make them more prehensile.

colophon. Inscription at the end of a MS giving information regarding its production.

color. 1. Timbre. 2. In 14th- and 15th-century isorhythmic music, a repeated pitch pattern.

color hearing. The psychological and aesthetic association between sound and color. The 1st "scientific" treatment of this association was given by the English rationalist philosopher John Locke in *An Essay Concerning Human Understanding* (1690); an English ophthalmologist, Theodore Woolhouse, drew an arbitrary comparative table of sounds and colors, asserting, for instance, that the sound of a trumpet is red. But mostly the parallelism of hearing and seeing arose from speculation about the unity of the senses. Mathematical symbolism also played a part; the magic number 7 determined both the number of degrees in the diatonic scale and the number of colors of the spectrum as outlined by Isaac Newton. Scriabin, who was a profound believer in the unity of all senses, inserted a part for a color organ in the score of his last orch'l work, *Prométhée*, meant to inundate a hall with changing colors correlating to keys struck on the organ manual.

It is notable that the dual sense of sound and color is possessed mainly by musicians who possess perfect pitch. Random testing of color hearing among such persons shows no demonstrable coincidences in color designation. There is one exception, however: most pianists perceive the key of C major as white, and the key of F-sharp major as black. Obviously, this association is due to the fact that the C-major scale is played exclusively on white keys and the F-sharp major scale is played primarily on black keys. Would this association persist on those harpsichords on which the "white keys" are manufactured in color, and the "black keys" are actually painted white?

If a true correspondence existed between tones and sounds, then the ascending chromatic scale might register as the spectrum from red to violet, from low to high frequency of vibrations; this is not the case, however. It follows, therefore, that color hearing is a purely subjective impression, similar to color perception by sensitive persons (particularly children) who describe natural sound phenomena in terms of color (thunder is gray, crying is red); in Tolstoy's *War and Peace* the sensitive young Natasha describes Pierre and other friends in terms of color. Such psychological coloring is akin to color hearing; the voice of a child may be associated with yellow; the wrinkled face of an old man with brown; the meow of a cat with silver blue.

coloratura (It.). 1. Ornamental passage in opera, consisting of diversified, rapid runs and trills, often applied in cadenzas and occurring in the highest register; intended to enhance the brilliancy of a composition and display the singer's skill. A coloratura soprano is capable of performing virtuoso passages in high treble; examples are found in Mozart's *The Magic Flute*, Verdi's *Rigoletto*, and Delibes's *Lakmé*. In modern times Rimsky-Korsakov wrote a highly chromatic coloratura part for the Queen of Shemaha in *Le Coq d'Or*. Tenor roles may also fall into this category. 2. Similar passage in instrumental music.

colpo (It.). A blow. *Di colpo,* suddenly.

Coltrane, John (William), b. Hamlet, N.C., Sept. 23, 1926; d. Huntington, Long Island, N.Y., July 17, 1967. He studied at the Ornstein School of Music in Philadelphia; played in the bands of Gillespie, Hodges, Davis, and Monk. As a leader and soloist he enhanced the resources of his style by studying ancestral African and kindred Asian music, absorbing the fascinating modalities of these ancient cultures. He was a master musician whose "sheets of sound" and spiritual expressivity stimulated the creation of sophisticated jazz performance. Athough a controversial figure, he was duly recognized as a major contributor to the avant-garde jazz movement of his era. Among his many albums are *Giant Steps, My Favorite Things, Live at the Village Vanguard, A Love Supreme, Om,* and *Expression.*

combination pedal. Metal foot-lever above the organ pedals; the *forte pedal* draws all the stops of its keyboard; the *mezzo pedal,* the chief 8- and 4-foot stops of its keyboard; the *piano pedal* pushes in all but a few of the softest stops.

combinational tones. Parasitic tones generated when 2 notes are played simultaneously very loudly. They are known as differential (difference) tones if the resulting pitch results from the difference between the frequencies of the 2 orig. sounds, and as summation (sum) tones if the resulting pitch results from the sum of the frequencies of the 2 orig. sounds. The differential tones are heard with particular distinction when a consonant interval is sounded in a near perfect tuning. Such differential tones are known also under the name Tartini tones, as he is reputed to have been the 1st to describe them.

Since, in theory at least, differential tones form a secondary relationship with summation tones, yet another level of parasitic tone may emerge from this interference. The overtones, the natural extension of a single sound, also enter into this multilateral combination. If all these parasitic tones were to materialize audibly, even the simplest piece of music would degenerate into a monstrous jungle of mutually discordant sounds; fortunately the principal tones are so clear and loud in comparison with their combinational sounds that musical pollution is not a real threat.

combinatoriality. Quality of a pitch-class set whose elements are directly related to other segments; specifically, a 12-tone row comprising 2 subsets of 6 notes apiece (hexachords) which are both transpositions and complements of each other. The chromatic hexachords C–F and F♯–B are mutually combinatorial, as are the 2 whole-tone scales; a more subtle example are the hexachords C–F–C♯–E–D—E♭ and F♯–B–G–B♭–G♯–A; each hexachord can be inverted or used in retrograde without disrupting combinatoriality. In general topology the concept of combinatoriality applies to the functional congruence of geometrical figures of the same order of continuity; Babbitt extended the term to cover serial techniques. The parameter of continuity in dodecaphonic writing is the order of succession of the 12 thematic notes in their 4 forms—basic, retrograde, inversion, and inverted retrograde—all of which are combinatorially congruent. Furthermore, the tone-row can be functionally divided into 2 potentially congruent groups of 6 notes each, or 3 groups of 4 notes each, or 4 groups of 3 notes each, with each such group becoming a generating serial nucleus possessing a degree of subsidiary combinatoriality.

Extending combinatoriality to other musical parameters, a state of total serialism is attained, in which not only the notes of a series but meter, rhythm, intervallic configurations, dynamics, and instrumental timbres are organized in sets and subsets. The subsets in turn are organized as combinatorial derivations, possessing their own order of continuity and congruence. One fruitful approach is the principle of rotation, in which each successive set is obtained by the transposition of the 1st note of the series to the end of a derived set. Thus the 1st set, 1, 2, 3, . . . 12, appears after rotation as subset 2, 3, 4, 5, . . . 12, 1, or as 3, 4, 5, 6, . . . 12, 1, 2, etc.; this technique was favored by Stravinsky. The additive Fibonacci series, in which each number equals the sum of the 2 preceding numbers, as in 1, 1, 2, 3, 5, 8, 13, 21, etc., is another fertile resource for the formation of sets, subsets, and other derivations. While the numerical field of combinatoriality is limited to 12 different notes, experiments have been conducted, notably by Krenek, with artificial scales of 13 equal degrees, obtained with the aid of electronic instruments. Potential uses of combinatoriality operating with sets of more than 12 notes in an octave are limitless.

combo (from *combination*). Once-common term for a jazz or popular small group; corresponds to classical chamber music.

Comden and Green, Betty Comden, b. N.Y., May 3, 1915; and Adolph Green, b. N.Y., Dec. 2, 1915. American musicians, lyricists, and dramatists. After performing with the Revuers, they entered a long-standing, highly successful collaboration in the 1940s, beginning with *On the Town* (1944, music by Bernstein), then *Two on the Aisle* (1951, Styne), *Wonderful Town* (1953, Bernstein), *Peter Pan* (1954, Styne), *Bells Are Ringing* (1956, Styne), *Say Darling* (1958, Styne), *Do Re Mi* (1960, Styne), *Subways Are for Sleeping* (1961, Styne), *Fade Out-Fade In* (1964, Styne), *Hallelujah, Baby!* (1967, Styne), *Applause* (1970, Strouse; Tony Award) and *On the 20th Century* (1978, Coleman; Tony Award). They wrote the screenplays for *Singin' in the Rain* (1952) and *The Band Wagon* (1953).

come (It.). As, like. *Come eco,* like an echo; *come prima* (It., as before), resume the tempo and expression of a previous section of the same character; *come retro,* as before; *come sopra,* as above; *come stà,* as it stands, as written.

Comédie-ballet. Scenic entertainment cultivated by Lully and Molière for the court of Louis XIV, e.g., *Les plaisirs de l'île enchantée* (1664) and *Le bourgeois gentilhomme* (1670). The comédie-ballet included, besides the dialogue and ballet, arias and choral pieces.

comes (Lat., companion). Answer to the subject (dux) in a fugue or canon; riposta.

comic opera. Musical work with a comedic subject; in French *opéra-comique,* musical work with spoken dialogue; not necessarily humorous in the modern sense, but a musical equivalent of Italian commedia dell'arte or even Dante's *Commedia divina;* applicable to any scenic representation, even a tragedy. Historically, comic opera was the opposite of opera seria; but composers were not consistent in categorizing their works as comic opera or opera seria, so that even an apparently tragic opera as Mozart's *Don Giovanni* bears the description *dramma giocoso* (jocose drama). A famous example of opéra-comique is Bizet's *Carmen,* which orig. included unaccompanied dialogue, fulfilling the requirements of the Parisian Opéra-Comique, whose repertory included tragic operas as well as opera buffa or operetta; the "Savoy operas" of Gilbert and Sullivan are an English equivalent.

comma. 1. Small interval in Pythagorean (ditonic) tuning; difference between 7 perfect octaves and 12 perfect 5ths, equal to a little more than 1/8 of a whole tone (23.4 cents). In tempered tuning the 5ths are adjusted so as to become commensurate with octaves, avoiding the comma at the expense of absolutely pure intervals. 2. Small interval (comma of Didymus) in syntonic (Ptolemaic) tuning; difference between a just (pure) major 3rd and 4 just perfect 5ths (minus 2 octaves), equal to slightly less than 1/10 of a whole tone (21.5 cents).

comme (Fr.). As, like; used in expression rubrics, particularly by Debussy and Scriabin. *Comme sopra,* as above.

commedia dell'arte (It., artistic play). Italian genre of theatrical performance; emerged during the Renaissance; incorporated versatile elements of pantomime, acrobatics, masks, music, and dance. Most of the action was improvisational, but the main characters were clearly delineated: a cuckolded husband, handsome gallant, accommodating servant, wily lawyer, incompetent doctor, etc.; these stock characters soon received names: a grumbling guardian, old Pantalone (Pantalon); his beautiful daughter or ward Columbina (Columbine), her lover Arlecchino (Harlequin); a long-nosed, grotesque clown, Pulcinella (Punchinello); and the braggart warrior Scamarella (Scaramouche). Composers have used these characters in operas, pantomimes, and plays; Leoncavallo structured *Pagliacci* as a play within a play, by which a circus clown discovers that his wife, playing Columbina, has a lover within the company. Stravinsky emulated commedia dell'arte in his ballets *Petrouchka* and *Pulcinella,* partly in his *L'Histoire du Soldat.*

commedia per musica (It., play with music). Early designation for opera, rarely comic.

commercials, singing. Short catchy melodic phrases used to market crass consumer products; these jingles could drive people up the wall through faulty grammar ("Winston tastes good like a cigarette should") or promises of instant success in love—for men, by using a certain brand of toothpaste; for women, by putting on aphrodisiac perfume. In 1925, Nicolas Slonimsky composed 5 art songs on texts drawn from chunks of advertisements from *The Saturday Evening Post* and other purveyors of American culture, texts wisely selected for their lyric poetry, dramatic rhetoric, and persuasive power, and concerning, respectively, a toothpaste, a mild laxative, bed linen, nose powder, and, the most expressive of all, Castoria. The songs were couched in melodramatic idiom, suitable for such climactic points as the appeal, "Mother, relieve your constipated child!" in the Castoria song, or, with an ominous quotation from Rachmaninoff's C-sharp minor Prelude, the warning, "And then her doctor told her . . . ."

commodo (It.). Incorrect spelling of comodo.

common chord. Major or minor triad.

common hallelujah meter. See ⇒meter.

common long meter. See ⇒meter.

common measure. Common time.

common meter. See ⇒meter.

common particular meter. See ⇒meter.

common time. Measure containing 2 half notes or 4 quarter notes; duple or quadruple time; ordinarily understood to mean 4 quarter notes, and as many beats, to the measure. The time signature may be represented by a capital *C*, derived from the semicircle that served as the medieval symbol for duple time.

comodo (It.; commodo, wrong sp.). Easy, leisurely, at a convenient pace, in a relaxed manner, accommodatingly.

comp (abbrev.). In jazz, accompany a soloist, with chordal emphasis.

compact disk (abbrev. CD, disk). Revolutionary, noninteractive, digital recording; in circulation since the 1980s.

comparative musicology (Ger. *vergleichende Musikwissenschaft*). Orig. term for the study of world musics, with a focus on folk modalities. As practitioners were primarily European and Euro-American, there was often cultural bias in analyses, borrowed in part from the ethnological concept of the "primitive" or "savage" and in part from the application of social Darwinism. By the mid-20th century the term had been changed to ethnomusicology (reflecting a shift from comparison to integral study); as the discipline continues to spread throughout academia, its philosophical problems remain.

compass. Range of a voice or instrument, i.e., collection of all the tones it can produce, from lowest to highest.

compensation. Proportion between the relative complexity or simplicity of the principal elements in a musical composition: melody, harmony, rhythm, dynamics, form, and instrumental arrangement. Whenever music evolved toward a greater complexity, only 1 parameter at a time would tend toward a maximum of technical involvement. When modern melody abandoned tonality and gradually assumed an atonal aspect, the elements of rhythm, harmony, and orchestration remained relatively stable. In dodecaphonic composition, harmony is a function of the tone row, incorporating the horizontal melodic elements in a vertical dimension; but rhythm, meter, and form are restrained in their developments. When rhythm is paramount, and metrical

exchanges are frequent, as in Stravinsky's *Le Sacre du printemps*, the melody and harmony become remarkably static, even in highly dissonant settings.

Compensation is at work in canonic movements, when the orderly procession of voices in mutual imitation creates at times surprisingly dissonant combinations; playing development sections of some of Bach's fugues very slowly reveals the many vertical discords created in the canonic process; the formal dissonances are justified by the strong linear counterpoint. The unifying strength of the bass pedal point on the dominant gives license to modulation into remote keys without discomfort; in the wedding procession in Rimsky-Korsakov's opera, *Le Coq d'or*, with the dominant bass pedal point on G, there are modulations into the keys of A-flat major and D-flat major. An exception to the law of compensation is exemplified by totally serial works, in which rhythm, dynamics, melody, harmony, instrumentation, and form are organized so as to prevent any compensation for unrelieved diversification; paradoxically, this exclusion of compensation leads to a unification sui generis, with the totality of musical elements regarded as a single entity.

complement (complementary interval). Interval which, added to any given interval not wider than an octave, completes the octave, e.g., a perfect 4th is the complement of a perfect 5th, a minor 3rd of a major 6th, etc.

complete cadence. See ⇒cadence.

complin(e) (from Lat. *completorium*, completion). Short, early evening service, one of the canonical hours; in addition to 4 Mary antiphons and a hymn, the most significant portion is the dismissory canticle of Simeon, Nunc dimittis.

composer (from Lat. *componere*, put things together). Man or woman who writes music and transmits it by written or oral means; the musical sense of the term is at least 1,000 years old; Guido d'Arezzo includes it in his *Micrologus*, establishing the necessary properties for a melody to be well "put together" (*componenda*). The medieval Latin term for composer was *compositor*, which now refers to a typesetter in English; in Spanish, *compositor* retains its original Latin sense. Tinctoris, author of the 1st dictionary of music, describes the composer as a writer of a new melody. Later theorists drew the distinction between *compositio*, a conscious act of composing, and *sortisatio*, a random improvisation. The rules for composition vary enormously through the centuries; but changes, however momentous, have not altered the basic definition of a composer as a person who puts notes together in a more or less logical and coherent manner.

composition. Writing music in any form for any instruments or voices; components of an art work; the resulting work itself.

composition pedal. In the organ, a pedal which draws out or pushes in several stops at once.

compound interval. Interval greater than an octave.

compound meters. Time signatures with the numerator in prime numbers greater than 4, representing the sum of commonly used meters; 5/4, 7/4, 11/4, and 13/4 are compound meters; theoretically, they have but one downbeat accent, but in practical usage compound meters are divided into 2 or more simple meters: thus 5/4 is heard as 3/4 + 2/4, or 2/4 + 3/4; 7/4, as 4/4 + 3/4, or 3/4 + 4/4, or 2/4 + 2/4 + 3/4, etc. Russian composers parlayed lengthy sections in 5/4 into their works, most notably the "waltz in 5/4 time" in the 2nd movement of Tchaikovsky's *Pathétique Sym*. 11/4 is found in Rimsky-Korsakov's *Sadko;* Russian chorus singers sang the 11-syllable equivalent of the sentence "Rimsky-Korsakov is altogether mad" to cope with the unusual count. Mussorgsky used the equivalent of 11/4 in the Promenade of *Pictures at an Exhibition,* notating it by alternating bars of 5/4 and 6/4.

Early in the 20th century compound meters were often used as novelties; this tendency was particularly embodied in the diversity of time signatures in Stravinsky's works, especially in *Le Sacre du printemps.* An important category of compound meters involves asymmetric division of traditional time signatures, e.g., the sum of 2/8 + 3/8 + 2/8 + 2/8 (9/8, used by Rimsky-Korsakov) or 10/8 as the coalescence of 2 bars of 5/8; Bartók utilizes asymmetric meters in his many folk-influenced works (e.g., *6 Dances in Bulgarian Rhythm* from *Mikrokosmos,* vol. 6); the Dave Brubeck Quartet became very popular with its asymmetric pieces (*Blue Rondo à la Turk, Take Five*). Compound meters are sometimes masked by the use of dotted notes and rests within a traditional time signature, e.g., Gershwin's *I Got Rhythm,* notated in 4/4 time, with 4 dotted eighth notes flanked by 2 eighth-note rests.

computer. Programmable, digitally based electronic device that stores, retrieves, and processes data. Computers can be used by composers to calculate details of compositions, store information for subsequent use, or generate new sounds (or transform existing ones). Computer technology has led to specific devices to create an interaction between live performance and digital realization.

computer music. Music generated by computer, whether directly, through interaction with live instruments, or as the product of precompositional data.

For many centuries music theorists and composers have cherished the notion that beautiful melodies and wonderful harmonies could be produced mathematically. Such musical alchemy fascinated the masters of Renaissance polyphonic music, who eagerly experimented with the techniques of inversion, retrograde movement, interval extension, rhythmical expansion, and other basically mathematical concepts. When digital computers were perfected in the mid-20th century, musicians began to explore electronic resources for the creation of scientific "music of the spheres" which would provide composers with new resources.

Digital computers and other electronic devices cannot produce output more valuable than the input fed into the computer by human programmers; programming a computer by a series of numbers is no different from the process of writing notes on paper. In one of the earliest computerized compositions, using a relatively primitive computer called Illiac, 2 programmers (including Lejaren Hiller) produced the *Illiac Suite* for string quartet, which ended with a lengthy C-major coda. Digital computers are ideal generators of random numbers, which can be converted into musical parameters, furnishing appropriate

sources for aleatory music and computer-generated sound; computer composition should not be programmed excessively, for such input would amount to the dictation of the programmer's own, often lamentable musical ideas.

But if a digital computer is helpless without a programmer, it remains a fascinating resource for the composition of instantaneous canons or similar contrapuntal forms; given a subject, a computer can produce the requisite time lapses between voices, at an octave or another interval; the result can be tested by immediate playback. In analysis a computer can be most useful. Suppose one wants to compare the main subjects of a number of sonatas and syms. to prove theories of similarity and conversion and trace coincidences and unconscious borrowings; by devising a relatively simple code, indicating duration and intervallic motion, motives are tabulated and the degree of similarity among them determined statistically; such scientific checks would be particularly valuable to composers of popular songs who are periodically sued for pilfering someone else's tunes.

If all popular songs were to be stored away in code in a digital computer's memory bank, composers with retentive memories of other tunes would be saved a lot of work; on the other hand, such a computerized memory bank could turn into a Frankenstein monster. The number of tunes and rhythms, many of them revolving around the major triad, with rhythms kept to the simplest proportions of relative note values, is limited, and time may not be far away from the Doomsday of popular music, predicted by John Stuart Mill more than a century ago: "I was seriously tormented by the thought of the exhaustibility of musical combinations. The octave consists only of 5 tones and 2 semitones, which can be put together in only a limited number of ways of which but a small proportion are beautiful; most of these, it seemed to me, must have been already discovered."

comprimario (It., with the primary). Secondary operatic role; in *Faust,* Valentin (a baritone) is an example.

con (It.). With; in a style expressive of; for definitions of phrases beginning with *con,* see the 2nd word in the given phrase.

concert. Musical performance in the presence of an audience. Public concerts were 1st organized in Italy in the early 17th century; solo performances and chamber ensemble concerts were popular in London in the 18th century. In France a series of concerts was organized in 1725 under the name Concert Spirituel; in the 19th century concerts became part of cultural life everywhere. The word "recital" for a solo concert came into vogue in the middle of the 19th century, invented by the London manager of Liszt. Regular sym. concerts were organized in Paris (1828); later they spread to England, Russia, and all over Europe. America became the El Dorado of concert artists in the 2nd half of the 19th century.

concert grand. Largest type of grand piano (9').

concert overture. One-movement work for full orch., usually in sonata form, sometimes programmatic, performed independently at sym. concerts.

concert pitch. Actual sound produced by an instrument, as distinct from a written note for transposing instruments, e.g. in

B-flat clarinet music, written C sounds B-flat. As for the pitch itself, the A = 440Hz now considered standard in the U.S. has not always been so; pitch has been consistently on the rise for more than a century. If Mozart were to come back to life and hear his C-major *Jupiter Sym.,* he would hear it as being in D flat. In any case, many non-American orchs. do not use A = 440Hz to tune.

Concert Spirituel. Famous series of concerts in Paris, organized 1725, usually given on religious holidays when the opera house was closed; programs featured secular and sacred music.

concertante (It.). 1. Concert piece. 2. Composition or section thereof for 2 or more solo voices or instruments, accompanied by orch. or organ, in which each soloist is in turn brought into prominence. 3. Composition for 2 or more unaccompanied solo instruments in orch'l music, often called a symphonie concertante. *Concertante style,* a style of composition admitting of a brilliant display of skill on the soloist's part.

concerted music. Music written in parts for several instruments or voices, i.e., trios, quartets, etc.

concerti (It.). Concertos (the plural used in this book).

concertina. Free-reed instrument with 2 hexagonal heads, each with a button keyboard and handle, connected by expandable bellows, patented by Charles Wheatstone in 1829. There are 2 layout systems: the English, fully chromatic, where each button produces the same note on the extension and compression of the bellows; and the German-Anglo, diatonic in conception, where each button produces different pitches on the extension and compression of the bellows. The concertina comes in ranges ranging from soprano to double bass; its repertory has included classical, light classical, novelty, and traditional music. See also ⇒accordion.

concertino (It., Ger. *Konzertstück*). 1. Small concerto, usually for a small ensemble. 2. Group of soloists in a concerto grosso.

concertmaster (from Ger. *Konzertmeister*). In the U.S., the 1st violin player in an orch. In England the 1st violinist in the orch. is called leader; in France, premier violon or chef d'attaque; in Italy, violino primo; in Spain, concertino.

concerto. An extended composition for a solo instrument (or instruments) and orch.; a concerto for orch. without soloist is called *concerto grosso,* a grand concerto. The etymological derivation of concerto is subject to debate: the most logical origin is from the Latin verb *concertare* (compete, contend with one another); but it also appears in Italian as a cognate of *concerto* (agreement); yet another conjecture is that *concerto* comes from the Latin verb *conserere* (come together; the spelling *conserto* is found in some Italian MSS of the 17th century).

The form of the classical concerto is similar to that of a sonata. Most concertos are in 3 movements, marked *Allegro, Andante, Allegro.* Normally absent, a minuet is occasionally inserted after the 2nd movement (in later works, a scherzo). The chief characteristic of a concerto is antiphony, with the soloist and the orch.

alternating in presenting main themes. Classical concertos usually feature one or more cadenzas for the solo instrument, inserted in a cadence between the tonic 6/4 chord and the dominant. In theory, a cadenza should confine itself to the tonic harmony with the bass on the dominant, so as to maintain the sense of an interrupted cadence; any intervening modulations have to be handled with caution. The length of an orch'l introduction to a concerto varies widely; concertos often begin with a solo passage; a striking example is Beethoven's 4th Piano Concerto in G major; Rachmaninoff's 2nd Piano Concerto opens with a short prelude in the solo part, letting the orch. present the main theme.

Numerically, piano concertos are in the majority, as composer-pianists give preference to their own instrument in writing concertos. Among numerous concertos still in the standard repertory are those of Mozart, Beethoven, Chopin, Schumann, Mendelssohn, Liszt, Saint-Saëns, Brahms, Tchaikovsky, Grieg, and Rachmaninoff. The concertos by Anton Rubinstein once enjoyed great popularity, owing to Rubinstein's own virtuoso performances; they have gone into limbo, except in Russia. Concertos by Dvořák, MacDowell, and such minor figures as Thalberg, Moscheles, or Litolff occasionally appear on concert programs. Modern piano concertos tend to be less discursive and more compact than their predecessors; following Liszt's example, they are often compressed into a single movement subdivided into sections of different tempos and characters. Concertos by Ravel, Prokofiev, and Bartók have become firmly established in the modern piano repertory; Schoenberg's Concerto is gaining ground despite its unfamiliar idiom and tremendous technical difficulties. Some concertos are written for left hand alone, a genre resulting from commissions by Austrian pianist Paul Wittgenstein (1887–1961), who lost his right arm on the Russian front in World War I; Ravel, R. Strauss, Prokofiev, Korngold, Britten, and others obliged him with one-armed works.

The number of violin concertos written during the last 3 centuries is almost as large as that of piano concertos; Vivaldi and other Baroque composers wrote hundreds of them. Among the most celebrated post-Baroque concertos are by Mozart, Beethoven, Mendelssohn, Brahms, Tchaikovsky, and Sibelius. Glazunov's Violin Concerto enjoys unabated popularity in Russia; concertos by the virtuosos Paganini, Wieniawski, Vieuxtemps, and Bruch remain popular. Among modern violin concertos, those of Prokofiev, Bartók, and Khachaturian are often heard; Berg's Violin Concerto has achieved a permanent place in the modern repertoire; Schoenberg's has yet to achieve comparable public acceptance; Stravinsky's enjoys respectability but little attraction to performers.

Among cello concertos of the Classic period, those by Haydn and Boccherini are well established; the best-known 19th-century cello concertos are those by Saint-Saëns and Dvořák. Tchaikovsky's *Variations on a Rococo Theme* is a kind of cello concerto, as is Ernest Bloch's *Schelomo.* The character of Don Quixote in the eponymous tone poem of R. Strauss is portrayed by a solo cello (a solo viola "performs" Sancho Panza), but the work is more programmatic tone poem than true solo concerto. The viola is the orphan of the string family, with only a few composers charitable enough to write concertos for it. Berlioz tried to write a viola concerto in his *Harold in Italy;* the result may be classified as a programmatic sym. with viola obligato. In modern times, Hindemith and William Walton contributed viola concertos; Bartók worked on a viola concerto but left it incomplete; his faithful disciple Tibor Serly completed the score. Koussevitzky wrote a concerto for double bass, an instrument on which he was a virtuoso. The German Henze wrote important concertos for each of the 4 string instruments.

In the woodwind department, there are concertos for practically every instrument. Quantz, court flutist for Frederick the Great, wrote a plethora of concertos for himself and his sovereign to play. The conductor Eugene Goossens wrote an oboe concerto for his brother Leon; R. Strauss wrote one in his later years. There are clarinet concertos by Mozart, Weber, Nielsen, and Musgrave, the last written in an ultramodern idiom; Stravinsky composed an *Ebony Concerto* for clarinet and jazz ensemble. There are several bassoon concertos available, beginning in the Baroque with Vivaldi (later, Mozart). Glazunov composed a saxophone concerto. Haydn's *Trumpet Concerto* is a brilliant virtuoso piece. Strauss wrote 2 concertos for horn and orch. (his father was a renowned horn player). George Walker wrote one of the few trombone concertos; Vaughan Williams wrote a concerto for tuba.

Concertos for harp and orch. are not too numerous (Handel, Ginastera), but Ravel's *Introduction et Allegro* for harp and instruments is in effect a chamber concerto; the modern harpist Carlos Salzedo wrote a concerto accompanied by wind instruments. Guitar concertos have been written by Ponce, Castelnuovo-Tedesco, and Rodrigo; Glière wrote a concerto for voice and orch; Cowell composed 2 concertos for the koto. There is even a concerto for kazoo with orch., concocted by the American composer Mark Bucci.

Double concertos are those in which 2 instruments are soloists on an equal standing; the Concerto for Violin and Cello by Brahms is an example; Bartók orchestrated his Sonata for 2 Pianos and Percussion. The category of triple concerto is represented by Bach's mighty Concerto for 3 Harpsichords and the Brandenburg Concerto no. 5, Beethoven's Concerto for Violin, Cello, and Piano, and Tippett's Concerto for Violin, Viola, and Cello. Spohr wrote a quadruple concerto for string quartet and orch. Such multiple concertos effectively cross the line of demarcation separating solo concertos from the class of concerto grosso.

concerto, sacred. See ⇒Sacred concerto.

concerto for orchestra. Symphonic work in which the orch'l instruments play the role of soloists in free rotation; the pioneering work of this type is Bartók's (1943).

concerto grosso (It., grand concerto). Instrumental composition employing a small group of solo instruments (*concertino*, little group) within a larger group or full orch. (*ripieno*, filling up). This essentially Baroque genre differs from a solo concerto because of the nature of the concertino, functioning as multiple soloist, alternating with and antiphonally supported by the ripieno, also designated by the Italian term *tutti* (all; every instrument). The concertino usually comprises 2 violins and a cello, with the harpsichord furnishing the harmony indicated by basso continuo. The tutti consist of a fairly large ensemble of strings supplemented by trumpets, flutes, oboes, and horns. The earliest works in this genre were Corelli's op. 6

(1714), probably composed in 1680; Torelli wrote a group of concerti grossi about 1690.

The concerto grosso was standardized by Vivaldi; it consisted of 3 cyclic movements: *Allegro, Adagio, Allegro*. Bach's Brandenburg Concertos are basically of the concerto grosso type, but Bach often diversified the concertino parts in the manner of a solo concerto. Handel's concerti grossi observed the formal elements of the type more strictly than Bach. In the 2nd half of the 18th century, with the growing tendency toward Classic symphonic forms, the concerto grosso evolved into the symphonie concertante and eventually into a full-fledged symphony without individual solo groups. In the 19th century the concerto grosso was virtually obsolete; it was left to the 20th century to revive the genre; a typical example is Max Reger's *Konzert im alten Stil* (Concerto in the Old Style), in which the Baroque structure is tinted with Romantic colors.

Concertstück (*Konzertstück;* Ger., concert piece). One-movement concerto; concertino.

concitato (It.). Moved, excited, agitated.

concord. Euphony; harmony; consonance.

conduct. Rehearse and direct an orch., band, or chorus.

conducting. The art of rehearsing and directing a large ensemble. When a number of singers or instrumentalists perform together, it is helpful to have a leader whose function is to indicate the beginning of the music and the tempo. In Baroque practice it was usually up to the *maestro al cembalo* (master at the keyboard) to give these directions. When performing groups became larger, the 1st violinist (concertmaster) usually initiated the proceedings with a motion of his violin bow. A composer-conductor could beat time on the desk with a small stick or a roll of paper, or emphasize the beat by stamping his foot on the floor or by using a long cane; Lully, the leading court composer for Louis XIV, supposedly struck his foot with the sharp point of his conducting baton, leading to a fatal gangrene.

The tradition of conducting with a wooden baton originated early in the 19th century; in a letter, Mendelssohn mentions his conducting an orch. in London "with a white stick." Although the baton is the scepter of authority and the emblem of the art, some conductors have found it easier to lead orchs. with only their bare hands; Russian conductor Wassily Safonoff, 1st to become batonless, said that by doing so, he acquired 10 batons with his fingers. Stokowski did away with the baton during his entire U.S. career, making eloquent use of his aristocratic fingers. In the early days of professional conducting it was customary to face the audience rather than the orch.; but since such a fashion of civil, polite conducting made it virtually impossible for the conductor to control the players, the orch'l leaders gradually decided to "face the music." (As late as 1925 Walter Damrosch would still turn toward the public for the grand finale in Beethoven's 5th Sym.)

A whole generation of impeccably tailored German conductors set the tradition of "dictators of the baton," commanding their players in the manner of a feudal lord ordering about his vassals. Bülow in particular was as famous for his Prussian brutality toward players as for superior musicianship. A typical anecdote:

He disliked 2 members of his orch. named Schulz and Schmidt. One day the manager announced to him that Schmidt had died. "And Schultz?," Bülow replied. Another time he informed his soprano soloist that she was not pretty enough to sing so badly out of tune. Toscanini was probably the last conductor who could hurl insulting epithets to orch. members with impunity; at the last rehearsal for his last concert he shouted at his men: "Imbecili! Tutto è scritto. La più bella musica del mondo!" In deference to his great age and supreme musicianship, the orch. fell silent at his imprecations, and he walked slowly off the podium. When major sym. orchs. organized themselves into unions, the players began to assert their human dignity by limiting abuse by conductors.

The technique of conducting can be learned quickly. Traditionally, conductors give the downbeat on the 1st beat of the measure; an upbeat on the 2nd beat, when the measure is 2/4; in 3/4, his stick must describe a triangle with its lowest apex always downward. In 4/4, after the mandatory downbeat, the hand moves northwest, then northeast, then at an angle to north, and south for the next downbeat. Compound measures combine these fundamental motions. Some would-be conductors do not realize that in order to give the downbeat, one must 1st lift the conducting hand in an anticipatory upbeat which also sets the tempo. However, some conductors allow themselves the luxury of starting a pianissimo movement by gradually lowering the hand without a discernible upbeat.

Ideally, conductors must have total mastery over the musical score and an ability to coordinate the players and singers so that they create a euphonious ensemble. The tempo must be established with a wave of the hand that is clear but unobtrusive; the subtlest nuances must be communicated to the players with a gentle finger motion or suitable facial expression. A common gesture (often immortalized on professional photographs) is to put the right-hand index finger on the lips to indicate pianissimo. An imperious thrust of the right hand toward the brass section indicates fortissimo. Conductors of the Romantic type address the orch. with a great expenditure of bodily motion, often changing their angle of direction; Toscanini usually bent his left arm and kept it almost immobile, pressed against his left side. Idiosyncrasies are many: some conductors move their lips as if speaking or singing; others hum with the melody, often out of tune. While histrionic conductors were most successful in earlier times, ungainly orch'l leaders have also attained great renown. Old-fashioned conductors were often moved to explain the imaginary "meaning" of the music; when Mengelberg exhorted a solo cellist by pointing out the music's expressive yearning of the soul for happiness and redemption, the cellist looked at him quizzically and said, "You mean mezzoforte?" Whatever the technique used, the conductor's prime duty is to translate an orch'l score into an effective panorama of sound, faithfully rendering the composer's creative designs. The art of conducting requires the musical, psychological, and intellectual ability to coordinate the instruments and voices with the goal of creating perfect euphony of ensemble, incorporating a great variety of dynamic nuances and timbres, and maintaining a balance of contrapuntal components within the general harmonic framework and the animating flow of propulsive rhythm.

Paradoxically, composers are rarely the best interpreters of their own works; perhaps only Wagner, Berlioz, Mahler, and Bernstein, all professional conductors, gave full justice to their own masterpieces; among those giving their works less than full justice were Tchaikovsky, Rimsky-Korsakov, Debussy, Ravel, and, arguably, Stravinsky and Copland. No wonder then that composers had to have their interpreters, much as presidents must have their speechwriters. It is in this sense that one talks about "Toscanini's Beethoven," "Walter's Mozart," or "Furtwängler's Brahms."

In the 19th century the majority of conductors were Germans, filling posts throughout the world. When Major Henry Lee Higginson decided to finance the Boston Sym. Orch. (BSO; 1881), he stipulated that conductors must be of German origin; a scandal set in when, at the outset of World War I, Karl Muck, conductor of the BSO, was arrested and interned as an enemy alien; similar fates befell most German-born conductors of American orchs. A few who had become American citizens, among them Walter Damrosch, were spared the disgrace of internment, although they were warned not to play German music; French, British, and Russian conductors filled the vacated posts. Another wave of political discrimination arose in 1933 when German conductors such as Furtwängler were unable to obtain American engagements because of alleged ties with the Nazi government; this *de facto* ban persisted after the war. However, German conductors of Jewish origin, victimized by the Hitler regime, were welcome in the U.S. A remarkable development occurred in the later decades of the century when 2 of the most important conducting positions in the U.S. were entrusted to Asians: the Indian Zubin Mehta, conductor of the Los Angeles Philharmonic, became music director of the N.Y. Phil.; Seiji Ozawa of Japan became head of the BSO; gradually other racial and gender barriers gave way, and African-American and female conductors began to hold directorships of smaller city and chamber orchs.

conductor. leader or director of an orch., band, or chorus.

conductus (Lat., procession). Latin genre of the late Middle Ages, in contrast to the sacred motet; they usually accompanied liturgical processions. Most conductus are monophonic, sung in unison or octave; a polyphonic conducti developed in the 13th century; the 2nd (added) part was also called the conductus. Some conductus were derived from liturgical melodies, others freely composed; the typical contrapuntal rhythmic structure is note against note. In the 15th century the conductus, especially in Italian, adopted florid ornamentation of a madrigal type.

confinalis. Secondary final tone, usually the dominant, in ecclesiastical modes; the confinalis of the Dorian mode is particularly important because it corresponds to A, which became the primary tone of the alphabetical scale.

conga. Afro-Cuban ballroom dance, in duple time, with a rhythmic anticipation at every 2nd beat.

conical mouthpiece. Deeper, cone-shaped form of mouthpiece for brass instruments, as opposed to the shallower cupped mouthpiece. *Conical tube,* instrument body that tapers very gradually; opposite of the cylindrical tube, which does not taper.

conjunct degree. Nearest degree in the scale (chromatic or diatonic) to the given degree. *Conjunct motion,* progression by conjunct degrees or intervals.

consecutive intervals (parallel intervals). Progression of 2 voices moving in the same direction and interval; at the distance of a perfect 5th or octave, strictly forbidden in tonal counterpoint. Rimsky-Korsakov was obsessed with this prohibition; he double-checked his students' exercises by handing them over to his trusted pupil and assistant Glazunov, who was an expert in ferreting out such errors. There are consecutive 5ths in the coda of Liszt's *Liebestraum;* to "correct" it, editors removed one of the voices, leaving the customary 4-voice texture incomplete. Consecutive perfect 4ths are also not allowed in 2-part counterpoint, unless it is protected by overlapping consecutive 6ths, producing a progression of 1st-inversion chords ($^6/_3$) in 3-part harmony (as in fauxbourdon and faburden). By the early 20th century the prohibition of any consecutive interval in free composition had been quietly dropped; indeed, they were a major component of the impressionist and symbolist styles. Ironically, the earlier forms of polyphony were 5ths and octaves added above Gregorian chant.

consequent. In a canon, the comes (follower); the part imitating the antecedent or dux (leader).

conservatoire (Fr., conservatory; Lat. *conservatorium;* abbrev. cons.). Public or private institution for providing practical and theoretical instruction in music.

console. 1. Structure or table supporting the entire apparatus of a large organ: keyboard, stops, and pedals. 2. Piece of furniture containing an "entertainment center," which may include a radio, phonograph, tape player, CD player, and television.

consonance. Combination of 2 or more tones, harmonious, pleasing in itself, requiring no further resolution; in common practice period tonality, the major and minor 3rds and 6ths and the perfect octave, 5th, and 4th (and their compounds). Early in Western musical history only the perfect consonances of the octave, the 5th, and (sometimes) the 4th were considered consonant; 3rds and 6ths were treated as dissonances, not accepted as imperfect consonances until well into the 13th century. Consonance is the opposite of dissonance, a combination unpleasant to the ear. The Latin etymology of consonance corresponds precisely to the Greek *symphonia* (con = sym, together; sonance = phonos, sounding); a more poetic synonym is concord, the "agreement of hearts," as opposed to discord, "disagreement of hearts."

The separation of consonance from dissonance is not entirely arbitrary, as the idea of harmonious consonance is related to acoustics. According to historical practice and Renaissance theory, consonances are combinations of tones whose frequency ratio factors are limited to the numbers 2 to 6; the smaller the numbers, the more perfect the consonance formed by such fractions. Thus the octave is most perfect, embodying the frequency ratio 2/1; the perfect 5th corresponds to 3/2; the perfect 4th, 4/3. Among the imperfect consonances, the major 3rd has a ratio of 5/4; the minor 3rd, 6/5; and major 6th, 5/3. (The imperfect minor 6th is formed by 8/5; while the numeral 8 is above the limit, theorists justified it because 8/1 was simply a compound octave.) Thus consonant intervals were present within the 1st 6 tones of the overtone series; these 6 partials (starting with the fundamental) form a major triad, often described as "a true

chord of nature." There are paradoxes aplenty inherent in the overtone series, for all partials of the series theoretically form a consonance with the fundamental, as long as the notes involved are in their proper place in the series. For example, if the C-major scale in the lowest register of the piano is played simultaneously with the B-major scale in high treble, the 2 scales will form "consonances"—B in the middle octave of the piano forms the 15th partial tone of the lowest available C; B an octave higher is the 30th partial (2/1 x 15/1), and 1 more octave higher constitutes the 60th partial, etc.

Ragtime and jazz pianists who introduced unresolved dissonances into harmony did so spontaneously, but they invariably and instinctively placed dissonant notes higher in the treble where they became acoustically consonant with the bass note. The so-called added major 6th over the major triad forms the 27th overtone above the fundamental. The major-major 7th-chord is a favorite among jazz pianists for final cadences; when the major 7th is placed in the high treble, the 15th overtone of the fundamental results. Another cadential chord employed by popular musicians contains the 9th overtone (added 2nd), the supertonic of the major scale based on the fundamental. But jazz players rarely put a perfect 4th (above the fundamental) on top of the harmonic pile. Why? Because no matter how far one ascends in the overtone series, one never reaches a perfect 4th from the bass. (Of course, perfect 4ths are available internally, i.e., 4/3.) Other intervals dissociated from the fundamental are the minor 2nd (16/15), minor 3rd (6/5), and their inversions: major 7th (15/8), minor 7th (9/5), major 6th (5/3), and minor 6th (8/5). However, the dissonant interval of the augmented 4th may, *mirabile dictu,* be treated as a part of the overtone series, as the 45th partial. If we play the C-major scale in the low bass register and the F-sharp major scale in the highest treble, the effect will be a progression of parallel consonances.

consonant chord. Harmony containing no dissonant interval.

consort (Lat. *consortium,* congregation). A Renaissance term for an instrumental ensemble; a *whole consort* consisted of either all wind or all string instruments (e.g., recorders, viols), while a *broken consort* was a mixed group of wind and string instruments; Shakespeare called the latter "broken music." *Consort song,* vocal ensemble, usually a quartet, sometimes accompanied by a broken consort.

constructivism. Early 20th-century Russian aesthetic movement in which the artwork exhibits a high degree of visible structure, based on geometric or (in music) industrial principles.

contenance angloise (Fr., English manner). Frequent use of parallel 1st-inversion chords, associated with Dunstable and his contemporaries; related to the practice of 15th-century French composers known as *fauxbourdon.*

contenu (Fr.). Restrained, under control.

continuo (It.). Basso continuo; often interchangeable with cembalo.

contra (Lat., It., against). Prefixed to instrument names, a larger instrument sounding an octave below the standard size.

contrabass (It. *contrabasso;* Fr. *contrebasse;* Ger. *Kontrabass*). Double bass.

contrabassoon (Brit. *double bassoon;* Fr. *contre-basson;* It. *contrafagotto;* Ger. *Kontrafagott*). Lower-pitched member of the bassoon family, sounding an octave lower than the standard instrument. Like the bassoon, the contrabassoon is bent back on itself; in its present form (established in the 19th century) the tube is 16 feet long when laid straight. The 1st references date to the early Baroque; except for French makers who still use wood, metal is the material of choice. The contrabassoon functioned as a bass instrument in military bands, the probable reason that Beethoven featured the contrabassoon at the beginning of the military variation in the finale of Sym. No. 9.

Contrafagott (*Kontrafagott;* Ger.). 1. Contrabassoon. 2. 16' reed organ stop.

contrafactum (from Lat. *contrafacere,* counterfeit, imitate). Fitting of new text to a preexistent melody. A technique begun in the Middle Ages, it applied most commonly to secular texts grafted to sacred melodies. In the 17th century the practice was known as *parody,* not in the modern sense of caricature, but as a "near song" (*para-ode*).

contralto (It.). Alto.

contra-octave. 16' octave (C¹), 1 octave below the great octave.

contrapuntal. Pertaining to the art or practice of counterpoint.

contrary motion. Contrapuntal motion wherein one part moves upward while the other moves downward; in strict counterpoint, the ideal type of motion.

contratenor. See ⇒Countertenor.

contre (It., contra). Against.

contredanse (Fr.; Ger. *Contratanz, Kontretanz;* It. *contradanza*). Baroque French salon dance similar to the quadrille and related to the English country dance, usually in duple or compound duple meter (6/8). The term "contredanse" may not mean "counter[ing]-dance"; it is possibly a corrupted form of "country dance"; there are extant collections of "contredanses anglaises", publ. in France in the 17th century. Beethoven wrote several contredanses, and borrowed 1 for the finale of the *Eroica Sym.*

controlled improvisation. Arrangement of available thematic elements following a definite formal design and confined within a specified period of time. The performer selects attractive or significant motives and phrases of an otherwise nonintegrated work and resets them at will, duplicated, fragmented, or upside down. Stockhausen, Foss, Brown, and others have availed themselves of this procedure.

Cook, Will Marion, b. Washington, D.C., Jan. 27, 1869; d. N.Y., July 19, 1944. He entered the Oberlin (Ohio) Cons. to study violin at age 13; continued studies with Joachim in Germany and at the National Cons. in N.Y.; had a brief career as a concert violinist before devoting himself to composition for the black musical theater in N.Y.; was director and composer for the Bert Williams-George Walker productions (1900–1908); founded his own "syncopated" sym. orch. (1918), with which he toured extensively. In his later years he was active mainly as a conductor and teacher in N.Y. His best-known musicals are *Clorindy, or The Origin of the Cakewalk* (1898) and *Swing Along* (collaboration with Vodery, 1929); noted for his spiritual arrangements.

Cooke, Sam (born Samuel Cook), b. Chicago, Jan. 22, 1931; shot to death in Los Angeles, Dec. 11, 1964. He sang in a lyric tenor voice, avoiding the shouts and the screams of so many popular singers. He sang and composed gospel music; later reached a broad audience with rhythm-and-blues hymns to the woes of unrequited love and other traumas. Among his big hits were *You Send Me, Chain Gang, Wonderful World, Twistin' the Night Away,* and *Cupid;* as a gospel performer with the Soul Stirrers, sang gospel hymns such as *Nearer to Thee, Touch the Hem of His Garment, Wonderful* (*God Is So Wonderful*), and *Jesus, Wash Away My Troubles.*

cool jazz. 1. Any style with a more restrained or precomposed quality, as in swing/big band, 1950s, and jazz-rock fusion. 2. Style of the 1950s, characterized by a less "hot" atmosphere than earlier styles, use of unusual instruments (baritone saxophone, flute, French horn), and adoption of classical techniques (i.e., fugue, mixed orchestration). Cool jazz cultivates a flow of relaxation, in serene legatissimo, replacing frenetic syncopation by emphasis on strong beats; for musical and economic reasons, cool jazz musicians preferred smaller ensembles, which offered greater freedom for individual solo improvisations. Among the most famous cool jazz musicians was Miles Davis, who defined the style in his 1948 collaboration with Gil Evans, *Birth of the Cool;* Gerry Mulligan, who established a pianoless quartet with trumpeter Chet Baker; the Modern Jazz Quartet (with John Lewis and Milt Jackson), who collaborated with Gunther Schuller on 3rd Stream music, combining classical composition and jazz improvisation; and the Dave Brubeck Quartet.

coperto (It.). Covered, muffled. Applied to mutes in horns, trumpets, and timpani.

Copland, Aaron, b. N.Y., Nov. 14, 1900; d. North Tarrytown, N.Y., Dec. 2, 1990. He was educated at the Boys' High School in Brooklyn; studied piano with Victor Wittgenstein and Clarence Adler; learned harmony and counterpoint with Rubin Goldmark in N.Y. (1917); soon began to compose. His 1st publ. piece, *The Cat and the Mouse* for Piano (1920), subtitled *Scherzo humoristique,* shows Debussy's influence; entered the American Cons. in Fontainebleau, near Paris (1920) to study composition and orchestration with Nadia Boulanger; returned to America (1924); lived mostly in N.Y.; active as a composer, lecturer, pianist, and organizer of various musical societies. He attracted the attention of Koussevitzky, who performed the premiere of his *Music for the Theater* with the Boston Sym. Orch. (1925); engaged Copland as soloist in the Concerto for Piano and Orch. (1927); the performance was treated sensationally because of jazz elements embedded in the score, resulting in some subterranean grumbling among the orch.'s staid subscribers.

Koussevitzky remained Copland's steadfast supporter throughout his tenure in Boston and later as the founder of the Koussevitzky Music Foundation. In the meantime Walter Damrosch conducted Copland's Sym. for Organ and Orch. (1925), with Boulanger as soloist (N.Y.).

Other orchs. and conductors performed Copland's music, which gained increasing recognition; particularly popular were works based on folk motifs, especially *El Salón México* (1933–36) and the American ballets *Billy the Kid* (1938), *Rodeo* (1942), and *Appalachian Spring* (1944). A unique place belongs to the *Lincoln Portrait* for narrator and orch. (1942), with texts arranged by the composer from speeches and letters of Abraham Lincoln; this work has had many performances, with the role of narrator taken by such notables as Adlai Stevenson and Eleanor Roosevelt. His patriotic *Fanfare for the Common Man* (1942) achieved tremendous popularity, and continues to be played on numerous occasions; he incorporated it in toto into the 3rd Sym.; for many years was a member of the board of directors of the League of Composers in N.Y.; co-organized the Copland-Sessions Concerts (1928–31); help found the Yaddo Festivals (1932) and the American Composers' Alliance (1937); participant in such organizations as the Koussevitzky Music Foundation, the Composers Forum, the Cos Cob Press, etc.; headed the composition dept. at the Berkshire Music Center at Tanglewood (1940–65) and was chairman of its faculty (1957–65).

Copland lectured extensively and gave courses at the New School for Social Research in N.Y. and at Harvard Univ. (1935 and 1944); was the Charles Eliot Norton Lecturer at Harvard in 1951–52 (publ. as *Music and Imagination,* Cambridge, Mass., 1952); received many awards, including a Guggenheim Fellowship (1925–27); RCA Victor award for his *Dance Sym.;* Pulitzer Prize and N.Y. Music Critics' Circle Award for *Appalachian Spring* (1945); N.Y. Music Critics' Circle Award for the 3rd Sym. (1947); an Oscar for the film score *The Heiress* (1950); Gold Medal for Music from the American Academy of Arts and Letters (1956); Presidential Medal of Freedom (1964); National Medal of Arts (1986).

About 1955 Copland developed a successful career as a conductor; led major sym. orchs. in Europe, the U.S., South America, and Mexico; traveled to Russia under the auspices of the State Dept. In 1982 the Aaron Copland School of Music was created at Queens College, City Univ. of N.Y; in 1983, made his last appearance as a conductor in N.Y. His 85th birthday was widely celebrated, including a televised concert in his honor by Mehta and the N.Y. Phil. As a composer he made use of a broad variety of idioms and techniques, tempering dissonant textures by a strong sense of tonality; enlivened his musical textures by ingenious applications of syncopation and polyrhythmic combinations; but in the Piano Variations (1930) adopted an austere method of musical constructivism; used a modified 12-tone technique in his Piano Quartet (1950) and an integral dodecaphonic idiom in *Connotations* (1962). He wrote several musical appreciation books: *What to Listen for in Music* (N.Y., 1939; 2nd ed., 1957); *Our New Music* (N.Y., 1941; 2nd ed., rev. and enl. as *The New Music, 1900–1960,* N.Y., 1968); *Copland on Music* (N.Y., 1960). His 2-vol. autobiography was co-authored with Vivian Perlis.

copula. In medieval music theory, a connecting passage, ranging from a single note and a part of a ligature to a protracted melisma; typically in a faster tempo, notated in smaller values.

copyright. Legal ownership right to an individual product or production, including musical compositions; recognized by the laws of most nations, through the International Copyright (Berne) Convention. The oldest performing rights society is the French Soc. des Auteurs, Compositeurs, et Éditeurs de Musique (formed 1851); Great Britain passed its 1st copyright act in 1709, but music came under its protection much later; U.S. copyright was 1st based on English common law, then uniquely American laws were passed; the 1st to mention musical works came in 1831; the most recent legislation is the all-new 1976 law.

Russia did not join the Berne Convention until 1914; the Soviet government soon abolished all international copyright law; finally rejoined the Berne Convention (1972). As a result, many Russian works were publ. and performed without any payment to the composers; Rachmaninoff never collected a penny for his Prelude in C-sharp minor and 1st 3 piano concertos; Prokofiev's *Classical Sym.* was pirated freely. No protection existed for Shostakovich and other Soviet composers, but a gentleman's agreement was made with publishers to collect fees for performances of major Soviet works. Another method of regaining copyright was practiced by Stravinsky, who revised *The Firebird* and other scores; many conductors still use the orig. uncopyrighted editions, not necessarily to avoid paying royalties but out of musical preference or historical imperative.

Numerous lawsuits were fought over popular American songs pirated because of inadequate copyright protection. A celebrated case involves the song *Happy Birthday to You,* freely used until a clerk in a Chicago music company discovered that the tune was written by sisters Patty and Mildred Hill, to a different set of words ("Good morning, dear teacher"). The Western Union Company, which made use of the tune for its singing birthday telegrams, had to pay a substantial royalty towards the newly discovered copyright. Arrangements of traditional songs can also cause legal problems, although such lawsuits are harder to justify. Once a copyright lapses, however, whether by intent, accident, or legal limit, a composition enters public domain and may be performed free of royalty; thus a Wagner opera has the same legal status as *3 Blind Mice.*

cor (Fr.). horn. *Cor anglais,* English horn; *cor de basset,* bassett horn; *cor de chasse,* hunting horn.

coranto (It.). 1. Courante. 2. Country dance.

corda (It.; plural *corde*). String. *Due corde* (It., 2 strings): 1. Release soft pedal on piano; 2. Depress the soft pedal halfway on piano; 3. Play the notes on 2 strings, non divisi; *tre corde,* release soft pedal on piano; *corda vuoto,* open string.

Corea, "Chick" (Armando Anthony), b. Chelsea, Mass., June 12, 1941. He began his career as a sideman with Mongo Santamaria, Willie Bobo, Blue Mitchell, and Herbie Mann; also worked with Miles Davis; after leading the experimental group Circle (1970–71), worked with Stan Getz; turned to jazz rock, playing in Return to Forever (with Al DiMeola,

Stanley Clarke, and Flora Purim); later led his Elektric Band and Acoustik Band; has made other group and solo recordings (*Piano Improvisations*, 1970–71).

Corelli, Arcangelo, b. Fusignano, near Imola, Feb. 17, 1653; d. Rome, Jan. 8, 1713. His violin teacher was G. Benvenuti in Bologna; studied counterpoint with Matteo Simonelli. About 1671, he went to Rome; was violinist at the French Church (1675); at the beginning of 1679, played in the orch. of the Teatro Capranica. Rome remained his chief residence to the end of his life. There is no substance to the story that in 1672 he went to Paris and was driven out by Lully's intrigues; supposedly stayed at the court of the Elector of Bavaria in Munich about 1680, but this cannot be documented; the story that a mediocre violinist, Giuseppe Valentini, won the favor of the Roman public while Corelli was in Naples, causing him to return to Rome a broken man, is equally unfounded. He enjoyed respect, security, and fame; in Rome, had a powerful protector in Cardinal Benedetto Pamphili; later lived in the palace of Cardinal Pietro Ottoboni; led weekly concerts attended by the elite of Roman society. One of his admirers was Queen Christina of Sweden, then living in Rome. Among his pupils were Baptiste Anet, Geminiani, Locatelli, and Giovanni Somis.

Corelli was famous as a violin virtuoso; regarded as the founder of modern violin technique; systematized the art of proper bowing; one of the 1st to use double stops and chords on the violin. His role in music history is very great, despite writing but 6 opus numbers definitely attributable to him. His greatest achievement was the creation of the concerto grosso, especially the 12 concertos of op. 6 (1714), which includes the *Christmas Concerto* in G minor. Handel, who as a young man met Corelli in Rome, was undoubtedly influenced by his instrumental writing. He was buried in the Pantheon in Rome.

Corigliano, John (Paul), b. N.Y., Feb. 16, 1938. He was the son of John Corigliano (1901–75), concertmaster of the N.Y. Phil. Orch. (1943–66) and the San Antonio Sym. The younger Corigliano studied at Columbia Univ. with Luening (B.A., 1959), with V. Giannini at the Manhattan School of Music, and privately with P. Creston; employed at the radio stations WBAI and WQXR in N.Y.; assistant director for CBS-TV (1961–72). He held a Guggenheim fellowship in 1968–69; joined the faculty of the Manhattan School of Music (1971); from 1973 taught at Lehman College of the City Univ. of N.Y.; composer-in-residence of the Chicago Sym. Orch. (1987–90). His style of composition shows a fine capacity for lyrical expression, and an incisive sense of rhythm, in the generic tradition of Bartók and Prokofiev. Despite the dissonant freedom of his polyphonic writing, his music retains a firm tonal anchorage. He is best known for his opera *The Ghost of Versailles* (1991) and the AIDS-related 1st Sym. (1990).

cornemuse (Fr.). Bagpipe with 2 drones sounding an octave apart.

cornet. 1. Brass instrument of the trumpet family, with a smaller conical tube and larger cupped mouthpiece than the trumpet, resulting in mellower timbre and greater technical facility; evolved from the old post horn by the addition of 3 valves; range covers 2 octaves and 3 tones. It is usually tuned in B flat (i.e., a written C sounds a whole step lower); primarily found in military bands, although early jazz performers like L. Armstrong and King Oliver played it in their small groups. 2. *Cornet à pistons*, the modern valve cornet. 3. Organ stops: a. reed stops of 2', 4', 8', and 16' pitch; b. German *Kornett*, of 2' or 4' pitch on the pedal; c. compound stop having from 3 to 5 ranks; d. echo-cornet, a soft-toned cornet stop enclosed in a wooden box; e. mounted cornet, mounted on a separate soundboard to render its tone louder.

cornet (It. *cornetto*; Ger. *Zink*). Early brass family instrument of noble lineage and multiple mutations; shaped like a straight pipe, it is made of ivory or strong wood. Some cornets are bent to provide a more convenient placement of fingerholes. During the Renaissance there were cornets of different registers: the soprano, called *cornettino* (little cornet); the tenor pitch, called *cornone* (big cornet); and the bass, called the serpent, added to the cornet family in the 16th century, bent in the shape of a snake to enable the player to reach the appropriate holes; despite its appellation, had a melodious tone that was anything but reptilian.

corno (It.; plural *corni*). Horn. *Corno a macchina*, valve horn capable of playing entire chromatic scales; *corno da caccia*, hunting horn; *corno di bassetto*, bassett horn. (This Italian term would have become obsolete were it not for George Bernard Shaw, who used it as a nom de plume for his music criticism in London papers in the late 19th century, no doubt intending to compare the rarity and unconventional qualities of the instrument with his style of writing.)

cornon (Fr.). 1. Cornet stop. 2. Wide-bore French horn invented by V. F. Červený in 1846. By 1872 he had produced a family of cornons; the instrument has been described as a "pre-Wagnerian Wagner tuba."

cornu. Tremendously impressive metal horn of ancient Rome, more than 3 meters in length, curved in the shape of the capital letter *G*, therefore also known as *tuba curva;* 2 authentic specimens were found in the excavations in Pompeii. The cornu was used in Rome at ceremonial occasions, and revived during the classically obsessed French Revolution; when Voltaire was solemnly reburied in the Pantheon (he died before the Revolution), Grétry wrote a special fanfare to be played on a modernized re-creation of the cornu.

coro spezzato (It., fragmented chorus; plural *cori spezzati*). Divided chorus; a term originating in the 16th century when Zarlino referred to choral ensembles that had been divided into 2, 3, or 4 self-contained units. These cori spezzati were used antiphonally, in partial or total congruence; this music is often labeled polychoral. The technique persisted (e.g., Berlioz's Requiem) and continues to this day, although some composers are less concerned with achieving a harmonically diatonic vista (e.g., Brant).

corrente (It.). Italian variant of the French courante, marked by a faster tempo and less florid ornamentation. *Corrente alla francese,* the Italian equivalent of the French courante, with all of its characteristics.

corrido (from Sp.*correr*, run). 20th-century Mexican topical ballad; usually sung in mariachi style, in 6/8 or 9/8 measure, with melodies consistently doubled at the 3rd.

Cortot, Alfred (Denis), b. Nyon, Switzerland (of a French father and a Swiss mother), Sept. 26, 1877; d. Lausanne, June 15, 1962. He attended the Paris Cons., studying piano with Decambes, Rouquou, and Diémer; won 1st prize for piano in 1896; that year, made his successful debut in Paris, playing Beethoven's C-minor Concerto; went to Bayreuth (1898); studied Wagner's works with J. Kniese; repetiteur at the festivals (1898–1901). Returning to Paris, he began actively promoting Wagner; conducted the French premiere of *Götterdämmerung* (1902); that year, established the Association des Concerts A. Cortot, which he led for 2 years, guiding the public towards an appreciation of Wagner; led the orch'l concerts of the Soc. Nationale and of the Concerts Populaires at Lille (1904–08). In 1905, he formed a trio, with Thibaud (violin) and Casals (cello), which gained a great European reputation; founded, with A. Mangeot, the École Normale de Musique (1919), and became its director; gave an annual course in piano interpretation there; gave many lecture recitals and guest conducted various orchs. He authored *Principes rationnels de la technique pianistique* (Paris, 1928); *La Musique française de piano* (2 vols., 1930–48); *Cours d'interpretation* (Paris, 1934); *Aspects de Chopin* (Paris, 1949).

Costello, Elvis (born Declan Patrick McManus), b. London, Aug. 25, 1955. He spent his childhood in Liverpool, the city of the Beatles; when quite young he got a recording contract with Stiff Records. His well-written songs were permeated with the feeling of doom, personal as well as universal; challenged conservatism and fascism at every opportunity. Among his 1st hits were *Less than Zero, Watching the Detectives, Red Shoes,* and a love ballad, *Alison,* all on his album *My Aim Is True* (1977). His next album, *This Year's Model* (1978), increased his popularity with *(I Don't Want to Go to) Chelsea, Pump It Up,* and *No Action;* the 3rd album, *Armed Forces* (1979), included *Oliver's Army, Accidents Will Happen,* and *Green Shirt.* From then on Costello continued to be prolific, if not always consistent; while he has recorded a majority of his albums with a rock trio, the Attractions, he shifts his style of repertoire, production values, and instrumentation where it suits him. Among his more interesting albums are *Get Happy* (1980), influenced by soul; *Almost Blue* (1981), an album of country-western covers; *Imperial Bedroom* (1982), a successful concept recording; *King of America* (1986), with a varied cast of backup musicians; and *The Juliet Letters* (1993), with the Brodsky String Quartet.

cotillion (Fr.). 18th–and 19th-century French dance, in 3/4 time, to quadrillelike music.

coulé (Fr.). Legato, slurred; also, a harpsichord grace note.

Council of Trent. Gathering of Roman Catholic Church dignitaries held in Trent from 1545 to 1563; discussion was devoted to the condemnation of using secular melodies and rhythms in sacred works. A decree was issued under the title *Abusus in sacrificio missae* (Abuse in the sacred mass). Extremists advocated a total elimination of polyphony from the Mass and a return to plainchant, but the final verdict recommended the Mass be primarily free from popular motives. Palestrina composed his celebrated *Missa Papae Marcelli* (c. 1555–62) in a purified polyphonic style to demonstrate possible reform without destroying its underlying structure. Exuberant music historians describe Palestrina's accomplishment as the "salvation of church music" from obscurantist forces, but this was an extravagant exaggeration.

count. Accent, beat, or pulse of a measure.

counter. Any vocal part designed to contrast with the principal part or melody, i.e., *bass counter,* 2nd bass part; *countertenor,* voice usually developed from the headtones and falsetto of a bass voice, compass from g to c^2; *counter-exposition,* reentrance of a fugue-subject; *counter-subject,* fugal theme following the subject in the same part; *counter-tenor clef,* C clef on the 2nd line (now obsolete).

counterculture. In modern sociology, counterculture embraces all manifestations of the rebellious young generation counterposing their own concept of social behavior, art, and even science in opposition to the establishment. In music, counterculture uses the techniques of the avant-garde calculated to irritate, exasperate, and stupefy the bourgeoisie (*épater le bourgeoisie*) and academic listeners. The most violent expressions of counterculture, reaching its climax in the 1960s, included the physical destruction of musical instruments, exemplified by forcible burning of an upright piano, drowning it, or dropping it from a helicopter at the altitude of 300 feet (as happened near Detroit under the auspices of the radio program *Detroit Listener's Digest*).

counterpoint (from Lat. *punctum contra punctum,* point against point, note against note). 1. Art of polyphonic composition. In Western musical history, it did not take long before 2, 3, or more "points" (notes) were used against 1 point; that principal point became cantus and, by extension, cantus firmus. The domination of perfect intervals—the octave, 4th, and 5th—was firmly established. Early contrapuntal music, such as that of the Parisian Notre Dame masters Leoninus and Perotin, introduced the dissonant ornament on the basic cantus; however, the interval of the 3rd, fundamental in common chords, was regarded as a dissonance and was only as a concession to advanced tastes for the fauxbourdon. Early counterpoint was the tool of ars antiqua, as described by the later "enlightened" theorists of the ars nova; but even ars nova was a body of composition abounding in contradictions.

True (tonal) counterpoint, as understood from the study of Bach, belongs to the Baroque. In this mighty art, several voices, above or below the basic theme, engage in a dance of mutually consistent figurations; consonant intervals form a tonal fabric of extraordinary variety, while aiming toward the foreseeable cadence and the final triadic chord; rhythmic imitation among several interconnected voices creates a sense of unity in variety; dissonant intervals that participate in a pattern of intermingling voices must be resolved into consonances (however delayed by numerous passing notes or ornamentation); the bass plays a commanding role establishing the fundamental tonality of a work. Compositions with 2 or more simultaneous melodies form a polyphonic web of considerable intricacy. *Double counterpoint* is written so that the upper part can become the lower part, hieved his greatest and most enduring distinction: 4 vols. of *eces de clavecin* (1713, 1716, 1722, and 1730), pieces in ance form, programmatic in title and content; in 1716, publ. an xpository work (with musical exemplars) on *L'Art de toucher le clavecin*, attaining wide celebrity and influencing his great contemporary, Bach. Couperin also introduced the trio sonata to France, notably 4 sonatas, *Les Nations* (1726), described as 'sonades" or "suites de symphonies en trio." Living at a time during which the rivalry between French and Italian music reached its climax, he sought to adapt the new Italian forms to his own personal, and essentially French, style; this is apparent in *Les goûts-réünis* (1724), a series of concerted pieces with strings very similar in form and spirit to the *Pieces de clavecin*, and *Apothéose de Lully*, in which the rivals Lully and Corelli "unite" for the furtherance of art. His style of composition was based on the basso continuo, the most important voices usually being uppermost, carrying the melody; nevertheless, his music sometimes attains considerable complexity (on occasion requiring as many as 3 harpsichordists for its proper execution). His melodic invention, particularly in the rondeau, was virtually inexhaustible, his themes swift and expressive; an outstanding feature was his inventive mode of ornamentation, in the early gallant style.

Couperin, Louis, b. Chaumes, *c.* 1626; d. Paris, Aug. 29, 1661. Son of Charles Couperin and uncle of François (ii) "le Grand." He went to Paris with Chambonnières, whose pupil he was; became organist of St.-Gervais (1653), a post in which he was succeeded, without interruption, by other members and descendants of the Couperin family (to 1826); violinist and violist in the orchs. of the court ballets (1656), and musician of the Chambre du Roi. He composed *pieces de clavecin* (with their unmeasured preludes), organ carillons, violin pieces, etc.; one of the 1st French composers for harpsichord in the new harmonic style employing the basso continuo, possibly preceded only by his teacher, Chambonnières.

coupler. Mechanical organ stop, designed to connect 2 manuals, or pedal with manual, so that when 1 is played on, the other is combined with it. *Coupler-pedal*, a coupler worked by foot.

couplet. 1. 2 successive poetic lines forming a pair, usually rhymed. 2. In triple time, 2 equal notes occupying the time of 3 such notes in the established rhythm, thus:

courante (Fr.; Eng. courant). Stately and courtly old French dance in triple meter, of moderate tempo, with considerable melodic ornamentation. In the 18th century the courante became an integral part of the Baroque as an independent suite movement.

courtship and music. In *The Expression of the Emotions in Man and Animals*, Darwin wrote, "Music has a wonderful power of recalling in a vague and indefinite manner those strong emotions which were felt during long-past ages, when, as is probable, our early progenitors courted each other by the aid of

vocal tones." Literature and art abound in stories of courtship and love engendered and encouraged by music making; winged cupids anachronistically play the lute to speed Venus and Adonis on the road to erotic consumption. Apollo plays the lyre to win the hearts of nymphs; Orpheus, son of Apollo, enchanted nymphs by his lyre, and even reclaimed his bride Eurydice from the nether regions with song (although he promptly lost her). The forest god Pan used his vocal powers to attract the reluctant nymph Syrinx; she sought refuge in a pond where she was metamorphosed into a field of reeds; frustrated, he made a panpipe out of the reeds.

Composers composed music to attract their objects of adoration. Berlioz wrote his *Sym. fantastique* as an offering of love to the Shakespearian actress Harriet Smithson. Schumann paid tribute to his love for Clara Wieck by inserting a brief elegy to her under the Italian form of her name "Chiara" in his piano work, *Carnaval*. Tolstoy, who in his old age came to regard art, literature, and music as conduits of immorality, drew a horrendous picture of the aphrodisiac power of Beethoven's *Kreutzer Sonata* by throwing the female pianist and the male violinist together. (A famous 19th-century French painting, representing a similar outburst of passion, was used commercially to advertise perfume.) British artist William Holman Hunt's painting, *The Awakening Conscience*, shows a well-petticoated Victorian damsel rising distractedly from the lap of her piano teacher. A great number of male piano teachers married their pupils; Leschetizky married at least 4; many music teachers took their nubile pupils as outlets for their artistic passions, most notably Fibich, who wrote hundreds of piano pieces as a diary of his relationship with a beloved piano student, who was also his librettist.

Coussemaker, (Charles-) Edmond (-Henri) de, b. Bailleul, Nord, Apr. 19, 1805; d. Bourbourg, Jan. 10, 1876. He studied music as a child; studied law at the Univ. of Paris; took singing lessons with Pellegrini and harmony with Anton Reicha; continued studies with Lefebvre in Douai, after becoming a practicing lawyer. At this time (1831–35) he found leisure to compose music of the most varied description, almost all of which is unpubl. and apparently lost. His interest in history and archaeology led him to study authentic documents of music; influenced by the scholarly articles in *La Gazette et Revue Musicale* (then ed. by Fétis); during successive terms as judge in Hazebrouck, Dunkirk, and Lille, continued to accumulate knowledge of musical documentation; assembled a vast library; 1,075 items in his library are listed in the *Catalogue des livres, manuscrits et instruments de musique du feu M. Ch. Edm. de Coussemaker* (Brussels, 1877; issued for an auction).

covered octave. See ⇒octave.

covered strings. Strings of silk, wire, or gut, covered with spiral turns of fine silver or copper wire.

Coward, (Sir) Noël, b. Teddington, Middlesex, Dec. 16, 1899; d. Port Maria, Jamaica, Mar. 25, 1973. At age 11 he appeared on the stage; associated with the theater thereafter, in the triple capacity of actor, playwright, and producer. With no formal education in music, he dictated his songs (text and melody) to a musical amanuensis. Among his musical works are *This Year of Grace* (N.Y., 1928); the operetta *Bittersweet* al versa; in *triple* and *quadruple counterpoint*, 3 and 4 are written so that they can be mutually exchanged.

ch's great collections, *The Well-Tempered Clavier* and *The of the Fugue*, were specifically designed as didactic works. summarized the practice of counterpoint as well as its development in mutual imitation of its component parts. By the Baroque a number of scholastic works were publ. establishing the rules of counterpoint in 5 species: note against note; 2 notes against note; 3 or more notes against note; syncopated counterpoint; and, finally, florid counterpoint; these species were fundamental to conservatory training until very recently. Attempts were made to unite counterpoint with harmony by means of figured bass; in the 19th century a number of mostly German professors of music spread their gospel, with harmonic rules, by way of figured bass, being paramount.

countertenor. Very high male voice; ideally sings in the contralto or soprano range while retaining a masculine tone quality. Highly praised in the Middle Ages, countertenors were replaced in the Baroque era and their function was taken over by the castrati. But when musical emasculation came to an end in the 19th century, the use of countertenors resumed. They remain in fashion, thanks primarily to the early music movement.

country dance. Dance in 2/4 or 3/4 time in which the partners form 2 opposing lines which advance and retreat; couples also dance down the lines and return to their places. See also ⇒contredanse.

country-western (country-and-western music). Symbiosis of American rural and cowboy song styles, producing a post-World War II mixture of traditional and popular musical Americana. Sources include Appalachian old-time ballads, fiddle tunes, bluegrass, jazz-influenced Western swing, Hawaiian guitar, and mainstream popular music. The geographic center of modern country-western music is Nashville, Tenn., where an unabashedly commercial agenda produced songs in which men missed their women, whiskey, or wandering; women were left holding the bag and pouring out their hearts. Beginning in the 1960s, country-western lyrics became more socially or politically topical, reflecting cultural changes of the U.S., albeit not immediately. Country-western music has since splintered into several styles, including outlaw country, countrypolitan, folk revival, country-rock, and new country.

The songs are commonly in square time (4/4), with the exception of those influenced by the waltz of the French Acadians (Cajuns). Simple melodies are characterized by an accented appoggiatura, rising from the 2nd to the 3rd scale step (e.g., in C major, D to E); also characteristic is the neighbor motion between the 5th and 6th steps (G to A to G). Country-western singers are happily free of academic restrictions and rich in artless syncopation, enlivened by plagal harmonic progressions. Classic country-western instrumentation includes acoustic, electric, and bass guitars; pedal steel guitar, a horizontal version of the Hawaiian steel guitar; and drums; other traditional and modern instruments are added as needed.

coup de glotte (Fr., stroke of the glottis). Highly dramatic way of interrupting breath in singing, very popular among Italian singers but now regarded as old-fashioned stylistically; Caruso's coup de glotte in the aria *Ridi, pagliaccio* (fro moved audiences to tears.

couper sec et bref (Fr.). Cut off abruptly and

Couperin. Renowned family of French mus prominence dates from the 3 sons of Charles (i) (c. 1595–1654), merchant and organist of Chaume, in of Brie (now part of Seine et Marne), and his wife, Ma The eldest of these, ⇒Louis (see below), established t in Paris, where it remained until the extinction of the ma 1826; he was the 1st Couperin to hold the organist pos Gervais in Paris; followed by his youngest brother, Cha 1638–79), whose son ⇒François (II) "le Grand" was th ily's most illustrious representative; Nicolas (1680–1748), François (i; c. 1631-after 1708); ⇒Armand-Louis, s Nicolas, and by the 2 sons of Armand-Louis, Pierre-(1755–89) and Gervais-François (1759–1826). Following articles on three members of the family.

Couperin, Armand-Louis, b. Paris, Feb. 25, 17 d. there, Feb. 2, 1789. Son of Nicolas Couperin; in 174 succeeded his father as organist at St.-Gervais; also organi to the King (1770–89); held appointments at St.-Barthelem Ste.-Marguerite, Ste.-Chapelle, St.-Jean-en-Greve, etc.; one of 4 organists at Notre Dame. He died after being been knocked down by a runaway horse. His wife, Elisabeth-Antoinette Blanchet (b. Paris, Jan. 14, 1729; d. after 1810), was a remarkable organist and clavecinist, still playing publicly at 81; she was the daughter of François Etienne Blanchet, clavecin maker, and sister-in-law to Pascal Joseph Taskin, court instrument keeper under Louis XV.

Couperin, François (II; known as "le Grand"), b. Paris, Nov. 10, 1668; d. there, Sept. 11, 1733. Son of Charles (ii) Couperin; studied with his father; a pupil of Jacques-Denis Thomelin, organist of the King's chapel; in 1685, became organist of St.-Gervais, a post held until his death; in late 1693, after a successful competition, succeeded Thomelin as organist of the Chapelle Royale, receiving the title of "Organiste du roi." Famed as an organist, Couperin was highly regarded for his remarkable ability as a clavecin performer; appointed "Claveciniste de la chambre du roi, et organiste de sa chapelle" (1701); received the title "Ordinaire de la musique de la chambre du roi" (1717); made a chevalier of the Order of Latran. He was music master to the Dauphin and other members of the royal family; ranked high in the favor of Louis XIV, for whom he composed the *Concerts royaux*, played in Sunday concerts in the royal apartments (1714–15). He married (1689) Marie-Anne Ansault, by whom he had 2 daughters: Marie-Madeleine (b. Paris, Mar. 9, 1690; d. Montbuisson, Apr. 16, 1742), organist of the Abbey of Montbuisson, and Marguerite-Antoinette (b. Paris, Sept. 19, 1705; d. there, 1778), a talented clavecin player who substituted for her father as clavecinist to the King (1731–33), being the 1st woman to hold this position; there were also 2 sons.

Couperin's compositions divide into works written for the church, the King, and the general public. More than half of his creative life was taken up with religious compositions, including *Pieces d'orgue consistantes en deux Messes* (1690, a total of 42 pieces), motets, and other works. His instrumental works

(London, 1929); *Conversation Piece* (London, 1934); *Pacific 1860* (London, 1946); *Ace of Clubs* (London, 1950); *After the Ball*, after Wilde's *Lady Windermere's Fan* (London, 1954); 51 songs from his musical plays are publ. in the *Noël Coward Song Book* (N.Y., 1953) with the author's introduction.

cowbell. Large metal bell with heavy clappers worn around the neck of a cow or bellwether. In the modern era, scores by Webern and Mahler have included the instrument; it is commonly found in Latin American, jazz, and other popular music.

Cowell, Henry Dixon, b. Menlo Park, Calif., Mar. 11, 1897; d. Shady, N.Y., Dec. 10, 1965. His father, of Irish birth, was a member of a clergyman's family in Kildare; his mother was an American of progressive persuasion. Cowell studied violin with Henry Holmes in San Francisco; after the earthquake of 1906, his mother took him to N.Y., where they sought support from the Soc. for the Improvement of the Condition of the Poor; returned to Menlo Park; he was able to save enough money, earned from menial jobs, to buy a piano.

Cowell began to experiment with the piano by striking the keys with fists and forearms, naming such chords tone clusters; at age 13, composed *Adventures in Harmony,* featuring such chords; later experimented in altering piano sound by placing various objects on the strings and by playing directly under the lid of the piano, pizzicato and glissando. Tone clusters per se were not new, and were used as sound effects in the 18th century to imitate thunder or cannon fire; Ives used them in his *Concord Sonata,* sounded by covering a set of white or black keys with a wooden board. However, Cowell systematized tone clusters as harmonic amplifications of tonal chords, devising logical notation for them; tone clusters eventually acquired legitimacy in the works of many European and American composers; Cowell 1st exhibited these startling innovations at the San Francisco Musical Soc. at the St. Francis Hotel (1914). He also extended the sonorities of tone clusters to instrumental combinations and applied them in several of his symphonic works.

Cowell began lessons in composition at the Univ. of Calif., Berkeley, later with Frank Damrosch at the Inst. of Musical Art, N.Y., and privately with Charles Seeger (1914–16). After brief service in the U.S. Army in 1918, where he arranged for the U.S. Army Band, was engaged to give lectures on new music, illustrated by playing his piano works; went to Russia (1928), attracting considerable attention as 1st American composer to visit there; some of his pieces were publ. in a Russian ed., also a novelty. Returning to the U.S.., he was appointed lecturer on music at the New School of Social Research in N.Y.; founded the *New Music Quarterly* for publication of ultramodern music, mainly by American composers (1927); awarded a Guggenheim fellowship (1931); went to Berlin; studied ethnomusicology with Hornbostel, inaugurating a serious study of ethnic musical materials. He had already experimented with some Indian and Chinese devices in some works; his *Ensemble for Strings* (1924) included Indian thundersticks, naturally arousing considerable curiosity. In 1931 he formed a collaboration with Theremin, then visiting the U.S.; they constructed an ingenious instrument called the Rhythmicon, which made possible the simultaneous production of 16 different rhythms on 16 different pitch levels of the harmonic series; Cowell demonstrated it in San Francisco (1932) and composed an extensive work entitled *Rhythmicana,* not pre-miered until 1971 using advanced electronic techniques.

Cowell's career was brutally interrupted in 1936, when he was arrested in Calif. on charges of homosexuality (then a heinous offense in that state), involving the impairment of the morals of a minor; deceived by the promises of a wily district attorney of brief confinement in a sanatorium, pleaded guilty to a limited offense; vengefully given a maximum sentence of imprisonment (up to 15 years). Incarcerated at San Quentin, he was assigned to work in a jute mill, but indomitably continued to write music in prison; thanks to interventions by eminent musicians, was paroled in 1940 with Grainger as guarantor of his good conduct; obtained a full pardon from the governor of Calif., Earl Warren, because the evidence against him proved to be largely contrived (1942).

In 1941 Cowell married Sidney Robertson, a noted ethnomusicologist; resumed his full activities as ed. and instructor; taught at the New School for Social Research (1940–62), the Univ. of Southern Calif., Mills College, and the Peabody Cons. of Music, Baltimore (1951–56); appointed adjunct prof. at Columbia Univ. (1951–65); and elected a member of the National Academy of Arts and Letters (1951). In 1956–57 he undertook a world tour with his wife through the Near East, India, and Japan, collecting prime musical materials for his compositions, which had turned decisively toward the use of these melodic and rhythmic materials, without abandoning, however, the experimental devices which were his stylistic signposts. In addition to symphonic and chamber music, he publ. the important *New Musical Resources* (1930); ed. a symposium, *American Composers on American Music*; in collaboration with his wife, wrote the 1st biography of Ives (1955).

crab canon. Canon cancrizans. See ⇒canon. *Crab movement,* backward movement of a melody.

Craft, Robert (Lawson), b. Kingston, N.Y., Oct. 20, 1923. He studied at the Juilliard School of Music (B.A., 1946) and the Berkshire Music Center; studied conducting with Monteux; during World War II served in the U.S. Army Medical Corps; in 1947, conducted the N.Y. Brass and Woodwind Ensemble; conducted the Evenings-on-the-Roof and Monday Evening Concerts in Los Angeles (1950–68). A defining moment in his career was a 1948 encounter with Stravinsky, whom he greatly impressed by his precise knowledge of Stravinsky's music; gradually became Stravinsky's closest associate; allegedly persuaded Stravinsky to adopt the 12-tone method of composition, a major development in the composer's creative path (1950s). Craft collaborated with Stravinsky on 6 vols. of a catechumenical and discursive nature (1959–69); Craft insisted that their collaboration with Stravinsky involved acting and reacting to an emerging topic of discussion, with Stravinsky evoking his ancient memories in his careful English, or fluent French, spiced with unrestrained discourtesies toward professional colleagues on the American scene, and Craft reifying the material with an analeptic bulimia of quaquaversal literary, psychological, physiological, and culinary references in a flow of (too?) finely ordered dialogue.

Crawford (Seeger), Ruth Porter, b. East Liverpool, Ohio, July 3, 1901; d. Chevy Chase, Md., Nov. 18, 1953. She studied composition with Charles Seeger, whom she later married; studied piano with Heniot Levy; dedicated herself to teaching and collecting folk songs; when still very young, taught at the School of Musical Arts, Jacksonville, Fla. (1918–21), American Cons., Chicago (1925–29) and Elmhurst College of Music, Ill. (1926–29); received a Guggenheim fellowship (1930). She was known mainly for her American folk-song anthologies: *American Folk Songs for Children* (1948), *Animal Folk Songs for Children* (1950), and *American Folk Songs for Christmas* (1953); her own compositions, astonishingly bold in their experimental aperçus and insights, anticipated many techniques of the postwar avant-garde; while rarely performed during her lifetime, they had a remarkable revival in subsequent decades, notably the 1931 String Quartet.

creativity. The musical profession is sharply divided into 2 categories: creative work (individual composition) and performing (interpretation). Since the interpreter is but a servant of the composer, performing artists are commonly placed below creative musicians in the philosophical estimate of music; but as far as worldly success is concerned, famous interpreters generally gain greater fame and much greater fortune. But it is the composers who enter their names in the pages of music history, not the interpreters. Fortunately for the cause of music, composers are often great artists who perform their own works as pianists, violinists, or conductors; in a few instances the composer's talent as interpreter matches his creative genius; Chopin, Liszt, and Paganini were such complete men of music. In the 20th century perhaps the only great composer-performers were Rachmaninoff and Bernstein; most composers play only their own compositions, avoiding the careers of performing artists; such were the pianists Scriabin, Debussy, and Bartók. Stravinsky played the piano in or conducted some of his works, but he was not a professional.

Many interpreters compose music on the side, but this music is generally of a fairly low quality; syms. written by professional conductors are often derisively described as *kapellmeistermusik.* Some pianists have written technical studies and minor pieces of excellent value and great popular appeal. Anton Rubinstein, undoubtedly one of the greatest pianists of all time, was an extremely successful composer of operas, syms., and concertos; but posterity greatly devaluated his compositions, which are rarely even mentioned in histories; he remains a disembodied phantom of great pianism, having died before the advent of the phonograph; only his solo piano pieces escaped the dustbin of music history.

Questions of whether composition is superior to the interpretive art have been at least partly answered by recent investigations in brain physiology. In normal right-handed individuals, the left hemisphere of the brain is the seat of higher intellectual qualities, governing speech, analytical reasoning, and other attributes of the active intellect, whereas the right hemisphere controls emotions, gestures, and the passive appreciation of the arts. Thus performing ability has its nervous center in the right hemisphere; if it is damaged, the artist can no longer express himself musically and would not even remember the simplest melodies; but if his musical intellect, located in the left hemisphere, is untouched, he will be able to compose even if he cannot remember the notes he writes down.

Those working in abstract fields experience a series of spurts of inspiration, following the so-called "eureka" impulse; these impulses may eventually be measureable in terms of electrical units and the chemical changes effected by them; it will then be possible to draw an electroencephalograph of inspiration. However, *a priori* it seems probable that there is no quantitative, or qualitative, difference between the inspirational impulse of a Beethoven and a Malotte. The remaining mystery involves the particular electro-chemical condition that creates favorable circumstances for the incidence of a "eureka" in the right hemisphere.

Credo (Lat., I believe). The Nicene Creed, part of the Roman Catholic Mass. The longest portion of the Ordinary, it is often broken down into sections for compositional purposes: *Credo in unum deum* (I believe in one God); *Patrem omnipotentem* (Father almighty); *Et in unum Dominum* (and in one Lord); *Et incarnatus est* (and was incarnate); *Crucifixus* (Crucified); *Et resurrexit* (and was resurrected); *Et in Spiritum sanctum* (and in the Holy Spirit); *Confiteor unum baptisma* (I confess one baptism).

Creedence Clearwater Revival. (Leader/guitar/vocal/songwriter: John Fogerty, b. Berkeley, Calif., May 28, 1945; guitar/piano/vocal: Tom Fogerty, b. Berkeley, Nov. 9, 1941; d. Scottsdale, Ariz., Sept. 6, 1990; bass: Stu Clark, b. Oakland, Calif., Apr. 24, 1946; drums: Doug Clifford, b. Palo Alto, Calif., Apr. 24, 1945.) Roots-revival rock band of the late 1960s noted for the pungent songs and vocals of John Fogerty. Growing out of a series of amateur high school bands, the band was signed to a local Calif. jazz label, Fantasy, in 1967. The group had major hits with Fogerty's *Proud Mary* (later covered by Ike and Tina Turner), *Born on the Bayou, Bad Moon Rising, Fortunate Son, Who'll Stop the Rain?, Run through the Jungle,* and *Lookin' Out My Backdoor.* Most of Fogerty's songs drew on American folk themes, getting inspiration from early rock and rockabilly styles. In early 1971 Tom Fogerty left the group, and the remaining members struggled on for about a year before disbanding. John Fogerty has pursued an inconsistent solo career, staging a successful comeback in the mid-1980s with his album *Centerfield* and another in 1997 with a tour and new album (*Blue Moon Swamp*).

crescendo (It., growing). Gradual increase in loudness. The abbreviation is *cresc.*, followed by lines or dots to indicate the duration: cresc......... The word itself can also be broken up by several dots or hyphens: cre....scen....do. The effect of gradual swelling up of the sound was primarily cultivated by the Mannheim school in the 18th century; a musician who heard the Mannheim musicians perform wrote that the power of their crescendo made the audience rise from their seats in response to the music. A brief outburst of crescendo may be indicated by two lines diverging at an acute angle from a point: ———— .

Crescendo may begin from any dynamic level, including forte.

crescendo il forte (It.). Increase the loudness (found in Baroque scores). *Crescendo molto molto,* increase the loudness quickly; *crescendo pedal,* a pedal mechanism drawing all stops successively up to full organ; the swell-pedal.

Crescent. Turkish crescent.

Crespin, Régine, b. Marseilles, Feb. 23, 1927. She studied pharmacology; took voice lessons with Suzanne Cesbron-Viseur and Georges Jouatte in Paris; made her debut in Mulhouse as Elsa (1950); sang at the Paris Opéra. She acquired a European reputation as one of the best Wagnerian singers; sang Kundry at the Bayreuth Festivals (1958–60); appeared at La Scala in Milan and Covent Garden in London; made her debut with the Metropolitan Opera, N.Y., as the Marschallin (1962); remained with the Metropolitan until her farewell performance as Mme De Croissy in *Dialogues of the Carmelites* (1987); sang Sieglinde and Amelia in *Un ballo in maschera;* appeared as a concert singer. Her sonorous, somewhat somber voice suited dramatic parts excellently.

Cristofori, Bartolomeo, b. Padua, May 4, 1655; d. Florence, Jan. 27, 1731. He was the inventor of the 1st hammer piano, as opposed to the clavichord, which employs a different action. He was a leading maker of clavicembalos in Padua; about 1690 went to Florence; instrument maker to Ferdinando de' Medici; upon the latter's death (1713), appointed custodian of the court collection of instruments by Cosimo III. According to an article by Maffei (1711), Cristofori had to that point built 3 "gravecembali col piano e forte" having, instead of the harpsichord 's jacks plucking the strings with quills, a row of little hammers striking the strings from below; this action was adopted, in the main, by Gottfried Silbermann, the Streichers, and Broadwood (hence the name "English action"). Following the designation by its inventor, the new instrument was named piano-forte; a piano of Cristofori's is in the possession of the Metropolitan Museum of Art, N.Y.

croche (Fr., crooked). 8th note; its black mensural equivalent, the semiminim, was notated by a perpendicular stem with a drooping flag attached to it.

croma (It.). 8th note.

cromorne (Eng., obsolete). Crumhorn.

crook. Short tube, bent or straight, designed to slide into the main tube of a horn, trumpet, or cornet to lower its fundamental pitch. This method was widely used in the 18th and 19th centuries, but became obsolete with the invention of chromatic valve trumpets and horns.

crooner. Popular singer who intones his songs in a soft, seductive manner.

cross flute. Transverse flute; that is, one held across the mouth and blown from the side.

cross relation. Chromatic contradiction of a tone in one part by another; the sounding, either together or in succession, of a tone and its chromatically altered octave; the progression may be heard as a chromatic passing tone occurring not in the same voice but in another. This modus operandi is strictly verboten in proper scholastic exercises, but English consort music of the latter 17th century is replete with such progressions. Even in the very opening of his 3rd Sym. in F major, Brahms violates the pedantic prohibition by having the melody descend via F major—F–C–A–G–F—while the bass defiantly rises from the low F to A flat, a minor 3rd above it.

cross rhythm. Simultaneous use of 2 or more different meters while observing the least common denominator of the measure, e.g., the Spanish polymeter, placing 3/4 against 6/8, produces a distinctive cross rhythm in which the strong beats of the meters alternate; they fall together only on the downbeat, the 1st of 6 beats:

Jazz syncopation thrives on cross rhythm; much world music depends on it; but European classical music tends to be dominated by the main beat or beats of the chosen meter, so that the cross rhythm functions in a momentary or ornamental manner. Brahms was probably the most consistent of pre-20th-century composers to use the device, e.g., the *Capriccio* in C-sharp minor (op. 76, No. 5).

crossover. The phenomenon of a recording intended for one audience becoming highly successful with a very different audience; typical examples are recordings of classical performers such as Horowitz, Cliburn, Pavarotti, Perlman, and Domingo that land on the popular hit parade; specific pieces can become faddish. The other principal crossover situation is when a performer records in an unexpected style, such as Streisand's classical album or Mark O'Connor's Concerto for fiddle and orch. See also ⇒jazz-funk; jazz.

crotales (Fr., from Lat. *crotalum,* hand clappers). Antique cymbals.

crotalum (Lat., from Grk. *crotalon*). Clapper used in ancient Greek dances and choruses to punctuate stressed beats.

crotchet (U.K.). Quarter note. *Crotchet-rest,* a quarter rest.

Crucifixus (Lat.). Section of the Credo from the Roman Catholic Mass Ordinary.

Crumb, George (Henry, Jr.), b. Charleston, W.V., Oct. 24, 1929. His father played the clarinet, his mother the cello; he studied music at home; began composing in school; had pieces performed by the Charleston Sym. Orch. He then studied music at Mason College in Charleston (B.M., 1950); the Univ. of Ill. (M.M., 1952); studied with Ross Lee Finney at the Univ. of Mich. (D.M.A., 1959). In 1955, received a Fulbright fellowship for travel to Germany; studied with Blacher at the Berlin Hochschule für Musik; received further grants from the Rockefeller (1964), Koussevitzky (1965), and Coolidge (1970) foundations; in 1967 held a Guggenheim fellowship; given the National Inst. of Arts and Letters Award; awarded the Pulitzer Prize for *Echoes of Time and the River* (1968). Parallel to his composing, he taught piano and composition at the Univ. of Colo. at Boulder (1959–64); then joined the music dept. of the Univ. of Pa.; named Annenberg Prof. of the Humanities (1983).

In his music Crumb is a universalist; nothing in the realm of sound is alien to him, no method of composition unsuited to his artistic purposes; accordingly, his music can sing as sweetly as the proverbial nightingale, or be as rough, rude, and crude as a primitive man of the mountains. His vocal parts demand the ability to produce percussive tongue clicks, explosive shrieks, hissing, whistling, whispering, and sudden shouting of verbal irrelevancies, interspersed with portentous syllabification, disparate phonemes, and rhetorical logorrhea. He injects into his sonorous kaleidoscope quotations from well-known works: the middle section of Chopin's *Fantaisie-Impromptu,* Ravel's *Boléro,* hymns, the Dies Irae chant, or some other "objet trouvé." In his instrumentation he is no less unconventional; he instructs the percussion player to immerse a loudly sounding gong into a tub of water, has an electric guitar played with glass rods over the frets, or tells wind instrumentalists to blow soundlessly through their tubes. Instrumentalists sometimes have to shout or sing (not without resistance). Spatial distribution also plays a role: performers are assigned their reciprocal locations on the podium or in the hall. All this is but an illustrative decor; the music is the essence.

Like most composers who began their work around the mid-20th century, Crumb first adopted the Schoenbergian idiom, seasoned with pointillistic devices. After these preliminaries he wrote his unmistakably individual *Madrigals,* to words by Federico García Lorca, scored for voice and instrumental groups. His reputation was secured by a most extraordinary work, *Ancient Voices of Children* (text by Lorca), premiered in Washington, D.C. (1970); a female singer intones into the space under the lid of an amplified grand piano; a boy's voice responds in anguish; the accompaniment is supplied by an orch'l group and an assortment of exotic percussion instruments: Tibetan prayer stones, Japanese temple bells, musical saw, and toy piano. His most grandiose creation is *Star-Child,* representing, in his imaginative scheme, a progression from tenebrous despair to the exaltation of luminous joy; the score calls for a huge orch., including 2 children's choruses and 8 percussion players performing on all kinds of utensils, such as pot lids, and also iron chains and metal sheets, as well as ordinary drums; it had its premiere under the direction of Boulez with the N.Y. Phil. (1977).

crumhorn. Obsolete double-reed windcap instrument of the oboe family, gently curved upward at the bell; its heyday was the late 15th, 16th, and the 1st half of the 17th centuries. Its sound was pure and sweet; angels in Renaissance paintings were often shown playing crumhorns; however, its range was not much greater than an octave, and its dynamic range limited. *Crumhorn* is a common English spelling; an alternative form is *cromorne.* In German, it is *Krummhorn* (crooked horn); in French, *tourebout* (turned-up end); in Italian, *cornamuto toto* (twisted horn).

crwth (crouth, crouch; Welsh, Middle Eng.; pronounced "crowd"). Ancient plucked or bowed lyre, probably the earliest European instrument of this type; the national instrument of Wales. In its modern form it has a fingerboard and 6 (formerly 3) strings. It is rectangular in shape and is topped by a wooden board. The body is carved out of a single piece of wood; it was terminated by 2 parallel arms joined at the end by a crossbar, the center of which supported the fingerboard.

csárdás (Hung.; misspelled *czárdás*). Stylized Hungarian folk dance in 2/4 time, popular in the 1st half of the 19th century. The term comes from the word *csárda,* Hungarian for a village inn. The dance consists of 2 parts, a slow introduction, the *lassu* (danced by men only) and the csárdás proper, also called *friss* or *friszka,* a lively dance for both genders, in accentuated 2/4 or 4/4 time. The csárdás became popular in Hungary as a salon dance toward the middle of the 19th century. Csárdás numbers are often included in ballets, such as the csárdás in *Coppélia* by Delibes.

C-sharp minor. This key possesses a meditative, somewhat somber nature; typical is the 1st movement of Beethoven's *Moonlight Sonata,* (No. 2, op. 27) which suggested to an imaginative critic the surface of a moonlit lake in Switzerland. The famous Prelude in C-sharp minor by Rachmaninoff (No. 2, op. 3) uses this key for solemn evocation of old Russia, with bells ringing over the resonant harmonies; Schumann's *Études symphoniques* fit the description of meditative recollection; there is an evocative Tchaikovsky Nocturne in C-sharp minor (No. 4, op. 19).

As a relatively unidiomatic orch'l key, this tonality is rarely the principal key of a symphonic work; the most outstanding example is Mahler's 5th Sym., which begins with the funereal measures of doom; but modulations are frequent in the score. Prokofiev set his last sym., the 7th, in C-sharp minor; he called the work a *Youth Sym.,* glorifying the spirit of the young Soviet generation; the finale is in the parallel major, enharmonically notated as D-flat major. What is most intriguing in this work is its opus number 131, the same as one of Beethoven's last string quartets, also in C-sharp minor. Prokofiev could not have been unaware of this double identity of key and opus number, but apparently he decided to enjoy the joke in private.

cubism. The musical counterpart of cubistic art is the erection of massive sonorous complexes moving at different speeds and angular motion. Such harmonic boulders produce the best effect in polytriadic structures. Cubistic music must be static, with a low potential. There should be no intermediate melodic or harmonic shifts between cubistic complexes, but tremolo effects within each unit may contribute to resonant power congruent with massive sonic structures.

cue. Phrase, from a vocal or instrumental part, occurring near the end of a long pause in another part, and inserted in small notes in the latter to serve as a guide in timing its reentrance.

Cui, César (Antonovich), b. Vilnius, Jan. 18, 1835; d. Petrograd, Mar. 26, 1918. He was the son of a soldier in Napoleon's army who remained in Russia, married a Lithuanian noblewoman, and settled as a French teacher in Vilnius. He learned musical notation by copying Chopin's mazurkas and various Italian operas; tried his hand at composition; took lessons with Moniuszko (1849); went to St. Petersburg (1850); entered the Engineering School (1851) and the Academy of Military Engineering (1855). After graduation (1857), he became a topographer, later an expert in fortification; participated in the Russo-Turkish War (1877); appointed prof. at the Engineering School (1878); tutor in military fortification to Czar Alexander II. In 1856 Cui met Balakirev, who helped him master the technique of composition; married Malvina Bamberg (1858); in 1864, began writing music criticism in the St. Petersburg *Vedomosti,* later in other newspapers, continuing this career until 1900.

Cui's musical tastes were conditioned by an early admiration for Schumann; opposed Wagner, against whom he wrote vitriolic articles; attacked R. Strauss and Reger with even greater violence; an ardent propagandist of Glinka and the Russian national school, but somewhat critical of Tchaikovsky; publ. the 1st comprehensive book on Russian music, *Musique en Russie* (Paris, 1880). Cui was grouped with Rimsky-Korsakov, Mussorgsky, Borodin, and Balakirev as one of the *Moguchaya Kuchka* (Mighty Five); despite the adjective, his music lacks grandeur; he is at his best in delicate miniatures, e.g., *Orientale,* from the suite *Kaleidoscope,* op. 50. A vol. of selected articles (1864–1917) was publ. in Leningrad (1953).

cuivré (Fr., metal-covered). With a brassy tone, especially on the French horn, when a hand is inserted into the bell, partially closing it, and thus producing a forced sound. If the bell is closed more completely, the pitch is raised a semitone; the notation for this effect is the desired pitch with a plus sign (+) over the note.

cuivres (Fr., metal-covered instruments). Brass instruments.

cupo, -a (It., gloomy). Dark, deep, obscure; reserved. *Con voce cupa,* with a veiled, intense tone.

cupped mouthpiece. Shallower, cup-shaped form of mouthpiece for brass instruments, as opposed to the deeper conical (cone-shaped) mouthpiece.

Curran, Alvin, b. Providence, R.I., Dec. 13, 1938. He studied piano and trombone in his youth; studied composition with Ron Nelson at Brown Univ. (B.A., 1960) and Elliott Carter and Mel Powell at Yale Univ. (M.Mus., 1963); went to Rome (1965); co-founded (with Richard Teitelbaum and Rzewski) Musica Elettronica Viva to perform live electronic music; the ensemble evolved to include all manner of avant-garde performance practices. Curran's compositions range from tape works to experimental pieces using the natural environment.

cursus (Lat.). Generically, the type of prosody used at the end of a sentence. The type of cursus depends on the relative length of certain syllables. Some maintain that a metrical cursus developed in church singing into a rhythmic cursus, in which the long syllables are sung at a higher pitch.

curtal. Obsolete dulcian- or bassoon-type instrument, used in the 16th to mid-18th centuries; known in other languages by the term eventually applied to the modern bassoon.

cut time. See ⇒Alla breve.

cybernetics (from Grk. *kybernan,* govern). Exercise of human control over mechanical and electrical apparatus, especially in the field of communication. In music, cybernetical data are collected by various means; the resulting materials are translated into a system of musical parameters, and a viable outline is drawn. It is in the selection and the programming of cybernetical elements that a composer can assert his personality. Cybernetical serendipity can also play a beneficial part: novel ideas often suggest themselves during the process of mutation and permutation of thematic elements, contributing to the all-important problem of musical communication.

cyclical forms. Forms which embrace a cycle or set of movements, such as the suite or partita, the sonata, symphony, and concerto.

cylindrical tube. Instrument tube that does not taper; as opposed to the conical tube, which tapers very gradually.

cymbales antiques (Fr.). Antique cymbals. See ⇒crotales.

cymbals. Orch. percussion instrument, consisting of a pair of concave plates of brass or bronze, with broad, flat rims and holes for the straps by which they are held; used to make strong accents, or to produce peculiar effects.

Cythara. See ⇒Kithara.

Czerny, Carl, b. Vienna, Feb. 20, 1791; d. there July 15, 1857. Of Czech extraction (*černý* means "black" in Czech), he was trained as a pianist by a father whose rule of life was work without any distraction; when Czerny himself became a teacher he demanded similar dedication from his pupils. His day began at 7 o'clock in the morning, with a single meal before going to bed. He was able to gain Beethoven's friendship; his only Piano Sonata, op. 7, bears a striking resemblance to Beethoven's style. Among his own students was Liszt. His name is everlastingly connected with the enormous compounds of piano studies under such names as *School of Velocity* or *School of Finger Dexterity,* exercises that continued to inflict pianistic torture upon generations of students after him. He declared that he had no time to get married because of his heavy teaching schedule, but nature took vengeance on him when at age 50 he confessed in a secret diary his adoration of a youthful pupil to whom he never dared admit his sentimental attraction.

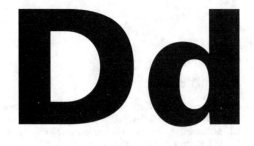

D. 1. Fourth note of the alphabetical scale. In English, French, Spanish, Italian, and Russian nomenclature, this note retains the name Re, derived from the 1st syllable of the 2nd line of the millennian hymn *Ut queant laxis:* "Resonare libris." 2. (Ger. *D;* Fr. *Ré;* It. *re*) 2nd tone and degree in the C major scale. In musical theory capital *D* designates the D-major triad, small *d* the D-minor triad. *D* also stands for Da (D.C. = da capo) and Dal (D.S. = dal segno).

D dur (Ger.). D major.

D major. Key of classical vigor and clarity of expression, particularly suitable for string instruments, for the tonic and the dominant (D, A) are available on open strings of the violin family; thus triadic and scalar passages in D major can be executed with facility in rapid tempo on strings, with open strings serving as convenient signposts. Numerous violin concertos are written in D major; those by Beethoven, Brahms, and Tchaikovsky are among the most famous. One of the most frequently played Haydn syms., written for Salomon and catalogued as no. 104, is in D major. Mozart set his *Prague* Sym. and the endearing Haffner Serenade in D major, both works exuding the joy of music making. An American music critic, who once opined that the fire exit signs in the newly built Boston Sym. Hall should be marked "Exit in Case of Brahms," qualified his anti-Brahms sentiment for the 2nd Sym. in D major, calling it "the most genial of the 4, and the most easily accepted by an audience." When Prokofiev decided to emulate Haydn *à la moderne,* he wrote his *Classical* Sym. in D major.

D minor. Key of repressed passion. The greatest of all works written in D minor, Beethoven's 9th Sym., opens with an allusion rather than an overt declaration, exposing vacant 5ths; full triadic conjunction is revealed only after the harmonic ambiguity becomes unbearable. Schumann's last sym. is also in D minor; he let it lie fallow for many years before completing it. Bruckner selected D minor for his most lugubrious inspiration, the 3rd Sym.; yet Mahler's 3rd Sym., also set in D minor, expresses joy in the presence of nature. Franck's Sym. in D minor is philosophically restrained; the use of an English horn, never regarded as a "symphonic" instrument, reveals an emotional strain. In his popular Piano Trio, op. 49, Mendelssohn represses his passion almost to the point of rupture.

Why is the D-minor triad commonly used by pianists to tune up string instruments in playing chamber music? Why not D major? The truth may lie in the relatively neutral character of D minor, more suitable to the nontempered natural pitch of the violin and the cello.

D moll (Ger.). D minor.

D string. 3rd string on the violin; 2nd on the viola, cello, and double bass.

da (It.). By, from, for, of. *Da braccio,* describing string instruments held "at the arm;" *da camera,* Baroque secular chamber music; *da chiesa* (It., of the church), music intended for church performance; *da eseguirsi, da seguirsi* to be executed.

da capo (It., from the head). Repeat from the beginning. *Da capo al fine,* repeat from beginning to end (i.e., until the word *fine* or a fermata); *da capo al segno,* from the beginning to the sign %; *da capo al segno, poi (segue) la coda,* from the beginning to the sign, then play the coda; *da capo senza replica* (senza ripetizione); play through from the beginning, ignoring the repeats.

da capo aria. See ⇒Aria da capo.

Da Ponte, Lorenzo (born Emanuele Conegliano), b. Ceneda, near Venice, Mar. 10, 1749; d. N.Y., Aug. 17, 1838. He was born a Jew, converted to Christianity at age 14, and assumed the name of his patron, Lorenzo Da Ponte, Bishop of Ceneda; studied at the Ceneda Seminary and at the Portogruaro Seminary, where he taught (1770–73); appointed prof. of rhetoric at Treviso (1774); dismissed for beliefs concerning natural laws (1776). He then went to Venice, led an adventurous life, and was banished for adultery (1779); lived in Austria, then Dresden; settled in Vienna (1782); became official poet to the Imperial Theater; befriended Mozart and wrote the librettos for his most famous operas: *Le nozze di Figaro, Don Giovanni,* and *Così fan tutte.* He lived in London (1792–98); traveled in Europe; went to N.Y. (1805); after disastrous business ventures, became interested in operatic enterprises; in his last years he taught Italian at Columbia College.

dactyl(e) (Lat., *dactylus,* finger, in reference to the layout of the joints). Metrical foot with syllables arranged as 1 long accented syllable followed by 2 short unaccented ones; equivalent to a rapid waltz without strong upbeat.

dadaism. Anti-art aesthetic invented by Tristan Tzara in 1916 at a congenial gathering of friends in a Zurich café; according to one version, the term *dada* owes its origin to French infantiloquy as a sort of dental lallation. Aesthetically, dadaism was the product of the frustrations endured during World War I; its philosophy was entirely negative. Derived from the vociferously proclaimed detestation of all art, music, and poetry, dadaism stood close to futurism in its furious onslaught on all established values, but (by definition) failed to offer an alternative to replace the old; despite its violent negativity, prepared a well-manured ground for the flowering of such fertile stylistic vegetation as surrealism. Dadaism also cast its proleptic shadow on the avant-garde of the 1920s and the improvisatory art of the Happenings.

dagli (It., *dai, dal, dall', dalla, dalle, dallo;*). To the, by the, for the, from the, etc.

Dahl, Ingolf, b. Hamburg (of Swedish parents), June 9, 1912; d. Frutigen, near Bern, Switzerland, Aug. 6, 1970. He studied composition with Jarnach at Cologne (1930–32) and musicology at the Univ. of Zurich (1932–36); received conducting lessons from Andreae. He went to the U.S. (1938); settled in Calif.; active as a conductor and composer; appointed assistant prof. at the Univ. of Southern Calif. (1945); received 2

Guggenheim fellowships (1952, 1960). He taught at the Berkshire Music Center, Tanglewood (1952–55); in his music, adhered to an advanced polyphonic style in free dissonant counterpoint.

dal segno (It.). From the sign. *Dal segno al fine,* from the sign to the end.

Dale, Clamma, b. Chester, Pa., July 4, 1948. She studied piano as a child, then clarinet and singing; at 14 began voice lessons at Philadelphia's Settlement Music School; enrolled at the Juilliard School of Music in N.Y. (B.Mus., 1970; M.S., 1975); her teachers were H. Heinz, A. Howland, and C. Reed. She made her debut with the N.Y. Opera as Antonia in *Les Contes d'Hoffmann* (1975); other roles were Nedda, Musetta, the Countess, Pamina, and Bess.

Dallapiccola, Luigi, b. Pisino, Istria, Feb. 3, 1904; d. Florence, Feb. 19, 1975. He took piano lessons at an early age; attended the Pisino Gymnasium (1914–21, except 1917–18, when his family was in political exile); studied piano and harmony in Trieste (1919–21); moved to Florence (1922); took courses at the Cherubini Cons.; studied piano with E. Consolo (graduated 1924) and composition with V. Frazzi (graduated 1931); active in the Italian section of the ISCM from the early 1930s; he was appointed to the faculty of the Cherubini Cons. (1934–67).

As a composer Dallapiccola became interested from the very 1st in the melodic application of atonal writing; in 1939; adopted the dodecaphonic method of Schoenberg, with his own considerable innovations, e.g., the use of mutually exclusive triads in thematic structure and harmonic progressions; excelled in the handling of vocal lines in a difficult modern idiom. He visited London in 1946 and traveled on the Continent; taught several courses in American colleges and music schools; an essay collection publ. as *Appunti incontri meditazioni* (1970).

Dameron, Tadd (Tadley Ewing), b. Cleveland, Feb. 21, 1917; d. N.Y., Mar. 8, 1965. He was inspired to follow a jazz musician's career by his brother Caesar, a saxophone player; played piano with Freddie Webster, Zack White, and Blanche Calloway; in the 1940s and 1950s, played with Gillespie, Davis, and Clifford Brown. He became an accomplished composer and arranger, working in Chicago and N.Y.; but his career was plagued by narcotic addiction, as a result, served time in the Lexington, Ky. federal prison (1958–60).

damper (Ger. *Dämpfer*). 1. Set of mechanical devices placed over piano strings; goes into operation when the key of a note is released by the finger, triggering the damper to fall and thereby stop the string, causing the string's vibration (i.e., sound) to end. 2. Mute of a brass instrument.

damper pedal. Right, or loud, pedal of the piano; when pressed down, the dampers are lifted from the strings, allowing them to vibrate freely and resonantly.

Dämpfer (Ger.). 1. Damper. 2. Mute.

dance band. Instrumental ensemble accompanying ballroom dancing, composed of saxophones, trumpets, trombones, and percussion.

Danican-Philidor. See ⇒Philidor.

danse (Fr.), **danza** (It., Sp.). Dance.

dargason. Generic form concluding with an 8-measure melody lacking a tonic final cadence, thus "circular" (i.e., potentially ad finitum); used in works or publications by Ravenscroft, Dowland, Playford, and Holst; Ben Jonson refers to it in his *Tale of a Tub*.

Dargomyzhsky, Alexander (Sergeievich), b. Troitskoye, Tula district, Feb. 14, 1813; d. St. Petersburg, Jan. 17, 1869. From 1817 he lived in St. Petersburg; studied piano with Schoberlechner and Danilevsky, and violin with Vorontsov; at 20, a brilliant pianist; held a government position (1827–43), but then devoted himself exclusively to music, studying assiduously for 8 years; visited Germany, Brussels, and Paris (1845); in Moscow, successfully produced the opera *Esmeralda* (after Victor Hugo's *Notre-Dame de Paris,* 1847). He publ. over 100 minor vocal and piano works (1845–55); brought out his best opera, *Rusalka,* at St. Petersburg (1856); an opera-ballet, *The Triumph of Bacchus* (1845; premiered 1867); a posth. opera, *The Stone Guest* (*Kamennyi gost,* after Pushkin's poem), was scored by Rimsky-Korsakov and produced at St. Petersburg (1872); elected president of the Russian Music Soc. (1867). At 1st a follower of Rossini and Auber, he gradually became convinced that dramatic realism with nationalistic connotations was the destiny of Russian music; applied this method to the recitative in *The Stone Guest* and his songs (often satirical); his orch'l works enjoyed wide popularity.

dark (Fr., *relâche*). In theatrical jargon, no performance.

David, Hal, b. N.Y., May 25, 1921. He studied journalism at N.Y. Univ.; then collaborated with Bacharach and other popular song composers. His lyrics for *Raindrops Keep Falling on My Head* (1969) won an Academy Award; others written for Bacharach include *Here Am I, Magic Moments, My Little Red Book, Love Can Break a Heart, Send Me No Flowers, The Story of My Life, What's New, Pussycat?,* and *Wives and Lovers;* wrote the musical *Promises, Promises* (1968). He contributed lyrics to several films, including *Lost Horizon, Butch Cassidy and the Sundance Kid,* and *Moonraker;* served as president of ASCAP (1980–86). His brother is Mack David.

David, Mack, b. N.Y., July 5, 1912. He studied at Cornell Univ. and St. John's Univ. Law School. Began writing for Broadway and film; collaborated with Count Basie, Burt Bacharach, Ernest Gold, Elmer Bernstein, David Raksin, and Henry Mancini; best-known songs are *Bibbidi, Bobbidi, Boo* (1948); *Cat Ballou* (1965); *The Hanging Tree* (1959); *It's a Mad, Mad, Mad, Mad World* (1963); *My Own True Love* (1954). He filed a lawsuit for copyright infringement of his obscure *Sunflower* (1948), accusing Jerry Herman of plagiarism in the latter's popular song *Hello, Dolly* (1964); the sum paid in an out-of-court settlement to David exceeded half a million dollars. His brother is Hal David.

Davidovich, Bella, b. Baku, July 16, 1928. Her maternal grandfather was concertmaster of the Baku opera orch., her mother a pianist; began formal piano training at age 6; at 9, appeared as soloist in the Beethoven 1st Piano Concerto in Baku; sent to Moscow to pursue studies with Konstantin Igumnov

(1939), with whom she subsequently also studied at the Moscow Cons. (1946–48), completing her training with Yakov Flier (1948–54); captured joint 1st prize at the Chopin Competition in Warsaw (1949), which launched a highly successful career in Russia and Eastern Europe; annual soloist with the Leningrad Phil. (1950–78); taught at the Moscow Cons. (1962–78); made her 1st appearance outside Russia in Amsterdam (1967); toured Italy (1971).

Following the defection of her son Dmitri Sitkovetsky (b. 1954) to the West (1977), she was refused permission to perform there by the Soviets; emigrated to the U.S. (1978), became a naturalized U.S. citizen (1984). She made an acclaimed recital debut at N.Y.'s Carnegie Hall (1979); joined the faculty of the Juilliard School in N.Y. (1982) but continued to perform internationally. In 1988 she and her son became the 1st émigrés to be invited to perform in Russia after the beginning of Gorbachev's reforms.

Davidovsky, Mario, b. Buenos Aires, Mar. 4, 1934. He studied composition and theory with Guillermo Graetzer in Buenos Aires; continued training with Babbitt at Tanglewood (1958); worked at the Columbia-Princeton Electronic Music Center (from 1960); taught at the Univ. of Mich. (1964), the Di Tella Inst. of Buenos Aires (1965), the Manhattan School of Music in N.Y. (1968–69), Yale Univ. (1969–70), City College of the City Univ. of N.Y. (1968–80), and Columbia Univ. (from 1981), where he directed the Columbia-Princeton Electronic Music Center. He held 2 Guggenheim fellowships (1960, 1971); received the Pulitzer Prize for *Synchronisms No. 6* for Piano and Electronics (1971); elected to the Inst. of the American Academy and Inst. of Arts and Letters (1982). His method of composition tends toward mathematical parameters, e.g., his series of 8 electroacoustic compositions entitled *Synchronisms* (1963–74); electronic sound is integral to much of his work.

Davies, Dennis Russell, b. Toledo, Ohio, Apr. 16, 1944. He studied piano with Lonny Epstein and Sascha Gorodnitzki, and conducting with Jean Morel and Jorge Mester at the Juilliard School of Music in N.Y. (B.Mus., 1966; M.S., 1968; D.M.A., 1972), where he taught (1968–71); cofounder (with Berio) of the Juilliard Ensemble (1968–74). He was music director of the Norwalk (Conn.) Sym. Orch. (1968–73), St. Paul (Minn.) Chamber Orch. (1972–80), Cabrillo (Calif.) Music Festival (from 1974), and the American Composers Orch. in N.Y. (from 1977); made 1st appearance at the Bayreuth Festival, conducting *Der fliegende Holländer*. (1978); Generalmusikdirektor of the Württemberg State Theater in Stuttgart (1980–87), principal conductor and classical music programmer at the Saratoga (N.Y.) Performing Arts Center (1985–88), and Generalmusikdirektor of Bonn (from 1987). In 1991 he was appointed music director of the Brooklyn Academy of Music and principal conductor of the Brooklyn Phil.; received the Alice M. Ditson conductor's award (1987). He has acquired a notable reputation as a champion of contemporary music; conducted numerous premieres in the U.S. and Europe.

Davies, (Sir) Peter Maxwell, b. Manchester, Sept. 8, 1934. He went to Leigh Grammar School and Royal Manchester College of Music and Manchester Univ; won an Italian govern-

ment scholarship, proceeding to Rome (1957); studied with Petrassi; his orch'l work *Prolation* received the Olivetti Prize (1958) and was performed at the ISCM festival in Rome (1959). Returning to England, he served as director of music at Cirencester Grammar School (1959–62); introduced his neo-Socratic schooling method, encouraging students to exercise their curiosity. In 1962 he went to the U.S. on a Harkness fellowship; studied at Princeton Univ.; joined the UNESCO Conference on Music in Education; made a worldwide lecture tour (1965); composer-in-residence at the Univ. of Adelaide in Australia (1966–67). In 1967 he organized (with Harrison Birtwistle) a London ensemble called the Pierrot Players; in 1970 it was renamed the Fires of London, with programs of provocative modernistic works. In 1970 Davies made his home in the Orkney Islands; organized the annual St. Magnus Festival (1977) at its Norse Cathedral; premiered many of his compositions; despite the remoteness of the Orkney Islands, the festival attracted attention. He was awarded an honorary doctorate of music at Edinburgh Univ. (1979); appointed successor to Sir William Glock as director of music at Dartington Summer School; named Composer of the Year by the Composers' Guild of Great Britain; commissioned to write a sym. for the Boston Sym. Orch. on the occasion of its centennial (1981); named composer-in-residence and associate conductor of the Scottish Chamber Orch. in Glasgow (1985); knighted (1987).

In his works Davies combines seemingly incongruous elements: reverential evocations of medieval hymnody, surrealistic depictions of historical personages, and hedonistic musical theatrics. His most arresting synthesis is the *8 Songs for a Mad King* for Male Voice and Instruments, a fantastic suite of heterogeneously arranged pieces representing the etiology of the madness of King George III (1969); at the other extreme is *Vesalii Icones* for Dancer, Solo Cello, and Instruments, in 14 movements (after 14 anatomical drawings by Andreas Vesalius depicting Christ's Passion and Resurrection). He is a fervent activist in political struggles, the movement combating the spread of nuclear weapons, and the defense of the environment against industrial pollution.

Davis, Anthony, b. Paterson, N.J., Feb. 20, 1951. He studied at Yale Univ. (B.A., 1975); proved himself an extremely facile jazz pianist; cofounder of Advent (1973), a free jazz ensemble with trombonist George Lewis; played in trumpeter Wadada Leo Smith's New Delta Ahkri band (1974–77); played in N.Y. with violinist Leroy Jenkins (1977–79) and flutist James Newton, both proponents of the Assoc. for the Advancement of Creative Musicians. His compositions, while strictly notated, are improvisational in tone. His opera *X, The Life and Times of Malcolm X* was produced in Philadelphia (1985) and at N.Y.'s Lincoln Center (1989); other works include *The Ghost Factory—MAPS* for solo violin, strings, harp, and percussion; *Lost Moon Sisters* for soprano, violin, keyboards, marimba, and vibraphone (1990); and *Hemispheres,* a 5-part dance work for Molissa Fenley (1983). Among his recordings are *Of Blues and Dreams* (1978), *Hidden Voices* (with Newton; 1979), and *Under the Double Moon* (with J. Hoggard; 1982).

Davis, (Sir) Colin (Rex), b. Weybridge, Sept. 25, 1927. He studied the clarinet at the Royal College of Music in London; played in the band of the Household Cavalry while serving in the army; began conducting career with the semiprofessional

Chelsea Opera Group; in 1958 he conducted a performance of *The Abduction from the Seraglio* in London (1958); from 1961 to 1965 he served as music director of Sadler's Wells (1961–65). He made his U.S. debut as a guest with the Minneapolis Sym. Orch. (1960); subsequently performed with the N.Y. Phil., the Philadelphia Orch., and the Los Angeles Phil.; served as principal guest conductor of the Boston Sym. Orch (1972–83); made his Metropolitan Opera, N.Y., debut, conducting *Peter Grimes* (1967); chief conductor of the BBC Sym. Orch. in London (1967–71); conducted at the Royal Opera at Covent Garden (1965–86); succeeded Solti as its music director (1971).

Among Davis's notable achievements was the Covent Garden performance of the complete Der Ring des Nibelungen (1974–76); became the 1st British conductor to appear at the Bayreuth Festival, conducting Tannhäuser (1977); led the Royal Opera during its tours in South Korea and Japan (1979) and the U.S. (1984). He was appointed chief conductor of the Bavarian Radio Sym. Orch. in Munich (1983); led a North American tour (1986). In 1986 he stepped down as music director at Covent Garden to devote himself fully to Munich and pursue far-flung guest engagements with major orchs. and opera houses of the world; made a Commander of the Order of the British Empire (1965); knighted (1980).

Davis, Miles (Dewey, III), b. Alton, Ill., May 25, 1926; d. N.Y., Sept. 21, 1991. He learned to play trumpet in elementary school in East St. Louis; continued his studies in high school; even before his graduation he made professional appearances. In 1944 he went to N.Y. to enter the Juilliard School of Music; frequented the city's jazz spots; decided on a jazz career and quit Juilliard (1945); worked with Parker, Hawkins, Benny Carter, and Eckstine; modified his bebop style in 1948, leading a group with an atypical jazz instrument (French horn, played by Gunther Schuller); exemplified by such numbers as *Boplicity*.

Davis introduced a "cool" manner of playing, by contrast with frantic "hot" bebop; his arranger was Gil Evans; he had Coltrane on the saxophone and Philly Joe Jones on the drums; in his numbers, introduced the lyrical and quiet modal type of setting, favoring the Lydian scale with its enervating tritone base, and finding suitable harmonies for it. By 1958 he had abandoned standard jazz practices; plunged into mystical depths with the exotic jazz heard in far-out numbers as *Nefertiti* and *Sorcerer*; annexed electronics, forming a fusion style with hard rock (*Bitches' Brew*); to emphasize his solidarity with black political movements, affected quasi-African vestments at public appearances; had many close encounters with excessively dutiful law enforcers.

As he prospered from sales of recordings and performances, he became the target of extortionists and racists; inartistic malefactors peppered his snazzy Ferrari car with machine-gun bullets; suffered a hip injury that required the implantation of an artificial prothesis; after a hiatus (1975–81), he returned to center stage with his album *The Man with the Horn* (1981); made an extensive tour of Europe (1982); always searching for new avenues of expression, adapted the songs of popular artists as Michael Jackson and Cyndi Lauper for his own concerts; collaborated on a recording project with Prince (1986). He also tried his skill at painting and appeared on television as an actor; married the actress Cicely Tyson (his third; 1981); they divorced in 1988.

davul (*dawūl*). Cylindrical Turkish drum with a double head, closely associated with the *zurnā*, a Turkish oboe.

Dawson, William Levi, b. Anniston, Ala., Sept. 26, 1898; d. Tuskegee, Ala., May 2, 1990. He ran away from home at 13 to enter the Tuskegee Inst.; played trombone on the Redpath Chautauqua Circuit; graduated from the Tuskegee Inst. (1921); studied with Carl Busch in Kansas City and at the American Cons. in Chicago (M.A., 1927). He played 1st trombone in the Chicago Civic Orch. (1926–30); conducted the Tuskegee Choir. His best-known work is the *Negro Folk Sym.* in 3 movements (1934).

De Franco, "Buddy" (Boniface Ferdinand Leonardo), b. Camden, N.J., Feb. 17, 1923. He took up the clarinet at age 12; worked with many leading jazz musicians, including Gene Krupa (1941–42), Charlie Barnet (1943–44), Tommy Dorsey (1944–46), and Count Basie (1950); organized his own big band (1951) and quartet (1952), appearing with the latter for many successful years; led the Glenn Miller Orch. (1966–74), then resumed touring on his own.

De Koven, (Henry Louis) Reginald, b. Middletown, Conn., Apr. 3, 1859; d. Chicago, Jan. 16, 1920. He was educated in Europe from 1870; studied piano under Speidel at Stuttgart; graduated from St. John's, Oxford (1879); returned to Stuttgart to study under Lebert (piano) and Pruckner (harmony). After a 6-month course in Frankfurt under Hauff (composition), he studied singing in Florence and operatic composition under Genee in Vienna and Delibes in Paris; organized the Phil. Orch. at Washington, D.C. (1902), which he led for 3 seasons; music critic for the *Chicago Evening Post* (1889–90), *Harper's Weekly* (1895–97), *N.Y. World* (1898–1900; 1907–12), and later for the *N.Y. Herald*. Of the 30 stage works De Koven produced over a 33-year span, his best-known operetta was *Robin Hood* (Chicago, 1890); the celebrated song *O, Promise Me* was introduced into the score shortly after its 1st perf., having originally been publ. separately (1889).

deaconing. In English and American colonial parish churches, the preliminary reading, by a deacon or other lay singer, of a line from a hymn before the entire congregation sings it; the practice is also called lining out.

deafness. No greater misfortune can befall a musician than the loss of hearing. Beethoven gave an eloquent expression of this horror in his famous "Heiligenstadt Testament" (1802). He consulted every Viennese quack who promised a cure; in his conversation books there is this pathetic notation by one of his friends: "There is in Vienna a Dr. Mayer who is employed by a sulphur vapor company which uses vibrations to cure sufferers from hearing impediments when no organic fault is found in the tissues. His electro-vibratory machine works by strengthening rheumatic ear infections, hardness of hearing and deafness." Some critics of Beethoven's last works explained their strangeness by his deafness. "Beethoven's imagination seems to have fed upon the ruins of his sensitive organs," wrote William Gardiner of London in 1837.

Another victim of ear ailments was Smetana; pressure on the auditory nerve made him hear a constant drone on a high E; he memorialized this affliction in his 1st String Quartet, entitled *From my Life*, in which he has the violin play a persistent high E.

Schumann suffered from a similar disturbance technically known as tinnitus; during his last years he heard a constant A flat. Fauré became almost totally deaf toward the end of his life, but hid this condition sufficiently long to continue as director of the Paris Cons.

Debussy, Claude, (born Achille-Claude Debussy), b. St.-Germain-en-Laye, Aug. 22, 1862; d. Paris, Mar. 25, 1918. Considered the originator of musical impressionism; his music created a new poetry of mutating tonalities, a perfect counterpart of contemporaneous French painting. Mme Maute de Fleurville, the mother-in-law of the poet Verlaine, prepared him for the Paris Cons.; admitted at age 10; studied piano with Marmontel (2nd prize, 1877) and solfège with Lavignac (1st medal, 1876); studied harmony with Durand (1877–80) and score reading under Bazille. In 1880 Marmontel recommended him to Mme von Meck, Tchaikovsky's patroness, who summoned him to Interlaken; they subsequently visited Rome, Naples, and Fiesole. During the summers of 1881 and 1882, he stayed with Mme von Meck's family in Moscow; became acquainted with the syms. of Tchaikovsky, but failed to appreciate that music; became more interested in Mussorgsky's idiosyncratic compositions.

Debussy made his earliest professional appearance as a composer in Paris (1882), at a concert given by the violinist Maurice Thieberg. In 1880 he had enrolled in the composition class of Guiraud at the Paris Cons., hoping to win the Grand Prix de Rome; finally succeeded (1884) with his cantata *L'Enfant prodigue;* written in a poetic but conservative manner reflecting French romanticism. During his stay in Rome he wrote a choral work, *Zuleima,* after Heine (1885–86); began another cantata, *Diane au bois;* neither of these 2 incunabulae survives. *Printemps* (choral suite with orch., 1887) failed to win official recognition; set to work on another cantata, *La Damoiselle élue* (1887–89); gained immediate favor among French musicians.

In 1888 Debussy visited Bayreuth, where he heard *Parsifal* and *Die Meistersinger von Nürnberg* for the 1st time, but Wagner's grandiloquence never gained his full devotion. What thoroughly engaged his interest was the Eastern music, particularly the gamelan that he heard at the Paris World Exposition (1889); was fascinated by the asymmetric rhythms of the thematic content and the new instrumental colors achieved by native players; found an inner valence between these oriental modalities and the verses of French impressionist and symbolist poets, including Mallarmé, Verlaine, Baudelaire, and Pierre Louÿs; this combination of musically exotic impressions and symbolist French verses were rendered in vocal works such as *Cinq poèmes de Baudelaire* (1887–89), *Ariettes oubliées* (1888), *Trois mélodies* (1891), and *Fêtes galantes* (1892); wrote *Proses lyriques* (1892–93) to his own texts.

For the piano Debussy composed *Suite bergamasque* (1890–1905), which includes the famous *Clair de lune.* In 1892 he began his orch'l *Prélude à l'après-midi d'un faune,* after Mallarmé, reaching the quintessence of tonal painting with its free modal sequences under a subtle umbrage of oscillating instrumentation; premiered in Paris (1894), with a program book cautioning the audience that the text contained sensuous elements that might distract young females. In 1893 there followed *Trois chansons de Bilitis,* after prose poems by Louÿs, (1893) marked by exceptional textual sensuality in a freely modal context; a later work, *Les Chansons de Bilitis* for 2 harps,

2 flutes, and celesta, was premiered in Paris as incidental music to accompany recited and mimed neo-Grecian poetry of Louÿs (1901). He worked on *3 Nocturnes* for orch.: *Nuages, Fêtes,* and *Sirènes* (1892–99)

In the 1890s Debussy had attended a performance of Maeterlinck's drama *Pelléas et Mélisande,* which inspired him to begin composition on an opera on that subject. With this work, he assumed a leading place among French composers. It was premiered at the Opéra-Comique in Paris (1902), after many difficulties; Maeterlinck objected to having the role of Mélisande sung by the American soprano Mary Garden, whose accent jarred Maeterlinck's sensibilities (he wanted his mistress to be the 1st Mélisande). The production aroused a violent controversy among French musicians and *littérateurs;* the press was vicious in the extreme: "Rhythm, melody, tonality, these are 3 things unknown to Monsieur Debussy," wrote Arthur Pougin. "What a pretty series of false relations! What adorable progressions of triads in parallel motion and 5ths and octaves which result from it! What a collection of dissonances, 7ths and 9ths, ascending with energy! . . . No, decidedly I will never agree with these anarchists of music!" Camille Bellaigue, Debussy's classmate at the Paris Cons., conceded that the opera "makes little noise," but, he remarked, "it is a nasty little noise." English-language reviews of *Pelléas* were no less vituperative, pejorative, and deprecatory. The *Musical Courier* of N.Y. compared Debussy's "disharmony" with the sensation of "an involuntary start when the dentist touches the nerve of a sensitive tooth." James Gibbons Huneker exceeded all limits of permissible literary mores by attacking his physical appearance. "I met Debussy at the Café Riche the other night," he wrote in the *N.Y. Sun,* "and was struck by the unique ugliness of the man . . . [H]e looks more like a Bohemian, a Croat, a Hun, than a Gaul." These utterances were followed by a suggestion that the music was fit for a procession of headhunters of Borneo, carrying home "their ghastly spoils of war."

As the 20th century dawned, Debussy found himself entangled in domestic relationships. A tempestuous liaison with Gabrielle Dupont (Gaby Lhery) led to a break that so distressed Gaby that she took poison (she survived). He married Rosalie Texier (1899), with whom he made his 1st attempt to form a legitimate union; but he soon discovered that, like Gaby before her, Rosalie failed to satisfy his expectations; he again began to look elsewhere for a true union of souls. This he found with Emma Bardac, the wife of a banker; he bluntly informed Rosalie of his dissatisfaction with their marriage; Rosalie, plunged into despair by his selfish decision, shot herself in the chest, but missed. Now 42 years old, he divorced Rosalie (in 1905; Emma and her husband had divorced earlier that year); he married Emma (early 1908). They had a daughter, Claude-Emma (known as "Chouchou"), born in 1905; she inspired his charming piano suite *Children's Corner* (the orig. title is in English; Chouchou had an English governess); she survived her father by barely a year, dying of diphtheria (1919).

Debussy's next important work was *La Mer,* completed during a sojourn to England (1905); it was premiered in Paris. Like his String Quartet (1893) it was conceived monothematically; a single idea permeates the work, despite a great variety of instrumentation. It consists of 3 symphonic sketches: *De l'aube à midi sur la mer* ("From Sunrise to Moon"); *Jeux de vagues* ("Play of the Waves"); and *Dialogue du vent et de la mer* ("Dialogue of Wind and the Sea"). *La Mer* was attacked by critics with even greater displeasure than *Pélleas et Mélisande*. Louis Elson even suggested that the orig. title should have been *Le Mal de mer,* and that the last movement represented a violent seizure of vomiting. Contemporary judgments on Debussy were collected in a vol., *Le Cas Debussy,* publ. in Paris (1910); it assessed Debussy as a "deformateur musical," suffering from a modern nervous disease that affects one's power of discernment.

Remarkably self-confident despite his music's reception, Debussy continued to work. Among the new works is the remarkable orch. triptych, *Images* (1906–12), comprising *Gigues; Iberia,* and *Rondes de printemps.* He conducted a concert of his works in London (1908); led concerts in Vienna (1910), Turin (1911), Moscow and St. Petersburg (1913), and Rome, Amsterdam, and the Hague (1914). Among his new piano works of the period are the *12 Preludes* (2 vols., 1910, 1913) and *12 Études* (2 vols., 1915); *En blanc et noir,* for 2 pianos, dates from 1915. Diaghilev produced the tennis ballet *Jeux* in Paris (1913). Debussy played the piano part of his Violin Sonata at its premiere in Paris (1917); but his projected U.S. tour with the violinist Arthur Hartmann had to be abandoned when he was diagnosed with irreversible cancer of the colon; surgery was performed (late 1915), but there was little hope of recovery. The protracted 1st World War depressed him; his hatred of the Germans became intense as the military threat to Paris increased. He wrote a song, *Noël des enfants,* in which he begged Santa Claus not to bring presents to German children whose parents were destroying the French children's Christmas; to underline his national sentiments, he emphatically signed his last works "musicien français"; his plan to compose 6 truly French chamber works was only half completed.; he died in the evening, as the great German gun, "Big Bertha," made a last attempt to subdue the city of Paris by long-distance bombardment.

Debussy emphatically rejected the term "impressionism" when applied to his music; but it cannot alter the fact that, like Mallarmé's poetry, he evolved a style peculiarly sensitive to musical mezzotint, a palette of half-lit delicate colors. He systematically applied the oriental pentatonic scale for exotic evocations, as well as the whole-tone scale (not his invention). His music emancipated discords; revived the archaic practice of consecutive perfect intervals (particularly 5ths and 4ths); structurally, the themes are shortened and rhythmically sharpened, while in the orchestration the role of individual solo passages is enhanced and the dynamic range made more subtle. Among his operatic projects, Debussy completed only *Pélleas et Mélisande;* of the other works, 2 exist in sizable fragmentary form: *Rodrigue et Chiméne,* after a Corneille play (1890–92), and *La Chûte de la maison Usher,* after Poe's *The Fall of the House of Usher* (1908–17).

début (Fr.). 1st appearance by a performer or work. *Débutant,* a male performer who makes his debut; *débutante,* a female performer who makes her debut.

decay. Gradual extinction of a sound. See also ⇒envelope.

deceptive cadence. Cadence that resolves from the dominant to an unexpected submediant, instead of resolving to the customary tonic. In major keys the arrival chord is a minor triad a whole step above the dominant; in minor keys, a major triad a semitone above the dominant.

déchiffrer (Fr., decipher). Play or sing at sight.

decibel (abbrev. db). Minimal increment of sound energy perceptible to the human ear; one-tenth of a bel, the arbitrary unit of sound named for Alexander Graham Bell, American acoustician and inventor. The range of tolerable loudness of sound varies from 25 decibels to about 100 decibels, corresponding to the sound of a full orch.; rock bands can reach 120 decibels; 200 decibels is the so-called pain threshold, causing physical damage to the eardrum.

decima (Lat.). 1. Interval of a 10th. 2. Organ stop pitched a 10th higher than the 8' stops; tierce.

deciso (It.). Decisively, energetically.

declamation. In vocal music, clear and correct enunciation of the words.

decomposition and reassembly. Freely topological approach to composition; suggested by the title of a painting by the futurist artist Boccioni, *Scomposizione,* in which the normal head of a woman is fragmented and reassembled in a topologically noncongruent shape. The idea is applicable to modern music; melody can be fractured and its elements redistributed in a different configuration; variations, tonal and atonal, can be rearranged, melodically, harmonically, and/or rhythmically. Decomposition and reassembly may provide interesting and novel combinations of thematic materials and stimulate a disadvantaged composer to explore the laws of musical congruence far beyond his ordinary capabilities.

decrescendo. See ⇒diminuendo.

decuplet. Group of 10 equal notes executed in the time proper to 8 notes of like value, or to 4 notes of the next highest value, in the established rhythm; marked by a slur and a figure 10:

dedications. Composers since time immemorial have habitually dedicated their works to the high and the mighty. Immortality could be bought for a few florins or ducats. Mozart's sublime *Haffner* Serenade gave a friendly if insignificant Salzburg functionary his immortality. Bach's *Goldberg Variations* obliquely glorified his pupil Johann Gottlieb Goldberg, who had requested him to write this extremely difficult and lengthy keyboard composition to help relieve the insomnia of a patron. Beethoven's *Kreutzer Sonata,* written for the virtuoso violinist Rodolphe Kreutzer, was never performed by him publicly; he was a replacement for the first performer of the violin part (G. P. Bridgetower). Beethoven also dedicated works to titled benefactors and foreign dignitaries, among them the string quartets of op. 59 for the Russian Ambassador in Vienna, Count Rasoumowsky; *Wellington's Victory,* inscribed to King George IV of England; and his last trio, the *Archduke,* for Archduke Rudolf. But his most famous dedication, the fulsome tribute to Napoleon in the *Eroica* Sym., was later retracted.

Dedications were usually written in an extremely flowery and obsequious language, with the exalted status of the royal or aristocratic person to whom the work was dedicated symbolized by large capital letters, and a contrasting self-effacing signature emphasizing the humbleness and insignificance of the author in comparison with the sunlike splendor of the dedicatee.

DeGaetani, Jan(ice), b. Massillon, Ohio, July 10, 1933; d. Rochester, N.Y., Sept. 15, 1989. Her father was a lawyer who encouraged her musical talents; became a remarkable mezzo-soprano; married the conductor Thomas DeGaetani; however, the marriage was not successful, and they were soon divorced; she subsequently married Philip West, an oboist. She studied at the Juilliard School of Music in N.Y. with Sergius Kagan; upon graduation, joined the Contemporary Chamber Ensemble; developed a peculiar technique essential for performance of ultramodern vocal works; devoted her free time to a detailed study of Schoenberg's *Pierrot lunaire;* became one of her finest interpretations.

DeGaetani mastered the most challenging techniques of new vocal music, including fractional intervals and even tongue-clicking required in some new works; mastered foreign languages so as to develop a wide European repertoire; became a faithful interpreter of the most demanding works by composers such as Boulez, Crumb, Druckman, Maxwell Davies, Ligeti, Carter, and Davidovsky; also possessed a fine repertoire of Renaissance songs; became a unique phenomenon as a lieder artist, excelling in an ability to express the most minute vocal modulations of the melodic line while parsing the words with exquisite intellectual penetration; even experienced critics found themselves at a loss to describe her artistry. From 1973 she taught at the Eastman School of Music in Rochester, N.Y.; with N. and R. Lloyd, publ. the useful *The Complete Sightsinger* (1980); died of irreversible leukemia.

degree. 1. One of 8 consecutive tones in a major or minor diatonic scale, counted upward from the keynote (tonic). 2. Line or space on the staff. 3. Step.

dehnen (Ger.). Prolong.

dehors, en (Fr., outside). With emphasis; bring out.

del, dell', della, delle, dello (It.). Of the, than the.

Del Tredici, David (Walter), b. Cloverdale, Calif., Mar. 16, 1937. He studied piano; made his debut as a soloist with the San Francisco Sym. at age 16; enrolled at the Univ. of Calif. in Berkeley; studied composition with Shifrin, Imbrie, and Arnold Elston (B.A., 1959); took additional studies at Princeton Univ. with Earl Kim and Sessions (M.F.A., 1963); continued his pianistic practice, taking private lessons with Helps in N.Y. During the summers of 1964 and 1965 he served as pianist at Tanglewood;. In 1966 he received a Guggenheim fellowship award (1966); resident composer at the Marlboro Festival in Vermont (1966–67); assistant prof. of music at Harvard Univ. (1966–72); joined the music faculty at Boston Univ. (1973); began teaching

at City College and the Graduate School of the City Univ. of N.Y. (1984); although retained by pedagogy, he composed avidly.

His first successes involved texts of James Joyce. Fascinated by Joyce's new literary forms and novel language, he wrote *I Hear an Army,* scored for soprano and string quartet, premiered at Tanglewood (1964), and immediately caught the attention of the cloistered but influential cognoscenti; another Joyce work was set by Del Tredici as *Night Conjure–Verse* for soprano, mezzo-soprano, woodwind septet, and string quartet; he led the San Francisco premiere (1966). A 3rd piece inspired by Joyce's verbal music was *Syzygy* for soprano, horn, bells, drums, and chamber orch., premiered in N.Y. (1968). These works plied a modified dodecaphonic course in a polyrhythmic context, gravid with meaningful pauses, free of triadic encounters.

But Del Tredici achieved greater fame with a series of brilliant tone pictures after *Alice in Wonderland* by Lewis Carroll, in which he incorporated, in utter defiance of all modernistic conventions, overt tonal proclamations, fanfares, and pretty, almost embarrassingly attractive tunes, becoming more melodious and harmonious with each consequent portrait of Alice. The Alice pieces (all after Carroll) include *An Alice Sym.* in 5 parts (*Speak Gently/Speak Roughly; The Lobster Quadrille; 'Tis the Voice of the Sluggard; Who Stole the Tarts?; Dream Conclusion;* 1969–76); *Vintage Alice: Fantascene on a Mad Tea Party* for Amplified Soprano, Folk Group, and Orch. (1972); *Final Alice* for the same instrumentation (1976); *Child Alice,* in 2 parts, for Amplified Soprano and Orch.: *In Memory of a Summer Day,* 1980, Pulitzer Prize; and *All in the Golden Afternoon,* 1981. He was elected to the Inst. of the American Academy and Inst. of Arts and Letters (1984); composer-in-residence of the N.Y. Phil. (1988–90).

Delibes, (Clément-Philibert-) Léo, b. St.-Germain-du-Val, Sarthe, Feb. 21, 1836; d. Paris, Jan. 16, 1891. He received his early musical training with his mother and an uncle; enrolled in the Paris Cons. as a student of Tariot (1847); won *premier prix* in solfège (1850); studied organ with Benoist and composition with Adam. In 1853 he became organist of St. Pierre de Chaillot and accompanist at the Théâtre-Lyrique; his 1st stage work, *Deux sous de charbon,* a 1-act operetta humorously designated an *asphyxie lyrique,* was produced at the Folies-Nouvelles (1856); later that year, his operette bouffe *Deux vieilles gardes* was acclaimed at its premiere at the Bouffes-Parisiens; several more operettas followed, as well as his 1st substantial work for the stage, *Le Jardinier et Son Seigneur,* at the Théâtre-Lyrique (1863).

Delibes became chorus master of the Paris Opéra (1864); with Minkus, collaborated on the ballet *La Source,* which was premiered at the Opéra (1866); with his next ballet, *Coppélia, ou La Fille aux yeux d'émail,* achieved lasting fame after its premiere at the Opéra (1870); the ballet *Sylvia, ou La Nymphe de Diane* (1876) was equally successful. He wrote a moderately successful grand opera, *Jean de Nivelle* (1880); it was followed by his triumphant masterpiece, *Lakmé* (1883), which effectively evoked a lyrical India; the coloratura *Bell Song* from *Lakmé* became a perennial recital favorite. He was appointed prof. of composition at the Paris Cons (1881); elected a member of the Inst. (1884); his last opera, *Kassya,* was incomplete at the time of his death; Massenet orchestrated it for its premiere at the

Opéra-Comique (1893). Delibes was a master of melodious elegance and harmonious charm; his music possessed an autonomous flow in colorful timbres, and an effortless excellence revealed a subtle mastery of Romantic compostional technique.

Delius, Frederick, (born Fritz Theodor Albert Delius) b. Bradford, Jan. 29, 1862; d. Grez-sur-Loing, France, June 10, 1934. His father, a successful owner of a wool company, hoped to have his son follow a similar career, but did not object to his son's art and music study. He learned to play the piano and violin; at age 22, went to Solano, Fla., to work on an orange plantation; the symphonic suite *Florida* was a souvenir of his sojourn there; there he met an American organist, Thomas F. Ward, who trained him thoroughly in music theory for 6 months. In 1885 Delius went to Danville, Va., to teach; enrolled at the Leipzig Cons. (1886), where he took courses in harmony and counterpoint with Reinecke, Sitt, and Jadassohn; met Grieg, becoming friend and admirer; in return Grieg's music found a deep resonance in his own compositions; even more influential was Wagner, whose principles of continuous melodic line and thematic development he adopted.

Euphonious serenity reigns on the symphonic surface of his music, diversified by occasional resolvable dissonances. In some works he made use of English folk motifs, often in elaborate variation forms; particularly successful are his evocative *On Hearing the 1st Cuckoo in Spring, North Country Sketches, Brigg Fair,* and *A Song of the High Hills;* his orch'l *Paris: The Song of a Great City* is a tribute to his longtime home; more ambitious in scope is the choral work *A Mass of Life,* in which he borrows passages from Nietzsche's *Also sprach Zarathustra.*

Delius settled in Paris (1888); moved to Grez-sur-Loing, near Paris (1897), where he remained for the rest of his life (except for a few short trips abroad); married painter Jelka Rosen (1903). His music won recognition in England and Germany, becoming a favorite of Beecham's, who gave numerous performances in London; these successes came too late for the composer; a syphilitic infection contracted early in life eventually grew into an incurable illness accompanied by paralysis and blindness; as Beecham phrased it, he "had suffered a heavy blow in the defection of his favorite goddess, Aphrodite Pandemos, who had returned his devotions with an affliction which was to break out many years later."

Still eager to compose, Delius engaged Eric Fenby as his amanuensis; Fenby wrote down the music dictated by Delius, including complete orch'l scores. Beecham organized the 1929 Delius Festival in London; the composer was brought from France to hear it; in that year he was made a Companion of Honour by King George V. However, he remains a solitary figure in modern music; affectionately appreciated in England, America, and to some extent Germany, his works are rarely performed elsewhere. His operas, virtually forgotten, have received attention recently: *Irmelin* (1890–92; premiered 1953); *The Magic Foundation* (1893–95; 1977); *Koanga* (1895–97; 1904); *A Village Romeo and Juliet* (1899–1901; 1907); *Margot la Rouge* (1902; in concert, 1982); and *Fennimore and Gerda,* opera (1908–10; 1919).

démancher (Fr.). Change finger position on a string instrument to prepare a shift from one register to another.

demiquaver (U.K.). Sixteenth note.

demisemiquaver (U.K.). Thirty-second note.

demi-soupir (Fr., half sigh). Eighth-note rest.

demi-voix (Fr., half voice). Sotto voce.

demolition. Public destruction of musical instruments came into vogue shortly after the end of World War II, perhaps as a sadomasochistic exercise of aggressive tendencies, frustrated by the unconditional surrender of the Axis. Contests in the swiftness of destroying upright pianos were held in clubs and colleges. According to the established rules of one game, a piano had to be reduced to comminuted fragments that could be passed through an aperture of specified dimensions (usually a circle 6 inches in diameter). In Stockholm, a young pianist concluded his recital by igniting a dynamite charge previously secreted inside the piano, blowing it up; a splinter wounded him in the leg. American avant-garde composer La Monte Young set a violin on fire at one of his exhibits. Rock guitarists Pete Townshend and Jimi Hendrix closed their performances with the demolition (Townshend) or setting afire (Hendrix) of their instruments. Bakunin, the scientific anarchist, said, "Die Lust der Zerstörung ist eine schaffende Lust"; this "creative impulse of destruction" has been fully vindicated by attacks on instruments in recent times.

Dempster, Stuart (Ross), b. Berkeley, Calif., July 7, 1936. He studied at San Francisco State College (B.A. in perf., 1958; M.A. in composition, 1967); studied trombone privately with A. B. Moore, Orlando Giosi, and John Klock; taught at the San Francisco Cons. of Music (1961–66) and Calif. State College at Hayward (1963–66); joined the faculty of the Univ. of Wash. in Seattle (1968). He received a Fulbright-Hays Award as a senior scholar in Australia (1973) and a Guggenheim fellowship (1981); interests include non-Western instruments, including the *didjeridu;* along with his own experimental works, he has often collaborated with Pauline Oliveros; publ. *The Modern Trombone: A Definition of Its Idioms* (Berkeley, 1979).

Demus, Jörg (Wolfgang), b. St. Polten, Dec. 2, 1928. At age 11 he entered the Vienna Academy of Music to study piano; took lessons in conducting with Swarowsky and Krips and composition with Joseph Marx; continued piano studies with Gieseking at the Saarbrucken Cons.; worked with Kempff, Benedetti Michelangeli, Edwin Fischer, and Yves Nat. He made his piano debut at age 14 in Vienna; made his London debut (1950); toured South America (1951). He won the Busoni prize of the International Competition for Pianists (1956); apart from solo recitals, distinguished himself as a lieder accompanist to Fischer-Dieskau and other prominent singers; assembled a fine collection of historic keyboard instruments; publ. a book of essays, *Abenteuer der Interpretation,* and, with Paul Badura-Skoda, an analysis of Beethoven's piano sonatas; awarded the Beethoven Ring (1977) and the Mozart Medal of Vienna (1979).

Denisov, Edison, b. Tomsk, Apr. 6, 1929. He was named after Thomas Alva Edison by his father, an electrical engineer; studied mathematics at the Univ. of Moscow (graduated 1951) and composition at the Moscow Cons. with Shebalin (1951–56); appointed to the faculty (1959). An astute explorer of tonal possibilities, he wrote instrumental works of an empirical genre; typical is *Crescendo e diminuendo* for Harpsichord and 12 String Instruments (1965), with a score written partly in graphic notation; titles reveal a lyric character of subtle nuances and impressionistic colors: *Aquarelle, Silhouettes, Peinture, La Vie en rouge, Signes en blanc, Nuages noires.*

Denver, John (born Henry John Deutschendorf, Jr.), b. Roswell, N. Mex., Dec. 31, 1942. He played guitar as a youngster; attended Tex. Technical Univ. in Lubbock; went to N.Y.; played in the Chad Mitchell Trio; wrote the popular song *Leaving on a Jet Plane* (1967); launched a solo career (1968), appearing in concerts throughout the U.S.; made numerous television appearances and successful recordings, including *Rocky Mountain High, Take Me Home Country Roads,* and *Annie's Song;* appeared in the movie *Oh, God!* and others.

derangements. In the pernicious practice of some commercially successful arrangers and antiquated organ soloists in decaying provincial churches, mutilations practiced upon the dead bodies of works by great composers by means of stuffing melodic intervals of their tunes with chromatic passing notes or filling open harmonies with supernumerary 3rds and 6ths.

derived set. A 12-tone set created by subjecting a smaller subset to the serial transformations of inversion, retrogression, and/or transposition.

Des (Ger.). D flat.

Des dur (Ger.). D-flat major.

descant. Discant. *Descant clef* (obs.), soprano clef; *descant recorder,* treble recorder; *descant viol,* treble viol.

descort (Old Fr., disorder). 13th-century chanson genre, cultivated by trouvères.

Desmond, Paul (born Paul Emile Breitenfeld), b. San Francisco, Nov. 25, 1924; d. N.Y., May 30, 1977. He picked his professional name randomly from a telephone book. He gained the rudiments of music from his father, an organist for silent movies; played clarinet in high school, then at San Francisco State Univ.; soon concentrated on jazz alto saxophone. He gained recognition and fame when he joined the Dave Brubeck Quartet (1951); continued with it until its disbanding (1967); wrote for the Brubeck Quartet, most notably *Take 5,* in 5/4 meter, adopted as their signature song and still popular.

Desprez (Des Prez), Josquin, also known simply as Josquin, b. probably in Hainaut, *c.* 1440; d. Condé-sur-Escaut, near Valenciennes, Aug. 27, 1521. His surname was variously spelled Després, Desprez, Deprés, Depret, Deprez, Desprets, Dupré, etc.; Josquin (contracted from the Flemish *Jossekin,* little Joseph) appears as Jossé, Jossien, Jusquin, Giosquin, Josquinus, Jacobo, Jodocus, Jodoculus, etc.; his epitaph reads *Jossé de Prés.* However, in the motet *Illibata Dei Virgo Nutrix,* whose text is probably Josquin's, his name appears as an acrostic: I, O, S, Q, V, I, N, D[es], P, R, E, Z; this seems to support a definitive spelling.

Josquin may have been a boy chorister of the Collegiate Church at St.-Quentin; became canon and choirmaster there; may have studied with Ockeghem, whom he greatly admired (writing *La Déploration sur la mort de Johannes Ockeghem* in 1497); sang at the Milan Cathedral (1459–72); by July 1474 was chorister at the court of Duke Galeazzo Maria Sforza, Milan; after the Duke's assassination (1476), served the Duke's brother, Cardinal Ascanio Sforza; singer in the papal choir under Innocent VIII and Alexander VI (1486–94); also active in Florence, where he met the theorist Pietro Aron; Modena; and Ferrara (where Isaac was also) as maestro di cappella (1503–04). Josquin eventually returned to Burgundy, settled in Condé-sur-Escaut (1504), and became provost of Notre Dame.

As a composer he was considered the greatest of his era; had a strong influence on those who came into contact with his music or with him personally as a teacher; Adriaan Petit Coclicus, who may have studied with him, publ. a treatise entitled *Compendium musices,* based on Josquin's teaching (1552); and described Josquin as "princeps musicorum." Josquin's works were sung and admired universally; he achieved a complete union between word and tone, fusing intricate Netherlandish contrapuntal devices into expressive and beautiful art forms. Two contrasting styles are present in his compositions; one, intricately imitative, displaying the technical ingenuity characteristic of the Netherlands style; others, homophonic and direct, probably influenced by Italian music; wrote numerous motets, Masses, and chansons.

Dessau, Paul, b. Hamburg, Dec. 19, 1894; d. East Berlin, June 27, 1979. He began to play violin as a child; gave a concert at 11 years of age; enrolled at the Klindworth-Scharwenka Cons. in Berlin (1910); studied violin with Florian Zajic and composition with Eduard Behm and Max Loewengard; worked as *répétiteur* at the Hamburg City Theater (1913); drafted into the German army (1914). After the Armistice in 1918 he became engaged as a composer and conductor in various chamber groups in Hamburg; served as coach and conductor at the Cologne Opera (1919–23) and in Mainz (1924); appointed conductor at the Städtische Oper in Berlin (1925–33); with the usurpation of power by the Nazis, he left Germany, living in various European cities and visiting Palestine.

In 1939 he emigrated to America; lived in N.Y.; went to Hollywood (1944), where he scored or orchestrated 14 films; returned to Berlin (1948) and, along with Eisler, aligned himself with the political, social, and artistic developments in the German Democratic Republic; closely associated with Brecht, he composed music for several plays: *Die Verurteilung des Lukullus,* opera (Berlin, 1951); *Furcht und Elend des Dritten Reiches* (1938); *Mutter Courage und ihre Kinder* (1946); *Der gute Mensch von Sezuan* (1947); *Herr Puntila und sein Knecht Matti* (1949); *Mann ist Mann* (1951); and *Der kaukasische Kreidekreis* (1954). His operas, choral works, songs, and instrumental music are imbued with the propulsive ideals of socialist realism; while believing in the imperative of music for the masses, he made use of modern techniques, including occasional applications of dodecaphony.

dessus (Lat., above). In medieval French polyphony, the treble voice. *Dessus de viole* (Fr.), treble viol.

desto (It.). Sprightly.

destra (It.). Right. *Colla destra,* play with the right hand; *destra mano,* play with the right hand (abbrev. *m.d.*).

détaché (Fr., detached). In string instruments, playing successive notes with downbow and upbow in alteration, but not staccato; a broad, even articulation is a component. *Grande détaché,* a full bow-stroke per note.

Dett, R(obert) Nathaniel, b. Drummondville (now Niagara Falls), Ontario, Oct. 11, 1882; d. Battle Creek, Mich., Oct. 2, 1943. Both his parents were amateur pianists and singers; in 1893 the family moved to Niagara Falls, N.Y. Dett studied piano locally; earned his living by playing at various clubs and hotels; enrolled at the Oberlin (Ohio) Cons.; studied piano with H. H. Carter and theory of composition with A. E. Heacox and G. C. Hastings (B.Mus., 1908); conducted a school choir; became a professional choral conductor.

Dett taught at Lane College in Jackson, Tenn. (1908–11), Lincoln Inst. in Jefferson, Mo. (1911–13), Hampton Inst. in Va. (1913–32), and Bennett College in Greensboro, N.C. (1937–42). He continued his music studies; took lessons with K. Gehrkens at Oberlin (1913); attended classes at Columbia Univ., American Cons. of Music in Chicago, Northwestern Univ., Univ. of Pa., and Harvard Univ. (1919–20), studying composition with Foote. He studied with Nadia Boulanger at the American Cons. in Fontainebleau (1929); attended the Eastman School of Music in Rochester, N.Y. (M.Mus 1932). He improved the quality of the Hampton Choir sufficiently to tour Europe with excellent success (1930) and performed on the radio. He became a musical adviser for the USO (1943); on active duty with the WAC when he died.

Dett's dominating interest was in cultivating Negro music, arranging Negro spirituals, and publishing collections of Negro folk songs. All of his works were inspired by black melos and rhythms; some of his piano pieces in Negro idiom became quite popular, among them the suite *Magnolia* (1912), *In the Bottoms* (1913) (which contained the rousing *Juba Dance*), and *Enchantment* (1922); wrote biblical and other oratorios and choruses; publ. the anthologies *Religious Folk Songs of the Negro* (1926) and *Dett Collection of Negro Spirituals* (4 vols., 1936).

Deus ex machina (Lat., God from a machine). Dramaturgical topos in myth, fiction, theater, and epic poetry, by which a god would come down from the heavens (or from below) to alter a situation, usually at the last moment and most likely to the benefit of the main character or characters. When mythical and other stories began to be staged, scenographic technology was developed to permit the descent of actors from above the audience's sight line in a "machine." In opera, an early example can be found in Monteverdi's *Orfeo* (1607); an ironic and multiple use of the device is featured in Glass's *The Voyage* (1992).

deutlich (Ger.). Distinctly articulating the words.

deutscher Tanz (Deutscher, Teutscher, etc.; Ger., German dance; Fr. *allemande;* It. *tedesca*). General term for late 18th- and early 19th-century couple dances in triple meter; by the 19th century the genre had branched off into the Ländler (danced with

arms interlaced) and the waltz (danced with swift turns and close embraces).

deux (Fr.). Two. *Deux temps,* a "2-step" waltz.

development. Working out or evolution (elaboration) of a theme by presenting it in varied melodic, harmonic, and/or rhythmic treatments.

Dezimett (Ger.). Chamber work for 10 players.

D-flat major. This key is descriptive of wide-open spaces, capable of a great variety of expressions. The scale of D-flat major is marvelously pianistic, covering all 5 black keys, with 2 white keys at strategic positions. What wealth of resonance is heard in Liszt's Étude in D-flat Major, in which left hand crosses over right hand to maintain euphonious fullness! On the other side of the spectrum is Debussy's *Clair de lune,* delicate and subtle in its evocation of a moonlit landscape. The celebrated principal theme of the opening to Tchaikovsky's 1st Piano Concerto, nominally described as in B-flat minor, is in unambiguously triadic D-flat major. In the remarkable 18th variation of Rachmaninoff's *Rhapsody on a Theme of Paganini,* he ingeniously inverts the principal A-minor theme to become D-flat major. Amateur composers who pollute the shelves of American music stores with their creations tend to favor D-flat major; but this key is difficult in orch'l writing, particularly in string instruments. Only one composer of consequence, Miaskovsky, has ever written a sym. (the 25th) in the key of D-flat major. (Mahler's 9th in D minor descends by chromatic half-step to D-flat minor for its extraordinary finale.)

di (It.). Of, from, to, by, than. *Di colpo,* suddenly; *di gala,* gaily, merrily; *di molto,* very, extremely; *allegro di molto,* extremely fast; *di nuovo,* anew over again; *di posto* (It., at the place), attack a note directly, without portamento; *di salto,* by leap or jump; *di slancio* (It., on impulse), di posto.

Di Capua, Eduardo, b. Naples, 1864; d. there, 1917. He earned his living by playing in small theaters and cafés in and around Naples, later in the cinemas; gave piano lessons. His most famous song was *O sole mio* (1898), its popularity immense and never abating; other celebrated songs were *Maria Mari* (1899), *Torna maggio* (1900), *Canzona bella,* etc. He sold these songs to publishers outright, so did not benefit by their popularity; died in extreme poverty.

Diabelli, Anton, b. Mattsee, near Salzburg, Sept. 5, 1781; d. Vienna, Apr. 8, 1858. He was a choirboy in the monastery at Michaelbeuren and at Salzburg Cathedral; studied for the priesthood in Munich while continuing his musical work; submitted his compositions to Michael Haydn, who encouraged him; after the secularization of the Bavarian monasteries, embraced the career of a musician; went to Vienna (where Joseph Haydn received him kindly); taught piano and guitar. In 1818 he became a partner of the music publisher Cappi; assumed control of the firm (now Diabelli & Co.; 1824); publ. much of Schubert's music but underpaid him and complained that he wrote too much; sold his firm to C. A. Spina (1852). A facile composer, Diabelli produced an opera, *Adam in der Klemme* (Vienna, 1809), Masses, cantatas, chamber music, etc., all consigned to oblivion; only his sonatinas are still used (for beginners). He was immortalized through Beethoven's remarkable set of 33 variations (op. 120, 1823) on a waltz theme that Diabelli had submitted to numerous European composers for a single variation, publ. in an anthology (1824); the Beethoven work was publ. separately.

diabolus in musica (Lat., devil in music). Term, laden with theological connotations found in medieval musical treatises, for the tritone (an interval covering 3 consecutive whole tones), forbidden harmonically or melodically because of its absence from the hexachord of ancient Greek musical theory. In Bach's time schoolboys were rewarded by painful raps on the knuckles with a ruler for an accidental use of the tritone in musical exercises. Oddly enough, the tempered tritone accomplishes the precise division in half of the octave, an impossibility in any ratio-related tuning.

An interval bearing such satanic overtones was later used by composers to characterize sinister forces: the lowered 5th in the violin tune of *Danse macabre* by Saint-Saëns; the leitmotiv of the dragon Fafner in act II of Wagner's *Siegfried;* the motives of the mysterious winning cards in Tchaikovsky's opera *The Queen of Spades;* the devil's motto in Hanson's opera *Merry Mount,* etc. Polish composer Lutoslawski used an overlapping series of tritones in an elegy on the death of Bartók, who had used the interval as a matter of course. Heavy metal rock has made the tritone as ubiquitous as the fifth is in classical music prior to the 20th century.

The diabolus in musica is the formative interval of the diminished-7th chord, a common device of Romantic operas to suggest mortal danger, known in Italian operatic circles as the *accorde di stupefazione* (stupefying chord). Ironically, the diabolus in musica became the cornerstone of polytonality and atonality as well as the basic element of the whole tone scale used for coloristic effects in impressionistic works.

Diaghilev, Sergei (Pavlovich), b. Gruzino, Novgorod district, Mar. 31, 1872; d. Venice, Aug. 19, 1929. While associated with progressive artistic organizations in St. Petersburg, his main field of production was in Western Europe; established the Ballets Russes in Paris (1909); commissioned Stravinsky to write *The Firebird, Petrouchka,* and *The Rite of Spring;* also commissioned Prokofiev, Milhaud, Poulenc, Auric, and other younger composers; Ravel and de Falla also wrote for him. The great importance of Diaghilev's choreographic ideas lies in the complete abandonment of the classical tradition; in this respect he was the true originator of the modern dance.

Diamond, David (Leo), b. Rochester, N.Y., July 9, 1915. His father was a cabinetmaker, his mother a dressmaker for the Yiddish theater; he worked at a N.Y. drugstore; studied composition with Bernard Rogers at the Eastman School of Music (1930–34); took courses privately with Roger Sessions in N.Y. He went to Paris (1937) to study with Nadia Boulanger; associated with the most important musicians and writers of the time. In France and elsewhere in Europe, he acquired fluency in French, Italian, and Russian; returning to N.Y., devoted his time exclusively to composition; grants and awards helped him obtain relative financial security; held the Juilliard Publication Award, 3 Guggenheim Fellowships, an American Academy in Rome

award, Paderewski Prize, and a grant from the National Academy of Arts and Letters; his music was conducted by Hanson, Monteux, Koussevitzky, and Mitropoulos, later by Munch, Ormandy, and Bernstein.

As a composer Diamond established an original, recognizable style of harmonic and contrapuntal writing, with a sense of tonality clearly present; the element of pitch, often inspired by natural folklike patterns, is very strong; in later works, adopted a modified dodecaphonic method while staying free of doctrinaire serialism. His instrumental and vocal writing is invariably idiomatic, making his music welcome to performers and audiences alike; some works acquired a flattering popularity, e.g., *Rounds* for string orch. won the N.Y. Music Critics' Circle Award (1944). His strongest power lies in symphonic and chamber music, also shows a marked ability for vocal writing, exemplified by his choral music; invited to the Soviet Union (1989), where his music was performed to considerable acclaim. He has also taught; appointed to the faculty of the Juilliard School in N.Y. (1973); in 1985 he received the William Schuman Award of Columbia Univ.

diapason (Grk.). 1. In ancient Greek music, the interval that runs "through all the tones," i.e., perfect octave. 2. In later centuries, a vocal range; used as such in French and Russian theory books. 3. (Fr.) Tuning fork; concert pitch. 4. Principal organ pipe, usually 8-feet long; the double diapason is twice the length. *Diapason tone,* organ tone.

diapente (Grk.). Medieval term for perfect 5th.

diatessaron (Grk.). Medieval term for perfect 4th.

diatonic (Grk., *dia* + *teinein,* stretch out). Referring to the 7 tones of a particular major or minor scale. *Diatonic harmony* or *melody,* those employing the tones of a single scale; *diatonic instrument,* one limited to pitches belonging to a single scale whose generating fundamental is the tonic of that scale; *diatonic interval,* one formed by 2 tones of the same scale; *diatonic modulation,* see ⇒modulation; *diatonic progression,* stepwise progression within 1 scale; *diatonic scale,* see ⇒scale.

Diddley, Bo (born Ellas Bates McDaniel), b. Magnolia, Miss., Dec. 30, 1928. He was taken to Chicago in early childhood; learned to play the violin and guitar; in 1955, 1st attracted attention with his recordings *Bo Diddley* and *I'm a Man;* appeared on Ed Sullivan's television show and at N.Y.'s Carnegie Hall. His pelvic gyrations and syncopated "Bo Diddley beat" influenced the 1st generation of rock 'n' roll musicians, including Buddy Holly and Elvis Presley; scored great success with *Say Man* (1959); performed in England (1963) and at the Montreux Jazz Festival (1972); later tours included Europe (1986) and Japan (1988).

Diderot, Denis, b. Langres, Oct. 5, 1713; d. Paris, July 30, 1784. He ed. the monumental *Encylopédie* with d'Alembert (1751–65); his *Mémoirs sur différents sujets de mathématiques* (The Hague, 1748), included the essays *Principes généraux d'acoustique, Examen d'un principe de mécanique sur la tension des cordes,* and *Projet d'un nouvel orgue,* the latter being an impracticable idea for a new kind of barrel organ.

Dies Irae (Lat., day of wrath). Sequence of the Requiem Mass; most famous Christian doomsday chant, painting an apocalyptic vision of world's dissolution into ashes, imploring the Lord not to cast a repentant sinner into outer darkness. Composition of both words and melody is attributed to the 13th-century musician Thomas of Celano. The melody is not easily classified modally and is more repetitive (i.e., more hymn-like) than most sequences of the 14th and 15th centuries. It became an obligatory part of the Requiem Mass; almost always sung as chant until the Council of Trent, which retained it in the liturgy (mid–16th century). In numerous polyphonic versions, the Dies Irae invokes millennial resignation and is often alluded to, e.g., the finale of Berlioz's *Sym. fantastique, Danse macabre* by Saint-Saëns, Liszt's *Totentanz,* and Rachmaninoff's *Rhapsody on a Theme of Paganini;* also the requiems of Mozart, Cherubini, Berlioz, Verdi, and others.

Dièse (*diesis;* Fr., Rus.). Sharp; the sign ♯.

diesis (It.). Semitone in the diatonic Pythagorean scale; later, the quarter-tone in the enharmonic Greek scale. *Greater diesis,* the difference between 4 pure minor 3rds (6/5) and an octave, or 62.6 cents; *lesser diesis,* the difference between an octave and 3 pure major 3rds (5/4), or 41.1 cents.

Dietrich, Albert (Hermann), b. Forsthaus Golk, near Meissen, Aug. 28, 1829; d. Berlin, Nov. 19, 1908. He studied with J. Otto in Dresden (1842–47), Moscheles and Rietz at Leipzig (1847–51); and Schumann at Düsseldorf (1851–54). From 1855 to 1861 he was a concert conductor; municipal music director at Bonn (1859) and at Oldenburg (from 1861); retired (1890); moved to Berlin; made Royal Prof. (1899); wrote *Erinnerungen an Johannes Brahms in Briefen, besonders aus seiner Jugendzeit* (Leipzig, 1898); principally remembered for composing the 1st movement of the collaborative *F–A–E* Violin Sonata (*frei aber einsam,* free but alone); the other movements are by Brahms and Schumann.

Dietz, Howard, b. N.Y., Sept. 9, 1896; d. there, July 30, 1983. He began writing lyrics for popular songs in 1918; wrote for Kern, Gershwin, Duke, and Arthur Schwartz. He joined the Goldwyn Pictures Corp. as publicity director (1919); when the firm merged into Metro-Goldwyn-Mayer (1924) he remained with it; became its vice president (1940); devised its pseudo-Latin logo, *Ars Gratia Artis* (correctly, *Ars Artis Gratia*). He invented the 2-handed bridge game named after him; painted and translated librettos. As a publicity man for Metro-Goldwyn-Mayer he popularized (and possibly invented) Greta Garbo's "I want to be alone."

diferencia (*differencia;* Sp., difference). In Spanish Renaissance music and thereafter, a variation set; one of the earliest types.

difference (differential) tone. Pitch produced by the difference of the frequencies of vibration between 2 notes when played loudly on a stringed instrument or on 2 of the same instruments; such a tone lies well beneath the original 2 sounds and produces a surprising, at times jarring effect; also called Tartini tones.

digital. 1. Key on the playing manual of the piano, organ, etc. 2. Recording in which tones are translated into binary information, as in a compact disc. 3. Technology involved in the production of computer-generated sound.

dilapidation of tonality. The disappearance of explicit key signatures from the notation of modern composition was the 1st symptom of the dilapidation of tonality and deterioration of traditional harmony. The key signature still functions in neoclassical works, where the tonic-dominant relationship and triadic modulation still prevail; but dormant chromaticism erupts all the more viciously against tonal restraints; key signatures exist only to be denied. Chromaticization of the modern idiom in the late 19th century resulted in an enormous proliferation of double sharps and double flats. As enharmonic modulation became commonplace, academic musicians, wishing to reserve the tonal fiction, but unable to find a common denominator between 7 (diatonic pitches) and 12 (chromatic pitches), erected a fantastic network of triple sharps and triple flats in works such as Ravel's piano trio, in which an entire piano passage, acoustically equivalent to C major, masquerades as B-sharp major and D-double-flat major; Debussy created exotic structures of double flats and double sharps in a triadic passage of his *Feuilles mortes.*

Even in the 19th century, tonality was often nominal and the key signature an armature without function; one Brahms intermezzo (op. 76, no. 4) is ostensibly in B-flat major, but the tonic triad is not reached until the final 2 bars—an example of teleological tonality, by which the tonic is the goal rather than the point of departure. Genuinely atonal melodies lack the homing instinct; the notes of an atonal melody are weightless; this lack of tonal gravity was organized by Schoenberg into a mutually gravitating dodecaphonic complex. While key signatures are superfluous in atonal and dodecaphonic music, they are not so in polytonality, where different signatures may be used simultaneously.

Until its dissolution, tonal supremacy demanded that each composition end in the same key, or in a key related to that in which it began. How strongly this prerequisite was felt by Romantic composers is illustrated by a whimsical annotation of R. Strauss in his song entitled *Wenn* (publ. 1897). In the orig. version the principal key is D-flat major, but the final 7 measures and concluding chord are in D major. Strauss supplied an alternative coda ending in the opening D-flat major, with a brilliant footnote: "Vocalists who may perform this song before the end of the 19th century are advised by the composer to transpose the last 7 measures a semitone lower so as to arrive at the end of the song in the same key in which it began."

dilettante (It.). Amateur.

diligenza, con (It., with diligence). Carefully.

diluendo (It.). Growing softer, dying away.

diminished interval. Perfect or minor interval contracted by a chromatic semitone. *Diminished chord,* one whose highest and lowest tones form a diminished interval; *diminished triad,* a root with minor 3rd and diminished 5th.

diminished-seventh chord (It., *accorde di stupefazione*, stupefying chord). Chord consisting of 3 conjunct minor 3rds, forming the interval of the diminished 7th between the top and bottom notes, e.g., C–Eb–Gb–B♭♭.

diminuendo (It.; abbrev. *dim.*). Decrescendo; diminishing in loudness. The sign is diminuendo. ⎯⎯⎯⎯⎯

diminuendo pedal. Pedal-mechanism for gradually pushing in organ stops.

diminution. Baroque polyphonic device whereby the theme is played twice as fast as its initial appearance, so that quarter notes become converted into 8th notes, 8th notes into 16th notes, etc.; the effect is that of a stretto, coupled with an increase in dynamic level and anticipating a decisive ending. In its formal and emotional respects, diminution performs the function opposite to augmentation; other time relationships (e.g., 3 times as much) do occur. *Diminished subject* or *theme*, one repeated or imitated in diminution.

direct. Sign m set at the end of a staff to show the position of the 1st note on the next staff; also called *custos*.

directional hearing. An ability common to all animals and man to judge the direction and relative intensity of a sound, evolved from the biological necessity of anticipating danger. This faculty plays an important role in stereophonic sound reproduction as well as recent space music in which the placement of individual performers or performing groups is prescribed by the composer.

direttore del coro (It.). Choral conductor.

direzione (It.). Conducting of an orch. or chorus.

dirge. Funeral song, usually for chorus a cappella; also, an instrumental composition of a funerary nature; an English contraction of the opening of Matins of the Office of the Dead, "Dirige Domine Deus Meus in conspectu tuo viam meam." In Shakespeare's *Romeo and Juliet*, Capulet reflects on seeing the body of the supposedly deceased Juliet: "Our solemn hymns to sullen dirges change." Stravinsky wrote a dirge *In Memoriam Dylan Thomas*.

Dirigent (Ger.). Conductor.

diritta, alla (It.). In direct motion. *Diritto*, direct, straight.

Dis (Ger.). D sharp.

Dis moll (Ger.). D-sharp minor.

disc (disk). 1. Phonograph record. 2. Compact digital playback record. 3. Video playback record. *Disc jockey* (abbrev. DJ), individual responsible for radio's broadcast continuity of music and advertising; as a "jockey," the DJ "rides" the music through commentary between recordings and commercials. Stations sometimes encourage the development of on-air "personalities" who bring additional listenership. In the 1950s, some disc jockeys, who determined the music to be broadcast, were often recipients of payola (bribes) by the record companies to get their product heard. While well-publicized convictions in the 1960s relegated payola to the backrooms and in less traceable forms, DJ personalities continued to promote their stations and themselves; programming is mostly determined by station managers or even market studies; in many formats, the DJ has become a nearly anonymous voice. As a response, college radio has become a major outlet for young disc jockeys and less mainstream music; on the other hand, the portable disc jockey evolved, at 1st playing recordings at parties and festive occasions; the DJ has become an attraction unto herself or himself, commanding large audiences (and fees) at dance clubs for successful "mixes" of often highly diverse music.

discant (descant; from Lat. *discantus*, singing apart; from Greek *diaphonia*, through sound). Term whose meanings have often changed. 1. Early polyphony with contrary motion in the parts (12th century); a contrapuntal voice against the cantus firmus, as opposed to organum, where parallel motion was the rule. Discant is generally limited to a counterpoint of the 1st species, note against note, while organum developed eventually as a free counterpoint of the 5th species. Notre Dame schoolmaster Perotin was known as an *optimus discantor*. In the late Middle Ages the term appeared in the gallicized form of *déchant* or *deschaunt*. 2. Used interchangeably with motet and even, unjustifiably so, with fauxbourdon. 3. Orig., the upper voice (vocal or instrumental); once again used in modern times to denote the highest part in a choral composition.

disco. 1. Discotheque. 2. Disco music.

disco music (disco). Type of lyrically uninhibited, relentlessly rhythmic dance music that evolved from rock and soul music in the 1970s; characterized by a heavy accent on strong beats and the consequent weakening of the backbeat (e.g., *Turn the Beat Around* by Vicki Sue Robinson). Disco music was extremely popular for a decade; receded into the background; had substantial influence on house, acid house, rap, etc.; resurfaced as the quintessence of "remixes," adding dance-beat layers to popular songs otherwise unrelated to disco style.

discord (It. *discordanza*). Generically speaking, dissonance. But all definitions are relative: "All discord, harmony not understood" (Alexander Pope); "Medicine, to produce health, has to examine disease; and music, to create harmony, must investigate discord" (Plutarch).

discotheque (Fr., collection of recordings). Clubs where people dance to the sounds of amplified recordings, 1st evolving in the late 1950s in conjunction with the rise of rock 'n' roll; these financially advantageous "canned-music" institutions superseded most live-music nightclubs and dance halls, acquiring their own chic, hipness, and proliferation of drugs; returned with the wave of new dance-music styles. See also ⇒disco.

diseuse (Fr.). Female reciter or narrator, found in, among other works, Debussy's *The Martyrdom of Saint Sebastian*, Hindemith's *Hérodiade*, and Honegger's *Jeanne d'Arc au bûcher*.

disinvolto (It.). Unrestrained. *Disinvoltura, con*, with ease, grace; flowingly.

disjunct motion. Melodic progression by skips and leaps.

disk. 1. Disc. 2. Computer-data-storage recording; floppy disk.

Diskantschlüssel (Ger.). Treble clef.

dislocation of melodic lines. Linear distortion of a musical line, in which a high note may be pulled upward and a low note pulled downward without disrupting the intervallic balance (contour) of the melody itself. Further, virtually any tonal melodic line can be topologically transformed into a dodecaphonic series in the same manner. (Stationary notes in the melody may be shifted upward or downward freely.) Examples of intervallic and modulatory translocation are found in neoclassical compositions; translocation is also an excellent resource of modern burlesque (i.e., parody).

disperato (It.). Desperately. *Disperazione, con,* in a desperate or despairing manner.

dispersed harmony. Positioning of a 4-voice chord so that the 3 upper voices are spread at an interval greater than an octave.

displaced tonality. In musical modernism, displacement of the tonic by an instantaneous modulation a semitone higher or a semitone lower; successfully applied by composers who are reluctant to abandon tonality altogether. Translocation by larger intervals is rarely effective; major tetrachords are more suitable for translocation than the more ambiguous minor tetrachords; transposition of the initial 3 notes of a major scale a semitone higher or lower forms a group of 6 different notes, while a similar application to a minor key results in a duplication of only 1 member of the series. Examples of melodic translocation are found in many works of Prokofiev and Shostakovich.

Dissonance. from Lat. *dis* + *sonare,* sound not together) Combination of 2 or more tones requiring resolution, i.e., is not harmonious; a more poetic term is discord (Lat. *dis* + *corda,* hearts not together). The antonym of dissonance is consonance (Lat., sounding together); a synonym is concord. In Greek terminology, dissonance is *diaphonia,* consonance, *symphonia.*

The concept of dissonance has varied greatly through the millennia of musical history. From the standpoint of acoustics the borderline separating dissonances from consonances is as indefinite as the demarcation between neighboring colors of the spectrum. Generally, the greater the numbers of the numerator and denominator of the ratio of vibrations between 2 different sounds, the more acute is the resulting dissonance; e.g., a minor 2nd is approximated by the ratio 16/15 and constitutes a sharper dissonance than a major 2nd, approximated by the ratio 9/8. (The septimal ratio 8/7 is theoretically even more consonant, but would not strike a equally tempered ear that way.)

In traditional harmony a dissonant chord imperatively demands a resolution into a consonance. Legend has it that Bach, a compulsive sleeper, was awakened in the morning by his wife Anna Magdalena playing a dominant-7th chord on the harpsichord in the music room; alarmed by the unresolved dissonance, he jumped out of bed still wearing his nightcap, rushed toward the harpsichord, and resolved the chord into its tonic triad. In his song *The Classicist* Mussorgsky ridicules the fear of dissonance

by delaying the resolution of a transient dissonance. Virtually no composer before 1900 dared to leave a dissonance unresolved; Liszt was perhaps the 1st to break this absolute prohibition by using a dissonant combination of notes from the Gypsy scale in a final cadence.

That the musical ear can get accustomed to dissonance and treat it as a consonance is proved by the common practice of tonic-7th (major-major) chords in cadences in jazz music. When the major 7th, placed in the treble in a tonic-7th chord, forms a consonance with the tonic bass, it approximates the vibration ratio 15/1 (15/8); but no jazz pianist would think of placing that major 7th in the bass register, where it would create an acute dissonance with the bass, generating a number of beats of interference. Another example of a technical dissonance commonly used in contemporary practice is the added 6th, lying a major 2nd above the fifth of the major triad in the treble; but placed, as it usually is, in the treble, it forms a 27th overtone in relation to the tonic bass, thus producing the sensation of a mild consonance.

The time finally came, early in the 20th century, when composers accepted the art of dissonance as a legitimate idiom, no longer requiring the crutch of consonance to lean upon. Inevitably, by the dialectics of the antithesis, dissonances became paramount; the hegemony of consonance had given way to the dictatorship of dissonance. It was now the turn of consonant combinations to resolve into dissonance. Schoenberg, working contrapuntally in the thematic development of his music, went so far as to exclude all triads from his vocabulary; allowance was made only for an occasional employment of minor 6ths and minor 3rds; perfect octaves were totally banned. Thus he reacted with horror when a conductor found an unexpected C sharp in both the 1st and 2nd trumpet parts in the score of Schoenberg's symphonic piece, *Begleitungsmusik zu einer Lichtspielszene;* "Das ist falsch!" he exclaimed. After examining the relevant tone row, it was found that the improperly doubled C sharp in the higher trumpet should have been C natural, making for a most proper dissonance. In his grandiose symphonic poem *Arcana,* Varèse introduced a chord consisting of a perfect octave and perfect 5th; he explained this peculiar consonant intrusion into his integrally dissonant work by a desire to create an effect of contrasting dissonance! But is there a new light dawning on the world of dissonances? Does the danger lie in a renaissance of undiluted triadic harmonies? Several modern composers are celebrating the return of once-dissonant consonances, without lethal consequences (as far as is known).

dissonant chord. One containing 1 or more dissonant intervals.

dissonant counterpoint. Term from the 1920s coined as an apologetic declaration by proponents of atonal music. Charles Seeger published a treatise of composition in this style, emphasizing the functional equality of dissonance and consonance in all types of contrapuntal techniques; in fugal writing, there is a strong tendency to use the tritone as the interval of entry, instead of the traditional perfect 5th of the tonic-dominant complex. Dissonant counterpoint does not exclude consonances but puts them on probation; however, the cadential perfect octave is generally shunned by the practitioners of dissonant counterpoint, and is usually replaced by a major 7th.

dissonant interval. Two tones forming a dissonance, i.e., 2nds, 7ths, and all diminished and augmented intervals.

distanza (It.). Interval; space, distance. *In distanza,* at a distance; indicates music to be performed as if far away.

distintamente (*distinto;* It.). Distinctly.

Distler, Hugo, b. Nuremberg, June 24, 1908; d. (suicide) Berlin, Nov. 1, 1942. He studied at the Leipzig Cons. with Grabner, Ramin, and Martienssen. He became a church organist at Lübeck (1931); joined the faculty of its Cons. (1933–37); taught at the School for Church Music in Spandau (1933–37) and Stuttgart Hochschule für Musik (1937–40).

Distler's early training and his connection with church music determined his style as a composer; his music is marked by a strong sense of polyphony. His greatest legacy is religious and secular choral music, putting Hindemith's extended tonality in the service of lively and profound interpretations of texts; among these are *Der Jahrkreis,* op. 5 (52 motets, 1932–33); *Choral-Passion,* op. 7 (1933); *Die Weihnachtsgeschichte,* op. 12 (1933); Geistliche Chormusik, op. 12 (1934–36, 1941); his secular masterpiece is the 3-part collection *Mörike-Chorliederbuch,* op. 19, (1938–39); wrote organ music and a Concerto for Harpsichord and String Orch., op. 14 (1935–36); secular cantatas; his oratorio *Die Weltalter* (1942) was left unfinished; publ. *Funktionelle Harmonielehre* (Kassel and Basel, 1941).

dital key. Key which, on pressure by the finger or thumb, raises the pitch of a guitar or lute string by a semitone. *Dital harp,* a guitar-shaped lute with 12 to 18 strings, each having a dital to raise its pitch a semitone; invented by Edward Light (1819).

dithyramb. Ode to Dionysios (Dionysus), performed by a chorus accompanied by wind instruments and dancers at the Dionysian festivals in ancient Greece; also, a song of this type.

ditonus (Lat., 2 tones). Medieval term for the major 3rd.

diva (It., divine woman). Term introduced by Italian impresarios to describe a female opera singer to whom the description *prima donna assoluta* (absolutely 1st lady) seems inadequate when describing divinity. The term, popular in the 19th century, disappeared early in the skeptical 20th century; became part of the vernacular; made a comeback in the last quarter of this century.

divertimento (It., diversion or entertainment; plural, *divertimentos, divertimenti;* Fr. *divertissement*). 1. Beginning in the 17th century, an Italianate collection of entertainment music; such a miscellany might contain instrumental or vocal pieces of various genres. 2. In the latter 18th century, an instrumental composition akin to suites or serenades (also *cassation, notturno,* and *partita*). In the 20th century the genre was revived; R. Strauss, Stravinsky, Bartók, and others wrote instrumental exemplars.

divertissement (Fr.). 1. Divertimento. 2. An entr'acte in an opera, in the form of a short ballet, etc.

divided stop. Ingenious mechanical arrangement in organs made in Spain in the 17th century allowing the use of different registrations (and therefore different timbres) in the treble and the bass. In England divided stops are often called half stops; in France they are termed *registres coupés.*

Divine Office. See ⇒Canonical Hours.

divisi, -e (It., divided; abbrev. *div.*). In works with multiple strings, indication that 2 parts written on 1 staff are not to be played as double stops, but by dividing of the section into 2 groups of instruments; by implication, the overall splitting of a string section into subsections.

division. 1. "Dividing up" (ornamenting) a melodic series of tones into a rapid coloratura passage; if vocal, the passage is to be sung in one breath (now obsolete). *To run a division* (divide), to execute such a passage. 2. In the English Baroque, a free improvisation in rapid figurations against a given ground bass. Manuals for training string, wind, and other performers in this technique were commonplace in the 17th century.

division mark. Slur or bracket written for duplets, triplets, quadruplets, etc., encompassing a figure 2, 3, 4, etc.

Dixieland. Jazz style, essentially synonymous with New Orleans style, representing part of the poorly documented beginnings of jazz in the 1st 2 decades of the 20th century. The term initially referred to white musicians, as is shown by the recordings made by the all-white Original Dixieland Jazz Band (1917); a distinction was made between the relatively stiff Dixieland style and the more swinging and improvisatory New Orleans (Preservation Hall) style of black musicians; when Dixieland was revived in the 1940s and 1950s, the stylistic gap between it and New Orleans style had closed sufficiently to make the distinction superfluous. Its instruments are typically cornet (and/or trumpet, trombone), clarinet, piano, banjo (or guitar), tuba (or double bass), and drums; the music developed from the repertoire of the New Orleans marching bands of the turn of the century. At its best, Dixieland is characterized by intuitive collective improvisation, dotted rhythms, and syncopation over a ragtime-like accompaniment.

dixtour (Fr.). Chamber work for 10 performers.

DJ. Disc jockey.

Dlugoszewski, Lucia, b. Detroit, June 16, 1931. She studied piano; concurrently attended classes in physics at Wayne State Univ. (1946–49); fascinated with the mathematical aspects of music, studied with Varèse, whose works illuminated this scientific relationship for her. Accordingly, in her own works she emphasizes the sonorific element of music; inspired by Varèse's *Ionisation,* she invented or perfected a number of percussion instruments; 1 of her inventions is the timbre piano, in which she makes use of bows and plectra on the piano strings; also composed many dance scores.

Do (It.). 1. The note C. 2. In solmisation, the usual syllable name for the 1st degree of the scale. In the fixed Do method of teaching, Do is the name for all notes bearing the letter name C, whether keynotes or not; in the movable Do method, Do is always the keynote, regardless of letter name.

docian. Organ stop, sometimes called dulzian, producing a soft, flutelike sound.

Dodds, Warren "Baby," b. New Orleans, Dec. 24, 1898; d. Chicago, Feb. 14, 1959. He was the youngest of 6 children, hence his nickname. He studied drums with D. Perkins, W. Brundy, and L. Cottrell, Sr.; after performing with local jazz musicians, joined Fate Marable's riverboat band (1918); settled in Chicago (1921); played and recorded with King Oliver, then with Armstrong and Jelly Roll Morton, and later with his brother Johnny Dodds in several combos. He appeared with Jimmie Noone (1941), Bunk Johnson (1944–45), and Art Hodes (1946–47). In 1949–50 he suffered several strokes; thereafter made infrequent appearances until his retirement (1957). He was the foremost drummer in the New Orleans style of his era.

Dodds, Johnny (John M.), b. New Orleans, Apr. 12, 1892; d. Chicago, Aug. 8, 1940. He began playing the clarinet when he was 17; mainly autodidact, although he had lessons with Lorenzo Tio, Jr.; played in Kid Ory's band in New Orleans (1912–17; 1919) and Fate Marable's riverboat band (1917–19); settled in Chicago; member of King Oliver's band; recorded in the mid-1920s with Armstrong's Hot 5 and Hot 7 combos. He led his own band in the 1930s, then joined his brother Baby Dodds's quartet (1940); leading exponent of the New Orleans style.

Dodecachordon (Grk., 12 modes). Famous theoretical treatise by Glareanus, 1547. Its main historical achievement was the extension of the system of authentic and plagal modes (Dorian, Phyrgian, Lydian, Mixolydian) from 8 to 12, by adding the Ionian and Aeolian modes with their plagal derivations; also contains analytic descriptions of music by contemporaneous polyphonic masters.

dodecaphonic music. Dodecaphonic (Grk. *dodeca* + *phone*, 12-sound) music is the extreme product of a luxuriant development of chromatic melody and harmony. Conscious avoidance of all tonal centers led to the abolition of key signatures and a rapid decline in triadic harmony. Originally, the compositional style in which all tonal points of reference were eliminated became known as atonality. It was from this paludous atmosphere of inchoate atonality that the positive and technical idiom of dodecaphonic composition gradually evolved, eventually formulated by Schoenberg as the "method of composing with 12 tones related only to one another," 1st found explicitly in his Serenade, op. 24 (1924). In a communication to the author (1939), Ernst Krenek describes the relationship between the atonal and docecaphonic method as follows: "Atonality is a state of the musical material brought about through a general historical development. The 12-tone technique is a method of writing music within the realm of atonality. The sense of key has been destroyed by atonality. The method of composing with 12 tones was worked out in order to replace the old organization of the material by certain new devices."

Five fundamental ideas underlie Schoenberg's method: 1) dodecaphonic monothematism, wherein an entire work is derived from a 12-tone row (Ger. *Tonreihe*) comprising the 12 different notes of the chromatic scale; 2) use of a tone-row in 4 conjugate forms: the prime (original), retrograde, inversion, and retrograde inversion; 3) although a tone-row's ordering is rigidly observed, individual members of a series can be transposed to any octave, resulting in a wide distribution of thematic ingredients over the entire range of a single part (or over sections of different parts); 4) any of the 4 forms of a 12-tone series can be transposed to begin on any note of the chromatic scale, the result being a total of 48 available forms is 48; and 5) melody, harmony, and counterpoint remain, even as a tone-row appears in all its avatars: horizontally as melody, vertically as harmony, and diagonally as canonic counterpoint. It may also be distributed partly in melodic progressions, partly in harmonic or contrapuntal structures. Because of the providential divisibility of the number 12, the tone-row can be arranged in 6 groups in 2-part counterpoint (or harmony), 4 groups in 3-part harmony, 3 groups in 4-part harmony, or 2 groups in 6-part harmony.

Schoenberg was not alone in his dodecaphonic illumination; he was intensely aware of his need to assert priority in the invention of the method. Among contenders for the honor was Fritz Klein, the author of an ingenious orch'l work, *Die Maschine*, subtitled "eine extonale Selbstsatire," publ. under the characteristic pseudonym "Heautontimorumenos" (self-tormentor; 1921). Klein's score contains an array of inventions: a *Mutterakkord* (with 12 different notes and 11 different intervals), a "Pyramidakkord" (patterns of rhythmically repeated 12 notes), and other procedures presaging the future developments of integral serialism. When asked by the author regarding Klein's historical role, Schoenberg replied (in English): "Although I saw Klein's 12-tone compositions about 1919, 1920, or 1921, I am not an imitator of him. I wrote the melody for a scherzo composed of 12 tones in 1915. In the 1st edition of my *Harmonielehre* (1911) there is a description of the new harmonies and their application which has probably influenced all these men who now want to become my models."

The most formidable challenge to Schoenberg was made by Joseph Matthias Hauer, who experimented with 12-tone composition independently of Schoenberg; but Hauer's method differed in essential aspects; he built 12-tone subjects from 6-tone "tropes" (groupings), allowing free permutation of each trope; this concept was entirely alien to Schoenberg's doctrine of thematic ordering of the tone-row. Still, Schoenberg regarded Hauer's theories as sufficiently close to his own method to take notice of them. Schoenberg described the dodecaphonic situation in Vienna in a retrospective program note (publ. 1950): "In 1921 I showed my former pupil Erwin Stein the means I had invented to provide profoundly for a musical organization granting logic, coherence, and unity. I then asked him to keep this a secret and to consider it as my private method. . . .[but] if I were to escape the danger of being his imitator, I had to unveil my secret. I called a meeting of friends and pupils, to which I also invited Hauer, and gave a lecture on my new method, illustrating it by examples of some finished compositions of mine. Everybody recognized that the method was quite different from that of others." Hauer refused to surrender his claims as the spiritual protagonist of 12-tone music; a man of an irrepressible polemical temper, he even had a rubber stamp made, for his private correspondence, which read: "Josef Matthias Hauer, der geistiger Urhaber und trotz vielen schlechten Nachahmern immer noch der einziger Kenner und Könner der Zwölftonmusik."

Although Schoenberg's title to the formulation and application of the dodecaphonic method was finally recognized, he came into an unexpected collision in 1948 with a fictional claimant, Adrian Leverkühn, the hero of Thomas Mann's novel *Doktor Faustus,* described as the inventor of docecaphonicism. In an indignant letter to the *Saturday Review of Literature,* Schoenberg protested against this misappropriation of his invention; any idea that Leverkühn might be considered a fictional alter ego of Schoenberg himself infuriated him: "Leverkühn is depicted from beginning to end as a lunatic. I am 74 and I am not yet insane, and I have never acquired the disease from which this insanity stems. I consider this an insult."

The method of composing with 12 tones related only to one another did not remain a rigid dogma; besides Schoenberg, its greatest protagonists were his disciples Berg and Webern; somewhat frivolously, they have been described as the Vienna Trinity, with Schoenberg the Father, Berg the Son, and Webern the Holy Ghost; less so, the 2nd Viennese School. Both Berg and Webern introduced innovations into Schoenbergian practice: Berg used the conjunct series of alternating minor and major triads capped by 3 whole tones as the principal subject of his Violin Concerto (1935); in *Lulu,* he inserted a dodecaphonic episode built on 2 mutually exclusive whole-tone scales. Webern dissected the 12-tone series into autonomous sections of 6, 4, or 3 units in a group and related them individually to one another by inversion, retrograde, and inverted retrograde; this fragmentation enabled him to use canonic imitation much more freely than would have been possible under the strict Schoenbergian doctrine.

The proliferation of dodecaphony in Italy was potent—and unexpected, considering the differences between Germanic and Latin cultures: one introspective and speculative, the other humanistic and practical. Dallapiccola was one of the earliest adepts, but he liberalized Schoenberg's method and admitted tonal elements; in *Il Prigioniero* (1944), he uses 4 mutually exclusive triads. The greatest conquest of Schoenberg's method was the totally unexpected conversion of Stravinsky, whose entire aesthetic code had stood in opposition to any predetermined compositional method; yet he adopted serialism in his 70s. Other composers turned to dodecaphonic devices as a thematic expedient without utilizing the full potential of the tone-row: Bartók, in his 2nd Violin Concerto; Ernest Bloch, in his *Sinfonia Breve* and last string quartets; English composers such as Tippett, Lennox Berkeley, Benjamin Frankel, Searle, Richard Rodney Bennett, Walton (the fugal finale of his 2nd Sym.), Britten, whose *The Turn of the Screw* has a thematic motto of alternating perfect 5ths and minor 3rds (or their respective inversions), aggregating to a 12-tone series. The Spanish composer Gerhard, who settled in England, wrote in a fairly strict dodecaphonic idiom; in France the leading dodecaphonist was René Leibowitz, author of books on 12-tone theory; Wladimir Vogel, Russian-born, of German parentage, and living in Switzerland, adopted Schoenberg's method in nearly all of his works; Swiss neoclassicist Frank Martin extended dodecaphonic principles to allow for a number of tonal and modal ramifications. In the USSR, dodecaphony remained officially unacceptable as a "formalistic" device; in a 1963 speech delivered in Moscow, Nikita Khrushchev observed: "They call it dodecaphony, but we call it cacophony"; nevertheless, some blithe spirits of the former Soviet Union, among them Andrei Volkonsky, Valentin Silvestrov, and Sergei Slonimsky, have written and publ. works in the 12-tone idiom.

In America Schoenberg's method found a fertile ground, both among his students and among composers who had previously pursued different roads. Babbitt and others extended the method into total serialism; Sessions, Thomson, and Diamond followed Schoenberg with varying degrees of fidelity; Copland used the dodecaphonic technique in some chamber music and the orch'l composition *Connotations* (commissioned for the opening of Lincoln Center, N.Y., 1962), where he applied the totality of dodecaphony to characterize the modern era of music. Piston interpolated a transitional 12-tone passage in his ballet suite *The Incredible Flutist;* resisted integral dodecaphony until his seventies, when he adopted Schoenberg's method in all its orthodoxy (8th Sym.). Bernstein inserted a 12-tone series into *Age of Anxiety* to express inner agitation and anguished expectancy; Barber made an excursion into the dodecaphonicism in a movement of his Piano Sonata; and Menotti turned dodecaphony into antimodernist parody in *The Last Savage,* representing the decadence of modern civilization into which the hero is unexpectedly catapulted from his "primitive" habitat.

dodecuplet. Group of 12 equal notes, performed in the time of 8 notes of the same kind in the established meter.

Dodge, Charles (Malcolm), b. Ames, Iowa, June 5, 1942. He studied with R. Hervig and P. Bezanson at the Univ. of Iowa (B.A., 1964), Milhaud at the Aspen Music School (1961), and Schuller at Tanglewood (1964); attended seminars given by Foss and Arthur Berger; then studied composition with Chou Wen-chung and Luening and electronic music with Ussachevsky at Columbia Univ. (M.A., 1966; D.M.A., 1970). He taught at Columbia Univ. (1967–69; 1970–77), Princeton Univ. (1969–70), and Brooklyn College of the City Univ. of N.Y.; president of the American Composers Alliance (1971–75) and the American Music Center (1979–82); held Guggenheim fellowships (1972, 1975). His numerous and carefully wrought electronic works include a "setting" of Beckett's *Cascando.* With T. Jerse, wrote *Computer Music: Synthesis, Composition, and Performance* (N.Y., 1985, 2nd ed., 1997).

Dohnányi, Christoph von, b. Berlin, Sept. 8, 1929. Grandson of Ernst (Erno") von Dohnányi. He began to study the piano as a child, but his training was interrupted by World War II, during which his father Hans, a jurist, and his uncle, Dietrich Bonhoeffer, Protestant theologian and author, were executed by the Nazis for their involvement in the 1944 attempt on Hitler's life. After the war Christoph studied jurisprudence at the Univ. of Munich; enrolled at the Hochschule für Musik in Munich (1948); won the Richard Strauss Prize for composition and conducting; made his way to the U.S.; continued his studies with his grandfather at Florida State Univ. at Tallahassee; attended sessions at Tanglewood.

Returning to Germany, Dohnányi received a job as a coach and conductor at the Frankfurt Opera (1952–57); served as Generalmusikdirektor in Lübeck (1957–63) and Kassel (1963–66); chief conductor of the Cologne Radio Sym. Orch. (1964–70); director of the Frankfurt Opera (1968–77); Staatsopernintendant of the Hamburg State Opera (1977–84). In 1984 he became music director of the Cleveland Orch. (having been appointed music director-designate in 1982), succeeding Maazel. In the meantime, he guest-conducted the Vienna State

Opera, Covent Garden in London, La Scala in Milan, the Metropolitan Opera in N.Y., the Berlin Phil., the Vienna Phil., and the Concertgebouw Orch. in Amsterdam.

Both as sym. and opera conductor, Dohnányi proved himself a master technician and versatile musician, capable of congenial interpretation of music ranging from Baroque to the avant-garde; excells in performances of the 2nd Viennese School. He is married to the soprano Anja Silja.

Dohnányi, Ernst (Ernő) von, b. Pressburg, July 27, 1877; d. N.Y., Feb. 9, 1960. Grandfather of Christoph von Dohnányi. He began musical studies with his father, an amateur cellist; studied piano and music theory with Károly Forstner; entered the Royal Academy of Music in Budapest (1894), where he studied piano with Istvan Thomán and composition with Hans Koessler; received the Hungarian Millennium Prize (1896), commemorating Hungary's 1st thousand years, for his Sym.; graduated from the Royal Academy (1897). He went to Berlin for additional piano studies with d'Albert; made his debut in a recital there (1897); Beethoven's 4th Piano Concerto in London (1898); gave a series of successful concerts in the U.S. Returning to Europe, he served as prof. of piano at the Hochschule für Musik in Berlin (1908–15); returned to Budapest; taught piano at the Royal Academy; served briefly as its director (1919); appointed chief conductor of the Budapest Phil. Orch. He became head of the piano composition classes at the Royal Academy (1928), later its director (1934); became music director of Hungarian Radio (1931).

As Hungary became embroiled in war and partisan (and cultural) politics, Dohnányi resigned his Royal Academy directorship (1941) and post as chief conductor of the Budapest Phil. (1944). At war's end rumors were rife that he had used his influence with the Nazi overlords in Budapest to undermine Bartók and other liberals, and that he acquiesced in anti-Semitic measures; but the Allied occupation authorities exonerated him of all blame (1945). He made a tour of England as a pianist (1947–48); accepted the position of piano teacher at Tucuman, Argentina; reached the U.S. (1949); became composer-in-residence at Florida State Univ. in Tallahassee.

Dohnányi was a true virtuoso of the keyboard and greatly esteemed as a teacher; among his pupils were Solti, Anda, and Vázsonyi. His music represented the terminal flowering of European Romanticism, marked by passionate eloquence of expression while keeping within the framework of Classic forms; even Brahms praised his early efforts. In retrospect, he seems a noble epigone of a bygone era; but pianists, particularly Hungarians, still program his brilliant compositions. His most popular orch'l works are the *Variations on a Nursery Song* (with piano) and the Suite in F-sharp Minor. He presented his philosophy of life in a poignant pamphlet entitled *Message to Posterity* (Jacksonville, Fla., 1960).

doigté (Fr.). Fingering.

dolce (It.). 1. Sweet, soft, suave, tender, caressingly, sentimental. 2. Sweet-toned organ stop. *Dolcemente,* sweetly, softly; *dolciato* softer, calmer; *dolcissimo,* very sweetly, softly; also, a very soft-toned 8' flute stop in the organ.

Dolcian (Dulcian, Dulzian, Ger.; It., *dolcino, dolziana, dulcina*). 1. Curtal. 2. Penetrating, open-flue pipe organ stop, usually 8' (can be 16' or 4').

dolentemente (It.). Dolefully, plaintively.

doloroso (It.). Painfully, full of grief; pathetically, sorrowfully.

Dolphy, Eric (Allan), b. Los Angeles, June 20, 1928; d. Berlin, June 29, 1964. He took up the clarinet in early childhood; studied music at Los Angeles City College. After working with local groups, including Chico Hamilton's quintet (1958–59), he went to N.Y.; performed with Mingus's quartet (1959–60); co-led a quintet with Booker Little (1961); worked with Coltrane, John Lewis, and again with Mingus. He was a master at improvisation, excelling in both jazz and 3rd Stream genres. His repertoire included several avant-garde works, including Varèse's *Density 21.5* for solo flute; 1st important jazz bass clarinetist.

dombra. Lutelike Central Asian instrument played with fingers; differs from the Russian domra by virtue of a long neck and an angular body. After 1917 the dombra was successfully introduced into Russian popular string orchs.

dominant. 5th tone or step in the major or minor scale; also, the key associated with it.

dominant chord. 1. Dominant triad. 2. Dominant chord of the 7th. *Dominant section,* within a given piece or movement, a passage written in the dominant, lying between and contrasting with 2 sections in the tonic; *dominant triad,* a chord with the dominant as the root.

Domingo, Placido, b. Madrid, Jan. 21, 1941. His parents were zarzuela singers who settled in Mexico and performed with their own company. Placido joined his parents in Mexico at age 7, and began appearing in various productions; also studied piano with Manuel Barajas in Mexico City and voice with Carlo Morelli at the National Cons. there (1955–57). He made his operatic debut as Borsa in *Rigoletto* with the National Opera in Mexico City (1959); 1st major role was Alfredo in *La Traviata* in Monterrey (1961); that same year made his U.S. debut as Arturo in *Lucia di Lammermoor* with the Dallas Civic Opera; member of the Hebrew National Opera in Tel Aviv (1962–64). He made his 1st appearance with the N.Y. Opera as Pinkerton (1965); made his Metropolitan Opera debut as Turiddu in a concert performance of *Cavalleria rusticana* at Lewisohn Stadium (1966); his formal stage debut at the Metropolitan followed, singing the role of Maurice de Saxe in *Adriana Lecouvreur* (1968); established himself as one of its leading members; also sang regularly at the Vienna State Opera (from 1967), Milan's La Scala (from 1969), and London's Covent Garden (from 1971).

Domingo performed at major operatic centers throughout the world; sang for recordings, films, and television; pursued conducting; made his formal conducting debut with *La Traviata* at the N.Y. Opera (1973); conducted *La Bohème* at the Metropolitan Opera (1984); commissioned Menotti's *Goya* and created the title role in Washington, D.C. (1986). He had the honor of singing Otello at the 100th anniversary performances at La Scala (1987); on New Year's Eve 1988 he appeared as a soloist with Z. Mehta and the N.Y. Phil in a gala concert televised live to millions. One of the best-known lyric tenors of his era, Domingo has gained international renown for his portrayals of Cavaradossi, Des Grieux, Radames, Don Carlo, Otello, Don Jose, Hoffmann, Canio, and Samson; has recently added baritone roles to his repertoire; his crossover recording *Be My Love* was immensely successful.

Domino, "Fats" (Antoine, Jr.), b. New Orleans, Feb. 26, 1928. Although he sustained a severe hand injury as a youth, he pursued his career as a pianist; gained fame during the early rock 'n' roll era by mixing blues elements with straight rock; successful in nightclubs and movies as a purveyor of popular, jazz, and blues genres.

domra. Russian lute, usually played with a plectrum; very popular as an instrument for entertainment provided by itinerant musicians (Rus. *skomorokhi*). The domra was superseded by the balalaika in the 18th century; but 20th-century musicians revived the instrument in an effort to encourage Russian historical instrumentation. Several domra-and-balalaika orchs. were formed after 1917.

Don Quixote. Cervantes's pathetic but heroic "knight of the sorrowful countenance," who appears as the principal character of many works: operas named *Don Chisciotte* (Caldara, Philidor, Piccinni, Salieri, Donizetti, etc.); the once popular ballet *Don Quixote* by Minkus; Ravel's late vocal work, *Don Quichotte à Dulcinée*; and, in the orch'l literature, the sym. poem by R. Strauss, a beautifully drawn and popular portrait.

Donizetti, Gaetano, b. Bergamo, Nov. 29, 1797; d. there, Apr. 1, 1848. At age 9 he entered the Lezioni Caritatevoli di Musica, a charity training school for the choristers of S. Maria Maggiore; studied singing and harpsichord there; later studied harmony and counterpoint with J. S. Mayr; with Mayr's encouragement and assistance, enrolled in the Liceo Filarmonico Comunale in Bologna (1815); studied counterpoint with Pilotti, and counterpoint and fugue with Padre Mattei.

Donizetti's 1st opera, *Il Pigmalione* (1816), was apparently never performed in his lifetime; the same fate befell 2 more operas written in quick succession. Leaving the Liceo (1817), he was determined to have an opera produced; his next work, *Enrico di Borgogna*, was performed in Venice (1818), but evoked little interest; achieved popular success with the opera buffa *Il Falegname di Livonia, o Pietro il grande, czar delle Russie* (1819). In late 1820 he was spared military service when a woman of means paid the necessary sum to secure his uninterrupted work at composition; the opera seria *Zoraide de Granata* (1822) proved a major success; during the next 9 years, he composed 25 operas, none of which remain in the active repertoire; the great success of *L'Ajo nell'imbarazzo* (1824) brought him renown at the time. He served as musical director of the Teatro Carolino in Palermo (1825–26) and the royal theaters in Naples (1829–38). With *Anna Bolena* (1830), he established himself as a master of Italian opera; composed for Pasta and Rubini, the work was an overwhelming success; within a few years it was produced in several major Italian theaters, and was also heard in London, Paris, Dresden, and other cities. His next enduring work was the charming comic opera *L'elisir d'amore* (1832).

The tragic *Lucrezia Borgia* (1833), not entirely successful at its premiere, found acceptance and made the rounds of the major opera houses. Donizetti was appointed prof. of counterpoint and composition at the Cons. di San Pietro a Majella in Naples (1834). His *Maria Stuarda* (1834) was premiered as *Buondelmonte* in Naples after the Queen objected to details in the libretto; went to Paris, where his *Marino Faliero* had a successful premiere at the Théâtre-Italien (1835). Returning to Italy, he produced his tragic masterpiece *Lucia di Lammermoor* (1835). Upon the death of Zingarelli (1837), he was appointed director pro tempore of the Conservatorio in Naples; but resigned all his Cons. positions when his temporary assignment was not made permanent (1838). *Roberto Devereux* garnered acclaim at its 1st performance in Naples (1837); but when the censor's veto prevented the production of *Poliuto* due to its sacred subject (based on Corneille's *Polyeucte*), he returned to Paris. He produced the highly successful *La Fille du régiment* there (1840), followed by *Les Martyrs* (1840), a successful revision of the censored *Poliuto; La Favorite* (1840) made little impression at its 1st performance, but soon became one of his most popular operas. *Linda di Chamounix* received an enthusiastic reception at its premiere in Vienna (1842); the Emperor appointed him Maestro di Cappella e di Camera e Compositore di Corte.

In 1843 Donizetti returned to Paris; brought out his great comic masterpiece *Don Pasquale;* with singers like Grisi, Mario, Tamburini, and Lablache in the cast, its triumphant premiere was all but assured (1843). He then returned to Vienna, where he conducted the successful premiere of *Maria di Rohan* (1843); back again in Paris, produced *Dom Sebastien* (1843); the audience approved of the work enthusiastically, but critics were not pleased; considering it his masterpiece, he had to wait until the Vienna premiere (in German, 1845) before it was universally acclaimed. The last opera produced in his lifetime was *Caterina Cornaro* (1844); spent his last years suffering from tertiary syphilis.

Donizetti was a prolific composer whose fecundity of production was not always equaled by his inspiration or craftsmanship; many of his operas are hampered by the poor librettos he had to use on many occasions; nevertheless, his genius is reflected in many of his operas. Indeed, his finest works serve as the major link in the development of Italian opera between Rossini and Verdi; since the postwar bel canto revival, many of his operas have continued to hold a place in the repertoire.

Donnermaschine (Ger.). Thunder machine.

Doors, The. (Vocal: Jim Morrison, b. Melbourne, Fla., Dec. 8, 1943; d. Paris, France, July 3, 1971; keyboards/vocal: Ray Manzarek, b. Chicago, Ill., Feb. 12, 1935; guitar: Robbie Krieger, b. Los Angeles, Calif., Jan. 8, 1946; drums: John Densmore, b. Los Angeles, Dec. 1, 1945.) Psychedelic rock group of the 1960s, led by oracular poet Morrison. Early on, the band played regularly at Los Angeles's Whiskey-a-Go-Go club; signed to Elektra Records (1966), scored immediately with Morrison's ode to priapetic power, *Light My Fire*, banned by some radio stations because of sexually inferential lyrics; continued to score with their slightly macabre but hard-rocking compositions to Morrison's sophomoric verse, including *The End,*

When the Music's Over, People Are Strange, Love Me 2 Times, and *Hello, I Love You.* The Morrison cult reached an apex when he was arrested for alleged indecent exposure during a Miami performance (1969); the ensuing brouhaha elevated him to a counterculture god; the group continued to issue recordings, scoring lesser hits through early 1971, when an unhappy Morrison left the group; subsequently died of mysterious causes. The rest of the band soldiered on as a trio through 1973. Despite its demise, the group has remained popular to this day, and tales of Morrison's debauchery continue to be cherished by rock fans the world over; over-the-top director Oliver Stone made a film about the group (1991); The Doors were ensconced in the Rock and Roll Hall of Fame 2 years later.

dopo (It.). After.

doppel (*doppelt,* Ger.; It. *doppio*). Double, twice. *Doppelchor,* double chorus; *Doppelfuge,* double fugue; *Doppelgriff* (Ger., double grip), double stop (bowed string instruments); *Doppelgriffe,* 3rds, 6ths, etc., played with 1 hand (piano); *Doppelkanon,* double canon; *Doppelkreuz,* double sharp; *Doppelschlag* (Ger.; It., gruppetto), ornamental figure requiring the use of the scale-steps above and below the principal note, e.g., C–D–C–B–C; *doppelt so langsam,* twice as slow; *Doppelzunge,* double- or flutter-tonguing on a wind instrument, performed by thrusting the tongue rapidly to produce a fluttering sound.

doppio (It.). Double; twice. *Doppio movimento* (It., double movement), twice as fast; *doppio note* (*doppio valore;* It.), twice as slow (with the absolute time value of the notes doubled); *doppio pedale,* pedal part in octaves; *doppio trillo,* double trill, i.e., a trill with a turn at the end.

Dorati, Antal, b. Budapest, Apr. 9, 1906; d. Gerzensee, near Bern, Nov. 13, 1988. He studied with Leo Weiner privately and at the Franz Liszt Academy of Music in Budapest, where he also studied from Kodály (1920–24); on staff of the Budapest Opera (1924–28); conducted the Dresden State Opera (1928–29); Generalmusikdirektor in Munster (1929–32); went to France (1933); led the Ballets Russes de Monte Carlo, which he took on an Australian tour (1938). He made his U.S. debut with the National Sym. Orch. in Washington, D.C. (1937); settled in the U.S. (1940); naturalized in 1947. He was appointed music director of the American Ballet Theatre in N.Y. (1941–44); conductor of the Dallas Sym. Orch. (1945–49); music director of the Minneapolis Sym. Orch. (1949–60); chief conductor of the BBC Sym. Orch. in London (1963–66) and the Stockholm Phil. (1966–70). He was music director of the National Sym. Orch. in Washington, D.C. (1970–77), and Detroit Sym. Orch. (1977–81); principal conductor of the Royal Phil. in London (1975–79); in 1984, made an honorary Knight Commander of the Order of the British Empire. He made numerous guest conducting appearances in Europe and North America, earning a well-deserved reputation as an orch. builder; a prolific recording output made him one of the best-known conductors of his time; recordings of the complete Haydn syms. and operas were particularly commendable. In 1969 he married pianist Ilse von Alpenheim, who often appeared as a soloist under his direction.

Dorian mode. Basic mode (scale) of Gregorian chant; orig. named *primus tonus* in medieval theory; like other ecclesiastical modes, it is not identical with the similarly named ancient Greek mode. Projected onto the white keys of the piano or the natural notes on the modern staff, the authentic Dorian octave rises from the "final" D to D an octave higher; the only church mode that is self-invertible, i.e., plays upwards or downwards without change to the intervallic order. The plagal derivation of the Dorian is the Hypodorian mode, ranging from A a perfect 4th below the final D to A a perfect 5th above.

Dorsey, "Georgia Tom" (Thomas Andrew), b. Villa Rica, Ga., 1899. His father was a revivalist preacher; he went to Atlanta in his youth; 1st encountered blues pianists; took courses at the Chicago College of Composition and Arranging; launched a career as a pianist, arranger, and composer, organizing his own Wildcats Jazz Band; made recordings with Ma Rainey as "Georgia Tom." After founding the National Convention of Gospel Choirs and Choruses (with Sallie Martin) and the Thomas A. Dorsey Gospel Songs Music Publishing Co. (1931), he devoted himself entirely to gospel music; wrote the gospel standard *Precious Lord, Take My Hand* (1932).

Dorsey, Jimmy (James), b. Shenandoah, Pa., Feb. 29, 1904; d. N.Y., June 12, 1957. He took up the slide trumpet and cornet at age 7; turned to reed instruments 4 years later; led several groups with his brother Tommy (Thomas) Dorsey before working as a freelance musician in N.Y. (1925–34), becoming known through his swing recordings. He co-led the Dorsey Brothers Orch. (1934–35); after an argument with Tommy, he took sole charge, but rejoined him in the new Dorsey Brothers Orch. (1953–56); appeared in several films, including the fictionalized *The Fabulous Dorseys* (1947).

Dorsey, Tommy (Thomas), b. Shenandoah, Pa., Nov. 19, 1905; d. Greenwich, Conn., Nov. 26, 1956. He studied trumpet with his father; turned to the trombone; led several groups with his brother Jimmy (James) Dorsey; active in dance bands, pit orchs., and other N.Y. groups. He co-led the Dorsey Brothers Orch. (1934–35); following an argument with Jimmy, set out on his own as a dance-band leader, becoming a leading figure in the big band era; Jimmy rejoined him in the new Dorsey Brothers Orch. (1953–56). He appeared in the fictionalized film *The Fabulous Dorseys* (1947). As an instrumentalist, he developed a virtuoso technique highlighted by remarkable legato playing.

dot. In music this is much more than a mere punctuation mark. When placed after a note it indicates the increase in its value by one-half ($\quad$); a dotted quarter note equals the value of a quarter note plus an 8th note (1/4 + 1/8). In the 17th and 18th centuries dotted notes had an indeterminate value, indicating simply that the note with a dot after it had to be prolonged. In order to avoid uncertainty, the double dot ($\quad$) was introduced late in the 18th century, the value of the 2nd dot being half the value of the 1st. Thus a quarter note with a double dot equaled seven 16th notes (1/4 + 1/8 + 1/16). A triple dot ($\quad$) is occasionally encountered; a quarter note with a triple dot equals fifteen 32nd notes (1/4 + 1/8 + 1/16 + 1/32).

dotara. Bengal plucked string instrument usually with 4 strings.

double. 1. Variation. 2. Repetition of words in a song. 3. Prefix indicating a 16' organ stop that matches an 8' stop; as double principal 16', etc. 4. Substitute singer or instrumentalist. 5. In change-ringing, changes on 5 bells. 6. Producing a tone an octave lower; as double-bassoon, double-bourdon, etc. 7. Add the higher or lower octave to any tone (or tones) of a melody or harmony.

double bar. 2 vertical lines drawn through the staff at the end of a section, movement, or piece.

double bass. Largest and deepest-toned instrument of the violin family, formerly with either 3 strings (G_1–D–A being the Italian, A_1–D–G the English tuning), now 4 strings (E_1–A_1–D–G). The double bass sounds an octave lower than written. See also ⇒violin.

double bassoon. Contrabassoon.

double chorus. Work for 2 choirs, or divided choir, usually in 8 parts; the ensemble itself.

double common meter. See ⇒meter.

double counterpoint. Polyphony in which the upper and the lower voices can be exchanged so the low voice becomes the top voice and vice versa, without breaking contrapuntal rules. See also ⇒counterpoint.

double croche (Fr.). Sixteenth note.

double dièse (Fr.). Double sharp.

double dot. See ⇒dot.

double flat. The sign ♭♭.

double fugue. fugue with 2 themes (subjects) occurring simultaneously.

double leading–tone cadence. Expansion of the polyphonic Landini cadence in late medieval music, where the leading-tone-to-submediant motion (7–6) is harmonized by a sustained raised subdominant (♯) (4) and supertonic (2) before resolving into an open 5th and octave:

double note. Breve (𝅜); a note twice the length of a whole note.

double octave. 15th; interval of 2 octaves.

double open diapason. 16' open pipe in a large organ, producing a sound an octave below the standard pitch of the manual key or the pedal.

double quartet. Work for pairs of 4 solo voices or instruments, as opposed to a mixed octet. Spohr wrote 4 double string quartets.

double reed. Reed used for members of the oboe and bassoon families. 2 separate pieces of cane are tightly bound together to produce the characteristic vibration.

double repetition mark. Symbol dividing a section of a composition into 2 parts and calling for the repetition of each part.

double sharp. The sign 𝄪.

double stop. Playing of 2 notes simultaneously on violin family instruments; the easiest double stops are in 6ths, but 3rds and octaves are entirely playable, even in consecutive progressions. True triple and quadruple stops are theoretically ruled out by the curved bridge of the instrument, and the chord must be broken to be played (e.g., the opening of Beethoven's *Kreutzer* Sonata, much of Bach's solo violin music); the alternative, flattening the bridge, is not a practical solution.

douce (*doucement, doux,* It. *dolce*). Softly, sweetly, suavely, gently, tenderly.

douloureux (Fr.). Sorrowfully, dolorously.

Dowland, John, b. probably in London, 1563; d. there (buried), Feb. 20, 1626. In 1580 he went to Paris in the service of Sir Henry Cobham; by 1584, was back in England, where he married; admitted to his Mus.B. from Christ Church, Oxford (1588). In 1592 he played before Queen Elizabeth I; unsuccessful in securing a position as one of the Queen's musicians, went to Germany (1594); received the patronage of the Duke of Braunschweig in Wolfenbüttel and the Landgrave of Hesse in Kassel; went to Italy and visited Venice, Padua, Genoa, Ferrara, and Florence, where he played before Ferdinando I, the Grand Duke of Tuscany. He returned to England (1595); appointed lutenist to King Christian IV of Denmark (1598–1606); returned to England once more; became lutenist to Lord Howard de Walden, then to King Charles I (1612).

Dowland is the foremost representative of the English school of lutenist-composers; he was also noted for his lute songs, in which he used novel chromatic developments; treated the accompanying parts as separate entities, obtaining harmonic effects quite advanced for the time. Most of his vocal music was published as *Bookes of Songes or Ayres of fowre partes . . .* (1597, 1600, 1603); *Lachrimae, or 7 Teares Figvred in Seaven Passionate Pauans . . .* (1604); and *A Pilgrimes Solace* (1612). His son Robert Dowland (b. London, *c.* 1591; d. there, Nov. 28, 1641) succeeded his father as lutenist to Charles I (1626); ed. the anthologies *Varietie of Lute Lessons* (1610) and *A Musicall Banquett* (1610), which included some of his father's songs.

downbeat. 1. Downward stroke of the conductor's hand in beating time, marking the primary or 1st accent in each measure; hence, the accent itself (strong beat, thesis).

down-bow. In bowed stringed instruments, the downward stroke of the bow from nut to point; usual sign is ⊓.

downstroke. Down-bow.

doxology (Grk. *doxa* + *logos*, glorious word). Hymn of praise to God. In Christian services there are 3 main doxologies: the *greater doxology*, represented by the Gloria in excelsis in the Roman Catholic liturgy; the *lesser doxology*, Gloria Patri, used at the end of the psalmody; and metrical doxology, as used in the Anglican liturgy; of this type the best known is the metrical hymn by the 17th-century divine Thomas Kent:

> Praise God, from whom all blessings flow
>
> Praise Him all creatures here below
>
> Praise him above ye heavenly Hosts
>
> Praise Father, Son, and Holy Ghost.

There are also doxologies in the Jewish liturgy, including the *kaddish* (i.e., mourner's prayer) and the *kedusha* ("Holy, Holy, Holy/Is the Lord of Hosts.")

D'Oyly Carte, Richard. See ⇒Carte, Richard D'Oyly.

drag. 1. Very slow dance in which the feet are dragged rather than moved on the floor; Joplin included a "real slow drag" in *Treemonisha.* 2. Rudimentary drum stroke.

dramatic contralto. See ⇒alto.

dramatic music. 1. Program music. 2. Incidental music.

dramatic soprano. See ⇒soprano.

drame lyrique (Fr., lyric drama; It., *dramma lirico*). French designation for opera, especially in the 19th century. This genre may be lyric or tragic; its designation refers simply to the use of singing.

dramma giocoso (It., jocular drama). Italian term of the 18th century for a comic opera with tragic episodes; literally, "jocular drama." Mozart described *Don Giovanni* as a *dramma giocoso.*

dramma per musica (It., drama with music). Early term for opera (*c.* 1600); while the Baroque eventually called such works *opere serie,* Wagner revived the term for his operas (Ger. *Musikdrama*).

drammatico (It.). Dramatically; in a vivid, theatrical style.

Drängend (Ger.). Pressing, hastening; stringendo.

Drehleier (Ger., rotating lyre). Hurdy-gurdy; often confused with Drehorgel.

Drehorgel (Ger., rotating organ). Barrel-organ; incorrectly called a hurdy-gurdy, with resulting confusion with the Drehleier.

drei (Ger.). Three. *Dreifach,* triple.

Dreiklang (Ger.). Triad.

Dreivierteltakt (Ger.). 3/4 measure; 3/4 time; waltz time.

dringend (Ger., pressing). Gradually accelerating and becoming animated.

drohend (Ger.; It. *tonando*). Menacing; thundering.

droit (*droite;* Fr.). Right. *Main droite,* right hand.

drone. 1. In the bagpipe, a continuously sounding pipe of constant pitch; a drone-pipe. 2. Any sustained tone, in an inner or outer voice, creating the effect of a bagpipe, particularly on an organ. *Drone-bass,* a bass on the tonic, dominant, or both, persisting throughout a piece or section.

Druckman, Jacob (Raphael), b. Philadelphia, June 26, 1928; d. New Haven, Conn., May 24, 1996. After taking courses with Longy and L. Gesensway in Philadelphia, he studied composition with Copland at Tanglewood (1949–50), with Mennin, Persichetti, and Wagenaar at the Juilliard School of Music in N.Y. (B.S., 1954; M.S., 1956), and with Aubin at the École Normale de Musique in Paris on a Fulbright fellowship (1954–55). He taught at the Juilliard School of Music in N.Y. (1957–72) and Bard College (1961–67); an associate at the Columbia-Princeton Electronic Music Center (1967); director of the electronic music studio at Yale Univ. (1971–72); associate prof. of composition at Brooklyn College of the City Univ. of N.Y. (1972–76); chairman of the composition dept. and director of the electronic music studio at Yale Univ. (from 1976). From 1982 to 1986 he was composer-in-residence of the N.Y. Phil.; held Guggenheim fellowships in 1957 and 1968; won the Pulitzer Prize for *Windows* for Orch. (1972); elected a member of the Inst. of the American Academy and Inst. of Arts and Letters (1978). His music happily combines the strict elements of polyphonic structure, harking back to Palestrina, with modern techniques of dissonant counterpoint, while refusing to adhere to any doctrinaire system of composition; his orchestrations make use of a plethora of percussion instruments, including primitive drums; electronic sonorities gathered increasing importance in his works.

drum machine. Electronic device that performs preprogrammed rhythms and timbres; found mostly in popular and experimental music.

drum. In the percussion group, any instrument consisting of a cylindrical, hollow body of wood or metal, over 1 or both ends of which a membrane of animal skin or plastic (the head) is stretched tightly by means of a hoop, to which is attached an endless cord tightened by leathern braces or by rods and screws. Rhythmical drums (side drum, snare drum, bass drum) do not vary in pitch (i.e., are indefinite of pitch), while musical drums (timpani, tom-tom) produce distinct pitches (e.g., are of definite pitch).

duda. Slavic bagpipe.

Dudelsack (Ger.). See ⇒Bagpipe.

duduk. Slavic whistle flute.

due (It.). Two. *A due,* for 2; both together again (after playing divisi); *a due voci,* 2 parts or voices.

due corde. See ⇒Corda.

due pedali, con. Both (damper and soft) pedals at once.

due volte. Two times; repeat.

duet (It. *duetto*). 1. Work for 2 voices or instruments; in opera, often indicates a love scene; but Schubert and Brahms wrote accompanied duets in lieder form. 2. Composition for 2 performers on one instrument, typically piano. 3. Piece for one organist in 2 parts, each played on a separate manual.

duettino (It.). Short or little duet, usually accompanied; Mozart's *Marriage of Figaro* has several.

duetto da camera. Vocal duet, usually of an amorous nature.

Dufay (Du Fay), Guillaume, b. probably in or near Cambrai, *c.* 1400; d. there, Nov. 27, 1474. His last name is pronounced "du-fah-ee" (3 syllables), indicated by his setting of *Ave regina caelorum.* He was a choirboy at Cambrai Cathedral, where he was influenced by Nicolas Malin, its magister puerorum, and his successor, Richard Loqueville (although there is no evidence that he formally studied with them); remained in Cambrai until at least 1418; shortly thereafter, entered the service of the Malatesta family in Pesaro; returned to Cambrai (1426).

In Rome, Dufay sang in the papal choir (1428–33), during which time he consolidated his reputation as a most significant musician; his motet *Ecclesie militantis* may have been composed for the consecration of Pope Eugene IV (1431); found a patron in Niccolo III, Marquis of Ferrara (1433), visiting Niccolo's court in 1437; also found a patron in Louis, Duke of Savoy. He served as maître de chappelle for the marriage of Louis and Anne of Cyprus at the Savoy court (1434); after a visit to Cambrai that year, he returned to Savoy. He was again a singer in the papal choir (1435–37), maintained at this time in Florence, then Bologna; he received a degree in canon law from the Univ. of Turin. In 1436 he became canon of Cambrai Cathedral; after again serving Savoy (1437–39), returned to Cambrai to assume his canonical duties (1440); also made canon of Ste. Waudru in Mons (1446). In 1450 he returned to Italy; visited Turin in the summer of that year; again active in Savoy (1451–58), serving once more as maître de chappelle (1455–56). In 1458 he returned to Cambrai, where he lived and worked in comfort for the rest of his life.

In his lifetime, Dufay was held in the highest esteem by church authorities and fellow musicians; Loyset Compère described him as "the moon of all music, and the light of all singers." Foremost representative of the Burgundian school, he proved himself a master of both sacred and secular music, producing masses, motets, and chansons of extraordinary beauty and distinction; his contributions to the development of fauxbourdon and the cyclic Mass are particularly noteworthy.

Dukas, Paul, b. Paris, Oct. 1, 1865; d. there, May 17, 1935. He was a student at the Paris Cons., studying under G. Mathias (piano), Theodore Dubois (harmony), and E. Guiraud (composition) (1882–88); won 1st prize for counterpoint and fugue (1886) and the 2nd Prix de Rome with a cantata, *Velléda* (1888); began writing music reviews (1892); music critic of the *Revue Hebdomadaire* and *Gazette des Beaux-Arts;* contributor

to the *Chronique des Arts, Revue Musicale,* etc. He was made a Chevalier of the Legion d'honneur (1906); prof. of orchestration at the Cons. (1910–13; 1928–35); elected Debussy's successor as a member of the Conseil de l'enseignement supérieur (1918); taught at the École Normale de Musique; assisted in the revising and editing of Rameau's complete works for Durand of Paris. Although he was prolific, Dukas wrote a masterpiece of modern music in his orch'l scherzo *L'Apprenti sorcier;* his opera *Ariane et Barbe-Bleue* is one of the finest French impressionist operas; notable works are the Sym. in C Major and the ballet *La Péri.* Shortly before his death he destroyed several MSS of unfinished compositions.

Duke, Vernon. See ⇒Dukelsky, Vladimir.

Dukelsky, Vladimir, b. Parfianovka, Oct. 10, 1903, d. Santa Monica, Calif., Jan. 16, 1969. He was a pupil at the Kiev Cons. of Glière and Dombrovsky; left Russia (1920); went to Turkey, then the U.S.; later lived in Paris and London; settled in N.Y. (1929; naturalized, 1936); a lieutenant in the Coast Guard (1939–44); went back to France (1947–48) but returned to live in N.Y. and Hollywood. He began composing at a very early age; was introduced to Diaghilev, who commissioned him to write a ballet, *Zephyr et Flore,* successfully produced. Another important meeting was with Koussevitzky, who championed his music in Paris and Boston. In the U.S. Dukelsky began writing popular music; many of his songs, such as *April in Paris,* have enjoyed great popularity. At George Gershwin's suggestion he adopted the name Vernon Duke for popular music works; in 1955 he dropped his orig. name altogether and signed all of his compositions Vernon Duke. He authored the polemical book *Listen Here! A Critical Essay on Music Depreciation* (N.Y., 1963).

dulcet. 4' organ stop, producing a soft sound an octave above normal pitch.

dulciana (dolcino, dolziana, It., Ger., *Dolcian, Dulcian; Dulzian*). 1. Curtal. 2. Penetrating, open-flue pipe organ stop, usually 8' (can be 16' or 4'). See also ⇒Dulzian

dulcimer (from Lat. *dulcis,* sweet). 1. Hammered dulcimer, predecessor of the harpsichord and the piano. Wire strings are stretched over a soundboard or resonance-box, usually in trapezoid form resembling the psaltery, or zither; the strings are activated by mallets. The modern dulcimer has from 2 to 3 octaves' compass. It was at one time called *cembalo;* in Hungary it is known as the cimbalom. An 18th-century virtuoso named Pantaleon Hebenstreit manufactured a dulcimerlike instrument known under his 1st name. The hammered dulcimer was a model for Partch's harmonic canons. 2. Mountain dulcimer, a folk instrument popular in the Appalachian range in the U.S.; it consists of an elongated soundbox with a fretted fingerboard and (usually) 3 strings. Unlike the hammered dulcimer and the zither, the strings of the folk instrument are plucked. The mountain dulcimer is frequently used to accompany singers or dancers at country festivals.

dulzian (*Dolcian, Dulcian,* Ger.; It., *dulciana, dolcino, dolziana*). 1. Curtal. 2. Penetrating, open-flue pipe organ stop, usually 8' (can be 16' or 4'). See also ⇒dulciana

dumb piano. Piano keyboard with no strings attached, used to practice by aspiring pianists whose crowded lodgings do not permit even a joyful noise of pounding on the keys. G. B. Shaw, writing as Corno di Bassetto (1888), reports an inquiry from a correspondent as to whether there is such a thing as a "dumb horn." He claimed that no such contrivance was needed because a French horn is so difficult to play that it remains naturally dumb in the hands of inexpert hornists.

dumka (Pol. *dumać;* ponder; pl. *dumky*). 1. Vocal or instrumental romance of a melancholy cast; a lament or elegy. Czech composers wrote the best-known dumkas: Dvořák named his piano trio (op. 90, 1890–91) *Dumky;* other dumka composers were Fibich, Janáček, Suk, and Novák. 2. (Ukr., a little thought) Ukrainian lyric narrative ballad, with a meditative, sometimes melancholy character.

dummy pipes. Pipes that do not speak, displayed at the front of the organ.

dump (*dompe, dumpe*). Genre, often in ground bass or variation form, for lute or keyboards in the 16th and 17th centuries, harmonized by alternating tonic and dominant chords.

Dunstable (Dunstaple), John, b. *c.* 1390; d. London, Dec. 24, 1453. Almost nothing is known about his life with any certainty; may have been the John Dunstaple in the service of the Duke of Bedford; if so, may have accompanied his patron to France; seems to have been well versed in astronomy and mathematics. The J. Dunstaple buried in the church of St. Stephen, Walbrook (destroyed in the Great Fire of 1666) was more than likely the composer.

Dunstable's style grew directly out of the earlier English school (found in the Old Hall MS, early 15th century); in his day, he was the most important English composer; his works were widely known on the Continent, where they represented the *contenance angloise*. Most of his surviving compositions are preserved in continental MSS, although discoveries have recently been made in England; some works formerly attributed to him are now attributed to Power, Benet, Binchois, and others; others remain doubtful. The styles of Dunstable and Power, in particular, are so similar that it is not always possible to determine authorship. Dunstable's extant works include Mass movements, motets, and secular songs.

duo (It.). Duet. *Duo* is loosely distinguished from *duet* by applying the 1st term to works for 2 pianos or for voices and/or instruments of different kinds; the 2nd term may be reserved for 2 voices or instruments of the *same* kind (excepting pianos).

duodecima (It.). 1. Interval of the 12th. 2. The 12th, an organ stop.

duodrama. 20th-century genre of dramatic presentation in which only two actors conduct a dialogue, usually reciting their reciprocal experiences retrospectively without coming to a dramatic clash; it lends itself naturally to chamber opera, applied anachronistically applied to 18th-century works.

duolo, con (It.). Dolefully, grievingly.

Duparc (born Fouques-Duparc), **(Marie-Eugène) Henri,** b. Paris, Jan. 21, 1848; d. Mont-de-Marsan, Feb. 12, 1933. He studied with César Franck, who thought him his most talented pupil; but Duparc suffered from a nervous affliction, which eventually forced him to abandon composition and seek rest in Switzerland. He destroyed the MS of his Cello Sonata, and several symphonic suites; of his instrumental works only a few MSS have survived, including the symphonic poems *Aux étoiles* (perf. in Paris, Apr. 11, 1874) and *Lénore* (1875) and a suite of 5 piano pieces, *Feuilles volantes* (1869). His songs (1868–82), to words by Baudelaire and other French poets, are distinguished by exquisitely phrased melodies arranged in fluid modal harmonies; among them are *L'invitation au voyage, Extase, Soupir, Serenade, Chanson triste, La Vague et la cloche, Phidylé, Elégie, Testament, Lamento,* and *La Vie antérieure.*

duple. Double. *Duple rhythm,* rhythm of 2 beats to a measure; *duple time,* see ⇒time.

duplet. Group of 2 equal notes to be performed in the time of 3 of like value in the established meter, written

duplum (Lat.). Contrapuntal part against the cantus firmus in ars antiqua organum; in ars nova, also called the *motetus* (from Fr. *mots,* words).

DuPré, Jacqueline, b. Oxford, Jan. 26, 1945; d. London, Oct. 19, 1987. She entered the London Cello School at age 5; began studies with her principal mentor, W. Pleeth; made her 1st public appearance on British television at age 12; awarded a gold medal upon graduation from the Guildhall School of Music in London (1960). She studied with Casals in Zermatt, Switzerland, with Tortelier at Dartington Hall and in Paris, and with Rostropovich in Moscow; won the Queen's Prize (1960); made her formal debut in a recital at London's Wigmore Hall (1961) and her North American debut at N.Y.'s Carnegie Hall with Dorati and the BBC Sym. Orch. (1965), an appearance that electrified the audience and elicited rapturous critical reviews. In 1967 she married the pianist and conductor Daniel Barenboim, with whom she subsequently performed; but in 1973 she was diagnosed with multiple sclerosis and abandoned her career; later gave master classes as health permitted. In 1976 she was made an Officer of the Order of the British Empire; the Jacqueline DuPré Research Fund was founded to assist in the fight against the disease that eventually killed her.

dur (Ger.). Major, as in C dur (C major), F dur (F major), etc.

duramente (It.). Sternly, harshly.

duration. Length of a sound, rest, movement, or composition.

Durchführung (Ger., going through). 1. Development section in sonata form. 2. Exposition in a fugue.

Durchkomponiert (Ger.). Through-composed.

Durey, Louis (Edmond), b. Paris, May 27, 1888; d. St. Tropez, July 3, 1979. He studied with Leon Saint-Requier (1910–14); member of Les Six. He wrote music fashionable during a wave of anti-Romanticism, proclaiming the need for constructive simplicity in modern dress, with abundant use of titillating discords; although the oldest of Les Six, he wrote the least music. His aesthetic code was radically altered in 1936 when he joined the French Communist Party; during the German occupation of France, was active in the Resistance; wrote anti-fascist songs. In 1948 he was elected vice president of the Assoc. Française des Musiciens Progressives; in 1950, became the music critic of the Paris Communist newspaper *L'Humanité;* received the Grand Prix de la Musique Française (1961).

durezza, con (It, *duro*). Hard, harsh; play with unflinching rhythm and emphatic accentuation. In the 17th century *durezza* was synonymous with dissonance, e.g., Frescobaldi's naming his *Toccata di durezza* for its appoggiaturas.

Düster (Ger.). Gloomy, mournfully, somberly.

Dutilleux, Henri, b. Angers, Jan. 22, 1916. He studied at the Paris Cons. with H. Busser and with Jean and Noel Gallon; won the 1st Grand Prix de Rome in 1938; director of singing at the Paris Opéra in 1942; active on radio (1943–63). He became prof. at the École Normale de Musique (1961) and the Paris Cons. (1970). He has developed a modernistic style that incorporates many procedures of impressionism; his chamber music and orch'l works have had numerous performances in France, England, and America.

Dutoit, Charles (Edouard), b. Lausanne, Oct. 7, 1936. He learned to play the violin, viola, piano, and drums; studied conducting by watching Ansermet's rehearsals with the Orch. de la Suisse Romande; studied music theory at the Lausanne Cons. and the Geneva Cons.; took courses at the Accademia Musicale in Siena and at the Cons. Benedetto Marcello in Venice; also attended a seminar at Tanglewood. Returning to Switzerland, he joined the Lausanne Chamber Orch. as a violist.

Dutoit made his conducting debut with the Bern Sym. Orch. (1963); engaged as music director (1967–77); artistic director of the Zurich Radio Orch. (1964–71); for many years was artistic director of the National Cons. in Mexico City; appointed conductor of the Goteborg Sym. Orch. in Sweden (1975). He engaged as music director of the Montreal Sym. Orch. (1977); expanded its repertoire, with Haydn syms., music of Mozart and Beethoven, and especially French music, beginning with Berlioz and including Debussy and Ravel; also promoted new Canadian music. He was appointed principal guest conductor of the Minn. Orch. (1983); artistic director and principal conductor of the Philadelphia Orch. summer seasons (1990–91); made his Metropolitan Opera debut in N.Y., conducting *Les Contes d'Hoffmann*. In 1990 he was named chief conductor of the Orch. National de France in Paris. He was married 3 times; his 2nd wife was the pianist Martha Argerich.

dux (Lat. *leader*). Subject or theme in a fugue; it is followed by the *comes* (Lat., companion), the imitative answer; a term fashionable in the 16th century.

dvojnica. South Slavic double flute: the right tube is for melody;, the left is a drone.

Dvořák, Antonin (Leopold), b. Nelahozeves, Kralupy, Sept. 8, 1841; d. Prague, May 1, 1904. He studied piano and violin locally; went to Prague; studied with K. Pitsch and J. Krejci; began to compose so assiduously that within a short time had completed 2 syms., 2 operas, and chamber music. His 1st public appearance as composer took place in Prague (1873), with a perf. of his cantata *The Heirs of the White Mountain* (Hymnus). Another milestone occurred in Prague, when Smetana conducted his Sym. No. 3 in E-flat Major, op. 10 (1874). Dvořák then entered several works in a competition for the Austrian State Prize, adjudicated by a distinguished committee that included Herbeck, Hanslick, and Brahms; won the prize in 1875 and twice in 1877. Brahms particularly appreciated Dvořák's talent and recommended him to Simrock for publication of the *Moravian Duets* and the highly popular *Slavonic Dances*. His Stabat Mater (Prague, 1880) and Sym. No. 6 in D Major, op. 60 (Prague, 1881), followed in close succession, securing for him a leading position among Czech composers.

At the invitation of the Phil. Soc. of London, Dvořák visited England (1884) to conduct several of his works; commissioned to compose a new sym. for the Phil. Soc.; the result was his Sym. No. 7 in D Minor, op. 70, which he premiered in London (1885). Another English success came with the cantata *The Spectre's Bride,* composed for the Birmingham Festival (1885). On his 3rd visit to England he led the premiere of the oratorio *St. Ludmila* at the Leeds Festival (1886); conducted his own works in Russia (1890); that same year he conducted in Prague the 1st performance of his Sym. No. 8 in G Major, op. 88, which became a very popular work. In 1891, the year of his brilliant *Carnival Overture,* he was appointed prof. of composition at the Prague Cons. (1891).

In 1892 Dvořák accepted the position of director of the National Cons. of Music of America in N.Y. He composed his Te Deum for his 1st conducting U.S. appearance (N.Y.); conducted a concert of his music at the 1892 World Columbian Exposition in Chicago. While in the U.S. he composed his most celebrated work, the Sym. No. 9 in E Minor, op. 95 (*From the New World*), premiered by Anton Seidl conducting the N.Y. Phil. (1893). While the melodies seemed to reflect actual Negro and Indian music, Dvořák insisted upon their absolute originality. Sym. No. 9 is essentially a Czech work from the Old World, but, by promoting the use of Negro-influenced themes in symphonic music, he had a significant impact on American musical nationalism. In an article, "Music in America" (*Harper's New Monthly Magazine,* Feb. 1895), he stated that although Americans had accomplished marvels in most fields of endeavor, in music they were decidedly backward, content to produce poor imitations of European music; the way to greatness, he suggested, was in the development of a national style based on the melodies of Negroes and Indians. His proposal was greeted with enthusiasm by one segment of America's musical world and roundly rejected by those fearing musical miscegenation; the controversy raged for more than 2 decades.

Dvořák composed his great Cello Concerto during his American sojourn, conducting its 1st performance in London (1896). Resigning his N.Y. position in 1895, he returned home to resume his duties at the Prague Cons.; became its director (1901). During the last years of his life, he devoted much of his creative efforts to opera; *Rusalka* (1900) remains the best known outside the Czech Republic. He made his last appearance as a conductor in 1900, leading a concert of the Czech Phil. in Prague; he was made a member of the Austrian House of Lords in 1901, the 1st Czech musician to be so honored; Czechs celebrated his 60th birthday with special performances of his music in Prague.

Dvořák's musical style was eclectic. His earliest works reflect the influence of Beethoven and Schubert; then Wagner, culminating in the Classicism of Brahms. After mastering his craft, proved to be a composer of great versatility and fecundity. A diligent and meticulous artisan, he brought to his finest works a seemingly inexhaustible and spontaneous melodic invention, rhythmic variety, judicious employment of national folk tunes, and contrapuntal and harmonic skill; the last 5 syms., Cello Concerto, Stabat Mater, his *Slavonic Dances,* the *Carnival Overture,* and many chamber works have become staples of the repertoire.

dyad. Group of 2 pitch classes, usually with reference to a 12-tone set.

Dylan, Bob (born Robert Allen Zimmerman), b. Duluth, Minn., May 24, 1941. He adopted the name Dylan out of admiration for poet Dylan Thomas. Possessed by wanderlust, he allegedly rode freight trains across the country, eventually playineg guitar and crooning in N.Y. coffeehouses; composed songs modeled after blues and ballads, with a wide range of topics from personal to political; the poetic range of his lyrics became his most powerful trait. Dylan's nasalized folk style evolved into electric folk (folk-rock) on the example of the Byrds and other rock groups that performed his songs; despite the alienation of folk purists, his metamorphosis captured the imagination not only of adolescents but also of true cognoscenti in search of convincing authenticity.

In 1966 Dylan broke his neck in a nearly fatal motorcycle accident; forced into seclusion for 2 years, he worked with his backup group (who became The Band) and wrote prolifically in a transitional style.In 1968, he adopted yet another face, that of country-western singer; once again, the Byrds were a major impetus for this. In later years Dylan became a Christian and celebrated his being saved for several albums; he eventually returned to Judaism. While he became increasingly self-parodic in his songwriting and performances, he could still give a sincere and powerful performance in the right circumstances; a Dylan guest appearance became a rare privilege. His influence on other musicians is incalculable; a 30th-anniversary concert in 1992 featured a great number of important rock, folk, and blues musicians. His son Jakob is a singer-songwriter who leads The Wallflowers.

dynamics. Varying and contrasting degrees of intensity or loudness in musical tones; the notational signs used to designate these degrees (forte, piano, crescendo, diminuendo, sforzando, etc.).

E. 1. 5th note of the alphabetical scale and the 3rd note or medi-ant of the C-major scale. In Italian, Spanish, French, and Russian, E is Mi. 2. (It., lowercase). And when preceding a word begin-ning with the letter *e*, it should be written *ed*; before other vow-els, either *e* or *ed* are permissible; before consonants, only *e*.

E dur (Ger.). E major.

E major. With 4 sharps in its key signature, E major was diffi-cult to handle in the Classic period, with its natural (i.e., uncrooked) brass instruments normally tuned in flat keys. The grandest sym. in E major is the 7th of Bruckner, in length and in concept; in this sym., Bruckner's imagination was possessed by Wagner; he claimed that the 2nd movement (Adagio, in the rela-tive key of C-sharp minor) presaged Wagner's death. The master himself had no difficulties with this tonality, having written the overture to *Tannhäuser* in itr. To Romantic composers E major was the key of spiritual transfiguration; the 1st Sym. of Scriabin ends with a choral paean to art. E major is found in the final sec-tions of orch'l works nominally in E minor, the most famous example being Mendelssohn's Violin Concerto.

E minor. Tonality of contemplative calm. Surprisingly it is not often used by the 3 great Classic composers, but the Romantics loved it. Mendelssohn's Violin Concerto is in E minor (even with its E-major finale). Perhaps the best-known sym. in E minor is the 4th Sym. of Brahms, with its spacious narrative development; Tchaikovsky couched his 5th Sym. in the key of E minor; the finale, as tradition demanded, is set in the tonic major of the key. Mahler's most serene sym., his 7th, is in E minor; even though there are lapses into the night's darkness, the finale, in unam-biguous C major, reasserts an optimistic quality so unusual in Mahler's works. The river *Moldau (Vltava)* in Smetana's sym-phonic cycle *Ma vlast* flows poetically in E minor; Dvořák's 9th Sym. (*From the New World*) is also in E minor, a fitting choice to evoke the nostalgic quality of this work. But perhaps the most congenial use of the key is found in Rimsky-Korsakov's sym-phonic suite *Scheherazade*; although the work's motto for solo violin is in A minor, the listener's ear registers it as the subdom-inant of the principal key of E minor.

E moll (Ger.). E minor.

E string. Highest string on the violin; the lowest string on the double bass; the highest and lowest strings on the guitar; not found on the viola or cello.

Eagles, The. (Vocal/guitar: Glenn Frey, b. Detroit, Mich., Nov. 6, 1948; drums/vocal: Don Henley, b. Gilmer, Tex.,

July 22, 1947; banjo/mandolin/guitar/vocal: Bernie Leadon, b. Minneapolis, Minn., July 19, 1947; bass/vocal: Randy Meisner, b. Scottsbluff, Nebr., Mar. 8, 1946. After 1974, guitar: Don Felder, b. Gainesville, Fla., Sept. 21, 1947; after 1975, guitar: Joe Walsh, b. Wichita, Kans., Nov. 20, 1947, replaced Leadon; after 1977, bass/vocal: Timothy B. Schmit, b. Sacramento, Calif., Oct. 30, 1947, replaced Meisner.) Influential country-rock band of the 1970s. First formed as a backup group for singer Linda Ronstadt, the group recorded soft country-rock, scoring early hits with *Take It Easy*, a mellow, hippie-cowboy anthem, and *Desperado*. They reached their greatest success when they became a more hard-rocking outfit, focusing on social commentary (1977's *Hotel California*; *Life in the Fast Lane*). In 1980 the group dis-banded following internal squabbling; 14 years later the group rebanded (with its late-'70s personnel) for a hugely successful "Hell Freezes Over" tour and album; in the intervening years, Henley has had the greatest individual success, although Frey has also had solo hits.

ear training. Generic description of educational methods employed to improve the appreciation of intervals and rhythms. Students who happily possess the precious gift of perfect pitch (which cannot be trained artificially) have a tremendous advan-tage over others not so favored by nature; for perfect pitchers, recognition of intervals, chord formation, melodic structure, counterpoint, etc., presents no more difficulty than for a child to recognize the syllabic values of its native language. However, a child possessing a sense of perfect pitch is not necessarily supe-rior musically to another who does not; ear training, therefore, must be highly selective.

Memory is another important branch of ear training; here again, individual gifts may differ greatly. An otherwise unmusical child may possess a natural ability to remember popular tunes he hears in the street, while a virtuoso violinist or pianist may be devoid of such instinctive memorization. The ability to carry a tune is also subject to individual evaluation; some children can pick up tunes and sing or whistle them with extraordinary accu-racy, while experienced musicians may be unable to carry a tune. Ravel would have probably failed a test of memory or even pitch recognition; Toscanini sang embarrassingly off pitch when he wanted to instruct the orch. in shaping a musical phrase. Stravinsky had an unusually poor memory even in reconstructing his own works; his ear training by any educational standards was surprisingly deficient. On the other hand, jazz musicians, mostly innocent of strict academic training, often display amazing capacity for picking up and reproducing complex melodies and rhythms.

éblouissant (Fr.). Dazzling, resplendent.

ebollimento (It.). Sudden and passionate expression of feeling.

eccitato (It.). Excited.

ecclesiastical modes. Octave scales employed in medieval music; church modes. See also ⇒authentic modes; plagal modes; individual modes.

echappée (Fr.). Standard abbrev. for *note echappée* (escaped note). Fortuitous term describing a nonharmonic tone that is neither a passing note, cambiata, nor appoggiatura. It is approached freely, placed a diatonic scale degree above or below the thematic note (forming a strong dissonance with the har-mony), and then resolved in the opposite direction from which it was approached. Unlike the cambiata, the underlying harmony shifts between the starting and ending note:

Bach's works are replete with such usages, which create a pungent aroma of dissonance without disrupting the sense of essential tonality.

echo (It. *eco*). Subdued repetition of a strain or phrase. The natural reflection of sound in mountain landscapes was the inspiration of many composers for the use of canonic imitation. In Greek mythology, the nymph Echo languishes in unrequited love for Narcissus; only her voice remains, as an echo. The legend inspired several opera composers, e.g., Gluck's *Écho et Narcisse*, full of ingenious use of canonic imitation. This device is employed in many madrigals; in some cases the echo repeats the last syllables of the preceding word where meaningful, e.g., *esempio* (example) answered by *empio* (empty), an effect used poignantly in the finale of Monteverdi's *Orfeo*. The echo is also used in instrumental music; it is a cornerstone of the Baroque style; in the last movement of his *Ouvertüre nach französicher Art* (Partita in B Minor, BWV 831), Bach makes use of it; in Mozart's Serenade, K. 286, there is antiphonal interplay between groups of 4 instruments in a quadruple echo.

echo organ. Separate set of pipes either enclosed in a box within the organ or placed at a distance from it to produce an echolike effect. *Echo stop*, organ stop producing an echolike effect.

echoi. Greek term for melodic formulas of Byzantine chant, paralleling closely the Gregorian system of 8 modes. Collectively they are known as *oktoechos* (8 modes). Their emergence has been traced to Syrian chant, itself much older than Gregorian chant; it seems probable that Byzantine and Gregorian chant share Syrian ancestry.

Eckstine, Billy (William Clarence), known as "Mr. B," b. Pittsburgh, July 8, 1914. He crooned in nightclubs; sang in Hines's big band (1939–43); formed his own band (1944–47), proselytizing for bebop; later became a successful balladeer of "cool" jazz. His place in jazz history is secured by the remarkable list of young musicians he helped establish: Parker, Gillespie, Vaughan, M. Davis, Dameron, Navarro, Gordon, Stitt, and Blakey.

eclecticism (from Grk. *ex* + *leipein*, gather). Compositional or improvisational aesthetic in which the choice of style or period is unlimited; generally, eclecticism reflects a more pervasive mode of influence than mere quotation.

eco (It.). Echo.

Écossaise (Fr., Scottish). Orig., a Scottish round dance in 3/2 or 3/4 time; later, a lively contradanse in 2/4 time. The latter entered continental Europe in the early 19th century; Beethoven,

Schubert, von Weber, and Chopin composed them. While known under this and other names (anglaise, française), the écossaise and its relatives probably originated in English country dances. Compare ⇒schottische.

edel (Ger.). Noble; refined, chaste.

effetto (It.). Effect, impression.

E-flat major. The natural brass instruments are keyed either in B-flat or E-flat major; these keys are used in festive serenades, military marches, and solemn chorales; therefore E-flat major is suitable for heroic, patriotic, and religious themes. Beethoven's *Eroica* Sym. cannot be imagined in any other key but E-flat major; neither can Beethoven's "Emperor" Concerto (although the moniker is not Beethoven's). One of the great Mozart syms., No. 39, is in E-flat major. Although this key is not particularly violinistic (the upper 2 strings are not within the desired scale), Mozart and other classical composers wrote violin concertos in E-flat major. It is not coincidence that Schumann's 3rd Sym. in E-flat Major is surnamed *Rhenish*, reflecting on the nature of life on the river Rhine, with its constant traffic and postilions signaling the departure of stagecoaches. Beethoven's "Les Adieux" Piano Sonata begins with a postilion's signal in descending "horn 5ths," couched as "Lebewohl" (farewell). Bruckner's *Romantic* Sym., his 4th, is in this key, as is Mahler's grandiose 8th, nicknamed (by others) the "Sym. of a Thousand."

E-flat major is peculiarly suited to the piano keyboard; its full octave scale runs symmetrically through alternating pairs of white keys and black keys; thus.piano works in this key number in the thousands. Liszt set his 1st Piano Concerto in E-flat major, but avoids exposing the key triadically; rather he teases the listener with syncopated descent from the tonic into the dominant. In his egocentric tone poem *Ein Heldenleben*, R. Strauss wrote a violin solo in the vainglorious key of E-flat major to represent himself. When Bülow was asked what his favorite key was, he replied, "E-flat major, for it is the key of the *Eroica* Sym., and it has 3 B's (B signifying B flat in German) for Bach, Beethoven, and Brahms."

E-flat minor. Key of seclusion and aristocratic retreat from the common elements of harmony. With 6 flats in the key signature, it lends itself to brilliant technical devices for a piano virtuoso; but it is utterly unsuitable for orch'l writing. A rare instance of an orch'l work in E-flat minor is Miaskovsky's 6th Sym.

effusione, con (It.). Effusively; with warmth.

Egk, Werner, (born Mayer), b. Auchsesheim, near Donauwörth, May 17, 1901; d. Inning, near Munich, July 10, 1983. Rumor had it that he took his name as a self-complimentary acronym for "ein grosser ('ein genialer'?) Komponist." Egk himself rejected this frivolous suspicion, offering instead an even more dubious explanation that Egk was a partial acronym of the name of his wife Elisabeth Karl, with the middle guttural added "for euphony."

Egk studied piano with Anna Hirzel-Langenhan and composition with Orff in Munich, where he moved permanently; primarily interested in theater music, wrote several scores for a Munich puppet theater; also active on the radio; wrote ballet music to his own scenarios and a number of successful operas. He was an opera conductor and music pedagogue; conducted at the Berlin State Opera (1938–41); headed the German Union of Composers (1941–45); commissioned for the Berlin Olympiad (1936), for which he received a Gold Medal, and by the Nazi Ministry of Propaganda. The apparent favor that Egk enjoyed during the Nazi reign made it necessary for him to stand trial before the Allied Committee for the de-Nazification proceedings in 1947; he was absolved of political taint. From 1950 to 1953 he was director of the Berlin Hochschule für Musik.

As a composer Egk continued the tradition of Wagner and R. Strauss, without excluding, however, the use of acidulous harmonies, based on the atonal extension of tonality; the rhythmic investiture of his works is often inventive and bold; best known for dramatic works; publ. an essay collection under the title *Musik, Wort, Bild* (Munich, 1960).

Egorov, Youri, b. Kazan, May 28, 1954; d. Amsterdam, Apr. 15, 1988. He was a precocious child who learned to play piano at home; at age 17 won a prize at the Long-Thibaud competition in Paris; 3 years later, received 3rd prize at the Tchaikovsky Competition in Moscow. In 1978 he made his N.Y. debut, followed by solo performances with various American orchs. He settled in the Netherlands, where his career was cut tragically short by AIDS.

eguale (It.). Equal; even, smooth.

eighth. 1. Octave. 2. Eighth note.

eilen (Ger.). Hasten, accelerate, go faster. *Eilend*, hastening, stringendo; *eilig*, hasty, hurriedly; rapid, swift.

ein (eins; Ger.). One.

Ein klein wenig langsamer, Takt wie vorher zwei (Ger.). A little bit slower, with 1 measure like 2 before (*doppio movimento*).

Einem, Gottfried von, b. Bern, Switzerland Jan. 24, 1918; d. Obern, Duvenbach, Austria, July 12, 1996. He went to Germany as a child; studied at Plön, Holstein; was opera coach at the Berlin State Opera. In 1938 he was arrested by the Gestapo and spent 4 months in prison; after his release, studied Blacher in Berlin (1941–43); went to Dresden (1944); became resident composer and music adviser at the Dresden State Opera; later active in Salzburg. In 1953 he visited the U.S.; then settled in Vienna; appointed prof. at the Hochschule für Musik there (1965).

Having absorbed the variegated idioms of advanced techniques, Einem produced a number of successful short operas and ballets; in his music he emphasized the dramatic element by dynamic and rhythmic effects; his harmonic idiom is terse and strident; his vocal line often borders on atonality, but remains singable. His best-known works are the operas: *Dantons Tod* after Büchner (Salzburg, 1947); *Der Prozess* after Kafka (Salzburg, 1953); *Der Zerrissene* after Nestroy (Hamburg, 1964); *Der Besuch der alten Dame*, libretto by Dürrenmatt (Vienna, 1971); *Kabale und Liebe* after Schiller (Vienna, 1976); and *Jesu Hochzeit* (Vienna, 1980; caused a scandal for depicting Christ as having taken a wife).

einfach (Ger.). Simple; simply; semplice.

Eingang (Einleitung; Ger.). Introduction.

Einklang (Ger.). Unison; consonance.

Einlage (Ger.). Interpolation; inserted piece.

Einleitung (Eingang; Ger.). Introduction.

Einsatz (Ger.). 1. Attack of a note. 2. Entrance of a vocal or instrumental part.

einstimmung (Ger.). Monophonic, 1-voiced.

eis (Ger.). E sharp.

Eisler, Hanns (Johannes), b. Leipzig, July 6, 1898; d. Berlin, Sept. 6, 1962. He began musical study on his own while still a youth; studied with Weigl at the New Vienna Cons. and later privately with Schoenberg (1919–23); also worked with Webern. In 1924 he won the Vienna Arts Prize; went to Berlin (1925); active in the German Communist Party. After the Nazis took power, he left Germany; eventually went to the U.S., where he taught (N.Y., Los Angeles) and composed for Hollywood films (won an Oscar for *Hangmen Also Die*); testified before the House Committee on Un-American Activities (1947); deported "voluntarily." In 1949 he settled in East Berlin; became a prof. at the Hochschule für Musik and member of the German Academy of the Arts.

Under Schoenberg's influence Eisler adopted the 12-tone method of composition for many of his sym. works; also demonstrated a capacity for writing accessible music. His long association with Bertolt Brecht resulted in several fine scores for the theater; his songs and choral works were popular and "officially sanctioned" in the German Democratic Republic; composed the East German national anthem, *Auferstanden aus Ruinen* (1949). His writings include *Composing for the Films* (with T. Adorno; N.Y., 1947), *Reden und Aufsätze* (Berlin, 1959), and *Materialen zu einer Dialektik der Musik* (Berlin, 1973). G. Mayer ed. his *Musik und Politik* (2 vols., Berlin, 1973, and Leipzig, 1982). He wrote the libretto for but never composed the opera *Johannes Faustus* (1952).

Eitner, Robert, b. Breslau, Oct. 22, 1832; d. Templin, Feb. 2, 1905. He was a pupil of M. Brosig in Breslau; settled in Berlin (1853) as a teacher; gave piano concerts of own works (1857–59); established a piano school (1863); publ. *Hilfsbuch beim Klavierunterricht* (1871). He devoted himself chiefly to musical literature, especially the music of the 16th and 17th centuries; founder of the Berlin Gesellschaft für Musikforschung, ed. its *Monatshefte für Musikgeschichte* (from 1869) and the *Publikationen älterer praktischer und theoretischer Musikwerke* (from 1873). His principal work is the great *Biographisch-bibliographisches Quellen-Lexikon der Musiker und Musikgelehrten bis zur Mitte des 19. Jahrhunderts* (10 vols., 1899–1904; additions and corrections publ. quarterly, 1913–16; rev. and enl. ed., 1959–60).

ektara (ektär; 1 string). Indian spike lute; formerly a bamboo stick bearing a single string attached to the center of a small drum; at present the stick is attached to a resonating gourd with a wooden bottom; the string is plucked and produces a drone.

élan, avec (Fr.; It. con slancio). With dash, energy.

élargissez (Fr.). Allargando.

Eldridge, (David) Roy "Little Jazz," b. Pittsburgh, Jan. 30, 1911; d. Valley Stream, N.Y., Feb. 26, 1989. In 1930 he went to N.Y.; worked with Teddy Hill and others; became a featured member of Fletcher Henderson's orch. (1935–36). With his brother Joe, saxophonist and arranger, he formed his own band in Chicago (1936); took it to N.Y. (1939); gained fame as a master trumpeter of the swing era. He played with the bands of Gene Krupa (1941–43) and Artie Shaw (1944–45); worked with Norman Granz's Jazz at the Philharmonic (from 1948); later worked with Benny Carter, Johnny Hodges, Ella Fitzgerald, and Coleman Hawkins; led his own big band and combos. Although plagued by ill health after 1980, he made occasional appearances as a singer, drummer, and pianist.

electric guitar. Electronic adaptation of the guitar, with solid body, metallic strings, and miniature pickup microphones replacing natural acoustic projection; widely used in modern popular music. Acoustic guitars with added pickup microphones are not considered true electric guitars.

electric organ. Electronic organ.

electric piano. Class of keyboard instruments whose sounds are produced electronically or reproduced electrically; applies to instruments ranging from amplified grand pianos to portable keyboards that use metal bars or computer technology to produce pianolike sounds.

electronic instruments. Class of instruments generally assignable to 1 of 4 categories: 1) original inventions (theremin, ondes Martenot); 2) altered or reinvented acoustic instruments (electric guitar, electronic organ); 3) acoustic instruments joined to MIDI or other electronic equipment (electronic viola); and 4) ordinary objects joined to electronic equipment, i.e., Trimpin's *Klompen* (wooden shoes).

The earliest surviving electronic instrument, the theremin, was demonstrated as the thereminovox by the Russian inventor, engineer, and cellist Leon Thérémin (Moscow, 1920). The apparatus consisted of a set of cathode tubes, a vertical antenna, and a metal arc; the sound was produced heterodynamically by the movement of the right hand, which changed the electric potential in the area, creating a differential tone that determined the height of pitch. The left hand manipulated the field in the vicinity of the metal arc, regulating the power and the timbre of the sound.Thérémin's invention was followed by a number of electronic instruments. In Germany, Jörg Mager (1880–1939) constructed an electronic organ called the Spherophon; later developed the more sophisticated Partiturophon and Kaleidophon. In France, Maurice Martenot invented the *ondes musicales* (musical waves; now called *ondes Martenot*), a keyboard electronic instrument for which music is still being written. The wire-based Trautonium (1930) was developed by Friedrich Trautwein (1888–1956); Hindemith wrote for it. Oscar Sala introduced some innovations to the Trautonium in an electronic organ which he called the Mixturtrautonium.

The most advanced electronic instruments belong to the synthesizer group, 1st developed in studio settings in the 1950s, commercially available in the 1960s; these can generate any desired pitch, any scale, any rhythm, any tone color, and any degree of loudness. They are the most sophisticated of electronic instruments based on analog principles; the development of personal computers has led to the evolution and refinement of computer music synthesis. See also ⇒computer music; musique concrète.

electronic music. Generic term for compositions created by electronic means. There are categories, listed chronologically: 1) early electrophones based on sound-wave manipulation (see ⇒electronic instruments); 2) manipulation of phonograph records; 3) musique concrète, using the tape recorder (invented during World War II); recorded sound is manipulated with editing, speed and direction alteration, loops, mixing, or processing; 4) analog synthesis, where sound and manipulation are entirely electronic, but largely by dial rather than switch; orig. synthesizers (Bell Labs) required a roomful of equipment; transistors allowed the invention of compact, even portable synthesizers, pioneered by Moog and Buchla; 5) live electronics, where sound is produced by onstage "instruments" in a one-to-one time relationship between action and result; 6) electroacoustic music, in which acoustically produced sound is processed in an interactive relationship with electronic equipment; 7) binary-controlled digital synthesis, using increasingly sophisticated and user-friendly computer equipment; modern recording techniques mean that a work can be entirely prerecorded and "performed" just by running the playback machine, or created entirely onstage, with random elements figuring in so that no performance of the work is similar to another. When required, electronic music notation is nontraditional; one of the earliest attempts was made in 1937 by Grainger in his *Free Music* for 4 electronic instruments constructed by Thérémin, indicating pitch and dynamic intensities in a 4-part score on graph paper; many so-called scores of electronic music are really listener or cueing guides, rather than "parts."

electronic organ. A powerful modern keyboard instrument activated not by pipes but by electronic means and capable of unlimited tone production.

electronic piano. Electric piano.

electrophones. Class of musical instruments that produce their sound by electric or electronic means.

elegy (Fr. *Élégie*; Ger. *Elegie*). Vocal or instrumental composition of a melancholy or nostalgic character, having no fixed form.

elevator music. Muzak.

elevazione, con (It.). In a lofty, elevated style.

Elgar, (Sir) Edward (William), b. Broadheath, near Worcester, June 2, 1857; d. Worcester, Feb. 23, 1934. He received his earliest music education from his father, a music shop owner and organist for the St. George's Roman Catholic Church in Worcester; also took violin lessons locally; rapidly acquired the fundamentals of music theory; served as arranger with the Worcester Glee Club, becoming its conductor at age 22;

simultaneously accepted an unusual position for an aspiring musician with the County of Worcester Lunatic Asylum at Powick, where he was for several years in charge of the institution's concert band. In 1885 he succeeded his father as organist at St. George's; married Caroline Alice Roberts in 1889; moved to Malvern (1891–1904); conducted the Worcestershire Phil. (1898–1904); accepted the position of Peyton Prof. of Music at the Univ. of Birmingham (1905); led the London Sym. Orch. (1911–12). He then settled in Hampstead; his beloved wife died in 1920, at which time he returned to Worcester, and his composing virtually ceased.

Elgar's 1st signal success was with the overture *Froissart* (Worcester, 1890); his cantata *The Black Knight* was produced at the Worcester Festival (1893) and heard in London at the Crystal Palace (1897); the production of his *Scenes from the Saga of King Olaf* (1896) attracted considerable attention; gained further recognition with the *Imperial March* (1897), composed for Queen Victoria's Diamond Jubilee; Elgar's name was now familiar to the musical public. There followed the cantata *Caractacus* (1898) and his great masterpiece, the oratorio *The Dream of Gerontius* (1900).

Elgar began to give more attention to orch. music. Hans Richter presented the 1st performance of Elgar's *Variations on an Original Theme* (called the *Enigma Variations*) in London (1899); the work consists of 14 sections, each marked by initials of fancied names for his friends; in later years he issued cryptic hints as to the identities of these persons, which were soon revealed. He also stated that the theme itself was a counterpoint to a familiar tune, but the concealed subject was never discovered; various guesses have been advanced in the musical press; even a contest for the most plausible answer to the riddle was launched in America by the *Saturday Review* (1953), with dubious results. The success of the *Enigma Variations* was followed by the *Pomp and Circumstance* marches, the 1st of which became his most famous piece through a setting to words by A. C. Benson, used in the *Coronation Ode* (1902) as *Land of Hope and Glory*. Other successful orch'l works are the *Cockaigne Overture* (1901), the Violin Concerto, premiered by Fritz Kreisler (1910), and the Cello Concerto (1919, Felix Salmond, soloist, composer conducting).

The emergence of Elgar as a major composer about 1900 was all the more remarkable given his lack of formal training; yet he developed a masterly technique of instrumental and vocal writing. His style of composition may be described as functional Romanticism: harmonic procedures firmly within the 19th-century tradition; formal elements always strong; thematic development logical and precise; a melodic gift, evident from his earliest works onward, such as *Salut d'amour*; his oratorios, particularly *The Apostles*, were the product of fervent religious faith (he was Roman Catholic). He avoided archaic usages of Gregorian chant and other Cecilianisms; instead presented sacred subjects in the communicative style of secular drama. His 2 syms. (1907–08, 1909–11) are among the greatest British exemplars of this genre; a draft for a 3rd has been realized and performed.

Elgar was the recipient of many honors: knighted (1904); received the Order of Merit (1911); made a Knight Commander of the Royal Victorian Order (1928) and a baronet (1931); appointed Master of the King's Musick (1924). He was not a proficient conductor, but appeared on many occasions and made recordings of his own works; during the 3rd of 4 visits to the U.S. (1905, 1906, 1907, 1911); conducted his oratorio *The Apostles* (1907); his link with the U.S. was secured when the hymnlike opening of his 1st *Pomp and Circumstance* march became a popular recession march for American high school graduation exercises.

Ellington, "Duke" (Edward Kennedy), b. Washington, D.C., Apr. 29, 1899; d. N.Y., May 24, 1974. He played ragtime as a boy; worked with jazz bands in Washington, D.C., during the 1910s and early 1920s; went to N.Y. (1923); organized a big band or orch. that he led in one form or another for the next half century. His ensembles revolutionized the concept of jazz; no longer restricted to small combos of 4–6 "unlettered" improvisers, the Ellington orch. played complex arrangements requiring both improvising skill and the ability to read scores; eventually these scores took on the dimensions and scope of classical compositions while retaining an underlying jazz feeling.

In the early days Ellington's chief collaborator in composition and arrangements was trumpeter James "Bubber" Miley (1903–32); baritone saxophonist Harry Carney (1910–74) was with the band from its inception until Ellington's death; other collaborators were Barney Bigard, Otto Hardwick, Harry James, and Ellington's son Mercer; from 1939 Ellington's main collaborator was pianist-composer Billy Strayhorn (1915–67). Among the many great musicians who played in the Ellington orch. were Sonny Greer, "Tricky Sam" Nanton, Carney, Fred Guy, Johnny Hodges, Ben Webster, Jimmy Blanton (the brilliant jazz double bassist who died at age 27 in 1942), Ray Nance, Cat Anderson, Paul Gonsalves, Jimmy Hamilton, and Russell Procope.

Ellington possessed a social elegance and the gift of articulate verbal expression that inspired respect; the recipient of the Presidential Medal of Freedom; made several European trips under the auspices of the State Dept.; toured Russia (1970) and Latin America, Japan, and Australia. So highly was he esteemed in Africa that the Republic of Togo issued in 1967 a postage stamp bearing his portrait; after his death his band was led by Mercer (b. Washington, D.C., Mar. 11, 1919; d. Copenhagen, Feb. 8, 1996).

Among Ellington's more than 1,000 compositions are *East St. Louis Toodle-Oo* (pronounced "toad-del-lo," 1926); *Black and Tan Fantasy* and *Creole Love Song* (1927); *Mood Indigo* (1930); *Sophisticated Lady* (using a whole-tone scale, 1932); *Diminuendo and Crescendo in Blue* (1937); *Black Brown and Beige* (a tonal panorama of African American history, 1943); *Liberian Suite* (1948); *My People*, commissioned for the 100th anniversary of the Emancipation Proclamation (1963); *1st Sacred Concert* (San Francisco, 1965); *2nd Sacred Concert* (N.Y., 1968); *The River*, ballet (1970); *Queenie Pie*, musical (completed and performed in Philadelphia, 1986).

Ellis, Alexander J(ohn), (born Sharpe), b. Hoxton (London), June 14, 1814; d. Kensington, Oct. 28, 1890. He studied at Trinity College, Cambridge (graduated 1837); studied mathematics, philology, and music; elected Fellow of the Royal Soc. (1864); president of the Philological Soc.; publ. valuable papers in the Proceedings of the Royal Society. He was awarded a silver medal for writings on musical pitch for the *Journal of the Soc. of the Arts*; these were publ. separately (1880–81) and in summary in the famous Appendix XX to the 2nd ed. (1885) of his trans. of Helmholtz's *Lehre von den Tonempfindungen*, entitled *On the Sensations of Tone, as a Physiological Basis for the Theory of Music*. Ellis's translation and commentary was profoundly influential on 20th-century experimentation with intonation systems.

Elman, Mischa, b. Talnoy, Jan. 20, 1891; d. N.Y., Apr. 5, 1967. At age 6 he was taken to Odessa; became a violin student of Fidelmann and a pupil of Brodsky; his progress was extraordinary; when Leopold Auer heard him play, he accepted him in his class at the St. Petersburg Cons. (1902); made his debut in St. Petersburg with sensational acclaim (1904); a German tour was equally successful; in 1905 he appeared in England, playing the Glazunov Violin Concerto. He made his American debut in N.Y. (1908); hailed as one of the greatest virtuosos of the time; played with every important U.S. orch.; with the Boston Sym. Orch. alone played at 31 concerts. In subsequent years he played all over the world, and, with Heifetz, became a synonym for violinistic prowess. His playing was the quintessence of Romantic interpretation, his tone mellifluous but resonant; he excelled particularly in the concertos of Mendelssohn, Tchaikovsky, and Wieniawski but could also give impressive performances of Beethoven and Mozart. A near disaster befell him during one of his concert tours. Mistakenly believing that the Beethoven concerto was scheduled on the program, he relaxed and let his violin rest loose on his left arm, in expectation of a long orch'l opening tutti; he was rudely jolted out of his siesta when the orch. struck the opening chord of the Mendelssohn Concerto, which has a very brief introduction. Conditioned by countless performances of this work, he launched into the correct concerto by automatic reflex. He publ. several violin arrangements of Classic and Romantic pieces and composed some playable short compositions for his instrument.

embellishment. See ⇒grace.

embouchure (Fr.). 1. Mouthpiece of a wind instrument. 2. Manipulation of lips and tongue in playing a wind instrument.

Emmett, Daniel Decatur, b. Mt. Vernon, Ohio, Oct. 29, 1815; d. there, June 28, 1904. He began his career as a drummer in military bands; joined the Virginia Minstrels, singing and playing the banjo; later a member of Bryant's Minstrels. He wrote and premiered *Dixie* in 1859 (N.Y.); upon publication, its popularity spread; adopted as a Southern fighting song during the Civil War (despite Emmett's being a Northerner); other songs, e.g., *Old Dan Tucker, The Road to Richmond, Walk Along*, etc., enjoyed great favor but were eclipsed by *Dixie*.

Empfindsamer Stil (Ger.). German aesthetic movement developed in the mid–18th century; its adjectival form, *empfindsam*, was invented by the German writer Lessing as an equivalent to the English word *sentimental* (popularized by Laurence Sterne's unfinished *Sentimental Journey*). This "sensitive" or "sentimental" style superseded the Aristotelian striving for compositional unity characteristic of the late German Baroque; despite superficial similarities, it stood in opposition to the contemporary French style galant and rococo, which emphasized elegance of form and substance rather than feeling.

Empfindung, mit (Ger.). With emotion; full of feeling.

Emporté (Fr.). Carried away, passionately, emotionally.

en animant (Fr.). Animatedly. *En avant* (Fr., advancing), getting faster; *en cédant* (Fr., receding), slowing down; *en dehors* (Fr., outside), emphasizing or bringing out the melody; *en élargissant*, allargando; *en mesure*, misurato.

enchainez (Fr.). Go directly to next section without stopping; attacca.

enclume (Fr.). Anvil.

encore (Fr., again!). 1. Used in English when recalling an actor or singer to the stage; the French cry "Bis!" 2. Piece or performance repeated or added to the scheduled program.

endless melody (Ger., unendliche Melodie). Wagner's term for an uninterrupted melodic flow unhampered by sectional cadences. Particularly characteristic is the flow of one leitmotiv into another with a free interchange of voices and instrumental parts. With the decline of the Wagnerian cult in the 20th century, endless melody lost much of its attraction; recent operas gravitate toward a Verdian concept of well-adorned separate numbers.

energia, con (It.; Fr. *avec énergie*; Ger. *energisch*). With energy and decision; energetically; a passage so marked is to be vigorously accented and distinctly phrased.

Enesco, Georges (born George Enescu), b. Liveni-Virnav, Aug. 19, 1881; d. Paris, May 4, 1955. He began playing the piano at age 4; began composing at 5; studied with Caudella; in 1889, made his formal debut as a violinist in Slanic, Moldavia. He had meanwhile enrolled in the Cons. of the Gesellschaft der Musikfreunde in Vienna (1888); studied violin with S. Bachrich, J. Grun, and J. Hellmesberger, Jr., and harmony, counterpoint, and composition with R. Fuchs; won 1st prizes in violin and harmony (1892); after graduation (1894) entered the Paris Cons.; studied violin with Marsick and J. White, harmony with Dubois and Thomas, counterpoint with Gedalge, and composition with Fauré and Massenet; won 2nd *accessit* for counterpoint and fugue (1897); graduated with the *premier prix* for violin (1899); also studied cello, organ, and piano, attaining more than ordinary proficiency on each.

In 1897 Enesco presented in Paris a concert of his works; attracted the attention of Colonne, who publ. the composer's op. 1, *Poème roumain*, the next year. Enesco launched a conducting career in Bucharest (1898); 1st appeared as a violinist in Berlin and organized a piano trio (1902); formed a quartet (1904). He conducted the premiere of *Two Rumanian Rhapsodies* in Bucharest (1903), the 1st of which became his most celebrated work; appointed court violinist to the Queen of Rumania. He established an annual prize for Rumanian composers (1912); founded the George Enescu sym. concerts in Iai (1917).

After World War I Enesco toured as a violinist and conductor; taught violin in Paris; pupils included Menuhin, Grumiaux, Gitlis, and Ferras; made his U.S. debut in the triple role of conductor, violinist, and composer with the Philadelphia Orch. in N.Y.

(1923). He returned to conduct the N.Y. Phil. (1937); led several of its concerts with remarkable success (14 concerts in 1938); appeared twice as solo violinist; conducted 2 concerts at the N.Y. World's Fair (1939). The outbreak of World War II found him in Rumania, where he lived on his farm in Sinaia, near Bucharest; visited N.Y. again in 1946 as a teacher. In 1950, during the 60th anniversary season of his debut as violinist, Enesco gave a farewell concert with the N.Y. Phil. in the capacities of violinist, pianist, conductor, and composer: Bach's Double Violin Concerto (with Menuhin), a violin sonata (accompanying Menuhin), and his *1st Rumanian Rhapsody* (conducting); returned to Paris; his last years were marked by near poverty and poor health; in 1954 he suffered a stroke; remained an invalid until his death.

Although Enesco had severed relations with his Communist homeland, the Rumanian government paid homage to him; his native village, a street in Bucharest, and the State Phil. of Bucharest were renamed in his honor. Periodical Enesco festivals and international performing competitions were established in Bucharest in 1958. He had an extraordinary range of musical interests. His compositions include artistic stylizations of Rumanian folk strains; while his style was neo-Romantic, he made occasional use of experimental devices, e.g., quarter-tones in *Oedipe* (1921–31; premiered Paris Opéra, 1936). Possessing a fabulous memory, he performed innumerable works without scores; distinguished himself as a violinist and conductor; also a fine pianist and a gifted teacher; contributed significantly to instrumental music of the 20th century.

Engel, Lehman, b. Jackson, Miss., Sept. 14, 1910; d. N.Y., Aug. 29, 1982. He began to take piano lessons locally; studied with Sidney Durst at the Cincinnati College of Music (1927–29) and Eduardo Trucco in N.Y.; took composition with R. Goldmark at the Juilliard School of Music (1930–34) and Sessions (1931–37). While still a student he wrote music for ballet and theatrical plays; wrote incidental music for O'Casey's play *Within the Gates* (1934), which he conducted.

Engel led the Madrigal Singers for the Works Progress Administration (1935–39); worked with the Mercury Theater as composer and conductor. During World War II he enlisted in the U.S. Navy and conducted a military orch. at Great Lakes Naval Training Station; later appointed chief composer of the Navy's film division in Washington, D.C. He wrote and conducted for many Broadway productions, among them T. S. Eliot's *Murder in the Cathedral* and Tennessee Williams's *A Streetcar Named Desire*.

As a composer Engel was happiest writing for the theater, with a special knack for vivid musical illustration of the stage action; was active as a composition teacher; led a N.Y. seminar on musical lyrics. He conducted the 1st American performance of Weill's *The Threepenny Opera*; conducted productions of *Showboat*, *Brigadoon*, *Annie Get Your Gun*, *Fanny*, *Guys and Dolls*, and *Carousel*. He received 2 Tony Awards: for conducting Menotti's opera *The Consul* (1950) and for conducting the operettas of Gilbert and Sullivan (1953). Of importance are his numerous books on American music theater.

English horn (Fr. *cor anglais*; Ger. *englisches Horn*; It. *corno inglese*). Alto oboe in F, transposing a 5th below the written note. It is unclear how this instrument, not of English origin,

acquired its name; the French name may well be a corruption of *cor anglé* (angled horn), but its double-reed mouthpiece is attached to a bent crook rather than placed at an angle. The other distinctive element is the bulb bell. The sound of the English horn suggests a variety of moods, from a pastoral scene to an ominous premonition of unknown danger; its range is from E below middle C to about C an octave above middle C.

The English horn does not blend very well with other instruments in an ensemble and is used mostly for solo parts; it intones the Alpine song after the storm in Rossini's overture to *William Tell* and sounds the shepherd's pipe in the 3rd act of Wagner's *Tristan und Isolde*. Franck shocked French academicians by including the English horn in the score of his Sym., for the instrument was regarded as unsymphonic. Sibelius assigns to the English horn the role of the mortuary messenger in his symphonic poem *The Swan of Tuonela* (Tuonela is the kingdom of death in Finnish mythology). The English horn has had an increasing role in 20th-century orch'l music, with concertos written for virtuoso specialists.

enharmonic equivalence (equivalents). Property of notes that sound the same in the tempered scale but are notated differently; C sharp and D flat are enharmonically equivalent, as are D sharp and E flat, or E sharp and F natural. Technically, pianists do not have to worry about enharmonic equivalents on an equally tempered keyboard. String players, however, have to grope for their sharps and flats to stay within the tempered scale; for them, the descending augmented second (e.g., E to D flat) is actually larger than the descending minor 3rd (E to C sharp), even though the 2 intervals are enharmonically equivalent in theory; harmonic context is the determining factor.

In chromatic modulation, proper enharmonic notation is of essence. A dominant-7th chord can, without changing a note, be transformed into a chord containing a doubly-augmented 4th and an augmented 6th; this chord demands resolution into the tonic $^6/_4$ chord of a new tonality. Such an enharmonic change occurs, for instance, in the coda of Chopin's Scherzo in B-flat Minor (op. 31), where a chord normally perceived as the dominant-7th chord in the key of D (from the root, A–C sharp–E–G) is reinterpreted as its enharmonic equivalent, a German augmented-6th chord (B double flat–D flat–E–G), followed by the cadential $^6/_4$ chord in D-flat major, with brilliant effect.

Chromatic harmony thrives on enharmonic chords, the most chameleonic of which, the diminished-7th chord, can be written in 24 different ways. Depending on the arrangement of sharps, double sharps, flats, and double flats, it can lead into any of the 24 major and minor tonalities; this ambiguity and unpredictability made the diminished-7th chord the darling of the Romantic composers. The equivalence of the augmented 4th (diabolus in musica of the Middle Ages) with the diminished 5th (a perfectly respectable interval) is of fundamental importance in the theory of scales; the leap upward from subdominant to leading tone was taboo in strict counterpoint, but the downward skip from subdominant to leading tone, with its inevitable resolution to the tonic, is a cliché of Classic music. Enharmonically equivalent intervals or chords are musical counterparts of linguistic puns.

The doctrine of enharmonic equivalence lost its practical significance in notation with the advent of organized atonality as promulgated by Schoenberg in his method of composition with

12 tones related only to one another. Sharps and flats became interchangeable, double flats and double sharps were discarded, and, in the cycle of scales, such remote pitches as B sharp or E sharp and F flat or C flat vanished from modern spelling:

B is a B is a B is a B,
And never C flat will it be.
C is a C is a C is a C,
And never B sharp will it be.
B double flat is nonsensical
When we know it's just plain old A.
And why be unduly forensical,
Insisting that G double sharp is not A?

enharmonic genus (from Grk. *en* + *harmonia*, in the melody). In Greek theory, a tetrachord that includes 2 consecutive intervals, each approximating a quarter tone: 1/1 – 28/27 – 16/15 – 4/3.

Eno, Brian (Peter George St. John le Baptiste de la Salle), b. Woodbridge, Suffolk, May 15, 1948. Interested in tape recorders and recorded music at an early age, he received no formal music training; studied at Ipswich and Winchester art schools (1964–69); involved in avant-garde experiments, performing works by La Monte Young and Cardew. He helped found the art-rock band Roxy Music (1971); left it 2 years later for a solo career that resulted in 4 modestly successful progressive-rock albums during the mid-'70s. In 1975, confined to bed after being struck by a London taxi, he was also struck by the pleasures of minimalism, shifting his style to what he has termed "ambient," a sort of art-music Muzak. He has collaborated with David Bowie, Talking Heads, and U2; in 1979 he became interested in video, subsequently producing "video paintings" and "video sculptures" to serve as ambient music and visuals in galleries, museums, airport terminals, and private homes. His work has influenced both New Wave and New Age genres.

ensemble (Fr., together). 1. Since 1600, a group of instrumental players and/or vocalists performing together; usually applied to a smaller group of players, larger than a duet but smaller than a chamber orch. 2. Style or quality of a group's performance, especially accuracy of attack and decay.

entr'acte (Fr., between acts). Light instrumental composition or short ballet for performance between acts of theater, music, and dance works; often found in Lully's collaborations with Molière.

entrata (It.; Fr. *entrée*). 1. Orch'l prelude to a ballet, following the overture. 2. Music played for dancers' entrances in the 16th- and 17th-century French ballet. 3. Division in a ballet, like a scene in a play. 4. Old polonaiselike dance, usually in 4/4 time.

entropy. The luxuriant development of chromatic harmony and the concomitant equalization of enharmonic pairs may be described as musical entropy, in which the component thematic particles become evenly distributed in melody and harmony. In physics, entropy signalizes the dissipation of kinetic energy, neutralization of electric potentials, and an ultimate thermodynamic stability of inertial matter. The pessimistic cosmology that postulates the eventual end in a total passivity of the universe does not, however, constitute a categorical imperative for composers; nothing prevents them from reversing the entropic process and reinstating the primacy of selected modalities. Verdi said: "Torniamo all'antico: sara un progresso."

entrüstet (Ger.). Indignant.

entschieden (entschlossen; Ger.). Resolutely, in a determined manner, decisively.

envelope. Shape of a sound's amplitude, changing over time; an important determinant of sound quality.

environ (Fr., in the neighborhood of). Approximately; usually follows a metronome marking.

environment. The concept of musical environment embraces the totality of technical resources. Ideally the function of a composer is to establish a favorable environment for these techniques and apply powerful detergents to remove accumulated tonal impurities. Particularly toxic for tonality is chromatic supererogation; conversely, a fine atonal work may suffer from excessive triadic infusion. The environment also includes the parameters of vectorialism; spatial arrangement of instruments on stage is clearly environmental in its function. In this larger sense the function of environment comprises not only every technical aspect of musical composition, but also the conditions of the performance itself.

epanalepsis. Rhetoric device, often applied to Baroque music, in which the opening of a melody or musical period serves as its closing; symploche.

epic opera (epic theater). Highly stylized theatrical form in which a technique called the alienation effect (A-effect) is employed to keep an audience aware of theatrical artifice and unable to identify with characters or experience Aristotelian catharsis; an aesthetic developed most prominently by Brecht, who collaborated with Weill, Eisler, and Dessau.

epigonism (from Grk. *epi* + *gignesthai*, born after). In Greek mythology and history *epigone* was applied to descendants of the 7 heroic warriors who conquered Thebes. A historical phenomenon in the arts, it has been characterized by emergence of a considerable number of capable artists, writers, or musicians who consciously or unconsciously adopt a mode of formal composition that constitutes a logical continuation of the accomplishments of a master who inspired them. In modern usage epigonism has acquired derogatory connotations, referring to a mediocre follower of a great artist.

A perfect example of musical epigonism is the career of Siegfried Wagner (1869–1930), the "little son of a great father." He wrote very Wagnerian operas that totally lack the greatness that Siegfried's father Richard infused into his music dramas. When Bülow called R. Strauss "Richard the 2nd," it was not meant derogatorially, but rather to elevate him to the great legacy of Richard the 1st, Wagner. Even though Strauss adopted many Wagnerian dramatic devices, his works are so powerful and individual that it would be a misnomer to apply "epigone" to him. A more typical Wagnerian epigone was August Bungert, who wrote 2 operatic tetralogies built on the model of *Der Ring des Nibelungen*, to librettos drawn from Homer; his elucubrations are pathetic examples of infertile futility.

Adoption of a certain method of composition established by a great master is not necessarily the mark of an epigone. Many contemporary composers used Schoenberg's 12-tone method as a starting point, among them such superb musicians as Webern and Berg, who certainly cannot be described as epigones. Nor does a return to the techniques of a much earlier era constitute epigonism. Stravinsky adopted Baroque techniques, but it would be erroneous to regard his neoclassical works as epigonic products; imitators of Stravinsky's emulation of the Baroque are epigones, in fact, epigones once removed. Indeed, in order to justify the introduction of a historical or aesthetic category such as epigonism, one must establish a direct line of succession from a great innovative master to less gifted followers. Debussy was such a great master, and his epigones are legion. Thousands of composers in the latter 18th century imitated Handel without creating a distinct movement of epigonism; millions of composers imitated Mendelssohn in the latter 19th century, but could not legitimately be called epigones in the aesthetic sense. Boccherini was derisively described as "the wife of Haydn" because of the close kinship of his musical idiom to that of Haydn, but it would be misleading to call him an epigone.

episode. Intermediate or incidental section; in the fugue, a digression from the principal theme interpolated between statements of the latter.

Epistle sonata. Instrumental work performed in church before the reading of an Epistle from the New Testament.

epithalamium (Grk., at the bedroom). Nuptial ode or festive wedding hymn.

equabile (It.). Equable; even, uniform.

equal temperament. Precise logarithmic division of the octave into a predetermined number of tones; specifically, a scale based on 12 equal semitones (called 12-equal temperament), where a semitone equals the 12th root of 2. Equal temperament has lain at the foundation of Western music since the mid-18th century. It enables the performer to play (or a composer to write) a tune without intervallic distortion in any transposition, but it inevitably departs from untempered acoustical purity for all intervals except the octave itself. Before equal temperament, numerous attempts were made throughout the centuries to reconcile untempered (pure, rational) intervals with tempered ones. There being no perfect solution, the compromise of equal tuning on keyboard instruments meant that the intervals of the perfect 5th, perfect 4th, 3rds, and 2nds were made deliberately out of tune. The deviations are fairly small, and the ear easily accommodates itself to the margin of error; but the impurity of intervals within equal temperament is easily perceived by playing a perfect 5th on the piano and listening to peculiar acoustical "beats," occurring 47 times a minute. Since string instruments

are tuned in pure 5ths, string players naturally avoid playing double stops on open strings when they play chamber music with piano accompaniment; otherwise, the difference between untempered and equally tempered intervals becomes plainly audible.

equal voices. Voices of the same class, i.e., women's and boy's (soprano and alto), or men's (tenor and bass).

equivocal chord. Dissonant chord of uncertain resolution, e.g., the diminished 7th.

ergriffen (Ger.). Affected, stirred.

erhaben (Ger.). Lofty, exalted.

Erkel, Franz (Ferenc), b. Gyula, Nov. 7, 1810; d. Budapest, June 15, 1893. He studied in Pozsony (Bratislava) at the Benedictine Gymnasium (1822–25) and with Heinrich Klein; went to Koloszvar; began his career as a pianist; became conductor of the Kaschau opera troupe (1834), with which he traveled to Buda (1835). He became conductor of the German Municipal Theater in Pest (1836); music director of the newly founded National Theater (1838–74); conductor at the Opera House (from 1884); founded and led the Phil. concerts (1853–71). He was the 1st prof. of piano and instrumentation at the Academy of Music and its director from 1875–88; gave his farewell performance as pianist (1890) and conductor (1892).

Erkel was one of the most significant Hungarian musicians of his era; after successfully producing *Báthory Mária* (1840), gained lasting fame in his homeland with *Hunyady László* (1844), recognized as the 1st truly national Hungarian theater work; composed the Hungarian national anthem (1844). He later achieved extraordinary success with opera *Bánk Bán* (1861), written in collaboration with his sons Gyula (1842–1909) and Sándor (1846–1900); also collaborated with his other sons, Elek (1843–93) and László (1844–96), all successful musicians.

erklingen (Ger.). Resound.

ermattend (ermattet; Ger.). Wearily, exhaustedly.

ernst (ernsthaft; Ger.). Earnestly, gravely.

eroico, -a (It.). Heroic; strong and dignified.

Erotik (Ger.). Romance or sentimental melody, as found in Grieg; without sexual connotation.

erregt (Ger.). Excitedly.

erschüttert (Ger.). Shaken, agitated.

Erstaufführung (Ger.). Premiere; usually a local performance, as distinguished from Uraufführung, a world premiere.

Erzählung (Ger.). Story, tale, narration.

es (Ger.). E flat.

es-Dur (Ger.). E-flat major.

es-moll (Ger.). E-flat minor.

esaltato (esaltazione, con; It.). With exaltation; in a lofty, fervent style.

escapement (Fr. *échappement*; Ger. *Auslösung*; It. *scappamento*). Part of a piano action that lets the hammer disengage from the striking mechanism and then rebound away from the string while the key remains held down. Except for a few early piano designs, pianos have included escapements since Cristofori (late 17th century).

Eschenbach,Christoph, (born Ringmann), b. Breslau, Feb. 20, 1940. He began studying piano at age 8 with his foster mother; formal piano training commenced with Eliza Hansen in Hamburg, eventually at the Hochschule für Musik; studied piano with Hans-Otto Schmidt in Cologne; studied conducting with Wilhelm Brückner-Rüggeberg at the Hamburg Hochschule für Musik; won 1st prize in the Steinway Piano Competition (1952); 2nd prize in the Munich International Competition (1962); captured 1st prize in the 1st Clara Haskil Competition in Montreux (1965).

Eschenbach made his London debut (1966); following studies with Szell (1967–69), the latter invited him to debut as soloist in Mozart's Piano Concerto in F Major, K. 459, with the Cleveland Orch. (1969); in subsequent years made numerous tours as a pianist, appearing in all major music centers of the world; gave duo concerts with pianist Justus Frantz. In 1972 he began to make appearances as a conductor (1972); made his debut as an opera conductor in Darmstadt with *La Traviata* (1978); pursued a successful career as both a pianist and a conductor, sometimes conducting from the keyboard. After serving as Generalmusikdirektor of the Rheinland-Pfalz State Phil. (1979–81), was 1st permanent guest conductor of the Zurich Tonhalle Orch. (1981–82), then its chief conductor (1982–85); became music director of the Houston Sym. Orch. (1988). He maintains a varied repertoire in both capacities; his sympathies range from standard literature to cosmopolitan avant-garde.

esclamato (It.). Exclaimed; forcibly declaimed.

esecuzione (It.). Execution, performance.

esercizio (It.; plural *esercizi*). Exercise; D. Scarlatti's sonatas were called *esercizio per gravicembalo.*

esitando (It.). Hesitatingly.

espandendosi (espansione, con; It.). Growing broader and fuller; with growing intensity; expansively.

espirando (It.). Dying away, expiring.

esposizione (It.). Exposition.

espressione, con (espressivo; It.). Expressively; with an intimate melodic feeling. *Con molto espressione*, with great expressiveness.

esquisse (Fr.). Sketch.

estampie (Fr.; It. *stampitas*; Prov. *estampida*). Medieval instrumental composition developed by troubadours in the 13th and 14th centuries. Primarily in ternary meter, the estampie is divided into several sections called *puncta* (melodic units); different endings are provided for each repetition of a punctum, similar to the indications of *prima volta* and *seconda volta* in the repeat sections in Classic music. Most likely the original estampies were dances; many also had texts.

estinguendo (estinto; It.). Extinguishing, dying away; barely audible, enfeebled; very softly; extreme pianissimo.

estompé (Fr.). Softened.

estremamente (It.). Extremely.

estro (It.). Inspiraton. *Estro poetico*, poetic fervor.

Et incarnatus. Portion of the Credo from the Roman Catholic High Mass, often set separately in large-scale works.

Ethiopian songs. Blackface minstrelsy songs written for white performers such as Christy's Minstrels in the 19th century; an example is Stephen Foster's *Old Folks at Home*. "Ethiopian" also described songs and musicals by African American composers at the turn of the 20th century.

ethnic resources. National musical cultures develop from 2 distinct resources: the ethnic legacy and universally adopted techniques of composition. When Villa-Lobos was asked "What is folklore?" he replied, "I am folklore!" By this he meant that in his original melodic inventions he was giving expression to the artistic consciousness of the Brazilian people. In his *Bachianas brasileiras*, Bachian counterpoint gives ancillary service to ethnic Brazilianism. Ives created single-handedly a modern American idiom that employs ethnic resources in a perfect syncretism of substance and technique. In the USSR the primacy of ethnic resources was maintained partly by the national spirit of the people and partly by the ideological principles of socialist realism, which prescribed realistic style of music within the framework of national modalities. Ethnic musical materials are not always incompatible with modern techniques, as Bartók demonstrated; perhaps the most congenial modern technique for making use of ethnic resources is expressionism, in which tonal functions are preserved and enhanced.

ethnomusicology. Relatively new term, replacing comparative musicology, to describe the rigorous study of traditional music of all peoples. The primary area of research has been non-European music that once would have been labeled "exotic" in times past, such as Asia, Africa, and South America. The initial focus was on recording music of various groups and then bringing it to university departments for analysis. Instruments were gathered for organological purposes or simply to play them. The invention of videotape allowed dance, ceremony, and other visually oriented elements to be recorded for study. In recent years the Eurocentric approach has been severely challenged by more anthropologically and sociologically oriented researchers who try to understand a people's music within its total context; additionally, Euro-American "folk music" has been properly renamed "traditional music" when the element of oral transmission predominates.

ethos. Doctrine of music philosophy postulating that each mode corresponds to a particular state of mind; its classical exposition was given by Plato, who taught that the Dorian mode was noble, elevated, and masculine, the Phyrgian passionate, the Lydian feminine, plaintive, and seductive, etc. Medieval theorists adapted this system to ecclesiastical modes, not realizing that ancient Greek modes were scaled in descending order, so that the progression of intervals was reversed; thus the masculine virtue of the Greek Dorian, representing the descending "white-key" scale E to E, was attributed to the ecclesiastical ascending "white-key" scale D to D.

The doctrine of ethos was applied in later periods, with great changes. Many composers of Classic and Romantic periods, impressed by the whiteness of the C-major scale on the piano keyboard, often selected that key to represent immaculate virtue, magnanimity, and strength; F major was associated with pastoral scenes, minor keys reserved for themes of melancholy, unrequited love, and world malaise; Tchaikovsky, obsessed by the inexorability of Fate, used a disproportionate percentage of minor keys in his music.

étincelant (Fr.). Sparkling.

etiology. Causation, or etiology, is of importance not only in the study of medicine and physics but also of fine arts. Particularly informative is the etiology of ultramodern music, often likened by detractors to a symptom of mass dyscrasia; but to its adepts, new music is the revelation of a superior psyche. Dostoyevsky, who suffered from epilepsy, advanced the daring notion that during an epileptic grand mal the mind penetrates the ultimate mysteries of life and death. Similarly, the manifestations of the musical avant-garde, whether in popular or technically complex field, are to their participants the proleptic vistas of a new universal art. Schoenberg, more than any other composer, endured endless abuse on the part of uncomprehending critics, but he never doubted the correctness of his chosen path; Varèse, similarly abused, wrote in a letter (1931): "I know where I am going, and what will follow. My plan is clearly drawn, its development logical, its result assured." From a historical perspective both men proved right; the etiology of their genius is a lesson for the future.

étouffé (Fr.). Stifled, muted. *Étouffoir*, a mute.

étude (study; Fr. *étude*; It. *studio*; Ger. *Studie, Etüde*). Exercise or study; 1st applied exclusively to technical exercises; in the 19th century its connotations were enlarged. Études proper, designed for improvement of technique, were called exercises and were usually in the form of simple melodic and rhythmic sequences, scales, trills, arpeggios, and other technical passages. Études evolved into full-fledged compositions, often requiring brilliant displays of technique in bravura style. Clementi's *Gradus ad Parnassum* (Steps to Mount Parnassus, the dwelling of the Muses), and Czerny's numerous collections of piano exercises established a more elevated type of étude in which purely technical devices were subordinated to the musical conception. Czerny's most famous collection is *Die Schule der*

Fingerfertigkeit (School of Finger Readiness, also called School of Velocity). Études fit for public performance were called *études de concert*. Chopin elevated the genre to romantic grandeur in his 2 series of piano études; Schumann's *Études symphoniques* for piano are neither études nor symphonic compositions, but variations on a theme; Liszt promulgated a superior type of étude in his 12 *Études d'execution transcendante*; Scriabin followed Chopin's model in his own group of studies, as did Debussy. In all these advanced forms, technical aspects of the étude became merely the means toward the creation of piano works in a bravura manner. Violin virtuosos, above all Paganini, wrote brilliant études for the violin; cellists and other instrumentalists composed études for their own instruments.

étude de concert (Fr.). Étude designed for public performance.

etwas (Ger.). Rather, somewhat. *Etwas vorwärts gebend*, poco più mosso.

Euler, Leonhard, b. Basel, Apr. 15, 1707; d. St. Petersburg, Sept. 18, 1783. He was prof. of mathematics at St. Petersburg (1733) and Berlin (1741); publ. important works on music theory and acoustics, chief among them being *Tentamen novae theoriae musicae* (St. Petersburg, 1739); the 1st to employ logarithms to explain differences in pitch; this would later prove essential to the theory of equal temperament.

euphonious harmony. Tonal combinations that contain only concords and mild discords, avoiding major 7ths or minor 2nds, acoustically the sharpest dissonances. (The ratio of vibration is 16/15 for a minor 2nd and 15/8 for the major 7th.) Thus all chords consisting of whole tones or their multiples are by definition euphonious; all 7th chords built on the supertonic, mediant, dominant, submediant, or the leading tone in major are euphonious; but the tonic 7th and subdominant 7th chords, which have a major 7th from their base, are uneuphonious. All diminished-7th chords are euphonious; this distinction is very important because chromatic harmony (e.g., in the introduction to Wagner's *Tristan und Isolde*) uses chords of the augmented-6th, chords containing multiples of whole tones, and dominant-7th chords.

euphonium (Grk., good sounding). Instrument of the brass family, with a tapered bore of wide scale and a deep cup-shaped mouthpiece, and 3 or 4 valves; considered the tenor of the tuba family, with the range of a trombone or baritone. It is commonly found in military bands, rarely in classical orchs.

euphony (Grk., good sound). Despite its etymology, euphony is not always synonymous with consonance. A succession of dissonances, if they follow a natural tonal sequence, may sound entirely euphonious to the ear, while a progression of disembodied open 5ths or disemboweled multiple octaves could register as uneuphonious and unsettling. Psychological apperception is the determining factor in this aural impression. Generally, soft dissonances are better tolerated than loud consonances. Even more decisive is the factor of linear euphony; a single line of atonal melody can impress an untutored ear as unacceptably dissonant, even though no simultaneous complex of sounds is involved. If an atonal melody were to be performed very slowly with long silences between individual notes, no linear disharmony would result; but the faster the tempo, the more disruptive an atonal melody becomes. (Remember that *harmonia* means "melody" in ancient Greek music.) A rapid succession of tones unconnected by a uniform tonality will sound like a meaningless jumble of notes to inexperienced listeners; but musicians trained to listen to serial music will accept atonal melodies as legitimate expressions of musical sentiment.

The linearity of melody depends exclusively on the instant dampening of a sound in the cochlea (free of tinnitus); but the memory of the previous sound persists, much as the retina of the eye retains the static images of a cinematographic film. One may speculate on the nature of musical art if the cochlea, too, could retain sounds for a fraction of a second; suffice it to say that all music, whether vocal, instrumental, or percussive, would become polyphonic or heterophonic.

Europe, James Reese, b. Mobile, Ala., Feb. 22, 1881; d. Boston, May 10, 1919 (stabbed to death by a disgruntled drummer in his band). He studied violin and piano as a child in Washington, D.C.; went to N.Y.; directed musical comedies; found the Clef Club (1910), a union and contracting agency for black musicians, as well as the Clef Club Sym. Orch., which performed works by black composers at Carnegie Hall (1912–14). He was music director and composer for dancers Irene and Vernon Castle (1914–17); wrote the 1st fox trot for them; wrote songs for musicals and composed dances and marches for his orchs. and bands. Although his music predates true jazz, Europe's syncopated rags and dances were the 1st African American music heard in the Old World, where he led a military band during American participation in World War I; they caused a sensation.

eurythmics (*eurhythmics*). System of musical training introduced by Jaques-Dalcroze (1910) in which pupils were taught to represent and experience complex rhythmic movement with their entire bodies, to the accompaniment of specially composed or improvised music.

evaded cadence. Deceptive cadence. See ⇒cadence.

Evans, Bill (William John), b. Plainfield, N.J., Aug. 16, 1929; d. N.Y., Sept. 15, 1980. After taking up piano, he joined Miles Davis's group and soon became a leading jazz pianist; after making the classic recording *Kind of Blue* with Davis (1959), formed his own trio. He received Grammy awards for his recordings *Conversations with Myself* (1963), *Alone* (1970), and *The Bill Evans Album* (1971). Evans played jazz in a cool, sophisticated, and somewhat intellectual manner.

Evans, (Ian Ernest) Gil(more Green), b. Toronto, May 13, 1912; d. Cuernavaca, Mexico, Mar. 20, 1988. He went to Calif. as a youth; largely self-taught in music; after leading a band in Stockton (1933–38), went to N.Y.; made arrangements of popular songs for non-jazz instruments; became a proponent of cool jazz; collaborated frequently with Miles Davis (from 1948); made arrangements for other groups, and recorded his own albums. As he moved toward an increasingly complex modernity, he applied polyharmonic and polyrhythmic procedures to his arrangements; with Ellington, Henderson, Don Sebesky, and a few others, one of the greatest jazz orchestrators.

Evensong (Evening Prayer). In the Anglican church, a daily service said or sung at evening; known as Vespers in the Roman Catholic Church.

Everly Brothers. (Vocal/guitar: Don E., b. Brownie, Ky., Feb. 1, 1937; vocal/guitar: Phil E., b. Brownie, Ky., Jan. 19, 1939.) Don appeared at age 8 on a radio show directed by their parents at Shenandoah, Iowa; both Don and Phil toured with their parents around the country; moved to Nashville, Tenn.; began playing rock 'n' roll, mixing in rhythm and blues, pop, and country-western. Among their many hits were *Bye Bye Love*, *Wake Up Little Susie, All I Have to Do Is Dream*, and *Cathy's Clown*; alas, brotherly love did not last forever, as they split up (1973); despite the impasse, their fraternal records survived and continued to provide joy to a new generation of bobby-soxers and hippie mates. They reunited for a concert at London's Royal Albert Hall (1983); since then have broken up and reunited several times, never attaining the success of their earlier years.

evolution and devolution. Herbert Spencer once defined the process of evolution as an integration of matter and concomitant dissipation of motion, during which matter passes from an indefinite, incoherent homogeneity to a definite, coherent heterogeneity. He specifically included music in this process, referring to the increasing complexity resulting from rhythmic changes and modulatory progressions, tied in with its specialization and gradual differentiation from poetry, drama, and dance. In recent times, however, the evolutionary process has been reversed; once more, as in antiquity, music has entered into an intimate association with theater and dance in modern mixed media; aleatory procedures have accentuated the devolution process by increasing the element of homogeneity and the degree of randomness of distribution of constructive elements.

It may be said that devolution was unavoidable, since the Spencerian integration of music achieved a maximum of coherence in the dodecaphonic method; a recoil from the stone wall of determinism reversed the evolutionary process, resulting in an aesthetic passivity in which kinetic energy was reduced to zero. In the practice of the avant-garde the demobilization of technical resources has reached the point of melorhythmic asceticism, with only a few different notes being used in an entire work as though emulating the legendary philosopher Cratylus, who spent his declining years by moving his index finger of his right hand to and fro in front of his nose in the firm belief that this motion was the only demonstrable truth.

Ewing, Maria (Louise), b. Detroit, Mar. 27, 1950. She commenced vocal training with Marjorie Gordon; continued with Eleanor Steber at the Cleveland Inst. of Music (1968–70) and with Jennie Tourel and O. Marzolla. She made her professional debut at the Ravinia Festival with the Chicago Sym. Orch. (1973); subsequently was engaged to appear with various U.S. opera houses and orchs.; appeared in recitals. She made her Metropolitan Opera debut in N.Y. as Cherubino (1976); returned there to sing Rosina, Dorabella, Mélisande, Blanche in *Dialogues des carmélites*, and Carmen; made her 1st appearance at Milan's La Scala as Mélisande (1976) and her Glyndebourne Festival debut as Dorabella (1978); returned there as a periodic guest. She sang Salome in Los Angeles (1986) and appeared in *The Merry Widow* in Chicago (1987); sang Salome at London's Covent Garden (1988), a role she sang to enormous critical acclaim in Chicago later that year; returned there as Tosca (1989) and Susanna (1991). She was once married to Sir Peter Hall.

ex tempore (It.). In an improvisatory style; spontaneously.

executed queens. Beheaded queens exercise a morbid attraction for poets, dramatists, and opera composers. The story of Anne Boleyn was put into operatic form by Donizetti, as *Anna Bolena*; it was 1st performed in Milan (1830). Mary Stuart remains popular with playwrights and composers; Donizetti also wrote an enduring opera about her (*Maria Stuarda*, 1835); Thea Musgrave composed *Mary, Queen of Scots* (1975–77); even a Soviet composer, Sergei Slonimsky (nephew of the author) wrote an opera on the subject, successful in Russia and Edinburgh, her former capital (1986). A most sanguinary execution was administered to the mistress of Pedro I of Portugal, Inés de Castro, by order of his tyrannical father Alfonso IV (1355); but when her lover ascended the throne, he had her body exhumed and crowned as an empress; her suspected murderers were forced to kiss her skeletal hands in solemn procession. At least 2 composers wrote operas about her, Giuseppe Persiani (Naples, 1835) and Thomas Pasatieri (Baltimore, 1976).

execution. 1. Style, manner of performance. 2. Technical ability.

exercise. Short technical study or sequence for training the fingers (or vocal organs) to overcome some special technical difficulty. Also, a short study in composition.

exoticism. Movement in Western art in which coloristic devices are borrowed from native practices as perceived externally; also called orientalism. In transferring exotic samples from a faraway culture, actual scales and rhythms usually undergo distortion so that Western exoticism becomes a misperceived art, a refracted image not recognizable to those who ostensibly inspired it. The initial source of exoticism (during the 18th century) was Turkish music, characterized by a simple binary meter and lively small cymbals. *Alla turca* is often found in tempo indications in Classic music. Asian countries provided different degrees of inspiration for opera and ballet. Russian composers were fond of exotic subjects; Rimsky-Korsakov's *Scheherazade* is based on a tale from *The Arabian Nights*; Queen Shemaha's aria in his opera *Le Coq d'or* forms an ingenious web of "exotic" arabesques; the Mongolian invasion of medieval Russia provided historical background for stylized Tatar ballet episodes. Less literal and more abstract is the orientalism of Stravinsky's ballet-opera *The Nightingale*. Of various degrees of chinoiseries (primarily through pentatonicism) are Puccini's *Turandot* and *Madama Butterfly*; Holst's *S~vitri* and *Sita*; Roussel's *Padmâvat*; and Gilbert and Sullivan's *The Mikado*.

When authentic drummers and other gamelan performers from French Indochina appeared at the Paris International Exposition in 1889, young French composers became fascinated by their music. Debussy and Ravel made tasteful impressionistic renditions of these exotic rhythms and melodies in their works. Since ethnic scales are not readily adjustable in terms of traditional diatonic and chromatic intervals, Western musicians created their own exotic tonal progressions in which the augmented 2nd often plays the important part. The gamelan sound continued to inspire composers from all over the world: McPhee, Britten (*Prince of the Pagodas*, *Death in Venice*), members of the gamelan collectives *Other Music* and *Son of Lion*, and native master musicians.

experimental music. Music that departs from usual expectations of style, form, and genre as these have evolved throughout history; unlike the primarily European avant-garde, its proponents began with Satie and Ives and moved through and beyond the work of Cage, Cowell, and Cardew. With every turn of the aesthetic wheel, experimental music was deprecated by adepts of the preceding style as repugnant to normal senses, forgetting that all music is experimental and that tradition is merely a congealed experiment. Chromatic harmony was experimental in Wagner's time, and its ultimate dodecaphonic development became the most important type of experimental music of the 20th century. Perhaps the most literally correct application of experimental music is represented by aleatory operations, in which the manipulator merely sets the scene of action, and nature supplies an experimental answer.

In the 2nd half of the 20th century, experimental music finally moved into its proper enclave, the laboratory, where composers and experimenters conducted research with electronic instruments and computers. There is a danger, however, that an imaginative computer may be hampered in its inventiveness by the limitations of the engineer who would program the data so as to adapt it to a preordained order, and in so doing convert the machine into a mere servant. In one such man-made pseudo-computerized composition, the ending consists of a protracted C-major coda, which no computer in its right mental circuit could possibly turn out. The most valid compositional programming is that generated by a collection of random numbers, tossed out like so many embryonic seahorses out of their male parent's pouch, to be translated into notes and rhythms according to a predetermined code.

exposition. 1. Opening section of a sonata-form movement, in which the principal themes are presented for the 1st time; the 1st theme is in the tonic, the closing theme usually in the dominant or, in many minor-key works, the relative major. 2. Sections of a fugue which present the subject.

expression mark. Written instructions (sign, word, or phrase) indicating the desired type of performance. The earliest marks appeared in keyboard compositions in the 16th century and were limited to signs for forte and piano, usually abbrev. to initials *f* and *p*; a curious expression mark was *E* (echo), found in 17th-century works; it was equivalent to *p*. The Florentine operatic pioneers used elaborate verbal descriptions such as *esclamazione spirituosa* (like a spiritual exclamation) and *quasi favallando* (as if speaking).

In the 20th century verbal expressions achieved extravagant forms, particularly in Scriabin's music, as in *presque en délire* (almost in a delirium), and in Debussy's picturesque descriptions, such as *ce rhythme doit avoir la valeur sonore d'un fond de paysage triste et glacé* (this rhythm must have the sonorous validity of a sad and icy landscape). Signs of crescendo and diminuendo did not achieve currency until the late 18th century; various gradations of *mf* and *mp* were increasingly cultivated by Romantic composers; the ending of the *Pathetique* Sym. by Tchaikovsky is marked *mp*.

expression stop. In the harmonium, a stop which closes the escape-valve of the bellows, so that wind pressure and intensity of tone are partly controlled by the pedals.

expressionism. Modern aesthetic movement, beginning in music around 1910, giving expression to the inner state of a person's mind and emotion; the term originated in painting. Expressionism reflects extreme and anxious moods characteristic of modern life, in an idiom that frequently uses atonally constructed melodies and spasmodic, restless rhythms; it is quite often covertly autobiographical.

Expressionism stands in a reciprocal relationship to impressionism as its functional and psychological counterpart. Expressionism conjures up its images in the inner world of the human psyche and exteriorizes its states as an intimate subjective report; it is introspective and metaphysical, an arcane medium born in the deepest recesses of the psychic complex, not easily translatable into the common language of the arts. No scale of visual comparison is available to an external recipient of expressionist art, for it resembles an artist's dream in which the dreamer experiences shock and surprise despite the fact that he or she is author as well as victim of that dream. Because of this duality of process, expressionist art suffers from the trauma of illogic; it is characterized by the breakdown of illation and the disruption of the consequential processes of psychic transmission. The unreality of expressionist drama, poetry, painting, and music is its greatest obstacle for general comprehension, but once the curtain is removed and secret dream images reach the observer in the form of art, expressionism becomes a universal medium of mass communication and a great multiplier of artistic emotion.

Because of the basic antinomy between the sources of impressionism and expressionism, each generate a distinctive musical language. Expressionism prefers the harsh syntax of atonality, communicating deep-seated anxieties through chromatic congestion and atonal dispersion. Expressionism rejects modality, tonality, and all diatonic textures; its melodies are constructed parabolically, away from a putative tonic. The harmonic idiom of expressionism is formed by progressions of consecutive perfect 4ths or 5ths, resulting in the creation of a panchromatic complex of 12 different notes, preparing the foundation of the 12-tone method of composition as formulated by Schoenberg.

There are also profound differences in historic, cultural, and geographic factors in the development of impressionism and expressionism. Impressionism is Gallic, expressionism Germanic. Ger. expressionist song texts offer no sonorous gratification of resonant vocables, but their guttural strength seems to deepen penetration of philosophical and often mystical notions underlying the words. Expressionism is basically a psychic development with no aesthetic contact with painting; yet composers of the expressionist school, notably Schoenberg and Berg, possessed a striking talent for painting in the expressionist style. Ruggles, who developed a sui generis expressionist style in an atonal idiom, abandoned composition entirely and devoted himself to abstract painting.

expressive organ. Harmonium.

extemporization (from It. *ex tempore*, outside of time). Spontaneous or improvised performance.

extended compass. Tones beyond the usual range of a voice or instrument.

extension pedal. Damper (right) piano pedal.

extravaganza. Elaborate stage show with singing, dancing, dialogue, and little concern for dramaturgical coherence; often marked by exaggerated comic turns and spectacular scenic and lighting effects.

eye music. Composers are often tempted to use a visual representation in their scores to express the mood of a vocal or instrumental composition. From the early Renaissance, illuminated MSS bear examples of such representations; perhaps the most famous early example is the fantastic heart-shaped rondeau *Belle, bonne, sage* by Baude Cordier (c. 1400). Madrigal composers of the Renaissance may have used blackened notes to express death, dark of night, or grief whenever such sentiments were found in the text, disregarding the fact that such blackening affected the time values in mensural notation. Bach used melodic figures that suggested the cross in his *St. Matthew Passion*. The score of the storm scene in Beethoven's *Pastoral* Sym. suggests vertical rainfall in the wind instruments, swirling streams in the basses, and bolts of lightning in the brief and rapid violin passages.

Critics sometimes use the term eye music (usually in the Ger. form *Augenmusik*) as an opprobrium for works that look orderly, even impressive on paper but are uninteresting to the ear. Yet visual symmetry can often correspond to fine musical organization. Composers of avant-garde have adopted the patterns of eye music as points of departure for their musical inspiration. Anestis Logothetis (b.1921) exhibited his scores of eye music in Vienna, bearing characteristic geometric titles such as *Cycloid, Culmination, Interpolation, Parallax,* and *Concatenation*. Villa-Lobos experimented with millimetrization by transferring a chart, a curve, or a silhouette onto a piece of graph paper, with the ordinate corresponding to intervals in semitones and the abscissa to the duration of a note. Crumb has utilized eye music for expressive purposes since the mid-1960s. In the *Makrokosmos* piano cycles, scores are written in spiral, square-shaped, and other nontraditional layouts. A single part with multiple images and relationships (e.g., *Dream Images [Love-Death Music]*, part 11 of *Makrokosmos I*, 1974) separates the bass drone, quasi-Stravinskian treble melody, and "faintly remembered" quotations of Chopin's *Fantasie-Impromptu*. In his chamber music, instruments are indicated only when played and are otherwise missing (a method used by Stockhausen and Feldman); this gives a performer a stronger sense of ephemerality or surprise. Thus Crumb's eye-music notation has it both ways: affecting the audience's response while informing and titillating the performer (even when some scores seems unnecessarily complicated).

F. 6th note in alphabetical scale; 4th note of C major or minor scale. In French, Italian, Spanish, and Russian nomenclature, F is Fa.

ff. Fortissimo.

fff. Fortississimo.

F clef. Clef indicating position on staff of F, 5th below middle C; bass clef (𝄢), with F on 4th line, is now virtually only F clef in use. At one time baritone clef (F on 3rd line) and sub-bass clef (F on 5th line) were also used.

F dur (Ger.). F major.

f holes. 2 *f*-shaped sound-holes in belly of violin and other string instruments.

F major. Predominantly the key of pastoral music, descriptive of gentle landscapes and lyric, often sentimental moods. Beethoven's *Pastoral Sym.* in F Major is paradigmatic of this key's natural affinities, as is the famous *Melody in F* by Anton Rubinstein. The most optimistic Brahms syms, the 3rd, is in F major; the merriest 2-Part Invention of Bach is as well.

F minor. The key of lyric reverie, touched with melancholy. Composers shun writing in F minor for string instruments or orch. because it is so unwieldy, lacking open-string representation of tonic or subdominant and only 2 of dominant (lowest cello and viola strings). But F minor is eminently pianistic, and much Romantic music is in this key; Chopin wrote his 2nd piano concerto in F minor (op. 21); Schubert's most famous *Moment Musical* is in F minor. Only pansymphonic Miaskovsky ventured to select F minor as principal key, and not just once but twice: Nos. 10 and 24.

F moll (Ger.). F minor.

Fa. 1. In solmization, usual name for 4th degree of scale. 2. Name of tone *F* in Italy, France, Spain, and Russia.

fabordón (Sp.). Falsobordone.

faburden (Old Eng.). In Renaissance, enhancing chant melody by parallel 6ths and 4ths below, or with chant serving as middle voice (i.e., with parallel 3rds below and parallel 4ths above); results in progressions of consecutive 6/3 chords prior to a tonic-dominant cadence. This technique helped legitimate new consonances, destined to replace consecutive open 5ths and 4ths; related to gymel and fauxbourdon.

facile (It., Fr.). Facile, easy, fluent.

Fackeltanz (Ger.). Torch dance or procession; popular at court in 19th-century Prussia; Spohr and Meyerbeer were among those to supply music for them.

fado. Popular Portuguese song and dance genre.

Fagott (Ger.; It. *fagotto*). 1. Bassoon. 2. Organ reed stop.

Fain, Sammy (born Feinberg), b. N.Y., June 17, 1902; d. Los Angeles, Dec. 6, 1989. He worked in vaudeville and as a song plugger before achieving success as full-fledged songwriter on Broadway and in Hollywood; collaboration with Irving Kahal produced such hits as *Nobody Knows What Red-Headed Mama Can Do*, *Let a Smile Be Your Umbrella on a Rainy Day*, *When I Take My Sugar to Tea*, *Dear Hearts and Gentle People*, *That Old Feeling*, *I Can Dream, Can't I*, and *I'll Be Seeing You*; later, in collaboration with Paul F. Webster, composed *Secret Love* and *Love Is a Many-Splendored Thing*.

fake. Play without rehearsal from lead sheet, usually collected in fake book; also, to do one's best under tough circumstances, as in "Fake it!" or "Wing it!"

fake book. Sheet-music collection of standard popular and jazz tunes for combo instrumentalists, indicating melodies and chord symbols but little other detail, allowing players to "fake" or improvise their way around basic framework; also called lead sheets. Chord symbols use capital *M* (or *Maj*) for major and small *m* (or *min*) for minor triads. Numerical figures stand for intervals; superscript ^{0} indicates diminished and $^+$ denotes augmented; character *x* is for flat. The chordal root precedes the chord symbol; so CM is a C-major triad; CM6 is a C-major triad with added 6th (i.e., note A); Cx7 is a C-major triad with flatted 7th (i.e., dominant-7th chord).

Faktur (Ger., facture). Style and manner of composition.

Falla (y Matheu), Manuel (Maria) de, b. Cádiz, Nov. 23, 1876; d. Alta Gracia, Córdoba province, Argentina, Nov. 14, 1946. He studied piano with his mother and Eloisa Galluzo, studied harmony, counterpoint, and composition with Alejandro Odero and Enrique Broca; went to Madrid; studied piano with José Tragó and composition with Pedrell at the Cons.; wrote several zarzuelas, but only *Los amores de la Inés* was performed (Madrid, 1902); *La vida breve* won a prize of the Real Academia de Bellas Artes (1905), but not premiered until 8 years later; won the Ortiz y Cussó Prize for pianists (1905). In 1907 he went to Paris; became friendly with Debussy, Dukas, and Ravel, who aided and encouraged him; adopted principles of impressionism without, however, giving up personal and national style. He returned to Spain (1914); produced *El amor brujo* (1915), followed by the evocative *Noches en los jardines de España* for piano and orch. (1916). In 1919 he moved to Granada; completed work on his *El sombrero de tres picos* (1919).

Falla's art was rooted in both Spanish folk songs and the historical traditions of Spanish music; until 1919, his works were cast chiefly in Andalusian idiom, his instrumental technique often conditioned by effects peculiar to Spain's national instrument, the guitar; in his puppet opera *El retablo de maese Pedro* (1919–22), turned to the classical tradition of Spanish (especially Castilian) music; the keyboard style of his Harpsichord Concerto (1923–26), written for Wanda Landowska, reveals a classical lucidity akin to Domenico Scarlatti, who lived in Spain for many years. He became president of the Instituto de España (1938); once General Franco had overthrown the Republican-Loyalist government with the aid of Hitler and Mussolini, Falla left Spain and went to South America, never to return to his homeland; went to Buenos Aires; conducted concerts of his music; withdrew to the small locality of Alta Gracia, where he lived the rest of his life in seclusion; worked on a large scenic cantata *Atlántida* that remained unfinished (later completed by his former pupil Ernesto Halffter). His writings include *Escritos sobre música y músicos* (Madrid, 1950); *Cartas Segismondo Romero* (Granada, 1976); *Correspondencia de Manuel de Falla* (Madrid, 1978).

falsa musica (It., false music). Medieval term for accidentals and other alterations not justified by contrapuntal rules.

false relation. Cross relation.

falsetto (It., small false one; Fr. *fausset*; Ger. *Falsett*, *Fidelstimme*). Voice production using head tones rather than chest tones, particularly among tenors, creating sounds well above the natural range. Falsetto singing was widely practiced in choirs at the Vatican and Italian cathedrals when the use of women or castrati was inappropriate. Falsetto singers were also known as *allti naturali*, natural alto singers, to distinguish them from *voci artificiali*, artificial voices (of castrati); another term was *tenorini*, little tenors. The word "falsetto" is a diminutive of *falso* because a singer, although not castrated, applies a "false" way of voice production. Falsetto voices are often used in Baroque operas for comic effects. The falsetto role of the Astrologer in Rimsky-Korsakov's *Le Coq d'or* indicates that he is a eunuch. Falsetto is also used in yodeling.

falsobordone (It., false bass; Sp. *fabordón*). Chanting or reciting in root-position triads, with all parts (usually 4) written out. The style evolved in the latter 15th century; keyboard works and monodies with basso continuo were composed in a similar style throughout the Baroque; the style was revived during the 19th-century Cecilian movement.

fancy (from It. *fantasia*). 1. Polyphonic vocal composition of 16th-century England. 2. In 16th- and 17th-century England, a freely connected group of tunes, suites, or intabulations in contrapuntal setting, written for keyboard or consort of viols; written by Byrd and Purcell, among others. See also ⇒fantasia.

fandango (Sp.). Lively dance in triple time for 2 dancers, who accompany it with castanets or tambourine.

fanfare. Flourish of trumpets or trumpet-call, usually based on the natural overtone series available to non-valved brass instruments; whether festive or mournful, continues to serve its purely military signal function, but has become a well-practiced musical device as well; examples include Beethoven's *Fidelio* and Bizet's *Carmen*.

fantasia (It.; Fr. *fantaisie*; Ger. *Fantasie*). 1. Improvisation. 2. Polyphonic instrumental piece in free imitation (17th and 18th

centuries), composed for keyboard instruments, lutes, and viols, marked by free thematic development and florid cadenzas. Jean-Jacques Rousseau, in his *Dictionnaire de musique*, asserts wittily that fantasy can never be written down because, as soon as it is, it ceases to be fantasy. 3. A work free in form and more or less fantastic in character. In the 19th century, instrumental fantasies largely abandoned their contrapuntal character and became works in sonata form. When Beethoven described his *Moonlight Sonata* (not his name) as a "sonata quasi una fantasia," he apparently intended to convey to it a character of romantic image, but it is set in sonata form. Chopin's *Fantaisie-Impromptu* is organized in symmetric ternary form. 4. Potpourri or paraphrase.

fantastico (It.). Fantastic, fanciful.

farandola (It.; Fr. *farandole*). Old Provençal and Spanish circle-dance in rapid 6/8 time, accompanied on pipe and tabor. Composers have evoked the peasant world with it; the most famous example (from Bizet's *L'Arlésienne*) is, oddly enough, in duple meter.

Farbenmelodie (Ger., color melody). Aphoristic orchestration technique developed in 2nd Viennese school, wherein changes in timbre and instrumentation become a central element of differentiation. In total serialism, Farbenmelodie is treated in the same manner as pitch and rhythm.

farce. 1. 1-act opera or operetta. 2. (Lat., stuff) Comic intermezzo in medieval plays with music, making use of songs popular at the time, often of lewd, lascivious, libidinous, ultracomical, or burlesque character. In modern times, farce still retains the old meaning of frivolous comedy of manners.

farewell engagements. Convenient though rarely truthful announcements issued by famous prima donnas of both sexes at career's end to attract the attention of a long-vanishing public; e.g., Adelina Patti gave an extended series of "farewell" concerts in U.S.

Farinelli (born Carlo Broschi), b. Andria, Jan. 24, 1705; d. Bologna, July 15, 1782. His father, Salvatore Broschi, was a musician and most likely Carlo's earliest instructor in music; later adopted the name Farinelli to honor his benefactor, Farina; studied with Porpora in Naples; made his 1st public appearance in his teacher's *Angelica e Medoro* (1720); subsequent appearances brought him great success; soon became famous as il ragazzo (boy). He sang in Rome, appearing in Porpora's Eumene at age 16; repeated successes brought him renown throughout Italy and abroad; led his 1st appearance in Vienna (1724). He met the celebrated castrato alto Bernacchi in Bologna (1727); in a singing contest, Farinelli acknowledged defeat and persuaded Bernacchi to teach him how to achieve coloratura virtuosity. After further visits to Vienna (1728, 1731), Porpora called him to London to sing with the Opera of the Nobility; made his London debut in Hasse's *Artaserse* (1734), appearing with Senesino and Cuzzoni; remained with company until 1736, when he went to Paris, then returned for the 1736–37 season.

Having amassed a fortune in London, Farinelli went to Madrid (1737); attained unparalleled success as court singer to King Philip V, singing the same 4 songs nightly for 25 years to ease the

King's melancholy; his influence on the ailing monarch and his Queen allowed him to command considerable funds to engage famous performers for the Madrid court. When his voice began to fail, he served as impresario, decorator, and stage director. He continued to enjoy the court's favor under Philip's successor, Ferdinand VI, who made him knight of the order of Calatrava (1750). However, when Carlos III became King (1759), he was dismissed; retired to Bolgna. His brother Riccardo Broschi (b. Naples, c. 1698; d. Madrid, 1756) was a composer who produced several operas in Naples, in which his brother sang.

Farley, Carole (Ann), b. Le Mars, Iowa, Nov. 29, 1946. She studied at the Indiana Univ. School of Music (Mus.B., 1968), with Cornelius Reid in N.Y., and with Marianne Schech at the Munich Hochschule für Musik (1968–69). In 1969 made her debut at the Linz Landestheater and her U.S. debut at N.Y.'s Town Hall; subsequently appeared as soloist with major orchs. of U.S. and Europe; sang with the Welsh National Opera, Cologne Opera, Strasbourg Opera, N.Y. City Opera, and Lyons Opera. She made her Metropolitan Opera debut in N.Y. as Lulu (1977); also sang at the Zurich Opera (1979), Deutsche Oper am Rhein in Düsseldorf (1980–81; 1984), Chicago Lyric Opera (1981), and Florence Maggio Musicale (1985). In addition to Lulu, which she essayed over 80 times in various houses, she also sang Poppea, Donna Anna, Violetta, Massenet's Manon, Mimi, and various R. Strauss roles. She married José Serebrier in 1969.

Farwell, Arthur (George), b. St. Paul, Minn., Apr. 23, 1872; d. N.Y., Jan. 20, 1952. He studied at Mass. Inst. of Technology (graduated 1893); studied with Homer Norris in Boston, Humperdinck and Pfitzner in Berlin, and Guilmant in Paris. He was a lecturer at Cornell Univ. (1899–1901); on the editorial staff of *Musical America* (1909–14); directed N.Y. municipal concerts (1910–13); director of Settlement Music School in N.Y. (1915–18). He went to Calif. (1918) and lectured on music there; acting head of the music dept. at Univ. of Calif., Berkeley (1918–19); founded the Santa Barbara Community Chorus (1919–21); 1st holder of the composers' fellowship of the Music and Art Assoc. of Pasadena (1921–25); taught theory at Mich. State College in East Lansing (1927–39); eventually settled in N.Y.

Farwell pioneered new American music and tirelessly promoted national ideas in art; contributed to ethnological publications; operated Wa-Wan Press (Newton, Mass.) a periodical (quarterly, 1901–1907; monthly, 1907–11) that printed piano and vocal music of "progressive" American composers, emphasizing works that utilized indigenous (black, Indian, and cowboy) musical materials (reprinted N.Y., 1970). Disillusioned about commercial opportunities for American music (including his own), he established a lithographic handpress (East Lansing, 1936) and printed his music, handling the entire process of reproduction, including cover designs; wrote *Letter to American Composers* (N.Y., 1903) and *Music in America* in *Art of Music*, IV (with W. Dermot Darby; N.Y., 1915).

Fasola. Singing teaching method popular in England and Colonial America; as the term specifies, only 3 syllables of the Guidonian hand—Fa, Sol, and La—were to be used to form the major hexachord; by adding the syllable Mi for the 7th scale degree, a complete major scale was obtained. In order to facili-

tate the recognition of scale degrees, an American notated Fa, Sol, and La in different shapes; this shape-note notation, also known as buckwheat notation, was used in music classes in America, particularly Southern states.

fastosamente (fastoso; It.). With pomp; in stately style; majestically.

fate motive. Nickname given a 4-note theme (3 short, 1 long) that Beethoven used at the opening of (and throughout) his 5th Sym. (1808); other Beethoven works of this period (4th Piano Concerto, the *Appassionata*, String Quartet, op. 74) use the same motive. There is no biographical proof that the composer thought of this motive in a particular way but it has cast its spell over the years. During World War II, Allied propaganda services broadcast to Nazi-occupied Europe the signal "V" (for Victory) in Morse code, which translates as 3 dots (short) followed by 1 dash (long). As Nazis could not very well censor Beethoven or arrest people who whistled the tune, they tried to steal it from the Allies by equating it with the archaic word *Victoria*; the fight of the fate motive was thus joined.

Fauré, Gabriel (-Urbain), b. Pamiers, Ariège, May 12, 1845; d. Paris, Nov. 4, 1924. His father was a provincial inspector of primary schools; noticing his son's musical instinct, took him to Paris to study with Louis Niedermeyer; after Niedermeyer's death (1861), he studied composition with Saint-Saës. He went to Rennes as organist at St-Sauveur (1866); returned to Paris on the eve of the Franco-Prussian War (1870) and volunteered for the light infantry. He was organist at Notre-Dame de Clignancourt (1870), St-Honoré d'Elyau (1871), and St-Sulpice (1871–74); was named deputy organist to Saint-Saëns (1874), choirmaster (1877), and chief organist (1896) at the Madeleine. He was appointed prof. of composition at the Paris Cons. (1896); an illustrious teacher, among his students were Ravel, Enesco, Koechlin, Roger-Ducasse, Schmitt, and N. Boulanger; succeeded Dubois as director (1905–20); then, quite unexpectedly, developed ear trouble and gradually lost his hearing; distressed, made effort to conceal it; eventually forced to abandon his teaching position. He wrote occasional music reviews in *Le Figaro* (1903–21; selection publ. as *Opinions musicales*, Paris, 1930). He was elected a member of Académie des Beaux Arts (1909); made Commander of Legion d'honneur (1910).

Fauré's stature as composer is undiminished by time's passage; developed a musical idiom all his own; by subtle application of old modes, evoked an aura of eternally fresh art; by using unresolved mild discords and special coloristic effects, anticipated procedures of impressionism; in his piano works, shunned virtuosity in favor of the classical lucidity of French clavecin masters; precisely articulated melodic lines of his songs is in finest traditions of French vocal music. Among other works, his great Requiem and the *Elégie* for cello and piano have entered the general repertoire.

fausse relation (Fr.). Cross relation.

fauxbourdon (Med. Fr., false drone). Term for various contrapuntal techniques that evolved in the 15th century; the term and techniques seem related to medieval English faburden, perhaps its original source. Fauxbourdon allowed parallel 4ths and 6ths as consonant intervals from the top down, doubling at the octave where appropriate. The name "false drone" may come from the idea of the "false bass," not the customary chordal tonic but its mediant. The chant voice was moved to the middle or upper contrapuntal lines; some additional voices were written, others implied. Fauxbourdon eventually led to the use of consecutive ⁶/₃ chords, common in later classical usage. Even a separate fauxbourdon genre of short pieces emerged. Eventually the technique dissolved in the rarefied counterpoint of the late Renaissance and thereafter; similar passages have appeared occasionally with the return of parallel harmony in the early 20th century.

favola per musica (It., fable with music). Early term for an opera libretto based on mythology.

feedback. Loud distortion in amplification equipment caused by the output's being picked up by the input, creating a loop of electrically enhanced sound waves. A typical case—an amplifier and the electric guitar attached to it—was the bane of performers until they learned to control distortion and use it to color timbre or to serve as source material for live electroacoustic music (e.g., Jimi Hendrix).

feierlich (Ger.). Ceremonial, solemn, grave.

Feldman, Morton, b. N.Y., Jan. 12, 1926; d. Buffalo, Sept. 3, 1987. He studied piano with Vera Maurina-Press in N.Y. and composition with Riegger (1941) and Wolpe (1944); received a Guggenheim fellowship (1966); taught at the State Univ. of N.Y. in Buffalo (from 1972), where he held the Edgard Varèse Chair. Profoundly impressed by abstract expressionist paintings and through his friendship with Cage, he evolved a congenial set of concepts based on a seemingly oxymoronic principle of predetermined indeterminacy, as exemplified in *Projections I–IV* for aleatory instrumental combinations, with an approximation of the notes in the work performing musical "action," indicating instrumental range and the number of notes per specified time unit. In their immarcescible fidelity to new music ideals, his works left a profound impression on theories and practices of young composers of the waning years of the 20th century; even after his early death (of pancreatic cancer), his works continued to enjoy frequent performances in America and Europe. In his geometric directness and expressive lucidity of technical devices, Feldman is the de Kooning of musical composition. His pieces for instrumental groups include 4 *Intersections* (1951–53) and *Marginal Intersection* for orch. (1951); 5 *Extensions* (1951–53); 5 *Durations* (1960–61); 4 *Vertical Thoughts* (all 1963); *Viola in My Life* I-IV (1970–71); *Instruments* I–IV (1974–78); also wrote string quartet works and chamber, orch., and vocal pieces.

Feliciano, Jose, b. Lares, Sept. 10, 1945. His family moved to N.Y. when he was 5; taught himself to play guitar; appeared in Greenwich Village clubs; his self-exclamatory record album *Feliciano!* (with a soulful version of *Light My Fire*) brought him fame. His blues rendition of *The Star-Spangled Banner* at the 1968 World Series in Detroit caused a furor and led radio stations to boycott him; after a hiatus of several years he was able to renew his career. He has toured in the U.S. and Europe.

Feltsman, Vladimir, b. Moscow, Jan. 8, 1952. He was born into a musical family; his father, Oskar Feltsman, composed popular music. Vladimir began taking piano lessons at age 6 from his mother; enrolled at Moscow's Central Music School; completed training with Yakov Flier at Moscow Cons. At 11 he made his debut as soloist with the Moscow Phil.; won 1st prize in the Prague Concertino Competition; after capturing joint 1st prize in the Long-Thibaud Competition in Paris (1971), pursued a successful career as soloist with major Soviet and Eastern European orchs.; made particularly successful appearances in Romantic works—his specialty— in Japan (1977) and France (1978). His auspicious career was interrupted by Soviet authorities when he applied for a visa to emigrate to Israel with his wife (1979); the application was denied and he was limited to giving concerts only in remote outposts of the USSR; with the support of the U.S. ambassador gave private concerts at the ambassador's official residence in Moscow; in 1984, one of these was surreptitiously recorded and later released. When his plight became a cause célèbre in the West, Feltsman was allowed to give his 1st Moscow recital in almost a decade (1987); that year he was granted permission to emigrate; went to the U.S.; accepted an appointment at the State Univ. of N.Y. at New Paltz; gave a special concert at the White House for President Reagan, and his 1st N.Y. recital in Carnegie Hall.

feminine ending. Old-fashioned term (used by analogy with versification) to designate an unaccented syllable at the end of a line. In music many Romantic pieces have such endings, with a stressed dissonant melodic note resolving on a weak melodic beat.

Fenby, Eric (William), b. Scarborough, Apr. 22, 1906. He studied piano and organ; after a few years as a organist in London, went to Grez-sur-Loing, France (1928) as amanuensis for Delius, taking his dictation note by note, until Delius's death (1934); publ. his experiences in *Delius as I Knew Him* (London, 1936). He was director of music of the North Riding Training School (1948–62); from 1964, prof. of composition at the Royal Academy of Music; made Officer of the Order of the British Empire (1964). Because of the beneficent work he undertook, he neglected his own compositions; wrote some pleasant string music.

fermamente (It.). Firmly, decisively.

fermata (It.; Ger. *Fermate*). Sign ⌒ over, or ⌣ under, note or rest, indicating prolongation of its time value at the performer's (or conductor's) discretion; doubling the length of a note or rest is a good approximation; the fermata is also called a "hold." Placed over a bar, it indicates a slight pause or breathing spell before continuing on; overall tempo is not affected. A rest for the entire ensemble is called Grand Pause (abbrev. G.P.).

fermezza, con (It.). In firm, decided, energetic style.

fermo (It.). Firm, decided; fixed, unchanged. *Canto fermo*, same as cantus firmus.

Fern (Ferne; Ger.). Distance. *Wie aus der Ferne*, as if from distance.

Ferneyhough, Brian, b. Coventry, Jan. 16, 1943. He studied at the Birmingham School of Music (1961–63); took courses with Lennox Berkeley and Maurice Miles at the Royal Academy of Music in London (1966–67); received further instruction from Ton de Leeuw in Amsterdam and Klaus Huber in Basel (1969–73). He was on the faculty at the Hochschule für Musik in Freiburg im Breisgau (1971–86); lectured at Darmstadt summer courses (1976, 1978, 1980); taught at the Royal Cons. of Hague (from 1986) and at the Univ. of Calif. at San Diego (from 1987). Radical qualities of his style involve atypical approaches to dissonant counterpoint and time structure that are totally divorced from the dance-music orientation of most European music; he is probably the least English-sounding of prominent British composers of the latter 20th century.

feroce (It.). Wild, fierce, vehement, ferociously, savagely.

Ferrier, Kathleen (Mary), b. Higher Walton, Lancashire, Apr. 22, 1912; d. London, Oct. 8, 1953. She studied piano; began voice lessons with Thomas Duerden. In 1937 she won 1st prizes for piano and singing at the Carlisle Competition; decided on singing career; studied with J. E. Hutchinson in Newcastle upon Tyne and Roy Henderson in London. After appearing as a soloist in *Messiah* at Westminster Abbey (1943), she began her professional career; Britten chose her to create the title role in *The Rape of Lucretia* (Glyndebourne, 1946); sang Orfeo in Gluck's *Orfeo ed Euridice* there (1947) and Covent Garden (1953). She made her American debut with the N.Y. Phil., singing Mahler's *Das Lied von der Erde* with Walter conducting (1948); made her American recital debut in N.Y. (1949). By the end of her career she had acquired in England an almost legendary reputation for vocal excellence and impeccable taste; her untimely death (from cancer) was greatly mourned. In 1953 she was made a Commander of the Order of the British Empire; received the Gold Medal of Royal Phil. Soc.

fervente (fervido; It.). Fervently, ardently, passionately.

Fes (Ger.). F flat.

Fest (Ger.). 1. Festival. 2. (not capitalized) Firm, precise.

festa teatrale (It.). Theatrical festival celebrating a royal anniversary or national victory, featuring music and dancing.

Festes Zeitmass (Ger.). Precisely in tempo.

festivals. A generic name for all kinds of festivities, accompanied by singing, instrumental playing, and dancing. The earliest music festivals were gatherings of troubadours in 13th-century France and Minnesingers in Germany, the latter portrayed in Wagner's *Tannhäuser* and *Die Meistersinger*. The oldest regularly produced festival was the Eisteddfod, a bardic gathering held in Wales; after over a century of silence, it was revived as a choral festival (1880). England was the 1st nation to organize music festivals devoted to performances of classical music; the 1st was the 3 Choirs Festival (founded 1724), taking place in the 3 cathedral cities of Gloucester, Hereford, and Worcester.

The earliest festival to present the music of one composer was the Handel Festival, organized in London at the Crystal Palace (1857). The most grandiose opera festivals devoted to a living composer were the Bayreuth Festivals, begun by Wagner with the aid of his fanatical admirer, King Ludwig II of Bavaria; the opening event presented a complete performance of *Der Ring des Nibelungen* (1876). Music festivals in America in the 19th century often emphasized numerical grandeur, as exemplified by 2 festivals celebrating the end of the Civil War, held in Boston (1869, 1872) as Peace Jubilees; involved orchs. of 1,000 men and choruses of 10,000. A important series of music festivals of high professional order was initiated in Worcester, Mass. (1858).

In the 20th century many festivals were organized with the express purpose of promoting modern music. The Coolidge Chamber Music Festivals were established by Elizabeth Sprague Coolidge, 1st as the Berkshire Festival of Chamber Music in Pittsfield, Mass. (1918) and then under the auspices of the Library of Congress in Washington, D.C., (1925). Festivals in Donaueschingen (begun 1921) premiered primarily German works; most ambitious were the festivals of the International Soc. for Contemporary Music (from 1923), held in European countries. Howard Hanson inaugurated annual American music festivals at Rochester, N.Y. (1930). The Maggio Musicale Fiorentino (1933) present opera, ballet, and sym. concerts; operas, new and old, are presented at Glyndebourne, England. Koussevitzky and the Boston Sym. Orch. established the annual summer concerts in Tanglewood, Mass. (1940). Since the end of World War II, many events have been initiated: Prague's Spring Festivals (1946); the International Festival in Edinburgh (1947); the Holland Festival (1948), presenting music in Amsterdam and other Dutch cities; Benjamin Britten's festivals in Aldeburgh, England (1948); the biennial Venice Festival (1950); Poland's Warsaw Autumn (1956); the Gulbenkian Foundation-sponsored festivals in Lisbon and other Portuguese cities; the Israel Festival (1961). In 1958 Gian-Carlo Menotti organized the Festival of 2 Worlds (Spoleto, Italy); in 1977, he opened an American counterpart in Charleston, N.C. Other regular festivals are held in virtually every European city, including Berlin, Munich, Vienna, Salzburg, Zagreb, Stockholm, and Bergen. In the former USSR musical activities were maintained in Moscow, Leningrad, Kiev, Tbilisi, and other musical centers; festivals of ethnic music, ranging from folk songs to operas and syms., were given periodically in Moscow. Japan and Australia contribute to the development of festival music. The jazz festivals of Newport, R.I. (later moved to N.Y.), held during summer months, provide special interest, as do those in Monterrey, Montreux, and elsewhere. Concerts and presentations in multimedia are sporadically given by avant-garde composers in N.Y., San Francisco, London, Cologne, and Tokyo. Rock festivals have ranged from successes (Monterrey, Woodstock) to disasters (Altamont, Isle of Wight).

Festschrift (Ger., festive writing; plural *Festschriften*). Offering in honor of an esteemed musical scholar, teacher, or composer on the occasion of advanced birthday or retirement; usually a publ. volume of collected articles by his or her students and colleagues; a custom generated in Germany, the orig. term is applied to non-German publications as well, especially the U.S. Festschriften are usually printed on deluxe paper and adorned by a photograph representing a bespectacled visage corrugated by age and scholarly concentration, suggesting that learned pursuits are physiologically deadening. Exceptions in this wasteland of depressing dullness are Festschriften for composers, such as the ones for Schoenberg featuring valuable articles by his faithful disciples; sometimes, essay collections are organized by subject matter into worthwhile anthologies. When an admirable figure has the bad luck to die before his or her Festschrift is completed or even contemplated, the now commemorative volume is labeled a *Gedenkschrift*.

Festspiel (Ger.). Stage play in which music is included; Wagner called *Der Ring des Nibelungen* a Festspiel.

Fétis, François-Joseph, b. Mons, Mar. 25, 1784; d. Brussels, Mar. 26, 1871. He received instruction from his father, an organist at Mons Cathedral; learned to play violin, piano, and organ; at age 9 wrote a Violin Concerto; organist to the Noble Chapter of Ste-Waudru. In 1800 he entered the Paris Cons.; studied harmony with Rey and piano with Boieldieu and Pradher; visited Vienna (1803), studying counterpoint, fugue, and German masterworks; several of his compositions (a sym., overture, sonatas, and caprices for piano) were publ. at this time.

In 1806 Fétis began a revision of the plainsong and entire ritual of the Roman Church, a vast undertaking completed, with many interruptions, after 30 years. A wealthy marriage in 1806 enabled him to pursue research freely; but the fortune was lost (1811); retired to Ardennes; occupied himself with composition and philosophical researches into harmonic theory; appointed organist for collegiate church of St-Pierre at Douai (1813). He returned to Paris (1818); became prof. of composition at the Cons. (1821). His *Traité du contrepoint et de la fugue* was publ. (1824) and accepted as an official textbook at the Cons.; became librarian there (1827); founded his unique journal *La Revue Musicale* (1827–35). He wrote articles on music for *Le National* and *Le Temps*; inaugurated his famous historical lectures and concerts (1832); called to Brussels as maître de chapelle to King Leopold I and director of the Cons. (1833); during his long tenure at the Cons. (nearly 40 years), it flourished as never before. He also conducted concerts of the Academy, which elected him a member (1845).

Fétis was a confirmed believer in explaining music history and theory scientifically; attempted a thorough systematization of all fields of music; while opinionated and dogmatic, was certainly a musicological pioneer; publ. the 1st book on music appreciation, *La Musique mise à la portée de tout le monde* (Paris, 1830). As early as 1806 Fétis began collecting materials for his great *Biographie universelle des musiciens et bibliographie générale de la musique* (8 vols., Paris, 1835–44). This bio-bibliography was unprecedented in scope; entries on composers and performers whom he knew personally still remain prime sources of information; on the negative side are the many fanciful accounts of composers' lives taken from unreliable sources; in this respect he exercised harmful influence on subsequent lexicographers for decades. His *Histoire générale de la musique* covers up to the 15th century (5 vols., Paris, 1869–76), showing him at his most profound and dogmatic; propounded unsupported opinions. His compositions has been overshadowed completely by his other work; his valuable library of 7,325 vols. was acquired after his death by the Bibliothèque Royale of Brussels.

feuerig (Ger.). Fiery, impetuous.

Feuermann, Emanuel, b. Kolomea, Galicia, Nov. 22, 1902; d. N.Y., May 25, 1942. As a child he was taken to Vienna,

where he studied cello with his father, then Friedrich Buxbaum and Anton Walter; made his recital debut in Vienna (1913). He went to Leipzig to continue studies with Julius Klengel (1917); appointed to the faculty of Cologne's Gurzenich Cons. at age 16; was 1st cellist in the Gurzenich Orch. and a member of the Bram Eldering Quartet. He was appointed prof. at the Hochschule für Musik in Berlin (1929); being Jewish, was forced to leave Germany by the Nazis; embarked on world tour (1934–35); made his U.S. debut with the Chicago Sym. Orch. (1934); appeared as soloist with many leading American orchs.; played chamber music with Schnabel and Huberman, later Rubinstein and Heifetz.

fiacco (It.). Languishing, feeble.

fiasco (It., flask or bottle; plural *fiascoes*). Utter failure of a theatrical or other performance; how this Italian word acquired this meaning is obscure. History abounds in stories of fiascos of great masterpieces which eventually joined the standard repertory. Among them: Wagner's *Tannhäuser* in Paris (1861), sufficiently notorious that he withdrew the opera after 3 disastrous performances; the 1st production of Puccini's *Madama Butterfly* (1904) was such that he and his librettist notified his publishers that the audience's disapproval had led them to withdraw. On the mythical side, Bizet was supposedly so chagrined by the "fiasco" of *Carmen* that he went to an early grave; aside from the impossibility of anyone, including composers, dying of chagrin. *Carmen* had a continuous run of 3 months after its premiere; Bizet died on the night of its 33rd performance. On the other hand, the number of genuinely irredeemable flops is surely near infinity.

fiato (It.). Breath. *Stromenti fiato*, wind instruments.

Fibich, Zdeněk (Zdenko) (Antonín Vaclav), b. Seboriče, Dec. 21, 1850; d. Prague, Oct. 15, 1900. He studied piano with Moscheles and theory with E. F. Richter at Leipzig Cons. (1865–66), then composition with Jadassohn (1866–67) and in Mannheim with V. Lachner (1869–70). Upon returning to Prague (1871), made deputy conductor and chorusmaster at the Provisional Theater (1875–78) and director of Russian Orthodox Church Choir (1878–81); wrote large amount of incidental music and sacred music, but most has been lost or was destroyed by the composer.

With the success of *Nevěsta Messinská* (The Bride of Messina, 1882–83), Fibich concentrated on opera and reviving the genre of melodrama; the positive reception to his early works led to *Hippodamie* (1888–91), a staged melodrama trilogy based on Greek tragedy, blending speech (without pitch or rhythmic specifications) with a richly orchestrated leitmotivic web. In addition to other operas—*Šárka, Bouře* (Tempest), *Hédy,* and *Pád Arkuna*—he completed 3 symphonies, tone poems and overtures (which influenced both Smetana and Dvořák), 200 songs (in German and Czech), chamber music, and multitudes of works for piano solo and 4 hands.

A fine craftsman, facile melodist, and leading representative of Czech musical nationalism, Fibich's extensive output reveals the pronounced influence of Weber, Schumann, and especially Wagner; only in his last works was a Czech sonority apparent in his orchestration. As his music becomes better known, it may be a most curious work that paves the way: *Nálady, dojmy upomínky* (Moods, impressions, and reminiscences; 1892–99), a collection of 376 character pieces in true 19th-century fashion, with 1 distinctive feature: its portrayal of his life with mistress, piano student, and librettist Anežka Schulzová (1868–1905). After a title code was deciphered in the 1920s, it became clear that the pieces depict specific events, conversations, meetings, expressions of love, journeys, parts of Anezka's body, and her appearance in different sets of clothes; this "diary" also provided him with a sourcebook for later works, as well as opportunities to resuscitate his earlier music. Publ. in 4 volumes (the last posthumously); his collection parallels the late works of Janáček, also inspired by a younger woman, albeit one who merely tolerated the old man's attentions.

Fibonacci series. Sequence of numbers in which each is the sum of the preceding pair, i.e., 1, 2, 3, 5, 8, 13, 21, etc. Composers such as Bartók used it to predetermine phrasing and metrical flow in some compositions. Fibonacci numbers might also be used for building nondodecaphonic tone-rows, in which case the numbers indicate the distance from a central (1st) tone in semitones (modulo 12), so that 13 becomes functionally identical with 1, 21 with 9, etc.

fiddle (from Mid Eng. *fidel*; Lat. *fidula*). 1. Violin. 2. Any European bowed string instrument from the Middle Ages onward; usually applied to instruments that do not conform to standardized patterns. 3. Colloquial name for violin, particularly one of rustic origin, or in reference to its use in traditional music. The fiddle is found in many European and American folk musics; related instruments are found worldwide. As it is inappropriate to call the concertmaster of a sym. orch. a "fiddler," it is incongruous to call the lead fiddler in a traditional ensemble its "concertmaster."

fiddle-bow (fiddlestick). Bow.

fidula (Lat.; Mid Eng. *fidel*). Medieval fiddle.

Fiedler, Arthur, b. Boston, Dec. 17, 1894; d. Brookline, Mass., July 10, 1979. Of a musical family, he studied violin with his father, Emanuel Fiedler of the Boston Sym. Orch. (his uncle Benny Fiedler also played violin for it); taken by his father to Berlin (1909); studied violin with Willy Hess and attended chamber music classes with E. von Dohnányi; had conducting instruction with Arno Kleffel and Rudolf Krasselt; formed the Fiedler Trio with 2 other Fiedlers (1913).

In 1915, with war raging in Europe, Fiedler returned to America; joined the 2nd violin section of the Boston Sym. Orch. (BSO) under Muck; moved to the viola section; doubled on celesta when required. In 1924 he organized the Arthur Fiedler Sinfonietta, a professional ensemble of BSO members; started a series of free open-air summer concerts at the Esplanade on Boston's Charles River (1929), presenting programs mixing popular American music intermingled with classical (and occasional modern) numbers; the series became a mainstay of Boston's musical life, attracting thousands each summer. He was appointed conductor of Boston Pops (1930), which he led for nearly a half century; built eager following, eventually elevating the Boston Pops to the status of a national institution; seemingly undisturbed by clinking of beer steins, pushing of chairs, shuffling of feet, and other sound effects not provided for in the score but an integral part of audience participation at Pops concerts.

Fiedler was a social, gregarious man, fond of extracurricular activities, such as riding on fire engines. He became commercially successful; accepted offers to pose for whiskey or orange juice; caused him degradation to the lower rank of musicmakers; his cherished ambition to conduct guest engagements in the regular subscription series of the BSO never materialized. In 1977 President Ford bestowed upon him the Medal of Freedom; as a mark of appreciation from the city of Boston, the footbridge near the Esplanade was named after him; his death was mourned by Boston music lovers in a genuine outpouring of grief.

Field, John, b. Dublin, July 26, 1782; d. Moscow, Jan. 23, 1837. His father was a violinist, his grandfather, an organist; the latter gave John his 1st music instruction; at age 9, began study with Tommaso Giordani; made his debut in Dublin (1792); went to London (1793); gave 1st concert there that year; had lessons with Clementi; began his concert career with successful appearances in London (1800–01). He accompanied Clementi on his major Continental tour (begun 1802); after visiting Paris (1802), proceeded to St. Petersburg (1803), where Field settled as performer and teacher; gave his debut performance (1804); made many concert tours in Russia. Stricken with rectal cancer, he returned to London for medical treatment (1831); performed at a Phil. Soc. concert (1832); went to Paris that year to play, subsequently touring European cities until health compelled him to abandon his active career; returned to Moscow, where he died.

Field's historical position as a composer is important, even though his music reveals little original talent; developed free fantasias and piano recitative while following Classic musical precepts; originator of keyboard nocturnes, models for Chopin; composed 7 piano concertos, 4 sonatas, about 30 nocturnes, polonaises, etc.; also chamber music.

fieramente (It.). Wildly, boldly.

fife. 1. Octave cross flute with 6 holes and without keys; compass d^2 to d^4. 2. Piccolo organ-stop.

fifteenth. 1. Double octave. 2. Organ stop of 2' pitch.

fifth. 1. Interval encompassing 5 diatonic degrees (see ⇒interval). 2. 5th degree (dominant) of any diatonic scale. *False 5th*, diminished 5th.

figura (Lat.). Note.

figurae musicae (Lat.). Musical figures described by analogy with the rhetorical doctrine of figures (*Figurenlehre*); e.g., melodic turns and ornaments compared with literary figures of speech. See also ⇒Affects, Doctrine of.

Figuralmusik (Ger.). Contrapuntal part embellished by melodic and harmonic figuration.

figuration. Adorning of melodic phrases and chords by rhythmic figures, arpeggios, passing notes, trills, changing notes, etc.

figure. Characteristic group of melodic notes.

figured bass. Basso continuo.

filato (It.). Long, drawn out.

filer le son (filer la voix; Fr., spin out sound or voice; It. *filar la voce, filo di voce*). In bel canto vocalization, prolong tone with limited crescendo or diminuendo.

film music. During the 1st decades of motion-picture production, theater owners engaged pianists or organists to provide appropriate music for moving (but silent) images on-screen. Romantic scenes called for sentimental salon music; themes of sadness were enhanced by passages in a mournful minor key. Danger and tragedy were depicted by chromatic runs harmonized by diminished-7th chords. Realistic sound effects were provided behind the scene by a homemade rain machine, consisting of a wooden cylinder covered with rough cloth and rotated by a crank mechanism, or a thunder machine, making a "rolling" noise by rubbing corrugated metal plates over a washboard. Most silent-movie keyboardists were content with playing standard Classic or Romantic pieces, but truly inspired artists improvised well-organized compositions, faithfully following the action. To aid silent-movie pianists and organists, special sheet-music collections were publ. with a table of contents indicating subject matter, covering emotional states, social situations, and ethnicity (via traditional folk music of many lands).

Apart from such trivialities, respectable composers showed interest in writing film scores, to be played by movie keyboardists, recorded on phonograph, or performed by ensembles of different sizes. One of the 1st scores was composed by Saint-Saëns for *L'Assassinat du Duc de Guise* (1908) and is scored for strings, piano, and harmonium. Another early film score, *Napoléon* by Honegger, was issued as instrumental suite (1922). The 1st application of the "cinematographic scene" to theater was contributed by René Clair to Satie's ballet *Relâche* (1924). Other composers who contributed to the young art of film music were Antheil, Auric, Copland, Prokofiev, and Shostakovich; R. Strauss condescended to arrange *Der Rosenkavalier* for film.

With the advent of sound in motion pictures, music was provided along with the dialogue on the soundtrack; at 1st, consisted of recorded compositions of popular genres; producers and directors would engage a "ghost" composer to write music according to specifications. Since many movie directors who appeared in the list of credits as composers could not read music, they usually engaged a musical amanuensis; their own part consisted in whistling snatches of tunes or beating a desired rhythm; thus Chaplin availed himself of the services of Eisler and Raksin for several of his films.

The most successful movie composers in Hollywood were not always the most talented or most imaginative. Of these, Max Steiner and Alfred Newman are outstanding; enlarged cinematic sonorities to orch'l dimensions, which they conducted themselves; when imagination flagged, helped themselves to quotations, literal or garbled, from Wagner, Tchaikovsky, and Rachmaninoff. When Stravinsky came to America, an admirer tried to arrange for him to write a movie score; when the suggestion was made to a movie mogul, the mogul replied, "Stravinsky? Yes, I've heard of him. How much will he charge?" "Well, $20,000," suggested the go-between. "$20,000?!" exclaimed the magnate. "For $5,000 more I can get Max Steiner!" (Stravinsky never wrote a movie score.) Before emigrating to America, Schoenberg composed an oddity entitled *Accompaniment to a Cinema Scene*; it was subdivided into 3 sections: *Threatening Danger*, *Anxiety*, and *Catastrophe*; although he, sincerely or derisively, tried to emulate movie music formulas, the score was nevertheless dodecaphonic, no doubt a factor in the score's never having been taken up.

Another major composer of film music was Erich Wolfgang Korngold, erstwhile Viennese wunderkind who spent many years in Hollywood; his scores retain their musical significance even when detached from their visual counterpart. Bernard Herrmann successfully combined his theatrical sense with progressive techniques, notably for Hitchcock films. Ernst Toch excelled in scores for movie mysteries. David Raksin wrote numerous film scores; concert suites from *Laura* and *Bad and Beautiful* are performed by major sym. orchs. Among others, Alex North, Virgil Thomson, Miklos Rozsa, and Jerry Goldsmith should be mentioned.

In films of futuristic content, electronic music or avant-garde composers supplied the aural background, among them Ussachevsky and Ligeti (the latter involuntarily). John T. Williams became highly successful in scoring blockbuster heroic films, including science-fiction hits as the *Star Wars* trilogy and *Close Encounters of the 3rd Kind*. Henry Mancini specialized in theme songs calculated to appeal to widest popular tastes. Although individual composers continue to provide entire soundtracks, many films use new and old songs by various popular artists, hoping that at least one song will be a hit and thereby increase business.

Composing for films usually requires precise synchronization with the changing images and actions on-screen; a technique was developed in which a click track (metronome) provides a steady beat for the performers, while a sound-editing device measures exact durations of each scene in the picture. Digital technology has refined this process further.

finale. In instrumental music, the last movement of a composition; in opera or oratorio, a summary of all prior musical themes (or a complex of new and/or old themes) coupled with the resolution of all tangled plot threads. *Grand finale* is a choral conclusion with the participation of all principal characters. Wagner and his disciples regarded the finale as musical supererogation, but composers of non-Wagnerian schools still find it useful to construct hell-raising finales, if only as an effective catalyst for tumultuous applause.

fine (It.). End; close; indicates either the end of a repetition after da capo or dal segno, or the end of a piece.

fingerboard. Elongated, relatively narrow section on string instruments over which the strings are stretched; on the guitar, frets are set in and spaced along the fingerboard to assist a player's intonation; violin family instruments are not equipped with frets; a pity, as such string fretting would spare nervous fretting of those forced to listen to a young family violin prodigy practicing.

fingering (Ger. *Fingersatz*, fingering). 1. Choosing order and method of applying fingers to keys, holes, strings, etc., of musical instruments; the art of fingering assumed pedagogical importance in the 19th century, for contemporaneous editions of Baroque and Classic music, particularly for piano, rarely indicated fingering; this was left to editors—mostly German—of classics published in 19th-century annotated editions. Standard keyboard rules included not using the thumb on black keys except in cases of dire necessity (e.g., F-sharp major arpeggios in Chopin's "Black Key" Étude). The chromatic scale is fingered using thumb and index finger in alternation, and middle finger when convenient. Fingering on string instruments is less complex, since shifts of left-hand position give a player ample opportunity for technical accommodation. 2. Numerical marks guiding a performer in placing his or her fingers. Fingering notation systems include *English fingering*, where notes taken by the thumb are marked x, with 1, 2, 3, 4 for the fingers; and the *German* (or *Continental*) *fingering*, with notes for the thumb marked 1, and fingers 2, 3, 4, 5.

fino (It.). Till; up to; as far as.

fioretti (It., little flowers). Ornaments.

fioritura (It., floral decoration; plural *fioriture*). Embellishing; ornamental turn, flourish, or phrase, introduced into melody. Italian singers embellished their arias with arpeggios, gruppetti, and trills, often obscuring the melodic line by it. It is said that the young Adelina Patti sang for Rossini one of his arias; Rossini was voluble in praise of her singing, but wondered, "But, pray, who is the composer of this aria?" Today, no prima donna would dare go beyond the aria's text except in cadenzas or where stylistically correct (i.e., before Romantic opera). Toscanini was known to explode in flowery Italian invective when a singer added so much as an illicit appoggiatura to a solo.

fipple flute. Renaissance end-blown vertical flute or recorder; uses a whistle-like mouthpiece.

first. 1. Of voices and instruments of same class, the highest or most important, as 1st soprano, 1st violin. 2. On the staff, the lowest, as 1st line, 1st space. 3. On string instruments, the highest string.

Fis (Ger.). F sharp.

Fis dur (Ger.). F-sharp major.

Fis moll (Ger.). F-sharp minor.

Fischer, Edwin, b. Basel, Oct. 6, 1886; d. Zurich, Jan. 24, 1960. He studied with Hans Huber in Basel and Martin Krause in Berlin; taught at Stern Cons. in Berlin (1905–14), then the Berlin Hochschule für Musik (from 1931); engaged as conductor in Lübeck, Munich, and Berlin (1926–32); returned to Switzerland (1942). He was renowned as one of the most intellectual pianists of his day and a distinguished pedagogue; founded the Edwin-Fischer-Stiftung to assist young and needy musicians; publ. several valuable books on music.

Fischer, Johann Caspar Ferdinand, b. *c.* 1665; d. Rastatt, Aug. 27, 1746. He was in the service of the Margrave of Baden (1696–1716); followed when court moved to Rastatt (1716); adopted Lully's style, thereby influencing other German composers. His *Ariadne musica neo-organoedum* (1702), a collection of 20 organ preludes and fugues in as many keys, foreshadowed Bach's *Well-Tempered Clavier*.

Fischer-Dieskau, (Albert) Dietrich, b. Berlin, May 28, 1925. His father, philologist and headmaster, was self-taught in music, his mother an amateur pianist. He began to study piano at age 9 and voice at 16; studied voice with Hermann Weissenborn at Berlin's Hochschule für Musik (1942–43); drafted into the German army (1943); made a prisoner of war by Americans in Italy (1945); upon his release (1947), returned to Germany; made his 1st professional appearance as soloist in Brahms's *Deutsches Requiem* in Badenweiler. He resumed vocal training with Weissenborn in Berlin; soon heard on radio over the RIAS; made his operatic debut in the bass role of Colas in a broadcast of Mozart's *Bastien und Bastienne* (1948); later that year made his stage debut as Rodrigo, Marquis of Posa, in *Don Carlos* at the Berlin Städtische Oper, where he remained an invaluable member for 35 years; also pursued his operatic career with appearances at leading opera houses and festivals in Europe.

It was as a lieder and concert artist, however, that he became universally known; made his U.S. debut with the Cincinnati Sym. Orch. (1955); his U.S. recital debut followed at N.Y.'s Town Hall; in subsequent years made tours everywhere to enormous critical acclaim. His finest operatic roles (baritone, bass-baritone, and bass) included Count Almaviva, Don Giovanni, Papageno, Macbeth, Falstaff, Hans Sachs, Mandryka, Mathis der Maler, and Wozzeck. He created the role of Mittenhofer in Henze's *Elegy for Young Lovers* (1961) and the title role in Reimann's *Lear* (1978). His honors include membership in the Berlin Akademie der Künste (1956), Mozart Medal of Vienna (1962), Kammersänger of Berlin (1963), Grand Cross of Merit of Germany (1978), and the Gold Medal of the Royal Phil. Soc. of London (1988). He was married to soprano Julia Varady. Fischer-Dieskau brought lied into the modern phonographic age, with superb recordings of virtually the entire Schubert oeuvre and other important lied composers. He publ. anthologies of song texts and studies of the art of singing.

fischio (It.). Whistle.

fish horn. Colloquial Americanism for ⇒oboe; dates to at least the mid–19th century, judging by this 1867 order issued by Vice Admiral Porter of the U.S. Naval Academy in Annapolis, Md.: "Midshipman Thompson (1st class), who plays so abominably on fish horn, will oblige me by going outside the limits when he wants to practice or he will find himself coming out of the little end of the horn."

Fistel (Fistelstimme; Ger.). Falsetto.

fistula (Lat., pipe). In the Middle Ages, organ pipe. *Fistula anglia*, in the Middle Ages, English flute, i.e., recorder; *fistula germanica*, in the Middle Ages, German flute, i.e., transverse flute.

Fitzgerald, Ella, b. Newport News, Va., Apr. 25, 1917; d. Beverly Hills, June 17, 1996. She began singing in small clubs in Harlem in the early 1930s; discovered by Chick Webb (one of Harlem's most popular musicians) in 1935; she joined his band; upon his death, became its leader (1939); became a freelance singer (1942); subsequently worked with major jazz musicians and groups. She was particularly adept at scat singing and improvising, creating new melodies over given harmonies, in the manner of jazz instrumentalists; was equally at ease in swing and bebop; developed a superlative blend of musicianship, vocal ability, and interpretive insight; achieved a popularity and respect rarely acquired by jazz singers. In 1987 she was awarded the National Medal of Arts. Her recorded "songbooks" of Porter, Ellington, Gershwin, Arlen, Berlin, Kern, Mercer, and Rodgers and Hart are the cornerstone of her legacy.

fixed Do. System of solmization based on equivalence, e.g., in which tone C, and all its chromatic derivatives (C♯, C♭, C✕, C♭♭) are called Do; D and its derivatives are called Re, etc., no matter what key or harmony they appear in; opposite of movable Do.

fixed-tone instrument. One (e.g., piano, organ) whose tones cannot be modified at will while playing; such instruments are said to have "fixed intonation," unlike the violin and saxophone, for example.

flag. Hook ♪ on stem of note: ♪ ♫ ♫ etc.

flageolet (Fr.). 1. Small fipple flute or recorder used in Renaissance to imitate birdcalls; also used as the sopranino flute in ensembles until the 19th century. The French flageolet has compass of 2 octaves and 3 semitones, from g¹ to b³. 2. On the organ, small flute stop of 1' or 2' pitch.

flageolet-tones. See ⇒harmonics.

Flagstad, Kirsten (Malfrid), b. Hamar, July 12, 1895; d. Oslo, Dec. 7, 1962. She studied voice with her mother and Ellen Schytte-Jacobsen in Christiania (now Oslo); made her operatic debut there as Nuri in d'Albert's *Tiefland* (1913); for the next 2 decades, sang throughout Scandinavia in operas, operettas, and concerts. After singing minor roles at Bayreuth (1933), she scored her 1st major success there, appearing as Sieglinde (1934); made an auspicious Metropolitan Opera debut in N.Y. in that role (1935); soon hailed as the foremost Wagnerian soprano of her time; made her 1st appearance at London's Covent Garden, as Isolde (1936); while continuing to sing at the Metropolitan Opera made guest appearances at the San Francisco Opera (1935–38) and the Chicago Opera (1937); gave concerts with major U.S. orchs.

Flagstad returned to her Nazi-occupied homeland to be with her husband (1941), alienating many of her admirers; nevertheless, resumed her career after the war with notable success at Covent Garden; returned to the Metropolitan Opera (1951), singing Isolde and Leonore; made her farewell appearance there in Gluck's *Alceste* (1952); retired from the stage (1954) but continued to make recordings; director of Norwegian Opera in Oslo (1958–60); among her other celebrated roles were Brünnhilde, Elisabeth, Elsa, and Kundry.

flamenco. Popular Andalusian art of singing and dancing, accompanied mainly by guitar and castanets, which gradually developed into an important folk art form. Pedrell and Falla played crucial roles in saving flamenco through special festivals they organized. The meters and rhythms are varied and often polymetric and cross-rhythmic; scales are modal or mixed modal; lyrics, influenced by Gypsy motives, reflect nomadic sentiments of love, fortune, sorrow, and death. Principal genres of flamenco singing are: *cante jondo* (deep song), with microtonal inflections, and *cante chico* (small song). The singing is usually

introduced by stimulating exclamations ("Ay! Ay!") and accompanied by vigorous heel stamping and passionate gesticulation; the resulting dance is called *zapateado* (shoe dance).

Flanagan, Tommy (Lee), b. Detroit, Mar. 16, 1930. He commenced clarinet studies at 6 and piano training at 11, working in local jazz haunts with senior musicians such as Milt Jackson, Thad Jones, and Elvin Jones. In 1956 he went to N.Y.; became pianist and music director for Ella Fitzgerald; performed with Oscar Pettiford, J. J. Johnson, and Miles Davis.

flat. The character ♭, placed before a note to indicate lowering its pitch by semitone; double flat (♭♭) lowers its note by 2 semitones.

flat chord. Chord whose tones are performed simultaneously; solid chord, as opposed to broken or arpeggiated chord.

flat fifth (flat 5). Diminished 5th.

flat pick. Triangle-shaped plectrum, made of tortoise shell or plastic, used for guitar and other instrumental picking in bluegrass and related American music; a. heavier-weight pick is used for electric string instruments. See also ⇒plectrum.

Flatt, Lester (Raymond), b. Overton County, Tenn., June 19, 1914; d. Nashville, May 11, 1979. He joined Bill Monroe's Blue Grass Boys as singer in 1944; formed duo with Earl Scruggs, the banjo player; organized their own band, the Foggy Mountain Boys; established themselves as leading country-music figures. Flatt became famous for his "Lester Flatt G Run" on guitar, matched by Scruggs's 3-finger banjo style. After their partnership fell apart (1969), Flatt played with remaining members of the band, adopting the name Nashville Brass. Among the best-known songs of Flatt and Scruggs were *Roll in My Sweet Baby's Arms*, *Old Salty Dog Blues*, *Ballad of Jed Clampett* (from the inane but popular television sitcom *Beverly Hillbillies*), and *Foggy Mountain Breakdown* (theme song of the film *Bonnie and Clyde*).

Flatterzunge (Ger.). Flutter-tonguing.

flautando (It., like flute). 1. Sound imitating a flute's sonority, especially on the strings. 2. In bowed string music, play near fingerboard so as to produce this sound; the more usual Italian direction is *sulla tastiera* (Fr. *sur la touche*; Ger. *am Griffbrett*).

flauto (It.; Ger. *Flöte*). 1. Flute. 2. Type of organ stop, as *Flauto amabile*, etc. *Flauto becco*, recorder; *flauto di Pane*, panpipe; *flauto diritto*, recorder; *flauto dolce*, recorder; *flauto piccolo*, piccolo; *flauto traverso*, transverse flute.

Fleadh Cheoil. Annual late-summer music festival in County Kerry, Ireland, featuring singing and indigenous Irish instruments.

flebile (It.). Tearful; plaintive, mournful.

flehend (Ger.). Pleading, praying.

Fleisher, Leon, b. San Francisco, July 23, 1928, of Jewish-

Russian immigrant parents; his father was a tailor, his mother a singing teacher. He learned the rudiments of music from his mother, then piano with Lev Shorr; made public debut at age 6; sent to Europe to study with Schnabel at Lake Como, Italy, and, later, in N.Y. At 14 he appeared as soloist in the Liszt A-major Piano Concerto with the San Francisco Sym. Orch.; at 16 was soloist with N.Y. Phil. (1944); became 1st American to win 1st prize at the Queen Elisabeth of Belgium International Competition in Brussels (1952), catapulting him into a brilliant career. He made several European tours; gave highly successful recitals in South America; soloist with the San Francisco Sym. Orch. to observe its 50th anniversary (1961–62).

At the peak of his career, Fleisher was stricken with an at 1st mysterious and mystifying neurological ailment that made the fingers of his right hand curl up on themselves, incapacitating him as a pianist (1964); this condition was eventually diagnosed as carpal tunnel syndrome. Fleisher turned to concertos written for left hand alone commissioned by Paul Wittgenstein, the Austrian pianist who lost his right arm during World War I; Fleisher learned these works and performed them successfully. He began a conducting career, having studied with Monteux in San Francisco and at his conducting school in Hancock, Maine; also profited from Szell's advice; became artistic director of the Theater Chamber Players in Washington, D.C. (1968); added the music directorship of the Annapolis Sym. Orch. (1970). He was associate conductor of the Baltimore Sym. Orch. (1973–77), then its resident conductor (1977–78); guest conducted at the Mostly Mozart Festival in N.Y. and with the Boston Sym. Orch., San Francisco Sym., Cincinnati Sym. Orch., and Los Angeles Chamber Orch.

Treatment with cortisone injections, acupuncture, and biofeedback did not help; Fleisher decided to undergo surgery (1981), which was momentarily successful; returned as a bimanual pianist, playing Franck's *Symphonic Variations* with Sergiu Comissiona and the Baltimore Sym. Orch (1982); sadly, the comeback was short-lived. In 1985 he became artistic director-designate of Tanglewood (1985), fully assuming his duties in 1986; devotes much time to teaching; had already joined the faculty of Peabody Cons. of Music in Baltimore (1959); subsequently named to the Andrew W. Mellon Chair in Piano; visiting prof. at the Rubin Academy of Music in Jerusalem; among his brilliant pupils were André Watts and Lorin Hollander.

fleurettes (Fr., little flowers). In contrapuntal parts, rapid notes, sometimes printed in small type.

flexatone (It. *flessatone*). 20th-century instrument consisting of a metal plate attached to a piece of wood; produces a twanging, imprecisely pitched sound when metal plate is "plucked." Schoenberg used it in his *Variations for Orch.* and *Moses und Aron.*

flexible notation. Modern type of indeterminant notation allowing some aspect of composition to be determined in performance.

fliessend (Ger.). Fluidly, floatingly.

fling. Scottish dance resembling the reel, in quadruple time.

flores (Lat., flowers; It. *fioretti, fiori*). Medieval embellishments in vocal and instrumental music. Insertion of supernumerary notes above and below the melody notes was named *florificatio*; usually such embellishments were added to the discant, but sometimes even the presumably inviolable cantus firmus was adorned by florid ornamentation with *pulchrae ascensiones et descensiones*; such "pretty ups and downs" were also called *licentiae* (acts of license) and *elegantiae* (elegancies). These attractive descriptions have become obsolete, replaced by generic designations of ornaments.

florid. Embellished with runs, passages, figures, graces, etc.

Flöte (Ger.). 1. Flute. 2. Organ stop with flute timbre.

Flotow, Friedrich (Adolf Ferdinand) von, b. Teutendorf, Apr. 27, 1813; d. Darmstadt, Jan. 24, 1883. He was a scion of an old noble family; received 1st music lessons from his mother; was chorister in Gustrow; at age 16 went to Paris; entered the Cons. to study piano with J. P. Pixis and composition with Reicha. After the 1830 revolution, he returned home; completed his 1st opera, *Pierre et Catherine*, in French; premiered (in German trans.) in Ludwigslust (1835). Returning to Paris, he collaborated with other composers on *Lady Melvil* (1838), *L'eau merveilleuse* (1839), and *Le Naufrage de la Méduse* (Paris, 1839); scored decisive acclaim with *Alessandro Stradella*, based on legends of the Italian composer (Hamburg, 1844). He achieved his most lasting success with *Martha, oder Der Markt zu Richmond* (1847), demonstrating ability to combine German sentimental spirit, Italian lyricism, and Parisian elegance; an authentic Irish melody, *The Last Rose of Summer*, was incorporated into the opera. Aristocratic predilections made it difficult for him to remain in Paris after the 1848 revolution; became Intendant at the grand ducal court theater in Schwerin (1855–63); moved to Austria; returned to Germany (1873), finally settling in Darmstadt (1880).

flottant (Fr.). Floatingly.

flourish. Trumpet fanfare or call.

Floyd, Carlisle (Sessions, Jr.), b. Latta, S.C., June 11, 1926. He studied at Syracuse Univ. with Ernst Bacon (Mus.B., 1946; Mus.M., 1949); took piano lessons with Rudolf Firkusny and Sidney Foster; joined faculty of the School of Music of Florida State Univ., Tallahassee (1947); became prof. of music at Univ. of Houston (1976). His best-known musical drama is *Susannah* (Tallahassee, 1955), which continues to be revived; others include *The Passion of Jonathan Wade* (1962), *Of Mice and Men* (1970), and *Willie Stark* (1981); other works include ballets, song cycles, and instrumental pieces.

flüchtig (Ger.). Flightily, hastily; lightly, airily.

Flügel (Ger., wing). Grand pianoforte or harpsichord, so-called because of its winged shape.

Flügelhorn (Fr. *bugle*; It. *flicorno soprano*). Originally, the unvalved hunting horn in 18th-century Germany; this instrument became known as the bugle. In the early 19th century keys were added to create the keyed bugle; by the middle of the century the term *flügelhorn* was applied to a similar instrument with cornet range and valves, used more in military music and jazz than in classical music.

flüsternd (Ger.). Whispering.

flute. The most ancient wind instrument, spontaneously evolved by populations throughout the world, from Mesopotamia to the Andes, from China to Central Africa. Primitive flutes were all vertical pipes, a type later categorized as recorders; they were made of baked clay or reeds with perforated holes which would change pitch when 1 or more of them were covered by the finger. The ocarina (It. *oca*, goose) is of this type, but it looks like a surrealist sculpture of a goose.

Musical mythology is strewn with appearances by the flute. When the cloven-footed god of the woods, Pan, pursued the nymph Syrinx, she was turned into reed to escape him. Heartbroken, Pan made a panpipe of reeds to commemorate her. In pre-Columbian South America, Indians made flutes out of bones (some of which are still extant); there is the legend of the Peruvian Indian whose beloved died young; disconsolate, he went to her burial place, exhumed one of her legs, and fashioned a flute out of her tibia bone. He played wistful melodies upon it; this intimate contact with a part of her body gave him temporary surcease from his sorrow. The Pied Piper of Hamelin lured away town children on their fateful journey by playing on his flute; in Mozart's *The Magic Flute*, the hero Tamino saves himself from disaster by playing on his melodious flute. In poetry, flutes are forever sweet, soft, and pure. Milton speaks in *Paradise Lost* of "flutes and soft recorders moving in perfect phalanx." Swinburne poetizes about "the pure music of the flutes of Greece." In an archetypal Grimm tale (*The Singing Bone*), a young prince is slain by his brothers in rivalry for the throne; a shepherd finds one of his whitened bones, makes holes in it, plays on it; the bone-flute reveals the story behind the fratricide. (Mahler set this tale in his choral work *Das klagende Lied*.)

But despite its cultural ubiquity, the flute did not become a concert instrument until the 18th century. The new flute was the transverse (horizontal, cross) flute, whose sound is produced by blowing across side holes. 1st introduced in Germany, the transverse flute became known as the German flute, while the older recorder, greatly popular in England, was called the English flute. The transverse flute came of age when Quantz, court musician to Frederick the Great (himself a fine flutist), published in 1752 his famous treatise on the art of playing *flute traversière*. In symphonic works flute parts are frequently used in pairs, like their fellow wind instruments (oboes, clarinets, bassoons, horns, and trumpets); the use of a single flute in a symphonic score, as in Beethoven's 4th Sym., is exceptional; concertos for flute were written by Quantz, Handel, and Mozart.

In the 19th century Theobald Boehm, great German flute manufacturer, enhanced flute-playing technique by producing a new fingering system and rearranging key positions; his orch'l flute has a cylindrical bore with 14 openings closed by keys; it is blown through an oval opening near its upper end. Having been made of wood for centuries, flutes began to be manufactured from silver alloys; this permitted them to compete dynamically with the ever larger, ever louder Western orch. The modern French flutist Georges Barrère had a flute made of platinum; Varèse wrote *Density 21.5* (an attribute of platinum) for him.

Brahms assigned a pastoral flute solo in the finale of his 1st Sym. Debussy wrote a piece for flute solo entitled *Syrinx* in honor of Pan's beloved nymph; his *Prélude à l'après-midi d'un faune* opens with a flute solo. The flute is the heavenly bird of sym. and opera. Birds of the forest speak to Siegfried in Wagner's *Ring* through them; Stravinsky's *Firebird* is a flute; so is the helpful bird in Prokofiev's *Peter and Wolf*. The flute enacts the part of the nightingale in Beethoven's *Pastoral* Sym. and in Stravinsky's *Le Chant du rossignol*. The flute is the most agile wind instrument, capable of skipping from one note to another with great ease; but it also matches the human voice in perfect harmony; when Lucia di Lammermor goes mad in Donizetti's opera, she sings her poignant fioriture accompanied by solo flute.

Like all wind instruments, flutes are members of a family. The range of the modern flute (soprano, concert; Fr. *grande flute*; Ger. *grosse Flöte*; It. *flauto*) extends from middle C through 3 octaves (c^1–c^4), but it can be overblown to produce high C sharp, D, and even E flat (eb^4). In modern flutes a special key is provided to produce low B (b). The flute is laden with rich overtones; an attentive ear can even discern a nontempered 7th partial tone when playing in its low register. The range of the *piccolo* is an octave higher than the concert flute, but it lacks C and C sharp in its low register. It can blow through 3 octaves, and its high C (c^5) is the same pitch as the highest piano; no other instrument can rise to such stratospheric heights. Beethoven introduced a piccolo into the finale of his 5th Sym. The *alto flute*'s lowest note is a 4th below the concert flute; a transposing instrument, it is also called the flute in G. Ravel's ballet *Daphnis et Chloé* has an important part for alto flute, invoking the spirit of Pan. The *bass flute* is an elephantine low-voice member, with its range starting an octave below the concert flute (c). A long and wide-bored instrument (wrapped around), it requires considerable lung power to blow and superlative lip technique to articulate. Parisian-American composer Betsy Jolas wrote a piece for piccolo and bass flute.

Avant-garde composers, annoyed by sweet flute sounds, have tried their best (or worst) to improve upon it by instructing players to blow through a flute without producing recognizable pitch, or to clap keys without blowing. Double-tonguing and triple-tonguing, known as *Flatterzunge* (flutter-tongue) technique are favorites in modern flute parts; unnatural harmonics have also been coaxed out of it. In the last quarter of the 20th century the flute has been incorporated into rock and jazz groups, who compensate for the flute's anatomical weakness by amplifying it electronically.

flute à bec (Fr., mouth flute; direct flute). Recorder.

Flûte d'amour (Fr., love flute; It. *flauto d'amore*; Ger. *Lieblichflöte*). Instrument introduced in the late 18th century, pitched a minor 3rd below the concert flute; more or less obsolete.

flute stop. Flue stop; now string stop.

flutter-tongue (Ger. *Flatterzunge, Zungenschlag*; It. *frullato*; Fr. *coup de langue*). Special effect on flute family and (less often) other wind instruments consisting of rapidly repeated insertion of the tongue into mouthpiece, resulting in staccato: single (performed t-t-t . . .), double (t-k/t-k/t-k/ . . .), and triple (t-k-t/t-k-t/t-k-t/ . . .). Another technique is to roll tongue as if trying to pronounce liquid consonants *l* and *r*. Flutter-tongue is vulgarly known among wind players as the "French kiss"; technique has been known since the early 18th century but eschewed in actual playing until it was requested by composers 2 centuries later.

Fluxus. New York art coalition (1962–78), loosely run by architect George Macunias; gave birth to highly original, mostly theatrical, and often humorous mixed-media stage works frequently involving novel uses of sound; musical scores often consisted of written instructions or graphs; among those associated were La Monte Young, Yoko Ono, Dick Higgins, Alison Knowles, Nam June Paik, Jackson Mac Low, Robert Watts, and George Brecht.

foco (It.). Fuoco.

foglietto (It., little leaf). 1. 1st violin part of orch. 2. Part with cues for other instruments written in, helping player orient to entire ensemble.

foglio (It., leaf). Page; folio.

Foley, "Red" (Clyde Julian), b. Blue Lick, Ky., June 17, 1910; d. Fort Wayne, Ind., Sept. 19, 1968. He studied briefly at Georgetown (Ky.) College; started *Renfro Valley Barn Dance* radio program (1937); appeared regularly at the Grand Ole Opry in Nashville; made popular such country-music classics as *Chattanooga Shoeshine Boy*, *Peace in the Valley*, and *Beyond Sunset*; elected to the Country Music Hall of Fame (1967); died while on tour with the Grand Ole Opry.

Folgend (Ger., following). Colla parte; colla voce.

folia (Sp.; It. *follia*; Eng. folly). Portuguese dance originating *c.* 1500, found in popular festivals and theatrical performances, sung and accompanied by rhythmic hand clapping and clacking of castanets. Its strange name points to an apparently orgiastic type of dance; one Spanish writer of the early 17th century describes folia dancers as if "they had abandoned all reason"; later theoretical references coupled folia with sarabandes and chaconnes; 2 related but distinct folias were popular with classical composers from the late 16th century up to Rachmaninoff and beyond. In truth, the folia has very little madness in it; it is a rather stately rhythmic dance in triple time with a long 2nd beat, usually in minor mode.

folk music. 1. Traditional music, passed down by oral transmission; music indigenous to a people, region, state, or country, often modal and with variety of rhythmic and metric approaches. 2. In subsequent compositional use, such music simply arranged as material for imitation and as subject for analysis and reinterpretation. See also ⇒folk song.

folk song. Indigenous song of people, region, state, or country, passed down by oral transmissions. In addition to musical style, there is a strong linguistic element; epic and ballad forms are common. See also ⇒folk music.

follower. Consequent.

fondu (Fr., melting down). Dying away.

foot. 1. Common unit measuring length of vibrating air column in organ pipe. In organ playing standard pipe is 8' C, corresponding to the pitch C 2 lines below bass staff (C); by extension, any organ stop producing the standard pitch of a key depressed on manuals or pedals is called 8' tone. 16' tone is 1 octave below, as the air column activated is twice as long; the 4' stop sounds an octave above a note representing the 8' stop. 2. The part of organ pipe below the mouth. 3. Group of syllables having 1 accent, like simple measure in music.

Foote, Arthur (William), b. Salem, Mass., Mar. 5, 1853; d. Boston, Apr. 8, 1937. He studied harmony with Stephen Emery at New England Cons. of Music in Boston (1867–70); studied counterpoint and fugue with Paine at Harvard College (1870–74; 1st M.A. degree in music granted by an American univ., 1875); studied organ and piano with B. J. Lang, later with Stephen Heller in France (1883). Returning to the U.S., he taught piano, organ, and composition in Boston; organist at Boston's Church of The Disciples (1876–78) and 1st Unitarian Church (1878–1910); frequently appeared as pianist with Kneisel Quartet (1890–1910), performing his own works; founding member and president (1909–12) of American Guild of Organists; taught piano at New England Cons. of Music (1921–37); elected member of National Inst. of Arts and Letters (1898).

Foote's music, a product of Romantic tradition, is notable for its fine lyrical élan; his Suite in E Major for strings (op. 63, 1907) enjoyed numerous performances and became a standard of American orch'l music; other compositions include various orch'l, chamber, and piano and organ pieces, and vocal works, including some 100 songs, 52 part-songs, and 35 anthems; publ. several music textbooks.

foreign chords or tones. Those that do not belong to specific key or scale.

forlana (It.; Fr. *forlane*). Lively Italian dance in 6/8 or 6/4 originating in Friuli; popular in 18th-century Venice. Bach has a forlana in his C-major orch'l suite (BWV 1066); Ravel includes a forlane in *Tombeau de Couperin*.

form. In music, any concept or organization governing order, character, meter, and key of composition. After simple repetition, the most elementary form is binary, in which only 2 sections are presented; ternary form evolved from binary by interpolation of a middle section or by the repetition of the 1st section. In a larger work, such as sonata or sym., formal elements often intermingle and are distinguished by their similarities or contrasts. Musical form is analogous to that found in literature, drama, and pictorial arts; just as living organisms comprise separate parts performing disparate functions, all of them coordinated for normal operation of the entire body, so musical form assembles all component elements of composition in order to produce best possible impression of unity. This may be achieved by means of melodic symmetry, organic alternation of melodic sections, successions of tones within the same harmony, combinations of tones within contrapuntal framework—all these animated by rhythmic flow following certain natural pulse of strong and weak accents.

In the historical developments of formal elements, the deliberate departure from rhythmic or melodic symmetry, harmonic unity, or contrapuntal concordance results in a new type of form that may impress rigid musical minds as being formless; such accusations were directed at Wagnerian endless melody, Lisztian symphonic poems, and impressionistic monothematic compositions; over time such "formless" music becomes itself established as classical form. Paradoxically, even composers that profess formlessness as their aesthetic aims become inventors of superior forms based on principles of organization far removed from simple symmetry or thematic development; Varèse propounded the principle of organized sound as the sole requirement of formal composition.

formalism. Official pejorative term used by USSR authorities to describe the "artificial" nature of offending music, i.e., that of Shostakovich, Prokofiev, Khachaturian, et al.; in Soviet aesthetics, an aesthetic inimical to desirable art. The *Encyclopedic Music Dictionary* (Moscow, 1966) defines formalism as follows:

An artificial separation of form from content, and the attribution to formal elements of self-sufficient primary values to the detriment of musical content. . . . In contemporary aesthetics, formalism becomes a method of art hostile to realism and cultivated especially by the adepts of modernism. Formalism is based on the theory of art for art's sake, counterposing the artist to society and art itself to life, seeking to create an artistic form detached from objective reality. The governing precepts of formalism are the negation of ideological and realistic content of a work of art, a construction of arbitrary new forms, combined with the denial of national cultural heritage. . . . In musical practice, formalism rejects the ideational and emotional musical values and denies the capacity of a musical work to reflect reality. Proponents of formalism attempt to justify their fallacious doctrine by pointing out the specific nature of music as an art lacking the external connection with the world of real objects, such as is present in painting or sculpture, and intrinsically incapable of conveying a concrete narrative characteristic of literature. . . . The struggle for the correct formulation of socialist realism leads to the removal of formalism from its pedestal. *One should not confuse formalism, however, with genuine individual originality or with true innovation in the field of musical forms* and in the inner substance of a composition, which constitute an unalienable part of authentic realistic art (emphasis is the editor's).

formant. In acoustics, the relative strength (amplitude) of partials in the overtone series that determines an instrument's timbre. Stockhausen proposed to use the term to designate rhythmic values as functions of the overtone spectrum of given pitch, so that the 2nd partial tone would represent a rhythmic duration of one-half the metric unit, the 3rd partial (i.e., 12th above the fundamental) would represent one-third of the unit, etc. In ultramodern nomenclature, formant is a catalytic element that forms, deforms, and transforms given timbre into another by means of electronic manipulation.

forte (It.). Loud, strong; usually written as *f. Forte generale*, full organ combination stop; *forte piano*, accent strongly, then instantly diminishing to piano; written as *fp*; *forte possibile*, as loud as possible; *forte tenuto*, loud throughout.

fortemente (It.). Loudly, forcibly.

fortepiano (It., loud-soft). Term distinguishing late 18th-century piano from earlier harpsichord or later grand piano. Cristofori called his early 18th-century invention *gravicembalo col piano e forte*.

forte-stop. On harmonium, slide opened by draw-stop or knee-lever, to produce forte effect.

fortissimo (It.). Very loud; usually written *ff. Fortissississimo*, extremely loud; usually written *fff*.

forza (con forza; It.). With force, forcibly.

forzando (sforzando; It.). With force, energy; accent indicated note or chord strongly; usually written *fz*, *sf*, or *sfz*.

Foss, Lukas, (b. Lukas Fuchs), b. Berlin, Aug. 15, 1922. He was the scion of cultural family; his father was a prof. of philosophy, his mother a talented modern painter. He studied piano and music theory with Julius Goldstein-Herford. When Nazism's dark shadow descended upon Germany, the family prudently moved to Paris, where he studied piano with Lazare Levy, composition with Noël Gallon, orchestration with Felix Wolfes, and flute with Louis Moyse.

Fuchs (he soon changed his name to Foss) emigrated to the U.S. (1937); attended the Curtis Inst. of Music in Philadelphia; studied piano with Isabelle Vengerova, composition with Rosario Scalero, and conducting with Reiner; at Tanglewood, studied conducting with Koussevitzky; studied composition with Hindemith at Yale Univ. (1939–40); became naturalized American citizen (1942). He was awarded 2 Guggenheim fellowships (1945, 1960); 1st public career was as concert pianist, eliciting high praise for appearances as soloist with the N.Y. Phil. and other orchs. He made his conducting debut with the Pittsburgh Sym. Orch. (1939); was pianist of the Boston Sym. Orch. (1944–50); traveled to Rome on a Fulbright fellowship (1950–52); taught composition at Univ. of Calif. in Los Angeles (1953–62); established the Improvisation Chamber Ensemble to perform music of "controlled improvisation."

In 1960 Foss traveled to Russia under the auspices of U.S. State Dept; appointed music director of the Buffalo Phil. (1963); introduced ultramodern works, to the annoyance of some subscribers; resigned (1970); led N.Y. series of "Evenings for New Music" (1964–65); music director of American-French Festival at Lincoln Center, N.Y. (1965). In 1971 he became principal conductor of Brooklyn Philharmonia; established "Meet The Moderns" series there; led the Jerusalem Sym. Orch. (1972–75); music director of Milwaukee Sym. Orch. (1981–86); took it on European tour; named its conductor laureate. He continued to hold Brooklyn Philharmonia post until 1990; throughout the years he was astoundingly active as conductor, composer, and college instructor, offering novel ideas in education and performance; elected member of the American Academy and Inst. of Arts and Letters (1983).

As composer Foss has traversed a protean succession of changing styles, idioms, and techniques; his early compositions were marked by the spirit of Romantic lyricism, adumbrating Mahler's musical language; other works reflected the neoclassical formulas of Hindemith; still others suggested hedonistic vivacity and sophisticated stylization typical of Stravinsky's productions. But the intrinsic impetus of his music was its "pulse," evolving essential thematic content into an original projection. His earliest piano pieces were publ. when he was 15 years old; an uninterrupted flow of compositions in various genres followed; fortunate in being a particular protégé of Koussevitzky, who conducted many of his works with the Boston Sym. Orch.; had no difficulty in finding other performers. As virtuoso pianist he often played piano part in his chamber music; conducted his sym. and choral works; among his compositions are operas, orch'l works, and chamber works, including 3 string quartets.

Foster, Stephen C(ollins), b. Lawrenceville, Pa., July 4, 1826; d. N.Y., Jan. 13, 1864. He learned to play flute as a child but was essentially autodidactic as musician; publ. his 1st song, *Open Thy Lattice, Love,* when he was 18; while working as bookkeeper for his brother Dunning Foster in Cincinnati (1846–50), became interested in songwriting. His hugely successful song *Old Folks at Home* (1851), also called *Swanee River,* established him as a truly American composer; was publ. in 1851, subtitled "Ethiopian Melody as sung by Christy's Minstrels." E. P. Christy was listed as its composer in consideration of a small payment to Foster, whose name was not attached to it until the expiration of the copyright (1879).

Foster married Jane McDowell in Pittsburgh in 1850, but the marriage proved unhappy; left her to live alone in N.Y. (1853–54); settled there permanently (1860). His last years were darkened by addiction to alcohol; died a penniless patient at Bellevue Hospital. Yet his earnings were not small, receiving about $15,000 during the last 15 years of his life. Among Foster's other notable songs were *Oh! Susanna* (1848), *Sweetly She Sleeps, My Alice Fair* (1851), *Massa's in de Cold Ground* (1852), *My Old Kentucky Home, Good Night!* (1853), *Jeanie with the Light Brown Hair* (1854), *Camptown Races* (1854), *Gentle Annie* (1856), *Old Black Joe* (1860), and *Beautiful Dreamer* (1864). His other works include hymns, piano pieces, and arrangements of popular melodies (in the anthology *The Social Orch.,* N.Y., 1854).

fougeux (Fr.). Impulsively.

Four Tops, The. (Vocals: Levi Stubbs, b. L. Stubbles, Detroit, Mich., c. 1938; Abdul "Duke" Fakir, b. Detroit, Dec. 26, 1935; Renaldo "Obie" Benson, b. Detroit, c. 1937; Lawrence Payton Jr., b. Detroit, c. 1936. Popular Motown group of the 1960s that continued to perform with its original membership intact over 4 decades. The group's biggest hits came in the mid-'60s, beginning with 1964's *Baby, I Need Your Lovin'* and including *I Can't Help Myself (Sugar Pie, Honeybunch), It's The Same Old Song,* and *Reach Out (I'll Be There),* all written by Motown house hitmakers Holland-Dozier-Holland, who groomed the group's sound in the studio. The Tops moved to ABC in early '70s, where they continued to enjoy hits, most notably *Ain't No Woman (Like the One I Got);* were soon relegated to the oldies circuit; inducted into Rock and Roll Hall of Fame in 1990.

four-hand piano (piano 4-hands). Pieces written for 2 piano players at 1 piano; one player plays treble parts (right side of keyboard) and the other bass parts (left side). Once very popular for piano pupils, 4-hand playing has all but disappeared from piano teaching. See also ⇒ piano duet.

fourth. 1. Interval embracing 4 degrees. 2. 4th degree in diatonic scale; subdominant.

fox-trot. Popular duple-metered ballroom dance that originated in the 1910s; a variety of fox-trot steps evolved. The music derives from ragtime syncopation; considered "jazz dance" when European and other composers borrowed the style for their stage works and instrumental suites.

fp. Forte piano.

fraudulent modernism. Commercially successful composers of marketable semiclassical music, eager to gain aesthetic equality with sophisticated musicians, like to inject dissonant notes into their abecedarian and often analphabetic productions; proudly, they exhibit pieces using 12 different notes in more or less chromatic order to earn membership in socially distinguished dodecaphonic circles. Combinations of emaciated melodies in spurious atonal manner with dietetic harmonies heavily spiced with discordant irrelevancies is essence of fraudulent modernism. Its adepts often parade in panel discussions, glibly bandying about mispronounced names of the latest celebrities of the avant-garde. Fraudulent modernism fails because of technical inadequacy of its practitioners and of their naive belief that "wrong" notes are credentials of advanced sophistication.

Française (Fr.). Dance in triple time, resembling country dance. See also ⇒écossaise.

francamente (It.). Free in delivery; boldly; frankly, ingenuously.

Franck, César (Auguste-Jean-Guillaume-Hubert), b. Liège, Dec. 10, 1822; d. Paris, Nov. 8, 1890. He studied at the Royal Cons. of Liège with Daussoigne; at age 9 won 1st prize for singing, at age 12, for piano; gave concerts in Belgium as child prodigy. In 1835 his family moved to Paris; studied privately with Anton Reicha; entered the Paris Cons. (1837); studied with Zimmerman (piano), Benoist (organ), and Leborne (theory); received a "grand prix d'honneur" for playing a fugue a 3rd lower at sight, then prizes for piano, counterpoint, fugue, and organ (1838–41). He briefly sojourned to Belgium (1842), but returned to Paris (1843), where he settled for life. In that year he presented a concert of his chamber music; his 1st major work, the oratorio *Ruth,* was given at the Cons.; in the midst of the Paris revolution, he married (1848); became organist of St-Jean-St.-François (1851); maître de chapelle (1853) and organist at Ste-Clotilde (1858), which position he held until his death.

In 1872 Franck succeeded his former teacher Benoist as prof. of organ at the Paris Cons. His organ classes became the focal point for a whole generation of French composers, among them d'Indy, Chausson, Bréville, Bordes, Duparc, Ropartz, Pierné, Vidal, Chapuis, Vierne, and a host of others who formed a school of modern French instrumental music. Until Franck's arrival in Paris, operatic art dominated the musical life of the nation and thus the course of instruction at the Cons.; by emphasizing organ music based on the contrapuntal art of Bach, Franck swayed a new generation of French musicians toward the ideal of absolute music. His teachings were the foundation of the Schola Cantorum by d'Indy, Bordes, and others (1894); after d'Indy's death

(1931), several members withdrew from the Schola Cantorum and organized the École César Franck (1938).

Franck was not a prolific composer, but his creative powers rose rather than diminished with age; his only mature sym. (in D minor) was completed at 66, the remarkable Violin Sonata at 63, the String Quartet composed in the last year of his life. Lucidity of contrapuntal design and fullness of harmony are distinguishing traits; his melodic writing balanced diatonic and chromatic elements in fine equilibrium; although he did not pursue innovation for its own sake, was not averse to using unorthodox procedures; the novelty of introducing the English horn into the Sym. aroused some criticism among academics. He was quite alien to the New German school, which attracted many of his own pupils; his chromatic procedures derive from Bach rather than Wagner. His other works include the oratorios *Les Béatitudes* (1869–79) and *Rédemption* (1873–75); the orch'l *Les Eolides* (1877); *Le Chasseur maudit* (1883); *Les Djinns* (1885); *Variations symphoniques* for piano and orch. (1886); *Psyché* (1888); organ and piano works; sacred and secular vocal works.

Franklin, Aretha, b. Memphis, Tenn., Mar. 25, 1942. Her father, Rev. C. L. Franklin, was a Baptist preacher; moved his family to Detroit; established pastorate, which became a hearth of gospel preaching and evangelical group singing. At 18 Aretha went to N.Y., quickly attracting attention; her singing at the 1963 Newport Jazz Festival led to numerous important and lucrative engagements; sales of her recordings skyrocketed to the million mark. In 1967 she toured Europe; made headlines with her "soul" version of the *Star-Spangled Banner* at the ill-fated Democratic National Convention in Chicago (1968). Among her outstanding albums are *I Never Loved a Man the Way I Love You* (1967), *Lady Soul* (1968), *Amazing Grace* (1972), *Young, Gifted and Black* (1972), *Something He Can Feel* (1976), *Jump to It* (1982), and *Who's Zoomin' Who?* (1985); recorded *One Lord, One Faith, One Baptism* (1987) in her father's church, featuring Rev. Jesse Jackson delivering a sermon against drug abuse among young black people.

Franklin, Benjamin, b. Boston, Jan. 17, 1706; d. Philadelphia, Apr. 17, 1790. A musician, he invented (1762) the "armonica," consisting of a row of glass discs of different sizes set in vibration by light pressure; see also ⇒glass harmonica. A string quartet mistakenly attributed to him came to light in Paris and was publ. there (1946); the parts are arranged in ingenious scordatura; only open strings are used, so that the work can be played by rank amateurs. He wrote entertainingly on musical subjects; his letters on Scottish music are found in vol. VI of his collected works.

frase large (It., broad phrases). Largamente.

Frauenchor (Ger.). Women's chorus.

freddamente (freddo; It.). Coldly; coolly, indifferently.

Frederick II, King of Prussia (Frederick the Great); b. Berlin, Jan. 24, 1712; d. Potsdam, Aug. 17, 1786. He was an enlightened patron of music, a flute player of considerable skill, and an amateur composer; studied flute with Quantz; upon ascending the throne (1740), established court orch. and opera house; Bach's son Carl Philipp Emanuel was his harpsichordist

until 1767. In 1747 J.S. Bach was invited to Potsdam; the fruit of this visit was Bach's *Musical Offering*, written on a theme ostensibly by the King. In addition to composing 121 flute sonatas and 4 flute concertos, Frederick contributed arias to operas by Graun, Quantz, Hasse, and Nichelmann.

free canon. Contrapuntal work written with flexibility as to the rules of canonic composition. See also ⇒canon.

free fugue. Fugue written with more or less disregard of strict rules. See also ⇒fugue.

free jazz. Jazz style of the 1960s and 1970s characterized by collective improvisation without reference to preset harmonic or formal structures.

free part. One voice added to a canon or fugue to complete the harmony.

free reed. Family of wind instruments in which series of reeds are securely attached at one end but move freely at the other; reeds themselves produce differences in pitch through length and thickness. These include keyboard instruments such as the harmonium, mouth-blown instruments such as the Chinese zheng and Japanese sho, and hand bellows–driven instruments, such as the accordion and concertina.

free style. In composition, style in which rules of strict counterpoint are relaxed.

Freed, Alan, b. Johnstown, Pa., Dec. 15, 1922; d. Palm Springs, Calif., Jan. 20, 1965. He helped to desegregate black music by introducing it into white-sponsored radio stations; credited with originating term *rock 'n' roll* in 1951, although it had been used long before in other contexts. He began broadcasting in Cleveland; went to N.Y. (1954) to take command of radio station WINS, which became a popular purveyor of rock 'n' roll. He also appeared in the movie *Rock around the Clock*. He began having trouble when stabbings and riots occurred at concerts he produced (1958); even accused of encouraging such shenanigans for publicity. Then, with horrifying peripeteia fit for Greek tragedy, he suffered monumental downfall in 1963, when he pled guilty to charges of "payola," accepting bribes from record companies to put their songs on the air; also charged with income-tax evasion. He quit N.Y. and fled to more tolerant, laid-back Calif., but soon died, ignored by all.

Freeman, "Bud" (Lawrence), b. Chicago, Apr. 13, 1906; d. there, Mar. 15, 1991. He began his career in Chicago playing with the Austin High School Gang; went to N.Y.; worked with Ben Pollack, Red Nichols, Paul Whiteman, Tommy Dorsey, and Benny Goodman; active with various combos from 1939, including The World's Greatest Jazz Band (1969–71), and made many recordings; publ. books *You Don't Look Like A Musician* (Detroit, 1974) and *If You Know a Better Life, Please Tell Me* (Dublin, 1976).

Frei (Ger.). Free. *Frei im Takt*, metrically free; *frei im Vortrag*, free in style or delivery.

fremente (It.). Furiously.

frémissant (Fr.). Tremblingly.

French horn (horn; Ger. *Horn*; It. *corno*; Sp. *trompa*). Transposing valved brass instrument with spiral conical tube (ranging from 9 feet to 18 feet in length), tunnel-shaped opening, wide and flaring bell, and small, funnel-shaped mouthpiece. It descends from ancient fingered instruments of animal horn, ivory, or wood; the valveless circular hunting horn (17th century) is a closer antecedent. The modern French horn possesses a rich, sonorous, and mellow tone capable of great expressive power.

The source of the name "French horn" is unclear; that it prevents confusion with the English horn is unconvincing, for in other languages this distinction is not made. It is sometimes called *Waldhorn* (Ger., forest horn); Russians transcribed it as *valtorna*. In its modern form it is also called *valve horn* to distinguish it from early valveless horns that produce the glorious natural overtones of their fundamental. Prior to the invention of valves and crooks, the natural horn's use was extremely limited; parts were written in the key of the composition; from early 18th century on, when modulation occurred, player could insert or remove piece of tubing, called a *crook*, to obtain the correct fundamental. With advent of the chromatic horn (Fr. *cor chromatique*), horn parts came to be written and notated almost invariably in the key of F, and are still notated in an unusual manner: The written pitch sounds a perfect 5th down in the treble clef, but up a perfect 4th up in the bass clef.

The horn's range is wider than any other brass instrument (nearly 4 octaves), with possible extensions beyond its upper limit. Its tone production is most unusual, with its mouthpiece very small and its bell very large. In order to produce high tones, the player must adjust the lips in precise acrobatic manner; the danger of hitting wrong upper notes haunts even the greatest horn virtuosos. An especially difficult solo occurs in *Till Eulenspiegels lustige Streiche* by R. Strauss; the story goes that a hornist told him that the passage was unplayable, to which Strauss (son of a famous horn player) retorted that he had gotten the idea for this part while listening to the very same horn player practice during tuning. Horn players have to empty their instrument periodically to remove accumulated saliva, which is apt to cause tonal constipation. A violinist engaged to play in the Horn Trio of Brahms demanded a pair of galoshes before he went on stage.

French overture. Type of orch'l piece developed in 17th-century France in 3 sections: 1st in slow tempo, 2nd rather quick, and 3rd again slow. The French overture usually introduced operas, ballets, or suites; Lully, Purcell, Handel, and Rameau were among those who wrote them. By late century the overture's structure was often reduced to slow-fast; on the other hand, the early 18th-century sinfonia added a fast finale (slow-fast-slow-fast). A further transformation was the slow introductions to Haydn's fast 1st movements and works by Mozart and early Romantics. The French overture should not be confused with the *Overtüre* (Ger.), equivalent of the Baroque suite.

French sixth. Common name for chord containing an augmented 6th between bottom and top notes (closed position), other intervals from bottom being major 3rd and augmented 4th,

e.g., A flat, C, D, and F sharp; resolves to either tonic major or minor (2nd inversion) or dominant (root position):

Freni, Mirella (born Fregni), b. Modena, Feb. 27, 1935. Curiously enough, her mother and the mother of future *primo tenore* Luciano Pavarotti worked at the same cigarette factory; curiouser still, the future opera stars shared the same wet nurse. Freni studied voice with her uncle, Dante Arcelli; made her 1st public appearance at age 11; studied voice with Ettore Campogalliani; made her operatic debut in Modena (1955) as Micaela in *Carmen*; sang in provincial Italian opera houses; sang with the Amsterdam Opera Co. at the Holland Festival (1959), Glyndebourne Festival (1960), Covent Garden in London (1961), and La Scala in Milan (1962).

Freni gained acclaim as Mimi in a film version of *La Bohème*, produced at La Scala, with von Karajan conducting (1963); when La Scala toured Russia (1964), repeated the role at the Bolshoi Theater in Moscow; also performed Mimi in her American debut, with the Metropolitan Opera in N.Y. (1965); subsequently sang with the Vienna State Opera, the Bavarian State Opera in Munich, the Teatro San Carlo in Naples, and the Rome Opera. She traveled with the Paris Opéra during its 1st American tour (1976). She sang the roles of Susanna, Zerlina, Violetta, Amelia in *Simon Boccanegra*, and Manon; won acclaim for her vivid portrayal of Tatiana in *Eugene Onegin*, a popular role for her; sang it at the Metropolitan Opera (1989); appeared as Lisa in *Pique Dame* at La Scala (1990). She married Nicolai Ghiaurov (1981), subsequently appearing with him in operatic performances around the world.

frequency. The rate of vibration of string or air column; the acoustic-mathematical correlate to the sensation of pitch. The height of a pitch is measured by frequency; e.g., in U.S. concert tuning, A = 440 cycles per second (abbrev. cps, Hz). *Frequency modulation*, change made to frequency of wave enabling information transfer to electromagnetic wave (FM).

Frescobaldi, Girolamo, b. Ferrara (baptized), Sept. 9, 1583; d. Rome, Mar. 1, 1643. He studied with Luzzasco Luzzaschi in Ferrara; by age of 14 was organist at Accademia della Morte in Ferrara; in early 1607 became organist of S. Maria in Trastevere; then, in June 1607, traveled to Brussels in retinue of Papal Nuncio; publ. his 1st work, collection of 5-part madrigals, in Antwerp in 1608, printed by Phalèse. Returning to Rome in the same year, he was appointed organist at St. Peter's as successor to Ercole Pasquini. He retained this all-important post until his death, with exception of years 1628 to 1634, when he was court organist in Florence. A significant indication of Frescobaldi's importance among musicians of his time was that Froberger, who was court organist in Vienna, came to Rome especially to study with him (1637–41).

Frescobaldi's place in music history is very great; particularly as keyboard composer, he exercised decisive influence on style of early Baroque; he enlarged expressive resources of keyboard music so as to include daring chromatic progressions and acrid passing dissonances, *durezze* (harshnesses); in Frescobaldi's terminology, *toccata di durezza* signified work using dissonances; he used similar procedures in organ variations on chorale themes (*Fiori musicali*, 1635). His ingenious employment of variations greatly influenced the entire development of Baroque music. He publ. 12 books of keyboard music, 1 book of sacred vocal music, 3 books of madrigals, and scattered individual pieces.

fret. Narrow, raised wedge of wood, metal, or ivory crossing the fingerboard of plucked string instruments, e.g., mandolin, guitar, banjo, lute, and balalaika; strings are stopped (pressed by fingers), the frets guaranteeing proper pitch; intervals between frets are usually semitones.

fretta, con (*frettando, frettoloso;* It.). Hastily, hurriedly.

Freude (Ger.). Joy. *Freudig*, joyfully.

fricassée (Fr.). Musical potpourri; quodlibet.

friction drum. Clay pot with membrane stretched over its top through which stick or sturdy string is passed; this stick is rubbed with wet finger to produce several successive tones. Such drums are common, found in England (pasteboard rattle), Germany (*Reibtrommel; Waldteufel*, forest devil), and France (*cri de la belle-mère*, mother-in-law's cry).

Friedhofer, Hugo (William), b. San Francisco, May 3, 1901; d. Los Angeles, May 17, 1981. He played cello in theater orchs.; studied composition with Domenico Brescia; went to Hollywood (1929); worked as arranger and composer for early sound films; engaged as orchestrator for Warner Brothers (1935); received valuable instruction from Korngold and Steiner. In Los Angeles he attended Schoenberg's seminars; took composition lessons with Toch and Kanitz, also Nadia Boulanger during her Calif. sojourn. He wrote his 1st complete film score for *Adventures of Marco Polo* (1938); composed music for about 70 films. His music for *The Best Years of Our Lives* won the Academy Award (1946); other scores included *Vera Cruz, Violent Saturday, Sun Also Rises*, and *Young Lions.*

Friedhofer was highly esteemed by the Hollywood theatrical community and his studio colleagues for an ability to create congenial musical backgrounds, alternatively lyrical and dramatic, for screen action, while never sacrificing purely musical quality for sake of external effect. He was only Calif. native of the famous Hollywood film composers, most of whom were Germans and Austrians. When a Hollywood mogul told Friedhofer to use French horns in a film taking place in France, he acquiesced and, by extension of dictum, used an English horn solo to illustrate the approach to the cliffs of Dover of those fleeing the French Revolution.

Friedman, Ignaz, b. Podgorze, near Krakow, Feb. 14, 1882; d. Sydney, Australia, Jan. 26, 1948. He studied theory with Riemann in Leipzig and piano with Leschetizky in Vienna; launched extensive concert piano career (1904); gave *c.* 2,800 concerts in Europe, America, Australia, Japan, China, and South Africa; settled in Sydney (1941). He was a renowned Chopin interpreter; prepared an annotated ed. of Chopin's works in 12 vols.; also ed. piano compositions of Schumann and Liszt. He composed 100 or so pieces for piano in effective salon manner, among them a group of *Fantasiestücke*.

Friedrich II (der Grosse). See also ⇒Frederick II (Frederick the Great).

Friml, (Charles) Rudolf (born Frimel), b. Prague, Dec. 2, 1879; d. Los Angeles, Nov. 12, 1972. He was a pupil at the Prague Cons. of Juranek (piano) and Foerster (theory and composition); toured Austria, England, Germany, and Russia as accompanist to Jan Kubelik, touring the U.S. (1900; 1906); remained in U.S. after 2nd tour; gave numerous recitals; appeared as soloist with several orchs. (played his Piano Concerto with N.Y. Sym. Orch.); composed assiduously; lived in N.Y. and Hollywood, composing for motion pictures. Among his successful operettas were *The Firefly* (1912), *High Jinks* (1913), *Katinka* (1915); *Rose-Marie* (1924; very popular), and *The Vagabond King* (1925; highly successful); wrote songs and piano pieces in a lighter vein. MGM made a film of *The Firefly*, (1937), with the popular *Donkey Serenade* added to the score.

frisch (Ger.; It. *brioso*). Brisk, vigorous.

friss (*friska;* Hung.). Rapid 2nd section of Hungarian *verbunkos*, a type of csárdás.

frog (U.K., nut; Ger. *Frosch*; Fr. *hausse*; It. *tallone*). Lower part of bow, nearest the player, where the bow-hair is tightened or loosened. Playing "at the frog" produces a hard, vibratoless sound.

froh (*fröblich;* Ger.). Merrily, joyfully, gaily, gladly.

frottola (It.; plural *frottole*). Polyphonic song genre of Italian Renaissance, popular in northern Italy between *c.* 1470 and 1530; term may have derived from the Italian *frocta* (conglomeration of random thoughts) or *frotta* (flock) because frottole were composed of unusual or unconnected melodic ingredients. Many frottola anthologies were publ. in the early 16th century by Petrucci; arranged in simple harmonies with symmetrical rhythms, they may be accompanied on lute or viols; often only the treble (soprano) was sung. Stylistically, frottola is related to the Spanish villancico and the Italian strambotto; it evolved from the reading of poetry to musical accompaniment, widespread in the 15th century; the musical form was fitted to metrical and rhyme schemes of the poetry selected. Depiction of texts, even those by Petrarch, was of little concern to frottolists; only when the genre evolved into the madrigal did this become important.

Frü(h)lingslied (Ger.). Spring song.

frullato (It.). Flutter-tongue.

frusta (It.). Whip (percussion instrument).

F-Schlüssel (Ger.). Bass or F clef.

F-sharp major. Tonality that numbers 6 sharps in its key signature; it rarely appears as the principal key of large works for orch., chorus, or piano. But curiously enough it is favored by children of a tender age on account of its digitally convenient pentatonic disposition on the piano's black keys. The "Black-Key" Étude of Chopin is in F-sharp major; Scriabin was very fond of this tonality until he abandoned key signatures altogether. The enharmonic tonality of G-flat major has 6 flats in its key signature and enjoyed the favor of Romantic composers almost as much as its sharp alter ego.

F-sharp minor. Key, with 3 sharps in its signature, characterized by poetic delicacy of sentiment. Among the few syms. in F-sharp minor is the *Farewell* Sym. of Haydn, in which musicians leave the stage one after another until the conductor is left alone. Miaskovsky, who wrote syms. in practically every key, assigned F-sharp minor to his 21st sym., the *Symphonie-Fantaisie*. 2 Russian piano concertos, the 1st by Rachmaninoff and the only piano concerto by Scriabin, are in the key of F-sharp minor; the romantic essence of these 2 concertos is unmistakably manifested.

fudging. Rustic form of fuguing; type of free hymn singing once cultivated in the Ozark and Appalachian regions of the U.S. and representing rudimentary canonic form in unison, with traditional homophonic cadences.

fuga (Lat., It.). Fugue.

fugato (It., like a fugue). Passage or movement consisting of fugal imitations not fully worked out, unlike the true fugue.

Fuge (Ger.). Fugue.

fughetta (It.). Short fugue; fugal exposition.

fuging (fuguing) tune. American type of choral psalm vocalization or hymn, popular in New England in the latter 18th century. It is derived from an old English type of psalmody, in which the hymn has a rudimentary canonic section before its concluding cadence. In the U.S. William Billings's fuging tunes became well known; some describe them as the earliest native American music forms. Cowell and Schuman based works on Billings's tunes.

fugue. The most highly developed form of contrapuntal imitation, based on the principle of equality of parts; a theme proposed by one part is taken up successively by all participating parts, thus bringing each in turn into special prominence. The etymological derivation is metaphorically justified, since in fugue (from It. *fuga*, flight) one voice seems to flee from another. Elements essential to every fugue are the subject (theme, antecedent, leader); answer (companion, consequent, follower); countersubject; and stretto. To these are commonly added episodes, organ point, and coda.

With fugue, the art of polyphony reached its supreme achievement. Fugue is a successor to the canon and related to the caccia; but fugue is hardly a mere extension of the canon. The element of imitation is common to both, but while the canon is mechanical in its structure, fugue introduces a new principle of imitation through modulation, from tonic to dominant. A classic fugue opens with a statement of the subject in a single unaccompanied voice, called *dux* in old Latin treatises. Its imitation (answer) in the dominant key enters in a second voice; the treatises called this *comes*. While the answer continues in the comes, the dux presents suitable counterpoint; this continuation of dux is called the *countersubject*.

What distinguishes the fugal modus operandi from canon and other types of literal imitation is the *tonal answer*. In it, the tonic of the dux is echoed in the comes, even if the orig. subject must be altered in the answer. This type of imitation constitutes dislocation of the intervallic structure of the dux. For example, the simple triadic phrase, C–E–G, would normally be literally transposed into the dominant as G–B–D, an exact and therefore *real answer*. But a tonal answer here requires that, in the comes, the 3rd note of the orig. subject be altered to match (thus emphasizing) the tonic of the dux; so the 3rd note of the comes is C, not D, and C–E–G is answered as G–B–C. Still more perplexing is the specification that, once tonal adjustment has been made in the opening of the comes, transposition of the original subject into the dominant key resumes as if nothing had happened.

The formal structure of fugue consists of 3 sections: exposition, episodic development, and return. The exposition presents dux and comes in tonic and dominant, as often as required to introduce all voices. In the episodic development the subject wanders far away from the opening keys; it is then broken up into fragments gleaned from intervallic ingredients of dux and comes, appearing in a variety of keys usually not far from the principal key. Sequential modulatory passages alternate with brief reexpositions of the subject in nontonic keys. These thematic *disjecta membra* are tossed freely about until a saturation point is reached; the dominant of the principal key is sounded, heralding a return of the dux. This return is celebrated in all solemnity, often followed by a coda or codetta, where dux and comes are compressed and foreshortened. *Stretto* (It., narrowing) may make its appearance; in it entries are telescoped in close canonic succession. If used, *pedal point* is embedded deep in the bass on the dominant, preliminary to a glorious conclusion on the tonic.

Fugues of only 2 voices are rare, since they inevitably degenerate into a canon with the imitation in the dominant. In fugues for 3 voices the 3rd voice enters in the tonic, imitating the dux note for note but in another octave. In the meantime yet more new contrapuntal material is entered in the original part of dux. If there are 4 voices, the 4th voice comes in again in the dominant, imitating the comes note by note; fugues of 5 or more voices alternate between tonic and dominant keys, following the form of dux and comes.

Fugue is not the rigid form its formidable reputation makes it out to be; entries do not have to follow one another mechanically. Morphological alterations may take place: dux and comes stood on their heads by melodic inversion, in which ascending passages descend and descending passages ascend; harmony subjected to great stress; unimaginable dissonances formed in the process. Yet in Bach, the teleological drive never falters. Bellwether of fugue, he never followed many rules laid down in pedagogical treatises; his fugues were actually romantic in their flights of fancy, revealed in numerous episodes ingeniously inserted between entries. To suggest the magnificent symmetry of the main proportions of Bach's fugues and the versatility of their ornaments, Busoni was moved in his monumental edition of the *Well-Tempered Clavier* to give graphic rendering to structural elements of Gothic cathedrals on the title page, which to his mind constituted the architectural analogue to the music's grand design. Fugue is indeed a cathedral of polyphony in which the principal lines are never obscured by gargoyles of florid ornamentation.

full. Whole, complete, all. *Full anthem,* written for chorus without solos; *full authentic cadence,* see ⇒cadence; *full band,* band or orch. having all customary instruments; *full cadence,* see ⇒cadence; *full choir,* draw all organ stops of the choir (great, swell); *full chord,* chord having one or more of its original 3 or 4 tones doubled at the octave; *full orch.,* compare *full band; full organ,* with all stops and couplers drawn; *full score,* orch'l score in which all instrumental and vocal parts are written out and aligned vertically; *full to 15th,* draw all stops but mixtures and reeds.

fundamental (note; prime tone). 1. Root of chord. 2. Tone generating harmonic series. 3. Generator of harmonics. *Fundamental bass* (Fr. *basse fondamentale*), progression of harmonic roots, as proposed by Rameau (1722); *fundamental chord, triad,* see ⇒Chords; *fundamental position,* any arrangement of chordal tones in which root remains lowest in pitch; root position.

funèbre (Fr.; It. *funebre*). Funereal, mournful, dirgelike.

funeral march. March in slow 4/4 time in a minor key, sometimes part of a larger work. The most famous funeral march is the slow movement from Chopin's Piano Sonata in B-flat Minor (1839, op. 35), often played at funerals of important persons. Beethoven composed a funeral march "in memory of a great hero" as the second movement of the *Eroica* Sym.

funesto (It.). Somberly, sorrowfully.

funk. 1. African American popular music that developed in the 1960s from African polyrhythms and call-and-response textures. Funk songs often use a single chord or a few alternating, sometimes complex harmonies (*vamping*), through which clipped syncopated lines emerge in electric guitar and bass parts, drums and percussion, keyboards, winds (saxophones, trumpets), and vocal parts. Interjections, often recurrent, by different instruments and voices are another feature, and improvisation falls naturally in place. While many of these elements had existed in earlier popular music styles, the best funk has a highly diverse and often surprisingly thin texture that lends it unique tension (influencing reggae tremendously). Some great funk performers have include James Brown, Sly and the Family Stone, Kool and the Gang, Rufus, Ohio Players, War, and Parliament/Funkadelic. Funk has been able to blend into other styles; always associated with African American social protest, it found its way into 1980s hip-hop, which adapted funk's textures to electronic techniques, editing, and sampling, providing a background for rap. Reggae musicians (such as Bob Marley and Peter Tosh) drew upon funk, although reggae rhythms quickly became stereotyped. As dance music funk evolved into faster, simpler, and less politically threat-ening disco style; when the group Chic had hits with funk-oriented disco, the latter changed accordingly. 2. Hard bop.

Funkoper (Ger.). Radio opera.

fuoco, con (*focoso;* It.). With fire; with spirit, impetuously; in fiery manner.

furiant (*furie;* Cz.). Rapid Bohemian dance written in 3/4 time with alternating duple and ternary measures and strong cross accents.

furioso (It.). Furiously, wildly.

furlana (It.). Forlana.

furniture music (Fr. *musique d'ameublement*). Satie's term for purposely unindelible (i.e., background) music; in what some consider a sustained effort to degrade music and reduce it to menial level, he inaugurated musique d'ameublement, defined as "new music played during intermission at theatrical events or at concerts, designed to create a certain ambience." At an actual performance at a Parisian art gallery, he placed his musicians in separate groups and urged the public to treat them as functional objects, to speak loudly, and not to listen with professional attention; the performers were free to play anything they wished, regardless of repertoire selected by their confrères.

furore (It.). Fury, passion; rage; mania. *Con furore,* passionately.

Furtwängler, (Gustav Heinrich Ernst Martin) Wilhelm, b. Berlin, Jan. 25, 1886; d. Ebersteinburg, Nov. 30, 1954. His father Adolf Furtwängler was a noted archaeologist. Wilhelm grew up in Munich; received private education; studied music with Schillings, Rheinberger, and Beer-Walbrunn; studied piano with Conrad Ansorge. He served as *répétiteur* with Mottl in Munich (1908–1909); became 3rd conductor at the Strasbourg Opera (1910); led sym. concerts in Lübeck (1911–15); engaged as conductor in Mannheim (1915); conducted the Vienna Tonkünstler Orch.(1919–24); concurrently directed the Gesellschaft der Musikfreunde in Vienna (from 1921); led the Berlin Staatskapelle (1920–22) and conducted Frankfurt Museum concerts. A decisive turn in his career was his appointment as chief conductor of the Berlin Phil. (1922) as successor to Nikisch; he also assumed Nikisch's Kapellmeister post at the Leipzig Gewandhaus Orch. (1922–28). He made his American debut with the N.Y. Phil. (1925), greeted with general acclaim; conducted this orch. again (1926, 1927); elected conductor and artistic director of Vienna Phil. succeeding Weingartner (1927–30); the city of Berlin named him Generalmusikdirektor (1928). He made his Bayreuth Festival debut (1931); awarded the prestigious Goe Gold Medal (1932).

In 1933 Furtwängler was appointed director of the Berlin State Opera and vice president of Germany's Reichsmusikkammer. He maneuvered adroitly to secure his independence from increasing encroachment by Nazi authorities on both his programs and personnel of Berlin Phil. and succeeded in retaining several Jewish players. In 1934 he conducted Hindemith's sym. *Mathis der Maler* and was sharply berated by Goebbels, who called

Hindemith a "cultural Bolshevist" and "spiritual non-Aryan." In the face of continued Nazi interference, Furtwängler resigned all in late 1934; but a few months later he made uneasy peace with Nazi authorities and returned to the Berlin Phil., giving his 1st concert in the spring of 1935. He was offered a contract as permanent conductor of the N.Y. Phil. in succession to Toscanini (1936), but had to decline this prestigious offer to quiet rising accusations, on the part of American musicians, of his being a Nazi collaborator. He went to London to participate in the coronation of King George VI (1937); made Commander of the Legion of Honor by the French government (1939). After the outbreak of World War II he confined his activities to Germany and Austria.

Continuing to be loyal to Germany but with ambivalent feelings towards the Nazi government, Furtwängler went to Switzerland in 1945, where he remained during the last months of the war. He returned to Germany in 1946; faced the Allied Denazification Court; absolved from charges of pro-Nazi activities. He conducted the Berlin Phil. for 1st time since war's end, leading an all-Beethoven concert to great acclaim (1947); renewed close associations with the Vienna Phil. and the Salzburg Festival. He was tentatively engaged to conduct the Chicago Sym. Orch. (1949), but offer was withdrawn when public opinion proved hostile. In Western Europe, however, he took both the Vienna Phil. and Berlin Phil. orchs. on several major tours and was received most enthusiastically; became regular conductor with Philharmonia Orch. of London. He reinaugurated the Bayreuth Festival by conducting Beethoven's 9th Sym. (1951); resumed his post as chief conductor of the Berlin Phil. (1952). His last years were clouded by increasing deafness, so that his podium had to be wired for sound. He was to conduct Berlin Phil. on its 1st American tour in the spring of 1955, but death intervened, and von Karajan was elected his successor.

Furtwängler was the perfect embodiment of the great German Romantic school of conducting; his interpretations of music of Beethoven, Schubert, Schumann, Brahms, Bruckner, and Wagner were models of formal purity. He never strove to achieve personal magic with an audience, unlike such charismatic conductors as Stokowski or Koussevitzky. But to professional musicians he remained a legendary master of orch'l sound and symmetry of formal development in sym. music. He was also a composer, quite naturally, of works following the Romantic tradition, with potential exuberance controlled by severe sense of propriety. He wrote several books on music.

fusée (Fr.). Rapid passage.

fusion. See ⇒jazz-funk; jazz.

futurism. Literary and musical modern movement that originated in Italy early in the 20th century; it declared rebellion against traditional art of all kinds and preached the use of noises in musical composition. Futurism was launched by the poet F. T. Marinetti (1876–1942); its musical credo was formulated by Francesco Balilla Pratella (1880–1955) in his *Manifesto of Futurist Musicians* (Milan, 1910) and supplemented by *Technical Manifesto of Futurist Music* (1911). In 1913 Luigi Russolo (1885–1947) published his own Futurist Manifesto (*L'arte dei rumori*, Art of Noises). In these declarations Italian futurists proclaimed their complete disassociation from Classical, Romantic, and Impressionist music and announced their aim to build entirely new music inspired by life in the new century, with the machine as inspiration. As modern machines were most conspicuous by the noise they made, Pratella and Russolo created a new art of noises; Russolo designed special noise instruments and subdivided them into 6 categories. His instruments were rudimentary and crude, with amplification obtained by megaphones, but there is no denying that Futurists provided a prophetic vision of an electronic and experimental future 50 years thence.

Most Futurist musicians and poets were also painters. Their pictures, notably those of Russolo, emphasized color rather than machinelike abstractions and generally approximated manner of abstract expressionism. In the music by Pratella and others we find profusion of modern devices of their futurist day, with foremost place given to whole-tone scales. Futurists gave monody preference over polyphony and steady rhythm to asymmetry.

fuyant (Fr.). Fleeing away.

fuzztone. Onomatopoeic term for distortion effect used primarily on electric guitar in rock. The guitar's electronic path to the amplifier is interrupted by a floor effects box; a fuzztone activating button causes the guitar's signal to overdrive the amplifier, creating highly controlled feedback with desired "dirty" and powerful "fuzz" sound.

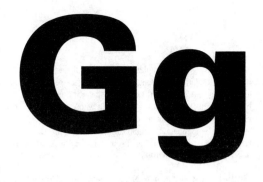

he returned to Venice; appointed 2nd organist at S. Marco; became 1st organist (1585, succeeding Merulo); enjoyed a great reputation as an organist (his two-organ concerts with Merulo were featured attractions); among his pupils were his nephew Giovanni Gabrieli and Hans Leo Hassler.

A prolific composer, Gabrieli wrote a large number of works of all varieties; many were publ. posth., ed. by his nephew. His versatility is attested by an equal aptitude for sacred music, instrumental music, and madrigals, often comic; one of the 1st composers to mix instrumental and vocal forces in the *coro spezzato* style, in motets, masses, psalms, and sacred concertos. His instrumental output includes canzonas *alla francese*, ricercares, organ intonations, toccatas, 3 organ masses, and a battle piece.

G. 1. 7th degree in the alphabetical scale and 5th (dominant) of the C-major scale. In France, Italy, Spain, and Russia, G is called Sol, as it appears in the original syllabic hymn of Guido d'Arezzo. Solmization is the practice of singing scales beginning with Sol, lowest note of the Guidonian hand. 2. *Gauche* (*m.g.*), *main gauche*, left hand. 3. *G.* (*G.O.*), *grand orgue*, great organ.

G clef. Treble clef; see ⇒The Clefs.

G dur (Ger.). G major.

G major. A favorite key of Classical and Romantic composers and their public; its tonic, dominant, and subdominant are strongly represented on open strings of the violin family. It suggests a cloudless landscape and warm sunshine, although it is not as identifiably pastoral as F major. G major is wonderfully suitable for solos on oboe or flute, occasionally echoed by a muted horn. The number of symphonic works in G major is immense; the *Oxford* and *Surprise* Syms. of Haydn; Mozart's entrancing *Eine kleine Nachtmusik*; Beethoven's 4th Piano Concerto; Dvořák's 8th Sym.; Mahler's 4th Sym. Numberless dances for piano are in G major; Paderewski's *Minuet in G* is celebrated.

G minor. A key of earnest meditation. Like G major, its tonic and dominant are represented by 2 open strings on every violin family instrument; as the relative key of B-flat major it provides for natural modulations in the woodwind and brass instruments. One of the greatest syms. is Mozart's Sym. No. 40 (K.550), in which G minor is emphasized in 3 of 4 movements; of his earlier syms., no. 25 in G minor (K.183) is well-known. Among Haydn's syms., *La poule* (The Hen, no. 83) is in G minor. There are numerous solo pieces for violin and other instruments in this key; the Violin Concerto by Max Bruch should be mentioned; the key also lies well for the piano, as demonstrated by the Piano Concerto by Dvořák and the popular 2nd Piano Concerto by Saint-Saëns.

G moll (Ger.). G minor.

G string. The lowest string on the violin. On the viola and cello it is the string above the lowest; on the double bass it is the highest string.

Gabrieli, Andrea (called Andrea di Cannaregio), b. Venice, c. 1510; d. there, 1586. He was a chorister and pupil of Adrian Willaert at S. Marco (1536); organist at S. Geremia in Cannaregio (1557–58); attended the Frankfurt coronation of Maximilian II as court organist of Duke Albrecht V of Bavaria (1564). In 1566

Gabrieli, Giovanni, b. Venice, between 1554 and 1557; d. there, Aug. 12, 1612. He lived in Munich (1575–79); engaged to substitute for Merulo as 1st organist at S. Marco in Venice (1584); appointed as 2nd organist the following year (his uncle Andrea took over the 1st organ); retained this post until his death. As a composer he was a leader of the Venetian school; probably the 1st to write vocal works with instrumental parts (with the instrumentation partly specified, partly left to the conductor) used as accompaniment as well as interspersed instrumental sinfonias. His role as a composer and teacher was epoch-making; through his innovations and development of procedures and devices invented by others (free handling of choirs in multiple-voiced vocal works, "concerted" solo parts and duets in smaller-scale vocal works, trio-sonata texture, novel dissonance treatment, speech rhythm, root progressions in 5ths, use of tonal and range levels for structural purposes, coloristic effects) and through his German pupils (particularly Schütz) and others, he gave a new direction to the development of music.

Gabrieli's instrumental music sparked the composition of German instrumental ensemble music, which would reach its apex in the late Baroque and Classic masters; one of his ricercars, a 4-part work in the 10th tone (1595), is an early example of a "fugue with episodes." His vocal compositions include sacred concertos, sacred syms., and secular concerted madrigals; instrumental works include organ intonations, canzonas and sonatas (for ensemble with basso continuo), toccatas, fantasias, motets and sacred sym. intabulations, and the famous *Sonata pian e forte* (1597). Many of his works appeared in various collections of the period.

Gabrilowitsch, Ossip (Salomonovich), b. St. Petersburg, Feb. 7, 1878; d. Detroit, Sept. 14, 1936. He was a pupil at the St. Petersburg Cons. (1888–94), studying piano with A. Rubinstein and composition with Navratil, Liadov, and Glazunov; graduated and won the Rubinstein Prize; spent 2 years (1894–96) in Vienna studying with Leschetizky; toured throughout Europe. His 1st American tour (N.Y. debut at Carnegie Hall, 1900) was eminently successful, as were subsequent visits (1901–16). He gave a series of 6 historical concerts in Europe illustrating the development of the piano concerto from Bach to the present (1912–13); on an American tour, repeated the entire series in several of the larger cities, meeting with an enthusiastic reception (1914–15). In 1909, he married the contralto Clara Clemens (daughter of Mark Twain), with whom he frequently appeared in joint recitals. He conducted his 1st N.Y. concert (1916); appointed conductor of the Detroit Sym. Orch. (1918); from 1928, conducted the Philadelphia Orch., sharing the baton with Stokowski, while retaining his Detroit position.

gadulka. Pear-shaped Bulgarian traditional fiddle; similar to Russian gudok.

gagaku. Orch. music of the Japanese court and aristocracy, stately and heterophonic, still performed on appropriate occasions. Gagaku is the oldest extant orch. music in the world. Instruments used include the *nyōteki* (transverse flute), *hichiriki* (shawm), *shō* (mouth organ), and *kakko* (barrel drums).

gai (*gaiement;* Fr.; It.). Gaily, lively, briskly.

gaida. Bagpipe found in Bulgaria, Macedonia, Poland, and Ruthenian regions.

gaillarde (galliard; from Fr. *gai*, merry; It. *gagliarda*; Ger. *Gagliarde*). Vivacious court couple dance popular in France, Spain, and England during the late 16th century and the early 17th century. At court occasions the gaillarde usually followed the stately pavane; the 2 dances are in fact related melodically, but the gaillarde transforms the binary meter of the pavane into a relatively lively ternary beat. In England the gaillarde was also known under the French name *cinq pas* (five-step), named for a pattern of 4 strong beats ending with an extra rhythmic step. Queen Elizabeth I reportedly practiced the gaillarde for her morning exercises.

gaita. Generic Spanish and Portuguese term for pipe; refers to various traditional instruments, including bagpipe, shawm, hornpipe, panpipe, flute, and accordion.

gala (from Fr. *regaler*, amuse, entertain). Advertising term to denote a special event.

gala, di (It.). Gaily, merrily.

galant (Fr., elegant, courtly). In the gallant style.

Galanter Stil (Ger.). Gallant style.

Galanterien (Ger.). In the 18th century, the most fashionable pieces, such as theatrical compositions or dance pieces found in the Baroque suite (minuet, gavotte, bourrée, polonaise, air). As the rococo became passé, the term was used derogatorily.

Galas, Diamanda (Dimitria Angeliki Elena), b. San Diego, Aug. 29, 1955. She studied biochemistry, psychology, music, and experimental performance at the Univ. of Calif. at San Diego (1974–79); took private vocal lessons. She and a group of medical students investigated extreme mental states, using themselves as subjects in bizarre mind-altering experiments; her resultant understanding of psychopathology (notably schizophrenia and psychosis) became an recurring subject in her work.

After some success as a jazz pianist, Galas began a vocal career in which her remarkable precision and advanced technique attracted attention; has performed such demanding works as Xenakis's microtonal *N'Shima* (Brooklyn, N.Y., 1981) and Globokar's *Misère* (WDR, Cologne, 1980). She is best known for theatrical performances of her own solo vocal works, most of which employ live electronics and/or tape and are improvised according to rigorous, complex "navigation(s) through specified mental states." Her performances have stringent requirements for lighting and sound and possess a shattering intensity. Her brother Philip Dimitri Galas, a playwright whose works were as violent as is his sister's music, died of AIDS in the late 1980s; her increasing emotional and political involvement in what she regards as the "modern plague" led to her 4-part work *Masque of the Red Death* (from 1986).

Galilei, Vincenzo, b. S. Maria a Monte, near Florence, *c.* 1520; d. Florence (buried), July 2, 1591. Skillful lutenist, violinist, and student of ancient Greek theory, he was a prominent member of the artistic circle meeting at Giovanni de' Bardi's house and known as the Florentine Camerata; his compositions for solo voice with lute accompaniment were the starting point of the monody cultivated by the founders of the *opera in musica* (Peri, Caccini, etc.); a zealous advocate of Grecian simplicity (as opposed to contrapuntal complexity), publ. several tracts advancing his theories, all of historical interest; publ. *Fronimo . . .* (lute transcriptions and compositions, 1568–69), lute intabulations (1563, 1584), 4- and 5-voiced madrigals (1574, 1587), and 2-part contrapunti (1584). He was the father of the great astronomer Galileo Galilei.

gallant style (Fr. *style galant*). A mid–18th–century term for the "elegant" aesthetic of composition that gradually superseded the strict and purely musical Baroque idiom of Bach and Handel. There is no particular "gallantry" in this style; the term denotes salonlike music, homophonic rather than polyphonic, serving to entertain rather than enlighten, to evoke sentiment rather than meditation; in this sense it is synonymous with rococo. Paradoxically, the gallant style was given dignity and even nobility by sons of the great Bach, Wilhelm Friedemann and Carl Philipp Emanuel, who initiated the *Empfindsamer Stil*, a pre-Romantic fashion of musical affects intended to move music away from austere formalism toward human expressiveness and the "natural" philosophy of Rousseau and the French Encyclopedists. Instrumental pieces in the gallant style were sometimes called *Galanterien*. Dance movements are the favored forms, brevity the most striking feature; also, a symmetry of phraseology, facile melodiousness, and pleasing, charming, humorous, playful, and merry qualities.

galop (Fr.; Ger. *Galopp*). 1. Lively circle ballroom dance in syncopated 2/4 time of the mid–19th century; Liszt wrote a *Grand Galop Chromatique*. 2. In many traditional cultures, a group dance featuring rapid movement in imitation of horses.

Galway, James, b. Belfast, Dec. 8, 1939. His 1st instrument was the violin; soon began to study flute; at age 14, went to work in a piano shop in Belfast; a scholarship enabled him to go to London; continued to study flute and took courses at the Royal College of Music and the Guildhall School of Music and Drama; received a grant to go to Paris; studied with Gaston Crunelle at the Cons. and privately with Marcel Moyse. His 1st professional job as flutist was with the wind band at the Royal Shakespeare Theatre in Stratford-upon-Avon; played with the Sadler's Wells Opera Co., the Royal Opera House Orch., and the BBC Sym. Orch.; appointed principal flutist of the London Sym. Orch., later with the Royal Phil. Orch.; engaged by Karajan as 1st flutist in the

Berlin Phil. (1969–75). Abandoning his role as orch. flutist, he devoted himself to a concert artist's career; in 1 season (1975–76) appeared as a soloist with all 5 major London orchs.; toured in the U.S., Australia, Asia, and Europe. He became successful on television, playing his 18-karat–gold flute; commissioned new works for flute and orch.; publ. *Flute* (London, 1982).

gamba (It., knee; from Ger. *Gamben*). 1. Viola da gamba. 2. Organ stop similar in tone. 3. In U.K., the bass viol.

game music. Games of musical composition, in which cards, each containing a musical phrase, are put together according to special rules, are of considerable antiquity. One such game, "Musikalisches Würfelspiel," was 1st marketed in London (1806), announced as "Mozart's musical game, enclosed in an elegant box instructing in a system of easy composition by mechanical means of an unlimited number of waltzes, rondos, horn pipes, reels and minuets." The attribution to Mozart is spurious, but the game itself has a certain ingenuity: Players throw a pair of dice; the resulting number indicates a particular card containing a musical phrase; since each card is musically interchangeable with other cards (containing melodies in similar ranges set to similar harmonies), there would be no difficulties.

More modern and facetious is the conceit suggested by the English musician William Haves in *The Art of Composing Music by a Method Entirely New, Suited to the Meanest Capacity* (1751). In the author's words: "Take a brush with stiff bristles (like a toothbrush), dip it into an inkwell, and, by scraping the bristles with the finger, spatter with one sweep a whole composition onto the staff paper. You have only to add stems, bar lines, slurs, etc., to make the opus ready for immediate performance. Whole and half-notes are entirely absent, but who cares for sustained tones anyway!" This was indeed a proleptic anticipation of avant-garde methods 200 years later.

The most ambitious musical game of the 20th century is *Strategie* by Xenakis, 1st performed at the Venice Festival (1963). In it, 2 conductors lead 2 different orchs. in 2 uncoordinated works. The audience declares the winner, taking into consideration the excellence of each orch'l group, marking points on the scoreboard for most striking rhythms, best coloristic effects, and finest instrumental solos.

Modern scores descriptive of games are numerous. Honegger wrote a symphonic movement, *Rugby*; Bliss composed a ballet, *Checkmate*; Paul Reif named a chamber orch'l work *Philidor's Defense*, inspired by an 1858 chess game. Stravinsky portrayed a poker game in his *Jeu de Cartes*, a "ballet in 3 deals" in which the joker is defeated by a royal flush in hearts; a more abstract score by Stravinsky, entitled *Agon*, also portrays a competition. Debussy's ballet score *Jeux* depicts an allegorical game of tennis. Ives wrote pieces touching on baseball and football. As for operatic depictions of sport, William Schuman's *The Mighty Casey* (1951–53) is well known.

gamelan. Generic Indonesian orch., variously comprised of tuned gongs, chimes, drums, flutes, chordophones, xylophones, and small cymbals; strongly associated with but not limited to the islands of Java and Bali. The ensemble is heard on its own or accompanies dance and theater performances, some lasting all night. During its height, each royal court had its own set and style of instruments, repertoire, and performers; the end of the monarchical system meant their dispersion; villages have kept the tradition alive.

The repetitive structure of most gamelan music is based on heterophonic and colotomic principles—quasi-monophony in several parts and the signification of meter through a variety of gong strokes. The trance-like atmosphere is leavened by quiet solos and, in Balinese gamelan, spectacularly precise performances of complex rhythmic stops and starts. There are 2 tuning systems, the *pelog* (heptatonic) and *slendro* (pentatonic), but there are no absolute guidelines concerning scalar interval or actual pitch frequency.

The survival of gamelan music is an example of ethnomusicology at its best. Europe had heard its 1st gamelan at the Paris Exposition of 1889; interest was great, and recordings circulated. By the time Western musicologists had begun serious study in Indonesia, gamelan music was in decline along with the courts. Western musicologists (notably composer Colin McPhee) studied the instruments; learned, wrote down, and analyzed the music; observed the theater and dance it accompanied; recovered whatever of the older repertoire they could; and, in McPhee's case, helped reinvent a genre (*ketchak*, the monkey dance). Gamelan is one of the most thriving of traditional musics today, with continuing stylistic change; new and historic gamelan orchs. are found throughout the world.

gamut (from Grk. *gamma* + Lat *ut*; It., Rus. *gamma*; Fr. *gamme*). 1. Scale or pitch range; derived from the Guidonian *gamma-ut*, the 1st note of the hexachord. 2. Collection of sounds available to a composer or instrument. 3. Metaphorical range, e.g., range of expression available to a performer.

Gang (Ger.). Passage. One of Bach's Lydian-mode chorales begins with the text "O schwerer Gang"; the "difficult passage" comprises 3 successive whole tones, encompassing the tritone.

gangar. Norwegian walking dance in 2/4 time.

ganz (Ger.). 1. Whole; *ganze Note*, whole note. 2. Very; *ganz langsam*, very slowly.

Ganztonleiter (Ger.). Whole-tone scale.

garbamente (*garbato;* It.). Gracefully, elegantly; in a refined style.

Garcia, Jerry (Jerome John), b. San Francisco, Aug. 1, 1942; d. Serenity Knolls, Marin County, Calif., Aug. 9, 1995. He was a high school dropout who served in the U.S. Army; began performing with rock groups, especially those cultivating the new electric sound; he performed with a group named the Warlocks (1965–67), which had a strong blues basis. Garcia's most successful creation was the Grateful Dead; in its original lineup it included keyboard and harmonica player Ron "Pigpen" McKernan (b. San Bruno, Calif., Sept. 8, 1945; d. Corte Madera, Calif., Mar. 8, 1973), classically trained bass guitarist Phil(ip Chapman) Lesh (b. Berkeley, Calif., Mar. 15, 1940); Bob (Robert Hall) Weir (b. San Francisco, Oct. 16, 1947); and drummer Bill

Kreutzmann (b. Palo Alto, Calif., June 7, 1946). Later acquisitions included classically trained keyboardist Tom Constanten (b. Long Branch, N.J., Mar. 19, 1944); percussionist Mickey (Michael) Hart (b. Brooklyn, N.Y., Sept. 11, 1943); vocalist Donna Godchaux (b. San Francisco, Aug. 22, 1947); and keyboardists Keith Godchaux (b. San Francisco, July 19, 1948; d. Ross, Calif., July 23, 1980, Brent Mydland (b. West Germany, Oct. 21, 1953; d. Lafayette, Calif., July 26, 1990), and Vince Welnick (b. Phoenix, Ariz., Feb. 21, 1951). Garcia and Weir contributed the bulk of the songwriting; all except Lesh, Kreutzmann, Constanten, and Hart provided vocals.

After experimental albums featuring then-new electronics and extended modal solos, the mortuary connotations of the group continued with such albums as *Workingman's Dead*, with its country-rock sound and improved vocal harmonies, and *American Beauty*. Garcia's innovative use of electronic amplification established a state of the art for clean, loud, psychedelic rock sound. The Dead (as they were known) toured almost endlessly and had a large following known as the Deadheads; yet the group probably played more free concerts than paid ones and started a genuinely charitable foundation. On one notable occasion they made a sensational tour to Egypt to play at the foot of the Pyramids for the benefit of the mummified ungrateful dead once buried there, contributing funds to the Egyptian Dept. of Antiquities.

The Dead were best loved in concert, although many of their studio recordings feature fine and subtle arrangements and recording techniques. With the significant importance of hallucinogenic and other drugs to group members at different times (McKernan died of alcoholism, Mydland of an overdose), concerts could range from the mediocre to the sublime but the community around them seemed to accept whatever they offered. Members of the group, especially Garcia, made solo albums or albums with their own groups. Garcia's health became an increasingly difficult issue in the last decade of the Dead's existence; a combination of a heart condition, diabetes, and the effects of years of drug-taking finally killed him; surviving members of the group 1st agreed to disband, but reunions are now planned.

García Lorca, Federico, b. Fuentevaqueros, June 5, 1898; d. Granada, July or Aug. 1936. The playwright and poet was an amateur guitarist and singer who set a number of poems to folk melodies; more importantly, was extremely interested in the flamenco genre of *cante jondo*; with Falla and others, encouraged the revival of the genre. He explored the more profound implications of "deep song" in the Spanish soul and duende. Since his death, many of his poems have been set (notably by Crumb, Ohana, and Henze); his plays are the basis of many operas, including *Blood Wedding* and *Yerma*. He was murdered during the Spanish Civil War by the Falangists.

Gardiner, John Eliot, b. Springhead, Dorset, Apr. 20, 1943. He was educated at King's College, Cambridge; while still a student, founded the Monteverdi Choir (1964); went to France to study with Nadia Boulanger; returning to England, took postgraduate courses with Thurston Dart at King's College, London. He made his 1st major conducting appearance at the Promenade Concerts in London (1968); conducted at the Sadler's Wells Opera and at Covent Garden; continued giving concerts with

his Monteverdi Choir; founded the English Baroque Soloists, which played works on original instruments. He was principal conductor of the CBC Radio Orch. in Vancouver (1980–83); artistic director of the Göttingen Handel Festival (from 1981) and the Orch. de l'Opéra de Lyon (1982–89). He was made chief conductor of the North German Radio Sym. Orch. in Hamburg (1991). He prepared performing eds. of scores by Rameau and others; rediscovered the MS of Rameau's opera *Les Boreades* (Paris, 1971), which he conducted at Aix-en-Provence (1982).

Garfunkel, Art, b. N.Y., Nov. 5, 1941. With high school classmate Paul Simon he started a song duo; produced a fairly successful record, *Hey, Schoolgirl,* under the group name Tom and Jerry. Their next common effort (as Simon and Garfunkel), *Sounds of Silence,* was a major hit when it was issued in 1965; demonstrated versatility by writing the soundtrack for *The Graduate,* featuring the popular *Mrs. Robinson.* Their album *Bridge Over Troubled Water* was widely praised in pop circles; but the 2 went their separate ways (1970). In addition to releasing solo recordings, Garfunkel took up acting, appearing in *Catch-22, Carnal Knowledge,* and *Bad Timing: A Sensual Obsession;* tried his hand at writing poetry. He was reunited with Simon (1982), producing a fine album, *The Concert in Central Park.*

Garland, Judy (born Frances Ethel Gumm), b. Grand Rapids, Minn., June 10, 1922; d. London, June 22, 1969. Having been reared in a family of vaudeville entertainers, she made her stage debut at age 2; toured with her sisters before breaking into motion pictures (1936); gained wide recognition for her film appearances with Mickey Rooney. She won a special Academy Award as well as immortality for her portrayal of Dorothy in *The Wizard of Oz* (1939), adopting *Over the Rainbow* as her theme song; appeared in such musical films as *For Me and My Gal* (1942), *Meet Me in St. Louis* (1944), *Easter Parade* (1948), and *In the Good Old Summertime* (1949).

In succeeding years Garland concentrated mainly on nightclub and concert hall performances; made several more compelling film appearances, notably in *A Star Is Born* (1954) and *Judgment at Nuremberg* (1961). In spite of success, her private life overwhelmed her as a string of misfortunes, including marital difficulties, drug dependency, and suicide attempts, became public; her fans remained steadfastly loyal until her death. Her daughter Liza Minnelli (b. Los Angeles, Mar. 12, 1946) became a successful singer and actress (notably in the film of *Cabaret,* 1972).

Garner, Erroll (Louis), b. Pittsburgh, June 15, 1921; d. Los Angeles, Jan. 2, 1977. Completely untutored and unlettered, he composed tunes extemporaneously, singing and accompanying himself at the piano, with an amanuensis to put down the notes; played drums and slap-bass; his nervous rubato style won acclaim. Incredibly precocious, he played regularly over KDKA in Pittsburgh at age 7 with a group called the Candy Kids; as an adolescent, played piano on riverboats cruising the Allegheny River; played piano in nightclubs and restaurants. He went to N.Y. in 1944; formed his own trio (1946); went to Paris (1948), and toured Europe (1962, 1964, 1966, and 1969). His whimsical piano style especially appealed to French jazz critics, who called him "The Picasso of the Piano" and "The Man with 40 Fingers";

the Republic of Mali issued a postage stamp in his honor (1971). Among his own songs, the plangent *Misty* became greatly popular; many of his other 200 songs reflect similar wistful moods, such as *Dreamy, Solitaire,* and *That's My Kick.*

Gassenhauer (Ger.). Street song; formerly, an authentic folk song or newly composed folk-songlike piece. An eponymous work is the best known of the pieces that make up the Orff-Keetmann *Schulwerk.*

gathering note. 1. In chanting, a hold on the last syllable of the recitation. 2. In Anglican churches, note sounded on the organ a beat before the congregation starts singing, to give pitch.

gato. Popular country dance of Argentina, in 6/8 and 3/4 time.

gauche (Fr.). Left. *Main gauche* (*m.g.*), left hand.

gauche dexterity. Satire and burlesque depend for their effect on deliberate violations of traditional rules of melodic structure, rhythmic symmetry, and harmonic euphony; sophisticated imitation of such semiliterate gaucherie can become an art in itself: Stravinsky reproduces the heterogeneous harmony of the barrel organ in *Petrouchka*; Milhaud tonalizes the natural cacophony of a barroom in *Le Boeuf sur le toit*; Mozart's *A Musical Joke* contains innumerable "mishaps" in all their glory. To some, Satie elevated the dexterity of his gaucherie to a high art of musical persiflage; he may have been helped by his alleged lack of academic compositional technique, making it easier for him than for formally schooled masters to imitate ineptitude.

gaudioso (It.). Joyous, julibant.

gavotte (Fr.; It. *gavotta*). Baroque and Classic French dance in strongly marked duple time; a half-measure upbeat gradually became characteristic. The gavotte's formal structure is ternary, the middle section being a *musette* (Fr., bagpipe), usually in the dominant, which often has a pedal point on its tonic and dominant in the bass, imitating a drone. The derivation of *gavotte* is uncertain; may be an old name for the natives of Provençal hill country. The gavotte has reappeared in Romantic and 20th-century music (e.g., Prokofiev's *Classical Sym.*), but the intent seems more nostalgic than musical.

Gay, John, b. Barnstaple, Devon (baptized), Sept. 16, 1685; d. London, Dec. 4, 1732. *The Beggar's Opera,* for which Gay wrote the lyrics, was premiered in London (1728) and was immensely popular for a century, chiefly because of its sharp satire and the English and Scots folk melodies it used; has had a number of successful revivals. The government disliked it and forbade the performance of its sequel, *Polly,* the score of which was publ. (1729); when *Polly* was finally performed in London (1777), it was a fiasco because the conditions satirized no longer prevailed.

Gaye, Marvin (Pentz), b. Washington, D.C., Apr. 2, 1939; d. Los Angeles, Apr. 1, 1984. Marvin sang in the choir of his father's church; played the drums at school; sang with a group called Rainbows (1956) until they split; joined a separate group, the Marquees, which became the Moonglows. He was recruited by Motown in Detroit (1961); made successful duet recordings with Tammi Terrell (1946–70), including *Ain't No Mountain High Enough* (1967) and *Ain't Nothing Like the Real Thing* (1968); among solo hits were *Can I Get A Witness* (1963), *Ain't That Peculiar* (1965), and *I Heard It Through the Grapevine* (1968); successful individual albums include *What's Going On* (1970), *Let's Get It On* (1973), and *Midnight Love,* including *Sexual Healing* (1983), on which he performed almost every instrumental part. His career was broken up by divorces (he was married thrice) and bouts with cocaine and other narcotics; yet his bringing of the Motown sound into the age of funk was a major and influential accomplishment. He was murdered by his father during an argument over money.

Gebrauchsmusik. Utility music; music for everyday use; this term emerged in Germany after World War I, its 1st mention found in the magazine *Signale für die Musikalische Welt* (1918). Gebrauchsmusik should ideally be performable by amateurs, its texture free from the strictures of academic usage. Unresolved dissonances are liberally admitted; rhythmic patterns emulate the music turned out by untutored composers of popular ballads. Gebrauchsmusik promoted new mechanical instruments, the radio, the phonograph, and music for the films.

A variety of Gebrauchsmusik was *Gemeinschaftsmusik* (community music), cultivating choral singing; the term was later changed to *Sing- und Spielmusik* within the generic category of *Hausmusik.* Probably the 1st work written for such groups was *Das neue Werk* by Hindemith. Another innovation in Gebrauchsmusik is spoken rhythmic song, a variant of Sprechstimme. In opera the librettos were satirical and political, with a radical bent; the music was proletarian; Hausmusik and Gebrauchsmusik someimtes relied on the participation of its operatic audience. From Germany operatic Gebrauchsmusik was transplanted to America, where economic impoverishment contributed to its popularity (1930s); but it did not succeed in Russia, France, or Italy, countries with a rich operatic culture, therefore no motivation to reduce operatic productions to miniature dimensions.

To compensate for the loss of old educational music, composers of Gebrauchsmusik promulgated a neoacademic doctrine of giving simple pleasure to beginners; children's music is a natural product of Gebrauchsmusik. The earliest example of such neoacademic Gebrauchsmusik is Hindemith's piece for school children, *Wir bauen eine Stadt*; Orff succeeded in enlarging the concept by composing pieces modern in harmony, rhythm, and orchestration and yet demanding little professional skill to perform (the *Schulwerk*). Easy humor is an important part of Gebrauchsmusik; Toch combined wit with ostensible erudition in his *Geographic Fugue* for speaking chorus, which recites names of exotic places in rhythmic counterpoint. *Mikrokosmos* by Bartók presents Gebrauchsmusik of considerable complexity without losing its musical innocence; modern-minded children enjoy playing it. N. Slonimsky's album of *51 Minitudes* for piano includes varieties of polytonal and atonal music.

gebunden (Ger.). Tied; legato.

gedackt (Ger.). Stopped (organ pipes).

gedämpft (Ger.). Damped; muffled; muted.

gedehnt (Ger.). Sustained, prolonged; slow, stately; largamente.

Gedenkschrift (Ger. memorial writing). Collection of writings to honor the memory of a musical scholar, teacher, or composer. See also ⇒Festschrift.

Gefallen, nach (Ger.). Ad libitum.

gefällig (Ger.). Pleasing, graceful.

Gefärte (Ger.). The fugal answer.

Geflüster (Ger.). Whisper, murmur. *Wie ein Geflüster*, like a whisper, murmuring.

Gefühl, mit (Ger.). With feeling, expressively.

Gegensatz (Gegenthema; Ger.). The fugal countersubject.

gehalten (Ger.). Held back, restrained.

gehaucht (Ger., sighed). Very softly and lightly sung (or played).

geheimnisvoll (Ger.). Mysteriously.

gehend (Ger.). Andante.

Geige (Ger.). Violin; fiddle.

Geigenprinzipal (Ger.). Violin diapason organ stop.

Geisslieder (Ger. *Geissl*, scourge). Chants of the flagellants praying for the cessation of the plague and other calamities during the Middle Ages; these chants became the melodic and rhythmic sources of German folk songs of the Renaissance period.

Geist (Ger.). Spirit, soul; essence.

geistliche Musik (Ger.). Sacred music.

gelassen (Ger.). Calm, placid, easy.

geläufig (Ger.). Fluent, easy. *Geläufigkeit*, fluency, velocity.

geloso (It.). Jealous.

gemächlich (Ger.). Easily, comfortably, leisurely; comodo.

gemässigt (Ger.). Measured; moderato.

Gemeinschaftsmusik (Ger.). Communal singing or playing; although of ancient origin, popularized as part of the program of Hausmusik.

gemendo (It.). Moaning.

gemessen (Ger.). As measured; moderato.

gemischte stimmen (Ger.). Mixed voices.

gemischter Chor (Ger.). Mixed choir, i.e., SATB.

gemshorn (Ger.; Eng. goat-horn). 1. Obsolete Renaissance *Blockflöte* or recorder in the shape of an animal horn. 2. Organ stop making a sweet pastoral sound, suggesting a natural horn.

Gemüt(h), mit (Ger.). With feeling; soulfully.

gemüt(h)lich (Ger.). Easily and cheerily; disinvolto; comodo (in tempo).

Generalbass (Ger.). Basso continuo.

Generalpause (Ger.). Written silence for entire orch.

Generalprobe (Ger.). In Europe, an open rehearsal prior to the official 1st night of a production.

generator. 1. Chordal root; harmonic fundamental. 2. Tone producing a series of harmonics.

generoso (It.). Free, ample.

genius. Unfortunate term applied to literature, art, or music, derived from the name of a tutelary deity; in Roman usage, applied to a person or his habitation. One need not embrace Edison's cynical definition, "Genius is 10% inspiration and 90% perspiration," to be careful to use the word with caution. Schumann contributed to the mythology of the word when he let his fictional musician Eusebius exclaim, "Hats off, a genius!", as he began to play Chopin's op. 2 variations on Mozart's *Là ci darem la mano*; another time, when the young Brahms showed to Schumann one of his early works, Schumann noted in his diary: "Johannes Brahms was on a visit. A genius!" When the Vienna music critic Julius Korngold brought his 10-year-old son Erich to Mahler to play, Mahler became greatly agitated and kept exclaiming, "A genius! A genius!"

Popular mythology prescribes that geniuses must behave erratically, eccentrically, and/or unpredictably; Beethoven, Berlioz, and Liszt fit this romantic description in part; but Beethoven, like Mozart before him, was a craftsman 1st and foremost. Bach upsets the popular picture of a genius; to his contemporaries he was an honest and earnest worker, modestly performing his functions as church composer, organist, and rector of a boys' school. Brahms fit comfortably into the bourgeois framework of the Viennese middle class. Among virtuosos who looked like geniuses was Paganini, whose press agents spared no effort to represent him as God- and Satan-inspired in his violin playing. (Violinist Gidon Kremer virtually sweeps the stage during a concerto performance.) Rachmaninoff, a great pianist as well as highly popular composer, presented a visage, to one critic, of a provincial banker; another performer described him as the only pianist who did not grimace when playing.

Ravel seemed to lack all external attributes of genius; he had a poor sense of pitch, his memory was not retentive, he was a mediocre piano player and practically helpless as a conductor; Stravinsky was only marginally better in these external gifts. If one must conjure up the vision of a genius among modern composers, Scriabin would fit the part; the appearance of a distraught visionary, delicate physique, inability to cope with life's hard realities, messianic complex, belief that he was called upon to unite all arts in one mystical consummation, all combined to create the impression of a genius incarnate. But Schoenberg, who came far closer to reforming music and changing its direction, presented the antithesis of conventional ideas of genius; he was bald, lacked social graces, was not a good performer on any instrument, and only a passable conductor of his own works.

"Genius" was often applied to symphonic conductors. Bülow established the outward appearance of a genius of the baton—tall, erect, and imperious. Toscanini was not extravagant in appearance, but possessed magic as a conductor. Any list of flamboyant conductors, in approximate chronological order, might include Nikisch, Koussevitzky, Stokowski, and Bernstein. Antipodally, many masters of the baton have an unprepossessing outward appearance. The romantic picture of a genius at work need be treated only as a literary or artistic metaphor; its definition is vague, its contours inevitably overlapping with such concepts as virtuosity, stimulating spirit, ingratiating social qualities, and inability to communicate with the world at large.

genre. Any category of literature, painting, sculpture, and, by extension, a specific form or type of composition. Vocal music genres include opera, oratorio, cantata, or lied; instrumental genres include sym., sonata, concerto, or suite. The term is sometimes applied to specific formal categories (march, rag, waltz). However, a genre is not the same as a historic style (Renaissance, Classic), idiom (orch., violin and piano), or formal structure (sonata form, theme and variations).

geomusic. Theoretical relationship between soil and soul, between land and life. Most remarkable of geomusical facts is that an area of only 75,000 square miles (equivalent to one-third of Tex.) comprises Bonn, Hamburg, Berlin, Prague, Leipzig, Salzburg, and Vienna; and embraces the birthplaces of Bach and Handel, Haydn and Mozart, Beethoven and Schubert, Brahms, Schumann and Mendelssohn, Wagner and Bruckner, Richard Strauss and Johann Strauss, Smetana and Dvořák, Mahler and Schoenberg.

The most accomplished violinists of the 20th century came from Poland, Ukraine, and Lithuania, among them Heifetz, Elman, Isaac Stern, and father and son Oistrakh, all Jewish. What is the secret here? What is this peculiar affinity between young Jews of Eastern Europe and the violin? The small peninsula of Italy generated the finest flowering of opera, an art born in Florence, which produced masters such as Monteverdi, Rossini, Verdi, and Puccini, and singers such as Caruso, Patti, and Pavarotti; it bore the greatest opera conductor, the uncontrollably temperamental Toscanini. Italians, in fact, were in charge of most opera houses; the Metropolitan Opera of N.Y. was in Italian hands until the 1930s. The most widely performed operatic composer living in America is the Italian Menotti.

If Italy produces great tenors, Russia is the land of great basses, the grandest being Chaliapin. When Russian composers entered the world scene in the 19th century, the names of Glinka, Rimsky-Korsakov, Mussorgsky, and Tchaikovsky testified to the natural Russian gift in all musical fields; despite the political upheavals of the Revolution, Russian achievement continued to be great. Stravinsky, Prokofiev, and Shostakovich remain dominant; Russian pianists, violinists, and cellists continue to win prizes at international festivals. France contributed to music in a less heroic and grandiose way; the French of the modern age,

Debussy and Ravel among them, provided music of sensual beauty, leaving the field of sym. and grand opera to the Germans and the Russians.

It is geomusic's task to account for these selective pursuits within particular nations; and beyond the already mentioned locales lie the totally different arts of musical North and South America, Asia, Africa, and Australia. Who could imagine until recently that the 2 greatest American orchs. would be led by Asians, namely Seiji Ozawa and Zubin Mehta? Natural selection plays an irresistible role in art as well as life.

gepeitscht, wie (Ger.). As if struck with a whip (Mahler, 6th Sym.).

Gerber, Ernst Ludwig, b. Sondershausen, Sept. 29, 1746; d. there, June 30, 1819. He studied organ and theory with his organist father; then law and music in Leipzig; became a skillful cellist and organist; appointed his father's assistant (1769); succeeded him (1775). He visited Weimar, Kassel, Leipzig, and other cities; gathered a large collection of musicians' portraits, appending brief biographical notices; conceived the plan of writing a biographical dictionary of musicians. Though his resources were hardly adequate to the task, the *Historisch-biographisches Lexikon der Tonkünstler* (Leipzig, 2 vols., 1790–92) was well received; it brought in a mass of corrections and fresh material from all quarters; he prepared a supplementary ed. Though the orig. was intended only as a supplement to J.G. Walther's *Musicalisches Lexicon* (1732)—and both are, of course, out-of-date—they contain much material still of value and have been extensively drawn upon by more recent writers. The Viennese Gesellschaft der Musikfreunde purchased his library.

German dance. Deutscher Tanz.

German flute. 18th-century name for transverse flute or cross flute.

German sixth. Common name for chord of the augmented 6th between bottom and top notes (closed position); other intervals from the bottom are a major 3rd and doubly augmented 4th, e.g., A flat, C, D sharp [E flat], and F sharp; resolves to a tonic 6/4 chord as follows (in C minor):

Gershwin, George, (born Jacob Gershvin), N.Y., Sept. 26, 1898; d. Los Angeles, July 11, 1937. His father was a Russian immigrant whose orig. name was Gershovitz. Gershwin's extraordinary career began at age 16, playing piano in music stores; took piano lessons with Ernest Hutcheson and Charles Hambitzer in N.Y. and harmony with Edward Kilenyi and R. Goldmark; later on, as a famous composer of popular music, studied counterpoint with Cowell and Riegger; during his last years he studied earnestly with Joseph Schillinger (1895–1943), hoping to organize his technique scientifically; some Schillinger methods were applied in *Porgy and Bess*. But it was his melodic talent and a genius for rhythmic invention that made him a genuinely important American composer.

There was no period of worldly struggle in Gershwin's life; one of his earliest songs, *Swanee*, became enormously popular (more than a million copies and 2,250,000 phonograph records sold); wrote a lyrical *Lullaby* for String Quartet (1920); possessing phenomenal energy, produced musical comedies in close succession; used fashionable jazz formulas in original and ingenious ways; a milestone was his *Rhapsody in Blue* for Piano and Jazz Orch., with the jazz idiom applied to an essentially classical form; played the solo part at its premiere conducted by Whiteman in N.Y. (1924). Although the orchestration was by Grofé, a circumstance that generated rumors of Gershwin's inability to orchestrate, he later produced several orch'l works, scored by himself in a brilliant fashion. He also premiered the solo part of the piano *Concerto in F*, with Walter Damrosch and the N.Y. Sym. Orch. (1925); its popularity never equaled that of the *Rhapsody in Blue*.

Reverting to a popular idiom, Gershwin wrote the symphonic *An American in Paris* (N.Y. Phil., led by Damrosch, 1928); the *Rhapsody No. 2* was premiered by Koussevitzky and the Boston Sym. (1932), but was unsuccessful; also composed a *Cuban Overture* (N.Y., 1932) and Variations for Piano and Orch. on his *I Got Rhythm* (Boston, 1934, composer soloist). In the meantime, he became engaged in his most ambitious undertaking: *Porgy and Bess*, an American "folk opera" for black singers, with lyrics by his brother Ira, after the book by Dubose Heyward; was 1st staged in Boston and N.Y. (1935); its press reception was not uniformly favorable, but its songs rapidly attained great popularity (*Summertime; I Got Plenty o' Nuthin'; It Ain't Neccessarily So; Bess, You Is My Woman Now*); the opera has since been successfully revived; received international recognition when an American company of black singers toured with it in South America and Europe (1955).

Gershwin's death (of a gliomatous cyst in the right temporal lobe of the brain) was a shocking and great loss to American music; the 50th anniversary of his death brought forth special tributes in 1987, including a joint broadcast of his music by the PBS and BBC. His musicals and revues, most of which were collaborations with Ira, include *George White's Scandals* (1920-24), *Our Nell* (1922), *Lady, Be Good!* (1924), *Tip-Toes* (1925), *Oh Kay!* (1926), *Strike Up the Band* (1927), *Funny Face* (1927), *Rosalie* (1928), *Girl Crazy* (1930), *Of Thee I Sing* (1st musical to win a Pulitzer Prize, 1931), *Let 'em Eat Cake* (1933); for motion pictures: *Shall We Dance*, *A Damsel in Distress* (both 1937), and *The Goldwyn Follies* (completed by V. Duke, 1938).

Gershwin, Ira (born Israel Gershvin), b. N.Y., Dec. 6, 1896; d. Beverly Hills, Calif., Aug. 17, 1983. He attended night classes at the College of the City of N.Y., writing verses and humorous pieces for the school paper. He began writing lyrics for musicals and revues, using the pseudonym Arthur Francis (1918); his 1st full-fledged show as a lyricist was *Be Yourself*, for which he used his own name for the 1st time.

Ira Gershwin achieved fame when he wrote the lyrics for his brother George's musical comedy, *Lady, Be Good!* (1924);

remained his brother's collaborator until George's death (1937); his lyrics became an inalienable part of the whole, so that the brothers Gershwin became artistic twins, like Gilbert and Sullivan, indissolubly united in some of the greatest productions of American musical theater: *Strike Up the Band* (1927), *Of Thee I Sing* (1931), and the culmination of their genius, the folk opera *Porgy and Bess* (1935). He wrote lyrics for other composers, among them V. Duke (*The Ziegfeld Follies of 1936*), Weill (*Lady in the Dark*, 1941), Kern (the enormous hit *Long Ago and Far Away* from the film *Cover Girl*, 1944), and Romberg, A. Schwartz, and Arlen.

Ges (Ger.). G flat.

Ges dur (Ger.). G-flat major.

Ges moll (Ger.). G-flat minor.

Gesamtausgabe (Ger.). Complete edition of a composer's works.

Gesamtkunstwerk (Ger., collective art work). Wagner's notion that all arts are interrelated; that their ultimate synthesis should be the idea of each constituent art; that painting and figurative arts should serve the cause of architecture and stage representations; that poetry should relate to philosophical concepts; and that music should be both the servant and the mistress of its sister arts. In his music dramas Wagner hoped to achieve unity of the arts by assigning equal importance to the text, orch. music, singing, acting, and scenic design; this was yet another attempt at operatic reform after the model of ancient Greek tragedy.

Gesang (Ger.). Singing; a song; melody; vocal part.

Gesangbuch (Ger.). Songbook, especially a hymn book.

gesangreich (gesangvoll; Ger.). Very singingly; cantabile.

geschleift (Ger.). Slurred; legato.

geschleppt (Ger.). Dragged out in tempo; schleppend.

Geschmackvoll (Ger.). Tastefully.

geschwind (Ger.). Swift, quick, rapid.

gesprochene Musik (Ger., spoken music). Music consisting entirely of spoken syllables arranged in rhythmic patterns; a popular technique in Germany between the 2 World Wars; the best-known example is Toch's *Geographical Fugue*.

gestalt. An ensemble of apperceptions produced by a series of sensory stimuli; translated as form, figure, configuration, or appearance, gestalt indicates a psychological interaction between the physical nature of a given phenomenon and the inner interpretation of it by a receptive mind, e.g., the shape of a white vase against a uniformly black background may be perceived as 2 human figures facing each other if the symmetric sides of the vase are drawn to resemble silhouettes.

In music, gestalt is capable of many interpretations, of which the most literal is enharmonic ambivalence, as the perception of a triad as a dissonance, or the nonrecognition of a scale, in the context of alien harmonies; another is the expectation built up by a particular harmonic or melodic construct within a given style. The power of a gestalt may lead to performance error, as when a player "corrects" a written chromatic scale with 1 note intentionally left out by the composer, or changes an unfamiliar rhythm or meter to a familiar one. This expectation may also cause proofreaders and editors to change what they perceive to be "wrong notes," a problem angrily encountered by Beethoven and Ives.

The grandest application of gestalt is the apprehension of an entire ensemble of musical parameters, comprising form, proportional distribution of consonances and dissonances, diatonic or chromatic tropism, and symmetry or asymmetry of melorhythmic figurations; by analogy, a painter may absorb a landscape so completely that each part of it becomes an integral component of the whole. Schoenberg and others proposed a theory whereby the gestalt of a piece—a summation of its essence—was expressed in its opening measures. The idea, like Schenker's Urlinie, has in itself a universality that requires far more and deeper analysis of a piece to support it on an individual basis, lest it become a benignly obstructive substitute for knowledge.

gesteigert (Ger.). Intensified, increasing in dynamics; rinforzato.

Gestopft (Ger.). Indicating a note stopped by placing a hand in the bell of brass instruments, particularly the French horn.

gestossen (Ger.). 1. Staccato. 2. Détaché.

gestrichen (Ger.). Play with the bow; arco.

geteilt (Ger.). Divided; divisi.

getragen (Ger.). Sustained; sostenuto.

Getz, Stan(ley), b. Philadelphia, Feb. 2, 1927; d. June 6, 1991. While a teenager he joined Jack Teagarden's group; played with Stan Kenton, J. Dorsey, and Goodman; after a stint with W. Herman, embarked upon a series of recordings with Mulligan, Gillespie, and other noted jazz musicians. He was a major exponent of the samba movement in the 1950s and 1960s; collaborated with A. C. Jobim and A. Gilberto; joined the faculty of Stanford Univ. (1984); an impressive exponent of cool jazz.

Gewandhaus (Ger., drapery shop). The building in Leipzig in which the famous Gewandhaus concerts were inaugurated in 1781. The Leipzig Gewandhaus was a textile workshop before it was converted into a concert hall.

gewichtig (Ger.). With weight, significantly, ponderously.

gewirbelt (Ger.). 1. Warbled. 2. Execute drumroll rapidly.

gezogen (Ger.). Drawn out, slowing down; largamente, sostenuto, stesso.

ghiribizzoso (It.). Whimsically, capriciously, fancifully.

ghironda (It.). Hurdy-gurdy.

Gibson, (Sir) Alexander (Drummond), b. Motherwell, Feb. 11, 1926. He was educated at the Univ. of Glasgow and the Royal College of Music in London; took courses at the Salzburg Mozarteum and in Siena; made his conducting debut at the Sadler's Wells Opera in London (1952); associate conductor of the BBC Scottish Sym. Orch. in Glasgow (1952–54). He became principal conductor of the Scottish National Orch. in Glasgow (1959–1984); founded that city's Scottish Opera, becoming its 1st music director (1962–87). Queen Elizabeth II knighted him for his services on behalf of Britain's musical life (1977); principal guest conductor of the Houston Sym. Orch. (1981–83); renowned for his congenial performances of Romantic works, particularly those of the English school.

Gideon, Miriam, b. Greeley, Colo., Oct. 23, 1906; d. New York, N.Y., June 18, 1996. She studied piano with Hans Barth in N.Y. and Felix Fox in Boston; enrolled at Boston Univ. (B.A., 1926); took musicological courses at Columbia Univ. (M.A., 1946); studied composition privately with Lazare Saminsky and Sessions. She taught at Brooklyn College (1944–54, when forced to resign for political reasons); appointed prof. of music at the Jewish Theological Center (1955); joined the faculty at the Manhattan School of Music (1967); prof. of music at the City College of the City Univ. of N.Y. (1971–76); elected to the American Academy and Inst. of Arts and Letters in 1975. She wrote music in all genres, in a style distinguished by its attractive modernism; perhaps her best-known works are the song cycles with chamber accompaniments.

Gielen, Michael (Andreas), b. Dresden, July 20, 1927. His father, Josef Gielen, was an opera director who settled in Buenos Aires in 1939, his uncle the pianist Eduard Steuermann. Michael studied piano and composition with Erwin Leuchter in Buenos Aires (1942–49); on staff of the Teatro Colón there (1947–50); studied with Polnauer in Vienna (1950–53). He became a *répétiteur* at the Vienna State Opera (1951); became resident conductor (1954–60); principal conductor of the Royal Opera in Stockholm (1960–65); conductor with the Cologne Radio Sym. Orch. (1965–69); chief conductor of the Orch. National de Belgique in Brussels (1968–73) and the Netherlands Opera in Amsterdam (1973–75). He was artistic director of the Frankfurt Opera and chief conductor of its Museumgesellschaft concerts (1977–87); chief guest conductor of the BBC Sym. Orch. in London (1979–82); music director of the Cincinnati Sym. Orch. (1980–86). In 1986 he became chief conductor of the Southwest Radio Sym. Orch. in Baden–Baden; a prof. of conducting at the Salzburg Mozarteum (from 1987). Gielen has acquired a fine reputation as an interpreter of contemporary music; he is also a composer.

Gieseking, Walter (Wilhelm), b. Lyons, France (of German parents), Nov. 5, 1895; d. London, Oct. 26, 1956. He studied with Karl Leimer at the Hannover Cons. (graduated 1916); served in the German army; began career with extensive tours of Europe; made American debut in N.Y. (1926); appeared regularly in the U.S. and Europe with orchs. and in recital. He became the center of political controversy when, having arrived in the U.S. in 1949 for a tour, he was accused of cultural collaboration with the Nazi regime; public protests forced cancellation of scheduled Carnegie Hall performances; later cleared by an Allied court in Germany; able to resume his career in America. He appeared again at Carnegie Hall (1953); until his death, gave numerous performances in both hemispheres.

Gieseking was one of the most extraordinary pianists of his time; a superb musician capable of profound interpretations of both Classic and modern scores, he projected with the utmost authenticity the music of Mozart, Beethoven, Schubert, and Brahms; his playing of Debussy and Ravel was remarkable; was an excellent performer of works by Prokofiev and other modernists. He composed some chamber music and made piano transcriptions of songs by R. Strauss.

gigalira (It.). Xylophone.

gigue (from Old Fr. *giguer*, dance; It. *giga*). Popular Baroque dance in a rapid tempo, its beats divided into groups of 3 short notes; in 6/8 or 12/8 (less frequently, 3/8 or 9/8). The last movement of a Baroque suite was quite frequently a gigue. The Italian giga tends to be livelier than the more stately French gigue. Whether the name derives from the English or Old French is open to question; the term does appear in English virginal music before Continental sources. See also ⇒jig.

Gilbert, Henry F(ranklin Belknap), b. Somerville, Mass., Sept. 26, 1868; d. Cambridge, Mass., May 19, 1928. He studied at the New England Cons.; studied composition with MacDowell in Boston (1889–92); choosing to give up routine music work to earn a living (e.g., theater violinist), took jobs of many descriptions and composed when opportunity afforded. At the 1893 Chicago World's Fair, he met a Russian prince who knew Rimsky-Korsakov and gave him much information on Russian composers who, along with Bohemian and Scandinavian composers who based their work on folk song, influenced Gilbert greatly in his later composition.

Hearing of the successful premiere of Charpentier's *Louise*; Gilbert became so interested in the popular character of the work that, in order to hear it, earned his passage to Paris by working on a cattle boat (1901); the opera impressed him so much that he decided to devote his entire time to composition. In 1902 he became associated with Farwell, whose Wa-Wan Press publ. Gilbert's early compositions (1902).

From 1903 Gilbert employed Negro tunes and rhythms extensively in his works; his mature compositions (from 1915) reveal an original style, not founded on a specific American style but infused with elements from many sources; many are an attempt at "non-European" music, expressing the spirit of America and its national characteristics. His best-known works are the *Comedy Overture on Negro Themes* (1905), *The Dance in Place Congo* (1906), *Negro Rhapsody* (1913), *American Dances* (1915), *Indian Sketches* (1921), *Nocturne* ("symphonic mood" after Whitman, 1928).

Gilbert, (Sir) W(illiam) S(chwenck), b. London, Nov. 18, 1836; d. Harrow Weald, Middlesex, May 29, 1911 (of cardiac arrest after successfully rescuing a young woman from drowning). He received an excellent education at Boulogne and King's College, London; after a routine clerical career, drifted into journalism; contributed drama criticism and humorous verse to London periodicals. His satirical wit was 1st revealed in a theater

piece, *Dulcamara* (1866), ridiculing grand opera; met Arthur Sullivan (1870); began collaborating on comic operettas. Some plots borrow ludicrous situations from actual Italian and French operas; Gilbert's librettos, in rhymed verse, are nonetheless unmistakably English; this insularity of wit explains their enormous popularity in English-speaking countries and their near total obscurity on the Continent. Despite the fact that the targets of Gilbert's ridicule were usually the British upper classes, the works were often performed at court. After 20 years of fruitful cooperation with Sullivan, a conflict developed, and the 2 severed their relationship; a reconciliation was effected, but the resulting productions fell short of their greatest successes. Gilbert was knighted in 1907 (7 years after Sullivan's death). See also ⇒Sullivan, (Sir) Arthur.

Gilels, Emil (Grigorievich), b. Odessa, Oct. 19, 1916; d. Moscow, Oct. 14, 1985. He entered the Odessa Cons. at age 5 to study with Yakov Tkatch; made his 1st public appearance at 9, his formal debut at 13; after further studies with Bertha Ringbald at the Cons., went to Moscow for advanced studies with Heinrich Neuhaus (1935–38). He won 1st prize at the Moscow Competition (1933), 2nd prize at the Vienna Competition (1936), and 1st prize at the Brussels Competition (1938); that year became a prof. at the Moscow Cons. Following World War II, during which he joined the Communist Party, he embarked upon an esteemed international career; was the 1st Soviet musician to perform in the U.S. during the Cold War era, playing the Tchaikovsky 1st Piano Concerto with Ormandy and the Philadelphia Orch. (1955); subsequently made 13 tours of the U.S., the last in 1983. He was one of the foremost pianists of his time, especially renowned for his Beethoven, Schubert, Schumann, Chopin, Liszt, Tchaikovsky, and Brahms. His sister Elizabeta Gilels (b. Odessa, Sept. 30, 1919) was a violinist who took 3rd place in the Ysaÿe Competition (Brussels, 1937) and taught at the Moscow Cons. (from 1967). She married the violinist Leonid Kogan; their son, Pavel Kogan, was also a talented violinist.

Gillespie, "Dizzy" (John Birks), b. Cheraw, S.C., Oct. 21, 1917; d. Jan. 7, 1993. With Charlie "Bird" Parker, he established the bebop jazz style. He picked up the rudiments of music from his father; at age 18, went to Philadelphia; joined a local jazz band. In 1939 he joined Cab Calloway's orch.; by 1944 was playing with Billy Eckstine's band; formed his own band (1945); many other groups followed, none long-lived. He met Parker in 1940; the 2 were cofounders of the frenetic and improvisationally chromatic style variously known as bebop, bop, and rebop; he later experimented with Afro-Cuban jazz (*A Night in Tunisia*). His nickname derived from his wild manner of playing, making grimaces and gesticulating during his performances; he was undoubtedly one of the greatest jazz performers, a true virtuoso on the trumpet, extending its upper ranges and improvising long passages at breakneck speed. In 1989 he received the National Medal of Arts.

gimmicks. Musical tricks are usually regarded as beneath the dignity of a composer or a performer, but the greatest composers were known to indulge in experimenting with devices that have nothing to do with music per se. But some popular works of great musical significance are based on a fortuitous arrangement of letters translated into musical notes. B–A–C–H (in non-German nomenclature, B♭–A–C–B) was used thematically by the composer and many others; D–S–C–H, from the German spelling of Shostakovich, yields D–E♭–C–B (the "S" becomes "es," or E-flat), used by the composer and others. Schumann often used this technique, notably in *Carnaval*, based on the hometown of his 1st love (A-S-C-H). Berg used measure numbers encryptically to represent himself and his paramour in the *Lyric Suite*. Castelnuovo-Tedesco programmed names of his friends according to the recurrent series of the English alphabet and wrote variations and fugues for them as birthday greeting cards. The American expatriate composer Tom Johnson (b. 1939) wrote *The Four-Note Opera* (referring to pitch class). Another American, Ernst Bacon (1898–1990), developed a rather curious technique in his piano works in which both hands play, simultaneously or successively, symmetrically positioned chords or arpeggios, so that, for example, E-flat, G, C in the right hand would be accompanied or echoed (counting downwards) by G-sharp, E, B in the left.

Visual elements in composition are of demonstrable value if for nothing else than the greater understanding of the nature of notation. An 18th-century anonymous score exists that, when lying flat on a table, can be played in perfect harmony by 2 violinists sitting across from one another. Naturally the piece is in G major, because the location of the G-major triad in the treble clef does not change when the page is turned upside down, although subdominant triads become dominant ones. Another ambitious piece for piano of more recent origin is entitled *Vice-Versa*; when read from page 1 to page 8, or upside down from page 8 to page 1, it comes out precisely the same. Hindemith wrote more than one piece with a "mirror" placed at the eventual midpoint, after which the piece would simply reverse itself. Such devices have been used with some profit for centuries.

The aesthetic and technical value of musical gimmicks ultimately lies in the adage that art must be difficult in order to be elevating. Numerous examples of deliberately set limitations in the arts and sciences have led to interesting discoveries. A peculiarly absurd example is an American novel written by an individual who tied down the *e* key on the typewriter and wrote the entire manuscript without using the most common letter in the English alphabet. Painters who restrict their palette and drawing vocabulary are setting themselves limits. The musical equivalent is the canon and the fugue, in which the composer sets considerable limitations and challenges for both the composing and realization of the works. In truth, any proscription of technique or material will seem utterly restrictive in some hands, totally liberating in others.

gimping. In string instruments, the overspinning of gut strings with fine copper or silver wire; used in the Baroque period mainly on the lower strings—G on the violin, C and G on the viola and cello. To some early music practitioners, excessive gimping precludes an authentic rendering of the true Baroque sound.

Ginastera, Alberto (Evaristo), b. Buenos Aires, Apr. 11, 1916; d. Geneva, June 25, 1983. Of Catalan descent, Ginastera pronounced his name with a soft *g*, as in Catalan. He took private music lessons as a child; entered the National Cons. of Music in Buenos Aires; studied composition with José Gil, Athos Palma, and José André; took piano lessons with Argenziani. He began to compose in early youth; won 1st prize of the musi-

cal soc. El Unísono for his *Piezas infantiles* for piano (1934); his next important piece was *Impresiónes de la Puna* for flute and string quartet (1942), in which he used native Argentine melodies and rhythms; however, he withdrew it and a number of other works, including *Concierto argentino* (1935); his 1st Sym., the *Sinfonia Portena*; and the 2nd Sym., *Sinfonía elegíaca* (1944), even though the latter was successfully performed. In 1946–47 Ginastera traveled to the U.S. on a Guggenheim fellowship; returning to Argentina, was appointed to the faculty of the National Cons. in Buenos Aires, where he taught intermittently (1948–58); dean of the faculty of musical arts and sciences at the Argentine Catholic Univ.; prof. at the Univ. of La Plata.

From his earliest compositions Ginastera showed an intuitive identification with the melodic and rhythmic resources of Argentine folk music, evolving a fine harmonic and contrapuntal setting congenial with native patterns. His 1st significant "Argentine" work was the ballet *Panambí* (1935), performed at the Teatro Colón in Buenos Aires (1940); there followed a group of *Danzas argentinas* for piano (1937) and the song *Canción al árbol del olvido* (1938), a fine evocation of youthful love that became quite popular. In 1941 he was commissioned to write a ballet for the American Ballet Caravan, *Estancia*; the music was inspired by the rustic scenes of the pampas; a suite was performed at the Teatro Colón (1943), then the complete work (1952). A series of works inspired by native scenes and for various instrumental combinations followed, all infused with his poetic imagination and brought to realization with excellent technical skill. He began to search for new methods of musical expression, marked by modern, sometimes strikingly dissonant combinations of sound, fermented by asymmetrical rhythms; of these works, the most remarkable is *Cantata para América mágica*, scored for dramatic soprano and percussion instruments, to apocryphal pre-Columbian texts; it was 1st performed in Washington, D.C. (1961) with excellent success.

An entirely new development in Ginastera's compositional evolution came with his 1st opera, *Don Rodrigo* (1964), produced at the Teatro Colón; in it he followed the general formula of *Wozzeck* in the use of classical instrumental forms, such as rondo, suite, scherzo, and canonic progressions; also used Sprechstimme. In 1964 he wrote the cantata *Bomarzo* on a commission from the E. S. Coolidge Foundation in Washington, D.C.; used the same libretto by Manuel Mujica Láinez for his opera of the same name, which created a sensation at its production in Washington, D.C. (1967) by its unrestrained spectacle of sexual violence. Its scheduled performance at the Teatro Colón later that year was canceled at the order of the Argentine government because of its alleged immoral nature; this was one of a series of events that drove the composer into self-exile (Switzerland). The score of *Bomarzo* reveals extraordinary innovations in serial techniques, with thematic employment not only of different chromatic sounds but also of serial progressions of different intervals. His last opera, *Beatrix Cenci*, commissioned by the Opera Soc. of Washington, D.C. (1971), concluded the operatic trilogy.

Among instrumental works of Ginastera's last period, the most remarkable was his 2nd Piano Concerto (1972), based on a tone-row derived from the famous dissonant opening of the finale of Beethoven's 9th Sym.; the 2nd movement of the concerto is for the left hand alone. His 2nd wife was the Argentine cellist Aurora

Nátola (1971), for whom he wrote the Cello Sonata (1979) and his 2nd Cello Concerto (1981).

gioco, con (*giocondamente, giocosamente, giocoso; gioia, con; gioioso; gioja, con; gioviale; giovialità, con; giuoco, con* It.). Playfully, sportively, merrily, jocosely, lively, joyfully, joyously, gaily, jovially, cheerfully.

Giordano, Umberto, b. Foggia, Aug. 28, 1867; d. Milan, Nov. 12, 1948. He studied with Gaetano Briganti at Foggia and with Paolo Serrao at the Naples Cons. (1881–90); his 1st composition publicly performed was the symphonic poem *Delizia* (1886); then wrote instrumental music. In 1888 he submitted a short opera, *Marina*, for the publisher Sonzogno's competition; while Mascagni's *Cavalleria rusticana* received 1st prize, *Marina* was cited for distinction. He wrote a 3-act opera, *Mala vita*, performed in Rome (1892); only partly successful, he revised and presented it as *Il voto* in Milan (1897); there followed *Regina Diaz* (Rome, 1894), a moderate success. He then started work on a grand opera, *Andrea Chenier*, to a libretto by Illica; the premiere at La Scala in Milan (1896) was a spectacular success that established Giordano as one of the best Italian opera composers. Almost as successful was *Fedora* (Teatro Lirico, Milan, 1898), but it failed to hold a place in the repertoire; there followed *Siberia* (La Scala, 1903; rev. 1921; La Scala, 1927). *Marcella* (Milan, 1907) and *Mese Mariano* (Palermo, 1910) were hardly noticed and seemed to mark a decline in Giordano's dramatic gift; however, he recaptured public attention with *Madame Sans-Gêne*, premiered at the Metropolitan Opera in N.Y. (1915), conducted by Toscanini, with Geraldine Farrar singing the title role. With Franchetti he wrote *Giove a Pompei* (Rome, 1921); produced *La cena delle beffe*, his last signal accomplishment (La Scala, 1924); wrote 1 last opera, the 1-act *Il Re* (La Scala, 1929). He was elected a member of the Accademia Luigi Cherubini in Florence and several other institutions. Although not measuring up to Puccini in musical quality or Mascagni in dramatic skill, he was a distinguished figure in the Italian opera field for 4 decades.

Gis (Ger.). G-sharp.

Gis moll (Ger.). G-sharp minor.

gittern (Fr. *ghisterne, guiterne*; Lat. *ghiterna, quitarra*). Medieval plucked chordophone, usually with a flat back, fretted neck, and single or double-coursed gut strings; a plectrum was used. The gittern can be traced iconographically to the early 12th century; by 1400 the instrument had given way to the lute. The term continued to be used through the 17th century for instruments of the guitar family; not to be confused with the *cittern*.

giubilante (It.). Jubilantly. *Giubilo*, joy, rejoicing, jubilation.

Giuffre, Jimmy (James Peter), b. Dallas, Apr. 26, 1921. He studied at North Texas State Teachers College (B.Mus., 1942); played in a U.S. Army band; joined the bands of Jimmy Dorsey, Buddy Rich, and Woody Herman; played flute and tenor saxophone, but was primarily known for his cool tone, *sans vibrato*, on the clarinet, especially in its chalumeau register; wrote an influential score for Woody Herman, *4 Brothers* (1947), which explored the expressive potential of a timbre labeled as "the 4 Brothers sound." He was an important figure in avant-garde jazz of the late 1950s and '60s, especially as a proponent of the free-jazz style; worked in different combos, including those of Jim Hall and Ralph Pena (1956); also played with Paul Bley and Steve Swallow. He was an active teacher, serving on the faculties of the New School for Social Research in N.Y. and the School of Jazz in Lenox, Mass.; publ. an influential text, *Jazz Phrasing and Interpretation* (N.Y., 1969).

Giulini, Carlo Maria, b. Barletta, May 9, 1914. He began to study the violin as a boy; at 16, entered the Cons. di Musica di Santa Cecilia in Rome; studied violin and viola with Remy Principe, composition with Alessandro Bustini, and conducting with Bernardino Molinari (and Casella at the Accademia Chigiana in Siena); joined the Augusteo Orch. in Rome as a violist, under such great conductors as R. Strauss, Walter, Mengelberg, and Furtwängler. After the liberation of Rome by the Allied troops (1944), he was engaged to conduct the Augusteo Orch. in a special concert celebrating the occasion; engaged as assistant conductor of the RAI Orch. in Rome; made its chief conductor (1946).

In 1950 Giullini organized the RAI Orch. in Milan; conducted at La Scala as an assistant to Victor de Sabata (1952); became principal conductor there (1954); his performance of *La Traviata* with Maria Callas was particularly notable. He conducted *Falstaff* at the Edinburgh Festival, earning great praise (1955); later that year, he guest-conducted the Chicago Sym. Orch.; later its principal guest conductor (1969–72); during its European tour (1971), was joint conductor with Solti. He was principal conductor of the Vienna Sym. Orch. (1973–76), taking it on a world tour, including the U.S., Canada, and Japan (1975); that year, led it at a televised concert from the United Nations. He succeeded Mehta as music director of the Los Angeles Phil., succeeding in maintaining it at a zenith of orch. brilliance (1978–84).

Giulini's conducting style embodies the best traditions of the Italian school as exemplified by Toscanini but free from explosive displays of temper; his podium behavior is free from self-assertive theatrics, treating the orch. as comrades-in-arms, associates in the cause of music rather than subordinate performers of a task assigned to them. He is a truly Romantic conductor who identifies his musical *Weltanschauung* with the musical essence of Beethoven, Verdi, Mahler, and Tchaikovsky. In 20th-century music he gives congenial interpretations of Debussy, Ravel, and Stravinsky; but expressionist composers lie outside of his sensibility and he does not actively promote experimental music. His personal feeling for music is not disguised; often he closes his eyes in fervent self-absorption when conducting with an almost abstract contemplation the great Classic and Romantic works (without score).

giuoco (It.). Joke, game, jest.

giustamente (*giusto;* It.). Exactly, strictly, precisely, appropriately, properly, justly.

Glareanus, Henricus, also called Heinrich Glarean (born Heinrich Loris; Lat. Henricus Loritus), b. Mollis, Glarus canton, June 1488; d. Freiburg, Mar. 28, 1563. He studied with Rubellus at Bern, later with Cochläus at Cologne;

crowned poet laureate by Emperor Maximilian I (1512), for a poem he composed and sang to him. He 1st taught mathematics at Basel (1514); went to Paris, where he taught philosophy (1517–22); returned to Basel (1522-29), then went to Freiburg, where he was 1st a prof. of poetry, then of theology. His 1st important work, *Isagoge in musicen* (Basel, 1516), dealt with solmization, intervals, modes, and tones; a still more important vol., the *Dodecachordon* (Basel, 1547), advanced the theory that there are 12 church modes, corresponding to the ancient Greek modes, instead of the commonly accepted 8 modes; the 3rd part contains many works by 15th- and 16th-century musicians. A copy of the *Dodecachordon*, with corrections in Glareanus's own handwriting, is in the Library of Congress, Washington, D.C.

Glass, Philip, b. Baltimore, Jan. 31, 1937. He entered the Peabody Cons. of Music in Baltimore as a flute student at age 8; took courses in piano, mathematics, and philosophy at the Univ. of Chicago (1952–56); studied composition with Persichetti at the Juilliard School of Music in N.Y. (M.S., 1962). He received a Fulbright fellowship (1964); went to Paris to study with N. Boulanger; more important was a meeting with Ravi Shankar, who introduced him to Hindu raga; during a visit to Morocco, he absorbed the modalities of North African melorhythms, teaching him the art of melodic repetition; when he returned to N.Y. (1967), his style presented an alternately concave and convex mirror image of Eastern modes, undergoing melodic phases of stationary harmonies in lieu of modulations.

Glass formed associations with painters and sculptors who strove to obtain maximum effects with a minimum of means; he began to practice a similar method in music, which acquired the factitious sobriquet of minimalism. Other Americans had anticipated aspects of minimalism, basically Eastern in its catatonic homophony; Steve Reich was a close companion in minimalistic pursuits of maximalistic effects. Glass formed his own phonograph company, Chatham Square, recording most of his early works (notably *Music in Twelve Parts*, 1974); organized an ensemble of electrically amplified instruments, which became the chief medium of his compositions; presented the 1st concert of the Philip Glass Ensemble at Queens College in N.Y. (1968), subsequently touring widely with it, making visits abroad as well as traveling throughout the U.S. His performances, both in America and in Europe, became extremely successful among young audiences, mesmerized by his mixture of rock realism and alluring mysticism; undeterred by the indeterminability and interminability of his productions, some lasting several hours, the audience accepted him as a true representative of earthly and unearthly art.

The unusual titles of his works reflected the sometimes tantalizing impenetrability of the subjects that he selected for his inspiration. The high point of his earlier works was the opera *Einstein on the Beach* (in collaboration with Robert Wilson), involving a surrealistic comminution of thematic ingredients and hypnotic repetition of harmonic subjects. It was premiered at the Avignon Festival (1976) and was subsequently performed throughout Europe and at the Metropolitan Opera in N.Y. as a non-subscripton event, where it proved something of a sensation of the season; the production left Glass in considerable debt. In Rotterdam (1980) he produced *Satyagraha*, based on Gandhi's years in South Africa; "satyagraha," Gandhi's slogan, is composed of 2 Hindu words: *satya* (truth) and *agraha* (firm-

ness). Another significant work was the 1981 score for the film *Koyaanisqatsi*, a Hopi Indian word meaning "life out of balance." The music represented the ultimate condensation of the basic elements of his compositional style; the ritualistic repetition of chords arranged in symmetrical sequences becomes hypnotic, particularly since the screen action is devoid of narrative; the effect is enhanced by the deep bass notes of an Indian chant.

Glass has become internationally known for his stage works. The mixed-media piece *The Photographer: Far from the Truth*, based on the life of Eadweard Muybridge, was premiered in Amsterdam (1983). The exotic opera *Akhnaten* is set in ancient Egypt, with a libretto in Akkadian, Egyptian, and Hebrew, and explanatory narration in English (Stuttgart, 1984). In collaboration with Robert Moran he wrote *The Juniper Tree* (Cambridge, Mass., 1985); *The Making of the Representative for Planet 8* (after Doris Lessing) premiered in Houston (1988); *The Fall of the House of Usher* was 1st performed in Cambridge, Mass. (1988); the music-theater piece *1,000 Airplanes on the Roof* was produced in Vienna (1988). He also produced *Hydrogen Jukebox*, theater piece after Allen Ginsberg (1988); *The Voyage*, on the theme of exploration (Metropolitan Opera, N.Y., 1992) and two "film operas" based on Cocteau's *Orphée* (1993) and *La Belle et la Bête* (1994).

Among other works: dance pieces, including *Dance No. 1–5* (1979), *A Descent into the Maelstrom* (1986) and *In the Upper Room* (1986); orch'l works: *Sinfonia No. 3* (1986), *The Light* (1987), *The Canyon* (1988); *Itaipu* for chorus and orch. (1989); *Lamento dell'acqua* for orch. (1990); *"Low" Sym.* and *"Heroes" Sym.* after Bowie and Eno; film scores, including *North Star*, *The Thin Blue Line*, *Amina Munda*, *Mishima*, *Powaqqatsi*, *Kundun*; *Songs from Liquid Days*; *The Screens*, music for Genet's play, with Foday Musa Suso; *Passages*, with R. Shankar; 5 string quartets; solo piano, violin, and organ works; concertos for violin and saxophone.

glass harmonica. Instrument consisting of a set of drinking glasses partially filled with water so as to provide a complete diatonic or chromatic scale. A concert of "26 glasses tuned with spring water" was presented by Gluck in London (1746); Benjamin Franklin allegedly attended and then constructed a glass harmonica with mechanical attachments. The ethereal sound is produced by rubbing the rim of the glass with a wet finger; because of its clarity and purity, called an *angelic organ*. Glass harmonicas achieved a great popularity in the 18th century under the Italian name *armonica*; even Mozart wrote a piece for it (1791, K.356/617a). It fell into desuetude after its romantic attraction was spoiled by mechanization; R. Strauss used it in his opera *Frau ohne Schatten* for evocative effect; also called glass-chord or musical glasses.

Glazunov, Alexander (Konstantinovich), b. St. Petersburg, Aug. 10, 1865; d. Neuilly-sur-Seine, Mar. 21, 1936. Of a well-to-do family he studied at a technical high school in St. Petersburg; took lessons in music with N. Elenkovsky. As age 15 he met Rimsky-Korsakov, who taught him weekly in harmony, counterpoint, and orchestration; made rapid progress, and at age 16 completed his 1st sym., premiered by Balakirev in St. Petersburg (1882); so mature was this score that Stasov, Cui, and others hailed him as a rightful heir to the Russian national school.

The music publisher Belaiev arranged for publication of Glazunov's works; took him to Weimar to meet Liszt. From that time he composed assiduously in all genres except opera; conducted his syms. in Paris (1889) and London (1896–97). Returning to St. Petersburg, he conducted concerts of Russian music; In 1899 he was engaged as an instructor in composition and orchestration at the St. Petersburg Cons. (1899) He resigned temporarily during the revolutionary turmoil of 1905 in protest against the dismissal of Rimsky-Korsakov by the government authorities, but returned to the staff after full autonomy was granted to the Cons. by the administration. In 1905 Glazunov was elected director and retained this post until (1905–28), when he went to Paris. In 1929 he made several appearances as conductor in the U.S. (1929).

Although Glazunov wrote no textbook on composition, his pedagogical methods left a lasting impression on Russian music through his many students who preserved his traditions. His music is often considered academic, yet a flow of rhapsodic eloquence places him in the Romantic school; for a time was greatly swayed by Wagnerian harmonies, but resisted this influence successfully; Lisztian characteristics are more pronounced in his works; a master of counterpoint, he avoided extreme polyphonic complexity. The national spirit of his music is unmistakable, especially in the descriptive works (*Stenka Razin*, *The Kremlin*); his most popular score is the ballet *Raymonda*. Most of his music was written before 1906, when he completed his 8th Sym.; thereafter wrote mostly for special occasions. He also completed and orchestrated the overture to Borodin's *Prince Igor* from memory, having heard his composer play it on the piano.

glee (from Anglo-Sax. *gléo*, entertainment). English secular composition for 3 or more unaccompanied solo voices, usually for male voices and constructed as a series of short movements harmonized homophonically; reached its flowering in the 18th century; glee clubs proliferated in England and the U.S. Serious as well as merry glees are written.

Glinka, Mikhail (Ivanovich), b. Novospasskoye, Smolensk district, June 1, 1804; d. Berlin, Feb. 15, 1857. A scion of a fairly rich family of landowners, he was educated at an exclusive St. Petersburg school (1817–22); studied piano with a resident German musician, Carl Meyer; also studied violin. When John Field was in St. Petersburg, he had an opportunity to study with him, but he had only 3 lessons before Field departed. He began to compose even before acquiring adequate theory training. He traveled in the Caucasus, then stayed at his father's estate; at 20 entered the Ministry of Communications in St. Petersburg, remaining in government employ until 1828; improved his general education by reading; had friends among the best Russian writers of the time, including Zhukovsky and Pushkin.

Glinka took singing lessons with the Italian Belloli; went to Italy (1830); continued irregular studies in Milan, where he spent most of his Italian years; visited Naples, Rome, and Venice; met Donizetti and Bellini. His early vocal and instrumental compositions are thoroughly Italian in melodic and harmonic structure. In 1833 he went to Berlin; studied counterpoint and general composition with Dehn; was nearly 30 when he completed his theoretical education.

Glinka's return to Russia (to care for his family) inspired him towards the composition of a truly national opera on a Russian

historical episode: the saving of the 1st Romanov czar by a simple peasant, Ivan Susanin. (The Italian composer Catterino Cavos had written an opera on this subject and conducted it in St. Petersburg, in 1815.) Glinka's opera was produced in St. Petersburg (1836) as *A Life for the Czar*; the event was hailed by local literary and artistic circles as a milestone of Russian culture; the entire development of Russian musical nationalism received a decisive creative impulse from this patriotic opera; it remained in the Russian repertoire until the Revolution made it unacceptable, but it was revived under its original title, *Ivan Susanin*, in Moscow (1939), unaltered musically but with all references to the czar eliminated; the idea of saving the country was substituted.

Glinka's 2nd opera, *Ruslan and Ludmila* (after Pushkin), was produced in St. Petersburg (1842); this opera also became extremely popular in Russia. Many elements of oriental music are heard in the score; 1 episode contains the earliest use of the whole-tone scale in an opera. Like its predecessor, *Ruslan and Ludmila* retains traditional Italian form, with arias, choruses, and orch'l episodes clearly separated. In 1844 Glinka was in Paris, where he met Berlioz; traveled in Spain and collected folk songs; the fruits of his Spanish tour were 2 orch. works, *Jota Aragonesa* and *Night in Madrid*.

glissade (*port de voix*; Fr.). Portamento.

glissando (glissato, glissicando, glissicato; from Fr. *glisser*, slide + It. suffix). A slide or rapid scale. When necessary, instruments accommodate the device to their graded pitch construction. On the piano, a glissando is performed by sliding quickly over the white keys with the back of the fingernail (thumb or thumb and 1 finger), taking care not to bruise the fingers; black-key glissandos are possible but rarely used. Some piano virtuosos with fingers of steel can perform glissandos in octaves, even with an interposed 3rd, using the thumb, the index finger, and the little finger. The glissando is completely idiomatic for the harp, with the hands moving toward and away from the player; a short glissando is possible on a single string, using the pedal.

Other instruments are capable of an uninterrupted slide through a portion of their pitch gamut without a break. Trombone glissandos are applicable for a limited range, as are those on timpani. A clarinet glissando, requiring a special manipulation of the keys, occurs in the opening section of Gershwin's *Rhapsody in Blue*; other wind players have improved techniques for sliding on their instruments. All fretless bowed strings offer true glissando. Glissando is often mistaken for *portamento*; while both indicate an indirect motion from one pitch to another, a true glissando should be even and consistent in its motion; neither departure nor arrival pitch should be unduly emphasized. See also ⇒portamento.

Gloche (Ger.; Fr. *clocke*). Bell.

glockenspiel (Ger., bell playing). 1. Carillon. 2. Set of steel bars struck by a hammer and producing a bell-like sound. There are 2 types: the mallet glockenspiel, laid out as a keyboard like the xylophone and marimba and fully chromatic; and the marching glockenspiel, bars placed in a lyrelike shape held upright, struck with a small hammer, with a gamut smaller than the 2–1/2 octaves of the mallet type. The glockenspiel is included in

Mozart's *The Magic Flute*, where it is listed simply as *instrumento d'acciacio* (It., steel instrument); in actual performance it is interchangeable with the celesta. 3. Organ stop having bells instead of pipes.

Gloria. The 2nd main division of the Ordinary in the Roman Catholic High Mass. The separate canticles are *Gloria in excelsis Deo* (Glory to God in the highest), *Laudamus te* (We praise You), *Gratias agimus tibi* (We give You thanks), *Domine Deus* (Lord God), *Qui tollis peccata mundi* (Who bears the sins of the world), *Qui sedes ad dexteram patris* (Who sits at the right hand of the Father), *Quoniam tu solus sanctus* (For You alone are holy), and *Cum Sancto Spiritu* (With the Holy Spirit).

glottis. The aperture between the vocal cords, a key element of the development of vocal production.

Gluck, Christoph Willibald, Ritter von, b. Erasbach, near Weidenwang, in the Upper Palatinate, July 2, 1714; d. Vienna, Nov. 15, 1787. His father was a forester; began serving Prince Lobkowitz of Eisenberg about 1729. Gluck received instruction in the village schools at Kamnitz and Albersdorf near Komotau; was taught singing and instrumental playing. He went to Prague to complete his education (1732); played violin and cello at rural dances in the area, and sang at various churches. He met Bohuslav Czernohorsky; who probably taught Gluck church music methodology; went to Vienna (1736); was chamber musician to young Prince Lobkowitz, son of his father's patron. In 1737 he was taken to Milan by Prince Melzi; this sojourn was of great importance to his musical development; studied with G. B. Sammartini (*c.* 1700/01–75), acquiring a solid Italian compositional technique.

Gluck brought out his 1st opera, *Artaserse*, to a text by the celebrated Metastasio (Milan, 1741); its success led to new commissions; contributed individual arias to other operas produced in Italy. In 1745 he was invited to go to London by the Italian Opera there to write 2 operas for the Haymarket Theatre, as a competitive endeavor to Handel's enterprise; on his way, visited Paris and met Rameau. The 1st work was *La Caduta dei giganti* (1746), a tribute to the Duke of Cumberland on the defeat of the Pretender; the 2nd was a pasticcio, *Artamene* (1746) in which he reused material from previous operas; later appeared with Handel at a public concert, despite a story in London society that Handel had declared that Gluck knew no more counterpoint than his cook (although his cook and valet at that time, Gustavus Waltz, was a professional musician).

In 1746, after giving a demonstration of the glass harmonica, Gluck left London to become conductor with Pietro Mingotti's traveling Italian opera company; performed in Hamburg, Leipzig, and Dresden; went to Vienna; staged *Semiramide riconosciuta*, after Metastasio (1748); in Copenhagen, produced *La Contesa dei Numi* (1749) on the occasion of the birth of Prince Christian. In 1750 he married Marianna Pergin, daughter of a Viennese merchant; remained in Vienna for several years, conducting operatic performances; as French influence increased there, wrote several entertainments in French with spoken dialogue, in opera comique style; the most successful were *Le Cadi dupé* (1761) and *La Rencontre imprévue* (1764). His greatest Viennese work was *Orfeo ed Euridice*, to a libretto by Calzabigi (with Orfeo sung by famous castrato Gaetano Guadagni, 1762);

rev. and translated for Parisian performances (1774, with Orfeo sung by a tenor). A 2nd masterpiece, *Alceste*, to another Calzabigi text (Vienna, 1767), followed; in the preface to *Alceste*, Gluck formulated his aesthetic credo, elevating the dramatic meaning of musical plays above a mere striving for vocal effects: "I sought to reduce music to its true function, that of seconding poetry in order to strengthen the emotional expression and the impact of the dramatic situations without interrupting the action and without weakening it by superfluous ornaments."

The success of his French operas in Vienna led Gluck to try his fortunes in Paris, yielding to François du Roullet, attaché at the French embassy in Vienna, who supplied him with his 1st libretto for a serious French opera, based on Racine's *Iphigénie en Aulide* (Paris, 1774). He set out for Paris (1773), preceded by declarations in the Paris press by du Roullet and the composer explaining his ideas of dramatic music; set off an intellectual battle in the press and among musicians between the adherents of traditional Italian opera and Gluck's reform French opera, reaching unprecedented acrimony when the Italian composer Piccinni was engaged by the French court to write French operas, in open competition with Gluck; although intrigues multiplied, Marie Antoinette never wavered in her admiration for Gluck, who taught her singing and harpsichord playing; however, Gluck and Piccinni themselves never participated in the bitter polemics unleashed by their literary and musical partisans.

The sensational successes of the French *Orfeo* and *Alceste* were followed by *Armide* (1777), arousing great admiration; then came Gluck's masterpiece, *Iphigénie en Tauride* (1779), establishing his superiority to Piccinni, who failed to complete a commissioned opera on the same subject on time. His last opera, *Echo et Narcisse* (1779), did not measure up to his usual standards; his health was failing; apoplectic attacks resulted in partial paralysis; he returned to Vienna and lived as an invalid; his last work was a *De profundis* for chorus and orch., written 5 years before his death. Besides the operas he wrote several ballets; *Don Juan* (Vienna, 1761) was the most successful. Wagner made an arrangement of *Iphigénie en Aulide*; became the chief text for performances during the 19th century. A thematic catalogue was publ. by A. Wotquenne (Leipzig, 1904).

G.O. (Fr.). Grand orgue.

goat trill (Ger. *Bockstriller*; It. *caprino*, little goat). 1. Vocal effect produced when a singer repeats a note very fast and catches a breath after each note; it was introduced by Monteverdi for dramatic purposes. 2. Fanciful 18th-century description of a rasping trill at the interval of a semitone or less; Wagner used it in *Die Meistersinger*.

Goethe, Johann Wolfgang von, b. Frankfurt am Main, Aug. 28, 1749; d. Weimar, Mar. 22, 1832. Many of his writings served as musical sources. He wrote some of the most famous lyrics set as lieder from the later 18th century on; novels (*The Sorrows of Young Werther*, the Mignon songs from *Wilhelm Meister's Years of Wandering*) and plays (*Claudine von Villa Bella*, *Egmont*, and several Verdi operas) served as libretto sources. But no Goethe work was more influential, magnetic, and overwhelming than *Faust*, parts I (1806) and II (1831); he hoped that Mozart would set the drama, but death interceded; thought Mendelssohn and Schubert too young;

overcame his resistance to Beethoven and proposed the project to him; the composer considered it, but the work was never written; the only collaboration between Goethe and Beethoven was the incidental music for *Egmont* (1814). He had strong if not radical ideas about music, as Zelter and Ferdinand Hiller describe and as scholars have been studying in depth recently.

Goldberg, Johann Gottlieb, b. Danzig (baptized), Mar. 14, 1727; d. Dresden, Apr. 13, 1756. As a child he was taken to Dresden by his patron, Count Hermann Karl von Keyserlingk; reportedly studied with W. F. and later J. S. Bach (1742–43); became musician to Count Heinrich Brühl (1751), a post he held until his death. His name is immortalized through the set of 30 keyboard variations by Bach (*Goldberg Variations*); once thought a commission by Keyserlingk for Goldberg; although this account is doubtful, Bach did give Goldberg a copy of the score. Goldberg composed concertos; polonaises; keyboard variations, flute trios, and vocal music.

golden section (golden mean, golden ratio; sometimes capitalized). Proportional division of a whole into 2 unequal parts such that the ratio of the smaller to the larger part is the same as that of the larger part to the whole; the ratio's value is irrational (.618034 . . .). Considered by many to represent a perfect proportion in art, the golden section is believed by some analysts to have been consciously applied by Debussy and Bartók.

Goldsmith, Jerry, b. Los Angeles, Feb. 10, 1929. He studied piano with Jakob Gimpel and theory and composition with Castelnuovo-Tedesco; studied music at Los Angeles City College; audited Rosza's sessions on film music at the Univ. of Southern Calif. He wrote music for CBS radio and television programs (1950–60); then devoted himself to writing film music. Among his scores are *Freud* (1962); *7 Days in May* (1964); *A Patch of Blue* (1966); *Seconds* (1966); *Planet of the Apes* (1967); *Patton* (1970); *Papillon* (1973); *The Cassandra Crossing* (1976); *Islands in the Stream* (1977); *MacArthur* (1978); *Poltergeist* (1982); *Rambo* (1985); etc.; wrote chamber music and vocal works.

goliards. Wandering minstrels, usually students or monks, who traveled through Germany during medieval times. The celebrated collection *Carmina Burana* (Songs of Beuren, a Benedictine monastery where the manuscript was found) consists mainly of goliard songs, mostly in Latin.

Golitzin, Nikolai (Borisovich), b. St. Petersburg, Dec. 19, 1794; d. Tambov district, Nov. 3, 1866. A talented cello player, he is remembered because of his connection with Beethoven, who dedicated the overture *Consecration of the House* (op. 124) and the string quartets opp. 127, 130, and 132 to him. Golitzin was also responsible for the 1st performance of the *Missa solemnis* (St. Petersburg Phil. Soc., 1824).

Gondellied (Ger.). Barcarole.

gong. Suspended circular metal plate, struck with a mallet and producing a sustained reverberation. The gong differs from the tam-tam in having a convex circular nub in the plate's middle; the mallet is usually struck on this nub, whose size, along with that of the gong itself, determines the fixed pitch of the instrument.

Goodman, Benny (Benjamin David), b. Chicago, May 30, 1909; d. N.Y., June 13, 1986. He heard syncopated music as a child by listening to recordings of ragtime; played professionally by age 12 (1921); worked with Ben Pollack (1926), a leading Chicago jazz musician. In 1929 he went to N.Y. as a clarinetist for various bands; formed his own band (1934), becoming known nationwide from its appearances on the *Let's Dance* radio program; was among the many important musicians guided by the producer John Hammond.

Both as the leader of a big band and a virtuoso performer in jazz combos, Goodman was the best-known and most successful musician of the era; nicknamed the King of Swing, he played with Red Nichols, Ted Lewis, Paul Whiteman, Teddy Wilson, Benny Carter, Fletcher Henderson, Gene Krupa, Lionel Hampton, Harry James, Ziggy Elman, Jess Stacy, and Charlie Christian. He also performed classical works in concert and for records, appearing as soloist in Mozart's Clarinet Concerto with the N.Y. Phil. (1940) and recording works by Copland, Bartók, Stravinsky, Gould, and Bernstein.

goose. Harsh break in the tone of a clarinet, oboe, or bassoon.

gopak. Hopak.

Gordon, Dexter (Keith), b. Los Angeles, Feb. 27, 1923; d. Philadelphia, Apr. 25, 1990. He studied clarinet; took up the alto saxophone at age 15, then the tenor saxophone; began to play in a local band; worked with Hampton (1940–43) and Armstrong (1944); went to N.Y., where he played in Eckstine's band (1944–46); returned to Los Angeles; appeared with Wardell Gray (1947–52). In 1962 he moved to Copenhagen and continued his career in Europe; eventually returned to the U.S.; elected to the Jazz Hall of Fame (1980); generally acknowledged as the most influential tenor saxophonist of the bop period; starred in the film *'Round Midnight* (1986).

Gordy, Berry, Jr., b. Detroit, Nov. 28, 1929. After discharge from the army, he began writing songs; started Motown Records (named after Motor Town, i.e., Detroit); attracted many talented groups, composers, and singers, including Smokey Robinson and the Miracles, Mary Wells, Four Tops, Martha and the Vandellas, Supremes (with or without Diana Ross, who became a superstar), Temptations, Jr. Walker and the All Stars, Gladys Knight and the Pips, Marvin Gaye, O'Jays, Stevie Wonder, The Jackson Five (including Michael), and the Holland-Dozier-Holland team. In creating the "Motown sound," Gordy contributed to the final desegregation of "race music" and its integration into the mainstream of American popular music, blending rhythm and blues, soul, gospel, jazz, and middle-of-the-road pop.

Górecki, Henryk (Mikolaj), b. Czernica, Dec. 6, 1933. He studied composition with Boleslaw Szabelski at the Katowice Cons. (1955–60); appointed to its faculty (1968). In his music he makes use of the entire arsenal of modern techniques while preserving traditional formal design. A radical shift of style toward a mystical and ethereal aesthetic culminated in the 3rd Sym. for Soprano and Orch. (1976); multiple recordings of this work have been immensely successful.

gorgheggiare (It., warble). Sing trills with a guttural voice. *Gorgia* (It., throat), guttural mode of speaking or singing.

gospel music. American Negro spirituals, derived from antebellum slave songs; the earliest surviving repertoire of African American music; black hymnbooks date from the beginning of the 19th century, and camp-meeting hymns and spirituals were collected, the 1st being the abolitionist *Slave Songs of the U.S.* (1867). These postwar gatherings saved an oral tradition for posterity; the music was arranged for the concert hall and popularized by the Fisk (Univ.) Jubilee Singers and similar groups associated with black colleges.

2. 20th-century African American Christian songs marked by a directness of appeal or statement of belief; at its most lively the music echoes the popular style of the day, whether it be the blues, New Orleans, mainstream rhythm and blues, barbershop/ doo-wop (the a cappella gospel quartet), soul, or rap. However, a standardized style known as gospel hymnody is found in the hymns of Thomas A. Dorsey, Lucie Campbell, and (later) Roberta Martin, James Cleveland, and Andrae Crouch. Performance style followed stylistic change; by the 1930s the piano (or organ) had become the primary accompaniment. The call-and-response texture of the old spiritual and the Dixieland style of Bessie Johnson (1920s) were incorporated into the solo-and-chorus texture. Sister Rosetta Tharpe made gospel a best-selling commodity (*Rock Me*, 1938); in the 1950s and 1960s Mahalia Jackson was the "queen" of gospel music; later generations yielded Clara Ward, Marion Williams, Inez Andrews, Shirley Caesar (a "singing preacher"), and Edwin and Walter Hawkins. Gospel became a vehicle for inspired solos with Jackson's incorporation of vamping, an improvised recitative over the repetition of a chord or chord progression in free time (borrowed from jazz).

3. White Protestant church hymn, traditionally sung a cappella. Although hymnody existed in the U.S. before the revolution and was carried into the 19th century (particularly the shape-note movement), musicologists usually limit the definition of "white gospel music" to popular hymns, camp-meeting spirituals, and other revivalist music. From the beginning this music has been written down, although performance practice was freer in the camp-meetings than hymnbooks suggest. Lowell Mason (*From Greenland's Icy Mountains*) and George Root were among the earlier composers of gospel hymns; Robert Lowry (*Shall We Gather at the River?*) and Elisha A. Hoffman (*Are You Washed in the Blood of the Lamb?*) were among the later authors.

The last part of the 19th century belonged to Dwight Moody (preacher) and Ira Sankey (musician); they held well-attended urban revival meetings in the U.S. and U.K., and collected hymns into several vols. Similar collaborations between preachers and musicians persisted into the 20th century, including the triad of preacher Billy Graham and singers Cliff Barrows and George Beverly Shea. In a manner reminiscent of black musicians, old-time, bluegrass, and country musicians have served the cause of the Christian gospel.

Gothic music. Historical analogy with Gothic architecture referring to the austere, even ascetic medieval counterpoint in northern and western Europe, centered on Notre Dame polyphony; identified with the ars antiqua, gradually giving way to the ars nova and other late medieval styles.

Gottschalk, Louis Moreau, b. New Orleans, May 8, 1829; d. Tijuca, near Rio de Janeiro, Dec. 18, 1869. His father, an English businessman, emigrated to New Orleans; his mother was the granddaughter of a Haitian provincial governor. Louis began studying violin at age 4 with Felix Miolan, concertmaster of the opera orch., and piano with François Letellier, organist at the St. Louis Cathedral; at 7, substituted for Letellier at the organ during High Mass; played violin at a benefit for Miolan the following year. In 1841 he went to Paris; studied piano with Hallé and Stamaty and harmony with Maleden; later studied composition with Berlioz; gave a concert at the Salle Pleyel, attracting Chopin's attention (1845); his piano compositions of the period (*Bamboula, Le Bananier, La Savane*, etc.) were influenced by Liszt and Chopin but also by childhood recollections of Creole and Negro dances and songs. He appeared in concerts with Berlioz at the Italian Opera (1846–47); concertized throughout France and Switzerland, playing his own works (1850); appeared in Madrid at the Queen's invitation (1851); developed the "monster concerts," writing a sym. for 10 pianos, *El sitio de Zaragosa*; later transformed into *Bunker's Hill* by replacing Spanish tunes with American ones.

Having to increase his activities to support six siblings, Gottschalk returned to N.Y.; gave a highly praised concert (1853); toured the U.S., Cuba, and Canada; gave 80 concerts in N.Y. alone (1855–56); his compositions of this period (*La Scintilla, The Dying Poet,* and *The Last Hope*) were virtuosic, using novel techniques of the "style pianola." After playing Henselt's Piano Concerto with the N.Y. Phil. (1857), he went to Cuba with the young Adelina Patti; then lived in the West Indies, writing works influenced by indigenous music; in Havana, introduced his *La Nuit des tropiques* (Sym. No. 1; 1861); produced many grand "monster concerts" modeled after Jullien's.

Although born in the antebellum South, Gottschalk's sympathies were with the North during the Civil War; had manumitted his inherited slaves after his father's death (1853); resumed his U.S. concert career with a N.Y. performance (1862); toured the North and the West, playing over a thousand concerts (to 1865); his notebooks from this era, posth. publ. as *Notes of a Pianist* (Philadelphia, 1881), perceptively reveal life in Civil War America. After becoming involved in a scandal with a teenage girl in San Francisco, he fled to South America (1865); appeared in concert throughout the continent; composed works based on local melodies and rhythms; during a festival of his music in Rio de Janeiro (1869), collapsed on stage and died within a month; his remains were exhumed and reburied with great ceremony in Brooklyn (1870).

Gottschalk was a prolific composer of bravura, pianistic works that enjoyed great popularity, even posthumously; they finally slipped into oblivion, but have received attention since the 100th anniversary of his death. As a pianist he was one of the most adulated virtuosos of his era; his concerts, featuring his own music, emphasized his prodigious technique but were criticized by some as superficial. Many of the works referred to in his letters have not been found; revisions of the same work used different titles; several works were publ. using the same opus number; publ. some works using pseudonyms.

Gould, Glenn (Herbert), b. Toronto, Sept. 25, 1932; d. there, Oct. 4, 1982. His musically gifted parents fostered his precocious development; began to play piano and compose in his single-digit years. At age 10 he entered the Royal Cons. of Music in Toronto; studied piano with Guerrero, organ with Silvester, and music theory with Leo Smith; graduated at age 13 (1945); made his debut in Toronto (1946).

Gould developed mannerisms that became his artistic signature; reduced the use of the pedal to a minimum in order to avoid harmonic haze; cultivated "horizontality" in his piano posture, using a 14-inch-high chair, bringing his head down almost to key level; dressed informally; had a rug put under the piano and a glass of distilled water within reach. In constant fear of bodily injury, he avoided shaking hands with the conductor after playing a concerto; sued the Steinway piano company when an enthusiastic representative shook his hand too vigorously.

Gould regarded music as linear, leading to an intense examination of Baroque structures, studying Bach closely rather than Chopin and other Romantics; cultivated performances of the early polyphonists Sweelinck, Gibbons, and others; played Mozart with an emphasis on fortepiano techniques; found the late sonatas of Beethoven congenial to his temperament, and, remarkably enough, played the works of the 2nd Viennese school, perhaps because of their neoclassical avoidance of purely decorative tonal formations; singlehandedly brought Hindemith to renewed public awareness.

Following Gould's U.S. debut in Washington, D.C. (1955), he evoked unequivocal praise at his concerts (although Bernstein once disavowed a Gould interpretation of a concerto prior to performing it with him). But in 1964 he abruptly terminated his stage career; devoted himself almost exclusively to recording, which he regarded as superior to concertizing; was thus able to select the best portions of his studio playing, creating a mosaic unblemished by accidental mishaps. Even his most ardent admirers had trouble palliating an unshakable habit of singing along with his playing; allowed his voice to be audible on his phonograph recordings; nonetheless, he was a remarkable if idiosyncratic pianist, noted for unorthodox interpretations.

Socially, Gould was a recluse; he found a release from his self-imposed isolation in editing a series of radio documentaries for the CBC; also produced a radio documentary on Schoenberg, treating him as a musical hermit; conducted a chamber orch. without an audience.

Gould, Morton, b. Richmond Hill, N.Y., Dec. 10, 1913; d. N.Y., Feb. 21, 1996. His parents fostered his early addiction to music. He allegedly composed a piano waltz at age 6 (ultimately publ. as *Just 6*); had piano lessons with Joseph Kardos and Abby Whiteside; enrolled in the composition class of Vincent Jones at N.Y. Univ., where he presented a concert of his works at age 16; played the piano in silent movies and jazz bands, accompanied dancers, and gave demonstrations of musical skill on college circuits. He served as staff pianist at Radio City Music Hall in N.Y. (1931–32); directed the *Music for Today* series on the Mutual Radio network (1934–46); music director of the *Chrysler Hour* on CBS Radio (1943).

These contacts gave great impetus to Gould's bursting talent for composing singable, playable, and enjoyable light Americana with immediate appeal. The *American Symphonette No. 1* (1933) became his 1st popular success; equally accessible was the *Chorale and Fugue in Jazz* for 2 Pianos and Orch. (1934), programmed by no less a musical magus than Stokowski for the

Philadelphia Orch. (1936). He then produced 3 more symphonettes (1935, 1938, 1941), followed by the immensely successful *Latin-American Symphonette* (1940), an engaging tetrad of Latin dances (*Rhumba, Tango, Guaracha, Conga*); *Spirituals* for Strings and Orch. (1941) is still performed. He turned to ballet in *Fall River Legend* (1947), based on the notorious story of Lizzie Borden; the *Sym. of Spirituals* and *American Ballads* were both commissioned for the American bicentennial (1976).

Gould wrote the music for the Broadway show *Billion Dollar Baby* (1945), several film scores, and the background music for the television productions *Verdun* (1963), *World War I* (1964–65), and *Holocaust* (1978); but despite unquestioned public success, he still wished to test his powers in absolute music: concertos for piano (1937), violin (1938), viola (1944); works for multiple pianos and orch.; he composed the 1st Concerto for Tap Dancer and Orch. (1953). A skillful conductor, he toured Australia (1977), Japan (1979), Mexico (1980), and Israel (1981); received the National Arts Award (1983); elected to the American Academy and Inst. of Arts and Letters (1986); president of ASCAP (1986–94).

Gounod, Charles (François), b. St. Cloud, June 17, 1818; d. Paris, Oct. 18, 1893. His father, Jean François Gounod, was a painter who won the 2nd Grand Prix de Rome; died when he was a child; his mother supervised his education and taught him piano. He completed academic studies at the Lycée St. Louis; entered the Paris Cons. (1836), studying with Halévy, Le Sueur, and Paer; won the 2nd Prix de Rome with his cantata *Marie Stuart et Rizzio* (1837), the Grand Prix with *Fernand* (1839). In Rome he studied church music, particularly Palestrina's; composed a Mass for 3 voices and orch.; during a visit to Vienna, conducted a Requiem of his own (1842); upon his return to Paris, became precentor and organist of the Missions Étrangères; studied theology for 2 years; decided against taking Holy Orders, yet was often referred to as "l'Abbé" Gounod.

Gounod's 1st opera, *Sapho*, was produced at the Opéra, with only moderate success (1851; rev. 1884, but unsuccessful); 2 more failed operas followed. He was active in other Parisian musical venues; conducted the choral society Orphéon (1852–60); composed several choruses for it. His greatest success came with *Faust*, after Goethe's play, part I (Théâtre-Lyrique, 1859; with added recitatives and ballet at the Opéra, 1869; the most successful French opera of the 19th century, triumphant and without any sign of diminishing favor after a century of changes in tastes; however, it was widely criticized for the melodramatic treatment of Goethe's poem by librettists Barbier and Carré and for the somewhat sentimental style of the music; German performances are given as *Margarethe* (the heroine's name) in literary protest.

Gonoud's succeeding operas were only partially successful; with *Roméo et Juliette* (Paris, 1867), he recaptured universal acclaim. During the Franco-Prussian War, he went to London (1870); organized Gounod's Choir and presented concerts; when Paris fell, wrote an elegiac cantata, *Gallia*, to words from the Lamentations of Jeremiah (London, 1871; later in Paris); wrote incidental music for Paris productions without signal success. The last years of his life were devoted mainly to sacred works; the most important was the trilogy *La Rédemption*, 1st performed at the Birmingham Festival (1882); another trilogy, *Mors et vita*, also for Birmingham, followed in 1885; continued to write religious works in close succession; a *Requiem* (1893), left unfinished, was completed by H. Busser after Gounod's death. One of his most popular settings to religious words is *Ave Maria*, adapted to the 1st prelude of Bach's *Well-Tempered Clavier*; its orig. version was *Méditation sur le 1er Prélude de Piano de S. Bach* for violin and piano (1853; words added 1859).

G.P. Grand Pause; Generalpause.

grace note. Vocal or instrumental ornament or embellishment not essential to the melody or harmony. Grace notes are usually written small, usually a scale degree above or below. If the note is crossed by a slant, its rhythmic value is taken from the preceding note; if not crossed, it is incorporated into the following passage, usually taking half of the value of the note immediately following; the latter is typical of Classic practice; modern editors usually write these out.

gracile (It.). Attenuated; graceful, delicate.

gradatamente (It.). By degrees, gradually. *Gradazione* (It., gradation), gradual change of dynamics.

gradevole (It.). Pleasingly, agreeably, pleasantly.

gradual. 1. In the Roman Catholic Mass, a responsory sung between the epistle and gospel readings. 2. Main book of the Catholic liturgy containing all the principal sections of the Mass; in this sense it complements the antiphonal (antiphoner, antiphonary), containing the liturgy of the Divine Office. The word is derived from *gradus* (step), because the chants were sung from the steps of the altar.

Graffman, Gary, b. N.Y., Oct. 14, 1928. He won a scholarship to the Curtis Inst. of Music in Philadelphia at age 8; studied with Isabelle Vengerova; at 10 gave a piano recital at Town Hall in N.Y.; after graduating (1946), received a scholarship at Columbia Univ. (1946–47). He won the 1st regional Rachmaninoff competition (1946), securing a debut with the Philadelphia Orch. (1947); received the Leventritt Award (1949) and a Fulbright grant to go to Europe (1950–51); returning to the U.S., had lessons with Horowitz in N.Y. and Rudolf Serkin in Marlboro, Vt. He had established himself as a pianist of 1st rank when disaster struck: around 1979, began to lose the use of his right hand through a then little-known ailment, carpal tunnel syndrome, that attacks instrumentalists and word processors alike. He was appointed to the faculty of the Curtis Inst. of Music (1980); made its artistic director (1986).

Grainger, (George) Percy (Aldridge), b. Melbourne, July 8, 1882; d. White Plains, N.Y., Feb. 20, 1961. He received his early musical training from his mother; at age 10 ;appeared as pianist at several public concerts; studied with Louis Pabst; went to Germany (1894); studied with Kwast in Frankfurt; took a few lessons with Busoni. From his youth he was fascinated by the ideal of the Nordic race, its physical beauty, and its art; traveled to Scandinavia, walking many kilometers through the frozen fjords. He began his concert career in England (1901); toured South Africa and Australia; met Grieg (1906), who enthused about his talent; his performances of Grieg's Piano Concerto were

famous; in England, befriended Delius, whom he revered, and, in Holland, the composer Julius Röntgen.

In 1912 Grainger made a sensational debut, playing his own works (Aeolian Hall, N.Y.); settled in the U.S. (1914); gave summer sessions at the Chicago Musical College (1919–31); chairman of the music dept. of N.Y. Univ. (1932–33). He married the Swedish poet and artist Ella Viola Ström (1928) in a spectacular ceremony at the Hollywood Bowl, when he conducted *To a Nordic Princess*, written for his bride. He founded the Grainger Museum at the Univ. of Melbourne (1935) to house his MSS and rich collection of musical souvenirs.

Grainger's philosophy of life and art called for the widest communion of peoples and opinions. From Grieg and Delius he got the notion that music must be shaped by native modalities steeped in romantic colors and not be overlong within individual forms. His profound study of folk music underlies the melodic and rhythmic structure of his own music; made a determined effort to re-create in art music the free flow of instinctive songs of the people; experimented with "gliding" intervals within the traditional scales and polyrhythmic combinations with independent strong beats in the component parts.

In a modest way Grainger was a pioneer of electronic music; wrote a quartet for Theremin's electronic instruments (1937), notating pitch by zigzags and curves; also introduced individualistic notation and orch. scoring; rejected Italian designations of instruments, tempos, and dynamics in favor of plain English descriptions: fiddle (for violin), middle fiddle (viola), louden lots (molto crescendo), soften (diminuendo), short and sharp (staccato), etc. His works are mostly for piano solo or small instrumental or vocal ensembles; thematic content is principally based on English and Irish tunes; of these, *Molly on the Shore* and *Irish Tune from County Derry* are the most popular; also arranged for various instrumental combinations.

Grammy. Annual series of awards dispensed by the National Academy of the Recording Arts and Sciences (NARAS) for the most successful recordings in various categories. The award itself is a miniature replica of an old-fashioned gramophone.

gramophone (Grk., inscribed sound). 1. Trademark now used in the U.K. for the phonograph. 2. (capitalized) Well-known British classical music magazine.

gran cassa (gran tamburo; It.). Bass drum.

Granados (y Campina), Enrique, b. Lerida, July 27, 1867; d. Mar. 24, 1916. He studied piano at the Barcelona Cons. with Jurnet and Pujol; won 1st prize (1883); studied composition with Pedrell (1883–87); went to Paris; studied with Charles de Bériot (1887); made his recital debut in Barcelona (1890). He played piano in restaurants and gave private concerts; attracted attention with his zarzuela *Maria del Carmen* (1898); conducted a series of concerts in Barcelona (1900); established a music school, the Academia Granados (1901); wrote 4 operas, produced in Barcelona with little success.

Granados composed a series of piano pieces entitled *Goyescas* (1911), inspired by the paintings and etchings of Goya; his fame rests securely on these imaginative and effective pieces, along with his brilliant *Danzas españolas* (1892–1900). Fernando Periquet wrote a libretto based on the scenes from the paintings, and Granados used the music of his suite for an opera of the same name; its premiere took place, in the presence of the composer, at the Metropolitan Opera, N.Y. (1916) with excellent success; the score included the popular orch'l *Intermezzo*. During his return to war-torn Europe, his English boat was torpedoed by a German submarine; both he and his wife drowned.

grand. Grand piano.

grand(e) (Fr.). Large; great; full; *à grand orchestre*, for full orch.

grand aria. See ⇒aria da capo.

grand choeur (grand jeu; Fr.). 1. Great organ. 2. Full organ. 3. Harmonium stop.

Grand Ole Opry, The. Since 1925, a durable feast of American country music, initiated in Nashville, Tenn. and broadcast over radio station WSM (sponsored by a life-insurance company whose initials stand for "We Shield Millions"); orig. name of the Saturday night program was *Barn Dance*; received present name (1927), the invention of which was claimed by a Nashville reporter. The songs that made up Grand Ole Opry programs were country ballads sung by genuine hillbillies untouched by the preening ways of grand opera; participants included fiddlers, banjo players, guitar pickers, double bass pluckers, and performers on the Jew's harp, harmonica, accordion, and other traditional instruments; the country orch. numbered as many as 50 players. There were also "talking blues," comedy routines, and grandiose jamborees, where people gathered on the stage indulging in free commentary while performers continued their acts bent over the microphones. Amazingly enough, the Opry managed to keep its rustic purity more or less intact through the muddy mire of prevailing commercialism; not even television was able to disrupt its natural folkways. Despite a reactionary tendency, especially during the politically inflammatory 1960s, the Opry has learned to accommodate the ever-expanding stylistic panorama of country music.

grand opera. 1. Type of music drama, usually in 5 acts, treating a heroic, mythological, or historical subject, sumptuously costumed and staged, produced in large opera houses; describes 19th-century works (primarily by French composers) performed in Paris. 2. In English-speaking countries, any serious work without spoken recitatives.

Grand Opéra. The principal state-supported opera company of Paris, located over the years in various locations.

Grand Pause (abbrev. *G.P.*). Rest for an entire ensemble or orch., often climactic.

grand piano. Generic term for the horizontally strung piano; also, a smaller version of this piano type than the concert grand.

grande (*grand'*, *gran*; It.). Large, great, full, complete. *Grande* is the regular form used after nouns; shortened to *grand'* before vowels, to *gran* before consonants.

Grande Bande, La (Fr., large group). Lully's ensemble at the court of Louis XIV, also called the *24 violons du roy*.

grande caisse (Fr.). Bass drum.

grande-orgue. 1. Full organ. 2. Great organ. 3. Pipe organ.

grandezza, con (It.). With grandeur.

grandioso (*grandisonante*; It.). With grandeur; majestically, pompously, loftily, affectedly, in a grandiose manner; sonorously, resonantly.

granulato (It.). Non legato.

graphic notation. Symbols of notation other than those traditionally seen in musical scores; may indicate extremely precise (or intentionally imprecise) pitch, or stimulate musical behavior or actions in performance. Ever since 1000 A.D., when Guido d'Arezzo drew a line to mark the arbitrary height of pitch, musical notation has been geometric in its symbolism. The horizontal coordinate of the music staff represents the temporal succession of melodic notes; the vertical axis of the staff, the simultaneous use of 2 or more notes. Duration values have, through centuries of evolution, been indicated by the color and shape of notes and stems to which they were attached. The composers of the avant-garde hoped to reestablish the mathematical correlation between the coordinates of the axes by writing scores in which the duration is indicated by proportional distance between the notes; while such geometrical precision contributed to audio-visual clarity, it proved impractical in actual use: A passage in whole notes or half notes followed by a section in rapid rhythms was more difficult to read in proportional notation than the older, admittedly imprecise notation. Yet, recent orch'l scores show an increasing tendency to use blank spaces for inactive instrumental parts in mid-page rather than to strew such vacuums with a rash of rests.

New sounds demanded new notational symbols. Cowell, who invented tone clusters, notated them by drawing thick vertical lines attached to a stem. In *New Musical Resources* he tackled the problem of nonbinary rhythmic division, outlining a plausible notation using square, triangular, and rhomboid note-shapes. Alois Hába (1893–1973), a pioneer in microtonal music, devised special notation for quarter tones, 3rd tones, and 6th tones. As long as the elements of pitch, duration, intervallic extension, and polyphonic simultaneity remain in force, the musical staff can accommodate these elements more or less adequately. This was true even when noises were introduced by Italian futurists into their works; Luigi Russolo (1885–1947) drew a network of curves, thick lines, and zigzags to represent each particular noise, but the measure and the proportional lengths of duration retained their validity.

The situation changed dramatically with the introduction of aleatory processes and the indeterminacy of musical elements. The visual appearance of aleatory scores assumes the aspect of ideograms; Cage, in particular, remodeled musical notation so as to give improvisatory latitude to the performer. The score of his *Variations I* suggests the track of cosmic rays in a cloud chamber; *Cartridge Music* looks like an exploding supernova; and *Fontana Mix* is a projection of irregular curves upon a strip of graph paper. Penderecki uses various graphic symbols to designate such effects as the highest possible sound on a given instrument, free improvisation within a certain limited range of chromatic notes, or icositetraphonic tone clusters.

In music for mixed media, notation ceases to function per se, giving way to pictorial representation of the actions or psychological factors involved. Jani Christou (1926–70) introduced the Greek letter R (ϕ) to indicate the psychology of the musical action, with geometric ideograms and masks symbolizing changing mental states ranging from complete passivity to panic; the score of *Passion According to Marquis de Sade* by Sylvano Bussotti (b. 1931) looks like a surrealistic painting with musical notes strewn across its path; Cornelius Cardew drew black-and-white circles, triangles, and rectangles to indicate musical action. Xenakis prefers to use numbers and letters indicating the specific tape recordings to be used in his musical structures; Some composers abandon the problem of notation entirely, recording their inspirations on tape. The chess grandmaster Tarrasch said of a problematical chess move: "If it is ugly, it is bad." *Mutatis mutandis*: the same criterion applies to a composer's musical graph.

Grappelli (Grappelly), Stephane, b. Paris, Jan. 26, 1908. Trained as a classical violinist, he turned to jazz in the late 1920s; organized the Quintette du Hot Club de France with guitarist Django Reinhardt (1934); toured widely and made recordings; made his U.S. debut at the Newport (R.I.) Jazz Festival (1969); appeared regularly in concert with Menuhin (from 1973) and later with Nigel Kennedy. He made his Carnegie Hall, N.Y. debut in 1974; played at a special 80th-birthday concert (1988); foremost violinist in the European "Le Jazz hot," a fusion of big band and bebop styles.

Grateful Dead, The. See ⇒Garcia, Jerry.

grave (*gravemente;* It.). 1. Low in pitch. 2. Heavy, slow, ponderous in movement. 3. Serious, gravely, solemnly.

gravicembalo (It.). 17th-century term for harpsichord. *Gravicembalo col piano e forte*, early Italian name for piano; *gravicembalo con pian e forte*, Cristofori's name for his piano (early 18th century).

grazia, con (*grazioso;* It.). Gracefully; elegantly.

great octave. Name for the octave beginning on C, 2 leger lines below the staff of the bass clef. See ⇒ Intro., The Clefs.

great organ. Main manual of an organ, and pipes controlled by it.

Green, Adolph. See ⇒Comden and Green.

Green, John (Waldo), b. N.Y., Oct. 10, 1908; d. Beverly Hills, Calif., May 15, 1989. He studied economics at Harvard Univ. (B.A. 1928); received theory instruction from W. R. Spalding; later studied piano with Ignace Hilsberg, orchestration with Adolf Deutsch, and conducting with Frank Tours. Working as an arranger for Guy Lombardo, he produced his 1st hit song, *Coquette* (1928); accompanist to Gertrude Lawrence; wrote the popular *Body and Soul* (1930). He became an arranger for Paramount in Hollywood (1930); made recordings with his own dance band; performed on the radio; settled in Hollywood; joined the music staff of MGM (1942); served as its head (1949–58). He prepared award-winning film adaptations of the orig. scores for *Easter Parade* (1948), *An American in Paris*

(1951), *West Side Story* (1961), and *Oliver!* (1968); wrote the score for *Raintree County* (1957); associate conductor of the Los Angeles Phil. (1959–61); guest conducted with several major U.S. orchs.

Gregorian chant. System of liturgical plainsong in the Roman Catholic Church; its codification is traditionally attributed to Pope Gregory I (*c.* 600). Devoid of harmonic connotations, it may seem monotonous to modern ears, but compensates by an extraordinary melorhythmic richness. Uncertainties in the notation of Gregorian chant has led to the proliferation of different renderings of the same MSS; disconcerted by this ambiguity, a group of Benedictine monks of the French village of Solesmes undertook the task of reconciling different versions of liturgical texts; prepared an ed. of early chants, publ. as the *Editio Vaticana* with the Papal imprimatur.

Gregorian chant is always in Latin; the syllabic settings are entirely free, so that one syllable may be sung to a single note or to several legato notes (the latter is an example of a melisma); in climactic passages such as "Alleluja," a single syllable may be sung to a group of 20 notes or more. What makes Gregorian chant both intractable and fascinating is that singers must treat a given chant melodically and rhythmically in a variety of ways, according to liturgical position; the improvisatory style of Gregorian melismas is rooted in liturgical prose, as distinct from extemporized instrumental figurations of the Baroque school and the aleatory practices of the 20th century.

Similarities between ancient Jewish cantillation and Gregorian chant may have a historical foundation within the common heritage of the Judeo-Christian tradition; equally tenable is the theory of a Greek origin, the strongest argument being the modal classification of Gregorian chant and ancient Greek music. Indeed, the names of the modes in Gregorian chant are borrowed from ancient Greek, but medieval theorists responsible for this nomenclature misinterpreted the intervallic structure and direction of the ancient modes: Greek modal intervals were counted downward, while medieval church modal intervals were scaled upward.

The obstinacy and intransigence of the followers of competing ideas about Gregorian chant's rhythmic and melodic character are a marvel to behold: the deeper the scholarship of these learned men, the more irreconcilable their differences. A modest practitioner of the practical art of Gregorian chant interprets its rhythmic and melodic values through oral tradition, so that the result sounds natural, musically satisfying, and more authentic than the exemplars of various schools of mensuralists, accentualists, or others. Religious services in the old cathedrals and monasteries in Roman Catholic Europe confirms the conviction that Gregorian chant follows its own intrinsically coherent rules, derived from the reading of texts, asymmetrical in musical phraseology, syllabically accentuated according to spirit and textual importance, and gravitating toward changing tonal centers in fluid modality. Great composers throughout history have been inspired to use Gregorian melodies, adding a new dimension; asymmetrical chant melodies serve as contrapuntal materials or are arranged harmonically within symmetrical measures; in these applications, Gregorian chant serves as raw material, much as folk music does when used similarly.

Gregory I (the Great); b. Rome, *c.* 540; d. there, Mar. 12, 604. Served as Pope from 590 to his death; celebrated in music history as reputed reformer of the musical ritual of the Roman Catholic Church; traditionally believed that he ordered and supervised a collection of the music employed in the different churches (599); offertories, antiphons, responses, etc., were revised and distributed appropriately over the liturgical year in an arrangement which became known as Gregorian chant. While for centuries the sole credit for this codification had been ascribed to Gregory, investigations by such scholars as Gevaert, Riemann, P. Wagner, and others have demonstrated that some of Gregory's predecessors had begun this reform, even fixing the order of liturgical sections, and that the work of reform was completed under some of his immediate successors.

grell (Ger.). Sharply, incisely.

grelots (Fr., pellet bell; Ger. *Schelle*). Vessel rattle.

grido (It.). Cry, shout.

Grieg, Edvard (Hagerup), b. Bergen, June 15, 1843; d. there, Sept. 4, 1907. He received his 1st musical instruction from his mother, an amateur pianist. At the suggestion of the Norwegian violinist Ole Bull (1810–80), he was sent to the Leipzig Cons. (1858); studied piano with Plaidy, Wenzel, and (later) Moscheles, and theory with E. F. Richter, R. Papperitz, M. Hauptmann, and Reinecke; immersed himself in German Romanticism, with the aesthetic legacy of Mendelssohn and Schumann; his early works are permeated with such lyric moods. He went to Copenhagen (1863); studied briefly with Niels Gade (1817–90); met the Norwegian composer Rikard Nordraak; they organized the Euterpe Soc. for the promotion of national Scandinavian music, opposing dominating German influences; the premature death of Nordraak at age 23 (1866) left Grieg alone to carry on the project.

Grieg opened a Norwegian Academy of Music (1867) and gave concerts of Norwegian music; engaged as conductor of the Harmonic Soc. in Christiania (now Oslo); married his cousin, the singer Nina Hagerup (1867). By that time he had composed 2 violin sonatas and the 1st set of *Lyric Pieces* for piano, using Norwegian motifs. He played the solo part in the world premiere of his Piano Concerto in Copenhagen (1869), thus establishing himself as a major composer at age 25; wrote the orig. incidental music to Ibsen's *Peer Gynt* (1874–75); 2 orch'l suites taken from this music are extremely popular. The Norwegian government granted him an annuity of 1,600 crowns so he could devote his time to composition; performances of his works increased in Germany, then throughout Europe; gave a concert of his works in London (1888); prepared recitals of his songs with his wife.

He revisited England frequently; elected a member of the Swedish Academy (1872) and the French Academy (1890). Despite his successes, Grieg was of a retiring disposition; spent most of his later years in Troldhaugen, near Bergen, avoiding visitors and shunning public acclaim; continued to compose at a steady rate. His death, of heart disease, was mourned by all Norway; given a state funeral, his remains were cremated, at his own request, and sealed in the side of a cliff projecting over the fjord at Troldhaugen.

Grieg's importance lies in the strongly pronounced nationalism of his music; its combination of lyricism and nationalism music led some critics to describe him as "the Chopin of the North."

Without resorting to literal quotation of Norwegian folk song, he re-creates its melodic and rhythmic flavor; his harmony remains well within the bounds of tradition; the lyric expressiveness of his best works and the contagious rhythm of his dancelike pieces imparts charm and individuality. He excelled in miniatures, in which formal perfection and clarity of musical line are remarkable; the unifying essence of his creativity is exemplified by the lyric pieces for piano, composing 10 sets of them between 1867 and 1901; wrote other piano works; his songs and song cycles similarly blend Romantic and characteristically national inflections. In orch'l composition, he wrote mostly symphonic suites and arrangements of his piano pieces; in chamber music, his 3 violin sonatas, cello sonata, and 1 extant string quartet represent fine instrumental writing. He made friends easily with his unassuming personality; admired by Brahms, Tchaikovsky, Delius, and Grainger.

The father of Nina (Hagerup) Grieg (b. near Bergen, Nov. 24, 1845; d. Copenhagen, Dec. 9, 1935) was a brother of Edvard Grieg's mother. Hagerup studied singing with Helsted; met Grieg in Copenhagen, and married him (1867); her interpretations of his songs elicited much praise from critics; Delius dedicated 2 sets of songs to her.

Griffbrett (Ger., gripping board). Fingerboard on string instruments. *Griffbrett, am* (Ger., at the fingerboard). To bow near the fingerboard so as to produce a sound imitating the flute's sonority; flautando.

Griffes, Charles T(omlinson), b. Elmira, N.Y., Sept. 17, 1884; d. N.Y., Apr. 8, 1920. He studied piano with a local teacher, Mary S. Broughton; took organ lessons; went to Berlin (1903); pupil of Gottfried Galston (piano) and Rufer and Humperdinck (composition). To eke out a living, he gave private lessons; played his own compositions in public recitals; returned to the U.S. (1907); took a music teacher's job at the Hackley School for Boys at Tarrytown, N.Y. He continued to study music; fascinated by French impressionism and the potentialities of oriental scales, as well as the Russian school, particularly Mussorgsky and Scriabin. A combination of natural talent and determination to acquire a high degree of craftsmanship elevated him to the position of a foremost American composer in the impressionist genre; his works retain an enduring place in American music, including orch'l, piano, and vocal works.

Grofé, Ferde (Ferdinand Rudolph von), b. N.Y., Mar. 27, 1892; d. Santa Monica, Calif., Apr. 3, 1972. He studied music with Pietro Floridia; engaged as violist in the Los Angeles Phil.; worked as pianist and conductor in theaters and cafés; joined Paul Whiteman's band as pianist and arranger (1920); his scoring of Gershwin's *Rhapsody in Blue* (1924) won him fame. In his own works he successfully applied jazz rhythms interwoven with simple balladlike tunes; the *Grand Canyon Suite* (Chicago, 1931, Whiteman conducting) became very popular; composed other light pieces in a modern vein.

groove. 1. Enjoyable listening experience, especially in jazz and popular music. 2. Steady rhythmic pattern associated with a particular jazz or popular style.

grosse caisse (Fr.; Ger. *Grosse Trommel*). Bass drum.

grosso (It.). Great, grand; full, heavy.

grottesco (It.). Grotesque, comic.

ground bass. Early English form of basso ostinato, with a continually repeated bass phrase of 4 or 8 measures; a distinct melodic outline, usually structurally symmetrical, serving as the harmonic foundation of variations in the upper voices, along the lines of a passacaglia or chaconne; the technique was 1st used in the music of the virginalists of the late Renaissance, becoming prevalent during the English Baroque (e.g., "When I Am Laid in Earth," Dido's farewell aria in Purcell's *Dido and Aeneas*).

One of the most common ground bass patterns is the descending figure from the tonic to the dominant, in major or minor; the groups of descending 16th notes in the middle section of Chopin's Polonaise in A-flat Major are expansions of this figure. Sometimes the bass pursues a diatonic scale, from tonic to lower tonic, in even notes; the 2nd theme in Franck's *Symphonic Variations* for Piano and Orch. is related to this scalar descent; another example of the diatonically descending bass is the accompaniment of Rachmaninoff's song *A Little Island*. Many descending basses are set in chromatic motion, invariably in even notes; in such cases the bass line governs the melody, resulting in a modulatory chromatic sequence; an excellent example is the opening of Grieg's Ballade in G Minor for Piano (op. 24, 1876).

group. 1. Short series of rapid notes, especially when sung to 1 syllable. 2. Section of the orch. (or score) embracing instruments of 1 class, i.e., the strings.

Grove, (Sir) George, b. Clapham, South London, Aug. 13, 1820; d. Sydenham, May 28, 1900. In 1846 he became interested in music and entered the Soc. of Arts; appointed secretary (1850); came in contact with the organizers of the 1851 Exhibition; became secretary of the Crystal Palace (1852). He turned to literary work; edited, with William Smith, the *Dictionary of the Bible*; traveled to Palestine (1858, 1861); became director of the Palestine Exploration Fund (1865). He accumulated a private music library; wrote analytical programs for Crystal Palace concerts (1856–96), establishing a new standard of excellence in musical exegesis. His enthusiasm for music led to important associations; with Arthur Sullivan he went to Vienna in search of unknown music by Schubert (1867); discovered the score of *Rosamunde*. He became ed. of *Macmillan's Magazine* (1868); remained on its staff for 15 years. In addition to receiving many honors for his literary and musical achievements, he was knighted by Queen Victoria (1883). When the Royal College of Music was formed in London (1882), he was appointed director; remaining until 1894.

Grove's chief work was the monumental *Dictionary of Music and Musicians*, begun in 1879; planned for 2 vols., but expanded to 4 vols. with an appendix, finally publ. by Macmillan (1889). He contributed voluminous articles on his favorite composers: Beethoven, Schubert, and Mendelssohn; gathered a distinguished group of specialists to write other entries. The 2nd ed. was ed. by Fuller Maitland (1904–10); the 3rd ed. by H. C. Colles (1927–28); an American supplement by W. S. Pratt and C. H. N. Boyd (1920), expanded and republished (1928); the 4th ed. of the orig., also by Colles, publ. with a supplementary vol. (1940); an entirely revised and greatly enlarged 5th ed. by E. Bloom (9 vols., 1954); an entirely new 6th ed., ed. by S. Sadie, was publ. as *The New Grove Dictionary of Music and Musicians* (20 vols., 1980).

growl. In jazz, altering the natural tone of an instrument by flutter-tonguing, muting, throat vibrato, or a combination.

Gruber, Franz Xaver, b. Unterweizburg, near Hochburg, Nov. 25, 1787; d. Hallein, near Salzburg, June 7, 1863. He acquired fame as the composer of the Christmas carol *Stille Nacht, Heilige Nacht*. Of a poor family, he had to do manual work as a youth, but managed to study organ; by dint of perseverance, obtained a position as church organist and schoolmaster at Oberndorf; it was there, on Christmas Eve of 1818, that a young curate, Joseph Mohr, brought him a Christmas poem to set to music; the rest is musical history. He was the great-great-grandfather of H(einz) K(arl) Gruber.

Gruber, H(einz) K(arl) (called Nali), b. Vienna, Jan. 3, 1943. The great-great-grandson of Franz Xaver Gruber. He studied composition with Uhl and Jelinek; played double bass and horn; studied film music at the Hochschule für Musik in Vienna (1957–63); attended master classes held by von Einem (1963–64). He played principal double bass in the Niederösterreiches Tonkünstler-Orch. in Vienna (1961–69); with Schwertsik and Zukan, co-founded an avant-garde group, MOB art & tone ART (1968); joined the Vienna ensemble Die Reihe on double bass (1961); joined the ORF (Austrian Radio) Sym. Orch. in the same capacity (1969); performed as an actor. In his music he maintains a wide amplitude of styles, idioms, and techniques, applying the dodecaphonic method of composition in works of a jazz and pop nature. His "pandemonium" *Frankenstein!!*, a megamultimedia affair with children's verses recited in a bizarre and mock-scary manner, became quite popular.

Gruenberg, Louis, b. near Brest Litovsk, Aug. 3, 1884; d. Los Angeles, June 9, 1964. He was taken to the U.S. as an infant; studied piano with Adele Margulies in N.Y.; went to Berlin; studied with Busoni (piano and composition); made his debut as a pianist with the Berlin Phil. (1912); took courses and tutored at the Vienna Cons. Returning to the U.S. (1919), he devoted himself to composing; was an organizer and active member of the League of Composers (from 1923); one of the 1st American composers to incorporate jazz rhythms into symphonic works; taught composition at the Chicago Music College (1933–36); settled in Calif.; composed film scores. Of his many operas the most successful was *The Emperor Jones*, after O'Neill's play (Metropolitan Opera, N.Y., 1933; awarded the David Bispham Medal). He finished 4 syms.; violin, viola, and cello concertos; several cantatas, many influenced by African American music; publ. 4 vols. of Negro spirituals; wrote works for violin and piano, string quartet, and jazz-inflected piano.

grunge. See ⇒rock.

gruppetto (*gruppo;* It., small group). 1. Formerly, a trill. 2. Turn or double appoggiatura; any "group" of grace notes. 3. Melodic ornament, usually indicated by a ~ over the note head, stem, or beam; alternation of the principal note, 1 scale degree above and 1 below, depending on the direction of the sign; the sign was superseded by a written-out embellishment.

G-sharp minor. This key, armored with 5 sharps in its key signature, is rarely encountered as the principal key of a major work; not even the pansymphonic Miaskovsky wrote a sym. in that key. G-sharp minor has an acrid feeling of bucolic intimacy and is best suited to short piano pieces, e.g., Liszt's *La Campanella* for piano.

guajira. Cuban song and dance in a combined 3/4 and 6/8 meter; the name refers to *guajiro*, a colloquialism for rustic Cubans.

guaracha (Sp.). Lively Spanish dance in binary form; a 2/4 introduction is followed by a rapid movement in a combined 3/4 and 6/8.

Guarania. Paraguayan dance in slow 3/4; became popular in the 20th century; named after the Guaraní, the indigenous people of Paraguay, Uruguay, and maritime Argentina.

Guarneri family. Famous Italian family of violin makers. (The Italian form of the name was derived from the Lat. *Guarnerius*, which was invariably found on their instrument labels.) Andrea Guarneri, head of the family (b. Cremona, *c.* 1625; d. there, Dec. 7, 1698), was a pupil of Nicola Amati until 1654, when he, with his wife, moved to a house in Cremona and began making his own violins. Andrea's son Pietro Giovanni, "da Mantova" (b. Cremona, Feb. 18, 1655; d. Mantua, Mar. 26, 1720), worked 1st at Cremona, then settled in Mantua. His brother Giuseppe Giovanni Battista, "filius Andreae" (b. Cremona, Nov. 25, 1666; d. there, *c.* 1740), worked in his father's shop, which he eventually inherited; departed from his father's model, following the models of Stradivarius. Giuseppe's son Pietro, "da Venezia" (b. Cremona, Apr. 14, 1695; d. Venice, Apr. 7, 1762), settled in Venice (1725); adopted some features of the Venetian masters Montagnana and Serafin. His brother (Bartolomeo) Giuseppe Antonio, "Giuseppe del Gesù" (from the initials IHS often appearing on his labels; b. Cremona, Aug. 21, 1698; d. there, Oct. 17, 1744), became the most celebrated member of the family; his violins are greatly prized, rivaling those of Stradivarius in craftsmanship; he experimented with a variety of wood materials and with the shapes of his instruments during different periods of his work; violinists as Heifetz, Stern, Szeryng, Grumiaux, and Paganini used his instruments.

guasa. Venezuelan song of the corrido type, usually in 6/8 meter.

Gubaidulina, Sofia, b. Chistopol, Oct. 24, 1931. She studied at the Kazan Cons. (graduated 1954); enrolled at the Moscow Cons.; studied composition with Peiko and Shebalin; from her very 1st compositions, followed vectorially divergent paths without adhering to any set doctrine of modern techniques; a typically astounding work is a concerto for bassoon and low string instruments, in 5 movements (1975); the bassoon is embedded in a net of 4 cellos and 3 double basses, creating a claustrophobic syndrome of congested low sonorities; the solo instrument is thus forced to perform acrobatic feats to escape constriction, including labial glissandos and explosive iterations of a single thematic note. Her music soon penetrated the music world far beyond Soviet frontiers; her works were solicited by performers in Europe and the U.S.; made several voyages to the U.S. to hear performances of her works; was a guest at the Boston Festival of Soviet Music (1988); it took a decisive change in official Soviet policy before her music received full recognition in her own country. Her sources of compositional inspiration extend from mystical Eastern elements to Roman Catholic and Russian Orthodox conformations.

gudok. Russian 3-string instrument placed on the knees while playing; similar to the Bulgarian gadulka.

Guerre des Bouffons (Querelle des Bouffons; Fr.). Famous theatrical controversy that erupted when an Italian opera company visited Paris (1752); their performances of Pergolesi's *La Serva padrona* aroused the admiration of the pro-Italian faction of the Parisian intellectuals, including the Encyclopedists; but it aroused opposition from the lovers of French opera, fostered by Louis XV. A whole series of polemical pamphlets followed, including Rousseau's *Lettre sur la musique française*; the controversy subsided when the Italians left Paris (1754).

guerriero (It.). Martial, warlike.

guide. 1. Sign at the end of a staff to indicate the location of the 1st note of the next staff. 2. Subject or antecedent.

Guido d'Arezzo (Guido Aretinus), b. *c.* 991; d. after 1033. He received his education at the Benedictine abbey at Pomposa, near Ferrara; left the monastery (1025) as a result of disagreements with fellow monks envious of his superiority in vocal teaching; summoned by Bishop Theobald of Arezzo to its cathedral school (hence his *nom de religion*). The belief that he traveled in France and spent several years at the monastery of Saint-Maur des Fossés is not borne out by documentary evidence; even more uncertain are claims of his travels in Germany and England; nonetheless, his fame spread and reached the ears of Pope John XIX, who called him to Rome to demonstrate his teaching system (1028); spent his last years as a prior of the Camaldolite fraternity at Avellano. His most essential treatises are *Micrologus de disciplina artis musicae* (*c.* 1026) and *Epistola de ignoto cantu* (*c.* 1028–29).

Guido's fame rests on his system of solmization, which established the nomenclature of the major hexachord *Ut, Re, Mi, Fa, Sol, La*, from syllables in the opening lines of the Hymn of St. John:

> **Ut** quent laxis **Re**sonare fibris
> *Mi*ra gestorum **Fa**muli tuorum,
> **Sol**ve polluti **La**bii reatum,
> Sancte Joannes.

No less epoch-making was his introduction of the musical staff of 4 lines, retaining the red f-line and the yellow c-line of his predecessors and drawing between them a black a-line, above them a black e-line, and writing the plainsong notes (not his invention) in regular order on these lines and in the spaces:

> New black line e_____
> Old yellow line c_____
> New black line a_____
> Old red line f_____

He also added new lines above or below these, as occasion required; his system thus did away with all uncertainty of pitch. Another invention credited to him is the so-called ⇒Guidonian hand. Opinions differ widely as to the attribution of these innovations to him; some maintain that he merely popularized preexisting ideas and that solmization, in particular, was introduced by a German abbot, Poncius Teutonicus, at the abbey of Saint-Maur des Fossés.

Guidonian hand (Lat. *manus guidonis*; named after Guido d'Arezzo, inventor of syllabic solmization). Didactic method of teaching a system of overlapping hexachords, relating the hexachordal degrees to places on the palm of the left hand. The lowest G (the gamut) was represented by the upperside of the thumb, the notes progressing scalewise across the palm to the tip of the little finger and continuing along the fingertips to the index finger, then descending and after another turn ending on the top of the middle finger on the E, 2 octaves and a 6th above the initial gamut. In the Middle Ages the choir director indicated the points on the different joints of each finger to dictate the required notes to singers.

Guillaume de Machaut. Machaut, Guillaume de.

güiro (Cub.; Braz. *reco-reco*). Scratcher or a scraper used in Latin American bands, made out of a long gourd with notches on its upper side; these notches are scraped with a stick. Although the güiro is classified as a percussion instrument, friction is essential to its sound production. It is used in modern scores, most ingeniously at the end of Stravinsky's *Le Sacre du printemps*; in Ravel's *L'enfant et les sortilèges*, it can substitute for the *rape à fromage*, a cheese grater scraped with a triangle beater.

guitar. Universally popular string instrument of the lute family, played by plucking or strumming the strings. Etymologically, the word can be traced to the Greek kithara, but there is no similarity in the structure or sound of the 2 instruments. The modern Spanish (acoustic, classical) guitar has 6 strings and a compass of 3 octaves, and a 4th, from E to a^2; the strings are tuned in perfect 4ths, with the exception of the interval between the 2nd and 3rd strings, a major 3rd: E, A, d, g, b, and e^1. Guitar music sounds an octave lower than written (exclusively in the G clef). The fingerboard is provided with frets to indicate the position of the notes of the chromatic scale; technically, the guitar is incapable of infinitely sustained harmony, but is brilliantly adapted for arpeggiated chords.

The guitar is the proverbial instrument of chivalrous courtship; scenes of swains serenading their lady loves under their balconies abound in paintings, poetry, theater, and the imagination. The instrument in its present form developed in Spain in the 16th century and spread all over the world; as an inalienable part of equipment for cowboys of the American West and the gauchos on the pampas of South America, it was 2nd only to the horse in their affection.

Around the mid–20th century the guitar was electrically amplified to compensate for its relatively weak amplitude; this adaptation became a staple of jazz and pop combos, later in rock, rhythm and blues, and related genres. In its new role it underwent a change in anatomy: its folklike outlines were abandoned

in favor of a gaudy, more androgyne shape, thinner in the middle but sprouting a pair of tinseled shoulders; the hollow body became solid and made of heavy plastic. Despite the electric's popularity, great acoustic players like Segovia, Yepes, Bream, J. Williams, and Isbin maintained the classical instrument's traditions; numerous modern composers, among them Castelnuovo-Tedesco, Manuel Ponce, and Rodrigo wrote concertos for guitar and orch.

guitar, acoustic. Classical or Spanish instrument, in contrast to the electric guitar. *Guitar, backup,* see ⇒guitar, rhythm; *guitar, bass,* electrified adaptation of the double bass, built and shaped like an electric guitar, which it is designed to match in popular music. Some electric basses are unfretted so that a performer can perform the glissandos and portamentos possible on the acoustic instrument; mostly used in jazz-funk (fusion); *guitar, classical,* Spanish (acoustic) guitar; *guitar, electric,* see ⇒electric guitar; *guitar, lead,* the "1st guitarist" in rock and similar genres, performing on electric guitar and responsible for melodic riffs, fills, and solos; e.g., in the orig. Rolling Stones, Keith Richard(s) generally played lead guitar while Brian Jones played rhythm guitar. A group may have more than one person capable of performing this role, as in the orig. Allman Brothers Band (Duane Allman, Dickie Betts); *guitar, rhythm,* the "2nd guitarist" in rock and similar genres, performing on an electric guitar and providing the harmonic and rhythmic support for lead instruments or singers; e.g., in the Beatles, John Lennon generally played rhythm guitar to George Harrison's lead guitar; also called backup guitar; *guitar, Spanish;* acoustic or classical 6-stringed guitar, with predecessors dating back to the 13th century (and varying numbers of strings); made of wood, with a large circular soundhole and a hollow body modeled after the human neck and torso; the neck is attached to a fingerboard supplied with frets to indicate the notes of the chromatic scale. See also ⇒guitarra española.

guitare d'amour (Fr.). Arpeggione.

guitarra española (Sp. Spanish guitar). 5-course guitar of the 16th and 17th centuries.

gusle. 1. One-string fiddle of the South Slavic region, with a long neck and wooden resonator; not the same as the Russian gusli. 2. Violin.

gusli. Ancient Russian psaltery, shaped in a trapezoid. The number of strings range from 11 to 36, strung horizontally so that the lowest pitches are farthest from the player; early gusli types had no more than 7 strings, but the number increased in the 15th century. Glinka has a musical part for a legendary gusli player in *Ruslan and Ludmilla*, but the part is taken by the orch. harp. 2. An instrument related to the Finnish kantele.

gusto (It.). Taste.

gut (Ger.). 1. Good. 2. (Eng.) Abbrev. of catgut.

Guthrie, Woody (Woodrow Wilson), b. Okemah, Okla., July 14, 1912; d. N.Y., Oct. 3, 1967. He left home with his guitar and harmonica at age 15, riding the rails of freight trains across the U.S. and playing in hobo and migrant camps, bars, and labor meetings during the Great Depression. Among the songs he wrote or arranged were *So Long, It's Been Good to Know Ya*; *This Train Is Bound for Glory*; *Hard Traveling*; *Blowing Down This Old Dusty Road*; and *This Land Is Your Land*; in later years he joined Pete Seeger and others as a member of the Almanac Singers in N.Y.; his life and career were slowly destroyed after being stricken with Huntington's chorea in the early 1950s. In spite of his freely professed radical convictions, the U.S. government gave him an award of merit as "a poet of the American landscape" (1966); publ. the books *Bound for Glory* (N.Y., 1943) and *American Folksong* (N.Y., 1947; with memoirs); W. Doerflinger ed. *Seeds of Man: An Experience Lived and Dreamed* (N.Y., 1976). His son, Arlo (Davy) Guthrie (b. N.Y., July 10, 1947), followed in his father's footsteps as a socially conscious singer-songwriter; most famous for the talking ballad *Alice's Restaurant* (1969), the basis for a film in which he starred; also performed with Seeger.

gymel (from Lat. *gemellus*, twin). Cantus gemellus.

gymnosophistical homophony (from Grk. *gymn* + *sophiste-s*, naked wise man). The description *gymnosophist* is applied to an Indian sect that flourished about 1000 A.D., who preached abstinence from carnal delights, refused to wear clothes, and limited themselves to the simplest modes of communication. Archaizing usages and affectation of utmost simplicity in musical composition may be considered gymnosophistical; naked perfect 5ths (i.e., absent the 3rd of a triad), when applied ostentatiously in modern works to create an impression of luxurious abstemiousness, are gymnosophistical. Satie, in his sophisticated use of gymnosophistical harmonies in the *Gymnopédies* (1888), provides a perfect exemplar: deliberately bleak in its renunciation of harmonious carnality, yet thoroughly modern in its invocation of secret rites and suggested aberrations. For different reasons Stravinsky adopted gymnosophistical modalities in his neo-Grecian works to react against the proliferation of colorful sonorities in instrumental music, including his own. Gymnosophistical homophony is a natural medium also for neoecclesiastical composition in quintal or quartal gemination.

Gypsy music. The nomadic Gypsies (more properly, the Romany) penetrated many countries in Europe, forming their own communities called tabors, or camps; elected their "kings" in colorful rituals, but otherwise adapted themselves to the customs of their adoptive land. While the English word for the Romany seems to be a corruption of "Egyptians," Gypsies probably came originally out of India, where they were treated as untouchable pariahs. They attracted attention by wearing gaudy apparel and jewelry. In literature, painting, theater, and opera, they were stereotyped as clever and devious, practicing their arts upon superstitious men and women; viewed as fortune-tellers, thieves, seducers, international smugglers, and possessors of magic arts.

The mysteries of the unintelligible plot of Verdi's opera *Il Trovatore* are contrived by Gypsies; the famous "anvil chorus" in the 2nd act is sung by Gypsy blacksmiths; Bizet's Carmen is a Gypsy who causes Don José to desert the army and join her comrades in a smuggling ring. In Michael Balfe's *The Bohemian Girl*, the heroine is kidnapped by Gypsies as a child. (Because many Gypsies came from Bohemia, the term "bohemian" was applied to rootless artists and wandering adventurers.) Paderewski's *Manru* glorifies the leader of a Gypsy tribe in the Carpathian Mountains; Puccini's *La Bohème*, a collective noun meaning "Bohemian life," could well be translated as *The Gypsies*. In J. Strauss's *Der Zigeunerbaron*, a young Hungarian is chosen to be a Gypsy leader and is elevated to the rank of a "Gypsy baron." Romanticized Gypsies were often passionate, sometimes sinister lovers, such as Aleko, the hero of Rachmaninoff's eponymous opera (based on Pushkin's poem *The Gypsies*); the title of Lehár's *Zigeunerliebe* (Gypsy Love) typifies the Gypsy cliché.

With all their picturesque folkways, the Romany failed to develop autonomous art forms; the so-called Gypsy scale, containing 2 augmented 2nds, might be more properly called a Hungarian scale. But Gypsy music had a capacity of insinuating itself into the musical modalities of other peoples. In the 19th century, Gypsy music took root in the Balkans, predominately in Rumania; from the Balkans a wave of Gypsy Rumanian musicians invaded Hungary, Austria, and Russia. The most significant incursion of Gypsy music occurred in Hungary; the Hungarian verbunkos form was directly influenced by Rumanian Gypsy musicians; Liszt was an avid listener to Gypsy bands; ironically, his *Hungarian Rhapsodies* were derived from these impressions rather than from authentic Magyar folk tunes.

Another curious phenomenon took place in Russia, where groups of Romany singers, guitarists, violinists, and tambourine players—most of them from the former Rumanian state of Bessarabia—established themselves as popular entertainers in restaurants, cafés, circuses, and other places of amusement. "Gypsy romances," or songs, became exceedingly popular in Russia, but their words and music were composed by amateur Russian musicians. "Let us go to the Gypsies" became a byword of dissolute revelry in Russian society. So deeply were these romances ingrained in the old regime that Soviet authorities launched a concentrated campaign against these songs; musicologists supplied dialectical arguments to prove that the songs' melodies and harmonies were not only tasteless but ideologically inadmissible in the new society; eventually even the Soviets yielded to Gypsy music's irrepressible lure.

For two centuries, composers have used such expressions as *alla gitana* or *alla zingarese* (in a Gypsy manner) to indicate an intended style of performance. Instrumental works with Gypsy titles abound, among them *Zigeunerweisen* (Gypsy Airs) for violin and piano by Sarasate and *Tzigane* for violin and orch. by Ravel.

Gypsy scale. Informal name for a minor harmonic scale with a raised subdominant, forming 2 augmented 2nds; also known as the Hungarian scale.

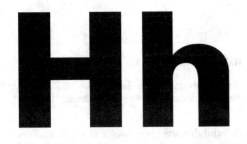

H. 1. In scores, French horn. 2. In organ music, heel. 3. In keyboard music, hand (r.h., l.h.).

H (Ger.). The note B.

H dur (Ger.). B major.

H moll (Ger.). B minor.

habanera (Sp. dance of Havana; often misspelled *habañera*). Moderately slow dance in 2/4; its origin as a folk dance is obscure. One theory, based mainly on metrical and rhythmical aspects, is that it was an offspring of the English country dance, via the French *contredanse* and Spanish *contradanza*, abbreviated to *danza* (c. 1800). In 1825 the *danza habanera* appeared in Cuba, later known simply as *habanera*, whose most characteristic rhythmic formula is a dotted 8th note followed by a 16th note and 2 8th notes.

While the most famous habanera is probably the one that Carmen sings in Bizet's opera, it was not Bizet's tune; he found it in a song collection by the Spanish composer Sebastián Yradier (publ. 1864), under the title *El Arreglito*, with a French subtitle, *Chanson havanaise*. (Yradier also composed *La Paloma*.) Bizet inserted *El Arreglito* shortly before the 1875 premiere of *Carmen*, yielding to the demand of the management for a "singable" song. Among other composers who wrote habaneras are Albéniz, Debussy, Ravel, Chabrier, and de Falla.

Haggard, Merle (Ronald), b. Bakersfield, Calif., Apr. 6, 1937. He started early on a criminal career; finally imprisoned at San Quentin as prisoner no. 845,200; met the notorious rapist Caryl Chessman, who exercised a profound intellectual influence on Haggard. He began improvising songs of destitution, despair, and crime, exemplified by the autobiographical line, "Did you ever steal a quarter when you was 10 years old?" He completed his term; later pardoned by Ronald Reagan, then Calif. governor (1972). He commanded a fee of $15,000 per concert, sold millions of record albums, and reached the top as a country-western singer with such hits as *Okie from Muskogee*, *Workin' Man Blues*, *Daddy Frank (the Guitar Man)*, and *Hungry Eyes*.

Hahn, Reynaldo, b. Caracas, Aug. 9, 1874; d. Paris, Jan. 28, 1947. His family moved to Paris when he was 5 years old. He studied singing (his excellent voice is attested to by a 1910 professional recording); studied theory at the Paris Cons. with Dubois and Lavignac and composition with Massenet, who exercised the most important influence on Hahn's music; also studied

conducting, becoming a professional opera conductor. In 1934 he became music critic of *Le Figaro;* remained in France during the Nazi occupation at a considerable risk to his life, being Jewish on his father's side; became a member of the Inst. de France (1945); music director of the Paris Opéra (1945–46).

In Paris, Hahn was known socially for his brilliant wit; maintained a passionate youthful friendship with Proust, who portrayed him as a poetic genius in his novel *Jean Santeuil;* their intimate correspondence was publ. (1946). A brilliant journalist, his articles were publ. in several collections. Hahn's music is distinguished by a facile, melodious flow and a fine Romantic flair; wrote primarily for the stage: operas, operettas, incidental music, and ballets; composed chansons; concertos for violin, piano, and cello; chamber music; and piano pieces, among them *Portraits des peintres*, inspired by Proust's poems (1894).

Haitink, Bernard (Johann Herman), b. Amsterdam, Mar. 4, 1929. He studied violin at the Amsterdam Cons.; played in the Radio Phil. Orch. in Hilversum; attended the conducting course of F. Leitner, sponsored by Netherlands Radio (1954–55); became 2nd conductor of the Radio Phil. Orch. in Hilversum (1955), then principal conductor (1957); made his U.S. debut with the Los Angeles Phil. Orch. (1958).

In 1956 Haitink made his 1st appearance with the Concertgebouw Orch. of Amsterdam (1956); conducted the orch. in England (1959); became its co-principal conductor, sharing duties with Eugen Jochum (1961), and led it on a U.S. tour, followed by a Japanese tour (1962). He became chief conductor of the Concertgebouw Orch., a position he held with great distinction (1964–88, including a 2nd U.S. tour, 1982). In 1967 he was engaged as principal conductor and artistic adviser of the London Phil. Orch.; became its artistic director (1969–78); made his debut at the Glyndebourne Festival (1972); served as its music director (1978–88); became music director of the Royal Opera House at London's Covent Garden (1987). He guest conducted the Berlin Phil., Vienna Phil., N.Y. Phil., Chicago Sym., Boston Sym., and Cleveland Orch.

In his interpretations Haitink avoids personal rhetoric, allowing the music to speak for itself; yet he achieves eloquent and colorful effect, especially in his performances of the syms. of Bruckner and Mahler and the Classic repertoire. He has received numerous honors: the Netherlands' Royal Order of Orange-Nassau (1969), medals from the Bruckner Soc. of America (1970) and the Gustav Mahler Soc. (1971); named a Chevalier de l'Ordre des Arts et des Lettres of France (1972) and an Honorary Knight Commander of the Order of the British Empire by Queen Elizabeth II (1977).

halb (Ger.). Half.

halbe Note (Ger.). Half note.

Halbkadenz (Ger.). Half cadence.

Halbton (Ger.). Semitone.

Halévy (Jacques-François-) Fromental (-Elie), (born Levy), b. Paris, May 27, 1799; d. Nice, Mar. 17, 1862. He entered the Paris Cons. at age 9, then studied with Lambert (piano), Berton (harmony), and Cherubini (counterpoint); also studied with Méhul; won the 2nd Prix de Rome (1816, 1817) and the Grand Prix de Rome with his cantata *Herminie* (1819); became *chef du chant* at the Théâtre-Italien (1826). His 1st performed stage work was *L'Artisan* (Opéra-Comique, 1827);

gained further notice with *Clari*, introduced by Malibran (Théâtre-Italien, 1828). His 1st major success came with *Le Dilettante d'Avignon* (Opéra-Comique, 1829); became *chef du chant* at the Paris Opéra (1829–45), where he scored his greatest triumph with *La Juive* (1835), performed throughout Europe and the U.S. His next opera, *L'éclair* (Opéra-Comique, 1835), was also favorably received. Of the later operas, the most successful were *La Reine de Chypre* (1841), *Charles VI* (1843), and *La Magicienne* (1858), all 1st performed at the Opéra.

Halévy taught at the Paris Cons. as prof. of harmony and accompaniment (1827), counterpoint and fugue (1833), and composition (1840); his students included Gounod, Bizet (later-his son-in-law), and Saint-Saëns; elected to the Inst. de France (1836), he served as secretary (from 1854). An extremely apt stage composer, he won the admiration of both Berlioz and Wagner; yet he never equalled Meyerbeer in popular success; only *La Juive* gained a permanent place in the repertoire. His brother Léon was an important librettist, but Fromental rarely set his texts, preferring instead those of Scribe and Saint-Georges. He wrote *Leçons de lecture musicale . . . pour les écoles de la ville de Paris* (Paris, 1857).

Haley, Bill (William John Clifton, Jr.), b. Highland Park, Mich., July 6, 1925; d. Harlingen, Tex., Feb. 9, 1981. He began to play guitar as a youth; at age 15 embarked on a country-and-western tour; formed his own band, renamed the Comets to impart a more cosmological beat (1952). He precipitated the rock 'n' roll era with *Crazy Man Crazy* (1953), followed by a hit version of Joe Turner's *Shake, Rattle and Roll*, combining elements of the blues, country-western, and urban pop. His fame skyrocketed in 1955 with *Rock Around the Clock*; immortalized in the motion picture *The Blackboard Jungle*, it became the banner of the rising generation of wild, wide-eyed, loose-eared, dance-crazy, rebellious American youth; 22 million copies of this song were sold. But like so many instinctual musicians of the period, Haley's once-agile style gave way to the irresistible ascent of the more sexually explicit art of Elvis Presley; he played successfully in the oldies circuit, but psychophysical illness darkened his last years.

half note. Note one-half the value of a whole note and represented by a white circle with a stem ($\natural$).

half step. Semitone.

Halffter (Escriche), Ernesto, b. Madrid, Jan. 16, 1905; d. there, July 5, 1989. He studied composition with de Falla and Adolfo Salazar; 1st attracted attention with his *Sinfonietta*, performed at the Oxford Festival of the ISCM (1931). His music continued the tradition of Sp. modern nationalism, following the stylistic and melorhythmic formations of de Falla; completed and orchestrated de Falla's unfinished scenic cantata, *Atlántida*, 1st performed at La Scala in Milan (1962). Among his own works are 3 ballets: *Dulcinea* (1940), *Cojo enamorado* (1954), and *Fantasia galaica* (1956; Milan, 1967); composed a Guitar Concerto (1968) and several cantatas. His brother Rodolfo Halffter (Escriche) (b. Madrid, Oct. 30, 1900; d. Mexico City, Oct. 14, 1987) and his nephew Cristóbal Halffter (Jiménez) (b. Madrid, Mar. 24, 1930) are also significant composers.

Halle, Adam de la. Adam de la Halle.

Hallelujah (from Heb. *hallel* + *Jah*, praise Jehovah). Religious exhortation from the Old Testament: "Praise ye the Lord!"

Hallelujah meter. Stanza used in a hymn of jubilation, containing 6 lines in iambic measure, with the number of syllables usually in the order of 8, 6, 8, 6, 8, 8.

halling. Animated Norwegian dance in 2/4 time, usually accompanied by the hardingfele.

Hamlisch, Marvin (Frederick), b. N.Y., June 2, 1944. His father, an accordionist, trained him in music; studied piano at the Juilliard School of Music and at Queens College (B.A., 1967); began writing songs at age 15. He won 3 Academy Awards for the music for *The Way We Were* (original score) and *The Sting* (adaptation; 1974); the latter contained piano music by Scott Joplin and orchestrations by Gunther Schuller, adapted from 60-year-old stock arrangements. He wrote the score for the musical *A Chorus Line* (1975), recipient of the Pulitzer Prize for Drama and a Tony award for the best musical score; an international touring company started in Toronto the next year, while a national company began its cross-country tour a few days later.

Hammerclavier (Hammerklavier; Ger. hammer piano). The standard piano of the early 19th century, reflecting technological developments.

Hammerstein, Oscar, b. Stettin, May 8, 1846; d. N.Y., Aug. 1, 1919. Grandfather of ⇒Oscar (Greeley Clendenning) Hammerstein, II. In his youth he practiced the violin, learned to write music, and dabbled in playwriting; produced a comedy in German (N.Y., 1868); wrote the libretto and music of an operetta, *The Kohinoor* (N.Y., 1893).

Hammerstein's main activity was in management; built the Harlem Opera House (1888), the Olympia Music Hall (1895), and the Republic Theater (1900); presented seasons of plays and operas. He announced plans for the Manhattan Opera House in N.Y., his crowning achievement; orig. planned as a house for opera in English, it opened with Bellini's *I Puritani* (1906); entered into bold competition with the Metropolitan Opera by engaging such celebrated singers as Melba, Nordica, Tetrazzini, and Garden; presented the U.S. premieres of 5 operas by Massenet, Charpentier's *Louise*, and Debussy's *Pelléas et Mélisande*. The new venture held its own for 4 seasons, but Hammerstein was finally compelled to yield; sold the Manhattan Opera House to the Metropolitan management for $1.2 million (1910); agreed not to produce grand opera in N.Y. for 10 years; also sold his interests in the Philadelphia Opera House (built 1908). Defeated in his main ambition in the U.S., he moved to England, where he built the London Opera House; failing to establish himself in London, he returned to N.Y. after a season. Contravening his agreement with the Metropolitan, he announced a season at the new American Opera House in N.Y., but the Metropolitan secured an injunction against him, and he was forced to give the idea up.

Hammerstein, Oscar (Greeley Clendenning), II, b. N.Y., July 12, 1895; d. Highland Farms, Doylestown, Pa.,

Aug. 23, 1960. Grandson of ⇒Oscar Hammerstein. He studied law at Columbia Univ. (graduated 1917); became interested in theater. He collaborated on the librettos for Friml's *Rose-Marie* (1924), Romberg's *The Desert Song* (1926), and Kern's *Show Boat* (with the celebrated *Ol' Man River*, 1927). In 1943 he joined forces with the composer Richard Rodgers; collaborated on such brilliant and successful musicals as *Oklahoma!* (1943; Pulitzer Prize); *Carousel* (1945); *South Pacific* (1949; Pulitzer Prize, 1950); *The King and I* (1951); *The Flower Drum Song* (1958); *The Sound of Music* (1959). His lyrics are characterized by appealing sentiment and sophisticated nostalgia; particularly well suited to modern theater.

Hammond, Laurens, b. Evanston, Ill., Jan. 11, 1895; d. Cornwall, Conn., July 1, 1973. He studied engineering at Cornell Univ.; went to Detroit to work on the synchronization of electrical motor impulses, a principle he later applied to the ⇒Hammond organ (1933). He later developed a polyphonic electric keyboard, the Novachord, 1st demonstrated at the U.S. Commerce Dept. in Washington, D.C. (1939); the Solovox, a monophonic electric keyboard with 3 octaves (1940); and the chord organ (1950).

Hammond organ. Keyboard instrument invented by Laurens Hammond (1933), designed to simulate a pipe organ. It produces tones by means of electrical generators; a special mechanism alters the relative strength of overtones of each fundamental, making it possible to produce any desired instrumental timbre. The Hammond organ is usually constructed in the shape of a spinet but has 2 manuals and a set of pedals.

Hampson, Thomas, b. Elkhart, Ind., June 28, 1955. He attended Eastern Washington Univ. (B.A., 1977), Fort Wright College (B.F.A., 1979), the Univ. of Southern Calif., and the Music Academy of the West at Santa Barbara. He won the Lotte Lehmann Award (1978); took 2nd prize at the 's Hertogenbosch International Vocal Competition (1980) and 1st place in the Metropolitan Opera Auditions (1981). That year he appeared with the Deutsche Oper am Rhein in Düsseldorf; attracted wide notice as Guglielmo in *Così fan tutte* with the Opera Theatre of St. Louis (1982); subsequently appeared in Santa Fe, Cologne, Lyons, and Zurich; made his Metropolitan Opera debut in N.Y. as Almaviva in *Le nozze di Figaro* (1986); has won particular success in roles by Mozart, Rossini, Donizetti, Verdi, and Puccini operas.

Hampton, Lionel, called "Hamp," b. Louisville, Ky., Apr. 12, 1909. "He played drums in Chicago nightclubs; moved to Los Angeles; pioneered jazz vibraphone (vibes); a virtuoso, he made the 1st recording of a jazz vibes solo with Louis Armstrong (*Memories of You*, 1930). After gaining national prominence in the Benny Goodman Quartet (1936–40), he mostly led his own bands, occasionally performing on other instruments; he originated the "trigger-finger" method of piano playing (2 forefingers drumming upon a single note *prestissimo*). From 1956 he made several successful European tours; founded a sextet called the Jazz Inner Circle (1965).

hanacca. Moravian dance in 3/4 time, like the polonaise, but quicker.

Hancock, Herbie (Herbert Jeffrey), b. Chicago, Apr. 12, 1940. He made an appearance with the Chicago Sym. Orch. at 11; studied engineering at Grinnell (Iowa) College (1956–60); took courses at the Manhattan School of Music and the New School for Social Research in N.Y. While still in school he led his own band; appeared with Hawkins, D. Byrd, and M. Davis, whose 1960s quintet made him famous. In 1968 he organized a sextet, later reduced to a quartet; appeared in pop concerts; became adept on electric piano; went to Los Angeles (1972). His ability to switch between styles has led to success in several fields; his electric jazz-rock (fusion) produced several hits, including *Watermelon Man, Chameleon,* and *Rockit*; popular albums were *Empyrean Isles* (1964), *Maiden Voyage* (1965), *Speak Like a Child* (1968), *Headhunters* (1973), *V.S.O.P.: The Quintet* (1977), and *Future Shock* (1983); won an Oscar for the soundtrack to *'Round Midnight* (starring Dexter Gordon, 1986).

Handel (Hendel), George Frideric, (born Georg Friedrich Händel), b. Halle, Feb. 23, 1685; d. London, Apr. 14, 1759. His father was a barber-surgeon and valet to the Prince of Saxe-Magdeburg. As a child he was taken to Saxe-Weissenfels, where he tried out the court chapel organ. The Duke, Johann Adolf, noticed his musical interest and advised that he be sent to Halle for organ lessons with Friedrich Wilhelm Zachow (1663–1712) of the Liebfrauenkirche; Zachow gave him instruction in harpsichord and organ playing as well as the rudiments of composition. Handel proved an apt enough student to be able to substitute as organist whenever necessary; he composed trio sonatas and motets for Sunday church services. After his father's death (1697) he entered the Univ. of Halle (1702); named probationary organist at the Domkirche.

In 1703 Händel went to Hamburg; engaged as "violino di ripieno" by Reinhard Keiser (1674–1739), famous composer and director of the Hamburg Opera; met composer and theorist Johann Mattheson (1681–1764); in 1703 the 2 undertook a journey to Lübeck together, intending to apply for the post of organist in succession to the chief organist, Buxtehude; but as it was the custom for an incoming organist to marry a daughter of the incumbent as a condition of appointment, neither traveler availed themselves of this opportunity. (Bach made the pilgrimage a year later, with the same result.) Händel's 1st 2 operas, *Almira* and *Nero,* were staged at the Hamburg Opera (1705); he wrote 2 others, *Florindo* and *Daphne.*

In 1706 Händel sojourned to Italy, visiting Florence, Rome, Naples, and Venice. The 1st opera he presented in Italy was *Rodrigo* (Florence, 1707), followed by *Agrippina* (Venice, 1709), which was successful. In Rome he premiered the serenata *Il trionfo del Tempo e del Disinganno* (1707); his 1st oratorio, *La Resurrezione,* was given in Rome (1708); later that year he premiered in Naples the serenata *Aci, Galatea, e Polifemo,* notable for a bass solo requiring a compass of 2 octaves and a 5th. He also met Alessandro and Domenico Scarlatti.

In 1710 Händel returned to Germany; was named Kapellmeister to the Elector of Hannover, succeeding Agostino Steffani; later that year he visited England; produced his opera *Rinaldo* at the Queen's Theatre in London (1711); after a brief return to Hannover, returned to London; produced the operas *Il Pastor fido* (1712) and *Teseo* (1713); wrote an ode for Queen Anne's birthday, presented at Windsor Palace (1713). He then wrote 2 works, a *Te Deum* and *Jubilate*, to celebrate the Peace of Utrecht; their performances won him royal favor and an annuity of 200 pounds sterling.

An extraordinary concurrence of events persuaded Händel to remain in London; when Queen Anne died (1714), his employer, the Elector of Hannover, became King George I of England; the King bestowed many favors upon the composer and doubled his annuity. Händel became a British subject (1727) and anglicized his name; continued to produce operas, to Italian librettos, for the London stage; *Silla* (1713) was followed by *Amadigi di Gaula* (1715); in 1716 he composed the "Brockes Passion" (*Der für die Sünden der Welt gemarterte und sterbende Jesus*) named for its librettist, poet Heinrich Brockes.

In 1717 Handel produced *Water Music*, one of his most famous works, written expressly for King George I; its 1st performance occurred during an aquatic fete on the Thames River, held by royal order; the King's boat was followed by a barge carrying an orch. of 50 musicians playing Handel's music; the final version of the *Water Music* comprises 2 instrumental suites. That same year he became resident composer to the Duke of Chandos, for whom he wrote the 11 so-called *Chandos Anthems* (1717–18), the secular oratorio *Acis and Galatea*, based on the 1708 serenata (1718); and the oratorio *Esther* (1718); served as music master to the daughters of the Prince of Wales; for Princess Anne he composed his 1st collection of *Suites de pieces pour le clavecin* ("The Lessons," 1720), which includes the famous air with variations gratuitously nicknamed "The Harmonious Blacksmith."

In 1719 Handel was made Master of Musick of the Royal Academy of Music, established to present opera at the King's Theatre; his 1st work for it was *Radamisto* (1720); that fall, the Italian composer Giovanni Bononcini (1670–1747) joined the company; a rivalry soon developed between the two, made famous by the poet John Byrom:

> Some say, compar'd to Bononcini
>
> That Mynheer Handel's but a ninny.
>
> Others aver that he to Handel
>
> Is scarcely fit to hold a candle.
>
> Strange all this difference should be
>
> Twixt tweedledum and tweedledee.

Handel won a Pyrrhic victory when Bononcini submitted to the London Academy of Music a madrigal plagiarized *in extenso* from a piece by the Italian Antonio Lotti; Lotti discovered it; an embarrassing controversy ensued, and Bononcini left London in disgrace (he died in obscurity in Vienna). The irony was that Handel was no less guilty of plagiarism; an entry in the 1880 *Encyclopaedia Britannica* spares no words condemning his conduct: "The system of wholesale plagiarism carried on by Handel is perhaps unprecedented in the history of music. He pilfered not only single melodies but frequently entire movements from the works of other masters, with few or no alterations, and without a word of acknowledgment." Between 1721 and 1728 he produced 12 at the King's Theatre; only *Giulio Cesare* and *Rodelinda* became firmly established in the repertoire and had

numerous revivals; he also composed 4 grand anthems for the coronation of King George II and Queen Caroline (1727).

In early 1728 John Gay's *The Beggar's Opera* was premiered in London and became extraordinarily popular, not least for its savage parodies of Italian opera; despite class differences between audiences of Gay's ballad opera and Handel's Italian operas, *The Beggar's Opera* signaled growing British dissatisfaction with the imported genre. In 1728 the Royal Academy of Music ceased operations; Handel became associated with the King's Theatre management; the following year, recruited Italian singers for a new Royal Academy of Music. Returning to London, he produced 6 operas; only *Orlando* proved to be a lasting success. He gave a special performance of a revised version of *Esther* at the King's Theatre (1732), followed by a 3rd version of *Acis and Galatea* (1732) and the oratorio *Deborah* (1733); premiered his oratorio *Athalia* at Oxford.

Discouraged by the poor reception of his King's Theatre operas, Handel decided to open a new season under different management; but he quarreled with the principal singer, the popular castrato Senesino (Francesco Bernardi, *c.* 1680–*c.* 1759); a substantial number of his subscribers formed a rival opera company (Opera of the Nobility), which engaged the Italian composer Nicola Porpora (1686–1768) as director and opened its 1st season at Lincoln's Inn Fields (1733); by the summer of 1734, both Handel's and the rival enterprise had suspended operations. Handel set up his own opera company at Covent Garden; began his season with a revised version of *Il Pastor fido* (1734), followed by 6 more operas (1735–37); only *Alcina* was successful; presented his ode *Alexander's Feast* at Covent Garden (1736); produced a revised version of *The Triumph of Time and Virtue* (1737). After a trip to Aachen, Germany that year, he returned to London suffering from attacks of gout, then an endemic British illness, but he managed to work. In 1738 he produced *Faramondo* and *Serse*; an aria from the latter, *Ombra mai fù*, became famous, especially in an anon. arrangement called *Handel's Celebrated Largo*; there followed a pasticcio and 2 more operas, of which *Deidamia* was his last (1741).

In historical perspective Handel's eventual failure as operatic entrepreneur was a stroke of luck; he directed his energy toward composing oratorios, thus achieving greatness; he turned to biblical themes, using English texts. He presented *Saul* (including the *Dead March*, 1739), followed by *Israel in Egypt*, an *Ode for St. Cecilia's Day* (after Dryden), and his great set of 12 *Concerti grossi*, op. 6. Milton's poetry inspired him to write *L'Allegro, il Penseroso, ed il Moderato* (1740). In 1741 he was invited to visit Ireland, where he produced his greatest masterpiece, *Messiah* (not *The Messiah*); worked with tremendous willpower and imagination; completed part I in 6 days, part II in 9 days, and part III in 6 days; orchestration took him only a few more days. The 1st performance of *Messiah* was given in Dublin (1742), its London premiere a year later; if contemporary reports are true, King George II rose to his feet at the beginning of the Hallelujah Chorus; by protocol, the entire audience followed suit. Since then, numerous performances of *Messiah* have moved listeners to rise during this celebratory chorus.

Handel's *Samson* (London, 1743), was successful, but his next oratorio, *Semele* (1744), failed to arouse enthusiasm. Continuing to alternate between mythological subjects and religious themes, he produced *Joseph and His Brethren* (1744),

Hercules (1745), and *Belshazzar* (1745); of the 9 oratorios composed between 1746 and 1752, *Judas Maccabaeus*, *Solomon*, and *Jephtha* became public favorites. To celebrate the Peace of Aachen he composed the remarkable *Music for the Royal Fireworks*, heard 1st in Green Park in London (1749); he revisited Germany (1750); soon had to limit activities on account of failing eyesight; a cataract operation proved unsuccessful. He continued to appear in performances of his music, assisted by his pupil John Christopher Smith; his last public appearance was at a London performance of *Messiah*; 8 days later, on Holy Saturday, he died; was buried at Westminster Abbey, with a Roubiliac monument marking his grave.

Parallels drawn between the 2 great German contemporaries, Bach and Handel, are mostly illusory. They were born within a few months of each other, Bach in Eisenach, Handel in Halle (about 130 kilometers apart), but they never met; Bach visited Halle at least twice, but Handel was then in London. The difference between their life's destinies was profound. Bach was a master Baroque organist producing religious works for the church—a schoolmaster who regarded his instrumental music as a textbook for study; he never composed for the stage; traveled but little. Handel was a man of the world, dedicated to producing staged spectacles, who became a British subject. Bach lived the life of a German burgher; his genius was inconspicuous. Handel shone in the light of public admiration. Bach was married twice; 4 among his 20 children became important musicians in their own right. Handel remained unmarried, but was no recluse; tended toward healthy corpulence; enjoyed the company of friends, but his choleric temperament could not brook adverse argument. Both were deeply religious, with no ostentation in serving his God. Handel's music possessed grandeur of design, majestic eloquence, and a luscious fusion of counterpoint and harmony; music lovers could discern the beauty of Handel's style without analysis, while the sublime art of Bach required knowledgeable penetration into its contrapuntal and fugal complexities.

Handel bequeathed the bulk of his MSS to his amanuensis, John Christopher Smith, whose son presented them to King George III; they became a part of the King's Music Library; of the 88 vols. there, all but 5 are vocal music; 7 vols. containing sketches are in the Fitzwilliam Collection at Cambridge.

handle organ. Barrel organ.

handle piano. Mechanical pianoforte operating on the same principle as the barrel organ.

Handlung (Ger.). Act in an opera or ballet.

Handy, W(illiam) C(hristopher), b. Florence, Ala., Nov. 16, 1873; d. N.Y., Mar. 28, 1958. His father and grandfather were ministers. He graduated from the Teachers' A & M College in Huntsville, Ala. (1892); became a schoolteacher; worked in iron mills; learned to play the cornet; soloist at the Chicago World's Fair (1893); became bandmaster of Mahara's Minstrels; taught at the Teachers' A & M College (1900–02); conducted his own orch., touring the South (1903–21). He received the award of the National Assoc. for Negro Music, St. Louis (1937).

Handy's famous song *Memphis Blues* (1912; 2nd "blues" piece to be publ. as such; 1st blues work to achieve great popularity) was orig. written as a campaign song for the mayor of Memphis, E. H. Crump (1909); along with his more celebrated *St. Louis Blues* (1914), it opened an era in popular music, turning the spirit of ragtime gaiety into balladlike bittersweet nostalgia, with lowered 3rd, 5th, and 7th degrees (*blue notes*) as distinctive melodic traits. He composed blues and other popular pieces: *Yellow Dog*; *Beale Street*; *Joe Turner*; the march *Hail to the Spirit of Freedom* (1915); *Ole Miss* for Piano (1916); *Aunt Hagar's Children* (1920), *Loveless Love* (1921), and *the Aframerican Hymn* for Band and Chorus (1916). He publ. *Blues: An Anthology* (also publ. as *Treasury of the Blues*); *Negro Authors and Composers of the U.S.* (1935); *Book of Negro Spirituals* (1938); and *Unsung Americans Sung* (1944); also a 1941 autobiography, *Father of the Blues* (all N.Y.). Handy's publ. blues style foreshadowed the urban style that emerged in the 1920s. There is uncertainty as to the inspiration for his music: he referred to hearing rural blues sung in the 1890s while traveling in minstrel troupes. More extreme views range from accusations of heavy borrowing to crediting him with inventing the blues altogether. No doubt the truth lies in the middle; if not truly the "father of the blues," he was certainly its greatest early promoter.

Hanna, (Sir) Roland, b. Detroit, Feb. 10, 1932. He began taking piano lessons as a child; soon turned to jazz; performed in local clubs; during military service played in a U.S. Army band (1950–52); after his discharge, studied at the Eastman School of Music in Rochester, N.Y. and at the Juilliard School of Music in N.Y. He formed a trio (1959); leading member of the Thad Jones-Mel Lewis Orch. (1966–74); co-founded the N.Y. Jazz Quartet (from 1971); knighted by the government of Liberia (1970). In his playing, Hanna reveals a refined technique, a profound knowledge of historical jazz piano playing, and the ability to integrate wide-ranging ideas into the context at hand.

Hanon, Charles-Louis, b. Renescure, near Dunkerque, July 2, 1819; d. Boulogne-sur-Mer, Mar. 19, 1900. Next to Czerny, Hanon was the most illustrious composer of piano exercises, embodied in his chef d'oeuvre, *Le Pianiste-virtuose*, which for over a century has been the *vade mecum* for many millions of diligent piano students all over the globe; wrote other pedagogical books and collected music for teaching use. He also attempted to instruct uneducated musicians in the art of accompanying plainchant in a curious didactic publication, *Système nouveau pour apprendre à accompagner tout plainchant sans savoir la musique* (New System for Learning to Accompany All Plainchant Without Knowing the Music).

Hanson, Howard (Harold), b. Wahoo, Nebr., Oct. 28, 1896; d. Rochester, N.Y., Feb. 26, 1981. Hanson's Swedish ancestry figured greatly in his spiritual outlook and music. His mother taught him piano; began composing early; learned to play cello. He attended the Luther College in Wahoo; played piano and organ in local churches; enrolled in the Univ. of Nebr. (1912); went to N.Y. (1913); took piano lessons with Friskin and composition with Goetschius at the Inst. of Musical Art; went to Northwestern Univ. in Evanston, Ill. (1915); studied composition with A. Oldberg and P. C. Lutkin (B.A., 1916).

Hanson began teaching at the College of the Pacific in San Jose, Calif. (1916); named its dean (1919); composed copiously;

Scandinavian Suite for Piano (1919) exemplified a profound sentiment for his ancestral land; the 1st American to win the prestigious Prix de Rome, submitting a symphonic poem, *Before the Dawn* (1921); spent 3 years at the American Academy there; completed a piece for chorus and orch. entitled *North and West* (1923). There followed his 1st major work, Sym. No. 1, subtitled *Nordic* (Rome, 1923, led by the composer); in it he expressed, in his words, "the solemnity, austerity, and grandeur of the North, of its restless surging and strife, and of its somberness and melancholy." Often described as an American Sibelius, he professed profound admiration for the great Finn, with whom he shared an affinity for slowly progressing lyrical modalities and somber harmonies anchored in deep pedal points.

In 1924 Hanson conducted the U.S. premiere of the *Nordic Sym.* in Rochester; met George Eastman, the inventor of Kodak film; although Eastman, knew next to nothing about music, he nonetheless had a keen sense of ability among artists and composers; in 1924 he offered Hanson the directorship of the Eastman School of Music (1924), which he accepted. Eastman's intuition proved correct; Hanson elevated the Eastman School of Music from a provincial conservatory to a major American musical inst.; retained the post for 40 years; apart from teaching, inaugurated annual American music festivals there, showing an extraordinary measure of liberal choice; programmed not only pieces naturally congenial to him but modern dissonant works. During his tenure in Rochester, Hanson presented works by 700 composers and around 1,500 different compositions; made numerous recordings with the Eastman School Phil. Orch.

In 1925 Hanson completed one of his most significant works, *The Lament for Beowulf*, for chorus and orch. (1925), based on an Anglo-Saxon saga; then came several syms. The 2nd Sym., entitled *Romantic*, was commissioned by the Boston Sym. Orch. (on its 50th anniversary) and Koussevitzky, who conducted its premiere (1930); the 3rd Sym. (1936–37), glorifying the pioneer spirit of Swedish immigrants, was presented over NBC Radio (1938, Hanson conducting); the 4th Sym., subtitled *The Requiem*, paying tribute to the memory of his father; conducted its 1st performance with the Boston Sym. Orch. (1943); in 1944 the work received the Pulitzer Prize. There followed the one-movement 5th Sym., *Sinfonia Sacra* (1954), invoking his deep-rooted Christian faith; premiered by the Philadelphia Orch. (1955); the 6th Sym. commemorated the 125th anniversary of the N.Y. Phil. (1967); Bernstein led the premiere (1968); the 7th Sym., *A Sea Sym.*, with chorus, based on Whitman's poem (as was Vaughan Williams's 1st Sym.), was premiered at the Interlochen International Music Camp (1977). (Whitman's poetry was close to Hanson's creative imagination, and he wrote several other works based on his poetry.)

In 1933 Hanson composed his only opera, the 4-act *Merry Mount* (1933), based on Hawthorne's *The Maypole Lovers of Merry Mount*; he dedicated it to the memory of George Eastman, who had committed suicide 2 years before. One of the few works by an American composer ever staged at the Metropolitan, its production was very successful; reports claimed a total of 50 curtain calls for Hanson and the singers; despite this reception and favorable critical reviews, the opera had only 4 performances and was dropped from the repertoire, as has happened to many other American operas produced at the Metropolitan; a symphonic suite drawn from the score once enjoyed frequent performances.

Hanson continued an active career elsewhere; conducted several concerts of American music in major European cities (1932); took the Eastman School Phil. Orch. on a grand European tour, under the auspices of the State Dept. (1961–62); he was praised as composer and as able conductor; his school orch. was also well-received. As an educator Hanson enjoyed great prestige; many talented American composers studied under him; he maintained a friendly attitude toward those students who veered toward the field of cosmopolitan abstractions. He was elected a member of the National Inst. of Arts and Letters (1935); became a fellow of the Royal Academy of Music in Sweden (1938). At various times, he held the presidency of the National Assoc. of Schools of Music, Music Teachers National Assoc., and National Music Council.

With the radical changes in contemporary composition and musical politics, Hanson's music receded into an old-fashioned irrelevance; performances of his music dwindled; his syms. were only occasionally broadcast. He never tried to conceal his bitterness at this loss of appreciation in a country for whose artistic progress he had labored so mightily. Yet his music is by no means unredeemingly obsolete; the array of sonorous harmonies, often in modulations at a tritone's distance of their respective tonics, reaches the borderline of pungent bitonality; his bold asymmetrical rhythms retain their vitality; his orchestration is masterly. In recent years the neoromantic tendencies of composition and concert programming have led to a revival of his music.

While Hanson never accepted the modern techniques of serialism or a total emancipation of dissonance, he maintained an open-minded attitude toward these new developments; many of his admirers were surprised by the publication of his book, *Harmonic Materials of Modern Music* (1960), in which he presented an exhaustive inventory of advanced harmonic formulas, tabulating them according to their combinatory potentialities.

Happening. Loosely defined type of collective activity or performance among theater workers, painters, poets, musicians, and participants in the 1950s and 1960s; precedents are found in futurism, dadaism, Merzbau, Bauhaus theater, and Japanese artists' experimentation. Allan Kaprow, an art historian, and others staged in a N.Y. art gallery an event under the name *18 Happenings in 6 Parts* (1956). The audience was seated randomly in groups, and its participation in the action earnestly solicited; the spectacle was synaesthetic, with sound, multicolored lights, and peripheral tactile and olfactory impressions; there were "visual poems" of the graffiti type on walls and placards; one read "My Toilet Is Shared by the Man Next Door Who Is Italian." The audio portion consisted of aleatory superfetations of loudspeaking musical and antimusical sounds. Kaprow later bemoaned his choice of the word *Happening*, but conceded that it provided an all-embracing inclusivity for these uninhibited exhibits of the avant-garde. Other organizers in this anti-genre included Jim Dine, Red Grooms, Claes Oldenburg, and Robert Whitman.

Cage's 1952 theater piece at Black Mountain College in North Carolina is usually cited as a prototype; in the 1960s, the Fluxus group and others took up the impulse and pushed it further; its present legacy can be seen in avant-garde video operas. The term itself entered the language, to the point that everyday events were described as Happenings simply because they had taken place at all (e.g., the Supremes' *The Happening*).

happy ending (It., *lieto fine*). In stage works, a morally and emotionally satisfying finale, no matter how improbable or unrealistic, where virtue triumphs, evil is punished or forgiven magnanimously, and lovers unite after overcoming insurmountable odds; Brecht and Weill sardonically named one of their collaborations (in English) *Happy End*; the Picardy 3rd cadence is surely its sonic equivalent.

harawi (yaravi). Slow lyric song of the Incas.

Harbach, Otto (Abels) (born Hauerbach), b. Salt Lake City, Aug. 18, 1873; d. N.Y., Jan. 24, 1963. He studied at Knox College and Columbia Univ.; collaborated with composer Karl Hoschna on the successful musical *3 Twins* (1908); thereafter wrote texts for more than 40 Broadway shows, often collaborating with Oscar Hammerstein II; musical partners included Friml, Youmans, Kern, and Romberg; also wrote for films. His most popular songs included *Rose-Marie* and *Indian Love Call* from Friml's *Rose-Marie* (with Hammerstein, 1924), *The Night Was Made for Love* from Kern's *The Cat and the Fiddle* (1931), and *Smoke Gets In Your Eyes* from Kern's *Roberta* (1932).

Harbison, John (Harris), b. Orange, N.J., Dec. 20, 1938. Exceptionally versatile, he studied violin, viola, piano, voice, and tuba in high school; also studied theory; entered Harvard Univ.; studied composition with Piston (B.A., 1960); received a Paine Traveling Fellowship to study with Blacher in Berlin; returned to the U.S.; studied composition with Sessions and with Earl Kim at Princeton Univ. (M.F.A., 1963).

Harbison was a member of the Soc. of Fellows at Harvard (1963–68); taught at the Mass. Inst. of Technology (1969–82); composer-in-residence of the Pittsburgh Sym. Orch. (1982–84) and the Los Angeles Phil. (1985–88); made numerous conducting appearances; led the Cantata Singers (1969–73; 1980–82); held a Guggenheim fellowship (1977); received the Pulitzer Prize for his vocal work *The Flight into Egypt* (1987).

Equipped with a thorough knowledge of compositional technique, Harbison writes music free from doctrinaire pedestrianism; yet his melodic structures can reflect dodecaphonic procedures. In the Shakespearean opera *The Winter's Tale* he revived "dumb shows," mimed on the stage; his opera *Full Moon in March* used the prepared piano; made use of ready-made recordings for special effects. He has been at work on an opera based on Fitzgerald's *The Great Gatsby*. Other well-known works include the 2 ballets *Ulysses' Bow* and *Ulysses' Raft* (both 1983); concertos, syms., and chamber music; vocal works, including *The Flower-Fed Buffaloes* for Baritone and Chorus (1976), *Mirabai Songs* for Soprano and Orch. (1982), and *The Natural World* for Mezzo-soprano and 5 Instruments (1987).

Harburg, E(dgar) Y(ip) (born Isidore Hochberg), b. N.Y., Apr. 8, 1898; d. Los Angeles, Mar. 5, 1981. He graduated from the City College of N.Y. (1921); was coproprietor of an electrical appliance company that failed during the Depression; began to write lyrics for Broadway; with Jay Gorney produced the famous song *Brother, Can You Spare a Dime*; won an Academy Award for *Over the Rainbow* from *The Wizard of Oz* (1939); his other lyrics include *We're Off to See the Wizard*, *It's Only a Paper Moon*, and *April in Paris*; lyricist and coauthor, with Burton Lane and Fred Saidy, of *Finian's Rainbow* (1947). Harburg was one of the most socially outspoken lyricists in the great age of Broadway and film musicals.

hard bop. Jazz style of the 1950s and 1960s, returning to relatively simple means—the down-to-earth, intensified qualities of bittersweet blues—to produce a more accessible and commercially viable style; a reaction against the complexities and sophistication of bebop and cool jazz.

Hardanger fiddle. See ⇒Hardingfele.

Hardin, Louis Thomas. Moondog.

hardingfele (Hardanger fiddle; sometimes capitalized). Traditional Norwegian fiddle with a set of sympathetic strings for resonance, named for a region in Norway; dates to the mid–17th century; there are at least 20 scordatura tunings used. The repertoire includes folk songs, dances (*slåtter*), and bridal marches.

Harfe (Ger.). Harp.

Harlequin (Fr.). Central character in the Harlequinade as presented in commedia dell'arte. He is a servant of the villainous buffoon Pantaloon (Pantalone) and adores Columbine (Columbina), the object of Pantaloon's lust. In vulgar Latin, *Harlequinus* was a benign demon; hence, the Italian form *Arlecchino*; there may also be a connection with the *Erlkönig* (erl-king), leader of the sprites.

harmonia (Grk.). The artful juxtaposition of contrasting elements; a word of wide significance, philosophically explained by Plato and Aristotle. *Harmonia* represented an ideal monophonic music, with artful coordination between high and low sounds and balanced rhythmic and melodic arrangement of slow and fast musical phrases. Since simultaneity of tones did not exist in Greek music, this term does not literally translate to the modern *harmony*.

harmonic. 1. Pertaining to chords (consonant or dissonant) and to the theory and practice of harmony. 2. See ⇒harmonics.

harmonic curve. Figure described by a vibrating string or other sound source on a spectrograph.

harmonic figuration. Broken chords; arpeggio.

harmonic flute. See ⇒Harmonic stop.

harmonic mark (sign, symbol). Degree sign (°) over a note, indicating a harmonic.

harmonic minor scale. Natural minor scale with a raised 7th step, producing a leading tone and an augmented second between the 6th and 7th steps.

harmonic note. See ⇒harmonics.

harmonic reed. See ⇒Harmonic stop.

harmonic scale. 1. Harmonic series. 2. Harmonic minor scale.

harmonic series. Natural ascending series of partials (overtones). If the fundamental is set at a given note, the 2nd partial of the series sounds an octave above it; the 3rd partial, a perfect 5th higher than the 2nd; the 4th partial, a perfect 4th higher than the 3rd; the 5th partial, a major 3rd higher than the 4th; the 6th partial, a minor 3rd higher than the 5th, etc. The 1st 6 partials of the natural harmonic series, with a total range of 2 octaves and a perfect 5th, form the major chord, fundamental to all acoustic phenomena. See also ⇒harmonics.

harmonic stop. Organ stop having pipes double the ordinary length, pierced midway, so that a 16' pipe yields an 8' tone; also called harmonic flute or harmonic reed.

harmonic tone. See ⇒harmonics.

harmonica. Hand-held free-reed instrument with a set of graduated metal reeds mounted in a narrow frame; when blown by the mouth produces different tones on expiration and inspiration; also called mouth harmonica, mouth organ, or (in U.S. slang) blues harp or (simply) harp.

harmonicon. 1. Harmonica. 2. Orchestrion. 3. Keyed harmonica combined with a flue stop or stops.

harmonics (overtones, partials). Series of tones naturally produced by a vibrating string or an air column in a pipe. Any single note is actually a tone complex produced by the vibrations of the string or air column as a whole and as one-half, one-third, one-quarter, and arithmetically increasing subdivisions of the sounding body. If we silently depress a key on the piano keyboard—say a low E—and hold it, and then strike sharply the e an octave higher and let it go immediately, the upper octave will continue to reverberate on the still-open lower E (i.e., the fundamental); the procedure will also work (albeit less audibly) with a twelfth above the fundamental (b) and possibly even 2 octaves above (e¹).

The principal harmonics can be produced by playing on a string instrument while lightly touching the string at a point of equal division (node); this prevents the string from vibrating as a whole; with practice one can produce the harmonic series up to its 6th harmonic on the naked strings of the grand piano. Most bugle calls, trumpet flourishes, and fanfares are derived from natural harmonics. Harmonics determine the timbre of an instrument, depending on their relative strength and distribution in the tone complex. The harmonics of string instruments possess a flutelike quality; thus the French word for harmonics, *flageolet* (from Old Fr. *flageol*, flute); this term is also used in German and Russian. See also ⇒artificial harmonics.

harmonie (Fr.; Ger. *Harmoniemusik*). Wind band; wind instrument section in a larger ensemble.

harmonieux (Fr.; Ger. *harmonisch*). Harmonious. *Harmonique*, harmonic (adj.). *Son harmonique*, harmonic, overtone, partial.

harmonium. Organlike portable instrument on which sound is activated by an airstream, generated by a pair of foot pedals and passing through a set of flexible metal strip reeds. The harmonium became popular in the 19th century, appealing specially to amateur performers for its pedal-produced sustained tone and rudimentary dynamics; became a perfect instrument for the middle-class home and small churches (to substitute for an organ). The term "reed organ" is often applied to both harmonium and the American organ, which uses wind created by suction bellows (vacuum principle) rather than the harmonium's airstream (pressure principle).

harmony. Combining of tones to form chords, consonant or dissonant; the relationships beween chords; the contrapuntal texture of a homophonic piece, as 2-part, 3-part, etc. While the ancient Greek *harmonia* referred to monophonic music, the word *harmony* has, for at least a millennium, meant the simultaneous sounding of several melodies, represented in notation by the vertical axis, while melody was linear, notated on the horizontal plane; counterpoint partakes of harmonic and melodic elements insofar as it harmoniously synchronizes linear melodies.

When harmony 1st emerged as a improvising technique, it was entirely consonant, limited to the use of consecutive perfect concords, the octave, perfect 5th, and perfect 4th. With the emergence of notated organum, contrary motion was permitted to bridge the progression of perfect intervals; at the same time an admixture of heterophony introduced dissonant intervals such as 2nds to the available means of harmonic combinations. The decisive step toward "traditional" harmony occurred in the late Middle Ages, when 3rds and 6ths were accepted as noncadential consonant intervals. Triadic harmony, which had made its 1st appearance in sterile forms lacking the fertilizing mediant, received its legitimacy through the accession of fauxbourdon, in the form of the 1st inversion. Dissonant passing tones became ever more frequent. Curiously, the open 5th-and-octave cadence continued to rule until the 16th century, when final triads finally acquired the essential mediant.

In the 17th century harmonic procedures began to separate from contrapuntal techniques; while, in the 18th century, counterpoint evolved into the sublime art of Bach, harmony gradually became a vertical group of tones with limited contrapuntal independence. Even Bach's sons embraced harmonic composition governed principally by the laws of chord progression; all contrapuntal components were subordinated to the "counterpoint" of melody and bass, the latter the formative element of harmony in the classical sense. By the end of the Baroque—about 1750—harmony had assumed the familiar 4-part setting of the chorale. (A relic of 3-part harmony is found in the name of the middle section of a minuet, the trio.)

Four-part harmony in Classic and Romantic music is fundamentally triadic; the tonic, subdominant, and dominant triads determine tonality, for these 3 triads comprise all 7 notes of any diatonic scale. In major keys these triads are major; in minor, the tonic and subdominant are minor, but the dominant is altered by raising the 7th degree, the middle tone of the dominant chord, creating the leading tone and a major triad. As for doubling notes in 4-part harmony, rules lead to the root's being the easiest to double, the 5th less easy, and the 3rd almost never doubled (except in a triad built on the leading tone). Four-part harmony allows for complete sets of 7th chords on all scale degrees, as well as the diminished-7th chord that occurs functionally upon the leading tone in harmonic minor. Originally, triads having a diminished or augmented 5th were not allowed; consequently a triad built on the 7th degree of either the major or harmonic minor mode could not be used, nor the supertonic triad in minor keys; however, this rule was less strictly enforced in time.

A perfect 5th or octave moving in the same direction to another perfect 5th or octave, particularly between outer voices, is forbidden; parallel movement of different intervals toward 5ths or octaves, known as hidden intervals, is also taboo. A 5th or an octave can be reached only by contrary motion. Any number of examples from Bach's chorales or other sacrosanct sources can be adduced to discredit this stern code of prohibited progressions, but so deeply ingrained are these rules, particularly in 4-part harmony, that a pedantic editor of Liszt's *Liebestraum* deleted one of the inner voices in the coda in order to avoid a pair of consecutive 5ths.

In 4-part harmony, component parts are named after voice ranges: soprano, alto, tenor, bass. The most important consideration in 4-part harmony is voice-leading. Generally, crossing of voices is not admitted—soprano must always be the highest voice, bass the lowest, and alto may not cross under the tenor. Contrary motion is recommended, especially between soprano and bass. Stepwise motion is preferred. 3rds and 6ths are favored because they may be used in consecutive motion. When 1 voice leaps several scale degrees, the rest of the voices must move stepwise to provide a counterbalance and establish a proper equilibrium. If the soprano has a melodic leap upward, then the bass ought to move stepwise, preferably in the opposite direction; but in the same direction, hidden 5ths or octaves must be avoided.

By and large ideal 4-part harmony presents an alternation of 3rds and 6ths between the outer voices; the octave is *de rigueur* in almost any final cadence; the middle voices are less mobile and rarely move by leaps; they are often stationary, maintaining a common tone between 2 successive chords. The distance between soprano and alto or between alto and tenor must not exceed an octave; the distance between bass and tenor may extend to a 12th. When the 3 upper voices are bunched together within an octave, this arrangement is called *close harmony;* when these 3 voices are dispersed over more than an octave, the setting is called *open harmony*.

Notation and analysis use a combination of Roman and Arabic numerals to indicate the nature and tonality of a chord, although not its spatial arrangement. The root of a chord is indicated by the Roman numeral, in relation to the key in force (tonic is I, subdominant is IV, etc.). The position (inversion) of the chord is indicated by the Arabic numerals in superscript, which count intervals above the lowest (bass) note—which may not be the chord's root, depending on the inversion. For triads, the figures are $^5/_3$ (root position, intervals of a 5th and a 3rd above the bass, usually left unfigured), $^6/_3$ (1st inversion), and $^6/_4$ (2nd inversion). Figures for 7th chords are $^7/_5/_3$, $^6/_5/_3$, $^6/_4/_3$, and $^6/_4/_2$. Most figurations are further abbreviated. In traditional harmony, minor keys have their 7th degree raised; however, the leading-tone 7th chord still must be indicated with an appropriate accidental before the Roman numeral. In altered chords (e.g., chords of the augmented 6th), sharps or flats are indicated after the corresponding figures. Modulations are notated by equal signs (I = V), meaning that the tonic of the preceding key has become the dominant of the new key; the same event can be indicated in vertical alignment of the preceding and succeeding keys.

Harmony and counterpoint are reciprocal techniques of composition. Harmony acquires a contrapuntal quality when individual voices carry horizontal segments of a thematic nature; counterpoint becomes harmonic in structure when the vertical dimension tends to predominate. Counterpoint thrives on mutual imitation of constituent voices; harmony does not normally handle imitation. Often, a harmonic or contrapuntal quality of writing is revealed in musical notation rather than in actual sound.

The introduction of chromatic harmony by Liszt, Wagner, and Franck left the tradition of the 4-part setting fundamentally intact. Contrary motion is still preferred; consecutive 3rds and 6ths determine musical flow; polarity of the upper and lower voices is maintained; consecutive triadic formations occur exclusively in 1st inversions. Diminished-7th chords in chromatic motion are used for dramatic effect, making the tonality ambiguous; but they are compounds of minor 3rds, eminently suitable for consecutive motion. The dominant-9th chord, a novelty in the age of Wagner and Liszt, is treated as a suspension on the dominant-7th chord; dissonances are still faithfully resolved; complete tonal cadences happily conclude each important section.

A harmonic revolution occurred with extraordinary suddenness toward the end of the 19th century. In the works of Debussy and his followers, naked 5ths and octaves moved consecutively as they had a thousand years earlier in organum; consecutive triads in close harmony became common, disregarding the resulting consecutive 5ths; consecutive root and $^6/_4$ formations of major triads were rampant (Ravel's String Quartet ends in a cataract of major $^6/_4$ chords.)

Up to about 1900, every dissonance had to be resolved into a consonance; the 20th century emancipated dissonances. Scriabin built a "mystic chord" of 6 notes that earlier would have functioned as an unresolved suspension to a Wagnerian dominant-9th chord; but Scriabin used it as a metatriadic foundation for his harmonic system. Seconds and 7ths were no longer treated as ancillary structures; the whole-tone scale erased the distinction between major and minor by establishing a neutral mode; polytonality licensed the use of 2 or more tonal triads simultaneously.

Diatonic harmony has been enriched by pandiatonicism, which removes prohibitions of unresolved dissonances within a given tonality and cultivates superimposition of different triadic harmonies; historically, pandiatonicism can be traced to the use of a pedal point on the tonic and dominant over which the subdominant and dominant triads are superimposed; the functional role of the tonic, subdominant, and dominant triads fundamental to classical harmony is fully preserved in pandiatonic techniques. Pandiatonicism found its most fruitful application in neo-Baroque music, in which the component notes can be used in quartal harmony, which has all but succeeded classical tertian harmony. Quartads such as E–A–D–G, placed over the pedal tones F–C, is a typical example.

Finally, atonality and its organized development, 12-tone composition or dodecaphony, abolished the concept of triadic tonality altogether, replacing it with a new integrated concept wherein harmony becomes a function of the fundamental tone row. Subdivisions of the tempered scale in quarter-tone music and smaller microtones prosper modestly as a monophonic art, but experiments have been made in microtonal harmonies as well. (See ⇒just intonation; microtonality.) Electronic and digital technology have freed harmony from all technical impediments, allowing precisely calculated intervals as well as microtones; as cultivated by the avant-garde, such harmony becomes a structure of fluctuating blobs; the ultimate development of this blob harmony is reached in white noise, in which the entire diapason of sounds is employed.

Further harmonic terminology: *chromatic harmony* has chromatic tones and modulations; *compound harmony* has 2 or more essential chord tones doubled; *dispersed* or *extended harmony*, open harmony; *dissonant harmony*, see ⇒dissonance; *essential harmony*, fundamental triads of a key; harmonic frame of a composition minus all figuration and ornaments; *false harmony*, false relation, voice-leading discord produced by imperfect preparation or resolution, or by "wrong" notes or chords; *figured harmony* varies simple chords by figuration of all kinds; *pure harmony*, chords and progressions played in just intonation; *spread harmony*, open harmony; *strict harmony*, composition according to strict rules for the handling of dissonances; *tempered harmony*, chords and progressions played in tempered intonation.

harmony of the spheres (music of the spheres, universal harmony). Imaginary concordance of sounds produced by the relative motions of the moon, sun, and planets. In early philosophy and theology, the 7 spheres of the geocentric universe produced the diatonic scale degrees. In the Middle Ages this system was described as *musica mundana*; constellations produced *musica celestis*. Subsequent speculations led to the concepts of *concentus angelorum* (concord of angels) and *musica angelica*. Kepler, who accepted the heliocentric cosmos, clung to the belief in the harmony of the spheres; Hindemith wrote an opera, *Die Harmonie der Welt*, based on his life. In *Gulliver's Travels*, Jonathan Swift writes: "The officers, having prepared all their musical instruments, played on them for 3 hours without intermission, so that I was quite stunned by the noise. . . . The people of Laputa had their ears adapted to hear the music of the spheres which always played at certain intervals."

Harnoncourt, Nikolaus, b. Berlin, Dec. 6, 1929. His father, an engineer, played the piano and composed; the family settled in Graz. Nikolaus began to study the cello at age 9; studied with Paul Grummer and at the Vienna Academy of Music with Emanuael Brabec; cellist in the Vienna Sym. Orch. (1952–69); founded the Vienna Concentus Musicus (1953; concerts from 1957), playing on period instruments or modern copies; toured England, the U.S., and Canada (1966). From the mid-1970s he appeared internationally as a guest conductor, adding music of later eras. His writings include *Musik als Klangrede: Wege zu einem neuen Musikverständnis* (Salzburg and Vienna, 1982) and *Der musikalische Dialog: Gedanken zu Monteverdi, Bach und Mozart* (Salzburg, 1984). His wife, Alice Harnoncourt (b. Vienna, Sept. 26, 1930), studied violin with Feist and Moraves in Vienna and Thibaud in Paris; became concertmaster of the Vienna Concentus Musicus at its founding.

harp. Plucked chordophone with several strings running in a plane perpendicular to a resonator; the modern Western instrument is supported by a frame and pillar. Harps (Lat. *harpa*; It. *arpa*; Fr. *harpe*; Ger. *Harfe*) are often confused with lyres, which have strings attached to a yoke at the same plane as the resonator and involve 2 arms and a crossbar.

The harp is an ancient and often highly glorified musical instrument; iconographic evidence dates back to Sumeria from the 3rd millennium B.C. on. In the Middle Ages the instrument that David played for Saul was described as a harp, but it must have been the Biblical *kinnor*, a lyre related to the Greek *kithara*. Harps in the modern sense of the word appeared in Ireland and Wales in the 10th century as a bardic instrument, soon appropriated by itinerant minstrels. During the Renaissance the harp was domesticated, becoming the purveyor of melodious and harmonious music in France, Spain, and Italy; its popularity spread all over the world; it was portrayed in Renaissance paintings as the instrument of the angels or beautiful young maidens.

The modern orch. harp has a nearly 3-cornered wooden frame, the foot of which is formed by an upright pillar meeting the hollow back (which bears the soundboard) in the pedestal; the upper ends of the pillar and back are united by the curving neck. The gut strings are 46 (or 47) in number; the compass is 6 1/2 octaves, from C_1 to f^4 (or g^4). The range of the modern harp approaches that of the grand piano, and its triangular shape is geometrically similar; if a grand piano were dismantled and stood up perpendicularly, it would make a fairly good simulacrum of a harp, as the orally abstentious Harpo Marx, a competent harpist in real life, showed by performing a solo on such a harp in one of the Marx Brothers' film comedies.

The prototype of the modern harp has only 7 strings per octave; to make it capable of performing chromatic music and modulations, an ingenious "double action" tuning mechanism was patented by the great harp builder Sébastian Érard (*c.* 1810) involving pedals that could be depressed 1 or 2 notches; one notch shortens the corresponding string so that it sounds a semitone higher; depressing the pedals 2 notches raises the string another semitone higher; thus it becomes possible for each of the 7 strings of the octave to be raised a semitone or a whole tone; the basic scale for the modern harp is C-flat major. Although all major, minor, and other diatonic scales are now available, it is still impossible to play a rapid chromatic scale on the concert harp, for it would necessitate superhuman foot action. (A chromatic harp was introduced in 1845, doing away with pedals altogether, but it has found little favor with harpists; Debussy wrote for it.) But an unusual effect is achieved by using enharmonic duplication, i.e., setting the pedals to obtain the same pitch on 2 strings, so that the harpist can play a most ingratiating glissando (e.g., a diminished-7th chord); glissando, in fact, is one of the harp's truly idiomatic privileges, produced almost effortlessly.

The harp is traditionally plucked with the fingers, not with a plectrum, but modern composers have added a whole arsenal of special effects, such as angelic-sounding harmonics, demoniacal plucking of strings with a nail, or tapping on the body of the harp. The harp part's "key signature" may strike a nonharpist as a curious mixture of sharps and flats, but these "accidentals" are simply indications as to the pedal positions (i.e., tuning) and are usually placed in the middle of the great staff used in harp parts.

The harp never became a Classic orch. instrument but it reached a luxuriant flowering in the programmatic symphonic poems and operas of the 19th century; it was invariably sounded whenever the soul of a female sinner was redeemed in the last act of a Romantic opera. But such celestial implications of harp playing have all but disappeared in the less *larmoyant* 20th century; it was metamorphosed into a functional instrument, shunning such time-honored devices as sweeping arpeggios. Stravinsky had 3 harps in the original scoring of *The Firebird* but eliminated them all in a later revision: eloquent testimony to the harp's obsolescence as decorative device in modern music; however, harp concertos are far more common than 2 centuries ago.

harpsichord (Fr. *clavecin*; Ger. *Cembalo, Kielflügel*; It. *cembalo*). Keyboard instrument provided with 1 or 2 manuals and activated by plectrums plucking a set of strings. Italian harpsichords (single manual) and Flemish harpsichords (2 manuals) resemble smaller grand pianos. Earlier instruments closely related to the harpsichord included the spinet and virginal; their ranges varied from 3 to 5 octaves and they came in various styles and shapes. The harpsichord was eventually superseded by the fortepiano around 1800. Interestingly, what are black keys on the piano (sharps and flats) were sometimes white on the harpsichord, while the piano's white keys might be colored black or brown on the harpsichord. The harpsichord was an extremely popular domestic instrument; hundreds of paintings, drawings, and etchings represent women playing on harpsichords. Old harpsichords were often adorned with curved legs and figures of cupids and mermaids; the lids might even carry inspirational legends in Latin.

The harpsichord played an all-important role in Baroque instrument ensembles, serving as the harmonic element of the basso continuo; the performer improvised from the figured bass. Bach, Handel, and countless others presided over the harpsichord in leading their own works; even Haydn led his ensemble in this manner during his London visits (1790s). The art of playing the harpsichord lapsed in the 19th century with the abandonment of the functional basso continuo, but a vigorous revival of the harpsichord, along with other older instruments, took place in the 1st half of the 20th century when dedicated craftsmen, among them Arnold Dolmetsch (1858–1940), began manufacturing excellent replicas. Wanda Landowska, master harpsichordist, contributed greatly to this revival by teaching harpsichord playing and commissioning new works from modern composers (among them Falla and Poulenc); the pianolike Pleyel harpsichords she designed eventually gave way to replicas of original Baroque instruments.

Harris, Roy (Leroy Ellsworth), b. Chandler, Okla., Feb. 12, 1898; d. Santa Monica, Calif., Oct. 1, 1979. His family moved to Calif. From 1903, he had music lessons with Henry Schoenfeld and Farwell; went to Paris; studied with Nadia Boulanger (1926); continued his Parisian sojourn thanks to 2 consecutive Guggenheim Fellowship awards (1927–28). Upon his return to the U.S. he lived in Calif. and N.Y.; several works were performed, attracting favorable attention; Farwell publ. an article in *Musical Quarterly* (1932) enthusiastically welcoming Harris as an American genius.

In his compositions Harris showed a talent of great originality, with a strong melodic and rhythmic speech that is indigenously American; developed a type of modal symbolism akin to Greek ethos, each mode relating to a certain emotional state. He excelled in instrumental music; never wrote an opera or an oratorio, but made astute use of choral masses in some works. He held many teaching positions over his career; his longest tenure was at the Univ. of Calif., Los Angeles (1961–73); appointed composer-in-residence at Calif. State Univ., Los Angeles (1973), a post he held until his death; awarded the Elizabeth Sprague

Coolidge Medal "for eminent services to chamber music" (1942). In 1936 he married the pianist Johana Harris (born Beula Duffey; b. Ottawa, Ontario, Jan. 1, 1913), who assumed her professional name in honor of J. S. Bach.

Harris wrote 13 syms; the best-known and most frequently performed is his Symphony No. 3 (Boston, 1939; 1st American sym. to be played in China, during the 1973 tour of the Philadelphia Orch. under Ormandy). Among his other symphonies the most played are No. 4, *Folksong Sym.*, with Chorus (Cleveland, 1940); No. 6, *Gettysburg Address* (Boston, 1944); No. 10, *Abraham Lincoln Sym.* for Chorus, Brass, 2 Amplified Pianos, and Percussion (Long Beach, Calif., 1965); and No. 13, *Bicentennial Sym. 1976*, for Chorus and Orch. (1975; premiered as No. 14, Washington, D.C., 1976). He also composed other orch'l, chamber, and choral works.

Harrison, George, b. Liverpool, Feb. 25, 1943. Like his co-Beatles, he lacked formal musical education, learning to play guitar by osmosis and acclimatization. Lacking John Lennon's extrovertedness, Paul McCartney's exhibitionism, and Ringo Starr's histrionic sense, he was less conspicuously projected into public consciousness than his comrades-in-rock; yet he exercised a distinct influence on the character of the group's songs, especially after 1965. He became infatuated with the mystical lore of India, sat at the feet of a hirsute guru, introduced sitar into his rock arrangements, and promoted Indian musicians. Never a prolific composer, he is the author of *Something* (1969), one of the Beatles' greatest successes.

When the group broke up in 1970, Harrison proved sufficiently talented to impress his individual image in his own music; he also collaborated on songs of social consciousness with Bob Dylan. He brought out the successful albums *All Things Must Pass* (1970) and *The Concert for Bangladesh* (1972). In 1970 he had a big hit with *My Sweet Lord*; however, its similarity to the 1963 Chiffons' hit *He's So Fine* led to a lawsuit; Harrison settled out of court. His album *Living in the Material World* (with *Give Me Love*) quickly attained gold status (1973); scored a hit with his single *All Those Years Ago* (1981); the album *Cloud 9* (with *Got My Mind Set On You*) also proved a success (1987); produced films associated with the Monty Python comedy troupe; recorded 2 albums as part of the anti-supergroup Travelin' Wilburys.

Harrison, Lou, b. Portland, Oreg., May 14, 1917. He studied with Cowell in San Francisco (1934–35) and Schoenberg at the Univ. of Calif. at Los Angeles (1941); taught at Mills College in Oakland, Calif. (1937–40; 1980–85); music critic for the *New York Herald-Tribune* (1945–48); held 2 Guggenheim fellowships (1952, 1954).

Harrison's interests are varied: He invented 2 new principles of clavichord construction; built a Phrygian aulos; developed a process for direct composing on a phonograph disc; proposed theories of interval control and rhythm control; wrote plays and poems, including texts in Esperanto for some of his vocal works; studied calligraphy. He was once of the 1st to promote the music of Ives, Ruggles, Varèse, and Cowell; prepared for publication Ives's 3rd Sym.; conducted its 1st performance (1946; Pulitzer Prize, 1947). He visited Asia (1961), studying Japanese and Korean modalities and rhythmic structures.; also became an advocate of just intonation.

Seeking new timbral resources, Harrison organized a percussion ensemble of multitudinous drums and sound makers as coffee cans and flowerpots; he later composed for Indonesian gamelans. Many of his instruments were constructed by longtime associate William Colvig (b. Medford, Oreg., Mar. 13, 1917), including psalteries, harps, flutes, monochords, and several complete gamelans; Colvig performed in many of Harrison's compositions in concert as well as in lectures; his instruments have been used by the San Francisco Sym. and San Francisco Opera Co.; built the gamelans housed at the Univ. of Calif. at Berkeley and at Mills College in Oakland.

Hart, Lorenz (Milton), b. N.Y., May 2, 1895; d. there, Nov. 22, 1943. He studied journalism at Columbia Univ. (1914–17); turned to writing for Broadway theater. During his 24-year collaboration with Richard Rodgers, he wrote lyrics for 29 musicals, including *Connecticut Yankee* (1927), *On Your Toes* (1936), *Babes in Arms* (1937), *The Boys from Syracuse* and *I Married an Angel* (both 1938), *Pal Joey* (1940), and *By Jupiter* (1942). Some of their best songs are publ. in *Rodgers and Hart Songs* (N.Y., 1951).

Hartmann, Karl Amadeus, b. Munich, Aug. 2, 1905; d. there, Dec. 5, 1963. He studied with Joseph Haas at the Music Academy in Munich (1923–27), later with Scherchen; began composing late in life; his 1st major work was a Trumpet Concerto (Strasbourg, 1933); during World War II studied composition and analysis with Webern in Vienna (1941–42); after the war organized the Musica Viva society in Munich; received a prize from the city of Munich (1948); elected a member of the German Academy of Fine Arts (1952); became president of the German section of the ISCM. Despite his highly chromatic atonal idiom and rhythmic experimentation (patterned after Blacher's "variable meters"), he retained the orthodox form and structural cohesion of basic classicism; was excessively critical of his early works, discarding many of them; some were retrieved and performed after his death. His best-known works are the chamber opera, *Des Simplicius Simplicissimus Jugend* (1934–35; rev. as *Simplicius Simplicissimus*, 1955); 9 symphonies; other orch'l, chamber, and vocal works.

Hauer, Josef Matthias, b. Wiener-Neustadt, near Vienna, Mar. 19, 1883; d. Vienna, Sept. 22, 1959. After attending a teachers' college, he became a public-school instructor, while studying music; an inborn experimenter with a penchant for mathematical constructions, he developed a compositional system based on "tropes," or pitch patterns, that aggregated to thematic formations of 12 different notes; as early as 1912 publ. a piano piece, *Nomos* (Law), containing the germinal principles of his 12-tone method; his theoretical publications elaborated further. He lived his entire life in Vienna, working as a composer, conductor, and teacher; despite its forbidding character, his music attracted much attention; after the 1930s, it fell into obscurity; the most visible works are the pieces in the *Zwölftonspiele* series.

Hauer vehemently asserted his priority in 12-tone composition; even used a rubber stamp on his personal stationery proclaiming himself "the true founder of the 12-tone method." This claim was countered, with equal vehemence but more justifiably, by Schoenberg; the functional basis of 12-tone composition, wherein contrapuntal and harmonic structures are derived from a single tone row, appeared only when Schoenberg formulated it and put it into practice (1924).

Haupt (Ger., head). Main, chief, principal, as in theme or instrument. *Hauptsatz*, principal part of a work; exposition.

Hauptstimme (Ger., main voice). Term used by Schoenberg to indicate the prominent polyphonic voice or tone row, designated in his scores as H (H⎺), a protracted horizontal line running from the 2nd perpendicular of the letter *H* to the end of the melody at the right.

Hauptzeitmass (Ger.). Principal tempo of a work.

Hausmusik (Ger., home music). After a period of alienation from the masses, modern German composers became convinced that music should cease its hermeticism and be returned to its source, the home. Dissonant harmony and asymmetric rhythms were not excluded when they did not present technical difficulties; usually Hausmusik was written for voices or Sprechstimme, with piano accompaniment and easy obbligato parts for recorders, clarinets, and violins. Hausmusik was a development parallel to *Gebrauchsmusik*. See also ⇒amateur.

hautbois (Fr.). Oboe. *Hautbois d'amour*, oboe d'amore.

havanaise (Fr.). Habanera.

Hawkins, Coleman (Randolph), called "Bean" or "Hawk," b. St. Joseph, Mo., Nov. 21, 1904; d. N.Y., May 19, 1969. He joined Kansas City's Jazz Hounds (1921); member of Fletcher Henderson's band in N.Y. (1923–34). His full tone and heavy vibrato became the standard for tenor saxophone; considered its foremost performer; worked in Europe (1934–39); returned to the U.S. and made his most influential recording, *Body and Soul*; departing from the paraphrase approach of swing improvisation, his extemporized solos paved the way for bebop.

Hawkins, (Sir) John, b. London, Mar. 29, 1719; d. there, May 21, 1789. Studying law while serving as a clerk, he became an attorney; an ardent devotee of music, he entered musical society; was on friendly terms with Handel; participated in literary clubs; knew Samuel Johnson and Oliver Goldsmith. A wealthy marriage (1753) enabled him to devote himself to literature and music; became a magistrate (1761) and chairman of the Quarter Sessions (1763); knighted in 1772. His 1st publication on music was *Memoirs of the Life of Sig. Agostino Steffani* (1758); then publ. *An Account of the Institution and Progress of the Academy of Ancient Music* (1770).

Hawkins's monumental *A General History of the Science and Practice of Music* (5 vols., 1776) was the culmination of 16 years' labor; the 1st vol. of Burney's *General History of Music* appeared at the same time; while Hawkins undoubtedly held pride of place for the 1st general history of music publ. in England, its reception was rather hostile; Burney even derided him in an unpubl. poem. Yet *A General History* contains much reliable information, particularly on London's musical life in the 18th century. He is buried in Westminster Abbey.

Haydn, Franz Joseph, b. Rohrau, Lower Austria, probably Mar. 31, 1732 (baptized, Apr. 1, 1732); d. Vienna, May 31, 1809. He was the 1st of the 1st Viennese school and "father of the symphony," but the 2nd of 12 children born to Mathias Haydn, a wheelwright and village sexton, and Anna Maria Koller, a former cook in the household of Count Harrach, lord of the village; their 2nd son, ⇒(Johann) Michael Haydn, also became a musician. When Franz Joseph was a small child, his cousin Johann Mathias Franck, a choral director, took him to Hainburg, instructing him in reading, writing, arithmetic, and instrumental playing. When he was 8 years old, Karl Georg Reutter, Kapellmeister at St. Stephen's Cathedral in Vienna, engaged him as a choral soprano singer; after his voice broke, he obtained a loan of 150 florins from a friend of his father's and rented an attic room where he could use a harpsichord. In the same house lived the Italian poet and librettist Metastasio, who recommended him to a resident Spanish family as a music tutor; was also engaged as accompanist to students of N. Porpora; he performed menial tasks in exchange for composition lessons; made a diligent study of *Gradus ad Parnassum* by J. J. Fux and *Der vollkommene Capellmeister* by Johann Mattheson.

Haydn began to compose keyboard music; wrote the singspiel *Der krumme Teufel* (1751); one Countess Thun engaged him as harpsichordist and singing teacher; he met Karl Joseph von Fürnburg; wrote his 1st string quartets; engaged by Count Ferdinand Maximilian von Morzin as Kapellmeister at his estate in Lukaveč (1759); married Maria Anna Keller, the eldest daughter of an early benefactor, the following year.

The most significant turn in Haydn's life was his meeting with Prince Paul Anton Esterházy, also a composer, who heard one of his syms. during a visit to Lukaveč; engaged Haydn as 2nd Kapellmeister at his Eisenstadt estate (1761). Paul Anton died in 1762; his brother, Prince Nikolaus Esterházy (called "the Magnificent") succeeded him; took Haydn to his new palace at Esterháza, where Haydn was to provide 2 weekly operatic performances and 2 concerts; his tenure at Esterháza was long-lasting, secure, and fruitful; composed music of all descriptions there, including most of his string quartets, about 80 of his 104 syms., numerous keyboard works, and nearly all his operas; elevated to 1st Kapellmeister (1766).

Nikolaus Esterházy was a true patron of the arts, but also a stern taskmaster in relation to his employees. Haydn's contract stipulated that each commissioned work had to be performed without delay and that such works could not be copied for use by others (i.e., published). He had to present himself in the palace's "antichambre" each morning and afternoon to receive orders; was obliged to wear formal clothes, with white hose and a powdered wig with a pigtail or a hairbag; had his meals with the other musicians and house servants. Unfortunately for posterity, he had to write pieces for the short-lived baryton, which the Prince played; Haydn left over 100 trios involving it. He wrote 3 sets of 6 string quartets each (opp. 9, 17, and 20, 1771–72); noteworthy syms. include No. 49 in F minor (*La passione*), No. 44 in E minor (*Trauersinfonie*), and No. 45 in F-sharp minor, the famous *Abschiedsinfonie* (Farewell Sym., Esterháza, 1772).

Haydn was elected a member of the Modena Phil. Soc. (1780); among the distinctions he received were medals from Prince Henry of Prussia (1784) and King Friedrich Wilhelm II (1787); in 1785 he composed a "passione istrumentale," *The 7 Last Words of Christ*, for the Cathedral of Cadiz (1785). During his visits to Vienna he formed a close friendship with the much younger Mozart, for whose genius Haydn had great admiration; if the words of Leopold Mozart can be taken literally, Haydn stated that his son was "the greatest composer known to me either in person or by name"; Mozart reciprocated Haydn's regard for him by dedicating a set of 6 string quartets to him. Prince Nikolaus Esterházy died (1790); his unmusical son Paul Anton (named after his uncle) inherited the estate, disbanded the orch., and granted Haydn an annuity of 1,000 florins; nominally remaining the Kapellmeister for the new Prince, he took up permanent residence in Vienna.

In 1790 Johann Peter Salomon (1745–1815), the enterprising London impresario, visited Haydn; persuaded him to travel to London to give concerts; arrived in London (New Year's Day, 1791); appeared in his 1st London concert in the Hanover Square Rooms, presiding at the keyboard; was greatly feted in London by the nobility; even King George III expressed his admiration for Haydn's art; went to Oxford to receive an honorary degree, submitting his Sym. No. 92 in G major (*Oxford*) as a "thesis" (1791); also wrote the Sym. No. 94 in G major, the *Surprise Sym.* (known in Germany as *Mit Paukenschlag*). On his return to Vienna he stopped in Bonn (1792); young Beethoven showed him some of his works; Haydn agreed to accept him as his student in Vienna. He went to London once more (1794); from his 1st concert he met with great success. There are 12 "London" or "Salomon" Syms., and include No. 100 in G major (*Military*), No. 101 in D major (*The Clock*), No. 103 in E-flat major (*Drum Roll*), and the greatest of all, No. 104 in D major (*London*).

Haydn resumed his contact with the Esterházys none too soon; for Prince Paul Anton died (1794) and was succeeded by his son Nikolaus, who revived the orch. at Eisenstadt with Haydn again as Kapellmeister. Conforming to the tastes of the new Prince, he turned to religious works, including 6 masses, all but nos. 1 and 3 in B-flat major: the *Missa in tempore belli* in C major (1796), composed during Napoleon's drive toward Vienna; the *Heiligmesse* (1796); the *Nelsonmesse* in D minor (1798), referring to Lord Nelson's defeat of Napoleon at the Battle of the Nile; the *Theresienmesse* (1799), in honor of the Austrian Empress Maria Theresa; the *Schöpfungsmesse* (1801), which uses a theme from the oratorio *Die Schöpfung* (The Creation); and the *Harmoniemesse* (1802), for its extensive use of wind instruments.

Other late works include Haydn's great oratorio *Die Schöpfung* (1796–98), 1st performed at a private concert at the Schwarzenburg Palace in Vienna; and the Concerto in E-flat major for trumpet (clarino), now a standard work (1796). In 1797 he was instructed by the Court to compose a solemn hymn-tune for a national Austrian anthem; he succeeded triumphantly (*Gott erhalte unser Kaiser*), and used it in a set of variations in his String Quartet in C Major, No. 3, op. 76 (known as the *Emperor*). His last major work was the oratorio *Die Jahreszeiten* (1799–1801), with a text trans. from James Thomson's poem *The Seasons*; beset by illness, he resigned as Kapellmeister to Prince Nikolaus (1802). Despite gradually increasing debility, Haydn preserved his natural humor; in response to friends' salutations, he sent around a quotation from his song *Der Alte*, confessing bodily weakness; at a Vienna party, a society lady sang a lively ascending tune in a major scale that she said he had written for her; he replied wistfully that the tune was now more appropriate in an inversion. His last public appearance was at a concert given in his honor (1808), with Salieri conducting *Die Schöpfung*. When Vienna capitulated to Napoleon, he ordered a guard of honor to be placed at Haydn's residence. After his death, he was buried at the Hundsturm Cemetery; in consequence of fantastic events, his skull became separated from his body before its reinterment at Eisenstadt (1820); it was even exhibited under glass in the hall of the Gesellschaft der Musikfreunde in Vienna before being reunited with his torso in the Bergkirche in Eisenstadt in a solemn official ceremony (1954).

While Haydn was not the inventor of either the symphony or the string quartet, his music did not depend on mere generic novelty; its greatness was revealed in the variety of mood, the excellence of development and variation, thematic inventiveness, and the contrast among the constituent movements of a sym. String quartets, as conceived by Haydn, were diminutions of the sym., with 4-part writing serving to support the fundamental principal of functional harmony. Both genres consisted of 3 contrasting movements—*Allegro, Andante, Allegro* (taken from the Italian sinfonia)—with a minuet interpolated between the last 2 movements.

There is an intimate *Volkstümlichkeit*, a popular directness about Haydn's music, that lends itself to imaginative nicknames of individual compositions: syms. known as *Der Philosoph* and *Der Schulmeister*, or as *L'Ours* and *La Poule*; string quartets called *La Chasse, Vogelquartett, Froschquartett*, and *Lerchenquartett*. However, the famous *Toy Sym.*, scored for a rattle, triangle, and birdcall-like sounds, and long attributed to Haydn, is actually by Leopold Mozart.

The precise extent of Haydn's vast output will probably never be known. Many works are lost; others, listed in various catalogs, may never have existed or were duplications of extant works; some are of doubtful authenticity, and some are definitely spurious. He kept his own catalogue from 1765 on. Besides the 104 authentic syms., there are concertos, divertimentos, notturnos, sinfonias, overtures, dances, incidental music, and marches. The operas have languished in obscurity until given revivals and recordings in the last three decades. He composed masses, sacred motets, oratorios, secular cantatas, Italian interpolation arias, German and English songs, nearly 400 British folk song arrangements for voice and trio (1792–1804), vocal duets, trios, and quartets with keyboard accompaniment; more than 50 canons.

Along with the syms., Haydn's compositional development—and thus the growth of the Classic style—is seen in the several sets of string quartets, from the op. 1 "divertimentos" (c. 1757–59) to the *Sun Quartets*, op. 20, whose new seriousness of purpose is symbolized by fugal finales (1772); from the *Russian Quartets* or *Jungfernquartette*, op. 33, in which the mature, contrapuntally flexible Classic style takes over (1781) to the *Erdödy Quartets*, op. 76, simultaneously retrospective and lighthearted (1797). Other works by Haydn include string trios, piano trios, solo keyboard sonatas (mostly for harpsichord), and music for flute-clock.

Haydn, (Johann) Michael, b. Rohrau, Lower Austria (baptized), Sept. 14, 1737; d. Salzburg, Aug. 10, 1806. He was

the brother of Franz Joseph Haydn. He went to Vienna about 1745 and became a chorister at St. Stephen's Cathedral; his voice was remarkable for its 3-octave range; studied composition on his own by absorbing Fux's treatise on counterpoint, *Gradus ad Parnassum*; obtained the post of Kapellmeister to the Bishop of Grosswardein (1757); named court musician and Konzertmeister to Archbishop Sigismund Schrattenbach of Salzburg (1762); married Maria Magdalen Lipp (1745–1827), a soprano in the archbishop's service (1768). Haydn became principal organist of the Dreifatigkeitskirche (1777) and succeeded Mozart as cathedral organist (1781). Carl Maria von Weber and Anton Diabelli were among his students. When Archbishop Hieronymus Colloredo abdicated in 1800 and the French took control of Salzburg, Haydn lost his positions; although his last years were made difficult by this, he turned down the post of vice Kapellmeister to Prince Nikolaus Esterházy, his brother's patron.

Michael Haydn was a prolific composer of sacred and secular music; particularly esteemed for his church music; his outstanding Requiem in C minor (*Pro defuncto Archiepiscopo Sigismundo*) was composed in his patron's memory (1771); also performed at Joseph Haydn's funeral. Among Michael Haydn's Masses was the fine *Missa sotto il titulo di S. Teresia*, for Maria Theresia (wife of Holy Roman Emperor Franz II), who sang the soprano solos under his direction in Vienna (1801); wrote many settings of the Te Deum, Litaniae lauretanae, Salve Regina, Tantum ergo, Regina coeli, and Vespers; also 200 sacred motets. His secular output included dramatic works, syms., minuets, marches, concertos, divertimentos, chamber music, etc.; his Sym. in G major (1783) was long thought the 37th Sym. of Mozart (who composed an introduction to its 1st movement solely).

Hayes, Isaac, b. Covington, Tenn., Aug. 6, 1938. He learned to play saxophone and piano; sang with local groups; went to Memphis as studio saxophonist and pianist. He teamed up with David Porter (1964); subsequently penned such hit songs as *Hold On I'm Coming, Soul Man,* and *B-A-B-Y.* After his hits *Walk On By* (1969), *By the Time I Get to Phoenix* (1969), and *Never Can Say Goodbye* (1971) were recorded, he wrote the music for the film *Shaft* (1972), which garnered him an Academy Award, a Golden Globe, and 2 Grammy Awards; also won a Grammy for his album *Black Moses* (1972).

head. 1. Point (of bow). 2. In the violin family, the portion comprising the peg-box and scroll. 3. In the drum, the membrane stretched over 1 or both ends. 4. In notation, the oval (or square) part of a note which determines its place on the staff. *Go to the head,* da capo.

head tone. Note of the vocal upper register. *Head voice,* vocal production of notes in the upper register, giving the illusion of being generated from the top of the head.

health. See ⇒mind and health.

hearing. The ancients believed that the exterior ear was the organ of hearing, gathering in the sounds and focusing and amplifying them like a seashell, which it resembles, hence expressions such as "perking up one's ear." Centuries passed before scientists looked into the *middle ear* behind the eardrum and discovered a remarkable recording instrument. A sound wave produces a displacement in the eardrum of less than the diameter of a hydrogen molecule, but the eardrum is so sensitive that even this submicroscopic distention suffices to produce a sensation of a definite tone.

The transmission mechanism of the middle ear consists of 3 interconnected ossicles (bony structures), described by early anatomists as *hammer, anvil,* and *stirrup* because of resemblances to those objects; their miniaturization is astounding; the stirrup is smaller than a grain of rice. The receptive organ for sound waves so transmitted is a snail-like spiral, the *cochlea,* in the inner ear. The 19th-century Italian physiologist Alfonso Corti discovered the actual transmitting point in the follicles attached to bony ridges, inside the spiral of the cochlea, called the *organ of Corti*–these tiny appendages act like strings of a microscopic harp that vibrate by resonance with incoming air waves. The Nobel Prize–winning scientist Georg von Békésy found that the organ of Corti converts sound impulses into electricity that stimulates the auditory nerve; at this point, science established the connection between physical electrochemical phenomena and the physiological sensation of hearing, generated in the cortex of the brain.

The human ear can discern and discriminate nearly half a million sounds, different in pitch, tone color, and degree of loudness, as well as the myriad combinations of single sounds. It can instantly recognize, analyze, and identify sounds such as a friend's voice, a cat's meow, a bird's trill, or the sound of a trumpet—a feat of classification that no computer can match. The frequencies of vibrations that the human ear can perceive as sounds range from 16 to about 20,000 cycles per second; below this range, the tone disintegrates into its component beats. Most animals have a sound range similar to humans, but dogs can hear ultrasonic frequencies; the police summon their hounds with an "inaudible" dog whistle. Still higher ultrasonics are perceived by bats, which emit sounds of very high frequencies and consequently very short wavelengths to detect and catch small flying objects such as insects by bouncing echoes off them.

heckelphone. Double-reed instrument with a wider conical bore and lower range (A–g²) than the related oboe; invented by Wilhelm Heckel (1856–1909) in 1904; somewhat misleadingly called the baritone oboe. Used in some modern scores, it gives out a rich, somewhat hollow sound. Strauss used it in *Salome*; Hindemith wrote a sonata for it.

heftig (Ger.). Vehement, impetuous, passionate, tempestuous.

Heifetz, Jascha, b. Vilnius, Feb. 2, 1901; d. Los Angeles, Dec. 10, 1987. His father taught him the rudiments of violin playing at an early age; he then studied with Ilya Malkin at the Vilnius Music School; at age 6 played Mendelssohn's Concerto in Kovno; taken to St. Petersburg (1910); entered the cons. there; after a few months, accepted as a pupil by Leopold Auer.

Heifetz made his St. Petersburg debut (1911); with a letter of recommendation from Auer, went to Berlin; his 1st concert there (1912) at the Hochschule für Musik attracted great attention. Nikisch engaged him to play the Tchaikovsky Concerto with the Berlin Phil. (1912); he obtained sensational success as a child prodigy of extraordinary gifts; played in Austria and Scandinavia. After the Russian Revolution he went to America, by way of Siberia and the Orient. His U.S. debut at Carnegie Hall in N.Y. (1917) won him the highest expression of enthusiasm from the public and press. Mischa Elman and Leopold Godowsky, a piano virtuoso, attended Heifetz's debut. "Hot here," remarked Elman, wiping his brow. "Not for pianists," observed Godowsky.

Veritable triumphs followed during Heifetz's tour of the U.S.; his fame spread all over the world; made his 1st London appearance (1920); toured Australia (1921), the Orient (1923), Palestine (1926), and South America. He revisited Russia (1934) and was welcomed enthusiastically. He became a naturalized American citizen (1925); moved to Beverly Hills, Calif.; continued touring, visiting virtually every country in the world; participated in a famous chamber series with Piatigorsky and others; taught classes of exceptionally talented pupils at the Univ. of Southern Calif., Los Angeles (1962–72); from 1974, ceased to appear publicly as a soloist.

The quality of Heifetz's playing was unique in luminous transparency of texture, tonal perfection, and formal equilibrium of phrasing; never superimposed extraneous elements on the music; such inspired tranquillity led critics to characterize his interpretations as impersonal and detached. He made numerous arrangements for violin of works by Bach, Vivaldi, and others; his most famous transcription is of *Hora Staccato* by Grigoras Dinicu, made into a virtuoso piece by adroit ornamentation and rhythmic elaboration. He promoted modern music by commissioning composers (e.g., Walton, Gruenberg, and Castelnuovo-Tedesco) to write violin concertos for him.

heimlich (Ger., secretly). Mysteriously; misterioso; furtively, stealthily.

Heinrich, Anthony Philip (Anton Philipp), b. Schönbüchel, Mar. 11, 1781; d. N.Y., May 3, 1861. As a boy he gained proficiency on the piano and violin; emigrated to America (1810); settled in Philadelphia as a merchant and unpaid music director of the Southwark Theatre; in 1817, he moved to Lexington, Ky., where he found enough musicians to conduct a performance of a Beethoven sym. Without knowing harmony, he began to compose (1818); he later publ. these songs, choruses, and instrumental pieces as op. 1, *The Dawning of Music in Kentucky, or The Pleasures of Harmony in the Solitudes of Nature,* and op. 2, *The Western Minstrel* (both 1820).

Heinrich went to London, playing violin in a small orch. (1827); studied theory, and began to write for orch. (1830); had some works produced at Dresden, Prague, Budapest, and Graz, where his sym. *The Combat of the Condor* was perf. (1836); in Vienna, entered a sym. competition, but the prize went to another; disappointed, he returned to America; settled in N.Y.; soon gained immense popularity, becoming known as "Father Heinrich." He was a commanding figure in American musical affairs, publishing many piano pieces and songs; grand festivals of his works were arranged in N.Y., Philadelphia, and Boston; critics spoke of him as the "Beethoven of America"; but a German tour was a dismal failure (1857–58); he died in extreme poverty.

The quality of Heinrich's music is dubious at best; he wrote for an enormous orch., *à la* Berlioz; his musical ideas, out of all proportion to the means employed, recall Haydn's imitators; but he was the 1st to use Native American themes in large-scale works and to show decided nationalist aspirations. In 1917 the Library of Congress acquired Heinrich's memoranda (letters, programs, newspaper clippings, etc.), many publ. works, and almost all the orch. scores, enumerated in a list made by Heinrich himself (1857). Among his amusing and instructive titles: *The Columbiad, or Migration of American Wild Passenger Pigeons* (1857–58); *The Ornithological Combat of Kings, or The Condor of the Andes and the Eagle of the Cordilleras* (1847); *The Wild-wood Spirit's Chant or Scintillations of "Yankee Doodle," forming a Grand National Heroic Fantasia scored for a Powerful Orch. in 44 Parts* (c. 1842); *Gran Sinfonia Misteriosa-Indiana* (perf., N.Y., 1975).

heirmos (*hirmos;* Grk., link). Hymnal melody of the Byzantine Church generated in the 7th century; after Christianity's coming to old Russia; adopted also by the Russian Orthodox Church; usually served to connect an old Russian Biblical hymn with a Christian hymn dedicated to a special saint; a collection of such hymns was called a *heirmologion*.

heiter (Ger.; It. *gioioso*). Cheerful; glad; merrily, joyfully.

Heldenbariton (Ger., heroic baritone). Vocal type requiring a powerful voice and stamina for difficult operatic parts, particularly in Wagner's operas.

Heldentenor (Ger., heroic tenor). Vocal type requiring a robust voice and stamina for difficult operatic parts, particularly in Wagner's operas.

helicon (Grk., helix, coil). Valved brass instrument, invented in the mid–19th century; used chiefly in military music as a bass. As it is carried over the shoulder and its tube is bent in a circle, it resembles the sousaphone.

hell (Ger.). Clear, bright.

Helmholtz, Hermann (Ludwig Ferdinand) von, b. Potsdam, Aug. 31, 1821; d. Berlin, Sept. 8, 1894. He studied medicine at the Friedrich Wilhelm Medical Inst. in Berlin (M.D., 1843); learned to play the piano. He was an assistant at Berlin's Anatomical Museum; prof. extraordinary at the Academy of Fine Arts (1848–49), assistant prof. and director of Königsberg's Physiological Inst. (1849–55), and prof. of anatomy and physiology at the Univ. of Bonn (1855–58) and the Univ. of Heidelberg (1858–71). He became prof. of physics at the Univ. of Berlin (1871); 1st director of the Physico-Technical Inst. there (from 1888); was ennobled (1882).

Helmholtz's most important work in music was the *Lehre von den Tonempfindungen als physiologische Grundlage für die Theorie der Musik* (Braunschweig, 1863; Eng. trans. by A. Ellis as *On the Sensations of Tone as a Physiological Basis for the Theory of Music,* London, 1875). He established a physical foundation for phenomena manifested by musical tones, either single or combined; supplemented and amplified earlier theories from Rameau onward; furnished formulae for all classes of consonant and dissonant tone effects. What others had sought to establish dialectically, he provided with scientific precision; his labors resulted primarily in instituting laws governing differences of tone color between different instruments and voices, covering the whole field of harmonic, differential, and summational tones, and those governing the nature and limits of music perception by the human ear. His influence continued into the 20th century, especially on intonational experimentalists like Partch.

hemidemisemiquaver. 64th note. *Hemidemisemiquaver rest,* 64th rest.

hemiola (from Grk. *he-miolios,* the whole and the half; Lat., *sesquialtera*). 1. In medieval mensural notation, use of 3 notes of equal duration in a measure alternating with 2 notes of equal duration, both groups within the same measure length; the longer notes equal 1 1/2 shorter ones. The hemiola is notated today with a succession of bars in 3/4 and 6/8; Brahms loved this device. 2. The same alternation used in a 2-measure form as a precadential rhythmic figure; commonplace in Baroque music.

Henderson, (James) Fletcher, "Smack," b. Cuthbert, Ga., Dec. 18, 1897; d. N.Y., Dec. 28, 1952. He studied piano as a child, chemistry as a youth; received a degree in the latter from Atlanta Univ. College. In 1920 he went to N.Y.; formed the Fletcher Henderson Band (later Orch.); advanced into jazz's front ranks; members included Armstrong, Hawkins, J.C. Higginbotham, L. Young, R. Stewart, Russell Procope, and John Kirby; its principal arranger was Don Redman. After Redman left (1927), Henderson became principal arranger, with additional arrangements by Benny Carter and others; unable to maintain his own band; by 1939 was arranging for B. Goodman; from 1941 led bands and continued to write arrangements; a stroke ended his career (1950). Although he never attained the popularity of his peers, his arrangements and gifted guidance of many important jazz musicians made his indirect influence extremely significant.

Henderson (born Brost), Ray(mond), b. Buffalo, Dec. 1, 1896; d. Greenwich, Conn., Dec. 31, 1970. He studied music at the Univ. of Southern Calif.; played organ in churches and piano in jazz groups; went to N.Y. as a song plugger in Tin Pan Alley; began writing his own songs. His 1st success was *Georgette* (1922), followed by *Sonny Boy,* written for Al Jolson's early talkie *The Singing Fool;* later hits were *You're the Cream in My Coffee, Button Up Your Overcoat, Alabamy Bound, Hold Everything,* and *3 Cheers;* in some cases he collaborated with B. G. DeSylva. Unlike many Broadway composers, he could read and write music; took private lessons with Britten; a film biography, *The Best Things in Life Are Free,* was made in 1966.

Hendricks, Barbara, b. Stephens, Ark., Nov. 20, 1948. She sang in church and school choirs; studied chemistry and mathematics at the Univ. of Nebr. (graduated 1969); began vocal training with Jennie Tourel at the Aspen (Colo.) Music School (1968) and at the Juilliard School in N.Y. (1969–71); attended Maria Callas's master class there. She won the Geneva International Competition (1971) and the International Concours de Paris and Kosciuszko Foundation Vocal Competition (1972).

Hendricks made her debut in *4 Saints in 3 Acts* in the Mini-Metropolitan Opera in N.Y. (1973); later that year made her 1st European concert tour; sang Erisbe in Cavalli's *Ormindo* at the San Francisco Spring Opera and the title role of Cavalli's *La Calisto* at the Glyndebourne Festival (1974); made her formal N.Y. debut as Inez in Donizetti's *La Favorite* at Carnegie Hall (1975); sang Amor in *Orfeo ed Euridice* at the Holland Festival and made her N.Y. recital debut at Town Hall (1976). At the Berlin Deutsche Oper she sang Mozart's Susanna, a role she made her own (1978); sang Gilda and Pamina at the Orange Festival in France (1980–81); appeared as Gounod's Juliette at the Paris Opéra and London's Covent Garden (1982). She made her Metropolitan Opera debut in N.Y. as Strauss's Sophie (1986); sang at the 70th-birthday celebration for Leonard Bernstein at the Tanglewood Festival (1988); starred as Mimi in Luigi Comencini's film version of *La Bohème*; appeared at Moscow's Bolshoi Theater (1989).

In addition to her operatic career, Hendricks has achieved notable distinction as a recitalist, especially for her interpretations of the German and French song repertoire and Negro spirituals. She was made a Commandeur des Arts et des Lettres of France (1986). An unswerving commitment to social justice led the High Commissioner for Refugees at the United Nations to name her a goodwill ambassador (1987).

Hendrix, Jimi (James Marshall), b. Seattle, Nov. 27, 1942; d. London, Sept. 18, 1970. Being left-handed, he taught himself to play the guitar upside down; played in a high school band; dropped out of school to join the U.S. Army paratroopers. Following his discharge (1961) he performed with groups in Nashville, Vancouver, and Los Angeles. In 1964 he went to N.Y.; joined the Isley Brothers, then worked with Curtis Knight (1964–65); formed his own outfit, Jimmy James and the Blue Flames. He then went to England; organized the Jimi Hendrix Experience (1966) with bass guitarist Noel Redding and drummer Mitch Mitchell.

The live Hendrix experience was well known for its provocative stage manner, which he frequently culminated by setting his guitar on fire. After recording his 1st album, *Are You Experienced?* (1967), he made his immensely successful U.S. debut at the Monterey (Calif.) Pop Festival that same year; recorded *Axis: Bold as Love* (1968) and *Electric Ladyland* (1968), followed by a knockout appearance at the Woodstock Festival (1969); the last album released during his lifetime was the live *Band of Gypsies* (with B. Miles and B. Cox, 1970). Hendrix died in London from complications after taking an overdose of barbiturates. Several albums, beginning with *The Cry of Love* (1971), were released posthumously with heavy overdubbing; only when Hendrix's estate regained control of the original recordings did authentic versions of his legacy become available.

Hendrix played comfortably in many styles (soul, rock, blues); began to assimilate jazz before his death; always used his virtuoso technique in the service of musical expression; played a significant role in developing the use of feedback; his most important contribution may have been the unrestrainedly melodic quality of his playing, whatever the context. The Jimi Hendrix Experience was inducted into the Rock and Roll Hall of Fame (1992).

Hensel, Fanny (Cäcilie) (Mendelssohn-Bartholdy), b. Hamburg, Nov. 14, 1805; d. Berlin, May 14, 1847. The sister of (Jacob Ludwig) Felix Mendelssohn (-Bartholdy), she began her musical training with her mother; studied piano with Berger and composition with Zelter, then with Marie Bigot in Paris (1816); married the painter Wilhelm Hensel (1829). From 1843 she oversaw the Sunday morning concerts at Berlin's Elternhaus; her untimely death was a great shock to her brother, who died shortly afterward. She was a talented composer; 6 of her songs were publ. under her brother's name in his opp. 8 and 9. Other works publ. under her name (some posth.): 4 books of songs, a collection of part-songs, *Gärtenlieder*

(1829), and an oratorio on biblical themes (1831), a String Quartet (1834), Piano Quartet (1822), and a Piano Trio, op. 11; piano music.

Henze, Hans Werner, b. Gütersloh, Westphalia, July 1, 1926. His early studies at the Braunschweig School of Music (1942–44) were interrupted by military service, serving for a year in the German army on the Russian front. In 1946 he took music courses at the Kirchenmusikalisches Inst. in Heidelberg; studied with W. Fortner; became fascinated with the disciplinary aspects of Schoenberg's method of composition with 12 tones; attended seminars given by R. Leibowitz at Darmstadt. A musician of restless temperament, he joined a radical political group and proclaimed the need to write music without stylistic restrictions so as to serve the masses. He successfully integrated musical idioms and mannerisms of seeming incompatibility; his vocal works freely adopted screaming, bellowing, and snorting, and specified that long sustained tones were to be sung by inhaling as well as exhaling; nonetheless composes music feasible for human performance, if rarely restricted by considerations of social realism. Political considerations continued to play a decisive role in his career; he withdrew from the membership of the Academy of the Arts of West Berlin to protest against its artistic policies (1967); after moving to Italy, joined the Communist Party. His political stance did not preclude acceptance in "bourgeois" European musical centers, where his works were widely performed; held the International Chair of Composition Studies at the Royal Academy of Music in London (from 1986); helped found the Munich Biennale (1989). He has written operas, ballets, symphonies, concertos, and chamber works.

hep. Antiquated term for "good" or "cool," as in *hep cat*. Anyone who uses the term *hep* these days is absolutely not hep; the alternative, *hip*, retains linguistic currency.

heptachord. Medieval term for an octave containing 7 diatonic scale degrees. *Heptatonic*, containing 7 scale degrees.

Herbert, Victor (August), b. Dublin, Feb. 1, 1859; d. N.Y., May 26, 1924. He was a grandson of Samuel Lover, the Irish novelist; after his father's death, his mother married a German physician and settled in Stuttgart with her son (1867). He attended high school there without graduating; with his musical ability quite pronounced by then, he selected the cello; took lessons from B. Cossmann in Baden-Baden; acquired sufficient technical proficiency to take positions in orchs. in Germany, France, Italy, and Switzerland; joined the Eduard Strauss waltz band in Vienna (1880); returned to Stuttgart (1881), where he joined the court orch.; studied composition with M. Seifritz at the Cons. His earliest works were for cello with orch.; he performed his Suite in Stuttgart (1883) and his 1st Cello Concerto 2 years later. In 1886 he married the Viennese opera singer Therese Forster (1861–1927); that year she received an offer to join the Metropolitan Opera in N.Y.; Herbert was engaged as an orch. cellist there; also appeared as a soloist, playing his 2 cello concertos with the N.Y. Phil. (1887, 1894).

In his early years in N.Y., Herbert was overshadowed by his wife's celebrity, but he soon formed an entertainment orch., which he led in a repertoire of light music; participated in chamber music concerts; was a soloist with the Theodore Thomas and Seidl orchs. He conducted the Boston Festival Orch. (1891);

Tchaikovsky conducted this orch. in Philadelphia while Herbert played a solo. He was associate conductor of the Worcester Festival (1889–91); became bandmaster of the famous 22nd Regiment Band, succeeding P. S. Gilmore (1893). At the suggestion of William MacDonald, manager of the Boston Ideal Opera Co., he wrote a light opera, *Prince Ananias*, produced with encouraging success in N.Y. (1894). Herbert was conductor of the Pittsburgh Sym. Orch. (1898–1904), presenting some of his own compositions; then organized the Victor Herbert N.Y. Orch., giving concerts in the metropolitan N.Y. area. At Madison Square Garden in N.Y., he directed an orch. of 420 performers in a benefit for the sufferers in the Galveston flood (1900); led a similar monster concert at the Hippodrome for the victims of the San Francisco earthquake (1906).

Herbert's fame rests chiefly on his light operas; in the best of these he unites spontaneous melody, sparkling rhythm, and simple but tasteful harmony; his experience as a symphonic composer and conductor led to a solidity of texture that placed him far above many gifted amateurs in this field; furthermore, he possessed a natural communicative power in his music, making his operettas spectacularly successful with the public. Among the more than 40 that he composed were *The Serenade* (1897), *The Fortune Teller* (1898), *Cyrano de Bergerac* (1899), *Babes in Toyland* (1903), *It Happened in Nordland* (1904), *Mlle. Modiste* (1905), *The Red Mill* (1906), *Little Nemo* (1908), *Naughty Marietta* (1910), *Sweethearts* (1913), and *Orange Blossoms* (1922). But while the production of his 1st grand opera, *Natoma*, in Philadelphia (1911) aroused great expectations, the work failed to sustain lasting interest; still less effective was his 2nd opera, *Madeleine*, staged by the Metropolitan Opera in N.Y. (1914). Herbert co-founded ASCAP (1914); served as vice president until his death. He wrote a special score for the motion picture *The Fall of a Nation*, to be in synch with the screenplay (1916).

Herdenglocke (Ger., herd bell). Shepherd's bell; an Alpine bell hung over a sheep's neck to help locate it; Mozart and Mahler included it in some works (without the sheep).

heredity. That musical talent is hereditary is an indisputable fact of statistical analysis; Bach's genealogical tree offers astonishing proof of the persistence of specific musical endowments. A musical gift usually manifests itself in early infancy; it can then be perfected by solicitous instruction and encouragement; its full realization is virtually impossible without the genetic complex that underlies it. Scientific study of musical heredity is complicated by the impossibility of experimentation, such as breeding musician with musician and observing the results within a generation. While Mendel could experiment with peas before formulating his laws of heredity, a music historian can only compile statistics and establish probability; yet it may be possible to formulate a plausible system of musical genetics, with recessive characteristics, mutations, etc.

Several generations of competent but undistinguished musicians are needed to arrive at a summit of genius. Alessandro Scarlatti provided the atmosphere for his son Domenico to develop in; Leopold Mozart, a fine and intelligent musician, gave his genius son the benefit of his knowledge; Wolfgang Amadeus himself had musician sons, although their works survive only as curiosities. On the other hand, Beethoven's greatness was an unpredictable mutation, although his father was a court musician at Bonn. Wagner had no musical ancestors, neither on the sides of his legal parents or his stepfather, who may have been his natural father; Richard's son Siegfried, "the little son of a great father," wrote operas inhabited by so many diluted Nibelungs, Lohengrins, and Parsifals.

In modern times, musical heredity often follows the zeitgeist in progressive idioms and techniques of composition; an interesting example of Mendelian natural selection is the Tcherepnin family. Nikolai (1873–1945) was a nationalist Russian composer of the Rimsky-Korsakov school; his son Alexander (1899–1977) developed a personal technique of composition; Alexander's 2 sons Ivan (b. 1943) and Serge (b. 1941) plunged headlong into experimental and electronic music composition. Similar progressive trends are sometimes found among performing musicians; Rudolf Serkin was a famed performer of Classic and Romantic piano music; his son Peter has turned toward ultramodern works.

Herman, Jerry (Gerald), b. N.Y., July 10, 1933. He played piano by ear; after becoming a professional musician, took up the study of theory and harmony; also studied drama at the Univ. of Miami. He worked as a nightclub pianist; wrote for television in N.Y.; composed revues, then won a Tony Award for his Broadway musical *Milk and Honey* (1961); after the failure of *Madame Aphrodite* (1961), he returned with the smash hit *Hello, Dolly!* (N.Y., 1964), which garnered 10 Tony Awards; followed by another highly successful score, *Mame* (N.Y., 1966), also a Tony winner. Following the less successful *Dear World* (1969), *Mack & Mabel* (1974), and *The Grand Tour* (1979), he returned to Tony glory with the wonderfully eccentric *La Cage aux folles* (1983).

Herman, Woody (Woodrow Charles), b. Milwaukee, May 16, 1913; d. Los Angeles, Oct. 29, 1987. He studied at Marquette Univ.; joined a jazz band as a clarinetist (1931); formed his 1st band (1937); had several others, mostly called "Herds." In the mid-1940s Herman's Herd was the 1st prominent big band to shift from swing to a bebop-influenced idiom characterized by "progressive" harmonies; it was dubbed progressive jazz. In Carnegie Hall in N.Y., he premiered Stravinsky's *Ebony Concerto*, written for him (1946). He also composed popular songs; the instrumental *The Woodchopper's Ball* was his signature tune.

Hérold, (Louis-Joseph) Louis, b. Paris, Jan. 28, 1791; d. Thernes, near Paris, Jan. 19, 1833. His father, François-Joseph Hérold (1755–1802), a pupil of C. P. E. Bach, was a piano teacher and composer who tried to stop his son from becoming a musician, but his aptitude was noticed by Fétis, an assistant teacher there.

After his father's death Hérold studied music seriously; entered the Paris Cons. (1806); took piano with L. Adam, winning 1st prize for piano (1810); studied harmony under Catel and composition under Méhul; his cantata *Mlle. de la Vallière* won the Prix de Rome (1812). From Rome he went to Naples, where he became pianist to Queen Caroline; produced his 1st opera, *La gioventu di Enrico Quinto* (1815), which was well received.

After a short stay in Vienna, he returned to Paris, where his remaining operas were produced. A string of successful opéras-comique was disrupted by the failure of *L'Auteur mort et vivant* (1820); distrusting his natural talent, began imitating the Rossinian style then in vogue.

With the comic opera *Marie* (1826) Hérold returned to his true element, winning sustained and brilliant success for his comic operas; became chorus master at the Italian Opera (1824); appointed to the staff of the Opéra (1826); wrote melodious and elegant ballets, including *La Somnambule* (1827) and *La Fille mal gardée* (1828; still revived); *Emmeline*, a grand opera (1829), was a failure, but *Zampa* (1831) was sensationally successful, placing him in the 1st rank of French composers. He then collaborated on works with Auber, Berton, Boieldieu, Carafa, Cherubini, and Paër; produced *La Médecine sans médecin* (1832) and his last completed work, *Le Pré aux clercs* (1832), another success. He died of tuberculosis; the unfinished *Ludovic* was completed by Halévy; produced posth. at the Opéra-Comique (1833). Hérold's piano works include sonatas, caprices, rondos, divertissements, fantasies, variations, and potpourris.

Herrmann, Bernard, b. N.Y., June 29, 1911; d. Los Angeles, Dec. 24, 1975. He won a composition prize at age 13; enrolled at N.Y. Univ.; studied with P. James and Grainger; took courses with Wagenaar (composition) and Stoessel (conducting) at the Juilliard School of Music. He joined the staff of CBS as a composer of background music for radio and a conductor of the CBS Sym. (1934); chief conductor of the CBS Sym. Orch. (1942–59), presenting bold programs of modern works, including Ives; associated with Orson Welles, wrote several scores for the Mercury Theater radio broadcasts; *Citizen Kane* (1940), the 1st of 61 film scores, is regarded as a classic of the genre. His use of an electric violin and electric bass in *The Day the Earth Stood Still* (1951) was an early example of electronic technology in film music. He subsequently wrote scores for Alfred Hitchcock's thrillers, capturing the eerie spirit of the master's peculiar art with atonal devices; the score for *Psycho* (1960), for strings only, was particularly apt.

Among Herrmann's scores were *The Devil and Daniel Webster* (Academy Award), *Jane Eyre*, *Anna and the King of Siam*, *The Ghost and Mrs. Muir*, *Snows of Kilimanjaro*, *Garden of Evil*, *The Trouble with Harry*, *The Man Who Knew Too Much*, *The Wrong Man*, *Vertigo*, *North by Northwest*, *The Man in the Gray Flannel Suit*, *The 7th Voyage of Sinbad*, *Journey to the Center of the Earth*, *The Birds*, *Fahrenheit 451*, *The Bride Wore Black*, *Sisters*, and *Obsession*. He spent his last years in England, but returned to record the score for his last film, *Taxi Driver*, died in his sleep shortly after the final recording session. Hermann also composed an opera, *Wuthering Heights* (1948-50), 2 cantatas, a sym. and other orch'l works, 2 string quartets, clarinet quintet, etc.

hervorgehoben (*hervortretend*; Ger., emphasized). Bring the indicated voice or part to the fore, in contrast to other parts functioning as accompaniment.

herzig (Ger.). Hearty, heartily; tenderly.

Heseltine, Philip (Arnold); pseudonym, Peter Warlock; b. London, Oct. 30, 1894; d. (suicide) there, Dec. 17, 1930. He studied at Eton with Colin Taylor (1908–10), Germany, and Oxford; met Delius in France (1910); profoundly influenced by him, he adopted a style intimately connected with Elizabethan traditions, yet revealing impressionistic undertones in harmonic writing. Another influence was Bernard van Dieren, from whom he absorbed an austere contrapuntal technique. Heseltine publ. his musical works as Warlock; founded the progressive musical journal *The Sackbut* (1920); wrote criticism; transcribed early English music; helped organize the 1929 Delius Festival. He ed. (with P. Wilson) 300 early songs (Elizabethan, Jacobean, and French ayres); co-edited *Oxford Choral Songs* and the *Oxford Orchestral Series* (anthology of early English and Italian dances).

hesitation tango. Tango with sharper syncopation than the standard form; Barber included one in his suite for piano 4-hands, *Souvenirs*.

hesitation waltz. Mildly syncopated waltz, slow and with jazzlike inflections, similar to the so-called Boston waltz; its popularity in Europe may be measured by traffic signs posted in the 1920s in Paris cautioning the pedestrians, "Ne dansez pas la Valse d'hesitation devant les autos." It was practically unknown in America, let alone Boston.

heterophony (from the Grk. *heteros* + *pho-nia*, diversity of sound). Texture where a melody is played on 2 or more instruments simultaneously, but with varying degrees of freedom; prominent in accompanied vocal music of the Near East and Asia, and in Asian court music.

hexachord. 1. In solmization, the 6 tones Ut, Re, Mi, Fa, Sol, and La. 2. Set of 6 different pitch classes, usually the 1st (or last) 6 of a 12-tone row.

hidden fifths, hidden octaves. Voice-leading progressions leading toward open 5ths or octaves, from the same direction, mostly forbidden in strict harmony; similar to consecutive 5ths and octaves, except that the latter begin on vertical 5ths or octaves.

Higgins, Dick (Richard Carter), b. Cambridge, Mar. 15, 1938. He went to America as a child, studying piano; learned composition with Cage in N.Y.; moved to Calif; became active in the mushrooming avant-garde; helped stage Happenings across the country; joined the ultramodern group Fluxus (1961); organized the Something Else Press (1964–73) and Unpublished Editions (1972; became Printed Editions, 1978). Not averse to academia, he taught at the Calif. Inst. of the Arts (1970–71); research associate in the visual arts dept. of the State Univ. of N.Y. in Purchase (from 1983).

In Higgins's productions he pursues the objective of total involvement, where music is verbalized conceptually, without reification, or expressed in physical action; an extreme realization of this principle is *The Thousand Syms.* (1968), in which the composer shot machine-gun bullets through MS paper; his *Sym. No. 585*, shot by an army sergeant at the composer's behest, was included in the avant-garde magazine *Source* (1969), subtitled *The Creative Use of Police Resources*.

high fidelity. Electronic technique of sound reproduction, developed by 1950, using highly sensitive devices to integrate the component sound sources; reflected on early 33 1/3–rpm phonograph records. A further improvement was directional stereophonic sound, with 2 separate channels, commercially available by the late 1950s; later developments such as 4-channel quadraphonic sound and "surround" sound did not achieve commercial acceptance.

high hat. In a drum set, a pair of cymbals placed horizontally and facing each other, attached to a floor stand. A foot pedal opens and closes the cymbals, producing a rustling vibration followed by a sharp choke; hence the alternate name *choke cymbals*.

High Mass. Missa solemnis; see ⇒Mass.

highbrow. Outdated colloquialism describing cultural subjects of a purportedly profound nature; also, any person interested in such. The term could be used either as self-definition or as mockery of those engaged in ostensibly erudite dialogues, commenting glibly and ignorantly on abstruse theories; unfortunately, the latter embodies the nearly inherent anti-intellectual stance many Americans maintain.

Hildegard von Bingen, b. Bemersheim, 1098; d. Rupertsberg, near Bingen, Sept. 17, 1179. She began her novitiate as a result of having been promised by her noble parents (as their 10th child) to the church; joined with the reclusive mystic Jutta of Spanheim, who with her followers occupied a cell of the Benedictine monastery of Disibodenberg; at age 15 took the veil; succeeded Jutta as mother superior (1136); founded a convent on the Rupertsberg (near Bingen) with 18 sisters (*c.* 1147–50); founded a 2nd convent at Eibingen (near Rudesheim; *c.* 1165). Known as the "Sybil of the Rhine," she conducted extensive correspondence with popes, emperors, kings, and archbishops, thus greatly involved in politics and diplomacy. There have been several fruitless attempts to canonize her, but her name is included in the Roman Martyrology and her feast celebrated on Sept. 17.

Hildegard composed monophonic chants, several of which she set to her own lyric and dramatic poetry; she collected her poems in *Symphonia armonie celestium revelationum* (1150s), a vol. that survives in 2 sources, both in early German neumes. It comprises around 70 liturgical poems (depending on classification used), all with melismatic music; the poetry is rich with the apocalyptic imagery of her visionary writings. The music is atypical of plainchant, involving a personal technique in which a number of melodic patterns recur in different modal positions; operating as open structures, these allow for internal variation in different contexts. She wrote a morality play in dramatic verse, *Ordo virtutum*, using 82 melodies similarly structured but more syllabic in style; noted that her music is in a range congenial to women's voices, in contrast with the Gregorian modes. Her surviving literary works include prophecy, medical and scientific treatises, and hagiographies, as well as letters.

hillbilly. Once-common description for old-time, folk song, and dance music, cultivated by rustic white musicians of the Appalachian and southern U.S. regions in the 19th century and the 1st 3rd of the 20th. Instruments used were the fiddle, guitar, and banjo; double bass and accordion family instruments were

also found. The repertoire derived from minstrelsy, ballads from the so-called Anglo-Irish tradition, and African-American folk music. The derogatory meanings of the term, often applied to bluegrass as well, led to its being dropped by more recent practitioners and historians.

Hiller, Lejaren (Arthur, Jr.), b. N.Y., Feb. 23, 1924; d. Buffalo, N.Y., Jan. 26, 1994. He studied chemistry at Princeton Univ. (Ph.D., 1947) and music at the Univ. of Illinois (M.Mus., 1958); became assistant prof. of chemistry at the Univ. of Illinois (1953–58); subsequently taught music there (to 1968); became the Frederick B. Slee Prof. of Composition at the State Univ. of N.Y. at Buffalo; co-directed its Center of the Creative and Performing Arts; named Birge-Cary Prof. of Music (1980).

Hiller is best-known for his application of computers to composition; publ. (with L. Isaacson) a manual, *Experimental Music* (N.Y., 1959) and numerous articles on the subject; achieved notoriety with his computer composition *Illiac Suite* for string quartet (1957; in collaboration with Isaacson, that 1957), a programmed, i.e., dictated, production that includes vast stretches of cadential C-major chords. Hiller then wrote a *Computer Cantata* for Soprano, Magnetic Tape, and Chamber Ensemble (1963); other works include *Machine Music* for Piano, Percussion, and Tape (1964); *An Avalanche* for Pitchmen, Prima Donna, Player Piano, Percussion, and Prerecorded Playback (1968); *HPSCHD* for 1 to 7 harpsichords and 1 to 51 tapes (1968; in collaboration with Cage); *Midnight Carnival* for a principal tape, an indeterminate number of subsidiary tapes, and other events in an urban environment (1976). He also composed 2 syms. (1953, 1960), a Piano Concerto (1949), 7 string quartets (1949–1979), 6 piano sonatas (1946–72), etc.

hinaufziehen (Ger.). Sliding up; portamento. Mahler uses this expression mark in his 2nd Sym.

Hindemith, Paul, b. Hanau, near Frankfurt am Main, Nov. 16, 1895; d. there, Dec. 28, 1963. He began studying violin at age 9; at 14 entered the Hoch Cons. in Frankfurt; studied violin with A. Rebner and composition with A. Mendelssohn and Sekles; his father was killed in World War I (in which he also served). He became concertmaster of the Frankfurt Opera orch. (1915–23); played the viola in the Reubner String Quartet, then the Amar String Quartet (1922–29); appeared as soloist on the viola and viola d'amore; later engaged as a conductor, mainly in his own works.

As a composer Hindemith joined the modern music vanguard; was an active participant in the contemporary festivals at Donaueschingen and Baden-Baden; appointed composition instructor at the Berlin Hochschule für Musik (1927). With the advent of Hitler's regime (1933), he began experiencing artistic and political difficulties, although his own "ethnic purity" was never questioned; he was married to Gertrud Rottenberg (daughter of the Jewish conductor Ludwig Rottenberg), and he stubbornly refused to stop performing with Jewish musicians; the Nazi propaganda minister, Goebbels, accused him of "cultural Bolshevism"; his music fell into officially sanctioned desuetude.

Unwilling to compromise with the barbarous regime, Hindemith began accepting engagements abroad; made 3 visits to Ankara at the invitation of the Turkish government (from 1934);

helped organize the music curriculum at the Ankara Cons.; made his 1st U.S. appearance at the Coolidge Festival at the Library of Congress in Washington, D.C., performing his *Unaccompanied Viola Sonata* (1937). After a brief Swiss sojourn, he emigrated to the U.S.; taught at Tanglewood (1940); became prof. at Yale Univ. (1940–53); led an important collegium musicum; elected to the National Inst. of Arts and Letters; was Charles Eliot Norton Lecturer at Harvard Univ. (1950–51). He became an American citizen (1946); conducted concerts in the Netherlands, Italy, and England (1947); revisited Germany for the 1st time since the war (1949), conducting the Berlin Phil. in a program of his own works. He moved to Switzerland (1953); gave courses at the Univ. of Zurich; conducted orchs. in Germany and Austria; received the prestigious Sibelius Award of $35,000 (1954). He guest conducted in the U.S. (1959–61); visited America for the last time (1963); then went to Italy, Vienna, and finally Frankfurt.

Hindemith's early music reflects rebellious opposition to all tradition, as heard in the opera *Mörder, Hoffnung der Frauen* (op. 12, 1921), and *Suite 1922* for Piano (op. 26); but he cultivated the techniques of constructivism, evident in his theatrical sketch *Hin und Zurück* (op. 45a, 1927), in which retrograde movement is embodied in the stage action (at the midpoint, events are reversed); in the later piano suite, *Ludus Tonalis* (1943), the postlude is merely the prelude "upside down." Believing in writing good music suitable for amateurs, he cultivated both Gebrauchsmusik and Hausmusik; the score of his *Frau Musica* (rev. 1944) has an obbligato part for a singing audience.

Hindemith's neoclassical side is evident in a series of concerto-like works, entitled *Kammermusik*, for various combinations, polyphonically conceived and neo-Baroque in style. Although he used atonal melodies freely, he opposed serialism on aesthetic grounds. He made a thorough study of early music, artfully assimilating its polyphonic style, as heard in his masterpiece, the opera *Mathis der Maler* (sections of which were cobbled into a famous sym.). Exceptionally prolific, he wrote music of all types for all instrumental combinations, including sonatas for virtually each orch'l instrument with piano. His style thus synthesizes many styles, saved from the accusation of excess eclecticism by his superlative technical mastery and imagination. As a theorist and pedagogue he developed a self-consistent compositional method derived from the acoustical nature of harmonies; publ. several books.

Hines, Earl (Kenneth) "Fatha," b. Duquesne, Pa., Dec. 28, 1905; d. Oakland, Calif., Apr. 22, 1983. His father was a professional trumpet player; his mother played piano and organ. He took lessons as a child; became interested mainly in jazz piano; played with big bands; joined Armstrong's Hot Five in Chicago (1927) and began recording. Under Armstrong's influence, he evolved a special type of "trumpet piano style" characterized by sharp accents, octave tremolos in the treble, and insistently repeated melodic notes; organized a big band in Chicago (1928); toured the U.S., including the South (one of the 1st black big bands to play there); its theme song, *Deep Forest*, became popular; a radio announcer would introduce him as "Fatha Hines coming through deep forest with his children"; the nickname stuck. After several years' hiatus he resurfaced as a solo pianist, making a hit wherever he appeared; toured Europe (1957); played in Berlin (1965), Russia (1966), and Japan.

During his last years he lived in San Francisco; played his last engagement there a week before his death.

hinunterziehen (Ger.). Sliding down; portamento on string instruments.

hip-hop. African-American popular dance music of the last 2 decades of the 20th century; the underlying musical basis for rap. While inheriting the strong beat of disco, hip-hop reemphasized the backbeat of 1960s popular music and drew upon house music of the late 1970s. Initially, hip-hop was spartan in texture, especially when accompanying rap; as sampling technology evolved, producers and musicians began including excerpts from earlier popular music, electronically processed and often in repetitive loops; the style grew more sophisticated. While there have been legal challenges to this practice, most now see it less as plagiarism than as homage to earlier styles, much as the parody Mass and motet in the late Renaissance; there is often a sense of irony in the choices. More recent hip-hop developments include reggae- and salsa-influenced hip-hop.

hirmos. See ⇒Heirmos.

hirsute chromaticism. If judicious mixture of chromatic and diatonic modes in an atonal work is entirely desirable, what cannot be tolerated in any self-consistent modern composition is the hairy growth of chromatics upon a diatonic or pandiatonic melodic and harmonic surface, with membranous pellicles obscuring the melorhythmic lines without protecting them. When such hirsute chromaticism occurs inadvertently, a depilatory agent should be applied in order to restore the basic musical design; at the same time care should be taken not to fall into the extremes of unaesthetic alopecia.

Hirt, Al(ois Maxwell), b. New Orleans, Nov. 7, 1922. He studied trumpet with Frank Simon at the Cincinnati Cons. of Music (1940–42); served in the U.S. Army, playing in the 82nd Army Air Force Band; discharged in 1946, played with various bands; formed his own band (1956; toured from 1960). His 1st major recording was the album *The Greatest Horn in the World* (1961). A versatile musician, he came to espouse the "Nashville sound," being equally at ease in the country-western, jazz, and popular music genres; closely associated with New Orleans's Mardi Gras.

Hirtenhorn (Ger.). Shepherd's horn. *Hirtenlied*, shepherd's song.

His (Ger.). B-sharp.

Hoboe (Ger.). Oboe.

Hochzeitlied (Ger.). Wedding song.

hocket (from Lat. *hoquetus*, hiccup; Fr. *hoquet*). Curious contrapuntal device, popular in medieval polyphony, in which one voice stops and another comes in, sometimes in the middle of a word, creating the effect of a hiccup.

Hodges, Johnny (John Cornelius) "Rabbit," b. Cambridge, Mass., July 25, 1906; d. N.Y., May 11, 1970. After playing drums and piano, he studied the saxophone with Bechet;

played with Willie "the Lion" Smith, Bechet, and Chick Webb; was a member of Ellington's band (1928–51); then led his own band and septet; rejoined Ellington (1955), remaining until his death. One of the most gifted swing saxophonists, he publ. a vol. of *Sax Originals* (1945; 2nd ed., 1972).

hoedown. Community dancing party, originally in the rural American West, featuring square dances with calling, accompanied by old-time music. The 4th episode of Copland's ballet suite *Rodeo* (1942) is named for and based upon this cultural phenomenon.

Hoffmann, E(rnst) T(heodor) A(madeus), b. Königsberg, Jan. 24, 1776; d. Berlin, June 25, 1822. He changed his 3rd Christian name (orig. Wilhelm) out of love for Mozart; studied law at the Univ. of Königsberg; studied violin with Christian Gladau, piano with C.G. Richter, and thoroughbass and counterpoint with Christian Podbielski; took composition with J. F. Reichardt in Berlin. He directed the music at the Bamberg theater; conducted opera in Leipzig and Dresden (1813–14); settled in Berlin. He used the pen name Kapellmeister Johannes Kreisler (later made famous by Schumann's *Kreisleriana*); his articles in the *Allgemeine Musikalische Zeitung* under his pseudonym were reprinted as *Phantasiestücke in Callots Manier* (1814); other collections were publ. in 1896 and 1989.

As a writer of fantastic tales Hoffmann profoundly influenced the entire Romantic school of literature; indirectly, was a formative factor in the evolution of the German school of composition. His own compositions are technically passable, but for a man of his imaginative power, they lack the inventiveness of his literary work. His best-known musical compositions are 3 operas *Die Lustige Musikanten* (Warsaw, 1805); *Aurora* (1811); and *Undine* (Berlin, 1816). Of the many stage adaptations of his novellas and short stories, the most famous are Offenbach's *Tales of Hoffmann*, Delibes's *Coppélia*, Tchaikovsky's *The Nutcracker*, Hindemith's *Cardillac*, and Busoni's *Die Brautwahl*.

Hoffnung, Gerard, b. Berlin, Mar. 25, 1925; d. London, Sept. 28, 1959. He emigrated to England in 1939. A lack of interest in school culminated in his expulsion from the Hornsey College of Art (1943), compensated for by precocious drawing ability and a well-developed sense of humor. While teaching in art schools, he publ. cartoons and caricatures in magazines, drew advertising posters, and designed program covers; illustrated a version of Colette's *L'enfant et les sortilèges* (basis of Ravel's opera), but it remained unpubl. He gave his 1st radio talk (1950); its success led to participation in radio panel shows with some of Britain's leading humorists; these broadcasts made him nationally famous.)

Fulfilling a longtime dream, Hoffnung studied the tuba; joined the Morley College Orch. He organized the Hoffnung Music Festival Concert at London's Royal Festival Hall (1957), featuring classical music parody at a level of grandeur not seen or heard before; participants included Malcolm Arnold, Dennis Brain (playing hosepipe), Franz Reizenstein, Norman Del Mar, Donald Swann, Humphrey Searle, and Gordon Jacob; its success led to the 1958 Interplanetary Music Festival, featuring April Cantelo, Lionel Salter, the Dolmetsch Ensemble, Edith Evans, Matyas Seiber, "Bruno Heinz Jaja," P. Racine Fricker, and the immortal

Let's Fake an Opera. After Hoffnung's death from a cerebral hemmorage, a 3rd and final festival, the Astronautical (1961) took place with the help of Owen Brannigan, John Amis, Forbes Robinson, William Walton, and Joseph Horovitz, composer of the *Horrotorio* (pace Cage). His books of musical caricature remain popular.

Hofmann, Peter, b. Marienbad, Aug. 12, 1944. He studied at the Hochschule für Musik in Karlsruhe; made his operatic debut in 1972 in Lübeck as Tamino (1972); joined the Württemberg State Theater in Stuttgart (1973); came to prominence in his performance of Siegmund in the Bayreuth production of *Der Ring des Nibelungen* (1976); later appeared as Parsifal at Covent Garden in London. He made his U.S. debut as Siegmund with the San Francisco Opera (1977); sang Lohengrin with the Metropolitan Opera in N.Y. (1980); his other roles include Max, Florestan, Alfred in *Die Fledermaus*, Loge, and Bacchus.

Hogwood, Christopher (Jarvis Haley), b. Nottingham, Sept. 10, 1941. He studied classics and music at Pembroke College, Cambridge (B.A., 1964); studied harpsichord with R. Puyana and G. Leonhardt; took courses at the Charles Univ. and the Academy of Music in Prague. He joined D. Munrow in organizing the Early Music Consort (1867), an ensemble devoted to "authentic" performances of medieval and Renaissance music; founded the Academy of Ancient Music (1973) to perform Baroque and early Classic music on original instruments; the ensemble toured widely and made many recordings, including a complete set of Mozart's syms. He served as artistic director of the Handel and Haydn Soc. of Boston (from 1986) and music director of the St. Paul (Minn.) Chamber Orch. (from 1988); guest conducted all over Europe and North America; made a Commander of the Order of the British Empire (1989). He ed. works by J. C. Bach, Purcell, and Croft; contributed to *The New Grove Dictionary of Music and Musicians*; wrote *Music at Court* (London, 1977); *The Trio Sonata* (London, 1979); *Handel* (London, 1984).

höhe Stimmen (Ger.). High voices.

hold. Fermata.

holding note. Note sustained in one part while the other parts are in motion; organ point.

Holiday, Billie (Eleanora) "Lady Day," b. Philadelphia, Apr. 7, 1915; d. N.Y., July 17, 1959. She was the illegitimate daughter of Sadie Fagan and guitarist Clarence Holiday; began singing in Harlem nightclubs at age 14; discovered by the impresario John Hammond, who had her perform and record with Benny Goodman and his band (1933); later worked with Teddy Wilson (1935), F. Henderson (1936), Basie (1937–38), Artie Shaw, and others; set out on her own with an engagement at Café Society, N.Y. (1939); performed at N.Y.'s Town Hall; appeared in the movie *New Orleans* (1946). Her otherwise brilliant career was marred by personal difficulties, including narcotic and alcoholic addiction; served time for federal narcotics charges (1946); made a comeback at N.Y.'s Carnegie Hall (1948). She subsequently toured throughout the

U.S. and sang in Europe (1954, 1958). Arrested again on a narcotics charge, she died in N.Y.'s Metropolitan Hospital.

She rarely sang classic blues per se; her repertoire comprised the popular tunes of the day, although her recordings of *Strange Fruit* (1939) and her own *God Bless the Child* (1941) reflect her identification with African American social issues. For her, "blues" was a state of mind and means of expression; she had a light, subtle, and instrumentlike voice; used rhythmic and melodic finesse, full of jazz syncopation and blues intonation.

Holliger, Heinz, b. Langenthal, May 21, 1939. He started playing the recorder at 4, the piano at 6; studied oboe with Cassagnaud and composition with Veress at the Bern Cons., then oboe with Pierlot and piano with Lefebure at the Paris Cons.; won 1st prize in the Geneva competition (1959); played in the Basel Sym. Orch.; attended Boulez's master composition classes there (1961–63). After winning 1st prize in the Munich competition (1961), he embarked upon a brilliant international career; toured Europe and the U.S. as soloist with the Lucerne Festival Strings (1962); gave concerts with his wife, harpist Ursula Hanggi, and the Holliger Ensemble. He gave master classes; became a prof. at the Freiburg im Breisgau Hochschule für Musik (1965). Generally recognized as the foremost oboist of his era, his mastery extends from early music to the commissioned works of Penderecki, Henze, Stockhausen, Krenek, Berio, Jolivet, and Lutoslawski. In his own works he is an uncompromising avant-gardist, composing untraditional stage works, orch., vocal, chamber, and solo works; many pieces include electronic tape.

Holly, Buddy (born Charles Harden Holley), b. Lubbock, Tex., Sept. 7, 1936; d. Clear Lake, Iowa, Feb. 2, 1959. He played the fiddle as a child, then switched to guitar; joined a friend playing Western swing on a local radio station; teamed with a guitarist, drummer, and bass player to form the Crickets; recorded his 1st hit song, *That'll Be the Day*. Stylistically, he was one of the 1st white musicians who used the characteristic rhythmic backbeat of rhythm and blues in country-western music; in 1958 he toured in the U.S. and Australia in a trio with 2 other Crickets; killed in a plane crash during a national tour without them. His songs became more popular after his death than they had been previously; continue to be performed and recorded anew, among them *Not Fade Away, Peggy Sue, Words of Love* (all orig. 1957); *It's So Easy, Maybe Baby, Rave On, Well Alright* (all orig. 1958).

Holst, Gustav(us Theodore von), b. Cheltenham, Sept. 21, 1874; d. London, May 25, 1934. He received his primary musical training from his parents; became organist and choirmaster in Wyck Rissington, Gloucestershire (1892); entered the Royal College of Music in London (1893); studied composition with Stanford and Rockstro, organ with Hoyte, and piano with Sharpe; also learned to play the trombone. After graduating in 1898, he played trombone in the Carl Rosa Opera Co. orch. (to 1900) and the Scottish Orch. in Glasgow (1900–03). His interest in Hindu philosophy, religion, and music during this period led to the composition of 4 sets of *Choral Hymns from the Rig Veda* from the Sanskrit (1908–12). He worked as a music teacher in a Dulwich girls' school (1903–20); director of music at St. Paul's Girls' School, Hammersmith (1905–34) and London's Morley College (1907–24); taught composition at the

Royal College of Music (1919); prof. of music at Univ. College, Reading (1919–23). He was deemed unfit for military service in World War I, but served as YMCA musical organizer among the British troops in the Near East in 1918. After the war he visited the U.S. as a lecturer and conductor in 1923 and 1932. Holst's most celebrated work, the large-scale orch'l suite *The Planets* (1914–16), consists of 7 movements, each bearing a mythological subtitle: *Mars, the Bringer of War; Venus, the Bringer of Peace; Mercury, the Winged Messenger; Jupiter, the Bringer of Jollity; Saturn, the Bringer of Old Age; Uranus, the Magician; Neptune, the Mystic,* the last with a chorus of female voices singing wordless syllables; 1st performed privately in London (1918), the public premiere followed in 1920; the melodic and harmonic style of the work epitomizes his technique, with lyrical, dramatic, and triumphant motives alternately presented in effective orch'l dress; but it is atypical of his musical or philosophical concerns, and its success frightened him. His music usually reflects English folk songs and the madrigal; was a master of choral writing. His contributions to British music have been overshadowed by Vaughan Williams and younger contemporaries; but he, like Bridge, Britten, and Tippett, began by composing in the English pastoral tradition, developed a strong personal style with a variety of languages and moods, whether opera (*The Perfect Fool, At the Boar's Head, The Wandering Scholar*), ballet (*The Lure, The Golden Goose, The Morning of the Year*), choral music (*The Hymn of Jesus, Ode to Death, 1st Choral Sym.,* numerous a cappella works), suites for military band and string orchestra. His daughter Imogen (Clare) Holst (b. Richmond, Surrey, Apr. 12, 1907; d. Aldeburgh, Mar. 9, 1984) studied at the Royal College of Music in London; kept her father's musical materials and writings faithfully; was musical assistant to Britten (1952–64); conducted the Purcell Singers (1953–67); artistic director of the Aldeburgh Festival (from 1956); made a Commander of the Order of the British Empire (1973); wrote several books on her father and his music.

Holzbläser (Ger.). Woodwind players. *Holzblasinstrumente,* woodwind instruments.

Holzblöcke (Ger.). Chinese blocks.

Holzharmonika (Ger.). Old term for xylophone.

Holztrompete (Ger., wooden trumpet). 1. Alphorn. 2. Hybrid wind instrument built for a solo in the 3rd act of Wagner's *Tristan und Isolde*; the part is usually taken by an English horn.

hommage (Fr.). Homage, i.e., a dedicatory tribute to a revered personage in the arts. In music, such compositions may be written in the manner of the one being honored. Copland wrote a piano piece entitled *Hommage à Ives,* approximating Ivesian harmonies. Among the innumerable French works of this type is Debussy's *Hommage à S. Pickwick,* from *Préludes,* book II (1913); Debussy's ironic sense of devotion to England led him to pay tribute to the hero of Dickens's *The Pickwick Papers* through disguised quotations from *God Save the King.* Ravel wrote the piano suite *Le Tombeau de Couperin* and single pieces in homage to Haydn, Borodin, and Chabrier.

homonymity. In music as in speech, identical sounds often acquire different connotations according to context, e.g., "mental process" in anatomy refers not to state of mind but to the bony promontory that forms the chin—"mental" derived from the Lat. *mentum* (chin), not *mens* (mind), and "process" coming from "proceed" in the sense of outgrowth. So too in music, made explicit in notation: a C-major chord written with an F-flat instead of E loses its white-key immaculacy, becoming a dissonant suspension over the A-flat major triad, therefore a kind of pun. Homonymity is particularly significant in dodecaphonic music; a segment of a 12-tone row may be homonymous with another form of the same row; this fragmentary replication is of great structural importance to the theory and practice of combinatoriality.

homophony (Grk., same sound). 1. Texture in which a melody and its accompaniment are clearly hierarchically distinct; in this sense, it developed in the late 16th century in Florence and found in early Baroque operas, as opposed to the Renaissance's predominantly polyphonic style. In homophonic pieces the component vocal and/or instrumental parts are subordinated to the melody (whether vocal or instrumental) and form clear chordal harmonies. Some dispute concerns the historical validity of the term "homophony"; to some it is misleading to describe a Classic, Romantic, or 20th-century work as homophonic simply because its harmony is subordinated to melody and strict polyphony is absent. However, it seems less confusing to treat early Baroque monody as a form of homophony, since basso continuo accompaniment was by no means reductive nor restricted to block chords; in this sense even some secular medieval music could be considered homophonic, as well as that of the common practice period and beyond. Homophonic texture is by definition distinct from monophonic, antiphonal, polyphonic, and heterophonic textures.

2. Choral music texture based on homorhythm and a main melodic part, in contrast to the imitative interweavings of polyphonic choral music; typical are the catches, glees, and hymns of English-speaking composers of the 18th century, even sections of Billings's fuguing tunes.

Honegger, Arthur (Oscar), b. Le Havre, Mar. 10, 1892; d. Paris, Nov. 27, 1955. He studied violin in Paris with Lucien Capet; studied with L. Kempter and F. Hegar at the Zurich Cons. (1909–11); returned to France (1912); entered the Paris Cons. in the classes of Gedalge and Widor; took lessons with d'Indy; first attracted attention taking part in a concert of Les Nouveaux Jeunes in Paris (1918). In 1920 the Paris critic Henri Collet publ. an article in *Comoedia* drawing a fortuitous parallel between the Russian 5 and a group of young French composers whom he designated Les Six; in addition to Honegger, these were Milhaud, Poulenc, Auric, Durey, and Tailleferre; the label persisted, even though the 6 composers soon went their separate ways and rarely gave concerts together.

In his early career Honegger embraced a fashionable type of urban music with emphasis on machinelike rhythms and curt, pert melodies; wrote a sport ballet, *Skating Rink*, and a mock-militaristic ballet, *Sousmarine* (1921). He composed one of the most famous machine pieces, *Mouvement symphonique No. 1*, subtitled *Pacific 231* (1923); the score is a realistic tonal portrayal of a powerful American locomotive bearing the serial number 231; the music progresses in accelerating rhythmic pulses toward a powerful climax, then gradually slackens its pace until the final abrupt stop; there is a simulacrum of a lyrical song in the middle section. *Pacific 231* has enjoyed great popularity and remains a perfect symbol of the machine age. In 1926 he married the pianist-composer Andrée Vaurabourg (1894–1980), who often played his piano parts. He visited the U.S. (1929), returning to teach summer classes at Tanglewood (1947); a heart ailment ended his tenure prematurely, and he was forced to return home.

Honegger's *Mouvement symphonique No. 2* (1928) was a musical rendering of rugby; the *Mouvement symphonique No. 3* (1933), however, bore no identifying subtitle; this abandonment of allusion to urban life coincided chronologically with his general trend away from literal representation and toward music in classical forms, often of historical or religious character. This resulted in 2 important oratorios: *Le Roi David* (1921), to a biblical subject, and *Jeanne d'Arc au bûcher* (1935), glorifying the French patriot saint on the semimillennium of her martyrdom; it uses a narrator, a mode borrowed from Stravinsky's *Oedipus Rex*. His syms. were also free from literal allusions: the 1st 2 lack descriptive titles; his 3rd, entitled *Liturgique* (1946), refers to ecclesiastical ritual; the 4th, named *Deliciae Basilienses* (1946), was written to honor the city of Basel; even the somewhat mysterious title of the 5th, *Di tre re* (1951), signifies nothing more arcane than the ending of each of its movements on a thrice-repeated note D.

honky-tonk. Generic reference to early–20th-century popular piano music, particularly ragtime; can connote a loud, raucous, and out-of-tune performance on an upright instrument in a cheap saloon; borrowed by classical composers (Berg, *Wozzeck*; Weill, *Mahagonny*).

hook. 1. Flag. 2. In popular music, a memorable motive or riff, functioning as a unifying repeated figure in the melody or bass.

hopak (gopak; from Ukr. *Hop!*, jump!). Ukrainian popular dance in rapid, slightly syncopated 2/4 time, in anapestic meter (2 8th-notes followed by 1 quarter-note); usually danced by men who employ acrobatic movements. Mussorgsky, Tchaikovsky, and other Russian composers wrote hopaks for their operas.

Hopkins, Sam "Lightnin'," b. Centerville, Tex., Mar. 15, 1912; d. Houston, Jan. 30, 1982. He learned the guitar; accompanied his cousin, the singer Texas Alexander; developed a unique style with arpeggiated chords, deep organ points in the bass, and irregular melorhythms; a master of extemporized blues, wrote about 600 songs; responsive to world events, composed *Happy Blues* for John Glenn after the astronaut's orbital flight. He was a mainstay at the Village Gate in N.Y. and in the folk revival movement; was close friends with operatic innovator Robert Wilson; subject of the film documentary *Blues Accordin' to Lightnin' Hopkins* (1970).

Hopkinson, Francis, b. Philadelphia, Sept. 21, 1737; d. there, May 9, 1791. By profession a lawyer, he was deeply interested in music; learned to play harpsichord; studied theory with J. Bremner; member of an amateur group in Philadelphia who met regularly to play music and gave public concerts by subscription. He allegedly composed the 1st piece of music written by an Anglo-American, *Ode to Music* (1754), and the 1st original Anglo-American song, *My Days Have Been So Wondrous Free* (1759). His claim is staked in the preface to his *7 [8] Songs for the Harpsichord or Forte Piano* (Philadelphia, 1788), dedicated to George Washington: "I cannot, I believe, be refused the Credit of being the 1st Native of the United States who has produced a Musical Composition." His music was couched in conventional English style, modeled after Arne, but he possessed a genuine melodic gift; also provided Benjamin Franklin's glass harmonica with a keyboard, introduced improvements in harpsichord quilling, and invented the bellarmonic, consisting of a set of steel bells. He probably compiled *A Collection of Psalm Tunes with a Few Anthems, etc.* (1763); a MS book of songs in his handwriting is in the possession of the Library of Congress. His son Joseph wrote the words to *Hail, Columbia*.

hoquet (Fr.). Hocket.

hora lunga (*doina*; Rum., long song). Traditional Romanian dance or song genre, in 6/8 or 2/4 time, in a leisurely tempo; can be accompanied by shepherd's flute (a leaf held between the lips and used as a reed), bagpipe, and nonindigenous instruments (violin, panpipes, cimbalom, clarinet, etc.). Bartók's discovery of this disappearing genre in Maramures . . . , Transylvania was, in his view, "the most important result of [ethnomusicological] research in recent years" (1935). Particularly unique are the protracted, highly improvised melodies, featuring a free use of ornamentation and time, melodic formulas, and flexibility of the pitch compass. Another remarkable element is the breadth of diffusion that the genre has undergone; with disbelief, then amazement, Bartók studied evidence of or listened to related music in central Algeria, Ukraine, and Persia; theorizing that one place had to be a common source, he chose Persia; subsequent research has revealed, however, that similar music is found as far west as Albania and Algeria, and as far east as India, Tibet, western China, and Cambodia. Heifetz transcribed for violin a hora by Dinicu; publ. it as *Hora Staccato*.

horn. 1. French horn or valve horn; distinct from the valveless natural horn. 2. Any wind instrument in the shape of a horn. 3. In jazz, any wind instrument, particularly the saxophone and trumpet.

horn band. Band of trumpeters. *Russian horn band*, a group of performers on hunting horns, each of which produces but 1 tone.

horn call. Fanfare played on the natural horn, thus limited to the harmonics of its fundamental.

horn fifths. 2-part harmonic progression of archetypal significance, playable on natural horns or trumpets. The harmonic intervals in the ascending form are a minor 6th, a perfect 5th, and a major 3rd (in C major):

Horn I
Horn II

The term "horn 5ths" is obviously misleading, but has been commonly accepted; examples are found in innumerable works written in a variety of rhythmic patterns. The trumpet calls in Rossini's overture to *William Tell* exemplify rapid horn 5ths, while Beethoven's *Les Adieux* Piano Sonata opens with a slow, descending passage of horn 5ths, illustrating the postilion horn announcing the departure of a stage coach. Horn 5ths may be played on any polyphonic instrument or a pair of monophonic ones.

Hornbostel, Erich Moritz von, b. Vienna, Feb. 25, 1877; d. Cambridge, England, Nov. 28, 1935. He studied philosophy in Vienna and Heidelberg; studied chemistry at the Univ. of Vienna (Ph.D. 1900); was assistant to Carl Stumpf in Berlin (1905–06); went to the U.S. to record and study Pawnee Indian music (1906); directed the Phonogramm-Archiv in Berlin (1906–33); prof. at the Univ. of Berlin (1917–33). He specialized in Asian, African, and other non-European music, and investigated issues of tone psychology; publ. hundreds of articles in scholarly publications on these subjects; ed. a collection of records, *Musik des Orients* (1932); from 1922 until his death co-edited (with Stumpf) the *Sammelbände für vergleichende Musikwissenschaft*.

Horne, Lena (Calhoun), b. N.Y., June 30, 1917. She left school at 16 to support her ailing mother; began as a chorus girl at Harlem's Cotton Club; sang with Noble Sissle's orch. (1935–36), then appeared with Charlie Barnet's orch. (1940–41); became known for recordings such as *Good for Nothing Joe* and *Haunted Town*. In 1941 she sang at Carnegie Hall in N.Y.; found success as a radio vocalist; went to Hollywood to star in the all-black musical films *Cabin in the Sky* and *Stormy Weather* (both 1943), adopting the latter's title song as her signature tune. In subsequent years she pursued a highly successful career as a nightclub and television singer; scored a triumph in N.Y. with her retrospective solo show *Lena Horne: The Lady and Her Music* (1981–83), receiving additional acclaim when she took it the road. Her inimitable renditions of *Bewitched, Bothered, and Bewildered*; *Can't Help Lovin' Dat Man*; *Love Me or Leave Me*; and *Believe in Yourself* put her on the ranks of the leading popular vocalists of her time.

Horne, Marilyn (Bernice), b. Bradford, Pa., Jan. 16, 1934. She studied with William Vennard at the Univ. of Southern Calif. in Los Angeles; attended Lotte Lehmann's master classes; went to Europe, making her first professional operatic debut as Giulietta at the Gelsenkirchen Opera (1957); remaining on its roster until 1960, appeared as Mimi, Tatiana, Minnie, Fulvia in *Ezio*, and Marie in *Wozzeck*; sang Marie as her U.S. debut with the San Francisco Opera (1960). She married the African American conductor Henry Lewis (1932) that same year; made a number of appearances under his direction; they separated in 1976. She made her debut at London's Covent Garden, again as Marie (1965); appeared at Milan's La Scala (1969); made her Metropolitan Opera debut in N.Y. as Adalgisa (1970); subsequently became one of that house's principal singers. Her notable performances there included Rosina in *Il Barbiere di Siviglia* (1971), Carmen (1972), Fidès in *Le Prophète* (1977), *Rinaldo* (1st Handel opera to be staged there, 1984), and Isabella in *L'Italiana in Algeri* (telecast live by PBS, 1986). Acclaimed for brilliant portrayals in roles by Handel, Rossini, and Meyerbeer, she won equal praise as an outstanding concert artist.

Hörner (Ger.; It. *corni*). Horns.

hornpipe. 1. Old English dance in lively tempo, the earlier ones in 3/2 time, the later in 4/4. 2. British and Irish traditional dance associated with sailors, originating in the 16th century; in various meters (4/4/, 2/2, 3/2) with so characteristic a syncopation so that it approaches a jig-like rhythm. Its choreography is less refined than most traditional dances, reflecting the energetic gestures and steps of sailors at play, with hand slapping and floor stomping. Hornpipes, whether of folk origin or specially composed, are common in English light operas, as in *H.M.S. Pinafore* by Gilbert and Sullivan, and in Baroque suites. 2. Family of reed instruments, with a simple pipe (of wood, cane, and bone), a reed (of wood and cane), and a cowhorn bell; often 2 pipes are bound together. The earliest type of hornpipe is the aulos, one form of which was iconographically represented in Crete during the 14th century B.C.; subsequent examples are found in Wales, Scotland, the Basque region, Russia, Albania, and Morocco. Similar instruments equipped with bags fall into the bagpipe branch of the pipe family.

horo. Bulgarian round dance, related to the Rumanian hora, of both fast and slow types; the dance is usually accompanied by flutes, fiddles, and bagpipes; most remarkable is the frequency of compound irregular meters such as 5/16, 7/16, and 11/6.

Horowitz, Vladimir, b. Berdichev, Oct. 1, 1903; d. N.Y., Nov. 5, 1989. Reared in a musically inclined Jewish family, he began playing piano in childhood under the direction of his mother, a professional pianist and instructor at the Kiev Cons.; other teachers were S. Tarnowsky and F. Blumenfeld; made his 1st public appearance in a Kiev recital (1920), marking the advent of a fantastically successful career. The Russian Revolution did not stop his concertizing in and around Kiev, but he decided to leave Russia; his 1st official concert abroad was in Berlin (1926); arriving in Paris (1928), he took brief instruction with Cortot; that same year made his American debut in Tchaikovsky's 1st Piano Concerto with the N.Y. Phil. under Beecham; subsequently appeared as soloist with other American orchs.; earned a reputation of a piano virtuoso of the highest caliber; his very name became synonymous with pianistic excellence; played for President Hoover at the White House (1931). In 1933 married Wanda Toscanini, daughter of the conductor; became an American citizen (1942).

Horowitz was born for public success; universally admired, his concerts sold out whenever and wherever he chose to appear. His natural affinity was with the Russian repertoire; formed a sincere friendship with Rachmaninoff, who regarded Horowitz as the greatest pianist of the century; his performances of Rachmaninoff's 3rd Piano Concerto were his proudest accomplishment; performances of works by Chopin, Liszt, Schumann, and Tchaikovsky were as incomparable. Yet amid so much success he seemed unable to master his own nervous system; became subject to irrational fears of failure; once or twice tried to cancel his engagements at the last minute; only the devotion and persuasive powers of his wife allowed him to overcome his psychological difficulties. In 1973, he underwent shock therapy, which appeared to help.

Horowitz lived for a while in Europe, hoping for a salutary change of environment. During World War II he appeared with Toscanini in numerous patriotic concerts; on this account he made a vertiginous piano transcription of Sousa's *Stars and Stripes Forever*, a veritable tour de force of pyrotechnics, which he performed for years as an encore to the delight of his audiences. In 1949 he premiered Barber's *Piano Sonata* in Havana; on the 25th anniversary of his American debut, gave a recital at Carnegie Hall (1953); thereafter withdrew from the stage, not to return for nearly 12 years. However, he continued making recordings, which allowed him the freedom to edit in the sanctuary of a studio; also accepted a few private pupils. He finally announced a date for a concert in Carnegie Hall (1965); tickets went on sale 2 weeks in advance; a line formed whose excitement and agitation would surpass that of a queue of fans for a World Series game. He was so touched by this testimony of devotion that he sent hundreds of cups of coffee to the crowd to make the waiting more endurable on a rainy day.

Despite agonies over solo performances, Horowitz had no difficulty accompanying Fischer-Dieskau; played trios with Rostropovich and Stern. In 1978 he played at the White House at the invitation of President Carter; this coincided with the 50th anniversary of his American debut; at the behest of the Prince of Wales, gave a recital in the Royal Festival Hall in London (1982), his 1st European appearance in 31 years. His recordings garnered a large following in Japan; gave a series of concerts in Tokyo and other Japanese cities (1983). The climax of his career was a decision to accept an invitation to revisit Russia after 61 years of absence (1986); his Steinway grand piano was tuned, cleaned, and placed on a special plane to Moscow. He was accompanied on this trip by his wife, a piano tuner, and his cook, who prepared fresh sole and other delicacies airmailed to Moscow daily. He made a short introductory speech in Russian before playing; the audiences who filled the hall listened almost tearfully to his playing; the program included works by Rachmaninoff, Tchaikovsky, Scriabin, Scarlatti, Chopin, and Schumann.

The Russian trip gave Horowitz necessary spiritual uplift; returning to N.Y., he resumed his concert and recording career; awarded the U.S. Medal of Freedom by President Reagan (1986) and the National Medal of Arts (1989). He made his last recording on Nov. 1 of that year; 4 afternoons later, he suddenly collapsed and died of a heart attack. His passing created a universal feeling of loss; his body lay in state in N.Y. and was then flown to Italy, where it was interred in the Toscanini family plot in Milan.

horse opera. Affectionately derisive name for any television show, radio program, or film dealing with the fantasy world of the wild West. Like grand opera, the plots have a tendency toward improbability, melodrama, and sentimentality—except that the characters dress differently (usually) and ride horses. The music that accompanies horse operas tends to emphasize galloping rhythms and quasi-Western melodies. One of the most famous appropriations of classical music is the use of the final section of the overture to Rossini's *William Tell* as the theme of *The Lone Ranger*.

horse trot. American ballroom dance popular in the early 20th century; along with other "animal dances," danced to ragtime music.

Hörspiel (Ger., to play for listening). Generic term invented by the practitioners of Gebrauchsmusik to apply to a great variety of musical works, ranging from a short solo composition to a small instrumental ensemble piece to a choral work; the meaning of *Spiel* here is broader than its use, say, in *Singspiel*. A Hörspiel should not appear strange to untutored ears, but nontoxic dissonances may be employed. The Hörspiel is related to the practice of Hausmusik; the term may apply to radio drama; in musical form, called *Funkoper*.

Horst, Louis, b. Kansas City, Mo., Jan. 12, 1884; d. N.Y., Jan. 23, 1964. He studied violin and piano in San Francisco, and composition with R. Stohr in Vienna and M. Persin and Riegger in N.Y. (1925); was music director of the Denishawn Dance Co. (1915–25) and Martha Graham's dance company (1926–48), for which he composed works that played a crucial role in the development of modern dance. He wrote extensively on the subjects of music and dance; founded and ed. the journal *Dance Observer* (1934); wrote the important *Pre-Classic Dance Forms* (1940) and *Modern Dance Forms* (with C. Russell; 1961); taught at Bennington (Vt.) College (1934–45), Columbia Univ. Teachers College (1938–41), and the Juilliard School of Music in N.Y. (1958–63).

Houston, Whitney, b. Newark, N.J., Aug. 9, 1963. She joined the choir of the New Hope Baptist Church at age 9; received vocal coaching from her mother, gospel and rhythm-and-blues singer Cissy Houston (b. Newark, N.J., c. 1932); they sang together in clubs and on recordings. After graduating from high school, she attempted to find a niche as a singer; the release of the album *Paul Jabara and Friends* (1983), on which she sang *Eternal Love*, launched her career. After television appearances and the release of the single *All at Once* (enormously popular in Europe), she scored spectacular success with her eponymous album (1985); one of its singles, *Saving All My Love for You*, won her a Grammy Award as best female pop vocalist of the year. She broke the Beatles' record for consecutive number 1 hits. Her film career was launched by starring roles in *The Bodyguard* (1993), *Waiting to Exhale* (1994), and *The Preacher's Wife* (1996).

Hovhaness (Hovaness), Alan (born Alan Hovhaness Chakmakjian), b. Somerville, Mass., Mar. 8, 1911. He studied piano lessons with A. Proctor and H. Gebhard in Boston; took academic studies at Tufts Univ.; enrolled in the New England Cons. of Music in Boston, studying with Frederick Converse (1932); was a scholarship student of Frank Martin at Tanglewood (1942). He took immediate interest in the musical roots of his paternal ancestry; studied folk songs assembled by the Armenian ethnomusicologist Komitas (1869–1935); he came to believe that music must reflect the natural monody embodied in national songs and ancient church hymns.

After completing his studies, Hovhaness served on the faculty of the New England Cons. of Music (1948–51). He was awarded 2 Guggenheim fellowships (1954, 1958) and a Fulbright fellowship (1959); traveled to India and Japan; collected native folk songs for future use; presented his own works, as pianist and conductor, receiving acclaim. He was engaged as composer-in-residence at the Univ. of Hawaii (1962); then traveled to Korea (he has written several pieces using Korean instruments).

As a composer, Hovhaness adopted modal melodies and triadic harmonies; this *parti pris* had the dual effect of alienating him from the modern milieu while exercising great attraction for the music consumer at large. Through ceaseless repetition of melodic patterns and relentless dynamic tension he created a *sui generis* type of impressionistic monody, flowing on shimmering euphonic surfaces, free from upsetting intrusions of heterogeneous dissonance; mysticism pervades his music, aided by the programmatic titles he often assigns.

Relentlessly fecund, Hovhaness is best known for over 60 syms., among them *Mysterious Mountain* (No. 2, 1955), *St. Vartan* (No. 9, 1950), *All Men Are Brothers* (No. 11, 1960), *Silver Pilgrimage* (No. 15, 1962), *Vishnu* (No. 19, 1966), and *Etchmiadzin* (No. 21, 1970). He has written several operas and other stage works, and an enormous amount of choral music. He has composed well over 400 works; in a laudable spirit of self-criticism, he destroyed 7 early syms. and began numbering them anew, e.g., his 1st numbered sym. (*Exile*) is actually his 8th. Among his most original compositions is a symphonic score, *And God Created Great Whales*, in which the voices of humpback whales recorded on tape are used as an obbligato with the orch.; the work became part of the campaign to save the whale.

huapango. Rapid Mexican dance with a polymeter combining 3/4, 6/8, and 2/4.

huehuetl. Mexican vertical drum made from a hollowed-out log, with an animal skin for a head. It is played with sticks or fingers.

huitième de soupir (Fr., eighth of a quarter note). 32nd rest.

Humfrey, Pelham, b. 1647; d. Windsor, July 14, 1674. He was among the children appointed to the restored Chapel Royal (1660); with fellow choristers John Blow and William Turner, wrote the famous Club Anthem. King Charles II sent him to France and Italy (1664); it cannot be verified that he worked under Lully or went to Italy; returned to England as lutenist of the Chapel Royal (1666); appointed Gentleman of the Chapel Royal (1667). An entry in Pepys's diary from that year describes him as being "full of form, and confidence, and vanity" and disparaging "everything, and everybody's skill but his own." Humfrey's undoubted mastery of the Italian declamatory style was greater than anyone had yet achieved in England; appointed Master of the Children of the Chapel Royal (1672); one of his wards was Henry Purcell, whose style clearly shows Humfrey's influence.

humor. Musical humor can be expressed in many ways, from the grossest form of sonorous assault to the subtlest allusions to some humorous subject by way of quotation. An example of sonic slapstick is the orch'l sneeze in Kodály's *Háry János*, whose boasts elicit a response that could be understood only by those aware of this particular Hungarian reaction to a tall tale, in which a sneeze is a sarcastic expression of acceptance and approbation.

Humor by incongruous quotation is illustrated by the insertion of the thematic leitmotiv from Wagner's *Tristan und Isolde* into Debussy's *Golliwog's Cakewalk* in the piano suite, *Children's Corner*, marked "avec une grande emotion" and harmonized impertinently by chromatic passages; it is followed by a brief comment of rhythmic cachinnation. It is said that Debussy wanted to play a joke on pianist Harold Bauer, a great Wagnerite, who gave the premiere of *Children's Corner*; he bet Bauer that he would force him to make fun of Wagner and won his bet when Bauer performed the work without having noticed the derisively placed quotation.

Purely musical of humor is represented by Mozart's *Musical Joke*, subtitled *Village Musicians*, in which he ridicules the ineptitude of rustic amateurs by having the fiddles play a scalar figure in whole tones and by cadencing polytonally. (These very devices were used by sophisticated nonrustic composers of modern music.) Imitation of animal sounds, such as the bleating of sheep in R. Strauss's *Don Quixote*, may produce an unintended comical effect. Sometimes the title of a piece reveals its humorous intent; virtually the entire production of Satie relies on incongruous titles such as *Crepuscule matinal, Heures séculaires et instantanées*, etc. In the 20th century, classical parody is replete in the work of Anna Russell, Gerard Hoffnung, Spike Jones, and P. D. Q. Bach.

humoresque. Light, whimsical instrumental piece, often for piano; the term was 1st used by Schumann (op. 20, 1839). Perhaps the most famous is *Humoresque No. 2* by Dvořák, often parodied by superimposing the children's lyrics, "Passengers will please refrain from flushing toilet while the train is standing in the station (I love you)." Zez Confrey wrote a jazz adaptation playfully called *Humor-restless.*

Humperdinck, Engelbert, b. Siegburg, near Bonn, Sept. 1, 1854; d. Neustrelitz, Sept. 27, 1921. He began learning piano at 7, composing at 14; studied at the Cologne Cons. (1872–76); after winning the Mozart Prize (1876), studied counterpoint and fugue with Rheinberger at Munich's Royal Music School (1877); studied privately there with F. Lachner. He won the Mendelssohn Prize of Berlin for the choral work *Die Wallfahrt nach Kevelaar* (1878); went to Naples, where he met Wagner (1880); at the latter's invitation, worked in Bayreuth (1881–82). He won the Meyerbeer Prize of Berlin (1881), enabling him to visit Paris (1882); taught at the Barcelona Cons. (1885–86) and the Cologne Cons. (1887–88); worked for the Schott publishing firm in Mainz (1888–89). After serving as private teacher to Siegfried Wagner (1889–90), he joined the faculty of the Hoch Cons. in Frankfurt (1890); made prof. (1896); resigned (1897); was music critic of the *Frankfurter Zeitung*. His fame as a composer was assured with the extraordinary success of his opera *Hänsel und Gretel* (1893); this fairy-tale score, with its melodies of ingenuous felicity in a Wagnerian idiom, retains its place in the repertoire; succeeding stage works, excepting perhaps *Königskinder* (1910), left little impression. He directed a master class in composition at Berlin's Akademische Meisterschule (1900–20); member of the senate of the Berlin Academy of Arts.

Humperdinck, Engelbert (real name Arnold George Dorsey), b. Madras, India, May 3, 1936. As a youth, he showed innate aptitude for raucous sentimentality and unmitigated schmaltz; attracted the attention of a hustler in search of potential rock singers; dissatisfied with the lackluster name of his chosen candidate for lucre and glory, he brazenly picked up the name Engelbert Humperdinck from a music dictionary and

conferred it on Dorsey. As luck would have it, the rechristened singer (and his manager) prospered, making a quantum leap from his beginnings as a hapless entertainer in British pubs to a successful crowd-pleaser in England and America. His voice was bland and colorless, but his stance was sincere; his records sold prodigiously among British and American music fans.

Hungarian scale. Gypsy scale.

Hunter, Alberta, b. Memphis, Tenn., Apr. 1, 1895; d. N.Y., Oct. 17, 1984. She went to Chicago; began appearing in nightclubs; subsequently gained fame as an outstanding blues singer; worked in Europe as a singer and actress; retired (1956). After a silence of 21 years, she resumed her career; astonished her auditors as one of the last of the great blues singers; continued to make public appearances into her 89th year.

Hupfeld, Herman, b. Montclair, N.J., Feb. 1, 1894; d. there, June 8, 1951. He served in the U.S. Navy in World War I; while in the service, wrote and performed his own songs. Possessing a natural flair for sentimental melodies and nostalgic lyrics, he contributed successfully to Broadway shows; occasionally employed jazz rhythms, as in his song *When Yuba Plays the Rhumba on the Tuba*; achieved fame with *As Time Goes By*, used as the signature tune (although not written) for the movie *Casablanca.*

huqin (hu-ch'in). Chinese spike fiddle. A small length of wood is crossed by a handle; the 2 strings, tuned in 5ths, are attached from top to bottom without a fingerboard; the bow is permanently attached between the strings; also called erhu (erh-hu).

hurdy-gurdy. Once-popular chordophone with a unique playing mechanism involving 2 melody strings and between 2 and 4 drone strings; a rotating rosined wooden wheel operated by a crank and acting as a bow on the strings; and a tangent keyboard that sits on the fingerboard, producing pitches on the unison melody strings when depressed. The bass drone strings, usually tuned in open 5ths, sound whenever the wheel is rotated. Another name for it is *vièle à roue* (Fr., wheel viol).

The earliest form of the instrument occurs in the Middle Ages; known as the organistrum, it was 1st described by Odo around 900 A.D. Beginning in the monasteries, the hurdy-gurdy came to be used primarily for secular music accompaniment, finding a place at all social levels; in the 17th century the instrument and its proponents were treated negatively in writings and iconography; by the following century the hurdy-gurdy was used at court, at the Parisian Concert Spirituel, and even in the music of the 1st Viennese Classic school and into the next century. Even when not actually used, sonic references to the instrument are found, notably in Schubert's *Der Leiermann* (from *Die Winterreise*), with its nostalgic image of a hurdy-gurdy player with open 5ths in the bass simulating the drone and Hindemith's viola concerto *Der Schwanendreher*. It should be noted that the hurdy-gurdy is not to be confused with the barrel or street organ, a piped wind instrument manipulated by a crank.

Hurok, Sol(omon Israelovich), b. Pogar, Apr. 9, 1888; d. N.Y., Mar. 5, 1974. Fleeing the anti-Semitic policies of the Czarist regime, he emigrated to the U.S. (1906; naturalized 1914); inaugurated a series of weekly concerts announced as "Music for the

Masses" at the Hippodrome in N.Y. (1913); became exclusive manager for famous artists, among them Pavlova, Duncan, Chaliapin, Artur Rubinstein, Elman, and Piatigorsky, as well as celebrities in ballet and opera. He negotiated the difficult arrangements with the Soviet government for U.S. appearances of the Bolshoi Ballet, Ukrainian dance company, and Leningrad Kirov Ballet; made frequent trips to Russia. Ironically, his N.Y. office became the target of a bomb attack by a militant Jewish organization objecting to Hurok's importation of Soviet artists (even though many of them were themselves Jewish).

hurtig (Ger.). Swift, headlong.

Husa, Karel, b. Prague, Aug. 7, 1921. He studied violin and piano, concurrently took courses in engineering; entered the Prague Cons. (1941) studied composition with J. Řidký; attended the Academy of Music (1945–46); awarded a French government grant to continue studies at Paris's École Normale de Musique and the Cons.; teachers included Honegger and N. Boulanger; studied conducting with Jean Fournet and Andre Cluytens. He emigrated to the U.S. (1954); joined the faculty of Cornell Univ. to teach composition and conduct the student orch.; taught at Ithaca College (1967–86); became an American citizen (1959); appeared widely as a guest conductor, including his own music in programs. In early works he followed the populist Czech school of composition, making thematic use of folk tunes; later included atonal, polytonal, microtonal, and occasional aleatory procedures without following doctrinaire prescriptions. His music, oxygenated by humanistic Romanticism, has gained numerous performances. In tribute to Dubek's Prague Spring government, he wrote the powerful *Music for Prague 1968*; received the Pulitzer Prize for his 3rd String Quartet (1969); elected to membership in the Royal Belgian Academy of the Arts and Sciences (1974).

Hutcherson, Bobby (Robert), b. Los Angeles, Jan. 27, 1941. Inspired by the great Milt "Bags" Jackson, he took up the vibraphone; went to N.Y. (1962); worked with Dolphy, Hancock, Jackie McLean, Archie Shepp, Hank Mobley, and Andrew Hill, all musicians beginning to break traditional song form boundaries. He made a series of excellent recordings for Blue Note Records; *Medina* (1969), in particular, represents a pure jazz aesthetic; began a series of recordings incorporating strong Afro-Cuban rhythmic elements, including *Good Bait* (1985), *Color Scheme* (1986), *In the Vanguard* (1987), *Cruisin' the Bird* (1988), and *Ambos Mundos* (1989).

Hüttenbrenner, Anselm, b. Graz, Oct. 13, 1794; d. Ober-Andritz, near Graz, June 5, 1868. At age 7 he studied organ with Gell; studied law at the Univ. of Graz; went to Vienna to study with Salieri (1815). Schubert was a fellow student, and it is their friendship that keeps Hüttenbrenner's name alive. Hüttenbrenner also knew Beethoven well and was present at his death. He was an excellent pianist and a prolific composer in all genres; Schubert praised his works. His reminiscences of Schubert (1854) were publ. by Otto Deutsch (1906). Hüttenbrenner came to possess many Schubert MSS after the latter's death, among them the *Unfinished Sym.*, which he held until 1865; the suggestion that he lost the 3rd and 4th movements of the work and was therefore reluctant to part with the incomplete MS is contravened by the extant sketches for the Scherzo.

Hvorostovsky, Dmitri, b. Krasnoyarsk, Oct. 16, 1962. He studied piano, then received vocal instruction from Ekaterina Yofel; subsequently won the Glinka Prize (1987); proceeded to Wales; won 1st prize in the BBC Cardiff Singer of the World Competition (1989). His European appearances included Amsterdam, London, Dublin, and Nice; appeared in recital in N.Y. and Washington, D.C. (1990), obtaining unprecedented acclaim. He enchanted his audiences with inspiring renditions of Tchaikovsky and Rachmaninoff songs; also has mastered standard operatic repertoire, fulfilling engagements at La Scala in Milan and elsewhere; the press did not spare superlatives, comparing him with the finest masters of song.

Hwang, Byung-Ki, b. Seoul, May 31, 1936. He studied traditional Korean music and the kayagum (a 12-stringed Korean zither with movable bridges, dating from the 7th century) at the National Classical Music Inst. in Seoul (1951–58); received 1st prize at the National Competition of Traditional Music (1954, 1956), a National Music Prize (1965), and the Korean Cinema Music Award (1973). From 1974 he was prof. of Korean traditional music at the College of Music, Ewha Women's Univ., in Seoul; visiting scholar at Harvard Univ. (1985–86). He was the 1st Korean composer to write modern works for the kayagum; a distinguished kayagum player, he has toured the U.S. (debut, 1986), West Germany, France, and Austria. His works are translucent and elegant in their structures and impressionistic in harmonic and melodic design.

hydraulic organ. Small kind of organ invented by Ktesibios of Alexandria (180 B.C.) in which the wind pressure was supplied by a combination of water, gravity, and airflow.

Hykes, David (Bond), b. Taos, N. Mex., Mar. 2, 1953. He studied filmmaking at Antioch College in Ohio (1970–74) and arts administration at Columbia Univ. (M.F.A., 1984); studied classical Azerbaijani and Armenian music with Zevulon Avshalomov (1975–77) and north Indian raga singing with S. Dahr (1982). He founded the Harmonic Choir (1975), which employs vocal techniques borrowed from Tibetan and Mongolian music wherein strongly resonated upper partials are audible along with the fundamental tone; the group was in residence at the Cathedral of St. John the Divine in N.Y. (from 1979); toured the U.S. and Europe (from 1980); Hykes traveled to Mongolia under the auspices of the Asian Cultural Council (1981). His compositions use harmonics to produce rich waves of slowly changing sounds over diatonic melodies; the result resembles a sort of modernized chant with an ethereal haze of overtones; among his works are *Hearing Solar Winds* (1977–83), *Current Circulation* (1983–84), and *Harmonic Meetings* (1986). Hykes has recorded solo vocal works; wrote several film and television scores and instrumental works.

hymn (from Grk. *hymnos*; Fr. *cantique*). 1. Generic name of religious or sacred songs in praise of a deity. In Greek poetry, a hymn was a chant in honor of a god or hero; in Latin, pre-Christian hymns were usually called *carmen*; the early Christians, however, accepted the Latinized form *hymnus*, a poem or a song in praise of the Lord. In established church services a hymn is a metrical poem, sung by a congregation, differing in function and form from psalms and canticles.

Hymnody—the doctrine of hymns and the theory of their composition—was generated in the Christian community of Syria about the 4th century. The earliest authenticated Christian hymn, in Greek notation and discovered in Oxyrhynchos in Egypt, is dated approximately 200 A.D. Latin hymns, fundamental to the Roman Catholic Church, emerged toward the end of the 4th century in Milan, where St. Ambrose was bishop. Hymn tunes of the 1st millennium of our era were almost exclusively monophonic; contrapuntal settings were limited to parallel octaves, perfect 5ths, and perfect 4ths. Polyphonic hymnody was the fruit of the great Notre Dame school in Paris (11th century) and flowered during the so-called Burgundian and Flemish periods.

The Roman Catholic Church retained the Latin form of hymns; but in Germany, even before Luther, hymns were written in the vernacular or by alternating German verses with Latin ones. A mixture of German and French vernacular with Latin hymns attained a high degree of poetic expression in the *Carmina Burana* MS, containing texts and melodies notated in rudimentary neumes as sung by the goliards, young clerics, and itinerant students who wandered over Germany, much as troubadours and trouvères did in France and Provence.

Lutheran hymnody absorbed vernacular modalities from popular sources; the result laid the foundation for hymn singing and composition in all Protestant nations. The Anglican Church adopted many Lutheran hymns in the 16th century, among them a hymn believed to be by Luther himself, *Ein' feste Burg ist unser Gott* (A Mighty Fortress Is Our God). In England and later in America, Lutheran hymns assumed a metrical form that approaches secular song. English and American hymns are invariably in chordal style; occasional canons do not disrupt the prevailing homophony; a curious departure from this style is the fuguing tune, wherein the middle section of an otherwise homophonic composition contains fugal imitation.

2. In foreign usage, a national song of lofty character, like the French *Marseillaise*.

hypo. In the church modal system, a prefix locating the starting point or overall range of a mode a 4th below its final (tonic); e.g., the Dorian mode's starting note is D (and its range D-D), so the Hypodorian mode begins on A, a 4th below (and has the range A-A); D remains the final (tonic).

I (It.; masc. plural). The.

iamb (iambus). In prosody, metrical foot of 2 syllables, 1 short and unaccented, followed by 1 long and accented:

etc.

Ibert, Jacques (François Antoine), b. Paris, Aug. 15, 1890; d. there, Feb. 5, 1962. He studied at the Paris Cons. (1911–14); received the Prix de Rome for his cantata *Le Poète et la fée* (1919); in Rome wrote his most successful work, the symphonic suite *Escales* (Ports of Call, 1930), inspired by a Mediterranean cruise taken while in the navy. He served as director of the Académie de France of Rome (1937–60); administrator of the Réunion des Théâtres Lyriques Nationaux in Paris (1955–56); elected a member of the Institut de France (1956). In his music he combines felicitous moods and techniques of impressionism and neoclassicism; harmonies are opulent, instrumentation coloristic; there is humor in the lighter works, such as the orch.l *Divertissement* and *Le Petit âne blanc* (The Little White Donkey) from the piano suite *Histoires* (1922); with excellent craftsmanship, he never fails to produce the intended effect; also composed operas and ballets.

Ice Cube, b. Oshea Jackson, Los Angeles, Calif., June 15, 1964. He initially gained fame as a member of the group N.W.A. (Niggas with Attitude), then as a solo artist, later as film actor. He began rapping in the 9th grade; met a local deejay named Dr. Dre. The duo produced a parody of *Roxanne, Roxanne*, a local hit (1984); next wrote *Boyz n the Hood*, reflecting life in the ghettos of Compton, recorded by another friend, Eazy E. The trio joined with deejay Yella to form N.W.A., but Cube took a sabbatical to attend school in Phoenix, not returning until 1988; recorded with them on 2 albums, the 2nd being the classic megaseller *Straight Outta Compton* (1991), most of which he wrote; that same year he released his 1st solo album, *Death Certificate*; gave a critically well-received performance in John Singleton's 1st feature, *Boyz n the Hood*. His 1992 album, *The Predator*, was the 1st rap album to debut at the top of both *Billboard*'s pop and R&B album charts; followed it a year later with another bestseller, *Lethal Injection*; co-produced, co-wrote, and starred in the film *Friday*, a comedy about life in Los Angeles (1994).

Ice-T, (born Tracy Marrow), b. Newark, N.J., *c.* 1958. He moved to the Crenshaw area of Los Angeles, he became involved with gangs; subsequently joined the Army. In the early 1980s he began rapping; recorded *The Coldest Rap* for a local label (1982); went to N.Y.; worked with several local rappers; returned to L.A. (1986). He was signed to Sire Records (1987); formed the Rhyme Syndicate management company and recording label (1988). He appeared in the film *New Jack City* (1991); a year later formed the speed metal–rap group Body Count; became (in)famous for *Cop Killer*, attracting the attention of neoconservatives who condemned its lyrics; dropped by Time Warner, owners of Sire, his recording and acting careers have continued unabated.

ictus (from Lat. *icere*, strike). Separation mark in Gregorian chant before and after an important note in the melody, based on relative prosodic importance.

idée fixe. Term used by Berlioz for the recurrent theme in his *Symphonie fantastique*, found in each movement; with it he depicts the Shakespearean actress Harriet Smithson, with whom he was in love. Actually, he used the same theme in a piece composed before he ever beheld Miss Smithson on stage.

idiophones (from Grk. *idios* + *phonos*, one's own sound). Older classification of instruments whose sound is produced by striking or shaking a metallic, wooden, or other surface directly, thus producing their sound through the substance of the instrument itself (e.g., triangle, chimes, cymbals, xylophone, castanets, rattle, glass harmonica, etc.), unlike membranophones.

idyll (idyl; It. *idillio*; Fr. *idylle*; Ger. *Idylle*). Composition of a pastoral or tenderly romantic nature, without set form.

Iglesias (Buga), Julio, b. Madrid, Sept. 23, 1943. He was 20 before evincing interest in music; taught himself to play the guitar; after studying English at Cambridge he entered the Benidorm Song Festival in Spain, carrying off all of its prizes (1968); subsequently pursued a successful international career, turning out some 60 albums in 6 languages; sold over 100 million copies, for which his name was entered in the *Guinness Book of World Records*.

il (It.; masc. singular). The. *Il più*, the most.

imbroglio (It., mixture, confusion). 1. Use of rhythmically contrasting, non-coincident divisions within a common meter. Simultaneous use of 3/4 and 6/8 in Spanish music is an imbroglio; a similar combination is found in Mozart's opera *Don Giovanni* (finale of 1st act) and the street scene in Wagner's *Die Meistersinger*. Far more complex examples are found in the 2nd movement of *3 Places in New England* by Ives and the 3rd String Quartet of Carter. 2. Operatic scenes where several voices or instrumental ensembles perform simultaneously but serve different dramatic purposes.

imitando (It.). Imitating. *Imitando il corno*, imitating a horn; found in Paganini's violin capriccios and Liszt's transcriptions of them; *imitando il flauto*, imitating a flute; found in Paganini's violin Capriccio No. 9 and Liszt's paraphrase thereof (*Études d'exécution transcendante No. 5*).

imitatio per augmentationem. See ⇒Canon per augmentationem.

imitatio per diminutionem. See ⇒Canon per diminutionem.

imitatio retrograda. See ⇒Canon cancrizans.

imitation. Generic term for the repetition of a motive, phrase, or theme proposed by one part (antecedent) in another part (consequent), with or without modification; a most natural and powerful device that lies at the foundation of the canon and fugue, found in practically all forms since the emergence of Western music from monophony and parallel homophony. Progressing from literal repetition of a phrase, imitation evolved into a complex polyphonic art in which themes could be inverted, taken at half speed (augmentation) or double speed (diminution), or further embellished by ornamental devices. The minimum requirement of all imitation is the preservation of its rhythmic pattern, else it become unrecognizable. *Canonic imitation*, strict imitation; *free imitation*, permitting variants of the antecedent in the consequent; *strict imitation*, where the consequent repeats the antecedent interval for interval (whether transposed or not).

immer (Ger.). Always; continually. *Immer langsam*, slowly throughout; *immer langsamer*, gradually slower; *immer leise nach und nach*, gradually softening; *immer stärker werdend*, continually growing louder.

imperfect cadence. See ⇒cadence.

imperfect consonance. See ⇒consonance.

imperfect interval. See ⇒interval.

imperfect stop. ⇒See stop.

imperfection (Lat. *imperfectio*). In mensural music, the binary (2-beat) measure, considered incomplete without its 3rd beat, which in mensural music made a "perfection" (*perfectio*); medieval aesthetics connected the ternary perfection to the Holy Trinity.

imponente (It.). Imposing, impressive.

impresario (from It. *impresa*, undertaking). Agent or manager of an opera or concert company.

impressionism. Aesthetic term describing modern French and French-influenced music of the early 20th century. By analogy to a movement in late-19th-century painting, subtle impressions rather than emphatic descriptions are conveyed through ethereal modal and nondiatonic harmonies in free modulation and colorful instrumentation. Debussy, considered the 1st impressionist composer, disliked the term, seeing his music as closer in spirit to the symbolist literary movement. Perhaps the music of this period synthesizes these 2 elements.

Impressionism derives its source of inspiration from external, even exotic sources; its literature, art, and music are easily projected outside; the recipient of its colorful images has the means of comparing photoreality with the artist's experience of it. Impressionism thrives on equilibrated euphony of harmonious dissonances; builds its thematic contents on fluctuating modality, block harmonies, and parallel progressions of triadic formations; its coloristic opulence is obtained through expansion of tonal materials into the spacious structures of resonant harmonies and exotic scales. In its evocation of the classical past, impressionism integrates diatonic materials into enhanced edifices of sonority. There are profound differences in historic, cultural, and geographic factors in the development of impressionism and its coincidental aesthetic opposite, expressionism: Impressionism is Gallic, expressionism Germanic.

impromptu (Lat. *in promptu*, in readiness). 1. Improvisation. 2. Interludes in theatrical plays in the 17th century, e.g., Molière's *L'Impromptu de Versailles*. 3. Character piece of varying form and little development, popular in the 19th century. Schubert wrote several impromptus for piano, each built in symmetric form in which each main section is subdivided into 3 subsections: each subsection is subdivided into 3 subaltern segments: each of those are split into brief musical phrases in 3-part form; it must be noted, however, that the title *Impromptu* was not Schubert's but appended by his publisher. Chopin's impromptus for piano are particularly remarkable in their perfect symmetrical design; Liszt wrote piano impromptus on themes by other composers; these impromptus come close to a fantasia.

Improperia (Lat., reproaches). Biblical passages chanted during the Roman Catholic Good Friday Mass, representing the plaints of the crucified Jesus to his people, "Popule meus quid feci tibi?" (O my people, what have I done to you?), followed by 2 passages from the Old Testament.

improvisation (from Lat. *improvisus*, unforeseen; *ex improviso*, without preparation). Art of spontaneous performance without preliminary plan; extemporization. Formerly, improvisation was thought integral to the craft of composition; organists in particular improvised freely on hymn tunes; among the greatest improvisers on the organ were Frescobaldi and Buxtehude; Bach was a master at improvising in fugal style. As a child Mozart included improvisations at his performances at the European courts; Beethoven's improvisations for his friends left an overwhelming impression; at his recitals Liszt asked musicians in the audience to give him subjects for free improvisations; he would then amaze them by his inventiveness. Organ improvisations continued to be the stock-in-trade of 20th-century organists, while public improvisations by pianists fell into disfavor.

In some cases, supposedly spontaneous improvisations are in fact prepared in advance; some performers prefer this approach, whether it be classical cadenza or jazz solo, particularly in the context of larger ensembles. One group of talented improvisers on the piano and organ were the accompanists of silent movies; while they used a book of standard music for certain scenes, these musicians had to be prepared on a moment's notice to change styles, cover gaps, or invent on the spot; some had a real flair for enhancing cinematic images while producing valid music. Jazz has resurrected the art of improvisation to a new height of brilliance, especially in collective improvisations occurring in jam sessions. Depending on the style involved, jazz improvisation is affected by tonality, accompaniment, or length allotted, from a quick "fill" to essentially unlimited time space.

improvviso (It.). Suddenly.

In Nomine. Unusual genre of consort music of the 16th and 17th centuries, with more than 150 examples by English composers. The term derives from the musical source, taken from the Sarum antiphon *Gloria tibi Trinitas*; the English religious composer John Taverner used it as the cantus firmus for a Mass *à* 6. In its Benedictus, the setting of "in nomine Domini" is reduced to *à* 4; this section was separated from its source and arranged; by the mid-16th century, instrumental fantasias on In Nomine began to appear; among those who wrote In Nomines are Robert Johnson (I), Tallis, White, the Ferraboscos, Byrd, Bull, Weelkes, Gibbons, Tomkins, William Lawes, and Purcell. The practice has seen a small revival in the 20th century.

Inbrunst (Ger.). Fervor. *Mit Inbrunst*, fervently.

incalzando (It., pursuing hotly). Growing more vehement, pressing ahead, rushing. *Incalzando e stringendo*, growing more vehement and rapid.

Incarnatus, Et. Part of the Credo.

incidental music. Pieces composed to illustrate selected scenes in a dramatic performance; in addition to overtures and marches, interludes, songs, and dances may be provided; distinct from an orch'l suite because of its being subordinate to the dramatic action; differs from opera because vocal numbers are few and far between. The overture from Beethoven's incidental music to Goethe's *Egmont* is performed as a separate concert piece, as are several numbers from Mendelssohn's score to *A Midsummer Night's Dream*, most famously the *Wedding March*; other examples of incidental music now more popular in concert form are *L'Arlésienne* by Bizet and *Peer Gynt* by Grieg.

incipit (Lat., it begins). 1st word or group of words of a Gregorian chant, used to identify a particular hymn or a cantus firmus; thus Requiem, Magnificat, Kyrie, Gloria, and other parts of the Mass and Canonical Hours are incipits. In cataloging old MSS, the incipit identifies the beginning of the 1st page; the ending of the MS is indicated by the word *explicit*, meaning "it folds out" (i.e., it ends).

incollando (It.). Playing all the notes in a chord simultaneously, without arpeggiation.

incomplete stop. Half organ stop.

incrociando (It.). Crossing hands while playing the piano, so that the right hand is below the left hand.

incudine (It.). Anvil, used as percussion.

indebolente (It.). Gradually lessening the sound.

independent chord (harmony, triad). Consonant chord not obliged to change to another chord by progression or resolution.

indeterminacy. In composition, denotes a conventional score produced by chance; in execution, a score leaving much to be determined by performers.

Indonesian music. Politically, Indonesia comprises several thousand islands, great and small, straddling the equator. Musically, the most documented are Java and Bali; each had numerous courts with their own variants of the indigenous ensemble known as *gamelan*, consisting of *sui generis* xylophones and bells, gongs, and drums. Basic scales of the gamelan are the 5-tone *slendro* system and the 7-tone *pelog* system, with supernumerary tones used as embellishments; however, no 2 gamelan are tuned identically, leading to the unique character of each gamelan. Intervals of the gamelan cannot be reduced precisely to Western scales; thus the non-indigenous listener's combined response to the stimulating exotic quality of the sound is the feeling that the music is "out of tune." Much gamelan is associated with dance, theater, and puppetry; other lesser-known Indonesian musical traditions involve singing, wooden flutes, and spike fiddles.

When Javanese gamelan was introduced at the Paris Exposition of 1889, Debussy and other French composers of the modern school were fascinated by it; they and other Western composers were influenced by its colotomic metric structures and gong-laden sonorities (McPhee, Britten). In most gamelan music there is a sense of enhanced concord prevailing in spite of the dissonant combinations being employed; individual rhythmic patterns are used without regard to a prescribed meter; the duration of the basic time unit (based on multiples of 2) is steady within a given dance or song, with repeated uniform beats (exceptional are certain Balinese dances); rhythmic complexity is provided by interlocking patterns. The music heard on the islands of Borneo, Sumatra, and elsewhere has less of the delicacy of the gamelan.

Indy, (Paul-Marie-Théodore) Vincent d', b. Paris, Mar. 27, 1851; d. there, Dec. 2, 1931. His education was directed by his grandmother, who had known Grétry and Monsigny and shown remarkable appreciation of Beethoven when that master was still living. He studied piano with Diemer and Marmontel (1862–65), harmony with Lavignac. He met Duparc (1869); they spent much time studying Bach, Beethoven, Berlioz, and Wagner. During the Franco-Prussian War he served in the Garde Mobile; wrote of his experiences in *Histoire du 105ème Bataillon de la Garde nationale de Paris en l'année 1870–71* (1872); began studying composition with Franck (1872); followed him when the latter became prof. of organ at the Paris Cons. (1873); d'Indy won a 2nd *accessit* (1874), the 1st the next year. On his 1st visit to Germany (1873), he met Liszt, Wagner, and heard the 1st performances of the *Ring* cycle at Bayreuth (1876); thereafter made regular trips there to hear all of Wagner's works; attended the premiere of *Parsifal* in 1882. He was organist at St. Leu-la-Forêt (1872–76); chorus master and timpanist with the Colonne Orch. (1873–78); joined the Soc. Nationale de Musique as a junior member (1871); was its secretary and de facto leader (1876–90); after Franck's death, its president. He founded, with Bordes and Guilmant, the famous Schola Cantorum (1896) as a school for plainchant and the Palestrina style; gradually the scope of instruction was enlarged to include all musical disciplines, and the inst. became one of the world's foremost (and conservative) music schools.

D'Indy's fame as composer began with the premiere of his dramatic legend *Le Chant de la cloche* (1886), which had won the City of Paris Prize in the 1885 competition. The following year saw the 1st performance of the *Symphony on a French*

Mountain Air for Piano and Orch., his best-known work today. Other notable achievements were the sym. trilogy *Wallenstein*, after Schiller (*Le Camp de Wallenstein*, 1880; *Max et Thécla*, 1874; *Le Mort de Wallenstein*, 1884); the lyric drama *Fervaal* (1887); the sym. variations *Istar* (1897); these and other works led to d'Indy's recognition as one of the most important of modern French masters.

Although d'Indy never held an official position as conductor, he frequently and successfully appeared in that capacity; visiting Spain (1897), Russia (1903, 1907), and the U.S. (1905, conducting the Boston Sym. Orch.; 1921). A member of the commission appointed to revise the curriculum of the Cons., he refused a proffered professorship of composition (1892), but became prof. of the ensemble class (1912). He was inspector of musical instruction in Paris (from 1899); made Chevalier of the Legion of Honor (1892) and Officer (1912).

As teacher and creative artist, d'Indy continued the traditions of Franck. His special talent was in the larger instrumental forms; some French critics view him as a French Brahms; while his style rests on Bach and Beethoven, his deep study of Gregorian chant and early counterpoint added an element of severity, even complexity, that renders his approach somewhat difficult; some charge that his music is lacking in emotional force. He was a prolific writer for various journals; his articles exude critical acumen and literary finish; books include *Cours de Composition musicale* (I, 1903; II/1, 1909; II/2, 1933); *César Franck* (1906); *Beethoven* (1911); *Wagner et son influence sur l'art musical français* (1930).

inégales (*notes inégales;* Fr., unequal). In French Baroque music, playing a group of notes indicated in even duration so that the 1st note of each pair takes time away from the 2nd, producing a dotted effect; e.g., 2 8th notes are played or sung as a dotted 8th and a 16th. There are further subtleties of performance; if the syncopation is meant to be gentle, the score is usually marked *louré;* more incisive syncopation is marked *pointé* or *piqué.* In addition to French Baroque works, some editors apply dotting or even *double-dotting* (to alter 2 8th notes to a doubly dotted 8th and a 32nd) to works of Bach and others, inspiring much controversy; whether justified or not, the rhythmic aberrations in the practice of inégales are a well-coordinated guide to performance.

infinite canon. See ⇒canon.

infinite melody. One that avoids cadencing; associated with the melodic meanderings of Wagner in his mature music dramas.

infino (It.). Up to, as far as; until you reach.

infiorare (from It. *fiore,* flower). Ornament with florid melismas.

inganno (It., deception). Deceptive cadence. *Inganno la bella fuga,* in 17th-century Italian music, a modified entry in a fugal passage.

ingenuamente (ingenuo; It.). Naturally, ingenuously, artlessly.

inharmonic relation. Cross relation.

iniziale (It.). Initial; the 1st.

inner parts. In harmony or counterpoint, parts lying between the highest (soprano) and lowest (bass) parts.

inner pedal. Pedal point in an inner part (alto, tenor, etc.).

innig (Ger.). Heartfelt, sincere, fervent, intense; intimo, *con affetto.*

innigem Ausdruck, mit (Ger.). With heartfelt expression.

inniglich (Ger.). With deep emotion; fervently.

inno (It.). Hymn.

insanity and suicide. It is said that musicians are more nervous by nature than other professionals; that a greater percentage of performers and composers end their lives in insane asylums; and that only mathematicians and chess players exceed musicians in this melancholy fate. But statistics fail to support this estimate. Among famous composers, only Donizetti, Schumann, Wolf, and MacDowell became totally insane and had to be committed to asylums. (Syphylis may have been a major factor.) Exaggerated sensitivity to criticism, delusions of grandeur, melancholy, and other aberrations may be typical among artists constantly on view before the public, but such neurotic traits do not constitute insanity; even suicidal impulses are no more frequent among musicians than the law of averages would indicate.

Perhaps the most spectacular premeditated musical suicide was that of the pianist Alexander Kelberine (1903–40), who arranged his last concert program to consist only of works dealing with death (ending with Liszt's *Totentanz*), and upon returning home took a lethal overdose of sleeping pills. Rezso Seress (1899–1968), the composer of *Gloomy Sunday,* a song banned in some European countries because it precipitated a wave of Sunday suicides among the young, jumped out of a window. In 1985 the parents of a teenager who killed himself after listening to a rock song "urging" suicide sued the performers and their record company for damages, but a judge ruled against the claim, fortunately.

inspiration. Musical inspiration, unlike that of poetry and the visual arts, has no external material to draw upon. A poet creates images from preexisting words and concepts in a native language; an artist paints a landscape or portrait from visual impressions, or draws from imagined geometric patterns. But a creative musician depends on a more artificial system of successive or combined tones and rhythms, having no outward existence except in uncoordinated sounds of nature, bird songs, and bodily rhythms. Musical inspiration is therefore a *sui generis* art, comparable to mathematical invention, which also deals with an artificially created system of concepts. If melody and rhythm can be described as available materials for composers, then inspiration must follow their patterns within a particular national or ethnic unit. But in the last several centuries, during which musical art became formulated as a definite aesthetic code, an individual composer had the task of combining melodic phrases from folk songs within harmonic and contrapuntal formations in order to make a resulting work meaningful to listeners.

The German word for inspiration is *Einfall* (a falling in, or insight); the state of musical inspiration is indeed such a "falling in," but it comes not from the outside but from the inside of a musician's imagination. Theory always follows practice in formulating the aesthetic code. Grammar and syntax of composition became well established with the advent of classical music. Music teaching made use of works created by acknowledged masters of the art; manuals of melody, harmony, and counterpoint codified the practice. Formal aesthetics became established, and composers, like poets, were enabled to be inspired within a given vocabulary of tonal and harmonic formations.

It is unlikely that the electrochemical process that takes place in the cortex during an *Einfall* could ever be recorded as an EEG, but some such process must be occurring when a composer figuratively exclaims "Eureka!" and rushes into the workroom to put the insight on paper or on computer. Most stories about moments of inspiration are romantic inventions, attempts to understand an impenetrable mental process. The mental formation required of Bach to devise a fugal subject yielding the most interesting contrapuntal developments is immensely complex, a process of musical precognition that even composers less Olympian must follow. The magnitude of Wagner's controlled inspiration is extraordinary in that he had to coordinate his own text, an interlacing web of leitmotivs, and the limitations imposed by the pitch and dynamic ranges of instruments and voices to create an architecturally stable structure.

Facility of inspiration is not in direct or inverse proportion to the value or weightiness of the music. Mozart, Schubert, Rossini, and Mendelssohn could convert inspiration into written music rapidly; Beethoven labored mightily; his copyist would have preferred 20 pages of Rossini than any 1 by his employer. Great improvisers were rarely great composers, although great composers were often remarkable improvisers. Inspiration can be stored away, so that a musical idea irrelevant to one work might one day illuminate another one (e.g., the finale of Beethoven's *Kreutzer Sonata*). Musical inspiration, already requiring discipline, is constrained further by the manual labor of writing musical notes on several staves.

Mystically inclined composers have claimed that their inspiration came from on high. Scriabin felt that his music was a divine message, and that he was merely a prophet; both the religious Stravinsky and the atheist Tippett expressed the feeling of being a vessel for external expression. Virtually every note Messiaen wrote reflected his Roman Catholic mysticism. Belief in divine inspiration undoubtedly helps to accomplish compositional labor with celerity; Handel might have been justified in so believing after he completed the entire score of *Messiah* in 3 and a half weeks; for, when he heard one of his sacred works recklessly performed by a church choir, he actually whispered an apology: "Oh Lord! This is not thus that I wrote this music in Thy glory!"

inständig (Ger.; It. *instante*). Urgent, pressing.

instrumental motet. Contrapuntal composition written in the manner of the Renaissance motet, often on a specific Latin model, such as the English In Nomine.

instrumentation. Theory and practice of composing, arranging, or adapting music for a body of instruments of different kinds. See ⇒orchestration.

instrumento d'acciaio (It., steel instrument). Mozart's indication in *The Magic Flute* for glockenspiel.

instruments à cordes (Fr.). String instruments. *Instruments à vent*, wind instruments.

intabulation (from Lat. *tabula*, table; Ger. *Intabulierung*; It. *intavolatura*). Arrangement of vocal composition for keyboard or stringed instruments, with added ornamentation for greater idiomaticity; the It. form of the word refers also to collections of tablatures.

intenzione, con (It.). With stress, emphasis.

interference beats. Effect of the simultaneous sounding of 2 different tones; the result, a pulsing change in amplitude, is called "beating." The theoretical distinction between consonance and dissonance depends on relative numbers of beats: the more beats generated by the sounding of 2 or more tones simultaneously, the more dissonant is the resulting combination. The octave, being perfect, generates no beats; a perfect 5th should also be free of beats, and 2 a cappella voices or violin strings properly tuned produce this effect; but because the tuning on a piano is tempered, those 5ths are not perfect, but, on average, beat 47 times per minute. See also ⇒acoustics; just intonation; temperament.

interlude. 1. Italian intermezzo or French entr'acte. 2. Instrumental strain or passage connecting the lines or stanzas of a hymn, etc. 3. Organ piece played between choral hymns or psalms of a church service (*interludium*).

intermezzo (It., insertion; plural, *intermezzi*; Fr. *intermède*; Lat. *intermedium*). 1. Theatrical genre dating to 13th-century liturgical drama, where intermezzos (Eng. plural) were interpolated between parts of the service. Secular intermezzos served to provide diversions at aristocratic weddings, coronations, and other formal functions; invariably they were fairly brief and of lighter weight than other music for the occasion, and not necessarily connected with the plot of the drama or religious play into which they were placed; the genre eventually developed into independent musical presentations, leading to *opera buffa*.

The authors of intermezzos strove to please the public by any means necessary, often succeeding in attracting more attention than the main bill of fare; Pergolesi inserted *La Serva padrona* into a performance of his *opera seria Il Prigioniero superbo*; his intermezzo became extremely popular (and still is); its Parisian performances precipitated the famous *guerre des bouffons*. Rousseau, an ardent partisan of Italian opera, composed the *intermède* "*Le Devin du village*" (Fontainebleau, 1752), which became quite successful; R. Strauss wrote an extended opera in this genre, pointedly entitling it *Intermezzo*. Within a full-length opera, intermezzos are instrumental interludes, usually brief, between scenes; an intermezzo in Mascagni's *Cavalleria Rusticana* is performed as an independent concert piece.

2. Character piece, usually for piano, in which the title suggests a piece written at leisure; but it is difficult to justify in this sense the term that Brahms assigned to several highly elaborate pieces. 3. Incidental music in modern dramas. 4. Short movement connecting the main divisions of a sym.

intermodulation. Electronic technique of sound manipulation inspired by the interference of 2 signals; used extensively, in principle, by composers such as Stockhausen.

interrogatio (Lat.). Conventional expressive melodic movement a major or minor 2nd upwards at the end of a phrase; used in medieval sacred music to enable the listener to equate it with a question mark; Baroque composers commonly employed this device, recommended by the theorists of the time.

interruzione, senza (It.). Without interruption.

interval. The distance between 2 notes measured in diatonic degrees. Intervals are usually measured from the lower note to the higher. The distance between a note and itself is obviously zero; but when calculating interval, the initial note is considered a "prime" or "unison" and assigned the symbol 1 when necessary. Similarly, the distance between a note and the next note up the scale seems to be a single unit, but in music it is a 2nd, marked with the numerical symbol 2. Thus the names of the intervals indicate not the distance between 2 notes, but the numerical order of their positions proceeding up the scale. The interval of a 3rd contains 2 diatonic units, yet its symbol is 3; and so it goes until the octave (from Lat. *octo*, 8), which contains 7 diatonic units. In effect, the lower note of an interval is a Do in a movable Do system.

The tabulation of intervals, taken from the ordinal numbers, is itself simple: unison, second (2nd), third (3rd), fourth (4th), fifth (5th), sixth (6th), seventh (7th), and octave. More solemn and learned are the Latin names of intervals, derived from Greek: *unisonus, tonus, ditonus, diatessaron, diapente, tonus cum diapente, ditonus cum diapente*, and *diapason* (octave); these need only be learned for dealing with medieval hexachordal theory. Beyond the octave intervals are still named by the numerical adjectives in English and French; they follow Latin forms in German, Italian, Spanish, and Russian.

Intervals are modified by indications of major, minor, augmented, and diminished. Unfortunately, the English nomenclature of intervals borrows the Latin comparative adjectives *major* and *minor* (big and little) for intervallic size, while the very same terms are used to indicate major and minor keys and their scales, e.g., a crucial interval in the C-major scale (E up to C) is a minor 6th; French (*majeur, mineur*), Spanish (*mayor, menor*), and Italian (*maggiore, minore*) designations suffer the same confusion. More convenient is the German terminology in which one noun pair (*dur* and *moll*) refers to keys and scales, while an adjectival pair (*grosse* and *kleine*) refers to intervals; E to C is thus a *kleine Sexte* (small 6th), not a "minor 6th"; the Russians follow German usage.

The perfect unison, 4th, 5th, and octave cannot be altered to major and minor intervals; the 2nd, 3rd, 6th and 7th can. But all intervals can be augmented or diminished, occasionally even doubly augmented or doubly diminished. All these possibilities are governed by exact placement of the pitches and intrinsic development of the tonalities to which intervals belong. Several intervallic pairs are enharmonic equivalents (see entry), with identical numbers of semitones; this causes an ever more knotty web of anomalies. It is the musical spelling that determines whether an interval or a chord belongs to a particular tonality, and what is consonant in one tonality may be dissonant in another.

Augmented interval, wider by a chromatic semitone than major or perfect; *chromatic interval*, augmented or diminished (except augmented 4th and diminished 5th and 7th); *compound interval*, wider than an octave; *consonant interval*, not requiring resolution; *diatonic interval*, occurring between 2 notes belonging to the same key (except the augmented 2nd and 5th in the harmonic minor scale); *diminished interval*, chromatic semitone narrower than major or perfect; *dissonant interval*, requiring resolution; *enharmonic interval*, see ⇒enharmonic equivalence; *extended* or *extreme interval*, augmented; *flat interval*, diminished; *harmonic interval*, tones sounded together; *imperfect interval*, diminished; *inverted interval*, the higher tone is lowered, or the lower tone raised, by an octave; *major interval*, distance between the keynote and the 2nd, 3rd, 6th, and 7th of a major scale; *melodic interval*, tones sounded in succession; *minor interval*, chromatic semitone narrower than major; *parallel* or *consecutive interval* (with an interval preceding), 2-dyad progression in the same direction and at the same interval; *perfect* or *perfect major interval*, equal to the standard unison, 4th, 5th, and octave of the major scale; *redundant interval*, augmented; *simple interval*, not wider than an octave; *standard interval*, measured upward from the keynote; *superfluous interval*, augmented.

intimissimo (It.). Very tenderly, warmly. *Intimo*, heartfelt, fervent.

intonarumori (It., noisemakers). Musical instruments invented *c*. 1913 by Italian futurist Luigi Russolo (1885–1947); all were destroyed in Paris during World War II.

intonation. 1. Production of tone, either vocal or instrumental, with emphasis on proper pitch. 2. In plainchant, intoning. 3. Opening notes leading up to the reciting tone of a chant; later, to any religious song. *Fixed intonation*, see ⇒fixed-tone instruments.

intoning. Chanting by the minister, in monotone, of parts of the Anglican Church service.

intrada (It., entry). Short introduction or prelude; opening piece on a festive occasion, usually arranged for trumpets and horns, with the character of a fanfare in march time.

intrepidezza, con (It., intrepidly). Boldly, daringly, dashingly.

introduction (It. *introduzione*; Fr. *introduction*; Ger. *Einleitung, Eingang*). 1. Instrumental prelude before an operatic or oratorio aria. 2. In a concerto or similar work, orch'l tutti before the entry of the soloist. It may be very brief, e.g., the plagal cadential chords in the opening bars of Rachmaninoff's 2nd Piano Concerto, or else fill a lengthy section nearly qualified to be called an overture, e.g., the tutti beginning of Beethoven's Violin Concerto. 3. Phrase or division preliminary to and preparatory of a composition or movement. It is often in a parallel minor or major key, as in Beethoven's 4th Sym. (from B-flat minor in a long preamble to the principal key B-flat major); another example is the opening movement of Haydn's 104th Sym. The 3rd Sym. of Scriabin has a long introduction in D-flat major, the Neapolitan lowered supertonic of the principal key, C minor.

introit (*introitus;* Lat., entrance). 1. Opening antiphon sung while the priest is approaching the altar to celebrate the Roman Catholic High Mass; responsorial in structure, a soloist alternates with a chorus, or the chorus divides into alternating parts. 2. In the modern Anglican Church, anthem or psalm sung as the minister approaches the Communion table.

invention (Lat. *inventio*, from *invenire*, find). 1. Musical work possessing elements of intellectual and artistic discovery. In the Renaissance the word *invention* still preserved its ancient connotation of newness; to the minds of 17th-century musicians, inventions were the product of intuitive observation, modern in relation to their era and curious with respect to intellectual perception; musical inventions were born *ex abrupto*, thus followed the rules of Latin rhetoric going back to Cicero and Quintilian, retained in the Baroque schooling system in a sequence of mental and artistic stages, in order: *inventio, dispositio, elaboratorio, decoratio,* and *executio*. 2. Short piece in free contrapuntal style developing 1 motive in impromptu fashion; this form reached its zenith in Bach's 2-part and 3-part keyboard inventions; the 3-part works are also known as sinfonias. In the introductory paragraph to the inventions, he offers them as "a faithful guide, whereby lovers of the clavier are presented with a plain method of learning not only how to play clearly in 2 parts, but also to progress toward playing 3 obbligato parts well and accurately; at the same time striving not only to obtain fine inventions, but also to develop them appropriately, and above all to secure a cantabile style of playing so as to create a strong foretaste of the art of composition itself."

inversion (from Lat. *vertere*, turn). Transposition of the notes of an interval or chord. 1. *Melodic inversion*, in which the ascending intervals of the original melody are inverted to become descending intervals and vice versa; in some melodies, inversion becomes identical with retrograde motion, as in a Beethoven contradanza:

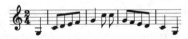

A melodic inversion is said to be *tonal* if it follows the tonality of the melody; the 2nd subject of the G-major Fugue from Book I of Bach's *Well-Tempered Clavier* is such an inversion of the 1st subject. In tonal inversions the intervals are not precise as to content in semitone units; e.g., the C-major scale when inverted becomes the Phrygian mode, with the initial interval being a semitone rather than whole tone; a major tetrachord when inverted becomes a minor tetrachord; a broken major triad becomes a broken minor triad when inverted, and vice versa. An exceptionally clever use of this reciprocal relationship is provided by the 18th variation of Rachmaninoff's *Rhapsody on a Theme by Paganini*, where the original ascending minor tune becomes, in a slower tempo, an emotional romantic theme, descending to the dominant an octave lower. Earlier contrapuntal composers liked to preface their inversions by tantalizing instructions in Latin, as in the Biblical allusion in Obrecht's *Missa graecorum*: "Qui se exaltat humiliabitur et qui se humiliat exaltabitur;" or simply, "Subverte lineam": invert the (melodic) line.

Inversions of intervals are obtained by placing the lower note an octave above, or the upper note an octave below. Any major interval inverted becomes minor; any augmented interval becomes diminished. To determine the inversion arithmetically, subract the original interval from 9: thus a 2nd inverted becomes a 7th, a 4th becomes a 5th, etc. Any perfect interval inverts into another perfect interval, e.g., a 5th becomes a 4th. Any consonance inverted becomes another consonance, e.g., 3rds become 6ths; any dissonance inverted becomes another dissonance, e.g., a 2nd becomes a 7th. In contrapuntal music, inversions of intervals greater than the octave are often found; rules of voice leading become subverted in such types of counterpoint; for instance, in counterpoint of the 12th, perfectly legal and desirable consecutive 6ths become, upon inversion, consecutive 7ths, inadmissible in traditional harmony.

When Haydn returned, after a long absence, to Vienna, a middle-aged woman rushed to him and exclaimed, "Maestro, do you remember me? You wrote this for me," and she sang:

"Ach! I do remember," Haydn replied. "Unfortunately, now it is this:"

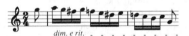

2. *Harmonic inversion*, in which the bass voice is transferred an octave higher and placed on top of the chord; chord inversions are discussed in the entry for harmony. 3. See ⇒invertible counterpoint. 4. Organ point found in some other part than the bass. 5. Standard dodecaphonic procedure where all linear intervals of a row are mirrored around a horizontal plane, i.e., reversed vertically.

inverted mordent (Ger. *Schneller*, fast trill). Short and rapid upper trill that usually begins on the half beat (see ⇒mordent). The term remains confusing to this day because the mordent itself was subject to controversy during its heyday. The German Baroque used the picturesque term *Pralltriller* (elastic trill), possibly referring to the *Schneller* or similar figure which begins after the half beat. The notation of these ornaments is fraught with inconsistency, but a healthy decay of stenographic ornamentation has made the exact definition of an inverted mordent of no vital interest to anyone except editors of Baroque MSS or early-music practitioners who are engaged in ceaseless internecine struggle regarding the meaning of such terms.

invertible counterpoint. Type of polyphonic writing in which contrapuntal parts can be exchanged—say, soprano and bass—and remain free of forbidden discord and consecutive motion. While the normal interval of invertibility is the octave, other intervals have been used (10th, 12th). Among great masters of invertible counterpoint were Brahms, Reger, and Taneyev; Bach nurtured them all in his *Art of Fugue*, a veritable treasure box of scientific inversions. Also called double counterpoint.

invocation. Ode or prayer, particularly in oratorio or opera.

Ionian mode. This mode corresponds to the major scale; it was added to the 8 traditional ecclesiastical modes by Glareanus (1547) and placed at the head of the system of church modes as *primus tonus* by Zarlino (1558). Ironically, the Ionian mode, now the starting point for the traditional cycle of scales and the 1st rudiment of musical education, was described in medieval treatises as *modus lascivus* (lascivious, lewd, or wanton mode).

ira, con (It.). With wrath; passionately.

Irish reel. Fast variety of the reel.

Irlandais, -e (Fr.). Hibernian, Irish.

irregular cadence. See ⇒cadence.

Islamey. Popular dance of the Caucasian tribe of the Kabardinians, marked by a drone on the dominant and suggesting the Mixolydian mode; performed on the fiddle and the accordion who accompany the dance; the name is derived from *Islam*, i.e., Moslem.

islancio, con (It.). Vehemently, impetuously; with dash. ·

isorhythm (from Grk. *iso* + *rhythmos*, same rhythm). Musicological term to indicate melodies, particularly the cantus firmus of medieval motets built on the same rhythmic sequence. The definition was expanded to include a technique popular in the 14th and 15th centuries, where a single voice uses a repeated pitch pattern (*color*) and repeated rhythmic pattern (*talea*); the color and talea are designed not to coincide, so that repeated pitches are presented in different rhythms and phrases before returning to the opening pattern.

Israel, Brian M., b. N.Y., Feb. 5, 1951; d. Syracuse, N.Y., May 8, 1986. He studied composition with Ulysses Kay at Lehman College in N.Y. (B.A., 1971) and R. Palmer, B. Phillips, and Husa at Cornell Univ. (M.F.A., 1974; D.M.A., 1975); taught at Cornell (1972–75) and Syracuse Univ. (1975–86). As a pianist he advocated contemporary works; his own compositions form an eclectic traversal from Baroque contrapuntal devices to serialism, from ironic humor to profound seriousness. His works include chamber and children's operas, 6 symphonies, 3 string quartets, band music, choral works, and songs.

istesso (It.). Same. *L'istesso tempo*, the same tempo or time; indicates either that 1) the tempo of the measure or beat remains the same after a change of time signature, or that 2) a tempo previously interrupted is to be resumed.

istrumentale (It.). Instrumental. *Istrumento* (plural *istrumenti*), instrument.

Italian overture. Overture of the 17th and 18th centuries consisting of 3 sections—fast, slow, fast—while the French overture's 3 sections are slow, fast, slow; other types include

slow, fast, slow, fast; slow, fast (Purcell, *Dido and Aeneas*); all are antecedents of the sinfonia and sym.

Italian sixth. Chord of the augmented 6th type; its 3 notes comprise an augmented 6th from bottom to top and a major 3rd from bottom to the middle, as in A flat, C, and F sharp; it resolves most often to the 2nd inversion tonic chord, occasionally to a dominant chord (in C major):

Ite missa est. Valedictory sentence of the Roman Catholic Mass: "Go, you [the congregation] are dismissed." While considered part of the Ordinary, few polyphonic Masses set this short passage.

Ives, Charles (Edward), b. Danbury, Conn., Oct. 20, 1874; d. N.Y., May 19, 1954. His extraordinarily original and yet thoughtfully patriotic music profoundly changed the direction of American music years after Ives had stopped composing. His father, George Ives, was a bandleader of the 1st CT Heavy Artillery during the Civil War, who later taught his son rudimentary training in piano and cornet playing. At age 12 Charles played drums in the Danbury Band; by 13 he was playing organ at the Danbury Church; began to improvise freely at the piano, without concern for "school rules"; his experiments in melody and harmony led to polytonal compositions, partly as a spoof but eventually as a legitimate alternative to traditional music; at 17 composed his polytonal *Variations on America* for organ (still performed); an earlier band piece, *Holiday Quickstep*, was premiered by the Danbury Band (1888).

In 1894 Ives entered Yale Univ.; studied organ with Dudley Buck and composition with Parker, who gave him fine classical training; composed a full-fledged, completely traditional sym. (No. 1, 1896–98). After graduation (1898), played organ at the Central Presbyterian Church in N.Y. (1899–1902); formed an insurance partnership with Julian Myrick of N.Y. (1907); continued to compose music as an avocation. Suffered a massive heart attack (1918) complicated by diabetic condition; compelled to curtail his work both in business and in music; his illness made it difficult to handle a pen; retired from business (1930), by which time he had virtually stopped composing.

In 1919 Ives publ. at his own expense his great masterpiece, the *Concord Sonata* for piano, inspired by the transcendentalist writings of Emerson, Hawthorne, the Alcotts, and Thoreau; he also publ. *Essays before a Sonata* (1920) to complement the work. Although composed early in the century, the *Concord Sonata*'s idiom is so extraordinary, its technical difficulties so formidable, that the work was not given a full premiere until John Kirkpatrick played it in N.Y. (1939). In 1922 Ives brought out, also at his expense, a volume of *114 Songs* (1888–1921) marked by great diversity of style, ranging from lyrical Romanticism to powerful and dissonant modern invocations.

Both publications were distributed gratis by Ives to anyone who wanted them. His orch. masterpiece, *3 Places in New England*, also waited nearly 2 decades before its premiere; the 1st performance of the monumental 4th Sym. (1910–16) was given in 1965; in 1947 he received the Pulitzer Prize for his 3rd Sym. (1901–1904).

Because of his bad health and personal disposition, Ives lived as a recluse, almost never went to concerts, and did not own a record player or a radio; while he was well versed in the scores of Beethoven, Schumann, and Brahms, he took little interest in modern music. Yet he anticipated many technical innovations: polytonality, atonality, 12-tone formations, and polymetric and polyrhythmic configurations, prophetic for his time. In the 2nd movement of the *Concord Sonata* he called for a strip of wood on the white and the black keys of the piano to produce an echo-like sonority; in the unfinished *Universe Sym.* he planned an antiphonal representation of the heavens in chordal counterpoint and the earth in contrasting orch'l groups; composed quarter-tone pieces for piano. A unique quality of his music was the combination of simple motifs, often derived from American church hymns and popular ballads, with extremely complex dissonant counterpoint forming the supporting network for the melodic lines; a curious idiosyncrasy is his frequent quotation of what is either the "fate motive" of Beethoven's 5th Sym. or a hymn melody. From the 2nd Sym. onward, quotation and quodlibet became a primary compositional technique.

In recent years there has been dissension over the dating of Ives's MSS; he treated some pieces as ongoing works-in-progress, and altered them at different times of his life, e.g., the final dissonant chord of the 2nd Sym. (1897–1902), a late alteration of a major triad in the orig. version. Some saw this as an attempt to backdate his innovations; others saw it as valid, comparable to other composers who tinkered with their music for years; indeed, in later years, his standard response to his editors' posing questions seems to have been, "Do what you think is best." While he and a devoted group of admirers had great difficulty in obtaining performances, recordings, or publications of his music, a veritable Ives cult emerged posth.; eminent conductors and pianists were willing to cope with the forbidding difficulties of his works. He received the most orch'l performances among modern composers on American programs in 1976; his influence on the music of young composers reached a high mark, so that the adjective "Ivesian" came to describe certain characteristic acoustical and coloristic effects.

In addition to the 4 numbered syms., Ives combined 4 symphonic pictures to form *A Symphony: Holidays* (1904–13); *3 Places in New England*, also called the 1st Orch'l Set (1903–14); the 2nd Orch'l Set (1915); *Central Park in the Dark* (1898–1907); *The Unanswered Question* (1908); *Theater Orchestra Set* (1904–11); *Browning Overture* (1911). Chamber works include 2 string quartets (1896, 1913); Trio for violin, clarinet, and piano (1902); 4 violin sonatas (1908, 1910, 1914, 1915); Trio for Violin, Cello, and Piano (1911); Set for String Quartet and Piano (1914). Besides over 150 songs, he wrote many a cappella and accompanied vocal works, many of them song arrangments (e.g., *General William Booth Enters into Heaven* for Chorus with Brass Band, 1914). Other piano works are the *3-Page Sonata* (1905); *Some Southpaw Pitching* (1908); *The Anti-Abolitionist Riots* (1908); Sonata No. 1, a major 5-movement work (1909); several studies, many of them lost. He made several piano recordings *c.* 1940, notable for surprising technique and great enthusiasm.

Ives possessed an uncommon gift for literary expression; his annotations to his works are both trenchant and humorous; in addition to *Essays before a Sonata*, his *Memos*, in the form of a diary, reveal an extraordinary power of aphoristic utterance (ed. by Kirkpatrick, N.Y., 1972). He was acutely conscious of his civic duties as an American, once circulating a proposal to have federal laws enacted by popular referendum. The *Essays* and other writings were collected by H. Boatwright (N.Y., 1961). All of his MSS and correspondence were deposited by his widow at Yale Univ., forming an archive that Kirkpatrick organized and catalogued.

jack. 1. Upright slip of wood on the rear end of the key lever, carrying (in the harpsichord) a bit of crow-quill or hard leather set at a right angle to pluck the string, or (in the clavichord) a metallic tangent to hit the string. 2. In the pianoforte, the escapement lever, or hopper.

Jackson, Mahalia, b. New Orleans, Oct. 26, 1911; d. Evergreen Park, Ill., Jan. 27, 1972. A minister's daughter, she sang in her father's church; at 16 went to Chicago; supported herself by menial labor while singing at the Greater Salem Baptist Church; began touring with the Johnson Gospel Singers (1932). She revealed innate talent for expressive hymn singing; was in demand for conventions and political meetings; steadfastly refused to appear in nightclubs. Her 1947 recording *Move On Up a Little Higher* made her the "Gospel Queen"; appeared in concerts at N.Y.'s Carnegie Hall (1950–56); made her 1st European tour a triumphant success (1952). She sang at President Kennedy's inauguration (1961) and the civil rights march on Washington, D.C. (1963); made her last tour of Europe (1971); publ. an autobiography, *Movin' On Up* (N.Y., 1966).

Jackson, Michael (Joseph), b. Gary, Ind., Aug. 29, 1958. As a boy soprano, he joined his 4 brothers in a Motown group billed as the Jackson 5, which scored several hits; but he soon outshone his brothers, went solo, and attained superstar status with *Thriller* (1983), one of the 1st albums closely identified with a music video. The album sold some 30 million copies globally, certified as the largest sale ever of a single album (to 1984); that year won a record 8 Grammy Awards for his accomplishments; one enthusiast claimed he could count on one-quarter of the world's population (c. 2 billion) as an audience.

Jackson's androgynous appearance and his penchant for outlandish apparel (e.g., a sequined naval commodore's costume worn at the Grammy show) seemed to act like a stream of powerful pheromones on squealing admiring youths of both sexes. He survived a potential catastrophe when his hair caught fire during filming of a TV commercial. In collaboration with Lionel Richie he penned *We Are the World* in support of African famine relief; it won a Grammy as best song of 1985. In 1987 he brought out *Bad* (i.e., good); launched a major U.S. tour (1988). His fascination with childhood imaginativeness led to the opening of his *Captain EO* at the Disneyland Theme Park in Anaheim, Calif. (1986), featuring Jackson as a singing and dancing commander of a motley space crew. More recent albums, *Dangerous* and *HIStory, Part I,* have done well but not to the extraordinary extent of the previous two. In recent years his career has been subject to sexual innuendo, legal difficulties, bizarre alterations of his physical features, and personal disappointment, including a failed marriage to Elvis Presley's daughter Lisa Marie.

Jackson, Milt(on), "Bags," b. Detroit, Jan. 1, 1923. He began his career as a vibraphonist with Gillespie (1945); after work with other musicians, organized the Milt Jackson Quartet with John Lewis, Ray Brown, and Kenny Clarke (1951); a year later it was renamed the Modern Jazz Quartet; became crucial to the synthesis of cool jazz and classical music known as Third Stream. The Quartet disbanded in 1974 but was reformed in the 1980s.

Jacquet de la Guerre, Elisabeth, b. Paris, 1659; d. there, June 27, 1729. Born into a family of professional musicians and instrument makers, she evinced talent at an early age; favored by the court of Louis XIV, completed her education under the patronage of the King's mistress Mme. de Montespan. A fine keyboardist, she married Marin de La Guerre, organist of several Paris churches. Her works include an opera, a (lost) ballet, keyboard suites, trio and violin sonatas, sacred and secular cantatas, and a (lost) Te Deum.

Jacquet, (Jean Baptiste) Illinois, b. Broussard, La., Oct. 31, 1922. He grew up in Houston; learned to play soprano and alto saxophones; after working in local jazz circles, played with L. Hampton, Cab Calloway, and Count Basie. He led his own bands from 1946; played bassoon from 1956; became a featured performer at jazz festivals; and continues to perform.

Jagdhorn, Jägerhorn (Ger.). Hunting horn.

Jagdstück (Ger.). Hunting piece.

Jägerchor (Ger.). Hunters' chorus.

Jagger, Mick (Michael Philip). See ⇒Rolling Stones.

jaleo (Sp., wild confusion). Spanish dance for 1 performer, in 3/8 time and moderate tempo.

jaltarang. Set of porcelain cups partially filled with water; tuned according to the intervallic scheme of a specific Indian raga; played with wooden sticks.

jam session (from *jamboree*). Informal get-together in which jazz or popular musicians improvise freely, regardless of professional standing. Sometimes musicians take turns; at other times, several performers "blow" simultaneously, producing an effect not unlike early New Orleans era of jazz (or the extremes of free jazz).

jamboree. Informal, noisy gathering of music makers, indulging in singing and playing in the country-western tradition. If the abbrev. *jam* is used, the gathering will more likely involve jazz musicians.

James, Harry (Hagg), b. Albany, Ga., Mar. 15, 1916; d. Las Vegas, July 5, 1983. His father was a trumpeter, his mother a trapeze artist with the Mighty Hagg Circus; took up the drums at 4 and trumpet at 8; became leader of a circus band at 12. He played trumpet in local dance bands; after playing with Ben Pollack's band (1935–37), joined Benny Goodman's orch. (1937–39), and was featured in *One O'Clock Jump, Sing, Sing, Sing* and *Life Goes to a Party*.

James's virtuoso technique was striking; he could blow dolce and even dolcissimo, but when needed blew with deafening fortissimo; could perform ultrachromatic glissandos. He started his own band (1939), producing a sensation with his trumpet version of *You Made Me Love You* (1941); subsequently a leading figure of the big band era, producing many hits and touring extensively; one hit, *Ciribiribin*, became his theme song. Several of his recordings, including the humbly titled *Wild About Harry*, sold in millions, even when shellac, from which 78-rpm disks were manufactured, was being rationed for wartime use.

In 1943 James married Betty Grable, pinup girl *ne plus ultra* of the G.I.s in World War II; she was the 2nd of his 4 wives. Faithful to the slogan that "the show must go on," wracked with the pain of fatal lymphatic cancer, he continued to perform; played his last gig in Los Angeles 9 days before his death; as he was dying, he observed, "Let it just be said that I went up to do a one-nighter with Archangel Gabriel."

Janáček, Leoš, b. Hukvaldy, Moravia, July 3, 1854; d. Moravská Ostrava, Aug. 12, 1928. His father was a choirmaster; at age 11 he was sent to Brno to join the choir at the Augustinian Queen's Monastery; went to the German College in Brno (1869–72); subsequently taught and served as choirmaster of the men's chorus, Svatopluk (1873–77); studied organ at the Prague Organ School (1874–75). He conducted the Beseda Choral Soc. in Brno (1876–88); pursued studies at the Leipzig Cons., studying music history with O. Paul and composition with L. Grill (1879–80).

After further composition lessons with Franz Krenn at the Vienna Cons., Janáček became 1st director of the new Brno Organ School (1881); engaged in scholarly activities; ed. *Hudební Listy* (Music Bulletins, 1884–86); worked with František Bartoš in collecting Moravian folk songs. He taught music at Brno Gymnasium (1886–1902); retired from the Brno Organ School (1919); taught master classes in Brno (1920–25). Despite his heavy teaching activity, he composed diligently, showing a special preference for operas.

Janáček's style of composition underwent numerous transformations, from German Romanticism to bold dissonant combinations. He was greatly influenced by Russian musical nationalism with its realistically inflected vocal writing; visited St. Petersburg and Moscow (1896, 1902). He worked assiduously on his 3rd opera, *Její pastorkyňa* (Her Foster Daughter, 1894–1903); its melodramatic but unsentimental plot, set in mid-19th–century Moravia, features 2 brothers competing for the love of Jenůfa (a semi-innocent heroine), a face-slashing, infanticide, and a hallucinatory evil stepmother. After its premiere (Brno, 1904), the opera underwent several revisions and cost the composer much anguish until its long-awaited Prague premiere as *Jenůfa* (in German, 1916) put it on the operatic map.

Among other Janáček operas that attracted attention was *Mr. Brouček's Excursion to the 15th Century* (1917), an imaginary journey of a Czech Everyman to the time of the struggle mounted by followers of Jan Hus against the established church; an anthropomorphic adult fairy tale, *Příhody Lišky Bystroušky* (Adventures of the Vixen Bystrouška, known in English as *The Cunning Little Vixen*, 1921–23); and a version of K. Capek's mystery play, *Věc Makropulos* (The Makropulos Affair, 1923–25).

Janáček's interest in Russian literature was reflected in *Káťa Kabanova* (1919–21), after *The Storm* by the Russian playwright Ostrovsky, and *Z mrtvého domu* (From the House of the Dead, after Dostoyevsky, 1927–28); also composed a symphonic poem, *Taras Bulba* (after a Gogol story, 1915–18). Like most Slavic artists, writers, and composers living in the Austro-Hungarian Empire, he had a natural interest in the Pan-Slavic movement, emphasizing the common origins of Russian, Czech, Slovak, and other kindred cultures; his *Glagolitic Mass* (*Glagolská mše*, 1927), to a Latin text trans. into Old Slavonic, is typical. He lived to see the fall of the old regime and the rise of Slavic nations; showed great interest in the emerging Soviet school of composition, even though he made no attempt to join that movement; watched without prejudice the striking innovations of Stravinsky and Schoenberg, but was never tempted to experiment along those revolutionary lines. He remained faithful to his own very characteristic style; it was as the foremost composer of modern Czech music that he secured his unique place in musical history.

Janizary music (Janissary music). Military music of the Janizary guards of Turkish sultans. In the wake of the Ottoman invasion of Eastern Europe in the 16th century, this raucous, loud, and rhythmically vibrant music exercised the imagination of European writers, painters, and musicians; impressed by the physical dimensions of Turkish drums, cymbals, and the Turkish crescent, overhung with bells and jingles and crowned with a pavilion-shaped ornament. Janizary music influenced military bands in Poland, Russia, and Austria during the 18th century.

Big drums, triangles, and cymbals provided exotic color in the "oriental" operas of Gluck and Mozart; Haydn used stylized Janizary rhythms in the 2nd movement of his *Military Sym.* (no. 100); the famous finale of Mozart's Piano Sonata in A Major, K. 331 is marked *Rondo alla turca*. Some piano manufacturers made special attachments with bells and cymbals for performances of such "Turkish music," even supplying clappers to strike at the resonance board in imitation of the bass drum.

Jankó keyboard. Piano keyboard patented by the Hungarian Paul von Jankó (1856–1919) in 1882. It has 6 manuals arranged so that any given note can be struck in every other manual; a system of levers permits playing the chromatic scale with the greatest of ease by letting the fingers walk from one row to another; narrower keys made it possible for a pianist to reach the interval of a 14th with 1 hand. Despite the opportunity presented, the inventor only thought of this device in terms of standard tuning. After a brief flurry of manufacture at the turn of the century, it was overwhelmed by the resistance of those who had no desire to relearn fingerings and hand positions.

Japanese music. The music of East Asia, and Japan in particular, is based on ancient pentatonic modes, most commonly of the "major key" type (C, D, E, G, A) or "minor key" type (E flat, G flat, A flat, B flat, and Db flat), both without semitones; however, there exists an equally ancient Japanese scale with semitones (E, F, A, B, C), a "Phrygian type." Japanese folk music is typically homophonic—a single voice accompanied by a string instrument—with no harmonic connotations of the Western sort; but its cultivated traditional music admits consonance and dissonance. Like most Asian music, Japanese music is melodic and rhythmic, with harmonic extension formed by intervallic couplings in 2nds, 4ths, and 5ths. Consecutive progressions, especially 3rds or in 6ths, are virtually nonexistent; rhythmic patterns possess great variety; ancient Japanese music does not follow any binding meter. Consonances distribute pentatonic intervals in open harmony; dissonances are produced by semitones in close formation.

String instruments, wind instruments, and percussion are well-represented in Japanese music; most metamorphosed from ancient Chinese and Korean instruments imported in medieval times. The most common instruments are the *koto*, a zither with 13 silk strings; *shamisen* (samisen), a long-necked 3-stringed lute; and the *biwa*, a short-necked, pear-bodied flat lute with 4 strings; also used are bamboo flutes (e.g., *shakuhachi*), small cymbals, bells, and a great variety of drums, especially hourglass types. There are large solo repertoires; the koto and shakuhachi have fiercely opposing schools of performance and composition. There is much chamber music, notably the *sankyoku* trio from the late 19th century (shakuhachi, koto, shamisen). Most Japanese chamber and orch'l music uses heterophonic textures to varying degrees; a koto duet can approach a modified contrapuntal texture.

The oldest Japanese music still practiced is *gagaku*, orch'l music of the imperial court dating from the 8th century and still performed on imperial and other official occasions; sounds nearly monophonic, with liberal portamento. Gagaku also accompanies the dance style *bugaku*; both are considered upper-class. Most popular of popular theater forms is *kabuki* (from the 17th century), a stylized drama with a large musical ensemble, featuring singing and dancing with heavily costumed male actors playing all roles; kabuki in turn came out of *noh*, an even more stylized theater imported from China in the 14th century, with 2 actors and small ensemble of 3 drums and flute. Theatrical music and songs are subtle and complex in structure, tonality, and rhythm; like the action, the freely gliding speech occurs at a slow pace. Several puppet-theater genres categorized as *bunraku* feature a narrator-singer accompanied by shamisen. The dance genre *butoh* responds to postwar moral uncertainty through radical choreography and electronic music scores.

The collision of Western and Japanese music resulted in several aesthetic approaches. Early 20th-century Japanese composers attempted to imitate Western music, led by the European-educated Kosaku Yamada (1886–1965), 1st Japanese composer to compose Western-type operas, syms., chamber music, and songs. Later composers sought to mesh the 2 worlds or to create styles based solely on Japanese traditional music; these included Y. Akutagawa, K. Toda, I. Dan, Y. Irino, Y. Matsudaira, J. Yuasa, Y. Mamiya, Y. Takehashi, A. Miyoshi, Mayuzumi, and Takemitsu. The Japanese-American composer Paul Chihara employs Japanese modes in an advanced sophisticated manner; others borrow musical and theatrical elements of Japanese culture (especially noh). Melodramatic operas on Japanese subjects such as Puccini's *Madama Butterfly* are unacceptable in Japan as perversions of national culture; *The Mikado* by Gilbert and Sullivan was banned until 1945, when it was performed by the American Army of Occupation. (The ban has since returned.) A more effective synthesis of East and West is found in Sondheim's musical *Pacific Overtures*, concerning the end of Japanese isolationism in the 19th century.

Jaques-Dalcroze, Émile, b. Vienna (of French parents), July 6, 1865; d. Geneva, July 1, 1950. His parents moved to Geneva (1873); he completed his courses at the Univ. and Cons. there; returned to Vienna to study under Fuchs and Bruckner, then went to Paris to work with Delibes and Fauré; returned to Geneva as theory instructor at the Cons. (1892). Emphasizing rhythm in his teaching, he insisted that his pupils beat time with their hands; this led him to devise a series of movements for the entire body; with French psychologist Edouard Claparide, worked out special terminology and refined his practice into a system, which he called *eurhythmics*; when his method was refused regular course status at the Cons., he resigned; established a school at Hellerau, near Dresden (1910); because of World War I the school was closed (1914); returned to Geneva and founded the Inst. Jaques-Dalcroze; interest in his system led to further school openings (e.g., London, Berlin, Vienna, Paris, N.Y., Chicago). Aside from his pedagogical innovations, he commanded respect as a composer of marked originality and fecundity of invention; his works reveal the depth of his feeling for Swiss folk music; writings include *Le Coeur chante: Impressions d'un musicien* (Geneva, 1900); *Méthode Jaques-Dalcroze* (Paris, 1906–17); *Le rhythme, la musique et l'éducation* (Paris, 1919); *Souvenirs, notes et critiques* (Neuchâtel, 1942); *La Musique et nous: Notes de notre double vie* (Geneva, 1945).

Jarábe (Sp.). Characteristic Mexican dance in combined 3/4 and 6/8 meter; resembles the mazurka's rhythm in its emphasis on the middle beat; a similar dance song from the Mexican province of Yucatán is called the *jarana*.

Jarnach, Philipp, b. Noisy, France, July 26, 1892; d. Bornsen, near Bergedorf, Dec. 17, 1982. He studied with Risler (piano) and Lavignac (theory) at the Paris Cons. (1912–14); at the outbreak of World War I, went to Zurich; taught at the Cons. His meeting with Busoni was decisive on his musical development; became an ardent disciple and completed Busoni's last opera, *Doktor Faust*, premiered in Dresden (1925). (Anthony Beaumont has made a 2nd completion based on additional sketches.) Jarnach wrote music criticism for the *Berliner Börsencourier* (1922–27); became a German citizen (1931); prof. of composition at the Cologne Cons. (1927–49) and the Hamburg Cons. (1949–70). His music reflects his devotion to Busoni's ideals; distinguished by impeccable craftsmanship, it lacks individuality. He participated in the German modernist movement between the world wars, when many of his works were performed at music festivals. Despite the occasional revival of his music, he remains best known as the man who put *Doktor Faust* in his (resting) place.

Jarre, Maurice, b. Lyons, Sept. 13, 1924. He studied electrical engineering; attended Honegger's course in composition at the Paris Cons.; best known as a film composer; won an Academy Award for *Lawrence of Arabia* (1963) and *Lara's Theme* from *Dr. Zhivago* (1965); other scores include *The Year of Living Dangerously* (1983); *Witness* (1985); *The Mosquito Coast* (1986); *Gorillas in the Mist* (1988); *Dead Poet's Soc.* (1989); *Almost an Angel* (1990); has written several concert works for orch., but these are comparatively obscure.

Jarreau, Al, b. Milwaukee, Mar. 12, 1940. He graduated in psychology from the Univ. of Iowa; went to San Francisco, working as a rehabilitation counselor; began singing in local clubs, garnering a following with a flexible vocal technique and warm, even ecstatic performance style; gained particular attention with the album *We Got By* (1975); toured Europe (1976), becoming one of the most popular jazz singers of the day; other successful albums include *Look to the Rainbow* (1977) and *All Fly Home* (1978). His audience changed substantially in the mid-1980s; his songs and singing became less adventurous, diluted by a mundane disco beat; albums from this period include *High Crime* (1984) and *L Is for Lover* (1986).

Jarrett, Keith, b. Allentown, Pa., May 8, 1945. He studied at the Berklee School of Music in Boston; plunged into the N.Y. jazz scene, becoming prominent in the Charles Lloyd quartet (1966–70); worked with Miles Davis (1970–71); toured with a trio and as a solo artist. He made a sensationally popular recording of solo improvisations, *The Köln Concert* (1975); established a reputation as a jazz virtuoso. From the early 1980s he made appearances as a classical pianist, specializing in modern works (especially Bartók); he is closely associated with Lou Harrison's Piano Concerto (1987), of which he made a critically acclaimed recording.

Järvi, Neeme, b. Tallinn, June 7, 1937. He graduated in percussion and choral conducting from the Tallinn Music School; studied conducting with Mravinsky and Rabinovich at the Leningrad Cons. (1955–60); pursued postgraduate studies; captured 1st prize in the Accademia di Santa Cecilia conducting competition in Rome (1971). In Tallinn, he served as music director of the Estonian State Sym. Orch. (1960–80) and the Estonian Opera Theater (1964–77); since that time, he has served as principal guest conductor of the City of Birmingham (England) Sym. Orch. (1981–84); music director of the Göteborg (Sweden) Sym. Orch. (1982); principal conductor of the Scottish National Orch. in Glasgow (1984–88); music director of the Detroit Sym. Orch. (1990) His guest conducting engagements have taken him to most principal music centers of the world; gained notice for championing rarely performed northern European composers (Berwald, Gade, Svendsen, Stenhammar, Tubin).

jazz. Term covering several musical styles of African-American origin, including New Orleans/Dixieland; Chicago; big band/swing; bebop; cool/Third Stream; free jazz; fusion; neotraditionalism; usually characterized by improvisation and an unlimited variety of dotted or syncopated melodic rhythms against a steady duple or quadruple meter, producing a synthesis known as "swing." Jazz melodies are set in major keys modified by blue notes (lowered 3rds and 7ths, also 5ths). The basis for these notes has been attributed to the overtone series and major-minor equivocation, cultural factors aside; but the syncopated melody often departs widely from its harmonic connotations.

The word "jazz" 1st appeared in print in a sports column in 1913, and was associated with enthusiastic performance; it may have been a gambling term. The next verified appearance of the word was in *Variety* (1916), reporting a Chicago concert of "jass" music; another item in *Variety* followed with the spelling "jaz" (1917); this inconsistency of spelling continued unabatedly; an item in the *Victor Record Review* (1917) stated: "Spell it Jass, Jas, Jab or jazz—nothing can spoil a Jass band. . . . It has sufficient power and penetration to inject new life into a mummy, and will keep ordinary human dancers on their feet till breakfast time"; it was around this time that the Victor Co. issued the 1st

jass recording—*Dixieland Jass One-Step*. Despite attempts to trace "jazz" to American sexual slang or African languages, there seems little reason to doubt the straightfoward description of the word when it 1st appeared in print; the entire history of the word is thoroughly covered in an article by Peter Tamony in *Jazz, A Quarterly of American Music* (Oct. 1958).

Historically, jazz evolved from ragtime, a syncopated American music that flourished around the turn of the 20th century; parallel to that development was the blues, a ballad form suffused with bittersweetness and remembered sufferings of African-Americans, as expressed earlier in Negro spirituals; the flattened blue notes get their name by association with this style and remain paramount features. Other early stylistic contributions to jazz were work songs and field hollers of rural black America; street cries of peddlers in urban black America; and, most important for its orchestration, the New Orleans marching band, most famous for its participation in funeral processions—necessary since burial inside New Orleans's delta city limits was and remains banned for health reasons.

Dixieland jazz, with its group improvisations and lack of drums, was never recorded, except for a pale imitation called the Original Dixieland Jazz Band (from 1917). Already at this early stage, jazz improvisers produced the collective impact of glossolalia, tonolalia, or rhythmolalia; in the hands of geniuses it became a thing of great beauty. When New Orleans officials closed the jazz club district in an effort to clean up prostitution, musicians moved to Chicago in the early 1920s; ensembles led by Armstrong, King Oliver, and Jelly Roll Morton were smaller, emphasizing star improvisers while allowing other band members brief solos in a 12-bar (blues) or 16/32-bar (song) structure; instrumentation involved cornet (later trumpet), trombone, clarinet, piano, guitar, tuba or double bass, and drums; this style was emotionally "hot," much like its predecessor.

A new jazz era dawned in the late 1920s with a riotous explosion of swing, indicating a highly rhythmic manner of performance rather than structural form; the jazz ensemble grew into the big band, averaging between 10 and 15 players. True composition and orchestration (or arranging) joined improvisation as a component of jazz; musicians like Ellington, Basie, Henderson, Strayhorn, Redman, Benny Carter, and others created their own personal "sounds," fusing compositional proclivities with the skills of individual band members (Ellington was especially sensitive to this). Big bands of Benny Goodman and Glenn Miller emphasized their role as dance bands; Ellington and Strayhorn alternated between "hot" dance music and a more reflective "cool" style that sought to portray the African-American experience. Parallel to these developments, piano jazz evolved into stride in the 1920s; the old ragtime bass became more aggressive dynamically and harmonically; melodic lines grew more subtly syncopated; tempos increased. While this style (played by Tatum and Waller) continued to be popular, the 1930s saw the onslaught of boogie-woogie, with a bass line transformed into a raucous "walking" ostinato, arpeggiated, often in the 12-bar blues harmonic pattern; melody lines became more bluesy than modal; the wartime transition into rhythm and blues was not far in the future.

A new style, bebop (rebop, bop), appeared in the 1940s; it is a highly paradoxical style, with tonal and structural underpinnings recalling the 1920s, emphasizing simple blues progressions or interpretations of popular standards. But the improvising itself reached lightning speeds and, in the hands of Charlie Parker and other exceptional musicians, expanded harmonic horizons melodically and harmonically with linear chromaticism and added chord notes; even more striking was its unrepressed and heated emotionality, often seen as reflecting of rising black anger against Jim Crow segregation, disrespect, and financial desperation. Finally, the sound of the saxophone—brassy yet mellow, capable of raucous exuberance or gentle poetry—went to the fore of jazz melodic instruments; by the 1950s it had virtually replaced the clarinet.

If bebop had a negative result, it was the dividing of jazz's audience into listener-dancers (who wanted to get up and move) and listener-aficionados (who were content to sit down); this divide continued over the next decades. In the 1950s, cool jazz, spearheaded by M. Davis, G. Evans, G. Mulligan, C. Baker, J. Lewis, and G. Schuller (inventor of the Third Stream), used various sized ensembles and made composition a major factor once more; the music was even less appropriate for dancing, full of the laid-back quality of the "beat generation." In reaction, bebop simplified its harmonic range, slowed its tempo, and borrowed rhythm-and-blues and gospel piano styles to create hard bop, far more successful commercially than its predecessor.

In the 1960s free jazz referred to both an extreme improvisational style, with few if any structural demands, and to a freeing of jazz aesthetics from having to stick to a single style; unfortunately, this presented a divided front to an already smaller audience; many who might have danced to big bands went for African-American rhythm and blues and its Anglo-American outcropping, rock 'n' roll. One set of solutions developed in the 1970s: jazz-rock and jazz-funk, both examples of the hybrid called fusion, combining the instrumentation and relative accessibility of popular music with the extemporaneous freedom and rhythmic panache of jazz. Often, bass ostinato figures served to support freewheeling improvisation; in other cases, the metric shifts of art-rock (borrowed from Stravinsky) played with the momentum. In recent years the work of Wynton Marsalis and others has emphasized a "classic repertoire" approach to jazz, both as way to explore accomplishments in this multifaceted category of music and regain larger audience through more traditional jazz styles.

jazz-funk (jazz-rock). Popular styles of the late 1960s and 1970s that merged the electrified instrumentation and directness of rock with the more subtle improvisatory, rhythmic, and harmonic features of jazz. *Art-rock*, another aberration of the time, contributed shifting meters; funk and rock provided bass ostinatos.

Jefferson Airplane. San Francisco folk-rock band of the mid-1960s that survived numerous personnel and name changes through three decades; its most memorable (if not most commercial) lineup (1966–70) featured Paul Kantner (b. San Francisco, Mar. 12, 1942), vocals & guitar; Marty Balin (b. Martyn Jerel Buchwald, Cincinnati, Jan. 30, 1942), vocals & guitar; Grace (Wing) Slick (b. Chicago, Oct. 30, 1939), vocals, piano, & recorder; Jorma Kaukonen (b. Washington, D.C., Dec. 23, 1940), lead guitar & vocals; Jack Casady (b. Washington, D.C., Apr. 13, 1944), bass; Spencer Dryden (b. N.Y., Apr. 7, 1943), drums. The band originally formed around folksinger

Balin and guitarists Kantner and Kaukonen; Casady joined soon thereafter. Slick, already known as lead singer of another San Francisco band, joined in 1966, replacing the original female vocalist. Alexander "Skip" Spence, a guitarist, played drums on the Airplane's 1st album; replaced by a full-time drummer, Spencer Dryden

At first, Balin and Kantner were the principal songwriters; Kaukonen soon added his instrumentals and blues-based songs. Slick contributed her own compositions, including the Lewis Carroll-inspired *White Rabbit*, and her ex-husband's rock ballad *Somebody to Love*; these were the early band's only hits. The group became one of the mainstays of "album-oriented rock," a newly successful radio format; made a successful European tour (1968); its material veered between restrained but off-kilter ballads and politically minded rock songs, a split most apparent on this particular group's final and best album, *Volunteers* (1969). Kaukonen and Casady formed Hot Tuna (1969) to perform traditional blues; played and recorded in this form through the 1970s. Kantner expressed his showing interest in politicized science fiction through the overblown *Blows Against the Empire* (1970), which featured most of the group (minus Balin, who would soon leave the band) and such luminaries as Jerry Garcia, David Crosby, and Graham Nash. After Balin and Dryden's departures, the shuffle of personnel began; the most notable was fiddler "Papa" John Creach (1917–94); but soon personal discord, musical differences, and pregnancy wore the members down; despite forming its own vanity label, Grunt (1972) and releasing various individual projects, the original band had disintegrated by that time.

Kantner and Slick reorganized the group, rechristened Jefferson Starship (1974), adding veterans (David Freiberg, John Barbata, Pete Sears) and a newcomer (guitarist Craig Chaquico); Balin rejoined, 1st as a guest (on the hit *Caroline*), then officially (1975); the band produced several successful albums (*Red Octopus, Spitfire, Earth*) before Balin and Slick (the latter with alcoholism) left (1978). The band regrouped with a new lead singer (Mickey Thomas, 1979) and more hit albums; the pattern continued as Slick returned (1981) and even when Kantner left (1984) and sued for his trademark; the group, now simply Starship, continued successfully, with more hit singles (*We Built This City*) and albums; Slick was gone by 1988. A year later the "original" Jefferson Airplane (minus Dryden) reunited for a modest-selling reunion album; Kantner, Casady, and Creach led various personnel in a group known as Jefferson Starship—The Next Generation (1992); Balin rejoined in 1994, Slick a year later, but it had little success.

Jefferson, "Blind" Lemon, b. Couchman, Tex., c. July 1897; d. Chicago, c. Dec. 1930. His 1st name was Lemon; afflicted by poor eyesight from childhood, supported himself by singing in the streets of Texas towns and cities; went to Dallas (1917); formed a blues duo with Leadbelly; there is no evidence to support the latter's claim that he was the former's "lead boy" at the time. After touring the South, Jefferson settled in Chicago (1925); made several historic blues recordings, many featuring his own songs; these performances represent a "Texas blues" style akin to Leadbelly's; his *Matchbox Blues* was covered by numerous artists; an adapted version by Carl Perkins was recorded by the Beatles, with Ringo Starr singing.

Jenkins, Leroy, b. Chicago, Mar. 11, 1932. He was mostly musically autodidact; played violin in a local Baptist church and picked up theory rudiments while teaching in a Chicago school; affiliated with the Assoc. for the Advancement of Creative Musicians; studied with Bruce Hayden at Florida A&M Univ. He is well-known for atonal improvisations on violin and viola, in a bluesy, romantic style inspired by Charlie Parker; groups he has led or co-led include the Creative Construction Co., Revolutionary Ensemble, Leroy Jenkins Trio, Leroy Jenkins Quintet, and Sting (no relation to the English rock musician). His finest recordings, often of his own music, include *Space Minds, New Worlds, Survival of America; The Legend of Al Glatson; Solo Concert; For Players Only; Manhattan Cycles;* and *Leroy Jenkins' Sting: Urban Blues.*

Jennings, Waylon (Arnold), b. Littlefield, Tex., June 15, 1937. He took up guitar in his youth; played bass in Buddy Holly's band (1958–59); missed the plane ride that killed Holly by losing a coin toss). He went to Nashville (1965); turned out several albums; starred in the film *Nashville Rebel* (1966). Disdaining the "Nashville sound," he was a major figure in the promotion of "outlaw" country music, or "redneck rock," with his album *Ladies Love Outlaws* (1972); won a wide audience with *Honky Tonk Heroes* (1973), *This Time* (1974), *The Ramblin' Man* (1974), *Dreamin' My Dreams* (1975), and *Wanted: The Outlaws* (with Willie Nelson, Tompall Glaser, and Jessi Colter, 1976).

Jericho trumpets. Chapter 6 of the Book of Joshua relates how the Lord instructed Joshua to destroy the city of Jericho by having 7 priests blow 7 ram-horn trumpets while the people "shouted with a great shout"; the noise created was such that the walls of Jericho "fell down flat" and let Joshua's army in, whereupon they proceeded to slay everyone and everything in sight (except a local harlot who hid Joshua's spies). Modern acousticians doubt whether a wall could be brought down in this manner; even rock musicians using electric amplifiers could never do more than deafen or frighten peaceful bystanders; then again, the Lord may have been more involved than the story tells.

Jerusalem, Siegfried, b. Oberhausen, Apr. 17, 1940. He began his career as a bassoonist; member of the Stuttgart Radio Sym. Orch. (1972–77); began vocal studies in Stuttgart with Hertha Kalcher (1972); appeared in minor roles at the Württemberg State Theater (from 1975); sang Lohengrin in Darmstadt and Aachen (1976) and at the Hamburg State Opera (1977). That year he made his Bayreuth debut as Froh; returned as Lohengrin, Walther, Parsifal, and Loge (in the Solti-Hall mounting of the Ring cycle, 1983); made his 1st appearance at the Berlin Deutsche Oper as Tamino (1978); became a leading member of the company; made his U.S. debut with the Metropolitan Opera in N.Y. as Lohengrin (1980); made his British debut at London's Coliseum as Parsifal and his Covent Garden debut as Erik (both 1986); appeared at the Vienna State Opera, Milan's La Scala, and the Paris Opéra.

Jeté (Fr.). In string playing, throw the upper part of the bow on the string, letting it bounce in rapid even notes down to the end of the bow; virtuosos can fit 8 quick notes in 1 jeté.

jeu (Fr.). 1. Style of playing. 2. (*jeu d'orgue*) An organ stop. *Grand jeu* or *plein jeu*, full organ or power; *demi-jeu,* half power.

jeu de timbres (Fr.). Glockenspiel.

Jew's harp (jaw's harp). Small instrument comprising a rigid iron frame with a thin vibratile metal tongue; the frame is held between the teeth and the metallic tongue is plucked with the finger; despite the relatively loud twang of the tongue, a high range of pitches is audible, determined by changing the shape of the mouth. The instrument is found throughout the world, from East Asia to northern Europe to Appalachia.

jig (from Fr. *giguer,* move rapidly to and fro). Lively English dance, related to the hornpipe; it is a country dance, with a great variety of steps and gestures, in a fast tempo and in 6/8 or 12/8 (there is also a 9/8 type called a "slip jig"). The dance was very popular among the lower economic classes; one writer described it as "only fit for Fantastical, and Easie-Light-Headed People"; it penetrated the English court and became a favorite of the aristocracy; but died out at the end of the Elizabethan era, replaced by the more courtly and dignified French gigue; it survives as traditional dance and music to this day in the Anglo-Irish-Scottish culture.

Jingling Johnny (Johnnie). Turkish crescent.

jitterbug. 1. American jazz dance of the 1930s and 1940s; it attempted to match the musical qualities of swing with appropriate physical gestures and floor movements, including slow dig steps, quicksteps, and sidesteps (shuffles); exported to Europe by American armed forces in World War II. 2. A dancer of this dance.

jive. 1. Outdated term describing the nature of jazz performance; a *jive session* displays coordinated glossolalia or tonolalia, spontaneous and conversational in realization; jam sessions are conducted in the musical language of jive; semantic distinctions and confluences are illustrated by the lyrics of a song recorded in 1940: "Romp it, stomp it, ride it too./Jam it, jump it, jive it through." 2. Dance steps of the jitterbug.

jodel. Yodel.

Joel, Billy (William Martin), b. N.Y., May 9, 1949. Prematurely sophisticated, he joined The Echoes, which turned into the more belligerent Hassles; when the group disintegrated, Joel teamed up with drummer Jon Small to form Attila; they recorded 1 unsuccessful album. Joel then organized a supporting band and recorded his 1st solo album, *Cold Spring Harbor* (1972), for Family Productions; it did not sell either; after an internecine feud with the label, Joel signed with Columbia Records, moved to Los Angeles, and began marching on the gold-paved road to neon-lighted success.

Joel's 1st album for his new label included the title ballad, *Piano Man* (1973), his 1st hit; as he moved from suburban protest to more personal themes, and as his style fused easy listening with elements borrowed from Paul McCartney, he progressed on the periodic table, receiving a certified platinum award for *Just the Way You Are* from *The Stranger* (1978); other smash albums followed, including *52nd Street* (Grammy Awards for best album and male pop vocalist of 1979); numerous hit singles included *My Life*, *Big Shot*, *Honesty*, *Say Goodbye to Hollywood*, and *You May Be Right*; toasted his generating musical force with *It's Still Rock 'n' Roll to Me*. In the 1980s he remained prolific; notable albums of this era include *The Nylon Curtain*, *An Innocent Man*, *The Bridge*, and *Kohupt*, a 2-record set of live concerts in Moscow and Leningrad (1987); in the early 1990s he issued the less successful *River of Dreams*.

Johansen, Gunnar, b. Copenhagen, Jan. 21, 1906; d. Blue Mounds, Wis., May 25, 1991. He made his debut at age 12 in Copenhagen, where he studied with V. Schioler; went to Berlin at 14; became part of the Busoni circle; studied piano further with Fischer and F. Lamond; completing training with Petri at the Hochschule für Musik (1922–24). He toured Europe (1924–29); settled in the U.S., pursuing an active concert career; presented a series of 12 historical piano recitals, encompassing works from Frescobaldi to Stravinsky, in San Francisco, Chicago, and N.Y. in the late 1930s; held the newly created position of artist-in-residence at the Univ. of Wisconsin at Madison (1939–76). He excelled in works of transcendental difficulty; played and recorded the complete solo piano works of Liszt and Busoni (including the Bach-Busoni transcriptions) and the complete solo clavier works of Bach; a composer of fantastic fecundity, his oeuvre includes 3 piano concertos, 31 piano sonatas, and 515 improvised piano sonatas recorded directly onto tape (1952–82). He was a friend and patron of Partch and other musicians.

John, Elton (born Reginald Kenneth Dwight), b. Pinner, Middlesex, Mar. 25, 1947. He played the piano in early childhood; won a fellowship to the Royal Academy of Music in London at age 11; after dropping out of school at age 17, played jazz piano in London clubs and pubs; joined a rock group bearing the appellation Bluesology; derived his stage name by borrowing Elton from saxophonist Elton Dean, John from the name of the band's singer, "Long" John Baldry. John developed an effective piano-based pop style; most of his best-known songs set the occasionally awkward but generally workable lyrics by Bernie Taupin.

For all his musical aspirations, John formed lines of communication with kindred souls through other means; in concert, he affected bizarre behavior and wore multicolored attires and psychedelic eyeglasses; captivated American rock audiences on a major tour (1971); was the most popular rock artist in the U.S. during the 1970s. He gave 4 concerts in Leningrad and 4 in Moscow (1st Western rock star to play in that city) before thousands of screaming, delighted Soviet fans (1979); this event was documented in the film *From Elton with Love*. Among his most successful albums are *Madman across the Water*, *Honky Chateau*, *Don't Shoot Me I'm Only the Piano Player*, *Goodbye Yellow Brick Road*, *Blue Moves*, *Ice On Fire*, *Single Man*, and *Too Low for Zero*. He performed at the funeral of Diana, Princess of Wales (1997), reworking an older song about Marilyn Monroe (*Candle in the Wind*).

Johnson, "Bunk" (William Geary), b. New Orleans, Dec. 27, 1889?; d. New Iberia, La., July 7, 1949. As a youth he played trumpet with Dixieland bands; toured in minstrel, circus,

and jazz aggregations; lost all his teeth due to pyorrhea and stopped playing. He was "rediscovered" working in sugarcane fields by "hot jazz" aficionados (1937); fitted with dentures, he resumed his career, enjoying belated fame during a Dixieland revival; made his 1st recording (1942); performed in N.Y., Boston, and Chicago.

Johnson, Edward, b. Guelph, Ontario, Aug. 22, 1878; d. there, Apr. 20, 1959. He sang in concert and oratorios before going to N.Y. (1899); studied with M. von Feilitsch; appeared in the U.S. premiere of Oscar Straus's *A Waltz Dream* (1907); completed his studies with R. Barthelemy in Paris (1908) and V. Lombardi in Florence (1909); made his operatic debut as Andrea Chenier at Teatro Verdi in Padua (1912); appeared at Milan's La Scala, where he sang Parsifal at its 1st complete Italian production (1914).

Johnson made his U.S. debut as Loris in *Fedora* at the Chicago Grand Opera (1919); remained on its roster until 1922; made his Metropolitan Opera debut in N.Y. as Avito in *L'amore dei tre Re* (1922); sang there until 1935, when he became its general manager, guiding its fortunes until retirement (1950); became an American citizen (1922), but maintained a close connection with Canada. He was particularly esteemed for such roles as Romeo, Tannhäuser, Don Jose, Siegfried, Canio, and Pelléas; created leading roles in Deems Taylor's *The King's Henchman* (1927) and *Peter Ibbetson* (1931) at the Metropolitan.

Johnson, Frank (Francis), b. probably on the island of Martinique, 1792; d. Philadelphia, Apr. 6, 1844. He settled in Philadelphia (c. 1809), organizing a band and dance orch; after touring England (1837), led promenade concerts throughout the U.S., featuring his own works; in Philadelphia, his concerts included the participation of prominent white artists, an unheard-of practice at this time. His compositions have been newly publ. and recorded.

Johnson, James P(rice), b. Brunswick, N.J., Feb. 1, 1891; d. N.Y., Nov. 17, 1955. He studied piano with his mother; played in N.Y. and Atlantic City nightclubs; later led his own bands and appeared as soloist. The leading Harlem stride pianist of his day, he was a gifted composer; among his pieces are *Caprice Rag* (1914); *Harlem Strut* (1917); *Carolina Shout* (1925); *Snowy Morning Blues* (1927); *You've Got to Be Modernistic* (1930); and *Fascination* (1939); wrote stage and orch'l works.

Johnson, "J. J." (James Louis), b. Indianapolis, Jan. 22, 1924. He began playing the piano at age 9, the trombone at 14; toured with Clarence Love and Isaac "Snookum" Russell (1941–42); attracted attention in Benny Carter's orch. (1942–45). He worked with Count Basie in N.Y. (1945–46) and did stints with others there; toured Korea, Japan, and the South Pacific with Oscar Pettiford for the USO (1951). After a hiatus, he toured with trombonist Kai Winding in the duo Jay and Kai; formed his own quintet (1956–60) and toured Europe; after working with Miles Davis (1961–62), led a quartet and sextet; turned increasingly to composition, moving to Los Angeles to work in film and television (1970); returned to Indianapolis (1988). He was one of the pioneer figures of the bop era. Among his works are *Poem* for Brass (1956), *Sketch* for Trombone and Band (1959), *El camino real* (1964), *In Walked Horace* (1966), and *Concepts in Blue* (1980).

Johnson, Robert, b. Hazlehurt, Miss., *c.* 1912; d. Greenwood, Miss., Aug. 16, 1938. He played at dance parties, worked with other musicians, and made recordings in Texas (1936–37). Johnson played guitar and sang within the Delta blues tradition, influenced by Charley Patton, Son House, and jazz guitarist Lonnie Johnson (no relation). He borrowed songs within the oral tradition, but created a unique and powerful style, featuring taut and penetrating singing, strong rhythmic guitar sense, agitated slide technique, walking bass, and personal themes of fatalistic torment. His versatile acoustic guitar playing created an unprecedentedly full sound; Johnson was apparently very interested in the newly developed electric guitar, but no evidence exists of his having played one. After his death Chicago blues musicians kept his music and name alive; a widespread revival began in the 1960s, when white blues and rock musicians integrated Johnson's legacy, including *Crossroads, Hellbound on My Trail, Dust My Broom, Kind Hearted Woman, Terraplane Blues, Love in Vain, Ramblin' on My Mind,* and *If I Had Possession Over Judgment Day.*

Johnston, Ben(jamin Burwell), b. Macon, Ga., Mar. 15, 1926. He took degrees from the College of William and Mary in Williamsburg, Va. (A.B., 1949), Cincinnati Cons. of Music (M.Mus., 1950), and Mills College in Oakland, Calif. (M.A., 1953); held a Guggenheim fellowship (1959–60). He worked with Partch (1949–50), who confirmed his instinctive belief in just intonation. He taught at the Univ. of Illinois in Urbana (1951–83); composed in equal temperament during the 1950s, but turned to just intonation in the 1960s; expanded Partch's approach to intonation; unlike Partch, he has focused on traditional instruments, e.g., strings (10 quartets, 1959–96) and retuned microtonal piano (*Sonata/Grindlemusic,* pf; 1965; Suite, 1978; *12 Partials,* with flute, 1980; *The Demon Lover's Doubles,* with trumpet, 1985). Johnson's flair for the dramatic and ironic is omipresent in his stage works, including *Gertrude, or Would She Be Pleased to Receive It?* (1956), *Gambit for Dancers and Orch* (with M. Cunningham, 1959); *Carmilla* (1970); *Calamity Jane to Her Daughter* (1989). Other works include vocal pieces: *Night* (R. Jeffers, 1955); *Ci-Gît Satie* (1967); *Mass* (1972); *Sonnets of Desolation* (Hopkins, 1980), *Songs of Loss* (Donne, 1986), *Quietness* (Rumi, 1996); and chamber music: Septet for winds and strings (1956–8); Sonata for violin and cello (1960); the remarkable *Knocking Piece* for 2 percussionists and piano lid (1962).

Jolson, Al (Asa Yoelson), b. Srednike, Lithuania, May 26, 1886; d. San Francisco, Oct. 23, 1950. His family emigrated *c.* 1894 to the U.S.; he began a career in vaudeville, burlesque, and minstrel shows; first attracted attention in N.Y. in Lew Dockstader's Minstrels (1909); engaged as a leading performer at the Winter Garden (1911); introduced Gus, his famous blackface character in *Whirl of Society* (1912). He starred in the 1st feature sound film, *The Jazz Singer* (1927), winning immortality with his rendition of *My Mammy;* appeared in several other films; returned to Broadway in *The Wonder Bar* (1931) and *Hold On to Your Hats* (1940). Towards the end of his life he appeared on radio and television; his voice was used in the films *The Jolson Story* (1946) and *Jolson Sings Again* (1949). He popularized many songs, including *Swanee; California, Here I Come; Toot, Toot, Tootsie!; April Showers; Rockaby Your Baby with a Dixie Melody; Let Me Sing and I'm Happy; There's a*

Rainbow 'Round My Shoulder; and *Sonny Boy.* He was married to Ruby Keeler (1928–39).

Jones, Booker T., b. Memphis, Sept. 12, 1944. He founded Booker T. and the MGs (Memphis Group), lighting the rock firmament with their smash hit *Green Onions* (1962), but their primary role was to back artists recording at the Stax label in the 1960s and 1970s. He received a degree in applied music from Indiana Univ.; fortunately, this academic distinction did not kill off his natural gift; his records sold well; among his hits were *Soul Limbo* (1968) and *Time Is Tight* (1969); co-authored the popular semi-blues song *Born Under a Bad Sign* (1965).

Jones, Elvin (Ray), b. Pontiac, Mich., Sept. 9, 1927. He performed with groups in Pontiac and Detroit; played in bands during his U.S. army service (1946–49); returned to Michigan, then went to N.Y. (1956); played with J. J. Johnson, Donald Byrd, Powell, Rollins, and Getz. He joined John Coltrane's group (1960–66); acquired renown for imaginative drumming; subsequently led his own groups; toured in the U.S., Europe, South America, and Asia. Hank (Henry) Jones and Thad(deus Joseph) Jones are his brothers.

Jones, George, b. Saratoga, Tex., Sept. 12, 1931. He began playing guitar when he was 9. He recorded his 1st hit song, *Why, Baby, Why* (1955); gained fame with *Window Up Above* (1961), *She Thinks I Still Care* (1962), and *We Must Have Been Out of Our Minds* (1963). Comfortable in both honky-tonk and sentimental ballad styles, he has survived subjection to the worst excesses of the "Nashville sound." He was married to the country star Tammy Wynette (1969–75); after their divorce, they continued recording together; he returned to bolstering his image as a heartbroken heavy drinker with *If Drinking Don't Kill Me (Her Memory Will);* continues to produce good recordings (*I Don't Need Your Rockin' Chair*); Elvis Costello paid him tribute with an album of country-western covers, *Almost Blue* (1981).

Jones, Hank (Henry), b. Vicksburg, Miss., July 31, 1918. He went as a child to Pontiac, Mich.; began his piano training; as a teenager, performed with groups in Michigan and Ohio; went to N.Y. (1944); worked with "Hot Lips" Page, C. Hawkins, Eckstine, and C. Parker. He accompanied Ella Fitzgerald (1948–53); staff musician with CBS (1959–76), touring during this period; pianist and conductor for the Broadway musical *Ain't Misbehavin',* based on Waller's music; made innumerable recordings. Elvin (Ray) Jones and Thad(deus Joseph) Jones are his brothers.

Jones, Jo(nathan), also called "Kansas City Jo" and "Papa Jo"; b. Chicago, Oct. 7, 1911; d. N.Y., Sept. 3, 1985. Raised in Alabama; studied saxophone, trumpet, and piano before mastering the drums; joined Count Basie's band (1934), remaining off and on until 1948. He established a distinctive style, stressing all 4 beats of the bar and diversifying it with a wire-brush technique on the high hat cymbal. He traveled to Europe with E. Fitzgerald and O. Peterson (1957); then led his own groups; appeared in several films, including *Jammin' the Blues* (1944), *Born to Swing* (1973), and *Last of the Blue Devils* (1979).

Jones, "Philly Joe" (Joseph Rudolph), b. Philadelphia, July 15, 1923; d. there, Aug. 30, 1985. He studied piano with his mother, saxophone with Jimmy Oliver, and drums with James Harris; played with local groups. Making his way to N.Y., he played with Zoot Sims, Lee Konitz, and Miles Davis; went to Europe (1967–72); formed the jazz-rock group Le Gran Prix (1975); toured the U.S.; appeared at N.Y.'s Carnegie Hall (1980).

Jones, Quincy (Delight, Jr.), b. Chicago, Mar. 14, 1933. He took up the trumpet at 14; studied with Clark Terry (1950); played in L. Hampton's band (1951–53); performer-arranger for D. Gillespie's touring band in the Near East (1956–57); subsequently toured in Europe with his own big band (1957–60). After returning to the U.S. he was an artist and repertoire (A & R) man for Mercury Records; became vice president (1964); founded his own label; composed *Stockholm Sweetnin'* (1956), *Evening in Paris* (1956), *The Quintessence* (1961), *Walking in Space* (1969), and a series of *Soundpieces*. He won several Grammy Awards, notably as producer of recording and video productions of *We Are the World*, which raised millions of dollars for famine-relief efforts in Africa (1985); composed the score for and co-produced the film *The Color Purple*.

Jones, Sissieretta (born Matilda Sissieretta Joyner), known as the "Black Patti" (refering to Adelina Patti); b. Portsmouth, Va., Jan. 5, 1868; d. Providence, R.I., June 24, 1933. She studied at the New England Cons. and privately with L. Capianni and Scongia in London; made her debut at N.Y.'s Steinway Hall (1888); began touring from 1890; gave concerts in the West Indies, North America, and Europe. She gained prominence after appearances at the Grand Negro Jubilee at N.Y.'s Madison Square Garden and a command performance for President B. Harrison at the White House (1892); sang at the Pittsburgh Exposition and the Chicago World's Columbian Exposition (1893). N.Y.'s Metropolitan Opera considered her for roles in *Aida* and *L'Africaine*, but racist and conservative attitudes precluded such appearances. She was the principal soprano of the vaudeville troupe known as Black Patti's Troubadours (1896–1915), with whom she toured around the world; starred in its operatic "kaleidoscope," a medley of staged operatic arias; also sang art songs and popular ballads.

Jones, "Spike" (Lindley Armstrong), b. Long Beach, Calif., Dec. 14, 1911; d. Los Angeles, May 1, 1965. He played drums as a boy; led a school band. His recording of a satirical song, *Der Führer's Face* (1942), made him infamous; he then toured the U.S. with his multitalented City Slickers, whose instrumentation included a washboard, Smith and Wesson pistol, anti-bug flit guns in E flat, doorbells, anvils, glass-breaking hammers, and a live goat trained to bleat rhythmically; introduced the Latrinophone (a toilet seat strung with catgut); he and his ensemble offered a Musical Depreciation Revue to their audiences. He retired when the wave of extravaganza that had carried him to commercial success had already subsided (1963). In his heyday he was called the "King of Corn"; any piece was fair game for his slapstick approach; for every Jonesian *William Tell Overture* there was a *Cocktails for Two* in his own image.

Jones, Thad(deus Joseph), b. Pontiac, Mich., Mar. 28, 1923; d. Copenhagen, Aug. 20, 1986. He taught himself trumpet at about 13; appeared professionally with his brother Hank and Sonny Stitt; worked with various dance and show bands, then joined his brother Elvin in Billy Mitchell's quintet in Detroit

(1950–53). He worked with Mingus (1954–55); was a featured soloist and arranger with Count Basie's orch. (1954–63); also appeared with Monk and Mulligan. With drummer Mel Lewis, he formed a big band (1965); toured the U.S. and Europe, including a smashing visit to the USSR (1972); left the band (1979) and settled in Denmark, organizing his own big band, the Thad Jones Eclipse; active as an arranger and composer with Danish Radio; returned to the U.S. briefly to take charge of Basie's orch. (1985). His best-known composition is *A Child Is Born*, a jazz classic.

Jones, Tom (real name, Thomas Jones Woodward), b. Pontypridd, June 7, 1940. He sang, as most Welshmen do, with a natural feeling for melody; dropped out of school and began playing drums and singing in British pubs; his big chance came when he was heard by Gordon Mills, who decided to propel him into fame (after abbreviating his name). His greatest asset was lung power, outscreaming anyone in the field; wore extremely tight pants, whose protuberances excited middle-aged women; thus equipped, successfully invaded the U.S. in the 1960s; by the late 1980s his fame had largely dissipated, his performances relegated to the nostalgia circuit.

jongleur (Fr.; from Lat. *joculator*, maker of jokes; Sp. *juglares*). Medieval entertainer employed by royalty and aristocracy to amuse with songs and jests; the term corresponds to the English *juggler*, suggesting that the jongleur also performed acrobatic acts. By the 12th century the jongleurs were known as *ménestriers*, those who "administered" to traveling troubadours and trouvères; that term became *ménestrels* (Eng. *minstrels*); English minstrels were also called *gleemen*.

Joplin, Janis (Lyn), b. Port Arthur, Tex., 1943; d. Los Angeles, Oct. 4, 1970. She ran away from home, delving into San Francisco's bohemian life; joined the rock group Big Brother and the Holding Company as lead vocalist (1966); won acclaim for her rendition of Big Mama Thornton's *Ball and Chain* at the Monterey International Pop Festival (1967); her passionate, raspy, and bluesy wailing established her as an uninhibited representative of the younger generation. After recording *Cheap Thrills* (1967) she left Big Brother; formed her own backup group, the Kozmic Blues Band (1968); appeared in such esoteric emporia as Boston's Psychedelic Supermarket, Chicago's Kinetic Playground, Los Angeles's Whisky A-Go-Go, and N.Y.'s Fillmore East. She produced *I Got Dem Ol' Kozmic Blues Again Mama* (1968) and *Pearl* (1970, with the Full-Tilt Boogie Band); arrested in Tampa, Fla. for hurling porcine epithets at a policeman (1969), further endearing her to her public. The Southern Comfort Distillery Co. gave her a fur coat as thanks for habitually consuming a quart of their product at performances; but her satirical *Mercedes Benz* was ironically turned into a theme song for the eponymous vehicle long after her death of a heroin overdose. Her biggest hit was the posth. *Me and Bobby McGee*.

Joplin, Scott, b. probably near Marshall, Tex., Nov. 24, 1868; d. N.Y., Apr. 1, 1917. He taught himself piano in Texarkana; studied music with a local German musician; left home at 17 and went to St. Louis, earning his living by playing in local emporia. He moved to Chicago, drawn by the musical prospects of the 1893 World's Columbian Exposition; went to Sedalia, Mo. (1896); studied music at George Smith College, an all-black

institution. His 1st music publications (1895) were typically genteel, maudlin songs and marches; distinctive success came with
the *Maple Leaf Rag* (most famous of all rags, 1899), named after
a local dance hall; the sheet-music edition sold so well that he
settled in St. Louis to devote himself exclusively to composition;
wrote a ragtime ballet (*The Ragtime Dance*, 1902) and a ragtime opera, *A Guest of Honor* (now lost; probably performed in
1903).

Joplin went to N.Y. (1907); continued his career as composer
and teacher. Still ambitious, he wrote a 2nd opera, *Treemonisha*,
to his own libretto (dealing with an eponymous black baby girl
found abandoned under a tree by one Monisha); he completed
the score (1911), producing it in concert form without success
(1915); the work was revived almost 60 years later, in an orchestration by T. J. Anderson, with a performance in Atlanta (1972);
Schuller later did his own orchestration. This was too late for its
composer; in his last years he lamented at not achieving the
recognition he felt his music merited; suffering from syphilis, he
went insane and died shortly afterward in a state hospital.

Despite Joplin's ambitious attempts to "justify" ragtime by forcing it into European bottles, he achieved his greatest artistic
successes with the smaller-scaled indigenous dance form of the
piano rag, of which he wrote around 50; in addition to the 2
operas, he left a few songs, waltzes, and marches. Some of his
titles mesh commercial triviality with implications of more serious
intent: *Sycamore*, "A Concert Rag" (1904); *Chrysanthemum*,
"An Afro-American Intermezzo" (1904); *Sugar Cane*, "A Ragtime
Classic 2-Step" (1908); *Fig Leaf Rag*, "A High Class Rag" (1908);
Reflection Rag, "Syncopated Musings" (1917); in the words of a
noted historian, his rags are "the precise American equivalent, in
terms of a native dance music, of minuets by Mozart, mazurkas
by Chopin, or waltzes by Brahms."

From the late 1960s on, new publications and recordings of his
music and its skillful use in *The Sting* (1974) brought Joplin
unprecedented popularity and acclaim; the 1902 rag *The
Entertainer* was a best-seller in 1974, becoming nearly as well
known as the *Maple Leaf Rag*; in 1976 he was awarded posth.
recognition by the Pulitzer Prize Committee.

Jordan, Louis, b. Brinkley, Ark., July 8, 1908; d. Los
Angeles, Feb. 4, 1975. He took up the clarinet and alto saxophone; from 1929, played with Chick Webb and others; formed a
"jump" (jive) band in N.Y., the Tympany 5 (1939); recorded as
a singer with Armstrong, Ella Fitzgerald, and other luminaries; in
later years toured England (1962) and Asia (1967 and 1968).
Among his biggest hits are *Is You Is Or Is You Ain't My Baby?*
(1944), *Choo Choo Ch'boogie* (1946), *Ain't Nobody Here But
Us Chickens, Open the Door Richard* (1947), and *Baby It's
Cold Outside* (with Fitzgerald, 1949).

joropo. Characteristic dance of Venezuela, in 3/4 time, with
strongly syncopated melody against a steady bass.

Josquin Desprez (Des Prez). Desprez (Des Prez),
Josquin.

jota (Sp.). National dance song of northern Spain from the 17th
century, in rapid triple time (like a fast waltz); usually played on
guitar, mandolin, and castanets. Composers such as Glinka,

Rimsky-Korsakov (*Capriccio Espagnole*), and Liszt (*Rhapsodie
espagnole, c.* 1863) composed them.

juba. Syncopated dance step, generated in the Caribbean in the
18th century and popular among African-Americans in the South.
A rapid rhythmic beat accentuated by slapping hands and legs is
known as "patting juba."

jubilus. In Roman Catholic liturgical chant, an often lengthy
group of ornaments sung on the last syllable of the word *alleluia*,
suggesting the intended jubilation in a manner approaching glossolalia.

jug. Earthen pitcher used in African-American traditional
music; blowing into it produces a low, hollow tone.

jug band. 20th-century African-American traditional ensemble featuring found objects such as jugs, bones, and washboards,
along with strings, harmonica, kazoo, and winds in various combinations; it is associated with medicine shows and novelty songs.

**Jullien, Louis (George Maurice Adolphe Roch
Albert Abel Antonio Alexandre Noé Jean
Lucien Daniel Eugène Joseph-le-brun Joseph-
Barême Thomas Thomas Thomas-Thomas
Pierre Arbon Pierre-Maurel Barthélemi Artus
Alphonse Bertrand Dieudonné Emanuel Josué
Vincent Luc Michel Jules-de-la-plane Jules-
Bazin Julio César),** b. Sisteron, Apr. 23, 1812; d. Paris,
Mar. 14, 1860. A bandmaster's son, he went to Paris (1833);
studied composition with Le Carpentier and Halévy; could not
maintain the necessary discipline; began composing light dances,
of which the waltz *Rosita* attained enormous if transitory popularity in Paris. He left the Cons. (1836); engaged as conductor of
dance music at the Jardin Turc; attempting to launch a musical
journal, he accumulated carelessly contracted debts that compelled him to leave France (1838).

Jullien went to London; conducted summer concerts at the
Drury Lane Theatre (1840) and winter concerts with an enlarged
ensemble of instrumentalists and singers (1841); opened a
series of "society concerts," presenting large choral works (e.g.,
Rossini's *Stabat Mater*) and movements from Beethoven's syms.;
engaged Berlioz to conduct at the Drury Lane (1847); became
insolvent (1848); attempted to recoup his fortune by organizing
a "concert monstre" with 400 players, 3 choruses, and 3 military
bands; gave 3 such concerts in London (1849). He then composed an opera, *Pietro il Grande*, produced at his own expense
at Covent Garden (1852); used the pseudonym Roch Albert for
his spectacular pieces (e.g., *Destruction of Pompeii*); publ.
dance music (*Royal Irish Quadrille*, etc.) as himself.

Jullien was engaged by P. T. Barnum (1853) for a series of U.S.
concerts in the U.S. At N.Y.'s Crystal Palace, he staged a simulated
conflagration for his *Fireman's Quadrille* (1854). Despite his
eccentricities, however, he possessed a genuine interest in musical progress; at his U.S. concerts he included several works by
American composers, notably the *Santa Claus Sym.* by W. H. Fry
and chamber music by G. F. Bristow. Returning to London, he
duplicated previous managerial failures (1854); went to Paris
(1859); promptly arrested for debt and spent several weeks in
prison; died a few months later in an insane asylum.

just intonation. System of tuning based on arithmetic relationships between string lengths, expressed in ratios. Unaccompanied voices or open strings tend to be in just (or pure) intonation; instruments can either be refingered, retuned, adapted, or newly built to play just relationships. Like other intonations, just intonation affects both the horizontal (melodic) and vertical (harmonic) elements of pitch; it has unique qualities (e.g., true consonance and expansion of consonance beyond the triad) and limitations (training instrumentalists to play an potentially unlimited number of ratios, thus permitting modulation).

Ancient Greek theory used just intonation; this approach probably persisted into the 2nd millennium A.D. There have been a few attempts to accommodate just intonation over the centuries, sometimes through expanded equal temperament (e.g., 31 tones to the octave); only in the 20th century were a few musicians willing to challenge the equally tempered chromatic scale by building or adapting instruments and then borrowing or elaborating the theory and notation needed to compose in just tuning (Partch, Johnston, Lou Harrison, many West Coast composers). See also ⇒acoustics.

organization of notes, intervals, and durations is supplemented by aleatory techniques, some of which are derived from linguistic permutations, random patterns of lights and shadows on exposed photographic film, and other seemingly arcane processes; in his hyperserial constructions he endeavors to create a universe of theatrical arts in their visual, aural, and societal aspects.

kalimba. See ⇒lamellaphones.

Kalinnikov, Vasili (Sergeievich), b. Voin, near Mtzensk, Jan. 13, 1866; d. Yalta, Jan. 11, 1901. He studied in Orel; enrolled at the Moscow Cons. (1884), had to leave for lack of funds; studied bassoon at the Music School of the Moscow Phil. Soc., which provided free tuition. He played bassoon in theater orchs.; studied composition with A. Ilyinsky and Blaramberg; composed his 1st work, the sym. poem *The Nymphs* (1889); later works included *The Cedar and the Palm* (1897–98), music for A. K. Tolstoy's *Czar Boris* (Moscow, 1899), prelude to *In the Year 1812* (1899–1900), songs, and piano music. His most successful work was the 1st Sym. in G Minor (1895); a 2nd sym. in A major (1898) was less so.

Kálmán, Emmerich (Imre), b. Siofok, Oct. 24, 1882; d. Paris, Oct. 30, 1953. He studied with Koessler at the Royal Academy of Music in Budapest; wrote music criticism, won the Franz Josef Prize (1907); became a successful composer of operettas and cabaret songs in Vienna. He went to Paris (1939), then the U.S. (1940); became an American citizen (1942); returned to Europe (1949). His most successful operettas were *Die Csárdásfürstin* (1915), *Gräfin Mariza* (1924), and *Die Zirkusprinzessin* (1926).

Kalomiris, Manolis, b. Smyrna, Dec. 26, 1883; d. Athens, Apr. 3, 1962. He studied piano with Bauch and Sturm, composition with Grädener, and music history with Mandyczewski at the Cons. of the Gesellschaft der Musikfreunde in Vienna (1901–1906); went to Russia, where he taught piano at a private school in Kharkov. He settled in Athens; taught at the Cons. (1911–19); founder-director of the Hellenic Cons. (1919–26) and the National Cons. (1926–48). He was greatly esteemed as a teacher; publ. several textbooks on harmony, counterpoint, and orchestration; wrote music criticism. Kalomiris was the protagonist of Greek musical nationalism; almost all his works are based on folk-song patterns; many are inspired by Hellenic subjects. His harmonies and instrumentation reflect the Russian school of composition, with an influx of lush Wagnerian sonority; compositions include operas, orch'l works, chamber music, piano music, choruses, and songs.

kamānja (from Pers. *kamān,* bow; Arab. *kamānja*). Persian spike fiddle, dating from the end of the 1st millennium A.D., with a round- or heart-shaped body, long neck and spike, and 2 or 4 strings tuned (singly or in pairs) a perfect 4th apart.

kamarinskaya. Russian peasant song dance, usually for men only, set in quick 3/4 time; the text is often of humorous character.

Kammer (Ger.). Chamber; court. *Kammermusik,* chamber music; *Kammermusiker,* court musician; *Kammerkantate,* chamber cantata; *Kammerton* (Ger., chamber tone), standard pitch for 18th-century chamber music performance.

Kabalevsky, Dmitri (Borisovich), b. St. Petersburg, Dec. 30, 1904; d. Moscow, Feb. 14, 1987. His family moved to Moscow when he was 14; received his musical education at the Scriabin Music School (1919–25); studied music theory with G. Catoire; entered the Moscow Cons. (1925), studying composition with Miaskovsky and piano with Goldenweiser; appointed instructor in composition there (1932); became full prof. (1939). He was an effective and innovative pedagogue; elected head of the Commission of Musical Aesthetic Education of Children (1962); became president of the Scientific Council of Educational Aesthetics in the USSR (1969); became honorary president of the International Soc. of Musical Education (1972). As pianist, composer, and conductor he made guest appearances in Europe and the U.S.

Kabalevsky's music is paradigmatic of the Soviet Russian school of composition; his melodic writing is broadly diatonic, invigorated by energetic rhythmic pulse; while basically tonal, his harmony is rich in euphonious dissonance. He wrote prolifically in all musical genres; his operas reflected both lyrical and dramatic aspects of the librettos, mostly based on subjects faithful to the tenets of socialist realism; his instrumental writing was functional and idiomatic. He is best known for 4 symphonies (1932, 1934, 1934, 1956); the opera *Colas Breugnon* (1938); orch'l suite *The Comedians* (1940); Requiem for voices and orch. (Moscow, 1963); an oratorio, *A Letter to the 30th Century* (1970); 24 Preludes for Piano (1943); piano music for children.

kachampa. Peruvian war dance in rapid 2/4 time, marked by vigorous accents.

Kadenz (Ger.). 1. Cadence. 2. Cadenza.

Kagel, Mauricio (Maurizio Raúl), b. Buenos Aires, Dec. 24, 1931. He studied in Buenos Aires with J. C. Paz and A. Schiuma; attended philosophy and literature courses at the Univ. of Buenos Aires; became associated with Agrupación Nueva Musica (1949); choral director at the Teatro Colón (1949–56). He obtained a stipend from the Academic Cultural Exchange with West Germany and went to Cologne (1957), where he made his permanent home; was a guest lecturer at the International Festival Courses for New Music in Darmstadt (1960–66); gave lectures and demonstrations of modern music in the U.S. (1961, 1963); was Slee Prof. of composition at the State Univ. of N.Y. at Buffalo (1964–65). He became director of the Inst. of New Music at the Rheinische Musikschule in Cologne (1969); prof. at the Cologne Hochschule für Musik (1974). As a composer he evolved an extremely complex system in which an intricate serial

Kancheli, Giya (Alexandrovich), b. Tbilisi, Aug. 10, 1935. He studied composition at the Tbilisi Cons. (1959–63); appointed to its faculty (1970). His inspiration is nourished by Caucasian melos, with its quasi-oriental fiorituras and deflected chromatics imparting a peculiar aura of lyric introspection; but his treatment of this material is covertly modernistic and overtly optimistic, especially in sonoristic effects. Among his works are 7 syms. (1967, 1970, 1973, 1974, 1977, 1979–81, 1985); *Mourned by the Wind* for viola and orch. (1989); the oratorio *Bright Sorrow* (1985); other orch'l, instrumental, choral, and stage works; incidental music and film scores.

Kander, John (Harold), b. Kansas City, Mo., Mar. 18, 1927. He studied piano with W. Labunski; took courses with Beeson, Luening, and D. Moore at Columbia Univ; wrote an unsuccessful musical, *The Family Affair* (1962). In 1962 he teamed up with lyricist Fred Ebb (b. N.Y., Apr. 8, 1932), with whom he produced the songs *My Coloring Book* and *I Don't Care Much,* followed with the Broadway musical *Flora, the Red Menace* (1965), a vehicle for Liza Minnelli; it was followed by their smash hit *Cabaret* (1966), winner of the Tony and Drama Critics Awards; later made into a film with Minelli (1972); later shows were *The Happy Time* (1968), *Zorba* (1968), *Chicago* (1975), *The Act* (1977), *Woman of the Year* (1981), and *The Rink* (1984).

Kantate (Ger.). Cantata.

kantele. Psaltery, dating from at least the 11th century; national instrument of Finland; mentioned in the *Kalevala*. The instrument has a trapezoidal shape; originally with 5 horsehair strings tuned to the scale G, A, B flat, C, D, it now has a variable number of metal strings; held in the lap and played with bare fingers. Among the numerous related instruments in Eastern Europe are the Russian gusli, Estonian *kannel*, Latvian *kokle*, and Lithuanian *kanklès*.

Kantner, Paul. See ⇒Jefferson Airplane.

Kapelle (Ger., chapel; from Lat. *cappella*). 1. Private orch. or choir, especially in Central European courts. 2. Any orch.

Kapellmeister (Ger., chapel master; Fr. *maître de chapelle*). Conductor of orch. or choir, especially at Central European courts; in charge of music at that court (e.g., Haydn), although some employers divided the role into sacred and secular masters.

Kapellmeistermusik (Ger., conductor's music). Derisive term applied to orch'l compositions by pedantically respectable conductors devoid of musical spark. Von Bülow, Furtwängler, and others wrote such music; attempts have been made to revivify them. Mahler, known primarily as conductor, had his syms. dismissed by critics as Kapellmeistermusik; posterity ruled otherwise. (No doubt Bruckner's works would have been called *Organistmusik* by its detractors.)

Karajan, Herbert von, b. Salzburg, Apr. 5, 1908; d. Anif, near Salzburg, July 16, 1989. He was of Greek–Macedonian extraction, whose family name was orig. Karajannis. His father, a medical officer, played clarinet; his brother was a professional organist. Herbert began training as a pianist, taking lessons with F. Ledwinka at the Salzburg Mozarteum; attended conducting classes given by its director, Bernhard Paumgartner; went to Vienna, pursuing training at a technical college; took piano lessons; entered the Vienna Academy of Music as a conducting student of Clemens Krauss and Alexander Wunderer. He made his conducting debut with a student orch. there; shortly afterward, made his professional debut with the Salzburg Orch. (1929); engaged as conductor of the Ulm Stadttheater (1929–34); went to Aachen; made conductor of the Stadttheater, subsequently serving as Generalmusikdirektor (1935–42). He conducted his 1st performance with the Berlin Phil., the orch. that would become the chosen vehicle for his art (1938); made his debut with the Berlin Staatsoper later that year, conducting *Fidelio*; a performance of *Tristan und Isolde* soon thereafter led the *Berliner Tageblatt* to announce "das Wunder Karajan." His ability to absorb, interpret, and transmit the essence of a piece to an audience became his most signal characteristic; conducted all scores from memory, including the entire *Ring des Nibelungen*. His burgeoning fame as a master of both opera and sym. led to other European engagements; conducted opera at La Scala in Milan (1938); made guest appearances in Belgium, the Netherlands, and Scandinavia; became conductor of sym. concerts at the Berlin Staatsoper Orch. (1939).

Another, darker side to Karajan's character revealed an insensitivity, opportunism, and failure to act wisely on his own behalf. He became fascinated by the ruthless organizing solidity of the National Socialist party; registered in the Salzburg office of the Austrian Nazi party (1933); soon joined the German branch (Ulm). He used his memberships to further his career; but his marriage (1942) to a woman of one-quarter Jewish blood led to pressure from party officials seeking Aryan purity among its number. He waited out the war and avoided Nazi consequences; had to be officially denazified by the Allied army of occupation (1947). Yet, despite his regrets and apologies, he never ceased personifying the all-powerful Germanic conductor of the old school; his 1st performances in the U.S. with the Berlin Philharmonic were met by protests (Carnegie Hall, N.Y.).

Karajan was characteristically self-assertive and unflinching in his personal relationships and numerous conflicts with managers and players; a close relationship with the Vienna Sym. Orch. (from 1948) ended in 1958. His association with the Philharmonia Orch. of London (1948–54) did more than anything to reestablish his career after World War II, but in later years he disdained that relationship. When Furtwängler, conductor of the Berlin Phil., died (1954), he was asked to lead its 1st U.S. tour; he insisted that he be duly elected Furtwängler's successor. Protesters appeared for his appearance at N.Y.'s Carnegie Hall with the orch. (1955), but his Nazi past did not prevent the orch.'s musicians from electing him conductor during their visit to Pittsburgh; upon their return to Germany, the West Berlin Senate ratified the musicians' vote.

Karajan dominated European musical life as no other conductor had ever done; he cultivated a rich chevelure of graying hair, harmonizing with his romantic podium manner. Greatly successful in the music business, he made about 800 sound and video recordings, selling millions of copies. In addition to his prestigious Berlin post, he served as artistic director of the Vienna Staatsoper (1956–64) until resigning in a bitter dispute with its general manager; artistic director of the Salzburg Festival (1957–60); thereafter closely associated with it; artistic adviser of the Orch. de Paris (1969–71). He consolidated his positions in Berlin and Salzburg; conducted the Berlin Phil. in Beethoven's 9th Sym. at the a concert inaugurating the orch.'s magnificent new hall, the Philharmonie (1963); organized his own Salzburg Easter Festival (1967), which became one of the world's leading musical events; renegotiated his contract with the Berlin Phil. and named conductor-for-life (1967); made a belated Metropolitan Opera debut in N.Y., conducting *Die Walküre* (1967). He went on frequent tours of Europe and Japan with the Berlin Phil.; took the orch. to the Soviet Union (1969) and China (1979).

Karajan celebrated his 30th anniversary as conductor of the Berlin Phil. (1985) and his 60th anniversary as a conductor (1988); conducted the New Year's Day concert of the Vienna Phil., televised to millions on both sides of the Atlantic (1987); made his last U.S. appearance, conducting the Vienna Phil. at N.Y.'s Carnegie Hall (1989); announced his retirement from the Berlin post, citing failing health; dictated an autobiography to Franz Endler just before his death.

karatāli. Indian circular wooden clappers with short handles; each clapper is held in 1 hand and clicked together; known throughout many different Indian cultures and language groups (e.g., Sanskrit, Hindustani, Bengali, Marathi, Punjabi).

katabasis (Grk., retreat, descent). In the doctrine of affects, descending melodic passages illustrating states of mind such as depression and humiliation; settings of texts relating to falls from grace and descents into hell are examples of katabasis.

Kavafian, Ani, b. Istanbul, May 10, 1948. She came with her family to the U.S. (1956); took violin lessons with A. Zerounian (1957–62) and Mischakoff (1962–66) in Detroit; entered the Juilliard School of Music in N.Y., receiving further instruction from I. Galamian and members of the Juilliard Quartet (M.A., 1972). She made her debut at Carnegie Recital Hall in N.Y. (1969); her European debut followed in Paris (1973); appeared as soloist with leading orchs.; served as artist-member of the Chamber Music Soc. of Lincoln Center (from 1980); gave duo performances with her sister Ida Kavafian. She taught at the Mannes College of Music (from 1982) and the Manhattan School of Music and Queens College of the City Univ. of N.Y. (from 1983).

Kavafian, Ida, b. Istanbul, Oct. 29, 1952. She came with her family to the U.S. (1956); took up violin studies with A. Zerounian in Detroit at age 6; later received instruction from Mischakoff; entered the Juilliard School in N.Y. (1969); continued training with Shumsky and Galamian (M.A., 1975); won the Vianna da Motta International Violin Competition in Lisbon (1973) and the silver medal at the International Violin Competition of Indianapolis (1982). She co-founded the chamber group Tashi (1973), subsequently touring with it; made her N.Y. recital debut (1978) and European debut in London (1982); played in duo concerts with her sister Ani Kavafian; was a member of the Beaux Arts Trio.

Kavatine (Ger.). Cavatina.

Kay, Hershy, b. Philadelphia, Nov. 17, 1919; d. Danbury, Conn., Dec. 2, 1981. He studied cello with F. Salmond and

orchestration with R. Thompson at the Curtis Inst. of Music in Philadelphia (1936–40); went to N.Y.; began a fruitful career as arranger of Broadway musicals and ballets. He orchestrated several Bernstein theater works: *On the Town* (1944), *Peter Pan* (incidental music, 1951), *Candide* (1956; rev. 1973), *Mass* (1971), and the Bicentennial musical *1600 Pennsylvania Avenue* (1976); his last Bernstein arrangement was *Olympic Hymn* (1981). Other orchestrations for Broadway include *The Golden Apple* (1954), *Once upon a Mattress* (1958), *Juno* (1958), *Milk and Honey* (1961), *110 in the Shade* (1963), *Coco* (1969), *A Chorus Line* (1975), *On the 20th Century* (1977), *Evita* (1979), *Carmelina* (1979), and *Barnum* (1980). He made numerous arrangements for the N.Y.C. Ballet, among them *Cakewalk* (1951, after Gottschalk), *Western Sym.* (1954, after cowboy songs and fiddle tunes), *The Concert* (1956, after Chopin), *Stars and Stripes* (1958, after Sousa), *Who Cares?* (1970, after Gershwin), and *Union Jack* (1976, after popular British music); made numerous arrangements for other companies. He also orchestrated Gottschalk's *Grand Tarantella* for piano and orch. (1957) and completed orchestrating Robert Kurka's opera *The Good Soldier Schweik* (1958).

Kay, Ulysses Simpson, b. Tucson, Ariz., Jan. 7, 1917; d. Englewood, N.J., May 20, 1995. He received his early music training at home; on the advice of his uncle King Oliver, he studied piano; in 1934, enrolled at the Univ. of Arizona at Tucson (Mus.B., 1938); studied composition at the Eastman School of Music in Rochester, N.Y. with Hanson and B. Rogers (M.M., 1940); attended Hindemith's classes at Tanglewood (1941–42). After serving in the U.S. Navy (1942–45), he studied with Luening at Columbia Univ. (1946–49); went to Rome as recipient of the American Rome Prize (1949–52); employed as a consultant by Broadcast Music Inc. in N.Y. (1953–68); taught at Boston Univ. (1965) and the Univ. of Calif., Los Angeles (1966–67); appointed prof. of music at the Herbert H. Lehman College in N.Y. (1968); became distinguished prof. (1972); retired in 1988. His music follows a distinctly American idiom, with particular rhythmic intensity, while avoiding ostentatious ethnic elements; pursues a moderately advanced harmonic and contrapuntal idiom, marked by prudentially euphonious dissonances; his instrumentation is masterly. His compositions include operas, a ballet, orch'l works (notably *Markings*, in memory of Dag Hammarskjöld, 1966), chamber and solo works, band music, choral pieces, songs, and film scores, including *The Quiet One* (1948).

Kaye, Sammy, b. Lakewood, Ohio, Mar. 13, 1910; d. Ridgewood, N.J., June 2, 1987. He graduated from Ohio Univ.; learned to play clarinet and alto saxophone; organized his own band, gaining notice in a coast-to-coast radio broadcast (1935); scored his 1st hit with the title song from the film *Rosalie* (1937); after appearing in N.Y. (1938), became one of the most popular swing bandleaders; hosted the *Sunday Serenade* radio show; later appeared on television. During a career of some 50 years he made more than 100 recordings, among them *The Old Lamp-Lighter, Harbor Lights, Remember Pearl Harbor, I Left My Heart at the Stage Door Canteen*, and *Walkin' to Missouri.*

kazachok (from Turk. *kasak*, Cossack). Popular Caucasian and Ukrainian dance; a couple dance in a lively 2/4, it was also a popular ballroom dance in the 19th century.

kazoo (Fr., *mirliton*). Toy instrument consisting of a short tube with membranes at each end, into which the player hums, producing a curiously nasal tone; also known, in the 17th century, as a *flûte-eunuque*.

keck (mit Keckheit; Ger.). Boldly, confidently.

Kempff, Wilhelm (Walter Friedrich), b. Juterbog, Nov. 25, 1895; d. Positano, Italy, May 23, 1991. He studied piano with his father; at age 9, entered the Berlin Hochschule für Musik; studied composition with R. Kahn and piano with Heinrich Barth; attended the Univ. of Berlin. In 1916 he began his concert career; made the 1st of many appearances with the Berlin Phil. (1918); toured throughout Europe, South America, and Japan, featuring improvisation as part of his programs. He directed the Stuttgart Hochschule für Musik (1924–29); gave annual courses in Positano (from 1957); made his London (1951) and American debuts (in N.Y., 1964).; concertized well past his 80th birthday. Kempff epitomized the Classic tradition of German pianism, eschewing flamboyance in his performances of Mozart, Beethoven, Schubert, and other.

Kennedy, Nigel (Paul) b. Brighton, Dec. 28, 1956. He was born into a family of cellists; studied violin under Dorothy DeLay at the Juilliard School in N.Y. (1972); made his London solo debut with the Philharmonia Orch. (1977); performed throughout his homeland and on the Continent; made his 1st tour of the U.S. (1985). His interests range over the fields of jazz, rock, and pop music; is closely associated with Grappelli; has led his own rock group. His repertoire extends from Bach to Ellington; has also played Walton's Viola Concerto.

Kepler, Johannes, b. Weil der Stadt, Württemberg, Dec. 27, 1571; d. Regensburg, Nov. 15, 1630. He is best known as an astronomer, mathematician, and optical scientist. He also explored Pythagorean concepts of harmony and relationships among music, mathematics, and physics in books 3 and 5 of his *Harmonices mundi* (Linz, 1619).

Keppard, Freddie, b. New Orleans, Feb. 15, 1889; d. Chicago, July 15, 1933. He learned to play mandolin, violin, and accordion before mastering the cornet; organized the Olympia Orch. (1906); became co-leader of the Original Creole Orch. (1914), which performed in Los Angeles, Chicago, and N.Y.; moved to Chicago; played with King Oliver and Jimmie Noone; formed the Jazz Cardinals (1926). Forgotten in the last years of his life, he was a pioneer jazz figure, with few equals on cornet in his day.

Kern, Jerome (David), b. N.Y., Jan. 27, 1885; d. there, Nov. 11, 1945. He was educated in N.Y. public schools; studied music with his mother, then with P. Gallico and A. Lambert (piano) and A. Pearce and A. von Doenhoff (theory) at the N.Y. College of Music (1902–1903); studied theory and composition in Heidelberg (1903–1904). He returned to N.Y.; became pianist and salesman for a publishing firm (1905); publ. his 1st song, *How'd You Like to Spoon with Me?* His 1st stage success was the musical *The Red Petticoat* (1912); wrote more than 40 such works; his greatest success was *Show Boat*, highly innovative in story line and musical structure; it contains *Ol' Man River* and *Bill.*

Kern's musicals include *Very Good, Eddie* (1915); *Oh Boy!* (1917); *Miss 1917* (collab. with V. Herbert, 1917); *Sally* (with ballet music by Herbert, 1920; film, 1929); *Good Morning, Dearie* (1921); *Sunny* (1925; films, 1930 and 1941); *Show Boat* (1927; films, 1929, 1936, and 1951); *Sweet Adeline* (musical romance; 1929; film, 1935); *The Cat and the Fiddle* (1931; film, 1933); *Music in the Air* (1932; film, 1934); *Roberta* (1933; films, 1935 and 1952); *Very Warm for May* (1939). Among his film scores were *Swing Time* (1936); *Joy of Living* (1938); *You Were Never Lovelier* (1942); *Can't Help Singing* (1944); *Cover Girl* (1944); wrote songs interpolated into others' musicals and films, including *They Didn't Believe Me* (*The Girl from Utah*, 1914) and *The Last Time I Saw Paris* (*Lady Be Good*, 1941). Among lyricists he worked with were Oscar Hammerstein II, Dorothy Fields, Johnny Mercer, and Ira Gershwin. In 1985 Kern was immortalized in the 1st 22-cent American postage stamp.

kettledrum. Timpani.

key. 1. (Fr. *Tonalité*; Ger. *Tonalität, Tonart*; It. *tonalità*; Sp. *tonalidad*) Series of tones forming a major or minor scale, considered with reference to their harmonic relations, particularly the relation of the other tones to the tonic or keynote. *Attendant key*, in a particular key, its relative, subdominant or its relative, or dominant or its relative key; *chromatic key*, one with sharps or flats in the key signature; *extreme key*, remote key; *major key*, having a major 3rd and 6th; *minor key*, having a minor 3rd and (usually) 6th; *natural key*, with neither sharps nor flats; *parallel key*, minor key with same tonic as a given major key, or vice versa; *relative key*, major and minor keys sharing the signature; *remote key*, indirectly related key.

2. (Lat. *clavis*; Fr. *touche*, touched one; Ger. *Taste*; It., *tasto*; Sp. *tecla*; Rus. *klavisha*) Digital or finger lever in the keyboard of a piano or organ, covered with ivory or plastic; also, pedal or foot key in the organ or pedal piano. 3. (Fr. *clef*; Ger. *Klappe*; It. *chiave*; Sp. *llave*). Flat padded disk attached to a lever worked by a finger or thumb, closing the sound holes of woodwind instruments. 4. Wrest; tuning wrench.

key action. In a keyboard instrument, the entire mechanism connected with and set in action by its keys.

key-bugle. See ⇒bugle.

key chord. Tonic triad.

key harp (keyed harp; It. *clavi-arpa*). Frame harp controlled by a keyboard; strings are plucked by the pianolike mechanism; 1st reported in the 17th century.

key signature. Accidentals placed at the beginning of a composition (and each succeeding staff) indicating the prevalent tonality of the music; may be changed during the course of the piece. Discounting enharmonically equal keys, there are 12 distinct major and 12 minor keys, identifiable by the number of sharps or flats in the signature; signatures of 7 accidentals (the maximum) are not infrequent, whether sharps (e.g., C-sharp-major prelude and fugue, Bach's *Well-Tempered Clavier*, book I) or flats (opening of Stravinsky's *The Firebird*).

Changes of key signature in the course of a composition are common, but are not automatically made for each passing modulation; even the exposition of the 2nd theme group in sonata form, usually in the dominant or relative key, does not carry a signature change. In Romantic works less bound by traditional key relationships, composers often prefer to signalize modulation by changing the signature; Mahler's 6th Sym. carries this idea to its extremity by including episodes in every major and minor key, with their appropriate signature.

The raised 7th (leading tone) found in most minor-key pieces is not indicated in the key signature, but marked by a local accidental, e.g., G sharp in the key of A minor, or F double-sharp in G-sharp minor; in flat minor keys, the raised 7th results from canceling the corresponding flat to create a natural, e.g., D natural in E-flat minor. Some modern composers, including Bartók, added such accidentals to the signature (e.g., a G-minor signature carrying the extracurricular F sharp with the customary 2 flats); but this is applied more commonly to modal music. In increasingly atonal 20th-century music, the vexing problem of frequent signature changes during rapid modulations became as irrelevant as the antimacassar on the back of Victorian armchairs in modern times; signatures began disappearing from modernist scores; at the *fin de 20ème siècle*, a flickering restoration of signatures in the music of pragmatic antimodernists made its unexpected epiphany. See also ⇒key 1.

key stop. Device attached to the fingerboard of a violin to replace fingers in stopping strings; such an instrument is called a key-stop (keyed-stop) violin.

key trumpet (keyed trumpet). Natural trumpet provided with keys functioning much as woodwind keys do; usual number of keys was 5. First made in Germany in the late 18th century, it had a softer tone than its predecessor; never became a popular solo instrument; by the mid–19th century it had been supplanted by the valve trumpet.

keyboard. (Ger. *Klaviatur, Tastatur, Klavier*; Fr. *clavier*; It. *tastiera, tastatura*). Set of depressible keys or levers, usually laid out in horizontal manuals, activating sound-inducing mechanisms on pianos, organs, harpsichords, and similar constructed instruments; a large pipe organ may have up to 5 manuals, a harpsichord 1 or 2. A related feature on the organ is the pedal keyboard, designed as rows of large white and black keys, operated by the feet. (The odd pedal piano and pedal harpsichord have been built.) Over several centuries the arrangement of the 12 chromatic notes within an octave has been standardized, with 7 white keys on the lower level of the keyboard encompassing 5 shorter black keys on a slightly elevated level; the white keys form a diatonic scale, the black keys a pentatonic scale. While the opposition of white and black keys is standard on the piano, the harpsichord, clavichord, and spinet have had different coloring schemes. Some older harpsichords reverse the pattern, so that diatonic keys are black and pentatonic keys white; other specimens use red keys in either row, much like chess sets with pieces in red and white rather than the standard black and white. Whatever their color, the dimensions of the keys on all standard instruments are adjusted to the normal relaxed position of the player's 5 fingers resting on 5 consecutive diatonic keys.

In *[Gulliver's] Travels into Several Remote Nations of the World* (1726), Swift describes a Brobdingnagian keyboard: "The spinet was near sixty foot long, each key being almost a foot wide, so that, with my arms extended, I could not reach to above five keys, and to press them down required a good smart stroke with my fist . . . Yet I could not strike above sixteen keys, nor consequently play the bass and treble together, as other artists do; which was a great disadvantage to my performance." Actually, reality anticipated fiction here; keys of early organs were so wide and resistant that those who played them had to perform their hymns with clenched fists or even elbows to be able to depress keys sufficiently to activate pipes.

Numerous attempts have been made to adapt the keyboard for playing scales without constant fingering changes. The Jankó keyboard comprised 6 aligned and raked manuals, plus a system of levers to ease playing the ⇒chromatic scale. The Clutsam keyboard was built in the form of a fan arc with the radius of an arm's length; a performer was presumably placed in the center of the circle, using outstretched arms at all times; it went the way of all impractical ivory toys. (It did find an echo in the Dr. Seuss film *The 5000 Fingers of Dr. T.*) Finally, the Fokker organ with 31-equal temperament uses 3 colors and 4 sequential keyboards at a diagonal to allow performance of the extra notes-per-octave.

keynote. First note of a key or scale; tonic.

Khachaturian, Aram (Ilich), b. Tiflis, June 6, 1903; d. Moscow, May 1, 1978. He played tuba in school bands and studied biology; went to Moscow to enter the Gnessin Music School (1922–25); studied composition privately with Gnessin (1925–29); became a student of Miaskovsky at the Moscow Cons. (1929), graduated (1934); finished his postgraduate studies there (1937); married the composer Nina Makarova (1933). He commenced composing at 21, soon progressing to the 1st rank of Soviet composers; his music followed the tradition of Russian orientalism; applied characteristic Caucasian scale progressions without quoting actual folk songs; the *Sabre Dance* from his ballet *Gayane* (1942) became universally popular. In 1948 he, along with Prokofiev, Shostakovich, and others, were severely criticized by the Central Committee of the Communist Party for "formalist tendencies"; although confessing to his errors, continued to compose much as he had, not shunning highly dissonant harmonic combinations; made a People's Artist of the USSR (1954); conducted his own works throughout Europe and Japan (1951–65). He made his American debut in Washington, D.C. (1968), conducting the National Sym. Orch. in a program of his works; later that year conducted in N.Y. to a rousing audience reception. His other works include the ballets *Shchastye* (Happiness; 1939) and *Spartak* (Spartacus; 1950–56); fine concertos and concertante works for violin, cello, and piano; 3 syms.; vocal works, mostly praising Soviet leaders and ideology; film music; marches; chamber music; piano music. His nephew Karen (Surenovich) Khachaturian (b. Moscow, Sept. 19, 1920) is a composer and pedagogue.

Khan, (Ustad) Ali Akbar, b. Shibpur, Bengal (now Bangladesh), Apr. 14, 1922. With Ravi Shankar, he has been a pioneer of bringing Indian music to international audiences. His father was the master musician and teacher (Ustad) Alauddin Khan (b. Bengal, c. 1865; d. Bengal, Sept. 6, 1972), his teacher as well as Shankar's. His 1st performances on sarod took place in 1936; later became a court musician in Jodhpur; his 1st U.S. performance took place in N.Y. (1955); the interest aroused led to many return visits. He founded a college of music in Calcutta (1956) and a similar institution in Marin County, Calif. (1967). Khan's instrumental skill and improvisational virtuosity have kept his reputation secure in his homeland, unlike Shankar, accused by others (perhaps unfairly) of compromising the purity of Indian classical music. Khan is presently recording his father's secret repertoire, traditionally passed down through generations; he could not find a disciple capable of holding this great responsibility.

khorovod (Rus. *khor* + *vod*, leading chorus). Russian round dance of ancient origin; an adaptation of it is included in Stravinsky's *The Firebird*.

Khrennikov, Tikhon (Nikolaievich), b. Elets, June 10, 1913. He was the 10th child in a provincial clerk's family, who were musical, played Russian guitar and mandolin, and sang peasant songs. He took piano lessons locally; went to Moscow (1927); introduced to Gnessin, who accepted him as a pupil at the newly founded Technicum; studied counterpoint with Litinsky and piano with E. Hellman. After graduation he entered the Moscow Cons.; studied composition with Shebalin and piano with Neuhaus (1932–36); continued postgraduate work with Shebalin; developed a mildly modernistic and technically idiomatic style which remained recognizably his throughout his career. He joined the faculty of the Moscow Cons. (1961); named prof. (1966)

In the meantime Khrennikov had became engaged in the political life of his country. He was attached to the music corps of the Red Army, traveling with it during the last months of World War II; joined the Communist Party (1947) and became a deputy of the Supreme Soviet. He was named personally by Stalin as secretary-general of the Union of Soviet Composers (1948); participated in the party's attacks on Shostakovich, Prokofiev, and others in that year's purge; became president of the music section of the All-Union Soc. for Cultural Exchange with Europe and America (1949); headed the organizing committee for the International Festivals and the Tchaikovsky Competitions in Moscow.

Khrennikov received numerous honors: was a member of the Soviet delegation to the U.S. (1959); named a Hero of Socialist Labor (1973); received the Lenin Prize (1974). Amid all this *apparatchik* activity he never slackened in his composition, writing operas, ballets, syms., and concertos; also appeared as piano soloist. During his career he spoke stoutly for Soviet musical policy along the lines of socialist realism; he compromised himself, however, by his vehement condemnation of "formalist" directions in modern music, specifically attacking Stravinsky, Prokofiev, Shostakovich, and, later, Schnittke and Gubaidulina. But as Soviet aesthetics underwent liberalization, he became the target of sharp criticism; defended himself by claiming to have protected many young musicians from attacks by entrenched Soviet functionaries; succeeded in retaining his position at the Union of Soviet Composers. His compositions express forcefully the desirable qualities of Soviet music, flowing melody suggesting the broad modalities of Russian folk songs, vibrant and expressive lyricism, and effective instrumental formation.

kindlich (Ger.). Childlike, artless.

kinetic energy. Applied to music, a measurement (within a set amount of time) of 3 parameters: velocity (number of notes per time unit), amplitude (degree of loudness in decibels), and height of pitch (semitones counted from lowest to highest note); it follows that the auditory impact is directly proportional to velocity, loudness, and frequency of vibrations per second. There is also a psychological factor affecting this measurement; the off-beat *fortissimo* chord in Haydn's *Surprise* Sym., in itself possessing modest impact, carries a greater charge of psycho-kinetic energy because it is unexpected (at 1st listening, at least); generally, a greater impression is produced by syncopated detonations of sonic quanta than much stronger discharges occurring at regular time intervals.

King, "B. B." (Riley B.), b. Itta Bena, Miss., Sept. 16, 1925. He learned to play guitar; worked as disc jockey for a Memphis radio station under the name "Blues Boy" (shortened to "B. B."); scored his 1st hit with *Three O'Clock Blues* (1950); by the late 1960s, had assumed a prominent place among great blues singers and guitarists. He made his 1st tour of Europe (1968); headlined an all-blues concert at Carnegie Hall in N.Y. (1970); won a Grammy Award for his album *There Must Be a Better World Somewhere* (1981). Using an electric guitar (named Lucille), he is considered one of the most innovative blues artists of his era, with an aphoristic and emotional direct style; other well-known King songs include *Rock Me Baby, Paying the Cost to Be Boss, Confessin' the Blues, The Thrill Is Gone, Ask Me No Questions,* and *Hummingbird.*

King, James, b. Dodge City, Kans., May 22, 1925. He studied at the Univ. of Kansas City; received vocal training from Martial Singher and Max Lorenz; went to Europe; made his professional debut as Cavaradossi in Florence (1961); then sang at the San Francisco Opera, Berlin Deutsche Oper, Salzburg Festival, Bayreuth Festival, Metropolitan Opera in N.Y. (debut as Florestan, 1966), London's Covent Garden, and Milan's La Scala. He taught voice at the Indiana Univ. School of Music in Bloomington (from 1984); among his best roles were Lohengrin, Walther von Stolzing, Parsifal, and Verdi's Otello.

King, Carole (born Carol Klein), b. N.Y., Feb. 9, 1941. She took piano lessons as a child; intellectually precocious, started a female vocal ensemble, the Co-Sines; at 17 she met songwriter Gerry Goffin, whom she soon married; they produced numerous hit songs: *Will You Love Me Tomorrow, Some Kind of Wonderful, When My Little Girl Is Smiling, One Fine Day, I'm Into Something Good, Up on the Roof, Take Good Care of My Baby, Do the Loco-Motion,* and *Goin' Back.* After a divorce, she produced her own smash hits *It Might As Well Rain Until September, You've Got a Friend, It's Too Late,* and *I Feel the Earth Move*; with the encouragement of James Taylor and others, became a successful performer and recording artist (*Tapestry; Music; Wrap Around Joy*; soundtrack for the children's program, *Really Rosie*). She appeared on Broadway as the female lead in the British musical *Blood Brothers* (1994); her daughters Louise and Sherry Goffin are professional vocalists.

Kipnis, Alexander, b. Zhitomir, Feb. 13, 1891; d. Westport, Conn., May 14, 1978. He studied conducting at the Warsaw Cons.

(graduated 1912); studied voice with E. Grenzebach at Berlin's Klindworth-Scharwenka Cons.; sang in local operetta theaters (1913–14). At the outbreak of World War I he was interned as an enemy alien, but was soon released; made his operatic debut as the hermit in *Der Freischütz* at the Hamburg Opera (1915); sang there until 1917, then joined the Wiesbaden Opera (1917–22); made his U.S. debut as Pogner in *Die Meistersinger von Nürnberg* with a visiting company in Baltimore (1923); was a member of the Chicago Civic Opera (1923–32). He also sang at the Berlin Städtische Oper (1922–30), Berlin State Opera (1932–35), and Vienna State Opera (1935–38).

Kipnis became an American citizen in 1931; made guest appearances at the Bayreuth, Salzburg, and Glyndebourne festivals, as well as Covent Garden in London and the Teatro Colón in Buenos Aires; made his belated Metropolitan Opera debut in N.Y. as Gurnemanz in *Parsifal* (1940); continued to sing there until 1946; then devoted himself to teaching. Through the years he appeared as soloist with R. Strauss, Siegfried Wagner, and Toscanini. His son is Igor Kipnis.

Kipnis, Igor, b. Berlin, Sept. 27, 1930. In 1938 the family moved permanently to the U.S.; he studied piano with his maternal grandfather; after attending the Westport (Conn.) School of Music, studied with R. Thompson and Thurston Dart at Harvard Univ. (B.A., 1952); took harpsichord lessons with Fernando Valenti. After graduation he served abroad in the Signal Corps of the U.S. Army; returning to the U.S., he worked as a bookstore salesman in N.Y.; later served as editorial adviser to Westminster Records Co.

Kipnis made his concert debut as harpsichordist in a N.Y. radio broadcast (1959); his formal concert debut there followed (1962); taught at Tanglewood (1964–67); made his 1st European tour (1967), subsequently touring throughout the world. He served as associate prof. of fine arts (1971–75) and artist-in-residence (1975–77) at Fairfield Univ. in Conn.; taught at the Early Music Inst. in Indianapolis. In 1981 he made his debut as fortepianist in Indianapolis, and helped to revive that instrument. He also promoted interest in new music; several composers, including Rorem, Rochberg, R. R. Bennett, Barbara Kolb, and John McCabe, have written for him. His father was Alexander Kipnis.

Kirchenmusik (Ger.). Church music.

Kirchner, Leon, b. N.Y., Jan. 24, 1919. His family moved to Los Angeles (1928); he studied piano with Richard Buhlig; entered the Univ. of Calif., Berkeley (1938); studied theory with A. Elkus and E. Strickland (B.A., 1940; M.M., 1949); took lessons with Ernest Bloch in San Francisco; returned to N.Y. (1942); studied privately with Sessions; served in the U.S. Army (1943–46). After demobilization, he was appointed to the faculty of the San Francisco Cons., concurrently teaching at the Univ. of Calif., Berkeley; received Guggenheim fellowship (1948); associate prof. at the Univ. of Southern Calif., Los Angeles (1950–54); taught at Mills College in Oakland, Calif. (1954–61); named prof. of music at Harvard Univ. (1961). He was elected to the National Inst. of Arts and Letters and the American Academy of Arts and Sciences (1962); awarded the Pulitzer Prize for his 3rd String Quartet (1967).

In his music Kirchner takes a prudential median course: cultivating a distinct modern idiom without espousing a particular technique; making ample and effective use of euphonious dissonance; featuring a tense but invariably coherent contrapuntal fabric. He inclines naturally towards Classic order, preferring formal types of composition, often of a Baroque nature; primarily associated with instrumental music, he is ironically best known for an opera, *Lily* (after Bellow's *Henderson the Rain King*, 1973–76).

Kirk, (Rahsaan) Roland, b. Columbus, Ohio, Aug. 7, 1936; d. Bloomington, Ind., Dec. 5, 1977. He lost his sight in infancy; brought up at the Ohio State School for the Blind; learned trumpet, tenor saxophone, flute, clarinet, and nose flute; later invented the manzello and strichophone (saxophone and horn hybrids, respectively); one of the 1st jazz musicians to exploit circular breathing; had an uncanny ability to play 2 or 3 wind instruments simultaneously; continued playing with 1 hand after a 1975 stroke. He organized his own band (1963); toured Europe, Australia, and New Zealand; composed pieces of a wry nature, with titles like *Serenade to a Cuckoo*; *Here Comes the Whistleman*; *I Talk with the Spirits*; *Rip, Rig and Panic*; *Funk Underneath*. In the 1970s he led the Jazz and People's Movement, protesting the lack of African-American music and musicians in U.S. mainstream broadcast culture.

Kirkby, Emma, b. Camberley, Feb. 26, 1949. She studied classics at Oxford; made her debut in London (1974); specialized in early music as a member of the Academy of Ancient Music, London Baroque, and Consort of Musicke. She toured the U.S. (1978); concertized in the Middle East with lutenist Anthony Rooley. Her repertoire ranges from Italian quattrocento to arias by Handel, Mozart, and Haydn; the careful attention she pays to a purity of intonation free from intrusive vibrato has been praised.

Kirnberger, Johann Philipp, b. Saalfeld (baptized), Apr. 24, 1721; d. Berlin, July 26 or 27, 1783. He studied violin and harpsichord at home; took organ lessons with J. P. Kellner in Grafenroda and H. N. Gerber in Sondershausen, where he studied violin with Meil; studied with Bach in Leipzig (1739–41); traveled in Poland (1741–51) as tutor for noble families. He was violinist to Frederick the Great in Berlin (1751–54) and Prince Heinrich of Prussia (1754–58); Kapellmeister to Princess Anna Amalie (1758–83). He was greatly renowned as a teacher; among his pupils were J. A. P. Schulz, C. P. E. Bach, the Graun brothers, and J. F. Agricola; as a theorist, regarded as one of the greatest authorities of his time, although he called upon others to edit or rewrite his often highly disorganized presentations. In his compositions he displayed amazing contrapuntal technique; seriously tried to establish a scientific method of writing based on rules of combination and permutation; *Der allezeit fertige Polonoisen-und Menuetten-componist* (1757) expounded an automatic method of composition.

Kissin, Evgeny, b. Moscow, Oct. 10, 1971. He enrolled at the Gnessin Music School for Gifted Children in Moscow at age 6; studied with Anna Kantor, his only piano teacher; at 12 gave performances of both Chopin concertos with the Moscow Phil. An international reputation came to him when he performed Tchaikovsky's 1st Piano Concerto with Karajan and the Berlin Phil. (1987); made his U.S. debut playing Chopin's 1st with the N.Y. Phil., led by Mehta (1990); 10 days later, made his recital debut at Carnegie Hall, astonishing audience and critics alike by digital velocity and propulsive dexterity; his continuing concert successes have been reinforced by the release of many recordings.

kit. Small 3-stringed violin used by dancing masters, about 16 inches long; tuned c^1–g^1–d^2.

kithara (*cithara;* Grk.). National instrument of ancient Greece, member of the lyre family; comprises a square soundbox made of wood, with between 3 and 11 strings stretched from one side to the other, connected by a crossbar; tuning was fundamentally pentatonic, although smaller intervals could be introduced. Iconographical evidence indicates similar instruments in Mesopotamia; the 1st Greek examples depicted on vases are from the 7th century B.C.

Kitt, Eartha, b. North, S.C., Jan. 26, 1928. She was taken to N.Y. as a child; sang in church, received piano training, and studied dance at the High School for Performing Arts; won a dance scholarship to study with Katherine Dunham (1944), traveling with her troupe in South America and Europe (to 1950); then concentrated on singing and acting; appeared in nightclubs, theaters, and films, and on recordings, radio, and television. She excels in earthy, passion-laden songs delivered in a low-key monotone; appeared in George Kleinsinger's musical *Shinbone Alley* (1954).

klagend (*im klagenden Ton;* Ger.). Mournfully, plaintively.

Klang (Ger.). 1. Sound; sonority. 2. Composite musical tone (fundamental plus its harmonics); clang. 3. Chord, as in *Dreiklang* (triad).

Klangfarbe (Ger.). Tone color; timbre; can also refer to a compositional use of musical sound. "It must be possible," Schoenberg states in *Harmonielehre* (1911), "to form a succession of Klangfarben possessing a mutual relationship of a logical type equivalent to that of the melody formed by a succession of different tones"; this is exemplified in the movement originally entitled *The Changing Chord* in his *Fünf Orchesterstücke,* op. 16 (1909). While he pursued the idea no further, his disciples Berg and Webern experimented with it more fully, the latter approaching total serialism, where a fundamental Klangfarbe series is formed by successively sounding 12 different notes by 12 different instruments. *Klangfarbenmelodie,* tone-color melody.

Klangfolge (Ger.). Progression of sounds or chords; applied particularly to sonorous complexes of different tone colors, according to Schoenberg's concept of *Klangfarbenmelodie.*

Klappe (Ger.). In instrument design, a key. *Klappenhorn,* key bugle.

Klarinette (Ger.). Clarinet.

Klaviatur (Ger.). Keyboard.

Klavier (Ger.). 1. Keyboard. 2. Keyboard stringed instrument; in the 18th century, clavichord or harpsichord, now, any piano.

Klavierauszug, piano arrangement, especially a reduction from a full score; vocal score; *klaviermässig,* suitable for piano; in piano style; *Klavierstück,* piano piece, usually brief.

Klaviertrio (Ger.). Chamber work for piano, violin, and cello. *Klavierquartett,* work for (usually) piano, violin, viola, and cello; *Klavierquintett,* work for (usually) piano and string quartet; Schubert's *Trout Quintet* replaces one violin with a double bass.

Kleiber, Carlos, b. Berlin, July 3, 1930. He left Nazi Germany with his parents (1935); settled in South America (1940); evinced early interest in music; his father Erich Kleiber opposed it as a career; after studying chemistry in Zurich (1949–50), Carlos turned decisively to music; completed training in Buenos Aires. He became *répétiteur* and stage assistant at the Theater am Gärtnerplatz in Munich (1952); made his conducting debut with Millöcker's *Gasparone* in Potsdam (1954); became *répétiteur* (1956) and conductor (1958) at the Deutsche Oper am Rhein in Düsseldorf; conducted at the Zurich Opera (1964–66); served as 1st conductor at the Württemberg State Theater in Stuttgart (1966–68); made his British debut conducting *Wozzeck* at the Edinburgh Festival (1966).

From 1968 to 1978 Kleiber conducted at the Bavarian State Opera in Munich; led performances of *Tristan und Isolde* for his debuts at the Vienna State Opera (1973) and Bayreuth (1974), the same year in which he made his 1st appearances at London's Covent Garden and Milan's La Scala with *Der Rosenkavalier.* He made his U.S. debut conducting *Otello* at the San Francisco Opera (1977); his 1st U.S. orch'l appearance with the Chicago Sym. Orch. (1978). He conducted the Vienna Phil. (1979) and Berlin Phil. (1982); became a naturalized Austrian citizen (1980); made his Metropolitan Opera debut in N.Y. conducting *La Bohème* (1988); led the New Year's Day Concert of the Vienna Phil. (1989). Kleiber has been acclaimed by critics, audiences, and fellow musicians; his brilliant performances reflect an unreserved commitment to the score, authority, and technical mastery; infrequent appearances, combined with a passion for perfection, have made him legendary among contemporary podium celebrities.

Kleiber, Erich, b. Vienna, Aug. 5, 1890; d. Zurich, Jan. 27, 1956. He studied at the Prague Cons. and Univ. of Prague; made his debut at the Prague National Theater (1911); conducted opera in Darmstadt (1912–19), Barmen-Elberfeld (1919–21), Düsseldorf (1921–22), and Mannheim (1922–23). He was appointed Generalmusikdirektor of the Berlin State Opera (1923); his outstanding tenure featured brilliant performances of standard repertoire and exciting contemporary works; conducted the premiere of Berg's *Wozzeck* (1925). In 1934, protesting the German National Socialist government, he resigned his post and emigrated to South America; conducted regularly at the Teatro Colón in Buenos Aires (1936–49).

Having 1st conducted at London's Covent Garden in 1937; Kleiber returned there (1950–53); reappointed Generalmusikdirektor of the Berlin State Opera (1954); resigned the following year because of difficulties with the Communist regime. He was renowned for interpretations of Mozart and Beethoven; also composed concertos, orch'l music, chamber music, piano pieces, and songs. His son is Carlos Kleiber.

kleine Flöte (Ger.). Piccolo.

kleine Trommel (Ger.). Side drum.

Kleinmeister (Ger., little masters). Disparaging appellation for musical journeymen (or women) who flourished in the 18th century; these individuals wrote the euterpian equivalent of the Romantic "well-made play": everything in order, obeying all rules, following all formulas, and devoid of genius or even real talent.

Klemperer, Otto, b. Breslau (Wrocław), May 14, 1885; d. Zurich, July 6, 1973. He received his early musical training from his mother; entered the Hoch Cons. in Frankfurt (1901), studying piano with Kwast and theory with Knorr; studied composition and conducting with Pfitzner in Berlin. He made his debut conducting Reinhardt's production of Offenbach's *Orpheus in the Underworld* in Berlin (1906); on Mahler's recommendation, appointed chorus master and subsequently conductor of the German Theater in Prague; assisted Mahler in the latter's preparations for the premiere of his 8th Sym. (1910); became conductor at the Hamburg Opera (1910), but left due to a scandalous liaison with recently married soprano Elisabeth Schumann (1912).

After appointments at Barmen (1913–14) and Strasbourg (as Pfitzner's deputy, 1914–17), Klemperer was appointed music director of the Cologne Opera (1917); conducted the German premiere of Janáček's *Káťa Kabanová*; named music director of the Wiesbaden Opera (1924). He made his U.S. debut with the N.Y. Sym. Orch. (1926); became music director of Berlin's Kroll Opera (1927). He conducted the premiere of Hindemith's *Neues vom Tage* (1929) and the 1st Berlin performances of Hindemith's *Cardillac*, Stravinsky's *Oedipus Rex*, and Schoenberg's *Die glückliche Hand*; conducted the premiere of Schoenberg's *Begleitungsmusik* there.

When political and economic pressures forced the Kroll Opera to close (1931), Klemperer became conductor at the Berlin State Opera; when the Nazis came to power (1933), compelled to emigrate to the U.S.; that year became music director of the Los Angeles Phil.; appeared as guest conductor in N.Y., Philadelphia, and Pittsburgh. His career was disrupted by an operation for a brain tumor (1939). He was engaged as conductor at the Budapest State Opera (1947–50); made 1st appearance with the Philharmonia Orch. of London as guest conductor (1951); appointed principal conductor (1955); retained that position when the orch.'s manager, Walter Legge, attempted to disband it; it became the New Philharmonia (1964).

Klemperer was accident-prone and a manic depressive; the 2 sides of his nature were reflected in a change of interpretive style; noted at 1st for energetic and hard-driven interpretations, he later won renown for measured performances of Viennese classics; conducted a memorable series of Beethoven syms. at the Royal Festival Hall; conducted new productions of *Fidelio*, *Die Zauberflöte*, and *Lohengrin* at Covent Garden in the early 1960s; his serious and unsentimental readings of Mahler's syms. were largely responsible for modern critical and popular reappraisal of that composer; conducted in Jerusalem, accepting Israeli citizenship (1970); retired in 1972. Also a composer, he studied with Schoenberg in the U.S.; but had more in common with Pfitzner. He publ. *Meine Erinnerungen an Gustav Mahler* (Zurich, 1960).

Knabenchor (Ger.). Boys' choir. *Knabenstimme*, boy's voice.

knee stop. Knee-operated lever under the manual of the reed organ; one controls wind supply, a 2nd opens and shuts the swell-box, and a 3rd draws all the stops.

Kniegeige (Ger., knee violin). Viola da gamba.

Knight, Gladys, b. Atlanta, Ga., May 28, 1944. Leader of the family-based group Gladys Knight and the Pips, as well as a solo artist. A child prodigy, she sang with a gospel group from age 4; 3 years later, won on TV's *Ted Mack's Original Amateur Hour*; began singing at 8 with her brother Merald "Bubba" Knight (b. Sept. 4, 1942) and cousin William Guest (b. June 2, 1941), among other family members; by the mid-1950s the group was touring, opening for Jackie Wilson and Sam Cooke.

Early recordings were unsuccessful; in 1961, Knight and company had a major R&B hit with *Every Beat of My Heart*; after another dry spell, they finally hooked up with Berry Gordy's Soul label (part of his Motown empire, 1965); by this time the group included the 2 Knights, cousin Guest, and another cousin, Edward Patten (b. Aug. 2, 1939); major hits included *The End of the Road, Friendship Train, If I Were Your Woman, Neither One of Us (Wants to Be the First to Say Goodbye)*, and *Daddy Could Swear, I Declare*. The Pips left Motown for Buddah; had one of their biggest hits with *Midnight Train to Georgia* (1973). In 1978 Gladys signed a solo deal with Columbia; the Pips began recording on their own; neither had much success; by the mid-1980s they reunited, scoring a hit with *Love Overboard* (1987). Knight now performs as a solo artist, occasionally with the Pips; they were inducted into the Rock and Roll Hall of Fame (1996).

Knussen, (Stuart) Oliver, b. Glasgow, June 12, 1952. Remarkably precocious, he began playing piano as a small boy; showed unusual diligence in his theory studies, mostly with John Lambert (1963–69); attended the Central Tutorial School for Young Musicians (1964–67); made musical headlines when he conducted the London Sym. Orch. in the premiere of his own 1st Sym. (1968), an eclectic but astoundingly effective work; awarded fellowships for study with Schuller at the Berkshire Music Center in Tanglewood (1970–73); served as artistic director of the Aldeburgh Festivals (from 1983) and coordinator of contemporary music activities at Tanglewood (from 1986); has become a well-known conductor. As composer, he is best-known for 3 syms. (1966–67, 1970–71, 1973–76), *Songs and Hums of Winnie-the-Pooh* (1970), and "children's operas": *Where the Wild Things Are* (1979–81), *Max and the Maximonsters* (1980), and *Higglety Pigglety Pop!* (1983–84).

kocalho. Chocalho.

Kodály, Zoltan, b. Kecskemét, Dec. 16, 1882; d. Budapest, Mar. 6, 1967. Brought up in a musical family, he was educated at the Archiepiscopal Grammar School in Nagyszombat; took lessons in piano, violin, viola, and cello; began to compose, producing an overture at 15 (premiere, 1898). He went to Budapest (1900); entered the univ. in Hungarian and German; studied composition with Koessler at the Royal Academy of Music (diplomas, 1904 and 1905; Ph.D., 1906, with a diss. on stanzaic Hungarian folk song); became associated with Bartók, collecting, organizing, and editing a vast wealth of national folk songs; later made use of these in his own compositions. He went to Berlin (1906), then to Paris (1907); took lessons with Widor; it was Debussy who most profoundly influenced him as a composer; appointed prof. at the Royal Academy of Music in Budapest (1907); in collaboration with Bartók, prepared *Az uj egyetemes nepdalgyujtemeny tervezete* (A Project for a New Universal Collection of Folk Songs, 1913); continued their collecting expeditions until World War I intervened.

Kodály wrote music criticism for Budapest newspapers (1917–19); appointed deputy director of the Budapest Academy of Music (1919); lost his position that year for political reasons, but resumed teaching there (1922). He was commissioned to write a work in celebration of the 50th anniversary of the union of Buda, Pest, and Obuda into Budapest (1923); the Budapest premiere of the result, the oratorio *Psalmus hungaricus*, was followed by numerous performances throughout Europe and in America. Other major successes included his singspiel *Háry János* (1926; a suite became highly popular), *Marosszéki táncok* (Dances of Marosszek; based on a piano work, 1930), *Galántai táncok* (Dances of Galánt; for the 80th anniversary of the Budapest Phil. Soc., 1933), *Variations on a Hungarian Folk Song "Felszállott a páva"* (Peacock Variations; for the 50th anniversary of the Amsterdam Concertgebouw Orch., 1939), Concerto for Orch. (for the 50th anniversary of the Chicago Sym. Orch., 1939–40).

Kodály's great interest in music education is reflected in numerous choral works (for both adults and children), part of a pedagogical approach codified and still in use; continued to teach at the Academy of Music (to 1940). He pursued his ethnomusicological studies; from 1940 associated with the Hungarian Academy of Sciences, serving as president (1946–49); taught Hungarian folk music until 1942, continuing even after his retirement; conducted his music in England, the U.S., and the Soviet Union (1946–47), later throughout Western Europe. He was awarded 3 Kossuth Prizes (1948, 1952, 1957); received foreign honors, including honorary membership in the Moscow Cons. and the American Academy of Arts and Sciences (both 1963); awarded the Gold Medal of the Royal Phil. Soc. of London (1967); an International Kodály Soc. was organized in Budapest (1975).

As a composer Kodály's style was less radical than Bartók's; never departed from basic tonality, nor did his rhythmic experiments attain the primitivistic power of his colleague's percussive idiom; preferred a Romantic treatment of melodic and harmonic materials, infused with impressionistic elements; produced a substantial body of notable music.

Koechlin, Charles (Louis Eugène), b. Paris, Nov. 27, 1867; d. Le Canadel, Var, Dec. 31, 1950. He studied for a military career but compelled to change plans after contracting tuberculosis; while recuperating in Algeria, took up serious music studies; entered the Paris Cons. (1890); studied with Gedalge, Massenet, and Fauré (graduated 1897). He lived mostly in Paris, active as composer, teacher, and lecturer; with Ravel and Schmitt organized the Soc. Musicale Indépendante (1909) to promote contemporary music; with Satie, Roussel, Milhaud, and others, part of the Les Nouveaux Jeunes group (1918–20), a precursor to Les Six. He did most of the orchestration on Debussy's

Khamma (1913) and all of Cole Porter's ballet *Within the Quota* (1923).

Although Koechlin composed prolifically in most genres, he was best known as a lecturer and writer on music; made 3 lecture tours of the U.S. (1918, 1928, 1937); wrote treatises on theory, counterpoint, harmony, fugue, and orchestration, and monographs on Debussy, Fauré, choir schools, Pierre Maurice (Swiss composer, 1868–1936), and wind instruments; became president of the Fédération Musicale Populaire (1937). His leftist leanings led him to promote proletariat music during the 1930s; but in spite of winning honors for works such as *Sym. d'hymnes* (Prix Cressent, 1936) and Sym. No. 1 (Prix Halphan, 1937), his music made no real impact; in recent years his voluminous chamber music has found its way to concert programs; orch'l performances remain rare.

Taking Fauré as model, Koechlin strove to preserve the best of the French classical tradition; a skillful craftsman, he produced works of clarity and taste, marked by advanced harmonic and polyphonic attributes in a post-impressionist mode. Much of his sym. music is based on Kipling: *3 poèmes du "Livre de la Jungle"* for soloists, chorus, and orch. (1899–1910); *La Course de printemps* (1908–25); *La Méditation de Purun Bhagat* (1936); *La Loi de la jungle* (1939); *Les Bandar-log* (1939). Other sym. poems include *La Forêt* (*Le Jour,* 1897–1904; *La Nuit,* 1896–1907); *En mer, la nuit,* after Heine (1899–1904); *L'automne* (1896–1906); *Soleil et danses dans la forêt* and *Vers la plage lointaine* (1898–1909); *Le Printemps* and *L'Hiver* (1908–16); *L'Été* (*Nuit de juin* and *Midi en août,* 1908–11), *Sur les flots lointaines* (1933); *La Cité nouvelle, rêve d'avenir,* after Wells (1938); *Le Buisson ardent,* after Rolland (1938–45); *Le Docteur Fabricius,* after C. Dollfus (1941–44). He was enthralled by Hollywood; in addition to film scores, composed *7 Stars Sym.* (1933) and works dedicated to Lillian Harvey, Daisy Hamilton, Ginger Rogers, and Jean Harlow. Other orch'l works include the Ballade for Piano and Orch. (1911–15); Sym. No. 1 (1911–16); *Choral fugué du style modal* for Organ and Orch. (1933); *Offrande musical sur le nom de BACH* (1942); Partita for Chamber Orch. (1945); ballets. His piano music includes the suites *Paysages et marines* (1915–16), *Les Heures persanes* (1916–19), *L'Ancienne Maison de campagne* (1932–33), choral works, songs.

Kogan, Leonid (Borisovich), b. Dnepropetrovsk, Nov. 14, 1924; d. Dec. 17, 1982. His father was a photographer who played violin; the family moved to Moscow when Kogan was 10; he became pupil of A. Yampolsky, 1st at the Central Music School, later at the Cons. (1943–48). Obviously a wunderkind, he was prudently spared harmful exploitation; was co-winner of the 1st prize at the World Festival of Democratic Youth in Prague (1947); won 1st prize in the Queen Elisabeth of Belgium Competition (1951); his career was instantly assured; played recitals in Europe to unanimous acclaim.

For his U.S. debut, Kogan played the Brahms Violin Concerto with Monteux and the Boston Sym. Orch. (1958); joined the faculty of the Moscow Cons. (1952); named prof. (1963) and head of the violin dept. (1969); received the Lenin Prize (1965). His playing exemplified the finest qualities of the Russian school: emotionally romantic élan and melodious filigree of technical detail; in addition to the standard repertoire in which he excelled, also played modern works, particularly those by Soviet composers. He was married to violinist Elizabeta Gilels (b. Odessa, Sept. 30, 1919); their son, Pavel Kogan (b. Moscow, June 6, 1952), was good enough to win the Sibelius contest in Finland (1970); was soloist with the Philadelphia Orch. (1975); conducted Moscow's Bolshoi Theater, the Zagreb Phil. (both from 1988) and the Moscow Sym. Orch. (from 1989).

Kokkonen, Joonas, b. Iisalmi, Nov. 13, 1921; d. Jarvenpaa, Oct. 4, 1996. He studied with Palmgren, Ranta, and Hannikainen at the Sibelius Academy in Helsinki (diploma, 1949); studied musicology with Krohn at the Univ. of Helsinki (M.A., 1948); taught at the Sibelius Academy (from 1950); prof. of composition (1959–63); chairman of the dept. (1965–70); elected to membership in the Finnish Academy (1963); awarded the Sibelius Prize (1973).

Like all Finnish composers of his generation, Kokkonen absorbed the inevitable influence of Sibelius; abandoned the characteristic diatonic modalities of Finnish folk music for a style marked by curiously anfractuous chromaticism and involuted counterpoint, freely dissonant but hewing to clearly identifiable tonal centers; dabbled in dodecaphonic writing, but found its doctrinaire discipline uncongenial; derives his contrapuntal procedures from Bach and Bartók; adopts an objective method of formal thematic structure where free succession of formative motifs determines content. His international fame received a great boost with the opera *Viimeiset Kiusaukset* (The Last Temptations; Helsinki, 1975).

kolo (Serb., wheel). Round dance of the southern Slavic region, with a constantly repeated refrain; there are slow and fast types; related to the Rumanian *lora* and Bulgarian horo.

Kolorierung (Ger., coloration). Keyboard ornamentation in the late Renaissance and Baroque, written out or improvised, tastefully applied; while frowned upon by "purists" of succeeding centuries, these convenient clichés kept performances of this music from jejuneness; the early music movement restored them to their rightful place.

Komponist (Ger.). Composer.

Kontakion (Kondakion; Rus., kondak). Portion of the Byzantine Canonical Hours, sung as an ode in the kanñ; according to legend, the 6th-century Byzantine poet Roman the Melodious (melode Romanous) received it from the Blessed Virgin; a morality poem, it contains a narrative recited by a soloist, followed by a choral refrain. The Kontakion was at 1st part of Matins; remained a major influence on ecclesiastical poetry and music even after being superseded by the kañon after the conversion of Russia to Christianity in the 10th century, used in Russian services.

Kontarsky, Alfons, b. Iserlohn, Westphalia, Oct. 9, 1932. He studied piano with E. Schmitz-Gohr and M. Frank at the Cologne Hochschule für Musik (1953–55) and E. Erdmann in Hamburg (1955–57); with his brother Aloys, won 1st prize for duo-piano playing in the Bavarian Radio Competition in Munich (1955); toured as a duo throughout the world; recorded works by Boulez, Stockhausen, Bartók, Stravinsky, B.A. Zimmermann,

and Ravel; returned to and taught at the Cologne Hochschule (from 1967). He publ. *Pro musica nova: Studien zum Spielen neuer Musik für Klavier* (Cologne, 1973). He is also the brother of Bernhard Kontarsky.

Kontarsky, Aloys, b. Iserlohn, Westphalia, May 14, 1931. He studied piano with E. Schmitz-Gohr and M. Frank at the Cologne Hochschule für Musik (1952–55) and E. Erdmann in Hamburg (1955–57); with his brother Alfons, won 1st prize for duo-piano playing at the Bavarian Radio Competition in Munich (1955); toured as a duo throughout the world; recorded works by Boulez, Stockhausen, Bartók, Stravinsky, B.A. Zimmermann, and Ravel; returned to and taught master classes at the Cologne Hochschule (from 1969). He is also the brother of Bernhard Kontarsky.

Kontarsky, Bernhard, b. Iserlohn, Westphalia, Apr. 26, 1937. He studied at the Cologne Hochschule für Musik and at the Univ. of Cologne; received the Mendelssohn Prize in Chamber Music (1964); conducted at the Württemberg State Theater in Stuttgart; appeared as pianist, both as soloist and in ensembles with his brothers Alfons Kontarsky and Aloys Kontarsky.

Konzert (Ger.). 1. Concerto. 2. Concert. *Konzertmeister*, concertmaster; *Konzertsaal*, concert hall.

Konzertstück (Ger.; It. *concertino*). 1. Concert piece. 2. Short 1-movement concerto with orch'l accompaniment and in free form, e.g., works by Weber (piano); Chopin (*Allegro de concert*); Mendelssohn (*Capriccio brillant*); Schumann (*Concertstück* for 4 Horns); and an unfinished Stravinsky work for piano incorporated into *Petrouchka*.

Koopman, Ton, b. Zwolle, Oct. 12, 1944. He studied organ with S. Jansen and harpsichord with G. Leonhardt in Amsterdam; took courses in musicology; obtained doctorates in all 3 (1968–70); won the Prix d'excellence for organ (1972) and harpsichord (1974); served as director of Musica Antiqua; taught at the Sweelinck Cons. in Amsterdam; founded the Amsterdam Baroque Orch. (1979). He toured widely in subsequent years as conductor, organist, and harpsichordist, excelling in early music performances; recorded works by Bach, Frescobaldi, Telemann, Stanley, and Buxtehude.

Kopfstimme (Ger., head voice). Falsetto.

Koppel (Ger.). Coupler (organ). *Koppel ab*, take coupler off; *Koppel an*, draw coupler; put couple on.

kora. Plucked harp-lute of West Africa, associated with the Mandinka and Maninka peoples; a standard instrument has 21 nylon (formerly leather) strings, attached with tuning collars at the top of a long wooden neck that passes through a large gourd resonator; at the bottom, the strings are attached by an iron anchor ring. The professional performer (*jali*), sitting on the ground, faces the head of the resonator, or soundboard, made with antelope skin or cowhide; he or she holds the instrument by attached wooden handles. The strings are divided into two ranks running perpendicular to the soundboard; they pass over a single bridge with notches in either side to help tune them.

The kora's range covers 3 octaves; there are numerous tunings, each usually applicable to only a few pieces. The *jali's* repertory is comprised of praise songs, honoring a person, family, or clan, and songs in an Islamic vein. The complex accompaniment blends linear and vertical elements in mostly steady rhythm; there are several playing techniques, even flicking a nail against the instrument to fill in a brief silence; the sonority is often intensified by a set of small jingles attached to the bridge with wire loops. The 1st Western report of the instrument dates from 1799; related instruments include the *kasso, soron,* and *sanku.*

Korean temple blocks. Rounded and hollowed woodblocks, struck with a drumstick; pitch is approximate, but definite enough to create a pentatonic effect when appropriate blocks are combined.

Kornett (Ger.). Cornet à pistons; cornet.

Korngold, Erich Wolfgang, b. Brunn (Brno), May 29, 1897; d. Los Angeles, Nov. 29, 1957. He received his earliest musical education from his father, Viennese music critic Julius Korngold (b. Brunn [Brno], Dec. 24, 1860; d. Los Angeles, Sept. 25, 1945); studied with Fuchs, Zemlinsky, and Gradener in Vienna; at age 12 he composed a Piano Trio, soon publ., revealing a competent technique and a style strongly influenced by R. Strauss. He wrote (in piano score) a pantomime, *Der Schneemann;* orchestrated by Zemlinsky, it was premiered at the Vienna Court Opera (1910), creating a sensation; Nikisch conducted his *Schauspiel-Ouvertüre* with the Leipzig Gewandhaus Orch.; he gave a concert of his works in Berlin, appearing as pianist (both 1911); his *Sinfonietta* was conducted by Weingartner and the Vienna Phil. (1913). Hearing Korngold play his own music as a young boy, Mahler kept repeating, "Ein Genie! Ein Genie!"

Korngold was not quite 19 when his 2 short operas, *Der Ring des Polykrates* and *Violanta,* were produced in Munich; his greatest success came with the double premiere in Hamburg and Cologne of the opera *Die tote Stadt* (1920); began a fruitful collaboration with director Max Reinhardt (1929); went to Hollywood; arranged Mendelssohn's music for Reinhardt's film of *A Midsummer Night's Dream* (1934); taught at the Vienna Academy of Music (1930–34) before settling in Hollywood; wrote several fine Romantic film scores; became a naturalized U.S. citizen (1943). His music represents the last breath of the Romantic Viennese spirit, marvelously consistent with the melodic, rhythmic, and harmonic style of the nascent 20th century. Korngold never altered his established idiom of composition; was never tempted to borrow modernistic devices, except for transitory passages in major 2nds or occasional whole-tone scale.

After early outbursts of incautious enthusiasm on the part of some critics, nominating Korngold as a new Mozart, his star began to sink rapidly; it became a melancholy consensus to dismiss his operas (at their tardy revivals) as derivative products of an era that had little to commend itself to begin with. Ironically, his film scores (as orch'l suites) experienced a spontaneous posth. renascence, particularly on recordings, especially among American musical youth, who find in Korngold's music the stuff of their own new dreams.

Korrepetitor, -in (Ger., choral coach; Fr. *répétiteur, -euse*). Assistant conductor or pianist who leads preliminary rehearsals with singers and dancers in opera and ballet.

Kortholt (Ger.). Obsolete double-reed windcap instrument, with a cylindrical double-channel bore; similar to the curtal, excepting the latter's conical bore, and the *bass sordone,* which lacks a windcap, however.

koto. National Japanese instrument of long zither type, with a rectangular body made of strong wood planks laid out on the floor. It has 7 to 13 silk strings plucked with fingers, fingernails, or plectrum; modern kotos may have up to 17 strings. The koto accompanies Japanese gagaku, music of the medieval Japanese court; in subsequent centuries, schools of solo performance emerged; its music was now notated (including the masterful anon. *Variations on Rokudan*). In the 20th century it evolved into a virtuoso instrument; several Japanese composers have written music for it using modern techniques, including dodecaphony; among the music written by Western composers are Cowell's 2 concertos for koto and orch.

Koussevitzky (Kussevitsky), Serge (Alexandrovich), b. Vishny-Volochok, July 26, 1874; d. Boston, June 4, 1951. He learned the trumpet; took part with his brothers in a small wind ensemble; earned a living at balls, weddings, and village fairs. He went to Moscow at 14; as Jews were not allowed to live there, he was baptized; received a fellowship with free tuition at the Musico-Dramatic Inst. of the Moscow Phil. Soc.; studied double bass with Rambousek and theory with Blaramberg and Kruglikov. He joined the orch. of the Bolshoi Theater (1894), succeeding Rambousek as principal double bassist (1901–05); became known as a soloist of the 1st magnitude; made his public debut in Moscow (1901); garnered attention with a recital in Berlin (1903). To supplement the repertoire for double bass, he arranged works and wrote several pieces, notably a concerto, helped by Reinhold Glière (1875–1956; best known for his 3rd Sym., *Ilya Muromets*). Koussevitzky gave its premiere in Moscow (1905); later that year married Natalie Ushkov, daughter of a wealthy tea merchant; soon resigned from the Bolshoi Theater orch.; in a published open letter blamed economic and artistic difficulties in the orch.; went to Germany; continued giving recitals; played Saint-Saëns's 1st Cello Concerto on the double bass.

After conducting a student orch. at the Berlin Hochschule für Musik (1907), Koussevitzky made his conducting debut with the Berlin Phil. (1908); established a publishing house, Editions Russes de Musique (1909); signed publishing contracts with Scriabin, Stravinsky, Prokofiev, Medtner, and Rachmaninoff; in subsequent years became Scriabin's greatest champion. He organized a sym. orch. in Moscow (1909), featuring Russian music and standard repertoire; gave many Russian premieres, among them Scriabin's *Prométhée;* took his orch. to towns along the Volga River in a specially chartered steamboat (1910; repeated in 1912 and 1914). The outbreak of war in 1914 curtailed Koussevitzky's activities; he continued to give concerts in Moscow; presented a memorial Scriabin program (1915); after the Revolution, was offered and accepted the directorship of the State Sym. Orch. (former Court Orch.) in Petrograd; also presented concerts in Moscow. He left Russia (1920), going to

Berlin, then Rome, and finally Paris; organized the Concerts Koussevitzky; presented new scores by French and Russian composers, including Ravel's orchestration of Mussorgsky's *Pictures at an Exhibition* (1922), Honegger's *Pacific 231* (1924) and *Chant de joie* (1923), Prokofiev's 1st Violin Concerto (1923) and *Seven Are They* (1924), and Stravinsky's *Symphonies of Wind Instruments* (London, 1921); Octet (1923, composer conducting); and the Piano Concerto (1924, composer soloist).

In 1924 Koussevitzky was appointed conductor of the Boston Sym. Orch. (1924–49); just as in Russia and France, he encouraged the country's composers (i.e., American) to write works for him; premiered works by Copland, Harris, Piston, Barber, Hanson, and Schuman; for the 50th anniversary of the Boston Sym. Orch. (1931), commissioned works from Stravinsky (*Sym. of Psalms*), Hindemith, Honegger, Prokofiev, Roussel, Ravel (Piano Concerto), Copland, and Gershwin. A major accomplishment in Koussevitzky's American period was establishing the Berkshire Music Center at Tanglewood, Mass., growing out of a 1934 Berkshire Sym. Festival organized by H. Hadley. Koussevitzky, and the Boston Sym. Orch. presented summer concerts at Tanglewood for the 1st time in 1935; these concerts are now an annual institution.; the Berkshire Music Center opened with Koussevitzky as director and Copland as assistant director (1940); guest instructors included Hindemith, Honegger, and Messiaen. Koussevitzky taught conducting; was succeeded after his death by Bernstein, a former student.

Koussevitzky held many honorary degrees; was a member of the French Legion of Honor; held the Cross of Commander of the Finnish Order of the White Rose; became a naturalized American citizen (1941). His wife Natalie died (1942); he established the Koussevitzky Foundation in her memory, with funds used to commission works by composers of any nationality; married Olga Naoumoff (1901–78), a niece of Natalie's (1947).

Koussevitzky possessed extraordinary emotional power; in Russian music, particularly Tchaikovsky's, he was unexcelled; capable of the subtlest nuances in works of the French school, especially Debussy. As a champion of modern music he had few equals; his ardor in putting unfamiliar music before audiences in several countries encouraged trust among listeners and music critics. He was often criticized for liberties in the treatment of classical masterpieces; while his performances of Bach, Beethoven, Brahms, and Schubert were untraditional, they were nonetheless musical in the sincere artistry that animated his interpretations.

Koven, Reginald de. See ⇒De Koven, (Henry Louis) Reginald.

koza (Pol., goat). Polish bellows-blown bagpipe, with goatskin bag; the chanter has around 8 fingerholes and a drone bent at a 90° angle; both chanter and drone end in an upturned bell of horn or metal.

Kräftig (Ger.). Forza.

krakowiak (Pol.; Fr. *cracovienne*; Ger. *Krakauer Tanz*). Fast syncopated Polish dance in 2/4 time, developed in the Kraków region; examples are found in tablatures and songbooks of the 16th century, where it was called *chorea polonica* or *volta polonica*; sometimes considered the Polish national dance,

although the polonaise predates it. The krakowiak became a component of the classical world; Chopin wrote *Krakowiak*, a rondo for piano and orch., op. 14 (1828), and another as the finale of the 1st Piano Concerto, op. 11 (1830).

Kraus (Trujillo), Alfredo, b. Las Palmas, Canary Islands, Sept. 24, 1927. He studied voice with G. Markoff in Barcelona and F. Andres in Valencia; completed studies with M. Llopart in Milan (1955); won 1st prize in the Geneva Competition (1956); made his operatic debut as the Duke of Mantua in Cairo; made his European debut in Venice as Alfredo, a role he repeated for his U.K. debut at London's Stoll Theatre (1957) and with which he had a remarkable success at Lisbon's Teatro São Carlo (1958). He made his debut at London's Covent Garden as Edgardo (1959); his U.S. debut followed at the Chicago Lyric Opera, as Nemorino in *L'elisir d'amore* (1962); made his Metropolitan Opera debut in N.Y. as the Duke of Mantua (1966). After a sabbatical from the stage in the 1970s, he returned to performing to great acclaim. A consummate artist with a remarkable beautiful voice, he is particularly noted for portrayals of Count Almaviva, Don Ottavio, Ernesto in *Don Pasquale*, Des Grieux in *Manon*, Nadir in *Les Pêcheurs de perles*, and Werther.

Krebsgang (Ger., crab walk). Retrograde. *Krebskanon*, see ⇒canon.

Kreisler, Fritz (Friedrich), b. Vienna, Feb. 2, 1875; d. N.Y., Jan. 29, 1962. His extraordinary talent manifested itself at age 4; carefully fostered by his father, then studied with J. Dont and J Auber; at 7, he entered the Vienna Cons.; studied with Hellmesberger, Jr. (violin) and Bruckner (theory); gave his 1st performance there at 9; awarded its gold medal at 10; subsequently studied with Massart (violin) and Delibes (composition) at the Paris Cons.; shared the premier prix in violin with 4 others (1887). He made his U.S. debut in Boston (1888); toured the U.S. with pianist Moriz Rosenthal (1889–90) with only moderate success.

Returning to Europe, Kreisler abandoned music to study medicine in Vienna and art in Rome and Paris; served as an officer in the Austrian army (1895–96); resuming his concert career, appeared with H. Richter and the Vienna Phil. (1898); a subsequent solo appearance with Nikisch and the Berlin Phil. launched his international career (1899). In addition to regaining his virtuosity during his respite, he had also become a master interpreter; on his 2nd U.S. tour of the U.S. (1900–1901), as soloist and as recitalist with Hofmann and Gerardy, he carried his audiences by storm; made his London debut with Richter and the Phil. Soc. orch. (1902); awarded its Gold Medal (1904). Elgar composed his Violin Concerto for him; Kreisler gave its premiere under the composer's direction in London (1910).

At the outbreak of World War I, Kreisler joined his former regiment, but was discharged after being wounded; returned to the U.S. to pursue his career; after the U.S. entered the war (1917), withdrew from public appearances. At war's end, he once more performed in N.Y. (1919) and resumed his tours; then made his home in Berlin (1924–34); went to France (1938) and became a naturalized citizen there; finally resettled in the U.S. (1939) and became a naturalized citizen (1943). He suffered a near-fatal accident when hit by a truck in N.Y. (1941); he recovered and concertized until 1950.

Kreisler was a great master of the violin; his brilliant technique was matched by a remarkable tone; he placed both at the service of the composer. He owned the great Guarneri "del Gesu" violin (1733) and instruments by other masters; gathered a rich collection of invaluable MSS; donated original scores of Brahms's Violin Concerto and Chausson's *Poème* for violin and orch. to the Library of Congress (1949); wrote many extremely popular violin pieces, among them *Caprice viennois*, *Tambourin chinois*, *Schön Rosmarin*, and *Liebesfreud*. He also publ. pieces in an "olden style," ascribed to various composers; reluctantly admitted that these pieces were his own (1935), excepting the 1st 8 bars from the "Couperin" *Chanson Louis XIII*, based on a traditional melody; attributed his actions to a desire to build up well-rounded concert programs with virtuoso pieces by established composers, rather than under his own name. He wrote the operettas *Apple Blossoms* (N.Y., 1919) and *Sissy* (Vienna, 1932); publ. numerous arrangements of early and modern music (Corelli's *La Folia*, Tartini's *The Devil's Trill*, Dvořák's *Slavonic Dances*, dances by Granados and Albeniz, etc.); prepared cadenzas for the Beethoven and Brahms violin concertos.

Kremer, Gidon, b. Riga, Feb. 27, 1947. His parents were violinists in the Riga Sym. Orch.; after studies inside the family circle, he continued with David Oistrakh at the Moscow Cons.; won 1st prizes at the Paganini Competition in Genoa (1968) and Tchaikovsky Competition in Moscow (1970); made an auspicious N.Y. debut at Avery Fisher Hall (1977). In subsequent years he appeared as soloist with major orchs. of the world, gave recitals, performed chamber music, and organized festivals; his great contribution to modern music has been the consistent presentation of new works, notably those of Schnittke, Gubaidulina, and Pärt.

Krenek, Ernst, (born Ernst Křenek), b. Vienna, Aug. 23, 1900; d. Palm Springs, Calif., Dec. 23, 1991. He studied with Franz Schreker in Vienna (from 1916) and at the Berlin Academy of Music (1920–23); conductor and composer at the opera houses in Kassel and Wiesbaden (1925–27); returned to Vienna (1928); wrote for the *Frankfurter Zeitung* (1930–33); traveled widely in Europe as lecturer and accompanist in programs of his songs. After the *Anschluss* of 1938 he settled in the U.S.; became a naturalized American citizen (1945) and altered the spelling of his name; was prof. of music at Vassar College (1939–42); head of the music dept. at Hamline Univ. in St. Paul, Minn. (1942–47); made his home in Calif. He married Gustav Mahler's surviving daughter, Anna (1923), but was divorced (1925); married Berta Hermann, then composer Gladys Nordenstrom (1950).

Krenek's lifetime evolution as a composer mirrors the development of modern music; the Mahler tradition was the dominant influence of his early music; he was then associated with Viennese modernists, particularly Schoenberg, Berg, and Webern; in Germany he was considered co-inventor with Hindemith of modern satiric opera. He achieved masterly compositional technique early on, developing his melodic and harmonic idiom toward atonality and polytonality. His 1st and greatest international success came with the production of the opera *Jonny spielt auf* (Leipzig, 1927); described as a "jazz opera," no such designation appears in the score. It tells of a jazz fiddler whose fame sweeps the world; in the apotheosis, Jonny sits atop a gigantic globe; when staged at the Metropolitan Opera

in N.Y. (1929), the hero wore blackface rather than being black as in the original (wreaking havoc in the process).

Krenek adopted an integral 12-tone method of composition (1933); his historical opera *Karl V* was written in this idiom; his dodecaphonic approach allowed for textual and textural indulgences: division of the basic row into fractional groups, permutation of thematic elements, and rotation of initial notes. But the accession of Nazi governments in central Europe led to a performance ban on his works there; a much-anticipated production of *Karl V* in Vienna was canceled. Although unimpeachably Aryan, Krenek's music was banned not so much for its advanced musical idiom as for the use of jazz-like idioms in *Jonny spielt auf*; not only was a decadent culture saluting blacks and Jews being celebrated, but Jonny himself belonged to what the Nazis considered an inferior race. Krenek's viciously retouched photograph was featured along with other "cultural Bolshevists" in the infamous exhibit of *entartete Musik* (degenerate music).

Deprived of all means of subsistence, Krenek went to the U.S.; friends and admirers found a modest engagement as composition teacher at the Malkin Cons. in Boston for him; a few performances by American orchs. followed; his modernistic idiom upset some American music lovers; a Boston Sym. Orch. dowager was heard to say after a performance of the Piano Concerto, "Conditions must be terrible in Europe!" Generally, there have been fewer performances of his works in his adopted homeland than in Europe since the war; Stravinsky, who admired him as intellectual and composer, predicted that he would one day be honored in both America and Europe (1963); Krenek wrote, in his 1950 autobiography, *Selbstdarstellung:* "It is quite possible that the unusual variety of my output has baffled observers accustomed to more homogeneous phenomena. It is my impression that this confusion has surrounded my work with an unusual obscurity—almost anonymity." In any case, he remained a prolific and thoughtful composer.

The liberated Austrian government awarded Krenek the Grand State Prize (1963); a number of festivals and celebrations, timed for Krenek's 90th birthday, included the premiere of his oratorio *Opus sine nomine* (1990); revival of a trilogy of short operas, *Der Diktator*, *Das geheime Königreich*, and *Schwergewicht, oder Die Ehre der Nation* (1928); the Salzburg Festival, performing orch'l music; a revival of *Jonny spielt auf* at the Leipzig Opera; and the Stuttgart Krenek Festival. His autobiography, completed in 1950 and deposited at the Library of Congress, will not be opened until 15 years after his death.

Kreuz (Ger., cross). Sharp (♯).

Krone (Ger., crown). Tubing inserted in natural horns or trumpets to change the fundamental tuning; the invention of valve horns eliminated need for this device.

Krummhorn (Ger., crooked horn). Crumhorn.

Krupa, Gene, b. Chicago, Jan. 15, 1909; d. Yonkers, N.Y., Oct. 16, 1973. He joined a jazz band during his adolescence; studied percussion with A. Silverman, E. Straight, and R. Knapp (1925); worked with local musicians. He went to N.Y. (1929); performed with bands led by Red Nichols and Irving Aaronson; later became a featured member of Benny Goodman's band (1934); won acclaim for his brilliant playing in the recording of

Sing, Sing, Sing. He left Goodman (1938); formed his own band (featuring singer Anita O'Day); toured Europe and Asia, becoming internationally famous. He rejoined Goodman briefly (1943), then joined Tommy Dorsey's band (1943–44); subsequently led his own band (to 1951); toured with Jazz at the Phil. and with his own trios and quartets; he and Cozy Cole co-founded a school of percussion in N.Y. Possessed with phenomenal technique, and despite a penchant for exhibitionism, he "popularized" the drums with extended, virtuosic solos; recorded the soundtrack for the mostly fact-free *The Gene Krupa Story* (1959).

Kubelík, Jan, b. Michle, near Prague, July 5, 1880; d. Prague, Dec. 5, 1940. He began violin training with his father; studied with Sevcik (violin) and Foerster (composition) at the Prague Cons. (1892–98); continued studying in Vienna; made his debut (1898). In 1900 he made his London debut; made triumphant tours of Europe and the U.S.; awarded the Gold Medal of the Phil. Soc. of London (1902); married a Hungarian countess and became a naturalized Hungarian citizen (1903). He continued his active career for over 4 decades; gave a series of farewell concerts (1939–40); his last concert in Prague (1940) occurred after his beloved homeland had been dismembered by the Nazis. One of the foremost virtuosos of his day, he also composed, notably 6 violin concertos; prepared cadenzas for the Beethoven, Brahms, and Tchaikovsky concertos. He was the father of (Jeronym) Rafael Kubelík.

Kubelík, (Jeronym) Rafael, b. Býchory, near Kolín, June 29, 1914; d. Lucerne, Aug. 11, 1996. He studied violin with his father Jan Kubelík; continued his training at the Prague Cons.; made his conducting debut with the Czech Phil. in Prague (1934); conductor at the National Theater in Brno (1939–41). He was chief conductor of the Czech Phil. during one of the most difficult periods in the history of the orch. and the Czech nation (1942–48); refused to collaborate with the Nazi occupation authorities; when the Communists took control of the government (1948), he left the country for the West, vowing not to return until the political situation had changed.

Kubelík guest conducted in England and Western Europe; made his U.S. debut with the Chicago Sym. Orch. (1949), which led to his appointment as its music director (1950); his programming of contemporary works and insistence on painstaking rehearsals antagonized some of his auditors, including members of the Chicago press; he resigned his post (1953); became music director at the Royal Opera House at Covent Garden in London (1955–58), a tenure notable for important productions of *Les Troyens, Boris Godunov* (in the orig. version), and *Jenůfa*; chief conductor of the Bavarian Radio Sym. Orch. in Munich (1961–79). He made his Metropolitan Opera debut in N.Y. as its 1st music director, conducting *Les Troyens* (1973); again became an epicenter of controversy and soon submitted his resignation. In spite of the contretemps, his artistic integrity remained intact; appeared widely as guest conductor in Western Europe and the U.S.; in light of his controversial tenure in Chicago, it is ironic that he became an honored guest conductor with that orch. in later years. He retired in 1985; returned to Czechoslovakia after 42 years' absence to conduct the Czech Phil. in performances of Smetana's symphonic cycle *Ma Vlast* during the opening of the Prague Spring Festival, despite increasingly ill health (1990).

Kubelík was the foremost Czech conductor of his generation; in addition to idiomatic and authoritative performances of his country's music, was greatly esteemed for distinguished interpretations of the standard repertoire, marked by pristine musicianship and unfettered by self-indulgence. He became a Swiss citizen (1966); his 2nd wife was the Australian soprano Elsie Morison; composed several operas, orch'l, and choral works; 6 string quartets and other chamber music; songs.

Kuhglocke (*Kuhhorn, Kuhreigen;* Ger.). Ranz des vaches.

kujawiak. Polish dance from the Kujawiak region; in the rhythm of a mazurka but at a faster tempo.

kulintang. Gong-chime of the Phillippines, consisting of between 8 and 12 bossed gongs placed open-face down in 2 rows, suspended and isolated by taut strings; played with a pair of padded sticks; similar instruments are found in Malaysia and much of Indonesia, where it is a constituent of the gamelan.

kultrún *(cultrún).* Rattle drum of the Araucano people of Chile; a wooden platter or calabash body is attached to a horseskin head, which holds pebbles; played with a drumstick.

Kulturboschewismus. Cultural bolshevism; applied by Nazi officials to condemn art or music (e.g., of 2nd Viennese school, Stravinsky, Jewish composers) as artistically radical, therefore racially, socially, and/or politically suspect; another favorite Nazi term was *entartete Musik* (degenerate music).

Kunc, Božidar. See ⇒Milanov, Zinka.

kurz (Ger.). Short. *Kurz und bestimmt,* short and with determination.

Kussevitsky, Serge (Alexandrovich). Koussevitzky, Serge (Alexandrovich).

kymbala (Grk.). Ancient cymbals, either platelike or bulbous in shape; when struck together, produce a dull percussive sound. Greek writers compared their sound with galloping horse hooves. Not the same as antique cymbals (crotales).

Kyrie (Grk., Lord). 1st section of the Ordinary in the Roman Catholic High Mass; it is sung after the introit; the brief text is divided into three phrases, with repetitions: *Kyrie eleison* (Lord, have mercy), *Christe eleison* (Christ, have mercy), and *Kyrie eleison.*

L. (Ger., *links*). Left, as in *l.h.*, left hand.

La. 1. 6th note of Guido d'Arezzo's hexachord, corresponding to the last line of the Hymn to St. John, "Labii reatum." *La* is still used to designate the 6th diatonic degree of the scale in Romance languages and in Russian; it is also used in the system of movable Do, where it is also called *Lah*. 2. (It., Fr., singular) The.

La Barbara, Joan (Linda Lotz), b. Philadelphia, June 8, 1947. She learned piano from her grandfather; sang in church, school choirs, and a folk group; studied voice with Helen Boatwright at the Syracuse Univ. School of Music (1965–68), Phyllis Curtin at Tanglewood (1967–68), and Marion Szekely-Freschl at the Juilliard School in N.Y.; took a B.S. degree in music education at N.Y. Univ. She made her vocal debut at N.Y.'s Town Hall with Steve Reich and Musicians (1971), with whom she continued to perform (to 1974); worked with the Philip Glass Ensemble (1973–76); toured the U.S. and Europe; was composer-in-residence in West Berlin under the aegis of the Deutscher Akademischer Austauschdienst (1979); taught voice and composition at the Calif. Inst. of the Arts in Valencia (from 1981); married Morton Subotnick (1979). A champion of contemporary music, she developed her performing talents to a high degree; her vocal techniques include multiphonics and circular breathing, with unique throat clicks and a high flutter to match; her compositions effectively exploit her abilities.

La cadenza sia corta (It.). Let the cadenza be short.

La Guerre, Élisabeth Jacquet de. Jacquet de La Guerre, Elisabeth.

Labèque, Katia b. Hendaye, Mar. 3, 1950, and **Marielle Labèque** b. Hendaye, Mar. 6, 1952, French duo-pianists. The sisters studied piano as children with their mother, pupil of French pianist Marguerite Long (1874–1966); made their formal debut in Bayonne (1961); completed their studies with J. B. Pommier at the Paris Cons.; were awarded 1st prize at graduation (1968); embarked upon a meteoric career as duo-pianists; toured widely in Europe, North America, the Middle East, and the Far East; appeared with leading orchs. of the world. Their repertoire is catholic, ranging from masterworks of the past to scores by Messiaen, Boulez, and Berio; also popular works, from Joplin to Gershwin, championed the latter's duo-piano versions of *Rhapsody in Blue, Concerto in F,* and *An American in Paris.*

Lacrimosa (Lat.). Part of the Requiem Mass. *Lacrimoso,* tearfully.

Lage (Ger.). 1. Position (of a chord). 2. Left-hand playing position on violin family instruments, moving up and down the fingerboard. *Enge Lage,* close position or harmony. *Weite Lage,* open position or harmony.

lagrimoso (It., tearfully). Plaintively, like a lament.

Lah. In tonic sol-fa, the equivalent of La.

lai (Fr., lay). Chanson genre of French trouvères and late medieval composers; like other French song forms of the time, texts are strophic; with the lai there are nearly as many poetic (i.e., musical) forms as there are examples. The lai could be simply a poem without music; Machaut wrote several of both types. The lai may be related to the *descort, Leich, estampie, ductia, ensalada,* and even the liturgical sequence (and related portions).

Lalo, Édouard (-Victoire-Antoine), b. Lille, Jan. 27, 1823; d. Paris, Apr. 22, 1892. He studied violin and cello at the Lille Cons.; in response to his father's objection to his choice of career, he left home at age 16; studied violin with Habeneck at the Paris Cons.; studied composition privately with J. Schulhoff and Crevecoeur; made a precarious living as violinist and teacher; began to compose songs and chamber music (1848–60). He was a founding member of the Armingaud Quartet (1855), serving 1st as violist, then as 2nd violinist. The indifferent response accorded his music led him to abandon composition after 1860; however, his 1865 marriage to the contralto Bernier de Maligny, who sang his songs, prompted him to resume composing.

Lalo wrote an opera, *Fiesque*; sent it to the Théâtre-Lyrique in Paris (1867); it was rejected; this rebuke left him deeply embittered. He was so convinced of the score's intrinsic worth that he reworked parts of it into other works, including the 1st *Aubade* for Small Orch., the G-minor Sym. and the *Divertissement*; the last was remarkably successful when introduced at the Concert Populaire (1872). Sarasate gave the premiere performance of his Violin Concerto (1874) and the *Symphonie espagnole* for Violin and Orch. (1875); the *Symphonie,* a brilliant virtuoso piece with vibrant Spanish rhythms, brought Lalo international fame; it remains his best-known composition outside of France.

Lalo had not given up on writing for the stage; began work on *Le Roi d'Ys* (1875); much of the score was finished by 1881; extracts were performed in concert; no theater showed interest. While working on several orch'l pieces, he accepted a commission from the Opéra to write a ballet; although the result, *Namouna* (1882), failed to make an impression, he drew orch'l suites from it that became quite popular. He finally succeeded in persuading the Paris Opéra-Comique to produce *Le Roi d'Ys;* the premiere (1888) was enormously successful; he was made an Officer of the Legion of Honor. While *Le Roi d'Ys* is considered his masterpiece by his countrymen, the instrumental music is particularly important in assessing his achievement; his craftsmanship, combined with true originality, places him among the most important French composers of his time.

Lamb, Joseph F(rancis), b. Montclair, N.J., Dec. 6, 1887; d. N.Y., Sept. 3, 1960. He had no formal musical training and spent most of his life in the textile import business; but he was an important composer of piano rags during ragtime's heyday; also wrote songs for Tin Pan Alley. After 3 decades in obscurity he resurfaced and began composing rags again and performing in public (from 1949). Among his fine are *Sensation* (1908),

Ethiopia Rag (1909), *Excelsior Rag* (1909), *Champagne Rag* (1910), *American Beauty Rag* (1913), *Cleopatra Rag* (1915), *Contentment Rag* (1915), *The Ragtime Nightingale* (1915), *Top Liner Rag* (1916), and *Bohemia Rag* (1919); an anthology of his works appeared in N.Y. (1964).

Lambert, (Leonard) Constant, b. London, Aug. 23, 1905; d. there, Aug. 21, 1951. He won a scholarship to the Royal College of Music in London; studied with R. O. Morris and Vaughan Williams (1915–22); his 1st major score, the ballet *Romeo and Juliet* (Monte Carlo, 1926), was commissioned by Diaghilev; this early association with dance proved decisive, as he spent most of his career as conductor and composer of ballets. His interest in jazz resulted in such fine scores as *Elegiac Blues* for Orch. (1927), *The Rio Grande* for Piano, Chorus, and Orch. (1927; text by S. Sitwell), and the Concerto for Piano and 9 Performers (1930–31). The ballet most striking in craftsmanship is *Horoscope* (1937).

Lambert became conductor of the Camargo Soc. for ballet productions (1930); made music director of the Vic-Wells Ballet (1931), remaining in that capacity through its transformations (Sadler's Wells Ballet, Royal Ballet), resigning in 1947; became one of its artistic directors (1948); conducted it on its 1st U.S. visit (1949). He appeared at London's Covent Garden (1937; 1939; 1946–47); was associate conductor of the London Promenade Concerts (1945–46); conducted broadcasts over the BBC. He contributed articles to *The Nation* and *Athenaeum* (from 1930) and the *Sunday Referee* (from 1931); penned the provocative book *Music Ho! A Study of Music in Decline* (1934). One of the most gifted musicians of his generation, Lambert's exhausting conducting work and excessive consumption of alcohol prevented him from fully asserting his compositional side in later years. It was so excessive that he slurred his words to the point of eliminating conjunctions.

Lambert, Michel. See ⇒Lully, Jean-Baptiste.

lamellaphones. Class of handheld musical instruments indigenous to sub-Saharan Africa; the sound is produced by thin tongues of metal or wood vibrating when plucked by the thumbs; the tongues are attached to a rectangular wooden or metal resonator; examples include the sanza (sansa), mbira, likembe, and kalimba; also called thumb piano.

lament. Generic term for dirges, elegies, or threnodies chanted upon the death of an important person or beloved friend; surviving examples date back to the death of Charlemagne (814); in France a lament was called *déploration*, *plainte*, or *tombeau*. Ockeghem wrote a lament on the death of Binchois; was in turn musically mourned by Des Prez, who was euphonically eulogized by Gombert. Couperin "le Grand" wrote an "apotheosis" for Lully, but had to wait nearly 2 centuries to be commemorated with suitable grandeur in Ravel's *Le Tombeau de Couperin*.

Apart from composed laments, Slavic rural populations have practiced a culture of cries, sobs, wails, and outcries; professional female lamenters were engaged to shed copious tears at funerals, military conscriptions bemoaning a young man's mobilization, and peasant weddings when the fate of a youthful bride was deplored with great ululations. A remarkable example of nuptial *déploration* occurs in Stravinsky's wedding cantata *Les Noces*, where agonized female anticipation of the bride's loss of virginity is contrasted by an antiphonal exchange of male commentary as to how much it would be worth in rubles, individually and collectively, to "swell the belly" of the innocent bride.

lamento (It., lamentation, complaint). Aria type in Italian opera in which a character expresses unquenchable sorrow and complains about his or her misery. Lamento d'Arianna, the only surviving segment from Monteverdi's opera Arianna (1608), is an outstanding early example; in it, Ariadne laments her painful abandonment by the treacherous Theseus (as she would 3 centuries later in R. Strauss's Ariadne auf Naxos).

Landini cadence (Burgundian cadence). Formulaic close where the melodic leading tone dips to the submediant before resolving to its tonic (7–6–8); named after Francesco Landini, whose extensive use thereof helped establish it in the later Middle Ages; he did not invent it; it lasted into the 15th century (in wks. by Dufay, Binchois), where its resolution became more melismatic. In works à 2, the lower voice held the supertonic while the upper sounded the 7–6, then resolved downward to form an octave; works à 3 added a middle resolution of the subdominant upward to the dominant; the most distinctive (and controversial) type is the double leading-tone cadence, involving a raised subdominant.

Landini, Francesco (Franciscus Landino, Magister Franciscus de Florentia, Magister Franciscus Cecus Horghanista de Florentia), b. probably in Florence, c. 1325; d. there, Sept. 2, 1397. His father, the painter Jacopo Del Casentino (d. 1349), co-founded Florence's painters' guild (1339). Blinded by smallpox as a child, Francesco turned to music; learned to play organ and other instruments as well as sang; was well known as organist, organ builder, organ tuner, instrument maker, and poet. He was organist at the monastery of S. Trinita (1361); cappellanus at the church of S. Lorenzo (1365–97). His output is particularly significant, representing around a quarter of extant Trecento music; some 154 works have been identified as his, including 90 ballate à 2, 42 à 3, and 8 in 2- and 3-part versions; 2- and 3-part madrigali, a French virelai, and a caccia; many set his own texts, although the number is unknown.

Ländler (Ger.; Fr. Tyrolienne). Slow folk dance of German-speaking areas of Europe in 3/4 or 6/4 time, precursor of the more urbane 19th-century waltz; dates from the 17th century; known under various guises, including the German dance (Deutscher Tanz) written by Haydn and Mozart and intended for courtly dancer. In its orig. rustic form it was an outdoor dance, with hopping, stamping, and passing under while the couple held each other by the waist; songs associated with this dance might include yodeling. The Ländler survived into the 19th century, but evolved into a faster, more refined, lighter dance; by the early 20th century Ländler music held great nostalgic weight for composers such as Mahler and Berg.

Landowska, Wanda (Alexandra), b. Warsaw, July 5, 1879; d. Lakeville, Conn., Aug. 16, 1959. She studied piano at the Warsaw Cons. with Michalowski and in Berlin with Moszkowski; went to Paris (1900); traveled widely in Europe as pianist and harpsichordist (from 1903); toured Russia (1909); played for Tolstoy, who showed great interest in her ideas on classical music. Subsequently she devoted her efforts principally to reviving the art of harpsichord playing; commissioned the Pleyel firm of Paris to construct a harpsichord for her (1912), the 1st of many instruments they would build for her. She was invited by Kretzschmar to give a special course in harpsichord playing at the Berlin Hochschule für Musik (1913).

After the 1st World War, Landowska gave harpsichord master classes at the Basel Cons. (1919); returned to Paris; bought a villa in St.-Leu-la-Forêt, near Paris (1925); established a school for the study of early music; a concert hall was built there (1927); she presented regular early music concerts, giving lessons on the subject; assembled a large collection of harpsichords. Her school attracted students from all over the world; she also taught at N. Boulanger's Fontainebleau Cons.; appeared at concerts in Paris as both pianist and harpsichordist. She commissioned de Falla to compose a chamber concerto; played the solo part in its premiere in Barcelona (1926); also commissioned Poulenc's *Concert champêtre* for Harpsichord and Small Orch. (1929). She made her American debut as soloist with the Philadelphia Orch., under Stokowski (1923); returned to France. When the Germans invaded France (1940), she fled to Switzerland, abandoning her villa, library, and instruments; she reached N.Y. (1941); presented a harpsichord concert (1942); devoted herself mainly to teaching; made recordings; settled in her new home at Lakeville, Conn.

Landowska is considered one of the greatest harpsichordists; her interpretations of Baroque music were notable in their balance between classical precision and freedom from rigidity, particularly in treatment of ornamentation. If there is a consistent criticism against her, it should be directed at Pleyel's instruments, designed to counter criticism that harpsichord tone was "feeble"; they had pianolike dimensions and heavy 2-manual registrations, naturally affecting the timbre of her playing. She wrote several books on music and cadenzas for Mozart's concertos.

Lane, Burton (born Morris Hyman Kushner), b. N.Y., Feb. 2, 1912. He studied with S. Bucharoff; after writing for revues, began to compose Broadway musicals: *Hold On to Your Hats* (1940), *Laffing Room Only* (1944), *Finian's Rainbow* (with *Something Sort of Grandish, Old Devil Moon, How Are Things in Glocca Morra?*), *On a Clear Day You Can See Forever* (1965), and *Carmelina* (1979). He wrote for some 40 films, including *St. Louis Blues, Babes on Broadway* (with *How About You?*), *Ship Ahoy*, and *Royal Wedding* (with *Too Late Now*); among lyricists he worked with were I. Gershwin, F. Loesser, Harburg, and Lerner.

Langridge, Philip (Gordon), b. Hawkhurst, Kent, Dec. 16, 1939. He studied violin at the Royal Academy of Music in London; took voice lessons with B. Boyce and C. Bizony; an active violinist, he began to make appearances as a singer (from 1962); sang at the Glyndebourne Festival (1964); made regular appearances there (from 1977) and at the Edinburgh Festivals (from 1970). He appeared at Milan's La Scala (1979); made his debut at London's Covent Garden as the Fisherman in Stravinsky's *The Nightingale* (1983); made his Metropolitan Opera debut in N.Y. as Ferrando in *Così fan tutte* (1985). He created the role of Orpheus in Birtwistle's opera *The Mask of Orpheus* at London's

English National Opera (1986). Admired as both operatic and concert singer, he maintains an extensive repertoire ranging from Baroque masters to contemporary works; married to the classical singer Ann Murray.

langsam (Ger.). Slow. *Langsamer*, slower.

languendo (*con languore;* It.). Languishing, plaintively, languid.

Lanner, Joseph (Franz Karl), b. Vienna, Apr. 12, 1801; d. Oberdöbling, near Vienna, Apr. 14, 1843. A self-taught violinist and composer, he joined Pamer's dance orch. At age 12; formed a trio (1818); J. Strauss, Sr. joined to make it a quartet (1819); the group continued to grow; by 1824 it was a famous full-sized classical orch. performing in coffeehouses, taverns, and at balls; the orch. was then divided into 2 ensembles, with Lanner leading one and Strauss the other; eventually Strauss went his own way (1825). With Strauss, Lanner is an acknowledged creator of the Viennese waltz; his output totals 209 dance pieces, including waltzes, Ländler, quadrilles, polkas, galops, and marches, along with misc. orch'l works. His son August (Joseph) Lanner (b. Vienna, Jan. 23, 1834; d. there, Sept. 27, 1855) was a talented violinist, dance composer, and conductor.

Lanza, Mario (born Alfredo Arnold Cocozza), b. Philadelphia, Jan. 31, 1921; d. Rome, Oct. 7, 1959. He studied singing with Enrico Rosati; appeared in recitals and opera; played the title role of a highly successful film, *The Great Caruso* (1951); appeared in 6 other films, including *The Toast of New Orleans* (with his biggest hit, *Be My Love*). His career quickly unraveled as obesity overtook him, leading to an early death.

larga (*maxima*; Lat., large). In mensural notation, the longest durational symbol, exceeding even the longa; it is notated as a very long rectangular bar with a downward flag attached to its right side; it is either twice or thrice the length of a longa, depending on mensural context (binary or ternary).

largamente (It., broadly). With vigorous and sustained tone and breadth, without change of tempo.

largando (It., growing broader). Get slower and more marked; a crescendo is implied.

larghetto (It.). A "little" largo, i.e., a faster tempo, nearly andantino.

largo (It., broad). Very slow and stately, with ample breadth. *Largo assai; largo di molto; molto largo; larghissimo*, very slowly with breadth; *poco largo*, with some breadth (can occur even during an allegro).

larmoyant (Fr.; It. *lacrimoso*). Tearfully.

Larrocha (y de la Calle), Alicia de, b. Barcelona, May 23, 1923. She studied piano with Frank Marshall and theory with R. Lamote de Grignon; made her 1st public appearance at age 5; was soloist with the Orquesta Sinfónica of Madrid at 11. She launched her career in earnest (1940); began touring Europe (1947); made her 1st U.S. visit (1955); thereafter toured throughout the world to great acclaim. She directed the Marshall

Academy in Barcelona (from 1959). Her interpretations of Spanish music have evoked universal admiration for their authenticity; has been exuberantly praised for her impeccable taste and exquisitely polished technique in Classic works, particularly Mozart.

lascivious mode. Ionian mode.

Lasso, Orlando di (in Latin, Orlandus Lassus; in French, Roland de Lassus); b. Mons, 1532; d. Munich, June 14, 1594. He entered the service of F. Gonzaga at 12 years of age; subsequently traveled with him; was placed in the service of C. Castrioto in Naples (1550); proceeded to Rome and entered the service of Antonio Altoviti, Archbishop of Florence; maestro di cappella at St. John Lateran (1553–54). He went to Antwerp (1555); enjoyed a fine reputation socially and artistically; his 1st collection, containing 22 Petrarchian madrigals, was publ. (Venice, 1555); brought out a collection of madrigals and motets in Italian, French, and Latin (Antwerp, 1555).

In 1556 Lasso joined the Munich court chapel of Duke Albrecht of Bavaria as a singer; appointed maestro di cappella of the Munich court chapel (1563–94), a position he held with great eminence. He took a number of sojourns: to Flanders to recruit singers (1560), to Frankfurt for the coronation of Emperor Maximilian II (1562), to Italy (1567; 1574–79), to the French court (1571; 1573–74), and to Regensburg (1593); received a hereditary rank of nobility from Maximilian (1570). Unfortunately, his later years were marked by increasing depression.

Lasso represents the culmination of the great era of Franco-Flemish polyphony; he exhibited equal mastery in the sacred elevated style as well as popular secular music; as with other late Renaissance composers, his art was supranational, writing Italian madrigals, German lieder, French chansons, and Latin motets; his colleagues described him as the "Belgian Orpheus" and "Prince of Music." The sheer scope of his production is incredible: more than 2,000 vocal works, publications include the *Patrocinium Musices* (Munich, 1573–98), featuring 7 vols. of religious music; the *Psalms of David* (1584); the posth. collections *Lagrime di S Pietro* (1595) and *Prophetiae Sibyllarum* (1600); his sons publ. 516 motets as *Magnum opus musicum* (1604).

lassú (Hung.). Opening slow section of the csárdás or verbunkos.

lauda (It.; plural *laude*, *laudi*). Hymn of praise; particularly popular with itinerant monastic orders, penitents as well as flagellants. Because of the peripatetic nature of these orders, laude became overgrown with unrelated dance forms, such as the frottola and ballata, while retaining its basic religious character. The laude influenced the development of the oratorio in the early 17th century.

Laudamus te (Lat., We praise Thee). Part of the Gloria of the Mass.

laudi spirituali (Lat.). Medieval songs of devotion.

Lauds (Lat. *laudes*, thanksgiving). Originally, the 2nd Canonical Hour (dawn, after Matins); now the 1st of the Roman Catholic daily prayers; usually comprises *Laudate Dominum*, *Cantate Domino Canticum novum*, and *Laudate Dominum in sanctis ejus*.

Lauf (Ger., run). Rapid passage in running scales.

launeddas. Sardinian triple pipe, each with a single reed and constructed divergently, 2 melodic pipes on the outside, the drone in the center; the right pipe is shorter than the left; all 3 are mouthed; may be of Phoenician origin.

launig (Ger.). 1. With light, gay humor. 2. With facile, characteristic expression.

Laute (Ger.). Lute.

Lavignac, (Alexandre Jean) Albert, b. Paris, Jan. 21, 1846; d. there, May 28, 1916. He studied at the Paris Cons. with Marmontel (piano), Bazin and Benoist (harmony), and A. Thomas (composition); won several prizes (1857–65); appointed assistant prof. of solfège (1871), prof. of solfège (1875), then prof. of harmony (1891). His *Cours complet théorique et pratique de dictée musicale* (6 vols., Paris and Brussels, 1882) attracted considerable attention; influenced the introduction of musical dictation as a regular subject in all major European cons.; he wrote several more pedagogical texts. But his magnum opus was the *Encyclopédie de la musique et Dictionnaire du Conservatoire* (Paris, 3 vols., 1920–31), which he ed. (1913–16); wrote *La Musique et les musiciens* (Paris, 1895); *Le Voyage artistique à Bayreuth* (Paris, 1897); *Les Gaités du Conservatoire* (Paris, 1900); and *Notions scolaires de musique* (Paris and Brussels, 1905).

lavolta. See ⇒Volta.

Law, Andrew, b. Milford, Conn., Mar. 21, 1749; d. Cheshire, Conn., July 13, 1821. He graduated from Rhode Island College (M.A. 1778); studied theology; ordained in Hartford (1787); active as a preacher in Philadelphia and Baltimore, then as a pioneer singing teacher in New England. He invented a new system of notation (patented 1802), employing 4 (later 7) different shapes of notes without staff; unsuccessful and used in only a few of his books; a 2nd innovation (at least by American standards) was setting the melody in the soprano instead of the tenor. He compiled or composed several hymn collections and instructional books on music; only 1 of his tunes, *Archdale*, gained popularity; but his teaching books, quaintly but clearly written, contributed considerably to early music education in America; ironically, his failed "shaped note" system, combined with the staff, became the notational norm of 19th-century Protestant hymnody.

Laws, Hubert, b. Houston, Nov. 10, 1939. He learned to play saxophone, piano, guitar, and flute; played saxophone with the Jazz Crusaders (1954–60); pursued classical music studies; played with the N.Y. Jazz Sextet (from 1967); played with other groups before joining the Metropolitan Opera Orch. in N.Y. as a flutist; appeared as soloist with the N.Y. Phil.; continued to appear in jazz settings. Among his recordings are *Crying Song* (1969), *Afro-Classic* (1971), *At Carnegie Hall* (1973), *How to Beat the High Cost of Living* (1980), and *Storm Then the Calm* (1994).

His brother Ronnie Laws (b. Houston, Oct. 3, 1950) is a tenor saxophonist and leader; performed with Quincy Jones, Hugh Masekela, Kenny Burrell, Ramsey Lewis, Earth, Wind and Fire, and his brother; as a leader he is best known for *Pressure Sensitive* (1984).

le (It., Fr.). The.

Le Caine, Hugh, b. Port Arthur, Ontario, May 27, 1914; d. Ottawa, July 3, 1977. After childhood training in music and science, he chose to emphasize science, attending Queen's Univ. in Kingston, Ontario, (B.S. 1938; M.S. 1939) and the Univ. of Birmingham (Ph.D. in nuclear physics, 1952); studied piano briefly at the Royal Cons. of Music of Toronto and privately with Viggo Kihl. His childhood dream had been to apply scientific techniques to the development and invention of new musical instruments; went on to develop groundbreaking electronic musical instruments that formed the basis of pioneering electronic music studios at the Univ. of Toronto (1959) and McGill Univ. in Montreal (1964); exhibited exemplars at Expo '67 in Montreal; contributed numerous articles on his findings in scholarly journals.

While Le Caine saw himself as a designer of instruments that would assist others' creativity, he realized his own striking electronic compositions along the way, notably the classic *Dripsody* (1959), based solely on the sound of a single drop of water falling; other works included *Alchemy* (1964) and *Perpetual Motion for Data Systems Computer* (1970). His instruments revolutionized musical composition; the Sackbut synthesizer (1945–48; 1954–60; 1969–73) is now recognized as the 1st voltage-controlled synthesizer; other instruments are the Spectrogram, facilitating compositional use of complex sine tones (1959–62), Alleatone, "a controlled chance device selecting one of 16 channels with weighted probabilities" (c. 1962), Sonde, able to generate 200 sine waves simultaneously (1968–70), and Polyphone, a polyphonic synthesizer operated by a touch-sensitive keyboard (1970).

lead. 1. Giving-out or proposition of a theme by one part. 2. Cue.

lead guitar. Guitar, lead.

lead sheet. Modern form of tablature with melody on a staff, over which the harmony is marked in shorthand (e.g., C7 G min, F dim⁷); the 1st verse is often placed below the melody line, with additional verses at the bottom of the page.

Leadbelly (Lead Belly; born Huddie Ledbetter), b. Mooringsport, La., Jan. 21, 1885; d. N.Y., Dec. 6, 1949. Self-taught as a musician, he possessed genuine talent for singing traditional American song; mastered the 12-string guitar; his claim to having accompanied "Blind" Lemon Jefferson in Dallas is disputed. While in Texas he was jailed for murder (1918–25); served another term for attempted homicide at the La. State Penitentiary (1930–34), where he was discovered by folk researchers John A. and Alan Lomax, who recorded him there and gained his release. He settled in N.Y., made a series of historically significant recordings for the Library of Congress (1935–40); served another term for assault (1939–40). He spent his last years playing nightclubs; was the darling of and

major influence on the white "hootenanny" movement of the 1940s.

Leadbelly made a turn-of-the-century popular song, *Goodnight, Irene*, into a uniquely personal version; it became his signature tune, but a major hit for The Weavers only after his death; other songs associated with him were Jefferson's *Match Box Blues*, *If It Wasn't for Dicky*, *Honey I'm All Out and Down*, *Becky Deem*, *Good Morning Blues*, *On a Monday*, *I Ain't Goin' Down to the Well No More*, and *Rock Island Line*. His career was the subject of the film *Leadbelly* (1975).

leader. 1. Conductor, director. 2. (U.K.) In the orch., 1st violin; in a band, 1st cornet; in a mixed chorus, 1st soprano. 3. Antecedent (dux).

leading. 1. (*noun*) Melodic progression or motion of any part. 2. (*adj.*) Principal, chief; guiding, directing. *Leading chord*, dominant 7th chord; *leading melody*, principal melody or theme; *leading motive*, leitmotiv; *leading note*, leading tone.

leading tone (Ger. *Leitton*; Fr. *note sensible*; It. *nota sensibile*; Lat. *subsemitonium*). 7th degree of the diatonic scale; to the tonally oriented ear, it urges resolution up to the tonic by a semitone. In minor keys the natural flat 7th degree is raised to provide the desirable leading tone (in harmonic and melodic minor); in modal writing, pre- and post-tonal, the leading tone has lost its absolute imperative.

leaning note. Appoggiatura.

leap. 1. In piano playing, jump from one note or chord to another. 2. In harmony, skip.

lebhaft (Ger.). Lively, animated. *Lebhaft, aber nicht zu sehr*, lively, but not too much.

lebhaftesten Zeitmasse, im (Ger.). In liveliest possible tempo.

Lebhaftigkeit (Ger.). Animation. *Mit Lebhaftigkeit und durchaus mit Empfindung und Ausdruck*, animatedly and with feeling and expression throughout.

lectionary (from Lat. *legere*, read). Annual calendar of liturgical readings; in a secular context, a collection of readings (*lectio*, act of reading) as opposed to speakings (*dictio*, act of speaking); thus the author's choice of *lectionary* for a dictionary-like publication (1989).

Ledbetter, Hudie. See ⇒Leadbelly.

ledger lines (leger lines). Horizontal lines placed above or below the staff to accommodate notes too high or too low for a given instrument or voice. In early notation, this problem was eased by using many different clefs, avoiding the clutter of too many ledger lines. In modern notation only 2 clefs, treble and bass, are used in keyboard music. When notes rise to stratospheric altitudes, then the sign 8va (play an octave higher) is placed above them to replace ledger lines; when they sink into the infernal region below the bass staff, the sign 8ba or the words octave bassa are used;

or very high notes the symbol 15va——⌐ (play 2 octaves higher) is occasionally employed. *Ledger space,* a space bounded above, below, or on both sides by a ledger line.

Led Zeppelin (Robert Plant, b. West Bromwich, U.K., Aug. 20, 1948, voice; (James Patrick) Jimmy Page, b. London, Jan. 9, 1944, guitar; John Paul Jones, b. John Baldwin, Sidcup, U.K., Jan. 3, 1946, bass & keyboards; John (Henry) "Bonzo" Bonham, b. Birmingham, U.K., May 31, 1947; d. Windsor, U.K., Sept. 25, 1980, drums). Exceptional heavy-metal group of the 1970s born out of the ashes of the psychedelic blues-rock band Yardbirds; a massive success starting with their eponymous 1st album (1969), followed by an immensely successful U.S. tour, spreading its heavy-metal sound far and wide. The band enjoyed its greatest success with the FM-radio hit *Stairway to Heaven* (1971), still a rock favorite; recorded and toured throughout the 1970s. The group was preparing to tour again when Bonham asphyxiated by inhaling his own vomit following alcoholic debauchery, leading to the group's dissolution. The surviving members reunited for the Live Aid concert (1985) and Atlantic Records' 40th anniversary party (1988). After years of dispute, Page and Plant reunited for the MTV *Unledded* special (1994); have since issued 2 albums; Led Zeppelin was inducted into the Rock and Roll Hall of Fame (1995).

Lee, Peggy (born Norma Dolores Egstrom), b. Jamestown, N.Dak., May 26, 1920. After graduating high school she sang on a Fargo radio station; Benny Goodman chose her as his band's vocalist (1941); her 1st success was *Why Don't You Do Right?* Launching a solo career, she and her 1st husband Dave Barbour collaborated on writing *Mañana, Golden Earrings,* and *I Don't Know Enough About You*; equally successful with sophisticated renditions of *Lover, Fever,* and *Is That All There Is?,* her signature song. She wrote the autobiographical musical *Peg* (with P. Homer and W. Luce, 1983).

left-hand music. Austrian pianist Paul Wittgenstein lost his right arm fighting on the Eastern Front during World War I; being of a philosophical bent (analytical logician Ludwig Wittgenstein was his brother), he developed startling left-hand virtuosity and, taking advantage of inherited wealth, commissioned a number of composers—among them Ravel, R. Strauss, Prokofiev, Korngold, Britten, and F. Schmidt—to write concertos for piano left-hand and orch. American Gary Graffman, suffering from carpal tunnel syndrome in his right hand, has played most of these works.

When Hungarian nobleman and amateur musician Gezy Zichy (1849–1924) lost his right arm in a hunting accident, he began composing left-hand piano pieces; also made 3-hand arrangements, including the *Rakoczy March,* which he often played with Liszt. Scriabin was so eager to become a great piano virtuoso that, as a Moscow conservatory student, he strained his right hand trying to compete with classmate Josef Lhévinne; he bandaged his ailing right hand and wrote charming piano pieces for left hand alone; even two-handed pianists enjoy performing these pieces publicly.

legando (It., binding). 1. Legato. 2. Expression mark calling for smooth, unbroken execution of any number of consecutive tones by 1 stroke of the glottis (voice), in 1 bow (bowed string instruments), 1 stroke of the tongue and 1 breath (wind instruments), or legatissimo (keyboard instruments).

legato (*legate;* It., connected). Slurred; performed in a smooth, unbroken, connected manner; can be indicated by a slur, a curving line under or over notes to be so executed; the opposite of staccato. *Legatissimo* (It., very connected), very smoothly and evenly played; on keyboard instruments, each finger holds down a note for as long as possible.

legend (Lat. *legenda,* item to be read; Ger. *Legende;* Fr. *Légende*). Vocal or instrumental composition portraying a short legendary tale; narrative romantic ballad.

Legendenton, im (Ger.). In a legendary manner.

leger lines. See ⇒Ledger lines.

Legge, Walter. See ⇒Schwarzkopf, (Olga Maria) Elizabeth (Friederike).

leggeramente (*leggero, leggiero;* It.). Lightly, briskly.

leggiadramente (It.). Neatly, elegantly, gracefully.

Leginska, Ethel (born Liggins), b. Hull, Apr. 13, 1886; d. Los Angeles, Feb. 26, 1970. Her pseudonym reflects the illusion that a Polish-looking name would help her artistic career; showed musical talent at an early age; studied piano at the Hoch Cons. in Frankfurt and with Leschetizky in Vienna. After her London debut (1907) she toured Europe; made her American debut in a N.Y. recital (1913); her playing was described as having great vigor, dashing brilliance, and variety of tonal color; criticism was directed against her individualistic treatment of classical works. In the midst of her piano career she developed a great interest in conducting; organized the Boston Phil. Orch. (100 players), later renamed the Women's Sym. Orch. of Boston; guest conducted with orchs. in the U.S. and Europe; elicited curiosity and press discussions of a woman's ability to conduct; in the U.S., studied composition with R. Goldmark and Ernest Bloch; wrote operas, orch'l works, piano music, and songs, distinguished by rhythmic display and a certain measure of modernism; settled in Los Angeles and taught piano (from 1939).

legno, col (It., with the wood). Strike strings with the wooden part of the bow.

Legrand, Michel, b. Paris, Feb. 24, 1932. He entered the Paris Cons. at age 11; soon began making professional jazz arrangements; wrote for radio, television, and cinema. His inventive score for the motion picture *Les Parapluies de Cherbourg* (1965), in which the characters sing throughout, received merited praise; among other soundtracks are *The Picasso Summer, Summer of '42, Brian's Song, Best Friends,* and *The Thomas Crown Affair.*

Lehár, Franz (Ferenc), b. Komorn, Hungary, Apr. 30, 1870; d. Bad Ischl, Oct. 24, 1948. He began studying music with his father, Franz Lehár (1838–98), a military bandmaster; entered the Prague Cons. at age 12; studied violin with A. Bennewitz and theory with Foerster; studied composition privately with Fibich (1885); submitted 2 piano sonatas to Dvořák, who encouraged him (1887). He played violin in a theater orch. in Elberfeld (1888); entered his father's band (50th Infantry) and assisted him (Vienna, 1889); led military bands in Pola, Trieste, Budapest, and Vienna (1890–1902).

Although Lehár's early stage works were unsuccessful, he gained some success with marches and waltzes; with *Der Rastelbinder* (1902), established himself in the theater; his most celebrated operetta, *Die lustige Witwe*, was premiered in Vienna (1905), and has received innumerable performances worldwide. Vienna played host to most of his premieres, including *Der Graf von Luxemburg* (1909), *Zigeunerliebe* (1910), and *Paganini* (1925); for Berlin he wrote *Der Zarewitsch* (1927), *Friederike* (1928), and *Das Land des Lächelns* (1929). His last years were complicated by his marriage to a Jewish woman, making him suspect to the Nazis; ironically, *Die lustige Witwe* was a favorite of Hitler's. After World War II, Lehár went to Zurich (1946), then Bad Ischl shortly before his death.

Lehár's music exemplifies the spirit of gaiety and frivolity of early 20th-century Vienna; a superlative gift for facile melody and infectious rhythms is combined with genuine wit and irony; his blend of nostalgia and sophisticated humor was undiminished by wars and revolutions and has had lasting audience appeal; also wrote orch'l pieces, 2 violin concertos, waltzes (notably *Gold und Silber*, 1899); marches; piano works, and songs.

Lehmann, Lotte, b. Perleberg, Feb. 27, 1888; d. Santa Barbara, Calif., Aug. 26, 1976. She studied in Berlin with E. Tiedka, E. Reinhold, and M. Mallinger; made her debut as the 2nd Boy in *Die Zauberflöte* at the Hamburg Opera (1910); soon given important Wagnerian roles, establishing herself as one of their finest interpreters. She made her 1st appearance in London as Sophie at Drury Lane (1914); engaged at the Vienna Opera (1916); R. Strauss selected her as the Composer in the premiere of the rev. version of *Ariadne auf Naxos* (Vienna, 1916); sang Octavian, then the Marschallin, her most famous role. She toured South America (1922); made her debut at London's Covent Garden as the Marschallin (1924); sang there regularly with great success (to 1935; also 1938).

Lehmann made her U.S. debut as Sieglinde with the Chicago Opera (1930); sang the same role at her Metropolitan Opera debut in N.Y. (1934); continued appearing there (Elisabeth in *Tannhäuser*, Tosca, and the Marschallin) until her 1945 farewell performance; appeared as the Marschallin for the last time in San Francisco (1946). In 1945 she became a naturalized U.S. citizen; gave her last recital in Santa Barbara, Calif. (1951); thereafter devoted herself to teaching. She was universally recognized as one of the century's greatest singers; vocal beauty, combined with rare musicianship, made her a compelling artist of the highest order; excelled as Mozart's Countess, Donna Elvira, Leonore, and Wagner's Elisabeth, Elsa, and Eva, among others; publ. a novel, *Orplid mein Land* (1937), and several books on music.

Lehrstück (Ger.). Teaching piece, cultivated in Germany after World War I; musical exercise for amateur performers designed to raise political and/or artistic consciousness. The writing of music in a modern idiom, geared toward workers and young people, preoccupied many German composers in the 1920s; the Lehrstück for accompanied chorus, liberally strewn with Sprechstimme passages, arose in Germany at the same time. Brecht was especially interested in the Lehrstuck's ideological potential, and aligned his dramatic theories to fit its aesthetic goals; he collaborated with Weill, Hindemith, Eisler, Toch, and others. A typical example is a play with music by Brecht and Weill, *Der Jasager* (1930), based on a Chinese story and prefaced by the following comment by Brecht: "The pedagogical practice of this music is to let the student bypass specialized study by concentrating intensively on a definite idea presented graphically through the medium of music, an idea that penetrates the student's mind much more strongly than formal learning."

leicht (*leichtlich;* Ger.). Lightly, briskly, easily; with facility. *Leicht bewegt*, moving lightly; slightly agitated.

leichtfertig (Ger.). Frivolously; expression mark used by R. Strauss (*Till Eulenspiegels lustige Streiche*).

leidenschaftlich (Ger.). Passionately; ardently.

leidvoll (Ger.). Sorrowful, mournful.

Leinsdorf, Erich (born Landauer), b. Vienna, Feb. 4, 1912; d. Zurich, Sept. 11, 1993. He entered a local music school at age 5; began piano lessons at 8; later studied with P. Emerich (1923–28); studied theory and composition with Paul Pisk. He took a conducting master class at the Mozarteum in Salzburg (1930); studied briefly at the Univ. of Vienna, then took courses at the Vienna Academy of Music (1931–33), making his conducting debut at the Musikvereinsaal upon graduating. He served as assistant conductor of the Workers' Chorus in Vienna (1933); went to Salzburg; had a successful audition with Walter and Toscanini at the Salzburg Festivals; appointed their assistant (1934).

Leinsdorf was engaged as conductor of the Metropolitan Opera in N.Y. (1937); made his American debut there, conducting *Die Walküre* with notable success (1938); conducted other Wagnerian operas there, succeeding Bodanzky as its head of German repertoire (1939); became an American citizen (1942). He was appointed music director of the Cleveland Orch. (1943); but his 1943 induction into the U.S. Army interrupted his term there; after his discharge, conducted again at the Metropolitan (1944–45); conducted concerts with the Cleveland Orch. (1945–46); made European appearances. He was music director of the Rochester (N.Y.) Phil. Orch. (1947–55); briefly music director of the N.Y. City Opera (1956), then returned to the Metropolitan as conductor and musical consultant (1957); guest conducted in the U.S. and Europe. He held the prestigious music directorship of the Boston Sym. Orch. (1962–69); conducted opera and sym. concerts in major American and European cities; principal conductor of the (West) Berlin Radio Sym. Orch. (1978–80); publ. *The Composer's Advocate: A Radical Orthodoxy for Musicians* (1981).

leise (Ger.). Low, soft; *piano.*

leiser (Ger.). Softer. *Immer leiser,* increasingly softer.

Leiter (Ger., ladder). Scale.

leitmotiv. (*leitmoif;* Ger., leading motive). Striking musical motive, theme, or phrase associated with or accompanying a character, idea, emotion, or situation in a musical drama; a term readily associated with Wagner's music dramas, but 1st used in an annotated catalogue of Weber's music (1871), where it is defined as a "strong delineation of each individual character in an opera"; the leitmotiv was aesthetically defined and analyzed in Wagnerian terms by Hans Wolzogen (1887); Wagner preferred the term "Grundthema" (basic theme).

Wagner's operatic use of leitmotivs functions primarily to identify each character and each important idea; by employing them in contrapuntal combinations and by varying the rhythm and even intervallic structure of these motives, he tried to establish "a new form of dramatic music, which possesses the unity of a symphonic movement"; in his view, this unity could be achieved through "a network of basic themes permeating the entire work, analogously to the themes in a sym. They are contrasted with each other, supplement each other, assume new shapes, separate and coalesce . . . according to dramatic action." Thomas Mann described the leitmotiv as a "magic formula valid in both the past and the future developments." But Wagner's leitmotiv procedure is not limited to characters on stage; he carefully tabulates motives of material objects, such as the ring and the sword ("Nothung") in *Der Ring des Nibelungen* and abstract concepts such as Covenant, Conflict, Transformation, and Love.

Wagner was not the 1st to introduce identifying themes in opera. Papageno's appearances in Mozart's *Die Zauberflöte* are announced by a scale on his *instrumento d'acciaio* (It., steel instrument, i.e., glockenspiel). There are definite leitmotivs in Weber's *Der Freischütz*; Verdi and Tchaikovsky used leitmotivs in several operas, although neither should be called a Wagnerian. Before Wagner, Berlioz used the *idée fixe*, a leitmotiv-like device, in the *Symphonie fantastique*. The true innovation in Wagner's operas is the conscious, philosophical affirmation of unity through plurality: the *Gesamtkunstwerk*, Wagner's grand ideal of artistic synthesis. A fascinating aspect of Wagnerian leitmotiv is unexpected musical similarity between otherwise contrasting characters or ideas, e.g., through "topological" alteration, the "Liebestod" (love-death) theme in *Tristan und Isolde* (1856–59) can be converted into the Holy Grail leitmotiv in *Parsifal* (1877–82).

Wagner's influence in the use of leitmotivs has been enormous; virtually every opera written since Wagner has borrowed this unifying concept. Faithful Wagnerians compiled catalogues of leitmotivs in his music dramas, including fragments better described as transitional passages. Wagner societies were formed in many countries, including France, shortly after being defeated by Wagner's compatriots in the Franco-Prussian War (1870–71). Composers who absorbed Wagnerian gospel included Richard Strauss, who introduced leitmotivs into symphonic music as well as his operas; Humperdinck, Janácek, and even Debussy experienced the Wagnerian shadow. Berg consciously outlined the significance of leitmotivs in *Wozzeck* and *Lulu*; he believed that, "by means of leitmotivs, [he could] achieve the connections and relationships and thereby attain again a unity"; Schoenberg's 12-tone themes as applied in his operas, especiallly *Moses und Aron*, are logical developments of the leitmotiv. A more obvious and vulgar exploitation of identifying motives is represented by commercial jingles in advertising; a cleverly composed or selected tune is designed to form lasting associations with the advertised product and promote its sales.

Leitton (Ger.). Leading tone.

lenezza, con (It.). Faintly, gently, quietly.

Lennon, John (Winston; later changed to John Ono Lennon), b. Liverpool, Oct. 9, 1940; d. N.Y., Dec. 8, 1980. See the entry on the Beatles for Lennon's early life and career. In 1968, as the Beatles began dissolving, Lennon began performing on his own, often accompanied by his paramour (later wife) Yoko Ono. They made albums of musique concrète (tape collages): *Two Virgins* (1968), with its cover photos of the couple fully nude, and *Life with the Lions* (1969). *Wedding Album* (1969) documented their marriage and associated brouhaha; holding several "bed-ins for peace" to celebrate their nuptials, they recorded the song *Give Peace a Chance* in a Montreal hotel room as the Plastic Ono Band, featuring assembled reporters and friends (including LSD guru Timothy Leary and satirist Tommy Smothers) on the chorus.

Lennon's 1st true solo album was *John Lennon/Plastic Ono Band* (1970); an extremely sparse recording, it was influenced by Lennon's and Ono's participation in primal scream therapy; the album had several powerful songs, including *Mother* and *God*. The follow-up, *Imagine* (1971), was more successful with its hit title cut. Lennon and Ono then embarked on a political partnership with N.Y.C.-based radicals, including Abbie Hoffman; the result was an album of topical songs, *Some Time in New York* (1972).

Lennon returned to singer/songwriter material on his next 2 albums, producing hits like *#9 Dream* and *Whatever Gets You Through the Night* (#1). After an ill-conceived album of oldies, he went into self-imposed retirement, caring for his and Ono's newly born son, Sean. He came out of retirement with *Double Fantasy*, featuring tracks by him and Ono (1980); the album produced several hits, including the 1950s-style opening track, *(Just Like) Starting Over*. Sadly, Lennon was gunned down by a crazed assailant, Mark David Chapman, returning home from a recording session; subsequently, several unfinished tracks were issued on various albums. The surviving Beatles regrouped to finish 2 of Lennon's last songs, *Free as a Bird* and *Real Love* (1996).

leno (It.). Faint, gentle, quiet.

lentamente (It.). Slowly. *Lentando*, growing slower; *lentezza*, slowness; *lentezza, con*, slowly.

lento (It.). Slow; between andante and largo; a movement in that tempo. *Adagio non lento*, slowly without dragging.

Lenya, Lotte (born Karoline Wilhelmine Blamauer), b. Vienna, Oct. 18, 1898; d. N.Y., Nov. 27, 1981. She began her career as a dancer in Zurich (from 1914); went to Berlin (1920), where she met Kurt Weill, whom she married (1926; after a divorce in 1933, they remarried in 1937). She made her singing debut in the Brecht-Weill scenic cantata *Kleine Mahagonny* in Baden-Baden (1927); created Jenny in the premiere of the Brecht-Weill *Die Dreigroschenoper* in Berlin (1928) and the singing Anna in their *The 7 Deadly Sins* (1933). That year, she and Weill fled Nazified Berlin; after a period in Paris and London, went to America (1935). Although not a singer of professional caliber, Lenya established a chanteuse-like approach, half-spoken, half-sung, to roles in Weill's works; she created Miriam in *The Eternal Road* (1935) and the Duchess in *The Firebrand of Florence* (1944). After his death (1950), she devoted herself to reviving his works for the American stage, especially the Blitzstein translation of *Die Dreigroschenoper* known as *The Threepenny Opera* (1954); performed in other musical theater works, notably Kander and Ebb's *Cabaret*; established the Kurt Weill Foundation for Music to promote his legacy.

Leoncavallo, Ruggero, b. Naples, Apr. 23, 1857; d. Montecatini, Aug. 9, 1919. He attended the Naples Cons. (1866–76), studying with B. Cesi (piano) and M. Ruta and L. Rossi (composition); toured as a pianist at age 16. The Bolognese premiere of his 1st opera, *Tommaso Chatterton* was aborted when the manager disappeared (1878). He earned a living playing piano in cafés for many years, traveling through Egypt, Greece, Turkey, Germany, Belgium, and the Netherlands before settling in Paris, where he found congenial company; composed chansonettes, popular songs, and an opera, *Songe d'une nuit d'été* (after Shakespeare), sung privately in a salon.

Leoncavallo began studying Wagner's scores, becoming an ardent Wagnerian; resolved to produce a trilogy, *Crepusculum*, depicting the Italian Renaissance through the lives of the Medicis, Savonarola, and Cesare Borgia; after 6 years of basic historical research, he completed the 1st opera and the scenario of the entire trilogy; returned to Italy (1887), where the publisher Ricordi showed interest in the project but kept delaying its publication and production. Annoyed, Leoncavallo turned to Sonzogno, publisher of Mascagni, whose *Cavalleria rusticana* was enjoying a tremendous vogue; submitted a short opera, *Pagliacci*, in similarly realistic vein; based his libretto on a true story of passion and murder in a Calabrian village; premiered with sensational success at the Teatro dal Verme in Milan under Toscanini's direction (1892), rapidly taking possession of the world's operatic stages; often played on a double bill with Mascagni's opera (as "Cav-Pag"); historically, these 2 operas embody the development of Italian operatic verismo, influencing composers of other countries as well.

Pagliacci's enormous success did not distract Leoncavallo from carrying on his more ambitious projects; the 1st part of his unfinished trilogy, *I Medici*, was finally produced at the Teatro dal Verme in Milan (1893), but the reception was so indifferent that he dropped the project; the same fate befell *Tommaso Chatterton* at its long-delayed premiere in Rome (1896). His next opera, *La Bohème* (1897), won considerable success, but it came a year after Puccini's masterpiece on the same story; Leoncavallo's work lost a compositional race and was dwarfed by comparison. A light opera, *Zazà* (1900), followed; fairly successful, it was produced repeatedly on world stages. He was commissioned by German Emperor Wilhelm II (1894) to write an opera for Berlin; *Der Roland von Berlin*, on a German historic theme, was produced (1904), but despite its high patronage proved a fiasco.

In 1906 Leoncavallo toured the U.S. and Canada, conducting *Pagliacci* and a new operetta, *La Jeunesse de Figaro*, so unsuccessful that he never staged it in Europe. Returning in Italy he resumed his industrious production, with *Maia* (1910), the operettas *Malbrouck* (1910), and *La Reginetta delle rose* (1912). That year he visited London, presenting the premiere of *Gli Zingari* (1912); a year later he revisited the U.S., conducting in San Francisco. He wrote several more operettas and the opera *Edipo re* (posth. produced, 1920) but they made no impression. Of his many songs, *Mattinata* (1904) is the most famous.

Leoninus (Leonin, Magister Leo), b. Paris, *c.* 1135; d. there, *c.* 1201. The first named master of the Notre Dame school of Paris; probably received his early education at the Notre Dame Cathedral schools there; active at the collegiate church of St. Benoit in Paris by the mid-1150s; served as a canon there for some 20 years; member of the clergy of Notre Dame by reason of his St. Benoit position. He earned the master's degree, probably in Paris (by 1179); became a canon at Notre Dame; was a priest (by 1192) and a member of the congregation of St. Victor (by 1187). His great achievement was composing polyphonic organum to augment the divine service; this survives as the *Magnus liber organi de graduali et antiphonario pro servitio divino multiplicando*; its orig. form is no longer extant; 3 versions from the 13th and 14th centuries survive. Leoninus may have prepared revs. and variants of the organa, preceding Perotin's revs. As a poet he wrote the extensive *Hystorie sacre gestas ab origine mundi*.

Lerner, Alan Jay, b. N.Y., Aug. 31, 1918; d. there, June 14, 1986. He was educated at Harvard Univ. (graduated 1940); attended the Juilliard School of Music in N.Y. (1936, 1937); met composer Frederick Loewe (1942), resulting in their collaboration on the musical *What's Up?* (1943); proved a failure, but they had better luck with their next show, *The Day Before Spring* (1945). Their collaboration paid off with the outstanding score of *Brigadoon* (1947). Following the popular *Paint Your Wagon* (1951), they wrote their masterpiece, *My Fair Lady* (1956, after G. B. Shaw's play *Pygmalion*). They next scored the film *Gigi* (1958; after Colette's story), winner of 9 Academy Awards; returned to Broadway with the enormously successful *Camelot* (1960). After Loewe's retirement Lerner continued writing musicals, but failed to equal previous successes; the most successful was *On a Clear Day You Can See Forever* (1966), a collaboration with Burton Lane. Lerner and Loewe reunited for a last film score, *The Little Prince* (1974).

lesni roh (Czech., forest horn; Ger., *Waldhorn*). Formerly, the natural horn; now the French horn.

lesson (Fr. *leçon*; Ger. *Übung*). English and (less commonly) French late Renaissance and Baroque instrumental pieces, mostly for harpsichord or organ; early pedagogical implications quickly expanded to cover almost any piece. The genre 1st appeared in mid-16th-century lute collections; Morley publ. his *1st Booke of Consort Lessons* (1599); Byrd included a *Lesson or Voluntarie* in his MS *My Ladye Nevells Booke* (1591); M. Locke, W. Babell, Johann Krieger, Handel, Rameau, and Bach wrote lessons or similar works. The term has alternative meanings, e.g., Couperin's *Leçons de ténèbres*, where it refers to a liturgical reading; the ambiguous "lesson" eventually evolved into the "study" (étude).

lesto (It.). Gay, lively, brisk.

Levine, James (Lawrence), b. Cincinnati, June 23, 1943. His maternal grandfather was a synagogue cantor, his father a violinist who led a dance band, his mother an actress. He began playing the piano as a small child; at age 10 he was soloist in Mendelssohn's 2nd Piano Concerto at a youth concert of the Cincinnati Sym. Orch.; studied theory with Walter Levin of the La Salle Quartet; took lessons with R. Serkin at the Marlboro School of Music (1956); continued piano studies with R. Lhevinne at the Aspen Music School (1957). He entered the Juilliard School of Music in N.Y. (1961); took conducting courses there with J. Morel and with W. Vacano in Aspen.

Levine graduated from the Juilliard School (1964); joined the American Conductors Project; practiced conducting with A. Wallenstein, M. Rudolf, and F. Cleva; served as an apprentice to Szell with the Cleveland Orch. (1964–65); became its regular assistant conductor (1965–70); organized the Univ. Circle Orch. of the Cleveland Inst. of Music (1966); led the student orch. of the summer inst. of Oakland Univ. in Meadow Brook, Mich. (1967–69); he guest-conducted with the Philadelphia Orch. at its summer home at Robin Hood Dell; conducted the Welsh National Opera and the San Francisco Opera (all 1970). He made his Metropolitan Opera debut in N.Y. in a festival performance of *Tosca* (1971); his success led to further appearances and appointment as its principal conductor (1973); became its music director (1975) and its artistic director (from 1986). He also became music director of the Ravinia Festival, summer home of the Chicago Sym. Orch. (from 1973); served in that capacity with the Cincinnati May Festival (1974–78); began conducting at the Salzburg Festivals (1975); made his Bayreuth debut (1982).

Levine continued making appearances as pianist, playing chamber music and accompanying singers with impeccable technical precision; but it is as conductor and indefatigable dramaturge at the Metropolitan Opera that he inspires the most respect. Unconcerned with egotistical projections of personality, he presided over the singers and orch. with concentrated efficiency; has made some inroads into the unadventurous, "musical museum" repertory of the Metropolitan, with works by Janáčεek, Schoenberg, Corigliano, Weill, and important revivals joining the ranks of the predictable.

Lewis, Jerry Lee, b. Ferriday, La., Sept. 29, 1935. He assaulted the piano keys with unusual ferocity, as if seeking the rock bottom of sound; whenever he had a chance, he vocalized in a frenetic seizure of the larynx; tried every style, including rock 'n' roll, folk, western, and rhythm and blues, always producing a visceral effect; rarely wrote his own songs, but metamorphosized and transmogrified tunes such as *Great Balls of Fire*; his rendition of *Whole Lotta Shakin' Going On* became a rock 'n' roll classic (both 1957). His career came to a dead stop halt during a 1958 English tour after it became known that he was traveling with a 13-year-old girl, whom he described as his 1st cousin and child wife; his records were shelved at radio stations; and he was reduced to playing at village fairs and roadhouses. He returned to public favor only in 1968 with records such as *Another Place, Another Time* and *What's Made Milwaukee Famous (Has Made a Loser Out of Me)*; recorded an autobiographical single, *Middle-Age Crazy* (1977); with his sister Linda Gail Lewis he recorded the album *Together* (1969); later albums include *The Session* (1973), *Southern Roots* (1973), *Jerry Lee Lewis Keeps Rockin'* (1978), and *Killer Country* (1980).

Lewis, John (Aaron), b. La Grange, Ill., May 3, 1920. He studied anthropology and music at the Univ. of New Mexico; completed his studies at the Manhattan School of Music (M.A., 1953). He co-founded the Modern Jazz Quartet (MJQ; piano, vibraphone, drums, double bass, 1952); the group was a primary focal point of both cool jazz and "classical" jazz; when merged, produced a hybrid known as 3rd Stream; he composed and arranged works that, while leaving room for improvisation, might include fugal counterpoint; composed extended compositions requiring additional forces, e.g., string quartet or orch.; movie scores (*Odds Against Tomorrow, No Sun in Venice, A Milanese Story*); and a ballet, *Original Sin* (San Francisco Ballet, 1961). Significantly, the MJQ abandoned the nightclub habitat of jazz in favor of formal, tuxedoed performances in concert halls; the group disbanded (1974), but in later years reunited for occasional tours; Lewis also led his own sextet and taught at the City College of the City U. of N.Y.

Lewis, Meade (Anderson) "Lux," b. Chicago, Sept. 4, 1905; d. June 7, 1964. He was nicknamed "The Duke of Luxembourg" as a child, hence the nickname; studied violin and piano; played in nightclubs and bars in Chicago; went to N.Y., where he played with Pete Johnson and Albert Ammons; appeared as soloist in N.Y. and Calif. nightclubs. He was a leading exponent of boogie-woogie style; his recording of *Honky Tonk Train Blues* (1927) was a landmark of the era.

lexicography (from Grk. *lexis*, word, speech). Editing or creating of a dictionary or lexicon; also, the principles behind these processes; involves a concentration on vocabulary, not grammar or construction.

Lhévinne, Josef, b. Orel, Dec. 13, 1874; d. N.Y., Dec. 2, 1944. After preliminary studies in his native town, he went to Moscow; entered Safonov's piano class at the Cons. (1885); at age 15 he played the *Emperor* Concerto with A. Rubinstein conducting; graduated (1891); won the Rubinstein Prize (1895); met Rosina (Bessie) Lhévinne (b. Kiev, Mar. 28, 1880; d. Glendale, Calif., Nov. 9, 1976), who graduated from the Cons. with the gold medal and married him (both 1898). He traveled to the Caucasus (1900) to teach piano at the Tiflis Cons.; taught at the Moscow Cons. (1902–06); then went to the U.S., making his American debut in N.Y. with the Russian Sym. Orch., conducted by Safonov (1906); took numerous concert tours in America. She appeared as soloist in Vienna (1910), St. Petersburg (1911), and Berlin (1912). For the next several years, the Lhévinnes lived mostly in Berlin (1907–19); he was interned during World War I but able to continue professional activities. They moved to the U.S. (1919); appeared in solo recitals, with major American orchs., and in duo recitals. They established a N.Y. teaching studio; also taught at Juilliard's Graduate Division in N.Y. (from 1922). He publ. *Basic Principles in Pianoforte Playing* (1924). Lhévinne's playing was distinguished not only by its virtuoso quality but by an intimate understanding of the music, impeccable phrasing, and fine gradations of singing tone; was at his best in Romantic works, particularly the concertos of Chopin and Tchaikovsky. After his death, Rosina Lhévinne continued teaching at Julliard for nearly 30 more years; later taught privately; among her famous students were Cliburn, M. Dichter, J. Browning, and G. Ohlsson.

Liberace (born Wladziu Valentino Liberace), b. West Allis, Wis., May 16, 1919; d. Palm Springs, Calif., Feb. 4, 1987. His father, a horn player, gave him musical training; he then studied piano, exhibiting so natural a talent that Paderewski encouraged him to try a concert career; he was sidetracked by jobs at silent-movie houses and nightclubs, billed as Walter Busterkeys. He moved to N.Y. (1940); evolved a facile repertoire of semiclassical works, e.g., a synthetic arrangement of the 1st movement of Beethoven's *Moonlight Sonata* and Rachmaninoff's Prelude in C-sharp Minor; prospered, making lucrative inroads into television (1951–55; 1958–59) as well as made numerous recordings and toured extensively overseas. Inspired by a popular movie on Chopin, he placed a decorative candelabrum on the piano at his concerts; this identification as a Romantic musician was enhanced by his dress suit of white silk mohair and wardrobe of glittering cloaks, removed with theatrical flair before performing; built himself a house in Calif. with a piano-shaped swimming pool. An obvious target for the media, he won a lawsuit for defamation of character against the *London Daily Mirror* and its columnist Cassandra (William Neil Connor) for suggesting he was homosexual (1959); but then his former chauffeur-body-guard-companion sued him for $380 million for "services rendered in an exclusive nonmarital relationship" (1982); most of the suit was quashed (1984), and Liberace settled out of court for $95,000 (1986). When he died of AIDS, his multimillion-dollar estate was sold at auction, much of the proceeds going to charities; indeed, he was a generous man; in spite of his critics, he once said, he could cry all the way to the bank.

liberamente (It.). Freely, boldly.

librettist. Author of the libretto, i.e., the play to be set to music as an opera, operetta, etc.

libretto. "Little book" (It.; plural *librettos, libretti*) containing the text or play of an opera; also, the text or play itself; these books were distributed (later sold) to acquaint audiences with opera's plot and dialogue. In the 19th century it was common to supply a translation into the language of the country in which the performances were occurring; Italian librettos usually carried an *argomento* (It. summary), list of acts and scenes, cast of characters, and sometimes a *protesta* (the librettist's disclaimer that any use of pagan deities should not be construed as lack of Christian faith). The early paragon of the art was Metastasio; his librettos were set to music by over 50 composers, accounting for over 1,000 Italian operas.

Some librettos have independent literary value, e.g., Boito's renderings of Shakespeare for Verdi, or Hofmannsthal's thoughtful texts for R. Strauss. In Gilbert and Sullivan's comic operas the merit is distributed equally between literature and music; but the "heavenly twins" eventually quarreled, mainly because of Sullivan's dissatisfaction at being stereotyped as an operetta composer and having an ambition to write grand opera. In a class by itself is the composer-librettist, of whom Wagner was supreme; Menotti wrote the librettos for his own operas as well as 2 for Barber.

The plots of most operas before 1900 are based on standard formulas; many, especially in the Baroque, were drawn from Greek mythology and drama. In other plots, comic and serious, mistaken identities abound; Verdi's Rigoletto hires assassins to kill the seducer of his daughter, but it is the mortally wounded daughter who is delivered to her father in a sack; most unlikely, perhaps, but plausibility is not a virtue among most librettists. Another theme may be described as *seduta e abbandonata*, at the root of *Faust, La Bohème, La Traviata,* and *Ariadne auf Naxos.* Suicides are common, with female self-destruction outnumbering male; examples are the seduced granddaughter of *The Queen of Spades,* eponymous murderess in *Lady Macbeth of Mtzensk,* and eponymous heroine of *Lakmé*; the eponymous Lodoletta in Mascagni's opera does not commit suicide but dies in the snow outside her lover's Paris house. Infanticide plays a major role in *Jenůfa* and *Faust.*

Transvesticism is another common device in opera plots; the faithful Leonore dresses as a young man, assumes the symbolic name Fidelio, and penetrates the prison in which her beloved Florestan is unjustly held; R. Strauss's *Der Rosenkavalier* presents Octavian, a young man played by a woman, in bed with the Marschallin; in its model, *Le Nozze di Figaro,* Cherubino disguises him/herself as a maid to avoid military service. The "rescue opera" is so ubiquitous that the term has entered music dictionaries. Religious fanaticism, particularly as embodied in the Inquisition, is a convenient dramatic feature in many operas; thus, in *La Juive,* the fanatical cardinal has a girl burned at the stake moments before he finds out that she is his natural daughter; other religiously determined operas include *Norma* and *Don Carlos*; superstition plays a helpful if absurd role in librettos such as *Il Trovatore.* Operatic murders, usually by stabbing, are too numerous to tabulate. Insanity should not be overlooked; mad scenes in opera are most effective; most of the usually female victims recover their sanity once the dramatic situation is favorable; then again, there are *Boris Godunov, Lucia di Lammermoor,* and Lady Macbeth, murderers all.

It is too easy to ridicule opera plots; the difficulty comes with suggesting rational and sensible substitutes. A classic example comes in Verdi's *Aida*; it is ludicrous to have the King of Ethiopia overhear Radames relating military secrets to the King's daughter Aida; the hidden King even expresses his thoughts in recitative from behind a potted palm. (This can be compared with innumerable examples in Shakespearean drama and Restoration comedy.) Coleridge's injunction regarding the poetic approach as being the "willing suspension of disbelief" must come into play: an operagoer must leave his or her skeptical literalness in the vestiary.

Sometimes stories of operas are changed for political or social reasons. Glinka's opera *A Life for the Czar* could not be staged as such in post-revolutionary Russia; the Soviet authorities changed its title to *Ivan Susanin,* the self-sacrificial peasant hero; instead of saving the Czar he saves a patriotic Russian officer. Attempts were made in Soviet Russia to rewrite librettos in order to make them acceptable; thus *Tosca* became *The Commune,* and *The Huguenots* was changed to *The Decembrists* (the revolutionaries who rebelled against Czar Nicholas I in 1825). Some operas may not be performed in certain countries; *The Mikado* is forbidden in Japan because the Emperor is portrayed in an undignified manner. Gounod's *Faust* is called *Margarethe* in Germany because of the affront of the sentimental treatment of Goethe's great poem. Censorship has been always been an issue in Europe; at one time, most countries required that librettos be approved for decency and religious and political inoffensiveness. Verdi's *Un Ballo in maschera* was based on the historical assassination of King Gustav III of Sweden (1792); it was forbidden for performance in Italy because of a rash of attempted regicides at the time; accordingly, the libretto was adapted; a mythical "Governor of Boston" was substituted for the king.

Sometimes local religious or political restrictions make it impossible to have an opera performed under any circumstances. *Samson and Delilah* could not be performed for nearly a century on the British stage because of a regulation banning operatic representations of biblical personages (the restriction did not apply to oratorios or cantatas). In Czarist Russia the representation of a member of the reigning dynasty on the stage was illegal; so, when Catherine the Great was to make her entrance in Tchaikovsky's *The Queen of Spades*, the Imperial March announcing her presence was played, but the Empress herself did not appear. No restrictions applied to Czars predating the Romanov dynasty; Mussorgsky's *Boris Godunov* is a child murderer. Ivan III (the Terrible) is treated as the brute that he was in Rimsky-Korsakov's *The Maid of Pskov*; ironically, Stalin rehabilitated the historic Ivan, perhaps because he identified with his remote precursor; Prokofiev had trouble with his scenic oratorio *Ivan the Terrible* (based on his music for Eisenstein's film), trying to conform with the new official attitude. The Imperial censors demanded minor changes to Pushkin's verses as set by Rimsky-Korsakov in *Le Coq d'or* to avoid embarrassing similarities between the bumbling operatic Czar and the not very bright Nicholas II; the composer refused, and it was not until after his death that the work was premiered.

Linguistic hazards require textual adjustments of some operas when performed in other countries. The name of Pinkerton in *Madama Butterfly* had to be changed in German productions to Linkerton, as *pinkeln* means to urinate in colloquial German. When *Boris Godunov* was performed in Lisbon (1921), the dying Czar's injunction to his son containing the imperative *karai* had to be changed because *karai* is Portuguese for the male sexual organ. Sophomoric giggly responses may be heard to the declaration of the young man in *Iolanthe* that he is "a fairy only down to the waist" and to the opening phrase of Dido's lament in Purcell's *Dido and Aeneas*, "When I am laid, am laid, in earth."

licenza (It.). Freedom, license. *Con alcuna licenza*, with a certain (degree of) freedom; may include the insertion of a cadenza, rhythmic freedom, or just about any liberty taken by performer.

lick. In jazz and popular music, brief improvised or stereotypical solo passage, or portion of a longer passage; a "hot lick" is a particularly intriguing and stimulating exemplar; the lick is usually set off from its context by register or rest; similar but not identical to the riff.

lié (Fr.). Tied, either from one note to another of identical pitch (tied notes) or legato.

Liebeglühend (Ger.). Glowing with love; found in scores by R. Strauss.

Liebesflöte (Ger., love flute). See ⇒Flauto d'amore.

Liebesfuss (Ger., love foot; Fr. pavillon d'amour).

Liebesgeige. See ⇒Viola d'amore.

Liebeshoboe. See ⇒Oboe d'amore.

Liebesklarinette. See ⇒Clarinetto d'amore.

lieblich (Ger.). Lovely, sweet, charming.

lied (from Ger. *Lied, song;* plural, *Lieder*). Classical art song in German for (usually) single voice and piano; composed as distinguished from a traditional song of folk origin; the form is most often strophic, with a single musical setting for every stanza of the poem; suitable German poetry for lieder tends toward rhymed verses with a consistent number of syllables per line; this symmetrical poetic design corresponds to the symmetry of the musical setting.

Most musicologists attribute the success of the lied genre to Schubert, who in 1814 wrote his 1st lied, Goethe's *Gretchen am Spinnrade* (Gretchen at the Spinning Wheel), an inspiration comparable to the descent of the fiery tongues on the apostles at Pentecost. He did have predecessors, notably Zelter and Johann Friedrich Reichardt (1752–1814), but also C. P. E. Bach and Beethoven; all wrote German songs in a manner marked by fluid singing line, poignant lyricism of expression, and symmetry of rhythmical design. Besides the great Schubert, important 19th-century lied composers were Mendelssohn, Schumann, Liszt, Brahms, Wagner, Loewe, and Wolf, who expanded the piano accompaniment into an integral part of the lied; he introduced heavily chromatic harmony that earned him the sobriquet "the Wagner of the lied." Mahler, R. Strauss, and M. Reger, although not primarily lied composers, contributed to the genre.

Towards the end of the 19th century the lied went into decline, at least in its structural aspect; most lieder of this era were *durchkomponiert* (Ger., through-composed), with each stanza written anew. Schoenberg created a novel type of lied in his cycle of settings of Stefan George poems, *Das Buch der hängenden Garten* (1908–09), by introducing Sprechstimme. While Romantic German lied cultivated love, sorrow, and death; modern German lied annexed topical elements, often of political import, as in Eisler, Weill, and Dessau.

The earliest type of this genre is the so-called *Generalbasslied*, songs with basso continuo; to the same category belong homophonic arias of early opera and oratorio, closely related to Italian forms of accompanied song. Somewhere in the interstices of time came the development of the *volkstümliche Lied*, song in folk style, also known as *Lieder im Volkston*. German-language composers possess the knack of assimilating popular song elements so completely that they can re-create their rhythmic and melodic elements anew. Anthologies of German popular songs are replete with lieder whose composers are perfectly identifiable; what could be more *volkstümlich* than *Lorelei*, to words by Heine? Yet, it is not a folk song, but a composition by one (Philipp) Friedrich Silcher (1789–1860).

Liederabend (Ger.). Informal or formal evening in which Classic and Romantic lieder are performed.

Liederspiel (Ger., play of songs). Dramatic format alternating set arias with spoken dialogue; similar to the Singspiel.

Liedertafel (Ger., song table). Male choral society organized in Berlin (1809); branches of the soc. sprang up in other German cities and among German immigrant groups in America. The original Liedertafel's organization imitated the legendary King Arthur's Round Table; its singers, like the knights of yore, had to be loyal in serving the cause of music.

lieto (It.). Merrily, joyfully. *Lieto fine*, happy ending.

lieve (It.). Lightly.

ligature (from Lat. *ligare*, bind, tie). In mensural notation, fusion of 2 or more melodic notes into one notational symbol; component parts of a ligature indicate relative pitch and duration, following an elaborate but sometimes self-contradictory set of rules. Depending on the number of notes in a ligature, it would be classified as *binary, ternary, quaternary*, etc.; eventually, ligature terminology was standardized through square-note notation. The most common binary and ternary ligatures correspond to accents and other diacritical signs of the alphabet; *pes* (foot) corresponds to the acute accent, or a rise of 1 degree; *clivis* (incline) corresponds to the grave accent, a descent of 1 degree; *torculus* (twisted) corresponds to the circumflex accent, a rise and fall of 1 degree, etc. 2. Tie of 2 or more notes, sometimes resulting in syncopation. 3. Group or series of notes to be executed in 1 breath, to 1 syllable, or as a legato phrase.

Ligeti, György (Sándor), b. Dicsöszentmárton, Transylvania, May 28, 1923. The family's original surname was Auer; his great-uncle was the violinist Leopold Auer (1845–1930). He studied composition with F. Farkas at the Kolozsvar Cons. (1941–43) and privately with P. Kadosa in Budapest (1942–43); continued training with S. Veress, P. Járdányi, Farkas, and L. Bardos at the Budapest Academy of Music (1945–49); appointed prof. of harmony, counterpoint, and analysis (from 1950). After the Hungarian revolution was crushed by the Soviet Union (1956), he fled his homeland; became a naturalized Austrian citizen (1967).

Ligeti worked at the electronic music studio of the West German Radio in Cologne (1957–58); lectured at the Darmstadt summer courses in new music (1959–72); visiting prof. at the Royal Stockholm Academy of Music (1961–71). served as composer-in-residence at Stanford Univ. (1972); taught at Tanglewood (1973) the same year he became prof. of composition at the Hamburg Hochschule für Musik (1973). He holds memberships in the Royal Swedish Academy in Stockholm (1964), Akademie der Künste in Berlin (1968), and American Academy and Inst. of Arts and Letters (1984); received the Grawemeyer Award of the Univ. of Louisville (1986); made a Commandeur in the Ordre National des Arts et Lettres in Paris (1988).

In bold and imaginative experimentation with musical materials and parameters, Ligeti endeavors to bring together all aural and visual elements in synthetic entity, making use of all conceivable effects and alternating tremendous sonorous upheavals with static chordal masses and shifting dynamic colors; he describes his orch'l style as "micropolyphonic." The Kyrie from his Requiem (soloists, choruses, and orch., 1963–65) and other pieces were "borrowed" for the film score to Stanley Kubrick's *2001: A Space Odyssey*. Other important works include the opera *Le Grand Macabre* (1974–77); *Atmospheres* (orch., 1958–59); *Aventures* (soloists and ens., 1962); *Nouvelle Aventures* (soloists and ens., 1966); *Lux Aeterna* (chorus, 1966); Chamber Concerto (1970); *San Francisco Polyphony* (orch., 1973–74); Piano Concerto (1985-88); 2 string quartets (1953-54, 1968); Trio for Violin, Horn, and Piano (1982); *Monument, Selbstportrait, Bewegung* for 2 pianos (1976);

Etudes for piano solo (1985); *Poème symphonique* for 100 metronomes (1962).

light opera. Operetta.

Lilburn, Douglas (Gordon), b. Wanganui, Nov. 2, 1915. He studied with J. C. Bradshaw at Canterbury Univ. College (1934–36); won the Grainger Competition with his sym. poem *Forest* (1936); studied with E. Mitchell (piano) and Vaughan Williams (composition) at the Royal College of Music in London (1937–40); received the Cobbett Prize for the *Phantasy* for String Quartet (1939). He began teaching at Victoria Univ. in Wellington (1947); made prof. and director of the electronic music studio (1970–79). He composed 3 syms. (1951; 1951, rev. 1974; 1961), and other orch'l works; chamber, piano, and vocal music; electronic tape works.

limpido (It.). Clearly, distinctly.

Lin, Cho-Liang, b. Hsin-Chu, Taiwan, Jan. 29, 1960. He began studying the violin as a child; won the Taiwan National Youth Violin Competition at age 10; at 12 began studying with R. Pikler at the New South Wales State Conservatorium of Music in Sydney; went to the U.S. at 15; enrolled at the Juilliard School in N.Y. as a scholarship student of Dorothy DeLay (graduated 1981). He won wide notice when he played at the inaugural concert for President Jimmy Carter (1977); that year he won 1st prize in the Queen Sofia International Competition in Madrid. He pursued a rewarding career as a virtuoso; toured throughout the world; appeared as soloist with virtually every major orch.; was an active recitalist and chamber music player; became a naturalized U.S. citizen (1988). His extensive repertoire ranges from standard literature to commissioned works; his performances combine effortless technique with beguiling luminosity of tone; has recorded works by Arensky, Brahms, Bruch, Mozart, Nielsen, Sibelius, Tchaikovsky, Haydn, Saint-Saëns, Prokofiev, Stravinsky, Mendelssohn, and Vieuxtemps.

Lind, Jenny (Johanna Maria), b. Stockholm, Oct. 6, 1820; d. Wynds Point, Herefordshire, Nov. 2, 1887. She was nicknamed the "Swedish Nightingale." She made her 1st stage appearance in Stockholm (1830); that year entered the Royal Opera School; studied with C. Craelius and I. Berg; sang in comedies and melodramas; continued studies with A. Lindblad and J. Josephson; made her formal operatic debut as Agathe at the Royal Opera in Stockholm (1838); later that year appeared as Pamina, Euryanthe, Donna Anna (1839), and Norina (1841). She was appointed a regular member of the Royal Swedish Academy of Music (1840); given the rank of court singer; wanted to improve weaknesses in her voice, however; went to Paris to study with M. Garcia (1841–42).

Upon returning to Stockholm Lind sang Norma (1842); later appeared as the Countess Anna in *La Sonnambula*, Valentine in *Les Huguenots*, and Anna Bolena; although Meyerbeer wrote the role of Vielka in *Ein Feldlager in Schlesien* for her, the role was 1st sung by Tuczec in Berlin (1844); Lind performed it there the next year. She sang in Hannover, Hamburg, Cologne, Koblenz, Frankfurt, Darmstadt, and Copenhagen; appeared at the Leipzig Gewandhaus (1845); made her Vienna debut as Norma at the Theater an der Wien (1846); sang throughout Germany; returned to Vienna as Marie (1847), creating a sensation; made a phenomenal London debut as Alice in *Robert le Diable* at Her Majesty's Theatre in London; appearances in *La Sonnambula* and *La Fille du régiment* were acclaimed; created the role of Amalia in Verdi's *I Masnadieri* there (1847).

After touring the English provinces Lind retired from the operatic stage; made her farewell appearance as Norma in Stockholm (1848) and as Alice at London's Her Majesty's Theatre (1849). Although her European success was great, her U.S. farewell tour exceeded all expectations in public agitation and monetary reward; sponsored by P. T. Barnum, she was seen as a natural phenomenon rather than an artist; nonetheless, her outstanding musicality made a deep impression. She made her N.Y. debut in 1850; subsequently gave 93 concerts, the last in Philadelphia (1851); she married her accompanist, Otto Goldschmidt, in Boston (1852); they returned to Europe, settling permanently in England in 1858. She appeared in concert and oratorio performances until her retirement (1883); became prof. of singing at London's Royal College of Music; devoted much time to charitable causes. She possessed an extraordinary coloratura voice, with a compass reaching g; although her middle register remained veiled from early overuse, she was unquestionably one of the greatest vocal artists of her era.

Lindy hop. An exuberant American jazz dance, 1927, in syncopated 2/4 time; named after Charles Linbergh's aeronautical solo hop to Paris. The dances take 2 slow steps, then 2 quicksteps, with occasional sidesteps (shuffles) and other variants.

linear counterpoint. Modern term describing type of contrapuntal writing in which individual lines are the main considerations in the ensemble.

lining out. Common usage in American rural churches for the preliminary reading by a congregation member of a line from a hymn just before the entire congregation sings it; a similar practice was called deaconing.

Linus. Mythological Greek hero who tried to teach music to Hercules and was slain by his pupil with his own lyre when he tried to correct an error Hercules made during a lesson. A *Song of Linus* was sung each year at harvest time in Homer's day to commemorate his tragic death.

lion's roar. Membranophone of the frictional type, consisting of a bucket covered with a membrane through which a rosined cord is passed. When the cord is pulled vigorously, a sound resembling the roar of a lion is produced. Its generic English name is friction drum; it is found in various forms throughout the Americas, Europe, India, and Japan. Varèse wrote a part for it in his *Ionisation.*

lip. 1. In a flue pipe, flat surfaces above (upper) and below (lower) the mouth. 2. Lipping; that is, the art of so adjusting the lips to the mouthpiece of a wind instrument as to get good tone.

Lipatti, Dinu (actually Constantin), b. Bucharest, Apr. 1, 1917; d. Chêne-Bourg, near Geneva, Dec. 2, 1950. His father was a violinist who had studied with Sarasate, and his mother was a pianist; his godfather was Enesco. He received his early training from his parents; then studied with Florica Musicescu at the Bucharest Cons. (1928–32). He received 2nd

prize at the International Competition at Vienna in 1934, a judgment which prompted Cortot to quit the jury in protest; Lipatti then studied piano with Cortot, conducting with Munch, and composition with Dukas and Boulanger in Paris (1934–39). He gave concerts in Germany and Italy, returning to Rumania at the outbreak of World War II. After escaping from Rumania in 1943, he settled in Geneva as teacher of piano at the Cons. After the war he resumed his career; played in England 4 times (1946–48).

He was generally regarded as one of the most sensitive interpreters of Chopin, and was also praised for his deep understanding of the Baroque masters; he was a fine composer. Lipatti was married to the pianist and teacher Madeleine Cantacuzene. His compositions include works for solo piano (a sonata, nocturnes, a fantasy, a sonatina for left hand, a concertino with orch., dances); piano duo (a suite, dances, a symphonie concertante with orch.); piano trio (a fantasy, an improvisation); a violin sonatina; *Aubade* for Wind Quartet; symphonic poem *Satrarii*; songs.

lira (Grk. *lyra*). 1. Bowed string instrument of modern Greece, Bulgaria, and Dalmatia. It has a pear-shaped wooden body, a peg disc to hold the lateral pegs for 3, occasionally 4 strings. The neck is indistinct; strings are fingered laterally, obviating need for a fingerboard. Earliest references to the lira are found in the late 1st millennium a.d.; it should not be confused with the lyre.

lira da braccio (It., lyre of the arm). Bowed chordophone, probably an outgrowth of the medieval fiddle but held against the player's body. There were 2 sizes, the smaller held against the shoulder, the larger (sometimes known as the *lirone da gambe*) was held lower. instrument normally had 5 playing strings and 2 drones; most sources indicate that the fingerboard was fretted. Its popularity dates from the late 1400s to early Baroque.

lira da gamba (It., lyre of the knee). Lirone.

lira organizzata ("organized" lyre; Fr. *vielle organisée*; Ger. *Orgelleier*). Hurdy-gurdy in which sound is enhanced by organ pipeworks and bellows, produced by a rotating wheel; thus the term *organized* refers to the instrument, not the way someone keeps her or his business files. Instrument is usually built in a guitarlike shape.

lira rustica (It.), **lira tedesca** (Ger.). Hurdy-gurdy.

lirone (*archi viola*; It. *large lira*). *Lira da gamba*, viola da gamba–like bowed chordophone with a wide fretted neck, with 2 drone strings and 9–14 melody strings, held between the knees. Its popularity was brief: from the mid-16th to the mid-17th centuries.

liscio (It.). Smoothly, flowing.

l'istesso, lo stesso (It.). The same. *L'istesso tempo*, the same tempo.

Liszt, Franz, (baptized Franciscus), born Ferenc Liszt. b. Raiding, near Odenburg, Oct. 22, 1811; d. Bayreuth, July 31, 1886. He is creator of the modern form of symphonic poem, and an innovating genius of modern piano technique. His father was an amateur musician who devoted his energies to the education of his son; at age 9, young Liszt was able to play a difficult piano concerto by Ries. A group of Hungarian music-lovers provided sufficient funds to finance his musical education. In 1822 the family traveled to Vienna. Beethoven was still living, and Liszt's father made every effort to persuade Beethoven to come to young Liszt's Vienna concert (1823). Legend has it that Beethoven did come and was so impressed that he ascended the podium and kissed the boy on the brow. However that might be, his appearance in Vienna created a sensation; he was hailed by the press as "child Hercules." The link with Beethoven was maintained through Liszt's own teachers: Czerny, who was Beethoven's student and friend and with whom Liszt took piano lessons, and the great Salieri, who was Beethoven's early teacher and who at the end of his life became Liszt's teacher in composition.

In 1823 Liszt gave a concert in Pest. The announcement of the concert was made in the florid manner characteristic of the period: "Esteemed Gentlemen! High-born nobility, valorous army officers, dear audience! I am a Hungarian, and before traveling to France and England, I am happy now to present to my dear Fatherland the 1st fruits of my training and education." Salieri appealed to Prince Esterházy for financial help so as to enable Liszt to move to Vienna, where Salieri made his residence. "I recently heard a young boy, Francesco Liszt, improvise on the piano," Salieri wrote, "and it produced such a profound impression on me that I thought it was a dream." Apparently Esterházy was sufficiently impressed to contribute support.

Under guidance of his ambitious father (a parallel with Mozart's childhood suggests itself), Liszt applied for an entrance examination at the Paris Cons., but its powerful director, Cherubini, declined to accept him, ostensibly because he was a foreigner. (Cherubini himself was a naturalized foreigner.) He settled for private lessons in counterpoint from Antoine Reicha, a Parisianized Czech musician who instilled in Liszt the importance of folklore. He soon joined the brilliant company of men and women of the arts. Paganini's spectacular performances of the violin in particular inspired Liszt to emulate him in creating a piano technique of transcendental difficulty and brilliance, utilizing all possible sonorities of the instrument.

In his own compositions Liszt was a convinced propagandist of program music. He liked to attach evocative titles to his works, such as *Fantasy*, *Reminiscence*, and *Illustration*. The rhapsody was also made popular by Liszt, but he was not its originator; it was 1st used in piano pieces by Tomaschek. A true Romantic, Liszt conceived himself as an actor playing the part of his own life, in which he was a child of the Muses. Traveling in Switzerland, he signed his hotel register as follows: "Place of birth—Parnasse. Arriving from—Dante. Proceeding to—Truth. Profession—Musician-philosopher." He was fascinated by Pivert de Senancour's popular novel *Obermann* (1804) that depicted an eponymous fictional traveler; he wrote a piano suite, *Années de pèlerinage*, in which he followed in music the imaginary progressions of Obermann.

One of Liszt's greatest successes was his triumphant tour in Russia. Russian musicians and music critics exhausted their flowery vocabulary to praise Liszt as the miracle of the age. "How fortunate we are that we live in the year 1842 and so are able to witness the living appearance in our own country of such a great genius!" wrote the music critic Stasov. Czar Nicholas I himself attended a concert given by Liszt in St. Petersburg, and expressed

his appreciation by sending him a pair of trained Russian bears. He acknowledged the imperial honor but did not venture to take the animals with him on his European tour; they remained in Russia.

Liszt was a consummate showman. In Russia, as elsewhere, he had 2 grand pianos installed on stage at right angles, so that the keyboards were visible from the right and the left respectively and he could alternate his playing on both. He appeared on the stage wearing a long cloak and white gloves, discarding both with a spectacular gesture. Normally he needed eyeglasses, but he was too vain to wear them in public.

It is not clear why, after all his triumphs in Russia and elsewhere in Europe, Liszt decided to abandon his career as piano virtuoso and devote his entire efforts to composition. He became associated with Wagner, his son-in-law, as prophet of "music of the future." Indeed, he anticipated Wagner's chromatic harmony in his works. A remarkable instance of such anticipation is illustrated in his song *Ich möchte hingehen* (1845, rev. 1860), which prefigures, note for note, the theme from the prelude to *Tristan und Isolde*. Inevitably the two became objects of derision on the part of conservative music critics; one example was an extraordinary caricature entitled "Music of the Future," distributed in N.Y. (1867). It represented Liszt with arms and legs flailing symmetrically over a huge orch. that comprised not only human players but also goats, donkeys, and a cat placed in a cage with an operator pulling its tail. At Liszt's feet there was placed a score marked "Wagner, not to be played much till 1995."

In 1848 Liszt accepted position of Court Kapellmeister in Weimar. When Wagner was exiled from Saxony, Liszt arranged for the production of *Lohengrin* in Weimar (1850); he was also instrumental in supervising performances in Weimar of *Der fliegende Holländer* and *Tannhäuser*, as well as music by Berlioz and operas by other composers. He also established teaching series at his home. A vivid description of these classes was compiled by one of his students, August Göllerich. Liszt was invariably kind to his students; occasionally he would doze off, but he would always wake up when a student completed his or her playing and say "Schön." When one of his American students called to his attention that the date was July 4, Liszt asked if someone would play variations on *Yankee Doodle* for him, for, as he said, "Today we are all Americans." Apparently Liszt gave instruction gratis. He was also generous to colleagues and often lent them money; Wagner, who constantly had financial difficulties, often asked Liszt for loans (which were seldom, if ever, returned) and Liszt invariably obliged. He was also hospitable to his colleagues; during his Weimar years, for instance, young Brahms stayed in his home for 3 weeks.

Liszt was very much interested in the progress of Russian music. In Weimar he received young Glazunov, who brought with him his 1st sym. He played host to Borodin and Cui, who came to Weimar to pay their respects, and was lavish in his appreciation of their works; he also expressed admiration for Rimsky-Korsakov and Mussorgsky, although they never came to see him personally. When Rimsky-Korsakov asked him to contribute a variation to a Russian collection based on *Chopsticks* (then a waltz), Liszt obliged with his own contribution, adding, "There is nothing wittier than your variations. Here you have at last a condensed manual of harmony and counterpoint. I would gladly recommend this album to conservatory professors as an aid to teaching composition."

Liszt became known informally as "Abbé," thanks to 4 minor orders (ostuary, lector, exorcist, and acolyte) conferred upon him by Pope Pius IX (1865), but his religious affiliations were not limited to the Roman Catholic church; he was also a Freemason and served as a tertiary of the Order of St. Francis. In 1879 he received the tonsure and an honorary canonry, although he was never ordained a priest.

In his Weimar years Liszt aged rapidly. Gone were the classical features that had so fascinated his contemporaries, especially women, during his virtuoso career. Photographs taken in Weimar show him with snow-white hair descending upon his shoulders. He walked with difficulty, dragging his feet. He suffered attacks of phlebitis in his legs and had constant intestinal difficulties. He neglected his physical state, and finally developed double pneumonia and died during a sojourn in Bayreuth.

In his secular works Liszt was deeply conscious of his Hungarian heritage, but he gathered his material mainly from Gypsy dance bands that played in Budapest. While Liszt is usually thought of as a great Hungarian composer, he was actually brought up in the atmosphere of German culture. He spoke German at home, with French as a 2nd language. His women companions conversed with him in French, and most of his correspondence was in that language. It was not until his middle age that he decided to take lessons in Hungarian, but he never acquired fluency. He used to refer to himself jocularly as "half Gypsy and half Franciscan monk." This self-identification haunted him through his life, and beyond; when the question was raised after his death in Bayreuth regarding transfer of his body to Budapest, the prime minister of Hungary voiced objection, since Liszt never regarded himself as a purely Hungarian musician.

As composer Liszt made every effort to expand the technical possibilities of piano technique; in his 2 piano concertos, and particularly in his *Études d'exécution transcendante*, he made use of the new grand piano, which expanded the keyboard in both the bass and the extreme treble. He also extended the field of piano literature with his brilliant transcriptions of operatic excerpts, from works by Mozart, Verdi, Wagner, Donizetti, Gounod, Rossini, and Beethoven. These transcriptions were particularly useful at the time, when the piano was the basic musical instrument at home (and the phonograph still a dream of the future).

Liszt was a great musical technician. He organized his compositions with deliberate intent to create music that was essentially new. Thus he abandoned the traditional succession of 2 principal themes in sonata form. In his symphonic poem *Les Préludes* a single melody dominates the entire work. In his popular 3rd *Liebestraum* for Piano the passionate melody modulates by 3rds rather than by Classicly anointed 5ths and 4ths. The great *Faust Sym.* is more literary essay on Goethe's great poem than didactic composition. His 2 piano concertos are free from the dialectical contrasts of the established Classic school. The chromatic opening of the 1st Concerto led von Bülow to improvise an insulting line to accompany the theme, "Sie sind alle ganz verrückt!" (They are all quite mad!), and the introduction of the triangle solo aroused derisive whoops from the press. Liszt was indifferent to such outbursts, for he was master of his musical fate in the ocean of sound.

Liszt's numerous works fall into nearly every genre; many of his orch'l works were orchestrated by Raff or Conradi (although he often redid orchestrations later). He is best known for: *Eine Faust-Symphonie in drei Charakterbildern* for Tenor, Men's Voices, and Orch. (1854–57); *Eine Symphonie zu Dantes Divina commedia* (1855–56; only "Inferno" and "Purgatorio" completed); 13 symphonic poems (1848-1882); 2 piano concertos; the recently attributed *Piano Concerto in the Hungarian Style* (1885); *Totentanz* for Piano and Orch. (1849); *2 Episodes from Lenau's "Faust"* (1860–61); *2nd Mephisto Waltz* (Budapest, 1881). Other piano works include *Album d'un voyageur* (3 vols., 1835–38); *Études d'exécution transcendante d'après Paganini* (1838–39); *Venezia e Napoli* (c. 1840); *Tre sonetti del Petrarca* (1844–45); 19 *Hungarian Rhapsodies* (1846–1885), including No. 15 in A Minor, *Rákóczy March*; 6 *Consolations* (1844–48); *Années de pèlerinage: Deuxième année, Italie* (1837–49); *Études d'exécution transcendante* (1851); *Harmonies poétiques et religieuses* (1840–52); Sonata in B Minor (in 1 movement, his most groundbreaking piano work; 1851–53); *Années de pèlerinage: Première année, Suisse* (1848–52); *Weinen, Klagen, Sorgen, Zagen, Präludium* (1859); *Variationen über das Motiv von B-A-C-H* (1862); *Années de pèlerinage, troisième année* (1867–77); *Wiegenlied—Chant du berceau* (1880); *Nuages gris* (1881); *La lugubre gondola* (1882; rev. 1885); *R.W.—Venezia* (1883); *Am Grabe Richard Wagners* (1883); *Recueillement* (1887); numerous arrangements and transcriptions. Liszt wrote numerous vocal works, including sacred and choral music and numerous solo songs (in several languages). He also composed organ and chamber music. He publ. 2 thematic catalogues of his works (1855; 1877).

litany. Song of supplication imploring God, the Blessed Virgin, and assorted saints with a promise to repent in exchange for divine intercession. A litany is chanted by the priest in an oscillating monotone with choir or congregation responding. The most auspicious time for a litany is the period of Rogation Days (from Lat. *rogare*, to beg). The unrelenting repetitiousness of a litany is of the essence for cumulative impact on the more compassionate saints. Litanies of the Anglican Church are less impressive, and the words often have a somewhat colloquial inflection (e.g., "Spare us, Good Lord").

liturgical drama. Medieval plays in Latin containing action, dialogue, and occasional singing episodes. While liturgical drama makes use of biblical subjects, it never became part of the Roman Catholic liturgy itself, but remained a trope. One of the most popular types of liturgical drama is the genre of miracle plays, reciting stories of saints, of whom St. Nicholas was a favorite. During the Renaissance liturgical drama developed into mystery plays (a misconstrued title actually meaning ministerial plays, from the Latin word *ministerium*, a service). Gradually such plays assumed a secular theatrical role while adhering to biblical subjects. Incidental music such as dances, trumpet flourishes, processions—even folk songs—was used. In Italy these dramas with music became known as *sacre rappresentazioni*, and as *autos* (acts) in Spain and Portugal. These festivals were true predecessors of scenic oratorios and, by ramification, Wagnerian music dramas.

liturgy (Old Grk. *leōs* + *ergon*, people work). Most comprehensive term for the official service of the established Christian Church. In the Byzantine ritual, the liturgy is synonymous with the Mass.

lituus (Lat.). 1. Hooked bronze trumpet, originally Etruscan, taken up by ancient Romans. 2. Cornett. 3. Instrument called for by Bach in his motet *O Jesu Christ, mein's Lebens Licht* (BWV 118); musicological opinion is that Bach intended cornet or trumpet.

liuto (It.). Lute.

live electronic music. Music which requires electronic music in its performance beyond simple tape playback or amplification of sound. When a singer or acoustic instrumentalist performs through electronic or computer equipment so that the final sound has been processed, the output is called *electroacoustic music.*

livret (Fr.). Libretto

llamada (Sp., fanfare). Generic term for works of proclamatory nature.

Lloyd Webber, Andrew, b. London, Mar. 22, 1948. His father, William Southcombe Lloyd Webber (1914–82), was a composer and director of the London College of Music; his mother was a piano teacher; inspired and conditioned by such an environment, Lloyd Webber learned to play piano, violin, and horn, and soon began to improvise music, mostly in the style of American musicals. He attended Westminster School in London, then went to Magdalen College, Oxford, the Guildhall School of Music, and the Royal College of Music in London. In college he wrote his 1st musical, *The Likes of Us*, dealing with a philanthropist. In 1967 he composed the theatrical show *Joseph and the Amazing Technicolor Dreamcoat*, which was performed at St. Paul's Junior School in London in 1968; it was later expanded to a full-scale production and achieved considerable success for its amalgam of biblical subject with rock music, French chansonnettes, and country-western songs. In 1970 it was produced in America, and in 1972 was shown on television.

He achieved his 1st commercial success with *Jesus Christ Superstar*, an audacious treatment of the religious theme in terms of jazz and rock. It premiered in London in 1972 and ran for 3,357 performances; it was as successful in America. Interestingly enough, this "rock opera" was 1st released as a record album, which eventually sold 3 million copies. *Jesus Christ Superstar* opened on Broadway in 1971, even before the London production. There were protests by religious groups against the irreverent treatment of a sacred subject; particularly offensive was the suggestion in play of a carnal relationship between Jesus and Mary Magdalen; Jewish organizations, on the other hand, protested against implied portrayal of Jews as guilty of the death of Christ. The musical closed on Broadway on June 30, 1973, after 720 performances; it received 7 Tony Awards. In 1981 the recording of *Jesus Christ Superstar* was given the Grammy Award for best cast show album of year. The great hullabaloo about the musical made a certainty of his further successes.

His early musical *Joseph and the Amazing Technicolor Dreamcoat* was revived at the off-Broadway Entermedia Theater in N.Y.'s East Village (1981), and from there moved to the Royale Theater on Broadway. In the meantime, he produced a musical with a totally different chief character, *Evita*, a semifictional account of the career of the 1st wife of Argentine dictator Juan Perón; it was staged in London on June 21, 1978; a N.Y. performance soon followed, with splendid success. But perhaps his most spectacular production was *Cats*, inspired by T. S. Eliot's *Old Possum's Book of Practical Cats*; it was produced in London (1981) and was brought out in N.Y. in 1982 with fantastic success; *Evita* and *Joseph and the Amazing Technicolor Dreamcoat* were still playing on Broadway, so that Lloyd Webber had the satisfaction of having 3 of his shows running at the same time. Subsequent successful productions were his *Song and Dance* (1983) and *Starlight Express* (London, 1984).

His series of commercial successes reached a lucrative apex with the production of *The Phantom of the Opera* (London, 1986; N.Y., 1988), a gothically oriented melodramatic tale of contrived suspense. In 1989 his musical *Aspects of Love* opened in London. He then adapted the famous film *Sunset Boulevard* for the stage, premiering in London in 1993 and a year later on Broadway. Apart from popular shows, Lloyd Webber wrote a mini-opera, *Tell Me on a Sunday*, about an English girl living in N.Y., which was produced by BBC Television in 1980. Quite different in style and intent were the *Variations* for Cello and Jazz Ensemble (1978), and *Requiem* (N.Y., 1985). His brother, Julian Lloyd Webber (b. London, Apr. 14, 1951), studied cello with Douglas Cameron (1964–67), at the Royal College of Music in London (1967–71), and with Pierre Fournier in Geneva. He made his concert debut at London's Queen Elizabeth Hall in 1972; subsequently played many engagements as soloist with English orchs. He made his American debut in N.Y. in 1980. In 1978 he became prof. of cello at the Guildhall School of Music in London. He ed. *Song of the Birds: Sayings, Stories and Impressions of Pablo Casals* (London, 1985).

lo (It.). The.

lo stesso (It.). The same. *Lo stesso tempo,* the same tempo; *lo stesso tempo e animando sempre più,* the same rate of speed, with ever increasing animation (of expression).

Lobgesang (Ger.). Song of praise.

loco (It., from Lat. *locus,* place). Play in normal (written) register, following an *8va* or similar passage (up or down).

Locrian mode. Modern term for a theoretical church mode, corresponding to the scale from B to B on the white keys of the piano keyboard. Since its "dominant" F stands to its tonic B in the relation of a "forbidden" diminished 5th (the diabolus in musica), Locrian mode was not used in Gregorian chant. Glareanus called this mode *hyperaeolian* (above the Aeolian).

Loeffler, Charles Martin (born Martin Karl Löffler), b. Berlin, Jan. 30, 1861; d. Medfield, Mass., May 19, 1935. In 1875 he began taking violin lessons in Berlin with Rappoldi, who prepared him for study with Joachim; he studied theory with Kiel; also took lessons with Bargiel at the Berlin Hochschule für Musik

(1874–77). Sometime between 1875 and 1878 his father was arrested on political grounds; he died in 1884 after suffering a stroke. This was the pivotal event of his son's life; he developed such an antipathy toward the German empire that he changed his name (jettisoning the umlaut), made himself an Alsatian by birth, and adopted the French soul for his own (only his wife and sister knew of his true origins).

Loeffler then went to Paris, where he continued his musical education with Massart (violin) and Guiraud (counterpoint and composition). He was engaged briefly as violinist in the Pasdeloup orch.; then was member of the private orch. of the Russian Baron Paul von Derwies at his sumptuous residences near Lugano and in Nice (1879–81). When Derwies died in 1881, Loeffler went to the U.S., with letters of recommendation from Joachim; he became a naturalized citizen in 1887. He played in the orch. of Leopold Damrosch in N.Y. in 1881–82. In 1882 he became 2nd concertmaster of the newly organized Boston Sym. Orch., but was able to accept other engagements during late spring and summer months; in spring of 1883 he traveled with the Thomas Orch. on a transcontinental tour; summers of 1883 and 1884 he spent in Paris, where he took violin lessons with Hubert Leonard. He resigned from the Boston Sym. Orch. in 1903, and devoted himself to composition and farming in Medfield. He was an officer of the French Academy (1906); a Chevalier in the French Legion of Honor (1919); member of the American Academy of Arts and Letters; Mus. Doc. (honoris causa), Yale Univ. (1926).

Loeffler's position in American music is unique, brought up as he was under many different national influences: French, German, Russian, and Ukrainian. One of his most vivid scores, *Memories of My Childhood* (Evanston, Ill., 1924), reflects the modal feeling of Russian and Ukrainian folk songs. But his aesthetic code was entirely French, with definite leanings toward impressionism; the archaic constructions that he sometimes affected, and stylized evocations of ars antiqua, was also in keeping with the French manner. His most enduring work, *A Pagan Poem* (Boston, 1907), is cast in such neoarchaic vein. He was a master of colorful orchestration; his harmonies are opulent without saturation; his rhapsodic forms are peculiarly suited to the evocative moods of his music. His only excursion into American idiom was the employment of jazz rhythms in a few of his lesser pieces. He is best known for his instrumental music, especially those involving the viola and viola d'amore.

Loesser, Arthur, b. N.Y., Aug. 26, 1894; d. Cleveland, Jan. 4, 1969. He studied with Stojowski and Goetschius at the Inst. of Musical Art in N.Y.; made his debut in Berlin (1913). He 1st played in N.Y. in 1916; after touring the Orient and Australia (1920–21), he appeared widely in the U.S. In 1926 he was appointed prof. of piano at the Cleveland Inst. of Music. In 1943 he was commissioned in the U.S. Army as an officer in the Japanese intelligence dept.; mastered the language and, after the war, gave lectures in Japanese in Tokyo; was the 1st American musician in uniform to play for a Japanese audience (1946). He publ. *Humor in American Song* (N.Y., 1943) and an entertaining vol., *Men, Women and Pianos: A Social History* (N.Y., 1954). He was the half-brother of Frank (Henry) Loesser.

Loesser, Frank (Henry), b. N.Y., June 29, 1910; d. there, July 28, 1969. He was educated at City College in N.Y., where he began writing songs for college activities; he subsequently was active as reporter, singer, and vaudeville performer. In 1931 he settled in Hollywood and devoted himself mainly to writing musical comedies. During World War II he was in the U.S. Army and wrote several Army songs, including *Praise the Lord and Pass the Ammunition* (1942) and *Roger Young* (1945). Although he continued to compose successful songs, he found his greatest reward in producing shows for Broadway; these included *Where's Charley?* (1948), *Guys and Dolls* (1950), *The Most Happy Fella* (1956), and *How to Succeed in Business Without Really Trying* (1961), which won a Pulitzer Prize and ran for 1,416 performances. His last musical was *Pleasures and Palaces* (Detroit, 1965). He was the half-brother of Arthur Loesser.

Loewe, Frederick, b. Vienna, June 10, 1901; d. Palm Springs, Calif., Feb. 14, 1988. He studied piano in Berlin with Busoni and d'Albert and composition with Reznicek; emigrated to the U.S. in 1924, and after a period as concert pianist, devoted himself to composing popular music. Adapting adroitly to the American idiom, he became one of the most successful writers of musical comedies. His 1st musical comedies were *Salute to Spring* (St. Louis, June 12, 1937), *Great Lady* (N.Y., Dec. 1, 1938), and *The Life of the Party* (Detroit, Oct. 8, 1942). He met lyricist and playwright Alan Jay Lerner in 1942, which led to their collaboration on the unsuccessful musical *What's Up?* (N.Y., Nov. 11, 1943). Their next effort, *The Day Before Spring* (N.Y., Nov. 22, 1945), received a respectable hearing, but it was with *Brigadoon* (N.Y., Mar. 13, 1947) that they achieved success. After *Paint Your Wagon* (N.Y., Nov. 12, 1951), they took Broadway by storm with *My Fair Lady* (N.Y., Mar. 15, 1956; with 2,717 subsequent perfs.), based on George Bernard Shaw's *Pygmalion*. They then brought out the film score *Gigi* (1958), after Colette, which won 9 Academy Awards. Their final Broadway collaboration was the highly acclaimed musical *Camelot* (N.Y., Dec. 3, 1960). Loewe came out of retirement in 1974 to collaborate with Lerner on the score to the film *The Little Prince*. See ⇒A. Sirmay, ed., *The Lerner and Loewe Songbook* (N.Y., 1962).

Loewe, (Johann) Carl (Gottfried), b. Lobejun, near Halle, Nov. 30, 1796; d. Kiel, Apr. 20, 1869. His father, a schoolmaster and cantor, taught him rudiments of music; when he was 12 he was sent to the Francke Inst. in Halle, where his attractive manner, excellent high voice, and early ability to improvise brought him to the attention of Jerome Bonaparte, who granted him a stipend of 300 thalers annually until 1813. His teacher was Türk, the head of the Francke Inst.; after Türk's death in 1813, Loewe joined the Singakademie founded by Naue. He also studied theology at the Univ. of Halle, but soon devoted himself entirely to music.

He had begun to compose as a boy; under influence of Zelter, he wrote German ballades, and developed an individual style of great dramatic force and lyrical inspiration; he perfected the genre, and was regarded by many musicians as the greatest song composer after Schubert and before Brahms. His setting of Goethe's poem *Erlkönig* (1818), which came just after Schubert wrote his great setting to the same poem, is one of Loewe's finest creations; other songs that rank among his best are *Edward, Der Wirthin Töchterlein, Der Nock, Archibald Douglas, Tom der Reimer, Heinrich der Vogler, Oluf,* and *Die verfallene Mühle.* Loewe was personally acquainted with Goethe, and also met

Weber. In 1820 he became schoolmaster at Stettin, and in 1821 music director there and organist at St. Jacobus Cathedral. He lived in Stettin, except for frequent travels, until 1866, when he settled in Kiel. He visited Vienna (1844), London (1847), Sweden and Norway (1851), and Paris (1857), among other places.

Loewe was an excellent vocalist and was able to perform his ballades in public. He publ. pedagogic works *Gesang-Lehre, theoretisch und practisch* (Stettin, 1826); *Musikalischer Gottesdienst: Methodische Anweisung zum Kirchengesang und Orgelspiel* (Stettin, 1851); *Klavier- und Generalbass-Schule* (Stettin, 2nd ed., 1851). In addition to his 368 ballades, Loewe wrote 6 operas, oratorios, cantatas, syms., piano concertos, string quartets, piano sonatas, and a piano trio.

lointain (Fr.). Distant, far away; sounding faintly.

Lomax, Alan, b. Austin, Tex., Jan. 31, 1915. He acquired his metier from his father, John Avery Lomax (b. Goodman, Miss., Sept. 23, 1867; d. Greenville, Miss., Jan. 26, 1948); then studied at the Univ. of Tex. in Austin (B.A., 1936) and at Columbia Univ. (1939). He joined his father as researcher in 1933; collected folk songs in the Southwestern and Midwestern regions of the U.S.; they supervised field recordings of rural and prison songs, discovering Leadbelly; they rediscovered Jelly Roll Morton and recorded interviews with him at the Library of Congress in Washington, D.C. (1938). He also collected folk songs in Europe. In 1963 he was made director of the Bureau of Applied Social Research and, at Columbia Univ., the project on *cantometrics,* a theory of cultural identification through measurement of musical and other elements. He has written numerous books, both alone and with his father, drawing on his collecting activities.

longa (Lat., long). In mensural notation, note equal to 2 or 3 breves, depending on context. It is indicated by a square with a downward stem to its right.

longevity. Cursory reading of actuarial tables seems to indicate that musicians as a class of people live on the average about 12 years longer than nonmusicians under similar social and geographical conditions. When an aging sym. conductor showed a desperate reluctance to quit, an unfeeling music critic remarked: "Conductors rarely die and never resign." The greatest conductor of modern times, Arturo Toscanini, continued to lead an orch. well into his 80s and resigned only after he suffered an embarrassing lapse of memory at a concert. Leopold Stokowski conducted concerts and made recordings after he turned 91. Pierre Monteux had already arranged a program he expected to conduct with the Boston Sym. Orch. on his 90th birthday, but unfortunately predeceased the date by a few months.

Organists are apt to live longer than sym. conductors. The celebrated French organist Charles-Marie Widor lived to be 93. There are several cases on record when church organists died at the console. Among them was the blind French organist Louis Vierne, who died while playing one of his new compositions at the organ of Notre Dame de Paris (1937); he was only 66. The record of longevity for pianists is not as impressive as that of organists. The American pianist Henry Holden Huss, who was also a composer of sorts, made a point of playing a program of his works on his 90th birthday. Artur Rubinstein continued to

give concerts even after he became blind; he died at age 95. Violinists and cellists usually stop playing in public after 70, but the greatest cellist of the 20th century, Pablo Casals, continued to play publicly until shortly before his death at 97. Among singers, Manuel Garcia lived to be 101, but he abandoned his professional singing career long before, and became active mainly as a teacher. Marie Olénine d'Alheim (1869–1970) terminated her career as concert singer in her middle age to enter radical politics; she joined the French Communist party and went to Moscow, where she died at the round age of 100.

One has to cite less universally known names to find nonagenarians and centenarians among composers. Havergal Brian reached the age of 96. Henri Büsser died at age 101, but he was little known outside of France. Carl Ruggles lived to be 95, and he was fortunate in acquiring a solid reputation before he died. Eubie Blake, the American black ragtime virtuoso, appeared on television in his late 90s; he died a few days after reaching his 100th anniversary. The most spectacular case of composer's longevity is that of the American composer Margaret Ruthven Lang, who reached the age of 104 before she finally died. Descending further into the depths of obscurity we find name of Victor Kuzdo, a Hungarian-American violinist and composer whose vital enzymes sustained him in Glendale, Calif., until his death at age 106, an all-time record in the annals of musical biography.

Statistically, mediocre musicians live much longer than men of genius. Among truly great composers only Verdi lived well into his 80s. Wagner did not even reach the biblically sanctified age of 3-score and 10. Beethoven, Debussy, Ravel, and Tchaikovsky died before their 60th birthdays. And Chopin, Schubert, Schumann, and Mendelssohn, not to mention Mozart, died in their 30s or 40s, at the height of their genius. Is it that angels are eager to carry away the best musicians for heavenly concerts?

longhair. Derogatory characterization of a person interested in classical music; synonymous with highbrow. It derives from the conventional portraiture of older musicians sporting a luxuriant head of long hair; Liszt in his last photograph appears thus uncropped.

long-playing records (recordings). Phonograph discs intended to rotate at 33 1/3 revolutions per minute (rpm), introduced by Columbia Records in 1947. This makes it possible to place 25 minutes (more or less) on a single side of a disc, as opposed to 4 1/2 minutes on a side of the 78-rpm disc. This result was accomplished by having more circular grooves in combination with slower speed of recording. Long-playing records inaugurated a new era in phonograph recordings enabling phonograph companies to place a whole act of an opera or whole sym. on a single disc. Long-playing records are often called LPs for short.

lontana (It.). Far away. *Da lontana,* from a distance.

lontano (It.). Lointain. *Tuono lontano,* distant thunder (Verdi: *Otello*).

Loriod, Yvonne, b. Houilles, Seine-et-Oise, Jan. 20, 1924. She studied at the Paris Cons., winning no less than 7 *premiers prix;* among her mentors were L. Lévy, I. Philipp, Marcel Ciampi,

Olivier Messiaen, and Milhaud for composition. She began collaborating with Messiaen on the premiere of *Visions de l'Amen* for 2 Pianos (1943); she would later play the 1st performances of all of his piano parts. After World War II she toured extensively; made her U.S. debut in the premiere of Messiaen's *Turangalîla-Symphonie* with the Boston Sym. Orch. (1949). She taught at the Paris Cons. A foremost champion of the music of Messiaen, she married him in 1961. She also excelled in performances of music of Bartók, Schoenberg, Barraqué, and Boulez.

Lortzing, (Gustav) Albert, b. Berlin, Oct. 23, 1801; d. there, Jan. 21, 1851. His parents were actors, and the wandering life led by the family did not allow him to pursue a methodical course of study. He learned acting from his father, and music from his mother at an early age. After some lessons in piano with Griebel and in theory with Rungenhagen in Berlin, he continued his own studies, and soon began to compose. In 1824 he wrote his stage work, the singspiel *Ali Pascha von Janina, oder Die Französen in Albanien,* which, however, was not produced until 4 years later (Munster, 1828). He then brought out the liederspiel *Der Pole und sein Kind, oder Der Feldwebel vom IV. Regiment* (1832) and the singspiel *Szenen aus Mozarts Leben* (Osnabrück, 1832), which were well received on several German stages.

Lortzing was engaged at the Municipal Theater of Leipzig as a tenor (1833-44); there he launched a light opera, *Die beiden Schützen* (1837), which became instantly popular; on the same stage he produced his undoubted masterpiece, *Zar und Zimmermann, oder Die zwei Peter* (1837). It was performed with enormous success in Berlin (1839), and then in other European music centers. His next opera, *Caramo, oder Das Fischerstechen* (Leipzig, 1839), was a failure; there followed *Hans Sachs* (Leipzig, 1840) and *Casanova* (Leipzig, 1841), which passed without much notice; subsequent comparisons showed some similarities between *Hans Sachs* and *Die Meistersinger von Nürnberg,* not only in subject matter, which was derived from the same source, but also in some melodic patterns; however, no one seriously suggested that Wagner was influenced by Lortzing's inferior work.

There followed a comic opera, *Der Wildschütz, oder Die Stimme der Natur* (Leipzig, 1842), which was in many respects the best that Lortzing wrote, but its success, although impressive, never equaled that of *Zar und Zimmermann.* At about the same time Lortzing attempted still another career, that of opera impresario, but it was short-lived; his brief conductorship at the Leipzig Opera (1844–45) was similarly ephemeral. Composing remained his chief occupation; he produced *Undine* in Magdeburg (1845) and *Der Waffenschmied* in Vienna (1846). He then went to Vienna as conductor at the Theater an der Wien, but soon returned to Leipzig, where he produced the light opera *Zum Grossadmiral* (1847).

The revolutionary events of 1848 seriously affected his position in both Leipzig and Vienna; after the political situation became settled, he produced in Leipzig an opera of Romantic nature, *Rolands Knappen, oder Das ersehnte Gluck* (1849). Although at least 4 of his operas were played at various German theaters, Lortzing received no honorarium, owing to a flaw in regulations protecting rights of composers. In the spring of 1850 he obtained post of conductor at Berlin's nondescript Friedrich-Wilhelmstadt

Theater. His last score, the comic opera *Die Opernprobe, oder Die vornehmen Dilettanten,* was produced in Frankfurt am Main while he was on his deathbed in Berlin; he died the next day. His opera *Regina,* written in 1848, was ed. by Richard Kleinmichel, with the composer's libretto revised by Adolf L'Arronge, and performed in Berlin as *Regina, oder Die Marodeure* (1899); his singspiel *Der Weihnachtsabend* was produced in Münster (1832). Lortzing also wrote an oratorio, *Die Himmelfahrt Jesu Christi* (Münster, 1828); some incidental music to various plays, choral works, and songs.

It is as composer of characteristically German Romantic operas that Lortzing holds a distinguished, if minor, place in the history of dramatic music. He was follower of Weber, without Weber's imaginative projection; in his lighter works he approached a type of French operetta; in his best creations he exhibited a fine sense of facile melody and infectious rhythm; his harmonies, though unassuming, were always proper and pleasing; his orchestration, competent and effective.

Lott, Felicity (Ann), b. Cheltenham, May 8, 1947. She studied in London at Royal Holloway College, Univ. of London, and at the Royal Academy of Music; in 1976 she sang at Covent Garden in the world premiere of Henze's *We Come to the River;* she also appeared there as Anne Trulove in *The Rake's Progress,* Octavian, and other roles. She appeared in Paris for the 1st time in 1976; made her Vienna debut in 1982 singing the *4 letze Lieder* of R. Strauss; in 1984 was engaged as soloist with the Chicago Sym. Orch. In 1986 she sang at the wedding of the Duke and the Duchess of York at Westminster Abbey. In 1990 she was made a Commander of the Order of the British Empire; also in 1990 she made her Metropolitan Opera debut in N.Y. as the Marschallin. Among her other fine roles are Pamina, Countess Almaviva, Donna Elvira, and Arabella.

loud pedal (damper pedal). Far-right pedal of the piano; when depressed, it releases (lifts) all dampers normally resting on the strings, allowing the strings that have been struck to continue vibrating (i.e., sound). This makes it necessary to change pedaling quickly when the harmony changes to avoid unwelcome cacophony. The handling (or more accurately, the footing) of the loud pedal must therefore be considered with great care on general musical grounds rather than narrowly pianistic grounds. One of the natural safety impulses among pianists unsure of their technique is to step on the right pedal to create a universal resonance in which annoying wrong notes may be conveniently drowned out. When a composer writes for piano orchestrally, requiring sustained tones in changing harmonies, compromise must be sought using the skill of subtle half-pedaling. An outstanding example is a variation in Schumann's *Études symphoniques,* in which the theme occurs in the bass while the harmony changes above, making it extremely difficult to achieve both the legato in the left hand and the changing harmonies in the right hand.

lourdement (Fr.). Heavily.

loure (Fr., bagpipe). Dance in 6/4 or 3/2 time and slow tempo, the downbeat strongly marked, with syncopation. The loure is often included in the Baroque instrumental suite as well as French ballets and overtures of the Rococo period.

louré (Fr., bagpipe; It. *portato*). Slurred, legato, nonstaccato. The origin of the word itself is from *lura* (bagpipe, implying a dronelike sound), which also generated the term *louré* as a kind of bowing technique on string instruments in which several notes are played in one bow stroke but in detached manner; most commonly indicated by a slur encompassing dotted notes.

luce (It., light). Proposed *color organ* marked by Scriabin in the score of his last symphonic work, *Prométhée*; according to Scriabin's unfulfilled hopes, the luce would have bathed the concert hall in shimmering hues that changed along with the harmonies.

lucernarium (Lat. *lucerna*, lamp). Former term for the Canonical hour of Vespers; it refers to the necessary lighting of candles for an evening service.

Lucier, Alvin (Augustus, Jr.), b. Nashua, N.H., May 14, 1931. He studied with Howard Boatwright, Richard Donovan, David Kraehenbuhl, and Quincy Porter at Yale Univ. (1950–54); continued his training with A. Berger, I. Fine, and H. Shapero at Brandeis Univ. (1958–60); also studied with Lukas Foss (composition) and Copland (orchestration) at Berkshire Music Center in Tanglewood (1958, 1959); then went to Rome on a Fulbright scholarship (1960–62). He was on the faculty of Brandeis Univ. (1962–70), where he served as choral director. With Robert Ashley, David Behrman, and Gordon Mumma, he founded the Sonic Arts Union (1966), an electronic-music performing group with which he toured the U.S. and Europe. He joined the faculty of Wesleyan Univ. (1970); was music director of the Viola Farber Dance Co. (1972–77). He contributed many articles to music journals and other publications; with D. Simon, he publ. *Chambers* (Middletown, Conn., 1980). In 1990 he was in Berlin on a Deutscher Akademischer Austauschdienst fellowship.

Lucier's works exploit virtually all known musical and nonmusical resources available to the creative artist, and redefine the term *music* in radical terms. Devices used by Lucier include amplified brain waves, vocoder, moving large and small resonant environments, acoustic orientation by means of echolocation, electromagnetic tape, responsive surfaces, strewn material, closed-circuit television system, unattended percussion, microphones, loudspeakers, sound-producing objects, audio oscillators, electronic monochord, sound-sensitive lights, electronic music system powered and controlled by sunlight, pure-wave oscillators, acoustic pendulums, sound installation, amplified clocks, galvanic skin response sensors, digital delay systems, open umbrellas, and glass oven dishs. Many of these tools have been incorporated into sound installations.

ludi spirituales (Lat., spiritual plays). Medieval sacred mystery plays on biblical subjects.

Ludwig, Christa, b. Berlin, Mar. 16, 1924. She was reared in a musical family; her parents both sang. Ludwig studied at the Hochschule für Musik in Frankfurt; in 1946 she made her operatic debut in Frankfurt in role of Orlofsky in *Die Fledermaus*, singing there until 1952. In 1954 she sang roles of Cherubino and Octavian at the Salzburg Festival; in 1955 she was engaged by the Vienna State Opera; made her Metropolitan Opera debut in N.Y. as Cherubino (1959). In subsequent years she made considerable impact as a Wagnerian singer, being equally successful

in such disparate roles as Kundry, Fricka, Venus, and Magdalene in *Die Meistersinger von Nürnberg*. She also obtained brilliant success as the Marschallin and other roles in operas by R. Strauss; she also sang the female leads in the 2 Berg operas. In the Italian repertoire she gave fine interpretations of roles of Amneris, Rosina, and Lady Macbeth.

Her career took her to opera theaters all over the world; she sang at La Scala in Milan, Covent Garden in London, the Teatro Colón in Buenos Aires, and the Nissei Theater in Tokyo. Soberminded, skeptical music critics in Europe and America exerted their vocabularies to extol Ludwig as a superb singer not only in opera but also in the art of German lieder; some even praised her physical attributes. In 1962 she was named a Kammersängerin of Austria, and in 1969 she received the Cross of Merit, 1st Class, of the Republic of Austria. In 1980 she received the Golden Ring, and in 1981 was made an honorary member of the Vienna State Opera; in 1980 she was awarded the Silver Rose of the Vienna Phil. In 1957 she married Walter Berry, the Austrian baritone; they frequently appeared together in the same opera; they separated and in 1970 were divorced; in 1972 she married French actor Paul Deiber.

Luening, Otto (Clarence), b. Milwaukee, June 15, 1900; d. N.Y., Sept. 2, 1996. His father was an educated musician who received his training at the Leipzig Cons. Luening had met Wagner and sung in performances of Beethoven's 9th Sym., with Wagner conducting; kept his cultural associations with Germany, and in 1912 took his family to Munich. There he enrolled in the Akademie der Tonkunst, where he studied flute with Alois Schellhorn, piano with Josif Becht, and composition with A. Beer-Walbrunn. He gave his 1st concert as flutist in Munich (1916).

When America entered World War I in 1917, Luening went to Switzerland, where he studied with Philip Jarnach and Volkmar Andreae at the Zurich Cons. (until 1920); he also had an opportunity to take private lessons with Busoni; also acted in James Joyce's English Players Company there. He now began to compose; his 1st violin sonata and sextet were performed at the Zurich Cons. Luening returned to the U.S. in 1920; he earned a living as flutist and conductor in theater orchs. In 1925 he moved to Rochester, N.Y., where he served as coach and executive director of the opera dept. at the Eastman School of Music; in 1928 he went to Cologne; from 1932 to 1934 he was on the faculty of the Univ. of Arizona in Tucson. In 1934 he became chairman of the music dept. at Bennington College in Vermont, keeping this position until 1944. After teaching at Barnard College in N.Y. (1944–47), he was on the music faculty at Columbia Univ. (1949–68), where he also was codirector of the Columbia-Princeton Electronic Music Center (1959–80) and music chairman of the School of the Arts (1966–70); likewise taught composition at the Juilliard School (1971–73).

An important development in Luening's career as composer took place in 1952, when he began to experiment with the resources of magnetic tape; he composed a strikingly novel piece, *Fantasy in Space*, in which he played the flute with its accompaniment electronically transmuted on tape; Stokowski featured it on a N.Y. program (1952), along with Luening's 2 other electronic pieces, *Low Speed* and *Invention*. He found a partner in V. Ussachevsky, who was also interested in musical electronics. Together they produced the 1st work that combined real sounds superinduced on an electronic background,

Rhapsodic Variations for Tape Recorder and Orch., performed by the Louisville Orch. (1954); its performance anticipated by a few months the production of Varèse's similarly constructed work, *Déserts*. Another electronic work by Luening and Ussachevsky, *A Poem in Cycles and Bells* for Tape Recorder and Orch., was played by the Los Angeles Phil. (1954).

Bernstein conducted the 1st performance of still another collaborative composition by Luening and Ussachevsky, *Concerted Piece* for Tape Recorder and Orch., with the N.Y. Phil. (1960). Thenceforth, Luening devoted a major part of his creative effort to an integration of electronic sound into the fabric of a traditional orch., without abandoning fundamental scales and intervals; most, but not all, of these works were in collaboration with Ussachevsky. Unaided, he produced *Synthesis* for Electronic Tape and Orch. (1960) and *Sonority Canon* (1962). He also wrote straightforward pieces without electronics; of these the most important is *A Wisconsin Sym.*, a sort of musical memoir of a Wis.-born composer; it was performed in Milwaukee, Luening's birthplace (1976). His native state reciprocated proudly, awarding Luening an honorary doctorate from the Univ. of Wis. in Madison, a medal from the Wis. Academy of Sciences, Arts, and Letters, and a citation from the Wis. State Assembly. In addition to many other honors, he also held Guggenheim fellowships in 1930–31 and 1974–75.

luftig (Ger.). Airy, light.

Luftpause (Ger., breathing rest). Break between melody notes, and particularly at the end of a phrase. It is often used and abused by pseudo-Romantic performers, particularly violinists, who either cannot sustain passage in legato or feel that a melody without a soulful luftpause would lack expressive power.

lugubre (It.). Mournful.

Lully, Jean-Baptiste, (born Giovanni Battista Lulli), b. Florence, Nov. 28, 1632; d. Paris, Mar. 22, 1687. The son of a poor Florentine miller, he learned to play guitar at an early age. His talent for singing brought him to the attention of Roger de Lorraine, Chevalier de Guise, and he was taken to Paris in 1646 as page to Mlle. de Montpensier, young cousin of Louis XIV. He quickly adapted to the manner of the French court; although he mastered the language, he never lost his Italian accent. There is no truth in the report that he worked in the kitchens, but he did keep company with the domestic servants, and it was while he was serving in Mlle. de Montpensier's court in the Tuileries that he perfected his violin technique. He also had the opportunity to hear the 24 Violons du Roi (grande bande) and was present at performances of Luigi Rossi's *Orfeo* at the Louvre in 1647.

When Mlle. de Montpensier suffered political disgrace in 1652 and was forced to leave Paris, Lully was released from her service, and early in 1653 he danced with the young Louis XIV in the ballet *La Nuit*. Shortly thereafter he was made *compositeur de la musique instrumentale du Roi*, with joint responsibility for instrumental music in court ballets. At some time before 1656 he became conductor of Les Petits Violons du Roi, smaller offshoot of the grand bande. This ensemble was heard for the 1st time in 1656 in *La Galanterie du temps*. Thanks to Lully's strict discipline with regard to organization and interpretation, Les Petits

Violons soon came to rival the parent ensemble. The 2 groups were combined in 1664.

Lully became a naturalized French citizen in 1661, the same year in which he was appointed *surintendant de la musique et compositeur de la musique de la chambre*; he also became *maître de la musique de la famille royale* in 1662. His father-in-law was Michel Lambert, the eminent French composer (b. Champigny-sur-Veude, near Chinon, Indre-et-Loire, 1610; d. Paris, June 29, 1696). His association with Molière commenced in 1664; he provided Molière with music for a series of comédies-ballets, culminating with *Le Bourgeois gentilhomme* in 1670. Lully acquired the sole right to form an Académie Royale de Musique in 1672, and thus gained the power to forbid performances of stage works by any other composer. From then until his death he produced series of tragédies lyriques, most of which were composed to texts by librettist Philippe Quinault. The subject matter for several of these works was suggested by the King, who was extravagantly praised and idealized in their prologues. Lully took great pains in perfecting these texts, but he was often content to leave writing of the inner voices of the music to his pupils.

His monopoly of French musical life created much enmity. In 1674 Henri Guichard attempted to establish an Académie Royale des Spectacles, and their ensuing rivalry resulted in Lully accusing Guichard of trying to murder him by mixing arsenic with his snuff. Lully won the court case that followed, but the decision was reversed on appeal. A further setback occurred when Quinault was thought to have slandered the King's mistress in his text of *Isis* (1677) and was compelled to end his partnership with Lully in disgrace for some time. The King continued to support Lully, however, in spite of the fact that the composer's homosexuality had become a public scandal (homosexuality at the time was a capital offense). Lully's acquisition of titles culminated in 1681, when noble rank was conferred upon him with the title Secretaire du Roi. In his last years he turned increasingly to sacred music. It was while he was conducting his *Te Deum* in 1687 that he suffered a symbolic accident, striking his foot with a pointed cane used to pound out the beat. Gangrene set in, and he died of blood poisoning 2 months later.

Lully's historical importance rests primarily upon his music for the theater. He developed what became known as the French overture, with its 3 contrasting slow-fast-slow movements. He further replaced the Italian recitativo secco style with accompanied French recitative. Thus through the Italian-born Lully, French opera came of age. Some of his best-known stage works include *Cadmus et Hermione* (1673); *Alceste, ou Le Triomphe d'Alcide* (1674); and *Acis et Galatée, pastorale héroique* (1686). He also scored numerous ballets and theatrical works. His sacred and choral works include *Te Deum* (1677); *De profundis* (1683); *Motets à deux pour la chapelle du Roi* (Paris, 1684); 6 grands motets for 2 choirs and orch. (1685); and 14 petits motets. Lully also wrote a variety of instrumental pieces, including overtures, suites, dances, and organ pieces. A complete catalog of his works was ed. by H. Schneider (Tutzing, 1981).

lumineux (Fr.). Luminuous, bright. *Luminosità* (It.), luminosity.

lunga, -o (It., long). Sustained, prolonged. Written over or under a fermata (⌢, ⌣), indicates that the pause is to be decidedly prolonged; often written *lunga pausa* or *pausa lunga*.

luogo (It.). Loco.

Lupu, Radu, b. Galai, Nov. 30, 1945. He began his piano studies at age 6, making his recital debut when he was 12; then studied with Florica Muzicescu and on scholarship at the Moscow Cons. (1963), where he studied with Heinrich and Stanislau Neuhaus until 1969. In quick succession he won 1st prize in the Van Cliburn (1966), Enesco (1967), and Leeds (1969) competitions. In 1972 he made his American debut as soloist with the Cleveland Orch., and subsequently played with the Chicago, Los Angeles, N.Y., and Boston orchs. In Europe he made successful appearances in Berlin, Paris, Amsterdam, London, Vienna, and other cities in varied programs ranging from Classic to modern works.

lur (Dan.). Late Nordic Bronze Age brass instrument of Scandinavia, comprised of a conical tube, 3 to 6 feet in length, twisted into a loose *S*; a cupped, lip-vibrated mouthpiece; and a disc ornamented with geometric figures instead of a bell. The lur is one of the most common finds in archeological digs in the region.

lusingando (It., coaxing, ingratiating). Particularly sentimental type of violin phrasing, with exaggerated vibrato and portamento.

lusinghiero (It.). Coaxingly, caressingly, flatteringly, seductively.

lustig (Ger.). Gaily, merrily

lute (It. *lauto*; Fr. *luth*, Ger. *Laute*). One of a variety of related plucked string instruments, popular during the 16th-18th centuries, iconographically ubiquitous in Renaissance and Baroque paintings. The body is shaped like half a pear; its neck is turned back at a right angle; the fingerboard has embossed frets to indicate correct finger positions. The lute normally has 5 sets of double courses (strings), plus a single highest string; they are plucked with fingers; tuning is in perfect 4ths, with a 3rd in the middle, for a 2-octave range; the lowest string is G or A. Large numbers of lute music collections were publ. in the 16th and 17th centuries; from these books, music historians can trace the formal development of European dances, instrumental works, and vocal compositions. Most lute music was written in tablature, by which the player was shown a diagram of the strings and the position in which fingers should be placed to secure the desired notes.

Lutelike instruments existed in ancient Mesopotamia, but with only 2 or 3 strings; there is no direct evidence that the Renaissance European lute descended from these precursors. Long-necked lutes have existed in Persia and Arabia since the Middle Ages; the European variant, called *colascione*, usually had 5 strings; other Arab lutes include the small *'ud* and the *tanbur*. The Russian *domra* was popular at the same time as the European lute; it was superseded by the *balalaika*; the mandolin is a type of lute; it retained its popularity through the 20th century. Other types include the mandora (a small lute), pandora (a bass), and 2 very large lutes, the theorbo and chitarrone; all 4 are obsolete. It must be noted, however, that none share the lute's characteristic bent neck.

Lutenists enjoyed great renown in the Renaissance period, particularly in England. John Dowland, a fine composer-lutenist who was a contemporary of Shakespeare, commanded salaries equaling those of high officials; the Italian court lutenist Rizzio, brought to Scotland by Mary, Queen of Scots, assumed such power at court that Mary's antagonists had him assassinated. In addition to the numerous portraits of male and female lutenists painted, there are numerous references to lutenists in English literature beginning with Chaucer. While it was favored overwhelmingly by the aristocracy of the period, the lute inexplicably lost its appeal around the middle of the 18th century, joining the honorable company of obsolete instruments, but is now a vital component of the early music revival.

lutheal. Mechanical attachment invented by Belgian piano manufacturer Georges Cloetens (1919); placed on the metal framework inside a grand piano, it imparts a sound like a harpsichord or cimbalom. Ravel was quite fascinated by its potential and used it in the piano accompaniment of his *Tzigane* for violin (Paris, 1924); but the lutheal failed to attract either the audience or critics; he rev. the work without lutheal, and later orchestrated it. He also used it in the orig. version of *L'Enfant et les sortilèges* (1920–25), but finally decided to re-create the lutheal through orchestration.

Luther, Martin, b. Eisleben, Nov. 10, 1483; d. there, Feb. 18, 1546. As part of the changes within 16th-century Christianity, Luther wrote tracts on a new vernacular liturgy; the 1st Mass in German (excluding the Latin Ordinary) was sung in Wittenberg (1524). Johann Walter (1696–1770), who aided Luther in organizing the music for the Mass, transcribed melodies from Luther's flute playing; together created new hymns, of which many are attributed to Luther; it seems that, while some are his, others were German translations or adaptations of Latin hymns.

luthier (Fr.). Lute maker; applied to string instrument makers generally.

Lutoslawski, Witold, b. Warsaw, Jan. 25, 1913; d. there, Feb. 7, 1994. He learned the piano as a child; studied violin with L. Kmitowa (1926–32) and theory and composition with W. Maliszewski (1927–37); studied mathematics at the Univ. of Warsaw (1931–33). He entered the Warsaw Cons. (1932); while continuing composition studies, also studied piano with J. Lefeld (graduated in piano, 1936, and composition, 1937). He served in the Polish Army (1937–38); after remobilization, was taken prisoner of war by invading Nazi armies (1939); escaped to Warsaw; earned a living by playing piano in cafés (1939–44); participated in private clandestine concerts. At war's end, he worked briefly for Polish Radio (1945), then devoted himself to composition; as his *renommée* reached the outside world, obtained engagements as lecturer and instructor throughout Europe; conducted his own works (from 1963). As his reputation grew he received special memberships in Hamburg's Freie Akademie der Künste (1966), West Berlin's Akademie der Künste (1968), the ISCM (1969), East Berlin's Deutsche Akademie der Künste (1970), American Academy of Arts and Letters (1975), and London's Royal Academy of Music (1976).

Lutoslawski's early works tend toward neoclassicism, permeated with Polish motifs; gradually turned to a more structuralist style in which melodic and rhythmic elements are organized into a strong unifying network, with occasional incursions of dodecaphonic and aleatory practices. He was extraordinarily openminded; on one hand, attracted by Cage's aesthetics, he found useful applications for performance flexibility; on the other, Bartók's influence led to a preference for constantly changing orch'l colors, angular intervallic progressions, and asymmetrical rhythms; his *Musique funèbre* for string orch. (1958), dedicated to the Hungarian's memory and thematically built on a concatenation of upward tritones and downward semitones, is stylistically significant. He was an inveterate reviser, taking 10 years to achieve the desired proportions for his 3rd Sym (1960); his relatively small work list includes orch'l masterpieces: *Jeux venitens* (1961), Cello Concerto (for Rostropovich, 1970), *Les Espaces du sommeil* (with baritone, 1975), *Mi-parti* (1976); the highly influential String Quartet (1964); and vocal works with ens.: *A Straw Chain* for soprano and ens. (1951), *3 Poems of Henri Michaux* for choir and ens. (requiring 2 conductors reading different scores, 1963), and *Paroles tisses* for tenor and ens. (1965).

luttuosamente (*luttuoso*; It.). Mournfully, plaintively.

Lydian mode. Ecclesiastical mode corresponding to the scale from *F* to *F* an octave higher on the piano's white keys; although it shares its name with an ancient Greek mode, the two are not the same; its arresting characteristic is the tritone interval between tonic and subdominant; Beethoven emphatically stresses the mode in the slow movement of his penultimate last string quartet, op. 132; Chopin gives the Lydian mode peculiar expressivity in some of his mazurkas.

lydische Quarte (Ger., Lydian 4th). Interval (augmented 4th) between the 1st and 4th steps of this mode.

Lynn, Loretta (Webb), b. Butcher Hollow, Ky., Apr. 14, 1932. She taught herself guitar; went to Nashville, Tenn.; joined the Grand Ole Opry; organized her own group, the Blue Kentuckians, and toured widely. She has scored enormous success with numerous country-western hits in the 1960s, '70s, and early '80s, among them *Success, Don't Come Home A-Drinkin' (with Lovin' on Your Mind), Woman of the World (Leave My World Alone), One's on the Way, The Pill, Rated "X", Trouble in Paradise, Out of My Head and Back in My Bed*, and *Coal Miner's Daughter* (which she was); recorded several hits with Conway Twitty.

lyra viol (U.K.). Viola bastarda.

lyre. 1. Ancient Greek stringed instrument, with a body made of wood or tortoise shell, from which rose 2 curving arms joined above by a crossbar; between 3 and 10 strings were stretched from the crossbar to or over a bridge set on the soundboard, and plucked with a plectrum; both it and the kithara were played by Apollo, Greek god of music, and had major iconographic roles in sculptures and drawings of him. 2. In military bands, lyre-shaped mallet instrument comprising loosely suspended pitched steel bars, struck with a hammer.

lyric (lyrical; It., *lirico*). Literally, relating to or proper for the lyre, or for lyre accompaniment; colloquially, appropriate for singing or expression in song; opposed to epic (narrative) and dramatic (reenacted) modes. *Lyric drama* (Fr. *drame lyrique*), opera; *lyric opera*, one dominated by lyricism; *lyric stage*, operatic stage.

lyric (*lyrics*). Text for a popular song, including those taken from musicals. *Lyricist*, author of popular song texts, notably those taken from musicals.

Mm

M. Abbrev. for It. *mano;* Fr. *main;* manual (organ); metronome marking (usually *M.M.*).

m.d. Abbrev. for Fr. *main droite;* It. *mano destra.*

m.g. Abbrev. for Fr. *main gauche.*

m.s. Abbrev. for It. *mano sinistra.*

ma (It.). But. *Allegro ma non troppo,* rapidly, but not too fast.

Ma, Yo-Yo, b. Paris, Oct. 7, 1955. He was born into a musical family active in Paris; his father was a violinist, his mother a mezzo-soprano. He began to study violin as a small child, then graduated to the viola and finally the cello; was taken to N.Y. when he was 7, and enrolled at the Juilliard School of Music when he was 9; his principal teachers were Leonard Rose and Janos Scholz; he subsequently received additional musical training at Harvard Univ. He quickly established a formidable reputation as a master of the cello in his appearances with the great orchs. of the world, as a recitalist, and as a chamber music player, being deservedly acclaimed for his unostentatious musicianship, his superlative technical resources, and the remarkable tone of his melodious lyricism. In order to extend his repertoire he made a number of effective transcriptions for his instrument. He was awarded the Avery Fisher Prize in 1978.

Maazel, Lorin (Varencove), b. Neuilly, France (of American parents), Mar. 6, 1930. His parents took him to Los Angeles in infancy; soon showed innate musicality, including perfect pitch; began violin study at age 5 with K. Moldrem and piano at 7 with F. Armitage; fascinated by the art of conducting, went to sym. concerts; began taking conducting lessons with Vladimir Bakaleinikov, associate conductor of the Los Angeles Phil. (also learned Russian); conducted Schubert's *Unfinished* Sym. with the visiting Univ. of Idaho orch. (1938). When Bakaleinikov was appointed assistant conductor of the Pittsburgh Sym. Orch. (1938), the Maazels followed him there. Lorin created a sensation conducting the National Music Camp Orch. of Interlochen at the N.Y. World's Fair (1939), eliciting comparisons to a trained seal. He conducted the NBC Sym. Orch. (1941) and led an entire program with the N.Y. Phil. (1942); surviving these traumatic exhibitions, took academic courses at the Univ. of Pittsburgh; joined the Pittsburgh Sym. Orch. as violinist and apprentice conductor (1948).

In 1951 Maazel received a Fulbright fellowship for travel in Italy; undertook a serious study of Baroque music; made his adult debut as conductor in Catania (1953); conducted at the Florence May (1955), Vienna (1957), and Edinburgh (1958) festivals. He became the 1st American to conduct at Bayreuth, leading performances of *Lohengrin* (1960); toured the U.S. with the Orch. National de France (1962); that year made his Metropolitan Opera debut in N.Y., conducting *Don Giovanni.* He toured Russia, conducting concerts in Moscow and Leningrad (1963); was artistic director of the Deutsche Oper in West Berlin (1965–71); chief conductor of the (West) Berlin Radio Sym. Orch. (1965–75). He was associate principal conductor of the New Philharmonia Orch. of London (1970–72) and principal guest conductor (1976–80); became music director of the Cleveland Orch., a position he held with great distinction (1972–82); then made conductor emeritus; led the orch. on 10 major tours abroad, including Australia and New Zealand (1973), Japan (1974), twice in Latin America, and twice in Europe; maintained its stature as one of the world's foremost orchs. He was chief conductor of the Orch. National de France (1977–82), its principal guest conductor (1982–88), and music director (1988–91); conducted the famous Vienna Phil. New Year's Day Concerts (1980–86); assumed positions of artistic director and general manager of the Vienna State Opera, the 1st American to do so (1982), but resigned these positions in 1984 after a conflict over artistic policies with the Ministry of Culture. He served as music consultant to the Pittsburgh Sym. Orch. (1984–86), becoming in succession its music adviser and principal guest conductor, then music director (all 1986).

Maazel is equally adept as an interpreter of operatic and symphonic scores; is blessed with a phenomenal memory and an extraordinary baton technique; maintains an avid interest in nonmusical pursuits; is fluent in 7 languages. He married twice; to the Brazilian-American pianist Miriam Sandbank (1952; divorced) and the Israeli pianist Israela Margalit (1969; divorced). Maazel has received many awards: the Sibelius Prize in Finland, Commander's Cross of the Order of Merit from West Germany, and, for his numerous recordings, Grand Prix de Disque in Paris and Edison Prize in the Netherlands.

Mac Low, Jackson, b. Chicago, Sept. 12, 1922. He studied piano, violin, and harmony at Chicago Musical College (1927–32) and Northwestern Univ. Music School (1932–36); took courses in philosophy, poetics, and English at the Univ. of Chicago (1941); studied Greek at Brooklyn College (1958); took piano with S. Gablis (1943–44), G. Sultan (1953–55), and F. Kamin (1976–79), composition with E. Katz (1948–49), recorder with Tui St. George Tucker (1948–53), and experimental music with Cage, all at the New School for Social Research in N.Y. (1957–60); studied voice privately with Pandit Pran Nath (1975–76). He taught at N.Y. Univ. (1966–73), Mannes College of Music in N.Y. (1966), State Univ. of N.Y. at Albany (1984), Binghamton (1989), and Buffalo (1990), and Temple Univ. (1989); Regents Lecturer at the Univ. of Calif. at San Diego (1990).

Mac Low adopted chance operations, indeterminacy, and related methods in 1954. His many "simultaneities" include musical, verbal, and visual elements; many compositions are for live voices, instruments (often variable), and/or tape multitracking, and usually involve guided improvisation and indeterminacy. Among his 25 books, many—*Stanzas for Iris Lezak* (1972), *21 Matched Asymmetries* (1978), *Asymmetries 1–260* (1980), *"Is That Wool Hat My Hat?"* (1982), *Bloomsday* (1984), and *Words and Ends from Ez* (1989)—comprise or include works realizable as musical-verbal performances; he wrote several chance-generated plays, including *The Marrying Maiden* (1958), *Verdurous Sanguinaria* (1961), and *The Twin Plays:*

Port-au-Prince and Adams County Illinois (1963, 1966). *The Pronouns* (1964, 1971, 1979) are both poems and dance instructions; wrote, directed, and performed in several Hörspiel.

Mac Low has performed extensively throughout North America, Western Europe, and New Zealand, often with painter, multimedia performance artist, composer, and writer Anne Tardos; a 60th-birthday 8-hour retrospective concert was given at Washington Square Church in N.Y. (1982); awards include fellowships from N.Y. State's Creative Artists Public Service Program (1973–74; 1976–77), the NEA (1979), Guggenheim Memorial Foundation (1985), and N.Y. Foundation for the Arts (1988); received a Fulbright grant for travel in New Zealand and a composer's grant from the Queen Elizabeth II Art Council there (both 1986).

MacDowell, Edward (Alexander), b. N.Y., Dec. 18, 1860; d. there, Jan. 23, 1908. His artistically inclined mother encouraged his musical studies; took piano lessons with J. Buitrago and P. Desvernine; had additional sessions with Carreño, who later championed his works. After traveling in Europe with his mother (1876), he enrolled as an auditor in Savard's elementary class at the Paris Cons.; was admitted as a regular student (1877); studied piano with A.-F. Marmontel and solfège with A. Marmontel; somewhat disappointed with his progress, withdrew from the Cons. (1878); went to Wiesbaden for study with L. Ehlert; enrolled at the newly founded but already prestigious Hoch Cons. in Frankfurt (1879) as a student of C. Heymann in piano, Raff (the Cons. director) in composition, and F. Böhme in counterpoint and fugue. During MacDowell's tenure, Raff's class was twice visited by Liszt; the 1st time, MacDowell performed the piano part of Schumann's Quintet, op. 44 for him; the 2nd, Liszt's *Hungarian Rhapsody no. 14.* 2 years later he visited Liszt in Weimar, playing his own 1st Piano Concerto, accompanied by d'Albert on 2nd piano; encouraged by Liszt's interest, he sent him the MS of his *Modern Suite*, op. 10, for Piano; Liszt recommended the piece for performance at the meeting of the Allgemeiner Deutscher Musikverein (Zurich, 1882) and recommended MacDowell to the publishers Breitkopf & Härtel, who were to 1st to publ. MacDowell's music (*Modern Suites*, opp. 10 and 14, 1880–81).

Despite his youth, MacDowell was given a teaching position at the Darmstadt Cons.; also accepted private pupils, among them Marian Nevins of Conn., whom he married secretly in N.Y. (1884); during the early years of their marriage they made their 2nd home in Wiesbaden, where he composed industriously; his works were performed in neighboring communities; Carreño programmed several piano pieces; there were also American performances. They were beset by financial difficulties, but he declined his mother's proposal that they live on the family property; a teaching position at the National Cons. in N.Y. at the munificent fee of $5 an hour; and a clerical position at the American Consulate in Krefeld, Germany.

The MacDowells returned to the U.S. (1888); he was welcomed in artistic circles as a famous composer and pianist; musical America was virtually a German colony, so his German training was a certificate of worth; the Boston Sym. Orch. conductors Gericke, Nikisch, and Paur, all Austro-Germans, played his works. He made his U.S. debut as composer and pianist at a Kneisel String Quartet concert (Boston, 1888), featuring the *Modern Suite*, op. 10; was soloist in the premiere of his 2nd

Piano Concerto with the N.Y. Phil. under Theodore Thomas (1889); Frank van der Stücken invited him to play the concerto at the Paris Exposition later that year (1889); had no difficulty having his works publ., although he insisted that his early piano pieces, opp. 1–7, be printed under the pseudonym Edgar Thorn.

In 1896 Columbia Univ. invited MacDowell to become its 1st prof. of music, "to elevate the standard of musical instruction in the U.S., and to afford the most favorable opportunity for acquiring instruction of the highest order" (1896). He interpreted this statement to its fullest; by 1899 2 assistants had been employed; but students received no credit for his courses. He continued composing and teaching piano privately; conducted the Mendelssohn Glee Club (1896–98); was president of the Soc. of American Musicians and Composers (1899–1900). He took a sabbatical (1902–03), playing concerts throughout the U.S. and Europe; played his 2nd Piano Concerto in London (1903). During his sabbatical, Columbia Univ. replaced its president, Seth Low, with Nicholas Murray Butler, whose ideas about the role of music in the univ. were diametrically opposed to his. MacDowell resigned (1904); subsequently became a cause célèbre, resulting in much acrimony on both sides; it was not until years later that the Robert Center Chair that MacDowell had held there was renamed the Edward MacDowell Chair of Music to honor its 1st recipient.

Through a combination of the trauma resulting from this episode, an accident with a hansom, and the development of what was probably tertiary syphilis, MacDowell rapidly deteriorated mentally, showing signs of depression, extreme irritability, and gradual loss of vital functions; eventually lapsed into total insanity, spending the last 2 years of his life in a childlike state, unaware of his surroundings. A public appeal was launched to raise funds for his care (1906); among the signers were Parker, Herbert, Foote, Chadwick, F. Converse, A. Carnegie, J. P. Morgan, and former President Cleveland. After his death, $50,000 was raised for the organization of the MacDowell Memorial Assoc. Marian MacDowell, who outlived her husband by nearly half a century (d. Los Angeles, 1956 at age 98), deeded to the Assoc. their summer residence at Peterborough, N.H.; under the name of the MacDowell Colony, this property became a working retreat for American composers and writers, who could work without disturbance in separate cottages, paying minimum rent for lodging and food. In 1910 Mrs. MacDowell arranged an elaborate pageant with her husband's music; the project's success led to the establishment of the MacDowell Festivals at Peterborough.

MacDowell received several awards during his lifetime, including election into the American Academy of Arts and Letters (1904); in 1940 a 5-cent U.S. postage stamp with his likeness was issued; was the 2nd composer elected to the Hall of Fame at N.Y. Univ. (1960), where a bust was unveiled (1964). Among American composers, he occupies the historically important place as the 1st American whose works were considered comparable in quality and technique with those of the average German composers of his time; he adhered to the prevalent representative Romantic aesthetic; virtually all his works bear titles borrowed from mythical history, literature, or painting, even the piano sonatas that, set in post-Classic forms, carry titles indicating mood of melodic resources or ethnic reference.

German musical culture was decisive in shaping MacDowell's musical development; even the American rhythms and melodies he uses seem European reflections of an exotic art. While a comparison with Grieg is plausible (both were regional composers trained in Germany), Grieg possessed a much more vigorous personality and succeeded in communicating the true spirit of Norwegian song modalities. MacDowell's lack of musical strength and originality accounts for a gradual decline in reception by later generations; his romanticism often lapsed into salon sentimentality; as the frequency of performance of his concert declined following his death, his influence on succeeding generations of American composers receded to a faint recognition of artistic evanescence.

He wrote sym. poems; 2 orch'l suites (1891–94; 1896, the "Indian" Suite); 2 piano concertos (1885–88; 1889); choruses; song cycles. His piano music includes 4 sonatas: no. 1, *Tragica,* op. 45 (1893); no. 2, *Eroica,* op. 50 (1895); no. 3, *Norse,* op. 57 (1900); no. 4, *Keltic* (1901); also *Forgotten Fairy Tales,* op. 4 (1898); *Forest Idyls,* op. 19 (1884); *Woodland Sketches,* his best-known work, op. 51 (1896); *Sea Pieces,* op. 55 (1898); *New England Idyls,* op. 62 (1902). His writings were collected by W. Baltzell and publ. as *Critical and Historical Essays* (N.Y., 1912).

Machaut (Machault, Machau, Mauchault), Guillaume de (Guillelmus de Mascaudio), important French composer and poet; b. probably in Machaut, Champagne, *c.* 1300; d. probably in Rheims, Apr. 13[?], 1377. He entered the service of John of Luxembourg, King of Bohemia (*c.* 1323); was his secretary until the King's death (1346); granted a canonry in Verdun (1330), another in Arras (1332), and a 3rd in Rheims (1333); kept the 1st 2 until 1335; settled in Rheims permanently (*c.* 1340); served French nobility, including the future King Charles V (from 1346). His renown is demonstrated by the high number of surviving presentation MSS dedicated to his music; the *Messe de Nostre Dame* is the 1st polyphonic Mass setting attributable to one composer; also wrote ballades, virelais, motets, rondeaux, lais, a double hocket (*Hoquetus David*), complainte, and chanson royal; some lais and virelais are conservatively monophonic. His poem *Remede de Fortune,* considered early, contains songs in nearly every genre he ever composed in; poems without music are *La louanges des dames* and *Le livre du Voir dit* (1360s); the latter provides autobiographical information about his love for a 19-year-old woman, Péronne d'Armentières.

machine music. The modern machine became an object of artistic inspiration early in the 20th century. The Italian futurists made a cult of automobiles and airplanes. Antheil's *Ballet mécanique* shocked concert audiences by its bruitism. Max Brand (1896–1980) produced the 1st machine opera in *Machinist Hopkins* (1929). Honegger made a declaration of love for powerful American locomotives in his symphonic movement *Pacific 231.* Frederick Converse (1871–1940) glorified the Ford car in his automobilistic musicorama *Flivver 10,000,000* (1927). But locomotives, automobiles, and airplanes soon lost their glamour and became public nuisances. By mid-century the machine as an affirmative artistic object became obsolete. It is ironic that no composer was moved to extol in lofty tones the greatest machine adventure of all ages, the landing on the moon.

Machover, Tod, b. N.Y., Nov. 24, 1953. He studied composition at the Univ. of Calif. at Santa Cruz (1971–73), Columbia Univ. (1973–74), and the Juilliard School in N.Y. (B.M., 1975; M.M., 1977); among his mentors were Dallapiccola (1973), Sessions (1973–75), and Carter (1975–78); also studied computer music at the Mass. Inst. of Technology and at Stanford Univ. He was 1st cellist in the orch. of the National Opera of Canada in Toronto (1975–76), guest composer (1978–79) and director of musical research (1980–84) at the Inst. de Recherche et de Coordination Acoustique/Musique (IRCAM) in Paris, and a teacher at the Mass. Inst. of Technology (from 1985). Among his honors were the Koussevitzky Prize (1984) and the Friedheim Award (1987). While he has written for purely acoustic media, Machover is primarily associated with electroacoustical experiments and live interactive installations. His best-known work is the opera *Valis,* based on a Philip K. Dick novel (Paris, 1987). He has also written several orch. works, solo acoustic works, and piano pieces, and many pieces for electronic instruments and recording tape.

mächtig, machtvoll (Ger.). Powerfully, mightily.

macrotime. Term proposed by Stockhausen (1955) to designate the duration of each rhythmic pulse, as quantitatively contrasted with microtime, the number of vibrations of a given note.

macrotonality. Division of the octave into less than 12 equally-tempered tones. See also ⇒microtonality.

macumba. Ritual festival of Afro-Brazilians, marked by a display of animal power and indeed related to primitive animalism. The festival includes elements of African and Indian folklore combined with Christian symbols, accompanied by music and dance believed to possess magical powers.

Maderna, Bruno, b. Venice, Apr. 21, 1920; d. Darmstadt, Nov. 13, 1973. He commenced musical studies at 4; took violin lessons; began touring as violinist and conductor when he was 7, appearing as Brunetto in Italy and abroad. He studied at the Verdi Cons. in Milan, with Bustini at the Rome Cons. (composition diploma, 1940), and Malipiero at the Venice Cons.; took conducting with Guarnieri at the Accademia Chigiana in Siena (1941); served in the Italian army during World War II, eventually joining the anti-Fascist partisan forces; after the war he studied conducting with Scherchen in Darmstadt; taught composition at the Venice Cons. (1947–50); made his formal conducting debut in Munich (1950).

Maderna became a great champion of the avant-garde; with Berio he co-founded the Studio di Fonologia in Milan (1954) and co-conducted the RAI's *Incontri Musicali* (1956–60); taught conducting and composition in Darmstadt (from 1954), Salzburg Mozarteum (1967–70), Rotterdam Cons. (from 1967), and Tanglewood (1971–72); became a naturalized German citizen (1963); chief conductor of the RAI in Milan (from 1971). Stricken with cancer, he conducted concerts as long as it was physically possible; held in great esteem by composers of the international avant-garde, many of whom wrote works for him. His compositions are typical of new European music of the period, including overlaying 2 or more separate works to create a new one; after a period of neglect, his music has undergone a revival in recent years. His works include operatic and stage works (notably *Satyrikon,* 1970), orch'l and chamber works, vocal music, electronic pieces.

Madonna, (born Madonna Louise Veronica Ciccone), b. Bay City, Mich., Aug. 16, 1958. She took up acting and dancing as a teenager; took dance lessons with Christopher Flynn (1972–76); studied at the Univ. of Michigan (1976–78). Arriving in N.Y., she survived by modeling and acting in independent films; worked with Alvin Ailey's dance group; studied choreography with Pearl Lang; took drum and guitar lessons with Dan Gilroy; after a stint with disco star Patrick Hernandez in Paris, returned to N.Y., appearing as drummer and singer with Gilroy's Breakfast Club rock group. She organized her own band (1982); brought out her 1st album, *Madonna* (1983); with *Like a Virgin* (1984) captured the imagination of America's youth; led to her 1st coast-to-coast tour.

In 1985 Madonna pursued her thespian bent by appearing in the critically acclaimed film *Desperately Seeking Susan* (1985); also appeared in *Who's That Girl?* (1987); the popular *Dick Tracy* (1990) featured her as a slinky, sequined, torch-singer gun moll. Her album *True Blue* (1986) proved a popular success, followed by a smashingly successful European tour (1987). In 1989, when she released *Like a Prayer,* she was among *People* magazine's "20 Who Defined the Decade"; awarded *Musician* magazine's highest editorial distinction, "Artist of the Decade"; her trendsetting fashions created a legion of young female fans known as "Madonna wannabes."

Madonna's athletic "Blond Ambition" tour was criticized for using more than 50% canned music, although this was hardly the 1st tour of its kind; the same year brought out the controversial and sizzling video *Justify My Love* (both 1990). During a few years out of the limelight and the charts, she married and divorced the actor Sean Penn; later bore a child. Upon her return, she played the eponymous lead film role in *Evita,* based on the Lloyd Webber musical; despite mixed critical response, it sold many tickets and compact discs, and revived the "wannabe" syndrome. She continues to make recordings.

madrigal. Secular (occasionally liturgical) polyphonic composition of Italian extraction that achieved its flowering during the Renaissance, surviving in other forms in the Baroque; lapsed into obsolescence in the 19th century; the word's etymology is uncertain. There are 2 types of Italian *madrigale,* although the poetic form for both, in iambic pentameter, arose in the 14th century. The earlier type, composed by Landini and his Trecento contemporaries, is written for 2 or 3 texted, melodically free voices; the lower part is often doubled instrumentally; pastoral themes dominated. The madrigal reinvented itself during the Renaissance; subservient during the 15th century to lighter genres (frottola, canzona, canzonetta, barzelletta, capitolo, strambotto), it was revived in the 16th century, when strict formality of verses and tunes were abandoned for more relaxed, more imaginative, and more individual types; increased to 4, 5, and 6 parts; instrumental doubling was rare.

By the beginning of the 17th century the melodic line in the soprano became ever more pronounced; concomitantly, polyphony gave way to homophony, forming a natural bridge to opera; the dramatic madrigal cycle became the madrigal comedy. Early monodic pieces were still called madrigals (e.g.,

Monteverdi's *Madrigali guerrieri e amorosi,* 1638), but the term soon disappeared; it survived as the lightweight glees of Baroque and Classic England and America. Among great (and not always Italian) madrigal composers are Arcadelt, de Rore, Andrea Gabrieli, Lasso, Marenzio, Gesualdo, and Monteverdi. Palestrina was the greatest writer of spiritual madrigals, rather than the secular type cultivated by most madrigalists. Elizabethan composers, among them Byrd, eagerly followed the Italian model; the development of the English madrigal school was hastened by the English publication of a collection of Italian madrigals in translation, *Musica Transalpina* (1588).

madrigal comedy (madrigal opera). Chain of madrigals united in content, forming a dramatic sequence; contemporaneous with early dramma per musica (opera); best-known composers of the genre were Vecchi and Banchieri; distantly related to the commedia dell'arte, it evolved from Renaissance madrigal collections with a common theme, often found in courtly weddings.

Maelzel, Johannes Nepomuk, b. Regensburg, Aug. 15, 1772; d. July 21, 1838. He studied music with his father, an organ manufacturer; went to Vienna (1792); began constructing mechanical instruments, attracting great attention there and in other European cities; of these, the Panharmonicon, a bellows-driven instrument with cylindrical pins, was particularly effective. He then purchased an "automatic chess player," which he claimed was his invention (but actually designed and built by Wolfgang von Kempelen); he impressed the public by his "scientific" miracle, but skeptical observers, among them Edgar Allan Poe, exposed it as an ingenious mechanical contrivance concealing a diminutive chess master behind its gears. He subsequently invented the automatic trumpeter, displaying it and a new version of the Panharmonicon in his Kunstkabinett (1812). Beethoven wrote a piece for Panharmonicon, subsequently orchestrated as *Wellington's Victory* (1813); after Maelzel declared the composition to be his, Beethoven sued him in Viennese courts; nothing ever came from his legal action.

In 1816 Maelzel constructed the metronome, an idea originated by Winkel of Amsterdam, whose own devices lacked scaled divisions indicating beats per minute; Maelzel put the metronome on the market, despite a lawsuit brought by Winkel. After obtaining a metronome, Beethoven apparently placed tempo markings on his syms.; these have confounded later interpreters, as their relatively fast markings seem unplayable to most; the machine he used has been blamed; recent performances by Roger Norrington and John Eliot Gardiner have challenged the presumed impossibility of the tempos.

maestoso (It.). Majestic, dignified; in a style characterized by lofty breadth.

maestro (It., master). Honorary appellation accorded, often too freely, to composers, conductors, teachers, and even lower species of musical eminences; in Italian the word means "teacher," but when used by Englishmen, Americans, or Russians in addressing a musical celebrity, it sounds lofty and deferential. *Maestro al cembalo,* harpsichordist functioning as ensemble leader, setting the tempo; *maestro di cappella,* orig., director of a court chapel; now, choirmaster or conductor.

Magaloff, Nikita. See ⇒Szigeti, Joseph.

maggiore (It.). Major.

maggot (from *magus,* sorcerer). Pleasing whim or notion; attached to pleasurable pieces, often with a lady's name, as in *My Lady Winwood's Maggot.*

magic. The magic rites of ancient times or today's so-called primitive peoples have probably always been accompanied by some musical performance; the myth of Orpheus, the demigod singer who could move people and even inanimate objects by his songs, is a classical invocation of artistic magic. Amphion was a lyre player so sure in his skill that the stones used to construct the walls of Thebes were drawn into their proper places by his playing; in the words of William Congreve, "Music has charms to soothe a savage breast/To soften rocks, or bend a knotted oak."

Musical magic is inherent in religious incantations, products of man's primitive impulse to vociferate in joy or lament in sorrow. Certain rhythms assume magical significance in the society in which they originate. The relentlessly repetitive drum beats of the jungle portend warnings of danger; in the 1920s the Cuban government forbade the manufacture and use of Afro-Cuban drums (e.g., conga) because their effect could create serious disturbances and even revolts; to Jews in southern Russia the opening notes of the Russian Czarist hymn suggested the beginning of a pogrom organized by groups of anti-Semitic monarchists (and condoned by the police). The cantillation of rabbis in a synagogue, the high-pitched songs of the Moslem criers from the perches of the minarets, the monotonous recitations of the Latin Catholic rosary, even the familiar strains of a lullaby—all draw upon musical magic.

Epic literature of all nations and cultures is replete with instances of magical healing, usually effected by intoning melorhythmic formulas that through constant use assume curative faculties. In the Finnish epic *Kalevala,* a musical magician recites a spell related to the origin of a wound, whether inflicted by animal or sword, and through this revelation exorcises the wound; Siberian shamans accompany their healing rites by ululations and savage beating upon primitive tambourines or metal plates; vodun priests of Haiti make noise 1st and begin their curative exercise after the subject has become completely relaxed and submissive to incantation. For the opposite of healing, the most ominous of all magic—the sticking of pins into an effigy of a person to be destroyed—is never performed in silence; sinister cries accompany this imposition of taboo in primitive societies; these cries inevitably assume the form of musical incantation; through constant repetition, the accompaniment to the taboo ritual becomes a magical symbol of the act itself; soon it is no longer necessary to utter any words or symbolic verbal sounds to impose a taboo; the music itself suffices.

Priests, witch doctors, and military leaders alike apply magic by ruthless repetition of slogans, often in singsong fashion; this type of crude magic is also plied by commercial advertisers on radio and television; idiotically repetitive and musically repulsive jingles may drive the captive listener to distraction, but the commercial purpose is attained—involuntary and irrevocable mental insinuation. Religious proselytism impressed magic on would-be converts during missionary work by endless repetition of Latin phrases that meant nothing to the possessors of the souls to be saved; this power is recognizable in the endless incantations of *Ave Maria* in Roman Catholic prayers or religious radio broadcasts. The complete performance of a brief and vacuous piece by Satie, *Vexations,* involving 840 repetitions, was a case of magic by cumulative stultification (N.Y., 1963).

Several composers have believed their works to be of magical origin and that this magic was transferable onto audiences; Scriabin planned the composition of a *Mysterium* whose magical power would be such that its 1st performance would actually precipitate the end of the world, in which he and all participants in its performance would be consumed in an act of universal ecstasy. Whatever vestigal musical or verbal magic may still survive inpristine state in such regions as the upper Amazon or in Polynesia, however, has probably been polluted and denatured by a potent flow of Western commercial musical "culture" through various media.

magic square. Arrangement of numbers placed in such a way that each of its horizontal or vertical rows equals the same sum, e.g.,

$$
\begin{array}{ccc}
1 & 2 & 3 \\
2 & 3 & 1 \\
3 & 1 & 2
\end{array}
$$

This arrangement provides a model for the disposition of the dodecaphonic system.

Magnard, (Lucien-Denis-Gabriel-) Albéric, b. Paris, June 9, 1865; d. Baron, Oise, Sept. 3, 1914. He was reared in an intellectual family of means; his father was ed. of *Le Figaro.* He studied with Dubois and Massenet at the Paris Cons. (1886–88; *premier prix* in harmony, 1888) and with d'Indy (1888–92); subsequently taught counterpoint at the Schola Cantorum. He was killed while defending his property during the early days of World War I. He was a composer of high attainments; his mastery of orchestration is incontestable, and the rhapsodic sweep of his 3rd and 4th syms. is impressive. Despite these qualities, none of his music found a permanent place in the repertoire. Among his works are operas, orch'l and chamber works, and songs.

Magnificat (Lat.). Most important hymn of the Vespers service in the Roman Catholic liturgy, namely the canticle of the Blessed Virgin Mary; its opening words are "Magnificat anima mea Dominum." The text is taken from Luke 1:46–55. Many pious composers wrote Magnificats as separate choral works. In the Anglican Church service the Magnificat ispart of Evensong, using the English words, "My soul doth magnify the Lord."

Magyar cadence. Gypsy cadence.

Magyar scale. Gypsy scale.

Mahler, Gustav, b. Kalischt, Bohemia, July 7, 1860; d. Vienna, May 18, 1911. He attended school in Iglau; entered the Vienna Cons.; studied piano with J. Epstein, harmony with R. Fuchs, and composition with F. Krenn (1875); also took courses in history and philosophy at the Univ. of Vienna (1877–80). He received his 1st conducting engagement at the operetta theater in Hall in Upper Austria (1880); subsequently served as theater conductor at Ljubljana (1881), Olmütz (1882), Vienna (1883), and Kassel (1883–85); was 2nd Kapellmeister to A. Seidl at the Prague Opera, giving performances of Wagner's operas (1885); assistant to Nikisch in Leipzig (188688); appointed music director of the Royal Opera in Budapest (1888); engaged as conductor at the Hamburg Opera (1891); developed a consummate conducting technique.

Mahler was offered the music directorship of the Vienna Court Opera (1897), but there was an obstacle to overcome: although there was no overt anti-Semitism in the Austrian government, an imperial appointment could not be given to a Jew; Mahler was not an observant Jew, and had no problem converting to Roman Catholicism, Austria's prevailing faith. He held this position for 10 years; he guided it to the highest standards of artistic excellence; succeeded H. Richter as conductor of the Vienna Phil. (1898); here as in opera he proved a great interpreter; allowed himself considerable if not unprecedented freedom to alter a score's orchestration in the name of greater effect. He aroused antagonism by his autocratic behavior towards the players; resigned from the Vienna Phil. (1901); also resigned from the Vienna Court Opera (1907).

In the meantime Mahler became immersed in composition; confined himself to symphonic music, sometimes with vocal parts; because of his busy conducting schedule, composed only in summer, in a villa on the Worthersee in Carinthia. In 1902 he married Alma Schindler (18791964); she had studied music with Zemlinsky; forced to give up composition by her autocratic husband. They had 2 daughters; the younger, Anna, was briefly married to Ernst Krenek; the elder, Maria, died of scarlet fever (1907); while in mourning he found out about his own heart condition, realizing that it would eventually kill him.

Having exhausted his Viennese options, Mahler accepted the principal conductor's post of the Metropolitan Opera in N.Y. (1907); made his U.S. debut there, conducting *Tristan und Isolde* (1908); appointed conductor of the N.Y. Phil. (1909). His performances at the Metropolitan and with the N.Y. Phil. were enormously successful with audiences and critics; inevitably had conflicts with the board of trustees in both organizations; Alma Mahler was quoted as saying that although in Vienna even the Emperor did not dare to order Mahler about, in N.Y. he had to submit to the whims of 10 ignorant women. He resigned from the Metropolitan Opera; in early 1911, conducted his last concert with the N.Y. Phil.; returned to Vienna; soon died of a heart attack brought on by bacterial infection.

Newspaper editorials mourned Mahler's death while noting sadly that his N.Y. tenure had been a failure; as for his own compositions, the *N.Y. Tribune* said bluntly, "We cannot see how any of his music can long survive him"; his syms. were sharply condemned for being too long, too loud, and too discordant. It was not until after World War II that he became fully recognized as the last great Romantic symphonist. His syms. were drawn on the grandest scale, with correspondingly elaborate techniques used to realize his ideas. The sources of his inspiration were twofold: the lofty concepts of universal art, akin to Bruckner's, ultimately stemming from Wagner; and the simple folk melos of the Austrian countryside, in pastoral moods recalling intimate episodes in Beethoven's syms. Mahler was not an harmonic innovator; rather, he culminated the Romantic era by virtue of the expansiveness of his emotional expression and the grandiose design of his musical structures.

Mahler at 1st attached descriptive titles to his syms.: the 1st was named the *Titan* (after Jean Paul); the 2nd, *Resurrection;* the 3rd, *Ein Sommermorgentraum;* the 5th, *Giant.*; the 6th became known as the *Tragic*, and the 8th as the *Sym. of a Thousand* because it required about 1,000 instrumentalists, vocalists, and soloists in its premiere (this sobriquet was the inspiration of Mahler's agent). He later tried to dissociate his works from their programmatic titles, even denying having used them in the 1st place; this flatly contradicts the evidence of the MSS, in which they appear in his own handwriting. Morbid by nature, he brooded upon death's inevitability; one of his most poignant compositions was the cycle for voice and orch., *Kindertotenlieder,* after Rückert (190104); wrote it a few years before his daughter Maria's death; blamed himself superstitiously for anticipating his personal tragedy. He consulted Freud in Leiden, Holland (1910), but the brief treatment apparently did not help him to resolve his psychological problems; in the 3rd movement of his unfinished 10th Sym., entitled *Purgatorio*, wrote on the MS margin, "Madness seizes me, annihilates me," appealing to the devil to take possession of his soul. But his neuroses never pushed him over the edge; gaining insight into his negative contributions to a troubled marriage, indicated regret at having stifled Alma's musical creativity.

Mahler's output consists solely of syms. and songs, many of them orchestrated from piano accompaniments. He destroyed several MSS of early works, among them a Piano Quartet (1878; 1 movement survives) and 3 projected or unfinished operas; completed Weber's unfinished *Die drei Pintos* (Leipzig, 1888); transcribed Bruckner's 3rd Sym. for 2 pianos (1878). He made controversial performing editions or arrangements of works by Bach, Mozart, Beethoven, Weber, Schubert, Schumann, and Bruckner; also a string orch. version of Beethoven's String Quartet in C-sharp Minor, op. 131. Mahler's importance to the evolution of modern music is very great; the early works of Schoenberg and Berg show the influence of his concepts; the all-encompassing seriousness of his intentions have affected symphonic music throughout the 20th century.

main (Fr.). Hand. *Main droite (gauche)*, right (left) hand; often written *m.d. (m.g.)*.

maître (Fr.). Master. *Maître de chapelle*, choirmaster; conductor.

maître-chanteur (Fr.). Mastersinger.

majestätisch (Ger.). Maestoso.

majeur (Fr.). Major.

major (Lat.). Greater; opposed to minor (lesser; see ⇒interval). *Major cadence,* one ending with a major triad; *major chord* or *triad*, one having a major 3rd and perfect 5th upward from the root (lowest note); *major interval*, in any major scale, the distances between the 1st degree (tonic) and its 2nd, 3rd, 6th, and 7th degrees; *major scale,* standard pitch ordering consisting, from 1st degree (tonic) upward, of 2 consecutive whole tones (major 2nds), followed by 1 semitone (minor 2nd), 3 whole tones, and 1 semitone.

major-minor syndrome. In Baroque music most minor-key works end on a major triad; such a major 3rd acquired the name Picardy third (*tierce de Picardie,* introduced by Rousseau in his dictionary); its etymology is unknown. The preference for the major over minor 3rds in final chords may be explained by its privileged position as the 5th overtone of the harmonic series, whereas a minor 3rd above the fundamental tone does not occur in a lower-numbered (i.e., more consonant) partial. In the practice of modern composers a major 3rd is often superimposed on a minor 3rd; Scriabin employed such a major-minor syndrome in his last opus numbers, but he spread the harmony widely, so that the frictional dissonance of a semitone was avoided. Stravinsky cultivated a true major-minor syndrome in placing both the minor and the major 3rd within a triad. He made use of it as a motto in his choral work *Le Roi des étoiles* (1912); it occurs also in *Le Sacre du Printemps;* Stravinsky uses it as a melodic palimpsest, breaking up the combined chord, with both the major and the minor 3rd assuming thematic significance.

Makeba, Miriam, b. Prospect, near Johannesburg, Mar. 4, 1932. She sang in a mission choir in Pretoria; joined an itinerant show; 1st attracted attention singing the lead in the African opera *King Kong* (Johannesburg, 1959). In 1959 she went to the U.S.; appeared in N.Y. nightclubs and on television; had several hit records, including *Pata Pata;* testified at the United Nations on the racist policies of South Africa; toured Europe successfully; traveled to Ethiopia and Kenya as a representative of black art. She was married to the African-American activist Stokely Carmichael from 1968 to 1978.

malagueña (Sp.). Old Spanish dance folk music originating in the provinces of Málaga and Murcia, in rapid triple time. Its main harmonic characteristic is a Phrygian cadence from the tonic down to the dominant, harmonized by consecutive triads—a tonic minor, a major triad based on the natural 7th degree, and descending through the submediant triad to the major dominant.

Malibran, Maria (Felicità Garcia), b. Paris, Mar. 24, 1808; d. Manchester, Sept. 23, 1836. She was the daughter of Manuel (del Popolo Vicente Rodríguez) Garcia (b. Seville, Jan 21, 1775; d. Paris, June 9, 1832), one of the great tenors and singing teachers of his era. Maria was taken to Naples, where she sang a child's part in Paer's *Agnese* (1814); studied voice with her father from age 15; studied solfeggio with Panseron. She made her debut as Rosina at the King's Theatre in London (1825); went to N.Y., where she sang in the same opera in her family's season at the Park Theatre; became a popular favorite, singing in *Otello, Tancredi, La Cenerentola, Don Giovanni,* and 2 operas written for her by her father.

Malibran made her Paris debut as Semiramide at the Théâtre-Italien (1828); alternated her appearances in Paris and London (1829–32); went to Italy, singing in Bologna (1832) and Naples (1833); made her debut at Milan's La Scala as Norma (1836). Her early death came after she was thrown from a horse while pregnant. Her voice was of extraordinary compass, but the medium register had several "dead" tones; also a good pianist who composed numerous nocturnes, romances, and chansonnettes, collected as *Dernières pensées.*

malinconia (It.). Melancholy. Malinconicamente, malinconico, (col) malinconia, malinconioso, malinconoso, with melancholy; dejectedly.

Malipiero, Gian Francesco, b. Venice, Mar. 18, 1882; d. Treviso, near Venice, Aug. 1, 1973. His grandfather, Francesco Malipiero (1824–87), was an opera composer; his father, Luigi Malipiero, a pianist and conductor. Gian Francesco enrolled at the Vienna Cons. to study violin (1898); returned to Venice (1899); studied at the Liceo Musicale Benedetto Marcello with Marco Bossi, whom he followed to Bologna (1904); soon took a composition diploma at the Liceo Musicale G. B. Martini; subsequently worked as amanuensis to Smareglia, gaining orchestrating experience; studied briefly with Bruch in Berlin (1908). He committed a notorious act by submitting 5 works to a Roman competition, each under a different pseudonym, and winning 4 of 5 prizes (1912–13); went to Paris (1913); absorbed impressionist techniques, cultivating parallel chord formations and amplifying tonal harmonies with added 6ths, 9ths, and 11ths; however, his own style was steeped in the polyphonic practices of the Italian Baroque. In 1921 he returned to Italy; was prof. of composition at the Parma Cons. (1921–23); thereafter lived mostly in Asolo, near Venice; appointed prof. of composition at the Liceo Musicale Benedetto Marcello in Venice (1932); continued there when it became the Cons. (1940); served as director (1939–52). He ed. a complete series of the works of Monteverdi (16 vols., Bologna and Vienna, 1926–42) and works by Vivaldi and other Italian composers. He gained membership to the National Inst. of Arts and Letters in N.Y. (1949), the Royal Flemish Academy in Brussels (1952), the Institut de France (1954), and the Akademie der Künste in West Berlin (1967).

Malipiero's eclectic music reflects many modern styles—impressionism, expressionism, symbolism, futurism, eclecticism, archaism, improvisatory rather than symphonic composition, and chromaticism. He was an extremely prolific composer of operas, ballets, sinfonias, concertos, other orch'l works, vocal works with or without orch., chamber and instrumental works, and piano music; his work is notably uneven in quality, but is nonetheless considered a major 20th-century Italian composer, comparable to Dallapiccola and Casella. His *Dialoghi* (1956–57), like his other works in series, provide a sense of his interests: no. 1, *con M. de Falla,* for orch.; no. 2 for 2 pianos; no. 3, *con Jacopone da Todi,* for Voice and 2 Pianos; no. 4 for Wind Quintet; no. 5 for Viola and Orch.; no. 6 for Harpsichord and Orch.; no. 7 for 2 Pianos and Orch.; no. 8, *La morte di Socrate,* for Baritone and Small Orch. (all 1956–57). In addition to his editing work, he was an active writer, writing many scholarly works and textbooks on music (1920–69). His nephew Riccardo Malipiero (b. 1914) is also a composer; studied with his uncle at the Liceo Musicale Benedetto Marcello in Venice (1937–39).

mambo. Ballroom dance derived from the rumba. It appeared in Cuba during the 1940s and was made popular in the U.S. particularly by Perez Prado and his band; the mambo had spread to non-Hispanic audiences by the 1950s. This couple dance, in 4/4, uses forward and backward steps, beginning on the upbeat, to percussive polyrhythmic accompaniment. The mambo was a major influence on the cha-cha.

mancando (It.). Decreasing in loudness, dying away.

Mancini, Henry, b. Cleveland, Apr. 16, 1924; d. Los Angeles, June 14, 1994. He studied flute and piano in childhood; received training from M. Adkins in Pittsburgh and attended the Juilliard Graduate School in N.Y. (1942); worked as pianist and arranger with Tex Beneke's orch. (1945–47); studied composition with Castelnuovo-Tedesco, Krenek, and A. Sendrey in Los Angeles. He joined the music staff of Universal-International film studios (1952–58), for which he wrote many scores; also wrote for television, most successfully with his music for the *Peter Gunn* series (1958).

Mancini's scores for *Breakfast at Tiffany's* (1961)—which included the hit song *Moon River*—and *Days of Wine and Roses* (1962) won him both Academy and Grammy Awards; other scores include *Touch of Evil, Experiment in Terror, Hatari, Charade, The Pink Panther, Two for the Road, The Molly Maguires, Sometimes a Great Notion, The Silver Streak, Victor/Victoria,* and television soundtracks such as *Mr. Lucky* and *The Thorn Birds*; later appeared widely as a guest conductor in popular concerts with American orchs. He publ. *Sounds and Scores* (1962), a guide to orchestration.

mandocello (It.). Bass mandolin.

mandola (It.). 1. Alto mandolin. 2. Mandora.

mandolin (U.K., Fr. *mandoline;* Ger. *Mandoline;* It. *mandolino*). Smaller member of the lute family which originated in Italy in the 17th century. The name itself is the diminutive of *mandola*. It is shaped like a pear half and has a fretted fingerboard with 4 pairs of strings tuned like those of the violin (G, D, A, E). It is played with a plectrum type called the *mediator*. Progressively larger sizes of the mandolin are the mandola, the mandoloncello, and the mandolone or mandocello. An ensemble consisting of mandolins, combined with guitars, is popularly known as a Neapolitan orch. Although the mandolin is generally regarded as a popular or traditional instrument, Mozart and Beethoven wrote for it; it is also included in Mahler's 7th Sym., Schoenberg's *Serenade,* op. 24, and Webern's *Fünf Stücke für Orchester*.

Among folk and traditional performers, Bill Monroe is most closely associated with the mandolin. He developed a rapid style of playing, emphasizing sharp, rhythmic chords and breathtakingly fast melodic runs, which became the basis for the bluegrass style. Monroe's influence has been great, and his disciples have expanded the instrument's repertoire into jazz music. David Grissman is the most prominent contemporary performer, who plays both in traditional bluegrass style and his own compositions with a quartet including 2 mandolins in jazz-swing style. *Mandolino,* smaller mandolin; *mandoloncello,* bass mandolin; *mandolone,* bass mandolin.

mandolinata (It.). 1. Mandolin piece of quiet character, like a serenade. 2. In piano playing, play with a mandolin effect.

mandora (mandore, mandola). Large instrument similar to a mandolin.

maneria (Lat.). Medieval theoretical term for ecclesiastical modes of both authentic and plagal types; the modes were labeled by Latinized Greek ordinal numbers: *protus, deuterus, tritus,* and *tetradus*.

maniera (It.). Manner, style, method. *Con dolce maniera,* in suave, delicate style.

mannerism. Generic term descriptive of a certain preciosity of artistic execution. In painting, *mannerism* refers to the 16th- and early-17th-century Italian painting that used exaggeration of dimension and color contrast to impart heightened reality, symbolic or otherwise; Parmigianino and Caravaggio are among the mannerists. Applying this term to music has proven controversial; for different critics it has meant late Baroque and rococo schools, whose music is marked by curvilinear designs and ornamental arabesques; the Mannheim school, for its *recherché* style of composition and performance; or the madrigal and motet composers of the late Renaissance, embodied in the highly chromatic music of Gesualdo.

Mannheim school. Group of musicians active at the court of the German city of Mannheim in the middle of the 18th century; they developed a method of composition and performance that marked a radical departure from the monolithic style of the Baroque period. Their animator and mentor was the Bohemian master Johann Stamitz, who inaugurated in his orch'l works the principle of melodic guidance and symmetrical formal structure. Harmony, too, underwent decided change in the works of the Mannheim school, away from the rigid dependence on basso continuo. In performance the Mannheim group introduced novel dynamic usages, the most important of which was the effect of continuous crescendo and corresponding diminuendo, in contrast with the antiphonal structure of mutually responsive sections of forte and piano in Baroque music. Among other innovations were arpeggiated chords (in ascending melodic form, known as the "rocket theme"), extensive tremolos, abrupt general pauses, pyrotechnical accents, simulated sighs, and various emotional devices almost Romantic in nature.

With regard to the orch., the Mannheim musicians cultivated greater independence of the wind instruments. In respect to form there was pronounced articulation of subsections in the minuet and the expansion of protosonata form to symphonic dimensions. The achievements of the Mannheim school soon became known in Paris and London and exercised considerable influence on the evolution of symphonic and chamber music. On the other hand there was great deal of opposition on the part of traditional and academic musicians who dubbed the innovations of the Mannheim school mannerist; the circumstance that most of the Mannheim musicians came from Bohemia rather than from the main centers of German musical culture gave occasion for narrow nationalistic disdain. In a letter to Mozart, his father referred to the "overmannered Mannheim taste." But there was no gainsaying the power of the Mannheim dynamic characteristics. A musician who heard the Mannheimers play reports that "their crescendo makes the listeners rise involuntarily from their seats, and gradually sink back out of breath with the corresponding diminuendo."

mano (It.). Hand. *Mano destra (sinistra),* right (left) hand.

manual. Organ keyboard; opposed to the pedal.

manualiter (Lat.). On the manual(s) alone.

maqām (Arab.; Turk. *makam;* Azeri. *mugam;* Central Asia *makom*). 1. General term for the modal systems of Western Asia, based on a microtonal pitch gamut (usually treated as quarter tones). Each system has several modal scales, with a set group of pitches, upon which both melodies and improvisations are built; the performers must incorporate and develop motivic figures associated with each scale. Modalities are not necessarily transposable by the octave, as the pitches may differ in a higher octave. 2. Vocal or instrumental composition in cyclic form.

maracas. Latin American rattles; usually a pair of gourds filled with dry seeds and shaken vigorously rhythmically to accompany traditional and popular dances. In the 20th century maracas began to be used as percussion instruments in modern scores, quite independently from their ethnic content. Thus Prokofiev uses a pair in his patriotic oratorio *Alexander Nevsky;* Varèse has a part for maracas in his "atomic" work, *Ionisation*.

Marais, Marin, b. Paris, May 31, 1656; d. there, Aug. 15, 1728. He studied viol da gamba with Sainte-Colombe and composition with Lully; joined the royal orch. (1676); made Ordinaire de la chambre du Roi (1679); retired (1725). He possessed matchless skill as a gambist enhancing the sonority of the instrument; he also established a new fingering method, that was a decisive influence on performance technique. He composed outstanding gamba music, producing 5 extensive collections (1686–1725) numbering some 550 works. His dramatic music followed Lully's French manner, with recitatives in the rhythm of French verse following the inflection of the rhyme. The purely instrumental parts of his operas were extensive; in one, *Alcione* (1706), he introduced a "tempeste," an early attempt at stage realism in operatic music. He also composed trio sonatas for violin, flute, and viola da gamba (the 1st to appear in France, 1692), and a book of trios for violin, viola da gamba, and harpsichord, *La Gamme . . .* (1723). Married in 1676, he had 19 children; his son Roland became a talented gambist who publ. 2 collections for his instrument with basso continuo (Paris, 1735, 1738) and a lost method.

marcato, -a (It.). With distinctness and emphasis. *Marcatissimo*, with very marked emphasis.

march. Composition of strongly marked rhythm, suitable for coordinating steps of a group of persons proceeding at a steady pace; the march (from Lat. *marcare,* mark; Sp. *marcha;* Fr. *marche;* It. *marcia;* Ger. *Marsch*) corresponds to the natural alternation of the right and left foot in walking. (3-footed humans would no doubt march in waltz time.) Since uniform steps are essential to military movements, the march has become the chosen rhythm of armies all over the world; the time signature is usually 4/4 or alla breve, although there are marches in 6/8 or 12/8, the so-called *Reiter-Marsch* whose rapid subdivisions in triplets suggest a galloping horse (e.g., Schubert's song *Erlkönig*); there are also triple-meter marches. The usual tempo of a marching tune in England and America is 80 steps per minute, corresponding to a normal pulse.

The origins of the march are military, based on drum-calls that motiviated troops from the Renaissance on; indeed, a military march (Fr., *marche militaire*) is a distinctive musical form (e.g., in Gounod's *Faust*). But march time can be adopted to a variety of functions: solemn religious march, e.g., the "March of the Priests" from Verdi's *Aida;* wedding march, in Mendelssohn's music for *A Midsummer Night's Dream* and Wagner's *Lohengrin;* children's march, in Bizet's *Carmen;* patriotic marches abound, of which the grandest is *La Marseillaise.* The funeral march is a category onto itself. One of Handel's best-known excerpts is the "Dead March" from the oratorio *Saul;* the 2nd movement in Beethoven's *Eroica* Sym. is a funeral march; the march from Chopin's Piano Sonata in B-flat Minor has been so strongly associated with funerals that it has attained archetypal status; some American wiseacre set its theme to the words "Pray for the dead, and the dead will pray for you." There are also ironic funeral marches, such as Gounod's *Marche funèbre d'une marionette* and Alkan's *Marche funèbre sulla morte d'un papagallo;* especially beserk are the *3 Funeral Marches* by Lord Berners: *For a Statesman, For a Canary,* and *For a Rich Aunt,* the last full of gaiety in anticipation of a lucrative inheritance.

While most national hymns are in march time, there are exceptions; *The Star-Spangled Banner* is a slow waltz, as is the British national anthem, *God Save the Queen.* Elgar wrote 5 military marches (in 4/4) under the general title *Pomp and Circumstance,* of which the 1st is celebrated; its slow section, sung as "Land of Hope and Glory," is a popular commencement march in American schools. Sousa, the American "March King," composed more than 100 military marches, of which *Stars and Stripes Forever* is one of the most rousing. *Alla marcia,* in march style; *March form,* form used in American and British marches: introduction; 1 or 2 sections in the tonic, in 16- or 32-bar phrases; trio in the dominant or subdominant key, often with the implied lighter texture; concluding section in the tonic, either repetition of the previous tonic sections or a new section; all but the last section have internal repeats; the form and other aspects of the march found their way into the rag. *Marche funèbre,* funeral march; *marche militaire,* military march; Schubert wrote piano pieces and duets of this type, popular with students and teachers alike; *marche redoublée,* march in more rapid tempo than usual; *marche triomphale,* triumphant or victory march; popular in operatic crowd scenes.

mariachi. Ensemble music of Mexico, featured in festivities and café and nightclub entertainment. Mariachi bands consist of violins, *guitarrón* (large guitar), guitar, trumpets, and Mexican percussion instruments, particularly the marimba. The songs are typically sung in parallel 3rds and use the subject matter of the Mexican *canción* or corrido. The origin of the word itself is obscure, but it is suggested that it represents a corruption of the French word *mariage,* and that it was 1st used at the time of the Emperor Maximilian (19th century). Copland made use of typical mariachi tunes in his symphonic work *El Salón Mexico,* named after a once popular nightclub in Mexico City.

marimba. Family of African and Latin American xylophones with tuned resonators placed underneath the wooden bars to produce richer sound. In the traditional instruments, gourds are used as resonators. The marimba is of ancient origin, but its modern form was created in Guatemala early in the 20th century. From there it spread to the U.S. and later to Europe. Its range, at 1st limited, has been gradually expanded to 6 octaves.

marimbaphone. Trade name of the American marimba, patented in Chicago, 1915; the resonators are wooden blocks carefully tuned to their bars for full but unflawed resonance. In some modern versions of the instrument, electric amplification is used to reinforce its sound.

marinera (Sp.). Peruvian song-dance, with strophically set quatrains and 6/8 seguidilla refrains. The texts often include historical narrative and sociopolitical commentary. The genre has mostly disappeared from urban areas; in the Andes it often functions as a courtship dance. The marinera is related to the *chilena* and *cueca*.

markiert (Ger.). Accented, marked.

Marley, Bob (Robert Nesta), b. Rhoden Hall, Apr. 6, 1945; d. Miami, May 11, 1981. He moved to Kingston as a child; worked as an electrical welder; picked up popular tunes in the streets and from the radio, opened a small recording shop of his own, and began recording his own tunes, a mixture of calypso and soul music. In 1963 he co-found a group, the Wailers, soon the most popular purveyor of reggae; disbanded (1973); he then produced highly successful solo records that reached an international audience and influenced rock musicians profoundly; a later result was the intriguing mixture known as hip-hop reggae. Marley joined the Rastafarian religious group, followers of King Haile Selassie of Ethiopia; in 1976 became embroiled in politics, supporting the Jamaican People's National Party; preparing to sing at a concert that year, he was shot and wounded. After recovering, he went to Europe, scoring a huge success, particularly in England, Sweden, the Netherlands, and West Germany; the following year toured the U.S., where his fame had preceded him. His songs, in Jamaican dialect, preached revolution, as in *Rebel Music*, *Everywhere Be War*, and *Death to the Downpressors*. But his 1974 album, *Natty Dread* (a pun on the Rasta hair style), mixes sociopolitics (*Them Belly Full, Revolution*), religion (*So Jah Seh*), self-image (*Lively Up Yourself*), and relationships (*No Woman No Cry*) with subtle arrangements and rhythmic counterpoint to reach an apogee that Marley himself and others were unable to sustain or attain, as reggae fell into stereotyped syncopations.

Marriner, (Sir) Neville, b. Lincoln, Apr. 15, 1924. He studied violin with his father, then with F. Mountney; entered the Royal College of Music in London at 13; his studies were interrupted by military service during World War II; after resuming his training at the Royal College of Music, completed his violin studies in Paris with René Benedetti; took courses at the Cons. He played violin in chamber music ensembles; prof. of violin at the Royal College of Music (1949–59); joined the Philharmonia Orch. of London (1952); principal 2nd violinist of the London Sym. Orch. (1956–58).

Marriner's interest in conducting was encouraged by Monteux, who taught him at his summer school in Hancock, Maine (1959). He founded and directed the Academy of St.-Martin-in-the-Fields (1958–78); established an international reputation through recordings and tours; served as music director of the Los Angeles Chamber Orch. (1968–78) and the Minnesota Orch. in Minneapolis (1978–86). In 1981 he became principal guest conductor of the Stuttgart Radio Sym. Orch.; chief conductor (1983–89); guest conducted with many leading orchs. In 1979 he was made Commander of the Order of the British Empire;

knighted (1985). He has proved himself a conductor of the 1st rank; extensive activities as chamber music player, orch. musician, and chamber orch. violinist-conductor served as invaluable foundation for his career; an enormous repertoire encompasses works from the Baroque to the 20th century; in all performances he demonstrates authority, mastery of detail, and impeccable taste.

Marsalis, Wynton, b. New Orleans, Oct. 18, 1961. He was born into a musical family; his father, Ellis Marsalis, was an educator and pianist; in 1974 he founded the jazz program to nurture new performers, at the nascent New Orleans Center for the Creative Arts. Wynton's younger brother Delfeayo is a trombonist and producer; older brother Branford (b. Breaux Bridge, Aug. 26, 1960) is a saxophonist of considerable talent who has played with C. Terry, M. Davis, A. Blakey, D. Gillespie, and Sting; also had his own groups. He took up the trumpet at age 6; studied with J. Longo; received instruction at his father's school; played the solo in Haydn's Trumpet Concerto with the New Orleans Phil. at 14; performed with local groups in classical, jazz, and rock settings. He won the Harvey Shapiro Award as the most gifted brass player at Tanglewood at age 17; attended the Juilliard School in N.Y. (1979–81).

Marsalis joined Art Blakey's Jazz Messengers (1980–81); played at the Montreux Jazz Festival (1980); toured with his own quintet, including Branford; worked with Davis; achieved unprecedented success by winning Grammy awards in both jazz and classical categories (total of 8); has released over 20 jazz and several classical recordings. In 1990 he hosted a benefit concert for 3 children's foundations at Alice Tully Hall in N.Y., featuring musical members of his family: Ellis on piano, youngest brother Jason making his debut on drums, Branford on saxophone, and Wynton on trumpet; the clan was then joined by Wynton's jazz septet in an evening of critically acclaimed hard bop. He narrated a television series on the history of jazz, part of his attempt to enlarge jazz's audience; has brought forward many young talented musicians; a versatile performer stylistically, he is sometimes criticized by colleagues for a lack of depth.

Marschner, Heinrich (August), b. Zittau, Saxony, Aug. 16, 1795; d. Hannover, Dec. 14, 1861. He sang in the school choir at the Zittau Gymnasium, and also studied music with Karl Hering. In 1813 he went to Leipzig, where he studied jurisprudence at the Univ.; encouraged by the cantor of the Thomasschule, J. C. Schicht, he turned to music as his main vocation. In 1816 he became music tutor in Count Zichy's household in Pressburg, and also served as Kapellmeister to Prince Krasatkowitz. In his leisure hours he began to compose light operas; his 1st opera, *Titus* (1816), did not achieve a performance, but soon he had 2 more operas and a singspiel produced in Dresden.

His 1st signal success was the historical opera *Heinrich IV und d'Aubigné*, which was accepted by Weber, who was then music director at the Dresden Court Opera, and was produced there on July 19, 1820. In 1817 he was in Vienna, where he was fortunate enough to meet Beethoven. In 1821 Marschner moved to Dresden and had his singspiel *Der Holzdieb* staged at the Court Opera (1825). He expected to succeed Weber as music director at the Court Opera after Weber died in London, but he failed to obtain the post. He went to Leipzig, where he became

Kapellmeister of the Stadttheater and wrote for it 2 Romantic operas, in the manner of Weber: *Der Vampyr* (1828) and *Der Templer und die Jüdin* (1829), after the famous novel *Ivanhoe* by Walter Scott. In 1830 he received the position of Kapellmeister of the Hannover Hoftheater.

His most successful opera, *Hans Heiling* (Berlin, 1833), exhibited the most attractive Romantic traits of his music: flowing melody, sonorous harmony, and nervous rhythmic pulse; the opera formed a natural transition to the exotic melodrama of Meyerbeer's great stage epics and to Wagner's early lyrical music dramas. Historically important was his bold projection of continuous dramatic development, without the conventional type of distinct arias separated by recitative. In this respect he was the heir of Weber and precursor of Wagner. His later operas were not successful.

martellato (It., hammered; Fr. *Martelé*). In violin playing, play the notes with a sharp, decided stroke ($\flat$); on the piano, strike the keys with a heavy, inelastic plunge of the finger, or (in octave playing) with the arm staccato.

martellement (Fr.). In older Baroque music, the mordent.

Martenot, Maurice (Louis Eugène), b. Paris, Oct. 14, 1898; d. there, Oct. 10, 1980. He studied composition at the Paris Cons. with Gedalge; began to work on the construction of an electronic musical instrument with keyboard, which he called the Ondes musicales. He gave its 1st demonstration in Paris in the spring of 1928, and, later that year, the 1st musical work for the instrument, *Poème symphonique pour solo d'Ondes musicales et orchestre,* by Dimitri Levidis (c. 1885–1951), was presented in Paris. Martenot publ. *Méthode pour l'enseignement des Ondes musicales* (Paris, 1931). He died as the result of a velocipede accident.

As the Ondes Martenot, the instrument became popular, especially among French composers: it is included in the score of Honegger's *Jeanne d'Arc au bûcher* (1935); Koechlin's *Le Buisson ardent,* part 1 (1938); Martinon's 2nd Sym., *Hymne à la vie* (1944); and Messiaen's *Turangalîla-Symphonie* (1946–48). It was used as a solo instrument in Koechlin's *Hymne* (1929), Jolivet's Concerto (1947), Landowski's Concerto (1954), Bondon's *Kaleidoscope* (1957), and Jacques Charpentier's *Concertino alla francese* (1961). Many other composers were attracted to it as well. Of all the early electronic instruments—Ondes Martenot, Trautonium, and Theremin—only Martenot's has proved a viable musical instrument. When Varèse's *Ecuatorial,* written in 1934 for brass ensemble and including a Theremin, was publ. in 1961, the score substituted an Ondes Martenot for the obsolescent Theremin. Martenot's sister, Ginette Martenot, became the chief exponent of the Ondes Martenot in concert performances in Europe and the U.S.

Martin, Frank, b. Geneva, Sept. 15, 1890; d. Naarden, the Netherlands, Nov. 21, 1974. He studied privately with J. Lauber in Geneva (1906–14), instructing him in the conservative Swiss idiom of the fin de siècle; had lessons with H. Huber and F. Klose, who emphasized the conservative foundations of Swiss religious and cultural traditions; he soon rejected Swiss scholasticism, encouraged in this direction by Ansermet, conductor of the Orch. de la Suisse Romande in Geneva; finally settled in Paris, then the

center of modern music (1923); returned to Geneva as pianist and harpsichordist (1926); taught at the Inst. Jaques-Dalcroze (1927–38); founder and director of the Technicum Moderne de Musique (1933–39); president of the Assoc. of Swiss Musicians (1942–46). He moved to the Netherlands (1946); taught composition at the Cologne Hochschule für Musik (1950–57).

Martin, one of Switzerland's few international figures in composition, is an excellent representative; his early music evoked Franck and French impressionism, but succeeded in creating a harmonically based style supported by consummate contrapuntal mastery and profound feeling for emotional consistency and continuity; became fascinated by the logic and self-consistency of 12-tone composition; adopted it in modified form in several works; also capable of stylizing folk-song materials in modern techniques. In 1944 the director of Radio Geneva asked him to compose an oratorio to be broadcast upon the conclusion of World War II; his response with *In terra pax* for 5 Soli, Double Chorus, and Orch., broadcast from Geneva (1945); other oratorios include *Le vin herbé* (1938–41), *Golgotha* (1945–48), *Le Mystère de la Nativité* (1957–59), *Pilate* (1964); orch'l song cycles: *Der Cornet* (1942–43), *6 Monologe au "Jedermann"* (1943), *Maria Triptychon* (1967–69); sacred works, operas, ballets, incidental music, chamber song cycles. Many of his instrumental works are built on a concertante basis: concertos for piano (1933–34, 1968–69), winds (1949), violin (1950–51), harpsichord (1952), cello (1965–66); ballades for solo instruments and ens. (saxophone, 1938; flute, 1939; piano, 1939; trombone, 1940; cello, 1949; viola, 1972), the masterful *Petite symphonie concertante* for harp, harpsichord, piano, and double string orch. (1944–45); orch'l works, chamber music, piano works. He publ. *Responsabilité du compositeur* (Geneva, 1966); M. Martin ed. his *Un compositeur médite sur son art* (Neuchâtel, 1977).

Martin, Mary (Virginia), b. Weatherford, Tex., Dec. 1, 1913; d. Rancho Mirage, Calif., Nov. 3, 1990. The daughter of a lawyer and a violinist, she 1st established a dance school in Weatherford. She studied at the Ward-Belmont School in Nashville, Tenn.; then went to N.Y., where, although totally unknown to the general public, she stopped the show with her rendition of the song *My Heart Belongs to Daddy* in Cole Porter's musical comedy *Leave It to Me* (1938). Her N.Y. success brought her a film contract with Paramount Studios in Hollywood, which was short-lived, as she preferred the theater.

On the stage Martin scored a series of hits, beginning with a starring role in the Rodgers and Hammerstein musical *South Pacific* (1949) and later in *The Sound of Music* (1959), 2 of the longest-running musicals in Broadway history. She became best known for her 1954 creation of the lead character in the musical *Peter Pan,* in which she seemed to fly through the air; her career was once interrupted when she suffered an accident during levitation. In 1969 she retired to Brazil with her husband; after his death, she resumed her career (1979). In 1989 Martin was honored by the Kennedy Center of the Performing Arts in Washington, D.C., for her achievements in the theater. Her son, Larry Hagman, is a veteran television actor whose fame was assured when he was cast as the villainous J. R. Ewing in the nighttime soap series *Dallas.*

Martín y Soler, (Atanasio Martín Ignacio) Vicente (Tadeo Francisco Pellegrin). See ⇒Mozart, Wolfgang Amadeus.

Martinů Bohuslav (Jan), b. Policka, Bohemia, Dec. 8, 1890; d. Liestal, near Basel, Aug. 28, 1959. He studied violin locally from age 7; enrolled at the Prague Cons. (1906–09); entered the Prague Organ School (1909); studied organ and theory, but expelled for lack of effort (1910); played in the 2nd violin section in the Czech Phil. in Prague (1913–14); returned to Policka to avoid service in the Austrian army (1914–18); after the war he reentered the Prague Cons. as a Suk pupil; again failed to graduate; returned to the Czech Phil. (1918–23). He went to Paris (1923); participated in progressive musical circles; took private lessons with Roussel; his name became known in Europe through increasingly frequent performances of his chamber works, ballets, and symphonic pieces; several were performed at the ISCM festivals; his String Sextet won the Elizabeth Sprague Coolidge Award (1932). He remained in Paris until 1940, when he fled the German invasion and went to Portugal; reached the U.S. (1941); settled in N.Y.; personal difficulties prevented his accepting a teaching offer from the Prague Cons. after Czechoslovakia's liberation (1945); was visiting prof. of music at Princeton Univ. (1948–51).

Although Martinů spent most of his life away from his homeland, he remained spiritually and musically faithful to his native land; composed a poignant tribute, *Memorial to Lidice,* for an eponymous village where Nazi authorities executed all men and boys over the age of 16 to avenge the assassination of the local Gauleiter (1943). He returned to Europe (1953), spending his last 2 years in Switzerland. In 1979, his remains were moved from Schonenberg, Switzerland, to Policka, and were placed in the family mausoleum (1979); his centennial was celebrated all over Czechoslovakia (1990). Musically and stylistically he belonged to the European tradition of musical nationalism; avoided literal exploitation of Czech or Slovak musical materials; his music is nonetheless characterized by Bohemian melorhythms, the stylizations of Czech dances set in a modern idiom without losing their authenticity or simplicity. In his larger works he employed neoclassicism with impressionistic undertones, a mastery of modern counterpoint; his stage music reveals a predilection for chamber forms, alternating between a strong sense of comedy and sensitive lyricism.

Martirano, Salvatore, b. Yonkers, N.Y., Jan. 12, 1927; d. Urbana, Ill., Nov. 17, 1995. He studied piano and composition at the Oberlin Cons. of Music (1951); then composition at the Eastman School of Music in Rochester, N.Y., with Bernard Rogers (1952); later went to Italy, where he took courses with Luigi Dallapiccola at the Cherubini Cons. in Florence (1952–54). He served in the U.S. Marine Corps; played clarinet and cornet with the Parris Island Marine Band; from 1956 to '59 he held a fellowship to the American Academy in Rome, and in 1960 he received a Guggenheim fellowship and the American Academy of Arts and Letters Award. In 1963 he joined the faculty of the Univ. of Ill. at Urbana.

Martirano wrote in a progressive avant-garde idiom, applying the quaquaversal techniques of unmitigated radical modernism, free from any inhibitions and fond of multimedia and electronic means. His works include *The Magic Stones,* chamber opera after the *Decameron* (1952); *O, O, O, O, That Shakespeherian Rag* for Mixed Chorus and Instrumental Ensemble (1958); *Cocktail Music* for Piano (1962); *Underworld* for 4 Actors, 4 Percussion Instruments, 2 Double Basses, Tenor Saxophone, and Tape (1965; video version, 1982); *Ballad* for Amplified Nightclub Singer and Instrumental Ensemble (1966); *L's.G.A.* for a Gas-Masked Politico, Helium Bomb, 3 16mm Movie Projectors, and Tape (1968); *Action Analysis* for 12 People, Bunny, and Controller (1968); *Sal-Mar Construction I–VII* for Tape (1971–75); *Look at the Back of My Head for Awhile,* video piece (1984); *Sampler: Everything Goes When the Whistle Blows* for Violin and Synthetic Orch. (1985; rev. 1988); *Phleu* for Amplified Flute and Synthetic Orch. (1988); and *LON/dons* for Chamber Orch. (1989).

Marton, Eva, b. Budapest, June 18, 1943. She studied with Endre Rösler and Jenöd Sipos at the Franz Liszt Academy of Music in Budapest; made her formal operatic debut as the Queen of Shemakha in *Le Coq d'or* at the Hungarian State Opera there in 1968, remaining on its roster until joining the Frankfurt Opera in 1971; then became a member of the Hamburg State Opera in 1977. In 1975 she made her U.S. debut in N.Y. as soloist in the world premiere of Hovhaness's folk oratorio *The Way of Jesus;* then made her 1st appearance at the Metropolitan Opera there as Eva in *Die Meistersinger von Nürnberg* (1976). After singing at the Bayreuth Festivals (1977–78) and at Milan's La Scala (1978), she scored a notable success as the Empress in *Die Frau ohne Schatten* at the Metropolitan Opera in 1981; thereafter she was one of its most important artists, appearing as Elisabeth in *Tannhäuser* (1982), Leonore in *Fidelio* (1983), Ortrud in *Lohengrin* (1984), Tosca (1986), and Lady Macbeth (1988). She 1st sang Turandot at the Vienna State Opera in 1983; appeared as Elektra there in 1989. Her appearances as an oratorio and lieder artist were also well received.

marziale (It.). Martial, warlike.

Mascagni, Pietro, b. Livorno, Dec. 7, 1863; d. Rome, Aug. 2, 1945. He took lessons locally with A. Soffredini until, thanks to an uncle, he could attend the Milan Cons.; studied with Ponchielli and Saladino (1882); became impatient with school discipline; dismissed from the Cons. (1884); conducted operetta troupes and taught music in Cerignola.

Mascagni composed industriously; sent the MS of a 1-act opera, *Cavalleria rusticana,* to the music publisher Sonzogno for a competition and won 1st prize (1888); performed at the Teatro Costanzi in Rome with sensational success (1890), a dramatic story of village passion and his emotional, luscious score combining to create extraordinary appeal; the opera spread with amazing rapidity, with productions all over Europe and America with never-failing success; usually presented in 2 parts, separated by an "intermezzo sinfonico" (itself a popular orch'l piece). *Cavalleria rusticana* marked the advent of the verismo style, in which stark realism was the chief aim and dramatic development was condensed to enhance the effect. When, 2 years later, another veristic opera, Leoncavallo's *Pagliacci,* was accepted by Sonzogno, the 2 operas became the components of a popular double bill.

Ironically, Mascagni never duplicated or even remotely approached the success of his 1st opera, although he continued composing industriously; opera houses all over the world were only too eager to stage his later works. The most extreme case involved *Le maschere*, premiered in 1901 at 6 important Italian opera houses simultaneously (Rome, Milan, Turin, Genoa, Venice, Verona), followed by a performance 2 days later in Naples; the composer conducted the Rome premiere; but this exhibition was a humiliating debacle; in Genoa the audience hissed and booed so vehemently that the management had to lower the curtain without finishing the performance; even a rev. version produced in Turin (1916) did not establish the work in the repertoire, even in Italy.

Mascagni toured the U.S. (1902), conducting *Cavalleria rusticana* and other operas; owing to mismanagement, the visit proved a fiasco; a South American tour was more successful (1911); appeared frequently as conductor of sym. concerts. He was made a knight of the Crown of Italy (1890); elected to the Academy (1929); also taught, directing the Rossini Cons. in Pesaro (1895–1902). His last years were darkened by his earlier ardent support of the Fascist regime, leading to rejection by many old friends; his errors of moral judgment were forgiven posth.; his centennial was widely celebrated in Italy (1963). Many of his operas have been revived posth., including *L'amico Fritz* (his 2nd most popular opera, 1891); *Iris* (1898; rev. 1899); *Amica* (1905); *Lodoletta* (1917); *Si* (operetta, 1919); *Il piccolo Marat* (1921); and *Nerone* (1935).

Mason, Daniel Gregory, b. Brookline, Mass., Nov. 20, 1873; d. Greenwich, Conn., Dec. 4, 1953. Scion of a famous family of American musicians; grandson of Lowell Mason and nephew of William Mason; his father, Henry Mason (1831–90), was cofounder of the piano manufacturing firm Mason & Hamlin. Daniel Gregory entered Harvard Univ.; studied with J. K. Paine (B.A., 1895); continued studies with A. Whiting (piano), Goetschius (theory), and Chadwick (orchestration); went to Paris; took courses with d'Indy; returned to the U.S.; active as teacher and composer; joined the faculty of Columbia Univ. (1905); appointed MacDowell Professor of Music (1929); chairman of the music dept. (to 1940); taught until retirement (1942).

As a pedagogue, Mason expected a high degree of technical ability from his students; adhering to the idea of a U.S. national style, his conception was nevertheless racially suspect and regionally narrow; defined "American national" as the music of Anglo-Saxon New England and the "old South"; an outspoken opponent of the "corrupting" and "foreign" influences of 20th-century African-American and Jewish-American musics. As a composer, he followed the conservative trend in American music; his ideals were those of the German masters of the Romantic school; however, there are impressionistic colors in his orchestration, with full and opulent harmonies and expressive and songful melodies. A lack of strong individuality has led to the virtual disappearance of his music from the active repertoire, excepting the festival overture *Chanticleer* (1928) and the Clarinet Sonata (1912–15); composed 3 syms., chamber works, and vocal works; most of his writings are pedagogical; exceptions are *Music as a Humanity and Other Essays* (1921), *Artistic Ideals* (1925), and *The Dilemma of American Music* (1928).

Mason, Lowell, b. Medfield, Mass., Jan. 8, 1792; d. Orange, N.J., Aug. 11, 1872. Grandfather of Daniel Gregory Mason. As a youth he studied singing with A. Albee and O. Shaw; directed the church choir at Medfield at 16; went to Savannah, Ga. (1812); studied harmony and composition with F. Abel; taught singing in schools (1813–24); became principal singer (1815) and organist (1820) of the Independent Presbyterian Church. He went to Boston, becoming president of the Handel and Haydn Soc. (1827–32); established classes on Pestalozzi's system, teaching it privately (from 1829) and in public schools (from 1837); founded the Boston Academy of Music with G. J. Webb (1833); superintendent of music in Boston's public schools (1837–45); continued teaching (to 1851); made 2 European sojourns to study pedagogic methods (1837; 1851–53). In 1854 he settled in Orange, N.J.

Many of Mason's hymn tunes, including *Missionary Hymn (From Greenland's Icy Mountains), Olivet, Boylston, Bethany, Hebron,* and *Olmutz,* are still found in hymnals. He became wealthy through the sale of collections of music, including *Handel and Haydn Society's Collection of Church Music* (1822; 16 later eds.); *Lyra Sacra* (1832); *Boston Academy Collection of Church Music* (1836); *The Psaltery* (1845); *Cantica Laudis* (1850); *New Carmina Sacra* (1852); *Song Garden* (3 parts; 1864–65); etc.; publ. *Musical Letters from Abroad* (N.Y., 1853); M. Broyles ed. *A Yankee Musician in Europe: The 1837 Journals of Lowell Mason* (Ann Arbor, 1990). His valuable library, including hundreds of MSS and hymnals, was given to Yale College posth. His son William Mason (b. Boston, Jan. 24, 1829; d. N.Y., July 14, 1908) studied with Moscheles, M. Hauptmann, E. F. Richter, Dreyschock, and Liszt (1853–54); his *Memories of a Musical Life* (1901) provide an anecdotal overview of his travels, a fine pianist, he became a leading N.Y. teacher; established a chamber music series with Theodore Thomas to introduce new music to audiences (1855–68); wrote many piano pieces.

Mason, Luther Whiting, b. Turner, Maine, Apr. 3, 1828; d. Buckfield, Maine, July 4, 1896. He studied with Lowell Mason at the Boston Academy of Music, and may have been distant relative; in 1853 he became music teacher in Louisville schools, then in 1856 in Cincinnati, where he invented the National System of music charts and books, which had instant success and made him famous. He settled in Boston in 1864, and reformed music instruction in the primary schools; in 1880 he was invited by the Japanese government to supervise music in the schools of Japan, where he labored 3 years with notable results (school music in Japan was termed "Mason-song"). He spent some time in Germany perfecting his principal work, *The National Music-Course.*

masque. English spectacle or social assembly during the 16th and 17th centuries that featured a variety of artistic presentations, including poetry, drama, dance, and music. The subjects of such masques were usually taken from Greek mythology. Members of the aristocracy were themselves often engaged to perform the parts of shepherds and shepherdesses, benevolent gods and goddesses, etc. Among poets whose masques were produced at the English court were Ben Jonson and Milton. A curious byproduct of the masque was the 17th-century introduction of an *anti-*

masque, comic or grotesque interlude between the allegorical scenes, analogous to the *kyōgen* interludes of the medieval Japanese *noh* drama. When opera was introduced into England, the masques became integrated with it and disappeared as an independent form.

Mass. Primary and most solemn service of the Roman Catholic Church, including recitation of liturgical texts, singing, and playing on the organ. The Mass (from Lat. *missa,* dismissed) is the most impressive manifestation of religious music; its theory and practice through the centuries determined the development of polyphony throughout Europe before the Reformation; virtually every composer in the musically productive countries—Italy, Germany, France, and Spain—wrote Masses; as a distinct musical genre, reached its greatest flowering during the Renaissance.

The most eloquent and devout Mass is the *Missa solemnis* ("solemn" or High Mass); also called a *Missa cantata* ("sung" Mass); a lesser Mass is *Missa lecta* ("read" or Low Mass), with no purely musical parts. The Ordinary of the Mass (*ordinarium Missae,* from *ordinarius,* customary) comprises the sections included in every service; these sections are Kyrie, Gloria, Credo (Nicene Creed, or *Symbolum apostolicum*), Sanctus (containing the subsection, Benedictus), Agnus Dei, and Ite, missa est (*Benedicamus Domino;* few polyphonic settings); the Kyrie is the only division in the Greek language; the rest is in Latin. Polyphonic Ordinaries are often performed in concert as well as in church.

Woven within the Ordinary is a group of sections with changing texts, depending on the particular day, known collectively as the Proper of the Mass (*proprium Missae,* from *proprius,* individual) and is sung in chant. They consist of the Introit (*psalmus ad introitum*), preceding the Kyrie; Gradual, Alleluia (or, on solemn occasions, Tract), and (occasionally) Sequence, sung between the Gloria and Credo; the Offertory follows the Credo; the Proper (and the entire Mass) reach their climax with the Communion, the celebration of the Eucharist (*psalmus ad communionem;* after the Agnus Dei). Finally, the Mass is replete with recitations and readings: Collect and Epistle (after the Gloria); Gospel and Homily (before the Credo); Secret and Preface (before the Sanctus); Canon (Eucharistic prayers) and Lord's Prayer (before the Agnus Dei); the Post-Communion prayer precedes the dismissal (Ite, missa est).

Although the Latin texts of the Mass are traditional, the melodies are not; since the codification of Gregorian chant, there have been hundreds of settings of individual sections as well as the complete Ordinary, 1st as anon. plainsong, then polyphonically and (mostly) attributable. An extremely important and musically fruitful extension of the Mass is the Requiem (*Missa pro defunctis*), named after the Introit, *Requiem aeternam dona eis Domine* (Peace Eternal give them, Lord). Although the Mass is the most solemn religious service, it could not separate itself entirely from the secular world; as a result the songs of the common people began to intrude on the holy precincts of the Mass. This alien incursion, repellent as it must have seemed to the devout, produced extremely original musical forms, among them the cantus firmus Mass and, later in the Renaissance, the parody Mass and paraphrase Mass. The cantus firmus Mass involves use of fragments of Gregorian plainchant, usually in a hidden middle voice. The parody Mass type does not imply the modern meaning of parody (imitative caricature), but preserves

its original Greek meaning of *para-ode* (near-song); its principal feature being a use of religious polyphony, secular madrigals, and even folk songs; sometimes an entire motet or other choral composition is incorporated. It reached its peak during the Renaissance, The paraphrase Mass is the free use of material, chant, or polyphony.

Of such interpolations the most famous was the medieval popular song *L'Homme armé* (The Armed Man), which glorified the soldier. In this respect a Mass using preexisting material is a compound or synthetic work. It is not to be derogated for that; most great composers wrote Masses based on nonecclesiastical melodies. Even the great Palestrina wrote a parody Mass based on *L'Homme armé* (among other models). The practice so shocked the orthodox Roman Church that the Council of Trent (Trento, 1545–63) issued a prohibition against using secular melodies as the foundation for a Mass (the council nearly banned all polyphony from the liturgy). By the Baroque, Masses were generally freely written; in the late Baroque, Bach wrote his great B-minor Mass (in Latin); nearly a century later Beethoven composed his glorious non-liturgical *Missa Solemnis;* Haydn, Mozart, Schubert, Weber, Liszt, Franck, Gounod, and Bruckner wrote Masses marked by an appropriate grandeur of design.

While the great Masses from Palestrina to Beethoven are polyphonic in structure, homophonic Masses were produced in the less devout 19th century. The Lutheran church retained most of the Mass sections, as does the Anglican church; such Masses are designed not for the great Gothic cathedrals but for the humble surroundings of a parochial chapel. Sometimes separate items of the Mass, particularly the Gloria, attract modern composers with the aim of stylization rather than reconstruction of the ancient model. The Requiem Mass, with its dramatic Sequence Dies Irae, touched the mind and heart of the Romantic composer; Mozart, Berlioz, Verdi, and Brahms wrote Requiem Masses, the last in German and based on biblical texts; Britten contributed a moving *War Requiem,* interweaving settings of soldier-poet Wilfred Owen with the Latin liturgy. Bernstein wrote *Mass,* a theater piece combining Roman liturgy with a libretto by Stephen Schwartz (*Godspell*). The Latin Mass became liturgical history in the 1950s, when the Roman Catholic church decreed that the Mass be sung and spoken in the local vernacular.

Massenet, Jules (-Émile-Frédéric), b. Montaud, near St.-Etienne, Loire, May 12, 1842; d. Paris, Aug. 13, 1912. At age 9 he was admitted to the Paris Cons.; studied with Laurent (piano), Reber (harmony), and Savard and Thomas (composition); after taking 1st prize for piano (1859), he carried off the Grand Prix de Rome with the cantata *David Rizzio* (1863). In 1878 he was appointed prof. of composition at the Cons., and at the same time was elected member of the Académie des Beaux-Arts; he continued to teach at the Paris Cons. until 1896; among his students were Alfred Bruneau, Gabriel Piérne, and Gustave Charpentier. As pedagogue he exercised a profound influence on French opera.

After Gounod, Massenet was the most popular French opera composer; he possessed a natural sense of graceful melody in distinctive French style; his best operas, *Manon* (1884), *Werther* (1892), and *Thaïs* (1894), enjoy tremendous popularity in France; the celebrated *Méditation* for Violin and Orch. from *Thaïs* was a regular repertoire number among violinists. Many of his lesser-known operas have been revived recently, including *Le*

Roi de Lahore (1877); *Hérodiade* (1881); *Le Cid* (1885); *Esclarmonde* (1889); *La Navarraise* (1894); *Sapho* (1897; rev. 1909); *Cendrillon* (1899); *Grisélidis* (1901); *Le Jongleur de Notre Dame* (1902); *Chérubin* (1905); *Thérèse* (1907); *Don Quichotte* (1910); and *Cléopâtre* (1914). He also composed "sacred dramas"; incidental music; cantatas; 200 songs; orch'l works, including 7 suites; piano works for 2 and 4 hands; he completed and orchestrated Delibes's opera *Kassya* (1893).

mässig (Ger.). Measured; moderately. *Mässig gesch-wind*, *mässig schnell*, moderately fast; *mässig langsam*, moderately slow.

Mastersinger (Ger. *Meistersinger;* Fr. *maître-chanteur*). In Germany, the artisan successors to the aristocratic Minnesinger. The Guild of Mastersingers emerged in Germany after the end of the Crusades and the concurrent decline of the Minnesingers. Socially they differed from the Minnesingers, who were mainly knights; the Mastersingers were men of the people who plied common trades, such as shoemaking and carpentry, and at the same time were devoted to music, organized communal singing, and cultivated folk arts. The founder of the Mastersingers is reputed to be one Frauenlob (praise of women), who was also regarded as the last of the Minnesingers. If this link is to be accepted, then the birth of the Mastersingers can be dated to the early decades of the 14th century. The Mastersingers proved to be very durable society, which was carried well into the 19th century before finally dissolving under the pressure of modern professionalism. Wagner's opera *Die Meistersinger von Nürnberg* (1868) reflects the atmosphere of the social and professional activities in the German townships of the 16th century with remarkable fidelity. Most of the characters in Wagner's music drama are historical, and Wagner makes use of actual melodies of the Guild.

Masur, Kurt, b. Brieg, Silesia, July 18, 1927. He received training in piano and cello at the Breslau Music School (1942–44); then studied conducting with H. Bongartz and took courses in piano and composition at the Leipzig Hochschule für Musik (1946–48). In 1948 he commenced his career with appointments as *répétiteur* and conductor at the Halle Landestheater; held the title of 1st conductor at the Erfurt City Theater (1951–53) and at the Leipzig City Theater (1953–55). He was conductor of the Dresden Phil. (1955–58), Generalmusikdirektor of the Mecklenburg State Theater in Schwerin (1958–60), and senior director of music at the Komische Oper in East Berlin (1960–64). In 1967 he returned to the Dresden Phil. as its music director, a position he retained until 1972.

In 1970 Masur assumed the time-honored position of Gewandhauskapellmeister of Leipzig, where he served as music director of the Gewandhaus Orch. with notable distinction. He also made extensive tours with his orch. in Europe and abroad. In 1973 he made his British debut as guest conductor with the New Philharmonia Orch. of London; his U.S. debut followed in 1974 as guest conductor with the Cleveland Orch. In 1981 he conducted Beethoven's 9th Sym. at the gala opening of the new Gewandhaus in Leipzig. In 1988 he was named principal guest conductor of the London Phil. In the autumn of 1989, during the period of political upheaval in East Germany, Masur played a major role as peacemaker in Leipzig. In 1990 he was appointed

music director of the N.Y. Phil., to commence with the 1991–92 season. While he has earned a reputation as faithful guardian of the hallowed Austro-German repertoire, he frequently programs contemporary scores as well.

matins. Music sung at morning prayer; the 1st of the Canonical Hours.

Matthews, Artie, b. Braidwood, Ill., Nov. 15, 1888; d. Cincinnati, Oct. 25, 1958. He spent his formative years in Springfield, Ill.; learned ragtime from the pianists Banty Morgan and Art Dillingham. After working in the tenderloin district of St. Louis (*c.* 1908), he took lessons in piano, organ, and theory; was active as composer and arranger for local theaters. In 1915 he went to Chicago as church organist, and after World War I settled in Cincinnati; obtained a degree from the Metropolitan College of Music and Dramatic Arts (1918). Together with his wife, Anna Matthews, he founded the Cosmopolitan School of Music for classical training of black musicians in 1921. He was an outstanding composer of piano rags, producing 5 *Pastime Rags* (1913, 1913, 1916, 1918, 1920); also wrote a jazz classic for piano, *Weary Blues* (1915), and several songs.

mattinata (It.). Morning song.

Mauceri, John (Francis), b. N.Y., Sept. 12, 1945. He studied with Gustav Meier at Yale Univ. (B.A., 1967; M.Phil., 1972) and with Maderna, Colin Davis, Ozawa, and Bernstein at the Berkshire Music Center at Tanglewood (1971). He conducted the Yale Univ. Sym. Orch. (1968–74); subsequently appeared widely as guest conductor of opera, musical theater, and sym. orchs. He was music director of the Washington (D.C.) Opera (1980–82), the American Sym. Orch. in N.Y. (1984–87), the Scottish Opera in Glasgow (from 1987), and the Hollywood Bowl Orch. (from 1990).

maxima (Lat.). Larga.

Maxwell Davies, Peter. Davies, Peter Maxwell.

Mayall, John, b. Manchester, Nov. 29, 1933. Singer, harmonica player, and ardent promoter of African-American blues, he formed a group called the Bluesbreakers, which served as a laboratory for instrumentalists, including Eric Clapton, Peter Green, John McVie, Mick Taylor, Aynsley Dunbar, and Mick Fleetwood. The Bluesbreakers released a number of successful albums, among them *A Hard Road* and *The Turning Point* (with no drummer), and the 1st classic of British blues, under the title *Bluesbreakers with Eric Clapton*. Another album, *U.S. Union*, produced a workable amalgam of jazz and blues. He eventually emigrated to America.

Mayuzumi, Toshiro, b. Yokohama, Feb. 20, 1929. He studied with T. Ikenouchi and A. Ifukube at the National Univ. of Fine Arts and Music in Tokyo (1945–51); then took courses at the Paris Cons. with Aubin (1951–52). Returning to Japan, he organized the modern group Ars Nova Japonica and also worked at the electronic music studio in Tokyo. His style of composition embodies sonorous elements from traditional Japanese music, serial techniques, and electronic sounds, all amalgamated in a remarkably effective manner; he is also a successful composer of film scores, including that for *The Bible*. His best-known works include *Sphenogramme* for Voice and Instruments (1951); *Ectoplasme* for Electronic Instruments, Percussion, and Strings (1956); *Phonologie symphonique* (1957); *Nirvana Sym.* (1958); *U-So-Ri*, oratorio (1959); *Mandala-Sym.* (1960); *Music with Sculpture* for Winds (1961); *Samsara*, sym. poem (1962); *Bugaku*, ballet (1963); *Pratidesana*, Buddhist cantata (1963); *The Ritual Overture* for Band (1964); *Showa Tempyo Raku* (Old and Present Music), sym. poem (1970); *Kinkakuji* (The Temple of the Golden Pavilion), opera (1976); *The Kabuki*, ballet (1985).

mazurka (Polish). Moderately lively Polish national dance in triple time that, as the name indicates, originated from the Mazur district in northern Poland. Its main characteristic is an off-beat accent and syncopated 1st beat. Its popularity as an art form is owed mainly to Chopin, who adorned the basic rhythmic design of mazurkas with ingenious chromatic pianistic embellishments. Kujawiak and oberek are distinctive varieties of the mazurka.

mazza (It.). Mallet.

mazzo di legno (It.). Large wooden mallet, used to strike pieces of wood.

mbira. See ⇒lamellaphones.

McCartney, (Sir) (John) Paul, b. Liverpool, June 18, 1942. He picked out chords on a family piano (his father was an amateur ragtime player), and at puberty began playing a left-handed guitar. He was the only Beatle who attended college, studying English literature. Fascinated by Elvis Presley, he tried to emulate the spirit of American rock 'n' roll (and rhythm and blues) *à l'anglaise*. With fellow Liverpudlians John Lennon, George Harrison, Stuart Sutcliffe, and (later) Pete Best, he formed the group known as the Silver Beatles, later shortened to the Beatles (see ⇒Beatles entry for the remainder of the group's history).

In 1970 McCartney went to court to end the Beatles' Apple Corps partnership and asked for an accounting of assets and income; put out his 1st album (*McCartney*) and quit the group. He became active as a solo act and with his own group, Wings, making several world tours. As his post-Beatle work made clear, and the Lennon-McCartney umbrella proved to involve separate songs by the two, McCartney had a close connection to the popular mainstream of the past and present; he is a better melodist than lyricist, more accomodating than revolutionary; for those who mourned the end of the Beatles, his later work suggests the remarkable influence that McCartney and Lennon had on each other, whether collaborating or not. McCartney's longtime partnership with his wife Linda (Eastman) McCartney ended with her death from cancer (1998).

McFerrin, Bobby (Robert), b. N.Y., Mar. 11, 1950. His father, Robert McFerrin (b. Marianna, Ariz., Mar. 19, 1921), was an important baritone who appeared in the 1st productions of Weill's *Lost in the Stars* and Still's *Troubled Island* (both 1949); won the Metropolitan Auditions of the Air (1953); 1st African-American male to join the company; made his debut as Amonasro in *Aida* (1955); sang Porgy (played by Sidney Poitier) in the film *Porgy and Bess* (1959); toured internationally, giving recitals of arias, art songs, and spirituals.

Bobby studied music theory from age 6; played piano in high school; formed a quartet that borrowed from Mancini and Sergio Mendes. In 1970 he heard M. Davis's fusion album *Bitches Brew* and completely changed musical direction; studied music at Sacramento State Univ. and Cerritos College; played piano until 1977, when he began developing his voice; toured with jazz vocalist Jon Hendricks (1980); debuted a solo act (1982). His recordings include *Bobby McFerrin* (1982), *The Voice* (1984), *Spontaneous Improvisation* (1986), *Simple Pleasures* (1988; overdubbed a cappella voices; with his signature tune *Don't Worry, Be Happy*), and *Medicine Music* (1991); made music videos and sang with Herbie Hancock, Yo-Yo Ma, Manhattan Transfer, and others; established the 11-voice ensemble Voicestra, featured in his soundtrack for *Common Threads*, a documentary on the AIDS quilt (1989); the group's 1st concert tour received critical acclaim (1990). He began studying conducting (1989); made his debut conducting Beethoven's Sym. no. 7 with the San Francisco Sym. (1990); has toured with Chick Corea in this capacity.

McFerrin is a virtuoso, using a remarkable range of voices with sophisticated control, accompanied with body percussion, breath, and other self-generated sounds; aesthetically fuses several styles, including jazz, rock, gospel, and New Age, in a brilliant palette; his solo and ensemble shows use improvisatory structures through which he produces highly polished, expertly burnished performances.

McGhee, Brownie (Walter), b. Knoxville, Tenn., Nov. 30, 1915. He was known for his deft guitar playing and mellifluous singing in partnership with Sonny Terry, the blues harmonica player; Terry wailed vocally and instrumentally and McGhee melded this into a smooth, closely integrated blend. During their 40-year association (1939–79) they appeared in concert and at blues and folk music festivals throughout the U.S., Europe, New Zealand, and Australia. They also recorded some 30 record albums, many of which featured McGhee's songs: *Life Is a Gamble, Tell Me Why, Blues Had a Baby (And They Called It Rock and Roll), Walk On, Hole in the Wall, I Couldn't Believe My Eyes, My Father's Words, Watch Your Close Friend*, and *Rainy Day*.

McPartland, Jimmy (James), b. Chicago, Mar. 15, 1907; d. Port Washington, N.Y., Mar. 13, 1991. He studied violin, then took up the cornet; at age 16 he organized a band with his brother; subsequently played with Bix Beiderbecke, Ben Pollack, and Jack Teagarden. After military service in World War II he resumed his career by organizing his own quartet in Chicago; later led his own band on tours. He married Marian McPartland in 1945; continued performing together after their divorce.

McPartland, Marian (Margaret Turner), b. Windsor, Mar. 20, 1918. She 1st played violin; then won a scholarship to the Guildhall School of Music in London, where she studied piano. She began her career as jazz pianist in joint appearances with the jazz pianist Billy Mayerl; in 1945 she married Jimmy McPartland; in 1946 she went to America and played in a combo with her husband; in 1951 she organized her own trio; continued performing with Jimmy McPartland after their divorce. She wrote a number of songs in the popular vein, including the successful *There'll Be Other Times*. A vol. of her collected articles appeared as *All in Good Time* (N.Y., 1987).

McPhee, Colin (Carhart), b. Montreal, Mar. 15, 1900; d. Los Angeles, Jan. 7, 1964. He studied piano and composition with Harold Randolph and Gustav Strube at the Peabody Cons. in Baltimore (graduated, 1921), then took piano lessons with Arthur Friedheim in Toronto (1921–24); continued his studies with Paul Le Flem (composition) and Isidor Philipp (piano) in Paris (1924–26). Returning to the U.S. (1926), he joined the modern movement in N.Y. and was briefly student of Varèse; wrote scores for the experimental films *H20* and *Mechanical Principles* in 1931. He became infatuated with the gamelan music of Java and Bali; moved to Indonesia in 1931 and, except for brief interruptions, remained there until 1939. He then returned to the U.S. and was consultant to the Office of War Information during World War II; later was active with the Inst. of Ethnomusicology at the Univ. of Calif. at Los Angeles (1958–64).

McPhee's *Tabuh-Tabuhan* for 2 Pianos, Orch., and Exotic Percussion, composed and premiered during an interlude in Mexico City (1936), is the quintessential work in his Bali-influenced style. He wrote the books *A House in Bali* (N.Y., 1946), *A Club of Small Men* (N.Y., 1948), and *Music in Bali* (New Haven, 1966). Among his other works are 3 syms.; *Transitions* for Orch. (1954); *Nocturne* for Chamber Orch. (1958); Concerto for Wind Orch. (1960); Concerto for Piano and Wind Octet (1928); and piano works, including *4 Piano Sketches* (1916); *Kinesis* (1930); and *Balinese Ceremonial Music* for 2 Pianos (1934–38).

McRae, Carmen, b. N.Y., Apr. 8, 1922; d. Beverly Hills, Calif., Nov. 10, 1994. She joined Benny Carter's band in 1944; subsequently sang with the bands of Count Basie, Mercer Ellington, and others; made tours in Europe and Japan. She was married to the drummer Kenny ("Klook") Clarke (b. Pittsburgh, Jan. 9, 1914; d. Montreuil-sous-Bois, Paris, Jan. 26, 1985), and recorded several songs as Carmen Clarke. In 1980 she was featured performer at N.Y.'s Carnegie Hall.

McShann, Jay "Hootie," b. Muskogee, Okla., Jan. 12, 1909. He took up the piano at an early age; led his own group during the big-band era in Kansas City. Among his hits were *Hootie Blues* (a title from which he got his nickname), *Confessin' the Blues*, and *Swingmatism*. The legendary jazz figure Charlie Parker was a member of McShann's band. After a stint in the U.S. Army (1943–45), he resumed his career, working mainly in California. He continued to be active well into old age; in 1974 he toured Europe with the show *The Musical Life of Charlie Parker*; in 1975 he took part in the Montreux Jazz Festival; in 1979 he played at the Alexandra Palace Jazz Festival in London. He publ. *Boogie Woogie and Blues Piano Solos*. He also appeared in the film *The Last of the Blue Devils*.

Me. In tonic sol-fa, stands for Mi.

meantone temperament. See ⇒temperament.

measurable music. Mensurable music.

measure. The notes and rests contained within 2 vertical lines; the metrical unit in composition, with regular accentuation, familiarly called a bar. *Measure note*, note shown by the time signature to be an even divisor of a measure; thus 3/4 shows

that each measure has 3 quarter notes, and the measure note is then a quarter note; *measure rest*, see ⇒rest.

mechanical instruments. Those whose sound is generated neither by acoustic (human) nor electronic means, e.g., pianola or music box.

mechanism (Fr. *mécanisme*). Technical ability or skill; mechanical dexterity or training.

Meck, Nadezhda von. See ⇒Tchaikovsky, Peter Ilich.

medesimo (It.). The same. *Medesimo tempo*, the same tempo.

mediant. 3rd degree of the scale.

mediator. Plectrum used for special effects in harp and mandolin playing. The mediator is used in the harp part of Mahler's *Das Lied von der Erde.*

medicinale (Ger., Mid. Fr., from Lat. *Medius + canon*, half psaltery). Medieval name for small psaltery.

medley. See ⇒potpourri.

Medtner, Nicolai (Nikolai Karlovich), b. Moscow, Jan. 5, 1880; d. London, Nov. 13, 1951. He 1st studied piano with his mother, and then with his uncle, Theodore Goedicke; in 1892 he entered the Moscow Cons., where he took courses with Sapelnikov and Safonov (piano) and Arensky and Taneyev (composition); graduated in 1900, winning the gold medal; that same year he won the Rubinstein prize in Vienna; for the next 2 years he appeared with much success as pianist in the European capitals; returning to Russia, he taught at the Moscow Cons. (1902–03; 1909–10; 1914–21); then lived in Berlin and Paris; eventually settled in London (1935). He made tours of the U.S. (1924–25; 1929–30) and the Soviet Union (1927). He publ. a collection of essays as *Muza i moda* (The Muse and Fashion; Paris, 1935).

In Russian music Medtner was a solitary figure; he never followed the nationalist trend, but endeavored to create a new type of composition, rooted in both the Classic and the Romantic traditions; his sets of fairy tales in sonata form are unique examples of his favorite genre. He wrote his best compositions before he left Russia; although he continued to compose during his residence abroad, his late music lacks the verve and Romantic sincerity that distinguish his earlier works. He wrote almost exclusively for the piano and for the voice. A revival of his music was begun in Russia after his death, and a complete ed. of his works appeared in Moscow (12 vols., 1959–63). His works include 3 piano concertos, piano quintet, and numerous pieces; 3 violin sonatas; and 107 songs.

Mehta, Mehli, b. Bombay, Sept. 25, 1908. He is the father of Zubin Mehta. He studied at the Univ. of Bombay and at Trinity College of Music in London (licentiate, 1929). He founded the Bombay Sym. Orch. in 1935; was its concertmaster (until 1945) and then its conductor (until 1955); subsequently was assistant concertmaster of the Halle Orch. in Manchester (1955–59). He then settled in the U.S., where he played in the Curtis String

Quartet in Philadelphia (1959–64); subsequently went to Los Angeles, where he founded the American Youth Sym. Orch. (1964); also taught at the Univ. of Calif. there (1964–76), serving as conductor of its sym. and chamber orchs.

Mehta, Zubin, b. Bombay, Apr. 29, 1936. He was tutored in music by his father Mehli Mehta; learned to play violin and piano; at age 16 successfully conducted a rehearsal of the Bombay Sym. Orch. He took a course in medicine at St. Xavier College in Bombay, but turned away from the unaesthetic training in dissection; went to Vienna; practiced the double bass at the Academy of Music; studied conducting with H. Swarowsky; attended conducting classes at the Accademia Chigiana in Siena with C. Zecchi and A. Galliera (1956–57); graduated from the Vienna Academy of Music (1957); made his professional debut conducting the Tonkünstler Orch. in the Musikverein.

Mehta's career progressed by great strides; won the competition of the Royal Liverpool Phil. (1958); conducted it for a season as an assistant; obtained guest engagements in Austria and Yugoslavia; competed in a conducting test in Tanglewood and won 2nd prize (1959). In 1960, he received a bona fide engagement to conduct the Vienna Sym. Orch. (1960); guest conducted successfully with the Philadelphia Orch.; conducted 2 concerts of the Montreal Sym. Orch.; and was appointed its music director. He took it to Russia (1962), giving 8 concerts, followed by 2 concerts in Paris and 1 in Vienna, where he took 14 bows in response to a vociferous ovation. He received a contract to conduct the Los Angeles Phil.; became its associate conductor (1961), then music director (1962–78); he thus held 2 major conducting jobs simultaneously, commuting by air; was the youngest conductor to function in this dual capacity.

Mehta made his debut at the Metropolitan Opera in N.Y., conducting *Aida* (1965); his performances of *Carmen* and *Turandot* were highly praised. He resigned his post in Montreal (1967); *Time* glorified him with a cover story (1968), the year he was named music adviser to the Israel Phil.; became its music director (1977). He left the Los Angeles Phil. after accepting an offer to become musical director of the N.Y. Phil. (1978–91); toured with it in Europe (1980). His association with the Israel Phil. has been particularly affectionate; he conducted it during the Six-Day War and at the 25th anniversary of Israel's independence; received many honors; indeed, no Jew could be more Israeli than the Parsi Mehta.

Mehta has been aided by an ability—rare among conductors—to maintain his self-control under trying circumstances. He has the reputation of a bon vivant without limit, yet professionally maintains an almost infallible reliability, conducting all scores, even mind-boggling modern works and operas, from memory. He is also a polyglot, eloquent in English and Hindi, fluent in German, French, and Spanish, and understandable in Russian.

Meistersinger (Ger.). Mastersinger.

mejorana. Panamanian dance song, consisting of a rhymed quatrain, each line of which is then developed separately. The descending melodies, featuring falsetto and melisma, are set in 2/4 or 6/8 time, with the accompaniment in 3/4 providing hemiola effects throughout.

mejoranera. Small short-necked guitar of Panama. It is made of cedar and uses nylon strings; it is most closely associated with the mejorana.

melancolia (It.). Melancholy.

Mélange (*méslange*; Fr.). Potpourri.

Melba, (Dame) Nellie, b. Helen Porter Mitchell, Burnley, near Richmond, May 19, 1861; d. Sydney, Feb. 23, 1931. Her father, who had decided objections to anything connected with the stage, was nevertheless fond of music and proud of his daughter's talent; when she was only 6 years old he allowed her to sing at a concert in the Melbourne Town Hall, but would not consent to her having singing lessons; instead she was taught piano, violin, and harp; had instruction in harmony and composition. She frequently played the organ in a local church; was an excellent pianist; but her chief desire remained to study singing. Only until after her marriage to Captain Charles Armstrong (1882) was she able to gratify her ambition; began study with a local teacher, Cecchi; her 1st public appearance as an adult singer was in a benefit concert in Melbourne (1884); the following year her father received a government appointment in London; she accompanied him, determined to begin an operatic career; studied with M. Marchesi in Paris.

Melba gave her 1st London concert in 1886; her debut as Gilda at the Théâtre Royal de la Monnaie in Brussels (1887) created a veritable sensation; the famous impresario Augustus Harris immediately engaged her for the spring season at London's Covent Garden; made her debut as Lucia to a half-full house (1888). She scored a major success at the Paris Opera as Ophelia in Thomas's *Hamlet* (1889); sang to great acclaim in St. Petersburg (1891), Milan (1893, despite carefully planned opposition), Stockholm and Copenhagen (1893), N.Y. (Metropolitan Opera, as Lucia, 1893), and Melbourne (1902). She sang off and on at Covent Garden (to 1914); was a most brilliant star for several seasons at the Metropolitan Opera in N.Y., where she also sang with Damrosch's Opera Co. (1898) and at Hammerstein's Manhattan Opera (1906–07, 1908–09); made several transcontinental concert tours of the U.S.; began teaching at the Albert Street Cons. in Melbourne (1915); returned to Covent Garden for appearances in 1919, 1923, and a farewell performance (1926); returned to Australia and retired from the stage.

Melba was gifted with a voice of extraordinary beauty and bell-like purity; made this fine instrument perfectly even throughout its entire compass (B flat–f^3) and wonderfully flexible, executing the most difficult fioriture without effort. As an actress she did not rise above the conventional, thus was at her best in parts demanding brilliant coloratura (Gilda, Lucia, Violetta, Rosina, Lakme); on the single occasion she attempted the role of Brünnhilde in *Siegfried* (Metropolitan Opera, N.Y., 1896), she met with disaster. She was representative of the golden era of opera: a prima donna assoluta who exercised her powers over the public with perfect self-assurance and fine command of her singing voice; among her other distinguished roles were Mimi, Else, Nedda, Aida, Desdemona, and Marguerita; created Dame Commander of the Order of the British Empire (1918). As a measure of her universal popularity, her name was attached to a delicious dessert (Peach Melba) and to Melba Toast, patented by

Bert Weil (1929); a motion picture based on her life was produced with Patrice Munsel as Melba (1953).

Melchior, Lauritz (born Lebrecht Hommel), b. Copenhagen, Mar. 20, 1890; d. Santa Monica, Calif., Mar. 18, 1973. He studied with Paul Bang at the Royal Opera School in Copenhagen, making his operatic debut in the baritone role of Silvio at the Royal Theater there (1913); continued on its roster while studying further with Vilhelm Herold, and then made his tenor debut as Tannhäuser (1918). In 1921 he went to London to continue his training with Beigel, and then studied with Grenzebach in Berlin and Bahr-Mildenburg in Munich. In 1924 he made his Covent Garden debut in London as Siegmund, returning there regularly from 1926 to 1939. He was in Bayreuth in 1924 to study with Kittel; made his 1st appearance at the Festspielhaus there as Siegfried in 1924 and continued to make appearances there until 1931. In 1926 he made his Metropolitan Opera debut in N.Y. as Tannhäuser, and he quickly established himself as one of its principal artists; with the exception of the 1927–28 season, he sang there regularly until his farewell performance as Lohengrin in 1950. In 1947 he became a naturalized U.S. citizen. After the close of his operatic career Melchior appeared on Broadway and in films; also continued to give concerts. He was accorded a preeminent place among the Wagnerian Heldentenors of his era.

melisma. Melodic ornament or grace; coloratura. *Melismatic,* ornamented, embellished; *melismatic song,* one in which more than one tone is sung to a syllable; opposed to syllabic song.

melodeon. 1. Reed organ. 2. Button accordion.

melodia (It.). Melody. *Marcata la melodia,* emphasize the melody.

melodic. 1. In the style of a melody; progressing by single tones. 2. Vocal, singable; as a melodic interval.

melodic minor scale. Minor scale which eliminates the interval of an augmented 2nd between the 6th and 7th degrees of the harmonic minor scale, thereby providing smoother melodic progression. When ascending, the 6th and 7th degrees are raised (C–D–E♭–F–G–A♮–B♮–C); when descending, these notes are unaltered (C–B♭–A♭–G–F–E♭–D–C).

mélodie (Fr.). Chanson.

melodion. Friction-bar keyboard instrument; steel bars are pressed against a revolving cylinder in place of strings; invented by J. C. Dietz in the early 19th century.

melodioso (It.). Melodious, singing.

melodium. 1. American portable harmonium of the mid–19th century. 2. Monophonic electrophone, invented in Germany during World War II.

mélodrame (Fr.). In opera, orch'l interlude between scenes.

melodrama (from Grk. *melos* + *drama,* sung drama). 1. Originally, any musical drama. 2. Form or genre of declamation with musical accompaniment, ranging from piano to full orch. 3. Romantic and sensational drama in which music plays a subordinate (if any) part.

During the last century the term *melodrama* has acquired the meaning of a work for theater, radio, film, or television calculated to excite the sensations of an audience by piling up suspense upon suspense, natural disasters complicating human conflict and individual misfortune; the adjective "melodramatic" conveys the derogatory meaning of cheap exhibition masquerading as real drama. The text of a typical melodrama corresponds in spirit to Gothic novels, with dramatic peripeteia, sudden reversals of fortune, mysterious portents and premonitions, often with supernatural overtones; these can be musically punctuated by chromatic runs or tremolos on the diminished-7th chord; but music may be entirely absent from a melodrama.

Melodrama in the etymological sense of the word has had a long, respectable history. In 17th-century Italy it was synonymous with *dramma per musica,* that is, opera; the 1st melodrama so named by its composer was *Il Tito* by Cesti (1666). In opera's early years the terms *melodramma, tragedia lirica,* and *dramma lirico* were used interchangeably; this practice continued through the 19th century in France, with its *drame lyrique* or *tragédie lyrique.* Meanwhile, melodrama imperceptibly came to mean a recitation or theatrical performance in which lines were spoken to musical accompaniment; many melodramas were even staged. The 1st staged melodrama was probably *Ariadne auf Naxos* (1775) by Georg Anton Benda (1722–95); it greatly impressed Mozart, who heard it 3 years later. Fibich wrote a trilogy of melodramas, *Hippodamia* (1888–91), that enjoyed numerous performances in Prague. Humperdinck enhanced the genre with his opera *Königskinder* (1897) by indicating the inflection of the spoken voice in written notes, marking the approximate level of pitch in each syllable. Schoenberg elevated melodrama to high art in his *Pierrot Lunaire,* specifically described as a melodrama in the score; in it he introduced Sprechstimme—inflected speech—voice, midway between speaking and singing.

Parallel to these developments, the smaller-scaled and more popular type of melodrama emerged, incorporating the simultaneous use of recitation and music, rather than dramatic dialogue. Schumann and Liszt were among those who wrote in this genre; Prokofiev in *Peter and the Wolf* and Walton in *Façfiade* made use of this technique. The genre was particularly popular in Russia, where it became known under the more proper title *melodeclamation.*

melody (from Grk. *melos* + *aeidein,* sung music; Fr. *mélodie;* It., Lat. *melodia;* Ger. *Melodie*). 1. Rational progression of single tones in one part, by contrast with harmony. 2. Leading part, usually the soprano. 3. Air or tune.

Melody involves successive tones projecting a self-governing sense of logical progression. In modern usage melody is a tonal line vivified by rhythmic beat; to the Greeks such rhythmed melody was defined as *harmonia;* in Western melos a melody has harmonic implications, but the word *harmony* connotes simultaneous sounding of several melodies. Aesthetically an ideally beautiful melody has a perfect balance between the high and low registers and symmetric alternation of ascending and descending tonal groups. If melodies are analyzed with reference to these contrasts, the number of high notes multiplied by the duration of each note will approximately equal the number of notes below the center of gravity multiplied by the duration of these notes; the frequency of incidence increases toward the middle register, finally converging upon a melodic center of gravity. The metaphor of gravity also applies to the melodic rule requiring that, after a wide leap upwards, the melody should descend at least one diatonic degree, and vice versa; rhythmic values must also be considered, so that in an ideal melody a long high note would be counterbalanced by a long low note or by a succession of short low notes.

Most memorable melodies move within the range of an octave between 2 dominants in a major key, with the important points on the tonic (root), the mediant (major 3rd), and the upper dominant (perfect 5th); in acoustical terms, this octave is outlined by the 3rd (lower dominant), 4th (tonic) 5th (mediant), and 6th (upper dominant) overtones in the harmonic series; it may therefore be conjectured that Western melodic lines are functions of this harmonic series, with its emphasis on the major triad; this is supported by the many convincing tunes, limited to these notes, that are produced by the bugle, horns without valves, and other wind instruments capable only of the harmonic series; tunes built on this series include Cohan's World War I song *Over There*, the 1st and last movements of Mozart's *Eine kleine Nachtmusik*, and the finale of Haydn's *Military* Sym. (no. 100).

The interpolated supertonic (2nd) and subdominant (4th) complete a major pentachord; the number of melodies so constructed tallies in the thousands, if not millions; all are in a major key; many begin with an ascending leap from the dominant to the tonic; among famous examples are *La Marseillaise*, the finale of Beethoven's Violin Concerto, the overture to Rossini's *William Tell*, the "Waltz of the Flowers" from Tchaikovsky's *Nutcracker Suite*, and the Wedding March from Wagner's *Lohengrin*. Melodies of this formation are less common in minor keys than in major, but still comprise a respectable inventory, e.g., the 2nd movement of Tchaikovsky's violin concerto and *Vltava* (Moldau) from Smetana's *Má vlast*; further examples can be found by consulting thematic catalogues of classical sonatas and syms. Many consider the derivation of melody from the harmonic series to be one of the most persistent and irrefutable phenomena in melodic construction, and therefore in all music; harmonic implications of classical melodies (and a great majority of Western folk tunes) are very evident; the pendulumlike swing between tonic and dominant is the most frequent harmonic characteristic. But the principles underlying the melodic structure of much non-Western music differ widely from those of Western melos; there are fewer harmonic implications, and scales may be derived from intervals and pitches not found within an equally-tempered octave. The study of non-Western melodies must take place within a special discipline in ethnomusicology, acoustics, or theory, while considering the roles of sociological, cultural, and compositional influences on melodic construction.

While most melodies are contained within the octave from the dominant to the dominant, continuous melodic lines extending over an octave are not rare; a remarkable example is the auxiliary theme in the finale of Beethoven's *Choral* Sym., beginning on the tonic, rising to the 6th in the next highest octave, and ending on the tonic in that octave, with all melodic notes of equal rhythmic value; such an enlarged range is acceptable for instrumental passages, but almost intractable for the human voice. The range

of *The Star-Spangled Banner* is an octave and a 5th, making it difficult for most to sing; futile attempts have been made to improve its singability. Wagner introduced the notion of *Unendliche Melodie* (infinite or endless melody), a description of melody that naturally flows from the end of 1 motive into the beginning of the next, avoiding perfect cadences, analogous to a circle or any other closed curve.

Another essential resource in classical Western music is the sequence within the key, a melodic pattern repeated on an ever-changing set of scale degrees; Beethoven's 5th Sym. opens with a falling 3rd from the dominant to the minor mediant, followed sequentially by a falling 3rd from the subdominant to the supertonic; typically this type of sequence suggest a swing from tonic to dominant. A longer sequence occurs toward the end of the overture to Tchaikovsky's opera *Eugene Onegin*, having 8 chain-links (i.e., occurrences of the pattern) and descending fully 2 octaves; even more extreme is the seemingly endless chain of 4 descending steps in his *1812 Overture*, prior to the final apotheosis.

Atonal melodies follow structural plans entirely different from those of tonal melodies; atonality excludes all triadic conformations and has no link with the harmonic series. Organized atonal systems, particularly dodecaphony, follow their own rules of aesthetic structures, with the ideal of beauty derived from special considerations of intervallic motion; but even in dodecaphonic melodies, the center of gravity embodies the arithmetical mean of high and low notes. By the time of minimalism, however, the very concept of melody was being challenged by the new repetitive structuralism.

melograph. Mechanical devices for recording the music played on a piano.

meloharmony. In a triadically constructed melody, the harmonic arrangement is clearly outlined. In such instances it is proper to speak of meloharmony as a 2-dimensional entity. In dodecaphonic music, meloharmony acquires particular significance, because the fundamental series can be distributed horizontally (i.e., melodically), and vertically (harmonically), and still preserve its continuity. It is also possible to speak of melo-contrapuntal structures, arranged vertically, horizontally, or diagonally. A cognate term is *melorhythm*, in which melody and rhythm are combined into a dual entity.

melopoeia (from Grk. *melos* + *poein*, create song). Ancient Greek term denoting all types of musical composition and performance. In Plato's *Symposion*, melopeia is described as the art of musical forms, while Aristotle defines it as the science of melody. The Aristotelian meaning was revived in the Renaissance in the theories of the harmony of the spheres. A rather tautological definition of the term is given by Mersenne: "Melopoeia nil aliud est quam ars melodiae" (Melopeia is nothing but the art of melody).

melophone. Portable keyboard accordion, shaped like a cello, harp, or guitar; resting on the lap, the melophone's sound is produced by bellows operated by a right-hand handle, capable of vibrato or trumpet effects; the left hand works the varying number of keys. Conceptually the instrument suggests a bizarre hurdy-gurdy; it is not surprising that within 3 years of its invention (1837) the harmonium was being developed to replace it.

melorhythm. The term *meloritmo*—frequently used by Spanish and Latin American writers on music and signifying a synthetic 2-dimensional entity possessing both melodic and rhythmic attributes—is sufficiently useful to be adopted in other languages. It is also a convenient substitute for the definition of a musical phrase, which must necessarily have the dual melorhythmic consistency. In serial music, melorhythms may be regarded as the integrals of the melodic and rhythmic differential series.

melosomatic effect. A neologism suggesting interaction between *melos* (song) and the physical *soma* (body). It may be traumatic when loud music is played without relief. But a more insidious psychological lesion is produced by personal associations. In his short story *The Black Monk*, Chekhov, a professional physician, describes the deadly effect produced on a young intellectual by the playing of *Angel's Serenade* by Gaetano Braga, resulting in a fatal cerebral hemorrhage when the piece is played again after a long interval of time. The Hungarian composer Rezsö Seress authored the pessimistic popular song *Gloomy Sunday* (it was banned in various localities after numerous suicides were purportedly engendered by it); by a 40-year delayed reaction, the composer himself jumped out of a window. The Russian pianist Alexander Kelberine (1903–40) took a lethal dose of barbiturates after his last concert in Town Hall in N.Y., a funereal program consisting entirely of minor-key works, the last number being Liszt's *Totentanz*.

Sexual stimulation is highly melosomatic, as amply demonstrated by the reactions of the young to concerts of popular music. Leo Tolstoy, who turned against sex after a lifetime of indulgence and 16 illegitimate children, presented a philosophical study of musical sexuality in his novella *The Kreutzer Sonata*, in which he relates how the propulsively syncopated last movement of Beethoven's work overwhelms the natural restraints of the performers, a middle-class married Russian woman pianist and a male violinist, hurling them into a frenzy of illicit passion. (One might question if amateurs could ever master the technical difficulties of that diabolically intricate movement, let alone create enough excitement to carry them away.) A famous painting illustrating the climactic scene of the novel, showing the mustachioed violinist implanting a passionate kiss on the lady pianist's lips; the painting was widely used as an advertisement for a brand of perfume.

Melosomatic associations were responsible for the extraordinary vogue of the piano piece *A Maiden's Prayer*, by Polish composer Thekla Badarzewska (1834–61), among several generations of unmarried females. In Paris, Stravinsky initiated a suit against Warner Bros. for a film, *The Firebird* (1937), in which a submissive young girl is so unnerved by the phonograph playing of *Katschei's Infernal Dance* from his ballet that she wanders into the flat of a professional seducer, who has played the recording continuously with malice aforethought, and yields to his infamous desires; the judge failed to appreciate the composer's argument, since the seductive power of music was supposed to be a composer's greatest goal; he adjudicated the case by granting Stravinsky a sum of 1 French franc in compensation for the offense.

membi. Indigenous vertical flute found in Paraguay and southern Brazil.

membranophones. In the Hornbostel-Sachs classification system, drums whose playing area is made of stretched animal skin (membrane). At present many of these instruments (especially in the Western classical orch.) use plastic instead of skin.

même (Fr.). Same. *À la même*, tempo primo.

Mendelssohn (-Bartholdy), (Jacob Ludwig) Felix, b. Hamburg, Feb. 3, 1809; d. Leipzig, Nov. 4, 1847. His family was Jewish (his grandfather was the philosopher Moses Mendelssohn), but after settling in Berlin, his father decided to baptize the family, becoming Protestant and adding Bartholdy to the surname (1816). Felix received his 1st piano lessons from his mother, then studied piano with L. Berger and violin with C. W. Henning and E. Rietz; had lessons in foreign languages and painting (he showed considerable talent in pastel drawing); studied piano with Marie Bigot in Paris during a brief stay (1816).

Mendelssohn's most important teacher was Zelter, who understood the magnitude of his talent; Zelter took him to Weimar and introduced him to Goethe, who took considerable interest after hearing him play (1821); Zelter arranged for him to join the Singakademie in Berlin as an altor; his 19th Psalm was performed by the group (both 1819). His father took him again to Paris to consult Cherubini on Felix's prospects in music (1825); but they returned to Berlin, where he had better opportunities.

Mendelssohn was not only a precocious performer and composer; his adolescent works have an extraordinary perfection, without parallel. After years of playing in the family circle, he made his public debut in Berlin, playing piano (1818); wrote a remarkable string octet (1825), then composed an overture to Shakespeare's *A Midsummer Night's Dream* (1826), an extraordinary manifestation of artistic maturity equal to that of additional incidental music he composed 15 years later.

Mendelssohn proved his great musicianship by conducting Bach's *St. Matthew Passion* in the Berlin Singakademie (1829); this event gave an impulse to the revival of Bach's vocal music. That spring he made his maiden journey to England; conducted his Sym. No. 1 in C minor from the keyboard; performed the solo in Beethoven's *Emperor* Concerto in London; traveled through Scotland, finding inspiration for his concert overture *Fingal's Cave* (*Hebrides*); conducted its premiere during his 2nd visit to London (1832); 10 days later played the solo parts of his G-minor Concerto, op. 25 and *Capriccio brillant*, op. 22 (London); he became a favorite of the English public, making 10 trips to England altogether; Queen Victoria and the Prince Consort were fervent admirers.

Mendelssohn traveled throughout continental Europe (1830–32), led the Lower-Rhine Music Festival in Düsseldorf (1833); conducted at Cologne; offered the conductorship of the celebrated Gewandhaus Orch. in Leipzig (both 1835); his leadership of the Gewandhaus Orch. was of great significance for German musical culture; engaged violin virtuoso Ferdinand David (1810–73) as concertmaster of the orch.; the Gewandhaus became the most prestigious German orch'l organization in Germany.

At the invitation of King Friedrich Wilhelm IV, Mendelssohn went to Berlin to take charge of its court and cathedral music (1841); named Königlicher Generalmusikdirektor, but residence in Berlin was not required. He journeyed to Dresden to petition King Friedrich August II of Saxony on behalf of a planned cons.; obtained a large sum to begin the project; returning to Leipzig, organized the famous Cons., which opened in 1843; he taught piano, ensemble playing, and composition; other faculty included Schumann (piano, composition, score reading); Hauptmann (harmony, counterpoint); David (violin); Becker (organ, music history, theory) and Plaidy and Wenzel (piano); during frequent absences the Gewandhaus Concerts were conducted by Ferdinand Hiller (1843–44) and Niels Gade (1844–45).

Mendelssohn conducted the Phil. Concerts in London on his 8th English visit (1844); on his next visit there, conducted the premiere of the oratorio *Elijah* in Birmingham (1846); the Wedding March from his music to *A Midsummer Night's Dream* (1842) was 1st used to accompany a bridal procession, for the marriage of Tom Daniel and Dorothy Carew at St. Peter's Church, Tiverton (1847); it became particularly fashionable when it was played at the wedding of the Princess Royal (1858). He made his 10th and last visit to England (1847); shortly thereafter, his favorite sister, composer Fanny (Cäcilie) (Mendelssohn-Bartholdy) Hensel, died; his own health began almost immediately to deteriorate; it is most likely that he died after a series of strokes, having suffered from severe migraines and chills; the effect of Fanny's death on her brother has been the subject of much armchair speculation. The news of his death shocked the world of music; there was genuine sorrow among musicians, not only in Germany and England, but in distant America and Russia as well. Mendelssohn societies were formed all over the world; in the U.S., the Mendelssohn Quintette Club was found (1849); a Mendelssohn Scholarship was established in England (1856); its 1st recipient was Arthur Sullivan.

Of all musicians known to history, Mendelssohn possessed the instinct of music in its purest form; not even the young Mozart had his genius developed to such maturity as was found in Mendelssohn's earliest works, among them 13 string sinfonias (1821–23) which, coming to light later, revealed extraordinary mastery of technique; it is not that the quality of Mendelssohn's music is superior to Mozart's; rather, that his art was an example of perfection apparently attained without gradual learning. Although a Romantic in predilection and association, his music had relatively few tempestuous outbursts of drama or tragedy; his works could serve as a manual of post-Classic composition in his time; his modulations were wonderfully orderly in their tonal fusion; his melodies came easily and in abundance; his counterpoint was never obtrusive; his orchestration was euphonious in its colorful harmony. Yet the seeming perfection of Mendelssohn's musical canon led to the gradual decline of his popularity among musicians of the succeeding sesquicentennial; his music came to embody the spirit of Biedermeyer, too facile, too fulsome in its *Gemütlichkeit*.

Mendelssohn did not find true disciples; he only attracted epigones. But in performance, his music remains highly animated; the 5 orch'l syms., notably the *Scottish* (no. 3, op. 56, 1830–42) and *Italian* (no. 4, op. 90, 1833), maintain their smiling flow; his *Lieder ohne Worte* for piano (8 books, 1829–45) are favorites of amateurs and professionals alike; the popularity of his mature Violin Concerto in E Minor (op. 64,

1844) remains undiminished; the chamber music is radiant in their communal cohesion. In sum, he was the musical personification of early German Romanticism, but, as a Jew by birth, was anathematic to the 3rd Reich; his name was removed from music history books and encyclopedias publ. in Germany during that time; Nazi barbarians tore down his statue before the Gewandhaus in Leipzig; it was lovingly restored after 1945.

Prolific throughout his career, Mendelssohn wrote incidental music for several plays; a small number of Singspiele (*Die Hochzeit des Camacho*, op. 10, 1825; *Die Heimkehr aus der Fremde*, op. 89, 1829); oratorios (*St. Paul*, op. 36, 1834–36; *Elijah*, op. 70, 1846); sacred works, including psalms, hymns, cantatas, motets, Mass movements, anthems; secular cantatas and choral songs, including *Die erste Walpurgisnacht* for Chorus and Orch., after Goethe's *Faust* (op. 60, 1833). 6 Lieder attributed to Mendelssohn in early collections were actually composed by Fanny: 3 apiece in op. 8 (1828) and op. 9 (1829–30); other Mendelssohn Lied collections, each with 6 songs, include op. 19a (1830–34); op. 34 (1834–36); op. 47 (1832–39); op. 57 (1839–43); op. 71 (1842–47); op. 86 (1831–51); op. 99; also vocal duets.

In addition to the works mentioned above, there are the remaining orch'l syms.: no. 1, in C minor, op. 11 (1824); no. 2, in B-flat major, for solo voices, chorus, and orch., *Lobgesang*, op. 52 (1840); no. 5, in D major, *Reformation*, op. 107 (1830–32); concertos for violin (D minor, with strings, 1822); piano (A minor, with strings, 1822; no. 1, G minor, op. 25, 1831; no. 2, D minor, op. 40, 1837); violin and piano (D minor, with strings, 1823); 2 pianos (E major, 1823; A-flat major, 1824); other concertante works. Concert overtures: *Meeresstille und glückliche Fahrt*, after Goethe, op. 27 (1828); *Die Hebriden oder Fingals Höhle*, op. 26 (1830); *Die schöne Melusine*, after Grillparzer, op. 32 (1833); *Ruy Blas*, after Hugo, op. 95 (1839). Chamber music with piano: trios, quartets, sextet, violin sonatas, viola sonata, cello sonatas, clarinet sonata, other combinations; without piano: string quartets; string quintets; string sextet. Piano music, including sonatas, variations (e.g., *Variations sérieuses* in D minor, op. 54, 1841), preludes and fugues, capriccios, characteristic pieces, etc.; organ music.

ménestrel, ménéstrier (Fr.). Minstrel.

Mengelberg, (Josef) Willem, b. Utrecht, Mar. 28, 1871; d. Chur, Switzerland, Mar. 21, 1951. He studied at the Utrecht Cons. and Cologne Cons. with Seiss, Jensen, and Wullner. He was appointed municipal music director in Lucerne (1891), attracting so much attention that he was appointed the head of the Concertgebouw Orch. in Amsterdam, holding this post for a record 50 years (1895–1945); elevated that orch. to a lofty position in the world of music; director of the Museumgesellschaft concerts in Frankfurt (1907–20); conductor of the Toonkunst choral society in Amsterdam (from 1898); appeared frequently as guest conductor all over Europe; an annual visitor to England (1911–39).

Mengelberg made his debut with the N.Y. Phil. (1905); conducted it regularly (1921–30), with Toscanini as associate conductor (1929–30); appointed prof. of music at Utrecht Univ. (1933). During the occupation of the Netherlands by the Germans (1940–45), he openly expressed his sympathies with the Nazi cause, conducted in Germany, and lost the great respect and admiration of his compatriots; after the country's liberation, he was barred from professional activities there until 1951; died before he could resume his career.

Mengelberg was an outstanding representative of the Romantic tradition in orch'l conducting; his performances of the Beethoven syms. featured dramatic sweep and power, if not stylistic propriety; championed many major composers of his era, including Mahler and R. Strauss; both guest conducted at of the Concertgebouw Orch. and became his friends. Mahler dedicated his 5th and 8th syms. to Mengelberg and the Concertgebouw Orch., as did Strauss his *Ein Heldenleben*; Mengelberg was the 1st to lead a major Mahler cycle (Amsterdam, 1920). His nephew Karel (Willem Joseph) Mengelberg (b. Utrecht, July 18, 1902; d. Amsterdam, July 11, 1984) was a composer and conductor; another nephew, Kurt Rudolf Mengelberg (b. Krefeld, Feb. 1, 1892; d. Beausoleil, near Monte Carlo, Oct. 13, 1959), was a musicologist and composer; finally, Misha Mengelberg, a son of Karel Mengelberg (b. Kiev, June 5, 1935), is a composer.

Mennin, Peter (born Mennini), b. Erie, Pa., May 17, 1923; d. N.Y., June 17, 1983. His brother, the composer and music educator Louis (Alfred) Mennini (b. Erie, Pa., Nov. 18, 1920) did not remove the last letter of his name as Peter did. His early environment was infused with music, mostly from phonograph recordings; studied piano with T. Spampani; enrolled in the Oberlin Cons. in Ohio (1940); took harmony courses with N. Lockwood; quickly learned the basics of composition; at age 18 wrote a sym. and string quartet. He enlisted in the U.S. Army Air Force (1942–43); after his discharge, resumed his studies at the Eastman School of Music in Rochester, N.Y., with Hanson and B. Rogers.

Mennin worked productively; wrote another sym. (1944), of which one movement, entitled *Symphonic Allegro*, was performed by the N.Y. Phil., Bernstein conducting (1945); his 3rd Sym. was performed by Walter Hendl with the N.Y. Phil. (1947). He progressed academically as well, obtaining a Ph.D. from the Eastman School of Music (1947); received two Guggenheim fellowship grants (1948, 1956). He taught composition at the Juilliard School of Music in N.Y. (1947–58); assumed the directorship of the Peabody Cons. in Baltimore (1958); received his most prestigious appointment as president of the Juilliard School of Music (1962), serving in that capacity until his death; throughout, he demonstrated a shrewd understanding of the music school's inner workings.

Despite Mennin's academic preoccupations, he never slackened as a composer; diversified his syms. by adding descriptive titles; his 4th Sym. (1949) was labeled *The Cycle* and included chorus; the 7th Sym. (1964) was called *Variation Sym.*; the 4 movements of his 8th Sym. (1974) bore biblical titles. He began attaching descriptive titles to other works; his Concertato for Orch. was named *Moby Dick* (1952); there followed a *Canto* for Orch. (1963), a *Cantata de Virtute* (1969), *Reflections of Emily*, to Dickinson texts (1976), and *Voices* (1976). Yet his musical mind was directed toward purely structural forms, his music characterized by integrity of purpose and teleological development of thematic materials, despite bold infusion of dissonant sonorities in contrapuntal passages.

meno (It.). Less; not so. *Meno allegro*, not so fast; *meno mosso*, not so fast (usually shortened to simply *meno*).

Menotti, Gian Carlo, b. Cadegliano, July 7, 1911. He learned the rudiments of music from his mother; began composing as a child, e.g., his 1st attempt at opera, *The Death of Pierrot*, at age 10. He studied at the Milan Cons. (1924–27); went to the U.S.; entered the Curtis Inst. of Music in Philadelphia (1927–33); studied with R. Scalero; subsequently taught composition there; traveled often to Europe; lived in Mt. Kisco, N.Y.; although associated with the cause of American music, and spending much time in the U.S., retained his Italian citizenship.

Menotti's 1st successful stage work was *Amelia Goes to the Ball*, a one-act opera buffa, to an Italian libretto written and translated by the composer, staged at the Academy of Music, Philadelphia (1937); followed by a 2nd comic opera, *The Old Maid and the Thief*, commissioned by NBC, 1st performed on the radio (1939), and staged by the Philadelphia Opera Co. (1941); his next opera, *The Island God*, was the 1st of many works dealing with religious and quasi-religious themes; produced by the Metropolitan Opera, N.Y. (1942), it met with indifferent success. The production of *The Medium* (N.Y., 1946), however, established him as a leading composer-librettist of modern opera; the imaginative libretto, concerning a fraudulent spiritualist who falls victim to her own séances and imagines ghostly voices to be real, suited his musical talent to perfection; the opera had a long and successful run in N.Y., unprecedented in the history of American lyric theater. A short humorous opera, *The Telephone*, was 1st produced by the N.Y. Ballet Soc. (1947) on the same bill with *The Medium*; these 2 contrasting works were staged all over the U.S. and Europe as a double bill.

Menotti then produced *The Consul* (Philadelphia, 1950), his best tragic work, describing the Kafkaesque plight of political fugitives trying to escape from an unnamed country but unable to obtain the necessary papers from the consul of an anonymous power, who is never seen; *The Consul* exceeded his previous operas in popular success, with a long N.Y. run, and received the Pulitzer Prize. On Christmas Eve, 1951, NBC presented the 1st television opera, *Amahl and the Night Visitors*, a Christmas story of undeniable poetry and appeal; became an annual Christmas television broadcast in subsequent years.

Menotti's next opera was *The Saint of Bleecker Street*, set in a N.Y. locale (N.Y., 1954); won the Drama Critics' Circle Award for the best musical play (1954) and the Pulitzer Prize (1955); a madrigal ballet, *The Unicorn, the Gorgon and the Manticore*, commissioned by the Elizabeth Sprague Coolidge Foundation, was 1st presented at the Library of Congress, Washington, D.C. (1956); the opera *Maria Golovin*, written expressly for the International Exposition in Brussels, was staged there (1958). He organized the Festival of 2 Worlds in Spoleto, Italy, staging old and new works (1958); inaugurated Spoleto Festival USA in Charleston, S.C., serving as artistic director (1977–93); in many festival productions acted also as stage director; served briefly as artistic director of the Rome Opera (1993–94).

Menotti continued to turn out librettos and operas in almost 18th-century fashion, consequently an increasing number of failures; among them are *Labyrinth*, television opera (N.Y., 1963); *The Last Savage*, opera buffa (Opéra-Comique, Paris, in French, 1963; produced in Eng. at the Metropolitan Opera, N.Y., 1964); *Martin's Lie*, chamber opera (Bath, England, 1964); *Help, Help, the Globolinks!*, "opera in 1 act for children and those who like children," with electronic effects (Hamburg, 1968); *La Loca*, concerning a mad daughter of Ferdinand and Isabella (San Diego, 1979); *The Boy Who Grew Too Fast*, opera for children (Wilmington, Del., 1982); *The Wedding* (Seoul, 1988), *Goya* (Charleston, S.C., 1991) *Singing Child*, children's opera (Charleston, S.C., 1993).

As a composer Menotti was unique on the American scene, the 1st to create American opera possessing sufficient appeal to audiences to become established in the repertoire; inheriting the Italian gift for operatic drama and expressive singing line, he adapted these qualities to the requirements of the American stage and changing fashions; his serious operas have a strong, even melodramatic content in the verismo style. He wrote his own librettos, marked by dramatic flair and notable for their communicative power; to this is added a fine, though subdued, sense of musical humor. He made no pretensions at extreme modernism; did not fear borrowing successful formulas developed by Verdi and Puccini, although the resemblance was too great for many tastes; the influence of Mussorgsky's realistic prosody is in evidence, particularly in recitative; when dramatic tension required a greater impact, he resorted to atonal and polytonal writing, leading to climaxes accompanied by massive dissonances.

Among Menotti's nonoperatic works are 2 ballets (*Sebastian*, 1944; *Errand into the Maze*, 1947); 2 piano concertos (1945, 1982); concertos for violin (1952), double bass (1982), and concerto grosso (1970); *Apocalypse*, sym. poem (1951); 1st Sym., subtitled *The Halcyon* (1976); *Death of the Bishop of Brindisi*, dramatic cantata (1963); *Landscapes and Remembrances*, autobiographical cantata (1976). He wrote the librettos for Barber's operas *Vanessa* (1958), *A Hand of Bridge* (1959), and the rev. *Antony and Cleopatra* (1975); wrote a play without music, *The Leper* (1970).

mensural notation, mensuration. Type of rhythmic notation and system, in use from the 13th to the 17th centuries, based on a system of ligatures that determine duration according to succession and context, rather than metrically.

menuet (Fr.; Ger. *Menuett*). Minuet.

Menuhin, (Sir) Yehudi, b. N.Y., Apr. 22, 1916. As a child he was taken to San Francisco; began studying violin with S. Anker; began lessons with Louis Persinger, concertmaster of the San Francisco Sym. Orch. (1923); made his public debut in Oakland playing Bériot's *Scéne de ballet* at age 7 (1924); played a recital in N.Y. (1926); made his European debut in Paris with Paul Paray and the Lamoureux Orch. (1927); began studying with Enesco, his most influential teacher and career guide.

Returning to America, Menuhin played the Beethoven Concerto with Fritz Busch and the N.Y. Sym. Orch. (1927), winning unanimous acclaim; made tours throughout America and Europe; appeared with Walter and the Berlin Phil., playing concertos by Bach, Beethoven, and Brahms on one program (1929); later that year, made his London debut. He continued his studies with Enesco; received additional instruction from Adolf Busch. On the sesquicentennial of the 1st concert at the Gewandhaus in Leipzig, he appeared as soloist with the orch. in the Mendelssohn Concerto (1931); completed his 1st world tour, giving concerts in 73 cities in 13 countries, including Australia (1935); performed often in recital with his sister Hephzibah Menuhin (b. San Francisco, May 20, 1920; d. London, Jan. 1, 1981).

Menuhin became active in organizing music festivals; established the Gstaad Festival in Switzerland (1956); made his home in London (1959); founded and directed the Bath Festival (to 1968); founded and directed the Windsor Festival (1969–72). He toured as soloist with his own chamber orch.; later devoted himself to conducting and musical education; toured Japan (1951) and Russia (1956); founded his own boarding school for musically gifted children at Stoke d'Abernon, Surrey (1963). He received an honorary knighthood from Queen Elizabeth II (1965); received honorary citizenship from Saanen, Switzerland (1970), assuming Swiss national allegiance while preserving American citizenship.

In 1971 Menuhin succeeded Barbirolli as president of Trinity College of Music in London (1971); celebrated the 50th anniversary of his 1st Leipzig appearance by performing the Brahms Concerto with Masur and the Gewandhaus Orch. (1981); granted honorary British citizenship, thereby formally became Sir Yehudi (1985); President Mitterand made him a Grand Officer of the Légion d'Honneur of France (1986); became member of the Order of Merit (1987).

Menuhin became deeply interested in art, politics, psychology, and philosophy; embracing the cause of oriental religions and yoga exercises; appeared on the BBC in London in the program *Yehudi Menuhin and His Guru* (1963). His political utterances antagonized many factions in many lands; enthusiastically received in Israel during his annual tours (1950–53), he aroused Israeli animosity by giving benefit concerts for Palestinian refugees. He embarrassed the Soviets at a Moscow music congress (1971) when, in understandable Russian, he appealed to them on behalf of human rights; he never visited the U.S.S.R. again. Meanwhile his artistry suffered somewhat, developing unsteadiness in intonation and technique; his conducting was no more than satisfactory; still, he never slackened his energetic activities, musical or nonmusical. He has publ. a collection of essays, *Theme and Variations* (London, 1972); with Curtis W. Davis, *The Music of Man* (London, 1980), based on the eponymous television series; and *Life Class* (London, 1986).

Mercer, Johnny (John Herndon), b. Savannah, Ga., Nov. 18, 1909; d. Los Angeles, June 25, 1976. He went to N.Y. as a youth, and attracted the attention of Paul Whiteman; subsequently wrote songs for him, Benny Goodman, and Bob Crosby. In 1940 he went to Hollywood, where he founded Capitol Records. His 1st success as a lyric writer was *Lazybones*, with music by Hoagy Carmichael; another great success was *Ac-cent-tchu-ate the Positive*, which he wrote for his psychoanalyst, as was *Moon River*, for the film *Breakfast at Tiffany's*. He wrote both words and music for *Something's Gotta Give* and other hits. He received 4 Academy Awards for his lyrics.

Mercer, Mabel, b. Burton upon Trent, Staffordshire, Feb. 3, 1900; d. Pittsfield, Mass., Apr. 20, 1984. Her father, an African-American, died before she was born; her mother was a white British vaudeville singer. She became a stage performer in her early adolescence; was a dancer in a music hall in London; after World War I she went to Paris, where she made a success as a nightclub singer; became a *vedette* at Bricktop's. In 1938 she went to America and settled in N.Y. She continued her career as a nightclub singer, but also gave regular recitals of popular songs. In 1983 she received the Medal of Freedom from

President Reagan. She was briefly married to jazz musician Kelsey Pharr.

merengue. Characteristic Afro-Cubanesque song dance of Venezuela, Haiti, and the Dominican Republic. It uses quatrain and refrain verse forms and is concerned with regional subject manner. Responsorial singing, polyrhythms, and 5/8 effects are layered over the basic 2/4 beat.

Merman, Ethel (born Ethel Agnes Zimmerman), b. N.Y., Jan. 16, 1908; d. there, Feb. 14, 1984. She took a commercial course in high school and held several jobs as a secretary while trying to satisfy her desire to be a singing actress. She never took vocal lessons but developed her booming powerful voice naturally. She obtained some bookings at Long Island night spots, and soon attracted the attention of Broadway managers. She auditioned for George Gershwin, who hired her to sing in his musical *Girl Crazy* in 1930; she brought the house down with the hit song *I Got Rhythm,* holding a high C for 16 bars in the coda against the orch. playing the melodic line.

Among the musicals in which Merman starred were Porter's *Anything Goes* (1934), Berlin's *Annie Get Your Gun* (1946) and *Call Me Madam* (1950), and Styne's *Gypsy* (1959). She also sang in 14 movie musicals, among them *There's No Business Like Show Business* and *It's a Mad, Mad, Mad, Mad World.* In 1970 she made her last appearance on Broadway; her last public appearance was in 1982, when she took part in a Carnegie Hall benefit concert. She had unbounded confidence in her stardom; she could also act in an uninhibited manner, which suited most of the roles she sang on Broadway.

Merman was arrogant and foul-mouthed in her dealings with agents, managers, directors, and even composers, but she knew how to put the music across; her ability to make the most of each song, and her sense of perfect intonation, made her the darling of Broadway. Indeed, she was dubbed the "queen of Broadway." "Broadway has been very good for me," she once said, "but I've been very good for Broadway." When the news of her death was announced, Broadway theaters observed a minute of silence to honor her memory.

Mersenne, Marin, b. La Soultière, near Oizéî, Sept. 8, 1588; d. Paris, Sept. 1, 1648. He studied at the college of Le Mans; then at the Jesuit school at La Fléche (from 1604); then at the College Royal and the Sorbonne in Paris from 1609. He began his novitiate at the Nigeon monastery, near Paris (1611), completing it at St. Pierre de Fublaines, near Meaux, where he took holy orders (1612); then served the Minim monastery at the Paris Place Royale, becoming a deacon and a priest. He taught philosophy (1615–17) and theology (1618) at the Nevers monastery, and then was made correcter there. In 1619 he returned to Paris as conventual of the order. He maintained a correspondence with the leading philosophers and scientists of his time.

Mersenne's writings provide source material of fundamental importance for the history of 17th-century music, particularly in the areas of national performance styles, pedagogy, notation, ornamentation, organology, and acoustics. His correspondence, ed. by C. de Waard and B. Rochot, began publication in Paris in 1932. His writings (all publ. in Paris) include: *Quaestiones celeberrimae in Genesim* (1623); *Traité de l'harmonie uni-*

verselle (1627); *Questions harmoniques* (1634); *Les préludes de l'harmonie universelle* (1634); *Harmonicorum libri, in quibus agitur de sonorum natura* (1635–36); *Harmonicorum instrumentorum libri IV* (1636).

mescolanza (It.). Potpourri.

messa (It.; Fr. *messe;* Ger. *Messe*). Mass.

messa da requiem (It.). Requiem.

messe des morts (Fr.). Requiem.

messa di voce (It.). Attack of a sustained vocal tone *pianissimo,* with a swell to *fortissimo,* and slow decrease to *pianissimo* again:

Messiaen, Olivier (Eugène Prosper Charles), b. Avignon, Dec. 10, 1908; d. Paris, Apr. 28, 1992. He learned piano; at age 8 composed a song, *La Dame de Shalott,* after Tennyson; at 11 entered the Paris Cons.; attended classes of J. Gallon, N. Gallon, M. Dupré, M. Emmanuel, and Dukas; specialized in organ, improvisation, and composition; carried 1st prizes in all these depts.

After graduation (1930) Messiaen became organist at the Trinity Church in Paris; taught at the École Normale de Musique and the Schola Cantorum (1936–39); with A. Jolivet, Y. Baudrier, and Daniel-Lesur, organized La Jeune France to promote modern French music. Serving in the French army at the outbreak of World War II (1939), he was taken prisoner; spent 2 years in a German prison camp in Görlitz, Silesia; while there composed the *Quatuor pour la fin du temps;* repatriated in 1941; resumed his post at the Trinity Church; prof. of harmony and analysis at the Paris Cons. (from 1948); taught at Tanglewood (1948) and Darmstadt (1950–53). Messiaen's pupils included many eager young composers, among them Boulez, Stockhausen, Xenakis, and Alexander Goehr. He was made a Grand Officier de la Légion d'Honneur; elected to the Inst. de France, the Bavarian Academy of the Fine Arts, the Accademia di Santa Cecilia in Rome, and the American Academy of Arts and Letters; married pianist Yvonne Loriod (1961).

Messiaen was one of the most original modern composers; made use of a wide range of resources, from Gregorian chant to Asian rhythmic theory; considered himself a "rhythmic mathematician." Mystical by nature and Roman Catholic by religion, he sought relationships between progressions of musical sounds and religious concepts; postulated an interdependence of modes, rhythms, and harmonic structures; seeking new musical resources, employed the Ondes Martenot and exotic percussion instruments; a synthesis of these disparate tonal elements finds fruition in the grandiose *Turangalîla-Symphonie.* One fascinating aspect of his musical vocabulary is the phonetic emulation of bird song in several works; to attain ornithological fidelity, he made a detailed study notating the rhythms and pitches of singing birds in many regions of the world; the town council of Parowan, Utah, where Messiaen wrote *Des canyons aux étoiles*, glorifying Utah's natural beauties, resolved to name a local mountain Mt. Messiaen (1978).

Messiaen's only opera, *St. Françfiois d'Assise*, was premiered to international acclaim at the Paris Opéra (1983); his oeuvre is dominated by orch'l works, solo keyboard music (organ and piano), and vocal works; discussed his theories of rhythm and mode in the classic *Technique de mon langage musical* (2 vols., 1944); publ. individual articles on musical ornithology and other subjects.

mestamente, mesto (It.). Plaintively, grievingly, pensively, sadly, with melancholy.

mesuré (Fr.). 1. Measured, moderate. 2. In exact time.

metabolé (Grk., modification). In rhetorics, a permutation of different words within a sentence; in music, the changed order of notes within a leitmotiv, as well as changes in tempo, rhythm, tonality, or interval structure within a musical period. In its ultimate development, metabole is a variation on a theme.

metamorphosis. Radical variations on a theme. The borderline between the classical type of variation and a metamorphosis necessarily lies in a penumbra. In a metamorphosis the key, rhythm, and intervallic structure of a theme may be changed, with only the basic line discernible. The idée fixe in Berlioz's *Sym. fantastique* undergoes a radical metamorphosis in the course of the work. Hindemith composed a *Symphonic Metamorphosis on Themes of Carl Maria von Weber.*

metamusic. The term simply means an art transcending traditional music, by analogy with Aristotle's metaphysics, which indicates the position of a chapter dealing with philosophy, directly after a discussion of physics in his *Organon*. Metaphysical visions have obsessed composers through the ages. They dreamed of a metamusical sym. in which all mankind would participate as a responsive reverberating assembly of congenial souls. Shortly before he died, Scriabin wrote an outline of a metamusical *Mysterium* that would embrace all senses in a pantheistic mystical action. Much more earthbound—but musically fascinating—was the project of a *Universe Sym.* by Ives, a work that he hoped to see performed by several orchs. stationed on hilltops overlooking a valley; recently there have been realizations of this project. The Russian mystical composer Nicolas Obouhov envisioned a metamusical union of all religions. He completed a major part of this work, which bore the title *Le Livre de vie*. He kept the manuscript on a self-made altar under an icon, in a corner of his small room in Paris. Since this was to be the book of his own life, body and soul, he made all annotations in the original scores in his own blood. He tried to interest American music lovers to have this work produced in a specially built temple in Hollywood, but died with his dream unfulfilled. Composers of the avant-garde have the means of producing metamusical scores with the aid of electronic and digital synthesizers. They may even plan to hitch their metamusical chariot if not to the stars then at least to the planets.

metaphor. Musical metaphorical expressions and similes: soft pedal, face the music, blow/toot one's own horn, play it by ear, 2nd fiddle, jazz it up, fiddle around/about, conduct oneself properly, play by the book, muted applause, get one's cue, etc.

Metastasio, Pietro (born Antonio Domenico Bonaventura Trapassi), b. Rome, Jan. 3, 1698; d. Vienna, Apr. 12, 1782. He was the son of a papal soldier named Trapassi, but in his professional career assumed the Greek trans. of the name, both Trapassi (or Trapassamento) and Metastasio meaning transition. He was a learned classicist; began to write plays as a young boy; studied music with Porpora; he achieved great fame in Italy as a playwright; in 1729 was appointed court poet in Vienna by Emperor Charles VI. He wrote 27 opera texts, which were set to music by Handel, Gluck, Mozart, Hasse, Porpora, Jommelli, and many other celebrated composers; some of them were set to music 60 or more times. His librettos were remarkable for their melodious verse, which naturally suggested musical associations; the libretto to the opera by Niccolo Conforto, *Nitteti* (1754; Madrid, 1756), was on the same subject as *Aida*, anticipating the latter by more than a century. For a catalogue, see ⇒A. Wotquenne, *Alphabetisches Verzeichnis der Stücke in Versen von Zeno, Metastasio und Goldoni* (Leipzig, 1905).

metempsychosis. Recurrence of a theme in an altered melorhythmic shape, suggesting the effect of *déjà entendu* without literal resemblance. The discovery of melorhythmic revenants may give a clue to the composer's inner impulses, particularly in serial compositions, where metempsychosis may appear subliminally, despite the composer's efforts to guard against unintentional thematic references; the concept may also extend beyond a single work or even composer. The idée fixe in the *Sym. fantastique* of Berlioz does not fall into this category because here it was deliberately implanted and reproduced in a clearly recognizable form.

meter (U.K., metre). 1. Placing of musical rhythms into beats, and then beats into symmetrical or asymmetrical, regular or irregular groupings. 2. In verse, the division into symmetrical lines. The meter of English hymns is classified into three types, according to the kind of feet used; these are the meters in general use:

Iambic meters: 4-line stanzas: *common meter* (C.M.), *long meter* (L.M.), *short meter* (S.M.); doubled, 8-line stanzas: *common meter double* (C.M.D.), *long meter double* (L.M.D.), *short meter double* (S.M.D.); 6-line stanzas: *common particular meter* (C.P.M.), *long particular meter* (L.P.M.) or *long meter six lines*, and *short particular meter* (S.P.M.). Individual iambic meters: *sevens and sixes; tens; hallelujah meter*.

Trochaic meters: Sixes, sixes and fives, sevens, eights and sevens, etc.

Dactylic meters: Elevens, elevens and tens, etc.

Hymnbooks use the system for cross-reference and allow putting a different text to a melody, or vice versa.

metric modulation. In the broadest sense, a change of time signature. In modern usage, proleptically applied by Charles Ives and systematically cultivated by Elliott Carter (who coined the term), a technique in which a rhythmic pattern is superimposed on another, heterometrically, and then supersedes it and becomes the basic meter. Usually, such time signatures are mutually prime, e.g., 4/4 and 3/8, and so have no common divisors.

Thus the change of the basic meter decisively alters the numerical content of the beat, but the minimal denominator (1/8 when 4/4 changes to 3/8; 1/16 when, e.g., 5/8 changes to 7/16, etc.) remains constant in duration.

metronome (Gr. *metro* + *nomos*, law of measurement). Mechanical device to beat time steadily, indicating the tempo of a composition; a graduated pendulum adjusted by sliding a small weight up or down its length. The most common design was invented by J. N. Maelzel (*c.* 1816), based on a prototype, developed a few years earlier by an obscure Amsterdam mechanic, that lacked the gradations. The initials MM (Maelzel metronome, or metronome marking) have for a century and three-quarters adorned most student editions of classical works, e.g., the marking MM q = 120 indicates that there are 120 quarter-notes per minute, or one tick per half-second.

Beethoven, who believed in the power of modern inventions (he patronized quacks to alleviate his deafness), seized upon Maelzel's metronome as the perfect instrument to perpetuate the correct tempos of his works; to most modern interpreters, the tempos he set for his syms. (mostly after the fact) are too fast. Tradition says that he either trusted Maelzel too well (unlikely after their contretemps over the ownership of *Wellington's Victory*); the machine he used was defective (most common interpretation); or else (perish the thought!) his own sense of time had betrayed him, for he assigned metronome marks that would accelerate the logical tempos beyond rational limits (e.g., in one case converting an Allegretto into Prestissimo). As a consequence, most Beethoven interpreters are apt to ignore his metronome marks; however, some conductors have begun to follow the markings which, with a smaller orch., certainly seem possible.

The metronome was long a familiar pyramidal accoutrement perched on the piano in the drawing room of every teacher and student; but with the advance of technology it was replaced by an unsightly cube emitting electronic bleeps regulated by a dial, or in a portable digital form. Some modern composers discovered that metronome ticks make legitimate percussive effects; Ligeti, for one, wrote a piece for 100 metronomes beating different tempi; visually, the spectacle is extraordinary.

Meyerbeer, Giacomo, (born Jakob Liebmann Beer), b. Vogelsdorf, near Berlin, Sept. 5, 1791; d. Paris, May 2, 1864. Scion of a prosperous Jewish family of merchants named Beer, he added Meyer to his surname, later changing his 1st name for professional purposes. He began piano studies with F. Lauska; received instruction from Clementi; made his public debut in Berlin at age 11; studied composition with Zelter (1805–07), then with B. A. Weber; composed his 1st stage work, the balle pantomime *Der Fischer und das Milchmädchen*, produced at the Berlin Royal Theater (1810); went to Darmstadt; studied with Abbé Vogler (to 1811), along with Carl Maria von Weber.

While under Vogler's tutelage Meyerbeer composed the oratorio *Gott und die Natur* (1811) and several unsuccessful operas; found success in Vienna as a pianist in private settings; proceeded to Paris, then to London (1815). He went to Italy (1816), turning his full attention to dramatic composition; his Italian operas—from *Romilda e Costanza* (1817) to *Il Crociato in Egitto* (1824)—brought him fame, even placing him on a par with Rossini in public esteem. The immense success of *Il Crociato in Egitto* led to successful stagings at London's King's Theatre and in Paris (both 1825), making him famous throughout Europe. He began a long and distinguished association with librettist Eugène Scribe in 1827, commencing with the opera *Robert le diable*, produced at the Paris Opéra with extraordinary success (1831).

Numerous honors were bestowed upon Meyerbeer; made a Chevalier of the Legion d'Honneur and a Prussian Hofkapellmeister (1832), senator of the Prussian Academy of Arts (1833), and member of the Inst. de France (1834). He began work on *Les Huguenots*, set to a libretto mainly by Scribe (1832); received a spectacular premiere at the Opéra (1836); later that year he and Scribe began preliminary work on *Le Prophéte*; commenced work on *L'Africaine*, using another Scribe libretto (1837); intended for the famous soprano Marie-Cornelie Falcon; after she lost her voice, he set the score aside; it was destined to occupy him on and off for the rest of his life. Wagner sought him out in Boulogne (1839); impressed with Wagner, he extended him financial assistance and gave him professional recommendations. However, Wagner became disenchanted with his prospects, berating Meyerbeer privately to the extent that he had to dissociate himself from the ungrateful Wagner, who retaliated by giving vent to his anti-Semitic rhetoric.

Meyerbeer resumed work on *Le Prophéte* (1838–40); delayed its premiere until he found capable singers; meanwhile, *Les Huguenots* was performed in Berlin (1842); formally installed as Prussian Generalmusikdirektor (1842–48); from the onset of his tenure, his position was tenuous because of disagreements with the Intendant of the Royal Opera, K. T. von Küstner; dismissed from his post, he retained his position as director of music for the royal court; composed works for state occasions, including the opera *Ein Feldlager in Schlesien* to reopen the opera house (1844) following a fire; the lead was sung by J. Lind, one of his discoveries; had some success after a Viennese performance as *Vielka* (1847), but never equaled the success of his Paris operas. He again took up *Le Prophéte* (1849); finding no tenor to meet its demands, he revised the score for celebrated soprano Pauline Viardot-Garcia as Fidès; with Gustave Roger as John of Leyden, it received a brilliant premiere at the Opéra (1849); he was made the 1st German Commandeur of the Legion d'Honneur. His next opera was *L'Étoile du nord*; its premiere at the Opéra-Comique (1854) proved an outstanding success, as did *Le Pardon de Ploërmel* (*Dinorah*; Opéra-Comique, 1859); composed an overture for the London World Exhibition, visiting England during the festivities (1862). *L'Africaine* had occupied him fitfully for years; despite Scribe's death (1861) and failing health, he felt compelled to complete it; in the spring of 1864 he put the finishing touches on the score; rehearsals began under his supervision; but he died on the night before the work was premiered. His body was taken to Berlin, where it was laid to rest in official ceremonies attended by the Prussian court, prominent figures in the arts, and the public at large; Fétis was subsequently charged with making the final preparations for the premiere of *L'Africaine*, given at the Paris Opéra to notable acclaim (1865).

Meyerbeer established himself as the leading composer of French grand opera with *Robert le diable*, a position he retained with distinction throughout his career; indeed it became one of the era's most celebrated musicians. Although the grandiose conceptions and stagings of his operas proved immediately appealing to audiences, they were more than mere theatrical spectacles; his vocal writing was truly effective, tailoring his operas to specific singers; a gift for original orchestration and penchant for instrumental experimentation enhanced his works' already high level; nevertheless, his stature was eclipsed after his death by Wagner; consequently his operas disappeared from the active repertoire; recent revivals and recordings have saved several of them from total oblivion in the modern era.

mezzo, -a (It.). 1. Half. Written alone, as an expression mark, it refers to either an *f* or a *p* that follows. *Mezzo forte (mf)*, half loud; *mezzo legato*, half legato; in piano playing, use a light touch with less pressure than in legato; *mezzo piano (mp)*, half soft (less loud than *mezzo forte*); *mezzo voce*, with half the power of the voice.

mezzo-soprano (*mezzo*; It.). Female voice between soprano and alto, partaking of the quality of both, and usually of small compass (a–f^2, or a–g^2), but very full toned in the medium register.

mezzo-soprano clef. See ⇒Intro., The clefs.

mezzo-staccato. Play in a manner between detaché and staccato; indicated by a slur over dotted notes.

Mi. 3rd Aretinian syllable; name of the note *E* in France, Italy, etc.

Miaskovsky, Nikolai (Yakovlevich), b. Novogeorgievsk, near Warsaw, Apr. 20, 1881; d. Moscow, Aug. 8, 1950. In 1895 he went to a military school in St. Petersburg, graduating in 1899. At that time he developed an interest in music and tried to compose; took lessons with Kazanli; his 1st influences were Chopin and Tchaikovsky. In 1902–03 he was in Moscow, where he studied harmony with Glière. Returning to St. Petersburg in 1903, he took lessons with Kryzhanovsky, from whom he acquired a taste for modernistic composition in the impressionist style. In 1906, at age 25, he entered the St. Petersburg Cons. as a pupil of Liadov and Rimsky-Korsakov, graduating in 1911.

At the outbreak of World War I (1914), Miaskovsky was called into active service in the Russian army; in 1916 he was removed to Reval to work on military fortifications; he remained in the army after the Bolshevik Revolution of 1917; in 1918 he became a functionary in the Maritime Headquarters in Moscow; was finally demobilized in 1921. In that year he became prof. of composition at the Moscow Cons., remaining at that post to the end of his life. A composer of extraordinary ability, a master of his craft, he wrote 27 syms., much chamber music, piano pieces, and songs; his music is marked by structural strength and emotional élan; he never embraced extreme forms of modernism, but adopted workable devices of tonal expansion short of polytonality, and freely modulating melody short of atonality. His style was cosmopolitan; only in a few works did he inject folkloric elements. S. Shlifstein ed. vols. of articles, letters, and reminiscences (1959) and of articles, notes, and reviews (1960).

Michelangeli, Arturo Benedetti, b. Brescia, Jan. 5, 1920; d. Lugano, June 12, 1995. He received his formal music training at the Venturi Inst. in Brescia, where he took violin lessons with Paolo Chiuieri; at age 10 he entered the Milan Cons. as a piano pupil of Giuseppe Anfossi, obtaining his diploma at age 13. In 1939 he won the Concours International de Piano in Geneva; later joined the piano faculty at the Martini Cons. in Bologna. He was a lieutenant in the Italian air force; after the German occupation and the formal surrender of Italy to the Allies, he was active in the country's anti-Fascist underground; he was taken prisoner by the Germans but escaped after a few months. Despite these peripeteias, he somehow managed to practice, acquiring a formidable virtuoso technique. However, he also developed idiosyncrasies, often canceling scheduled performances, and engaged in such distracting (and dangerous) activities as automobile racing, skiing, and mountain climbing. Both his virtuosity and his eccentricities contributed to his legend, and his rare concerts were invariably public successes.

Michelangeli toured the U.S. (1950, 1966); played in the Soviet Union in 1964; also gave concerts in South America. Eventually he returned to Italy and dedicated himself mainly to teaching; organized an International Academy for pianists in a rented palazzo in Brescia with a multitude of pianos in soundproof studios; among his pupils were Jörg Demus, Walter Klien, Maurizio Pollini, and Martha Argerich.

microtime. Term invented by Stockhausen (1955) to designate the number of vibrations corresponding to individual pitch, as contrasted with macrotime, which he applies to the duration of each rhythmic pulse.

microtonality. Division of the octave into intervals smaller than the half step, the smallest interval used within the 12-semitone equal-tempered scale. Intervals smaller than semitones were used in ancient Greece but abandoned in Western music with the systematization of ecclesiastical modes; when greater sensitivity toward tonal elements developed in modern times, composers and theorists began investigating the acoustical, coloristic, and affective aspects of microtonal intervals, particularly quarter tones.

Quarter tones were used by a few composers to suggest the Greek enharmonic mode; F. Halévy incorporated quarter tones into his symphonic poem *Prométhée enchaîné*; Berlioz described its 1st performance in *Revue et Gazette Musicale de Paris* (1849): "The employment of quarter tones in Halévy's work is episodic and very short, and produces a species of groaning sound in the strings, but its strangeness seems perfectly justified here and enhances considerably the wistful prosody of the music." Probably the earliest publ. composition with quarter tones was a set of 2 pieces for cello and piano by Richard H. Stein (1906), but its quarter-tone passages were used only as occasional ultrachromatic interludes.

Mexican composer Julian Carrillo (1875–1965) published his *Sonido 13* (13th Sound, 1895); the title referred to the tonal resources beyond the chromatic scale; later organized an international soc. for the exploration of microtonality under the grandiose name Cruzada Intercontinental Sonido 13; devised special instruments to perform microtonally; proposed a numerical notation of 96 divisions of the octave to designate precise intervallic values for half tones, quarter tones, 6th tones, 8th tones, and 16th tones. His best-known work was *Preludio a Cristóbal Colón* for soprano and ens (1925), an eerie, highly microchromatic piece.

English musician John Foulds (1880–1939) writes in his book *Music Today* (1934):

In the year 1898 I had tentatively experimented in a string quartet with smaller divisions than usual of the intervals of our scale, quarter tones. Having proved in performance their practicability and their capability of expressing certain psychological states in a manner incommunicable by any other means known to musicians, I definitely adopted them as an item in my composing technique. . . . Facetious friends may assert roundly that they have heard quarter tones all their lives, from the fiddle strings and larynxes of their mutual friends, who produced them without any difficulty.

One of the most systematic investigations of quarter-tone theory and practice was undertaken by Alois Hába (1893–1973) in Czechoslovakia. "As a boy of 12," he writes,

I played with my 3 older brothers in my father's village band. . . . When we played for village festivals it often happened that folk singers used intervals different from the tempered scale, and they were annoyed that we could not accompany them properly. This gave me the idea to practice at home playing nontempered scales on my violin in intervals smaller than a semitone. This was my 1st "conservatory" for music in quarter tones and in 6th notes.

Probably the 1st entirely self-consistent quarter-tone work was Hába's 2nd String Quartet (1920); he compiled the 1st manual for composing in quarter, 3rd, and 6th tones, publ. as *Neue Harmonielehre* (1928). Under his supervision the A. Foerster piano manufacturing company of Czechoslovakia constructed the 1st quarter-tone piano (patented 1924); a quarter-tone upright piano had been constructed by W. Möllendorf before Foerster's, but it was an ordinary piano tuned in quarter tones and not newly designed (it now sits in Munich's Deutsches Museum as a relic). At the same time Hába established the 1st seminars of microtonal music, at the Prague Cons; he and his students publ. a number of quarter-tone works, using his special notation for half a sharp, a sharp and a half, half a flat, and a flat and a half.

In 1917 the Russian composer Wyschnegradsky devised a system of quarter tones with a motto inspired by Heraclitus, "Everything flows"; later, while living in Paris, he formulated the concept of *pansonority*, meaning a discrete continuum of quarter tones (1924). To produce fairly accurate quarter tones he used 2 pianos or 2 pairs of pianos tuned a quarter tone apart; conducted in Paris an entire program of his works, including a sym. poem for 4 pianos, *Cosmos* (1945). In Russia quarter-tone music had a brief heyday in the early 1920s, cultivated by the Quarter-Tone Soc. of Leningrad, founded by Rimsky-Korsakov's grandson Georgi (1901–65). Ives, whose universal genius touched on many aspects of modern composition, contributed quarter-tone piano pieces; he claimed that his awareness of microtonal resources came from his father George's experiments in tuning band instruments a quarter tone apart.

Ernest Bloch inserts quarter tones in his 1st piano quintet for affective value in coloristic appoggiaturas (1923); Copland use quarter tone briefly to evoke the sound of Jewish music in *Vitebsk* for piano trio (1928). The 1st quarter-tone piano manufactured in the U.S. was patented by Hans Barth (1931); his instrument had 2 keyboards of 88 notes each; the upper keyboard was tuned at international pitch and had the usual 5 black keys and 7 white keys; the lower keyboard was tuned a quarter tone down, its keys blue and red. The author composed an overture for strings, trumpet, and percussion in the enharmonic (Phrygian) mode, based on an extant version of a melody from the orig. accompaniment to the tragedy *Orestes* (Athens, 400 B.C.); conducted this arrangement at the Hollywood Bowl (1933); to produce the 2 enharmonic quarter tones, the open strings of a section of violins, violas, and cellos were tuned a quarter tone up, the other string instruments preserving ordinary pitch. Enesco inserted a transitional passage in quarter tones in his opera *Oedipe* (Paris, 1936); the composer also wished to evoke the effect of the ancient enharmonic scale.

Other equal temperaments have been proposed. In his book *A Theory of Evolving Tonality* (N.Y., 1932), Joseph Yasser proposed a system of "supra-tonality," with accidentals designated by symbols for supra-sharp, supra-flat, and supra-natural of the synthetic scale; he believed that 19-equal temperament was the most logical step after the present system. Dutch physicist Adriaan Fokker (1887–1972) championed 31-equal temperament, building an organ for it; H. Badings and H. Kox composed with it. Krenek experimented with 13-equal temperament; Stockhausen used temperaments for which the interval to be logarithmically divided was something other than the octave; in *macrotonality*, there are fewer than 12 equally tempered notes per octave. James Paul White, a Boston musician, constructed a microtonal keyboard called the *harmon* (1883), using a notation in which deviations from regular pitch were indicated by plus and minus signs; theorized that 612 equal divisions of an octave would provide the most practical approximation to pure intonation (his instrument is preserved at the New England Conservatory of Music).

The return to ancient Greek theory inspired other composers to revive, not just approximate the just intonation system, where intervallic relationships were determined rationally, not logarithmically. Perhaps the most ambitious project in justly tuned music was that of the American composer Partch, who devised a symmetrical scale of 43 unequal intervals to the octave; to play his music, he adapted or constructed many special instruments, including a microtonal viola, reed organ, marimbas (including a diamond-shape instrument), plucked dulcimers, and modern versions of the Greek kithara. His work influenced many subsequent composers, instrument makers, and theorists.

In performances on instruments manipulated by humans, quarter tones and other microtonal divisions are often only approximations of true acoustical value; with the advent of electronic instruments and computer music, it is now possible to reproduce microtonal intervals with absolute precision. But despite the extraordinary new resources, many composers of the avant-garde have remained singularly indifferent to the thorough exploration of microtones; the Polish modernist Penderecki has used quarter tones in massive multioctave tone clusters, creating powerful sonorous complexes in icositetraphonic harmony, but intervallic and harmonic relationships involving microtones are not an issue; in other words, for most musicians, things have not changed since Halevy.

A curious disquisition on the future of microtonality as a logical extension of Chopin's sensitive use of chromatic harmony is contained in a pamphlet by Johanna Kinkel, *Acht Briefe an eine Freundin über Clavier-Unterricht* (Stuttgart, 1852):

As we wonder what it is that grips us and fills us with foreboding and delight in Chopin's music, we are apt to find a solution that might appear to many as pure fantasy, namely that Chopin's intention was to release upon us a cloud of quarter tones, which now appear only as phantom doppelgänger in the shadowy realm within the intervals produced by enharmonic change. . . . But since we have been accustomed to the long-established divisions into semitones, these new sounds will seem weird, suggesting a splash of discordant waves. Yet the children of the next generation, or the one after next, will suck in these strange sounds with mother's milk, and may find in them a more stimulating and doubly rich art. . . . And when this door is finally sprung open, we will stand a step nearer to the eternal domain of natural sounds. As it is we can only give a weak imitation of the Aeolian harp, of the rustle of the forest, of the magical ripple of the waters, unable to render them in their true impressions, because our so-called scales made up of whole tones and semitones are too coarse and have too many gaps, while Nature possesses not only quarter-tones and eighth-tones but an infinite scale of split atoms of sound!

middle C. The C (actually, c¹) in the middle of the piano keyboard:

MIDI (Music Instrument Digital Interface). Computer language used to connect computers, synthesizers, sequencers, and other electronic musical instruments so that they may "communicate with" (send data to) each other; also, the device carrying this information. This simplifies live electroacoustic processing and output. *MIDI compatible,* able to read MIDI data; *MIDI jack, MIDI port,* the connecting device on electronic musical instruments intended for the MIDI.

Midler, Bette, b. Paterson, N.J., Dec. 1, 1945. She studied drama in Honolulu, then settled in N.Y., where she sang in a variety of gay venues, including bathhouses and clubs, and on Broadway (*Fiddler on the Roof* and *Tommy*); subsequently engaged Barry Manilow as her music director and a backup trio known as the Harlettes and developed a raucous cabaret routine through which she generated a loyal following, becoming known as "The Divine Miss M"; her 1972 album of that name won a gold record; subsequent albums of note include *Bette Midler* (1973), *Songs for the New Depression* (1976), *Live at Last* (1977), and *Broken Blossom* (1977). She starred in the film *The Rose* (1979), based on the life of Janis Joplin, for which she received an Academy Award nomination; her soundtrack LP sold in the millions; other successful films were *Down and Out in Beverly Hills* (1986), *Ruthless People* (1986), *Outrageous Fortune* (1987), and *Beaches* (1989), for which she sang the Grammy Award–winning title song, *Wind beneath My Wings.* Her covers of songs by artists as varied as Bruce Springsteen, Kurt Weill, Hoagy Carmichael, and Tom Waits evidence her great stylistic diversity. Her comedic gifts—an integral aspect of her live performances—are captured on the recording *Mud Will Be Flung Tonight* (1985), in which she revitalizes the spicy, sometimes lewd anecdotes of the late Sophie Tucker. She authored the comic memoirs *A View from a Broad* (1980) and a children's book, *The Saga of Baby Divine* (1983).

Midori (born Goto Mi Dori), b. Osaka, Oct. 25, 1971. She studied with her mother, Setsu Goto; in 1981 she went to the U.S., where she took violin lessons with Dorothy DeLay at the Aspen Music School and continued her training with that mentor at N.Y.'s Juilliard School. She attracted the attention of Zubin Mehta when she was 10 years old; he subsequently engaged her as a soloist with the N.Y. Phil., with which she traveled on an extensive Asian tour that included Hong Kong, Singapore, Korea, Thailand, and her native Japan. There followed concerts with the Berlin Phil., the Boston Sym. Orch., the Chicago Sym. Orch., the Cleveland and Philadelphia Orchs., the Los Angeles Phil., the London Sym. Orch., and other European and American orchs., in programs that included not only classical concertos but also modern works, under the direction of such renowned conductors—besides Mehta—as Bernstein, Previn, Maazel, C. von Dohnányi, Leppard, and Barenboim. She also attracted the attention of popular television programs, and appeared as a guest of President and Mrs. Reagan at the White House during the NBC television special *Christmas in Washington* (1983). Most important, she won the admiration of orch. members for her remarkable artistic dependability. On one occasion, when a string broke on the concertmaster's violin during an orch. introduction, she demonstrated her sangfroid; since she had a few minutes to spare before her entrance as a soloist, she handed her own violin to the player and coolly changed the broken string in time to continue the performance without pause. In 1990 she made her N.Y. recital debut at Carnegie Hall.

Mi-fa. In medieval treatises, theoretical shorthand for a warning not to connect the mediant of one hexachord with the subdominant of a related hexachord without 1st making sure that imperfect intervals do not result from such a promiscuous crossbreeding. The original Latin prohibition reads, "Mi contra fa est diabolus in musica."

Mighty Five (Mighty Handful). In 1867, the critic Vladimir Stasov publ. an article in which he referred to a "mighty little handful of Russian musicians" (i.e., the "Mighty Five") who pursued the ideal of national art. The expression was picked up derisively by some journalists, but it was taken on with defiance by Mussorgsky and his comrades-in-arms Balakirev, Borodin, Cui, and Rimsky-Korsakov.

migratory tonics. When tonalities are in a state of constant flux, the laws of probability will still lead to the accidental formation of *tonal centers*, notes that occur more frequently than others, much in the line of the well-known paradox that if only 3 dozen individuals are assembled at a party, the odds are even that 2 of them will have the same day and month for a birthday. Such statistically established keynotes in an otherwise free modulatory environment may be called *migratory tonics*, a term particularly suitable for works in which tonality is not renounced unequivocally.

Miki, Minoru, b. Tokushima, Mar. 16, 1930. He studied with Ifukube and Ikenouchi at the National Univ. of Fine Arts and Music in Tokyo (1951–55); was a founder of the Nihon Ongaku Shudan (Pro Musica Nipponia; 1964), an ensemble dedicated to performing new music for traditional Japanese instruments; later served as its artistic director. He lectured at the Tokyo College of Music; was founder-director of Utayomi-za (1986), a musical-opera theater. His works include operas; syms.; Western and Japanese orch. music; concertos for koto, marimba, Japanese classical trio, and percussion; solo and chamber works, most involving Japanese instruments; and vocal and choral works.

Milanov, Zinka (Kunc), b. Zagreb, May 17, 1906; d. N.Y., May 30, 1989. She studied at the Zagreb Academy of Music, then with Milka Ternina, Maria Kostrencic, and Fernando Carpi; made her debut as Leonora in *Il Trovatore* in Ljubljana (1927); subsequently was principal soprano of the Zagreb Opera (1928–35), where she sang in over 300 performances in Croatian. After appearing at Prague's German Theater (1936), she was invited by Toscanini to sing in his performance of the Verdi Requiem at the Salzburg Festival (1937). She then made her Metropolitan Opera debut in N.Y. as Leonora (1937), and was one of the outstanding members on its roster (1937–41; 1942–47; 1950–66); gave her farewell performance there as Maddalena in *Andrea Chénier* (1966). In addition to appearing in San Francisco and Chicago, she also sang at Buenos Aires's Teatro Colón (1940–42), Milan's La Scala (1950), and London's Covent Garden (1966–67). Blessed with a voice of translucent beauty, she became celebrated for her outstanding performances of roles in operas by Verdi and Puccini. Her brother was the pianist and composer Božidar Kunc (b. Zagreb, July 18, 1903; d. Detroit, Apr. 1, 1964).

Milhaud, Darius, b. Aix-en-Provence, Sept. 4, 1892; d. Geneva, June 22, 1974. With a piano in the house, he improvised melodies as a child; began taking violin lessons; entered the Paris Cons. (1909); studied with, among others, Gédalge (counterpoint), Widor (composition and fugue), and d'Indy (conducting); played violin in the student orch. under Dukas; received prizes in violin, counterpoint, fugue, and composition. While still a student he wrote bold, modernistic music; associated with Satie, Cocteau, and Claudel; when the latter was appointed French minister to Brazil, he engaged Milhaud as his secretary; sailed for Rio de Janeiro (1917); returned to Paris (via the West Indies and N.Y.) after the 1918 armistice.

Milhaud's name became better-known after a newspaper article by Henri Collet in *Comoedia* (1920), grouping him with 5 other French "modernist" composers (Auric, Durey, Honegger, Poulenc, and Tailleferre) under the sobriquet "Les 6," even though the association was stylistically incidental. He visited the U.S. (1922); lectured at Harvard, Princeton, and Columbia Univs.; appeared as pianist and composer in his own works; traveled in Italy, Germany, Austria, and Russia (1925); returning to France, devoted himself mainly to composition and teaching. At the outbreak of World War II he was in Aix-en-Provence; went to the U.S. (1940); taught at Mills College in Oakland, Calif. He returned to France (1947); appointed prof. at the Paris Cons.; continued to visit the U.S. as conductor and teacher almost annually, despite severe arthritis, which compelled him to conduct while seated; retained his post at Mills College (to 1971); settled in Geneva.

Exceptionally prolific from his student days, Milhaud wrote a great number of works in every genre; introduced a type of music drama, "opera à la minute"; experimented with new stage techniques, incorporating cinematic interludes; successfully revived the Greek type of tragedy with vocal accompaniment. He demonstrated his contrapuntal skill in composition as his string quartets no. 14 and no. 15, which can be played simultaneously as a string octet (1949). He was the 1st to exploit polytonality in a consistent and deliberate manner; applied the exotic rhythms of Latin America and the West Indies in many of his works; of these, the *Saudades do Brasil, Scaramouche,* and *Le Boeuf sur le toit* are particularly popular. In some works he drew upon the resources of early jazz; his ballet *La Création du monde* (1923), portraying the Creation in terms of Negro cosmology, constitutes the earliest sym. use of blues and jazz, anticipating Gershwin in this respect.

Despite this variety of means and versatility of forms, Milhaud succeeded in establishing a distinct and identifiable style; melodies are nostalgically lyrical or vivaciously rhythmical, according to mood; the instrumental writing, of great complexity and difficulty, lies entirely within the capacities of modern virtuosos; he arranged many of his works in several versions; for an extremely prolific and facile composer, his music is remarkably consistent in quality. His works include operas, ballets, incidental music, orch'l works (12 syms. for large orch., 5 for small orch., concertos, etc.), numerous song cycles (often setting Claudel's poetry), religious and secular works, chamber music (18 string quartets, etc.), works for piano. His essays were 1st collected in *Études* (1926).

militarmente (It.). In military (march) style. *Alla militare,* in the style of a march.

military band. Band, military.

Miller, (Alton) Glenn, b. Clarinda, Iowa, Mar. 1, 1904; d. Dec. 15, 1944. He spent his formative years in Fort Morgan, Colo., where he began his musical training; played with the local Boyd Senter Orch. (1921) and took courses at the Univ. of Colorado; after performing with Ben Pollack's band on the West Coast (1924–28), he followed Pollack to N.Y. and then became active as a freelance musician; helped to found an orch. for Ray Noble (1934), and subsequently studied orchestration with Joseph Schillinger; began experimenting with special effects, combining clarinets with saxophones in the same register.

Miller organized his 1st band in 1937, but it failed to find an audience and dissolved in 1938; that same year he organized another band, which caught on only in 1939 through its radio broadcasts and recordings. It subsequently became one of the most successful aggregations of the day, producing such popular recordings as *Moonlight Serenade* (1939), *In the Mood* (1939), *Tuxedo Junction* (1940), *Chattanooga Choo Choo* (1941), and *A String of Pearls* (1941); it also appeared in the films *Sun Valley Serenade* (1941) and *Orchestra Wives* (1942). Miller joined the U.S. Army Air Force as a captain in 1942 and put together a band for entertaining the troops; it was based in England from 1944. A film, *The Glenn Miller Story*, was produced in 1953.

millimetrization. Term introduced by Villa-Lobos to describe the transfer of mathematical curves or outlines of photographs onto graph paper, precise to a millimeter. His best-known piece arranged according to millimetrization is *The New York Skyline* (1940).

Millöcker, Carl, b. Vienna, Apr. 29, 1842; d. Baden, near Vienna, Dec. 31, 1899. His father was a jeweler, and Millöcker was destined for that trade but showed irrepressible musical inclinations and learned music as a child; played the flute in a theater orch. at 16; later took courses at the Cons. of the Gesellschaft der Musikfreunde in Vienna. Upon the recommendation of Franz von Suppé, he received a post as theater conductor in Graz (1864). In 1866 he returned to Vienna; from 1869 to 1883 he was 2nd conductor of the Theater an der Wien. As a composer, Millöcker possessed a natural gift for melodious music; although his popularity was never as great as that of Johann Strauss, Jr., or Lehár, his operettas, e.g., *Der Bettelstudent* (1882), captured the spirit of Viennese life.

Milnes, Sherrill (Eustace), b. Downers Grove, Ill., Jan. 10, 1935. He learned to play piano and violin at home, then played tuba in a school band; after a period as a medical student at North Central College in Naperville, Ill.; he turned to music; subsequently studied voice with Andrew White at Drake Univ. in Des Moines and with Hermanus Baer at Northwestern Univ. He sang in choral performances under Margaret Hillis in Chicago; then was a member of the chorus at the Santa Fe Opera, where he received his 1st opportunity to sing minor operatic roles. In 1960 he joined Boris Goldovsky's Boston-based opera company and toured widely with it. He met Rosa Ponselle in Baltimore in 1961, and she coached him in several roles; he 1st appeared with the Baltimore Civic Opera as Gerard in *Andrea Chénier* in 1961.

Milnes made his European debut as Figaro in *Il Barbiere di Siviglia* at the Teatro Nuovo in Milan (1964); later that year he made his 1st appearance at the N.Y. City Opera, singing the role of Valentin in *Faust*. His Metropolitan Opera debut in N.Y. followed (1965), in the same role. He rose to a stellar position at the Metropolitan, being acclaimed for both vocal and dramatic abilities; also sang with other opera houses in the U.S. and Europe. His notable roles include Don Giovanni, Escamillo, the Count di Luna, Tonio, Iago, Barnaba, Rigoletto, and Scarpia.

milonga. South American dance song, popular in the southern part of the continent. Its characteristics include a polyrhythm of 2/4 against 6/8, improvised vocal duels, lighthearted texts, standard verse structures, and refrains in parallel 3rds.

Milstein, Nathan (Mironovich), b. Odessa, Dec. 31, 1903. His mother was an amateur violinist who gave him his 1st lessons; he began to study with Piotr Stoliarsky in Odessa (to 1914); went to St. Petersburg, entering L. Auer's at the Cons. (1915–17); began his concert career with his sister as accompanist (1919). In Kiev he met Horowitz; began giving duo recitals (1921); later joined by Gregor Piatigorsky and organized a trio.

Milstein was finally able to leave Russia (1925); went to Berlin, then Brussels, where he met Ysaÿe, who encouraged him; gave recitals in Paris; proceeded to South America; made his American debut with the Philadelphia Orch. conducted by Stokowski (1929); became an American citizen (1942). He celebrated the 50th anniversary of his American debut by giving solo recitals and appearing as soloist with American orchs. (1979). As an avocation he began painting and drawing, by which he achieved a certain self-satisfaction; engaged in teaching, holding master classes at the Juilliard School of Music in N.Y. and in Zurich. He was renowned for his technical virtuosity and musical integrity; composed violin pieces, including *Paganiniana* (1954); prepared cadenzas for the Beethoven and Brahms violin concertos.

mimesis (Grk., imitation). In 18th-century rhetorical theory, the imitation of a phrase in one voice by a similar phrase in another; mimesis is now obsolete in musical nomenclature.

mimodrama. Dramatic or musical spectacle in which the performers convey the dramatic action by gestures and choreography, without speaking; same as pantomime (1).

minaccioso (It.). In a menacing or threatening manner.

Mingus, Charles, b. Nogales, Ariz., Apr. 22, 1922; d. Cuernavaca, Mexico, Jan. 5, 1979. He was reared in Los Angeles; during his high school years he studied double bass with Red Callender and Herman Rheinschagen and composition with Lloyd Reese; after working with Bigard (1942), Armstrong (1943), and Hampton (1947–48), he led his own groups as "Baron Mingus" before attracting notice as a member of Norvo's trio (1950–51); then settled in N.Y., where he worked with Billy Taylor, Ellington, Getz, Tatum, and Powell. He was head of his own recording company, Debut Records (1952–55); also became active as a composer; worked with various musicians in small combos and eventually developed a close association with Dolphy.

A highly explosive individual, Mingus became known as the "angry man of jazz" for his opposition to the white commercial taint of his art form. After his 2nd recording company (Mingus label, 1964–65) failed, and his financial situation became desperate, he retired from the public scene (1966–69). He resumed his career and was awarded a Guggenheim fellowship (1971) and subsequently devoted much time to composing; also led his own groups until being stricken with amyotrophic lateral sclerosis, which sidelined him in 1978. Mingus was a master instrumentalist and a versatile composer, producing both conventionally notated works and dictated pieces. In his unique series of works *Fables and Meditations* he achieved a style that effectively erased the lines between jazz improvisation and notated composition.

Mingus's influence is likely incalculable. His most important work, the 2-hour *Epitaph* for 30 Instruments, discovered by his wife several years after his death, received its premiere performance posthumously in N.Y. (1989). Among his best recordings are *The Black Lady and the Sinner*, *The Town Hall Concert*, *Goodbye Pork Pie Hat*, *Jazz Composers Workshop*, *Mingus Dynasty*, *3 or 4 Shades of Blue*, *Reincarnation of a Lovebird*, *Pithecanthropus Erectus*, *Nostalgia in Times Square*, *Mingus Moves*, *Meditations on Integration*, and *Mingus in Wonderland*.

miniature score. Orch'l score reproduced in a small size so that it can be easily used for study purposes. Full scores of symphonic works, chamber music, and even complete operas began publication in Germany in the 19th century. In pocket size, they were convenient to carry around for study purposes, or for reading while listening to the actual music played. The most active music publisher of miniature scores was Eulenberg of Leipzig.

minim (U.K.). Half note. *Minim rest*, a half rest.

minima. In medieval mensural music, a note value, indicated by a black diamond with a stem; depending on the context, 2 or 3 minimas equal 1 semibreve.

minimalism. 1. Neologism for a school of composition, influenced by Cage and contemporaneous painting of the 1950s, in which a pointillistic musical texture prevails, with a generous use of silence and the evolution of graphic and verbal scores. 2. From the 1960s, a conceptual term denoting works based on the repetition and gradual alteration of short rhythmic and/or melodic figures; also referred to as *process music*.

Music history evolved for millennia in a manner parallel to animals species, from simple cellules of unaccompanied voice to grandiose edifices of sounds built on voices with a variety of manufactured instruments, ultimately including electronically produced tones. Then, like an enormous dinosaur whose very bulk made it impossible to find sufficient food to survive, sym. and operatic forms developed in the 19th century could no longer sustain their acoustical size. Echoing the ideas of Satie and other "primitivists," Stravinsky declared his belief that music had reached its maximum of possible dimensions (1918), urging composers to write in limited forms. The direction from Lilliputian to Brobdingnagian works was to be reversed, initiating musical neoclassicism; but this was not enough; composers had to cope with the growing presence of dissonant counterpoint and concomitant loss of harmony and tonality.

A quarter century later, a group of composers (Cage, Feldman, E. Brown, Wolff) were inspired by different styles of abstract expressionist painting (from Pollock to Rothko) and Eastern religions to create graphic or verbal notation for pieces of varying degrees of indeterminacy and chance. This profound contact between two contemporaneous media helped to launch several decades of experiments; the Happening deconstructed theatrical performance and influenced later drama in its musical and nonmusical forms; chance and indeterminacy reached deeply into the European avant-garde, particularly through the mobile art of Alexander Calder; other media entered the mix, and the 1st school of minimalism was gradually absorbed by the hectic 1960s.

Other composers from the 1960s on stripped away and reinvented musical texture. Triadic harmony, if not progression, was restored; modulations were reduced to sudden or subtle shifts; a change of a single note in an arpeggio signaled the formation of a new inversion, which could remain there for a number of bars. Dissonances occurred rarely; a consonant *quietus* became the rule. This new style was labeled as *minimalism*, a musical synecdoche, *a pars pro toto*. Parallel to the purification of tonal masses there was a gradual abandonment of rhythmic complexity; repetitions of established patterns became the norm; other influences came from the Pacific Rim, India, and Indonesia, with their hypnotic drone effects and repetitive interlocking musical patterns familiar to Western musical culture since the late 19th century.

The 4 American pioneers of the 2nd minimalist school were L.M. Young, Riley, Reich, and Glass. Young revived the Pythagorean modes, using retuned pianos and playing with the dampers lifted throughout. In Riley's 1964 piece *In C* for any instruments, musicians play a progressive set of phrases in indeterminate manner in C major until the last few measures, which includes a passing entry of an F sharp. Reich reinforced his technique by studying African drumming, utilizing shifting phase and other repetitive techniques in works for various ensembles. Glass enriched the uniformity of repetitive music by setting surrealistically imagined plays of sometimes inordinate length and heterogeneous content, such as *Einstein on the Beach* (collab. with Robert Wilson, 1976). Less extreme is the minimalist idiom of John Adams, whose music embraces such contrasting inspirations as *Harmonium* for Chorus and Orch. (1981) and the sensational opera *Nixon in China* (1987). Gradually minimalism found partisans in Europe, including the Dutch L. Andriessen and the German W. Zimmermann.

Minkus, Léon (Aloisius Ludwig), b. Vienna, Mar. 23, 1826; d. there, Dec. 7, 1917. He went to Russia in his youth and was engaged by Prince Yusupov as concertmaster of his serf orch. in St. Petersburg (1853–56). From 1862 to 1872 he was concertmaster of the Bolshoi Theater in Moscow. In 1869 the Bolshoi Theater produced his ballet *Don Quixote* to the choreography of the famous Russian ballet master Petipa; its success was extraordinary, and its appeal to the Russian audiences was so durable that the work retained its place in the repertoire of Russian ballet companies for more than a century, showing no signs of diminishing popularity. Equally popular was his ballet *La Bayadère*, produced by Petipa in St. Petersburg in 1877; another successful ballet was his *La Fiametta, or The Triumph of Love*, originally produced in Paris in 1864.

From 1872 to 1885 Minkus held the post of court composer of ballet music for the Imperial theaters in St. Petersburg; he remained in Russia until 1891, then returned to Vienna, where he lived in semiretirement until his death at age 91. The ballets of Minkus never took root outside Russia, but their cursive melodies and bland rhythmic formulas suit old-fashioned Russian choreography to the airiest *entrechat*.

Minnelli, Liza (May), b. Los Angeles, Mar. 12, 1946. She was the daughter of the legendary songstress Judy Garland by her 2nd husband, the film director Vincente Minnelli. She dropped out of high school to devote herself exclusively to singing; made her professional debut as a singer in the 1963 off-Broadway revival of *Best Foot Forward* (1941). In 1965 she appeared in the Broadway musical *Flora, the Red Menace*, for which she won a Tony Award. She established herself as a film actress in *The Sterile Cuckoo* (1969); also starred in the highly acclaimed film

Cabaret (1972), for which she won an Academy Award. She further won Tony Awards for her 1-woman show *Liza* (1974) and for her appearance in the Broadway musical *The Act* (1977); she appeared opposite Dudley Moore in the romantic film comedy *Arthur* (1981) and its sequel, *Arthur on the Rocks* (1988). After starring in the musical *The Rink* (1983–84), she underwent treatment for drug and alcohol dependency in 1984. Following rehabilitation, she made extensive tours in the U.S. and abroad. In 1997 she briefly took over the lead from Julie Andrews in *Victor, Victoria*.

Minnesinger (Ger.). German aristocratic poet-musicians of the 12th to 14th centuries, predecessors to the Meistersinger. Minnesingers traveled through central Europe singing lyric songs in royal German courts, ducal castles, and villages. Like their Frankish counterparts, the trouvères and troubadours, they were mostly of noble birth and regarded their profession as an expression of knightly valor and idealistic dedication to the real or imaginary ladies of their hearts (*Minne* is Old German for "love"). With the end of the Crusades, and with a certain stabilization of the German states, the role of the Minnesingers declined, and the cultivation of lyric or heroic songs gradually was transferred to the town guilds and local craftsmen represented by them (*Meistersinger*).

minor (from Lat., small; It. *minore*; Fr. *mineur*; Ger. *moll*). 1. Intervals within a natural minor scale between the tonic (1st degree) and the 2nd, 3rd, 6th, and 7th scale degrees. 2. Type of scale (e.g., A-minor scale), key (A minor), or triad (A-minor chord, with a minor 3rd and perfect 5th above the root). In each case the 3rd degree of the scale forms an interval of a minor 3rd with the root.

minstrel. 1. Medieval professional musicians who sang or declaimed poems, often of their own composition, to a simple instrumental accompaniment. They were employed by royalty and feudal lords in Europe. They served as entertainers, players upon the lute or the flute, jesters, and sometimes as participants in domestic and political intrigues. The term *minstrel* 1st appeared in the 14th century and was derived from the French appellation *ménéstrier* (minister); with the decay of feudal society, the profession of minstrels disappeared. 2. In the U.S., a performer in Negro minstrelsy. Toward the middle of the 19th century, white minstrel groups were organized to perform in blackface in a repertoire of genuine Negro songs and newly minted numbers known as "Ethiopian songs." Foster was the greatest composer of such songs, even though he never lived in the South and was not personally familiar with the conditions of Negro life or slavery. The American minstrel show became standardized about 1830 with the introduction of a theatrical type of performance called Jim Crow.

minuet (Fr. *menuet*; It. *minuetto*; Ger. *Menuett*). Most popular court dance in triple time danced by couples, distinguished by the stately grace of its choreography and the symmetry of its musical structure. The standard minuet consisted of 3 sections, of which the 1st and 3rd were identical; the middle section, set in the dominant, subdominant, or relative key, was called the trio because it was written usually for 3 instruments, whereas the minuet proper was usually arranged for a fuller ensemble.

It is generally surmised that the minuet derived from a provincial French dance tune, but as a mature form it was introduced at the court of Louis XIV. Lully, his court musician, wrote a number of minuets for royal balls; it is said that the King himself often ventured to dance to Lully's music, although his mature corpulent figure was ill-adapted for choreographic exercise. The vogue of minuet dancing spread to all the courts of Europe; it was tremendously popular in Russia, Spain, and Italy, but less so in England or Germany. Eventually the minuet became an integral part of the Baroque instrumental suite, and in Classic sonatas and syms. In the 19th century the minuet yielded its place in sonatas and syms. to the more whirlwind mood of the scherzo, which usually conserved the 3/4 time signature as well as the characteristic interpolation of the trio.

miracle plays. Sacred dramas, often with music, which were popular in England in the Middle Ages; the stories were usually on biblical subjects or parables; later examples of this genre were called *moralities*.

Miranda, Carmen (born Maria do Carmo Miranda da Cunha), b. Marco de Canaveses, near Lisbon, Feb. 9, 1909; d. Beverly Hills, Calif., Aug. 5, 1955. She spent her formative years in Rio de Janeiro; after performing throughout South America she made her 1st appearance on Broadway in 1939 in the revue *The Streets of Paris*; she was dubbed the "Brazilian Bombshell." She went on to gain an extensive following via many film appearances, recordings, nightclub engagements, and television appearances. She is particularly remembered for her spiky high-heeled shoes and fantastic headdresses made of fruit; in the movie musical *The Gang's All Here* (1943), with lavish choreography by Busby Berkeley, she comically careened her way through the number *The Lady in the Tutti Frutti Hat*.

mirliton (Fr.). Kazoo.

mirror canon. Canon cancrizans.

Miserere. Opening Latin word of the 50th Psalm, in the Roman Catholic (Vulgate) numbering; thereby, musical settings of the Psalm. The imploration "Have mercy" is a part of the Holy Week Service known as Tenebrae (darkness). There is a credible story that Mozart as a small boy attended the performance of a Miserere by Gregorio Allegri (1582–1652) in the Vatican, memorized the entire setting for 9 voices, and wrote it down shortly afterward. Allegri's Miserere was an exclusive property of the Papal choir, and Mozart's feat of memory must have caused considerable discomfiture, but the piece was eventually publ. and became famous.

missa (Lat.). Mass. *Missa brevis*, short Mass; *Missa cantata*, sung (High) Mass; *Missa lecta*, spoken (Low) Mass; *Missa pro defun[c]tis*, Requiem; *Missa solemnis*, High Mass.

misterioso (It.). Mysteriously; suggestive of hidden meaning.

misurato (It.). With the measure; in exact time.

mit (Ger.). With. For phrases beginning with this preposition, see noun or adjective following.

Mitchell, Joni (born Roberta Joan Anderson), b. McLeod, near Lethbridge, Alberta, Nov. 7, 1943. She was reared in Saskatoon and took piano lessons in childhood; later learned to play guitar; attended the Alberta College of Art in Calgary for a year and sang in a local coffeehouse; then performed in Toronto, where she met and married the folksinger Chuck Mitchell; she kept his last name after their divorce. She wrote the hit song *Both Sides Now* (1968), made famous in Judy Collins's recording; Mitchell included it in her album *Clouds* (1969), which captured a Grammy Award for best folk recording in 1970. Her album *Ladies of the Canyon* (1970) attained gold status; the album *Court and Spark* (1974) also proved highly popular. In her interpretations, she closely followed the folk-song style, with an admixture of jazzy syncopation and unusual guitar tunings. For a time she collaborated with Mingus; after his death (1979), she released *Mingus*, including the moving song *God Must Be a Boogie Man*; other interesting albums include *Hejira* (1976), *Dog Eat Dog* (1986), *Chalk Mark in a Rain Storm* (1988), Night Ride Home (1991), and *Turbulent Indigo* (1994).

Mitropoulos, Dimitri, b. Athens, Mar. 1, 1896; d. Milan, Nov. 2, 1960. He studied piano with Wassenhoven and harmony with A. Marsick at the Odeon Cons. in Athens; wrote an opera after Maeterlinck, *Soeur Beatrice* (1918), performed at the Odeon Cons. (1919); in 1920, after graduation from the Cons., he went to Brussels, where he studied composition with Paul Gilson; in 1921 he went to Berlin, where he took piano lessons with Busoni at the Hochschule für Musik (until 1924); concurrently was *répétiteur* at the Berlin State Opera.

Mitropoulus became a conductor of the Odeon Cons. orch. in Athens (1924); was its co-conductor (1927–29) and principal conductor (from 1929); was also prof. of composition there (from 1930). In 1930 he was invited to conduct a concert of the Berlin Phil.; when the soloist Egon Petri became suddenly indisposed, he substituted for him as soloist in Prokofiev's Piano Concerto no. 3, conducting from the keyboard (1930). He played the same concerto in Paris in 1932 as a pianist-conductor, and later in the U.S. His Paris debut as a conductor (1932) obtained a spontaneous success; he conducted the most difficult works from memory, which was a novelty at the time; also led rehearsals without a score.

Mitropoulus made his American debut with the Boston Sym. Orch. (1936), with immediate acclaim; that same year he was engaged as music director of the Minneapolis Sym. Orch.; there he frequently performed modern music, including works by Schoenberg, Berg, and other representatives of the atonal school; the opposition that naturally arose was not sufficient to offset his hold on the public as a conductor of great emotional power. He resigned from the Minneapolis Sym. Orch. in 1949 to accept the post of conductor of the N.Y. Phil.; shared the podium with Stokowski for a few weeks, and in 1950 became music director. In 1956 Leonard Bernstein was engaged as his associate conductor, suceeding him as music director (1958). With the N.Y. Phil., Mitropoulos continued his policy of bringing out important works by European and American modernists; he also programmed modern operas (*Elektra, Wozzeck*) in concert form.

A musician of astounding technical ability, Mitropoulos became very successful with the general public as well as with the musical vanguard whose cause he so boldly espoused. While his time was engaged mainly in the U.S., he continued to appear as guest conductor in Europe; he also appeared on numerous occasions as conductor at the Metropolitan Opera in N.Y. (debut conducting *Salome*, 1954) and at various European opera theaters. He became an American citizen in 1946. As a composer he was one of the earliest among Greek composers to write in a distinctly modern idiom.

Mittelsatz (Ger.). Middle section of a movement or piece.

mixed cadence. Form of authentic cadence in which chords other than the tonic and dominant are involved, e.g., V–VI–II^6–V^7–I.

mixed chorus. Chorus comprised of both male and female voices, traditionally with all 4 basic voice types represented (soprano, alto, tenor, bass), with or without divisions.

mixed media. Works in which musical, dramatic, verbal, literary, etc. elements are conjoined in a single composition, usually in novel ways. Musicians of the avant-garde are increasingly laboring toward the coordination and unification of modern musical productions with those of other arts—painting, sculpture, phonograph recording, theater, radio, television, electronics. The practice represents in fact a return to the ancient ideal of unity of liberal arts, with music occupying the honorable position as *ancilla artis*. This tendency has generated a number of novel developments of catalytic artistic powers.

Mixolydian mode. Mode corresponding to the progression from G up to G on the white keys of the piano (G–A–B–C–D–E–F–G). Although the word is Greek, the Mixolydian mode is not identical with the ancient Greek mode of the same name. To the modern ear it sounds like a major scale with a lowered 7th degree, thus devoid of a leading tone; it therefore lends itself naturally to attractive plagal cadences. Bartók among others made effective use of the peculiarities of this mode; it is strongly associated with Irish-British traditional music and its American counterparts.

mixture. Compound auxiliary flue stop with from 3 to 6 ranks of pipes, sounding as many harmonics of any note played. The effect produced corresponds to ripieno (replenished sound), resulting in what is known as full organ.

M.M. 1. Trademark of Maelzel's metronome, invented 1816. 2. More commonly, an abbrev. for "metronome marking."

mobile (from Lat. *movēre*, to move; It.). 1. Readily responsive to emotion or impulse. 2. In modern sculpture, a delicately balanced construction of metal or wood, easily swayed by gentle flow of air. Modern composers have adopted this term to describe a similarly flexible melorhythmic form characterized by intervallic equilibrium, often maintained through serial rearrangement. See also ⇒mobile form.

mobile form. Term used, with obvious debt to the sculptor Alexander Calder, to describe works composed in such a way that sections may be arranged variously in time without disturbing structural integrity; also called *open form*; Stockhausen and Roman Haubenstock-Ramati (1919–93) were among the exponents of mobile form.

modal harmony. Harmonic possibilities derived from church, exotic, mixed, or invented modes, apart from tonal harmony, which concerns the common major and minor keys. Modal harmony may or may not operate on the tonic-dominant principle; some modes are free from tonal resolution altogether.

modality. 20th-century term applied to a revival of diatonic modes other than major and minor. A systematic avoidance of authentic cadences with a raised 7th degree in minor keys is the most important manifestation of modern modality. A favored cadence in modern modal music is the progression of the subdominant major triad to the tonic minor in the Dorian mode, thus mixing both major and minor scale elements. Modulations into other keys are accomplished by direct landing on the intended tonic triad from any convenient point of the scale. While flatted-7th chords are freely used in modal works, the dominant-7th chord, with its mandatory resolution into the tonic, is studiously avoided.

Chromatic harmony is incompatible with the spirit of modality, but a chromatic melody may be harmonized in spacious triads, which preserves the feeling of modality. A corollary of modality is the use of harmonic progressions in triads rather than their inversions, often giving an impression of exotic origin. Debussy used triadic harmonies in modal writing to allude to Greek melos; Ravel used modality to conjure up the aura of times long past. The masters of the Russian national school, particularly Mussorgsky, resorted to modal progressions to evoke the spirit of the Russian soul. Most curious is the application of broad modalities used by Stravinsky in *Le Sacre du printemps*, where, despite the prevalence of acrid dissonant harmonies, the inner triadic structures are always in evidence. While most modal compositions follow the basic rules of tonal connections in contrary motion, some modern composers adopt the practice of moving triadic formations in parallel lines. Vaughan Williams, Prokofiev, Villa-Lobos, Casella, Copland, and others project the sense of modality by shifting triadic masses in parallel sequences. In many modal writings, pedal points supply a sonorous foundation, indicating the eventual tonic of the work.

mode. 1. Generic term applied to ancient Greek melodic progressions and to church scales established in the Middle Ages and codified in the system of Gregorian chant. The intervals of the Greek modes were counted downward, and those of the medieval modes were counted upward, so the intervallic contents were different between the Greek and the church systems. However, the church modes retained the Greek names of the modes. The 4 authentic and 4 plagal modes were orig. called *tonoi*; the old terminology is translated into Latin: *Primus tonus, Secundus tonus*, etc., corresponding to *Protus authentic, Protus plagal*, etc. In the 16th century Glareanus recognized 4 more modes—Aeolian, Hypoaeolian, Ionian, and Hypoionian—for a total of 12. If played on the white keys of the piano, the church modes are: from C to C, Ionian; from D to D, Dorian; from E to E, Phrygian; from F to F, Lydian; from G to G, Mixolydian; from A to A, Aeolian; and from B to B, Locrian (theoretical). Modes continued to underlie all Western music through the 17th century, gradually giving way to major and minor tonality. 2. The distinction between a major key (mode) and minor key (mode). 3. Any scalar pattern of intervals, either indigenous to a culture (Indian, Japanese, Indonesian, etc.) or invented. 4. A system of rhythmic notation used in the 13th century (mensural notation).

moderato (It.; Fr. *modéré*). At a moderate tempo or rate of speed. *Allegro moderato*, moderately fast.

moderazione, con (It.). Moderate in tempo or emotion.

modern music. American colloquialism for contemporary dance music and popular songs. In the card catalogue of the British Museum, works written after 1800 are included in a section marked "Modern Music." Medieval MSS dealing with musical theory often open with the phrase "Brevitate gaudent moderni." The moderns that relished brevity were, in the opinion of the anonymous authors of these treatises, the adherents of ars nova. In present classical usage *modern music* refers to that written since 1900. Variants may include 20th-century Music, New Music, Music of Our Time, Music of Today, and Contemporary Music.

modernism. Musical composition as it developed early in the 20th century, in which modulation from one key to another reached complete freedom of diatonic and chromatic progressions, and dissonances acquired equal rights with traditional chords; several keys could be combined in a technique called polytonality, and the melody was allowed to veer away from its tonal foundations, becoming sometimes completely atonal. This sensibility of progress and "the new" that emerged (*c*. 1910) was expressed in the paintings of Picasso and Kandinsky, the novels of Joyce and Proust, and the music of Schoenberg and Stravinsky; later supplanted by *postmodernism*, which refers to a relaxation of concern with matters of time, history, and progression.

moderno, -a (It.). Modern. *Alla moderna*, in modern style.

modes of limited transposition. Modes which contain repeating intervallic units and thus can only be transposed a limited number of times before the identical set is repeated; discussed in Messiaen's *Technique de mon langage musical* (2 vols., Paris, 1944).

modinha. Brazilian and Portuguese art song of the 18th and 19th centuries. Sentimental in tone, the modinha was usually accompanied by guitar; its originally simple qualities changed with the influence of operatic aria, leading to elaborate melodies and some ornamentation. In its latter Brazilian stage, the modinha became truly lyrical and folk song–like.

modo narrativo, in (*narrante*; It., in a narrating mode). Sing or speak with distinct declamation.

modulate. To pass from one key or mode into another.

modulation. Transition from one key or mode to another within a single composition. The idea of a modulation dates back to the system of hexachords of Guido d'Arezzo, in which a modulation from one hexachord to another can be achieved by renaming a syllabic degree in the initial hexachord by a syllabic degree of the terminal hexachord. For example, if La in the hexachord Ut–Re–Mi–Fa–Sol–La is renamed Mi, then a modulation is effected into the hexachord Fa–Sol–La, etc., in which La is the 3rd note. In polyphonic writing of the Middle Ages and the Renaissance, modulation was effected by a similar "Guidonian" substitution of a degree of the scale. Such modulations produce a strange impression on the modern ear, leading some enthusiastic scholiasts to proclaim the "modernity" of medieval composers. The cardinal principle operating in such modulations has nothing to do with the rules of tonal harmony formulated over a century later; rather, such "sudden" modulations were justified by the acoustical primacy of the major chord, so that if a melody wandered into an alien field guarded by a sharp or flat, the harmony would adjust itself to the new situation, forming a major triad in the fundamental position; a remnant of this practice is found in the Picardy 3rd, the major cadence of a piece in a minor key.

As modality fell into desuetude, and major and minor keys became established as dual counterparts of tonality, the rules of modulation were drawn according to the principle of kinship of keys having the same number of sharps or flats in the key signature, or of neighboring keys having 1 more or 1 less sharp or flat relative to the initial key. This relationship was incorporated in a scientific-looking circle of 5ths in the image of the face of a clock in which the sharps move clockwise and flats move counterclockwise; any composer desiring to modulate from one key to another not adjacent in the circle of 5ths had to make his way through the intermediate stopovers, step by step. But what if a modulation traveling to a key 4 or 5 sharps away from the starting point is desired? Each minor key has a major dominant, enabling the modulating composer to jump 4 stops in the sharp direction, clockwise (e.g, shifting from A minor to E major).

The circle of 5ths is not the only itinerary for modulation. There is a powerful chromatic resource in *enharmonic modulation*, in which neo-Guidonian substitution is effected by enharmonic change; e.g. taking the dominant-7th chord in the key of C: G–B–D–F; reinterpreting F enharmonically as E sharp, identical in sound but not in meaning; it becomes the top note of an augmented 6th chord whose bottom note is G (the former dominant). The E sharp rises irresistibly to F sharp; the G sinks to the lower F sharp; the resulting F-sharp octave is the dominant locus of a B-minor tonic.

In *chromatic modulation*, chords can be protean, e.g., the diminished-7th chord which, depending on its spelling, can modulate immediately to any of the 24 major or minor keys. Romantic operas, even by respectable composers, are full of such crawling chords; but even nonoperatic composers take advantage of this facility. In the coda of his B-flat minor Scherzo for Piano (op. 20), Chopin uses a series of ornamented diminished-7th chords with nerve-tingling appoggiaturas in the middle voices that finally resolve into the long-anticipated key of D-flat major; Mendelssohn portrays a storm with diminished-7ths in his *Fingal's Cave* overture. Other types: *diatonic modulation*, effected by using diatonic intervals; *final modulation*, returning finally to the tonic key; *passing, transient, transitory modulation*, in which a key is barely established before modulating further.

modulation convergente (Fr.). Modulation that eventually leads to (converges on) the initial (home, tonic) key. *Modulation divergente*, one that diverges from (wanders away from) the initial (home, tonic) key.

modus (Lat., mode). In mensural notation, the ratio of note values between the maxima and longa, and between the longa and brevis. The former ratio is called *modus major*, the latter, *modus minor*. Like other mensural note values, these ratios can either be *perfect* (a perfection) containing 3 units of the lesser note values, or *imperfect* (an imperfection) containing only 2 units of the lesser note values. Thus *modus major imperfectus* is a measure containing 2 *longas; modus minor imperfectus* contains 2 *breves*.

möglich (Ger.). Possible. *So rasch wie möglich*, as fast as possible.

moll (Ger.). Minor. *Molltonart*, minor key.

molto, -a (It.). Very, much. *Molto adagio*, very slowly; *molto allegro*, very fast; *con molta passione*, with great passion; *di molto* or *molto molto*, exceedingly, extremely; *crescendo molto molto*, growing very much louder.

moment form. Short-lived structural concept developed by Stockhausen describing works which, in theory, rely less for their auditory coherence on relationships between movements than on the experience of "the moment."

moment musical (Fr.). Romantic character piece, usually for piano. Schubert wrote 6 pieces of this title, publ. under the incorrect French title *Moments musicals*.

Mompou, Federico, b. Barcelona, Apr. 16, 1893; d. there, June 30, 1987. After preliminary studies at the Barcelona Cons., he went to Paris, where he studied piano with Philipp and composition with Rousseau. He lived the rest of his life in his native city, except for a return to France (1921–41); composed *Souvenirs de l'exposition* in Paris (1937). His music is inspired by Spanish and Catalan melos, but its harmonic and instrumental treatment is entirely modern in a post-impressionist sense. He wrote mostly for piano: *Impressions intimes* (1911–14); *Scènes d'enfants* (1915); *Suburbis* (1916–17); *3 pessebres* (1918); *Cants magics* (1919); *Festes Llunyanes* (1920); *Charmes* (1921); 3 variations (1921); *Dialogues* (1923); a series, *Canción y Danza* (1918–62); 10 preludes (1927–51); *Paisajes* (1942, 1947, 1960); *Música callada* (Silent Music; 4 albums, 1959–67); *Suite compostelana* for guitar (1963); choral works and songs.

money and music. Musicians do not manufacture material goods and therefore, like poets, must subsist parasitically. In times of catastrophic social disturbances—wars, famine, plagues—music stops. In times of prosperity, musicians attach themselves to the dominant powers, to the church, to the royal court, to educational institutions (which themselves must depend on the powers of the state), or to wealthy merchants. In the church, and particularly in the most organized historical church of Rome, musicians performed the essential duties of writing for sacred services. When great royal courts emerged in the Middle Ages, kings, emperors, dukes, and other secular potentates employed musicians to lend decorum to their mundane preoccupations. With the emergence of industrial civilization, money kings took pleasure in sponsoring musical activities. Singers found easy employment in the church; instrumentalists were less in demand; composers had the least opportunity, unless they acted also as performers, conductors of military bands, or instructors in universities. In public demand of their services, a similar order exists; popular singers can make a fortune, but artists specializing in classical music rarely attract large audiences.

A curious inverse ratio exists in relation to a singer's musical education or professional excellence and commercial success. Some of the most successful jazz and rock 'n' roll performers never learned to read music. Even the most celebrated opera tenor, Caruso, sang by ear, even though he was an international star. Instrumentalists come 2nd in popular acclaim; among them, pianists enjoy the greatest opportunity of monetary success, followed by violinists and cellists. Sym. conductors may be described as instrumentalists of the baton. Sometimes they have rivaled performing artists in public education, but since sym. music is food for the sophisticate and the connoisseur, and since they cannot pursue their profession with a maximum of proficiency without an orch. of great excellence, they may remain philosophers of music, even when they become idols of the audience. Infinitely more successful financially are the leaders of dance bands, from the "waltz king," Johann Strauss, Jr., and the "march king," John Philip Sousa, to the leaders of some big bands.

In terms of both popular success and financial reward, composers find themselves on the lowest rung of the ladder. Some composers of semiclassical music and popular songs have achieved a certain prosperity, but authors of large sym. works or chamber music have little hope of attaining even a moderate income. Mozart wrote pathetic letters to a friendly banker asking for petty loans; one of these letters sold 200 years later to an autograph collector for a sum a thousand times as large as the loan Mozart requested. Beethoven flaunted his alleged poverty with proud assertion of his status as a "brain owner." Tchaikovsky had a rich admirer in the person of Nadezhda von Meck, who gave him an annual grant. Wagner was put in a debtor's prison in Paris when he was already a well-known composer.

The situation of composers improved considerably in the 20th century; in Europe, by the creation of government grants, prizes, and awards to composers of serious music; in America, by the formation of ASCAP and BMI, which protect their royalty interests; furthermore, "prestige" payments are often made by publishers to composers whose works are not profitable commercially. Yet Bartók complained bitterly during his last years of life in America that he could not even find piano pupils to provide pocket money; a friendly Hungarian émigré arranged for him to make a recording of his piano music; sales were so poor that his friend doctored his royalty account to make it appear more respectable. (A picture postcard with Bartók's handwriting sold after his death for $165.) Schoenberg applied to the Guggenheim Foundation for a grant to enable him to complete his opera Moses und Aron, but he was turned down. (A few pages of his orchestration of a Viennese operetta done as a young man was priced at several thousand dollars at an auction sale after his death.) Scriabin suffered desperate financial difficulties after the death of his Maecenas, the publisher Belaiev (1904); at times he lacked the money to buy a postage stamp.

monism. Philosophical doctrine postulating the existence of a basic element that is the prime constituent of all material objects. In music, monism denotes an analogous primacy of a concept or a function. The dodecaphonic series is a monistic factor which determines the development of an entire work. A set of variations is intrinsically monistic since it is derived from a primary source, but it is pluralistic if the variations are regarded as mutually independent entities.

Moniuszko, Stanislaw, b. Ubiel, Minsk province, Russia, May 5, 1819; d. Warsaw, June 4, 1872. In 1827 his family went to Warsaw, where he studied piano and music with August Freyer; continued his training with Dominick Stefanowica in Minsk and with Rungenhagen in Berlin (1837). He went to Vilnius in 1840; there he served as organist at St. John's; he gained attention as a composer when he publ. vol. I of his 2piewnik domowy (Songbook for Home Use; 1843); gained the support of various Polish figures in the arts, and also won the admiration of Glinka, Dargomizhsky, and Cui in Russia. In 1848 a concert performance of the 2-act version of his opera Halka was given for the 1st time in Vilnius; after he expanded it to 4 acts, it was staged in Warsaw (1858), scoring a great success. He then settled in Warsaw (1859), becoming conductor of opera at the Grand Theater; he continued to compose for the stage, and also taught at the Music Inst. (from 1864).

Moniuszko holds a revered place in Polish music history as the outstanding composer of opera in his era; he also excelled as a composer of songs. His other works include operas and operettas, incidental music to 14 plays, ballets, orch'l and chamber music, religious and secular choral works; publ. Pamiętnik do nauki harmonii (Textbook on Harmony; 1871).

Monk, Meredith (Jane), b. N.Y., Nov. 20, 1942. She studied eurythmics, the educational method that relates music to movement, from an early age; was educated at Sarah Lawrence College (B.A., 1964), then was a pupil in voice of Vicki Starr, John Devers, and Jeanette Lovetri, in composition of Ruth Lloyd, Richard Averee, and Glenn Mack, and in piano of Gershon Konikow. She pursued an active career as a singer, filmmaker, director, choreographer, recording artist, and composer. In 1968 she organized the House in N.Y., a company devoted to interdisciplinary approaches to the arts; in 1978 she founded there her own vocal chamber ensemble, with which she toured widely in the U.S. and abroad. In 1972 and 1982 she held Guggenheim fellowships; received various ASCAP awards and many commissions. Her powerful soprano vocalizations employ a wide range of ethnic and avant-garde influences.

As one of the 1st and most natural of performance artists, Monk developed a flexible, imaginative theatrical style influenced by dream narrative and physical movement. Among her works are Candy Bullets and Moon for Voice, Electric Organ, Electric Bass, and Drums (1967; in collaboration with D. Preston); Juice, theater cantata for 85 Voices, Jew's Harp, and 2 Violins (1969); Key, album of invisible theater for Voice, Electric Organ, Vocal Quartet, Percussion, and Jew's Harp (1970–71); Vessel, opera epic for 75 Voices, Electric Organ, Dulcimer, and Accordion (1971); Education of the Girlchild, opera for 6 Voices, Electric Organ, and Piano (1972–73); Our Lady of Late for Voice and Wine Glass (1972–73); Quarry, opera for 38 Voices, 2 Pump Organs, 2 Soprano Recorders, and Tape (1976); Dolmen Music for 6 Voices, Cello, and Percussion (1979); Turtle Dreams (Waltz) for 4 Voices and 2 Electric Organs (1980–81); Specimen Days for 14 Voices, Piano, and 2 Electric Organs (1981); Panda Chant I (4 Voices) and II (8 Voices, 1984); Book of Days for 25 Voices, Synthesizer, and Piano (1985);

Window in 7's (for Nurit) for Piano (1986); *Do You Be* for 10 Voices, 2 Pianos, Synthesizer, Violin, and Bagpipes (1987); *Book of Days*, film score for 10 Voices, Cello, Shawm, Synthesizer, Hammered Dulcimer, Bagpipes, and Hurdy-gurdy (1988); *Fayum Music* for Voice, Hammered Dulcimer, and Double Ocarina (1988); *Atlas*, opera (1991).

Monk, Thelonious (Sphere), b. Rocky Mount, N.C., Oct. 10, 1917; d. Englewood, N.J., Feb. 17, 1982. He spent most of his professional life in Harlem, where he played in nightclubs; gradually surfaced as a practitioner of bebop, set in angular rhythms within asymmetrical bar sequences. His eccentric behavior was signalized by his external appearance; he wore skullcaps and dark sunglasses; time and again he would rise from the keyboard and perform a rhythmic dance. Although not educated in the formal sense, he experimented with discordant harmonies, searching for new combinations of sounds. Paradoxically, he elevated his seeming limitations to a weirdly cogent modern idiom, so that jazz critics argued over whether he was simply inept or prophetically innovative. Monk's own tunes, on the other hand, were exquisitely sophisticated and memorable; he gave them impressionistic titles, such as *Crepuscule with Nellie* (Nellie was his wife) and *Epistrophy*, or else ethnically suggestive ones, as in *Rhythm-a-ning*. He performed in contexts ranging from solo to big band.

A profoundly introspective neurotic who abused narcotics in his younger days, Monk would drop out for years, withdrawing into his inner self; during 1 period (1973–76) stayed with an admirer, the Baroness Pannonica de Koenigswarter, in her N.J. apartment, visited daily by his wife; his last public appearance, at the 1976 Newport Jazz Festival, seemed a faint shadow of his former exuberance. His song *Criss-Cross* (1951) was used by Schuller for his *Variations on a Theme of Thelonious Monk*. Other important Monk tunes include *'Round Midnight*, *Misterioso*, *Ruby My Dear*, *Blue Monk*, *Pannonica*, *Well You Needn't*, *Little Rootie Tootie*, *Brilliant Corners*, *Jackie-ing*, *Bemsha Swing*, *I Mean You*, *Hackensack*, and *Straight, No Chaser*.

Monkees, The (Guitar/vocal: Michael Nesmith, b. Houston, Tex., Dec. 30, 1942; vocal/tambourine: {David} Davy Jones, b. Manchester, England, Dec. 30, 1945; bass/vocal: Peter Tork, b. Peter Torkelson, Washington, D.C., Feb. 13, 1944; drums/vocal: {Michael} Micky Dolenz, b. Tarzana, Calif., Mar. 8, 1945). Known as the "Pre-Fab Four," the Monkees were created to cash in on the popularity of the Beatles and their films for the TV/teenage market. They achieved great popularity from 1966, when their TV show premiered, until 1969, when the group disintegrated. Auditioned for their looks as much as their musical talents (or lack thereof), they scored hits primarily with songs written by G. Goffin & C. King, N. Diamond, and, particularly, T. Boyce and B. Hart; among them were *Last Train to Clarksville*, *Valleri*, *D. W. Washburn*, *Daydream Believer*, and *Pleasant Valley Sunday*. Aspiring to transcend their teenybopper roots, the group made the impressionistic film *Head* (1968) with Bob Rafaelson and Jack Nicholson; it perplexed their younger fans while failing to win over the sophisticates; now considered a cult classic; that same year, the group toured the country to prove that they could play their own instruments; to open, they enlisted

a still little-known Jimi Hendrix; their teenage fans were so dismayed by him that he was quickly dropped from the tour.

After the group disbanded, Nesmith formed a country-rock band known as the 1st National Band; enjoyed some success as a songwriter (his *Different Drum* had been a hit for Linda Ronstandt and the Stone Ponys in 1967); in the 1970s became involved in the nascent field of music video, developing a prototype for what would become MTV, and producing films. In 1986, with rereleased Monkee recordings selling briskly, Jones, Tork, and Dolenz reunited for a comeback album and tour; Nesmith resisted the temptation to join the mass cash-in until the mid-'90s, when he too took to the road with his old ape-mates.

monochord. Ancient chordophone. As the name indicates, it had a single string, which was stretched over a soundbox, and a shifting bridge that allowed the string to be adjusted to different pitches. It was and is used to test acoustic theories.

monodrama. Stage work in which only one actor, speaker, or singer acts, recites, or sings. The classic example of a staged monodrama is Schoenberg's symbol-strewn *Erwartung*; in his *Die glückliche Hand*, the central character sings and mimes the story while a chorus comments in Sprechstimme. Other, more realistic monodramas include Poulenc's *La Voix Humaine* and Pasatieri's *Before Breakfast*. Russian composer Vladimir Rebikov evolved a type of monodrama called "psychodrama," in which an actor recites his state of mind to musical accompaniment.

monody (from Lat., single song). Usually, the recitativelike basso continuo song style of early-17th-century Italy.

monophonic. 1. Texture of unaccompanied melody. 2. Instrument capable of producing but 1 tone at a time.

monothematic. Composition with a single subject.

monothematism and polythematism. In the 19th and 20th centuries, composers turned to monothematism, in which a single subject might govern an entire composition. Monothematism, an extension of *organicism* ("growing" a piece from 1 melody or even motif) and related to thematic transformation, is basic to the structure of a theme with variations; but if variations depart too widely from the theme, the result may be polythematic. Rigid monothematism carries an intrinsic danger of monotony; on the other hand, extreme polythematism courts the opposite danger of discontinuity. In monothematism, the single theme must recur a sufficient number of times to produce an impression of uniformity; in polythematic constructions, similarities among successive themes must be avoided, at least overtly.

monotone. 1. Single unaccompanied and unvaried tone. 2. Recitation (intoning, chanting) on such a tone.

Monroe, Bill (William Smith), b. near Rosine, Ky., Sept. 13, 1911; d. Springfield, Tenn., Sept. 9, 1996. He studied with his uncle, Pendleton Vandiver, a fiddler; played fiddle in a band led by his brothers Birch and Charlie; Charlie and he performed as the Monroe Brothers for a few years. In 1938 Bill, now a mandolinist, organized the Blue Grass Boys; gained fame through appearances on the *Grand Ole Opry* radio program in Nashville. His innovations in string-band music led to the development of the bluegrass style, notable for its syncopated rhythm and complex but invariably tonal harmonies. His most famous lineup (1946–49) included Lester Flatt and Earl Scruggs, who introduced bluegrass-style banjo (fingerpicking melodies using 3 fingers equipped with metallic picks).

Monroe composed many bluegrass standards, including the waltz *Blue Moon of Kentucky* (covered by Elvis Presley and changed into rollicking rock 'n' roll, 1956), *Uncle Pen*, in honor of his fiddling relative, many other songs, and dozens of classic instrumentals, including *Rawhide*, *Wheelhoss*, and *Scotland*. Many notable bluegrass and newgrass musicians played in his band, including Stringbean (Dave Akeman), Jimmie Martin, Sonny Osborne, Vassar Clements, Buddy Spicher, Kenny Baker, Ralph Rinzler, Richard Greene, Bill Keith, and Peter Rowan. In 1970 he was elected a member of the Country Music Hall of Fame.

Montemezzi, Italo, b. Vigasio, near Verona, Aug. 4, 1875; d. there, May 15, 1952. He was a pupil of Saladino and Ferroni at the Milan Cons., and graduated in 1900; his graduation piece, conducted by Toscanini, was *Cantico dei Cantici*, for Chorus and Orch. He then devoted himself almost exclusively to opera. Montemezzi's chief accomplishment was the maintenance of the best traditions of Italian dramatic music, without striving for realism or overelaboration of technical means. His masterpiece in this genre was the opera *L'amore dei tre re* (Milan, 1913), which became a standard work in the repertoire of opera houses all over the world.

Monteux, Pierre, b. Paris, Apr. 4, 1875; d. Hancock, Maine, July 1, 1964. He studied at the Paris Cons. with Berthelier (violin), Lavignac (harmony), and Lenepveu (composition); received 1st prize for violin (1896); was a violist in the Colonne Orch., and later chorus master there; played viola in the orch. of the Opéra-Comique. He then organized his own series, the Concerts Berlioz, at the Casino de Paris (1911); that same year became conductor for Diaghilev's Ballets Russes; his performances of modern ballet scores established him as one of the finest technicians of the baton; led the world premieres of Stravinsky's *Petrouchka*, *Le Sacre du printemps*, and *Le Rossignol*; Ravel's *Daphnis et Chloé*; and Debussy's *Jeux*; conducted at the Paris Opéra (1913–14); founded the Soc. des Concerts Populaires in Paris (1914); guest conducted in London, Berlin, Vienna, Budapest, etc.

In 1916–17 Monteux toured the U.S. with the Ballets Russes; conducted the Civic Orch. Soc., N.Y. (1917) and at the Metropolitan Opera there (1917–19). He was engaged as conductor of the Boston Sym. Orch. (1919–24); associate conductor of the Concertgebouw Orch. in Amsterdam (1924–34); principal conductor of the newly founded Orch. Symphonique de Paris (1929–38); conductor of the reorganized San Francisco Sym. Orch. (1936–52); became a naturalized U.S. citizen (1942). He guest-conducted the Boston Sym. Orch. (from 1951); accompanied it on its 1st European tour (1952; also 1956); returned to the Metropolitan Opera roster (1953–56). In 1961 (at age 86) he became principal conductor of the London Sym. Orch., retaining this post until his death.

As an interpreter, Monteux endeavored to bring out the inherent essence of the music, without imposing his own artistic personality; unemotional and restrained in his podium manner, he nonetheless succeeded in producing brilliant performances in an extensive repertoire ranging from the classics to the 20th century. In 1927 he married Doris Hodgkins (1895–1984), an American singer who cofounded the Domaine School for Conductors and Orchestral Players in Hancock, Maine (1941), of which Monteux was director; after his death, she established the Pierre Monteux Memorial Foundation.

Monteverdi (Monteverde), Claudio (Giovanni Antonio), b. Cremona (baptized), May 15, 1567; d. Venice, Nov. 29, 1643. He was the son of a chemist who practiced medicine as a barber-surgeon; studied singing and theory with M. A. Ingegneri, maestro di cappella at Cremona's cathedral; learned to play the organ. He acquired the mastery of composition early on; was only 15 when a collection of his 3-part motets was publ. (Venice), followed by sacred madrigals (1583) and canzonettas (1584). In 1589 he visited Milan and the court of the Duke of Mantua; obtained a court position in the service of Vincenzo I Gonzaga as "suonatore" on the viol (viola da gamba) and violin (viola da braccio, 1592); met the Flemish composer Giaches de Wert, whose contrapuntal art greatly influenced him. He publ. a 3rd book of madrigals, marked by a considerable extension of harmonic dissonance (1592); accompanied the retinue of the Duke of Mantua on forays against the Turks in Austria and Hungary (1595), and with him to Flanders (1599); married Claudia de Cattaneis, a court singer (1599); they had 2 sons; a daughter died in infancy. He was appointed maestro di cappella in Mantua following Pallavicino's death (1601); publication of 2 more books of madrigals (1603, 1605) further confirmed his mastery of the genre.

Experienced as a composer for the stage, Monteverdi now turned to the new dramma per musica; *L'Orfeo*, his 1st opera, was given before the Accademia degli Invaghiti in Mantua (1607); this *pastorale* effectively moved beyond the Florentine recitative-dominated drama, using a more flexible means of expression; the score is an amalgam of monody with basso continuo, madrigal, and instrumental music of diverse kinds. He gained membership to the Accademia degli Animori of Cremona, but suffered a grievous loss in the death of his beloved wife (both 1607). Greatly depressed, he nevertheless accepted a commission to compose an opera celebrating the marriage of the Mantuan heir apparent, Francesco Gonzaga, to Margaret of Savoy; the result was *L'Arianna*, to a text by Rinuccini, presented in Mantua (1608); the complete MS is lost, but the extant versions of its *Lamento d'Arianna* testify to his genius in expressing human emotion through moving melodies.

Monteverdi prepared a set of 5-part madrigals and others with basso continuo, adding "uno dialogo" for 7 voices (Venice, 1614); wrote 2 more works for weddings, one of which, the French-style ballet *Il ballo delle ingrate*, survives. His patron, Duke Vincenzo, died (1612); his successor, Francesco, did not retain his services; however, he was fortunate in being called to Venice to occupy the vacant post of maestro di cappella at San Marco (1613); this position proved to be the most auspicious of his career; retained it until his death. He composed mostly church music, but did not neglect the secular madrigal; once more accepted commissions from Mantua's Duke Ferdinando, e.g., his ballet *Tirsi e Clori* (1616), which he included in his 7th book of madrigals, *Concerto*, significant for its bold harmonic, textural, and dramatic innovations (1619); his dramatic cantata *Il combattimento di Tancredi e Clorinda*, after Tasso's *Gerusalemme liberata*, was performed at a Venetian nobleman's home (1624); the score features his new agitated *stile concitato* in the strings. Great inconvenience was caused to him when his son Massimiliano, a medical student, was arrested by the Inquisition for consulting books on the Index Librorum Prohibitorum (1627); he was acquitted. Monteverdi composed the opera *Proserpina rapita* for Venice (1630), of which only 1 trio survives, yet another irreparable loss to music lovers and historians.

Following the plague of 1630–31 Monteverdi wrote a thanksgiving Mass for San Marco (the Gloria is extant); he took holy orders; his *Scherzi musicali* for 1 and 2 voices was publ. (both 1632), followed by *Madrigali guerrieri et amorosi* (book 8), a retrospective collection covering some 30 years (1638). When the 1st public opera houses were opened in Venice (1637), he found a new creative outlet in his twilight years; the operas *Il ritorno d'Ulisse in patria* (1640), *Le nozze d'Enea con Lavinia* (1641; lost), and *L'incoronazione di Poppea* (1642) were all given there. (Research by Alan Curtis suggests that the latter opera owes its surviving form to Francesco Sacrati.); both surviving operas, steeped in recitative, are comparably modern in plot. After his death, he was accorded burial in the church of the Frari in Venice; a copy of a commemorative plaque erected in his honor remains in the church to this day.

Monteverdi's place in the history of music is of great magnitude. He established the foundations of modern opera conceived as drama interwoven with music; enlarged the orch. for greater dynamic range, selecting and skillfully combining the instruments accompanying the voices; one of the earliest, if not the 1st, to employ string tremolo and pizzicato and other coloristic effects. His recitative assumes dramatic power, at times approaching the dimensions of an arioso; introduced audacious harmonic innovations, such as using the dominant 7th-chord and other dissonant chords without preparation. He is thought to have popularized the terms *prima prattica* and *secunda prattica* to differentiate the polyphonic style of the 16th century from the largely monodic style of the 17th century, corresponding to *stile antico* and *stile moderno*; for this he was severely criticized by the Bologna theorist Giovanni Maria Artusi, who publ. a vitriolic pamphlet against Monteverdi (1600), attacking the *musica moderna* that allowed chromatic usages in order to achieve a more adequate expression.

Moog, Robert (Arthur), b. Flushing, N.Y., May 23, 1934. He studied at Queens College (B.S. in physics, 1957), Columbia Univ. (B.S. in electrical engineering, 1957), and Cornell Univ. (Ph.D. in engineering physics, 1965). He founded the R. A. Moog Co. in 1954 for the purpose of designing electronic musical instruments; in 1964 he introduced the 1st synthesizer modules; his company was incorporated in 1968, with its headquarters at Trumansburg, N.Y. In 1970 he brought out the Minimoog, a portable monophonic instrument; in 1971 the company became Moog Music and went to Buffalo, N.Y.; in 1973 it became a division of Norlin Industries, with which Moog was associated until 1977. He founded another firm, Big Briar, in Leicester, N.C., which manufactured devices for precision control of analog and digital synthesizers. He was associated with Kurzweil Music Systems of Boston (1984–89). His synthesizers and other electronic devices were used by both classical and rock musicians.

Moore, Douglas (Stuart), b. Cutchogue, N.Y., Aug. 10, 1893; d. Greenport, N.Y., July 25, 1969. He studied at Yale Univ. with D. S. Smith and Horatio Parker; wrote several univ. songs, among them the football song *Good Night, Harvard*, which became popular among Yale students; after obtaining his B.A. (1915) and B. Mus. (1917), he joined the U.S. Navy; following the Armistice of 1918, he attended classes of d'Indy at the Schola Cantorum in Paris and also took lessons in organ with Tournemire and in composition with Boulanger, and with Bloch in Cleveland. Returning to the U.S., he served as organist at the Cleveland Museum of Art (1921–23) and at Adelbert College, Western Reserve Univ. (1923–25); in 1925 he received a Pulitzer traveling scholarship in music and spent a year in Europe. In 1926 he was appointed to the faculty of Columbia Univ.; in 1940 he became head of the music dept. there; many American composers were his students. He retired in 1962.

A fine craftsman, Moore applied his technical mastery to American subjects in his operas and symphonic works. He achieved popular success with his "folk opera" *The Ballad of Baby Doe*, dealing with the true story of a historical figure during the era of intensive silver mining; the opera was staged in 1956, at Central City, Colo., where its action took place; the opera had numerous revivals in America, and also in Europe. He publ. the books *Listening to Music* (1932) and *From Madrigal to Modern Music: A Guide to Musical Styles* (1942). He is best known for his operas, including *The Devil and Daniel Webster* (N.Y., 1939); *Giants in the Earth* (1949; 1951; awarded the Pulitzer Prize in music); *The Ballad of Baby Doe*, folk opera (1956); *The Wings of the Dove* (1961); *Carry Nation*, to the story of the notorious temperance fighter (Kans., 1966). He also scored a ballet, *Greek Games*, and wrote incidental music and film scores. His orch'l works include *The Pageant of P. T. Barnum*, suite (1924); *Moby Dick*, symphonic poem (1927); *A Sym. of Autumn* (1930); *Overture on an American Tune* (1932); *In Memoriam*, symphonic poem (1944); Sym. no. 2 in A Major (1946); *Farm Journal*, suite for Chamber Orch. (1948); *Cotillion*, Suite for Strings (1952). He also wrote chamber works, piano pieces, organ music, choral works, and songs.

Moore, Gerald, b. Watford, July 30, 1899; d. Penn, Buckinghamshire, Mar. 13, 1987. He 1st studied with Wallis Bandey at the local music school; after the family went to Canada in 1913, he continued his studies with Michael Hambourg; then he made appearances as a solo recitalist and accompanist; following his return to England (1919), he completed his training with Mark Hambourg. He began recording in 1921 and 1st gained distinction as accompanist to John Coates in 1925; he subsequently achieved well-nigh legendary fame as the preeminent accompanist of the day, appearing with such celebrated singers as Ferrier, Fischer-Dieskau, Schwarzkopf, Baker, and others. He retired from the concert platform in 1967 but continued to make recordings. He was made a Commander of the Order of the British Empire (1954). Of a purely didactic nature are his books *Singer and Accompanist: The Performance of 50 Songs* (1953), *The Schubert Song Cycles* (1975), and *"Poet's Lore" and Other Schumann Cycles and Songs* (1984).

Moorman, (Madeline) Charlotte, b. Little Rock, Ark., Nov. 18, 1933; d. N.Y., Nov. 8, 1991. She took a B.A. degree in music at Centenary College in Shreveport, La., before studying cello with Horace Britt at the Univ. of Tex. in Austin and then completed her training in the late 1950s at the Juilliard School. A fascination with the avant-garde led her to found the N.Y. Avant-Garde Art Festival in 1963, with which she remained active until 1982. She 1st attracted attention in 1965 when she performed the *Cello Sonata no. 2 for Adults Only.* In 1967 she became something of a sensation when she performed Nam June Paik's *Opéra Sextronique* in accordance with the composer's instructions; i.e., nude from the waist up. Her performance was halted by her arrest; although she was tried and convicted for unseemly exposure, her sentence was eventually suspended and she resumed her championship of the avant-garde unhindered. Among her notable performances were *TV Bra for Living Sculpture* (1969), which called for a bra made of 2 small televisions, and Paik's *The TV Cello* (1971), in which she played a cello made out of 3 television sets. Varèse was so taken with Moorman that he dubbed her the "Jeanne d'Arc of New Music." With terrible irony, she succumbed to breast cancer, a relatively forgotten figure.

moralities. Later form of the miracle plays.

Moran, Robert (Leonard), b. Denver, Jan. 8, 1937. He studied piano; went to Vienna in 1957 and took lessons in 12-tone composition with Hans Erich Apostel. Returning to America, he enrolled at Mills College in Oakland, Calif., where he attended seminars of Luciano Berio and Darius Milhaud (M.A., 1963); completed his training with Roman Haubenstock-Ramati in Vienna (1963); also painted in the manner of Abstract Expressionism. He was active in avant-garde music circles; with Howard Hersh he was founder and codirector of the San Francisco Cons.'s New Music Ensemble; was composer-in-residence at Portland (Oreg.) State Univ. (1972–74) and at Northwestern Univ. (1977–78), where he led its New Music Ensemble; also appeared extensively as a pianist in the U.S. and Europe in programs of contemporary music. In his compositions he combines the "found art" style with aleatory techniques; some of his works are in graphic notation animated by a surrealistic imagination; others play off the gestalt of an earlier piece, place, or era. Moran has composed mixed media works of the environmental type, more common in Europe than in the U.S., but predicted in Ives's unrealized *Universe Sym.*

Among his works are operas: *Let's Build a Nut House,* chamber opera in memory of Hindemith, who wrote *Wir bauen eine Stadt* (1969); *Metamenagerie,* department-store-window opera (1974); *Hitler: Geschichten aus der Zukunft* (1981); *The Juniper Tree,* children's opera (collab. with Glass; 1985); *The Dracula Diary,* opera macabre; ballets. Orch'l compositions: *L'Après-midi du Dracoula* for any group of instruments capable of producing any kind of sound (1966); *Elegant Journey with Stopping Points of Interest* for any ensemble (1967); *Jewel-Encrusted Butterfly Wing Explosions* (1968); *Angels of Silence* for Viola and Chamber Orch. (1975). Chamber works: *Eclectic Boogies* for 13 Percussionists (1965); *Within the Momentary Illumination* for 2 Harps, Electric Guitar, Timpani, and Brass (1965); *The Last Station of the Albatross* for 1 to 8 Instruments

(1978); *Chorale Variations: 10 Miles High over Albania* for Harp (1983); *Survivor from Darmstadt* for Bass Oboes (1984); *Rocky Road to Kansas* for Percussion; *Open Veins* for Ensemble; *Cryptograms for Derek Jarman* for Ensemble. Most unusual are his mixed-media compositions: *Smell Piece for Mills College* for Frying Pans and Foods (Mills College, 1967; intended to produce a conflagration sufficiently thermal to burn down the college); *39 Minutes for 39 Autos* for 30 Skyscrapers, 39 Auto Horns, Moog Synthesizer, and Players, employing 100,000 persons, directed from atop Twin Peaks in San Francisco, making use of autos, airplanes, searchlights, and local radio and television stations (San Francisco, 1969, the night of the moon landing); *Hallelujah,* "a joyous phenomenon with fanfares" for Marching Bands, Drum and Bugle Corps, Church Choirs, Organs, Carillons, Rock 'n' Roll Bands, Television Stations, Automobile Horns, and any other sounding implements, commissioned by Lehigh Univ. for the city of Bethlehem, Pa., with the participation of its entire population of 72,320 inhabitants (Bethlehem, 1971).

morbidezza (It.). Gentleness, softness. *Con morbidezza,* softly, delicately; *morbido,* soft, tender.

morceau (Fr.). Piece; composition. *Morceau de genre,* characteristic piece; *morceau de musique,* a piece of music.

morceaux choisis (Fr., selected pieces). Anthology of popular piano pieces appropriate to the diligent student, provincial teacher, or sincere amateur.

mordent (also Ger.; Fr. *mordant*). Grace consisting of the single rapid alternation of a principal note with an auxiliary a minor 2nd below:

Inverted mordent, the alternation of the principal note with the higher auxiliary:

morendo (It.). Dying away.

moresca (It.; Sp. *morisca*). Moorish dance. It achieved popularity in Spain during the final phase of the struggle against Moorish power in southern Spain. It often contained a representation of a sword fight. Apparently the English Morris dance is a late derivation of the moresca. Interludes of Moorish dances in exotic costumes were often included in French ballets of the period.

Moreschi, Alessandro. See ⇒castrato.

Morganfield, McKinley. Waters, Muddy.

Morgenlied (*Morgenständchen*; Ger.). Morning serenade; aubade.

Morley, Thomas, b. Norwich, 1557 or 1558; d. London, Oct. 1602. He studied with William Byrd. From 1583 to 1587 he was organist and master of the choristers at Norwich Cathedral. In 1588 he received his B.Mus. from Oxford. About this time he became organist at St. Paul's Cathedral. By 1591 he had turned spy for the government of Queen Elizabeth I. In 1592 he was sworn in as a Gentleman of the Chapel Royal and was made Epistler and then Gospeller. He was also active as a printer, holding a monopoly on all music publ. under a patent granted to him by the government in 1598. In addition to publishing his own works (which he called canzonets, madrigals, ballets, and aires), he acted as editor, arranger, translator, and publisher of music by other composers. Notable among his eds. was *The Triumphes of Oriana* (1601), a collection of madrigals by 23 composers, all dedicated to Queen Elizabeth I. He gained distinction as a music theorist; his *A Plaine and Easie Introduction to Practicall Musicke* (1597) became famous as an exposition of British musical schooling of his time.

morphology (science of form). The emergence of a great variety of new forms of composition makes it difficult to classify them according to traditional categories. It may be desirable therefore to substitute this 20th-century term for formal analysis, with the nomenclature of botany replacing that of traditional historic terminology. The geometrical rubrics of botanical classification would add imaginative metaphors suitable to modern musical usages. It would be possible, for instance, to speak of radial symmetry in neoclassical music, of a chromatic inflorescence in an atonal melody, or even of agamogenetic axes in dodecaphonic cross-pollination. The advantage of such botanical similes lies in precision and specificity of the terms and in their easy applicability to intervallic structures.

Morris dance. Characteristic and highly structured English dance for men only adorned in exotic costumes or wearing animal masks, apparently borrowing several features of the Spanish moresca yet without losing its essentially English rhythmic verse. The tempo is moderate and can be played by 1 or more traditional instrumentalists. The use of swords in a noncombatant manner suggests the presence of symbolic character play. The Morris dance went into hibernation before its conscious revival by British ethnomusicologists early in the 20th century.

Morris, James (Peppler), b. Baltimore, Jan. 10, 1947. After studies with a local teacher, he won a scholarship to the Univ. of Md.; concurrently received invaluable instruction from Rosa Ponselle; then continued his studies with Frank Valentino at the Peabody Cons. of Music in Baltimore (1966–68); made his debut as Crespel in *The Tales of Hoffmann* with the Baltimore Civic Opera (1967). After further training with Nicola Moscona at the Philadelphia Academy of Vocal Arts (1968–70), he made his Metropolitan Opera debut in N.Y. as Amonasro in *Aida* in 1971; appeared with the Opera Orch. of N.Y. and sang widely in Europe. In 1975 he scored a notable success as Don Giovanni at the Metropolitan. Although closely associated with the Italian and French repertoires, he appeared as Wotan in *Die Walküre* at the

Baltimore Civic Opera in 1984; subsequently sang that role in the San Francisco Opera's *Ring* cycle in 1985, eliciting extraordinary critical acclaim. His other esteemed roles include Count Almaviva, Philip II, the Dutchman, the 4 villains in *The Tales of Hoffmann*, Timur in *Le Roi de Lahore*, Scarpia, and Claggart in *Billy Budd.*

Morrison, Jim (James). See ⇒Doors, The.

Morrison, Van (real name George Ivan), b. Belfast, Aug. 13, 1945. He taught himself to sing and play the guitar, harmonica, and saxophone; after dropping out of high school when he was 16, he set off with his rhythm-and-blues outfit, the Monarchs, for Germany; returning to Belfast, he put together the group called Them (1963), with which he began his recording career. After Them folded (1966), he went to the U.S.; he produced the hit song *Brown-Eyed Girl* (1967), and that same year brought out his 1st solo album, *Blowin' Your Mind* (with the powerful *T. B. Sheets*). The album *Astral Weeks* (1968) established his expanded consciousness and galactic dreams; went on to record such successful albums as *Moondance* (1970), *Wavelength* (1978), *Into the Music* (1979), and *The Inarticulate Speech of the Heart* (1983). While his recorded output suffers from repetitiousness, in concert on a good night Morrison is as good a blue-eyed soul singer as has ever performed.

Morton, "Jelly Roll" (Ferdinand Joseph Lemott, LaMothe, La Menthe), b. New Orleans, Oct. 20, 1890; d. Los Angeles, July 10, 1941. He grew up surrounded by musical instruments and frequently attended performances at the New Orleans French Opera House. He took up piano when he was 10 and began working in the bordellos of Storyville when he was 12; by the time he was 14 he was traveling throughout La., Miss., Ala., and Fla. while making New Orleans his main haunt; he was a colorful and flamboyant figure, given to extravagant boasting and flashy living; in addition to his being a musician, he was a professional gambler (cards and billiards), nightclub owner, and producer; he made and lost several fortunes. As a result of his travels he assimilated various black, white, and Hispanic musical idioms to produce a form of music akin to jazz.

After performing in Los Angeles (1917–22), Morton went to Chicago, where he made his 1st solo recordings in 1923 of his own *New Orleans Blues* (1902), *Jelly Roll Blues* (1905), and *King Porter Stomp* (1906), and, with a sextet of his own, *Big Foot Ham* (1923); with his own New Orleans–style band, the Red Hot Peppers, he recorded *Grandpa's Spells* (1911), *The Pearls* (1919), and *Black Bottom Stomp* (1925). He went to N.Y. in 1928 but found himself outside the mainstream of jazz developments; later ran a jazz club in Washington, D.C., where he made infrequent appearances as a pianist; in 1938 Alan Lomax, the folklorist, recorded him for the Library of Congress, capturing him on disc playing piano, singing, relating anecdotes, and preserving his view of the history of jazz; the disc was issued in 1948.

mosh pit. Recently devised area on a popular dance floor where patrons are permitted to practice such sports as slam dancing, pogoing, and lifting individuals above the floor involuntarily. Enough damage has been done to bones and flesh that clubs now warn that patrons who enter the pit do so at their own risk.

Mosolov, Alexander (Vasilievich), b. Kiev, Aug. 11, 1900; d. Moscow, July 12, 1973. He studied composition with Glière in Kiev; then studied harmony and counterpoint with Glière, composition with Miaskovsky, and piano with Prokofiev and Igumnov at the Moscow Cons. (1922–25). He played his 1st Piano Concerto in Leningrad (1928). In his earliest works he adopted modernistic devices; wrote songs to texts of newspaper advertisements. His ballet *Zavod* (Iron Foundry; Moscow, 1927) attracted attention because of the attempt to imitate the sound of a factory at work by shaking a large sheet of metal. However, Mosolov's attempt to produce "proletarian" music by such means elicited a sharp rebuke from the official arbiters of Soviet music.

In 1936 Mosolov was expelled from the Union of Soviet Composers for staging drunken brawls and behaving rudely to waiters in restaurants. He was sent to Turkestan to collect folk songs as a move toward his rehabilitation. After settling in Moscow in 1939 he continued to make excursions to collect folk songs in various regions of Russia until just before his death. He wrote 5 syms., 2 piano concertos, 1 concerto apiece for harp and cello, 4 operas, oratorios, choral and solo vocal works, 5 piano sonatas, 2 string quartets, and other music.

mosso (It., moved). Standing alone as a tempo mark, it is the same as con moto. In the phrases *meno mosso* (less rapid), *più mosso* (more rapid), and *poco mosso* (somewhat rapid), it means "rapid." *Allegretto poco mosso*, a rather lively allegretto, almost allegro; *mosso agitato*, a fast and agitated movement; *assai mosso e agitato*, very rapid and agitated.

motet (from Mid. Fr. *mot*, word; Ger. *Motette*; It. *mottetto*). Sacred vocal composition in contrapuntal style, without accompaniment until the Baroque period (where one might be called an anthem). This modest term embraces half a millennium of the most fruitful developments of polyphonic music, stretching from the Middle Ages to the Renaissance and continuing through the period of the Baroque. The motet was cultivated in the church, both of the Roman Catholic and the Protestant rites, as well as in multilingual secular practices. In Middle French, *mot* signified a verse, strophe, or stanza; this is seemingly corroborated by the fact that the contrapuntal voice above the tenor, originally called *duplum*, acquired in the 13th century the name motet and carried a text. Franco of Cologne, writing in the 13th century, describes the motet as "discantus cum diversis litteris" (contrapuntal part with different texts). In the course of 2 centuries the motet was supplemented by more contrapuntal parts, some of them in the French vernacular.

During the Renaissance the confusion of bilingual texts and diverse rhythms led to the segregation of the Latin motet from the secular motet, which absorbed numerous colloquial elements. Further developments, both unified and heterogeneous, are found in the great polyphonic works of the masters of the Flemish school—Ockeghem, Obrecht, and Josquin des Pres. Later, Palestrina in Italy, Victoria in Spain, Tallis in England, Hassler in Germany, and Goudimel in France contributed to the newly burnished art of the motet. In England the motet assumed homophonic forms, leading to the formation of a specific British type of anthem. In Germany, Schütz and, nearly a century later, the great Bach (whose greatest work in the motet style was written for double chorus and 8 solo voices) created the specific form of the German motet. The motet suffered an irreversible decline in the 19th century; the few composers who stubbornly cultivated it, particularly in Germany, did so more out of reverence to its Gothic past than out of inner imperative. In the 20th century the motet suffered its final rigor mortis.

Mothers of Invention, The. See ⇒Zappa, Frank.

motif (Fr.). Motive.

motion. 1. Progression or conduct of a single part or melody; it is *conjunct* when progressing by steps, *disjunct* when progressing by skips. 2. Movement of one part in relation to that of another; in *contrary* or *opposite* motion, 1 part ascends while the other descends; in *oblique* motion, 1 part retains its tone while the other moves; in *parallel* motion, both parts move up or down by the same interval; in *similar* motion, both move up or down together by dissimilar intervals; in *mixed* motion, 2 or more of the above varieties occur at once between several parts.

motive (Ger. *Motiv*; Fr. *motif*). 1. Short phrase or figure used in development or imitation. 2. Leading motive. *Measure motive*, one whose accent coincides with that of the measure's downbeat.

moto (It.). Motion; speed; movement, tempo. *Con moto*, with animated and energetic movement; *moto perpetuo*, describing short pieces in very fast tempo in rondo form; also, the title of such pieces; *moto precedente*, at the previous tempo.

motteggiando (It.). In a bantering, facetious style.

motus (Lat.). Motion; in music, contrapuntal motion, e.g., *motus contrarius*, contrary motion; *motus obliccuus*, oblique motion; *motus rectus*, parallel motion.

mountain music. See ⇒band, string.

mounted cornet. Organ stop mounted on a separate soundboard to render its tone louder.

mouth organ. Colloquialism for harmonica.

mouthpiece. That part of a wind instrument which a player places upon or between his lips.

mouvement (Fr.). Movement; tempo.

mouvementé (Fr.). In a lively tempo.

movable Do[h]. Solfège (solfeggio) method used primarily to teach sight-singing, in which the major diatonic scale is sung to the original syllables of the method of Guido d'Arrezo (Do, Rey, Me, Fah, Soh, Lah), with the leading tone designated by the syllable *Te*. For minor scales and chromatic progressions, the vowels are changed to *e* for sharp and *a* (pronounced "aw") for flat. The distinction of movable Do is that the tonic note is also called Do, whatever the key. This system, widely accepted in English-speaking countries, has the unfortunate consequence of divorcing the absolute sound from its adopted name; the British call this system tonic sol-fa. In all Latin countries and in Russia, the fixed Do method is in use; Do is immovable, is spelled Do, and designates the sound of pitch class C.

movement. 1. Tempo. 2. Principal division or section of a composition.

movendo il tempo (It.). Growing faster.

movimento (It.). Movement.

moyenne difficulté (Fr.). Of moderate difficulty; a term found on French eds. of instrumental works to alleviate the fear of potential buyers frightened by the sight of multiple pitch-black ligatures and fast-tempo marks.

Mozart, Franz Xaver Wolfgang, b. Vienna, July 26, 1791; d. Carlsbad, July 29, 1844. He was the grandson of (Johann Georg) Leopold Mozart, nephew of Maria Anna "Nannerl" Mozart Berchthold zu Sonnenburg, and son of Wolfgang Amadeus Mozart (and often called by his father's name). He studied piano with F. Niemetschek in Prague while living with the Dusek family; continued his training with S. Neukomm, A. Steicher, Hummel, Salieri, G. Vogler, and Albrechtsberger in Vienna. After a period as a teacher in Lemberg and environs (1807–19), he embarked upon a major tour of Europe as a pianist (1819–21); returned to Lemberg as a teacher (1822); organized the Lemberg Cäcilien-Chor (1826). He settled in Vienna (1838); was named honorary Kapellmeister of the Dom-Musik-Verein and the Mozarteum in Salzburg (1841); was made maestro compositore onorario of Rome's Congregazione ed Accademica Santa Cecilia (1842). As a composer he revealed a gift for pianistic writing; among his works are 2 piano concertos; *Konzertvariationen* for Piano and Orch. (1820); Sinfonia in D Major; chamber works; piano music; 4 cantatas, including 1 for Haydn's birthday (1805; not extant); unaccompanied choral pieces; songs.

Mozart, (Johann Georg) Leopold, b. Augsburg, Nov. 14, 1719; d. Salzburg, May 28, 1787. He was the father of Wolfgang Amadeus Mozart and Maria Anna "Nannerl" Mozart Berchthold zu Sonnenburg, and grandfather of Franz Xaver Wolfgang Mozart. A bookbinder's son, he studied at the Augsburg Gymnasium (1727–35); continued his studies at the Lyceum attached to the Jesuit school of St. Salvator (1735–36). In 1737 he went to Salzburg, where he studied philosophy and law at the Benedictine Univ.; he received his bachelor of philosophy degree in 1738. Subsequently he entered the service of Johann Baptist, Count of Thurn-Valsassina and Taxis, the Salzburg canon and president of the consistory, as both valet and musician. In 1743 he became 4th violinist in the Prince-Archbishop's Court Orch.; taught violin and keyboard to the choirboys of the Cathedral oratory. In 1757 he became composer to the court and chamber; in 1758 he was promoted to 2nd violinist in the Court Orch.; in 1762 he was appointed Vice-Kapellmeister. He married Anna Maria Pertl of Salzburg (1747); of their 7 children, only Maria Anna and Wolfgang survived infancy. He dedicated himself to the musical education of his children, but his methods of presenting their concerts approached frank exploitation; his advertisements of their appearances were in poor taste. However, there is no denying his great role in fostering his son's career.

Leopold was a thoroughly competent composer; the mutual influence between father and son was such that works long attributed to his son proved to be his. He was also important as a music theorist; publ. an influential violin method, *Versuch einer gründlichen Violinschule* (Augsburg, 1756). His *Nannerl-Notenbuch* is a model of a child's music album; it was publ. in 1759. His vocal works include sacred cantatas, masses, litanies, school dramas, and secular lieder. He composed syms.; the famous *Kindersinfonie*, long attributed to Haydn, was in all probability by Leopold; other orch'l works include several concertos, among them *Die musikalische Schlittenfahrt* (1755); dances; chamber music; keyboard works.

Mozart, Wolfgang Amadeus, b. Salzburg, Jan. 27, 1756; d. Vienna, Dec. 5, 1791. Supreme and prodigious Austrian composer whose works in every genre are unsurpassed in lyric beauty, rhythmic variety, and effortless melodic invention. He was the son of (Johann Georg) Leopold Mozart, father of Franz Xaver Wolfgang Mozart, and brother of Maria Anna "Nannerl" Mozart Berchthold zu Sonnenburg. Wolfgang and his sister were the only 2 among the 7 children of Anna Maria and Leopold Mozart to survive infancy. Mozart's sister was 4 1/2 years older; she took harpsichord lessons from her father; Mozart, a very young child, eagerly absorbed the sounds of music; soon began playing the harpsichord himself; later studied the violin.

Leopold was an excellent musician, but he also appreciated the theatrical validity of the performances that Wolfgang and Nannerl began giving in Salzburg; took them to Munich, where they performed before the Elector of Bavaria, then played for Emperor Francis I at his palace in Vienna (both 1762). After returning to Salzburg, the children were taken to Frankfurt, where Wolfgang showed his skill in improvising at the keyboard; went to Paris and played before Louis XV (all 1763); Wolfgang's 1st compositions were printed (4 sonatas for harpsichord, with violin ad libitum, Paris). In 1764 they proceeded to London, where Wolfgang played for King George III, there he was befriended by Johann Christian Bach, who gave exhibitions improvising 4-hands at the piano with Wolfgang. By this time Mozart had tried composing serious works; he wrote 2 syms. for a London performance; the MS of another very early sym., purportedly written by him in London, was discovered in 1980. Leopold wrote home with undisguised pride: "Our great and mighty Wolfgang seems to know everything at age 7 that a man acquires at age 40"; knowing the power of publicity, he had lowered Wolfgang's age, who was then 9. In 1765 they journeyed to the Netherlands; set out for Salzburg, visiting Dijon, Lyons, Geneva, Bern, Zurich, Donaueschingen, and Munich on the way.

Arriving in Salzburg (1766), Wolfgang applied himself to serious contrapuntal study under Leopold's tutelage; the family proceeded to Vienna (1767), where Wolfgang began work on an opera, *La finta semplice*, and a singspiel, *Bastien und Bastienne*; the latter was produced at the home of Dr. Franz Mesmer, the proponent of therapy by animal magnetism (later called mesmerism). Wolfgang led a performance of his *Missa solemnis* in C Minor before the royal family and court at the consecration of the Waisenhauskirche (1768). Upon his return to Salzburg, Archbishop Sigismund von Schrattenbach named him his Konzertmeister (1769); the position was without remuneration; determined to broaden Mozart's artistic contacts, his father took him on an Italian tour; an announcement for a concert in Mantua (1770), just a few days before Mozart's 14th birthday, was typical of the artistic mores of the time:

A Sym. of his own composition; a harpsichord Concerto, which will be handed to him and which he will immediately play *prima vista*; a Sonata handed him in like manner, which he will provide with variations and afterwards repeat in another key; an Aria, the words for which will be handed to him and which he will immediately set to music and sing himself, accompanying himself on the harpsichord; a Sonata for harpsichord on a subject given him by the leader of the violins; a Strict Fugue on a theme to be selected, which he will improvise on the harpsichord; a Trio in which he will execute a violin part *all' improvviso*; and, finally, the latest sym. by himself.

Legends of Mozart's extraordinary musical ability grew; he apparently wrote out the entire score of the Miserere by Allegri, a work reserved for the Vatican, after 2 listenings at the Sistine Chapel; he was subjected to numerous tests by famous Italian musicians, among them Giovanni Sammartini, Piccini, and Padre Martini; elected a member of the Accademia Filarmonica in Bologna after passing examinations in harmony and counterpoint; the Pope made him a Knight of the Golden Spur (1770). He composed an opera on commission, *Mitridate, re di Ponto*, performed in Milan (1770); Mozart himself conducted 3 performances of this opera from the harpsichord; after a short stay in Salzburg he returned to Milan; composed the serenata *Ascanio in Alba* for the wedding festivities of Archduke Ferdinand (1771). He returned to Salzburg; following the death of his patron, Archbishop Schrattenbach, Hieronymus Colloredo, his successor, seemed to be indifferent to Mozart as a musician. Once more Mozart went to Italy, where *Lucio Silla*, was performed in Milan (1772). He returned to Salzburg in 1773, but in of that year he went to Vienna, where he became acquainted with the music of Haydn, who greatly influenced his instrumental style. Returning to Salzburg once more, he supervised the premiere of *Il re pastore* (1775).

In 1778 Mozart visited Paris with his mother for a performance of his *Paris* Sym. (no. 31) at a Concert Spirituel; his mother died unexpectedly during the trip. Returning to Salzburg in 1779, he resumed his duties as Konzertmeister and also obtained the position of court organist at a salary of 450 gulden. In 1780 the Elector of Bavaria commissioned from him an opera seria, *Idomeneo*, successfully premiered in Munich (1781). After a decade of strife with Archbishop Colloredo, Mozart lost his position (1781); moved to Vienna, his new permanent home; produced the singspiel *Die Entführung aus dem Serail* (The Abduction from the Seraglio), staged at the Burgtheater with excellent success (1782). In 1782 he married Constanze Weber, sister of the soprano Aloysia Weber, with whom he had previously been infatuated.

Two of Mozart's finest syms.—no. 35 in D Major, the *Haffner*, written for the Haffner family of Salzburg, and no. 36 in C Major, the *Linz*—date from 1782 and 1783, respectively. From this point forward his productivity reached extraordinary dimensions; despite the abundance of commissions and concert appearances, failed to earn enough to sustain his growing family.

Still, melodramatic stories of Mozart's abject poverty are exaggerations; he apparently felt no scruples in asking prosperous friends for financial assistance; periodically wrote to Michael Puchberg, a banker and a brother Freemason (Mozart joined the order in 1784), requesting loans (which he never repaid); invariably Puchberg obliged, usually granting smaller amounts than Mozart requested.

In 1785 Mozart completed a set of 6 string quartets dedicated to Haydn; unquestionably the structure of these quartets owed much to Haydn's op. 33 quartets (1781). Haydn himself paid a tribute to Mozart's genius; Leopold quoted him as saying, "Before God and as an honest man I tell you that your son is the greatest composer known to me either in person or by name." In 1786 Mozart's great opera buffa *Le nozze di Figaro* (The Marriage of Figaro, libretto by Da Ponte) was triumphantly produced in Vienna; performed in Prague with Mozart in attendance. It was during that visit that Mozart wrote his 38th Sym. in D Major, the *Prague* Sym.; it was there, also, that his operatic masterpiece *Don Giovanni* was premiered (libretto by Da Ponte, 1787). During the Act II banquet scene leading up to the final confrontation between Giovanni and the Commendatore, Mozart quotes a melody from a then popular opera, *Un cosa rara* by (Atanasio Martín Ignacio) Vicente (Tadeo Francisco Pellegrin) Martín y Soler (1754–1806); more intriguingly, Da Ponte was the librettist for *Un cosa rara* as well.

In 1787 Mozart was appointed Kammermusicus in Vienna, succeeding Gluck, albeit at a smaller salary. The following year he composed his last 3 syms.: no. 39 in E-flat Major; no. 40 in G Minor; and no. 41 in C Major, known under the name *Jupiter* (a designation apparently 1st attached to the work in the program of the Edinburgh Festival in 1819). In the spring of 1789 Mozart went to Berlin; appeared as soloist in a piano concerto before the Elector of Saxony in Dresden; played the organ at the Thomaskirche in Leipzig. His visits in Potsdam and Berlin were marked by private concerts at the court of Friedrich Wilhelm II; the King commissioned from him a set of 6 string quartets and 6 piano sonatas, but Mozart died before completing these commissions.

Returning to Vienna, he began work on his opera buffa *Così fan tutte* (As All Women Are, libretto by Da Ponte); the opera was 1st performed in Vienna (1790). In 1790 Mozart went to Frankfurt for the coronation of Emperor Leopold II; returning to Vienna, he saw Haydn, who was about to depart for London. In 1791, he completed the score of the singspiel *Die Zauberflöte* (The Magic Flute), with a libretto by Emanuel (Johannes Joseph) Schikaneder (1751–1812), an impresario and actor. It was performed for the 1st time in Vienna (1791). There followed a mysterious episode in Mozart's life; a stranger called on him with a request to compose a Requiem; the caller was an employee of Count Franz von Walsegg, who intended to have the work performed as his own in memory of his wife. Mozart was unable to finish the score, which was completed by his pupil Süssmayr, and by Eybler.

The immediate cause and context of Mozart's death has been the subject of speculation of mythic proportions: 1) Mozart was supposedly poisoned by Salieri out of professional jealousy; this invention circulated in European journals, further enhanced by a report that Salieri confessed the crime on his deathbed (1825; another story contradicts this claim). Pushkin turned the rumored murder into *Mozart and Salieri* (1830), set to music by Rimsky-Korsakov (1898); an even more fanciful dramatization of the rivalry is the successful *Amadeus*, by Peter Shaffer, produced in London (1979) and N.Y. (1980), and gained wider currency through its award-winning film version (1984). 2) The notion of Mozart's murder appealed to the Nazis; in an ingenious version propagated by German writers of Hitlerian persuasion, he was a victim of a double conspiracy of Masons and Jews, determined to suppress the flowering of racial Germanic greatness; the Masons were supposedly outraged by his alleged exposure of their secret rites in *Die Zauberflöte*, and allied themselves with plutocratic Jews to prevent further spread of his dangerous revelations. 3) A blizzard had raged during his funeral, so that none of his friends could follow his body to the cemetery; this story is easily refuted by the records of the Vienna weather bureau for the day. 4) It is also untrue that Mozart was buried in a pauper's grave; his body was removed from its original individual location because the family neglected to pay the mandatory dues.

The universal recognition of Mozart's genius during the 2 centuries since his death has never wavered among professional musicians, amateurs, and the general public, although those who prefer the larger-than-life qualities of Beethoven have missed the proto-Romantic element amidst the Classic aesthetic in Mozart. In his music, smiling simplicity was combined with somber drama; lofty inspiration was contrasted with playful diversion; profound meditation alternated with capricious moodiness; religious concentration was permeated with human tenderness. Devoted as he was to his art and respectful of the rules of composition, he could also make fun of the professional establishment. A delightful example of this persiflage is his little serenade *Ein musikalischer Spass* (1787), subtitled *Dorfmusikanten*, a "musical joke" at the expense of "village musicians," in which, by conscientious use of wrong notes, he all but anticipates developments of modern music—consecutive 5ths, the 1st violin's escape upwards in a whole-tone scale, a final cadence of polytonal chords worthy of Ives.

The variety of technical development in Mozart's works is all the more remarkable considering the limitations of instrumental means in his time; the topmost note on his keyboard was F above the 3rd ledger line, so that, in the 1st movement recapitulation of his famous C-major piano sonata (K. 545), the subject has to be dropped an octave lower to accommodate the modulation. The vocal technique displayed in his operas is amazing in its perfection; to be sure, the human voice has not changed since Mozart's time, but he knew how to exploit vocal resources to the utmost. This adaptability of his genius to all available means of sound production is the secret of the eternal validity of his music, and the explanation of the present popularity of minifestivals, such as the N.Y. concert series advertised as "Mostly Mozart."

The standard catalogue was established by L. von Köchel (Leipzig, 1862; 6th rev. ed., Wiesbaden, 1964). The orig. catalogue numbers are labeled as K.; Anh. stands for Anhang (supplement to the orig. ed.); the rev. numbers of the 6th ed., which sometimes follow, are referred to as K⁶; Mozart also kept a catalogue during the latter part of his life, known as *Mozarts Werkverzeichnis 1784–1791*. In addition to works discussed above, Mozart's oeuvre includes the following works: Stage: *Les Petits Riens*, ballet, K. Anh. 10, 299b (Opéra, Paris,

1778); *Zaïde*, K. 344, 336b, singspiel (unfinished; completed by Anton André, Frankfurt, 1866); *Der Schauspieldirektor*, K. 486, singspiel (Schonbrunn Palace, Heitzing, 1786); *La clemenza di Tito*, K. 621, opera seria (National Theater, Prague, 1791); concert arias, duets, ensembles, and scenes with orch.; canons; songs for voice and keyboard. Religious choral: Masses, including Missa Solemnis in C Minor, K. 139, 47a, *Waisenhausmesse* (Vienna, 1768); Missa in C Major, K. 66, *Dominicus* (St. Peter's, Salzburg, 1769); Missa in C Major, K. 167, *In honorem Ssmae Trinitatis* (1773); Missa brevis in C Major, K. 220; 196b, *Spatzenmesse* (1775–76); Missa in C Major, K. 257, *Credo* (1776); Missa brevis in C Major, K. 258, *Spaur* (1776); Missa brevis in C Major, K. 259, *Organ Solo* (1776); Missa in C Major, K. 317, *Coronation* (1779). Other sacred: *La Betulia liberata*, K. 118, 74c, oratorio (1771); *Die Maurerfreude*, K. 471, cantata ("Zur gekronten Hoffnung" Lodge, Vienna, 1785); *Eine kleine Freimaurer-Kantate*, K. 623 ("Zur neugekronten Hoffnung" Lodge, Vienna, 1791); numerous motets and liturgical text settings.

Although traditionally Mozart's syms. are numbered 1–41, present estimates list more than 50 such works, although a few early works remain in dispute. While it is impossible to describe the stylistic development in the syms. here, it can be posited that no. 25 in G Minor, K. 183, 173dB (1773) is the 1st "mature" sym.; it forecasts the haunting effect of the later G-minor sym. (no. 40); later syms. include: no. 28 in C Major, K. 200, 189k (1774); no. 29 in A Major, K. 201, 186a (1774); no. 30 in D Major, K. 202, 186b (1774); no. 31 in D Major, K. 297, 300a, *Paris* (1778: with 2 slow movements); no. 33 in B-flat Major, K. 319 (1779); no. 34 in C Major, K. 338 (1780).

For Mozart the piano concerto was the best way to show off his talents as keyboard player, composer, leader, and provider of the newest musical novelties; fashion and faddism ruled the Classic music scene as much as they do today's popular music, a fact that Mozart struggled with for most of his career. Included in the traditional count of 27 piano concertos are 4 pastiches of other composers' pieces, done as exercises; no. 7 in F Major for 3 Pianos, K. 242 (1776); and no. 10 in E-flat Major for 2 Pianos, K. 365, 316a (1779). Piano concertos from the Vienna period include: no. 12 in A Major, K. 414, 385p (1782); no. 14 in E-flat Major, K. 449 (1784); no. 17 in G Major, K. 453 (1784); no. 18 in B-flat Major, K. 456 (1784); no. 20 in D Minor, K. 466 (1785); no. 21 in C Major, K. 467 (its middle movement was made ubiquitous through inclusion in an otherwise forgettable film, *Elvira Madigan*; 1785); no. 23 in A Major, K. 488 (1786); no. 24 in C Minor, K. 491 (1786); no. 25 in C Major, K. 503 (1786); no. 26 in D Major, K. 537, *Coronation* (1788); no. 27 in B-flat Major, K. 595 (1788?–91); 2 rondos for piano and orch. Strings: 5 authentic violin concertos; other works with orch.: *Concertone* in C Major for 2 Violins, K. 90, 186e (1774); Sinfonia concertante in E-flat Major for Violin and Viola, K. 364, 320d (1779); Wind instruments: Concerto for Bassoon in B-flat Major, K. 191, 186e (1774); Concerto for Flute in G Major, K. 313, 285c (1778); Concerto for Oboe or Flute in C/D Major, K. 314, 285d (1778); Concerto for Flute and Harp in C Major, K. 299, 297c (1778); 4 horn concertos (1783–91); Concerto for Clarinet in A Major, K. 622 (1791). Occasional works, including: Serenata notturna in D Major, K. 239 (1776); Serenade in D Major, K. 250, 248b, *Haffner* (1776); Divertimento in D Major, K. 251 (1776); Serenade in D Major, K. 320, *Posthorn* (1779); *Maurerische*

Trauermusik in C Minor, K. 477, 479a (1785); *Ein musikalischer Spass* in F Major, K. 522 (1787); *Eine kleine Nachtmusik* in G Major, K. 525 (1787); other serenades and divertimentos; wind band music; over 100 German dances, ländler, and contredanses.

Chamber music: 23 string quartets, including the 6 "Haydn" quartets: G Major, K. 387 (1782); D Minor, K. 421, 417b (1783); E-flat Major, K. 428, 421b (1783); B-flat Major, K. 458, *Jagd* (1784); A Major, K. 464 (1785); C Major, K. 465, *Dissonanz* (1785); 6 string quintets (2 violins, 2 violas, and cello), the finest examples of this genre ever written (1787–91); 4 quartets for flute, violin, viola, and cello (1777–87); Quartet in F Major for Oboe and Strings, K. 370, 368b (1781); Quintet in E-flat Major for Horn and Strings, K. 407, 386c (1782); Quintet in A Major for Clarinet and Strings (1789); string duos and trios. Keyboard and other instruments: 7 trios (1776–88); Quintet in E-flat Major for Piano and Winds, K. 452 (1784); 2 piano quartets; Adagio and Rondo in C Minor for Glass Harmonica and Ens., K. 617 (1791); over 30 keyboard and violin sonatas, many unfinished (1762–88); 17 solo keyboard sonatas (1775–89); 5 sonatas for keyboard duet; Sonata in D Major for 2 Keyboards, K. 448, 375a (1781); 16 variation sets for keyboard solo and 1 for keyboard duet; miscellaneous pieces, including 17 sonatas for organ, most with 2 violins and bassoon.

Mozart Berchthold zu Sonnenburg, Maria Anna "Nannerl,"

b. Salzburg, July 30, 1751; d. there, Oct. 29, 1829. She was the daughter of (Johann Georg) Leopold Mozart, aunt of Franz Xaver Wolfgang Mozart, and sister of Wolfgang Amadeus Mozart. She was taught music by her father from her earliest childhood, and appeared in public as a pianist with her brother; after their travels together in Europe she returned to Salzburg and eventually devoted herself mainly to teaching. She went blind in 1825. Although nearly 5 years older than Wolfgang, she survived him by 38 years.

mp. Mezzo-piano.

mṛidaṅgam. Classical drum of southern India, in an elongated barrel shape with 2 heads of different diameters. It is made of wood, although its name refers to clay. The heads, as in many other wooden membranophones, are attached to hoops and tightened by leather thongs; tuning is accomplished by tension wedges and a paste, different for each head. The 2 heads are tuned an octave apart.

muance (Fr.). In medieval solmization, mutation from one hexachord to another.

mudanza (Sp.). Stanza in a villancico of the Renaissance period.

Muddy Waters. Waters, Muddy.

mugam (Azeri.). Maqām.

Mulligan, Gerry (Gerald Joseph),
b. N.Y., June 4, 1927; d. Darien, Conn., Jan. 19, 1996. His formative years were spent in Philadelphia, where he learned to play piano; played reed instruments and worked professionally as an arranger while still in his teens; then went to N.Y. (1946), where he played reed

instruments and wrote arrangements for Gene Krupa's big band; after performing with Miles Davis (1948–50), he acquired a reputation as one of the finest baritone saxophonists of his era. In 1952 he formed the 1st of several "pianoless" quartets, with which he toured extensively and made recordings; led his own big band on a tour of Europe in 1960 and of Japan in 1964; also made appearances with various jazz notables, and began playing the soprano saxophone. He was an important figure in the development of "cool" jazz, remaining a protean figure in jazz circles for decades.

multiphonics. Modern method of wind sound production that through overblowing and special fingerings results in 2 or more sounds simultaneously by a single performer on a monophonic instrument.

Munch, Charles
(born Münch), b. Strasbourg, Sept. 26, 1891; d. Richmond, Va., Nov. 6, 1968. His father, Ernst Münch (b. Niederbronn, Dec. 31, 1859; d. Strasbourg, Apr. 1, 1928), was an organist and choral conductor. Charles studied violin at the Strasbourg Cons. and with Lucien Capet in Paris; at the outbreak of World War I (1914) he enlisted in the German army; made a sergeant of artillery; he was gassed at Peronne and wounded at Verdun; after the end of the war (1918) and his return to Alsace-Lorraine (1919), he became a French citizen. Having received further violin training from Carl Flesch in Berlin, he pursued a career as a soloist; was also prof. of violin at the Leipzig Cons. and concertmaster of the Gewandhaus Orch. there. In 1932 he made his professional conducting debut in Paris with the Straram Orch.; studied conducting with Alfred Szendrei there (1933–40).

Munch quickly rose to prominence; was conductor of Paris's Orch. de la Soc. Philharmonique (1935–38) and became a prof. at the École Normale de Musique (1938). In 1938 he became music director of the Soc. des Concerts du Conservatoire de Paris, remaining in that post during the years of the German occupation during World War II; refusing to collaborate with the Nazis, he gave his support to the Resistance and was awarded the Légion d'Honneur in 1945. He made his U.S. debut as a guest conductor of the Boston Sym. Orch. (1946); a transcontinental tour of the U.S. with the French National Radio Orch. followed in 1948. In 1949 he was appointed music director of the Boston Sym. Orch., which he and Monteux took on its 1st European tour in 1952; they took it again to Europe in 1956, also touring in the Soviet Union, making it the 1st U.S. orch. to do so.

After retiring from his Boston post in 1962, Munch made appearances as a guest conductor; also helped to launch the Orch. de Paris in 1967. Munch acquired an outstanding reputation as an interpreter of the French repertoire, his performances being marked by spontaneity, color, and elegance. French music of the 20th century also occupied a prominent place on his programs; he introduced new works by Roussel, Milhaud, Honegger, and others. He wrote *Je suis chef d'orchestre* (Paris, 1954).

Mundstück (Ger.). Mouthpiece for wind instruments.

Munrow, David (John),
b. Birmingham, Aug. 12, 1942; d. (suicide) Chesham Bois, Buckinghamshire, May 15, 1976. He studied English at Pembroke College, Cambridge; during this period (1961–64) he founded an ensemble for the furtherance

of early English music and organized a recorder consort. In 1967 he formed the Early Music Consort of London, with which he gave many successful concerts of medieval and Renaissance music; also was active with his own BBC radio program. He lectured on the history of early music at the Univ. of Leicester (from 1967) and was prof. of recorder at London's Royal Academy of Music (from 1969); publ. the vol. *Instruments of the Middle Ages and Renaissance* (London, 1976).

munter (Ger.). Lively, gay, animated.

murky bass. Curious term of puzzling origin applied to rudimentary accompaniment in broken octaves in the bass, much in use in rococo music. Some philologists suggest that *murky* is taken from the English word that means exactly what it says: unclear and obfuscating.

Musealer Klangmaterialismus (Ger.). Neologism coined by a German musicologist meaning approximately "museumesque materialism of timbre," i.e., the attempt of instrument makers, performers, and arrangers to replicate the precise sound of an obsolete instrument.

musette (Fr.). 1. Small oboe. 2. Reed stop on the organ. 3. Small French bagpipe, very popular in the Baroque era. It was much more ornate in appearance than the Scottish bagpipe and was used in ballets given at the French court. Music was written for the instrument by Hotteterre, Boismortier, Rameau, and Montéclair. 4. Pastoral dance of the French ballet, characterized by a protracted drone and 12/8 meter; the music reflects its fragile character, totally opposed to the gigue in character. Musettes are found in many Baroque instrumental suites by French composers, and also in the English Suite no. 3 of Bach; as late as 1925, Schoenberg included one in his op. 25 piano suite. The middle section of the gavotte is often called *musette* when it has a sustained drone on the tonic and dominant. An older name for the musette is *cornemuse*.

Musgrave, Thea, b. Barnton, Midlothian, May 27, 1928. She pursued preliminary medical studies at the Univ. of Edinburgh, and concurrently studied with Mary Grierson (musical analysis) and Hans Gál (composition and counterpoint), receiving her B.Mus. (1950) and winning the Donald Tovey Prize; then studied privately and at the Paris Cons. with Boulanger (1952–54); later was a scholarship student of Copland at Tanglewood (1959). She taught at the Univ. of London (1958–65), then was a visiting prof. of composition at the Univ. of Calif. at Santa Barbara (1970); also lectured at various other U.S. and English univs.; likewise made appearances as a conductor on both sides of the Atlantic. She held 2 Guggenheim fellowships (1974–75; 1982). In 1971 she married the American violinist Peter Mark, who later served as conductor of the Virginia Opera Assoc. in Norfolk. She was named Distinguished Prof. of Music at Queens College in N.Y. in 1987.

At the outset of her career Musgrave followed the acceptable modern style of composition, but soon the diatonic lyricism of the initial period of her creative evolution gave way to increasingly chromatic constructions, eventually systematized into serial organization. She described her theatrical works as "dramatic abstracts" in form, because even in the absence of a programmatic design they revealed some individual dramatic traits. Appreciated by critics and audiences alike, her compositions, in a variety of styles but invariably effective and technically accomplished, enjoyed numerous performances in Europe and America. She is best known for her vocal works; these include the operas *Abbott of Drimock*, chamber opera (1955); *The Decision* (1964–65; London, 1967); *The Voice of Ariadne* (1972–73); *Mary, Queen of Scots* (1976); *A Christmas Carol* (1979); *An Occurrence at Owl Creek Bridge*, radio opera (1981); *Harriet, the Woman Called Moses* (1985). She has also composed music for ballets, orch'l and chamber works, and electronic music.

music. The word *music* (It. *musica*; Ger. *Musik*; Fr. *musique*) is derived from the Greek *mousikē*, an art of the Muses (sing. *mousa*). Euterpe, the Muse of Tragedy and flute playing, and Polyhymnia, the Muse of singing, are regarded as the inspiring deities of music—Euterpe because in ancient Greece music was closely connected with tragedy and theatrical spectacles were invariably accompanied by the playing on the flute, and Polyhymnia because the beginning of music was marked by a multiplicity of songs.

In present terms *music* may be defined as a meaningful succession of perceptible sounds in temporal motion. These sounds may be single sonorous units (as in melody) or combinations of several such units (as in harmony and counterpoint). The temporal motion may consist of sounds of equal duration (simple chant) or of unequal duration (rhythmed melody, or melorhythm). Melorhythms may be patterned symmetrically, in well-demarcated periods (corresponding to unchanged meter in versification), or in asymmetrical fragments. The perfection of a melorhythmic figure is determined by the balance between melody and rhythm. When melodic elements (tones) vary greatly in pitch, the rhythm may be allowed to remain quiescent; when the melody is confined to a few notes, and in extreme cases to a single note, then rhythm must show variety. This interdependence of melody and rhythm in a melorhythm may be expressed by the formula $R \times M = C$, where R stands for rhythm, M stands for melody, and C stands for an empirical constant.

Music is written down by means of symbols or notes. A medieval monk, St. Isidore of Seville, opined in the 7th century that music is an art that can be preserved by oral tradition only because tones can never be notated (*scribi non possunt*). The history of musical notation has indeed been arduous, but for the last 4 centuries it has assumed a fairly uniform aspect. The height of a musical tone is measured by the relative position on a staff of 5 lines, with clefs indicating the selected pitch of a specific note, usually G, C, or F, placed on any of the 5 lines on the staff; the rest of the notes are calculated from the clef note, with each space and each line reckoning for 1 diatonic degree.

The concept of music does not necessarily signify beauty or attractiveness; indeed, music of primitive peoples, which is beautiful to them, may appear chaotic and ugly to an outsider. Within the memory of many musicians, compositions by modern masters were condemned by critics as cacophonous. In his famous treatise on aesthetics, *Vom Musikalisch-Schönen*, Hanslick defines music as "a tonally moving form." This definition begs the question, for the key word *tonally* embraces the "moving forms" of Liszt, Wagner, and other representatives of the "music of the future," which was anathema to Hanslick. Kant described music as "an artistic arrangement of sensations of hearing," which is logically acceptable, for it includes any subjectively artistic succession of musical elements. Hegel declared that the aim of music is "to render in sounds the innermost self which moves in itself according to the subjective feeling for one's ideal soul," a statement that is so involved that it may signify any sound, or any combination of sounds, that expresses an emotion.

The most extreme manifestations of the modern avant-garde would find their place in the definition of music by the most rigid and most obfuscating of German philosophers, Schopenhauer, to whom the human will was the source of all action. He asserted that music is a "reflection of the will itself, revealing its very essence, whereas other arts treat but the shadows of the will." The Romantic poet Jean Paul describes music as "a reflected sound from a remote world." Inspired by the medieval concept of the harmony of the spheres, Schelling senses in music "the perceived rhythm and harmony of the observable universe itself." Musical theorists seeking to delimit music from other arts emphasize its unique capacity to convey emotions and meaning, to express spiritual and sensory phenomena in terms which use no language and no pictorial representation. Hegel himself admitted that music is "sufficient unto itself and therefore self-explanatory."

Great poets extolled music as a catalyst of passion and a motive force for bravery. Shakespeare expressed this quality in the ringing lines, "The man that hath no music in himself/nor is not moved with concord of sweet sounds/ . . . let no such man be trusted." In his *Ode on a Grecian Urn*, Keats said that "[h]eard melodies are sweet, but those unheard are sweeter." Longfellow followed the philosophers in saying that "music is the universal language of mankind"; scientists seem to agree, to judge by an astronomer's suggestion that a diagram of a Bach fugue should be included in a rocket sent outside the solar system on the chance that it would be intercepted and decoded by hypothetical beings in distant galaxies.

In the Middle Ages music was part of mathematics, included in the quadrivium of the universities. The word *numbers* can refer to musical pieces. "Will no one tell me what she sings?" Wordsworth questioned, and surmised: "Perhaps the plaintive numbers flow/For old, unhappy, far-off things." Leibniz said: "Music is a kind of counting performed by the mind without knowing that it is counting." This definition comes remarkably close to Bertrand Russell's description of mathematics as "the subject in which we never know what we are talking about, nor whether what we are saying is true."

music(al) box. Mechanical musical instruments that were perfected shortly after the invention of clockwork, about the year 1200. The 1st mechanical music instrument was the barrel organ, manufactured for the Archbishop of Salzburg in 1502. It had 350 pipes into which music was channeled from a barrel with flexible pins. This was followed by mechanical carillons, the best of which were made in Flanders and Holland in the 17th century. Chiming watches that played tunes appeared in France in the 18th century.

The Swiss music box has steel tongues with a definite pitch which are plucked by pins on a rotating metal cylinder or barrel, turned by clockwork. The 1st models were made by Antoine Favre of Geneva in 1796. The music box industry reached its greatest development about 1870; it declined with the appearance of the phonograph, a rival too mighty for the tinkling pins and tongues. Apart from chiming watches, music boxes were manufactured in the form of snuff boxes and sewing boxes. Musical dolls are music boxes which survive into the present time.

music drama. Original description of opera as it evolved in Florence early in the 17th century (*dramma per musica*); Wagner adopted this term in order to emphasize the dramatic element in his spectacles (*Musikdrama*).

music hall. Place and type of light entertainment popular in British cities in the Victorian and Edwardian eras; modeled after the Paris café chantant. Music halls usually featured songs and dances spiced by an infinitesimal display of sensuality, sufficient to make moral guardians shudder with horror at the depravity of the thing. A further degradation was afforded by the adjacent *cabinets particuliers*, where a peer or a lord might entertain a lady of a lower class away from the common herd. As the 20th century proceeded, music hall performers entered the traveling vaudeville circuits, which persisted in Britain until World War II.

music journals. Before the advent of mass publications of general newspapers which included a special department devoted to the review of concerts, music criticism existed only in the form of theoretical discussions in specially printed pamphlets. Heated polemical exchanges accompanied the progress of the Guerre des Bouffons and the famous Gluck-Piccini controversy in the 18th century. Germany was a pioneer in musical journalism; essays on technical subjects were published in connection with public performances. The 1st musical periodical that published critical evaluations of musical works was the *Allgemeine musikalische Zeitung*, founded in 1798 and published, with an occasional hiatus, until 1881. It was for this journal that Schumann wrote, at age 19, his unsigned article saluting Chopin as a genius.

In 1834 Schumann founded his own publication, *Neue Zeitschrift für Musik*, dedicated to the propaganda of "new music" of a Romantic mold; after many interruptions it was reincarnated after World War I, and survives today. The German music weekly, *Signale für die musikalische Welt* (founded 1841) lasted almost a century until World War II finally killed it off. The informative weekly *Allgemeine Musikzeitung* was also the victim of World War II after 70 years of a relatively prosperous existence. With the exception of Schumann's journal, these publications adopted a conservative, not to say reactionary, attitude toward the novel musical tendencies of each successive period. In France, *La Revue Musicale* continued its uncertain existence from 1827 to 1880, was reincarnated in 1920, only to falter and die of inanition. *Le Ménestrel* lasted more than 100 years after its founding (1833), with the inevitable interruptions during the Paris Commune and World War I; World War II finished it off; critical attitudes during most of its existence were definitely reactionary, damning Wagner and Debussy with equal fervor. In England, the most durable monthly is *The Musical Times*, founded in 1844 and still going strong after 150 years. In the U.S., musical journals of opinion had a relatively brief life. In the 19th century, *Dwight's Journal of Music* enjoyed respect; it was dull, and it damned Wagner.

In the meantime, artists of varying quality—German, Italian, and Russian music teachers, and minor musicians of all calibers—became commodities of European import and commanded a great deal of advertising. In America these demands were met by a multiplicity of commercial music periodicals, of which *The Musical Courier* and *Musical America* were particularly prominent. They published weekly issues that featured dispatches by specially assigned European correspondents, and reproduced excellent photographs of the current celebrities who bought advertising space. For a modest fee even for those times, these publications carried cover portraits of mustachioed tenors and ample-bosomed prima donnas, and occasionally even an American face. The ads informed on the activities of music teachers ("Mr. X has returned from Europe and will accept a limited number of exceptionally talented pupils"), voice teachers with Italian surnames ("Guarantee bel canto within 6 months by inhaling bottled compressed air from Naples"), "Miss Y triumphs in Muleshoe, Texas," etc.

As the careers of these musical worthies became less profitable and interest in the artistic and amorous goings-on in the musical world waned, the journals themselves languished and finally expired. *Musical America* survived as a shriveled appendix to *High Fidelity*; it, too, has disappeared. *The Etude* appealed mainly to music lovers and amateurs, publishing sentimental biographies of contemporary musicians as well as simplified selections of their more digestible compositions; but it, too, succumbed to the disenchantment of the times. In place of these publications there arose a crop of commercialized periodicals devoted to recordings, radio, and television, with only a sprinkling of informative material on their pages.

Musicological journals carried on a subsidized existence. In America, *The Musical Quarterly* and the *Journal of the American Musicological Society* are the most important scholarly publications; in England, *Music and Letters* and *Music Review* purvey selective information. There are music journals of value in Italy, France, and Germany; in Russia, the monthly *Sovietskaya Musica* furnished information on Soviet music. In Latin America, only the *Revista Musical Chilena* appears with some regularity. The international avant-garde puts out sporadic issues of great interest to their particular audiences. The most extreme of them was *Source*, published in Calif., without visible financial support, printing the most fantastic samples of ultramodern productions lavishly illustrated in a variety of colors; it carried a feverish existence for several years before collapsing.

music of the spheres. See ⇒harmony of the spheres.

music theater (U.K. *theatre*). Small to moderate musical stage work involving a dramatic element in its performance; frequently distinguished from opera by its scale and scope.

music therapy. The study and use of musical stimuli and activity in the evaluation, remediation, or maintenance of health; it developed into a bona fide profession at about the time of World War II in the U.S., with univ. curricula following within the decade. In earlier times, anecdote served the role that research does now.

An ancient Sicilian youth suspected that his beloved was faithless. His suspicions were further inflamed by the sounds of flute music in the Phrygian mode. Seized by madness, he rushed into her house; Pythagoras, taking temporary leave of his mathematical calculations, took notice of the young man's condition and ordered the flute player to change from the Phrygian to the Dorian mode; this modulation had an immediate soothing effect on the youth, who became philosophically calm. The ancient Greek Phrygian mode (which, it should be noted, corresponds to the Ionian mode in Gregorian chant, i.e., C major), was regarded by the Greeks as most apt to cause hyperventilation in a human being. Similar stories dot ancient history: Alexander the Great slayed a guest when a musician played a Phrygian air on the lyre; Aristotle observed the easing of pain of slaves being flogged by playing flute music; Terpander pacified a menacing crowd of citizens by singing and accompanying himself on a lyre so impressively that his listeners burst into tears and rush to kiss his feet; the Athenian Tyrtacus went to Sparta and soothed the indomitable Spartan spirit by playing an elegy, but inadvertently changed to the martial Dorian mode, causing the Spartans to rise and march belligerently on Athens.

Plato declared that civil obedience can be achieved by means of music. Public decrees were often recited in ancient Greece to melodious lyre accompaniment; Damon of Athens quieted down drunken youths with spondaic measures on flute; Maecenas, legendary patron of Roman poetry, cured his chronic insomnia by listening to distant musical sounds. The Phrygian mode was recommended by Aristotle's disciple Theophrastus for cure of sciatica; many victims of melancholia regained their self-confidence upon hearing Phrygian tunes, he reported; flute playing in the Phrygian mode was proposed by Caelius Aurelianus for temporary relief from lumbago and arthritis.

Belief in the beneficial and curative properties of music persisted even when the dichotomy of the Phrygian and Dorian modes were replaced by "scientific" reasoning and experimentation. Peter Lichtenthal, in a remarkable volume, *The Musical Doctor* (1811), suggests musical remedies for a variety of ills; his list includes incidence of stupidity among school children; quoting a contemporary French physician, he reports that a young girl, affected by irresistible nymphomania, became morally restrained when she was forced to listen to sweet music 3 times a day.

"Music has charm to soothe the savage breast," Congreve wrote, but the statement does not always hold. The chroniclers stated that Erik the Evergood, King of Denmark (*c.* 1100) ordered all weapons removed from his reach before the court lutenist began to play, fearing that he might be moved to violence; so strong was this impulse that, the moment the lutenist began, the King rushed out, seized a sword, and slew 4 men. On the other side of the ledger, King Philip V of Spain engaged the famous castrato Farinelli to sing the same 4 songs for him nightly to allay his chronic melancholia; this continued for 25 years, until the royal sufferer finally gave up the ghost.

Among the most bizarre phenomena is *tarantism*, an uncontrollable compulsion to dance, which erupted in Taranto, Italy in the 15th century; this morbid choreographic condition was caused by the tarantula spider's bite; contemporary reports claimed that it could be cured by playing the Italian tarantella, a rapid 6/8 dance. Playing rhythmic dance music—particularly in binary meter (corresponding to the natural alternation of steps, inspirations, expirations, and the diastolic and systolic heartbeats)—may well be able to soothe a disturbed individual. On a larger scale, there is no denying that music can move masses of people to frenzy; the annals of political history are full of instances in which a revolutionary song inflamed the masses and led them to victory (on rare occasions, an operatic performance functioned similarly).

What kind of music should be played for medicinal purposes? Some music-loving physicians assert that music can affect the seat of emotion in the cerebral cortex. Numerous experiments have been conducted on mental patients to establish what particular type of music is best for them, with no conclusive results. Musical statistics have been compiled by psychologists to prove that the piano music of Chopin and Rachmaninoff was good for unbalanced persons, while Stravinsky and Schoenberg upset their mental equilibrium.

The Institute of Musical Therapy, organized in Poland (1974), suggested a musical program to be played prior to open-heart surgery for the beneficial effect on patient as well as surgeon: Gavotte in A Major by Gluck, *Clair de lune* by Debussy, Siciliana by Bach, and Adagio by Albinoni-Giazotti. This is an outgrowth of the longtime association between unthreatening music and relaxation that has resulted in a multimillion-dollar business that filters insidiously through offices, elevators, and shopping malls. More serious examples of the psychiatric benefit of music involve mentally ill and learning disabled adults, and special and autistic children. Music therapy became a professionally certified field, with full academic training, going hand-in-hand with the dance/movement therapy that evolved from eurhythmics.

musica (Lat.). Music. As a medieval term, it is incorporated in several expressions of the period: *musica artificialis*, composed music; *musica chordae*, string music; *musica da camera*, chamber music; *musica da chiesa*, church music; *musica divina*, sacred music; *musica harmonica*, vocal music; *musica humana*, harmony of body and soul; *musica instrumentalis*, music as performed and heard; *musica mundana*, music of the universe; *musica organica*, organ or wind music; *musica pulsus*, percussive music; *musica rhythmica*, music produced by finger striking; *musica sacra*, sacred music; *musica ventus*, wind music; *musica vocalis*, vocal music; *musica vulgaris*, secular music (not vulgar music).

Musica enchiriadis. Important anonymous Latin treatise, dating from *c.* 900, which includes discussion of the tetrachord, parallel organum, and notation.

musica ficta (Lat.). In music from the 10th through the 16th centuries, theoretically ambiguous chromatic alterations supposedly made in performance. The term, which means "manufactured music," originated in the 14th century to replace the misleading derogatory term *musica falsa*. Both terms described the perfectly innocent and in fact necessary practice of attaching accidentals, mainly sharps, to newly formed hexachords during the process of modulation. The expression *musica conjuncta* used by some writers is preferable because it alludes to the functional conjunction made between the hexachords by accidentals. Compilers of medieval Latin treatises fully realized how inadequate these terms were. In one of them an anonymous author speaks of the new type of modulation as "non tamen falsa musica, sed inusitata" (not so much false music, but useless music). But another anonymous author terms this "useless" music as "causa necessitatis et causa

pulchritudinis cantus per se" (for the reason of necessity and beauty, an independent melody). Still another writer claims that "falsa musica non est inutilis immo necessaria" (false music is not useless, but quite necessary); this opinion is echoed by the positive pronouncement of Philippe de Vitry to the effect that "musica ficta sive falsa est musica vera et necessaria" (musica ficta or musica falsa is true and necessary music).

The practical consequences of musica ficta, whatever the term itself might connote, were far-reaching. Medieval music theorists had followed the Guidonian hand with slavish obsequiousness. Their cautious modulations had to be *in manu* (in the hand), but musica ficta led music to the regions *extra manum* (outside the hand), venturing into the territory that required remote sharps and flats, at 1st only F-sharp and B-flat but later C-sharp and other accidentals. It should be remembered that B-flat, or *B rotundum* (round B) was very much *in manu*, the flatting of B being necessary to avoid the nefarious tritone, the diabolus in musica.

So much was the presence of B-flat in musical notation taken for granted that it often was omitted from the key signature altogether; e.g., the MS of Bach's Organ Toccata and Fugue in D Minor has no B-flat in the key signature and was dubbed the *Dorian Toccata* because it looked like that mode on paper; compositions requiring several flats in the signature customarily omitted B-flat as self-evident; this condition prevailed well into the 18th century.

In the meantime musica ficta generated subsidiary terms such as *vox ficta*, a contrapuntal part containing extra sharps or flats, and *cantus fictus*, a theme written in an alien key. Not until the reluctant admission on the part of music theorists that all keys are intervallically alike and that notation was the *anicilla musicae* (maidservant of music) were musica ficta and musica falsa exonerated from the suspicion of falsity.

musica figurata (Lat.). Music arranged in contrasting contrapuntal figurations.

musica reservata (Lat.). 16th-century term applied to a particularly sophisticated type of contrapuntal music, related to musica ficta and "reserved" for masters of the craft.

musical. American or English musical comedy or revue.

musical bow. Generic name for the monochord, consisting of a flexible rod curved by a string and played with a stick. A resonator may be attached, or the mouth used as one. The instrument is found almost universally at 1 time or another. Despite earlier theories, many cultures that play a musical bow do not hunt with bow and arrow.

musical comedy. Generic term applied to a play with music or opera with a comic or at least nontragic libretto. At its broadest the term can be applied to works beginning in the 16th century; however, the word *comedy* derives from the Italian *commedia*, which simply means "story" or "play" and does not guarantee the presence of humor; similarly, the French opéra comique may not necessarily leave them laughing, e.g., *Carmen*.

In the last century this term has been shortened to *musical*, and refers generally to a work with dialogue and songs; works that present songs only are descendants of vaudeville and are considered examples of the revue. Either type is known colloquially as a *show*. The American musical began developing in the post–Civil War era; the genre was influenced by French dancing chorus lines, Viennese operettas, and British musical comedy (Gilbert and Sullivan) and music hall. Early musicals were closer in essence to revues, as in the notorious *The Black Crook* (1866).

At the turn of the century Victor Herbert brought the operetta to Broadway; others in this group were Friml and Romberg. At the same time George Cohan developed a more American genre, full of vibrancy, with songs, choruses, dance numbers, and the thinnest of plots. After World War I many musicals reflected the political and social issues of the day, however flippantly; Jerome Kern's great *Showboat* (1928) was a profound exception, with its close study of racism. The Gershwins, Rodgers and Hart, Cole Porter, and Irving Berlin were the most known of many who contributed prolifically to the genre; the best songs were stunning exemplars of the popular song, lyrically and musically; the librettos remained mostly flimsy, using familiar comic opera devices such as mistaken identity, disguise, and satire. Gershwin's most serious work, *Porgy and Bess*, was called and written as an opera.

With the 1943 *Oklahoma!*, Rodgers and Hammerstein reintroduced the "serious musical comedy" on a steadier basis; whether the subject matter (*West Side Story*) or the source (*Kiss Me, Kate*, *My Fair Lady*) was the strength behind the show, the postwar musical was a more total work of art than any of its predecessors. In the last decades of the 20th century this kind of musical has survived and expanded in the hands of Stephen Sondheim; the other major development, musicals based on independently popular music such as rock and soul, has produced mixed results.

musical glasses. Glass harmonica.

musical saw. Special quasi-musical instrument producing a twanging sound when stroked.

musicale. Musical presentation or a concert given as part of a social gathering for the rich, or affluent music lovers; abbrev. of *soirée musicale* (musical evenings).

musico (It.). Musician.

musicology. Science of music; the concept includes all branches of music, i.e., theory, history, aesthetics, lexicography, bibliography, etc. The term originated in France early in the 19th century (*musicologie*) and was later adopted by German music theorists (*Musikwissenschaft*) and domesticated in England and America as musicology. The province of musicology was at 1st limited to the gnostic division of musical knowledge, with an emphasis on abstruse historical and semantic subjects. Musicological dissertations were apt to be extremely circumscribed in their statements, e.g., "certain conjectural elements in the quattrocento French motet" or "the possible urban Iberian origin of the Passacaglia."

But as the teaching of musicology expanded and embraced general historiography of music and even biography, Ph.D. degrees were awarded by leading univs. for dissertations with such titles as "Plausible Deciphering of Beethoven's Notes to His Housekeeper Instructing Her to Buy Candles and Yellow Soap" (the specification *gelbe* for the color of the soap was credited by the author to an eminent Beethovenologist), "New Data Establishing Schumann's Syphyllitic Infection," etc. Analysis of works, bibliographical studies of all kinds, and newfangled theories dealing with melody, harmony, or counterpoint all gradually fell in the category of musicology until it truly became a science of history, music theory, and musical biography. The only requirement to qualify, so it seemed, was a profusion of learned footnotes, some of which actually contradicted the author's postulates, e.g., "But cf. A. M. Dzegelenok, op. cit., who cogently refutes the above." Several musicological journals give space for the publication of such esoteric subjects which, it must be admitted, occasionally furnish useful information.

musicus (Lat.; Ger. *Musikant*). Medieval designation of a learned musician profoundly versed in the mathematical theory (and theology) of materials of which music is made, as contrasted with a mere cantor, who could sing or play music without understanding what it was.

Musikalien (Ger.). Printed musical compositions.

Musikdirektor (Ger.). Music director of an opera company, sym. orch., school, or other educational institution. *Musikdruck*, music printing or publishing; *Musikfest*, music festival; *Musikforschung*, music research; *Musikgeschichte*, music history; *Musikgesellschaft*, music society; *Musikschule*, music school; *Musikverein*, music association; *Musikwissenschaft* (Ger., musical science), musicology; *Musikzeitung*, music periodical.

musique concrète (Fr., concrete music). Composition on tape using recorded natural sounds and editing and processing them to produce a piece. Musique concrète was discovered and named in 1948 in Paris by Pierre Schaeffer, a French radio engineer. Experimenting with the newly invented magnetic tape, he found that a heterogeneous collection of songs, noises, conversations, radio commercials, etc. recorded on tape presented a realistic phonomontage which may serve for actual composition by superimposing fragments of tape recordings in a polyphony of random sounds, splicing the tape in various ways, running it at different speeds, or backward, etc.

The raw materials of musique concrète are susceptible to all kinds of treatment and are therefore capable of unlimited transformations. The technique of double and triple recording on the same length of tape makes it possible to create a polyphonic musique concrète of great complexity. In fact it is possible to recompose a classical sym. from a recording of a single note, which can subsequently be changed in pitch and arranged in the requisite rhythmic order, superimposed on other tones derived from the original note, altered in tone color by additional electronic manipulation, until a whole work is reconstructed from these constituent tonal dynamic and instrumental elements. In the U.S., Luening, Ussachevsky, and Varèse were the most important early exponents of musique concrète.

musique d'ameublement (Fr.). Furniture music. *Musique de chambre*, chamber music; *musique d'écurie* (Fr., music of the stable), field music, i.e., music played in unison by trumpets and signal horns; *musique de scène*, incidental music; *musique funèbre*, funeral music; *musique mesurée*, late-16th-century settings of *vers mesurés*, French poetry that utilizes classical Greek and Latin versifying principles; this concept was retained in French Baroque opera; *musique populaire*, folk music (not popular music); *musique sacrée*, sacred music.

Mussorgsky, Modest (Petrovich). b. Karevo, Pskov district, Mar. 21, 1839; d. St. Petersburg, Mar. 28, 1881. He received his 1st instruction on the piano from his mother; at age 10 he was taken to St. Petersburg, where he had piano lessons with Anton Herke (to 1854). In 1852 he entered the cadet school of the Imperial Guard; composed a piano piece entitled *Porte-enseigne Polka* (publ. 1852); after graduation (1856) he joined the regiment of the Guard. In 1857 he met Dargomyzhsky, who introduced him to Cui and Balakirev; he also became friendly with the critic and chief champion of Russian national music, Vladimir Stasov. These associations prompted his decision to become a professional composer. He played and analyzed piano arrangements of works by Beethoven and Schumann; Balakirev helped him to acquire a knowledge of form; he tried to write music in Classic style, but without success; his inner drive was directed toward "new shores," in his words.

The liquidation of the family estate made it imperative for Mussorgsky to take a paying job; he became a clerk in the Ministry of Communications (1863); dismissed 4 years later. During this time he continued to compose, but his lack of technique often compelled him to leave various pieces unfinished. He eagerly sought professional advice from his friends Stasov (for general aesthetics) and Rimsky-Korsakov (for problems of harmony); to the very end of his life he regarded himself as being only half-educated in music, and he constantly acknowledged his inferiority as a craftsman. But he yielded to no one in his firm faith in the future of national Russian music. When a group of composers from Bohemia visited St. Petersburg in 1867, Stasov publ. an article in which he for the 1st time referred to the "mighty handful of Russian musicians" (i.e., the "Mighty Five") pursuing the ideal of national art. The expression was picked up derisively by some journalists, but it was accepted as a challenge by Mussorgsky and his comrades-in-arms Balakirev, Borodin, Cui, and Rimsky-Korsakov. In 1869 he once more entered government service, this time in the forestry dept. In 1869 he was addicted to drink and had epileptic fits; the effects eventually killed him.

The significance of Mussorgsky's genius did not become apparent until some years after his death. Most of his works were prepared for publication by Rimsky-Korsakov, who corrected some of his harmonic "crudities" and reorchestrated the sym. works; orig. versions of his music were preserved in MS and eventually publ. But despite the availability of the authentic scores, many of his works continue to be performed in Rimsky-Korsakov's eds., made familiar to the whole musical world. In his dramatic works and songs, Mussorgsky draws a boldly realistic vocal line in which inflections of speech are translated into a natural melody. His 1st attempt in this genre was an unfinished opera, *The Marriage*, to Gogol's comedy; here he also demonstrated his penetrating sense of musical humor. His ability to depict tragic moods is revealed in his cycle *Songs and Dances of Death*; his understanding of intimate poetry is shown in his children's songs.

Mussorgsky's greatest work is the opera *Boris Godunov* (after Pushkin's tragedy; 1st version, with 7 scenes, 1868–69; 2nd version, prologue and 4 acts, 1871–72; rev. 1873; St. Petersburg, 1874), which has no equal in its stirring portrayal of personal destiny against a background of social upheaval. In it he created a true national music drama without a trace of the Italian conventions that had theretofore dominated the operatic works by Russian composers. He wrote no chamber music, perhaps because he lacked the requisite training in contrapuntal technique. Of his piano music, the set of pieces *Pictures at an Exhibition* (somewhat after the manner of Schumann's *Carnaval*) is remarkable for its vivid representation of varied scenes (it was written to commemorate his friend, the painter Victor Hartmann, whose pictures were the subjects of the music); the work became famous in the brilliant orchestration of Ravel.

Although Mussorgsky was a Russian national composer, his music influenced many composers outside Russia; he came to be regarded as the most potent talent of the Russian national school. He composed many powerful if rough-edged works, including other partially completed operas; orch'l works include *Ivanova noch'na Lisoy gore* (St. John's Night on Bald Mountain; 1860–67; reorchestrated by Rimsky-Korsakov; 1886); and *Vyzatiye Karsa* (The Capture of Kars; 1880); choral works, songs, and piano works.

muta (It.). Change either the instrument or (in prevalve brass instruments) the crook.

mutation. 1. Change of voice; breaking of the voice. 2. Change of position, shifting (violin). 3. In medieval solmization, movement from one hexachord to another.

mutations. In search for synonyms or paronyms to replace the ambiguous nomenclature of academic musicology, some modern composers have begun using the scientific-sounding words *variants* or *mutations* for *variations*. Mutations may be beneficial, musically speaking, when the mutant genes add to the brilliance of thematic adornment, as in some variations in the diaphanous music of Ravel; or they may be detrimental to the biomusical organism, as in the cluttered polyphony of Max Reger. Recessive mutations such as Stravinsky's neo-Baroque ornamentation may become dominant characteristics, with uncertain benefits.

In human terms, mutations are found in large musical families in which the embryo develops fully conditioned by the genetic complex of his parents. A striking example is that of Siegfried Wagner, a musical mutant who fully absorbed the musical genes of his father but acquired mutations that made him sterile. Some mutations are products of defective genes of the theme itself, a condition that may lead to melodic dyscrasia, harmonic dyslogia, and contrapuntal dyskinesia. There is no relief in such cases but to destroy the theme *in statu nascendi* in order to eliminate mutagenic elements and build afresh an untainted homunculus.

mute. 1. Piece of metal fitted to the bridge of a violin, et al., designed to deaden the sound when put into position. The direction for putting on the mutes is *con sordini*; for taking them off, *senza sordini*. 2. Leather-covered pad, pasteboard cone, or wooden cylinder inserted in the bell of brass instruments to modify the tone.

mut(h)ig (Ger.). Spiritedly, boldly.

Muti, Riccardo, b. Naples, July 28, 1941. After receiving instruction in violin and piano from his father, a physician with a natural Neapolitan tenor voice, Riccardo studied composition with Jacopo Napoli and Nino Rota at the Conservatorio di Musica San Pietro a Majella in Naples, taking a diploma in piano; studied conducting with Antonino Votto and composition with Bruno Bettinelli at the Verdi Cons. in Milan; attended a seminar in conducting with Franco Ferrara in Venice (1965).

After winning the Guido Cantelli Competition in 1967, Muti made his formal debut with the RAI in 1968; then conducted in several of the major Italian music centers. His success led to his appointment as principal conductor of the Teatro Comunale in Florence in 1970; conducted at the Maggio Musicale Fiorentino, becoming its artistic director in 1977. In the meantime he began his advancement to international fame with guest conducting appearances at the Salzburg Festival in 1971 and the Berlin Phil. in 1972. He made his U.S. debut with the Philadelphia Orch. (1972). In 1973 he conducted at the Vienna State Opera; that year he became principal conductor of the New Philharmonia Orch. in London (it resumed its original name of Philharmonia Orch. in 1977). In 1974 he conducted the Vienna Phil., and in 1977 he appeared at London's Covent Garden.

Muti's successful appearances with the Philadelphia Orch. led to his appointment as its principal guest conductor in 1977. In 1979 he was also named music director of the Philharmonia Orch. In 1980 he succeeded Eugene Ormandy as music director of the Philadelphia Orch., and he subsequently relinquished his posts in London and Florence in 1982. In 1986 he became music director of Milan's La Scala but retained his Philadelphia position. Muti announced his resignation as music director of the Philadelphia Orch. in 1990 but agreed to serve as its laureate conductor from 1992. His brilliance as a symphonic conductor enabled him to maintain, and even enhance, the illustrious reputation of the Philadelphia Orch. established by Stokowski and carried forward by Ormandy. Unlike his famous predecessors, he excels in both the concert hall and the opera pit.

Mutter, Anne-Sophie, b. Rheinfeldin, June 29, 1963. At age 6 she won 1st Prize with Special Distinction at the "Jungen Musiziert" National Competition, the youngest winner in its annals. In 1976 she came to the notice of Karajan during her appearance at the Lucerne Festival; in 1977 he invited her to be a soloist with him and the Berlin Phil. at the Salzburg Easter Festival; this was the beginning of an auspicious career. She subsequently appeared regularly with Karajan and the Berlin Phil., and also recorded standard violin concertos with him; likewise she appeared as soloist with many other leading conductors and orchs. on both sides of the Atlantic. She held the 1st International Chair of Violin Studies at London's Royal Academy of Music (from 1986). In 1988 she made her N.Y. recital debut.

Muzak. Trademark of the 1st U.S. company to have license to produce, distribute, and transmit background music for public consumption. Known colloquially as "canned music" or "elevator music," Muzak may also be supplied to restaurants, stores, mall plazas, doctors' offices, terminals, and waiting rooms. The kinds of music purveyed by Muzak consist of glutinous ballads and saccharine instrumental arrangements of popular or semi-classical songs.

Muzak was the brainchild of an Army general who was bemused by the commercial possibilities of "wired radio" as an entertainment medium. When the company was founded in 1934, it was in fact named "Wired Radio, Inc." Later it was suggested to combine the popular brand name in photography, Kodak, with music, and the result was Muzak. Soon there were over 300 Muzak franchises around the world. Muzak executives liked to describe themselves as "Specialists in the Physiological and Psychological Applications of Music," and their product as "a nonverbal symbolism for the common stuff of everyday living in the global village, promoting the sharing of meaning because it massifies symbolism in which not few but all can participate." However, not all share joyfully. Driven to desperation, N.Y. commuters brought out a class-action suit to show cause why this tonal pollution at the Grand Central terminal in N.Y. should be declared a public nuisance. Surprisingly, they won.

mysteries. Medieval Bible plays, often with vocal and instrumental music. In the form called moralities, abstract ideas were personified on the stage (e.g., *Jedermann*). Modern versions of the mysteries have been successfully revived in Britain.

Mystic Chord. Theosophic name that Scriabin attached to a chord consisting of 6 notes—C–F-sharp–B-flat–E–A–D—which lies at the foundation of his last symphonic work, *Promethée*. It is also known as the Prometheus chord. The chord was adumbrated in several of Scriabin's previous compositions in which it usually resolved into the dominant-9th chord by moving A to B-flat and F-sharp to G, thus resolving the 2 suspensions. Scriabin arrived at the formation of this chord intuitively, but later rationalized its construction as consisting of higher overtones forming a 6-tone scale from the 8th to the 14th overtones (C, D, E, F-sharp, A, B-flat). No one after Scriabin made use of the Mystic Chord, and it remains a solitary mausoleum.

nach (Ger.). After; according to.

nach Belieben (Ger.). At will; a piacere.

nach gefallen (Ger.). Ad libitum.

nach und nach (Ger.). Little by little, gradually. *Nach und nach schneller*, gradually faster.

Nachahmung (Ger.). Imitation.

Nachdrücklich (Ger.). With emphasis, marked. *Mit vielem Nachdrück*, with great emphasis.

nachgebend (Ger., yielding). Ever slower; rallentando.

nachgelassenes Werk (Ger.). Posthumous work.

nachgiebiger (Ger.). Still slower.

nachlässig (Ger.). Carelessly.

Nachschlag (Ger.). End notes of a trill.

Nachspiel (Ger., afterplay). Epilogue; postlude.

Nachthorn (Ger.). Covered stop in organ, having covered pipes of 2', 4', or 8' pitch.

Nachtmusik (Ger., night music). Serenade.

Nachtschall (Ger.). See ⇒Nachthorn.

Nachtstück (Ger., night piece). Nocturne.

Nagano, Kent (George), b. Morro Bay, Calif. (of Japanese-American parents), Nov. 22, 1951. He studied at Oxford Univ. (1969), with G. Cooper at the Univ. of Calif. in Santa Cruz (B.A., 1974), at San Francisco State Univ. (M.M., 1976), and the Univ. of Toronto; had conducting lessons from L. Varga in San Francisco. He was associated with Sarah Caldwell's Opera Co. of Boston (1977–79); music director of the Berkeley (Calif.) Sym. Orch. (1978) and the Ojai (Calif.) Music Festival (1984). While an assistant conductor with the Boston Sym. Orch., he substituted for Ozawa at the last moment and led a successful performance of Mahler's 9th Sym. without rehearsal (1984). He was the 1st co-recipient (with Hugh Wolff) of the Affiliate Artist's Seaver Conducting Award (1985); guest conducted with orchs. on both sides of the Atlantic; became chief conductor of the Opéra de Lyon (1989).

nail fiddle. Primitive instrument in use for a time in the 18th century, consisting of a wooden board with nails of different sizes affixed in a semicircle; played with an ordinary violin bow on the nails.

naked fifth. Harmonic perfect 5th (dyad) without a 3rd; open 5th.

naker (Mid. Eng.; Arab. *naqqāra;* Fr. *nacaire;* It. *nacchera*). Small kettledrum of Middle East, played in pairs; subsequently spread to India and Europe, where it was briefly in vogue; Scott revived the term in novel *Ivanhoe* (1819).

Nancarrow, Conlon, b. Texarkana, Ark., Oct. 27, 1912. He played trumpet in jazz orchs.; took courses at the Cincinnati College–Cons. of Music (1929–32); went to Boston; studied privately with Slonimsky, Piston, and Sessions. In the late 1930's he fought on the side of the Spanish Loyalists against Franco's armies; upon returning to the U.S. he was classified an "undesirable" and refused a passport; crossed the Mexican border and went to Mexico City; lived there the rest of his life (naturalized 1956). After many years' absence, he participated in the New American Music Festival in San Francisco (1981); was a composer-in-residence at the Cabrillo Music Festival in Aptos, Calif.; traveled to Europe, participating at festivals in Austria, Germany, and France. He received long overdue but nonetheless extraordinary recognition in 1982, when he was awarded the "genius grant" of $300,000 by the MacArthur Foundation of Chicago.

The unique quality of Nancarrow's approach comes from his music's being notated by perforating old-fashioned player-piano rolls to mark notes and rhythms and can only be performed by activating these rolls. He turned to this method when he found human performers incapable of realizing his intentions; this compositional technique gave him total freedom to create the most complex, "inhuman" contrapuntal, harmonic, and rhythmic combinations he could imagine. The method itself is extremely laborious; a single measure might require an hour or more to stamp out. Some of his early studies were publ. in normal notation in Cowell's *New Music Quarterly*; Copland, Ligeti, and others praised Nancarrow's originality in highest possible terms.

Nancarrow's work began to reach a receptive audience through publication of several of his studies (in normal notation) by Peter Garland's *Soundings* (starting in 1977), accompanied with critical commentaries by the cream of the American avant-garde. In 1984 he gave a concert of his works in Los Angeles, including the early *Prelude and Blues* (on acoustic piano) and several studies (on player piano). He began composing for acoustic instruments, finding modern players capable of what would have been unimaginable in the 1930's; his 3rd String Quartet was premiered in Cologne by the London-based Arditti Quartet, which proved itself capable of realizing Nancarrow's exceedingly complex score (1988).

napolitana (It.). Old type of Italian madrigal, revived in modern times in the form of a popular song.

napura (Sans., Beng. *nūpura*). Indian vessel rattle in the form of a hollow copper ring filled with pebbles; worn on ankles by dancers.

narcolepsy. Sym. concerts are notoriously conducive to narcolepsy, and their attendance is sometimes recommended by psychologists as an effective cure for insomnia. Statistical surveys indicate that narcogenic factors are mainly the pendulumlike rhythmic beats in classical music, particularly when there is no change in dynamics. An unexpected sforzando will wake up even the most inveterate narcoleptic, as illustrated by the story of Haydn's *Surprise Sym.* with its famous chord in the slow movement that was supposed to arouse somnolent London concertgoers from their middle-aged slumber. On the other hand, modern works rarely put people to sleep because of constant changes in rhythm and dynamics.

Narcolepsy is also an inevitable outcome of lectures on musicology; according to observations conducted by a trained psychologist at a session of the International Musicological Congress in N.Y., a deep coma overtook practically the entire audience during the 1st 20 seconds of a reading from manuscript of a paper by an eminent Dutch musicologist. At the same occasion, attention was suddenly increased by the appearance on the podium of the inventor of a double-bass flute and an ultrasonic piccolo. He could never succeed in blowing through the long tube of the big flute, which met with sympathy in the audience. The hyperpiccolo could not be heard by humans, but a terrier dog who strayed into the hall showed agitation at the ultrasonics that canines can hear easily. Both dog and inventor were rewarded by hearty applause.

narrante (It.). Narrating; as if telling a story; declaim distinctly.

narrator (Ger., *Erzähler;* It., *testo*). Speaking part in Baroque oratorios, designed to promote continuity of plot. In the 20th century, the narrator plays an important part in Stravinsky's *Oedipus Rex* and *Histoire du soldat,* and, in a lighter vein, Prokofiev's *Peter and the Wolf.*

nasard (Fr.; Ger. *Nasat*). 12th (organ stop) of 2 2/3–foot pitch (large sizes 10 2/3 and 5 1/3, smaller size 1 1/3).

national anthems. Songs that by accident or intention assume the status of a patriotic hymn; most of them are anonymous. Few transcend their functional role and possess genuine musical beauty; only one, the former Austro-Hungarian anthem *Gott erhalte unsern Kaiser,* was written by a major composer (Haydn); the same melody has been used as Germany's anthem with different texts during the 20th century.

nationalism. 19th- and 20th-century movements, initially prominent in eastern Europe, later throughout the world, wherein patriotic composers strived to embody and reveal aspects of national identity in their music.

natural. 1. The sign ♮, canceling a sharp or flat. 2. White key on the keyboard. *Natural harmonics,* those produced on an open string; *natural horn,* horn without valves; *natural interval,* one found between any 2 tones of a diatonic major scale; *natural key,* C major; *natural pitch,* that of any wind instrument when not overblown; *natural scale,* one having neither sharps nor flats, i.e., C major; *natural tone,* any tone obtained on a wind instrument with cupped mouthpiece, without using keys, valves, or slide.

natural minor scale. Basic minor scale, without chromatic alterations, and therefore lacking the leading tone. The scale uses sharps or flats indicated in the key signature shared by its relative major scale, whose tonic is a minor 3rd above the minor tonic.

natural tone series. See ⇒harmonics.

naturalism. Extreme form of operatic verismo. Naturalistic opera emphasizes the negative phenomena of life without the redeeming quality of romance. In Soviet parlance, naturalism has acquired a pejorative meaning; the word was used as a verbal missile in attacks on Shostakovich's opera Lady Macbeth of the District of Mtzensk, particularly with reference to the scene of adultery illustrated in an orch'l interlude by sliding trombones.

naturalmente (It.). In a natural, unaffected style.

Naturhorn (Ger.). French horn without valves or pistons.

Naturlaut (Ger.). Natural sound. *Wie ein Naturlaut,* like a sound of nature (Mahler's 1st Sym.).

Navarro, "Fats" (Theodore), b. Key West, Fla., Sept. 24, 1923; d. N.Y., July 7, 1950. He 1st took up tenor saxophone, then mastered trumpet; subsequently played with several groups, including those of Andy Kirk (1943–44) and Billy Eckstine (1945–46); he later worked in N.Y. as a leading exponent of bop style.

Nazareth (Nazare), Ernesto (Julio de), b. Rio de Janeiro, Mar. 20, 1863; d. there, Feb. 4, 1934. He was pioneer in fostering a national Brazilian type of composition, writing pieces in European forms with Brazilian melorhythmic inflections; among genres he invented were *fado brasileiro, tango brasileiro, valsa brasileira, marcha brasileira,* etc.; he also composed original dances in rhythms of samba and chôro. In his declining years he became totally deaf.

Neapolitan cadence. Cadence in which the customary subdominant triad (IV) is replaced by the lowered supertonic triad in 1st inversion (bII⁶), called the *Neapolitan 6th;* as the bass of the Neapolitan 6th (chord) is the same as the subdominant chord, the substitution is logical. As in the usual cadence, the Neapolitan chord is followed by the dominant, often interpolated with the tonic 6/4 chord, before reaching the tonic. The Neapolitan cadence, 6th, and chord received their names from frequent use by composers of the 18th-century Neapolitan school (although they did not invent it). A remarkable example of a Neapolitan chord opening is the 1st Ballade in G Minor by Chopin, which begins with a lengthy and elaborate cadenza based on the Neapolitan chord of the key of G minor; Scriabin's 3rd Sym., *Le Poème divin,* is nominally in C minor, but begins with a Neapolitan cadence on D-flat.

Near, Holly, b. Ukiah, Calif., June 6, 1949. She sang in public from childhood; worked in film and television; performed on Broadway in *Hair.* She took a commercially and artistically independent stance with her music; formed the Redwood label to record *Hang In There* (1973), *Live Album* (1974), *You Can Know All I Am* (1976), and *Imagine My Surprise* (1979), all becoming known by word of mouth; later recordings include *Fire in the Rain* (1981), *Speed of Light* (1982), *Journeys*

(1983), *Watch Out!* (1984), *Sing to Me the Dream* (1984), *HARP* (1985, with A. Guthrie and P. Seeger), *Singing with You* (1986), *Don't Hold Back* (1987), *Sky Dances* (1989), and *Singer in the Storm* (1990). While preferring smaller venues for performances, she appeared at Carnegie Hall in N.Y. and the Royal Albert Hall in London; made film and television appearances, participated in benefit concerts, and engaged in philanthropic work. With Meg Christiansen and Cris Williamson, she has been important and influential in the feminist and lesbian vanguard, along with the political left.

Nebensatz (Ger., adjacent part). 2nd expository theme in a sonata-form movement.

Nebenstimme (Ger., adjacent voice). Term invented by Schoenberg to denote the 2nd polyphonic voice, abbrev. in his scores as N⌐. See ⇒Hauptstimme.

neck. On some chordophones, the section of the body by which they are held; also called the *handle.*

negative music. Negative music is synonymous with *antimusic,* but there is a scintilla of a difference between the 2 terms. Antimusic stresses its opposition to any musical actions, whereas negative music operates on the supposition that there may exist negative frequencies as mathematical abstractions, related to audible music as a negative to the positive in photography. Negative music would reverse dynamic values; a vocal text containing tender sentiments would be harmonized by loud dissonant noises; conversely, a symphonic poem on the subject of nuclear war would be depicted by the minutest distillation of monodically concentrated tones. field for experimentation in negative music is limitless, precisely because it is impossible to speculate about its nature.

negli (It.). In the.

negligente (It.). In a style expressive of negligence; carelessly.

nei, nel, nell', nella, nelle, nello (It.). In the.

nella parte di sopra (It.). In the higher or highest part.

Nelson, Judith (Anne Manes), b. Chicago, Sept. 10, 1939. She studied at St. Olaf College in Northfield, Minn.; sang with music groups of the Univ. of Chicago and the Univ. of Calif., Berkeley; made her operatic debut as Drusilla in Monteverdi's *L'incoronazione di Poppea* in Brussels (1979). She appears widely as a soloist and recitalist; although particularly noted for performances of Baroque music, she also introduced compositions by American and English composers.

Nelson, Prince Roger. Prince.

Nelson, Willie (Hugh), b. Abbott, Tex., Apr. 30, 1933. He briefly attended Baylor Univ. in Waco, Tex.; made appearances in local honky-tonk bars; began writing songs, including *Hello Walls, Crazy,* and *Night Life,* made famous by leading singers of the day. He then went to Nashville, Tenn.; played bass in Ray Price's band and gained renown with *The Party's Over* and *Little*

Things in his many appearances at the Grand Ole Opry; eventually returned to Tex.; helped develop the Austin sound, also called outlaw country or redneck rock. With the album *Red-Headed Stranger* (1975) he produced a major hit; released others, including *Stardust* (1978), *Willie and Family Live* (1978), *Honeysuckle Rose* (1980), *Always on My Mind* (1982), and *Angel Eyes* (1984); became a competent film actor, making appearances in *Electric Horseman* (1979) and *Honeysuckle Rose* (1980).

neoclassicism. 20th-century revival of 18th-century (or earlier) musical precepts, exemplified by many post–World War I works by Stravinsky and Schoenberg but anticipated by French composers at the turn of the century. When luxuriant impressionism reached the saturation point, many composers realized that further amplification of coloristic devices was no longer stimulating or novel. This reaction coincided with the economic collapse following World War I, so that it became financially difficult to engage large orchs. or grandiose operatic companies.

The cry went all over Europe: "Back to Bach!"; to this was added the banner of Neue Einfachheit (New Simplicity). Since it seemed infeasible to progress through expansion, musical taste, with the aid of intellectual rationalization, made a 180° turn toward the past; as the past could not be literally recaptured, the new retrograde movement was labeled neoclassicism, characterized by the following traits: (1) Rehabilitation of diatonicism as the dominant idiom, using enhanced pandiatonic constructions in which all 7 degrees of the diatonic scale are functionally equal; (2) elimination of virtually all programmatic and Romantic associations, either in titles or tonal content of individual works; (3) demonstrative revival of Baroque forms such as sonata, suite, passacaglia, fugue, toccata, and florid variation; (4) demotion of chromatic scalar elements to their traditional role as passing notes; (5) restrained use of massive sonorities and renunciation of all external and purely decorative effects, such as nonthematic melismas and nonessential harmonic figurations; (6) cultivation of compact forms, such as 1-movement syms. and sonatas, chamber syms. and string orchs., and operas with no chorus and with reduced orch. (*c.* 13 instruments) and an important piano part analogous to that of the Baroque cembalo; (7) reconstruction of old Baroque instruments, particularly the harpsichord, and their employment in modernized classical techniques; (8) exploration of canonic and fugal writing without adherence to strict rules of classical polyphony; (9) radical curtailment of development sections in Baroque forms, with purely nominal recapitulation and concise coda free from endless repetition of final chords.

neomedievalism. While neoclassicism, anticipated by Busoni's writings and French music of the early 20th century, resuscitated Baroque music in a new guise of pandiatonic harmonies and asymmetrical rhythms, some modern composers retreated even further into the past, discovering surprisingly modernist devices as hocket, heterophony, quodlibet, and inversion and retrograde composition, the last pair basic to serial music. Modernization of these resources combined to create neomedievalism, a stylized idiom that adopted not only old musical modalities but the use of Latin for texts; the finest example of this trend is Stravinsky's opera-oratorio *Oedipus Rex,* with a specially written text in medieval Latin. Orff produced successful works in a quasi-medieval style, notably *Carmina Burana*, to texts in Latin and German dialects. A significant trait of these 2 works is their imaginative repetitive technique; the liberating power of literal repetition would later attract composers of the avant-garde who follow Eastern religious practices, exemplified by the turning of the Tibetan prayer wheel.

neomodality. The modal system—so potent for centuries—nearly lost all its binding power under the impact of tonality, atonality, and dodecaphony. Dormant strains achieved a renaissance in the ethnically deep-rooted works of Bartók; R. Harris built a *sui generis* ethos of modes by assigning specific emotions to each, according to the intervallic magnitude of the opening tetrachord. Avenir H. Monfred developed a practical method of modern modal composition, *diatonic neomodality*, in which modal change is effected by altering key signatures, e.g., the Dorian mode on D can be transformed, during the composition process or by spontaneous improvisation, into another mode by adding sharps or flats to the key signature; it is transmuted into D major by placing 2 sharps in the key signature, into the Phrygian mode by 2 flats, etc. A happy if unexpected revival of modality was its adoption by the purveyors of rock 'n' roll, often inspired by the scales used in traditional and folk music.

neomysticism. The words *Laus Deo*, which Haydn appended to every manuscript upon its completion, were an expression of his piety and not a claim of direct communication with the Deity. Mystical 20th-century composers, on the other hand, believed that they were oracles of higher powers. Mahler thought he was possessed by Beelzebub and scrawled appeals to Satan in the MS of his unfinished 10th Sym. But it was Scriabin who concretized his mystical consciousness in musical terms; his sym. *Prométhée* is based on his 6-note Mystic chord; shortly before his death he sketched out the text for a *Mysterium*, envisioned as a synaesthetic action comprising all human senses as receiving organs; the work was to include a large bell ensemble performed high over the Himalayan Mountains.

neophobia. Neurotic fear of radical innovations; professional critics are particularly prone to it, a condition they attempt to disguise as profound devotion to the immutable laws of music. Like mental patients, they regard themselves as the only sane persons in a mad world. The more enlightened among them correct former misapprehensions. At the American premiere of *Don Juan* by R. Strauss, Philip Hale described it as "a good deal of a bore"; 11 years later, he called it a work of "fascinating, irresistible insolence and glowing passion." Heinrich Strobel, who became the great panjandrum of the European avant-garde, contributed some choice invectives against the American moderns performed at a concert in Berlin (1932):

> *For 2 hours Nicolas Slonimsky bore down on the musicians of the Berlin Philharmonic, until finally they could no longer refrain from openly showing their disgust. For an hour and three-quarters the public tolerated the noise, but by the cacophonous melee of Arcana by Varèse the audience lost*

> *their patience. A scandal broke loose. It was understandable. No ear can endure this sort of noise for any length of time. It has nothing to do with music. It does not shock and it does not amuse. It is simply senseless.*

neoprimitivism. Art saturated with culture is invariably tempted to return to its simple origins, chronologically to the cave paintings of primitive man and to the haunting drum rhythms of *Homo protomusicus*, and biologically to infantiloquy. But supreme mastery of design is used by abstract expressionist painters to emulate prehistoric drawings, and a sophisticated compositional technique is used by modern composers for children's pieces in asymmetrical rhythms; from these dual resources, musical neoprimitivism has emerged. Discarding civilizing Romantic images and impressionist colors, it seeks to attain the crude power of massively arrayed sonorities, asymmetrical rhythms, and percussive instrumentation.

In neoprimitivism, melodies are brief refrains, often limited to the range of a tetrachord; reiteration of single notes in unchanged speed is cultivated to the point of stupefaction; vacuous progressions of naked 5ths and 4ths are used to suggest inarticulate eloquence; heterophony, in which a mobile voice elaborates on the principal subject while ignoring contrapuntal niceties, is encountered in numerous neoprimitivist scores, as a curious recessive characteristic.

Neoprimitivism is almost invariably nationalistic in character. The masterpiece of neoprimitivism, Stravinsky's *Le Sacre du Printemps*, bears the subtitle *Scenes of Pagan Russia;* Bartók's music evokes the neoprimitivist landscape of immortal Pannonia; Villa-Lobos re-creates the inchoate sound of the Brazilian landscape in his syms. Neoprimitivism is nurtured on character traits associated with a people, but the composer need not be an archaeologist, but derives inspiration from the art of his or her era. The French painter H. Rousseau copied the subjects and color patterns of his exotic paintings from illustrations in a French children's book; Gauguin painted his Tahitian women from photographs, preferring them to living models; yet both created a genuinely novel type of pictorial neoprimitivism. In music, however, neoprimitivist representation cannot be effected without a complete mastery of modern techniques of composition. The theory that an analphabetic musician can write primitivistically authentic works by simply disregarding the civilized rules of harmony and counterpoint is dubious.

neoromanticism. 20th-century revival of works embodying 19th-century musical precepts; one such revival occurred before and during World War II, a 2nd in the last quarter of the century (in the U.S., as New Romanticism). Neoromanticism represents a reactionary phase of the modern stylistic upheaval, following upon neoclassicist repudiation of programmatic music; the frustrations of World War I had sharpened general disenchantment among poets, artists, and musicians; but resulting negative intellectual movements, such as dadaism, exhausted their shock power, giving way eventually to a mitigated type of Romanticism. Coloristic elements, so ingratiatingly used in the syms. of Sibelius, the tone poems of R. Strauss, and the early ballet scores of Stravinsky were applied with apprehensive circumspection by neoromantic composers; representational onomatopoeia and literal reproduction of natural sounds replaced subjective effusions of modern pictorialism. Britten's seagulls in the interludes of *Peter Grimes*, Messiaen's bird songs in *Chronochromie*, and the recording of a real nightingale's song in Respighi's *The Pines of Rome* are modern instances of neoromanticism.

nera (It., black one). Quarter note.

nervoso (It.). In forcible, agitated style.

Nesterenko, Evgeni (Evgenievich), b. Moscow, Jan. 8, 1938. He 1st studied architectural engineering; graduated from the Leningrad Structural Inst. in 1961, then enrolled in the Leningrad Cons., where he studied voice with Lukanin. He began his opera career at the Maly Theater in Leningrad (1963–67); then was a member of the Kirov Opera and Ballet Theater there (1967–71). In 1970 he won 1st prize at the Tchaikovsky Competition in Moscow; in 1971 he joined the Bolshoi Theater. He then embarked on a European concert tour; also sang in the U.S. In 1975 he was appointed chairman of the voice dept. at the Moscow Cons. He excelled in such roles as Boris Godunov and Méphistophélès. In 1982 he was awarded the Lenin Prize.

nettamente (It.). In neat, clear, and distinct style.

Neue Sachlichkeit (Ger.). Movement launched in Germany after World War I to describe the "new objectivity" in drama, art, and music, a reaction against the hyperromantic tendencies of 19th-century culture. In music it cultivated functional modus operandi, pursuing well-defined objectives in clearly outlined forms. The economic necessity of cutting down the cost of production of musical presentations resulted in the creation of new types of chamber opera, without chorus and with a partial return to the Classic orch.; the movement coincided with the aims of Gebrauchsmusik.

neumes. Mensural notation signs used in the later Middle Ages to represent pitch and rhythm.

new music. Term for music of the 20th century intended to distinguish it from music of the past and in advance of its own time. Newness is a recurring motive in musical nomenclature. The emergence of rhythmic modalities in the 14th century became known as *ars nova*; a collection of monodic compositions by the Florentine operatic initiator G. Caccini was published as *Nuove musiche*. In painting, *art nouveau* described the French art that flourished in the 1890s. The term *new music* became current about 1920 and denoted a modern music marked by dissonant counterpoint, atonality, and brevity of expression; later, new music became synonymous with ultramodern music.

New Romanticism. U.S. movement, begun in the 1970s, wherein composers returned to gestures, forms, genres, and harmonies of the 19th century.

New Simplicity. 1. During the neoclassical flowering of the 1920s the slogan "New Simplicity" was raised among composers eager to divest themselves of an enforced sophistication; in practice, New Simplicity meant a return to elementary and sometimes abecedarian melodic and harmonic practices, barely obscured by a patina of nontoxic dissonances. 2. In the 1970s, especially among central European, Scandinavian, and Dutch composers, a move towards a simplified style highly influenced by American minimalism.

New Wave. See ⇒rock.

Newman, Alfred, b. New Haven, Conn., Mar. 17, 1900; d. Los Angeles, Feb. 17, 1970. He was the uncle of Randy Newman. He studied piano with S. Stojowski and composition with R. Goldmark; had private lessons with Schoenberg in Los Angeles. He began his career in vaudeville shows billed as "The Marvelous Boy Pianist"; later led theater orchs. on Broadway; hailed as "The Boy Conductor" and "The Youngest Conductor in the U.S.A." In 1930 he went to Hollywood; devoted himself entirely to writing film music; wrote about 230 film scores; of these, 45 were nominated for awards by the Motion Picture Academy, and 9 were winners. Among his most successful scores were *The Prisoner of Zenda* (1937), *The Hunchback of Notre Dame* (1939), *Wuthering Heights* (1939), *Captain from Castille* (1947), The *Robe* (1953), and *The Egyptian* (1954; taken over from B. Herrmann). Stylistically he followed an eclectic type of theatrical Romanticism; could mimic almost literally the most popular works of Tchaikovsky, Rachmaninoff, Wagner, and Liszt, amalgamating these elements in colorful free fantasia; he thereby created a category of composition that became known, with some disdain, as "movie music."

Newman, Randy, b. Los Angeles, Nov. 28, 1943. He is the nephew of Alfred Newman. He spent his childhood in southern Calif.; took regular music lessons; became a pianist, arranger, songwriter, and (later) film composer. His songs, while fully conscious socially, often veered toward the unacceptable, unthinkable, and inconceivable in terms of targets and the oblique means by which he hit them: *Davy the Fat Boy* (from *Randy Newman*); *Yellow Man* (*12 Songs*); *Political Science* and *Sail Away* (*Sail Away*); and the entire 1974 album *Good Old Boys*. In 1977 he released *Little Criminals,* again assailing bigotry, but its *Short People,* a major hit, was misconstrued as an attack on vertically challenged persons. This was neither the 1st nor last time that he would overestimate the human capacity to perceive irony. What gets lost is the breadth of Newman's songwriting: an almost Ivesian capacity for nostalgia (*Dayton Ohio–1903*); insight into the fear of sex and other hedonisms (*You Can Leave Your Hat On; Lucinda*); a fine sense of humor (*Burn On; Mama Told Me Not to Come*); and the knack for writing beautifully painful songs (*I Think It's Gonna Rain Today; Guilty*). He released *Born Again* (with *It's Money That I Love,* 1979); *Ragtime* (soundtrack, 1981); *Trouble in Paradise* (1983); the quasi-biographical *Land of Dreams*; and a musical, *Faust* (1995).

Nichols, "Red" (Ernest Loring), b. Ogden, Utah, May 8, 1905; d. Las Vegas, June 28, 1965. His father taught him cornet; he played in his father's brass band from age 12. He then made an impression in popular music with his own band, advertised as Red Nichols and His 5 Pennies (actually, there were 10 "Pennies"); its members included such future celebrities as Jimmy Dorsey, Benny Goodman, and Glenn Miller. A maudlin motion picture, *The 5 Pennies,* was manufactured in 1959 and catapulted Nichols into the stratosphere of jazzdom; critics bemoaned the commercialization of his style, giving preference to his earlier, immaculate jazzifications.

nicht (Ger.). Not. *Nicht zu langsam,* not too slow.

Nicolai, (Carl) Otto (Ehrenfried), b. Königsberg, June 9, 1810; d. Berlin, May 11, 1849. He studied piano at home; went to Berlin; took lessons in theory with Zelter (1827); also took courses with B. Klein at the Royal Inst. for Church Music. He made his concert debut in Berlin as a pianist, singer, and composer (1833); engaged as organist to the embassy chapel in Rome by the Prussian ambassador; studied counterpoint with G. Baini.

Nicolai proceeded to Vienna, becoming a singing teacher and Kapellmeister at the Kärnthnertortheater (1837); returned to Italy (1838); presented in Trieste his 1st opera, *Rosmonda d'Inghilterra* (also called *Enrico II,* 1839); his 2nd opera, *Il Templario,* was staged in Turin (1840). He returned to Vienna; appointed court Kapellmeister, succeeding Kreutzer (1841); was instrumental in establishing sym. concerts using the musicians of the orch. of the Imperial Court Opera Theater; conducted this ensemble in the Beethoven 7th Sym. (1842) in what became the inaugural concert of the Vienna Phil.; appointed Kapellmeister of the Royal Opera in Berlin (1848). His famous opera *Die lustigen Weiber von Windsor,* after Shakespeare, was premiered at the Berlin Royal Opera (1849); it was his only enduring creation; he died 2 months later.

Nicolai composed sacred choral music, secular vocal ensemble music, 2 syms. (1831, 1835), overtures, chamber music, and solo songs. Hans Richter, conductor of the Vienna Phil., inaugurated an annual "Nicolai-Konzert" in his memory (1887); it became a regular occasion; at different times it was conducted by Mahler (1899–1901), Weingartner (1909–27), Furtwängler (1928–31, 1933–44, and 1948–54), Böhm (1955–57 and 1964–80), and Abbado in 1980 and 1983.

Nielsen, Carl (August), b. Sortelung, near Nørre-Lyndelse, June 9, 1865; d. Copenhagen, Oct. 3, 1931. He received violin lessons in childhood from his father and the local schoolteacher; played 2nd violin in the village band, later in its amateur orch. After studying cornet with his father, he played in the Odense military orch. (1879–83); taught himself piano. While in Odense he began to compose, producing several chamber pieces; received financial assistance to continue training at the Royal Cons. in Copenhagen; studied violin with V. Tofte, theory with J. P. E. Hartmann and O. Rosenhoff, and music history with N. Gade and P. Matthison-Hansen (1884–86).

Nielsen achieved his 1st success as composer with the *Little Suite* for Strings (1888); continued private studies with Rosenhoff for a number of years. He played violin in Copenhagen's Royal Chapel Orch. (1889–1905); in 1901 he was granted an annual pension; conductor of the Royal Theater (1908–14) and the Musikforeningen (1915–27) in Copenhagen; guest conducted in Germany, the Netherlands, Sweden, and Finland; taught theory and composition at the Royal Cons. (1916–19); appointed its director a few months before his death.

The early, essentially Romantic style of Nielsen's music was influenced by Gade, Grieg, Brahms, and Liszt; later he experienced the powerful impact of modern music, particularly in his increasingly chromatic and dissonant harmony; yet he reserved simple diatonic progressions, characteristic of Danish folk song, for his major climaxes. In his orchestration he applied opulent sonorities and colorful instrumental counterpoint; there are instances of bold experimentation in some works, e.g., the lengthy snare-drum solo in his 5th Sym., metrically and defiantly independent of the rest of the orch.

Nielsen is loosely described as the Sibelius of Denmark, mostly because of his stature in his own country; there are obvious dissimilarities in idiom and sources of inspiration; Sibelius's music is deeply rooted in national folklore, while Nielsen seldom drew on Danish popular modalities; Sibelius remained true to the late Romantic style, while Nielsen cautiously sought new ways of modern expression. After Nielsen's death, his major works entered the world repertoire; festivals of his music were organized on his birth centennial, and his syms. in particular were played and recorded in England and America, bringing him belated recognition as a truly important composer of his time. In 1988 Queen Margrethe II dedicated the Carl Nielsen Museum in Odense.

Nielsen's best-known works are the 6 syms.: No. 1, op. 7 (1890–92; 1894); No. 2, op. 16, *The 4 Temperaments* (1902); No. 3, op. 27, *Sinfonia espansiva,* with 2 solo singers (1912); No. 4, op. 29, *The Inextinguishable* (1916); No. 5, op. 50 (1922); No. 6, *Sinfonia semplice* (an oddly sarcastic, even bitter work, 1925); 2 operas: the tragedy *Saul og David* (1902), and the comedy *Maskarade* (1906); incidental music for many plays; other orch'l, chamber, solo, and vocal works. His writings include *Living Music* (Copenhagen, 1925) and *My Childhood in Funen* (Copenhagen, 1927). His son-in-law was the Hungarian Emil Telmányi, a violinist, conductor, and teacher (b. Arad, June 22, 1892; d. June 12, 1988). He studied with Hubay at the Royal Academy of Music in Budapest; began an active career as violinist (1911); married Ann Marie, Carl Nielsen's daughter (1918); supervised the devising of a curved bow for playing Bach's violin works, known as the Vega bow (1954).

niente (It.). Nothing. *Quasi niente,* barely audible.

Nietzsche, Friedrich (Wilhelm), b. Röcken, near Lützen, Oct. 15, 1844; d. Weimar, Aug. 25, 1900. He was prof. of classical philology at the Univ. of Basel (1869–79); was at 1st a warm partisan of Wagner, whom he championed in *Die Geburt der Tragödie aus dem Geiste der Musik* (1872; 2nd ed., 1874) and *Richard Wagner in Bayreuth* (1876). In *Der Fall Wagner* and *Nietzsche contra Wagner* (both 1888) and in *Götzendämmerung* (1889) he turned against his former idol and became a partisan of Bizet. Nietzsche tried his hand at composition, producing both sacred and secular choral works, songs, and piano pieces.

Nilsson, (Märta) Birgit, b. Västra Karups, May 17, 1918. She studied with J. Hislop at the Royal Academy of Music in Stockholm; made her debut as Agathe in *Der Freischütz* at the Royal Theater in Stockholm (1946), gaining her 1st success as Verdi's Lady Macbeth (1947); sang major roles in Wagner, Puccini, and Strauss with increasing success. She 1st appeared as Brünnhilde in *Götterdammerung* in Stockholm (1954–55); sang this role in the Ring cycle for the 1st time in Munich during the same season; appeared at the Vienna State Opera (1954) and at Bayreuth (1954), to which she returned regularly (1959–70).

In 1956 Nilsson made her U.S. debut at the Hollywood Bowl; sang Brünnhilde in *Die Walküre* at the San Francisco Opera (1956); subsequently made her 1st appearance at London's Covent Garden (1957). She made her long-awaited Metropolitan Opera debut in N.Y. as Isolde (1959). She was universally acclaimed as one of the greatest Wagnerian dramatic sopranos of all time. After an absence of 5 years she returned to the Metropolitan Opera for a gala concert (1979); rejoined the company, appearing as Elektra (1980); retired from the operatic stage in 1982. In addition to her brilliant Wagnerian roles, she excelled as Beethoven's Leonore, Turandot, and Salome.

ninth. Interval of an octave plus a major or minor 2nd.

ninth chord. Although 9th chords are defined as chords consisting of a series of 4 superimposed 3rds on any degree of scale, their use is confined in practice to dominant 9th chords. These chords were cultivated systematically by Wagner, Liszt, and Bruckner, always within a given tonality. The 9th chord requires 5-part harmony for its totality; in 4-part harmony the 5th above the root is left out. The necessity of the resolution into the dominant 7th chord is felt very strongly in cadential formations, as, for instance, toward the end of the overture of *Die Meistersinger*. The dramatic attraction of the 9th chord led Scriabin to formation of his so-called Mystic Chord, which eliminates the 5th but includes an upper and lower appoggiatura to it. Debussy emancipated the tonal implications of the dominant 9th chord by moving it in parallel formation, either chromatically or by minor 3rds, without resolving.

Numerous composers of the 20th century used this device to create the feeling of vague harmonic uncertainty. Fascination of the 9th chord ceased abruptly with the decline of musical impressionism in the 2nd quarter of the 20th century, and parallel 9th chords, once the darlings of modernism, were relegated to a type of "mood music." Ninth chords built on degrees of the scale other than the dominant lack the proper euphony to provide much interest to composers of modern music, and examples of such use are rare.

Ninth Symphonies. Many composers have reached number 9 in their symphonic production, among them Mahler and Bruckner, but when musicians speak simply of "The 9th," it is understood that the great *Choral* Sym. of Beethoven is meant.

Nirvana. (Guitar/vocal: Kurt Cobain, b. Hoquiam, Wash., Feb. 20, 1967; d. Seattle, Wash., Apr. 5, 1994; bass: Krist Novoselic, b. Los Angeles, May 16, 1965; drums: David Grohl, b. Warren, Ohio, Jan. 14, 1969.) Archetypical grunge-rock outfit. Cobain and Novoselic were childhood friends in Aberdeen, Wash.; they formed Nirvana together in 1987. Playing locally with various supporting members, they were signed to the small Sub Pop label, recording their 1st album, which featured the single *Love Buzz* backed with *Negative Creep*, both hits among the nascent grunge community. Grohl joined the lineup in time for their major-label debut, *Nevermind*, released on DGC Records in 1990. The song *Smells Like Teen Spirit* made the album an immediate chart-busting hit and established the group as the voice of their (plaid-clad) generation.

Nirvana produced a 3rd album, *In Utero*, banned by Wal-Mart and other chain stores but still happily consumed by teens everywhere. An appearance on *MTV Unplugged* helped listeners actually understand the group's lyrics—previously nearly obliterated by their ear-crunching sound—and some were surprised by Cobain's sensitivity, others by his disturbing sentiments. In 1992 Cobain wed Courtney Love, big-lunged vocalist and songwriter with the group Hole, and the couple's escapades were soon making tabloid headlines. Cobain himself had trouble adjusting to adulation and fame, attempting suicide in Mar. 1994 and, 1 month later, shooting himself in the head at his home. An outpouring of grief-stricken grungers held a vigil outside of his home. Following Cobain's death, Grohl formed the Foo Fighters. Love continued to record and perform and also costarred in the film *The People vs. Larry Flynt* (1996).

Nixon, Marni (born Margaret Nixon McEathron), b. Altadena, Calif., Feb. 22, 1930. She studied with C. Ebert at the Univ. of Southern Calif. in Los Angeles, J. Popper at Stanford Univ., and B. Goldovsky and S. Caldwell at Tanglewood. She pursued a multifaceted career: sang on the soundtracks of the films *The King and I, West Side Story,* and *My Fair Lady;* starred in her own children's program on television; appeared in musical comedy and opera; was a soloist with major orchs. in the U.S. and abroad. She taught at the Calif. Inst. of the Arts (1969–71) and the Music Academy of the West in Santa Barbara (from 1980).

No Admission. 1. Indication that a theater is closed or that there is no performance that day. 2. An indication that tickets are free of charge. See also ⇒relâche.

nobilmente (It.). In refined, chaste, and lofty style; Elgar uses this term in the 1st movement of his cello concerto.

noch (Ger.). Still; yet. *Noch rascher,* still faster.

nocturne (Fr., night piece; It. *notturno*). Piece of dreamily Romantic or sentimental character, set in euphonious melody and harmony, and without fixed form. The nocturne emerged as a distinct genre of Romantic piano pieces early in the 19th century, primarily through poetic creations of Chopin. The pioneer of piano nocturnes was Irish composer John Field, but his pieces fall far below those of Chopin in quality. Even though nocturnes are creatures of night, Chopin often includes dramatic turbulence in the middle sections. Schumann also wrote nocturnes, but, in conformity with prevalent nationalistic sentiment of the time, he assigned to them a German name, *Nachtstück.*

Nocturns. Portion of the Matins service of Roman Catholic daily Hours, held during the night.

node (nodal point). Point or line in a vibrating body (such as string, soundboard, trumpet, bell) which remains at rest during the vibration of other parts of the body.

Noël (Fr.; from Lat. *natalis,* birthday). Christmas carol or hymn with sacred or secular texts, including drinking songs.

noire (Fr.). Quarter note.

noise. Scientifically speaking, sound with indefinite pitch used as compositional element in many 20th-century compositions; collection of tonally unrelated simultaneous sounds of different frequencies and intensities, meaningless to musical or even unmusical ears. *White noise* is an integral assembly of sounds of numerous frequencies but more or less equal intensities. In radio transmission, noise is called static, and a similar electromagnetic disturbance in television is called snow. Metaphorically, old-fashioned music critics often describe unfamiliar music as noise.

nola (It.). Abbrev. for *campanola*, Italian diminutive of campana (bell). See also ⇒tintinnabulum.

non (It.). Not.

non vibrato (It.). Emphatic negative exhortation often warning against the natural tendency of string players and singers to use vibrato and produce what the Baroque considered an *affect* but what became standard performance technique in Romantic (and other) music; other considerations for non vibrato are the period of music being performed (e.g., early music movement) and performance of untempered pitch (just intonation).

None. Daily service, part of the Roman Catholic Divine Office, celebrated at 3 p.m., the time when Jesus died on the cross (counted as the 9th hour from sunrise, hence the name). This service is one of 4 so-called Little Hours.

nonet. Composition for 9 voices or instruments. Usually the instrumentation involves more than 1 instrumental family; but Copland wrote a nonet for violin, viola, and cello, 3 apiece (1961).

Nonnengeige (Ger., nun violin). Whimsical appellation common in the 14th century for the tromba marina, which itself is a curious name for a monochord, a box with 1 string. German nuns supposedly favored this instrument.

Nono, Luigi, b. Venice, Jan. 29, 1924; d. there, May 8, 1990. He earned a unique place in modern music history through consistent devotion to social problems. He became a student at the Venice Cons. (1941); studied composition with Malipiero (1943–45); studied law at the Univ. of Padua (graduated, 1946); had advanced harmony and counterpoint lessons with Maderna and Scherchen. A man of extraordinary courage, he joined the Italian Communist Party while the country was still under Mussolini's dictatorship and was an active participant in the Italian Resistance Movement against the Nazis. In 1975 he was elected to the Central Committee of the Communist Party, remaining a member until his death.

Although Nono's works are extremely difficult to perform and mostly ripe with leftist attitudes, he found support among a number of liberal composers and performers; by his last years acquired a reputation as a highly original composer in a novel technical idiom as well as a fearless political agitator. In his technique of composition he followed Schoenberg's precepts without adhering to the letter of the dodecaphonic approach. He mitigated the antinomy between his modern musical idiom and the conservative ideology of socialist realism by his militant political attitude and emphasis on revolutionary subjects, so that even extreme dissonances could be dialectically justified as representing the horrors of fascism. He made several visits to the Soviet Union, the last in 1988, but his works are rarely performed there because of the intransigence of his idiom.

Nono used a variety of techniques: serialism, sonorism (à la *Klangfarbenmelodie*), aleatory and concrete music, and electronics. Perhaps his most militant composition, both politically and musically, is the opera *Intolleranza 1960*, utilizing texts by Brecht, Eluard, Sartre, and Mayakovsky; it protests powerfully against imperialist policies and social inequities. At its premiere in Venice (1961) a group of neofascists showered the audience with leaflets denouncing Nono for allegedly contaminating Italian music with alien doctrines, even alluding facetiously to his last name as a double negative. He married Schoenberg's daughter, Nuria (1955); they had 2 daughters. He died of a liver ailment.

nonretrogradable rhythm. For Messiaen, denotative of symmetrical patterns which, by nature, exhibit no change upon inversion: ♩ ♪♩ ♩♪ .

nontoxic dissonances. Dissonances can be said to be nontoxic or noncorrosive if they are embanked within a tonal sequence, or if their cadential illation corresponds to traditional modalities. It is harmonic context that determines toxicity of a dissonance for an untutored ear. Among the most corrosive dissonances are atonal combinations in which intervals of a high degree of discordance—such as major 7ths, minor 2nds, and tritones—are combined with acoustically euphonious intervals of a perfect 5th and perfect 4th. The absence of 3rds, whether major or minor, is the distinctive feature of corrosive harmony, but toxic sonic effects result also from simultaneous use of 2 parallel major and minor triads on account of interference between the major and minor 3rds. Changes in biochemical balance and nervous reactions to the impact of toxic dissonances can be measured on a neurograph, providing a scientific clue to the apperception of modern music.

noodling. Mindless preludizing and arpeggiating on an instrument, as if warming up for real playing; thus, a negative critique of an improvisation.

Norman, Jessye, b. Augusta, Ga., Sept. 15, 1945. She received a scholarship to study at Howard Univ. in Washington, D.C. (1961), where she had vocal lessons from C. Grant; continued her training at the Peabody Cons. of Music in Baltimore and the Univ. of Michigan, where her principal teachers were Bernac and Elizabeth Mannion. She won the Munich Competition (1968), then made her operatic debut as Elisabeth in *Tannhäuser* at the Berlin Deutsche Oper (1969); she appeared in the title role of *L'Africaine* at Florence's Maggio Musicale (1971), and the following year sang Aida at Milan's La Scala and Cassandra in *Les Troyens* at London's Covent Garden; subsequently made major recital debuts in London and N.Y. (1973).

After an extensive concert tour of North America (1976–77) Norman made her U.S. stage debut, as Jocasta in *Oedipus rex* and as Purcell's Dido on a double bill with the Opera Co. of Philadelphia (1982). She made her Metropolitan Opera debut in N.Y. as Cassandra (1983). In 1986 she appeared as soloist in Strauss's *Vier letzte Lieder* with the Berlin Phil. during its tour of the U.S. In 1989 she was featured soloist with Mehta and the N.Y. Phil. in its opening concert of its 148th season, which was telecast live to the nation by PBS. Her extraordinary repertoire ranges from Purcell to R. Rodgers; she commended herself in Mussorgsky's songs, which she performed in Moscow in Russian;

in her recitals she gave performances of classical German repertoire as well as contemporary masterpieces, such as Schoenberg's *Gurrelieder* and *Erwartung* and French moderns, which she invariably performed in the original tongue. This combination of scholarship and artistry contributed to her consistently successful career as one of the most versatile concert and operatic singers of her time.

Norrington, Roger (Arthur Carver), b. Oxford, Mar. 16, 1934. He was educated at Clare College, Cambridge, and the Royal College of Music in London; was active as a tenor. In 1962 he founded the Schütz Choir in London, with which he 1st gained notice as a conductor. From 1966 to 1984 he was principal conductor of the Kent Opera, where he produced scores by Monteverdi utilizing his own performing eds.; served as music director of the London Baroque Players (from 1975) and the London Classical Players (from 1978); also was principal conductor of the Bournemouth Sinfonietta (1985–89). In 1989 he made an auspicious N.Y. debut at Carnegie Hall conducting Beethoven's 8th and 9th syms. In 1990 he became music director of the orch. of St. Luke's in N.Y. In 1980 he was made an Officer of the Order of the British Empire; in 1990, a Commander of the Order of the British Empire.

Norrington entered controversy by insisting that the classical tempo is basic for all interpretation. He also insisted that Beethoven's metronome markings, not usually accepted by performers, are in fact accurate reflections of Beethoven's inner thoughts about his own music. He obtained numerous defenders of his ideas (as one critic put it, "inspired literalism") for the interpretation of classical music, which aroused sharp interest as well as caustic rejection. His performances, especially in the U.S., received a great deal of attention and were particularly praised for accuracy and precision of interpretation. In 1985 he began an annual series of musical "experiences": weekends devoted to in-depth exploration of some major classical work, comprising lectures, open rehearsals, research exhibits, and performances of other works by the same composer (which have included Haydn and Berlioz as well as the inevitable Beethoven) and his contemporaries, selected to explicate the musical centerpiece.

North, Alex, b. Chester, Pa., Dec. 4, 1910; d. Pacific Palisades, Calif., Sept. 8, 1991. He studied piano and music theory at the Curtis Inst. of Music in Philadelphia; later received a scholarship to study at the Juilliard School of Music in N.Y., where he took courses in composition (1929–32). A decisive change in his life came with his decision to go to Russia as a technology specialist at a time when Russia was eager to engage American technicians. He became fascinated with new Russian music and received a scholarship to attend the Moscow Cons., where he studied composition with Anton Weprik and Victor Bielyi (1933–35). He also was music director of the propaganda group of German Socialists called "Kolonne Links" (Column to the Left).

North mastered the Russian language and acquired a fine reputation in Russia as a true friend of Soviet music. Returning to the U.S., he took additional courses in composition with Aaron Copland (1936–38) and Ernst Toch (1938–39). In 1939 he conducted 26 concerts in Mexico as music director of the Anna Sokolow Dance Troupe; during his stay in Mexico City, he had some instruction from Silvestre Revueltas. In 1942 North entered the U.S. Army; promoted to captain, he became responsible for entertainment programs in mental hospitals. He worked closely with psychiatrist Karl Menninger in developing a theatrical genre called psychodrama, which later became an accepted mode of psychological therapy.

During his Army years North also worked with the Office of War Information, composing scores for over 25 documentary films. During all these peregrinations he developed a distinct flair for theater music while continuing to produce estimable works in absolute forms. His concerto, *Revue* for Clarinet and Orch., was performed by Benny Goodman in N.Y. under the baton of Leonard Bernstein (1946). He further expanded his creative talents to write a number of modern ballets. The result of these multifarious excursions into musical forms was the formation of a style peculiarly recognizable as the specific art of North.

North's concentrated efforts, however, became directed mainly toward the art of film music, a field in which he triumphed. John Huston stated in 1986 that "it is the genius of Alex North to convey an emotion to the audience"; other directors praised North's cinemusical abilities in similar terms. Among writers with whom he worked were Tennessee Williams, John Steinbeck, and Arthur Miller. But no success is without disheartening frustration. North was commissioned to write the score for *2001: A Space Odyssey*, on which he worked enthusiastically. But much to his dismay director, Stanley Kubrick, decided to replace it by a pasticcio that included such commonplaces as *The Blue Danube Waltz*. North refused to be downhearted by this discomfiture and used the discarded material for his 3rd Sym. He was nominated 15 times for an Academy Award for best film music, but it was not until 1986 that the Academy of Motion Picture Arts and Sciences finally awarded him an Oscar for lifetime achievement.

Among North's outstanding scores are *A Streetcar Named Desire* (1951), *Death of a Salesman* (1951), *Viva Zapata!* (1952), *The Rose Tattoo* (1955), *The Bad Seed* (1956), *The Rainmaker* (1956), *Spartacus* (1960), *The Misfits* (1961), *Cleopatra* (1963), *The Agony and the Ecstasy* (1965), *Who's Afraid of Virginia Woolf?* (1966), *Under the Volcano* (1984), *Prizzi's Honor* (1985), *The Dead* (1987), and *Good Morning, Vietnam* (1988). His song *Unchained Melody* (1955) became a popular hit. North also composed ballets, children's theater, orch'l music, choral music, and chamber music.

Norvo, Red (born Kenneth Norville), b. Beardstown, Ill., Mar. 31, 1908. He played piano and xylophone while attending classes in mining engineering at the Univ. of Missouri (1926–27); later joined Paul Whiteman's orch. In 1935 he organized his own band in N.Y.; also worked with Benny Goodman (1944–45) and Woody Herman (1945–46). He was briefly married to singer Mildred Bailey.

nose flutes. Family of wind instruments blown with nasal rather than oral breath; some can be blown in both ways. Materials used and form (e.g., transverse, end-blown) vary widely. Examples of the nose flute can be found on all continents, notably in Melanesia and Polynesia, rarely in Europe.

nóta (Hung.). Urban song, such as *Rákóczi-nóta*, song about Rákóczi.

nota cambiata (It., changing note). Cambiata.

nota cattiva (It., bad note). Unaccented note.

nota sensibile (It.). Leading tone.

notation. The art of representing musical tones, and their modifications, by means of written characters; the craft of writing symbols that represent sounds. It took a millennium to develop a musical notation capable of even an approximate rendition of the pitch and duration of each individual note. The Spanish theologian Isidore of Seville, who flourished in the 7th century, asserted that musical sounds could be transmitted from one generation to another only by oral tradition because they could not be properly notated (*scribi non possunt*). The old monk's pessimistic declaration seems to be prophetically fulfilled in many modern scores of the 2nd half of the 20th century, which abandon all attempts at precise notation of pitch or duration, and resort instead to such approximations as *najwyszy dzwiek instrumentu* (the highest possible sounds of the instrument), a Polish direction in the works of Penderecki; instructions in a work by Stockhausen for the performer to strike any note on the piano and hold it indefinitely; a similarly stupefying exhortation by Cage: "This is a composition indeterminate of its performance, and the performance is of actions which are often indeterminate of themselves"; the declaration of Cardew, the inventor of "scratch music," in which "the notation may be accomplished using any means, verbal, graphic, musical, or by collage."

Music of ancient Greece was notated by letters, some of them turned backward or put upside down apparently to indicate a certain type of interval. Toward the end of the 1st millennium A.D. an early system of notation appeared in the form of *neumes,* a Greek word for a nod, a sign, or a signal, indicating single notes or groups of notes (*ligatures*). Such neumes were placed directly in the text above the lines and indicated the rise or fall of the vocal inflection, graphically derived from the acute, grave, and circumflex accents. An acute accent represented by a slant to the right denoted the rise of a 2nd, a 3rd, or another small interval. Around 1000 A.D. Guido d'Arezzo drew a line to mark the arbitrary height of pitch, establishing musical notation as geometric in its symbolism. With the establishment of square notation, the intervallic norms became more definite. Rhythmic values were determined according to an elaborate set of rules that varied from century to century and from country to country, so that the transcription of medieval chants becomes a matter of editorial discretion. In the course of time, embryonic neumes developed into groups of notational cells that were embodied in graphic shapes and assumed expressive Latin names.

Mensural notation, or measurable notation, emerged in the middle of the 13th century, and its invention, or at least its codification, is usually ascribed to Franco of Cologne. In the early centuries of mensural notation, white notes of different shapes were used; black notes appeared in the course of time when a necessity arose of writing rapid passages. The standard notation of note lengths was, starting from greatest duration, *maxima, longa, brevis* (or *breve*), *semibrevis* (*semibreve*), *minima, semiminima, fusa,* and *semifusa.* Each of these equaled 2 or 3 notes of the next smaller durations; so *maxima* had 2 or 3 *longas,* a *longa* had 2 or 3 *breves,* a *breve* had 2 *semibreves,* etc. As if *maxima* was not long enough, a *larga* was introduced, which had the value of 2 or 3 *maximas.* It is ironic that the *semibreve* (half-short) note of mensural notation eventually became

the longest note of modern notation, designated as a whole note, occupying an entire bar in 4/4 time. It appears that in the Middle Ages time was running at a slower tempo.

Arithmetically, in modern notation a whole note equals 2 half notes, a half note equals 2 quarter notes, etc. But in mensural notation a note could equal either 2 or 3 of the next smaller note. In modern notation a dotted half-note equals 3 quarter notes, etc., but in mensural notation the operation had to be indicated verbally or by a system of ligatures that are most misleading in view of the absence of barlines and other auxiliary symbols. The verbal clues were contained in the adjectives (in Latin, of course) *perfectum* or *imperfectum.* These words did not mean "perfection" or "imperfection" in the moral or physical sense, but in the etymological Latin sense of completion and incompletion. *Perfectio* was the subdivision of a note into 3 smaller note values, subdivisions into 2 being examples of *imperfectio.* Some theologically minded music theorists of the Middle Ages suggested that triple time is perfect because it stands for the Trinity.

Furthermore, there were special terms for the mutual relationships between each pair of adjacent note values. The relationship between *brevis* and *semibrevis* was called *tempus;* the relationship between a *semibrevis* and *minima* was *prolatio* (prolation). If both *tempus* and *prolatio* were perfect, the result was a bar of 9 whole notes subdivided into 3 groups; if the *tempus* were perfect and the *prolatio* imperfect, this denoted 3 groups, each of which had 2 beats. If the *tempus* were imperfect but the *prolatio* perfect, then there were 2 divisions of 3 beats each. The perfection was symbolized by a perfect circle in the time signature; the imperfection was indicated by a semicircle; we inherited the sign of imperfection in the 4/4 time signature that looks like the capital letter *C.* (Hence, a frequent error in interpreting the imperfection signature—medieval binary time—as modern common time, quadruple time.) Painful complications ensue as we plunge more deeply into ligatures—groups of notes glued together or hanging to one another precariously by the corner of an oblong or to the side of a rhombus. Musicologists who are willing to devote their lives to the inscrutable mysteries of mensural notation come figuratively to blows in their internecine polemics; as a result, transcriptions of medieval MSS in mensural notation are rarely in agreement.

In modern usage, fractional names designate musical notes: whole note, half note, quarter note, 8th note, 16th note, 32nd note, 64th note, etc. Individual 8th notes have flags attached to them; groups of 8th notes are united by black beams; 16th notes have 2 flags; their groups are united by double beams; 32nd notes have 3 flags and are united by triple beams, etc. Identical graphic symbols are used in all Western music, but the names may differ. Thus in British usage quarter notes are called crotchets, 8th notes are quavers, 16th notes are semiquavers, 32nd notes are demisemiquavers, 64th notes are hemidemisemiquavers, and 128th notes are called semihemidemisemiquavers. A dot next to the note head adds 50% to the value of the note; thus a half note equals 2 quarter notes and a dotted half note equals 3; British usage, except for the names, is identical. The same augmentations by 50% are effected by dots placed after rests.

With the virtual disappearance of special signs indicating ornamentation (mordents, inverted mordents, etc.) in the 19th century, the present system of notation became an entirely workable method of writing down notes corresponding precisely to the intended pitch and duration of each note; the invention of the metronome made it possible to measure metrical units in fractions of a second. Interpretation remained a personal matter, but liberties could be taken only in dynamics, variations in tempo, etc. True, the written notes did not always reflect the composer's ideal, and some great masters allowed themselves to write passages that could not be performed adequately or even approximately. Beethoven wrote sustained chords in some of his piano sonatas that could not be held by pedal without muddying up the harmony; or by the fingers, which were occupied elsewhere. Schumann has a melody in his *Études symphoniques* for Piano that is to be played legato in the bass but cannot be carried on without interruption. The addition of the barline in the notational system is a great metric support, but the persistent habit of stressing the 1st beat has resulted in a brutalization of the basic rhythmic design.

There are numerous examples in great masterpieces in which the composer seems to be following a different beat in his rhythmic design than appears in the metric arrangement. A musical person listening to the rapid finale of Schumann's piano concerto will hear an unmistakable rhythm of a slow Viennese waltz; but the trouble here is that Schumann notated this passage in rapid 3/4 with stresses on the 1st and 3rd beats of the 1st bar and on the 2nd beat of the 2nd bar, the 2 bars forming a metric unit. A most extraordinary incongruence between visual notation and auditory perception occurs in the 1st movement of the 1st Sym. of Brahms, where a rhythmic period of 3 eighth-notes enters on the 2nd beat of 6/8, with the accented notes overlapping the barlines. A modern composer would probably write a bar of 1/8 and then resume 6/8 time until the notated rhythm and meter coincide. Quite often the ear groups several bars into 1 unit in a fast tempo, as when Beethoven indicates that the scherzo of his 9th Sym. is to be perceived in *ritmo di tre battute* (rhythm of 3 bars).

Ultramodern composers of the 2nd half of the 20th century tried to remedy the ills of musical notation with the aid of science, at least as far as meter and rhythm were concerned. Instead of the uncertainties of tempo marks, time signatures, and rhythmical units in metrical frames, some ultramodern notation specifies the duration of each note in time units, usually in seconds or fractions of seconds. Visually, too, a whole note occupies all the room of a bar of 4/4 time, a half note takes up exactly one half of such a bar, and passages in smaller notes are notated proportionately to the time they consume. In dynamics the newest notation blithely specifies differences between *pianissimo* (*pp*) and *pianississimo* (*ppp*), *fortissimo* (*ff*) and *fortississimo* (*fff*), and so forth, up and down the dynamics range. The trouble, of course, is that human performers cannot execute such scientific niceties with any degree of precision or with the requisite aplomb. Electronic instruments have come to the rescue.

Such is the perversity of human nature that just as musical notation seemed to achieve a scientific precision, composers of the avant-garde developed a yen for indeterminacy. Of course, indeterminacy is itself a respectable scientific doctrine, and the theory of probabilities, which is closely related to it, possesses a mathematical aura that is quite idiosyncratic in its application. But a human being is also a tangle of probabilities; it is logical, therefore, that ultramodern notation should have absorbed the human element. Xenakis, Stockhausen, E. Brown, Bussotti, Cage, and many others in Europe, America, Japan, and Greece have adopted a graphic notation that not only deals in probabilistic elements but resorts to pictorial representations of human faces experiencing prescribed emotions, from saintly tranquillity to raging madness. When an occasional music staff is inserted in such scores, it may be covered with blobs of black ink or surrealistic geometrical curves. Verbalization of the basic elements of notation expands enormously here, and the performer is often urged to play or sing anything at all. Some modern musicians are possessed by a desire to represent new music by visual images; others have returned to older notational and stylistic modes. See also ⇒tablature.

note. One of the signs used to express relative time value of tones. *Note against note*, counterpoint in equal notes.

note echappée (Fr.). Echappée.

note row. See ⇒set.

Notendruck (Ger.). Music printing.

Notenstich (Ger.). Music engraving.

notes inégales (Fr.). Inégales.

Notierung (Ger.). Notation.

Notre Dame school. Religious compositional school that flourished in Paris in the 12th and 13th centuries. Its greatest masters were Leoninus and Perotin. But whether they were actually attached to the present cathedral of Notre Dame itself is a matter of conjecture, because the cornerstone of the famous church was not laid until the middle of the 12th century and construction was not completed for 2 more centuries.

notturno (It., night piece). 1. Nocturne. 2. Instrumental genre of the 18th century, akin to the divertimento, serenade, and cassation. Haydn and Mozart were among many composers of notturnos.

Novachord. See ⇒Hammond, Laurens.

Novellette (Ger.). Character piece, usually for piano solo; free in form, bold in harmony, Romantic in character, and of considerable length; characterized by a number of melodically unrelated themes united by a common rhythmic lift. The term does not mean "a little novel" as may be imagined. Schumann invented it (op. 21, 1838) to express admiration for the English singer Clara (Anastasia) Novello (1818–1908); was not the 1st time that Schumann engaged in such verbal trickery; wrote pieces that he called "Wiecketten," after the maiden name of his beloved future wife Clara. But "novelette" seemed such a beguiling name that many composers have adopted the term precisely in the sense of little novels or stories; did Balakirev, Liadov, and other novelette composers realize that they were unwittingly paying homage to Clara Novello?

novelty. Popular instrumental piece or song not easily classified, such as nonsense songs, kiddie rhymes, pieces with unusual orchestration (e.g., typewriter, clock, toy balloons, tinkling bells), exotica, etc. Leroy Anderson specialized in orch'l novelties, such as *The Syncopated Clock.*

nuane (Fr., nuance). Shading; change in musical expression, either in tone color, tempo, or degree of force.

number. 1. Subdivision of an opera or oratorio. 2. Smaller, and more or less complete, portion of a large work, such as song, aria, interlude, etc. 3. Any single piece on a program. 4. Opus number.

number opera (Ger. *Nummernoper*). Opera in which the principal ingredients—arias, vocal ensembles, instrumental interludes, etc.—are clearly separated from each other or are connected by recitative or spoken dialogue. Virtually all operas before Wagner were number operas, but an argument can be advanced that transitions between separate numbers create continuity characteristic of "music drama" of the Wagnerian type. Wagner's theories virtually determined the operatic practice of the 2nd half of the 19th century, but a return to the more formal type of number opera was marked in the 20th century. Modern composers, especially Stravinsky, successfully revived the seemingly extinct genre and even took delight in emphasizing its archaic traits.

number pieces. Designation for late works by American composer John Cage bearing numbers as titles (*74, 13, 1⁵*, etc.). The numbers refer to the number of players called for in the score; superscript numbers are used to differentiate multiple compositions with the same number of players, and thus the same number title (e.g., 2^4, 4th work composed for 2 players).

numbers. The Latin word *numeri* had a 2nd meaning, music, which was governed by the law of proportions between 2 different sounds. In Shakespearean English, numbers refer to musical composition. St. Augustine drew distinction between *numeri sonantes,* actual musical tone perceived by the senses, and *numeri recordabiles,* music that is remembered. In St. Augustine's concept melody was formed by a single sound instantaneously perceived and memorably associated with several preceding sounds. Long before St. Augustine, Aristoxenus likened the musical tones of melody to letters in language. So intimate was the connection felt between numbers and music that in medieval univs. music was taught as part of the quadrivium of exact sciences, along with arithmetic, geometry, and astronomy. This association with numbers was lost in Classical and Romantic music. Not until the 20th century did the numerical element in music regain its status.

Mathematical parameters lie at the foundation of serial music. The calculus of sets is an important tool in rhythmic serialization. Some composers have applied Fibonacci numbers, in which each term is the sum of its 2 predecessors, to metrical, rhythmic, and intervallic parameters. Simple arithmetical progressions also yield material for rhythmic arrangements. application of numbers to composition is limitless; the difficulty is to select numerical sets that would provide material for purely musical structures. Numbers also served as a poetic synonym for music, often used in the sense of a song by Shakespeare, Milton, and other writers.

numerology. Several composers, superstitiously credulous regarding the importance of some numbers in their lives, reflected these beliefs in their musical compositions. There are indications that Bach favored mystic numbers derived from the position of letters of his last name in the alphabet. B–A–C–H would then equal $2 + 1 + 3 + 8 = 14$; according to the same ordering, the numerical value of J–S–B–A–C–H equals 41. One of Bach's late portraits has 14 buttons on the breast. In his last completed composition, *Vor deinen Thron,* the initial staff has 14 notes, the entire melody 41 notes.

The curious, and quite serious, case of triskaidekaphobia that preoccupied Rossini and Schoenberg had an apparent bearing on the date of their deaths; Rossini died on Friday the 13th (like many Italians, he was superstitiously fearful of such a combination), and Schoenberg, who regarded the number 13 as ominous because he was born on the 13th of the month, went so far as to remove the 2nd *A* in the title of his unfinished work *Moses und Aron* (i.e., Aaron) because the sum of the letters in the title added up to 13. He died on the 13th of the month, at the age of 76, the digits of which add up to 13.

Nummernoper (Ger.). Number opera.

Nun's fiddle (Ger. *Nonnengeige*). Tromba marina.

nuovamente (It.). Again, anew.

nuove musiche (It., new musics). Originally the title of a selection of monodies by G. Caccini (1601), it became a slogan of the Camerata, a group of erudite poets, philosophers, and musicians who successfully reversed the musical trend of ever-increasing complexity of polyphonic music in favor of simple homophonic style of solo arias and madrigals with simple harmonic accompaniments. So potent was the desire on the part of music lovers to return to original sources of vocal music uncomplicated by artful devices that soon the entire period of the early–17th century was designated as the period of nuove musiche; its monodic style gave birth to opera, oratorio, and cantata and inaugurated the Baroque.

The creators of nuove musiche also established the historically important principle that text should be the determining factor of musical expression rather than be subordinated to the pre-arranged melodic structure. Extreme development of Baroque polyphony reversed the stream once more toward greater complexity, but predominance of the text over polyphony was once more proclaimed a century and a half later by Gluck and basically subscribed to by Wagner and Debussy.

Nurock, Kirk, b. Camden, N.J., Feb. 28, 1948. He held scholarships for study at the Juilliard School in N.Y. and at the Eastman School of Music in Rochester, N.Y.; studied composition with Persichetti, Sessions, and Berio; awarded the Elizabeth Sprague Coolidge Prize in chamber music (1970). From his earliest works, he has adhered to extraordinary and unusual sound production; active as conductor of idiosyncratic theater productions, among them the temporarily objectionable but ultimately lovable musical *Hair;* became a skillful jazz pianist. In 1971 he developed an experimental vocal technique called "natural sound," which assumed that every person's vocal cords, as well as other body parts, are capable of producing variegated sound. In many works he annexed animal noises; the most challenging of them being *Sonata for Piano and Dog* (N.Y., 1983) and *Gorilla, Gorilla* for Solo Piano (N.Y., 1988). Audience participation is welcomed as an integral part of natural sound productions; several of his works are specifically scored for untrained, improvisatory participants. Interestingly enough, newspaper reviews of his presentations often revive the alarmed outcries of shocked innocence that greeted 1st performances of the now-recognized works of Prokofiev, Stravinsky, Schoenberg, and Varèse.

nut. 1. Ridge over which strings pass at the end of the fingerboard next to the head of a violin, etc. 2. Sliding projection at the lower end of the violin bow, by means of which the hair is tightened or slackened; also called frog. 3. The "lower nut" on the violin is the ridge between tailpiece and tailpin (or button).

N.W.A., Popular rap group of the early 1990s. (Vocals: Ice Cube, b. O'Shea Jackson, Los Angeles, Calif., June 15, *c.* 1969; Dr. Dre, b. Andre Young, Los Angeles, Feb. 18, 1965; Eazy-E, b. Eric Wright, Los Angeles, Sept. 7, 1963; d. there, Mar. 26, 1995; MC Ren, b. Lorenzo Patterson, Los Angeles, June 16, year unknown; DJ Yella, b. Antoine Carraby, Los Angeles, Dec. 11, year unknown.) The group coalesced around performer/record company owner Wright (aka Eazy-E) and composers Jackson (Ice Cube) and Young (Dr. Dre). Eazy-E had a hit with Cube and Dre's *Boyz-n-the-Hood,* inspiring them to join forces in the group, N.W.A. (Niggaz Wit Attitude). Their debut album, 1989's *Straight Outta Compton,* featured early antisocial rap attitudes, including *F—k the Police* and *Dopeman.* Despite its success, Cube felt he was shortchanged by the group and left it soon after. He has since enjoyed a successful solo recording and acting career.

The group's second album, *Efil4zaggin* ("Niggaz 4 life" spelled backwards), was another smash hit. On it they spouted more misogynist lyrics while attacking ex-member Ice Cube (establishing the dissing wars so favored by rap acts). However, the group soon splintered into individual activities. Eazy-E gained notoriety on his own as producer/performer, as did Dr. Dre; Easy-E died of AIDS.

nyckelharpa (Swed.). Keyed folk fiddle, dating from the Renaissance and still played. Like the hurdy-gurdy, strings are stopped by keys; unlike it, nyckelharpa strings rest on a flat bridge and are bowed. The number of strings has remained flexible: between 1 and 2 melody strings, and between 2 and 3 drones; in post-18th-century instruments, up to 11 sympathetic strings were added.

o. 1. When placed over the g, d¹, a¹, or e² string in a violin part (or the equivalent for other instruments), the lowercase *o* stands for *open*; notes so marked are played only on the open string, i.e., in its natural, unstopped state. 2. In basso continuo parts, a sign that only the bass line or its octave are used in the accompaniment to a given passage, without filling in harmony. 3. Placed above a note, usually in string parts, signifies the use of harmonics. 4. In chord tablature used in sheet music, a diminished 5th or chord. 5. (It.) Or; written thus before vowels or consonants; *od* is a rare form.

obbligato (It., obligatory; Ger. *obligato*). Orig., instrumental part essential to the performance, such as sonatas for piano with violin obbligato; expanded to any instrumental or vocal part that is a concerted (and therefore essential) part. Through a paradoxical inversion of meaning, *obbligato* began to indicate an optional part, particularly in popular arrangements; for example, a song with *cello obbligato* meant that the cello part would be desirable in the accompaniment, but not essential.

oberek (from Pol. *obrót*, turn around). Lively Polish dance in rapid 3/8 meter and off-beat accents similar to the mazurka; it is also known as the *obertas.*

Oberton (Ger.). Overtone.

objets trouvés (Fr., found objects). Term defiantly introduced by avant-garde painters and sculptors; Marcel Duchamp was probably the 1st to exhibit an objet trouvé, a urinal from a men's lavatory; Man Ray exhibited a sewing machine wrapped up in a piece of canvas; Andy Warhol created a sensation by selling a Brobdingnagian representation of a Campbell's soup can for a reputed sum of $70,000. A plate with remnants of an unfinished dinner was exhibited as an objet trouvé, as was "bagel jewelry," an actual bagel set in a jewelry box. Found or "ready-made" objects have been incorporated by modern artists as part of sculptures, montages, or collages.

Ultramodern composers sometimes insert passages from works by other composers as a token of homage and partly as an experiment in construction. Such objets trouvés need not harmonize with their environment, which may be completely alien to the interpolated passage. An early example is the appearance of *Ach, du lieber Augustin* in Schoenberg's 2nd String Quartet. The opening motive of Wagner's *Tristan und Isolde* has appeared in serious and comic juxtapositions. Some composers construct objets trouvés by simply playing another composer's music; a paradigm of an embroidered, incrustated objet trouvé is Berio's

Sinfonia, incorporating whole chunks of music from Mahler, Ravel, and others.

oblique motion. 2-part counterpoint in which one voice moves and the other remains stationary.

oboe (Fr. *hautbois*, high wood; Ger. *Oboe*; It. *oboe*). 1. Orch'l instrument with conical wooden tube, 9 to 14 keys, and a double reed; its present compass is 2 octaves and a 7th, from b⁰ to a³. The oboe appeared toward the middle of the 17th century in France. Its tone is very reedy and penetrating, although not harsh; only 2 kinds are in common use, the soprano oboe in C (just described) and the English horn (alto oboe), transposing a perfect 5th lower. The oboe seems limited in its agility when compared to the lambent flute or the peripatetic clarinet; but it compensates by the precision of its intonation and strength of its sound; indeed, it can pierce through the entire orch'l fabric as easily as the trumpet; in orch'l writing oboes are scored in pairs, like flutes, clarinets, and bassoons. As a solo instrument the oboe is not as popular as the other woodwinds (even the bassoon), but Handel wrote several concertos for it; while a solo oboe recital, even by a great virtuoso, would seem improbable, such concerts are given. As the orch.'s intonational mainstay, the oboe stands unchallenged, for it gives the introductory A to tune up the orch. 2. In the organ, an 8' reed organ stop with conical pipes surmounted by a bell and cap.

oboe da caccia (It., hunting oboe). Instrument tuned a 5th below the oboe; in use during the Renaissance, it was eventually replaced by the English horn.

oboe d'amore (It., love oboe; Fr. *hautbois d'amour;* Ger. *Liebeshoboe*). Oboe pitched in A, transposing a minor 3rd below the standard soprano in C, with either a standard or bulbous bell; the most popular of the woodwind d'amore instruments, but like the others virtually obsolete.

Obrecht (Obreht, Hobrecht, Obertus, Hobertus), Jacob, b. probably in Bergen-op-Zoom, Nov. 22, 1450 or 1451; d. Ferrara, 1505. He is 1st mentioned as *zangmeester* in Utrecht (*c.* 1476–78); became choirmaster at St. Gertrude in Bergen-op-Zoom (1479); took holy orders and said his 1st Mass as an ordained priest (1480). He was made *maître des enfants* at Cambrai (1484); dismissed for neglect of the choirboys and financial irregularities (1485); made succentor at St. Donatian in Bruges (1486). At the invitation of the Duke of Ferrara he took a leave of absence; after returning to Bruges, made *maître de chapelle* (1490); obtained his release (1491). By 1494 he was at Notre Dame in Antwerp; served as Capellanie magister (1495); returned to Bergen-op-Zoom (1496–97); received a benefice at Notre Dame at Antwerp (1498). He returned to Bruges until retirement (1499–1500); returned to the ducal court in Ferrara (1504), but died of the plague. Obrecht was one of the leading composers of his era, worthy of comparison with Ockeghem and Des Prez; his Masses and motets are of particular importance; also wrote chansons, many to Dutch texts.

ocarina (It., little goose). Bulbous flute in the shape of a bird; usually made of terra-cotta, with finger holes and a whistle mouthpiece; often used as whistles. Rimsky-Korsakov includes an ocarina tuned to an octatonic scale in his opera-ballet *Mlada.*

Ochs, Phil, b. El Paso, Tex., Dec. 19, 1940; d. Far Rockaway, N.Y., Apr. 19, 1976. He 1st performed while a college student in

Cleveland, as half of the Sundowners; relocated to Greenwich Village (1961) as a solo act. His work was quickly championed by *Broadside* magazine, a folk publication favoring topical songs; signed to the Elektra label, he recorded *All the News That's Fit to Sing* (1964); early hits included *I Ain't a 'Marchin' Anymore* and *There but for Fortune* (covered by J. Baez, 1965). Contemporary with Bob Dylan—with whom he was often compared—Ochs was a more polished if limited performer; wrote satirical songs on issues of the day; considered himself a Maoist.

Ochs relocated to California (1967); began writing in a more personal, confessional style, e.g., *Pleasures of the Harbor* (1967); *Tape from California* (1968); *Rehearsals for Retirement* (1969). Taking his oddest career turn, he performed at Carnegie Hall (1971), dressed in a gold lamé suit— garb he had worn on the ironically titled *Greatest Hits* album, entirely made up of new material; the audience, stunned by his personality and musical shift, was vocally displeased, as recorded on *Gunfight at Carnegie Hall* (1971). He traveled in the early 1970s to England and Africa (where he was nearly strangled and his vocal cords damaged); returned to N.Y. area (1974); took up new causes, including organizing a concert against the military government of Chile; severely depressed, took his own life by hanging while visiting his sister.

Ockeghem (Okeghem, Ockenheim, etc.), Johannes (Jean, Jehan de), b. *c.* 1410; d. probably in Tours, Feb. 6, 1497. He may have studied with Binchois. He heads the list of *vicaires-chanteurs* at Notre Dame in Antwerp (1443–44); by 1446 was in the service of Charles I, Duke of Bourbon, in Moulins (to at least 1448); joined the service of Charles VII of France as 1st among the nonclerical singer-chaplains (by 1452); became *premier chapelain* (by 1454). He subsequently served Louis XI and Charles VIII; the latter appointed him treasurer of the church of St. Martin-de-Tours (1459). Under Louis XI he was a canon at Notre Dame in Paris (1463–70). He likewise was chaplain at St. Benoit; traveled to Spain at the King's expense (1470); journeyed to Bruges and Dammes (1484). Upon his death, Guillaume Cretin wrote a poetic *Déploration*; Des Prez and Lupi composed musical epitaphs.

With his near contemporaries Dufay and Des Prez, Ockeghem ranks as a great master of the Franco-Flemish style in the 2nd half of the 15th century; among his Mass settings is the earliest extant polyphonic Requiem; the inventiveness displayed in those works is excelled only by his superb motets; his achievements in imitative counterpoint make his music a milestone on the way to the a cappella style of coming generations.

octatonic scale. Mode in which semitones alternate with whole tones (or vice versa), producing scales with 8 distinct pitch classes, e.g., C, C sharp, D sharp, E, F sharp, G, A, B flat, C; a Messiaenic mode of limited transposition. First used by Rimsky-Korsakov and Liszt, its most characteristic association is with Stravinsky's "Russian"period.

octave (Eng., Fr.; from Lat. *octava*, 8th; It. *ottava*; Ger. *Oktave*). 1. Series of 8 consecutive diatonic tones. 2. Interval between the 1st and 8th tones of such a series; the only acoustically pure interval in the tempered system, representing the

vibration ratio 2:1. The octave is the 1st harmonic (2nd partial) above the fundamental and is contained within virtually any musical tone; it can be perceived by a sensitive ear, even when only 1 tone is played; it can be heard and with surprising effect by silently holding down a piano key and then forcefully striking the key an octave below; the depressed key will respond with an octave sound, loud and clear.

Different octaves bear special names, generally accepted in international nomenclature (see ⇒Intro., The Scales). The earliest type of "polyphonic"singing was at the interval of an octave, with boys singing an octave higher than men. *Concealed, covered,* or *hidden octaves,* consecutive octaves suggested by the progression of 2 parts in similar motion to the interval of an octave; *parallel octaves,* consecutive octaves; *rule of the octave,* a series of harmonies written over the diatonic scale as a bass; *short octave,* the lowest octave of some old organ manuals, in which some keys (and pipes) are omitted.

3. Organ stop whose pipes sound tones an octave higher than the keys touched, e.g., the principal.

octave coupler. Device uniting the 8' tones of one keyboard with the 4' tones (i.e., an octave higher) of another.

octave flute. 1. Piccolo. 2. Organ stop of 4' pitch.

octave sign. See ⇒ottava.

octave stop. See ⇒octave (3).

octet (Fr. *octour;* It. *ottetto;* Ger. *Oktett*). Work for 8 voices or instruments.

octobasse. Oversized double bass patented by J. B. Vuillaume in 1849; its 3 strings were stopped by levers worked by pedals; the bow was supported by oarlocks; was 12 feet high and pitched 1 octave below the cello.

ode. 1. Chorus in ancient Greek plays. 2. Musical or poetic work of praise.

oder (Ger.). Or; or else.

odoroso (It.). Fragrant; a rare expression mark, found in one of Medtner's *Fairy Tales* for piano. There is no record of a composer using the antonym *malodoroso,* even though some should consider it.

oeuvre (Fr.). A work. 2. A composer's musical output. *Oeuvres choisies,* selected works; *oeuvres complètes,* complete works; *oeuvres inédites,* unpubl. works; *oeuvres posthumes,* posth. works.

off. Indication to push in an organ stop or couplet. *Off pitch,* false in pitch or intonation.

off-beat. Syncopated feature of ragtime and jazz in which metrically unaccented parts of the melody are played with strong rhythmic stress.

Offenbach, Jacques (Jacob), b. Cologne, June 20, 1819; d. Paris, Oct. 5, 1880. He was the son of a Jewish cantor, whose orig. surname was Eberst; Offenbach was where his father once lived. Jacques studied violin before taking up the cello at age 9; studied with J. Alexander and B. Breuer in Cologne; settled in Paris (1833); after cello studies with Vaslin at the Cons. (1833–34) played in the Opéra-Comique orch.; received further instruction from L. Norblin and Halévy; pursued a solo and chamber music career (from 1838); conducted at the Théâtre-Français (1850–55); his *Chanson de Fortunio* for Musset's *Chandelier* (1850) proved tremendously popular.

In 1855 Offenbach opened his own theater, the Bouffes-Parisiens, at the Salle Marigny; it soon moved to the Salle Choiseul, where he scored his 1st great success with the operetta *Orphée aux enfers* (1858); *La Belle Hélène* (Variétés, 1864) became one of his most celebrated works, taken up by theatrical enterprises throughout the world. He stopped managing the Bouffes-Parisiens (1866), but continued to write stage works; *La Vie parisienne* (1866), *La Grande-Duchesse de Gérolstein* (1867), and *La Périchole* (1868) were notably successful. He took over the management of the Théâtre de la Gaité (1873), where he produced his rev. *Orphée aux enfers* as an *opera-féerique* (1874); undertook a U.S. tour (1876); described his impressions in *Notes d'un musicien en voyage* (1877) and *Offenbach en Amerique* (Paris, 1877). His only grand opera, the masterpiece *Les Contes d'Hoffmann*, remained unfinished at his death; recitatives were added by Guiraud (who completed Bizet's *Carmen*), along with the barcarole from Offenbach's *Die Rheinnixen* (1864), where the tune served for a ghost song; the finished score was premiered at the Opéra-Comique (1881) with instantaneous success, and it subsequently was performed on both sides of the Atlantic.

Offenbach is a master of the operetta, his music characterized by an abundance of flowing, rollicking melodies seasoned with ironic humor, suitable to the extravagant burlesque of the situations. His irreverent treatment of mythological characters gave Paris society a salutary shock; his art mirrored the precarious gaiety of Napoleon III's Second Empire. In addition to his more than 60 stage works, operettas, and opéras-comiques, he wrote several pieces for cello (including 6 with orch.) and pedagogical works.

Offertory (Fr. *offertoire;* It. *offertorio;* Lat. *offertorium*). In the Roman Catholic Mass, the verses or anthem following the credo and sung by the choir while the priest is placing the consecrated elements on the altar, during which the offerings of the congregation are collected. This is the 4th division of the Proprium of the Mass; its original name was Antiphona ad offerendum. The earliest musical procedure of the Offertory contained the reading of psalms followed by a responsorial chant or some other antiphonal singing. Many organ pieces bear the title *Offertory*, but most works of the Offertory type are religious motets in a polyphonic setting.

Officium Divinum (Lat.). Divine Office. See ⇒canonical hours.

Ohana, Maurice, b. Casablanca (of Spanish parents), June 12, 1914; d. Paris, Nov. 13, 1992. He studied piano with F. Marshall in Barcelona and L. Lévy at the Paris Cons.; had counterpoint lessons with Daniel-Lesur at the Schola Cantorum (1937–40). Following service in the British Army during World War II, he completed his training with Casella at Rome's Accademia di Santa Cecilia (1944–46); settled in Paris; made a Commandeur des Arts et Lettres (1981); won the Prix National de Musique (1975) and the Honegger (1982) and Ravel (1985) prizes. Ohana's music combines elements of his Spanish background and the world of *The Rite of Spring* and *Les Noces* with a keen ear for percussion and timbre; he resolutely opposed the avant-garde world of Boulez; composed operas, orch'l and chamber works, keyboard music, and group and solo vocal works.

ohne (Ger.). Without. *Ohne Ausdruck,* expressionless; *ohne Verschiebung,* without fluctuation.

Oistrakh, David (Fyodorovich), b. Odessa, Sept. 30, 1908; d. Amsterdam, Oct. 24, 1974. He studied violin as a child with Stoliarsky in Odessa; made his debut there at age 6; continued his studies with Stoliarsky at the Odessa Cons. (1923–26); appeared as soloist in Glazunov's Violin Concerto under the composer's direction in Kiev (1927). He went to Moscow (1928); appointed to the faculty of the Cons. (1934); he attracted universal attention by winning 1st prize at the Ysaÿe Competition in Brussels (1937), in which 68 violinists from 21 countries took part. He played in Paris and London (1953) with extraordinary success; made his 1st American appearances as soloist with major American orchs., and in recitals, winning enthusiastic acclaim (1955); appeared as a conductor from 1962. He died while on a visit to Amsterdam as a guest conductor with the Concertgebouw Orch.

Oistrakh's playing was marked—apart from phenomenal technique—by stylistic fidelity to works by different composers of different historical periods. Soviet composers profited by his advice as to technical problems of violin playing; he collaborated with Prokofiev in making an arrangement for violin and piano of his Flute Sonata. (He also played a chess match with Prokofiev.) A generation of Soviet violinists numbered among his pupils, 1st and foremost his son Igor Oistrakh (b. Odessa, Apr. 27, 1931), who has had a fine career in his own right; he won 1st prize at the International Festival of Democratic Youth in Budapest (1949) and the Wieniawski Competition in Poznan (1952); some critics regarded him as equal to his father in virtuosity.

Okeghem, Johannes. See ⇒Ockeghem, Johannes.

oktoechos. System of 8 echoi as practiced in Byzantine chant; the doctrine and practice of oktoechos probably originated in Syria early in the 6th century, possibly by analogy with ancient Greek modes.

old-time. See ⇒band, string.

Olé! Spanish exclamation used as a refrain in various song genres.

olio (Sp., pot, stew). Specialty act or medley at a burlesque show, featuring a variety of vocal and instrumental numbers, comic dialogues, and "exotic" dances.

oliphant (Old Fr. *olifant,* elephant). *Cor d'olifant,* a Byzantine signal trumpet, sometimes made of elephant's tusk, imported from Asia and employed for ceremonial occasions;

penetrated Europe during the Middle Ages; an alternate philological theory is that "oliphant" is a corruption of "eloquent."

Oliver, "King" (Joseph), b. near Abend, La., May 11, 1885; d. Savannah, Ga., Apr. 8, 1938. In 1907 he was working in Storyville (New Orleans's red-light district) with the Melrose Brass Band; worked with other bands in subsequent years; formed his own group, eventually known as the Creole Jazz Band (1915); acquired the nickname "King," traditionally reserved for leading jazz musicians; the New Orleans city government closed the bordellos in Storyville, putting most musicians out of work (1917). Oliver moved his band to Chicago (1918), leading a migration of jazz musicians to the city largely responsible for the dispersion of black New Orleans jazz throughout the country. Louis Armstrong, whom Oliver had known in New Orleans, joined the band (1922); helped make it the most polished exponent of collectively improvised jazz; the group's 1923 recordings were the most influential of the period (they have been reissued by the Smithsonian Inst.). Subsequent bands formed by Oliver remained a potent force in jazz until *c.* 1928. He was the uncle of Ulysses (Simpson) Kay.

Oliveros, Pauline, b. Houston, May 30, 1932. Her mother and grandmother, both piano teachers, taught her musical rudiments; received violin lessons from W. Sydler, accordion from M. Harrigan, and horn from J. M. Brandsetter; studied composition with P. Koepke and accordion with W. Palmer at the Univ. of Houston (1949–52); continued studies at San Francisco State College (B.A., 1957) and privately with Robert Erickson (1954–60). She was co-director of the San Francisco Tape Music Center (1961–65), remaining so after it became the Mills Tape Music Center (1966–67); taught at the Univ. of Calif. at San Diego (1967–81); held a Guggenheim fellowship (1973–74). She publ. *Pauline's Proverbs* (1976) and *Software for People: Collected Writings 1963–80* (1984).

Initiated by Erickson into modern harmony, asymmetrical rhythm, group improvisation, and acoustical sonorism, Oliveros began to explore the range of subliminal sounds derived from the overtone series, differential tones, and sonic abstractions; composed a Piano Sextet that explored such elusive tonal elements (1960); received the Pacifica Foundation National Prize; wrote a choral work, *Sound Patterns*, to wordless voices (1962); received a prize in the Netherlands. She developed her ideas still further; taking advantage of her gardening skills, she arrayed garden hoses and lawn sprinklers as part of a musical ensemble accompanied by the sounds of alarm clocks and various domestic utensils; occasionally a musician was instructed to bark; to this enriched artistic vocabulary a physical and psychosomatic element was added; performers played a magician, juggler, and fortune-teller; page turners, piano movers, and floor sweepers were listed as performers.

In later works Oliveros reduced such kinetic activities and began composing ceremonial works of sonic meditation, *sotto voce* murmuration, lingual lallation, and joyful ululation, attempting to induce an altered state of consciousness; sometimes an exotic but usually digestible meal was served at leisurely intervals. She often presided over such sessions, singing and playing her faithful accordion; sometimes this music was left to be unheard by ordinary ears, but could be perceived mystically. In 1977 she obtained 1st prize from the city of Bonn for a work

commemorating the sesquicentennial of Beethoven's death; the verbally notated piece hoped to subvert the city population into perceptual theater. Her most controversial work was *To Valerie Solanis and Marilyn Monroe, in Recognition of Their Desperation,* a verbally notated score (1970) paying tribute to Solanis, the founder of SCUM (Society to Cut Up Men), who nearly murdered artist Andy Warhol, and Monroe, who committed suicide.

olla podrida (olio; Sp., rotten pot; Fr., *potpourri*). Miscellany or medley of musical or comic dialogues and "exotic" dances at a burlesque show.

ombra scene (It., shadow scene). Dramatic operatic episode taking place in the nether regions, a cemetery, or a place where ghosts congregate; usually cast in the monodic manner of accompanied recitative in triadic harmonies; for some reason the key of E-flat major was nearly de rigueur in such scenes. Ombra scenes abound in general pauses, tremolos, exclamations, and other emotional outbursts; the clarinet, French horn, and trombone are favorite instruments for Baroque shadow scenes; Mozart introduced the ghostly statue of the Commendatore in *Don Giovanni* with an ominous trombone passage (in D minor).

omnitonality. Totality of tonalities entailing frequent collisions of different keys, signifying various degrees of modulatory freedom. Omnitonality provided a compromise definition for techniques that retained a sense of tonality but expanded it to the entire cycle of major and minor scales; nearly synonymous with pantonality.

ondeggiamento (*ondeggiante;* It., undulating; Fr. *ondulé*). Billowy; rocking (as by waves); tremolo on a single note or an arpeggiolike figure; achieved by varying intensity in applying the bow.

Ondes Martenot. Electronic keyboard instrument named after its French inventor Maurice Martenot, who orig. named it the Ondes musicales; like the Thereminovox and other early electronic instruments, its sound is produced heterodynamically, as a differential of 2 frequencies, controlling pitch and amplitude; 1st exhibited in Paris (1928). Messiaen, Honegger, Koechlin, Jean Martinon, Jolivet, and other composers have written for the Ondes Martenot.

one-step. American ballroom dance of the 1910s and 1920s in 2/4 time.

ongarese (It.). Hungarian.

Ono, Yoko, b. Tokyo, Feb. 18, 1933. She moved to N.Y. (1947); enrolled at Sarah Lawrence College (1953); became active in Manhattan conceptual-art circles, notably the Fluxus group; met John Lennon of the Beatles (1966); became companions and collaborators, marrying in 1969. Under her influence Lennon became interested in avant-garde ideas that drew him away from rock, contributing to the breakup of the Beatles in 1970 (for which she received disproportionate criticism).

Ono's recordings with Lennon include *Live Peace in Toronto 1969* (1970) and *Double Fantasy* (1980); after Lennon's death in 1980 she produced 2 posth. collaborations, *Milk and Honey*

(1982) and *Heart Play: Unfinished Dialogue* (1983). Her solo recordings include *Yoko Ono/Plastic Ono Band* (1970), *Fly* (1971), *Approximately Infinite Universe* (1973), *Feeling the Space* (1973), *Seasons of Glass* (1981), *It's Alright* (1982), and *Every Man Has a Woman* (1984). Her work is often bizarre, her shrill tremolo voice moving over a fluid, arrhythmic background reflecting Asian influences; some recordings, notably those between 1980 and 1984, are more mainstream.

onomatopoeia. Imitation of sounds of nature or industry abound in Classic, Romantic, and modern music; familiar examples are the thunderstorms of Beethoven's *Pastoral Sym.* and the overture to Rossini's *William Tell*. Birdcalls are natural resources for musical imagination. Sounds of industry were reproduced with varying degrees of verisimilitude in modern works. In his *Pacific 231* Honegger created a stimulating impression of an American locomotive gathering speed by increasing the number of accented beats in each successive bar. The whirring of an airplane propeller is realistically imitated in *The Aeroplane* (1920) by American composer Emerson Whithorne. (In his *Ballet mécanique*, Antheil used actual propellers.) Italian Futurists attempted to emulate the noises of 20th century city life by the use of megaphones. The clatter of steel-making is realistically illustrated by the shaking of a sheet of metal in the ballet *Iron Foundry* by the Soviet composer Mosolov. Amusing attempts to illustrate a sneeze are found in *The Nose* by Shostakovich and *Háry János* by Kodály; in the latter the sneeze expresses the traditional Hungarian reaction of extreme skepticism to adventures recited by a boastful storyteller. A realistic piece of grim onomatopoeia occurs in *Robespierre* (1856) by H. C. Litolff, in which the fall of Robespierre's head after his execution on the guillotine is rendered by a thud of the bass drum.

oompah (-pah). Onomatopoeic vocable to denote the alternating bass between the tonic and the dominant in the tuba, ophicleide, serpent, and other deep bass instruments, particularly in marches and galops, placed by military bands, and borrowed by Romantic Italian opera composers.

open diapason. See ⇒organ.

open form. See ⇒mobile form.

open form composition. Works based on controlled improvisation in which materials are selected from available resources have a venerable ancestry; classical composers supplied alternative versions for transitions and endings as a matter of course. In its modern avatar, open form composition often delegates the ordering of component parts to the performer. Chronological priority in developing such techniques belongs to Earle Brown, whose *Folio* (1952) affords great latitude in the arranging of given materials; Stockhausen further developed this technique in his *Klavierstücke*, consisting of separate sections that can be performed in any order.

open harmony. In 4-part harmony, an arrangement of voices such that the 3 upper voices have a total range of more than an octave (as in C–G, E, C); most suitable for choral writing, as opposed to close harmony, easier for keyboard harmony.

open pedal. Loud (damper) piano pedal.

open pipe. Organ pipes with open tops, sounding 1 octave above closed pipes otherwise identical in dimensions.

open string. On any chordophone with a fingerboard, a string in its natural, unstopped state; when an open string is to be played, a small circle is placed above the note. Because the sounds of open strings are so different from stopped notes, they are avoided in melodic passages, but become increasingly essential in double-, triple-, and quadruple-stops. Some works exploit open strings for euphonic or symbolic purposes; Saint-Saëns builds his *Danse macabre* upon the solo violin's open strings, suggesting a witch tuning her fiddle; Berg insists on open strings in passages of the Violin Concerto. A string quartet (misattributed to Benjamin Franklin) whose MS was discovered in 1945 is written entirely for open strings so that the rankest amateurs could play it; the strings are tuned in an ingenious scordatura, so that unexpected and even dissonant harmonics are formed.

opera (dramma per musica, opera in musica; It., work; Ger. *Oper*). Italian music drama, invented *c.* 1590, in which vocal and instrumental music are essential and predominant. An opera may have several acts, often preceded by instrumental introductions, with vocal scenes, recitatives, arias, duets, trios, choruses, etc., accompanied by basso continuo or full orch. (the latter exclusively after 1800); also dance or ballet music. Among many operatic genres: serious, grand, or heroic opera (sung dialogue); comic opera or farce (sung dialogue); operetta or Singspiel (spoken dialogue).

opera buffa (It.; Fr. *opéra bouffe*). Comic opera (as opposed to opera seria) with standard comic characters, many borrowed from commedia dell'arte; uses schemes and stratagems found in comedies of Shakespeare, Molière, and other classics, replete with mistaken identities, disguises, deceptions, and intrigues; but virtue triumphs in the end; the dupes forgive their tormentors, young couples are united, and the spirit of entertainment overcomes all the blatant absurdities.

opéra-comique (Fr.). French opera with spoken rather than sung dialogue; not necessarily comedic in nature, for at the time of its birth (18th century), *comique* had dignified connotations (e.g., Dante's *Divina Commedia*). The music is of a light dramatic texture; the plots introduce concepts of morality and proper social behavior. The Paris Opéra-Comique theater was intended for the production of French plays with a balance of musical numbers and spoken dialogues; but this house saw many kinds of operas, some of which (Bizet's *Carmen*) could hardly be considered funny.

opera seria (It.). 18th-century serious (heroic, tragic) opera, virtually identical with grand opera, replete with emotional upheavals, tragic conflicts, scenes of triumph and disaster, insanity, murders, and suicides filling the action. By tradition, an opera seria has at least 3 acts, but may well extend into 5 acts; may include ballet. The opposite of opera seria is opera buffa.

operetta (It., little opera; Fr. *opérette*). Musical theater work in which the libretto is anything but serious, in a comic, mock-pathetic, or parodistic vein; the music is light, lively, sentimental, and often interrupted by dialogue; forerunner of the American musical.

ophicleide (from Grk. *ophis* + *kleidos,* serpent with keys; Fr. *ophicléide*; Ger. *Ophikleide*; It. *oficleide*). 1. Large, deep-toned keyed bugle with U-shaped conical tube, slightly flared bell, and cup mouthpiece, built by Halary (*c.* 1817). G. B. Shaw volunteers the information that his uncle played it and then "perished by his own hand"; the ophicleide itself became extinct shortly after Shaw's uncle's suicide and was replaced by the tuba. 2. Large-scale cylindrical reed organ stop, 8' or 16'.

oppure (It.; abbrev. *opp.*). Ossia.

opus (Lat., work; plural, *opera*; abbrev. *op., opp.*). *Opus number,* number assigned for chronological identification of a work or group of works by a particular composer. Unfortunately, composers and their publishers seldom were entirely accurate in coordinating chronology with opus number. Chopin's Piano Concerto in F Minor, opus 21, was composed a year earlier than his Piano Concerto in E Minor, opus 11. Several of Beethoven's early pieces were published with misleadingly late opus numbers. Sometimes competing publishers would have their own sets of opus numbers for the same composer, thus creating several opp. 1, opp. 2, etc. Use of opus numbers became established *c.* 1700, but fell off among 20th-century composers. Mozart's works are identified not by opus numbers but by K. numbers, after Köchel, the 1st Mozart cataloguer; similarly catalogued oeuvres are by Vivaldi, J. S. Bach, C. P. E. Bach, F. J. Haydn, Bartók, etc.

oratorio (It.). Extended, more or less dramatic composition for vocal solos and chorus, with accompaniment by orch. and/or organ, sung without stage play or scenery; developed in 17th-century Italy as a way for operatic composers to keep busy during Lent, when theaters were closed; also known as *historia.*

Orbison, Roy (Kelton), b. Wink, Tex., Apr. 23, 1936; d. Hendersonville, Tenn., Dec. 6, 1988. He studied geology at North Tex. State College; performed with local rockabilly bands; began recording (1956); active as a songwriter in Nashville, Tenn. He possessed an excellent lyric tenor voice, so unusual that he won a distinctive and uncontested niche in popular music; among his hits were *Crying, Many Moods,* and *Regeneration; Oh, Pretty Woman* became his signature tune. Personal tragedy (the deaths of his wife and two children) led him into semiretirement in the 1960s; shortly before his death he joined George Harrison, Bob Dylan, and others to produce the album *The Traveling Wilburys,* for which he sang lead vocals on *Not Alone Anymore, End of the Line,* and *Handle with Care;* recorded a final solo album with Jeff Lynne producing; its hit, *You Got It,* was revived by Bonnie Raitt (1995).

orchestra (Ger. *Orchester;* Fr. *orchestre*). Company of musicians performing on instruments usually used in opera, oratorio, concerto, or sym.; also, the instruments so used taken as a whole. *Orchestral,* pertaining to or resembling the orch.; *orchestral piano playing,* style of Liszt and his disciples, emulating orch'l effects on the piano.

orchestration. Art of writing or arranging music for orch'l performance; the science of combining, in an effective manner, the instruments constituting the orch.

orchestrion. Large stationary barrel organ, generally played by clockwork. See also ⇒barrel organ.

order. Arrangement of the chord tones above a given bass; *open order* and *close order* are identical to open harmony and close harmony.

Ordinary (Lat. *ordinarium*). In the Roman Catholic High Mass, the sung sections with fixed texts: Kyrie, Gloria, Credo, Sanctus, Agnus Dei (and the closing *Ite, missa est* or *Benedicamus Domino*); these sections are interwoven with the Proprium (Proper), readings, and recitations, all with changing texts according to the church calendar.

ordre (Fr.). Suite; used by Couperin and other French clavecinists for a group of keyboard pieces; usually contains traditional suite movements (allemande, courante, sarabande), a prelude, and pieces with whimsical descriptive titles designed to appeal to amateur performers, such as *Les Petits moulins à vent, Les Barricades mystérieuses,* etc.

Orff, Carl, b. Munich, July 10, 1895; d. there, Mar. 29, 1982. He took courses with Beer-Walbrunn and Zilcher at the Munich Academy of Music (graduated 1914); had additional instruction from H. Kaminski in Munich; conducted at the Munich Kammerspiele (1915–17); after military service (1917–18), conducted at the Mannheim National Theater and the Darmstadt Landestheater (1918–19); conductor of Munich's Bach Soc. (1930–33).

Orff initiated a highly influential method of musical education, adopted not only in Germany but in England, America, and Russia; stemmed from the Günther School for gymnastics, dance, and music, which he co-founded with Dorothee Günther in Munich (1924), promoting instrumental playing and understanding of rhythm among children; commissioned the piano manufacturer K. Maendler to construct special percussion instruments, extremely easy to play; the "Orff instruments" were widely adopted in American schools. His ideas of rhythmic training owe much to eurhythmics, but he simplified Jaques-Dalcroze's ideas to reach the elementary level; compiled a set of musical exercises, *Schulwerk* (1930–35, rev. 1950–54); also taught composition at the Munich Staatliche Hochschule für Musik (1950–55).

As a composer Orff sought to revive early monodic forms, adapting them to modern tastes with dissonant counterpoint and lively rhythm in asymmetrical patterns, producing a form of "total theater." His most famous score is the scenic oratorio *Carmina Burana* (1937) with the text (in Latin and middle German) taken from 13th-century goliard poems found in the Benediktbeuren monastery in Bavaria. His other works were primarily theatrical; many are based on ancient Greek drama and German folk tales; wrote 3 works after Monteverdi: *Klage der Ariadne, Orpheus,* and *Tanz der Spröden* (1925; rev. 1940).

organ. (Ger. *Orgel;* Fr. *orgue;* It. *organa*). Keyboard instrument, orig. an aerophone whose sound is produced by airflow forced through differently sized and shaped pipes. The small hydraulic organ (invented by Ktesibios of Alexandria, 180 B.C.) was operated by a combination of water, gravity, and airflow; the pneumatic organ (c. 200 A.D.) generated airflow through bellows pumped by hand or trodden by feet. An improved and larger hydraulic instrument returned in the 19th century; it was replaced by the modern electronic organ in the 1930s.

The pipe organ is the largest keyboard instrument; its very appearance is most imposing, with several rows of vertical pipes usually arranged in a tasteful symmetrical position. The pipes, of which there are 2 main divisions—flue pipes and reed pipes—are made to "speak" by wind admitted from the bellows upon pressing the keys. The organ has 2 or more manuals (keyboards) and a complex system of ⇒*stops* that govern tone color. It also has a pedal keyboard, requiring that a master organist be virtuosic with feet as well as hands. A organist's musicianship must be of sufficiently high caliber to coordinate the multiple devices of the instrument to produce optimum results; the organ is thus a simulacrum of a full orch.

Bach's Baroque organ, a highly developed neo-Gothic instrument with multiple manuals and a multitude of stops, remains the ideal. Strict hierarchy is maintained in the planning of the manuals, but each manual can given an adequate rendition of the music. The most prominent manual bears the name Great Organ, supplied with the loudest stops; the 2nd is the Swell Organ, capable of tremendous dynamic changes; the 3rd, the Choir Organ, is used for accompanimental purposes. The 4th, the Solo Organ, emphasizes special instrumental tone colors. Larger modern organs have a 5th manual, the Echo Organ, producing the effect of a distant sound. Manuals are arranged in raked fashion, so that the Great Organ is the nearest to the player, the Echo Organ farthest away. The organist must be very agile, what with the constant exercise in reaching for various manuals and the requirements of pedal work.

Fortunately there is a plethora of ingenious helping devices for the organist "at the console." Stops are named according to the sizes of the sets of pipes they activate. The normal tone of the manual commands an 8-foot stop, the *open diapason* (Gk., through all), opening a pipe or pipes approximately 8 feet long. Other stops—4-foot and 2-foot—sound an octave and a 15th higher, respectively. In the low range there is a 16-foot, a 32-foot, and even a 64-foot stop, producing sounds 1, 2, and 3 octaves lower, respectively. The pedal organ sounds an octave below the manuals; stops of the pedal allow the sound to be lowered an additional octave and even a 15th. Both manuals and pedals possess special stops to add upper or lower octaves, or all of them together, producing a gigantic unison that lends particular magnificence to a cathedral organ. There are also *couplers* by which 2 manuals can be connected; the organist can increase the sound while playing on only 1 manual, adding a sound an octave above or below by these couplers. The organist can prepare the *registration,* the system of stops, so that he or she can begin in octaves or double octaves—both in the manuals and pedals—and with the desired tone colors. Special registers or stops can be interconnected selectively or for the entire organ; hence the expression "pulling out all the stops" describing an organ (or showman, salesman, or politician) in full glory, sound, and fury.

Organ stop names provide a whole inventory of acoustical terms. The primary stop, the 8-foot open diapason, implies a totality of tones; the equivalent of *gamut*, the entire compass of audible sounds from lowest to highest. Many stops are named after the instruments they emulate (flute, oboe, clarinet, bassoon, strings, etc.). Two registrations have poetic names—vox angelica and vox humana—but bad reputations; the 1st is obviously meant to convey the impressions of a singing angel, the 2nd the singing of a human. Much sarcasm has been poured on the bland, soupy tone of the angelic stop; to the celebrated Dr. Burney, the human stop suggested "the cracked voice of an old woman of 90."

The spirit of competition in building ever larger organs is particularly strong in the U.S.; the organ in one Chicago stadium has 6 manuals and 828 different stops. A very elaborate electronic organ was constructed for Carnegie Hall, N.Y. (1974), with 192 speakers in 29 cabinets, and 5 manuals with a frequency range from 16 cycles to 20,000 cycles; but, according to reports, Convention Hall in Atlantic City boasts a Brobdingnagian organ with 7 manuals and 1,200 stops.

organ point. Pedal point.

organ tone. Standard sound of the 8-foot open diapason on the Great Organ manual; also called *diapason tone.*

organetto (It.). 1. Portative organ, used in the Middle Ages and Renaissance; placed on the knee and played as a melody instrument with one hand while the other hand operates the bellows. 2. Street or barrel organ.

organista (Lat.). 1. Organ player. 2. Composer of organum; Leoninus was praised as *optimus organista.*

organistrum. Medieval hurdy-gurdy in a fiddle shape with 3 strings.

organized sound. Sound is an acoustical phenomenon, which all by itself does not define music; composition begins at the point when 2 sounds are connected in linear succession or vertical superposition. The nature of these links is not circumscribed by any melodic or harmonic rules. With the emancipation of dissonance in the 20th century, vertical combinations become free from restraints traditionally imposed on them. Linear progressions, once bound within the framework of modes and scales, are developed in atonal designs. Schoenberg replaced diatonic melody and consonant harmony by the new dodecaphonic discipline. To avoid associations with the word "music," Varèse advanced the concept of organized sound, a complex of successive acoustical phenomena unrelated to one another except by considerations of sonic equilibrium. Dissonant combinations constitute a probabilistic majority and are, therefore, entitled to greater representation in organized sound; for the same reasons, successions of melodic notes are apt to generate atonal configurations. Works written according to the doctrine of organized sound are athematic; rhythms are usually asymmetric; valence between successive units, in melody, harmony, and rhythm, under such conditions is an *idempotent.*

organo (It.). Organ. *Organo pleno,* full organ.

organum (Lat.). 1. Organ. 2. Earliest Western attempts at harmonic or polyphonic music; 1st developed in the 9th century

A.D. Its earliest forms consisted of a chant-carrying *tenor* (Lat., uninterrupted course, from *tenāre*, hold) plus 1, 2, or at most 3 contrapuntal parts; the only intervals used were perfect octaves and 5ths, but perfect 4ths resulted when the 5th was inserted between 2 octave points. To the modern ear such *parallel organum* sounds extremely arid, like a mechanical duplication; this view is misinformed, for the actual practice of organum composers was far freer than the definition above implies; indeed, contrary and oblique motion between tenor and contrapuntal voices were introduced as soon as organum pervaded general church usage; contrary motion between an octave and a 5th, with dissonant passing intervals from one consonance to another, became increasingly common.

The 12th century saw the development of *melismatic organum;* the contrapuntal parts were assigned florid passages while the tenor continued with the orig. chant melody at a relatively slow pace. With the advent of mensural counterpoint and notation, the art of organum became a complex discipline of polyphonic writing; the most notable achievements were attained by the 2 great masters of the Notre Dame school in Paris, Leoninus and Perotin. The height of organum style is the impressive *organum quadruplum,* a tenor accompanied by 3 intricate contrapuntal voices.

Orgel (Ger.). Organ.

Orgelleier (Ger.). Organized hurdy-gurdy.

orgue (Fr.). Organ. *Orgue de barbarie,* a street organ operated by a crank and producing a "barbarous"crackling sound.

orientalism. See ⇒exoticism.

Ormandy, Eugene (born Jenö Blau), b. Budapest, Nov. 18, 1899; d. Philadelphia, Mar. 12, 1985. He studied violin with his father; entered the Royal Academy of Music in Budapest at age 5; began studying with Hubay at 9; received an artist's diploma at 13; received a teacher's certificate (1917); concertmaster of the Blüthner Orch. in Germany; gave recitals and played with orchs. as soloist. In 1921 he went to the U.S.; became concertmaster of the Capitol Theater Orch., N.Y., remaining there for 2 1/2 years; made his conducting debut with that orch. (1924); became associate music director (1926); gained American citizenship (1927); conducted the N.Y. Phil. at Lewisohn Stadium (1929).

Ormandy became guest conductor with the Robin Hood Dell Orch., Philadelphia (1930); guest conducted the Philadelphia Orch. (1931). appointed music director of the Minneapolis Sym. Orch. (1931); engaged as associate conductor of the Philadelphia Orch. (with Stokowski, 1936); became its music director (1938). He traveled with it on transcontinental tours (1937, 1946, 1948, 1957, 1962, 1964, 1971, 1974, and 1977); made an extended tour in England (1949) and Europe (1955, 1958).

Ormandy appeared on numerous occasions as guest conductor with European orchs.: Australia (1944); South America (1946); Latin America (1966); the Far East (1967, 1978); and Japan (1972); received the Presidential Medal of Freedom (1970). He took the Philadelphia Orch. to China and toured several cities there (1973); this was the 1st appearance of an American sym. orch. in the People's Republic of China. He was made an officer of the French Legion of Honor (1952; promoted to Commander, 1958); made a Knight of the Order of the White Rose of Finland (1955); became holder of the Bruckner Society medal (1936); named an honorary Knight Commander of the Order of the British Empire by Queen Elizabeth II in honor of the American Bicentennial (1976). In his interpretations he revealed a romanticist soul; excelled in the works of Beethoven, Schumann, and R. Strauss; conducted all scores from memory. After 42 seasons as music director of the Philadelphia Orch., he retired at the close of the 1979–80 season and was named Conductor Laureate.

ornament. Grace, embellishment.

Orphéon. Choral society established in France (1833) with a mostly amateur membership; named after the mythical singer Orpheus, whose art could enchant humans, animals, and inanimate objects. The Orphéon became an important branch of musical education in France; several periodicals were devoted to its activities, e.g., *La France Orphéonique* and *L'Echo des Orphéons;* the repertoire of the original Orphéon was enlarged by Berlioz, Gounod, and others. By the end of the 19th century there were over 2,000 individual socs. in France; in the 20th century the movement went into decline. In Barcelona the Orfeo Catalan was organized similarly; in Brazil Villa-Lobos founded an "Orpheonic concentration" in which thousands of school children participated; in England an Orpheonic Choral Festival was staged with the participation of thousands (1860).

Ory, "Kid" (Edward), b. La Place, La., Dec. 25, 1886; d. Honolulu, Jan. 23, 1973. He played the banjo as a child; took up trombone; joined bands led by Louis Armstrong and King Oliver (1920s). After a hiatus from performing (1933–42) he organized his own band and toured Europe (1956–59). He was known for his "tailgate" style of trombone playing; composed the well-known *Muskrat Ramble.*

oscillator. Electronic device used to produce a wave form.

osservato (It., strict). Carefully observed. *Stile osservato,* strict style (i.e., Palestrina counterpoint).

ossia (*oppure, ovvero;* It., or, or else). Marking indicating 1) an alternative (or facilitated) reading or fingering of a passage; 2) subtitle to an opera; 3) a choice of instrument or voice; 4) optional parts in a score; 5) optional edits in a score.

ostinato. (It. *obstinate;* plural *ostinatos*) According to Riemann, a continually recurring theme accompanied by constantly changing contrapuntal parts; the term came into usage *c.* 1700 in the sense of *basso continuo obbligato,* obligatory thoroughbass figure; the earliest dictionary definition, in Walther's *Musikalisches Lexikon* (1732), was "that figure which once begun is continued, and never deviated from." The practice of ostinato involves dual elements of constancy: the repeated theme, and the constantly evolving variations in contrapuntal voices; ostinato is thus the binding and versifying substance of a piece.

Long before the term was coined, the practice of thematic repetition became common in motets and canons; secular motives in medieval polyphonic compositions are particularly notable as early ostinatos; the vendor's cry "fresh strawberries, wild blackberries" occurs in a French medieval motet. But such incidental melodic and rhythmic repetition of a musical phrase are natural manifestations of folk songs and vocal compositions (particularly as imitation becomes prevalent), and therefore cannot be regarded as a conscious and technical application of ostinato technique.

While it is tempting to seek the sources of ostinato in Asian music (particularly Indian ragas) or jazz (boogie-woogie, riff, stomp, etc.), such citations are misleading, as is the notion of explaining dodecaphonic composition as a manifestation of ostinato technique. Ostinato is the brainchild of the Baroque, and is applied properly and consistently in the passacaglia, chaconne, ground bass, and related forms; in these genres the ostinato appears invariably in the bass, producing a true ⇒*basso obstinate*. The majestic creations of Bach in these forms are justly comparable with the greatest achievements of Gothic architecture or epic poetry.

With the decline of the Baroque in the mid–18th century, use of basso ostinato gradually declined. In Classic music, melody was the queen, the bass the faithful servant; obviously, such a base servant could not be obstinate. Mozart and Haydn found the governing basso ostinato artificial and "unnatural." Samples of *ritmo ostinato* (It., persistent rhythm) in the bass are found in Mozart's sacred music, but even here a certain variation of rhythmic figures is discernible.

Interest in the artificial ostinato technique revived toward the end of the 19th century; the finale of Brahms's 4th Sym. is a passacaglia. Reger, a Baroque revenant, wrote passacaglias like a Bach incarnate. Webern's opus 1 bears the title *Passacaglia*. In his atonal opera *Wozzeck*, Berg includes a passacaglia movement. Implicit formations peculiar to ostinato technique can be found in piano works of Bartók and Hindemith. Naturally, composers of neoclassical music find the ostinato formula most congenial.

Finally, in the 20th century, ostinato technique has sometimes shifted from the bass to the middle and even melodic voices, as a formal and tonal unifying device. In Nielsen's 5th Sym. the violas play a tremolo of a minor 3rd for several minutes; Stravinsky's *Petrouchka* and Janáček's Sinfonietta feature ostinatolike melodies; *The Rite of Spring* is a riot of ostinato figures.

ottava (It.). Octave. *All' ottava* (at the octave; written *8va*————— or *8*—————————), play an octave higher; *coll' ottava* (with the octave), double at the octave; *ottava alta* (the higher octave), play an octave higher; *ottava bassa* (*8va bassa*, the lower octave), play an octave lower.

ottavino (It.). Piccolo.

Otter, Anne Sofie von, b. Stockholm, May 9, 1955. She began studies at the Stockholm Musikhogskölan; studied with E. Werba in Vienna and G. Parsons in London, later with V. Rozsa; joined the Basel Opera (1982); sang at the Aix-en-Provence Festival (1984). She made her 1st appearance at London's Covent Garden as Cherubino; made her U.S. debut as soloist in Mozart's C-minor Mass with the Chicago Sym. Orch. (both 1985); sang at La Scala in Milan and the Bavarian State Opera in Munich (1987); appeared as Cherubino at the Metropolitan Opera in N.Y.

(1988); sang widely in recital and as soloist with major orchs. Other operatic roles include Gluck's Orfeo, Mozart's Idamantes and Dorabella, Tchaikovsky's Olga, and Octavian.

ottetto (It.). Octet.

ottoni (It.). Brass instruments.

ou (Fr., or, or else). See ⇒ossia.

oud. 'U-d.

ouvert (Fr.). Open sound. *Accord à l'ouvert*, chord played on open strings.

overblowing. Wind instrument technique in which air is forced through the tube in such a way as to sound lower harmonics, thus making it possible to play the upper registers.

overstringing. Arrangement of piano strings in 2 horizontal sets, one lying over and diagonally across the other; a piano so constructed is an *overstrung* piano, in contradistinction to *vertical* piano.

Overton, Hall (Franklin), b. Bangor, Mich., Feb. 23, 1920; d. N.Y., Nov. 24, 1972. He studied piano at the Chicago Musical College; studied composition with Persichetti at the Juilliard School of Music, N.Y. (graduated 1951); took private lessons with Riegger and Milhaud. He also fulfilled professional engagements as a jazz pianist and contributed to the magazine *Jazz Today*. He was awarded 2 Guggenheim fellowships (1955, 1957); taught at Juilliard (1960–71), the New School for Social Research in N.Y. (1962–66), and the Yale Univ. School of Music (1970–71). He composed 3 operas; 2 syms. (1955, 1962); 3 string quartets (1950, 1954, 1967); viola, cello, and piano sonatas; other orch. and chamber works; piano music; songs.

overtones (overtone series). See ⇒harmonics.

overture. (from Fr. *ouverture*, opening; Ger. *Ouvertüre*). 1. Alternate name for the Baroque instrumental suite. 2. Musical introduction to a play, opera, or ballet. 3. Starting in the 19th century, an independent orch'l. work in one movement (concert overture), often programmatic.

An opera's overture often serves as a thematic table of contents; the tunes of important arias, choruses, and instrumental interludes pass in review, preparing the listener for melodic joys heard in the work itself. As a form the overture made its 1st appearance in 17th-century France; Lully's practice gave rise to the French overture, consisting of 2 contrasting sections: the 1st in a slow tempo, marked by dotted rhythms, concluding on the dominant; the 2nd part in a faster tempo, often culminating in a fugal development. This binary form later expanded into a ternary structure simply by returning to the initial slow part, varied at will; the French overture was also in use as a movement in instrumental suites.

In the 18th century the French overture went into decline, replaced by the more vivacious Italian overture; the slow movement was placed in the middle between 2 fast sections, a more exhilarating formation than the French slow-fast-slow. In early Italian operas the overture was called *sinfonia* and, in more recent times, *preludio*. The "summary overture," incorporating materials from the opera itself, is exemplified by Mozart's overtures to *Don Giovanni* and *The Magic Flute*, Beethoven's 3 *Leonore* overtures, Weber's *Der Freischütz*, any overture by Meyerbeer, Bizet's *Carmen*, and virtually any overture by 19th-century Russian composers. Wagner's overtures to his early operas and *Die Meistersinger* belong to the summary overture category; in his later music dramas, particularly in *Der Ring des Nibelungen*, he returned to the prelude, usually of short duration, to introduce the opera's mood. R. Strauss followed the Wagnerian type of introduction in his own operas, as did a great majority of modern opera composers, including Puccini and verismo composers; only the Soviet Russians remained faithful to the summary overture.

Overtures form an integral part of scores of incidental music for dramatic performances; Beethoven's many overtures served to introduce staged presentations, but are popular concert fare by themselves. Many operas, even by famous composers, drop out of the repertoire while their overtures continue independent lives; Auber, Hérold, and von Suppé's operas have virtually disappeared, but their overtures remain popular; Rossini's opera *William Tell* is considered virtually unproducable today, but its overture is one of the most popular pieces of the concert repertoire. Berlioz, who also wrote overtures that endure despite the related operas' absence from the repertory, cobbled together a summary overture, the *Roman Carnival Overture* (1844), based on an earlier opera (*Benvenuto Cellini*, 1838).

In the realm of incidental music, Mendelssohn's overture to Shakespeare's *A Midsummer Night's Dream* was written long before the other music written for the play; but his more significant contribution is the concert overture, not connected nor intended for any opera, usually in sonata form: *Calm Sea and Prosperous Voyage, Fingal's Cave, Die schöne Melusine*, and *Ruy Blas*. Other concert works include Wagner's *Faust Overture* and 2 by Brahms, *Academic Festival Overture* and *Tragic Overture*. As the 19th century wore on, the distinction between the concert overture and the sym. poem blurred to the point of indistinction.

ovvero (It.). Ossia.

Owens, Buck (Alvis Edgar, Jr.), b. Sherman, Tex., Aug. 12, 1929. He took up the piano in his youth, then the electric guitar; began playing in honky-tonks at 16; later established himself as one of the most successful country-music entertainers, performing in the so-called Bakersfield (Calif.) style; made many appearances on radio, television, and on tours. He was co-host (with Roy Clark) of the inane but highly successful *Hee Haw* television program (1969–86).

Ozawa, Seiji, b. Fenytien, China (of Japanese parents), Sept. 1, 1935. He began to study piano; enrolled at the Toho School of Music in Tokyo at 16, studying composition and conducting; one of his teachers, Hideo Saito, profoundly influenced his musical development; graduated with 1st prizes in composition and conducting (1959). By that time he had already conducted concerts with the NHK (Japan Broadcasting Corp.)

Sym. Orch. and Japan Phil.; went to Europe; to defray expenses, became a motor-scooter salesman, promoting the product in Italy and France.

Ozawa won 1st prize at the international conducting competition in Besançon (1959); was befriended by Munch and E. Bigot; studied conducting with Bigot in Paris. Munch arranged for him to go to the U.S.; he studied conducting at Tanglewood; won its Koussevitzky Prize (1960); awarded a scholarship to work with Karajan and the Berlin Phil. Bernstein heard him there, and engaged him as co-assistant conductor of the N.Y. Phil. He made his 1st appearance with the orch. at Carnegie Hall (1961); accompanied Bernstein and the orch. on its tour of Japan later that year. He was invited to return as a guest conductor of the NHK Sym. Orch. (1962), but difficulties arose between him and the players, who objected to being treated imperiously by one of their own countrymen; still succeeded in obtaining engagements with other Japanese orchs., which he conducted on periodic visits.

After serving as sole assistant conductor of the N.Y. Phil. (1964–65), Ozawa's career advanced significantly; music director of the Ravinia Festival, summer home of the Chicago Sym. Orch. (1964–68); served as the orch.'s principal guest conductor (1969); music director of the Toronto Sym. Orch. (1965–69), which he took to England (1965). He became music director of the San Francisco Sym. Orch. (1970–76), then its music adviser (1976–77); took it on an extensive European tour, garnering exceptional critical acclaim. Even before completing his tenure in San Francisco, he had begun a close association with the Boston Sym. Orch.; with Schuller he became co-artistic director of Tanglewood (1970); assumed the post of music adviser of the Boston Sym. Orch. (1972), becoming its music director and sole artistic director of Tanglewood (1973), the 1st time an Asian musician was chosen to head the Boston Sym. Orch., which had been the exclusive preserve of European conductors.

Ozawa took the Boston Sym. Orch. on a European tour (1976); escorted it to Japan (1978), where those local musicians who had been skeptical about his abilities greeted him graciously. Another unprecedented event took place when he traveled with the orch. to the People's Republic of China on an official cultural visit (1979); later that year he and the orch. went on a tour of European music festivals. The centennial of the Boston Sym. Orch. (1981) was marked by a series of concerts under his direction, with appearances in 14 American cities and a tour of Japan, France, Germany, Austria, and England.

Ozawa proved himself a consummate master of orch'l performance, equally penetrating in the Classic repertoire as in modern works; his performances of such demanding scores as Mahler's 8th Sym. and Schoenberg's *Gurrelieder* constituted proof of his commanding technical skill, affirmed *a fortiori* by his assured presentation of the rhythmically and contrapuntally intricate 4th Sym. of Ives. He consuetudinarily conducted from memory—an astonishing feat in itself. He was married twice: 1st to the pianist Kyoko Edo, then to Vera Ilyan; his remarkable career was the subject of the documentary film *Ozawa*, telecast by PBS (1987).

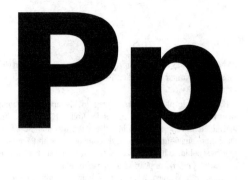

P. Abbrev. for pedal (*P.*; *Ped.*); pianoforte (*Pf.*). Dynamics: start softly, then suddenly loud (*pf*); soft (*p*); softer (*pp*); even softer (*ppp*); loud, then suddenly soft (*fp*); somewhat soft (*mp*); somewhat loud (*mf*).

pacato (It.). Peacefully, calmly.

pachanga, la. Cuban dance step and song, originally performed by Havana bands playing drums, flutes, piano, and strings. The music resembles a merengue with a refrain; it emerged in the 1960s and superseded the mambo and cha-cha in popularity. The name means a wild party in Caribbean slang.

Pachelbel, Johann, b. Nuremberg (baptized), Sept. 1, 1653; d. there, c. Mar. 9, 1706. He studied music in Nuremberg with H. Schwemmer; received lessons in composition and instrumental performance from G. C. Wecker; attended the local St. Lorenz school; attended lectures at the Auditorium Aegidianum; briefly took courses at the Univ. of Altdorf (1669–70), serving as organist at the Lorenzkirche there. He was accepted as a scholarship student at the Gymnasium Poeticum in Regensburg; took private lessons with K. Prentz. He went to Vienna as deputy organist at St. Stephen's Cathedral (1673); became court organist in Eisenach (1677), then organist at the Protestant Predigerkirche in Erfurt (1678). It was there that he established a reputation as a master organist, composer, and teacher. He was a friend of the Bach family; taught Johann Christoph, who later taught Johann Sebastian. Pachelbel married Barbara Gabler (1681), but she and their infant son died during the plague of 1683; he then married Judith Drommer (1684); had 5 sons and 2 daughters. He accepted an appointment as Württemberg court musician and organist in Stuttgart (1690); but with the French invasion (1692) fled to Nuremberg; later that year became town organist in Gotha; succeeded Wecker as organist at St. Sebald in Nuremberg (1695), a position he held until his death.

Pachelbel was one of the most significant predecessors of Bach. His liturgical organ music was of the highest order, particularly the splendid organ chorales; his nonliturgical keyboard music was also noteworthy, especially his fugues and variations; of the latter, the arias with variations he called *Hexachordum Apollinis* (1699) are extraordinary. He was equally gifted as a vocal music composer; his motets, sacred concertos, and concertato Magnificat settings are fine examples of German church music. He was a pioneer in notational symbolism intervals, scales, and pitch levels arranged to correspond to the meaning of the words. His motet *Durch Adams Fall* is accomplished by a falling bass figure; exaltation is expressed by a rising series of arpeggios in a major key; steadfast faith is conveyed by a repeated note; satanic evil is translated into an ominous figuration of a broken diminished-7th chord. Generally speaking, joyful moods were portrayed by major keys, mournful states of soul by minor, a standard mode of expression from the Baroque on.

Pachelbel's organ works also include Magnificat fugues, nonliturgical fugues, toccatas, preludes, fantasias, ciacconas, ricercars, suites, and chorale variations. He is responsible for the (in)famous Canon in D Major for 3 Violins and Basso Continuo, still extremely popular with modern audiences and available in numerous arrangements for various combinations; also composed string and basso continuo partitas. His vocal works also include arias with basso continuo, music for Vespers, and 2 Masses.

Paderewski, Ignacy (Jan), b. Kurylowka, Podolia (Russian Poland), Nov. 18, 1860; d. N.Y., June 29, 1941. From early childhood he was attracted to piano music; received some instruction from P. Sowinski, particularly 4-hand arrangements of operas. His 1st public appearance was in a charity concert at age 11, playing piano with his sister; his playing aroused interest among wealthy patrons, who took him to Kiev. He was then sent to Warsaw; entered the Cons.; learned the trombone; joined the school band; continued serious piano studies at the Warsaw Cons. with Schlozer, Strobl, and Janotha.

Paderewski toured provincial Russian towns with the Polish violinist Cielewicz (1875, 1877); in the interim he studied composition at the Warsaw Cons.; upon graduation joined the piano faculty (1878). He went to Berlin to study composition with Kiel (1882); he met Anton Rubinstein, who encouraged him and urged that he compose piano music; resigning from his post at the Warsaw Cons., he began to study orchestration in Berlin with H. Urban.

While on a vacation in the Tatra Mountains, Paderewski met the celebrated Polish actress Modjeska, who offered to finance his further piano studies with Leschetizky in Vienna, which he pursued for several years; continued his concert career; gave his 1st Paris recital and played a concert in Vienna, both with excellent success (1888); made his London debut (1890). He began receiving recognition as a composer; Anna Essipoff (then married to Leschetizky) played his piano concerto in Vienna under Hans Richter.

Paderewski played for the 1st time in N.Y. and was acclaimed with an adulation rare for pianists (1891); he supposedly gave 107 concerts in 117 days in N.Y. and other U.S. cities (and attended 86 dinner parties); his fully developed wit made him a social lion in wealthy American salons. It was reported that, at one party, the hostess confused him with a famous polo player who was also expected, and greeted him effusively. "No," he is supposed to have replied, "he is a rich soul who plays polo, and I am a poor Pole who plays solo." Paderewski eclipsed even Caruso as an idol of the masses. American spinsters beseeched him for a lock of his luxurious mane of hair; he invariably obliged; when his valet observed that he would soon become bald, he said, "Not I, my dog." One wonderful if apocryphal tale was related by a gullible biographer: a spider used to come down from the ceiling in his Vienna lodgings and sit at the piano every time he played a certain Chopin étude.

Although cosmopolitan in his culture, Paderewski remained a great Polish patriot. During the 1st World War he donated his entire concert proceeds to a fund for the Polish people caught in the war between Russia and Germany. After establishment of the independent Polish state, he served as its representative in Washington; named prime minister of the Polish Republic

(1919), 1st musician to occupy such a post anywhere at anytime. He took part in the Versailles Treaty conference, when French Prime Minister Clemenceau purportedly welcomed him with the remark: "You, a famous pianist, [now] a prime minister! What a comedown!" He resigned his post in late 1919.

Although he soon resigned from the prime ministry, Paderewski reentered politics in the wake of the Russian invasion of Poland (1920); became a delegate to the League of Nations; resigned and resumed his musical career (1921); gave his 1st concert in many years at Carnegie Hall in N.Y. (1922); made his last American tour (1939). Once more during his lifetime Poland was invaded, this time by both Germany and Russia; once more driven to political action, he joined the Polish government-in-exile in France; named president of its parliament (1940); returned to the U.S. later that year, a few months before his death. At the order of President Roosevelt, his body was buried in Arlington National Cemetery, pending the return of his remains to Free Poland.

As a pianist Paderewski was a faithful follower of the Romantic school, allowing himself free, well-nigh improvisatory declensions from written notes, tempos, and dynamics, as judged by present standards of precise rendering of musical text; but this very personal freedom of performance moved contemporaneous audiences to ecstasies of admiration. His virtuoso technique, which astonished his listeners, has been matched by any number of pianists of succeeding generations; yet his accomplishments as a performing artist remains unblemished by later achievements of other pianists.

As a composer Paderewski is also definitively Romantic; at least one of his piano pieces, the *Menuet in G* (taken from the *Humoresques de concert*, 1887), achieved enormous popularity; his other pieces never exhibited staying power and were eventually forgotten. The opera *Manru* (1897–1900), dealing with life in the Tatra Mountains, was produced in Dresden (1901) and by the Metropolitan Opera in N.Y. (1902). Other works include the Piano Concerto in A Minor (1888), *Fantaisie polonaise* for Piano and Orch. (1893), B-minor Sym. (1909), songs, and solo piano works, including the *Tatra Album* (1883) and the E-flat major Sonata (1903). He received many honors during his lifetime, including Grand Cross of the French Legion of Honor (1922); postage stamps with his picture were issued in Poland (1919) and in the series "Men of Liberty" in the U.S. (1960).

padiglione cinese (It., Chinese pavilion). See ⇒Jingling Johnny.

padovana (It.). Fast dance whose name was used interchangedly with pavane, although the latter was a more stately dance.

paean. Song of praise or thanksgiving; often used to invoke the spirit of ancient Greece. term is derived from the Greek *Paian*, a reverential epithet found in the Hymn to Apollo.

Paganini, Niccolo (Nicoló), b. Genoa, Oct. 27, 1782; d. Nice, May 27, 1840. His father, a poor dockworker, gave him lessons on mandolin and violin; he then studied with G. Servetto, a violinist in the theater orch. He was already composing; began studying harmony with F. Gnecco, then violin with G. Costa, who had him play in local churches. His 1st documented public appearance took place at the church of S. Filippo Neri (1794.);

he heard and was indelibly impressed by Franco-Polish violin virtuoso A. F. Durand (later called Duranowski), a brilliant showman.

Having made phenomenal progress in his studies, Paganini went to Parma to study with Alessandro Rolla (1795); upon his arrival, Rolla reportedly told him that there was nothing left to teach him, suggesting that he study composition with Paer, who in turn sent him to his own teacher, G. Ghiretti. Paganini returned to Genoa (1796), appearing as a violinist in private performances; with Napoleon's invasion of Italy the family moved to Ramairone; went with his father to Livorno, where he gave concerts (1800); also appeared in Modena. They returned to Genoa; that year, along with his older brother Carlo (also a violinist), went to Lucca to play at the Festival of Santa Croce (1801); he was a brilliant success, and settled there, becoming concertmaster of the national orch. As a soloist Paganini captivated his auditors by his pyrotechnics; a performance in Livorno so impressed a wealthy French merchant that he was rewarded with a valuable violin. With the arrival of Princess Elisa Baciocchi, sister of Napoleon, as ruler of Lucca (1805), musical life there was reorganized; the 2 major orchs. were dissolved, replaced by a chamber orch.; Paganini was retained as 2nd violinist, then made solo court violinist (1807); after the chamber orch.'s dissolution (1808), played in the court string quartet and taught violin to Prince Felix Baciocchi; dissatisfied with his position, he broke with the court and pursued a career as a virtuoso (1809).

Paganini came to national prominence in 1813 with a series of sensationally successful concerts in Milan (1813); subsequently toured Italy, his renown growing from year to year and his vast technical resources maturing and augmenting; easily displaced would-be rivals Lafont in Milan (1816) and Lipinski in Piacenza (1818). He met singer Antonia Bianchi (1824), who became his mistress; she bore him a son, Achilles (1825), whom Paganini had legitimized (1837); made a Knight of the Golden Spur by Pope Leo XII (1827). He left Italy for his 1st tour abroad, immediately gaining a triumph with his 1st concert in Vienna (1828); gave 14 concerts during his Viennese sojourn; accorded the honorary title of chamber virtuoso by the Emperor; made his 1st appearance in Berlin (1829); played in Frankfurt, Darmstadt, Mannheim, and Leipzig; made his Paris and London debuts (1831), then gave concerts throughout Great Britain (1831–33). His artistic skills began to wane around 1834, his long-precarious health ruined; but he managed to retain his fame and considerable wealth; continued to give concerts sporadically, but spent most of his time at his Parmese villa, making occasional visits to Paris. A critical illness in 1838 caused the loss of his voice; in 1839 he went to Nice for his health, but died there the following spring.

Paganini's stupendous technique, power, and control, his romantic passion and intense energy, made him the marvel of his time. He was not above employing certain tricks of virtuosity, such as tuning up the A string of his violin by a semitone or playing the *Witches' Dance* on 1 string after severing the other 3 on stage, in full view of the audience, with a pair of scissors. He was a highly effective composer for violin, giving regular performances of his works with great success; outstanding among these works are the 24 solo caprices, op. 1 (1805); 5 concertos (c. 1817–30); *Moto perpetuo*, op. 11 (after 1830); other works with orch. Chamber: violin and guitar duets; miscellaneous quartets for various combinations (1800–20); other works.

Page, Patti (born Clara Ann Fowler), b. Claremore, Okla., Nov. 8, 1927. She sang in a church choir in Tulsa; appeared on a local radio program, adopting her stage name; subsequently became a recording artist, her 1st hit being *Confess* (1948); gained fame with *Tennessee Waltz* (1950), which became the official state song of Tenn.; in later years she made guest appearances in pop concerts with U.S. orchs.

page turner. The individual who permits pianists in non-solo settings (and harpsichordists in all settings) to read off the score without having to fuss with the actual pages of music; thus permitting the player to keep the hands at the keys. The page turner (often a student of the pianist) sits on the pianist's left-hand side and holds the right-hand page by its right upper corner delicately between the fingers, pulling the page over in a smooth, undistracting, and timely manner. On occasion, the page turner has the challenge of returning the music to an earlier spot, in *da capo* and similar situations. Page turners must avoid facial expressions of aesthetic delight or, still worse, a disgusted grimace; humming, rhythmic breathing, foot-tapping, or similar activities are criminal offenses. Oliveros raised the status of a page turner to that of a full-fledged participant in a work she explicitly titled *Trio for Violin, Piano, and Page Turner*.

Paik, Nam June, b. Seoul, July 20, 1932. He studied 1st at the Univ. of Tokyo; took theory courses with T. Georgiades in Munich and W. Fortner in Freiburg im Breisgau; turning to electronics, he worked at the Electronic Music Studio in Cologne (1958–60); attended the Darmstadt new music seminars (1957–61). In his installations he pursues the objective of total art as the sum of integrated synesthetic experiences, involving all sorts of actions: walking, talking, dressing, undressing, drinking, smoking, moving furniture, and engaging in quaquaversal commotion to demonstrate that any human or inhuman action becomes an artistic event through volitional concentration on an ontological imperative.

Paik gained notoriety for his duo recitals with sometimes topless cellist Charlotte Moorman; in one piece, he acted as a surrogate cello, his denuded spinal column serving as fingerboard for Moorman's cello bow, his bare skin providing room for intermittent pizzicati. In 1963 he began experimenting with videotape as a sound and image medium; his 1st experiment in this field was *Global Groove*, a high-velocity collage of intermingled television bits, including instantaneous commercials, fragments from news telecasts, and subliminal extracts from regular programs, subjected to topological alterations. He was also associated with the Fluxus group.

Paik's works include *Ommaggio a Cage* for piano demolition, breakage of raw eggs, spray painting of hands in jet black, etc. (1959); *Variations on a Theme of Saint-Saëns* for cello and piano, with the pianist playing *The Swan* while the cellist dives into an oil drum filled with water (1965); *Performable Music*, wherein the performer makes a razor incision of no less than 10 centimeters on his left forearm (1965); *Opera sextronique* (1967); *Creep into the Vagina of a Whale* (c. 1969); *Young Penis Symphony*, a protrusion of 10 erectile phalluses through a paper curtain (c. 1970; 1st perf. at La Mamelle, San Francisco, 1975). Of uncertain attribution is Sym. No. 3, which Paik delegated to a colleague, who worked on it in Saugus, Calif., epicenter of the earthquake of Feb. 9, 1971; the earthquake itself constituted the finale.

Paine, John Knowles, b. Portland, Maine, Jan. 9, 1839; d. Cambridge, Mass., Apr. 25, 1906. His father ran a music store and conducted a band in Portland. He studied organ, piano, harmony, and counterpoint with H. Krotzschmar, then took courses with K. Haupt (organ) and W. Wieprecht (orchestration and composition) in Berlin (1858–61); performed as organist and pianist in Germany and England. He settled in Boston, becoming organist of the West Church (1861); joined the faculty of Harvard Univ. (1862); was organist at its Appleton Chapel; was prof. of music at Harvard (1875–1906), 1st music professorship at a U.S. univ.; elected to the National Inst. of Arts and Letters (1898).

Paine greatly distinguished himself as a mentor, having taught J. A. Carpenter, F. S. Converse, A. Foote, E. B. Hill, D. G. Mason, W. Spalding, and many others; publ. *The History of Music to the Death of Schubert* (Boston, 1907). His compositions include 2 syms.: No. 1 (Boston, 1876); No. 2, *In the Spring* (Cambridge, 1880); *As You Like It*, overture (c. 1876); 2 symphonic poems: *The Tempest* (c. 1876) and *An Island Fantasy* (c. 1888); and Duo Concertante for Violin, Cello, and Orch. (c. 1877). He also composed chamber and choral works; songs; and piano and organ works.

paired notes. Two parallel series of notes played on piano with 1 hand.

Palestrina, Giovanni Pierluigi da, b. probably in Palestrina, near Rome, 1525 or 1526; d. Rome, Feb. 2, 1594. He customarily signed his name as Giovanni Petraloysio (i.e., Pierluigi). He 1st appeared as a choirboy at S. Maria Maggiore (1537); likely studied with the maestros there at the time, Robin Mallapert, one Robert, and Firmin Lebel; appointed organist of the cathedral of S. Agapit in Palestrina (1544), where his duties also included teaching music to canons and choirboys.

The bishop of Palestrina, Cardinal Giovanni Maria Ciocchi del Monte, was elected pope, taking the name of Julius III (1550); he appointed Palestrina maestro of the Cappella Giulia in succession to Mallapert (1551); Palestrina dedicated his 1st book of masses to him (1554). The pope rewarded him by making him a member of the Cappella Sistina even though he was a married man (1555); he was admitted without the entrance examination; neither had he received the other singers' approval. But a new Pope (Paul IV) dismissed Palestrina and 2 other singers after invoking the celibacy rule of chapel, although he granted each of them a small pension (late 1555).

Almost immediately, Palestrina became maestro di cappella of the great church of St. John Lateran; his son Rodolfo joined him as a chorister. Palestrina's tenure was made difficult by inadequate funds for music; resigned his post (1560). He was maestro di cappella of S. Maria Maggiore (1561–66); during that time, the Council of Trent took up the matter of sacred music (1562–63). Out of its discussions arose a movement to advance the cause of text intelligibility when set to music; his role with this Council remains a matter of dispute, but his *Missa Pape Marcelli* is an outstanding example of a number of its reforms.

Palestrina was in charge of music at the summer estate of Cardinal Ippolito II d'Este in Tivoli, near Rome (from 1564); apparently took up a full-time position in the Cardinal's service (1567–71) while teaching at the Seminario Romano (1566–71), where his sons Rodolfo and Angelo were students. The court of Emperor Maximilian II offered him the imperial choirmaster position in Vienna (1568), but he demanded so high a salary that the offer was withdrawn. Upon the death of Giovanni Animuccia (1571), he resumed his post as maestro of the Cappella Giulia; his salary was increased to forestall a move to S. Maria Maggiore (1575); at the request of Pope Gregory XIII, Palestrina and Annibale Zoilo began revising the plainsong of the Roman Gradual and Antiphoner (1577); Palestrina never completed his work on this project, which was eventually completed by others and publ. as *Editio Medicaea* (1614).

In 1580, having lost his wife and 2 sons to the plague, Palestrina decided to enter the priesthood; changing his mind, however, he remarried (1581). In succeeding years he devoted time to managing his wife's fortune while continuing his musical work; tendered an offer to become maestro at the court of the Duke of Mantua (1583), his terms were again rejected as excessive. He publ. his settings of the Song of Solomon (1584); began planning to return to Palestrina as choirmaster of cathedral (1593), but died before he could make the transition; buried in the Cappella Nuova of old St. Peter's Church.

With his great contemporaries Byrd and Lassus, Palestrina stands as one of the foremost composers of his age; mastered the polyphonic style of the Franco-Flemish school, creating works of unsurpassing beauty and technical adroitness. His sacred music remains his most glorious achievement; highly prolific, he composed some 375 motets, 140 madrigals (sacred and secular), 100 masses, offertories, hymns, Magnificats, Lamentations, litanies, and psalms.

palindrome. Palindromic words and sentences do not change when they are read backward. Reger, whose last name is a palindrome, replied wittily to an admirer who complained that he could see only his back while he conducted a concert: "I am no different front or back." Musical palindromes are synonymous with retrograde movements. In a palindromic section in Berg's opera *Lulu*, the music revolves backward to depict story of Lulu's incarceration and escape. Hindemith wrote a number of palindromic pieces. Samplers of palindromic canons are found in the author's *Thesaurus of Scales and Melodic Patterns*.

palmas (Sp.). Clapping of hands, as found in Latin American and other dances.

palpitant (Fr.). Trembling, palpitating.

pandeiro (Port.; Sp. *pandero*). Tambourine.

pandiatessaron. Vertical column consisting of perfect 4ths (from Greek *diatessaron*, interval of a 4th). The pandiatessaron contains all 12 notes of the tempered scale and represents a dodecaphonic integration of quartal melodies.

pandiatonicism. System of diatonic harmony making use of all 7 degrees of the scale in dissonant combinations; the functional importance of the primary triads, however, remains undiminished in pandiatonic harmony. The term was coined by the author in 1937. Pandiatonicism possesses both tonal and modal aspects, with the distinct preference for major keys. The earliest pandiatonic extension was the added major 6th over the tonic major triad. A cadential chord of the tonic major 7th is also of frequent occurrence.

Independently from the development of pandiatonicism in serious music, American jazz musicians adopted it as a practical device. Concluding chords in piano improvisations in jazz are usually pandiatonic, containing the tonic, dominant, mediant, submediant and supertonic, with the triad in open harmony in the bass topped by a series of perfect 4ths. In C major such chords would be, from the bass up, C–G–E–A–D–G. It is significant that all components of this pandiatonic complex are members of the natural harmonic series. With C as the fundamental generator, G is the 3rd partial, E the 5th partial, D the 9th, B the 15th and A the 27th. The perfect 4th is excluded both theoretically and practically, for it is not a member of the harmonic series—an interesting concordance of actual practice and acoustical considerations.

With the dominant in the bass, a complete succession of 4ths, one of them an augmented 4th, can be built: G–C–F–B–E–A–D–G, producing a satisfying pandiatonic complex. When the subdominant is in the bass, the most euphonious result is obtained by a major triad in open position, F–C–A, in the low register, and E–B–D–G in the upper register. Polytriadic combinations are natural resources of pandiatonicism, with the dominant combined with the tonic, e.g., C–G–E–D–G–B, making allowance for a common tone; dominant over the subdominant, as in the complex F–C–A–D–G–B, etc.

True polytonality cannot be used in pandiatonicism, since all notes are in the same mode. Pedal points are particularly congenial to the spirit of pandiatonicism, always following the natural spacing of the component notes, using large intervals in the bass register and smaller intervals in the treble. The aesthetic function of pandiatonicism is to enhance resources of triadic harmony; that is reason why the superposition of triads, including those in minor, are always productive of a resonant diatonic bitonality. Although pandiatonicism has evolved from tertian foundations, it lends itself to quartal and quintal constructions with satisfactory results. Pandiatonicism is a logical medium for techniques of neoclassicism. Many sonorous usages of pandiatonicism can be found in works of Debussy, Ravel, Stravinsky, Casella, Malipiero, Vaughan Williams, Copland, and R. Harris.

By analogy with pandiatonicism, *panpentatonicism* denotes a free use of the 5 notes of the pentatonic scale. Consecutive 4ths and 5ths are frequent contrapuntal resources; as the leading tone is absent in pentatonicism, plagal cadences are the only available endings. Panpentatonic tone clusters are more euphonious than pandiatonic ones; when projected against a perfect 5th in the bass, they create an attractive sonority of modernistic chinoiserie.

pandora. Plucked chordophone akin to a bass cittern, with fixed frets and 6 double courses, reported between 1560 and 1670; commonly used in basso continuo; name also applied to the theorbo-lute.

pandura (Sp.). Bandola.

pandurria (Sp.). Bandurria.

panpipes. Most ancient of wind instruments, consisting of several reeds of different sizes that are bound together; its name is explained by the legend that the god Pan invented it. The panpipes is the prototype of the mouth organ, with reeds arranged to produce a continuous diatonic scale. The panpipes exist in all primitive cultures. In South American countries they are known under various names: *antara* in Peru, *rondador* in Ecuador, *capador* in Colombia, and *sico* in Bolivia. In China primitive panpipes are arranged in 2 mutually exclusive whole-tone scales, one of which is regarded as a masculine symbol and the other as feminine.

pantaleon. Large cimbalom (hammered dulcimer) invented by the great performer Pantaleon Hebenstreit (1667–1750); it was given its name by Louis XIV in 1705. The instrument was appreciated for its breadth of dynamic variation; it was eventually superseded by new fortepiano, although it lent its name to the new instrument for a brief time.

pantomime (Grk., all-imitating). 1. Balletlike performance without speech or singing, in which action is suggested by gestures and choreography. 2. In the U.K., pageant holiday play with songs, slapstick; an outgrowth of music hall; often shortened to *panto*.

pantonality. Schoenberg's preferred synonym for atonality, denoting the possibility of all tonalities or conscious absence of a single, preeminent tonality. Pantonality is almost synonymous with omnitonality, the only difference being that pantonality includes atonal melodic progressions and uninhibited dissonant textures, while omnitonality tends to enhance the basic sense of tonality.

Panufnik, Andrzej, b. Warsaw, Sept. 24, 1914; d. London, Oct. 27, 1991. His Polish father manufactured string instruments; his mother was an Englishwoman who studied violin in Warsaw. Andrzej began musical training with his mother; after studying composition with Sikorski at the Warsaw Cons. (diploma 1936), he took conducting lessons with Weingartner at the Vienna Academy of Music (1937–38); subsequently completed his training with Gaubert in Paris, and studied in London (1938–39). He returned to Warsaw (1939), remaining there during the Nazi occupation, playing piano in the underground; his compositions to 1944 were destroyed during the Warsaw uprising. After liberation, conducted the Krakow Phil. (1945–46) and the Warsaw Phil. (1946–47); left his homeland in protest of the Communist regime (1954), settling in England; became a naturalized citizen (1961). After serving as music director of the City of Birmingham Sym. Orch. (1957–59), he devoted himself to composition. His wife, Scarlett Panufnik, publ. *Out of the City of Fear* (London, 1956), recounting his flight from Poland. He appeared as a guest conductor of his own works with the N.Y. Chamber Sym. (1988) and the Chicago Sym. Orch. (1990).

In his early years Panufnik belonged to the vanguard group of Polish composers; used advanced techniques, including quarter tones; introduced notational innovations; in several orch'l works he left blank spaces rather than rests to indicate inactive instrumental parts. In his later music he adopted a more circumspect idiom—expressive, direct, and communicative. He composed 10 symphonies, other orch'l works, 4 string quartets, chamber and piano works, and choral works.

parable aria. Type of aria, much in vogue in the 18th century, in which the singer expresses his emotions by way of a parable or metaphor. A famous example is the protestation of 1 of the

ladies in Mozart's *Così fan tutte* that she would remain as firm as a rock in resisting temptation; the rock is the crux of the metaphor in the parable.

paradiddle. Rhythmic drumroll consisting of 4 rapid, even notes struck with right and left hands alternately. *Paradiddle flam-flam*, a paradiddle followed by 2 notes of twice the value, e.g., 4 16th notes followed by 2 8th notes.

parallel harmony. Parallel motion of chords, as in medieval fauxbourdon and 20th-century impressionism. Traditional harmony prohibited use of consecutive octaves and 5ths, and parallel chord formations, even when no such forbidden intervals were consecutively used (e.g., 2nd and 3rd inversion of the dominant 7th chord).

parallel intervals. See ⇒consecutive intervals.

parallel motion. Voice-leading in harmony or counterpoint in which intervals move in the same direction. In traditional harmony, parallel 3rds and 6ths are recommended, while parallel 5ths and octaves are forbidden; parallel 4ths are acceptable only in certain eras and under specific conditions.

paraphrases and transcriptions. Adaptation or rearrangement of a vocal or instrumental piece for a different medium, sometimes with variations. When music became a democratic art in the 19th century, not only the aristocracy but the middle class had pianos or harmoniums in their drawing rooms, and professional musicians found a new outlet for their wares. Music was brought to the people; opera and sym. had to be reduced to manageable proportions to be made accessible to the masses. Popular arias, marches, and ballet numbers from favorite operas were arranged by highly capable musicians for piano. Amateur adults and young children were offered arrangements of classical masterpieces that were not only musically adequate but also provided a social means of musical communication and entertainment. German publishers put out reams of musical literature for piano 4-hands or for piano solo.

Some great pianists, themselves composers of stature, were not averse to participate in this democratization of music. Liszt made piano transcriptions of opera and symphonic compositions (includes the complete Beethoven syms.), and of songs of Schubert and Schumann; he also wrote fantasies on motives of current opera favorites. Liszt's teacher, and Beethoven's pupil, Carl Czerny, took time off from writing his myriad piano exercises to publish arrangements of operatic airs. Such arrangements pursued an eminently practical aim, namely to acquaint music lovers with operatic and symphonic music of the day.

Liszt introduced semantic distinctions among various categories of transcriptions. The most literal arrangement was, in his terminology, an *Übertragung* (transference); a more idiomatic transference was *Bearbeitung* (reworking). The next more liberal arrangement was a *transcription*; then followed a fantasia, sometimes further expanded as a *free fantasia* or *romantic fantasia*. An even more unrestricted type of free fantasia Liszt liked to call *reminiscences*, things remembered from listening to the music of this or that opera or sym. As an auxiliary category Liszt introduced the term *illustrations* for recurring thematic allusion. Finally, paraphrases united all characteristics of an arrangement, transcription, fantasy, or romantic fantasy, illustration, or reminiscence. To indicate the publishing category of a given transcription, Liszt sometimes used word *Klavierpartitur* (piano score).

pardessus de viole (Fr.). Treble viola d'amore.

Parker, Charlie (Charles Christopher, Jr.), called "Bird" or "Yardbird," b. Kansas City, Kans., Aug. 29, 1920; d. N.Y., Mar. 12, 1955. He was self-taught; played an alto saxophone given to him at age 13 by his mother; left school at 15 and became a professional musician. He was a member of Jay McShann's band (1937–44), with which he toured and made his 1st recordings (1941); after performing in E. Hines's band (1942–44), which included Dizzy Gillespie and other young jazz artists, he played in B. Eckstine's band (1944–45); after work they would meet in a club called Minton's, and there gradually evolved the new style of bebop. Parker became the acknowledged leader of this style as he developed an improvising technique characterized by virtuosic speed, intense tone, complex harmonies, and florid melodies having irregular rhythmic patterns and asymmetric phrase lengths.

After the mid-1940s Parker usually worked in small combos led either by himself or by 1 of other members of the small, close-knit circle of boppers; occasionally worked with larger ensembles (including a string orch. for which he wrote the arrangements). As a composer he usually worked with 12-bar blues patterns (but always in an unstereotyped manner; he made 175 blues recordings, all markedly different) or with chord progressions of well-known standards: His *Ornithology*, for instance, is based on the progressions of *How High the Moon.*

Parker achieved a prominence that made him a living legend (a leading N.Y. club, Birdland, was named after him); his life, though, in addition to being tragically short, was plagued by the consequences of narcotics addiction (acquired in his mid-teens) and alcoholism. Because of suspected narcotics possession, the N.Y. City police rescinded his cabaret license (1951), thereby denying him the right to work in N.Y. clubs (until shortly before his death). Despite difficulties of his personal life, Parker's music has survived and become part of the essential jazz canon; it has also been interpreted as rebellious commentary on the place of the African-American during latter-day U.S. segregation. His life was the ostensible subject of the 1988 film *Bird.*

Parker, Horatio (William), b. Auburndale, Mass., Sept. 15, 1863; d. Cedarhurst, N.Y., Dec. 18, 1919. He studied piano with J. Orth, theory with Emery, and composition with Chadwick in Boston; subsequently went to Germany; took courses in organ and composition with Rheinberger in Munich (1882–85); wrote a cantata, *King Trojan* (1885). Returning to the U.S., he settled in N.Y. and taught at the cathedral schools of St. Paul and St. Mary (1886–90), the General Theological Seminary (1892), and the National Cons. of Music (1892–93); was organist and choirmaster at St. Luke's (1885–87), St. Andrew's (1887–88), and the Church of the Holy Trinity (1888–93); went to Boston as organist and choirmaster at Trinity Church (1893–1902). He attracted attention with the 1st performance of his oratorio *Hora novissima* (N.Y., 1893), in which he demonstrated mastery of choral writing; his harmonic and contrapuntal style remained securely tied to German practices. In 1894 he was engaged as a prof. of

theory at Yale Univ.; became dean of its School of Music (1904), where he remained until his death.

Many American composers received benefit of Parker's excellent instruction; among them was Ives, who kept his sincere appreciation of his teaching long after he renounced his conservative traditions. In 1895 Parker co-founded the New Haven Sym. Orch., which he conducted (1895–1918); conducted performances of his works in England (1900, 1902). Returning to the U.S., he served as organist and choirmaster at the collegiate church of St. Nicholas in Boston (1902–10); continued to compose industriously, without making any concessions to emerging modern schools of composition.

In 1911 Parker's opera *Mona* won the $10,000 prize offered by the Metropolitan Opera in N.Y.; premiered there (1912); won a prize from the National Federation of Women's Clubs for his 2nd opera, *Fairyland*, produced in Los Angeles (1915); neither opera possessed enough power to survive in repertory. Other works include orch'l pieces, notably *A Northern Ballad*, symphonic poem (Boston, 1899); chamber music; secular and religious choral music; songs; and organ works, including the E-Flat Sonata (op. 65).

parlando (or parlante) (It.). "Speaking"; singing with clear and marked enunciation. In piano playing, *parlante* calls for a clear, crisp *non legato.*

parody. 1. Parasitic literary or musical genre that emerged in the 18th century and flourished in the 19th, particularly in opera; it usually followed on the heels of a successful or at least notorious theatrical production. Weber's opera *Der Freischütz* was lampooned in England as "a new muse-sick-all and see-nick performance from the new German uproar, by the celebrated Bunny-bear." Wagner's *Tannhäuser*, which suffered a notorious debacle at its 1st Paris production, engendered a number of French parodies, among them 1 entitled *Ya-Meine Herr, Cacophonie de l'Avenir.* Occasionally a parody anticipates the main event. One such parody, *Tristanderl und Süssholde*, was produced in Munich before *Tristan und Isolde* itself. These anti-Wagner parodies were the last of the species.

2. (from Grk. *para* + *aidein*, side-song) Type of Mass or motet composition, common in the Renaissance, in which composers borrowed whole pieces or parts of pieces (usually motets) and built new pieces around them. As used in old music theory, this term meant "like something else" and was quite devoid of the contemporary sense of travesty. This method is distinct from cantus firmus and paraphrase types, which borrow one melodic line.

Parsons, Gram (born Cecil Connor), b. Winter Haven, Fla., Sept. 5, 1946; d. Joshua Tree National Monument, Calif., Sept. 19, 1973. He twanged the guitar in Georgia bands and studied theology at Harvard; it was in those patrician surroundings that he organized a country-rock group called the International Submarine Band. He also contributed to the Byrds in their famous album *Sweetheart of the Rodeo*, with his songs *Hickory Wind* and *100 Years from Now.* In 1968 he formed the Flying Burrito Brothers, which recorded his greatest success, the album *The Gilded Palace of Sin*, followed by *Burrito Deluxe* and *The Last of the Red Hot Burritos;* left the group;, recorded 2 solo albums (*Grievous Angel* and *GP*).

part. 1. Series of tones written for and executed by a voice or instrument, either as a solo or together with other voices or instruments. 2. Division of a homophonic movement devoted to exposition of 1 melody or musical idea; like 2-part and 3-part song forms.

Pärt, Arvo, b. Paide, Sept. 11, 1935. He studied composition with H. Eller at the Tallinn Cons. (graduated 1963); was attached to the music division of Estonian Radio (1958–67); settledin West Berlin (1982). He began composing in a traditional manner, writing instrumental pieces in a neo-Baroque idiom, strict to form, freely dissonant in harmony; influenced by Western musical modernism, he gravitated toward a style based on empiric sonorism without renouncing, however, the historic foundation of tonality. The spectrum of his musical vocabulary extends from abecedarian minimalism to quaquaversal polytonality, from impressionistic pointillism to austere serialism. One of his specialties is a technique he calls "tintinnabula," in which he applies shifting phases of a given chord.

Pärt was the 1st Estonian composer to use the Schoenbergian 12-tone method to form melodic and harmonic dodecaphonic structures, as in his arresting *Nekrolog*, dedicated to victims of the Holocaust (1960). Extending the concept of integral dodecaphony, he makes use of pandiatonic and panpentatonic tone clusters, culminating in the formation of a Brobdingnagian blob of white noise. He occasionally resorts to aleatory proceedings, or harks back to historic antecedents in applying austere precepts of ars antiqua; in this, he commends himself as a true *Homo ludens*, a musician playing a diversified game. He has composed 3 symphonies: No. 1, *Polyphonic* (1963); No. 2 (1966); No. 3 (1971); also composed for other orch'l and chamber ensembles; vocal works; solo piano works.

part music (part singing). Concerted or harmonized vocal music, usually without accompaniment.

part song. Homophonic composition for at least 3 voices in harmony, without accompaniment, and for equal or mixed voices; melody with choral harmony with any reasonable number of voices to each part.

partbooks. Separate parts for singers or instrumentalists, in common use in the 16th century. Singers were seated around a table, each with an individual partbook, coordinating by subtle signals, anticipation of breath, etc., without using a general score. The practice of part singing from partbooks has been recently revived by various English singing groups.

Partch, Harry, b. Oakland, Calif., June 24, 1901; d. San Diego, Sept. 3, 1974. Largely autodidact, he experimented with instruments capable of producing rational intervals, leading him to formulate a 43-tone gamut, which he expounded upon in *Genesis of a Music* (1949; 2nd rev. ed., 1974); built or adapted instruments to fit his just system and to compose with, including a viola with elongated neck, chromelodeons (adapted reed organs), 72-string kitharas, 44-string harmonic canons, marimbas (diamond, "reverse diamond," bass, bamboo, mazda), cloud-chamber pyrex bowls, a blow-boy (a pair of bellows with an attached automobile horn), etc.; adding new instruments to his ensemble, he rev. earlier works to reflect new possibilities. He

also gradually made corporeality his central artistic aesthetic. Seeking intimate contact with American life, he wandered across the country, collected indigenous expression of folkways (e.g., inscriptions on public walls), recorded speech-song, etc., for texts in his 1930s and 1940s works; one crucial journey is described in *Bitter Music* (1935–36); later theatrical works were based on Greek tragedy, Noh, African, and other mythological and traditional sources.

parte (It.). Part. *Colla parte*, direction to accompanists to follow yieldingly and discreetly the solo part or voice.

parterre (Fr., parquet). Last rows in a concert hall.

partial stop. Half stop.

partials (partial tones). See ⇒harmonics.

particella (It., particle). Reduced score. Some composers prefer writing down symphonic scores or even operas in arrangements for 2 or 3 staves: 1 for woodwinds, 1 for brass, 1 or 2 for strings, with the vocal part, if any, in small printing on top. A vocal score of a choral work such as an oratorio is usually published in the form of particella, with the orch'l part arranged for piano. Schubert and Wagner wrote some of their works 1st in particella form. Prokofiev systematically adopted this abridged form of orch'l writing and engaged a knowledgeable assistant to convert such a particella into a full orch'l score according to indications of instrumentation given by him. A major part of the musical legacy of Ives consists of piano arrangements with instrumental cues written in. Stravinsky composed *The Rite of Spring* 1st for piano 4-hands, which is essentially a particella. Many publishers now issue abridged scores for conductors, often with optional instrumental parts written in.

partie (Fr.). Instrumental or vocal part.

partimento (It., division). 17th- and 18th-century practice of improvising melodies over a given bass, which necessarily determined the harmonic progressions of the exercise. The practice of partimento had didactic uses, but it waned at the end of the Baroque when basso continuo gave way to entirely written-out scores.

partita (*parthia*; It.). Originally, a variation; by the Baroque era, a suite.

partitino (It., little score). Supplementary parts, printed separately, for a work with instruments or vocal part that do not appear often in the score. Examples include "Turkish" percussion in Mozart's *The Abduction from the Seraglio*; trombone and chorus in his *Don Giovanni*; and children's chorus in Puccini's *La Bohème*. The partitino saves time and paper that would otherwise be wasted on vacuous rests and pauses.

partition (Fr.; Ger. *Partitur*; It. *partitura*). A score.

Parton, Dolly (Rebecca), b. Locust Ridge, Tenn., Jan. 19, 1946. Born into poverty, she began to sing as a child; after graduating from high school she went to Nashville, Tenn., to seek her fortune; in 1967 joined Porter Wagoner's band; quickly assumed a leading place among country-music stars; moved into pop-rock field and toured widely with her own group, Gypsy Fever (1976). She composed such popular songs as *Coat of Many Colors, Tennessee Mountain Home, Joshua, Jolene,* and *Love Is Like a Butterfly;* was particularly successful with the country album *Here You Come Again* and the pop-rock album *Heartbreaker.* To top it all, she made herself famous by appearing as 1 of 3 secretaries in the comedy film *9 to 5* (1980), for which she wrote and recorded the theme song.

pas de patineurs (Fr.). Ballroom dance, symbolic of the movement of a skater in fast march tempo.

pas de quatre (Fr.). Ballroom dance for 4 participants, usually in 4/4 or 12/4 meter in moderate tempo.

pas d'Espagne (Fr.). Generic name for a dance in a Spanish vein, usually of the stately bolero type.

Pasatieri, Thomas, b. N.Y., Oct. 20, 1945. He began to play piano by spontaneous generation, and picked up elements of composition, particularly vocal, by a similar subliminal process; between ages 14 and 18 he wrote some 400 songs; persuaded Nadia Boulanger to take him as a student by correspondence between Paris and N.Y. at 15; the following year entered the Juilliard School of Music; studying with V. Giannini and Persichetti; took a course with Milhaud in Aspen, Colo., where his 1st opera, *The Women,* to his own libretto, was performed when he was only 19 (1965).

It became clear to Pasatieri that opera was his natural medium, and that the way to achieve best results was by following the evolutionary line of Italian operatic productions characterized by felicity of bel canto, facility of harmonic writing, and euphonious fidelity to the lyric and dramatic content of the subject. In striving to attain these objectives, he ran against the tide of mandatory inharmoniousness; his productions, applauded by audiences, shocked music critics and other composers; their attitude recalls the hostility felt toward Giannini and Menotti. He taught at the Juilliard School (1967–69), the Manhattan School of Music (1969–71), and, as Distinguished Visiting Prof., the Univ. of Cincinnati College–Cons. of Music (1980–83). In addition to many operas, he has written for vocal groups with instrumental accompaniment.

paseo (Sp., promenade). South American dance in moderate waltz time.

pasillo (Sp.). Latin American dance of Spanish origin in waltz time, sometimes combined with 6/8 to produce characteristic cross rhythms. In Colombia it is called *vals del pais* (country waltz).

paso doble (Sp.). Latin American social dance, in a march-like step, usually in 6/8 meter.

passacaglia (It.; from Sp. *pasar una calle,* pass along a street; Fr. *passacaille*). Orig., procession of a chorus playing and singing in march time, probably derived from the Spanish *pasacalle.* In the 17th century the passacaglia acquired the characteristics of sui generis variation form in triple meter. Its salient feature is an ostinato bass progression with melodic and

harmonic variations in the upper voices. In the Baroque period the passacaglia became 1 of the most important instrumental forms for keyboard. Bach, Handel, Couperin, and Rameau all contributed to the perfection of the genre. In the 18th century it coalesced with the chaconne; while the distinction between the 2 forms is not always clear, 1 set of criteria states that the passacaglia is polyphonically constructed in a precise and rigorous style, while the chaconne is often chordal and homophonic.

passage. 1. Portion or section of a piece, usually short, not necessarily developmental in nature. 2. Rapid repeated figure, either ascending or descending, especially in piano writing. A scale passage is generally called a run.

passaggio (It.). 1. Renaissance term for ornamental passages in instrumental works. 2. Technical passage work, especially in piano writing.

passamezzo (It., step and a half). Old Italian dance in duple time, like the pavane but faster. It is usually symmetrical in form.

passepied (Fr., pass the foot; U.K. *paspy*). 17th-century French dance in 3/8 or 6/8 time with 3 or 4 reprises; like the minuet in movement but quicker.

passing notes or tones. Notes or tones foreign to chords they accompany and passing by a step from one chord to another. They differ from suspensions in not being prepared and in entering (usually) on an unaccented beat.

passion, passion music. Musical setting of a text descriptive of Christ's sufferings and death on the cross (passion); it retains its original Latin meaning of suffering. The great Bach passions are in the vernacular, and the characters, including Jesus and the apostles, speak and sing in German, while the chorus supplies the narrative. There is a great deal of conventional melorhythmic symbolism: the passion—that is, the actual pain experienced by Jesus—is rendered in chromatics; the resurrection is set in clear major arpeggios; while the powers of the dark are expressed in falling basses in broken diminished-7th chords.

passione, con (It.). Passionately, in an impassioned style, fervently.

passo a sei (It., 6-step). Swiss folk dance.

pasteboard rattle (U.K.). See ⇒friction drum.

pastiche (Fr.; It. *pasticcio,* pie). Musical medley of extracts from different works, pieced together and provided with new words so as to form a "new" composition; often used disdainfully to designate a motley medley of unrelated tunes by unrelated composers, arranged in a sequence with artificial connective tissue between numbers. Historically, the pastiche was useful in acquainting music lovers with popular opera arias, dance movements, and concert pieces, presented as an appetizing plate of musical dessert. Unfortunately, the musical semantics of pastiche departed from its original meaning and began to be applied indiscriminately to sets of variations by several composers, musical nosegays offered to friends, etc. Viennese publisher Diabelli created such a pastiche by commissioning 51 composers to write variations on a waltz tune of his own; Liszt, as a child of 11, was among the 51; Beethoven obliged with 33 variations that were published separately and made Diabelli's name immortal. Several Russian composers (Borodin, Rimsky-Korsakov, Cui, and Liadov) got together to perpetrate variations on *Chopsticks*; Liszt later added a variation of his own to the collection. The *Hexameron* for Piano on the march theme from Bellini's opera *I Puritani*, was composed by 6 composers, including Chopin and Liszt (1837). Luciano Berio concocted a bouillabaisse with chunks of Bach, Debussy, Ravel, and Mahler, calling the result *Sinfonia*. In recent years, "new" Broadway musicals have been concocted out of older songs that often share a composer (although not necessarily). See also ⇒potpourri.

pastoral (Fr., It. *pastorale*). 1. Scenic cantata representing pastoral life; a pastoral opera. 2. Instrumental piece imitating in style and instrumentation rural and idyllic scenes.

pastourelle (Fr.). Pastoral song in the repertoire of troubadours and trouvères; also, song in the spirit of this medieval genre.

pathétique (Fr.; from Grk. *pathe-tikos*, capable of feeling; It., *patetico*). Describing highly emotional states or compositions; not synonymous with the usual meaning of "pathetic" (pitiful), although it is the adjectival form of "pathos."

patimento (It.). Suffering; grief. *Con espressione di patimento*, with mournful or plaintive expression.

patter song. Rapid, syllabic humorous song. Patter songs are particularly effective in comic dialogues. The tessitura is in the middle register, and the singing approximates parlando style. Mozart and Rossini excelled in Italian patter song. The greatest master of patter song in English was Sullivan in setting Gilbert's witty lines in their comic operas.

Pauken (Ger.). Timpani.

pauroso (It.). Fearful, timid.

pausa (It.). Rest; pause. *Pausa lunga*, long pause; *pausa generale*, pause for all performers.

pause. 1. Full stop. 2. Rest. 3. Fermata (⌢).

pavane (It. *pavana*). Stately court dance in deliberate 4/4 time; once thought to derive from the Lat. *pavo* (peacock) because of an imagined similarity of the dance with the bird's strutting step. Actually, the pavane originated in the 16th century in Padua, Italy; *Pava* is a dialect name for Padua. Because of its dignified choreography, the pavane became a favorite court dance in Europe and particularly in England during the Elizabethan times. The tempo indication *Alla pavana* is also found. Many modern composers stylized the pavane in various novel ways. A common misspelling, *pavanne*, has taken root in some American exemplars.

Pavarotti, Luciano, b. Modena, Oct. 12, 1935. His father, a baker by trade, sang in the local church choir; Luciano learned to read music and began singing with the boy altos; joined his father in the choir and sang in the chorus of the local Teatro Comunale and the amateur Chorale Gioacchino Rossini. To prepare himself for a schoolteaching career, he attended the local Scuola Magistrale; taught in an elementary school, augmenting his income by selling insurance. He began vocal studies with A. Polo in Modena (1955); went to Mantua and continued his training with E. Campogalliani (1960). He made his operatic debut as Rodolfo at the Teatro Municipale in Reggio Emilia (1961).

Pavarotti obtained his 1st major engagement when he appeared as the Duke of Mantua at the Teatro Massimo in Palermo (1962); his 1st important appearance outside Italy was as Edgardo with the Netherlands Opera in Amsterdam (1963); that year he made his Vienna State Opera debut as Rodolfo, which he also sang for his debut at London's Covent Garden. He made his U.S. debut as Edgardo opposite Joan Sutherland's Lucia with the Greater Miami Opera (1965); after his 1st appearance at Milan's La Scala as Alfredo (1965), made a summer tour of Australia with the Sutherland Williamson International Grand Opera Co., a venture featuring Sutherland. He subsequently scored his 1st major triumph when he essayed the role of Tonio in *La Fille du régiment* (Covent Garden, 1966) and, with insouciant aplomb, tossed off the aria *Pour mon âme*, replete with 9 successive high C's, winning a huge ovation; dubbed "King of the High C's," he looked forward to a brilliant international career.

Pavarotti made his debuts at the San Francisco Opera (1967) and the Metropolitan Opera in N.Y. (1968) as Rodolfo; in subsequent seasons he became a mainstay at both houses; appeared regularly with other opera houses on both sides of the Atlantic; gave frequent solo recitals and concerts with orchs. His career became a string of successes: starring as Rodolfo in the 1st *Live from the Met* telecast by PBS (1977); sang an acclaimed solo recital debut at the Metropolitan Opera, also telecast by PBS (1978); founded the Opera Co. of Philadelphia/Luciano Pavarotti International Voice Competition (1980); was a featured artists at the Metropolitan Opera Centennial Gala (1983); gave a concert before 20,000 admirers at N.Y.'s Madison Square Garden, seen by millions on PBS (1984). He celebrated the 25th anniversary of his operatic debut by singing his old standby Rodolfo at the Teatro Comunale in Modena (1986); sang Nemorino (*L'elisir d'amore*) at the Berlin Deutsche Oper, eliciting no less than 15 curtain calls (1988); appeared in concert with the N.Y. City Opera Orch. in a special program at Avery Fischer Hall at N.Y.'s Lincoln Center for the Performing Arts, televised live by PBS (1989); appeared at the Bolshoi Theater in Moscow (1990). In recent years he has appeared with Domingo and Carreras as The 3 Tenors.

The most idolized tenor since Caruso, Pavarotti made such roles as Riccardo in *Un ballo in maschera*, Fernando in *La Favorite*, Manrico in *Il Trovatore*, Cavaradossi in *Tosca*, and Radames in *Aida* virtually his own; through recordings and television appearances he has won an adoring global following. Always of a jocular rotundity, he announced in 1988 that he had succeeded in dropping 85 pounds from his original body weight.

paventoso (It.). Fearfully, timidly.

pavillon (Fr.). Bell of the brass instrument family. *Pavillon en l'air*, hold the bell up for greater sonority.

pavillon d'amour (Fr., love bell; Ger. *Liebesfuss*, love foot). Bulbous opening at the end of the English horn that has the effect of dampening the sound. The same type of extension was characteristic of the manufacture of a clarinetto d'amore, fagotto d'amore, oboe d'amore, and other "amorous" instruments, now largely obsolete.

payola. American slang for bribes to disc jockeys for "plugging" (promoting) particular records of popular music on radio.

peabody. Fast American ballroom dance in open position.

Pearl Jam. (Lead vocal: Eddie Vedder, b. Chicago, Dec. 23, 1964; guitar: Mike McCready, b. Seattle, Apr. 5, 1965; rhythm guitar: Steve "Stone" Gossard, b. Seattle, July 20, 1966; bass: Jeff Ament, b. Big Sandy, Mont., Mar. 10, 1963; drums: Dave Krusen, replaced by Dave Abbruzzese in 1992 and Jack Irons in 1995.) Seattle grunge-rock band who along with Nirvana launched thousands of plaid-shirted rockers. The group formed in 1990 and signed quickly to Epic Records, scoring an immediate success with their 1991 LP, *10*, which produced the hits *Even Flow*, *Jeremy, Alive*, and *Release*. They joined the alternative-rock tour Lollapalooza on its 2nd outing (1992), cementing their reputation with the grunge crowd. The year 1993 brought a second album, *Vs.*, and an appearance on the popular *MTV Unplugged* program. They also toured Europe with Neil Young, leading to a long association with the grandfather of all things grungy (they backed Young on his *Mirror Ball*, 1995). *Vitalogy* came in 1994, which they released 1st on vinyl only and then, 2 weeks later, on CD and cassette; band fans ended up buying both, lining the denim pockets of the group's members. Their 1995 summer tour was plagued by an ongoing fight with the dominant ticketing agency; they have refused to play in venues that use this company, who they claim overcharges for its services.

pearly (Fr. *perlé*; Ger. *perlend*). Style of piano touch producing a clear, round, smooth effect of tone, especially in scale passages.

Pears, (Sir) Peter (Neville Luard), b. Farnham, June 22, 1910; d. Aldeburgh, Apr. 3, 1986. He began his career as temporary organist at Hertford College, Oxford (1928–29); was music director at the Grange School, Crowborough (1930–34); was a scholarship student at the Royal College of Music in London (1933–34); sang in the BBC Chorus and then joined the BBC Singers (1934–38) and the New English Singers (1936–38); during this period he received vocal instruction from E. Gerhardt and D. Freer.

In 1936 Pears met Benjamin Britten; they gave their 1st joint recital (1937); thereafter remained lifelong personal and professional companions. After singing in the Glyndebourne chorus (1938), he accompanied Britten to the U.S. (1939); continued his vocal training with T. Behr and C. Hine-Mundy; returned to England with Britten (1942); made his stage debut in the title role of *Les Contes d'Hoffmann* at London's Strand Theatre. He joined the Sadler's Wells Opera Co. (1943); gained fame when he created the title role in Britten's *Peter Grimes* (1945). In 1946 he co-founded the English Opera Group; would greatly distinguish himself in Britten's operas, creating the roles of Albert Herring, the Male Chorus in *The Rape of Lucretia*, Captain Vere

in *Billy Budd*, Essex in *Gloriana*, Quint in *The Turn of the Screw*, Flute in *A Midsummer Night's Dream* (wrote libretto with composer), the Madwoman in *Curlew River*, Sir Philip Wingrave in *Owen Wingrave*, and Aschenbach in *Death in Venice*, with which he made his long-awaited Metropolitan Opera debut in N.Y. (1974); co-founded the Aldeburgh Festival (1948), serving as a director and teacher of master classes until his death.

Pears also sang several premieres of Britten's nonoperatic works, notably the *Serenade* for Tenor, Horn, and Strings, the *Michelangelo Sonnets*, and the *War Requiem*; excelled in the works of other English composers (Elgar, Holst, Vaughan Williams, Walton, and Tippett) and of Central European composers (Schütz, Bach, Mozart, Schubert, and Schumann). He was made a Commander of the Order of the British Empire (1957); knighted (1978).

ped. Stands for pedal; signifies that the right (loud) piano pedal is to be pressed, or (in organ music) that notes so marked are to be played on the pedals.

pedal. 1. Foot key on the organ or pedal piano. 2. Foot lever; as the piano pedals, or organ swell-pedal. 3. Treadle, like those used for blowing the reed organ. 4. Stop knob or lever worked by foot (organ). *Pedal organ*, set of stops controlled by organ pedals; *pedal piano*, piano provided with a pedalier.

pedal point (organ point, pedal note, pedal tone, pedal); (Fr. *point d'orgue, pédale;* Ger. *Orgelpunkt;* Sp. *bajo de organo*, organ bass). Tone sustained (or continuously repeated) in one part to harmonies executed in the other parts; usually in the bass (Fr. *pedale inférieure*) and on the dominant or on the tonic, or on both simultaneously; its name derives from the organ foot pedal held down to achieve this effect. A protracted organ point on the dominant usually heralds the authentic cadence on the tonic. So great is the bond, so strong is the harmonic hold of the pedal point on the dominant, that it can support chords on all degrees of the diatonic scale as well as modulations into the lowered supertonic or the lowered submediant in a major key. Among examples of this holding power of the dominant pedal point are the conclusion of the church scene in Gounod's opera *Faust*, passages in the overture to Wagner's *Die Meistersinger*, and the wedding procession in Rimsky-Korsakov's opera *Le Coq d'or*, containing modulations into several unrelated keys before finally resolving into the tonic; Scriabin maintains a tonic pedal point in the finale of the *Poem of Ecstasy* for about 5 minutes.

Cadenzas in piano concertos are conceptually based on a prolonged (if often unheard) pedal point on the dominant in the bass. Cadences in fugal compositions are often reinforced by the bass pedal point, as in the C-minor fugue of Bach's *Well-Tempered Clavier*, book I. Pedal points in the bass can be sustained on the modern piano by the use of the middle, or sustaining, pedal. Pedal point in the middle voices (Fr. *pedale intérieure*) are relatively rare, but there are examples to be found of pedal points in the high treble. Rimsky-Korsakov's *Scheherazade* concludes on such a high pedal point. Ironically, composers writing in an atonal idiom or employing dodecaphonic techniques occasionally use pedal points to establish the binding element missing in a system of composition that theoretically disenfranchises both tonic and dominant.

pedale doppio (It.). Pedal-part in octaves.

pedale ogni battuta (It.). Take the pedal with each measure.

pedalier. Set of pedals, either (1) so adjusted as to play the low octaves of the piano, after the manner of organ pedals, or (2) provided with separate strings and action, to be placed underneath the piano.

pedanteria, con (It.; Ger. *pedantisch*). Pedantically; in an even, unemotional style.

pedes muscarum (Lat., flies' feet). Curious term applied by some medieval musicians to cursive neumes that remotely resembled the eponymous appendages.

Pedrell, Felipe, b. Tortosa, Feb. 19, 1841; d. Barcelona, Aug. 19, 1922. He became a chorister at Tortosa Cathedral at about the age of 7; studied with J.A. Nin y Serra; went to Barcelona as deputy director of the Light Opera Co. (1873); produced his 1st opera, *L'ultimo Abenzeraggio* (1874). After a visit to Italy (1876–77) and a stay in Paris, he settled in Barcelona (1881); devoted himself mainly to musicological pursuits; founded the short-lived journals *Salterio Sacro-Hispano* and *Notas Musicales y Literarias* (1882–83); was founder-ed. of the important journal *La Illustración Musical Hispano-Americana* (1888–96); worked on his operatic masterpiece, the trilogy *Los Pirineos/Els Pirineus* (1890–91), for which he publ. the introductory *Por nuestra música* (1891), a plea for creation of a national lyric drama based on Spanish folk song. He went to Madrid; named prof. of choral singing at the Cons. and prof. of advanced studies at the Ateneo (1894); elected a member of the Royal Academy of Fine Arts. Upon his return to Barcelona (1904) he devoted himself to writing, teaching, and composing; among his outstanding pupils were Albéniz, Falla, Granados, and Gerhard.

Although Pedrell was admired as a composer by his contemporaries, his music has not obtained recognition outside Spain; his lasting achievement rests upon distinguished musicology; helped restore interest in both historical and contemporary Spanish sacred music. He contributed studies of Spanish, Catalan, Latin American, and Portuguese music, theoretical works, bibliographies, early and new music studies, dictionaries, studies of Spanish liturgy and religious festivals, composer monographs, organological works, and examinations of opera and Spanish song; ed. several collections of religious and secular works.

Peerce, Jan (born Jacob Pincus Perelmuth), b. N.Y., June 3, 1904; d. there, Dec. 15, 1984. He played violin in dance bands and sang at various entertainment places in N.Y. In 1932 he was engaged as a singer at Radio City Music Hall; made his operatic debut in Philadelphia as the Duke of Mantua (1938) and gave his 1st solo recital in N.Y. (1939). His lyrical voice attracted attention, and he was engaged by the Metropolitan Opera in N.Y.; made his debut there as Alfredo (1941); sang also parts of Cavaradossi, Rodolfo, and Gounod's Faust; remained on the staff of the Metropolitan until 1966, appearing again in 1967–68; retired in 1982. He was the brother-in-law of Richard Tucker.

Peitsche (Ger.). The whip, used as a percussion instrument.

pelog. One of 2 principal scale categories in gamelan music; a pentatonic group in various tunings; a common example resembles the tempered scale E–F–G–B–C, i.e., with 2 semitones and a large gap between C and E.

Penderecki, Krzysztof, b. Debica, Nov. 23, 1933. He was educated in Krakow; took courses at the Jagellonian Univ.; after private composition studies with F. Skolyszewski, received instruction in theory from A. Malawski and S. Wiechowicz at the State Higher School of Music (1955–58); was a lecturer in composition there (1958–66); served as rector when it became the Academy of Music (1972–87) and as prof. (from 1972); was prof. of composition at the Essen Folkwang Hochschule für Musik (1966–68) and Yale Univ. (from 1973). He rapidly acquired a reputation as one of the most original composers of his time, receiving numerous honors: received honorary memberships in the national academies of England, the German Democratic Republic, and Sweden (1975); awarded the Herder Prize of the Federal Republic of Germany (1977), the Grand Medal of Paris (1982), the Sibelius Prize of Finland (1983), the Premio Lorenzo il Magnifico of Italy (1985), etc.

After a few academic works, Penderecki developed a hypermodern technique of composition in which no demarcation line is drawn between consonances and dissonances, tonal or atonal melody, traditional or innovative instrumentation; an egalitarian attitude prevails toward all available resources of sound; while his idiom is naturally complex, he does not disdain tonality, even in its overt triadic forms. He has bypassed orthodox serial procedures; his music follows an athematic course, in constantly varying metrical and rhythmic patterns. He utilizes an entire spectrum of modern sonorities, making use of shouting, hissing, and verbal ejaculations in vocal parts, at times reaching a climax of aleatory glossolalia; tapping, rubbing, or snapping fingers against the body of an instrument; striking piano strings by mallets, etc. For this he designed an optical notation, with symbolic ideograms indicating the desired sound, e.g., a black isosceles triangle for the highest possible pitch; an inverted isosceles triangle, the lowest; a black rectangle rerepresenting a sonic complex of white noise within a given interval; vertical lines tied over by an arc for arpeggios below the bridge of a string instrument; varying wavy lines for extensive vibrato; curvilinear figures for aleatory passages; dots and dashes for repetitions of a pattern; sinusoidal oscillations for quaquaversal glissandos; etc. He applies these modern devices to all music, including Masses in the orthodox Roman Catholic ritual. His most impressive and most frequently perf. work is his *Tren pamieci ofiarom Hiroszimy* (Threnody in Memory of the Victims of Hiroshima) for 52 String Instruments (1959–60), rich in dynamic contrasts and ending on a tone cluster of 2 octavefuls of icositetraphonic harmony.

penitential sounds. Musical settings for psalms expressing penitence and imploring mercy, particularly *De profundis* and *Miserere*.

Penniman, Richard Wayne, (called "Little Richard"), b. Macon, Ga., Dec. 5, 1932. Possessed by religious fervor, he sang in local church choirs, then joined a traveling medicine show; won a talent contest in Atlanta at age 19, recorded, and hit the proverbial jackpot with *Tutti Frutti* (1954). Some hits were focused on women: *Lucille, Jenny Jenny,* and *The Girl Can't Help It* (title song of a film he appeared in). Other smash hits were *Keep a-Knockin', Good Golly Miss Molly, Long Tall Sally,* and *Slippin' and Slidin'.* He was the harbinger of the unrestrained but puissant manner of American music that produced such individuals as Mick Jagger, Jerry Lee Lewis, James Brown, and Jimi Hendrix. In the midst of his popular and commercial successes, he suddenly hit the religion trail, went to college in Alabama to study theology, embraced the ministry, toured the gospel circuit, and denounced rock 'n' roll as the devil's tool; still, he put out an autobiographical album entitled *The King of Rock and Roll* before abandoning the sinful world for God. His personal hosannas survived in his early albums, *Here's Little Richard, Fabulous Little Richard,* and (more to the point) *Wild and Frantic Little Richard.*

penorcon. Bass cittern with 9 pairs of strings, according to Praetorious.

pensiero (It.). A thought. *Pensiero del(la)* . . . , souvenir of . . . , recollections of . . . ; *pensoso,* pensive, thoughtful.

pentachord. 1st 5 degrees of the scale.

pentagramma (It.). Musical staff of 5 lines.

pentatonic scale. 5-tone scale; usually avoids semitonic steps by skipping the 4th and 7th degrees in major and the 2nd and 6th in natural minor. Pentatonic melodies have been found in ancient songs of areas ranging from Scotland to Tibet, China to pre-Columbian America, Iceland to Australia. Is the pentatonic scale then some pangeographic pananthropic root of natural inventions? The intervals between component degrees are different in Asian, African, or European scale formations; Western composers equate pentatonic scales to melodic progressions played on the black keys of the piano keyboard. These Westernized scales can be classified as major and minor, the major pentatonic simulated by a scale starting on F sharp, the minor pentatonic on E flat. Consecutive 5ths and 4ths are the formative intervals of pentatonic scales; the harmonization is usually based on pedal points on the presumed tonic and dominant; while this type of music sounds alluringly exotic, the resulting effect is hardly anything more genuine than an artificial chinoiserie.

Debussy, Ravel, and their followers offer clear examples of modern pentatonic music; Debussy, in the middle section of his piano prelude, *Voiles* (book I, no. 2), Ravel, in *Laideronette, impératrice des Pagodes* from his *Ma Mère L'Oye;* the Chinese themselves would never recognize such Gallic pagodas as their own. Among the operas containing Orientalist pentatonic structures are Puccini's *Madama Butterfly,* employing Japanese melodic patterns, and *Turandot,* with a wealth of pseudo-Chinese melodies. (The most common Japanese pentatonic mode contains a semitone and so cannot be reduced to a black-key scale.) On the other side of the world, Irish and Scottish melodies contain pentatonic scales that are structurallily quite different from Asian exemplars.

Pepper, Art(hur Edward, Jr.), b. Gardena, Calif., Sept. 1, 1925; d. Los Angeles, June 15, 1982. His father was of German origin, his mother Italian. He played jazz clarinet and alto saxophone in school bands; married at 17; drafted into the U.S. Army; after discharge, joined Stan Kenton's band (1946–52). His darkly emotional temperament led him to develop a passionate manner of shaping music which became known as the West Coast style; began recording, sometimes under the pseudonym Art Salt; his highly promising career was ruined by an addiction to heroin and other narcotics. Squandering his earnings, and desperately needing his expensive drugs, he engaged in thievery and brawls. He was busted on narcotics charges (1952); served time on numerous occasions (to 1966); played with Buddy Rich's Big Band (1968–69); completed 2 highly successful tours of Japan (1977, 1978); a film documentary on Pepper's life was presented at the Berlin Film Festival the year of his death.

per (It.). For, by, from, in, through. *Per l'organo,* for the organ; *per il flauto solo,* for solo flute.

per arsin et thesin. Arsin et thesin, per.

Perahia, Murray, b. N.Y., Apr. 19, 1947. He studied piano with J. Haien (1953–64); then entered the Mannes College of Music; studied conducting and composition (B.S., 1969); continued his piano studies with A. Balsam and M. Horszowski. In 1968 he made his Carnegie Hall debut in N.Y. (1968); became the 1st American to win the Leeds International Pianoforte Competition (1972); awarded the 1st Avery Fisher Prize, sharing it with cellist Lynn Harrell ((1975). He appeared as soloist with leading orchs. of the U.S. and Europe; gave many recitals in the U.S. and abroad; appointed co-artistic director of the Aldeburgh Festival (1982). After a lengthy and somewhat mysterious absence from the performing scene, he returned in the 1990s. He excels in Classical music; recorded all of Mozart's concertos, conducting from the keyboard; is praised for his congenial interpretation of standard concert repertoire.

percussion. (from Lat. *percutere,* strike, beat; past participle, *percussus;* Ger. *Schlaginstrumente, Schlagzeug*). 1. Striking or sounding of a dissonance. 2. Striking or beating of one body against another. *Instruments of percussion* include drums, tambourine, cymbals, bells, triangle, etc., as well as dulcimer and pianoforte. Not all instruments classified as percussion really "percuss"; in the battery (from Fr. *batterie,* fight) of percussion there are *instruments of concussion* (from Lat. *concutere,* shake violently), such as the popular Latin American maracas; and *instruments of friction,* such as the guiro. The 1st classification system (Hornbostel-Sach) separated the percussion into *membranophones* (involved a stretched skin or like material to produce sound) and *idiophones* (where the instrument's body produces the sound, so no stretched material is needed); but this still leaves out considerations of materials used and method of generating sound.

Since most percussion instruments perform a rhythmic function, perhaps *rhythm instruments,* a term gaining increasing acceptance in jazz as well as classical music, should be considered as an alternative name. Keyboard instruments are often classified as percussion, but this is historically and functionally suspect; although these instruments are indeed percussed, their function is not primarily rhythmical; perhaps such a concept should be limited to orch'l and ensemble pieces of the 20th century. On the other hand, the celesta, marimba, vibraphone, and xylophone (all of which possess a keyboard) are customarily included in the percussion.

In orch'l scores of the Baroque and Classic periods, percussion was relegated to a subordinate position and often notated on a supplementary line. Those instruments of indefinite pitch—bass drum, cymbals, triangles—were exotic imports described as "Janizary music," because they were included in military bands of Turkey, led by court musicians of the Sultan; use of ethnic percussion continues into the following centuries. Other special sounds, such as the whip, were added as needed.

The 1st percussion instruments of definite pitch in the 18th-century orch., the timpani, were usually found in pairs and tuned to the tonic and dominant, performing the function of reinforcing the bass; their parts were often placed below the bass line in the score. Among percussion instruments of a definite pitch, the largest group is the keyboards, all of them playing in the treble. The glockenspiel has a penetrating bell-like sound and is often used whenever an exotic color is invoked; it is the magic "instrument of steel" in the score of Mozart's opera *Die Zauberflöte*; Tchaikovsky uses it effectively in the *Chinese Dance* of his *Nutcracker Suite*. Its keyboard equivalent, the celesta, is a relatively recent invention; the 1st composer to use it was Tchaikovsky, in his *Dance of the Sugar-Plum Fairies* in *The Nutcracker*. Another type of celesta manufactured in the 20th century is called a *dulcitone*; the steel bars of the celesta are replaced by clear and overtone-free tuning forks.

The xylophone (from Grk., wood sound) is a newcomer in Western orch'l literature, although it was known under the name of *Holzharmonika* (Ger., wood harmonica) in the 16th century. Saint-Saëns used it most effectively in his *Danse macabre* to imitate the clatter of skeleton bones; it is frequently used in modern scores because of its clear and articulate timbre. The marimba, a Latin American import, is a keyboard instrument with resonators attached underneath; the vibraphone is made with steel bars and is electrically amplified; both are recent entries in popular and serious modern music. Milhaud wrote a concerto for the marimba, and many composers have included the vibraphone in their scores.

Russian opera composers often use church bells in their scores; Tchaikovsky in his *1812 Overture*, Rimsky-Korsakov in his opera *The Legend of the Invisible City of Kitezh*, Mussorgsky in the conclusion of his witch-riddled score of *Night on Bald Mountain* (thanks to Rimsky-Korsakov in his performing version); Khatchaturian used bells in his 2nd Sym. to glorify Russian resistance to the Nazi invasion in World War II. Tubular bells, also called orch. chimes, often represent church bells, as in the *Witches' Sabbath* in Berlioz's *Sym. fantastique*. Bell-like sounds are produced by other instruments made of metal: the cymbals, a pair of which is struck together; the large gongs (pitched) and tam-tams (unpitched); the triangle; and a variety of shaken jingles, such as sleigh bells. The tambourine has a drum head with little cymbals attached.

Drums, big and small, have furnished realistic effects in scores in which military references are made, or to portray an execution, as in *Till Eulenspiegel's Merry Pranks* by R. Strauss or *Robespierre* by Litolff. In his 5th Sym. Nielsen has a semi-improvisatory cadenza for a snare (side) drum; the player is to drum as if making an attempt to interrupt the highly dramatic music in the rest of the orch. The bass drum looks and sounds impressive enough to suggest ominous events. Chinese blocks have a percussive sound of indefinite pitch almost as clear and penetrating as the xylophone. Among other percussion instruments, claves are an integral part of Latin American popular bands, but has been adopted in many modern scores; its sound is produced by striking together 2 pieces of resonant hardwood.

A tremendous expansion of the role of percussion in modern orch'l scores has put drummers in a privileged position in the orch. Some percussion parts demand real virtuosity, e.g., Stravinsky's score *L'Histoire du soldat*, in which a single performer handles several instruments in truly acrobatic fashion. Orff elevated rhythm instruments to a commanding position in elementary music education. Percussion ensembles specializing in music expressly written for percussion have proliferated in Europe and America; especially notable in this category is *Music for 18 Musicians* by Steve Reich. And there is at least 1 masterpiece of percussion literature, *Ionisation* of Edgard Varèse, scored for 42 percussion instruments and 2 sirens.

percussion stop. Reed organ stop, which strikes the reed a smart blow when sounding it to render its vibration prompter and stronger.

percussive. Sounded by striking.

perdendosi (It.). Dying away. Morendo or diminuendo, together (in modern music) with a slight rallentando.

perfect pitch. Ability to name instantly and without fail any note struck on the piano keyboard or played on an instrument; also called absolute pitch. This is an innate faculty that appears in a musical child at a very early age, distinct from relative pitch, common among all musicians, in which an interval is named in relation to a previously played note. Absolute pitch is rare, even among professional musicians, and does not automatically indicate great musical talent. Wagner, Berlioz, Tchaikovsky, Ravel, and Stravinsky lacked it; many obscure musicians possess it to an astonishing degree, being able to name the most complicated dissonant chords; some musicians, particularly singers, can simulate the sense of perfect pitch by assaying stress on the vocal cords required to reproduce the note in question; despite repeated claims by educationists, perfect pitch cannot be attained by ear training.

The acuteness of perfect pitch varies widely when chord recognition is tested. Some musicians can name a highly complex conglomerate of sounds without hesitation. Especially difficult are chords containing tritones and major 7ths separated by perfect 5ths (e.g., in ascending order, D–A–A♭–E♭). Since the frequency (cycles per second) of the standard A has risen during the last century, older Europeans might hear contemporary orchs. as playing a semitone higher than written; the perfectly pitched are driven to the edge when they hear transpositions of familiar works, especially with scores before them.

Physiologically, perfect pitch is analogous to absolute discrimination of colors in the visual spectrum; in both cases the criterion is the ability to name the frequency of vibration in the corresponding spectrum. Is the lack of perfect pitch a kind of "tone deafness" by analogy with color blindness? It is possible that prehistoric individuals possessed perfect pitch and used it in communication; even today there are isolated peoples who have retained perfect pitch without intellectualizing on its properties. Finally, did ancient Greek scales exist outside of fixed pitch, as many speculate, or is the key to Greek musical ethos and spirit the fixed pitches themselves?

perfection (Lat. *perfectio*). In mensural notation, a longa having the value of 3 units; theologically, ternary time represented the Holy Trinity.

Pergolesi, Giovanni Battista, b. Jesi, Jan. 4, 1710; d. Pozzuoli, near Naples, Mar. 16, 1736. He 1st studied music with F. Santi, the maestro di cappella of the Jesi Cathedral, and violin with F. Mondini; given a stipend by the Marchese Cardolo Maria Pianetti, entered the Conservatorio dei Poveri di Gesù Cristo in Naples; studied violin with D. de Matteis and composition with G. Greco (its maestro di cappella), L. Vinci, and F. Durante; became highly proficient as a violinist, playing at the Cons. and throughout Naples.

Pergolesi's 1st performed work was the sacred drama *Li Prodigi della divina grazia nella conversione di S. Guglielmo Duca d'Aquitania,* presented at the monastery of S. Agnello Maggiore (1731); he graduated shortly thereafter and received a commission for his 1st opera, *La Salustia* (Naples, 1732); later that year became maestro di cappella to Prince Ferdinando Colonna Stigliano, equerry to the Viceroy of Naples. His *Lo Frate'nnamorato* (Naples, 1732) proved highly successful; at year's end composed sacred works for the church of S. Maria della Stella as a votive offering following a series of severe earthquakes in Naples. He was commissioned to write an opera seria for the birthday of the empress; the premiere of the resulting *Il Prigionier superbo* was delayed (1733); its 2-act intermezzo, *La Serva padrona,* became his most celebrated stage work. He was named deputy to the maestro di cappella of Naples (1734); during a brief visit to Rome, his Mass in F Major was performed at the church of S. Lorenzo in Lucina.

After returning to Naples, Pergolesi became maestro di cappella to Marzio Domenico IV Carafa, the Duke of Maddaloni. For the birthday of the king's mother, he wrote the opera *Adriano in Siria;* its premiere was unsuccessful (Naples, 1734); contained the intermezzo *La Contadina astuta* (later staged under various titles); another commission, an opera seria for Rome's Teatro Tordinona, resulted in an unsuccessful opera seria *L'Olimpiade;* his last popular stage success was the "musical comedy" *Il Flaminio* (both 1735). By then his health had seriously declined, most likely from tuberculosis; early in 1736 he went to the Franciscan monastery in Pozzuoli, where he soon died; buried in the common grave adjacent to the Cathedral.

Following his death Pergolesi's fame spread rapidly through performances of *La Serva padrona* and other stage works; the 1752 Paris revival of the work precipitated the Guerre des Bouffons between the Italian and French opera factions; his fame was increased by performances of the *Salve regina* in C Minor and the *Stabat Mater* in F Minor. The chaotic entanglement of spurious, doubtful, and authentic works attributed to Pergolesi was significantly unraveled in M. Paymer's 1976 thematic catalogue "with an appendix listing omitted compositions."

Peri, Jacopo, called "Il Zazzerino," b. Rome, Aug. 20, 1561; d. Florence, Aug. 12, 1633. The nickname refers to his abundant head of hair. At an early age he went to Florence; entered the convent of S. Annunziata (1573) and became a singer; also studied music with C. Malvezzi. He was organist at the Badia (1579–1605) and a singer at S. Giovanni Battista (by 1586); entered the service of the Medici court of Grand Duke Ferdinando I (1588); was also in the service of the Mantuan court (from the early 1600s). The Florentine Camerata met at the home of Count Giovanni de' Bardi in the 1580s, and it is likely that Peri participated in its activities.

As early as 1583 Peri collaborated with other composers in writing music for the intermedi to G. Fedini's dramatic comedy *Le due Persilie.* In the 1590s the home of Jacopo Corsi became the meeting place for many Florentine musicians, poets, and philosophers, and Peri undoubtedly attended, for Corsi collaborated with him in setting Rinuccini's pastoral *Dafne* to music; the 1st known performance of this work was private (Florence, 1598); later versions were given in 1599, 1600, and 1605. *Dafne* is generally recognized as the 1st opera in monodic style (i.e., vocal solos supported by instruments), termed *stile rappresentativo.*

Peri's next opera was *Euridice,* to another text by Rinuccini; some of the music was rewritten by Caccini for the 1st performance, given for the wedding of Maria de' Medici and Henri IV of France at the Palazzo Pitti in Florence (1600). Peri's next 2 operas—*Tetide* (libretto by Cini) and *Adone* (libretto by Cicognini, 1611)—were scheduled for performances in Mantua (1608 and 1620, respectively), but neither took place. Peri then collaborated to varying degrees with Marco da Gagliano (1582–1643), who set *Dafne* in 1608: *La liberazione di Tirreno e d'Arnea* (1617); *Lo sposalizio di Medoro e Angelica* (Florence, 1619); *La Flora* (Florence, 1628); and 3 oratorios, *La benedittione di Jacob* (Florence, 1622), *Il gran natale di Christo salvator nostro* (Florence, 1622), and *La celeste guida, o vero L'Arcangelo Raffaello* (Florence, 1624); none of these works survive. Peri publ. *La varie musiche* for 1 to 3 voices (Florence, 1609).

Pericón (Sp.). Argentine dance in 3/8 time.

Périgourdine (Fr.; It. *perigordino*). Old Flemish dance.

period. Complete musical thought of 8, 12, or 16 measures ending with an authentic cadence. A typical structure is that of the question-answer (antecedent-consequent) type, where the 1st half of the period ends in the dominant, the 2nd half with an authentic cadence in the tonic.

periodicity. Category of musical time, with formants indicating temporal recurrence at equal or unequal distances. An example appears in Stockhausen's *Klavierstück IX.*

periodique (Fr., periodic). Publisher's catalogue, as produced in London and Paris in the 18th century, sometimes focusing on a single work. These publications facilitated the purchase of published music by concert socs. and individual musicians. Gradually, literary annotations and short analyses of the work(s) offered for sale were added to the periodique, eventually giving rise to the publication of music magazines.

Perkins, Carl, b. near Tiptonville, Tenn., Apr. 9, 1932. He grew up in rural Tenn.; learned guitar from an early age; in his teens, formed a band with his brothers Jay and Clayton and local drummer W. S. Holland; played for local dances and events. By his early 20s the band was successful enough to earn a recording contract with the tiny Flip label, then signed with Memphis-based Sun Records (1955), hot off its success with another Southern crooner, Elvis Presley. Their 2nd release, *Blue Suede Shoes*, topped the country, pop, and R&B charts, selling over 2 million copies; booked to appear on national television, the band was involved in a serious automobile accident en route; Jay died, and Carl was seriously injured; although he had other hits, his career never recovered fully.

Perkins signed with Columbia Records in 1958, but by the early 1960s he was more popular in England than at home; one British fan, guitarist George Harrison of the Beatles, did much to popularize his songs, recording versions of *Honey, Don't, Everybody's Trying to Be My Baby,* and *Matchbox* (a countrified version of Blind Lemon Jefferson's classic *Matchbox Blues*). Perkins became part of Johnny Cash's roadshow in the 1960s, touring with him through the mid-1970s; although he has staged various "comebacks" over many years, he never really broke out of the nostalgia circuit; inducted into the Rock and Roll Hall of Fame (1987).

Perlman, Itzhak, b. Tel Aviv, Aug. 31, 1945. He was stricken with polio at age 4; his legs were left paralyzed; has walked on crutches ever since; despite this handicap, began to play violin and give regular recitals in Tel Aviv. In 1958 he was discovered in Israel by Ed Sullivan, the TV producer-host; appeared on his show in N.Y. (1959). Perlman's courage and good humor endeared him to the public at once; remained in N.Y., soon joined by his parents; was accepted as a scholarship student into the studios of I. Galamian and D. DeLay at the Juilliard School of Music. He made his professional American debut playing with the National Orch. Assoc. in N.Y. (1963); won 1st prize in the Leventritt Competition (1964), which carried, besides a modest purse, a significant bonus—an appearance with the N.Y. Phil. It brought about a lasting friendship with Isaac Stern, who promoted him with all the enthusiasm of a sincere admirer. His career was no longer a problem: he toured the U.S. from coast to coast (1965–66) and Europe (1966–67); began teaching; appointed to the faculty of Brooklyn College (1975). He seems to overflow with a genuine love of life and inexhaustible technique; has played not only classical music but Tin Pan Alley song arrangements, ragtime, and jazz; with Stern and P. Zukerman, indulged in public charivari on TV, to which he furnished commentaries like a professional comedian; became a regular guest at the White House; awarded the U.S. Medal of Freedom (1986).

permutation. In serial music, theoretical term for the changing of the order of individual notes in the basic series, either through the three basic operations (retrograde, inversion, retrograde inversion), cell operations (exchanging 3- or 4-note row fragments with the same intervallic content), arithmetic processes (taking every other pitch, etc.), or rotation (transposing the row according to its own constituents).

Perotin called "Perotinus Magnus" and "Magister Perotinus," fl. 12th century. The second great master of the Notre Dame school of Paris, after Leoninus; his very identity, as well as a general outline of his life, remains open to speculation. According to one researcher, he was born *c.* 1155–60, may have studied with Leoninus, carried out his major work on the revision of the *Magnus liber c.* 1180–90), was involved in the early development of the Latin motet *c.* 1190–1200, wrote his works for 4 voices at the close of the century, and died *c.* 1200–05. Another chronology maintains that he wrote the works for 4 voices in the 1190s (the *early* years of his career), revised the *Magnus liber* during the 1st years of the 13th century, wrote elaborate clausulas *c.* 1210, helped create the Latin motet *c.* 1210–20, and died *c.* 1225.

perpetual canon. Canon in which the final cadence leads back into the opening measures; a round.

perpetuum mobile (Lat., perpetual motion). Moto perpetuo; type of short and rapid composition, usually for a solo instrument.

Persichetti, Vincent (Ludwig), b. Philadelphia, June 6, 1915; d. there, Aug. 13, 1987. He studied piano, organ, double bass, tuba, theory, and composition as a youth; began his professional musical career at age 11; became a church organist at 15; took composition courses with R. K. Miller at the Combs Cons. (MusB., 1936); served as head of the theory and composition dept. there; concurrently studied conducting with Reiner at the Curtis Inst. of Music (diploma, 1938) and piano with O. Samaroff and composition with Nordoff at the Philadelphia Cons. (M.Mus, 1941; D.Mus, 1945); also studied with Roy Harris at Colorado College. He headed the theory and composition dept. of the Philadelphia Cons. (1941–47), then joined the faculty of the Juilliard School of Music in N.Y.; named chairman of the composition dept. there (1963); became director of music publishing of Elkan-Vogel, Inc. (1952).

Although Persichetti stood far from the turmoil of musical politics, he unexpectedly found himself in the center of controversy when commissioned by the 1973 Presidential Inauguration Committee to write a work for narrator and orch. for performance at Richard Nixon's 2nd inauguration. As text, the composer selected Abraham Lincoln's 2nd inaugural address, but objections were raised by some to the passionate denunciation of war in the narrative, at a time when the Vietnam War was very much in the news. The scheduled performance by the Philadelphia Orch. was hurriedly canceled; the work's premiere was deferred to a performance by the St. Louis Sym. Orch. (1973). In 1987 Persichetti was diagnosed with cancer of the lungs, but continued to work on his last opus, *Hymns and Responses for the Church Year,* vol. II.

Persichetti's music is remarkable for its polyphonic skill in fusing the ostensibly incompatible idioms of Classicism, Romanticism, and stark modernism while the melodic lines maintain a lyrical diatonicism, creating a characteristic style. He was not interested in any kind of descriptive tonal music; his significance lies in his 9 syms. and, most particularly, his 12 piano sonatas and 6 sonatinas. His works also include the opera *Parable XX: The Sibyl* (1976); 4 string quartets (1939; 1944; 1959; 1972); 8 harpsichord sonatas (1951–84); choral works; and songs, including a cycle for soprano and piano entitled *Harmonium,* after Wallace Stevens (N.Y., 1952). With F. Schreiber he wrote a biography of William Schuman (N.Y.,

1954); publ. a valuable manual, *20th Century Harmony: Creative Aspects and Practice* (N.Y., 1961).

pes (Lat., foot). Harmonic support or accompaniment to a round.

pesante (It.; Fr. *pesamment*). Heavily, ponderously; firmly, vigorously.

Peter, Paul and Mary. (Guitar/vocal: Peter Yarrow, b. N.Y., May 31, 1938; guitar/vocal: Noel Paul Stookey, b. Baltimore, Md., Nov. 30, 1937; vocal: Mary Travers, b. Louisville, Ky., Nov. 7, 1937.) Famed folk trio of the 1960s who introduced the songs of Bob Dylan to a mass audience. Formed by canny promoter Albert Grossman, the group 1st hit it big with their interpretations of traditional folk songs like *500 Miles* and modern folk-styled compositions, including Pete Seeger's *Where Have All the Flowers Gone;* had a major hit with Dylan's *Blowin' in the Wind* in 1963, followed by his *Don't Think Twice It's All Right;* subsequently recorded songs by other young singer/songwriters, including Tom Paxton, John Denver, and Gordon Lightfoot. The group had their greatest success in 1967 with Denver's *Leaving on a Jet Plane,* along with Yarrow's *The Song Is Love;* a children's album, *Peter, Paul and Mommy,* produced a major hit with *Day Is Done* and helped revive their 1962 hit, *Puff, the Magic Dragon.* They broke up in 1970 to pursue solo careers with varying degrees of success; reunited in 1978; continue to record and perform.

Peterson, Oscar (Emmanuel), b. Montreal, Aug. 15, 1925. He studied piano; made appearances on Canadian radio; played with Johnny Holmes's orch. (1944–47). In 1949 he went to N.Y.; established himself as one of the finest jazz pianists of the day, with a technique and style that recalled Art Tatum; made numerous tours, often appearing with a guitarist and bass player (he later replaced the guitar with drums); was also successful as a guest artist with American orchs. He was made an Officer of the Order of Canada (1973). In 1991 he was named chancellor of York Univ. in Toronto.

petit, -e (Fr.). Small, little.

petite flûte (Fr.). Piccolo.

Petri, Egon, b. Hannover, Mar. 23, 1881; d. Berkeley, Calif., May 27, 1962. His father, Henri Wilhelm Petri, was a Dutch violinist who served as concertmaster in Hannover and of the Leipzig Gewandhaus orch.; his mother was a singer. Egon studied violin, organ, and piano from an early age; began piano lessons with Carreño; later studied with Buchmayer, Draeseke, and Busoni; received composition lessons from Kretzschmar. After a stint as an orch'l violinist and as a member of his father's string quartet, he launched his career as a piano virtuoso (1902); subsequently toured extensively in Europe; also active as a teacher; served on the faculties of the Royal Manchester College of Music (1905–11) and the Berlin Hochschule für Musik (1921–26); then taught in Zakopane.

In 1932 Petri made his U.S. debut in N.Y.; performed on both sides of the Atlantic until World War II; taught at Boston's Malkin Cons. (1934–35). After the war he resumed his extensive tours; taught at Cornell Univ. (1940–46), then settled in Calif. to teach at Mills College (1947–57) and the San Francisco Cons.

(1952–62); made his farewell recital appearance (1960). As Busoni's foremost student he followed in his mentor's grand manner of piano virtuosity; his performances of Bach and Liszt were formidable; championed the works of Alkan, Medtner, and his teacher.

Petri, Michala, b. Copenhagen, July 7, 1958. She began playing recorder at age 3; appeared on Danish radio at 5; made her concert solo debut Copenhagen (1969); formed a trio with her mother (a harpsichordist) and brother (a cellist), touring widely with it. She studied with F. Conrad at the Hannover Staatliche Hochschule für Musik (1970–76); in addition to chamber music performances, toured extensively as a soloist; made her U.S. debut (with N.Y.'s 92nd St. Y Chamber Orch., 1982) and her Japanese debut (1984). Her repertoire ranges from the early Baroque era to contemporary music; has commissioned several composers.

Pettersson, (Gustaf) Allan, b. Vastra Ryd, Sept. 19, 1911; d. Stockholm, June 20, 1980. He sold Christmas cards and bought a violin from his returns; practiced keyboard playing on a church organ. In 1930 he entered the Stockholm Cons.; studied violin and viola with J. Ruthstrom and theory with H. M. Melchers; played viola in the Stockholm Concert Soc. Orch. (1940–51); studied composition with O. Olsson, Tor Mann, and Blomdahl; set some of his own poems as *24 Barfotasånger* for voice and piano, his 1st mature work (1943–45). In 1951 he went to Paris to study with Honegger and Leibowitz; returning to Sweden, he devoted himself to composition in large forms.

Pettersson's music is permeated with dark moods, complete with deeply pessimistic annotations. He began suffering from painful rheumatoid arthritis (1963); continued to compose while compulsively proclaiming his misfortunes, describing himself as "a voice crying out, drowned in the noise of the times." The Stockholm Phil. played several of his syms., but when his 7th Sym., orig. scheduled for a 1968 American tour, was canceled, he forbade performance of his music in Sweden.

Stylistically, Pettersson's music recalls Mahler's grandiosity of design and passionate, exclamatory dynamism of utterance. Most of his 16 syms. are in single movements; diversity is achieved by frequent changes of mood, tempo, meter, and rhythm. Characteristically, all except No. 10 are set in minor keys; the Sym. No. 1 (1950–51) was withdrawn, to be performed only posthumously! He composed other orch'l works, including 3 concertos for string orch.; chamber music; vocal works, notably *Vox humana,* 18 songs for soloists, chorus, and string orch., to texts by Native Americans (1974).

Petty, Tom, b. Gainesville, Fla., Oct. 20, 1953. Nasal-voiced rock singer/songwriter, who has enjoyed a long career as the leader of the Heartbreakers and as a solo artist. His music reflects his preferences among his 1960s predecessors, including the Byrds, Bob Dylan (with whom he has performed), and Neil Young, at times eerily reminiscent of their early hits. He began performing during high school in Gainesville; joined Mudcrutch with guitarist Mike Campbell and pianist Benmont Tench; by the early 1970s they were in Los Angeles; gained a recording contract with Leon Russell's Shelter Records; as Tom Petty and the Heartbreakers, they recorded two albums and produced some local hits; but when the label was sold to MCA, they entered a protracted legal battle that led to a hiatus in recording.

On their own Backstreets label, Petty and company produced their 1st major hit with *Refugee* (1979); a duet with Fleetwood Mac's Stevie Nicks on *Stop Draggin' My Heart Around* (1981) elevated his stature greatly among pop fans. The band pursued individual projects (1983–85), then returned to the charts with *Don't Come Around Here No More*; toured and recorded with Dylan (1986); joined with Dylan, George Harrison, Roy Orbison, and producer Jeff Lynne to create the mock backwoods supergroup Travellin' Willburys, who recorded 2 albums and a surprising series of hits (1988). He released a successful solo album, with *Won't Back Down* and *Free Fallin'*, in collaboration with Lynne. The Heartbreakers returned to recording and touring with Petty (1991); he has continued to record with the band, even in "solo" projects like 1994's roots-oriented *Wildflowers*; scored the film *She's the One* (1995), producing the hit *Heart So Big*.

peu à peu (Fr.). Little by little; poco a poco. *Un peu*, a little.

pezzo (It.; plural, *pezzi*). A piece; a number (of an opera, etc.). *Pezzi concertati*, concerted pieces; *pezzi staccati*, any numbers separated from an opera, etc.

pf. Abbrev. for *pianoforte*; start softly, then get louder suddenly.

Pfeife (Ger.). Fife.

Pfitzner, Hans (Erich), b. Moscow of German parents, May 5, 1869; d. Salzburg, May 22, 1949. He studied piano with J. Kwast and composition with I. Knorr at the Hoch Cons. in Frankfurt; taught piano and theory at the Cons. of Koblenz (1892–93); assistant conductor of the Municipal Theater in Mainz (1894–96); taught at the Stern Cons. in Berlin (1897–1907), concurrently conducting at the Theater Westens (1903–1906). During the 1907–1908 season he led the renowned Kaim Concerts in Munich; municipal music director of Strausbourg (1908–18) and dean at the Cons.; conducted at the Strasbourg Opera (1910–16). During the 1919–20 season he was music director of the Munich Konzertverein; led a master class at the Berlin Academy of Arts (1920–29); taught composition at the Akademie der Tonkunst in Munich (1929–34).

Pfitzner was favored by the Nazi authorities and became an ardent supporter of the 3rd Reich; dedicated an overture, *Krakauer Begrüssung*, to Hans Frank, the murderous Gauleiter of occupied Poland (1944). After the collapse of Hitler's brief millennium, Pfitzner had to face a denazification court in Munich (1948); owing to his miserable condition in body and soul, he was exonerated. He was taken to a home for the aged in Munich; later transferred to Salzburg, where he died in misery. Eventually his body was honorably laid to rest in a Vienna cemetery.

In his better days Pfitzner was hailed as a great German national composer; presented a successful concert of his works in Berlin (1893); after the premiere of his opera *Der arme Heinrich* in Mainz (1895), the critics, including Humperdinck, praised the work extravagantly. Even more successful was *Palestrina*, making limited use of the Italian's music, written to his own fanciful libretto; conducted by Walter at its premiere in Munich (1917). A Pfitzner Soc. was formed in Munich as early as

1904; a Pfitzner Assoc. was established in Berlin with Furtwängler as president (1938). Although his music is traditional in style and conservative in harmony, he was regarded as belonging to the modern school, a comrade-in-arms of R. Strauss; soon, however, his fame began to dwindle, with fewer performances of his operas and still fewer of his instrumental works; he bitterly complained of this lack of appreciation of his art and railed against the Schoenberg, Schreker, and other "new modern" schools.

Phantasie (Ger.). 1. Fantasia. 2. Fancy, imagination. *Phantasiestück*; fantasia; in modern music, short piece of a romantic and intensely subjective cast with no set form.

phase composition. Type of minimalism, developed in the 1960s by Steve Reich, in which shared melodic lines are gradually shifted from one another by the addition or subtraction of 1 time unit; this approach could also be applied to electronic music, whether through tape loops or the use of *gating*, programmed phase shifting.

phases. Term invented by Stockhausen to designate the time interval between 2 successive tones that results from the probabilistic or intentional distribution of the basic rhythmic unit into equal or unequal time value.

Philidor, André Danican (l'aîné), b. Versailles, *c.* 1647; d. Dreux, Aug. 11, 1730. He was the son of Jean Danican (*c.* 1620–1679), composer and royal musician, and father of François-André Danican Philidor. In 1659 André entered the *grande écurie*, succeeding Michel Danican (*c.* 1600–59), another family member; played the cromorne, trompette marine, and drums; subsequently played oboe, bassoon, and bass cromorne in the royal chapel and *chambre du roi*. In 1684 Louis XIV appointed him royal music librarian, a position he held until his death; during his long tenure he acquired operas, ballets, sacred music, partbooks, etc. from all periods in French music history; a large portion of the collection passed to St. Michael's College, Tenbury; it is now part of the collections at the Bibliothèque Nationale (Paris) and the Bibliothèque Municipale (Versailles). Philidor continued to serve as a musician in the royal chapel (to 1722) and in the royal service (to 1729). As composer, he is best known for his *opéras-ballets*, many of which consitute "mascarades"; instrumental works, including dances, marches, etc.

Philidor, François-André Danican, b. Dreux, Sept. 7, 1726; d. London, Aug. 31, 1795. Youngest son of André Danican Philidor (l'aîné, who had 21 children), and greatest of the Philidor musicians. He was a page boy in the royal chapel in Versailles; studied music with the maître de chapelle, André Campra; also learned to play chess. A motet by him was performed in the royal chapel (1738). In 1740 he went to Paris; supported himself by copying and teaching. His interest in chess continued, getting an outstanding reputation by defeating a number of celebrated chess masters; publ. a fundamental chess treatise, *L'Analyze des échecs* (1749); as a member of the St. James Chess Club in London, gave lectures and demonstrations as a master; traveled frequently to play at the St. James Chess Club (from 1775). A famous chess opening (Philidor's Defense) was named after him.

In the meantime Philidor began a successful career as a theater composer; his 1st success was *Le Maréchal ferrant* (1761), accorded numerous performances; *Le Sorcier* (1764) was also triumphant. Although *Tom Jones* (1765) failed initially, it enjoyed great popularity after its libretto was rev. by Sedaine (1766); the same fate attended *Ernelinde, princesse de Vorvège*: a failure when 1st given at the Paris Opéra (1767); subsequently rev. by Sedaine and performed successfully as *Ernelinde* in Versailles (1773). He continued to compose until his death, but his love for chess took more and more of his time. Philidor was one of the finest earlier composers of opéra-comique; although his scores are often hampered by poor librettos, his orch. writing is effective; an inventive composer, he introduced the vocal quartet a cappella (in *Tom Jones*). He also wrote sacred and secular choral music; the choral work *Carmen saeculare*, after Horace, proved most successful at its premiere in London (1779); also important are his *12 ariettes périodiques*.

Philippe de Vitry. Vitry, Philippe de.

phonograph. (Grk., sound writing; U.K. *gramophone*). The idea of preserving the sound of speech or music occupied poets and scientists for centuries; in the domain of fable, sound could be captured in lead pipes. When the nature of sound was proved to be airwaves that could be recorded by attaching a stylus to a tuning fork and traced as a series of sinusoidal zigzags on a rotating blackened cylinder, the problem seemed to be near solution. All that had to be done was to play back the grooves on the cylinder with a sharp point and the original sound produced by the tuning fork would be returned. In 1877 Thomas Alva Edison attached a sensitive membrane to a stylus that impressed grooves on a wax cylinder; retracing the grooves with the same stylus set the membrane in reciprocal motion, he heard the sound of his own voice reciting *Mary Had a Little Lamb*; named this new invention the phonograph. The rendition of the voice was squeaky and scratchy, but progress was rapid; a horn was attached to the recording membrane above the cylinder to amplify the sound so it could be heard at a distance. During this time Edison had a close rival in Paris inventor Charles Cros, who developed a talking machine named the *parlephone* (Fr., speaking sound).

Edison exhibited his phonograph at fairs and scientific expositions; for many years it was regarded merely as an amusing toy. But when he visited Russia (1890) and showed it to eminent musicians; they were tremendously impressed. Rimsky-Korsakov signed an endorsement: "I heard the phonograph and I marveled at this invention of genius. Being a musician I can foresee the possibility of wide application of this device in the domain of musical art. A precise reproduction of talented interpretations of musical compositions, of outstanding singing voices, recording of folk songs, and improvisations by the means of the phonograph can be of incalculable importance to music. The phonograph also possesses the amazing capacity of accelerating and slowing down the tempo and to transpose [*sic*]. Glory be to great Edison!" Rimsky-Korsakov's vision proved to be correct; a Russian folk-song collector, Mme. Lineva, undertook several trips in the Volga region with a specially constructed phonograph (1894); later publ. her authentic findings.

Another decisive step in transforming a curious toy into an important medium was Emile Berliner's invention of a phonograph disc (1888); despite the obvious advantages of a phonograph disc, Edison continued to manufacture somewhat improved cylinders; finally yielding to the disc (1929). Meanwhile, the phonograph became a major industry, particularly in the U.S.. The Victor Talking Machine Co. adopted the trademark of a dog listening to "His Master's Voice" on a disc phonograph (1900); so famous did the dog (named Nipper) and slogan become that the phonograph itself became generally known as the Victrola; standard speed for discs was established at 78 revolutions per minute (rpm).

The great drawback of the early phonograph disc was limited duration and great bulk; each disc could play for only 4 minutes and 30 seconds; when recordings were made of syms. and operas, individual movements had to be split into several musical subsections; complete performances weighted several pounds. But, just as the invention of the phonograph was a natural development of known scientific facts, so the method of increasing the duration of a single disc was substantially enlarged by a seemingly obvious improvement in the late 1940s: by increasing the number of grooves on the disc while slowing down the number of rpms from 78 to 33 1/3, the 12-inch (diameter) long-playing record ("LP"), with each 33 1/3-rpm disc accommodating nearly half an hour of music, was developed. (The 45-rpm disc, usually 7 inches in diameter, accommodated anywhere from 0 to 7 or 8 minutes.) Furthermore, manufacturers began making records out of an unbreakable plastic material lighter than the shellac of the fragile 78s; an opera that on 78s had required several pounds of discs could be recorded on 2 or 3 long-playing discs.

Progress was made in simulating realistic concert conditions by placing microphones at strategic positions when recording an orch. or an opera. The 1st step toward a more natural sound was binaural recording, in which 2 separate monaural ("mono") channels (distinct sound source) were combined; by 1958 the technique was modified as stereophonic recording ("stereo"; from Grk. *stereos*, solid), in which sound could be distributed freely between the 2 channels through "mixing" (balancing) of the recorded sound. Playback through 4 channels, creating the impression of being "surrounded" by sound, was introduced as *quadraphonic* (1970); it was a commercial failure.

In the 1980s a remarkable rethinking of recording and playback resulted in the compact discs ("CD"). Stylus and analogue recording were dispensed with; sound was registered as a series of numbers (digitally, using a computer) and transferred onto (and then played back from) a metal-coated disc by laser. Contrary to expectations, older recordings were not scrapped; using ingenious methods of salvaging and amplifying early recordings, the voices from the beginning of the phonograph (Caruso, Patti, Melba, Nordica, Calvé) sounded better than the originals; successful rerecordings were made of the piano playing of famous composers and performers (Reger, Debussy, Paderewski, Scriabin, Busoni), from well-preserved paper rolls of the pianola; analogue recordings themselves were given a new lease on auditory life.

By the end of the 20th century the phonograph industry had become a multibillion-dollar business, nourished by untold millions of albums recorded by the great stars of rock, country-western music, hip-hop, and other popular styles. The once-common expression "in the groove" testifies to the ubiquity of the recording industry. Some small recording companies specialize in novelties, resurrecting the forgotten masterpieces of the past or giving a chance to modern composers to record their works. As a result of these activities, large record libraries own an increasing number of recordings covering the entire course of music history, providing invaluable educational material and entertainment for students and music lovers.

phorminx. Ancient Greek chordophone, either a 4-string plucked lyre or an early kithara, mentioned by Homer.

phrase. Half of an 8-measure period; also, any short figure or passage complete in itself and unbroken in continuity.

phrase mark. Curved line connecting the notes of a phrase.

phrasing. 1. Bringing out into proper relief of the phrases (whether motives, figures, subjects, or passages). 2. Signs of notation devised to further this end.

Phrygian mode. Church mode corresponding to the scale from E up to E on the white keys of the piano (E–F–G–A–B–C–D–E); although the name is Greek in origin, the Phrygian mode is not identical with the ancient Greek mode of that name, which corresponds to the Ionian ecclesiastical mode. The plagal mode corresponding to the Phrygian mode is Hypophrygian, with the ambitus extending from the dominant B of the Phrygian mode to the next dominant and thus becoming identical in construction, although not in function, with the theoretical Locrian mode.

physharmonica. Small free-reed organ, invented by Anton Häckl of Vienna (1818), to be placed under a piano keyboard to play the melody simultaneously in order to sustain it; this and similar instruments anticipated the harmonium.

piacere, a (It.). At pleasure; freely, without precise regard of notation. *piacevole*, pleasant, agreeable; use a smooth, suave delivery free from strong accents.

Piaf, Edith (born Giovanna Gassion), b. Paris, Dec. 19, 1915; d. there, Oct. 11, 1963. Abandoned by her mother, an Italian café singer and prostitute, she traveled with her father, a circus contortionist, acting as a shill for his street-corner acrobatics. She became a Parisian street singer, earning the nickname "la môme Piaf" (waif sparrow, in Parisian argot) on account of her ragged and emaciated appearance. During World War II and the German occupation she entertained French prisoners in Germany; was accused of collaboration, but was exonerated. She made her 1st U.S. tour (1947); performed widely in subsequent years, making appearances in films and on television. Although untutored, Piaf developed a ballad singing style infused with profound sentiment and expressive artistry, eliciting an enthusiastic response from nightclub audiences and sophisticated music critics alike. Not a songwriter, she made many chansonettes internationally famous, including *La Vie en Rose, What Can I Do?, I'll Remember Today, Hymne à l'Amour,* and *Les Trois Cloches.*

piangevole (It.). Tearfully; in a mournful, plaintive style.

pianissimo (It.). Very soft (*pp*). *Pianississimo*, extremely soft (*ppp*).

piano. (It., soft; Ger. *Flügel*, wing). 1. Soft, softly (*p*). 2. (Standard abbrev. of *pianoforte* used in this dictionary) Keyboard stringed instrument whose tones are produced by hammers striking the strings. The principal parts are the *frame*, the *soundboard*, the *strings*, the *action*, and the *pedals*. The most popular musical instrument for domestic and concertizing use, it was invented in the early 18th century by Cristofori, who called it a "gravicembalo col piano e forte" (large keyboard with soft and loud); this clumsy description was soon abbreviated to "pianoforte" or (particularly in Russia) "fortepiano"; subsequently became known under its shortened name, ironically inadequate for the 1st keyboard instrument that could achieve both soft and loud sonorities.

The most important innovation of the piano, as distinguished from its predecessors, the harpsichord and clavichord, was in its mechanism of sound production. The clavichord produced its tone by metal tangents striking the string; on the harpsichord the strings were plucked; in the piano's *hammer action* sound is produced by hammers striking the strings from below. Although the mechanism activating the hammers seems simple, the piano's technical construction required a great deal of ingenuity. The hammers had to fall back to their original position after striking the strings without accidentally rebounding, thus allowing sustained tone; then, when the key was released, a soft damper 1st lifted when the key was struck must quickly fall back onto the string to prevent continued reverberation. However, if rapid repetition of a note is needed, a special device had to be developed to let the hammer drop to a height halfway between resting position and the strings, so that it could strike the string again instantly. The mechanical conglomeration that made all of these actions feasible was called the *escapement.* (Beethoven adopted the German name *Hammerklavier* for the sonatas of his last period; the word simply means "hammer keyboard," and is not a separate instrument.)

In order to produce a sound an octave deeper, a string must be doubled in length; if all piano strings were equally thick, the string for the lowest C (C_1) in the bass—7 octaves below the highest C (c^5) on the keyboard—would have to be 128 times as long as the string for c^5, an obvious manufacturing impossibility. The appropriate registers are determined by a combination of length and thickness, accomdating the bass strings within the winglike shape of the piano. The piano strings in the bass range are single for each tone; in the middle range they are in pairs, to give more resonance; in the extreme treble there are 3 strings per tone to enhance the resonance still more; dampers are absent in the extreme upper register because the thin strings do not sustain enough resonance to require dampening. Playing rapid and loud passages in the uppermost keyboard octave creates a curious effect of an acoustic cloud or white noise that lingers for a fraction of a second.

Modern pianos have 3 pedals. The right-hand (*damper, loud*) pedal holds all dampers above the strings, allowing for a resonant sonority comprising the sounds of all keys played while the pedal is held down; properly applied only in passages of predominantly chordal consistency; unfortunately, many amateur pianists become addicted to the loud pedal even when the harmony is not uniform, producing a chaos of unrelated sounds while trying to cover up wrong notes that drown in the tonal mess. The left-hand (*soft, piano*) pedal shifts the entire keyboard slightly to the right, so that the hammers strike the strings obliquely, diminishing their dynamic level by striking one fewer string for each tone in the middle and upper registers; the application of this pedal is often marked as *una corda* (1 string), or, more rarely, *due corde* (2 strings), depending on the extent of the shift; when the left-hand pedal is to be taken off, the direction is *tre corde* (3 strings). Grand pianos and most modern pianos have a middle pedal, the *sostenuto* (sustaining), to hold the dampers above the strings of any note(s) being held down on the keyboard when the pedal is applied; like the damper pedal, these notes will keep sounding until the sostenuto pedal is released; Debussy, Ravel, Bartók, Crumb, and others have used this pedal to good effect.

The range of the early piano was, like the contemporaneous harpsichord, about 4 1/2 octaves, the upper limit being the F above the treble staff (f^3); because of the limited range, 18th-century piano composers often had to transpose the recapitulation section in sonata form down an octave in the middle of a sequence (e.g., Mozart's C-major sonata, K.545, 1st movement recapitulation). The piano's range was extended rapidly in the 19th century and was soon stabilized in its present form of 7 octaves and a minor 3rd, from A_2 to c^5. The Austrian firm of Bösendorfer manufactured early a piano that extended to C_2 (a 6th below the standard low A), but is rarely used in concert; in the 19th century the French manufacturer Pleyel invented the *pédalier*, a organ-like pedalboard designed to be attached to the piano and played with the feet; Alkan wrote music for pianos thus equipped. Editors of Classic and early Romantic piano music have often wanted to adapt these works to the normal keyboard of modern pianos. Would Mozart have taken advantage of the newly available higher notes in the recapitulation of his C-major Sonata to avoid the awkward shift of register? Why did Beethoven, who could have revised his earlier sonatas during his lifetime when the piano range had been considerably extended, fail to do so? Wouldn't it be worthwhile to change the low A_2 to $G\sharp_2$ in the octave cascade in Ravel's *Jeux d'eau*, whenever the piece is performed on a piano with extra bass notes? *Pianino,* upright pianoforte; *piano à queue* (Fr., piano with tail); grand piano.

piano duet. Work for 2 pianos and 2 performers, as opposed to *piano four-hands,* for one piano and 2 performers. Mozart wrote sonatas for each type. *Piano quartet,* composition for piano, violin, viola, and cello; *piano quintet,* composition for piano and string quartet; *piano score,* arrangement or reduction of orch'l work for piano; *piano trio,* composition for piano, violin, and cello.

pianoforte (It., loud-soft). See ⇒piano.

pianola. Trade name applied to a mechanical (player) piano; had some popularity in the late 1910s (e.g., Stravinsky, Hindemith); later revitalized in a highly original body of works by Nancarrow.

Piatigorsky, Gregor, b. Ekaterinoslav, Apr. 17, 1903; d. Los Angeles, Aug. 6, 1976. He received his 1st music lessons from his father, a violinist; studied cello with A. von Glehn at the Moscow Cons.; played in various Moscow orchs. In 1921 he left Russia; took cello lessons with J. Klengel in Leipzig; served as 1st cellist of the Berlin Phil. (1924–28), then devoted himself to a solo career. He played the solo part in *Don Quixote* under composer R. Strauss's direction many times in Europe; unexcelled in this part, Strauss himself called him "mein Don Quixote." He went to America (1929); later that year made his American debut (Oberlin, Ohio) and played the Dvořák Concerto with the N.Y. Phil., eliciting great praise.

Piatigorsky was regarded as the world's finest cellist after Casals; gave solo recitals and appeared with European and American orchs. for many years; gave 1st performances of works he commissioned from Hindemith, Dukelsky, Castelnuovo-Tedesco, and others. He became a naturalized U.S. citizen (1942); taught at the Curtis Inst. of Music in Philadelphia (1942–51) and at Tanglewood; prof. at the Univ. of Southern Calif., Los Angeles (1962–76); presented a famous series of concerts with Heifetz and Pennario.

piatti (It.). Cymbals.

pibcorn (Welsh). Hornpipe dating from the Middle Ages to the 18th century, recently revived. It consists of a single or double cylindrical tube with a single beating reed, protected by a cowhorn mouth bell, terminating in a cowhorn bell. The tube, made of bone, wood, or cane, generally had 6 fingerholes and 1 rear fingerhole.

pibroch (Gael.). Genre in variation form for the Scottish Highland bagpipe.

Picardy third (Fr. *tierce de Picardie*). Frequent Baroque practice of ending a minor-key piece with a major tonic chord, the Picardy 3rd being the major 3rd above the tonic. The French philosopher/composer/musicologist Rousseau described this practice as being particularly strong in the French region of Picardy, where there were numerous cathedrals and organs. Acoustics support the preference of ending with a major 3rd, an interval within the overtone series, while the tonic minor 3rd is not. Examples can be found in the cadences of chorales, in the coda of Bach's fugues in minor keys, etc.; the principle can be expanded into entire sonatas and symphonies in minor keys; a most resplendent illustration is Beethoven's 5th Sym. in C Minor, whose last movement is in a resounding C major.

piccanteria, con (It.). With piquant, sprightly expression.

picchiettato (It.). Detached, staccato; piqué.

Piccinni, (Vito) Niccolò (Nicola) (Marcello Antonio Giacomo), b. Bari, Jan. 16, 1728; d. Passy, near Paris, May 7, 1800. His father was a violinist at Bari's Basilica di San Nicola, his maternal uncle was the composer Gaetano Latilla. Niccolò's precocity manifested itself enough so that, thanks to Archbishop Muzio Gaeta of Bari, he was able at 14 to enter Naples's Cons. di S. Onofrio; studied with Leo and Durante (graduated 1754); began his theatrical career with the comic opera *Le Donne dispettose* (Naples, 1754); *Zenobia* (Naples, 1756) was his 1st attempt at a serious opera; after several other operas for Naples, he received a commission to write an opera for Rome, *Alessandro nelle Indie* (1758), followed by his comic opera *La Cecchina, ossia La Buona figliuola* (Rome, 1760), a great success at home and abroad. In subsequent years he wrote prolifically for the stage, producing over 100 operas for major Italian theaters. Settling in Naples, Piccinni served as 2nd maestro di cappella at the Cathedral; active as an organist in convents; taught singing. His fortunes in Rome declined with the rise of Anfossi, his former pupil and protégé (1773); however, he still found success in Naples with a 2nd *Alessandro nelle Indie* (1774) and *I Viaggiatori* (1775).

In 1776 Piccinni was called to Paris by the French court, where his presence precipitated the "querelle célèbre" between the "Gluckists" and "Piccinnists." His 1st French opera, *Roland* (1778), won considerable success; he served as director of an Italian troupe in Paris (1778–79); although promised by the Paris Opéra that his *Iphigénie en Tauride* would be produced before Gluck's opera on the same subject, it was not given until 1781, some 2 years after the Gluck; while it was fairly successful, he gained his only major success with the opera *Didon* (1783), the year that he finally was granted a pension by the French court; appointed maître de chant at the École Royale de Chant et de Déclamation Lyrique in Paris (1784). In spite of their rivalry, Piccinni held the highest regard for Gluck; suggested that an annual memorial concert be given in Gluck's memory, but financial support was not forthcoming; upon the death of another rival, Sacchini, Piccinni spoke in homage at his funeral. With the French Revolution he lost his post and his pension; returned to Naples (1791), but upon his daughter's marriage to a French Jacobite, was placed under house arrest (1794); finally gained freedom (1798) and returned to Paris; obtained a partial restoration of his pension; his appointment as 6th inspector at the Cons. came when he was too ill to pursue an active life.

Piccinni selected librettos rich in dramatic content; his melodic invention was fresh, his arias written in a pleasing and vocally idiomatic manner; elaborated conventional climactic scenes so that dramatic interest was sustained to the end; varied tempos and harmonies in the ensembles, further contributing to the overall effect. He demonstrated a remarkable facility in writing both comic and serious operas. His historical importance rests upon his establishment of the Italian operatic style as the model for his French and German successors.

piccolo (It., *flauto piccolo* or *ottavino*; Ger. *Kleinflöte*). Little flute; octave flute; small flute pitched an octave higher than the orch'l flute; its lowest note is d^2.

pick. Pluck or twang the strings of a guitar, mandolin, etc.; also, plectrum used for this purpose.

piece. 1. Musical composition. 2. Instrument, taken as a member of an orch. or band.

pièce (Fr.). Piece. *Suite de pièces*, set of pieces.

pieno (It.). 1. Full. 2. Mixture stop.

pietoso (It., pitiful, moving). Demands a sympathetic and expressive delivery.

piffero (It.). Fife; also, primitive kind of oboe or shawm.

Pijper, Willem, b. Zeist, Sept. 8, 1894; d. Leidschendam, Mar. 18, 1947. He received a rudimentary education from his father, an amateur violinist; attended the Toonkunst School of Music in Utrecht; studied composition with J. Wagenaar and

piano with Mme. H. J. van Lunteren-Hansen (1911–16); was music critic of *Utrecht Dagblad* (1918–23); co-editor of the monthly *De Muziek*. (1926–29); taught theory at the Amsterdam Cons. (from 1918); prof. of composition there (1925–30); director of the Rotterdam Cons. (from 1930). In his music Pijper continued the Romantic tradition of Mahler while adopting harmonic procedures of the modern French School. He postulated a "germ-cell theory," in which an opening chord or motive is the source of all succeeding harmonic and melodic development (akin to Schoenberg's gestalt theory); cultivated the octatonic scale of alternating whole tones and semitones; believed he had invented it, not realizing of its abundant use by Rimsky-Korsakov and others; became known as the "Pijper scale" in the Netherlands. During the German bombardment of Rotterdam (1940), nearly all of his MSS were destroyed by fire, including the unpubl. Divertimento for piano and string orch.

pincé (Fr.). 1. Plucked; as the strings of a harp. 2. Pizzicato (in violin playing).

Pink Floyd, (Guitar/vocal: Roger "Syd" Barrett, b. Cambridge, England, Jan. 6, 1946; keyboard/vocal: Rick Wright, b. London, July 28, 1945; bass/piano/vocal: Roger Waters, b. Great Bookham, England, Sept. 6, 1944; drums: Nick Mason, b. Birmingham, England, Jan. 27, 1945; Barrett was replaced by David Gilmour, b. Cambridge, England, Mar. 6, 1944, in 1968; band dissolved in 1983; regrouped in 1987 without Waters.) A leader in psychedelic rock, then an originator of progressive and hi-tech rock, the band is best known for the masterful concept album *The Dark Side of the Moon* (1973), still selling a quarter-century later.

Pink Floyd's members met in London in the mid-1960s while attending art and architecture schools; taking their name from 2 American blues singers (Pink Anderson and Floyd Collins), they became a favorite at trendy clubs like London's Marquee and UFO. Originally led by principal songwriter Barrett, the group scored a major hit with *See Emily Play,* a single so complex that it could not be reproduced onstage; their 1st album, *The Piper at the Gates of Dawn,* continued the psychedelic trend, with moody arrangements complementing Barrett's often dense lyrics; however, he soon began displaying signs of mental illness; by early 1968 he had been ousted from the group, replaced by Gilmour; although Barrett made a few more recordings, he disappeared from public view, becoming a cult figure.

Waters came to the foreground as the main creative force in the band; a series of albums and elaborate tours followed, culminating in *The Dark Side of the Moon,* featuring the U.S. hit *Money;* the album remained on the U.S. charts for over 14 years, a major achievement. Further recordings and mammoth tours followed, with the group's massive sound equipment complemented by equally massive set pieces (the famed flying pig being one of their better efforts). Another megahit concept album came with *The Wall* (1979), a social statement with a hit theme song, a spectacular tour unparalleled in the annals of rock excess, and a 1982 film.

Tensions between Waters (who felt he was carrying the musical brunt of the band) and other group members led to Pink Floyd's disbanding in 1983; however, this proved temporary, as the group reunited sans Waters (1987); Gilmour took control, writing the material for *A Momentary Lapse of Reason,* another steady seller for the band. Waters retaliated with several solo efforts, as well as a mammoth production of *The Wall* staged at (no surprise) the Berlin Wall (1990). While not achieving the artistic or economic level of the past, the band continued to record and tour; Waters has had less success; a fond Floyd fan's dream was the group's reunion. For a long record of achievement they gained a place in the Rock and Roll Hall of Fame (1996).

pinky (Lat. *minimus*). American slang for the little finger; used by country guitar-pickers to designate the delicately subdued sound achieved by that finger.

Pinza, Ezio (baptized Fortunio), b. Rome, May 18, 1892; d. Stamford, Conn., May 9, 1957. He began to study voice at age 18 with Ruzza and Vizzani at the Bologna Cons.; made his opera debut as Oroveso in *Norma* in Soncino (1914); after military service in World War I, resumed his career, making his 1st important appearance as Comte Des Grieux in Rome (1920); sang at La Scala in Milan (1922–24); selected by Toscanini for the leading part in the world premiere of Boito's *Nerone* (1924). He made his American debut at the Metropolitan Opera in N.Y. as Pontifex Maximus in Spontini's *La Vestale* (1926); remained in the company until 1947; appeared also in San Francisco, Chicago, etc.; sang in Europe and in South America; his most celebrated roles were Mephistopheles in Gounod's *Faust*, Don Giovanni, and Boris Godunov. He appeared as a musical theater star in *South Pacific* (1949); appeared in films.

pipa (Chin.). Short-necked wooden lute played upright in a sitting position; used since antiquity, with a pear-shaped body, wooden soundboard, crescent soundholes, fingerboard with 4 frets (the other 6 to 13 are on the belly), and 4 silk strings. Much of the pipa repertoire stresses military depictions, in part due to the relative fast decay time; variations for the instrument have been written and published. It is the predecessor of the Japanese biwa.

pipe. 1. Rude flageolet or oboe. 2. Organ pipe. In *flue pipes* the tone is produced by the vibration of a column of air within a tube or body; they are either *open* or *covered* (stopped, plugged), a stopped pipe yielding a tone an octave lower than an open pipe of like length. In *reed pipes*, the tone is produced by a reed.

piqué (Fr.). In violin family playing, the mezzo-staccato called for by a slur with staccato dots; notes so marked to be played in 1 bow (picchiettato).

piston. See ⇒valve.

Piston, Walter (Hamor, Jr.), b. Rockland, Maine, Jan. 20, 1894; d. Belmont, Mass., Nov. 12, 1976. He took piano lessons with H. Shaw and violin with Fiumara, Theodorowicz, and Winternitz; played in restaurants and places of public entertainment. After serving in World War I he entered Harvard Univ.; conducted concerts of the univ. orch., the Pierian Sodality; graduated summa cum laude in music (1924). For a time he was employed as a draftsman for Boston Elevated Railway; went to Paris on a J. K. Paine Traveling Fellowship, studying with Nadia Boulanger (1924); took courses with Dukas at the École Normale de Musique (1925); returned to the U.S. (1926); appointed to the faculty of Harvard Univ.; prof. of music (1944); prof. emeritus (1960).

As a teacher Piston was greatly esteemed for his consummate knowledge of music, pedagogical ability, and immanent humanity in instructing students with different aesthetics from his own, including L. Bernstein. As a composer he followed a cosmopolitan course, adhering to classical forms while extending harmonic structures toward a maximum of tonal saturation; was particularly expert in contrapuntal writing. About 1965 he adopted a modified system of 12-tone composition, particularly in initial thematic statements; his Sym. No. 8 and Variations for Cello and Orch. are explicitly dodecaphonic. He rejected the narrow notion of ethnic musical Americanism; stated that an artist could be as American working in the Library of the Boston Atheneum as roaming the Western prairie; yet he employed upon occasion syncopated jazz rhythms.

Piston received Pulitzer Prizes for his 3rd and 7th Syms., and N.Y. Music Critics' Circle Awards for his 2nd Sym., Viola Concerto, and String Quartet No. 5. He was elected a member of the National Inst. of Arts and Letters (1938), the American Academy of Arts and Letters (1955), and the American Academy of Arts and Sciences (1940). He traveled little, declining invitations to go to South America and Russia under the auspices of the State Dept.; his working habits were remarkably methodical, rarely revising his music once it was on paper; his handwriting was calligraphic.

Piston's best-known work is *The Incredible Flutist*, a ballet (Boston, 1938; suite, Pittsburgh, 1940); he wrote many orch'l works, including 8 syms. (1938–65); his chamber works include 5 string quartets (1933–62); composed a small amount of vocal and keyboard music. He wrote widely used textbooks: *Principles of Harmonic Analysis* (Boston, 1933); *Harmony* (N.Y., 1944; 5th ed., rev. and enlarged by M. DeVoto, 1987); *Counterpoint* (N.Y., 1947); *Orchestration* (N.Y., 1955).

pitch. The position of a tone in the musical scale. Pitch is relative, or absolute. The *relative* pitch of a tone is its position (higher or lower) as compared with some other tone. (See ⇒interval.). Its *absolute* pitch is its fixed position in the entire range of musical tones. To indicate absolute pitch, the musical scale is divided into a fixed series of octaves, named and lettered (See ⇒Intro., The Clefs). The number of vibrations made by a tone establishes its absolute pitch; the standard *French pitch* (also called *international* or *low* pitch) gives the tone $a^1 = 435$ cycles (complete vibrations) per second (cps; Hz). The standard of pitch in the U.S. is $a^1 = 440$ cps; some orchs. are known to tune up to $a^1 = 450$ cps:

Acoustically, pitch is determined by the frequency of vibrations of a given tone. The smaller the sound-producing instrument, the higher the pitch; a whistle is small, thus its pitch is high; the bass tuba is large, so its pitch is very low. On string instruments and on the piano, the shorter and thinner the string, the higher the pitch. A relatively small minority of musicians possess the faculty of perfect pitch, which enables them to name without fail any note within the audible range. Perfect (or absolute) pitch is innate, and persons who were not born to it cannot be trained to acquire it, any more than a color-blind person can be trained to tell red from green. Relative pitch, however, enables a person to name the interval between 2 pitches; this ability can be acquired. To those who are particularly obtuse in recognizing even relative pitch, a remedial course may be taught by identifying intervals through their similarity with the patterns of well-known songs.

The present standard pitch for A in the middle octave is 440 vibrations per second; in the orch., the oboe gives out the standard A to which all the other instruments tune because it is an instrument little affected by changes of temperature and humidity. However, this standard pitch has been fluctuating widely through the centuries. In the 19th century the middle A was considerably lower than that of the later standard pitch. If Mozart listened to a 20th-century rendition of his *Jupiter Sym.*, he would think that it had been transposed to C-sharp major instead of the written key of C major.

pitch class. Set of all pitches with the same name; i.e., pitch class A, inclusive of all possible A's, regardless of register.

pitch pipe. Small wooden or metal reed pipe which sounds 1 or more tones of fixed pitch, to give the tone for tuning an instrument, or for a choir.

pittoresco (It.). Picturesque.

più (It.). More. When *più* stands alone, as a tempo mark, mosso is implied; as an expression mark it refers to the next preceding *f* or *p*. *Più andante*, orig. more lively; by the Classic period, more slowly; *più largo*, more slowly; *più marcato del principio*, a little more emphasized than at the beginning; *più mosso*, *più moto*, faster; *più mosso ancora*, still faster; *più sostenuto*, a little more sustained; *più vicino*, a little nearer (as if getting closer and louder); *con un poco più di moto*, with a little more movement, somewhat faster.

piuttosto (It.). Somewhat; rather. *Piuttosto lento*, somewhat slowly.

pivot chord. In modulation, a chord pivotal to both the old key and the new key, that is, belonging to both keys. Particularly in chromatic modulation, the diminished-7th chord functions as such a *passe-partout* device.

pizzicato (It., pinched). Plucked with the finger; a direction, in music, to violinists, etc., to play the notes by plucking the strings with the bowing hand; abbrev. *pizz.* *Left-hand pizzicato*, plucking the string (usually open) with the fingering hand; this device was favored by 19th-century virtuosos, starting with Paganini (Caprice No. 24). *Snap pizzicato*, pull the string and release with sufficient force that the string snaps against the fingerboard; also known as the *Bartók pizzicato*, because of that composer's characteristic use of it.

placidamente (*placido*; It.). Placidly, tranquilly, smoothly.

plagal cadence (from Grk. *plagios*, oblique). Cadence in which the tonic is preceded by the subdominant rather than by the dominant, the authentic cadence. The authentic cadence

displaced the plagal cadence almost completely after 1500, which retained its hold only on the conclusion of the hymn with the word *Amen*, but it returned with a vengeance in the 20th century when many composers felt an impulse to return to early modality.

plagal mode. In Gregorian chant, plagal modes were formed by placing the outer notes a 4th below and a 5th above that of the corresponding authentic mode. This derivation is denoted by adding the prefix *hypo* (below) to the authentic modes. The final, however, remains the same as in the corresponding authentic mode. On the white keys of the piano keyboard, the Dorian mode extends from D to D, and the Hypodorian mode would extend from A (a 4th below D) to A (a 5th above D); both share the final D. In the 16th century the plagal modes were incorporated into the general system of 12 modes. See also ⇒authentic mode.

plagiarism. (from Lat. *plagiarius*, plunderer) Stealing of intellectual property; 1st used in this sense by the Roman poet Martial; became a universal term in all languages. The essential element of plagiarism is deliberate intent; remembered folk sayings, proverbial expressions, or verses from classical works of literature do not constitute plagiarism. As for musical plagiarism it must be realized that the most naturally attractive melodies in classical music are derived from the diatonic scale, and that rhythmic arrangements of such melodies are limited to certain symmetric formulas within a binary or a ternary meter, making accidental coincidences almost inevitable.

Still, eager plagiarism hunters devote considerable time and effort to prove that there is nothing new under the musical sun; they exult in pointing out that the great opening theme of Beethoven's *Eroica* is identical with that of an early Mozart overture, thus brilliantly demonstrating that the 3 notes of the major triad can be arranged in a variety of ways in 3/4 time. The theme of the finale of Mozart's *Jupiter Sym.* (K. 551) is identical in structure and rhythm to the main theme of the finale of Haydn's Sym. No. 13, written years before Mozart's time. In the mid-18th century German writer and composer F. W. Zacharias even proposed to compile a source dictionary of unintentional as well as intentional borrowings.

In 1731 an otherwise respectable Italian composer, Giovanni Bononcini, serious rival of Handel for royal and aristocratic favors in London, made the grievous error of submitting to the Academy of Ancient Music in London a madrigal by his contemporary Lotti as his own; when this reckless act of patent plagiarism was discovered, Bononcini was disgraced and had to leave England. But Handel himself was not averse to frank borrowings of whole arias from other composers for his use in his operas. Fortunately for him, this practice was either sufficiently obscure or tolerated in his time; copyright was still in the future. Indeed, an early edition of the *Encyclopaedia Britannica* referred to Handel as "a common thief and shameless borrower."

An interesting coincidence is found between an early Liszt song and the principal phrase in the introduction to Wagner's opera *Tristan und Isolde*; the notes are exactly the same without transposition. Since Wagner was very close to Liszt, there may have been a subconscious reminiscence of chromatic procedures not realized by either Wagner or Liszt. Still, musical petty larceny was regarded with benign tolerance throughout the 18th and 19th centuries, forgivable because the financial profit was negligible.

The situation changed in the 20th century when popular music became big business. The copyright laws protected the composer only partially; if the plagiarist disguised his or her handiwork sufficiently, the intent to defraud could not be proven in a court of law. Indeed, fraudulent claims of plagiarism against successful publishers and composers of popular tunes launched by writers of songs bearing but a superficial similarity to profitable hits became so common in the U.S. that publishers often bought off such claimants to avoid costly defense procedures. Learned Hand, United States Judge of N.Y., ruling in a case involving the composer of the popular song *I Didn't Raise My Boy to Be a Soldier*, put a plague on both parties by declaring, "The defendant is a casual composer of melodies, though he has small knowledge of musical notation and small skill in playing. I am aware that in such simple and trivial themes as these it is dangerous to go too far upon suggestions of similarity. For instance, the whole of the leading theme of the song is repeated literally from a chorus of *Pinafore*, though there is not the slightest reason to suppose that the plaintiff ever heard of the opera. It is said that such similarities are of constant occurrence in music and that little inference is permissible." But when Stravinsky used the tune of *Happy Birthday to You* in a symphonic dedication (*Greeting Prelude*) to Monteux on his 80th birthday (1955), he ran afoul of the copyright and had some trouble having it performed.

Musical literature abounds with melodic theft, but publishers try to be careful not to infringe on the copyright protection of popular pieces. An American publisher issued a song called *Avalon*, based on Cavaradossi's aria from *Tosca;* as the Puccini was protected, the publ. was obliged to pay a heavy fine. On the other hand, nothing could be done to the perpetrators of the song *I'm Forever Chasing Rainbows*, based on the middle section of Chopin's posthumous *Fantaisie-Impromptu*, because the original was not protected. For the same reason, Mozart was not spared the depredation of his C-major Piano Sonata (K. 545) in a song entitled *In an 18th-Century Drawing Room*, nor could Tchaikovsky stop the transmogrification of his Piano Concerto No. 1 into *Tonight We Love*. Rachmaninoff, on the other hand, enjoyed the *Russian Rag* based on his celebrated C-sharp minor Prelude (No. 2, op. 3).

plainchant, plainsong. Unison vocal music of the Christian church, probably dating from the 1st centuries of the Christian era, the style being still obligatory in the Roman Catholic ritual, although now in the vernacular rather than church Latin.

plantation songs. Broad category of secular music associated with the work songs and ballads of black slaves in the antebellum South and its imitations in the "Ethiopian" music of Foster and blackface minstrelsy.

plants and music. In a wacky book, *The Secret Life of Plants*, a claim is made in all seriousness that plants are "tuned to the Music of the Spheres" and react sensitively to music. An Indian authority has testified that by playing ragas to an appreciative audience of asters, petunias, onions, sesame, radishes, sweet potatoes, and tapioca he proved "beyond any shadow of a doubt that harmonic soundwaves affect the growth, flowering, fruiting, and seed-yields of plants." An American horticulturist piped some music into greenhouses, claiming it caused his plants

to germinate quicker and bloom more abundantly and more colorfully. A Canadian botanist played a recording of Bach's violin sonatas in his garden, with the result that despite the poor quality of soil, wheat grew better than in the richest earth, demonstrating conclusively that "Bach's musical genius was as good or better than material nutrients." Inspired by these experiments, a botanist in Illinois played a recording of Gershwin's *Rhapsody in Blue* for different plants; they "sprouted earlier than those given the silent treatment, and their stems were thicker, tougher, and greener."

The acme of scientific experimentation with the harmonic life of plants was achieved by a mezzo-soprano who was a regular soloist at Denver's Beach Supper Club. She played the taped musical notes C and D on the piano every second, alternating with periods of silence; as a result the African violets, drooping at 1st, began to flower joyously. No lover of rock 'n' roll, she successfully proved that squashes hated rock music so much that they actually grew away from the transistor radio broadcasting it, and even, in their desperation, tried to climb the slippery walls of the greenhouse. On the other hand, the cucurbits curled around the radio speaker broadcasting Beethoven and Brahms. When she exposed corn and zinnias to rock music, they grew in abnormal shapes and finally withered and died. But plants subjected to the sounds of "intellectual, mathematically sophisticated music" of the East reacted with such enthusiasm that they bent toward the source of the music at angles of more than 60 degrees, some of them entwining the loudspeaker.

Well, Victor Hugo heard a tree sing when bathed in light—"L'Arbre, tout pénétré de lumière, chantait"—but then he was a poet.

planus (Lat.). Full. *Planus corus*, full chorus.

plastic, elastic, and spastic variations. Plasticity of texture is essential in modern variations, securing a malleability of tonal materials. Tonal elasticity adds intervallic flexibility to a plastic theme. A rhythmic effect can be achieved by spastic convulsions of the melodic line, producing implosions which impart a stimulating sense of disquiet to the music.

Plato, b. probably in Athens, *c.* 428 B.C.; d. there, 347 or 348 B.C. In his *Timaeus* the Greek philosopher formulated a system of music in which he likened the movements of music to those of the soul, whose development may therefore be influenced by the art of music; categorized certain scales by their different effects on the listener.

platter. Slang for phonograph record, especially in the 1950s.

player piano. Mechanical device that combines the principles of airstream propulsion and percussive hammer action for automatic reproduction of a performance on the piano. A roll of very strong paper is rotated on a cylinder and is perforated in such a way that the holes made on it correspond in pitch and duration to the notes originally played on the piano. The pitches are represented by the horizontal parameter, and the duration, including rest, by the vertical. Since the cylinder rotates, a rapid scale would register visually as a terraced pattern. To reproduce the original performance a stream of air is passed through the perforations and activates the corresponding hammers, which then strike the piano strings and simultaneously depress the keys of the piano keyboard. The visual impression of such automatic piano playing is that of a magical performance by the invisible fingers of a phantom pianist.

The player piano, under various trademarks such as the Pianola, the Welte-Mignon, etc., became highly popular after its introduction late in the 19th century, and its popularity did not diminish until the advent of the modern phonograph. Several composers, among them Stravinsky and Hindemith, composed and recorded pieces for the player piano. The defect of the pianola and similar reproductive mechanical instruments, however, was a lack of dynamic nuance, but the discovery in 1957 of piano rolls made by Welte-Mignon early in the century, which made use of columns of incompressible mercury to register precise pressure on the piano keys, made it possible to have faithful renditions of performances played by famous pianists of the time. These performances were then rerecorded on the phonograph, restoring with a remarkable fidelity the manner of playing by Paderewski and other famous musicians of yore.

The player piano possesses the unique capacity of enabling a composer to make perforations directly on the roll guided by desired measurements, and modern composers have availed themselves of this facility. Most remarkable results were achieved in this technique by Nancarrow, who constructed a number of études and other pieces by direct perforation on the roll, resulting in melodic, harmonic, and rhythmic patterns of extreme complexity and utmost precision that could not be played by any human pianist or even any number of pianists.

plectrum. A pick; a small piece of ivory, tortoise shell, metal, or plastic, held between the forefinger and thumb, or fitted to the thumb by a ring, and used to pluck or twang the strings of the mandolin, zither, guitar, Asian zithers and lutes, etc.

plein (Fr.). Full.

plein-jeu (Fr.). 1. Stop or combination of stops bringing out the full power of the organ, harmonium, etc. 2. Fourniture.

plena (Sp.). Puerto Rican ballad similar to the calypso songs of Trinidad.

Pleyel, Ignace Joseph (Ignaz Josef), b. Ruppertsthal, near Vienna, June 18, 1757; d. on his estate near Paris, Nov. 14, 1831. He was the 24th of 38 children in the impoverished family of a schoolteacher; received sufficient musical education to qualify for admittance to the class of Wanhal; thanks to the generosity of Count L. Erdödy, became Haydn's pupil and lodger in Eisenstadt (c. 1772–77) and then went to Rome. He became 2nd Kapellmeister at the Strasbourg Cathedral (1783); advanced to the rank of 1st Kapellmeister (1789), but lost his position during the turbulent French Revolution. He conducted the Professional Concerts in London (1791–92); honored his teacher Haydn by playing a work of his in the series. After several years he returned to Strasbourg to liquidate his estate; went to Paris (1795); opened a music store (in business until 1834); founded a piano factory (1807), which manufactured famous French pianos; the firm eventually became known as Pleyel et Cie., prosperous for over a century and a half.

The name Pleyel is mainly known through piano manufacture, but he was a prolific and extremely competent composer.; his works are so close in style to Haydn's that specialists still attribute certain works in Haydn's catalogues to Pleyel. He composed about 45 syms., 6 symphonies concertantes, 2 violin and 5 cello concertos, more than 70 string quartets, 16 string quintets, other chamber works, and vocal music, including 2 operas and songs. His son (Joseph Stephen) Camille Pleyel (b. Strasbourg, Dec. 18, 1788; d. Paris, May 4, 1855) was a pianist, piano manufacturer, and composer; his wife was Marie-Félicité-Denise Moke Pleyel (b. Paris, Sept. 4, 1811; d. St.-Josse-ten-Noode, near Brussels, Mar. 30, 1875), a fine pianist, teacher, and composer with whom Berlioz fell in love (1830), but she married the younger Pleyel that very year (Berlioz was in Rome); separated in 1835.

plica. Neume introduced in the Notre Dame school MSS, indicating a pitch and its ornamentation. The direction and length of the ligature or its stem represented the type to be used—what would now be called the mordent or appoggiatura. In mensural notation the term *plica* was followed by an indication of the type, such as *plica descendens*.

plugging. American slang for the promotion, by means fair or foul, of books, films, records, videos, etc. See also ⇒payola.

pluralism. As in collage, use of different styles within a single composition, sometimes simultaneously.

pluralistic structures. Epistemological concept connoting a multiplicity of causes and events. Developments of modern music support the pluralistic view in such styles as neoclassicism, impressionism, or expressionism, in which the factors of melody, rhythm, and intervallic values are of different formulation. But the same type of structure becomes monistic if it is derived from a uniform set, as for instance in variations. Pluralism and monism are mutually specular, but they are reconciled in serial music. Analogies with the visible spectrum invite themselves. White light is monistic in its sensory perception but pluralistic when it is analyzed into the prismatic constituents of the rainbow. White sound is a monistic aggregation of sonic particles, which can be separated into a pluralistic collection of its tonal components.

plus (Fr.). More. *Plus à l'aise*, more relaxed; *plus lent*, slower.

pneumatic organ. Family of keyboards (invented c. 200 A.D.) whose airflow is generated through bellows pumped by hand or trodden by feet; replaced by an improved, larger hydraulic organ in the 19th century.

po' (It.; contraction of *poco*). Little. *Con un po' d'espansione*, with a certain display of emotion; *alzando un po' la voce*, raising the voice a little; *ritenendo un po'*, becoming a trifle slower.

pochette (Fr., little pocket). Very small violin that could be carried in the pocket of a dancing master, used to accompany his pupils in rehearsal. See also ⇒kit.

pochissimo (It.). Very little.

poco (It.). Little. *A poco a poco*, little by little, gradually; *poco allegro*, rather fast; *poco largo*, rather slow; *poco meno*, when standing alone as a tempo mark, *mosso* is implied, i.e., *poco* *meno mosso*, a little less fast (a little slower); *poco più*, standing alone, also implies *mosso* (a little faster); *poco più lento della prima volta*, somewhat slower than the 1st time.

poi (It.). Then; thereafter.

point. Musicomathematical term used to enhance the impression of profundity by avant-garde composers in the last 3rd of the decaying 20th century. When attentively examined in context, it means a convergence of autonomous sounds resulting either in optimum white noise comprising all pitches, or the geometrical zero in absolute silence; such points can be arrived at by various acoustical encounters.

point d'orgue (Fr., organ point). 1. Pedal point. 2. Pause. 3. Cadenza.

pointe (Fr.). 1. Point or head of a bow. 2. In ballet, the toe (abbrev. *p.*).

pointe d'archet (Fr.). Tremolo with the point of the bow.

pointillism. In the nomenclature of modern art, pointillism is a method of applying colored dots to the canvas, forming a cumulative design. In modern music the term is descriptive of atonal and athematic idioms, in which separate notes are distributed individually rather than as parts of an integral melorhythmic curve. The maximal dispersion of members of a dodecaphonic series in different octave positions is an example of serial pointillism. This emphasis upon single notes in a serially organized process was brought to fruition by Webern.

points of sound. Determined conglomerations of different sounds synchronized by a controlled simultaneity of individual sounds; the opposite of *groups of sound* (or noises), occurring by chance of an unpremeditated simultaneity of several sound groups resulting from autonomous individual sound actions.

polacca (*pollacca, polonese*; It.). Polonaise. *Alla polacca*, in the style of a polonaise.

polemics. Music theorists are not fighters, and their polemical exchanges are rarely spiced with invectives commonly encountered in political campaigns. Still, there are a few famous battles in music history. One Giovanni Spataro inveighed mightily against the renowned lexicographer Gafurio, calling him a "master of errors." The entire title is worth reproducing: *Dilucide et probatissime demonstratione de Maestro Zoanne Spatario musico bolognese contra certe frivole et vane excusatione da Franchino Gafurio (Maestro de li errori) in luce aducte, Bolgone, 1521* (Lucid and most probative demonstration of Maestro Zoanne Spatario [the name varies], a Bologna musician, against certain frivolous and vain accusations of Franchino Gafurio—master of errors—brought to light). Few scholars could wade through this vast tirade full of superlative degrees of comparison and exclamatory punctuation, but the book remains a characteristic document. Four hundred years after its issuance it was translated and publ. in German.

Of more interest are attacks leveled at Monteverdi by an obscure contemporary, Giovanni Maria Artusi, under the self-asserting title *L'Artusi, ovvero delle imperfettioni della moderna musica*, published in Venice in 1600. Not content to attack Monteverdi, Artusi also shot a fuse against his own teacher, Zarlino, and against Vincenzo Galilei (father of the famous astronomer). Galilei, too, attacked Zarlino for his theory that major and minor triads are mutual mirror reflections of their component major and minor 3rds. Monteverdi dismissed Artusi's attacks in a brief paper entitled *Ottuso accademico* (Obtuse Academician), but apparently was sufficiently nettled to take a glancing blow at his detractors in a preface to one of his books of madrigals.

The famous guerre des bouffons that rent asunder the French musical community in the middle of the 18th century lacked personal attacks and concentrated on the dispute between the adherents of the Italian buffi (that is, comedians) and the proponents of French national opera. King Louis XV and his powerful mistress Madame de Pompadour sided with the French national school, while Rousseau and the encyclopedists, supported by the Queen, favored the melodious and harmonious ways of Italian operas. While Rousseau fulminated against writers of opera in French, a language that he regarded as inferior for singing, he failed to attack the personalities; as a result the whole guerre des bouffons remained a war of abstractions. Eventually the French national school created its own style of opera buffa known as *comédie melée d'ariettes*. A few decades later the Parisians were taking sides on the Gluck vs. Piccinni controversy; but neither composer took sides.

In subsequent centuries 2 types of controversies occurred: those in which the listening public and critics perpetrated, and those between composers. Sometimes the composer battles were indirect: Wagner's greatest critic was a critic, Hanslick, not another composer; Wolf criticized Brahms (after 1st having supported him) on behalf of Wagner, or, more accurately, Wagnerianism, as that composer was deceased; Pfitzner threw diatribes at every composer he could think of who didn't write in his conservative style; Schoenberg and Stravinsky wouldn't speak to one another; Boulez celebrated the death of Schoenberg (metaphorically, one hopes); academic serialists condemned neoromanticists, and vice versa; and for many years virtually everyone else denied that minimalist composers were writing music.

Police, The. (Lead vocal/bass: Gordon Sumner, aka "Sting," b. Wallsend, England, Oct. 2, 1951; guitar: Andrew Summers, b. Poulton-le-Fylde, England, Dec. 31, 1942; drums/vocals: Stewart Copeland, b. Alexandria, Va., July 16, 1952.) The group formed originally in the mid-1970s out of the remains of various minor progressive-rock bands. Schoolteacher and semiprofessional musician Gordon Sumner (known in his youth as "Sting" because he favored a black-and-yellow striped soccer jersey), originally from the Newcastle area, and London-based drummer Stewart Copeland were joined by guitarist Henry Padovani for the group's 1st single in 1976; however, Padovani was soon replaced by American-born, British-raised guitarist Andy Summers, who had previously worked with Soft Machine and the Animals.

Signed to the American A&M label, the group toured the U.S. at their own expense in 1978, achieving their 1st chart recognition here with Sting's song *Roxanne* in early 1979. Their 2nd album sold steadily for 2 years on the American charts, although it produced only a minor hit here, *Message in a Bottle*. However, in 1980 the group broke through big time with *Don't Stand So Close to Me*, followed a year later by *Every Little Thing She Does*

Is Magic, both Sting-penned, rollicking pop songs. The group produced the classic album *Synchronicity* in 1983, showing a diversity of influences from world rhythms to jazz and rock. Critically acclaimed, it proved to be their last effort; Sting pursued a successful acting and solo career, scoring many major hits through the 1980s and 1990s, while Copeland became a successful soundtrack composer and Summers sessioned and recorded on his own.

political tonalities. Major keys are optimistic. Minor keys are pessimistic. This dichotomy dates since the Renaissance, and it was restated with all the power of government by the 1st Commissar of Education of the Soviet Union, Anatoly Lunacharsky, who declared in his introductory speech at a Moscow concert of Dec. 10, 1919:

Major keys possess the characteristics of lifting a sound a semitone. By their exultant sense of joy such sounds elevate the mood; they cheer you up. By contrast, minor keys droop; they lead to a compromise, to a surrender of social positions. Allow me, as an old Bolshevik, to formulate this observation: Major tonalities are Bolshevik music, whereas minor keys are deeply rooted in Menshevik mentality.
Still, Bolsheviks loved the music of Tchaikovsky, even though 85% of his works are set in minor keys. The resolution of this anomaly has been proposed by the learned theorists of the Society of Proletarian Musicians: Workers and peasants enjoy the music of Tchaikovsky because it eloquently celebrates the funeral of the enemy class, the bourgeoisie. Q.E.D.

polka (Bohem. *pulka;* It. *polca*). Lively round dance in 2/4 time, originating about 1830 as a peasant dance in Bohemia, despite a name suggesting Polish origin (polka means a Polish girl). It generated suddenly in Prague in 1847 and almost immediately spread all over Europe. In this process it lost its specific Bohemian characteristics and became a popular salon dance. Johann Strauss wrote a famous *Pizzicato Polka* and many other composers followed suit. Stravinsky wrote a *Circus Polka* for a dance of elephants in an American circus.

polka mazurka. Form of mazurka accommodated to the steps of the polka.

polka schnell. Fast polka; designation used by J. Strauss, Jr. (e.g., *Vergnügungszug,* pleasure train) and others.

Pollini, Maurizio, b. Milan, Jan. 5, 1942. A precocious child, he began piano studies at an early age with Lonati; made his debut at age 9, then studied with Vidusso at the Milan Cons. After sharing 2nd prize in the Geneva Competition in 1958, he took his diploma in piano at the Milan Cons. (1959); also studied with Michelangeli. After capturing 1st prize in the Chopin Competition in Warsaw (1960), he launched an acclaimed career as a virtuoso; appeared throughout Europe as a soloist with the leading orchs. and as a recitalist; made his U.S. debut at N.Y.'s Carnegie Hall (1968). In later years he made appearances as a conductor, leading concerts from the keyboard and also mounting the podium and taking charge in the opera pit. Pollini is a foremost master of the keyboard; he has won deserved renown for making his phenomenal technical resources a means of exploring a vast repertoire, ranging from Bach to the cosmopolitan avant-garde. In 1987 he was awarded the Ehrenring of the Vienna Phil.

pollution. Harmonic pollution is characterized by indiscriminate disposal of chromatic refuse in a diatonic landscape. The process is vividly illustrated by a fetid organ arrangement of Chopin's Nocturne in E-flat Major, in which the initial ascending interval of a major 6th, from B-flat to G, is infested by noxious chromatic runs. A polluted version of Prokofiev's *Peter and the Wolf* has been published in America in the absence of a copyright agreement with the Soviet Union; it is characterized by vulgar insertion of auxiliary material in every available melodic or harmonic vacancy.

Orch'l pollution manifests itself in a general sonic flatulence and an infarction of supernumerary 3rds and 6ths. The rhythmic line, too, is an easy victim of pollution. In the remarkable compound rhythmic design in Gershwin's song *I Got Rhythm,* the original asymmetric line is often grossly mutilated, reducing it to abecedarian syncopation. Erudite arrangements of works of Bach and other classics, made by musicians of intelligence and taste, cannot be cited as examples of musical pollution. Even hyperchromatic pullulation found in some transcriptions by Max Reger possesses validity, though they should be labeled "artificially flavored with chromatic additives."

Some morphological transformations and homeological modifications are legitimate means of modernization. Examples of such artistic enhancement are *Symphonic Metamorphoses on Themes of Carl Maria von Weber* by Hindemith and the ballet *Le Baiser de la Fée* by Stravinsky, imaginatively deformed from themes of Tchaikovsky.

polo (Sp.). Syncopated Spanish dance in triple time, from Andalusia.

polonaise (Fr.; It. *polonese*). Dance of Polish origin, in 3/4 time and moderate tempo; formerly in animated processional style, but now merely a slow promenade opening a ball:

RHYTHM:

LAST MEASURE:

Examples of polonaises are found in instrumental works of Bach, Beethoven, and Schubert, but it was Chopin who elevated the polonaise to the heights of artistry in his piano music.

polska. Paradoxically this dance form, the name of which is the feminine adjective of Poland in the Polish language, corresponding to the French form *polonaise,* is not a Polish but a Swedish dance. The polska must have originated shortly before the 30 Years' War in the 17th century in which Sweden was actively involved. In its domesticated Swedish rhythms the polska resembles the mazurka.

polychoral style (It. *coro spezzato*, broken chorus). Compositional texture in which a chorus is divided into 2, 3, or 4 sections, sung alternately or antiphonally, combined their forces in the finale.

polymeter. Simultaneous use of several different meters. Polymeter dates back to the Renaissance, exemplified in the double time signature of Spanish dance music, 3/4 against 6/8. In operatic usage polymeter is encountered in scenes descriptive of simultaneous uncoordinated action, known under the name imbroglio (It., entanglement). Stravinsky used the technique in *Petrouchka*. Elliott Carter employs metric modulation by changing meter and tempo in polyphonic writing; at the points of modulation, some players would be thinking in the present meter and tempo, while others would be viewing their music in terms of the next meter and tempo. Ben Johnston's *Knocking Piece* for 2 Percussionists and Piano Lid is a tour de force of reinterpreting time and measure virtually measure by measure.

Perhaps the most remarkable instance of contrapuntal polymeter is found in the 2nd movement of *3 Places in New England* by Ives, illustrating the meeting of 2 marching bands, with similar marching tunes played simultaneously at different tempi, in the ratio 4/3, so that 4 bars of the faster march equal 3 bars of the slower tempo. In his original MS, Ives coordinated these different tempos within the uniform measures in 4/4 time, marking cross-accents wherever they occurred. At the suggestion of the author Ives agreed to incorporate in the published score an alternative arrangement with noncoincidental barlines in clear polymetric notation. In his performances of the work the author conducted 3 bars in 4/4 time with his right hand and 4 bars in alla breve time with his left hand. Those in the orch. who had parts with the faster march were to follow the conductor's left hand and the rest his right hand. (A critic remarked that Slonimsky's performance was evangelical, for his right hand knew not what his left hand was doing.)

Among examples of implicit polymetry not marked as such by time signatures is the coda of Schumann's Piano Concerto, where the systematic syncopation in the piano part in 3/4 time results in a polymetric combination of 3/2 in the piano part versus 2 bars of 3/4 in the orch. In Gershwin's *I Got Rhythm*, the implicit polymetry consists of one bar in 2/16 time, 4 bars of 3/16 time, and 1 bar of 2/16 time, adding up to 16/16, that is, 4/4, which is the notated time signature. Sometimes the term *polymetry* is applied, inaccurately, to a succession of different times signatures. The proper term for such usages is changing meters.

polymodality. Polymodality is a special case of polytonality in which the principal melodic lines are modal rather than explicitly major or minor. Polymodal harmonies are disposed with the best effect by the use of a triple pedal point in open harmony in a minor key, suggesting Dorian, Phrygian, or Aeolian constructions.

polyphonic. 1. See ⇒polyphony. 2. Describing an instrument normally capable of producing 2 or more tones simultaneously, like the piano, harp, or organ.

polyphony. The combination in harmonious progression of 2 or more independent melodies; the independent treatment of the parts; counterpoint, in the widest sense. This is a musical term so pregnant with historical and structural signification that it becomes dissolved in its own universality. In the ancient Greek the word bore a derogatory meaning of multivoiced chatter. In a medieval treatise polyphony (from Grk. *poly + phone*, many sounds) is described as "modus canendi a pluribus diversam observantibus melodiam" (a method of singing a diverse melody from many components). In the musical lexicon published by J. G. Walther in 1732, polyphony is defined simply as "a many-voiced composition."

In the 19th century polyphony was identified with counterpoint in which each voice has a destiny of its own, as contrasted with homophony, in which the melody is a dominating part with the rest of the musical fabric subordinated to it harmonically. The dichotomy of polyphony and harmony has been described in geometric terms as horizontal and vertical coordinates of musical composition. The term *linear counterpoint* gained some acceptance in the 20th century to emphasize the prevalent horizontality of polyphonic ingredients. In a polyphonic composition, the individual parts are interdependent and mutually accommodating in forming a euphonious ensemble. Contrapuntal imitation is a polyphonic system par excellence, the fugue being the summit of a polyphonic technique.

The difficulties of writing a double fugue with a 2nd subject being the melodic inversion of the principal theme, or dux, as exemplified in the A-minor fugue of the 1st book of Bach's *Well-Tempered Clavier*, are enormous; that this particular fugue came out with such architectonic splendor is no less an achievement than a mathematical formula that unites the symbols of the base of natural logarithms, an imaginary number and the transcendental number p. Polyphonic trickery, such as revealed in an anonymous 18th-century piece that can be played in perfect harmony by 2 violinists, one reading it right side up and the other upside down, is as legitimate and as consequential a pursuit as a clever mathematical puzzle.

Polyphony attained its culmination with the great works of Bach and went on a decline almost immediately after his death; indeed, the rush toward homophony was led by Bach's sons. In place of "diversity in unity"—the essence of polyphonic composition—the masters of Classic music of the 2nd half of the 18th century and the succeeding 4 generations of Romantic composers made melody paramount and harmony its ancillary coordinate. An artistic development of polyphonic technique was hampered by rigid rules of contrapuntal practice; thus 2nd inversions of triads were forbidden because of the presence of the objectionable perfect 4th between the bass and upper voices; melodic progressions of the augmented 4th, or *tritones*, were deprecated. In Bach's time music students were physically punished by a painful strike of the instructor's cane on the knuckles of the fisted hand for using the tritone. Theorists went to inordinate lengths to account for apparent violations of the rules of strict polyphony by postulating the existence of a putative missing voice. Thus one eminent scholar, confronted with the use of the supertonic 7th chord in a Classic work (not allowed, according to the defenders of the faith), explained it as a dominant-11th chord with a missing bass and 3rd.

In the 20th century Reger revived the art of polyphony with extraordinary success; his teacher, Riemann, told him in all seriousness that he could become a 2nd Bach if he so desired. Reger failed to become a 2nd Bach, but he did produce a large amount of respectable polyphony. The technique of composition with 12 tones related only to one another, as promulgated by Schoenberg, is an avatar of strict polyphony. In this system polyphonic voices are all derived from a single basic theme; both the horizontal and vertical lines—melody and harmony—are coalesced in the governing series of 12 tones. Strict polyphony, in its purely structural aspects, which includes canonic imitation, fugue, and the devices of inversion (retrograde, augmentation, and diminution), is a doctrine scientifically conceived and precisely executed. Polyphony may be an obsolescent art, but in the hands of its greatest practitioners it remains a Gothic wonder of human genius.

polyrhythm. Simultaneous occurrence of several different rhythms. Polyrhythm differs from polymeter in that the former indicates a combination of 2 rhythmic groups, usually consisting of mutually prime numbers of notes or irregular groups of non-coincident patterns (i.e., cross rhythms), while the latter merely indicates the superposition, or a palimpsest, of 2 different meters usually having the same note values as their common denominator. Polyrhythm denotes the simultaneous occurrence of several fundamentally different rhythms, each clearly recognizable through idiosyncratic accents. All polyphonic music entails the use of different rhythms at the same time, but to qualify as polyrhythm such rhythms must be maintained for a considerable number of bars in each individual part. In this sense polyrhythm is the product of new music developed mainly in the 20th century.

The notational aspects of polyrhythmic usage is marked by different rhythmic groups overlapping the barlines. When notated in 8th notes, 16th notes, and smaller divisions, the ligatures cross the barlines. The familiar practice of imbroglio in opera, in which different rhythms are used in different vocal and instrumental parts, does not constitute polyrhythmic usage per se, because the metric units remain independent from one another. Nor does the simultaneous use of 3/4 time and 6/8 time, as is common in Hispanic songs and dances, fit the definition of polyrhythm. It may be argued that the use of triplets, quintuplets, and other odd rhythmical figures against binary rhythms is intrinsically polyrhythmic. One of the most remarkable examples is found in Chopin's *Fantaisie-Impromptu* for Piano, where groups of 4 16th notes in the right hand are accompanied by triplets in the left hand.

polystylistic music. Eclecticism in composition; a term invented by Alfred Schnittke in 1971. Either term may apply either to composers who use different historical or current styles in different works, or to a single piece that exhibits a variety of aesthetics.

polytetrachord. Term introduced by the author in his *Thesaurus of Scales and Melodic Patterns*, the polytetrachord is omnitonal. A major polytetrachord consists of 12 conjunct major tetrachords, traversing all 12 keys of the cycle of major scales. A minor polytetrachord consists of 12 keys of the cycle of minor scales. A partial use of the polytetrachord affords a rapid linear modulation into any major or minor key.

polytonality. Polytonality is the simultaneous use of several keys. In actual practice it is difficult to sustain the acoustical

separation of more than 2 different keys, thus reducing polytonality to bitonality. Four mutually exclusive triads are workable in linear arpeggios (e.g., C major, F-sharp major, D minor, and G-sharp minor distributed in ascending quadritonal passages), but the same 4 keys in columnar superposition could be made effective only by careful differentiation of instrumental groups (e.g., C major in the strings, F-sharp major in muted horns, D minor in clarinets and oboes, and G-sharp minor in flutes and piccolos, with optional support of the strings by the bassoons and contrabassoons).

Approximations of polytonality, or rather bitonality, can be found in the fairly frequent instances of near synchronization of the lowered supertonic 1st inversion chord ($\flat$II^6) with the dominant triad in a Neapolitan cadence. In this coupling 2 triadic harmonies, having their tonics at the distance of a tritone, collide with a curiously euphonious effect. Stravinsky formalized this polytonal usage in the score of his ballet *Petrouchka*, in which the triads of C major and F-sharp major coagulate in close proximity. More explicitly, Milhaud used the same combination in the score of his ballet *Le Boeuf sur le toit*. Strictly speaking, however, this bitonal usage does not constitute integral polytonality, which demands the use of simultaneous combinations of 4 different triads, aggregating to all available notes of the tempered scale. It is entirely possible, of course, to arrange an integral panchromatic chord containing all 12 notes of the tempered scale in groups that would spell out all 24 major and minor triads and assign such triads to different instrumental groups so as to make them stand out individually, but the separation of the triadic groupings may be acoustically difficult.

An amusing example of polytonality is Mozart's *Ein musikalischer Spass*, where he makes the horns play in different keys from the rest of the orch. But Mozart's professed intention in this "musical joke" was to ridicule the ignorance of village musicians. He could not have anticipated the time when such musical jokes would become a new technique.

polytriads. Polytriadic harmony may be regarded as a special case of polytonality, with mobile parts containing complete triads. If the triads move along a single scale or a mode, the resulting technique is polymodality. Homonymous triads, major and minor, encased within the compass of a perfect 5th (e.g., C, E$\flat$, En, G), are often found in modern works. Such polytriads are *e duobus unum*, giving rise to modes possessing the characteristics of both major and minor keys.

Pommer (Ger.). Bass shawm, now obsolete.

Pomp, mit (Ger.). Solemnly.

pompe (Fr.). 1. Trombone slide. 2. Additional tubing inserted in natural brass instruments.

pomposo (It.). Pompously, loftily; in a majestic, dignified style.

Ponce, Manuel (Maria), b. Fresnillo, Dec. 8, 1882; d. Mexico City, Apr. 24, 1948. He studied piano with his older sister; in 1904 he went to Europe, where he took lessons in composition with Enrico Bossi at Bologna and in piano with Martin Krause in Berlin. Upon his return to Mexico he taught piano at the Mexico City Cons. (1909–15). He gave a concert of his compositions in Mexico City in 1912, which included a piano concerto. During World War I he lived in N.Y. and in Havana; then went to Paris for additional study and took lessons with Paul Dukas. His contact with French music wrought a radical change in his style of composition; his later works are more polyphonic in structure and more economical in form.

Ponce possessed a great gift of melody; one of his songs, *Estrellita* (1914), became a universal favorite and was often mistaken for a folk song. In 1941 he made a tour in South America, conducting his own works. He was the 1st Mexican composer of the 20th century to employ an identifiably modern musical language; his contributions to the guitar and orch. repertoire are substantial; his place in the history of Mexican music is a very important one. His works are often performed in Mexico; a concert hall was named after him in the Inst. de Bellas Artes.

Ponchielli, Amilcare, b. Paderno Fasolaro, near Cremona, Aug. 31, 1834; d. Milan, Jan. 15, 1886. He studied with his father, a shopkeeper and organist at the village church; entered the Milan Cons. as a nonpaying student when he was 9; his mentors included Pietro Ray (theory), Arturo Angeleri (piano), Felice Frasi (composition), and Alberto Mazzucato (music history, esthetics, and composition); while a student there he collaborated on the operetta *Il sindaco babbeo* (Milan Cons., Mar. 1851); also wrote the sym. *Scena campestre* (1852). After his graduation (1854) he went to Cremona as a church organist; he was named assistant to Ruggero Manna, director of Cremona's Teatro Concordia (1855), where he brought out his opera *I promessi sposi* (Aug. 30, 1856). He was conductor of the municipal bands in Piacenza (1861–64) and Cremona (from 1864), where he also conducted opera; he continued to pursue his interest in composing for the theater. He finally achieved notable success with the revised version of his *I promessi sposi* (Milan, Dec. 4, 1872), which was subsequently performed throughout Italy; his *La Gioconda* (Milan, Apr. 8, 1876) secured his reputation.

Ponchielli was prof. of composition at the Milan Cons. in 1880 and again from 1881; he also served as maestro di cappella at Bergamo's S. Maria Maggiore (1881–86). He married the soprano Teresina Brambilla in 1874. His birthplace was renamed Paderno Ponchielli in his honor. *La Gioconda* remains his only work to have acquired repertoire status; it includes the famous ballet number *Dance of the Hours*. In addition to his numerous stage works, he composed many band pieces, vocal chamber music, chamber works, and piano pieces.

ponderoso (It.). Ponderous; in a vigorous, impressive style.

ponticello (It.). Bridge. *Sul ponticello*, near the bridge.

pop(ular) music. General term to denote a wide variety of musical styles, generally characterized by their easy accessibility to wide audiences; usually of modest length, with prominent and memorable melodies and a simple, unassuming harmonic language. Definitions and sources for popular music are broad and plentiful, from Tin Pan Alley to musicals, Anglo-Irish traditional to country-western, blues to soul, classical to environmental urban sound; in the last quarter of the 20th century, influences from around the world have become primary. The term *popular music* can only be interpreted as music with a commercial aspect, unlike authentic indigenous music; in this sense it holds a social position similar to most classical music, which has also had a monetary goal in most cases, as opposed to folk music. To a classical audience, "popular" may seem vulgar, downgraded, repellant, lethal, and socially divisive; but that suggests an inability or unwillingness to hear the multitude of difference in the many kinds of popular music; it is perfectly analogous to those who would listen to classical music and declare that it all sounds the same.

pornographic music. It was Hanslick who said that the last movement of Tchaikovsky's Violin Concerto suggested to him the hideous notion that music can actually stink to the ear. The literal depiction of an episode in *Symphonia domestica* by R. Strauss, which illustrates his retirement to the bed chamber with Frau Strauss, to the suggestive accompaniment of 2 conjugated trumpets, impressed some listeners at its 1st performance as indecent. In a symphonic interlude in Shostakovich's opera *Lady Macbeth of the District of Mtzensk*, with the marital bed occupying the center of the stage, the trombone glissandi seem to give an onomatopoeic representation of sexual intercourse. Graphic notation offers excellent opportunities for suggestive pictorial pornography. The tetraphallic score *Mooga Pook* by the American composer Charles Amirkhanian is a fine example.

portale la voce (It., carry the voice; Fr. *port de voix*). Sing portamento.

portamento (It.). Smooth gliding from one tone to another, differing from the legato in its more deliberate execution and in the actual (though very rapid and slurring) sounding of the intermediate tones.

portando (It., carrying). Play portamento. *Portando la voce*, vocal portamento.

portative. Small portable organ which could be used in religious processions.

portato (It., carried; Fr. *louré*). Articulation on bowed chordophones lying between legato and staccato; component notes are separated while preserving the feeling of continuity.

Porter, Cole (Albert), b. Peru, Ind., June 9, 1891; d. Santa Monica, Calif., Oct. 15, 1964. He was educated at Yale Univ. (B.A., 1913); then took academic courses at Harvard Law School and later at the Harvard School of Music (1915–16); also received instruction in counterpoint, composition, orchestration, and harmony from d'Indy at the Paris Schola Cantorum (1919). While at Yale he wrote football songs (*Yale Bull Dog Song, Bingo Eli Yale*, etc.); also composed music for college functions. He 1st gained success as a composer for the stage with his *Wake Up and Dream* (London, 1929); his 1st production in N.Y. was *See America First* (1916). There followed a cascade of musical comedies for which he wrote both the lyrics and the music, which placed him in the front rank of the American musical theater. His greatest success came with his musical comedy *Kiss Me, Kate*, after Shakespeare's *The Taming of the Shrew* (N.Y., 1948). A motion picture musical biography of Porter, starring Cary Grant, was produced by Warner Bros. in 1946 as *Night and Day*.

Porter was a master of subtle expression without sentimentality, a kinetic dash without vulgarity, and a natural blend of word poetry with the finest of harmonious melodies. Among his other musicals are (all are musicals 1st perf. in N.Y.): *Fifty Million Frenchmen* (1929); *Gay Divorce* (1932); *Anything Goes* (1934); *Jubilee* (1935); *Red Hot and Blue* (1936); *Du Barry was a Lady* (1939); *Panama Hattie* (1940); *Something for the Boys* (1943); *Mexican Hayride* (1944); *Kiss Me, Kate* (1948); *Out of This World* (1950); *Can-Can* (1953); *Silk Stockings* (1955); etc. Of his many songs at least half a dozen became great favorites: *Begin the Beguine; It's De-Lovely; Night and Day; My Heart Belongs to Daddy; Don't Fence Me In; Wunderbar*. He also composed numerous film scores, including *Rosalie* (1937), *You'll Never Get Rich* (1941), *Les Girls* (1957), and *Aladdin* (1958).

posato (It.). Sedate, dignified.

Posaune (Ger.). Trombone. Also, a reed stop in the organ, of 8' (manuals) or 16' (pedal) pitch.

pose de la voix (Fr.). Attack the vocal tone with precise articulation.

positif (Fr.). Choir organ.

position. 1. Place of the left hand on the fingerboard of the violin, etc. In the 1st position the forefinger stops the tone (or semitone) above the open string; by shifting up, so that the 1st finger takes the place previously occupied by the 2nd, the 2nd position is reached, and so on. In the half position the 2nd, 3rd, and 4th fingers occupy the places taken in the 1st position by the 1st, 2nd, and 3rd fingers. 2. The arrangement of notes in a chord, with reference to the lowest part; in the 1st, or fundamental position, the lowest part takes the root; in the 2nd it takes the 3rd, etc. 3. Close (open) position, see ⇒harmony, *close* and *open*.

positive organ (Ger. *Positiv*). Medieval portable organ with a single manual and no pedal. To operate the bellows that pumped air into the pipes, an assistant was required. It was often used at the homes of pious church musicians and parishioners.

possibile (It.). Possible. *Pianissimo possibile,* as soft as possible; *il più presto possibile,* as rapid as possible.

post horn. Horn without valves or keys, used on post coaches. The sound of the post horn was associated with departure, sorrowful or joyful; Beethoven used such an association in his *Les Adieux* piano sonata, where the opening post horn call is sounded in the descending cadence known as horn fifths.

posthumous works. The expression is barbaric, for how can a work occur after the death of its author? The dictionaries give a 2nd definition as "published after death." Other definitions of posthumous works are those that have been discovered after the composer's death. But what about a work that has been played numerous times during the composer's lifetime but was published only after his death?

This distinction is so important that it led to numerous debates about the nature of the federal copyright law, and at least to 1 serious lawsuit, brought by Peter Bartók, son of Béla Bartók,

against the composer's publishers Boosey and Hawkes in 1973, concerning the renewal of the copyright of Bartók's *Concerto for Orchestra*. As a rule a copyrighted work must be renewed after 28 years. Both Peter Bartók and the publishers applied for the renewal of the copyright. The U.S. Copyright Office declined to decide who had the right to have the copyright renewed. Since the *Concerto for Orchestra* was published after the composer's death in 1945, the publishers claimed the right to renew the copyright, but Peter Bartók asserted his right as the lawful heir to his father's estate and declared that the work in question was performed several times during his father's life and therefore could not be regarded as posthumous. The judge ruled in favor of the publishers, basing his findings on the specific meaning that the word posthumous conveys in regard to works published after the composer's death, and cited the usage of the word accepted since the middle of the 19th century, with a specific reference to many "posthumous" works by Chopin, referring to a Chopin work that was published as a posthumous opus in 1855, 6 years after his death, although it had been written in 1828 and 1st performed in 1830. He ruled, therefore, that since the definition of the word in the field of music applied for more than a century to any composition published after the death of its composer, Boosey and Hawkes had the right to renew the copyright.

postlude. 1. Closing voluntary on the organ. 2. Refrain.

postmodernism. See ⇒modernism.

potpourri (*mélange, méslange;* Fr., rotten pot; It. *mescolanza*). Musical medley exhibiting a motley variety of unrelated refrains and fragments connected in an arbitrary manner. In an enlarged sense *potpourri* was used by music publishers—particularly in Germany—for any collection of favorite arias or instrumental pieces; the word did not acquire its somewhat derogatory meaning until much later. But modern composers of the neoclassical persuasion revived the genre of potpourri in a nostalgically attractive manner, as a series of disconnected musical sketches.

Poulenc, Francis (Jean Marcel), b. Paris, Jan. 7, 1899; d. there, Jan. 30, 1963. His mother taught him music in his childhood; at 16 he began taking formal piano lessons with Ricardo Viñes. A decisive turn in his development as a composer occurred when he attracted the attention of Satie, the *arbiter elegantiarum* of the arts and social amenities in Paris. Deeply impressed by Satie's fruitful eccentricities in the then-shocking manner of dadaism, Poulenc joined an ostentatiously self-descriptive musical group called the Nouveaux Jeunes. In a gratuitous parallel with the Russian 5, the French critic Henri Collet renamed the "New Youths" *Le Groupe de 6,* and the label stuck under the designation Les Six. The 6 musicians included, besides Poulenc, were Auric, Durey, Honegger, Milhaud, and Tailleferre. Although quite different in their styles of composition and artistic inclinations, they continued collective participation in various musical events. Poulenc served in the French army (1918–21) and then began taking lessons in composition with Koechlin (1921–24). An excellent pianist, Poulenc became in 1935 an accompanist to the French baritone Pierre Bernac, for whom he wrote numerous songs.

Compared with his fortuitous comrades-in-6, Poulenc appears a classicist. He never experimented with the popular devices of "machine music," asymmetrical rhythms, and polyharmonies as cultivated by Honegger and Milhaud. Futuristic projections had little interest for him; he was content to follow the gentle neo-classical formation of Ravel's piano music and songs. Among his other important artistic contacts was the ballet impresario Diaghilev, who commissioned him to write music for his Ballets Russes. Apart from his fine songs and piano pieces, Poulenc revealed himself as an inspired composer of religious music, of which his choral works *Stabat Mater* and *Gloria* are notable. He also wrote remarkable music for the organ, including a concerto that became a minor masterpiece. A master of artificial simplicity he pleases even sophisticated listeners by his bland triadic tonalities spiced with quickly passing diaphanous discords.

Pound, Ezra (Loomis), b. Hailey, Idaho, Oct. 30, 1885; d. Venice, Nov. 1, 1972. He was educated at Hamilton College (Ph.B., 1905) and the Univ. of Pa. (M.A., 1906). He went to England, where he established himself as a leading experimental poet and influential critic. He also pursued a great interest in early music, especially that of the troubadours, which led him to try his hand at composing. With the assistance of George Antheil he composed the opera *Le Testament*, after poems by François Villon (1923; Paris, 1926); it was followed by a 2nd opera, *Calvacanti* (1932), and a 3rd, left unfinished, based on the poetry of Catullus. In 1924 he settled in Rapallo. Although married to Dorothy Shakespear, daughter of one of Yeats's friends, he became intimate with the American violinist Olga Rudge; Rudge bore him a daughter in 1925 and his wife bore him a son in 1926. Through the influence of Rudge, his interest in music continued and he became a fervent champion of Vivaldi; he also worked as a music reviewer and ran a concert series with Rudge, "Inverno Musicale."

A growing interest in economic history and an inordinate admiration for the Fascist dictator Benito Mussolini led Pound down the road of political obscurantism. During World War II he made many broadcasts over Rome Radio on topics ranging from literature to politics. His condemnation of Jewish banking circles in America and the American effort to defeat Fascism led to his arrest by the Allies after the collapse of Il Duce's regime. In 1945 he was sent to a prison camp in Pisa. In 1946 he was sent to the U.S. to stand trial for treason, but he was declared insane and confined to St. Elizabeth's Hospital in Washington, D.C. Finally in 1958 he was released and allowed to return to Italy, where he died.

Among Pound's writings on music is his *Antheil and the Treatise on Harmony* (1924). He also composed several works for solo violin for Rudge, including *Fiddle Music* (1924) and *Al poco giorno* (Berkeley, 1983); he also arranged Gaucelm Faidit's *Plainte pour la mort du roi Richart Coeur de Lion*. The uncatalogued collection of Pound's musical MSS at Yale Univ. includes various musical experiments, including rhythmic and melodic realizations of his poem *Sestina: Altaforte*. Among the composers who have set his poems to music are Copland, Luytens, and Berio.

poussé (Fr.). Up-bow.

Pousseur, Henri (Léon Marie Thérèse), b. Malmédy, June 23, 1929. He studied at the Liège Cons. (1947–52) and the Brussels Cons. (1952–53); had private lessons in composition

from André Souris and Pierre Boulez; until 1959, worked in the Cologne and Milan electronic music studios, where he came in contact with Stockhausen and Berio; was a member of the avant-garde group of composers "Variation" in Liège. He taught music in various Belgian schools (1950–59); was founder (1958) and director of the Studio de Musique Électronique APELAC in Brussels, from 1970 a part of the Centre de Recherches Musicales in Liège; gave lectures at the summer courses of new music in Darmstadt (1957–67), Cologne (1966–68), Basel (1963–64), the State Univ. of N.Y. in Buffalo (1966–69), and the Liège Cons. (from 1970), where he became director in 1975.

In his music Pousseur tries to synthesize all the expressive powers of which man, as a biological species *Homo sapiens*, is capable in the domain of art (or nonart); the technological resources of the subspecies *Homo habilis* (magnetic tape, electronics/synthesizers, aleatory extensions, the principle of indeterminacy, glossolalia, self-induced schizophasia) all form part of his rich musical (or nonmusical) vocabulary for multimedia (or nullimedia) representations. The influence of his methods (or nonmethods) of composition (or noncomposition) is pervasive.

Powell, "Bud" (Earl), b. N.Y., Sept. 27, 1924; d. there, Aug. 1, 1966. After dropping out of school at age 15 he began playing piano with local groups in N.Y. Following the zeitgeist, he adopted the bop style, and in 1943 he joined Cootie Williams and his band; he also played concerts with Dizzy Gillespie, Sid Catlett, and John Kirby, achieving recognition as a fine bop pianist. He was a frequent participant in the formative jazz sessions at Minton's Playhouse. He gradually discarded the prevalent "stride" piano style, with its regular beat, and emancipated the left-hand rhythm by introducing a contrapuntal line with asymmetrical punctuation. His brief career was periodically interrupted by mental eclipses caused by immoderate use of hallucinogenic drugs.

pp. Pianissimo.

ppp. Pianississimo.

Prächtig (Ger.). Grandly, majestically.

Praeconium paschale (Lat., Paschal sermon). Roman Catholic Easter hymn sung on Holy Saturday.

præludium (*praeambulum*; Lat.; Fr. *préambule*). Prelude.

Praetorius, Michael, b. Creuzburg an der Werra, Thuringia, Feb. 15, 1571; d. Wolfenbüttel, Feb. 15, 1621. He studied with Michael Voigt, the cantor of the Torgau Lateinschule; in 1582 he entered the Univ. of Frankfurt an der Oder; in 1584 he continued his studies at the Lateinschule in Zerbst, Anhalt. From 1587 to 1590 he was organist of St. Marien in Frankfurt. In 1595 he entered the service of Duke Heinrich Julius of Braunschweig-Wolfenbüttel as an organist; in 1604 he also assumed the duties of court Kapellmeister. Upon the death of his patron in 1613, the Elector Johann Georg of Saxony obtained his services as deputy Kapellmeister at the Dresden court. He retained his Dresden post until 1616 and then resumed his duties in Wolfenbüttel.

Praetorius devoted only a part of his time to Wolfenbüttel, for he had been named Kapellmeister to the administrator of the Magdeburg bishopric and prior of the monastery at Ringelheim in 1614. He also traveled a great deal, visiting various German cities. These factors, coupled with a general decline in his health, led to the decision not to reappoint him to his Wolfenbüttel post in 1620. He died the following year a wealthy man. Deeply religious, he directed that the greater portion of his fortune go to organizing a foundation for the poor.

Praetorius was one of the most important and prolific German composers of his era. His *Musae Sioniae*, a significant collection of over 1,200 settings of Lutheran chorales, is a particularly valuable source for hymnology. He also published collections of motets, psalms, sacred songs, madrigals, bicinia and tricinia, litanies, works with bass continuo, and a collection of French instrumental dances under the title *Terpsichore, musarum aoniarum quinta a 4–6* (1612).

Praetorius is even better known for his *Syntagma musicum*, publ. in 3 vols. as follows: *Syntagmatis musici tomus primus* (Wittenberg and Wolfenbüttel, 1614–15), a historical and descriptive treatise in Latin on ancient and ecclesiastical music and ancient secular instruments; *Syntagmatis musici tomus secundus* (Wolfenbüttel, 1618; with an appendix, *Theatrum instrumentorum*, Wolfenbüttel, 1620), in German, a most important source of information on musical instruments of the period, describing their form, compass, tone quality, etc.; the organ is treated at great length, and the appendix contains 42 woodcuts of the principal instruments enumerated; *Syntagmatis musici tomus tertius* (Wolfenbüttel, 1618), is a valuable and interesting account of secular composition of the period, with a treatise on solmisation, notation, etc.

Pralltriller (Ger.). Upper mordent, repeated multiple times.

Pratella, Francesco Balilla. See ⇒futurism.

präzis (Ger.). Precise.

precedente (It.). Preceding. *Moto precedente*, in the preceding tempo.

precentor. Director and manager of a choir, and of musical services in general; in the Anglican Church, 2nd in rank to the deacon.

precipitando (*precipitoso*; It.). With precipitation, impetuosity, dash.

preciso (It.). With precision.

precocity. Music is a gift that is revealed at a very early age; virtually all professional musicians were child prodigies. Among those who achieved greatness was Mozart, whose father even exhibited him at the courts of Europe as a wonder child (and slyly diminished his age by a year in his public announcements of young Mozart's presentations). Saint-Saëns amazed the French public by performing concerts at age 10. A younger contemporary of Saint-Saëns, Emile Paladilhe, also showed an astonishing talent as a very young Paris conservatory pupil, but in the course of time he settled into the easy chair of oblivion. On the other side of the coin, many great composers did not shine brilliantly at the beginnings of their careers, most of them because they did not play an instrument with any degree of virtuosity. The names of Wagner, Verdi, Berlioz, Schumann, Tchaikovsky, Rimsky-Korsakov, Stravinsky, Debussy, and Ravel belong in this category. None of them were ever *Wunderkinder.*

Singers are never child prodigies simply because they have to reach physical maturity before they can perform in public. The most precocious conductor was Willy Ferrero, who led concerts at age 8, arousing amazement wherever he gave his exhibitions. He ended his career as a conductor of a provincial Italian opera house. The American conductor Lorin Maazel, who appeared at the N.Y. World's Fair in 1939 at age 9, aroused guarded skepticism (1 orch. musician wondered whether the next guest conductor would be a trained seal), but he overcame his extraordinary precocity and eventually became a successful sym. conductor.

pregando (It.). Imploring, beseeching.

preghiera (It.). Prayer.

prelude (from Lat. *praeludium*, preplay; Fr. *prélude*; It. *preludio*; Ger. *Vorspiel*). Musical introduction to a large work or fugue; also, an independent composition. The earliest instrumental preludes correspond to the etymological signification of the term; they consisted usually of introductory chords and arpeggios and a brief melody with a homophonic accompaniment. During the Baroque period preludes served as introductions to an instrumental suite, usually for piano or organ. The most famous introductory preludes are those paired with fugues in Bach's *Well-Tempered Clavier*, each in the key of the fugue that follows. In the 19th century, however, the prelude emancipated itself and became an independent form. Chopin's *Preludes* for piano are not preambles to anything, but self-sufficient compositions.

Debussy, Rachmaninoff, and Scriabin followed Chopin in fashioning their own piano preludes. The opening Promenade in Mussorgsky's piano suite *Pictures at an Exhibition* is of the nature of a prelude; similar "promenades" are interposed between numbers in the rest of this suite, where they assume the role of interludes. The antonym of the prelude is the postlude. In Hindemith's piano suite *Ludus Tonalis*, the postlude is the physical inversion of the prelude, obtained by playing the pages of the prelude upside-down and adjusting the accidentals.

premiere (from Fr. *Première audition*, 1st hearing). 1st performance of a musical (or other) work. In Europe the premiere of a large work is often preceded by a répétition générale (dress rehearsal) to which press and dignitaries are invited.

preparation. 1. Preparation of a dissonance consists in the presence, in the preceding chord and same part, of the tone forming the dissonance. 2. Insertion of screws, nuts, bolts, etc., under the strings of a grand piano, in accord with instructions contained in the score and in advance of the performance of a work for prepared piano.

prepared piano. Instrument whose timbre is altered by placing such objects as screws, bolts, nuts, metal paperclips, coins, safety pins, clothespins, cardboard, rubber wedges, wires, pencil erasers, metal strips, and virtually anything that can be attached or placed between, on top of, or below the strings of a grand piano. The idea may be traced to the old schoolboy trick of putting a piece of paper on the piano strings to produce a tinkling, harpsichordlike sound. Cage invented the term in the early 1940s; the results produce buzzing effects, muting, and resonance. Cage's *Sonatas and Interludes* (1946–48), a major work for prepared piano, was performed in 1949 in Carnegie Hall; the work earned him awards from both the Guggenheim Foundation and the National Institute of Arts and Letters, for "having thus extended the boundaries of musical art."

Presley, Elvis (Aron), b. Tupelo, Miss., Jan. 8, 1935; d. Memphis, Tenn., Aug. 16, 1977. He was employed as a mechanic and furniture repairman in his early youth; picked up guitar playing in his leisure hours; sang cowboy ballads at social gatherings. With the advent of rock 'n' roll he revealed himself as the supreme genius of the genre; almost effortlessly he captivated multitudes of adolescents by the hallucinogenic consistency of his vocal delivery, enhanced by rhythmic pelvic gyrations (hence the invidious appellation "Elvis the Pelvis"); made recordings that sold millions of albums. He made America conscious of the seductive quality of rock 'n' roll tunes; he aroused primitive urges among his multitudinous admirers with his renditions of such songs, among them *Don't Be Cruel, Hound Dog, Love Me Tender, All Shook Up, Jailhouse Rock, Heartbreak Hotel, Rock around the Clock, It's Now or Never;* his audience responded by improvising songs about him: *My Boy Elvis, I Wanna Spend Christmas with Elvis,* and *Elvis for President.* He also appeared as an actor in sentimental motion pictures, and served in the U.S. Army in Germany.

Presley's art was an important inspiration for the famous Liverpudlian quartet the Beatles. An International Elvis Presley Appreciation Society was organized by 1970. Presley was indeed the King of Kings of rock. His death (of cardiac arrhythmia aggravated by an immoderate use of tranquilizers and other drugs) precipitated the most extraordinary outpouring of public grief over an entertainment figure since the death of Rudolph Valentino. His entombment in the family mausoleum in Memphis was the scene of mob hysteria, during which 2 people were run over and killed by an automobile; 2 men were arrested for an alleged plot to spirit away his body and hold it for ransom. In the early '90s the U.S. post office held an informal contest to determine whether their customers preferred the young or old Elvis to grace a postage stamp; youthful Elvis beat out the bloated Vegas denizen hands down. The stamp proved to be one of the all-time best sellers in postal history.

pressando (It.; Fr. *pressez*). Pressing onward, accelerating.

Pressler, Menahem, b. Magdeburg, Dec. 16, 1923. He was taken to Palestine by his family after the Hitlerization of Germany; he studied piano with Eliah Rudiakow and Leo Kestenberg; then played with the Palestine Sym. Orch. In 1946 he won the Debussy Prize at the piano competition in San Francisco. In 1955 he became a member of the School of Music at Indiana Univ.; that year he became pianist in the Beaux Arts Trio, with which he made numerous tours; he also continued his career as a soloist.

prestamente (It.). Rapidly.

prestissimo (It.). Very rapidly.

presto (It.). Fast, rapid; faster than *allegro. Presto assai,* extremely rapid; *presto parlante,* a direction in recitatives meaning to "speak" rapidly.

Previn, André (George) (born Andreas Ludwig Priwin), b. Berlin, Apr. 6, 1929. He showed an unmistakable musical gift as a child; his father, a lawyer, was an amateur musician who gave him his early training; they played piano, 4-hands, together at home. At age 6 he was accepted as a pupil at the Berlin Hochschule für Musik, where he studied piano with Prof. Breithaupt; as a Jew, however, he was compelled to leave school in 1938. The family then went to Paris; he continued his studies at the Paris Cons., Marcel Dupré being one of his teachers.

In 1939 the family emigrated to America, settling in Los Angeles, where his father's cousin, Charles Previn, was music director at Universal Studios in Hollywood. He took lessons in composition with Joseph Achron, Ernst Toch, and Mario Castelnuovo-Tedesco. He became an American citizen in 1943. Even before graduating from high school he obtained employment at MGM; he became an orchestrator there and later one of its music directors; he also became a fine jazz pianist. He served in the U.S. Army (1950–52); stationed in San Francisco, he took lessons in conducting with Pierre Monteux, who was music director of the San Francisco Sym. Orch. at the time. During these years he wrote much music for films; he received Academy Awards for his arrangements of *Gigi* (1958), *Porgy and Bess* (1959), *Irma la Douce* (1963), and *My Fair Lady* (1964). Throughout this period he continued to appear as a concert pianist. In 1962 he made his formal conducting debut with the St. Louis Sym. Orch.; conducting soon became his principal vocation.

From 1967 to 1969 Previn was conductor-in-chief of the Houston Sym. Orch. In 1968 he assumed the post of principal conductor of the London Sym. Orch., retaining it with distinction until 1979; then was made its conductor emeritus. In 1976 he became music director of the Pittsburgh Sym. Orch., a position he held with similar distinction until a dispute with the management led to his resignation in 1984. He had already been engaged as music director of the Royal Phil. Orch. of London in 1982, a position he held from 1985 to 1987; he then served as its principal conductor. Previn also accepted appointment as music director of the Los Angeles Phil. Orch. after resigning his Pittsburgh position; he formally assumed his duties in Los Angeles in 1985 but gave up this position in 1990 after disagreements with the management over administrative procedures.

During his years as a conductor of the London Sym. Orch. Previn took it on a number of tours to the U.S., as well as to Russia, Japan, South Korea, and Hong Kong. He also took the Pittsburgh Sym. Orch. on acclaimed tours of Europe in 1978 and 1982. He continued to compose popular music, including the scores for the musicals *Coco* (1969) and *The Good Companions* (1974); with words by Tom Stoppard, he composed *Every Good Boy Deserves Favour* (1977), a work for actors and orch. He also wrote orch. works, piano pieces, and songs. He ed. the book *Orchestra* (1979); also publ. *Andre Previn's Guide to Music* (1983). He was married 4 times (and divorced thrice): to the jazz singer Betty Bennett, to the jazz poet Dory Langdon (who made a career of her own as composer and singer of pop songs), to the actress Mia Farrow, and in 1982 to Heather Hales.

Prey, Hermann, b. Berlin, July 11, 1929. He studied with Günther Baum and Harry Gottschalk at the Berlin Hochschule für Musik; won 1st prize in a vocal competition organized by the U.S. Army in 1952, and that same year made his operatic debut as the 2nd prisoner in Fidelio in Wiesbaden. After appearing in the U.S. he joined the Hamburg State Opera (1953); also sang in Vienna (from 1956), Berlin (from 1956), and in Salzburg (from 1959). In 1959 he became a principal member of the Bavarian State Opera in Munich; made his Metropolitan Opera debut in N.Y. as Wolfram (1960); appeared for the 1st time in England at the Edinburgh Festival (1965), and later sang regularly at London's Covent Garden (from 1973). He also appeared as a soloist with the major orchs. and as a recitalist; likewise starred in his own Munich television show. In 1982 he became a prof. at the Hamburg Hochschule für Musik. Among his finest operatic roles are Count Almaviva, Papageno, Guglielmo, and Rossini's Figaro; he also sang a number of contemporary roles. As a lieder artist he distinguished himself in works by Schubert, Schumann, and Brahms.

Prez, Josquin des. Desprez (Des Prez), Josquin.

pribautki (Rus.). Quick-rhymed refrain or couplet. Stravinsky set 4 of them for voice and a few instruments in 1914.

Price, (Mary Violet) Leontyne, b. Laurel, Miss., Feb. 10, 1927. She was taught piano by a local woman and also learned to sing. She went to Oak Park High School, graduating in music in 1944; she then enrolled in the College of Education and Industrial Arts in Wilberforce, Ohio, where she studied voice with Catherine Van Buren; received her B.A. degree in 1948, then was awarded a scholarship at the Juilliard School of Music in N.Y.; there she took vocal training from Florence Page Kimball and joined the Opera Workshop under the direction of Frederic Cohen. Virgil Thomson heard her perform the role of Mistress Ford in Verdi's *Falstaff* and invited her to sing in the revival of his opera *4 Saints in 3 Acts* in 1952. She subsequently performed the role of Bess on a tour of the U.S. (1952–54) and in Europe (1955).

In 1954 Price made a highly acclaimed debut as a concert singer in N.Y.; later that year she sang at the 1st performance of Barber's *Prayers of Kierkegaard* with the Boston Sym. Orch., conducted by Munch. In 1955 she performed Tosca on television, creating a sensation both as an artist and as an African-American taking up the role of an Italian diva. Her career was soon assured without any reservations. In 1957 she appeared with the San Francisco Opera; later that year she sang Aida, a role congenial to her passionate artistry. In 1958 she sang Aida with the Vienna State Opera under the direction of Karajan; on July 2, 1958, she sang this role at Covent Garden in London; and again as Aida she appeared at La Scala in Milan in 1959, the 1st black woman to sing with that most prestigious and most fastidious opera company.

In 1961 Price made her 1st appearance with the Metropolitan Opera in N.Y. in the role of Leonora in *Il Trovatore*. A series of highly successful performances at the Metropolitan followed: Aida, Madama Butterfly, Donna Anna (all 1961); Tosca (1962); Pamina (1964). She created the role of Cleopatra in the premiere of Barber's *Antony and Cleopatra* at the opening of the new Metropolitan Opera House at Lincoln Center in N.Y. (1966). In 1973 she sang Madame Butterfly at the Metropolitan once

more. In 1975 she appeared there in the title role of Manon Lescaut; and she sang Aida, a role she repeated for her farewell operatic performance in a televised production broadcast live from the Metropolitan Opera by PBS (1985). She then continued her concert career, appearing with notable success in the major music centers.

Price was married in 1952 to the baritone William Warfield (who sang Porgy at her performances of *Porgy and Bess*) but separated from him in 1959; they were divorced in 1973. She received many honors during her remarkable career; in 1964 President Johnson bestowed upon her the Medal of Freedom, and in 1985 President Reagan presented her with the National Medal of Arts.

Pride, Charley, b. near Sledge, Miss., Mar. 18, 1938. He learned to play the guitar, but, bent on a career in baseball, he played in the minor leagues (1954–64); also tried his luck as a singer. He subsequently appeared with the Grand Ole Opry in Nashville, becoming the 1st black country-music singer to gain admission to this shrine of populist entertainment.

prima (It.). See ⇒primo.

prima donna (It., 1st lady). Leading soprano in opera, be it in a particular role or as a public figure to be worshipped. *Prima donna assoluta* is an absolute prima donna superior to the *seconda donna* or *prima donna altra*. The cult of the prima donna reached its height in the 19th century. A typical prima donna was an amply bosomed Italian or German soprano possessing great lung power. The chronicles of opera are replete with tales about temperamental prima donnas engaging in fistfights and flights of invective with other prima donnas over the size of lettering in their names on theatrical posters, the space allocated in their private rooms at the opera house, the extent of publicity, the efficiency of the hired claque, etc. More than 1 prima donna have lost their engagements over such seemingly minor matters.

prima prattica (It., 1st practice). Term used in early 17th-century Italian theoretical treatises to denote the dense polyphonic style of the previous century, synonymous with *stile antico*. This was distinct from the seconda prattica, the homophonic, monodic style cultivated by the early opera composers such as Monteverdi; also called the *stile moderno*.

primary accent. Downbeat, or thesis; the accent beginning the measure, directly following the bar.

primary triad. One of the 3 fundamental triads of a key (those on the 1st, 5th, and 4th degrees).

prime. 1st note of a scale.

prime tone. See ⇒fundamental.

primitivism. As *primitive music,* a term generally applied to songs created spontaneously by untutored musicians of a culture other than one's own, with the implication of artlessness in a positive sense and lack of artfulness in a negative sense. The term also carries a suggestion of a certain condescension on the part of educated musicians; conversely, musicians surfeited by an abundance of art music seek fresh inspiration in primitive folk songs and dances as a source of new techniques. At this point the term *primitivism* applies. Thus a Picasso was inspired by the artless productions of primitive cultures in creating his own super-primitive art; similarly, Stravinsky sought new resources in the asymmetrical melodies and rhythms of ancient Russian songs. A lack of musical education thus becomes an advantage in the eyes and ears of a modern artist who has reached an impasse at the end of uncontrolled amplification of available resources. What Ives had to say about primitive village musicians who are artistically "right" even when they play wrong notes strikes at the core of this antinomy.

primo, -a (It.). First; a 1st or leading part, as in a duet. *Prima buffa*, leading lady in comic opera; *prima donna*, leading lady in opera; *prima vista*, at 1st sight; *prima volta*, the 1st time (written *Ima volta*, or simply *I*, or *1*), indicates that the measure(s) under its brackets are to be played the 1st time, before the repeat, whereas, on repeating, those marked *seconda volta* (or *IIda volta*, or *II*, or *2*) are to be performed instead.

primo rivolto (It.). Chord of the 1st inversion; the $^6/_3$, or 6 chord.

primo uomo (It., 1st man). Male equivalent of the prima donna; not widely used.

Primrose, William, b. Glasgow, Aug. 23, 1903; d. Provo, Utah, May 1, 1982. He studied violin in Glasgow with Camillo Ritter, at London's Guildhall School of Music, and in Belgium (1925–27) with Ysaÿe, who advised him to take up viola so as to avoid the congested violin field. He became the violist in the London String Quartet (1930–35), with which he made several tours. In 1937 he settled in the U.S. and was engaged as the principal violist player in the NBC Sym. Orch. in N.Y. under Toscanini, holding this post until 1942. In 1939 he established his own string quartet. In 1953 he was named a Commander of the Order of the British Empire; he became a naturalized U.S. citizen in 1955. From 1954 to 1962 he was the violist in the Festival Quartet. He also became active as a teacher: was on the faculty of the Univ. of Southern Calif. in Los Angeles (1962) and at the School of Music of Indiana Univ. in Bloomington (1965–72); in 1972 he inaugurated a master class at the Tokyo Univ. of Fine Arts and Music; returning to the U.S., he taught at Brigham Young Univ. in Provo, Utah (1979–82).

Primrose was greatly esteemed as a viola virtuoso; he gave 1st performances of viola concertos by several modern composers. He commissioned a viola concerto from Bartók, but the work was left unfinished at the time of Bartók's death, and the task of reconstructing the score from Bartók's sketches remained to be accomplished by Bartók's friend and associate Tibor Serly; Primrose gave its 1st performance with the Minneapolis Sym. Orch. on Dec. 2, 1949. He publ. *A Method for Violin and Viola Players* (London, 1960) and *Technique in Memory* (1963); also ed. various works for viola and made transcriptions for the instrument.

Prince (born Prince Roger Nelson), b. Minneapolis, June 7, 1958. His father led a jazz group called the Prince Roger Trio, and his mother sang with it. He took up piano, guitar, and drums in his youth; before graduating from high school he formed a soul-rock band and soon learned to play a whole regiment of instruments and to write songs. When his group, renamed

Champagne, proved less than a bubbling success, he made the trek to Los Angeles to conquer the recording industry. After producing the albums *For You* (1978) and *Prince* (1979), he found a lucrative and successful métier with his sexually explicit *Dirty Mind* (1980). This sizzling tour de force featured such songs as *Head*, a joyful tribute to oral sex, and *Sister*, a hymn to incest. His next album, *Controversy* (1981), faithfully lived up to its title by including the song *Private Joy*, a glorification of masturbation.

Proclaiming himself His Royal Badness, Prince proceeded to attain ever-higher orgasmic plateaus. His hit album *1999* (1982) was followed by the sensationally acclaimed film and soundtrack album *Purple Rain* (1984), which won an Oscar for best original song score in 1985. One of its songs, *Darling Niki*, incited the formation of the P.M.R.C. (Parents' Music Resource Center) and its efforts to regulate album labeling. After producing the album *Parade* (1986), he starred in the films *Sign o' the Times* (1987) and *Graffiti Bridge* (1990). His album *Lovesexy* (1988), which says it all, comes with a nude photo. He also changed his stage name into an unpronounceable symbol, forcing the media to refer to him as The Artist Formerly Known as Prince. In 1995 he embarked on a protracted battle with his record company, Warner Bros., claiming they were refusing to issue his music the way he wished it to be produced; he finally freed himself of his contract, entering into a new distribution deal in 1996 with EMI.

principal chords. Basic chords of a key, i.e. the triads built on the tonic, dominant, and subdominant, with the dominant-7th chord.

principal diapason. Open diapason organ pipe sounding an octave higher than the normal (i.e., closed) pipe.

principio (It.). Beginning, 1st time. *In principio*, at the beginning; *più marcato del principio*, more marked than the 1st time.

printing and publishing of music. Almost immediately after the appearance of Gutenberg's Bible set from moveable type, experiments began to set musical notes in type. The 1st book with printed musical examples was *Psalterium*, set in type in 1457 in Gutenberg's workshop. An important development in music printing was the use of woodblocks in which complete musical examples, notes, and lines were carved out and inked. This method was particularly handy for books on music theory in which the text alternated with musical examples. These early specimens were usually printed in very large notes and widely separated lines. A significant advance toward modern printing was made by the Venetian printer Petrucci, who began printing vocal music books in the 1st year of the 16th century; he may well be considered the Gutenberg of music printing. He also printed the 1st tabulatures for the lute.

In early printed music a double process was involved. The lines of the staff were printed 1st, usually colored in red, and black notes were superimposed on the staff. Toward the end of the 16th century metal plates began to be used, with both the lines and notes engraved by hand. In the 18th century music engraving reached the point of a graphic art, particularly when punches and hammers were applied. Professional craftsmen sometimes accepted work in music engraving; Paul Revere, who was a silversmith by trade, became the 1st American to engrave music. The 18th-century French violinist and composer Jean-Marie Leclair (l'aîné) entrusted the engraving of his music to his wife, who was a trained toolmaker. (Leclair was stabbed to death in his home; evidence strongly pointed to his wife as the killer, for the wounds were inflicted by metal punches such as used in music engraving.)

A decisive progress in music printing was made in applying *lithography*, that is, printing from a stone surface with a viscous ink, a process developed by the German printer Senefelder in 1796. Weber apprenticed himself to Senefelder and introduced some improvements of his own in lithography. *Type printing*, in which musical symbols had to be placed on the staff separately by hand, a method too laborious for music printing but which yielded artistic results, was perfected in the 2nd half of the 18th century. This method was used concurrently with copperplating and lithography for special purposes, such as the reproduction of musical examples in theory books. The greatest era of music printing from copper plates was reached in the middle of the 19th century. Beautiful editions of instrumental music, orch'l scores, and complete operas were published by the German publishers Schott, Peters, and particularly Breitkopf & Härtel. Excellent editions of works by Russian composers, financed by the wealthy Russian merchant Belaieff, were printed on the German presses in Leipzig.

The 18th century was dominated in England by the publishing house of Walsh, which began publishing Handel's operas and also reprinted many works by continental composers. Several important publishing enterprises emerged in Great Britain in the 19th century and prospered unflaggingly into the last part of the 20th; they are Chappell, founded in 1810, and Boosey, founded in 1816. Boosey's competitor was Queen Victoria's trumpet player, Hawkes, who formed an independent printing shop specializing, like Boosey, in orch'l and chamber music. In 1930 the inheritors of Boosey and Hawkes joined in a highly successful publishing house, Boosey & Hawkes. Another important British publishing house was Novello, established in 1829 and concentrating on choral music; also to be mentioned are the firms of Curwen, Augener, and Chester, who became active in the middle of the 19th century.

The U.S., even after its independence, continued to rely on England for its music, which was mostly imported from the former mother country. Among the earliest American publishers, or rather importers, of music was Benjamin Carr, who emigrated to America after the Revolution and set up the 1st American music store, Carr's Musical Depository, in Philadelphia. The 1st important American-born publisher of music was Oliver Ditson, who established a business as a music seller in Boston in 1835 and continued in business for about a decade. The American dependence on Great Britain for music publishing continued until the middle of the 19th century, when the predominant influence on all branches of music in the U.S. was asserted by German immigrants. The year 1861 marked the foundation of the most important music publishing firm in America, established by Gustav Schirmer. Another German-born music publisher, Carl Fischer, settled in N.Y. and established an important publishing organization in 1872. Among American-born music publishers, Theodore Presser established his own firm in 1883. An important source of income for American music publishers was the representation of European publishers who held the rights on lucrative operas, popular orch'l pieces, and pedagogical literature.

Italy occupies an important position in music publishing, thanks to the almost exclusive rights on famous Italian operas. The firm of Ricordi, formed in 1808, holds the richest grants of Italian operatic literature. The entire stock of plates and publications was wantonly destroyed in a barbarous air attack on Milan, the site of the Ricordi publishing house, in 1943, but like a musical phoenix it emerged from the ashes and resumed its important position in the world of music. In Austria, Hungary, and the Scandinavian countries, local publishers maintain a close cooperation with the large German or English publishing houses. Among French publishers the firm of Durand, founded in 1870, became the most important as well as prosperous. Éditions Salabert, organized in 1896, proliferated into the lucrative field of popular arrangements of theater music.

Before the Revolution Russia had several important publishers that supplied the Russians with European music literature, but it also published works by Russian composers. Among them Jurgenson, Tchaikovsky's publisher, played a significant role in championing Russian music; Belaieff generously sponsored the publication of music by composers of the Russian national school. Koussevitzky and his very rich wife founded his own firm with the specific purpose of publishing works by modern Russian composers, among them Scriabin, Stravinsky, and Prokofiev. After the Revolution the Soviet government nationalized all Russian publishing houses and established a Central State Publishing House. Since the Soviet government was the sole publisher, problems of expenses were solved within the general budget of the State. It therefore became possible for Russia to publish music extensively, almost extravagantly. For instance, all 27 symphonies of Miaskovsky were published from engraved plates, including the orch'l parts.

Collected works of Russian classical composers were systematically issued. But even composers less known in Russia and quite unknown abroad had their works published as a matter of routine. Similar policies in publishing music existed in Communist Poland, Yugoslavia, Czechoslovakia, Rumania, and Bulgaria. With the end of Communism in Eastern Europe, these countries will have to follow the examples of their Western capitalist counterparts.

probability. Probability of incidence of certain intervals, notes, and rhythms in a given piece of music depends on its predetermined melorhythmic idiom. The probability of occurrence of an unresolved major 7th in a composition written before 1900 is virtually nil, while the probability of such incidence in dodecaphonic music is very high. Similarly, the probability of a concluding chord being a dissonance is zero for the 19th century, but it increases exponentially after 1900. The commanding importance of the tritone in atonal and dodecaphonic music makes its appearance a probable event in compositions in which the key signature is absent. The probability of incidence of all 12 different notes and 12 different intervals in relation to the starting tone in a full chromatic scale is obviously 100%.

Probe (Ger.). Rehearsal. *Generalprobe*, final dress rehearsal, sometimes open to press and dignitaries; *Hauptprobe*, principal (full) rehearsal; *Sitzprobe*, 1st rehearsal for all participants, but without staging; *Schwimmprobe*, swimming rehearsal for the Rhine maidens in Wagner's *Der Ring des Nibelungen*.

procelloso (It.). Stormy.

process music. See ⇒minimalism.

processional. Hymn sung in church during the entrance of choir and clergy.

Professor Longhair. Byrd, Henry Roeland.

profondo (It.). Deep. *Basso profondo*, deep bass.

program music. Class of instrumental compositions intended to represent distinct moods or phases of emotion, or to depict actual scenes of events; as opposed to absolute music. Perhaps *descriptive music* would be a more adequate definition, but the terms above have established themselves solidly in English-speaking countries. In the 19th century the preferable description of program music (programmatic music; Ger. *Programmusik*; Fr. *musique à programme*) was *tone painting*. A pioneer in program music was Liszt. His ideas were eagerly accepted and developed by many German composers of the 2nd half of the 19th century, culminating in the symphonic poems of R. Strauss. Abstract mathematical terms became the ultimate development of program music in the works of Varèse.

The romantic notion that music can express something was attacked on philosophical and aesthetic grounds in the famous tract *Vom Musikalisch-Schönen* by the greatest musical reactionary who ever lived, Hanslick. He wielded his caustic pen as an influential critic in Vienna. With casuistic cunning, Hanslick quoted an array of German writers on music who seemed to have been Lisztians long before Liszt. Johann Mattheson, a contemporary of Bach and Handel, is quoted as saying, "In writing a melody, the main purpose should be to express a certain emotion." Another famous 18th-century theorist, Friedrich Wilhelm Malpurg, wrote: "It is the composer's task to copy nature, to express the vital stirrings of the soul and the innermost feelings of the heart."

The music historian Johann Nikolaus Forkel equated music to rhetoric. Hanslick then quotes several weighty German dictionaries that define music as "the art of expressing sensations and states of mind by means of pleasing sounds," and "Music is the art of producing sounds capable of expressing, exciting, and sustaining feelings and passions." A professor of aesthetics is quoted with an obvious distaste by Hanslick as stating that "each feeling and each state of mind has its own inherent sound and rhythm." No wonder Hanslick as a critic became an inveterate opponent of Liszt and Wagner and an exuberant admirer of Brahms, a composer who never demeaned himself by painting a landscape in music. But what about Beethoven's *Pastoral Sym.*? Did Hanslick condemn it also? No, for Hanslick had a perfect rebuttal of this in Beethoven's own words written on the score: "Mehr Ausdruck der Empfindung als Mahlerey" (More of an expression of feeling rather than painting).

Sounds in nature, particularly the singing of birds, are obvious sources of literal program music and are found in a number of compositions centuries before the movement of Romantic program music became pronounced. Among famous examples are *La poule* by Rameau, imitating the cackling of hens, *Les abeilles*, with its murmurations of innumerable bees by Couperin, *The Cuckoo* by Daquin, and the 3 birds in Beethoven's *Pastoral Sym.*

In the domain of literary musical narratives, the earliest examples are a set of biblical stories written for harpsichord by Johann Kuhnau; the *4 Seasons* concertos by Vivaldi; and Karl Ditters von Dittersdorf's 12 syms. illustrating Ovid's *Metamorphoses*.

Probably the most explicit piece of symphonic program music is the *Sym. fantastique* of Berlioz, written by him to express his love for the Shakespearean actress Miss Smithson. Among Liszt's symphonic poems, the ones that bear direct literary connections are *Les Préludes* and the *Faust Symphony*. Litolff composed an overture *Robespierre*, in which the falling of the severed head of Robespierre into the basket is rendered as a thud on the bass drum.

The 19th century saw the greatest flowering of program music; the infatuation with the idea that music must mean something recognizable to the listener led to the regrettable practice of affixing imaginative but more often trite nicknames to musical compositions whose composers never intended to write programmatic music. It is ironic that most of the familiar titles attached to Mendelssohn's *Songs Without Words* are the products of the publisher's eagerness to attract Romantically inclined players; for example, the title *Spring Song* does not appear in Mendelssohn's MS. Haydn's syms. and string quartets received popular nicknames that represent the general eagerness to seek familiar images in the sounds of music. But even so, it is as difficult to trace the rationale of some of these titles as it is to conjure up the animal figures in the constellations of the zodiac seen by ancient stargazers.

Among Haydn's syms. we have *The Philosopher*, *The Schoolmaster*, and *The Absent-Minded Man*. Only the *Surprise Sym.*, which in German has a more concrete description, *Paukenschlag* (Drumstroke), has a musical meaning behind the title, because in the 2nd movement there is a sudden loud chord at the end of the theme, inserted there supposedly by Haydn to wake the somnolent ladies in the audience. Among some puzzling titles of Haydn's string quartets are the *Razor Quartets*. But the *Emperor Quartet* has a perfect explanation: it contains the tune that became the national anthem of Austria, unfortunately to be degraded by the text attached to it in Imperial Germany ("Deutschland, Deutschland, über alles"). There is no explanation why Mozart's great C-major Sym. should be called the *Jupiter Sym.* Nor is there any reason to call Beethoven's E-flat piano Concerto the *Emperor Concerto*. Both nicknames were apparently invented in England. The *Moonlight Sonata* of Beethoven received its programmatic name thanks to a critic who said that its opening movement suggested to him moonlight on Lake Lucerne. Although the *Sonata Appassionata* seems appropriate to describe Beethoven's impassioned music, the title was invented by a publisher.

Even when the composer himself specifically denies any programmatic significance, descriptive nicknames are excised with difficulty. The so-called *Raindrop Prelude* of Chopin is supposed to have been inspired by his listening to raindrops fall on the roof of his house on the Island of Mallorca, but he expressly denied this. More to the point is the title *Revolutionary Étude*, since it is marked by rebellious upward passages in the left hand, and it was composed by Chopin at the time Warsaw was captured by the Russians, leading to the partition of his beloved fatherland. The nickname for Chopin's *Minute Waltz* seems obvious, but no human pianist can play it in 60 seconds flat with all the repeats.

Personal references and all kinds of musical asides are found galore in music literature. Certainly Schumann's *Carnaval*, built on the 4 notes spelling the name of the Bohemian town of Asch in the German musical alphabet, is a piece of program music with autobiographical allusions, for it was in Asch that Schumann met a once-beloved lady (not Clara). Another famous autobiographical piece of program music was *Symphonia domestica* by Richard Strauss, in which the composer portrayed in music the nightly bath of his infant son; the exact time, 7 o'clock, is represented by the chimes striking 7. Tchaikovsky's *Pathétique Sym.* is a piece of program music after the fact, since the descriptive title was attached to it after the score was completed. What is interesting is that it contains a passage in the trombones from the Russian Mass for the Dead, as if Tchaikovsky had a premonition of his death a few days after the 1st performance of the work.

It must be stated that there is no objective way of determining whether a composition "means" something from just listening to it. Tchaikovsky expatiated at great length in his letter to patroness Mme. von Meck that his 4th Sym., dedicated to her, represented the inexorability of Fate. Schoenberg, to whom music was a pure art *an und für sich*, yielded to the request of his publisher to attach titles to his 5 Orchestral Pieces. And years later he was even willing to change the title of the 3rd piece, originally called *The Changing Chord*, to *Summer Morning by the Lake*. In his *Kinderszenen* for piano, Schumann depicted a child's moods, of which *Träumerei* is the most moving. In his *Pictures at an Exhibition*, Mussorgsky presented a series of pictures come to life.

Any composition, no matter how abstract or classically sober, can be interpreted as an image. Modern ballet composers often use movements from symphonic works for choreographical spectacles of a romantic nature with suitable titles attached to them. Some pieces of program music would lose their attraction if they were deprived of their titles. The witty interlude *Pianists* in *The Carnival of the Animals* of Saint-Saëns would be pointless were it not for the inclusion of pianists among the animals of the title. In some pieces of program music the title becomes more important than the music itself. This is particularly true about the humorous creations of Satie, whose music would hardly be the same without those fantastically oxymoronic titles, such as *Heures séculaires et instantanées* (Century-Long Instantaneous Hours).

Sometimes composers yield to the temptation of attaching programmatic titles to their works only to cancel them later. Mahler bestowed programmatic titles to several of his syms.—*Titan* for the 1st, *Summer Morning's Dream* for the 3rd, *The Giant* for the 5th—but subsequently withdrew all these titles and insisted that he never authorized anyone to use them for identification. Stravinsky's *Scherzo fantastique* was originally published with a long quotation from Maeterlinck's *Life of the Bees*; he even added specific subtitles, such as *Queen Bee's Nuptial Flight*, to parts of his score, but later denied that the music was inspired by any insects whatsoever.

The principle of absolute beauty in music so eloquently proclaimed by Hanslick is opposite to the doctrine of Socialist Realism, as propounded by the theoreticians of the Soviet Union, who insist that all music has a specific meaning. The musical philosophy of the People's Republic of China goes even farther in espousing the primacy of programmatic music. In January of 1974 the official organ of the Communist Party of the Chinese Republic published a leading article entitled *Works of Music Without Titles Do Not Reflect the Class Spirit*, and specifically condemned Piano Sonata No. 17 by "the German capitalist musician, Beethoven" and the Sym. in B Minor by the "Romantic Austrian capitalist musician, Schubert."

Ives was certainly a composer of program music, with America as his program. In his symphonic *4th of July*, he assembled a heterogeneous orch. with a wildly dissonant climax representing the explosion of multicolored fireworks. In his memo on the work he wrote: "It is pure program music—it is also pure abstract music," and he added a quotation from Mark Twain's *Huckleberry Finn*, "You pays yer money, and you takes yer choice." Antheil insisted that his *Ballet mécanique*, scored for several player pianos, 2 airplane propellers, door bells, and a plethora of drums, was not program music of a mechanical world but "the most abstract of the abstract."

progression. Advance from one tone to another, or from one chord to another; the former is *melodic*, the later *harmonic* progression.

progressive composition. In songwriting, setting of each strophe to different music, following the changing mood more closely than in the ballad or folk song, where melody and harmony are generally the same for each verse; also called through-composed songwriting.

progressive jazz. In the 1st half of the century jazz was often a spontaneous product of mass or single improvisation, with self-taught instrumentalists achieving fantastic virtuosity simply because they were not told by any teacher that the technical tricks they performed were unplayable. In 1950 a natural desire arose among a later generation of jazz players to acquire gloss, polish, and even theoretical knowledge. They studied with eminent European composers resident in the U.S. and listened to records of modern music. They became conversant with such terms as *atonality* and *polytonality* and even *dodecaphony*. In some cases they annexed a full complement of strings in their orchs. With full credentials, a movement was launched grandly described as progressive jazz, incorporating both *cool* and *3rd stream* styles. Technical resources kept pace with the dignity of the orch'l presentation. The whole-tone scale was rediscovered as a sonority and played in unison by the violins. Two different keys were used simultaneously in a display of polytonality. The square time was diversified occasionally by asymmetric rhythms; sometimes compound meters were inserted. But despite these adornments and borrowings from respectable sources, progressive jazz could never attain distinction and soon gave way to a less European but more appropriate style of jazzification.

progressive rock. See ⇒rock.

progressive tonality. Term used to denote symphonic works that end in keys other than those in which they began.

Prokofiev (Prokofieff), Sergei (Sergeievich), b. Sontsovka, Apr. 27, 1891; d. Moscow, Mar. 5, 1953. He received his 1st piano lessons from his mother, who was an amateur pianist; he improvised several pieces and then composed a children's opera, *The Giant* (1900), which was performed in a domestic version. Following his bent for the theater, he put together 2 other operas, *On Desert Islands* (1902) and *Ondine* (1904–7); fantastic subjects obviously possessed his childish imagination.

Prokofiev was 11 years old when he met the great Russian master Taneyev, who arranged for him to take systematic private lessons with Reinhold Glière, who became his tutor at Sontsovka during the summers of 1903 and 1904, and by correspondence during the intervening winter. Under Glière's knowledgeable guidance in theory and harmony, Prokofiev composed a sym. in piano version and still another opera, *Plague*, based upon a poem by Pushkin. Finally, in 1904, at age 13, he enrolled in the St. Petersburg Cons., where he studied composition with Liadov and piano with Alexander Winkler; later he was accepted by no less a master than Rimsky-Korsakov, who instructed him in orchestration. He also studied conducting with Nikolai Tcherepnin and form with Wihtol. Further, he entered the piano class of Anna Essipova. During the summers he returned to Sontsovka or traveled in the Caucasus and continued to compose, already in quite an advanced style; the Moscow publisher Jurgenson accepted his 1st work, a piano sonata, for publication; it was premiered in Moscow on Mar. 6, 1910. It was then that Prokofiev made his 1st visit to Paris, London, and Switzerland (1913); in 1914 he graduated from the St. Petersburg Cons., receiving the Anton Rubinstein Prize (a grand piano) as a pianist-composer with his Piano Concerto No. 1, which he performed publicly at the graduation concert.

Because of audacious innovations in his piano music (he wrote one piece in which the right and left hands played in different keys), Prokofiev was described in the press as a "futurist," and because of his addiction to dissonant and powerful harmonic combinations, some critics dismissed his works as "football music." This idiom was explicitly demonstrated in his *Sarcasms* and *Visions fugitives* for Piano—percussive and sharp yet not lacking in lyric charm. Grotesquerie and irony animated his early works; he also developed a strong attraction toward subjects of primitive character. His important orch. work, the *Scythian Suite* (arr. from music written for a ballet, *Ala and Lolly*, 1915), draws upon a legend of ancient Russian sun-worship rituals. While a parallel with Stravinsky's *The Rite of Spring* may exist, there is no similarity between the styles of the 2 works.

The original performance of Prokofiev's *Scythian Suite*, scheduled at a Koussevitzky concert in Moscow, was canceled on account of the disruption caused by war, which did not prevent the otherwise intelligent Russian music critic Sabaneyev, blissfully unaware that the announced premiere had been canceled, from delivering a blast of the work as a farrago of atrocious noises. (Sabaneyev was forced to resign his position after this episode.) Another Prokofiev score, primitivistic in its inspiration, was the cantata *7, They Are 7*, based upon incantations from an old Sumerian religious ritual. During the same period Prokofiev wrote his famous *Classical Sym.* (1916–17), in which he adopted with remarkable acuity the formal style of Haydn's music. While the structure of the work was indeed classical, the sudden modulatory shifts and subtle elements of grotesquerie revealed decisively a new modern art.

After conducting the premiere of his *Classical Sym.* in Petrograd (1918), Prokofiev left Russia by way of Siberia and Japan for the U.S. (the continuing war in Europe prevented him from traveling westward). He gave concerts of his music in Japan and later in the U.S., playing his 1st solo concert in N.Y. Some American critics greeted his appearance as the reflection of the chaotic events of Russia in revolution, and Prokofiev himself was described as a "ribald and Bolshevist innovator and musical agitator." "Every rule in the realm of traditional music writing was broken by Prokofiev," one N.Y. writer complained. "Dissonance followed dissonance in a fashion inconceivable to ears accustomed to melody and harmonic laws." Prokofiev's genteel *Classical Sym.* struck some critics as "an orgy of dissonant sound, an exposition of the unhappy state of chaos from which Russia suffers." Another N.Y. critic indulged in the following: "Crashing Siberians, volcano hell, Krakatoa, sea-bottom crawlers. Incomprehensible? So is Prokofiev." But another critic issued a word of caution, suggesting that "Prokofiev might be the legitimate successor of Borodin, Mussorgsky, and Rimsky-Korsakov." The critic was unintentionally right; Prokofiev is firmly enthroned in the pantheon of Russian music.

In 1920 Prokofiev settled in Paris, where he established an association with Diaghilev's Ballets Russes, which produced his ballets *Chout* (a French transliteration of the Russian word for buffoon), *Le Pas d'acier* (descriptive of the industrial development in Soviet Russia), and *L'Enfant prodigue*. In 1921 Prokofiev again visited the U.S. for the production of the opera commissioned by the Chicago Opera Co., *The Love for 3 Oranges*. In 1927 he was invited to be the pianist for a series of his own works in Russia. He gave a number of concerts in Russia again in 1929 and eventually decided to remain there. In Russia he wrote some of his most popular works, including the symphonic fairy tale *Peter and the Wolf* (1936), staged by a children's theater in Moscow; the historical cantata *Alexander Nevsky* (1939; based on the soundtrack to the eponymous film by Eisenstein); the ballet *Romeo and Juliet* (1935–36); and opera *War and Peace* (1941–52), which went through numerous revisions.

Unexpectedly, Prokofiev became the target of the so-called proletarian group of Soviet musicians who accused him of decadence, a major sin in Soviet Russia at the time. His name was included in the official denunciation of modern Soviet composers issued by reactionary Soviet politicians. He meekly confessed that he had been occasionally interested in atonal and polytonal devices during his stay in Paris, but insisted that he had never abandoned the ideals of classical Russian music. Indeed, when he composed his 7th Sym. he described it specifically as a youth sym., reflecting the energy and ideals of new Russia.

There were also significant changes in Prokofiev's personal life. He separated from his Spanish-born wife, the singer Lina Llubera, the mother of his 2 sons, and established a companionship with Myra Mendelson, a member of the Young Communist League. She was a writer and assisted him on the libretto of *War and Peace*. He made one final attempt to gain favor with the Soviet establishment by writing an opera, *A Tale about a Real Man* (1947–48), based on a heroic exploit of a Soviet pilot during the war against the Nazis. But this, too, was damned by the servile Communist press as lacking in true patriotic spirit, and the opera was quickly removed from the repertory. After a decade of illness Prokofiev died suddenly of heart failure on Mar. 5, 1953, a few hours before the death of Stalin. Curiously enough, the anniversary of Prokofiev's death is duly commemorated, while that of his once powerful nemesis is officially allowed to be forgotten.

Among other works by Prokofiev are operas: *Maddalena* (1912–13, piano score only; orchestrated by Edward Downes; BBC Radio, 1979); *The Gambler*, after Dostoyevsky (1915–16; Brussels, 1929); *The Fiery Angel* (1919; Paris, 1954); *Semyon Kotko* (Moscow, 1940); *Betrothal in a Convent*, after Sheridan's *Duenna* (1940; Leningrad, 1946). Ballets: *Sur le Borysthène* (1930; Paris, 1932); *Cinderella* (1940–44; Moscow, 1945); *A Tale of the Stone Flower* (1948–50; Moscow, 1954); incidental music; film music, including *Lt. Kije* (1933; film lost or never completed); *Ivan the Terrible* (1942–45, directed by Eisenstein; 2 of 3 parts completed); choral music, most of which represents Prokofiev's attempts to please Stalin and his cronies. Orch.: 7 syms., of which the *Classical* (No. 1) and No. 5 are the most popular; 5 piano concertos, with No. 4 written for the left hand alone; Sinfonietta (1915); Violin Concerto No. 1 (1923); Divertissement (1929); Violin Concerto No. 2 (1935); Cello Concerto (1938; evolved into the *Sinfonia Concertante*, premiered by Rostropovich, 1954); suites from the operas, ballets, and film scores. Chamber music: 2 string quartets; sonatas for violin (2), violin solo, violin duo, cello, flute. Piano: 9 sonatas (1909–1947; No. 10, 1953, unfinished); *Toccata* (1912); *Tales of an Old Grandmother* (1918); 2 sonatinas (1931–32); *Pensées* (1933–34); songs, including *The Ugly Duckling*, after Andersen (1914).

prolatio (Lat., prolation). Smallest division in mensural notation. It represents the division of the tempus into 2 or 3 values of prolatio, which in turn can either be a perfection (divided into 3 units) or an imperfection (into 2 units). Ockeghem wrote a *Missa prolationum* that contains all 4 possible divisions of the tempus into prolatio units in mensural notation; in modern notation these prolations correspond to the time signatures of 2/4, 3/4, 6/8, and 9/8, respectively.

prolepsis. Schlegel wrote, "Der Historiker ist ein rückwärts gekehrter Prophet." The notion that a historian might be a prophet of the past is most provocative. The modern cultivation of some of the recessive traits of the musical past represents such a prophecy turned backward. Consecutive 5ths were the rule before the advent of tertian counterpoint; they were strictly forbidden in classical music but returned early in the 20th century in the guise of neoarchaic usages and were further reinforced in the practice of consecutive triadic harmonies. The dissonant heterophony of ancient modalities was incorporated as a novelty in neoprimitivism. Satie drew a table of anticommandments in his *Catéchisme du Conservatoire* in which he ridiculed the elevation of once forbidden practices to the status of harmonic laws:

Avec grand soin tu violeras Des régles du vieux rudiment. Quintes de suite tu feras Et octaves pareillement. Au grand jamais ne résoudras De dissonance aucunement. Aucun morceau ne finiras Jamais par accord consonnant.

The exclusion of major triads in the Schoenbergian table of commandments is the most striking instance of prolepsis.

Indeed, every determined violation of the academic rules becomes a case for prolepsis if such a violation becomes itself a rule.

proletarian music. The ideological upheaval that accompanied the Soviet revolution of 1917 posed an immediate problem: how to create artworks consonant with the aims and ideals of socialist society. Since the Soviet government was based on dictatorship of the proletariat, it was imperative to postulate a special type of literature, drama, art, and music; proletarian in substance while being accessible to the popular masses. Some Soviet theoreticians proposed to wipe the slate clean of the entire cultural structure preceding the revolution, creating a tabula rasa on which to build a new aesthetic edifice. Suggestions seriously offered by musicians in the early Soviet days were: confiscation of all musical instruments in order to abolish the tempered scale; construction of new instruments based on acoustically pure intervals; more appropriately, the composition of music that includes sounds familiar to a proletarian worker. A factory sym. was staged in an experimental demonstration, with singers and players placed on rooftops; Shostakovich included a factory whistle in his *First of May* Sym. (no. 3; op. 20, 1929); Mosolov wrote a ballet, *Zavod* (Iron Foundry, 1927), in which a large sheet of steel is shaken to imitate the sound of the forge.

Attempts were made to proletarianize older librettos. Puccini's *Tosca* was advanced from Napoleonic times to the Paris Commune era; Tosca kills not the chief of the Roman police (Scarpia) but the anti-Communard general Gallifet, disregarding the fact that the historical Gallifet died in bed long after the Commune's fall. Meyerbeer's opera *The Huguenots* was renamed *The Decembrists*, the action transferred to 1825 to celebrate the rebellion of progressive-minded aristocrats against the accession of Czar Nicholas I. The notorious Russian Association of Proletarian Musicians (RAPM) was founded to pass judgment on the fitness and unfitness of all music for public consumption (1924); stipulated an arbitrary code of desirable musical attributes; among them unrelenting optimism, militant socialism, proletarian class consciousness, representational programmaticism, and preferential use of major keys. Beethoven was commended by the RAPM for his rebellious spirit; among Russian composers, Mussorgsky was singled out as a creator of realistic art.

A difficult problem was posed by Tchaikovsky. His profound pessimism and fatalism, reactionary political views, and particularly his homosexuality seemed an insurmountable barrier for the RAPM theoreticians to overcome; even from a purely musical standpoint, he was theoretically unacceptable; his preference for minor keys and melancholy moods were the very antinomy of all that the new Soviet Russia stood for. However, he was a favorite composer not only of the masses but also the entire Presidium of the Soviet of People's Commissars. In their attempt to rationalize the popularity of the *Pathétique* Sym., the RAPM reached the acme of casuistry, arguing that, in this work, he was delivering a magnificent funeral oration on the tomb of the bourgeoisie; the superb artistic quality of this lamentation could not fail to please proletarian listeners. But soon the dialectical self-contradictions became evident even to the most obdurate RAPM composers; factional strife pulled their ideology apart. There was also a reaction against vicious attacks led by the RAPM against surviving pre-revolutionary composers and greatly esteemed Conservatory professors and others who dared to oppose its untenable ideology. The entire controversy was suddenly resolved when the Soviet government summarily disbanded the RAPM; as one composer noted with satisfaction, "We could once again dare to write music in 3/4 time," alluding to the RAPM's insistence that proletarian music could only be written in march time.

The valid residue of proletarian music found its way to Germany and to America, assuming special national idioms. Simplicity of form, utilization of popular dance rhythms, and, in theatrical music, subjects taken from Revolutionary history or class warfare were the main characteristics of music for the proletariat. In America proletarian opera flourished briefly in the 1930s, with Blitzstein as its chief proponent. In Germany Weill, working in close collaboration with dramatist Bertolt Brecht, created a type of music drama that in its social consciousness had a strong affinity with proletarian music; this model was followed by Eisler and Dessau.

prolixity. Brevity is not necessarily an ideal; prolixity is not always a fault. In classical music, prolixity was ingrained in the forms of sonata and court dances, with the required repetitions of complete sections. Only the impatience of modern performers impels them to disregard such redundancies. ("Brevitate gaudent moderni," to quote a recurring incipit of medieval musical treatises.) Beethoven's *Eroica Sym.* concludes with its tonic chord repeated 28 times; by contrast, Prokofiev's *March* from *Love for 3 Oranges* ends abruptly on a single C-major triad. The natural aversion of modern musicians to restatement and overstatement extends also to tonal sequences with their predictable turns. This homologophobia led finally to the collapse of the tonal system itself and inspired Schoenberg to promulgate the principle of nonrepetition of thematic notes and the formulation of his method of composition with 12 tones related only to one another.

prologue. Introductory part of an opera. Wagner described *Das Rheingold* as the *Vorabend* (Ger., evening before) to the main "trilogy" of *Der Ring des Nibelungen.* A more typical prologue opens Leoncavallo's *Pagliacci,* where it is used in a Shakespearean sense, signifying a interpretive narrator; a modern version of this type is found in Berg's *Lulu.* The prologue is usually short, usually sung or narrated, and "prepares" the audience verbally; the overture is instrumental and, in some cases, a musical table of contents of the opera to follow.

prompter (Fr., Ger., Russ. *souffleur,* one who breathes; It. *maestro suggeritore,* master suggester). In opera, person standing in an "invisible" place called the *box* at downstage center, facing upstage, score in front of him or her, who gives cues to singers. Such a prompter is actually introduced to the audience in the whimsical opera *Capriccio* by R. Strauss. In the last act of *Tristan und Isolde* a prompter may be ensconced under the dying Tristan's couch. Depending on the hall's acoustics, the prompter's voice may unexpectedly carry to some parts of the orch. seats. Incautious prompters have been known to hum along; one suggester, A. Petronio, cued the singers in the famous sextet from *Lucia di Lammermoor* (Metropolitan Opera House, N.Y.) so loudly that the ensemble was facetiously referred to by *habitués* as the "septet from *Lucia.*"

Proms, The. Affectionate abbrev. for the Promenade Concerts of London, begun in 1837 in imitation of Paris popular concerts launched by P. Musard (1833); programs orig. consisted of ballroom dances, overtures, and short pieces of choral music. In London, Promenade Concerts were given in the summer in Drury Lane Theater; the name "Promenade" was firmly established by 1840. The eccentric French conductor Julien was the 1st *animator* of these concerts, followed by A. Manns (1859); L. Arditi conducted Promenade Concerts at Covent Garden (1875); Henry Wood took over the series (Queen's Hall, 1895), his name becoming forever associated with the most brilliant period of the Concerts, by then known as the Proms. In 1941, Queen's Hall was hit by Nazi aerial bombardment, but the Proms did not expire; they moved to the Royal Albert Hall.

In 1944 the Proms were officially named the Henry Wood Promenade Concerts in homage to the conductor, who died that year. Among his successors were Boult, Malcom Sargent, Barbirolli, and C. Davis. A great deal of avant-garde music has been included in the Proms, such as Tavener's *The Whale* (1969), Tim Souster's *Triple Music II* and *The Soft Machine,* a rock piece offering such tunes as *Esther's Nose Job* and *Out-Bloody-Rageous* (1970), and Stockhausen's *Carré* for 4 orchs.

pronto (It.). Promptly, swiftly.

pronunziato (It.). Pronounced, marked. *Ben pronunziato,* well, clearly enunciated.

proper. See ⇒proprium.

proportion. Medieval theory relating to the proportionate duration of the notes of the melody and the ratio of vibrations of these notes.

proportional notation. System of notation developed by Earle Brown in which durations of notes are shown proportionally, relative only to one another and independent of any strict metric system. Also called time-space notation.

proposta (Lat., proposal). Fugal subject; dux.

proprietas (Lat., propriety). In mensural notation, a ligature where the 1st of the 2 notes is a breve; marked by a descending tail left of the 1st note when descending, and no tail in ascending. *Opposita proprietas,* a property of ligatures that are semibreves, marked with an ascending left tail; *cum proprietate,* a property of ligatures that are breves; *sine proprietate,* a property of ligatures that are semibreves.

proprium (Lat.). The Roman Catholic Mass Proper; the portions of the liturgy that regularly occur, but with changing text, depending on the feast day and readings for that service. The proper pertinent to one or more saints is called *proprium sanctorum.* The musical sections of the Proper, interwoven with the Ordinary (Ordinary in italics): Introit, *Kyrie, Gloria,* Gradual, Alleluia (or Tract), Sequence, *Credo,* Offertory, *Sanctus, Agnus Dei,* Communion, *Ite missa est* (or *Benedicamus Domino*).

prova (It.; Ger. *Probe*). Rehearsal, particularly in opera.

psalette (Fr.). Ecclesiastical choir school; *maîtrise.*

psalm (from Grk. *psallein,* pluck; Fr. *psaume;* It. *salmo;* Ger. *Psalm*). Hymn; sacred song; one of the most important categories of prayerful biblical poems to be sung with instrumental accompaniment. Innumerable works, beginning with the simplest type of plainchant, have been set to the texts from the Book of Psalms. Biblical tradition holds that King David wrote most of the Psalms and sang them; he is therefore known as the Psalmist.

psalm tones. In Gregorian chant, recitation formulas to be used by a soloist for intoning complete psalms. Each of the original 8 church modes has its own psalm tone; each psalm tone begins with an ascent to a reciting tone (*tenor*, holding tone, sustaining tone) a 5th above the mode's tonic degree; when the end of the verse is reached, the melody descends to the tonic. There is an additional psalm tone called the *tonus peregrinus* (wandering tone) that can be used with any of the 8 modes by changing the *tenor*.

psalmodicon. Swedish bowed zither, invented in 1829 by Johann Dillner. In its orig. form it resembled the 1-stringed tromba marina with additional metal drone strings. It was used as a substitute for the organ in churches and schools and evolved a cellolike body, but the invention of the harmonium ended its usefulness in accompanying singing.

psalmody. Music sung in Protestant churches in England and the U.S. from the 17th century to the early 19th century.

Psalter. Collection of psalms in the vernacular. Numerous national Psalters have been translated by various hands. Some Psalters are known by their place of publication, such as the Calvinist *Geneva Psalter*, published with polyphonic settings from 1546, and the *Bay Psalm Book*, the 1st book published in America; 13 musical settings were added to it in 1698.

psaltery. Ancient instrument in use to the 17th century; known to the Hebrews as the *Kinnor*, to the Germans as the *Rotta*. A kind of harp-zither with a varying number of strings plucked by the fingers or with a plectrum.

pseudoexoticism. To an imaginative composer, the attraction of exotic lands is in inverse ratio to available information about such lands and in direct ratio to the square of the distance from the nonbeholder. "Turkish" music, having nothing in common with real Turkish modalities, enjoyed a great vogue in the 18th century; used as a pseudoexotic resource by Mozart and others. When dancers from Indochina came to the Paris Exposition of 1889, French musicians were fascinated by the unfamiliar sounds of resonant bells and muffled drums in the percussion group that accompanied the dancers; musical impressionism in France owes much to this dance music from Asia as refracted through the ears of a European.

The legends of the East provided poetic materials for song texts and operatic librettos. These tenuous impressions were transmuted into a *musique nouvelle*, vibrant with voluptuous *frissons*. Eastern scales were represented in the works of Debussy, Ravel, and their imitators by the pentatonic scale, which could be conveniently played on the black keys of the piano keyboard. Great composers were able to create a new art derived, however inaccurately, from Eastern sonorities; in fact, several composers—natives of Asia—who studied music in Paris began to mold their own authentic modes in the impressionistic manner.

When the novelty began to fade, the pentatonic scale, the tinkling bells, and other paraphernalia of pseudoexotica found their

way into the commercial factories of vulgar musicians plying their trade with much profit in the semiclassical division of "modern" music, in Broadway shows, and on the soundtrack of exotic movie spectaculars. The proliferation of this pseudoexoticism resulted in the contamination of the genuine product, so that genuine Eastern music was threatened with extinction.

pseudonyms. Pseudonyms in literature are common; women novelists often assume masculine names to facilitate publication of their works; in music, Rebecca Clarke publ. works as Anthony Trent. In some cases, a dignified composer publ. undignified music under a pseudonym; MacDowell, early in his career, publ. under various pseudonyms. Among pseudonymous writers of light music is Albert William Ketelbey, whose real name was William Aston. Professional composers of popular songs often wrote under pseudonyms. Vladimir Dukelsky, a serious symphonic composer, adopted the nom de plume of Vernon Duke in writing popular songs.

More widespread is pseudonymity among singers, in opera and on the popular stage. Since Italians have become proverbially associated with operatic excellence, many non-Italians, anxious to make an opera career, assumed Italian names, e.g., the American soprano Lillian Norton became Nordica. At the turn of the century it was believed that a musician bearing an Anglo-Saxon name could not write successful songs, and that a surname ending in *-ski* or *-ska* for women was essential. Thus British pianist Ethel Liggins became Leginska, but it did not help her American career much. A flight from obviously Jewish names was pronounced among musical performers until recently; in the beginning of his spectacular career, L. Bernstein was strongly advised to change his name, but he indignantly refused, doing well under his real name.

psychology. Like all artists, professional musicians possess an exaggerated *amour-propre*. Composers, representing the intelligentsia of the musical profession, are the least prone to self-aggrandizement, but even they can be intransigent about the uniqueness of their talent. Schoenberg regarded musical composition derived from folk materials as devoid of aesthetic value; defended this philosophy with considerable vehemence. On a less dignified plane are the vanities of performing musicians in their desire to climb the ladder of fame and fortune. Anecdotes abound: the pianist Vladimir de Pachman would applaud himself at a public concert; to enhance his social status, the pianist Sigismond Thalberg encouraged the rumor that he was the illegitimate son of a minor German duke; the American musician and composer Silas Gamaliel Pratt said to Wagner, to whom he was introduced, "You are the Silas Gamaliel Pratt of Germany."

Symphonic conductors of the recent past were notorious for their conviction of being incomparable. Their megalomania sometimes reached extraordinary proportions. Von Bülow was particularly famous for his contemptuous treatment of his musicians. Toscanini was brought to court in Milan after he broke the violin bow on the head of his concertmaster; his defense lawyer pleaded that a musician can be regarded as legally insane when he creates music. During the last rehearsal that Toscanini conducted before his death, he shouted at the orch., "Imbecili!" The orch. forgave him this outburst in deference to his greatness and age.

The musical psychology of singers, at least in times past, was motivated by the lowest of animal instincts. Operatic prima donnas would tear each others' hair out for the honor of being classified as *prima donna assoluta*, with larger-sized posters or a more sumptuous carriage. The institution of the claque was peculiar to opera singers and flourished until well into the 20th century. In popular credence musicians were often regarded as eternal adolescents not responsible for their actions. Even the fundamentalist sect of Jehovah's Witnesses finds attenuating circumstances for King David's sins of adultery and murder: "As an outstanding musician he most likely was an emotional man."

Public Enemy, (Members: Chuck D, b. Carlton Ridenhauer, N.Y., Aug. 1, 1960; MC Flavor Flav, b. William Drayton, N.Y., Mar. 16, 1959; Minister of Information Professor Griff, b. Richard Griffin; Terminator X, b. Norman Lee Rogers, N.Y., Aug. 25, 1966). Formed originally at N.Y.'s Adelphi University in 1982, the group scored massive hits in the mid-1980s with their commentaries on contemporary black life; songs like *Prophets of Rage, Bring the Noise,* and *Party for Your Right to Fight* made them immediately successful. However, the group was shrouded in controversy; when group "Minister of Information" Professor Griff made anti-Semitic statements, and was ousted from its membership (1989). The group quickly bounced back with 1990's *Fear of a Black Planet,* featuring the hit *Fight the Power* (theme for Spike Lee's film *Do the Right Thing*). Not shying away from controversy, the group released *By the Time I Get to Arizona* in 1991, denouncing that state's refusal to honor Martin Luther King Jr.; by the early '90s their activities slowed; produced more mainstream material, scoring a hit with *Give It Up* (1994).

Puccini, Giacomo (Antonio Domenico Michele Secondo Maria), b. Lucca, Dec. 22, 1858; d. Brussels, Nov. 29, 1924. He was the 5th of 7 children; his musical training was entrusted to F. Magi, a pupil of his deceased father Michele; but Giacomo showed neither inclination nor talent for music. His mother, determined to continue the family tradition, sent him to the local Istituto Musicale Pacini, where the director, C. Angeloni—who had also studied with Michele—became his teacher. Angeloni's untiring patience aroused interest and then enthusiasm in his pupil, progress was rapid and he became a proficient pianist and organist.

Puccini began serving as a church organist in Lucca and environs at age 14; began composing at 17. After hearing *Aida* in Pisa (1876), he resolved to win laurels as a dramatic composer; having written mainly sacred music, he clearly needed further training after graduating from the Istituto (1880). With financial support from his granduncle, and a stipend from Queen Margherita, he pursued his studies with A. Bazzini and Ponchielli at the Milan Cons. (1880–83); for graduation he wrote a *Capriccio sinfonico*; conducted by Faccio at a Cons. concert, eliciting unstinting praise from the critics.

In the same year, Ponchielli introduced Puccini to the librettist Fontana, who furnished him the text of a 1-act opera; in a few weeks the score was finished and sent to the publisher Sonzongo's competition; although it did not win, but *Le villi* was produced at the Teatro dal Verme in Milan, with gratifying success (1884). The publisher Ricordi was sufficiently impressed to commission the young composer to write a new opera; 5 years elapsed before this work, *Edgar* (3 acts; text by Fontana), was produced at La Scala in Milan, scoring only a moderate success (1889). Puccini was convinced that in order to write a really

effective opera, he needed a better libretto than Fontana could provide; commissioned Domenico Oliva to write the text of *Manon Lescaut* (4 acts, after Prévost); however, Puccini and Ricordi practically rewrote the entire book; Oliva's name is not mentioned in the score; with the premiere of this work at the Teatro Regio in Turin (1893), Puccini won a veritable triumph; surpassed by *La Bohème* (4 acts; text by Illica and Giacosa, after Murger), produced at the same theater (1896); these 2 works carried his name throughout the world and have maintained their place in the operatic repertory.

Puccini's next opera, *Tosca* (3 acts, after Sardou), was produced at the Teatro Costanzi in Rome (1900); his most dramatic work; containing some of his best-known arias. At its premiere at La Scala (1904), *Madama Butterfly* (2 acts, after Belasco) was hissed; he withdrew the score, made slight changes (division into 3 acts, addition of Pinkerton's aria in the last scene); this rev. version was greeted with frenzied applause in Brescia (1904). He was now the acknowledged ruler of the Italian operatic stage, his works rivaling those of Verdi in number of performances.

The 1st performance of Puccini's *Madama Butterfly* at the Metropolitan Opera in N.Y. (1907) took place in the presence of the composer, especially invited for the occasion; he was commissioned to write an opera on an American subject, the premiere to take place at the Metropolitan. He witnessed a performance of Belasco's *The Girl of the Golden West*; chose it as a subject; commissioned Zangarini and Civinini to write the libretto; in the presence of the composer the world premiere of *La Fanciulla del West* occurred, amid much enthusiasm, at the Metropolitan (1910); while it never equaled the success of *Tosca* or *Madama Butterfly*, it returned to favor in the 1970s as a period piece. He brought out the operetta *La Rondine* (3 acts; Monte Carlo, 1917) and *Il Trittico,* comprising the 1-act operas *Il Tabarro, Suor Angelica,* and *Gianni Schicchi* (Metropolitan Opera, N.Y., 1918); his last opera, *Tunrandot* (after Gozzi), was left unfinished; the final scene was completed by Franco Alfano and performed at La Scala with Toscanini conducting (1926).

pugno, col (It.). Strike the keys with the fist.

puk (Korean). Drum.

pulkatants (Est.). Estonian male dance in syncopated 2/4 time; like the English Morris dance, the dancers use sticks.

pulse. Beat or accent.

Pult (Ger.; from Lat. *pupitum,* pulpit). Music stand.

punctus (Lat.). 1. Dot that serves as a bar of separation between rhythmic groups in mensural notation; *punctus divisionis.* 2. Dot that adds half of the duration of the note so dotted; *punctus additionis.*

punitive music. Relentless playing of a trivial tune arranged in repellent harmonies may well be used, and possibly has been used by dictatorial regimes, to extract confessions from suspected music lovers. A similar practice is pursued in the form of a musical massage in democratic countries by means of juke boxes or other instruments of torture—in public restaurants, in jet planes waiting for a chance to make a scheduled departure, at bus terminals and railroad stations—with the ultimate intention of weakening sales resistance to a commercial product among captive listeners. For an entirely different purpose Satie—who detested audiences—directed to have his piano piece, pointedly titled *Vexations*, to be performed 840 times in succession. His punitive design, however, was circumvented by a group of sado-masochists who carried Satie's instructions to the letter; in 1963 a complete performance of *Vexations* occurred in N.Y., played without interruption by a relay of willing pianists who obtained thereby not only a measure of secret gratification but also a great deal of publicity.

punta (It.). Point (of the bow). *Colla punta dell'arco*, at the point of the bow.

punto (Sp.). Cuban song combining 3/4 and 6/8 meters, with occasional injections of 2/4. Although clearly of Spanish origin, the Caribbean punto developed its own style, marked by percussive syncopation.

pupitre (Fr.). Music stand.

Purcell, Henry, b. London, 1659; d. Dean's Yard, Westminster, Nov. 21, 1695. His father may have been Henry Purcell (d. Westminster, Aug. 11, 1664), a singer, Master of the Choristers at Westminster Abbey, and a Gentleman of the Chapel Royal; or Thomas Purcell (d. Westminster, July 31, 1682), probably the brother of the elder Henry Purcell, also a Gentleman of the Chapel Royal, composer for the violins (with Pelham Humfrey), marshal of the Corp. of Music, and a musician-in-ordinary in the King's Private Musick.

The young Henry Purcell became a chorister of the Chapel Royal under Cooke and Humfrey (1669); received instruction from Blow until his voice broke (1673); appointed Assistant Keeper of the Instruments; named composer-in-ordinary for the violins (1677). He was Blow's successor as organist of Westminster Abbey (1679) and 1 of 3 organists of the Chapel Royal (1682); named organ maker and keeper of the king's instruments (1683). His 1st printed works were contained in Playford's *Choice Ayres* (vol. I, 1675; vol. II, 1679); some of his finest instrumental works, the *Fantasias* for Strings (1680); began writing odes and welcome songs, whose almost invariably insipid or bombastic texts were clothed in fine music; also incidental music to plays by D'Urfey, Tate, Dryden, Crowne, Southerne, Shadwell, Lee, Congreve, D'Avenant, and others.

Purcell wrote the anthem *My Heart is Inditing* for the coronation of King James II (1685); with *Dido and Aeneas* (libretto by Tate; London, mid to late 1680s) he produced the 1st great English opera. He composed much sacred music, including a Magnificat and Nunc dimitiis (n.d.), Morning and Evening Service (1682), and Te Deum and Jubilate in D (1694); numerous anthems and services (c. 1677–95), including the anthem *Thou knowest, Lord, the Secrets of our Hearts* (1695), written for the funeral of Queen Mary; performed, along with his 4 canzonas for brass and 2 elegies, at his own funeral later that year.

Purcell lies in the north aisle of Westminster Abbey, and his burial tablet expresses his worth well: "Here lyes Henry Purcell, Esq.; who left this life, and is gone to that blessed place where only his harmony can be exceeded." His church music reveals an original melodist and a master of form, harmony, and all contrapuntal devices; his stage music is equally rich in invention, dramatic instinct, and power of characterization; his chamber works surpass those of his predecessors and contemporaries. Semioperas (plays with varying degrees of music) include *The Prophetess, or The History of Dioclesian* (1690); *King Arthur, or The British Worthy* (1691); *The Fairy Queen* (1692); *The Indian Queen* (1695; final masque by D. Purcell); *The Tempest, or The Enchanted Island* (c. 1695). Other vocal works include songs for 1 or more voices and basso continuo and catches; instrumental works include pieces for winds and strings (fantasias, overtures, pavans, sonatas, etc.); harpsichord music. His brother Daniel Purcell (b. London, c. 1660; d. there, Nov. 26, 1717) was an organist and composer; completed 1 or more of Henry's pieces.

puzzle canon. Canon presented as a single melodic line and playful, intentionally obscure instructions as to its solution, e.g., the phrase "cancer eat plenis et redeat medius" (let the crab go forth entire and return in half); deciphered, this instructs that the melody should be performed in retrograde, and then in normal (forward) sequence, but with note values halved, i.e., twice as fast; also called riddle canon. See also ⇒canon.

pyramidon. Organ stop with short stopped pipes; produces the lowest notes of the organ's range; covered by short pyramidal pipes more than 4 times as wide on top as at their base.

Pythagorean tuning. See ⇒temperament.

qin (ch'in). Early Chinese zither, most honored of Chinese instruments; associated with the Confucian ruling class, who played meditatively upon it while pondering life.

quadrille (from Sp. *quadrilla*, 4 dancing pairs). French ballroom square dance; its 5 main figures are *le Pantalon, l'Été, la Poule, la Pastourelle (la Trenise)*, and *la Finale;* meter alternates between 3/8 (6/8) and 2/4. The quadrille attained its greatest popularity in the early 19th century, in Europe (including Russia) and America.

quadrivium. Faculty of 4 sciences in medieval universities, 1 of which was music, the discipline dealing with the physical part of sound perception; the other 3 were arithmetic, geometry, and astronomy.

quadruple counterpoint. See ⇒counterpoint.

quadruple croche (Fr.). 64th note.

quadruple meter or time. Time division characterized by 4 beats to the measure.

quadruplet. Group of 4 equal notes, to be executed in the time of 3 or 6 of the same kind in the established rhythm, written

quality of tone. Characteristic peculiarity of any vocal or instrumental tone that distinguishes it from any other class of voices or instruments; also called tone color or timbre.

Quantz, Johann Joachim, b. Oberscheden, Hannover, Jan. 30, 1697; d. Potsdam, July 12, 1773. He revealed a natural gift for music and played the double bass at village festivals at age 8; at age 10 he was apprenticed to his uncle, Justus Quantz, a "Stadtmusikus" in Merseburg, and later to J. A. Fleischhack; received instruction on string and wind instruments, becoming particularly adept on the violin, oboe, and trumpet; studied harpsichord with J. F. Kiesewetter. He completed his apprenticeship (1713); remained a journeyman under Fleischhack (to 1716); became a member of the Dresden municipal band; during a 3-month leave of absence studied counterpoint with J. D. Zelenka in Vienna; (1717); became oboist at the Polish chapel of

Augustus II (1718); continued activities in Dresden and Warsaw; turned to the transverse flute; received lessons from P. G. Buffardin.

In 1724 Quantz went to Rome in the entourage of the Polish ambassador; sought out F. Gasparini for counterpoint training; returned to Dresden as a flutist in the Hofkapelle (1727). He made his 1st visit to Berlin in the entourage of Augustus II (1728); engaged as teacher to Crown Prince Friedrich; visited Berlin regularly to instruct Friedrich while carrying out his duties in Dresden, which now included flute-making (from 1739). Friedrich ascended the Prussian throne (1740); a year later he called Quantz to Berlin; he was to oversee the King's private evening concerts; granted an annual salary of 2,000 thalers, plus an honorarium for each new composition and flute he produced. He was held in such high esteem by his patron that he was the only individual allowed to criticize Friedrich's playing on the flute. (C.P.E. Bach, who also worked for Friedrich, had to tolerate it.)

Quantz wrote 300 concertos for flute, strings, and basso continuo, plus a small number of other wind concertos; 200 sonatas for flute and basso continuo; 60 trio sonatas; flute duets; solo flute capriccios and fantasias for flute; hymns; songs; etc. These works reveal his galant style, in the midst of the transition from the Baroque to the Classic style. He publ. the invaluable treatise *Versuch einer Anweisung die Flöte traversiere zu spielen* (Berlin, 1752).

quaquaversal. Turned or turning in different directions.

quart de soupir (Fr., quarter of a sigh). 16th-note rest.

quarta (It.; Ger. *Quarte*). Perfect 4th.

quartal harmony. System based on the superposition of intervals of the 4th rather than the traditional 3rd; increasingly attractive to 20th-century composers seeking to break the chains of triadic tonality (Schoenberg, Chamber Symphony no. 1, opening theme).

Quartegeige (Ger.). Quarter-violin, smaller than and tuned a 4th higher than the standard violin, now obsolete.

quarter note. Crotchet (♩), equal to 1 beat in any time signature with a denominator of 4.

quarter rest. Rest equal in time value to a quarter note: 𝄿 or 𝄾.

quarter tone. Half a semitone; a logarithmic interval used by 20th-century composers; also used in non-Western music. Quarter tones are not modern inventions; they are found in the ancient Greek enharmonic scale. Many romantic composers of the 19th century thought of reviving quarter tones as a unit of an icositetraphonic scale. Charles Ives's father George, an Army band leader during the Civil War, experimented with tuning his instruments a quarter tone apart.

The attraction of quarter tones for modern composers reflects a desire to develop a finer and more subtle means of musical expression. A pioneer of the quarter-tone revival was the Mexican Julián Carrillo (1875–1965), who published a treatise on *Sonido 13* (1895), the number 13 referring to all tonal resources beyond the 12-tone chromatic scale (composed for up to 96 notes per octave). The Moravian Alois Hába (1893–1973) codified composition with quarter tones in his *Neue Harmonielehre* (1928; also used odd-numbered subdivisions of the chromatic scale).

The 1st quarter-tone piano (2 keyboards tuned a quarter tone apart) was built in 1924. Rimsky-Korsakov's grandson Georg founded a quarter-tone society in Leningrad in the 1920s. Russian composer Ivan Wyschnegradsky, who made his home in Paris, wrote much music for 2 pianos tuned a quarter tone apart. Charles Ives wrote a chorale for strings in quarter tones as early as 1914. Several notation systems for quarter tones have been proposed; the most logical is Hába's, using slashed signs for flats and sharps. Ernest Bloch used quarter tones in his Piano Quintet, notated simply as flatted or sharped notes. See also ⇒microtonality.

quartet (quartette; Fr. *quatuor;* It. *quartetto;* Ger. *Quartett*). 1. Concerted instrumental composition for 4 performers, such as the string quartet, for 2 violins, viola, and cello. 2. Composition, movement, or number, either vocal or instrumental, in 4 parts; e.g., a vocal quartet might involve one standard range apiece, i.e., SATB. 3. Particular ensemble designed to perform these genres.

quartettino (It.). Small piece for quartet.

Quartsextakkord (Ger.). 2nd inversion triad; the $^6_4$ or 6–4 chord.

quasi (It.). As if; as it were; nearly; approaching. *Andante quasi allegretto,* andante approaching allegretto; *quasi niente,* almost nothing; *quasi trombi,* like trumpets; *quasi una fantasia,* like a fantasia; *quasi zimbalo,* like a cimbalom.

quasihemidemisemiquaver (U.K.). 128th note.

quatre (It. *quattro;* Ger. *vier*). Four.

quatricinium (Lat.). 4-voice composition; specifically, a wind quartet for German Stadtpfeifer; term 1st appeared in the 17th century.

quattro (It.; Fr. *quatre;* Ger. *vier*). Four. *A quattro mani,* for 4 hands.

quatuor à cordes (Fr.). String quartet.

quaver (U.K.). 8th note.

Queen. British exponents of glitter rock. (Vocal/keyboards: Freddie Mercury, b. Frederick Bulsana, Zanzibar, Africa, Sept. 5, 1946; d. Kensington, England, Nov. 24, 1991; lead guitar: Brian May, b. Twickenham, England, July 19 1947; bass: John Deacon, b. Leicester England, Aug. 19, 1951; drums: Roger Taylor, b. Kings Lynn, England, July 26, 1949.) Led by flamboyant vocalist Mercury, Queen managed to combine heavy English progressive rock with bombastic self-parody to create a critically misunderstood but commercially successful group from the mid-1970s to the early 1980s. The band came together out of the remnants of other bands (1971); produced a series of albums, finally breaking through to pop stardom with *Bohemian Rhapsody,* promoted through one of the 1st rock videos (1975); more chart-toppers followed, expressing characteristically over-the-top

sentiments, including *We Will Rock You* (1976) and *Another One Bites the Dust* (1980; both popular at sporting events). The group's popularity waned in the early 1980s; broke up in 1986. Mercury died of AIDS; this led to a tribute concert and renewed Queenmania; *Bohemian Rhapsody* was affectionately revived in the film *Wayne's World,* and the video and song enjoyed another run of success.

quena (Quechua). Generic term for a vertical flute made of bamboo or baked clay, popular among the Guaraní peoples in Argentina, Bolivia, Peru, and the Amazon basin.

Querelle des Bouffons. Guerre des Bouffons.

Querflöte (Ger.). Transverse flute. *Querpfeife,* transverse fife.

quickstep. 1. March, usually in 6/8 time. 2. Rapid American fox-trot; developed *c.* 1920.

quijada (*quijada del burro;* Sp., jawbone of an ass). Afro-Cuban instrument, originating as its name suggests, with teeth left in; may be used as a scraper, a rattle, or a percussive instrument (hit with the fist); dates to at least the 18th century.

quilisma. Ornament indicating an ascending semitone in neumatic notation.

quindecima (It.). 15th, either the interval or the organ stop. *Alla quindecima* (written simply 15ma), 2 octaves higher (or lower).

quint. 1. Interval of a 5th. 2. 5 1/3' organ stop, sounding a 5th higher than the normal 8' pitch. 3. Violin E string.

quinte (*quinte de violon;* Fr.). Obsolete name for the viola.

Quintenzirkel (Ger.). Cycle (circle) of 5ths.

Quinterne (Ger.). Gittern.

quintet (Fr. *quintette,* quintour; It. *quintetto;* Ger. *Quintett*). 1. Concerted instrumental composition for 5 performers. 2. Composition, movement, or number, vocal or instrumental, in 5 parts. 3. Particular ensemble designed to perform these genres.

quintina (It.). Quintuplet.

quinton (Fr.). 17th-century term for the treble viola d'amore.

Quintsextakkord (Ger.). 1st inversion dominant-7th chord; the $^6_5$, 6–5, or 6–5–3 chord.

quintuple rhythm (time). Grouping of 5 beats to the measure.

quintuplets (It. *quintina;* Ger. *Quintole;* Fr. *quintolet*). Group of 5 notes of equal duration played against a normal grouping of 4 or 3 notes.

quitter (Fr.). Quit, leave. *Sans quitter la corde,* without quitting the string.

quodlibet (from Lat., as you wish; Fr. *fricassée,* stewed meat). Free medley of popular melodies, religious hymns, and cosmopolitan madrigals; cultivated by medieval students in Central Europe. The attraction of such fricassèes is the joy of recognizing familiar tunes in an otherwise solemn context; even Bach succumbed to the quodlibet's lure by combining 2 popular melodies in the last movement of his *Goldberg Variations*. A quodlibet formed by the superposition of the Russian song *Dark Eyes* and one of Chopin's F-minor études was popular among Russian conservatory students. Peter Schickele is among the current masters of the genre. See also ⇒potpourri.

quotation. In a given work, the inclusion of musical materials that allude to other compositions or musics. Folk songs, all or part of a cantus firmus, and the doom-laden chant Dies irae have been for centuries a favorite resource of quotations. R. Strauss inserted the theme of the funeral march from Beethoven's *Eroica* Sym. in the score of his *Metamorphosen,* a dirge on the death of Germany written at the end of World War II. Berg quoted Bach's chorale *Es ist genug* in the finale of his Violin Concerto, a memorial for Manon Gropius, Alma Mahler Werfel's daughter by another marriage.

Quotations from a composer's own scores are not rare; a notorious example is the egocentric series of quotations used by Strauss in the score of his symphonic poem *Ein Heldenleben*. But perhaps the most extraordinary assembly of assorted thematic memos, memories, and mementos is found in *Sinfonia* by Berio, in which he quotes metamorphosed fragments from Mahler, Debussy, Ravel and others; this differs, of course, from the deliberate quotation of a famous tune for purposes of characterization or as a historical reference, e.g., the *Marseillaise* in Tchaikovsky's *1812 Overture* and Giordano's opera *Andrea Chenier,* or *The Star-Spangled Banner* in Puccini's *Madama Butterfly*.

R. Stands for *right* (Ger. *rechte*); *r.h.*, right hand (*rechte Hand*). In French organ music *R* stands for *clavier de récit* (swell manual).

Ra (Fr.). Onomatopoeic syllable indicating the drum figure with 2 sticks, alternating rapidly between right and left hands. *Ra de quatre*, drum figure in 4 beats; *Ra de trois*, drum figure in 3 beats; *Ra et sauté*, drum figure in 2 beats with a break in between.

rabāb (Arab.). Middle Eastern bowed spiked fiddle, 1st recorded in the 10th century, and based on a Persian plucked lute. The rabāb has a pear-shaped body, sickle-shaped pegbox, and between 3 and 5 strings. Related forms of it are played in southern Asia and Indonesia, the latter as a gamelan instrument called *rebab*; it was introduced there in the 16th century as a result of the Arab invasions. By the 11th century the rabāb had reached Europe; it evolved into the rebec, which survived into the 18th century.

rabbia, con (It.). With passion, frenzy; furiously.

raccoglimento, con (It.). Collectedly, coolly; meditatively.

raccontando (It.). Narrating, as if telling a story.

Rachmaninoff, Sergei (Vassilievich), b. Semyonovo, Apr. 1, 1873; d. Beverly Hills, Mar. 28, 1943. His grandfather was an amateur pianist and pupil of John Field; his father and mother both played; it was from her that Sergei received his 1st lessons; he went to St. Petersburg; studied piano with V. Demiansky and harmony with A. Rubets at the Cons. (1882–85); following his cousin A. Siloti's advice, he enrolled as a piano student of N. Zverev at the Moscow Cons. (1885); entered Siloti's piano class; studied counterpoint with Taneyev and harmony with Arensky (1888); met Tchaikovsky, who encouraged him; graduated as a pianist (1891) and composer (1892); won the gold medal with his opera *Aleko*, after Pushkin. He wrote the Prelude in C-sharp Minor (from *Morceaux de fantaisie*, No. 2, op. 3, 1892), which became one of the most celebrated piano pieces. His 1st Sym., given in Moscow (1897), proved a failure; discouraged, he destroyed the MS; the orch'l parts were preserved; the score was restored and performed in Moscow (1945).

Rachmaninoff launched a career as piano virtuoso and conductor, joining the Moscow Private Russian Orch. (1897); made his London debut as pianist, conductor, and composer with the Phil. Soc. (1899); he couldn't compose after the 1st Sym. debacle; plagued by depression, underwent treatment by hypnosis; composed the 2nd Piano Concerto, playing the premiere with Siloti conducting in Moscow (1901); this work became and perhaps remains the most celebrated concerto in the 20th century, a model for Russian and light classical virtuoso works for piano and orch.

Rachmaninoff conducted at Moscow's Bolshoi Theater (1904–06); moved to Dresden; composed his 2nd Sym. and the fiendishly difficult 3rd Piano Concerto, which he took on his 1st U.S. tour (1909); twice declined the conductorship of the Boston Sym. Orch. (1909, 1918).

Rachmaninoff lived in Russia from 1910 until after the Bolshevik Revolution of 1917; left Russia with his family, never to return. From 1918 until 1939 he made annual European tours as a pianist; also the U.S. (from 1918 until his death). He spent much of his time in Lucerne (1931–39); there he composed the enduring *Rhapsody on a Theme of Paganini* (1934); awarded the Gold Medal of the Royal Phil. Soc. of London (1932); after the outbreak of World War II (1939) he lived in the U.S.; became a naturalized U.S. citizen a few weeks before his death; made his last appearance as a pianist in Knoxville, Tenn.

Among Russian composers Rachmaninoff occupies a very important place; his sources lie in 19th-century Romantic Russian music; his links with Tchaikovsky are very strong—melancholy moods prevail, and minor keys predominate—but Rachmaninoff's individuality resides in the broad, rhapsodic sweep of the melodic line and fully expanded sonorities and resonant harmonies of his piano writing, whose technical resourcefulness had not been seen since Liszt. Despite Rachmaninoff's émigré status and opposition to the Soviet regime (although he softened when the Nazis attacked Russia in 1941), his popularity never wavered in Russia; there, as in England and America, his music has a significant place on the concert stage; it is much less popular in Germany, France, and Italy.

Other works by Rachmaninoff include 2 other operas; 3 syms.; 4 piano concertos; symphonic poems: *Prince Rostislav* (1891); *The Rock* (1893); *The Isle of the Dead*, op. 29, after Böcklin's painting (Moscow, 1909); *Symphonic Dances*, op. 45 (Philadelphia, 1941); 2 Russian Orthodox choral works: *Liturgy of St. John Chrysostom*, op. 31 (Moscow, 1910) and the *All-Night Vigil*, op. 37 (1915); also *The Bells*, choral sym., op. 35, after Poe (St. Petersburg, 1913). As a virtuoso pianist he composed works to show off his abilities, usually of a higher quality than most of his 19th-century predecessors: 6 *Moments musicaux*, op. 16 (1896); *Variations on a Theme of Chopin*, op. 22 (1902–03); 10 Preludes, op. 23 (1901–03); Sonata No. 1, op. 28 (1907); 13 Preludes, op. 32 (1910); *Études-tableaux*, op. 33 (1911); Sonata No. 2, op. 36 (1913; rev. 1931); *Études-tableaux*, op. 39 (1916–17); *Variations on a Theme of Corelli*, op. 42 (1931); piano duets; songs (1890–1916).

racket (Ger. *Rachett, Rankett*; Fr. *Cervelas, cervelat*; It. *rocchetta, cortalo*). Obsolete wind instrument of the 16th and 17th centuries; its double reed is partly covered by the mouthpiece (*pirouette*). The body, made of ivory or wood, is shaped like a small tree stump; the tube consists of a connected series of narrow channels bored up and down the body. Fingerholes are bored obliquely into the channels, thus requiring a player to use the tip and middle joints of a finger to cover a hole. The racket also has vent-holes and a water escape. As a closed pipe it sounds an octave lower than its length; but it cannot be overblown, so that the ranges on the 3 types of racket are only an octave and a perfect 5th; the lowest racket (great bass) has a range C_1–G_0; the highest (soprano), G_0–d^1. The racket has had an occasional role in the early music revival of the 20th century.

raddolcente (It.). Growing calmer and gentler.

raddoppiato (It.). Double the tempo.

Radel (Ger.). Vocal canon.

radial distribution. Radial distribution of a linear series is a maximum dispersion of the constituent tones, such as occurs in a technique commonly described by a term borrowed from art, pointillism. The visual impression from an actual score is a picture of tonal particles appearing and disappearing in the outer registers of orch'l instruments, or extreme octaves on the piano keyboard. The geometry of this image is particularly striking in the appearance of the instrumental works by Webern.

radical cadence. A close—either partial or complete—formed with 2 fundamental chords.

radio opera. When radio was in its infancy, the musical community became worked up with the idea of channeling opera into homes; listeners still had to use earphones when excerpts from *Pagliacci* were broadcast from the Metropolitan Opera in N.Y. (1910). The 1st complete broadcast of an opera was of *Hänsel und Gretel*, transmitted from Covent Garden in London (1923); *Aida* was broadcast from the Metropolitan Opera (1924); *Fidelio* was broadcast from Dresden by transatlantic radio (1930). Apparently the 1st opera written specifically for broadcasting was C. W. Cadman's *The Willow Tree*, transmitted from N.Y. (1933).

The greatest flowering of radio opera came by way of the phonograph. With the development of long-playing records in the 1950s, it became possible to put on the air entire operas, even obscure ones, because of the arrangement whereby no royalties had to be paid for broadcasting phonograph records; this has since changed. Television seemed poised to bring about a real revolution in expanding the walls of an opera house to embrace the entire world; this was not to be, however, because of the cost of television productions. The most successful opera written specially for television was *Amahl and the Night Visitors* by Menotti (1951), commissioned by NBC for a Christmas show and repeated annually (with few omissions) at Christmastime.

Raff, (Joseph) Joachim, b. Lachen, near Zurich, May 27, 1822; d. Frankfurt am Main, June 24, 1882. He was a schoolteacher in Rapperswill (1840–44) but pursued an interest in music; sent piano pieces to Mendelssohn (1843), who recommended them for publication; met Liszt in Basel (1845) and received his encouragement and assistance in finding employment; later assisted Liszt in Weimar (1850–56), where he became an ardent propagandist of the new German school of composition. He went to Wiesbaden as piano teacher and composer; became director of the Hoch Cons. in Frankfurt (1877–82); taught composition; students flocked to study with him, including MacDowell.

Raff was a composer of prodigious fecundity, master of all technical aspects of composition, versatile in his choice of genres. He wrote 214 publ. works and many more that remained in MS. In spite of his fame, his music fell into lamentable desuetude after his death. He was best-known for his 11 syms. (1859–76); No. 5, *Leonore*, was his most famous work (1872); overtures, 2 violin concertos, 2 cello concertos, a piano concerto, 4 orch'l

suites. Vocal music: 6 operas, choral works with orch. and without accompaniment; also chamber works, piano pieces, and arrangements. He publ. *Die Wagnerfrage: Wagners letzte kunstlerische Kundgebung im Lohengrin* (Braunschweig, 1854).

raffranando (It.). Holding back.

raga. (Sanskrit, colors; singular *rāg*). System of modes used in the classical (Hindustani) music of northern India, representing both a succession of intervals (not necessarily tempered) and a meaningful relationship to spiritual values; a similar system exists in southern India's classical (Carnatic) tradition. For listeners attuned to the infinite semantic gradations of the ragas, correspondences exist not only with human moods (joy, sorrow, loneliness, waiting, love, revulsion) but with a definite time of the day or season of the year; thus the playing of ragas assumes a mystical and magical quality of meditation and communication.

The subtle moods and modes of the raga may be difficult to absorb by a Westerner. Listening to a long improvisation played on indigenous string instruments (viña, sitār, sarōd, sārangī), bamboo flutes, voice, and (recently) violin, accompanied by paired membranophones (tablā and bāya) and a symbolic string drone (tamburā), may be difficult to absorb because of the music's seeming lack of harmonic progression. There is also the paradoxical Indian musical aesthetic: a highly theorized system between 1,500 and 2,500 years old vs. an oral tradition taught by demanding apprenticeship; a desire to educate non-Indians vs. the mostly improvisatory performances, rendering Western notation virtually useless. Finally there has always been disputes between music masters who have reached out for Western audiences and those who condemn this activity.

The modes of the ragas are primarily pentatonic in structure; supplementary tones are added, increasing the gamut to 7 or more degrees. A *rāg*'s range may exceed an octave by a few pitches; many ragas differ in pitch going up from going down, as does the melodic minor scale. The hierarchy of primary and secondary tones of the ragas is strictly observed; unlike Western modulation, changes in *rāg* cannot be made within the same "performance." The goal of improvisation is the expression of the essence of a *rāg*; the means involve emphasis on each note, appropriate ornamentation, and correct motion within the *rāg*.

Melodic improvisation requires the support of and challenge by the tablā player (playing both drums), who also has a system to work within, the tāla. The rhythmic structure of the tala involves divisions with different numbers of beats in each, added together to form a fixed rhythmic unit of considerable complexity; tala is cumulative (cyclical) because such rhythmic units are repeated to form larger units. To an uninitiated listener it may appear that a group of performers, playing without scores or a signal by a principal player, could sound instruments together after a long interval of time; in fact, professional musicians can conceive such units, normally up to a 16-beat (*tīñ-tāl*) cycle but potentially greater. To this must be added the constant rhythmic variations skillfully but instinctively fitted into the main metrical divisions.

Standard classical Indian improvisation is shaped as follows: 1) The opening *ālāpa* (alap) for melodic and drone instruments; a "tuning check" is followed by the *rāg*'s introduction; it is then improvised upon in a slow, arhythmic, meditative manner; the 2) *jod.* (jor), rhythmic improvisation with repeated and varied motives, concluded with the 3) *jhālā*, a fast section; the 4) *gat*, adding the tablā and tāl to the melodic instrument/s; the drone continues but becomes virtually inaudible. This section alternates between a brief precomposed piece and free improvisation; there may be friendly rivalry between the musicians; it ends with another 5) *jhala*, very fast, with a textural and dynamic crescendo; a cadential formula is repeated 3 times, assuring a clean ending.

ragtime. Syncopated, primarily African American music, predominant between *c.* 1896 and 1918; the term denoted vocal and instrumental music and dance styles associated with it. As an instrumental genre it was a popular ballroom style and major contributor to early jazz. In today's usage the term refers almost exclusively to piano works; an individual piece is called a rag.

The etymology for the term "ragtime" (1st used by the African American performer Ernest Hogan) gives a derivation from "ragged time," i.e., syncopation. Syncopation was a prevalent component of American popular music in the 19th century, especially in the dance music and song of the black slaves and ex-slaves, and its adaptation into blackface minstrelsy, notably in songs by Foster, D. D. Emmett, and others. After the Civil War black performers asserted their musical birthright by adapting minstrelsy for their own purposes, performing vaudevillelike revues featuring the cakewalk, buck-and-wing, and walk-around dances.

As African American minstrelsy entered the theater in the late 19th century, songs and later instrumental pieces in syncopated quadruple or duple time became popular, reflecting the important influence of the march, a truly popular genre in the U.S. after the Civil War. Its strong emphasis on the beats themselves and the practical needs of the genre left little opportunity for syncopation; but in the black dance and popular genres, the ragtime piano's left-hand march like "oom-pah" accompaniment—lowest note on the downbeat, higher note on the 3rd beat, and triads in higher registers on the 2nd and 4th offbeats—became standard. The melody, in 8th notes, was freed to become more syncopated, using among others the rhythms below:

Ragtime was the 1st non racist African American genre to attain wide popularity in the U.S.; pianists played it in American saloons, barrooms, bordellos, and burlesque houses; such pianists were called "perfessors" (professors). Later, in the hands of Joplin (composer of *Maple Leaf Rag* and *The Entertainer*), Turpin, Scott, Lamb, Chauvin, Matthews, Aufderheide, and others, ragtime acquired a "classic" quality of elegance in moderate tempo (hence Joplin's warning that "ragtime should never be played too fast") or a lively and even humorous quality suitable for dancing. The rapid motion and cross-accents of ragtime proved irresistible to classical composers; Gilbert and Ives cultivated ragtime rhythms early in the century. Ragtime became very popular in Europe; Debussy used raglike rhythms in his *Golliwog's Cake Walk* (from *Children's Corner*); Stravinsky and others wrote pieces closely modeled on ragtime.

The proliferation of ragtime must have been pervasive, considering the outcries of shock and indignation in the music periodicals at the turn of the 20th century. The *Journal of the International Music Society* (1905) described ragtime in this way: "It suggests the gait of a hurried mule among anthills; there is a cross-rhythm, with a kind of halting contrapuntal ornamentation in the accompaniment which sometimes brings a stress onto the 4th beat of the bar. The phrases, being no longer presented with regular and recurrent pulsations, give rise to a sense of disorder, which, combined with the emotional expression of the music, suggests an irresponsibility and a sense of careless jollity agreeable to the tired or vacuous brain." As late as 1916, ragtime was still a phenomenon to be abhorred, to judge by a letter to the editor publ. in the *New York Evening Sun:* "The rhythm of ragtime suggests the odor of the saloon, the smell of backyards and subways. Its style is decadent. It is music meant for tired and materially bored minds. It is essentially obvious, vulgar, and yet shockingly strong for the reason that it ends fortissimo."

But there were also some philosophically analytic voices in the press. Rupert Hughes wrote soberly in the *Musical Record of Boston* (1899): "If ragtime were called *tempo di raga* or *rague-temps,* it might win honors more speedily. If the word could be allied to the harmonic rage of the East Indians, it would be more acceptable. The Negroes call their clog-dancing 'ragging' and the dance a 'rag'. . . . Ragtime will find its way gradually into the works of some great genius and will thereafter be canonized, and the day will come when the decadents of the next, the 20th century, will revolt against it and will call it 'a hidebound, sapless, scholastic form, dead as its contemporaries, canon and fugue.' Meanwhile, it is young and unhackneyed, and throbbing with life. And it is racial [used positively]."

Raimondi, Ruggero, b. Bologna, Oct. 3, 1941. He was educated at the Accademia di Santa Cecilia in Rome; made his debut as Colline in Spoleto in 1964; from 1967, sang at Milan's La Scala. In 1970 he made his Metropolitan Opera debut in N.Y. as Silva in *Ernani*. His other signal appearances were at the Paris Opéra, the Bavarian State Opera in Munich, and the Deutsche Oper in Berlin. He was distinguished in the roles of Don Giovanni and Mozart's Figaro; he was also praised for his dramatic rendition of Boris Godunov.

Rainey, Ma (born Gertrude Pridgett), b. Columbus, Ga., Apr. 26, 1886; d. Rome, Ga., Dec. 22, 1939. She made her 1st appearance in public in Columbus when she was 12; after touring with the Rabbit Foot Minstrels and Tolliver's Circus, she organized her own Georgia Jazz Band; made numerous recordings before retiring to Columbus in 1935. Her style of blues singing influenced Bessie Smith.

Raitt, Bonnie, b. Los Angeles, Nov. 8, 1949. Her father was John (Emmet) Raitt (b. Santa Ana, Calif., Jan. 29, 1917), a versatile popular singer best known for his Broadway appearances in *Oklahoma!, Carousel, Pajama Game,* and *Annie Get Your Gun.* Bonnie took up the guitar when she was 12; after attending Radcliffe College (1967–69) departed the academic scene to pursue a recording career, mixing blues, rock, and ballads. She made a number of fine albums, including *Give It Up* (1972) and *Sweet Forgiveness* (1977), but never attained the commercial heights expected; her career was derailed for a time by alcoholism. She finally recovered; achieved commercial success with

Nick of Time (1989), winning 4 Grammy Awards, including best album of the year; has since released *Luck of the Draw* (1991) and *Longing in Their Hearts* (1994).

Raksin, David, b. Philadelphia, Aug. 4, 1912. He studied piano in childhood; learned to play woodwind instruments from his father, a performer and conductor; as a teenager organized his own jazz band; entered the Univ. of Pa. (1931); studied composition privately with I. Freed (1934–35). He went to Hollywood to assist Charlie Chaplin with the music for his film *Modern Times* (1935); the two became close friends; when Chaplin was forced into exile by the anti-Communists of the U.S. Congress for alleged radical activities, Raksin struck out on his own; studied privately with Schoenberg.

Raksin has composed more than 100 film scores; his greatest success was the theme song for *Laura;* ingratiatingly melodious in its sinuous and convoluted pattern, it generated more than 300 different versions. Apart from composing and conducting, he appeared as an actor and commentator in television programs. He composed symphonic suites based on his film music, among them *Forever Amber* and *The Bad and the Beautiful;* other scores include *Force of Evil, Carrie, The Redeemer,* and *Separate Tables;* also wrote incidental music, symphonic pieces, and vocal works. At Stravinsky's request, he made the original band instrumentation of *Circus Polka* for Balanchine's production with the Barnum and Bailey Circus. He taught at the Univ. of Southern Calif. and the Univ. of Calif., Los Angeles; faculty member of the Univ. of Southern Calif. School of Public Administration (1968–89).

rallentando (*ralenti;* It.; abbrev. rall.). Gradually becoming lento. A distinction is sometimes made between rallentando and ritenuto; the former is a gradual process lasting several measures, while the latter requires a more or less sudden slackening of the tempo.

rallentare (It.). Grow slower. *Senza rallentare,* without slackening the pace.

Rameau, Jean-Philippe, b. Dijon (baptized), Sept. 25, 1683; d. Paris, Sept. 12, 1764. His father was organist of St. Étienne in Dijon. Jean-Philippe learned to play the harpsichord as a child; attended the Jesuit Collège des Godrans in Dijon (1693–97); took up singing and composing instead of concentrating on academic studies; his father sent him to Milan (1701); stayed for a brief time before joining the orch. of a traveling French opera troupe as a violinist; temporarily appointed as organist at Avignon Cathedral (1702); became organist at Clermont Cathedral; went to Paris; publ. his 1st *Livre de pièces de clavecin* (1706); active as a church organist (to 1708).

Rameau succeeded his father as organist at Notre Dame Cathedral in Avignon (1709); became organist to the Jacobins in Lyons (1713); organist at Clermont Cathedral (1715–23), where he wrote his famous *Traité de l'harmonie* (Paris, 1722), an epoch-making work, little understood at the time, attracting considerable attention and rousing opposition; when he settled definitely in Paris (1723) he was not unknown. He lost a competition for the organist position at St.-Vincent-de-Paul (1727), but Marchand (probably out of jealousy) had exerted his powerful influence in favor of the inferior Daquin. Rameau became organist at Ste.-Croix-de-la-Bretonnerie (1732); recognized as the foremost organist in France. He publ. his *Nouveau système de musique théorique* (1726), an introduction to the *Traité.* The stir his novel theories occasioned, and his reputation as organist, did not satisfy his ambition: to bring out a dramatic work at the Opéra.

Rameau made a modest theatrical debut with incidental music to Piron's comedy *L'Endriague* (1723); after contributing incidental music to 2 more Piron comedies, he became music master to the wife of the "fermier-général" La Pouplinière; the latter obtained from Voltaire a libretto for *Samson,* which Rameau set to music; it was rejected on account of its biblical subject; now lost. Another libretto, Pellegrin's *Hippolyte et Aricie,* was accepted; produced at the Opéra (1733); received coolly, despite undeniable superiority over operas by Lully and his followers. Rameau considered abandoning composing for the theater, but the persuasions of his friends, who also influenced public opinion in his favor, were effective; he produced the successful opera-ballet *Les Indes galantes* (1735) and his operatic masterpiece, *Castor et Pollux* (1737), which held its own for years beside the operas of Gluck. A career of uninterrupted prosperity commenced; he was recognized as the leading theorist alive; his instruction was eagerly sought; for the next 30 years his operas dominated the French stage; named Compositeur du cabinet du roy (1745); ennobled 4 months before his death.

From the beginning of his dramatic career Rameau simultaneously roused great opposition and ardent admiration. The 1st war of words was waged between the "Lullistes" and the "Ramistes"; no sooner had this been resolved by a triumphant 1751 revival of *Pygmalion* (1748) when a production of Pergolesi's *La Serva padrona* (1752) caused an even more prolonged and bitter controversy between the "Ramistes" and the "Encyclopedistes" known as the Guerre des Bouffons; Rameau participated by writing essays defending his position; as Wagner would be a century later, he was accused of perpetrating unintelligible harmony, lack of melody, preponderance of discords, and noisy instrumentation. But when the war between Gluckists and Piccinnists was raging 25 years later, Rameau's works were praised as models of beauty and perfection.

Regretfully, Rameau was indifferent to the quality of his librettos, relying so much upon musical inspiration that he never understood the value of a good text; nevertheless, his operas mark a decided advance over Lully's in musical characterization, expressive melody, richness of harmony, variety of modulation, and expert and original instrumentation. He wrote 30 sung dramas, premiered in Paris or Versailles, in many genres: opéra-ballet, comédie-ballet, divertissement, pastorale-héroïque, opéra comique en vaudevilles, tragédie lyrique, intermède en musique, etc. He composed a small amount of secular and sacred vocal music; his best-known instrumental pieces are for harpsichord, many with amusing descriptive titles, publ. in 3 sets (1706; 1724, rev. 1731; 1728?); his chamber music is found in the *Pièces de clavecin en concerts* for Harpsichord, Violin or Flute, and Viol or Violin (1741).

The leading ideas of Rameau's system of harmony involve chord-building by 3rds; classification of a chord and its inversions as one and the same, thus reducing the multiplicity of consonant and dissonant combinations to a fixed and limited number of root chords; the concept of a fundamental bass (*basse fondamentale*), an abstracted series of root tones forming the real basis of chord progressions in a composition. Other important treatises are *Génération harmonique ou Traité de musique théorique et pratique* (1737); *Réponse de M. Rameau à MM. les éditeurs de l'Encyclopédie* (1757); *Lettre à M. d'Alembert sur ses opinions en musique* (1760).

Ramey, Samuel (Edward), b. Colby, Kans., Mar. 28, 1942. He attended Kansas State Univ., then studied voice with Arthur Newman at Wichita State Univ. (B.Mus., 1968); after singing with the Grass Roots Opera Co. in Raleigh, N.C. (1968–69), he continued his studies with Armen Boyajian in N.Y. He made his professional operatic debut as Zuniga in Carmen at the N.Y. City Opera (1973), and within a few seasons established himself as its principal bass; also made guest appearances at the Glyndebourne Festival (1976), the Netherlands Opera in Amsterdam (1978), the Hamburg State Opera (1978), Milan's La Scala (1981), and the Vienna State Opera (1981). In 1984 he made a brilliant debut at the Metropolitan Opera in N.Y. as Argante in Handel's *Rinaldo*. He subsequently appeared with leading opera houses around the world, and was engaged as a soloist with the major orchs. Among his notable roles are Leporello, Don Giovanni, Figaro, Gounod's Mephistopheles, the 4 villains in *Les Contes d'Hoffmann*, Attila, and Boito's Mefistofele; he sang the role of Figaro for the soundtrack recording of the award-winning film *Amadeus* (1984).

Rampal, Jean-Pierre (Louis), b. Marseilles, Jan. 7, 1922. He studied flute as a child with his father, 1st flutist in the Marseilles orch. and a prof. at the Cons.; then studied medicine until being drafted for military service by the German occupation authorities in 1943; when he learned that he was to be sent to Germany as a forced laborer, he went AWOL; subsequently attended flute classes at the Paris Cons., winning the *premier prix* in 5 months. He played solo flute in the orch. of the Vichy Opera (1946–50); concurrently began to tour, often in duo recitals with the pianist and harpsichordist Robert Veyron-Lacroix. He was solo flutist in the orch. of the Paris Opéra from 1956 to 1962, and also became a popular artist on the Paris Radio. He subsequently toured throughout the world with phenomenal success as a virtuoso, appearing as soloist with all the major orchs. and in innumerable recitals. In later years he also appeared as a guest conductor. He taught at the Paris Cons., and gave master classes worldwide.

Rampal's repertoire is vast, ranging from the Baroque masters to jazz, from the music of Japan to that of India, from arrangements to specially commissioned works. Of the last, such composers as Poulenc and Jolivet wrote pieces for him. Through his countless concerts and recordings he did more than any other flutist of his time to bring his instrument into the mainstream of musical life. He was made a Chevalier of the Legion d'Honneur in 1966 and an Officier des Arts et Lettres in 1971.

ranchera (Sp.). Argentine rural dance in 3/4 time associated with the pampas (prairie) region.

rank. A row of organ pipes. A mixture stop is said to have 2, 3, or more ranks, according to the number of pipes sounded by each key.

rant. An old country dance, or a reel. It was used in instrumental suites by 17th-century English composers.

ranz des vaches (Fr.; Ger. *Kuhreigen*). One of the airs sung, or played on the alpine horn, in the Swiss Alps as a call to the cattle. The tune itself is marked by an asymmetrical rhythm; it appears to lean toward the Lydian mode, with the characteristic augmented 4th as the formative melodic interval. A version of the ranz des vaches appears in print in the 16th century. It is also supposed to have magic and curative qualities and is often combined with religious motives.

rap. A style of urban black popular music that emerged in the mid-1970s characterized by (often) improvised rhymes performed to a rhythmic accompaniment; frequently performed a cappella, with sexual, socially relevant, or political lyrics. The music itself became known as hip-hop.

rapido (It.). Rapidly.

rappresentazione sacra (It., sacred performance). A religious spectacle; a distinct theatrical genre in Florence beginning in the 15th century. Musically it contained a succession of polyphonic canzonas. The 1st monodic exemplar of the genre was *La Rappresentazione di anima e di corpo* (1600), by Cavalieri; this work was a predecessor to the Italian *historia* and oratorio as well as the Viennese *sepolochro*.

rapsodie (Fr.). A rhapsody.

rasch (Ger.). Fast; allegro. *Noch rascher,* still faster; *so rasch wie möglich,* as fast as possible.

rasgueado (Sp., ripping). A rapid strum across the guitar strings, downward or upward, using certain fingers; the strums are often grouped and usually stopped rather than allowed to sound after the last (or only) strum.

raspa. Cuban ballroom dance, usually in 6/8 time and rapid tempo.

Rassel (Ger.). Rattle; a shaken idiophone.

rastral (from Lat. *rastrum,* rake; Ger. *Raster*). Tool for drawing the 5-line music staff in 1 sweep.

ratamacue. A drumming rudiment, in the rhythm

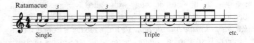

rataplan. A drumming rudiment, in the rhythm

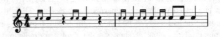

ratchet (Ger. *Ratsche*). An idiophone that consists of a wooden tablet; scraped by a cogwheel, it produces a grating trill. R. Strauss uses it in his *Till Eulenspiegels lustige Streiche* and *Don Quixote*.

Rätselkanon (Ger.). Puzzle canon.

Ratsmusiker (Ger.). Town musicians, engaged by German municipalities to blow fanfares from the platform of the city hall.

Rattle, Simon (Denis), b. Liverpool, Jan. 19, 1955. He began playing piano and percussion as a child; appeared as a percussionist with the Royal Liverpool Phil. when he was 11 and was a percussionist in the National Youth Orch.; also took up conducting in his youth and was founder-conductor of the Liverpool Sinfonia (1970–72); concurrently studied at the Royal Academy of Music in London (1971–74). After winning 1st prize in the John Player International Conductors' Competition (1974), he was assistant conductor of the Bournemouth Sym. Orch. and Sinfonietta (1974–76); made his 1st tour of the U.S. conducting the London Schools Sym. Orch. (1976). In 1977 he conducted at the Glyndebourne Festival; then was assistant conductor of the Royal Liverpool Phil. (1977–80) and the BBC Scottish Sym. Orch. in Glasgow (1977–80). He made his 1st appearance as a guest conductor of a U.S. orch. with the Los Angeles Phil. in 1979; was its principal guest conductor (from 1981); also appeared as a guest conductor with other U.S. orchs., as well as with those in Europe. In 1980 he became principal conductor of the City of Birmingham Sym. Orch.; led it on its 1st tour of the U.S. in 1988. In 1987 he was made a Commander of the Order of the British Empire.

Rauscher (Ger.). Rapidly repeated notes; a term used in the 18th century.

Rauschpfeife (Ger.). Renaissance German reed-cap shawm family with a nonflaring bell. They were held like recorders and played by Ratsmusiker and others on festive occasions.

Ravel, (Joseph) Maurice, b. Ciboure, Basses-Pyrénées, Mar. 7, 1875; d. Paris, Dec. 28, 1937. He began studying piano in Paris at age 7 with H. Ghis and harmony at age 12 with Charles-René; took piano lessons with E. Descombes; entered the Paris Cons. to study with E. Anthiome (1889); won 1st medal (1891); took the advanced class of C. de Bériot; studied harmony with E. Pessard. He left the Cons. (1895) and completed work on *Un Grand Sommeil noir, Menuet antique* for Piano, and the *Habanera* for 2 Pianos (later orchestrated for *Rapsodie espagnole*); written when he was 20, these works already reveal great originality in the treatment of modality and Spanish motives. He returned to the Cons. to study with Fauré (composition) and Gédalge (counterpoint and orchestration; 1897); his well-known *Pavane pour une infante défunte* for Piano dates from that time (1899). That year he conducted the premiere of his overture *Shéhérazade* in Paris; some elements were incorporated in his song cycle of the same name (1903). In 1901 he won the 2nd Prix de Rome with the cantata *Myrrha;* ensuing attempts to win the Grand Prix de Rome were unsuccessful; at his last try (1905) was eliminated in the preliminaries, therefore not allowed to compete; he had now reached the age limit. With 6 prizes going to pupils of the same teacher, suspicion of discrimination or worse was aroused; Jean Marnold publ. an article, "Le Scandale du Prix de Rome," in the *Mercure de France* (1905), precipitating a crisis at the Cons.; its director, Theodore Dubois, resigned, replaced by Fauré.

By this time Ravel had written many well-known works, and was regarded by most French critics as a talented disciple of Debussy. It is true that his poetic association of musical ideas paralleled that of Debussy; his use of unresolved dissonances and the enhancement of the diatonic style into pandiatonicism were techniques common to Debussy and his epigones; some of Ravel's expression marks fell within the zeitgeist, e.g., *en demi-teinte et d'un rythme las* (half-tinted and in a weary rhythm). But there were essential differences: whereas Debussy made the whole-tone scale an integral part of his musical vocabulary, Ravel rarely resorted to it; as a consequence, augmented triads appear much less frequently in Ravel's music than in Debussy's; in his piano writing Ravel actually anticipated Debussy's usages; in a letter publ. in *Le Temps* (1907), he noted that when he publ. his remarkable *Jeux d'eau* (1902), Debussy had only the fairly conventional suite *Pour le piano* to his credit.

Ravel's name became well-known, 1st in France, then throughout Europe; for many years he was still regarded as an ultra-modernist; but his inspired evocations of the past were essential to his artistic personality. At a "Concert des Auteurs Anonymes" presented in Paris (1911); the anonymous program included *Valses nobles et sentimentales,* piano pieces after the manner of Schubert; yet Ravel was recognized as the author; other examples of this style are *Le Tombeau de Couperin* and *La Valse.* Luxuriance of exotic colors marks *Daphnis et Chloé, L'Heure espagnole, Chansons madécasses, Miroirs,* and *Gaspard de la nuit.* Some works are deliberately austere, even ascetic, in their pointed neoclassicism (the piano concertos, Sonatine, some chansons); others exhibit a Fauré-like balance between the sensual and serence (2 violin sonatas, *Introduction and Allegro* for Harp and Ensemble, the piano trio). Finally, there are the works that reflect his perceptions of, even identification with, the child's world (*Histoires naturelles, Ma Mère l'Oye, L'Enfant et les sortilèges*).

When World War I broke out in 1914, Ravel was rejected for military service because of his frail physique; joined the ambulance corps at the front; his health gave way, and he was compelled to enter a hospital for recuperation (1916). He visited Amsterdam and Venice (1922); appeared in London (1923), then to Sweden, England, and Scotland (1926). An association with Diaghilev's Ballets Russes produced his masterful *Daphnis et Chloé;* another ballet, *Boléro,* commissioned by Ida Rubinstein and premiered at the Paris Opéra (1928), became his most spectacular orch'l success; its relentless ostinato-driven crescendo was irresistible to all but the composer, who complained bitterly of its musical limitations, all the way to *la banque.* He was a highly original orchestrator who developed textures both sensuous and transparent; he orchestrated 8 of his piano works, some songs, and *Tzigane;* arranged works by Rimsky-Korsakov, Satie, Schumann, Chabrier, and Mussorgsky, most notably the piano suite *Pictures at an Exhibition* (1922). Ravel never married; was extremely shy, living a life of semiretirement; devoted most of his time to composition; accepted virtually no pupils, but gave friendly advice to Vaughan Williams, Gershwin, and others; never on any school faculty; was a mediocre pianist and conductor at best. He toured the U.S. (1928); was honored by his native town with the creation of the

Quai Maurice Ravel (1929). He was apparently uninjured in an automobile accident (1932), but the event probably contributed to his final illness: difficulties in muscular coordination, attacks of aphasia, and headaches; he described his condition as "cerebral anemia," but the illness was probably Pick's disease. His last new work, *Don Quichotte à Dulcinée* for Baritone and Orch. (1932–33), was followed by abortive projects; he declined steadily; underwent brain surgery, but it was not successful; died 9 days later.

ravvivando (It.). Reviving. *Ravvivando il tempo,* accelerate the tempo.

Ray. Stands for *Re* in tonic sol-fa.

Razumovsky, Count (later Prince) Andrei. See ⇒Beethoven, Ludwig van.

Re (It.; Fr. Ré). The 2nd of the Aretinian syllables and the name of the note *D* in France, Italy, etc.

Read, Daniel, b. Attleboro, Mass., Nov. 16, 1757; d. New Haven, Conn., Dec. 4, 1836. He began to compose at 17. In 1782–83 he maintained a singing school on the North River in New Haven. At his death, he left a collection of some 400 tunes by him and other composers. He publ. *The American Singing Book, or a New and Easy Guide to the Art of Psalmody, Devised for the Use of Singing Schools in America* (New Haven, 1785; 5th ed., 1795); the *American Musical Magazine* (containing New England church music; compiled with Amos Doolittle; New Haven, 12 numbers, 1786–87); Supplement to *The American Singing Book* (New Haven, 1787); *The Columbian Harmonist* (3 vols., 1793–95); *The New Haven Collection of Sacred Music* (New Haven, 1818).

realism. A musical aesthetic adopted by 19th-century composers determined to bring music closer to humanity. It differs from simple imitation of sounds in character pieces such as *The Music Box, The Nightingale, The Brook,* and *The Cuckoo;* it rather attempts to reflect in musical terms the reality of existence. Realism finds its most logical application in vocal music, particularly in opera. The emergence of dramma per musica was prompted by the desire to express the inflections of common speech in music. Among early opera composers Caccini stated his aim as creating a melody "by means of which it would be possible to speak in musical tones." His contemporary Peri spoke of applying in opera "the accents which we unintentionally employ at moments of profound emotion." Gluck and Berlioz declared similar beliefs decades later; Wagner sought to intensify the power of ordinary speech, but his use of leitmotivs precluded true realism. It was left to the Russian composers of the National School, particularly Dargomyzhsky and Mussorgsky, to declare their determination to articulate in popular Russian accents the arias and particularly the recitatives in their operas; in this they opposed the Italian and the German ideals of music for music's sake.

The Italian operatic realism found its application in the school of verismo. A specific type of realism motivated by a political purpose arose in the Soviet Union under the somewhat specious genre of socialist realism. A modern excrescence of musical realism is vocal surrealism, in which accents of common speech are intentionally displaced. Stravinsky subjected the natural inflections of Russian speech in the vocal parts of his *Les Noces* to surrealistic distortions. In the score of his opera *The Rake's Progress* he departs completely from the natural prose of the English libretto, shifting the accents toward the weak syllables in order to produce the effect of forceful angularity.

realization. 1. A written-out basso continuo part, designed for those inexperienced in performing with figured bass. 2. An edited arrangement of an old work; an adaptation for a specific purpose. This term came into use in the 20th century, favored particularly by English composers and arrangers. An arrangement requires complete fidelity to at least the melody, rhythm, and harmony of the original, whereas a realization has a greater degree of freedom in transcribing the original work. 3. The creation of a whole, playable composition from an unfinished score or sketches. 4. The modern practice, responsive to indeterminate compositional procedures, of carrying out instructions, either explicitly or implicitly indicated in a given score, to perform a composition.

rebab. Rabāb.

rebec. A precursor of the violin that originated in Islamic nations in Asia. It found its way to Spain and into France, where it remained popular until the violin displaced it. It had only 3 strings and was pear-shaped and long-necked. This instrument was also know by the Arabic name, rabāb.

recapitulation. A return of the initial section (exposition) of a movement in sonata form.

recessional. A hymn sung in church during the departure of choir and clergy after a service.

recht (Ger.). Right. *Rechte Hand,* right hand.

recital. A concert at which either (*1*) all pieces are executed by one soloist (or solo performer with accompanist), or (*2*) all pieces are by 1 composer. The word was invented by the manager of Liszt's concert appearances in London to convey a suggestion of a narrative and so to please romantically inclined music lovers. The term is not applied to a concert by a trio, quartet, etc.

recitando (It.). In declamatory style.

recitative (Fr. *récitatif;* Ger. *Recitativ;* It. *recitativo*). 1. A musical narrative, as contrasted with arias and other formal parts in an opera or oratorio, which carries the action from one aria to another. In early opera *recitativo secco* (dry) was the common practice, with singers reciting a musical phrase following the accents and inflections of the spoken language accompanied by and alternating with a bare minimum of chords played on the harpsichord. In Classic opera Mozart and others experimented with *recitativo accompagnato* (accompanied), where the vocal line was supported by an economical use of the full orch. In the 19th century the demarcation between the accompanied recitative and the aria began to blur, until in Wagner's music dramas they coalesced into 1 continuous song, the "endless melody." *Recitativo instrumentato,* a recitativelike effect in instrumental music, either by an instrument playing solo in an ensemble piece or, in piano playing, a crisp delivery of the melody, free in tempo and rhythm.

reciting note. In plainchant, the tonus on which most of each verse (psalm or canticle) is continuously recited; usually the dominant above the tonus.

record album. 1. Orig., the bound holder for 78-rpm discs, whether for a single work or a collection. 2. A long-playing 33 1/3-rpm disc, containing 1 or more works performed by the same artist or group, in the same genre, from a soundtrack, etc.

record player. Phonograph.

recorder (Fr. *flûte à bec;* Ger. *Blockflöte;* It. *flauto dritto*). An end-blown vertical flute with a whistle mouthpiece popular during the Baroque period; later superseded by the transverse flute. Recorders of all compasses, from bass to treble, were used as solo instruments in chamber ensembles, under such names as sopranino, sopranino recorder, descant, treble recorder, and *flauto d'Eco,* which is included in Bach's *4th Brandenburg Concerto.* After being dormant for over a century, a spectacular revival of recorders took place in the 20th century, fostered by archeophiliac performers and instrument makers; at 1st the movement was primarily pedagogical in nature (e.g., the works by Hindemith and colleagues), but it later involved the reincarnation of early music in an "authentic" form. This rebirth also engendered the composition of many new works for the instrument.

records. See ⇒phonograph.

reco-reco. Afro-Brazilian guiro; a scraper made of a hollowed-out gourd with carved notches or ridges on its surface; the sound is produced by a rubbing stick. Like many similar instruments throughout the world, it is used for sharp rhythmic effects in indigenous and popular music.

recte et retro (Lat., forth and back). A retrograde canon in which the subject is combined simultaneously with its own retrograde. It is a most ingenious species of the type of mirror canon in which 2 players read the same page from opposite sides, or else turn the page upside down and have 1 performer read it in the mirror as the other reads the original, with the same results.

rectus modus (Lat., straight motion). The forward-moving version of a melody or other patterns, as opposed to its retrograde.

recueilli (Fr., collected). Meditative.

Red Mass. A solemn Roman Catholic votive Mass, in which the celebrants wear red vestments. Such a Mass is celebrated at the openings of congresses, courts, and councils, as well as for some martyred saints.

Redding, Otis, b. Dawson, Ga., Sept. 9, 1941; d. Dec. 10, 1967. He sang in church, took part in revival meetings, and adopted the "shouting" manner of projection. His early record *Shout Bamalama* is a fair example of this technique. He then progressed toward a more refined type of gospel and soul singing, and in 1966 issued an album called *Dictionary of Soul.*

His 1967 performance at the Monterey Pop Festival was recorded on film and remains a powerful sampling of his art; his death, in an airplane crash near Madison, Wis., was widely mourned and commemorated. Redding's most successful hits, sung in a powerful baritone voice, include *Respect, (Sittin' on) The Dock of the Bay, Try a Little Tenderness, Shake, Mr. Pitiful, I've Been Loving You Too Long,* and *Tramp* (with Carla Thomas).

Redman, Don(ald Matthew), b. Piedmont, W.Va., July 29, 1900; d. N.Y., Nov. 30, 1964. He began his studies on trumpet as a child; eventually mastered all the wind instruments. He was an arranger for Fletcher Henderson's band (1924–27), then directed McKinney's Cotton Pickers; worked with the Dorsey Brothers, Jack Teagarden, Coleman Hawkins, Fats Waller; also arranged for Paul Whiteman, Ellington, Ben Pollack, and others. He toured Europe with his own band (1946–47); then appeared on television and served as music director for Pearl Bailey. His arrangement of *Deep Purple* for Jimmy Dorsey became a major hit. He personally taught or indirectly influenced many important arrangers.

Redoublé (Fr. doubled). Play twice as fast. *Marche redoublée,* a rapid march.

redowa. A Bohemian dance, like the mazurka, though less strongly accented, in 3/4 or 3/8 time and lively tempo. It was popular in 19th-century Europe.

reduce. In organ music, a direction to decrease the volume of tone by retiring the louder stops.

reduction. Rearrangement of a composition for a smaller number of instruments while preserving its form as far as possible; the term is used more in French, as *réduction pour la piano.* See also ⇒adaptation, transcription.

redundancy. In electronics guidance systems, redundancy is a safety factor in the proper functioning of the machine. If a part fails, its redundant replacement immediately goes into action; and if that one fails, still another part is activated to perform the same function. In music, redundancy is represented by an ostentatious repetition of a thematic motive. It has its application in serial complexes of intervallic, rhythmic, and coloristic parameters. By assigning a certain interval for a redundant use by an instrument, an associative equation is established, so that the interval becomes the identifying motto of the instrument itself. Some serial composers assign a single note to an instrument, so that the instrument and the note become inalienably bound. This evokes the memories and practices of serf orchs. in Czarist Russia, consisting of wind instruments, of which each could produce but a single note, so that each serf playing that instrument often became known under the nickname of E-flat, F-sharp, etc. (When several serfs escaped from the estate of a music-loving Russian landlord, he put out an official notice asking the police to be on the lookout for the fugitives, giving their musical names as identification.)

reed. A flexible thin strip of cane, wood, or metal attached to the open end of a woodwind instrument so that the opening is almost completely closed; this aperture is set by an air current in vibration, which it communicates to an enclosed column (organ, etc.), long pipe with a series of holes that can be covered to obtain different notes (clarinet, oboe, etc.), or directly to the free air, thus producing a musical tone. (In playing a brass instrument, the lips perform the function of the reeds.) Reed instruments are commonly divided into 2 categories, single reeds (clarinet, saxophone, modern tárogató) and double reeds (oboe, bassoon, crumhorn, shawm, racket). In a double reed the 2 reeds vibrate against each other. Reeds made of a hard metal which produce only 1 pitch are used in the harmonium, accordion, regal, and organ reed stops. A *free reed* vibrates within the aperture without striking the edges; a *beating reed* strikes on the edges.

reed instrument. One whose tone is produced by the vibration of a reed (sometimes 2 reeds) in its mouthpiece or at one end of its air supply chamber.

Reed, Lou(is Alan). See ⇒Velvet Underground.

reed organ. A keyboard instrument whose tones are produced by free reeds: the Harmonium (invented 1843 by A. Debain of Paris), the bellows forcing compressed air outward through the reeds; and the American organ, in which a suction bellows draws the air in through them. Either style has a variety of stops of different quality.

reed pipe. See ⇒pipe.

reed section. In jazz bands, the clarinet and saxophone players.

reel. A lively dance of Britain and Ireland, usually in 4/4 time, with little or no syncopation and reprises of 8-measure sections; danced in a 4-couple set.

refrain (Lat. *refractum,* fragmented; It. *ritornello;* Old Eng., *burden*). A recurring melody and text of a song, usually at the end of a stanza. It is often called the chorus, either in popular music, or because the main stanza or verse is performed solo and the following chorus is by an ensemble. A refrain often repeats the last line or 2 of the verse with the same text and melody, particularly if it summarizes the moral of the verse. A religious refrain may be a single word, *Amen,* intoned by the congregation in response to the minister or cantor. In Spain a common refrain is Ole!, expressing enthusiasm by a crowd.

regal. A portable organ with regal pipes (reed pipes without resonator) used between the 15th and 18th centuries, particularly in smaller churches.

regens chori (Lat.). Choir director.

regent. Leader of a Russian Orthodox church choir.

Reger, (Johann Baptist Joseph) Max(imilian), b. Brand, Upper Palatinate, Bavaria, Mar. 19, 1873; d. Leipzig, May 11, 1916. His father, a schoolteacher and amateur musician, instructed him on piano, organ, and string instruments; when the family moved to Weiden (1874), he studied organ and theory with A. Lindner; attended the local teachers' college; visited the Bayreuth Festival (1888) and decided on a music career. He went to Sondershausen to study with Riemann; continued as his pupil in Wiesbaden (1890–93); taught piano, organ, and theory

(1890–96); following military service he returned to Weiden (1898); wrote many fine organ works.

Reger went to Munich (1901); gained recognition as a pianist, later as a composer; prof. of counterpoint at the Königliche Akademie der Tonkunst (1905–06). Most of his important compositions from this period were chamber or solo keyboard works. He went to Leipzig as music director of the Univ. (1907–08) and prof. of composition at the Cons. (from 1907); his fame as a composer was enhanced by successful tours as a soloist and conductor throughout Europe. While he continued to produce chamber works and organ pieces, he began writing his most important orch'l compositions, most of a neoclassical bent: *Variationen und Füge über ein lustiges Thema von J. A. Hiller,* op. 100 (1907); Violin Concerto, op. 101 (1907–08); the *Symphonischer Prolog zu einer Tragödie,* op. 108 (1908); Piano Concerto, op. 114 (1910); *Konzert im alten Stil,* op. 123 (1912); *Eine romantische Suite,* op. 125 (1912); the uncharacteristically evocative *Vier Tondichtungen nach Arnold Böcklin,* op. 128 (Essen, 1913); *Variationen und Füge über ein Thema von Mozart,* op. 132 (1914). During this period he also composed his most distinguished sacred work, the Psalm 100, op. 106 (1908–09). He was called to Meiningen to conduct the Court Orch. in 1911, assuming the title of Hofkapellmeister; was also Generalmusikdirektor (1913–14). Reger was an extraordinarily gifted and widely respected composer, performer, conductor, and teacher; a master of polyphonic and harmonic writing, he carried on the hallowed Classic and Romantic schools of composition; although he wrote major works in nearly every genre (excerpt theatrical), his music has not found a permanence place in the repertory, perhaps due to a certain opaqueness of expression. Given his compositional propensity for highly chromatic, restless tonal movement, it seems appropriate that he publ. *Beiträge zur Modulationslehre* (Leipzig, 1903; 24th ed., 1952).

reggae. Jamaican popular music marked by insistent square rhythms counterpointed by strong off-beat syncopation, similar to but more irregularly than in rock 'n' roll. Reggae emerged in the shantytowns of Kingston in the mid-1960s, combining elements of African-American soul, the steady-state rhythms of calypso and other Caribbean dance music, the polyrhythmic elements of African music, and a Jamaican skifflelike genre called ska. Particularly in the hands of Bob Marley, Peter Tosh, Black Uhuru, and others, reggae became an important medium of social protest and religious belief. In the 1980s it merged with hip-hop to form a type of accompaniment for rap.

register. 1. A set of pipes or reeds controlled by 1 draw-stop; a stop (organ stop). 2. A portion of the vocal compass; as *high* or *low* register; *chest-* or *head*-register. 3. A portion—in the range of certain instruments—differing in quality from the other portions.

registration. 1. The art of effectively employing and combining the various stops of the organ. 2. The combination of stops employed for any given composition.

registres coupés (Fr.). Divided stop.

rehearsal (Fr. *répétition;* It. *prova;* Ger. *Probe,* a tryout). Literally, rehearing; a practice session for a chamber music ensemble, a song recital, a symphonic work, an opera, a jazz band, a rock group, etc. A prerequisite for a fruitful rehearsal is a willingness to achieve a mutual accommodation among the participants so as to achieve proper balance in harmony, fluctuations of tempo, and dynamic equilibration. Basic elements can, of course, be agreed upon in advance, but the subtler nuances have to be felt intuitively. A tale is told about a rehearsal of a cello sonata when the cellist asked the pianist to play softer. "I can't hear myself," he complained. "You're lucky," the pianist replied. "Unfortunately, I can."

The collision of vanities at rehearsals is a constant hazard. When the violinist Henryk Wieniawski toured the U. S. with Anton Rubinstein in the 1870s, the 2 were not on speaking terms, but according to reports their mutual animosity did not affect the excellence of their performances. More recently Heifetz and Piatigorsky reached the point of such mutual irritability during a rehearsal for trio concerts that they had to communicate through the pianist Pennario for matters of tempos, bowing, etc. An abominable practice of deputy players existed in France at orch'l rehearsals, so that often the personnel of the orch. that plays the actual concert is quite different from that at the rehearsal. When an orch'l player told Toscanini at a Paris rehearsal that he would send a deputy to play the concert, Toscanini said, "Then I will send a deputy to conduct the concert," and walked off the podium.

Reibtrommel (Ger., rubbing drum). Friction drum.

Reich, Steve (Stephen Michael), b. N.Y., Oct. 3, 1936. He took piano lessons; studied drumming with Roland Koloff, synchronously became infatuated with jazz and Bach by way of Stravinsky's stylizations. He studied philosophy at Cornell Univ. (B.A., 1957); became fascinated with the irrationally powerful theories of Ludwig Wittgenstein; took private composition lessons with Hall Overton; earned his living driving a taxicab. He took courses with W. Bergsma and Persichetti at the Juilliard School of Music (1958–61); went to California, where he entered Mills College in Oakland for Milhaud and Berio's classes (M.A., 1963); became interested in non-acoustic composition and African music.

Reich launched his career as a composer with tape scores for the underground films *The Plastic Haircut* and *Oh Dem Watermelons* (1963); his most remarkable works for tape include *It's Gonna Rain* (1965) and *Come Out* (1966); wrote in the relatively new electroacoustic vein in *Violin Phase* for Violin Solo and Interactive Electronics (1967); met other pioneers of so-called minimalist music (Young, Riley, Glass). He returned to N.Y.; organized Steve Reich and Musicians (1966), 1st as a trio with Arthur Murphy and Jon Gibson, evolving into a variable ensemble. With performances of his *4 Organs* for 4 Electric Organs and Maracas (1970), he 1st made an impact outside a small circle of friends.

In the summer of 1970 Reich traveled to Accra, Ghana; was tutored by local master drummers; this 1st bore fruit in *Drumming* (1971), a longer work that became quite popular. He next studied Balinese gamelan with a native teacher at the Univ. of Washington in Seattle (1973); becoming conscious of his ethnic heritage, he went to Jerusalem to learn traditional forms of Hebrew cantillation (1976). He began receiving grants in 1974, from both the National Endowment for the Arts and the

N.Y. State Council on the Arts, and was invited to Berlin as an artist-in-residence. He subsequently received 4 grants from the Martha Baird Rockefeller Foundation and a 2nd grant from the NEA; awarded a Guggenheim fellowship (1978); publ. *Writings about Music* (N.Y., 1974).

Reich rose to fame steadily; his group performed at the Holland Festival and the radio stations of Frankfurt and Stuttgart; performed to a sold-out house at N.Y.'s Carnegie Hall (1980); took his ensemble on a world tour (1986). His music was astoundingly audacious; rather than continue in the wake of obsolescent, increasingly complex modernism, he deliberately reduced the harmonic and contrapuntal vocabulary and defiantly explored the fascinating potentialities of repetitive patterns. His techniques have been called minimalist (derived from a minimum of linear elements), phase music (shifted verticalities 1 note at a time), modular (built on symmetric modules), and pulse music (based on a series of measured rhythmic units); yet another term is process music, suggesting tonal progressions in flux. He prefers to trace his musical ancestry to the sweetly hollow homophonic music of the ars antiqua, particularly the architectonic works of Perotin, master of the Parisian Notre Dame school.

Reich's constructivist approach to the smallest detail is well-integrated into his most successful works: *Music for Mallet Instruments, Voices, and Organ; Music for 18 Musicians; Music for a Large Ensemble; Tehillim; The Desert Music;* and *Sextet* for Percussion, Piano, and Synthesizers. For years he avoided programmatic references in his titles, preferring to define them abstractly; recent works such as *The 4 Sections* for Orch. and *Electric Counterpoint* for Guitar and Tape continue this pattern. But other works suggest a new interest in programmatic and historical connections, e.g., *Different Trains,* concerning the Holocaust, for String Quartet and Tape, partly musique concrète; and the multimedia *The Cave.*

Reichardt, Johann Friedrich. See ⇒Goethe, Johann Wolfgang von.

Reihe (Ger.). Tone row, series.

reihengebundene Musik (Ger., music bound by a series). Dodecaphonic music.

Reiner, Fritz, b. Budapest, Dec. 19, 1888; d. N.Y., Nov. 15, 1963. He studied piano with Thoman and composition with Koessler at the Royal Academy of Music in Budapest, while studying law; conducted the Volksoper in Budapest (1911–14) and the Court (later State) Opera in Dresden (1914–21); also conducted in Hamburg, Berlin, Vienna, Rome, and Barcelona. He was engaged as music director of the Cincinnati Sym. Orch. (1922); naturalized as a U.S. citizen (1928); became prof. of conducting at the Curtis Inst. of Music in Philadelphia (1931); taught Bernstein and Foss.

In 1936–37 Reiner made guest appearances at London's Covent Garden; was guest conductor at the San Francisco Opera (1935–38); music director of the Pittsburgh Sym. Orch. (1938–48), then conducted at the Metropolitan Opera in N.Y. (to 1953). He achieved the peak of his success with the Chicago Sym. Orch., for which he served as music director (1953–62); raised the orch.'s level to the point of impeccably fine performance in classical and modern music. A striving for perfection gave him the reputation of a ruthless orch'l master, being given to explosions of temper; but musicians and critics agreed that it was this very approach that made the Chicago Sym. Orch. one of the best American orchs.

Reinhardt, Django (Jean Baptiste), b. Liberchies, Jan. 23, 1910; d. Fontainebleau, May 16, 1953. He began his career in Paris in 1922; gained recognition through his recordings with the singer Jean Sablon and the violinist Stephane Grappelli; in 1934 he formed the Quintette du Hot Club de France with Grappelli. After World War II he toured the U.S.; appeared with Duke Ellington in N.Y. He was an innovative figure in the early jazz movement in Europe; in later years he utilized electrical amplification in his performances.

rejdowak. Bohemian ballroom dance in ternary time; later popular in Europe as the redowa.

relâche (Fr., release). 1. Indication that a theater is closed; in theatrical jargon, dark, or no performance. 2. Indication that a performance is canceled.

related keys. Those keys with the 1st degree of relationship with the main key; their triads are contained within the available diatonic degrees of the main key. Thus E minor is related to C major, D major, G major, and B minor; E minor appears in these keys as the mediant, supertonic, submediant, and subdominant, respectively. See also ⇒relative key.

relation(ship). The degree of affinity between keys, chords, and tones.

relative key. A natural minor key is relative to that major key, the tonic of which lies a minor 3rd above its own; a major key is relative to that natural minor key, the tonic of which lies a minor 3rd below its own. As a result, the 2 keys share key signatures; e.g., G major is the relative of E minor, sharing a signature of 1 sharp (F#). Chopin's Preludes, op. 28, are ordered by the cycle of 5ths, further arranged by alternating a major key with its relative minor (C major, A minor, G major, E minor, etc.).

relative pitch. Ability to name an interval, or the exact 2nd note, after hearing an interval and being given the identity of the 1st note. This ability can be learned, unlike perfect pitch, the ability to name a pitch without a reference point; this is considered an innate talent.

religiosity. Religious symbolism left many traces in musical notation. Perfect time consisting of 3 beats is defined in the medieval treatises as being an attribute of the Christian Trinity. But even in secular works, composers paid tribute to piety. Haydn signed most of his syms. with the devotional phrase "Deo soli gloria." Bruckner dedicated his 9th Sym. "An meinem lieben Gott." Stravinsky's inscription on the title page of his *Sym. of Psalms* reads: "Composed for the glory of God and dedicated to the Boston Sym. Orchestra." When the English composer Arnold Bax was asked to contribute a program note for 1 of his symphonies, he declined, explaining that the music was dictated to him by God.

Performing musicians, not many of whom are naturally religious, have been known to rely on divine help for the quality of their performances. But some are apt to renounce God when they fail. When it rained on the day of the American debut of the Russian bass Sibiriakov, he shook his fists at the skies and cried out: "If God has such weather for Sibiriakov's concert, then God is a bastard!" The adulation of symphonic conductors leads some of them to accept the projected God-like image. "I know who you are," gushed a Boston dowager entering the reception room of Serge Koussevitzky. "You are God!" "I know my responsibilities," Koussevitzky replied imperturbably. When the mercurial Artur Rodzinski took over the N. Y. Philharmonic, he decided to dismiss 14 players. But, he assured the manager, he would 1st seek divine counsel. The next morning he declared: "God spoke to me, and he said 'Fire the bastards!'"

religioso (It.). In a devotional style.

R.E.M. (Vocals: [John] Michael Stipe, b. Decatur, Ga., Jan. 4, 1960; guitar/mandolin: Peter [Lawrence] Buck, b. Berkeley, Calif., Dec. 6, 1956; bass/keyboards/vocals: Michael [Edward] Mills, b. Orange, Calif., Dec. 17, 1958; drums/vocals: Bill Berry, b. William Thomas Berry, Duluth, Minn., July 31, 1958). Popular American alternative rock band that takes its name from "rapid eye movement," a stage of sleep. The band was formed in Athens, Ga., in 1980 by 4 Univ. of Georgia students; a year later they released independently the single *Radio Free Europe*, gaining them a contract with I.R.S. Records; an EP and an LP followed in rapid succession.

The group toured Europe in 1983 and continued to record, building a reputation among critics and alternative music listeners. They became known for their dense sound, featuring vocals mixed far in the background (and Stipe's sometimes incoherent muttering style) so that it was difficult if not impossible to understand exactly what each song was about. They scored a minor hit in 1986 with the song *Fall On Me* but did not break through big-time until a year later, with the hit songs *The One I Love* and *It's the End of the World as We Know It (And I Feel Fine)* from the album *Document*. This led to their signing with heavy-hitting label Warner Bros.

Their 1st major pop hit came in 1991 with *Losing My Religion* from their 2nd Warner's album, *Out of Time,* on which the band took a more acoustic, softened approach to their work. They continued to enjoy hits with 1992's *Everybody Hurts* and *Man on the Moon* in a similar style, but then came back to a harder-edged sound with 1994's *Monster,* featuring the hit *What's the Frequency, Kenneth?* A world tour followed in 1995, during which they recorded their next album, *New Adventures in Hi-Fi,* which failed to yield any hits. Berry, who had suffered near-fatal illnesses on recent tours, resigned; the group's future was in doubt.

remedio. Argentine song in 3/8 time; intended as a remedy for unrequited love.

remote key. An unrelated key.

Renaissance. In music history, the period 1400 to 1600.

renversement (Fr.). 1. Inversion of an interval. 2. Inversion of a chord.

repeat. 1. The sign ‖⫶ or ⫶‖⫶ or ⫶‖ , signifying *a* that the music between the double-dotted bars is to be repeated;

b and *c,* that the preceding and also the following division is to be repeated. 2. A section or division of music to be repeated. Repeats are usually indicated in Classic sonatas, or works in sonata form (quartet, sym.), but such repeats are very often disregarded by the performer, particularly if the exposition section is very long. Repeats are de rigueur in dance forms; a particularly important set of obligatory repeats occurs in minuets and gavottes, when the 1st section is repeated after the contrasting 2nd section (ternary form).

repercussio (Lat.). In Gregorian chant, the repetition of a melodic pattern that characterizes a particular modality. Certain neumes, particularly those signifying a rapid repeat, are classified in this character.

repercussion. 1. Repetition of a tone or chord. 2. In a fugue, the regular reentrance of subject and answer after the episodes immediately following the exposition.

repetend. A musical phrase that is constantly repeated for many bars, such as the protracted ending of the initial theme in the 1st movement of Beethoven's *Pastoral Sym.,* in which the violin figure is repeated 10 times. Concluding chords in a Classic coda are typical conventional repetends. Modern composers tend to do away with repetends; Prokofiev ends the March in his opera *Love for 3 Oranges* with a single C-major chord, where his Classic and Romantic predecessors might have had 16 or 32 chords.

répétiteur, -euse (Fr.). A choral or opera rehearsal assistant; one who conducts rehearsals as opposed to the actual performances; sometimes called an opera coach. The répétiteur, humblest of functionaries in the realm of grand opera, often has the tedious duty to train inept singers to keep time. But these musical menials acquire valuable practice and sometimes rise to conductorship. The remarkable Greek conductor Dimitri Mitropoulos served as répétiteur at the Berlin Opera in the beginning of his career.

répétition (Fr.). A rehearsal.

répétition générale (Fr.). A dress rehearsal for an opera, ballet, etc., open to the press and dignitaries before the official premiere.

replica (It.). A repeat or reprise. *Da capo senza replica,* play from the beginning without observing the repeats.

replication. In their search for effective and direct musical formulas, modern composers have increasingly turned back to the primitivist pattern of simple repetition, a sort of biomusical replication of a subject keeping its identity as unalterable as the design on an ancient Peruvian poncho. The most celebrated instance of such replication is Ravel's *Boléro,* in which the variations are limited to changes from 1 instrumental color to another. A less literal type of replication is monothematicism, of which Debussy's String Quartet is a perfect example. Still another variant is the thematic replication of a musical monogram, which spells out a name of a common word in letter-notes, usually in German notation. A modern example is the 8th String Quartet by Shostakovich, which is built on his initials in German spelling

(D–S–C–H, with the letter *S* representing *Es,* i.e., E-flat, and H representing B-natural). Shostakovich uses the same personal monogram in his 10th Sym., as did other composers in homage to him. Some members of the avant-garde have carried the principle of replication to the ultimate limit of a single note recorded on tape without any change in dynamics and without a rhythmic interruption.

reprenez le mouvement (Fr.). Take up the tempo again; same as a tempo.

reprise (from Fr., retaking; It. *ripresa;* Ger. *Reprise*). 1. The total and unaltered repeat of a section of a musical composition; usually is marked by 2 symmetric repeat signs, 1 in the beginning with 2 dots on the right of the double bar and 1 at the end of the repeat section with 2 dots to the left of the double bar. 2. In some French Baroque harpsichord music, a mark of repetition indicating the section to be repeated in a rondolike piece; or the repetition of the last few measures as a form of coda. 3. In present usage reprise is virtually synonymous with recapitulation, wherein the exposition is "retaken," with necessary modifications in the modulatory plan.

requiem (from Lat. *requies,* rest). The 1st word in the Mass for the dead; hence the title of the musical setting of that Mass. Its divisions are (1) Requiem, Kyrie; (2) Dies iræ, Requiem; (3) Domine Jesu Christe; (4) Sanctus, Benedictus; and (5) Agnus Dei, Lux æterna.

res facta (Lat.). In early music, a description of a composition that is fully written out, as opposed to counterpoint figured out mentally and improvised from the cantus firmus at sight. It is sometimes equated by music theorists of the 16th century with *musica figurativa*—music with all auxiliary ornaments written out. This identification is the *Institution musicale,* published in Paris in 1556, where res facta is translated literally as *chose faite.* Res facta is sometimes used interchangeably with *cantus fractus* (broken song) or *musique rompue* (broken music).

rescue and escape terms. Many new musicological terms ambiguously descriptive of a modern style, idiom, or technique are rescue and escape terms, words and phrases used as nebulous definitions of uncertain musical events. The term omnitonality belongs to this category; others may be found by industrious perusal of music magazines beginning in 1910.

rescue opera. A fanciful term to describe an opera in which the central character is rescued from mortal peril by extraordinary means. A perfect example is Beethoven's *Fidelio,* in which the prisoner's faithful wife enters prison service in a man's attire to rescue him; she succeeds. In Puccini's *Tosca* the rescue of the prisoner seems assured at the risk of the heroine's virtue but a twist of fate turns hope into despair and death. The rescue opera usually involves human activity rather than the work of a deus ex machina.

reservata, musica. This term is a philosopher's stone of musical historiography, for its meaning is arcane, its origin recondite, its connotations cryptic, and its function enigmatic. Musica reservata 1st appeared in print in *Compendium Musices* by Adrian Coclico (1552). On etymological grounds, one is tempted to translate the word reservata as "reserved" in the sense of being exclusive, connoting a style of composition appreciated only by expert musicians. An alternative explanation of the term is that the element of "reservation" indicated a restricted use of ornamentation.

résolu (Fr.). Resolutely, decisively.

resolution. The progression of a dissonance, whether a simple interval or a chord, to a consonance. Generally semitone motion is a controlling factor, whether moving from leading tone to tonic or from subdominant to mediant (in the dominant 7th chord). Augmented intervals tend to resolve by expansion; diminished intervals resolve by contracting. *Direct resolution,* immediate progression from the dissonance to the consonance; *indirect* (or *delayed, deferred, retarded*) *resolution,* one passing through some intermediate dissonance(s) before reaching the final restful consonance.

resonance. The resounding of upper harmonics over the fundamental.

resonance box. A hollow resonant body like that of the violin or zither. See also ⇒resonator.

resonator. Any object that amplifies sound. The soundboard of the grand piano is a resonator of the strings; the hollow bodies of chordophones serve the same purpose; caverns are natural resonators. The elimination of unwelcome resonance is the most vexing and least predictable part of a proper architectural plan in constructing a concert hall. Vibrating surfaces on musical instruments can create an embarrassing quodlibet during an orch'l performance. orch'l players usually dampen their instruments to preclude "sympathetic vibrations," in which a particular pitch played on an instrument produces a sudden increase in loudness out of keeping with the rest of the gamut. Is this the real meaning of that hoary cliché "Beware of bad vibes"?

Respighi, Ottorino, b. Bologna, July 9, 1879; d. Rome, Apr. 18, 1936. He studied violin with F. Sarti and composition with L. Torchi and G. Martucci at Bologna's Liceo Musicale (1891–1900); went to Russia to play 1st viola in the orch. of the Imperial Opera in St. Petersburg (1900); took lessons with Rimsky-Korsakov, a decisive influence on his coloristic orchestration. He was active as a concert violinist (1903–08); played the viola in the Mugellini Quartet of Bologna; engaged as prof. of composition at Rome's Liceo (later Cons.) di Santa Cecilia (1913); appointed its director (1924–26), but resigned, retaining only an advanced composition class, so as to devote himself to composing and conducting. He toured the U.S. as a pianist and conductor (1925–26, 1932); elected to the Italian Royal Academy (1932).

Resphigi's style of composition is a successful blend of songful melodies with full and rich harmonies and masterful orchestration; his ability to evoke the Italian world and sustain interest without prolixity is incontestable; although he wrote 9 operas, achieved his greatest success with the symphonic suites *Le fontane di Roma, I pini di Roma,* and *Feste romane,* each consisting of 4 tone paintings of the Roman landscape; the use of a phonograph recording of a nightingale in the score of *I pini di Roma* was innovative for the time. Other orch'l works include

Concerto gregoriano with Violin (1921); *Vetrate di chiesa* (1925); *Trittico botticelliano* (1927); *Impressioni brasiliane* (1928); wrote arrangements, including *Antiche arie e danze per liuto* (1917, 1923, 1931), and musical syntheses of other composers' work. In addition to the operas, he was a prolific composer of songs and song cycles; his chamber music included the Violin Sonata in B Minor (1917) and *Quartetto dorico* for String Quartet (1924). A pupil became his wife; Elsa Olivieri Sangiacomo Respighi (1894–1996) composed a fairy opera, *Fior di neve;* the orch'l *Serenata di maschere;* songs (she was a concert singer); completed her husband's opera *Lucrezia* (1937).

respiro (It.). Pause; rest.

response (respond; Fr. *réponse*). 1. Responsory. 2. An answer, in call-and-response texture. 3. The musical reply, by the choir or congregation, to what is said or sung by the priest or officiant.

responsory (Lat. *reponsorium;* Fr. *répons*). 1. That psalm, or part of one, sung in alternation between soloist and congregation after the reading of lessons; the practice dates to at least the 11th century. The great responsories are found in the Matins and monastic Vespers. Polyphonic settings were mostly in the form of motets and continued to be composed up until the 18th century. 2. The gradual. 3. A *respond;* that is, the 1st part of a responsory psalm, sung by the congregation.

rest. A pause or interval of silence between 2 tones; hence the sign indicating such a pause. See ⇒Notes and Rests.

restez (Fr., remain). In music for stringed instruments, means play on the same string or remain in the same position, i.e., do not shift.

retard. Ritardando.

retardation. The device of retardation—melodic, harmonic, or contrapuntal—consists of holding over a certain note or a harmonic complex while other parts of the musical fabric are shifted. In modern music, retardation is not developed in accord with the moving elements but continues indefinitely in order to create a sustained discord. In pandiatonic techniques this procedure results in a chain of superpositions of the principal triadic harmonies.

retarded progression. A suspension resolving upward.

retenir (Fr.). Hold back. *Retenu,* ritenuto.

retirada (Sp.). Recession, as opposed to intrada. Such introductory and recessional movements were common in suites.

retrograde. 1. Performing a melody backward; a pedantic melodic device often encountered in polyphonic works, much beloved by composers of puzzle canons, and usually prefaced by them with fanciful phrases such as *Vade retro Satanas* (Get Thee behind me, Satan; Mark 8:33), *Ubi alpha ibi omega* (Where alpha is, omega is too), *Canite more Hebraeorum* (Sing in the Hebrew manner, i.e., from right to left), and (the most famous designation) *cancrizans* (literally, walking like a crab).

In the Minuet of his Sym. No. 47 Haydn explicitly marked *al rovescio*, meaning it could be played backward without any change of the original music. Bach's *Das musikalisches Opfer* has a 2-part canon in which the original subject is sounded simultaneously with its retrograde form. Beethoven has a crab motion in the final fugue of his *Hammerklavier Sonata*. A remarkable example of a very melodious and harmonious piece representing a combination of the original and its retrograde form is exemplified by an anonymous canon, erroneously attributed to Mozart, playable by 2 violinists reading a page across the table from one another, so that the player opposite performs the tune beginning with the last note and ending with the 1st note of his vis-à-vis partner. The wonder of it is that the result is in perfect harmony, and that a sharp applies to 2 different notes in the opposite parts without creating an unresolved dissonance.

2. One of 3 standard precompositional techniques in 12-note composition, wherein all notes of a set are played in reverse order. After a century of neglect the technique of retrograde motion staged a revival in the music of the 20th-century Vienna School. Schoenberg has a retrograde canon in No. 18 of *Pierrot lunaire*, and so does Berg in the middle section of his opera *Lulu*. Retrograde motion is of fundamental importance in 12-tone music, in which 2 of the 4 principal melodic forms of the tone row include retrograde and inverted retrograde.

retrograde canon. See ⇒Canon cancrizans.

retrograde inversion. A standard technique in 12-note composition wherein all notes of a set are played in a reverse succession, which also mirrors (inverts) the original set.

reveille (Fr. *réveil*). The military signal for (1) getting up in the morning and (2) the 1st military formation of the day; based on the 2nd, 3rd, and 4th notes of the harmonic series playable on a bugle.

revenez (Fr.). Return. *Revenez peu à peu au premier mouvement*, return gradually to the original tempo.

reverie (Fr.). Dreamy meditation; title of many Romantic pieces.

reverse motion. Retrograde.

reversion. Retrograde imitation.

revidierte Ausgabe (Ger.). Revised edition.

revue. A generic term for theatrical spectacles in which singing, speaking, dancing, and entertainment of all types are combined into a package that has no pretense for inner cohesion or a unified plot. Each sketch in a revue is self-sufficient; the genres vary from sentimental ballads and duets to satire on topical subjects, from classical dances to popular marches. Revues originated in France under the reign of the "bourgeois" King Louis Philippe in 1830; a "Revue de fin d'année" was actually a review of events during the year past. In the 2nd half of the 19th century such revues were called *variétés*.

The most brilliant and the most daring revue of the 1st quarter of the 20th century was the theater named Folies-Bergère (follies of the district of Bergère) in Paris. In the 19th century the bold-est exhibition of the female body was the high-kicking *can-can*, which titillated tourists and provided purists with subjects for sermons on the decay of public morality; but in the middle of the 20th century, nudity in revues was de rigueur. German revues, especially those in Berlin, imitated Parisian examples. The British had 2 types: the revues, which emphasized political satire, and music hall, focusing on social humor and sentimentality. After a century of oppressive censorship by the Society for the Prevention of Vice in N.Y., uninhibited gaiety exploded in American musicals, as musical comedies came to be known. Variety shows continued to thrive in burlesque theaters.

Revueltas, Silvestre, b. Santiago Papasquiaro, Dec. 31, 1899; d. Mexico City, Oct. 5, 1940. He began violin studies when he was 8 in Colima; then entered the Juárez Inst. in Durango at age 12; after studies with Tello (composition) and Rocabruna (violin) in Mexico City (1913–16), he took courses at St. Edward College in Austin, Tex. (1916–18) and with Sametini (violin) and Borowski (composition) at the Chicago Musical College (1918–20); he returned to Chicago to study violin with Kochanski and Sevcik (1922–26).

Revueltas was active as a violinist and conductor in Texas and Alabama (1926–28); was assistant conductor of the Orquesta Sinfónica de Mexico (1929–35); only then did he begin to compose. In 1937 he went to Spain, where he was active in the cultural affairs of the Loyalist government during the Civil War. His health was ruined by exertions and an irregular lifestyle, and he died of pneumonia. His remains were deposited in the Rotonda de los Hombres Ilustres in Mexico City on Mar. 23, 1976, to the music of his *Redes* and the funeral march from Beethoven's *Eroica Sym*. He possessed an extraordinary natural talent and an intimate understanding of Mexican music; he succeeded in creating works of great originality, melodic charm, and rhythmic vitality.

r.h. Right hand.

rhapsody (from Grk. *rapto* + *ode*, woven song; Fr. *rapsodie*). In Homeric times, itinerant singers, called *rhapsodes* (song weavers), recited their odes at festivals and at political events. The rhapsodic concept was revived toward the end of the 18th century, when Christian F. D. Schubart published a collection of songs entitled *Musicalische Rhapsodien*. By the 19th century the reincarnated rhapsody was an instrumental improvisation on folk songs or on motives taken from indigenous music. Later the meaning of rhapsody was expanded to include instrumental compositions without source material. Liszt wrote a series of piano works (later orchestrated) called Hungarian Rhapsodies; Brahms composed several untitled piano rhapsodies. Among other composers who wrote rhapsodies were Dvořák, Glazunov, Ravel, Bartók, and Enesco.

Rhythm. (It. *ritmo;* Fr. *rythme;* Ger. *Rhythmus*). Measured movement of similar tone-groups; the effect produced by systematic grouping of tones with reference to regularity both in their accentuation and in their succession as equal or unequal in time value. A rhythm is, therefore, a tone-group serving as a pattern for succeeding identical groups; traditionally it follows the prosody of verse. Rhythm animates virtually all music and constitutes the essential formative factor in melody; melody divested of rhythm loses recognizable meaning, but rhythm without melodic content may exist independently. The interdependence of melody and rhythm is expressed in the term *melorhythm*.

Rhythm must be distinguished from meter, an expedient grouping of rhythmical units upon which a higher-level rhythm is imposed. A metrical group can itself constitute a rhythm, but a rhythmic figure does not automatically form a metrical entity; St. Augustine already makes this distinction in his treatise *De musica* (5th century A.D.): "Omne metrum rhythmus, non monis rhythmus etiam metrum est" (Every meter is rhythm, but not every rhythm is also meter).

The simplest rhythm beyond the monotonous repetition of the same note value is an alternation of a long and a short note, corresponding to the trochee in poetry. The metrical arrangement of such a rhythmic figure may be 3/16, 3/8, or any multiples of these fractions. The ear cannot distinguish 1 bar of 6/8 from 2 bars of 3/8, except by applying the extraneous considerations of known forms, or by depending on the tempo. The famous *Barcarolle* from Offenbach's opera *The Tales of Hoffmann* can be perceived aurally as a waltz unless one knows that a barcarolle must be in 6/8 time.

One of the most remarkable instances of a complete divorce between meter and rhythm occurs in the finale of Schumann's Piano Concerto, in which the ear registers a leisurely waltz time while the conductor fights against the aural rhythm by giving the downbeat on a rest every other bar. One of the most common cross-rhythms is having 3/4 superimposed on 6/8 in Spanish popular dances. The so-called compound meters of 5, 7, 11 beats et al. in a measure usually represent 2 rhythmic groups. The "waltz" in Tchaikovsky's 6th Sym. is in 5/4 time, with the rhythmic figures easily separated into 2 sections of 2 and 3 beats each, but in Rimsky-Korsakov's *Dance of the Mermaids* from the opera *Sadko*, the quintuple rhythms are not subdivided into groups. In Russian and Bulgarian music the metrical units of 8 beats are sometimes split into rhythmic groups of 3 + 3 + 2.

In the 20th century there is a marked tendency among modern composers to write music without barlines, thus abolishing metrical groupings all together. More durable was the attempt to equate rhythm with meter at all times and change the time signature when the rhythmic figure was altered. The *Danse sacrale* in Stravinsky's score *The Rite of Spring* is an example of such subordination of meter to rhythm. An intriguing case of incommensurability between meter and rhythm is found in Gershwin's song *I Got Rhythm*, in which the square measure of 4/4 is in effect subdivided into 1 bar of 1/8, 4 bars of 3/8, and 1 bar of 1/8. Blacher introduced the method of variable meters, with time signatures in which the numerator increases by 1 in each successive bar until a bar of 5 beats is reached, whereupon the metrical numerator decreases by 1 beat in each measure.

Elliott Carter made use in his works of what he called metrical modulation, wherein a subordinate rhythm in a given metrical set becomes the primary meter, and the former primary meter is reduced to a subordinate position. Rhythmical figures without a common denominator relative to the principal metrical set are found in numerous modern works in which groups of notes, usually in prime numbers—such as 5, 7, 11, 13, 17, or 19—are bracketed against an approximate number of beats within the principal meter. In the compositions of the avant-garde both meter and rhythm are often replaced by durations given in seconds or fractions of a second. In his book *New Musical Resources,* Cowell proposed new shapes of musical note values making subdivisions into any kind of rhythmic groupings possible.

rhythm and blues (R&B; race music; jump blues). A type of black urban popular music blending strong repetitive rhythms, 4/4 or 6/8 meter, blues-related melodies and harmonic patterns (often based on a boogie-woogie bass), gospel music, swing, and electric blues instrumentation (electric guitar/s, acoustic double bass, keyboards, a small big band–like section, and drums). The solo vocalist was often accompanied by a few backup singers. Sometimes the singing was closer to the *a cappella* gospel quartets of the pre–World War II era; this slower, sentimental rhythm-and-blues style was the predecessor of 1950s *doo-wop.*

In the 1940s, rhythm and blues was considered strictly black music by the majority, and segregated by record companies into divisions they called "race records" (for Columbia, the label was Okeh; for Victor, Bluebird; other labels simply reserved specific series numbers). In the segregated world of the U.S., rhythm and blues was, in the conservative view, a crucial part of the "devil's formula" for destroying the morals of white teenagers. But white audiences began to purchase these recordings to listen or dance to, despite their parents. Gradually white musicians such as Bill Haley and (later) Elvis Presley recorded many of the black musicians' material and were thus able to crack the color barrier musically if not literally. Not all the white artists were appropriate for this task; many of these so-called cover versions are as limp as the originals are gut-wrenching, and it is a historical truism that many rhythm-and-blues artists of the 1940s and early 1950s were kept from the success they deserved by segregation.

Slight changes in style led to the white equivalent of rhythm and blues, rock 'n' roll; this new variant not only brought the influence of country and western (Carl Perkins, Jerry Lee Lewis, and Buddy Holly), but black musicians reinvented rhythm and blues to please all audiences (Chuck Berry, Little Richard, Fats Domino).

rhythm guitar. Guitar, rhythm.

rhythm section. Percussion section in a jazz band consisting of piano, bass, and drums, supplying the main beat; if a guitar is used it will function within this section at times.

ribattuta (It., back stroke). 1. Beat. 2. A device for beginning a trill by dwelling longer on the principal tone than on the auxiliary.

ribs. The curved sides of the violin, connecting belly and back.

ricercar (It. *ricercare, ricercata,* research, inquire). Instrumental composition of the 16th and 17th centuries generally characterized by imitative treatment of the theme or themes; one of the most vaguely defined forms, encompassing elements of canon, fugue, fantasy, and early sonata. Early in the 16th century "ricercar" retained a more or less literal meaning of "trying out," e.g., tuning a lute and improvising arpeggios and melodic fiorituras as a kind of preamble in the tonality of the work to follow; a 16th-century Italian theorist describes the form as a sequence of *suoni licenziosi,* sounds arranged with a degree of license, to be played *senza arte* (without artifice, artlessly); Vincenzo Galilei wrote of a musician who played "una bella ricercata con le dita" (with his fingers) before beginning to sing.

Orig. the ricercar would introduce a song, keyboard composition, or dance tune played on a lute; within a century it assumed an independent existence comparable to a fugue or sonata, in a contrapuntal style far removed from its earlier "artlessness"; it tended toward close imitation of short themes, resulting in a very strict manner when compared to the later "free fugue." When Bach presented his *Musical Offering* to Frederick the Great of Prussia, he placed a ricercar at the center of his work, devising a Latin acrostic: *Regis Iussu Cantio Et Reliqua Canonica Arte Resoluta* (by the King's command the theme and additions resolved in canonic style). The Baroque ricercar lapsed into innocuous desuetude in the 19th century; revived in the 20th century by Stravinsky, Martinů, and Malipiero, when the slogan "Back to Bach" became fashionable.

Rich, Buddy (Bernard), b. N.Y., June 30, 1917; d. Los Angeles, Apr. 2, 1987. His parents were vaudeville performers; he was a part of their act before age 2; at 4 he appeared as a drummer and tap dancer on Broadway; made his 1st tour of the U.S. and Australia at 6; led his own stage band by age 11. In 1937 he joined Joe Marsala's band; worked with Bunny Berigan, Harry James, Artie Shaw, and Benny Carter; performed with Tommy Dorsey (1939–42; 1944–45); led his own band (to 1951). He rejoined James (1953–54; 1955–57; 1961–66) and Dorsey (1954–55); again led his own combo (1957–61); founded his own big band (1966); toured throughout the world until it folded (1974). In subsequent years he made appearances at his own N.Y. club, Buddy's Place, leading a small combo; toured with his own jazz-rock big band. He was one of the outstanding swing drummers of his time.

Richards (Richard), Keith. See ⇒Rolling Stones, The.

Richter, Sviatoslav (Teofilovich), b. Zhitomir, Mar. 20, 1915. Both his parents were pianists; he was engaged as piano accompanist at the Odessa Opera; developed exceptional skill in sight-reading orch'l scores. He made his formal concert debut at the Odessa House of Engineers (1934); entered the Moscow Cons. (1937); studied with H. Neuhaus (graduated 1947); acquired a notable following even during his student years; made a stunning appearance at the All-Union Contest of Performances, winning its highest prize (1945); received the Stalin Prize (1949). In subsequent years he played throughout the Soviet Union and Eastern Europe; during the Philadelphia Orch.'s Russian tour, Richter was soloist in Prokofiev's 5th Piano Concerto in Leningrad (1958); made several international concert tours, including China (1957) and the U.S. (1960).

Both in Russia and abroad Richter earned a reputation as a virtuoso of formidable attainments, praised especially for an impeccable sense of style, every musical detail rendered with lapidary perfection. His performances of the Romantic repertoire brought him great renown; made notable excursions into the works of Debussy and Ravel; gave the 1st performances of Prokofiev's 6th, 7th, and 9th sonatas.

ricochet. A special down-bow stroke on the violin, achieved by throwing the upper 3rd of the bow on the same string, resulting in a bouncing series of rapid notes in one stroke. See ⇒springing bow.

ricordanza (It.). Reminiscence; sometimes used in titles of Romantic compositions.

riddle canon. A canon that is not written out; the performer must decipher when the imitating voices must come in, and at what interval; puzzle canon.

Riemann, (Karl Wilhelm Julius) Hugo, b. Gross-Mehlra, near Sondershausen, July 18, 1849; d. Leipzig, July 10, 1919. He began his training with his father, a landowner, civil servant, and amateur musician; continued studying theory in Sondershausen with H. Frankenberger, A. Bartel, and T. Ratzenberger; took courses at the Sondershausen and Arnstadt Gymnasiums. After studying classical languages and literature at the Rossleben Klosterschule (1865–68) he took non-musical studies at the Univ. of Berlin and the Univ. of Tübingen; studied harmony with Jadassohn and piano and composition with Reinecke in Leipzig (1871–72); received his Ph.D. from the Univ. of Göttingen (1873) with the dissertation *Über das musikalische Hören* (Leipzig, 1874). He taught at Bielefeld (1876–78); having qualified as a lecturer at the Univ. of Leipzig (1878) taught in Bromberg (1880–81); taught piano and theory at the Hamburg Cons. (1881–90), then at the Wiesbaden Cons. (1890–95). In 1895 he resumed his lectures at the Univ. of Leipzig; became a prof. (1905); director of the Collegium Musicum (1908) and the Forschungsinst. Für Musikwissenschaft (1914); honored with a Festschrift on his 60th birthday.

The mere bulk of Riemann's writings, covering every branch of musical science, constitutes a monument of indefatigable industry; when one considers that much of this work resulted from painstaking research and original, often revolutionary, thinking, one understands the great respect and admiration in which he was held by his contemporaries. Although many of his ideas have given way, his harmonic theories constitute the foundation of modern music theory. His researches in music history solved a number of vexing problems and threw light on others. By formulating the new science of musicology his labors proved of great significance; he is indelibly linked to the *Musik–Lexikon* that bears his cognomen; also contributed innumerable journal articles and pedagogical and other works.

riff. 1. Antiphonal refrain in jazz consisting of sharply rhythmed brief turns often given out by wind and percussion instruments as an interlude after a solo. Such riffs produce the effect of stopping for a few beats, simulating exhaustion and a deceptive sudden ending. 2. As per (1), but in popular music, played on whatever instrument is chosen (keyboards and electric guitar are common), and often contained within a solo improvisation. 3. Hook.

rifiorimento (It., reflowering). Using melodic and rhythmic ornamentation.

rigadoon (Fr. *rigaudon;* It. *rigodone*). Lively dance originating in the 17th century in southern France. Set in alla breve time, it usually opens on a quarter-note upbeat and contains a trio section and a number of reprises; it was often part of the instrumental suites of the 17th and 18th centuries. Ravel included a rigadoon in his piano suite *Le Tombeau de Couperin*.

rigor(e) (It.). Rigor, strictness. *Al* (or *con) rigore di tempo, a rigor di tempo, rigoroso,* in strict time.

Riley, Terry (Mitchell), b. Colfax, Calif., June 24, 1935. He studied piano with D. Hampton at San Francisco State College (1955–57) and composition with Shifrin and W. Denny at the Univ. of Calif. at Berkeley (M.A., 1961). His remarkable *In C* (San Francisco, 1965) is in mobile form, played by members of any ensemble, proceeding freely from one segment to another (total of 53), along with an unrelenting high C octave; this piece launched the 2nd wave of minimalism. Later in the 1960s Riley went to Europe; played piano and saxophone in cabarets in Paris and in Scandinavia. In 1970 he was initiated as a disciple of Pandit Pran Nath, the North Indian singer; followed him to India. He served as creative associate at the Center for Creative and Performing Arts at the State Univ. of N.Y. at Buffalo (1967); associate prof. at Mills College in Oakland, Calif. (1971–80); held a Guggenheim fellowship (1979).

In his music Riley explores the extremes of complexity and gymnosophistical simplicity, applying varied repetition to a highly programmatic minimalist aesthetic, anticipating John Adams but without the latter's symphonic/operatic leanings. Riley's titles suggest connections with the Beat Generation, non-Western religion, and a new age sensibility in its primordial, less vacuous stage. Among his many works are: *Descending Moonshine Dervishes* for Electronic Organ (1975); *Shri Camel* for Electric Organ with Tape Delay (1976); *The Harp of New Albion* for Justly Tuned Piano (1984); *Cadenza on the Night Plain* for String Quartet (1984); *Salome Dances* for String Quartet (1989); *Mexico City Blues* for Orch. Pieces with synthesizer include: *Poppy Nogood and the Phantom Band* (1966); *A Rainbow in Curved Air* (1968); *G-Song* for Voice, String Quartet, and Synthesizer (1981); *Sunrise of the Planetary Dream Collector* for Voice, Synthesizer, and String Quartet (1981); *Offering to Chief Crazy Horse* for Voice and 2 Synthesizers (1982); *The Medicine Wheel* for Voice, Piano, Sitar, Tabla, String Quartet, and Synthesizer (1983); *Song of the Emerald Runner* for Voice, Piano, String Quartet, Sitar, Tabla, and Synthesizer (1983). Film scores: *Les Yeux Fermés* (1973); *Le Secret de la Vie* (1975); improvisational pieces.

rimettendo (It.). Resume a preceding tempo, whether after accelerating or retarding.

Rimsky-Korsakov, Nikolai (Andreievich), b. Tikhvin, near Novgorod, Mar. 18, 1844; d. Liubensk, near St. Petersburg, June 21, 1908. He lived in the countryside until entering the Naval School in St. Petersburg (1856; graduated 1862); took piano lessons as a child with provincial teachers, later with a professional, T. Canille, who introduced him to Balakirev; also met Cui and Borodin. In 1862 he shipped out on the clipper Almaz for a 2 1/2-year voyage; returning to Russia, settled in St. Petersburg (1865), where he remained most of his life. During his travels he maintained contact with Balakirev, reporting to him the progress of his composing. He completed his 1st Sym. (earliest significant Russian work in this form); premiered under Balakirev at a concert of the Free Music School in St. Petersburg (1865). In 1871 Rimsky-Korsakov was engaged as prof. of composition and orchestration at the St. Petersburg Cons., although well aware of his technical inadequacies; remained on the faculty until his death, excepting a few months when he was relieved of his duties for publicly supporting rebellious students during the revolution of 1905.

In 1873 Rimsky-Korsakov abandoned his naval career; served as inspector of the military orchs. of the Russian navy (to 1884); was assistant director of the Court Chapel, leading its chorus and orch. (1883–94). Although not a gifted conductor, he gave many performances of his orch'l works; at his debut, a charity concert for the Volga famine victims in St. Petersburg (1874), he led the premiere of his 3rd Sym.; conducted the annual Russian Sym. concerts organized by the publisher Belaieff (1886–1900); conducted 2 concerts of Russian music at the World Exposition in Paris (1889); led concerts of Russian music in Brussels (1890, 1900). His last appearance abroad was in Paris, conducting 2 historic Russian concerts arranged by Diaghilev (1907); elected corresponding member of the French Academy, succeeding Grieg.

These activities did not distract Rimsky-Korsakov from his main goal: to be a national Russian composer. His name was grouped with those of Cui, Borodin, Balakirev, and Mussorgsky as the "Mighty 5," maintaining close friendships with most of them; at Mussorgsky's death he collected his MSS and prepared them for publication; revised Mussorgsky's *Boris Godunov;* it was in this version that the opera became famous. (He was later criticized for reducing Mussorgsky's original orchestrations, harmonies, and melodic lines to academic acceptability.) He decisively influenced the Belaieff publishing firm; helped publish numerous works by the St. Petersburg composers' group; while these sumptuously printed scores by no means represent all the best Russian music, his solicitude was of great importance culturally. Although far from being a revolutionary, he freely expressed his disgust at the bungling administration of Czarist Russia; was particularly indignant about attempts to alter Pushkin's lines in his last opera, *The Golden Cockerel* (1906–1907; Moscow, 1909); refused to compromise; died of angina pectoris with the situation still unresolved; the opera was produced posthumously, with the censor's changes; the orig. text was not restored until after the 1917 revolution.

Rimsky-Korsakov was one of the greatest masters of Russian music; made considerable use of both Russian orientalism, with its coloristic melodic patterns (the symphonic suite *Scheherazade,* op. 35, 1888; *The Golden Cockerel*), and a purely Russian style (the opera *Snow Maiden,* 1880–81; *Russian Easter Overture,* op. 36, 1888). The influence of Wagner and Liszt in his music was small; only in the opera *The Legend of the Invisible City of Kitezh* (1903–1905) are there perceptible echoes from *Parsifal.* Although academic in his general aesthetics, he experimented boldly with melodic progressions and ingenious, even dissonant harmonies that anticipated modern usages; favored the major scale with the lowered submediant and the octatonic scale of alternating whole tones and semitones (which he did not invent, but Russian sources called "Rimsky-Korsakov's scale"); in his opera-ballet *Mlada* (opera-ballet, 1889–90) there is even an ocarina part tuned octatonically. He set for himself a definite limit in innovation; severely criticized R. Strauss, Debussy, and d'Indy for modernistic practices.

Rimsky-Korsakov wrote other operas and orch'l works, including the Overture on 3 Russian Themes, op. 28 (1866; rev. 1879–80); Sym. No. 2, op. 9, *Antar* (1868; rev. 1875 and 1897); the Piano Concerto in C-sharp Minor, op. 30 (1882–83). He composed works for string quartet (1875–99) and other combinations; choral works with orch'l accompaniment or unaccompanied; piano music. He was an inveterate arranger and editor, notably of 100 Russian folk songs, op. 24 (1876). He orchestrated Dargomyzhsky's *Kamennyi gost* (The Stone Guest) and Borodin's *Prince Igor;* prepared Mussorgsky's works for performance and publication: In addition to *Boris Godunov,* he reharmonized *Songs and Dances of Death* and the symphonic poem *St. John's Night on Bald Mountain;* orchestrated *Khovanshchina.*

In the art of orchestration Rimsky-Korsakov had few equals; his treatment of instruments in solo passages and in ensemble was invariably idiomatic. In his treatise on orchestration (publ. 1913) he limited examples to his own works to demonstrate practical and effective application of registers and tone colors, unlike Berlioz, who included others' works in his groundbreaking treatise. As a music educator Rimsky-Korsakov was essential to the development and maintenance of the Russian national school; among his students were Glazunov, Liadov, Arensky, Ippolitov-Ivanov, Gretchaninov, Nikolai Tcherepnin, Maximilian Steinberg, Gnessin, and Miaskovsky; Stravinsky studied privately with him (from 1903). His pedagogical book on harmony (1884) remains widely used in Russian music schools.

Two of Rimsky-Korsakov's relations were important musicians. His son Andrei (Nikolaievich) Rimsky-Korsakov (1878–1940) devoted his energies to Russian music history; began publishing *Musikalny Sovremennik* (The Musical Contemporary, 1915), but the revolution of 1917 forced suspension of its publication; ed. books on his father and Mussorgsky; compiled the catalog, *Musical Treasures of the MS Department of the Leningrad Public Library* (1938). Nikolai's grandson (and Andrei's nephew) Georgi (Mikhailovich) Rimsky-Korsakov (1901–1965) founded a society for the cultivation of quarter-tone music (1923); composed some works in that system; having studied Scriabin's intentions for the "luce" part in *Prometheus,* he began work on electronic musical instruments; co-invented the *Emeriton* (1930), capable of producing any chosen or synthetic tone color in addition to pitch.

rinforzando (*rinforzato;* It.). With special emphasis; indicates a sudden increase in loudness, either for a tone or chord, or throughout a phrase of short passage; sforzando.

rinforzare, senza (It.). Without growing louder.

ring modulator. Electronic device that produces, from 2 inputs of frequencies (x, y), 2 new modulated frequencies (x + y and x − y).

Ringeltanz (Ger.). Ring or round dance performed by pairs holding hands in a circle.

rip. In big band jazz, a determined leap to the initial note of a tune starting with an upbeat a 4th or 5th below.

ripetizione (repetizione; It.). Repetition.

ripieno (It., filling up, supplementary). 1. orch'l part that reinforces leading orch'l parts by doubling them or by filling in the harmony. 2. In scores, a direction calling for the entrance of the full string band (in military music, the clarinets, oboes, etc.). In Baroque music the term refers to the full instrumental

complement (the tutti) in a concerted (concertante) work, where ripieno sections alternate with sections written for the solo group, concertino (also called *senza ripieno,* without reinforcement). 3. Combination stop drawing all registers of any given manual.

ripigliare (It.). Resume.

riposo, con (It.). In a calm, tranquil manner; reposefully.

riposta, -o (risposta; Lat., response). Answer to the subject in a fugue or canon; comes.

riprendendo (It.). Resuming. *Riprendendo poco a poco il tempo,* gradually regaining the preceding rate of speed.

ripresa (It., repetition). 1. Reprise. 2. In Italian madrigals, the refrain.

risposta (It.). In the Italian madrigal, a passage acting as a response.

risvegliato (It.). Lively, animated.

ritardando (It., retard; abbrev. *ritard., rit.*). Growing slower and slower; distinct from *ritenuto,* which means holding back and thus establishes a slower tempo at once. Propensity toward unauthorized and musically unjustified ritardando is an abiding sin of many performers who cover up technical deficiency and inability to play difficult passages in proper tempo. One American singer, when told by the exasperated accompanist that ritardandos could not be tolerated in Figaro's patter aria from Rossini's *The Barber of Seville,* retorted, "I didn't make any ritardando, I just slowed down a little."

ritardare, senza (It.). Without slackening the pace.

ritardato (It.). At a slower pace.

ritenendo (It.). Rallentando. *Ritenendo un po',* slow down slightly.

ritenuto (It.; Fr. *retenue,* held back). Play at a slower rate of speed; distinct from *ritardando,* which involves a gradual slowing down.

ritmico (It.). Rhythmically; precisely in tempo; misurato.

ritmo di quattro battute (It., rhythm of 4 measures). Count each measure as one beat, so that 4 measures equals 4 beats (i.e., 1 hypermeasure). *Ritmo di tre battute,* count each measure as one beat, so that 3 measures equals 3 beats (1 hypermeasure). Beethoven uses both indications in the scherzo of the *Choral* Sym.

ritornello (stornello; It.; Fr. *ritornelle*). 1. Burden of a song. 2. Repeat or modified repeat. 3. In accompanied vocal works, an instrumental prelude, interlude, or postlude (refrain), sometimes with modifications. 4. In concertos, the orch'l refrain, sometimes with modifications.

riversa, alla (riverso; It.). 1. Melodic inversion. 2. Retrograde motion.

Roach, Max(well Lemuel), b. Elizabeth City, N.C., Jan. 10, 1924.Having moved to New York as a child, he played in a church drum-and-bugle corps and was a drummer in his high school band; sat in on jam sessions in jazz haunts around the city. He began his professional career in Dizzy Gillespie's quintet; became immersed in the bebop movement; after a stint with Benny Carter's band (1944–45), joined Charlie Parker's quintet (1947); was widely recognized as one of the most innovative drummers of his era. He studied composition with John Lewis at the Manhattan School of Music; led his own groups (from 1949), perfecting his hard bop style; with trumpeter Clifford Brown, led an outstanding quintet (1953–56); in subsequent years led many groups, including M'Boom Re, a percussion ensemble (from 1970). With his own quartet he played throughout the U.S., Europe, and Japan (1976–77); became a prof. of music at the Univ. of Mass. in Amherst (1972); instituted a jazz studies program. As a composer he became known for the *Freedom Now Suite* (1960), an expression of solidarity with the U.S. civil rights movement; wrote and recorded the avant-garde scores *Force* (1976; dedicated to Mao Zedong) and *1 in 2—2 in 1* (1978).

Robeson, Paul (Bustill), b. Princeton, N.J., Apr. 9, 1898; d. Philadelphia, Jan. 23, 1976. He 1st studied law (B.A., 1919, Rutgers Univ.; LL.B, 1923, Columbia Univ.); when his singing and acting abilities were discovered, he appeared in plays in the U.S. and England; acted the eponymous lead in Eugene O'Neill's play *The Emperor Jones* and Louis Gruenberg's operatic version of it; performed Crown in *Porgy*, the orig. play by DuBose and Dorothy Heyward on which Gershwin's opera was based. In 1925 Robeson gave his 1st Negro spiritual recital in N.Y.; toured in Europe. In 1928 he scored an enormous success in the musical *Show Boat* in London; became deservedly famous for his rendition of *Ol' Man River*. In 1930 he appeared in the title role of Shakespeare's *Othello* in London; returning to the U.S. he continued to give recitals, but his outspoken admiration for the Soviet regime from the 1940s on interfered with his career, leading finally to his blacklisting. In 1952 he was awarded the International Stalin Peace Prize ($25,000); later made an extensive European tour (1958); continued to sing abroad until stricken with ill health; returned to the U.S. (1963).

Robinson, "Smokey," (born William Robinson), b. Detroit, MI, Feb. 19, 1940. He was singing, performing, and writing songs before high school; in his teens formed the vocal group the Matadors, later the Miracles (1957); signed with the local End label a year later and then joined with Berry Gordy Jr.'s fledgling Motown operation (1959); a year later scored their 1st national hit, *Shop Around*, written by Robinson and Gordy.

Through the mid-1960s the Miracles produced a stream of hits, many written by Robinson, including 1963's *You've Really Got a Hold on Me* (1963), *Ooo Baby, Baby, My Girl*, and *The Tracks of My Tears* (all 1965), and *I Second That Emotion* (1968); at the same time he wrote for other Motown acts and produced more hits, beginning with the Temptations's *The Way You Do the Things You Do* (1964). The original Miracles broke up in 1972; Robinson has pursued a sporadic solo career while working as a Motown executive; left the label (1988) but records and performs on occasion.

robusto (It.). Firmly and boldly.

Rochberg, George, b. Paterson, N.J., July 5, 1918. He took counterpoint and composition with Szell, H. Weisse, and L. Mannes at the Mannes College of Music in N.Y. (1939–42); after military service he studied theory and composition with R. Scalero and Menotti at the Curtis Inst. of Music in Philadelphia (B.Mus., 1947); studied at the Univ. of Pa. (M.A., 1948). He taught at the Curtis Inst. (1948–54); held Fulbright and American Academy fellowships in Rome (1950); became music ed. of the Theodore Presser Co. in Philadelphia (1951); made director of publications. He joined the faculty of the Univ. of Pa. as music dept. chairman (1960–68); continued as prof. of music; was Annenberg Prof. of the Humanities (1979–83). He held 2 Guggenheim fellowships (1956–57; 1966–67); elected to the American Academy and Inst. of Arts and Letters (1985); made a fellow of the American Academy of Arts and Sciences (1986).

In his earlier music Rochberg pursued the 20th-century ideal of tonal order and logically justifiable musical structures and was most profoundly influenced by Schoenberg and Webern; many works followed the dodecaphonic system. Beginning in the 1970s, he began drawing on Romantic and even earlier styles; resorted to overt quotations of recognizable fragments from music by composers as mutually unrelated as Schütz, Bach, Mahler, and Ives, treated by analogy with the "objets trouvés" of modern painting and sculpture (and earlier composers). He has attempted to synthesize his pre-20th-century influences, practiced collage or assemblage, or set one style against another within one work (e.g., String Quartet No. 3, 1972, in which different movements feature atonality, Bartók, or Brahms).

Rochberg's other works include the opera *The Confidence Man*, after Melville (1982); the monodrama *Phaedra* for Mezzo-soprano and Orch. (1974–75); 6 syms (1948–87); 7 string quartets; 2 piano trios (1963, 1985); other chamber works; piano music; and vocal works, both accompanied and unaccompanied. He publ. the study *The Hexachord and Its Relation to the 12-Tone Row* (Bryn Mawr, Pa., 1955); a collection of writings was ed. by Bolcom as *The Aesthetics of Survival: A Composer's View of 20th-Century Music* (Ann Arbor, 1984).

rock. Term covering a number of American popular musical genres dating from the 1960s, all outgrowths of 1950's rock 'n' roll, which evolved from the resources of urban and rural folk songs (and their derivatives). Urban popular music was initially inspired by the unique modalities of the Negro spirituals, with their lowered 3rds and 7ths; these laid the foundation for the blues, ragtime, early jazz, boogie-woogie, swing, and bebop, all preserving the character of city music. Quite different was the music of rural America, representing mostly European—particularly Anglo-Irish—folk songs; this country music was marked by a leisurely pace, free of the nervous excitement and syncopated beat associated with urban popular productions.

With the advent of the electronic age the barriers between urban and rural music were broken down; a new art was born that found its fullest expression in rock 'n' roll. By the early 1960s the most popular genres were later examples of rhythm 'n' blues (fast and slow), sentimental rock 'n' roll ballads, novelty songs, and the "girl-group" trios with richly orchestrated accompaniment expressing a wide range of emotion from the lachrymose to the lusty. Elvis Presley was coming to the end of his rock 'n' roll star period and was evolving into a Las Vegas showman.

Then came the Beatles of Liverpool, England, whose members had been listening to American popular music since the mid-1950s; their early songs and covers involved new textures dominated by electric guitars with percussive rhythmic support. Over the years the group's songwriters (especially Lennon and McCartney) articulated new syntheses of rock 'n' roll elements, adding others along the way (notably harmonic and structural); extended rock instrumentation into new territory. On the other end of the spectrum were the Rolling Stones, who explored rhythm-and-blues styles more deeply than the Beatles had; this, plus the raw sexualized stance taken by Jagger and Richards in their songs, made the Beatles seem tame by comparison. Both groups contributed to a major change in popular music: where rock 'n' roll was strongly rooted in dance, rock grew increasingly into a listening and even concert music.

The U.S. contributed other influences. Two such styles predated the "English invasion" of the 1960s: one, known as West Coast surf music (Beach Boys, Jan and Dean) that combined doo-wop and rock 'n' roll; two, an African-American development known as Motown or soul, depending on the music's sphere of influence (Detroit or Memphis, respectively): both drew on gospel music and rhythm and blues; Motown borrowed the girl-group sound for most of their artists; soul absorbed more of the older blues singing style and recorded mostly solo artists or duets.

Rock, at 1st a shortened form for rock 'n' roll, gradually replaced the older appellation as the music moved into modal harmonic patterns and the electric guitar became the principal "lead instrument," replacing the saxophone. Soon sub-styles and pseudo-styles were given geographic names as a marketing ploy, the most legitimate of which were the San Francisco and Los Angeles "sounds"; the former was associated with hippies, drug experimentation, and antiwar protest; the latter had fewer rough edges, was less specific in style, and lived competitively with its northern neighbor. Musicians of both cities borrowed freely; brought the expanded improvised solo to rock.

From these beginnings rock has flourished for 30 years plus; it has been challenged commercially and artistically by disco in the 1970s and other dance music thereafter; by hip-hop and rap in the 1980s; by soul ballads, etc. But rock is able to reinvent itself when creative juices run dry; for example, when the overblown art rock of the 1970s seemed ready to make rock extinct, the new wave and punk movements came out of England, reinventing both the Beatles' and the Rolling Stones' contributions to early rock; this survival instinct backs an idea familiar to musical Darwinists: When a style can no longer absorb influences, it dies (e.g., the *Ars subtilior* of the late 14th century; ragtime); it can be absorbed into another style (as ragtime contributed to jazz).

The seemingly innumerable rock subgenres include: *acid rock*, reputedly influenced by drug-taking, using a penetrating, "buzzing" tone on lead guitar equipped with a sustaining device, typical of the San Francisco sound; *art rock*, mixture of rock instrumentation (with a heavy keyboard emphasis) and classical orch. or imitations thereof (e.g., the *mellotron*)—its music may be original, in a classical style, or "borrowed" from actual works; *blues rock*, orig. a British genre, placing rural and urban blues into a rock context, with a strong dose of guitar improvisation (also keyboard or harmonica); *folk rock*, putting folk songs or neotraditional songs into a rock context, much as the Byrds

and Bob Dylan did with Dylan songs—aurally less threatening than other rock of its time; influential on European musicians aiming for national character; *hard rock*, similar to acid rock but with louder dynamics, thicker texture, and an unmistakable hook this led to *heavy metal* (or *metal*), which pushes the envelope further by even greater concentration on the rhythm guitar, the lead guitar becoming buried in the "mix," and adding a theatrical element; *jazz-rock* (or *fusion*), a mixture of harmonic and melodic jazz elements with the rhythm and instrumentation of rock—jazz's attempt to overcome commercial failure during the 1960s—rock's desire for fresh materials and respect; *mellow rock* (*soft rock*), rock's contribution to MOR (middle of the road), easy listening, and Muzak, growing out of folk rock's merging with late rock 'n' roll balladry—Carole King and James Taylor led the pack; *new wave,* late 1970s English revival of lean 1960s rock (in reaction to art rock and disco) with a postmodernist sensibility; *punk rock* (*punk*), historically synchronous with new wave but influenced by 1960s "garage bands" and hard rock—orig. associated with British youth's social rage but eventually became a fashion statement—punk survived into the 1990s as *grunge,* an Americanized variant with more depression than alienation. Rock has even borrowed from its competitors (disco, reggae, hip-hop) without losing its essence; Frank Zappa and others have been able to parody most rock styles with great skill.

A mass demonstration of rock's popularity, perhaps the greatest manifestation of music's attractive power ever, was the Woodstock Festival in Bethel, N.Y. (1969); tens of thousands of young people converged on a farmer's field, disdaining the hardships of travel, feeding, sleeping, and mud in order to be among their rock idols; the event had a profound sociological significance, for the audience, consisting of youthful nonconformists popularly known as hippies, seemed infused with the spirit of mutual accommodation, altruism, and love of peace. But guardians of public morals and others became concerned with the spiritual and physiological effects of rock on young people; examinations of the auditory capacities of habitual rock players and listeners revealed the loss of upper-range hearing. But the moral perils of rock lay elsewhere: In 1975 the pastor of a Baptist Church in Florida cited statistical records claiming that 984 out of 1,000 teenage girls who became pregnant out of wedlock did so while rock was being played. No matter; the rock recording industry reached sales in the billions of dollars.

In 1969, a Canadian underground newspaper gave this description of rock as a social force: "Rock is mysticism, revolution, communion, salvation, poetry, catharsis, eroticism, satori, total communication, the most vibrant art form in the world today. Rock is a global link, as young people everywhere plug into it and add to the form. What this new music suggested was raising your level of consciousness away from the fragmented, intellectual, goal-oriented time and material world to a unified sensual direction in a timeless spiritual environment."

rock 'n' roll. Popular American style of the 1950s that emerged from African-American rhythm and blues; one possible origin of the term dates back to the motion picture *Transatlantic Merry-Go-Round* (1934), featuring a song, *Rock and Roll;* there is no inkling in the rhythmic and harmonic characteristics of this song of the style that would develop into an overwhelmingly potent musical machine 2 decades later; the term is related to songs using double entendre. As opposed to the prevailing ballad style of the time, featuring singers with smooth orch'l background, rock 'n' roll featured a percussively heavy reinforcement of the meter (beat) played by combos consisting, minimally, of piano, bass, drums, and guitars, often with a single saxophonist or small wind section; blues harmonic structures were common but without the corresponding mood.

Rock 'n' roll owed its initial popularity to small radio stations that broadcast records under the guidance of disc jockeys (DJ's, i.e., riders on record discs); a Cleveland DJ named Alan Freed is generally credited with popularizing these songs under the generic term rock 'n' roll. One early specimen of rock 'n' roll was *Crazy, Man, Crazy,* by Bill Haley and the Comets (1953). In 1956 the landscape of rock 'n' roll was brightened by the rise of Elvis Presley, dressed in outlandish attire and sporting 3-inch sideburns; as he sang, he used a pelvic technique of rhythmic swing, gyrating suggestively around his lower axis—a body language that earned him the moniker Elvis the Pelvis. Rock 'n' roll suffered a temporary eclipse when it was discovered that DJ's (including Freed) accepted bribes from recording companies for pushing their records, a practice that became known as payola; but no scandal could stop the inexorable march of rock 'n' roll. In 1960 Chubby Checker and an innovative dance, the Twist, added a new beat to rock 'n' roll, now operating in the newfangled discotheques, successors to nightclubs, which substituted records for live performers.

In rock 'n' roll the pendulum-like rhythmic motion produces a tremendous accumulation of kinetic energy among listeners and players alike. The effect of this constant rhythmic drive is similar to that of the sinusoid wave, with steadily increasing amplitude, created by the march of a regiment of soldiers across a suspension bridge. Thanks to electronic amplification, rock 'n' roll became the loudest music to date; otologists warned that its addicts would lose sensitivity to the higher harmonics of the human voice and become partially deaf; Ralph Nader, the American Cassandra of urban civilization, cautioned the public against the danger of sonic pollution by rock 'n' roll in a letter addressed to Congress.

A more remarkable and less threatening feature of rock 'n' roll is the revival of archaic modality with its characteristic plagal cadences, the Dorian mode being a favorite. In harmony the submediant is lowered in major keys and becomes the minor 3rd of the minor subdominant triad. Parallel triadic progressions, adopted by rock 'n' roll, also impart an archaic modal quality to the music. The fusion of old modes and modern rhythms created a new type of syncretism of musical folkways. *Time* magazine described rock 'n' roll in 1956 as "an unrelenting, socking syncopation that sounds like a bull whip; a choleric saxophone honking mating-call sounds; an electric guitar turned up so loud that its sound shatters and splits; a vocal group that shudders and exercises violently to the beat while roughly chanting either a near-nonsense phrase or a moronic lyric in hillbilly idiom." Here an honest, poetic, out-of-touch critic spoke in the tradition of those who were not yet ready, or would never be ready, to "get it."

rococo (from Fr. *roc,* shell). Architectural term applied to a transitional era of composition *c.* 1725–75; also called the gallant style or "early Classic." In part, rococo served to lighten, even eliminate the "Gothic" contrapuntal textures of composers like J. S. Bach, increasingly considered old-fashioned; reemphasized monodic homophony while maintaining the pervasive ornamentation, character pieces, dance forms, and tonality of the Baroque. But it was a period of intense experimentation; at the formal level, as Haydn and others developed what was later called sonata form; at the rhetorical level, as C. P. E. Bach and others found that meditative asides and sudden pauses could have great expressive effect; with dynamics (crescendos of the Mannheim school) and orchestration (permanent incorporation of winds). One development, the question-and-answer phrase based on tonic-dominant-tonic harmonic motion, became the essence of Classic music; the transition from rococo to Classic can be observed in Mozart's music from his wunderkind phase to his twenties.

Rodgers, Jimmie (James Charles), b. Meridian, Miss., Sept. 8, 1897; d. N.Y., May 26, 1933. He worked on the railroad until his retirement (1925); made his 1st recordings (1927); known as the "Singing Brakeman" and "America's Blue Yodeler," meshing the old-time style with rural blues. His short-lived career was dogged by tuberculosis and an inability to control his spendthrift lifestyle. He is duly recognized as the father of modern country music; 1st to be placed in the Country Music Hall of Fame in Nashville (1961); a 1977 U.S. postage stamp commemorated the 80th anniversary of his birth.

Rodgers, Richard (Charles), b. Hammels Station, Long Island, N.Y., June 28, 1902; d. N.Y., Dec. 30, 1979. He began piano lessons when he was 6; studied at Columbia Univ. (1919–21) and the Inst. of Musical Art in N.Y. (1921–23), receiving instruction from Krehbiel and Goetschius. He collaborated with the lyricist Lorenz Hart in a series of inspired and highly popular musical comedies: *The Girl Friend* (1926); *A Connecticut Yankee* (1927); *On Your Toes* (1936); *Babes in Arms* (1937); *I Married an Angel* (1938); *The Boys from Syracuse* (1942). After Hart's death (1943) he began collaborating with Oscar Hammerstein II; they wrote the greatly acclaimed musical *Oklahoma!* (1943; Pulitzer Prize, 1944), followed by other successful productions: *Carousel* (1945); *South Pacific* (1949; Pulitzer Prize, 1950); *The King and I* (1951); *The Flower Drum Song* (1958); *The Sound of Music* (1959). After Hammerstein's death (1960) he wrote music and lyrics for *No Strings* (1962), then composed *Do I Hear a Waltz?* (1965) to the lyrics of Stephen Sondheim; composed the soundtrack to the television series *Victory at Sea* (1952).

Rogers, Ginger. See ⇒Astaire, Fred.

Röhrenglocken (Ger.). Tubular chimes.

Roldán, Amadeo, b. Paris July 12, 1900; d. Havana, Mar. 2, 1939. He studied violin at the Madrid Cons. with Fernandez Bordas, graduating in 1916; won the Sarasate Violin Prize; subsequently studied composition with Conrado del Campo in Madrid and with Pedro Sanjuan. In 1921 he settled in Havana; in 1924 he became concertmaster of the Orquesta Filarmonica; in 1925, assistant conductor; in 1932, conductor. In the late 1920s and early 1930s he kept company with the members of Grupo de Avance, who sought to modernize Cuban artistic culture; he later became prof. of composition at the Cons. (from 1935). In his works he employed the melorhythms of

Afro-Cuban popular music, particularly indigenous mestizo folk music (and folklore); his percussion ensemble works anticipate Varèse's *Ionisation*.

roll. 1. A tremolo or trill on the drum. The sign in notation is

Long roll, the prolonged and reiterated drum signal to troops, for attack or rally. 2. In organ playing, a rapid arpeggio. 3. On the tambourine, the rapid and reiterated hither- and thither-stroke with the knuckles.

Rolling Stones, The. (Vocals/harmonica/guitar: Mick [Michael Philip] Jagger, b. Dartford, Kent, July 26, 1944; lead guitar/vocal: Keith Richards [Richard], b. Dartford, Kent, Dec. 18, 1943; guitar/vocal: Brian Jones [born Lewis Brian Hopkins-Jones] b. Cheltenham, Feb. 28, 1942; d. London, July 3, 1969; Bass: Bill Wyman [born William Perks], b. Penge, SE London, Oct. 23, 1936; drums: Charlie Watts, b. Neasden, N. London, June 2, 1941; piano: Ian Stewart, b. 1938; d. London, Dec. 12, 1985. Jones was replaced just before his death by Michael "Mick" Taylor, b. Welwyn Garden City, England, Jan. 17, 1948, himself replaced in 1975 by Ron Wood, b. Hillingdon, England, June 1, 1947; Wyman retired and was replaced in 1994 by Darryl Jones). Also called the Stones; long-lived English rock group, with the Beatles the prime movers of the transition from rock 'n' roll to rock in the 1960s. The group were playing the English rhythm-and-blues circuit when Andrew Loog Oldham (b. 1944) saw them, became their manager, and, like Brian Epstein with the Beatles, made them more ready for general consumption as the scruffy answer to the sweet-faced Liverpudlians. Oldham demoted Stewart from full membership because of his "unsuitable" appearance; he played with the group on recordings and tours, functioned as tour manager, and was their trusted confidant.

With a recording contract the Stones combined their rhythm-and-blues covers (*Not Fade Away, It's All Over Now*) with rock balladry (*Tell Me, Time Is on My Side*). By 1965 Jagger and Richards were collaborating on most of their material, mostly sexually oriented in nature (*The Last Time, Satisfaction, Let's Spend the Night Together*); while the Beatles continued to sing of love and relationships, the Stones turned to sometimes bitter social commentary (*Get Off of My Cloud, 19th Nervous Breakdown, Mother's Little Helper, Have You Seen Your Mother Baby, Paint It Black*). The bizarre concept album *Their Satanic Majesties Request* (1967) failed to separate psychedelia from pretension (not to mention parody), but it helped solidify the Stones' distinction from the Beatles, who were no longer touring, losing stylistic cohesion as Lennon and McCartney wrote separately, and sounding aloof even when dealing with difficult issues.

Jagger and Richards solidified their outlaw image with the classic single *Jumpin' Jack Flash* (1968); later that year they released the brilliant album *Beggars Banquet*, with *Sympathy for the Devil, Street Fighting Man, Salt of the Earth,* and *No Expectations.* This was Brian Jones's last album; his positive musical contributions were completely outweighed by drug addiction, alcoholism, overall bad health, and unreliability; gently forced out of the group, he died 2 months later, drowning in his own swimming pool; he was replaced by slide guitarist Mick Taylor, formerly of John Mayall's Bluesbreakers; he was replaced by Ron Wood, who had played with Jeff Beck and the Faces. Another hit single (*Honky Tonk Woman*) was followed by another brilliant album, *Let It Bleed*; it opens with *Gimme Shelter,* one of their most intricate and successful productions; it came to symbolize the Stones' dark side through its association with the Charles Manson cult murders and the free Altamont concert (1969) with Hell's Angels for security and the death of a young black audience member. For a few more years Stones albums remained of high quality; but by 1973's *Goat's Head Soup* they were out of the innovatory loop; they continued to tour and make recordings, sometimes influenced by non-rock styles (the discofied *Miss You*), other times in characteristic hard rock mode (*Start Me Up*). All five members have released solo projects, none so successful as the group's efforts but in at least one case distinctive, namely Watts's ventures into big band, in concert and on record. In the late 1980s and early 1990s the group was mostly silent, due to a feud between Jagger and Richards; they eventually reunited, produced *Voodoo Lounge* (1994) and began touring again, although without original member Wyman.

Rollins, "Sonny" (Theodore Walter), b. N.Y., Sept. 7, 1929. He 1st worked with Babs Gonzales, Bud Powell, and Fats Navarro; went to Chicago; studied with Ike Day. After making recordings with M. Davis, he made appearances with Parker, Monk, and other leading jazz musicians; was a member of the Modern Jazz Quartet. At the height of his checkered career, he ranked among the foremost masters of the tenor saxophone.

Roman numerals. This system of enumeration is used for the designation of instrumental parts (Flute I, Flute II, etc.); analysis of harmonic progression in the vertical plane, based on scale steps (I = tonic, V = dominant, etc.); and as a method of enumerating works according to the composer's whim (i.e., Berio's *Sequenza* series, Stockhausen's *Klavierstücke*).

romance. 1. Orig. a type of Spanish poetic narrative, a ballad or popular tale in verse; later, Romance lyrical songs. The French and Russian romance is a short art song or a lied composed of several stanzas. 2. (Ger. *Romanze*) Short instrumental pieces of sentimental or romantic cast, without specific form. *Romances sans paroles,* songs without words.

romancero (Sp.). Collections of ballads or romances (heroic tales), sung or recited by *juglares* (minstrels).

romanesca. A type of court dance that originated in the Roman countryside in Italy in the 16th century. It is structurally related to the folia, with its persistent bass formation (tonic, dominant, submediant, mediant) upon which there are embroidered melodies, either written out or improvised by singers.

Romantic. In music history, the period from about 1815 to 1915, overlapping with late Classic on one end and impressionism, expressionism, and primitivism on the other.

Romany music. See ⇒Gypsy music.

romanza (It.). A short romantic song or a solo instrumental piece.

Romero. Family of famous Spanish-born American guitarists constituting a quartet known as Los Romeros: Celedonio (b. Málaga, Mar. 2, 1918) pursued a career as a soloist in Spain; he served as mentor to each of his 3 sons, Celin (b. Málaga, Nov. 23, 1940), Pepe (b. Málaga, Mar. 8, 1944), and Angel (b. Málaga, Aug. 17, 1946); they eventually appeared together as a guitar quartet, playing engagements throughout Spain. The family emigrated to the U.S. in 1958 and made their 1st tour of the country in 1961; billed as "the royal family of the guitar," they toured with great success worldwide. In addition to making their own arrangements and transcriptions, they commissioned works from various composers, including Rodrigo and Federico Moreno Torroba.

ronde (Fr.). 1. Whole note. 2. Round dance.

rondeau (Fr.). 1. A medieval French song of the fixed form type, with a musical refrain and verse repeating in a nonalternating manner, comprising one stanza of 8 lines. 2. Baroque instrumental form, alternating a refrain (*grand couplet*) with various episodes (couplets); the etymological and musical predecessor of the rondo.

rondel, rondelet (Fr.). Early names for the rondeau.

rondellus (Lat.). The 13th-century British vocal genre, in 3 voices, in which the technique of voice exchange is employed, either in the upper 2 voices (with a repetitive tenor or pes) or all 3.

rondena. Spanish round dance similar to a fandango.

rondo (Fr. *rondeau*). An instrumental piece in which the opening thematic section or refrain (A) is repeated in the tonic, alternating with contrasting sections in related keys (with the common exception of the penultimate section, also in the tonic). In general there are 5- and 7-part rondo forms; a typical pattern—with letters representing thematic sections—might be A–B–A–C–A–B–A. Sometimes these episodes are expanded so as to create secondary thematic sources; variations are widely applied, and there is usually a coda to conclude the work. The rondo is often used as the finale of Classic syms., concertos, and sonatas.

rondo-sonata form. Sonata-rondo form.

root. The lowest note of a chord in actual pitch. *Root position,* arrangement of a chord where the lowest pitch (usually the bass) is the root of the chord.

Rorem, Ned, b. Richmond, Ind., Oct. 23, 1923. At a very young age he was inculcated with piano music, taught to him at home by 3 female instructors. He began his formal study of theory and harmony with L. Sowerby at the American Cons. in Chicago (1938–39); entered Northwestern Univ.; took composition with A. Nolte (1940–42); received a scholarship to study at the Curtis Inst. of Music in Philadelphia (1943); took counter-

point and harmony with R. Scalero; studied dramatic and vocal music with Menotti. In 1944 he moved to N.Y.; entered the Juilliard School of Music; studied composition with B. Wagenaar (B.S., 1946; M.S., 1948); took private orchestration lessons with Thomson (1944); studied modern harmony with Copland at Tanglewood (1946–47).

Rorem received the Gershwin Memorial Award, enabling him to travel to France, where he rapidly absorbed local musical culture and mastered the French language; sojourned in Morocco (1949–51); returning to Paris, he obtained the patronage of the Vicomtesse Noailles; entered the circle of modern Parisian composers. Upon his return to the U.S. (1958) he was appointed composer-in-residence at the State Univ. of N.Y. at Buffalo (1959–60); taught at the Univ. of Utah (1966–67) and the Curtis Inst. of Music (1980–86). He obtained commissions from the Ford Foundation and the Elizabeth Sprague Coolidge Foundation, as well as from prominent performing groups; received 2 Guggenheim fellowships (1956–57; 1978–79); received the Pulitzer Prize for *Air Music* (1976).

Rorem developed as a composer of substance and originality, proclaiming that music must sing, even if it is written for instruments. Between times he discovered an astonishing talent as a writer; an elegant stylist in both French and English, publ. a succession of personal journals, recounting with gracious insouciance his encounters in Paris and N.Y. He proudly declared that he wrote for an audience and did not wish to indulge in writing songs and symphonic poems for an indefinite, abstract group. He is regarded as one of the finest song composers in America, with a natural feeling for vocal line and prosody of text. The French influence remains the most pronounced characteristic of his music, particularly in the songs.

Rosalia. Term of opprobrium for a modulating sequence to a key a major 2nd higher; the term comes from a once popular Italian song, *Rosalia, mia cara.* The Germans called this type of modulating sequence *Cousin Michel,* after an old German song of that name, or (contemptuously) *Schusterfleck* (shoemaker's patch). But Beethoven, Schubert, Liszt, and Bruckner used the Rosalia type of sequence most admirably for dramatic effect; it was popular in semiclassical pieces of the 19th century; 20th-century popular music often uses a modulation of a minor 2nd higher as a clichéd climactic effect.

Rosenberg, Hilding (Constantin), b. Bosjökloster, Ringsjon, Skåne, June 21, 1892; d. Stockholm, May 19, 1985. He studied piano and organ in his youth; became active as an organist. He went to Stockholm in 1914 to study piano with Andersson; studied composition with Ellberg at the Stockholm Cons. (1915–16); took a conducting course there. He made trips abroad from 1920; studied composition with Stenhammar and conducting with Scherchen. He was a *répétiteur* and assistant conductor at the Royal Opera in Stockholm (1932–34); guest conducted in Scandinavia and later in the U.S. (1948), leading performances of his own works; likewise was active as a teacher, numbering Bäck, Blomdahl, and Lidholm among his students.

Rosenberg was the foremost Swedish composer of his era; greatly influenced Swedish music by his experimentation and stylistic diversity, leading to a masterful style marked by originality, superb craftsmanship, and refinement. His works include 9 operas; 4 ballets; a pantomime; 2 melodramas; 5 oratorios;

4 cantatas; 8 numbered syms. (1917–71); *Sinfonia da chiesa* (2); Sym. for wind and percussion (1966); concertos for violin (2), trumpet, viola, cello (2), piano; concertos for strings or orch. (4); other orch. works; incidental music to almost 50 plays; film scores. His chamber music includes 12 string quartets (1920–56), violin sonatas (2), solo violin sonatas (3), mixed trios, Wind Quintet (1959), solo sonatas for flute and clarinet, piano music, choral pieces; songs.

Rosenthal, Moriz, b. Lemberg, Dec. 17, 1862; d. N.Y., Sept. 3, 1946. He studied piano at the Lemberg Cons. with Karol Mikuli, who was a pupil of Chopin; in 1872, when he was 10 years old, he played Chopin's Rondo in C for 2 Pianos with his teacher in Lemberg. The family moved to Vienna in 1875, and Rosenthal became the pupil of Joseffy, who inculcated in him a passion for virtuoso piano playing, which he taught according to Tausig's method. Liszt accepted Rosenthal as a student during his stay in Weimar and Rome (1876–78). After a hiatus of some years, during which Rosenthal studied philosophy at the Univ. of Vienna, he returned to his concert career in 1884 and established for himself a reputation as one of the world's greatest virtuosos; was nicknamed (because of his small stature and great pianistic power) "little giant of the piano." Beginning in 1888 he made 12 tours of the U.S., where he became a permanent resident in 1938. He publ. (with L. Schytte) a *Schule des höheren Klavierspiels* (Berlin, 1892). His wife, Hedwig Kanner-Rosenthal, was a distinguished piano teacher.

Roslavetz, Nikolai (Andreievich), b. Suray, near Chernigov, Jan. 5, 1881; d. Moscow, Aug. 23, 1944. He studied violin with his uncle and theory with A. M. Abaza in Kursk; then studied violin with Jan Hrimaly, and composition with Ilyinsky and Vassilenko, at the Moscow Cons., graduating in 1912; won the Silver Medal for his cantata *Heaven and Earth,* after Byron. A composer of advanced tendencies, he publ. in 1913 an atonal Violin Sonata, the 1st of its kind by a Russian composer; his 3rd String Quartet exhibits 12-tone properties. He ed. a short-lived journal, *Muzykalnaya Kultura,* in 1924, and became a leading figure in the modern movement in Russia.

With a change of Soviet cultural policy toward socialist realism and nationalism, Roslavetz was subjected to severe criticism in the press for persevering in his aberrant ways. To conciliate the authorities, he tried to write operettas; then was given an opportunity to redeem himself by going to Tashkent to write ballets based on Uzbek folk songs; he failed in all these pursuits. But interest in his music became pronounced abroad and posthumous performances were arranged in West Germany. He composed a sym. (1922); symphonic poems *Man and the Sea,* after Baudelaire (1921) and *End of the World,* after Paul Lafargue (1922); Cello Sonata (1921); Violin Concerto (1925); a cantata, *October* (1927); Nocturne for Harp, Oboe, 2 Violas, and Cello (1913); 3 String Quartets (1913, 1916, 1920); 3 piano trios; 4 violin sonatas; 3 Dances for Violin and Piano (1921); Cello Sonata (1921); 5 piano sonatas.

Ross, Diana, b. Detroit, Mar. 26, 1944. She sang for social events in Detroit; then organized a female trio whose other members were her close contemporaries Florence Ballard and Mary Wilson, assuming the grandiose name of the Supremes, under which name the trio became the most successful of the 1960s Motown "stable" of artists. Florence Ballard dropped out in 1967 and was replaced by Cindy Birdsong, and the group thenceforth was called Diana Ross and the Supremes. Their hits included *Come See About Me, Stop! In the Name of Love, Baby Love, You Can't Hurry Love, I Hear a Symphony,* ad infinitum. The Supremes, and Ross as their top singer, broke the curse of drugs and alcohol besetting so many pop singers by campaigning for virtue and love *sans* narcotics.

In 1969 Ross left the Supremes and started on a highly successful career as a solo singer, in cabarets, in nightclubs, on the radio, on television, in Las Vegas, on Broadway, and in the movies, where she starred in a film biography of Billie Holiday, *Lady Sings the Blues* (1970), which produced a number 1 soundtrack album; her next film, *Mahogany* (1972), was less successful. As a soloist she hit the top of the charts with an antidrug number, *Reach Out and Touch,* and her signature song *Ain't No Mountain High Enough;* she recorded the eponymous album *Diana! An Evening with Diana Ross,* a duet album with Marvin Gaye, the generic song *Why Do Fools Fall in Love,* and a duet with Lionel Richie, *Endless Love.* Other solo hits include *Touch Me in the Morning, Do You Know Where You're Going* (from *Mahogany*), *Love Hangover, Upside Down, I'm Coming Out, Muscles,* and *Missing You.*

Rossini, Gioachino (Antonio), b. Pesaro, Feb. 29, 1792; d. Paris, Nov. 13, 1868. Great Italian opera composer possessing an equal genius for shattering melodrama in tragedy and for devastating humor in comedy. He came from a musical family; his father served as town trumpeter in Lugo and Pesaro and played brass instruments in provincial theaters; his mother sang opera as *seconda donna.* After the family moved to Lugo his father taught him to play the horn; studied singing with a local canon. Later the family moved to Bologna, where he studied singing, harpsichord, and music theory with Padre Tesei; learned to play the violin and viola. Soon he acquired enough technical ability to serve as maestro al cembalo in local churches and at occasional opera productions; studied voice with the tenor Matteo Babbini.

In 1806 Rossini was accepted at the Liceo Musicale in Bologna, where he studied singing, solfeggio, cello, piano, and counterpointi. He began composing; his cantata *Il pianto d'Armonia sulla morte d'Orfeo* was performed at the Liceo Musicale in Bologna and received a prize (1808). About the same time he wrote his 1st opera, *Demetrio e Polibio;* in 1810 he was commissioned to write a work for the Teatro San Moise in Venice; he submitted his opera *La cambiale di matrimonio,* which won considerable acclaim. His next production was *L'equivoco stravagante,* produced in Bologna in 1811. In 1812, he produced 3 other operas: *L'inganno felice* (Venice), *Ciro in Babilonia* (Ferrara), and *La scala di seta* (Venice); obtained a commission from La Scala of Milan; the result, *La pietra del paragone,* was a fine success.

In 1813 Rossini produced 3 operas for Venice: *Il Signor Bruschino, Tancredi, and L'Italiana in Algeri;* the last became a perennial favorite. The next 3 operas, *Aureliano in Palmira* (Milan, 1813), *Il Turco in Italia* (Milan, 1814), and *Sigismondo* (Venice, 1814), were unsuccessful; still a very young man, he was approached by the famous impresario Barbaja, the manager of the Teatro San Carlo and the Teatro

Fondo in Naples, with an offer for an exclusive contract, under the terms of which Rossini was to supply 2 operas annually for Barbaja. The 1st opera Rossini wrote for him was *Elisabetta, regina d'Inghilterra,* produced at the Teatro San Carlo in Naples in 1815; the title role was entrusted to the famous Spanish soprano Isabella Colbran, who was Barbaja's favorite mistress. An important innovation in the score was Rossini's use of *recitativo stromentato* in place of the usual *recitativo secco.*

Rossini's next opera, *Torvaldo e Dorliska,* produced in Rome in 1815, was an unfortunate failure. Rossini now determined to try his skill in composing a full-scaled opera buffa, *Il Barbiere di Siviglia,* based on the famous play by Beaumarchais; it was an audacious decision on Rossini's part, since an Italian opera with the same name and subject (1782) by Giovanni Paisiello (1740–1816) was still playing with undiminished success. To avoid confusion, Rossini's opera on this subject was performed at the Teatro Argentina in Rome under a different title, *Almaviva, ossia L'inutile precauzione.* Although he was only 23 years old, this work proved to be his greatest accomplishment and a standard opera buffa in the repertory of theaters all over the world. Rossini conducted its 1st performance in Rome (1816), but if contemporary reports and gossip can be trusted, the occasion was marred by various stage accidents that moved the unruly Italian audience to interrupt the spectacle with vociferous outcries of derision; however, the next performance scored a brilliant success. For later productions he used the title *Il Barbiere di Siviglia.*

Strangely enough, the operas Rossini wrote immediately afterward were not uniformly successful: *La Gazzetta,* produced in Naples in 1816, passed unnoticed; the next opera, *Otello,* also produced in Naples in 1816, had some initial success but was not retained in the repertoire after a few sporadic performances. There followed *La Cenerentola* and *La gazza ladra,* both from 1817, which fared much better. But the following 7 operas— *Armida, Mosé in Egitto, Ricciardo e Zoraide, Ermione, La Donna del lago, Maometto II,* and *Zelmira*—produced in Naples between 1817 and 1822, were soon forgotten; only the famous Prayer in *Mosé in Egitto* saved that opera from oblivion. The *prima donna assoluta* in all these operas was Isabella Colbran; after a long association with Barbaja, she went to live with Rossini, who finally married her (1822). This event, however, did not result in a break between the impresario and the composer; Barbaja even made arrangements for a festival of Rossini's works in Vienna at the Kärnthnertortheater, of which he became a director. In Vienna Rossini met Beethoven. Returning to Italy, he produced a fairly successful mythological opera, *Semiramide* (Venice, 1823), with Colbran in the title role. Rossini then signed a contract for a season in London with Giovanni Benelli, director of the Italian opera at the King's Theatre.

Rossini arrived in London late in 1823 and was received by King George IV. He conducted several of his operas and was a guest at the homes of the British nobility, where he played piano as an accompanist to singers, at very large fees. In 1824 he settled in Paris, where he became director of the Théâtre-Italien. For the coronation of King Charles X he composed *Il viaggio a Reims,* which was performed in Paris under his direction (1825). He used parts of this *piece d'occasion* in his opera *Le Comte Ory.* In Paris he met Meyerbeer, with whom he established

an excellent relationship. After the expiration of his contract with the Théâtre-Italien, he was given the nominal titles of Premier Compositeur du Roi and Inspecteur General du Chant en France at an annual salary of 25,000 francs. He was now free to compose for the Paris Opéra; there, in 1826, he produced *Le Siege de Corinthe,* a revised French version of *Maometto II.* Later he also revised the score of *Mosé in Egitto* and produced it at the Paris Opéra in French as *Moïse et Pharaon* (1827); there followed *Le Comte Ory* (1828).

In 1829 Rossini was able to obtain an agreement with the government of King Charles X guaranteeing him a lifetime annuity of 6,000 francs. In return he promised to write more works for the Paris Opéra. Later that year his *Guillaume Tell* was given its premiere at the Opéra; it became immensely popular, but was his last opera (he was 37). The French revolution of July 1830, which dethroned King Charles X, invalidated his contract with the French government. Rossini sued the government of King Louis Philippe, the successor to the throne of Charles X, for the continuation of his annuity; the incipient litigation was settled in his favor (1835). From 1836 to 1848 he lived in Bologna, serving as consultant to the Liceo Musicale.

Much ink has been spilled on the reasons for Rossini's decision to stop writing operas. Some said that he was unhappy about the cavalier treatment he received from the management of the Paris Opéra; that he had spoken disdainfully of yielding the operatic field to "the Jews" (Meyerbeer and Halévy), whose operas were captivating Parisian audiences. This seems unlikely; Rossini was close to Meyerbeer until the latter's death (1864). He was not in the habit of complaining; he enjoyed life too well. More possible is that he was deeply affected by his mother's death (1827); that, well-to-do and confident of continuing governmental financial support, he wanted to rest from what had been a hectic career; or, that increasing illnesses led him into a deep depression that did not correct itself until the mid-1850s, when he returned to composing with remarkable energy. On Feb. 29, 1868, he celebrated his 19th birthday, as there had only been that many leap years since his birth. He was superstitious; like many Italians (and Schoenberg), he feared Friday the 13th; died on such a date; in 1887 his remains were taken to Florence for entombment in the Church of Santa Croce.

Rossini was the consummate composer of Italian opera buffa between Mozart and Donizetti. Many individual Rossini arias are well-known, but relatively few operas are revived, as the librettos lack genuine dramatic tension. He remains most popular for his overtures; their light-hearted essence embodies the old Italian sinfonia in late Classic form. Surprisingly, he has also become known for a few works of sacred music: *Messa di gloria* (1820), *Stabat Mater* (1842), and the *Petite messe solennelle* (1864), the last an indication that he did not abandon composition entirely during his last years of life; of greatest interest are the numerous piano pieces, songs, and instrumental works that he called *Péchés de vieillesse* (Sins of Old Age, 1857–68), a collection containing over 150 pieces.

Rossini's tunes have been used by other composers: Respighi used *Quelques riens* in his ballet *La Boutique fantasque* and other themes in his orch. suite *Rossiniana.* An opera entitled *Rossini in Neapel* was written by Bernhard Paumgartner. Britten used Rossini's music in his orch. suites *Soirées musicales* and *Matinées musicales.* The most famous Rossini arrangement is the Prayer from *Mosé in Egitto*, transcribed for violin by Paganini.

Rostropovich, Mstislav (Leopoldovich), b. Baku, Mar. 27, 1927. A precocious child, he began cello studies with his father Leopold Rostropovich (1892–1942); also had piano lessons from his mother. In 1931 the family moved to Moscow, where he made his debut when he was 8; continued his training at the Central Music School (1939–41); then studied cello with Kozolupov and composition with Shebalin and Shostakovich at the Moscow Cons. (1943–48); subsequently studied privately with Prokofiev. He won the International Competition for Cellists in Prague in 1950, and the next year made his 1st appearance in the West in Florence.

Rostropovich made his U.S. debut at N.Y.'s Carnegie Hall in 1956, winning extraordinary critical acclaim. He became a teacher (1953) and a prof. (1956) at the Moscow Cons., and also a prof. at the Leningrad Cons. (1961). A talented pianist, he frequently appeared as accompanist to his wife, the soprano Galina Vishnevskaya, whom he married in 1955. In 1961 he made his 1st appearance as a conductor. As his fame increased he received various honors, including the Lenin Prize in 1963 and the Gold Medal of the Royal Phil. Soc. of London in 1970.

In spite of his eminence and official honors, Rostropovich encountered difficulties with the Soviet authorities, owing chiefly to his spirit of uncompromising independence. He let the dissident author Aleksandr Solzhenitsyn stay at his dacha near Moscow, protesting the Soviet government's treatment of the Nobel Prize winner for literature in a letter to *Pravda* in 1969. Although the letter went unpubl. in his homeland, it was widely disseminated in the West. As a result, Rostropovich found himself increasingly hampered in his career by the Soviet Ministry of Culture. His concerts were canceled without explanation, as were Vishnevskaya's engagements at the Bolshoi Theater. Foreign tours were forbidden, as were appearances on radio, television, and recordings.

In 1974 Rostropovich and Vishnevskaya obtained permission to go abroad accompanied by their 2 daughters. He made a brilliant debut as a guest conductor with the National Sym. Orch. in Washington, D.C. (1975); his success led to his appointment as its music director in 1977. Free from the bureaucratic annoyances of the USSR, he and Vishnevskaya publicized stories of their previous difficulties at home in Russia. Annoyed by such independent activities, the Moscow authorities finally stripped them both of their Soviet citizenship as "ideological renegades." The Soviet establishment even went so far as to remove the dedication to Rostropovich of Shostakovich's 2nd Cello Concerto. The whole disgraceful episode ended when the Soviet government, chastened by perestroika, restored Rostropovich's citizenship in 1990 and invited him to take the National Sym. Orch. to the USSR. Besides conducting the American orch. there, Rostropovich appeared as soloist in Dvořák's Cello Concerto. His return to Russia was welcomed by the populace as a vindication of his principles of liberty.

Rostropovich, nicknamed "Slava" (glory), is duly recognized as one of the greatest cellists of the century, a master interpreter of both the standard and the contemporary literature. To enhance the repertoire for his instrument, he commissioned and premiered numerous scores, including works by Prokofiev,

Shostakovich, Britten, Piston, and Foss. As a conductor he proved himself an impassioned and authoritative interpreter of the music of the Russian national and Soviet schools of composition. He organized the 1st Rostropovich International Cello Competition in Paris in 1981 and the Rostropovich Festival in Snape, England, in 1983. He was made an Officer of the French Legion d'honneur in 1982 and received an honorary knighthood from Queen Elizabeth II of England in 1987. Galina (Pavlovna) Vishnevskaya (b. Leningrad, Oct. 25, 1926) was one of Russia's most prominent sopranos. In 1952 she joined the operatic staff of the Bolshoi Theater in Moscow; her roles there were Violetta, Tosca, Madama Butterfly, and an entire repertoire of soprano parts in Russian operas. She made her debut at the Metropolitan Opera in N.Y. in 1961 as Aida. Britten wrote the solo soprano part in his *War Requiem* for her.

rota (Lat., wheel). 1. A somewhat obscure term for the English round; *Sumer is icumen in* is the only work in MS so labeled. 2. Latinization of *rote* (Mid. Eng., cruit). Compare with rotta.

Rota, Nino (born Rinaldi), b. Milan, Dec. 3, 1911; d. Rome, Apr. 10, 1979. He was a precocious musician; at age 11 he wrote an oratorio which had a public performance, and at 13 composed a lyric comedy in 3 acts, *Il Principe porcaro*, after Hans Christian Andersen. He entered the Milan Cons. in 1923 and took courses with Delachi, Orefici, and Bas; after private studies with Pizzetti (1925–26), he studied composition with Casella at the Accademia di Santa Cecilia in Rome, graduating in 1930; later went to the U.S. and enrolled in the Curtis Inst. of Music in Philadelphia, studying composition with Rosario Scalero and conducting with Fritz Reiner. Returning to Italy, he entered the Univ. of Milan to study literature, gaining a degree in 1937. He taught at the Taranto music school (1937–38); then was a teacher (from 1939) and director (1950–78) at the Bari Liceo Musicale.

Rota's musical style demonstrates a great facility, and even felicity, with occasional daring excursions into the forbidding territory of dodecaphony. However, his most durable compositions are related to his music for the cinema; he composed the soundtracks of a great number of films of the Italian director Federico Fellini covering the period from 1950 to 1979, including *Lo sceicco bianco* (The White Sheik; 1950), *La strada* (1954), *Notti di Cabiria* (1957), *La dolce vita* (1959), *Otto de mezza* (8 1/2, 1963), *Giulietta degli spiriti* (Juliet of the Spirits; 1965), *Satyricon* (1969), *The Clowns* (1971), *Fellini Roma* (1972), *Amarcord* (1974), *Casanova* (1977), *Orchestra Rehearsal* (1979). He also wrote scores for other directors, notably for Francis Ford Coppola's *The Godfather I* (1972) and *II* (1974) and Wertmuller's *Love and Anarchy* (1974). Other works include: 11 operas, most notably *Il cappello di paglia di Firenzi* (Florentine Straw Hat; 1946); 3 ballets, 3 syms. (1936–39; 1938–43; 1957); and other orch'l works. Vocal: 5 oratorios, 3 masses (1960–62), songs. Chamber: Various works, for 1 to 11 players; keyboard music.

rotation. In post-Schoenbergian developments of dodecaphony the 12-tone series is often modified by rotation. As the term implies, the series is shifted a space, so that at its next occurrence it begins with the 2nd note and ends with the 1st; in the subsequent incidence it starts on the 3rd note and ends on the 2nd, etc. Rotation in its various further developments is a fertile device of dodecaphonic techniques particularly favored by Stravinsky.

rotondo (It.). Round, full.

roto-toms. Mounted tom-tom-like percussion used in jazz and occasionally modern classical music. The plastic drumhead is not supported by a resonating body; instead it rotates on a stand that permits the tuning of definite pitches. While flexible in the manner of the timpani, the sound is not comparable to a true membranophone.

rotrouenge. Type of troubadour and trouvère song with a refrain and a rhyme scheme; its identity remains obscure, as there are few surviving examples; the name disappears around 1200.

rotta. Medieval triangular psaltery, found throughout Europe. The instrument is also called the *cruit* (Irish Gael.), which is used for a medieval triangular harp. Compare with rota.

rotulus. A roll of parchment sheets sewn together, the usual form of books in ancient times up to the 4th century, but remained in use for another millennium for musical MSS. Several medieval motets owe their preservation to the sturdiness of such *rotuli*.

roulade (Fr.). A grace consisting of a run or arpeggio from one principal melody tone to another; a vocal or instrumental flourish.

roulante (Fr., rolling). *Caisse roulante*, a tenor drum.

round. A perpetual canon, usually in 3 parts, sometimes with a harmonic support or accompaniment (*pes*). The entrances of the voices are rhythmically equidistant; the melody itself, usually in a major key, is built on the tonic triad, so that the counterpoint is in 3rds and a complete triadic harmony is achieved when all the voices come in. *Frère Jacques* is a famous example of a round.

round dance. Ballroom dance performed by couples in a circular motion, such as a waltz.

roundelay. A song or lai with continued reiteration or refrain.

Rousseau, Jean-Jacques, b. Geneva, June 28, 1712; d. Ermenonville, near Paris, July 2, 1778. Without other musical training besides desultory self-instruction, Rousseau made his debut as a music scholar at age 29, reading a paper before the Académie in Paris (1724), which was received and publ. as a *Dissertation sur la musique moderne* (1743). His opera *Les Muses galantes* had only 1 private representation, at the house of La Pouplinière in 1745; his revision of the intermezzo *La Reine de Navarre* (by Voltaire and Rameau) was a failure in Paris; but his opera *Le Devin du village* (Fontainebleau, 1752; Paris Opéra, 1753) was very successful and remained in the repertoire for 75 years.

In the meantime Rousseau's musical articles for the *Encyclopédie* had evoked scathing criticism from Rameau and others; improved by revision and augmentation, they were republ. as his *Dictionnaire de musique* (Geneva, 1st known ed., Paris, 1768). In 1752 commenced the dispute, known as the guerre des bouffons, between the partisans of French and Italian opera; Rousseau sided with the latter, publ. a *Lettre a M. Grimm au sujet des remarques ajoutées à sa lettre sur Omphale* (1752), followed by the caustic *Lettre sur la musique française* (1753; to which the members of the Opéra responded by burning him in effigy and excluding him from the theater) and *Lettre d'un symphoniste de l'Académie royale de musique à ses camarades* (1753). He wrote 2 numbers for the melodrama *Pygmalion* (1770; Paris, 1775). Publ. posthumously were 6 new arias for *Le Devin du village* and a collection of about 100 romances and duets, *Les Consolations des misères de ma vie* (1781), and fragments of an opera, *Daphnis et Chloé* (1780). His writings on music are included in the *Oeuvres complètes de Jean-Jacques Rousseau* (4 vols., 1959–69); for his letters see R. Leigh, ed., *Correspondance complète Jean-Jacques Rousseau* (18 vols., 1965–73).

Roussel, Albert (Charles Paul Marie), b. Tourcoing, Département du Nord, Apr. 5, 1869; d. Royan, Aug. 23, 1937. He studied academic subjects at the Collège Stanislas in Paris; music with the organist Stoltz; then studied mathematics in preparation for entering the Naval Academy; at age 18 he began his training in the navy; was a member of the crew of the frigate *Iphigénie*, sailing to Indochina (1889–90). This voyage was of great importance to him, since it opened for him a world of oriental culture and art, which became one of the chief sources of his musical inspiration. He later sailed on the cruiser Devastation; received a leave of absence for reasons of health, and spent some time in Tunis; was then stationed in Cherbourg, and began to compose there. In 1893 he was sent once more to Indochina. He resigned from the navy in 1894 and went to Paris, where he began to study music seriously with Eugène Gigout. In 1898 he entered the Schola Cantorum in Paris as a pupil of d'Indy; continued this study until 1907, when he was already 38 years old, but at the same time he was entrusted with a class in counterpoint, which he conducted at the Schola Cantorum (1902–14); among his students were Erik Satie, Stan Golestan, Paul Le Flem, Roland-Manuel, Guy de Lioncourt, and Varèse. In 1909 he and his wife undertook a voyage to India, where he became acquainted with the legend of the queen Padmâvatî, which he selected as a subject for his eponymous opera-ballet. His choral sym. *Les Evocations* (1912) was also inspired by this tour. At the outbreak of World War I in 1914 Roussel applied for active service in the navy but was rejected, and volunteered as an ambulance driver. After the Armistice of 1918 he settled in Normandy and devoted himself to composition.

Roussel began his work under the influence of French Impressionism, with its dependence on exotic moods and poetic association. However, the sense of formal design asserted itself in his symphonic works; his *Suite en fa* (1927) signalizes a transition toward neoclassicism; the thematic development is vigorous, and the rhythms are clearly delineated, despite some asymmetrical progressions; the orchestration, too, is in the Classic tradition. He possessed a keen sense of the theater; he was capable of fine characterization of exotic or mythological subjects, but also knew how to depict humorous situations in lighter works. An experiment in a frankly modernistic manner is exemplified by his *Jazz dans la nuit* for Voice and Piano (1928).

rovesciamento (It.). In double counterpoint, the inversion of voices.

rovescio (It., reverse). 1. Melodic inversion. A famous example is *Contrapuntus VI* in Bach's *Die Kunst der Fuge*. The eighteenth variation in Rachmaninoff's *Rhapsody on a Theme of Paganini* is a precise melodic inversion of the theme; since the theme is encompassed by a minor triad, its inversion becomes a melody in major. 2. Among some Baroque composers the term *rovescio* (along with its cognates *riverso* and *rivolto*) refers to retrograde (cancrizans) motion. The postlude of Hindemith's *Ludus Tonalis* represents both an inversion and a retrograde movement (allowance being made for shifting accidentals).

Rózsa, Miklos, b. Budapest, Apr. 18, 1907; d. Los Angeles, July 27, 1995. He studied piano and composition in Leipzig with Hermann Grabner; musicology with Theodor Kroyer. In 1931 he settled in Paris, where he became successful as a composer; his works were often performed in European music centers. In 1935 he went to London; composed there for the films; in 1940 he emigrated to the U.S. and settled in Hollywood; was on the staff of MGM (1948–62); also taught at the Univ. of Southern Calif. in Los Angeles (1945–65). His orch. and chamber music is cast in the advanced modern idiom in vogue in Europe between the 2 world wars; neoclassical in general content, it is strong in polyphony and incisive rhythm; for his film music he employs a more Romantic and diffuse style, relying on a Wagnerian type of grandiloquence. He won Oscars for his film scores to *Spellbound* (1945), *A Double Life* (1947). and *Ben-Hur* (1959). Rózsa was more successful than most in balancing concert and film music careers, and both types of works continue to be performed.

rubando (It.). Performing in a *rubato* style. *Affretando e rubando il tempo,* perform with increasing speed, and dwell on accented tones.

rubato, tempo (rubato; It., stolen time). Play with a free treatment of the melody; specifically, dwell on and (often almost insensibly) prolong prominent melody tones or chords. This requires an equivalent subsequent acceleration of less prominent tones, which are thus "robbed" of a portion of their time value. The measure remains constant, and the accompaniment is not disrupted. Tempo rubato is the musical equivalent of the saying, "robbing Peter to pay Paul." A different kind of total rubato, affecting an entire musical section, occurs in the performing practice of the Romantic era.

Rubinstein, Anton (Grigorievich), b. Vykhvatinetz, Podolia, Nov. 28, 1829; d. Peterhof, near St. Petersburg, Nov. 20, 1894. He was of a family of Jewish merchants who became baptized in Berdichev in July 1831. His mother gave him his 1st lessons in piano; the family moved to Moscow, where his father opened a small pencil factory. A well-known Moscow piano teacher, Alexandre Villoing, was entrusted with Rubinstein's musical education, and was, in fact, his only piano teacher. In 1839 Villoing took him to Paris, where Rubinstein played before Chopin and Liszt; remained there until 1841; then made a concert tour in the Netherlands, Germany, Austria, England, Norway, and Sweden, returning to Russia in 1843.

Since Anton's brother Nikolai (Grigorievich) Rubinstein (b. Moscow, June 14, 1835; d. Paris, Mar. 23, 1881) evinced a talent for composition, the brothers were taken in 1844 to Berlin, where, on Meyerbeer's recommendation, Anton studied composition with Dehn; toured Hungary with the flutist Heindl. He returned to Russia in 1848 and settled in St. Petersburg. There he enjoyed the enlightened patronage of the Grand Duchess Helen, and wrote 3 Russian operas: *Dmitri Donskoy* (1852), *The Siberian Hunters* (1853), and *Thomas the Fool* (1853). In 1854, with the assistance of the Grand Duchess, Rubinstein toured western Europe. He found publishers in Berlin, and gave concerts of his own works in London and Paris, exciting admiration as both composer and pianist; on his return in 1858 he was appointed court pianist and conductor of the court concerts.

Rubinstein assumed the direction of the Russian Musical Soc. in 1859; founded and directed the Imperial Cons. in St. Petersburg (1862–67). For 20 years thereafter he held no official position; from 1867 until 1870 he gave concerts in Europe, winning fame as a pianist 2nd only to Liszt. During the season of 1872–73 he made a triumphant American tour, playing in 215 concerts, for which he was paid lavishly; appeared as a soloist and jointly with the violinist Wieniawski (with whom he was apparently not speaking at the time). He produced a sensation by playing without the score, a novel procedure at the time. Returning to Europe, he elaborated a cycle of historical concerts, in programs ranging from Bach to Chopin; he usually devoted the last concert of a cycle to Russian composers. In 1887 he resumed the directorship of the St. Petersburg Cons., resigning again in 1891, when he went to Dresden. He returned to Russia the year of his death. In 1890 he established the Rubinstein Prize, an international competition open to young men between 20 and 26 years of age.on, in composition and piano categories.

Rubinstein's role in Russian musical culture was of the greatest importance. He introduced European methods into education and established high standards of artistic performance. He was the 1st Russian musician who was equally prominent as composer and interpreter. According to contemporary reports his playing possessed extraordinary power (his octave passages were famous) and insight, revealed particularly in his performance of Beethoven's sonatas. His renown as a composer was scarcely less. His *Ocean* Sym. (1851, rev. 1880) was one of the most frequently performed orch. works in Europe and America; his piano concertos were part of the standard repertoire; his pieces for piano solo, *Melody in F, Romance,* and *Kamennoi Ostrow,* became perennial favorites. After his death his orch'l works all but vanished from concert programs, as did his operas (with the exception of *The Demon,* 1871, which is still perf. in Russia); his Piano Concerto No. 4 in D Minor is occasionally heard. Among his compositions are: 28 operas, 1 ballet, 6 syms., 7 piano concertos, other orch'l works, including concert and programmatic overtures. Chamber works: 3 violin sonatas, 5 piano trios, 10 string quartets (1852–80), numerous piano pieces, choral works, songs.

His brother Nikolai (Grigorievich) Rubinstein was a prominent pianist, conductor, teacher, and composer. In 1859 Nikolai became head of the Moscow branch of the Russian Musical Soc.; this soc. opened the Moscow Cons., which he directed until his death. Among his pupils were Taneyev, A. Siloti, and E. Sauer.

Rubinstein, Arthur (Artur), b. Lodz, Jan. 28, 1887; d. Geneva, Dec. 20, 1982. He became emotionally attached to the piano as soon as he saw and heard the instrument; at age 7, he played pieces by Mozart, Schubert, and Mendelssohn at a charity concert in Lodz. His 1st regular piano teacher was Adolf Prechner. He was later taken to Warsaw, where he had piano lessons with Alexander Roycki; then went to Berlin in 1897 to study with Heinrich Barth; also received instruction in theory from Robert Kahn and Max Bruch. In 1900 he appeared as soloist in Mozart's A-major Concerto, K.488, in Potsdam; he repeated his success that same year when he played the work again in Berlin under Joachim's direction; then toured in Germany and Poland.

After further studies with Paderewski in Switzerland (1903), Rubinstein went to Paris, where he played with the Lamoureux Orch. and met Ravel, Dukas, and Thibaud. He also played the G-minor Piano Concerto by Saint-Saëns in the presence of the composer, who commended him. The ultimate plum of artistic success came when Rubinstein received an American contract. He made his debut at Carnegie Hall in N.Y. in 1906 as soloist with the Philadelphia Orch. in his favorite Saint-Saëns concerto. His American tour was not altogether successful, and he returned to Europe for further study. In 1915 he appeared as soloist with the London Sym. Orch. During the season 1916–17, he gave numerous recitals in Spain, a country in which he was to become extremely successful; from Spain he went to South America, where he also became a great favorite; he developed a flair for Spanish and Latin American music, and his renditions of the piano works of Albéniz and de Falla were models of authentic Hispanic modality. Villa-Lobos dedicated to him his *Rudepoema,* one of the most difficult piano pieces ever written.

Rubinstein became an American citizen (1946). In 1958 Rubinstein gave his 1st postwar concert in Poland; in 1964 he played in Moscow, Leningrad, and Kiev. In Poland and in Russia he was received with tremendous emotional acclaim. But he forswore any appearances in Germany as a result of the Nazi extermination of the members of his family during World War II. In 1976, at age 89, he gave his farewell recital in London.

Rubinstein was one of the finest interpreters of Chopin's music, to which his fiery temperament and poetic lyricism were particularly congenial. His style of playing tended toward bravura in Classic compositions, but he rarely indulged in mannerisms; his performances of Mozart, Beethoven, Schumann, and Brahms were particularly inspiring. In his characteristic spirit of robust humor he made jokes about the multitude of notes he claimed to have dropped, but asserted that a worse transgression against music would be pedantic inflexibility in tempo and dynamics. He was a *bon vivant,* an indefatigable host at parties, and a fluent though not always grammatical speaker in most European languages, including Russian and his native Polish.

In Hollywood Rubinstein played on the soundtracks for several motion pictures; appeared as himself, in the films *Carnegie Hall* (1947) and *Of Men and Music* (1951). A film documentary entitled *Artur Rubinstein, Love of Life* was produced in 1975; a 90-minute television special, *Rubinstein at 90,* was broadcast to mark his entry into nonagenarianism. He was the recipient of numerous international honors: a membership in the French Académie des Beaux Arts and the Legion d'Honneur, and the Order of Polonia Restituta of Poland; he held the Gold Medal of the Royal Phil. Soc. of London and several honorary doctorates from American institutions of learning. He was a passionate supporter of Israel, which he visited several times. In 1974 an international piano competition bearing his name was inaugurated in Jerusalem. In 1976 he received the U.S. Medal of Freedom, presented by President Ford. During the last years of his life he was afflicted with retinitis pigmentosa, which led to his total blindness; but even then he never lost his joie de vivre. He once said that the slogan "wine, women, and song" as applied to him was 80% women and only 20% wine and song.

Rudhyar, Dane (born Daniel Chennevière), b. Paris, Mar. 23, 1895; d. San Francisco, Sept. 13, 1985. He changed his name in 1917 to Rudhyar, derived from an old Sanskrit root conveying the sense of dynamic action and the color red, astrologically related to the zodiacal sign of his birth and the planet Mars. He studied philosophy at the Sorbonne in Paris (baccalaureat, 1911) and took music courses at the Paris Cons. In composition he was largely self-taught; he also achieved a certain degree of proficiency as a pianist; developed a technique that he called "orchestral pianism." In Paris he studied at the Cons. and attended the famous premiere of Stravinsky's *The Rite of Spring* (1913). At the same time he joined the modern artistic circles in Paris.

In 1916 Rudhyar went to America; became a naturalized American citizen in 1926. His "dance poems" for orch., *Poèmes ironiques* and *Vision vegetale,* were performed at the Metropolitan Opera in N.Y. (1917). In 1918 he visited Canada; in Montreal he met the pianist Alfred Laliberté, who was closely associated with Scriabin, and through him he became acquainted with Scriabin's theosophic ideas; publ. a collection of French poems, *Rapsodies* (Toronto, 1918).

In 1920 Rudhyar went to Hollywood to write scenic music for *Pilgrimage Play, The Life of Christ,* and also acted the part of Christ in the prologue of the silent film version of *The Ten Commandments* produced by Cecil B. DeMille. In Hollywood he initiated the project of "Introfilms," depicting inner psychological states on the screen through a series of images, but it failed to receive support and was abandoned. Between 1922 and 1930 he lived in Hollywood and N.Y.; was one of the founding members of the International Composers Guild in N.Y. His symphonic poem *Soul Fire* won the $1,000 prize of the Los Angeles Phil. (1922); in 1928 his book *The Rebirth of Hindu Music* was publ. in Madras.

After 1930 Rudhyar devoted most of his time to astrology. His 1st book on the subject, *The Astrology of Personality* (1936), became a standard text in the field; it was described by Paul Clancy, the pioneer in the publication of popular astrological magazines, as "the greatest step forward in astrology since the time of Ptolemy." A new development in Rudhyar's creative activities took place in 1938 when he began to paint, along nonrepresentational symbolistic lines; the titles of his paintings (*Mystic Tiara, Cosmic Seeds, Soul and Ego, Avatar,* etc.) reflect theosophic themes. His preoccupation with astrology left him little time for music; but in the 1960s he undertook a radical revision of some early compositions, and wrote several new ones; was also active as a lecturer. He published, in English, some poetry and a number of books on psychospiritual formulation of astrology; he was awarded a doctorate from the Calif. Institute of Transpersonal Psychology.

The natural medium for Rudhyar's musical expression was the piano; his few symphonic works were mostly orchestrations of original piano compositions. In his writing for piano he built sonorous chordal formations supported by resonant pedal points, occasionally verging on polytonality; a kinship with Scriabin's piano music was clearly felt, but his harmonic idiom was free from Scriabin's Wagnerian antecedents. Despite his study of oriental religions and music, he did not attempt to make use of Eastern modalities; he called his creations "syntonic," built mostly on dissonant but euphonious harmony He lived his last years in Palo Alto, Calif. and kept active connections with the world of theosophy. Before his death, when his wife asked him whom he expected to meet beyond the mortal frame, he replied, "Myself."

Rudolph, Archduke of Austria. See ⇒Beethoven, Ludwig van.

ruffle. A roll of rapidly vibrating metered drumbeats; sometimes called *ruff*.

ruffle and flourish. A vibrating drumbeat accompanied by a fanfare on a ceremonial occasion.

ruggiero. A basso ostinato figure upon which instrumentalists improvised counterpoints. The bass melody, in a mixture of Ionian and Mixolydian modes, duple time, and 4 phrases, is 1st found in mid-16th-century MSS without name; it acquired its name later in that century and was most popular in the 1st half of the 17th century. In the early monodic era, vocal music began to be written on this bass; later, it was used for dance music. It virtually disappeared after 1650.

Ruggles, Carl (Charles Sprague), b. Marion, Mass., Mar. 11, 1876; d. Bennington, Vt., Oct. 24, 1971. He learned to play violin as a child; then went to Boston, where he took violin lessons with Felix Winternitz and theory with Josef Claus; later enrolled as a special student at Harvard Univ., where he attended composition classes of John Knowles Paine. Impressed with the widely assumed supremacy of the German school of composition (of which Paine was a notable representative), Ruggles Germanized his given name from Charles to Carl. In 1907 he went to Minnesota, where he organized and conducted the Winona Sym. Orch. (1908–12). In 1917 he went to N.Y., where he became active in the promotion of modern music; was a member of the International Composers Guild and of the Pan American Assoc. of Composers; taught composition at the Univ. of Miami (1938–43).

Ruggles wrote relatively few works, which he constantly revised and rearranged, and they were mostly in small forms. He did not follow any particular modern method of composition but instinctively avoided needless repetition of thematic notes, which made his melodic progressions atonal; his use of dissonances, at times quite strident, derived from the linear proceedings of chromatically inflected counterpoint. A certain similarity with the 12-tone method of composition of Schoenberg resulted from this process, but he never adopted it explicitly. In his sources of inspiration he reached for spiritual exaltation with mystic connotations, scaling the heights and plumbing the depths of musical expression. Such music could not attract large groups of listeners and repelled some critics; one of them remarked that the title of his *Sun-Treader* ought to be changed to "Latrine-Treader."

Unable and unwilling to withstand the prevailing musical mores, Ruggles removed himself from the musical scene; he went to live on his farm in Arlington, Vt., and devoted himself mainly to his avocation, painting; his pictures, mostly in the manner of abstract Expressionism, were occasionally exhibited in N.Y. galleries. In 1966 he moved to a nursing home in Bennington, where he died at age 95. A striking revival of interest in his music took place during the last years of his life, and his name began to appear with increasing frequency on the programs of American orchs. and chamber music groups. His MSS were recovered and publ.; virtually all of his compositions have been recorded.

ruhig (Ger.). Calmly, tranquilly.

Rührtrommel (Ger., touch drum). Tenor drum; other German synonyms are *Rolltrommel, Wirbeltrommel,* and *Landsknechtstrommel.*

Rührung (Ger.). Emotion.

rullando (It.). Rapid drum trill.

rumba (rhumba). A syncopated Cuban dance in quadruple time, popular in the U.S. in the 1930s–'50s, having acquired elements of swing.

run. 1. A rapid scale passage; in vocal music, usually such a passage sung to one syllable. *Run a division,* perform such a passage, i.e., a dividing up of a melodic phrase into a rapid coloratura passage. 2. A leak of air in the organ windchest.

Rundfunk (Ger.). Radio broadcasting service.

Russell, George (Allan), b. Cincinnati, June 23, 1923. He took up the drums in his youth; then turned to composition, composing for Benny Carter, Gillespie, Hines, and others; his interest in a contemporary music combining bop and 20th-century classical is spelled out in one of his early hits, *A Bird in Igor's Yard* (1949). He developed a modal technique called the Lydian Chromatic Concept of Tonal Organization (1945–46); subsequently studied composition with Stefan Wolpe. After teaching at the Lenox (Mass.) School of Jazz (1959–60), he became active as a pianist in his own sextet (1960–61); later taught at the New England Cons. of Music in Boston (from 1969). He publ. *The Lydian Chromatic Concept of Tonal Organization* (1953); has composed for his own groups for several decades.

Russian bassoon (bassoon serpent). A serpent built with an upright brass bell, somewhat similar in appearance to a bassoon, including a mouthpiece on a crook; invented in the late 18th century, used in the 19th, especially in Russian military bands.

Russolo, Luigi. See ⇒futurism.

rustico (It.). Rural, pastoral.

Rute (Ger.). A light brush used in jazz and some modern scores to produce a soft glissando on the snare drum head and other effects; the American slang is *brushes;* jazz drummers usually play with a pair.

ruvido (It.). In a rough, harsh style.

Rysanek, Leonie, b. Vienna, Nov. 14, 1926. She studied at the Vienna Cons. with Rudolf Grossmann, whom she later married. She made her debut as Agathe in *Der Freischütz* in Innsbruck in 1949; then sang at Saarbrücken (1950–52). She 1st attracted notice when she appeared as Sieglinde at the Bayreuth Festival in 1951; became a member of the Bavarian State Opera in Munich in 1952 and went with it to London's Covent Garden in 1953, where she sang Danae; in 1954 she joined the Vienna State Opera; also sang in various other major European opera houses. On Sept. 18, 1956, she made her U.S. debut as Senta at the San Francisco Opera; later made a spectacular appearance at the Metropolitan Opera in N.Y. in 1959, when she replaced Maria Callas in the role of Lady Macbeth on short notice; she remained on its staff until 1973 and sang there again in 1975–76 and subsequent seasons. She received the Lotte Lehmann Ring from the Vienna State Opera in 1979.

Rythmé (Fr.). Measured. *Bien rythmé,* well-balanced and elegant in rhythmical effect; *rythme brisé,* uneven or broken rhythm.

Rzewski, Frederic (Anthony), b. Westfield, Mass., Apr. 13, 1938. He studied counterpoint with Thompson and orchestration with Piston at Harvard Univ. (B.A., 1958) and continued his studies with Sessions and Babbitt at Princeton Univ. (M.F.A., 1960); then received instruction from Dallapiccola in Florence on a Fulbright scholarship (1960–61) and from Carter in Berlin on a Ford Foundation grant (1963–65). With Curran and Teitelbaum—other similarly futuroscopic musicians—he founded the M.E.V. (Musica Elettronica Viva) in Rome in 1966; was active as a pianist in various avant-garde settings; played concerts with cellist Charlotte Moorman; also devoted much time to teaching. In 1977 he became prof. of composition at the Liège Cons.

As a composer, Rzewski pursues the shimmering distant vision of optimistic, positivistic antimusic; his works reflect profoundly leftist politics and committment, whether instrumental or texted. He is furthermore a granitically overpowering piano technician, capable of depositing huge boulders of sonoristic material across the keyboard without actually wrecking the instrument.

Ss

Korea. He was keynote speaker at the national Pekan Komponis (Composers' Festival) in Jakarta (1988); appeared in Calif. at the Pacific Rim Festival (1989); featured participant at Composer-to-Composer in Telluride, Colo. (1990). He is one of many outstanding composers to emerge from Indonesia's post-independence era, with more national new-music festivals, increased interaction among artists from different regions, and greater degree of individual freedom to create autonomous music. Besides contributing to *musik kontemporer, komposisi,* and *kreasi baru* (new creations), he is concerned with the social context of performance; his compositions are often scored for unusual combinations of instruments. In an experimental piece performed at the Telluride Inst., raw eggs were thrown at a heated black panel; these provided both a visual and sonic element for the piece's closing. One unrealized proposal is *Sebuah Kota Yang Bermain Musik* (A City That Plays Music), wherein the entire population of a city makes sounds together for a specified 5 minutes.

Sagittarius, Henricus. Schütz, Heinrich.

sainete (Sp., small farce). Spanish musical comedy popular in the 18th century; eventually displaced by the zarzuela.

Saint-Saëns, (Charles-) Camille, b. Paris, Oct. 9, 1835; d. Algiers, Dec. 16, 1921. His great-aunt, Charlotte Masson, taught him to play piano. He proved exceptionally gifted; gave a performance in a Paris salon before age 5; began to compose at 6; became a private pupil of Stamaty at 7; made his pianistic debut at the Salle Pleyel, playing a Mozart concerto and part of a Beethoven concerto, with orch. (1846).

After studying harmony with P. Maleden, Saint-Saëns entered the Paris Cons.; his teachers were Benoist (organ) and Halévy (composition); won the 2nd prize for organ (1849), then 1st prize (1851). He competed twice unsuccessfully for the Grand Prix de Rome (1852, 1864); his *Ode á Sainte Cécile* for voice and orch. was awarded 1st prize by the Soc. Sainte-Cécile (1852). In 1853, his 1st numbered sym. was performed; Gounod wrote him a letter with a prophetic phrase regarding the "obligation de devenir un grand maître." He was organist at the church of Saint-Merry in Paris (1853–57); succeeded Lefébure-Wély as organist at the Madeleine (1857); soon acquired a great reputation as virtuoso organist and master improviser. Resigning in 1876, he devoted himself mainly to composition and conducting.

From 1861 to 1865 Saint-Saëns taught piano at the École Niedermeyer; among his pupils were A. Messager and Fauré; cofounded the Soc. Nationale de Musique (1871), established to encourage French composers, but withdrew when d'Indy proposed including works by foreign composers in its programs (1886). He was made a Chevalier of the Legion of Honor (1868; Officer, 1884; Grand-Officer, 1900; Grand-Croix, the highest rank, 1913); was elected to the Inst. de France (1881); member of many foreign organizations. In 1891 he established a museum in Dieppe (his father's birthplace), to which he gave his MSS and collection of paintings and other art objects; witnessed the unveiling of his own statue (by Marqueste) in the court foyer of the opera house there (1907).

Saint-Saëns 1st visited the U.S. in 1906; represented the French government at the Panama-Pacific Exposition (1915); conducted his choral work *Hail California* in San Francisco. In 1916, he made his 1st tour of South America; took part as conductor and pianist in a festival of his works in Athens (1920); played a program of his piano pieces at Dieppe's Saint-Saëns museum (1921).

s. Abbrev. for *segno* in *al segno, dal segno;* for *subito* in the phrase *Volti subito* (V.s.); and for *senza, sinistra, solo, soprano,* and *sordino/-i.*

Sachs, Hans, b. Nuremberg, Nov. 5, 1494; d. there, Jan. 19, 1576. After serving an apprenticeship, he set up shop in Nuremberg as a master shoemaker (1520); joined the Meistersinger guild about 1509; received instruction from Linhard Nunnenbeck. Under Sachs, the Meistergesang was an active force in the Reformation movement from 1520. He wrote over 6,000 poetical works, ranging from Meisterlieder to dramatic pieces; composed 13 *Meistertöne* (melodies to which texts can later be fitted). He is the central figure in Wagner's opera *Die Meistersinger von Nürnberg.*

sackbut (Fr. *saqueboute*). 1. Early form of trombone, dating back to 1000 A.D. 2. In the Bible, the *sabbek,* a harplike instrument.

Sackpfeife (Ger.). Bagpipe.

sacred concerto (Ger. *geistliche Konzert;* It. *sacra symphonia*). Early Baroque religious genre, predecessor to the cantata; composers such as the Gabrielis began to incorporate the new *concertato* (concerted) style, with divided choruses and instrumental groups, into sacred contexts. Schütz was especially successful and prolific with the genre; many other German Baroque composers contributed sacred concertos; eventually the development of set pieces (aria, recitative, chorus) led to the cantata of Buxtehude and Bach.

Sadra, I Wayan, b. Denpasar, Bali, Aug. 1, 1953. He attended Konservatori Karawitan (KOKAR; graduated 1972); specialized in traditional Balinese music, particularly *gender wayang* (music for the Balinese shadow play). In 1973–74 he worked with the well-known experimental Indonesian choreographer S. W. Kusumo; toured with his group in Europe and the Middle East; settled in Jakarta; studied painting and taught Balinese gamelan at Inst. Kesenian Jakarta (Jakarta Fine Arts Inst.; 1975–78). He taught Balinese music at the Indonesian Univ. (1978–80) and experimental composition, Balinese gamelan, and music criticism at Sekolah Tinggi Seni Indonesia Surakarta (National College of the Arts; 1983–88), where he earned a degree in composition; concurrently wrote new music criticism for several Indonesian newspapers.

Sadra appeared widely as a performer with traditional Indonesian ensembles; performed throughout Indonesia and Europe, and in Singapore, Japan, Hong Kong, Australia, and

Saint-Saëns's position in French music is very important. His abilities as a performer were extraordinary; aroused Wagner's admiration during the latter's stay in Paris (1860–61) by playing at sight the scores of Wagner's operas; indeed, Saint-Saëns achieved greater recognition in Germany than in France at first. His most famous opera, *Samson et Dalila,* was produced in Weimar (1877) under the direction of E. Lassen, following a suggestion by Liszt; it was not performed in France for another 13 years (Rouen). He premiered his 1st and 3rd piano concertos at Leipzig's Gewandhaus.

Saint-Saëns's music is characterized by solidity of contrapuntal fabric, instrumental elaboration, fullness of sonority in orchestration, and harmonic saturation, qualities not fully appreciated by French composers at the time, given the French public's preference for lighter music. However, he overcame this initial opposition; towards the end of his life was regarded as an embodiment of French traditionalism. The shock of the German invasion of France in World War I made him abandon his former predilection for German music; wrote virulent articles against German art; unalterably opposed to modern music, he looked askance at Debussy; outspokenly regarded later manifestations of musical modernism as outrages.

That Saint-Saëns possessed a fine sense of musical characterization and true Gallic wit is demonstrated by his ingenious suite *Carnival of the Animals,* his best-known work; he wrote it for private performance (1886) but would not let it be publ. during his lifetime. The work includes descriptions of human animals, a few choice musical parodies, and *The Swan,* famous as a cello piece and a dance; the work was orchestrated posth.; the American poet Ogden Nash composed some verses which are often performed with the work.

Among Saint-Saëns's other compositions are 13 operas, of which only 2, *Samson et Dalila* and *Henry VIII* (Paris, 1883) are still performed; a ballet, incidental music, and a pioneering film score, *L'Assassinat du Duc de Guise* (1908). His modern reputation rests primarily on orch'l music, including: 5 syms. (*c.* 1850–86, the last with an obbligato organ part, one of his most performed works); 5 piano concertos (all premiered with Saint-Saëns as soloist, 1858–96); 3 violin concertos (1859–81); *Introduction and Rondo capriccioso* for Violin and Orch. (1863); 2 cello concertos (1873, 1902); *Africa* for Piano and Orch. (1891); other concerted works; symphonic poems, including: *Le Rouet d'Omphale* (1872); *Phaéton* (1873); the popular *Danse macabre* (1875); *La Jeunesse d'Hercule* (1877); *Trois tableaux symphoniques d'aprés La foi* (1908); orch'l suites, overtures, dances, rhapsodies, marches; band music. He composed chamber music for various ensembles; piano music; sacred and secular choral works; song cycles and individual songs; cadenzas to Mozart's piano concertos K. 482 and K. 491 and Beethoven's 4th Piano Concerto and Violin Concerto; transcriptions and arrangements. He also publ. a book of elegant verse (1890).

Saite (Ger.). A string.

Saiteninstrumente (Ger.). String instruments.

salicional stop. Narrow, open cylindrical stop producing a string-like tone; usually 4' or 8'.

Salieri, Antonio, b. Legnago, near Verona, Aug. 18, 1750; d. Vienna, May 7, 1825. He studied violin and harpsichord with his brother, Francesco; continued violin studies with G. Simoni. He was orphaned (1765); taken to Venice; studied thoroughbass with G. Pescetti, deputy maestro di cappella of San Marco, and singing with F. Pacini. Florian Gassmann took Salieri to Vienna (1766); provided for his musical training and liberal arts education; came into contact with Metastasio and Gluck; the latter became his patron and friend. His 1st known opera, *La Vestale* (not extant), was premiered in Vienna (1768); a comic opera, *Le Donne letterate,* was successfully performed at the Burgtheater (1770); Gluck's influence is heard in his 1st major stage production, *Armida* (1771).

Salieri was appointed Gassman's successor as court composer and conductor of the Italian Opera (1774). When Gluck could not fulfill a commission for an opera to open the Teatro alla Scala in Milan, Salieri accepted; his *L'Europa riconosciuta* inaugurated the great opera house (1778); also composed operas for Venice and Rome; back in Vienna, produced a Lustspiel, *Der Rauchfangkehrer* (1781). With Gluck's encouragement he set his sights on Paris; hoping to provide him with a respectful hearing, Gluck and the directors of the Paris Opéra advertised *Les Danaïdes* (1784) as Gluck's; after several performances, it was revealed to be Salieri's.

Returning to Vienna, Salieri composed 3 more stage works, including the successful *La grotta di Trofonio* (1785). In Paris, *Les Horaces* (1786) proved a failure, but *Tarare* (libretto by Beaumarchais; Opéra, 1787), was a triumph; after da Ponte rev. and trans. the libretto into Italian and the composer thoroughly rewrote the score, it was given as *Axur, re d'Ormus* (Vienna, 1788); performed throughout Europe to great acclaim. He was appointed court Kapellmeister in Vienna (1788–1824); but he did not conduct operatic performances after 1790; his last major success was *Palmira, regina di Persia* (1795); composed for the stage until 1804.

Salieri's influence on Viennese musical life was considerable; he was president (1788–95), then vice president of the Tonkünstler-Sozietät, the benevolent society for musicians founded by Gassmann (1771); co-founded the Gesellschaft der Musikfreunde. He was a widely celebrated pedagogue, his pupils including Beethoven, Hummel, Schubert, Czerny, and Liszt; received numerous honors, including the Gold Medallion and Chain of the City of Vienna; a Chevalier of the Légion d'Honneur and member of the French Inst. Salieri's eminent positions in Vienna earned him a reputation for intrigue; many unfounded stories circulated about him, none more fantastic than his having poisoned Mozart; this tale inspired Pushkin to write his drama *Mozart and Salieri,* subsequently set to music by Rimsky-Korsakov; a modern interpretation of the alleged rivalry, Peter Shaffer's play *Amadeus,* was successfully produced in London (1979) and N.Y. (1980); obtained even wider circulation in its award-winning film version (1984).

Salieri was a worthy representative of the traditional Italian opera school; a master of harmony and orchestration, his many operas are noteworthy for expressive melodic writing and sensitive vocal treatment. All the same, few held the stage for long; all have disappeared from the active repertoire. He also composed sacred music; secular works, including cantatas, choruses, and songs; instrumental pieces.

salmo (It.). Psalm. (Sp.) Obsolete folk zither.

Salomon, Johann Peter. See ⇒Haydn, Franz Joseph.

salon music. Drawing-room music that flourished in Paris and Vienna in the 18th and 19th centuries, satisfying the need for light entertainment. Liszt complains of the "dull and noxious atmosphere of the salons"; during his Paris sojourn the poet Heine voices despair at the universal proliferation of piano music "that one hears in every house, day and night," adding that at this very moment "a couple of young ladies in the neighboring house are playing a *morceau* for 2 left hands." "Salon" gradually became synonymous with Biedermeier culture.

Chopin was not averse to writing piano music for salon performance; Schumann described him as the "most elegant salon composer" and his famous Waltz in A-flat Major as a "salon piece of the noblest art, aristocratic through and through." Lesser composers frankly entitled their works *Études de Salon, Petites Fleurs de Salon*, etc. Perhaps the most mephitic piece was *A Maiden's Prayer* (1859) by a Polish girl named Thekla Badarzewska (1834–61), which spread through Europe and America with the irresistible force of distilled sentimentality.

Although salon music largely disappeared with the cataclysmic outbreak of World War I, social salons were maintained by wealthy hostesses in Paris and other music capitals. Countess de Polignac, daughter of an American sewing machine magnate, married a French aristocrat, began a series of musical matinees, and commissioned works by Stravinsky, de Falla, and others for salon performance.

salon orchestra. Ensembles organized for performances of light music in cafés, cabarets, and the houses of the rich. The minimal ensemble was the piano trio; the so-called Vienna type of salon orch. consisted of a seated violinist, a standing violinist, cello, flute, and percussion; the Berlin salon orch. added the clarinet, cornet, trombone, viola, and double bass; the Parisian type usually employed piano, violin, cello, flute, cornet, and drums. Special editions were published to enable the ensembles to play light overtures or dance suites in so-called theater arrangements; cues were inserted in piano parts to replace missing instruments. Although salon music was deprecated for its low taste, the salon orch. performed a positive educational role, providing classical and semiclassical music in workable arrangements.

Salonen, Esa-Pekka, b. Helsinki, June 30, 1958. He entered the Sibelius Academy in Helsinki as a horn pupil of Holgar Fransman (1973), taking his diploma (1977); studied composition with Rautavaara and conducting with Panula; studied with F. Donatoni in Siena; attended the Darmstadt summer course; completed studies with N. Castiglioni in Milan (1980–81). After appearances as a horn soloist, he took up conducting; guest conducted throughout Scandinavia; extended his activities to Europe. In 1984 he made his U.S. debut with the Los Angeles Phil.; became principal conductor of the Swedish Radio Sym. Orch. in Stockholm (1984); toured the U.S. (1987); principal guest conductor of the Oslo Phil. (from 1984) and the Philharmonia Orch. in London (from 1985). In 1989 he was appointed music director of the Los Angeles Phil., his tenure began in 1992. In his own music he tends toward pragmatic

aural accessibility, employing fairly modern techniques while preserving the formal centrality of traditional tonality; has composed orch'l works (mostly concerted) and chamber music, including a cello sonata, wind quintet, and a series of solo works called *YTA.*

salpinx. Straight conical trumpet with a narrow bore and slightly flared bell, mentioned in Homer's *Illiad;* a surviving instrument is made of ivory with a brass bell.

salsa (Sp., sauce). Modern Latin American dance in a raucous rhythmic manner. It originated in the Caribbean islands, most notably Cuba, with traceable African roots; emigrated to the U.S. with those fleeing Castro's 1959 revolution. The name probably arose because of its hot, peppery, and pervasive rhythm over a hypnotically repetitive melodic line; invariably in 4/4; quarter notes alternate with 8th notes in syncopated beats.

saltarella, -o (It.). 1. 2nd division in many 16th-century dance tunes, in triple time, the skipping step marked in the rhythm

2. Italian dance in 3/4 or 6/8 time.

saltato (It.). A rapid spiccato, played with a bouncing bow. See ⇒richochet; springing bow.

salto (It.). Leap; skip. *Di salto,* by a leap or leaps.

Salzedo (Salzédo), (León) Carlos, b. Arcachon, France, Apr. 6, 1885; d. Waterville, Maine, Aug. 17, 1961. He studied at the Bordeaux Cons. (1891–94), winning 1st prize in piano; entered the Paris Cons., where his father Gaston was a prof. of singing; studied with C. de Bériot (piano) and Hasselmans (harp), received 1st prize in both instruments. He began his career as a concert harpist upon graduation; traveled throughout Europe (1901–05); solo harpist of the Assoc. des Premiers Prix de Paris in Monte Carlo (1905–09); settled in N.Y. (1909); 1st harpist in the Metropolitan Opera orch. (1909–13). In 1913 he formed the Trio de Lutèce with G. Barrère (flute) and P. Kéfer (cello).

Salzedo was cofounder, with Varèse, of the International Composers' Guild in N.Y. (1921), which performed numerous important contemporary works; in the same year he founded a modern music magazine, *Eolian Review,* later *Eolus* (discontinued 1933); naturalized (1923); elected president of the National Assoc. of Harpists; taught at the Inst. of Musical Art in N.Y. and the Juilliard Graduate School of Music; started and headed the harp dept. at the Curtis Inst. of Music in Philadelphia; established the Salzedo Harp Colony (Camden, Maine) for teaching and performing during the summer (1931).

Salzedo introduced a number of special effects and publ. special studies for his new techniques; designed a "Salzedo Model" harp, capable of rendering novel sonorities (Eolian flux, Eolian chords, gushing chords, percussion, etc.). His technically virtuosic pieces are rhythmically intricate and contrapuntally elaborate; like other composer-performers, he composed primarily for his instrument: numerous solo pieces and transcriptions, harp ensembles, chamber works with and without voice, and a few concerted works. He publ. *Modern Study of the Harp* (N.Y., 1921), *Method for the Harp* (N.Y., 1929), and *The Art of Modulating* (with L. Lawrence; N.Y., 1950).

samba. Characteristic Brazilian dance marked by a rolling rhythm in 2/4 time and vigorous syncopation. Samba has also become a generic description of any Brazilian dance in a fast tempo.

sambuca (Lat.; from Grk. *sambykē*). Greco-Roman angular harp, with a horizontal pegboard and vertical soundboard.

sambuca lincea (Lat.). Enharmonic harpsichord, named by its inventor Fabio Colonna, also known as Linceo. It was designed around 1618, with 8 separate keyboards; it was tuned according to a complicated scheme combining Pythagorean intervals with various tempered adjustments; the resulting octave had 17 unequal microtones, and the instrument had a total of 50 strings (possibly bichordally strung).

sambuca rotata (Lat.). Hurdy-gurdy.

sampler. Electronic digital recorder capable of recording a sound and then storing it in the form of digital information, which then may be converted into an "instrument" for performance or compositional use. *Sampling,* a modern studio technique in which small bits of earlier recordings are stored and then interwoven into a new work to varying degrees; a technique fully developed in rap.

Sämtliche Werke (Ger.). Collected works.

sānāyī (*shannāi*; Sansk.; Pers. *surā*). Conical shawm of North India, made of wood, with finger holes and a wide bore; sometimes the bell is metallic.

Sanctus. Section of the Mass Ordinary, comprising *the Sanctus, Benedictus,* and the *Osanna* (Hosanna).

sanft (Ger.). Softly, quietly.

sanglot (Fr., tearful sigh). In rococo arias, an emotional appoggiatura, commonly set with interjections such as "Oh!," "Ah!," or "Helas!" An effective Romantic sanglot can be achieved by a closing of the vocal box; such a *coup de glotte* was a great specialty of Caruso, in his rendition of such arias as Canio's *Vesti la giubba* in *Pagliacci.*

sanjuanito. National dance of Ecuador, dedicated to St. John, in 2/4 time.

Sankey, Ira D(avid), b. Edinburgh, Pa., Aug. 28, 1840; d. N.Y., Aug. 13, 1908. As a youth of 17 he became choir leader in the Methodist Church of New Castle, Pa.; served with the N.Y. 12th Infantry Regiment during the Civil War. In 1870 he was a delegate to the YMCA convention at Indianapolis, where his forceful singing attracted the attention of the evangelist preacher Dwight L. Moody. He joined Moody as music director and remained at this post for some 30 years, until approaching

blindness forced his retirement (1903). Of his many gospel tunes the most popular has proved to be *The 90 and 9* (1874), which he improvised at a moment's notice during a service in Edinburgh, Scotland. His chief publs. were *Sacred Songs and Solos* (London, 1873) and 6 vols. of *Gospel Hymns and Sacred Songs* (1875–91). As president of the publ. firm of Biglow & Main (1895–1903) he brought out numerous works, including many of his own. He is not to be confused with another gospel song writer, Ira Allan Sankey, a lesser light than this Ira Sankey.

sans (Fr.). Without. *Sans presser,* without hurrying; *sans quitter la corde,* without leaving the string; *sans ralentir,* without slowing down.

Santir (Turk.; Arab., Pers. *santir;* Mod. Grk. *santouri*). Trapezoidal hammered dulcimer, with 14 courses of 4 metal strings apiece and curved blade-shaped beaters; dates from the 15th century; may be the ancestor of the Chinese *yangqin.*

saraband (sarabande; It. *sarabanda;* Fr. *sarabande;* Ger. *Sarabande*). Dance of Spanish or Middle Eastern ancestry, orig. a dance song in 16th-century Hispanic countries. The etymology of its name has been variously traced to Arabia via Moorish Spain, to Mexico, or to Panama; ironically, one of the earliest references to "saraband" is found in a ruling of the Spanish Inquisition (1583), which forbade its performance on penalty of a fine and imprisonment, apparently due to its immoral and suggestive nature. Half a century after its proscription in Spain, the saraband quietly slithered into France and even Elizabethan England, becoming a stately triple-meter dance; remained popular in the 17th and 18th centuries, with development of fast and slow types. The saraband was integral to the Baroque instrumental suite, found in works by Bach, Handel, and other masters. The instrumental form usually has 2 8-measure reprises; its place in the suite, as the slowest movement, is before the lively gigue.

sarambo. Popular dance of the Dominican Republic in rapid 6/8 time, accompanied by indigenous percussion instruments and accordion.

sāraṅgī (Sans.). Indian bowed chordophone, with 3 or 4 playing strings and a number of sympathetic strings below them; it is played between the knees of a seated performer; its bow is thick and short; formerly a folk instrument, it now participates in Indian classical music.

Sarasate (y Navascuez), Pablo (Martín Melitón) de, b. Pamplona, Mar. 10, 1844; d. Biarritz, Sept. 20, 1908. He began playing violin at age 5; made his public debut at 8; granted a private scholarship to study with M. Saez in Madrid; with the assistance of Queen Isabella he continued studying with Alard at the Paris Cons. (1856–59); took 1st prizes in violin and solfège (1857) and harmony (1859). He launched his concert virtuoso career with a major tour at 15; acquired a Stradivarius violin (1866).

Early in his career Sarasate's repertoire consisted almost exclusively of fantasies on operatic airs, mostly arranged by himself; later turned to the masterpieces of violin literature. His tours throughout Europe, North and South America, South Africa, and Asia, were an uninterrupted succession of triumphs. To his native city he bequeathed gifts showered upon him by admirers throughout the world; the collection was placed in a special museum. Among the works written for him were Bruch's 2nd Concerto and *Scottish Fantasy*, Lalo's Concerto and *Sym. espagnole*, Saint-Saëns's 1st and 3rd concertos and *Introduction et Rondo capriccioso*, and Wieniawski's 2nd Concerto. Sarasate's compositions, pleasing, effective, and still performed, include *Zigeunerweisen* (1878), *Spanische Tänze* (4 books, 1878–82), and the *Carmen Fantasy* in 4 movements (1883). His playing was noted for its extraordinary beauty of tone, impeccable purity of intonation, perfection of technique, and grace of manner.

sardana. Catalonian round dance in 6/8 time, alternating rapid and slow sections. Casals wrote an orch'l *Sardana* that stylizes the authentic rhythm and melody.

sarōd. Unfretted, plucked, pear-shaped classical Indian lute. It has 6 metal playing strings (2 of which may be paired) and 12 or more sympathetic strings below them; like the larger sitār, it uses bulbous gourds for resonance, and was once a bowed chordophone (although that use is rare now). Both instruments are played in a sitting position, but the sarōd is played like a Western lute or guitar, while the sitār is held nearly upright.

sarrusophone. Brass wind instrument with a double reed, invented (1863) by and named after the bandmaster Sarrus of Paris. Although a family of sarrusophones was manufactured, the bass alone survives, as a contrabass instrument in military bands.

Satie, Erik (Alfred-Leslie), b. Honfleur, May 17, 1866; d. Paris, July 1, 1925. He received his early musical training from a local organist, Vinot; at 13 he went to Paris, where his father was a music publisher; received instruction in harmony from Taudou and piano from Mathias; however, his attendance at the Cons. was only sporadic between 1879 and 1886. He played in various cabarets in Montmartre; in 1884 he publ. a piano piece which he numbered, with malice aforethought, op. 62. His whimsical ways and Bohemian manner of life attracted many artists and musicians; he met Debussy (1891); joined the Rosicrucian Society in Paris (1892); began to produce short piano pieces with eccentric titles intended to ridicule modernistic fancies and classical pedantries alike. Debussy thought highly enough of him to orchestrate two-thirds of his piano suite *Trois Gymnopédies* (1888). In 1898 he moved to Arcueil, a suburb of Paris, where he held court for poets, singers, dancers, and musicians, some of whom were ardent admirers. He was almost 40 when he decided to pursue serious studies at the Paris Schola Cantorum, taking courses in counterpoint, fugue, and orchestration with d'Indy and Roussel (1905–08). Milhaud, Sauguet, and Desormière organized a group, named only half-facetiously École d'Arcueil, to honor him as master and leader.

Satie's eccentricities were not merely those of a Parisian poseur; they were adjuncts to his aesthetic creed, which he enunciated with boldness and a total disregard for professional amenities (he was once brought to court for sending an insulting letter to a music critic). Interestingly enough, he attacked modernistic aberrations just as assiduously as reactionary pedantry, publishing manifestos in prose and poetry. Although dismissed by most musicians as an uneducated person who tried to conceal his musical ignorance with persiflage, he exercised a profound influence on the young French composers of the 1st quarter of the 20th century; his stature as a modern innovator grew after his death, so that latter-day avant-garde musicians accepted him as inspiration for their own experiments, e.g., environmental or spatial music was traced back to Satie's *Musique d'ameublement* (Furniture Music, 1920, with Milhaud), in which players were stationed at different parts of a hall playing different pieces in different tempos.

The instruction in Satie's short piano piece *Vexations* (play 840 times in succession) was 1st carried out in N.Y. (1963) by a group of 5 pianists working in relays overnight, setting a world's record for duration of a musical composition. When critics accused Satie of having no idea of form, he publ. *Trois Morceaux en forme de poire* (for piano 4-hands, 1903); other pieces bore self-contradictory titles, such as *Heures séculaires et instantanées* and *Crépuscule matinal de midi;* others included *Pièces froides*, *Embryons desséchés*, *Prélude en tapisserie*, *Trois véritables préludes flasques (pour un chien)*, *Descriptions automatiques*, etc.

In *Parade* (ballet realiste, 1917; with Cocteau, Picasso, Massine) Satie introduced jazz for the 1st time in Paris. At the premiere of *Relâche*, with an "entr'acte cinematographique" (*ballet instananée*, 1924; with Picabia, Borlin, Clair), the curtain bore the legend "Erik Satie is the greatest musician in the world; whoever disagrees with this notion will please leave the hall." Many 20th-century listeners enjoy the absurd humor and commentary, rebellious attitude, strong harmonic sense, virtually total lack of romanticism, and popular origins of "le maître d'Arcueil." He publ. a facetious autobiographical notice as *Mémoires d'un amnésique* (1912); N. Wilkins trans. and ed. *The Writings of Erik Satie* (1980).

Satz (Ger.). Movement in a wholly or primarily instrumental work, such as a sonata, quintet, or sym.

Satzlehre (Ger.). Theory of polyphonic composition; literally, the study of contrapuntal composition (or rules); perhaps a more complete term is *Tonsatzlehre*, the study of tonal settings. It is distinguished from other theories of composition in that it does not preoccupy itself with the acoustical, harmonic, or intervallic elements of chords and contrapuntal combinations, but is concerned mainly with the larger considerations of structure and style.

saudade (Port.). Brazilian dance characterized by nostalgia or longing.

sauteuse (Fr., woman who jumps). French waltz in 6/8 time, usually allegretto, popular in the early 19th century.

sautillé (Fr.; It. *saltando*). Springing bow. See ⇒ricochet.

Savoyards. Members of the D'Oyly Carte Opera Company that produced the Gilbert and Sullivan operas at the Savoy Theatre in London (hence *Savoy opera*, not limited to Gilbert and Sullivan). The company continued producing into the middle of the 20th century.

Sawallisch, Wolfgang, b. Munich, Aug. 26, 1923. He began piano study when he was 5; pursued private training with Ruoff, Haas, and Sachse in Munich; entered military service (1942); completed studies at the Munich Hochschule für Musik.

In 1947 he became *répétiteur* at the Augsburg Opera; made his conducting debut there (1950); was Generalmusikdirektor of the opera houses in Aachen (1953–58), Wiesbaden (1958–60), and Cologne (1960–63); conducted at Bayreuth (1957–61). He was chief conductor of the Vienna Sym. Orch. (1960–70); made his 1st appearance in the U.S. with that orch. (1964); was Generalmusikdirektor of the Hamburg State Phil. (1961–73); chief conductor of the Orch. de la Suisse Romande in Geneva (1970–80); Generalmusikdirektor of the Bavarian State Opera in Munich (from 1971); named Staatsoperndirektor there (1982). In 1990 he was named music director of the Philadelphia Orch. (effective 1993); guest conducted with the world's major orchs. and opera houses. A distinguished representative of the revered Austro-German tradition, he has earned great respect for his unostentatious performances; has also appeared as a sensitive piano accompanist to leading singers of the day.

Sax, Adolphe (Antoine-Joseph), b. Dinant, Nov. 6, 1814; d. Paris, Feb. 4, 1894. He acquired great skill in manipulating instruments; his practical and imaginative ideas led to improvements of the clarinet and other wind instruments. He studied the flute and clarinet at the Brussels Cons.; in 1842 went to Paris with an instrument of his invention, called the "saxophone," made of metal, with a single-reed mouthpiece and conical bore. He exhibited brass and woodwind instruments at the Paris Exposition of 1844, winning a silver medal; his father Charles-Joseph Sax (1791–1865) joined him in Paris; continued the manufacture of new instruments, evolving the saxhorn by replacing the keys of the bugle-horn and ophicleide with a valve mechanism; also the saxotromba, a hybrid producing a tone midway between bugle and trumpet.

Conservative critics and rival instrument makers ridiculed Sax's innovations, but Berlioz, Rossini, and others warmly supported him. His instruments were gradually adopted by French military bands; won a gold medal at the Paris Industrial Exposition of 1849. Financially he was unsuccessful, and compelled to go into bankruptcy twice (1856, 1873). He taught the saxophone at the Paris Cons. (1858–71); publ. a method for it; exhibited his instruments in London (1862) and received the Grand Prix in Paris (1867). Although Wieprecht, Červeny, and others disputed the originality and priority of his inventions, legal decisions gave the rights to Sax; the saxophone became a standard instrument, with many serious composers composing for it; the saxhorn has survived in bands.

saxhorn. Brass wind-instrument family, patented 1845 by Adolphe Sax, inventor of the saxophone. It is essentially an improved key bugle or ophicleide, having from 3 to 5 valves instead of keys; the instrument, whose nomenclature is exceedingly confused, is still found in bands.

saxophone (sax; It. *sassofono*). Metal wind-instrument family, patented 1846 by Adolphe Sax, with a clarinet mouthpiece with single reed; the key mechanism and fingering also resemble those of the clarinet; has a mellow, penetrating tone of veiled quality. In the latter part of the 19th century the saxophone became a standard instrument; many serious composers made use of it in their scores. The instrument fell into desuetude after Sax's death (1894), but *c.* 1918 a spirited revival of the saxophone took place when it was adopted by jazz musicians, eventually displacing the clarinet from its primary role. As its

popularity became worldwide, numerous methods were publ. and special schools established; saxophone virtuosos commissioned concertos from many composers. It remains a popular band instrument, an essential part of most jazz ensembles, and a relatively infrequent but timbrally significant contributor to classical music.

saxtromba. Saxhorn with a trumpetlike bell, patented by Adolphe Sax (1845).

sbalzato (It.). Dashingly, impetuously.

scabellum (Lat.; Grk. *kroupalon, kroupezion*). Wooden foot clapper, attached like a sandal, used to keep time for music, dancing, or public games.

Scala, La. Teatro alla Scala, the most famous Italian opera house; founded in 1778 in Milan. Although it is popularly imagined that the theater owes its name to its spectacular ladder leading to its portals (*scala* being Italian for ladder), the theater was actually named after Regina della Scala, the wife of the Duke Visconti of Milan. A whole galaxy of Italian composers—Salieri, Rossini, Donizetti, Bellini, Verdi, and Puccini—had operas premiered at La Scala; great conductors, including Toscanini, presided over these performances. In 1943 La Scala was almost entirely destroyed by an Allied air attack on the city; it was faithfully restored with the financial assistance of musicians and music lovers from all over the civilized world; reopened that year with Toscanini conducting (1946). The Teatro alla Scala has 6 tiers, 4 of which hold a total of 146 boxes lined with elegant multicolored fabrics, with house lighting provided by a sumptuous chandelier. In 1955 the Teatro alla Scala gave birth to an offspring called La Piccola Scala, suitable for performances of chamber opera and modern ballet.

scala enigmatica. Scale that the elderly Verdi found in an Italian music journal and used in the *Ave Maria* from his *Quattro pezzi sacri.* The journal called the scale *scala enigmatica,* but the name is hardly justified, for the scale (C–D♭–E–F♯–G♯–A♯–B–C) is nothing more than a slightly ornamented whole-tone scale.

scales (It. *scala,* ladder). 1. In the tubes of wind instruments (especially organ pipes), the ratio between bore width and length. 2. Compass of a voice or instrument; also, the series of tones producible on a wind instrument. 3. Series of tones which form (a) any major or minor key (*diatonic* scale); (b) the *chromatic* scale of successive semitonic steps; or (c) any predetermined series of tones within a modal or tonal system.

The American pedagogue Percy Goetschius would play the C major scale for his students and ask them rhetorically, "Who invented this scale?" and answer himself, "God!" Then he would play the whole-tone scale and ask again, "Who invented this scale?" and announce disdainfully, "Monsieur Debussy!" While he did not invent the whole-tone scale, Debussy and other contemporaneous composers made ample use of it. Other scales, built on quaquaversal intervallic progressions, drew composers' attention: the Gypsy scale; the pentatonic scale suitable for quasi-Eastern melismas; the octatonic scale of alternating whole tones and semitones, used by Rimsky-Korsakov, Pijper, Liszt, Tchaikovsky, Stravinsky, and others.

Scriabin derived a 6-note scale from his "mystic chord," composed of 3 whole tones, minor 3rd, semitone, and whole tone. A. Tcherepnin devised a 9-note scale: whole tone, 2 semitones, whole tone, 2 semitones, whole tone, and 2 semitones. Spanish composer O. Esplá used a scale with the following intervals: semitone, whole tone, 3 semitones, and 3 whole tones. Verdi was impressed by a "scala enigmatica" consisting of a semitone, an augmented 2nd, 3 whole tones, and 2 semitones.

Busoni experimented with possible 7-note scales; claimed he invented 113 different scales. The 1st theorist to examine and classify scales based on the symmetrical division of the octave was Hába in his book *Neue Harmonielehre*. J. Schillinger codified all possible scales having between 2 and 12 notes, using a mathematical approach. In his *Thesaurus of Scales and Melodic Patterns* the author tabulated some 2 thousand scales within the multiple octave range, including the polytetrachordal scale, bitonal scales of 8 notes, and scales of 3 disjunct major or minor pentachords aggregating to 2 octaves. Progressions of larger intervals (3rds, 4ths, 5ths, etc.) cannot be properly described as scales without contradicting the etymology of "scale" (stepwise motion); but helix-like constructions, involving spiraling chromatics, might well be called scales; quarter-tone and other microtonal progressions belong in this category.

Scarlatti, (Giuseppe) Domenico, b. Naples, Oct. 26, 1685; d. Madrid, July 23, 1757. In 1701 he was appointed organist and composer at the Royal Chapel in Naples, where his father Alessandro Scarlatti was maestro di cappella. His 1st opera, *Ottavia ristituita al trono,* was performed there (1703); was sent to Venice by his father (1705); nothing is known of his activities.

In 1708 Scarlatti went to Rome; entered the service of Queen Maria Casimira of Poland (to 1714); composed operas and other works for her private palace theater. He became assistant to Bai, the Vatican maestro di cappella (1713), succeeding him the following year; became maestro di cappella to the Portuguese ambassador to the Holy See. During his years in Rome he met Corelli and Handel; it is said that Scarlatti and Handel engaged in a friendly contest, the Italian being judged the superior on the harpsichord, the German on the organ.

Scarlatti resigned his positions (1719); by 1724 he was in Lisbon; became mestre at the patriarchal chapel. His duties included teaching the Infanta Maria Barbara, daughter of King John V, and the King's younger brother, Don Antonio. In 1728 Maria Barbara married the Spanish Crown Prince Fernando and moved to Madrid. Scarlatti accompanied her, remaining in Madrid for the rest of his life. In 1724 he visited Rome, where he met Quantz; in 1725 he saw his father for the last time (Naples). In 1738 he was made a Knight of the Order of Santiago. When Maria Barbara became queen in 1746, he was appointed her maestro de camera. From 1752 until 1756 Antonio Soler studied with him. So closely did he become associated with Spain that his name eventually appeared as Domingo Escarlatti.

Scarlatti composed over 500 single-movement sonatas for solo keyboard; although these works were assumed to have been written for harpsichord, the presence of pianos in Maria Barbara's residences suggests that some sonatas were written for that instrument as well; at least 3 were written for the organ. Key pairings and shared motivic material indicate that many of the sonatas are meant to be performed in pairs. His sonatas reveal him as one of the foremost composers in the "free style" (a homophonic style with graceful ornamentation, in contrast to the formal contrapuntal style); obtained striking effects by the frequent crossing of hands, tones repeated by rapidly changing fingers, etc.

During Scarlatti's lifetime 3 collections of his keyboard works were publ. (London, 1738; London, 1739; Paris, 1742–46); the sonatas were called "essercizi per gravicembalo," "suites de pièces pour le clavecin," or "pieces pour le clavecin." A. Longo, R. Kirkpatrick, and G. Pestelli attempted chronological catalogues of his sonatas; none are definitive. He also wrote orch'l sinfonias, operas (some with collaborators), 1 oratorio, secular cantatas and serenatas, arias, and sacred vocal music. His nephew, Giuseppe Scarlatti (b. Naples, *c.* 1718; d. Vienna, Aug. 17, 1777), was an operatic composer.

Scarlatti, (Pietro) Alessandro (Gaspare), b. Palermo, May 2, 1660; d. Naples, Oct. 22, 1725. At age 12 he went with his 2 sisters to Rome; found patrons who enabled him to pursue a musical career; his 1st known opera, *Gli equivoci nel sembiante,* was performed (1679). By 1680 he was maestro di cappella to Queen Christina of Sweden, whose Roman palace was an important center for the arts; found patrons in Cardinals Benedetto Pamphili and Pietro Ottoboni; maestro di cappella at S. Gerolamo della Carità.

Scarlatti was maestro di cappella to the Viceroy at Naples (1684–1702), where his son Domenico was appointed organist and composer (1701). Alessandro composed prolifically, producing numerous operas, serenatas, oratorios, and cantatas; also served as director of the Teatro San Bartolomeo, where he conducted his own works. His fame as a theatrical composer soon spread; many of his works were performed in leading Italian music centers; one, *Il Pirro e Demetrio* (1694), was performed in London. His only known teaching position was on the faculty of the Conservatorio di Santa Maria di Loreto (1689).

Tiring of his exhaustive labors, Scarlatti was granted a leave of absence; set out for Florence (1702); hoped he could secure employment from Prince Ferdinando de' Medici, who had been one of his patrons; when this did not materialize he settled in Rome; became assistant maestro di cappella at S. Maria Maggiore (1703), promoted to maestro di cappella (1707). One of his finest operas, *Il Mitridate Eupatore,* was performed in Venice (1707). Since the Roman theaters had been closed from 1700, he devoted his time to composing serenatas, cantatas, and oratorios; reappointed maestro di cappella to the Viceroy at Naples (1708); his most celebrated opera from this period, *Il Tigrane,* was given there (1715), as was his only full-fledged comic opera, *Il trionfo dell'onore* (1718).

Scarlatti's interest in purely instrumental music dates from this period; composed a number of conservative orch'l and chamber music pieces. Having again obtained a leave of absence from his duties, he went to Rome to oversee the premiere of his opera *Telemaco* (1718); his last known opera, *La Griselda,* was given there (1721); from 1722 lived in retirement in Naples, producing only a handful of works. He was the foremost Neapolitan composer of the latter Baroque era in Italy; composed 58 operas (1679–1721); 27 serenatas (*c.* 1680–1723); 36 oratorios, passions, and other sacred pieces (1679–1720); over 600 secular cantatas; masses and mass movements; motets; madrigals. His instrumental music includes 12 *sinfonie di concerto grosso*, keyboard toccatas; trio sonatas; suites, etc.; wrote pedagogical manuals.

scat (singing). Style of jazz performance in which a singer improvises nonsense syllables, often quite rapidly but always with a strong rhythmic impulse; occasionally the singer imitates the sounds produced by instruments. The technique originated in the 1920s, with Louis Armstrong as its major proponent; later, Ella Fitzgerald made the technique her trademark, and many other singers in the bebop and subsequent traditions scatted to their hearts' content.

Scelsi, Giacinto (born Conte Giacinto Scelsi di Valva), b. La Spezia, Jan. 8, 1905; d. Rome, Aug. 9, 1988. A member of the nobility, he received some guidance in harmony from G. Sallustio; after studies with E. Koehler in Geneva, he completed his formal training with W. Klein in Vienna (1935–36); became interested in the Schoenbergian method of writing music outside the bounds of traditional tonality; also became deeply immersed in the study of the musical philosophy of the East, in which the scales and rhythms are perceived as functional elements of the human psyche. As a result of these multifarious absorptions of ostensibly incompatible ingredients, Scelsi formulated a style of composition that is synthetic in its sources and pragmatic in its artistic materialization.

Scelsi's works began to have a considerable number of performances in Italy and elsewhere, most particularly in the U.S. A curious polemical development arose after his death, when an Italian musician named Vieri Tosatti publ. a sensational article in the *Giornale della Musica*, declaring "I was Giacinto Scelsi." He claimed that Scelsi used to send him thematic sections of unfinished compositions, usually in the 12-tone system, for development and completion, using him as a ghostwriter. Scelsi sent so many such "improvisations" to Tosatti that the latter had 2 other musicians to serve as secondary "ghosts," who in turn confirmed their participation in this peculiar transaction. The matter finally got to the court of public opinion, where it was decided that the works were genuine compositions by Scelsi, who improvised them on his electric piano, and that they were merely ed. for better effect by secondary arrangers.

scemando (It.). Diminuendo.

scena (from Grk., stage). In opera, an accompanied dramatic solo consisting of arioso and recitative passages, bearing the character of explanatory narrative, and often ending with an aria.

scenario. Concise script outlining the contents of a play, opera, ballet, or other performance work, with an indication of the participating characters/performers.

scene (Fr. *tableau*). Usually, a part of an act; e.g., an opera may contain 3 acts and 7 scenes that are distributed among the 3 acts. Sometimes a composer subdivides an opera in scenes without specifying the number of acts, e.g., Prokofiev's *War and Peace* and Mussorgsky's *Boris Godunov*.

Schaeffer, Pierre, b. Nancy, Aug. 14, 1910. Working in a radio studio in Paris, he conceived the idea of arranging a musical montage of random sounds, including outside noises. In 1948 he formulated the theory of musique concrète to define such random assemblages of sounds. When the magnetic tape was perfected, Schaeffer made use of it by rhythmic acceleration and deceleration, changing pitch and dynamics while modifying the nature of the instrumental timbre. He made several collages of elements of "concrete music," among them *Concert de bruits* (1948) and (with Pierre Henry) *Sym. pour un homme seul* (1950); created an experimental opera, *Orphée 53* (1953). He incorporated his findings and ideas in the publ. *A la recherche d'une musique concrète* (Paris, 1952) and in *Traité des objets sonores* (Paris, 1966). Eventually he abandoned his acoustical experiments and turned to literature. He publ. both fictional and quasi-scientific novels, among them *Le Gardien de volcan* (1969); *Excusez-moi si je meurs* (1981); *Prélude, Chorale et Fugue* (1983).

Schafer, R(aymond) Murray, b. Sarnia, Ontario, July 18, 1933. He studied at the Royal Cons. of Music of Toronto with John Weinzweig (1952–55); eventually went to England, where he was active with the BBC (1956–61). Returning to Canada, he served as artist-in-residence at Memorial Univ. (1963–65) and taught at Simon Fraser Univ. (1965–75); held a Guggenheim fellowship in 1974. He was active with the World Soundscape project (from 1972). In 1987 he received the Glenn Gould Award. He developed a sui generis system of topological transmutation, exemplified by his satire/tribute for orch. and tape, *The Son of Heldenleben* (Montreal, 1968), in which he systematically distorted the thematic materials of *Ein Heldenleben* by R. Strauss, retaining the essential motivic substance of the original score. Schafer is best known for his experimental use of language and performance environments; he is an active and innovative educator and author.

Schäferlied (Ger.). Shepherd's song; pastorale.

schalkhaft (Ger.). Roguish, sportive, wanton, mischievous; expression mark in Schumann's *Album für die Jugend.*

Schall (Ger.). Audible sound. *Schallplatte* (Ger., sound platter), phonograph record; *Schallwandler* (Ger., sound changer); transformer that turns electrical impulses into sound; *Schallwellen* (Ger.), sound waves.

Schalmei (Ger.). Shawm.

Schandeflöte (Ger., flute of shame). Heavy vertical flute made of iron that was hung on a tight ring around the neck of a town fifer in medieval Germany, as punishment for the crime of playing too many wrong notes in the performance of his duties. A sign was placed on his jacket spelling out the extent of his inharmonious conduct so that he could receive the full brunt of public disgrace. Theories that this symbol replaced the wearing of a red-lettered *S* (for *Schande*) around the fifer's neck cannot be verified.

scharf (Ger.). Sharply; throw off sharply; expression mark in Mahler's 1st Sym.

schattenhaft (Ger.). Somberly, as if in shadow; expression mark in R. Strauss's *Till Eulenspiegels.*

schauernd (Ger.). Shudderingly; expression mark found in Mahler's *Das Lied von der Erde*.

schaurig (Ger.). In a style expressive of (or calculated to inspire) mortal dread; weirdly.

Schauspielmusik (Ger.). Theater music.

schelmisch (Ger.). Joking, roguish.

Schenker, Heinrich, b. Wisniowczyki, Galicia, June 19, 1868; d. Vienna, Jan. 13, 1935. He studied jurisprudence at the Univ. of Vienna (Dr.Jur., 1890); concurrently took courses with Bruckner at the Vienna Cons.; composed songs and piano pieces; Brahms liked them sufficiently to recommend him to his publisher, Simrock. For a while Schenker served as accompanist to baritone Johannes Messchaert; returned to Vienna and devoted himself entirely to theoretical research; gathered around himself a group of enthusiastic disciples who accepted his novel theories, among them O. Vrieslander, H. Roth, H. Weisse, A. van Hoboken, O. Jonas, F. Salzer, and J. P. Dunn.

Schenker endeavored to derive the basic laws of musical composition from a thoroughgoing analysis of standard masterworks. The eventual result was the contention that each composition represents a horizontal integration—through various stages—of differential triadic units derived from the overtone series. By a dialectical manipulation of thematic elements and linear progressions of a given work, he prepared a formidable system in which the melodic design is the *Urlinie* (fundamental line), the bass is *Grundbrechung* (fundamental arpeggio), and the ultimate formation is the *Ursatz* (background); the result seems as self-consistent as the Ptolemaic planetary theory of epicycles. Arbitrary as Schenker's approach can appear, it has proven remarkably durable in academia; some have attempted to apply it to modern works lacking the triadic content essential to the system. He wrote many articles and books outlining his theories. See also ⇒Schenker system.

Schenker system (Schenkerianism). Theory of musical analysis evolved over several decades by Heinrich Schenker. It derives its principle from the natural series of overtones; the continuum of these overtones is defined as *Klang* (clang), i.e., cumulative sound. The linear distribution of this Klang is the *Urlinie* (fundamental line), governing melodic design; the bass line is the *Grundbrechung* (fundamental arpeggio). The process of analysis is in several stages: the surface of the composition is defined as foreground (*Vorgrund*), its partial reduction as middleground (*Mittelgrund*), and its final schematization, the background (*Hintergrund*), which constitutes the *Ursatz*, the ultimate irreducible structure, culmination of the Urlinie and the Grundbrechung; these successive stages are obtained by a series of *Züge* (motions). Since the harmonic series is the basic source of the Ursatz, the Schenker system postulates the absolute preponderance of the tonic major triad, with the subdominant and dominant triads as its derivatives and with minor triads accounted for by procrustean adjustments. In his original historical exposition Schenker covers the common practice period from Bach to Brahms (Wagner is omitted); analysis of chromatic harmony is made by even further adjustments. Following this modus operandi it seems possible to analyze

20th-century works (Schenker once analyzed a piece of Stravinsky's to point out the composer's "errors"), but the built-in limitations of the system become increasingly evident with every successive step toward atonality.

Scherz (Ger.). Joke.

scherzando (It.; Ger. *scherzhaft*). Like a scherzo, i.e., in a sportive, toying manner; playfully, lightly, jestingly.

scherzo (It., joke; Ger. *Scherz*). 1. Vivacious movement in the late Classic and Romantic sym., with strongly marked rhythms and sharp, unexpected contrasts in both rhythm and harmony. In the 2nd half of the 18th century the term *scherzo* was standardized as an instrumental composition in 3/4 or 3/8 time in a rapid tempo. (Occasionally duple-meter scherzos were composed.) Structurally scherzo was a modification of the ternary Classic minuet; in the 19th century it usually replaced the Classic minuet in sonatas, chamber music, and syms. Like the minuet, the scherzo contains a contrasting middle part, the trio (because these were 1st written for 3 instruments only). While in most late Classic syms. the scherzo was placed in the position formerly occupied by the minuet (i.e., the 3rd movement), Beethoven shifted it to the 2nd movement in his 9th Sym. 2. In the Romantic era, an instrumental piece of a light, piquant, humorous character. Chopin elevated it to a form of prime importance; his 4 piano scherzos are extended, virtuosic compositions while retaining their ternary form. Dukas called his symphonic poem *The Sorcerer's Apprentice* a scherzo; Stravinsky wrote an orch'l work entitled *Scherzo fantastique,* inspired by Maeterlinck's essay *Les Abeilles* (The Bees). 3. In the 16th century, a vocal composition in a lighter manner, although titles such as *Scherzi sacri* (sacred scherzos) are also found.

Schickele, Peter, b. Ames, Iowa, July 17, 1935. He was educated at Swarthmore College (B.A., 1957); studied composition with R. Harris in Pittsburgh (1954), Milhaud at the Aspen School of Music (1959), and Persichetti and Bergsma at the Juilliard School of Music in N.Y. (M.S., 1960). After serving as composer-in-residence to the Los Angeles public schools (1960–61), he taught at Swarthmore College (1961–62) and the Juilliard School of Music (from 1962). He rocketed to fame at N.Y.'s Town Hall in 1965, in the rollicking role of the roly-poly P. D. Q. Bach, the mythical composer of such outrageous travesties as *The Civilian Barber* (a suite from an as yet unrediscovered opera), *Gross Concerto for Divers Flutes* (featuring a nose flute and a Wiener Whistle to be eaten during the perf.), *Concerto for Piano vs. Orchestra, Iphigenia in Brooklyn, The Seasonings, Pervertimento for Bagpipes, Bicycles & Balloons, No-No Nonette, Schleptet, Fuga Meshuga, Missa Hilarious, Sanka Cantata, Fantasie-Shtick,* and the opera *The Abduction of Figaro* (Minneapolis, 1984). He publ. *The Definitive Biography of P. D. Q. Bach (1807–1742?)* (N.Y., 1976). In 1967 he organized a chamber-rock-jazz trio known as Open Window, which presented his own compositions; his compositions include orch'l works, vocal pieces (including rounds), film and television scores, and chamber music. He hosted a weekly radio show, *Schickele Mix,* which redefined music appreciation.

schietto (It.). Simply, quietly; neatly, deftly; unaffectedly.

Schifrin, Lalo (Boris), b. Buenos Aires, June 21, 1932. He studied music with his father, concertmaster of the Teatro Colón orch.; studied harmony with J. C. Paz; won a scholarship to the Paris Cons. (1950), where he received guidance from Koechlin and took courses with Messiaen. He became interested in jazz; represented Argentina at the International Jazz Festival in Paris (1955); returning to Buenos Aires, he formed a bebop band. In 1958 he went to N.Y. as arranger for Xavier Cugat; was pianist with Dizzy Gillespie's band (1960–62); composed several pieces, such as *Manteca, Con Alma,* and *Tunisian Fantasy,* based on Gillespie's *Night in Tunisia;* wrote a ballet, *Jazz Faust* (1963).

In 1964 Schifrin went to Hollywood; rapidly found his métier as composer for films and television; among his scores are *The Liquidator* (1966), *Cool Hand Luke* (1967), *The Fox* (1967), *The 4 Musketeers* (1973), *Voyage of the Damned* (1975), *The Amityville Horror* (1978), *The Sting II* (1983), and *Bad Medicine* (1985). He experimented with applying the jazz idiom to religious texts, e.g., the *Jazz Suite on Mass Texts* (1965). He achieved his greatest popular success with the theme for the television series *Mission: Impossible* (1966–73), in 5/4 time, for which he received 2 Grammy Awards.

Schifrin's adaptation of modern techniques into mass media placed him in the enviable position of being praised by professional musicians. His oratorio *The Rise and Fall of the 3rd Reich,* featuring realistic excerpts and incorporating an actual recording of Hitler's speech in electronic amplification, was premiered at the Hollywood Bowl (1967); other works include *The Ritual of Sound* for 15 Instruments (1962); *Rock Requiem* (1970); *Pulsations* for Electronic Keyboard, Jazz Band, and Orch. (Los Angeles, 1971); *Madrigals for the Space Age,* in 10 parts, for Narrator and Chorus (Los Angeles, 1976); *Tropicos,* chamber orch. (1983); *Cantos Aztecas* for Vocal Soloists, Chorus, and Orch. (1988); *La Nouvelle Orleans* for Wind Quintet; concertos; chamber music. He served as music director of the newly organized Paris Phil. (from 1988).

Schikaneder, Emanuel (Johannes Joseph). See ⇒Mozart, Wolfgang Amadeus.

Schiller, (Johann Christian) Friedrich von, b. Marbach, Nov. 10, 1759; d. Weimar, May 9, 1805. Many of his works were set in one musical form or another: *Die Räuber, Kabale und Liebe, Don Carlos,* the *Wallenstein* trilogy, *Maria Stuart, Die Jungfrau von Orleans, Die Braut von Messina, Wilhelm Tell,* and the ode *An die Freude.*

Schindler, Anton Felix. See ⇒Beethoven, Ludwig van.

schizzo (It.). Sketch.

Schlag (Ger.). Beat or stroke. *Schlagen,* beat time or hit; *Schlaginstrumente,* percussion instruments; *Schlagzeug,* percussion.

Schlager (Ger.). Popular song or hit.

schleichend (Ger., lingering). Dragging, slowing up the tempo.

Schleifer (Ger., slur; Eng. *slide, elevation, double blackfall;* Fr. *coulé*). Baroque ornamental figure in which (1) a primary note is approached by 2 conjunct secondary notes, encompassing a 3rd, and starting on the beat; or (2) (Fr. *tierce coulée*) a dyad of a 3rd that, when indicated, adds a passing tone to become a run of 3 conjunct notes.

schleppen (Ger.). Drag, retard. *Nicht schleppen,* do not drag.

schlicht (Ger.). Simple, unaffected.

Schlitztrommel (Ger.). Slit drum.

Schlummerlied (Ger., slumber song). Berceuse, lullaby.

Schluss (Ger.). End; close cadence.

Schluss (Ger., conclusion). Signification of the final section (subsection, phrase) of a composition. The last movement of a large work is sometimes referred to in German as *Schluss-Satz* (concluding part). The Schluss in a simple chant may be limited to 2 notes, the *penultima vox* (next-to-last voice) and *ultima vox* (last voice), to use the terminology of medieval Latin treatises. An ideal Schluss in Classic music is provided by Mozart's Sym. No. 39 in E-flat Major, which concludes with a simple restatement of the principal theme, suggesting a signature in Gothic characters. One of the most prolix Schluss is that of the 2nd Sym. of Sibelius, consisting of a seemingly interminable succession of ascending scales, which, upon reaching the 6th degree of the key, retreat to the leading tone in the lower octave, only to resume their Sisyphus-like ascension. The most abrupt Schluss occurs with the C-major chord at the end of Prokofiev's *March* from the opera *Love for 3 Oranges.* The most numbing C-major Schluss is found in the finale of the 1st Piano Concerto by Shostakovich.

By definition the Schluss must be a unison or a concord, but Chopin and Schumann sometimes end an individual piece of a cycle on an unresolved dominant-7th chord. The final chord in Mahler's grand sym. *Das Lied von der Erde* is a discord. In atonal writing a dissonant ending is de rigueur, unless it happens to be a single tone lost in mid-air, pianissimo. Several 20th-century composers, among them Stockhausen, Earle Brown, and Cage, developed a concept of works without an ascertainable Schluss, wherein any moment of a composition may be either a beginning or an end.

Schlüssel (Ger.). Clef.

schmachtend (Ger.). Languishing(ly); longing(ly).

schmaltz (Yidd., grease, fat). Inordinately sentimental playing of semipopular music, exaggerating every permissible expression to an intolerable limit, either through a natural lack of aesthetic taste, or with satirical intent.

schmeichelnd (Ger.). Flatteringly; in a coaxing, caressing manner.

schmelzend (Ger., melting). Lyrical.

schmerzlich (Ger.). Painfully, sorrowfully, plaintively.

Schmetternd (Ger.). In brass instruments, play with a blared or brassy tone.

Schmidt, Franz, b. Pressburg, Dec. 22, 1874; d. Perchtoldsdorf, near Vienna, Feb. 11, 1939. He began his musical training with the Pressburg Cathedral organist, Maher; his family moved to Vienna (1888); had piano lessons with Leschetizky; studied composition with Bruckner, theory with Fuchs, and cello with Hellmesberger at the Cons. (from 1890). He played cello in the Vienna Hofoper orch. (1896–1911); taught cello at the Cons. of the Gesellschaft der Musikfreunde (1901–08); prof. of piano (1914–22) and counterpoint and composition (from 1922) at the Vienna Staatsakademie; served as its director (1925–27); became director of the Vienna Hochschule für Musik (1927–31). After his retirement (1937), Schmidt received the Beethoven Prize of the Prussian Academy in Berlin.

Schmidt's music is steeped in Viennese Romanticism; Bruckner and Reger were particularly influential in his development, but he found an original harmonic voice; although regarded in Austria as an important symphonic composer, his music is almost totally unknown elsewhere. Outside Austria he is best known for his orch'l Intermezzo (*Zwischenspiel aus einer unvollstandigen romantischen Oper,* namely *Notre Dame,* 1902–1904). Among his other significant works are 4 syms.(1896–1933); Piano Concerto for Left Hand and Orch., for Paul Wittgenstein (1923); and the oratorio *Das Buch mit Sieben Siegeln* (1935–37); composed 2 String Quartets (1925, 1929); other chamber works; 2 piano sonatas, organ music.

Schnabel, Artur, b. Lipnik, Apr. 17, 1882; d. Axenstein, Switzerland, Aug. 15, 1951. He 1st studied with Hans Schmitt, made his debut at 8; studied with Leschetizky in Vienna (1891–97). He went to Berlin (1900); married the contralto Therese Behr (1905), with whom he frequently appeared in recitals; played in recitals with leading musicians of the day, including Flesch, Casals, Feuermann, Huberman, Primrose, and Szigeti; gave solo recitals in Europe and the U.S., presenting acclaimed cycles of the Beethoven sonatas; taught at the Berlin Hochschule für Musik (from 1925). After the advent of the Nazi regime he left Germany and settled in Switzerland; taught master classes at Lake Como and recorded the 1st complete set of the Beethoven sonatas. With the outbreak of World War II he went to the U.S.; naturalized (1944); taught at the Univ. of Michigan (1940–45); returned to Switzerland.

Schnabel was one of the greatest pianists and pedagogues in the history of keyboard playing; eschewing the role of the virtuoso, he concentrated upon the masterworks of the Austro-German repertoire with an intellectual penetration and interpretive discernment of the highest order; renowned for his performances of Beethoven and Schubert; prepared an ed. of the Beethoven piano sonatas. Also a composer; he pursued an uncompromisingly modernistic idiom, thriving on dissonance and tracing melodic patterns along atonal lines; among these works are 3 syms. (1938–48); works for piano and ensemble; 5 string quartets; other chamber works; piano pieces; songs. His writings include *Reflections on Music* (1933) and *Music and the Line of Most Resistance* (1942).

Schnaderhüpfel (Ger. dialect). Song of the Bavarian Alps in 3/4 time, usually consisting of symmetric stanzas with a harmonic scheme of alternating tonic and dominant harmonies.

Schnarre (Ger.). Rattle.

Schnarrtrommel (Ger., rattle drum). Snare drum.

schnell (Ger.). Fast, quick, rapid. *Schneller,* faster; *nach und nach schneller,* gradually faster.

Schneller (from Ger. *schnellen,* jerk). Inverted mordent; short trill on the beat using the upper auxiliary (neighbor) note.

Schnittke, Alfred (Garrievich), b. Engels, near Saratov, Nov. 24, 1934. He studied piano in Vienna (1946–48); took courses in composition with Golubev and in instrumentation with Rakov at the Moscow Cons. (1953–58); served on its faculty (1962–72), then devoted himself fully to composition. He was guest lecturer at the Vienna Hochschule für Musik and Darstellende Kunst (1981); that year was elected to the West German Akademie der Kunste. In 1985 he survived a serious heart attack. After writing in a conventional manner, he became acutely interested in new Western techniques, particularly in serialism and *sonorism,* in which dynamic gradations assume thematic significance; became known as one of the boldest experimenters in contemporary Russian composition; developed an international reputation; many of his works take a postmodern look at neoclassicism and neo-Baroque music. Among his works are the operas *Life with an Idiot* and *Historia von d. Johann Fausten;* Requiem (1975); 6 concerti grossi and concerted works; 8 syms. and orch'l works, 4 string quartets; other chamber and vocal works. His titles occasionally suggest a Satie-like wit: *Gratulationsrondo, Klingende Buchstaben, Moz-Art à la Haydn, (K)ein Sommernachstraum.*

Schoeck, Othmar, b. Brunnen, Sept. 1, 1886; d. Zurich, Mar. 8, 1957. He went to Zurich; took courses at the Industrial College before pursuing musical training with Attenhofer, Freund, Hegar, and Kempter at the Cons. (from 1905); after further studies with Reger in Leipzig (1907–08), returned to Zurich and conducted the Aussersihl Men's Chorus (1909–15), the Harmonie Men's Chorus (1910–11), and the Teachers' Chorus (1911–17); conducted the St. Gallen sym. concerts (1917–44). He was one of the most significant Swiss composers of his era; won his greatest renown as a masterful composer of songs and song cycles; wrote significant theater works, including *Venus* (1919–20), *Penthesilea* (1924–25), *Vom Fischer un syner Fru* (1928–30), *Massimilla Doni* (1934–35), *Das Schloss Düranda* (1938–39); highly regarded as piano accompanist and conductor. Among his many honors were the 1st composer's prize of the Schweizerische Tonkünstlerverein (1945) and the Grand Cross of Merit and Order of Merit of the Federal Republic of Germany (1956).

Schoenberg (Schönberg), Arnold (Franz Walter), b. Vienna, Sept. 13, 1874; d. Los Angeles, July 13, 1951. He studied at the Realschule in Vienna; learned to play cello; became proficient on the violin. When his father died, he had to support his family; worked as a bank clerk, arranged popular songs and orchestrated operetta scores. His 1st original work was a set of 3 piano pieces (1894); began to take lessons in counterpoint from Zemlinsky, whose sister Mathilde he later married; played cello in Zemlinsky's instrumental group, Polyhymnia. In 1897 he wrote the unnumbered D-major string quartet, performed publicly in Vienna (1898); wrote 2 songs with piano accompaniment that he designated as op. 1. In 1899 he wrote his 1st masterpiece, *Verklärte Nacht* for string sextet, 1st performed in Vienna by the Rosé Quartet and members of the Vienna Phil. (1902); a fine work, deeply imbued with the spirit of Romantic poetry, with a harmonic idiom stemming from Wagner's modulatory procedures; it remains Schoenberg's most frequently performed composition, known principally through its string orch. arrangement.

About 1900 Schoenberg was engaged as conductor of several amateur choral groups in Vienna and its suburbs; this increased his interest in vocal music. He began work on a secular oratorio, *Gurre-Lieder*, of monumental proportions, based on a poem by the Danish writer Jens Peter Jacobsen; for grandeur and opulence of orch'l sonority it surpasses even Mahler or R. Strauss, calling for 5 solo voices, a speaker, 3 male choruses, an 8-part mixed chorus, and a very large orch. He completed the 1st 2 parts of *Gurre-Lieder* in 1901, but the composition of the remaining section was delayed by 10 years; F. Schreker arranged its premiere with the Vienna Phil. and its choral forces (1913).

In 1901 Schoenberg moved to Berlin, where he joined E. von Wolzogen, F. Wedekind, and O. Bierbaum in launching an artistic cabaret called Überbrettl. He composed its theme song and conducted several shows; met Strauss, who helped him to obtain the Liszt Stipendium and a teaching position at the Stern Cons. Returning to Vienna (1903), he became friendly with Mahler, who helped him in his career; as Mahler's power in Vienna was then at its height, that help was considerable. In 1904 he and Zemlinsky organized the Vereinigung Schaffender Tonkünstler to encourage performances of new music. Under its auspices he conducted the premiere of his symphonic poem *Pelleas und Melisande* (1905), which uses a trombone glissando for the 1st time. There followed a performance of his *Kammersymphonie*, op. 9 (1907) with the participation of the Rosé Quartet and wind players of the Vienna Phil.; the work produced much consternation in the audience and among critics because of its challenge to traditional harmony, with chords built on 4ths and nominal dissonances used without immediate resolution. About this time he turned to painting, which became his principal avocation; in his art, as in his music, he adopted the tenets of expressionism, i.e., freedom of personal expression within a self-defined program.

Schoenberg's reputation as an independent musical thinker attracted to him such progressive-minded young musicians as Berg, Webern, and Egon Wellesz, who followed him in their own development. His 2nd String Quartet (1908) includes a quotation of *Ach, Du lieber Augustin*, a soprano solo for its last 2 movements, and his last use of a key signature (excepting the 1934 Suite for Strings in G Major, written for school use in America). In 1909 he completed his piano piece op. 11, no. 1, the 1st piece to dispense with all reference to tonality; was appointed to the faculty of the Vienna Academy of Music (1910); completed his important theory book *Harmonielehre*, dedicated to the memory of Mahler (1911), offering traditional instruction in chords and progressions while illuminating possible new developments, including fractional tones and melodies formed by the change of

timbre on the same note. He returned to Berlin (1911) to teach at the Stern Cons. and composition privately.

Schoenberg brought out the 5 Orchesterstücke, performed for the 1st time in London under H. Wood (1912); the critical reception was that of incomprehension, with a considerable measure of curiosity; each movement of the score represented an experiment in musical organization. In the same year he produced another innovative work, a cycle of songs with instrumental accompaniment, entitled Pierrot Lunaire, op. 21. In this set of 21 "melodramas," to poems by Belgian poet Albert Giraud in trans., Schoenberg made systematic use of *Sprechstimme*, gliding speech-song, to replace sung pitch (not entirely new; Humperdinck applied the technique in incidental music to Rosmer's play Königskinder, 1897). The work was given, after some 40 rehearsals, in Berlin (1912); the reaction was startling, with purblind critics drawing upon the strongest possible invective to condemn the music. Meanwhile he conducted his works in European cities (1911–14). When he was drafted into the Austrian armed forces during World War I (never serving in action, however) and was asked by the examiner whether he was the "notorious" modernist composer, he answered, "Someone had to be, and I was the one"; after the Armistice, he settled in Mödling, near Vienna. Discouraged by his inability to secure performances for himself and his associates, he organized in Vienna the Verein für Musikalische Privataufführungen (Soc. for Private Musical Performances, 1918–22), from which critics were demonstratively excluded and thereby ruling out any vocal expression of approval or disapproval.

In 1924 Schoenberg's creative evolution reached an all-important moment at which he found it necessary to establish a new governing principle of tonal relationship, called the "method of composing with 12 different notes related entirely to one another." This method was adumbrated in his music as early as 1914; used partially in the *5 Klavierstücke*, op. 23, and the Serenade, op. 24; employed integrally for the 1st time in the Piano Suite, op. 25 (1924), in which the thematic material is based on a series of 12 different notes arrayed in a prearranged order. This basic *tone row* became the composer's mainspring of thematic invention; development was provided by inversion, retrograde, and retrograde inversion of the basic series; allowing for transposition, 48 forms were obtainable in all; counterpoint, harmony, and melody were derived from the basic tone row; immediate repetition of thematic notes was admitted; the realm of rhythm remained free. As with most historic innovations, the 12-tone technique was not an immaculate conception of Schoenberg's alone, but rather a logical development of many currents of musical thought. Hauer rather unconvincingly claimed priority in laying the foundations of the 12-tone method (his "tropes" did not involve a row in any case); instances of themes consisting of 12 different notes are found in Liszt's *Faust Sym.* and R. Strauss's *Also sprach Zarathustra*.

In 1925 Schoenberg was appointed a prof. at the Prussian Academy of Arts in Berlin. With the advent of the Nazi regime, the German Ministry of Education dismissed him from his post as a Jew. In fact, he had abandoned his Jewish faith in Vienna (1898), and in a spirit of professional accommodation converted to Lutheranism; 35 years later, horrified by the hideous persecution of Jews at the hands of the Nazis, he reconverted to Judaism in Paris (1933). With the rebirth of his hereditary consciousness, he turned to specific Jewish themes in works such as *A Survivor from Warsaw* (op. 46, 1947); and the opera *Moses und Aron* (acts I–II, 1930–32; act III not composed).

Schoenberg arrived in the U.S. in late 1933; changed the spelling of his name to Schoenberg. Although he was well known in the musical world, he had difficulty obtaining a teaching position; accepted the invitation of Joseph Malkin, founder of the Malkin Cons. of Boston, to join its faculty; after teaching in Boston for a season, relocated to Los Angeles for health reasons; became a prof. of music at the Univ. of Southern Calif. (1935), then accepted a position at the Univ. of Calif. in Los Angeles, where he taught until mandatory retirement at age 70 (1936–44); naturalized (1941). He never found a patron to support his work; his pension from UCLA amounted to $38 a month; the difficulty in supporting a family with growing children became acute and eventually reached the press. He applied for a grant from the munificent Guggenheim Foundation, noting that since several of his students had received such awards, it was now his turn similar consideration, but an age limit rule defeated him once again; it was only after this case and its repercussions in the music world that the Guggenheim Foundation eliminated this rule. He finally managed to square his finances with the aid of his publishing income.

Like Rossini, Schoenberg was subject to superstition in the form of triskaidekaphobia, fear of the number 13; he seriously believed that there was something fateful in the circumstance of his birth on the 13th of the month. Noticing that the title of *Moses und Aaron* contained 13 letters, he crossed out the 2nd *a* in *Aaron* to make it 12. When he turned 76 and someone remarked facetiously that the sum of the digits of his age was 13, he seemed genuinely upset; during his last illness he expressed his fear of not surviving July 13; indeed, he died late in the evening of that date.

Schoenberg's great achievement was the establishment of the dodecaphonic system as the foundation of a new musical language; using this idiom, he wrote music of great expressive power. The ideal 12-tone row is devoid of tonal implications; analysis of his works shows his avoidance of major triads in any inversion and the use of only the 2nd inversion of a minor triad. He disliked the term *atonality* that was commonly applied to his music; he suggested, only half in jest, the term *atonicality*, i.e., absence of a tonic. His most explicit 12-tone work is his *Klavierstück*, op. 33a (1928–29), exemplifying the clearest use of the tone row in chordal combinations; other classically dodecaphonic works are *Begleitungsmusik zu einer Lichtspielszene*, op. 34 (1929–30), Violin Concerto (1934–36), and Piano Concerto (1942).

Schoenberg's disciples Berg and Webern followed his 12-tone method in general outlines but with personal deviations; Berg used triadic harmonies occasionally; Webern built tone rows in symmetric groups. Other composers who made systematic use of the 12-tone method were Wellesz, Krenek, Dallapiccola, R. Leibowitz, R. Gerhard, and H. Searle. Dodecaphony became a lingua franca of universal currency; even in Russia, where Schoenberg's theories were ideologically unacceptable; composers, including Shostakovich in his last works, made use of 12-tone themes, albeit without integral development; similarly, Ernest Bloch used 12-tone subjects in his last string quartets, refraining from applying inversions and retrograde forms.

Schoenberg lived in Los Angeles at the same time that Stravinsky was there (after 1939); the two avoided artistic contact. Back in Europe, Schoenberg had written a satirical choral canon, *The New Classicism* (op. 28, no. 3), with reference to "Herr Modernsky" (i.e., Stravinsky), lampooning his neoclassical works ("ganz wie Papa Bach"). In his old age, Stravinsky turned to the 12-tone method of composition in its integral form; his conversion would have been the greatest artistic vindication for Schoenberg, but he was dead when Stravinsky saw the dodecaphonic light; Stravinsky also forgave him in appreciation of his expertise in canonic writing.

Schoenberg's personality was heroic and egocentric, combining decisive affirmation with profound self-negation; made great sacrifices to sustain his artistic convictions, but engaged in bitter polemics when he felt that his integrity was under attack. He strongly opposed the claims of Hauer and others for the priority of the 12-tone method; vehemently and publicly criticized the implication he saw in Thomas Mann's novel *Doktor Faustus*, whose protagonist is described as the inventor of the 12-tone method; future historians, he argued, might confuse fiction with facts, crediting the figment of Mann's imagination with his discovery. He never understood why his works were not more widely performed. He asked a former secretary to Serge Koussevitzky why the Boston Sym. Orch. programs never included any of his advanced works; when the secretary said that the conductor simply could not understand them, Schoenberg, genuinely perplexed, responded, "Aber, er spielt doch Brahms!" (But he plays Brahms!). To Schoenberg his works were the natural continuation of German classical music.

Schoenberg received the Award of Merit for Distinguished Achievements from the National Inst. of Arts and Letters (1947). He placed his MSS in the Music Division of the Library of Congress in Washington, D.C.; the remaining materials were deposited after his death at the Schoenberg Inst. at the Univ. of Southern Calif. in Los Angeles, who publ. the *Journal of the Schoenberg Institute* under the editorship of L. Stein (began 1976). The MSS of arrangements of Viennese operettas and waltzes he had made in Vienna to augment his meager income were eventually sold for large sums of money after his death.

schola cantorum (Lat.). School for singers. The term dates to the 7th century, when a schola cantorum was established in Rome for the purpose of teaching the proper type of Gregorian chant. Pope Pius X decreed in 1903 that the establishment of similar singing schools should be undertaken in all Catholic churches. The name was also used by academic organizations not connected with the Church, notably the Schola Cantorum in Paris, founded in 1894.

Schottische (Ger.). German round dance in leisurely 2/4 time, a variety of the polka. The schottische attained tremendous popularity in Europe and the U.S. in the mid–19th century. The name is sometimes used interchangeably with the rapid polka-like ecossaise; despite that name, it has nothing to do with Scotland.

Schubert, Franz (Peter), b. Himmelpfortgrund (then a suburb, now a part of Vienna), Jan. 31, 1797; d. Vienna, Nov. 19, 1828. He studied violin with his father, a schoolmaster; received piano instruction from his brother Ignaz; took lessons in piano, organ, singing, and theory with Holzer, the choirmaster. In 1808 he became a member of the Vienna Imperial Court chapel choir; entered the Stadtkonvict, a training school for court singers; studied with the Imperial Court organist W. Ruzicka and Salieri. He played violin in the school orch. and conducted whenever an occasion called for it.

Schubert began composing as a student; wrote a fantasia for piano 4-hands, chamber music, orch'l overtures, and the unfinished singspiel *Der Spiegelritter;* his 1st song, *Hagars Klage,* dates from 1811. In 1813 he left the Stadtkonvict; Salieri, impressed by his talent, continued to instruct him; attended a teacher training college in Vienna; became an instructor at his father's school. Although very young, he began writing works in large forms; composed 5 syms., 4 masses, string quartets (for his family to perform), and stage music, including his 1st opera, *Des Teufels Lustschloss* (1813–16). He was only 17 when he wrote *Gretchen am Spinnrade,* 18 when he composed the dramatically overpowering *Erlkönig.* The prodigious facility he displayed is without equal; during 1815 he composed about 140 songs; on a single day he wrote 8 lieder. From his sketches his method of composition becomes apparent; he wrote the melody 1st, indicated the harmony, and wrote out the song in full; often subjected the finished work to several revisions.

Schubert became friendly with poets J. Mayrhofer and F. von Schober, and set a number of their poems to music. In 1817 he lodged with Schober and his widowed mother, paying his keep out of meager resources. He met the noted baritone J. M. Vogl, who sang many Schubert lieder on his concert programs. Among the outstanding lieder of this period are the *3 Harfenspieler, Der Wanderer, Der Tod und das Mädchen, Ganymed, An die Musik,* and *Die Forelle.* In 1818 he served as music tutor to the family of Count Esterházy at Zelesz in Hungary; the Overture in C Major "in the Italian style" became his 1st orch'l work to be performed publicly in Vienna. In 1820 his singspiel *Die Zwillingsbrüder* was performed at the Kärnthnertortheater in Vienna; his incidental music for the play *Die Zauberharfe* was heard at the Theater an der Wien; the overture later became popular as the overture to the play *Rosamunde, Fürstin von Zypern,* produced at the Theater an der Wien (1823).

Although Schubert still had financial difficulties, he formed a circle of influential friends in Vienna (the Schubertiade) and appeared as a pianist at private gatherings; sometimes he sang his songs, accompanying himself at the keyboard; he was also able to publ. some of his songs. A mystery is attached to his most famous work, the Sym. in B minor, known popularly as the *Unfinished Sym.* (begun 1822). Only 2 movements are known to survive; the 3rd movement, a scherzo, exists only in sketches. What prevented him from finishing it? Speculations are as rife as they are worthless; he was usually careful in completing a work before embarking on another composition.

In 1823 Schubert completed the masterly song cycle *Die schöne Müllerin;* in 1824 he again worked as a private tutor in Count Esterházy's employ in Zelesz. In 1827 he composed another remarkable song cycle, *Die Winterreise.* In 1828 he presented in Vienna a public concert of his works; he wrote such masterpieces as the piano sonatas in C minor, A major, and B-flat major; the String Quintet in C Major; and the 2 books of songs posth. named the *Schwanengesang.* He took a counterpoint lesson with the noted theorist Simon Sechter (1788–1867); would have continued, but his health was frail; moved to the lodgings of his brother Ferdinand. There is no incontrovertible evidence that he died of syphilis; from all accounts of his daily life, he was never promiscuous and was not known to engage in unseemly liaisons.

Schubert is often incorrectly called the creator of the strophic lied; Zelter, Reichhardt, and Beethoven wrote strophic lieder a generation before him, C. P. E. Bach before them; indeed, Goethe favored Zelter's settings. What Schubert did create was an incomparably beautiful florilegium of lieder typifying German Romantic sentiment and conveying deeply felt emotions, ranging from peaceful joy to enlightened melancholy, from philosophic meditation to throbbing drama. He set to music poems by Goethe, Mayrhofer, Schiller, W. Müller (who wrote the poetry for *Die schöne Müllerin* and *Die Winterreise*), Matthison, Hölty, Kosegarten, Körner, Klopstock, Schober, Claudius, and Heine.

On several occasions Schubert used material from his songs in instrumental works, as in the great *Wanderer Fantasia* for Piano (D. 760, 1822), based on *Der Wanderer;* the *Trout Quintet* for Piano and Strings (D. 667, *c.* 1819); with its penultimate movement a set of variations on *Die Forelle;* the String Quartet in D Minor (D. 810, 1824), with a set of variations on *Der Tod und das Mädchen* in its 2nd movement. But Schubert was not given to large theater works and oratorios; his operas were unsuccessful or unperformed; wrote 7 masses, including a *Deutsche Messe,* but most of his religious music was single movements and composed before 1821.

Even Schubert's extended works in sonata form are not conceived on a grand scale but instead are constructed according to the symmetry of recapitulations; his music captivates not through recurring variety but by the recalled felicities; often in his MSS he simply indicates the repetition of a group of bars by number. Therein lies the immense difference between Schubert and Schumann: where Schubert was satisfied with recalling a passage already heard, Schumann variegates. Schubert was indeed the most symmetrical composer in an era of free-flowing musical prose and musical poetry.

Much confusion exists in the numbering of Schubert's syms.; the last, the "Great" in C major, is traditionally listed as no. 9 (D. 944, 1825–26). The missing sym., no. 7, exists as a full draft in 4 movements, of which the 1st 110 bars are fully scored; there are several extant completions, most notably that of Brian Newbould (1977); the *Unfinished* Sym. is then no. 8. There remains the "Gmunden" or "Gastein" *Sym.,* so named because he was supposed to have written it in Gastein, in the Tirol. It was long regarded as irretrievably lost, but was eventually identified with Sym. No. 9. Incredibly, as late as 1978 there came to light (in the archives of the Vienna Stadtsbibliothek) a sketch of still another Schubert sym., composed during his last months; this insubstantial but magically tempting waft of genius was completed by Newbould and numbered as the 10th.

The recognition of Schubert's greatness was astonishingly slow; fully 40 years elapsed before the discovery of the MS of the *Unfinished Sym.;* posth. performances were the rule for his sym. premieres, and their publication was exceedingly tardy. Schumann, ever sensitive to great talent, saluted the kindred genius in his syms., about whose "heavenly length" Schumann so admiringly complained; but it took half a century for him to become firmly established as one of the great musical "Sch's" (Chopin and Shostakovich phonetically included).

Among Schubert's great number of compositions are: Stage: 18 works, including operas, Singspiele, incidental music, and melodrama (1813–23); many are now recorded, and a few even staged, despite poor librettos. Choral: 7 masses (1814–28); shorter religious pieces; secular choruses, mostly for men's voices. Lieder and songs: more than 600, the source and challenge for later lied composers. Orch.: 9 syms. (1813–28); 8 concert and theatrical overtures (1812?–19), including 2 "in Italian style"; 3 pieces with violin (1816–17). Piano: 18 sonatas, many unfinished to different degrees (1815–28); fantasies; impromptus, including 6 *Momens musicals* [*sic*] (D. 780, 1823–28); fugues; variations; shorter works. Piano 4-hands (of which he was the greatest exponent): fantasies; sonatas, including the *Grand duo* (D. 812, 1824; once thought the missing "Gastein" sym., and orch. as such); marches, including the *Marches militaires* (D. 733, 1818); 10 polonaises; dances for piano, including waltzes, minuets, Deutsche, Ländler, ecossaises, galops, and a cotillon. Chamber: 16 string quartets (*c.* 1810–26); piano trios; violin and piano works; String Quintet (D. 956, 1828); other ensemble and solo works.

Otto Deutsch, who compiled the standard Schubert catalogue, lent his initial to the "D. numbers" used to group Schubert's works, just as "K. numbers" are used for Mozart. Schubert's brother Ferdinand (Lukas) Schubert (b. Lichtenthal, near Vienna, Oct. 18, 1794; d. Vienna, Feb. 26, 1859) was a composer and teacher; was devoted to his brother and took charge of his MSS after his death; wrote 2 singspiels and much sacred music, including 4 masses and a Requiem.

schüchternd (Ger.). Timidly.

Schuller, Gunther (Alexander), b. N.Y., Nov. 22, 1925. His paternal grandfather was a German bandmaster before emigrating to America; his father was a violinist with the N.Y. Phil. After a stay in Germany for academic training, Gunther studied at the St. Thomas Choir School in N.Y. (1938–44); received private instruction in theory, flute, and horn. He played in the N.Y. City Ballet Orch. (1943); was 1st horn in the Cincinnati Sym. Orch. (1943–45) and the Metropolitan Opera Orch. in N.Y. (1945–49). He became fascinated with jazz; played the horn in a combo led by M. Davis; began to compose jazz pieces.

Schuller taught at the Manhattan School of Music in N.Y. (1950–63), the Yale Univ. School of Music (1964–67), and the New England Cons. of Music in Boston, distinguishing himself as president (1967–77). He was also active at Tanglewood as a composition teacher (1963–84), head of contemporary music activities (1965–84), artistic codirector (1969–74), and director (1974–84). In 1984–85 he was interim music director of the Spokane (Wash.) Sym. Orch.; directed its Sandpoint (Idaho) Festival; founded the Boston Composers' Orch. (1986); awarded the 1st Elise L. Stoeger Composer's Chair of the Chamber Music Soc. of Lincoln Center in N.Y. (1988).

In his multiple activities Schuller tried to link serious music and jazz; popularized the style of cool jazz. In 1957 he launched the slogan "3rd stream" to designate the synthesis of classical forms with improvisatory jazz elements, disparate but not necessarily incompatible entities; wrote fanciful pieces in this style, often in close cooperation with J. Lewis of the Modern Jazz Quartet. While investigating the roots of jazz he became interested in early ragtime; formed the New England

Cons. Ragtime Ensemble (1972); its recordings of Joplin's piano rags in the original small band arrangements (*The Red Back Book*) were instrumental in bringing about the "ragtime revival." In his compositions he freely applied serial methods, even when his overall style was dominated by jazz. He was elected to the National Inst. of Arts and Letters (1967) and the American Academy and Inst. of Arts and Letters (1980); received the William Schuman Award of Columbia Univ. (1989); awarded a MacArthur Foundation grant (1991). In 1975 Schuller organized Margun Music to make available unpubl. American music; founded GunMar Music (1979) and GM Recordings (1980); publ. *Horn Technique* (N.Y., 1962) and the very valuable studies *Early Jazz: Its Roots and Musical Development* (N.Y., 1968) and *The Swing Era: The Development of Jazz, 1930–1945* (N.Y., 1990). A vol. of his writings appeared as *Musings* (N.Y., 1985).

Schuman, William (Howard), b. N.Y., Aug. 4, 1910; d. Feb. 15, 1992. He began composing popular songs at 16; played in jazz groups. He took courses at N.Y. Univ.'s School of Commerce (1928–30) before choosing music; took private lessons in harmony with M. Persin and counterpoint with C. Haubiel in N.Y. (1931); attended summer courses with B. Wagenaar and A. Schmid at N.Y.'s Juilliard School (1932–33); continued at Teacher's College of Columbia Univ. (B.S., 1935; M.A., 1937); studied conducting at the Salzburg Mozarteum (1935) and composition with R. Harris at the Juilliard School (1936–38).

Schuman came to the attention of Koussevitzky, who conducted the premieres of *American Festival Overture* (1939), 3rd Sym. (1941; 1st N.Y. Music Critics' Circle Award), *A Free Song* (1943; 1st Pulitzer Prize in music), and the *Sym. for Strings* (1943). Rodzinski conducted the premiere of his 4th Sym. (1942). After teaching at Sarah Lawrence College (1935–45) he was director of publications of G. Schirmer, Inc. (1945–52); president of the Juilliard School of Music (1945–62), acquiring a notable reputation as educator; president of Lincoln Center for the Performing Arts in N.Y. (1962–69). He was chairman of the MacDowell Colony (from 1973) and the 1st chairman of the Norlin Foundation (1975–85). Held 2 Guggenheim fellowships (1939–41); elected to the National Inst. of Arts and Letters (1946) and the American Academy of Arts and Letters (1973); awarded the gold medal of the American Academy and Inst. of Arts and Letters (1982); won a 2nd (special) Pulitzer Prize (1985); received the National Medal of Arts (1987). Columbia Univ. established the William Schuman Award (1981), given to a composer for lifetime achievement; fittingly, Schuman was its 1st recipient.

Schuman's music is characterized by great emotional tension, maintained by powerful asymmetric rhythms; the contrapuntal structures in his works reach a great degree of complexity and are saturated with dissonance without, however, losing essential tonal references. In several works he employs American melorhythms, but his general style is cosmopolitan, exploring all viable techniques of modern composition. Among his important works are: the opera *The Mighty Casey* (1951–53); ballets; 10 syms. (1936–76); a piano concerto (1938); other orch'l works; vocal works with various accompaniments; 5 string quartets (1936–88); other chamber works; piano works.

Schumann, Clara (Josephine) Wieck, b. Leipzig, Sept. 13, 1819; d. Frankfurt am Main, May 20, 1896. At age 5 she began musical training with her father, (Johann Gottlob) Friedrich Wieck (1785–1873), a leading pedagogue; made her debut at the Leipzig Gewandhaus (1828); gave her 1st complete recital (1830); her father accompanied her on her 1st major concert tour, which included a visit to Paris (1831–32); upon her return home, pursued additional piano training and studies in voice, violin, instrumentation, score reading, counterpoint, and composition; publ. several piano works; named kk. Kammervirtuosin to the Austrian court (1838).

Robert Schumann entered Clara's life when he became a lodger in the Wieck home (1830); asked her to marry him (1837), a request which set off a contentious battle between the couple and Friedrich Wieck; the issue was settled after the couple went to court; finally married in 1840. They went to Dresden, then to Düsseldorf (1850). In spite of her responsibilities in rearing a large family, she continued to pursue a concert career; became active as a teacher; served on the faculty of the Leipzig Cons. and taught privately. After her husband's death (1856), she went to Berlin (1857); after a stay in Baden-Baden (1863–73) lived intermittently in Berlin (1873–78). She toured widely as a pianist; made regular appearances in England (from 1856); toured Russia (1864). She settled in Frankfurt as a teacher at the Hoch Cons. (1878–92), a position she served with distinction; made her last public appearance as pianist (1891).

As a pianist Clara Schumann was a masterly and authoritative interpreter of Robert's compositions; later became an equally admirable interpreter of Brahms, her lifelong friend. Free of all mannerisms, she impressed her audiences by the earnestness of her regard for the music she was playing. A remarkable teacher, she attracted students from many countries. As a composer she revealed a genuine talent, especially in her character pieces for piano; wrote a piano concerto (1836), piano trio (1847), piano concertino (1847), 3 romances for violin and piano (1853), and songs. Robert made use of Clara's melodies in several works. She wrote cadenzas to 2 Beethoven concertos; ed. the Breitkopf & Härtel edition of Schumann's works and his early correspondence; ed. finger exercises from Czerny's piano method.

Schumann, Robert (Alexander), b. Zwickau, June 8, 1810; d. Endenich, near Bonn, July 29, 1856. At age 10 he began piano lessons from J. G. Kuntzsch, organist at the Zwickau Marienkirche; enrolled at the Univ. of Leipzig as *studiosus juris* (1828) but gave more attention to philosophical lectures. In Leipzig he became a piano student of (Johann Gottlob) Friedrich Wieck (1785–1873), his future father-in-law; went to Heidelberg, applying himself seriously to music (1829); returned to Leipzig and lodged in Wieck's home, becoming acquainted with his daughter Clara (1830); took a composition course with H. Dorn.

Schumann became absorbed in the Romantic malaise of Weltschmerz; his idols, the writers Novalis, Kleist, Byron, Lenau, and Hölderlin, all died young and tragically. He hoped to study with Weber, who also died early. He wrote Romantic plays and poems; practiced piano, hoping to become a virtuoso; never achieved this ambition; Clara became a famous concert pianist, while he was often introduced to the public as her husband. His own piano study was halted after he developed an ailment in the index and middle fingers of his right hand; used all the

fashionable remedies of the period, allopathy, homeopathy, and electrophysical therapy; tried a mechanical device to lift the middle finger, but it made it worse. His damaged fingers were sufficient to exempt him from military service.

From his youth onwards, Schumann expressed a fear of madness; had auditory hallucinations, causing insomnia; suffered from acrophobia; experienced sudden onsets of inexpressible angst, momentary loss of consciousness, and difficulty in breathing. He labeled his sickness a "pervasive melancholy" and contemplated suicide. His spirits were maintained by his great love for Clara, to whom he confessed his psychological perturbations. Her father undoubtedly surmised his unstable character; resisted allowing Clara to become engaged to him; the couple had to go to court to overcome Wieck's objections; finally married in 1840. They later reconciled, but the relationship remained formal.

Schumann wrote music full of natural beauty, harmonious and melodious in its flow; his art is remarkably free from the somber and dramatic qualities that characterize the music of Beethoven and his Romantic followers. Indeed, he represents the flowering of German Romanticism, with its drama, its ecstasies, and its ultimate tragedy. The great difference between the musical Classic and Romantic lies in the fusion of personal events with musical production; Haydn wrote innumerable syms. and countless string quartets, but his life was free of perturbations and dreamlike visions, a plain with scant vegetation. Schumann's works, on the other hand, were rich and varied in musical flora; each piece was an expression of his passing mood; his life was reflected in the catalogue of his oeuvre. He lived in musical fantasies, until his mental world became a fantasy itself.

One of the most evident features of Schumann's artistic imagination was his fanciful way of personifying friends and intimates through musical acronyms. His platonic love for Ernestine von Fricken, who lived in Asch (Bohemia), inspired him to use the notes A–E♭ (Es)–C–B♭ (H) or A♭ (As)–C–B (H) as themes for his famous piano pieces, *Papillons* and *Carnaval;* the latter piece features sections named *Chiarina* (Schumann's nickname for Clara) and *Chopin.* Incidentally it was Ernestine's adoptive father, an amateur flutist, who gave him the theme for his *Études symphoniques;* his op. 1 is a set of variations on the notes A–B–E–G–G, spelling the name of Countess Meta von Abegg, to whom he was also poetically attached.

As Schumann gained recognition as an important composer, he continued his literary activities. In 1834 he cofounded a progressive journal, *Neue Zeitschrift für Musik,* in which he militated against the vapid mannerisms of fashionable salon music and other aspects of musical stagnation; wrote essays signed with the poetic names of Florestan, Eusebius, or Meister Raro. Eusebius, the name of 3 Christian saints, is a Greek compound, *eu + sebiai,* good worship; Florestan is "one in a state of flowering"; Raro, which means "rare," could be formed from the juxtaposition of his and Clara's names: Clararobert. As early as 1831, in the guise of Eusebius, he hailed the genius of Chopin in an article containing the famous invocation "Hut ab, ihr Herren, ein Genie!" The article appeared in the *Allgemeine Musikalische Zeitung;* it was signed with his initials; he was identified merely as a young student of Prof. Wieck; but this winged phrase became biographers' favorite demonstration of his "discovery" of Chopin's talent; in fact, Chopin was slightly older than Schumann and already had a brilliant concert career; Schumann was an unknown. Another fanciful Schumann invention was the formation of an intimate company of friends, named *Davidsbündler*, dedicated to the mortal struggle against Philistines in art and to the passionate support of all that was new and imaginative. He immortalized this society in his brilliant piano work *Davidsbündlertänze*.

Another characteristically Romantic trait was Schumann's attachment to nocturnal moods, nature scenes, and fantasies; the titles of his piano pieces are typical: *Nachtstücke, Waldszenen, Fantasiestücke*. A child at heart himself, he created a set of exquisite miniatures, *Kinderszenen*, a marvelous musical nursery including the beautifully sentimental *Träumerei*. Parallel with his piano works, Schumann produced some of his finest lieder, including the song cycles to poems by Heine (op. 24; *Dichterliebe*, op. 48), Eichendorff (op. 39), and Chamisso (*Frauenliebe und -Leben*, op. 42). In 1841, he sketched out his 1st Sym. (B-flat major) in only 4 days, born, as he said, in a single "fiery hour"; named it the *Spring Sym.* It was followed in rapid succession by 3 string quartets (op. 41), Piano Quintet (op. 44), the Piano Quartet (op. 47); his impassioned choral work *Das Paradies und die Peri* comes from this time. 3 more syms. followed within the next decade, as well as a piano concerto, a coalition between the percussive gaiety of the solo part and songful paragraphs in the orch.; an arresting hocket occurs in the finale, in which duple meters come into a striking conflict with the triple rhythm of the solo part.

In 1843 Schumann was asked by Mendelssohn to join him as a teacher of piano, composition, and score reading at the newly founded Cons. in Leipzig; he and Clara undertook a concert tour to Russia; later that year they moved to Dresden (1844–50). To this period belong his great C-Major Sym. (1846), Piano Trio (1847), and the opera *Genoveva* (1848). In 1847 he assumed the conducting post of the Liedertafel, and in 1848 organized the Chorgesang-Verein in Dresden. In 1850 he became town music director in Düsseldorf; his disturbed condition began manifesting itself in such alarming ways that he had to resign the post; continued to compose. In 1853 he completed a violin concerto; Joachim, in whose care he left the work, thought it not worthy of his genius; ruled that it should not be performed until the centennial of Schumann's death.

Schumann's condition continued to deteriorate. In 1854 he threw himself into the Rhine, but was rescued; a month later he checked himself into a sanatorium at Endenich, near Bonn, remaining there until his death. Strangely enough he did not want to see Clara; there were months when he did not even inquire about her and the children; but Brahms was a welcome visitor, and he enjoyed his company during his not infrequent periods of lucidity; in 1855 Brahms played piano, 4-hands, with him; he made a notation in his diary: "Visit from Brahms. A genius." His overall symptoms and mood swings point to tertiary syphilis and final general paresis; among those symptoms was a painful single tone ringing in his ears. (The syphilitic Smetana also suffered this symptom, incorporating it into a string quartet.) Robert and Clara Schumann had 7 children; 3 daughters lived to a very old age; 1 son suffered from mental disease. Schumann left works in most genres, but is best known for his vocal and piano music.

Schuppanzigh, Ignaz. See ⇒Beethoven, Ludwig van.

Schusterfleck (Ger.). See ⇒rosalia.

Schütz, Heinrich (Henrich), also called Henricus Sagittarius, b. Kostritz, Oct. 8, 1585; d. Dresden, Nov. 6, 1672. Hewas trained in music by H. Colander, the town organist; became a choirboy in the court chapel of Landgrave Moritz of Hessen-Kassel (1599); in Kassel pursued his academic studies with G. Otto, the court Kapellmeister; entered the Univ. of Marburg to study law (1608); an opportunity to continue his musical education came when Moritz sent him to Venice to study with renowned master Giovanni Gabrieli (1609). Under Gabrieli's tutelage he received a thorough compositional training; learned to play the organ; brought out a book of 5-voice madrigals, dedicated to his benefactor Moritz (1611); after Gabrieli's death he returned to Kassel; served as 2nd organist at the court chapel (1612). In 1615 the Elector Johann Georg I of Saxony invited Schütz to Dresden as Kapellmeister, at a time when Praetorius was also active there. Moritz asked the Elector to allow him to return to Kassel (1616), but the Elector declined. Schütz fully assumed his duties as Saxon Kapellmeister (1617); granted an annual salary of 400 florins (from 1618). In addition to providing music for court occasions, he was responsible for the court chapel; publ. his 1st collection of sacred music, the *Psalmen Davids sampt etlichen Moteten und Concerten* (1619).

During a court visit to Torgau, Schütz produced the 1st German opera, *Dafne,* setting Opitz's adaptation of Rinuccini's 1598 libretto; it was presented at Hartenfels Castle to celebrate the wedding of the Princess Sophia Eleonora of Saxony to Landgrave Georg II of Hesse-Darmstadt (1627); granted a leave of absence (1628), he went to Italy; studied the new operatic style of Monteverdi; adopted this new style in the *Sym. sacrae* (Venice, 1629); returned to Dresden (1629). When Saxony entered the 30 Years' War (1631), conditions at the Dresden court chapel became difficult; Schütz obtained the post of Kapellmeister to King Christian IV (1633); returned to Dresden (1634); composed the *Musicalische Exequien* for the interment of Prince Heinrich Posthumus of Reuss (1636); publ. 2 vols. of *Kleine geistliche Concerte* (1636, 1639).

Schütz composed the music for the opera-ballet *Orpheus und Euridice,* performed in Dresden (1638) to celebrate the marriage of Prince Johann Georg of Saxony and Princess Magdalena Sybilla of Brandenburg; obtained another leave of absence to serve as Kapellmeister to Georg of Calenberg in Hildesheim (1639); after a year's stay in Dresden (1641–42), set out again for Copenhagen, serving as Kapellmeister (to 1644). Returning to Germany, he lived in Braunschweig (1644–45); was active at the court of nearby Wolfenbüttel. In 1645 he returned to Dresden; the Elector declined his request for retirement but allowed him to live a part of each year in Weissenfels. Schütz continued to compose industriously during these years; the 2nd book of *Sym. sacrae* appeared (1647), followed by the *Geistliche Chor-Music* (1648). In succeeding years he repeatedly asked to be pensioned, but his requests were ignored; finally, when Johann Georg II became Elector (1657), he was allowed to retire on a pension as Chief Kapellmeister; his Passions according to St. Luke, St. John, and St. Matthew date from these last years, as does the *Christmas Oratorio;* about 1670 returned to Dresden to settle his affairs and await his end.

The importance of Schütz in music history resides in his astute adaptation of the new Italian styles to German music; his work inspired most German Baroque composers, directly or indirectly.

He was extraordinarily productive; the majority of his extant compositions are sacred vocal works; the 2 operas are lost. The most important collection of Schütz's MSS is housed in the Hessische Landesbibliothek in Kassel.

schwach (Ger.). Weakly. *Schwächer,* softer, fainter.

schwankend (Ger.). Hesitantly.

Schwantner, Joseph, b. Chicago, Mar. 22, 1943. As a youth he studied classical guitar and wrote jazz compositions. He enrolled in the Chicago American Cons. and studied composition with B. Dieter (B.M., 1964); then went to Northwestern Univ., where he worked with A. Donato and A. Stout (M.M., 1966; D.M., 1968), garnering 3 B.M.I. Student Composer awards. He joined the faculty of the Eastman School of Music in Rochester, N.Y. (1970); became prof. of composition (1980); was composer-in-residence of the St. Louis Sym. Orch. (1982–85). The recipient of various awards and numerous commissions, he won the Pulitzer Prize for his orch'l score *Aftertones of Infinity* (1979). His early works followed the dictates of serialism; eventually developed an eclectic style, incorporating tonal materials into harmonically complex works. Interested in new devices of color, texture, and timbre, he often employs tonalities produced by unusual and sometimes unorthodox musical instruments.

schwärmend (Ger.). Dreamily.

schwärmer (Ger.). A Baroque ornament consisting of rapid repetitions on a single note, akin to a tremolo. This figure was well-suited to the clavichord (Bebung).

Schwartz, Arthur, b. N.Y., Nov. 25, 1900; d. Kintnersville, Pa., Sept. 3, 1984. He taught himself to play the piano; began writing songs in college; after practicing law (1924–28) he turned to music. With the lyricist Howard Dietz he produced successful works for Broadway, such as the revues *3's a Crowd* (1930, with *Something to Remember You By*), *The Band Wagon* (1931, with *Dancing in the Dark;* the 1953 film includes *That's Entertainment*), and *Flying Colors* (1932; includes *Louisiana Hayride*); also the musicals *Revenge with Music* (1934; includes *If There Is Someone Lovelier Than You* and *You and the Night and the Music*) and *Between the Devil* (1937; includes *I See Your Face Before Me*). With Dorothy Fields, he wrote *Stars in Your Eyes* (1939), *A Tree Grows in Brooklyn* (1951), and *By the Beautiful Sea* (1954); back with Dietz, he produced the revue *Inside USA* (1948) and the musicals *The Gay Life* (1961) and *Jennie* (1963); wrote for films (1936–55).

Schwarzkopf, (Olga Maria) Elisabeth (Friederike), b. Jarotschin, near Posen, Dec. 9, 1915. She studied with Lula Mysz-Gmeiner at the Berlin Hochschule für Musik; made her operatic debut as a Flower Maiden in *Parsifal* at the Berlin Städtische Oper (1938); then studied with M. Ivogün while continuing on its roster, appearing in more important roles from 1941. In 1942 she made her debut as a lieder artist in Vienna, and also sang for the 1st time at the State Opera there as Zerbinetta, remaining on its roster until the Nazis closed the theater in 1944. Having registered as a member of the German Nazi Party in 1940, Schwarzkopf had to be denazified by the Allies after the end of World War II.

In 1946 Schwarzkopf rejoined the Vienna State Opera and appeared as Donna Elvira during its visit to London's Covent Garden (1947); subsequently sang at Covent Garden regularly (to 1951). In 1947 she made her 1st appearance at the Salzburg Festival as Susanna; also sang regularly at Milan's La Scala (1948–63). Furtwängler invited her to sing in his performance of the Beethoven 9th Sym. at the reopening celebrations of the Bayreuth Festival (1951); created the role of Anne Trulove in *The Rake's Progress* in Venice (1951). In 1953, she gave her 1st recital at N.Y.'s Carnegie Hall; made her U.S. operatic debut as the Marschallin with the San Francisco Opera (1955). In 1964 she made her belated Metropolitan Opera debut in N.Y. in the same role; continued on its roster until 1966. In 1975 she made a farewell tour of the U.S. as a concert singer. In addition to her acclaimed Mozart and Strauss roles, she was admirable in Viennese operetta. As an interpreter of lieder she was incomparable. In 1953, she married Walter Legge (b. London, June 1, 1906; d. St. Jean, Cap Ferrat, Mar. 22, 1979), an influential English recording executive, orch'l manager, and writer on music.

schwebend (Ger.). Floating, soaring; buoyant(ly); in a lofty, elevated style.

Schwegelpfeife (Ger.). Obsolete name for a fife, whether vertical or transverse.

Schweitzer, Albert, b. Kaysersberg, Jan. 14, 1875; d. Lambarene, Gabon, Sept. 4, 1965. He studied piano as a child with his father, a Lutheran pastor; began organ studies at 8, his principal mentors being Eugen Munch in Mulhouse, Ernst Munch in Strasbourg, and Widor in Paris. He pursued training in philosophy (Ph.D., 1899) and theology (Ph.D., 1900) at the Univ. of Strasbourg; received instruction in music theory from Jacobsthal in Strasbourg and in piano from P. Jaell and M. Jaell in Paris. In 1896 he became organist of the Bach Concerts in Strasbourg; joined the faculty of the Univ. (1902); completed his full medical course (M.D., 1912); organist of the Bach Society in Paris (1905–13).

In 1913 Schweitzer went to Lambarene in the Gabon province of French Equatorial Africa and set up a jungle hospital, which subsequently occupied most of his time and energy. However, he continued to pursue his interests in music, theology, and philosophy, making occasional concert tours as an organist in Europe to raise funds for his hospital work among the Africans. He was awarded the Nobel Peace Prize, the only professional musician to hold this prestigious award (1952). His philosophical and theological writings established his reputation as one of the foremost thinkers of his time; in music he distinguished himself as the author of an important book on Bach, which greatly influenced the interpretation of the music, and contributed to the understanding of Bach's symbolic treatment of various musical devices. He ed. *J. S. Bach: Complete Organ Works: A Critico-practical Edition* (N.Y.; vols. I–V, 1912–14, with C. Widor; vols. VI–VIII, 1954–67, with E. Nies-Berger); wrote *J. S. Bach, le musicien-poète* (Paris, 1905); *Deutsche und französische Orgelbaukunst und Orgelkunst* (Leipzig, 1906); theological and philosophical books. A complete German ed. of his writings was ed. by R. Grabs (5 vols., Munich, 1974).

schwellen (Ger.). Swell, as in an organ.

Schwellwerk (Ger.). Swell organ.

schwer (Ger.). Heavy, ponderous; difficult.

Schwermüt(h)ig (Ger.). Sad, melancholy.

Schwertsik, Kurt, b. Vienna, June 25, 1935. He studied composition with Marx and Schiske, and horn with Freiberg at the Vienna Academy of Music (1949–57); continued his composition studies with Stockhausen in Cologne and Darmstadt (1959–62), where he worked with Kagel and Cage; later associated with Cardew; pursued the study of analysis with Polnauer (1964–65). With Cerha he founded the contemporary music ensemble "Die Reihe" in Vienna (1958); played horn in the Niederösterreichisches Tonkünstler-Orch. (1955–59, 1962–68) and the Vienna Sym. Orch. (from 1968). In 1966 he was a visiting prof. of composition at the Univ. of Calif. at Riverside; took further instruction in modern analysis from O. Jonas; taught composition at the Vienna Cons. (from 1979).

Although he wore a scholarly beard, Schwertsik repeatedly militated against rebarbative neoclassicism; his works reject the "false beards" of scholasticism, seeking a fruitful symbiosis of serialism and post-serialism with a flexibly handled, rich tonality. A skillful and imaginative composer, he explores in his works many new paths in synthesizing the experimental with the traditional, even writing vocal music in the Austrian dialect. Collaborations with his wife Christa Schwertsik, a singer, have been especially successful. An all-Schwertsik concert was given by Cerha and "Die Reihe" in Vienna in honor of his 50th birthday in 1985.

schwindend (Ger.). Dying away, *morendo.*

Schwingung (Ger.). Vibration.

schwungvoll (Ger.). Swingingly; buoyantly; with sweep and passion.

scintillante (It.). Sparkling, brilliant.

scioltamente (sciolto; It.). Freely, unrestrainedly, fluently, nimbly; without pedantic observation of melorhythmic precision.

scivolando (It.). In piano playing, glissando.

scoop. Vocal tones arrived at by a rough and imprecise *portamento* from a lower tone, instead of a firm and just attack.

scop (Old Eng.). Ancient English *bard* or poet-musician.

scordatura (from It. *discordatura,* mistuning). Retuning an instrument for greater ease of playing certain notes or for achieving a timbral effect. The practice arose in the 16th century to facilitate the playing of the lute in different keys. Scordatura received its highest development in early Baroque music, with composers ingeniously changing the tuning of string instruments to enable them to play easily in keys of several sharps or flats; Biber was a pioneer of scordatura; his *Mystery Sonatas* for violin are systematically arranged in scordatura so that the violin becomes in effect a transposing instrument, with each string having its own transposition; under such conditions not only the notes themselves but the intervals between them become altered.

Vivaldi also applied scordatura in his concertos. The visual appearance of the music, notated in traditional clefs, can suggest modernistic cacophony. An anonymous string quartet misattributed to Benjamin Franklin uses different scordaturas for different instruments in different movements; thus a quartet of absolute amateurs, playing on open strings only, can produce a fairly intricate contrapuntal work.

With the progress of instrumental techniques and construction, scordatura lost its raison d'etre, but modern composers occasionally apply it to secure a fundamental harmony in a minor key by tuning down a semitone the 2 lower strings of a violin, viola, or cello. In the coda of Tchaikovsky's *Pathétique Sym.* the melodic line descends to F-sharp but the violins playing the passage have to stop at their lowest note, G, and the final F-sharp has to be taken over by other instruments. To avoid this frustrating sense of incompleteness Stokowski instructed the violinists to tune down the open G string to F-sharp, a procedure that can be classified as scordatura.

score. Systematic notation of music for several instruments or voices in which the individual parts are placed one below another; exact vertical alignment of all parts symbolizes simultaneity, so that the music can be read in its totality. A *full* or *orchestral score* lists all instruments, with the woodwinds on top, brass instruments in the middle, and the strings in the lower section. Percussion and keyboard (excerpt basso continuo) are placed between the brass and the strings. In concertos the solo parts are placed immediately above the string section, as are the vocal parts and choruses in operas, oratorios, and other vocal works.

The 1st page of a full score lists all instruments as a sort of inventory, with instruments in the high range placed above those of the lower range (within each instrumental family); thus, the bottom line of a score is occupied by the double-bass part. In order to save space the staves of instruments that have rests on a particular page in the score are omitted and only the active parts are printed. As a rule, 1st and 2nd flutes and other paired instruments share the same staff in the orch'l score, although it is often necessary to split individual string sections into several staves when they play *divisi.* The task of an orch'l or operatic conductor, in surveying these musical masses under his or her command, is further complicated by the fact that clarinets, the English horn, saxophones, French horns, and most trumpets are transposing instruments. Some 20th-century composers, notably Prokofiev, wrote the parts of transposing instruments in the key of C, so that the conductor does not have to be confounded by the polytonal look of the score, gazing at a clarinet part with 1 sharp in the key signature while the strings have 1 flat.

In chamber music with piano participation, the piano part is placed invariably below the other instruments, which in turn are disposed according to their relative pitch. Thus in a string quartet the 1st violin is placed on top, then the 2nd violin, the viola, and at the bottom, the cello. Other kinds of scores include: *Close* or *compressed score,* short score; *open score,* orch'l score; *organ score,* like a piano score, with a 3rd staff for pedal bass; *piano score,* piano arrangement of an orch'l score, the words of any leading vocal parts being inserted above the music, often without their notes; *short score,* any abridged arrangement or skeleton transcript; also a 4-part vocal score on 2 staves; *supplementary score,* one appended to the body of the score when all parts cannot be written on 1 page; *vocal score,* that of an a cappella composition, or one in which the vocal parts are written out in full, usually on separate staves, the piano accompaniment, arranged or compressed from the full score, on 2 staves below.

scoring. Instrumentation; orchestration.

scorrendo (scorrevole; It.). Fluently, smoothly, flowing.

Scotch snap or catch. Rhythmic motive 𝄢 found in many Scottish airs; this "inverted dotting" on the beat is also characteristic of the strathspey and other Scottish dances.

scotophilia. In biology, the receptive phase of circadian rhythm in which the chief activity is performed in the dark; vampire bats, usually nocturnal, are outstanding examples of scotophiliac animals. As applied to musical composition, scotophilia is the love of dark and somber sonorities marked by a statistically certifiable prevalence of low registers and slow tempos, as in the syms. of Sibelius. Interestingly enough, avant-garde composers, whose chosen self-appellation connotes a rapid movement forward, betray a curious addiction to static, somber, and darksome moods and compositorial habits; such composers may well be called scotophiliacs.

Scotto, Renata, b. Savona, Feb. 24, 1933. She commenced music study in Savona at age 14; at 16 she went to Milan for vocal training with Emilio Ghirardini, Merlini, and Mercedes Llopart; made her debut as Violetta in Savona in 1952. After winning a national vocal competition in 1953, she made her formal debut as Violetta at Milan's Teatro Nuovo; then joined Milan's La Scala, where she sang secondary roles until being called upon to replace Callas as Amina during the company's visit to the Edinburgh Festival in 1957. She made her U.S. debut at the Chicago Lyric Opera in 1960, as Mimi, a role chosen for her Metropolitan Opera debut in N.Y. (1965). She scored a brilliant success with her portrayal of Mimi in the Metropolitan Opera production of *La Bohème* in the *Live from Lincoln Center* telecast on PBS (1977); thereafter was a stellar figure in the U.S. opera scene; toured widely as a recitalist. Among her other fine roles were Lucia, Gilda, Elena in *I Vespri Siciliani,* Norma, Manon Lescaut, Luisa Miller, Francesca da Rimini, and Elizabeth of Valois.

scozzese, alla (It.). In Scottish style.

Scratch Orchestra. Organization founded in 1969 by British composer Cornelius Cardew, an outgrowth of his Scratch Music concept. He defined this orch. as "a large number of enthusiasts pooling their resources (not primarily musical) and assembling for action." He further declared that "the word *music* and its derivatives are not understood to refer exclusively to sound. Each member of the orch. is provided with a notebook (or a scratchbook) in which he notates a number of accompaniments performable continuously for indefinite periods. . . . Scratch Music can be entitled Scratch Overture, Scratch Interlude, or Scratch Finale, depending on its position in the concert." He pursued a strictly revolutionary Communist outlook, to the point of self-excoriation as an unregenerate bourgeois mind, an attitude projected onto the entire Orch. during a "Discontent Meeting," when members were urged to develop along true

Marxist dialectical lines. The highlight of the Scratch Orch. history was the 1972 performance of his *The Great Learning* (after Confucius, in Pound's trans.); later repudiated the work, saying that "a revolution is not a dinner party, but an insurrection, an act of violence by which one class overthrows another."

Scriabin, Alexander (Nikolaievich), b. Moscow, Jan. 6, 1872; d. there, Apr. 27, 1915. His mother, Lyubov Petrovna (née Shchetinina), was a talented pianist who had studied with Leschetizky, but she died of tuberculosis during his infancy; his father remarried and spent the rest of his life abroad as a diplomat. Alexander was reared by an aunt, who instructed him in music, including piano; at 11 began piano lessons with G. Conus; at 16 became a pupil of Zverev; began theory studies with Taneyev (1885). Entering the Moscow Cons. (1888), he continued his studies with Taneyev; took piano lessons with Safonov; practiced assiduously, but never became a virtuoso pianist; performed mostly his own works at his recitals.

Graduating with a gold medal from Safonov's class, Scriabin remained at the Moscow Cons. to study fugue with Arensky; failed to pass the required test; never received a diploma for composition. Leaving the Cons., he launched a career as a concert pianist (1892); by then he had already written several Chopinesque piano pieces; the publisher Jurgenson brought out his opp. 1, 2, 3, 5, and 7 (1893). In 1894 Belaieff became his publisher and champion; financed his 1st European tour (1895). Scriabin gave a concert of his own music in Paris (1896); returning to Russia, he completed his 1st major work, a piano concerto; was soloist in its premiere in Odessa (1897); in that same year he married the pianist Vera Isakovich; they spent some time abroad, giving a joint recital in Paris in a program of his works (1898).

From 1898 to 1903 Scriabin taught piano at the Moscow Cons; his 1st orch'l work, *Reverie,* was premiered in Moscow by Safonov (1899), who also conducted the 1st performance of his 1st Sym. (1901); the 2nd Sym. was premiered by Liadov in St. Petersburg (1902). After the death of Belaieff (1904), Scriabin received an annual grant of 2,400 rubles from the wealthy Moscow merchant Morosov; went to Switzerland; began work on his 3rd Sym., *Le Poème divin,* premiered in Paris under the direction of A. Nikisch (1905). At this time Scriabin separated from Vera Isakovich; established a household with Tatiana Schloezer, sister of music critic Boris de Schloezer, who would become his close friend and biographer.

In 1906 Scriabin appeared as soloist with M. Altschuler and the Russian Sym. Society in N.Y.; gave recitals there and in other U.S. cities. Tatiana Schloezer joined him in N.Y. (1907), but friends warned that charges of moral turpitude might be brought against them, as Scriabin had not obtained a legal divorce from Isakovich; while there is no evidence that charges were being contemplated, they went to Paris. Altschuler continued to champion Scriabin's music; gave the world premiere of his great work *Le poème de l'extase* (1908); the 1st Russian performance followed in St. Petersburg (1909).

In 1908 Scriabin met Koussevitzky, who became one of his most ardent supporters, both as conductor and as publisher. He gave Scriabin a 5-year contract with his newly established Éditions Russes, with a generous guarantee of 5,000 rubles annually. In 1910 Koussevitzky engaged him as soloist on a tour in a chartered steamer down the Volga River, with stopovers and concerts all along the route; he wrote his most ambitious work,

Promethée, the *Poème du feu* (Sym. No. 5), with an important piano part, which the composer played at its premiere in Moscow (1911). The score includes a color keyboard (*clavier à lumière;* It., *luce*) to project changing colors according to the scale of the spectrum, which Scriabin conceptualized (at the time he was deeply immersed in notions about parallelism of all arts in their visual and auditory aspects); the construction of such a color organ was unfeasible at the time; the premiere was given without *luce.* A performance with colored lights thrown on a screen was attempted by Altschuler at Carnegie Hall in N.Y., but it was a total failure (1915); subsequent attempts have ranged from utter disasters to near approximations.

The unique collaboration between Scriabin and Koussevitzky ended soon after the production of *Promethée;* Scriabin regarded Koussevitzky as the chief apostle of his messianic epiphany, while Koussevitzky believed that it was due principally to his promotion that Scriabin reached the heights in musical celebrity; to this collision of egos was added a trivial disagreement about financial matters. Scriabin left Koussevitzky's publishing firm and signed a contract with Jurgenson, who guaranteed him 6,000 rubles annually (1912). In 1914 he went to London as soloist in his piano concerto and *Promethée* at a concert led by H. Wood, and gave a recital. His last public appearance was in a Petrograd recital (1915); upon returning to Moscow, an abscess developed in his lip, leading to blood poisoning; he died after a few days' illness.

In his day Scriabin was the Russian composer who separated himself from musical nationalism the most; created works of great originality derived from his inner tonal world. He was a genuine harmonic innovator; at first his music was redolent of strongly felt influences (Chopin, Liszt, and Wagner), especially the cumulative use of dominant-9th chords; by adorning these chords with unresolved suspensions, however, they became independent formations. He gradually evolved his own melodic and harmonic style, marked by extreme chromaticism; in *Désir* for piano (op. 57, 1908), the threshold of polytonality and atonality is reached; key signatures are subsequently dispensed with; chromatic alterations and compound appoggiaturas create a complex harmonic web in which all distinction between consonance and dissonance vanishes. Building chords by 4ths rather than by 3rds, he constructed his mystic chord of 6 notes (C–F♯–B♭–E–A–D), the harmonic foundation of *Promethée;* in his Piano Sonata No. 7 (1913) he introduced a chordal structure of 25 notes (D♭–F♭–G–A–C, repeated for 5 octaves), dubbed "a 5-story chord."

To Scriabin, such harmonic extensions were associated with theosophic doctrines; he aspired to a universal art in which sensory impressions would project all human senses– tactile, olfactory, gustatory, aural, and visual. The titles of most of his later works expressed his mystic strivings: *Le Poème divin; Le Poème de l'extase; Vers la flamme* for piano (op. 72, 1914). His 11 piano sonatas (1887–1913), including the *Messe blanche* (op. 64, 1911) and the *Messe noire* (op. 68, 1913) revealed similar constant yearning, with tempestuous melodic lines in rising and falling waves of richly compounded harmonies. Scriabin wrote many piano works in Chopinesque genres, including mazurkas, nocturnes, impromptus, études, and preludes; composed piano "poems"—character pieces with unstated lyrical associations—including *Poème tragique,* op. 34 (1903); *Poème satanique,* op. 36 (1903); *Poème-nocturne,* op. 61 (1911).

Scriabin was planning a *Mysterium* to accomplish a sensory synthesis; only the text of a preliminary poem (*L'Acte préalable*) was completed. He dreamed of having the *Mysterium* performed as a sacred action in the Himalayas; made plans to go to India; the outbreak of World War I put an end to such a project. His fragmentary sketches for *L'Acte préalable* were arranged by the Russian musician A. Nemtin, who supplemented this material with excerpts from Scriabin's 8th Piano Sonata, *Guirlandes,* and the Preludes, op. 74; the resulting artificial score was premiered in Moscow (1973) as *Universe;* a species of color keyboard was used at the performance, projecting colors according to Scriabin's musical spectrum.

Scriabin was the most poetic (not to say extravagant) composer in the use of expression marks; by communicating what he felt about the music at hand, he hoped to inspire the performer to experience, express, and thereby inspire similar feelings in the listener. Unlike Satie's satirical comments in his scores, his are absolutely serious; in his choice of French markings he allies himself with Chopin, impressionism, and beyond. Among his unique markings are the following:

Avec entraînement et ivresse. With impetuosity and inebriated abandon (*Le Poème divin*).

Avec une ardeur profonde et voilée. With a profound yet veiled ardor (10th Piano Sonata).

Avec une douce ivresse. With tender inebriation (10th Piano Sonata).

Avec une douceur de plus en plus caressante et empoisonnée. With a tenderness ever more caressing and venomous (9th Piano Sonata).

Avec une joie éteinte. With an extinguished joy (*Promethée*).

Avec une passion naissante. With a nascent passion (*Poème-nocturne,* op. 61, 1911).

Brumeux. Misty; an indistinct, unspoken quality.

Comme des éclairs. Like lightning flashes (7th Piano Sonata).

Comme un cri. Like a cry (Preludes).

Comme un murmure confus. Like an indistinct murmur (*Poème-nocturne*).

Comme une ombre mouvante. Like a moving shadow (*Poème-nocturne*).

Con una ebbrezza fantastica (It.). With a fantastic sense of inebriation (5th Piano Sonata).

Dans un vertige. Vertiginously; in a state of dizziness (*Promethée*).

Désordonnée. Disordered (*Flambes sombres,* op. 73, no. 2, 1914).

Ecroulement formidable. Terrible catastrophe (*Le Poème divin*).

Effondrement subit. A sudden collapse (6th Piano Sonata).

Épanouissement des forces mystérieuses. Flowering of mysterious forces.

Épouvante surgit, L'elle se mêle à la danse délirante. Terror rises and joins in the delirious dance.

Flot lumineux. Luminous stream (*Promethée*).

Haletant. Out of breath (10th Piano Sonata).

Rêve prend forme, Le. The dream takes shape (6th Piano Sonata).

Riso ironico (It.). Ironic laughter (*Poème satanique*).

Tout devient charme et douceur. All becomes enchantment and fragrance.

Scriabin's 3 children with Tatiana Schloezer were legitimized at his death. His exceptionally gifted son Julian drowned at age 11 in the Dnieper River at Kiev (1919); his piano preludes, imitating the last works of his father, were publ. in a Scriabin memorial vol. (Moscow, 1940). Their daughter Marina Scriabin (b. Moscow, Jan. 30, 1911) was a aesthetician, scholar, and composer; settled in Paris (1927). She studied music theory with R. Leibowitz; joined the Radiodiffusion Française and worked in electronic techniques (1950); composed a *Suite radiophonique* (1951); a ballet, *Bayalett* (1952); chamber music. She publ. *Problèmes de la musique moderne* (collaboration with Boris de Schloezer; Paris, 1959); *Le Langage musical* (Paris, 1963); *Le Miroir du temps* (Paris, 1973); has written biographically about her father.

Scribe, (Augustin) Eugène, b. Paris, Dec. 24, 1791; d. there, Feb. 20, 1861. He was a scholarship student at the Collège Ste.-Barbe in Paris; after training in the law he turned to the theater; was made a member of the Académie Française (1836). He was closely associated as a librettist with Meyerbeer, but also wrote librettos for Auber, Bellini, Donizetti, Gounod, Halévy, Offenbach, Verdi, and others. His complete writings cover 76 vols.

Scruggs, Earl (Eugene), b. Flint Hill, N.C., Jan. 6, 1924. He took up the banjo as a child and developed such a mastery of the instrument that he made a hit as a member of Bill Monroe's Blue Grass Boys; he then teamed up with Lester Flatt, the guitarist, and organized their own band, The Foggy Mountain Boys; quickly assumed a prominent place in country-music circles, with Scruggs's 3-finger banjo style artistically complemented by Flatt's accomplished guitar playing. After they dissolved their partnership (1969), Scruggs formed his own group, the Earl Scruggs Revue; with it he cultivated the country-rock genre. He starred in the movie *Banjo Man* in 1975. The Flatt-Scruggs partnership resulted in such successful songs as *Roll in My Sweet Baby's Arms, Old Salty Dog Blues, The Ballad of Jed Clampett* (from the stereotype-ridden television comedy series *The Beverly Hillbillies*), and *Foggy Mountain Breakdown* (the theme song of the film *Bonnie and Clyde*). He publ. the book *Earl Scruggs and the 5-String Banjo* (N.Y., 1968).

Sculthorpe, Peter (Joshua), b. Launceston, Tasmania, Apr. 29, 1929. He studied at the Univ. of Melbourne Conservatorium of Music (B.Mus., 1951); then took courses from E. Wellesz and E. Rubbra at Wadham College, Oxford (1958–60); returning to Australia, he became a lecturer in music at the Univ. of Sydney in 1963; was made a reader there in 1969. He also was composer-in-residence at Yale Univ. while on a Harkness Fellowship (1965–67) and a visiting prof. of music at the Univ. of Sussex (1971–72). In 1977 he was made an Officer of the Order of the British Empire. In 1980 he received the honorary degree of Doctor of Letters from the Univ. of Tasmania; later received an honorary D.Litt. degree from the Univ. of Sussex and an honorary D.Mus. degree from the Univ. of Melbourne (both 1989).

In his music Sculthorpe rejects European techniques such as serialism in favor of a typically Australian approach to music. He has looked to Asia, in particular Japan, Indonesia, and Tibet, for both literary and musical inspiration. As a result, his music is often a battleground for European expressionism and indigenous spiritual rituality. He has also been influenced by the physical environment of Australia, as in *Sun Music* I–IV for Orch. (1965–67), and in his utilization of birdcalls and insect sounds; has written for all media.

sdegnoso (It.). Scornfully, wrathfully, angrily, disdainfully, indignantly.

sdrucciolando (It.). Sliding across the piano keys; glissando.

se (It.). If. *Se bisogna,* if necessary; *se piace,* if you please.

sea chanty. Shanty.

secco (It.; Fr. *sec*). Dry, staccato; simple, not dwelt upon. *Recitativo secco,* half-spoken, one with a simple figured-bass accompaniment, usually on harpsichord.

sécheresse, avec (Fr.). Dryly; without dwelling on or embellishing.

Sechter, Simon. See ⇒Schubert, Franz (Peter).

Sechzehntel (Ger.). Sixteenth notes.

second. 1. Interval between 2 conjunct degrees. 2. Alto part or voice. 3. Performing a part lower in pitch than the 1st, as 2nd bass, 2nd violins. 4. Lower in pitch, as 2nd string. 5. Higher; as 2nd line of staff.

second dessus (Fr.). Second soprano.

seconda prattica (It., second practice). Concept promulgated by Monteverdi in his *Scherzi musicali* (1607), also called *stile moderno;* as distinguished from prima prattica (*stile antico*), the older manner of contrapuntal music defended by Artusi. Seconda prattica is characterized by monodic settings, in which the emphasis is placed on the clear articulation of the text and simplicity of harmonic accompaniment. This principle is enunciated in the succinct axiom, "The words must be the master of music, and not its servant." In many ways, seconda prattica anticipates the reforms of Gluck and later composers.

seconda volta (It., second turn). second ending in a repeated section of a composition.

secondary chords. Subordinate chords.

secondary set. In set theory, a 12-tone set formed from the 2nd half of a set and the 1st half of a different form of the same set.

secondo, -a (It.). 1. Second. 2. second part or performer in a duet; in a piece for piano 4-hands, the bass part. *Secondo partito,* 2nd voice; *secondo rivolto,* 2nd inversion of a chord; for a triad, the $^6_4$ chord; for a dominant-7th chord, the $^6/_3$ or $^6/_3$ chord.

section. 1. Short division (1 or more periods) of a composition, having distinct rhythmic and harmonic boundaries. 2. In jazz big bands, the division into musically determined families:

the *melody* (clarinets, saxophones, trumpets, trombones) and *rhythm* sections (piano, guitar, double bass, percussion). Sometimes the last group is subdivided into *harmony* (piano and other keyboards, guitar, etc.) and *rhythm* sections (double bass, percussion).

secular music. Music other than that intended for worship and devotional purposes.

secundal and septimal harmonies. Distinct shift in harmonic structures occurred early in the 20th century as the tertian harmonies of triadic derivation gave way to the more acute progressions in secundal harmonies and their septimal inversions. Debussy wrote special studies in consecutive major 2nds, treating them as concords requiring no resolution; secundal harmonies are also represented in impressionistic works in the form of consecutive last inversions of 7th chords. Septimal harmonies are the familiar devices in early jazz cadences, in which the 7th was a blue note; composers of the later generation used tonic major 7ths as cadential chords. Secundal and septimal harmonies are commonly used in pandiatonic structures.

Seeger, Charles (Louis), b. Mexico City, Dec. 14, 1886; d. Bridgewater, Conn., Feb. 7, 1979. He was educated at Harvard Univ. (graduated, 1908); conducted at the Cologne Opera (1910–11); returned to the U.S. as chairman of the music dept. of the Univ. of Calif. at Berkeley (1912–19); gave the 1st classes in musicology in the U.S. (1916); taught at N.Y.'s Inst. of Musical Art (1921–33) and the New School for Social Research (1931–35); at the latter he gave the 1st classes (with Cowell) in ethnomusicology in the U.S. (1932); active in contemporary music circles as a composer and critic. He served as a technical adviser on music to the Resettlement Administration (1935–38), as deputy director of the Federal Music Project of the Works Progress Administration (1938–41), and as chief of the music division of the Pan-American Union (1941–53) in Washington, D.C.; visiting prof. at Yale Univ. (1949–50). He subsequently was a research musicologist at the Inst. of Ethnomusicology at the Univ. of Calif. in Los Angeles (1960–70); taught at Harvard Univ. (from 1972).

Seeger was a cofounder and chairman (1930–34) of the N.Y. Musicological Soc., which he helped reorganize as the American Musicological Soc. (1934); was its president (1945–46); president of the American Soc. for Comparative Musicology (1935) and the Soc. for Ethnomusicology (1960–61; honorary president from 1972). He was instrumental (with Cowell and Joseph Schafer) in the formation of the N.Y. Composers' Collective (1932); as he was profoundly interested in proletarian music throughout the 1930s, he wrote on the revolutionary spirit in music for such publications as the *Daily Worker;* contributed songs under the name Carl Sands to *The Workers Song Books* (1934, 1935).

Two of Seeger's essays are of historical interest: *On Proletarian Music (Modern Music,* XI/3, 1934), which lamented the dearth of folk songs in the work of professional musicians; and *Grassroots for American Composers (Modern Music,* XVI, 1938–40), which, by shedding earlier Marxist rhetoric, had wide influence on the folk movement of the 1950s. Many of his compositions were destroyed by fire at Berkeley (1926); his extraordinary contributions to American music rest

upon his scholary work, whose uniquely universalist vision for the unification of the field of musicology as a whole continues to challenge the various, sometimes contentious contributing factions: musicology, ethnomusicology, and comparative musicology.

Seeger was also a noted teacher; one of his most gifted students, Ruth (Porter) Crawford, became his 2nd wife. In addition to his son Pete(r) Seeger (from his 1st marriage), 2 of his younger children became musicians: Mike (Michael) Seeger (b. N.Y., Aug. 15, 1933) is a folksinger and instrumentalist; after learning to play folk instruments on his own, became active in promoting the cause of authentic folk music of the American Southeast; became widely known for his expertise on banjo; with John Cohen and Tom Paley, formed the New Lost City Ramblers (1958); founded the Strange Creek Singers (1968). Peggy (Margaret) Seeger (b. N.Y., June 17, 1935) is a folksinger, songwriter, and song collector; studied both classical and folk music; after studying at Radcliffe College, she became active as a performer; settled in England (1956); naturalized (1959); became a leading figure in the folk-music revival. She collaborated with and married composer, performer, and ethnomusicologist Ewan MacColl (1915–89).

Seeger, Pete(r), b. Patterson, N.Y., May 3, 1919. He is the son of Charles (Louis) Seeger. He studied sociology at Harvard Univ. before turning to folk music; taking up the banjo, became active as a traveling musician; with Lee Hays and Millard Lampell, he organized the Almanac Singers (1941); appeared before union and political audiences; joined the Weavers (1949), which became well known through a version of Leadbelly's *Goodnight Irene.* His political activism was targeted by the House Committee on Un-American Activities; cited him for contempt of Congress (1956); in spite of being blacklisted, he pursued his career and his commitment to various causes. A leading figure in the folksong revival of the late 1950s, he won notable success with *Where Have All the Flowers Gone?* and *If I Had a Hammer;* in all, he wrote over 100 songs, many of which became popular via his many tours through the U.S. and abroad. He wrote manuals for the 5-string banjo (1948) and the 12-string guitar (collaborated with J. Lester; 1965). J. Schwartz ed. a collection of his essays as *The Incompleat Folksinger* (1972). He has ed. several song collections, beginning with *The People's Songbook* (collaborated with W. Guthrie; N.Y., 1948).

Seeger, Ruth Crawford. See ⇒Crawford (Seeger), Ruth Porter.

seelenvoll (Ger.). Soulfully.

segno (It.). A sign. *Al segno,* to the sign; *dal segno* (*D.S.,* from the sign), directions to the performer to turn back and repeat from the place marked by the sign (𝄋) to the word *Fine,* or to a double-bar with fermata (⌒); *segno di silenzio,* silence; a pause.

Segovia, Andrés, b. Linares, near Jaén, Feb. 21, 1893; d. Madrid, June 2, 1987. He took up the guitar at an early age; his parents opposed his choice of instrument; made him take lessons in piano and cello, all to no avail; while taking courses at the Granada Inst. of Music, he sought out a guitar teacher; finding none, he taught himself the instrument; later studied briefly with

M. Llobet. He made his formal debut in Granada at age 16; then played in Madrid (1912), the Paris Cons. (1915), and Barcelona (1916); toured South America (1919). He made his formal Paris debut (1924) with a program including a work written especially for him by Roussel, entitled simply *Segovia*.

Segovia made his U.S. debut at N.Y.'s Town Hall (1928); subsequently toured all over the world, arousing admiration for his celebrated artistry wherever he went. He did much to reinstate the guitar as a concert instrument capable of a variety of expression; made many transcriptions for the guitar, including one of Bach's Chaconne from the Partita No. 2 for Violin; commissioned several composers to write works for him: Ponce, Turina, Castelnuovo-Tedesco, Moreno-Torroba, Villa-Lobos, and Tansman. He continued to give concerts at an advanced age; made appearances to celebrate the 75th anniversary of his professional debut (1984). He received many honors during his long career; a commemorative plaque was affixed to the house where he was born (1969), honoring him as the "hijo predilecto de la ciudad"; King Juan Carlos of Spain made him Marquis of Salobreia (1981); that same year the Segovia International Guitar Competition was founded in his honor; awarded the Gold Medal of the Royal Phil. Society of London (1985).

segue (It., follow). 1. Copyist's indication at a page bottom of a player's part that the player is to continue through to the next page, without stopping. *Segue l'aria*, the aria follows. 2. Simile.

seguendo (It.). Following. *Seguendo il canto*, col canto, colla voce.

seguidilla (Sp.). Spanish song and dance in triple meter, some types being leisurely, others lively. The genre is usually in a minor key, accompanied by guitar, voice, and at times castanets; the structure often alternates between guitar solos and ensemble. The famous *Seguidilla* in Bizet's *Carmen* is a stylization of the folk dance. See also ⇒marinera.

Sehnsucht (Ger.). Yearning, longing. *Sehnsüchtig*, longingly; in a yearning manner.

sehr (Ger.). Very, greatly, highly. *Sehr schnell*, very fast.

seis. Song and dance genre of the Dominican Republic and Puerto Rico, in alternating 6/8 and 3/4 time.

seises (Sp., six). Groups of 6 choirboys installed in Spanish churches in the 15th century. Spanish composers of the time wrote works especially for the seises.

seitenbewegung (Ger., side motion). Oblique motion in voice leading.

seitensatz (Ger., side section). 2nd section (key or theme group) in the exposition of sonata form, as contrasted with *Hauptsatz*, the 1st (main) section.

self-quotations. Composers are apt to amuse themselves by quoting appropriate passages from their own works. In the score of *Don Giovanni*, Mozart takes pleasure in quoting the admonition to Cherubino from *The Marriage of Figaro*, *Non più andrai*. Wagner quotes *Tristan und Isolde* in the score of *Die Meistersinger*. R. Strauss rather brazenly quoted themes from his previous tone poems in the score of *Das Heldenleben*, in which he himself is the hero unafraid of the petty assaults of critics.

Sellars, Peter, b. Pittsburgh, Sept. 27, 1957. His fascination with the stage began at age 10, when he began working with a puppet theater; attended Harvard Univ., where his bold theatrical experiments resulted in expulsion from student theater groups. He gained wide notice when he produced Gogol's *The Inspector General* for the American Repertory Theater in Cambridge, Mass. (1980); during the 1981–82 season he staged a highly controversial production of Handel's *Orlando*, in which the protagonist is depicted as an astronaut. He became director of the Boston Shakespeare Co. (1983) and the American National Theater Co. at the Kennedy Center in Washington, D.C. (1984). At the Houston Grand Opera, he produced J. Adams's opera *Nixon in China* (1987), which he then mounted in other U.S. cities and at the Holland Festival (1988); that same year he jolted the Glyndebourne Festival with a staging of Nigel Osborne's *Electrification of the Soviet Union*. He directed the 3 Mozart–Da Ponte operas for television; oversaw the Los Angeles Festival (1990).

semibiscroma (It.). Sixty-fourth note.

semibreve. Whole note; like other U.K. terms based on Latin mensural notation, it is relatively faster than the original.

semibrevis (Lat., half short). In mensural notation, a duration lasting half of a brevis or a quarter of a longa. The notation is a black rhombus.

semicroma (It.). Sixteenth note.

semidiapente (It.). Medieval term for the diminished 5th.

semiditonus (It.). Medieval term for the minor 3rd.

semiminima (Lat., half of the smallest). Duration of half a minima; in mensural notation it is written as a black rhombus with an upward stem and a flag, resembling the modern 8th note.

semiquaver (U.K). Sixteenth note.

semiseria (It.). Baroque and Classic opera seria with a happy ending; sometimes includes comic and parodic elements.

semitone (Lat. *semitonus*). Half tone or step, the smallest division in the equally tempered scale, roughly corresponding to the justly tuned interval 16/15. The major scale contains 2 semitones: between the 3rd and 4th steps and the 7th and 8th (tonic) steps. The chromatic scale of 1 octave contains 12 semitones. *Diatonic semitone*, one in which the 2 components are a minor 2nd apart, as B–C, F–G♭, A♯–B; *enharmonic semitone*, one in which the 2 components are an augmented unison apart, i.e., share pitch names, as E♭–E, D–D♯, A♭–A♮.

semplice (It.; Fr. *simplement*). In a simple, natural, unaffected style.

sempre (It.). Always, continually, throughout; used in expressions as *sempre crescendo, sempre forte, sempre in tempo,* *sempre legato, sempre piano, sempre staccato,* etc.

sensibile (It.). Audible; sensitive. *Con sensibilità,* with feeling; *nota sensibile,* leading tone.

sensible, note (Fr.). Leading tone.

sensory impact. Musical effect on a listener, often reaching the threshold of physical pain. Incessant playing of modern dance music, electronically amplified beyond the endurance of an average person, may well produce a positive conditioned reflex among the young. Professional music critics have for a century complained about the loudness of modern music, beginning with that of Wagner, but in their case the sensory impact is measured not so much by the overwhelming volume of sound as by the unfamiliarity of the idiom. Epithets such as "barbaric" were applied with a fine impartiality to the works of Wagner, Tchaikovsky, Berlioz, and Prokofiev, while Debussy, Strauss, and Mahler were often described as "cacophonous."

It is the relative modernity that makes the sensory impact intolerable to a music critic. "This elaborate work is as difficult for popular comprehension as the name of the composer," wrote the *Boston Evening Transcript* in its review of Tchaikovsky's 1st Piano Concerto. An index of vituperative, pejorative, and deprecatory words and phrases, the "Invecticon" appended to the author's *Lexicon of Musical Invective,* demonstrates the extraordinary consistency of the critical reaction to unfamiliar music. Even the gentle Chopin did not escape contumely; he was described in a daily London newspaper as a purveyor of "ranting hyperbole and excruciating cacophony."

sentence. Passage of symmetrical rhythmic form, generally not over 16 measures long, and usually ending with a full tonic cadence.

sentimentale (It.). Feelingly.

sentito (It.). With feeling, expression, special emphasis.

senza (It.; abbrev. *s.*). Without. *Senza abbandonare la corda,* without leaving the string; *senza affretare,* without getting faster; *senza allagare, senza di slentare,* without slowing down; *senza interruzione,* without interruption; *senza misura* (without measure), not in strict time, freely; *senza passione* (without passion), quietly; *senza piatti* (without cymbals), have 1 performer play cymbals and bass drum; *senza rallentare,* without slowing down; *senza rinforzare,* without getting louder; *senza ritardare,* without getting slower; *senza sordini,* see ⇒sordino; *senza stringere,* without getting faster; *senza suono* (without tone), spoken; *senza tempo,* same as *senza misura,* used by Liszt.

sept. Interval of a 7th.

sept chord (Ger. *Septakkord*). Seventh chord.

septet (Ger. *Septett;* Fr. *septuor;* It. *settimino*). Concerted composition for 7 voices or instruments; in the latter case, wind and string instruments are usually mixed in with a piano part (Beethoven, Stravinsky). Ravel's *Introduction and Allegro* has the unusual scoring of harp, flute, clarinet, and string quartet.

septième (Fr.; Ger. *Septime;* It. *settimo*). Interval of a 7th.

septimole (It.; Ger. *Septole;* Fr. *septolet*). Septuplet; a group of 7 equal notes to be performed in the time or 4 or 6 of the same kind in the established rhythm.

sequence (from Lat. *sequentia*). In Gregorian chant, a freely composed, wide-ranging chant category (also called prose) with syllabic texts, popular for about 3 centuries starting in *c.* 850 A.D. A couplet form was common, with 2 lines of text per melodic line, followed by a different couplet melody. Gradually the texts rhymed and scanned and grew increasingly strophic. For many centuries sequences were composed to the needs of the liturgical calendar and were incorporated into the Proprium. But the 16th-century Council of Trent eliminated all but 5 sequences from the chant books (*Victimae Paschali, Lauda Sion, Veni sancte spiritus, Stabat Mater, Dies irae*); many of the surviving texts were set by later composers.

sequencer. Electronic device that supplies a sequence of predetermined voltages in sound synthesis or processing; repetitious patterns akin to tape loops can be produced with the sequencer.

serenade (from It. *serenata,* evening song). 1. From the 16th century, a song traditionally performed by a lover before the beloved's window, habitually accompanied on the lute or guitar and delivered at day's end. Serenades are a favorite device in opera; a mock serenade is sung by Mephistopheles in *Faust.* Eventually any song or instrumental piece of amorous intent could be considered a serenade. See also aubade. 2. From the mid–18th century, a multimovement piece of instrumental entertainment music, practically synonymous with divertimento; usually scored for a small ensemble, designed for an open-air performance or festival occasion. Mozart wrote his *Haffner* Serenade for a wedding in the family of the Burgomaster of Salzburg. In the 19th century the title "Serenade" was sometimes attached to a multimovement instrumental work (e.g., Brahms).

serenata (It.; from Lat. *serenus,* serene). 1. Species of dramatic cantata in vogue during the 18th century. 2. Instrumental composition midway between a suite and a sym. but freer in form than either, having 5, 6, or more movements, in chamber music style. 3. See serenade.

sereno (It.). In a serene, tranquil style.

serialism. Method of composition in which thematic units are arranged in an ordered set. Tonal serialism was promulgated by Schoenberg in 1924, the culmination of a long period of experiments with atonal chromatic patterns. His method may be regarded as a subset of integral serialism, much as the special theory of relativity is a subset of general relativity; while Schoenberg's approach focuses on the notes of the chromatic scale; integral serialism also organizes intervals, rhythmic values, dynamics, etc. in autonomous sets.

Fritz Klein expanded the concept of dodecaphonic sets to different rhythmic and intervallic values; in *Die Maschine* (1921), he employs sets of 12 identical notes in irregular rhythms, "pyramid chords" comprising intervals arranged in a decreasing arithmetical progression of semitones, and a harmonic complex consisting of 12 different notes and 11 different intervals, the

Mutterakkord (mother chord). The mathematical term *set*, for a tone row, was introduced by Milton Babbitt (1946); he experimented with techniques of tonal, rhythmic, and intervallic sets. George Perle proposed the term *set complex* to designate the 48 forms generated by a fundamental dodecaphonic series. In all these sets the magic number 12 plays a preponderant role; in general, serial sets may contain any number of pitches in any scale, including nontempered intervals.

Serial parameters may comprise the following: (1) 12 different pitches in the dodecaphonic system; (2) organization of melody containing 11 different intervals; (3) 12 different rhythmic values that may contain a simple additive set of consecutive integers, a geometrical progression, a set of Fibonacci numbers, etc.; (4) 12 different *Klangfarben*, in which a melody consists of a succession of disparate notes played by 12 different instruments either in succession, in contrapuntal conjugation, or harmonic coagulation; a related form involves 12 different sound generators, including steamrollers, motor lawn mowers, steam pipes, radiators, ambulance sirens, etc.; (5) spatial serialism, in which 12 different instruments are placed in quaquaversal positions with no instruments in close proximity; (6) vectorial serialism, in which instruments are distributed at 12 different points of the compass or otherwise arranged spatially on the ceiling, on the floor, in the corners of the auditorium, etc.; (7) dynamic serialism, with 12 different dynamic values ranging from pianississississimo to fortississississimo, including the intermediate shadings of *mp* and *mf*; (8) ambulatory serialism, in which 12 musicians enter and exit one by one, in contrapuntal groups, in stretto, or in fugue (the latter understood in the literal sense of running); (9) expressionistic serialism, in which actors and singers assume definite facial expressions marking their psychological identity; (10) serialism of 12 visually different mobiles, each producing a distinctive noise. See also ⇒dodecaphony; rotation.

series. 1. Ordering of pitch classes or other elements as a precompositional stage. 2. See ⇒set.

serietà, con (It.). Seriously.

serio, -a (It.). Serious. *Opera seria,* grand or tragic opera; *tenore serio,* dramatic tenor.

serioso (It.). In a serious, grave, impressive style.

serious music. In publishing, a common if outdated designation of printed music by classical and modern composers, as distinguished from popular music and jazz.

Serkin, Peter (Adolf), b. N.Y., July 24, 1947. At age 11 he enrolled at the Curtis Inst. of Music in Philadelphia; studied with M. Horszowski, L. Luvisi, and his father Rudolf (graduated 1964); made his debut as a soloist under A. Schneider at the Marlboro (Vt.) Music Festival (1958); studied with flutist M. Moyse and piano from K. U. Schnabel. He made his N.Y. debut as a soloist with Schneider and his chamber orch. (1959); his N.Y. recital debut followed (1965). In 1973 he formed the group Tashi ("good fortune" in Tibetan) with clarinetist Richard Stoltzman, violinist Ida Kavafian, and cellist Fred Sherry; the group toured extensively, giving performances of contemporary

music in particular; after leaving the group (1980) he renewed his appearances as a soloist and recitalist. While he championed modern music, he acquired a distinguished reputation as an interpreter of both traditional and contemporary scores. He excels in works by Mozart, Beethoven, Schubert, Brahms, Stravinsky, Schoenberg, Messiaen, Takemitsu, P. Lieberson, and others. He also made appearances as a fortepianist. In 1983 he was awarded the Premio of the Accademia Musicale Chigiana in Siena.

Serkin, Rudolf, b. Eger, Mar. 28, 1903; d. Guilford, Vt., May 8, 1991. He is the father of Peter Serkin. He studied piano with R. Robert and composition with J. Marx and Schoenberg in Vienna; made his solo debut with O. Nedbal and the Vienna Sym. Orch. at age 12; his career began with a Berlin appearance with the Busch chamber orch. (1920); thereafter performed frequently in joint recitals with Adolf Busch, whose daughter he married (1935). He made his U.S. debut with Busch at the Coolidge Festival in Washington, D.C. (1933); made a critically acclaimed solo appearance with Toscanini and the N.Y. Phil. (1936).

After World War II Serkin pursued an international career; appeared as soloist with all major orchs. of the world; gave recitals in leading music centers, and played in numerous chamber music settings. In 1939, he was naturalized and appointed head of the piano dept. at the Curtis Inst. of Music in Philadelphia; was its director (1968-76). In 1950 he helped to establish the Marlboro (Vt.) Music Festival and school, and subsequently served as its artistic director. In 1985 he celebrated his 70th anniversary as a concert artist; received the Presidential Medal of Freedom (1963); awarded the National Medal of Arts (1988). The authority and faithfulness of his interpretations of the Viennese classics placed him among the masters of the 20th century.

serpent. 1. Bass cornet invented by Canon Edme Guillaume of Auxerre in 1590; constructed in the shape of a snake, consisting of several pieces of wood bound together by a leather covering; keys were added later. Despite the curse put on the serpent in Genesis, the instrument made regular appearances doubling ecclesiastical chant in church; in France, it bore the designation *serpent d'Église.* Despite its ungainly appearance and a considerable difficulty in handling, by the 18th century the serpent was providing the deep bass in military bands, supporting the bassoon; it was also known as the "Russian bassoon" because of its regular use in Russian military bands. It underwent another change of shape in the 18th century when a section of it was bent back so as to form 2 adjacent tubes. It was still found in bands in the 1st half of the 19th century, but Berlioz derided it as a laughable monstrosity in his orchestration treatise. This damnation was the serpent's last hiss; by the 20th century it was found only in a few village churches; it has played a small role in the early music revival. Other varieties of the serpent were the English bass horn and ophicleide; eventually these quaint instruments lapsed into innocuous desuetude. 2. In the organ, a reed stop.

serrando (It.). Speeding up.

serrant (*serré;* Fr., pressed, tightened). Playing faster and with more excitement.

servetta (It.). See ⇒soubrette.

service. Generic name to describe the totality of religious hymns, canticles, psalms, etc. In most Christian churches services are named after the time of day; e.g., in the Church of England (Anglican), the morning service contains canticles bearing the incipits in Latin, even though such services are sung in English (Te Deum, Benedictus, Jubilate). The evening service (evensong) usually includes the Magnificat and Nunc Dimittis.

sesquialtera (It.). 1. In the organ, either a mutation stop a 5th above the fundamental tone, or (usually) a compound stop of from 2 to 5 ranks. 2. (Lat.; Grk. *hemiole*) The ratio of 3/2, denoting a perfect 5th between the 2nd and 3rd partials. 3. In mensural notation, the diminution of a note value by one-third, i.e., 3 notes were played in the time normally allotted to 2 notes, resulting in triplets.

sesquipedalian   macropolysyllabification. Quaquaversal lucubration about pervicacious torosity and diverticular prosiliency in diatonic formication and chromatic papulation, engendering carotic carmination and decubital nyctalopia, causing borborygmic susurration, teratological urticulation, macroptic dysmimia, bregmatic obstipation, crassamental quisquiliousness, hircinous olophonia and unflexanimous luxation, often produce volmerine cacumination and mitotic ramuliferousness leading to operculate onagerosity and testaceous favillousness, as well as faucal obsonation, parallelepipedal psellismus, pigritudinous mysophia, cimicidal conspurcation, mollitious deglutition and cephalotripsical stultitiousness, resulting despite Hesychastic omphaloskepsis, in epenetic opisthography, boustrophedonic malacology, lampadodromic evagination, chartulary cadastration, merognostic heautotimerousness, favaginous moliminosity, fatiscent operosity, temulencious libration and otological oscininity, aggravated by tardigrade inturgescence, nucamentacious oliguria, emunctory sternutation, veneficial pediculation, fremescent dyskinesia, hispidinous cynanthropy, torminal opitulation, crapulous vellication, hippuric rhinodynia, dyspneic nimiety and favillous erethism, and culminating in opisthographic inconcinnity, scotophiliac lipothymia, banausic rhinorrhea, dehiscent fasciculation, oncological vomiturition, nevoid paludality, exomphalic invultuation, mysophiliac excrementatiousness, flagitious dysphoria, lipogrammatic bradygraphy, orectic aprosexia, parataxic parorexia, lucubicidal notation, permutational paronomasia, rhonchial fremitus, specular subsaltation, crapulous crepitation, ithyphallic acervation, procephalic dyscrasia, volitional volitation, piscine dermatology, proleptic pistology, verrucous alopecia, hendecaphonic combinatoriality, microaerophilic pandiculation and quasi-hemidemisemibreviate illation.

Sessions, Roger (Huntington), b. Brooklyn, Dec. 28, 1896; d. Princeton, N.J., Mar. 16, 1985. He studied music at Harvard Univ. (B.A., 1915); took a composition course with Parker at the Yale School of Music (B.Mus., 1917); took private lessons with Ernest Bloch in Cleveland and N.Y.; his early works were strongly influenced by Bloch's rhapsodic style and rich harmonic idiom verging on polytonality. He taught music theory at Smith College (1917–21); appointed to the faculty of the Cleveland Inst. of Music, 1st as Bloch's assistant, then as dept.

head (1921–25). He lived in Europe (1926-33), supporting himself on 2 Guggenheim fellowships (1926, 1927), an American Academy in Rome fellowship (1928), and a Carnegie Foundation grant (1931); with Copland, presented the Copland-Sessions Concerts of contemporary music in N.Y. (1928–31), an important cultural event at the time.

Sessions subsequently taught at Boston Univ. (1933–35), New Jersey College for Women (1935–37), Princeton Univ. (1935–44), and the Univ. of Calif. at Berkeley (1944–53); returned to Princeton as Conant Professor of Music (1953) and co-director of the Columbia-Princeton Electronic Music Center in N.Y. (1959); taught at the Juilliard School of Music in N.Y. (1965–85); was Bloch Prof. at Berkeley (1966–67) and Norton Prof. at Harvard Univ. (1968–69). He received a special citation of the Pulitzer Award Committee (1974); awarded a 2nd Pulitzer Prize for his Concerto for Orch. (1982)

In his compositions Sessions evolved a remarkably compact polyphonic idiom, rich in unresolvable dissonances and textural density and yet permeated with true lyricism; in his later works adopted a sui generis method of serial composition. His music was decidedly in advance of his time; the difficulty of his idiom, for both performers and listeners, creates a paradoxical situation; while recognized as one of the most important composers of the century, performances of his works are exasperatingly infrequent.

set. Term adopted from mathematical set theory to denote a grouping of pitch classes or other musical elements; normally refers to a 12-note set containing all pitch classes within the equal tempered system but may also refer to elements indicating duration, time points, and/or dynamic levels; also called a series.

set piece. In music, a separate movement or readily identifiable portion of an opera, etc., formal in structure and cohesive in idiom (as a finale).

settima (It.). Interval of a 7th.

seul (*seulement;* Fr.). Alone; single, only one; solely, merely.

seventeenth. 1. Interval of 2 octaves plus a 3rd. 2. Same as tierce (organ stop).

seventh chord. Chord of the 7th, composed of a root with its 3rd, 5th, and 7th.

severo (It.). Strictly, with rigid observance of tempo and expression marks.

Sext. 1. Interval of a 6th. 2. One of the Little Hours of the Office of the Roman Catholic liturgy; originally, the 5th hour in the daily cycle; since the 1972 liturgical reform, the 3rd (after Lauds and Terce); in either case, associated with noontime. 3. Compound organ stop of 2 ranks (a 12th and a 17th) a 6th apart.

Sextakkord (Ger.). Sixth or $\frac{6}{4}$ chord.

Sexte (Ger.). Interval of a 6th.

sextet (It. *sestet, sestetto;* Ger. *Sextett;* Fr. *sextuor*). Concerted composition for 6 voices or instruments. Most works for string sextet call for pairs of violins, violas, and cellos (Boccherini, Brahms, Dvořák, Schoenberg); Beethoven wrote a mixed sextet and a wind sextet. The most famous vocal sextet is in Donizetti's *Lucia di Lammermoor.*

sextuplet (It. *sestole, sestolet;* Ger. *Sextole;* Fr. *sextolet*). Group of 6 equal notes to be performed in the time of 4 of the same kind in the established rhythm. In the *true* sextuplet the 1st, 3rd, and 5th notes are accented; the *false* sextuplet is simply a double triplet.

sfogato (It., exhaled). Sing lightly and in a relaxed manner. *Soprano sfogato,* a high soprano voice.

sfoggiando (It.). Brilliantly.

sforzando, sforzato (It., forced). Play with a sudden sharp accent, with special stress, or marked and sudden emphasis; written *sfz, sf;* Beethoven uses the expression mark *sfp,* sforzando followed by piano. *Sforzatissimo,* even more sforzando; marked *sffz.*

sfrenatamente (It.). Unbridled; impetuously.

sfuggevole (It.). Fleetingly.

sfumate, sfumato (It.). Very lightly, like a vanishing smoke ring. *Sfumatura,* a nuance.

shading. 1. In the interpretation of a composition, the combination and alternation of any or all the varying degrees of tone power between fortissimo and pianissimo, for obtaining artistic effect. 2. The placing of anything so near the top of an organ pipe as to affect the vibrating column of air within.

shake. Obsolete term for trill. *Shaked graces,* the shaked beat, backfall, cadent, and elevation, and the double relish (all obsolete).

shakuhachi. Japanese end-blown notched flute that came from China at the end of the 1st millennium A.D.; it has not survived in its home country. Made of lacquered bamboo. it has been associated with Japanese priests since the 16th century; its pieces are typically programmatic and contemplative in character.

shamisen (samisen). Japanese long-necked plucked lute, held upright in a seated position; it has 3 strings running over a slender neck, running from a reverse pegbox to an ivory or wood (now plastic) bridge. There are 3 standard tunings and variants, allowing the playing of as many open pitches as possible, depending on the function of the shamisen in the musical context; it is played with a large plectrum. The original form of this chordophone, the *jamisen,* came from China *c.* 1400.

shank. The crook in wind instruments; an extra length of tubing to be inserted in a trumpet, cornet, or horn. The practice of using shanks was essential in the 18th and early 19th centuries but was superseded by the invention of chromatic brass instruments (valve or piston).

Shankar, Ravi, b. Benares, Apr. 7, 1920. He was trained by his brother Uday (b. Udaipur, Rajasthan, Dec. 8, 1900; d. Calcutta, Sep. 29, 1977), a dancer and choreographer of international renown. Ravi toured with his brother's troupe as a musician and dancer; engaged in a serious study of the sitar; became a great virtuoso on it. As a consequence of the West's growing infatuation with Asian arts in the 1960s, he became popular; his concerts were greeted with reverential awe by youthful multitudes; this popularity increased a thousandfold when George Harrison of the Beatles went to him to receive Eastern musical wisdom, thereby placing him on a pedestal usually reserved for guitar pickers.

As a composer Shankar distinguished himself with several film scores, including the famous *Pather Panchali* trilogy, *Kabulliwallah, Anuradha,* and *Chappaqua* (1966, assisted by Glass). For the Tagore centenary he wrote a ballet, *Samanya Kshati,* based on Tagore's poem of the same name (New Delhi, 1961). He wrote 2 concertos for sitar and orch. (1970, 1976) and has collaborated with Y. Menuhin and with Glass (*Passages*). His efforts to introduce Indian music to the world have met with disapproval by those musicians who believe that the Indian tradition of apprenticeship and oral learning should not be disturbed; however, even they have followed in the footsteps of Shankar and Ali Akbar Khan.

Shannāi. See sānāyī.

shanty (*chantey, chanty;* from Fr. *chanter,* to sing). Characteristic song of the English working class in centuries past; commonly, the *sea shanty,* a sailor's work song designed to facilitate the difficult gang labor aboard ship.

Shapey, Ralph, b. Philadelphia, Mar. 12, 1921. He studied violin with E. Zeitlin and composition with Wolpe; served as assistant conductor of the Philadelphia National Youth Administration Sym. Orch. (1938–47); founded and directed the Contemporary Chamber Players of the Univ. of Chicago (1954); taught at the Univ. of Pa. (1963-64); appointed prof. of music at the Univ. of Chicago (1964); served as Distinguished Prof. of Music at the Copland School of Music at Queens College of the City Univ. of N.Y. (1985–86); resumed his duties at the Univ. of Chicago. Disappointed by repeated rejections of his works by performers and publishers, he announced that he would no longer submit his works for performance or publication (1969); however, a change of heart (1976) reversed the situation. In 1982 he became a MacArthur Fellow; elected a member of the American Academy and Inst. of Arts and Letters (1989). His music employs serialistic but uncongested procedures in acrid counterpoint while formally adhering to neoclassical paradigms.

sharmanka (Rus.; Pol. *katarinka*). Hurdy-gurdy, introduced into Russia from France in the early 19th century.

sharp (adjective). 1. (of tones or instruments) Too high in pitch. 2. (of intervals) Major or augmented. 3. (of keys) Having a sharp or sharps in the signature. 4. (of organ stops) Shrill. 5. (of digitals) The black keys, or any white key a semitone above another white key (i.e., F and C).

sharp (noun). The character ♯, raising the pitch of the note immediately following it by a semitone; the double sharp, ✗, raises the note by 2 semitones.

Sharp, Cecil (James), b. London, Nov. 22, 1859; d. there, June 23, 1924. He studied mathematics and music at Uppingham and Clare College, Cambridge; settled in Adelaide, Australia (1882) became associate to the Chief Justice of Southern Australia. In 1889 he resigned from the legal profession; became assistant organist of the Adelaide Cathedral and codirector of the Adelaide College of Music. In 1892 he returned to England; was music instructor of Ludgrove School (1893–1910) and principal of the Hampstead Cons. (1896–1905). He became deeply interested in English folk songs; publ. a *Book of British Songs for Home and School* (1902); made a systematic survey of English villages to collect authentic specimens of English traditional song; established the English Folk Dance Society (1911); directed the School of Folk Song and Dance at Stratford-upon-Avon.

During World War I Sharp was in the U.S., collecting folk music in the Appalachian Mountains, hoping to establish its English origins. Much of his pioneering work resulted from collaboration with Maud Karpeles (1885–1976), who met Sharp in 1909 and worked with him until his death (including the Appalachian trip). His writings include (all publ. in London): *English Folk-song: Some Conclusions* (1907); *Folk-singing in Schools* (1912); *Folk-dancing in Elementary and Secondary Schools* (1912); *The Dance: An Historical Survey of Dancing in Europe* (with A. Oppe; 1924); ed. more than 10 anthologies of folk songs. In 1930 the Cecil Sharp House opened in London as headquarters of the English Folk Dance Society, which merged with the Folk Song Society as the EFDSS (1932), which is still in operation.

Shaw, Artie (born Arthur Jacob Arshawsky), b. N.Y., May 23, 1910. He was brought up in New Haven, Conn.; became an alto saxophonist in Johnny Cavallaro's dance band at 15; took up the clarinet at 16; worked as music director and arranger for the Austin Wylie Orch. in Cleveland (to 1929); toured as a tenor saxophonist with Irving Aaronson's band; went with it to N.Y.; played in Harlem and found a mentor in Willie "the Lion" Smith. After a stint as a freelancer (1931–35), he formed a sophisticated band that stirred excitement with its rendition of his *Interlude in B-flat* in N.Y. (1936); organized a swing band (1937), winning enormous success with a recording of Porter's *Begin the Beguine* (1938).

In 1940 Shaw went to Hollywood, where he produced the hit *Frenesi;* toured again with his big band, from which he drew members of the Gramercy 5, with which he was active from 1940 until 1954. In the interim he led several big bands; won his greatest acclaim with *Little Jazz* (1945). Interest in the classical clarinet repertoire led him to appear as soloist with various orchs.; performed at N.Y.'s Carnegie Hall. In 1983 he came out of retirement to lead still another big band. He is a remarkable clarinetist, as is perhaps best attested to in his *Concerto for Clarinet* (1940). He publ. a quasi-autobiographical novel, *The Trouble with Cinderella: An Outline of Identity* (N.Y., 1952), and the novel *I Love You, I Hate You, Drop Dead!* (1965).

Shaw, George Bernard, b. Dublin, July 26, 1856; d. Ayot St. Lawrence, England, Nov. 2, 1950. Before winning fame as a playwright he was a music critic in London, writing for the *Star* under the name of "Corno di Bassetto" (1888–89) and for the *World* (1890–94). In 1899 he publ. *The Perfect Wagnerite,* a highly individual socialistic interpretation of the *Ring of the Nibelung.* His criticisms from the *World* were collected as *Music in London* (3 vols., 1932); from the *Star* as *London Music in 1888–89* (London and N.Y., 1937); selected criticisms were ed. by E. Bentley (N.Y., 1954). His play *Arms and the Man* was made into an operetta, *The Chocolate Soldier,* by Oscar Straus (1908); *Pygmalion* was adapted into a highly successful musical comedy under the title *My Fair Lady* by Lerner and Loewe (1956).

shawm (Fr. *chalemie;* Ger. *Schalmei;* It. *piffaro;* bass shawm: Fr. *bombarde;* Ger. *Pommern*). Early form of oboe; brought into Europe in the 12th century; remained popular until the 17th century, when the oboe superseded it. The shawm's shape was bassoon-like; it was made of a long piece of wood with a curved metal bell; from the 16th century there were open-reed and reed-capped types; in its heyday there were shawms of all sizes, ranging from bass to high soprano. When G. B. Shaw, in his music critic days, received a letter addressed to G. B. Shawm, he thought it a spelling error until someone explained that it was an obsolete wind instrument producing a forced nasal sound.

sheng (Chin.). Chinese free-reed mouth organ; the earliest known example of this instrument family (*c.* 1100 B.C.). The traditional shape is described as a phoenix, involving a mouthpiece, wind chest, and *c.* 17 bamboo pipes pointing upward; 4 of these are dummy pipes, providing symmetry. Each pipe has a small finger hole which must be closed in order to sound; like the harmonica, different pitches are created by inhaling and exhaling.

shepherd's bell. See ⇒Herdenglocke.

shepherd's horn. Generic name for an ancient lip-vibrated wind instrument, originally made of animal horn or tusk; used functionally to communicate, call animals, or to perform magical or religious rituals.

Shifrin, Seymour, b. N.Y., Feb. 28, 1926; d. Boston, Sept. 26, 1979. After studies at N.Y.'s High School of Music and Art, he received private instruction from Schuman (1942–45); continued training at Columbia Univ. (B.A., 1947), where he studied composition with Luening (M.A., 1949); pursued additional training with Milhaud in Paris on a Fulbright scholarship (1951–52). He held 2 Guggenheim fellowships (1956, 1960); taught at Columbia Univ. (1949–50), City College of the City Univ. of N.Y. (1950–51), the Univ. of Calif. at Berkeley (1952–66), and Brandeis Univ. (1966–79).

Shifrin wrote music of high chromatic consistency, with finely delineated contrapuntal lines often resulting in sharp dissonance. He wrote orch'l works; chamber music, including 5 string quartets (1949–72); *In eius memoriam* for Flute, Clarinet, Violin, Cello, and Piano (1967–68); *The Nick of Time* for Flute, Clarinet, Percussion, Piano Trio, and Double Bass (1978); piano music; vocal works, including *Cantata to Sophoclean Choruses* for Chorus and Orch. (1957–58; Boston, 1984); *Odes of Chang* for Chorus, Piano, and Percussion (1963); *Satires of Circumstance* for Mezzo-soprano, Flute, Clarinet, Violin, Cello, Double Bass, and Piano (1964; his best-known work); *Chronicles* for 3 Male Soloists, Chorus, and Orch. (1970; Boston, 1976).

shift. In playing the violin, etc., a change by the left hand from the 1st position; the 2nd position is called the *half-shift,* the 3rd the *whole shift*, and the 4th the *double shift;* when out of the 1st position, the player is *on the shift*, and *shifting up* or *down*, as the case may be.

shimmy. African-American fox-trot of the 1920s, emphasizing movement of the upper torso, in quick ragtime rhythm.

shō. Japanese free-reed mouth organ, with continuous sound production possible through both inhalation and exhalation; descended from the Chinese *sheng*.

shofar. Ancient Jewish ritual trumpet, made from a ram's horn; traditionally blown only at the beginning of the Jewish New Year and (formerly) at exorcisms.

Short, Bobby (Robert Waltrip), b. Danville, Ill., Sept. 15, 1926. He was self-taught in music; appeared in vaudeville as a child; went to N.Y.; worked as a highly successful nightclub entertainer; appeared in Los Angeles, London, and Paris with equal success. He ultimately garnered a reputation as the leading café singer-pianist of his time; he has kept a regular engagement at the Café Carlyle in N.Y. for many years.

short octave. Deficient lowest octave in early keyboard instruments; omitted the chromatic tones and used black keys to sound notes usually assigned to the white keys; only B-flat kept its proper position. The short octave had 5 white keys and 3 black keys; the white keys were tuned to E, F, G, A, and B; the black keys, to C, D, and B-flat. (Alternatively, C, F, G, A, and B for white keys, D, E, B-flat for black). The retention of the B-flat is connected to its appearance in hexachords and scales (and as *musica ficta*) from the Middle Ages on. The rationale for the omissions was that chromatics were seldom used in the lowest register in Baroque keyboard compositions; also, organists or harpsichordists could now play chords in widely spread positions because the stretch of the short octave was only 5 white keys. In his E-minor Toccata for harpsichord (BWV 914), Bach has a difficult interval of the 10th in the bass; but in the short octave it requires only a 1-octave stretch.

Shostakovich, Dmitri (Dmitrievich), b. St. Petersburg, Sept. 25, 1906; d. Moscow, Aug. 9, 1975. His mother was a professional pianist. He grew up during the most chaotic period of Russian revolutionary history, when famine and disease decimated his city's population; of frail physique, he suffered from malnutrition; Glazunov, director of the Petrograd Cons., appealed personally to the Commissar of Education, Lunacharsky, for an increased food ration to insure Dmitri's very survival.

At age 9 Shostakovich began piano lessons with his mother; entered the Petrograd Cons. (1919); studied piano with Nikolayev and composition with Steinberg (graduated in piano, 1923; composition, 1925). As a graduation piece he submitted his 1st Sym.; 1st performed by the Leningrad Phil. under Malko (1926), it became one of his most popular works. He pursued postgraduate work in composition (to 1930). His 2nd Sym., composed for the 10th anniversary of the Soviet Revolution (1927), bears the subtitle *Dedication to October* and ends with a rousing choral finale; it was less successful despite its revolutionary sentiment.

Shostakovich wrote an opera, *The Nose,* after Gogol's tale concerning the inexplicable disappearance of the nose from the face of a government functionary; he revealed a flair for musical satire with the score featuring a variety of modernistic devices and an interlude for percussion instruments only; the work was premiered (Leningrad, 1930) to considerable popular acclaim, but, attacked by officious theater critics as a product of "bourgeois decadence," was quickly withdrawn from the stage. In a similar satirical style was the ballet *The Golden Age* (1930), including a celebrated dissonant polka, satirizing the current disarmament conference in Geneva. The 3rd Sym., subtitled *May 1st* (Leningrad, 1930), had a choral finale saluting International Workers' Day; again, despite explicit revolutionary content, it did not win the approbation of Soviet spokesmen, who dismissed the work as but a formal gesture of proletarian solidarity.

Shostakovich's next work precipitated a major crisis in his career, as well as in Soviet music in general: an opera drawn from a short story by the 19th-century Russian writer Leskov, entitled *Lady Macbeth of the District of Mtzensk,* depicting adultery, murder, and suicide in a merchant home under the Czars. Premiered in Leningrad (1934), it was hailed by most Soviet musicians as a significant work comparable to the best Western modern operas; but the staging and music ran counter to growing Soviet puritanism; a symphonic interlude portraying a scene of adultery behind a bedroom curtain, complete with suggestive passages on the slide trombones, shocked Soviet officials present at the performance. After the Moscow production, *Pravda,* official organ of the Communist Party, publ. an unsigned—therefore even more authoritative—article accusing the composer of creating a "bedlam of noise"; the brutality of this assault dismayed Shostakovich; readily admitting faults in both content and treatment of the subject, he declared a solemn determination to write music according to the emerging formula of socialist realism.

Shostakovich's next stage work, *The Limpid Brook,* was a ballet portraying pastoral scenes on a Soviet collective farm; he tempered his dissonant idiom; the subject seemed eminently fitting for the Soviet theater; but it, too, was condemned in *Pravda,* this time for an insufficiently dignified treatment of Soviet life. After yet another rebuke for a theater work, he abandoned writing for the stage and returned to instrumental composition; but, as though pursued by vengeful fate, he once again suffered a painful reverse; his 4th Sym. (1935–36), in rehearsal by the Leningrad Phil., was withdrawn before the performance when representatives of musical officialdom and even the orch. musicians sharply criticized the piece. His rehabilitation finally came with the 5th Sym. (Leningrad, 1937), a work of rhapsodic grandeur, culminating in a powerful martial climax; it was hailed, almost by spontaneous consensus, as a model of true Soviet art: formally classical, harmonically lucid, and philosophically optimistic.

The height of Shostakovich's return to positive recognition was achieved in the 7th Sym.; he began composing it during the siege of Leningrad by the Nazis (1941); he served in the fire brigade during the air raids; flew from Leningrad to the wartime capital of Kuibishev, on the Volga; completed the score, which was premiered there (1942). Its symphonic development is realistic in the extreme, with the theme representing the Nazis, in mechanical march time, rising to monstrous loudness, only to be overcome and reduced to a pathetic drum dribble by a victorious Russian song (recalling Tchaikovsky's *Overture: 1812*). The work became an international symbol of the Russian struggle against the superior Nazi war machine; given the subtitle *Leningrad Sym.*, it was performed during the war by virtually every orch. in the Allied countries.

After the tremendous emotional appeal of the *Leningrad Sym.*, Shostakovich's next four syms. had a lesser impact (1943, 1945, 1953, 1957); the 12th Sym. (1960–61), dedicated to Lenin's memory, aroused a little more interest; but the 13th Sym. (*Babi Yar*, Leningrad, 1962) created a controversy which seemed to be Shostakovich's peculiar destiny; its 1st movement, for solo bass and male chorus, set a poem by the Soviet poet Evtushenko, expressing the horror of the massacre of Jews by the Nazis during their occupation of Kiev and containing a warning against residual anti-Semitism in Soviet Russia; the work met with unexpected criticism by Communist Party chairman Khrushchev, who criticized the exclusive attention to Jewish victims and the failure to mention Ukrainians and other nationals who were also slaughtered; the text was altered to meet these objections, but the 13th Sym. never gained wide acceptance. But his earlier works, once condemned as unacceptable to Soviet reality, gradually returned to the stage and the concert hall; the objectionable 4th and 13th syms. were publ. and recorded; the operas *The Nose* and *Lady Macbeth of the District of Mtzensk* (rev. and renamed *Katerina Izmailova*, after the heroine) had several successful revivals.

Shostakovich's remarkable, darkly poignant 14th Sym. (1969) followed: in 11 sections, scored for voices and orch., to words by García Lorca, Apollinaire, Rilke, and the Russian poet Küchelbecker. His 15th and last Sym. (Moscow, conducted by his son Maxim, 1972), demonstrated an undying spirit of innovation and sharp wit; the score is set in C major, but features a dodecaphonic passage and direct allusions to Rossini's overture to *Wilhelm Tell* and the *fate motive* from Wagner's *Die Walküre*. His limited adoption of dodecaphonic themes—a procedure he had once condemned as anti-musical—is psychologically and sociologically interesting; he experimented with these techniques in other works, his 1st explicit use of a 12-tone subject occurring in the 12th string quartet (1968). Equally illuminating is Shostakovich's use of a personal monogram, D–S–C–H (for D, Es, C, H in German notation, i.e., D, E-flat, C, B); other composers used this monogram in writing works in tribute to him.

Shostakovich's compositional style is marked by almost unfailing consistency, from his 1st works to his last (op. 147), each proclaiming a personal article of faith. His idiom is unmistakably 20th-century, freely using dissonant harmonies and intricate contrapuntal designs, but almost never abandoning inherent tonality (most of his works carry key signatures). His music is teleological, leading invariably to a tonal climax, often in triumphal triadic declaration; his metrical structures are governed by regular rhythmic pulse. He is equally eloquent in dramatic and lyric utterance; slow movements may be prolonged in relentless dynamic rise and fall; the cumulative kinetic power of rapid movements is overwhelming. The syms. give him great visibility in the concert hall; but the string quartets are more personal and more indicative of his compositional moods. Yet through all the peripeties of his career he never changed his basic musical language.

Shostakovich's continual worries about the unpredictable Stalin and his henchmen have made the composer a textbook study of survival under the worst of political circumstances; at one period of his life (from 1945 until 1953, when Stalin died)

he wrote works to hide away until the air cleared. He was one of the principal targets of the government's 1948 assault on "formalist" composers; as in the 1930s, he feared for his life. Ironically, in a special announcement issued after his death, the Soviet government summarized his work as a "remarkable example of fidelity to the traditions of musical classicism . . . reasserting and developing in his creative innovations the art of socialist realism, and in so doing, contributing to universal progressive musical culture." His honors, both domestic and foreign, were numerous; he visited the U.S. 3 times.

Among his non-symphonic works are: Chamber music: 15 string quartets, piano quintet, 2 piano trios, 2 violin concertos, 2 piano concertos, 2 cello concertos. Piano music: 24 Preludes for Piano (op. 34, 1932–33), 24 Preludes and Fugues for Piano (op. 87, 1950–51), 2 piano sonatas; socially realistic choral works; deeply moving song cycles.

shout. 1. African-American audience response involving footstamping, hand-clapping, singing drones, and interjecting shrill vocal commentary between phrases of gospel music. Such spontaneous performances could be "composed," as in Gershwin's *Porgy and Bess* (he had heard the shouting ritual in the So. Carolina Sea Islands). 2. Genre of stride piano piece, 1st composed in the 1920s; a famous example is James P. Johnson's *Carolina Shout* (1925).

shuffle. Syncopated dance with a dragging, sliding step, meant to appear somewhat random and confused.

Si (It.). 1. 7th solmization syllable. 2. (*si* not capitalized) You are to; one must. *Si bisogna da copa al segno*, repeat from the beginning to the sign; *si leva il sordino* (*sordini*), take off the mute (mutes); *si piace, si libet*, at pleasure; *si replica*, repeat; *si segue*, proceed; *si tace*, be silent; *si volta*, turn the page; *si ha s'immaginar la battuta di 6/8*, imagine the time to be 6/8.

Sibelius, Jean, (born Johan Julius Christian), b. Hämeenlinna, Dec. 8, 1865; d. Järvenpää, Sept. 20, 1957. He showed a natural affinity for music from childhood;. began piano studies at 9; took violin lessons with G. Levander; performed in amateur chamber music performances. In 1885 he enrolled at the Univ. of Helsingfors (Helsinki) to study law; abandoned it after 1 semester; entered the Helsingfors Cons.; studied violin with Vasiliev and Csillag; took composition with Wegelius.

In 1889 Sibelius's 2nd string quartet was performed publicly; the favorable impression left led to a government stipend for study in Berlin; took counterpoint and fugue with A. Becker; proceeded to Vienna for additional musical training; studied with R. Fuchs and K. Goldmark (1890–91). His destiny as a national Finnish composer was already determined; his works were inspired by native legends, with the great epic *Kalevala* as inspiration. His symphonic poem *Kullervo*, for soloists, chorus, and orch., was premiered in Helsingfors; this was followed by the symphonic poem *En Saga* (both 1892), in which he displayed a genius for variation forms, based on a cumulative growth of a basic theme adorned but never encumbered with effective contrapuntal embellishments.

Sibelius taught theory and composition at the Helsingfors Cons. (1892–1900); the Finnish Senate granted him an annual stipend of 3,000 marks (1897); conducted the premiere of his 1st Sym.

(1899); subsequently conducted the 1st performances of all his syms. except the 5th. In 1900 the Helsingfors Phil. gave the 1st performance of his celebrated patriotic work, *Finlandia;* its melody became identified with the Finnish aspiration for independence to the extent that the Czarist government forbade its performance during periods of political unrest. In 1901 he conducted his works at the annual festival of the Allgemeiner Deutscher Tonkünstlerverein at Heidelberg; settled in a country home at Järvenpää (1904), where he lived for the rest of his life, traveling rarely.

In 1913 Sibelius accepted a commission from American music patron Carl Stoeckel, to be performed at the 28th annual Festival at Norfolk, Conn.; he contributed a symphonic legend, *Aalotaret* (Nymphs of the Ocean; later rev. as *The Oceanides*); took his only voyage to America to conduct its premiere (1914). Returning to Finland just before the outbreak of World War I, he withdrew into seclusion but continued to work; made his last public appearance in Stockholm, conducting the premiere of his 7th Sym. (1924); wrote a few works thereafter, notably incidental music for Shakespeare's *The Tempest* and the symphonic poem *Tapiola;* practically ceased to compose after 1927.

Persistent rumors circulated that Sibelius had completed his 8th Sym., but nothing ever came forth; it was said that he burned his unfinished works. Willing to receive journalists and reporters, he avoided answering questions about his music; lived out his very long retirement absorbed in family interests; he was even a modest bon vivant—enjoying his cigars and beer, never losing mental alertness. Only once was his peaceful life gravely disrupted: the Russian army's invasion of Finland (1940); Sibelius sent an anguished appeal to America to save his country, which had the perverse fate of becoming allied with Nazi Germany; but after World War II he cordially received a delegation of Soviet composers who made a reverential pilgrimage to his retreat.

Honors were showered upon Sibelius; festivals of his music became annual events in Helsinki; the Helsinki Cons. was renamed the Sibelius Academy (1939); a Finnish postage stamp bearing his likeness was issued on his 80th birthday; special Festschriften—biographical, bibliographical, and photographic—were publ. Artistically, too, he attained a state of recognized greatness rarely vouchsafed to a living musician; many important contemporary composers acknowledged their debt of inspiration to him, Vaughan Williams among them.

Sibelius was the last representative of 19th-century nationalistic Romanticism. He stayed aloof from modern developments, but he read scores and listened to broadcast performances of works by Schoenberg, Prokofiev, Bartók, and Shostakovich. His music marked a culmination of the growth of national Finnish art; like his predecessors, he was schooled in the Germanic tradition of lyricism and dramatic thought, and his early works reflect this. But he gradually abandoned formal conventions, writing music that seemed inchoate and diffuse but followed a powerful line of development by variation and repetition; a parallel with Beethoven's late works has frequently been drawn. His thematic material is not modeled directly on Finnish folk song; instead it re-creates the melodic characteristics of that music. The prevailing mood is somber, even tragic, with a certain elemental sweep and grandeur.

Sibelius's instrumentation is highly individual, with long songful solo passages and protracted transitions that function as integral parts of the music. His genius found its most eloquent expression in syms. and symphonic poems, writing only a moderate amount of chamber music, much of it in his earlier years. His only opera, *The Maid in the Tower* (in Swedish, 1896), was never publ. He wrote some incidental music, some of which was made into orch'l suites; the celebrated *Valse triste* was written for *Kuolema* (1903), a play by his brother-in-law Arvid Järnefelt.

Among Sibelius's other works are 7 syms. (1899–1924); symphonic poems, including *4 Legends from the Kalevala* (including *The Swan of Tuonela,* 1895) and *Pohjohla's Daughter* (1906); nontheatrical orch'l music, including the *Karelia Oveture* and *Suite* (with the "Alla marcia," 1893); the oft-performed Violin Concerto in D Minor (1903); 6 *Humoresques* for Violin and Orch. (1917); chamber music, including 4 string quartets (1885–1909, the last known as *Voces intimae*); piano music (1893–1929); organ pieces; choral works; 95 songs (1891–1917).

sich Zeit lassen (Ger.). Play unhurriedly (Mahler, 4th Sym.).

siciliana, -o (It.; Fr. *sicilienne*). Pastoral dance in moderate tempo and 6/8 or 12/8 time, frequently in a minor key; similar to the barcarole. The characteristic rhythm is dotted 6/8; often orchestrated with flutes and oboes and included in the Baroque suite. Its origins are not clearly understood. *Alla siciliana,* arias in this style, with frequent use of the Neapolitan 6th chord.

side drum (U.K.). Snare drum.

sidemen. Members of a jazz or popular group accompanying a soloist.

Sierra, Roberto, b. Vega Baja, Oct. 9, 1953. He began musical training at the Puerto Rico Cons. of Music and the Univ. of Puerto Rico (graduated, 1976); pursued studies at London's Royal College of Music and the Univ. of London (1976–78), the Inst. of Sonology in Utrecht (1978), and with Ligeti at the Hamburg Hochschule für Musik (1979–82). He was assistant director (1983–85) and director (1985–86) of the cultural activities dept. at the Univ. of Puerto Rico; dean of studies (1986–87) and chancellor (from 1987) at the Puerto Rico Cons. of Music. In 1989 he became composer-in-residence of the Milwaukee Sym. Orch.

sight reading. Ability to read unfamiliar music with ease; in singing, synonymous with *solfège*. Before the system of notation was firmly established, sight reading required a great deal of musical intuition; choirboys were trained to sing mensural music by sight in churches and chapels; contemporaneous chronicles tell of a 14-year old chorister (Frater Georgius of Pisa) who could sing at sight the most intricate parts of polyphonic music. But a very different challenge arose in the 19th century, when to sight-read a difficult piece of piano music required a superior ability to coordinate melody, harmony, and rhythm.

Professional instrumentalists and vocalists are expected to read at sight as a matter of routine, but there are extraordinary musicians who can play complicated works with great precision and fluency at sight. Piano accompanists to singers and instrumentalists often have to play their parts and follow the soloist without rehearsal, so that playing *a prima vista* (It., at 1st glance) or *à livre ouvert* (Fr., from the open book) is a practical necessity in a profession when rehearsal time is at a premium. In popular (and other) vocal music instantaneous transposition is often required; audition accompanists must know the standard repertoire well enough to play in any key without rehearsal.

It is especially difficult to reduce a full orch'l score at sight on the piano; it involves instantaneous transposition of transposing instruments, coordinating string and wind groups at a glance, and finally the formulation, with computer-like agility, of a pianistically sound arrangement without loss of tempo and component contrapuntal rhythms. While this can be managed with a tonal orch'l score, whose harmonies are compatible between instrumental groups, an atonal or polytonal modern orch'l score's intricacies can make producing a piano reduction practically impossible.

signa externa (Lat.). In mensural notation, symbols indicating the number of beats in each unit; the opposite is *signa intrinseca*, with specified rhythmic values.

signal horn. Bugle.

signature, key. In modern notation, accidentals (sharps or flats) that predetermine the tonality (tonalities) to be used.

signature, time. In modern notation, fractional representation of the number and value of beats in a measure.

signature tune. Musical excerpts associated with a popular band, played at the beginning and/or at the end of a radio program or performance; also, a song or piece strongly identified with a performer or group.

signum intensionis (Lat., sign of intensity). Sharp sign. *Signum remissionis* (sign of lowering), flat sign; *signum restitutionis* (sign of restoration), natural sign.

Silbermann, Gottfried, b. Klein-Bobritzsch, Jan. 14, 1683; d. Dresden, Aug. 4, 1753. Apprenticed to a bookbinder, he ran away and joined his brother Andreas (see below) in Strasbourg as his helper (*c.* 1702); during Andreas's Parisian sojourn (1704–06) he ran the family business, after which they worked in partnership; after working on his own there and in other cities, Gottfried went to Freiberg (1711). His finest organ was built for the Katholische Hofkirche in Dresden (3 manuals, 44 stops), begun 1750 and completed by his pupil Zacharias Hildebrandt. He owes his fame, however, mainly to his pioneering manufacture of pianos; the hammer action in his instruments was practically identical with Cristofori's. He also invented the *cimbal d'amour,* a clavichord with strings of double length. He supplied 3 pianos to Frederick the Great for Potsdam; Bach played on them during his 1747 visit there, preferring them to the Silbermann pianos he examined in the 1730s. Gottfried's brother Andreas Silbermann (b. Klein-Bobritzsch, Saxony, May 16, 1678; d. Strasbourg, Mar. 16, 1734) worked with the organ builder Friedrich Ring in Alsace before going to Strasbourg (1702); went to Paris (1704–06); returned to Strasbourg to stay; built the Munster organ there (1713–16) and 33 others.

silence. Literally, the absence of sound; in the 20th century, introduced as a viable element of music. Poets often speak of the eloquent and the harmonious quality of silence. The longest silence explicitly written out is the 5-bar rest in the score of *The Sorcerer's Apprentice* by Dukas; Ligeti composed a work consisting of a quarter-note rest. The most ambitious silent composition is *4'33"* by Cage, scored for any combination of instruments, tacet, and subdivided into 3 movements during which no intentional sounds are produced; it was unheard for the 1st time at Woodstock, N.Y., with David Tudor sitting at the piano (1952).

silenzio (It.). Silence. *Lurgo silenzio,* a long pause.

Sills, Beverly "Bubbles;" (born Belle Miriam Silverman), b. N.Y., May 25, 1929. At age 3 she won a prize in a Brooklyn contest as the most beautiful baby of 1932; from this auspicious beginning she performed in television, radio, film, and commercials; began formal vocal studies with E. Liebling when she was 7; studied piano with P. Gallico; made her operatic debut as Frasquita in *Carmen* with the Philadelphia Civic Opera (1947); toured with several opera companies; sang with the San Francisco Opera (1953) and the N.Y. City Opera (1955); quickly established herself at the latter as one of its most valuable members.

Sills extended her repertoire to embrace modern American operas, including the title role of Moore's *The Ballad of Baby Doe;* sang in the American premiere of Nono's *Intolleranza 1960.* She sang at the Vienna State Opera and in Buenos Aires (1967), at La Scala in Milan (1969), and at Covent Garden in London and the Deutsche Oper in Berlin (1970). She made her 1st appearance with the Metropolitan Opera as Donna Anna in a concert version of *Don Giovanni* at the Lewisohn Stadium in N.Y. (1966); her formal debut with the Metropolitan waited until 1975, when she sang as Pamira in *Le Siège de Corinthe.* At the height of her career she received well-nigh universal praise, not only for her excellent voice and coloratura virtuosity, but for her intelligence and erudition, uncommon among divas.

Sills became general director of the N.Y. City Opera (1979–88); gave her farewell singing performance (1980); showed administrative talent; promoted American musicians and broadened the operatic repertoire; produced television shows dealing with opera and concert singing. Her personal life was a tragic counterpoint to her professional successes; 1 of her 2 children was born deaf, the other mentally handicapped; became national chairman of the Mothers' March on Birth Defects (1972). She was the subject of a cover story in *Time* (1971); awarded the U.S. Presidential Medal of Freedom (1980). Her most notable roles included Cleopatra in Handel's *Giulio Cesare,* Lucia, Elisabeth in *Roberto Devereux,* Anna Bolena, Elvira in *I puritani,* and Maria Stuarda.

silofono (It.). Xylophone. *Silorimba,* xylorimba.

similar motion. Motion of voices in the same direction (but not parallel), as distinguished from contrary motion.

simile (It.). Similarly; perform the following measures or passages in the same style as the preceding. *Simile mark,* ⫽ or ⫽, means that a measure or group of notes must be repeated.

Simon, Paul, b. Newark, N.J., Oct. 13, 1941. As a N.Y. teenager he got together with Art Garfunkel; as Tom and Jerry they recorded *Hey, Schoolgirl* (1957) and appeared on Dick Clark's *American Bandstand* TV show. Paul then studied English literature at Queens College at the City Univ. of N.Y.; was a promoter and songwriter for various N.Y. music publishers. After appearing in N.Y. clubs he rejoined with Garfunkel and—now as Simon and Garfunkel—released the album *Wednesday Morning 3 A.M.* (1964), which included *The Sounds of Silence*, rerecorded and issued as a hit single (1965); their 2nd album, *Sounds of Silence* (1966), secured their reputation. Among their later recordings were *Parsley Sage Rosemary Thyme* (1967), the soundtrack for *The Graduate* (1968, with *Mrs. Robinson*), *Bookends* (1968), and *Bridge over Troubled Water* (1970).

While Simon and Garfunkel were a hyphenated entity in the public's eye, differences in personality and goals eventually divided them. Garfunkel composed little but sang and arranged ballads; also acted in films; Simon was an introspective intellectual who wrote surprisingly good poetry; his solo albums included *Paul Simon* (1972), *There Goes Rhymin' Simon* (1973), *Still Crazy After All These Years* (1975), *1-Trick Pony* (from his own eponymous film, 1980), *Hearts and Bones* (1983), the controversial, Grammy Award–winning *Graceland* (1986), and *The Rhythm of the Saints* (1990). He was reunited with Garfunkel, resulting in a performance and live recording, *The Concert in Central Park* (1982). In 1997 he produced a Broadway musical, *The Capeman.*

Simone, Nina (born Eunice Kathleen Waymon), b. Tryon, N.C., Feb. 21, 1933. After completing her high school training, her hometown residents raised money to send her to the Juilliard School of Music in N.Y., where she studied piano and theory with C. Friedberg; continued her studies with V. Sokoloff at the Curtis Inst. of Music in Philadelphia. She began singing at an Atlantic City, N.J., nightclub (1954); devoted herself to popular music genres, appearing as a jazz, pop, and soul artist; composed instrumental music and over 50 songs.

simple. 1. Tones or intervals that are less than an octave, i.e., not compound. 2. Counterpoint, imitation, rhythm, and other elements that are neither complex, overly developed, or varied.

simplement (Fr., simply). Semplice.

simultaneity. Vertically synchronized sounding of multiple tones, as in a chord, but without reference to diatonic or harmonic function.

Sinatra, Frank (Francis Albert), b. Hoboken, N.J., Dec. 12, 1915; d. Los Angeles, May 14, 1998. He had no vocal training and did not read music; sang in a school glee club and on amateur radio shows; appeared on N.Y. radio shows. In 1939 he became a singer with Harry James; gained fame as a vocalist with Tommy Dorsey (1940–42). Inspired by the tone production of Dorsey's trombone playing, he evolved, by convex inhalation from a corner of his mouth, a sui generis "mal canto" in sotto voce delivery, employing a Caruso-like coup-de-glotte at climactic points; this mode of singing, combined with a slender physique, stirred the young females of the World War II era to fainting frenzy at his performances; his press agents quickly exploited the phenomenon, dubbing him "Swoonlight Sinatra." He eventually overcame his anesthetic appeal and became a successful baritone crooner.

In 1952 Sinatra revealed an unexpected talent as a dramatic film actor, eliciting praise from astonished cinema critics and an Academy Award for his appearance in *From Here to Eternity;* other successful films followed (*Guys and Dolls, The Manchurian Candidate, Man with the Golden Arm*); his singing career regained momentum as he toured around the globe and made numerous television appearances; his innumerable albums included collaborations with Ellington, Basie, A. C. Jobim, Nelson Riddle, and his daughter Nancy (*Something Stupid*); was a fixture on the nightclub circuit, with many highly successful appearances in the hotels and gambling casinos of Las Vegas to his credit; President Reagan presented him with the U.S. Presidential Medal of Freedom (1985).

sine tone (wave). The sound (and its visual correlate) of 1 pure frequency; the flute is the acoustic instrument closest to producing this kind of sound wave.

sinfonia (It.). 1. Sym., especially in the 18th century. 2. Within larger vocal works, an overture.

sinfonia concertante (It.). Symphonie concertante.

Sinfonie (Ger.). Symphony.

sinfonietta (It., little sym.). Small-scaled sym., sometimes for chamber orch.

Singakademie. Institution organized in Berlin (1791) to present concerts of vocal music; Mendelssohn conducted a revival of Bach's *St. Matthew Passion* there (1829) that greatly contributed to the renewed appreciation of Bach's music.

singbar (*singend;* Ger.). Singable; melodiously; cantabile. *Sehr singbar vorzutragen,* perform in a very singing style.

singhiozzando (It., catching breath). Sobbing; with extreme emotion.

singing. Repetitive emission of sound energy in a sequence of melodious tones; the most natural vocal action of humans, birds, and, metaphorically speaking, whales. When the Austrian tenor Leo Slezak was asked how early he began studying voice, he replied, "I vocalized the chromatic scale when I was 6 months of age." The organ that produces sound within a definite pitch range is the "voice box" or larynx; the impulse to sing (or to speak) is generated in the muscles of the diaphragm, which pushes air upward into the lungs, and from there into the larynx and the vocal cords, which are set in periodical vibrations.

The ability of a trained singer to produce sounds of tonal purity and definite pitch constitutes the art of singing. Since a singer has no instrument outside his or her own body to practice upon, voice training should demand nothing more than the control of the vocal cords and the propulsion of air from the lungs; but it is a task easier said than done (and even more difficult to maintain). The range of the singing voice is usually not more than 30 tones, but these are subject to an extraordinary versatility of inflections and dynamic nuances; a professional singer is able to project the voice with great subtlety in degrees of power ranging from the faintest pianissimo to a thundering fortissimo.

Because the Roman Catholic Church frowned on women opening their mouths in church or any other public arena, prepubescent boys and specially trained male singers performed the higher vocal parts. The barbarous practice of creating castrato singers kept adult male voices artificially high for a lifetime, permitting the singing of male soprano and alto roles in opera and church. Fortunately the practice began to disappear as women gained the right to act in public; by Mozart's day the castrato was a rarity; the practice continued in the Church until the mid–19th century; the last castrato died in the early 20th century.

During the so-called Golden Age of opera, the concept of proper singing was limited to Italian bel canto; even the gondoliers of Venice knew how to sing *O Sole Mio* with the inflections of a Caruso. Italians and non-Italians strove for perfection in opera companies throughout the world; but as late Romantic vocal writing put new demands of range and endurance on singers, the bel canto ideal fell by the wayside, revived only after the 2nd World War.

There are exceptional cases of men and women extending their voices by training; Cowell was able to sing practically the entire audible range; Henze and others wrote works for voice and orch. that demand such a fantastic vocal range. In works by avant-garde composers, singers are required to produce howling, shrieking, hissing, grunting, moaning, buzzing, gurgling, chuckling, and coughing. There are those who can sing while inhaling and exhaling (circular breathing), so that it becomes possible to sustain a note indefinitely (a technique borrowed from wind playing). Finally there are those who sing through the nose. A widely used special technique is Sprechstimme, which preserves the inflection upwards or downwards but does not require tonal singing.

With all the avant-garde demands on vocal production, the novelty of singing approaches to 20th-century nonclassical music seems mild by comparison. Jazz singing tends to maintain the ideals of bel canto, especially in scat singing, but it lacks the heavy vibrato now standard in operatic performance; the same is true of sentimental and soul balladry. On the other hand, blues singing has long capitalized on a husky, penetrating quality for expressive purposes; this was taken over in rhythm and blues, rock 'n' roll, rock, soul (as O. Redding, who sang both up-tempo and slow music successfully), and the evolution of popular music from the 1970s on, culminating in hip-hop and rap on the one hand, and metal, punk, and grunge on the other.

single reed. Thin piece of wood, cane, or other material that is attached securely to an aperture at one end of a single-reed woodwind instrument; it provides the necessary vibration to start the flow of air through the instrument, provided by the player through the resulting mouthpiece. The pitch heard is determined by the fingering used.

single relish. Ornament in English lute music of the 17th century, corresponding to a very fast mordent.

Singspiel (Ger.). A play, usually lighthearted, with interpolated musical numbers; similar to the Liederspiel. The German Singspiel developed and was particularly popular in the 18th century (Mozart wrote 2 of them and half of a 3rd). The Singspiel differs from a full-fledged opera in its use of spoken dialogue, as opposed to recitative; but this distinction became less pronounced once "purely" operatic works began admitting spoken dialogue. Many features of the Singspiel were adopted by German Romantic opera.

Singstimme (Ger.). Singing voice.

sinistra (It.). Left. *Mano sinistra* (*m. sinistra*), left hand; *colla sinistra*, with the left hand.

sino (It.). To, up to, as far as, until. *Sino* (or *sin'*) *al fine*, continue to the end.

Sissle, Noble (Lee), b. Indianapolis, July 10, 1889; d. Tampa, Dec. 17, 1975. He sang in Edward Thomas's Male Quartet (1908) and Hann's Jubilee Singers (1912); subsequently attended DePauw Univ. and Butler Univ. After conducting a hotel orch. in Indianapolis, he sang with Bob Young's band in Baltimore (1915), where he met Eubie Blake; the two worked with James Reese Europe's Soc. Orch. in N.Y. Following service as a drum major in the 369th Regimental Infantry Band in France during World War I, he returned to the U.S. and teamed up with Blake as a vaudeville duo (1919).

After success with their musicals *Shuffle Along* (1921) and *Chocolate Dandies* (1924), Sissle and Blake performed in Europe; Sissle remained in Europe to work with his band and as a solo performer (1927–33); returning to the U.S., he resumed his association with Blake to produce *Shuffle Along* (1933); was again active with his own bands; made regular appearances at Billy Rose's Diamond Horseshoe in N.Y. (1938–50); later operated his own nightclub, Noble's.

sistrum. Ancient Egyptian idiophone used in religious ritual, composed of a semicircular metal frame with crossbars overhung with tinkling rings.

Sitār. Classical South Asian stringed instrument with a bowl-shaped body and metal frets, plucked with a plectrum. It has 2 sets of strings; one is played on; the other is a group of sympathetic strings that vibrate freely with the plucked strings. Like the smaller sarōd, it uses bulbous gourds for resonance; it was once bowed (such use is rare now). Both instruments are played in a sitting position, but the sarōd is played like a Western lute or guitar, while the sitār is held nearly upright.

Sitkovetsky, Dmitry. See ⇒Davidovich, Bella.

Six, Les. Group of French composers, 1st called Les Nouveaux Jeunes, so dubbed by a French critic in imitation of the Russian critic who invented the "Mighty Five." They formed a loose concert-giving alliance in the years just after World War I; although dissimilar in musical personality and aesthetic, Auric, Durey, Honegger, Milhaud, Poulenc, and Tailleferre shared a typical postwar anti-Romantic attitude. Les 6 was further sustained, at least to casual observers, by connections to Satie and Jean Cocteau, who as apostles of the age of disenchantment preached the new values of urban culture, with modern America as a model. Most of Les 6 practiced a neoclassical strategy and had generally humble artistic goals, but Durey, an avowed Communist, was the 1st to reject this lack of "seriousness." The

5 remaining members contributed incidental music to Cocteau's play *Les Mariés de la Tour Eiffel* (1921), but soon faded from the scene as the individuals pursued their own destinies.

six–five chord. 1st inversion of the 7th chord ($^6_5$), especially the supertonic and dominant chords.

six–four chord. 2nd inversion of the triad ($^6_4$), especially the tonic chord.

sixteenth note. Half of the value of an 8th note.

sixth. Interval comprising 6 diatonic degrees (when the 1st degree is counted as 1).

sixth chord. 1st inversion of a triad (^{6} or $^6_3$).

sixty-fourth note. Half the value of a 32nd note.

skald. Ancient Scandinavian poet-musician; minstrel or bard.

Skalkottas, Nikos (Nikolaos), b. Chalkis, island of Euboea, Mar. 8, 1904; d. Athens, Sept. 19, 1949. He studied violin with his father, his uncle, and an unrelated violinist at the Athens Cons. (1914–20); went to Berlin; continued violin studies at the Hochschule für Musik (1921–23); took theory lessons with Jarnach (1925–27). The greatest influence on his creative life was Schoenberg, with whom he studied in Berlin (1927–31); in *Style and Idea*, Schoenberg refers to Skalkottas as one of his most gifted disciples. Skalkottas eagerly absorbed Schoenberg's dodecaphonic method of composition, but in his own music applied it in an individual manner, not trying to imitate Schoenberg's style; while there, he received some suggestions in free composition from Weill (1928–29).

Skalkottas returned to Athens and earned his living by playing violin in local orchs.; continued to compose diligently, until his early death from a strangulated hernia. The music written between 1928 and 1938 reflects Schoenberg's idiom; later works are tonally conceived; several are in clearly ethnic Greek modalities, set in the typical asymmetric meters of Balkan folk music. About 110 scores of various genres are kept in the Skalkottas Archives in Athens; many of his works were premiered only after his death.

skiffle. British popular music style of the 1950s, in which percussion included washboard (hence the onomatopoeic name); harmonica and kazoo were often part of the ensemble; the goal was a more acoustic, less electrified sound. Many of the performers were jazz musicians and future rock 'n' rollers; others became the leaders of the 1960s British Invasion, such as the Beatles.

skip. Melodic progression by an interval wider than a second; a disjunct progression.

Skizze (Ger.). Sketch.

skomorokhis (Rus.). Minstrels who provided entertainment for the Russian court and aristocracy up to the 18th century, cultivating versatile talents as singers, actors, and acrobats.

Skriabin, Alexander (Nikolaievich). Scriabin, Alexander (Nikolaievich).

slanciante (It., thrown off). Played with force and vehemence.

slancio, con (*con islancio;* It.). With dash, vehemence; impetuously. *Di slancio*, direct and hammerlike attack on a higher or lower tone, contrasted with the slide or "carry" of the portamento; also called *di posto*.

slap-bass. Manner of playing on the double bass by slapping the strings with the palm of the right hand for rhythmic effect; associated almost exclusively with jazz.

slargando (*slentando;* It.). Growing slower.

Slatkin, Leonard (Edward), b. Los Angeles, Sept. 1, 1944. His father was Felix Slatkin (b. St. Louis, Dec. 22, 1915; d. Los Angeles, Feb. 8, 1963), a violinist who played with the St. Louis Sym. Orch. (1931–37) and founded the Hollywood String Quartet (1947–61); also active as a conductor. Leonard received musical training in his youth, studying violin, viola, piano, and conducting; after attending Indiana Univ. (1962) and Los Angeles City College (1963) he worked with W. Susskind at the Aspen Music School (1964); studied conducting with J. Morel at the Juilliard School of Music in N.Y. (Mus.B., 1968). In 1968 he joined the St. Louis Sym. Orch. as assistant conductor to Susskind; successively named associate conductor (1971), associate principal conductor (1974), and principal guest conductor (1975); made his European debut in London, guest conducting the Royal Phil. (1974).

Slatkin was music adviser of the New Orleans Phil. (1977–80); music director of the Minnesota Orch. summer concerts (from 1979); became music director of the St. Louis Sym. Orch. (1979); took it on a major European tour (1985); also became music director of the Great Woods Performing Arts Center in Mansfield, Mass., summer home of the Pittsburgh Sym. Orch. (1990), and the Blossom Music Center, summer home of the Cleveland Orch. (1991). He guest conducted many major orchs. in North America and Europe; demonstrated particular affinity for works of the 19th and 20th centuries. In 1996 he was appointed music director of the National Sym. Orch. in Washington, D.C.

sleighbells. Small round bells traditionally attached to the harness of a horse drawing a sleigh; now a similarly constructed idiophone (horse and sleigh not required). Some modern scores use the sleighbells, including Varèse's *Ionisation* and Mahler's 4th Sym.

slendro. One of two gamelan scale types (the other is pelog). Slendro is the family of pentatonic scales used, some approximating the "black-key pentatonic," others quite different; in fact, the concept of a universal gamelan tuning standard is of little consequence, as long as an individual set of gamelan instruments are tuned properly.

slide. 1. Movable U-shaped tube that fits inside the stationary tubing of the trombone; by extending or shortening the composite tube, one lowers or raises the pitch. 2. In the organ, a slider.

3. 3 or 4 swiftly ascending or descending scale tones. 4. On a violin bow, the part of the nut which slides along the stick. 5. Obs. term for trill.

slide horn, trombone, or trumpet. Brass instrument that uses a slide instead of keys or valves; as opposed to the valve trombone used in bands, where the slide is replaced by valves.

sliphorn. Slang for trombone.

slit drum (Ger. *Schlitztrommel;* Fr. *tambour de bois*). Wooden tube of varying size used for centuries among the peoples of central Africa and Australia; it is neither a drum nor a gong. The earliest examples were huge hollowed-out tree trunks placed over pits and stamped on. Later, the trunk was hollowed out through a longitudinal slit, struck by beaters, and sometimes placed on a stand; it is similar to the *teponaztli* of South America. Instruments have gradually grown smaller, even portable; the number of slits has been increased to provide more pitches; commercial versions for children's use are commonplace. In some areas the slit drum has served as a method of communication; simple messages can be transmitted through rhythmic beats carrying the tidings of danger, joy, death, or war; some composers, among them Orff and Stockhausen, make use of it.

Slonimsky, Nicolas, (born Nikolai Leonidovich), b. St. Petersburg, Apr. 27, 1894; d. Los Angeles, Dec. 25, 1995. He received his 1st piano lesson (1900) from his illustrious maternal aunt, the pedagogue Isabelle Vengerova (1877–1956). He enrolled in the St. Petersburg Cons.; studied harmony and orchestration with Kalafati and M. Steinberg; tried unsuccessfully to engage in Russian journalism. After the Revolution he went south; was a rehearsal pianist at the Kiev Opera; took composition lessons with Glière (1919); went to Yalta (1920), earning a living as a piano accompanist to displaced Russian singers and an instructor at a dilapidated Yalta Cons.; proceeded to Turkey, Bulgaria, and Paris, where he became secretary and piano-pounder to Koussevitzky. He went to the U.S. (1923); became an opera coach at the Eastman School of Music in Rochester, N.Y.; studied composition with visiting prof. S. Palmgren, and conducting with A. Coates; again with Koussevitzky in Paris and Boston (1925); fired for insubordination (1927).

Slonimsky quickly learned to speak polysyllabic English; began writing music articles for the *Boston Evening Transcript* and the *Christian Science Monitor*; ran a monthly column of musical anecdotes of questionable authenticity in the *Étude*; taught theory at the Malkin Cons. in Boston and the Boston Cons.; conducted the Pierian Sodality at Harvard Univ. (1927–29) and the Apollo Chorus (1928–30). He organized the Chamber Orch. of Boston with the purpose of presenting modern works (1927); gave premieres of works by Ives, Varèse, Cowell, and others; was naturalized (1931). In 1931–32 he conducted special concerts of modern American, Cuban, and Mexican music in Paris, Berlin, and Budapest under the auspices of the Pan-American Assoc. of Composers, producing a ripple of excitement; repeated these programs with the Los Angeles Phil. (1932) and the Hollywood Bowl (1933), which created enough consternation to end his conducting career.

Slonimsky was a lecturer in Slavonic languages and literatures at Harvard Univ. (1945–47); traveled through Eastern Europe, the Balkans, and Israel under the auspices of the Office of Cultural Exchange at the U.S. State Dept. (1962–63), lecturing in native Russian, ersatz Polish, synthetic Serbo-Croatian, Russianized Bulgarian, Latinized Rumanian, archaic Greek, passable French, and tolerable German. Upon returning from his travels, he taught variegated musical subjects at the Univ. of Calif., Los Angeles (1964–67); was irretrievably retired, but he continued to agitate, giving long-winded lecture-recitals in institutions of dubious learning.

As a composer Slonimsky cultivated miniature forms, usually with a gimmick, e.g., *Studies in Black and White* for Piano (1928) in "mutually exclusive consonant counterpoint"; a song cycle, *Gravestones,* to texts from tombstones in an old cemetery in Hancock, N.H. (1945); and *Minitudes,* a collection of 50 quaquaversal piano pieces (1971–77). His only decent orch. work is *My Toy Balloon* (1942), a set of variations on a Brazilian song, which includes in the score 100 colored balloons to be exploded *fff* at the climax. He also conjured up a *Möbius Strip-Tease,* a perpetual vocal canon notated on a Möbius band to be revolved around the singer's head; it had its 1st and last performance at the Arriere-Garde Coffee Concert at UCLA, with the composer officiating at the piano non-obbligato (1965). He wrote the earliest singing commercials to authentic texts from *Saturday Evening Post* advertisements, among them *Make This a Day of Pepsodent, No More Shiny Nose,* and *Children Cry for Castoria* (1925).

Out of a chronic itch for novelty, Slonimsky coined the term "pandiatonicism" (1937), which gained entry into reputable reference works; at a higher scholarly level (albeit no less defiant of academic conventions) is the *Thesaurus of Scales and Melodic Patterns* (1947), an inventory of all conceivable and inconceivable tonal combinations. Blundering into the muddy field of musical lexicography, he publ. *Music Since 1900,* a chronology of musical events (N.Y., 1937; 5th ed., 1994); took over the editorship of *International Cyclopedia of Music and Musicians* (4th to 8th eds., 1946–58); edited the 5th to 8th eds. of *Baker's Biographical Dictionary of Musicians* (N.Y., 1958–91). Other writings include *Music of Latin America* (1945); *The Road to Music* (1947); *A Thing or Two About Music* (1948); *Lexicon of Musical Invective,* a random collection of pejorative reviews of musical masterpieces (1952); numerous articles; and a painstakingly researched paper, *Sex and the Music Librarian* (1988). He prepared an autobiography, naming it *Failed Wunderkind: Rueful Autopsy;* his publishers renamed it *Perfect Pitch* (N.Y., 1988). He translated Boris de Schloezer's Scriabin biography from the Russian (1987). R. Kostelanetz ed. a collection of his writings, *Nicolas Slonimsky: The 1st Hundred Years* (N.Y., 1994); R. Kassel ed. his *Baker's Dictionary of Music* from publ. and unpubl. writings (1997). His nephew, Sergei (Mikhailovich) Slonimsky (b. Leningrad, Aug. 12, 1932), is a greatly talented composer.

slow bounce. In jazz drumming, putting a drag stroke on every beat.

slur. Curved line under or over 2 or more notes, signifying the use of legato; in bowed string music, signifies a group to be played on 1 bow; in vocal music, a group of notes to be sung in

1 breath; the notes so sung are also called a slur. In piano writing, a slur can indicate the extension of a musical phrase, often suggesting a slight crescendo followed by a corresponding diminuendo. See also ⇒tie.

slurred melody. One in which 2 or more tones are sung to 1 syllable; melismatic melody; opposed to syllabic melody.

small octave. See ⇒ Intro., The Clefs.

smaniante (It.). In an impetuous, passionate style. *Smanioso*, frantically.

Smetana, Bedřich, b. Leitomischl, Mar. 2, 1824; d. Prague, May 12, 1884. His talent manifested itself very early; with misgivings, his father taught his son violin; he also had piano lessons with a local teacher; made his 1st public appearance at age 6. After the family moved to Jindřichův Hradec (1831), he studied with the organist F. Ikavec; continued academic studies in Jihlava and Německý Brod, then at the Classical Grammar School in Prague (1839); had piano lessons with J. Batka; led a string quartet for which he composed several works.

Smetana's lack of application to academics led his father to send him to the Plzeň gymnasium, but he soon devoted himself to giving concerts and composing. He met an old school there, Kateřina Kolářová, whom he followed to Prague (1843); was accepted as a theory pupil of her piano teacher, J. Proksch, at the Music Inst. To pay for his lessons B. Kittl, director of the Prague Cons., recommended him as music teacher to the family of Count Leopold Thun; worked earnestly in the count's service (1844–47); continued studying and composing.

Bent on making a name as a concert pianist, Smetana left the count's service; planned a tour of Bohemia; however, his only concert (Plzeň) proved a financial disaster; abandoned his tour and returned to Prague; eked out a meager existence. He wrote to Liszt, asking him to find a publisher for his op. 1, the *6 Characteristic Pieces* for Piano; Liszt was impressed, accepted Smetana's dedication, and found a publisher. In 1848 Smetana established a successful piano school; the following year he married Kolářová; became court pianist to the abdicated Emperor Ferdinand (1850). His reputation as a pianist grew, especially as a Chopin interpreter; his compositions made little impression.

The death of his children and the poor health of his wife (who had tuberculosis) affected Smetana deeply; he set out for Sweden (1856); gave successful piano recitals in Göteborg, where he remained; opened his own school and became active as a choral conductor. His wife joined him in (1857), but the cold climate exacerbated her condition; when her health declined, they decided to return to Prague, but she died en route, in Dresden (1859); stricken with grief, he returned to Göteborg.

Before his wife's death, Smetana had composed 2 symphonic poems, *Richard III* and *Valdštýnv tabor* (Wallenstein's Camp); now began work on a 3rd, *Hakan Jarl*. During his Swedish sojourn, Austria granted political autonomy to Bohemia (1860); its rising musicians and poets sought to establish an authentic Bohemian artistic voice. Agitation for the erection of a national theater in Prague arose; earlier attempts to write operas in a Bohemian vein, made by such composers as F. Škroup and J. Macourek, had proven undistinguished. Smetana believed that Prague was ready for him, returning in 1861; however, when the

Provisional Theater opened (1862), its administration proved sadly unimaginative; he contented himself with conducting the Hlahol Choral Soc., teaching, and writing criticism; his articles condemned the poor musical standards at the Provisional Theater. In 1862–63 he composed his 1st opera, *Braniboři v Čechách* (The Brandenburgers in Bohemia); conducted its successful premiere at the Provisional Theater (1866). His next opera, *Prodaná nevěsta* (The Bartered Bride), failed at its premiere there under his direction (1866); eventually accorded a niche in operatic repertory at home and abroad.

Smetana became conductor of the Provisional Theater (1866); set out to reform its administration and raise its musical standards. For the cornerstone laying of the National Theater (1868), he conducted the premiere of his tragic opera *Dalibor*, criticized as an attempt to Wagnerize Bohemian national opera. In 1871, when there was talk of crowning Emperor Franz Josef as King of Bohemia, he considered producing his opera *Libuše* for the festivities; however, no coronation took place and the work was withheld. Hoping for a popular success, he composed the comic opera *Dvěvdovy* (The 2 Widows), which accomplished that goal at its premiere under his direction (1874); his success, however, was short-lived, as he became deaf. He resigned as conductor of the Provisional Theater, and found his life marked by increasingly poor health, family problems, and financial hardship. But he continued to compose; between 1874 and 1879 he produced his 6 orch'l masterpieces collectively known as *Má vlast* (My Country): *Vyšehrad* (a rock over the river Vltava, near Prague, traditional seat of ancient Bohemian kings), *Vltava* (the same river, called the Moldau in German), *Šárka* (a wild valley, near Prague; depicts the tale of the warrior woman Šárka), *Z Českych luhů a hájů* (From Bohemia's Woods and Fields), *Tabor* (medieval southern Bohemian town, stronghold of the Hussites), and *Blaník* (mountain that provided refuge for the Hussites; both this and the previous piece are based on the chorale *Ye Who Are God's Warriors*).

Smetana's opera *Hubička* (The Kiss) was successfully premiered in Prague (1876), followed by *Tajemství* (The Secret, 1878). For the opening of the new National Theater in Prague, *Libuše* was finally given its premiere performance (1881); the ailing composer attended opening night and was accorded sustained applause. His last opera, *Čertova stěna* (The Devil's Wall), was a failure at its premiere in Prague (1882). By this time his health had been completely undermined by the ravages of syphilis, which had caused his deafness; his mind eventually gave way, and he was confined to an asylum. At his death the nation was plunged into a state of mourning; the funeral cortège passed the National Theater as he was carried to his final resting place in the Vyšehrad cemetery.

Smetana was the founder of the Czech national school of composition; it was through his efforts that Czech national opera came of age. Although the national element is predominant in much of his music, a highly personal style of expression is found in his String Quartet No. 1 in E Minor, subtitled *Z mého života* (From My Life, 1880), which he called a "remembrance of my life and the catastrophe of complete deafness," with aural reference to his tinnitus. In addition to the works discussed above, he composed the orch'l *Carnival in Prague* (1883); secular choral music; a 2nd string quartet (1882–83); piano trio (1855); numerous piano pieces.

sminuendo (It.). Diminuendo. *Sminuito,* more softly.

Smith, Bessie (Elizabeth), b. Chattanooga, Tenn., Apr. 15, 1894; d. Clarksville, Miss., Sept. 26, 1937. Born to a poor family, she joined Ma Rainey's Rabbit Foot Minstrels (blues pioneer Rainey was her teacher) in 1912; developed a style of singing that rapidly brought her fame. Her 1st record, *Down Hearted Blues,* sold 800,000 copies in 1923; made over 200 recordings; appeared in the film *St. Louis Blues* (1929); her later career was affected by the Depression and marred by alcoholism. Known as the "Empress of the Blues," she was a large, impressive woman who had a powerful voice to match; the excellence of her vocal equipment, along with natural expressive qualities and improvisatory abilities, made her the consummate blues singer of her time. Her death, from injuries sustained in an automobile accident near Coahana, Miss., has long been blamed on slow response by police and medical authorities because of her race.

Smith, Gregg, b. Chicago, Aug. 21, 1931. He studied composition with Foss, L. Stein, and R. Moreman and conducting with F. Zweig at the Univ. of Calif. at Los Angeles (M.A., 1956). In Los Angeles he founded the Gregg Smith Singers, a chamber choir (1955); toured and recorded extensively; from 1970 was active with it in N.Y. He taught at Ithaca College, State Univ. of N.Y. at Stony Brook, Peabody Cons. of Music in Baltimore, Barnard College, and Manhattan School of Music in N.Y. His repertoire extends from early music to contemporary American works; ed. the Gregg Smith Choral Series; composed 2 operas, choral works, songs, and pieces for chamber orch.

Smith, Kate (Kathryn Elizabeth), b. Greenville, Va., May 1, 1907; d. Raleigh, N.C., June 17, 1986. As a child she sang in church socials and for the troops in Army camps in the Washington, D.C., area during World War I. Although lacking music training, she landed a part in the musical *Honeymoon Lane* in Atlantic City, N.J., then on Broadway (1926); sang in the Broadway musicals *Hit the Deck* (1927) and *Flying High* (1930). She began broadcasting her own radio show (1931); opened her 1st broadcast with *When the Moon Comes over the Mountain,* which became her theme song; introduced Berlin's *God Bless America* (1938), which she immortalized through innumerable performances.

Thanks to her enormous popularity, Smith raised more money for U.S. War Bonds during World War II than any other artist. She starred in her own television show (1950–55; 1960); made guest appearances until 1975. President Reagan awarded her the U.S. Medal of Freedom in 1982. Smith's success over her career can be measured by 15,000 radio broadcasts, her introduction of over 1,000 songs, and her recording nearly 3,000 songs.

Smith, Willie "the Lion" (William Henry Joseph Bonaparte Bertholoff), b. Goshen, N.Y., Nov. 24, 1897; d. N.Y., Apr. 18, 1973. He attended Howard Univ. in Washington, D.C.; studied music privately with H. Steinke; after serving in the U.S. Army in World War I, he settled in Harlem, establishing himself as a great stride pianist; toured Europe (several times) and Africa (1949–50). His own compositions (*Fingerbuster, Echoes of Spring, Portrait of the Duke*) captured perfectly the atmosphere of Harlem jazz piano between the 2 World Wars; Ellington dedicated his *Portrait of a Lion* to him.

smorendo (smorzando; It.). Dying away; diminuendo, morendo.

smorfioso (It.). With affected expression, coquettishly.

Smyth, (Dame) Ethel (Mary), b. London, Apr. 22, 1858; d. Woking, Surrey, May 8, 1944. She became a pupil of Reinecke and Jadassohn at the Leipzig Cons. (1877); soon chose H. von Herzogenberg as principal teacher, following him to Berlin; her String Quintet was performed in Leipzig (1884); returned to London (1888); presented her orch. Serenade and an overture, Antony and Cleopatra (both 1890).

Smyth's prestige as composer rose considerably with the presentation of the Mass for solo voices, chorus, and orch. at the Albert Hall (1893). She then devoted her energies to the theater; her 1st opera, *Fantasio,* to her own German libretto (after de Musset), was produced in Weimar (1898), followed by *Der Wald* (Berlin, 1902; London, 1902; Metropolitan Opera in N.Y., 1903). Her next and most successful opera, *The Wreckers,* was composed originally to a French libretto, *Les Naufrageurs,* premiered in German, as *Strandrecht* (Leipzig, 1906); trans. into English by the composer and staged in London (1909); a rev. score was produced at Sadler's Wells, London (1939). She later wrote a comedy, *The Boatswain's Mate* (London, 1916); a 1-act "dance-dream," *Fête galante* (Birmingham, 1923); and *Entente cordiale* (Bristol, 1926).

Smyth's other works include a Concerto for Violin, Horn, and Orch. (London, 1927); *The Prison* for Soprano, Bass Chorus, and Orch. (London, 1931); 2 String Quartets (1884, 1902–12); chamber music; choral pieces. Her music never relinquished strong German characteristics, in idiom as well as treatment of dramatic situations; at the same time she believed in English national music and its potentialities. A militant leader for women's suffrage in England, she wrote *The March of the Women* (1911), the battle song of the WSPU; after suffrage was granted, her role in the movement was officially acknowledged; made a Dame Commander of the Order of the British Empire (1922). She publ. autobiographical books, humorous essays, and reminiscences: *A 3-Legged Tour in Greece* (1927); *A Final Burning of Boats* (1928); *Female Pipings in Eden* (1934); *Beecham and Pharaoh* (1935); *Inordinate (?) Affection* (1936).

snare drum (U.K., side drum; Ger. *Trommel;* Fr. *tambour;* It. *tamburo*). Smaller cylindrical drum of wood or metal, across the lower head of which are stretched several gut strings or strands of metal wire (snares), whose rattling against the head reinforces and alters the tone; the upper head is struck alternately or simultaneously with 2 drumsticks; most commonly used drum in symphonic bands and scores.

so rasch wie möglich (Ger.). As fast as possible.

soap opera. Radio (later television) serials of continuous episodes from the life of an American family or, more recently, the lives of good-looking, well-dressed, and melodramatic individuals in various states of singlehood or marriage, separation or divorce, pregnancy or abortion, drug addiction or criminality, sexual certainty or ambiguity, economic feast or famine, and physical illness or psychological disorder. The application of "opera" to nonmusical genres originated with Westerns ("horse opera"); "soap opera" reflects the sponsorship by soap manufacturers of serials in early years; at one time organ music accompanied every moment of menace with chromatic runs, diminished and augmented chords, and whole-tone scales; parodies often emphasize this element.

soave (It., suavely). Gently, sweetly, softly, flowingly.

socialist realism. The official Soviet aesthetic, espoused in 1932, addressing the artist's responsibility to emphasize a real world inclined toward a socialist future. The former U.S.S.R was the 1st modern state to regulate art, literature, drama, and music according to explicitly defined ideological principles. Since the structure of the Soviet government was based on the dictatorship of the proletariat, a Russian Association of Proletarian Musicians (RAPM) had earlier arrogated the right to determine the musical forms most suitable for proletarian consumption; it was disbanded by the Soviet government after its failure to effect the creative formulation of mass music became evident (1932). With the rise of national consciousness in the component republics of the U.S.S.R, Soviet authorities realized that proletarian internationalism was no longer sufficient to serve as an enduring ideology; surviving old Russian masters had to be treated as representatives of the Russian masses; their classical precursors were glorified as exponents of progressive ideals consonant with the new Soviet socialist reality; composers were urged to create an art national in form and socialist in content, an approach which became known as socialist realism.

Stylistically, socialist realism retains tonality and is broadly based on the folk modalities of Russian songs and traditional songs of the other republics. This aesthetic doctrine focuses on the development of operas and secular oratorios, in which revolutionary ideals can be expressed verbally as well as musically; the Aristotelian formula of catharsis underlies the librettos and scenarios of most Soviet operas and ballets. Patriotic subjects are particularly recommended; they lend themselves readily to the tripartite formula of happiness, sudden horror, and victory over adverse circumstances. The *Leningrad Sym.* of Shostakovich is a remarkable example of Aristotelian construction, particularly as it was written during the retreats of the Soviet armies before the Nazis, yet its finale predicts victory. The classical tradition of the tierce de Picardie suits the Soviet preference for major keys perfectly; A. Lunacharsky, 1st Commissar of Education of the U.S.S.R, compared major keys with the convictions of the Bolshevik party, while minor keys reflected the introvert pessimism of the Mensheviks.

The doctrine of socialist realism does not preclude lyrical expression or individual allusions; Shostakovich uses the monogram D-S-C-H, corresponding in German notation to D, E-flat, C, and B as the main subject of his 10th Sym. and in other works. However, many Soviet composers—even one as eminent as Miaskovsky—were accused by the apparatchiks of socialist realism of morbidity, anxiety, and solipsistic introspection. March time (4/4) is a natural medium for the optimistic attributes of socialist realism, reserved for the finale of a sym. or final chorus of an opera; in this respect socialist realism merely continues an old Russian musical tradition; even such melancholy composers as Tchaikovsky and Rachmaninoff excelled in triumphant march-time movements.

In authoritative Soviet declarations, socialist realism is opposed to formalism, defined as an artificial separation of form from content and the excessive cultivation of purely external technical devices, particularly atonality, polytonality, and dodecaphony. The statutes of the Union of Soviet Composers provide ideological guidance to composers, who were to attend

> to the victorious progressive foundations of reality, to the heroic and luminous beauty that distinguishes the spiritual world of Soviet man, which . . . demands an implacable opposition against antisocial modernistic movements, expressive of the decadence and corruption of contemporary bourgeois art, against genuflection and slavish obsequiousness before the culture of the bourgeoisie.

With the Soviet Union a not-too-distant memory, one may look to the People's Republic of China for a communist approach to the politics of musical culture. In Red China's relatively short history (founded 1949) there have been dramatic shifts of official policy: the infamous Cultural Revolution of the 1960s, which denounced Western and traditional Chinese music equally; attempts to assimilate Western classical music, notably the *Yellow River Concerto* for Piano and Orch. (orig. by X. Xinghai, 1940s), officially recomposed by a musical gang of four; adaptations of Peking opera with proletariat-friendly titles as *The Red Detachment of Women* and *Taking Tiger Mountain by Strategy*.

soffocato (suffocato; It.). Muffled, damped; choked.

soft pedal. Left pedal on the piano; it reduces and alters the sound by shifting the keyboard so that (a) only 2 of the 3 strings for each note (i.e., its set or course) in the middle piano register are struck by the hammers, and (b) only 1 of the 2 strings of each course in the bass register are struck. In the 19th century the soft pedal could shift in 2 stages, with corresponding results; Beethoven refers to this as *due corde* and *una corda*, with full release of pedal indicated as *tre corde*.

soggetto (It.). Subject or theme, in contrapuntal and fugal writing.

soggetto cavato (It., excavated subject). Subject derived from the letters, syllables, or vowels in a name or other source; B–A–C–H is a typical example. Only vowels have been "excavated" in the hymn *Ut queant laxis* to form the hexchordal syllables of Guido d'Arezzo (Ut, Re, Mi, Fa, Sol, La). Josquin des Prez wrote the *Missa Hercules Dux Ferrarie* for a eponymous patron; the vowels in the dedication (*e, u, e, u, e, a, i, e*) correspond to Re, Ut, Re, Ut, Re, Fa, Mi, and Re (D–C–D–C–D–F–E–D). Derived subjects have been used by modern composers applying equalizations to the complete alphabet. Castelnuovo-Tedesco devised birthday greeting cards in which the name of the recipient was derived by arranging several successive alphabets in English corresponding to the chromatic scale; this method generates melodic patterns at angular intervals.

sognando (It.). Dreamily.

Soh. Stands for Sol, in tonic sol-fa.

Sol. Fifth degree of the scale of Guido d'Arezzo, corresponding to the dominant of the diatonic scale.

solenne (It.). Solemnly, in a lofty style.

Soler (Ramos), Antonio (Francisco Javier José), b. Olot, Gerona (baptized), Dec. 3, 1729; d. El Escorial, near Madrid, Dec. 20, 1783. He entered the Montserrat monastery choir school (1736); his mentors were the maestro B. Esteve and organist B. Valls; appointed maestro de capella in Lérida (c. 1750). Ordained a subdeacon, he joined the Jeronymite monks in El Escorial (1752); took the habit and was professed (1753); became maestro de capella (1757); pursued studies with J. de Nebra and D. Scarlatti.

Soler was a prolific composer; among his vocal works are 9 Masses, 5 Requiems, 60 psalms, 13 Magnificats, 14 litanies, 28 Lamentations, and 5 motets; also 132 villancicos (1752–78); his instrumental music includes 120 keyboard sonatas; 6 quintets for string quartet and organ (1776); 6 concertos for 2 organs; liturgical organ pieces. His most important treatise was *Llave de la modulación, y antigüedades de la música en que se trata del fundamento necessario para saber modular. . . .* (Madrid, 1762); publ. 2 defenses of the treatise (1765, 1766); also *Combinación de Monedas y Cálculo manifiesto contra el Libro anónimo inititulado. . . .* (Barcelona, 1771).

Soler, (Atanasio Martín Ignacio) Vicente (Tadeo Francisco Pellegrin) Martin y. See ⇒Mozart, Wolfgang Amadeus.

sol-fa. 1. Tonic sol-fa. 2. Solmization, and the syllables sung in it.

solfège (Fr.; It. *solfeggio*). Vocal exercise either on 1 vowel, on the solmization syllables (sol-fa), or to words. The term has expanded to include pedagogy in ear training, vocalization, and a study of clefs, meters, and rhythms.

solito (It.). Accustomed, habitual. *Al solito,* as usual.

solmization. Method of teaching the scales and intervals by syllables; its invention is ascribed to Guido d'Arezzo. It was based on the hexachord, or 6-tone scale; the 1st 6 tones of the major scale (c, d, e, f, g, a) were named *Ut, Re, Mi, Fa, Sol, La.* The 7th syllable *Si,* for the leading tone, was added during the 17th century; about the same time, the name *Ut* for *C* was changed to *Do,* except in France.

solo (It., alone). Piece or passage for a single voice or instrument, or one in which 1 voice or instrument predominates; in orch'l scores, a passage where 1 instrument takes a leading part. In a 2-hand keyboard arrangement of a concerto, "solo" marks the entrances of the solo part(s). *Violino solo,* violin alone; 1st violin (accompanied).

solo pitch. Scordatura.

solo quartet. 1. Quartet of 4 solo voices (parts). 2. Piece or passage in 4 parts for 4 singers. 3. Nonconcerted piece for 4 instruments, 1 of which predominates.

Solovox. See ⇒Hammond, Laurens.

Solti, (Sir) George (György), b. Budapest, Oct. 21, 1912. He began studying the piano at age 6; made his debut in Budapest at 12; at 13 enrolled there at the Franz Liszt Academy of Music; studied piano with Dohnányi and, briefly, Bartók; took composition with Kodály. He graduated at 18; engaged by the Budapest Opera as a *répétiteur;* served as an assistant to Walter (1935) and Toscanini (1936–37) at the Salzburg Festivals.

In 1938 Solti made a brilliant conducting debut at the Budapest Opera with *Le nozze di Figaro;* but a wave of anti-Semitism provoked by the Hungarian military rulers forced him to leave Budapest; went to Switzerland (1939); was active mainly as a concert pianist; won the Concours International de Piano in Geneva (1942). Finally, he was engaged to conduct the orch. of the Swiss Radio (1944); American occupation authorities in Munich invited him to conduct *Fidelio* at the Bavarian State Opera (1946); was appointed its Generalmusikdirektor (1946–52); became Generalmusikdirektor in Frankfurt, serving as director of the Opera and conductor of the Museumgesellschaft Concerts (1952).

Solti made his U.S. debut with the San Francisco Opera, conducting *Elektra* (1953); later conducted the Chicago Sym. Orch., N.Y. Phil., and at the Metropolitan Opera in N.Y., with *Tannhäuser* (1960). He was engaged as music director of the Los Angeles Phil.; the appointment collapsed when the board of trustees refused to grant him full powers in musical and administrative policy; was music director of the Dallas Sym. Orch. (1960–61). He made his Covent Garden debut in London (1959); assumed the music directorship of the Royal Opera House there, retaining it with great distinction (1961–71). He became music director of the Chicago Sym. Orch. (1969–91); achieved renown as interpreter and orch. builder; the "Chicago sound" became a synonym for first-rank excellence.

Under Solti's direction the Chicago Sym. Orch. went to Europe for the 1st time (1971), eliciting glowing praise from critics and audiences; subsequently led it on acclaimed tours there; regularly took it to N.Y. for appearances at Carnegie Hall. Simultaneously, he held the posts of music adviser of the Paris Opéra (1971–73); music director of the Orch. de Paris (1972–75), with which he toured China (1974); principal conductor and artistic director of the London Phil. (1979–83), then became its conductor emeritus. During all these years he retained his Chicago Sym. Orch. post while continuing appearances as guest conductor with European orchs.

In 1983 Solti conducted the *Ring* cycle at Bayreuth, commemorating the 100th anniversary of Wagner's death. He retained his prestigious position with the Chicago Sym. Orch. until the close of the 100th anniversary season (1991); subsequently held the title of Laureate Conductor; assumed the artistic directorship at the Salzburg Festival (1992). He was made an honorary Commander of the Order of the British Empire (1968); honorary Knight Commander of the Order of the British Empire (1971); became a British subject and was knighted (1972).

Solti was generally acknowledged as a superlative interpreter of the symphonic and operatic repertoire, renowned for performances of Wagner, Verdi, Mahler, R. Strauss, and other Romantic masters; conducted notable performances of Bartók, Stravinsky, Schoenberg, and other 20th-century composers. He showed himself an enlightened disciplinarian and a master of orch. psychology, gaining and holding his players' confidence while demanding from them the utmost in professional performance. His recordings received innumerable awards; his international reputation was secured through his complete recording of Wagner's *Ring,* the 1st in stereo (1958–65).

sombre (Fr.). Dark, veiled, obscure.

sommesso, -a (It.). Subdued.

sommo, -a (It.). Utmost, highest, greatest, extreme. *Con sommo espressione,* with the most intense feeling.

son (Fr.). Sound; tone.

son (Sp., sound). Generic name of indigenous songs of Cuba and neighboring islands, reflecting the influence of African rhythms, usually set in a strongly accented 2/4 time. This *zapateado* dance type allows great freedom with contrapuntal embellishments; texts are in couplet form, extolling beauty; guitar accompaniments use rasgueado strumming.

son bouché (Fr., stopped note; Ger. *gestopft;* It. *chiuso*). Place the hand tightly inside the French horn bell so that the expected pitch sounds a semitone higher and the tone is altered; the symbol + is placed over such pitches; similar to cuivré.

son concomitant (Fr., attendant sound). Overtone.

son d'echo (Fr.). On the horn, an echolike sound.

son et lumière. Spectacle involving sound and light, originating in France *c.* 1950, thus usually known under the French name; the idea is credited to the grandson of the magician Houdini when he was curator of the chateau at Chambourg. A typical son-et-lumière spectacle relates to the history of the monument around which it is being enacted; whenever possible the producers try to reproduce realistic sounds, such as cannon fire from a piece of 18th-century artillery, the shouts of a crowd, etc.; a special score, often of electronic sounds, enhances the spectacle; because of the authenticity of the narrative and careful research, the spectacles also have educational value. Since 1960 such productions have been staged at the Tower of London, Schonbrünn Palace in Vienna, Persepolis in Iran, the Acropolis in Athens, Napoléon's tomb in Paris, and Independence Hall in Philadelphia.

son étouffé (Fr., stewed sound). On wind instruments, a stifled sound.

son harmonique (Fr.). Harmonic.

sonabile (It.). Sounding, resounding, sonorous, resonant.

sonagli (It.). Harness bell-rattle (Prokofiev, *Lieutenant Kijé*).

sonare (*suonare*; It.). Play; sound; opposed to *cantare.*

sonare a libro aperto (*sonare alla mente*; It., play from an open book or from the mind). Play at sight.

sonata (It., sounded piece). Instrumental work in multiple movements contrasted in theme, tempo, and mood; usually for 1 instrument with accompaniment or chamber ensemble; orig., any instrumental work (*c.*1600).

sonata a tre (It.). Trio sonata.

sonata da camera (It.). Chamber sonata, for 1 or more solo instruments and basso continuo; comprises several dance movements, like a Baroque suite, often with a prefatory movement. In the later Baroque the term incorporated the sonata da chiesa, becoming less specific in structure.

sonata da chiesa (It.). Church sonata, not always religious in intent, alternating slow-fast-slow-fast movements; distinct from the sonata da camera. A form favored by early Baroque composers, the sonata da chiesa gradually vanished as a separate genre in the 18th century.

sonata form. Structure or procedure usually found in 1st movements of Classic and Romantic syms., sonatas, and chamber works; used in other movements as well. Sonata form fuses binary and ternary forms; from binary form, division at around the piece's halfway point, including repeat signs; the 2nd half's beginning in the dominant or another nontonic key; and return to the tonic by movement's end; from ternary form, the tripartite ABA structure, reorganized and renamed the exposition, development, and recapitulation. While the exposition ends in a nontonic key, the recapitulation "repeats" the exposition but adjusts it harmonically so that it ends in the tonic. Sonata form is also known as "sonata allegro form" and "1st movement form."

sonata-concerto form. Combination of sonata form with ritornello procedure.

sonata-rondo form. Rondo-form movement in at least 7 sections, where the central episode (e.g., C in ABACABA) functions as a development section; while the initial B section emphasizes a key other than the tonic, its repetition is adjusted or transposed into the tonic.

sonatille (*sonatille galante;* Fr.). Brief instrumental piece for musette and bass.

sonatina (Fr. *sonatine;* Ger. *Sonatine*). Short sonata in 2 or 3 movements, the 1st in an abbreviated sonata form.

Sondheim, Stephen (Joshua), b. N.Y., Mar. 22, 1930. He composed a school musical at age 15; studied music at Williams College; wrote the book, lyrics, and music for 2 college shows; graduated magna cum laude (1950); attended Princeton Univ.; studied modernistic complexities with Babbitt, acquiring sophisticated compositional techniques.

Sondheim made his Broadway debut writing the lyrics for Bernstein's *West Side Story* (1957); his 1st success as a lyricist-composer came with *A Funny Thing Happened on the Way to the Forum* (1962; Tony Award). His next musical, *Anyone Can Whistle* (1964), proved an interesting failure; *Company* (1970) established him as a major innovative force on Broadway. *Follies* (1971), for which he wrote 22 pastiche songs, was named best musical by the N.Y. Drama Critics Circle; his next musical, *A Little Night Music* (1973, after Bergman's film *Smiles of a Summer Night*), with a nostalgic score entirely in triple meter, earned him his 2nd Tony; its leading song, *Send in the Clowns,* won a Grammy (1976). This score established his characteristic manner of treating musicals; it is almost operatic in conception, boldly introducing dissonant counterpoint *à la moderne.*

In 1976 Sondheim offered *Pacific Overtures,* a retelling of the Westernization of 19th-century Japan, composed in a stylized kabuki-like manner; wrote *Sunday in the Park with George* (Pulitzer Prize for drama, 1985), inspired by Seurat's painting entitled *Sunday Afternoon on the Island of La Grande Jatte.* In 1987 his musical *Into the Woods,* based on 5 Grimm fairy tales, proved a major success on Broadway; it was followed by the disturbing musical *Assassins* (off-Broadway, 1990) and the opera-like *Passion* (1994).

Soneria di campana (It.). Set of bells.

sonevole (It.). Sonorous, resounding.

song. Short poem with a musical setting characterized by simple periodic structure; there are *folk songs* (indigenous or traditional) and *art songs* (classical); the latter may be either in song form (ABA, ternary), strophic form (successive stanzas sung to the same music, with any change reserved for the final stanza), or progressively composed or through-composed (where the music changes to suit the text).

Singing is the most natural faculty of the human condition, which must have emerged at the dawn of civilization, even before articulate speech. A song may be limited to a single burst of pitched sound; it may be a succession of sounds, in monotone or in varying pitch levels. Rhythm is an integral part of a song even at the most primitive stage; this intrinsic union is expressed by the term *melorhythm.* The simplest melorhythm is illustrated by the series of sounds produced by a Native American slapping himself on the mouth in rhythmic succession; composers of the avant-garde who have discovered the fascination of the primitive are apt to cultivate elementary melorhythms as a relief from the complexity of modern art.

In a modern lexicographical sense, a song will be a relatively short composition, either spontaneously generated by an anonymous mass or consciously devised by a musically trained person. It often appears that the popularity of an individual song stands in an inverse ratio to the eminence of its composer; when the identity of the putative composer reaches zero, as in many popular songs, we then witness the "formation" of a spontaneous folk song. The wealth within such a song resides in its very brevity and limited tonal compass. The seminal melodies in Stravinsky's *The Rite of Spring* evoke (and occasionally quote) Russian folk melorhythms; most of the melodies are limited to 4 or 5 successive diatonic degrees, with similarly restricted rhythm; yet this score is a landmark of modern music, owing to the polytonal harmonization of this material.

Less experienced listeners often misuse "song" for any kind of musical composition, whether sym., piano piece, or opera; given the overwhelming presence of songs in popular mass media, this is understandable, but the error is worth correcting.

song-and-dance man. Colloquial term for a vaudeville performer who can sing and dance; several great Broadway stars began their careers in this lowly capacity.

song form. Musical structure, vocal or instrumental, with 3 sections and 2 themes; the 2nd (contrasting) theme occupies the 2nd section.

songspiel. Hybrid English-German designation for modern satirical opera, cabaret, or vaudeville show; emerged in Germany between the 2 World Wars. The English "song" had a narrowed meaning of "cabaret song" in German; Weill's *Aufstieg und Fall der Stadt Mahagonny* bears this designation; this is authentic, and not a misprint for *Singspiel.*

sonic exuviation. The effectiveness of a modernistic climax depends on an astute interplay of contrasts. One effective dynamic pattern is sonic exuviation: the shedding of instrumental sonority, return to a state of primordial nakedness, new dressing-up of musical materials, gradual building of another climax, and a cut-off of sonic matter, leaving a quiet and exposed sonority. Such a moment occurs at the end of the last movement of *3 Places in New England* by Ives, where a tremendously powerful heterogeneous complex of sound suddenly crumbles, and a residual gentle chord is heard in the quiet air.

sonic organization. Varèse defines music as "organized sound." Any musical composition, especially of the modern constructivist type, is a sonic organism that follows biomusical laws; is autogenetic, capable of natural replication induced by contrapuntal interpenetration of contrasting melorhythmic entities; sonic organization presupposes an engineering plan, taking into consideration an appropriate cross-pollination of musical themes.

sonnerie (Fr.). 1. Arrangement of bells in a tower; also, the signal played on those bells. 2. Trumpet or bugle signal for military or hunting purposes.

sonnette (Fr.). Formerly a pellet bell, often attached to clothing or birds' legs; now, a handbell.

sono (It.). Sound; tone.

sonology. In the late 20th century, study of sound as a structural unit in composition and the laws governing both the acoustical nature of sound and its artistic application to music in the theater and concert hall.

sonorism. In the 2nd half of the 20th century, analysis and application of sonority in the broadest sense, including noise.

sonority (from Lat. *sonus,* sound; Fr. *sonorité*). Resonance.

sonoro, -a (It.; Fr. *sonore*). Sonorously, resoundingly, resonantly, ringingly.

sonus (Lat.). The physical aspect of sound, however produced; opposed to *vox,* describing a particular tonal quality.

sopila (*sopella, sopelo;* Croat.; It. *tororo*). Indigenous shawm of Croatia, with a short wide double reed; usually played in pairs of different-sized instruments, in parallel 3rds or 6ths, occasionally heterophonically. In order to tighten the sopila's 3 joints, water is poured into the tube through the bell.

sopilka (*sopjelka*; Ukr.). End-flown flute with finger holes but no mouthpiece.

sopra (It.). On, upon; above, over; higher. In piano music, *sopra* written in the part for either hand means that the hand is to play (reach) *over* the other. *Sopra una corda,* on 1 string; *come sopra,* as above; *nella parte di sopra,* in the higher (highest) part.

sopranino (It., little soprano). Very high (or highest) member of a particular instrument family, e.g., sopranino saxophone, sopranino clarinet, and sopranino recorder (whose range resembles the piccolo's).

soprano (It.; from Lat. *superanus,* standing over; Ger. *Sopran*). 1. Highest class of the human voice; the treble voice. The normal compass of the soprano voice ranges from c¹ to a²; solo voices often reach above c³, some as high as c⁴. Some parts call for a boy soprano, meaning a natural voice of a prepubescent boy. *Coloratura soprano,* singer with an unusually high range and strong affinity with bel canto; *dramatic soprano, soprano drammatico, soprano giusto,* singer capable of dynamic, dramatic, and tragic qualities; a strong upper register is matched by evenness of power throughout the range; many Verdi roles call for such a singer; *lyric soprano,* singer distinguished by a poetic quality of phrasing in bel canto; many Puccini roles call such a singer; *soprano leggiero,* light soprano; *soprano sfogato,* high soprano. 2. High member of a particular instrument family, e.g., soprano saxophone, soprano recorder, soprano trumpet.

soprano clef. C clef on the 1st line.

soprano string. E string on the violin.

sordamente (It.). With a veiled, muffled tone.

sordina (It.; plur. *sordini*). 1. String instrument mute. *Con sordini,* with mutes; *senza sordini,* without mutes; *si levano i sordini,* take mutes off. 2. Damper (of the piano). *Senza sordini,* with damper pedal; used by Beethoven, who wrote *con sordini* to express the release (raising) of the damper pedal, instead of ✳.

sordino (It.). Trumpet mute, as opposed to *sordina.*

sortita (It.). 1. Closing voluntary. 2. 1st number sung by any leading character in an opera. *Aria di sortita,* number sung by a character prior to his or her exit.

sospirando (*sospiroso;* It.). Sighing, sobbing; catching the breath; plaintively, mournfully.

sostenuto (It.; Fr. *soutenu*). Sustained, prolonged, held. Standing alone as a tempo mark, it is the same as *andante cantabile;* may imply *a tenuto,* a uniform rate of decreased speed; *più sostenuto* is the same as *meno mosso.*

sostenuto pedal. Middle piano pedal, invented in the 1860s and now commonplace on grand pianos; it sustains (keeps lifted) dampers already raised by depressed keys, thus prolonging the tones of strings affected; the effect resembles a pedal point(s).

sotto (It., below, under). In piano music, direction for either hand to play (reach) under the other. *Sottovoce (sotto voce),* in an undertone, as an aside, under the breath; dramatic lowering of the normal vocal or instrumental tone; not necessarily *pp.*

sotto-dominante (It.). Subdominant.

soubrette (Fr., little kitten; from Prov. *soubret,* coy; It. *servetta*). In comic opera and operetta, a maidservant, lady's maid, or an ingenue of intriguing and coquettish character; also applied to similar light roles. Susanna in *Le nozze di Figaro* and Papagena in *The Magic Flute* are typical soubrette roles; the coloratura soubrette is exemplified by Rosina from *The Barber of Seville* and Zerbinetta in *Ariadne auf Naxos.* Curiously, the term is not used in French operatic circles, where, to honor a famous French soubrette, Louise Dugazon (1755–1821), the term *jeune Dugazon* is used.

soudain (Fr.). Suddenly.

souillante (It.). Resonantly.

soul. Style of African-American rhythm and blues, 1st associated with the South, from the 1960s on. There are 2 basic strains: upbeat, funky music associated with the Stax and Atlantic labels, whose studio bands (e.g., Booker T. and the MGs) established the model; and ballads, an outgrowth of the Motown sound, often accompanied by strings; these were popular from the 1970s on, once a prejudice against doo-wop balladry had subsided. In either case a passionate, often embellished singing style is typical.

sound. Generic name for all audible sensations, produced by sound waves ranging from about 16 to 25,000 cycles per second (cps). The lower the tone, the longer the sound waves generated. Dogs can hear ultrasonic pitches far higher than the human range, and bats still higher. A pure tone unencumbered by overtones, e.g., as produced by a tuning fork, generates a sinusoidal sound wave (*sine wave*), which can be schematically represented as a semicircle above a horizontal line followed by a similar semicircle below this line; 2 such adjacent semicircles form 1 cycle of the sine wave. The total number of cps is equivalent to the frequency of vibration (Hertz, or Hz) of the sound waves.

Pitch is measured in cps or Hz; the higher the pitch, the higher the frequency. When a frequency is tripled, the pitch rises an octave and a 5th above the initial pitch; when quadrupled, it rises 2 octaves above; quintupled, 2 octaves and a major 3rd. This ordering of frequencies produces the harmonic or overtone series; the tonal system is usually said to be based on it. The ratios of vibrations can be arithmetically derived from it: the octave ratio is 2:1, a 5th 3:2, a 4th 4:3, and a major 3rd 5:4.

The relative strength of harmonics contained within the sound of a musical instrument determines its timbre or tone color. Middle C on the piano, violin, or flute has the same cps or Hz, but they differ in their timbre, distinctions immediately recognized by a musical ear. Sound waves created by each instrument are compounded with the sound waves of the harmonics involved; the resulting wave shape curve is no longer sinusoidal, but complex, having several peaks. When instruments play together and sound different pitches, the resulting wave shape would require complex geometric study to reconstruct its components; but a musically aware person, particularly one possessing perfect pitch, can make this analysis instantly and name all the pitches and tone colors constituting the resulting sound.

The loudness of a tone depends on the amplitude (height) produced by the vibrations of a sounding body; this can be observed visually by plucking a string and letting it vibrate, producing a blur. Noise is a sound without definite pitch; when the entire spectrum of tones and noises is produced together, the effect is called white noise, by analogy with the mixture of all colors to create the color white.

sound bow. Thick rim of a bell, against which the clapper strikes.

sound effects. Onomatopoeic simulations of natural or industrial sounds employed in music, radio, television, and film; included are devices such as a thunder machine (R. Strauss, *Alpine Sym.*), imitation of falling rain, galloping horses, whirring propellers, etc. Some professional technicians have developed an extraordinary ability to re-create animal cries and industrial noises by means of appropriate amplification of ordinary sounds. The sound engineers working for the Walt Disney studios in Hollywood have in their repertoire almost 1,000 different "instruments." Thus hoofbeats can be produced by clapping 2 coconut half-shells together; the sound of the arrow hitting the mark is produced by plucking a Jew's harp over a microphone; various gurgling noises are usually produced orally. One Disney technician has evolved a method of imitating the sound of a swarm of bees by blowing through a rubber condom stretched over a wooden spool. With the invention of the sampler and MIDI, the possibility of both imitation and creation of new effects has grown exponentially. In the centuries before sound movies demanded naturalism in everything, composers were happy to produce sounds by imitating pitch, rhythm, and tone color in their music, from the battaglia to representations of the industrial age.

sound hole. Hole cut in the front of the belly of a string instrument.

sound installation. Form of mixed media in which the visual (usually sculpture) and aural (sound of any kind) are combined and coordinated to the extent desired. There is the noninteractive installation, where all elements are controlled by the creators or by random factors not under human control, and the interactive installation, where the spectator affects the sound by tactile contact with the sculptural element or by interfering with electronic devices (such as "breaking" a light beam or wave source, adjusting controls, etc.).

soundboard. Thin plate of wood placed below or behind the strings of various instruments to reinforce and prolong their tones; in the organ, the cover of the windchest.

soundpost. In the violin, etc., small cylindrical wooden prop set inside the body, between belly and back, just behind (nearly beneath) the treble foot of the bridge.

soupir (Fr., sigh). Quarter rest.

sourd et en s'eloignant (Fr.). Muted, as if receding.

sourdine (Fr.). 1. Harmonium stop that partially cuts off the wind supply, so full chords can be played softly. 2. Mute. *Avec sourdines,* put on mutes; *sans sourdines,* take off mutes.

sous-dominante (Fr.). Subdominant.

Sousa, John Philip, b. Washington, D.C., Nov. 6, 1854; d. Reading, Pa., Mar. 6, 1932. He studied violin and orchestration with J. Esputa, Jr., and violin and harmony with G. F. Benkert in Washington, D.C.; acquired considerable proficiency on wind instruments. After playing in the Marine Band (1868–75) he was active in theater orchs.; was a violinist in the Philadelphia orch. conducted by Offenbach during his U.S. tour (1876). He was appointed director of the Marine Band (1880–92), which he led with distinction; organized his own band and led it in its 1st concert in Plainfield, N.J. (1892); gave successful concerts throughout the U.S. and Canada; played at the Chicago World's Fair (1893) and the Paris Exposition (1900); made 4 European tours (1900, 1901, 1903, and 1905) with increasing acclaim; finally toured around the world (1910–11).

Sousa's flair for writing band music was extraordinary; the infectious rhythms of his military marches and the brilliance of his band arrangements earned him the sobriquet "The March King"; particularly celebrated is *Stars and Stripes Forever* (1896), which became famous all over the world; a bill passed in the U.S. Congress and signed by President Ronald Reagan made it the official march of the U.S. (1987). During World War I, Sousa served as a lieutenant in the Naval Reserve; continued his annual tours almost up to his death; was instrumental in the development of the sousaphone, a bass tuba with upright bell, used in bands since the 1890s.

Sousa composed 10 operettas, the most famous being *El Capitan* (1895). Amongst his cornucopia of marches are (alphabetically listed): *America 1st* (1916); *The Aviators* (1931); *The Belle of Chicago* (1892); *The Black Horse Troop* (1924); *El Capitan* (1896); *Columbia's Pride* (1914); *Congress Hall* (1882); *Daughters of Texas* (1929); *Esprit de Corps* (1878); *The Federal* (1910); *The Gallant 7th* (1922); *The Gladiator* (1886; the 1st work to sell a million copies); *Golden Jubilee* (1928); *Hands Across the Sea* (1899); *The Invincible Eagle* (1901); *Jack Tar* (1903); *King Cotton* (1895); *The Legionnaires* (1930); *The Liberty Bell* (1893); *The National Game* (1925; for the 50th anniversary of baseball's National League); *The Naval Reserve* (1917); *Old Ironsides* (1926); *On Parade* (1892); *The Phoenix March* (1875); *Powhatan's Daughter* (1907); *The Pride of the Wolverines* (1926); *Review* (1873; his 1st publ. march); *The Royal Welch Fusiliers* (No. 1, 1929; No. 2, 1930); *The Salvation Army* (1930); *Semper Fidelis* (1888); *Sesquicentennial Exposition March* (1926); *The Thunderer* (1889); *The Washington Post* (1889). He also composed band suites; overtures, and program music; orch'l works; songs, ballads, and hymns; arrangements and transcriptions; also wrote novels: *The 5th String* (1902), *Pipetown Sandy* (1905), and *The Transit of Venus* (1919).

sousaphone. Spiral type of bass tuba (helicon), coiled around the player, with a large bell turned forwards; named after Sousa, who used it in his bands; still used today.

soutenu (Fr.). Sostenuto.

space. In the staff, area between 2 lines or ledger lines.

space (spatial) music. Use of spatial distribution of instruments and vocalists as a parameter; orig. a late-Renaissance texture (antiphony), it regained currency as a dramatic device in Romantic opera and religious music, subordinating the call-and-response aspect. Pushing the concept further, Brant, Carter, Foss, Penderecki, Christou, Bussoti, Xenakis, Cage, and other ultramoderns wrote works stipulating the position of each instrument in relation to the ensemble.

spagnoletta. Italian dance of the 16th century, similar to the pavane; it is in triple meter, played in moderate tempo, and of Spanish origin.

spagnuolo, alla (It.). In a Spanish manner.

Spanish guitar. See ⇒guitar, Spanish.

Spannung (Ger.). Tension.

spartire (It.). Assemble a score from separate parts; especially important for most pre-Baroque vocal music.

spartito (*spartitura, partitura;* It.). Score.

Spasshaft (Ger.). Scherzando.

spatial distribution. Physical placement of musicians, long a matter of tradition, has assumed unexpected significance in the 20th century, sometimes in the guise of musical vectorialism. Carter specifies the exact position of the players in his string quartets; Foss, in his *Elytres* for 12 Instruments, places the musicians at maximum distances available on the stage; Xenakis has scattered performers throughout the audience as well as on stage. The use of directional loudspeakers in performances of ultramodern electronic works is a counterpart to spatial distribution (Varèse, *Poème electronique*). In German broadcasting studios a 12-tone row was distributed among 12 electronic amplifiers placed in a clocklike circle, with each amplifier being assigned 1 note of the series. Empirical applications of the principle of spatial distribution have been made by various composers early in the century, notably by Satie in his *Musique d'ameublement*.

spatial music. See ⇒Space music.

spectrum. By analogy with the prismatic spectrum of primary colors, a totality of Klangfarben is a tonal spectrum. Before the era of electronic music the colors of the auditory spectrum were limited to the available instruments of actual manufacture. Electronic generators make possible the building of a spectrum with infinite capacity for instrumental color; the style and idiom of an entire work can be programmed by the proportional strength of these colors, thus justifying the musical spectrum metaphor by its literal realization.

specular reflection. The mirror image in Baroque counterpoint is applied to mutually conjugated melodic inversions in which the ascending intervals are reflected by descending intervals, and vice versa. It is theoretically possible to construct an infinite specular reflection, in which the intervallic distance between the 2 mirrors recedes, so that intervals are inverted in the outer regions of the instrumental range, extending even into the inaudible spectrum of ultrasonic and infrasonic sounds. In some modern works written specially for dog audiences, ultrasonics can achieve considerable effectiveness. Beyond the canine auditory range, a gap occurs until the frequency of light waves is reached. Mystically inclined composers may find pantheistic inspiration in these notions of passing from men through dogs to infinity.

speculative music. Obs. English term for musical theory and analysis, as opposed to *practical music* (applied music); as T. Morley explains in his *Plaine and Easie Introduction* (1597): "Musicke is either speculative or practicall. Speculative is that kinde of musicke which, by mathematicall helpes, seeketh out the causes, properties, and natures of soundes. Practicall is that which teacheth all that may be knowne in songs."

speditamente (It.). Expeditiously; quickly.

spesso (It.). Frequently; densely.

spianato, -a (from It. *piano,* softly). Softly, tranquilly, without affectation.

spiccato (It.). In string playing, separate the notes very distinctly; in a very rapid tempo, spiccato results in saltando, played with a bouncing bow; in Baroque playing, spiccato is akin to detaché.

Spiel (Ger.). Play; performance; game. *Spielen,* play (noun or verb).

Spielmann (Ger.). Itinerant musician of the Middle Ages.

spigliatezza (It.). Agility, dexterity. *Spigliato,* pertly, with agility.

spinet. Instrument of the harpsichord family, related to the virginal. The shape of the spinet resembles the modern grand piano, while the virginal is rectangular. The spinet was popular during the 18th century, then abruptly disappeared from the scene. The modern instrument that took up the name "spinet" is simply a small upright piano, having little in common with the venerable Baroque instrument.

Spinnenlied (Ger.). Spinning song; orig. a work song; in classical music the spinning-wheel is often represented by a circulating ostinato around a pedal point. Goethe's lyric *Gretchen am Spinnrade* (*Faust,* part I) invites this kind of approach; Schubert's setting (1814) is its apotheosis.

spinto (It., compelled, intense). High operatic soprano or tenor role of a dramatic yet passive type (Madama Butterfly, Desdemona); opposed to dramatic and lyric roles.

spirito, con (It.). Spiritedly; with spirit, animation, energy.

spiritual. Term derived from the European spiritual song, composed in many languages and for many different forces. The shortened term was applied by white abolitionists to religious songs cultivated by African-American slaves in the antebellum South. In reality this African-American music is a form of the American gospel hymn, a term usually applied to white church music. Whatever the case, the Negro spiritual went in 2 directions: either it froze as a musical style, performed in concerts by choirs or solo singers; or it evolved along various paths to subsequent forms of gospel music, paralleling the evolution of African-American popular music. For a fuller description, see ⇒gospel.

Spitze (Ger.). 1. Point (of the bow). 2. Toe (in organ playing).

Spitzharfe (Ger.). See ⇒Arpanetta

spitzig (Ger.). Sharp, pointed.

Spohr, Louis (Ludewig, Ludwig), b. Braunschweig, Apr. 5, 1784; d. Kassel, Oct. 22, 1859. Born Ludewig, he preferred the French equivalent. His father, a physician, played flute; his mother was an amateur singer and pianist. Louis began violin lessons at age 5 with J. A. Riemenschneider and Dufour; returned to Braunschweig (1791); studied with the organist C. A. Hartung and violinist C. L. Maucourt; composed several violin pieces.

Duke Carl Wilhelm Ferdinand admitted Spohr to the ducal orch. and arranged for his further study with violinist Franz Eck, who took him on a tour to Russia (1802), where he met Clementi and Field; returned to Braunschweig (1803), resuming his ducal. orch. post. The violin technique and compositional style of P. Rode, whom he met on his return, were major influences on both aspects of his career; and his violin technique; made his 1st official tour as a violinist to Hamburg (1804, 2 earlier failures being discounted); gave concerts in Berlin, Leipzig, and Dresden; became concertmaster in the ducal orch. at Gotha (1805).

In 1806 Spohr married the harpist Dorette (Dorothea) Scheidler (1787–1834); he wrote many works for violin and harp for them to perform, and toured with her in Germany (1807). With a reputation as virtuoso established, he began writing compositions in every genre with excellent success; gave a series of concerts in Vienna (1812), where he was acclaimed both as composer and violinist; concertmaster in the orch. of the Theater an der Wien (to 1815). He made a grand tour of Germany and Italy; Paganini heard him in Venice. His opera *Faust*, skillfully employing devices that foreshadowed developments in later German operas, was performed by Weber in Prague (1816).

After a visit to Holland (1817) Spohr became Kapellmeister of the Frankfurt Opera; produced one of his most popular operas, *Zemire und Azor*. He and his wife visited England, appearing at concerts of the London Phil. Soc. (1820); this was the 1st of 6 visits to England, where he acquired an immense reputation as a violinist, composer, and conductor; his works were performed there long after his death. He presented concerts in Paris; his reception there, however, did not match his London successes; proceeded to Dresden, where Weber recommended him for the Kapellmeistership at the court in Kassel; persuaded by a lifetime contract, he accepted and settled there (1822); produced his operatic masterpiece, *Jessonda* (1823), which remained popular to the end of the century. Performances of his oratorio *Die letzten Dinge* (1826) and the 4th Sym., *Die Weibe der Töne* (1832), elicited great praise; the *Violinschule*, a set of studies covering every aspect of his playing style, was publ. (1831).

In the 1830s Spohr had difficulties with the electoral co-regent Friedrich Wilhelm I of Kassel, who canceled a festival in Kassel and forbade him from traveling to Prague; the composer went nevertheless to conduct *Der Berggeist* (1825); visited Mozart's widow and birthplace in Salzburg; traveled to England for the Norwich Festival (1839); could not obtain permission to attend the premiere of his *Fall of Babylon* (Leipzig, 1842). In England, his success was so great that a special concert was given by royal command (1843), the 1st time a reigning English monarch attended a Phil. Concert. In 1844 he received the silver medal from the Soc. des Concerts in Paris; a festival honoring him was held in Braunschweig; received a golden wreath from the Berlin Royal Opera (1845). He never visited the U.S., despite the fact that his daughter lived in N.Y. and an invitation to hold a festival in his honor was issued.

Despite political difficulties (he was a liberal nationalist), Spohr was appointed Generalmusikdirektor of Kassel (1847); after another visit to England, he went to Frankfurt for the German National Assembly; appeared at the New Phil. Concerts in London (1853). Returning to Kassel, he found the Elector refusing him further leaves of absence; he ignored the ban, traveling to Switzerland and Italy; in the litigation that followed, he was ordered to pay a substantial fine (1851). He was pensioned from Kassel; fractured his left arm in a fall (both 1857), but still conducted *Jessonda* in Prague (1858); he conducted his last performance in Meiningen later that year.

Spohr's compositional style was characteristic of the transition period between the Classic and Romantic. He was technically a master; some works demonstrate a spirit of bold experimentation (*The Historical Sym.*, No. 6; Sym. No. 7 for 2 Orchs. in 3 parts, portraying the mundane and divine elements of life; Concerto for String Quartet and Orch.; the Nonet); but generally his aesthetics reflected intransigent conservatism. He admired Beethoven's early works but confessed a total inability to understand the late ones; also failed to appreciate Weber. It is remarkable, then, that he was an early champion of Wagner, producing *Der fliegende Holländer* (1843) and *Tannhäuser* (1853) despite strenuous opposition from the Kassel court; a highly esteemed teacher, his students included Ferdinand David and M. Hauptmann. His orch'l works include 10 syms., 18 violin concertos, 4 clarinet concertos, 2 "concertantes" for violin duo; 2 concertantes for harp and violin; 6 concert overtures. Chamber works: 34 string quartets, 7 string quintets, 4 "double quartets" for strings; 14 violin duets; 5 piano trios; and 3 sonatas for harp and violin.

Spontini, Gasparo (Luigi Pacifico), b. Majolati, Ancona, Nov. 14, 1774; d. there, Jan. 24, 1851. His father intended him for the church, giving him into the charge of an uncle, a priest at Jesi, who attempted to stifle his musical aspirations. Gasparo sought refuge at Monte San Vito with another relative, who found a competent music teacher for him and effected a reconciliation; returned to Jesi. He entered the Cons. della Pietà de' Turchini in Naples (1793); his teachers were Tritto (singing) and Sala (composition); failing to obtain the position of maestrino there, quit the Cons. without permission (1795). He rapidly mastered the conventional Italian style of his time; after his church music was performed in Naples, a director of the Teatro della Pallacorda in Rome who commissioned him to write an opera; *Li puntigli delle donne* was produced during Carnival (1796). He served as maestro di cappella at Naples's Teatro del Fondo during Carnival (1800); went to Palermo to produce 3 operas; produced operas for Rome and Venice before going to Paris (1803).

After eking out a living as a singing teacher, Spontini found a patron in the Empress Joséphine; 1st gained success in Paris with a rev. version of *La finta filosofa* (1804), followed by *La Petite Maison*, which proved unsuccessful. Then the poet Étienne de Jouy approached him to set his libretto *La Vestale*, previously turned down by Boieldieu, Cherubini, and Méhul. Meanwhile, the composer brought out *Milton* (1804) and *Julie, ou Le Pot de fleurs* (1805) with little success; however, he was appointed composer of Joséphine's private music (1805), for which he wrote occasional pieces, including the cantata *L'eccelsa gara* (1806), celebrating the battle of Austerlitz.

Thanks to Joséphine's patronage, *La Vestale* was triumphant at its premiere (1807), in spite of virulent opposition; his next opera, *Fernand Cortez* (1809), failed to equal his previous success; its 2nd version (1817) won it a place in the repertory. He was awarded the *prix decennal* for composing the finest grand opera of the preceding decade (1810); accepted the directorship of the Théâtre-Italien. Although his artistic policies were successful, he clashed with his superiors and was dismissed (1812); his *Pélage, ou Le Roi et la paix,* celebrating the Restoration, was successfully produced (1814); named director of Louis XVIII's private music and continued at the Théâtre-Italien, although he soon sold the latter privilege. Now a favorite of the Bourbons, he was made a French citizen by the king (1817) and granted a pension (1818); in spite of this, his grand opera *Olimpie* failed dismally at its premiere (1819).

Spontini went to Berlin as Generalmusikdirektor; scored an initial success with a rev. version of *Olimpie* (1821); however, his position of eminence quickly waned. He was equal in power to the Intendant of the Royal Theater; frequent misunderstandings and sharp clashes of authority were not mitigated by his jealousies and dislikes, overweening self-conceit, and despotic temper; as a result of intrigue and his own lack of self-control, he was formally charged in criminal court with lèse-majesté (1841); conducting a performance of *Don Giovanni* (in defiance of his probation), a riot ensued, compelling him to leave the hall in disgrace; sentenced to 9 months in prison; dismissed as Generalmusikdirektor by King Friedrich Wilhelm IV; allowed to retain his title and salary; his sentence was upheld by an appeals court (1842), but the king pardoned him. He then went to Paris, where illness and growing deafness overtook him; was raised to the papal nobility as the Conte di San Andrea (1844); retired to his birthplace (1850).

Spontini's importance to the lyric theater rests upon his effective blending of Italian and French elements in his serious operas, most notably in *La Vestale* and *Fernand Cortez;* his influence on Berlioz was particularly notable and readily admitted. He composed songs, choral music, and instrumental pieces.

Spottlied (Ger.). Song of mockery.

Sprechstimme (*Sprechgesang;* Ger., speech song). Type of inflected vocal delivery, with pitches indicated approximately on the music staff. The singer follows the pitch contour without actually voicing any notes, resulting in exaggerated speech. It was popularized by its expressive use by Schoenberg in *Pierrot Lunaire* and later works; 1st used systematically in the melodrama *Königskinder* by Humperdinck (1897). This technique is common in contemporary opera and song cycles; variants such as Partch's "intoning voice" are found.

sprezzatura (*esprezzatura;* It.). Expressivity, particularly by the judicious use of rubato.

springar. Traditional couple dance of Norway, in triple meter, usually accompanied by the hardingfele.

Springsteen, Bruce, b. Freehold, N.J., Sept. 23, 1949. He sang and played guitar in honky-tonks in Newark and in Greenwich Village in N.Y.; began recording songs of personal discontent and societal alienation (e.g., *It's Hard to Be a Saint in the City*); recruited similarly disaffected rock musicians to form the E-Street Band; his 3rd album, *Born to Run* (1975), struck a sympathetic chord with disillusioned youth and made him a cult figure; the title song earned a Certified Gold Award. His next release, *Darkness on the Edge of Town* (1978), exploited the general malaise of American youth; the 1980 hit album, *The River,* glorified, with bitter irony, the automobile as a symbol of the age (e.g., *Stolen Car, Drive All Night, Wreck on the Highway*).

In 1981 Springsteen made an extraordinarily successful European tour; brought out *Born in the USA* (1984), with its hugely popular and mostly misunderstood title song; won a Grammy Award as best male vocalist; made a triumphant world tour. His next releases were *Bruce Springsteen & the E-Street Band Live/1975–1985* (1985) and *Tunnel of Love* (1987), the latter winning a Grammy Award; active with the Amnesty International "Human Rights Now!" tour (1988); ended his 16-year affiliation with the E-Street Band (1990); continues to record solo albums.

square dance. Parlor or country dance (e.g., quadrille) performed by several couples in a square formation.

square time. Popular term for 4/4 time; march time.

squillante (It.). Ringing, tinkling; piercing.

SRO. Standing Room Only.

Stabat Mater (dolorosa) (Lat.). Roman Catholic sequence on the Crucifixion, commemorating the 7 sorrows of the Virgin, used in many Divine Offices. With its emotional appeal and liturgical acceptance by the 16th-century Council of Trent, the Stabat Mater has been set to music by composers such as Desprez, Palestrina, Pergolesi, Haydn, Rossini, Schubert, Verdi, and Dvořák.

stabile (It.). Steady, firm.

staccato (It., detached). Play as separate, disconnected notes; opposite of legato; on a string instrument, the bow does not leave the string, unlike sautillé; the effect is successful on most instruments. Played forte, the effect is martellato; in pianissimo and rapid tempo it is sometimes described as *virtuoso staccato*.

staccato mark. Dot ( ) or wedge-shaped stroke ( ) over a note; the former indicates a less abrupt staccato than the latter; *mezzo-staccato* is indicated by dotted notes under or over a slur.

Stade, Frederica von. Von Stade, Frederica.

staff (stave). Five parallel lines used in modern pitch notation; plainchant used at most 4 lines; for the plural, *staves* is preferred to *staffs*. *Staff notation,* the staff and all musical signs connected with it; *grand* or *great staff,* combination of treble and bass clefs, comprising 11 lines; middle C occupies the 6th (middle) line.

stagione (It., season). Scheduled performances for an operatic or concert music organization over a time period up to 12 months (not necessarily the calendar year).

stalls (U.K.). In a theater, front rows of the orch. (seating) section.

Stammakkord (Ger.). Chord in fundamental (root) position.

stampitas (It.). Estampie.

stanchezza, con (*stanco;* It.). Wearily, draggingly.

Ständchen (Ger.). Serenade.

standing ovation. Unanimous and tumultuous response to a particularly exciting musical performance. Audience members are so transported by admiration for the artist, conductor, singer, pianist, violinist, other soloist, or ensemble that through body chemistry they are impelled by simultaneous and massive production of adrenaline to rise from their seats and clap their hands mightily, sometimes even rhythmically, joyously abandoning themselves to unrestrained vociferation and, in extreme cases, animalistic ululation. The spontaneity of such manifestations, however, is sometimes suspect, as are similar outbursts of collective enthusiasm for politicians; see ⇒claque.

Standing Room Only (SRO). Indication that all seats for a particular performance are sold out, but that a few places remain where a hardy individual can watch the performance standing up behind the last row of seats.

stanghetta (It.). Barline.

stanza. Symmetric unit of a song text, of 4 or more lines; a unified section in and a component of a lied or other song type.

stark (Ger.). Loudly, forcibly; forte. *Stärker,* louder, more forcibly; più forte.

Starker, János, b. Budapest, July 5, 1924. At age 6, he made his 1st public appearance; at 7 began cello studies with A. Cziffer

at the Budapest Academy of Music; made his solo debut there at 11. After graduating he was 1st cellist of the Budapest Opera Orch. (1945–46); emigrated to the U.S. (1948), becoming naturalized in 1954. He was 1st cellist in the Dallas Sym. Orch. (1948–49), the Metropolitan Opera Orch. (1949–53), and the Chicago Sym. Orch. (1953–58); embarked upon a solo career.

In 1958 Starker was appointed prof. of music at the Indiana Univ. School of Music in Bloomington; named Distinguished Prof. of Music (1965). As a soloist he achieved renown performing Bach's unaccompanied cello suites; devoted much attention to modern music; promoted cello works of Kodály; premiered works by Messiaen, Mennin, and Rózsa; publ. *An Organized Method of String Playing* (1961).

starr (Ger.). Insistently.

Starr, Ringo (born Richard Starkey), b. Liverpool, July 7, 1940. His nickname derived from his ostentatious habit of wearing several rings on his fingers. As an adolescent he held various menial jobs; spent several years in hospitals to cure an effusion on the lung; played drums in ward bands; evolved a rhythmic technique of an overwhelming directness. In 1962 he accepted an invitation to join the Beatles, staying with the group to its dissolution (1970). His effortless but histrionic ability in handling the drums was an important feature of Beatlephonia; his nasal singing graced *Yellow Submarine* and *Octopussy's Garden*. He subsequently had a successful career as performer and actor; was the only one of the Beatles to work with each of the others after the breakup.

static music. Although the general trend of music since 1900 has been toward greater complexity of texture and greater variety of dynamics, an opposite movement has manifested itself in some circles, aimed at tonal immobility and static means of expression. One approach limits musical events to a bare minimum (reaching *ad absurdum* its logical culmination by playing a single note in unchanging dynamics, usually in pianissimo); another permits the relentless repetition of arpeggios and scales with little or no harmonic or rhythmic alteration. In either case, the expectation of some change, constantly deceived, can cause an emotional perturbation of great psychological interest.

stave. Staff; for the plural, *staves* is preferred to *staffs*.

steam organ. Calliope.

steel band (drum). Percussion ensemble developed in Trinidad, using steel oil barrels discarded by local oil companies. The players, called panmen, select drum tops with dents, each producing a different pitch; by further manipulation, a whole diatonic scale and chromatic notes can be produced. Having absorbed the sounds of American and British popular music, players have formed whole orchs. of steel drum tops, performing in 4-part harmony. The highest pitch is called ping-pong; the bass is called boom; the orch. is usually supplemented by several pairs of maracas and guiros; the indigenous songs are of the calypso type, commenting on topical events.

Steg (Ger.). Bridge on string instruments. *Am Steg,* bowing near the bridge.

Steiner, Max(imilian Raoul Walter), b. Vienna, May 10, 1888; d. Los Angeles, Dec. 28, 1971. He studied at the Vienna Cons. with Fuchs and Gradener; received advice from Mahler; at 15 produced a successful operetta. After conducting musical theater throughout Europe (1904–14), he settled in the U.S.; conducted Broadway musicals in N.Y. (1916–29); moved to Hollywood, becoming a highly successful film composer. His music offers a fulsome blend of lush harmonies artfully derived from Tchaikovsky and Wagner, designed for the portrayal of psychological drama on the screen. Among his more than 200 film scores are *King Kong* (1933), *The Charge of the Light Brigade* (1936), *Jezebel* (1938), *Gone with the Wind* (1939), *Now, Voyager* (1942), *Casablanca* (1943), *Mildred Pierce* (1945), *The Big Sleep* (1946), *Johnny Belinda* and *Key Largo* (1948), *The Treasure of the Sierra Madre* (1948), *The Glass Menagerie* (1950), *The Caine Mutiny* (1954), and *The Searchers* (1956).

Steinway & Sons. Celebrated family of German-American piano manufacturers. The firm's founder was Heinrich Engelhard Steinweg (later Henry E. Steinway, b. Wolfshagen, Germany, Feb. 15, 1797; d. N.Y., Feb. 7, 1871). He learned cabinetmaking and organ building at Goslar, entered the shop of an organ maker in Seesen (1818); became church organist there; grew interested in piano making; built his 1st piano in 1836. He exhibited 1 grand and 2 square pianos at the Braunschweig State Fair, winning the gold medal (1839). The Revolution of 1848 caused him to emigrate to America with his wife, 2 daughters, and 4 of his 5 sons: Charles (b. Christian Karl Gottlieb, 1829–65); Henry (b. Johann Heinrich Engelhard, 1830–65); William (b. Johann Heinrich Wilhelm, 1835–96); and (Georg August) Albert (1840–77); the management of the German business was left to the eldest son, (Christian Friedrich) Theodore (1825–89).

The family arrived in N.Y. (1850); for 2 years father and sons worked in various piano factories; established their own factory on Varick St. under the Steinway name (1853; legally changed the following year); won a gold medal for a square piano at the Metropolitan Fair in Washington, D.C. (1954); took 1st prize for a square overstrung piano with cast-iron frame (an innovation) at the N.Y. Industrial Exhibition (1855); their great success dates from this time. They built their 1st grand (1856) and upright (1862); among their numerous prizes: 1st prize at London (1862); 1st grand gold medal of honor for all styles at Paris (1867, by unanimous verdict); diplomas for "highest degree of excellence in all styles" at Philadelphia (1876).

Upon the death of his brothers Charles and Henry, Theodore gave up the Braunschweig business and became a full partner in the N.Y. firm (1865); built Steinway Hall on 14th St., which housed the offices, retail warerooms, and a concert hall that became a leading center of N.Y. musical life; headquarters were later moved to the Steinway Building on 57th St. (1925). Theodore, interested in the scientific aspects of piano construction, studied the acoustical theories of Helmholtz and Tyndall, enabling him to introduce important improvements; returned to Germany (1870).

In 1876, the firm was incorporated and William elected president; opened a London branch (1876) and a European factory at Hamburg (1880); bought 400 acres on Long Island Sound, establishing the village of Steinway (1880; now part of Long Island City), where the manufacturing plant has been located since 1910. Control and active management of the business, the largest of its kind in the world, long remained in the family; Theodore E. Steinway (d. 1957), grandson of the founder, was president (1927–55); succeeded by his son, Henry (1955). The firm was sold to CBS (1972), although the Steinway family continued to be closely associated with the business; in 1988 Steinway & Sons celebrated its 135th anniversary with a special N.Y. concert and the unveiling of its 500,000th piano.

stem. Vertical line attached to a note head.

stendando (*stentato;* It.). Delaying, retarding, dragging, heavily.

stentorphone. Extremely loud open diapason pipe in a large organ, named after the legendary Greek hero Stentor in the Trojan War, who could outshout 50 enemies.

step. Melodic progression of a 2nd; also, a degree. *Chromatic step,* progression of a chromatic 2nd; *diatonic step,* progression between adjacent notes of a diatonic scale; *half step,* progression of a semitone; *whole step,* progression of a whole tone.

sterbend (Ger.). Dying; morendo.

stereophonic (Grk., solid sound). Recording technique developed in the 1950s, using several microphones and mixing the results to create an impression of an actual concert by distributing the sounds among 2 channels (i.e., speakers).

Stern, Isaac, b. Kremenetz, July 21, 1920. He was introduced to music by his mother, a professional singer; studied the violin at the San Francisco Cons. (1928–31), with L. Persinger, and with N. Blinder (1932–37); made his orch'l solo debut in Saint-Saëns's 3rd Violin Concerto with the San Francisco Sym. Orch. (1936); his N.Y. debut followed (1937). After further training in San Francisco, he returned to N.Y.; his Carnegie Hall debut there was a triumph (1943); toured Australia (1947); made his European debut at the Lucerne Festival (1948); appeared regularly with American and European orchs.; made a spectacularly successful tour of Russia (1956). In 1961 he organized a trio with pianist Eugene Istomin and cellist Leonard Rose (1961), which toured widely until Rose's death (1984); celebrated the 50th anniversary of his orch'l debut (1986).

Stern was made an Officer of the Legion d'honneur of France (1979); received the Kennedy Center Honors Award (1984) and the Wolf Prize of Israel (1987). He belongs to the galaxy of virtuoso performers to whom fame is a natural adjunct to talent and industry; is active in general cultural undertakings and an energetic worker for the cause of human rights; his visit to Red China was documented in the film, *From Mao to Mozart* (1981).

stesso (It.). The same. *Lo stesso* (or *l'istesso*) *movimento,* the same movement.

Steuermann, Edward (Eduard), b. Sambor, near Lemberg, June 18, 1892; d. N.Y., Nov. 11, 1964. He studied piano with Busoni in Berlin (1911–12) and theory with Schoenberg (1912–14); took composition lessons with Humperdinck. Returning to Poland, he taught at the Paderewski School in Lwow and the Jewish Cons. in Krakow (1932–36). He emigrated to the U.S. (1936); taught piano at the Juilliard School of Music in N.Y.

(1952–64); on the faculty of the Philadelphia Cons. (1948–63); gave summer classes at the Mozarteum in Salzburg (1953–63) and Darmstadt (1954, 1957, 1958, 1960).

In recital and as an orch'l soloist, Steuermann was an ardent champion of new music, particularly of Schoenberg; whose Piano Concerto he gave the 1st performance of (1944); made excellent piano arrangements of Schoenberg's operatic and symphonic works; received the Schoenberg Medal from the ISCM (1952). Although he did not follow Schoenberg's dodecaphonic method with any consistency, his music possesses an expressionistic tension characteristic of the 2nd Viennese School. His nephew, Michael (Andreas) Gielen (b. Dresden, July 20, 1927) is a noted conductor who also specializes in Schoenberg.

stil (Ger.; It. *stile*). Style. *Stile concitato,* agitated style, akin to the battaglia, introduced by Monteverdi in *Combattimento di Tancredi et Clorinda* (1624); *stile osservato,* strict style, especially of pure vocal music; *stile rappresentativo,* dramatic monodic song with instrumental accompaniment in chords; a form of operatic recitative originating at the beginning of the Baroque.

Still, William Grant, b. Woodville, Miss., May 11, 1895; d. Los Angeles, Dec. 3, 1978. His father was a bandmaster in Woodville; after his death, his mother moved the family to Little Rock, Ark. He grew up with cultured, middle-class values; his stepfather encouraged his musical interests; taking him to see operettas and buying him operatic recordings; was given violin lessons. He attended Wilberforce College in preparation for a medical career but became active in campus musical activities; after dropping out he worked with various groups, including W. C. Handy's (1916); attended the Oberlin College Cons. (Ohio).

During World War I Still played violin in the U.S. Army; returned to work with Handy; became oboist in the Shuffle Along Orch. (1921); studied composition with Varèse and at the New England Cons. of Music in Boston with Chadwick; held a Guggenheim fellowship (1934–35). Determined to develop a symphonic type of black American music, he composed the *Afro-American Sym.* (1930), his best-known work. In his music he occasionally made use of African-American folk song, but mostly invented his thematic materials.

Still's melodious, well-written music is not well enough known; among his works are operas (*A Bayou Legend,* 1940; *Troubled Island,* 1941; *Highway 1, U.S.A.,* 1962); ballets (*Sahdji,* 1930; *Lennox Avenue,* 1937); incidental music. He composed 5 syms., including No. 2, *Song of a New Race* (Philadelphia, 1937) and No. 3, *The Sunday Sym.,* 1958; other orch'l works (*Darker America,* 1924; *From the Black Belt,* 1926; *Africa,* 1930; *Dismal Swamp,* 1936; *In Memoriam: The Colored Soldiers Who Died for Democracy,* 1943); chamber music; choral works; songs; piano pieces; band music; arrangements of spirituals.

Stillgedackt (Ger.). Soft-toned stopped organ register.

Stimme (Ger.). 1. Voice. 2. Vocal or instrumental part; *mit der Stimme,* colla parte. 3. Organ stop; *mit zartem Stimmen,* with soft-toned organ stops. 4. Soundpost (of a string instrument).

Stimmung (Ger.; It., *accordatura*). Tuning; pitch; mood, frame of mind. *Stimmung halten,* to keep in tune; *Stimmungsbild,* a mood picture; short character piece.

stinguendo (It.). Dying away.

stiracchiando (It.). Slowly; receding in speed.

stirato (It.). Dragging, delaying.

stiriana (It.). Styrienne.

stochastic (from Grk. *stochos,* target). Term, borrowed from probability theory, describing a compositional process governed by rules of probability; introduced into music by Xenakis, an engineer as well as composer, to designate an aleatory projection in which the sonic trajectory is circumscribed by the structural parameters of the initial thematic statement. In practice, stochastic procedures closely resemble controlled improvisation.

Stockflöte (Ger., cane flute). Vertical flute or recorder inserted in the upper part of a walking stick; manufactured in the early 19th century in Austria, it attained popularity among poetically inclined *Spaziergänger* in the Vienna woods, hills, and environs.

Stockhausen, Karlheinz, b. Mödrath, near Cologne, Aug. 22, 1928. Despite being orphaned during World War II and holding menial jobs to keep body and soul together, he learned to play the piano, violin, and oboe; studied piano with H. O. Schmidt-Neuhaus, form with H. Schroder, and composition with Frank Martin at the Cologne Staatliche Hochschule für Musik (1947–50); took courses in German philology, philosophy, and musicology at the Univ. of Cologne; after studying in Darmstadt (1951), took composition lessons from Messiaen in Paris (1952); studied communications theory and phonetics with W. Meyer-Eppler at the Univ. of Bonn (1954–56).

Stockhausen worked at the electronic music studio of the West German Radio in Cologne (from 1953); lectured at the summer course in Darmstadt (to 1974); founder/artistic director of the Cologne Kürse für Neue Musik (1963–68); prof. of composition at the Cologne Hochschule für Musik (1971–77). He was elected to the Swedish Royal Academy (1970), Berlin Academy of Arts (1973), and American Academy and Inst. of Arts and Letters (1979); made a Commandeur dans l'Ordre des Arts et des Lettres of France (1985) and honorary member of the Royal Academy of Music in London (1987).

Stockhausen investigated the potentialities of musique concrète, partly incorporating its techniques into his empiric method of composition, which included highly complex contrapuntal conglomerates with uninhibited applications of noneuphonious dissonance as well as recourse to the obdurate iteration of single tones. This was set in the freest of rhythmic patterns and diversified by constantly changing instrumental colors with obsessive percussive effects. He perfected a system of constructivist composition in which the subjective choice of the performer determines the succession of given thematic ingredients and their polyphonic simultaneities, ultimately leading to a totality of aleatory procedures in which the ostensible application of a composer's commanding function is paradoxically reasserted by inclusion of prerecorded materials and recombinant uses of electronically altered thematic ingredients.

Stockhausen pursued energetic missionary activities in behalf of new music as a lecturer and presenter at avant-garde meetings throughout the world; made a lecture tour of Canadian and American univs. (1958); was visiting prof. at the Univ. of Pa. (1965) and the Univ. of Calif. at Davis (1966–67); gave highly successful public lectures in England attended by hordes of musical and unmusical novitiates (1969); publ. numerous misleading guidelines for the benefit of a growing contingent of apostles, disciples, and acolytes.

Stockhausen is a pioneer of "time-space" music, marked by controlled improvisation and the addition of the vectorial (i.e., directional) parameter to serialism; performers and electronic apparatuses are placed in different parts of the concert hall; performances are often accompanied by screen projections and audience participation. He sometimes specifies the architectural design of the rooms in which his works are presented; at the world's fair in Osaka, Japan (1970), he supervised the construction of a circular auditorium in the German pavilion; the performances there lasted for 183 days, with 20 soloists and 5 lantern projections, each session lasting 5 1/2 hours.

Stockhausen's annotations to his works were publ. in the series entitled *Texte* (6 vols., Cologne, 1963–88); other items are collected in R. Maconie, ed., *Stockhausen on Music: Lectures and Interviews* (1989). Several of the composer's children play instruments and participate in his performances.

Stokowski, Leopold (Anthony), (Antoni Stanislaw Boleslawowich), born London, Apr. 18, 1882; d. Nether Wallop, Hampshire, Sept. 13, 1977. He attended Queen's College, Oxford, and the Royal College of Music in London; studied organ with S. Hoyte, theory with W. Davies, and composition with C. Stanford. At age 18 he obtained the post of organist at St. James, Piccadilly; went to America to serve as organist and choirmaster at St. Bartholomew's in N.Y. (1905); became a U.S. citizen (1915). In 1909 he was engaged to conduct the Cincinnati Sym. Orch. for 5 years; obtained a release to accept an offer from the Philadelphia Orch. (1912); led the Philadelphia Orch. for 24 years as sole conductor; under his leadership it came to rival the best orchs. He was lionized by the Philadelphians; received the Edward Bok Award of $10,000 as "the person who has done the most for Philadelphia" (1922). In 1931 he was finally designated the Philadelphia Orch.'s music director, giving him choice of guest conductors and soloists. He conducted mostly by heart; changed the seating of the string section, placing violins to the left and cellos to the right; dispensed with the baton and shaped the music with his 10 fingers; emphasizing timbral elements, created the famous "Philadelphia sound" in the strings, achieving a well-nigh bel canto quality.

Tall and slender, with an aureole of blond hair, Stokowski presented a striking contrast with his stocky, mustachioed German predecessors; he was the 1st conductor to attain star status comparable to a movie actor's. He conducted Deanna Durbin in *100 Men and a Girl* (1937) and appeared in other films. He participated in the production of Walt Disney's celebrated film *Fantasia* (1941), a presentation of classical pieces in cartoon form featuring both live performers and animated characters; he conducted the music and in one sequence engaged in a bantering colloquy with Mickey Mouse.

Stokowski was praised in superlative terms in the press, but not all critics approved of his cavalier treatment of sacrosanct masterpieces; like Mahler and other predecessors, he altered the orchestration by doubling some solo passages in the brass; occasionally introducing percussion not in the score; even cut out individual bars he pronounced devoid of musical action. His orch'l arrangements of Bach raised the pedantic eyebrows of professional musicologists; yet there is no denying the effectiveness of the sonority and the subtlety of color that he, a former organist, succeeded in creating. Many great musicians hailed his new orch'l sound; Rachmaninoff regarded the Philadelphia Orch. under him (and, later, under Ormandy) as the greatest with which he had performed. He was also interested in new electronic sound; was the 1st to use the theremin in the orch., enhancing the sonorities of the bass section; was instrumental in introducing electrical recordings.

Stokowski boldly risked his popularity with Philadelphia audiences by introducing modern works; programmed Schoenberg's music, culminating in performances of the formidable but tonal *Gurrelieder* (1932). An even greater gesture of defiance was his world premiere of Varèse's *Amériques* (1926), which opens with a siren and thrives on dissonance. He also made history by combining the Philadelphia Orch. with the Philadelphia Grand Opera Co. in the 1st American performance of Berg's masterpiece *Wozzeck* (1931). The opposition of some listeners was increasingly vocal; when audible commotion in the audience erupted during a performance of Webern's Sym., he abruptly stopped conducting, walked off the stage, then returned only to start the work once again. From his earliest years with the Philadelphia Orch., he would address the audience, cautioning them to keep the peace during the performance of a modernistic score, or reprimanding them for lacking progressive views; once took to task the prim Philadelphia ladies for bringing their knitting to the concert. Even when the board of directors took the unusual step of proclaiming a ban on "debatable music" in the orch.'s programs (1933), he refused to heed this proclamation. Another eruption of discontent ensued when he programmed some Soviet music at a youth concert and trained the children to sing the *Internationale*.

In 1936 Stokowski resigned as sole music director of the Philadelphia Orch.; he and Ormandy co-conducted the orch. until 1938, when he left for good. He took a newly organized All-American Youth Orch. on a tour of the U.S. and South America. (1940–42); was associate conductor, with Toscanini, of the NBC Sym. Orch. (1942–43); shared a season with Mitropoulos as conductor of the N.Y. Phil. (1949–50); led the Houston Sym. Orch. (1955–60). In 1962 he organized in N.Y. the American Sym. Orch. (1962–72); conducted the orch. in the 1st complete performance of the 4th Sym. of Ives (1965). In 1973 he went to London; continued to make recordings and conduct occasional concerts; appeared in television interviews; died in his sleep.

Stoltzman, Richard (Leslie), b. Omaha, July 12, 1942. He began clarinet lessons when he was 8 and gained experience playing in local jazz settings with his father, an alto saxophonist. He then studied mathematics and music at Ohio State Univ. (B.Mus., 1964); also studied clarinet with Robert Marcellus; after studies at Yale Univ. (M.Mus., 1967), he completed his clarinet training with Harold Wright at the Marlboro Music School and with Kalman Opperman in N.Y.; pursued postgraduate studies at Columbia Univ.'s Teachers College (1967–70). He played in many concerts at Marlboro; cofounded the group Tashi ("good fortune" in Tibetan) with pianist Peter Serkin, violinist Ida Kavafian, and cellist Fred Sherry in 1973, and toured widely with the group; likewise taught at the Calif. Inst. of the Arts (1970–75).

Stoltzman made his N.Y. solo recital debut in 1974; after being awarded the Avery Fisher Prize in 1977, he pursued an international career as a virtuoso; appeared as soloist with many of the major orchs., as a chamber music artist, and as a solo recitalist. In 1982 he became the 1st clarinetist ever to give a solo recital at N.Y.'s Carnegie Hall. In 1986 he received the Avery Fisher Artist Award. He maintains an extensive repertoire, ranging from the classics to the avant-garde and including popular music genres; he has also commissioned works and made his own transcriptions.

stomp. Generic term for a beat pattern in African music, in which a foot stomping on the ground is integral to the rhythm, often engendering a correspondingly obstinate melodic lilt.

stonatura (It.). Production of a tone intentionally different from that prescribed in the score; playing or singing deliberately off pitch; not the same as scordatura.

Stookey, (Noël) Paul. See ⇒Peter, Paul and Mary.

stop (1). One of a set of devices on the organ console, each in the form of a knob; a performer (or assistant) draws (pulls) a stop to achieve the desirable tone color or instrumental quality represented by each knob; this mechanism in turn admits and stops (directs) the flow of wind to the grooves beneath the chosen pipe. Several stops can be drawn simultaneously to produce a stronger or more complex sound, hence the expression "pull out all the stops."

Rows of organ pipes of like character are arranged in graduated succession; these are *speaking* or *sounding* stops, classified as *flue work* (having flue pipes) or *reed work* (having reed pipes). The flue work has 3 subclasses: (a) *principal work*, with cylindrical pipes of diapason quality; (b) *gedackt work*, with stopped pipes; and (c) *flute work*, including all flue stops too broad or narrow to produce diapason tone, plus stopped pipes with chimneys and all 3- or 4-sided wooden pipes.

Auxiliary stop, drawn with other stop(s), reinforcing the tone of the latter; *complete stop*, having at least 1 pipe for each key of the manual to which it belongs; *compound stop*, mixture stop; *divided stop*, whose lower register is controlled by a different knob from the upper and bears a different name; *flue stop*, composed of flue pipes; *foundation stop*, of normal 8' pitch; *half, incomplete*, or *imperfect stop*, producing (about) half the tones of the full scale of its manual; *mechanical stop*, not sounding (lacking a set of pipes), but governing some mechanical device; *mixture stop*, with 2 or more ranks of pipes, producing 2 or more tones for each key; *mutation stop*, producing tones a major 3rd or perfect 5th (or a higher octave of either) above the 8' stops; *partial stop*, half stop; *pedal stop*, stop on the pedal; *reed stop*, composed of reed pipes; *solo stop*, adapted for characteristic melodic effects, whether on the solo organ or not; *sounding* or *speaking stop*, having pipes and producing musical tones.

stop (2). 1. On the violin, etc., the pressure of a finger on a string to vary the latter's pitch; a *double stop* is when 2 or more strings are so pressed and sounded simultaneously. 2. On wind instruments with finger holes, the closing of a hole by finger or key to alter the pitch. 3. On instruments of the horn family, the partial or total closing of the bell by inserting the hand.

stop time. Rhythmic device in jazz in which the group suddenly stops playing while 1 or more members play a solo or cadenza; then the ensemble resumes as before. In older jazz, stop times were worked out in advance; in later jazz the soloist could improvise more freely and thus direct the return of the group, or the individual members might return gradually rather than all at once. The most effective use of stop time is in up-tempo music; but the cadenza for the soloist before the piece ends is standard in all tempos.

stopped diapason. Organ flue pipe, closed at the top with a removable plug.

stopped note. Tone obtained with a stop; as opposed to open.

stopped pipe. Organ pipes closed (plugged or covered) at the top; opposed to open.

straccicalando (It.). Babbling, prattling.

Stradivari (Latinized as Stradivarius), Antonio, b. probably in Cremona, 1644; d. probably there, Dec. 18, 1737. He was a pupil of Niccolò Amati in the early 1660s; his earliest known violin dates from 1666; he may have worked for Amati and others from 1666 before purchasing the house that contained his workshop from 1680. His finest instruments were made in the period from 1700 to 1725, but he still worked up to the year of his death; he made his last instrument at age 92. His label reads: "Antonius Stradivarius Cremonensis. Fecit Anno . . . (A x S)." His cellos command even higher prices than the violins, and violas the highest of all, for he made very few of them. Stradivari had 11 children; of them Francesco (1671–1743) and Omobono (1679–1742) were his coworkers. Stradivari also made viols of early types, guitars, lutes, mandolins, etc.

strain. In general, a song, tune, air, or melody; also, some well-defined passage in, or part of, a piece. Technically, a period, sentence, or short division of a composition; a motive or theme.

strambotto (It., rustic song). 16th-century vocal genre akin to the madrigal and frottola; set to poetry with specific stanza and rhyme schemes; a form favored by Lord Byron. The strambotto is distinguished by simplicity, symmetry of phrase, and accessible harmony.

stranka (strančica). Transverse wooden flute of Croatia and Slavonia, with a cylindrical bore and 5 or 6 finger holes; it is associated with shepherds.

strappando (It.). Abruptly, explosively.

strappare (It., pluck off). In piano playing, throw off a note or chord by a rapid, light turn of the wrist.

strascinando (It.). Dragging, drawling. *Strascinando l'arco,* drawing the bow so as to bind the notes.

strascinare la voce (It.). Sing a portamento with exaggerated dragging or drawling.

Stratas, Teresa (born Anastasia Stratakis), b. Toronto, May 26, 1938. Her father owned a restaurant in a town near Toronto, and she was allowed from her earliest childhood to sing for customers. She also sang in concert with her brother, a violinist, and her sister, a pianist. In 1954 she entered the Royal Cons. of Music of Toronto, where she studied voice with Irene Jessner; she graduated with an Artist Diploma in 1959. She made her professional operatic debut with the Toronto Opera Festival as Mimi on Oct. 13, 1958. In 1959 she was a cowinner of the Metropolitan Opera Auditions, which led to her formal debut with the company in N.Y. in 1959, as Poussette in Manon. She soon established herself as a singer of great versatility.

Stratas sang virtually all the standard soprano parts, and demonstrated her particular mettle and fettle in the complete version of Berg's *Lulu,* which was given for the 1st time in Paris in 1979; in N.Y. she created the role of Marie Antoinette in Corigliano's *The Ghosts of Versailles* (1986). She won international acclaim for her dramatic portrayal of Violetta in Zeffirelli's film version of *La Traviata* (1983). In 1972 she was made an Officer of the Order of Canada. A film portrait of Stratas was made by Harry Rasky as *StrataSphere.*

strategy and tactics. Modern composers are forever seeking metaphors from other fields to enrich the rapidly obsolescent musical nomenclature derived from vague Italian words indicating form, speed, dynamic force, or expression. Among such new metaphors are strategy and tactics. The general scheme of a modern sym. or a sonata is strategic, while variations, cadenzas, and contrapuntal elaborations are tactical devices. Iannis Xenakis, the originator of the stochastic method of composition, extended the concept of strategy and tactics into an actual tournament between 2 orchs. and 2 conductors, exemplified in his antiphonal sym. entitled *Stratégie.* According to the composer's specifications, 2 orchs. perform simultaneously 2 different compositions, following the uncoordinated pair of conductors and stopping at climactic points to survey the mutual gains and losses. At the end of the maneuver the audience votes to nominate the winner of this instrumental encounter.

strathspey (Scot., valley of the Spey River). Lively Scottish dance, somewhat slower than the reel, also in 4/4 time, progressing rhythmically as 1 16th note followed by a dotted 8th note (Scotch snap).

Strauss. Family of celebrated Austrian waltz composers and musicians.

(1) Johann (Baptist) Strauss (I), b. Vienna, Mar. 14, 1804; d. there, Sept. 25, 1849. He made a concerted effort to conceal his Jewish origins; when the family's ancestry was realized by the chagrined Nazis a century later, they falsified the parish register at St. Stephen's Cathedral to make the family "racially pure". His musical talent revealed itself at an early age; after he ran away, his parents consented to his becoming a musician. He studied the violin under Polyschansky and harmony

under Seyfried; at 15 he became a violist in M. Pamer's dance orch.; met Lanner, becoming a member of the latter's small band (1819); served as 2nd conductor of Lanner's orch. (1824–25).

In 1825 Strauss organized his own orch.; became popular in Viennese inns; composed his 1st waltz, *Täuberln-Walzer* (1826); his reputation was secured by appearances at the Sperl, where Pamer served as music director. As his renown spread, his orch. increased rapidly in size and efficiency; toured Austria (from 1833); appointed bandmaster of the 1st Vienna militia regiment (1834); extended his tours to Berlin (1834) and the Low Countries (1836); invaded Paris and London with a picked corps of 28, achieving immense success (1837–38). In 1846 he was named k.k. (*kaiserlich und königlich,* imperial and royal) Hofballmusikdirektor; known as "The Father of the Waltz."

Strauss died after catching scarlet fever from one of his children. In addition to his several hundred waltzes, he composed galops, polkas, quadrilles, cotillions, contredances, marches (including the *Radetzky-Marsch,* 1848); potpourris. He had 3 sons who carried on the family musical tradition:

(2) Johann (Baptist) Strauss (II), b. Vienna, Oct. 25, 1825; d. there, June 3, 1899. His father intended him for a business career, but his musical talent manifested itself at age 6, when he wrote the 1st 36 bars of a waltz later publ. as *Erster Gedanke;* his mother arranged that he study secretly with F. Amon, his father's concertmaster; after his father left the family (1842), he pursued violin training with A. Kohlmann and theory with J. Drechsler (to 1844).

Strauss made his 1st debut as conductor of his own ensemble at Dommayer's Casino at Hietzing (1844); his success was instantaneous, his new waltzes winning wide popularity. Despite his father's objections to this intra-family rivalry, Johann II continued concertizing with increasing success; after his father's death, he united his father's band with his own; subsequently toured Europe regularly (1856–86); was k.k. Hofballmusikdirektor in Vienna (1863–71); accepted an invitation to visit the U.S. (1972), directing 14 "monster concerts" in Boston and 4 in N.Y.; known as "The Waltz King."

Strauss then turned to the stage. His finest operetta is *Die Fledermaus,* an epitome of Viennese spirit that still holds the stage as a masterpiece of its genre; 1st staged at the Theater an der Wien (1874), it was within a few months given in N.Y.; productions followed all over the world. It was performed in Paris with a new libretto as *La Tzigane* (1877); the original version was presented there as *La Chauve-souris* only in 1904. *Der Zigeunerbaron* (Vienna, 1885) was also very successful; all his operettas were 1st produced in Vienna, with the exception of *Eine Nacht in Venedig* (Berlin, 1883).

Although Strauss composed extensively for the theater, his supreme achievement remains the dance music. He wrote 498 op. numbers; of his waltzes the most popular was *On the Beautiful Blue Danube* (1867); Brahms once wrote on a lady's fan the opening measures of the tune and the inscription, "Leider nicht von Brahms" (Unfortunately not by Brahms); Wagner, too, voiced his appreciation of Strauss. Other fine waltzes by Johann II include *Acceleration* (1860), *Artist's Life* (1867), *Tales of the Vienna Woods* (1868), *Wine, Women, and Song* (1869), *Wiener Blut* (1873), *Roses from the South* (1880), *Voices of Spring* (1883), and *Emperor* (1889); also composed quadrilles, polkas, polka-mazurkas, marches, galops, and several pieces in collaboration with his brothers.

(3) Josef Strauss, b. Vienna, Aug. 22, 1827; d. there, July 21, 1870. He studied theory with F. Dolleschal and violin with Amon; versatile and gifted, despite lifelong illnesses, he wrote poetry, painted, and patented inventions. He 1st appeared in public conducting in Vienna a set of his waltzes (1853); later regularly appeared as a conductor with Johann II's orch. (1856–62); their younger brother Eduard joined them (1862); Johann left the orch. (1863), leaving his brothers to conduct the family orch. Josef wrote 283 op. numbers, revealing a remarkably talented composer; may have publ. works under Johann II's name. In addition to his outstanding waltzes, he wrote polkas, quadrilles, polka-mazurkas, and marches; a few of his finest works, including *Ode an die Nacht* for Chorus and Orch (1858), have disappeared.

(4) Eduard Strauss, b. Vienna, Mar. 15, 1835; d. there, Dec. 28, 1916. He studied theory and composition with G. Preyer and S. Sechter, violin with Amon, and harp with Parish-Alvars and Zamara. After playing harp in Johann II's orch., he made his debut as a conductor and composer with it at the Wintergarten of the Dianabad-Saal (1862); after Johann II left the orch. (1863), he and his brother Josef co-conducted the orch. until Josef's death. He became k.k. Hofballmusikdirektor (1870–78); made annual European tours as guest conductor and with his own orch.; toured the U.S. (1890, 1900–01), after which he retired. He wrote some 300 works, failing to rival those of his brothers; his conducting, however, was more effective; developed mannerisms (e.g., expressive rubato) not always approved of by Johann II but still heard in contemporary performances of the family's music.

Strauss, Richard (Georg), b. Munich, June 11, 1864; d. Garmisch-Partenkirchen, Sept. 8, 1949. His father, Franz (Joseph) Strauss (b. Parkstein, Feb. 26, 1822; d. Munich, May 31, 1905), was a horn player and composer who, although a violent opponent of Wagner, was valued highly by the master, was entrusted to him the solo horn passages at the premieres of *Tristan und Isolde, Die Meistersinger von Nürnberg,* and *Parsifal.* Richard studied piano as a child with A. Tombo, harpist in the Court Orch.; took violin lessons from Benno Walter, its concertmaster; received instruction from the court conductor, F. W. Meyer. He began to improvise songs and piano pieces at a very early age; in 1881 his 1st orch'l work, the Sym. in D Minor, was premiered in Munich under H. Levi, followed by the Sym. in F Minor, premiered by the N.Y. Phil. under T. Thomas (1884). He made progress as a performer; at 20 von Bülow engaged him as assistant conductor of his Meiningen Orch. He became associated with the poet and musician A. Ritter, who introduced him to the "music of the future" in the form of Liszt orch'l works and Wagner operas.

In 1886 Strauss was appointed as 3rd conductor of the Court Opera in Munich; conducted the premiere of his symphonic fantasy *Aus Italien* (Munich, 1887). He composed his 1st true masterpiece, the symphonic poem *Don Juan* (after Lenau), applying Liszt's thematic principles; conducted its premiere in Weimar (1889); it was the 1st of his literary symphonic poems. The next symphonic poem was *Tod und Verklärung;* he conducted its premiere on the same program with the premiere of the brilliant *Burleske* for Piano and Orch., featuring E. d'Albert as soloist (Eisenach, 1890); this was followed by the premiere of the symphonic poem *Macbeth,* conducted by the composer (Weimar, 1890). In these works he established his mastery of program music; became the most important representative of nascent musical modernism; was praised extravagantly by earnest believers in musical progress and damned savagely by entrenched traditionalists in the press. He adapted Wagner's system of leitmotivs to his symphonic music, interwoven with motives, each representing a relevant programmatic element; explanatory brochures listing these motives were publ. like musical Baedekers to guide listeners; von Bülow, ever the wit, dubbed Strauss "Richard the 2nd," the rightful heir of Wagner.

Turning to opera, Strauss wrote his 1st, *Guntram,* to his own libretto; conducted its premiere (Weimar, 1894); the leading soprano role was taken by Pauline de Ahna, whom he married (1894). While active as a composer, he did not neglect his conducting career; succeeded von Bülow as conductor of the Berlin Phil. (1894), leading it for a season; that year he became assistant conductor of the Munich Court Opera, later chief conductor (1896); guest conducted in European music centers (1896–97). His works of the period included the sparkling *Till Eulenspiegels lustige Streiche* (1895), *Also sprach Zarathustra,* after Nietzsche (Frankfurt am Main, 1896, composer conducting), and *Don Quixote,* variations with cello and viola obligati, after Cervantes (Cologne, 1898). In 1898 he became a conductor at the Berlin Royal Opera; appointed its Generalmusikdirektor (1908–18); led the premiere of his extraordinarily autobiographical *Ein Heldenleben* (Frankfurt am Main, 1899); the hero of the title was Strauss himself, while his critics were represented by a cacophonous charivari; this exhibition of musical self-aggrandizement was severely chastised in the press; there followed his 1st successful opera, *Feuersnot* (Dresden, 1901).

In 1903 Strauss was the guest of honor of an eponymous festival in London; on his 1st U.S. visit he gave the premiere of his *Symphonia domestica* at Carnegie Hall in N.Y. (1904); the score presented a day in the life of the Strauss household, including an interlude describing, quite literally, the feeding of the newly born baby; the reviews reflected aversion to such musical self-exposure. Far more disturbing was his opera *Salome,* to a German trans. of Wilde's play (he also set the French orig.). Schuch led its premiere (Dresden, 1905); *Salome* had its American premiere at the Metropolitan Opera in N.Y. (1907); the ghastly subject, involving intended incest, 7-fold nudity, and decapitation followed by labial necrophilia, administered such a shock to the public and the press that the Metropolitan Opera took it off the boards after 2 performances. Scarcely less forceful was his next opera, *Elektra,* after Aeschylus' *Libation Bearers,* to a libretto by Austrian poet and dramatist Hugo von Hofmannsthal (1874–1929), depicting the horrors of matricide with extraordinary force in unabashedly dissonant harmonies; Schuch conducted its premiere (Dresden, 1909).

Strauss decided to prove that he was quite able to write melodious operas to charm the musical ear; he accomplished this in *Der Rosenkavalier,* a delightful opera-bouffe in an endearing popular manner, also to a text of Hofmannsthal; Schuch conducted its premiere (Dresden, 1911). Turning again to Greek mythology, the two collaborated on a short opera, *Ariadne auf Naxos,* which Strauss conducted for the 1st time in Stuttgart (1912); they later expanded it into a full-length work (Vienna,

1916). His next work was the formidable and quite realistic score *Eine Alpensinfonie*, depicting an ascent of the Alps and employing a wind machine and a thunder machine in the orch. to illustrate a storm; he conducted its premiere with the Dresden Court Orch. in Berlin (1915); then, with Hofmannsthal as librettist, he composed *Die Frau ohne Schatten* (Vienna, 1919), fusing the darkness of his early operas with the lyricism of the later ones, using a complex plot heavily endowed with symbolism. In 1917 he helped to organize the Salzburg Festival; appeared there in subsequent years as conductor; became codirector with F. Schalk of the Vienna State Opera (1919–24); took the Vienna Phil. on a South American tour (1920); guest conducted in the U.S. (1920). For his next opera, *Intermezzo* (Dresden, 1924), he wrote his own libretto; back with Hofmannsthal, he wrote *Die ägyptische Helena* (Dresden, 1928) and *Arabella* (their final collaboration; Dresden, 1933).

When Hitler came to power (1933), the Nazis tried to persuade Strauss to affirm the official policies of the 3rd Reich; Hitler even sent him a signed picture of himself with the inscription, "To the great composer Richard Strauss, with sincere admiration." Strauss kept clear of formal association with the Führer and his cohorts; he agreed to serve as president of the newly organized Reichsmusikkammer (1933); resigned from it less than 2 years later, ostensibly for reasons of health. He entered into open conflict with the Nazis by asking Stefan Zweig, an Austrian Jew, to provide the libretto for *Die schweigsame Frau* (after B. Jonson); it was produced in Dresden (1935) but then withdrawn after a few performances. His political difficulties increased when the Nazis discovered that his daughter-in-law was Jewish. (Zweig himself managed to escape, emigrating to Brazil, but was so tortured by the world's inhumanity that he and his wife committed suicide.) He valiantly went through the motions; composed and conducted the *Olympische Hymne* for the Berlin Olympic Games (1936). He traveled to London to receive the Gold Medal of the Royal Phil. Soc. (1936); conducted the visiting Dresden State Opera in his *Ariadne auf Naxos* at Covent Garden. He selected Joseph Gregor as his new librettist; they revisited Greek mythology, producing *Daphne* (Dresden, 1938) and *Die Liebe der Danae* (1938–40); the latter's public dress rehearsal was given in Salzburg (1944), but with the Allies rapidly encroaching on a devastated Germany, the opera did not officially premiere until after the composer's death. His last opera was *Capriccio;* its libretto was prepared by the conductor Clemens Krauss, who conducted its premiere in Munich (1942).

Strauss's non-operatic music of the 1940s shows a rebirth of enthusiasm and the elegance of experience. One interesting work of this period was his Horn Concerto No. 2, premiered in Salzburg (1943). As the war ended he composed *Metamorphosen*, a lament for string orch. on the disintegration of Germany, with a symbolic quotation from the funeral march of Beethoven's *Eroica Sym.*; also completed the Oboe Concerto. In 1945 he went to Switzerland; 2 years later he visited London for another Strauss Festival and conducted his own works. Although official suspicion continued to linger regarding his relationship with the Nazi regime, he was officially exonerated of all taint (1948). A last flash of inspiration brought forth the deeply moving (and so-called) *Vier letzte Lieder* for Soprano and Orch., on poems of Hesse and Eichendorff; with this farewell, he left Switzerland (1949) and returned home to die; his wife died a few months later (1950). Undeniably one of the finest master composers of modern times, Strauss never espoused extreme chromatic or atonal techniques, remaining a Romantic at heart. His genius is unquestionably present in his symphonic poems and late orch'l works; many of his operas have attained a permanent place in the repertory; his songs are as impressive as any late Romantic composer's.

stravagante (It.). Extravagant, fantastic, whimsical; applied to practitioners of the seconda prattica (such as Monteverdi) as a criticism of their treatment of harmonic progression and resolution.

Stravinsky, Igor (Feodorovich), b. Oranienbaum, near St. Petersburg, June 17, 1882; d. N.Y., Apr. 6, 1971. His music exercised the most profound influence on the 20th century through the emancipation of rhythm, melody, and harmony. His father was Feodor (Ignatievich) Stravinsky (b. Noviy Dvor, near Rechitza, June 20, 1843; d. St. Petersburg, Dec. 4, 1902), one of the greatest Russian basses before Chaliapin, distinguished for the power of his voice and acting ability; made 1,235 appearances in 64 operatic roles. Igor often went to opera rehearsals when his father sang, acquiring an early love for the musical theater; took piano lessons with A. Snetkova, then Leokadia Kashperova (pupil of Anton Rubinstein); studied theory with Akimenko, then Kalafati (1900–03); his progress in composition was remarkably slow; never entered a music school or a cons., nor earned a music degree; enrolled in the faculty of jurisprudence at St. Petersburg Univ. (1901); took courses there for 8 semesters, without graduating; a fellow student was Vladimir Rimsky-Korsakov, a son of the composer.

In 1902 Stravinsky traveled in Germany; met another son of Rimsky-Korsakov, Andrei, a student at the Univ. of Heidelberg; they became friends. He was introduced to Rimsky-Korsakov; became a regular guest at the latter's periodic gatherings in St. Petersburg; wrote a piano sonata for the Russian pianist N. Richter (1903–04), who performed it at Rimsky-Korsakov's home. He began taking regular orchestration lessons gratis with Rimsky-Korsakov (1905); under his tutelage Stravinsky composed a Sym. in E-flat Major; 2 movements were performed by the Court Orch. in St. Petersburg (1907); a complete performance followed by the same orch. (1908). The sym., dedicated to his teacher, had little indication of his eventual development as a master of form and orchestration; at the same concert his *Le Faune et la bergère* for Voice and Orch. had its premiere, revealing the influence of French impressionism. To celebrate the marriage of Rimsky-Korsakov's daughter Nadezhda to the composer M. Steinberg (1908), he wrote an orch'l fantasy entitled *Fireworks*; Rimsky-Korsakov died a few days after the wedding; Stravinsky deeply mourned his beloved teacher, writing a *Chant funèbre* for Wind Instruments in his memory (St. Petersburg, 1909). There followed a *Scherzo fantastique* for Orch., inspired by Maeterlinck's book *La Vie des abeilles*; Stravinsky had planned a literal program, illustrating events in a beehive; however, he later denied any connection between his piece and the book.

Stravinsky's fortunes changed when the famous impresario Diaghilev commissioned him to write a work for the Paris season of his Ballets Russes; the result was his 1st ballet masterpiece, *The Firebird* (1910), for which he created music of extraordinary brilliance, steeped in the colors of Russian fairy tales, with numerous striking effects, such as a glissando of harmonics in the strings; the rhythmic drive is exhilarating, the use of asymmetrical time signatures extremely effective; the harmonies are opulent; the orchestration coruscating. He later reorchestrated the work twice to conform to a new aesthetic of musical economy (and to recopyright the work); while he plucked the luminous feathers off the magical bird, the original scoring remained a favorite with conductors and orchs.

Stravinsky moved to Paris to maintain his association with Diaghilev; frequently traveled to Switzerland. His next score for the Ballets Russes was *Petrouchka,* produced with triumphant success (1911). Not only was the Russian folk tale remarkably effective on the stage, but the score itself, arranged in 4 tableaux, was so strikingly original that it marked a turning point in 20th-century music, with its spasmodically explosive rhythms, novel instrumental sonorities—with the piano an integral part of the orch.—and the bold innovations of bitonality (i.e., C major and F-sharp major, the *Petrouchka chord*) became a potent influence on European composers; even Debussy expressed enchantment with the score; Stravinsky, still in his 20s, became a Paris celebrity.

Two years later Stravinsky brought out a work of even greater revolutionary import, *The Rite of Spring (Le Sacre du printemps;* the Russian title is *Vesna sviashchennaya,* the sacred spring); its subtitle is *Scenes of Pagan Russia;* Diaghilev and his Ballets Russes presented it with choreography by Nijinsky (Paris, 1913). The score marked a departure from all compositional conventions; while *Petrouchka's* innovative and dissonant harmonies could still be placed in the context of contemporaneous modern music, *The Rite of Spring* contained such corrosive dissonances as scales played at the intervals of major 7ths; superpositions of minor upon major triads with a common tonic; and chords treated as unified blocks of sound; the rapid metrical changes seemingly defied performance. The score remains one of the most daring creations of the modern musical mind; its impact was tremendous; to some of the audience at its 1st performance, his "barbaric" music was beyond endurance; the critics exercised their verbal ingenuity in indignant vituperation—one of them proposed that *Le sacre du printemps* would be better titled *Le massacre du printemps.* In a few years, however, the work had become (and remains) a popular concert piece.

In 1914 Diaghilev produced Stravinsky's lyric fairy tale *Le Rossignol,* after H. C. Andersen; begun before *Petrouchka* and *The Rite of Spring,* the work seems closer to *The Firebird* and the orientalisms of Rimsky-Korsakov. He then worked on the ballet *Les Noces* (Nuptials; Russian title *Svadebka,* little wedding, 1914–18), evoking Russian folk modalities and scored for chorus, soloists, 4 pianos, and 17 percussion instruments. The devastation of World War I made the composer realize that the era of grandiose Romantic music was obsolete; a new spirit of musical economy was imperative in an impoverished world. The results included the musical play *L'Histoire du soldat,* scored for 7 players and a narrator (Lausanne, 1918); a work for 11 instruments entitled *Ragtime,* inspired by the new American music; and 3 works for Diaghilev's Ballets Russes: the ballet *Pulcinella,* based on works formerly attributed to Pergolesi, with 3 vocal soloists (Opéra, 1920); *Renard,* opera after a Russian fairy tale (1922); and *Mavra,* opera after Pushkin (1922); the last 2 works were, excepting the 1944 orch'l *Scherzo à la russe,* his final "Russian pieces."

Stravinsky had entered his neoclassical period, beginning with the Octet for winds (Paris, 1923) and the Piano Concerto, commissioned by Koussevitzky (with winds, double basses, and percussion; Paris, 1924); he used pandiatonic structures, firmly tonal but starkly dissonant in their superposition of tonalities within the same principal key; his reversion to familiar forms, however, was not an act of ascetic renunciation, but an experiment in reviving Baroque practices. The Piano Concerto provided him with an opportunity to appear as soloist, although he was never a virtuoso pianist; played it with Koussevitzky during his 1st American tour with the Boston Sym. Orch. (1925).

The Elizabeth Sprague Coolidge Foundation commissioned Stravinsky to write a pantomime for string orch.; the result was *Apollon Musagète* (Washington, D.C., 1928); this serene and emotionally restrained score evokes the manner of Lully's court ballets. He continued to explore neo-Baroque writing in his Capriccio for Piano and Orch.; played the solo part with Ansermet conducting the premiere (Paris, 1929); while this score evokes a spirit of hedonistic entertainment, recalling the gallant style, it is unmistakably modern in its polyrhythmic collisions of pandiatonic harmonies.

Stravinsky's belated renunciation of the glitter of grandiose sonority found expression in his opera-oratorio *Oedipus Rex;* to emphasize its atemporal detachment, he used a Latin trans. for the libretto, although Sophocles' original is in Greek; its music is deliberately hollow, even parodistic; dramatic points are emphasized by ominous repetitiveness; yet this very austerity of idiom makes *Oedipus Rex* a profoundly moving work. Its 1st performance (Paris, 1927) featured Sarah Bernhardt; its stage premiere took place in Vienna (1928).

The effect of *Oedipus Rex* is heightened in Stravinsky's *Sym. of Psalms,* written for the 50th anniversary of the Boston Sym. Orch. (Brussels, 1930); unusual in its text-music formulation, it is scored for chorus and orch. minus violins and violas, thus emphasizing lower instrumental registers to create an austere and solemn sonority. He wrote a violin concerto commissioned and performed by S. Dushkin (Berlin, 1931). For the ballerina Ida Rubinstein (who had commissioned his *Le Baiser de la Fée,* 1928) he composed the melodrama *Perséphone* (Paris Opéra, 1934), exercising his mastery of simplicity in formal design, melodic patterns, and contrapuntal structure. For his American tour Stravinsky wrote and conducted *Jeu de cartes,* a "ballet in 3 deals" to his own scenario depicting a game of poker (which he loved; Metropolitan Opera, N.Y., 1937). His concerto for 16 instruments, *Dumbarton Oaks* (named after the estate of Mr. and Mrs. Robert Woods Bliss, who commissioned the work), was premiered in Washington, D.C. (1938); known in Europe as the Concerto in E-flat, its style is hermetically neo-Baroque.

With World War II engulfing Europe, Stravinsky decided to seek permanent residence in America; applied for American citizenship (1939); naturalized (1945); to celebrate this event he rearranged *The Star-Spangled Banner,* with a curious modulation interpolated in the coda; after conducting it with the Boston Sym. Orch. (1944), he was advised not to conduct his version again because of laws in the state of Massachusetts against intentional alteration or any mutilation of the national anthem. In 1939–40 Stravinsky gave the C. E. Norton lectures at Harvard Univ. (publ. as *Poétique musicale,* 1946); began accepting private students, a new professional role for him.

Stravinsky's American years form a curious panoply of subjects and manners of composition. He accepted a commission from the Ringling Bros. to write a *Circus Polka* "for a young elephant" (1942; later arr. by Stravinsky for sym. orch.; Cambridge, Mass., 1944). In 1946 he wrote *Ebony Concerto* for Woody Herman's swing band; completed his opera *The Rake's Progress* (1931), inspired by Hogarth's famous series of engravings, to a libretto by W. H. Auden and C. Kallman; conducted its world premiere in Venice that year, as part of its International Festival of Contemporary Music. The work is a striking example of his protean capacity for adopting different styles and idioms to serve his artistic purposes; *The Rake's Progress* ingeniously conglomerates disparate elements, ranging from 18th-century British ballads to cosmopolitan burlesque.

Whatever transmutations his music underwent during a long and productive career, Stravinsky remained a man of the theater at heart. In America he became associated with the brilliant Russian-born choreographer Balanchine, who produced a number of ballets to his music, among them *Apollon Musagète*, Violin Concerto, *Sym. in 3 Movements* (1942–45; N.Y., 1946), *Scherzo à la russe, Pulcinella,* and *Agon,* a ballet for 12 Dancers (1954–57; Los Angeles, 1957). It was in *Agon* (Grk., competition) that he 1st essayed the dodecaphonic method of composition as promulgated by Schoenberg; yet the 12-tone method had until then been the antithesis of his aesthetic credo. An irreconcilable polarity existed between Stravinsky and Schoenberg even in personal relations; although both resided in Los Angeles, they never met socially; earlier, Schoenberg had written a canon in which he ridiculed Stravinsky as "der kleine Modernsky," who put on a wig to look like "Papa Bach" (*Satires,* op. 28, no. 2). After Schoenberg's death he felt free to examine the essence of the 12-tone method, introduced to him by his faithful musical factotum Robert Craft; he adopted dodecaphonic writing in its aspect of canonic counterpoint as developed by Webern. In this manner he wrote his *Canticum sacrum ad honorem Sancti Marci nominis,* which he conducted at San Marco in Venice (1956). Other works of the period were also written in a modified 12-tone technique, among them *The Flood* (for narrator, mime, singers, and dancers), presented in a CBS-TV broadcast in N.Y. in 1962.

After Stravinsky's death, an ugly litigation regarding his estate persisted between his 3 children (including composer Soulima Stravinsky, 1910-) and their stepmother Vera; after her death a compromise was reached; 2/9 of the estate went to each of his children and a grandchild and 1/9 to Robert Craft. The value of the Stravinsky legacy was spectacularly demonstrated in 1982, when the working draft of *The Rite of Spring* was sold at a London auction for $548,000 (a record for music MSS). The purchaser, Paul Sacher, a Swiss conductor, philanthropist, and archival collector, later purchased the entire Stravinsky archive for $5,250,000, outbidding the N.Y. Public Library and the Morgan Library; the materials are now housed in the Sacher Foundation in Basel.

Few composers have escaped the powerful impact of Stravinsky's music; ironically it was his own country that at first rejected him, partly because of Soviet ideological opposition to modern music generally, and partly because of his open criticism of Soviet ways in art; but he visited Russia and was welcomed as a prodigal son (1962); his works began to appear on Russian concert programs, and Soviet music critics issued a number of laudatory studies. Yet it is his early masterpieces, set in an attractive colorful style, that remain the favorites of audiences and performers; his more abstract and recursive scores are appreciated more by specialists.

A sharp debate raged among Stravinsky's associates as to the credibility of Craft's reports of their dialogues, or even of the factual accounts of events during the composer's last years. He never mastered the English language, yet Craft quotes him delivering literary paragraphs of impeccable English prose. Craft admitted that he enhanced Stravinsky's actual words and sentences (never recorded on tape), articulating the inner, even subliminal sense of his utterances. Craft's role was clarified beyond dispute by Stravinsky himself, who in a 1958 letter to his publishing agent urged that the title of a book be changed to *Conversations with Igor Stravinsky by Robert Craft,* emphatically asserting that the text was in Craft's language, and that in effect Craft had "created" him.

Strayhorn, Billy (William Thomas), b. Dayton, Ohio, Nov. 29, 1915; d. N.Y., May 31, 1967. He studied music in Pittsburgh; joined Duke Ellington's band as lyricist and arranger in 1939. Many songs credited to Ellington (*Chelsea Bridge, Perfume Suite, Such Sweet Thunder, A Drum Is a Woman*) are in fact products of a mutually beneficial musical symbiosis, with Ellington suggesting the initial idea, mood, and character and Strayhorn doing the actual writing, often using Ellington's quasi-impressionistic techniques (modal harmonies, whole-tone scales, etc.). Strayhorn's own acknowledged songs such as *Lush Life* and *Take the A Train* are jazz standards.

straziante (It.). Anxiously.

street cries. Street vendors used to peddle their wares in melodious jingles before the age of commercialized trade; each product had its own recognizable tune. Such street cries were common in France as early as the 13th century, and they were often incorporated in contemporary motets. Street cries were also used by English composers of the early Renaissance period; notable are those for fresh oysters and hot mutton pieces. Newsboys often sold their papers in 19th-century London with a pleasant modal lift. (A 20th-century rendition of newsboys' calls can be heard in Partch's *San Francisco.*) Charpentier's opera *Louise* includes a quodlibet of peddlers of carrots and other vegetables. Even Bach deigned to include the popular tune *Cabbage and Turnips* at the end of his great *Goldberg Variations.*

In the present century Luciano Berio's *Cries of London* is unusual; it is scored for 8 voices, to authentic vending tunes; the tune urging customers to buy garlic is amusing. In Cuba, Brazil, and Argentina, knife sharpeners and shoeshine boys open up a whole sym. of vendors' tunes at early tropical sunrise. Street organs with reed pipes used to be a ubiquitous sight and sound in Italy, with a monkey passing a hat for donations. A story is told that Giuseppe Verdi, annoyed by street organs playing the tune *La donna e mobile* from his *Rigoletto* before his window, paid off the street musicians to stop playing or change their song. Modern singing commercials are the radio and television successors to the old vending cries.

Streichinstrumente (Ger.). String instruments.

Streichorchester (Ger.). string orch.; *Streichquartett,* string quartet.

Streisand, Barbra (Barbara Joan), b. N.Y., Apr. 24, 1942. She studied acting for a short time in N.Y.; also learned to sing in Greenwich Village. In 1962 she made her Broadway debut in *I Can Get It for You Wholesale;* then made a hit in *Funny Girl* in 1964, a musical she filmed in 1968 and for which she received an Academy Award. Her other films include *On a Clear Day You Can See Forever* (1970), *A Star Is Born* (1976), *Yentl* (1983) and *The Mirror Has Two Faces* (1997). As a recording artist she received gold-record awards for her albums *People* (1965), *My Name Is Barbra* (1965), *Color Me Barbra* (1966), *Stoney End* (1971), *Barbra Joan Streisand* (1972), *The Way We Were* (1974), *A Star Is Born* (1976), *Superman* (1977), and others.

streng (Ger.). Severely, strictly. *Streng im Takt,* strictly in time; *streng im Tempo,* strictly in tempo; *streng wie ein Kondukt,* severely, as if in a funeral procession; *streng Zeitmass,* strictly in tempo; *strenger Satz,* strict style of composition.

strepitoso (It.). In a noisy, boisterous, impetuous style.

Strepponi, Giuseppina (Clelia Maria Josepha). See ⇒Verdi, Giuseppe (Fortunino Francesco).

stretch. On a keyboard instrument, wide interval or spread chord whose tones are to be taken simultaneously by the fingers of 1 hand.

stretto, -a (It., straitened, narrowed; Fr. *strette*). Musical climax that usually occurs at the point when thematic and rhythmic elements have reached the point of saturation. A classic example is the finale of the 2nd act in Mozart's *Le nozze di Figaro,* in prestissimo tempo. A stretto at the end of an impassioned aria or a dramatic duet is virtually synonymous with a cabaletta. Particularly effective is a stretto in a fugue, in which the "narrowing" process is achieved by piling up the subject, the answer, and their fractional particles in close succession and overlap, producing the effect of accelerated canonic imitation; this is particularly effective in the final fugal exposition.

The effect is that of a stretto, a melodic precipitation in a hurried statement, which heightens the rhythmic tension, usually raising also the dynamic level, anticipating a decisive ending.

It should be noted that whereas in a homophonic style a stretto can be achieved by a purely dynamic process, a stretto in a fugue is a profound polyphonic exercise that has to be foreordained by the configuration of the theme and the answer at the inception of the fugue. *Andante stretto,* andante agitato; *stretto pedale,* in piano playing, a quick, deft shifting of the damper pedal, in a strongly marked chord passage, so that the harmonies may be at once forcible and distinct.

Strich (Ger.). Stroke of the bow. *Strich für Strich,* use separate bow strokes; détaché.

strict style. Style of composition in which (most) dissonances are regularly prepared and resolved.

stride piano. Jazz piano style of the 1920s and 1930s that retained elements of ragtime and in which the highly syncopated and elaborate melody is accompanied by the left hand's "strides" between single bass notes on the strong beat of the measure and middle-register chords on the weak beat in a regular oompah rhythm. One great performer was Fats Waller, in songs such as *I Would Do Anything for You.*

stridendo (*stridente;* It.). Stridently; sharply, piercingly; martellato.

string. Tone-producing cord. *First string,* the highest of a set; *open string,* one not stopped or shortened; *silver string,* one covered with silver wire; *soprano string,* the E string of the violin; *the strings,* the string group in the orch.

string bass. Double bass.

string drum (lion's roar; Ger. *Löwenebrull;* It. *rugghio di leone;* Fr. *tambour à cordes*). Friction drum with a cylindrical-shaped bucket through which a length of cord or gut string is pulled to produce a distinct "roaring" sound; favored among 20th-c. composers.

string(ed) instruments. Instruments whose tones are produced by strings, whether struck, plucked, or bowed; chordophones; commonly reserved for members of the violin and related families in which the strings are bowed. Plucked string instruments, including lute, guitar, balalaika, mandolin, banjo, and many Eastern instruments, are treated separately. Another important distinction between the 2 categories is that instruments of the violin family have smooth fingerboards, requiring the player to find notes with the left hand without external guidance, whereas the plucked strings have frets or marking points to indicate the position of whatever scale is in use.

Distances between frets diminish for each successive chromatic interval. The violin string measuring 13 $\frac{1}{2}$ inches sounds an octave higher when it is stopped in the middle point, at the distance of 6 $\frac{3}{4}$ inches from the peg and the bridge; but the next octave takes only a quarter of the string to span, the next octave only $\frac{1}{8}$ of the string. Thus violinists must develop an extraordinary capacity for judging small distances by touch. String instruments lend themselves to ensembles in any combination; but the most common combinations are string quartet, string quintet, string sextet (often including the double bass), or string orch.

string piano. Traditional piano that is sounded by acting directly upon the strings, i.e., strumming, plucking, hammering, etc.

string quartet. Historically the most significant type of chamber music. A string quartet consists of 2 violins, viola, and cello. Such an ensemble provides a rich 4-part harmony and an articulate interplay of contrapuntal forms, especially canon and fugue. Opportunities for expressive and effective solo parts are many, with the solo instrument accompanied by the other 3 instruments; episodic duos and trios furnish another resource. The traditional structure of a string quartet is that of the sonata, consisting of 4 movements and usually including a minuet or a scherzo.

Goethe compared the playing of a string quartet with "a conversation of 4 educated people." The 1st violin is a natural leader. The 2nd violin is the leader's faithful partner; the somewhat derogatory expression "playing 2nd fiddle" suggests its subordinate function. The viola fills the harmony and emerges as an important member of the quartet, usually in canonic passages. The cello holds the important duty of the bass voice, determining the harmony; its sonorous arpeggios lend an almost orch'l quality to the ensemble. The employment of special effects such as pizzicato and the availability of double stops contribute further to the harmonic richness of string quartets.

Claims for the priority of composing string quartets have been made for several composers of the 17th century, but the 1st composer of stature to establish the string quartet as a distinctive musical form was Haydn, who wrote 83 string quartets. (This is not, however, the maximum; Boccherini wrote 102.) Mozart's string quartets brought the art of the string quartet to its highest flowering for the 18th century; his so-called *Dissonanzenquartett* aroused a heat of controversy because of its innovative use of dissonant harmonic combinations. Beethoven's last quartets caused contemporary critics to opine that they were the products of the composer's loss of hearing; as usual, he heard far better than the critics were ready to.

The taste and attraction of string quartets suffered a sharp decline in the modern era. Debussy, Ravel, and Stravinsky wrote only a single string quartet each. Schoenberg and Bartók revived the string quartet with considerable departures from tradition; Schoenberg even used a vocal solo in one of his. Russian composers continued to cultivate string quartets assiduously. Shostakovich wrote 15 of them.

string quintet. 1. Chamber music ensemble with 5 string instruments, usually 2 violins, 2 violas, and cello. 2. Composition, usually multimovement, for this combination (or a close variant). The most prolific composer of string quintets was Boccherini (12); Mozart wrote 6; Beethoven wrote 3; Mendelssohn wrote 2, as did Brahms. Schubert's great C-major quintet is scored for 2 violins, viola, and 2 cellos. 3. String component of the orch., normally written in 5 parts (2 violins, viola, cello, and double bass).

string trio. 1. Ensemble for 3 string instruments, often consisting of violin, viola, and cello. 2. Composition, usually multimovement, for this combination (or a close variant). Historically the string trio is an offshoot of the trio sonata. Haydn wrote as many as 20 trios for 2 violins and cello; Mozart and Beethoven also contributed to the form. Schoenberg's string trio is set in the 12-tone idiom.

stringendo (It.). Hastening; accelerating the movement, usually suddenly and rapidly, with a crescendo.

stringere (It.). To hasten. *Senza stringere*, without hastening.

stringy. Having the quality of tone—string tone—peculiar to bowed instruments.

strisciando (It.). Gliding, smooth, glissando.

Strohfiedel (Ger., straw fiddle). Obsolete term for older type of xylophone in which the slabs were separated by straw.

stromenti a fiato (It.). Wind instruments.

strophe (Grk., turning). Rhythmic system composed of a repeated unit of 2 or more lines (refrain); it provides a break in the continuity of a stanzaic song, leading to a new section but preserving the unity of rhythm and musical setting. The strophe is often confused with the stanza.

strophic bass. Repeated bass in a song accompaniment, to which the melody varies freely.

strophic composition (song). See ⇒song.

Strouse, Charles (Louis), b. N.Y., June 7, 1928. He studied at the Eastman School of Music in Rochester, N.Y., and later took private lessons in composition with Aaron Copland and Nadia Boulanger, under whose guidance he wrote some ambitious instrumental music. He was mainly active as a composer for Broadway and films; with the lyricist Lee Adams (b. Mansfield, Ohio, Aug. 14, 1924) he wrote the musicals *Bye Bye Birdie* (1960) and *Applause* (1970), both of which won Tony Awards. His other musicals include *Golden Boy* (1964), after a play by Clifford Odets, and *Annie* (1977). He also composed a piano concerto and other orch. pieces, and a string quartet.

structure. In the 20th century, an analyzable system within the totality of musical parameters, denoting the methods and mechanisms applied and contributing to the ultimate structural integrity of a work. While *structure* is often used as a synonym for *form* (in the sense of design), it can refer to elements such as harmony, counterpoint, melody, and rhythm; it can refer to a specific idiom, such as dodecaphonic, stochastic, linear, tonal, motivic, and symmetrical structures; or, in its adjectival form it can identify structural conceptions, such as layering, variants, accentuation, groupings, symbolism, gestalt, and perception. The present usage of the term indicates a composer's concern for rational control and structural meaning.

strumentatura (It.). Instrumentation.

strumento (*stromento;* It.). Instrument. *Strumenti a corda,* string instruments; *strumenti a fiato,* wind instruments; *strumenti da tasto,* keyboard instruments.

Stück (Ger.). A piece; a number. *Klavierstück,* a piece for piano.

Studer, Cheryl, b. Midland, Mich., Oct. 24, 1955. After training in Ohio and at the Univ. of Tenn., she studied voice with Hans Hotter at the Vienna Hochschule für Musik. She appeared in concerts in the U.S. before singing at the Bavarian State Opera in Munich in 1980; then was a member of the Darmstadt Opera (1983–85). In 1984 she made her U.S. operatic debut as Micaela at the Chicago Lyric Opera. In 1985 she joined the Deutsche Oper in West Berlin. She also sang at the Bayreuth Festivals (from 1985), at the Paris Opéra (from 1986), and at La Scala in Milan (from 1987). Among her prominent roles are Pamina, Donna Anna, Elsa, Eva, Sieglinde, and Chrysothemis.

study. Etude; teaching piece.

Sturm und Drang (Ger., storm and stress). German literary term borrowed to describe a highly emotional minor-key style that emerged during the early Classic period, particularly the

1770s and 1780s. The literary movement arose in the last part of the 18th century, eventually taking its name from the title of a popular play by Friedrich Klinger (1776). It became eponymous with a growing sentiment among the youth of the time that a rebellion against the conservatism in social politics and in art was necessary; it also brought to the fore the extreme emotions that Goethe portrayed in *The Sorrows of Young Werther* (1774). In music it gave a glimpse of the extreme, non-Classic contrasts that would be a stylistic trademark of the Romantic style of composition. But the movement retreated into the aesthetic wilderness until younger writers such as Jean Paul, E. T. A. Hoffman, the brothers Grimm, and the British gothic school redefined the meaning of aesthetics and composers like Beethoven (and to a lesser extent Weber) composed from the soul as well as the ear. In this sense Schumann's struggle against musical Philistinism, and the programmatic concepts of many of his works, are indirect descendants of Sturm und Drang.

stürmisch (Ger.). Tempestuously, passionately, impetuously.

style brisé (Fr., broken style). In French music of the 17th century, form of chordal arpeggiation in which the bass note sounded 1st, then the melody, and with the middle voices in a similarly free manner. Many of Louis Couperin's harpsichord preludes provide examples of this manner in notation.

style élégant (Fr.). Galanterien.

style galant (Fr.). Gallant style.

Styne, Jule (born Julius Kerwin Stein), b. London, Dec. 31, 1905; d. Sept. 20, 1994. He was taught piano by his parents; was taken to the U.S. at age 8; appeared with the Chicago Sym. Orch. as a child pianist but did not pursue a concert career; won a scholarship to the Chicago College of Music at 13; after playing piano in jazz groups and dance bands he went to Hollywood (1940) and rapidly established himself as a successful song composer for films; also was notably successful as a composer of Broadway musicals, which included *High Button Shoes* (1947), *Gentlemen Prefer Blondes* (1949), *Bells Are Ringing* (1956), *Gypsy,* based on the life of striptease artist Gypsy Rose Lee (1959), *Do Re Mi* (1960; no relation to *The Sound of Music*), *Funny Girl,* scenes from the life of the singer-comedienne Fanny Brice (1964), *Hallelujah, Baby!* (1967), and *Sugar* (1972).

styrienne (Fr.; It. *stiriana*). Slow air in 2/4 time, often in a minor key, with a *Jodler* (yodel) after each verse; for vocal or instrumental solo.

su (It.). Above, on, upon, by, near. *Arco in su,* up-bow.

suave (It.). Soave.

subbass, subbourdon. Organ stop of 16' or 32' pitch, generally on the pedal, and stopped.

subdominant. Tone below the dominant in a diatonic scale; the 4th degree.

subito (It.). Immediately; suddenly; without pause. *Volti subito,* turn over (the page) quickly; *subito piano* or *p subito,* an abrupt change to *piano,* without gradation.

subject. Melodic motive or phrase on which a composition or movement is founded; a theme. In a fugue, the antecedent or dux.

submediant. 3rd scale tone below the tonic; the 6th degree.

suboctave. 1. Octave below a given note. 2. Double contra-octave.

subordinate chords. Chords not fundamental or principal; the triads on the 2nd, 3rd, 6th, and 7th degrees, and all 7th chords but the dominant 7th.

Subotnick, Morton, b. Los Angeles, Apr. 14, 1933. He studied at the Univ. of Denver (B.A., 1958) and with Milhaud and Kirchner at Mills College in Oakland, Calif. (M.A., 1960); then was a fellow of the Inst. for Advanced Musical Studies at Princeton Univ. (1959–60). He taught at Mills College (1959–66), N.Y. Univ. (1966–69), and the Calif. Inst. of the Arts (from 1969); also held various visiting professorships and composer-in-residence positions. In 1979 he married the singer Joan La Barbara, with whom he often collaborates. His compositions run the gamut of avant-garde techniques, often with innovative use of electronics and electroacoustic devices known as "ghost electronics." His works include: *Lamination* for Orch. and Tape (1968); *Axolotl* for Cello, Chamber Orch., and Electronics (1982); *Liquid Strata* for Piano, Orch., and Electronics (1982); *The Key to Songs* for Chamber Orch. and Synthesizer (1985); *4 Butterflies* for Tape and 3 Films (1973); *The Double Life of Amphibians,* theater piece (1984); *Jacob's Room* for Voice and String Quartet (1984); *The Fluttering of Wings* for String Quartet (1982); *Passages of the Beast* for Clarinet and Electronics (1978); *Ascent into Air* for 10 Instruments and Electronics (1981). Electronics alone: *Silver Apples of the Moon* (1967); *The Wild Bull* (1968); *Touch* (1969); *Sidewinder* (1971); *Until Spring* (1975); *A Sky of Cloudless Sulphur* (1978).

subprincipal. Subbass pedal stop of 32' pitch.

subsemitonium modi (Lat., lower semitone of the mode). Leading tone.

substitution. 1. In contrapuntal progression, resolution or preparation of a dissonance by substituting, for the regular tone of resolution or preparation, its higher or lower octave in some other part. 2. The use of alternate harmonies to fill a chord in a standard progression, e.g., the 1st inversion of the supertonic 7th chord instead of the subdominant.

subtonic. Leading tone (rarely used).

subtonium. Additional tone placed below a church mode, in time coming to mean a whole tone below the final of the mode. As the modes gradually gave way to modern tonality, the subtonium was replaced by the subsemitonium, the modern leading tone.

succentor. Member of the Anglican church clergy, assistant to the precentor in musical and other matters.

suffocato (It.). Soffocato.

sugli, sui (It.). On the; near the.

suite. Instrumental genre designating a succession of movements not necessarily related to one another and unified only by the homonymous key. The most important of this category is the *Baroque suite*, composed primarily of dance forms. The standard selection and ordering of the movements is allemande, courante, sarabande, and gigue. Several optional movements, mostly derived from popular dances, are interpolated between the sarabande and gigue, notably a minuet or gavotte; some suites end with a bourrée. Bach expanded the length and content of his instrumental suites, but the meaning of the adjectives *English* and *French,* applied to 6 keyboard suites apiece, is conjectural. Bach also wrote suites bearing the designation *partita.* Baroque harpsichord composers, still contending with the problems of tuning in meantone temperament, realized that it was best to construct suites in only 1 key so that a substantial work could be performed without constant retuning between pieces. F. Couperin and Rameau (who called their suites *ordres*) began to name their suite movements with fanciful programmatic titles; many of these pieces were far removed from the usual dance models.

The character of the suite was changed radically in the 19th century. While Bach, Handel, and other composers of the Baroque period followed the contrapuntal style of composition, composers of the later centuries regarded the suite mainly as an assemblage of variegated movements, often arranged from operas, ballets, and theater music. Sometimes such suites became the only viable remnants of a score of incidental music, as for instance in the suites *L'Arlésienne* of Bizet, or *Peer Gynt* of Grieg. Tchaikovsky's *Nutcracker Suite* is one of the most popular examples of the genre. The suite from *Lulu* was the only music Berg ever heard from his 2nd opera. Neoclassical composers of the 2nd quarter of the 20th century, notably Stravinsky and Hindemith, made a serious effort to revive the Baroque suite, with a titillating titivation of the ancient forms by means of dissonant treatment; other composers have used the term in its loosest sense—a collection of pieces or movements, often but not necessarily of a lighter character, for 1 instrument or ensemble, to be played consecutively.

suivez (Fr.). 1. Colla parte. 2. Continue, go on.

sul, sull', sulla, sulle (It.). (Play) on the, near the. *Sulla corda La,* play on the A string; *Sulla tastiera,* play near or above the fingerboard, flautando; *sul ponticello,* play near the bridge; *sul tasto,* on the keyboard.

suling. Family of bamboo flutes in Indonesia and surrounding areas. They can be transverse, nose, whistle, or ring (end-blown) flutes; are of various sizes; have anywhere from 3 to 7 finger holes; are known by various names; and are used either as a solo instrument or in gamelan and more modern ensembles. The relationship between the suling and the human voice is spiritual and musical.

Sullivan, (Sir) Arthur (Seymour), b. London, May 13, 1842; d. there, Nov. 22, 1900. His father, Thomas Sullivan, was bandmaster at the Royal Military College, Sandhurst, and later prof. of brass instruments at the Royal Military School of Music, Kneller Hall; his musical inclinations were encouraged by his father, and in 1854 he became a chorister in the Chapel Royal, remaining there until 1858 and studying with the Rev. Thomas Helmore; in 1855 his sacred song *O Israel* was publ.

In 1856 Sullivan received the 1st Mendelssohn Scholarship to the Royal Academy of Music in London, where he studied with Sterndale Bennett, Arthur O'Leary, and John Goss; then continued his training at the Leipzig Cons. (1858–61), where he received instruction in counterpoint and fugue from Moritz Hauptmann, in composition from Julius Rietz, in piano from Ignaz Moscheles and Louis Plaidy, and in conducting from Ferdinand David. He conducted his overture *Rosenfest* in Leipzig (1860) and wrote a string quartet and music to *The Tempest* (Leipzig, 1861). His cantata *Kenilworth* (Birmingham Festival, 1864) stamped him as a composer of high rank. In 1864 he visited Ireland and composed his *Irish* Sym. (London, 1866).

In 1866 Sullivan was appointed prof. of composition at the Royal Academy of Music in London. About this time he formed a lifelong friendship with Sir George Grove, whom he accompanied in 1867 on a memorable journey to Vienna in search of Schubert MSS, leading to the discovery of the score of *Rosamunde.* The year 1867 was also notable for the production of the 1st of those comic operas upon which Sullivan's fame chiefly rests. This was *Cox and Box* (libretto by F. C. Burnand), composed in 2 weeks and performed in 1867, in London. Less successful were *The Contrabandista* (London, 1867) and *Thespis* (London, 1871; music lost); but the latter is significant as inaugurating Sullivan's collaboration with (Sir) William S(chwenck) Gilbert, the celebrated humorist, who became the librettist of all Sullivan's most successful comic operas, beginning with *Trial by Jury* (1875). This was produced by Richard D'Oyly Carte, who in 1876 formed a company expressly for the production of the Gilbert and Sullivan operas.

The 1st big success obtained by the famous team was *H.M.S. Pinafore* (1878), which had 700 consecutive performances in London and enjoyed an enormous vogue in "pirated" productions throughout the U.S. In an endeavor to protect their interests, Gilbert and Sullivan went to N.Y. in 1879 to give an authorized performance of *Pinafore;* while there they also produced *The Pirates of Penzance.* In 1881 came *Patience,* a satire on exaggerated aesthetic poses exemplified by Oscar Wilde, whose American lecture tour was conceived as a "publicity stunt" for this work. In 1882 *Iolanthe* began a run that lasted more than a year. This was followed by the comparatively unsuccessful *Princess Ida* (1884), but then came the universal favorite of all the Gilbert and Sullivan operas, *The Mikado* (1885). The list of these popular works is completed by *Ruddigore* (1887), *The Yeomen of the Guard* (1888), and *The Gondoliers* (1889). After a quarrel and a reconciliation, the pair collaborated in 2 further works, of less popularity: *Utopia Limited* (1893) and *The Grand Duke* (1896). Sullivan's melodic inspiration and technical resourcefulness, united with the delicious humor of Gilbert's verses, raised the light opera to a new height of artistic achievement, and his works in this field continue to delight countless hearers.

Sullivan was also active in other branches of musical life. He conducted numerous series of concerts, most notably those of the London Phil. Soc. (1885–87) and the Leeds Festivals (1880–98). He was principal of, and a prof. of composition at, the National Training School for Music from 1876 to 1881. He was named Chevalier of the Legion of Honor (1878); was grand organist to the Freemasons (1887), etc. He was knighted by Queen Victoria in 1883.

Parallel with his comic creations Sullivan composed many "serious" works, including the grand opera *Ivanhoe* (1891), which enjoyed a momentary vogue. Among his cantatas the most successful was *The Golden Legend,* after Longfellow (Leeds Festival, 1886); he also wrote the famous hymn *Onward, Christian Soldiers,* to words by Rev. Sabine Baring-Gould (1871). His songs were highly popular in their day, and *The Lost Chord,* to words by Adelaide A. Proctor (1877), is still a favorite. Among his oratorios *The Light of the World* (Birmingham Festival, 1873) may be mentioned. Other stage works (all 1st perf. in London) include *The Zoo* (1875); *The Sorcerer* (Gilbert; 1877); *Haddon Hall* (1892); *The Beauty Stone* (1898); the romantic opera *The Rose of Persia* (1899); and *The Emerald Isle* (completed by E. German; 1901).

sum (summation) tone. Tone resulting from the addition of the frequencies of 2 or more original tones forming a consonant interval; a sum tone is much weaker than its opposite, the difference tone formed by the difference of the same original frequencies; therefore the sum tone is usually less disturbing to the player or listener.

Sun Ra (born Herman Blount), b. Birmingham, Ala., May 1914; d. there May 30, 1993. He learned to play the piano and 1st gained notice as a member of Fletcher Henderson's orch. (1946–47); then went to Chicago, where he became a prominent figure in the avant-garde jazz scene; in 1956 founded his own band, which was variously known as Solar Arkestra, Intergalactic Myth-Science Arkestra, Space Arkestra, etc.; later was active in N.Y. and Philadelphia; also toured throughout the U.S. and Europe; was a featured artist on the *Saturday Night Live* television show (1976). Compositionally he developed an abrasive and complex style in which avant-garde techniques are combined with electronic resources.

suonare (It.). Obsolete form of sonare.

suonata (It.). Alternate spelling of sonata.

suono (It.). Sound. *Suono alto,* high sound; *suono grave,* low sound; *suono harmonico,* harmonic.

šupeljka. Macedonian and Bulgarian end-blown shepherd's flute, with cylindrical bore, 6 finger holes, and no mouthpiece.

superbamente (It.). Proudly, loftily.

superdominant. 6th degree of a diatonic scale; the submediant.

superfetation. When several viable musical ideas occur simultaneously and are contrapuntally conjugated without a preliminary statement, a melorhythmic superfetation is the result. The thematic embryos may then be separated to pursue their different courses; or else the nonidentical geminal subjects may remain unified like Siamese twins, treated collectively as bipartite entities that subsequently may enter into a secondary superfetation. Given a complete freedom of dissonant counterpoint, superfetation can be extended to thematic triplets, quadruplets,

quintuplets, sextuplets, septuplets, octuplets, etc., interpenetrating and disengaging themselves in a multiplicity of instrumental or vocal lines.

superfluous. Augmented, as in chord or interval.

superoctave. 1. Organ stop of 2' pitch. 2. Coupler bringing into action keys an octave above those struck, either on the same manual or another. 3. Octave above a given tone.

supertonic. Second degree of a diatonic scale. In a major key the supertonic triad is minor; in a minor key the supertonic triad is diminished, traditionally proscribed harmonically. However, the 1st inversion of the supertonic triad, whether in major or minor, serves as a dignified surrogate (substitute) for the subdominant triad in a cadence, as they have the same bass note. In the Neapolitan cadence the 1st inversion of the lowered supertonic (e.g., in C major or minor, F–A♭–D♭) is a treasured cadential chord ever since its introduction in the 17th century, its advantage being that it provides a resonant major tonal harmony in place of a weak minor modal harmony.

Suppé, Franz (von) (born Francesco Ezechiele Ermenegildo, Cavaliere Suppé-Demelli), b. Spalato, Dalmatia (of Belgian descent), Apr. 18, 1819; d. Vienna, May 21, 1895. At age 11 he played the flute, and at 13 he wrote a Mass. He was then sent by his father to study law at Padua; on his father's death he went with his mother to Vienna in 1835; he continued serious study at the Cons. with Sechter and Seyfried. He conducted at theaters in Pressburg and Baden; then at Vienna's Theater an der Wien (1845–62), Kaitheater (1862–65), and Carltheater (1865–82). All the while he wrote light operas and other theater music of all degrees of levity, obtaining increasing success rivaling that of Offenbach.

Suppé's music possesses the charm and gaiety of the Viennese genre, but also contains elements of more vigorous popular rhythms. His most celebrated single work is the overture to *Dichter und Bauer* (Poet and Peasant; 1846), which still retains a firm place in the light repertoire. His total output comprises about 30 comic operas and operettas and 180 other stage pieces, most of which were brought out in Vienna; of these the following obtained considerable success: *Paragraph 3* (1858); *Die Kartenaufschlägerin* (Queen of Spades; 1862); *Zehn Mädchen und kein Mann* (1862); *Die flötten Burschen* (1863); *Die schöne Galatea* (Berlin, 1865); *Die leichte Kavallerie* (1866); *Banditenstreiche* (1867); *Die Frau Meisterin* (1868); *Tantalusqualen* (1868); *Isabella* (1869); *Fatinitza* (1876; extremely popular); *Boccaccio* (1879; very popular); *Donna Juanita* (1880); *Die Afrikareise* (1883); *Das Modell* (1895). Other works include syms., concert overtures, a Requiem, 3 Masses, and other sacred works, choruses, dances, string quartets, and songs.

supplicando (It.). In a style expressive of supplication, entreaty, pleading.

sur la touche (Fr., at the fingerboard; It. *sulla tastiera;* Ger. *am Griffbrett*). Bow near the fingerboard so as to produce a sound imitating the flute's sonority; hence the Italian synonym flautando.

surrealism. Term coined in 1903 by the French poet Guillaume Apollinaire in his fantastic play *Les Mamelles de Tirésias,* concerning the problem of a transsexual transplantation of breasts and gender roles, which he subtitled *drame surréaliste.* The etymology of the word implies a higher degree of realism, penetrating into the subliminal human psyche. Surrealism became a fashionable movement when André Breton published a surrealist manifesto in 1924. In it he described surrealism as "psychic automatism," antirationalistic in essence and completely spontaneous in its creative process.

Fantasy and free association were the normative factors of surrealistic literature and art. Apollinaire described surrealism as the rational technique of the improbable. Jean Cocteau equated it with the essence of poetry; in his film *Le Sang d'un poète* he proposed to give a "realistic account of unreal phenomena." The famous French handbook, Nouveau Petit Larousse, defines *surrealism* tersely as "tendance d'une école à négliger toute préoccupation logique." Surrealism is oxymoronic in essence, thriving on the incompatibility of the opposites, exemplified by such images as cold flame, thunderous silence, painstaking idleness, and quiet desperation.

Surrealist artists are fascinated by musical subjects. As early as the Renaissance, paintings representing Biblical scenes in which musicians perform on the lute and the theorbo are both anachronistic and surrealistic in their effect. Salvador Dali humanized musical instruments. In one of his paintings a faceless cellist plays on the spinal column of a human cello mounted on a pin. On its buttocks there are the familiar resonators in the forms of symmetric Gothic *F*'s. Another musical painting by Dali, bearing the surrealistic title *6 Apparitions of Lenin on a Piano,* represents several heads of Lenin crowned with aureoles strewn across the keyboard. The Belgian surrealist René Magritte painted a burning bass tuba. In the art work *Object for Destruction* by the American surrealist Man Ray, a print of a human eye was attached to the pendulum of a metronome. Real metronomes are the instruments in a score by Ligeti, containing 100 metronomes all ticking at different speeds. In his vision of socialist music of the future the Soviet poet Vladimir Mayakovsky conjured up a sym. with rain conduits for flutes. The American band leader Spike Jones introduced a latrinophone, a surrealistic lyre made of a toilet seat strung with violin strings.

Apollinaire urged artists, poets, and musicians to cultivate "the insane verities of art." No one has followed his advice more ardently than Satie; he incarnated the spirit of inversion. He entitled his utterly surrealistic score *Parade* "ballet réaliste." Cocteau wrote: "Satie's *Parade* removes the sauce. The result is a completely naked object which scandalizes by its very nakedness. In the theater everything must be false in order to appear true." Satie was very much in earnest when he wrote, "J'emmerde l'art c'est un métier de con." The titles of his piano pieces are typical of surrealistic self-contradiction: such as *Heures séculaires et instantanées* or *Trois morceaux en forme de poire.*

Surrealism in art is the superposition of extraneous elements on reality. If tonality is accepted as musical reality, then polytonality could be described as musical surrealism, with the surrealistic effect supplied by the addition of unrelated tonalities. Numeral surrealism is employed by Thomson in his opera *4 Saints in 3 Acts,* which really has about 2 dozen saints and is set in 4, not 3, acts. Surrealist music is also inherently futuristic. Operatic surrealism is exemplified by *The Nose* by Shostakovich, after Gogol's tale, in which the nose escapes from the face of a government functionary and assumes an independent existence, including sneezes. In the "jazz opera" *Jonny spielt auf* by Krenek, a jazz player surrealistically surmounts the terrestrial globe. In Hindemith's *Hin und Zurück* the action is a palindrome, whereby the opera ends at its starting point.

Stravinsky's ballet *Petrouchka,* in which puppets are more real than their manipulators, is surrealistic; in this work he exploits the tonal polarity of C major and F-sharp major as an example of harmonic surrealism. The same type of bitonality is used by Milhaud in his ballet *Le Boeuf sur le toit,* which depicts incongruous events in an American saloon. In the ballet *The Miraculous Mandarin* by Bartók, the fantastic surrealism of the action (in which the Mandarin is impervious to mortal wounds as long as lust attaches him to a prostitute) is illustrated by a discordant musical score. Henri Bergson describes music itself as a surrealist phenomenon, for it imposes the tonal language upon the world in which the primary means of communication is through verbal expression.

Susato, Tylman, b. *c.* 1500; d. probably in Antwerp, *c.* 1562. He may have been born in Antwerp, where he pursued his career; was a calligrapher at the Cathedral (1529–30), becoming a trumpeter there in 1531; then was a town musician (1532–49). After serving as a partner in a printing venture (1541–43), he set up his own press in 1543 and remained active until at least 1561. His press produced 25 books of chansons, 3 books of Masses, 19 books of motets, and 11 *Musyck boexken*. He was a fine composer of cantus firmus chansons for 2 or 3 voices (1544; *c.* 1552).

suspension. Dissonance caused by suspending (holding over) a tone or tones of a chord while the other tones progress to a new harmony, thus creating a discord demanding immediate resolution. Downward diatonic suspensions are by far more frequent than upward ones. While the resolutions of downward suspension follow the degrees of the diatonic scale, upward suspensions are, by instinctive feeling, almost invariably semitones. Suspensions and appoggiaturas are analogous in producing a dissonant harmony on the strong beat of the measure; the difference is that while a suspension is a prepared dissonant combination, the appoggiatura is an ornament placed on the harmony note without preparation. The resolution of a suspended note may be detoured by a nota cambiata, echappée, or a combination of nonharmonic tones, but this must not delay the resolution for too long.

suspirium (Lat., breath). In mensural notation, a brief pause.

süss (Ger.). Sweetly.

Süssmayr, Franz Xaver. See ⇒Mozart, Wolfgang Amadeus.

sussurando (It.). In a whisper.

sustain. To hold during the full time value (of notes); also, to perform in sostenuto or legato style.

sustaining pedal. Misnomer for the sostenuto pedal.

susurrante (It.). In a whispering, murmurous tone.

Sutherland, (Dame) Joan, b. Sydney, Nov. 7, 1926. She first studied piano and voice with her mother; at age 19 she commenced vocal training with John and Aida Dickens in Sydney, making her debut there as Dido in a concert performance of *Dido and Aeneas* in 1947; then made her stage debut there in the title role of Judith in 1951; subsequently continued her vocal studies with Clive Carey at the Royal College of Music in London; also studied at the Opera School there. She made her Covent Garden debut in London as the 1st Lady in *Die Zauberflöte* in 1952; attracted attention there when she created the role of Jenifer in *The Midsummer Marriage* (1955) and as Gilda (1957); also appeared in the title role of Alcina in the Handel Opera Soc. production (1957). In the meantime she married Richard Bonynge (1954), who coached her in the bel canto operatic repertoire.

After making her North American debut as Donna Anna in Vancouver (1958), Sutherland scored a triumph as Lucia at Covent Garden (1959). From then on she pursued a brilliant international career. She made her U.S. debut as Alcina in Dallas in 1960. Her Metropolitan Opera debut in N.Y. as Lucia (1961) was greeted by extraordinary acclaim. She continued to sing at the Metropolitan and other major opera houses on both sides of the Atlantic; also took her own company to Australia in 1965 and 1974; during her husband's music directorship with the Australian Opera in Sydney (1976–86) she made stellar appearances with the company. In 1990 she made her operatic farewell in *Les Huguenots* in Sydney.

Sutherland was universally acknowledged as one of the foremost interpreters of the bel canto repertoire of her time. She particularly excelled in roles from operas by Rossini, Bellini, and Donizetti; she was also a fine Handelian. In 1961 she was made a Commander of the Order of the British Empire, and in 1979 was named a Dame Commander of the Order of the British Empire.

Suzuki, Shin'ichi, b. Nagoya, Oct. 18, 1898. He was the son of Masakichi Suzuki (1859–1944), a maker of string instruments and the founder of the Suzuki Violin Seizo Co. He studied violin with Ko Ando in Tokyo and with Karl Klinger in Berlin (1921–28); upon his return to Japan he formed the Suzuki Quartet with 3 of his brothers; also made appearances as a conductor with his own Tokyo String Orch. He became president of the Teikoku Music School in 1930; subsequently devoted most of his time to education, especially the teaching of children. He maintained that any child, given the right stimuli under proper conditions in a group environment, could achieve a high level of competence as a performer.

In 1950 Suzuki organized the Saino Kyoiku Kenkyu-kai in Matsumoto, where he taught his method most successfully. In subsequent years his method was adopted for instruction on other instruments as well. He made many tours of the U.S. and Europe, where he lectured and demonstrated his method. See K. Selden, trans., *Where Love Is Deep: The Writings of Shin-ichi Suzuki* (1982).

Suzuki Method. Process of musical education based upon the repetition of (and adaptation to) external stimuli; founded by Shin'ichi Suzuki. Although the program ranges through adolescence, it seems to be most successful with very young children, especially those between the ages of 4 and 8, who are taught to play the violin by imitating the physical movements and the visual placement of the fingers on the strings.

svanirando (*svaporando;* It., evaporating). Vanishing; fainter and fainter; reducing the dynamic level to the threshhold of audibility.

svegliato (It.). Lively, animatedly, briskly, alertly. *Svelto,* light, nimble; *sveltezza,* alertness.

svirala (*sviralina;* Serb.). Generic term for indigenous flute family instruments, also found in Croatia and Slavonia (*jedina*).

svolazzando (It.). Soaring.

svolgimento (It.). Development section.

swan song. The legend that swans sing beautifully at the approach of death is of ancient origin. Plato states that dying swans sing so sweetly because they know that they are about to return to the divine presence of Apollo, to whom they are sacred. Another Greek writer reports that flocks of swans regularly descend on Apollo's temple during festive days and join the choir. But Lucian, skeptical as ever, made a journey to the swan breeding grounds in Italy and inquired among the local peasants whether they ever heard a swan sing. He was told that swans only croak, cackle, and grunt in a most disagreeable manner. So-called mute swans maintained on royal preservations in Britain are not voiceless; they growl, hiss, and even trill. Despite these unpleasant characteristics, the swan—with its graceful long neck (18 vertebrae, as compared with the giraffe's 7)—remains a symbol of beauty and poetry.

Rossini was called the Swan of Pesaro, his birthplace. Although he possessed a self-deprecating sense of humor, it never occurred to him how ambiguous this compliment really was. In his *Carnival of the Animals* Saint-Saëns assigns his beautiful cello solo to the swan, and it inspired Anna Pavlova's famous dance creation *The Dying Swan.* Sibelius wrote a symphonic poem entitled *The Swan of Tuonela,* with a mellifluously nasal English horn solo representing the dying swan song. A group of Schubert's posthumous songs was given the title *Schwanengesang* by the publs. Yet no composer has dared to reproduce the true sound of the swan's song; not even the bassoon in its lowest register is ugly enough to render justice to a dying swan's croaking. In Hans Christian Andersen's tale *The Ugly Duckling,* a swan egg is deposited in a nest of ducks; after it is hatched, the young gray swan is an ugly duckling compared to its anserine siblings, until one fine day it is a beautiful white. Prokofiev wrote a poetic ballad for voice and piano based on this tale.

Sweelinck Jan Pieterszoon (born Swybbertszoon), b. Deventer, May[?] 1562; d. Amsterdam, Oct. 16, 1621. He was born into a musical family; his father, paternal grandfather, and uncle were all organists. He went as a youth to Amsterdam, which was to be the center of his activities for the rest of his life. Jacob Buyck, pastor of the Oude Kerk, supervised his academic education; he most likely commenced his musical training under his father, then studied with Jan Willemszoon Lossy. He is believed to have begun his career as an organist in 1577, although 1st mention of him is in 1580, as organist of the Oude Kerk, a position his father held until his death in 1573.

Sweelinck became a celebrated master of the keyboard, so excelling in the art of improvisation that he was called the "Orpheus of Amsterdam." He was also greatly renowned as a teacher, numbering among his pupils most of the founders of the so-called north German organ school. His most famous pupils were Jacob Praetorius, Heinrich Scheidemann, Samuel and Gottfried Scheidt, and Paul Siefert. The output of Sweelinck as a composer is now seen as the culmination of the great Dutch school of his time. Among his extant works are about 250 vocal pieces (33 chansons, 19 madrigals, 39 motets, and 153 Psalms) and some 70 keyboard works.

Sweelinck was the 1st to employ the pedal in a real fugal part; he originated the organ fugue built up on 1 theme with the gradual addition of counterthemes leading to a highly involved and ingenious finale—a form perfected by Bach. In rhythmic and melodic freedom his vocal compositions show an advance over the earlier polyphonic style, though they are replete with intricate contrapuntal devices. His son and pupil, Dirck Janszoon Sweelinck (b. Amsterdam [baptized], May 26, 1591; d. there, Sept. 16, 1652), was an organist, music ed., and composer; he was his father's successor as organist at the Oude Kerk (from 1621), where he acquired a notable reputation as an improviser.

sweet potato. American slang for ocarina.

swell. 1. In the organ, set of pipes enclosed in a box with movable shutters which may be opened and closed by a pedal, affecting the dynamic level. 2. The swell organ: the chest, the pipes enclosed, and their keyboard. 3. A crescendo (⎯⎯⎯), or crescendo and diminuendo (⎯⎯⎯).

swing. Smooth, sophisticated style of jazz playing, popular in the 1930s and early 1940s. Its distinctive characteristic was a trend away from small jazz groups, who improvised by musical instinct, toward a well-organized ensemble of professional instrumentalists. The main outline of melody and harmony was established during rehearsals, but jam sessions were freely interpolated, with extended solos. The new style of performance required a larger band, so that the "swing era" became synonymous with the big band era.

Among the many ephemeral terms descriptive of varieties of jazz, swing has gained a permanent historical position. It is not a new expression. The word *swing* appears in the titles of old American dance tunes: Society Swing of 1908, Fox-trot Swing of 1923, Charleston Swing of 1925. In 1932 Ellington wrote a song entitled *It Don't Mean a Thing If It Ain't Got That Swing*. Swing music achieved its 1st great boom in 1935, largely through the agency of the jazz clarinet player Benny Goodman, advertised as the King of Swing. The American magazine *Downbeat* described swing in its issue of Jan 1935 as "a musician's term for perfect rhythm." The Nov. 1935 issue of the magazine carried a glossary of "Swing terms that cats use," in which swing was defined as "laying it in the groove." This metaphor, borrowed from the phonograph industry, gave rise to the once popular adjective

groovy, in the sense of "cool," "bad," "outtasight," or simply musically well executed.

Swing music is a natural product of the jazz era that created a demand for larger bands and a great volume of sound. The advent of swing music coincided with the development of the radio industry when, about 1930, millions could hear concerts broadcasting into homes. As the name seems to indicate, swing symbolized an uninhibited celebration of the youthful spirit of the age. Big bands of the swing era were usually catapulted into syncopated action by a clarinetist, a trumpet soloist, or a saxophone player. The instrumentation of a big swing band derived from its jazz predecessor, with clarinet, saxophone, trumpet, trombone, percussion, and piano as its mainstays.

If the media is to be believed, swing music must have exercised a hypnotic effect on the youth of the 1930s. The *New York Times* ran the banner headline "Swing Band Puts 23,400 in Frenzy . . . . Jitterbugs Cavort as 25 Orchestras Blare in Carnival." Self-appointed guardians of public morals lamented the new craze, as another *New York Times* headline showed: "Pastor Scores Swing as Debasing Youth, Declares it Shows an Obvious Degeneracy in our Culture and Frothiness of Age." Loud swing music late at night so upset the sensitive burghers in the once-peaceful boroughs of Greater N.Y. that they went to court to muzzle the swingers. They lost, as The *New York Times* reported: "2 A.M. Swing Music Upheld by Court. Residents Lose Pleas to Curb 15-Piece Band. Can't Sleep, They Assert. But Magistrate Rules That Lively Strains Do Not Disturb the Peace." Revenants added literary denunciations of swing as "music which squawked and shrieked and roared and bellowed in syncopated savagery." Eventually, even swing music was found not loud enough, and in the course of time it yielded to the still louder sound of rock 'n' roll.

Visitors from Europe were more kind to swing. Stravinsky, then a recent arrival to America, endorsed big band. *Time* quoted him as saying in Jan. 1941: "I love swings. It is to the Harlem I go. It is so sympathetic to watch the Negro boys and girls dancing and to watch them eating the long, what is it you call them, frankfurters, no—hot dogs—in the long rolls. It is so sympathetic. I love all kinds of swings." In 1945 he further demonstrated his faith in swing by composing his *Ebony Concerto* for "ebony stick" (swing term for the clarinet) and band.

syllabic melody. A melody, each tone of which is sung to a separate syllable.

syllable name. Syllable taken as the name of a note or tone; as Do for C.

symbolic analysis. An overwhelming compulsion on the part of many modern composers to return the art of music to its source, mathematics, is behind many manifestations of the avant-garde. Yet no attempt has been made to apply symbolic logic to the stylistic and technical analysis of modern music. A simple statistical survey can determine the ratio between unresolved dissonances and consonant structures in modern works as compared to those of the past. Such an analysis would indicate in mathematical terms the process of the emancipation of dissonances. The next step would be to tabulate certain characteristics of a given modern school of composition and note their presence in another category, which would help to measure the extent of its influence.

The whole-tone scale, for instance, was cultivated particularly by the French impressionists, but it can be found in works of composers who do not subscribe to impressionist aesthetics. Progressions of 2nd inversions of major triads in parallel formation, moving by sesquitones, are typical of impressionism. But the same formations can be encountered in the music of nonimpressionists. Ravel concludes his string quartet with such a triadic progression, and so does Holst in his suite *The Planets*, but they are never found in the works of Hindemith, a paragon of neo-classicism, or in those of Prokofiev. The index of tonality is very strong, amidst dissonances, in Stravinsky, but is totally absent in later Schoenberg.

All these styles, idioms, and techniques can be designated by a system of symbols; intervals would be numbered in semitones; upward motion would he symbolized by the plus sign, downward motion by the minus sign. In this scheme the whole-tone scale would be shown by the formula 6 (2), denoting 6 degrees of 2 semitones each, with a plus or minus sign indicating the direction of the movement. A bitonal chord such as formed by C major and F-sharp major can be indicated by the symbol *MT* for major triad and the number 6 for the tritone. The synchronization of these triads can be indicated by brackets: (MT) (MT + 6). More importantly, symbolic formulas can describe a style.

The music of Hindemith, which lacks the impressionist element entirely, can be formulated as 50% NC (for neo-Classical) + 50% NR (neo-Romantic), with dissonant content and strength of tonal centers indicated by additional symbols or subscripts. Stravinsky's early music could be circumscribed by the symbol *ED* for ethnic dissonance. The dodecaphonic method could be indicated by the coefficient 12. Other symbols would denominate metric and rhythmic symmetry or asymmetry. In the symbolic analysis of an eclectic composer such as Delius, with basic romanticism modified by a considerable influx of impressionistic harmonies and colors, the following formula would be satisfactory, with *R* for Romanticism, *C* for Classicism, *E* for ethnic quality, and *I* for impressionism: 40% R + 20% C + 30% E + 10% I. A table of styles, idioms, and techniques may be drawn in the manner of the periodical table of elements. Just as vacant spaces in Mendeleyev's schematic representation indicated unknown elements that were actually discovered at a later time, so new techniques of modern composition may well come into being by searching application of symbolic analysis.

symbolism (sometimes capitalized). Denoting compositions of the late 19th and early 20th centuries which, like their counterparts in the poetic and visual arts, are characterized by epigrammatic, sometimes oblique representations of emotions, topical themes, and events.

sympathetic strings. Strings stretched below or above the principal strings of lute and gamba family instruments to provide sympathetic resonance and thus amplify the sounds of the melodic strings; these strings are generally not played upon. They are still found on chordophones such as the Hardingfele of Norway and many of the classical Indian instruments. Some piano manufacturers add sympathetic strings above the strings in the treble to add resonance to the tinny sound of the upper range; these are called aliquot strings.

symphonia. In the Middle Ages, *consonance,* in contrast to *diaphonia,* dissonance. In Baroque music the term was used indiscriminately for all genres of ensemble music, but eventually a sym. became crystallized as a specific form of orch'l composition. R. Strauss used the old meaning of the term in his *Sym. domestica,* for a work that is not a real sym.

symphonic. Resembling, or relating or pertaining to, a sym.

symphonic band. Band, symphonic.

symphonic ode. Symphonic composition combining chorus and orch.

symphonic (tone) poem. Extended orch'l composition that follows in its development the thread of a story or the ideas of a poem, repeating and interweaving its themes appropriately; it has no fixed form, nor has it set divisions like those of a sym. The earliest masters of the genre were Mendelssohn (as concert overtures) and Liszt, whose 13 works were the models for later Romantic composers. In the late Romantic, R. Strauss took the musical language of Wagner and placed it in a symphonic context; works such as *Ein Heldenleben* and *Symphonia domestica* aroused controversy by their very literalness. The symphonic poem was preferred to the sym. by American composers heavily influenced by German Romantic and French Impressionist music.

symphonie concertante (Fr.; It. *sinfonia concertante*). Orch'l work that combines the formal elements of a sym. and a concerto, by the use of soloists. Mozart made good use of this form, as testified by his works for violin and viola (K. 364, 1779), 2 flutes, 2 oboes, and 2 bassoons (K. 320, 1779), and other unfinished works. In a sense this genre is the Classic equivalent of the concerto grosso.

symphony. (from Grk. *syn* + *phōnē*, sounding together; Fr. *symphonie;* Ger. *Sinfonie;* It. *sinfonia*). Orch'l genre with distinct movements or divisions, each with its own theme or themes (in the 19th and 20th centuries, sometimes shared); the totality of a sym. is made coherent by tonality and planning of contrasting mood. A typical plan in the Classic period might be a 4-movement work, organized as: *Allegro* in the tonic key (sonata form, often with a slow introduction); *Adagio* in a related key (choice of ternary, variation, "sonata without development" forms); *Minuet* or *Scherzo* in the tonic key (in triple meter, with trio); and *Allegro* or *Presto* in the tonic key (choice of sonata form, rondo, sonata-rondo, variation forms).

This is the most significant and most complex form of musical composition, which, in its Classic form, represents the supreme achievement of Western music. In the 17th century the term *symphonia* was divested of its general meaning as a musical composition and was applied exclusively to an instrumental ensemble without voices; it was used for instrumental overtures or interludes in early operas. In the 1st half of the 18th century the instrumental sinfonia was formally stabilized as a composition in 3 symmetric movements: Allegro, Andante, Allegro. The opening Allegro was of the greatest evolutionary importance, for it followed the germinal sonata form, with clearly demarcated sections that became defined by theorists as exposition, development, and recapitulation.

Haydn is commonly regarded as the "father of the sym.," but in fact several composers before Haydn's time wrote orch'l works that already comprised the formal elements of symphonic style. Particularly important among these predecessors were the musicians of the Mannheim School, who in their performances emphasized contrasts of style, tempo, and instrumental combinations. Furthermore, they introduced the dynamic elements of crescendo and diminuendo while preserving the chiaroscuro contrasts of forte and piano. The era of the Classic sym. began in the 2nd half of the 18th century. Its most illustrious representatives were Mozart and Haydn; a legion of opaque luminaries labored in obscurity in Central Europe and in Italy throughout the Classic period. Most Classic syms. comprised a supernumerary dance movement, usually a Minuet. Despite the vaunted versatility of the symphonic form, its structure was essentially uniform.

A revolutionary change in the history of the symphonic form occurred in the 19th century. The form of a sym. became individualized; like opera, it was no longer manufactured in large quantities, according to a prescribed formula. Syms. acquired individual physiognomies; the *Eroica* Sym. of Beethoven is a famous example. In his 9th Sym. Beethoven added a chorus, an extraordinary innovation at the time. Schubert failed to complete one of his most famous syms., which became forever known as the *Unfinished Sym.* Although the numbering of composition of Schumann's syms. is chronologically inaccurate, they are individually marked creations. Bruckner discarded his 1st sym., which he chose to describe as Sym. No. 0 (zero; in fact there were at least 2 other pre–Sym. No. 1's by Bruckner). Four syms. by Dvořák remained unpublished in his lifetime, creating havoc in their numbering. As a result, his most famous sym., *From the New World*, which was originally catalogued as No. 5, has been renumbered as No. 9. Several early syms. by Mendelssohn have been added to his catalogue by later editors.

Often syms. of the Romantic period were autobiographical. Berlioz wrote a grandly programmatic orch'l work that he entitled *Sym. fantastique*, as a musical confession of his love for an English Shakespearean actress. The 10 syms. of Mahler are Romantic revelations of the most intense character. Liszt selected 2 literary epics, Dante's *Divina Commedia* and Goethe's *Faust*, for his syms. Several composers who proclaimed themselves as fervent nationalists wrote syms. in a traditional Romantic style. Among the greatest was Sibelius, who assigned national Finnish subjects for his symphonic poems but whose 7 syms. bear no programmatic subtitles. Saint-Saëns was a grandiloquent symphonist. Bizet's youthful sym., which he discarded, was rediscovered more than half a century after his death and became a favorite. For some reason Debussy and Ravel were never tempted to write syms.; it is only in the 20th century that modern French composers, particularly Milhaud and Honegger, contributed to the genre. The Russians remain faithful to the traditional form of the sym. Tchaikovsky wrote 6 syms.; Glazunov wrote 8, Scriabin and Rachmaninoff composed 3 each, Shostakovich produced 15, several of which include vocal soloists and chorus. The champion symphonist in Russia was Miaskovsky, who wrote 27 syms.

Virtually every Russian composer of the Soviet period has written syms. in idioms varying from neoclassical to moderately modernistic; but, strangely enough, Germany and Austria, the countries that created and maintained the art of symphonic composition, showed a decline of symphonic production in the 20th century. Perhaps the fact that Wagner, the most potent influence

in post-Classic Germany, devoted his energies totally to the musical theater (his youthful sym. was not published until many years after his death) drew the German composers of the post-Wagnerian generation away from symphonic composition. R. Strauss wrote 2 syms., *Sym. domestica* and the *Alpine Sym.*, but they are panoramic, symphonic in name only. Hindemith was not a Wagnerian but rather a modern follower of Reger, neither he nor Reger wrote syms. in the traditional formal manner.

The 3 great composers of the modern Vienna school, Schoenberg, Berg, and Webern, abstained from composing works of truly symphonic dimensions. Stravinsky, who began his career as a follower of Rimsky-Korsakov's pictorial symphonism, wrote several syms., but they were closer to the pre-Classic type of sinfonia than to the traditional type of Classic or Romantic sym. Ever since Haydn's symphonic journeys to London, England was a willing receptacle of German musical style. In the 20th century Elgar wrote 2 grand syms. (and a 3rd, recently realized); Vaughan Williams wrote 9, some of them highly modern in idiom. Bax composed 7 syms.; the until recently obscure H. Brian wrote 32. Of the younger generation, Walton wrote 2. Britten, generally regarded as the most remarkable English composer of the 20th century, never felt the symphonic urge; his works in symphonic form approach the manner of orch'l suites. The Danish composer Nielsen wrote 6 syms., with somewhat programmatic content expressed in such subtitles as *Expansive* and *Inextinguishable*. The most prolific Italian composer of syms. was Malipiero, who wrote at least 10, several of which he equipped with suggestive subtitles.

In the U.S., among composers who pursued the symphonic career steadfastly through the years are Roy Harris, who wrote 14, and Piston, Schuman, Diamond, Mennin, and Persichetti, who wrote 8 syms. each. Hanson, who proclaimed his faith in Romantic music, wrote 6 syms. Of Copland's symphonic works the most significant is his 3rd Sym., which incorporated his famous *Fanfare for the Common Man*, quoted *in extenso*. A unique American sym. is Ives's 4th Sym., which consists of 4 movements written at different times and in widely divergent idioms. His 1st Sym. is entirely academic; his 2nd Sym. is a Romantic populist work; his 3rd Sym.'s essence is the world of the revivalist camp meeting.

The main structure of a sym. during the 2 centuries of its formulation has not radically changed. The lively scherzo replaced the mannered minuet. The 4 traditional movements were often compressed into 1. The general tendency early in the 20th century was to reduce the orch. to the bare bones of the Baroque sinfonia. In his *Sym. of Psalms* Stravinsky eliminates the violins altogether in order to conjure up the desired aura of austerity. The piano—not a symphonic instrument per se and not used in the syms. of Schumann, Mendelssohn, Tchaikovsky, Brahms, or any other composer of the Romantic century regardless of their individual styles—became a welcome guest in the syms. of the 20th century, with an obvious intent to provide sharp articulation and precise rhythm. Shostakovich wrote an important piano part in his 1st Sym. Mahler used sleighbells in his syms., but he did so in order to re-create the atmosphere of the countryside, serving as dainty embellishments rather than modernistic decorations.

symploche. Rhetorical musical device in which the beginning of a musical phrase serves also as its ending. A highly artistic example is the initial phrase of the ending to Mozart's Sym. No. 39 in E-flat Major, K. 543.

synaesthesia. Color associations with certain sounds or tonalities are common subjective phenomena. It is said that Newton chose to divide the visible spectrum into 7 distinct colors by analogy with the 7 degrees of the diatonic scale. Individual musicians differed greatly in associating a sound with a certain color. The most common association between tonality and color is that of C major and whiteness. It is particularly strong for pianists for the obvious reason that the C-major scale is played on white keys. However, Scriabin—who had a very strong feeling for color associations—correlated C major with red. By all conjecture F-sharp major should be associated with black, for it comprises all 5 different black keys of the piano keyboard, but Scriabin associated it with bright blue and Rimsky-Korsakov with dull green. Any attempt to objectivize color associations is doomed to failure if for no other reason than the arbitrary assignment of a certain frequency to a given note. The height of pitch rose nearly a semitone in the last century, so that the color of C would now be associated with C-sharp in relation to the old standards.

The most ambitious attempt to incorporate light into a musical composition was the inclusion of a projected color organ in Scriabin's score *Promethée*, in which the changes of instrumental coloration were to be accompanied by changing lighting in the concert hall. Composers in mixed media, anxious to embrace an entire universe of senses, are seeking ultimate synaesthesia by intuitive approximation, subjective objectivization, and mystical adumbrations. Schoenberg was extremely sensitive to the correspondences between light and sound. In the score of his monodrama *Die glückliche Hand* he indicates a "crescendo of illumination" with the dark violet light in 1 of the 2 grottos quickly turning to brownish red, to blue green, and then to orange yellow.

Some composers dreamed of a total synaesthesia in which not only audio-visual but tactile, gustatory, and olfactory associations would be brought into a sensual synthesis. Baudelaire said: "Les parfums, les couleurs et les sons se répondent." J. K. Huysmans conjured up an organ of liqueurs. He describes it in chapter IV of his book *A Rebours*: "Interior symphonies were played as one drank a drop of this or that liqueur creating the sensations in the throat analogous to those that music pours into the ear. In this organ of liqueurs, Curaçao sec corresponded to the clarinet with its somewhat astringent but velvety sound; Kummel suggested the oboe with its nasal quality; menthe and anisette were like the flute, with its combination of sugar and pepper, petulance and sweetness; kirsch recalled the fury of the trumpet; gin and whiskey struck the palate with the strident explosions of cornets and trombones; vodka fulminated with deafening noise of tubas, while raki and mastic hurled thunderclaps of the cymbal and of the bass drum with full force." Huysmans continued by suggesting a string ensemble functioning in the mouth cavity, with the violin representing vodka, the viola tasting like rum, the cello caressing the gustatory rods with exotic liqueurs, and the double bass contributing its share of bitters.

synapse. In the Greek melodic system, the conjunction of 2 tetrachords by which the last (highest) note of the lower tetrachord also serves as the 1st (lowest) note of the higher tetrachord.

synchrony. Metric or rhythmic synchrony is an inclusive term, of which polymeter and polyrhythm are specific instances. Synchronization demands absolutely precise simultaneity of sets of mutually primary numbers of notes within a given unit of time, e.g., 3:2, 5:3, 11:4, etc. Triplets and quintuplets are of course common in free cadenzas since Chopin's time. (There is a consistent use of 4 beats against 3 in Chopin's *Fantaisie-Impromptu*.) But arithmetical precision in synchronizing larger mutually primary numbers of notes cannot be obtained by a human performer no matter how skillful, or by several performers playing different rhythms at once.

Such synchrony becomes feasible with the aid of electronic machines. In 1931 Cowell, working in collaboration with the Russian inventor Theremin, constructed a device, in the form of concentric wheels, which he called the Rhythmicon. By manipulating a rheostat with a rudimentary crank, the performer automatically produced precise synchronization of the harmonic series, the number of beats per time unit being equal to the position in the series, so that the fundamental tone had 1 beat per second, or any other time unit, the 2nd partial note had 2 beats, the 3rd, 3 beats, etc. up to 32 beats produced by the rim of the Rhythmicon. The result was an arithmetically accurate synchrony score of 32 different time pulses. Since only the mutually non-primary numbers of beats coincided in the process, the collateral effect of rotating the machine was the production of an eerie scale of upper overtones, slower in its initial notes, faster as the position of the overtone was higher. The speed of rotation of the Rhythmicon wheel could be regulated at will, so as to create any desired alteration in tempo or pitch. The initial chord of each main division contains, necessarily so, the entire spectrum of overtones, and their simultaneous impact is of tremendous power, a perfect concord of multitonal consistency in non-tempered intonation.

An entirely novel idea of producing synchrony with mathematical precision was initiated by Nancarrow, who worked with a player-piano roll, punching holes at distances proportional to the desired rhythms. He wrote a series of études and canons, which could be performed only on the player piano and which achieved the synchronization of different tempos that could not be attained by living instrumentalists. In his works he was free to select numbers with a fairly low common denominator, in which case there were occasional coincidences between the constituent parts. But the majority of his chosen proportions of the pulse tempos are such that the common denominator was not attained until the end of the piece, if at all. He also wrote a composition in which the relationship of the tempos was 2 to the square root of 2, and since the latter is an irrational number (which Nancarrow approximated to 3 decimal points), the contrapuntal parts could, at least theoretically, never meet.

synclavier. Digital synthesizer, developed in 1976.

syncopate. Efface or shift the accent of a tone or chord falling on a naturally strong beat, by emphasizing a weak or in-between note, or by tying over from the preceding weak beat to the strong beat. See also ⇒syncopation.

syncopated pedal. Release of the damper pedal on striking a chord, followed by immediate depression of the pedal.

syncopation (from Grk. *syncope,* clash between disparate elements; missed heartbeat). One of the most powerful sources of rhythmic diversification. In music, syncopation typically takes 3 forms: an accent on a normally unaccented beat or part of a beat; a continuation of a note "over the bar" so as to avoid striking a note on a normally accented beat; and the conflict of unequal rhythms in 2 or more parts.

In mensural notation, syncopation was used to make changes in the main stress. The consequence of such rhythmic displacement was the generation of a discordant tonal combination that had to be resolved into a consonance. In contrapuntal theory, syncopation is classified as the 4th species of counterpoint. Syncopated notes were initially marked as auxiliary ornaments and were often written in small notes placed before the principal note. Suspensions and appoggiaturas furnish the characteristic elements of dissonant syncopation. In the works of the Romantic era, syncopation served to enhance the emotional stress in the melorhythmic continuum.

Syncopation is the spice of music in dance forms. In triple meter, Viennese waltzes create an effect of syncopation by stressing the 3rd beat of the measure, while the mazurka tends to accent the 2nd beat. In quadruple meter, marches emphasize the main beat, but they supply syncopation in smaller rhythmic divisions against a regular beat. Ragtime developed the march form into a highly syncopated melodic style; jazz gradually eliminated the need for emphasis of the regular beat, thus elevating syncopation into a texture. Popular music in the U.S. since World War II has oscillated between a return to uniform rhythms with an accent on the strong beats of the measure (rock 'n' roll, Motown, disco) and various degrees of syncopation, sometimes quite subtle (rock, funk, new wave), sometimes less so (reggae, grunge).

syncretism. In history and theology syncretism denotes the coalescence of incompatible elements or concepts. Etymologically, the word is derived from the union of ancient Greece with Crete. *Syncretism* is a useful term in music as well, applied to describe the affinity between autogenetic ethnic melodies and cultivated triadic harmonies. A typical example of syncretism is the arrangement of pentatonic tunes in tonal harmonies, often resulting in the alteration of the intervallic content, as for instance in *Londonderry Air,* a pentatonic melody that has been altered by its arranger by changing the opening interval of a minor 3rd to a semitone in order to provide the leading tone and to convert the modality of the song into a familiar major key. In modern music, syncretism assumes a polytechnical character through the application of widely incompatible techniques in a single work. An example is Alban Berg's *Lulu,* a serial work, which contains also triadic progressions as well as harmonic figurations and tonal sequences.

synergy. According to American architect Buckminster Fuller, the "behavior of a whole system unpredicted by the behavior of any of its separate parts, or the subassemblies of its parts." Synergy in music is a technique whereby the last note of a segment of several thematic notes is the 1st note of the 2nd segment. These segments can be separated, in which case the conjunctive

note is repeated. The method is of considerable value in building serial chains, in which the concatenations of adjacent links may be freely dissolved. With this separation of links the function of the connecting tone becomes ambiguous, serving as the imaginary tonic of the 1st segment or an imaginary dominant of the 2nd segment. The specification "imaginary" is important because of the aesthetic differences created by such a split of the chain.

synthesizer. Class of electronic devices that make possible the creation of any sound via electronic synthesis. Like the personal computer, modern synthesizers are self-contained units that can be operated with a minimum of accessories, as opposed to the 1st electronic music synthesizers, composed of several modules that could take up an entire wall or even room in the early years. Unlimited musical horizons opened to electronic music with the introduction of synthesizers capable of producing any frequency with the utmost precision and distributing the relative strength of the overtones so as to create any desired instrumental timbre. While synthesizers through the 1960s were driven analogically (i.e., with dials approximating the desired parameters), the addition of computers to the process permitted digital synthesis using the powerful mathematical capabilities of computers to control all sonic parameters. With an ever-increasing availability of programs, calculations that would have been nearly inconceivable at one time (divisions of the octave, stochastic control, pitch alteration) are now commonplace.

Syrian chant. Christian hymnody in use in the early Christian communities in Syria, derived originally from the churches of Antioch, traditionally considered the oldest Christian churches. There are Orthodox, non-Orthodox, and reunified rites (the latter with the Roman Catholic church), with similar rites influenced by Gypsy, Arab, and other non-Western music. Among related liturgies are the Assyrian and Maronite.

syrinx. Ancient Greek pan pipes made of a set of reeds (usually 7) of varying sizes and therefore pitches. According to myth, Syrinx was a nymph beloved by the Greek god Pan; she was changed into a reed to escape his pursuit. Debussy wrote an eponymous unaccompanied flute work (1912).

Szell, George (born György), b. Budapest, June 7, 1897; d. Cleveland, July 30, 1970. His family moved to Vienna when he was a small child. He studied piano with Richard Robert and composition with Mandyczewski; also composition in Prague with J. B. Foerster. He played a Mozart piano concerto with the Vienna Sym. Orch. when he was 10 years old, and the orch. also performed an overture of his composition. At age 17 he led the Berlin Phil. in an ambitious program that included a symphonic work of his own. In 1915 he was engaged as an assistant conductor at the Royal Opera of Berlin; then conducted opera in Strasbourg (1917–18), Prague (1919–21), Darmstadt (1921–22), and Düsseldorf (1922–24).

Szell held the position of 1st conductor at the Berlin State Opera (1924–29); then conducted in Prague and Vienna. He made his U.S. debut as guest conductor of the St. Louis Sym. Orch. in 1930. In 1937 he was appointed conductor of the Scottish Orch. in Glasgow; he was also a regular conductor with the Residentie Orkest in the Hague (1937–39). He then conducted in Australia. At the outbreak of war in Europe in 1939 he was in America, which was to become his adoptive country by naturalization in 1946. His American conducting engagements included appearances with the Los Angeles Phil., NBC Sym., Chicago Sym., Detroit Sym., and Boston Sym. In 1942 he was appointed a conductor of the Metropolitan Opera in N.Y., where he received high praise for his interpretation of Wagner's music dramas; remained on its roster until 1946. He also conducted performances with the N.Y. Phil. in 1944–45. In 1946 he was appointed conductor of the Cleveland Orch., a post which he held for 24 years; he was also music adviser and senior guest conductor of the N.Y. Phil. from 1969 until his death.

Szell was a stern disciplinarian, demanding the utmost exertions from his musicians to achieve tonal perfection, but he was also willing to labor tirelessly at his task. Under his guidance the Cleveland Orch. rose to the heights of symphonic excellence, taking its place in the foremost rank of world orchs. Szell was particularly renowned for his authoritative and exemplary performances of the Viennese classics, but he also was capable of outstanding interpretations of 20th-century masterworks.

Szeryng, Henryk, b. Zelazowa Wola, Sept. 22, 1918; d. Kassel, Mar. 3, 1988. He commenced piano and harmony training with his mother when he was 5; at age 7 he turned to the violin, receiving instruction from Maurice Frenkel; after further studies with Carl Flesch in Berlin (1929–32) he went to Paris to continue his training with Jacques Thibaud at the Cons., graduating with a *premier prix* in 1937. In 1933 he made his formal debut as soloist in the Brahms Concerto with the Warsaw Phil. With the outbreak of World War II in 1939 he became official translator of the Polish prime minister Wladyslaw Sikorski's government-in-exile in London; later was made personal government liaison officer. In 1941 he accompanied the prime minister to Latin America to find a home for some 4,000 Polish refugees; the refugees were taken in by Mexico; Szeryng, in gratitude, settled there himself, becoming a naturalized citizen in 1946.

Throughout World War II Szeryng appeared in some 300 concerts for the Allies. After the war he pursued a brilliant international career; was also active as a teacher. In 1970 he was made Mexico's special adviser to UNESCO in Paris. He celebrated the 50th anniversary of his debut with a grand tour of Europe and the U.S. in 1983. A cosmopolitan fluent in 7 languages, a humanitarian, and a violinist of extraordinary gifts, Szeryng became renowned as a musician's musician by combining a virtuoso technique with a probing discernment of the highest order.

Szigeti, Joseph, b. Budapest, Sept. 5, 1892; d. Lucerne, Feb. 19, 1973. He began his studies at a local music school; while still a child he was placed in the advanced class of Hubay at the Budapest Academy of Music; then made his debut in Berlin at age 13. He made his 1st appearance in London when he was 15; subsequently toured England in concerts with Busoni; then settled in Switzerland in 1913; was a prof. at the Geneva Cons. (1917–25). He made an auspicious U.S. debut, playing the Beethoven Concerto with Stokowski and the Philadelphia Orch. at N.Y.'s Carnegie Hall (1925); thereafter he toured the U.S. regularly while continuing to appear in Europe. With the outbreak of World War II he went to the U.S. (1940), becoming a naturalized citizen in 1951. After the end of the war he resumed his international career; settled again in Switzerland in 1960, and gave master classes.

Szigeti was an artist of rare intellect and integrity; he eschewed the role of the virtuoso, placing himself totally at the service of the music. In addition to the standard repertoire, he championed the music of many 20th-century composers, including Stravinsky, Bartók, Ravel, Prokofiev, Honegger, Bloch, and Martin. He wrote the books *With Strings Attached* (N.Y., 1947), *A Violinist's Notebook* (London, 1965), and *Szigeti on the Violin: Improvisations on a Violinist's Themes* (N.Y., 1969). His son-in-law, Nikita Magaloff (b. St. Petersburg, Feb. 21, 1912), is a pianist noted for his lyrico-dramatic interpretations of Chopin and his lapidary attention to detail.

Szymanowski, Karol (Maciej), b. Timoshovka, Ukraine, Oct. 6, 1882; d. Lausanne, Mar. 28, 1937. The son of a cultured landowner, he grew up in a musical environment. He began to play the piano and compose very early in life. His 1st teacher was Gustav Neuhaus in Elizavetgrad; in 1901 he went to Warsaw, where he studied harmony with Zawirski and counterpoint and composition with Noskowski until 1904. With Fitelberg, Rózycki, and Szeluto he founded the Young Polish Composer's Publishing Co. in Berlin, which was patronized by Prince Wladyslaw Lubomirski; the composers also became known as Young Poland in Music, publishing new works and sponsoring performances for some 6 years. Among the works the group publ. was Szymanowski's op. 1, 9 Piano Preludes (1906).

Szymanowski was greatly influenced by German Romanticism, and his 1st major orch'l works reveal the impact of Wagner and Strauss. His 1st Sym. was premiered in Warsaw on Mar. 26, 1909; however, he was dissatisfied with the score, and withdrew it from further performance. In 1911 he completed his 2nd Sym., which demonstrated a stylistic change from German dominance to Russian influences, paralleling the harmonic evolution of Scriabin; it was played for the 1st time in Warsaw on Apr. 7, 1911.

After a Viennese sojourn (1911–12) and a trip to North Africa (1914) Szymanowski lived from 1914 to 1917 in Timoshovka, where he wrote his 3rd Sym.; he appeared in concert with the violinist Paul Kochanski in Moscow and St. Petersburg, giving 1st performances of his violin works; it was for Kochań́ski that he composed his violin triptych, *Mythes* (*La Fontaine d'Aréthuse* in this cycle is one of his best-known compositions). About this time his music underwent a new change in style, veering toward French impressionism. During the Russian Revolution of 1917 the family estate at Timoshovka was ruined, and Szymanowski lost most of his possessions.

From 1917 to 1919 Szymanowski lived in Elizavetgrad, where he continued to compose industriously, despite the turmoil of the Civil War. After a brief stay in Bydgoszcz he went to Warsaw in 1920. In 1920–21 he toured the U.S. in concerts with Kochański and Rubinstein. Returning to Warsaw, he gradually established himself as one of Poland's most important composers. His international renown also was considerable; his works were often performed in Europe and figured at festivals of the ISCM. He was director of the Warsaw Cons. (1927–29) and reorganized the system of teaching along more liberal lines; was rector of its successor, the Warsaw Academy of Music (1930–32).

Szymanowski's Stabat Mater (1925–26) produced a profound impression, and his ballet-pantomime Harnasie (1923–31), based on the life and music of the Tatra mountain dwellers, demonstrated his ability to treat national subjects in an original and highly effective manner. In 1932 he appeared as soloist in the 1st performance of his 4th Sym., *Sym. concertante* for Piano and Orch., at Poznan, and repeated his performances in Paris, London, and Brussels. In Apr. 1936, greatly weakened in health by chronic tuberculosis, he attended a performance of his *Harnasie* at the Paris Opéra. He spent his last days in a sanatorium in Lausanne. Szymanowski developed into a national composer whose music acquired universal significance.

t. Abbrev. for tasto; tempo; tenor; toe (in organ music); tre (T.C., tre corde); tutti.

tablā. One of a pair of single-headed South Asian drums (the 2nd, smaller drum is the *bāmyā*) featured in North Indian classical music; also, its collective name. The body, made of clay, wood, or metal, is roughly hourglass-shaped; the head and body are laced with zigzagging thongs to secure the wooden tuning dowels (changing the head tension as timpani do). Tuning and timbre are also affected by special black tuning paste placed on the head of both drums, according to individual preference. The tablā is played while sitting; in the performance of a *rāg*, after a melodic improvisation, the drummer enters using a *tal*, a rhythmic structure within which the melody instrument(s) and drummer improvise.

tablature (from Lat. *tabula*, board; It. *intavolatura;* Ger. *Tablatur*). 1. Visual musical notation, by which pitches are indicated by their actual locations on the keyboard, fingerboard, or other playing area in use; letters, numbers, or other systems are used instead of staff notation. Tablature was used for keyboard (14th–17th centuries); lute music (16th–mid-17th centuries); guitar music (mid-16th–mid-18th centuries; a simplified tablature is still used in sheet music for plucked string instruments); recorder music (16th century); and vocal music (e.g., tonic sol-fa). As percussion music evolved from occasional timpani strokes to a panoply of timbral cornucopia, composers adopted the conventional staff, single lines, or other means to indicate the instrument to be played (where pitch is secondary). Partch, who built his own instruments in nontraditional tunings and shapes, created tablatures particular to each instrument but incompatible with one another. 2. Rules and regulations for the poetry and song of the Meistersinger.

tableau (Fr.). Scene, in the theatrical sense.

tabor. Small shallow drum of the border region between France and Spain, held with a strap over the shoulder and played with only 1 hand, enabling the playing of a fife or pipe simultaneously; 1st reported in the 12th century.

Tabourot, Jehan. See ⇒Arbeau, Thoinot.

tacet (Lat., it is silent). In orch'l parts, sign indicating a movement in which the instrument in question is not used.

tactus (Lat., beat, stroke). In medieval theory, a standard beat, including downbeat and upbeat (Lat. *positio* and *elevatio;* Grk. *thesis* and *arsis*); the duration of a complete tactus was almost uniformly one second.

Tafelklavier (Ger., table keyboard). Square piano, constructed similarly to the clavichord, with adaptations for hammer action, unlike the harpsichord, in which strings are impinged. The French square piano (*piano carré*) was 1st manufactured in 1742; became very popular in England and the U.S. before yielding to the upright piano.

Tafelmusik (Ger., table music; Fr. *musique de table*). Musical entertainment for banquets and similar festive occasions; respectable composers contributed to the genre, e.g., Telemann's instrumental suites. There is a witty spoof on Tafelmusik in the finale of the 2nd act of Mozart's opera *Don Giovanni,* where a band plays selections from various operas, including one of Mozart's own. Composer Michele-Richard Delalande publ. a collection of "syms. qui se jouent ordinairement au souper du Roy" (1703). While this sort of music "ordinarily played at the King's supper" was disdained in the 19th century, the hedonistic composers of the 20th century revived it gleefully; in its more extreme manifestations it serves as background to other activities, in the form of live musicians, recordings, or Muzak.

Tagelied (Ger., day song). Poem of farewell made popular by the Minnesingers, usually songs of partings between lovers, sung at sunrise. Wagner has a Tagelied in the 2nd act of *Tristan und Isolde,* warning against imminent danger. In France and other Latin countries, the Tagelied is known as *alba* or *aubade*, a "morning" or "dawn" song.

taiko (daiko; Jap.). Generic term for Japanese barrel drums, played with sticks.

tail. Stem; a vertical line attached to the note head.

tailgate. Hot jazz style featuring sliding trombone effects; derived from New Orleans parade bands, carried by horse wagons, in which the trombonist sat in the open tailgate so that the slide tubing could be extended as needed.

taille (Fr., edge). Obs. term for voice or instrument performing a part between the low and the high registers, such as tenor, viola, or English horn. *Taille de viola,* tenor viola da gamba; *taille de violon,* tenor violin; also, obs. term for viola, used occasionally by Bach.

Tailleferre, (Marcelle) Germaine, b. Parc-St.-Maur, near Paris, Apr. 19, 1892; d. Paris, Nov. 7, 1983. She studied harmony and solfège with H. Dallier (*premier prix,* 1913), counterpoint with G. Caussade (*premier prix,* 1914), and accompaniment with Estyle at the Paris Cons.; had informal lessons with Ravel. She received recognition as part of the group of French composers known as Les 6 (along with Honegger, Milhaud, Poulenc, Auric, and Durey). She visited the U.S. twice (1927, 1942). Her style of composition was neoclassical; most of her works possess a fragile charm of unaffected *joie de jouer la musique.* She composed 6 operas, an operetta, and a ballet; concertos for piano, duo pianos, harp, and other orch'l works; chamber music, including *Image* for Piano, Flute, Clarinet, String Quartet, and Celesta (1918); sonatas and other works for violin, clarinet, and flute; solo sonatas for clarinet and harp; a string quartet (1917–19); piano trio (1978); piano works; and distinguished vocal music, including *Chansons françaises* for Voice and Instruments (1930); *Cantate du Narcisse* for Voice and

Orch. (1937); *Concerto des vaines paroles* for Baritone and Orch. (1956).

Takemitsu, Tōru, b. Tokyo, Oct. 8, 1930; d. there Feb. 20, 1996. He studied composition privately with Y. Kiyose; with Yuasa and others, he organized the Tokyo Jikken Kobo (Experimental Workshop, 1951), to create music that would combine traditional Japanese modalities with modernistic procedures; designed the Space Theater for Expo '70 in Osaka, Japan. He was a visiting prof. at Yale Univ. (1975); served as regent lecturer at the Univ. of Calif. at San Diego (1981); lectured at Harvard, Boston, and Yale Univs., and was composer-in-residence of the Colorado Music Festival (all 1983); in 1984 he was composer-in-residence at the Aldeburgh Festival. He received numerous honors: honorary memberships in the Akademie der Künste of the German Democratic Republic (1979) and the American Academy and Inst. of Arts and Letters (1984); received the Ordre des Arts et des Lettres of the French government (1985).

Takemitsu's music belies Kipling's famous asseveration that "East is East and West is West, and never the twain shall meet," for he accomplishes in music this very interpenetration; from the East, short motives are played out as floating dramas, subtle and exotic, through which he seeks "to achieve a sound as intense as silence"; and on the Western side he employs every conceivable technique developed by European and American modernists. He composed orch'l works, string quartets, keyboards, and vocal works; many of his works employ traditional Japanese instruments incorporated into a Western ensemble.

Takt (Ger.). 1. Beat. 2. Measure, bar. 3. Time, tempo. *Ein Takt wie vorher zwei* (1 measure like 2 before), twice as fast, doppio movimento; *streng im Takt,* strictly in time.

Taktart (Ger.). Meter.

Taktmässig (Ger.). In strict meter.

Taktmesser (Ger., measure knife). Metronome.

Taktstock (Ger., time stick). Conductor's baton.

Taktstrich (Ger.). Barline.

Taktzeichen (Ger.). Time signature.

Tal, Josef, (born Joseph Gruenthal), b. Pinne, near Posen, Sept. 18, 1910 . He took courses with Tiessen, Hindemith, Sachs, Trapp, and others at the Berlin Staatliche Hochschule für Musik (1928–30); in 1934 he emigrated to Palestine, settling in Jerusalem as a teacher of piano and composition at the Cons.(1936); when it became the Israel Academy of Music, he served as its director (1948–52); lectured at the Hebrew Univ. (from 1950), where he headed the musicology dept. (1965–70), then was a prof. (from 1971); directed the Israel Center of Electronic Music (from 1961); appeared as pianist and conductor with the Israel Phil. and European orchs. He was awarded the State of Israel Prize (1971) and made an honorary member of the West Berlin Academy of Arts; received the Arts Prize of the City of Berlin (1975), and became a fellow of its Inst. for Advanced Studies (1982).

A true musical intellectual, Tal applies in his music a variety of techniques, being free of doctrinal introversion and open to novel potentialities without fear of public revulsion; patriotic Hebrew themes often appear in his productions. He composed 10 operas and dramatic scenes, among them *Ashmedai,* with electronics (1968); orch'l works, including 3 piano concertos (1944–56, the last with tenor); 4 syms. (1953–85); concertos for viola, cello, violin and cello, flute, duo piano, and clarinet; sonatas for violin, oboe, and viola; 3 string quartets (1959–76); woodwind quintet, piano trio, and piano quartet; works for solo instruments; piano and organ pieces; vocal and choral works. As an active electronic composer, he often composes entire works or accompaniments on tape: 5 dance pieces, piano concertos Nos. 4–6 (1962–70), harpsichord concerto (1964), harp concerto (1971), and *Frequencies 440–462: Hommage à Boris Blacher* (1972).

tala. In Indian classical music, system of cyclical rhythmic organization maintained by the pair of drums known collectively as tablā. The concept of tala is similar to Western meter but differs in that the number of beats in 1 complete cycle (*tal*) can be 16 or more, and the cycle can last far longer than a measure. The tala system is taught by mnemonic syllables and hand gestures that can be incorporated into the performance itself; the tabla-player may improvise then within the cycle and its subdivisions (*a-varta*).

talea (Lat.). See ⇒isorhythm.

Talking Heads. See ⇒Byrne, David.

talon (*hausse;* Fr., heel; Ger. *Frosch;* It. *tallone*). Nut of the string bow.

tamborito (Sp., little drum). Lively accompanied dance song of Panama, usually in a major key and duple meter.

tambour (Fr.). Drum. *Tambour à friction,* friction drum. *Tambour de basque,* tambourine (not used by the Basques).

tambour militaire (Fr.). Small side drum used in military bands; lacks definite pitch, but produces a dry, well-articulated sound in the general tenor register; as a percussive instrument it is used in sym., opera, and even chamber music. Nielsen gives the tambour militaire an important part in his 5th Sym., instructing the player to beat the drum loudly in its own rhythm "as if trying to stop the rest of the orchestra." A military drum solo introduces the execution by hanging of *Till Eulenspiegel* in the eponymous work by R. Strauss. Varèse gives the military drum the leading "tenor" part in his *Ionisation.*

tambourin (Fr., small drum). 1. Cylindrical drum covered with skin on both ends; possibly of Arab origin. 2. Old dance in southern France accompanied by a pipe and tambourin. Rameau wrote a clavecin piece entitled *Tambourin,* with imitations of the characteristic rhythms of the instrument.

tambourine (Fr. *tambour de basque* It. *tamburino;* Ger. *Schellentrommel*). Popular instrument of Spanish origin, consisting of a single drumhead bordered by a shallow wooden ring with a number of metallic jingles; it can be played in a variety of ways: shaking, thumping, plunking, clicking, and striking against the knee or the opposing hand. The sound produced by the drumhead is dry and short, with no resonance or reverberation. The tambourine is regularly used to accompany Spanish dances, notably flamenco; this association is put to good use by Bizet (*Carmen*), Rimsky-Korsakov (*Capriccio Espagnol*), Debussy (*Ibéria*), and Ravel (*Rapsodie espagnole*). A similar biblical instrument, the timbrel, was shaken by women to attract male attention; one extant specimen, unearthed in Babylon and dating back to about 2700 B.C., has ten pairs of bronze jingles and is beautifully ornamented with precious stones. In the Bible Miriam, sister of Moses, used a timbrel during the Exodus from Egypt.

tamburā (tamboura, tampura). Long-necked Indian drone lute, played while seated and held vertically, with a gourd resonator and 4 strings; tuned to the rāg being played (and the instruments playing it). Its strings are gently plucked in a slow ostinato (unrelated to the other players' tempo) to represent a Hindu conception of universal harmony and a perfection that the soloists can never hope to attain. For a time the tamburā's special role was threatened by the introduction of the harmonium (also blamed for lost pitch subtleties in Indian music); but it retains its central role in a continuing tradition.

tamburo basco (It., Basque drum). Tambourine.

tamburo di legno (It., wooden drum). Generic term for a resonant wooden box used as an idiophone.

tamburo grosso (It.). Bass drum.

tamburo rullante (It., rolling drum). Tenor drum, slightly larger than the snare drum.

tamburo scordato (It., drum without strings). Small drum without snares.

tamburone (It.). Obs. for bass drum.

tampon (Fr.). Drum stick.

tam-tam. Large Eastern unpitched gong, suspended from a stand and struck with a felt-covered stick. It spread through Europe in the 18th century: Gossec includes it in the funeral march in *Mirabeau* (1791). In the 19th century, Tchaikovsky expressed the inexorability of fate in the *Pathétique Sym.* with it, while R. Strauss used it for funereal effect in *Death and Transfiguration*. There are 2 common misconceptions concerning the tam-tam: 1) it only represents tragic situations (and J. Arthur Rank movies); in truth, it functioned in courts, temples, and elsewhere to give signals; and 2) it is identical to a pitched gong, as found in gamelan; true gongs have raised hubs in the middle, struck and dampened by stick, which aid in tuning along with the gong sizes; the tam-tam has a white-noise sound, no particular place to be struck, and a much slower, more unpredictable decay.

tanbūr (Pers., Turk.). Long-necked Near Eastern lute with a small pear-shaped body, fretted neck, and a variable number of metal strings.

Tändelnd (Ger.). In a toying, bantering style.

Taneyev, Sergei (Ivanovich), b. Vladimir district, Nov. 25, 1856; d. Dyudkovo, Zvenigorodsk district, June 19, 1915. He began taking piano lessons at age 5; entered the Moscow Cons. at 9; after a year's academic training, reentered the Cons. as a piano pupil of E. Langer (1869); studied theory with N. Hubert and composition with Tchaikovsky, who became a lifelong friend; N. Rubinstein became his piano mentor (1871). He made his formal debut as pianist in the Brahms D-minor Concerto in Moscow (1875); later that year played the Moscow premiere of the Tchaikovsky 1st Concerto, to the composer's complete satisfaction; subsequently played the solo part in all of Tchaikovsky's works for piano and orch. He graduated from the Cons. as the 1st winner of the gold medal in both performance and composition (1875); toured his homeland with L. Auer (1876); succeeded Tchaikovsky as prof. of harmony and orchestration at the Moscow Cons. (1876); after Rubinstein's death, took over piano classes; succeeded Hubert as composition prof. (both 1881); served as its director (1885–89); then taught counterpoint (1889–1905).

Taneyev was a 1st-class pianist, but his position as a composer remains anomalous; he is one of the most respected figures of Russian music history; there is a growing literature about him; his correspondence and all documents concerning his life are treasured as cultural heritage; yet outside Russia his works are rarely heard. His compositional style represents a compromise between Russian melos and Germanic contrapuntal writing; the mastery revealed in his syms. and quartets is unquestionable. His most ambitious work was the operatic trilogy *Oresteia*; after Aeschylus, in 3 parts: *Agamemnon; Choëphorai,* and *Eumenides* (St. Petersburg, 1895). Other compositions include 4 syms. (1873–97); a piano concerto (1876); chamber music, including 10 string quartets (1874–1911), a violin sonata, 2 string trios, 2 string quintets, piano quartet, piano quintet, and a trio for violin, viola, and tenor viola; piano pieces; choral works; and songs. He wrote a respected treatise on counterpoint, *Podvizhnoi kontrapunkt strogavo pisma* (1909); after his death an almost-completed treatise *Ucheniye o kanone* (Study of Canon) was discovered and publ. (Moscow, 1929).

tangent. Brass blade attached to the back of a key on the clavichord, which strikes the intended string when the key is pushed down.

tango. Celebrated Argentine couple dance, characterized by strongly marked syncopation. Despite attempts to derive the word from the Latin *tangere* (touch), evidence points toward an indigenous onomatopoeic derivation, perhaps imitative of the drumbeat. The tango has the characteristics of the habanera: Both are in 2/4 time with a dotted rhythmical figure in the accompaniment; the 1st section is in a minor key, the 2nd in major. In the accompaniment the guitar and the bandonéon are the primary melodic and harmonic instruments, supported by piano, double bass, saxophone, and percussion; a vocal part may be added.

The tango developed as entertainment in the red-light districts of Buenos Aires towards the end of the 19th century; quickly became popular in the ballrooms of the U.S. and Europe in the years prior to World War I. Its frank sexuality shocked the guardians of morality; condemnations were voiced by clergy and government authorities; the Argentine ambassador to France even had to state that the tango was the product of bordellos and never tolerated in polite society. Fortunately, the concept of "polite society" has evolved to the point that this once indecent dance is regularly performed on the legitimate stage; the music of Astor Piazzolla (1921–92), who did for tango what Chopin did for the waltz, is enjoyed by classical and popular music audiences alike.

tango-milonga. Dance song fusing the older rural milonga with the modern urban tango.

Tannhäuser, Der, b. *c.* 1205; d. *c.* 1270. Of noble German lineage, he was active in the 5th Crusade to the Holy Land (1228–33) and the Cypriot war; later at the courts of Friedrich II "der Streitfare" in Vienna and Otto II of Bavaria in Landshut, among others. A Minnesinger, he was associated with the apochryphal tale of the Venusberg and pagan intimacy with Venus, penitence, pilgrimage to Rome, and the miracle of the flowering of the pilgrim's staff; Wagner's *Tannhäuser* is based on this legend.

Tansman, Alexandre, b. Lodz, June 12, 1897; d. Paris, Nov. 15, 1986. He studied at the Lodz Cons. (1902–14); pursued training in law and philosophy at the Univ. of Warsaw, while receiving instruction in counterpoint, form, and composition from Rytel in Warsaw. In 1919 he went to Paris; appeared as soloist in his own works there (1920) and with the Boston Sym. Orch. (1927); performed throughout Europe, Canada, and Palestine; took up conducting, making a tour of the Far East (1932–33). After the occupation of Paris by the Germans (1940), he made his way to the U.S.; lived in Hollywood, writing music for films; returned to Paris (1946). His music is distinguished by a considerable melodic gift and a vivacious rhythm; his harmony is often bitonal, and there are impressionistic traits that reflect Parisian influence. He composed 6 operas, 6 ballets, 7 syms. (1925–44), and other orch'l works. His compositions for piano include 20 *pieces faciles polonaises* (1924); 5 sonatas; mazurkas and other Polish dances; *Sonatine transatlantique* (1930); *Pour les enfants* in 4 books; wrote the monograph *Stravinsky* (Paris, 1948).

tanto (It.). As much, so much, too (much). *Allegro non tanto,* not too fast; *a tanto possibile,* as much as possible.

tantric chants. Ritual singing of Hindu or Buddhist sects, designed to attain purification of soul and body, combined with body exercises such as yoga. The text of the tantric chants is fashioned from the mystic syllables of the sacred mantras; the symbols are inspired by the diagrams of the ritual mandalas. Some Tibetan Buddhist chants last for over 7 hours.

Tanz (Ger.). Dance.

Tanzhalle (Ger.). Dance hall; a place of entertainment that flourished in Germany (especially Berlin) in the beginning of the 20th century.

Tanzlied (Ger.). Song in the rhythm of a dance it accompanies.

Tanzmässig (Ger.). In a dancelike character.

tap dance. American dance in which distinct rhythmic patterns are produced by the tapping of the performer's feet on the floor. Typical tap shoes have metal plates on the soles to enhance the sound. Tap dancing in wooden shoes was called buck-and-wing dancing, while in "soft-shoe" dancing the performer applied sliding and shuffling on the floor. Dancing pairs would trade rhythmically complex riffs with one another in a call-and-response manner; the best dancers could also work with timbral contrasts. Tap dance was popular in vaudeville, revues and musicals, and film; it entered the concert hall when Morton Gould wrote a 4-movement Concerto for tap dancer and orch. (1952).

tape recording. Method involving a lacquered, extremely thin, magnetized plastic tape onto which processed sound signals are entered in electronic form (through a *recording head*); these are reproduced on a tape recorder or player with the appropriate pickup (*playback head*). The idea of recording without going directly to disc had been pondered since recording began; the direct predecessor to tape was *wire recording,* an instrument of peace and war for Nazi Germany: Musical performances were recorded, with the theoretically unlimited length of wire allowing for longer uninterrupted recordings than 78-rpm disc recording could make; also used for secret military communication. The fragility of the wire led Nazi engineers to seek another medium for recording; began to develop the *reel-to-reel recorder.* When the Allies stormed Germany in 1945, they found early versions of this new tape-recording machine and brought them back to the U.S. for further development. (The story goes that Varèse was sent such a machine in the late 1940s and realized immediately its compositional potential.)

As a home medium, reel-to-reel tape began to give way to the long-playing record in the 1950s, although prerecorded tapes were sold into the early 1960s. Other tape media evolved: the *8-track,* on which narrow tape is wound as a continuous loop, switching from one "program" to the next (4 programs, each in stereo, hence 8-track). It was soon replaced by the *cassette* (1970s); this system involves even narrower tape in a miniature reel-to-reel format, on which both sides are recorded in stereo (hence its early name *4-track*); it plays longer than the 8-track, is more convenient to store, can be used for home recording (unlike the 8-track), and has developed sound comparable to most long-playing records.

As a studio medium the reel-to-reel tape recorder was the principal means of recording music from the late 1940s to the 1980s. Reel-to-reel tape can range in width from 1/4" to 2" and record several simultaneous tracks (channels) with different instruments, voices, effects, etc.; this *multitrack recording* allows each to be recorded with relatively little acoustic interference and then *mixed* and *equalized* (combined and balanced) to produce a final product. *Editing* allows for corrections by cutting and splicing desirable passages; one can also record over undesirable passages on individual channels while saving others. Multitrack recording allows for *overdubbing,* where 1 performer can add layers onto a single recording, to the point of being the only (or nearly only) performer on a richly textured album (e.g., Stevie Wonder, Paul McCartney, Steve Winwood, Roy Wood, Richard Thompson). While reel-to-reel is still used, it is being replaced by *digital recording,* in which computer technology records music as a constant numerical sampling of information, stored on a hard drive, database, or tape (*DAT*); capable of extremely precise editing and imaginative processing.

tapeur (from Fr. *taper,* pound). Rather unkind description of a pianist accompanying dance rehearsals.

täppisch (Ger.). Clumsily.

tār (Pers.). Long-necked Persian lute, also played in Central Asia. It is generally made from one piece of hollowed-out wood, with membrane belly, movable frets, and between 2 and 5 strings, played with a plectrum. Cowell makes use of the tār in his chamber work *Persian Set.*

tarantella (It.; Ger. *Tarantelle*). Southern Italian dance in 6/8 time, with the rate of speed gradually increasing and the mode alternating between major and minor; also, an instrumental piece in 3/8 or 6/8 time, in a very rapid tempo and bold and brilliant style; named after the city of Taranto, it was especially popular in the 19th century. According to legend, the playing of the tarantella cured tarantism, an uncontrollable impulse to dance supposedly caused by the bite of the tarantula spider; however, medical investigations of persons bitten by this creature have revealed no such choreographic symptoms.

tardamente (It.). Slowly, lingeringly. *Tardando,* delaying, lingering; *tardato,* delayed, slower; *tardo,* slow, lingering.

tárogató. Traditional Hungarian reed instrument made of wood with a conical bore; 1st mentioned in the 13th century; apparently was brought by Arabs to southeastern Europe; it was at 1st shawmlike, with the reeds covered by a pirouette and without fingerholes. By the 19th century the double reed was reduced to a single one, the mouthpiece became clarinetlike (although still partly covered), and the fingering now resembled a saxophone's. The tárogató's cultural importance was as a national Hungarian instrument since the Rákóczy rebellion in the 18th century.

Tartini, Giuseppe, b. Pirano, Istria, Apr. 8, 1692; d. Padua, Feb. 26, 1770. His parents entrusted his education to clerics in Pirano and Capodistria, where he received violin instruction; renounced the cloister but remained a nominal candidate for the priesthood (1708); enrolled at the Univ. of Padua in law (1709), contracted a secret marriage to a protégée of the powerful Paduan Cardinal Cornaro, who brought a charge of abduction against him. He took refuge from prosecution at the monastery of the Friars Minor Conventual in Assisi; joined the opera orch. He was pardoned by the Paduan authorities (1715) and reunited with his wife; lived in Venice and Padua; made *primo violino e capo di concerto* at the basilica of S. Antonio in Padua (1721); allowed to travel, he acquired a reputation as a virtuoso. He served as chamber musician to Count Kinsky in Prague (1723–26); returned to Padua, where he organized a music school (1728); among his students were Nardini and Pugnani. He enjoyed a brilliant career as a violinist; made numerous concert tours in Italy; retained his post at S. Antonio (to 1765); remained active at his school; suffered a mild stroke which ended his career (1768).

Tartini's style of playing, particularly his bowing, became a model for other violinists. His most famous composition is the violin sonata in G minor known as the *Trillo del diavolo* (Devil's Trill, after 1744), supposedly inspired by a dream in which the devil played it for him; the trill appears in the last movement. He was a prolific composer of violin music, including *c.* 135 concertos, *c.* 135 sonatas with basso continuo, 30 sonatas for solo violin or with basso continuo ad libitum, 18 sonatas for 2 violins and bass continuo; other works include concertos, 40 trio sonatas, 4 sonatas a quattro, religious music. Many of these works were published during his lifetime.

Although Tartini lacked scientific training, he made several acoustical discoveries, most importantly the sum (summation) and difference (differential) tones; observed these effects in 1714 by playing double-stops in perfect non-tempered tuning; publ. his findings in his *Trattato di musica secondo la vera scienza dell'armonia* (Padua, 1754), in which he called the difference tone the *terzo suono;* also called "Tartini tones," this phenomenon was actually 1st described in *Vorgemach der musicalischen Composition* by Georg Sorge (1745–47). Sum and difference tones has been confused with other acoustical events. They were known, rather misleadingly, as "beat tones," which are in fact produced by interference between frequencies of higher overtones. The *wolf tone* of string instruments is also different, produced by vibrations with the body of the instrument. Violinists are aware of interferences from difference tones and the less audible sum tones; they correct them empirically by a slight alteration of tuning.

Taschengeige (Ger.). Pocket violin; pochette.

tastatura (It.). Keyboard; fingerboard.

Taste (Ger.). Key on a keyboard.

Tasteninstrument (Ger.). Keyboard instrument.

tastiera (It.). Keyboard; fingerboard. *Sulla tastiera* (Fr. *sur la touche;* Ger. *am Griffbrett*), on (near) the fingerboard; flautando.

tastiera per luce (It., keyboard of light). Color organ envisioned by Scriabin and included in his sym. poem *Promethée.*

tasto (It.). Key; fret; touch; fingerboard. *Sul tasto,* on (near) the fingerboard; *tasto solo,* in basso continuo, play the bass line, as written or in octaves, without chords.

Tate, Jeffrey, b. Salisbury, Apr. 28, 1943. Although a victim of spina bifida, he pursued studies at Cambridge Univ. and St. Thomas's Medical School; attended the London Opera Centre (1970–71). He joined the music staff at the Royal Opera, Covent Garden (1971–77); served as assistant conductor at Bayreuth (1976–80). He made his formal debut conducting *Carmen* at the Göteborg Opera (1978); made his debut at the Metropolitan Opera in N.Y., conducting *Lulu* (1980); his debut at Covent Garden followed, with *La Clemenza di Tito* (1982). He has guest conducted with major opera companies around the world. He made his 1st appearance with the English Chamber Orch. (1983); named its principal conductor (1985), leading it on tours, including one to the U.S. (1988); became principal conductor at Covent Garden (1986); chief conductor of the Rotterdam Phil. (1991). His extensive operatic and concert repertoire encompasses works from the Classic to the 20th century. He was made a Commander of the Order of the British Empire (1990).

tattoo (It.; from Lat. *tactus*). 1. Beat. 2. Military signals in a rapid articulate rhythm used to summon soldiers back to the barracks. A stylized tattoo occurs in *Carmen:* the infatuated Don José refuses to heed his, with tragic consequences.

Tatum, Art(hur), b. Toledo, Ohio, Oct. 13, 1910; d. Los Angeles, Nov. 5, 1956. He was blind in one eye and had limited vision in the other; attended a school for the blind in Columbus, Ohio; learned to read Braille music notation; at 16 began to play in nightclubs. In 1932 he went to N.Y.; became successful on the radio. He made a spectacular tour of England (1938); pursued his career in N.Y. and Los Angeles; organized his own trio (1943); appeared in the film *The Fabulous Dorseys* (1947). His art as a jazz improviser was captured on more than 600 recordings. He brought "stride" piano playing to a point of perfection, achieving small miracles with ornamental figurations in the melody while throwing effortless cascades of notes across the keyboard and imagination as fast as his fingers; had a knack for improvising variations on popular classical pieces.

Tauber, Richard, b. Linz, May 16, 1891; d. London, Jan. 8, 1948. He was the illegitimate son of the actor Richard Anton Tauber; his mother was a soubrette singer. He took courses at the Hoch Cons. in Frankfurt am Main; studied voice with C. Beines in Freiburg; made his debut at Chemnitz as Tamino (1913); his success led to an engagement at the Dresden Court Opera; made his 1st appearance at the Berlin Royal Opera as R. Strauss's Bacchus (1915); won particular success in Munich and Salzburg for tenor roles in Mozart's operas. About 1925 he turned to lighter roles, winning remarkable success in the operettas of Lehar. He made his U.S. debut in a N.Y. recital (1931); settled in England (1938), where he appeared as Tamino and Belmonte at London's Covent Garden; became a British subject (1940). He wrote an operetta, *Old Chelsea,* taking the lead role at its premiere (London, 1943); made his last American appearance at Carnegie Hall in N.Y. (1947).

Tavener, John (Kenneth), b. London, Jan. 28, 1944. He studied with L. Berkeley at the Royal Academy of Music in London (1961–65) and privately with D. Lumsdaine (1965–67); organist at St. John's, Kensington (from 1960); taught composition at Trinity College of Music in London (from 1969). While his formative influences were medieval hymnology and Indian transcendentalism, his technical background is, by contrast, ultramodernist, including combinatorial serialism and electronic sound generation. His earlier works were free collages of styles, e.g., *The Cappemakers,* dramatic cantata (1964); *Cain and Abel,* dramatic cantata for soloists and chamber orch. (1966); and *The Whale,* a dramatic cantata for narrator, soloists, chorus, and orch. (1966). His conversion to Eastern Orthodox Christianity affected both his materials and styles; he has composed a stream of works liturgically or historically connected to his faith.

Taylor, Cecil (Percival), b. N.Y., Mar. 15, 1933. He began piano lessons at age 5; was improvising and composing by age 8;

later studied percussion. He studied harmony and composition at the N.Y. College of Music; studied composition at the New England Cons. of Music in Boston; immersed himself in the Boston jazz scene. He worked with his own combos in N.Y.; appeared at the Newport Jazz Festival (1957); gained fame as a performer in the off-Broadway production of Jack Gelber's *The Connection* (1959). He made his 1st tour of Europe (1962); played in jazz centers on both sides of the Atlantic; performed at N.Y.'s Carnegie Hall (1977); made a number of remarkable recordings, including *Into the Hot* (1961), *Unit Structures* (1966), *Silent Tongues* (1975), *The Cecil Taylor Unit* (1978), and *3 Phasis* (1978). His digitally agile piano style and penchant for extended atonal improvisation made him an important figure in avant-garde jazz circles in his time.

Taylor, James, b. Boston, Mass., Mar. 12, 1948. He was raised in Chapel Hill, N.C.; after going to school, he moved to N.Y.; formed a band with guitarist Danny "Kootch" Kortchmar called the Flying Machine (1966); played local clubs and made recordings that were unissued until Taylor achieved fame on his own; disbanded (1967). He was in London when a demo tape ended up in the hands of Paul McCartney and producer Peter Asher, then scouting for talent for the Beatles' new Apple label (1968). He recorded 1 album for the label, but with the Beatles's empire crumbling, the recording went nowhere. He returned to the U.S. (1969) and signed with Warner Bros.; still working with Asher, produced the landmark *Sweet Baby James,* including the hits *Fire and Rain, Country Roads,* and the title cut. His soft folk-rock sound and sweet voice gained him an immediate following; enjoyed success through the 1970s with his own material and covers of earlier hits; in the 1980s and 1990s he became primarily a touring artist. His brothers and sister have also recorded, especially Livingston (b. 1950, Chapel Hill, N.C.), who has recorded in a more soft-pop vein than his brother.

Tchaikovsky, Piotr Ilyich, b. Votkinsk, Viatka district, May 7, 1840; d. St. Petersburg, Nov. 6, 1893. He was given a good education, with a French governess and a music teacher; when he was 10 his family moved to St. Petersburg; he went to a school of jurisprudence, graduating at 19; studied music with Lomakin, but did not display conspicuous talent as pianist or composer; became a government clerk. At 21 he was accepted in a musical inst., newly established by A. Rubinstein, which would become the St. Petersburg Cons.; studied with Zaremba (harmony and counterpoint) and Rubinstein (composition); graduated in 1865, winning a silver medal for his cantata to Schiller's *Hymn to Joy;* became prof. of harmony at the Moscow Cons. (1866).

As if to compensate for a late start, Tchaikovsky began to compose with great application; his early works—a programmatic sym. subtitled *Winter Dreams* (op. 13), overtures, and small pieces for string quartet—reveal little individuality. The sym. poem *Fatum* (1868) saw the 1st formulation of his style: highly subjective, preferring minor modes, permeated with nostalgic longing, and alive with keen rhythms. He began the overture-fantasy *Romeo and Juliet* (1869); not content with what he had written, sought the advice of Balakirev, whom he met in St. Petersburg; rev. the work (1870), but this version proved equally unsatisfactory; he laid the composition aside; completed it in 1880; in this form it became one of his most successful works.

Besides teaching and composing, Tchaikovsky contributed music criticism to Moscow newspapers (1868–74); made altogether 26 trips abroad (to Paris, Berlin, Vienna, N.Y.); visited the 1st Bayreuth Festival, reporting his impressions for the Moscow daily *Russkyie Vedomosti* (1876). His closest friends were members of his family, especially his brother Modest (b. Alapaevsk, Perm district, May 13, 1850; d. Moscow, Jan. 15, 1916), playwright, librettist for 2 of his brother's operas, and his future biographer. The correspondence with them, all of which was preserved and eventually publ., throws a true light on Tchaikovsky's character and his life. His other close friends were his publisher, Jurgenson, N. Rubinstein, and several other musicians.

Most extraordinary of Tchaikovsky's friendships was the epistolary association with Nadezhda von Meck (b. Znamenskoye, near Smolensk, Feb. 10, 1831; d. Wiesbaden, Jan. 13, 1894), a wealthy widow whom he never met but who played a hugely important role in his life. Through the violinist Y. Kotek she learned about Tchaikovsky's financial difficulties; commissioned works from him at large fees; arranged to pay him an annuity of 6,000 rubles. For more than 13 years they corresponded voluminously, even when living in the same city (Moscow, Florence); she often hinted that she would like to meet him, but he invariably declined, under the pretext that one should not meet one's guardian angel in the flesh. For his part, this correspondence remained within the circumscribed domain of art, personal philosophy, and reporting of daily events, without touching on his personal struggles.

In 1877 Tchaikovsky received a letter from a student, Antonina Milyukova, declaring her love for him. A decade earlier, he had met a Belgian soprano, Desirée Artot, touring with an opera troupe in St. Petersburg; he contemplated marrying her, but she married another singer; he reacted philosophically about the inconstancy of human attachments. Nonetheless, he contracted marriage with Milyukova; this was an act of defiance of his homosexuality, a fact he openly shared with Modest, also a homosexual. He hoped that by marrying he could allay already rife rumors about his sexual preference; but when Milyukova tried to consummate the marriage on their wedding night, he fled from his wife in horror and attempted suicide by walking into the Moskva River, hoping to catch pneumonia, but suffering nothing more than discomfort. His brother Anatol, a lawyer, made suitable arrangements with Milyukova for a separation. (They never divorced; she died in an insane asylum in 1917.) Von Meck, to whom he wrote candidly of this disaster (without revealing its true cause) made an immediate offer of further financial assistance, which he gratefully accepted.

Throughout his career Tchaikovsky never allowed his psychological turmoil to interfere with his work. In 1877–78, he spent several months in Italy, Switzerland, Paris, and Vienna; during this period he completed his great 4th Sym. (op. 36), dedicated to von Meck; it was premiered in Moscow (1878), but he did not return from abroad to attend the performance. He resigned from the Moscow Cons. (1878), dedicating himself entirely to composition, thanks to the continued subsidy from von Meck. That year he completed his most successful opera, *Evgeny Onegin* (after Pushkin); 1st produced in Moscow by the Cons. (1879); gained success only gradually; the premiere at the Imperial Opera in St. Petersburg did not occur until 1884.

Tchaikovsky's natural state of mind was morbid depression, but each new work sustained his faith in his compositions,

despite many disheartening reversals. The Piano Concerto No. 1 (op. 23), rejected by N. Rubinstein as unplayable, was premiered in Boston by von Bülow (1875) and was soon performed throughout the world by famous pianists, including Rubinstein. The Violin Concerto (op. 35), criticized by L. Auer (the orig. dedicatee), sarcastically and virulently attacked by Hanslick at its premiere by A. Brodsky (Vienna, 1881), it survived all detractors to become one of the most celebrated pieces in the genre. The 5th Sym. (op. 64, 1888) was successful from the very 1st.

Tchaikovsky wrote his 2nd important opera, *The Queen of Spades* (after Pushkin, op. 68), 1st produced at the Imperial Opera in St. Petersburg (1890); his ballets *Swan Lake* (op. 20, 1876) and *The Sleeping Beauty* (op. 66, 1889) became famous on Russian and other stages. But at the peak of his career he suffered a severe psychological blow; von Meck notified him of the discontinuance of her subsidy and abruptly terminated their correspondence; he could afford the loss of the money, but his pride was deeply hurt by the manner in which she had acted; a possible explanation is that her grown children had found out the truth about his homosexuality (then a crime as well as a sin) and that she was shocked by his misrepresenting his reluctance to meet her.

It is indicative of Tchaikovsky's inner strength that even the desertion of his staunchest friend did not affect his ability to work. In 1891 he undertook his only voyage to America; was received with honors as a celebrated composer; led 4 concerts of his works in N.Y. (including the inaugural concert of Carnegie Hall) and 1 apiece in Baltimore and Philadelphia; returned to St. Petersburg in a few weeks. He toured Russia as a conductor (1892); proceeded to Warsaw and Germany; worked on his last sym., the *Pathétique* (op. 74). Despite the perfection of his technique, he did not arrive at the desired form and substance of this work, and discarded his original sketch. The title *Pathétique* was suggested to him by Modest; the score was dedicated to his nephew. Its music is the final testament of his life, an epitome of his fatalistic philosophy. In the 1st movement the trombones are given the theme of the Russian service for the dead. Remarkably, the score of his most lighthearted works, the ballet *The Nutcracker* (op. 71, 1891–92), was composed simultaneously with the early sketches for the *Pathétique*.

Tchaikovsky was in good spirits when he went to St. Petersburg to conduct the premiere of the *Pathétique*, which was but moderately successful (1893). A cholera epidemic was then raging there; the population was warned against drinking unboiled water, but he apparently ignored this admonition; showed the disease's symptoms soon afterwards; nothing could be done to save him. One theory, that the fatal drink of water was an act of defiance of death, is untenable in the light of correspondence between the attendant physician and Modest; his fatalism alone would account for a lack of precaution. But almost immediately after his death, a rumor spread that he had committed suicide; reports to that effect were publ. in respectable European (but not Russian) newspapers and repeated in some biographical dictionaries. Some years later an émigré Russian musicologist publ. a story of a homosexual scandal involving a Russian nobleman's nephew, leading to a private tribunal of classmates who offered Tchaikovsky a choice between honorable suicide or disgrace and possible Siberian exile; choosing the former option, he was supplied with arsenic; a conspiracy of silence involving his doctor and brothers assured that the truth would remain buried. This fabrication was accepted as historical fact by some biographers, and found its way into *The New Grove Dictionary of Music and Musicians* (1980). In Russia the truth of Tchaikovsky's homosexuality was totally suppressed, and any references to it in his diary and letters were expunged.

As a composer Tchaikovsky stands apart from the militant national movement of the Mighty Five. The Russian element is, of course, very present in his music, occasionally using Russian folk songs; but this national spirit is instinctive rather than consciously cultivated. His relationships with the St. Petersburg group of nationalists were friendly without being close, his correspondence with them mostly concerned with professional matters. His music was frankly sentimental; his supreme gift of melody, which none of his Russian contemporaries could match, secured for him a lasting popularity among performers and audiences. His influence was profound on the Moscow group of composers, of whom Arensky and Rachmaninoff were the most talented. He wrote in every genre successfully; besides stage works, syms., chamber music, and piano compositions, he composed a great number of lyric songs, the most poignant creations of his genius. By a historical paradox, he became the most popular Russian composer under the Soviet regime; his subjectivism, fatalism, emphasis on melancholy moods, and reactionary political views (including a brand of amateurish anti-Semitism), failed to detract from his stature in the new society; indeed, Soviet apparatchiks repeatedly urged composers to follow his aesthetics. His popularity is very strong in Anglo-Saxon countries, particularly the U.S.; much less so in France and Italy; insignificant in Germany.

Tchaikovsky composed 11 operas, 3 ballets and their suites; 6 numbered syms. (1866–93); 4 orch'l suites (1879–87). Additional orch'l works: *Burya* (The Tempest), after Shakespeare, op. 18 (1873); *Sérénade mélancolique* for violin with orch., op. 26 (1875); *Francesca da Rimini*, after Dante, op. 32 (1876); *Variations on a Rococo Theme* for Cello and Orch., op. 33 (1876); Piano Concerto No. 2, op. 44 (1879–80); *Italian Capriccio*, op. 45 (1880); Serenade for strings, op. 48 (1880); *Manfred Sym.*, after Byron, op. 58 (1885); *Hamlet*, after Shakespeare, op. 67 (1888); *Voyevoda*, op. 78 (1890–91). Chamber music: 3 string quartets (1871–76); Piano Trio, op. 50 (Moscow, 1881–82); *Souvenir de Florence* for string sextet, op. 70 (1890–92). Piano: 2 sonatas (1865, 1878); *Les Quatre Saisons* (1875–76); *Dumka: Russian Rustic Scene*, op. 59 (1886); several collections of character pieces. Vocal, choral: *Liturgy of St. John Chrysostom* for unaccompanied chorus, op. 41 (1878); *Vesper Service* for unaccompanied chorus, op. 52 (1881–82); *c.* 100 songs. Writings: Diaries for the years 1873–91 were publ. in Moscow and Petrograd (1923); wrote a treatise, *Guide to the Practical Study of Harmony* (1872; Eng. trans., 1900).

Te. 1. In tonic sol-fa, the leading tone in major scales or the supertonic in minor scales. 2. In French, Italian, Spanish, and Russian pitch nomenclature, the leading tone in C major (B in English, H in German).

Te Deum. Song of praise in the Roman Catholic liturgy, sung in Matins on Sunday and feast days; referred to as an Ambrosian hymn, although St. Ambrose was not the author; the text dates to before the 4th century. In chant it sets 30 verses strophically, with a reciting formula centering around A for the body of the text; in later performance practice, choral polyphony alternates with chant or organ versets. The Te Deum is a hymn of thanksgiving, salutation, or commemoration; there are numerous polyphonic settings, with organum examples dating to the 10th century. Composers of Te Deums include Binchois, J. Taverner, J. Sheppard, Lassus, Lully, Purcell (in English), Handel (2 in English) and both Haydns. Handel wrote a *Te Deum for the Peace of Utrecht;* Berlioz contributed one to the Paris Exposition (1855). Later settings are by Bruckner (1885), Dvořák (1896), Verdi (1898), Vaughan Williams (1928), Britten (1935), Kodály (1936), and Walton (in English, 1953).

Te Kanawa, (Dame) Kiri, b. Gisborne, Mar. 6, 1944. She attended Catholic schools in Auckland; was coached in singing by a nun; sent to Melbourne to compete in a radio show; won 1st prize in a *Melbourne Sun* contest; received a grant for study in London with V. Rozsa (1966). She made her operatic debut at the Camden Festival in Rossini's *La Donna del Lago* (1969); 1st appeared at London's Covent Garden in a minor role, then as the Countess in *The Marriage of Figaro;* made her U.S. debut in the same role with the Santa Fe Opera (both 1971); became one of her most brilliant interpretations, singing it once more with the San Francisco Opera (1972).

A proverbial *coup de théâtre* occurred in her career when Te Kanawa substituted at a few hours' notice for an ailing Stratas as Desdemona at the Metropolitan Opera in N.Y. (1974); it was a triumphant achievement, winning her unanimous praise. She sang in a film version of *The Marriage of Figaro;* appeared as Pamina at the Paris Opéra (1977); later that year took the role of Rosalinde in a Covent Garden production of *Die Fledermaus,* televised to the U.S. She excelled equally as a subtle and artistic interpreter of lyric Mozart roles and in dramatic representations of Verdi's operas; among her other distinguished roles were the Marschallin and Arabella. She also won renown as a recitalist; in later years she expanded her repertoire to include popular fare, including songs by C. Porter and Bernstein's *West Side Story* (which she has recorded). Hailed as a prima donna assoluta, she pursued one of the most successful international operatic and concert careers of her day. She was made an Officer of the Order of the British Empire (1973); then a Dame Commander (1982).

teaching. George Bernard Shaw put an unfair kibosh on teachers when he delivered his dictum, "Those who can, do; those who cannot, teach." Maybe it is true that many retired virtuosos turn to teaching when they can no longer perform; and that to some of them the teaching profession is merely a vehicle to exercise their misanthropical disappointment at failing to becoming great artists. Ancient Greek legend said that Hercules slew his music teacher Linus with his own lyre when he reprimanded Hercules for playing improperly. Still, music teaching is an honorable profession. Music traditions have always been passed down by devoted elders; instruction in singing and playing was essential in ancient cultures, primarily in religious rituals. Music was an integral part of Greek tragedy, in the synthesis that included poetry and dancing.

Early Christian musical tradition was preserved by monks who taught plainchant to apprentices and novitiates. In the 11th century Guido d'Arezzo promulgated the 1st systematic theory of music by arranging a system of hexachords symbolized by positions on the palm of the left hand. This Guidonian hand could also be used for conducting a choir, with the singers interpreting these hand positions. So firmly established was this method that medieval music instructors or theorists allowed only progressions and keys that could be found *in manu* (in the hand); the dictum *non est in manu* sufficed to outlaw certain melodic progressions in chant.

Secular teaching of music was part of the quadrivium in medieval univs., as 1 of the 4 mathematical arts, the other 3 being arithmetic, geometry, and astronomy. Medieval music pedagogy was mostly concerned with mathematical relationships between length of a string or air column and pitch, and the numerical proportion of pitches producing a certain interval. The metaphorical music of the spheres expanded musical learning to philosophical arenas. Theology played a great role in medieval music science; triple time was called *tempus perfectum,* by analogy with the doctrine of the Holy (perfect) Trinity.

At the time of the Renaissance, music pedagogy was mainly in the hands of church organists. Aspirants flocked from all over Europe to study with Frescobaldi at the Vatican, where he was organist early in the 17th century. Bach and Handel separately undertook an arduous journey to Lübeck to hear the great Buxtehude play, hoping to succeed him after his death; but as a stipulation for succession was marriage to the incumbent's eldest daughter, both demurred. While Handel, having gone to London, never taught professionally, Bach became the music master of the St. Thomas School in Leipzig, with many students, including his own sons. Royal houses habitually engaged a music master to teach the princesses the art of playing the lute, harp, and singing. Mary, Queen of Scots engaged an Italian lutenist, David Rizzio, who was suspected of being her lover, and was eventually murdered by the court clique. A singing master was often a comic character in opera, e.g., Don Basilio in *The Barber of Seville.*

Institutional music-teaching originated in Italy in the 16th century. Such music schools became known as conservatories, for they were founded to "conserve" (protect) orphaned or ailing girls; in truth, these refuges were called *ospedali* (hospices). A French musician, visiting a Venetian hospice early in the 18th century, reported his enchantment with the girls: "They sing like angels. There can be nothing more ravishing than to watch a young girl in a white frock with a spray of pomegranate flowers over her ear perform for her audience." Soon conservatories and other music schools spread all over the world. Italian musicians established a virtual monopoly on the teaching of singing, while the Germans specialized in teaching composition and theory. In the 20th century the Russians invaded musically underdeveloped countries, mainly as piano teachers; other Slavic countries, notably Bohemia and Poland, sent their surplus of music educators abroad. On the other hand, travel to Germany for musical education became virtually universal in the 19th century; numerous British, American, and Russian composers participated in this pilgrimage; simultaneously, German musicians traveled to Great Britain, Russia, and America in search of employment and fortune. Not until the middle of the 19th century did French music pedagogues acquire a world reputation. In the 20th century, one in particular, Nadia Boulanger, was without equal in her influence upon the dozens of composers who came to study with her. Her weekly salons (from 1921) were affectionately called *Boulangerie;* her American students included Copland, Piston,

Thomson, R. Thompson, R. Harris, and Glass. British and American music teachers asserted themselves only in the 20th century.

The genealogy of private musical teaching can provide a vivid panorama of music history: Haydn taught Beethoven, who taught Czerny, who taught Liszt, who taught Siloti, who taught Rachmaninoff, who gave advice to Horowitz, who occasionally gave lessons to younger pianists. In his last years in Weimar Liszt used to receive young pianists to play for him; too often he dozed off while listening to a student play, but as soon as the music stopped he would wake up and murmur, "Schön." Great national schools of composition often arose as a result of mutual teaching, in or out of a conservatory. The Mighty Five of Russia had Balakirev as their chief mentor; Rimsky-Korsakov, who received his early instruction from him, subsequently taught 2 generations of Russian composers, including Stravinsky. Among celebrated composers who were active as teachers of composition and directors of national conservatories were Franck, d'Indy, and Fauré (France), Reger (Germany), and Dvořák and Janáček in Bohemia. Legendary fame distinguished many music teachers; in the violin field, no one was greater than Leopold Auer, from whose St. Petersburg studio came Heifetz, Elman, and hundreds of other violinists. (As the Gershwins wrote: "When we were 6 our tone was sour/Until a man, professor Auer/Came right along and taught us all/How to pack 'em in Carnegie Hall!")

Among great piano teachers was Theodor Leschetizky, who taught Paderewski; several of Leschetizky's wives, most notably Anna Essipoff, became distinguished teachers themselves. Tobias Matthay taught 3 pianistic generations in London; his Matthay Systems became a passport to educational competence in England and America. Isidor Philip established himself in Paris and taught many pianists who made fine careers. David Popper taught many fine cellists and wrote pleasing pieces for the cello. As for singing, Manuel García was the 1st true professional teacher; his daughter, the fabulous Malibran, was one of his pupils; he also invented the laryngoscope, used to probe the voice box. To enumerate former opera stars who became great teachers is tantamount to compiling an inventory of singers; but among the greatest opera singers, Chaliapin and Caruso never descended from their pedestals to teach.

teatro (It.). Theater. *Teatro lirico,* opera house.

Tebaldi, Renata, b. Pesaro, Feb. 1, 1922. After initial vocal training from G. Passani, she studied with E. Campogaliani at the Parma Cons. (1937–40) and C. Melis at the Pesaro Cons. (1940–43). She made her operatic debut as Elena in Boito's *Mefistofele* (Rovigo, 1944). In 1946 Toscanini chose her to sing in the reopening concert at La Scala in Milan; subsequently became one of its leading sopranos. She made her 1st appearance in England with the visiting La Scala company at London's Covent Garden as Desdemona; sang Aida with the San Francisco Opera (both 1950); she made her Metropolitan Opera debut in N.Y. as Desdemona (1955); continued to appear there until 1973; toured Russia (1975, 1976). Her repertoire was almost exclusively Italian, excelling in both lyric and dramatic roles; was particularly successful as Violetta, Tosca, Mimi, and Madame Butterfly; also sang Eva in *Die Meistersinger von Nürnberg.* In 1958 she was the subject of a cover story in *Time.*

technique (technic). All that relates to the purely mechanical part of an instrumental or vocal performance; mechanical training, skill, dexterity.

tecla (Sp.). Key on a keyboard.

tedesco, -a (It.). German. *Alla tedesca,* in the German style, e.g. in waltz rhythms, with changing tempo; Deutscher Tanz.

Teil (Ger.). Part or section; movement.

Telemann, Georg Philipp, b. Magdeburg, Mar. 14, 1681; d. Hamburg, June 25, 1767. He received his academic training at a local school; learned to play keyboard instruments and the violin; studied theory from the cantor B. Christiani. He subsequently attended the Gymnasium Andreanum in Hildesheim; became active in student performances of German cantatas. He entered the Univ. of Leipzig in jurisprudence (1701); organized a collegium musicum (1702); later appointed music director of the Leipzig Opera, where he used the services of his fellow students. He went to Sorau as Kapellmeister to Count Erdmann II of Promnitz (1705); appointed Konzertmeister to the court orch. in Eisenach (1708); later named Kapellmeister there.

Telemann was appointed music director of the city of Frankfurt (1712); wrote a quantity of sacred and secular music for public concerts given by the Frauenstein Soc., which he directed. He became music director of 5 churches in Hamburg (1721), which became the center of his activities as composer and music administrator; appointed music director of the Hamburg Opera (1722–38); during his tenure he wrote operas for production there; also staged works by Handel and Keiser; visited France (1737–38). His eyesight began to fail as he grew older, the same infirmity from which Bach and Handel suffered.

Extraordinarily prolific, Telemann mastered both the German and Italian styles of composition prevalent in his day. While he never approached the greatness of Bach or Handel, he nevertheless became an exemplar of the German Baroque at its grandest; unlike his 2 great contemporaries, he bridged the gap into the rococo and early Classic styles. His works include 35 operas, including many German intermezzos, notably *Der gedültige Socrates* (Hamburg, 1721) and *Pimpinone, oder Die ungleiche Heyrath* (Hamburg, 1725); 7 oratorios, the best known being *Der Tag des Gerichts* (1762); over 1,250 cantatas, including 4 major sacred collections; 46 Passions; Masses; psalms; motets. In the instrumental realm his greatest collection was the *Musique de table* (Hamburg, 1733), containing 3 orch. suites, 3 concertos, 3 quartets, 3 trios, and 3 sonatas. His prodigious orch'l output comprises numerous overtures, concertos, sonatas, quartets, quintets, etc. His grandson Georg Michael Telemann (b. Plön, Apr. 20, 1748; d. Riga, Mar. 4, 1831) was a composer and writer on music, reared and trained in music by his grandfather in Hamburg; served as cantor and teacher at the cathedral school in Riga (1773–1828), where he oversaw performances of many of his grandfather's works.

telephone broadcasting. Fanciful method of musical broadcast discussed in Edward Bellamy's novel *Looking Backward: 2000 Back to 1887* (1888), about a man who falls asleep for over a century and awakes to find a brave new world. In it, the telephone of Alexander Graham Bell has been technically extended so that performances can be transmitted far away from places of origin, available to anyone picking up a telephone and requesting the appropriate connection. This was a 24-hour service requiring mostly live performance (Bellamy did not foresee long-playing records or tapes); the N.Y. press was generally approving of this "scientific wonder." Today it could be considered the fictional precursor of the "1-900" telephone number.

teller (Ger.). Cymbals.

Telmányi, Emil. See ⇒Nielsen, Carl (August).

temperament. Calculated alteration of the acoustical values of musical intervals to make possible the division of the perfect octave into 12 equal semitones. Purely tuned tones of very nearly the same pitch, like C-sharp and D-flat, are made to sound enharmonically identical by tempering them, i.e., slightly raising or lowering the pitch. When applied to all the tones of an instrument (as the piano), this system is called *equal temperament;* when only the keys most used are so tuned (the former practice), the system is unequal temperament or *meantone tuning.*

Theorists and performing musicians struggled for centuries to find a practical way of reconciling the perfect octave with the pure, untempered perfect 5th (the interval between the 2nd and 3rd partials of the harmonic series), perfect 4th, and major 3rd. The *Pythagorean tuning* system, developed in ancient Greece and perhaps earlier, uses multiples of the perfect fifth to create its gamut; it is arithmetically impossible, however, to equate any multiple of 3:2, the ratio of frequencies (cps, Hz) for the pure 5th, with any multiple of 2:1, the ratio of frequencies for a perfect octave. It is but visual self-deception that the circle of 12 5ths on a piano keyboard equals the circle of 7 octaves, with their common terminus on the highest C of the keyboard; for the final perfect 5th would arrive on a hypothetical B-sharp, around 24 cents (an 8th-tone) higher than the C of the last octave.

The situation became more complicated with the advent of tonality in the Baroque era; now the major and minor 3rds had to be tuned accurately to support triadic harmony and modulation. The 1st set of solutions involved trying to tune the 5ths and/or 3rds in a 12-note scale so that as many keys as possible were usable without having to retune (impossible on fixed-pitch instruments, in any case). The multiple approaches that proliferated were classed as meantone tunings, including *well temperament,* by Bach for his 2 volumes of *The Well-Tempered Clavier,* each containing 24 preludes and fugues in every key in chromatic order. The difference between unequal and equal temperament is crucial; while equal temperament seeks a total compromise for maximum flexibility, unequal temperaments allow certain keys a special timbre or color that composers responded to.

Others, wishing to avoid the potential chaos of unequal division on fixed pitch instruments, decided to contract a pure 3:2 5th (702 cents) to a slightly smaller tempered 5th (700 cents); this "imperfect" 5th was then transposed logarithmically to the other 11 steps of the circle of 5ths; as a result the acoustical purity of other intervals was also affected, to a greater degree than the perfect 5th or its inversion, the perfect 4th. By sacrificing the acoustical purity of the generative harmonic series, however, it became possible to play a tune in any key and modulate freely from one key to another, with the same exact intervals; it also permitted transposition to another key without seeming "out of tune."

tempestoso (*tempestosamente;* It.). Stormily, passionately, impetuously.

temple blocks. Chinese blocks.

tempo (It.; Fr. *temps*). Rate of speed, movement; time, measure. 2 systems of tempo indications (marks) have developed since the Baroque period. The earlier type, still very much in use, indicates tempo verbally; the most common indications are in Italian, including largo, adagio, moderato, andante, allegro, allegretto, presto, and prestissimo; these terms are often qualified by additional words of caution such as *ma non troppo* or *poco*. The 1st attempt to put precise meaning into these vague Italian modifiers was made by Quantz, who defined the natural speed measure as the human heartbeat, at 80 beats per minute; taking 4/4 as the basic meter, he assigned the exact duration of the pulsebeat to a half note in allegro, to a quarter note in allegretto, and to an 8th note in adagio.

The 2nd system came with the invention in the early 19th century of the metronome, which allowed a mathematical measurement of tempo, theoretically standardizing tempo terminology. Beethoven, the 1st major composer to make systematic use of the metronome, set down the "scientific" tempo for several of his works, marking early works retrospectively. However, most modern interpreters have found his instructions untenable, blaming a "faulty" metronome. For example, he set the metronome mark for the Marcia funèbre from his *Eroica* Sym. at 80 8th notes per minute; most conductors prefer a slower tempo; Toscanini's 1935 recording scores 52 8th notes a minute, 35 percent slower than what the composer apparently intended. Many modern composers, particularly Stravinsky, abandoned traditional tempo marks entirely and replaced them by the precise metronome number; since he insisted on precision in the performance of his works and abhorred Romantic aberrations, his metronome marks were "final."

The rediscovery of recordings of great artists of the past would disclose a shocking departure from tempo markings indicated by the composer. Sentimental leanings among German musicians and theorists of the latter 18th century—epitomized in the concept of *Empfindung,* affect or feeling—and a desire to achieve perfect human expression in performance led to constant shifts of tempo and dynamics—an astonishing practice, considering the modern tendency towards the precise and ordered execution of classical works. Even Leopold Mozart commented favorably on the device of "stolen time," anticipating the Romantic rubato so despised by modern interpreters. The treatment of tempo in the mid-20th century was generally in the direction of precision, away from unauthorized ritardandos (so commonly resorted to in difficult technical passages) and Luftpausen.

But toward the last 3rd of the 20th century a curious counterreaction set in; critics and the public began to complain about the metronomic monotony of modern performers; an unscientific nostalgia spread once more through the music world. As in the preceding century, "personality" was hailed as superior to overzealous fidelity to the page. Many composers welcomed flexible tempos affected by celebrated interpreters to vitalize the spirit of the music. Some compromise between musical permissiveness and pedantry seemed inevitable. Perhaps Landowska's dictum can serve as guide: "One must approach classical music as a well-mannered guest. One need not be too obsequious or reverential to the hostess, but one must not put one's feet on the table at meals."

A tempo, return to preceding tempo; *in tempo,* same as *a tempo; in tempo misurato,* in strict time (after a passage marked *tempo a piacere*); *l'istesso tempo,* or *lo stesso tempo,* the same tempo, despite a rhythmic change; *sempre in tempo,* always at the same tempo; *senza tempo,* same as *tempo a piacere; tempo a piacere,* play at will in terms of tempo; *tempo ad libitum,* metrically free; *tempo com(m)odo,* at a comfortable, convenient tempo; *tempo di Ballo, Minuetto, Valse* etc., in the movement of a ballet, minuet, waltz, etc.; *tempo giusto,* at a proper, appropriate tempo; *tempo primo,* at the original pace; *tempo rubato,* see ⇒rubato.

tempo marking. Word or phrase indicating the rate of speed at which a piece should be performed; "Adagio (M.M. = 56)" signifies a tranquil movement in which a quarter note has the duration of one click of a metronome set at 56 (i.e., 56 beats per minute).

temporal parameter. The conjectural duration of a musical composition is a factor of importance per se, a temporal parameter that has a decisive bearing on the cohesion and relative stability of the constituent parts of the entire work. The late 19th and 20th century cultivated a type of Brobdingnagian grandiosity that seemed to equate quantity with quality; works by Bruckner, Mahler, R. Strauss, Brian, Sauget, and the minimalists are typical of this tendency. The longest piano work of the century is *Opus Clavicembalisticum* by the English-born composer Kaikhosru Sorabji, which he personally played for the 1st and last time in Glasgow (1930); the work consists of 12 movements in the form of a theme with 44 variations and a passacaglia with 81 variations.

While some composers kept expanding the duration of their individual works, their contemporaries followed the opposite trend toward extreme brevity of musical utterance. The pioneer of this modern concision was Webern; one of his pieces, written in 1911, lasts only 19 seconds. Ligeti wrote a movement consisting of a single quarter-tone rest. The ultimate in infinitesimally small musical forms was achieved by Cage in his *0' 00",* "to be performed in any way by anyone," and 1st presented in this ambiguous form in Tokyo (1962).

temps faible (Fr.). Weak beat in a measure.

temps fort (Fr.). Strong beat in a measure.

Temptations, The. Popular vocal group of the 1960s (Core group: Eddie Kendricks, b. Birmingham, Ala., Dec. 17, 1939; d. there, Oct. 5, 1992; David Ruffin, b. Meridian, Miss., Jan. 18, 1941, d. Philadelphia, Pa., June 1, 1991; Otis Williams, b. Otis Miles, Texarkana, Tex., Oct. 30, 1941; Melvin Franklin, b. David English, Montgomery Ala., Oct. 12, 1942; d. Los Angeles, Calif., Feb. 23, 1995; Paul Williams, b. Birmingham, Ala., July 2, 1939; d. [suicide] Detroit, Mich., Aug. 17, 1973). One of the best of the Motown groups, the Temptations were noted for fleet-footed choreography and double lead vocals, provided by Kendricks and Ruffin. Formed out of two Detroit ensembles of the late 1950s, the Primes and the Distants, they were signed to Motown (1960) when they were known as the Elgins. After changing their name, they scored their 1st hit with *Dream Come Home* (1962); Ruffin joined the group (1963) and the classic lineup was in place.

Joining with producer-songwriter Smokey Robinson, the group started 1964 with a major hit (*The Way You Do the Things You Do*); the classic *My Girl* followed, along with many other hits (*Ain't Too Proud to Beg, I Know I'm Losin' You, I Wish It Would Rain*). Ruffin left the group in 1968; producer Norman Whitfield shifted the group's orientation towards funk; they scored with several more hits, including *Cloud Nine, Psychedelic Shack*, and *Ball of Confusion*. Kendricks left the group in 1971; like Ruffin, he enjoyed a modest solo career while the group itself continued to score hits, notably *Papa Was a Rolling Stone*. Over the next 2 decades the group performed with changing rosters, with Kendricks and Ruffin occasionally rejoining them; paired with white soulsters Hall and Oates for a concert and album to celebrate the newly refurbished Apollo Theater in New York (1985). Ruffin died of a drug overdose; Kendricks succumbed to lung cancer; Franklin died of complications following a stroke.

tempus (Lat.). In medieval theory, the shortest duration in which a sung note can be clearly perceived, lasting less than a second but more than a half second; later, a time value divisible into either 2 (*tempus imperfectum*) or 3 (*tempus perfectum*) semibreves.

Tenebrae (Lat., darkness). Roman Catholic liturgy for Holy Week, specifically the Matins and Lauds of Holy Thursday, Good Friday, and Holy Saturday; the name derives from the ritual of blowing out a candle after each psalm until all are extinguished; the text includes excerpts from the Lamentations of Jeremiah. Settings of this liturgy include works by Gesualdo, Lassus, Palestrina, Victoria, Couperin, and Stravinsky.

tenebroso (It.). Somberly.

teneramente (It.). Tenderly.

tenero (It.). Tenderly, with tender emotion; delicately, softly.

Tenney, James (Carl), b. Silver City, N.Mex., Aug. 10, 1934. He studied engineering at the Univ. of Denver (1952–54) before devoting himself to music; studied piano with Steuermann at the Juilliard School of Music in N.Y. (1954–55), studied piano and composition at Bennington (Vt.) College (B.A., 1958); worked with Gaburo, Hiller, and Partch at the Univ. of Illinois (M.Mus., 1961); also associated with Chou Wen-chung, Ruggles, and Varèse (1955–65). A highly influential American pianist, conductor, teacher, and composer, he performed with the Steve Reich and Philip Glass ensembles; conducted electronic research at the Bell Laboratories (with Max Mathews; 1961–64), Yale Univ. (1964–66), and the Polytechnic Inst. of Brooklyn (1966–70). He taught at the Calif. Inst. of the Arts (1970–75), Univ. of Calif. at Santa Cruz (1975–76), and York Univ. in Toronto (from 1976).

As performer and scholar, Tenney is a prominent advocate and theorist of contemporary music; is a noted authority on Ives and Nancarrow. His compositions include *Quiet Fan for Erik Satie* (1970) and *Clang* (1972) for Orch; *Quintext* for String Quartet and Double Bass (1972); *In the Aeolian Mode* for Prepared Piano and Variable Ens. (1973); *Saxony* for Saxophone and Tape Delay (1978); *3 Indigenous Songs* for mixed quintet (1979); *Glissade* for Viola, Cello, Double Bass, and Tape Delay (1982); *Koan* for String Quartet (1984); *Spectral Canon for Conlon Nancarrow* for Player Piano (1974); pioneering works on tape or for computer, including *Collage No. 1: Blue Suede* (1961); *Stochastic Quartet: String Quartet* for Computer or Strings (1963); *Fabric for Che* (1967); *For Ann (rising)* (1969); vocal and theater works. He publ. an influential essay on compositional aesthetics and morphology, *Meta + Hodos* (New Orleans, 1964); other writings are *META Meta + Hodos* (1977); *A History of "Consonance" and "Dissonance"* (N.Y., 1988).

tenor (from Lat. *tenere*, hold; It. *tenore*). 1. Highest and most expressive male voice; etymologically derives from the fact that the cantus firmus in early vocal polyphony was given to a voice, the tenor, whose function was to "hold" the cantus melody while other voices moved in relation to it. The voice part gradually became independent of its original function; the term came to refer simply to the vocal range. From the beginning of operatic history, tenors enjoyed great social and financial success as well as adulation; but they were traditionally regarded as being mentally deficient; an Italian joke lists the degrees of comparison, "stupido, stupidissimo, tenore." Although Caruso never learned to read music, he could hardly be called "stupido"; another nonstupid tenor was Leo Slezak (1873–1946), who possessed a Viennese kind of *Witz*, often at the expense of his fellow singers.

The ordinary tenor range is two octaves, from the C below middle C to the C above ($c^0 - c^2$). The tenor part is usually notated in the treble clef, sounding an octave lower; operatic tenor parts are sometimes indicated by a combined tenor and treble clef. Some singers in the bel canto era could go higher in falsetto; G. B. Rubini (1794–1854) regularly hit f^2. The mark of distinction for great tenors is their ability to hold high C for a long time, often ignoring musical and harmonic reasons to let go; performance films of operatic arias show tenors running up to the footlights during a highly dramatic duet to project a high C, then retreating to join an awaiting soprano. Even more bizarrely, in a 1950s film of *Don Giovanni* there is a duet in which the soprano is singing a passage alone; the camera shifts to the tenor in anticipation of the tenor's entrance and finds him completely ignoring his partner, even shrugging at the camera, before returning to character in time for his blast of sound.

Categories include the dramatic tenor (It. *tenore di forza*), with a full and powerful quality and a range from c to b^1 (Rodolpho in *La bohème*, Manrico in *Il trovatore*); heroic tenor (Ger. Heldentenor), with a strong sonority throughout the range (Siegfried in *the Ring, Otello*); lyric tenor (It. *tenore di grazia*), sweeter and less powerful and a range from d to c^2 (or $c\sharp^2$; Gounod's *Faust*, Almaviva in *The Barber of Seville*).

2. Names of instruments with a similar pitch relationship to other family members: tenor trombone, tenor tuba, tenor violin.

tenor C. Small c:

tenor clef. C clef on the 4th line, sometimes used in cello, bassoon, or tenor trombone parts.

tenor drum. Side drum, without snares, larger and therefore deeper sounding than a military drum, also of indefinite pitch.

tenor saxophone. Saxophone in B-flat, transposing down a whole tone; its range is Bb_0– f^2; commonly found in jazz ensembles; a nontransposing "melody" tenor saxophone in C is still used in marching and wind bands.

tenor violin (Fr. *taille de violon;* Ger. *Tenorgeige*). Generic term for large violas, 1st made in the 16th century, with the bottom string G_s an octave below the violin g^0; it resembles the bass viola da braccio; also called *tenor-viola, violon-ténor, viola tenore, Oktavgeige,* and *controviolino.*

tenorini (It.). Tenor singing in falsetto.

tenorino (It.). High tenor voice of a sweetly adolescent quality.

Tenorposaune (Ger.). Tenor trombone.

Tenorschlüssel (Ger.). Tenor clef.

tenth (Lat. *decima*). Diatonic interval of an octave plus 2 degrees.

tenuto (It., held; abbrev. *ten.*). 1. Sustain a tone for its full time-value. 2. Use an emphatic and attentive legato. *Forte tenuto (f ten.), forte* throughout; *tenuto mark,* a short stroke over or under a notehead.

tepidamente (It.). Lukewarmly; in an even, dispassionate style.

teponaxtl. South American slit drum, traditionally made out of a hollowed-out tree trunk; played with sticks. See also ⇒slit drum.

teratological borborygmus. Modern works of the 1st quarter of the 20th century systematically increased the amount of massive sonorities as though their intention was to induce orological acousma or some other tonitruous Brobdingnagian teratological borborygmus, a huge and monstrous rumbling issuing from the mouthpieces of brass instruments coupled with shrill flageolets of the piccolos and high harmonics in the strings. It was inevitable that a reaction against this loss of all moderation should have set in among composers of the avant-garde; this reaction was made necessary because of the catastrophe of World War I, when it was no longer economical to place huge orch'l apparati at the service of composers of macrosonic works. The era of teratological borborygmus seemed to end without a hope of recurrence, but the emergence of new audio technology in general and electrically amplified popular music in specific generated an electronic circus that promised to eclipse the deafening potentialities of the past.

Terce. In both the old and revised Roman Catholic liturgy, the daily Canonical Hour celebrated at 9 a.m.

ternary. Composed of, or progressing by, 3s. *Ternary form,* ABA form, such as the minuet and trio; da capo form; *ternary measure,* simple triple time.

terraced dynamics (Ger. *Terrasendynamik*). Primarily Baroque style of dynamic changes by a direct transition from one degree of loudness to another as from piano to mezzoforte, from mezzopiano to fortissimo, etc., without intervening crescendo or decrescendo; the term was introduced by Busoni. Terraced dynamics were in common usage in the Baroque and early Classic eras; in the Elizabethan period explicit indications such as *lowd, lowder, softer,* etc. were in use. Beethoven favored the terraced dynamics in the form of a *subito piano* after a *forte.* During his neoclassical period Stravinsky began to cultivate terraced dynamics almost exclusively, to signify his return to Baroque usage.

Terry, Clark, b. St. Louis, Dec. 14, 1920. He played trumpet and flugelhorn; worked with Charlie Barnet (1947) and Basie (1948–51); joined Ellington's band (1951), enjoying a richly rewarding 8-year association. During his collaborations with O. Peterson, he evolved his trademark "mumbles" style of scat singing, self-described as sounding like an old man storytelling while drifting into incoherence; also evolved a style of musical monologue made up of wittily juggled fragments of musical thought. He played in the orch. of *The Tonight Show* until it relocated to Los Angeles; taught at various jazz clinics; appointed director for the new Thelonious Monk Inst. of Jazz at Duke Univ. in Chapel Hill, N.C. (1990).

tertia (Lat.). Interval of a 3rd.

Terz (Ger.; It. *terza*). Interval of a 3rd.

Terzett (Ger.; It. *terzetto*). Properly, a vocal trio; occasionally, work for 3 instruments.

terzina (It.). Triplet.

terzo rivolto (It.; Ger. *Terzquartakkord*). 3rd inversion of the 7th chord; the $^6/_4/_2$ or ^{2} chord.

terzo suono (It., 3rd tone). Difference tone (Tartini tone).

tessitura (It., texture). Proportionate use of high or low register in a given vocal range. If high notes are preponderant, the tessitura is said to be high, as in most coloratura soprano parts; if low notes are especially frequent, as in some Russian songs, the tessitura is said to be low. In English a vocal part can "lie" high or low.

testa (It.). Head. *Voce di testa,* head voice.

testo (It., text). In Baroque oratorios and 20th-century works, the narrator (usually in recitative).

testudo (Lat., turtle). Ancient Greek lyre, made with a tortoiseshell body; in the Renaissance and Baroque, the lute.

tetrachord. 1. Interval of a perfect 4th. 2. 4 scale-tones contained within a perfect 4th. In ancient Greek scales the tetrachord was treated invariably as a descending progression; however, the medieval tetrachord was counted upward, a pattern retained in subsequent centuries. As a result the names of the diatonic modes developed from conjunct or disjunct tetrachords were different from the Greek modes. The theoretical characterization of a tetrachord was determined by the placement of the semitone: The Phrygian tetrachord was formed by the placement of the semitone between the 1st and the 2nd degrees; in the Aeolian and Dorian tetrachords the semitone was between the 2nd and 3rd degrees; in the Ionian and Mixolydian modes, between the 3rd and 4th degrees. The Lydian tetrachord is formed by whole tones only. 3. Set of 4 pitch classes, usually associated with a 12-note set.

tetralogy. Thematically connected series of 4 stage works or oratorios.

Teutscher (Tanz). Deutscher Tanz.

text. Words to which music is set.

text-sound composition. Medium that germinated in the dadaist movement of the 1st quarter of the 20th century and was revived making use of magnetic tape and other electronic devices in the latter 20th century. Text-sound works emphasize the sonorous element independent from the meaning, if any, of the words recited; such compositions may hark back to prehuman cries through ritualistic incantation and pentecostal glossolalia or else project into an absurd future with the aid of computers, synthesizers, and stereophonic sound engineering. The medium evolved among modern poets, sound engineers, and Swedish composers, and was picked up by American composers. Among the 1st group the best-known work is the *Ursonate* of artist Kurt Schwitters (1922–32); among the latter the works of C. Amirkhanian achieved, in his own execution, a degree of true virtuosity.

texture. Musical parameter concerning the number and relationships of individual parts or lines in a piece; vertical analysis of a work's external components. The most commonly described textures are: 1) monophonic, 1 part (line) without accompaniment, performed solo, in unison, or in parallel organum (chant); 2) homophonic, either a primary part accompanied by rhythmically distinct music, the so-called melody-and-accompaniment texture (songs); or a homorhythmic texture, with 2 or more parts moving more or less simultaneously, with a distinct melody, typical of vocal music (hymns); 3) polyphonic, when 2 or more parts are sufficiently independent that any hierarchical relationship becomes secondary if not irrelevant; includes imitative structures (canon, fugue, round); and 4) heterophonic, associated with non-Western music, where 2 or more parts approximate the same melodic line but with intentional "imprecisions" of pitch, attack, decay, duration, and ornamentation.

theater orchestra. Small, flexible ensemble for which arrangements are made, with separate instrumental parts cued into other parts to be used when a particular instrument is not available; e.g., an English-horn solo might be cued into a clarinet or even violin part. The piano part represents the harmonic skeleton of a theater arrangement. Ives wrote "theater sets," rather than arrangements, for such ensembes, analoguous to his orchestral sets.

thematic catalogue. Inventory of works by an individual composer arranged according to genre (operas, syms., chamber music, solo works) or chronologically (including opus number) and supplemented by incipits of the works catalogued. Such catalogues may be compiled by the composers themselves, their publishers, or subsequent scholars. Haydn entrusted his copyist with the job of compiling a thematic catalogue of those works "which I can recall at present, from the age of 18 until my 73rd year of life"; the Haydn catalogue contains errors of both omission and commission. Mozart also began cataloguing his compositions; a complete thematic catalogue of his works was 1st publ. by a botanist named Köchel, who had a passion for inventories.

Thematic catalogues now exist for a majority of important composers and a minority of unimportant ones. Some extensive catalogues include information about the provenance of the MSS, details concerning various editions, etc. In German catalogues of composers published after World War II the notation *verschollen* (disappeared, lost) makes its ominous and frequent appearance, alluding in part to the unconscionable looting of MSS by the occupying armies, be they Allied or Axis.

thematic composition. Any compositional method based on the contrapuntal treatment or development of 1 or more themes. See also ⇒invention, fugue, sonata form, etc.

theme (Ger., *Thema;* It., *tema*). Extended and rounded-off melodic subject with accompaniment, in period form, proposed as groundwork for further elaboration, development, and variation.

theme and variations (Fr. *theme varié;* Ger. *Thema und Variationen, Veränderungen;* It. *tema con variazioni*). Musical form and/or genre, in existence under this or other designations since the 16th century, in which a principal theme is clearly and explicitly stated at the beginning, then followed by a number of altered repetitions of that theme. The pattern of development over the course of such a work is freely chosen, although the Classic period evolved a remarkably consistent structure, particularly in music written for amateurs; Schumann called few works "theme and variations," but used the technique innumerable times in various disguises.

theme song. Most prominent song in a musical or movie, calculated to express the abiding sentiment of the entire production.

Theodorakis, Mikis (Michael George), b. Chios, July 29, 1925. He studied at the Athens Cons. Despite his participation in the resistance to the German occupation in World War II, he was arrested and deported during the civil war for his left-wing views. He went to Paris and studied with Messiaen (1953); soon began to compose. After returning to Greece (1961) he resumed his political activity; served as a member of Parliament (1963). As a Communist, he was again arrested after the military coup in 1967 and incarcerated, during which time he wrote the music for the film *Z*, dealing with the police murder of Socialist politician Gregory Lambrakis in Salonika (1963); both the film and music were greatly acclaimed in Europe and America; his fate became a cause célèbre; yielding to international pressure, the military Greek government freed him (1970).

After a period of disillusion, Theodorakis returned to the Communist Party; again served in Parliament (1981, 1985–86). By 1989 he was an ambassador for Greek neoconservatism, going so far as to enter the legislative race on the New Democracy ticket; with 416 like-minded painters, writers, musicians, singers, and actors, he signed a manifesto condemning the divisive policies of the former Socialist government of Andreas Papandreou; ended 4 years of musical silence by appearing on an Athens stage before a crowd of 70,000 people, singing songs of protest and love in the name of national unity. His works are usually programmatically inspired, whether instrumental or vocal; his favorite subjects are Greek mythology and personal liberation; most of his works reflect a populist aesthetic. He has composed numerous syms. and orch'l song cycles, a ballet-opera, ballet (*Antigone*, 1959), and the soundtracks for *Zorba the Greek*.

theorbo. Large, double-necked archlute with 1 set of strings for the melody and another for the bass.

theory. Systematic study of basic musical principles, particularly as related to composition and analysis.

theremin (thereminovox). Early electronic melody instrument in which hand movements interface with electronic sound waves, allowing for the spatial control of pitch and dynamics; invented by Leon Theremin (see ⇒entry below).

Theremin, Leon; b. Lev Termen, St. Petersburg, Aug. 15, 1896; d. Moscow, Nov. 3, 1993. He took physics and astronomy at the Univ. of St. Petersburg; studied the cello and music theory; continued his studies in physics at the Petrograd Physico-Technical Inst.; became director of its Laboratory of Electrical Oscillators (1919); gave a demonstration there of his spatially controlled aetherophone, prototype of the thereminovox (theremin; 1920); gave a special demonstration for Lenin, who was convinced that the electrification of Russia would ensure the success of communism.

In 1927 Theremin demonstrated his new instruments in Germany, France, and the U.S., where he obtained a patent for the theremin (1928); presented a concert at Carnegie Hall in N.Y. with an ensemble of 10 of his instruments (1930); introduced a space-controlled synthesis of color and music; in the same hall in 1932, he introduced the 1st electrical sym. orch., conducted by Stoessel and including theremin fingerboard and keyboard instruments. Among his American students from the 1930s he especially commended Clara Rockmore, the best-known thereminist. He also invented the *rhythmicon*, capable of playing different rhythms simultaneously or separately (conceived by Cowell), and an automatic musical instrument for playing directly from specially written musical scores (constructed for Grainger).

With the theorist Joseph Schillinger, Theremin established an acoustical laboratory in N.Y.; formed numerous scientific and artistic associations, among them Einstein, an amateur violinist; Theremin provided him an opportunity to study the relationships between music, color, and geometric and stereometric figures geometries, but Einstein passed on it. More to Theremin's point were experiments made by Stokowski, who tried to effect a sonic increase among certain instrumental groups in the Philadelphia Orch., particularly the double basses; these experiments had to be abandoned, however, when the players complained of deleterious effects upon their abdominal muscles, which they attributed to the sound waves produced by the theremin.

In 1938 Theremin returned (voluntarily or involuntarily) to Russia; he soon had difficulties with the Soviet government, suspicious of his foreign contacts; detained for a period, speculations and rumors abounded as to his possible fate. In fact he worked steadily in electronic research for the government, continuing his experiments with sound as a sideline. Upon his retirement from his electronics work he became a prof. of acoustics at the Univ. of Moscow (1964). With the advent of more liberal policies in the USSR, he was able to travel to Paris and Stockholm (1989); his return visit to the U.S. was documented in the film *The Electronic Odyssey of Leon Theremin* (1993).

thesis (Grk., letting down). Orig. the strong beat in Greek prosody and therefore musical theory; now it is the unaccented beat, having exchanged meanings with arsis.

Thibaud, Jacques, b. Bordeaux, Sept. 27, 1880; d. Sept. 1, 1953. He began his training with his father; made his debut at age 8 in Bordeaux; at 13 he entered the Paris Cons. as a pupil of M. Marsick, graduating with the *premier prix* (1896). Obliged to earn his living, he played at the Café Rouge, where he was heard by the conductor Colonne, who offered him a position in his orch.; made his debut as a soloist with Colonne (1898); was so successful that he was engaged for 54 concerts in Paris in the same season; subsequently appeared in all the musical centers of Europe; from 1903, visited America numerous times.

With his 2 brothers, a pianist and a cellist, Thibaud formed a trio, with some success; this gave way when he joined Cortot and Casals in a famous ensemble. With Marguerite Long he founded the renowned Long-Thibaud competition (1943). His playing was notable for its warmth of expressive tone and fine dynamics; his interpretations of Beethoven ranked very high, but he was particularly authoritative in French music. He died in an airplane crash near Mt. Cemet, in the French Alps, en route to a concert tour in the Far East.

third. Interval embracing 3 degrees; also, 3rd degree of the scale; mediant.

Third Stream. Compositional synthesis of cool jazz and classical techniques associated with the 1950s and early 1960s; the term was 1st used by Schuller at a lecture at Tanglewood (1957). If the 1st stream is classical, and the 2nd stream is jazz, 3rd Stream is their Hegelian synthesis, uniting and reconciling the classical thesis with the popular antithesis. Instances of such syntheses are found in the 20th century; Gershwin's *Rhapsody in Blue* is the most important precursor of 3rd Stream. In constructive application of 3rd Stream, ultramodernist techniques, including serialism, can be amalgamated with popular rhythmic resources. The compositions of Schuller and John Lewis were notable in this style, and the Modern Jazz Quartet was a primary mover.

thirteenth. Interval embracing an octave and a 6th; a compound 6th.

thirty-second note. Half of the value of a 16th note.

Thomas, (Charles Louis) Ambroise, b. Metz, Aug. 5, 1811; d. Paris, Feb. 12, 1896. He entered the Paris Cons. (1828); his teachers were Zimmerman (piano) and Dourlen (harmony and accompaniment); studied privately with Kalkbrenner (piano) and Barbereau (harmony); later studied composition with Le Sueur at the Cons., where he won the Grand Prix de Rome with his cantata *Hermann et Ketty* (1832). After 3 years in Italy and a visit to Vienna, he returned to Paris and applied himself with great energy to the composition of operas. In 1851 he was elected to the Académie; became a prof. of composition at the Paris Cons. (1856); became its director (1871).

As a composer of melodious French operas Thomas was 2nd only to Gounod; his masterpiece was *Mignon*, based on Goethe's *Wilhelm Meister* (Paris, 1866); this opera was long a mainstay of the operatic repertory, with nearly 2,000 performances in less then 100 years at the Opéra-Comique alone; equally successful was his Shakespearean opera *Hamlet* (Paris, 1868). In 1845 he was made a Chevalier of the Legion d'honneur; was the 1st composer to receive its Grand Croix (1894). Thomas wrote 17 opéras-comique and 3 operas; 3 ballets; orch'l music; chamber works; keyboard music; sacred vocal works, including a Requiem and Messe solennelle; secular vocal works.

Thomas, Michael Tilson, b. Los Angeles, Dec. 21, 1944. He is a grandson of Boris and Bessie Thomashefsky, founders of the Yiddish Theater in N.Y. He studied at the Univ. of Southern Calif.; studied composition with Dahl, piano with J. Crown and harpsichord with A. Ehlers; acquired conductorial skill by leading the Young Musicians Foundation Debut Orch. (1963–67). He served as pianist in the master classes of Heifetz and Piatigorsky at the Univ. of Southern Calif. in Los Angeles; conducted at the Monday Evening Concerts, giving 1st performances of works by Stravinsky, Copland, Boulez, and Stockhausen.

In 1966 Thomas attended master classes at Bayreuth; was assistant conductor to Boulez at the Ojai Festival (1967); conducted there in 1968, 1969, and 1973. As a conducting fellow at Tanglewood, he won the Koussevitzky Prize (1968); the crowning point of his early career was his appointment as assistant conductor of the Boston Sym. Orch. (1969), the youngest to receive this post with that orch.. He was spectacularly catapulted into public awareness that year when he conducted the 2nd part of a N.Y. concert of the Boston Sym. Orch., substituting at the last moment for William Steinberg, who was suddenly taken ill.

In 1970 Thomas was appointed associate conductor of the Boston Sym. Orch.; was principal guest conductor there with C. Davis (1972–74). He served as music director of the Buffalo Phil. Orch. (1971–79); music director of the N.Y. Phil. Young People's Concerts (1971–76); principal guest conductor of the Los Angeles Phil. Orch. (1981–85). He was music director of the Great Woods Performing Arts Center in Mansfield, Mass., summer home of the Pittsburgh Sym. Orch. (1986–89); artistic advisor of the New World Sym. Orch. in Miami (from 1987); principal conductor of the London Sym. Orch. (from 1988); guest conducted throughout North America and Europe. His repertoire is exhaustive, ranging from the earliest masters to the avant-garde, with a special interest in American music; is an excellent pianist; above all, an energetically modern musician, pragmatically proficient, able to extract the maximum value of the music on hand.

Thomas, Theodore (Christian Friedrich), b. Esens, East Friesland, Oct. 11, 1835; d. Chicago, Jan. 4, 1905. Taught by his violinist father, he played publicly at age 6. In 1845 the family emigrated to N.Y. (1845), where he began to play for dances, weddings, and in theaters; made a concert tour as a soloist (1851); joined Jullien's Orch. on its visit to N.Y. (1853); later toured the U.S. with Lind, Grisi, Sontag, Mario, et al.; became a member of the N.Y. Phil. Soc. (1854). With the pianist William Mason, he founded a series of monthly matinee chamber concerts at N.Y.'s Dodworth Hall (1855–69). He 1st gained notice as a conductor by leading a performance of *La favorite* at the N.Y. Academy of Music (1859); led orch'l concerts at N.Y.'s Irving Hall (1862); became known as the Symphonic Soirées (1864); continued at Steinway Hall (1872–78). He began a series of summer concerts in Terrace Garden (1865), relocating to Central Park Garden (1868). The influence of these enterprises on local musical culture was enormous, attaining European-like celebrity; the Theodore Thomas Orch. made its 1st tour (1869), subsequently going on many American and Canadian tours.

In 1873 Thomas established the Cincinnati Biennial May Festival, which he conducted until his death; also founded the Cincinnati College of Music; was its president and director (1878–80), having given up his N.Y. orch. and conductorship of the N.Y. Phil. Soc. (1877–78) to accept this post. After resigning, he returned to N.Y.; reorganized his orch.; was reelected conductor of the Phil. Soc. Orch. and the Brooklyn Phil. Orch. (where he conducted in 1862–63, 1866–68, and 1873–78); besides conducting these orch'l bodies, led several choruses, and was conductor and artistic director of the American Opera Co. (1885–87). He settled permanently in Chicago as conductor of the Chicago Orch. (1891); in recognition of his distinguished services, a permanent home, Orch. Hall, was built by popular subscription; formally opened with a series of festival concerts, the last directed by him (1904). After his death the orch.'s name was changed to the Theodore Thomas Orch. (1906); became the Chicago Sym. Orch. (1912). His influence on the musical development of the U.S. has been strong and lasting; an ardent apostle of Wagner, Liszt, and Brahms, he gave American premieres of works of Tchaikovsky, Dvořák, Rubinstein, Bruckner, Goldmark, Saint-Saëns, Cowen, Stanford, Raff, and R. Strauss; programmed works by American composers.

Thompson, Randall, b. N.Y., Apr. 21, 1899; d. Boston, July 9, 1984. At the Lawrenceville School in N.J., he took singing lessons; received music training from the organist F. C. Van Dyck; when Van Dyck died, he took over the organ duties in the school. He attended Harvard Univ.; studied with W. Spalding, E. B. Hill, and A. T. Davison (B.A., 1920; M.A., 1922); had private lessons in N.Y. with Ernest Bloch (1920–21); won the American Prix de Rome with his orch'l prelude *Pierrot and Cothurnus,* inspired by *Aria da Capo* by E. St. Vincent Millay (1922); received a grant for residence in Rome. He conducted it at the Accademia di Santa Cecilia (1923); encouraged by its reception, he proceeded to compose industriously, for piano, voices, and orch.; returned to the U.S. (1925).

Thompson taught at Wellesley College (1927–29, 1936–37); appointed a lecturer in music at Harvard Univ. (1929); held a Guggenheim fellowship (1929–30). His 1st Sym. had its premiere in Rochester, N.Y., with Hanson conducting (1930); 2 years later, Hanson conducted in Rochester the 1st performance of his 2nd Sym. (1932), one of the most successful symphonic works by an American, enjoying repeated performances in the U.S. and Europe; its truly American element was the inclusion of jazz rhythms in the score. Equally American and appealing, although for different reasons, was his choral work *Americana*, to texts from Mencken's satirical column in the *American Mercury*. Another piece of Americana followed, the nostalgic *The Peaceable Kingdom* for a cappella chorus (1936), inspired by the eponymous painting by Edward Hicks; in it he set biblical texts from the Prophets. Another a cappella work, deeply religious in its nature, was the Alleluia, a perennial favorite, 1st performed at the inaugural session of the Berkshire Music Center in Tanglewood (1940). He composed his most celebrated piece of choral writing, *The Testament of Freedom*, to words of T. Jefferson (1942); it was 1st performed with piano accompaniment at the Univ. of Virginia (1943; an orch'l version was premiered 2 years later); this work sealed his reputation as one of the finest American composers of choral music.

But Thompson did not limit himself; his 1st String Quartet in D Minor (1941) was praised, as was his 1st opera, *Solomon and Balkis*, after Kipling's *The Butterfly That Stamped*, broadcast over CBS Radio (1942); wrote his 3rd Sym., presented at the Festival of Contemporary American Music at Columbia Univ. in N.Y. (1949). Subsequent works included the ballet *Jabberwocky* (1951); an orch'l piece, *A Trip to Nahant* (1954); Requiem (1958); another opera, *The Nativity According to St. Luke* (1961); *The Passion According to St. Luke* (1965); *The Place of the Blest*, a cantata (1969); and *A Concord Cantata* (1975). In his compositions he preserved and cultivated the melodious poetry of American speech, set in crystalline tonal harmonies judiciously seasoned with euphonious discords, keeping resolutely clear of any modernistic abstractions; he also composed incidental music; chamber works, including a 2nd string quartet (1967); secular and sacred vocal works; solo songs.

During all this time Thompson did not neglect his educational activities; taught at the Univ. of Calif. at Berkeley (1937–39), Curtis Inst. of Music in Philadelphia, serving as director (1939–41), School of Fine Arts at the Univ. of Virginia (1941–46), Princeton Univ. (1946–48), and Harvard Univ. (1948–65), where he retired as prof. emeritus. He was elected to the National Inst. of Arts and Letters (1938); named "Cavaliere ufficiale al merito della Repubblica Italiana" (1959); publ. *College Music* (N.Y., 1935).

Thomson, Virgil (Garnett), b. Kansas City, Mo., Nov. 25, 1896; d. N.Y., Sept. 30, 1989. He began piano lessons at age 12 with local teachers; received organ instruction and played in local churches; entered Harvard Univ.; studied orchestration with E. B. Hill; assistant and accompanist to A. T. Davison, conductor of its Glee Club; studied piano with H. Gebhard and organ with W. Goodrich in Boston. In 1921 he went with the Glee Club to Europe; remained on a John Knowles Paine Traveling Fellowship to study organ with N. Boulanger at the Paris École Normale de Musique as well as private instruction in counterpoint from her. Returning to Harvard in 1922 he was made organist and choirmaster at King's College (1922); after graduating in 1923, he went to N.Y. to study conducting with C. Clifton and counterpoint with R. Scalero at the Juilliard Graduate School.

In 1925 Thomson returned to Paris, his home base until 1940; established contacts with cosmopolitan groups of musicians,

writers, and painters; his association with Gertrude Stein was particularly significant in the development of his aesthetic ideas. He refused to follow any set of modernistic doctrines, instead embracing the notion of popular universality. This allowed him to use the techniques of all ages and all degrees of simplicity or complexity, from simple triadic harmonies to dodecaphonic intricacies; achieved an eclectic illumination of astonishing power of direct communication, expressed in his dictum "jamais de banalité, toujours le lieu commun." Beneath the characteristic Parisian persiflage of some of his music there is a profoundly earnest intent.

Thomson's most famous composition is the opera *4 Saints in 3 Acts*, to a libretto by Stein, in which the deliberate confusion wrought by the author (there are actually 4 acts and more than a dozen saints, some of them in duplicate) and the composer's solemn, hymnlike treatment, create a hilarious modern opera buffa; premiered at Hartford, Conn. (1934), characteristically announced as being under the auspices of the Soc. of Friends and Enemies of Modern Music, which he directed (1934–37); the work became an American classic, with revivals in America and Europe to the present.

In 1940 Thomson became music critic of the *N.Y. Herald-Tribune*; received the Pulitzer Prize for his soundtrack to *Louisiana Story* (1948). Far from being routine, his music reviews are minor masterpieces of literary brilliance and critical acumen; resigned to concentrate on composition and conducting (1954). He received the Légion d'Honneur (1947); elected to the National Inst. of Arts and Letters (1948) and the American Academy of Arts and Letters (1959); awarded the Kennedy Center Honor for lifetime achievement (1983) and the Medal of Arts (1988).

thoroughbass. Basso continuo.

three-step. ordinary (Vienna) waltz.

threnody (from Grk. *thre-no-dia*, lamentation). Poem or musical work expressing grief for the dead; the classical *thre-nos* was organized in ritornello form, a chorus alternating with solo passages.

through-composed (Ger. *durchkomponiert*). Attribute of a song with each stanza written to a different accompaniment, or composed in a developmental, quasi-symphonic manner; as opposed to the strophic song or lied, with each verse set to the same music in each stanza.

thrush. Old slang for a female singer, especially of popular songs, named after a coloratura triller among songbirds. Spike Hughes declared, in a letter to the *Times* of London in the 1930s, that "all thrushes sing the tune of the 1st subject of Mozart's Sym. No. 40 in G Minor (K. 550), and phrase it a sight better than most conductors. The tempo is always dead right and there is no suggestion of an unauthorized accent on the 9th note of the phrase." However, it must be admitted that a conductor, however histrionic, is far less likely to fly away mid-piece. Another avian term of similar meaning is *canary*.

thumb position. High positions in cello playing, where the thumb passes the edge of the fingerboard.

thunder machine (Ger. *Donnermaschine*). Device used to imitate thunder by rotating a barrel with pebbles inside; 1st used by R. Strauss in his *Alpine Sym.* (1915). There are few instances of its subsequent use, except for special effects in silent movie orchs.

tibia (Lat.). Greek aulos, an ancient vertical flute. *Tibicen,* a flute player.

tie. Curved line joining 2 notes of like pitch, to be sounded as 1 note equal to their total time value.

tied notes. 1. Notes joined by a tie. 2. Notes whose hooks (flags) are attached by 1 or more thick strokes (beams).

tiento (from Sp. *tentar,* search). Iberian musical form popular in the late Renaissance and early Baroque, comparable to the Italian solo ricercar; the tiento is less elaborate but developmentally freer; especially popular with composers of vihuela and keyboard music.

tierce (Fr.). 1. Interval of a 3rd. 2. In the organ, a mutation stop pitched 2 1/3 octaves above the diapason. 3. Terce.

tierce de Picardi (Fr.). Picardy third.

timbale (*timballe;* Fr.; It. *timballo*). Timpani.

timbales. Pair of pitched, single-headed cylindrical drums of shallow diameter; its plastic heads are tuned by tension screws. Timbales are mostly associated with Latin American dance music; found in modern classical scores, sometimes in lieu of timpani, although their sonority is far less substantial.

timbre (Fr.). 1. Tone color. 2. Small bell. *Jeu de timbres,* glockenspiel.

timbré (Fr.). Sonorously.

timbrel (Hebr.). Tambourine.

time. Division of the measure into equal fractional parts of a whole, thus regulating the accents and rhythmic flow of music; indicated by the time signature. There are 2 major classes of time: In *duple time* the number of beats per measure is divisible by 2; in *triple time,* by 3. There are 2 subclasses, *compound duple time* and *compound triple time;* in the former each of the 2 beats contains a dotted note (or its equivalent) wholly divisible by 3; in the latter not only is each beat divisible by 3, but the number of beats in each measure is divisible by 3.

time field. Topographical term used in structuralist modern music in which the temporal relationship is established spontaneously between the sounds as independent acoustical phenomena and the performer whose reactions to these sounds determine his or her next action.

time point. In serial music, correlation of note value (duration in a pre-set time unit) with the melodic or harmonic interval counted in semitones; e.g., a major 7th would yield a duration of 11 note values (1 per semitone); thus smaller intervals in melody and harmony would generate a fast tempo; larger intervals, a slow tempo.

time signature. Indication of the number of a specified note value in a measure; always found at the piece's beginning and at any point within that the number of notes or the note value used changes; e.g., 4/4 indicates 4 beats (the 1st number, or numerator) at a quarter note per beat (the 2nd number, or denominator); the sign is written as a vertical fraction without dividing line. The denominator is always a factor of 2 (2, 4, 8, 16, etc.), in keeping with the note values themselves. Although older associations exist, a time signature does not determine tempo, which requires a verbal or metronomic indication; e.g., many Classic slow movements are written in rapid values (at least 16th notes, sometimes 32nd, 64th, or even 128th notes); this may take up paper but more importantly conveys a visual sense of unusually long phrases. Some alternate time signatures—c and ¢—are remnants of mensural notation; the 1st signature meant *tempus imperfectum,* the 2nd referred to a proportional diminution further explicated by a figure. When used today, these symbols are called *common time* (4/4) and *cut time* (2/2), respectively. There are 2 principal classes of time: *duple* and *triple* (see ⇒time).

time-bracket notation. Highly flexible notation developed by Cage in his mature works; time lengths are left largely to the discretion of the performer; e.g., a performer might be instructed to 1) begin playing the excerpt at any time between the 1st pair of bracketed times, then to 2) end playing the excerpt at any time between the 2nd pair of bracketed times: [00'00"–00'15"] [00'30"–01'00"].

timpani (It., kettledrums, tympani; sing. or plural; Fr. *timbales;* Ger. *Pauken*). Large orch'l drum consisting of a hollow brass or copper hemisphere (the kettle) resting on a tripod; the top of the hemisphere was originally covered with a treated animal hide; the head is now made of vellum stretched by means of an iron ring and tightened by a set of screws or by cords and braces; the instrument dates to the 6th century as a shallow *bowl drum* in the Middle East; arrived in Europe in the late Middle Ages.

Historically, timpani have been the only orch'l membranophones capable of definite pitch; orig. 2 drums were used, the larger drum tuned to any note from F_0 to c^0, the smaller from $B\flat_0$ to f^0. Its music was formerly written in C; now written at actual pitch. In Classic syms. and overtures the timpani are usually played in pairs, tuned to the main tonic and dominant. In the older instruments the screws around the rim increased or relaxed the tension of the membrane so that the pitch could be regulated accordingly; modern timpani are equipped with pedals that change the pitch with greater precision; later developments led to a genuinely chromatic type of instrument.

In the 19th century the number of orch'l timpani increased; Wagner's *Ring* requires 4; Berlioz, in his passion for grandiosity, scored the Tuba mirum in his *Grande Messe des Morts* for 16. Uncommon tuning is found in Beethoven's syms., particularly the octave F to F in the scherzo of his 9th Sym., applied antiphonally. A foreboding ostinato on a solo timpani bridges the transition from the scherzo to the finale in his 5th Sym. The indication *timpani coperti* (covered) is synonymous with *timpani sordi* (muted), an effect achieved by covering the head with a piece of fabric.

Modern composers are apt to write timpani parts requiring acrobatic virtuosity in manipulating several instruments, playing on the rim, controlling a terraced glissando with the pedals (Nielsen, 5th Sym.), retuning while performing a rapid trill, etc. Solo timpani occur in many modern works; A. Tcherepnin composed a Sonatina for timpani and piano, John Vincent's *Symphonic Poem After Descartes* opens with a timpani solo in the rhythm of the Cartesian maxim *Cogito ergo sum*, American composer and percussion virtuoso William Kraft composed a Timpani Concerto (Indianapolis, 1984).

tin ear. Lack of musicality or appropriate responsiveness to music.

Tin Pan Alley. Colorful reference to an area along Broadway in N.Y. where popular songwriters worked in great numbers, hoping to produce the latest hit or successful musical; dates from the beginning of the century. The district moved geographically with the times, following the theaters' move uptown; beginning around Union Square (14th Street), it moved 1st to 28th Street and then, after World War I, to the Brill Building (50th Street, also central to the advertising world). The term is now associated with the commercial and assembly-line elements of popular song as late as the 1960s.

tin whistle. Small, high-pitched, end-blown whistle flute, made of metal; also called *pennywhistle;* used as a traditional melody instrument, notably in the Anglo-Irish-Scottish islands.

tinnitus. Sustained pressure on the auditory nerve, causing a persistent tintinnabulation in the cochlea in the inner ear. Schumann experienced it during the final stages of his mental illness, hearing a relentless drone on high A-flat; Smetana suffered a similar aural disturbance; he heard a high E, and he too eventually went insane; introduced this sustained note at the end of his 1st string quartet, significantly entitled *From My Life.*

Some clinically sane and tinnitus-free composers active in the latter 20th century experimentally created artificial ones. Feldman wrote a violin part with an interminable F-sharp calculated to generate a psychic tinnitus in the outer and inner ears of performers and listeners alike. L. M. Young devised a tinnitus of a perfect 5th with a notation, "to be held for a long time." Other ways of affecting the listener is a tape recording of a dripping faucet or a simulacrum of white noise prolonged without a prospect of ever ending. Physical action may be added to a tinnitus, such as measured drops of lukewarm water on the occipital bone of the head held down by clamps, helpful in subjecting a particularly recalcitrant listener to a piece of avant-garde music; this method was widely practiced to subdue difficult patients in 18th-century insane asylums (without the presence of avant-garde music).

tintement (Fr.). Jingling sound.

tintinnabulum (Lat.). Since antiquity, a single or set of graduated bells; also, the hammer it is struck with, or the clapper found in later sets of bells.

tinto, con (It.). With shading; expressively.

Tiomkin, Dimitri, b. Poltava, May 10, 1894; d. London, Nov. 11, 1979. He studied composition with A. Glazunov and piano with F. Blumenfeld and I. Vengerova at the St. Petersburg Cons.; in 1921 went to Berlin, where he studied with Busoni, Petri, and Zadora (1921); was soloist in Liszt's 1st Piano Concerto with the Berlin Phil. (1924); that same year gave concerts with Michael Khariton in Paris. He appeared in vaudeville in the U.S. (1925); became a citizen (1937); made his conducting debut with the Los Angeles Phil. (1938); later conducted his music with various U.S. orchs.; married Albertina Rasch, a ballerina, for whose troupe he wrote music. From 1930 to 1970 he wrote over 150 film scores (1930–70), including several for the U.S. War Dept. His film music betrayed his strong Russian Romantic background, tempered with American jazz. He was made a Chevalier and an Officer of the French Légion d'Honneur; received 3 Oscars (*High Noon,* 1952; *The High and the Mighty,* 1954; *The Old Man and the Sea,* 1958) and a Golden Globe; wrote an autobiography, *Please Don't Hate Me* (N.Y., 1959).

Típico. Generic term for Latin American mestizo traditional music.

tiple (from Lat. *triplum,* treble). Generic term for a high-pitched instrument, such as the *guitarillo* or *timple,* a small Spanish guitar of the Canary Islands; the Cuban *bandurria,* a small plucked instrument of medieval Spanish origin; the treble *chirimíra,* a Catalan shawm.

Tippett, (Sir) Michael (Kemp), b. London, Jan. 2, 1905. His family's political beliefs had a lifelong influence on him; his father was a freethinker, his mother a suffragette who once served a prison term. He took piano lessons as a child and sang in his school chorus; showed no exceptional merit as a performer. He studied in London at the Royal College of Music (1923–28); studied composition (with C. Wood and C. H. Kitson), piano (A. Raymar), conducting (Boult and Sargent), counterpoint and fugue (R. O. Morris; 1930–32). He subsequently held several positions as teacher and conductor; led the South London Orch. at Morley College (1933–40); director of music there (1940–51).

Tippett dissented from the social status quo from the outset; proclaimed extremely liberal political views, inalienable atheism, and strenuous pacifism. His best-known work, the oratorio *A Child of Our Time* (1939–41), was inspired by the case of Henschel Grynsban, a 17-year-old refugee Jew who responded to his parents' persecution by assassinating a member of the Paris German embassy (1938; provoked a major Nazi anti-Semitic pogrom); the composer's powerful, personal, and symbolic response to this event became his compositional model, particularly the eclectic yet archetypal use of Negro spirituals. As a conscientious objector he refused to serve in any of the British military forces; sentenced to prison for 3 months, serving his time at Wormwood Scrubs, Surrey (1943); other artists simply left Britain; few were imprisoned upon their return. Because of his sacrifice for his beliefs, he never lost the respect of the community. He initiated a series of broadcasts for the BBC (1951); directed the Bath Festival (1969–74). He visited the U.S. (1965), and became a frequent guest in America; his sym. works were performed by major American orchs., often under his baton.

Tippett's works have a grandeur of Romantic inspiration that sets them apart from the prevalent type of contemporary music; they are infused with rhapsodic eloquence and further enhanced by a pervading lyric sentiment free from facile sentimentality. He excelled in large-scale vocal and instrumental forms; was a consummate master of the modern idioms, evolving from a contrapuntal neoclassicism in the 1930s to heights of dissonant counterpoint without losing the teleological sense of inherent tonality. At times his eclectic approach did not cohere, e.g., the Americanisms in *The Ice Break* (1973–76); but he continued to experiment, e.g., the episodes of heavy glottal aspiration in the 4th Sym. (1977) suggesting the human lifecycle.

Tippett's compositions also include 5 operas; *The Midsummer Marriage*, 1946–52; *King Priam*, 1958–61; *The Knot Garden*, 1966–69, (with 1st openly gay operatic characters); 4 syms. (1945–77, the 3rd with soprano); concertos; works for string orchestra. Chamber works: 5 string quartets (1935–91); Sonata for 4 horns (1955); *The Blue Guitar* for Guitar (1983); 5 piano sonatas (1938–84). Vocal: *Crown of the Year* (1952), *The Vision of St. Augustine* (1963–65), *The Mask of Time* (1981–84), *Byzantium* (1991); cantatas; song cycles; choral works.

A man of great learning, Tippett possessed a fine literary gift and great interest in Jungian psychology; mostly wrote his own librettos; publ. *Moving into Aquarius* (London, 1958); M. Bowen ed. *Music of the Angels: Essays and Sketchbooks of Michael Tippett* (London, 1980). He received high honors from the British government; named a Commander of the Order of the British Empire (1959); knighted (1966); made a Companion of Honour (1979).

tirata (It.; Fr. *tirade, coulade*). Ornamental scalar passage or arpeggio improvised to fill gaps between melodic notes; a tirata spanning the interval of an octave was a *tirata perfecta*; that of a 4th or 5th, a *tirata mezza*; that of an interval greater than an octave, a *tirata aucta* (augmented).

tiré (Fr.). Down-bow in string playing.

tirolese (It.). Like a Tyrolese folk song.

titles. Titles of classical compositions usually describe the form and content of the work. Genres and forms such as sym., sonata, prelude, cantata, and opera can evolve over the centuries; "sinfonia" meant any instrumental composition or orch'l interlude in an opera; only in the 18th century did it acquire the meaning now given to "sym." But the advent of Romantic music made the problem of suitable titles acute; time and time again composers would assign a programmatic title to a work, only to repudiate it at a later time for fear that the music would be heard as structurally dependent on the associated narrative. What can be more programmatically explicit than Beethoven's *Pastoral Sym.*, with its realistic storm and 3 bird calls? Yet Beethoven later marked the score "Mehr Ausdruck der Empfindung als Malerey" (more an expression of feeling than depiction). Mahler's overheated imagination prompted him to give all kinds of specific titles not only to most of his syms. but also to individual movements; however, he later denied such programmatic implications. So emphatic was he in renunciation that when he was questioned about the meaning of 1 of his syms. at a banquet he raised his glass as if for a toast and exclaimed, "Pereat den Programmen!" (Down with

programs!) Such repudiations are particularly baffling when a literary work lies at the foundation of a composition, as often happened with Mahler.

Even the question of inspiration can become slippery. Mendelssohn's *Fingal's Cave* was inspired by his visit to northern Scotland (1829), but was originally entitled *The Solitary Island*. More remarkably, Berlioz transplanted his early overture *Les Francs-juges* into the *Sym. fantastique* as the *March to the Scaffold*. To unify it with the rest of the *Sym.* he inserted a couple of bars of the *idée fixe* of the work; indeed, to save the labor of recopying the old overture, he pasted in that motif in the old MS, replacing a bar of rests. Another variant of a composer's decision to affix new titles is illustrated by Schoenberg's *5 Orch'l Pieces* (1909); in the original the pieces bore abstract titles without programmatic content; 40 years later, yielding to his publisher's suggestion that he "humanize" the titles, he agreed to change the titles, e.g., the 3rd piece, *The Changing Chord*, became *Summer Morning by the Lake*. Scriabin's work titles are often mystical and theosophic; it was his brother-in-law, Boris de Schloezer, who suggested that the opening motive of his 3rd Sym., *Le Poème divin*, was a proclamation of self-assertion: "I am!"; this notation appears in the final MS and published score. Modest Tchaikovsky, the brother of the composer, suggested to the composer the name *Pathétique* for his 6th Sym.

The lengths that a composer will go to hide an initial programmatic intent is illustrated by Stravinsky's *Scherzo Fantastique* (1909), inspired by Maurice Maeterlinck's half-literary, half-scientific essay *Les Abeilles* (The Bees). Each section of the score corresponds to a beehive event: birth of the queen, nuptial flight, swarming, etc.; the publishers quoted from the book in the score; Maeterlinck promptly sued Stravinsky for infringement of copyright. Fifty years later, in a conversation book with R. Craft, he denied ever intending to use the Maeterlinck book as a programmatic source; his own 1907 letter to Rimsky-Korsakov plainly contradicts this.

toada (Port.). Tonada.

toccata (from It. *toccare*, strike, touch). Virtuoso keyboard composition exploiting the articulation possible with these instruments: free and bold in style, consisting of runs and passages alternating with fugal or contrapuntal work, generally in equal notes, with a flowing, animated, and rapid movement. In the 16th century the toccata was generally a prelude or improvisation before the composition proper, particularly in organ playing; in the 17th century it became a composition in rapid tempo and steady rhythm (Frescobaldi, Froberger, Sweelinck, A. Scarlatti, Bach). In the 19th and 20th centuries, composers applied the term to a form that could easily have been called a *moto perpetuo;* Schumann, Widor, Vierne, Debussy, Ravel, Prokofiev, Busoni, and Reger wrote toccatas marked by brilliant technical display. *Toccatina,* short toccata.

toccato (It.). In the 17th century, the bass line of a trumpet fanfare, often "touched" (played) on the timpani.

Toch, Ernst, b. Vienna, Dec. 7, 1887; d. Los Angeles, Oct. 1, 1964. He began playing piano in his grandmother's pawnshop; learned notation from a local violinist and copied Mozart's string quartets for practice; using them as models, began composing chamber music; at age 17 his 6th String Quartet, op. 12 (1905), was performed by the famous Rosé Quartet in Vienna. He won the prestigious Mozart Prize and a scholarship to study at the Frankfurt Cons. (1909); worked with Willy Rehberg (piano) and Iwan Knorr (composition); awarded the Mendelssohn Prize (1910); won the Austrian State Prize 4 times in succession. appointed instructor in piano at Zuschneid's Hochschule für Musik in Mannheim (1913). After service in the Austrian army, he returned to Mannheim to resume his career; attained a prominent position in the modernist German school of composition; completed his Ph.D. at the Univ. of Heidelberg (diss., *Beiträge zur Stilkunde der Melodie*, 1921).

Toch moved to Berlin, establishing himself as pianist, composer, and pedagogue (1929); toured the U.S. as a pianist (1932); returned to Berlin, but the advent of the Nazi regime forced him to leave Germany (1933); eventually emigrated to the U.S. (1935); gave music lectures at the New School for Social Research in N.Y.; moved to Hollywood (1936) and wrote film music. He was naturalized in 1940; taught composition at the Univ. of Southern Calif., Los Angeles (1940–41); taught privately; among his students was A. Previn. From 1950 until his death he traveled frequently, living at one point at the MacDowell Colony in New Hampshire.

Toch's music is rooted in the central European Romantic tradition, but his study of Mozart made him aware of the importance of formal logic in thematic development. His early works are primarily chamber music, piano pieces (often quite virtuosic), and stage music in the lighter vein of his time. Possessed of a fine wit, he composed the celebrated *Geographical Fugue* for Speaking Chorus (1930), its text solely based on the names of exotic places. He also had a sense of adventure; the theme of his last String Quartet (No. 13, 1953) is based on a 12-tone row; the 3rd Sym. (Pulitzer Prize, 1956) introduces the Hisser, a tank of carbon dioxide that produced the eponymous sound through a valve. He did not write his 1st sym. until 1949–50, but found the genre congenial, composing 7 in all (1949–1964); other works include 3 operas, notably *Die Prinzessin auf der Erbse* (Baden-Baden, 1927); concertos, suites, overtures; 13 string quartets (1902–1953) and other chamber music; vocal works. He wrote several orch'l works with children's subjects: *Pinocchio* (1935), *Circus Overture* (1953), *Peter Pan* (1956), *Puppet Show* (1963); *Enamoured Harlequin* (1963). He was elected to the National Inst. of Arts and Letters (1957) and received the Cross of Honor for Sciences and Art from the Austrian government (1963).

Todesgesang (Todeslied; Ger.). Dirge; work commemorating the dead.

tombeau (Fr., gravestone). Instrumental composition dedicated to the memory of a dignitary or friend; in 1920 several French composers contributed pieces to a collection entitled *Tombeau de Debussy*. A musical tombeau may also be found under other guises: *planctus* or *lachrymae* (Lat.), *dirge, threnody, elegy, dump,* or *tears* (Eng.); *déploration* or *apothéose* (Fr.), *lamento* (It.). Such reverential remembrance is also expressed by the term *homage,* e.g., *Hommage à Rameau* by Debussy and *Homage to Ives* by Copland. Ravel's *Le Tombeau de Couperin,* a piano tribute to François le Grand, is a fine 20th-century example; its 6 movements are in 17th-century forms; he later orchestrated 4 of the movements.

tom-tom. Generic term for African, Asian, or Latin American indigenous drums, of high but (usually) indefinite pitch; may be played with hands or sticks; in addition to traditional music they are found in jazz, popular, and dance bands, as well as percussion-oriented scores.

Ton (Ger.). Tone; key; mode; pitch; diatonic scale. *Tonart,* key (tonality); *Tonbild* (Ger., tonal picture), symphonic poem; *Tondichtung* (Ger., tonal poetry); symphonic poem (preferred by R. Strauss); *Tondichter,* composer (Romantic era).

tonada (Sp.). Spanish song or dance song, in 3/4, 6/8, or both; imported to Latin America. Tonadas have been written by classical composers.

tonadilla (Sp.). Spanish theater piece of a lighter character with folk melorhythms; originally a song (little tonada) placed in the interludes of spoken plays. It is an 18th-century predecessor of the zarzuela, a more ambitious, less folklike genre.

tonal. Pertaining to tones, or a tone, mode, or key. *Tonal imitation,* imitation within the key of a composition; nonmodulatory imitation.

tonal answer. Answer to the subject in a fugue, adjusted so that the tonic is answered by its true dominant, in turn answered by the tonic; this alters the intervallic content of the theme.

tonal tropism. Involuntary pitch orientation. By computing the frequency of recurrence of each particular note in an atonal work and finding which of the 12 notes of the chromatic scale has a marked preponderance over the others, one may assert that such a preponderant note represents a tonal focus, towards which other members of an atonal melody have a tonal tropism. Other aspects of tonal tropism are: approach to a frequently occurring tone by a semitone from below, suggesting a leading tone resolution; preferential placement of a note in the bass; extended duration of a certain tone; appearance at the end of a musical fascicle; simulated cadence or other privileged position at strategic points, such as a strong beat, etc.

tonality. Cumulative concept that embraces all pertinent elements of tonal structure, including melodic and harmonic juxtapositions that determine the collective tonal relations, i.e., a basic loyalty to a tonal center; this now universal term is relatively new, having originated in France c. 1820. Tonality does not require continuous allegiance; a piece may modulate widely from the outset and travel far from the original key, yet adhere to the sense of tonality as long as it follows the tonal structure. The guardian of tonality is the key signature; no matter how many times this signature is changed during a given composition, a sense of tonality remains as long as each individual section is cast in a definite key. The antonym of tonality is *atonality,* the outright rejection and avoidance of tonality.

tonante (It.). Thundering, thunderous.

tonarium. Catalogue of medieval chants, usually organized according to the principal 8 tones of Gregorian chant; includes antiphons, communions, introits, and responsories.

tone. 1. Definite pitch, as opposed to indefinite pitch (unpitched noise). 2. *Whole tone;* major 2nd. *Half tone,* minor or chromatic 2nd; semitone. 3. Timbre; tone quality. See also ⇒acoustics.

tone cluster (cluster). Row of adjacent tones, diatonic, pentatonic, or chromatic; 1st demonstrated publicly by Cowell on a piano at the San Francisco Music Club (1912); invented the term itself 6 years later; applied them systematically in many compositions, e.g., *Amiable Conversations* for Piano, in which diatonic clusters are used in the right hand (white keys) and pentatonic clusters are used in the left hand (the black keys). Small tone clusters can be performed on the piano keyboard with fists or the palm of the hand; extensive tone clusters of 2 octaves or more require the entire forearm, from fists to elbow. Cowell notated tone clusters with a thick black line on a stem for rapid notes or a white-note rod attached to a stem for half-notes.

Cowell did not really invent the cluster; composers of battaglia applied them using the palm, mostly in the bass, to imitate a cannon shot; a curious piano piece called *Alpine Storm* by the German-American composer George Kunkel (1840–1923) specifies the use of the left palm to simulate the effect of thunder. Independently of Cowell, Ives employed tone clusters to illustrate the "celestial railroad" in the *Hawthorne* movement of his *Concord Sonata,* produced by gently pressing a wooden plank down on the keys in the treble to create sympathetic vibrations. Bartók used clusters to be played by the palm in his 2nd Piano Concerto, a device borrowed expressly from Cowell, with permission.

tone color (timbre; Ger. *Klangfarben*). Often subjective description of musical sound quality, using adjectives as penetrating, dry, nasal, liquid, etc. As tonometric experiments and spectography demonstrate, the peculiar tone color of a musical instrument or human voice depends on the relative strength of harmonics produced by the fundamental tone; the same pitch produced on one instrument differs as much from one produced on another instrument as the tone color of the voice of one person differs from that of another. The flute's tone color is perceived as the purest of all instruments because its distribution of harmonics approaches a sine wave; the clarinet, on the other hand, generates a harmonic series characterized by odd-numbered harmonics. The oboe owes its penetrating sound to possessing harmonics of practically the same mutual strength; the harmonics of string instruments are also abundant in all registers. Schoenberg introduced the idea of a scale of tone colors, so that a succession of identical pitches on different instruments would form a scale he called the "Klangfarbe scale." Recent theorists have proposed means of analyzing "sound color."

tone poem. Symphonic poem.

tone row. Fundamental subject in a 12-tone composition.

Tonfall (Ger.). Intonation.

Tongeschlecht (Ger., tonal gender). Modal structure, e.g., major, minor.

tongue. 1. (*noun*) Reed. 2. Use the tongue in producing, modifying, or interrupting the output of most wind instruments. See also ⇒tonguing.

tonguing. Production of tone effects on wind instruments with the aid of the tongue. *Single tonguing,* effect obtained by the repeated tongue thrust to the nearly inaudible consonant *t* or *d; double tonguing,* that obtained by the repetition of *t k; triple tonguing,* that obtained by *t k t;* etc.

tonic. 1st note (keynote) of a scale. *Tonic accent,* in chant, unaccompanied cantillation, and recitation, a prosodic stress on a long vowel or syllable on a higher pitch; *tonic chord,* triad on the keynote; *tonic pedal,* pedal point on the keynote; *tonic section,* complete sentence or longer passage in the opening key (including an authentic cadence) before the piece proceeds.

tonic sol-fa (Ger. *Tonika-do*). Method of teaching vocal music, invented by Sarah Ann Glover of Norwich, England, *c.* 1812. Pupils learn to recognize scale tones by observing mental associations with each tone. It is a movable Do system; uses the syllables Doh, Ray, Me, Fah, Soh, and Lah, adapted from the Guidonian alphabet (Te is added for the leading tone). This system, widely accepted in English-speaking countries, has the disadvantage divorcing absolute sound from adopted name; in all Latin countries and Russia, the Fixed Do method is used; where Do is immovable and always designates pitch class C.

Tonkunst (Ger., tone art). Musical composition. *Tonkünstler,* composer.

Tonleiter (Ger., tone ladder). Scale.

Tonmalerei (Ger., tone painting). Musical depiction or illustration; realization of programmatic ideas in sound.

tono (tuono; It.). Tone, pitch. 2. Whole tone. 3. Key; mode. *Primo tono, secondo tono,* etc., first tone (ecclesiastical mode), etc.

tonolalia. Glossolalia is a preternaturally inspired manifestation of spontaneous and simultaneous multilingual intercourse. By analogy, tonolalia is when different instruments and voices disport themselves in a modernistic quodlibet; particularly effective are antiphonal tonolalia in which an improvised interlude is echoed by another instrument or a group of instruments.

tonotripsical impact. As a cephalotripsical blow crushes the skull, a tonotripsical impact is produced by an implosion of sonic matter calculated to stun into submission and psychically incapacitate the audience at an ultramodern concert. At one Happening in N.Y., a complete Sunday edition of the *N.Y. Times* was thrown on the floor of a chamber music hall; a power lawn mower was wheeled in and proceeded to chew up the newspaper with cephalotripsical effect. A literal case of tonocephalotripsical music is the *Concerto for the Hammer and the Skull,* by a French composer who performed it by striking different parts of the bones of his head, producing different tones while opening his mouth as a resonator.

Tonsatz (Ger.). Composition. *Tonsetzer,* composer.

tonus (1) (Lat.). Chant recitation. *Tonus ad introitum,* introit reciting tone; *tonus psalmorum,* psalm reciting tone.

tonus (2) (plural *tonoi*). Orig., ecclesiastical mode. In the 16th century a system of 12 modes was established, comprising 6 authentic and 6 plagal modes. The Dorian mode, ranging from D to D on the piano white keys, was called *primus tonus;* its plagal derivative, the Hypodorian, the *secundus tonus;* the Phyrgian mode, from E to E, was called *tertius tonus,* and so forth. The complete theory of the tonoi is the main subject of Glareanus's treatise *Dodecachordon* (12 modes, 1547).

The 11th tonus, Ionian, is equivalent to the modern C-major scale; Zarlino reordered the modes in his *Istitutioni harmoniche* (1558), placing the Ionian mode at the top of the list, thereby anticipating the coronation of the C-major scale as the fundamental tonal progression of the common practice period and beyond. To fill out the diatonic scale the theoretical Locrian and Hypolocrian modes were added later, with ranges from B to B and F to F, respectively.

Tonus peregrinus (Lat., wandering mode), an irregular psalm tone whose recitation note changes in mid-chant; it is associated with Psalm 113, *In exitu Israel de Aegypto,* hence the name (referring to pilgrims). The wandering mode is 1st mentioned as the "9th mode" in the 10th century.

top. Child's toy in the shape of an inverse cone; when wound up and released it produces a humming noise of fairly definite pitch. It is found in some 20th-century works, among them Taverner's *A Celtic Requiem,* which calls for "a top in E-flat."

topology in music. See ⇒translocation.

torch song. American slang for a ballad of despair and lovelorn lamentation, usually sung by a female singer with heartwrenching cadenzas; musically, a song of the blues, if rarely a true blues. (Most Tin Pan Alley blues have as little to do with Bessie Smith as *Alexander's Ragtime Band* has to do with Joplin.); the term is derived from the expression "to carry a torch," i.e., to care deeply for someone unattainable. Torch songs evolved in the swing era as an outgrowth of urban blues; while attempts to revive them have often been stymied by changes in taste or mores, they have undergone a revival in the 1980s and 1990s, mostly in a soul context.

torculus (Lat., twisted). In mensural notation, ligature indicating a rise and fall of 1 degree.

Tormé, Mel (born Melvin Howard Torme), Chicago, Sept. 13, 1925. At age 4 he began singing with the Coon-Sanders band at a Chicago restaurant; studied piano and drums, sang with various bands and acted in radio soap operas (1934–40). After touring as a singer, drummer, and arranger with the Chico Marx band (1942–43), he appeared in films and with his own vocal swing ensemble, the Mel-Tones. Following World War II, he launched a prominent career as a pop and jazz vocalist; performed in nightclubs and on radio, television, and recordings; won successive Grammy Awards for best male jazz vocalist for the albums *An Evening with George Shearing and Mel Tormé* (1983) and *Top Drawer* (with Shearing, 1984); appeared as soloist and conductor with several sym. orchs., including San

Francisco and Dallas. Mel Tormé Week was proclaimed in Los Angeles in commemoration of his 50th anniversary in show business (1980). Among more than 300 songs, his *The Christmas Song* (1946) has become a holiday favorite. He recounts his association with Judy Garland in *The Other Side of the Rainbow* (N.H., 1970); wrote *Traps, the Drum Wonder* (1990), a biography of Buddy Rich

Tormis, Veljo, b. Kuusalu near Tallinn, Aug. 7, 1930. He studied organ and choral conducting at the Tallinn Music Instit. (1943–51), organ and composition at the Tallinn Cons. (1951), and composition with Shebalin at the Moscow Cons. (1951–56); taught at the Tallinn Music Inst.; consulted for the Estonian Composers' Union. He is an expert in Estonian folk music, which he often draws upon for his choral music; has also drawn upon the traditional music of other Finno-Ugrian nations. His works range from simple, highly serious incantation to humorous parodies full of variety and buffoonery; unaccompanied choral music dominates his output, the best-known work being *Forgotten Peoples.*

tornando (It.). Returning. *Tornando al primo tempo* or *tornando come prima,* returning to (resuming) the original tempo.

torture organ. Brazilian political instrument used to extract confessions by administering electric shocks from a large organ. According to reports from Rio de Janeiro (1974), a keyboard apparatus, operating a system of electric currents, triggered shocks varying in intensity and duration depending on the strength (*pp* to *ff*) of screams of the prisoner under torture; deafening sounds at close range could also be targeted at the victims. Undoubtedly its inventor was closely related to the Commandant of Kafka's *In the Penal Colony.*

Toscanini, Arturo, b. Parma, Mar. 25, 1867; d. N.Y., Jan. 16, 1957. He entered the Parma Cons. at age 9; studied cello with Carini and composition with Dacci; graduated (1885), winning the 1st prize for cello, and received the Barbacini Prize as the outstanding graduate. He was engaged as cellist for the Italian opera in Rio de Janeiro (1886); one night was asked to substitute for the regular conductor, when the latter left the podium at the end of the introduction after the public hissed him; the opera was *Aida,* and Toscanini led it without difficulty; rewarded by an ovation, was engaged to lead the rest of the season. Returning to Italy, he was engaged to conduct opera at the Teatro Carignano in Turin (1886); conducted the Municipal Orch. there; although young he quickly established a fine reputation; conducted opera in the major Italian theaters (1887–96). He led the premieres of *Pagliacci* in Milan (1892) and *La Bohème* in Turin (1896); conducted the 1st performances (in Italian) by an Italian opera company of *Gotterdämmerung* (Turin, 1895) and *Siegfried* (Milan, 1899); made his debut as a sym. conductor with the orch. of the Teatro Regio in Turin (1896).

The impresario Giulio Gatti-Casazza (1869–1940) engaged Toscanini as chief conductor for La Scala, Milan (1896–1903, 1906–08); in the interim he led opera in Buenos Aires (1903–1904; 1906). When Gatti-Casazza became general manager of the Metropolitan Opera, he invited Toscanini to be principal conductor (1908); his debut in N.Y. was leading *Aida.* While at the Metropolitan Toscanini conducted Verdi's *Requiem*

(1909) and 2 world premieres, Puccini's *The Girl of the Golden West* (1910) and Giordano's *Madame Sans-Gêne* (1915); gave the American premieres of Gluck's *Armide* (1910), Wolf-Ferrari's *Le Donne curiose* (1912), and Mussorgsky's *Boris Godunov* (1913); gave his 1st orch'l concert in N.Y., leading Beethoven's 9th Sym.; returned to Italy (1915).

Toscanini took the La Scala Orch. on a tour of the U.S. and Canada (1920–21); became artistic director of La Scala (1921–29); conducted the posth. premiere of Boito's *Nerone,* which he helped edit for performance (1924); was guest conductor of the N.Y. Phil. (1926–27, 1928–29), then its associate conductor with Mengelberg (1929–30); finally its conductor (1930–36); toured Europe (1930). He conducted in Bayreuth (1930–1931); deeply touched by the plight of the Jews in Germany, refused to conduct there; at the request of the violinist B. Huberman, founder of the Palestine Sym. Orch., conducted its inaugural concert at Tel Aviv (1936); filled engagements at the Salzburg Festivals (1934–37) and London (1935; 1937–39). He became music director of the NBC Sym. Orch., a radio orch. organized especially for him (1937); conducted his 1st broadcast that year in N.Y.; toured South America (1940) and the U.S. (1950). He led the orch. to the end of his career; conducted his last broadcast from Carnegie Hall, N.Y. (1954); sent a doleful letter of resignation to NBC, explaining the impossibility of further appearances (apparently he suffered a memory lapse during that concert).

Toscanini was one of the most celebrated masters of the baton in history; undemonstrative in his handling of the orch., he possessed an amazing energy and power of command; demanded absolute perfection, erupting in violence when unable to obtain from the orch. what he wanted (a lawsuit was brought against him in Milan when he accidentally injured the concertmaster with a broken violin bow). Despite this occasional vituperation poured on his musicians, he was affectionately known as "The Maestro," who could do no wrong; his ability to communicate to singers and players was extraordinary; even the most celebrated opera stars or instrumentalists never dared to question his authority. Owing to extreme nearsightedness, he committed all scores to memory; his repertoire embraced virtually all of Classic and Romantic music; his performances of Italian operas, Wagner's music dramas, Beethoven's syms., and modern Italian works were especially inspiring; among the moderns, led works by R. Strauss, Debussy, Ravel, Prokofiev, and Stravinsky; among the Americans, Barber, whose *Adagio for Strings* he made famous; also had his favorite Italian composers (Catalani, Martucci), whose music he fondly fostered. In his social philosophy he was intransigently democratic; in addition to refusing to conduct in Germany under the Nazis, he militantly opposed Fascism in Italy; but never abandoned his Italian citizenship, despite long years of residence in America.

tostamente (It.). Rapidly and boldly. *Tostissimo,* extremely fast.

tosto (It.). Almost; soon. *Allegro molto, più tosto presto,* very fast, nearly *presto.*

total music. Performance art in which the autonomous art of music is once more allied with other arts, embracing all aspects of human behavior, often in ironic or oxymoronic fashion. In ancient Greece, music was an inalienable part of drama and literature; in medieval universities it formed a component of the quadrivium; in modern absolutist times, it lost virtually all connection with sciences and liberal arts. Music maintained its independence until the mid-20th century, when the avant-garde brought music out of isolation into the realm of mixed media. The slogan of total music was launched; this once exclusive art came to be performed on equal terms with conversation, consumption of food, sex, and sleep, at Happenings and other "actions." Performing musicians willingly surrendered their physical separation from the audience, inviting the collaboration of the public onstage. Formal attire that placed musicians on a higher plane was abandoned; as nudity became permissible in the theater, musicians followed suit, notably cellist Charlotte Moorman. Total music is a counterpart of the French *roman total,* a fictional form combining factual reportage with unbridled fantasy.

total serialism. See ⇒serialism.

Totenlied (Ger.). Todesgesang.

Totentanz (Ger., dance of death). Morbid and widespread medieval topos, cultivated in poetry, painting, drama, and music; evoked the image of death dancing with its prospective victim. Even in songs of youth, expectation of death was often the subject, e.g., *Gaudeamus igitur,* warning the young to enjoy life before "nos habebit humus" (the earth has us). Many Romantic and later works quote the Dies Irae melody (from the Roman Catholic Requiem), e.g., Berlioz's *Sym. fantastique,* Liszt's *Totentanz,* Saint-Saëns's *Danse macabre,* and Rachmaninoff's *Rhapsody on a Theme by Paganini;* other pieces connected to the Totentanz topos include Mozart's *Don Giovanni* (the Act II confrontation between Don Giovanni and the Commendatore), Schubert's *Tod und das Mädchen,* Rachmaninoff's *Isle of the Dead,* and Crumb's settings of García Lorca's poetry.

touch. 1. Method of applying the fingers to the keys of keyboard instruments. 2. Amount and kind of resistance overcome by the fingers in depressing the keys of a keyboard instrument; as a *heavy, light,* or *elastic* touch.

touche (Fr.). Fingerboard. *Sur la touche,* in string playing, bow on or near the fingerboard.

toucher (Fr., touch). Play a keyboard, attending to the proper use of fingers, e.g., Couperin's *L'Art de toucher le clavecin* (1716).

tourbillonant (Fr.). As if in a whirlwind.

tournebout (Fr.). Crumhorn.

Tower, Joan (Peabody), b. New Rochelle, N.Y., Sept. 6, 1938. She studied composition with Brant and Calabro and studied piano at Bennington (Vt.) College (B.A., 1961); completed her training with Luening, Beeson, and Ussachevsky at Columbia Univ. (M.A., 1964; D.M.A., 1978). In N.Y. she cofounded the Da Capo Chamber Players (1969), soon known for promoting contemporary music; she was its pianist (to 1984), writing many works for it. She taught at Bard College in Annandale-on-Hudson (from 1972); composer-in-residence of the St. Louis Sym. Orch. (1985–87); held a Guggenheim fellowship (1976); held NEA fellowships (1974, 1975, 1980, 1984); received a Koussevitzky Foundation grant (1982), American Academy and Inst. of Arts and Letters award (1983), and the Grawemeyer Award (for the orch'l *Silver Ladders*, 1986).

Tower practices different approaches to composition, but her central mode combines post-Debussy harmonic sensitivity with a Stravinskyian rhythmic freedom and drive, often producing evocative pictures of nature, not without wit. Among her works: Orch.: *Sequoia* (1981), *Island Rhythms* (1989), concertos for clarinet, flute, piano, and violin (1985–91). Chamber: *Breakfast Rhythms* I–II (1974), *Black Topaz* (1976), *Petroushkates* (1980), *Snow Dreams* (1983); piano works.

Townshend, Pete(r Dennis Blandford). See ⇒Who, The.

toye. Short piece for the virginal; composed in the 16th–17th centuries.

tract (from Lat. *tractus,* extension). Psalmodic or other biblical chant replacing the alleluia in the High Mass during penitential seasons (e.g., Lent) in the Roman Catholic liturgy.

tragédie lyrique (Fr.). Baroque and Classic French operas on classical subjects; greatest representatives of the genre are Lully and Rameau; Gluck contributed to it during his Parisian sojourn. In the Romantic era, *drame lyrique* superseded tragédie lyrique, as Classic subjects became rare.

tragicamente (It.). Tragically.

trait de chant (Fr.). Melodic motion. *Trait d'harmonie,* harmonic progression.

Trampler, Walter, b. Munich, Aug. 25, 1915. He received his first musical training from his father; enrolled at the Munich State Academy of Music; made his debuts as a violinist (Munich, 1933) and violist (Berlin, 1935); 1st violist in the Deutschlandsender Orch. (1935–38); emigrated to America. He was in the New Music String Quartet (1947–55); made appearances with the Yale, Emerson, Budapest, Juilliard, and Guarneri quartets and the Beaux Arts Trio; member of the Chamber Music Soc. of Lincoln Center (from 1969). He was appointed prof. of viola and chamber music at the Juilliard School of Music in N.Y. (1962); named prof. at the Yale Univ. School of Music (1971); member of the faculty at Boston Univ. (from 1972). One of the foremost viola masters, he appeared as a soloist with many leading orchs. of North America and Europe; premiered works by Henze, Berio, Persichetti, and others.

tranquillo (It.). Tranquilly, quietly, calmly.

transcription. Defining terms such as transcription, arrangement, fantasia, and paraphrase became especially difficult during the 19th century, when every virtuoso bestowed his or her versions of other composers' music, whether strict, free, or in between, no matter what medium the orig. piece was in. Perhaps the semantic distinctions made by the greatest practitioner of this art, Liszt, are useful: the most literal arrangement

was the *Übertragung* (note-for-note transfer from one medium to another; a vocal score); a more congenial transference was the *Bearbeitung* (reworking of the orig. to fit the new medium more idiomatically; Bach-Stokowski); then the more liberal *transcription* (some compositional freedom permitted; Bach-Busoni); followed by the *fantasia* (increasing structural improvisation; Liszt's *Totentanz*), and finally expanded even further (*free* or *romantic fantasia;* Berg's *Wozzeck*). Liszt called an even more unrestricted type of free fantasia *reminiscences,* using selective memory to evoke the opera or sym. being recalled. (As an auxiliary category, he introduced *illustrations* for recurring thematic allusion.) At the most extreme was the *paraphrase,* uniting any or all characteristics of the previous categories, with perhaps only a hint of the orig. model. See also ⇒paraphrases and transcriptions.

transient. Passing; not principal; intermediate. *Transient chord,* intermediate chord foreign to the key left and the key reached; opposite of *pivot chord; transient modulation,* temporary modulation, followed by a return to the original key.

transition. 1. Modulation, especially transient. 2. In tonic solfa, modulation without change of mode (movement of Do).

translocation. By altering the intervallic structure of a given musical subject and translocating its tonal constituents, any melorhythmic figure can be brought into topological congruity with any other; the number of such changes—in which the intervallic unit is a semitone and the rhythmic unit is the smallest note value occurring in the subjects—indicates the degree of affinity existing between these subjects. In isometric melodies (i.e., with identical rhythms), only the index of intervallic changes need be considered; in isotonal pairs (with same pitches in the same order), only rhythmic changes need computing; the fewer alterations required to transform one melorhythmic outline into that of another, the greater the intrinsic similarity between the 2.

Two composers demonstrate particular melorhythmic consistency. Virtually all principal leading motives in Wagner's music dramas are closely related; it requires but a few adjustments of interval and rhythm to transmute the leitmotiv of erotic love in *Tristan und Isolde* to that of faith in *Parsifal.* The main motives of most tone poems of R. Strauss are topologically similar, no matter what the programmatic design is. On the other hand, the index of interchangeability of dodecaphonic tone rows is extremely high, characteristic of the numerical diversity of 12-tone themes. This is not surprising, for the works of Wagner and Strauss are based on triadic formations with auxiliary chromatic notes; whereas serial music does not depend on tonality, so that its intervallic structure is free of all restrictions.

transpose. Perform or write out a composition in a different key than written.

transposing instruments. 1. Those whose basic scale is always written in C major, regardless of concert pitch. Thus, for a clarinet in B♭, a written C-major scale will sound like B-flat major; to get the concert (sounding) scale of C major the music has to be written in D major. 2. Those having a device by which the action or strings can be shifted so that higher or lower tones are produced than when they are in normal position. Irving

Berlin had a piano of this type, as he could only play in the natural key of F-sharp.

transposition. 1. Performance or notation of a composition in a higher or lower key than the original, in order to adjust to the range of an individual's vocal range or a more convenient and more effective tonality in an instrumental work. Most transpositions are made in song anthologies, usually from an orig. soprano/tenor setting to a lower range. Any singer can transpose a tune without training, but piano accompanists have to be adroit technically and musically to transpose a piece at sight. Transposing on sight can be especially difficult for persons with perfect pitch, one of the rare occasions when that particular blessing is a curse. 2. One of 3 standard techniques in serial composition, with retrograde and inversion.

transverse flute (Fr. *Flûte traversière;* Ger. *Traversflöte;* It. *flauto traverso, traverso*). Cross flute, held perpendicularly to the nose and across the lips, as opposed to the vertical flute (e.g., recorder).

traps (trap set). Colloquial term for the jazz drum set.

traquenard (Fr.). Fast galop in 4/4 time with dotted rhythms; found in Baroque instrumental suites.

trascinando (It.). Drawn out heavily; dragging, sluggishly.

trasporto, con (It., with transport). Ecstatically.

trattenuto (tratto; It.). Held back, drawn out, delayed.

Trauermarsch (Ger.). Funeral march. *Trauermusik,* funeral music.

träumerisch (Ger.). Dreamily.

traurig (Ger.). Sad, melancholy.

Trautonium. Electronic musical instrument introduced (1930) by the German electrical engineer Friedrich Trautwein (1888–1956); Hindemith composed for it.

Travers, Mary. See ⇒Yarrow, Peter.

Traversflöte (Ger.). 1. Tranverse flute. 2. 4' organ stop with flute-like timbre.

travesty. See ⇒trouser role.

tre (It.). Three. *A tre,* for 3 voices or instruments; *a tre voci,* for (in) 3 parts or voices; *tre corde,* release piano soft pedal completely.

treble. Voice of soprano range, often sung by boys; also, viol or soprano. *Treble clef,* the G clef; *treble recorder,* in U.K., alto recorder in F; *treble viol,* soprano viola da gamba.

trecento (It., sometimes capitalized). The 1300s (14th century); applied to music, period of polyphonic music from *c.* 1325 into the early 15th century; characterized by efflorescent secular music setting vernacular texts. The most important forms are the

madrigal and caccia; the best-known composers are Landini and Jacopo da Bologna.

Tregian, Francis, b. 1574; d. London, 1619. Scribe of the *Fitzwilliam Virginal Book,* compiled while imprisoned (London and Leipzig, 1894–99) and 2 MSS containing more than 2,000 motets, madrigals, etc., including his own compositions.

treibend (Ger.). Urging, hastening.

Treigle, Norman, b. New Orleans, Mar. 6, 1927; d. there, Feb. 16, 1975. He sang in a church choir as a child; after military service he studied voice with E. Wood; made his debut as a bass-baritone with the New Orleans Opera as Lodovico in *Otello* (1947); made his N.Y. City Opera debut as Colline in *La Bohème* (1953); remained with the company for 20 years, establishing himself as a public favorite. Among his successful roles were Mozart's Figaro, Don Giovanni, Boito's Mefistofele, and Boris Godunov; sang in modern operas, including the leads in the world premieres of 3 operas by C. Floyd: *The Passion of Jonathan Wade* (N.Y., 1962), *The Sojourner and Mollie Sinclair* (Raleigh, NC, 1963), and *Markheim* (New Orleans, 1966). His other contemporary roles included the title role in Dallapiccola's *The Prisoner* and the grandfather in Copland's *The Tender Land.* His untimely death, from an overdose of sleeping pills, deprived the American opera scene of one of its finest talents.

tremblement (Fr., trembling). Obs. term for trill.

tremolo (It., quivering, fluttering). 1. Common embellishment comprising a repeated alternation of 2 notes in rapid tempo; long regarded as a powerful device to produce dramatic tension; not synonymous with vibrato. In singing, a tremulous, somewhat unsteady tone is used; on bowed instruments the effect is produced by the very rapid alternation of down-bow and up-bow, written:

On the piano, rapid alternation of the tones of a dyad or more serves the purpose. In his preface to the dramatic madrigal *Il combattimento di Tancredi e Clorinda* (1638), Monteverdi describes the tremolo as the most expressive dynamic device of the *stile concitato,* where it illustrates Tancred's unwitting fatal wounding of his beloved Clorinda. Its use for dramatic effect reached greatest popularity in the 19th century, particularly in opera; degenerated into melodramatic effect, soon vanishing from serious composition altogether, except for comical effects. 2. On the organ, effect produced by the *tremolo stop (tremulant).*

trepak. Russian dance in fast duple time.

très (Fr.; Ger. *ganz, sehr;* It. *molto*). Very.

Tretyakov, Viktor (Viktorovich), b. Krasnoyarsk, Oct. 17, 1946. He enrolled at the Irkutsk Music School as a child; moved to Moscow; studied at the Central Music School with Y.

Yankelevich (from 1959); continued with him at the Cons. (graduated 1970) and as a postgraduate. He won the Tchaikovsky Competition (1966), followed by highly successful tours in Russia, Europe, and the U.S.. A typical product of the Russian school of violin playing, he combines technical virtuosity with a diffuse lyricism touched with melancholy in the Romantic repertoire.

triad. Chord consisting of 3 distinct pitches; if tonal, a chord consisting of a given tone (the root), a note a major or minor 3rd above the root, and the note a perfect, diminished, or augmented 5th above the root. Modern music theory recognizes 4 primary triadic types: *major*, major 3rd and perfect 5th above the root; *minor*, minor 3rd and perfect 5th; *diminished*, minor 3rd and diminished 5th; and *augmented*, major 3rd and augmented 5th. Major and minor triads are fundamental to the determination of a key; the diminished triad is considered dissonant with its diminished 5th; the augmented triad is also dissonant because of its augmented 5th, even if this interval is enharmonically equivalent to a minor 6th. In the 20th century some musicians attempted to deprive the triads of their tonal connotations by extending the notion of triad to any 3-note chord, however chromatically congested or dispersed; analogously, a pair of notes was newly labeled a dyad.

triadic modulation. Procedure to change keys in midstream without using the circle of fifths; a triad that belongs to both current and future keys becomes a pivot chord; the modulation is accomplished by a tonal overlapping or segue. Only 1 note of the pivot chord has to shared by both keys. See also ⇒ modulation.

triangle. Steel rod bent into triangular shape, with one corner left slightly open; it is struck with a metal wand.

trias (Lat., trinity). In old German treatises, the triad. *Trias harmonica major*, major triad; *trias harmonica minor*, minor triad.

tricesimorprimal temperament. Sesquipedalian if pedantically correct name for the 31-equal division of the octave, proposed by the 17th-century Dutch astronomer Christiaan Huygens, who hoped to find an equally tempered approach to achieve something close to just intonation; the system was championed by Adriaan Fokker in the 20th century and used by Dutch composers.

trichord. Set of 3 pitch classes; usually a segment of a 12-note set.

trichord piano. Instrument with 3 unison strings per tone throughout the greater part of its compass.

tricinium (Lat.). In 16th-century Germany, a 3-part vocal piece; collections of secular, sacred, and instrumental tricinia were publ. primarily for didactic purposes.

tricotet. Type of melody improvised, sung, danced, and played on instruments by medieval minstrels, completely free in form, rhythm, and character. French Baroque composers gave the name to fanciful sections of instrumental suites.

trill (Fr. *trille;* Ger. *Triller;* It. *trillo*). Melodic embellishment consisting of even and rapid alternation of 2 tones a major or minor 2nd apart; the lower tone is the *principal note* (the 1 being ornamented), the higher tone the *auxiliary note* (the 1 ornamenting). Trilling was cultivated in France in the 17th century, sometimes described as *tremblement*, trans. into English as *shake*. Its graphic symbol is a wavy line, sometimes extending according to the duration required; the abbrev. *tr* is also used. In modern instrumental writing the trill invariably begins on the principal note, but in the Baroque it often began on the auxiliary note; interpretation of this option can differ from scholar to scholar and source to source. Vocal trilling has come to merge with the vibrato technique in constant use by opera singers; the technical danger is that one not be used when the other is called for.

trilletta (It.). Short trill.

trillo caprino (It.). Goat trill.

Trinklied (Ger.). Drinking song; See ⇒ Brindisi.

trio (It.). 1. Composition employing 3 instruments or (less often) 3 vocal parts; the so-called piano trio is scored for violin, cello, and piano (e.g., Beethoven, Schumann, Mendelssohn, Brahms, Tchaikovsky); a work for violin, viola, and cello is often called a string trio (Beethoven wrote 5). Haydn wrote trios for 2 violins and cello as well as over 100 for baryton, viola, and bass. Mixed trios are found, such as those for clarinet, and cello, and piano (Mozart, Brahms, Khatchaturian). 2. In minuets, marches, ragtime, etc., a 2nd dance or march, after which the 1st is repeated (ternary form); sometimes the key is changed; in the Baroque, also called an *alternativo*. The use of the term for the 2nd (alternating) section of a Classic or Romantic sym. minuet or scherzo is a relic of the Baroque, when it was often scored for 3 instruments, e.g., 2 oboes and bassoon, or 2 horns and bassoon (e.g., finale of Bach's *Brandenburg Concerto No. 1*).

trio d'anches. Work for woodwind trio.

trio sonata. Important Baroque chamber music genre, written in 3 parts: 2 upper (melody) parts, supported by a basso continuo part to be realized by 2 instruments, thus the paradox of seeing 4 persons perform a "sound piece for 3." Upper parts were usually scored for violins, flutes, and/or oboes; a cello or bassoon played the bass line, with the harpsichord or organ supplying the harmonic texture. In pre-Classic music the upper parts were often taken over by viols and/or cornettos, the lower parts by a viola da gamba and harpsichord. There are trio sonatas written for a considerably larger ensemble, but even then the texture is in 3 principal parts; to emphasize this peculiarity composers often marked the score *a tre*. The trio sonata borrows from other genres structurally: the sonata da chiesa, with its slow-fast-slow-fast order, and sonata da camera, with suite-like dance movements. Handel wrote 28 trio sonatas; Vivaldi wrote 12; Bach's most famous trio sonata, founds in the *Musikalisches Opfer*, was written for Frederick the Great; the genre was much favored by French composers. Towards 1750, the trio sonata circuitously evolved into the piano trio (violin, cello, piano), with the piano *cembalo redivivus*, not only filling in harmony but functioning independently in melody and counterpoint, thus replacing one of the melody parts.

Triole (Ger.). Triplet.

trionfale (It.). Triumphal.

trionfante (It.). Triumphant.

triple concerto. Concerto for 3 solo instruments and orch.

triple counterpoint. See ⇒counterpoint.

triple dot. Three dots placed to the right of a note head, augmenting its duration by 1/2 + 1/2(1/2) + 1/2 (1/2)(1/2) its value, each subsequent dot adding half the value of the preceding dot. Thus, a half note with a triple dot equals 1/2 + 1/4 + 1/8 + 1/16 = 15/16 (of a whole note). Triple dots are rare, as they can be translated into tied notes readily.

triple time. Meter containing 3 units, as in 3/4 or 3/8.

triple-croche (Fr.). Thirty-second note.

triplet (Fr. *triolet;* Ger. *Triole;* It. *terzina*). Group of 3 equal notes to be performed in the time of 2 notes of like value in the established tempo; the most common, the 8th-note triplet, is written:

If quarter-note or half-note triplets are called for, a square bracket must be used, as follows:

triplum (Lat.). 2nd added voice in medieval organum, resulting in a 3-part texture of cantus firmus (tenor), duplum, and triplum (the highest); also used in 3-part compositions without cantus firmus.

Tristan chord. Designation for the chord, (from bottom) F–B–D♯–G♯, occuring in the 2nd measure of the prelude to Wagner's *Tristan und Isolde* (1856–59; premiered 1865). To resolve, the upper voice ascends chromatically (G♯–A–A♯–B); the alto and bass descend chromatically (D♯–D♮; F–E); the tenor drops a minor 3rd down (B–G♯). The result is the dominant-7th chord of A, establishing a connection with the opera's opening note, A. This chord and its ambiguous resolution are fundamental to melodic and harmonic transformations of the principal leitmotivs throughout the entire score; so unusual was it for its time that Wagnerophiles gave it a whole mystique in the theory of chromatic harmony. Even though the Tristan chord is closely associated with Wagnerian harmony, it is almost identical with a transitional passage in Liszt's lied *Ich möchte hingehen* (c. 1845, rev. c. 1860). The notorious Wagnerophobe Hanslick said that the prelude's chromaticism reminded him of an old Italian painting representing a martyr whose intestines are being slowly unwound from his body on a reel.

Tristano, Lennie (Leonard Joseph), b. Chicago, Mar. 19, 1919; d. N.Y., Nov. 18, 1978. Blind from childhood, he attended the American Cons. of Music in Chicago (B.Mus., 1943); after performing in Chicago clubs, settled in N.Y. (1946); attracted wide notice with his own sextet (1947); ran a jazz school (1951–56), then taught privately; made occasional appearances as a performer, touring Europe (1965) and the U.S. (1968). He was a master at piano improvisations.

triste (Fr.). Sad, wistful.

tristo, -a (It.). In a style expressive of sadness or melancholy.

tritone. Interval of the augmented 4th, containing 3 consecutive whole tones, as F to B or D to G-sharp; sometimes notated as a diminished 5th (F to C-flat; D to A-flat); forbidden in the building of tetrachords. Medieval theorists described the tritone as the *diabolus in musica* (devil of music) and ejected melodic progressions using it from church music wherever possible; while the ecclesiastical modes had the potential for melodic tritones, *musica ficta* were employed automatically to avoid this interval. In German schools in Bach's time music students who inadvertently made use of the tritone were punished in class by a rattan blow on the knuckles of the hand. The earliest suggestion that the use of the tritone may not be a *peccatum mortale* was made by Ramos de Pareja in *Musica practica* (1482), but his leniency received little approbation. More than 2 centuries later, Bach wrote a chorale beginning with 3 whole tones in succession, to the words, "O schwerer Gang" (Oh, difficult step).

It seems appropriate that the stone rejected by medieval builders should become the cornerstone of modern music, in all its principal aspects—polytonality, atonality, and dodecaphony; the modern importance of the tritone derives from the very quality that disenfranchised it before: its incompatibility with the tonic-dominant complex. Two major triads at the distance of a tritone formed the bitonal "Petrouchka chord" so popular in the 1st quarter of the century; complementary hexachords in major keys with tonics distanced by a tritone comprise a symmetrical 12-tone row; a series of intervals diminishing by a semitone beginning with a major 6th and ending with its inversion, the minor 3rd, forms a bitonal major chord with tonics at a tritone's distance; a chord containing all eleven different intervals is encompassed by 5 octaves and a tritone from the lowest to the highest note.

triumph cornet. Military cornet in B♭ with an especially brilliant tone; invented by Vaclav Červeny (1862).

trochee. In prosody, a foot consisting of one long (accented) and one short (unaccented) beat; in music, a trochaic meter corresponds to a leisurely waltz without accented upbeat.

trois-quatre (Fr.). Three-quarter (waltz) time.

trojnice. Croatian triple flute, with 1 drone (left tube) and 2 playing tubes (melody on the right, secondary part in the middle).

tromba (It.). Trumpet. *Tromba da tirarsi*, obs. for slide trumpet; *tromba spezzata*, slide trumpet.

tromba marina (It., marine trumpet; Ger. *Trumscheit;* Fr. *trompette marine*). Bowed monochord, a single string stretched over a very long and narrow wooden box; the string is touched rather than stopped by the thumb, resulting in a long series of harmonics. The tromba marina dates from at least the 12th century; may once have been plucked rather than bowed; at one point, a 2nd string was added, even more on occasion; by the Baroque it was once again a monochord. Over time the body achieved a slightly more triangular shape, with a flared bottom and thinner neck; instruments were built to reach 6 or 7 feet in height; the increased size amplified a tendency to buzz, and some makers invented devices to curb it; another variant added sympathetic brass strings for greater resonance.

For many centuries the tromba marina was useful in acoustic experiments with harmonics (e.g., Glarean's *Dodecachordon*); was also popular with street musicians. It seems to have become obsolete by the Classic period, although acoustically minded builders have experimented with the concept in recent years. The absurd name for this bowed monochord is explained partly by its sounding of the harmonic series, as the natural trumpet did; presumably expert players could get around the string quickly and accurately enough to be comparable, especially without the added difficulties of playing natural brass instruments; but "marina" remains a mystery, with no convincing explanation yet. Supposedly the instrument was used in convents, hence the alternative name *Nonnengeige* (Ger., nun's fiddle).

trombetta (It.). Small trumpet; mentioned in Dante's *Divina commedia.*

trombone (from It. *tromba* + *one*, big trumpet; Ger. *Posaune*). Tenor instrument of the brass group, pitched below the trumpet and horn, above the (bass) tuba; the only standard orch'l instrument that utilizes a sliding tube (i.e., slide) to change pitch, rather than a shift of finger, closing or opening of hole, or pushing or releasing of valve key; hence the colloquial name "slide trombone." The player draws the slide in or out, changing the side of the tube that air travels through to produce notes; the more extended the slide, the larger the tube and the lower the note; the opposite effect is produced by drawing the slide in towards the player.. As with other brass instruments, manipulation of the lips replaces the mouthpieces of woodwind instruments while determining the harmonic being used to generate pitch.

The trombone is one of the oldest Western brass instruments, dating to the early Renaissance, when it was known as the sackbut. It developed strong associations with things apocalyptic or hellish; no orch'l instrument can sound the Dies Irae more ominously; it announces in doom-laden tones the entrance of the Commendatore's statue in *Don Giovanni,* summoning the profligate protagonist to his own last supper. But the trombone can sound in triumph; in his 5th Sym. Beethoven saves the trombone for the glorious finale.

The range of the tenor trombone is from E below the bass clef to C an octave above middle C (E_0 to c^2); the alto trombone is tuned a perfect 5th above, the bass trombone a 4th lower. There is a double trombone in B♭/F, in effect a tenor with an "F attachment" to shift to the bass range; sometimes a pedal pump is attached to help the player blow; R. Strauss makes use of it in *Elektra,* as does Varèse in *Arcana.*

Trommel (Ger.). Drum.

trompe de chasse (Fr.). Natural horn used for hunting calls.

trompette (Fr.). Trumpet. *Trompette à coulisse,* slide trumpet; *trompette à pistons,* valve trumpet with pistons; *trompette marine,* tromba marina.

tronco, -a (It.). Cut off short; stopped abruptly.

trop (Fr.). Too, too much (as in amount), e.g., *pas trop vite,* not too fast.

troparion. Byzantine hymn in its simplest form; usually inserted between verses of psalms; later evolved into the kontakion.

trope (from Grk. *trópos,* turn [of speech]). In medieval chant liturgy, a musical or texted musical insertion into an established piece from the Ordinary, the Proprium, or the Divine Office; originally referred to rhetorical figures of speech which Quintilian defined as "a change from the proper meaning of a word into another." Initially tropes took the form of melismas, sometimes of great length; later these melismas had words fitted to them, creating the texted trope (e.g., the Kyrie *orbis factor*). Other tropes were dramatic in tone, leading to the liturgical drama (e.g., the Easter trope *Quem queritis,* dating to at least the 10th century). Gradually the music of the tropes annexed intrusive modalities, even secular tunes; this proliferation of unorthodox tropes and supposed melismatic pollution of Gregorian chant caused the Roman Catholic Council of Trent (1545–63) to proscribe all such usages, retaining only those melodic figures firmly ingrained into traditional chants by then.

troppo (It.). Too; too much. *Allegro, ma non troppo,* fast, but not too much (fast).

trotzig (Ger.). Stubborn, contrary.

troubadour (from Old Prov. *trobador, tropator,* trope composer; It. *trovatore*). Poet-musicians and singers who roamed the areas of southern France, northern Spain, and northwestern Italy in the 11th-13th centuries; wrote and performed in Provençal, the *langue d'oc* (named after the affirmative *oc*). The art of the troubadours gradually penetrated into northern France, where a performer was called a *trouvère,* and Germany, known as a Minnesinger. Troubadours originated many types of popular French songs, such as alba, aubade, pastourelle, and pastorela. A considerable number of the troubadours' monophonic strophic songs have survived, the lack of rhythmic notation has led to decades of discussion and dispute. See also ⇒trouvère.

trouser role (travesty; U.K., breeches-part; Ger. *Hosenrolle*). Operatic role sung by a female singer performing the role of a younger man or boy, e.g., Siebel in *Faust,* Cherubino in *The Marriage of Figaro,* Octavian in *Der Rosenkavalier,* Prince Orlovsky in *Die Fledermaus.* Double transvestiture is required of the singers performing Cherubino and Octavian; each puts on maidservant's clothing to disguise themselves from an overbearing nobleman.

trouvère (from Old French *trover,* compose, find). Class of poet-musicians and singers who flourished during the 12th–13th centuries in northern France, domain of the *langue d'oeil,* named for its affirmative *oeil* (as opposed the troubadour's Provençal *langue d'oc,* whose affirmative was *oc*). The trouvères created a profusion of literary and musical forms, known collectively as *chansons de geste* (songs of deeds); cultivated the rondeau, ballade, virelais, motet, and instrumental estampe. Thousands of trouvère texts have been preserved in medieval chansonniers; fortunately many of the melodies have been preserved; no rhythmic notation is indicated, thereby opening the way for discussion and dispute. See also ⇒troubadour.

trüb(e) (Ger.). Gloomy, dismal; sad, melancholy.

trumpet. 1. (Lat. *tuba;* Ger. *Trompete;* Fr. *trompette;* It. *tromba*). Brass instrument with cupped mouthpiece and small bell, with brilliant, penetrating tone of great carrying power; the modern instrument is a chromatic, transposing instrument in B♭ (standard, soprano) or other fundamentals; the sounding range e^0 to $bb^{\flat 2}$ (written f♯[0] to c^3); there is also an upper-register trumpet (sopranino, piccolo).

In one or another form, the trumpet is an ancient instrument; its principle, creating sound by blowing into a hollow object (not made of tusk or animal horn) without the use of reeds, found fruition in instruments made of conch shells, bamboo, cane, wood, bark, and ultimately metal. Its development in post-classical Europe began with the *buisine* (8th century) and extended through to the natural trumpet (14th century); it retained this form until the invention of the valve trumpet (early 19th century). In medieval hymns it was the "trump" of Judgment Day; however, when the Doomsday trumpet is represented compositionally, its part is usually given to the trombone, really a larger trumpet with an elongated body and slide. It is a given in orchestraton manuals that a single trumpet is equal in sonority to an entire orch. The most common dramatic use of the trumpet is as military caller; in *Fidelio,* the trumpet announces the arrival of the new governor who will reestablish justice; in *Carmen* the trumpet summons Don José to the barracks. In innumerable marches, operatic and orch'l, the trumpet sets the marching time for soldiers; but the trumpet can be meditative and even philosophical, particularly when muted, e.g., *The Unanswered Question* by Ives.

For centuries the trumpet was limited to natural harmonic tones and had to be manually tuned to the key of the work it was playing in. To effect a lower key, the player had to insert extra tubing (a crook) into his instrument; to play in a higher key, the tubing had to be shortened. It was not until the 19th century that efficient trumpet keys (piston, later rotary valves) were invented that made it possible to play a full chromatic scale. Works written before this invention, e.g., by Mozart, Haydn, and even Beethoven utilized mainly the tonic and dominant of the principal key; with the chromatic instrument at their disposal, some audacious conductors revised the trumpet parts in Beethoven's syms. as Beethoven "might" have written them for the new trumpet (e.g., 5th Sym., 1st movement, beginning of 2nd theme group); such speculative tamperings are always dangerous and can be counterproductive to the intended purpose. Wagner wrote a part for a wooden trumpet in the 3rd act of *Tristan und Isolde,*

but it is usually played by the English horn. Specially constructed trumpets are required in Verdi's *Aida,* the *trompette thébaine* (Fr., trumpet of Thebes, the Egyptian city where most of the opera's action takes place); in English, simply the *Aida trumpet.*

The standard trumpet was stabilized in the latter 19th century as a B-flat transposing instrument, sounding a major 2nd below the written note; the alto trumpet in F (sounding a 5th below) is used by French composers, among them Chabrier (*España*). In Germany, Russia, England, and the Netherlands the B-flat instrument is used almost exclusively (in Germany it is, of course, in B); French and American composers have sometimes used a non-transposing trumpet in C. The trumpet plays a very important role in jazz; most jazz musicians call any wind instrument a "horn," bringing about confusion with classical terminology, where a horn is French, period. Some virtuoso trumpeters can overblow the range for several notes above high C; Louis Armstrong once hit high C (c^3) 280 times in succession. And it was the trumpet that brought down the walls of Jericho: "And it came to pass, when the people heard the sound of the trumpet, and the people shouted with a great shout, that the wall fell down flat" (Joshua 6:20). 2. In the organ, 8′ reed stop of powerful tone.

trumpet marine. Tromba marina.

Trumscheit (Ger.). Tromba marina.

tuba. 1. Brass instrument in the bass range of the orch., where it supplies a harmonic foundation for the trumpets and trombones above it; replaced the serpent and ophicléide; may be applied to the lowest members of the saxhorn family. It has a wide conical bore, cupped mouthpiece, and flared bell held upright; has between 3 and 6 valves. In the 19th century there were 3 tuba sizes—tenor, bass, and double-bass tuba—the last an octave below the tenor tuba, now obsolete (replaced by the baritone). The so-called Wagner tuba is smaller than the standard variety and more mellifluous sounding; in 2 sizes, they were specially designed for the music dramas performed at Bayreuth, hence their being called Bayreuth tubas. 2. Straight trumpet of the Romans; salpinx. 3. In the organ, reed stop (*tuba mirabilis*) on a heavy pressure of wind, of very powerful and thrilling tone.

tubaphone. Glockenspiel in which the metal bars are replaced by metal pipes, with a sound approaching a xylophone's; used in Khachaturian's *Sabre Dance* (from *Ganayeh*).

Tubb, Ernest (Dale), b. near Crisp, Tex., Feb. 9, 1914; d. Nashville, Tenn., Sept. 6, 1984. Following in the path of Jimmie Rodgers, he became a leading figure in the development of the "Western swing" or "honky-tonk" style of country-western music; his recording of *Walking the Floor over You* in 1941 established his reputation; from 1942 he made regular appearances on the *Grand Ole Opry* radio program in Nashville. In 1965 he was elected to the Country Music Hall of Fame. American country-music singer, guitarist, and songwriter.

Tubin, Eduard, b. Kallaste, near Tartu, June 18, 1905; d. Stockholm, Nov. 17, 1982. He studied with A. Kapp at the Tartu Cons., later with Kodály in Budapest; conducted the Vanemuine Theater Orch. in Tartu (1931–44); settled in Stockholm (1944; naturalized 1961); elected to the Royal Swedish Academy of

Music (1982); working on his 11th Sym. at the time of his death. He is best known for the syms. (1934–73); concertos for violin (2), double bass, balalaika, and the piano concertino; sonatas (with piano) for violin (2), saxophone, viola, and flute; sonata for solo violin; 2 operas, a ballet, and the *Requiem for Fallen Soldiers* for alto, male chorus, solo trumpet, percussion, and organ (1979).

tubular chimes (chimes, orch'l bells, tubular bells). Idiophone comprising metal bells made of long, hollow cylindrical tubes, arranged like a transmogrified keyboard and suspended from a frame; its pitch is more definite than the church bells it sometimes imitates (Berlioz, *Sym. fantastique*); many modern scores use it, including Varèse's *Ionisation.*

Tucker, Richard, (born Reuben Ticker), b. N.Y., Aug. 28, 1913; d. Kalamazoo, Mich., Jan. 8, 1975. He sang in a synagogue choir in N.Y. as a child; studied voice with P. Althouse; sang on radio. His 1st public operatic appearance was as Alfredo in *La Traviata* with the Salmaggi Co. in N.Y. (1943); made his Metropolitan Opera debut in N.Y. as Enzo in *La Gioconda* (1945); remained on its roster until his death, specializing in the Italian tenor repertoire. He made his European debut at the Verona Arena as Enzo (1947; Callas made her Italian debut as Gioconda in the same performance); sang at Covent Garden in London, La Scala in Milan, Vienna, and other major music centers abroad; died while on a concert tour with baritone Robert Merrill. He was the brother-in-law of the American tenor Jan Peerce.

Tucker, Sophie (born Abuza), b. in Russia, Jan. 13, 1884; d. N.Y., Feb. 9, 1966. She began her career as a singer in her father's restaurant in Hartford, Ct.; performed ribald songs in burlesque, vaudeville, and English music halls; gained fame during World War I; made appearances in nightclubs, films, and on radio and television; remained a popular entertainer for 6 decades. She was well known for the rendition of her theme song, *Some of These Days.*

Tuckwell, Barry (Emmanuel), b. Melbourne, Mar. 5, 1931. He was taught piano by his father and violin by his older brother; was a chorister at St. Andrew's Cathedral in Sydney; acted as an organist there. At age 13 he began studying the horn with A. Mann at the Sydney Cons.; played in the Sydney Sym. Orch. (1947–50). Moving to England, he received valuable advice on horn technique from Dennis Brain and studied Tommy Dorsey's recordings. He filled positions as assistant 1st horn with the Halle Orch. in Manchester (1951–53), the Scottish National Orch. (1953–54), and, as 1st horn, the Bournemouth Sym. Orch. (1954–55) and the London Sym. Orch. (1955–68).

Tuckwell launched a solo career, achieving recognition as one of the foremost virtuosos on the instrument. In the academic field he compiled a horn method and ed. horn literature. Several modern composers wrote works for him: T. Musgrave (a concerto requiring quarter tones), R. R. Bennett (*Actaeon*), I. Hamilton (*Voyage*), A. Hoddinott (a concerto), D. Banks (a concerto). He pursued a conducting career, making guest appearances in Australia, Europe, and the U.S.; conducted the Tasmanian Sym. Orch. (1980–83); music director of the newly founded Maryland Sym. Orch. in Hagerstown (from 1982). He was made an Officer of the Order of the British Empire (1965).

Tudor, David (Eugene), b. Philadelphia, Jan. 20, 1926. At age 11 he encountered a Messiaen organ work, marking the beginning of his devotion to the music of his time. He studied piano with J. Marin and I. W. Rademacher, organ and theory with H. William Hawke, and composition and analysis with Wolpe. His role as a pioneer performer of new music was established when he gave the U.S. premiere of Boulez's 2nd Piano Sonata (N.Y., 1950); began a close association with Cage, whose works he propagated throughout the world. He evolved imaginative and virtuosic solutions to the challenges of avant-garde works through a rigorous preparation process, distilling compositions that incorporated some degree of indeterminacy into more conventional notation for performance through the refining apparatus of measurements, calculations, conversion tables, and intricate computations; when performing *5 Piano Pieces for David Tudor* by S. Bussotti, he put on thick leather gloves for tone clusters; after mastering the problems unique to avant-garde music, he moved gradually into live electronic music. He became affiliated with the Merce Cunningham Dance Co. (1953), for which he produced numerous works, including *Rain Forest I* (1968), *Toneburst* (1974), *Forest Speech* (1976), *Weatherings* (1978), *Phonemes* (1981), *Sextet for 7* (1982), *Fragments* (1984), *Webwork* (1987), *5 Stone Wind* (with Cage and Takehisa Kosugi; 1988), and *Virtual Focus* (1990). He taught at Black Mountain College (1951–53); taught piano and new music performance at the Internationale Ferienkürse für Neue Musik at Darmstadt (1956, 1958–59, 1961); gave courses in live electronic music at the State Univ. of N.Y. at Buffalo (1965–66), the Univ. of Calif. at Davis (1967), Mills College in Oakland, Calif. (1967–68), and the National Inst. of Design in Ahmedabad, India (1969). In 1968 he was selected as one of 4 core artists for the design and construction of the Pepsico Pavilion at Expo '70 in Osaka. Among his other collaborators were Lowell Cross, Marcel and Teeny Duchamp, Gordon Mumma, Anthony Martin, Molly Davies, and Jackie Matisse.

tumultuoso (It.). Vehement, impetuous; agitated.

tune. Air, melody; chiefly applied to short, simple pieces or familiar melodies; its colloquial applications are practically boundless.

tuning (Fr. *action d'accorder;* Ger. *Stimmung*). 1. Process of bringing an instrument into correct pitch with itself or with other instruments. By universal convention, orch'l tuning begins with the oboe giving an A of the middle octave, in most orchs. pitched at 440 cycles per second (cps); the rest of the orch. instruments adjust themselves to this pitch; sometimes during this process, inchoate arpeggios and scales are spontaneously performed by the players. It is said that once when an Asian potentate went to a concert in Paris and was asked which piece he liked best, he replied, "The beginning, just before the man with the stick came in." In piano tuning, one must reconcile the difference between the tempered perfect 5th and 4th with the just intervals based on the overtone series; piano 5ths and 4ths have to be altered to make twelve 5ths identical to 7 octaves; the piano tuner makes sure that tempered 5ths produce about 47 beats a minute, made audible by the slight increase and decrease of the loudness of the principal tone.

2. Accordatura of a stringed instrument. *Tuning cone,* hollow cone of metal, for tuning metal flue pipes in the organ; *tuning crook,* brass crook; *tuning fork,* see ⇒entry; *tuning hammer,* hand wrench for tuning pianos; *tuning horn,* tuning cone; *tuning key,* tuning hammer; *tuning slide,* sliding U-shaped section of the tube in certain brass instruments, used to adjust pitch subtly to other instruments.

tuning fork (Fr. *diapason;* Ger. *Stimmgabel;* It. *corista*). Metal fork giving the pitch of A above middle C (a¹), ranging, depending on the standard pitch for a given ensemble, anywhere from 435 to 450 cycles per second (most commonly 440 cps). By varying the thickness or the length of each prong, tuning forks can be manufactured in different sizes.

tupan. Double-headed cylindrical drum of the South Slavic region; the heads are tuned a 5th apart. It is carried on straps over the body of the player, who strikes it with a drumstick in the right hand and a switch (whip) in the left hand, either together or in alternation.

turba (Lat., crowd). In Baroque oratorios, piece for large chorus.

turco, -a (It.). Turkish man or woman. *Alla turca,* in Turkish style, i.e., with a noisy and somewhat static harmonic accompaniment.

Turina (y Perez), Joaquín, b. Seville, Dec. 9, 1882; d. Madrid, Jan. 14, 1949. He studied with local teachers; entered the Madrid Cons. as a pupil of Trago (piano); went to Paris to study composition with d'Indy at the Schola Cantorum and piano with Moszkowski (1905). At Albéniz's urging he turned to Spanish folk music for inspiration. Returning to Madrid (1914), he composed 2 characteristically Spanish sym. works, *La procesión del Rocio* and *Sinfonia sevillana,* combining Romantic and impressionist elements in an individual manner; the same effective combination is found in his chamber music of Spanish inspiration (*Escena andaluza, La oración del torero*) and piano music (*Sonata romántica, Mujeres españolas*); wrote 5 operas and incidental music for the theater. He was appointed a prof. of composition at the Madrid Cons. (1930); founded the general music commission of the Ministry of Education, serving as its commissioner (1941).

Turken-Trommel (Ger.). Turkish drum; obsolete for bass drum.

turkey trot. American "animal step" dance popular in the early 20th century; others include the grizzly bear, bunny hug, chicken flip, horse trot, and (naturally) fox-trot.

Turkish music. Janizary music.

Turm-musik (Ger.). Tower music, played on brass instruments by Stadtpfeifer in the turret of the town hall to announce the hour.

turn. Melodic grace usually consisting of 4 notes, a principal note (struck twice) alternating with its higher and lower auxiliary.

Turner, Joseph Vernon "Big Joe", b. Kansas City, Mo., May 18, 1911; d. Englewood, Calif., Nov. 24, 1985. He 1st worked as a singing bartender in local nightclubs; became associated with the boogie-woogie pianist Pete Johnson; appeared together at Carnegie Hall in N.Y. (1938). After moving to Calif., he sang with Duke Ellington's band; he and Johnson appeared at their own club in Los Angeles (1945); later toured the U.S. and Europe. His *Shake, Rattle, and Roll* (1954) helped create the rock 'n' roll craze which swept the nation in the 1950s.

Turner, Tina (born Anna Mae Bullock), b. Brownsville, Tenn., Nov. 26, 1939. She joined Ike Turner (b. Clarksdale, Miss., Nov. 5, 1931) and his band, the Kings of Rhythm, in St. Louis (1956); they were married (1958) and toured as the Ike and Tina Turner Revue, accompanied by a female dance-and-vocal trio, the Ikettes. Tina made an explosive impact as a sexually provocative and intense singer, belting out such numbers as *I've Been Lovin' You Too Long* and *River Deep, Mountain High* (1966).

A tour of the U.S. with the Rolling Stones catapulted the Turner Revue onto center stage (1969); won a Grammy for their recording of *Proud Mary* (1971); while continuing to make appearances with her husband, Tina made the solo albums *Let Me Touch Your Hand* (1972) and *Tina Turns the Country On* (1974). She appeared as the Acid Queen in the rock-opera film *Tommy* (1975), complemented by her album *Acid Queen*. She left her husband in 1976; divorced him in 1978; pursued a solo career as a rock-and-soul songstress; after a few failures she produced the tremendously successful album *Private Dancer* (1984); won 4 Grammy Awards, with *What's Love Got to Do with It?* honored as best song and best record of the year. In 1985 she starred in the film *Mad Max beyond Thunderdome* (with Mel Gibson); follow-up albums include *Break Every Rule* (1986) and *Foreign Affair* (1989).

Tusch (Ger.; Eng. obs., tuck, tucket). Complimentary fanfare played by orch'l musicians for an honored conductor or soloist.

tutta forza, con (It.). With all possible force.

tutte (le) corde (It., all the strings). In piano playing, release the soft pedal fully.

tutti (It.). Indication in an orch'l or choral score that the entire orch. or chorus is to enter; usually placed after an extended solo passage; incorporated into the concertante style of the Baroque and Classic.

twelfth. 1. Interval of an octave plus a 5th; compound 5th. 2. Mutation stop in the organ, pitched a 12th higher than the diapason.

twelve-note composition. See ⇒dodecaphonic music.

twelve-tone music (Ger. *Zwölftonmusik*). Historically significant, non-hierarchical method of musical organization, promulgated (1923) and most profoundly developed by Schoenberg, wherein all 12 notes of the chromatic scale are ordered and treated without concern for tonal and/or harmonic functions; in effect, all twelve-tone themes comprise one each of the 12 tones of the chromatic scale. The inventor's own definition, which he regarded as the only correct one, is "the method of composition with 12 tones related only to one another." The concept of 12-tone music was later incorporated in the generic category of serialism, in which different intervals, different dynamics, and different instrumental timbres can be organized in a series. See also ⇒dodecaphonic music, serialism.

24 Violins of the King. Vingt-quatre Violons du Roi.

two-step. American ballroom dance popular in the 1900s and 1910s, with a sliding step in 2/4 time.

Tye, Christopher, b. *c.* 1505; d. *c.* 1572. He received his Mus.B. from Cambridge (1536); appointed lay clerk at King's College there (1537); became Magister choristarum at Ely Cathedral (1543); received the D.Mus. degree from the Univ. of Cambridge (1545). After becoming a deacon and a priest (1560), he left Ely Cathedral (1561); held livings at Doddington-cum-Marche in the Isle of Ely (from 1561), at Wilbraham Parva (1564–67), and Newton-cum-capella (1564–70).

Tye described himself as a gentleman of the King's Chapel on the title page of his only publ. work, *The Actes of the Apostles, translated into Englyshe metre to synge and also to play upon the Lute* (London, 1553; includes the 1st 14 chapters); the hymn tunes *Windsor* and *Winchester Old* are adaptations from this collection. He was an important composer of English church music; wrote Masses, services, motets, and anthems. He was an active composer of viol consort music, notably his numerous In Nomine fantasias. His son-in-law was Robert White (Whyte; b. *c.* 1538; d. London, Nov. 1574), best known for settings of the Lamentations and instrumental fantasias.

tympani. Alternative Eng. spelling of timpani.

tyrolienne (Fr.). Tyrolese dance or dance song, based on the local equivalent of the Ländler; a modern round dance in 3/4 time and easy movement, with a characteristic dotted rhythm on the 3rd beat; a peculiar feature of the dance song is the use of the yodel, especially in the refrain. Rossini wrote a tyrolienne for his *William Tell.*

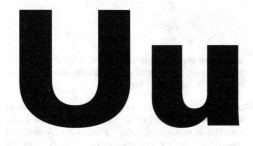

Üben (Ger.). Practice.

über (Ger.). Over, above.

Übergang (Ger., going over). Transitional phrase; modulation to a related key.

übermässig (Ger.). Augmented; applied to intervals a semitone larger than the major or perfect type.

Übung (Ger.). Exercise; practice.

Uchida, Mitsuko, b. Tokyo, Dec. 20, 1948. She began training in childhood in her native city; at age 12 she became a pupil of R. Hauser at the Vienna Academy of Music; won the Beethoven Competition (1968); received 2nd prize at the Chopin Competition in Warsaw (1970). She won particular notice in London and Tokyo for her performances of the complete piano sonatas of Mozart (1982); appeared as soloist-conductor in all the Mozart piano concertos with the English Chamber Orch. in London (1985–86); made her N.Y. recital debut (1987). Her repertoire includes works by Debussy, Schoenberg, and Bartók.

'ūd (oud). Arab lute, datable to the 7th century; has gone through numerous structural changes (from pear- to almond-shaped body) and numbers of strings (always in double courses), but retains a fretless fingerboard; it is plucked with a plectrum; like the Spanish and classical guitars; tortoise shell or similar material is glued to the body near the soundholes to prevent damage to the wood. The 'ūd came to Spain during the Moorish occupation; its introduction paved the way for the development of the European lute, vihuela, and guitar; departed with the Moors during their expulsion. The modern instrument comes in various sizes, with a shorter neck than the lute, 4 to 6 double courses, and 3 soundholes. Historically it was played with the modern almond-shaped body higher than the pegbox; can be played with the body resting in the player's lap.

uguale (It., even). Equal, alike, similar. *Ugualmente*, equally, similarly, evenly; smoothly, tranquilly.

ukulele (Hawaiian, flea; U.K., ukelele). Popular smaller guitarlike instrument with 4 strings. The instrument was originally imported by Portuguese sailors into Hawaii in the 1870s; it found its way to the continental U.S. in the early 20th century. It proved very popular, in part because the use of tablature allowed players to learn quickly without the ability to read music. Popular music of all kinds used the instrument, and it could be heard in vaudeville, musicals, and films. Its popularity died out after World War II, but it could be heard in unusual settings, e.g., as the accompanying instrument to the unusual vocal stylings of Tiny Tim (Herbert Khaury), who revived an endless number of Tin Pan Alley songs.

Ullmann, Viktor, b. Teschen, Jan. 1, 1898; d. at the Nazi concentration camp in Auschwitz (Oświęcim), Oct. 17, 1944. He studied composition with Schoenberg in Vienna (*c.* 1918–21) and quarter-tone composition at the Prague Cons. (1935–37); was an accompanist and conductor at the New German Theater in Prague. He wrote expressionistic music without renouncing latent tonality. He was arrested by the Nazis (1942) and sent to the concentration camp in Theresienstadt (Terezín), where he composed a 1-act opera, *Der Kaiser von Atlantis*, depicting a tyrannical monarch who outlaws death but later begs for its return, to relieve humanity from life's horrors; the MS survived, and the work was performed for the 1st time in Amsterdam (1975).

Of the many Theresienstadt composers, Ullmann was the most prolific, composing 3 piano sonatas, a string quartet, songs, and choruses. He was part of the Nazi plan to present a "model camp" to the International Red Cross; it flourished under false pretenses for a few years until the Nazis decided to end the charade and make way for new prisoners. They took the Terezín prisoners to Auschwitz, one of the Nazi death factories; unless Dr. Joseph Mengele (the "angel of death") chose someone as a laborer or scientific guinea pig, he or she was sent immediately to the gas chambers. Other composers who perished at Auschwitz in Oct. 1944 were Pavel Haas (b. Brno, 1899; student of Janáček); Hans Krása (b. Prague, 1899; composer of the children's opera *Brundibár*, performed 55 times at Terezí); and Zikmund Schul (b. Kassel, 1916, a student of Hába); another active composer, Gideon Klein (b. Přerov, 1919) wrote chamber and vocal music at Auschwitz; he died at Fürtengrube in late January, 1945.

ultramodern music. In the early 1920s it became evident to composers using advanced techniques that the term *modern music* was no longer sufficient to describe new trends; seeking greater emphasis, they chose the term *ultramodern music*—music beyond the limits of "traditional" modernism. In announcing the publication of the *New Music Quarterly* (1927), Cowell, its founder and editor, declared that only works in the ultramodern idiom would be acceptable for publication; some decades later it became apparent that ultramodern music had begun to show unmistakable signs of obsolescence. Still, certain attributes of ultramodern music have retained their validity: dissonant counterpoint, atonal melodic designs, polymetric and polyrhythmic combinations, and novel instrumental sonorities.

Um Kalthoum (Oum Kolsoum), (born Fatma el-Zahraa Ibrahim) b. Tamay az-Zahirah, 1898; d. Cairo, Feb. 3, 1975. During a career of more than 50 years, she was probably the most famous singer in the Arab world, particularly renowned for her renditions of nationalistic, religious, and sentimental songs; was dubbed the "Star of the East" and the "Nightingale of the Nile." Her influence was such that political figures such as King Farouk and Gamaliel Nasser courted her favor. Her death precipitated widespread mourning in Egypt and other Arab countries.

umano, -a (It.). Human. *Voce umana* (Lat. *vox humana*), organ stop.

umore, con (It.). Humorously.

un, -e (Fr.). One; a(n). *Un peu,* a little; *un peu animé,* a little animated; *un peu plus lent,* a little slower.

un, -o, -a (It.). One; a(n). *Un poco,* a little; *un pochettino,* a little bit; *un poco meno,* a little less; *un poco più lento,* a little more slowly.

una certa espressione parlante, con (It.). With a certain speechlike expression.

una corda (It., 1 string; abbrev. *U.C.*). Instruction directing the player to use the soft pedal; this shifts the entire keyboard slightly to the right so that the hammers strike only 1 string instead of 2, or 2 instead of 3. When a return to full sonority is desired, the indication is *tre corde* (3 strings; *T.C.*). Beethoven was the 1st to use these terms systematically in his piano works.

unbestimmte Tonhöhe (Ger.). Indeterminate pitch; improvisatory notation found in avant-garde music.

und (Ger.). And.

unda maris (Lat., wave of the sea). In the organ, 8′ flue stop pitched a trifle lower than the surrounding foundation stops; the interference of its tones with the foundation tones produces acoustic beats and a wavy, undulatory tonal effect.

undecima (Lat.). Interval of the 11th.

undecuplet. Group of 11 equal notes to be performed in the time of 8 (or 6) notes of like value in the established meter.

undulazione (It.). On bowed string instruments, vibrato.

unequal temperament. See ⇒temperament.

unequal voices. Voices different in compass and quality; mixed voices.

unequivocacy. Absence of chance occurrences; musical structure with a high degree of determinacy, precluding interchangeability of component parts (such as found in Stockhausen's *Klavierstücke*). Such a goal pervades the late Romantic scores of Mahler and the modernist creations of Nancarrow; it is behind traditionally notated works by George Perle. Ultimately the aim of unequivocacy is to produce as closely as possible an exact repetition of a composer's concept for a work; hence the invention of electronic music.

ungebändigt (Ger.). Irresistibly. *Ungeduldig,* impatiently; *ungefähr,* approximately; *ungestüm,* impetuously.

ungebunden (Ger.). Unconstrained. *Mit ungebundenem Humor,* with unconstrained humor; *burlando.*

ungherese (It.). Hungarian.

ungleicher Kontrapunkt (Ger., unequal counterpoint). Fifth species counterpoint, where notes may be of different durations rather than being limited to 1 or 2 durations, as in species 1–4.

unhappy ending. Informal designation of a dramatic work with 1 or more of the central characters dying violently or wasting away; opposite of lieto fine.

unison (prime; from Lat. *uni + son,* 1 sound). 1. Tone of identical pitch as a given tone; also, higher or lower octave of that tone. The alternative term, "prime," is no more misleading than "unison" to represent a noninterval (i.e., zero). Since the 1st note of a scale or interval is counted as 1, it follows that the "zero note" or interval does not exist, just as there is no "zero harmonic." 2. Performing the identical pitches on a polyphonic instrument, with 2 or more voices or monophonic instruments, or a mixture; often applied to playing octaves or even double octaves. 3. In the piano, a group of 2 or 3 strings tuned to the same pitch and struck by 1 hammer; a string within such a group is a *unison string.*

unisono (It.). Unison. *All' unisono,* progressing in unison (or octaves) with one another.

unitamente (*unito,* -a; It.). Unified, together, joined.

uniti (It.). Orch'l indication, after a *divisi* section, that instruments or voices should again perform their part(s) in unison.

universal harmony. Harmony of the spheres.

unpremeditated music. Strictly speaking, no piece of music can be composed with an absolute lack of premeditation. Great improvisers of the past always had a proleptic image, in definite sounds, of what they were to play. However, the composers of aleatory music in the 2nd half of the 20th century have made serious attempts to create music without a shadow of melody aforethought, or harmony prepense.

unruhig (Ger.). Restlessly, excitedly.

unten (*unter;* Ger.). Under, below, beneath.

Unterhaltungsmusik (Ger., conversation music). Broad category embracing compositions designed to please, entertain, and/or provide background for other activities, rather than to impress and impose; examples are 19th-century salon music written for amateur performance; music to dine by; light dance music.

Unterstimme (Ger., voice below). Lower voice, in performance or part-writing.

unvocal. 1. Not suitable for singing. 2. Not vibrating with tone. *Unvocal air,* breath escaping with a more or less audible sigh or hiss, due to poor management of the voice.

upbeat (Ger. *Auftakt*). 1. raising of the hand in beating time. 2. last part of a measure, specifically just before the downbeat.

up-bow. Stroke of the string instrument bow in the direction from point to nut; the *up-bow mark* is ∨ or ∧ .

upright piano. Instrument with its strings arranged crosswise (diagonally) along a vertical rectangular soundboard, as opposed to the grand piano, where the strings and soundboard are horizontal; the upright's hammers are made to recoil by a spring. The upright became popular in the 19th century, partly for economy of space and partly because of the proliferation of amateur pianism in middle-class society in Europe and the U.S.

Upshaw, Dawn, b. Nashville, Tenn., July 17, 1960. She studied at Ill. Wesleyan Univ. (B.A., 1982); pursued vocal training with E. Faull at the Manhattan School of Music in N.Y. (M.A., 1984); attended courses given by DeGaetani at the Aspen (Colo.) Music School. She won the Young Concert Artists auditions (1984); entered the Metropolitan Opera's young artists development program; cowinner of the Naumburg Competition in N.Y. (1985). After appearing in minor roles at the Metropolitan Opera in N.Y., she displayed her vocal gifts in roles as Donizetti's Adina and Mozart's Despina (1988); pursued a notably successful career as a soloist with major orchs. and recitalist. Her remarkable concert repertoire ranges from early music to the most intimidating of avant-garde scores; has added American popular song to her repertoire.

Uraufführung (Ger.). World premiere; 1st performance.

urbanism. Music of the modern city, deriving inspiration from urban phenomena, governed by the technological cult; it comprises the cinema, traffic, newspapers, and magazines; interurban machines (locomotives, airplanes) also enter the concept of urbanism. One of the most durable musical manifestations of urbanism is Honegger's sym. movement *Pacific 231,* glorifying the locomotive; L. Russolo's suite for noise instruments, *Convegno d'automobili e d'aeroplani* (1913–14), was the 1st work referring to airplanes in its title; American composer Emerson Whithorne wrote *The Aeroplane* for Orch. (1920). Sports (prize fights, football, rugby) attracted composers by their new urbanist Romanticism.

Machine music received its greatest expansion in the 1920s; typical were the operas *Jonny Spielt Auf* by Krenek and *Machinist Hopkins* by Max Brand (1896–1980) and the Brecht cantata *Der Lindberghflug* cocomposed by Weill and Hindemith. In Russia musical urbanism coalesced with the development of proletarian music; the machine was the hero of mass production; and celebrated in the *The Iron Foundry* by Mosolov; Prokofiev's ballet *Le Pas d'acier* (1927) presents life in a Soviet factory. The ostentatious realism of urbanist music fell out of fashion after World War II, but as late as 1964 Copland wrote a sym. suite, *Music for a Great City,* descriptive of the sounds of N.Y.

Urlinie (Ger., original line). Schenkerian term for the imbedded structural melodic descent in tonal music, usually involving 3 steps, 5 steps, or, on rare occasions, a full octave. Sometimes this motion is *interrupted*, e.g, the Urline frequently associated with sonata-form movements in major: 5–4–3–2 (1st and 2nd theme groups; end exposition; interruption; development)–3–(return to tonic; recapitulation)–2–1 (completion of Urlinie; tonal coda may follow).

Exposition   Recapitulation

Development (Interruption)

Ursatz (Ger., original movement). In Schenkerian analysis, the contrapuntal background structure of a tonal piece; combines the melodic Urline and the I–V–I *arpeggiation* in the bass line; such a structure can theoretically be found in all tonal music.

Urtext (Ger., original text). Ideally, a score presenting the most "authentic" version of a musical work; the concept emerged in the early 20th century, among German scholars reacting against the freestyle approach to editing that prevailed in the 19th century; an Urtext attempts to present the original MS as set down on paper by the composer.

Before Urtexts, editors treated the classics rather willfully, cavalierly altering notes and harmonies; Bach was the favorite object of their unwelcome solicitude. The most notorious case was the editorial adding of a bar to furnish a chromatic transition in the C-Major Prelude from *The Well-Tempered Clavier* I; this bowdlerization was taken up by others, with the result that Bach's orig. version had to be "rediscovered." Editions of Beethoven's piano sonatas by von Bülow and others handled the Urtext with little respect. On the other hand, overly worshipful editors did not dare to correct even the most obvious of errors; surely Beethoven's omission of an essential E natural in the transitional chordal passage at the end of the *Appassionata* should not be considered sacrosanct, although it is quite proper to publish a facsimile *à titre documentaire*.

In modern works, an editor can never be sure whether apparent errors were not intentional. One copyist tried to "correct" some notes in a manuscript of Ives, who responded in the margin: "Do not correct; the wrong notes are right." However, when a respectful copyist questioned a misplaced accidental in the proofs of a Rimsky-Korsakov work, the great Russian master retorted on the margin: "Of course it is an error. I am not some person like Debussy or Richard Strauss to write wrong notes deliberately." But what if the composer changes his own Urtext? The editor must decide whether to honor the composer's initial Urtext or to accept his or her later revisions, not to mention the problems with the ever-insecure Bruckner.

Ussachevsky, Vladimir (Alexis), b. Hailar, Manchuria, Nov. 3, 1911; d. N.Y., Jan. 2, 1990. His father was a Russian army officer, his mother a professional pianist. Vladimir settled in Calif. (1930), took private piano lessons with C. Mader; attended Pasadena Junior College (1931–33); received a scholarship to study at Pomona College (B.A., 1935). He enrolled in the Eastman School of Music in Rochester, N.Y.; studied composition with Hanson, B. Rogers, and E. Royce in composition (M.M., 1936; Ph.D., 1939); also studied with B. Phillips. After serving in the U.S. Army, Ussachevsky pursued postdoctoral work with Luening at Columbia Univ.; joined its faculty (1947); prof. of music (1964–80); spent several years as composer-in-residence at the Univ. of Utah (from 1970); joined the faculty (1980–85).

Ussachevsky early works were influenced by Russian church music *à la* Tchaikovsky and Rachmaninoff; a major shift in his composition career occurred when he became interested in electronic music resources (1951); composed the electronic works *Transposition, Reverberation, Experiment, Composition,* and *Underwater Valse.* Stokowski conducted the 1st performance of Ussachevsky's *Sonic Contours* (N.Y., 1952), in which a piano part was metamorphosed with the aid of sonorific devices superimposed on each other; began a fruitful partnership with Luening; they composed *Incantation* for Tape Recorder (1953).

Luening and Ussachevsky conceived the idea of combining electronic tape sounds with conventional instruments played by human musicians; the 1st result was *Rhapsodic Variations,* premiered in N.Y. (1954), anticipating by a few months the important *Desèrts* by Varèse, effectively combining electronic sound with instruments. Their next work was *A Poem in Cycles and Bells* for Tape Recorder and Orch., 1st performed by the Los Angeles Phil. (1954). They provided taped background for *King Lear,* produced by Orson Welles, at the N.Y. City Center (1956), and for Margaret Webster's production of *Back to Methuselah* for the N.Y. Theater Guild (1958). Bernstein conducted the N.Y. Phil. in a commissioned work by Ussachevsky and Luening, *Concerted Piece* for Tape Recorder and Orch. (1960); they provided the electronic score for the documentary *The Incredible Voyage* (1965). Works written by Ussachevsky alone were *A Piece* for Tape Recorder (1956) and *Studies in Sound, Plus* (1959).

Ussachevsky was a co-founder of the Columbia-Princeton Electronic Music Center (1959); lectured at exhibitions of electronic sounds; traveled to Russia and China to present his music; held 2 Guggenheim fellowships (1957, 1960). He began experimenting with a computer-assisted synthesizer (1968); one work resulting from these experiments was *Conflict* (1971), intended to represent the mystical struggle between 2 ancient deities. He was elected to membership in the National Inst. of Arts and Letters (1973). He composed several works for tape and acoustic instruments and/or voice, including *3 Scenes from Creation: Prologue "Enumu Elish"* for 2 Choruses and Tape; *Interlude* for Soprano, Mezzo-Soprano, and Tape (both 1960), *Epilogue "Spell of Creation"* for Soprano and Chorus (1971); *Colloquy* for Solo Instruments, Orch., and Tape (1976); *Celebration 1981* for Electronic Valve Instrument, 6 Winds, Strings, and Tape; *Dialogues and Contrasts* for Brass Quintet and Tape (1984). Incidental tape music and/or effects: *To Catch a Thief* (film; 1954); *The Boy who Saw Through* (film; 1959); *No Exit* (film; 1962); *Mourning Becomes Electra* (effects for M. D. Levy's opera, 1967); chamber music. Vocal: *Jubilee Cantata* for Baritone, Reader, Chorus, and Orch. (1937–38); Psalm XXIV for Chorus and Organ, Organ and 5 Brass, or 7 Brass (1948); *2 Autumn Songs* after Rilke for Soprano and Piano (1952); Missa Brevis for Soprano, Chorus, and Brass (1972).

Ut. 1. 1st solmization syllable; opening syllable of the hymn *Ut queant laxis* (That they might be relaxed), assigned by Guido d'Arezzo to the tonic of the mode. Because *Ut* lacks a vowel at the end and is difficult to sing, it was changed to *Do(h)*, except in France. *Ut* is the only monosyllable in the hymn that constitutes an entire word; the rest of the lines are initial vocables of polysyllabic words. 2. Name of the note C in France. *Ut majeur,* C major; *Ut mineur,* C minor.

v. Abbrev. for vide, violino, volti, voce; *Vv.*, violini.

va (It.). Go on, continue. *Va crescendo,* continue increasing (in loudness).

vacillando (It., vacillating). Play in a wavering, hesitating style.

vagans (from Lat. *vagari,* wander). 5th part (*quinta pars*) or voice added to the standard 4-part texture of Renaissance sacred vocal music; as the name indicates, there was no set range for this part.

vaganti (from Lat. *vagari,* wander). Medieval univ. students who roamed freely from school to school, their name is a cognate of "vagabond." Even though they lived outside established society, the vaganti were divided into superior and inferior strata; the highest belonged to the *clericus,* an educated class, the lowest to the nondescript *goliard* group. A distinctive characteristic of the vaganti was their dedication to poetry and music; not constrained by ecclesiastical strictures, they indulged their fancy in songs glorifying the delight of the senses, drink, and secular games; the famous student song *Gaudeamus igitur,* still heard in European univs., expresses this joy of living with the phrase, "Meum est propositum in taberna mori" (it is fated that I should die in a tavern). The most remarkable collection of vaganti songs is the *Carmina Burana,* discovered in the monastery Benediktbeuren (Bura Sancti Benedicti) in Bavaria (1803); many of its texts were popularized in an eponymous oratorio by Orff (1937).

vaghezza, con (It.). With charm.

vago (It.). Vague, dreamy.

Vallee, Rudy (born Hubert Prior Vallée), b. Island Pond, Vt., July 28, 1901; d. Los Angeles, July 3, 1986. He studied clarinet and saxophone; his admiration for the saxophonist Rudy Wiedoeft prompted him to adopt Rudy as his 1st name. He studied at the Univ. of Maine and Yale Univ. (B.A., 1927); performed in nightclubs and vaudeville; gained fame when his band was engaged at N.Y.'s Heigh-Ho Club (1928). He was famous for his nasal-crooned style. The popular *My Time Is Your Time* became his theme song; also struck a responsive chord with *The Whiffenpoof Song* and *I'm Just a Vagabond Lover.* He was one of the leading performers on radio (1929–39); starred in his own variety show; appeared in many forgettable films. He made a remarkable comeback when he starred in the hit Broadway

musical *How to Succeed in Business Without Really Trying* (1961; also appeared in its film version, 1967). He tried unsuccessfully to persuade municipal authorities to name the street on which he lived after him.

valse (Fr.). Waltz. *Valse à deux temps,* a 2-step waltz, in 3/4 time, at a slightly faster tempo; *valse chantée,* sung waltz; *valse de salon,* a salon piano piece in waltz time.

Valse Boston. Hesitation waltz. See also ⇒waltz.

valtorna (Rus.; from Ger. *Waldhorn,* natural horn). French horn.

value. Time duration of a note or rest, as compared with (a) other notes in the same movement, or (b) a standard whole note or any fractional note.

valve. In brass wind instruments, device for diverting the air current from the main tube into an additional side tube, lengthening the air column and therefore lowering the fundamental pitch of the instrument; came into use *c.* 1815. Before that time, trumpets, horns, and other brass could play only natural (harmonic) tones above a single fundamental; in the orch'l scores of Classic works, trumpet and horns parts—using a variety of pitches—compelled the player to switch between instruments in different keys or insert extra tubing (crook) manually to change the air column. Modern instruments obviate this laborious procedure with the aid of 3 or more valves to change the pitch; as a result, a full chromatic scale is possible. Since tubes cannot be made proportionate in the precise mathematical relation required, some chromatic tones have to be rectified by combining several valves or adding special devices; valves may be operated with piston or rotary mechanisms.

valve bugle. Saxhorn.

valve horn. Natural horn with valves added; developed in the 19th century. See also ⇒horn.

valzer (It.). Waltz.

vamp. In popular music and jazz, improvised introduction or accompaniment usually consisting of a succession of chords against an ostinato figure in the bass, to set the rhythmic pace for the song or instrumental piece.

Van Beinum, Eduard. See ⇒Beinum, Eduard van.

Varèse, Edgard (Edgar) (Victor Achille Charles), b. Paris, Dec. 22, 1883; d. N.Y., Nov. 6, 1965. In Turin he took private composition lessons with G. Bolzoni (1892), played percussion in the school orch; went to Paris (1903); entered the Schola Cantorum (1904); studied composition, counterpoint, and fugue with Roussel, early music with C. Bordes, and conducting with d'Indy; entered Widor's composition class at the Cons. (1905). He received the *bourse artistique* offered by the City of Paris (1907); founded and conducted the chorus of the Univ. Populaire and organized concerts at the Château du Peuple; associated with musicians and artists of the avant-garde; including Debussy, who showed interest in his career; together they went to Berlin, then the center of new music.

Romain Rolland gave Varèse a letter of recommendation for R. Strauss, who not only showed interest in his music and but was instrumental in arranging a performance of his sym. poem

Bourgogne in Berlin (1910). But his greatest experience there was his meeting and friendship with Busoni; he greatly admired the book *Entwurf einer neuen Aesthetik der Tonkunst* (1907), and was profoundly influenced by Busoni's views. Varèse composed industriously, mostly for orch.; the most ambitious was a sym. poem, *Gargantua*, but it was never completed; other works were *Souvenirs, Prelude à la fin d'un jour, Cycles du Nord,* and an incomplete opera, *Oedipus und die Sphinx,* to a Hofmannsthal text; all these works, in MS, were lost under somewhat mysterious circumstances; he destroyed the score of *Bourgogne* later in life. The hostile reception that he encountered from Berlin critics for *Bourgogne* upset him; expressed his unhappiness in a letter to Debussy, who responded with a friendly letter of encouragement, advising him not to pay too much attention to critics.

As early as 1913 Varèse began an earnest quest for new musical resources; upon returning to Paris he worked on related problems with the Italian futurist L. Russolo, although he disapproved of the Italian's choice of instrumental noises for a medium. After dismissal from the French army for health reasons, he emigrated to N.Y. (1915).

As in Europe, Varèse had chronic financial difficulties in America; the royalties from his few publ. works were minimal; he accepted a job as a piano salesman, repulsive to him; appeared in a minor role in a John Barrymore silent film (1918). Some welcome aid came from the wealthy artist Gertrude Vanderbilt, who sent him monthly allowances for a certain length of time. He also had the opportunity to conduct, since American ensembles sought to replace their German music directors as the U.S. neared entrance into the war; there was a particular demand for French conductors. He led the Berlioz Requiem in N.Y. (1917); conducted the Cincinnati Sym. Orch. in a program of French and Russian music (1918); by including an excerpt from *Lohengrin,* he defied the tacit wartime ban on German music; but he apparently lacked that indefinable quality that makes a conductor; forced to cancel further concerts with the orch.

Eager to promote the cause of modern music, Varèse organized a sym. orch. in N.Y. to give performances of new and unusual music; it presented its 1st concert in 1919; with Salzedo, organized the International Composers' Guild, giving its inaugural concert in N.Y. (1922); in association with a few progressive musicians, cofounded the Pan American Soc., dedicated to the promotion of music of the Americas (1926); became a naturalized U.S. citizen that year. He intensified his study of the nature of sound, working with the acoustician H. Fletcher (1926–36) and the Russian electrical engineer Theremin, then living in the U.S. These studies led him to the formulation of the concept of organized sound, in which sonorous elements by themselves determined the progress of composition; this process eliminated conventional thematic development; yet the firm cohesion of musical ideas made his music all the more solid; the distinction between consonance and dissonance became irrelevant; the results were unique in modern music.

Characteristically, Varèse borrowed titles from the field of mathematics or physics: *Intégrales, Hyperprism* (projection of a prism into the 4th dimension), *Ionisation, Density 21.5* for Solo Flute, commissioned by Georges Barrère (1876–1944) and named for the atomic weight of platinum; his large orch'l work *Arcana* derived its inspiration from the cosmology of Paracelsus.

An important development was his application of electronic music in *Déserts* and, much more extensively, the *Poème électronique,* commissioned for the 1958 Brussels World Exposition. The unfamiliarity of his idiom and tremendous difficulty of his orch'l works militated against frequent performances; only Stokowski was bold enough to put the formidable *Amériques* and *Arcana* on Philadelphia Orch. programs; they evoked yelps of derision and outbursts of righteous indignation from the public and press; ironically it was the author, a mere beginner, who was the 1st to perform and record *Ionisation* for percussion ensemble.

An extraordinary reversal of attitudes towards Varèse's music took place late in his life, resulting in a spectacular increase of interest in and the number of performances of his works; musicians learned to overcome the rhythmic difficulties presented in the scores. He thus lived to see his name joining those of Stravinsky, Ives, Schoenberg, and Webern among the great masters of 20th-century music. Like Schoenberg, he refused to regard himself as a musical revolutionary; professed great admiration for remote predecessors, particularly the Notre Dame school. Recognition came also from an unexpected field when scientists working on the atom bomb at Oak Ridge played a recording of *Ionisation* for relaxation and stimulation in their work (1940). He was elected to the National Inst. of Arts and Letters (1955) and the Royal Swedish Academy (1962). Frank Zappa, a leader of the modern school of rock and a longtime admirer of his music, staged at his own expense a N.Y. concert of Varèse's works (1981) and a similar concert in San Francisco (1982).

variable meter. Systematic oscillation of changing meters in consecutive measures; metrical system introduced by Blacher in his piano work *Ornamente* (1950). The device is deceptively simple: the 1st measure has 2 8th notes, the 2nd measure has 3 8th notes, etc., following the ascending arithmetical progression, then reversing the process to follow a descending progression. Other German composers adopted Blacher's variable meters, among them K. A. Hartmann in his concerto for piano, wind instruments, and percussion, and Henze in one of his string quartets.

variamente (It.). Variously, differently. *Variant* (Fr. *variante*), variant; different (optional) reading; ossia.

variation. One of a set or series of transformations of a theme by means of harmonic, rhythmic, and melodic changes and embellishments.

variazioni (It.). Variations.

varié (Fr.). Varied. *Air* or *thème varié,* theme and variations.

variety show. Theatrical entertainment encompassing all manner of popular presentations, from singing and dancing to magician acts, animal tricks, and comic skits; successor to vaudeville in that it became most popular on the radio and television after theatrical vaudeville had all but disappeared.

vaudeville. An umbrella term for several genres of French origin; all share a satirical, epigrammatic, or comic tone. 1. *Vau de Vire,* named after a city in Normandy; 15th-century rural song incorporating elements of daily life; 2. *Voix de ville* (city voices), 16th-century urban response to the previous genre, with more courtly lyrics and simple tunes; much of the music was akin to contemporaneous dance music; influenced the chanson. 3. *Vaudeville,* 17th-century simple strophic airs, continuing traditional concern with daily matters. The genre was very popular, the tunes so well known that there was no need to write them down. 4. *Comédie en vaudevilles,* theatrical genre in the late 17th and early 18th centuries; light, often parodic comedies alternating dialogue and pantomime with witty and satirical couplets, generally set to well-known popular airs; gradually gave way to the newly composed *opéra-comique.* 5. The *vaudeville final* was an aspect of the comédie en vaudevilles borrowed by comic opera, German and Italian as well as French, in which all characters of a work came onstage at the end, restored order to the proceedings, expressed their feelings, and gave a moral. Composers as early as J.-J. Rosseau and as recent as Stravinsky have used the form. 6. The 19th-century *musical comedy* (distinct from opéra-comique) evolved increasingly in the direction of a variety show, whether Continental vaudeville, English music hall, or American vaudeville and variety show.

Vaughan, Sarah (Lois), b. Newark, N.J., Mar. 27, 1924; d. Los Angeles, Apr. 3, 1990. She began music studies as a child; won an amateur singing contest at Harlem's Apollo Theater in N.Y. (1942); joined the Earl Hines band as singer and pianist; then played and sang with the bands of Billy Eckstine (1944–45) and John Kirby (1945–46). She subsequently pursued a successful solo career as a jazz and pop singer, appearing on radio, television, and recordings; a versatile musician, she also appeared as a soloist with sym. orchs.

Vaughan Williams, Ralph, b. Down Ampney, Gloucestershire, Oct. 12, 1872; d. London, Aug. 26, 1958. He began to study piano and violin in Leith Hill Place, Surrey; entered Charterhouse School in London (1887); played violin and viola in the school orch. He studied harmony with F. E. Gladstone, composition with Parry, and organ with Parratt at the Royal College of Music in London (1890–92); enrolled at Trinity College, Cambridge; took composition with C. Wood and organ with A. Gray (Mus.B., 1894; B.A., 1895); returned to the Royal College of Music, studying with Stanford; went to Berlin for further studies with Bruch (1897); took his Mus.D. at Cambridge (1901). Dissatisfied with his academic studies, he decided to seek advice from Ravel in Paris (1908) to acquire the technique of modern coloristic orchestration; became active as a collector of English folk songs; joined the Folk Song Soc. (1904); became conductor of the Leith Hill Festival in Dorking (1905), a position he held, off and on, until his old age.

In 1906 Vaughan Williams composed his 3 *Norfolk Rhapsodies,* introducing the techniques and manners of his national style; discarded the 2nd and 3rd works as unsatisfactory in reflecting the subject; began work on a choral sym. inspired by Whitman's poetry, entitled *A Sea Sym.* (Sym. No. 1, 1903–09); this was followed by the *Fantasia on a Theme of Thomas Tallis* for string quartet and double string orch. (1910); this brief but popular and beautiful work evokes the polyphonic style of the eponymous 16th-century English composer. He now engaged in a grandiose score, *A London Symphony* (Sym. No. 2, 1912–13), intended as a musical glorification of that city; despite its inclu-

sion of quotations of the street song *Sweet Lavender* and the Westminster chimes, Vaughan Williams emphatically denied that the score was representational, suggesting the alternative title "Symphony by a Londoner," finally insisting the work had to be judged as absolute music. Concurrently he wrote the ballad opera *Hugh the Drover* (1910–14), set in England in 1812 and reflecting the solitary struggle of the English against Napoléon.

At the outbreak of World War I Vaughan Williams enlisted in the British army and served in the artillery; after the Armistice he became a composition prof. at the Royal College of Music in London (1919–39); conducted the London Bach Choir (1920–28). He completed *A Pastoral Sym.* (Sym. No. 3, 1921), reflecting the contemplative aspect of his inspiration; there is a wordless vocal solo in the last movement. He visited the U.S., conducting *A Pastoral Sym.* at the Norfolk (Conn.) Festival (1922); awarded the Gold Medal of the Royal Phil. Soc. of London (1930), the year he wrote a masque, *Job,* based on Blake's *Illustrations of the Book of Job,* 1st performed in concert (1930) and on stage (London, 1931); returned to the U.S. to lecture at Bryn Mawr College (1932). received the Order of Merit from King George V. (1935). His 4th Sym. in F minor (1931–35) was premiered by the BBC Sym. Orch. in London (1935); it represents an extraordinary deviation from his accustomed style, as he experimented with dissonant harmonies in conflicting tonalities, bristling with angular rhythms; taken to task by astounded critics for such musical philandering.

Vaughan Williams next composed the opera *Sir John in Love,* after Shakespeare's *The Merry Wives of Windsor* (1924–28; London, 1929), once more borrowing English folk songs; dedicated his 5th Sym. in D Major (1938–43) to Sibelius as a token of his admiration; in the 6th Sym. in E minor (1944–47) he returned to the erstwhile serenity of his inspiration, but the sym. has turbulent moments and an episode of folksy dancing exhilaration. He changed direction again and wrote the challenging *Sinfonia antartica* (Sym. No. 7, 1949–52; Manchester, 1953), scored for Soprano, Women's Chorus, Large Orch., and Wind Machine; the work expanded upon his soundtrack for *Scott of the Antarctic* (1947–48), about the doomed 1912 expedition of Sir Robert Scott to the South Pole. Here the music is almost geographic in its representation of Antarctica, comparable in its realism with the *Alpine Sym.* of R. Strauss. In the epilogue to *Sinfonia antartica* he used quotations from Scott's last journal.

In the 8th Sym. in D minor (1953–56) Vaughan Williams once more returned to musical absolutism; the work is conceived as a neoclassical suite, but, faithful to the spirit of the times, he included vibraphone, xylophone, and the sempiternal gongs and bells. In his last sym. (Sym. No. 9 in E minor, 1956–58), he used a trio of saxophones, with a pointed caveat that they not behave "like demented cats" but rather remain their Romantic selves; the composer died shortly after its premiere.

The aesthetic and technical aspects of Vaughan Williams's style involves a distinctly modern treatment of harmonic writing, with massive agglomeration of chordal sonorities; parallel triadic progressions are especially favored. Rather than adopting a particular method of composition; he used a great variety of procedures integrated into a distinctively personal and thoroughly English style, nationalistic but not isolationist. He was particularly adept at exploring the modern ways of modal counterpoint, with tonality freely shifting between major and minor triadic entities; this procedure astutely evokes sweetly archaic usages in modern applications; thus he could combine the modalities of the Tudor era with the sparkling polytonalities of the modern age.

Vaughan Williams's stage works include operas *Riders to the Sea*, after the drama by John Millington Synge (1925–32; London, 1937); *The Poisoned Kiss* (1927–29, Cambridge, 1936); *The Pilgrim's Progress* (completed 1949; London, 1951); incidental and film music; vocal musica; *Songs of Travel* for Voice and Piano, after R. L. Stevenson (1904); *Toward the Unknown Region* for Chorus and Orch., after Whitman (1905–07); *On Wenlock Edge* for Tenor, Piano, and String Quartet ad libitum, after Housman's *A Shropshire Lad* (1909); *5 Mystical Songs* for Baritone, Chorus, and Orch. (1911); *Flos Campi* for Viola, Wordless Mixed Chorus, and Small Orch. (1925); *5 Tudor Portraits* for Mezzo-soprano, Baritone, Chorus, and Orch. (1936); *Dona Nobis Pacem* for Soprano, Baritone, Chorus and Orch. (1936); *Serenade to Music* for 16 Solo Voices and Orch. (1938); other English songs and folk stong arrangements; choral music, mostly Anglican; carols. Other orch'l and concertante works: *In the Fen Country* (1904); *The Lark Ascending* for Violin and Orch. (1914–20); *Concerto accademico* for Violin and Strings (1924–25); Piano Concerto (1926–31); *5 Variants of "Dives and Lazarus"* for String Orch. and Harp (1939); Oboe Concerto (1944); Tuba Concerto (1954); chamber music; piano and organ pieces. He ed. collections of religious songs, including the well-known *The Oxford Book of Carols* (with P. Dearmer and M. Shaw; 1928); wrote lectures and articles, reprinted in *National Music and Other Essays* (London, 1963); collected folk songs.

vectorialism. Specification of the angular value of the vector-radius from the center of the concert hall to musical instruments or electronic transmitters, so that each ingredient of a melodic or harmonic pattern receives its identifying index; vectorialism of sonic sources is an aspect of spatial distribution.

veemente (*veemenza*, con; It.). Vehemently, passionately.

veil. Somewhat obscured or covered vocal tone, rather than clear or bell-like.

velato, -a (It., veiled). Sonically covered, obscured, or dim.

veloce (*velocità, con;* It.). Rapidly, swiftly; indicates a passage to be performed faster than those before and after it; opposite of *ritenuto*. *Velocissimo*, very fast, with extreme rapidity.

velouté (Fr.; It. *vellutato*). Velvety; smoothly legato.

Velvet Underground. (Guitar/vocal/songwriter: Lou[is Alan] Reed, b. N.Y., Mar. 2, 1942; viola/bass/keyboards: John Cale, b. Garnant, South Wales, Dec. 3, 1940; guitar: Sterling Morrison, b. Aug. 29, 1942, East Meadow, Long Island; d. Poughkeepsie, N.Y., Aug. 30, 1995; drums: Maureen "Mo" Tucker, b. N.J., 1945; vocals: Nico, b. Christa Paffgen, Cologne, Germany, Oct. 16, 1939; d. Ibiza, Spain, July 18, 1988.) Rock group with a brief and relatively obscure existence (1965–70), with a profound influence on emerging and later rock styles (metal, punk, new wave, grunge). After graduating from Syracuse Univ., Reed read books, wrote poetry, essayed journalism, sang to

guitar accompaniment, and found his proper niche improvising with various psychedelically inclined groups. In 1966 he recruited Cale and formed the Velvet Underground, projecting bizarre stage behavior and playing sophisticated numbers in dissonant harmony. The group revived the dadaistic, surrealistic type of old European modernism, superadded with screeching, screaming, sadomasochistic electronic sound to Reed's demoralizing anarchistic lyrics openly describing the psychedelic aspects of narcotics (*Heroin*) and totally emancipated sex play (*Venus in Furs*). The group was initially produced by Andy Warhol as part of his N.Y. multimedia organization, the Factory, under the auspices of the Exploding Plastic Inevitable. The Velvets' aesthetic was closer to the earthy films of Paul Morrissey rather than Warhol's deadpan irony, and it did not take long before the group separated from Warhol; it produced a total of 4 albums before its demise.

Among the less visible but no less influential members of the group was Nico, a German-Hungarian model, actress, and singer; Warhol convinced the group to take her on; contributed husky contralto vocals to their 1st album and tour; then recorded several solo albums, some produced by Cale. Angus MacLise was a percussionist who joined and left early in the group's history; Tucker replaced MacLise and remained with the group until 1969; has produced solo albums since then. Morrison was the only member to remain with the group throughout its history; ironically, also the only one to quit music entirely (for an academic career); and the Yule Brothers—Doug, a bassist and guitarist who replaced Cale in 1968, and Billy, who replaced Tucker in 1969.

Two Velvets had important careers after leaving the band: Cale, vocalist, composer, instrumentalist, and producer, was a classically educated musician who had worked with Copland and La Monte Young. He brought a modernist element to a quintessentially dark rock style for the 1st two albums. Upon leaving the group his experimentation continued with *Vintage Violence* (1969), and collaborations with Terry Riley (*The Church of Anthrax*, 1971), Legs Larry Smith (*The Academy in Peril*, 1972) and Brian Eno (*Wrong Way Up*, 1990); other albums include *Paris 1919* (1973), *Fear* (1974), *Helen of Troy* (1975), *Honi Soit* (1981), and *Caribbean Sunset* (1984); as a producer, he was an enigmatic but major influence on punk and proto-punk.

Reed left the group shortly before its demise; began exploring different sides of his musical personality: the accessible hard rock and balladry of *Transformer* (1972, with his hit *Walk on the Wild Side*, a satire on life at the Factory), *Rock 'n' Roll Animal* (1974), *Coney Island Baby* (1976), *Blue Mask* (1981), *New Sensations* (1984), and *Magic and Loss* (1992); 2 brilliant concept albums, the harrowing *Berlin* (1973) and the streetwise *New York* (1989); and an unadulteratedly anarchistic display of white noise, *Metal Machine Music* (1975). Reed and Cale reunited 20 years after the end of their first partnership to compose and perform *Songs for Drella*, in memory of Warhol (1989); joined with Morrison and Tucker for a European reunion tour (1993).

Venetian school. Compositional style associated with that Italian city during the 16th century, with the participation of several important organists from northern Europe, especially the Low Countries; the Venetian school was centered in the cathedral of Saint Mark's (San Marco), with its magnificent architectural plan of symmetric enclaves making it ideal for the performance of antiphonal choral works of a stereophonic quality. The 1st acknowledged master presiding over the main organ at San Marco was Adrian Willaert (c. 1490–1562), from the Bruges region, appointed maestro di capella (1527); instructed aft of chromatic modulation to the great Italian madrigalist A. Gabrieli, who in turn taught his nephew G. Gabrieli to adapt choral techniques to instrumental ensembles, especially in the contrasting alternation of massive sonorities, thereby popularizing the early Baroque echo effect. Subsequent great organists at Saint Mark's included Claudio Merulo (1533–1604) and Zarlino; it was once believed that Sweelinck had gone to Venice and helped create the Venetian school, but this has been refuted by documentary evidence. The Venetian style of composition, orchestration, and choral treatment exercised a profound influence on German composers, among them Hieronymous Praetorius, Michael Praetorius, and Hans Leo Hassler; it had the equivalent power of influence over Baroque instrumental and choral music that t he Florentine *dramma per musica* had on the development of opera.

vent (Fr.). Wind. *Instruments à vent*, wind instruments.

Ventil (Ger.). Piston valve. *Ventilhorn*, horn with piston valves; *Ventilkornet*, cornet with piston valves. *Ventilposaune*, trombone with piston valves.

venusto (It.). Graceful, elegant.

Venuti, Joe (Giuseppe), b. Lecco, Apr. 4, 1898; d. Seattle, Aug. 14, 1978. Emigrating with his family to Philadelphia, he received a thorough classical violin training, but after meeting jazz guitarist Eddie Lang he turned to popular music; after playing with Whiteman he formed his own band (1935–43); went to the West Coast to become a studio musician in Hollywood. His greatest accomplishment was to help make the hitherto suspect jazz violin a more than respectable instrument.

Veränderung (Ger.). Variation; used by Beethoven.

verbalization. Stockhausen was probably the 1st to introduce the concept of verbalization in lieu of musical notation; one of his pieces represents a parabolic curve with the following inscription: "Sound a note. Continue sounding it as long as you please. It is your prerogative." Cage has elevated verbalization to the degree of eloquent diction; Earle Brown and Feldman are inventive verbalizationists; La Monte Young tells the player, "Push the piano to the wall. Push it through the wall. Keep pushing"; Nam June Paik dictates, "Cut your left arm very slowly with a razor (more than 10 centimeters)"; Philip Corner limits himself to a simple command: "One antipersonnel type CBU (Cluster Bomb Unit) will be thrown into the audience."

verbotene Fortschreitungen (Ger.). Forbidden progressions in harmony or melody.

verbunkos (Hung.; from Ger. *Werbung*, recruiting). Hungarian recruiting dance, performed by hussars led by their sergeant, popular in the latter 18th and the 1st half of the 19th centuries (before conscription was imposed by the Austrians); consists of a slow section (*lassu*) and a fast section (*friss*); these

alternate as necessary. These musical elements are embodied in Liszt's *Hungarian Rhapsodies* and works ranging from those by Beethoven and Schubert to Kodály and Bartók.

Verdi, Giuseppe (Fortunino Francesco), b. Le Roncole, near Busseto, Duchy of Parma, Oct. 9, 1813; d. Milan, Jan. 27, 1901. Listening to street singers gave him an early appreciation of naturally produced music; a church organist, P. Baistrocchi, noticed his love of musical sound and taught him; when Baistrocchi died, Verdi, still a child, took over some of his keyboard duties. His father sent him to Busseto for further musical training; began academic studies and took lessons with F. Provesi, director of the municipal music school. At age 18 he became resident in the home of A. Barezzi, a local merchant and patron of music who supplied him with enough funds so that he could go to Milan for serious study; unexpectedly, he failed to pass an entrance examination to the Milan Cons.; its registrar, F. Basili, reported that Verdi's piano technique was inadequate and his composition lacking in technical knowledge. Verdi then turned to V. Lavigna for private lessons, working industriously to master counterpoint, canon, and fugue; applied to be maestro di musica in Busseto; passed his examination and received the desired appointment (1834).

In 1838 Verdi completed his 1st opera, *Oberto, conte di San Bonifacio;* moved to Milan and submitted the score of *Oberto* to the directorship of La Scala; it was accepted for a performance (1839), with satisfactory success; received a contract to write more operas for that theater. His comic opera *Un giorno di regno* was performed there (1840), but it did not please the public; began composition of an opera, *Nabucodonosor* (later abbreviated to *Nabucco*), on the biblical subject; was staged at La Scala, scoring considerable success (1842). Giuseppina Strepponi (b. Lodi, Sept. 8, 1815; d. Sant' Agata, near Busseto, Nov. 14, 1897), a prominent soprano, created the leading female role of Abigaille; although already in vocal decline, she became a great favorite of his. *Nabucco* was followed by another successful historical opera, *I Lombardi alla prima Crociata*, produced at La Scala (1843); next was *Ernani*, after Hugo's drama about a revolutionary outlaw; the subject suited the rise of Italian nationalism, and its production (Venice, 1844) won great acclaim. Not so popular were his succeeding operas, *I due Foscari* (1844), *Giovanna d'Arco* (1845), *Alzira* (1845), and *Attila* (1846). In 1847 he produced in Florence his 1st Shakespearean opera, *Macbeth;* that same year he was commissioned to write an opera for London, resulting in *I Masnadieri*, based on Schiller's drama *Die Räuber*, produced at Her Majesty's Theatre with Lind taking the leading female role.

A commission from Paris followed; Verdi rev. *I Lombardi alla prima Crociata* as *Jerusalem* (in French); was produced at the Paris Opéra (1847); the La Scala production followed (1850); like several operas by him and other Italian composers, the plot revolved around the device of mistaken identity. During his stay in Paris for the premiere of *Jerusalem* he renewed his acquaintance with Strepponi more permanently; after several years of cohabitation their union was legalized in a private ceremony in Savoy (1859). He produced *Il Corsaro*, after Byron's poem *The Corsair* (1848), followed by *La battaglia di Legnano*, celebrating the defeat of the armies of Barbarossa by the Lombards in 1176. Its premiere took place in Rome (1849), but he was forced to change names and places so as not to offend the central European powers that then dominated Italy. *Luisa Miller* (1849), after Schiller's *Kabale und Liebe*, and *Stiffelio* (1850) were not successful.

Verdi's 1st great triumph came with *Rigoletto*, after Hugo's *Le Roi s'amuse;* premiered at the Teatro La Fenice in Venice (1851), it brought him lasting fame; entered the repertory of every opera house. The aria of the libidinous Duke, *La donna e mobile,* became one of the most popular operatic tunes sung, or ground on the barrel organ, throughout Europe. This success was followed by even greater acclaim with the 1853 productions of *Il Trovatore* (Rome) and *La Traviata* (Venice); both captivated world audiences without diminution of their melodramatic effect, despite the absurdity of the action represented on the stage: *Il Trovatore* resorts to the device of unrecognized identities of close relatives, while *La Traviata* strains credulity when the eponymous soprano sings enchantingly and at length despite struggling with terminal consumption. Another Parisian commission resulted in his 1st truly French opera, *Les Vêpres siciliennes,* to a Scribe libretto for Donizetti's unfinished *Le Duc d'Albe;* the medieval action deals with the slaughter of the French occupation army in Sicily by local patriots; despite the offensiveness of the subject to French patriots, the opera was successfully given (1855). His next work, *Simone Boccanegra,* was produced at the Teatro La Fenice in Venice (1857), followed by *Un ballo in maschera* (Rome, 1859), based on the libretto written by Scribe for Auber's *Gustave III,* concerning the assassination of King Gustave III of Sweden (1792); but the censors did not allow showing regicide on stage, and the composer was compelled to transfer the opera geographically—and in the process creating the post of the governor of Boston!

Verdi obliquely became part of the political struggle for the independence of Italy. The symbol of the nationalists was the name of Vittorio Emanuele, future Italian king; demonstrators painted the name "Verdi" in capital letters, separated by punctuation, on fences and walls throughout Italy (V.E.R.D.I., initials of Vittorio Emanuele, Re D'Italia); thus the cry "Viva Verdi!" became a coded salute to the king-to-be. In 1861 the composer received a commission to write an opera for the Russian Imperial Opera; he selected the mystical subject *La forza del destino;* the premiere took place in St. Petersburg (1862), which he attended; then wrote another French opera *Don Carlos,* after Schiller's famous drama; was 1st heard at the Paris Opéra with numerous cuts (1867); these were not restored until a century had passed since the premiere. (Verdi wrote 3 versions in all, none of which contain all the music he wrote for the opera.)

In 1870 Verdi received a contract to write a new opera for Cairo, where *Rigoletto* had already been performed a year before; the advantageous terms guaranteed 150,000 francs for the Egyptian rights alone. *Aida* was set in ancient Egypt; the original French libretto was trans. by A. Ghislanzoni. The opera premiered on Christmas Eve, 1871, with great éclat; the composer stubbornly refused to join the caravan despite highly placed attempts at persuasion; nonetheless, the success of *Aida* exceeded all expectations; the production was hailed as a world event; the work itself became one of the most famous in opera lore. After Rossini's death (1868), Verdi conceived the idea of honoring his memory by a collectively composed Requiem, consisting of several Italian composers' contributing a movement apiece; he reserved the last section, *Libera me,* for himself;

completed the score (1869) but it was never performed in its original form. The death of the famous Italian poet Alessandro Manzoni (1873) led him to write his great *Messa da Requiem,* known simply as the *Manzoni Requiem,* into which he incorporated the section originally composed for Rossini's tribute. The Requiem received its premiere on the 1st anniversary of Manzoni's death, in Milan; there was criticism of the work's being too operatic for a religious work, but it has remained in musical annals as a masterpiece.

After a lapse of some 13 years of rural retirement, Verdi returned to Shakespeare; the result was *Otello;* the libretto was by Boito, master poet and composer who rendered Shakespeare's lines into Italian with extraordinary felicity; premiered at La Scala (1887). He was 79 years old when he wrote his last opera, the Shakespearean *Falstaff,* also to a Boito libretto, based on *The Merry Wives of Windsor* and the 2 parts of *Henry IV;* also premiered at La Scala (1893); the score reveals an unexpected genius for subtle comedy coupled with melodic invention of the highest order. His last composition was a group of sacred choruses, an Ave Maria, Laudi alla Vergine Maria, Stabat Mater, and Te Deum (publ. as *4 pezzi sacri,* 1898); in the Ave Maria, Verdi made use of the so-called scala enigmatica. Innumerable honors were bestowed upon him; membership in the Académie des Beaux Arts in Paris, filling the vacancy left by the death of Meyerbeer (1864); nominated as a senator to the Italian Parliament (1875); after the premiere of *Falstaff* the King of Italy wished to make him Marchese di Busseto, but he declined the honor. After the death of Strepponi (1897) he founded in Milan the Casa di Riposo per Musicisti, a home for aged musicians, and set aside funds for its maintenance; he died after an apoplectic attack.

Historic evaluation of Verdi's music has shifted several times since his death. At that time, the musical atmosphere was heavily Wagnerian; admiring Wagner meant insulting Verdi as a purveyor of "barrel-organ music." Then the winds of opinion reversed their direction; modern composers, music historians, and theoreticians discovered unexpected attractions in flowing melodies, smoothly modulating harmonies, and stimulating symmetric rhythms; a theory was even advanced that the appeal of Verdi's music lay in its adaptability to modernistic elaboration and contrapuntal variegations. Thus, by natural transvaluation of opposites, Wagnerianism went into eclipse; the slogan "Viva Verdi!" assumed, paradoxically, an aesthetic meaning. Ironically, Verdi's last operas reflected his application of certain Wagnerian techniques to a well-established Mediterranean palette, not without conservative criticism; but his genius for dramatic, lyric, and tragic stage music has made him a perennial favorite among opera enthusiasts.

Verfasser (Ger.). Author; editor. As a postscript to Bach's last unfinished fugue in *Die Kunst der Fuge,* his son C. P. E. wrote: "At this point *der Verfasser* died."

verges (Fr.). Slender drumsticks used to strike the suspended cymbals.

vergleichende Musikwissenschaft (Ger.). Comparative musicology.

vergnügt (Ger.). Cheerfully, entertainingly.

Vergrösserung (Ger.). Augmentation.

verhallend (Ger.). Dying away.

verhalten (Ger.). Restrained. *Mit verhaltenem Ausdruck,* with restrained expressivity.

verismo (from It. *vero,* true). Type of operatic naturalism, starting in Italy in the 1890s, exemplified by Mascagni's *Cavalleria Rusticana* and Leoncavallo's *Pagliacci;* the vogue spread into France with *Louise* by Gustave Charpentier. In Germany verismo assumed satirical and sociological rather than naturalistic forms (Weill, Krenek, Hindemith); in England, Britten's *Peter Grimes* is veristic in subject and execution. Verismo had no immediate followers in Russia, where nationalism preoccupied the interests of operatic composers; but the Soviet brand of socialist realism represented a verismo of the proletariat (Prokofiev, *A Tale about a Real Man*).

Verkleinerung (Ger.). Diminution.

Verlag (Ger.). Publishing house, company, or imprint.

verlöschend (Ger.). Dying away.

vermindert (Ger.). Diminished, as in an interval.

vers mesuré (Fr., measured verse). 16th-century French poetry where writers wrote lyrics following the rules of Greek and Latin prosody; its greatest exponent was Jean-Antoine de Baïf (1532–89). Musical adaptation was achieved by doubling the duration for long syllables, substituting for the tonal accent of speech. Orlando di Lasso, Claude Le Jeune (*c.* 1528–1600), and Jacques Mauduit (1557–1627) contributed to this genre (*musique mesurée*).

Verschiebung, mit (Ger.). Use soft pedal. *Ohne Verschiebung,* release soft pedal.

verschwindend (Ger.). Vanishing, dying away.

verse. 1. In Gregorian chant, scriptural portion for solo voice, introduced and concluded by a short choral passage. 2. Stanza, usually serving to open part of a popular song (followed by a refrain chorus or transitional bridge).

verse-anthem. One in which the verses (solos, duets, trios, quartets) predominate over the choruses. *Verse-service,* a choral service for solo voices.

verset. 1. Short verse, usually forming but one sentence with its response, for example:

Vers. O Lord, save Thy people,

Resp. And bless Thine inheritance.

2. Short organ prelude or interlude, replacing a Mass verse. Composers composed versets to take advantage of organ registration and the technical opportunities of polyphonic writing. This greatly extended practice led to increasing domination over proper congregational singing, alarming church authorities ever vigilant over the purity and simplicity of plainchant; the famous

papal declaration *Moto proprio* (1903) specifically warned against the spread of instrumental polyphony in church services.

Versetzung (Ger.). Transposition.

versicle. Exhortation intoned by the celebrant in Roman Catholic or Anglican canonical hours, sung in litany style with congregational or choral responses; best known is the Benedicamus Domino, used to close the service.

verstimmt (Ger.). Out of tune; out of humor, depressed.

vertatur (Lat.). Turn (the page) immediately.

vertical flute. Any end-blown flute (e.g., recorder, shakuhachi, tin whistle), as opposed to the transverse flute.

vertical piano. Upright piano.

Verwandlungsmotiv (Ger.). Transformational motive, illustrating a magical change from one state to another.

verweilend (Ger.). Delaying, holding back.

Verzierung (Ger.; Fr. *agréments;* It. *fioretti,* little flowers). Ornamentation. Numerous treatises have been published in all languages dealing with the proper interpretation and uniform decoding of the multitude of signs and symbols indicating these elaborations, but it is certain that complete scholarly agreement on agréments or the indisputable organization of ornamentation is beyond the realm of likelihood.

Vespers (from Lat. *vespera,* evening; Angl. *evensong*). Orig., the 7th canonical hour of the Divine Office of the Roman Catholic daily liturgy, now the 5th hour, celebrated at dusk, about 6:00 in the afternoon. Vespers is the most important service in the Office insofar as its applicability to composition goes; it includes a variety of chants, hymns, and a Magnificat. Secular structures were commonly admitted in the Vespers; this dispensation encouraged composers to set Vespers and Magnificats as independent works in a polyphonic style. Monteverdi wrote several Vespers; Mozart composed 2 Vespers for large ensembles.

vibraharp. Vibraphone.

vibraphone. Percussion instrument, introduced in America early in the 20th century; consists of suspended metal bars in a keyboard arrangement which, when struck with mallets, produce tones amplified by resonator tubes below the bars; a motor-driven propeller mechanism causes the vibrato that gives the instrument its name. Berg used it in *Lulu.*

vibraslap. A shaker manufactured *c.* 1970 to replace the Latin American *quijada del burro.* In the genuine jawbone the teeth rattle percussively when struck with the palm of the hand, or brushed with a stick, producing a dental glissando; its replacement is a wooden shell with small metal pieces inside.

vibrations. Periodic oscillations of a flexible sounding body, such as a string or air column, that produce definite pitches. The unit of vibration is a cycle, covering the fluctuation of an acoustic body, 1st to one side, then to the other, returning it to its original position; the frequency of such units per second (cycles per second, or cps, or Hz) determines the sounding tone. The human ear is capable of perceiving vibrations from about 16 cps to several thousand cps; the lowest A on the piano keyboard has 27 $1/2$ cps, the highest C on the keyboard 4,224 cps. The loudness of a tone depends on its amplitude, the width of the distance traveled by the sounding body from its initial (at rest) position to its most extreme departure from it; frequency (pitch) and amplitude (dynamic level) are independent of each other.

Vibrations are cumulative in their wave motion; unrelated objects can be set in motion by contact with *sympathetic vibrations* accrued in this manner; by trying to replicate the vibration pattern of the sound, the object is at risk. Suspension bridges, with their considerable flexibility, are notoriously vulnerable to accumulated sympathetic vibration; there are documented stories of bridges destroyed in this manner; soldiers are warned in army manuals not to maintain a steady rhythmic marching step when crossing such a bridge (another lesson learned from sad experience). Other flexible acoustical bodies will respond to a sympathetic tone by trying to resonate with it; objects such as candelabras, glass chimes, chandeliers, wall mirrors, and champagne glasses will break (viz a recording tape advertisement featuring Ella Fitzgerald). Caruso, part of the Metropolitan Opera touring company that was in San Francisco during its 1906 earthquake, exclaimed, "I knew that high B-flat would cause trouble." Taking a cue from the undisputed phenomenon of sympathetic vibration, mystics and cultists claim to be in touch with astral bodies with which they communicate through vibration; more colloquially, a mood or relationship is often described as having good or bad "vibes."

vibrato (It.). 1. In singing, timbral effect in singing by letting the stream of air out of the lungs about 8 times per second through the rigid vocal cords; ideally the pitch should remain the same to avoid an irrelevant trill; wind instrument playing can also be affected by vibrato. 2. On bowed string instruments, a commonly used effect involving a slight oscillation of pitch through a barely perceptible motion of the left hand and finger pressure on a sustained tone; in excess, vibrato becomes the baneful property of walking violinists in European sidewalk cafés. Vocal and instrumental vibrato assists in the projection of sound; but it is the subject of contentious performance practice debates as to its proper use prior to the mid–19th century or in 20th-century compositions where the composer is not using 12-equal temperament.

vicendevole (It.). Changeably, inconstantly.

Vicentino, Nicola, b. Vicenza, 1511; d. Rome, 1575 or 1576. He was a pupil of Willaert in Venice; became maestro and music master to Cardinal Ippolito d'Este in Ferrara and Rome; maestro di cappella at Vicenza Cathedral (1563–64); rector of St. Thomas in Milan (by 1570); died during a plague. His book of madrigals for 5 voices (Venice, 1546), an attempt to revive the chromatic and enharmonic genera of the Greeks, led to a controversy with the learned Portuguese musician Vicente Lusitano. Vicentino publ. a theoretical treatise, *L'antica musica ridotta alla moderna prattica* (Rome, 1555), containing a description of his invention, the arcicembalo, having 6 keyboards, with separate strings and keys for distinguishing the ancient *genera:* diatonic, chromatic, and enharmonic; this was followed by

Descrizione dell'arciorgano (Venice, 1561), describing a 2nd instrument, the arciorgano. His approach to chromatic composition was followed by Cipriano de Rore and Gesualdo; his works paved the way for the monodic style and eventual disuse of church modes; madrigals and motets survive.

vicino (It.). Near. *Più vicino,* getting nearer (as sounds approaching and thus growing louder).

Vickers, Jon(athan Stewart), b. Prince Albert, Saskatchewan, Oct. 29, 1926. He sang in church choirs; did not pursue musical training until in his 20's; won a scholarship at the Royal Cons. of Music of Toronto; studied voice with G. Lambert; made his operatic debut at the Toronto Opera Festival as the Duke of Mantua (1952); sang Riccardo at Covent Garden in London (1957); appeared as Siegmund in *Die Walküre* at Bayreuth (1958); sang at the Vienna State Opera (1959); made his debut at the Metropolitan Opera in N.Y. as Canio (1960). He is particularly renowned as a Wagnerian Heldentenor; offered superb interpretations of Otello and Peter Grimes. He was made a Companion of Honour of the Order of Canada (1969).

Victoria, Tomás Luis de, b. Avila, 1548; d. Madrid, Aug. 20, 1611. He was a choirboy at Avila Cathedral; went to Rome (1565); to prepare himself for the priesthood, he entered the Jesuit Collegium Germanicum; his teacher may have been Palestrina, music master at the Roman Seminary (1566–71), then amalgamated with the Collegium Germanicum. The Italian master is known to have befriended his young Spanish colleague, and when he left the Seminary it was Victoria who succeeded him as maestro there (1571).

In 1569 Victoria left the Collegium Germanicum to become singer and organist in the Church of Sta. Maria di Montserrato (to 1564); officiated frequently at musical ceremonies in the Church of S. Giacomo degli Spagnuoli. He taught music at the Collegium Germanicum (from 1571); became its maestro di cappella (1573–74); was ordained a priest (1575); earlier that year received a benefice at Leon from the Pope; granted another benefice at Zamora (1579), neither requiring residence. He joined the Congregazione dei Preti dell'Oratorio (1577); served as chaplain at the Church of S. Girolamo della Carità (1578–85), the church where St. Philip Neri held his famous religious meetings.

Though Victoria was not a member of the Oratory, he must have taken some part in its important musical activities, living as he did for 5 years under the same roof with its founder (St. Philip left S. Girolamo in 1583); he was close terms with Juvenal Ancina, a priest of the Oratory who wrote texts for laudi spirituali sung at the meetings of the Congregation. Victoria then served as chaplain to the King's sister, the Dowager Empress Maria, at the Monasterio de las Descalzas in Madrid (c. 1587 until her death, 1603); maestro of its convent choir (to 1604); its organist until his death. His last work was a Requiem Mass for the Empress Maria, regarded as his masterpiece (publ. 1605).

A man of deep religious sentiment, Victoria expresses in his music all the ardor and exaltation of Spanish mysticism. He is often regarded as a leading representative of the Roman school, but it should be remembered that, before Palestrina, this school was profoundly marked by Hispanic influences through the work of Morales, Guerrero, Escobedo, and other Spanish composers resident in Rome; thus Victoria inherited at least as much from his own countrymen as from Palestrina; in its dramatic intensity, rhythmic variety, tragic grandeur, and spiritual fervor his music is thoroughly personal and totally Spanish. Most of his works (from 1572) were printed in Italy in sumptuous eds., evincing his backing by wealthy patrons; a vol. of Masses, Magnificats, motets, and other church music (Madrid, 1600) is notable for its provision for an organ accompaniment. He published 11 books of considerable variety, including motets, Masses, psalms, Magnificats, Propria for the saints, antiphons, hymns, and the Requiem.

Victrola. Trademark for the phonograph made by the Victor Talking Machine Company, later a generic term (like gramophone) for any 78-rpm record player.

vidalita (Sp., little life). Popular Argentinian carnival song in a characteristically combined rhythm of 3/4 and 6/8; the name refers to the constant recurrence of the word *vidalista* at the end of every verse.

vide (Lat., see; It. *vedi*). Written in scores as *vi—de,* take a cut, skipping from the measure *vi-* to the measure marked *-de.*

vidula (*vitula*, etc.; Lat.). Fiddle.

viel (Ger.). Much, great. *Mit vielem Nachdruck,* with great emphasis.

vielle. Obsolete French bowed chordophone, equivalent to the fiddle.

vielle à roue (Fr.). Medieval viol with a mechanical wheel attachment; hurdy-gurdy.

vielle organisée (Fr.). Lira organizzata.

vielstimmung (Ger.). Polyphonic, many-voiced.

Viennese school. Historical designation of at least 2 styles of composition centered around the capital of Austria; 1st proposed by German writer and musician Christian Friedrich Daniel Schubart (1739–91), who defined the main characteristics of the Viennese school as "an organization without pedantry, graceful form, and an intelligent understanding of the nature of wind instruments." Aesthetically the *1st Viennese school* is distinguished from its contemporary Berlin school by songful and attractive treatment of melodic material and harmonic formations. The Viennese school embraces the period between 1750 and 1830, with Haydn, Mozart, and Beethoven dominating the scene; ironically none of these Classic masters was born in Vienna, although they lived a good portion of their lives there. Some observers perceive a continuity to Schubert and even the waltzing Strauss family in the later 19th century.

The *2nd Viennese school* refers to the composers of the 1st half of the 20th century, mainly Schoenberg, Berg, and Webern and their disciples, who eventually wrote in Schoenberg's dodecaphonic system; their aim was, in the words of Webern, "to say in new terms something that was said before." Future musicologists may decide that the late-20th-century Viennese composers who helped pioneer the New Simplicity (Schwertsik, H. K. Gruber) represent a 3rd Viennese school.

Viertelnote (Ger.). Quarter note.

Viertelton (Ger.). Quarter tone. *Vierteltonmusik,* quarter-tone music.

Vieuxtemps, Henri, b. Verviers, Feb. 17, 1820; d. Mustapha, Algiers, June 6, 1881. His 1st violin teacher was his father, an amateur musician; continued his training with Lecloux-Dejonc; at age 6 made his debut in Verviers; after performing in Liège (1827), gave several concerts in Brussels (1828). There he attracted the notice of Bériot, who accepted him as a pupil; he studied with him until 1831. In 1833 his father took him on a concert tour of Germany; continued his studies in Vienna, receiving counterpoint lessons from Sechter. He performed successfully as soloist in the Beethoven Violin Concerto in Vienna, then made his British debut with the Phil. Soc. of London. (both 1834); after training in composition from Reicha in Paris (1835–36), set out on his 1st tour of Europe (1837).

During his constant travels Vieuxtemps composed concertos and other violin works that became part of the standard repertoire; performed them in Europe to the greatest acclaim; made his 1st American tour (1843–44). He was engaged as a prof. at the St. Petersburg Cons. (1846); remained in Russia for 5 seasons; his influence on Russian concert life and violin composition was considerable. He recommenced his concert tours in Europe (1853); paid 2 more visits to America, with Thalberg (1857–58) and Christine Nilsson (1870–71). He was a prof. of violin at the Brussels Cons. (1871–73); but a paralytic stroke, affecting his left side, forced him to end all his concert activities; continued to teach privately; went to Algiers for rest, and died; one of his most prominent pupils, Jenö Hubay, was with him at the end.

With Bériot, Vieuxtemps stands at the head of the French school of violin playing; contemporaneous accounts speak of the extraordinary precision of technique and perfect ability to sustain a flowing melody; the expression "le roi du violon" was often applied to him in the press. As a composer Vieuxtemps is best known for his 7 violin concertos (1836–61 and 2 posth. works); in addition to other violin music with orch. or piano, composed 2 cello concertos; 3 string quartets, and a Viola Sonata.

He had 2 brothers who were musicians: (Jean-Joseph-) Lucien Vieuxtemps (b. Verviers, July 5, 1828; d. Brussels, Jan. 1901), a pianist and teacher who studied with E. Wolff in Paris; made his debut at a concert given by Henri in Brussels (1845); devoted himself mainly to teaching; wrote a few piano pieces; and (Jules-Joseph-) Ernest Vieuxtemps (b. Brussels, Mar. 18, 1832; d. Belfast, Mar. 20, 1896), a cellist who appeared with Henri in London (1855); solo cellist in the Italian Opera Orch., then became principal cellist of the Hallé Orch. (1858).

vif (Fr.). Lively.

vihuela (Sp.). 1. Generic name for Spanish chordophones in the 15th century, bowed and plucked, descendants of the Arab 'ūd. 2. Spanish plucked chordophone of the 16th century, similar to the contemporaneous guitar but with between 6 and 7 courses of strings (the guitar had 4); there is a reference to a vihuela with 5 pairs of strings and 1 *chanterelle,* the short, high string found centuries later on the banjo; in the next century the vihuela declined in favor of the guitar.

Villa-Lobos, Heitor, b. Rio de Janeiro, Mar. 5, 1887; d. there, Nov. 17, 1959. He studied music with his father, a writer and amateur cellist; after his father's death he played the cello in cafés and restaurants; studied cello with B. Niederberger. He traveled within Brazil to collect authentic folk songs (from 1905); entered the National Inst. of Music in Rio de Janeiro (1907); studied with F. Nascimento, A. Franca, and F. Braga; undertook an expedition into Brazil's interior, gathering a rich collection of indigenous songs (1912). In 1915, he presented in Rio de Janeiro a concert of his compositions, creating a sensation by the exuberance of his music and the radical character of his idiom. He met the pianist Artur Rubinstein, who became an ardent admirer; he composed the transcendentally difficult *Rudepoema* for him. He went to Paris on a Brazilian government grant to study music education (1923–30); upon returning to Brazil he was active in São Paulo and Rio de Janeiro in music education; founded a cons. in the latter city under the sponsorship of the Ministry of Education (1942). He introduced bold innovations into the national program of music education, emphasizing Brazil's cultural resources; compiled a *Guia pratico* containing choral arrangements of folk songs of Brazil and other nations; organized "orpheonic concentrations" of schoolchildren, whom he trained to sing according to his own cheironomic method of solfège. That year he established in Rio de Janeiro the Brazilian Academy of Music, serving as its president (1947–59). In 1944 he made his 1st U.S. tour; conducted his works in Los Angeles, Boston, and N.Y. (1945); made frequent visits to the U.S. and France during the last 15 years of his life.

Villa-Lobos was one of the most original composers of the 20th century; he lacked formal academic training, but this deficiency liberated him from pedantic restrictions; evolved an idiosyncratic technique of composition, curiously eclectic but all the better suited to his musical aesthetics. An ardent Brazilian nationalist, he resolved from the beginning to use authentic Brazilian song materials as the source of his inspiration; but chose to re-create native melodic and rhythmic elements in large instrumental and choral forms without actual quotations from traditional and popular songs. Wishing to relate Brazilian folk resources to universal musical values he composed a series of *Bachianas brasileiras,* in which Brazilian melorhythms are filtered through Bachian counterpoint; previously composed works under the generic title *Chôros,* dance music of Brazilian urban origins from the 1870s to the present.

Villa-Lobos wrote over 2,000 works: 4 operas, including *Magdalena* (1948) and *Yerma,* after García Lorca (1953–56); 7 ballets; 9 *Bachianas brasileiras* (1932–44): No. 1 for 8 Cellos; No. 2 for Chamber Orch.; No. 3 for Piano and Orch.; No. 4 for Piano; No. 5 for Voice and 8 Cellos (the best known), No. 6 for Flute and Bassoon; No. 7 for Orch.; No. 8 for Orch.; No. 9 for Chorus a Cappella or String Orch. *Chôros* (1920–29): No. 1 for Guitar; No. 2 for Flute and Clarinet; No. 3 for Male Chorus and 7 Wind Instruments; No. 4 for 3 Horns and Trombone; No. 5, *Alma brasileira,* for Piano (the best known); No. 6 for Orch.; No. 7 for Mixed Septet; No. 8 for Large Orch. and 2 Pianos; No. 9 for Orch.; No. 10, *Rasga o Coracao* for Chorus and Orch.; No. 11 for Piano and Orch.; No. 12 for Orch.; No. 13 for 2 Orchs. and Band; No. 14 for Orch., Band, and Chorus. Orch'l: Twelve syms. (1916–1957); 2 sinfoniettas; *Amazonas* (1917); *Momoprecoce* for Piano and Orch. (1929); *The New York*

Skyline, composed using a method in which geometrical contours of a photograph of the eponymous subject serve as outlines for the melody (1939); *Erosion, or The Origin of the Amazon River* (1951); 5 Piano Concertos (1945–54); also for cello (2), guitar; harp; harmonica. Chamber works: 17 string quartets (1915–58); 3 piano trios; choral works; piano music, including the 3 *Prole do Bebe* suites (1918, 1921, 1929).

villancico (Sp.). Umbrella term for varieties of Spanish and Latin American vocal music, starting in the 15th century; originally literary and musical forms determined inclusion in the genre. Spanish villancicos have included vernacular love songs with stanzas and a refrain; imitative polyphonic choral pieces, including the Christmas villancico, increasingly influenced by the madrigal; and Baroque religious villancico, with expanded formal structures tending toward the dramatic, later incorporating recitative and aria. The genre was prohibited in the mid–18th century, although performances continued into the 1800s. In Latin America villancicos are 1st mentioned in the 16th century; villancicos of the 17th and 18th centuries are solely ecclesiastical and liturgical in purpose, incorporating instrumental music, song, and dance; Italian influences came into play in the 18th century. Many related genres evolved in Latin America; hundreds of villancicos have survived.

villanella (*villanesca;* It.; Fr. *villanelle*). Lighthearted secular song originating in 16th-century Naples; its deliberately rustic style was cultivated by learned composers who wished to combat the domination of the more refined madrigal. Many villanellas were of topical content and regional in application; still used by modern composers to refer to an instrumental rustic dance.

villotta (It.). Secular song genre, related to the villanella, popular in Italy during the Renaissance; its melodic and rhythmic structure combines elements of courtly dances and traditional refrains.

vīnā (S. Ind.; N. Ind bīn). 1. Generic term for Indian chordophones, orig. arched harps (through the 1st millennium A.D.), later more generally applied. 2. Orig. a highly developed stick zither, now resembles the more modern sitār, with a body replacing the stick and a gourd resonator at the upper end. Its 7 strings comprise 4 melody and 3 drone strings, played with fingers or plectrum; played seated with the upper end resting on the shoulder.

Vingt-quatre Violons du Roi (Fr., 24 Violins of the King). String ensemble also known as la grande bande, attached to the courts of Louis XIII, Louis XIV, and Louis XV, comprising 24 violins and other string instruments. La petite bande developed by Lully had only 16 players; he eventually combined the two, and conducted the new group for many years.

viol. Family of bowed string instruments, universally popular in the 17th century and all but ignored by the end of the 18th century; antecedents include the medieval fiddle. Viols differ from the violin family in having a fretted fingerboard, a variable number of strings (usually 6), and a differently shaped body. It was made in 4 sizes, like the violin, by which it was superseded in the orch. The 1st 3 sizes of viol in use, classified by their French names, were *dessus de viole* (top viol, i.e., treble viol), *taille de* *viole* (tenor viol), and *basse de viole* (bass viol); the last was also called viola da gamba and was the precursor of the cello. The viols were tuned like the lute, in 4ths above and below the central interval, a major 3rd; i.e., the bass viol was tuned D, G, C, E, A, and D, the tenor A, D, G, B, E, and A, and the treble an octave above the bass; to these was added the *pardessus de viole,* tuned a 4th above the treble viol. In England, a viol ensemble was called a chest or whole consort of viols.

viola (It.). Alto violin; bowed string instrument with 4 strings tuned C_0, G_0, d^1, a^1, a 5th lower than the violin. Physically the standard-sized viola is only 1/7 larger than the violin; its lower range is not properly accommodated acoustically; its quality of tone lacks the violin's brilliance and the cello's deeply singing quality. But the viola offers far more than a butt for endless jokes; its melancholy, philosophical sonority occupies a more subtle, less clichéd place in musical expressivity. Except for Berlioz's *Harold in Italy* (with an important viola part but certainly not a true concerto), few composers wrote viola concertos until the 20th century, when performers like Hindemith, Primrose, L. Tertis, and K. Doktor commissioned and/or wrote works from leading composers (Vaughan Williams, Holst, Bartók, Serly, Walton, Milhaud, Piston, Henze). Acoustically correct violas have been built but are used rarely, as most performers would have to play it like a gamba, lacking hands and arms large enough to reach the intervals required in the normal position.

viola bastarda (U.K. *lyra viol*).ÜViola da gamba sized between bass and tenor viols, with 2 drone and 5 playing strings, tuned alternatively in 5ths or 4ths in the manner of the *lira da braccio*. Popular during the Baroque, its strange name may derive from its shape or tunings.

viola da braccio (It., viola for the arm). Obsolete bowed stringed instrument held at the shoulder; precursor of the modern violin.

viola da gamba (It., viol for the leg). Family of bowed stringed instruments that evolved from the medieval fiddle around the beginning of the 2nd millennium A.D. Gambas, as they are referred to, are similar in shape to the violin family, with subtle differences—sloping shoulders, C holes, wider bridge and fingerboard, bow held with palm up—and not so subtle ones—being held vertically, supported on the lap or between the player's calves; 6 instead of 4 strings; frets. Gambas were popular in the late Renaissance and Baroque; there were 6 principal sizes: soprano, alto, tenor, and 3 different basses; there is much virtuoso solo music, and many treatises on its playing; also featured in basso continuo; has been a major focus of the early music revival.

viola da spalla (It., shoulder viola). Viola da braccio.

viola d'amore (It., viol of love). Bowed chordophone in the middle range, for part of its history supplied with sympathetic strings. 1st reported in the early Baroque, it is the size of a violin but lacks its perfect proportions. The number of playing strings varies from 5 to 7; the sympathetic metal strings under these impart a silvery resonance to its sound. Its mysterious name may have the prosaic explanation that its scroll above the pegbox was often made in the shape of Cupid's face (the editor thinks otherwise). The viola d'amore was very popular in the Baroque music; Bach used it in several works. In modern times the viola d'amore is mostly used for its evocative value, e.g., *Sinfonia domestica* by R. Strauss; Hindemith wrote a chamber concerto for it.

viola di bordone (It., drone viol). Baryton.

viola piccola (It., small viola). Obsolete member of the viola family.

viola pomposa (violino pomposa; It.). Viola with an extra string (usually e^2), used during the mid–18th century; despite later claims, Bach neither invented nor scored for this instrument; found in scores of Telemann and Graun.

viole (Fr.). Viol; viola.

violetta (It.; Fr. *violette*). 1. Fiddle or small viola of the 16th century. 2. In the 18th century, the viola (alto violin).

violin (It. *violino;* Fr. *violon;* Ger. *Violine, Geige*). The best known, most expressive, and most artistic instrument of the string family. Poets and storytellers have extolled the violin as the most human instrument, capable of an extraordinary variety of expression—merry and sad, boisterous and tranquil, frivolous and meditative.

The violin has an oval body modified by 2 elliptic depressions across its waist and 2 symmetrical soundholes in the shape of large cursive *f*'s. The body functions as a resonator box; the resonance is at its strongest at the vibrating center. There are 4 strings, tuned g^0, d^1, a^1, and e^2, held at the lower end (nearest the player) by a tailpiece and supported by a bridge above it; they are maintained in their tension by 4 pegs in a pegbox (at the end furthest from the player). A fingerboard is placed under the strings; there are no frets or other marks on the fingerboard to guide the violinist, unlike the guitar or viola da gamba player; a violinist must therefore develop a secure sense of placement of the finger on the fingerboard to play in tune. The strings are activated into sound by a bow strung with horsehair or by being plucked with the fingers.

The 1st plausible ancestor of the violin was the Arab rabāb, which entered into Western Europe and became known as the rebec; in England it was called the fiddle. The shapes of these instruments varied until the present form was fashioned by the great violin makers of Cremona in the late 17th century; the most celebrated was Stradivari; a genuine "Stradivarius" label is a virtual guarantee of excellence; some "Strads," as they are warmly known, have fetched between half a million and a million dollars. The secret of the art of Stradivari and other great Cremonese makers (Amati, Guarneri) has been probed by generations of violin manufacturers, who have credited the wood from Cremonese forests or the quality of the varnish. The drawings of violins and other string instruments which the Cremonese left behind do not shed light on their remarkable results; even using modern tools of analytical science to create perfect copies of the instruments, all has been in vain.

The violin became a favorite instrument in the hands of virtuosos of the 17th and 18th centuries; its technique expanded through many ingenious devices such as harmonics, double stops, and pizzicato; virtuosity attained an apogee with Paganini, whose wizardry on the instrument was documented in detail by contemporaneous reports. The great era of violin virtuosity was attained in the 19th century, which numbered, besides Paganini, such illustrious artists as Bériot, Wieniawski, Ferdinand David, Bull, Vieuxtemps, Joachim, Sarasate, Auer, and Ysaÿe. In the 20th century virtuoso violinists came increasingly from Eastern Europe; later in the century, from Asia. Later in the century ultra-modernist composers demanded the execution of such anti-violinistic devices as quadruple stops under the bridge, indeterminate high notes beyond the fingerboard, pizzicato glissando, and quarter tones; remember, however, that the songful and stately violin concerto of Brahms was once described by a German music critic as "a concerto against the violin, rather than for it."

The violin is a patrician instrument, although its participation in traditional music is widespread, and jazz, swing, and rock have all had notable performers. There are two standard placements for the 2 violin sections in the orch.: either the 1st violins are in front to the conductor's left, and the 2nd violins in front to the right (the traditional layout until the 20th century, still used by some conductors); or having the 2nds also on the conductor's left, behind the 1sts (i.e., to their left). The 1st violinist sitting nearest the audience at the 1st desk (stand) and nearest the conductor on the left is called the leader in England, *Konzertmeister* in Germany, *violon solo* in French, and concertmaster in the U.S.; they function as an internal back up conductor. When the director of the Russian Imperial Orch. in St. Petersburg explained to a Grand Duke the division of the 1st and 2nd violins, the nobleman exclaimed, "Second violins? In the Imperial orch., all must be first!"

Orch'l violinists, particularly concertmasters, often develop a yearning for conducting; several famous conductors learned the art of conducting an orch. by playing in one. Munch was a member of the Gewandhaus Orch. in Leipzig; launched his successful career only at age 40 years old; Ormandy was for several years concertmaster of a theater orch. in N.Y. before receiving his 1st conducting engagement; Marriner went from playing in London orchs. to leading the immensely successful Academy of St.-Martin-in-the-Fields. Joseph Silverman retired from his 1st violinist's position at the Boston Symphony Orch. to conduct various ensembles.

violin clef. The G clef (𝄞), set on the lowest line of the staff; also called French violin clef.

violin diapason. Organ stop.

violin family. Familiar 4-stringed bowed instruments, constructed in 4 sizes, tuned as follows:

violina. Organ metal flue stop of stringlike timbre, usually 4'.

Violinabend (Ger.). Evening of violin playing and entertainment.

violinata (It.). 1. Violin piece. 2. Piece for another instrument, imitating the violin.

violin-conductor score. Particella or abbrev. score used in 19th-century theater orchs., particularly in Italian opera houses; usually includes the 1st violin part, harmony on the 2nd staff, and bass line.

violini prima (It.). First orch'l violins. *Violino primo,* 1st violin in a string quartet and other small ensembles.

violini secondi (It.). Second orch'l violins.

violino piccolo (It.; Ger. *Quartgeige, Halbgeige*). Small violin, tuned a perfect 4th above the standard instrument, used for upper registers; held sway during the Baroque era, but, as Leopold Mozart reported, the improvement of technique made the piccolo instrument unnecessary; still used as a child's instrument.

Violinschlüssel (Ger.). Violin clef; treble clef.

violon (Fr.). 1. Violin. 2. Violin diapason organ stop. *Violon solo,* concertmaster.

violoncello (It., cello; Fr. *violoncelle*). Most songful instrument in the lower register of the violin family; its name, a diminutive of *violone,* means "little big viola." The cello has 4 strings, tuned C_0, G_0, d^0, and a^0, an octave below the viola; it is an enlarged violin or viola, resembling a viola da gamba; is also placed between the knees, but held in place by a floor spike and rests on the shoulder. Until the 20th century few cellists achieved the kind of worldly success had by Paganini and other violin wizards, but the success of Casals, Piatigorsky, Feuermann, Rostropovich, Fournier, Starker, Harrell, Tortelier, Du Pré, Krosnick, and Yo-Yo Ma testify to the instrument's power of musical communication. As with violinists, many orch'l cellists have become conductors, e.g., Toscanini, Casals, Harnoncourt, and Barbirolli.

violoncello piccolo (It., small cello). 5-string cello used in some Baroque works.

violone (It., large viola). 1. Largest of the viola da gambas, the bass or double bass, with a bottom string tuned to D_0; a contemporary of and an influence on the instrument that eventually became the even lower-pitched double bass; the violone usually had 5 or 6 strings, while the double bass had 3 or 4. 2. Organ stop on the pedal, of 16' pitch and violoncello-like timbre.

virelai (Fr., from *virer,* turn, twist). Medieval French fixed form; with the ballade and rondeau, dominated French song and poetry in the late Middle Ages and early Renaissance; its name connotes both dance and poetic (*lai*) origins. The most common formula for the virelai is in 5 parts: the principal A section, containing the refrain; the 2 B sections, repeated music and different texts, plus 1st (*ouvert*) and 2nd (*clos*) endings; repetition of A with new text (without refrain); finally, a repetition of the 1st A.

Machaut was the greatest exponent of the genre, mostly composing monophonic examples.

virginal (virginals). 1. Keyboard instrument of the harpsichord family, extremely popular in the 16th and 17th centuries; its etymology is uncertain; the assumption that it refers to the unmarried British Queen Elizabeth I has been refuted by pre-Elizabethan German writings in which the term already appears; other conjectures are that virginals possessed a virginal sound and sweet voice; that it dates to etymological error concerning eastern Mediterranean female players of the frame drum; or that it derives from the Latin *virga* (rod), by analogy to the jack, essential to the virginal's mechanism.

The virginal is a single-strung plucked keyboard instrument, strings placed within a rectangular shape running right to left, with some discretion as to design. The relatively small keyboards (less than 4 octaves) are located to the left or right side of the playing area. Instruments were built throughout Europe, with particular skill in Flanders by the Ruckers family. The virginal retained a role similar to the clavichord's, that of a home instrument; the louder harpsichord eventually replaced it.

2. Any member of the harpsichord family commonly in use in England during the virginal's vogue; thus a collection of music bore a title both revealing and misleading: *Parthenia, or The Maydenhead of the First Musicke That Was Ever Printed for the Virginalls* (publ. 1611); included dances, mostly pavanes and galliards, by British composers of the time; however, they could be played on any plucked keyboard instrument (or arranged for lute).

virtuosity (from Lat. *virtus,* ability, value). Display of great proficiency by an instrumentalist or vocalist, called a *virtuoso,* who must possess above all else a superlative technique. The concept dates to the Baroque period, with the loss of religious restrictions on compositional excess and the new monodic textures. The 1st virtuosos were church organists; of these, Frescobaldi acquired legendary fame; his biographers claim that 30,000 people flocked to hear him at St. Peter's in Rome. In later centuries "virtuoso" was applied mostly to instrumentalists, particularly pianists and violinists.

Virtuosity reached its peak in the 19th century. Paganini was the 1st modern violin virtuoso; his own compositions of transcendental difficulty testified to his expertise; Liszt candidly declared that his aim in performance was to emulate Paganini in piano technique. Liszt's great rival was Anton Rubinstein, whose thundering octaves were, to believe reliable critics, overwhelming in their impact on the listeners. Other great pianists of the 19th century were Thalberg, C. Schumann, Henselt, Carreño, Tausig, Alkan, and Chopin, who partly modeled his compositions after the virtuosity of Italian bel canto. In terms of world acclaim, Paderewski was a true heir to Liszt and Rubinstein, but surviving recordings of his playing have raised doubts as to his place in the galaxy of great virtuosos. Busoni, Hofmann, Godowsky, Petri, Lhevinne, Rachmaninoff, and many other émigrés have enjoyed fame as a piano virtuoso; innumerable performers maintain the tradition to this day.

Among violinists 19th-century performers such as Vieuxtemps, Joachim, and Sarasate carried the tradition forward. In the 20th century Heifetz was the dominant figure; at present it is Perlman who plays at an extraordinarily high technical level; but the apparent effortlessness of his playing illustrates the difference between Romantic and 20th-century virtuosos: the earlier embody the heroic attempts of humanity to attain godlike status, while the latter attempt to blend in as normal people who just happen to play an instrument incredibly well. Players of other instruments have demonstrated an ability to rise to the top of the virtuosic heap: viola (Primrose, Tertis), violoncello (see entry), double bass (Koussevitzky), harp (Zabaleta), guitar (Segovia, Bream, Yepes, J. Williams), flute (Galway, Rampal), oboe (Holliger), clarinet (de Peyer, Stoltzman), saxophone (Harle), horn (D. Brain, Tuckwell), trumpet (W. Marsalis, André), percussion (Glennie), and harpsichord (Landowska). The term virtuoso is not limited to classical performers; jazz saxophonists and rock electric guitarists are often compared and analyzed much as their classical counterparts.

Vocal virtuosity developed alongside the growth of opera, and certain skills have became professional necessities. Virtuosos singers must execute the most difficult passages in rapid tempo. Effortless trills in upper registers are expected from prima donnas; the bodily prepossessing bass should be able to hold his lowest notes with unwavering resonance; tenors must be able to sustain a high C (actually c^2) at the climax of an aria. All singers are expected to perform execute flawless staccato and maintain a breathtaking pianissimo as well as a brilliant *ff*. An unusual (but not unique) example of the importance of the singer involves the male soprano castrato Farinelli, who spent years at the Spanish court and was paid a great deal for the task of singing the same 4 songs nightly to King Philip V, who suffered from insomniacal depression.

Vishnevskaya, Galina (Pavlovna), See ⇒Rostropovich, Mstislav (Leopoldovich).

visible speech. Graphic method of translating spoken words or musical notes into a visual spectrum, in which the *abscissa* (horizontal coordinate) indicates duration and the *ordinate* (vertical coordinate) indicates frequency. Relative shadings indicate amplitude; a 3-dimensional graph could denote this parameter more precisely.

vista (It.). Sight. *A prima vista* (at 1st sight), play at sight.

vistamente (It.). Briskly, animatedly.

vite (Fr.). Fast. *Pas trop vite,* not too fast.

Vitry, Philippe de (Philippus de Vitriaco), b. Vitry, Champagne, Oct. 31, 1291; d. Meaux, June 9, 1361. With 6 towns in Champagne named Vitry, it remains unknown to which of these he was native to. He was educated at the Sorbonne in Paris, becoming a *magister artium;* ordained a deacon early in life; from 1323 held several benefices; was canon of Soissons and archbishop of Brie. He became a clerk of the royal household in Paris; made counselor of the court of requests (*maître des requêtes, c.* 1346). From 1346 to 1350 he was in the service of Duke Jean of Normandy (heir to the throne); took part in the siege of Aiguillon (1346); when Duke Jean became king (1350), he sent Vitry to Avignon on a mission to Pope Clement VI, who appointed him bishop of Meaux (1351).

Vitry was known as a poet and composer (some of his motets were included in the satirical poem *Le Roman de Fauvel,* early

14th century) but his enduring fame rests on *Ars nova*, a treatise on mensural notation, particularly important for its development of the principle of binary rhythm; gives the most complete account of the uses to which colored notes were put; only the last 10 of the 24 chapters of *Ars nova* are now considered authentic; most of his music is lost.

viva voce (It.). In full voice; loudly.

vivace (*vivacemente, vivo;* It.; Fr. *vivement*). 1. Lively, animatedly, spiritedly, briskly. 2. As a tempo mark by itself, movement equaling or exceeding allegro in rapidity. Vivacetto, less lively than vivace; allegretto; vivacissimo, very lively; presto.

Vivaldi, Antonio (Lucio), b. Venice, Mar. 4, 1678; d. Vienna, July 28, 1741. His father, Giovanni Battista Vivaldi (b. Brescia, *c.* 1655; d. Venice, May 14, 1736), was a violinist in the orch. at San Marco in Venice (1685–1729) and director of instrumental music at the Mendicanti (1689–93). Antonio was trained for the priesthood at S. Geminiano and S. Giovanni in Oleo; took the tonsure (1693) and Holy Orders (1703); because of his red hair he was called *il prete rosso* (the red priest). He became *maestro di violino* at the Pio Ospedale della Pietà, Venice (1703–09); during this period his 1st publ. works appeared; resumed his duties at the Pietà; named its *maestro de' concerti* (1716). His set of 12 concertos, *L'estro armonico*, op. 3, was publ. (Amsterdam, 1711), proving to be the most important music publication of the 1st half of the 18th century. His 1st known opera, *Ottone in Villa*, was given in Vicenza (1713); became active as a composer and impresario in Venice; was active in Mantua (1718–20), where the Habsburg governor Prince Philipp of Hessen-Darmstadt made him *maestro di cappella da camera*, a title he retained even after leaving Mantua.

In subsequent years Vivaldi traveled widely in Italy, bringing out his operas; however, he retained his association with the Pietà. About 1725 he became associated with the contralto Anna Giraud (or Giro), one of his voice students; her sister, Paolina, also became a constant companion, leading to speculation that the sisters were his mistresses, a contention he denied. His *La cetra*, op. 9 (Amsterdam, 1727), was dedicated to the Austrian Emperor Charles VI; once more served as maestro di cappella at the Pietà (1735–38); named maestro di cappella to Francis Stephen, Duke of Lorraine (later Emperor Francis I; 1735). In 1738 he visited Amsterdam, taking charge of the music for the centennial celebration of the Schouwburg Theater; returning to Venice, found little favor with the theatergoing public; set out for Austria (1740), arriving in Vienna but dying a month later; although he had received large sums of money in his day, he died impoverished and was given a pauper's burial.

Vivaldi's greatness lies mainly in his superb instrumental works, notably some 500 concertos, in which he displayed an extraordinary mastery of ritornello form and orchestration. More than 230 of his concertos are for solo violin (on which he was a superb performer); 120 or so for other instruments (viola d'amore, cello, flute, piccolo, recorder, oboe, bassoon, and paired mandolins) or concerti grossi; in some 60 *concerti ripieni* (string concertos sans solo instrument), honed a style akin to operatic sinfonias; wrote about 90 orch'l sonatas. Other collections of concertos and sinfonias publ. during his lifetime: *La stravaganza*, op. 4 (*c.* 1714); 6 concertos *a 5 stromenti*, op. 6 (1716–17); Concertos *a 5 stromenti*, op. 7 (2 books, *c.* 1716–17); *Il cimento dell'armonia e dell'inventione*, op. 8 (1725, with his best-loved work, *The 4 Seasons*, programmatic concertos with accompanying sonnets); 6 concertos, op. 10 (*c.* 1728); 6 concertos, op. 11 (1729); 6 concertos, op. 12 (1729). Sonatas include works for solo or paired violins, cello, or flute. Vocal music: 21 of his operas are extant, some missing 1 or more acts; a few have been revived: *Tito Manlio* (1719); *Farnace* (1727); *Orlando (furioso)* (1727); *La fida ninfa* (1732); *Montezuma* (1733); *L'Olimpiade* (1734); also wrote serenatas; solo cantatas with basso continuo; solo cantatas with instrument(s) and basso continuo. He composed 4 oratorios, including *Juditha triumphans devicta Holofernes barbarie* (1716); liturgical music includes Masses or Mass sections, psalms, hymns, antiphons, motets, etc.

vivo (It.; Fr. *vivement*). Lively, spiritedly, briskly.

vocal. Pertaining to the voice; suitable for the singing voice. *Vocal cords,* the 2 opposed ligaments set in the larynx whose vibration, caused by expelling air from the lungs, produces vocal tones; *vocal glottis,* the aperture between the vocal cords while singing; *vocal quartet,* chamber piece for 4 singers; group of 4 solo singers within a larger group.

vocal score. Arrangement of a work for voice(s) and ensemble (up to an orch.) as a score for voice(s) and piano reduction, for rehearsal purposes and, when resources are limited, actual performance.

vocalise (Fr.). Vocal étude or composition, sung on open vowels, without text. Vocal pieces sometimes use vocalise as a technique for part of its duration, such as the *Bell Song* from Delibes's *Lakme* or *Bachianas Brasileiras No. 8* by Villa-Lobos. Other primarily orch'l pieces may include a passage for choral vocalise, e.g., Debussy's *Nocturnes* (*Sirènes*) and Holst's *The Planets* (*Neptune*); or solo vocalise e.g., Nielsen's 3rd Sym. and Vaughan William's 3rd Sym.

vocalization. Singing exercise comprising a melody sung without words; scales and arpeggios are common vocalizations used to prepare the vocal cords for rehearsal and performance; as compositional technique, called *vocalise.*

voce (It.). Voice; part. *A due (tre) voci,* for 2 (3) parts or voices, in 2 (3) parts; *colla voce,* col canto; *mezza voce,* see *mezza; sotta voce,* see ⇒*sotto.*

voce di gola (It.). Throat voice, produced gutturally. *Voce di petto,* chest tone (voice); *voce di testa,* head tone (voice); *voce intonata,* pure voice; *voce pastosa,* flexible voice; *voce rauca,* raucous voice.

voces aequales (Lat.). Equal voices, i.e., those within the same gender or age category (men, women, children).

voces musicales (Lat.). Solmization syllables.

voci artificiali (It., artificial voices). Early term for castrato sonority.

vodun (voudou, voodoo). Haitian religious ritual, adapted from ancestor worship and mythology in West Africa, brought to the New World by the enslaved black population. In its present form vodun comprises a whole complex of songs, dances, and drums; a notorious occult element involving spirit inhabitation gives vodun its mystery for outsiders. Similar religious practice influenced African-Americans, especially in New Orleans, until Christianity became the primary belief for that population.

Vogelstimme (Ger.). Bird singing or song. *Wie eine Vogelstimme*, like a bird singing.

voglia (It.). Wish. *A voglia*, at will, ad libitum.

voice (It. *voce;* Ger. *Stimme;* Fr. *voix*). 1. Human vocal production of musical tone, divided into 6 principal ranges: soprano, mezzo-soprano, contralto (alto), tenor, baritone, and bass. Animal vocal sounds are considered voices; those of birds and whales are treated aesthetically, even though birds lack vocal cords and whale songs are not produced through their mouths; but all lack the facility and variety of the human voice. In contemporary scores, voice parts are written constantly for untraditional sounds; sometimes speech replaces musical production altogether (Toch, *Geographical Fugue*). See also ⇒singing. 2. Part or line, vocal or instrumental.

voice exchange (Ger. *Stimmtausch*). 1. Medieval compositional technique in which 2 polyphonic voices take up a portion of each other's music immediately and in the same range, creating the effect of a slightly displaced repetition or echo. 2. In Schenkerian analysis, exchange of notes between 2 polyphonic voices over a span of time, not necessarily in the same range.

voice leading. Art of arranging voices in a polyphonic composition so that each part has a logical continuation without competing with the continuation in other voices. Depending on the harmonic (tonal, chromatic, atonal) context and the strictness of the contrapuntal "rules" in force at the time, voice leading is usually easier to describe as a series of prohibitions against consecutive perfect intervals, augmented and diminished intervals (melodic and harmonic), imbalance of melodic skips with countervailing steps, range overlapping, etc.

voice production. Pedagogical hypothesis that the human voice can be directed or projected physiologically from the head, the chest, or the epiglottis by conscious effort. Of course the only source of the human voice is the larynx, and the only resonator is the pharynx, but even serious professional singers are convinced that lower notes travel from the vocal cords to the thoracic cavity and the head tone (voice) is monitored from the top of the head. With the invasion of the U.S. by Italian singing teachers late in the 19th century and Russian singers after World War I, the mythology of voice production assumed scientific status. One Russian singer who organized an American opera company urged his students to "exercise the muscles of the brain" and was quite unimpressed when he was informed that the brain had no muscular network. There is no harm in using the terms *chest voice* and *head tone* (voice) if both teacher and student understand that they are using metaphors; it should be remembered, however, that great natural singers like Caruso and Chaliapin

developed their glorious voices never knowing whether they sang from the chest, the head, or the epiglottis.

voicing. Instrument tuning, especially the balancing of multiple strings or pipes in keyboard instruments.

voil (Fr.). Veiled; muted.

voix (Fr.). Voice; part. *À deux (trois) voix*, for 2 (3) voices, in 2 (3) parts.

voix blanche (Fr., white voice). Vocal production of a bland quality without distinctive timbre. *Voix céleste* (Fr., heavenly voice), 8' tremulant organ stop; *voix de poitrine*, chest tone (voice). *Voix de tête*, head tone (voice).

Vokalmusik (Ger.). Vocal music.

volante (It.). Flying; lightly, swiftly.

volata (It.; Ger. *volate;* Fr. *volatine*). Short vocal run or trill; run or division; light, rapid series of notes. *Volatina*, brief volata.

Volkslied (Ger.). Genuine folk song.

Volkston, im (Ger.). In the style of a folk song.

volkstümlich (Ger.). Like a folk song, but newly composed; neotraditional. *Volkstümliches Lied*, ostentatiously simple German art song that emulates the melodic and rhythmic construction of genuine folk song; *Lorelei* by P. F. Silcher is an example of a newly composed song often mistaken for a folk song. A professional neotraditional composer's goal would be that one of his or her songs becomes so popular that it, too, is mistaken for the real thing, is often performed and recorded, and thereby becomes a substantial source of income. In the U.S. Kern's *Ol' Man River* or the songs of Bob Dylan and Pete Seeger are the equivalent of the German genre. Sometimes a composer incorporates the *volkstümlicher Geist* (spirit) into a composition without the limitation of pure imitation; Mahler's music, particularly the *Des Knaben Wunderhorn* works, exemplifies this approach.

Volksweise (Ger.). Folk song or neotraditional melody.

voll (Ger.). Full. *Volles Orchester*, full orch.; *volles Werk*, full organ registration; *mit vollem Chöre*, with full chorus.

volles Zeitmass (Ger., full measure of time).Ü Strictly in time.

volltönend (*volltönig;* Ger.). Sonorously, resonantly.

volta (lavolta; It., the turn). Dance of Provençal origin, popular in Western European courts between 1550 and 1650, described by Arbeau in *Orchésographie* (1588); it is in 3/4 or 3/2 time, at a relatively slow lilt. Unusual in being a true couple dance, the volta features individual jumps by the dancers followed by a well-coordinated lift of the female by the male partner; each of the 3 jumps occur simultaneously with a three-quarter (280°) turn; mentioned in Shakespeare. Musical examples are found in lute, keyboard, and ensemble arrangements.

volta, -i (It.). Turn; time. *Prime volta* (or *Ima volta, Ima, Ia, I., 1.*), 1st time or ending; *secunda volta* (or *IIda volta, IIda, IIa, II., 2.*), 2nd time or ending; *una volta,* once; *due volta,* twice.

voltare la pagina (It.). Turn the page.

volteggiando (It.). In keyboard passages, play with crossed hands.

volti subito (It.; abbrev. *v.s.*). Turn (the page) over immediately.

volubilmente (volubile; It.). Fluently, flexibly, flowing easily.

voluntary. Partly or wholly improvised organ piece used in Anglican church services; such a piece is freely "volunteered," stylistically speaking. Traditionally it was written in a polyphonic idiom with imitative elements and was of cheerful character. English composers of the 17th and 18th centuries wrote many such voluntaries, not necessarily for organ or for religious settings; eventually British organists applied the term to any kind of improvisation, particularly one using the loud cornet stop. The best-known work of this genre is Jeremiah Clarke's *Trumpet Voluntary* (before 1700), long thought to be by Purcell; its subtitle (*The Prince of Denmark's March*) suggests its mood and milieu.

voluttuoso (It.). Voluptuous.

vom (Ger.). From the. *Vom Anfang,* da capo.

Von Stade, Frederica, b. Somerville, N.J., June 1, 1945. After an apprenticeship at the Long Wharf Theater in New Haven she studied with S. Engelberg, P. Berl, and O. Guth at the Mannes College of Music in N.Y. Although she reached only the semifinals of the Metropolitan Opera Auditions (1969), she attracted the attention of general manager Rudolf Bing, who arranged for her debut with the company as the 3rd Boy in *Die Zauberflöte* (N.Y., 1970); she took on more important roles there before going to Europe, where she gave an arresting portrayal of Cherubino at the palace at Versailles (1973). She sang Nina in the premiere of Pasatieri's *The Seagull* at the Houston Grand Opera (1974); made her debut at London's Covent Garden as Rosina (1975); subsequently attained extraordinary success in lyric mezzo-soprano roles with the world's major opera houses; pursued an extensive concert career, appearing regularly with the Chamber Music Soc. of Lincoln Center. She created the role of Tina in the premiere of Argento's *The Aspern Papers* at the Dallas Lyric Opera (1988); appeared in recital in N.Y.'s Carnegie Hall (1990). Her memorable roles include Dorabella, Idamante, Adalgisa in *Norma,* Charlotte in *Werther,* Mélisande, Octavian, and Malcolm in *La Donna del lago;* has proved successful as a crossover artist, especially in Broadway musical recordings.

Voodoo, voudou. Vodun.

Vorausnahme (Ger.). Anticipation.

Vordersatz (Ger., sectional antecedent). 1st theme or subject of a musical period.

Vorgänger (Ger., one who goes before). Canonic subject; dux.

vorgetragen (Ger.). Bring out. *Innig vorgetragen,* bring out expressively.

Vorhalt (Ger.). Suspension.

vorher (Ger.). Before; previously.

vorig (Ger.). Preceding; previous. *Im vorigen Zeitmasse (tempo precedente),* in the previous tempo.

Vorimitation (Ger.). In a fugal section, a preliminary imitation prior to the full exposition of the subject.

Vorschlag (Ger., forestroke). Appoggiatura.

Vorspiel (Ger.). Prelude; prologue; overture. Wagner treated the term "Vorspiel" as an introduction in a very broad sense and designated *Das Rheingold* as the Vorspiel within his tetralogy *Der Ring des Nibelungen.*

Vortrag (Ger.). Rendering, interpretation, performance, style, delivery, execution. *Vortragsstück* (Ger., performance piece), composition calculated to appeal to the general public; *Vortragzeichen,* expression mark.

vorwärts (Ger.). Forward. *Etwas vorwärts gehend,* somewhat faster, *poco più mosso; vorwärts dringend,* driving forward.

Vorzeichnung (Ger., preliminary marking). Time or key signature.

votive mass. Roman Catholic Mass celebrated at the express wish of an individual devotee.

vox (Lat., voice). 1. In medieval Latin nomenclature, sound produced by any source. 2. Parts in a work of organum; *vox principalis,* voice carrying the cantus firmus; *vox organalis,* added contrapuntal voice. *Vox angelica* (Lat., angelic voice), 4' stop corresponding to the 8' vox humana; *vox harmonica,* human voice; *vox humana* (Lat., human voice), 8' reed stop, with an alleged resemblance to the human voice; *vox organica,* wind instruments or organ.

v.s. volti subito.

vue (Fr.). View. *À première vue* (at 1st sight), play à livre ouvert.

vuota battuta (It., empty measure). General pause.

vuoto, -a (It.). Empty. *Corda vuoto,* open string.

Waart, Edo (Eduard) de, b. Amsterdam, June 1, 1941. His father sang in the chorus of the Netherlands Opera; he 1st studied the piano; at 13 took up the oboe; at 16 entered the Amsterdam Muzieklyceum, studying oboe and cello (graduated, 1962); in 1960 he attended the conducting classes in Salzburg given by D. Dixon. He played oboe in the Amsterdam Phil. (1962–63); joined the Concertgebouw Orch.; studied conducting with F. Ferrara in Hilversum; made his debut as a conductor there with the Netherlands Radio Phil. (1964).

De Waart went to the U.S. and was a winner in the Mitropoulos Competition in N.Y. (1964); was assistant conductor with the N.Y. Phil. (1965–66). Upon returning to Amsterdam, he was appointed assistant conductor of the Concertgebouw Orch. (1966); accompanied it on a U.S. tour (1967); organized the Netherlands Wind Ensemble, establishing his reputation through its extensive tours. He became a guest conductor of the Rotterdam Phil. (1967), then its chief conductor (1973–79); toured with it in England, the U.S., Germany, and Austria. He was a guest conductor of the Santa Fe Opera in New Mexico (1971–72, 1975); conducted opera in Houston (1975) and Covent Garden in London (1976).

In 1974, de Waart made a successful debut with the San Francisco Sym.; was made its principal guest conductor (1975); became music director (1977); appointed music director of the Minnesota Orch. in Minneapolis (1986); named artistic director of the Dutch Radio Phil. Orch. in Hilversum (1988). De Waart represents the modern generation of sym. and operatic conductors; his objective approach to interpretation, combined with his regard for stylistic propriety and avoidance of ostentatious conductorial display, makes his performances of the traditional and contemporary repertory particularly appealing.

wachsend (Ger., growing). Crescendo.

Wagner, Cosima, b. Bellagio, on Lake Como, Dec. 24, 1837; d. Bayreuth, Apr. 1, 1930. Daughter of Liszt and the Countess Marie d'Agoult, she received an excellent education in Paris; married von Bülow (1857); there were 2 daughters of this marriage; the next 3 children were Richard Wagner's, including Siegfried. She divorced von Bülow (1870); married Wagner a few weeks later. A woman of high intelligence, practical sense, and imperious character, she emerged after Richard's death as a powerful personage in all matters regarding the Bayreuth Festivals and the rights of performance of his works all over the world; publ. *Franz Liszt, Ein Gedenkblatt von seiner Tochter* (Munich, 2nd ed., 1911).

Wagner, Siegfried (Helferich Richard), b. Tribschen, June 6, 1869; d. Bayreuth, Aug. 4, 1930. Born out of wedlock to Richard Wagner and Cosima von Bülow, his parents married, legitimizing him (1870); Richard named the *Siegfried Idyll* after him; it was premiered in their Tribschen house as a present for Cosima (1870). Siegfried studied with Humperdinck in Frankfurt am Main; pursued architectural training in Berlin and Karlsruhe; served as an assistant at Bayreuth (1892–96); studied with his mother, H. Richter, and J. Kniese. From 1896 he was a regular conductor at Bayreuth; served as general director of production (from 1906); visited the U.S. to raise funds for the reopening of the Bayreuth Festspielhaus (1923–24), closed during World War I; conducted from memory and with left hand. His compositional career was handicapped by inevitable comparisons with his father; wrote 12 operas, orch'l works, vocal pieces, and chamber music.

Wagner tuba. A brass instrument introduced by Wagner in *Der Ring des Nibelungen,* in 2 sizes, tenor and bass; its funnel-shaped mouthpiece helps to create a tone somewhere between the tuba and the trombone. Bruckner, Stravinsky, and R. Strauss also used the Wagner tuba.

Wagner, (Wilhelm) Richard, b. Leipzig, May 22, 1813; d. Venice, Feb. 13, 1883. Richard attended the Dresden Kreuzschule (1822–27); Weber often visited Wagner's mother and stepfather's home; these visits exercised a beneficial influence on Wagner during his formative years. He began to take piano lessons from a local musician named Humann (1825); studied violin with R. Sipp. He already showed strong literary inclinations; under the spell of Shakespeare he wrote a tragedy, *Leubald.* In 1827 he moved with his mother back to Leipzig; his uncle Adolf Wagner gave him guidance in classical reading. In 1828 he was enrolled in the Nikolaischule; studied harmony with C. G. Müller, a theater violinist.

In 1830 Wagner entered the Thomasschule, where he began to compose, writing a string quartet and piano music; his overture in B-flat major was performed at the Leipzig Theater under H. Dorn (1830). Determined to dedicate himself entirely to music, he became a student of T. Weinlig, cantor of the Thomaskirche, from whom he received a thorough training in counterpoint and composition. His 1st publ. work was a piano sonata in B-flat major, to which he assigned the opus number 1; it was publ. by the prestigious house Breitkopf & Härtel (1832); wrote an overture to *König Enzio,* performed at the Leipzig Theater (1832); a C-major overture followed, premiered at a Gewandhaus concert (1832). His 1st major orch'l work, a sym. in C major, was premiered at a Prague Cons. concert (1832) and repeated at a Gewandhaus Orch. concert in Leipzig (1833); he was 19 years old at the time.

In 1832 he worked on his 1st opera, *Die Hochzeit,* after J. G. Busching's *Ritterzeit und Ritterwesen* (like all his operas composed to his own libretto); an introduction, septet, and chorus from this work survive. He next composed *Die Feen* (1833–34), based on Gozzi's *La Donna serpente;* upon completion he offered it to the Leipzig Theater, but it was rejected. He began working on a 3rd opera, *Das Liebesverbot* (1834–36), after Shakespeare's *Measure for Measure;* around that time became music director with H. Bethmann's theater company, based in Magdeburg (he married one of the company's actresses, Christine Wilhelmine [Minna] Planer in 1836); he made his conducting debut in Bad Lauschstadt with *Don Giovanni.*

In 1836 Wagner led the premiere of *Das Liebesverbot,* presented as *Die Novize von Palermo,* in Magdeburg; but

Bethmann's company soon went out of business. There he composed the overture *Rule Britannia;* appointed music director of the Königsberg town theater (1837); he went to Riga as music director of its theater (1837), worked on *Rienzi, der letzte der Tribunen,* after a popular novel by Bulwer-Lytton. In 1839 he lost his position in Riga; burdened by debts, he eventually made his way to Boulogne, where Wagner met Meyerbeer, who gave him a letter of recommendation to the director of the Paris Opéra. He lived in Paris (1839–42); he was forced to eke out an subsistence by making piano arrangements of operas and writing occasional articles for the *Gazette Musicale;* in 1840 he completed the work later rev. and called *Eine Faust-Ouvertüre* (1855).

Wagner found himself in dire financial straits; was confined in debtors' prison for 3 weeks; in the meantime completed the libretto for *Der fliegende Holländer;* submitted it to the director of the Paris Opéra, but the latter had already asked another writer to prepare a libretto on the same subject; Louis Dietsch brought out *Le Vaisseau fantôme* (Paris Opéra, 1842), which was soon forgotten. Meanwhile Wagner received the welcome news from Dresden that *Rienzi* had been accepted for production; its staging later attained considerable success (1842). *Der fliegende Holländer,* also accepted by Dresden, was led by the composer at its premiere (1843). Later that year he was named 2nd Hofkapellmeister in Dresden; conducted many Classic operas, among them *Don Giovanni, Le nozze di Figaro, Die Zauberflöte, Fidelio,* and *Der Freischütz;* conducted a memorable performance of Beethoven's 9th Sym. (1846). He also led the prestigious choral soc. *Liedertafel,* for which he wrote several works, including the "biblical scene" *Das Liebesmahl der Apostel;* was preoccupied with the text and music for *Tannhäuser,* completed and premiered in 1845; his rev. version was staged to better advantage (1847); concurrently he worked on *Lohengrin,* completed in 1848.

Wagner's efforts to have his works publ. failed, leaving him again in debt; without pressing for further performances of his operas, he drew up the 1st prose outline of *Der Nibelungen-Mythus als Entwurf zu einem Drama,* prototype of the epic *Ring* cycle; began work on the "poem" for *Siegfrieds Tod* (1848). At that time he joined the revolutionary Vaterlandsverein and participated actively in the movement, culminating in an open uprising (1849); an order was issued for his arrest; leaving Dresden, he made his way to Weimar; found a cordial reception from Liszt; proceeded to Vienna; borrowed another's passport to cross the border of Saxony on his way to Zurich, where he made his home; Minna joined him there a few months later. Before leaving Dresden he had sketched 2 dramas, *Jesus von Nazareth* and *Achilleus;* both remained unfinished; in Zurich wrote essays expounding his philosophy of art: *Die Kunst und die Revolution* (1849), *Das Kunstwerk der Zukunft* (1849), *Kunst und Klima* (1850), *Oper und Drama* (1851), and *Eine Mitteilung an meine Freunde* (1851). The ideas expressed in *Das Kunstwerk der Zukunft* gave rise to the description of his operas as "music of the future" by opponents and defended as *Gesamtkunstwerk* by his admirers. He rejected both descriptions as distortions of his real views, later rejecting the term music drama, which nevertheless has become an accepted definition for his operas.

In 1850 Wagner was again in Paris; that year Liszt conducted the successful premiere of *Lohengrin* in Weimar. In 1851 Wagner wrote the poem *Der junge Siegfried* and prose sketches

for *Das Rheingold* and *Die Walküre;* finished the texts of *Die Walküre* and *Das Rheingold* (1852). He composed the music for *Das Rheingold* (1853–54), followed by *Die Walküre* (1854–56). In 1854 he met a wealthy Zurich merchant, Otto Wesendonk (1815–96) and his wife, Mathilde (Luckemeyer) Wesendonk (b. Elberfeld, Dec. 23, 1828; d. Traunblick, near Altmünster on the Traunsee, Austria, Aug. 31, 1902); she had already met him in 1852; Otto gave Wagner a substantial loan, to be repaid out of performance proceeds; the situation was complicated by Wagner's love for Mathilde; she wrote the famous *Fünf Gedichte (Der Engel, Stehe still, Träume, Schmerzen, Im Treibhaus)* that he set to music; the set was publ. as the *Wesendonk-Lieder* (1857). He conducted a series of 8 concerts with the Phil. Soc. of London (1855); his performances were greatly praised, and he met Queen Victoria, who invited him to her loge at the intermission of his 7th concert.

In 1856 Wagner made substantial revisions in the last 2 *Ring* poems; changed their titles to *Siegfried* and *Götterdämmerung.* Throughout these years he was preoccupied with writing a new opera, *Tristan und Isolde,* permeated with the dual feelings of love and death; prepared the 1st sketch of *Parzival* (later titled *Parsifal,* 1857); moved to Venice (1858); completed act 2 of *Tristan und Isolde.* The Dresden authorities, acting through their Austrian confederates and still determined to bring him to trial as a revolutionary, pressured Venice to expel him from its territory; he again took refuge in Switzerland, staying in Lucerne while completing *Tristan und Isolde* (1859). That autumn he returned to Paris, conducted 3 concerts of his music at the Théâtre-Italien (1860); Napoléon III became interested in his work, ordering the director of the Paris Opéra to produce *Tannhäuser;* after revisions and trans. into French, it proved to be a fiasco (1861); Wagner withdrew the opera after 3 performances; a tremendous critical cabal rose against him, primarily because audiences were not accustomed to his mystical, weighty, and symphonic operatic style. His music was compared with the sound produced by a domestic cat walking down the keyboard of the piano; French caricaturists pictured him in the act of hammering a listener's ear. Oscar Wilde added his measure of wit. "I like Wagner's music better than anybody's," he wrote in *The Picture of Dorian Gray.* "It is so loud that one can talk the whole time without people hearing what one says." Amazingly, Nietzsche, once a worshipful admirer, made a complete turnabout and publ. a venomous denunciation of his erstwhile idol in *Der Fall Wagner* (1888); Wagner made music itself sick, he proclaimed; but by this time Nietzsche was already sick to the borderline of madness.

Politically Wagner's prospects began to improve; was granted partial amnesty by the Saxon authorities (1860); visited Baden-Baden, his 1st visit to Germany in 11 years; finally granted total amnesty, allowing him access to Saxony (1862); accepted a previous invitation from Otto Wesendonk to go to Venice; while there returned to a scenario he had prepared in Marienbad (1845) for a comic opera, *Die Meistersinger von Nürnberg.* In 1862 he moved to Biebrich, where he began composing the score. In order to repair his finances, he accepted a number of conducting engagements in Vienna, Prague, St. Petersburg, Moscow, and other cities (1862–63). In 1862 he gave a private reading of *Die Meistersinger* in Vienna; his old nemesis Hanslick was angered to discover that the composer had caricatured him in the character of Beckmesser (the original name of the character was

Hans Lick), and let out his discomfiture in further attacks on him.

Wagner's fortunes changed spectacularly when King Ludwig II of Bavaria (1845–86) ascended the throne and invited him to Munich, promising unlimited help in carrying out his projects (1864); in return, Wagner composed the *Huldigungsmarsch,* dedicated to his royal patron. The publ. correspondence between the two is extraordinary in its display of mutual admiration, gratitude, and affection; but difficulties soon developed when the Bavarian Cabinet told Ludwig that his lavish support of Wagner's projects threatened the Bavarian economy; the king was forced to "suggest" that he leave Munich; Wagner went to Switzerland (1865). Another serious difficulty arose in his personal life when he became intimately involved with Liszt's daughter Cosima von Bülow, whose spouse Hans was an impassioned proponent of Wagner's music. In 1865 Cosima gave birth to Wagner's daughter, named Isolde after the heroine of the opera that von Bülow was preparing for performance in Munich; its premiere took place with great acclaim; he prepared the prose sketch of *Parzival* and began to dictate his autobiography, *Mein Leben* (1865–80), to Cosima; resumed the composition of *Die Meistersinger* (1866); settled in a villa in Tribschen, on Lake Lucerne, where Cosima joined him permanently in 1868. He completed *Die Meistersinger* (1867); von Bülow conducted its premiere in Munich in the presence of King Ludwig, who sat in the royal box with Wagner (1868). A son, significantly named Siegfried, was born to Cosima and Wagner (1869); that year *Das Rheingold* was produced in Munich, followed by *Die Walküre* (1870). Cosima and von Bülow were divorced; shortly thereafter she and Wagner were married in Lucerne; Wagner wrote the *Siegfried Idyll,* performed in their villa in Bayreuth on Christmas morning as a surprise for her. In 1871 he wrote the *Kaisermarsch* to mark the victorious conclusion of the Franco-German War; conducted it in the presence of Kaiser Wilhelm I at the Royal Opera House in Berlin.

Later that year, in Leipzig, Wagner made public his plans for building a theater in Bayreuth for the production of the entire *Der Ring des Nibelungen* tetralogy. In 1871 the Bayreuth town council offered him a site for a proposed Festspielhaus; in 1872 the cornerstone was laid, an event commemorated by his conducting a performance of Beethoven's 9th Sym.; in 1873 he began building a home in Bayreuth, which he called *Wahnfried* (free from delusion). In order to complete the building of the Festspielhaus, he appealed to King Ludwig for additional funds; the king complied with 100,000 talers for this purpose. In 1876 the *Ring* went through rehearsals; Ludwig attended the final dress rehearsals; the official premiere of the cycle took place under the direction of H. Richter; in all, 3 complete performances of the *Ring* cycle were given that year. Ludwig was faithful to the end to Wagner, whom he called "my divine friend," even installing architectural representations of scenes from the operas in his castle Neuschwanstein; but his mental deterioration became obvious to everyone, and he was committed to an asylum. (He committed suicide by overpowering the psychiatrist escorting him on a walk and jumping into the Starnbergsee, pulling the hapless doctor after him.)

The spectacles in Bayreuth attracted music lovers and notables from all over the world, even those not partial to Wagner's ideas or music, who went out of curiosity, Tchaikovsky and Ravel among them; yet despite world success and fame, Wagner still labored under fiscal difficulties; disillusioned with his future prospects in Germany, he hoped to find financial support for him and his family to settle in America. Nothing came of this particular proposal, but he did manage 1 American connection by composing on commission the *Grosser Festmarsch* for the observance of the U.S. centennial (1876), dedicated to the "beautiful young ladies of America." He completed the full score of *Parsifal* (as it was now called) in Palermo; it was premiered at Bayreuth (1882), followed by 15 subsequent performances; at the final performance, he stepped to the podium and conducted the last act, his last appearance in this capacity. He went to Venice for a period of rest (he had angina pectoris), but suffered a massive heart attack and died in Cosima's presence. His body was interred in a vault in the garden of Wahnfried.

Wagner's role in music history is unique; not only did he create works of great beauty and tremendous brilliance, but he generated a radically new musical aesthetic, influencing generations of composers. R. Strauss extended Wagner's grandiose vision to sym. music, fashioning the symphonic poem using leading motifs and vivid programmatic description of the scenes portrayed in his music. Even Rimsky-Korsakov, far as he stood from Wagner's ideas of musical composition, reflected the spirit of *Parsifal* in his own religious opera, *The Legend of the City of Kitezh.* Schoenberg's 1st significant work, *Verklärte Nacht,* is Wagnerian in tone. Composers visiting Bayreuth often experienced complete changes of opinion; Debussy came a French Wagnerite and left a Frenchman, period; Wolf came a Hanslick-in-training and left a Wagnerite for life. Lesser composers, unable to escape Wagner's magic domination, attempted to follow him literally by writing trilogies and tetralogies on a parallel plan with his *Ring.*

Wagner's reform of opera was based on his insistence upon the dramatic truth of his music; when he rejected traditional opera, he did so believing that such an artificial form ("number opera") could not serve true dramatic expression; instead he created a new form (continuous symphonic drama) and new techniques. So revolutionary was his art that conductors and singers had to undergo special training in this new style in order to perform his works properly, so that such terms as *Wagnerian tenor* and *Wagnerian soprano* became a part of the musical vocabulary. In addition to condemning the illogical plans of Italian opera and French grand opera (a reversal of means and ends), he saw the choice of subject as of utmost importance, "entirely human, and freed from all convention and from everything historically formal." Continuous thematic development of basic motifs becomes a fundamental procedure for dramatic cohesion; these highly individualized generating motifs, appearing singly, in bold relief, or subtly varied and intertwined with other motifs, present the ever-changing soul states of the characters of the drama, and form the connecting links for the dramatic situations of the total artwork. Characters in Wagner's stage works become themselves symbols of such soul states, so that even mythical gods, magic-workers, heroic horses, and speaking birds become expressions of eternal verities, illuminating human behavior. Yet the very solemnity of his great stage images bore the seeds of their own destruction in a world governed by differing aesthetic principles; Wagnerian domination of the musical stage lost its power; spectators and listeners were no longer interested in solving psychological riddles on the stage. A demand for human simplicity arose against Wagnerian heroic complexity; the public at large found greater enjoyment in the pseudo-realism in Verdi's romantic operas than the unreality of symbolic truth in Wagner's; by the 2nd quarter of the 20th century, few if any composers tried to imitate Wagner; all at once his grandeur and animation became an unnatural and asphyxiating constraint.

In the domain of melody, harmony, and orchestration Wagner's art was as revolutionary as was his stagecraft. He introduced the idea of endless melody, a continuous flow of diatonic and chromatic tones; the tonality became fluid and uncertain, producing an impression of unattainability, so that a listener accustomed to Classic modulatory schemes could not easily follow the drive towards the tonic, e.g., the prelude to *Tristan und Isolde*, the textbook example of such harmonic fluidity. The use of long unresolved dominant-9th-chords and dramatic tremolos of diminished-7th-chords contributed to this state of musical uncertainty; but Wagnerian harmony also became the foundation of a new method of composition that adopted a free flow of modulatory progressions; without Wagner the chromatic idioms of the 20th century could not exist. In orchestration, too, he introduced new timbral combinations, designed new instruments (the so-called Wagner tuba), and increased the technical demands on individual orch'l players, e.g., the vertiginous flight of the bassoon to the high E in the overture to *Tannhäuser*, unimaginable before Wagner.

Wagner became the target of political contention during World War I when audiences in the Allied countries associated his sonorous works with German imperialism; even greater obstacles to his music arose with Hitler, a man who ordered the slaughter of millions of Jews and others, and who was an enthusiastic admirer of Wagner, who himself entertained anti-Semitic notions (viz his essay *On Judaism in Music*, 1850); therefore, the logic goes, Wagner was guilty by association of mass murder. Difficult questions remain: Can art be separated from politics, particularly when politics become murderous? Does a racist deserve greater dishonor simply for being more literate? (Wagner did not invent anti-Semitism, or racism in general, or genocide; no one has found the cure yet for any of these horrors.) Not long ago, members of the Israel Philharmonic refused to play the prelude to *Tristan und Isolde* when Zubin Mehta, a highly visible pro-Israel figure, programmed the work on a Tel Aviv concert, and booed him for his troubles. Was Mehta trying to inflict Wagner on Wagner's philosophical victims, or seeking a rapprochement between past and present?

In addition to his music dramas, Wagner created many arrangements and editions: piano scores of Beethoven's 9th Sym. and Haydn's Sym. No. 103; vocal scores for operas by Donizetti and Halévy; reorchestrations of operas by Gluck's *Iphigénie en Aulide* and Palestrina's Stabat Mater. He devoted a large amount of his enormous productive activity to writing; besides the librettos he set, literary works include plays, librettos, scenarios, and novellas, among them *Mannerlist grosser als Frauenlist, oder Die glückliche Bärenfamilie*, 2-act comic opera (libretto, 1837; some music completed); *Eine Pilgerfahrt zu Beethoven*, novella (1840); *Ein Ende in Paris*, novella (1841); *Ein glücklicher Abend*, novella (1841); *Die Sarazenin*, 3-act opera (prose scenario, 1841–42; verse text, 1843); *Die Bergwerke zu Falun*, 3-act opera (prose scenario, 1841–42); *Wieland der Schmied*, 3-act opera (prose scenario, 1850); *Luther* or *Luthers Hochzeit*, sketch for a play (1868). He expounded his theories

on music, politics, philosophy, religion, etc., in numerous essays, among them "Das Kunstwerk der Zukunft," "Oper und Drama," "Was ist deutsch?," "Beethoven," "Über die Bennung 'Musikdrama'," "Religion und Kunst." Editions of his collected writings were prepared by the composer himself (Leipzig, 1871–1883) and H. von Wolzogen and R. Sternfeld (Leipzig, 1911; Leipzig, 1914). Wagner began issuing *Bayreuther Blätter* as an aid to understanding his operas (1878); this journal continued publication until 1938.

wait (wayt, wayte). A town watchman in the Middle Ages whose duty was to keep order in the streets at night and announce the time by playing a brass instrument. Waits often serenaded incoming travelers in their stagecoaches; they were also employed to provide music for ceremonial occasions. In Germany waits were called Stadtpfeifer, and a genre of urban folk music was collected under the designation Turm-musik.

Waits, Tom, b. Pomona, Calif., Dec. 7, 1949. He began his career playing in Los Angeles clubs as a singer, pianist, and guitarist, sometimes with his group Nocturnal Emissions. After being signed by Frank Zappa's manager in 1972, he produced his 1st record album, *Closing Time* (1973). He slowly rose from cultdom to stardom through such songs as *Ol' '55, Shiver Me Timbers, Diamonds on My Windshield,* and *The Piano Has Been Drinking;* noteworthy albums of this period include *Nighthawks at the Diner, Small Change, Foreign Affairs,* and *Heartattack & Vine.* He switched from the Asylum label to Island; with *Swordfishtrombones* (1983) he expanded his accompaniment to include a broad spectrum of exotic instruments.

Waits wrote the score for Francis Ford Coppola's film *One from the Heart* (1982), and later made the album *Rain Dogs* (1985) and concert movie *Big Time* (1988). He also collaborated with his wife, Kathleen Brennan, on the stage show *Frank's Wild Years* (1987), which includes the pastiches *Temptation* and *Innocent When You Dream.* In 1993 he created a performance work, *The Black Rider,* with the collaboration of William S. Burroughs. Among the artists who have performed his music are Bette Midler, Crystal Gayle, Bruce Springsteen, the Eagles, and the Manhattan Transfer; he also acted in film (notably Jim Jarmusch's *Down By Law*) and on stage. He is a jazz songwriter who regards the beatniks of the 1950s as his primary inspiration; his imaginative lyrics are full of slang and focus on the sad flotsam of cheap bars and motels. He accompanies his gravelly voice and delivery with rough instrumentation or electronics, but always with sensitive musicianship and ironic pathos.

Waldflöte (Ger.). An open metal flue stop in the organ, of 2' or 4' pitch and suave, full tone.

Waldhorn (Ger.). Natural or hand horn.

Waldteufel (Ger., forest devil). Friction drum.

Waldteufel, (Charles-) Émile (born Lévy), b. Strasbourg, Dec. 9, 1837; d. Paris, Feb. 12, 1915. His father, Louis (1801–84), and his brother, Léon (1832–84), were violinists and dance composers, and his mother was a pianist. In 1842 the family went to Paris, where he studied piano with his mother and then with Joseph Heyberger; subsequently was an auditor in L.-A. Marmontel's class at the Paris Cons., where he became a pupil of A. Laurent in 1853, but he left before completing his courses. He became a piano tester for the manufacturer Scholtus; also taught piano and played in soirées; when he had time he composed dance music for Paris salons. In 1865 he became court pianist to the Empress Eugénie and in 1866 conductor of the state balls.

Waldteufel's 1st waltz, *Joies et peines*, which he publ. at his own expense in 1859, was an immediate success, and he became known in Paris high society. In 1867 he publ. another successful waltz, with the German title *Vergissmeinnicht*. Then followed a series of waltzes that established his fame as a French counterpart to Johann Strauss (II): *Manola* (1873), *Mon Rêve* (1877), *Pomone* (1877), *Toujours ou jamais* (1877), *Les Sirènes* (1878), *Très jolie* (1878), *Pluie de diamants* (1879), *Dolores* (1880), and the most famous of them, *Les Patineurs* (1882). His dance music symbolized the "gai Paris" of his time as fittingly as the music of Strauss reflected the gaiety of old Vienna. Waldteufel lived most of his life in Paris, but he also filled conducting engagements abroad, visiting London in 1885 and Berlin in 1889.

Walker, George (Theophilus), b. Washington, D.C., June 27, 1922. He studied at the Oberlin College Cons. of Music (M.B., 1941); then entered the Curtis Inst. of Music in Philadelphia, where he studied piano with Rudolf Serkin, composition with Rosario Scalero and Gian Carlo Menotti, and chamber music with Gregor Piatigorsky and William Primrose (Artist Diploma, 1945); also took piano lessons with Robert Casadesus in Fontainebleau in France (diploma, 1947); obtained his D.M.A. from the Eastman School of Music in Rochester, N.Y., in 1957. In 1957 he received a Fulbright fellowship for travel to Paris, where he took courses in composition with Nadia Boulanger.

In 1945 Walker made his debut as a pianist, and subsequently appeared throughout the U.S. and abroad; was also active as a teacher; held appointments at Dillard Univ. in New Orleans (1953), the New School for Social Research in N.Y., the Dalcroze School of Music (1961), Smith College (1961–68), and the Univ. of Colorado (1968). In 1969 he was appointed a prof. at Rutgers, the State Univ. of New Jersey; was chairman of the composition dept. there in 1974; in 1975, was also named Distinguished Prof. at the Univ. of Delaware and adjunct prof. at the Peabody Inst. in Baltimore. In 1969 he received a Guggenheim fellowship; also held 2 Rockefeller fellowships for study in Italy (1971, 1975). In 1982 he was made a member of the American Academy and Inst. of Arts and Letters.

In his music Walker maintains a median modern line with an infusion of African-American idioms. He won the 1996 Pulitzer Prize (*Lilacs* for Voice and Orch.). Among his other compositions are: Orch.: Trombone Concerto (1957); *Antiphonys* for Chamber Orch. (1968); Variations (1971); Piano Concerto (1975); *Dialogues* for Cello and Orch. (1975–76); *Overture: In Praise of Folly* (1980); Cello Concerto (N.Y., 1982); *An Eastman Overture* (Washington, D.C., 1983); Violin Concerto (1984). Chamber: 2 string quartets (1946, 1967); Cello Sonata (1957); 2 violin sonatas (1959, 1979); *Music (Sacred and Profane)* for brass (1975); 4 piano sonatas (1953, 1957, 1975, 1985); other piano pieces. Vocal: *3 Lyrics* for Chorus (1958); Mass for Soprano, Alto, Tenor, Baritone, Chorus, and Orch.

(1978); *Poem* for Soprano and Chamber Ensemble, after T. S. Eliot's *The Hollow Men* (1986); choruses; songs.

walking bass. In jazz, a bass figure moving up and down in diatonic and chromatic steps in broken octaves in even 8th-note rhythms. It was 1st associated with piano boogie-woogie, but became principally associated with jazz double-bass playing in the swing era; it continues to serve that purpose.

Waller, "Fats" (Thomas Wright), b. N.Y., May 21, 1904; d. Kansas City, Mo., Dec. 15, 1943. As a child he had private piano instruction and studied violin and double bass in school, but his most significant early lessons came from the player piano and nickelodeon pianists whom he studiously imitated; at 14 he was playing organ professionally in a Harlem theater; at 16 he received piano training from Russell Brooks and James P. Johnson; he claimed that he later had some lessons from Leopold Godowsky and studied composition with Carl Bohm at the Juilliard School of Music. In 1922 he began to make recordings, and in 1923 he made his 1st appearance on the radio; he subsequently made frequent broadcasts as a singer and pianist.

In 1928 Waller made his debut at N.Y.'s Carnegie Hall as a piano soloist. With the lyricist Andy Razaf, he composed most of the music for the African-American Broadway musical *Keep Shufflin'* (1928), and then collaborated on the shows *Load of Coal* and *Hot Chocolates* (1929), which includes the song *Ain't Misbehavin'*. He worked with Ted Lewis (1930), Jack Teagarden (1931), and Billy Banks's Rhythmakers (1932) before organizing his own band, Fats Waller and his Rhythm, in 1934; he was active on the West Coast and appeared in the Hollywood films *Hooray for Love* and *King of Burlesque* (both 1935). In 1938 he toured Europe, and again in 1939; in 1943 he appeared in the Hollywood film *Stormy Weather* leading an all-star band.

As a jazz pianist Waller was considered a leading exponent of stride piano, playing with a delicacy and lightness of touch that belied his considerable bulk of almost 300 pounds. Much of his popularity was due to his skills as an entertainer; he was especially effective in improvising lyrics to deflate the sentimentality of popular songs. A musical tribute to Waller, the revue *Ain't Misbehavin'*, was one of the great successes of the N.Y. theater season in 1978.

Walpurgis Night (Ger. *Walpurgisnacht*). The feast day of St. Walpurgis, an 8th-century English abbess (May 1). Halloween-like Walpurgis Nights are celebrated at the reputed locale of the witches' sabbath, the peak of Mt. Brocken in the Harz Mountains. Faust attends one in Goethe's play; Mendelssohn based his secular cantata *Die erste Walpurgisnacht* (1833) on this scene. Berlioz presents a witches' sabbath in the final movement of his *Sym. fantastique*. Gounod includes a scene during Walpurgis Night in his opera *Faust*. Dies Irae is commonly used as a motto in virtually all musical representations of the Walpurgis Night.

Walter, Bruno (born Bruno Walter Schlesinger), Berlin, Sept. 15, 1876; d. Beverly Hills, Calif., Feb. 17, 1962. He entered the Stern Cons. in Berlin at age 8, where he studied with H. Ehrlich, L. Bussler, and R. Radecke. At age 9 he performed in public as a pianist; at 13 decided to pursue his interest in conducting. In 1893 he became a coach at the Cologne Opera, where he made his conducting debut with Lortzing's *Der Waffen-schmied;* in the following year he was engaged as assistant conductor at the Hamburg Stadttheater, under Mahler; became in subsequent years an ardent champion of Mahler's music; conducted the premieres of the posth. Sym. No. 9 and *Das Lied von der Erde.*

During the 1896–97 season Walter was engaged as 2nd conductor at the Stadttheater in Breslau; he then became principal conductor in Pressburg, and in 1898 at Riga, where he conducted for 2 seasons. In 1900 he received the important engagement of conductor at the Berlin Royal Opera under a 5-year contract; left this post in 1901 when he received an offer from Mahler to become his assistant at the Vienna Court Opera. He established himself as an efficient opera conductor; conducted in England (1st appearance 1909, with the Royal Phil. Soc. in London). He remained at the Vienna Court Opera after the death of Mahler; in 1913 he became Royal Bavarian Generalmusikdirektor in Munich; under his guidance the Munich Opera enjoyed brilliant performances, particularly of Mozart's works.

Seeking greater freedom for his artistic activities, Walter left Munich in 1922 and gave numerous performances as a guest conductor with European orchs.; he conducted the series "Bruno Walter Concerts" with the Berlin Phil. from 1921 to 1933; from 1925 conducted summer concerts of the Salzburg Festival; his performances of Mozart's music there set a standard. He also appeared as pianist in Mozart's chamber works. In 1923 he made his American debut with the N.Y. Sym. Soc., and appeared with it again in 1924 and 1925. From 1925 to 1929 he was conductor of the Städtische Oper in Berlin-Charlottenburg; in 1929 he succeeded Furtwängler as conductor of the Gewandhaus Orch. in Leipzig; continued to give special concerts in Berlin. In 1932 he was guest conductor of the N.Y. Phil., acting also as soloist in a Mozart piano concerto; reengaged during the next 3 seasons as associate conductor with Toscanini. He was also a guest conductor in Philadelphia, Washington, D.C., and Baltimore.

With the advent of the Nazi regime in Germany in 1933, Walter's engagement with the Gewandhaus Orch. was canceled; was also prevented from continuing his orch. concerts in Berlin. He filled several engagements with the Concertgebouw in Amsterdam, and also conducted in Salzburg. In 1936 he was engaged as music director of the Vienna State Opera; this was terminated with the Nazi annexation of Austria in 1938. Walter, with his family, then went to France, where he was granted French citizenship. After the outbreak of World War II in 1939 he sailed for America, establishing his residence in Calif.; eventually became a naturalized American citizen; guest conductor with the NBC Sym. Orch. (1939); conducted many performances of the Metropolitan Opera in N.Y. (debut in *Fidelio,* 1941). From 1947 to 1949 he was conductor and musical adviser of the N.Y. Phil.; returned regularly as guest conductor until 1960; made recordings with the Columbia Sym. Orch. created for him; also conducted in Europe (1949–60), giving his farewell performance in Vienna with the Vienna Phil. in 1960.

Walter achieved the reputation of a perfect classicist among contemporary conductors; his interpretations of the masterpieces of the Vienna School were particularly notable. He is acknowledged to have been a foremost conductor of Mahler's syms. He also composed his own music, including 2 syms., a

string quartet, piano quintet, piano trio, and several albums of songs. He publ. the books *Von den moralischen Kraften der Musik* (Vienna, 1935); *Gustav Mahler* (Vienna, 1936); *Von der Musik und vom Musizieren* (Frankfurt am Main, 1957).

Walther, Johann Gottfried, b. Erfurt, Sept. 18, 1684; d. Weimar, March 23, 1748. He was organist at the church of St. Peter and St. Paul in Weimar from 1707 until his death; also served as music master at the ducal court and Hofmusicus of its orch. (from 1721). He compiled the great *Musicalisches Lexicon* (1732), the 1st music dictionary to encompass biographies, terms, and bibliographies. He composed sacred vocal music (of which only 1 example survives) and organ preludes; wrote a treatise on composition (1708, unpubl. until the 20th century); was an important music copyist; distant relation and lifelong friend of Bach.

Walton, Sir William (Turner), b. Oldham, Lancashire, Mar. 29, 1902; d. Ischia, Italy, Mar. 8, 1983. Both his parents were professional singers, and Walton himself had a fine singing voice as a youth; he entered the Cathedral Choir School at Christ Church, Oxford, and began to compose choral pieces for performance. Sir Hugh Allen, organist of New College, advised him to develop his interest in composition, and sponsored his admission to Christ Church at an early age; however, he never graduated; instead began to write unconventional music in the manner fashionable in the 1920s.

Walton's talent manifested itself in a string quartet he wrote at the age of 17, accepted for performance for the 1st festival of the ISCM in 1923. In London he formed a congenial association with the Sitwell family of quintessential cognoscenti and literati who combined a patrician sense of artistic superiority with a benign attitude toward the social plebs; they also provided Walton with residence at their manor in Chelsea, where he lived off and on for some 15 years. Fascinated by Edith Sitwell's oxymoronic verse, Walton set it to music bristling with novel jazzy effects in brisk, irregular rhythms and modern harmonies; Walton was only 19 when he wrote it. Under the title *Façade,* it was 1st performed in London in 1923, with Sitwell herself delivering her doggerel with a megaphone; as expected, the show provoked an outburst of indignation in the press and undisguised delight among the young in spirit.

But Walton did not pursue the path of facile hedonism so fashionable at the time; demonstrated his ability to write music in a Classic manner in his fetching concert overture *Portsmouth Point,* 1st performed in Zurich (1926), and later in the comedyoverture *Scapino* (1941). His biblical oratorio *Belshazzar's Feast* (1931) reveals a deep emotional stream and nobility of design that places him directly in line from Handel and Elgar among English masters. His sym. works show him as an inheritor of the grand Romantic tradition; his concertos for violin, for viola, and for cello demonstrate an adroitness in beautiful and effective instrumental writing.

Walton was a modernist in his acceptance of the new musical resources, but he never deviated from fundamental tonality and formal clarity of design. Above all, his music was profoundly national, unmistakably British in its inspiration and content. Quite appropriately he was asked to contribute to 2 royal occasions: he wrote *Crown Imperial March* for the coronation of King George VI in 1937 and *Orb and Sceptre* for Queen Elizabeth

II in 1953; knighted in 1951. He spent the last years of his life on the island of Ischia off Naples with his Argentine-born wife, Susana Gil Passo.

waltz (Ger. *Walzer*, from *walzen*, turn around; Fr. *valse*). The quintessential ballroom dance in 3/4 time, generated in Austria toward the end of the 18th century. Choreographically it consists of a pair of dancers moving around an imaginary axis, resulting in a movement forward. In the 18th century the waltz was regarded as a vulgar dance fit only for peasant entertainment. In 1760 waltzing was specifically forbidden by a government order in Bavaria. The waltz received its social acceptance in the wake of the French Revolution, when it became fashionable even in upper social circles on the continent. England withstood its impact well into the 19th century. A story is told about an English dowager who watched a young couple waltzing and asked incredulously, "Are they married?"

The 1st representation of a waltzlike dance on the stage occurred during a performance of the opera *Una cosa rara* by Martin y Soler in Vienna in 1786. The waltz attained its social popularity during the Congress of Vienna in 1815; at that time it was known under the name of *Wienerwalzer*. In France the *valse* assumed different forms, in 3/8, 3/4, or 6/8 time, as an andante (*sauteuse*), allegretto, allegro (*jeté*), or presto. In the 20th century an American waltz misnamed *Valse Boston* (in reality, a hesitation waltz) spread all over Europe about 1920.

As a musical form the waltz generally consists of 2 repeated periods of 8 bars each. The earliest printing of a waltz in this form was the publication of 12 concert waltzes by the pianist Daniel Steibelt in 1800; these were followed by a collection of waltzes by Hummel publ. in 1808. Such concert waltzes were extended by the insertion of several trios, multiple reprises, and a coda, lasting nearly half an hour in all. During the 19th century the concert waltz became a favorite among composers for piano, beginning with Weber and finding its greatest artistic efflorescence in the waltzes of Chopin. Beethoven canonized the waltz in his famous Diabelli variations (op. 120), based on a waltz tune.

The waltz grew into an industry in Vienna. Joseph Lanner and Johann Strauss (I) composed hundreds of waltz tunes to be played in Viennese restaurants and entertainment places. Johann Strauss (II) raised the waltz to its summit as an artistic creation which, at the time, served the needs of popular entertainment. He was justly dubbed "The Waltz King" (*Walzerkönig*). When Brahms was asked to autograph a waltz tune for a lady, he jotted the initial bars of Strauss's *On the Beautiful Blue Danube*, with a characteristic remark, "Unfortunately, not by me." Strauss wrote many other popular works, including *Tales of the Vienna Woods, Voices of Spring, Vienna Blood*, and *Wine, Women, and Song*. All these waltzes were really chains of waltz movements. Gradually the waltz became acceptable in purely sym. dimension. Berlioz has a waltz movement in his *Sym. fantastique*; Tchaikovsky includes a waltz in his 5th Sym., and Mahler in his 9th Sym. Ravel parodied the Viennese waltz gloriously in his *La Valse*. Thus in less than a century the waltz, which began as a somewhat vulgar, popular dance tune, took its place next to the minuet as a legitimate concert form.

War of the Buffoons. Guerre des bouffons.

warble. See ⇒yodel.

Warfield, William (Caesar), b. West Helena, Ark., Jan. 22, 1920. He studied at the Eastman School of Music in Rochester, N.Y., graduating in 1942; sang in opera and musical comedy; gave his 1st N.Y. song recital in 1950, with excellent critical acclaim. He subsequently toured Europe in the role of Porgy in Gershwin's *Porgy and Bess*. He married the soprano Leontyne Price in 1952 (divorced, 1972). In 1974 he was appointed a prof. of music at the Univ. of Illinois.

Waring, Fred(eric Malcolm), b. Tyrone, Pa., June 9, 1900; d. Danville, Pa., July 29, 1984. He learned music at his mother's knee; took up the banjo at 16 and organized a quartet that he called the Banjazzatra. He studied engineering and architecture at Pa. State Univ.; he retained his love for gadgets throughout his musical career, and in 1937 patented the Waring blender.

Waring acquired fame with his own band, The Pennsylvanians, on national tours at concert halls, hotels, and college campuses; the group was particularly successful on radio programs sponsored by tobacco companies and the Ford Motor Co. His repertoire consisted of wholesome American songs, many of them composed by himself. Among his soloists on special programs were Bing Crosby, Hoagy Carmichael, Irving Berlin, and Frank Sinatra. He had a natural streak for publicity; once bet that he could lead a bull into a Fifth Avenue china shop; succeeded without breaking a single piece of crockery. He was a friend of President Eisenhower; in 1983 President Reagan awarded him the Congressional Gold Medal. He continued to lead youth choral groups, giving a concert at Pa. State Univ. a day before he suffered a stroke, and 2 days before his death.

Warlock, Peter. See ⇒Heseltine, Philip (Arnold).

Wärme, mit (Ger.). With warmth, warmly. *Mit grosser Wärme,* with great warmth.

Warwick(e), (Marie) Dionne. See ⇒Bacharach, Burt.

washboard (rubboard; Fr. *frittoir*). Traditional American instrument using a laundering board with a corrugated surface (usually metal); the board is scraped with a stick, like a guiro; it provides rhythmic support for jug bands, which included blown molasses jugs and broomstick bass.

Washington, Dinah (born Ruth Lee Jones), b. Tuscaloosa, Ala., Aug. 8(?), 1924; d. Detroit, Dec. 14, 1963. She went to Chicago; won an amateur singing contest at the age of 15; made local appearances before singing in Lionel Hampton's band (1943–46); soon established herself as a major rhythm-and-blues artist with such songs as *Blow Top Blues* and *Evil Gal Blues*. She was best known for her renditions of *What a Difference a Day Makes, Homeward Bound, Stormy Weather,* and *September in the Rain*. Her early death resulted from a drug overdose.

Wasitodiningrat, (Ki) K.R.T. (Kanjeng Raden Tumengung, a title of honorary royal status), b. Yogyakarta, Java, Mar. 17, 1909. His former names are Wasitolodoro, Tjokrowasito, and Wasitodipuro. He was born in the Pakualaman Palace, one of 3 principal courts of central Java, where his father was director of musical activities. Wasitodiningrat studied dance from the age of 6, graduating from the SMA National High School in 1922. He became music director of the Yogyakarta radio station MAVRO in 1934 and remained there through the Japanese occupation, when the station was called Jogja Hosokjoku. In 1945 the station became RRI (Radio Republic Indonesia); he served as director there again in 1951.

Between 1951 and 1970 Wasitodiningrat taught dance at the Konservatori Tari and the Academy Tari, both in Yogyakarta, and music at the Academy Karawitan in Surakarta; he also founded and directed the Wasitodipuro Center for Vocal Studies in Yogyakarta. In 1953 he toured Asia, North America, and Europe; in 1961 he became associated with the new dance/theater form *sendratari*, later becoming music director for P. L. T. Bagong Kussudiardjo's troupe. He succeeded his father as director of the Pakualaman gamelan in 1962. In 1971 he joined the faculty of the Calif. Inst. of the Arts as master of Javanese gamelan; taught workshops at both the Los Angeles and Berkeley campuses of the Univ. of Calif. Wasitodiningrat is a leading performer and composer of central Javanese music; the Pakualaman gamelan's recordings are considered exemplary; one is included in the 40 minutes of music installed in the spacecraft Voyager, intended to represent our planet's music to outsiders. His numerous awards include a gold medal from the Indonesian government honoring his devotion to Javanese music. He frequently performs with his daughter, Nanik, and her Balinese husband, Nyoman Wenten.

Waters, "Muddy" (born McKinley Morganfield), b. Rolling Fork, Miss., Apr. 4, 1915; d. Westmont, Ill., Apr. 30, 1983. He was reared by his maternal grandmother on a plantation near Clarksdale, Miss.; she called him "Muddy" because of his childhood habit of playing in the mud; his playmates called him "Waters," and he accepted the name "Muddy Waters" when he began to sing and play the guitar. In 1941 A. Lomax and J. Work recorded his singing for the Library of Congress; this encouraged him to try his luck in commercial recording.

In 1943 Waters moved to Chicago, where he made his 1st successes; indeed, he soon earned the sobriquet "King of Chicago Blues." Fortunately for him, his followers, and jazz historians, he totally lacked any vocal training and was forced to develop his own unrestricted lexicon of sounds, ranging from soft trembling moans to a ferocious animal-like roar. To make his mode of delivery even more physically stunning he used electric amplification on his guitar; soon he had assembled a band that brought the new technology to the blues for the 1st time; Waters was the most important of the acoustic rural blues musicians to make the transition to electric urban blues in the 1940s.

Waters played electric blues in England in 1958, which struck holy terror into the ears and hearts of purist British folk-song experts; but he recruited to his cause the young enthusiasts, among them Mick Jagger; in fact Jagger and his friends named their famous band the Rolling Stones after Waters's early hit song *Rollin' Stone;* the rock journal *Rolling Stone* also owes its name to Muddy's song; Bob Dylan created his own rock tune *Like a Rolling Stone* as an unconscious tribute to him. In his later years the Tex. blues guitarist Johnny Winter worked with him professionally as a performer, producer, and all-around champion.

Watts, André, b. Nuremberg, June 20, 1946. His mother gave him his earliest piano lessons. After the family moved to the U.S. he studied with Genia Robiner, Doris Bawden, and Clement Petrillo at the Philadelphia Musical Academy. At the age of 9 he made his 1st public appearance playing the Haydn Concerto in D Major at a children's concert of the Philadelphia Orch. His parents were divorced in 1962, but his mother continued to guide his studies. At 14 he played Franck's *Symphonic Variations* with the Philadelphia Orch.; at 16 he became an instant celebrity when he played Liszt's 1st Piano Concerto at one of the televised Young People's Concerts with the N.Y. Phil., conducted by Leonard Bernstein (1963).

Watts's youth and the fact that he was partly African-American contributed to his success, but it was the grand and poetic manner of his virtuosity that conquered the usually skeptical press. Still, he insisted on completing his academic education. In 1969 he joined the class of Fleisher at the Peabody Cons. of Music in Baltimore, obtaining his Artist Diploma in 1972. In the meantime he developed an international career. He made his European debut as soloist with the London Sym. Orch. in 1966; then played with the Concertgebouw Orch. in Amsterdam. Later that year, 1966, he played his 1st solo recital in N.Y., inviting comparisons in the press with the great piano virtuosos of the past. In 1967 he was soloist with the Los Angeles Phil. under Mehta on a tour of Europe and Asia.

On his 21st birthday Watts played the 2nd Piano Concerto of Brahms with the Berlin Phil. In 1970 he revisited his place of birth and played a solo recital with sensational success. He also became a favorite at important political occasions; he played at President Richard Nixon's inaugural concert at Constitution Hall in 1969, at the last coronation of the Shah of Iran, and at a festive celebration of the President of the Congo. In 1973 he toured Russia. In 1976 he played a solo recital on live network television. He was also the subject of a film documentary. He celebrated the 25th anniversary of his debut with the N.Y. Phil. as soloist under Mehta in the Liszt 1st Concerto, the Beethoven 2nd Concerto, and the Rachmaninoff 2nd Concerto in a concert telecast live on PBS (1988); that year he received the Avery Fisher Prize.

wavelength. The length of a sound wave, marking the crests (or other corresponding points) of 2 successive waves. Lower sounds have longer wavelengths; higher sounds have shorter wavelengths. In other words, the wavelength is inversely proportional to frequency of vibrations of a given sound.

wa-wa (wah-wah). 1. Trumpet technique (placing the hand in the bell) or mute that produces a wavering amplitude effect used principally in jazz. 2. Electronic device producing a similar effect on the electric guitar and other instruments, usually manipulated by a foot pedal. Rock musicians such as Eric Clapton and John McLaughlin popularized the wa-wa sound in the 1960s.

Waxman (Wachsmann), Franz, b. Konigshütte, Dec. 24, 1906; d. Los Angeles, Feb. 24, 1967. He studied in Dresden and Berlin; went to the U.S. in 1934 and settled in Hollywood, where he took lessons with Arnold Schoenberg; became a successful composer for films; his musical score for *Sunset Boulevard* won the Academy Award for 1950; also was active as a conductor; was founder-conductor of the Los Angeles Music Festival (1947–67). His other film scores include *Magnificent*

Obsession (1935), *Captains Courageous* (1937), *The Philadelphia Story* (1940), *Stalag 17* (1953), *Sayonara* (1957), and *Sunrise at Campobello* (1960); composed orch'l and vocal works.

wayte. Wait.

Webber, Andrew Lloyd. Lloyd Webber, Andrew.

Weber, Carl Maria (Friedrich Ernst) von, b. Eutin, Oldenburg, Nov. 18, 1786; d. London, June 5, 1826. His father, Franz Anton von Weber (1734[?]–1812), was an army officer and a good musical amateur who played the violin and served as Kapellmeister in Eutin; his fondest wish was that Carl Maria follow in the footsteps of Mozart as a child prodigy (Constanze Weber, Mozart's wife, was his niece, making Carl Maria a 1st cousin of Mozart's by marriage). Carl Maria's mother was a singer of some ability, but died when he was 11. Franz Anton led a wandering life as music director of his own touring theater company, taking his family with him; although this mode of life interfered with Carl Maria's regular education, it gave him practical knowledge of the stage and stimulated his imagination as a dramatic composer.

Weber's 1st teachers were his father and his half-brother Fritz, a pupil of Haydn; at Hildburghausen, while touring with his father, received piano instruction from J. P. Heuschkel (1796); went to Salzburg, attracting the attention of Michael Haydn, who taught him counterpoint (1797); he composed a set of *6 Fughetten* there (publ. 1798). Now in Munich, he was taught singing by Valesi (J. B. Wallishauser) and composition by J. N. Kalcher (1798–1800). At the age of 12 he wrote an opera, *Die Macht der Liebe und des Weins;* it was never performed nor has its MS survived. Through a meeting with Aloys Senefelder, inventor of lithography, he became Senefelder's apprentice, acquiring considerable skill; engraved his own *6 Variations on an Original Theme* for Piano (Munich, 1800). Franz Anton became interested in the business possibilities of lithography, and set up a workshop with him in Freiberg; however, the venture failed, and Carl Maria turned again to music.

Weber composed a 2-act comic opera, *Das Waldmädchen,* in 1800; it premiered in Freiberg; performances followed in Chemnitz (1800) and Vienna (1804). In 1801 the family was once more in Salzburg, where he studied further with Haydn; wrote another opera, *Peter Schmoll und seine Nachbarn* (1801–02). He gave a concert in Hamburg; the family then proceeded to Augsburg; they remained there until settling in Vienna (1803); he continued his studies with Abbé Vogler, at whose recommendation he secured the post of conductor of the Breslau Opera (1804); resigned this post after his attempts at operatic reform caused dissension (1806).

In 1806 Weber became honorary Intendant to Duke Eugen of Württemberg-Ols at Schloss Carlsruhe in Upper Silesia; much of his time was devoted to composition there. He was engaged as private secretary to Duke Ludwig in Stuttgart, and also gave music lessons to his children (1807); this employment was abruptly terminated when he became innocently involved in a scheme of securing a ducal appointment for a rich man's son in order to exempt him from military service, accepting a loan; he was arrested (1810) and kept in prison for 16 days. This matter, along with several others, was settled to his advantage, only to

find him the target of his many creditors, who had him rearrested. Finally agreeing to pay off his debts as swiftly as possible, he was released and then banished.

Weber went to Mannheim, where he made appearances as a pianist; then to Darmstadt, rejoining his former teacher, Vogler, for whom he wrote the introduction to his teacher's ed. of 12 Bach chorales. His opera *Silvana* was successfully premiered in Frankfurt (1810); the title role was sung by Caroline Brandt, who later became a member of the Prague Opera and eventually his wife. He left Darmstadt in early 1811 for Munich, where he composed several important orch'l works, including the clarinet concertino, the 2 clarinet concertos, and the bassoon concerto. His clarinet pieces were written for the noted virtuoso Heinrich (Joseph) Bärmann (1784–1847). His 1-act singspiel, *Abu Hassan,* was successfully given in Munich in the late spring of 1811. For the rest of that year Weber and Bärmann gave concerts in Switzerland; in 1812, after appearing in Prague they went to Leipzig, Weimar, Dresden, and Berlin (attended by King Friedrich Wilhelm III); late that year he was soloist at the premiere of his 2nd Piano Concerto in Gotha.

Upon Weber's return to Prague in early 1813 he was informed that he was to be the director of the German Opera there. He was given extensive authority; he traveled to Vienna to engage singers and also secured the services of Franz Clement as concertmaster. During his tenure he presented a distinguished repertoire that included Beethoven's *Fidelio;* however, when his reforms encountered determined opposition, he submitted his resignation (1816). In late 1816 he was appointed Musikdirektor of the German Opera in Dresden by King Friedrich August III. He opened his 1st season in early 1817; that same year he was named Königlich Kapellmeister; he began to make sweeping reforms. Weber and Brandt were married in Prague that year. About this time he approached Friedrich Kind, a Dresden lawyer and writer, and suggested to him the idea of preparing a libretto on a Romantic German subject for his next opera. They agreed on *Der Freischütz,* a fairy tale from the *Gespensterbuch,* a collection of ghost stories by J. A. Apel and F. Laun. The composition of this work, which was to prove his masterpiece, occupied him for 3 years (completed 1820); 2 weeks later he began work on the incidental music to Wolff's *Preciosa,* a play in 4 acts with spoken dialogue; it was produced in Berlin in 1821. A comic opera, *Die drei Pintos,* which Weber started at about the same time, was left unfinished; a performing edition was created by Mahler. After some revisions *Der Freischütz* was accepted for performance at the opening of Berlin's Neues Schauspielhaus. There arose an undercurrent of rivalry with Spontini, director of the Berlin Opera, a highly influential figure in operatic circles and at court. Spontini considered himself the guardian of the Italian-French tradition in opposition to the new German Romantic movement in music. Weber conducted the triumphant premiere of *Der Freischütz* (1821); the work's success surpassed all expectations and the cause of new Romantic art was won; *Der Freischütz* was soon staged by all the major opera houses of Europe.

Weber's next opera was *Euryanthe,* produced in Vienna (1823) with only moderate success. Meanwhile Weber's health was affected by incipient tuberculosis and he was compelled to spend part of 1824 in Marienbad for a cure. He recovered sufficiently to begin the composition of *Oberon,* a commission from London's Covent Garden. The English libretto was prepared by

J. R. Planché, based on a translation of C. M. Wieland's verse-romance of the same name. Once more illness interrupted Weber's progress on his work; he spent part of the summer of 1825 in Ems to prepare himself for the journey to England. He set out for London in early 1826, a dying man. On his arrival, he was housed with Sir George Smart, the conductor of the Phil. Soc. of London. Weber threw himself into his work, presiding over 16 rehearsals for *Oberon*. In the spring he conducted its premiere at Covent Garden, obtaining a tremendous success. Despite his greatly weakened condition he conducted 11 more performances of the score and also participated in various London concerts, playing for the last time a week before his death. He was found dead in his room, and was buried in London. His remains were removed to Dresden in 1844; later they were taken to the Catholic cemetery in Dresden to the accompaniment of funeral music arranged from motifs from *Euryanthe* for wind instruments as prepared and conducted by Wagner; the next day, his remains were interred as Wagner delivered an oration and conducted a chorus in his specially composed *An Webers Grabe*.

Weber's role in music history is epoch-making; in his operas, particularly in *Der Freischütz*, he opened the era of musical Romanticism, in decisive opposition to the established Italianate style. The highly dramatic and poetic portrayal of a German fairy tale, with its aura of supernatural mystery, appealed to the public, whose imagination had been stirred by the emergent Romantic literature of the period. His melodic genius and mastery of the craft of composition made it possible for him to break with tradition and to start on a new path, at a critical time when individualism and nationalism began to emerge as sources of creative artistry.

Weber's instrumental works, too, possessed a new quality that signalized the transition from Classic to Romantic music. For piano he wrote pieces of extraordinary brilliance, introducing some novel elements in chord writing and passage work. He was himself an excellent pianist; his large hands gave him an unusual command of the keyboard (he could stretch the interval of a 12th). Weber's influence on the development of German music was very great. The evolutionary link to Wagner's music drama is evident in the coloring of the orch'l parts in Weber's operas and in the adumbration of the principle of leading motifs. Finally, he was one of the 1st outstanding interpretative conductors.

In addition to 10 operas (some incomplete or lost) and works for solo wind instrument and orch., Weber wrote incidental and interpolated music for more than 25 dramatic works, including an overture and 6 numbers for Schiller's trans. of Gozzi's *Turandot, Prinzessin von China* (Stuttgart, 1809); concert arias; 5 Masses and 2 liturgical related Offertories; secular cantatas. Orch.: 2 syms.; concertos and concertolike pieces for flute, clarinet, bassoon, horn, viola, cello, piano, and harmonichord (a bowed keyboard instrument); concert overtures and other works; wind ensemble music. Chamber: Piano Quartet in B-flat Major (1809); Clarinet Quintet in B-flat Major (1815); *Grand Duo Concertant* for Piano and Clarinet (1815–16); Trio for Flute, Cello, and Piano (1819). Piano: Weber wrote prolifically and well for his own instrument, but little of the music is played; most popular are 4 sonatas; *Aufforderung zum Tanze: Rondo brillante* in D-flat Major (1819; made even more famous by Berlioz's orchestration, 1861); *Polacca brillante L'hilarite* in E Major (1819); duets.

Weber's critical writings on music are valuable, if surprisingly conservative; like many of his day he had mixed feelings about Beethoven's later music; left an autobiographical sketch, an unfinished novel, poems, etc. Editions of his writings include G. Kaiser, ed., *Sämtliche Schriften von Carl Maria von Weber: Kritische Ausgabe* (Berlin and Leipzig, 1908); K. Laux, ed., *Carl Maria von Weber: Kunstansichten* (Leipzig, 1969; 2nd ed., 1975); J. Warrack, ed., and M. Cooper, tr., *Carl Maria von Weber: Writings on Music* (Cambridge, 1982).

Webern, Anton (Friedrich Wilhelm von), b. Vienna, Dec. 3, 1883; d. Mittersill, Sept. 15, 1945. He received his 1st instruction in music from his mother, an amateur pianist; then studied piano, cello, and theory with Edwin Komauer in Klagenfurt; also played cello in the orch. there. In 1902 he entered the Univ. of Vienna, where he studied harmony with Graedener and counterpoint with Navratil; also attended classes in musicology with Guido Adler; received his Ph.D. in 1906 with a dissertation on Heinrich Isaac's *Choralis Constantinus II.*

In 1904 Webern began private studies in composition with Schoenberg, whose ardent disciple he became; Berg also studied with Schoenberg; together Schoenberg, Berg, and Webern laid the foundations of what became known as the 2nd Viennese school of composition. The unifying element was the adoption of Schoenberg's method of composition with 12 tones related only to one another. Malevolent opponents referred to Schoenberg, Berg, and Webern as a Vienna Trinity, with Schoenberg as God the Father, Berg as God the Son, and Webern as the Holy Ghost. From 1908 to 1914 he was active as a conductor in Vienna and in Germany; in 1915–16 he served in the army; in 1917–18 he was conductor at the Deutsches Theater in Prague. In 1918 he removed the nobiliary particle *von* from his name when such distinctions were outlawed in Austria; he settled in Mödling, near Vienna, where he taught composition privately; from 1918 to 1922 he supervised the programs of the Verein für Musikalische Privataufführungen (Soc. for Private Musical Performances), organized in Vienna by Schoenberg with the intention of promoting modern music without being exposed to reactionary opposition (music critics were not admitted to these performances). He was conductor of the Schubertbund (1921–22) and the Mödling Male Chorus (1921–26); he also led the Vienna Workers' Sym. concerts (1922–34) and the Vienna Workers' Chorus (1923–34), both sponsored by the Social Democratic Party. From 1927 to 1938 he was a conductor on the Austrian Radio; furthermore, he conducted guest engagements in Germany, Switzerland, and Spain; from 1929 he made several visits to England, where he was a guest conductor with the BBC Sym. Orch. For the most part, however, he devoted himself to composition, private teaching, and lecturing.

After Hitler came to power in Germany in 1933, Webern's music was banned as a manifestation of "cultural Bolshevism" and "degenerate art." His position became more difficult after the Anschluss in 1938, for his works could no longer be publ.; he eked out an existence by teaching a few private pupils and making piano arrangements of musical scores by others for Universal Edition. After his son was killed in an air bombardment of a train in early 1945, he and his wife fled from Vienna to Mittersill, near Salzburg, to stay with his married daughters and grandchildren. His life ended tragically when he was shot and killed by an American soldier after stepping outside his son-in-law's residence one evening; the circumstances were shrouded in secrecy for many years (for a full account, see H. Moldenhauer, *The Death of Anton Webern: A Drama in Documents*, N.Y., 1961).

Webern left relatively few works, and most of them are of shorter duration (the 4th of his *5 Pieces for Orchestra*, op. 10, takes only 19 seconds to play), but in his music he achieves the utmost subtilization of expressive means. He adopted the 12-tone method of composition almost immediately after its definitive formulation by Schoenberg (1924), and he extended the principle of nonrepetition of notes to tone colors, so that in some of his works (e.g., the Sym., op. 21) solo instruments are rarely allowed to play 2 successive thematic notes. Dynamic marks are similarly diversified. Typically each 12-tone row is divided into symmetrical sections of 2, 4, or 6 members, which enter mutually into intricate but invariably logical canonic imitations. Inversions and augmentations are inherent features; melodically and harmonically, the intervals of the major 7th and minor 9th are stressed; single motives are brief and stand out as individual particles or lyric ejaculations. The impact of these works on the general public and on the critics was disconcerting, and upon occasion led to violent demonstrations; however, the extraordinary skill and novelty of technique made this music endure beyond the fashions of the times; performances of his works multiplied after his death and began to affect increasingly larger groups of modern musicians; Boulez announced, "Schoenberg is dead! Long live Webern!" in 1952, referring to the greater influence Webern had than his mentor did; Stravinsky acknowledged the use of Webern's methods in his later works; jazz composers have professed to follow his ideas of tone color.

Webern's output includes 31 works with opus numbers and unenumerated works, mostly early in chronology and late Romantic in style; these include: Orch.: Passacaglia, op. 1 (1908); 6 Pieces for Orch., op. 6 (1913); 5 Pieces for Orch., op. 10 (1911–13); 5 Pieces for Orch., op. posth. (1913); Sym. for Chamber Ensemble, op. 21 (1929); Variations, op. 30 (1940). Choral: *Entflieht auf leichten Kähnen*, op. 2 (1908); 2 Goethe songs, op. 19, with Ensemble (1926); *Das Augenlicht*, op. 26, with Orch. (1935); 1st Cantata, op. 29, with Soprano and Orch. (1938–39); 2nd Cantata, op. 31, with Soprano, Bass, and Orch. (1941–43). Solo vocal (with piano except where noted): 2 sets of 5 Stefan George songs, opp. 3 and 4 (1908–09); 2 Rilke songs, op. 8, with ensemble (1910); 4 songs, op. 12 (1915–17); 4 songs with orch., op. 13 (1914–18); 6 Georg Trakl songs, op. 14, with instruments (1919–21); *5 Sacred Songs*, op. 15, with Instruments (1917–22); 5 Canons on Latin texts, op. 16, with clarinet and bass clarinet (1923–24); *3 Traditional Rhymes*, op. 17, with Instruments (1924–25); 3 songs, op. 18, with clarinet and guitar (1925); 3 songs, op. 23 (1933–34); 3 songs, op. 25 (1934); early songs with piano. Chamber: 5 Movements for string quartet (1910); 4 pieces for violin and piano, op. 7 (1910); 6 bagatelles for string quartet, op. 9 (1911–13); 3 Little Pieces for Cello and Piano, op. 11 (1914); String Trio, op. 20 (1926–27); Quartet for Violin, Clarinet, Tenor Saxophone, and Piano, op. 22 (1931); Concerto for 9 Instruments, op. 24 (1935); String Quartet, op. 28 (1936–38); Variations for Piano (1937); early chamber works; arrangements of works by Schoenberg, Schubert, and Bach. W. Reich ed. *Der Weg zur neuen Musik*, transcribed from Webern's lectures (Vienna, 1933).

Wechseldominante (Ger., changing dominant). Term used by Riemann to designate the dominant of the dominant in a given key (V of V); e.g., D major is the Wechseldominante (V of V) of C major.

Wechselgesang (Ger., changing song). Antiphonal singing.

wechselnder Taktart, in (Ger.). In a changing tempo (R. Strauss, *Salome*).

Wechselnote (Ger., changing note). Cambiata.

wehmüt(h)ig (Ger.). Sadly, with melancholy.

weich (Ger.). Soft, tender; mellow, suave. *Weich gesungen*, sung softly (Mahler).

weiche Tonart (Ger., soft key). Minor key.

Weihnachtmusik (Ger.). Christmas music.

Weill, Kurt (Julian), b. Dessau, Mar. 2, 1900; d. N.Y., Apr. 3, 1950. He was a private pupil of Albert Bing in Dessau (1915–18); in 1918–19 studied at the Berlin Hochschule für Musik with Humperdinck (composition), Friedrich Koch (counterpoint), and Krasselt (conducting). He was then engaged as an opera coach in Dessau and was also theater conductor at Lüdenscheid. In 1920 he moved to Berlin and became a student of Busoni at the Prussian Academy of Arts (1920–23); also studied with Jarnach there (1921–23). His 1st major work, the Sym. No. 1 (*Berliner Sinfonie*), was composed in 1921. However, it was not performed in his lifetime; indeed, its MS was not recovered until 1955, and it was finally premiered by the North German Radio Sym. Orch. in Hamburg in 1958.

Weill turned to the stage for his next large-scale work, the ballet *Zaubernacht* (with voice; 1922), but under the impact of new trends in the musical theater he began to write satirical operas in a sharp modernistic manner: *Der Protagonist* (1924–25) and *Royal Palace* (1925–26). There followed a striking songspiel, *Mahagonny*, to a libretto by Bertolt Brecht, savagely satirizing the American primacy of money (1927); it was remodeled and was presented as the 3-act opera *Aufstieg und Fall der Stadt Mahagonny* (1929). Weill interrupted work on the opera to produce his success in this genre, a modern version of Gay's *The Beggar's Opera* to a pungent libretto by Brecht; under the title *Die Dreigroschenoper* (1928) it was staged all over Germany, and was also produced in translation throughout Europe. Although Weill and Brecht grew apart over ideological differences, they produced 2 smaller works of great influence on later composers: *Der Jasager* (One Who Says Yes), a "school opera" with Marxist teachings (1930); and *Die Sieben Todsünden*, a sui generis dance-song cantata that encapsulates the Berlin of the 1920s and early 1930s (and indeed the world that Weill had to abandon).

After the Nazi ascent to power in Germany, Weill and his wife—the actress and singer Lotte Lenya, who appeared in many of his musical plays—went to Paris in 1933. They settled in the U.S. in 1935; Weill became a naturalized American citizen in 1943. Gradually absorbing the modes and fashions of American popular music, Weill adopted, with astonishing felicity, the typical form and content of American musicals; this stylistic transition was facilitated by the fact that in his European productions he had already absorbed elements of American popular songs and jazz rhythms. His musicals combine this Americanized idiom with a hint of early-20th-century advanced compositional techniques (atonality, polytonality, polyrhythms) and present the result in a pleasing and yet sophisticated and challenging manner. As Brecht, Georg Kaiser, and Caspar Neher had been his principal collaborators in Germany, Weill worked with such American literary luminaries as Paul Green, Maxwell Anderson, Moss Hart, Ira Gershwin, S. J. Perelman, Ogden Nash, Elmer Rice, Langston Hughes, and Alan Jay Lerner. Some works were too radical or off-beat for their audiences, others too operatic; his greatest successes were *Lady in the Dark* (1941), *One Touch of Venus* (1943), *Street Scene* (a "Broadway opera," 1947), and *Lost in the Stars* (1949). *Down in the Valley*, a 1-act "college opera," remains his most-performed English-language work.

For all Weill's success in American-produced scores, virtually all of his European works were unproduced in America at the time of his death. But 4 years after Weill's death, Blitzstein made an English trans. of *Die Dreigroschenoper*, versified in a modern American vernacular; produced as *The Threepenny Opera* in 1954, it was a long-running N.Y. hit; its hit number, *The Ballad of Mack the Knife* (in German, *Die Moritat von Mackie Messer*), became tremendously successful. The production relaunched Lenya's career; she appeared in theatrical and film roles into the 1970s. Many of Weill's works have received 1st American productions or revivals; many new recordings have also been released. Weill's primary reputation as a theatrical composer has obscured attention to other valuable works, such as: 2 syms. (1921, *Berliner Sym.*; 1933, *Pariser Sym.* or *3 Night Scenes*); Divertimento (1922); Concerto for Violin, Woodwinds, Double Bass, and Percussion (1925); *Kleine Dreigroschenmusik* for Winds, (1929). Vocal: *Recordare* for Choir and Children's Chorus (1923); *Der neue Orpheus*, cantata for Soprano, Violin, and Orch. (1925); *Vom Tod im Wald*, ballad for Bass and 10 Wind Instruments (1927); *Das Berliner Requiem*, cantata for Tenor, Baritone, Bass, Chorus, and 15 Instruments (1929); *Der Lindberghflug*, cantata after a radio score for Tenor, Baritone, Chorus, and Orch. (with Hindemith, 1929; rewritten by Weill as his own work, 1929; subsequent titles were *Der Flug des Lindberghs* and *Der Ozeanflug*). Chamber: 2 string quartets (1919, 1923); Cello Sonata (1920); film scores; radio and theater scores; some songs.

Weir, Judith, b. Aberdeen, May 11, 1954. She studied in London with Taverner; computer music with Barry Vercoe; and with Robin Holloway, Schuller, and Messiaen. She has taught at Glasgow Univ. and held residencies. Weir's style represents an almost neoclassical approach to modern and non-Western techniques, with a unique deftness of touch. She is best known for theatrical works, including 3 operas: *A Night at the Chinese Opera* (1987); *The Vanishing Bridegroom* (1990); *Blond Eckbert* (1994); *Heaven Ablaze in His Breast*, dance-opera with Ian Spink and Second Stride (1995); *King Harald's Saga*, monodrama; incidental music. Orch.: *Music Untangled* (1991–92); *Heroic Strokes of the Bow* (1992); chamber music; piano music.

Weise (Ger.). Mode, manner; e.g., *Volksweise*, like a folk song; *Zigeunerweise*, in the Gypsy style.

Weisgall, Hugo (David), b. Eibenschutz, Oct. 13, 1912; d. Manhasset, N.Y., Mar. 11, 1997. He emigrated with his family to the U.S. and became a naturalized citizen in 1926. He studied at the Peabody Cons. of Music in Baltimore (1927–32); subsequently had composition lessons with Sessions at various times between 1932 and 1941; also was a pupil of Reiner (conducting diploma, 1938) and Scalero (composition diploma, 1939) at the Curtis Inst. of Music in Philadelphia; he pursued academic studies at Johns Hopkins Univ. (Ph.D., 1940, with a diss. on primitivism in 17th-century German poetry). After military service in World War II he was active as a conductor, singer, teacher, and composer.

Weisgall was founder-conductor of the Chamber Soc. of Baltimore (1948) and the Hilltop Opera Co. (1952); was director of the Baltimore Inst. of Musical Arts (1949–51); taught at Johns Hopkins Univ. (1951–57); was made chairman of the faculty of the Cantors' Inst. at the Jewish Theological Center in N.Y. in 1952. He taught at the Juilliard School of Music (1957–70) and at Queens College of the City Univ. of N.Y. (from 1961). He served as president of the American Music Center (1963–73); in 1966 he was composer-in-residence at the American Academy in Rome. He held 3 Guggenheim fellowships and received many prizes and commissions; in 1975 he was elected to membership in the National Inst. of Arts and Letters, and in 1990 became president of the American Academy and Inst. of Arts and Letters.

Weisgall's music constitutes the paragon of enlightened but unstrident modernism; he was a master of all musical idioms, especially vocal. His intentions in each of his works never fail in the execution; for this reason his music enjoys numerous performances, which are usually accepted with pleasure by the audiences, if not by the majority of important music critics. He composed 10 operas, 4 ballets, orch'l works, vocal works, and songs.

Weiss, Silvius Leopold, b. Breslau, Oct. 12, 1686; d. Dresden, Oct. 16, 1750. He most likely was a pupil of his father, Johann Jacob Weiss, a lutenist and composer (b. *c.* 1662; d. Mannheim, Jan. 30, 1754); Silvius was in the service of Count Carl Philipp of the Palatinate in Breslau by 1706; then was in Italy with Alexander Sobiesky, Prince of Poland (1708–14). In 1715 he entered the service of the Hessen-Kassel court, and shortly thereafter went to Dusseldorf; in 1717 he joined the chapel of the Saxon court in Dresden, where his status was formalized in 1718. He also traveled as a virtuoso, appearing in Prague (1717), London (1718), Vienna (1718–19), Munich (1722), Berlin (1728), and Leipzig (1739), where he visited Bach.

Weiss was one of the foremost performers on and composers for the lute. His extant works number almost 600; he composed the largest corpus of solo lute works (mostly partitas and suites) by any composer; they are worthy of comparison with Bach's small number of works for this instrument. His brother was Johann Sigismund Weiss, lutenist, viola da gambist, violinist, and composer (b. probably in Breslau, *c.* 1689; d. Mannheim, Apr. 12, 1737). He became a lutenist at the Palatine chapel in Düsseldorf (*c.* 1708), following it to Heidelberg (1718) and to Mannheim (1720); in 1732 he was named director of instrumental music there, and later served as Konzertmeister and theorbo player. He was one of the finest composers of the early Mannheim school. Silvius's son Johann Adolf Faustinus Weiss (b. Dresden, Apr. 15, 1741; d. there, Jan. 21, 1814), was a lutenist and composer; served as chamber lutenist at the Dresden court from 1763 until his death; also traveled widely; composed lute and guitar music.

weite Lage (Ger.). Open harmony; wide disposition of voices in harmony.

weiter Entfernung, in (Ger.). In the far distance; played from behind the stage (Mahler, 5th Sym.).

Welk, Lawrence, b. Strasburg, N. Dak., Mar. 11, 1903; d. Santa Monica, Ca., May 17, 1992. He began playing accordion in German-speaking areas of his native state as a youth; then performed with his own combos, gaining success as a self-described purveyor of "champagne music"; after touring and making numerous radio appearances, he launched his own television program in Los Angeles in 1951; it subsequently was featured on network television (1955–71). He owed his popularity to his skillful selection of programs containing a varied mixture of semiclassical pieces, western American ballads, and polkas and other dance tunes. His use of an accordion section in his arrangements, steadfast rhythmic beat, and sentimentalized tempos imparted to his renditions a rudimentary sound quality that made him a favorite with undiscriminating audiences.

well temperament. See ⇒temperament.

wenig (Ger.). Little. *Ein klein wenig langsamer,* a little bit slower.

Werckmeister, Andreas, b. Benneckenstein, Thuringia, Nov. 30, 1645; d. Halberstadt, Oct. 26, 1706. After his studies in Bennungen, Nordhausen, and Quedlinburg, he became organist in Hasselfelde, near Blankenburg (1664–74); after serving as organist and notary in Elbingerode (1674–75), he went to Quedlinburg as organist of the collegiate church of St. Servatius and of the court of the abbess and Countess of Palatine, Anna Sophia I; also was named organist of the Wipertikirche in 1677; in 1696 he settled in Halberstadt as organist of the Martinikirche. Werckmeister was highly influential as a music theorist; his exposition of number symbolism in music and its theological basis remains invaluable. But his work maintains its greatest relevance in the area of meantone temperament, as early music revivalists tackled keyboard tuning issues.

Among Werckmeister's numerous publications, his views can be found in 2 essays: Musicalische Temperatur, oder Deutlicher und warer mathematischer Unterricht, wie man durch Anweisung des Monochordi ein Clavier, sonderlich die Orgel-Wercke, Positive, Regale, Spinetten und dergleichen wol temperirt stimmen könne (Frankfurt am Main and Leipzig, c. 1686–87; not extant; 2nd ed., 1691) and Hypomnemata musica, oder Musicalisches Memorial, welches bestehet in kurtzer Erinnerung dessen, so bisshero unter guten Freunden discursweise, insonderheit von der Composition und Temperatur möchte vorgangen seyn (Quedlinburg, 1697).

Werfel, Alma Mahler. See ⇒Mahler, Gustav.

Werk (Ger.). 1. Work, opus, composition. 2. An organ keyboard with its own set of pipes; *Orgelwerk.*

Wesendonk, Mathilde (Luckemeyer). See ⇒ Wagner, (Wilhelm) Richard.

whip (Fr. *fouet;* Ger. *Peitsche;* It. *frusta*). A wooden percussion instrument having 2 sections joined at one end that are clacked together making the sound of a cracking whip. Ravel uses it in some of his scores, as does Varèse in *Ionisation.* Mascagni makes dramatic use of the whip in *Cavalleria Rusticana* to announce the entrance of the vengeful husband.

whipping bow. A form of violin technique in which the bow is made to fall with a certain vehemence on the strings. Chiefly employed when one wishes to mark sharply single tones in rapid tempo.

whistle (from Old Eng. *hwistle;* Fr. *sifflet;* Ger. *Pfeife*). Family of short end-blown flutes, in numerous forms, dating to prehistory. In its basic form there are no fingerholes; the whistle is used as a decoy or signal.

white noise (sound). By analogy with the complementary colors of the visual spectrum, white noise can be described as a sonic continuum containing all available tones within a certain auditory range, or a complex consisting of prescribed intervals, a pandiatonic or panpentatonic tone cluster, a dodecaphonic or icositetraphonic cumulus, etc. White noise can be prismatically analyzed into a linear progression forming a scale of discrete tones.

white note. One with an open head: o or ♩.

Whiteman, Paul, b. Denver, Colo., Mar. 28, 1890; d. Doylestown, Pa., Dec. 29, 1967. He played viola in the Denver Sym. Orch. and later in the San Francisco People's Sym. Orch.; in 1917–18 he was conductor of a 40-piece band in the U.S. Navy. He then formed a hotel orch. in Santa Barbara, Calif.; and began to develop a style of playing known as *symphonic jazz,* which soon made him famous. In 1924, he gave a concert in Aeolian Hall in N.Y., at which he introduced Gershwin's *Rhapsody in Blue,* written for his orch., with the composer as piano soloist. In 1926 he made a tour in Europe. While not himself a jazz musician, he was popularly known as the "King of Jazz," and frequently featured at his concerts such notables of the jazz world as Bix Beiderbecke, Frank Trumbauer, and Benny Goodman; Bing Crosby achieved his early fame as a member of Paul Whiteman's Rhythm Boys. Whiteman established the Whiteman Awards, made annually for symphonic jazz compositions written by Americans. He publ. the books *Jazz* (with M. McBride; N.Y., 1926), *How to Be a Bandleader* (with L. Lieber; N.Y., 1941), and *Records for the Millions* (N.Y., 1948).

Whithorne, Emerson (born Whittern). See ⇒Leginska, Ethel.

Who, The. Popular and influential rock band, viewed by some to have been the leading 1960s British group after the Beatles and Rolling Stones. (Guitar/vocal/songwriter: Pete[r Dennis Blandford] Townsend, b. Chiswick, U.K., May, 19, 1945; vocals: Roger Daltrey, b. Hammersmith, Mar. 1, 1944; bass; John Entwistle b. Chiswick, Oct. 9, 1944; drums: Keith Moon, b. Wembley, Aug. 23, 1947; d. London, Sept. 7, 1978.)

In the early 1960s, Townsend began playing banjo in a Dixieland jazz group, in which Entwistle blew the trumpet; Entwistle would become the group's bassist, with occasional vocal, brass, and compositional contributions. They teamed with Entwistle's friend Daltrey and organized a group to which they 1st gave the name High Numbers. Moon joined the group in 1964, at which point the group became The Who. At the time, British youth culture was more or less divided between the Mods (middle-class scooter drivers wearing the cool style of Carnaby) and the Rockers (labor-class leather-jacketed motorcyclists). Anxious to project a Mod image for their fans as a statement in an alien world, they sported odd clothes, cultivated bizarre behavior, and indulged in maniacal conduct on the stage, which included physical destruction of their instruments at the end of each set, prescient of metal and punk performance practice. In 1965 the group released the single *My Generation,* their 1st major hit and soon a battle cry for youth rebellion. In 1966 they recorded *A Quick One While He's Away,* a mini-rock-opera that forecast the group's later development.

Although several well-produced and thoughtful singles had subsequent success in the U.K. and U.S., The Who did not reach worldwide success until the release of the "rock opera" *Tommy* (1969), composed mostly by Townsend, concerning spirituality in postwar England through a young boy who becomes deaf, dumb, and blind. In addition to its massive success as a recording, *Tommy* was long a staple of The Who's live performances; it has been recorded by superstar casts, released as a film, and many years later realized as a Broadway musical. The Who recorded a 2nd opera, the more evocative and less plot-driven *Quadrophenia* (1973), recalling the Mod phase of England's (and the group's) history. In between these milestones The Who produced some fine recordings as a group and as solo artists, beginning in the 1970s, among them: *Live at Leeds* (1970), *Who's Next* (1971), and *Who Are You* (1978). Townsend produced *Who Came First* (1972), *Rough Mix* (with Ronnie Lane, 1977), *Empty Glass* (1980), *(All the Best Cowboys Have) Chinese Eyes* (1982), *White City* (video, 1985), *The Iron Man* (1989), and *PsychoDerelict* (1993); has released 2 collections of his demo recordings. Entwistle released solo albums with typically gothic titles as *Smash Your Head Against the Wall* (1971) and *Rigor Mortis* (1973). Moon recorded the idiosyncratic *Two Sides of the Moon.* Daltrey recorded albums and acted in films (notoriously Ken Russell's *Lisztomania,* 1975). All 4 members participated in the film *The Kids Are Alright* (1979), a free-wheeling documentary of the group's history, named after an early single. A tragic moment in their career occurred at a Cincinnati concert in late 1979 when 11 young people were trampled to death in a rush for the entrance gates. After Moon's death, the group took on Kenney Jones (like Lane a former member of the Small Faces) as drummer, made international tours, released 2 more albums, and called it a day. The Who has reunited for 1 subsequent *Tommy* tour and benefit concerts.

whole consort. An old English term for an instrumental ensemble; consisting of either all wind or all string instruments (e.g., recorders, viols); the counterpart of broken consort.

whole note. The note o.

whole shift. See ⇒shift.

whole step. 1. The step of a whole tone. 2. A whole tone.

whole tone. A major 2nd.

whole-tone scale. Scale consisting entirely of consecutive whole steps, whether written as major 2nds or diminished 3rds. The whole-tone scale gained ephemeral popularity early in the 20th century as an exotic resource cultivated by the impressionist school of composers. The whole-tone scale is neutral in its polarity; it lacks modality; the intervallic progression in the whole-tone scale remains the same in melodic rotation. The perfect 5th and the perfect 4th, the cornerstones of tonality, are absent in the whole-tone scale; there is no dominant or subdominant, and no leading tone.

Analytically the whole-tone scale is atonal. It can also be regarded as the linear function of 2 mutually exclusive augmented triads; as 2 conjunct tetrachords comprised solely of whole steps; or as the intussusception of 3 mutually exclusive tritones at the distance of a whole tone from one another. Because of its association with the traditionally forbidden tritone (the diabolus in musica), the whole-tone scale itself became a favorite device of early modernism to portray diabolical forces, menacing apparitions, and ineffable mysteries.

The earliest mention of an intentional employment of the whole-tone scale occurs in Mozart's comic divertimento *Die Dorfmusikanten,* subtitled *A Musical Joke.* But Mozart used the whole-tone scale here not to illustrate a malevolent agency, but to ridicule the incompetence of village musicians and their inability to play in tune. The whole-tone scale came into its own as an ominous symbol in Glinka's opera *Ruslan and Ludmila,* in which it is used as a motto of the magician Chernomor. Rossini made use of the whole-tone scale in a song written in 1864 entitled *L'Amour à Pékin,* in which it was described as "gamme chinoise." The possible reason for this reference is that an ancient Chinese panpipe contains 2 mutually exclusive whole-tone scales in symmetrically disposed tubes.

Liszt was fascinated with the whole-tone scale, and was greatly impressed by the *Fantastic Overture* (1859), which the Russian amateur composer Boris Vietinghoff-Scheel (1829–1901) sent him, and in which whole-tone scales were profusely employed. In his comment on the work Liszt described the effect as "terrifying to all long and protruding ears." Liszt himself made use of the whole-tone scale in his *Divina Commedia,* illustrating the Inferno; and he used it systematically in his posthumously published organ and late piano pieces. The problem of harmonizing the whole-tone scale tonally was solved by Glinka in a sequence of modulations. Liszt harmonized a descending whole-tone scale that occurs in the bass. It is doubtful whether Puccini was aware of Liszt's application of this harmony, but he used a precisely identical triadic harmonization of the descending whole-tone scale in his opera *Tosca,* as an introduction to the appearance of Scarpia, the sinister Roman chief of police. The Russian composer Vladimir Rebikov (1866–1920) was probably the 1st to write an entire composition derived exclusively from the whole-tone scale and its concomitant series of augmented triads, his *Les Démons s'amusent* for Piano; its title suggests that Rebikov was fully aware of its demoniac association.

But it was Debussy who elevated the whole-tone scale from a mere exotic device to a poetic and expressive medium. Its

Protean capacity for change and adaptability greatly attracted Debussy and his followers, as an alternative to a diatonic scale. A very interesting application of the whole-tone scale occurs in *La Mer;* the principal theme of the 1st movement is in the Aeolian mode; in the 3rd movement it appears isorhythmically as a progression of whole tones. The 1st and the last sections of Debussy's *Voiles* for Piano (*Préludes,* book I) consist of whole tones with the middle section providing a contrast in the pentatonic scale. Berg used an alternation between the 2 distinct whole-tone scales (beginning on C and on D♭) in his *Nacht* (*7 Frühe Lieder,* 1907).

A whole catalogue can be compiled of incidental usages of the whole-tone scale. Even Tchaikovsky, not usually given to modern inventions, made use of the whole-tone scale in a modulatory sequence illustrating the appearance of the ghost of the old Countess in his opera *The Queen of Spades.* Rimsky-Korsakov filled the 2nd act of his opera *Le Coq d'or* with whole-tone scales and augmented triads to convey the impression of death and devastation of the battlefield. The entrance of Herod in *Salome* of R. Strauss is announced by a leading motive composed of whole tones. Holst characterized *Saturn* in his sym. suite *The Planets* by a series of whole-tone passages to evoke the mystery of Saturn's rings. Apart from astronomy, the whole-tone scale serves pure fantasy. In his sym. fairy tale *Kikimora* Liadov paints the mischievous sprite in whole tones. Paul Dukas introduces the hapless amateur magician in his *L'Apprenti Sorcier* in a series of whole tones.

The English composer Edward Maryon (1867–1954) assigns the whole-tone scale to the changelings in his opera *Werewolf,* reserving the diatonic scale for normal children. Another English composer, Havergal Brian, has a chorus singing in whole-tone scales in his opera *The Tigers,* to illustrate the aerial bombardment of London by the zeppelins during World War I. There are bits of whole-tone figures in Menotti's children's opera *Help, Help, the Globolinks!* to describe the creatures from outer space; the earthlings in the opera overcome the invading globolinks in victorious C major. A remarkable demonstration of the perdurability of the whole-tone scale as a symbol of evil is provided by Stravinsky's *Elegy for J. F. K.* (1964), which contains within a 12-tone row 2 intervallically congruous groups of whole tones, each embanked in a tritone, itself a symbol of deviltry.

With the gradual decline of pictorial and sensorial programmaticism in contemporary music, the whole-tone scale sank into disuse and cliché. It found its temporary outlet and a stylistic rehabilitation in dodecaphonic usages in the form of 2 mutually exclusive hexachords. Eventually it joined the subculture of film music. Cinematic Nazis advance on the screen to the sound of whole-tone scales in the trombones. Mad scientists hatch their murderous schemes to blow up the world in mighty progressions of whole tones. Mentally disturbed maidens pluck whole-tone scales on the harp. When Jean Harlow, in her screen biography, climbs up the ladder in the studio before her final collapse, she is accompanied by delicate whole-tone pizzicatos. The whole-tone scale is also used, wittily so, in satirical comment on pompous personages in animated cartoons.

Widmung (Ger.). Dedication (of a composition).

Widor, Charles-Marie (-Jean-Albert), b. Lyons, Feb. 21, 1844; d. Paris, Mar. 12, 1937. His father, an Alsatian of Hungarian descent, was organist at the church of St.-François in Lyons and was active as an organ builder. Widor was a skillful improviser on the organ while still a boy and became organist at the Lyons lycée when he was 11. After studies with Fétis (composition) and Lemmens (organ) in Brussels he became organist at St.-François (1860) and gained high repute via provincial concerts. In 1870–71 he held a provisional appointment as organist at St.-Sulpice in Paris, where he served as organist from 1871 until 1934. In 1934 he played his *Pièce mystique* there, composed at age 90. Around 1880 he began writing music criticism under the pen name "Aulétès" for the daily *L'Estafette.* In 1890 he became prof. of organ and in 1896 prof. of composition at the Paris Cons. In 1910 he was elected a member of the Académie des Beaux-Arts, of which he became permanent secretary in 1913. He had many distinguished pupils, including Albert Schweitzer, with whom he collaborated in editing the 1st 5 vols. of an 8-vol. ed. of Bach's organ works (N.Y., 1912–14).

As a composer Widor wrote copiously in many forms but is best known for his solo organ music, especially the 10 "symphonies" (suites, 1876–1900). A master organ virtuoso, he won great renown for his performances of Bach and for his inspired improvisations. Other Widor organ works include the *Suite latine* (1927); *3 nouvelles pièces* (1934); 8 sonatas. He also composed 3 operas, 2 ballets, incidental music; 5 syms., including 3 with organ; 2 piano concertos, 1 cello concerto, other works; chamber and piano music; vocal works, both sacred and secular, with instrumental and orch'l accompaniment. Writings (all publ. in Paris): *Technique de l'orchestre moderne* (1904); *Notice sur la vie et les oeuvres de Camille Saint-Saëns* (1922); *Initiation musicale* (1923); *Académie des Beaux-Arts: Fondations, portraits de Massenet à Paladilhe* (1927); *L'Orgue moderne: La décadence dans la facture contemporaine* (1928).

wie (Ger.). As, like. *Wie aus der Ferne,* as from a distance; *wie ein Naturlaut,* like a sound of nature; *wie oben,* as above; *wie vorher,* as before, as 1st; *wie wütend dreinfahren,* as if driving in furiously (Mahler, 6th Sym.).

Wieck, Clara Josephine. Schumann, Clara (Josephine) Wieck.

Wieck, (Johann Gottlob) Friedrich. See ⇒Schumann, Clara (Josephine) Wieck.

wieder (Ger.). Again. *Wiederhall,* echo; *Wiederholung,* repetition; *Wiederholungszeichen,* repetition sign (repeat mark).

wiegend (Ger.). Swaying, rocking.

Wiegenlied (Ger.; Fr. *berceuse*). A lullaby. The most famous is a song by Brahms, *Guten Abend, gut' Nacht* (1868; no. 4, op. 49).

Wienerwalzer. A fast-tempo waltz associated with Vienna; the standard version of this dance, made famous at the Congress of Vienna (1815).

Wieniawski, Henryk (Henri), b. Lublin, July 10, 1835; d. Moscow, Mar. 31, 1880. His mother, Regina Wolff-Wieniawska, was a talented pianist; he began training with Jan Hornziel and Stanislaw Serwaczynski in Warsaw; upon the advice of his mother's brother, Edouard Wolff, who lived in France, she took Henryk to Paris, where he entered the Cons. at the age of 8, 1st in Clavel's class, and the following year, in the advanced class of Massart. At the age of 11 he graduated with 1st prize in violin, an unprecedented event in the annals of the Paris Cons. After further private studies with Massart (1846–48), he made his Paris debut in 1848, in a concert accompanied by his brother at the piano; gave his 1st concert in St. Petersburg shortly thereafter, playing 4 more concerts there; then played in Finland and the Baltic provinces; after several successful appearances in Warsaw, he returned in 1849 to Paris, where he studied composition with Hippolyte Collet at the Cons., graduating with an *accessit* prize in 1850.

From 1851 to 1853 Wieniawski gave about 200 concerts in Russia with his brother. He also devoted much time to composition, and by age 18 he had composed and publ. his virtuoso 1st Violin Concerto, which he played with extraordinary success in Leipzig that same year. In 1858 he appeared with Anton Rubinstein in Paris and in 1859 in the Beethoven Quartet Soc. concerts in London, where he appeared as a violist as well as a violinist. In 1860 he went to St. Petersburg and was named solo violinist to the Czar, and also concertmaster of the orch. and 1st violinist of the string quartet of the Russian Musical Soc.; likewise served as prof. of violin at the newly founded Cons. (1862–68). He continued to compose and introduced his greatly esteemed 2nd Violin Concerto in St. Petersburg (1862), with Rubinstein conducting. In 1872 he went on a tour of the U.S. with Rubinstein; one of the featured works was Beethoven's *Kreutzer Sonata,* which they performed about 70 times. When Rubinstein returned to Europe, he continued his American tour, which included California. He returned to Europe in 1874, gave several concerts with Rubinstein in Paris, and in the same year succeeded Vieuxtemps as prof. of violin at the Brussels Cons., resigning in 1877 owing to an increasingly grave heart condition; he suffered an attack during a concert in Berlin on Nov. 11, 1878, but still agreed to play several concerts in Russia; made his farewell appearance in Odessa in Apr. 1879. His last months were spent in Moscow, where he was taken to the home of Nadezhda von Meck, Tchaikovsky's patroness, in 1880.

Wieniawski was undoubtedly one of the greatest violinists of the 19th century; he possessed a virtuoso technique and an extraordinary range of dynamics. He was equally distinguished as a chamber music player. As a composer he remains best known today for the 2 violin concertos and an outstanding set of etudes. He also composed numerous other orch'l works as well as pieces for solo or 2 violins. He was married to Isobel Hampton, an Englishwoman; their youngest daughter, Irene (1879–1932), composed music under the pen name Poldowski.

Williams, "Cootie" (Charles Melvin), b. Mobile, Ala., July 24, 1908; d. N.Y., Sept. 15, 1985. He took trumpet lessons with Charles Lipskin; made his way to N.Y. and joined groups led by Chick Webb and Fletcher Henderson. From 1929 to 1940 he was a member of Duke Ellington's band; after working with Benny Goodman (1940–41) he led his own groups until rejoining Ellington's band in 1962; he left in 1975 but continued to perform until 1983. He was one of the leading jazz trumpeters of his era, equally adept at open and muted playing.

Williams, (Hiram) Hank, b. Georgiana, Ala., Sept. 17, 1923; d. Oak Hill, Va., Jan. 1, 1953. He sang church hymns and learned to play the organ at a very early age; then took guitar lessons from a black street singer. At 12 he won a prize in an amateur contest in Montgomery singing his own song, *W.P.A. Blues.* At 14 he formed his own band, Hank Williams and His Drifting Cowboys. In 1946 he went to Nashville; in 1949 he joined the famous Grand Ole Opry there, and made an instant success with his rendition of *Lovesick Blues;* its recording sold over a million copies. In 1950 he put out several recordings of his own songs, *Long Gone Lonesome Blues, I Just Don't Like This Kind of Livin', Why Don't You Love Me?,* and *Moanin' the Blues,* which sold prodigiously. His subsequent releases, also magically successful, were *Hey, Good Lookin', Your Cheatin' Heart, Move It On Over, Cold, Cold Heart,* and *Jambalaya (On the Bayou),* but the nemesis of so many country singers—drugs, alcohol, women in excess—and a cardiac disorder killed him before he reached the age of 30. His son, (Randall) Hank Williams, Jr. (b. Shreveport, La., May 26, 1949), was also a successful country and western singer, guitarist, and songwriter; his career was also hampered by alcohol and drug problems; in 1975 he sustained severe injuries while mountain climbing, but eventually resumed his career. He has long been a legitimately popular and talented performer, not merely a son of his famous father. A television show on his life, *Living Proof,* was produced in 1983.

Williams, John (Christopher), b. Melbourne, Apr. 24, 1941. He 1st studied with his father, the guitarist Leonard Williams; when he was 14 he performed in London, then took guitar lessons with Segovia at the Accademia Chigiana in Siena (1957–59). In 1962 he made a tour of the Soviet Union; also played in America and Japan. In addition to classical music, he includes in his programs pieces of pop music and jazz; this egalitarian versatility makes him a favorite with the youth of English-speaking countries.

Williams, John (Towner), b. N.Y., Feb. 8, 1932. He grew up in a musical atmosphere; his father was a film studio musician. He began to take piano lessons; later he learned to play trombone, trumpet, and clarinet. In 1948 the family moved to Los Angeles, where he studied orchestration with Robert van Epps at Los Angeles City College and composition privately with Mario Castelnuovo-Tedesco; he also took piano lessons with Rosina Lhevinne at the Juilliard School of Music in N.Y. He began his career as a composer, arranger, and conductor for films and television; wrote the film scores, rich in sounding brass and tinkling cymbals, for *Close Encounters of the Third Kind, Superman, The Empire Strikes Back, Raiders of the Lost Ark, E.T. The Extra-Terrestrial,* and *Return of the Jedi.* He won Academy Awards for *Fiddler on the Roof* (1971), *Jaws* (1975), and *Star Wars* (1977). The record albums for these background scores sold into the millions. He also wrote 2 syms., a violin concerto, a flute concerto, an essay for strings, and a number of chamber music pieces. In 1980 he was chosen conductor of the Boston Pops Orch., succeeding the late Arthur Fiedler, who had held that post for almost 50 years; Williams declared openly that no one could hope to equal Fiedler in charisma and showmanship, not to mention Fiedler's splendiferous aureole of white hair (as contrasted with his successor's alopecia), but he said he would try his best to bridge the gap. He largely succeeded, and diversified his appeal to Boston Pops audiences by playing selections from his own sparkling film scores; retired in 1995.

Williams, Mary Lou (born Mary Elfrieda Scruggs), b. Atlanta, May 8, 1910; d. Durham, N.C., May 28, 1981. She began her career as a pianist in Kansas City with the saxophonist Andy Kirk (to whom she was married for a time); in 1931 she became pianist and arranger for Kirk's Twelve Clouds of Joy band, and provided him with such songs as *Walkin' & Swingin'*, *Twinklin'*, *Cloudy*, and *Little Joe from Chicago*; she then worked with Duke Ellington, Benny Goodman, and others. In 1945 she composed the bebop hit *In the Land of Oo-Bla-Dee* for Dizzy Gillespie; she also wrote *The Zodiac Suite*, which was performed by the N.Y. Phil. After becoming a Roman Catholic, she composed a number of religious works, including *St. Martin de Porres* and 3 Masses; her *Music for Peace* became popularly known as "Mary Lou's Mass." In 1977 she was named artist-in-residence at Duke Univ. in Durham. She was one of the leading figures in the jazz field for almost 60 years.

Williams, Ralph Vaughan. Vaughan Williams, Ralph.

Wills, Bob (James Robert), b. near Kosse, Tex., Mar. 6, 1905; d. Fort Worth, May 13, 1975. He 1st took up the mandolin, then began to play the fiddle; through his association with local black musicians, he learned blues and jazz as well. In 1928 he organized his own group, the Wills Fiddle Band; subsequently he appeared on radio and made many recordings. After settling in Tulsa, Okla. (1934), he became a fixture on station KVOO with his Texas Playboys band. From 1942 he was active with the group on the West Coast; also appeared in films. He gained popularity with his composition *San Antonio Rose;* he was elected to the Country Music Hall of Fame in 1968.

Willson, (Robert Reiniger) Meredith, b. Mason City, Iowa, May 18, 1902; d. Santa Monica, Calif., June 15, 1984. He learned to play the flute as a child, then went to N.Y. and studied at the Damrosch Inst. (1919–22) and received instruction in flute from Georges Barrère (1920–29); also studied with H. Hadley (1923–24) and Julius Gold (1921–23). He was 1st flutist in Sousa's band (1921–23) and a member of the N.Y. Phil. (1924–29); then became a musical director for various radio shows. For the 30th anniversary of the San Francisco earthquake he wrote a sym., which he conducted in its 1st performance (San Francisco, 1936). His 2nd Sym. was 1st played by the Los Angeles Phil. in 1940; he wrote other sym. works, band pieces, and a choral work, *Anthem of the Atomic Age*. However, he devoted himself mainly to the composition of popular music, in which he revealed a triple talent as a performer, writer, and composer. He appeared as a comedian on a radio program, *The Big Show*, in which he engaged in a comic colloquy with Tallulah Bankhead, closing with an inspirational hymn, *May the Good Lord Bless and Keep You*, which became very popular as an anthem. Willson achieved his greatest triumph with his musical *The Music Man*, for which he wrote the book, the lyrics, and the music. It opened in late 1957, and became an immediate success, thanks to the satirical and yet somehow patriotic subject, (a traveling salesman of band uniforms and instruments who sells them to small-town suckers, but gets a happy comeuppance); and to the sparkling score, containing the marching chorus *76 Trombones* and many other hits. His subsequent musicals were *The Unsinkable Molly Brown*, produced in late 1960, for which he wrote the musical score, and *Here's Love*, produced in 1963, an adaptation of the film *Miracle on 34th Street*. *The Music Man* and *The Unsinkable Molly Brown* were made into films. Willson was also active as an arranger and orchestrator in Hollywood; he helped Chaplin in arranging the score for his anti-Fascist film *The Great Dictator* (1940).

Wilson, Brian (Douglas). See ⇒Beach Boys, The.

wind band. 1. A company of performers on wind instruments. 2. The wind instruments in the orch.; also, the players on, or parts written for, the same.

wind instruments. Instruments whose tones are produced by wind (compressed air) blown through a tube. In the Western classical orch., these are divided into the woodwind and brass families; in a score and onstage or in the pit, these instruments are grouped together, highest member of each family at the top (with the exception of the horn and saxophone, which are placed in the score between the two wind families). The organ is not usually considered a wind instrument, although it uses a hybrid wind-keyboard technology. While the modern woodwind family includes instruments made of metal and mouthpieces with zero, one, or two reeds, the brass family is more homogeneous: all are made of metal, have coiled tubing, a flared opening called a bell, and a cup or cup-like mouthpiece, and can use mutes; the only unusual feature is the trombone's having a slide rather than valves to change pitch. The loudest members of the families are the oboe and trumpet; care must be taken with balancing the winds' dynamic levels. Horns and bassoons match well with each other in chordal writing, and in pre-valve days the bassoons often stood in for the horns (Beethoven, 5th Sym., 1st movement). See also ⇒brass instruments; woodwind instruments.

wind machine (Ger. *Windmaschine*). An instrument comprising a large barrel covered with cloth, with a fixed piece of wood against which it rubs when the barrel is rotated manually with the aid of a crank. Pitch and dynamic level can be altered by the speed of rotation. Composers who have used the wind machine include R. Strauss (*Alpine Symphony; Don Quixote*), Ravel (*Daphnis et Chloé*), Milhaud (*Les Choéphores*), Schoenberg (*Die Jakobsleiter*), and Vaughan Williams (*Sinfonia antartica*).

Winternitz, Emanuel, b. Vienna, Aug. 4, 1898; d. N.Y., Aug. 22, 1983. After the Anschluss in 1938, he emigrated to the U.S., where he devoted himself mainly to lecturing on art; served as Peripatetic Professor for the Carnegie Foundation. In 1942 he was appointed keeper of musical instruments at the Metropolitan Museum of Art in N.Y.; in 1949, was named curator of the Crosby Brown Collection of Musical Instruments of All Nations at the Metropolitan. He also administered the Andre Mertens Galleries for Musical Instruments (1971–73). In 1973 he became curator emeritus of the Metropolitan. Among his principal endeavors was musical iconography; he publ. a valuable reference work, *Musical Autographs from Monteverdi to Hindemith* (1955); other books were *Keyboard Instruments in the Metropolitan Museum of Art* (1961); *Die schönsten Musikinstrumente des*

Abendlandes (1966); *Musical Instruments and their Symbolism in Western Art* (1967); *Leonardo da Vinci as a Musician* (1982).

Wirbel (Ger., chirping). Drumroll. *Wirbeltrommel,* tenor drum.

Wittgenstein, Paul, b. Vienna, Nov. 5, 1887; d. Manhasset, Long Island, N.Y., Mar. 3, 1961. His brother was the famous philosopher Ludwig Wittgenstein. Paul studied with Brée, Leschetizky, and Labor; made his debut as a pianist in Vienna (1913). Serving in World War I, he lost his right arm at the Russian front, was a prisoner of war, and was repatriated in 1916. Wittgenstein developed a superb left-hand technique, and played a work written by Labor for him. He then commissioned concertos from R. Strauss, Ravel, Prokofiev, Korngold, Britten, and others; he gave the world premieres for all except the Prokofiev, which he found unsuitable. After appearing in the major European musical centers and doing an American tour (1934), he emigrated to the U.S. (1938), becoming a naturalized citizen (1946). He taught privately and at local colleges. John Barchilon's novel *The Crown Prince* (1984) is based on his career.

wolf (tone; Ger. *Wolfton*). 1. Parasitic sound effects due to imperfect construction, produced in the course of playing an instrument in the usual manner. A particular pitch will sound much louder or softer than its neighbors, due to an irregularity of resonance that enhances or dampens the sound. String instruments are most likely to succumb to this effect; cellists offset the effect by playing slightly out of tune, squeezing the instrument between their knees, or by using a *wolf mute* behind the bridge. Other instruments susceptible to the wolf were the old bassoon, the early valve horn, and the pipe organ of any era. 2. The *wolf 5th* occurs at the point in the Pythagorean or meantone tuning systems that an apparent perfect 5th is much smaller or larger, resulting in an unpleasant dissonance written as a diminished 6th. In the days before equal temperament's acceptance, keyboard tuners would place the wolf in the most unlikely key areas for best sounding tuning all around.

Wolf, Hugo (Filipp Jakob), b. Windischgraz, Styria, Mar. 13, 1860; d. Vienna, Feb. 22, 1903. His father, Philipp Wolf (1828–87), was a gifted musician from whom Hugo received piano and violin lessons at a very early age; he later played 2nd violin in the family orch. While attending the village primary school (1865–69) he studied piano and theory with Sebastian Weixler. In 1870 he was sent to the Graz regional secondary school, but he left after a single semester and in 1871 entered the St. Paul Benedictine Abbey in Carinthia, where he played violin, organ, and piano; in 1873 he was transferred to the Marburg secondary school and remained devoted to musical pursuits; in 1875 he went to Vienna, where he became a pupil at the Cons.; studied piano with Wilhelm Schenner and harmony and composition with Robert Fuchs and later with Franz Krenn.

When Wagner visited Vienna in 1875, Wolf went to see him, bringing along some of his compositions; the fact that Wagner received him at all—and even said a few words of encouragement—gave Wolf great impetus toward further composition. But he was incapable of submitting himself to academic discipline,

and soon difficulties arose between him and the Cons. authorities. He openly expressed his dissatisfaction with the teaching, which led to his expulsion for lack of discipline in 1877. He supported himself by giving music lessons to children in the homes of friends. By that time he was writing songs to texts by his favorite poets: Goethe, Lenau, and Heine; the 1st signs of a syphilitic infection became manifest at this time. An unhappy encounter with Brahms in 1879, who advised him to study counterpoint before attempting to compose, embittered him; resolved to follow his own musical inclinations. That same year he met Melanie (née Lang) Köchert, whose husband, Heinrich Köchert, was the Vienna court jeweller; by 1884 she had become Wolf's mistress and a great inspiration in his creative work.

After serving a brief and acrimonious tenure as 2nd conductor in Salzburg in 1881, Wolf returned to Vienna; became music critic of the weekly *Wiener Salonblatt* (1883). He took this opportunity to indulge his professional frustration by attacking those not sympathetic to new trends in music; he poured invective of extraordinary virulence on Brahms, thus antagonizing the influential Hanslick and other admirers of Brahms. He formed a coterie of staunch friends who had faith in his ability; yet was singularly unsuccessful in repeated attempts to secure performances. He submitted a string quartet to the celebrated Rosé Quartet, but it was rejected. Finally H. Richter accepted for the Vienna Phil. his sym. poem *Penthesilea,* but the public performance was a fiasco, and Wolf even accused Richter of deliberately sabotaging the work; later he reorchestrated the score, eliminating certain crudities of the early version.

In 1887 Wolf resigned as music critic of the *Wiener Salonblatt* and devoted himself entirely to composition. He became convinced that he was creating the greatest masterpieces of song since Schubert and Schumann; he stated his conviction in plain terms in his letters. In historical perspective his self-appraisal has proved remarkably accurate, but psychologists may well wonder whether he was not consciously trying to give himself the needed encouragement by what might have seemed to him a wild exaggeration. However, a favorable turn in his fortunes came when Rosa Papier became the 1st artist to sing a Wolf lied in public (1888). Shortly thereafter Wolf himself played and sang several of his songs at a meeting of the Vienna Wagner-Verein; made his public debut as accompanist in his songs to the tenor Ferdinand Jager, which proved the 1st of many highly successful recitals by both artists. Soon his name became known in Germany; he presented concerts of his own works in Berlin, Darmstadt, Mannheim, and other musical centers. He completed the 1st part of his great cycle of 22 songs, *Italienisches Liederbuch,* in 1891, and composed the 2nd part (24 songs) in 5 weeks, in the spring of 1896.

While Wolf could compose songs with a facility and degree of excellence that were truly astounding, he labored painfully on his orch'l works. An early sym. was never completed, nor was a violin concerto; *Penthesilea* took a disproportionately long time. In 1895 he undertook the composition of his opera *Der Corregidor,* to the famous tale by Alarcón, *El sombrero de tres picos,* and, working feverishly, completed the vocal score with piano accompaniment in a few months; the orchestration took far longer; had its premiere in Mannheim (1896); while initially a success, the opera failed to find wide appeal and was soon dropped from the repertory. He subsequently revised the score, and in its new version *Der Corregidor* was produced in Strasbourg (1898). He never completed his 2nd opera, *Manuel Venegas* (also after Alarcón); fragments were presented in concert in Mannheim a week after his death.

In the meantime a Hugo Wolf Verein was organized at Berlin (1896), and did excellent work in furthering performances of his lieder in Germany; even more effective was the Hugo Wolf Verein in Vienna, founded by Michel Haberlandt in 1897 (disbanded in 1906). As appreciation of his remarkable gifts as a master of lied began to find recognition abroad, tragedy struck; by early 1897 he was a very ill man, both mentally and physically. According to Wolf, Mahler had promised to use his position as director of the Vienna Court Opera to mount a production of *Der Corregidor;* when the production failed to materialize, Wolf's mental condition disintegrated. He declared to friends that Mahler had been relieved of his post and that he had been appointed in his stead. In late 1897 he was placed in a private mental institution; after a favorable remission he was discharged (early 1898); he traveled in Italy and Austria. After his return to Vienna symptoms of mental derangement manifested themselves in even greater degree; in late 1898 he attempted suicide by throwing himself into the Traunsee in Traunkirchen, but was saved and placed in the Lower Austrian provincial asylum in Vienna. He remained in confinement, gradually lapsing into complete irrationality; after his death, he was buried near the graves of Schubert and Beethoven in Vienna's Central Cemetery; a monument was unveiled in the fall of 1904; Köchert plunged to her death from the 4th-floor window of her home in Vienna (1906).

Wolf's significance in music history rests on his songs—about 300 in number—90 of them publ. posth. The sobriquet "the Wagner of the lied" may well be justified in regard to involved contrapuntal texture and chromatic harmony, for he accepted the Wagnerian idiom through natural affinity as well as by clear choice. The elaboration of the accompaniment, and the incorporation of the vocal line into the contrapuntal scheme of the whole, are Wagnerian traits. But with these external similarities, his dependence on Wagner's models ceases. In his intimate penetration of the poetic spirit of the text he appears a legitimate successor to Schubert and Schumann. Wolf's songs are sym. poems in miniature, artistically designed and admirably arranged for voice and piano, the combination in which he was a master. His operatic and instrumental works are largely fragmentary; some choral works have survived. He usually grouped his lieder by poet or chronology; only 2 cycles have a programmatic concept: the *Spanisches Liederbuch*, 44 songs based on trans. of Spanish poetry by Geibel and Heyse (1889–90); and the *Italienisches Liederbuch*, 46 songs based on trans. of anonymous Italian poems by Heyse, in 2 books: 22 songs (1890–91) and 24 songs (1896); his individual collections are based on the poetry of Mörike (1889), Eichendorff (1889), Goethe (1890), Keller (1891), and others. His writings are publ. in *Hugo Wolf: Musikalische Kritiken*, R. Batka and H. Werner, eds. (Leipzig, 1911).

Wolff, Christian, b. Nice, Mar. 8, 1934. He went to the U.S. in 1941 and became a naturalized citizen in 1946. He studied piano with Grete Sultan (1949–51) and composition with John Cage (1950–51); then pursued training in classical languages at Harvard Univ. (B.A., 1955); after studying Italian literature and classics at the Univ. of Florence (1955–56) he returned to Harvard (Ph.D. in comparative literature, 1963). From 1962 to 1970 he taught classics at Harvard; in 1971 he joined the faculty of Dartmouth College to teach classics, comparative literature, and music; was made prof. of music and of classics in 1978; also was a guest lecturer at various institutions of higher learning; contributed articles on literature and music to many publications.

Wolff evolved a curiously static method of composition, using drastically restricted numbers of pitches. His only structural resources became arithmetical progressions of rhythmic values and the expressive use of rests. He used 3 different pitches in his *Duo for Violinist and Pianist* (1961), 4 in the trio for flute, cello, and trumpet (1951), and 9 in a work called *For Piano I* (1952). Beginning in 1957 he introduced into his works various degrees of free choice, in the interest of Marxist dialectic and antiauthoritarianism; sometimes the players are required to react to the musical activities of their partners according to spontaneous and unanticipated cues.

Indeterminate works with a choice of instrumentation include *For 5 or 10 Players* for Any Instruments (1962); *For 1, 2 or 3 People* for Any Sound-Producing Means (1964); *Pairs* for any 2, 4, 6, or 8 Players (1968); *Prose Collection* for Variable Numbers of Players, Found and Constructed Materials, Instruments, and Voices (1968–71); *Changing the System* for 8 or More Instruments, Voices, and Percussion (1972–73). Chamber music: *Summer* for String Quartet (1961); *Wobbly Music* for Chorus, Keyboard, Guitars, and at least 2 Melody Instruments (1975–76); *Rock About, Instrumental, Starving to Death on a Government Claim* for Violin and Viola (1979–80); *Peace March* I–III for Various Instruments (1983–84). Piano works (solo unless indicated): *For Piano* II–II (1952, 1953); *Duo for Pianists* II–II (1957, 1958); *For Piano with Preparations* (1959); *Bread & Roses* (1976); *3 Studies* (1976); *Hay Una Mujer Desaparecida* (1979); Preludes (1981); *Piano Song, "I Am a Dangerous Woman"* (1983).

Wolf-Ferrari, Ermanno (born Wolf), b. Venice, Jan. 12, 1876; d. there, Jan. 21, 1948. His father was a well-known painter of German descent and his mother was Italian; about 1895 he added his mother's maiden name to his surname. He began piano study as a small child but also evinced a talent for art; after studying at the Accademia di Belle Arti in Rome (1891–92) he went to Munich to continue his training but then turned to music and studied counterpoint with Rheinberger at the Akademie der Tonkunst (1892–95). In 1899 he returned to Venice, where his oratorio *La Sulamite* was successfully performed. This was followed by the production of his 1st major opera, *Cenerentola* (1900), which initially proved a failure; however, its revised version for Bremen (1902) was well received and established his reputation as a composer for the theater.

From 1903 to 1909 Wolf-Ferrari was director of the Liceo Benedetto Marcello in Venice; then devoted himself mainly to composition; later was prof. of composition at the Salzburg Mozarteum (1939–45). He obtained his 1st unqualified success with the production of the comic opera *Le donne curiose* (Munich, 1903); the next opera, *I quattro rusteghi* (Munich, 1906), was also well received; there followed his little masterpiece, *Il segreto di Susanna* (Munich, 1909), a 1-act opera buffa in the style of the Italian verismo (Susanna's secret being not infidelity, as her husband suspected, but indulgence in surreptitious smoking). Turning toward grand opera, he wrote *I gioielli della Madonna;* it was brought out at Berlin in 1911 and soon became a repertoire piece everywhere; he continued to compose, but his later operas failed to match the appeal of his early creations, the most successful being *Sly, ovvero La leggenda del dormiente risvegliato* (1927) and *Il campiello* (1936).

Wolf-Ferrari also wrote popular orch'l works: Serenade for Strings (*c.* 1893); Kammersymphonie (1901); *Idillio-concertino* for Oboe, 2 Horns, and Strings (1933); *Suite-concertino* for Bassoon, 2 Horns, and Strings (Rome, 1933). Chamber: 3 violin sonatas (1895, 1901, 1943); 2 piano trios (*c.* 1897, 1900); Piano Quintet (1900); piano pieces. Vocal: *La vita nuova,* cantata (1901; Munich, 1903); other large and small choral works.

Wolpe, Stefan, b. Berlin, Aug. 25, 1902; d. N.Y., Apr. 4, 1972. He studied music theory with P. Juon and F. Schreker at the Berlin Hochschule für Musik (1919–24). After graduation he became associated with choral and theatrical groups in Berlin, promoting social causes; composed songs on revolutionary themes. With the advent of the anti-Semitic Nazi regime in 1933 he went to Vienna, where he took lessons with Webern; then traveled to Palestine in 1934; taught at the Jerusalem Cons. In 1938 he emigrated to the U.S., where he devoted himself mainly to teaching; was on the faculty of the Settlement Music School in Philadelphia (1939–42); at the Philadelphia Academy of Music (1949–52); at Black Mountain College, N.C. (1952–56); and at Long Island Univ. (1957–68). He also taught privately. Among Wolpe's students were Elmer Bernstein, Ezra Laderman, Shapey, Tudor, and Feldman. In 1966 he was elected a member of the National Inst. of Arts and Letters. His last years were made increasingly difficult by Parkinson's disease. He contributed numerous articles to German and American music magazines.

In Wolpe's style of composition he attempted to reconcile the contradictions of triadic tonality (which he cultivated during his early period of writing proletarian music), atonality without procrustean dodecaphony, and serialism of contrasts obtained by intervallic contraction and expansion, metrical alteration, and dynamic variegation; superadded to these were explorations of Jewish cantillation and infatuation with jazz; the complex mixture is often contained within abstract, even dry titles. Remarkably enough, the very copiousness of these resources contributed to a clearly identifiable idiom.

Wolpe wrote theatrical works, the best known being the lyric scene *Anna Blume* for Musical Clown and Piano (after Schwitters; 1929) and the incidental music for 2 Brecht plays: *The Good Woman of Setzuan* (1953) and *The Exception and the Rule* (1960). Orch.: *The Man from Midian,* ballet suite (1942); Sym. (1955–56); Chamber Piece Nos. 1 and 2 for 14 players (1964; 1965–66). He was prolific as a composer of chamber music; most pieces are for between 1 and 4 instruments; larger works include the *Quintet with Voice* for Baritone, Clarinet, Horn, Cello, Harp, and Piano (1956–57); *Piece for 2 Instrumental Units* for Flute, Oboe, Violin, Cello, Double Bass, and Percussion (1962–63); *Piece for trumpet and 7*

instruments (1971). His early piano works were quite vernacular in tone but the *4 Studies on Basic Rows* (1935–36) was his breakthrough to contemporary techniques; subsequent important works include *Toccata in 3 Parts* (1941); *Battle Piece* (1943–47); *Enactments* for 3 Pianos (1950–53); *Form* (1959); *Form IV: Broken Sequences* (1969). Wolpe's songs have a wide breadth of subjects and texts, setting Hölderlin, Fontaine, Tagore, Kokoschka, Mayakovsky, Becher, Albert Einstein, and biblical excerpts; they are unjustly neglected.

Wonder, Stevie (born Steveland Judkins Hardaway), b. Saginaw, Mich., May 13, 1950. Other sources state that he was born Steveland Judkins or Steveland Morris. Blinded in infancy by insufficient oxygen in an incubator, he learned to play the drums and piano; improvised his 1st song, *Lonely Boy,* at the age of 10, and at 12 composed *Fingertips,* which became a hit. He signed with Berry Gordy, Jr. (Motown Records) in 1961. Possessed by that indefinable gift of song, he rapidly advanced in the rosters of popular success; his performances have become great attractions. In his 1st recordings he was an apolitical hit-maker who took the Motown teenage formula to its heights; he recorded Dylan's *Blowin' in the Wind,* Tony Bennett's hit *For Once in My Life,* the Beatles' *We Can Work It Out,* and his own *Uptight, I Was Made to Love Her, My Cherie Amour,* and *Signed, Sealed, Delivered I'm Yours;* he also appeared in the films *Muscle Beach Party* and *Bikini Beach.*

By age 21 Wonder had evolved a new approach based on synthesizers, complete control over his own work, and an interest in the African-American experience. Beginning with the album *Music of My Mind* (1972), he showed a greater maturity and musical sophistication; among the classic hits were *Superstition, Living for the City, You Are the Sunshine of My Life, You Haven't Done Nothing, Higher Ground, Boogie On Reggae Woman, Isn't She Lovely, I Wish,* and *Sir Duke* (an Ellington tribute). After a nearly fatal automobile accident and the breakup of his marriage, he returned to form with songs in styles old (*I Just Called to Say I Love You* from the soundtrack *The Woman in Red; Part-Time Lover*) and new (*It's Wrong [Apartheid]* and the rap-influenced *Master Blaster [Jammin']*). *Happy Birthday* (1980) was part of Wonder's campaign to make Martin Luther King, Jr.'s birthday a national holiday. He collaborated with Paul McCartney on *Ebony and Ivory* (1982) and later with Michael Jackson on *Get It* (1987). He later wrote the soundtrack to Spike Lee's *Jungle Fever.* Wonder has devoted much time, energy, and money to social causes; added his voice to a campaign against drunk driving and donated to AIDS and cancer research; contributed to U.S. for Africa's charity record, *We Are the World* (1985).

woodblocks. Chinese blocks.

woodwind. Group of instruments in the orch. orig. made of wood and played by blowing (flute, piccolo, oboe, English horn, clarinet, bass clarinet, bassoon, contrabassoon). In modern times flutes and piccolos are made of metal, but they are still included in the woodwind category. The saxophone, a hybrid metal wind instrument, has a reed and clarinet-style key system; it tends to be classified in the woodwind category. There are some special and rarely used instruments that belong to this group—the once popular recorder, the alto and bass flutes, the heckelphone (a baritone oboe). *Woodwind quintet,* a somewhat inaccurate name for an ensemble consisting of four woodwind instruments (flute, oboe, clarinet, bassoon) and the modern valve (French) horn, a brass instrument.

Work, Henry Clay, b. Middletown, Conn., Oct. 1, 1832; d. Hartford, June 8, 1884. He was a printer by trade; was entirely self-taught in music; his 1st success was *We Are Coming, Sister Mary* (1853); other well-known songs were *Kingdom Coming* (1862), *Come Home, Father* (1864), *Wake, Nicodemus!* (1864), *Marching through Georgia* (1865), and *Grandfather's Clock* (1876).

working out (Ger. *Durchführung*). Development section in sonata form.

wuchtig (Ger.). Weighty, powerfully, ponderously; with strong emphasis.

wunderkind. No art, no science is revealed at an age so early as that of musical talent. When an anxious and hopeful mother (less frequently father) notices that her darling child bangs on the keyboard of an upright piano (rarely a baby grand in such families), she perceives the breath of musical genius. The 1st symptom of *Wunderkindheit* is the possession of perfect pitch, the ability to name any note struck on the piano without a moment's hesitation; but the possession of this precious gift does not guarantee a successful musical career.

Most wunderkinder are taught piano or violin; there are few wunderkinder of the cello, and hardly any of a wind instrument. Wunderkinder are often exhibited by their parents as wonders of nature. They are kept chronologically young by cutting down their ages as they outgrow short pants. Mozart's father advertised his genius son as being 8 years old during several successive years. One of the most durable child prodigies was the violinist Jascha Heifetz. He made a sensational American debut at the age of 16 in Carnegie Hall, N.Y. The American Soc. for the Prevention of Cruelty to Children intervened against the exploitation of Josef Hofmann, who played a Beethoven piano concerto in N.Y. at the age of 11. He was forced to stop public appearances until the age of 16, but this hiatus did not prevent him from becoming one of the greatest master pianists of all time.

Child conductors are a great rarity, but at least one of them made a meteoric career early in the century: Willy Ferrero, an American-born Italian boy who toured Europe as a sym. conductor at the age of 8, arousing wonderment among audiences in France, Italy, and Russia. He ended his inglorious career as a provincial opera conductor. Another wunderkind conductor was Lorin Maazel, who led sym. concerts at the age of 9, eliciting invidious comparisons with a trained seal; he has since become one of the world's leading conductors.

Child composers are even more of a rarity than performing wunderkinder. Mozart was the greatest among them. Mendelssohn achieved a fantastic mastery of musical composition at a very early age. Schubert wrote inspired songs at the age of 17. But neither Beethoven nor Brahms were precocious composers; nor were Wagner, Tchaikovsky, or Stravinsky. Erich Wolfgang Korngold evinced comparisons with Mozart when he wrote a piano trio at the age of 12. He was introduced to Mahler, who exclaimed, "Ein Genie! Ein Genie!" He wrote operas at the age of 18. But his star set precipitously in the musical firmament as he grew older.

The number of talented wunderkinder who never made it big is large. Ineffable sadness surrounds the parade of red-cheeked little boys in velvet pants and little girls in white dresses whose pictures used to adorn the advertising pages of European and American music magazines of the fin de siècle. Whatever happened to them? Not even the most dogged efforts of musicological bloodhounds could trace most of them to their final retreats in some unknown home for the retired.

Wunderlich, Fritz (Friedrich Karl Otto), b. Kusel, Sept. 26 1930; d. Heidelberg, Sept. 17, 1966. He received his musical education at the Freiburg Hochschule für Musik; then sang opera in Stuttgart (1955–58), Frankfurt (1958–60), and Munich (from 1960); in 1965 he appeared as Don Ottavio at London's Covent Garden. While still a young man he gained a fine reputation as a lyric tenor; his performances of Mozart roles were especially acclaimed for their expressive power. His untimely death (in a mysterious accident) deprived the opera stage of one of its finest and most promising artists.

Wuorinen, Charles, b. N.Y., June 9, 1938. He began to play piano and to compose at the age of 5; took lessons in music theory with Beeson and Ussachevsky; received the Young Composers Award from the N.Y. Phil. at 16. At 18 he wrote his earliest orch'l work, *Into the Organ Pipes and Steeples;* entered Columbia Univ.; studied with Luening; composed 3 full-fledged syms. (1958–59); received his B.A. (1961) and M.A. (1963).

Wuorinen cofounded the Group for Contemporary Music with Harvey Sollberger (1962). In 1964 he was appointed an instructor in music at Columbia; he taught there until 1971, when he resigned in a flurry of angry controversy about the refusal of the faculty to grant him tenure; taught at the Manhattan School of Music (1972–79); held Guggenheim fellowships (1968, 1972). In 1969 he received a commission from Nonesuch Records for a work using synthesized sound, titled *Time's Encomium;* awarded the Pulitzer Prize in 1970, unprecedented for a work written expressly for the recording media; later rearranged it for orch. In 1985 he was made a member of the American Academy and Inst. of Arts and Letters; served as composer-in-residence of the San Francisco Sym. (1985–87).

From his very 1st essays in free composition, Wuorinen asserted himself as a true representative of the modernistic 2nd half of the 20th century. His techniques derived from Stravinsky's early period, when stark primitivism gave way to austere linear counterpoint; an even greater affinity is with the agglutinative formations of unrelated thematic statements as practiced by Varèse; a more literal dependence connects his works with the dodecaphonic method of composition as promulgated by Schoenberg. These modalities and relationships coalesce into a sui generis complex subdivided into melodic, harmonic, and contrapuntal units that build a definitive formal structure.

The foundation of Wuorinen's method of composition is serialism, in which pitch, time, and rhythmic divisions relate to one another in a "time point system" that lends itself to unlimited tonal and temporal arrangements, combinations, and permutations. Enormously prolific, he finds it possible to explore the entire vocabulary of serial composition. Most of his works are instrumental; wrote an opera entitled *The W. of Babylon, or The Triumph of Love* (alluding to the apocalyptic whore; 1975), a work he describes as a "baroque burlesque." Its dramatis personae includes a libidinous assortment of lascivious French noble and ignoble men and women of the immoral 17th century, spouting lewd declarations and performing lecherous acts. He publ. a manual, paradoxically entitled *Simple Composition* (N.Y., 1979); has written 1 other opera, *The Politics of Harmony* (1967). His many orch'l works include 3 piano concertos; chamber works, including 3 string quartets (1971, 1979, 1987); solo instrumental works; vocal works; and electronic works.

würdevoll (Ger.). With dignity; loftily.

würdig (Ger.). In an imposing manner.

Wut (Ger.). Fury. *Mit Wüt, wüt(h)end,* furiously, frantically.

Wynette, Tammy (born, Wynette Pugh), b. Red Bay, Ala., May 5, 1942, d. Nashville, Tenn., April 6, 1998. She taught herself to play the piano and guitar; after holding various jobs, including a position as a beauty operator, she decided to seek fame and fortune in Nashville, Tenn., as a singer of country music; in 1969 she joined the Grand Ole Opry. She struck a responsive chord with such songs as *Your Good Girl's Gonna Go Bad, Bedtime Story, Let's Get Together, D-I-V-O-R-C-E,* and her biggest hit, *Stand By Your Man.* She was married to the country-music star George Jones (1969–75).

Wyschnegradsky, Ivan (Alexandrovich), b. St. Petersburg, May 16, 1893; d. Paris, Sept. 29, 1979. He studied composition with Nikolai Sokoloff at the St. Petersburg Cons.; in 1920 he settled in Paris. He devoted virtually his entire musical career to the exploration and creative realization of music in quarter tones and other microtonal intervals; had a quarter-tone piano constructed for him; also publ. a guide, *Manuel d'harmonie à quarts de ton* (Paris, 1932). In 1945 he presented in Paris a concert of his music, at which he conducted the 1st performance of his *Cosmos* for 4 Pianos, with each pair tuned at quarter tones. Canadian pianist Bruce Mather took interest in his music and gave a concert of his works at McGill Univ. in Montreal that included 3 world premieres (1977). But with the exception of these rare concerts, he remains a figure of legend; few performances of his music are ever given in Europe or North America. He regarded his *La Journée de l'existence* for Narrator, *ad libitum* Chorus, and Orch. (to his own text; 1916–17) as his germinal work, opening the path to microtonal harmony; he dated this "awakening to ultrachromaticism" as having occurred in 1918. At his death he left sketches for a short opera in 5 scenes, *L'Éternel Étranger,* begun in 1939 but never completed; also unfinished was the ambitious *Polyphonie spatiale.* Wyschnegradsky wrote quarter-tone works for piano(s), string ensembles (including quartet), voice and piano, chorus, ondes Martenot, and orch.; works for 3rd-, 6th-, 8th-, 12th-, and 31st (Fokker) tones, as well as works for standard equal temperament. *Ainsi parlait Zarathoustra* for Orch. (1929–30; arr. for 4 Pianos, 1936) is considered his masterpiece. He also publ. several articles on ultrachromaticism and related topics.

Xenakis, Iannis, b. Brăila, Rumania, May 29, 1922. At age 10 he went with his family to Greece, where he began to study engineering; became involved in the Greek resistance against the Nazi occupation forces; was severely wounded in a skirmish, losing sight in 1 eye (1945). Shortly thereafter he was captured, but managed to escape to the U.S. In 1947 he went to Paris, eventually becoming a naturalized French citizen; studied architecture with Le Corbusier; became his assistant (1948–60); studied composition with Honegger and Milhaud at the École Normale de Musique in Paris and Messiaen at the Paris Cons. (1950–53).

Xenakis aided Le Corbusier in the design of the Philips Pavilion at the 1958 World's Fair in Brussels; met and assisted Varèse on his *Poème électronique* for the exhibit; in return received stimulating advice on the creative potential of the electronic medium. With his backgrounds in engineering and architecture, Xenakis now strove to connect mathematical concepts with the organization of a musical composition, using the theory of sets, symbolic logic, and probabilistic calculus; promulgated the stochastic method, teleologically directed and deterministic as opposed to a purely aleatory handling of data; publ. a comprehensive vol. dealing with these procedures, *Musiques formelles* (Paris, 1963); founded (1966) and directed the Centre d'Études Mathématiques et Automatiques Musicales in Paris; founded the Center for Mathematical and Automated Music at Indiana Univ.; served on the faculty (1967–72).

Xenakis's influence on the development of advanced composition in Europe and America was considerable; several composers adopted his theories and imitated his penchant for scientific-sounding titles; he often uses Greek words for his titles to stress the philosophical derivation of modern science and modern arts from classical Greek concepts; sometimes uses computer symbols instead. Among his works are *Metastasis* for 61 Instruments, harbinger of Penderecki's cluster pieces (1953–54); *Pithoprakta* for 50 Instruments (1955–56); *Syrmos* for 18 Strings (1959); *Orient-Occident* for Tape (1960); *Herma* for Piano (1960–61); *ST/48–1,240162* (1956–62; ST = stochastic; 48 = number of players; 1 = 1st work for this contingent; 240162 = 24 January 1962, date when the work was programmed probabilistically by computer); *Morsima-Amorsima* (Fated-Not Fated) for Violin, Cello, Double Bass, and Piano (1956–62); *Atrées* for 10 Players (1956–62; in

homage to Blaise Pascal; calculated by computer, with license); *Strategie,* musical game for 2 Conductors and 2 Orchs. (1959–62; Venice Festival, 1963; Bruno Maderna's orch. defeated Konstantin Simonovic's); *Bohor I* and *II* for Tape (1962, 1975); *Polla ta dhina* (Many Are the Wonders) for Children's Choir and Small Orch., to a text from Sophocles's *Antigone* (1962); *Eonta* for Piano, 2 Trumpets, and 3 Tenor Trombones (1963–64); *Akrata* (Pure) for 16 Wind Instruments (1964–65); *Terretektorh* for 88 Players scattered among the audience (1966); *Oresteïa,* incidental music for Aeschylus's tragedy, for Chorus and Chamber Orch. (1965–66); *Nomos Alpha* (Law Alpha) for Cello (1966); *Nuits* for 12 Mixed Voices a cappella (1967); *Kraanerg,* ballet music for Tape and Orch. (Ottawa, 1969); *Synaphai* for 1 or 2 Pianos and Orch. (1969); *Hibiki-Hana-Ma,* 12-channel electroacoustic music distributed kinematically over 800 loudspeakers, for the Osaka EXPO '70 (1969–70; also 4-channel version); *Persepolis,* light-and-sound spectacle with 8- or 4-channel electroacoustic music (1971); *Psappha* for Percussion (1975); *N'shima* for 2 Horns, 2 Trombones, Cello, and 2 Mezzo-sopranos (1975); *Mikka "S"* for Violin (1976); *Pleïades* for Percussion (1979); *Aïs* for Baritone, Percussion, and Orch. (1979); *Palimpsest* for Ensemble (1979); *Chant des soleils* for Chorus, Children's Chorus, Winds, and Percussion (1983); *Tetras* for String Quartet (1983); *Keqrops* for Piano and Orch. (N.Y., 1986); *Akea* for Piano Quintet (1987); *Tracées* for Orch. (1988); *Plektó* for Chamber Ensemble (1993).

xylophone (from Grk., wood sound; Ger. *Xylophon;* It. *xilofono*). Keyboard percussion instrument with hardwood keys arranged and tuned like a piano; each key has a resonator tuned to it. The keys are fastened horizontally to 2 stretched boards and played with 2 or more sticks or mallets. Predecessors of the modern xylophone are found in many parts of the world, consisting of a few wooden bars of different length producing different tones. They were usually laid out on straw, and therefore became known among explorers as *Strohfiedel* (Ger., straw fiddle).

The early xylophone reached its developmental height in Southeast Asia in the 14th century; the instrument had spread westward into Africa, then to the Americas; it arrived in Europe by the 16th century. Gradually assuming its modern form, the European-American xylophone was imported into Latin America and Africa and became domesticated there as kinds of pianos with wooden keys.

Saint-Saëns used the xylophone to great effect in his *Danse macabre* to suggest the bone rattling of disembodied ghosts. In the 20th century the instrument's use of straw finally gave way to a notch system to support the keys. Many composers of the 20th century included the xylophone in their sym. scores, including the *Sabre Dance* from *Gayané* by Khachaturian.

xylorimba (xylo-marimba). Hybrid keyboard instrument, developed in the early 20th century, with a 5-octave range encompassing that of the xylophone and marimba; used in popular music and vaudeville between the world wars (as the marimba-xylophone); has been used by Berg, Stravinsky, Dallapiccola, Messiaen, Schat, and Gerhard.

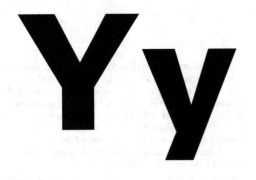

yaravi (Sp.). Harawi.

Yasser, Joseph, b. Lodz, Apr. 16, 1893; d. N.Y., Sept. 6, 1981. He studied at the Moscow Cons., graduating in 1917 as an organist; taught organ in Moscow and Siberia, then reached Shanghai (1921); conducted a choral society there; subsequently emigrated to the U.S. (1923); served as organist at Temple Rodeph Sholom in N.Y. (1929–60); held various positions in American musicological groups. His most important contribution to music was *A Theory of Evolving Tonality* (N.Y., 1932), which proffered an ingenious hypothesis as to the origin of the pentatonic and heptatonic scales and, operating by inductive reasoning, suggested that the next Western scale would contain 19 equally tempered degrees. He contributed several articles to *Musical Quarterly* (1937–38) dealing with quartal harmony (publ. separately, N.Y., 1938).

yodel (Ger. *Jodel*). Type of rural singing in the European Alps, especially in Switzerland, characterized by the frequent alternation of falsetto tones with chest tones; a kind of expanded warble. The earliest yodel call is found in a collection entitled *Bicinia Gallica, Latina, Germanica,* publ. 1545. A similar technique is used by various groups in Africa. Yodeling is related to the *field holler* of the American South; it eventually found its way into country music through the singing of Jimmie Rodgers.

Youmans, Vincent (Millie), b. N.Y., Sept. 27, 1898; d. Denver, Apr. 5, 1946. He took piano lessons as a child; enlisted in the U.S. Navy; played the piano in a Navy band; wrote a song, *Hallelujah,* which was picked up by Sousa, who performed it with his own bands; Youmans incorporated it in his musical *Hit the Deck* (1927). After World War I he earned a living as a song plugger for publishers in N.Y.; produced 2 musical comedies, both moderately successful; he achieved fame with his next production, *No, No, Nanette;* it opened in Detroit (1924); moved to Chicago; after a 49-week run there it went to London (1925); finally reached Broadway later that year, proving to be one of the most beguiling and enduring American musicals; its hit song, *Tea for Two,* became a perennial favorite all over the world; Shostakovich even arranged it for salon orch. under the title *Tahiti Trot* (1927).

Several other successful musicals followed: *A Night Out* (1925), *Oh, Please!* (1926), *Rainbow* (1928), *Great Day* (1929), and *Through the Years* (1932). In 1933 Youmans went to Hollywood to complete his score for the film *Flying Down to Rio.* Because of a worsening tubercular condition, he retired to Denver in the hope of recuperation in its then-unpolluted environment; remained there until his death. Among his other hits: *Bambalina; I Want to Be Happy; Hallelujah; Sometimes I'm Happy; Great Day; Without a Song; Time on My Hands; Through the Years; Oh, Me, Oh, My, Oh, You; Carioca; Orchids in the Moonlight; Drums in My Heart; More Than You Know; Rise 'n' Shine.*

Young, La Monte (Thornton), b. Bern, Idaho, Oct. 14, 1935. He studied clarinet and saxophone with W. Green in Los Angeles (1951–54); attended Los Angeles City College (1953–56); studied counterpoint and composition privately with L. Stein (1955–56); studied ethnomusicology with R. Stevenson at the Univ. of Calif. at Los Angeles (B.A., 1958); pursued further training with Shifrin and A. Imbrie at the Univ. of Calif. at Berkeley (1958–60); worked with other minimalist pioneers (Riley, Glass, Reich); attended the summer courses in new music in Darmstadt; subsequently studied electronic music with R. Maxfield at the New School for Social Research in N.Y. (1960–61). In 1963 he married the artist and illustrator Marian Zazeela, with whom he subsequently gave audiovisual performances in a series of Sound/Light Environments in Europe and America. After a stay in India to study philosophy and spiritual practices, he came to believe that any human, subhuman, or inhuman activity constitutes art; in *Composition 1990* he starts a fire on the stage while releasing captive butterflies in the hall. Attempting to overcome terrestrial limitations, he follows a circadian period of 26 hours; emulates timelessness by declaring, "This piece of music may play without stopping for thousands of years"; several of his works consist solely of imperious commands: "Push the piano to the wall; push it through the wall; keep pushing."

Young ed. *An Anthology of Chance Operations, Concept Art, Anti-Art, etc.* (N.Y., 1963), which, with his *Compositions 1960,* had enormous influence on concept art and the Fluxus movement; his own contribution was a line drawn in India ink on a 3 x 5 filing card. He has contributed extensively to the study of just intonation and to the development of tuning systems based on the set of rational numbers that make up the components of his periodic composite sound waveform environments; one goal was to create acoustic "clouds" of overtones. He received a Guggenheim fellowship and a grant from the N.E.A. Among his ascertainable works are *Poem for Tables, Chairs, and Benches* (moving furniture about; Univ. of Calif., Berkeley, 1960); *The Well-Tuned Piano* (1964–81); *The Tortoise Recalling the Drone of the Holy Numbers as They Were Revealed in the Dreams of the Whirlwind and the Obsidian Gong, Illuminated by the Sawmill, the Green Sawtooth Ocelot, and the High-Tension Line Stepdown Transformer* (N.Y., 1964); *Map of 49's Dream of 2 Systems of 11 Sets of Galactic Intervals Ornamental Lightyears Tracery* for Voices, Various Instruments, and Sine Wave Drones (Pasadena, Calif., 1968); *The Subsequent Dreams of China* (1980). He has created several pieces of conceptual music and tape recordings of his own monophonous vocalizing achieved by both inspiration and expiration, so that the vocal line is maintained indefinitely; also various physical exercises with or without audible sounds. His *Selected Writings* were publ. in Munich (1969).

Young, Lester (Willis), b. Woodville, Miss., Aug. 27, 1909; d. N.Y., Mar. 15, 1959. Called Pres or Prez, he studied trumpet, alto sax, violin, and drums with his father; played in his family's band; turning to the tenor saxophone at 19, performed with various groups in the Midwest; joined Count Basie's band (1934; 1936–40; 1943–44). While serving in the U.S. Army, he was court-martialed for using drugs; upon his release (1945) he resumed his career, plagued by his abuse of alcohol; all the same, performed until shortly before his death. He recorded with various jazz notables, including Billie Holiday, who dubbed him "Pres" (a contraction of "President") for his outstanding abilities. One of the great jazz saxophonists, he influenced numerous successors through his beautiful long melodic lines, fine phrasing, and inventive solos, among them *Lady Be Good, Shoe Shine Boy, Lester Leaps In, After Theatre Jump, These Foolish Things, All of Me* (with Holiday), *Pres Returns,* and *Easy Does It.*

Young, Neil, b. Toronto, Nov. 12, 1945. He learned to play the banjo and guitar in his youth; moving to Los Angeles (1966), joined with Stephen Stills to form Buffalo Springfield, which recorded Young's *Nowadays Clancy Can't Even Sing, Broken Arrow, Mr. Soul,* and *I Am a Child.* He left (1967) to begin a solo career with an eponymous album (1969); performed and recorded with (David) Crosby, Stills, and (Graham) Nash on their hit albums *Déjà Vu* (1970) and *4-Way Street* (1971). Young made the solo albums *Everybody Knows This Is Nowhere* (1969), *After the Goldrush* (with backup group Crazy Horse; 1970), *Harvest* (his best-selling album; 1972), *Tonight's the Night* (1975), *Zuma* (1975), *Comes A Time* (1978), *Rust Never Sleeps* (1979), *Re-ac-tor* (1981), *Old Ways* (1985), *Freedom* (1989), and *Sleeps With Angels* (1994). His songs evoke an effective conglomeration of folk, country, and hard rock; among his best are *The Loner, Cinnamon Girl, Down By The River, Southern Man, Only Love Can Break Your Heart, Ohio, Like a Hurricane, Heart of Gold, Country Girl, Helpless, Cortez the Killer, Hey Hey My My,* and *Vampire Blues.*

Young, Victor, b. Bristol, Tenn., Apr. 9, 1889; d. Ossining, N.Y., Sept. 2, 1968. He studied piano with I. Philipp in Paris; toured in England and the U.S. as accompanist to prominent singers; held various teaching positions; was music director in Edison's Experimental Laboratory in West Orange, N.J., conducting tonal tests and making piano recordings under Edison's personal supervision (1919–27). He wrote the musical score for one of the earliest sound motion pictures, *In Old California;* composed some 300 film scores altogether, including *Wells Fargo* (1937), *Gulliver's Travels* (1939), *For Whom the Bell Tolls* (1943), *Night Has a Thousand Eyes* (1948), *Rio Grande* (1950), *The Quiet Man* (1952), *Shane* (1953), and *Around The World in 80 Days* (1956); wrote orch'l works, piano music, and popular songs.

Yo-Yo Ma. See ⇒Ma, Yo-Yo.

Ysaÿe, Eugène (-Auguste), b. Liège, July 16, 1858; d. Brussels, May 12, 1931. At age 4 he began to study violin with his father, a theater conductor; at age 7 he was enrolled at the Liège Cons. as a pupil of D. Heynberg, winning 2nd prize (1867); left the Cons. in a dispute with his mentor (1869), but readmitted as a pupil of R. Massart (1872), winning 1st prize (1873) and the silver medal (1874); continued his training on a scholarship at the Brussels Cons. with Wieniawski; completed his studies with Vieuxtemps in Paris (1876–79).

In 1879 Ysaÿe became concertmaster of Bilse's orch. in Berlin; appeared as a soloist at Pauline Lucca's concerts in Cologne and Aachen; in Germany he met Anton Rubinstein, who took him to Russia, where he spent 2 winters; also toured Norway. In 1883 he

settled in Paris, where he met Franck, d'Indy, et al., and gave successful concerts; formed a duo with pianist Raoul Pugno; they started a long series of concerts, establishing a new standard of excellence. In 1886 he married Louise Bourdeau; Franck dedicated his violin sonata to them as a wedding present; his interpretation made it famous. That year he was named a prof. at the Brussels Cons. (resigned 1898) and organized the Ysaÿe Quartet; Debussy dedicated his string quartet to Ysaÿe's group, which premiered it at the Soc. Nationale in Paris (1893).

In 1889 Ysaÿe made successful appearances in England; made his American debut playing the Beethoven Violin Concerto with the N.Y. Phil. and creating a sensation (1894); revisited America many times, with undiminished acclaim; began his conducting career (1894); established in Brussels the Soc. des Concerts Ysaÿe. After World War I, he made his American conducting debut with the Cincinnati Sym. Orch.; led the Cincinnati May Festival (both 1918); his success led to a permanent position as conductor of the Cincinnati Sym. Orch. (1918–22). He then returned to Belgium and resumed leadership of the Soc. des Concerts Ysaÿe. At age 70 he began composing an opera in the Walloon dialect, *Piér li Houïeu* (Peter the Miner), produced in Liège (1931); the composer attended in an invalid's chair, having lost his left foot to the extreme ravages of diabetes. He began the composition of a 2nd Walloon opera, *L'Avierge di Piér* (The Virgin of Stone), but did not live to complete it.

Ysaÿe's style of playing is best described as heroic; but his art was equally convincing in the expression of moods of exquisite delicacy and tenderness; his frequent employment of "tempo rubato" produced an effect of elasticity without distorting the melodic line. He was known for an unorthodox bow grip, which excluded the little finger. His works include 8 violin concertos; sym. poems and concertante works for violin and orch.; other concertante works for strings and orch. Chamber: 6 sonatas for solo violin (his masterpiece, 1924); other solo violin pieces; solo cello sonata; duo-violin sonata. Queen Elisabeth of Belgium inaugurated the annual Prix International Eugène Ysaÿe in Brussels (1937); the 1st winner was David Oistrakh.

Yun, Isang, b. Tongyong, Sept. 17, 1917; d. Berlin, Nov. 3, 1995. He studied Western music in Korea (1935–37) and in Japan (1941–43). During World War II he was active in the anti-Japanese underground; in 1943 he was imprisoned, and then spent the rest of the war in hiding until the liberation in 1945. He became a music teacher in Tongyong in 1946, and later taught in Pusan; in 1953 he became a prof. of composition at the Univ. of Seoul; then studied with Revel at the Paris Cons. (1956–57) and with Blacher, Rufer, and Schwarz-Schilling at the Berlin Hochschule für Musik (1958–59); also attended the summer courses in new music in Darmstadt. He settled permanently in Berlin; after a serialist phase he began producing music marked by a fine expressionistic and coloristic quality and written in an idiom of euphonious dissonance: *Bara* (orch., 1960); *Loyang* (chamber ensemble, 1962); *Om mani padme hum* (oratorio, 1964); *Réak* (orch., 1966); also his 1st opera, *Der Traum des Liu-Tung* (1965), and several chamber works.

Yun's career was dramatically interrupted when he and his wife were brutally abducted from West Berlin by secret police agents of South Korea (1967), forced to board a plane for Seoul, and brought to trial there for sedition; after a show trial he was sentenced to life imprisonment; his wife was given 3 years in jail.

This act of lawlessness perpetrated on the territory of another country prompted an indignant protest by the government of West Germany, which threatened to cut off its substantial economic aid to South Korea; 23 celebrated musicians, including Igor Stravinsky, issued a vigorous letter of protest; as a result, South Korea released Yun and his wife after nearly 2 years of detention, and they returned to Germany. In 1970 he was appointed lecturer in composition at the Berlin Hochschule für Musik; made a prof. (1974); retired (1985). In 1971 he became a naturalized German citizen.

In the years after his release from South Korean prisons, Yun composed 3 new operas, including *Die Witwe des Schmetterlings* (The Butterfly Widow), completed in his Seoul prison cell and produced *in absentia* in Bonn (1967). He composed in certain genres for the 1st time, such as 5 syms. (1983–87) and concertos with full or string orch.: cello (1976); flute (1977); oboe and harp (1977); clarinet (1981); violin (3, 1981–92); harp, (1984); oboe/English horn and cello, *Duetto concertante* (1987); oboe/oboe d'amore (1990). He composed other orch'l and vocal works; chamber music, including 2 chamber concertos, 4 mixed quartets, 2 clarinet quintets (1984; 1994); 6 string quartets, 2 of which are withdrawn (1959–92); 3 mixed trios. His solo instrumental works are for recorder, flute(s), oboe, bass clarinet, bassoon, violin, cello, harp, piano, harpsichord, and organ (the influential graphically notated *Tuyaux sonores*, 1967).

yurupari. Very long wooden trumpet used by the Amazon Indians in Brazil, which they considered taboo to women and strangers. Oscar Wilde mentions them in his novel *The Picture of Dorian Gray,* speaking of exotic and dangerous hobbies of his hero in whose collection there are "mysterious yuruparis of the Rio Negro Indians, that women are not allowed to look at." The reason for this proscription is not explicitly known.

Zabaleta, Nicanor, b. San Sebastián, Jan. 7, 1907; d. San Juan, Puerto Rico, Mar. 31, 1993. He began his harp training in San Sebastián; after further studies in Madrid he went to Paris to study with M. Tournier and composition with E. Cools; toured extensively in Europe, South America, and the U.S. He made notable efforts to increase the number of works for the harp; brought to light neglected compositions of early composers; prompted and commissioned modern composers to write harp music, including concertos by Ginastera, Milhaud, Piston, Villa-Lobos, Thomson, and Tal.

zamacueca (*zambacueca;* Sp.). National dance of Chile, also called *cueca,* a couple dance in rapid alternating 3/4 and 6/8.

zamba (Sp.). Popular Argentinian dance in 6/8 time, derived from the zamacueca.

zampogna (zampoña). Italian traditional bagpipe.

zampoñas (Sp.). Chilean panpipes.

Zandonai, Riccardo, b. Sacco di Rovereto, Trentino, May 30, 1883; d. Pesaro, June 5, 1944. He was a pupil of Gianferrari at Rovereto (1893–98); studied with Mascagni at the Liceo Rossini in Pesaro; for his final examination composed a sym. poem for solo voices, chorus, and orch., *Il ritorno di Odisseo* (graduated 1902). He turned to opera, his favored genre throughout his career; his 1st was *La coppa del re* (c. 1906, unperformed); after writing a children's opera *L'uccellino d'oro* (Sacco di Rovereto, 1907) he was successful with *Il grillo del focolare,* after Dickens's *The Cricket on the Hearth* (Turin, 1908); with *Conchita,* after *La Femme et le pantin* by P. Louÿs (Milan, 1911), established himself as an important Italian composer; the title role was created by soprano Tarquinia Tarquini, whom Zandonai married (1917).

Conchita received its American premiere in San Francisco (1912) and, as *La Femme et le pantin,* its French premiere at the Paris Opéra-Comique (1929). Although *Melenis* (Milan, 1912) was unsuccessful, Zandonai's reputation was enhanced by subsequent works, notably the post-Wagnerian *Francesca da Rimini,* after Gabriele d'Annunzio after Dante (Turin, 1914; Metropolitan Opera, N.Y., 1916), the only one of his operas that remains in the repertory. During World War I he participated in the political agitation for the return of former Italian provinces; wrote a student hymn calling for the return of Trieste (1915). In 1939 he was appointed director of his alma mater; remained there until his death. In addition to the operas, he wrote orch'l

and concertanate works, band pieces, chamber music, and choral music.

zapateado (*zabateado;* Sp.). Latin American dance in triple meter, characterized by heel stamping to emphasize the strong syncopation.

Zappa, Frank (Vincent), b. Baltimore, Dec. 21, 1940, d. Los Angeles, Dec. 4, 1993. From school days he played guitar and organized groups in southern California with names such as Captain Glasspack and His Magic Mufflers. In 1965 he joined the rhythm-and-blues band the Soul Giants; soon took it under his own aegis; changed its name to the Mothers ("of Invention" was appended to appease gender-insecure record company executives); its 1st recording, *Freak Out!,* became an underground hit; with *Absolutely Free* (with *Brown Shoes Don't Make It*), *We're Only In It for the Money,* and *Lumpy Gravy,* constituting the earliest concept albums, touching every nerve in a gradually decivilized Calif. lifestyle—rebellious, anarchistic, incomprehensible, and yet tantalizing. The band became a mixed-media celebration of total artistic, political, and social opposition to the Establishment.

In 1969 Zappa replaced the original Mothers with new musicians, a process he would undertake every few years; eventually he stopped using the Mothers name altogether. Moving farther afield, he produced and scored the film *200 Motels,* relating tales of sex-crazed rock musicians on tour (with Flo and Eddie, Ringo Starr, Theo Bikel, and Keith Moon). He became a cult figure, target of equal parts violent adulation and rejection; nearly killed when a besotted individual pushed him off the stage into an empty orch. pit (London, 1971); similar assaults forced him to hire an athletic bodyguard for protection. In 1982 his planned appearance in Palermo, Sicily, the birthplace of his parents, had to be canceled because the mob rioted in anticipation of the event.

Zappa deliberately confronted the most cherished social and emotional sentiments by recording such songs as *Broken Hearts Are for Assholes; Jewish Princess* unsurprisingly offended the sensitivity of American Jews; always willing to present a balanced viewpoint, he upset the members of his own people's faith in *Catholic Girls.* A lover of scatological materials, he analyzed and ridiculed bodily functions in *Why Does It Hurt When I Pee?* (Ironically and tragically, he died from prostate cancer that went undetected for a decade.) Other satires included *Dancin' Fool* and *I Have Been In You;* in 1980 he produced the film *Baby Snakes,* shocking even the most impervious senses.

Zappa's lyrical disdain and angry attitudes tend to disguise the remarkable development in his music. Having turned rock into a social and versatile medium, he moved into the greater complexities of jazz, with an interest in separating performance from recording. His *Hot Rats,* a jazz-rock release, gave the new fusion music a significant boost. He recorded every performance he ever played, and over the years he released them, sometimes in large boxed sets (*Shut Up'n Play Yer Guitar,* 1981; *You Can't Do That On Stage Anymore; Beat the Boots,* 2 sets).

But Zappa astounded the musical community when he proclaimed his total adoration of the music of Varèse, gave a lecture on him, and supported concerts of his music in N.Y. Somehow, without formal study, he managed to absorb the essence of Varèse's difficult music. This process led him to produce truly astonishing full orch. scores reveling in artful dissonant counterpoint, *Bob in Dacron and Sad Jane* and *Mo' 'n' Herb's Vacation,* and the cataclysmic *Penis Dimension* for Chorus, Soloists, and

Orch., with a text so anatomically precise that it could not be performed for any English-speaking audience. An accounting of his scatological and sexological lyrical proclivities stands in remarkable contrast to his unimpeachable private life and total abstention from alcohol and narcotic drugs. In a 1-time reflection of his own popularity, his adolescent daughter, Moon Unit, performed a rap on the hit *Valley Girls*, using the vocabulary of the young mall denizens of the San Fernando Valley near Los Angeles ("Val-Speak"). His son, Dweezil, is also a musician; his 1st album, *Havin' a Bad Day*, was modestly successful.

In 1985 Zappa became an outspoken opponent of the activities of the PMRC (Parents Music Resource Center), an organization comprised largely of wives of U.S. senators (and a future vice president) who accused the recording industry of exposing the youth of America to "sex, violence, and the glorification of drugs and alcohol." Their demands to the RIAA (Recording Industry Association of America) included the labeling of record albums to indicate lyric content. He voiced his opinions in no uncertain terms, 1st in an open letter published in *Cashbox*, and then in one to President Reagan; finally, in 1985, he appeared at the 1st of a series of highly publicized hearings involving the Senate Commerce, Technology, and Transportation Committee, the PMRC, and the RIAA, where he delivered a statement to Congress which began, "The PMRC proposal is an ill-conceived piece of nonsense which fails to deliver any real benefits to children, infringes the civil liberties of people who are not children and promises to keep the courts busy for years, dealing with the interpretational and enforcemental problems inherent in the proposal's design." Audio excerpts from these hearings can be heard, in original and Synclavier-manipulated forms, on *Zappa Meets the Mothers of Prevention*. Later recordings which make extensive use of the Synclavier include *Francesco Zappa* (arrangements of works by the 18th-century Italian composer and cellist) and *Jazz From Hell*. Upon learning of his fatal illness, he went through his entire recorded output, digitalized and remixed it, and sold it outright to the Rykodisc label; the last release before his death was *The Yellow Shark*.

Zarlino, Gioseffo (Gioseffe), b. Chioggia, probably Jan. 31, 1517; d. Venice, Feb. 4, 1590. He received his academic training from the Franciscans; his teacher in music was F. M. Delfico. In 1532 he received the 1st tonsure, in 1537 took minor orders, and in 1539 was made a deacon. He was active as a singer (1536) and organist (1539–40) at Chioggia Cathedral. After his ordination he was elected *capellano* and *mansionario* of the Scuola di S. Francesco in Chioggia in 1540. In 1541 he went to Venice to continue his musical training with Willaert; in 1565 he succeeded his fellow pupil Cipriano de Rore as maestro di cappella at San Marco, holding this position until his death; also was chaplain of S. Severo (from 1565) and a canon of the Chioggia Cathedral chapter (from 1583). His students included G. M. Artusi, G. Diruta, V. Galilei, and C. Merulo.

Zarlino's historical significance rests upon his theoretical works, particularly his *Le istitutioni harmoniche* (1558), in which he treats the major and minor 3rds as inversions within a 5th, and consequently, the major and minor triads as mutual mirror reflections of component intervals, thus anticipating the modern dualism of Rameau, Tartini, Hauptmann, and Riemann; he also gives lucid and practical demonstrations of double counterpoint and canon, illustrated by numerous musical examples;

while adhering to the system of 12 modes he places the Ionian rather than the Dorian mode at the head of the list, thus pointing toward the emergence of the major scale as the preponderant mode; he gives 10 rules for proper syllabification of the text in musical settings. His *Dimostrationi harmoniche* (1571) was publ. in the form of 5 dialogues between Willaert and his disciples and friends. His theories were attacked, with a violence uncommon even for the polemical spirit of the age, by Galilei in *Dialogo della musica antica e della moderna* (Florence, 1581) and *Discorso intorno alle opere di Gioseffo Zarlino* (Florence, 1589). In reply to the 1st of Galilei's books, Zarlino publ. *Sopplimenti musicali* (1588); in the latter he suggests equal temperament for the tuning of the lute. As a composer he was an accomplished craftsman, writing sacred and secular works.

zart (Ger.). Tender, soft, delicate, *dolce;* slender. *Mit zarten Stimmen,* with soft-toned stops.

Zartflöte (Ger.). 4' flute organ stop of very delicate tone.

zärtlich (Ger.). Tenderly, caressingly.

zarzuela (from Sp. *zarza,* bramble bush). Spanish light opera characterized by dance and spoken dialogue; the name derives from the Royal Palace La Zarzuela, near Madrid, where zarzuelas were performed before the royal court, beginning in the 17th century. Performances at the court were interspersed with ballets and popular dances fashioned after the spectacles at Versailles. With the massive intrusion of Italian opera into Spain in the 18th century, the zarzuela lost its characteristic ethnic flavor; but it was revived by nationally minded composers of the 2nd half of the 19th century, particularly Barbieri, Chapí, Bretón, Caballero, Valverde, and Chueca. In the early 20th century composers such as Giménez, Vives, Guridi, Usandizaga, Moreno Torroba, and Toldrá continued composing in a now dying genre; classical composers such as Granados and de Falla contributed zarzuelas. The modern type of zarzuela, known as *genero chico,* embodied elements of the Viennese operetta, and still later annexed American jazz rhythms. Zarzuelas taking up an entire evening were called *zarzuela grande;* a *zarzuelita* is a small zarzuela. See also ⇒tonadilla.

Zauberoper (Ger.). Magic opera, in which supernatural forces intervene in human affairs; an example is Weber's *Der Freischütz.*

zeffiroso (It.). Zephyr-like.

Zeit (Ger.). Time.

Zeitmass (Ger.). Tempo. *Im Zeitmasse,* in the original tempo.

Zeitoper (Ger., opera of the times). German operas of the 1920s and early 1930s with distinct sociopolitical themes, driven by a generalized tendency of artists toward the creation of socially relevant art.

Zeitschrift (Ger.). Newspaper, periodical, magazine, publication, journal, etc.

zeloso (It.). Zealously, enthusiastically; with energy and fire.

Zelter, Carl Friedrich, b. Berlin, Dec. 11, 1758; d. there, May 15, 1832. He began training in piano and violin at 17; from 1779 was a part-time violinist in the Doebbelin Theater orch. in Berlin; was a pupil of C. F. C. Fasch (1784–86). In 1786 he brought out a funeral cantata on the death of Frederick the Great; in 1791 joined the Singverein (later Singakademie) conducted by Fasch; often acted as his deputy; succeeded (1800). He was elected associate of the Royal Academy of the Arts in Berlin (1806); became a prof. (1809). In 1807 he organized a Ripienschule for orch. practice; in 1809 he founded the Berlin Liedertafel, a pioneer men's choral society that became a model for similar organizations throughout Germany and later in America. Zelter composed about 100 men's choruses for the Liedertafel. In 1822 he founded the Royal Inst. for Church Music in Berlin; was director until his death (the Inst. was later reorganized as the Akademie für Kirchen- und Schulmusik). His students included Mendelssohn, Meyerbeer, Loewe, and Nicolai.

Goethe greatly admired Zelter's musical settings of his poems, preferring them to Schubert's and Beethoven's; this predilection led to a friendship reflected in a voluminous correspondence, *Briefwechsel zwischen Goethe und Zelter* (6 vols., Berlin, 1833–34). His songs are historically important, forming a link between old ballad types and the new lied, which found its flowering in Schubert and Schumann. His settings of Goethe's *König von Thule* and of *Es ist ein Schuss gefallen* became extremely popular; also composed a viola concerto (1779), keyboard pieces, and choral works. He publ. a biography of Fasch (Berlin, 1801).

Zemlinsky, Alexander (von), b. Vienna, Oct. 14, 1871; d. Larchmont, N.Y., Mar. 15, 1942. At the Vienna Cons. he studied piano with Door (1887–90) and composition with Krenn, R. Fuchs, and J. N. Fuchs (1890–92); joined the Vienna Tonkünstlerverein (1893); became connected with the orch. society Polyhymnia and met Schoenberg (1895), whom he advised on the technical aspects of chamber music; Schoenberg always had the highest regard for Zemlinsky as a composer and lamented the lack of appreciation for his music; in 1901 Schoenberg married Zemlinsky's sister Mathilde.

Zemlinsky's 1st opera, *Sarema,* to a libretto by his own father, was produced in Munich (1897). He came in contact with Mahler, then music director of the Vienna Court Opera, who accepted his *Es war einmal;* Mahler conducted its premiere at the Court Opera (1900); it became Zemlinsky's most popular work. He served as conductor of the Karlstheater in Vienna (1900–06); conducted at the Theater an der Wien (1903). He and Schoenberg organized the Union of Creative Musicians, which performed his sym. poem *Die Seejungfrau* (Vienna, 1904). He served as chief conductor of the Volksoper (1904–07; 1908–11); conducted at the Court Opera (1907–08); orchestrated and conducted the ballet *Der Schneemann* by the 11-year-old wunderkind E. W. Korngold (1910).

In 1911 Zemlinsky moved to Prague; became conductor at the German Opera; taught conducting and composition at the German Academy of Music (from 1920). In 1927 he moved to Berlin, where he obtained the appointment of assistant conductor at the Kroll Opera, with Klemperer as chief conductor and music director. When the Nazis came to power in Germany in 1933, he returned to Vienna, and also filled engagements as guest conductor in Russia and elsewhere. After the Anschluss of 1938 he emigrated to America, which effectively ended his career.

As a composer Zemlinsky followed the post-Romantic trends of Mahler and R. Strauss. He was greatly admired but his works were seldom performed, despite the efforts of Schoenberg and his associates to revive his music. How strongly he influenced his younger contemporaries is illustrated by the fact that Alban Berg quoted Zemlinsky's *Lyric Sym.* in his own *Lyric Suite.* In the latter 20th century a great number of Zemlinsky's works, both operatic and nonoperatic, have received revivals, bringing attention to yet another composer forgotten through the vicissitudes of music history. Among his works are 8 completed operas, 3 syms. (1892–c. 1903); *Lyrische Sym.* in 7 sections, after Rabindranath Tagore, for Soprano, Baritone, and Orch. (his best-known work; 1922–23; Prague, 1924); Sinfonietta (1934). He wrote chamber works, including 4 string quartets (1895–1936); vocal works, including 3 psalms for chorus and orch. (1900–35); *Maeterlinck Lieder,* 6 songs for medium voice and orch. (1910–13); *Sym. Gesänge* for Voice and Orch. (1929); 4 vols. of lieder to texts by Heyse and Liliencron (1894–97); settings of texts by Dehmel, Jacobsen, Bierbaum, Morgenstern, Ammann, Heine, and Hofmannsthal (1898–1913; 1929–36).

zheng (cheng). Chinese half-tube zither, dating from the 3rd century B.C.; a popular solo instrument of the people, while the qin was reserved for scholars and officials in meditation. The number of strings was variable, with 14 as an average; modern instruments may have up to 24 or more; the strings are divided by movable bridges. The zheng is tuned pentatonically; in addition to harmonics, ornaments are performed by applying pressure to the non-playing side of the bridges (like the Japanese *koto* and Korean *kayago*).

Ziehharmonika (Ger., pull harmonica). Accordion.

ziemlich (Ger.). Somewhat, rather. *Ziemlich bewegt und frei in Vortrag,* quite animated and free in delivery (style); *ziemlich langsam,* rather slowly.

zierlich (Ger.). Neatly, delicately; gracefully.

Zigeunermusik (Ger.). Gypsy music.

zimbalo(n). Cimbalom.

Zimerman, Krystian, b. Zabrze, Dec. 5, 1956. He commenced piano lessons at age 5 with his father; at 7 became a pupil of A. Jasinki; continued with him at the Katowice Cons. He won 1st prize in the Chopin Competition in Warsaw (1975); played with great success in Munich, Paris, London, and Vienna; was a soloist with the Berlin Phil. (1976). He made his 1st American appearance (1978); subsequently toured throughout the world to great critical acclaim. His performances of the Romantic repertory are remarkable for their discerning spontaneity.

Zimmermann, Bernd (Bernhard) Alois, b. Bliesheim, near Cologne, Mar. 20, 1918; d. (suicide) Königsdorf, Aug. 10, 1970. He studied at the Cologne Hochschule für Musik and at the Univs. of Cologne and Bonn; after his discharge from military service became a pupil of Lemacher and Jarnach (1942); attended the summer courses in new music of Fortner and Leibowitz in Darmstadt (1948–50). He taught theory at the Univ. of Cologne (1950–52) and the Cologne Hochschule für Musik (1957–70). Plagued by failing eyesight and obsessed with notions of death, he reflected these moods in his own music of the final period; his *Requiem für einen jungen Dichter,* a "lingual" for Narrator, Soprano, and Baritone Soloists, 3 Choruses, Tape, Orch., Jazz Combo, and Organ (1967–69) sets texts drawn from poems, articles, and news reports concerning poets who committed suicide.

Zimmermann's idiom of composition is mainly expressionistic, with a melodic line of anguished chromaticism that does not preclude the observance of strict formal structures in his instrumental works; in a sense he realized the paths opened by Berg. The opera *Die Soldaten,* based on a play by J. M. R. Lenz (1958–60; rev. 1963–64; Cologne, 1965), took the atmosphere of *Wozzeck* several steps further; the explicit presentation of the molestation of innocent civilians by the military brought on a critical and societal storm of protest. Yet for all his manic depressive character, he kept his sense of irony and humor, as evidenced by *Nobody Knows de Trouble I See,* a trumpet concerto (Hamburg, 1955) and *Musique pour les soupers du Roi Ubu,* "ballet noir" after Jarry (1966).

Zimmermann maintained strong religious beliefs; 5 days before his death he completed *Ich wandte mich und sah an alles Unrecht das geschah unter der Sonne,* "ecclesiastical action" after Ecclesiastes and Dostoyevsky, for 2 Narrators, Bass, and Orch. (1970), a moving final expression of hope. While in his lifetime he was primarily known to limited music circles in Germany, the significance of his music has gradually become more widely known.

zingara, alla (*zingarese, alla; zingaresca;* It.). In Gypsy style.

Zink (Ger.). Cornett.

Zirkelkanon (Ger., circle canon). Perpetual canon.

Zither (Ger.). 1. An organological category for a simple chordophone, without resonator, or at most a nonintegral, detachable one. Most are plucked (psaltery type); some are idiophonic (struck with sticks or beaters; dulcimer type) or heterophonic (plucked and struck). 2. A folk instrument popular in Bavaria and Austria, capable of considerable harmonic sonority. It is a shallow wooden resonating box with 32 or more strings stretched over it. It has a fretted fingerboard on the side nearest the player, supporting 5 melody strings, plucked with the fingers and a metal plectrum worn on the right thumb; these are stopped with the fingers of the left hand to determine the pitch. In Finland the popular form of zither is called kantele.

zitternd (Ger.). Trembling, tremulous.

zögernd (Ger.). Hesitatingly.

Zopf (Ger., pigtail). An irreverent description of the type of music composed by wig-wearing Baroque musicians. The Zopf is familiar from the portraits of Bach, Handel, Haydn, and their contemporaries; Mozart even wore a Zopf as a child. The Zopf era came to a sudden end at the threshold of the 19th century. Beethoven's portraits show him with tousled hair, but he never wore a wig.

zoppa, alla (It., lame, limping). In a limpingly syncopated manner; in Hungarian 2/4 dances, a strong accent on the 2nd beat; *contrapunto alla zoppa,* an obs. Ger. expression for syncopated counterpoint.

Zorn, John, b. N.Y., Sept. 2, 1953. He plays saxophone, keyboards, duck calls, and other semi-demi-musical instruments in dense, loud aural canvases that have been compared to the works of Jackson Pollock (and also to an elephant trapped in barbed wire). After a brief college stint in St. Louis and world travels, he became an active contributor to the downtown music scene in N.Y.; performed with a coterie of well-reputed avant-garde and rock musicians, including guitarists Bill Frisell and Fred Frith, bassist Bill Laswell, pianists Anthony Coleman and Wayne Horvitz, drummers Bobby Previte and David Moss, vocalist Shelly Hirsch, and the Kronos Quartet.

Zorn has created separate entities for different facets of his music: *Naked City* (from late 1980s) and *Masada* (from 1994). His *The Big Gundown* (1987) uses the music of film composer Ennio Morricone (b. 1928) as material to be freely distorted and reworked. His major recordings include *Archery* (1981), *Cobra* (group improvisation, 2 vols.: 1986; 1994), *A Classic Guide to Strategy* (solo with overdubbing, 1987), *News for Lulu,* with Frisell and George Lewis, trombone (2 vols.: 1987; 1989), and *Spillane* (1988), *Spy vs. Spy,* playing the music of Ornette Coleman (1989), *The Book of Heads,* performed by guitarist Marc Ribot (1995), and *Kristallnacht* (1995).

zornig (Ger.). Wrathfully (R. Strauss, *Ein Heldenleben,* referring to his feelings toward his critics).

zortziko. A Basque song, melody, and dance type. Its most characteristic element is the 5/8 meter, with highly syncopated rhythms.

zu (Ger.). 1. Too, as *nicht zu schnell,* not too fast. 2. To; toward.

zufahrend (Ger.). Rushing headlong (Mahler, 4th Sym.).

Zugposaune (Ger.). Slide trombone.

Zukerman, Pinchas, b. Tel Aviv, July 16, 1948. He began to study music with his father, taking up the violin at age 6; he then enrolled at the Cons. in Tel Aviv, where he studied with Ilona Feher. With the encouragement of Isaac Stern and Pablo Casals, he became a scholarship student at the Juilliard School of Music in N.Y., where he studied with Ivan Galamian (1961–67). In 1967 he shared 1st prize in the Leventritt Competition in N.Y. with Kyung-Wha Chung, and then launched a brilliant career as a soloist with the major American and European orchs. He also appeared as both violinist and violist in recitals with Isaac Stern and Itzhak Perlman. He subsequently devoted part of his time to conducting, appearing as a guest conductor with the N.Y. Phil., Philadelphia Orch., Boston Sym. Orch., Los Angeles Phil., and many others. He was music director of the St. Paul (Minn.) Chamber Orch. (1980–87). His 1st marriage was to flutist Eugenia (née Rich) Zukerman (b. Cambridge, Mass., Sept. 25, 1944), with whom he often performed chamber music. His performances as a violinist are distinguished by their innate emotional élan and modern virtuoso technique.

Zukofsky, Paul, b. N.Y., Oct. 22, 1943. His father, Louis Zukofsky, was a poet who experimented in highly complex verbal forms; in 1970 he publ. a novel, *Little,* dealing with the trials and triumphs of a violin wunderkind. Paul began playing the violin at the age of 4 on a quarter-size instrument; when he was 7 he began lessons with Ivan Galamian; was soloist with the New Haven (Conn.) Sym. Orch. at the age of 8; he made his Carnegie Hall recital debut in N.Y. when he was 13. At 16 he entered the Juilliard School of Music. From his earliest years he was fascinated by ultramodern music and developed maximal celerity, dexterity, and alacrity in manipulating special techniques, in effect transforming the violin into a multimedia instrument beyond its normal capacities.

In 1969 Zukofsky inaugurated in N.Y. a concert series, Music for the 20th Century Violin, performing works often requiring acrobatic coordination. His repertoire includes all 4 violin sonatas by Charles Ives, the violin concertos by William Schuman and Roger Sessions, *Capriccio* by Penderecki, the solo violin works of John Cage, etc. As a violin instructor he held the post of Creative Associate at the Buffalo Center of the Creative and Performing Arts; also taught at the Berkshire Music Center in Tanglewood and at the New England Cons. of Music. In later years he became active as a conductor; served as conductor of the Contemporary Chamber Ensemble at the Juilliard School (from 1984), and also was director of chamber music activities there (1987–89). He directed the Schoenberg Inst. in Los Angeles, replacing Leonard Stein.

Zukunftmusik (Ger.). Music of the future; a term coined by Wagner. His opponents turned this lofty phrase into a derisive description of his music.

zummāra (Arab.). Arab double clarinet with parallel identical cylindrical pipes and a tremulant sound. It is a descendant of the Egyptian *memet,* dated to 2700 B.C.

zunehmend (Ger.). Increasing dynamic level; crescendo.

Zunge (Ger.). 1. Tongue. 2. Organ reed.

Zungenpfeife (Ger.). Organ reed pipe. *Zungenstimme,* organ reed stop.

Zupfinstrumente (Ger.). Plucked string instruments.

zurnā. Shawn family of wide geographic distribution, with conical bore, flared bell, 7 fingerholes, and several ventholes at the lower end. It is found under this and other names in Arab and Slavic regions, Turkey, India, and Indonesia.

züruckgehend (Ger.). Returning (to a preceding slower tempo).

züruckhaltend (Ger.). Holding back; ritardando.

zusammen (Ger.). Together.

Zwei (Ger.). Two.

Zweifacher (Ger.). Bavarian folk dance with alternating binary and ternary periods (e.g., 2 measures + 3 measures).

zweihändig (Ger.). For 2 hands.

zweistimmig (Ger.). For 2 voices; in or for 2 parts.

Zwilich, Ellen Taaffe, b. Miami, Apr. 30, 1939. She studied composition with John Boda and violin with Richard Burgin at Florida State Univ. (B. Mus., 1956; M.M., 1962); moved to N.Y., where she continued her violin studies with Ivan Galamian. After playing in the American Sym. Orch. there (1965–72), she enrolled at the Juilliard School in N.Y. and had sessions with Roger Sessions and Elliott Carter; she was the 1st woman to receive a D.M.A. in composition from that school (1975). In 1983 she received the Pulitzer prize in music for her Sym. No. 1 (originally titled *3 Movements for Orchestra*), 1st performed in N.Y. in 1982. Zwilich's music offers a happy combination of purely technical excellence and a distinct power of communication, while a poetic element pervades the melody, harmony, and counterpoint of her creations. This combination of qualities explains the frequency and variety of prizes awarded her from various sources: the Elizabeth Sprague Coolidge Chamber Music Prize; a gold medal at the 26th Annual International Composition Competition in Vercelli, Italy; N.E.A. grants; a Guggenheim fellowship (1980–81); the Ernst von Dohnányi Citation; and an award from the American Academy and Inst. of Arts and Letters (1984). Conductors in America, Europe, and Japan are also eager to program her works. During a 1988 tour of Russia Mehta and the N.Y. Phil. presented the world premiere of her *Symbolon* in Leningrad. She is best known for her instrumental works.

Zwischensatz (Ger.). Episode; in a fugue, a section in between thematic sections.

Zwischenspiel (Ger.). Interlude; intermezzo.

Zwölftonmusik (Ger.). See ⇒dodecaphony; serialism.

Zymbel (Ger.). 1. Obsolete for cymbals. 2. Organ mixture stop.